2007 Baseball register

EVERY PLAYER, EVERY STAT

EDITED BY: Zach Bodendieck, Tom Gatto.
COVER DESIGN AND PAGE LAYOUT BY: Chad Painter.

PHOTO CREDITS: On the cover: photos of Albert Pujols, David Wright and Vlad Guerrero by Albert Dickson; photo of David Ortiz by Robert Seale.

Major league statistics compiled by STATS, Inc., a News Corporation company, 8130 Lehigh Avenue, Morton Grove, IL 60053. STATS is a trademark of Sports Team Analysis and Tracking Systems, Inc.

Minor league statistics provided by SportsTicker; MLB.com also contributed/delivered stats; Hitting/pitching zones provided by Baseball Info Solutions.

ISBN: 0-89204-866-2

10 9 8 7 6 5 4 3 2 1

CONTENTS

EXPLANATION OF FOOTNOTES AND ABBREVIATIONS

NOTE FOR STATISTICAL COMPARISONS: Player strikes forced the cancellation of games in the 1972 season (10 days missed), the 1981 season (50 days missed), the 1994 season (52 days missed) and the 1995 season (18 games missed). Positions are listed in descending order of games played; because of limited space, pinch hitter and pinch runner are listed in the regular-season section only if a player did not play a defensive position.

*   Led league. For fielding statistics, the player led the league at the position shown.

•   Tied for league lead. For fielding statistics, the player tied for the league lead at the position shown.

†   Led league, but number indicated is total figure for two or more positions.

‡   Tied for league lead, but number indicated is total figure for two or more positions.

§   Led or tied for league lead, but total figure is divided between two different teams.

...   Statistic unavailable, inapplicable, unofficial or mathematically impossible to calculate.

—   Manager statistic inapplicable.

LEAGUES: A.A., Am. Assoc.—American Association. **A.L.**—American. **App., Appal.**—Appalachian. **Ariz., AZL**—Arizona Rookie League. **Atl.**—Atlantic. **BSL**—Big South **Cal., Calif.**—California. **Can-Am.**—Canadian-American. **Car., Caro., Carol.**—Carolina. **Cent.**—Central. **DSL**—Dominican Summer. **East.**—Eastern. **Fla. St., FSL**—Florida State. **Fron.**—Frontier **GCL**—Gulf Coast. **I.L., Int'l.**—International. **Jp. Cen., Jp. Cn.**—Japan Central. **Jp. East.**—Japan Eastern. **Jp. Pac., Jap. Pac.**—Japan Pacific. **Jp. West.**—Japan Western. **Kor.**—Korean. **Mex., Mx.**—Mexican. **Mid., Midw.**—Midwest. **N.L.**—National. **Nor., North.**—Northern. **N. Cen. Pra.**— **N'west, N'West, NW, NWL**—Northwest. **NY-Penn, N.Y.-Penn, NY-P, NYP**—New York-Pennsylvania. **PCL**—Pacific Coast. **Pio., Pion.**—Pioneer. **S. Atl., SAL**—South Atlantic. **Sou., South.**—Southern. **Tai.**—Taiwan. **Tex.**—Texas. **Tex.-La.**—Texas-Louisiana. **VSL**—Venezuelan Summer. **West.**—Western.

TEAMS: Aguas., Aguascal.—Aguascalientes. **Alb./Colon., Alb./Colonie**—Albany/Colonie. **Ariz.**—Arizona. **Ariz. D-backs**—Arizona League Diamondbacks. **Belling.**—Bellingham. **Birm.**—Birmingham. **Brevard Co.**—Brevard County. **Cant./Akr.**—Canton/Akron. **Ced. Rap., Cedar Rap.**—Cedar Rapids. **Cent. Ore., Cen. Oregon**—Central Oregon. **Central Vall.**—Central Valley. **Char., Charl.**—Charleston. **Chatt.**—Chattanooga. **Chiba Lot.**—Chiba Lotte. **Ciu. Alianza**—Ciudad Alianza **Ciu. Juarez**—Ciudad Juarez. **Colo. Spr., Colo. Springs**—Colorado Springs. **Dall./Fort W.**—Dallas/Fort Worth. **Day. Beach.**—Daytona Beach. **Dom.**—Dominican. **Dom. Inds.**—Dominican Indians. **Dom. B. Jays**—Dominican Blue Jays. **Dom. Orioles/WS**—Dominican Orioles/White Sox. **Elizabeth.**—Elizabethton. **Fort Lauder., Fort Laud.**—Fort Lauderdale. **GC**—Gulf Coast. **GC Whi. Sox**—Gulf Coast White Sox. **Greens.**—Greensboro. **Jacksonv.**—Jacksonville. **Johns. City**—Johnson City. **Kane Co.**—Kane County. **M.C., Mex. City**—Mexico City. **M.C. R. Dev.**—Mexico City Red Devils. **M.C. Tigers.**—Mexico City Tigers **Monc.**—Monclova. **Montgom.**— Montgomery. **Niag. F., Niag. Falls**—Niagara Falls. **Okla. City**—Oklahoma City. **Prince Will., Prin. Will., Prin. William**—Prince William. **Ral./Dur.**—Raleigh/Durham. **Rancho Cuca.**—Rancho Cucamonga. **Salt.**—Saltillo. **Salt.-Monc.**—Saltillo-Monclova. **San. Dom., San. Domingo**—Santo Domingo. **San Bern.**—San Bernardino. **San Fran.**—San Francisco. **Scran./W.B.**—Scranton/Wilkes-Barre. **S.C.**—South Carolina. **S. Oregon**—Southern Oregon.

EXPLANATION OF FOOTNOTES AND ABBREVIATIONS cont.

Spartan.—Spartanburg. **St. Cath., St. Cathar.**—St. Catharines. **St. Pete.**—St. Petersburg. **Stock.**—Stockton. **Union Lag.**—Union Laguna **Ven.**—Venezuelan. **Wash.**—Washington. **Whi. Sox.**—Gulf Coast White Sox. **W. Mich.**—West Michigan. **Will.**—Williamsport. **Win.-Salem**—Winston-Salem. **Wis. Rap., Wis. Rapids**—Wisconsin Rapids. **W.P. Beach**—West Palm Beach. **W.Va.**—West Virgina. **Yo. Bay, Yoko. Bay**—Yokohama.

STATISTICS: A—assists. **AB**—at-bats. **Avg.**—average (average allowed for pitchers). **BB**—bases on balls. **CG**—complete games. **CS**—caught stealing. **E**—errors. **ER**—earned runs. **ERA**—earned run average. **G**—games. **GDP**—grounded into double play. **GS**—games started. **H**—hits. **HBP**—hit by pitch. **Hld.**—holds. **HR**—home runs. **IBB**—intentional bases on balls. **IP**—innings pitched. **L**—losses. **OBP**—on-base percentage. **OPS**—on-base plus slugging percentage. **Pct.**—winning percentage. **PO**—putouts. **Pos.**—position. **R**—runs. **RBI**—runs batted in. **SB**—stolen bases. **ShO**—shutouts. **SLG**—slugging percentage. **SO**—strikeouts. **Sv.**—saves. **Sv.Opp.**—save opportunities. **W**—wins. **WHIP**—walks plus hits divided by innings pitched. **2B**—doubles. **3B**—triples.

2007 PLAYERS LIST

▶ Year-by-year major and minor league statistics for every player who played in at least one major league game in 2006

▶ Career transactions and biographical information

▶ 2006 major league lefty-righty splits for every batter and pitcher

MAJOR LEAGUE PLAYERS

A

AARDSMA, DAVID — P

PERSONAL: Born December 27, 1981, in Denver. ... 6-5/200. ... Throws right, bats right. ... Full name: David Allan Aardsma. ... High school: Cherry Creek (Denver). ... College: Penn State, then Rice. **TRANSACTIONS/CAREER NOTES:** Selected by San Francisco Giants organization in first round (22nd pick overall) of 2003 free-agent draft. ... Traded by Giants with P Jerome Williams to Chicago Cubs for P LaTroy Hawkins (May 28, 2005).
CAREER HITTING: 0-for-2 (.000), 0 R, 0 2B, 0 3B, 0 HR, 0 RBI.

Year — Team (League)	W	L	Pct.	ERA	WHIP	G	GS	CG	ShO	Hld.	Sv.-Opp.	IP	H	R	ER	HR	BB-IBB	SO	Avg.
2003— San Jose (Calif.)	1	1	.500	1.96	1.15	18	0	0	0	...	8-...	18.1	14	4	4	2	7-0	28	.212
2004— San Francisco (N.L.)	1	0	1.000	6.75	2.81	11	0	0	0	1	0-1	10.2	20	8	8	1	10-0	5	.417
—Fresno (PCL)	6	4	.600	3.09	1.37	44	0	0	0	...	11-...	55.1	46	21	19	2	30-3	53	.223
2005— Norwich (East.)	6	2	.750	2.93	1.24	38	0	0	0	0	0-0	46.0	44	17	15	2	13-0	30	.256
—West Tenn. (Sou.)	4	1	.800	3.91	1.58	33	0	0	0	7	2-4	50.2	48	22	22	3	32-3	43	.259
2006— Iowa (PCL)	2	3	.400	3.22	1.27	29	0	0	0	8	8-13	36.1	31	15	13	1	15-2	36	.240
—Chicago (N.L.)	3	0	1.000	4.08	1.30	45	0	0	0	5	0-0	53.0	41	25	24	9	28-0	49	.214
Major League totals (2 years)	4	0	1.000	4.52	1.55	56	0	0	0	6	0-1	63.2	61	33	32	10	38-0	54	.254

2006 LEFTY-RIGHTY SPLITS

vs.	Avg.	AB	H	2B	3B	HR	RBI	BB	SO	OBP	Slg.	vs.	Avg.	AB	H	2B	3B	HR	RBI	BB	SO	OBP	Slg.
L	.190	63	12	2	0	2	6	10	15	.297	.317	R	.225	129	29	3	0	7	19	18	34	.320	.411

ABAD, ANDY — OF/1B

PERSONAL: Born August 25, 1972, in Palm Beach, Fla. ... 5-11/196. ... Bats left, throws left. ... Full name: Fausto Andres Abad. ... Junior college: Middle Georgia College.
TRANSACTIONS/CAREER NOTES: Selected by Boston Red Sox organization in 16th round of 1993 free-agent draft. ... Signed by Kintetsu Buffaloes of Japan Pacific League (2000). ... Signed by Oakland Athletics organization (November 15, 2000). ... Signed as a free agent by Florida Marlins organization (November 20, 2001). ... Signed by Red Sox organization (January 10, 2003). ... Released by Red Sox (November 17, 2003). ... Signed by Pittsburgh Pirates organization (January 8, 2004). ... Signed as a free agent by Cleveland Indians organization (November 25, 2004). ... Signed as a free agent by Cincinnati Reds organization (December 19, 2005).

Year — Team (League)	Pos.	G	AB	R	H	2B	3B	HR	RBI	BB	SO	HBP	GDP	SB-CS	Avg.	OBP	SLG	OPS	E	Avg.
						BATTING													FIELDING		
1993— GC Red Sox (GCL)	1B-OF	59	230	24	57	9	2	1	28	25	27	2	2	2-2	.248	.322	.317	.639	1	.995
1994— Sarasota (Fla. St.)	1B-OF	111	354	39	102	20	0	2	35	42	58	5	9	2-12	.288	.367	.362	.729	5	.975
1995— Trenton (East.)	OF	89	287	29	69	14	3	4	32	36	58	3	6	5-7	.240	.328	.352	.680	2	.987
—Sarasota (Fla. St.)	1B-OF	18	59	5	17	3	0	0	10	6	13	0	0	4-3	.288	.354	.339	.693	2	.980
1996— Sarasota (Fla. St.)	1B-OF-P	58	202	28	58	15	1	2	41	37	28	3	6	10-3	.287	.402	.401	.803	5	.985
—Trenton (East.)	1B-OF	65	213	33	59	22	1	4	39	33	41	0	4	5-3	.277	.369	.446	.815	1	.997
1997— Trenton (East.)	1B-OF	45	165	37	50	13	0	8	24	33	27	2	2	2-4	.303	.423	.527	.950	3	.986
—Pawtucket (Int'l)	1B-OF	68	227	28	62	7	0	9	32	36	47	2	4	3-2	.273	.376	.423	.799	8	.978
1998— Pawtucket (Int'l)	1B-OF	111	365	71	112	18	1	16	66	68	70	3	7	10-6	.307	.415	.493	.908	5	.994
1999— Pawtucket (Int'l)	1B-OF	102	377	61	112	21	4	15	65	51	50	2	9	7-2	.297	.381	.493	.874	6	.980
2000— Kintetsu (Jp. West.)		61	233	35	72	12	1	8	48	30	18	2	2	3-0	.309	.392	.472	.864	...	...
—Kintetsu (Jp. Pac.)		32	92	7	15	1	0	4	13	9	17	0	0	0-0	.163	.238	.304	.542	...	...
2001— Sacramento (PCL)	OF-1B	124	462	72	139	19	2	19	82	58	67	1	12	4-2	.301	.379	.474	.853	6	.974
—Oakland (A.L.)	1B	1	0	0	0	0	0	0	0	0	0	0	0	0-0	.000	.000	.000	.000	0	1.000
2002— Calgary (PCL)	OF-1B	111	352	50	106	28	2	11	70	57	44	4	7	0-3	.301	.402	.486	.888	3	.991
2003— Pawtucket (Int'l)	1B-OF-DH	134	504	78	153	35	3	13	93	55	67	4	15	0-3	.304	.372	.462	.834	5	.994
—Boston (A.L.)	1B-OF	9	17	1	2	0	0	0	2	5	0	0	1	0-1	.118	.211	.118	.328	1	.973
2004— Nashville (PCL)		99	301	45	88	15	1	12	49	40	52	5	9	4-1	.292	.382	.468	.850	...	...
2005— Buffalo (Int'l)	OF-1B-DH																			
	P	121	423	68	124	29	1	20	85	44	60	3	16	3-4	.293	.361	.508	.869	6	.988
2006— Louisville (Int'l)		82	266	36	71	12	0	9	32	26	31	6	6	0-1	.267	.344	.414	.758	3	.988
—Cincinnati (N.L.)		5	3	0	0	0	0	0	0	2	0	0	0	0-0	.000	.400	.000	.400	0	...
American League totals (2 years)		10	18	1	2	0	0	0	2	5	0	0	1	0-1	.111	.200	.111	.311	1	.974
National League totals (1 year)		5	3	0	0	0	0	0	0	2	0	0	0	0-0	.000	.400	.000	.400	0	...
Major League totals (3 years)		15	21	1	2	0	0	0	4	5	0	0	1	0-1	.095	.240	.095	.335	1	.974

2006 LEFTY-RIGHTY SPLITS

vs.	Avg.	AB	H	2B	3B	HR	RBI	BB	SO	OBP	Slg.	vs.	Avg.	AB	H	2B	3B	HR	RBI	BB	SO	OBP	Slg.
L	.000	0	0	0	0	0	0	0	0	.000	.000	R	.000	3	0	0	0	0	0	2	0	.400	.000

ABERCROMBIE, REGGIE — OF

PERSONAL: Born July 15, 1980, in Columbus, Ga. ... 6-3/225. ... Bats right, throws right. ... Full name: Reginald Damascus Abercrombie. ... College: Lake City (Fla.) C.C.
TRANSACTIONS/CAREER NOTES: Selected by Los Angeles Dodgers organization in 23rd round of 2000 free-agent draft. ... Traded by Dodgers with P Bill Murphy and C Koyie Hill to Arizona Diamondbacks for OF Steve Finley and C Brent Mayne (July 31, 2004). ... Claimed on waivers by Florida Marlins (April 5, 2005).
2006 GAMES PLAYED BY POSITION (MLB): OF—93.

Year — Team (League)	Pos.	G	AB	R	H	2B	3B	HR	RBI	BB	SO	HBP	GDP	SB-CS	Avg.	OBP	SLG	OPS	E	Avg.
						BATTING													FIELDING		
2000— Great Falls (Pio.)		54	220	40	60	7	1	2	29	22	66	8	1	32-8	.273	.360	.341	.701	...	...
2001— Wilmington (S. Atl.)		125	486	63	110	17	3	10	41	19	154	12	3	44-11	.226	.272	.335	.607	...	...
2002— Vero Beach (Fla. St.)		132	526	80	145	23	13	10	56	27	158	9	3	41-17	.276	.321	.426	.747	...	...
—Jacksonville (Sou.)		1	4	1	1	0	0	0	0	0	1	0	0	1-0	.250	.250	.250	.500	...	...
2003— Jacksonville (Sou.)		116	448	59	117	25	7	15	54	16	164	9	3	28-9	.261	.298	.449	.747	...	...
2004— Jacksonville (Sou.)		41	168	17	29	6	4	4	20	4	66	1	2	3-3	.173	.193	.327	.520	...	...
—Vero Beach (Fla. St.)		34	133	18	36	4	5	5	12	6	33	1	1	16-5	.271	.305	.489	.794	...	...
—Lancaster (Calif.)		29	120	24	41	10	2	3	19	2	24	1	1	8-1	.342	.358	.533	.891	...	...
2005— Jupiter (Fla. St.)	OF	76	299	51	82	12	3	15	45	14	87	5	1	19-6	.274	.317	.485	.802	10	.977
—Carolina (Southern)	OF	49	178	28	45	7	2	10	23	11	40	6	1	7-5	.253	.315	.483	.798	8	.966
2006— Florida (N.L.)	OF	111	255	39	54	12	2	5	24	18	78	3	2	6-5	.212	.271	.333	.604	5	.973
Major League totals (1 year)		111	255	39	54	12	2	5	24	18	78	3	2	6-5	.212	.271	.333	.604	5	.973

2006 LEFTY-RIGHTY SPLITS

vs.	Avg.	AB	H	2B	3B	HR	RBI	BB	SO	OBP	Slg.	vs.	Avg.	AB	H	2B	3B	HR	RBI	BB	SO	OBP	Slg.
L	.220	82	18	5	0	1	5	6	26	.281	.317	R	.208	173	36	7	2	4	19	12	52	.266	.341

ABREU, BOBBY — OF

PERSONAL: Born March 11, 1974, in Aragua, Venezuela. ... 6-0/211. ... Bats left, throws right. ... Full name: Bob Kelly Abreu. ... Name pronounced: ah-BRAY-you. **TRANSACTIONS/CAREER NOTES:** Signed as a non-drafted free agent by Houston Astros organization (August 21, 1990). ... On disabled list (May 25-July 1, 1997); included rehabilitation assignments to Jackson and New Orleans. ... Selected by Tampa Bay Devil Rays in first round (sixth pick overall) of expansion draft (November 18, 1997). ... Traded by Devil Rays to Philadelphia Phillies for SS Kevin Stocker (November 18, 1997). ... Traded by Phillies with P Cory Lidle to New York Yankees for SS C.J. Henry, Ps Matt Smith and Carlos Manastrios and C Jesus Sanchez (July 30, 2006). **HONORS:** Won N.L. Gold Glove as outfielder (2005). ... Named outfielder on N.L. Silver Slugger team (2004). **STATISTICAL NOTES:** Career major league grand slams: 6.

2006 GAMES PLAYED BY POSITION (MLB): OF—154, DH—2.

										BATTING									FIELDING	
Year	Team (League)	Pos.	G	AB	R	H	2B	3B	HR	RBI	BB	SO	HBP	GDP	SB-CS	Avg.	OBP	SLG	OPS	E	Avg.
1991— GC Astros (GCL)		OF-SS	56	183	21	55	7	3	0	20	17	27	1	3	10-6	.301	.358	.372	.729	5	.943
1992— Asheville (S. Atl.)		OF	135	480	81	140	21	4	8	48	63	79	3	5	15-11	.292	.375	.402	.777	11	.943
1993— Osceola (Fla. St.)		OF	129	474	62	134	21	17	5	55	51	90	1	8	10-14	.283	.352	.430	.782	8	.961
1994— Jackson (Texas)		OF	118	400	61	121	25	9	16	73	42	81	3	2	12-10	.303	.368	.530	.898	4	.967
1995— Tucson (PCL)		OF-2B	114	415	72	126	24	17	10	75	67	120	1	6	16-14	.304	.395	.516	.911	7	.970
1996— Tucson (PCL)		OF-DH	132	484	86	137	14	16	13	68	83	111	2	5	24-18	.283	.389	.459	.847	7	.969
— Houston (N.L.)		OF	15	22	1	5	1	0	0	1	2	3	0	1	0-0	.227	.292	.273	.564	0	1.000
1997— Houston (N.L.)		OF	59	188	22	47	10	2	3	26	21	48	1	0	7-2	.250	.329	.372	.701	2	.978
— Jackson (Texas)		OF	3	12	2	2	1	0	0	0	1	5	0	0	0-0	.167	.231	.250	.481	0	1.000
— New Orleans (A.A.)		OF	47	194	25	52	9	4	2	22	21	49	0	4	7-4	.268	.335	.387	.721	1	.990
1998— Philadelphia (N.L.)		OF	151	497	68	155	29	6	17	74	84	133	0	6	19-10	.312	.409	.497	.906	8	.973
1999— Philadelphia (N.L.)		OF-DH	152	546	118	183	35	•11	20	93	109	113	3	13	27-9	.335	.446	.549	.995	3	.989
2000— Philadelphia (N.L.)		OF	154	576	103	182	42	10	25	79	100	116	1	12	28-8	.316	.416	.554	.970	4	.989
2001— Philadelphia (N.L.)		OF	•162	588	118	170	48	4	31	110	106	137	1	13	36-14	.289	.393	.543	.936	8	.976
2002— Philadelphia (N.L.)		OF	157	572	102	176	* 50	6	20	85	104	117	3	11	31-12	.308	.413	.521	.934	5	.983
2003— Philadelphia (N.L.)		OF	158	577	99	173	35	1	20	101	109	126	4	13	22-9	.300	.409	.468	.877	6	.981
2004— Philadelphia (N.L.)		OF	159	574	118	173	47	1	30	105	127	116	5	5	40-5	.301	.428	.544	.971	6	.982
2005— Philadelphia (N.L.)		OF-DH	•162	588	104	168	37	1	24	102	117	134	6	7	31-9	.286	.405	.474	.879	4	.986
2006— Philadelphia (N.L.)		OF-DH	98	339	61	94	25	2	8	65	91	86	2	8	20-4	.277	.427	.434	.861	1	.995
— New York (A.L.)		OF-DH	58	209	37	69	16	0	7	42	33	52	1	5	10-2	.330	.419	.507	.926	2	.984
American League totals (1 year)			58	209	37	69	16	0	7	42	33	52	1	5	10-2	.330	.419	.507	.926	2	.984
National League totals (11 years)			1427	5067	914	1526	359	44	198	841	970	1129	24	89	261-82	.301	.412	.507	.919	47	.983
Major League totals (11 years)			1485	5276	951	1595	375	44	205	883	1003	1181	25	94	271-84	.302	.412	.507	.919	49	.983

DIVISION SERIES RECORD

Year	Team (League)	Pos.	G	AB	R	H	2B	3B	HR	RBI	BB	SO	HBP	GDP	SB-CS	Avg.	OBP	SLG	OPS	E	Avg.
1997— Houston (N.L.)		PH	3	3	0	1	0	0	0	0	0	2	0	0	1-0	.333	.333	.333	.667	...	...
2006— New York (A.L.)		OF	4	15	2	5	1	0	0	4	2	2	0	0	0-0	.333	.412	.400	.812	0	1.000
Division series totals (2 years)			7	18	2	6	1	0	0	4	2	4	0	0	1-0	.333	.400	.389	.789	0	1.000

ALL-STAR GAME RECORD

			G	AB	R	H	2B	3B	HR	RBI	BB	SO	HBP	GDP	SB-CS	Avg.	OBP	SLG	OPS	E	Avg.
All-Star Game totals (2 years)			2	3	0	1	0	0	0	0	1	1	0	0	0-0	.333	.500	.333	.833	0	...

2006 LEFTY-RIGHTY SPLITS

vs.	Avg.	AB	H	2B	3B	HR	RBI	BB	SO	OBP	Slg.	vs.	Avg.	AB	H	2B	3B	HR	RBI	BB	SO	OBP	Slg.
L	.293	167	49	11	2	3	26	31	47	.403	.437	R	.299	381	114	30	0	12	81	93	91	.433	.472

ABREU, WINSTON — P

PERSONAL: Born April 5, 1977, in Cotui, Dominican Republic. ... 6-2/155. ... Throws right, bats right. ... Full name: Winston Leonardo Abreu. ... High school: Cotui (Dominican Republic). **TRANSACTIONS/CAREER NOTES:** Signed as a non-drafted free agent by Atlanta Braves organization (July 2, 1993). ... Traded by Braves to San Diego Padres (September 6, 2001), completing deal in which Padres traded P Rudy Seanez to Braves for a player to be named (August 31, 2001). ... Traded by Padres to Chicago Cubs for IF Keto Anderson (March 20, 2002). ... Released by Cubs (April 30, 2003). ... Signed by Kansas City Royals organization (May 9, 2002). ... Signed as a free agent by New York Yankees organization (November 22, 2002). ... Released by Yankees (March 21, 2003). ... Signed by Los Angeles Dodgers organization (January 12, 2004). ... Released by Dodgers (June 10, 2004). ... Signed by Arizona Diamondbacks organization (June 15, 2004). ... Loaned to Oaxaca of the Mexican League (June 2005-August 21, 2005). ... Signed as a free agent by Baltimore Orioles organization (October 27, 2005). ... Signed as a free agent by Washington Nationals organization (November 6, 2006).

CAREER HITTING: 0-for-0 (.000), 0 R, 0 2B, 0 3B, 0 HR, 0 RBI.

Year	Team (League)	W	L	Pct.	ERA	WHIP	G	GS	CG	ShO	Hld.	Sv.-Opp.	IP	H	R	ER	HR	BB-IBB	SO	Avg.
1994— GC Braves (GCL)		0	8	.000	4.08	1.41	13	11	0	0	...	0-...	57.1	57	35	26	2	24-0	53	.254
1995— Danville (Appal.)		6	3	.667	2.31	0.91	13	13	1	0	...	0-...	74.0	54	29	19	5	13-0	90	.209
1996— Macon (S. Atl.)		4	3	.571	3.00	1.27	12	12	0	0	...	0-...	60.0	51	29	20	4	25-1	60	.232
1997—		Did not play.																		
1998— Eugene (Northwest)		0	4	.000	6.35	1.54	17	10	0	0	...	0-...	45.1	39	36	32	6	31-0	52	.232
1999— Macon (S. Atl.)		7	2	.778	1.69	0.97	14	14	0	0	...	0-...	69.1	41	17	13	4	26-0	95	.172
— Myrtle Beach (Carol.)		3	2	.600	3.28	1.37	13	12	0	0	...	0-...	68.2	53	26	25	7	41-0	76	.218
2000— Greenville (Sou.)		0	1	.000	2.25	1.75	1	1	0	0	...	0-...	4.0	4	1	1	0	3-0	5	.286
— GC Braves (GCL)		0	0	...	3.00	1.33	2	2	0	0	...	0-...	3.0	2	1	1	1	2-0	2	.182
— Macon (S. Atl.)		2	1	.667	1.88	0.59	11	1	0	0	...	3-...	28.2	11	6	6	2	6-0	48	.113
— Richmond (Int'l)		0	1	.000	7.00	1.89	3	0	0	0	...	0-...	9.0	7	8	7	2	10-0	5	.241
2001— Greenville (Sou.)		3	5	.375	4.64	1.37	34	7	0	0	...	0-...	73.2	56	40	38	9	45-2	93	.214
2002— West Tenn (Sou.)		1	0	1.000	7.20	1.93	11	0	0	0	...	0-...	15.0	9	12	12	2	20-0	20	.170
— Wichita (Texas)		3	0	1.000	3.32	1.23	23	1	0	0	...	2-...	40.2	29	16	15	1	21-3	52	.199
2003—		Did not play.																		
2004— Las Vegas (PCL)		1	2	.333	7.83	1.74	14	1	0	0	...	0-...	23.0	20	20	20	5	20-0	23	.227
— Jacksonville (Sou.)		1	1	.500	5.59	1.76	3	2	0	0	...	0-...	9.2	10	7	6	4	7-0	12	.270
— Tucson (PCL)		1	0	1.000	5.68	1.56	28	0	0	0	...	3-...	44.1	44	28	28	10	25-1	41	.249
2005— Tucson (PCL)		2	3	.400	6.48	1.56	27	0	0	0	2	2-4	33.1	37	24	24	6	15-0	42	.274
— Oaxaca (Mex.)		4	0	1.000	1.35	0.75	18	0	0	0	...	10-13	20.0	10	4	3	0	5-0	32	.141
2006— Ottawa (Int'l)		9	4	.692	2.48	1.13	46	0	0	0	11	1-4	65.1	54	22	18	4	20-6	78	.220
— Baltimore (A.L.)		0	0	...	10.13	2.00	7	0	0	0	...	0-0	8.0	10	10	9	1	6-1	6	.294
Major League totals (1 year)		0	0	...	10.13	2.00	7	0	0	0	...	0-0	8.0	10	10	9	1	6-1	6	.294

2006 LEFTY-RIGHTY SPLITS

vs.	Avg.	AB	H	2B	3B	HR	RBI	BB	SO	OBP	Slg.	vs.	Avg.	AB	H	2B	3B	HR	RBI	BB	SO	OBP	Slg.
L	.286	14	4	2	0	1	4	5	1	.474	.643	R	.300	20	6	4	0	0	2	1	5	.348	.500

ACCARDO, JEREMY — P

PERSONAL: Born December 18, 1981, in Phoenix. ... 6-2/190. ... Throws right, bats right. ... Full name: Jeremy Lee Accardo. ... High school: Mesa (Ariz.). ... College: Illinois State. **TRANSACTIONS/CAREER NOTES:** Signed as a non-drafted free agent by San Francisco Giants organization (August 12, 2003). ... Traded by Giants to Toronto Blue Jays for IF Shea Hillenbrand and P Vinnie Chulk (July 22, 2006). **CAREER HITTING:** 1-for-7 (.143), 0 R, 0 2B, 0 3B, 0 HR, 0 RBI.

Year	Team (League)	W	L	Pct.	ERA	WHIP	G	GS	CG	ShO	Hld.	Sv.-Opp.	IP	H	R	ER	HR	BB-IBB	SO	Avg.
2004—	San Jose (Calif.)	1	2	.333	4.25	1.31	50	0	0	0	...	27-...	55.0	57	28	26	3	15-1	43	.257
—	Norwich (East.)	2	1	.667	5.40	1.32	7	0	0	0	...	1-...	8.1	9	5	5	1	2-1	5	.265
2005—	Norwich (East.)	1	0	1.000	0.93	0.93	8	0	0	0	0	4-5	9.2	8	3	1	0	1-0	15	.211
—	San Jose (Calif.)	0	0	...	0.00	1.00	2	0	0	0	0	1-1	2.0	1	0	0	0	1-0	3	.143
—	Fresno (PCL)	2	0	1.000	1.95	1.08	25	0	0	0	5	3-3	32.1	25	7	7	0	10-1	30	.214
—	San Francisco (N.L.)	1	5	.167	3.94	1.18	28	0	0	0	4	0-1	29.2	26	13	13	2	9-1	16	.232
2006—	Fresno (PCL)	0	0	...	1.80	1.20	3	0	0	0	0	0-0	5.0	5	1	1	0	1-0	8	.278
—	San Francisco (N.L.)	1	3	.250	4.91	1.21	38	0	0	0	8	3-6	40.1	38	23	22	2	11-3	40	.247
—	Toronto (A.L.)	1	1	.500	5.97	1.64	27	0	0	0	2	0-2	28.2	38	19	19	5	9-2	14	.325
American League totals (1 year)		1	1	.500	5.97	1.64	27	0	0	0	2	0-2	28.2	38	19	19	5	9-2	14	.325
National League totals (2 years)		2	8	.200	4.50	1.20	66	0	0	0	12	3-7	70.0	64	36	35	4	20-4	56	.241
Major League totals (2 years)		3	9	.250	4.93	1.33	93	0	0	0	14	3-9	98.2	102	55	54	9	29-6	70	.266

2006 LEFTY-RIGHTY SPLITS

vs.	Avg.	AB	H	2B	3B	HR	RBI	BB	SO	OBP	Slg.	vs.	Avg.	AB	H	2B	3B	HR	RBI	BB	SO	OBP	Slg.
L	.241	108	26	4	0	3	12	13	25	.322	.361	R	.307	163	50	11	1	4	34	7	29	.331	.460

ADAMS, MIKE — P

PERSONAL: Born July 29, 1978, in Corpus Christi, Texas. ... 6-5/190. ... Throws right, bats right. ... Full name: Jon Michael Adams. ... High school: Sinton (Texas). ... College: Texas A&M-Kingsville. **TRANSACTIONS/CAREER NOTES:** Signed as a non-drafted free agent by Milwaukee Brewers organization (May 15, 2001). ... Traded by Brewers to New York Mets for P Geremi Gonzalez (May 26, 2006). ... Claimed on waivers by Cleveland Indians (July 7, 2006). ... Traded by Indians to San Diego Padres for P Brian Sikorski (July 18, 2006). **CAREER HITTING:** 0-for-0 (.000), 0 R, 0 2B, 0 3B, 0 HR, 0 RBI.

Year	Team (League)	W	L	Pct.	ERA	WHIP	G	GS	CG	ShO	Hld.	Sv.-Opp.	IP	H	R	ER	HR	BB-IBB	SO	Avg.
2001—	Ogden (Pion.)	2	2	.500	2.81	1.00	23	0	0	0	...	12-...	32.0	26	10	10	4	6-1	44	.220
2002—	Beloit (Midw.)	0	0	...	2.93	0.98	11	0	0	0	...	5-...	15.1	13	6	5	1	2-0	21	.228
—	High Desert (Calif.)	2	1	.667	2.57	1.14	10	0	0	0	...	5-...	14.0	9	6	4	2	7-0	23	.173
—	Huntsville (Sou.)	1	0	1.000	3.38	1.39	13	0	0	0	...	1-...	18.2	14	11	7	3	12-0	17	.209
2003—	Huntsville (Sou.)	3	7	.300	3.15	1.22	45	0	0	0	...	14-...	74.1	58	30	26	6	33-1	83	.208
2004—	Indianapolis (Int'l)	2	0	1.000	2.61	0.87	10	2	0	0	...	0-...	31.0	23	10	9	4	3-0	37	.209
—	Milwaukee (N.L.)	2	3	.400	3.40	1.21	46	0	0	0	12	0-5	53.0	50	21	20	5	14-2	39	.248
2005—	Milwaukee (N.L.)	0	1	.000	2.70	1.65	13	0	0	0	2	1-2	13.1	12	4	4	2	10-1	14	.235
—	Nashville (PCL)	3	4	.429	5.75	1.31	26	0	0	0	4	2-5	36.0	35	23	23	3	12-0	45	.263
2006—	Norfolk (Int'l)	0	0	...	4.91	1.36	13	0	0	0	2	0-0	14.2	13	8	8	0	7-0	12	.245
—	Portland (PCL)	0	2	.000	4.18	1.52	17	0	0	0	2	0-1	23.2	29	16	11	1	7-0	15	.299
—	Milwaukee (N.L.)	0	0	...	11.57	2.57	2	0	0	0	0	0-0	2.1	4	3	3	1	2-0	1	.364
—	Nashville (PCL)	0	0	.500	3.31	1.53	15	0	0	0	1	2-3	16.1	17	8	6	2	8-0	18	.274
—	Buffalo (Int'l)	0	0	...	1.93	0.86	3	0	0	0	0	0-0	4.2	4	1	1	0	0-0	3	.250
Major League totals (3 years)		2	4	.333	3.54	1.34	61	0	0	0	14	1-7	68.2	66	28	27	8	26-3	54	.250

2006 LEFTY-RIGHTY SPLITS

vs.	Avg.	AB	H	2B	3B	HR	RBI	BB	SO	OBP	Slg.	vs.	Avg.	AB	H	2B	3B	HR	RBI	BB	SO	OBP	Slg.
L	.000	4	0	0	0	0	0	1	1	.200	.000	R	.571	7	4	1	0	1	6	1	0	.625	1.143

ADAMS, RUSS — 2B/SS

PERSONAL: Born August 30, 1980, in Laurinburg, N.C. ... 6-1/180. ... Bats left, throws right. ... Full name: Russ Moore Adams. ... High school: Scotland (Laurinburg, N.C.). ... College: North Carolina. **TRANSACTIONS/CAREER NOTES:** Selected by Toronto Blue Jays organization in first round (14th pick overall) of 2002 free-agent draft. **2006 GAMES PLAYED BY POSITION (MLB):** 2B—50, SS—36, DH—1.

Year	Team (League)	Pos.	G	AB	R	H	2B	3B	HR	RBI	BB	SO	HBP	GDP	SB-CS	Avg.	OBP	SLG	OPS	E	Avg.
2002—	Auburn (NY-Penn)	SS	30	113	25	40	7	3	0	16	24	11	1	1	13-1	.354	.464	.469	.933	5	.963
—	Dunedin (Fla. St.)	SS	37	147	23	34	4	2	1	12	18	17	2	1	5-2	.231	.321	.306	.628	9	.947
2003—	Dunedin (Fla. St.)	SS	68	258	50	72	9	5	3	16	38	27	6	5	9-2	.279	.380	.388	.768	19	.941
—	New Haven (East.)	SS	65	271	42	75	10	4	4	26	30	37	0	5	8-1	.277	.349	.387	.736	16	.944
2004—	Syracuse (Int'l)	SS-DH	122	483	58	139	37	3	5	54	45	62	5	9	6-2	.288	.351	.408	.753	33	.939
—	Toronto (A.L.)	SS	22	72	10	22	2	1	4	10	5	5	1	3	1-0	.306	.359	.528	.887	5	.936
2005—	Toronto (A.L.)	SS	139	481	68	123	27	5	8	63	50	57	3	5	11-2	.256	.325	.383	.707	26	.952
2006—	Syracuse (Int'l)		42	161	21	50	9	3	0	15	17	23	0	3	3-2	.311	.374	.404	.778	9	.951
—	Toronto (A.L.)	2B-SS-DH	90	251	31	55	14	1	3	28	22	41	1	5	1-2	.219	.282	.319	.600	12	.960
Major League totals (3 years)			251	804	109	200	43	7	15	101	77	103	5	13	13-4	.249	.314	.376	.690	43	.953

2006 LEFTY-RIGHTY SPLITS

vs.	Avg.	AB	H	2B	3B	HR	RBI	BB	SO	OBP	Slg.	vs.	Avg.	AB	H	2B	3B	HR	RBI	BB	SO	OBP	Slg.
L	.135	37	5	0	0	1	4	3	7	.200	.216	R	.234	214	50	14	1	2	24	19	34	.295	.336

ADKINS, JON — P

PERSONAL: Born August 30, 1977, in Huntington, W.Va. ... 5-11/210. ... Throws right, bats left. ... Full name: Jonathan Scott Adkins. ... High school: Wayne (W.Va.). ... College: Oklahoma State. **TRANSACTIONS/CAREER NOTES:** Selected by Oakland Athletics organization in ninth round of 1998 free-agent draft. ... Traded by A's to Chicago White Sox for 2B Ray Durham and cash (July 25, 2002). ... Signed as a free agent by San Diego Padres organization (March 13, 2006). **CAREER HITTING:** 0-for-1 (.000), 0 R, 0 2B, 0 3B, 0 HR, 0 RBI.

Year	Team (League)	W	L	Pct.	ERA	WHIP	G	GS	CG	ShO	Hld.	Sv.-Opp.	IP	H	R	ER	HR	BB-IBB	SO	Avg.
1998—					Did not play.																
1999—	Modesto (California)	9	5	.643	4.76	1.40	26	15	0	0	...	1-...	102.0	113	65	54	6	30-1	93	.276
2000—	Ariz. A's (Ariz.)	1	1	.500	3.00	1.20	4	2	0	0	...	0-...	15.0	15	6	5	1	3-0	17	.234
—	Sacramento (PCL)	0	1	.000	9.00	1.75	1	1	0	0	...	0-...	4.0	6	4	4	2	1-0	2	.333
—	Modesto (California)	5	2	.714	1.81	1.17	9	7	1	0	...	0-...	49.2	41	17	10	1	17-0	38	.225
2001—	Midland (Texas)	8	8	.500	4.46	1.33	24	24	1	0	...	0-...	137.1	147	71	68	9	36-1	74	.273

Year Team (League)	W	L	Pct.	ERA	WHIP	G	GS	CG	ShO	Hld.	Sv.-Opp.	IP	H	R	ER	HR	BB-IBB	SO	Avg.
—Sacramento (PCL)	1	0	1.000	4.26	1.97	3	2	0	0	...	0-...	12.2	17	9	6	1	8-0	7	.333
2002— Modesto (California)	0	1	.000	8.10	1.80	1	1	0	0	...	0-...	6.2	11	7	6	0	1-0	4	.379
—Sacramento (PCL)	7	6	.538	6.03	1.77	20	20	0	0	...	0-...	97.0	139	74	65	9	33-0	76	.338
—Charlotte (Int'l)	4	2	.667	3.69	1.27	8	7	1	0	...	0-...	46.1	47	20	19	4	12-0	31	.260
2003— Charlotte (Int'l)	7	8	.467	3.96	1.25	26	19	1	1	...	1-...	122.2	119	65	54	11	34-1	59	.254
—Chicago (A.L.)	0	0	...	4.82	1.61	4	0	0	0	0	0-0	9.1	8	5	5	1	7-0	3	.250
2004— Chicago (A.L.)	2	3	.400	4.65	1.53	50	0	0	0	5	0-0	62.0	75	35	32	13	20-3	44	.305
2005— Chicago (A.L.)	0	1	.000	8.64	2.04	5	0	0	0	0	0-0	8.1	13	8	8	0	4-2	1	.351
—Charlotte (Int'l)	4	9	.308	5.37	1.50	23	21	0	0	0	0-0	127.1	148	81	76	20	43-1	92	.295
2006— Portland (PCL)	1	0	1.000	1.38	1.15	13	0	0	0	0	7-7	13.0	12	2	2	0	3-0	11	.255
—San Diego (N.L.)	2	1	.667	3.98	1.38	55	0	0	0	8	0-0	54.1	55	26	24	3	20-4	30	.271
American League totals (3 years)	2	4	.333	5.08	1.59	59	0	0	0	5	0-0	79.2	96	48	45	14	31-5	48	.305
National League totals (1 year)	2	1	.667	3.98	1.38	55	0	0	0	8	0-0	54.1	55	26	24	3	20-4	30	.271
Major League totals (4 years)	4	5	.444	4.63	1.51	114	0	0	0	13	0-0	134.0	151	74	69	17	51-9	78	.292

2006 LEFTY-RIGHTY SPLITS

vs.	Avg.	AB	H	2B	3B	HR	RBI	BB	SO	OBP	Slg.	vs.	Avg.	AB	H	2B	3B	HR	RBI	BB	SO	OBP	Slg.
L	.287	87	25	3	1	1	14	12	10	.370	.379	R	.259	116	30	11	0	2	11	8	20	.315	.405

AFFELDT, JEREMY — P

PERSONAL: Born June 6, 1979, in Phoenix. ... 6-4/215. ... Throws left, bats left. ... Full name: Jeremy David Affeldt. ... Name pronounced: AFF-felt. ... High school: Northwest Christian (Spokane, Wash.). **TRANSACTIONS/CAREER NOTES:** Selected by Kansas City Royals organization in third round of 1997 free-agent draft. ... On disabled list (June 9-August 1, 2002); included rehabilitation assignment to Omaha. ... On disabled list (April 20-May 6, 2003; and June 27-August 21, 2004); included rehabilitation assignment to Omaha. ... On disabled list (April 16-June 4; and June 20-July 7, 2005); included rehabilitation assignments to Omaha. ... Traded by Royals with P Denny Bautista to Colorado Rockies for IF Ryan Shealy and P Scott Dohmann (July 31, 2006).

CAREER HITTING: 2-for-9 (.222), 0 R, 0 2B, 0 3B, 0 HR, 2 RBI.

Year Team (League)	W	L	Pct.	ERA	WHIP	G	GS	CG	ShO	Hld.	Sv.-Opp.	IP	H	R	ER	HR	BB-IBB	SO	Avg.
1997— GC Royals (GCL)	2	0	1.000	4.50	1.38	10	9	0	0	...	0-...	40.0	34	24	20	3	21-0	36	.243
1998— Lansing (Midw.)	0	3	.000	9.53	2.29	6	3	0	0	...	0-...	17.0	27	21	18	1	12-0	8	.355
—GC Royals (GCL)	4	3	.571	2.89	1.32	12	9	0	0	...	0-...	56.0	50	24	18	1	24-0	67	.243
1999— Char., W.Va. (SAL)	7	7	.500	3.83	1.53	27	24	2	1	...	0-...	143.1	140	78	61	4	80-0	111	.261
2000— Wilmington (Caro.)	5	15	.250	4.09	1.47	27	26	0	0	...	0-...	147.1	158	87	67	7	59-0	92	.275
2001— Wichita (Texas)	10	6	.625	3.90	1.37	25	25	0	0	...	0-...	145.1	153	74	63	9	46-0	128	.276
2002— Kansas City (A.L.)	3	4	.429	4.64	1.57	34	7	0	0	1	0-1	77.2	85	41	40	8	37-4	67	.274
—Wichita (Texas)	0	0	...	1.50	0.67	3	3	0	0	...	0-...	6.0	1	1	1	0	3-0	3	.059
2003— Kansas City (A.L.)	7	6	.538	3.93	1.30	36	18	0	0	3	4-4	126.0	126	58	55	12	38-1	98	.261
2004— Omaha (PCL)	0	0	...	0.50	0.50	1	0	0	0	0	3-...	4.0	2	0	0	0	0-0	5	.154
—Kansas City (A.L.)	3	4	.429	4.95	1.61	38	8	0	0	0	13-17	76.1	91	49	42	6	32-2	49	.302
2005— Omaha (PCL)	0	1	.000	6.48	1.80	9	0	0	0	1	0-0	8.1	9	7	6	1	6-0	9	.290
—Kansas City (A.L.)	0	2	.000	5.26	1.71	49	0	0	0	12	0-0	49.2	56	35	29	3	29-2	39	.277
2006— Kansas City (A.L.)	4	6	.400	5.91	1.61	27	9	0	0	2	0-0	70.0	71	51	46	9	42-0	28	.262
—Colorado (N.L.)	4	2	.667	6.91	1.61	27	0	0	0	3	1-3	27.1	31	23	21	4	13-3	20	.277
American League totals (5 years)	17	22	.436	4.77	1.52	184	42	0	0	18	17-22	399.2	429	234	212	38	178-9	281	.274
National League totals (1 year)	4	2	.667	6.91	1.61	27	0	0	0	3	1-3	27.1	31	23	21	4	13-3	20	.277
Major League totals (5 years)	21	24	.467	4.91	1.52	211	42	0	0	21	18-25	427.0	460	257	233	42	191-12	301	.274

2006 LEFTY-RIGHTY SPLITS

vs.	Avg.	AB	H	2B	3B	HR	RBI	BB	SO	OBP	Slg.	vs.	Avg.	AB	H	2B	3B	HR	RBI	BB	SO	OBP	Slg.
L	.212	113	24	5	1	5	19	17	17	.315	.407	R	.289	270	78	13	0	8	50	38	31	.376	.426

AGUILA, CHRIS — OF

PERSONAL: Born February 23, 1979, in Redwood City, Calif. ... 5-11/180. ... Bats right, throws right. ... Full name: Christopher Louis Aguila. ... High school: McQueen (Reno, Nev.). **TRANSACTIONS/CAREER NOTES:** Selected by Florida Marlins organization in third round of 1997 free-agent draft.

2006 GAMES PLAYED BY POSITION (MLB): OF—31, DH—1.

Year Team (League)	Pos.	G	AB	R	H	2B	3B	HR	RBI	BB	SO	HBP	GDP	SB-CS	Avg.	OBP	SLG	OPS	E	Avg.
1997— GC Marlins (GCL)	3B	46	157	12	34	7	0	1	17	21	49	1	3	2-1	.217	.309	.280	.590	22	.843
1998— GC Marlins (GCL)	3B	51	171	29	46	12	3	4	29	19	49	2	4	6-2	.269	.349	.444	.793	15	.850
1999— Kane Co. (Midw.)	OF	122	430	74	105	21	7	15	78	40	127	9	9	14-4	.244	.320	.430	.750	5	.977
2000— Brevard County (Fla. St.)	OF	136	518	68	125	27	3	9	56	37	105	1	11	8-8	.241	.292	.357	.649	5	.985
2001— Brevard County (Fla. St.)	OF	73	272	44	75	15	3	10	34	21	54	2	7	8-4	.276	.328	.463	.791	3	.984
—Portland (East.)	OF	64	241	25	62	16	1	4	29	18	50	3	4	5-7	.257	.312	.382	.694	3	.969
2002— Portland (East.)	OF	130	429	62	126	28	4	6	46	48	101	4	8	14-8	.294	.369	.420	.788	3	.988
2003— GC Marlins (GCL)	OF	1	4	1	3	0	0	1	2	0	1	0	0	0-0	.750	.750	1.500	2.250	0	...
—Carolina (Southern)	OF	93	337	58	108	13	3	11	55	36	67	2	6	6-2	.320	.384	.499	.883	2	.989
2004— Albuquerque (PCL)	OF-DH	97	330	61	103	23	2	11	56	37	82	2	8	8-3	.312	.380	.494	.870	3	.986
—Florida (N.L.)	OF	29	45	10	10	2	1	3	5	2	12	0	0	0-0	.222	.255	.511	.766	2	.909
2005— Albuquerque (PCL)	OF	35	138	27	49	13	2	7	25	14	21	0	3	8-2	.355	.412	.630	1.042	1	1.000
—Florida (N.L.)	OF	65	78	11	19	3	0	0	4	3	19	0	0	0-1	.244	.272	.282	.554	0	1.000
2006— Albuquerque (PCL)		78	302	53	96	15	3	11	61	26	54	1	4	7-3	.318	.369	.497	.866	2	.984
—Florida (N.L.)	OF-DH	47	95	5	22	8	1	0	7	9	26	0	2	2-1	.232	.298	.337	.635	0	1.000
Major League totals (3 years)		141	218	26	51	13	2	3	16	14	57	0	2	2-2	.234	.280	.353	.633	2	.981

2006 LEFTY-RIGHTY SPLITS

vs.	Avg.	AB	H	2B	3B	HR	RBI	BB	SO	OBP	Slg.	vs.	Avg.	AB	H	2B	3B	HR	RBI	BB	SO	OBP	Slg.
L	.195	41	8	2	0	0	1	4	11	.267	.244	R	.259	54	14	6	1	0	6	5	15	.322	.407

ALBERS, MATT — P

PERSONAL: Born January 20, 1983, in Houston, Texas. ... 6-0/205. ... Throws right, bats left. ... Full name: Matthew James Albers. ... Junior College: San Jacinto (Tex.). **TRANSACTIONS/CAREER NOTES:** Selected by Houston Astros organization in 23rd round of 2001 free-agent draft.

CAREER HITTING: 0-for-4 (.000), 0 R, 0 2B, 0 3B, 0 HR, 0 RBI.

Year Team (League)	W	L	Pct.	ERA	WHIP	G	GS	CG	ShO	Hld.	Sv.-Opp.	IP	H	R	ER	HR	BB-IBB	SO	Avg.
2002— Martinsville (App.)	2	3	.400	5.13	1.66	13	13	0	0	...	0-...	59.2	61	38	34	2	38-0	72	.274

A

Year Team (League)	W	L	Pct.	ERA	WHIP	G	GS	CG	ShO	Hld.	Sv.-Opp.	IP	H	R	ER	HR	BB-IBB	SO	Avg.
2003—Tri-City (N.Y.-Penn.)	5	4	.556	2.92	1.09	15	14	0	0	...	0-...	86.1	69	37	28	1	25-0	94	.214
2004—Lexington (S. Atl.)	8	3	.727	3.31	1.37	22	21	0	0	...	0-...	111.1	95	51	41	3	57-0	140	.237
2005—Salem (Carol.)	8	12	.400	4.66	1.50	28	27	0	0		0-0	148.2	161	86	77	15	62-0	146	.278
2006—Corpus Christi (Texas)	10	2	.833	2.17	1.23	19	19	0	0		0-0	116.0	96	40	28	4	47-2	95	.223
—Round Rock (PCL)	2	1	.667	3.96	1.36	4	4	0	0		0-0	25.0	24	11	11	2	10-0	26	.253
—Houston (N.L.)	0	2	.000	6.00	1.60	4	2	0	0		0-0	15.0	17	10	10	1	7-0	11	.298
Major League totals (1 year)	0	2	.000	6.00	1.60	4	2	0	0		0-0	15.0	17	10	10	1	7-0	11	.298

2006 LEFTY-RIGHTY SPLITS

vs.	Avg.	AB	H	2B	3B	HR	RBI	BB	SO	OBP	Slg.	vs.	Avg.	AB	H	2B	3B	HR	RBI	BB	SO	OBP	Slg.
L	.333	27	9	3	0	0	4	7	6	.471	.444	R	.267	30	8	1	0	1	5	0	5	.267	.400

ALEXANDER, MANNY — 3B/SS

PERSONAL: Born March 20, 1971, in San Pedro de Macoris, Dominican Republic. ... 5-10/180. ... Bats right, throws right. ... Full name: Manuel Alexander. **TRANSAC-TIONS/CAREER NOTES:** Signed as a non-drafted free agent by Baltimore Orioles organization (February 4, 1988). ... On disabled list (March 25-May 2, 1995). ... Traded by Orioles with IF Scott McClain to New York Mets for P Hector Ramirez (March 22, 1997). ... On disabled list (June 13-July 10 and July 28-August 11, 1997). ... Traded by Mets to Chicago Cubs (August 14, 1997), completing deal in which Mets traded OF Lance Johnson and two players to be named to Cubs for OF Brian McRae and Ps Mel Rojas and Turk Wendell (August 8, 1997); Cubs acquired P Mark Clark to complete deal (August 11, 1997). ... Traded by Cubs to Boston Red Sox for OF Damon Buford (December 10, 1999). ... On disabled list (September 29, 2000-remainder of season). ... Signed as a free agent by Seattle Mariners organization (February 16, 2001). ... Signed as a free agent by New York Yankees organization (February 4, 2002). ... Released by Yankees (March 13, 2002). ... Acquired by Milwaukee Brewers organization from Cordoba of the Mexican League (August 10, 2002). ... Traded by Brewers to Texas Rangers for cash (March 25, 2003). ... Traded by Rangers to San Diego Padres for P Juan Jiminez (August 31, 2005). ... Released by Padres (October 11, 2005). **STATISTICAL NOTES:** Career major league grand slams: 1. ... Career major league pitching: 0-0, 67.5 ERA, 1 G, 0.2 IP, 1 H, 5 R, 5 ER, 4 BB, 0 SO.

2006 GAMES PLAYED BY POSITION (MLB): 3B—13, SS—9.

Year Team (League)	Pos.	G	AB	R	H	2B	3B	HR	RBI	BB	SO	HBP	GDP	SB-CS	Avg.	OBP	SLG	OPS	E	Avg.
1988—					Did not play.														
1989—Bluefield (Appal.)	SS	65	274	49	85	13	2	2	34	20	49	3	2	19-8	.310	.361	.394	.755	32	.908
1990—Wausau (Midw.)	SS	44	152	16	27	3	1	0	11	12	41	1	2	8-3	.178	.238	.211	.449	11	.938
1991—Hagerstown (East.)	SS	3	9	3	3	1	0	0	2	1	3	1	0	0-0	.333	.417	.444	.861	0	1.000
—Frederick (Carolina)	SS	134	548	81	143	17	3	3	42	44	68	2	4	47-14	.261	.318	.319	.637	32	.951
1992—Hagerstown (East.)	SS	127	499	69	129	23	8	2	41	25	62	6	10	43-12	.259	.300	.349	.648	36	.929
—Rochester (Int'l)	SS	6	24	3	7	1	0	0	3	1	3	0	0	2-2	.292	.320	.333	.653	1	.974
—Baltimore (A.L.)	SS	4	5	1	1	0	0	0	0	0	3	0	0	0-0	.200	.200	.200	.400	0	1.000
1993—Rochester (Int'l)	SS	120	471	55	115	23	8	6	51	22	60	1	11	19-7	.244	.283	.365	.648	18	.966
—Baltimore (A.L.)	DH	3	0	1	0	0	0	0	0	0	0	0	0	0-0	...	...	...	...	...	...
1994—Rochester (Int'l)	SS-2B	111	426	63	106	23	6	6	39	16	67	3	7	30-8	.249	.278	.373	.651	33	.939
1995—Baltimore (A.L.)	2B-SS-3B-DH	94	242	35	57	9	1	3	23	20	30	2	1	11-4	.236	.294	.318	.612	10	.969
1996—Baltimore (A.L.)	SS-2B-3B-OF-DH-P	54	68	6	7	0	0	0	3	4	27	0	0	3-3	.103	.141	.103	.244	5	.936
1997—New York (N.L.)	2B-SS-3B	54	149	26	37	9	3	2	15	9	38	1	3	11-0	.248	.291	.389	.680	4	.979
—St. Lucie (Fla. St.)	SS	1	4	0	1	0	0	0	0	0	1	0	0	0-0	.250	.250	.250	.500	0	1.000
—Chicago (N.L.)		33	99	11	29	1	1		7	8	16	2	3	2-1	.293	.346	.374	.720	7	.949
1998—Chicago (N.L.)	SS-2B-3B-DH-OF	108	264	34	60	10	1	5	25	18	66	1		4-1	.227	.277	.330	.606	7	.970
1999—Chicago (N.L.)	OF	90	177	17	48	11	2	0	15	10	38	0	1	4-0	.271	.309	.356	.664	7	.954
2000—Boston (A.L.)	3B-SS-2B-DH	101	194	30	41	4	3	4	19	13	41	0	1	2-0	.211	.261	.325	.586	7	.962
2001—Tacoma (PCL)	2B-SS-3B-OF	97	344	46	97	26	2	8	51	14	55	2	6	5-9	.282	.311	.439	.750	13	.961
2002—Indianapolis (Int'l)	3B-SS-2B	22	85	11	25	6	1	1	7	4	17	0	2	5-3	.294	.326	.424	.749	3	.944
2003—Oklahoma (PCL)	SS-2B-3B-DH	120	450	52	116	17	6	4	48	30	75	4	11	27-10	.258	.309	.349	.658	15	.973
2004—Oklahoma (PCL)	SS	93	361	65	104	29	4	10	49	27	45	1	6	8-4	.288	.338	.474	.811	18	.965
—Texas (A.L.)	2B-SS-3B	21	21	3	5	2	0	0	3	1	7	0	0	0-0	.238	.273	.333	.606	3	.914
2005—Oklahoma (PCL)	SS-3B-1B-DH-OF-P	108	417	64	129	23	6	12	67	38	66	4	8	27-9	.309	.368	.480	.847	23	.955
—Portland (PCL)	SS	4	16	0	4	2	0	0	1	1	4	0	0	0-1	.250	.294	.375	.669	1	.933
—San Diego (N.L.)	2B-SS-1B-3B	10	18	0	2	1	0	0	2	5	1	0	0	0-0	.111	.238	.167	.405	1	.950
2006—Portland (PCL)		102	430	78	114	21	0	7	37	35	58	3	13	14-4	.265	.323	.363	.686	11	.977
—San Diego (N.L.)	3B-SS	22	34	2	6	1	1	0	4	2	5	0	0	0-0	.176	.216	.265	.481	2	.960
American League totals (6 years)		277	530	76	111	15	4	7	49	37	108	2	4	16-7	.209	.264	.292	.556	25	.960
National League totals (5 years)		317	741	90	182	35	8	8	66	49	168	5	13	21-3	.246	.295	.347	.642	28	.964
Major League totals (11 years)		594	1271	166	293	50	12	15	115	86	276	7	17	37-10	.231	.282	.324	.606	53	.962

DIVISION SERIES RECORD

Year Team (League)	Pos.	G	AB	R	H	2B	3B	HR	RBI	BB	SO	HBP	GDP	SB-CS	Avg.	OBP	SLG	OPS	E	Avg.
1996—Baltimore (A.L.)	DH	3	0	2	0	0	0	0	0	0	0	0	0	0-0	...	...	...	...	0	...
1998—Chicago (N.L.)	SS	2	5	0	0	0	0	0	0	1	0	0	0	0-0	.000	.000	.000	.000	0	1.000
Division series totals (2 years)		5	5	2	0	0	0	0	0	1	0	0	0	0-0	.000	.000	.000	.000	0	1.000

2006 LEFTY-RIGHTY SPLITS

vs.	Avg.	AB	H	2B	3B	HR	RBI	BB	SO	OBP	Slg.	vs.	Avg.	AB	H	2B	3B	HR	RBI	BB	SO	OBP	Slg.
L	.182	22	4	1	1	0	4	2	1	.240	.318	R	.167	12	2	0	0	0	0	0	3	.167	.167

ALFONSECA, ANTONIO — P

PERSONAL: Born April 16, 1972, in La Romana, Dominican Republic. ... 6-5/250. ... Throws right, bats right. ... Name pronounced: al-fon-SAY-kah.
TRANSACTIONS/CAREER NOTES: Signed as a non-drafted free agent by Montreal Expos organization (July 3, 1989). ... Selected by Florida Marlins organization from Expos organization in Rule 5 minor league draft (December 13, 1993). ... On disabled list (May 15-June 15, 1995; and July 12-September 3, 1996; and May 14-31, 1998). ... Traded by Marlins with P Matt Clement to Chicago Cubs for Ps Julian Tavarez, Jose Cueto and Dontrelle Willis and C Ryan Jorgensen (March 27, 2002). ... On disabled list (March 21-May 5, 2003); included rehabilitation assignment to Iowa. ... On suspended list (September 5-12, 2003). ... Signed as a free agent by Atlanta Braves (December 23,

2003). ... Signed as a free agent by Marlins (December 17, 2004). ... On disabled list (April 22-July 26, 2005); included rehabilitation assignment to Jupiter. ... Signed as free agent by Texas Rangers organization (January 27, 2006). ... On disabled list (May 19-June 6, 2006); included rehabilitation assignments to Frisco and Oklahoma. ... Released by Rangers (June 19, 2006). **HONORS:** Named N.L. Fireman of the Year by THE SPORTING NEWS (2000).
CAREER HITTING: 2-for-13 (.154), 0 R, 0 2B, 0 3B, 0 HR, 2 RBI.

Year Team (League)	W	L	Pct.	ERA	WHIP	G	GS	CG	ShO	Hld.	Sv.-Opp.	IP	H	R	ER	HR	BB-IBB	SO	Avg.
1990—Dom. Expos (DSL)	3	5	.375	3.60	1.53	13	13	1	0	...	0-...	60.0	60	29	24	...	32-...	19	...
1991—GC Expos (GCL)	3	3	.500	3.88	1.39	11	10	0	0	...	0-...	51.0	46	33	22	2	25-0	38	.240
1992—GC Expos (GCL)	3	4	.429	3.68	1.36	12	10	1	1	...	0-...	66.0	55	31	27	0	35-0	62	.233
1993—Jamestown (NYP)	2	2	.500	6.15	1.57	15	4	0	0	...	1-...	33.2	31	26	23	3	22-1	29	.250
1994—Kane Co. (Midw.)	6	5	.545	4.07	1.15	32	9	0	0	...	0-...	86.1	78	41	39	5	21-1	74	.234
1995—Portland (East.)	9	3	.750	3.64	1.28	19	17	1	0	...	0-...	96.1	81	43	39	6	42-1	75	.229
1996—Charlotte (Int'l)	4	4	.500	5.53	1.51	14	13	0	0	...	1-...	71.2	86	47	44	6	22-0	51	.296
1997—Charlotte (Int'l)	7	2	.778	4.32	1.34	46	0	0	0	...	7-...	58.1	58	34	28	8	20-3	45	.264
— Florida (N.L.)	1	3	.250	4.91	1.79	17	0	0	0	...	0-2	25.2	36	16	14	3	10-3	19	.324
1998—Florida (N.L.)	4	6	.400	4.08	1.53	58	0	0	0	9	8-14	70.2	75	36	32	10	33-9	46	.281
1999—Florida (N.L.)	4	5	.444	3.24	1.39	73	0	0	0	...	21-25	77.2	79	28	28	4	29-6	46	.274
2000—Florida (N.L.)	5	6	.455	4.24	1.51	68	0	0	0	...	*45-49	70.0	82	35	33	7	24-3	47	.291
2001—Florida (N.L.)	4	4	.500	3.06	1.35	58	0	0	0	...	28-34	61.2	68	24	21	6	15-3	40	.281
2002—Chicago (N.L.)	2	5	.286	4.00	1.47	66	0	0	0	...	19-28	74.1	73	34	33	5	36-3	61	.257
2003—Iowa (PCL)	0	1	.000	4.91	1.90	3	0	0	0	...	0-...	3.2	6	2	2	0	1-0	5	.353
— Chicago (N.L.)	3	1	.750	5.83	1.55	60	0	0	0	9	0-4	66.1	76	43	43	7	27-3	51	.290
2004—Atlanta (N.L.)	6	4	.600	2.57	1.34	79	0	0	0	13	0-1	73.2	71	24	21	5	28-5	45	.255
2005—Jupiter (Fla. St.)	0	0	...	3.00	1.00	3	1	0	0	...	0-0	3.0	3	1	1	1	0-0	4	.300
— Florida (N.L.)	1	1	.500	4.94	1.57	33	0	0	0	...	0-2	27.1	29	15	15	2	14-4	16	.299
2006—Oklahoma (PCL)	0	1	.000	6.00	1.67	3	0	0	0	1	0-0	3.0	4	2	2	0	1-0	1	.400
— Frisco (Texas)	0	0	...	0.00	0.00	1	0	0	0	0	0-0	1.0	0	0	0	0	0-0	0	...
— Texas (A.L.)	0	0	...	5.63	1.88	19	0	0	0	8	0-0	16.0	23	10	10	3	7-0	5	.348
American League totals (1 year)	0	0	...	5.63	1.88	19	0	0	0	8	0-0	16.0	23	10	10	3	7-0	5	.348
National League totals (9 years)	30	35	.462	3.95	1.47	512	0	0	0	44	121-159	547.1	589	255	240	49	216-39	371	.279
Major League totals (10 years)	30	35	.462	3.99	1.48	531	0	0	0	52	121-159	563.1	612	265	250	52	223-39	376	.281

DIVISION SERIES RECORD

Year Team (League)	W	L	Pct.	ERA	WHIP	G	GS	CG	ShO	Hld.	Sv.-Opp.	IP	H	R	ER	HR	BB-IBB	SO	Avg.
1997—Florida (N.L.)	Did not play.																		
2003—Chicago (N.L.)	0	0	...	0.00	1.00	1	0	0	0	0	0-0	1.0	1	0	0	0	0-0	0	.250
2004—Atlanta (N.L.)	1	0	1.000	4.91	1.09	4	0	0	0	0	0-0	3.2	2	2	2	0	2-0	0	.154
Division series totals (2 years)	1	0	1.000	3.86	1.07	5	0	0	0	0	0-0	4.2	3	2	2	0	2-0	0	.176

CHAMPIONSHIP SERIES RECORD

Year Team (League)	W	L	Pct.	ERA	WHIP	G	GS	CG	ShO	Hld.	Sv.-Opp.	IP	H	R	ER	HR	BB-IBB	SO	Avg.
1997—Florida (N.L.)	Did not play.																		
2003—Chicago (N.L.)	0	0	...	0.00	1.71	3	0	0	0	0	0-0	2.1	2	0	0	0	2-1	0	.333

WORLD SERIES RECORD

Year Team (League)	W	L	Pct.	ERA	WHIP	G	GS	CG	ShO	Hld.	Sv.-Opp.	IP	H	R	ER	HR	BB-IBB	SO	Avg.
1997—Florida (N.L.)	0	0	...	0.00	1.11	3	0	0	0	0	0-0	6.1	6	0	0	0	1-0	5	.250

2006 LEFTY-RIGHTY SPLITS

vs.	Avg.	AB	H	2B	3B	HR	RBI	BB	SO	OBP	Slg.	vs.	Avg.	AB	H	2B	3B	HR	RBI	BB	SO	OBP	Slg.
L	.452	31	14	1	0	3	8	3	0	.486	.774	R	.257	35	9	3	0	3	4	5		.333	.343

ALFONZO, EDGARDO   3B/2B

PERSONAL: Born November 8, 1973, in Soapire, Venezuela. ... 5-11/187. ... Bats right, throws right. ... Full name: Edgardo Antonio Alfonzo. ... High school: Cecilio Acosto (Venezuela). ... Cousin of Eliezer Alfonzo, catcher, San Francisco Giants. **TRANSACTIONS/CAREER NOTES:** Signed as non-drafted free agent by New York Mets organization (February 19, 1991). ... On disabled list (August 11, 1995-remainder of season; and May 4-19, 1998). ... On disabled list (June 14-July 3, 2001); included rehabilitation assignment to Norfolk. ... On disabled list (August 4-24, 2002). ... Signed as a free agent by San Francisco Giants (December 15, 2002). ... On disabled list (June 14-July 22, 2005); included rehabilitation assignment to Fresno. ... Traded by Giants to Los Angeles Angels of Anaheim for OF Steve Finley (December 21, 2005). ... Released by Angels (May 20, 2006). ... Signed by Toronto Blues Jays organization (May 25, 2006). ... Released by Blue Jays (June 12, 2006). ... Signed by Bridgeport of independent Atlantic league (July 7, 2006). ... Signed by Mets organization (July 15, 2006). **RECORDS:** Shares major league record for runs scored, 9-inning game (6, August 30, 1999). **HONORS:** Named second baseman on THE SPORTING NEWS N.L. All-Star team (1999). **STATISTICAL NOTES:** Hit three home runs in one game (August 30, 1999). ... Career major league grand slams: 4.
2006 GAMES PLAYED BY POSITION (MLB): 3B—15, 2B—12, 1B—2, DH—1.

Year Team (League)	Pos.	G	AB	R	H	2B	3B	HR	RBI	BB	SO	HBP	GDP	SB-CS	Avg.	OBP	SLG	OPS	E	Avg.
1991—GC Mets (GCL)	2B-3B-SS	54	175	29	58	8	4	0	27	34	12	2	1	6-4	.331	.433	.423	.856	9	.958
1992—St. Lucie (Fla. St.)	2B	4	5	0	0	0	0	0	0	0	0	0	0	0-0	.000	.000	.000	.000	0	1.000
— Pittsfield (NYP)	SS	74	298	44	106	13	5	1	44	18	31	0	6	7-5	.356	.388	.443	.830	26	.933
1993—St. Lucie (Fla. St.)	SS	128	494	75	145	18	3	11	86	57	51	5	13	26-16	.294	.366	.409	.774	29	.954
1994—Binghamton (East.)	1B-2B-SS	127	498	89	146	34	2	15	75	64	55	0	9	14-11	.293	.369	.460	.829	27	.958
1995—New York (N.L.)	3B-2B-SS	101	335	26	93	13	5	4	41	12	37	1	7	1-1	.278	.301	.382	.683	7	.973
1996—New York (N.L.)	2B-3B-SS	123	368	36	96	15	2	4	40	25	56	0	4	2-0	.261	.304	.345	.649	11	.973
1997—New York (N.L.)	3B-SS-2B	151	518	84	163	27	2	10	72	63	56	6	4	11-6	.315	.391	.432	.823	12	.970
1998—New York (N.L.)	3B-SS	144	557	94	155	28	2	17	78	65	77	3	11	8-3	.278	.355	.427	.782	9	.976
1999—New York (N.L.)	2B	158	628	123	191	41	1	27	108	85	85	3	14	9-2	.304	.385	.502	.886	5	.993
2000—New York (N.L.)	2B-DH	150	544	109	176	40	2	25	94	95	70	5	12	3-2	.324	.425	.542	.967	10	.985
2001—New York (N.L.)	2B	124	457	64	111	22	0	17	49	51	62	5	7	5-0	.243	.322	.403	.725	7	.987
— Norfolk (Int'l)	2B	2	8	0	0	0	0	0	0	0	0	0	0	0-0	.000	.000	.000	.000	0	1.000
2002—New York (N.L.)	3B	135	490	78	151	26	0	16	56	62	55	7	5	6-0	.308	.391	.459	.850	12	.969
2003—San Francisco (N.L.)	3B-2B	142	514	56	133	25	2	13	81	58	41	4	14	5-2	.259	.334	.391	.726	11	.968
2004—San Francisco (N.L.)	3B-2B	139	519	66	150	26	1	11	77	46	40	5	15	1-1	.289	.350	.407	.757	14	.961
2005—Fresno (PCL)	3B-DH	14	15	2	7	2	0	1	0	0	0	0	0	0-0	.467	.467	.600	1.067	1	1.000
— San Francisco (N.L.)	3B-2B	109	368	36	102	17	1	2	43	27	34	2	11	2-0	.277	.327	.345	.672	8	.968
2006—Los Angeles (A.L.)	3B-1B-DH	18	50	1	5	1	0	0	1	2	3	0	1	0-0	.100	.135	.120	.255	0	1.000
— New Hampshire (East.)		3	8	0	0	0	0	0	0	1	0	0	0	0-0	.000	.000	.000	.000	0	1.000
— Toronto (A.L.)	2B	12	37	4	6	1	0	0	4	5	1	1	0	0-0	.162	.279	.189	.468	0	1.000
— Bridgeport (Atl.)		4	14	1	4	2	0	0	4	3	1	...	...	0-1	.286	.412	.429	.841	1	...
— Norfolk (Int'l)		42	141	10	34	6	0	3	19	16	15	2	4	0-1	.241	.323	.348	.670	0	1.000
American League totals (1 year)		30	87	5	11	2	0	0	5	7	4	1	2	0-0	.126	.200	.149	.349	0	1.000
National League totals (11 years)		1476	5298	772	1521	280	18	146	739	589	613	40	108	53-17	.287	.359	.429	.789	106	.977
Major League totals (12 years)		1506	5385	777	1532	282	18	146	744	596	617	41	110	53-17	.284	.357	.425	.782	106	.978

A

Year Team (League)	Pos.	G	AB	R	H	2B	3B	HR	RBI	BB	SO	HBP	GDP	SB-CS	Avg.	OBP	SLG	OPS	E	Avg.
DIVISION SERIES RECORD																				
1999— New York (N.L.)	2B	4	16	6	4	1	0	3	6	3	2	0	0	0-0	.250	.368	.875	1.243	0	1.000
2000— New York (N.L.)	2B	4	18	1	5	2	0	1	5	1	2	0	0	0-1	.278	.316	.556	.871	0	1.000
2003— San Francisco (N.L.)	3B	4	17	3	9	4	0	0	5	1	1	0	0	0-0	.529	.556	.765	1.320	0	1.000
Division series totals (3 years)		12	51	10	18	7	0	4	16	5	5	0	0	0-1	.353	.411	.725	1.136	0	1.000
CHAMPIONSHIP SERIES RECORD																				
1999— New York (N.L.)	2B	6	27	2	6	4	0	1	1	9	0	0	0	0-0	.222	.250	.370	.620	1	.971
2000— New York (N.L.)	2B	5	18	5	8	1	1	0	4	1	1	0	0	0-0	.444	.565	.611	1.176	0	1.000
Champ. series totals (2 years)		11	45	7	14	5	1	0	5	5	10	1	0	0-0	.311	.392	.467	.859	1	.979
WORLD SERIES RECORD																				
2000— New York (N.L.)	2B	5	21	1	3	0	0	0	1	1	5	1	0	0-0	.143	.217	.143	.360	0	1.000
ALL-STAR GAME RECORD																				
All-Star Game totals (1 year)		1	2	0	0	0	0	0	0	0	1	0	0	0-0	.000	.000	.000	.000	0	1.000

2006 LEFTY-RIGHTY SPLITS

vs.	Avg.	AB	H	2B	3B	HR	RBI	BB	SO	OBP	Slg.	vs.	Avg.	AB	H	2B	3B	HR	RBI	BB	SO	OBP	Slg.
L	.118	34	4	2	0	0	1	2	1	.167	.176	R	.132	53	7	0	0	0	4	5	3	.220	.132

ALFONZO, ELIEZER — C

PERSONAL: Born February 7, 1979, in Puerto la Cruz, Venezuela. ... 6-0/225. ... Bats right, throws right. ... Full name: Eliezer Jesus Alfonzo. ... Cousin of Edgardo Alfonzo, third baseman with Los Angeles Angels of Anaheim and Toronto Blue Jays in 2006. **TRANSACTIONS/CAREER NOTES:** Signed as a non-drafted free agent by St. Louis Cardinals organization (July 13, 1996). ... Traded by Cardinals with P Matt Parker to Milwaukee Brewers (June 13, 2000), completing deal in which Brewers traded 2B Fernando Vina to Cardinals for P Juan Acevedo and two players to be named (December 29, 1999). ... Released by Cubs (March 29, 2003). ... Signed as a free agent by Chicago Cubs organization (November 24, 2002). ... Released by Cubs (March 29, 2003). ... Signed as a free agent by Florida Marlins organization (January 9, 2004). ... Signed as a free agent by San Francisco Giants organization (December 16, 2004).

2006 GAMES PLAYED BY POSITION (MLB): C—84.

Year Team (League)	Pos.	G	AB	R	H	2B	3B	HR	RBI	BB	SO	HBP	GDP	SB-CS	Avg.	OBP	SLG	OPS	E	Avg.
															BATTING				**FIELDING**	
1996— St. Louis (DSL)		24	80	6	26	5	1	1	16	5	21	1	...	2-0	.325	.368	.450	.818	0	...
1997— Johnson City (App.)		38	120	15	33	11	1	2	15	7	34	6	...	0-1	.275	.346	.433	.779	4	...
1998— New Jersey (NYP)		48	175	16	43	4	1	2	19	6	49	2	...	1-0	.246	.274	.314	.588	4	...
1999— New Jersey (NYP)		46	178	14	58	12	2	3	28	3	39	4	...	3-4	.326	.349	.466	.815	6	...
2000— Beloit (Midw.)		60	221	22	59	10	0	5	27	8	58	3	...	2-2	.267	.299	.380	.679	6	...
— Peoria (Midw.)		49	175	28	54	16	0	5	21	6	35	6	...	2-0	.309	.349	.486	.835	4	...
2001— Beloit (Midw.)		106	397	52	110	28	2	14	48	13	65	8	...	0-1	.277	.311	.463	.775	14	...
2002— High Desert (Calif.)		12	43	7	15	2	0	2	9	3	14	2	...	0-0	.349	.417	.535	.952	2	...
— Huntsville (Sou.)		69	244	23	63	15	1	7	38	9	55	3	...	2-3	.258	.292	.414	.706	7	...
2003— St. Paul (North.)		68	253	46	76	15	1	9	46	11	44	9	...	0-0	.300	.347	.474	.821	8	...
2004— Jupiter (Fla. St.)		105	399	51	112	12	2	18	70	22	105	12	...	6-4	.281	.335	.456	.791	7	...
— Carolina (Southern)		4	4	0	0	0	0	0	0	0	4	0	...	0-0	.000	.000	.000	.000	0	...
2005— San Jose (Calif.)	C-DH	53	196	35	70	16	0	13	45	11	49	8	2	1-3	.357	.410	.638	1.048	8	.983
— Norwich (East.)	C-DH	49	176	30	55	9	0	9	31	4	39	4	5	4-5	.313	.354	.517	.872	3	.990
— Fresno (PCL)	C	4	14	3	4	0	1	3	1	2	1	1	0-0	.286	.375	.571	.946	0	1.000
2006— Fresno (PCL)	C	24	74	5	14	0	1	2	6	4	18	6	0	0-0	.189	.282	.297	.580	1	.993
— Connecticut (East.)	C	20	65	8	18	3	0	0	7	7	16	1	0	1-0	.277	.351	.323	.674	0	1.000
— San Francisco (N.L.)	C	87	286	27	76	17	2	12	39	9	74	7	10	1-0	.266	.302	.465	.767	5	.992
Major League totals (1 year)		87	286	27	76	17	2	12	39	9	74	7	10	1-0	.266	.302	.465	.767	5	.992

2006 LEFTY-RIGHTY SPLITS

vs.	Avg.	AB	H	2B	3B	HR	RBI	BB	SO	OBP	Slg.	vs.	Avg.	AB	H	2B	3B	HR	RBI	BB	SO	OBP	Slg.
L	.246	61	15	2	0	1	4	0	11	.246	.328	R	.271	225	61	15	2	11	35	9	63	.316	.502

ALOMAR, SANDY — C

PERSONAL: Born June 18, 1966, in Salinas, Puerto Rico. ... 6-5/235. ... Bats right, throws right. ... Full name: Santos Alomar Jr.. ... Name pronounced: AL-uh-mar. ... High school: Luis Munoz Rivera (Salinas, Puerto Rico). ... Son of Sandy Alomar, coach, New York Mets, and infielder with six major league teams (1964-78); brother of Roberto Alomar, second baseman with seven teams (1989-2004). **TRANSACTIONS/CAREER NOTES:** Signed as a non-drafted free agent by San Diego Padres organization (October 21, 1983). ... Traded by Padres with OF Chris James and 3B Carlos Baerga to Cleveland Indians for OF Joe Carter (December 6, 1989). ... On disabled list (May 15-June 17 and July 29, 1991-remainder of season); included rehabilitation assignments to Colorado Springs. ... On disabled list (May 2-18, 1992). ... On suspended list (July 29-August 2, 1992). ... On disabled list (May 1-August 7, 1993); included rehabilitation assignment to Charlotte. ... On disabled list (April 24-May 11, 1994). ... On disabled list (April 19-June 29, 1995); included rehabilitation assignment to Canton/Akron. ... On disabled list (May 11-September 6, 1999); included rehabilitation assignments to Akron and Buffalo. ... On disabled list (April 19-May 8, 2000). ... Signed as a free agent by Chicago White Sox (December 18, 2000). ... On disabled list (August 8-September 18, 2001). ... On disabled list (June 13-July 1, 2002); included rehabilitation assignment to Charlotte. ... Traded by White Sox to Colorado Rockies for P Enemencio Pacheco (July 29, 2002). ... Signed as a free agent by White Sox (December 20, 2002). ... On disabled list (May 31-June 23, 2003); included rehabilitation assignment to Charlotte. ... On disabled list (August 16-September 1, 2004). ... Signed as a free agent by Texas Rangers (December 8, 2004). ... Signed as a free agent by Los Angeles Dodgers (December 14, 2005). ... Traded by Dodgers to Chicago White Sox for P B.J. LaMura (July 23, 2006). **RECORDS:** Shares major league record for most doubles, game (4, June 6, 1997). **HONORS:** Named Minor League co-Player of the Year by THE SPORTING NEWS (1988). ... Named Minor League Player of the Year by THE SPORTING NEWS (1989). ... Named A.L. Rookie Player of the Year by THE SPORTING NEWS (1990). ... Named A.L. Rookie of the Year by Baseball Writers' Association of America (1990). ... Won A.L. Gold Glove at catcher (1990). **STATISTICAL NOTES:** Career major league grand slams: 2. **MISCELLANEOUS NOTES:** Batted as switch hitter (1984-86).

2006 GAMES PLAYED BY POSITION (MLB): C—35, DH—2.

Year Team (League)	Pos.	G	AB	R	H	2B	3B	HR	RBI	BB	SO	HBP	GDP	SB-CS	Avg.	OBP	SLG	OPS	E	Avg.
															BATTING				**FIELDING**	
1984— Spokane (N'west)	1B-C	59	219	13	47	5	0	0	21	13	20	1	7	3-0	.215	.260	.237	.497	8	.985
1985— Char., S.C. (SAL)	C-OF	100	352	38	73	7	0	3	43	31	30	3	9	3-1	.207	.276	.253	.529	18	.979
1986— Beaumont (Texas)	C	100	346	36	83	15	1	4	27	15	35	1	16	2-6	.240	.271	.324	.595	18	.969
1987— Wichita (Texas)	C	103	375	50	115	19	1	8	65	21	37	5	12	1-5	.307	.346	.427	.772	15	.978
1988— Las Vegas (PCL)	C-OF	93	337	59	100	9	5	16	71	28	35	4	11	1-1	.297	.354	.496	.849	14	.978
— San Diego (N.L.)	PH	1	1	0	0	0	0	0	0	0	1	0	0	0-0	.000	.000	.000	.000		...
1989— Las Vegas (PCL)	C-OF	131	523	88	160	33	8	13	101	42	58	2	23	3-1	.306	.358	.474	.832	12	.984
— San Diego (N.L.)	C	7	19	1	4	1	0	1	6	3	3	0	1	0-0	.211	.318	.421	.739	0	1.000
1990— Cleveland (A.L.)	C	132	445	60	129	26	2	9	66	25	46	2	10	4-1	.290	.326	.418	.744	* 14	.981

Year Team (League)	Pos.	G	AB	R	H	2B	3B	HR	RBI	BB	SO	HBP	GDP	SB-CS	Avg.	OBP	SLG	OPS	E	Avg.
1991— Cleveland (A.L.)	C-DH	51	184	10	40	9	0	0	7	8	24	4	4	0-4	.217	.264	.266	.530	4	.987
— Colo. Springs (PCL)	C	12	35	5	14	2	0	1	10	5	0	0	0	0-0	.400	.463	.543	1.006	1	.833
1992— Cleveland (A.L.)	C-DH	89	299	22	75	16	0	2	26	13	32	5	7	3-3	.251	.293	.324	.618	2	.996
1993— Cleveland (A.L.)	C	64	215	24	58	7	1	6	32	11	28	6	3	3-1	.270	.318	.395	.713	6	.984
— Charlotte (Int'l)	C	12	44	8	16	5	0	1	8	5	8	1	1	0-0	.364	.440	.545	.985	0	1.000
1994— Cleveland (A.L.)	C	80	292	44	84	15	1	14	43	25	31	2	7	8-4	.288	.347	.490	.837	2	.996
1995— Cant./Akr. (Eastern)	C-DH	6	15	3	6	1	0	0	1	1	1	0	1	0-0	.400	.438	.467	.904	1	.958
— Cleveland (A.L.)	C	66	203	32	61	6	0	10	35	7	26	3	8	3-1	.300	.332	.478	.810	2	.995
1996— Cleveland (A.L.)	C-1B	127	418	53	110	23	0	11	50	19	42	3	20	1-0	.263	.299	.397	.696	9	.988
1997— Cleveland (A.L.)	C	125	451	63	146	37	0	21	83	19	48	3	16	0-2	.324	.354	.545	.900	* 12	.985
1998— Cleveland (A.L.)	C-DH	117	409	45	96	26	2	6	44	18	45	3	15	0-3	.235	.270	.352	.622	6	.992
1999— Cleveland (A.L.)	C-DH	37	137	19	42	13	0	6	25	4	23	0	1	0-1	.307	.322	.533	.855	7	.974
— Akron (East.)	C	10	29	8	9	0	0	1	6	3	2	0	0	1-0	.310	.353	.414	.767	1	.929
— Buffalo (Int'l)	C-DH	10	33	9	9	2	1	2	10	6	3	1	1	0-0	.273	.400	.576	.976	3	.921
2000— Cleveland (A.L.)	C-DH	97	356	44	103	16	2	7	42	16	41	4	9	2-2	.289	.324	.404	.728	8	.989
2001— Chicago (A.L.)	C	70	220	17	54	8	1	4	21	12	17	2	6	1-2	.245	.288	.345	.634	4	.990
2002— Chicago (A.L.)	C	51	167	21	48	10	1	7	25	5	14	1	5	0-0	.287	.309	.485	.794	2	.994
— Charlotte (Int'l)	C	3	8	0	1	0	0	0	0	0	0	0	1	0-0	.125	.125	.125	.250	0	1.000
— Colorado (N.L.)	C	38	116	8	31	4	0	0	12	4	19	0	6	0-0	.267	.292	.302	.593	0	1.000
2003— Charlotte (Int'l)	C-DH	5	15	2	4	0	0	0	1	1	1	0	2	0-0	.267	.313	.267	.579	0	1.000
— Chicago (A.L.)	C	75	194	22	52	12	0	5	26	4	17	0	4	0-0	.268	.281	.407	.689	1	.997
2004— Chicago (A.L.)	C-DH	50	146	15	35	4	0	2	14	11	13	2	4	0-0	.240	.298	.308	.606	3	.990
2005— Texas (A.L.)	C	46	128	11	35	7	0	0	14	5	12	1	3	0-0	.273	.306	.328	.634	2	.992
2006— Los Angeles (N.L.)	C	27	62	3	20	5	0	0	9	0	7	0	3	0-0	.323	.323	.403	.726	1	.988
— Chicago (A.L.)	C-DH	19	46	5	10	3	0	1	8	3	7	0	0	0-0	.217	.255	.348	.603	1	.990
American League totals (17 years)		1296	4310	507	1178	238	10	111	561	205	466	41	122	25-24	.273	.310	.410	.721	85	.989
National League totals (4 years)		73	198	12	55	10	0	1	27	7	30	0	10	0-0	.278	.302	.343	.646	1	.997
Major League totals (19 years)		1369	4508	519	1233	248	10	112	588	212	496	41	132	25-24	.274	.310	.407	.717	86	.989

DIVISION SERIES RECORD

Year Team (League)	Pos.	G	AB	R	H	2B	3B	HR	RBI	BB	SO	HBP	GDP	SB-CS	Avg.	OBP	SLG	OPS	E	Avg.
1995— Cleveland (A.L.)	C	3	11	1	2	1	0	0	1	0	1	0	0	0-0	.182	.182	.273	.455	0	1.000
1996— Cleveland (A.L.)	C	4	16	0	2	0	0	0	3	0	2	0	0	0-1	.125	.125	.125	.250	1	.978
1997— Cleveland (A.L.)	C	5	19	4	6	1	0	2	5	0	2	0	0	0-0	.316	.316	.684	1.000	1	.967
1998— Cleveland (A.L.)	C	4	13	2	3	3	0	0	2	1	4	0	3	0-0	.231	.286	.462	.747	1	.967
1999— Cleveland (A.L.)	C	5	14	1	2	0	0	0	1	2	6	0	0	0-0	.143	.235	.143	.378	1	.971
Division series totals (5 years)		21	73	8	15	5	0	2	12	3	15	0	3	0-1	.205	.234	.356	.590	4	.975

CHAMPIONSHIP SERIES RECORD

Year Team (League)	Pos.	G	AB	R	H	2B	3B	HR	RBI	BB	SO	HBP	GDP	SB-CS	Avg.	OBP	SLG	OPS	E	Avg.
1995— Cleveland (A.L.)	C	5	15	0	4	1	1	0	1	1	1	0	0	0-0	.267	.313	.467	.779	1	.971
1997— Cleveland (A.L.)	C	6	24	3	3	0	0	1	4	1	3	0	1	0-0	.125	.160	.250	.410	0	1.000
1998— Cleveland (A.L.)	C	5	16	1	1	0	0	0	0	0	2	1	0	0-0	.063	.118	.063	.180	2	.938
Champ. series totals (3 years)		16	55	4	8	1	1	1	5	2	6	1	1	0-0	.145	.190	.255	.444	3	.974

WORLD SERIES RECORD

Year Team (League)	Pos.	G	AB	R	H	2B	3B	HR	RBI	BB	SO	HBP	GDP	SB-CS	Avg.	OBP	SLG	OPS	E	Avg.
1995— Cleveland (A.L.)	C	5	15	0	3	2	0	0	1	0	2	0	0	0-0	.200	.200	.333	.533	0	1.000
1997— Cleveland (A.L.)	C	7	30	5	11	1	0	2	10	2	3	0	2	0-0	.367	.406	.600	1.006	0	1.000
World series totals (2 years)		12	45	5	14	3	0	2	11	2	5	0	2	0-0	.311	.340	.511	.852	0	1.000

ALL-STAR GAME RECORD

	G	AB	R	H	2B	3B	HR	RBI	BB	SO	HBP	GDP	SB-CS	Avg.	OBP	SLG	OPS	E	Avg.
All-Star Game totals (6 years)	6	12	2	5	0	0	0	1	0	1	0	1	0-0	.417	.417	.667	1.083	0	1.000

2006 LEFTY-RIGHTY SPLITS

vs.	Avg.	AB	H	2B	3B	HR	RBI	BB	SO	OBP	Slg.	vs.	Avg.	AB	H	2B	3B	HR	RBI	BB	SO	OBP	Slg.
L	.327	52	17	5	0	1	10	1	5	.327	.481	R	.232	56	13	3	0	0	7	2	9	.259	.286

ALOU, MOISES — OF

PERSONAL: Born July 3, 1966, in Atlanta, Ga. ... 6-3/220. ... Bats right, throws right. ... Full name: Moises Rojas Alou. ... Name pronounced: MOY-zes ah-LOO. ... High school: C.E.E. (Santo Domingo, Dominican Republic). ... Junior college: Canada College (Calif.). ... College: Canada College (CA). ... Son of Felipe Alou, manager, San Francisco Giants in 2006, and outfielder with six major league teams (1958-1974); nephew of Jesus Alou, outfielder with four major league teams (1963-75 and 1978-79); nephew of Matty Alou, outfielder with six major league teams (1960-74). **TRANSACTIONS/CAREER NOTES:** Selected by Pittsburgh Pirates organization in first round (second pick overall) of January 1986 free-agent draft. ... Traded by Pirates to Montreal Expos (August 16, 1990), completing deal in which Expos traded P Zane Smith to Pirates for P Scott Ruskin, SS Willie Greene and a player to be named (August 8, 1990). ... On disabled list (March 19, 1991-entire season; July 7-27, 1992; September 18, 1993-remainder of season; August 18-September 5 and September 11, 1995-remainder of season; and July 8-23, 1996). ... On suspended list (August 23-27, 1996). ... Signed as a free agent by Florida Marlins (December 12, 1996). ... Traded by Marlins to Houston Astros for Ps Oscar Henriquez and P Manuel Barrios and a player to be named (November 11, 1997); Marlins acquired P Mark Johnson to complete deal (December 16, 1997). ... On disabled list (April 3, 1999-entire season; April 27-May 14, 2000; and March 29-April 16, 2001). ... Signed as a free agent by Chicago Cubs (December 19, 2001). ... On disabled list (March 31-April 15, 2002); included rehabilitation assignment to Daytona. ... Signed as a free agent by San Francisco Giants (January 5, 2005). ... On disabled list (April 7-22; and August 3-19, 2005). ... On disabled list (May 6-June 6, 2006). ... On disabled list (June 18-July 6, 2006). **HONORS:** Named outfielder on THE SPORTING NEWS N.L. All-Star team (1994 and 1998). ... Named outfielder on N.L. Silver Slugger team (1994 and 1998). **STATISTICAL NOTES:** Hit three home runs in one game (July 4, 2003). ... Career major league grand slams: 3.
2006 GAMES PLAYED BY POSITION (MLB): OF—92, DH—1.

Year Team (League)	Pos.	G	AB	R	H	2B	3B	HR	RBI	BB	SO	HBP	GDP	SB-CS	Avg.	OBP	SLG	OPS	E	Avg.
1986— Watertown (NYP)		69	254	30	60	9	8	6	35	22	72	1	5	14-8	.236	.300	.406	.705	7	.952
1987— Macon (S. Atl.)	OF	4	8	1	1	0	0	0	0	2	4	0	0	0-0	.125	.300	.125	.425	0	1.000
— Watertown (NYP)	OF	39	117	20	25	6	2	4	8	16	36	4	0	6-3	.214	.324	.402	.725	2	.957
1988— Augusta (S. Atl.)	OF	105	358	58	112	23	5	7	62	51	84	5	6	24-12	.313	.399	.464	.863	9	.962
1989— Salem (Carol.)	OF	86	321	50	97	29	2	14	53	35	69	3	6	12-5	.302	.374	.536	.910	10	.947
— Harrisburg (East.)	OF	54	205	36	60	5	2	3	19	17	38	0	1	8-4	.293	.344	.380	.724	2	.978
1990— Harrisburg (East.)	OF	36	132	19	39	12	2	3	22	16	21	1	5	7-4	.295	.373	.485	.858	1	.990
— Buffalo (A.A.)	OF	75	271	38	74	4	6	5	31	30	43	2		9-4	.273	.345	.387	.733	8	.957
— Pittsburgh (N.L.)	OF	2	5	0	1	0	0	0	0	0	0	0	1	0-0	.200	.200	.200	.400	0	1.000
— Indianapolis (A.A.)	OF	15	55	6	12	1	0	0	6	3	7	0	...	4-3	.218	.254	.236	.491	0	1.000
— Montreal (N.L.)	OF	14	15	4	3	0	0	0	0	0	5	0	0	0-0	.200	.200	.333	.533	0	1.000

Year Team (League)	Pos.	G	AB	R	H	2B	3B	HR	RBI	BB	SO	HBP	GDP	SB-CS	Avg.	OBP	SLG	OPS	E	FIELDING Avg.
1991— Montreal (N.L.)			Did not play.																	
1992— Montreal (N.L.)	OF	115	341	53	96	28	2	9	56	25	46	1	5	16-2	.282	.328	.455	.783	4	.978
1993— Montreal (N.L.)	OF	136	482	70	138	29	6	18	85	38	53	5	9	17-6	.286	.340	.483	.824	4	.985
1994— Montreal (N.L.)	OF	107	422	81	143	31	5	22	78	42	63	2	7	7-6	.339	.397	.592	.989	3	.986
1995— Montreal (N.L.)	OF	93	344	48	94	22	0	14	58	29	56	9	9	4-3	.273	.342	.459	.801	3	.981
1996— Montreal (N.L.)	OF	143	540	87	152	28	2	21	96	49	83	2	15	9-4	.281	.339	.457	.797	3	.989
1997— Florida (N.L.)	OF	150	538	88	157	29	5	23	115	70	85	4	13	9-5	.292	.373	.493	.866	3	.988
1998— Houston (N.L.)	OF-DH	159	584	104	182	34	5	38	124	84	87	5	14	11-3	.312	.399	.582	.981	5	.980
1999— Houston (N.L.)			Did not play.																	
2000— Houston (N.L.)	OF-DH	126	454	82	161	28	2	30	114	52	45	2	* 21	3-3	.355	.416	.623	1.039	6	.970
2001— Houston (N.L.)	OF-DH	136	513	79	170	31	1	27	108	57	57	3	18	5-1	.331	.396	.554	.949	2	.991
2002— Daytona (Fla. St.)	OF	2	8	0	5	1	0	0	2	1	1	0	0	0-0	.625	.667	.750	1.417	0	1.000
— Chicago (N.L.)	OF-DH	132	484	50	133	23	1	15	61	47	61	0	15	8-0	.275	.337	.419	.757	2	.991
2003— Chicago (N.L.)	OF-DH	151	565	83	158	35	1	22	91	63	67	7	16	3-1	.280	.357	.462	.819	6	.972
2004— Chicago (N.L.)	OF-DH	155	601	106	176	36	3	39	106	68	80	0	12	3-0	.293	.361	.557	.919	8	.969
2005— San Francisco (N.L.)	OF-DH	123	427	67	137	21	3	19	63	56	43	3	11	5-1	.321	.400	.518	.918	8	.966
2006— San Francisco (N.L.)	OF-DH	98	345	52	104	25	1	22	74	28	31	1	15	2-1	.301	.352	.571	.923	4	.978
Major League totals (15 years)		1840	6660	1054	2005	400	38	319	1229	708	860	44	181	102-36	.301	.368	.516	.884	61	.980

DIVISION SERIES RECORD

Year Team (League)	Pos.	G	AB	R	H	2B	3B	HR	RBI	BB	SO	HBP	GDP	SB-CS	Avg.	OBP	SLG	OPS	E	Avg.
1997— Florida (N.L.)	OF	3	14	1	3	1	0	0	1	0	3	0	1	0-0	.214	.214	.286	.500	0	1.000
1998— Houston (N.L.)	OF	4	16	0	3	0	0	0	0	0	2	0	1	0-0	.188	.188	.188	.375	0	1.000
2001— Chicago (N.L.)	OF	3	12	0	2	1	0	0	1	1	0	0	0	0-0	.167	.167	.250	.417	0	1.000
2003— Chicago (N.L.)	OF	5	20	3	10	1	0	0	3	1	4	0	1	1-0	.500	.524	.550	1.074	0	1.000
Division series totals (4 years)		15	62	4	18	3	0	0	5	1	10	0	3	1-0	.290	.302	.339	.640	0	1.000

CHAMPIONSHIP SERIES RECORD

Year Team (League)	Pos.	G	AB	R	H	2B	3B	HR	RBI	BB	SO	HBP	GDP	SB-CS	Avg.	OBP	SLG	OPS	E	Avg.
1997— Florida (N.L.)	OF	5	15	0	1	0	0	0	1	1	3	0	1	0-0	.067	.125	.133	.258	0	1.000
2003— Chicago (N.L.)	OF	7	29	4	9	1	0	2	5	2	1	0	2	0-0	.310	.355	.552	.907	0	1.000
Champ. series totals (2 years)		12	44	4	10	2	0	2	6	3	4	0*	3	0-0	.227	.277	.409	.686	0	1.000

WORLD SERIES RECORD

Year Team (League)	Pos.	G	AB	R	H	2B	3B	HR	RBI	BB	SO	HBP	GDP	SB-CS	Avg.	OBP	SLG	OPS	E	Avg.
1997— Florida (N.L.)	OF	7	28	6	9	2	0	3	9	3	6	0	0	1-0	.321	.387	.714	1.101	0	1.000

ALL-STAR GAME RECORD

		G	AB	R	H	2B	3B	HR	RBI	BB	SO	HBP	GDP	SB-CS	Avg.	OBP	SLG	OPS	E	Avg.
All-Star Game totals (6 years)		6	10	2	5	2	0	1	3	3	0	0		0-0	.500	.545	.700	1.245	0	1.000

2006 LEFTY-RIGHTY SPLITS

vs.	Avg.	AB	H	2B	3B	HR	RBI	BB	SO	OBP	Slg.	vs.	Avg.	AB	H	2B	3B	HR	RBI	BB	SO	OBP	Slg.
L	.349	83	29	10	0	6	19	8	8	.407	.687	R	.286	262	75	15	1	16	55	20	23	.334	.534

ALVAREZ, ABE   P

PERSONAL: Born October 17, 1982, in Los Angeles. ... 6-2/190. ... Throws left, bats left. ... Full name: Abraham Alvarez. ... High school: Fontana (Calif.). ... College: Long Beach State. **TRANSACTIONS/CAREER NOTES:** Selected by Boston Red Sox organization in second round of 2003 free-agent draft. ... On disabled list (September 19, 2006-remainder of season).
CAREER HITTING: 0-for-1 (.000), 0 R, 0 2B, 0 3B, 0 HR, 0 RBI.

Year Team (League)	W	L	Pct.	ERA	WHIP	G	GS	CG	ShO	Hld.	Sv.-Opp.	IP	H	R	ER	HR	BB-IBB	SO	Avg.
2003— Lowell (NY-Penn)	0	0		0.00	0.58	9	9	0	0		0-...	19.0	9	2	0	0	2-1	19	.138
2004— Boston (A.L.)	0	1	.000	9.00	2.60	1	1	0	0		0-0	5.0	8	5	5	2	5-0	2	.400
— Portland (East.)	10	9	.526	3.59	1.21	26	26	0	0	...	0-...	135.1	132	65	54	13	32-0	108	.252
2005— Boston (A.L.)	0	0		15.43	2.57	2	0	0	0	0	0-0	2.1	6	4	4	1	0-0	1	.462
— Pawtucket (Int'l)	11	6	.647	4.85	1.20	26	26	0	0	0	0-0	144.2	143	84	78	17	31-0	109	.255
2006— Boston (A.L.)	0	0		12.00	2.33	1	0	0	0	0	0-0	3.0	5	4	4	2	2-0	2	.385
— Pawtucket (Int'l)	6	9	.400	5.64	1.49	22	21	0	0	0	0-0	118.0	136	79	74	22	40-0	71	.288
Major League totals (3 years)	0	1	.000	11.32	2.52	4	1	0	0	0	0-0	10.1	19	13	13	5	7-0	5	.413

2006 LEFTY-RIGHTY SPLITS

vs.	Avg.	AB	H	2B	3B	HR	RBI	BB	SO	OBP	Slg.	vs.	Avg.	AB	H	2B	3B	HR	RBI	BB	SO	OBP	Slg.
L	1.000	4	4	0	0	2	4	1	0	1.000	2.500	R	.111	9	1	1	0	0	0	1	2	.200	.222

AMEZAGA, ALFREDO   OF/IF

PERSONAL: Born January 16, 1978, in Obregon, Mexico. ... 5-10/165. ... Bats both, throws right. ... Name pronounced: ah-MEZZ-ah-guh. ... High school: Miami Senior (Miami). ... Junior college: St. Petersburg (Fla.). **TRANSACTIONS/CAREER NOTES:** Selected by Colorado Rockies organization in 36th round of 1997 free-agent draft; did not sign. ... Selected by Colorado Rockies organization in 44th round of 1998 free-agent draft; did not sign. ... Selected by Anaheim Angels organization in 13th round of 1999 free-agent draft. ... Claimed on waivers by Colorado Rockies (December 17, 2004). ... Claimed on waivers by Pittsburgh Pirates (April 20, 2005). ... Signed as a free agent by Florida Marlins (November 22, 2005). **STATISTICAL NOTES:** Career major league grand slams: 2.
2006 GAMES PLAYED BY POSITION (MLB): OF—78, 2B—23, SS—11, 3B—4, 1B—2.

Year Team (League)	Pos.	G	AB	R	H	2B	3B	HR	RBI	BB	SO	HBP	GDP	SB-CS	Avg.	OBP	SLG	OPS	E	FIELDING Avg.
1999— Butte (Pion.)	2B-SS	8	34	11	10	2	0	0	5	5	5	1	0	6-2	.294	.400	.353	.753	0	1.000
— Boise (N'west)	2B-SS	48	205	52	66	6	4	2	29	23	29	5	7	14-3	.322	.402	.420	.821	12	.953
2000— Lake Elsinore (Calif.)	2B-SS	108	420	90	117	13	4	4	44	63	70	4	4	73-21	.279	.374	.357	.731	22	.961
2001— Arkansas (Texas)	SS	70	285	50	89	10	5	4	21	22	55	4	0	24-15	.312	.370	.425	.794	13	.964
— Salt Lake (PCL)	SS	49	200	28	50	5	4	1	16	14	45	3	2	9-6	.250	.307	.330	.637	11	.954
2002— Salt Lake (PCL)	SS-2B	128	518	77	130	25	7	6	51	45	100	8	15	23-14	.251	.317	.361	.678	24	.962
— Anaheim (A.L.)	SS-DH	12	13	3	7	2	0	0	3	0	1	0	1	1-0	.538	.538	.692	1.231	0	1.000
2003— Salt Lake (PCL)	SS-2B-DH	75	317	55	110	20	5	3	45	20	39	4	3	14-8	.347	.391	.470	.861	7	.982
— Anaheim (A.L.)	SS-3B	37	105	15	22	3	2	1	7	9	23	1	2	2-2	.210	.278	.333	.612	5	.962
2004— Salt Lake (PCL)	SS-3B-2B	32	135	15	35	4	2	2	14	13	18	1	2	7-0	.259	.329	.370	.699	7	.961
— Anaheim (A.L.)	DH	73	93	12	15	2	0	2	11	3	24	3	1	3-2	.161	.212	.247	.459	3	.978
2005— Colorado (N.L.)	3B	2	3	1	1	0	0	0	0	0	1	0	0	0-0	.333	.333	.333	.667	0	...

Year	Team (League)	Pos.	G	AB	R	H	2B	3B	HR	RBI	BB	SO	HBP	GDP	SB-CS	Avg.	OBP	SLG	OPS	E	Avg.
	— Pittsburgh (N.L.)	SS	3	3	1	0	0	0	0	0	1	0	0	0	1-0	.000	.250	.000	.250	0	1.000
	— Indianapolis (Int'l)	SS-2B-OF 3B	64	185	28	63	12	2	1	12	17	27	2	1	14-7	.341	.398	.443	.841	9	.959
2006—	Florida (N.L.)	OF-2B-SS 3B-1B	132	334	42	87	9	3	3	19	33	46	3	5	20-12	.260	.332	.332	.664	6	.978
	American League totals (3 years)		122	211	30	44	7	2	4	20	12	48	4	5	6-4	.209	.264	.318	.582	8	.972
	National League totals (2 years)		137	340	44	88	9	3	3	19	34	46	3	5	21-12	.259	.331	.329	.660	6	.979
	Major League totals (5 years)		259	551	74	132	16	5	7	39	46	94	7	10	27-16	.240	.306	.325	.631	14	.975

DIVISION SERIES RECORD

Year	Team (League)	Pos.	G	AB	R	H	2B	3B	HR	RBI	BB	SO	HBP	GDP	SB-CS	Avg.	OBP	SLG	OPS	E	Avg.
2004—	Anaheim (A.L.)	2B	2	2	0	0	0	0	0	0	0	2	0	0	0-0	.000	.000	.000	.000	0	1.000

2006 LEFTY-RIGHTY SPLITS

vs.	Avg.	AB	H	2B	3B	HR	RBI	BB	SO	OBP	Slg.	vs.	Avg.	AB	H	2B	3B	HR	RBI	BB	SO	OBP	Slg.
L	.091	55	5	1	0	0	3	8	11	.227	.109	R	.294	279	82	8	3	3	16	25	35	.354	.376

ANDERSON, BRIAN N. — OF

PERSONAL: Born March 11, 1982, in Tucson, Ariz. ... 6-2/215. ... Bats right, throws right. ... Full name: Brian Nikola Anderson. ... High school: Canyon Del Oro (Tucson, Ariz.). ... College: Arizona. **TRANSACTIONS/CAREER NOTES:** Selected by Chicago White organization in first round (15th pick overall) of 2003 free-agent draft. ... On suspended list (June 21-26, 2006).
2006 GAMES PLAYED BY POSITION (MLB): OF—134.

Year	Team (League)	Pos.	G	AB	R	H	2B	3B	HR	RBI	BB	SO	HBP	GDP	SB-CS	Avg.	OBP	SLG	OPS	E	Avg.
2003—	Great Falls (Pio.)	OF	13	49	6	19	2	1	2	13	9	10	1	1	3-1	.388	.492	.592	1.084	0	1.000
2004—	Win.-Salem (Car.)	OF	69	254	43	81	22	4	8	46	29	44	3	3	10-1	.319	.394	.531	.925	1	.933
	— Birmingham (Sou.)	OF	48	185	26	50	9	3	4	27	19	30	3	3	3-2	.270	.346	.416	.762	1	1.000
2005—	Charlotte (Int'l)	OF-DH	118	448	71	132	24	3	16	57	44	115	4	11	4-2	.295	.360	.469	.829	8	.986
	— Chicago (A.L.)	OF	13	34	3	6	1	0	2	3	0	12	0	2	1-0	.176	.176	.382	.559	0	1.000
2006—	Chicago (A.L.)	OF	134	365	46	82	23	1	8	33	30	90	5	3	4-7	.225	.290	.359	.649	2	.994
	Major League totals (2 years)		147	399	49	88	24	1	10	36	30	102	5	5	5-7	.221	.281	.361	.642	2	.994

2006 LEFTY-RIGHTY SPLITS

vs.	Avg.	AB	H	2B	3B	HR	RBI	BB	SO	OBP	Slg.	vs.	Avg.	AB	H	2B	3B	HR	RBI	BB	SO	OBP	Slg.
L	.226	159	36	10	1	2	9	16	35	.298	.340	R	.223	206	46	13	0	6	24	14	55	.284	.374

ANDERSON, DREW — OF

PERSONAL: Born June 9, 1981, in Kearney, Neb. ... Bats left, throws right. ... Full name: Drew Thomas Anderson. ... College: Nebraska. **TRANSACTIONS/CAREER NOTES:** Selected by Milwaukee Brewers organization in 24th round of 2003 free-agent draft.
2006 GAMES PLAYED BY POSITION (MLB): OF—2.

Year	Team (League)	Pos.	G	AB	R	H	2B	3B	HR	RBI	BB	SO	HBP	GDP	SB-CS	Avg.	OBP	SLG	OPS	E	Avg.
2003—	Helena (Pion.)		61	214	33	68	11	3	2	38	35	39	4	4	9-5	.318	.420	.425	.845	...	...
2004—	Beloit (Midw.)		123	456	64	140	22	5	5	59	45	95	6	6	12-4	.307	.372	.410	.782	...	...
2005—	Brevard County (Fla. St.)	OF-DH	129	508	69	158	17	7	6	62	39	95	3	7	19-8	.311	.360	.407	.767	6	.986
2006—	Nashville (PCL)		16	63	16	21	5	1	1	9	2	12	0	0	3-1	.333	.348	.492	.841	0	1.000
	— Huntsville (Sou.)		108	402	60	117	24	4	6	43	39	80	5	7	17-8	.291	.359	.415	.775	3	.987
	— Milwaukee (N.L.)	OF	9	9	3	1	0	0	0	0	1	4	0	0	0-0	.111	.200	.111	.311	0	1.000
	Major League totals (1 year)		9	9	3	1	0	0	0	0	1	4	0	0	0-0	.111	.200	.111	.311	0	1.000

2006 LEFTY-RIGHTY SPLITS

vs.	Avg.	AB	H	2B	3B	HR	RBI	BB	SO	OBP	Slg.	vs.	Avg.	AB	H	2B	3B	HR	RBI	BB	SO	OBP	Slg.
L	.000	1	0	0	0	0	0	0	1	.000	.000	R	.125	8	1	0	0	0	0	1	3	.222	.125

ANDERSON, GARRET — OF

PERSONAL: Born June 30, 1972, in Los Angeles. ... 6-3/225. ... Bats left, throws left. ... Full name: Garret Joseph Anderson. ... High school: John F. Kennedy (Granada Hills, Calif.). **TRANSACTIONS/CAREER NOTES:** Selected by California Angels organization in fourth round of 1990 free-agent draft. ... Angels franchise renamed Anaheim Angels for 1997 season. ... On disabled list (April 22-June 10, 2004); included rehabilitation assignment to Rancho Cucamonga. ... Angels franchise renamed Los Angeles Angels of Anaheim for 2005 season. **HONORS:** Named A.L. Rookie Player of the Year by THE SPORTING NEWS (1995). ... Named outfielder on THE SPORTING NEWS A.L. All-Star team (2002 and 2003). ... Named outfielder on A.L. Silver Slugger team (2002 and 2003). **STATISTICAL NOTES:** Hit three home runs in one game (June 4, 2003). ... Career major league grand slams: 7.
2006 GAMES PLAYED BY POSITION (MLB): OF—94, DH—45.

Year	Team (League)	Pos.	G	AB	R	H	2B	3B	HR	RBI	BB	SO	HBP	GDP	SB-CS	Avg.	OBP	SLG	OPS	E	Avg.
1990—	Ariz. Angels (Ariz.)	OF	32	127	5	27	2	0	0	14	2	24	2	3	3-0	.213	.231	.228	.460	2	.965
	— Boise (N'west)	OF	25	83	11	21	3	1	1	8	4	18	0	3	0-1	.253	.284	.349	.633	2	.950
1991—	Quad City (Midw.)	OF	105	392	40	102	22	2	2	42	20	89	0	16	5-6	.260	.295	.342	.637	10	.943
1992—	Palm Springs (Calif.)	OF	81	322	46	104	15	2	1	62	21	61	1	9	1-1	.323	.366	.391	.758	6	.959
	— Midland (Texas)	OF	39	146	16	40	5	0	2	19	9	30	0	8	2-1	.274	.316	.349	.665	1	.986
1993—	Vancouver (PCL)	OF-1B	124	467	57	137	34	4	4	71	31	95	0	15	3-4	.293	.334	.409	.743	2	.991
1994—	Vancouver (PCL)	OF-DH-1B	123	505	75	162	42	6	12	102	28	93	1	7	3-3	.321	.356	.499	.855	2	.990
	— California (A.L.)	OF	5	13	0	5	0	0	0	1	0	4	0	0	0-0	.385	.385	.385	.769	0	1.000
1995—	California (A.L.)	OF-DH	106	374	50	120	19	1	16	69	19	65	1	8	6-2	.321	.352	.505	.857	5	.978
	— Vancouver (PCL)	OF-DH	14	61	9	19	7	0	0	12	5	14	0	0	0-0	.311	.364	.459	.790	1	.957
1996—	California (A.L.)	OF-DH	150	607	79	173	33	2	12	72	27	84	0	22	7-9	.285	.314	.405	.719	7	.979
1997—	Anaheim (A.L.)	OF-DH	154	624	76	189	36	3	8	92	30	70	2	20	10-4	.303	.334	.409	.743	3	.992
1998—	Anaheim (A.L.)	OF	156	622	62	183	41	6	15	79	29	80	1	13	8-3	.294	.325	.455	.780	6	.983
1999—	Anaheim (A.L.)	OF-DH	157	620	88	188	36	2	21	80	34	81	0	15	3-4	.303	.336	.469	.806	3	.993
2000—	Anaheim (A.L.)	OF-DH-1B	159	647	92	185	40	3	35	117	24	87	0		7-6	.286	.307	.519	.827	4	.990
2001—	Anaheim (A.L.)	OF-DH	161	672	83	194	39	4	28	123	27	100	0	12	13-6	.289	.314	.478	.792	2	.994
2002—	Anaheim (A.L.)	OF-DH	158	638	93	195	•56	4	29	123	30	80	0	11	6-4	.306	.332	.539	.871	2	.994
2003—	Anaheim (A.L.)	OF-DH	159	638	80	201	•49	4	29	116	31	83	0	15	6-3	.315	.345	.541	.885	1	.997

Year Team (League)	Pos.	G	AB	R	H	2B	3B	HR	RBI	BB	SO	HBP	GDP	SB-CS	Avg.	OBP	SLG	OPS	E	Avg.
2004—Rancho Cuca. (Calif.)	OF	3	9	1	4	0	0	1	1	1	1	0	0	0-0	.444	.500	.778	1.278	0	1.000
—Anaheim (A.L.)	OF-DH	112	442	57	133	20	1	14	75	29	75	1	3	2-1	.301	.343	.446	.789	2	.991
2005—Los Angeles (A.L.)	OF-DH	142	575	68	163	34	1	17	96	23	84	0	13	1-1	.283	.308	.435	.743	5	.976
2006—Los Angeles (A.L.)	OF-DH	141	543	63	152	28	2	17	85	38	95	0	8	1-0	.280	.323	.433	.756	0	.989
Major League totals (13 years)		1760	7015	891	2081	431	31	241	1128	341	986	5	161	70-43	.297	.327	.470	.797	40	.989

DIVISION SERIES RECORD

Year Team (League)	Pos.	G	AB	R	H	2B	3B	HR	RBI	BB	SO	HBP	GDP	SB-CS	Avg.	OBP	SLG	OPS	E	Avg.
2002—Anaheim (A.L.)	OF	4	18	5	7	2	0	1	4	1	3	0	1	0-0	.389	.421	.667	1.088	0	1.000
2004—Anaheim (A.L.)	OF	3	13	1	2	0	0	0	0	0	3	0	0	0-0	.154	.154	.154	.308	0	1.000
2005—Los Angeles (A.L.)	OF	5	19	2	5	0	1	2	7	0	0	0	0	0-0	.263	.250	.684	.934	0	1.000
Division series totals (3 years)		12	50	8	14	2	1	3	11	1	6	0	1	0-0	.280	.288	.540	.828	0	1.000

CHAMPIONSHIP SERIES RECORD

Year Team (League)	Pos.	G	AB	R	H	2B	3B	HR	RBI	BB	SO	HBP	GDP	SB-CS	Avg.	OBP	SLG	OPS	E	Avg.
2002—Anaheim (A.L.)	OF	5	20	3	5	1	0	1	3	1	0	0	0	0-1	.250	.286	.450	.736	0	1.000
2005—Los Angeles (A.L.)	OF	5	17	2	3	0	1	2	1	5	0	0	0	0-0	.176	.211	.353	.563	0	1.000
Champ. series totals (2 years)		10	37	5	8	1	0	2	5	2	5	0	0	0-1	.216	.250	.405	.655	0	1.000

WORLD SERIES RECORD

Year Team (League)	Pos.	G	AB	R	H	2B	3B	HR	RBI	BB	SO	HBP	GDP	SB-CS	Avg.	OBP	SLG	OPS	E	Avg.
2002—Anaheim (A.L.)	OF	7	32	3	9	1	0	0	3	0	3	0	1	0-0	.281	.281	.313	.594	1	.947

ALL-STAR GAME RECORD

	G	AB	R	H	2B	3B	HR	RBI	BB	SO	HBP	GDP	SB-CS	Avg.	OBP	SLG	OPS	E	Avg.
All-Star Game totals (3 years)	3	10	1	3	1	0	1	3	0	2	0	0	0-0	.300	.300	.700	1.000	0	...

2006 LEFTY-RIGHTY SPLITS

vs.	Avg.	AB	H	2B	3B	HR	RBI	BB	SO	OBP	Slg.	vs.	Avg.	AB	H	2B	3B	HR	RBI	BB	SO	OBP	Slg.
L	.248	165	41	11	1	3	26	8	35	.280	.382	R	.294	378	111	17	1	14	59	30	60	.341	.455

ANDERSON, MARLON — 2B/OF

PERSONAL: Born January 6, 1974, in Montgomery, Ala. ... 5-11/200. ... Bats left, throws right. ... Full name: Marlon Ordell Anderson. ... High school: Prattville (Ala.). ... College: South Alabama. **TRANSACTIONS/CAREER NOTES:** Selected by Philadelphia Phillies organization in second round of 1995 free-agent draft; choice received from St. Louis Cardinals as part of compensation for Cardinals signing Type A free-agent P Danny Jackson. ... Signed as a free agent by Tampa Bay Devil Rays (January 16, 2003). ... On suspended list (July 29-August 1, 2003). ... Signed as a free agent by St. Louis Cardinals (January 9, 2004). ... Released by Cardinals (November 19, 2004). ... Signed by New York Mets organization (December 23, 2004). ... Signed as a free agent by Washington Nationals (November 18, 2005). ... Traded by Nationals with cash to Los Angeles Dodgers for P Jhonny Nunez (August 31, 2006). **STATISTICAL NOTES:** Hit home run in first major league at-bat (September 8, 1998). ... Career major league grand slams: 1.

2006 GAMES PLAYED BY POSITION (MLB): 2B—33, OF—32, DH—3, 1B—2.

								BATTING											FIELDING	
Year Team (League)	Pos.	G	AB	R	H	2B	3B	HR	RBI	BB	SO	HBP	GDP	SB-CS	Avg.	OBP	SLG	OPS	E	Avg.
1995—Batavia (NY-Penn)		74	312	52	92	13	4	3	40	15	20	4	2	22-8	.295	.331	.391	.722	14	.965
1996—Clearwater (Fla. St.)	2B	60	257	37	70	10	3	2	22	14	18	2	4	26-1	.272	.315	.358	.673	16	.958
—Reading (East.)	2B	75	314	38	86	14	3	3	28	26	44	1	5	17-9	.274	.330	.366	.697	18	.957
1997—Reading (East.)		137	553	88	147	18	6	10	62	42	77	10	8	27-15	.266	.328	.374	.703	29	.961
1998—Scran./W.B. (I.L.)		136	575	104	176	32	14	16	86	28	77	7	11	24-12	.306	.343	.494	.837	28	.959
—Philadelphia (N.L.)		17	43	4	14	3	0	1	4	1	6	0	0	2-0	.326	.333	.465	.798	1	.978
1999—Philadelphia (N.L.)	2B	129	452	48	114	26	4	5	54	24	61	2	6	13-2	.252	.292	.363	.652	11	.979
2000—Scran./W.B. (I.L.)	2B	103	397	57	121	18	8	8	53	39	43	5	2	24-10	.305	.370	.451	.821	14	.969
—Philadelphia (N.L.)	2B	41	162	10	37	8	1	1	15	12	22	0	5	2-2	.228	.282	.309	.590	2	.989
2001—Philadelphia (N.L.)	2B	147	522	69	153	30	2	11	61	35	74	2	12	8-5	.293	.337	.421	.758	12	.982
2002—Philadelphia (N.L.)	2B	145	539	64	139	30	6	8	48	42	71	5	16	5-1	.258	.315	.380	.696	*20	.970
2003—Tampa Bay (A.L.)	2B-DH-OF	145	482	59	130	27	3	6	67	41	60	3	6	19-3	.270	.328	.376	.703	15	.973
2004—St. Louis (N.L.)	2B-OF-1B-DH	113	253	31	60	12	0	8	28	12	38	1	5	6-2	.237	.269	.379	.649	7	.961
2005—New York (N.L.)	1B-OF-DH	123	235	31	62	9	0	7	19	18	45	1	2	6-1	.264	.316	.391	.708	3	.990
2006—Wash. (N.L.)	2B-OF-DH-1B	109	215	31	59	13	2	6	23	18	41	1	1	2-4	.274	.331	.423	.754	8	.951
—Los Angeles (N.L.)	OF-2B	25	64	12	24	3	2	7	15	7	8	0	3	2-2	.375	.431	.813	1.243	1	.957
American League totals (1 year)		145	482	59	130	27	3	6	67	41	60	3	6	19-3	.270	.328	.376	.703	15	.973
National League totals (8 years)		849	2485	300	662	134	17	53	267	169	366	12	50	46-19	.266	.314	.398	.712	65	.977
Major League totals (9 years)		994	2967	359	792	161	20	59	334	210	426	15	56	65-22	.267	.316	.394	.710	80	.976

DIVISION SERIES RECORD

Year Team (League)	Pos.	G	AB	R	H	2B	3B	HR	RBI	BB	SO	HBP	GDP	SB-CS	Avg.	OBP	SLG	OPS	E	Avg.
2004—St. Louis (N.L.)		3	3	0	0	0	0	0	0	0	0	0	0	0-0	.000	.000	.000	.000	0	...
2006—Los Angeles (N.L.)	OF	3	13	2	4	1	0	0	1	0	1	0	0	0-0	.308	.308	.385	.692	0	1.000
Division series totals (2 years)		6	16	2	4	1	0	0	1	0	2	0	0	0-0	.250	.250	.313	.563	0	1.000

CHAMPIONSHIP SERIES RECORD

Year Team (League)	Pos.	G	AB	R	H	2B	3B	HR	RBI	BB	SO	HBP	GDP	SB-CS	Avg.	OBP	SLG	OPS	E	Avg.
2004—St. Louis (N.L.)	2B	5	3	1	1	1	0	0	0	1	0	1	0	0-0	.333	.600	.667	1.267	0	...

WORLD SERIES RECORD

Year Team (League)	Pos.	G	AB	R	H	2B	3B	HR	RBI	BB	SO	HBP	GDP	SB-CS	Avg.	OBP	SLG	OPS	E	Avg.
2004—St. Louis (N.L.)	2B-DH	4	6	0	1	1	0	0	0	0	0	0	0	0-0	.167	.167	.333	.500	0	1.000

2006 LEFTY-RIGHTY SPLITS

vs.	Avg.	AB	H	2B	3B	HR	RBI	BB	SO	OBP	Slg.	vs.	Avg.	AB	H	2B	3B	HR	RBI	BB	SO	OBP	Slg.
L	.254	63	16	1	0	2	5	3	16	.284	.365	R	.310	216	67	15	4	10	33	22	33	.373	.556

ANDINO, ROBERT — SS

PERSONAL: Born April 25, 1984, in Miami. ... 6-0/170. ... Bats right, throws right. ... Full name: Robert Lazaro Andino. ... High school: Southridge (Miami). **TRANSACTIONS/CAREER NOTES:** Selected by Florida Marlins organization in second round of 2002 free-agent draft.

2006 GAMES PLAYED BY POSITION (MLB): SS—9.

								BATTING											FIELDING	
Year Team (League)	Pos.	G	AB	R	H	2B	3B	HR	RBI	BB	SO	HBP	GDP	SB-CS	Avg.	OBP	SLG	OPS	E	Avg.
2002—GC Marlins (GCL)	SS	9	27	2	7	0	0	0	2	5	6	0	1	3-0	.259	.364	.259	.623	1	.974
—Jamestown (NYP)	SS	9	36	2	6	1	1	0	3	1	9	0	2	1-0	.167	.189	.250	.439	1	.976

										BATTING									FIELDING	
Year	Team (League)	Pos.	G	AB	R	H	2B	3B	HR	RBI	BB	SO	HBP	GDP	SB-CS	Avg.	OBP	SLG	OPS	E	Avg.
2003— Greensboro (S. Atl.)		SS	119	416	45	78	17	2	2	27	46	128	1	6	6-5	.188	.266	.252	.518	28	.945
2004— Greensboro (S. Atl.)		SS	76	295	27	83	10	1	8	46	18	83	1	5	9-2	.281	.321	.403	.724	21	.475
— Jupiter (Fla. St.)		SS-2B	49	196	18	55	7	2	0	15	7	43	0	3	6-2	.281	.304	.337	.641	7	.000
2005— Carolina (Southern)		SS-2B	127	516	63	139	30	0	5	48	37	111	6	11	22-7	.269	.324	.357	.680	27	.952
— Florida (N.L.)		SS	17	44	4	7	4	0	0	1	5	8	0	2	1-0	.159	.245	.250	.495	2	.956
2006— Albuquerque (PCL)			120	498	70	127	18	6	8	46	33	100	4	13	13-11	.255	.303	.363	.667	20	.965
— Florida (N.L.)		SS	11	24	0	4	1	0	0	2	1	6	0	0	1-0	.167	.185	.208	.394	1	.964
Major League totals (2 years)			28	68	4	11	5	0	0	3	6	14	0	2	2-0	.162	.224	.235	.459	3	.959

2006 LEFTY-RIGHTY SPLITS

vs.	Avg.	AB	H	2B	3B	HR	RBI	BB	SO	OBP	Slg.	vs.	Avg.	AB	H	2B	3B	HR	RBI	BB	SO	OBP	Slg.
L	.111	9	1	0	0	0	0	1	3	.200	.111	R	.200	15	3	1	0	0	2	0	3	.176	.267

ANDRADE, STEVE — P

PERSONAL: Born February 6, 1978, in Woodland, Calif. ... 6-1/220. ... Throws right, bats right. ... Full name: Stephen Michael Andrade. ... College: Stanislaus State. **TRANSACTIONS/CAREER NOTES:** Selected by Anaheim Angels organization in 32nd round of 2001 free-agent draft. ... Claimed on waivers by Toronto Blue Jays (December 6, 2004). ... Selected by Tampa Bay Devil Rays in Rule 5 major league draft (December 8, 2005). ... Traded by Devil Rays to San Diego Padres for cash (December 8, 2005). ... Claimed on waivers by Kansas City Royals (March 28, 2006). ... Signed as a free agent by Padres organization (June 15, 2006).
CAREER HITTING: 0-for-0 (.000), 0 R, 0 2B, 0 3B, 0 HR, 0 RBI.

Year	Team (League)	W	L	Pct.	ERA	WHIP	G	GS	CG	ShO	Hld.	Sv.-Opp.	IP	H	R	ER	HR	BB-IBB	SO	Avg.
2001— Provo (Pion.)		0	0	...	0.00	1.50	1	0	0	0	...	0-...	2.0	3	0	0	0	0-0	5	.333
— Cedar Rap. (Midw.)		2	1	.667	6.52	1.41	20	0	0	0	...	0-...	29.0	33	24	21	3	8-0	31	.284
2002— Cedar Rap. (Midw.)		1	1	.500	1.16	0.85	46	0	0	0	...	11-...	54.1	30	7	7	1	16-1	93	.162
2003— Rancho Cuca. (Calif.)		0	0	...	0.00	1.00	3	0	0	0	...	1-...	3.0	3	0	0	0	3-0	7	.000
— Arkansas (Texas)		5	1	.833	2.65	0.88	36	0	0	0	...	7-...	51.0	26	16	15	2	19-1	74	.147
2004— Salt Lake (PCL)		0	1	.000	4.61	1.68	12	0	0	0	...	3-...	13.2	15	7	7	1	8-0	17	.288
— Arkansas (Texas)		2	2	.500	2.44	1.02	35	0	0	0	...	9-...	48.0	37	14	13	4	12-0	59	.204
2005— New Hampshire (East.)		3	2	.600	1.97	0.77	35	0	0	0	4	3-6	50.1	33	12	11	3	16-0	71	.134
2006— Omaha (PCL)		1	2	.333	4.63	1.24	12	0	0	0	0	0-1	23.1	21	13	12	3	8-0	22	.233
— Portland (PCL)		3	0	1.000	2.44	1.24	26	0	0	0	0	0-0	44.1	33	13	12	1	22-1	45	.209
— Kansas City (A.L.)		0	0	...	9.64	1.93	4	0	0	0	1	0-0	4.2	5	5	5	0	4-0	5	.278
Major League totals (1 year)		0	0	...	9.64	1.93	4	0	0	0	1	0-0	4.2	5	5	5	0	4-0	5	.278

2006 LEFTY-RIGHTY SPLITS

vs.	Avg.	AB	H	2B	3B	HR	RBI	BB	SO	OBP	Slg.	vs.	Avg.	AB	H	2B	3B	HR	RBI	BB	SO	OBP	Slg.
L	.286	7	2	0	0	0	2	2	3	.444	.286	R	.273	11	3	0	0	0	0	2	2	.385	.273

ANKIEL, RICK — OF

PERSONAL: Born July 19, 1979, in Fort Pierce, Fla. ... 6-1/215. ... Bats left, throws left. ... Full name: Richard Alexander Ankiel. ... Name pronounced: ann-KEEL. ... High school: Port St. Lucie (Fla.). **TRANSACTIONS/CAREER NOTES:** Selected by St. Louis Cardinals organization in second round of 1997 free-agent draft. ... On disabled list (March 29-June 5, 2002). ... On disabled list (March 25-September 1, 2004); included rehabilitation assignments to Palm Beach and Memphis. ... Released by Cardinals (April 4, 2005). ... Re-signed by Cardinals organization (April 6, 2005). ... On disabled list (March 31, 2006-entire season). **HONORS:** Named Minor League Player of the Year by THE SPORTING NEWS (1999). ... Named N.L. Rookie Pitcher of the Year by THE SPORTING NEWS (2000). **MISCELLANEOUS NOTES:** Appeared in one game as pinch runner (2000). ... Struck out three times in three appearances as pinch hitter (2000).
CAREER HITTING AS MAJOR LEAGUE PITCHER: 18-for-87 (.207), 9 R, 1 2B, 1 3B, 2 HR, 9 RBI.

Year	Team (League)	W	L	Pct.	ERA	WHIP	G	GS	CG	ShO	Hld.	Sv.-Opp.	IP	H	R	ER	HR	BB-IBB	SO	Avg.
1998— Peoria (Midw.)		3	0	1.000	2.06	.077	7	7	0	0	...	0-0	35.0	15	8	8	0	12-0	41	.134
— Prince Will. (Car.)		9	6	.600	2.79	1.02	21	21	1	0	...	0-0	126.0	91	46	39	8	38-0	181	.205
1999— Arkansas (Texas.)		6	0	1.000	0.91	0.83	8	8	1	1	...	0-0	49.1	25	6	5	2	16-0	75	.145
— Memphis (PCL.)		7	3	.700	3.16	1.35	16	16	0	0	...	0-0	88.1	73	37	31	7	46-1	119	.223
— St. Louis (N.L.)		0	1	.000	3.27	1.21	9	5	0	0	0	1-1	33.0	26	12	12	2	14-0	39	.215
2000— St. Louis (N.L.)		11	7	.611	3.50	1.30	31	30	0	0	1	0-0	175.0	137	80	68	21	90-2	194	.219
2001— St. Louis (N.L.)		1	2	.333	7.13	2.08	6	6	0	0	0	0-0	24.0	25	21	19	7	25-0	27	.275
— Memphis (PCL)		0	2	.000	20.77	4.62	3	3	0	0	0	0-0	4.1	3	10	10	0	17-0	4	.200
— Johnson City (App.)		5	3	.625	1.33	0.68	41	14	1	0	...	0-...	87.2	42	20	13	1	18-0	158	.140
2002— Peoria (Midw.)		Did not play																		
— St. Louis (N.L.)		Did not play																		
2003— Tennessee (Sou.)		2	6	.250	6.29	1.70	20	10	1	0	...	0-...	54.1	45	42	38	5	49-1	64	.232
2004— Palm Beach (Fla. St.)		0	1	.000	2.08	0.58	3	3	0	0	0	0-0	8.2	5	4	2	0	0-0	11	.167
— Tennessee (Sou.)		1	0	1.000	0.00	0.56	2	2	0	0	0	0-0	9.0	3	1	0	0	2-0	7	.100
— Memphis (PCL.)		1	0	1.000	0.17	0.17	1	1	0	0	0	0-0	6.0	1	1	0	0	0-0	5	.053
— St. Louis (N.L.)		1	0	1.000	5.40	1.10	5	0	0	0	2	0-0	10.0	10	6	6	2	1-0	9	.256
Major League totals (4 years)		13	10	.565	3.90	1.36	51	41	0	0	3	1-1	242.0	198	119	105	32	130-2	269	.226

DIVISION SERIES RECORD

Year	Team (League)	W	L	Pct.	ERA	WHIP	G	GS	CG	ShO	Hld.	Sv.-Opp.	IP	H	R	ER	HR	BB-IBB	SO	Avg.
2000— St. Louis (N.L.)		0	0	...	13.50	3.75	1	1	0	0		0-0	2.2	4	4	4	0	6-0	3	.400

CHAMPIONSHIP SERIES RECORD

Year	Team (League)	W	L	Pct.	ERA	WHIP	G	GS	CG	ShO	Hld.	Sv.-Opp.	IP	H	R	ER	HR	BB-IBB	SO	Avg.
2000— St. Louis (N.L.)		0	0	...	20.25	4.50	2	1	0	0	0		1.1	1	3	3	0	5-0	2	.333

										BATTING									FIELDING	
Year	Team (League)	Pos.	G	AB	R	H	2B	3B	HR	RBI	BB	SO	HBP	GDP	SB-CS	Avg.	OBP	SLG	OPS	E	Avg.
2001— Johnson City (App.)		DH	41	105	21	30	7	0	10	35	11	26	...		0-0	.286	...	.638		...	...
2005— Quad Cities (Mid.)		OF-DH	51	185	33	50	10	1	11	45	27	37	5	4	0-0	.270	.368	.514	.881	6	.949
— Springfield (Texas)		OF-DH	34	136	18	33	7	0	10	30	10	29	0	4	0-0	.243	.295	.515	.809	2	.981
2006— St. Louis (N.L.)		Did not play.																			

AQUINO, GREG — P

PERSONAL: Born January 11, 1978, in Palenque, Dominican Republic. ... 6-1/188. ... Throws right, bats right. ... Full name: Gregori Emilio Aquino. ... Name pronounced: uh-KEE-no. ... High school: Americo Lugo (Santo Domingo, D.R.). **TRANSACTIONS/CAREER NOTES:** Signed as a non-drafted free agent by Arizona Diamondbacks organization

A

(November 8, 1995). ... On disabled list (April 9-June 12, 2005); included rehabilitation assignment to Tucson. ... On disabled list (August 8-September 1, 2006); included rehabilitation assignment to Tucson.

CAREER HITTING: 0-for-2 (.000), 0 R, 0 2B, 0 3B, 0 HR, 0 RBI.

Year	Team (League)	W	L	Pct.	ERA	WHIP	G	GS	CG	ShO	Hld.	Sv.-Opp.	IP	H	R	ER	HR	BB-IBB	SO	Avg.
1999—Ariz. D'backs (Ariz.)		1	2	.333	3.79	1.58	13	2	0	0	...	0-...	19.0	17	11	8	0	13-0	20	.246
2000—South Bend (Mid.)		5	7	.417	4.46	1.47	29	18	0	0	...	0-...	119.0	119	67	59	9	56-0	93	.260
2001—Lancaster (Calif.)		2	5	.286	8.14	1.98	25	4	0	0	...	0-...	42.0	59	40	38	7	24-0	39	.331
—Yakima (N'west)		4	2	.667	3.30	1.14	8	8	0	0	...	0-...	46.1	39	18	17	2	14-1	39	.229
2002—Yakima (N'west)		1	1	.500	2.06	1.23	6	6	0	0	...	0-...	35.0	26	9	8	0	17-0	34	.213
—Lancaster (Calif.)		4	1	.800	3.67	1.39	8	8	0	0	...	0-...	49.0	50	20	20	3	18-0	50	.267
2003—El Paso (Texas)		7	3	.700	3.46	1.43	20	20	0	0	...	0-...	106.2	115	43	41	5	38-1	91	.278
2004—Tucson (PCL)		1	3	.250	6.37	1.72	21	2	0	0	...	1-...	29.2	33	25	21	2	18-0	19	.270
—Arizona (N.L.)		0	0	.000	3.06	1.16	34	0	0	0	1	16-19	35.1	24	15	12	4	17-2	26	.194
2005—Tucson (PCL)		1	0	1.000	1.04	0.46	6	0	0	0	...	0-0	8.2	4	1	1	0	0-0	7	.129
—Arizona (N.L.)		0	1	.000	7.76	1.88	35	0	0	0	3	1-3	31.1	42	29	27	7	17-1	34	.318
2006—Tucson (PCL)		2	0	1.000	0.00	0.86	9	0	0	0	1	1-2	11.2	6	0	0	0	4-0	15	.154
—Arizona (N.L.)		2	0	1.000	4.47	1.61	42	0	0	0	2	0-0	48.1	54	27	24	8	24-2	51	.283
Major League totals (3 years)		2	3	.400	4.93	1.55	111	0	0	0	6	17-22	115.0	120	71	63	19	58-5	111	.268

2006 LEFTY-RIGHTY SPLITS

vs.	Avg.	AB	H	2B	3B	HR	RBI	BB	SO	OBP	Slg.	vs.	Avg.	AB	H	2B	3B	HR	RBI	BB	SO	OBP	Slg.
L	.280	93	26	5	0	2	13	11	20	.362	.398	R	.286	98	28	6	0	6	17	13	31	.386	.531

ARDOIN, DANNY — C

PERSONAL: Born July 8, 1974, in Ville Platte, La. ... 6-0/218. ... Bats right, throws right. ... Full name: Daniel Wayne Ardoin. ... Name pronounced: ar-DWAH. ... High school: Sacred Heart (Ville Platte, La.). ... Junior college: Texarkana (Texas) C.C. ... College: McNeese State. **TRANSACTIONS/CAREER NOTES:** Selected by Boston Red Sox organization in 41st round of 1993 free-agent draft; did not sign. ... Selected by Cleveland Indians organization in 39th round of 1994 free-agent draft; did not sign. ... Selected by Oakland Athletics organization in fifth round of 1995 free-agent draft. ... Traded by A's to Minnesota Twins for 1B/OF Mario Valdez (July 31, 2000). ... Signed as a free agent by Kansas City Royals organization (December 22, 2001). ... Released by Royals (May 16, 2002). ... Signed as a free agent by Texas Rangers organization (May 17, 2002). ... Signed as a free agent by Colorado Rockies organization (December 14, 2004). ... On disabled list (May 26-July 31, 2006); included rehabilitation assignments to Modesto and Colorado Springs. ... Claimed on waivers by Baltimore Orioles (August 30, 2006). ... Signed as free agent by Washington Nationals organization (November 6, 2006).

2006 GAMES PLAYED BY POSITION (MLB): C—40.

							BATTING										FIELDING	
Year	Team (League)	Pos.	G	AB	R	H	2B	3B	HR	RBI	BB	SO	HBP	GDP	SB-CS	Avg.	OBP	SLG	OPS	E	Avg.
1995—S. Oregon (N'west)	C	58	175	28	41	9	1	2	23	31	50	9	2	2-1	.234	.370	.331	.701	14	.971
1996—Modesto (California)	1B-3B-C	91	317	55	83	13	3	6	34	47	81	9	9	5-7	.262	.371	.379	.749	21	.968
1997—Visalia (Calif.)	1B-3B-C																			
—Huntsville (Sou.)	OF	43	145	16	34	7	1	3	19	21	39	4	3	0-1	.234	.347	.359	.706	5	.987
1998—Huntsville (Sou.)	3B-C	57	208	26	48	10	1	4	23	17	38	3	7	2-3	.231	.296	.346	.642	10	.972
1999—Vancouver (PCL)	1B-C-OF	109	363	67	90	21	0	16	62	62	87	7	10	8-4	.248	.367	.438	.805	12	.982
2000—Sacramento (PCL)	C-3B-1B	109	336	53	85	13	2	8	46	50	78	9	12	3-3	.253	.364	.375	.739	10	.984
—Modesto (California)	C-1B-3B	67	234	42	65	16	1	6	34	34	72	8	5	6-0	.278	.385	.432	.817	8	.980
—Salt Lake (PCL)	C	4	10	1	3	1	0	0	2	0	4	1	0	0-0	.300	.364	.400	.764	1	.960
—Minnesota (A.L.)	C	3	9	1	2	0	0	0	0	3	4	0	0	0-0	.222	.417	.222	.639	1	1.000
2001—Edmonton (PCL)	C	15	32	4	4	1	0	1	5	8	10	0	0	0-0	.125	.300	.550	.550	1	.989
2002—Omaha (PCL)	C-OF	88	302	37	77	18	1	5	37	22	81	1	8	2-6	.255	.304	.371	.675	6	.989
—Tulsa (Texas)	C-1B	25	77	10	16	3	0	3	10	11	25	0	1	1-0	.208	.297	.364	.660	3	.984
—Oklahoma (PCL)	C	8	21	1	3	0	0	0	0	4	9	0	1	0-0	.143	.280	.143	.423	0	1.000
2003—Oklahoma (PCL)	C-OF	33	106	10	24	5	0	2	11	10	31	2	2	0-0	.226	.303	.330	.633	4	.984
2004—Texas (A.L.)	C-3B-DH	74	239	35	58	11	2	7	35	21	58	3	9	0-2	.243	.311	.393	.704	10	.973
—Oklahoma (PCL)	C	6	8	1	1	0	0	0	1	3	2	0	0	0-0	.125	.364	.125	.489	1	.958
2005—Colo. Springs (PCL)	C	68	237	50	73	12	0	10	44	41	66	8	0	1-1	.308	.422	.485	.907	11	.976
—Colorado (N.L.)	C-1B-DH	44	142	27	48	12	2	6	24	20	38	6	4	3-1	.338	.438	.577	1.015	2	.994
2006—Modesto (California)	C	80	210	28	48	10	0	6	22	20	69	9	8	1-1	.229	.320	.362	.681	6	.988
—Colo. Springs (PCL)		7	26	4	2	2	0	0	2	8	2	2	0	0-0	.077	.200	.154	.354	2	.941
—Colorado (N.L.)		6	15	2	4	2	0	0	2	2	5	1	0	0-0	.267	.389	.400	.789	1	.952
—Baltimore (A.L.)	C	35	109	12	21	5	1	0	8	8	27	2	2	0-0	.193	.261	.257	.517	3	.986
	C	5	13	2	1	0	0	0	1	1	6	1	1	0-0	.077	.200	.077	.277	0	1.000
American League totals (3 years)		26	53	7	6	1	0	1	7	12	18	1	1	0-0	.113	.288	.189	.477	2	.987
National League totals (2 years)		115	319	40	69	15	1	6	24	28	96	11	10	1-1	.216	.300	.326	.626	9	.988
Major League totals (4 years)		141	372	47	75	16	1	7	31	40	114	12	11	1-1	.202	.298	.306	.605	11	.987

2006 LEFTY-RIGHTY SPLITS

vs.	Avg.	AB	H	2B	3B	HR	RBI	BB	SO	OBP	Slg.	vs.	Avg.	AB	H	2B	3B	HR	RBI	BB	SO	OBP	Slg.
L	.250	12	3	0	1	0	1	1	5	.357	.417	R	.173	110	19	5	0	0	6	0	28	.242	.218

ARIAS, JOAQUIN — IF

PERSONAL: Born September 21, 1984, in Santo Domingo, Dominican Republic. ... 6-1/160. ... Bats right, throws right. ... Full name: Joaquin Arias. ... **TRANSACTIONS/CAREER NOTES:** Signed as a non-drafted free agent by New York Yankees organization (July 12, 2001). ... Traded by Yankees to Texas Rangers (March 23, 2004), completing deal in which Rangers traded SS Alex Rodriguez to Yankees for 2B Alfonso Soriano and a player to be named (February 16, 2004).

2006 GAMES PLAYED BY POSITION (MLB): SS—5, 3B—1.

							BATTING										FIELDING	
Year	Team (League)	Pos.	G	AB	R	H	2B	3B	HR	RBI	BB	SO	HBP	GDP	SB-CS	Avg.	OBP	SLG	OPS	E	Avg.
2002—GC Yankees (GCL)		57	203	29	61	7	6	0	21	12	16	0	4	2-4	.300	.338	.394	.732	...	...
2003—Battle Creek (Midw.)		130	481	60	128	12	8	3	48	26	44	3	7	12-5	.266	.306	.343	.649	...	...
2004—Stockton (Calif.)		123	500	77	150	20	8	4	62	31	53	5	3	30-14	.300	.344	.390	.740	...	...
2005—Frisco (Texas)	SS-DH	120	499	65	157	23	8	5	56	17	46	1	5	20-10	.315	.335	.423	.757	29	.952
2006—Oklahoma (PCL)		124	493	56	132	14	10	4	49	19	64	4	6	26-10	.268	.296	.361	.657	24	.957
—Texas (A.L.)	SS-3B	6	11	4	6	1	0	0	1	0	0	0	0	0-1	.545	.583	.636	1.220	0	1.000
Major League totals (1 year)		6	11	4	6	1	0	0	1	0	0	0	0	0-1	.545	.583	.636	1.220	0	1.000

2006 LEFTY-RIGHTY SPLITS

vs.	Avg.	AB	H	2B	3B	HR	RBI	BB	SO	OBP	Slg.	vs.	Avg.	AB	H	2B	3B	HR	RBI	BB	SO	OBP	Slg.
L	.333	6	2	1	0	0	0	0	0	.429	.500	R	.800	5	4	0	0	0	1	0	0	.800	.800

ARMAS, TONY — P

PERSONAL: Born April 29, 1978, in Puerto Piritu, Venezuela. ... 6-3/225. ... Throws right, bats right. ... Full name: Antonio Jose Armas. ... Name pronounced: AR-mus. ... Son of Tony Armas, outfielder with four major league teams (1976-89); nephew of Marcos Armas, outfielder with Oakland Athletics (1993). **TRANSACTIONS/CAREER NOTES:** Signed as a non-drafted free agent by New York Yankees organization (August 16, 1994). ... Traded by Yankees with a player to be named to Boston Red Sox for C Mike Stanley and SS Randy Brown (August 13, 1997); Red Sox acquired P Jim Mecir to complete deal (September 29, 1997). ... Traded by Red Sox to Montreal Expos (December 18, 1997), completing deal in which Red Sox traded P Carl Pavano and a player to be named to Expos for P Pedro Martinez (November 18, 1997). ... On disabled list (April 1-28 and July 19-September 6, 2000); included rehabilitation assignments to Jupiter and Ottawa. ... On disabled list (July 27-August 19, 2002; and April 21, 2003-remainder of season). ... On disabled list (March 26-May 31, 2004); included rehabilitation assignments to Brevard County and Edmonton. ... Expos franchise transferred to Washington, D.C., and renamed Washington Nationals for 2005 season (December 3, 2004). ... On disabled list (March 28-May 9; and September 17, 2005-remainder of season). ... On disabled list (June 23-July 17, 2006); included rehabilitation assignments to Harrisburg and GCL Nationals.

CAREER HITTING: 23-for-239 (.096), 6 R, 1 2B, 1 3B, 0 HR, 8 RBI.

Year Team (League)	W	L	Pct.	ERA	WHIP	G	GS	CG	ShO	Hld.	Sv.-Opp.	IP	H	R	ER	HR	BB-IBB	SO	Avg.
1995— GC Yankees (GCL)	0	1	.000	0.64	1.29	5	4	0	0	...	0-...	14.0	12	9	1	1	6-0	13	.226
1996— Oneonta (NYP)	1	1	.500	5.74	1.60	3	3	0	0	...	0-...	15.2	14	12	10	1	11-0	14	.230
— GC Yankees (GCL)	4	1	.800	3.15	1.18	8	7	0	0	...	1-...	45.2	41	18	16	1	13-0	45	.236
1997— Greensboro (S. Atl.)	5	2	.714	1.05	0.95	9	9	2	1	...	0-...	51.2	36	13	6	3	13-0	64	.190
— Tampa (Fla. St.)	3	1	.750	3.33	1.28	9	9	0	0	...	0-...	46.0	43	23	17	1	16-3	26	.257
— Sarasota (Fla. St.)	2	1	.667	6.62	1.70	3	3	0	0	...	0-...	17.2	18	13	13	2	12-0	9	.281
1998— Jupiter (Fla. St.)	12	8	.600	2.88	1.30	27	27	1	1	...	0-...	153.1	140	63	49	11	59-0	136	.244
1999— Harrisburg (East.)	9	7	.563	2.19	1.29	24	24	2	1	...	0-...	149.2	123	62	48	10	55-0	106	.226
— Montreal (N.L.)	0	1	.000	1.50	1.67	1	1	0	0	0	0-0	6.0	8	4	1	0	2-1	2	.320
2000— Jupiter (Fla. St.)	0	0	...	0.00	0.86	1	1	0	0	0	0-0	4.2	4	0	0	0	0-0	8	.222
— Ottawa (Int'l)	1	2	.333	3.79	1.37	4	4	0	0	0	0-0	19.0	22	11	8	3	4-0	12	.286
— Montreal (N.L.)	7	9	.438	4.36	1.31	17	17	0	0	0	0-0	95.0	74	49	46	10	50-2	59	.218
2001— Montreal (N.L.)	9	14	.391	4.03	1.38	34	34	0	0	0	0-0	196.2	180	101	88	18	91-6	176	.247
2002— Montreal (N.L.)	12	12	.500	4.44	1.38	29	29	0	0	0	0-0	164.1	149	87	81	22	78-12	131	.243
2003— Montreal (N.L.)	2	1	.667	2.61	1.06	5	5	0	0	0	0-0	31.0	25	9	9	4	8-0	23	.225
2004— Brevard County (Fla. St.)	0	1	.000	6.75	1.29	3	3	0	0	0	0-...	9.1	5	7	7	1	7-0	7	.179
— Edmonton (PCL)	0	0	...	1.80	1.20	2	2	0	0	0	0-...	10.0	11	4	2	0	1-0	8	.268
— Montreal (N.L.)	2	4	.333	4.88	1.54	16	16	0	0	0	0-0	72.0	66	41	39	13	45-6	54	.247
2005— New Orleans (PCL)	1	2	.333	4.38	1.46	5	5	0	0	0	0-0	24.2	26	13	12	3	10-3	21	.268
— Wash. (N.L.)	7	7	.500	4.97	1.52	19	19	0	0	0	0-0	101.1	100	57	56	16	54-4	59	.258
2006— Harrisburg (East.)	0	0	...	7.71	1.71	1	1	0	0	0	0-0	2.1	3	2	2	0	1-0	4	.300
— GC Nationals (GCL)	0	1	.000	5.40	1.80	1	1	0	0	0	0-0	5.0	8	3	3	0	1-0	7	.348
— Wash. (N.L.)	9	12	.429	5.03	1.50	30	30	0	0	0	0-0	154.0	167	96	86	19	64-7	97	.279
Major League totals (8 years)	**48**	**60**	**.444**	**4.45**	**1.42**	**151**	**151**	**0**	**0**	**0**	**0-0**	**820.1**	**769**	**444**	**406**	**102**	**392-38**	**601**	**.250**

2006 LEFTY-RIGHTY SPLITS

vs.	Avg.	AB	H	2B	3B	HR	RBI	BB	SO	OBP	Slg.	vs.	Avg.	AB	H	2B	3B	HR	RBI	BB	SO	OBP	Slg.
L	.274	274	75	12	1	8	37	35	40	.360	.412	R	.284	324	92	22	2	11	49	29	57	.357	.466

ARROYO, BRONSON — P

PERSONAL: Born February 24, 1977, in Key West, Fla. ... 6-5/190. ... Throws right, bats right. ... Full name: Bronson Anthony Arroyo. ... Name pronounced: ah-ROY-yoh. ... High school: Hernando (Fla.). **TRANSACTIONS/CAREER NOTES:** Selected by Pittsburgh Pirates organization in third round of 1995 free-agent draft. ... Claimed on waivers by Boston Red Sox (February 4, 2003). ... On suspended list (May 17-25, 2005). ... Traded by Red Sox to Cincinnati Reds for OF Wily Mo Pena (March 20, 2006). **MISCELLANEOUS NOTES:** Appeared in one game as pinch runner and grounded out in only appearance as pinch hitter (2000).

CAREER HITTING: 13-for-136 (.096), 7 R, 5 2B, 0 3B, 2 HR, 7 RBI.

Year Team (League)	W	L	Pct.	ERA	WHIP	G	GS	CG	ShO	Hld.	Sv.-Opp.	IP	H	R	ER	HR	BB-IBB	SO	Avg.
1995— GC Pirates (GCL)	5	4	.556	4.26	1.32	13	9	0	0	...	1-...	61.1	72	39	29	4	9-0	48	.277
1996— Augusta (S. Atl.)	8	6	.571	3.52	1.17	26	26	0	0	...	0-...	135.2	123	64	53	11	36-0	107	.242
1997— Lynchburg (Caro.)	12	4	.750	3.31	1.17	24	24	3	1	...	0-...	160.1	154	69	59	17	33-0	121	.250
1998— Carolina (Southern)	9	8	.529	5.46	1.65	23	22	1	0	...	0-...	127.0	158	91	77	18	51-0	90	.310
1999— Altoona (East.)	15	4	.789	3.65	1.47	25	25	2	1	...	0-...	153.0	167	73	62	15	58-1	100	.280
— Nashville (PCL)	0	2	.000	10.38	2.46	3	3	0	0	...	0-...	13.0	22	15	15	1	10-0	11	.367
2000— Nashville (PCL)	8	2	.800	3.65	1.21	13	13	1	0	...	0-...	88.2	82	43	36	7	25-3	52	.251
— Pittsburgh (N.L.)	2	6	.250	6.40	1.73	20	12	0	0	0	0-0	71.2	88	61	51	10	36-6	50	.302
— Lynchburg (Caro.)	0	0	...	3.86	1.43	1	1	0	0	0	0-0	7.0	8	3	3	0	2-0	3	.267
2001— Pittsburgh (N.L.)	5	7	.417	5.09	1.51	24	13	1	0	2	0-0	88.1	99	54	50	12	34-6	39	.289
— Nashville (PCL)	6	2	.750	3.93	1.18	9	9	1	0	...	0-...	66.1	63	32	29	6	15-1	49	.247
2002— Nashville (PCL)	8	6	.571	2.96	1.08	22	21	3	2	...	0-...	143.0	126	57	47	10	28-1	116	.236
— Pittsburgh (N.L.)	2	1	.667	4.00	1.67	9	4	0	0	1	0-0	27.0	30	14	12	1	15-3	22	.283
2003— Pawtucket (Int'l)	12	6	.667	3.43	1.10	24	24	1	1	...	0-...	149.2	148	66	57	9	23-0	155	.252
— Boston (A.L.)	0	0	...	2.08	0.81	6	0	0	0	0	1-1	17.1	10	5	4	0	4-2	14	.164
2004— Boston (A.L.)	10	9	.526	4.03	1.22	32	29	0	0	0	0-0	178.2	171	99	80	17	47-3	142	.249
2005— Boston (A.L.)	14	10	.583	4.51	1.30	35	32	0	0	0	0-0	205.1	213	116	103	22	54-3	100	.266
2006— Cincinnati (N.L.)	14	11	.560	3.29	1.19	35	•35	3	1	0	0-0	*240.2	222	98	88	31	64-7	184	.243
American League totals (3 years)	**24**	**19**	**.558**	**4.19**	**1.24**	**73**	**61**	**0**	**0**	**0**	**1-1**	**401.1**	**394**	**220**	**187**	**39**	**105-8**	**256**	**.254**
National League totals (4 years)	**23**	**25**	**.479**	**4.23**	**1.37**	**88**	**64**	**4**	**1**	**3**	**0-0**	**427.2**	**439**	**227**	**201**	**54**	**149-22**	**295**	**.266**
Major League totals (7 years)	**47**	**44**	**.516**	**4.21**	**1.31**	**161**	**125**	**4**	**1**	**3**	**1-1**	**829.0**	**833**	**447**	**388**	**93**	**254-30**	**551**	**.260**

DIVISION SERIES RECORD

Year Team (League)	W	L	Pct.	ERA	WHIP	G	GS	CG	ShO	Hld.	Sv.-Opp.	IP	H	R	ER	HR	BB-IBB	SO	Avg.
2004— Boston (A.L.)	0	0	...	3.00	0.83	1	1	0	0	0	0-0	6.0	3	2	2	1	2-0	7	.143
2005— Boston (A.L.)	0	0	...	18.00	4.00	1	0	0	0	0	0-0	1.0	2	2	2	1	2-0	1	.400
Division series totals (2 years)	**0**	**0**	**...**	**5.14**	**1.29**	**2**	**1**	**0**	**0**	**0**	**0-0**	**7.0**	**5**	**4**	**4**	**2**	**4-0**	**8**	**.192**

CHAMPIONSHIP SERIES RECORD

Year Team (League)	W	L	Pct.	ERA	WHIP	G	GS	CG	ShO	Hld.	Sv.-Opp.	IP	H	R	ER	HR	BB-IBB	SO	Avg.
2003— Boston (A.L.)	0	0	...	2.70	1.20	3	0	0	0	0	0-0	3.1	2	1	1	1	2-0	5	.167
2004— Boston (A.L.)	0	0	...	15.75	2.50	3	1	0	0	0	0-0	4.0	8	7	7	2	2-0	3	.421
Champ. series totals (2 years)	**0**	**0**	**...**	**9.82**	**1.91**	**6**	**1**	**0**	**0**	**0**	**0-0**	**7.1**	**10**	**8**	**8**	**3**	**4-0**	**8**	**.323**

WORLD SERIES RECORD

Year Team (League)	W	L	Pct.	ERA	WHIP	G	GS	CG	ShO	Hld.	Sv.-Opp.	IP	H	R	ER	HR	BB-IBB	SO	Avg.
2004— Boston (A.L.)	0	0	...	6.75	1.88	2	0	0	0	0	0-0	2.2	4	2	2	0	1-0	4	.333

ALL-STAR GAME RECORD

Year Team (League)	W	L	Pct.	ERA	WHIP	G	GS	CG	ShO	Hld.	Sv.-Opp.	IP	H	R	ER	HR	BB-IBB	SO	Avg.
All-Star Game totals (1 year)	**0**	**0**	**...**	**9.00**	**1.00**	**1**	**0**	**0**	**0**	**0**	**0-0**	**1.0**	**1**	**1**	**1**	**0**	**1-0**	**4**	**.250**

A

2006 LEFTY-RIGHTY SPLITS

vs.	Avg.	AB	H	2B	3B	HR	RBI	BB	SO	OBP	Slg.	vs.	Avg.	AB	H	2B	3B	HR	RBI	BB	SO	OBP	Slg.
L	.282	450	127	25	3	22	57	37	62	.340	.498	R	.206	462	95	16	0	9	36	27	122	.252	.299

A

ASENCIO, MIGUEL — P

PERSONAL: Born September 29, 1980, in Villa Mella, Dominican Republic. ... 6-2/190. ... Throws right, bats right. ... Full name: Miguel Depaula Asencio. ... Name pronounced: ah-SEN-see-oh. ... High school: Liceo Tiro Al Blanco (La Victoria, Dominican Republic). **TRANSACTIONS/CAREER NOTES:** Signed as a non-drafted free agent by Philadelphia Phillies organization (March 2, 1998). ... Selected by Kansas City Royals from Phillies organization in Rule 5 major league draft (December 13, 2001). ... On disabled list (May 16-September 5, 2003); included rehabilitation assignment to AZL Royals and Wichita. ... On disabled list (March 26, 2004-entire season). ... Signed as a free agent by San Diego Padres (January 18, 2005). ... On disabled list (March 9-June 10, 2005); included rehabilitation assignment to Lake Elsinore. ... Released by Padres (July 18, 2005). ... Signed by Colorado Rockies organization (January 25, 2006).
CAREER HITTING: 0-for-5 (.000), 0 R, 0 2B, 0 3B, 0 HR, 0 RBI.

Year	Team (League)	W	L	Pct.	ERA	WHIP	G	GS	CG	ShO	Hld.	Sv.-Opp.	IP	H	R	ER	HR	BB-IBB	SO	Avg.
1998—	Dom. Phillies (DSL)	0	2	.000	6.55	2.32	11	4	0	0	...	0-...	22.0	39	29	16	...	12-...	7	...
1999—	GC Phillies (GCL)	1	4	.200	5.97	1.78	9	5	0	0	...	0-...	28.2	35	24	19	1	16-0	14	.304
2000—	Clearwater (Fla. St.)	2	1	.667	2.73	1.18	5	5	0	0	...	0-...	33.0	22	10	10	2	17-0	24	.191
—	Batavia (NY-Penn)	2	2	.500	4.99	1.24	7	7	1	0	...	0-...	39.2	32	23	22	3	17-0	28	.224
2001—	Clearwater (Fla. St.)	12	5	.706	2.84	1.25	28	21	2	1	...	0-...	155.1	124	62	49	7	70-1	123	.218
2002—	Kansas City (A.L.)	4	7	.364	5.11	1.62	31	21	0	0	0	0-0	123.1	136	73	70	17	64-2	58	.282
2003—	Kansas City (A.L.)	2	1	.667	5.21	1.55	8	8	1	0	0	0-0	48.1	54	29	28	4	21-0	27	.295
—	Royals-1 (Ariz.)	0	0	...	2.84	1.90	3	3	0	0	...	0-...	6.1	11	3	2	0	1-0	3	.367
—	Wichita (Texas)	0	0	...	0.00	0.50	1	1	0	0	...	0-...	4.0	1	0	0	0	1-0	3	.077
2004—				Did not play.																
2005—	Lake Elsinore (Calif.)	1	0	1.000	1.80	1.20	1	1	0	0	0	0-0	5.0	2	1	1	0	4-0	2	.125
—	Portland (PCL)	0	3	.000	9.42	2.30	3	3	0	0	0	0-0	14.1	27	17	15	1	6-1	7	.409
2006—	Colo. Springs (PCL)	8	7	.533	5.03	1.51	38	16	0	0	4	1-3	111.0	127	69	62	13	41-0	71	.294
—	Colorado (N.L.)	1	0	1.000	4.70	1.70	3	1	0	0	0	0-0	7.2	9	8	4	1	4-0	7	.281
American League totals (2 years)		6	8	.429	5.14	1.60	39	29	1	0	0	0-0	171.2	190	102	98	21	85-2	85	.286
National League totals (1 year)		1	0	1.000	4.70	1.70	3	1	0	0	0	0-0	7.2	9	8	4	1	4-0	7	.281
Major League totals (3 years)		7	8	.467	5.12	1.61	42	30	1	0	0	0-0	179.1	199	110	102	22	89-2	92	.286

2006 LEFTY-RIGHTY SPLITS

vs.	Avg.	AB	H	2B	3B	HR	RBI	BB	SO	OBP	Slg.	vs.	Avg.	AB	H	2B	3B	HR	RBI	BB	SO	OBP	Slg.
L	.133	15	2	1	0	0	3	2	3	.235	.200	R	.412	17	7	3	0	1	5	2	4	.500	.765

ASTACIO, EZEQUIEL — P

PERSONAL: Born November 4, 1979, in Hato Mayor, Dominican Republic. ... 6-3/150. ... Throws right, bats right. ... Full name: Ezequiel F. Astacio. **TRANSACTIONS/CAREER NOTES:** Signed as a non-drafted free agent by Philadelphia Phillies organization (February 22, 1998). ... Traded by Phillies with Ps Brandon Duckworth and Taylor Buchholz to Houston Astros for P Billy Wagner (November 3, 2003).
CAREER HITTING: 3-for-21 (.143), 0 R, 0 2B, 0 3B, 0 HR, 0 RBI.

Year	Team (League)	W	L	Pct.	ERA	WHIP	G	GS	CG	ShO	Hld.	Sv.-Opp.	IP	H	R	ER	HR	BB-IBB	SO	Avg.
1998—	Philadelphia (DSL)	0	3	.000	7.71	2.29	15	4	0	0	...	0-...	21.0	26	29	18	3	22-1	16	.283
1999—	Philadelphia (DSL)	5	2	.714	2.67	1.20	12	12	0	0	...	0-...	64.0	50	24	19	4	27-0	42	.221
2000—	Philadelphia (DSL)	7	5	.583	2.20	1.00	15	15	0	0	...	0-...	90.0	70	40	22	1	20-0	97	.207
2001—	GC Phillies (GCL)	4	2	.667	2.30	1.23	9	9	0	0	...	0-...	47.0	48	16	12	2	10-0	42	.268
2002—	Lakewood (S. Atl.)	10	7	.588	3.31	1.35	25	25	1	0	...	0-...	152.1	159	61	56	9	46-1	100	.275
2003—	Clearwater (Fla. St.)	15	5	.750	3.29	1.14	25	22	2	1	...	0-...	147.2	140	60	54	9	29-0	83	.247
2004—	Round Rock (Texas)	13	10	.565	3.89	1.20	28	28	1	0	0	0-...	176.0	155	89	76	12	56-1	185	.240
2005—	Round Rock (PCL)	4	4	.500	3.02	0.99	13	12	0	0	0	1-1	65.2	53	25	22	6	12-0	57	.220
—	Houston (N.L.)	3	6	.333	5.67	1.54	22	14	0	0	0	0-0	81.0	100	56	51	23	25-2	66	.301
2006—	Round Rock (PCL)	8	4	.667	4.86	1.49	21	17	0	0	2	0-0	92.2	95	51	50	15	43-2	76	.262
—	Houston (N.L.)	2	0	1.000	11.12	2.29	6	0	0	0	0	0-0	5.2	7	7	7	2	6-3	6	.292
Major League totals (2 years)		5	6	.455	6.02	1.59	28	14	0	0	0	0-0	86.2	107	63	58	25	31-5	72	.301

CHAMPIONSHIP SERIES RECORD

Year	Team (League)	W	L	Pct.	ERA	WHIP	G	GS	CG	ShO	Hld.	Sv.-Opp.	IP	H	R	ER	HR	BB-IBB	SO	Avg.
2005—	Houston (N.L.)	0	0	...	0.00	0.00	1	0	0	0	0	0-0	1.0	0	0	0	0	0-0	2	.000

WORLD SERIES RECORD

Year	Team (League)	W	L	Pct.	ERA	WHIP	G	GS	CG	ShO	Hld.	Sv.-Opp.	IP	H	R	ER	HR	BB-IBB	SO	Avg.
2005—	Houston (N.L.)	0	1	.000	27.00	9.00	1	0	0	0	0	0-0	0.2	4	2	2	1	2-0	0	.800

2006 LEFTY-RIGHTY SPLITS

vs.	Avg.	AB	H	2B	3B	HR	RBI	BB	SO	OBP	Slg.	vs.	Avg.	AB	H	2B	3B	HR	RBI	BB	SO	OBP	Slg.
L	.182	11	2	1	0	0	0	2	2	.308	.273	R	.385	13	5	0	0	2	4	4	4	.529	.846

ASTACIO, PEDRO — P

PERSONAL: Born November 28, 1969, in Hato Mayor, Dominican Republic. ... 6-2/210. ... Throws right, bats right. ... Full name: Pedro Julio Astacio. ... Name pronounced: ah-STAH-see-oh. ... High school: Pilar Rondon (Dominican Republic). **TRANSACTIONS/CAREER NOTES:** Signed as a non-drafted free agent by Los Angeles Dodgers organization (November 21, 1987). ... Traded by Dodgers to Colorado Rockies for 2B Eric Young (August 19, 1997). ... Traded by Rockies to Houston Astros for P Scott Elarton and a player to be named (July 31, 2001); Rockies acquired P Garrett Gentry to complete deal (September 27, 2001). ... On disabled list (August 29, 2001-remainder of season). ... Signed as a free agent by New York Mets (January 16, 2002). ... On disabled list (March 21-April 24 and May 22, 2003-remainder of season); included rehabilitation assignment to St. Lucie. ... Signed as a free agent by Boston Red Sox organization (June 30, 2004). ... On suspended list (September 29-October 2, 2004). ... Signed as free agent by Texas Rangers organization (February 4, 2005). ... On disabled list (March 25-April 10, 2005). ... Released by Rangers (June 21, 2005). ... Signed by San Diego Padres organization (June 30, 2005). ... On disabled list (August 29-September 13, 2005). ... Signed as free agent by Washington Nationals (March 10, 2006). ... On disabled list (April 2-July 1, 2006); included rehabilitation assignments to Potomac, New Orleans and Harrisburg. ... Released by Nationals (October 3, 2006). **MISCELLANEOUS NOTES:** Struck out in both appearances as pinch hitter and appeared in one game as pinch runner (1999).
CAREER HITTING: 90-for-677 (.133), 31 R, 8 2B, 1 3B, 0 HR, 28 RBI.

Year	Team (League)	W	L	Pct.	ERA	WHIP	G	GS	CG	ShO	Hld.	Sv.-Opp.	IP	H	R	ER	HR	BB-IBB	SO	Avg.
1988—	Dom. Dodgers (DSL)	4	2	.667	2.08	1.28	8	7	1	0	...	0-...	47.2	43	21	11	...	18-...	20	...
1989—	GC Dodgers (GCL)	7	3	.700	3.17	1.16	12	12	1	0	...	0-...	76.2	77	30	27	3	12-0	52	.258
1990—	Vero Beach (Fla. St.)	1	5	.167	6.32	1.64	8	8	0	0	...	0-...	47.0	54	39	33	3	23-0	41	.286
—	Yakima (N'west)	2	0	1.000	1.74	0.63	3	3	0	0	...	0-...	20.2	9	8	4	0	4-0	22	.123
—	Bakersfield (Calif.)	5	2	.714	2.77	1.17	10	7	1	0	...	0-...	52.0	46	22	16	3	15-1	34	.238
1991—	Vero Beach (Fla. St.)	5	3	.625	1.67	0.88	9	9	3	1	...	0-...	59.1	44	19	11	0	8-0	45	.209
—	San Antonio (Texas)	4	11	.267	4.78	1.60	19	19	2	1	...	0-...	113.0	142	67	60	9	39-3	62	.318

Year — Team (League)	W	L	Pct.	ERA	WHIP	G	GS	CG	ShO	Hld.	Sv.-Opp.	IP	H	R	ER	HR	BB-IBB	SO	Avg.
1992— Albuquerque (PCL)	6	6	.500	5.47	1.61	24	15	1	0	...	0-...	98.2	115	68	60	8	44-1	66	.293
— Los Angeles (N.L.)	5	5	.500	1.98	1.22	11	11	4	4	0	0-0	82.0	80	23	18	1	20-4	43	.255
1993— Los Angeles (N.L.)	14	9	.609	3.57	1.25	31	31	3	2	0	0-0	186.1	165	80	74	14	68-5	122	.239
1994— Los Angeles (N.L.)	6	8	.429	4.29	1.27	23	23	3	1	0	0-0	149.0	142	77	71	18	47-4	108	.252
1995— Los Angeles (N.L.)	7	8	.467	4.24	1.27	48	11	1	1	2	0-1	104.0	103	53	49	12	29-5	80	.261
1996— Los Angeles (N.L.)	9	8	.529	3.44	1.29	35	32	0	0	0	0-0	211.2	207	86	81	18	67-9	130	.261
1997— Los Angeles (N.L.)	7	9	.438	4.10	1.29	26	24	2	1	0	0-0	153.2	151	75	70	15	47-0	115	.256
— Colorado (N.L.)	5	1	.833	4.25	1.29	7	7	0	0	0	0-0	48.2	49	23	23	9	14-0	51	.262
1998— Colorado (N.L.)	13	14	.481	6.23	1.52	35	34	0	0	0	0-0	209.1	245 *	160 *	145	• 39	74-0	170	.294
1999— Colorado (N.L.)	17	11	.607	5.04	1.44	34	34	7	0	0	0-0	232.0	258	140	130	* 38	75-6	210	.285
2000— Colorado (N.L.)	12	9	.571	5.27	1.50	32	32	3	0	0	0-0	196.1	217	119	115	32	77-5	193	.281
2001— Colorado (N.L.)	6	13	.316	5.49	1.43	22	22	4	1	0	0-0	141.0	151	91	86	21	50-3	125	.276
— Houston (N.L.)	2	1	.667	3.14	1.19	4	4	0	0	0	0-0	28.2	30	10	10	1	4-0	19	.280
2002— New York (N.L.)	12	11	.522	4.79	1.33	31	31	3	1	0	0-0	191.2	192	106	102	* 32	63-5	152	.262
2003— St. Lucie (Fla. St.)	0	2	.000	2.08	1.00	4	4	0	0	0	0-...	17.1	15	6	4	0	3-0	15	.231
— New York (N.L.)	3	2	.600	7.36	1.77	7	7	0	0	0	0-0	36.2	47	30	30	8	18-1	20	.311
2004— GC Red Sox (GCL)	1	0	1.000	0.00	0.90	2	1	0	0	0	0-...	4.2	3	0	0	0	0-0	6	.211
— Portland (East.)	0	0	...	0.00	1.00	1	1	0	0	0	0-...	4.0	3	0	0	0	1-0	4	.214
— Pawtucket (Int'l)	0	1	.000	2.89	1.07	2	2	0	0	0	0-...	9.1	9	4	3	1	1-0	7	.250
— Boston (A.L.)	0	0	...	10.38	2.08	5	1	0	0	0	0-0	8.2	13	10	10	2	5-0	6	.342
2005— Texas (A.L.)	2	8	.200	6.04	1.34	12	12	0	0	0	0-0	67.0	79	45	45	13	11-1	45	.292
— Portland (PCL)	0	1	.000	15.75	2.50	1	1	0	0	0	0-0	4.0	10	7	7	0	0-0	1	.500
— San Diego (N.L.)	4	2	.667	3.17	1.34	12	10	0	0	0	0-0	59.2	54	21	21	4	26-3	33	.247
2006— Potomac (Carol.)	0	0	...	0.00	1.00	1	1	0	0	0	0-0	3.0	3	0	0	0	0-0	2	.250
— New Orleans (PCL)	1	1	.500	6.43	1.43	3	3	0	0	0	0-0	14.0	17	10	10	1	3-0	4	.304
— Harrisburg (East.)	0	0	...	2.25	0.25	1	1	0	0	0	0-0	4.0	1	1	1	0	1-0	2	.077
— Wash. (N.L.)	5	5	.500	5.98	1.55	17	17	1	1	0	0-0	90.1	109	64	60	14	31-3	42	.301
American League totals (2 years)	2	8	.200	6.54	1.43	17	13	0	0	0	0-0	75.2	92	55	55	15	16-1	51	.298
National League totals (14 years)	127	116	.523	4.60	1.37	375	330	31	12	2	0-1	2121.0	2200	1158	1085	276	710-53	1613	.270
Major League totals (15 years)	129	124	.510	4.67	1.37	392	343	31	12	2	0-1	2196.2	2292	1213	1140	291	726-54	1664	.271

DIVISION SERIES RECORD

Year — Team (League)	W	L	Pct.	ERA	WHIP	G	GS	CG	ShO	Hld.	Sv.-Opp.	IP	H	R	ER	HR	BB-IBB	SO	Avg.
1995— Los Angeles (N.L.)	0	0	...	0.00	0.30	3	0	0	0	0	0-0	3.1	1	0	0	0	0-0	5	.091
1996— Los Angeles (N.L.)	0	0	...	0.00	0.00	1	0	0	0	0	0-0	1.2	0	0	0	0	0-0	1	.000
2005— San Diego (N.L.)	0	1	.000	4.50	1.50	1	1	0	0	0	0-0	4.0	3	4	2	0	3-0	4	.200
Division series totals (3 years)	0	1	.000	2.00	0.78	5	1	0	0	0	0-0	9.0	4	4	2	0	3-0	10	.129

2006 LEFTY-RIGHTY SPLITS

vs.	Avg.	AB	H	2B	3B	HR	RBI	BB	SO	OBP	Slg.	vs.	Avg.	AB	H	2B	3B	HR	RBI	BB	SO	OBP	Slg.
L	.270	174	47	9	4	7	30	18	23	.332	.489	R	.330	188	62	15	0	7	27	13	19	.374	.521

ATKINS, GARRETT — 3B

PERSONAL: Born December 12, 1979, in Orange, Calif. ... 6-3/210. ... Bats right, throws right. ... Full name: Garrett Bernard Atkins. ... High school: University (Irvine, Calif.). ... College: UCLA. **TRANSACTIONS/CAREER NOTES:** Selected by New York Mets organization in 10th round of 1997 free-agent draft; did not sign. ... Selected by Colorado Rockies organization in fifth round of 2000 free-agent draft. ... On disabled list (April 3-26, 2005); included rehabilitation assignment to Colorado Springs. **STATISTICAL NOTES:** Career major league grand slams: 3.
2006 GAMES PLAYED BY POSITION (MLB): 3B—157, 1B—3.

Year — Team (League)	Pos.	G	AB	R	H	2B	3B	HR	RBI	BB	SO	HBP	GDP	SB-CS	Avg.	OBP	SLG	OPS	E	Avg.
2000— Portland (N'west)	1B-3B	69	251	34	76	12	0	7	47	45	48	2	3	2-0	.303	.411	.434	.846	6	.983
2001— Salem (Carol.)	1B-3B	135	465	70	151	43	5	5	67	74	98	8	8	6-4	.325	.421	.471	.892	7	.995
2002— Carolina (Southern)	3B-1B	128	510	71	138	27	3	12	61	59	77	2	12	6-6	.271	.345	.406	.751	19	.951
2003— Colo. Springs (PCL) 3B-DH-1B		118	439	80	140	30	1	13	67	45	52	3	9	2-4	.319	.382	.481	.863	20	.942
— Colorado (N.L.)	3B	25	69	6	11	2	0	0	4	3	14	1	1	0-0	.159	.205	.188	.394	6	.850
2004— Colo. Springs (PCL) 3B-1B-DH		122	445	88	163	43	3	15	94	57	45	4	20	0-0	.366	.434	.578	1.012	21	.933
— Colorado (N.L.)	3B-1B-OF	15	28	3	10	2	0	1	8	4	3	0	0	0-0	.357	.424	.536	.960	1	1.000
2005— Colo. Springs (PCL)	3B	5	21	4	7	1	0	1	3	2	4	0	0	0-0	.333	.391	.524	.915	1	.917
— Colorado (N.L.)	3B	138	519	62	149	31	1	13	89	45	72	5	18	0-2	.287	.347	.426	.773	18	.950
2006— Colorado (N.L.)	3B-1B	157	602	117	198	48	1	29	120	79	76	7	• 24	4-0	.329	.409	.556	.965	19	.953
Major League totals (4 years)		335	1218	188	368	83	2	43	221	131	165	13	43	4-2	.302	.373	.479	.852	43	.949

2006 LEFTY-RIGHTY SPLITS

vs.	Avg.	AB	H	2B	3B	HR	RBI	BB	SO	OBP	Slg.	vs.	Avg.	AB	H	2B	3B	HR	RBI	BB	SO	OBP	Slg.
L	.341	91	31	10	0	6	24	24	12	.475	.648	R	.327	511	167	38	1	23	96	55	64	.395	.540

AURILIA, RICH — IF

PERSONAL: Born September 2, 1971, in Brooklyn, N.Y. ... 6-1/189. ... Bats right, throws right. ... Full name: Richard Santo Aurilia. ... Name pronounced: uh-REEL-yuh. ... High school: Xaverian (Brooklyn, N.Y.). ... College: St. John's. **TRANSACTIONS/CAREER NOTES:** Selected by Texas Rangers organization in 24th round of 1992 free-agent draft. ... Traded by Rangers with IF/OF Desi Wilson to San Francisco Giants for P John Burkett (December 24, 1994). ... On disabled list (September 24, 1996-remainder of season; July 4-20, 1998; May 20-June 4, 2002; and August 4-19, 2003). ... Signed as a free agent by Seattle Mariners (January 9, 2004). ... Traded by Mariners to San Diego Padres for a player to be named or cash (July 19, 2004). ... Signed as a free agent by Cincinnati Reds organization (January 24, 2005). ... On disabled list (May 11-29, 2005); included rehabilitation assignment to Louisville. ... On disabled list (May 4-19, 2006). **HONORS:** Named shortstop on THE SPORTING NEWS N.L. All-Star team (2001). ... Named shortstop on N.L. Silver Slugger team (2001). **STATISTICAL NOTES:** Career major league grand slams: 3.
2006 GAMES PLAYED BY POSITION (MLB): 3B—52, 1B—47, SS—26, 2B—10, DH—1.

Year — Team (League)	Pos.	G	AB	R	H	2B	3B	HR	RBI	BB	SO	HBP	GDP	SB-CS	Avg.	OBP	SLG	OPS	E	Avg.
1992— Butte (Pion.)	SS	59	202	37	68	11	3	3	30	42	18	0	2	13-9	.337	.447	.465	.913	14	.943
1993— Charlotte (Fla. St.)	SS	122	440	80	136	16	5	5	56	75	57	3	9	15-18	.309	.408	.402	.810	24	.964
1994— Tulsa (Texas)	SS	129	458	67	107	18	6	12	57	53	74	4	8	10-13	.234	.315	.378	.693	24	.962
1995— Shreveport (Texas)	SS	64	226	29	74	17	1	4	42	27	26	1	8	10-3	.327	.398	.465	.863	14	.962
— Phoenix (PCL)	SS	71	258	42	72	12	0	5	34	35	29	0	4	2-2	.279	.361	.384	.745	9	.975
— San Francisco (N.L.)	SS	9	19	4	9	3	0	2	4	1	2	0	0	1-0	.474	.476	.947	1.424	0	1.000
1996— Phoenix (PCL)	SS-2B	7	30	9	13	7	0	0	4	2	3	0	1	1-1	.433	.469	.667	1.135	1	.972
— San Francisco (N.L.)	SS-2B	105	318	27	76	7	1	3	26	25	52	1	4	4-1	.239	.295	.296	.590	10	.975

Year	Team (League)	Pos.	G	AB	R	H	2B	3B	HR	RBI	BB	SO	HBP	GDP	SB-CS	Avg.	OBP	SLG	OPS	E	Avg.
1997—San Francisco (N.L.)	SS		46	102	16	28	8	0	5	19	8	15	0	3	1-1	.275	.321	.500	.821	3	.979
—Phoenix (PCL)	SS		8	34	9	10	2	0	1	5	5	4	0	1	2-1	.294	.385	.441	.826	0	1.000
1998—San Francisco (N.L.)	SS		122	413	54	110	27	2	9	49	31	62	2	3	3-3	.266	.319	.407	.726	10	.979
1999—San Francisco (N.L.)	SS		152	558	68	157	23	1	22	80	43	71	5	16	2-3	.281	.336	.444	.780	*28	.957
2000—San Francisco (N.L.)	SS		141	509	67	138	24	2	20	79	54	90	0	15	1-2	.271	.339	.444	.783	21	.967
2001—San Francisco (N.L.)	SS		156	636	114	*206	37	5	37	97	47	83	0	14	1-3	.324	.369	.572	.941	17	.975
2002—San Francisco (N.L.)	SS		133	538	76	138	35	2	15	61	37	90	4	15	1-2	.257	.325	.413	.718	11	.980
2003—San Francisco (N.L.)	SS-DH		129	505	65	140	26	1	13	58	36	82	1	18	2-2	.277	.325	.410	.735	13	.974
2004—Seattle (A.L.)	SS		73	261	27	63	13	0	4	28	22	43	2	10	1-0	.241	.304	.337	.641	3	.990
—San Diego (N.L.)	3B-2B-SS-1B		51	138	22	35	8	2	2	16	15	28	2	2	0-0	.254	.331	.384	.715	7	.937
2005—Louisville (Int'l)	SS		1	3	2	1	1	0	0	1	2	1	0	0	0-0	.333	.600	.667	1.267	0	1.000
—Cincinnati (N.L.)	2B-SS-3B		114	426	61	120	23	2	14	68	37	67	1	8	2-0	.282	.338	.444	.782	10	.979
2006—Cincinnati (N.L.)	3B-1B-SS-2B-DH		122	440	61	132	25	1	23	70	34	51	1	10	3-0	.300	.349	.518	.867	7	.988
American League totals (1 year)			73	261	27	63	13	0	4	28	22	43	2	10	1-0	.241	.304	.337	.641	3	.990
National League totals (12 years)			1280	4602	635	1289	246	19	165	627	368	693	17	106	21-17	.280	.333	.449	.783	137	.974
Major League totals (12 years)			1353	4863	662	1352	259	19	169	655	390	736	19	116	22-17	.278	.332	.443	.775	140	.975

DIVISION SERIES RECORD

Year	Team (League)	Pos.	G	AB	R	H	2B	3B	HR	RBI	BB	SO	HBP	GDP	SB-CS	Avg.	OBP	SLG	OPS	E	Avg.
2000—San Francisco (N.L.)	SS		4	15	0	2	1	0	0	0	0	3	0	0	0-0	.133	.133	.200	.333	1	.955
2002—San Francisco (N.L.)	SS		5	21	4	5	1	0	2	7	1	5	0	0	0-0	.238	.273	.571	.844	0	1.000
2003—San Francisco (N.L.)	SS		4	15	4	2	1	0	0	1	3	3	0	0	0-0	.133	.278	.200	.478	2	.926
Division series totals (3 years)			13	51	8	9	3	0	2	8	4	11	0	0	0-0	.176	.236	.353	.589	3	.958

CHAMPIONSHIP SERIES RECORD

Year	Team (League)	Pos.	G	AB	R	H	2B	3B	HR	RBI	BB	SO	HBP	GDP	SB-CS	Avg.	OBP	SLG	OPS	E	Avg.
2002—San Francisco (N.L.)	SS		5	15	4	5	1	0	2	5	2	2	1	0	0-0	.333	.421	.800	1.221	1	.955

WORLD SERIES RECORD

Year	Team (League)	Pos.	G	AB	R	H	2B	3B	HR	RBI	BB	SO	HBP	GDP	SB-CS	Avg.	OBP	SLG	OPS	E	Avg.
2002—San Francisco (N.L.)	SS		7	32	5	8	2	0	2	5	1	9	0	1	0-0	.250	.273	.500	.773	0	1.000

ALL-STAR GAME RECORD

	G	AB	R	H	2B	3B	HR	RBI	BB	SO	HBP	GDP	SB-CS	Avg.	OBP	SLG	OPS	E	Avg.
All-Star Game totals (1 year)	1	2	0	0	0	0	0	0	0	0	0	0	0-0	.000	.000	.000	.000	0	1.000

2006 LEFTY-RIGHTY SPLITS

vs.	Avg.	AB	H	2B	3B	HR	RBI	BB	SO	OBP	Slg.	vs.	Avg.	AB	H	2B	3B	HR	RBI	BB	SO	OBP	Slg.
L	.347	147	51	14	1	11	28	16	18	.406	.680	R	.276	293	81	11	0	12	42	18	33	.318	.437

AUSMUS, BRAD — C

PERSONAL: Born April 14, 1969, in New Haven, Conn. ... 5-11/190. ... Bats right, throws right. ... Full name: Bradley David Ausmus. ... Name pronounced: AHHS-muss. ... High school: Cheshire (Conn.). ... College: Dartmouth. **TRANSACTIONS/CAREER NOTES:** Selected by New York Yankees organization in 48th round of 1987 free-agent draft. ... Selected by Colorado Rockies in third round (54th pick overall) of expansion draft (November 17, 1992). ... Traded by Rockies with P Doug Bochtler and a player to be named to San Diego Padres for Ps Bruce Hurst and Greg W. Harris (July 26, 1993); Padres acquired P Andy Ashby to complete deal (July 27, 1993). ... Traded to Padres with SS Andujar Cedeno and P Russ Spear to Detroit Tigers for C John Flaherty and SS Chris Gomez (June 18, 1996). ... On suspended list (September 4-5, 1996). ... Traded by Tigers with Ps Jose Lima, C.J. Nitkowski and Trever Miller and IF Daryle Ward to Houston Astros for OF Brian L. Hunter, IF Orlando Miller, Ps Doug Brocail and Todd Jones and cash considerations (December 10, 1996). ... Traded by Astros with P C.J. Nitkowski to Tigers for C Paul Bako, Ps Dean Crow, Mark Persails and Brian Powell and 3B Carlos Villalobos (January 14, 1999). ... Traded by Tigers with Ps Doug Brocail and Nelson Cruz to Astros for C Mitch Meluskey, P Chris Holt and OF Roger Cedeno (December 11, 2000). **HONORS:** Won N.L. Gold Glove at catcher (2001-02 and 2006). **STATISTICAL NOTES:** Career major league grand slams: 3.

2006 GAMES PLAYED BY POSITION (MLB): C—138, 2B—2, 1B—1.

Year	Team (League)	Pos.	G	AB	R	H	2B	3B	HR	RBI	BB	SO	HBP	GDP	SB-CS	Avg.	OBP	SLG	OPS	E	Avg.
1988—GC Yankees (GCL)	C		43	133	22	34	2	0	0	15	11	25	2	4	5-2	.256	.320	.271	.590	9	.979
—Oneonta (NYP)	C		2	4	0	1	0	0	0	0	0	2	0	1	0-0	.250	.250	.250	.500	0	....
1989—Oneonta (NYP)	3B-C		52	165	29	43	6	0	1	18	22	28	0	2	6-4	.261	.348	.315	.663	7	.984
1990—Prince Will. (Car.)	C		107	364	46	86	12	2	0	27	32	73	3	7	2-8	.236	.303	.280	.583	5	.993
1991—Prince Will. (Car.)	C		63	230	28	70	14	3	2	30	24	37	0	2	17-6	.304	.366	.417	.783	5	.990
—Alb./Colon. (East.)	C		67	229	36	61	9	2	1	29	27	36	1	8	14-3	.266	.345	.336	.681	4	.992
1992—Alb./Colon. (East.)	C		5	18	0	3	0	1	0	1	2	3	0	1	2-1	.167	.250	.278	.528	1	.970
—Columbus (Int'l)	C-OF		111	364	48	88	14	3	2	35	40	56	1	14	19-5	.242	.317	.313	.630	9	.988
1993—Colo. Springs (PCL)	C		76	241	31	65	10	4	2	33	27	41	1	6	10-6	.270	.342	.369	.711	6	.987
—San Diego (N.L.)	C		49	160	18	41	8	1	5	12	6	28	0	2	2-0	.256	.283	.413	.696	8	.975
1994—San Diego (N.L.)	C-1B		101	327	45	82	12	1	7	24	30	63	1	8	5-1	.251	.314	.358	.672	7	.991
1995—San Diego (N.L.)	C-1B		103	328	44	96	16	4	5	34	31	56	2	6	16-5	.293	.353	.412	.765	6	.992
1996—San Diego (N.L.)	C		50	149	16	27	4	0	1	13	13	27	3	4	1-4	.181	.261	.228	.489	6	.982
—Detroit (A.L.)	C		75	226	30	56	12	0	4	24	26	45	2	4	3-4	.248	.328	.354	.682	4	.992
1997—Houston (N.L.)	C		130	425	45	113	25	1	4	44	38	74		8	14-6	.266	.326	.358	.684	7	.992
1998—Houston (N.L.)	C		128	412	62	111	10	4	6	45	53	60	3	18	10-3	.269	.356	.357	.713	7	.992
1999—Detroit (A.L.)	C		127	458	62	126	25	6	9	54	51	71	14	11	12-9	.275	.365	.415	.779	2	.998
2000—Detroit (A.L.)	C-1B-2B-3B		150	523	75	139	25	3	7	51	69	79	6	19	11-5	.266	.357	.365	.722	8	.992
2001—Houston (N.L.)	C		128	422	45	98	23	4	5	34	30	64	1	13	4-1	.232	.284	.341	.625	3	.997
2002—Houston (N.L.)	C		130	447	57	115	19	3	6	50	38	71	6	*30	2-3	.257	.322	.353	.675	3	.997
2003—Houston (N.L.)	C		143	450	43	103	12	2	4	47	46	66	4	8	5-3	.229	.303	.291	.594	3	.997
2004—Houston (N.L.)	C		129	403	38	100	14	1	5	31	33	56	2	13	2-2	.248	.306	.325	.631	5	.995
2005—Houston (N.L.)	C-2B-SS		134	387	35	100	16	0	3	47	51	48	5	17	5-3	.258	.351	.331	.682	1	.999
2006—Houston (N.L.)	C-2B-1B		139	439	37	101	16	1	2	39	45	71	6	21	3-1	.230	.308	.285	.593	2	.998
American League totals (3 years)			352	1207	167	321	62	9	20	127	146	195	22	34	26-18	.266	.354	.382	.736	14	.994
National League totals (12 years)			1364	4349	485	1087	178	22	53	420	414	688	36	148	69-32	.250	.318	.338	.656	58	.994
Major League totals (14 years)			1716	5556	652	1408	240	31	73	547	560	883	58	182	95-50	.253	.326	.347	.673	72	.994

DIVISION SERIES RECORD

Year	Team (League)	Pos.	G	AB	R	H	2B	3B	HR	RBI	BB	SO	HBP	GDP	SB-CS	Avg.	OBP	SLG	OPS	E	Avg.
1997—Houston (N.L.)	C		2	5	1	2	1	0	0	0	0	1	0	1	0-0	.400	.400	.600	1.000	0	1.000

Year	Team (League)	Pos.	G	AB	R	H	2B	3B	HR	RBI	BB	SO	HBP	GDP	SB-CS	Avg.	OBP	SLG	OPS	E	Avg.
1998—Houston (N.L.)		C	4	9	0	2	0	0	0	0	0	4	0	0	0-0	.222	.222	.222	.444	0	1.000
2001—Houston (N.L.)		C	3	8	1	2	0	0	1	2	0	0	0	1	0-0	.250	.250	.625	.875	0	1.000
2004—Houston (N.L.)		C	5	9	3	3	0	0	1	1	3	3	0	0	0-0	.333	.500	.667	1.167	0	1.000
2005—Houston (N.L.)		C-1B	4	18	3	4	1	0	1	1	2	4	0	2	0-0	.222	.300	.444	.744	0	1.000
Division series totals (5 years)			18	49	8	13	2	0	3	6	5	12	0	4	0-0	.265	.333	.490	.823	0	1.000

CHAMPIONSHIP SERIES RECORD

Year	Team (League)	Pos.	G	AB	R	H	2B	3B	HR	RBI	BB	SO	HBP	GDP	SB-CS	Avg.	OBP	SLG	OPS	E	Avg.
2004—Houston (N.L.)		C	7	19	0	2	0	0	0	0	2	8	0	0	0-0	.105	.190	.105	.296	0	1.000
2005—Houston (N.L.)		C	6	22	3	7	2	0	0	1	1	6	0	0	1-0	.318	.333	.409	.742	0	1.000
Champ. series totals (2 years)			13	41	3	9	2	0	0	1	3	14	0	0	1-0	.220	.267	.268	.535	0	1.000

WORLD SERIES RECORD

Year	Team (League)	Pos.	G	AB	R	H	2B	3B	HR	RBI	BB	SO	HBP	GDP	SB-CS	Avg.	OBP	SLG	OPS	E	Avg.
2005—Houston (N.L.)		C	4	16	1	4	1	0	0	0	1	3	1	1	0-0	.250	.333	.313	.646	0	1.000

ALL-STAR GAME RECORD

			G	AB	R	H	2B	3B	HR	RBI	BB	SO	HBP	GDP	SB-CS	Avg.	OBP	SLG	OPS	E	Avg.
All-Star Game totals (1 year)			1	1	0	0	0	0	0	0	0	0	0	0	0-0	.000	.000	.000	.000	0	1.000

2006 LEFTY-RIGHTY SPLITS

vs.	Avg.	AB	H	2B	3B	HR	RBI	BB	SO	OBP	Slg.	vs.	Avg.	AB	H	2B	3B	HR	RBI	BB	SO	OBP	Slg.
L	.266	94	25	3	0	1	10	9	17	.333	.330	R	.220	345	76	13	1	1	29	36	54	.302	.272

AYALA, LUIS — P

PERSONAL: Born January 12, 1978, in Los Mochis, Mexico. ... 6-2/186. ... Throws right, bats right. ... Full name: Luis Ignacio Ayala. ... Name pronounced: eye-YA-lah. **TRANSACTIONS/CAREER NOTES:** Contract purchased by Colorado Rockies organization from Saltillo of the Mexican League (October 14, 1999). ... Loaned by Rockies organization to Saltillo (April 13, 2000-entire season). ... Contract sold by Rockies to Saltillo (May 15, 2001). ... Contract purchased by Montreal Expos from Saltillo (August 13, 2002). ... Signed as a free agent by Arizona Diamondbacks organization (October 23, 2002). ... Selected by Montreal Expos from Diamondbacks organization in Rule 5 major league draft (December 16, 2002). ... On disabled list (June 22-July 21, 2003); included rehabilitation assignment to GCL Expos. ... Expos franchise transferred to Washington, D.C., and renamed Washington Nationals for 2005 season (December 3, 2004). ... On disabled list (March 27, 2006-entire season). **MISCELLANEOUS NOTES:** Singled in only appearance as pinch hitter (2005).

CAREER HITTING: 4-for-13 (.308), 0 R, 1 2B, 0 3B, 0 HR, 0 RBI.

Year	Team (League)	W	L	Pct.	ERA	WHIP	G	GS	CG	ShO	Hld.	Sv.-Opp.	IP	H	R	ER	HR	BB-IBB	SO	Avg.
1997—Saltillo (Mex.)		7	5	.583	4.62	1.56	37	2	0	0	...	0-...	62.1	76	37	32	3	21-4	30	...
1998—Saltillo (Mex.)		7	8	.467	5.62	1.80	47	4	0	0	...	7-...	83.1	105	52	52	2	45-13	29	...
1999—Saltillo (Mex.)		7	3	.700	1.71	0.96	61	0	0	0	...	41-...	79.0	54	17	15	1	22-5	28	...
2000—Saltillo (Mex.)		5	3	.625	2.76	1.26	55	0	0	0	...	25-...	65.1	69	22	20	4	13-1	38	...
2001—Saltillo (Mex.)		1	2	.333	2.03	1.13	33	0	0	0	...	21-...	40.0	34	11	9	2	11-0	34	...
—Salem (Carol.)		0	1	.000	4.05	1.80	13	0	0	0	...	7-...	13.1	19	10	6	0	5-0	10	.358
2002—Saltillo (Mex.'l)		3	5	.375	1.68	1.08	49	0	0	0	...	23-...	53.2	43	16	10	2	15-0	43	...
—Ottawa (Int'l)		0	0	...	3.52	1.43	6	0	0	0	...	0-...	7.2	7	3	3	1	4-0	6	.250
2003—GC Expos (GCL)		0	0	...	0.00	1.09	2	2	0	0	...	0-...	3.2	2	0	0	0	2-0	2	.154
—Montreal (N.L.)		10	3	.769	2.92	1.10	65	0	0	0	19	5-8	71.0	65	27	23	8	13-3	46	.244
2004—Montreal (N.L.)		6	12	.333	2.69	1.18	81	0	0	0	21	2-7	90.1	92	30	27	6	15-2	63	.268
2005—Wash. (N.L.)		8	7	.533	2.66	1.25	68	0	0	0	22	1-3	71.0	75	23	21	7	14-4	40	.286
2006—Wash. (N.L.)		Did not play.																		
Major League totals (3 years)		24	22	.522	2.75	1.18	214	0	0	0	62	8-18	232.1	232	80	71	21	42-9	149	.266

AYBAR, ERICK — SS

PERSONAL: Born January 14, 1984, in Bani, Dominican Republic. ... 5-11/187. ... Bats both, throws right. ... Full name: Erick Johan Aybar. ... Name pronounced: EYE-bar. ... Brother of Willy Aybar, infielder, Atlanta Braves. **TRANSACTIONS/CAREER NOTES:** Signed as a non-drafted free agent by Anaheim Angels organization (February 4, 2002). ... Franchise renamed Los Angeles Angels of Anaheim for 2005 season.

2006 GAMES PLAYED BY POSITION (MLB): SS—19, DH—5, 2B—3.

Year	Team (League)	Pos.	G	AB	R	H	2B	3B	HR	RBI	BB	SO	HBP	GDP	SB-CS	Avg.	OBP	SLG	OPS	E	Avg.
														BATTING						FIELDING	
2002—Provo (Pion.)			67	273	64	89	15	6	4	29	21	43	11	4	15-10	.326	.395	.469	.864	...	...
2003—Cedar Rap. (Midw.)			125	496	83	153	30	10	6	57	17	54	13	6	32-9	.308	.346	.446	.792	...	...
2004—Rancho Cuca. (Calif.)			136	573	102	189	25	11	14	65	26	66	13	3	51-36	.330	.370	.485	.855	...	...
2005—Arkansas (Texas)		SS	134	535	101	162	29	10	9	54	29	51	14	13	49-23	.303	.350	.445	.795	32	.953
2006—Salt Lake (PCL)			81	339	63	96	20	3	6	45	21	36	3	5	32-18	.283	.327	.413	.740	12	.946
—Los Angeles (A.L.)		SS-DH-2B	34	40	5	10	1	1	0	2	0	8	0	1	1-0	.250	.250	.325	.575	4	.907
Major League totals (1 year)			34	40	5	10	1	1	0	2	0	8	0	1	1-0	.250	.250	.325	.575	4	.907

2006 LEFTY-RIGHTY SPLITS

vs.	Avg.	AB	H	2B	3B	HR	RBI	BB	SO	OBP	Slg.	vs.	Avg.	AB	H	2B	3B	HR	RBI	BB	SO	OBP	Slg.
L	.250	8	2	0	0	0	1	0	2	.250	.250	R	.250	32	8	1	1	0	1	0	6	.250	.344

AYBAR, WILLY — 3B/2B

PERSONAL: Born March 9, 1983, in Bani, Dominican Republic. ... 6-0/175. ... Bats both, throws right. ... Full name: Willy Del Jesus Aybar. ... Name pronounced: EYE-bar. ... Brother of Erick Aybar, shortstop, Los Angeles Angels of Anaheim. **TRANSACTIONS/CAREER NOTES:** Signed as a non-drafted free agent by Los Angeles Dodgers organization (January 31, 2000). ... Traded by Dodgers with P Danys Baez to Atlanta Braves for SS Wilson Betemit (July 28, 2006). ... On disabled list (August 12-September 1, 2006); included rehabilitation assignment to Richmond.

2006 GAMES PLAYED BY POSITION (MLB): 3B—61, 2B—15.

Year	Team (League)	Pos.	G	AB	R	H	2B	3B	HR	RBI	BB	SO	HBP	GDP	SB-CS	Avg.	OBP	SLG	OPS	E	Avg.
														BATTING						FIELDING	
2000—Great Falls (Pio.)		3B	70	266	39	70	15	1	4	49	36	45	0	3	5-5	.263	.349	.372	.721	6	.908
2001—Wilmington (S. Atl.)		3B	120	431	45	102	25	2	4	48	43	64	3	4	7-9	.237	.307	.332	.639	18	.948
—Vero Beach (Fla. St.)		3B	2	7	0	2	0	0	0	0	1	2	0	0	0-0	.286	.375	.286	.661	0	1.000
2002—Vero Beach (Fla. St.)		3B	108	372	56	80	18	2	11	65	69	54	3	7	15-8	.215	.339	.363	.702	15	.943
2003—Vero Beach (Fla. St.)		3B	119	445	47	122	29	3	11	74	41	70	3	3	9-9	.274	.336	.427	.763	17	.947
2004—Jacksonville (Sou.)		3B	126	482	56	133	27	0	15	77	50	77	3	11	8-10	.276	.346	.425	.771	15	.867
2005—Las Vegas (PCL)		3B-2B-DH	108	401	49	119	26	4	5	60	40	56	1	8	1-6	.297	.356	.419	.775	10	.967
—Los Angeles (N.L.)		3B-2B	26	86	12	28	8	0	1	10	18	11	1	0	3-1	.326	.448	.453	.901	2	.967

Year Team (League)	Pos.	G	AB	R	H	2B	3B	HR	RBI	BB	SO	HBP	GDP	SB-CS	Avg.	OBP	SLG	OPS	E	Avg.
2006— Las Vegas (PCL)		50	197	30	62	12	1	10	41	22	24	1	6	1-3	.315	.383	.538	.921	2	.989
— Los Angeles (N.L.)	3B-2B	43	128	15	32	12	0	3	22	18	17	3	5	1-0	.250	.356	.414	.770	6	.955
— Richmond (Int'l)		3	10	2	3	1	0	0	1	2	3	0	1	0-0	.300	.417	.400	.817	0	1.000
— Atlanta (N.L.)	3B	36	115	17	36	6	0	1	8	10	19	1	2	0-2	.313	.373	.391	.764	3	.947
Major League totals (2 years)		105	329	44	96	26	0	5	40	46	47	5	7	4-3	.292	.387	.416	.803	11	.956

2006 LEFTY-RIGHTY SPLITS

vs.	Avg.	AB	H	2B	3B	HR	RBI	BB	SO	OBP	Slg.	vs.	Avg.	AB	H	2B	3B	HR	RBI	BB	SO	OBP	Slg.
L	.328	64	21	3	0	1	8	7	8	.403	.422	R	.263	179	47	15	0	3	22	21	28	.350	.397

BACKE, BRANDON P

PERSONAL: Born April 5, 1978, in Galveston, Texas. ... 6-0/180. ... Throws right, bats right. ... Full name: Brandon Allen Backe. ... Name pronounced: back-EE. ... High school: Ball (Galveston, Texas). ... Junior college: Galveston (Texas). **TRANSACTIONS/CAREER NOTES:** Selected by Milwaukee Brewers organization in 36th round of 1996 free-agent draft; did not sign. ... Selected by Tampa Bay Devil Rays organization in 18th round of 1998 free-agent draft. ... Played three seasons as an outfielder in Devil Rays organization (1998-2000). ... Traded by Devil Rays to Houston Astros for IF Geoff Blum (December 14, 2003). ... On disabled list (July 27-September 3, 2005); included rehabilitation assignment to Corpus Christi. ... On disabled list (April 14-July 22, 2006); included rehabilitation assignment to Round Rock. ... On disabled list (August 19, 2006-remainder of season). **MISCELLANEOUS NOTES:** Scored a run in only appearance as pinch runner (2003). ... Made an out in only appearance as pinch hitter (2004). ... Made outs in both appearances as pinch hitter (2005). ... Appeared in one game as pinch runner (2006).

CAREER HITTING: 17-for-75 (.227), 9 R, 2 2B, 2 3B, 1 HR, 12 RBI.

Year Team (League)	W	L	Pct.	ERA	WHIP	G	GS	CG	ShO	Hld.	Sv.-Opp.	IP	H	R	ER	HR	BB-IBB	SO	Avg.
2001— Char., S.C. (SAL)	2	1	.667	2.92	0.97	16	0	0	0	...	7-...	24.2	17	8	8	2	7-1	20	.200
— Bakersfield (Calif.)	1	0	1.000	1.09	0.85	17	0	0	0	...	3-...	24.2	13	7	3	1	8-0	33	.149
— Orlando (South.)	1	0	1.000	5.73	1.41	14	0	0	0	...	0-...	22.0	20	14	14	1	11-0	20	.253
2002— Orlando (South.)	4	6	.400	4.68	1.39	20	14	3	1	...	2-...	92.1	91	58	48	9	37-1	45	.250
— Tampa Bay (A.L.)	0	0	...	6.92	1.69	9	0	0	0	0	0-0	13.0	15	10	10	3	7-0	6	.288
2003— Durham (Int'l)	2	1	.667	4.64	1.40	16	2	0	0	...	0-...	33.0	33	21	17	1	13-0	27	.250
— Tampa Bay (A.L.)	1	1	.500	5.44	1.46	28	0	0	0	5	0-0	44.2	40	28	27	6	25-1	36	.247
2004— New Orleans (PCL)	6	5	.545	2.80	1.29	19	9	0	0	...	0-...	64.1	57	26	20	7	26-1	74	.241
— Houston (N.L.)	5	3	.625	4.30	1.52	33	9	0	0	3	0-0	67.0	75	33	32	10	27-4	54	.290
2005— Corpus Christi (Texas)	0	1	.000	2.25	0.63	2	2	0	0	0	0-0	8.0	4	2	2	1	1-0	11	.143
— Houston (N.L.)	10	8	.556	4.76	1.46	26	25	1	1	0	0-0	149.1	151	82	79	19	67-1	97	.263
2006— Round Rock (PCL)	1	2	.333	5.31	1.77	4	4	0	0	0	0-0	20.1	23	12	12	1	13-0	13	.311
— Houston (N.L.)	3	2	.600	3.77	1.42	8	8	0	0	0	0-0	43.0	43	18	18	4	18-0	19	.261
American League totals (2 years)	1	1	.500	5.77	1.51	37	0	0	0	5	0-0	57.2	55	38	37	9	32-1	42	.257
National League totals (3 years)	18	13	.581	4.48	1.47	67	42	1	1	3	0-0	259.1	269	133	129	33	112-5	170	.270
Major League totals (5 years)	19	14	.576	4.71	1.48	104	42	1	1	8	0-0	317.0	324	171	166	42	144-6	212	.267

DIVISION SERIES RECORD

Year Team (League)	W	L	Pct.	ERA	WHIP	G	GS	CG	ShO	Hld.	Sv.-Opp.	IP	H	R	ER	HR	BB-IBB	SO	Avg.
2004— Houston (N.L.)	1	0	1.000	3.00	1.17	1	1	0	0	0	0-0	6.0	5	2	2	1	2-1	5	.227
2005— Houston (N.L.)	0	0	...	8.44	1.69	2	1	0	0	0	0-0	5.1	6	5	5	1	3-0	3	.300
Division series totals (2 years)	1	0	1.000	5.56	1.41	3	2	0	0	0	0-0	11.1	11	7	7	2	5-1	8	.262

CHAMPIONSHIP SERIES RECORD

Year Team (League)	W	L	Pct.	ERA	WHIP	G	GS	CG	ShO	Hld.	Sv.-Opp.	IP	H	R	ER	HR	BB-IBB	SO	Avg.
2004— Houston (N.L.)	0	0	...	2.84	0.79	2	2	0	0	0	0-0	12.2	6	4	4	1	4-0	10	.140
2005— Houston (N.L.)	0	0	...	1.59	0.88	1	1	0	0	0	0-0	5.2	2	1	1	0	3-0	7	.118
Champ. series totals (2 years)	0	0	...	2.45	0.82	3	3	0	0	0	0-0	18.1	8	5	5	1	7-0	17	.133

WORLD SERIES RECORD

Year Team (League)	W	L	Pct.	ERA	WHIP	G	GS	CG	ShO	Hld.	Sv.-Opp.	IP	H	R	ER	HR	BB-IBB	SO	Avg.
2005— Houston (N.L.)	0	0	...	0.00	0.71	1	1	0	0	0	0-0	7.0	5	0	0	0	0-0	7	.192

2006 LEFTY-RIGHTY SPLITS

vs.	Avg.	AB	H	2B	3B	HR	RBI	BB	SO	OBP	Slg.	vs.	Avg.	AB	H	2B	3B	HR	RBI	BB	SO	OBP	Slg.
L	.317	82	26	8	0	1	7	12	7	.400	.451	R	.205	83	17	4	0	3	11	6	12	.280	.361

BAEK, CHA SEUNG P

PERSONAL: Born May 29, 1980, in Pusan, South Korea. ... 6-4/190. ... Throws right, bats right. ... High school: Pusan (Pusan, South Korea). **TRANSACTIONS/CAREER NOTES:** Signed as a non-drafted free agent by Seattle Mariners organization (September 25, 1998). ... On disabled list (September 25, 2006-remainder of season).

CAREER HITTING: 0-for-0 (.000), 0 R, 0 2B, 0 3B, 0 HR, 0 RBI.

Year Team (League)	W	L	Pct.	ERA	WHIP	G	GS	CG	ShO	Hld.	Sv.-Opp.	IP	H	R	ER	HR	BB-IBB	SO	Avg.
1999— Ariz. Mariners (Ariz.)	3	0	1.000	3.67	1.33	8	4	0	0	...	0-...	27.0	30	13	11	2	6-0	25	.283
2000— Wisconsin (Midw.)	8	5	.615	3.95	1.36	24	24	0	0	...	0-...	127.2	137	71	56	13	36-0	99	.275
2001— San Bern. (Calif.)	1	0	1.000	3.43	0.90	5	4	0	0	...	0-...	21.0	17	10	8	2	2-0	16	.224
2003— Inland Empire (Calif.)	5	1	.833	3.65	1.13	13	10	0	0	...	1-...	56.2	55	27	23	3	9-0	50	.249
— San Antonio (Texas)	3	3	.500	2.57	1.18	9	9	0	0	...	0-...	56.0	49	18	16	2	17-1	46	.238
2004— Ariz. Mariners (Ariz.)	0	0	...	1.29	0.57	2	2	0	0	...	0-...	7.0	3	2	1	0	1-0	5	.125
— San Antonio (Texas)	0	0	...	0.00	0.40	1	1	0	0	...	0-...	5.0	2	0	0	0	0-0	5	.125
— Tacoma (PCL)	5	4	.556	4.21	1.50	14	14	0	0	...	0-...	72.2	85	41	34	7	24-0	56	.290
— Seattle (A.L.)	2	4	.333	5.52	1.48	7	5	0	0	0	0-0	31.0	35	23	19	5	11-1	20	.278
2005— Tacoma (PCL)	8	8	.500	6.41	1.61	25	21	0	0	0	0-0	113.2	147	87	81	19	36-0	73	.313
2006— Tacoma (PCL)	12	4	.750	3.00	1.16	24	24	0	0	0	0-0	147.0	133	57	49	17	37-0	103	.241
— Seattle (A.L.)	4	1	.800	3.67	1.14	6	6	0	0	0	0-0	34.1	26	15	14	6	13-0	23	.208
Major League totals (2 years)	6	5	.545	4.55	1.30	13	11	0	0	0	0-0	65.1	61	38	33	11	24-1	43	.243

2006 LEFTY-RIGHTY SPLITS

vs.	Avg.	AB	H	2B	3B	HR	RBI	BB	SO	OBP	Slg.	vs.	Avg.	AB	H	2B	3B	HR	RBI	BB	SO	OBP	Slg.
L	.211	57	12	3	0	3	8	9	6	.318	.421	R	.206	68	14	1	0	3	5	4	17	.270	.353

BAEZ, DANYS P

PERSONAL: Born September 10, 1977, in Pinar del Rio, Cuba. ... 6-3/225. ... Throws right, bats right. ... Name pronounced: DAN-ees BUY-ez. **TRANSACTIONS/CAREER NOTES:** Signed as a non-drafted free agent by Cleveland Indians organization (November 5, 1999). ... Signed as a free agent by Tampa Bay Devil Rays (January 6, 2004). ... Traded by Devil Rays with P Lance Carter to Los Angeles Dodgers for Ps Edwin Jackson and Charles Tiffany (January 14, 2006). ... Traded by Dodgers with 3B Willy Aybar to Atlanta Braves for SS Wilson Betemit (July 28, 2006). ... On disabled list (August 23, 2006-remainder of season).

CAREER HITTING: 0-for-3 (.000), 0 R, 0 2B, 0 3B, 0 HR, 0 RBI.

Year Team (League)	W	L	Pct.	ERA	WHIP	G	GS	CG	ShO	Hld.	Sv.-Opp.	IP	H	R	ER	HR	BB-IBB	SO	Avg.
2000— Kinston (Carol.)	2	2	.500	4.71	1.31	9	9	0	0	...	0-...	49.2	45	29	26	5	20-0	56	.236
— Akron (East.)	4	9	.308	3.68	1.27	18	18	0	0	...	0-...	102.2	98	46	42	6	32-0	77	.259
2001— Buffalo (Int'l)	2	0	1.000	3.20	1.07	16	0	0	0	...	3-...	25.1	18	9	9	2	9-0	30	.200
— Akron (East.)	0	0	...	0.00	0.50	1	0	0	0	...	0-...	2.0	1	0	0	0	0-0	2	.143
— Cleveland (A.L.)	5	3	.625	2.50	1.07	43	0	0	0	14	0-1	50.1	34	22	14	5	20-4	52	.191
2002— Cleveland (A.L.)	10	11	.476	4.41	1.46	39	26	1	0	0	6-6	165.1	160	84	81	14	82-5	130	.256
2003— Cleveland (A.L.)	2	9	.182	3.81	1.16	73	0	0	0	5	25-35	75.2	65	36	32	9	23-0	66	.229
2004— Tampa Bay (A.L.)	4	4	.500	3.57	1.31	62	0	0	0	1	30-33	68.0	60	31	27	6	29-4	52	.237
2005— Tampa Bay (A.L.)	5	4	.556	2.86	1.33	67	0	0	0	0	41-49	72.1	66	27	23	7	30-0	51	.244
2006— Los Angeles (N.L.)	5	5	.500	4.35	1.29	46	0	0	0	6	9-16	49.2	53	29	24	3	11-2	29	.283
— Atlanta (N.L.)	0	1	.000	5.40	1.30	11	0	0	0	0	0-1	10.0	7	6	6	0	6-1	10	.189
American League totals (5 years)	26	31	.456	3.69	1.32	284	26	1	0	20	102-126	431.2	385	200	177	41	184-13	351	.239
National League totals (1 year)	5	6	.455	4.53	1.29	57	0	0	0	12	9-17	59.2	60	35	30	3	17-3	39	.268
Major League totals (6 years)	31	37	.456	3.79	1.31	341	26	1	0	32	111-143	491.1	445	235	207	44	201-16	390	.243

DIVISION SERIES RECORD

Year Team (League)	W	L	Pct.	ERA	WHIP	G	GS	CG	ShO	Hld.	Sv.-Opp.	IP	H	R	ER	HR	BB-IBB	SO	Avg.
2001— Cleveland (A.L.)	0	0	...	2.45	1.09	3	0	0	0	0	0-0	3.2	4	1	1	0	0-0	6	.267

2006 LEFTY-RIGHTY SPLITS

vs.	Avg.	AB	H	2B	3B	HR	RBI	BB	SO	OBP	Slg.	vs.	Avg.	AB	H	2B	3B	HR	RBI	BB	SO	OBP	Slg.
L	.295	105	31	10	0	2	15	10	15	.358	.448	R	.244	119	29	7	0	1	22	7	24	.308	.328

BAGWELL, JEFF — 1B

PERSONAL: Born May 27, 1968, in Boston, Mass. ... 6-0/215. ... Bats right, throws right. ... Full name: Jeffrey Robert Bagwell. ... Name pronounced: BAG-well. ... High school: Xavier (Middletown, Conn.). ... College: Hartford. **TRANSACTIONS/CAREER NOTES:** Selected by Boston Red Sox organization in fourth round of 1989 free-agent draft. ... Traded by Red Sox to Houston Astros for P Larry Andersen (August 31, 1990). ... On disabled list (July 31-September 1, 1995); included rehabilitation assignment to Jackson. ... On disabled list (May 13-28, 1998). ... On disabled list (May 10-September 9, 2005); included rehabilitation assignment to Corpus Christi. ... On disabled list (March 25, 2006-entire season). **RECORDS:** Shares major league records for most doubles, game (4, June 14, 1996), and most bases on balls, extra-inning game (6, August 20, 1999, 16 innings). **HONORS:** Named N.L. Rookie Player of the Year by THE SPORTING NEWS (1991). ... Named Major League Player of the Year by THE SPORTING NEWS (1994). ... Named first baseman on THE SPORTING NEWS N.L. All-Star team (1994, 1996-97 and 1999). ... Named N.L. Rookie of the Year by Baseball Writers' Association of America (1991). ... Named N.L. Most Valuable Player by Baseball Writers' Association of America (1994). ... Won N.L. Gold Glove at first base (1994). ... Named first baseman on N.L. Silver Slugger team (1994, 1997 and 1999). **STATISTICAL NOTES:** Hit three home runs in one game (June 24, 1994; and April 21 and June 9, 1999). ... Hit for the cycle (July 18, 2001). ... Career major league grand slams: 6.

Year Team (League)	Pos.	G	AB	R	H	2B	3B	HR	RBI	BB	SO	HBP	GDP	SB-CS	Avg.	OBP	SLG	OPS	E	Avg.
1989— GC Red Sox (GCL)	2B-3B	5	19	3	6	1	0	0	3	3	0	0	1	0-0	.316	.409	.368	.778	2	.875
— Winter Haven (Fla. St.)	1B-2B-3B	64	210	27	65	13	2	2	19	23	25	3	7	1-1	.310	.384	.419	.803	12	.931
1990— New Britain (East.)	3B	136	481	63	160	34	7	4	61	73	57	7	15	5-7	.333	.423	.457	.881	34	.914
1991— Houston (N.L.)		156	554	79	163	26	4	15	82	75	116	*13	12	7-4	.294	.387	.437	.824	12	.991
1992— Houston (N.L.)	1B	•162	586	87	160	34	6	18	96	84	97	12	17	10-6	.273	.368	.444	.812	7	.995
1993— Houston (N.L.)	1B	142	535	76	171	37	4	20	88	62	73	3	20	13-4	.320	.388	.516	.903	9	.993
1994— Houston (N.L.)	1B-OF	110	400	*104	147	32	2	39	*116	65	65	4	12	15-4	.368	.451	*.750	1.201	9	.991
1995— Houston (N.L.)	1B	114	448	88	130	29	0	21	87	79	102	6	9	12-5	.290	.399	.496	.894	7	.994
— Jackson (Texas)	1B-DH	4	12	0	2	0	0	0	3	2	1	0	0	0-0	.167	.375	.167	.542	0	1.000
1996— Houston (N.L.)	1B	*162	568	111	179	*48	2	31	120	135	114	10	15	21-7	.315	.451	.570	1.021	*16	.989
1997— Houston (N.L.)	1B-DH	*162	566	109	162	40	2	43	135	127	122	16	10	31-10	.286	.425	.592	1.017	11	.993
1998— Houston (N.L.)	1B	147	540	124	164	33	1	34	111	109	90	7	14	19-7	.304	.424	.557	.981	7	.995
1999— Houston (N.L.)	1B-DH	*162	562	*143	171	35	0	42	126	*149	127	11	18	30-11	.304	.454	.591	1.045	8	.994
2000— Houston (N.L.)	1B-DH	159	590	*152	183	37	1	47	132	107	116	15	19	9-6	.310	.424	.615	1.039	9	.994
2001— Houston (N.L.)	1B	161	600	126	173	43	4	39	130	106	135	6	20	11-3	.288	.397	.568	.966	12	.992
2002— Houston (N.L.)	1B-DH	158	571	94	166	33	2	31	98	101	130	10	16	7-3	.291	.401	.518	.919	7	.995
2003— Houston (N.L.)	1B	160	605	109	168	28	2	39	100	88	119	6	25	11-4	.278	.373	.524	.897	9	.994
2004— Houston (N.L.)	1B-DH	156	572	104	152	29	2	27	89	96	131	8	12	6-4	.266	.377	.465	.842	6	.995
2005— Corpus Christi (Texas)		3	9	1	2	0	0	0	1	3	3	0	1	0-0	.222	.417	.222	.639	0	....
— Houston (N.L.)	1B	39	100	11	25	4	0	3	19	18	21	1	2	0-0	.250	.358	.380	.738	0	1.000
2006— Houston (N.L.)	Did not play.																			
Major League totals (15 years)		2150	7797	1517	2314	488	32	449	1529	1401	1558	128	221	202-78	.297	.408	.540	.948	129	.993

DIVISION SERIES RECORD

Year Team (League)	Pos.	G	AB	R	H	2B	3B	HR	RBI	BB	SO	HBP	GDP	SB-CS	Avg.	OBP	SLG	OPS	E	Avg.
1997— Houston (N.L.)	1B	3	12	0	1	0	0	0	0	1	5	0	0	0-0	.083	.154	.083	.237	2	.920
1998— Houston (N.L.)	1B	4	14	0	2	0	0	0	4	1	6	1	0	0-0	.143	.250	.143	.393	0	1.000
1999— Houston (N.L.)	1B	4	13	3	2	0	0	0	0	5	4	1	0	0-0	.154	.421	.154	.575	0	1.000
2001— Houston (N.L.)	1B	3	7	0	3	0	0	0	1	5	1	0	0	0-1	.429	.667	.429	1.095	0	1.000
2004— Houston (N.L.)	1B	•5	22	5	7	2	0	2	5	3	3	0	1	0-0	.318	.400	.682	1.082	1	.981
2005— Houston (N.L.)	PH	2	2	1	1	0	0	0	0	1	0	0	0	0-0	.500	.500	.500	1.000	0	....
Division series totals (6 years)		21	70	9	16	2	0	2	10	15	19	2	1	0-1	.229	.379	.343	.722	3	.983

CHAMPIONSHIP SERIES RECORD

Year Team (League)	Pos.	G	AB	R	H	2B	3B	HR	RBI	BB	SO	HBP	GDP	SB-CS	Avg.	OBP	SLG	OPS	E	Avg.
2004— Houston (N.L.)	1B	7	27	1	7	2	0	0	3	4	5	0	1	1-1	.259	.355	.333	.688	0	1.000
2005— Houston (N.L.)	PH	1	1	0	0	0	0	0	0	0	0	0	0	0-0	.000	.000	.000	.000	0	....
Champ. series totals (2 years)		8	28	1	7	2	0	0	3	4	5	0	1	1-1	.250	.344	.321	.665	0	1.000

WORLD SERIES RECORD

Year Team (League)	Pos.	G	AB	R	H	2B	3B	HR	RBI	BB	SO	HBP	GDP	SB-CS	Avg.	OBP	SLG	OPS	E	Avg.
2005— Houston (N.L.)	DH	4	8	0	1	0	0	0	0	0	1	2	0	0-0	.125	.300	.125	.425	0	....

ALL-STAR GAME RECORD

	G	AB	R	H	2B	3B	HR	RBI	BB	SO	HBP	GDP	SB-CS	Avg.	OBP	SLG	OPS	E	Avg.
All-Star Game totals (4 years)	4	12	1	3	0	0	0	0	0	4	0	0	0-0	.250	.250	.250	.500	0	1.000

BAJENARU, JEFF — P

PERSONAL: Born March 21, 1978, in Pomona, Calif. ... 6-1/190. ... Throws right, bats right. ... Full name: Jeffrey Michael Bajenaru. ... Name pronounced: Bah-juh-NAIR-oh. ... High school: Ayala (Chino Hills, Calif.). ... Junior college: Riverside (Calif.) C.C. ... College: Oklahoma. **TRANSACTIONS/CAREER NOTES:** Selected by Oakland Athletics organization in 13th round of 1998 free-agent draft; did not sign. ... Selected by Chicago White Sox organization in 36th round of 1999 free-agent draft. ... Traded by White Sox to Arizona Diamondbacks for SS Alex Cintron (March 8, 2006).

CAREER HITTING: 0-for-0 (.000), 0 R, 0 2B, 0 3B, 0 HR, 0 RBI.

Year	Team (League)	W	L	Pct.	ERA	WHIP	G	GS	CG	ShO	Hld.	Sv.-Opp.	IP	H	R	ER	HR	BB-IBB	SO	Avg.
2000—	Bristol (Appal.)	1	1	.500	3.77	1.05	12	0	0	0	...	5-...	14.1	10	6	6	2	5-0	31	.179
—	Win.-Salem (Car.)	2	0	1.000	4.38	0.97	10	0	0	0	...	2-...	12.1	7	6	6	1	5-0	15	.167
2001—	Birmingham (Sou.)	0	0	...	0.00	1.62	2	0	0	0	...	0-...	4.1	4	0	0	0	3-0	5	.222
—	Win.-Salem (Car.)	2	4	.333	3.35	1.31	35	0	0	0	...	10-...	40.1	32	16	15	3	21-2	51	.216
2003—	Birmingham (Sou.)	4	2	.667	3.20	1.25	50	0	0	0	...	14-...	64.2	53	29	23	2	28-3	62	.225
2004—	Birmingham (Sou.)	2	0	1.000	1.34	0.89	32	0	0	0	...	12-...	33.2	19	9	5	3	11-0	51	.158
—	Charlotte (Int'l)	1	2	.333	1.80	0.75	16	0	0	0	...	10-...	20.0	12	6	4	2	3-0	16	.171
—	Chicago (A.L.)	0	1	.000	10.80	2.52	9	0	0	0	0	0-0	8.1	15	10	10	0	6-1	8	.405
2005—	Charlotte (Int'l)	4	6	.400	1.41	1.05	61	0	0	0	3	19-23	70.1	45	14	11	4	29-5	83	.185
—	Chicago (A.L.)	0	0	...	6.23	0.92	4	0	0	0	0	0-0	4.1	4	3	3	2	0-0	3	.222
2006—	Tucson (PCL)	4	3	.571	4.50	1.49	52	3	0	0	5	7-11	80.0	79	47	40	6	40-1	72	.258
—	Arizona (N.L.)	0	1	.000	36.00	4.00	1	0	0	0	0	0-1	1.0	4	4	4	0	0-0	0	.571
American League totals (2 years)		0	1	.000	9.24	1.97	13	0	0	0	0	0-0	12.2	19	13	13	2	6-1	11	.345
National League totals (1 year)		0	1	.000	36.00	4.00	1	0	0	0	0	0-1	1.0	4	4	4	0	0-0	0	.571
Major League totals (3 years)		0	2	.000	11.20	2.12	14	0	0	0	0	0-1	13.2	23	17	17	2	6-1	11	.371

2006 LEFTY-RIGHTY SPLITS

vs.	Avg.	AB	H	2B	3B	HR	RBI	BB	SO	OBP	Slg.	vs.	Avg.	AB	H	2B	3B	HR	RBI	BB	SO	OBP	Slg.
L	.667	3	2	0	0	1	1	0	0	.667	1.667	R	.500	4	2	0	0	2	3	0	0	.500	2.000

BAKER, JEFF — IF/OF

PERSONAL: Born June 21, 1981, in Badkissagen, West Germany. ... 6-2/210. ... Bats right, throws right. ... Full name: Jeffrey Glen Baker. ... College: Clemson.
TRANSACTIONS/CAREER NOTES: Selected by Colorado Rockies organization in fourth round of 2002 free-agent draft.
2006 GAMES PLAYED BY POSITION (MLB): OF—12, 1B—1.

Year	Team (League)	Pos.	G	AB	R	H	2B	3B	HR	RBI	BB	SO	HBP	GDP	SB-CS	Avg.	OBP	SLG	OPS	E	Avg.
2003—	Asheville (S. Atl.)	3B	70	263	44	76	17	0	11	44	30	79	9	2	4-2	.289	.377	.479	.856	16	.902
2004—	Visalia (Pion.)		72	267	60	88	23	1	11	64	47	70	6	5	1-0	.330	.439	.547	.986	...	...
—	Tulsa (Texas)	3B	24	91	10	27	5	1	4	20	7	22	0	3	1-0	.297	.343	.505	.848	5	.000
2005—	Colorado (N.L.)	3B	12	38	6	8	4	0	1	4	5	12	0	1	0-0	.211	.302	.395	.697	1	.958
—	Colo. Springs (PCL)	3B	61	228	40	69	16	1	10	41	16	44	1	7	3-1	.303	.348	.513	.861	13	.917
2006—	Colo. Springs (PCL)		128	482	71	147	30	4	20	108	46	110	5	14	7-1	.305	.369	.508	.877	3	.985
—	Colorado (N.L.)	OF-1B	18	57	13	21	7	2	5	21	1	14	0	0	2-0	.368	.379	.825	1.204	0	1.000
Major League totals (2 years)			30	95	19	29	11	2	6	25	6	26	0	1	2-0	.305	.347	.653	.999	1	.975

2006 LEFTY-RIGHTY SPLITS

vs.	Avg.	AB	H	2B	3B	HR	RBI	BB	SO	OBP	Slg.	vs.	Avg.	AB	H	2B	3B	HR	RBI	BB	SO	OBP	Slg.
L	.438	16	7	2	0	3	9	1	1	.471	1.125	R	.341	41	14	5	2	2	12	0	13	.341	.707

BAKER, SCOTT — P

PERSONAL: Born September 19, 1981, in Shreveport, La. ... 6-4/220. ... Throws right, bats right. ... Full name: Timothy Scott Baker. ... College: Oklahoma State.
TRANSACTIONS/CAREER NOTES: Selected by Minnesota Twins organization in second round of 2003 free-agent draft.
CAREER HITTING: 0-for-3 (.000), 0 R, 0 2B, 0 3B, 0 HR, 0 RBI.

Year	Team (League)	W	L	Pct.	ERA	WHIP	G	GS	CG	ShO	Hld.	Sv.-Opp.	IP	H	R	ER	HR	BB-IBB	SO	Avg.
2003—	Quad City (Midw.)	3	1	.750	2.49	1.05	11	11	0	0	...	0-...	50.2	45	16	14	4	8-0	47	.234
2004—	Fort Myers (Fla. St.)	4	2	.667	2.40	1.02	7	7	0	0	...	0-...	45.0	40	13	12	1	6-0	37	.234
—	New Britain (East.)	5	3	.625	2.43	0.81	10	10	2	2	...	0-...	70.1	44	23	19	2	13-2	72	.174
—	Rochester (Int'l)	1	3	.250	4.97	1.47	9	9	0	0	...	0-...	54.1	65	31	30	3	15-1	36	.295
2005—	Rochester (Int'l)	5	8	.385	3.01	1.11	22	22	1	1	0	0-0	134.2	123	50	45	15	26-1	107	.241
—	Minnesota (A.L.)	3	3	.500	3.35	1.16	10	9	0	0	1	0-0	53.2	48	21	20	5	14-0	32	.241
2006—	Rochester (Int'l)	5	4	.556	2.67	1.21	12	12	1	0	0	0-0	84.1	77	26	25	4	25-4	68	.246
—	Minnesota (A.L.)	5	8	.385	6.37	1.56	16	16	0	0	0	0-0	83.1	114	63	59	17	16-1	62	.324
Major League totals (2 years)		8	11	.421	5.19	1.40	26	25	0	0	1	0-0	137.0	162	84	79	22	30-1	94	.294

2006 LEFTY-RIGHTY SPLITS

vs.	Avg.	AB	H	2B	3B	HR	RBI	BB	SO	OBP	Slg.	vs.	Avg.	AB	H	2B	3B	HR	RBI	BB	SO	OBP	Slg.
L	.349	175	61	14	2	9	31	12	25	.382	.606	R	.299	177	53	10	1	8	28	4	37	.326	.503

BAKO, PAUL — C

PERSONAL: Born June 20, 1972, in Lafayette, La. ... 6-2/215. ... Bats left, throws right. ... Full name: Gabor Paul Bako II. ... Name pronounced: BAH-koh. ... High school: Lafayette (La.). ... College: Southwestern Louisiana. **TRANSACTIONS/CAREER NOTES:** Selected by Cincinnati Reds organization in fifth round of 1993 free-agent draft. ... Traded by Reds with P Donne Wall to Detroit Tigers for OF Melvin Nieves (November 11, 1997). ... Traded by Tigers with Ps Dean Crow, Mark Persails and Brian Powell and 3B Carlos Villalobos to Houston Astros for C Brad Ausmus and P C.J. Nitkowski (January 14, 1999). ... Traded by Astros to Florida Marlins for cash (April 11, 2000). ... Claimed on waivers by Atlanta Braves (July 21, 2000). ... Traded by Braves with P Jose Cabrera to Milwaukee Brewers for C Henry Blanco (March 20, 2002). ... On disabled list (June 9-24, 2002). ... Traded by Brewers to Chicago Cubs for a player to be named (November 26, 2002); Brewers acquired IF Ryan Gripp to complete deal (December 16, 2002). ... Signed as a free agent by Los Angeles Dodgers (January 13, 2005). ... On disabled list (May 27, 2005-remainder of season). ... Signed as a free agent by Kansas City Royals (December 16, 2005). ... On disabled list (July 8-August 2, 2006); included rehabilitation assignment to Wichita.
2006 GAMES PLAYED BY POSITION (MLB): C—53, DH—1.

Year	Team (League)	Pos.	G	AB	R	H	2B	3B	HR	RBI	BB	SO	HBP	GDP	SB-CS	Avg.	OBP	SLG	OPS	E	Avg.
1993—	Billings (Pion.)	1B-C	57	194	34	61	11	0	4	30	22	37	1	5	5-1	.314	.382	.433	.815	6	.984
1994—	Win.-Salem (Car.)	C	90	289	29	59	9	1	3	26	35	81	4	6	2-2	.204	.299	.273	.572	15	.977
1995—	Win.-Salem (Car.)	C	82	249	29	71	11	2	7	27	42	66	1	6	3-1	.285	.389	.430	.819	6	.989
1996—	Chattanooga (Sou.)	C	110	360	53	106	27	0	8	48	48	93	5	5	1-0	.294	.381	.436	.817	13	.984
1997—	Indianapolis (A.A.)	C	104	321	34	78	14	1	8	43	34	81	2	7	0-5	.243	.316	.368	.683	6	.991
1998—	Toledo (Int'l)	C	13	48	5	14	3	1	1	6	1	13	0	1	0-0	.292	.300	.458	.758	1	.988
—	Detroit (A.L.)	C	96	305	23	83	12	1	3	30	23	82	0	3	1-1	.272	.319	.348	.667	6	.989
1999—	New Orleans (PCL)	C	12	47	2	9	4	1	1	4	11	10	1	0	0-0	.191	.208	.362	.570	1	.984
—	Houston (N.L.)	C	73	215	16	55	14	1	2	17	26	57	0	4	1-1	.256	.332	.358	.690	6	.983
2000—	Houston (N.L.)	C	1	2	0	0	0	0	0	0	1	0	0	0	0-0	.000	.000	.000	.000	0	1.000
—	Florida (N.L.)	C	56	161	10	39	6	1	0	14	22	48	1	4	0-0	.242	.335	.292	.627	3	.991
—	Atlanta (N.L.)	C-1B	24	58	8	11	4	0	2	6	5	15	0	2	0-0	.190	.254	.362	.616	1	.992

Year Team (League)	Pos.	G	AB	R	H	2B	3B	HR	RBI	BB	SO	HBP	GDP	SB-CS	Avg.	OBP	SLG	OPS	E	Avg.
													BATTING						FIELDING	
2001— Atlanta (N.L.)	C	61	137	19	29	10	1	2	15	20	34	0	3	1-0	.212	.312	.343	.655	3	.991
2002— Milwaukee (N.L.)	C	87	234	24	55	8	1	4	20	20	46	0	4	0-2	.235	.295	.329	.624	4	.991
2003— Chicago (N.L.)	C	70	188	19	43	13	3	0	17	22	47	1	2	0-1	.229	.311	.330	.641	6	.987
2004— Chicago (N.L.)	C	49	138	13	28	8	0	1	10	15	29	2	4	1-0	.203	.288	.283	.571	4	.989
2005— Los Angeles (N.L.)	C	13	40	1	10	2	0	0	4	7	12	0	0	0-0	.250	.362	.300	.662	1	.985
2006— Wichita (Texas)		3	12	3	2	0	0	0	2	0	1	0	0	0-0	.167	.167	.167	.333	0	1.000
— Kansas City (A.L.)	C-DH	56	153	7	32	3	0	0	10	11	46	0	3	0-0	.209	.261	.229	.489	2	.993
American League totals (2 years)		152	458	30	115	15	1	3	40	34	128	0	6	1-1	.251	.300	.308	.608	8	.990
National League totals (7 years)		434	1173	110	270	65	7	11	103	137	289	4	23	3-4	.230	.311	.326	.637	28	.990
Major League totals (9 years)		586	1631	140	385	80	8	14	143	171	417	4	29	4-5	.236	.308	.321	.629	36	.990

DIVISION SERIES RECORD

Year Team (League)	Pos.	G	AB	R	H	2B	3B	HR	RBI	BB	SO	HBP	GDP	SB-CS	Avg.	OBP	SLG	OPS	E	Avg.
2000— Atlanta (N.L.)	C	2	1	0	0	0	0	0	0	0	1	0	0	0-0	.000	.000	.000	.000	1	.800
2001— Atlanta (N.L.)	C	3	7	1	2	1	0	0	3	1	0	0	0	0-0	.286	.375	.857	1.232	0	1.000
2003— Chicago (N.L.)	C	3	4	0	0	0	0	0	1	2	2	0	0	0-0	.000	.333	.000	.333	0	1.000
Division series totals (3 years)		8	12	1	2	1	0	0	4	3	3	0	0	0-0	.167	.333	.500	.833	1	.976

CHAMPIONSHIP SERIES RECORD

Year Team (League)	Pos.	G	AB	R	H	2B	3B	HR	RBI	BB	SO	HBP	GDP	SB-CS	Avg.	OBP	SLG	OPS	E	Avg.
2001— Atlanta (N.L.)	C	3	3	0	0	0	0	0	0	0	0	0	0	0-0	.000	.000	.000	.000	0	1.000
2003— Chicago (N.L.)	C	6	16	4	4	1	0	0	1	1	7	0	0	0-0	.250	.294	.313	.607	0	1.000
Champ. series totals (2 years)		9	19	4	4	1	0	0	1	1	7	0	0	0-0	.211	.250	.263	.513	0	1.000

2006 LEFTY-RIGHTY SPLITS

vs.	Avg.	AB	H	2B	3B	HR	RBI	BB	SO	OBP	Slg.	vs.	Avg.	AB	H	2B	3B	HR	RBI	BB	SO	OBP	Slg.
L	.200	10	2	0	0	0	0	0	4	.200	.200	R	.210	143	30	3	0	0	10	11	42	.265	.231

BALDELLI, ROCCO — OF

PERSONAL: Born September 25, 1981, in Woonsocket, R.I. ... 6-4/187. ... Bats right, throws right. ... Full name: Rocco Daniel Baldelli. ... High school: Bishop Hendrickson (Warwick, R.I.). **TRANSACTIONS/CAREER NOTES:** Selected by Tampa Bay Devil Rays organization in first round (sixth pick overall) of 2000 free-agent draft. ... On disabled list (August 14-September 1, 2004; and March 25, 2005-entire season). ... On disabled list (April 1-June 7, 2006); included rehabilitation assignment to Durham. **STATISTICAL NOTES:** Career major league grand slams: 1.

2006 GAMES PLAYED BY POSITION (MLB): OF—91.

Year Team (League)	Pos.	G	AB	R	H	2B	3B	HR	RBI	BB	SO	HBP	GDP	SB-CS	Avg.	OBP	SLG	OPS	E	Avg.
													BATTING						FIELDING	
2000— Princeton (Appal.)	OF-3B	60	232	33	50	9	2	3	25	12	56	5	3	11-3	.216	.269	.310	.579	4	.966
2001— Char., S.C. (SAL)	OF	113	406	58	101	23	6	8	55	23	89	11	7	25-9	.249	.303	.394	.697	9	.964
2002— Bakersfield (Calif.)	OF	77	312	63	104	19	1	14	51	18	63	7	2	21-6	.333	.382	.535	.917	3	.975
— Orlando (South.)	OF	17	70	10	26	3	1	2	13	5	11	2	1	3-2	.371	.413	.529	.941	1	.967
— Durham (Int'l)	OF	23	96	13	28	6	1	3	7	0	23	0	1	2-5	.292	.292	.469	.760	0	1.000
2003— Tampa Bay (A.L.)	OF-DH	156	637	89	184	32	8	11	78	30	128	8	10	27-10	.289	.326	.416	.742	5	.989
2004— Tampa Bay (A.L.)	OF-DH	136	518	79	145	27	3	16	74	30	88	8	12	17-4	.280	.326	.436	.762	8	.978
2005— Tampa Bay (A.L.)			Did not play.																	
2006— Durham (Int'l)		12	47	7	19	5	0	0	4	4	10	0	1	0-1	.404	.451	.511	.962	1	.917
— Tampa Bay (A.L.)	OF	92	364	59	110	24	6	16	57	14	70	7	2	10-1	.302	.339	.533	.871	5	.979
Major League totals (3 years)		384	1519	227	439	83	17	43	209	74	286	23	24	54-15	.289	.329	.451	.780	18	.983

2006 LEFTY-RIGHTY SPLITS

vs.	Avg.	AB	H	2B	3B	HR	RBI	BB	SO	OBP	Slg.	vs.	Avg.	AB	H	2B	3B	HR	RBI	BB	SO	OBP	Slg.
L	.297	74	22	7	2	1	11	5	15	.342	.486	R	.303	290	88	17	4	15	46	9	55	.338	.545

BALFOUR, GRANT — P

PERSONAL: Born December 30, 1977, in Sydney, Australia. ... 6-2/188. ... Throws right, bats right. ... Full name: Grant Robert Balfour. ... High school: William Clarke College (Kellyville, Australia). **TRANSACTIONS/CAREER NOTES:** Signed as non-drafted free agent by Minnesota Twins organization (January 19, 1997). ... On disabled list (April 4-May 14 and July 26-August 17, 2004). ... On disabled list (March 25, 2005-entire season). ... Signed as free agent by Cincinnati Reds (January 12, 2006). ... On disabled list (March 31, 2006-entire season); included rehabilitation assignments to Dayton, GCL Reds and Sarasota. ... Claimed on waivers by Milwaukee Brewers (October 5, 2006).

CAREER HITTING: 0-for-0 (.000), 0 R, 0 2B, 0 3B, 0 HR, 0 RBI.

Year Team (League)	W	L	Pct.	ERA	WHIP	G	GS	CG	ShO	Hld.	Sv.-Opp.	IP	H	R	ER	HR	BB-IBB	SO	Avg.
1997— GC Twins (GCL)	2	4	.333	3.76	1.39	13	12	0	0	...	0-...	67.0	73	31	28	1	20-0	43	.292
1998— Elizabethton (App.)	7	2	.778	3.36	1.25	13	13	0	0	...	0-...	77.2	70	36	29	7	27-0	75	.240
1999— Quad City (Midw.)	8	5	.615	3.53	1.12	19	14	0	0	...	1-...	91.2	66	39	36	7	37-0	95	.204
2000— Fort Myers (Fla. St.)	8	5	.615	4.25	1.40	35	10	0	0	...	6-...	89.0	91	46	42	8	34-2	90	.263
2001— New Britain (East.)	2	1	.667	1.08	0.96	35	1	0	0	13-...	50.0	26	6	6	1	22-2	72	.149
— Minnesota (A.L.)	0	0	...	13.50	2.25	2	0	0	0	0	0-0	2.2	3	4	4	2	3-0	2	.333
— Edmonton (PCL)	2	2	.500	5.51	1.71	11	0	0	0	...	0-...	16.1	18	11	10	2	10-1	17	.305
2002— Edmonton (PCL)	2	4	.333	4.16	1.26	58	0	0	0	...	8-...	71.1	60	34	33	3	30-1	88	.231
2003— Rochester (Int'l)	5	2	.714	2.41	0.90	21	11	0	0	...	5-...	71.0	48	21	19	6	16-0	87	.188
— Minnesota (A.L.)	1	0	1.000	4.15	1.42	17	1	0	0	1	0-1	26.0	23	12	12	4	14-2	30	.235
2004— Minnesota (A.L.)	4	1	.800	4.35	1.42	36	0	0	0	4	0-1	39.1	35	19	19	4	21-1	42	.238
2005— Minnesota (A.L.)			Did not play.																
2006— Sarasota (Fla. St.)	0	0	...	7.94	1.94	5	0	0	0	...	0-0	5.2	8	7	5	0	3-0	7	.320
— Dayton (Midw.)	0	0	...	0.00	0.00	2	0	0	0	...	0-0	2.0	0	0	0	0	0-0	3	...
— GC Reds (GCL)	0	0	...	13.50	3.00	2	2	0	0	...	0-0	1.1	1	2	2	0	3-0	2	.250
Major League totals (3 years)	5	1	.833	4.63	1.46	55	1	0	0	5	0-2	68.0	61	35	35	10	38-3	74	.240

DIVISION SERIES RECORD

Year Team (League)	W	L	Pct.	ERA	WHIP	G	GS	CG	ShO	Hld.	Sv.-Opp.	IP	H	R	ER	HR	BB-IBB	SO	Avg.
2004— Minnesota (A.L.)	0	0	...	0.00	0.00	2	0	0	0	0	0-0	2.2	0	0	0	0	0-0	2	.000

BANNISTER, BRIAN — P

PERSONAL: Born February 28, 1981, in Scottsdale, Ariz. ... 6-2/200. ... Throws right, bats right. ... Full name: Brian P. Bannister. ... College: Southern California ... Son of Floyd Bannister, pitcher with six major league teams (1977-92). **TRANSACTIONS/CAREER NOTES:** Selected by New York Mets organization in seventh round of 2003 free-agent draft. ... On disabled list (April 28-August 25, 2006); included rehabilitation assignments to Norfolk and St. Lucie.

CAREER HITTING: 4-for-12 (.333), 2 R, 3 2B, 0 3B, 0 HR, 2 RBI.

Year Team (League)	W	L	Pct.	ERA	WHIP	G	GS	CG	ShO	Hld.	Sv.-Opp.	IP	H	R	ER	HR	BB-IBB	SO	Avg.
2003—Brooklyn (N.Y.-Penn.)	4	1	.800	2.15	0.98	12	9	0	0	...	1-...	46.0	27	12	11	0	18-0	42	.173
2004—St. Lucie (Fla. St.)	5	7	.417	4.24	1.25	20	20	0	0	...	0-...	110.1	111	63	52	6	27-1	106	.270
—Binghamton (East.)	3	3	.500	4.06	1.40	8	8	0	0	...	0-...	44.1	45	23	20	2	17-0	28	.283
2005—Binghamton (East.)	9	4	.692	2.56	1.08	18	18	1	1	0	0-0	109.0	91	36	31	11	27-0	94	.232
—Norfolk (Int'l)	4	1	.800	3.18	1.35	8	8	0	0	0	0-0	45.1	48	19	16	0	13-0	48	.270
2006—Norfolk (Int'l)	3	3	.500	3.86	1.29	6	6	1	0	0	0-0	30.1	34	15	13	4	5-0	24	.279
—St. Lucie (Fla. St.)	1	0	1.000	1.50	1.17	2	2	0	0	0	0-0	12.0	10	4	2	0	4-0	5	.233
—New York (N.L.)	2	1	.667	4.26	1.47	8	6	0	0	0	0-0	38.0	34	18	18	4	22-2	19	.239
Major league totals (1 year)	2	1	.667	4.26	1.47	8	6	0	0	0	0-0	38.0	34	18	18	4	22-2	19	.239

2006 LEFTY-RIGHTY SPLITS

vs.	Avg.	AB	H	2B	3B	HR	RBI	BB	SO	OBP	Slg.	vs.	Avg.	AB	H	2B	3B	HR	RBI	BB	SO	OBP	Slg.
L	.286	77	22	3	1	2	12	11	10	.359	.429	R	.185	65	12	3	1	2	6	11	9	.321	.354

B

BARAJAS, ROD — C

PERSONAL: Born September 5, 1975, in Ontario, Calif. ... 6-2/220. ... Bats right, throws right. ... Full name: Rodrigo Richard Barajas. ... Name pronounced: bar-AH-hoss. ... High school: Sante Fe Springs (Calif.). ... Junior college: Cerritos (Calif.). **TRANSACTIONS/CAREER NOTES:** Signed as a non-drafted free agent by Arizona Diamondbacks organization (January 23, 1996). ... Loaned by Diamondbacks organization to Oakland Athletics organization (April 5-June 16, 1996). ... On disabled list (April 7-28 and July 5-23, 2003); included rehabilitation assignments to Tucson and Lancaster. ... Signed as a free agent by Texas Rangers organization (January 15, 2004). **STATISTICAL NOTES:** Career major league grand slams: 2.

2006 GAMES PLAYED BY POSITION (MLB): C—94, 1B—5.

Year Team (League)	Pos.	G	AB	R	H	2B	3B	HR	RBI	BB	SO	HBP	GDP	SB-CS	Avg.	OBP	SLG	OPS	E	Avg.
1996—Visalia (Calif.)	C	27	74	6	12	3	0	0	8	7	21	1	3	0-0	.162	.244	.203	.447	0	1.000
—Lethbridge (Pion.)	1B-C	51	175	47	59	9	3	10	50	12	24	2	6	2-1	.337	.378	.594	.973	5	.986
1997—High Desert (Calif.)	1B-C	57	199	24	53	11	0	7	30	8	41	1	7	0-2	.266	.297	.427	.724	3	.993
1998—High Desert (Calif.)	C	113	442	67	134	26	0	23	81	25	81	7	13	1-1	.303	.345	.518	.863	14	.983
1999—El Paso (Texas)	C-DH-1B	127	510	77	162	41	2	14	95	24	73	8	8	2-0	.318	.354	.488	.842	14	.985
—Arizona (N.L.)	C	5	16	3	4	1	0	1	3	1	1	0	0	0-0	.250	.294	.500	.794	0	1.000
2000—Tucson (PCL)	C-1B-3B	110	416	43	94	25	0	13	75	14	65	5	13	4-3	.226	.253	.380	.633	14	.980
—Arizona (N.L.)	C	5	13	1	3	0	0	1	3	0	4	0	0	0-0	.231	.231	.462	.692	0	1.000
2001—Arizona (N.L.)	C	51	106	9	17	3	0	3	9	4	26	0	0	0-0	.160	.191	.274	.464	1	.995
—Tucson (PCL)	1B-C-3B	45	162	23	52	13	0	9	32	9	23	3	2	3-1	.321	.366	.568	.934	3	.990
2002—Arizona (N.L.)	C-1B	70	154	12	36	10	0	3	23	10	25	3	4	1-0	.234	.288	.357	.645	1	.997
—Tucson (PCL)	C-1B	5	16	2	7	1	0	1	1	1	2	0	0	0-0	.438	.471	.688	1.158	0	1.000
2003—Tucson (PCL)	C-DH	4	16	3	7	1	0	1	4	1	1	2	0	0-0	.438	.471	.688	1.158	0	1.000
—Lancaster (Calif.)	C-DH	3	12	2	5	0	0	0	3	1	2	0	0	0-0	.417	.462	.417	.878	0	1.000
—Arizona (N.L.)	C	80	220	19	48	15	0	3	28	14	43	1	6	0-0	.218	.265	.327	.592	0	1.000
2004—Texas (A.L.)	C-1B	108	358	50	89	26	1	15	58	13	63	3	0	0-1	.249	.276	.453	.728	7	.990
2005—Texas (A.L.)	C-1B	120	410	53	104	24	0	21	60	26	70	6	6	0-0	.254	.306	.466	.771	9	.988
2006—Texas (A.L.)	C-1B	97	344	49	88	20	0	11	41	17	51	4	9	0-0	.256	.298	.410	.708	10	.985
American League totals (3 years)		325	1112	152	281	70	1	47	159	56	184	13	18	0-1	.253	.294	.444	.738	26	.988
National League totals (5 years)		211	509	44	108	29	0	11	66	29	99	4	10	1-0	.212	.257	.334	.591	2	.998
Major League totals (8 years)		536	1621	196	389	99	1	58	225	85	283	17	28	1-1	.240	.282	.410	.692	28	.991

DIVISION SERIES RECORD

Year Team (League)	Pos.	G	AB	R	H	2B	3B	HR	RBI	BB	SO	HBP	GDP	SB-CS	Avg.	OBP	SLG	OPS	E	Avg.
2001—Arizona (N.L.)	C	1	0	0	0	0	0	0	0	0	0	0	0	0-0	...	...	...	...	0	...
2002—Arizona (N.L.)	C	2	4	1	1	0	0	0	1	1	0	1	0	0-0	.250	.250	1.000	1.250	0	1.000
Division series totals (2 years)		3	4	1	1	0	0	0	1	1	0	1	0	0-0	.250	.250	1.000	1.250	0	1.000

CHAMPIONSHIP SERIES RECORD

Year Team (League)	Pos.	G	AB	R	H	2B	3B	HR	RBI	BB	SO	HBP	GDP	SB-CS	Avg.	OBP	SLG	OPS	E	Avg.
2001—Arizona (N.L.)			Did not play.																	

WORLD SERIES RECORD

Year Team (League)	Pos.	G	AB	R	H	2B	3B	HR	RBI	BB	SO	HBP	GDP	SB-CS	Avg.	OBP	SLG	OPS	E	Avg.
2001—Arizona (N.L.)	C	2	5	1	2	0	0	1	1	0	0	0	0	0-0	.400	.400	1.000	1.400	0	1.000

2006 LEFTY-RIGHTY SPLITS

vs.	Avg.	AB	H	2B	3B	HR	RBI	BB	SO	OBP	Slg.	vs.	Avg.	AB	H	2B	3B	HR	RBI	BB	SO	OBP	Slg.
L	.156	64	10	4	0	3	9	5	9	.217	.359	R	.279	280	78	16	0	8	32	12	42	.316	.421

BARD, JOSH — C

PERSONAL: Born March 30, 1978, in Ithaca, N.Y. ... 6-3/215. ... Bats both, throws right. ... Full name: Joshua David Bard. ... Name pronounced: baahrd. ... High school: Cherry Creek (Englewood, Colo.). ... College: Texas Tech. **TRANSACTIONS/CAREER NOTES:** Selected by Minnesota Twins organization in 35th round of 1996 free-agent draft; did not sign. ... Selected by Colorado Rockies organization in third round of 1999 free-agent draft. ... Traded by Rockies with OF Jody Gerut to Cleveland Indians for OF Jacob Cruz (June 2, 2001). ... On disabled list (March 28-July 5, 2004); included rehabilitation assignments to Akron and Buffalo. ... Traded by Indians with OF Coco Crisp and P David Riske to Boston Red Sox for 3B Andy Marte, P Guillermo Mota and C Kelly Shoppach (January 27, 2006). ... Traded by Red Sox with RHP Cla Meredith and cash to San Diego Padres for C Doug Mirabelli (May 1, 2006). ... On suspended list (July 21-22, 2006).

2006 GAMES PLAYED BY POSITION (MLB): C—78.

Year Team (League)	Pos.	G	AB	R	H	2B	3B	HR	RBI	BB	SO	HBP	GDP	SB-CS	Avg.	OBP	SLG	OPS	E	Avg.
1999—			Did not play.																	
2000—Salem (Carol.)	C	93	309	40	88	17	0	2	25	32	33	1	6	3-1	.285	.352	.359	.711	10	.987
—Colo. Springs (PCL)	C	4	17	0	4	0	0	0	1	0	2	0	0	0-0	.235	.235	.235	.471	1	.923
2001—Carolina (Southern)	C	35	124	14	32	13	0	1	24	19	23	1	1	0-1	.258	.359	.387	.746	2	.993
—Akron (East.)	C	51	194	26	54	11	0	4	25	16	27	2	4	0-0	.278	.338	.397	.735	4	.986
—Mahoning Valley (N.Y.-Penn.)	C	13	44	7	12	4	0	2	8	6	2	1	1	0-1	.273	.373	.500	.873	3	.769
—Buffalo (Int'l)	DH	1	4	0	0	0	0	0	0	0	0	0	0	0-0	.000	.000	.000	.000	...	...
2002—Buffalo (Int'l)	C	94	344	36	102	26	2	6	53	20	45	0	13	0-0	.297	.332	.436	.768	11	.984
—Cleveland (A.L.)	C	24	90	9	20	5	0	3	12	4	13	0	6	0-0	.222	.255	.378	.633	2	.988
2003—Buffalo (Int'l)	C-DH	35	115	14	38	7	0	5	21	14	17	1	5	1-2	.330	.408	.522	.929	1	.995
—Cleveland (A.L.)	C-DH	91	303	25	74	13	1	8	36	22	53	0	9	0-2	.244	.293	.373	.666	5	.991
2004—Akron (East.)	DH-C	10	30	5	5	1	0	0	5	7	4	0	2	0-0	.167	.324	.200	.524	0	1.000

Year	Team (League)	Pos.	G	AB	R	H	2B	3B	HR	RBI	BB	SO	HBP	GDP	SB-CS	Avg.	OBP	SLG	OPS	E	Avg.
	— Buffalo (Int'l)	C-DH	40	156	25	41	10	0	4	18	11	23	0	7	0-0	.263	.310	.404	.713	3	.988
	— Cleveland (A.L.)	C	7	19	5	8	2	0	1	4	3	0	0	0	0-0	.421	.478	.684	1.162	0	1.000
2005—	Cleveland (A.L.)	C	34	83	6	16	4	0	1	9	9	11	0	2	0-0	.193	.266	.277	.543	3	.983
2006—	Boston (A.L.)	C	7	18	2	5	1	0	0	0	3	3	0	0	0-0	.278	.381	.333	.714	0	1.000
	— San Diego (N.L.)	C	93	231	28	78	19	0	9	40	27	39	1	9	1-0	.338	.406	.537	.943	3	.993
	American League totals (5 years)		163	513	47	123	25	1	13	61	41	80	0	17	0-2	.240	.293	.368	.661	10	.990
	National League totals (1 year)		93	231	28	78	19	0	9	40	27	39	1	9	1-0	.338	.406	.537	.943	3	.993
	Major League totals (5 years)		256	744	75	201	44	1	22	101	68	119	1	26	1-2	.270	.329	.421	.750	13	.991

DIVISION SERIES RECORD

Year	Team (League)	Pos.	G	AB	R	H	2B	3B	HR	RBI	BB	SO	HBP	GDP	SB-CS	Avg.	OBP	SLG	OPS	E	Avg.
2006—	San Diego (N.L.)	C	3	7	0	1	0	0	0	0	1	2	1	0	0-0	.143	.333	.143	.476	0	1.000

2006 LEFTY-RIGHTY SPLITS

vs.	Avg.	AB	H	2B	3B	HR	RBI	BB	SO	OBP	Slg.	vs.	Avg.	AB	H	2B	3B	HR	RBI	BB	SO	OBP	Slg.
L	.333	66	22	4	0	3	10	5	13	.384	.530	R	.333	183	61	16	0	6	30	25	29	.411	.519

BARFIELD, JOSH — 2B

PERSONAL: Born December 17, 1982, in Barquisimeto, Venezuela. ... 6-0/185. ... Bats right, throws right. ... Full name: Joshua LaRoy Barfield. ... Son of Jesse Barfield, outfielder with two major league teams (1981-92). **TRANSACTIONS/CAREER NOTES:** Selected by San Diego Padres organization in fourth round of 2001 free-agent draft. ... Traded by Padres to Cleveland Indians for IF Kevin Kouzmanoff and P Andrew Brown (November 8, 2006). **STATISTICAL NOTES:** Career major league grand slams: 1.
2006 GAMES PLAYED BY POSITION (MLB): 2B—147.

Year	Team (League)	Pos.	G	AB	R	H	2B	3B	HR	RBI	BB	SO	HBP	GDP	SB-CS	Avg.	OBP	SLG	OPS	E	Avg.
2001—	Idaho Falls (Pio.)		66	277	51	86	15	4	4	53	16	54	3	7	12-4	.310	.350	.437	.787	20	...
2002—	Fort Wayne (Midw.)		129	536	73	164	22	3	8	57	26	105	4	13	26-8	.306	.340	.403	.743	24	...
	— Lake Elsinore (Calif.)		6	23	2	2	0	0	0	4	1	4	0	1	0-0	.087	.120	.087	.207	1	...
2003—	Lake Elsinore (Calif.)		135	549	99	185	46	6	16	128	50	122	4	11	16-4	.337	.389	.530	.919	20	...
2004—	Mobile (Sou.)		138	521	79	129	28	3	18	90	48	119	5	6	4-2	.248	.313	.417	.730	13	...
2005—	Portland (PCL)	2B	137	516	74	160	25	1	15	72	52	108	1	10	20-5	.310	.370	.450	.819	13	.980
2006—	San Diego (N.L.)	2B	150	539	72	151	32	3	13	58	30	81	2	8	21-5	.280	.318	.423	.741	9	.987
	Major League totals (1 year)		150	539	72	151	32	3	13	58	30	81	2	8	21-5	.280	.318	.423	.741	9	.987

DIVISION SERIES RECORD

Year	Team (League)	Pos.	G	AB	R	H	2B	3B	HR	RBI	BB	SO	HBP	GDP	SB-CS	Avg.	OBP	SLG	OPS	E	Avg.
2006—	San Diego (N.L.)	2B	4	8	0	2	1	0	0	0	1	2	0	0	0-0	.250	.333	.375	.708	0	1.000

2006 LEFTY-RIGHTY SPLITS

vs.	Avg.	AB	H	2B	3B	HR	RBI	BB	SO	OBP	Slg.	vs.	Avg.	AB	H	2B	3B	HR	RBI	BB	SO	OBP	Slg.
L	.331	121	40	10	0	7	20	10	15	.378	.587	R	.266	418	111	22	3	6	38	20	66	.299	.376

BARKER, KEVIN — 1B

PERSONAL: Born July 26, 1975, in Bristol, Va. ... 6-3/205. ... Bats left, throws left. ... Full name: Kevin S. Barker. ... High school: Virginia (Bristol, Va.). ... College: Virginia Tech. **TRANSACTIONS/CAREER NOTES:** Selected by Milwaukee Brewers organization in third round of 1996 free-agent draft. ... Traded by Brewers to San Diego Padres for C Dusty Wathan (March 24, 2002). ... Released by Padres (September 30, 2002). ... Signed by Detroit Tigers organization (January 24, 2003). ... Released by Tigers (March 24, 2003). ... Signed by Florida Marlins organization (May 30, 2003). ... Signed as a free agent by Philadelphia Phillies organization (January 23, 2004). ... Signed as a free agent by Toronto Blue Jays organization (April 3, 2005).
2006 GAMES PLAYED BY POSITION (MLB): DH—5, 1B—2, OF—1.

Year	Team (League)	Pos.	G	AB	R	H	2B	3B	HR	RBI	BB	SO	HBP	GDP	SB-CS	Avg.	OBP	SLG	OPS	E	Avg.
1996—	Ogden (Pion.)	1B	71	281	61	89	19	4	9	56	46	54	3	4	0-2	.317	.412	.509	.921	11	.982
1997—	Stockton (Calif.)	1B	70	267	47	81	20	5	13	45	25	60	0	6	4-3	.303	.362	.562	.924	6	.988
	— El Paso (Texas)	1B	65	238	37	66	15	6	10	63	28	40	2	5	3-3	.277	.352	.517	.868	9	.982
1998—	El Paso (Texas)	1B	20	85	14	26	6	0	5	14	3	21	2	2	2-1	.306	.337	.553	.890	1	.995
	— Louisville (Int'l)	1B-OF	124	463	59	128	26	4	23	96	36	97	3	11	2-5	.276	.330	.499	.829	9	.991
1999—	Louisville (Int'l)	1B-OF	121	442	89	123	27	5	23	87	59	94	4	13	2-2	.278	.363	.518	.881	10	.991
	— Milwaukee (N.L.)	1B	38	117	13	33	3	0	3	23	9	19	0	...	1-0	.282	.331	.385	.715	1	.996
2000—	Milwaukee (N.L.)	1B	40	100	14	22	5	0	2	9	20	21	1	...	1-0	.220	.352	.330	.682	2	.993
	— Indianapolis (Int'l)	1B	85	286	41	56	10	1	11	44	52	76	1	6	0-1	.196	.316	.353	.669	3	.995
2001—	Indianapolis (Int'l)	OF-1B	51	159	12	30	5	0	4	20	20	40	1	3	0-0	.189	.282	.296	.577	0	1.000
	— Huntsville (Sou.)	1B-OF	66	232	42	75	16	1	8	38	35	51	1	2	0-0	.323	.410	.504	.914	4	.992
2002—	Portland (PCL)	1B-OF	113	390	54	98	14	1	14	48	46	70	3	10	1-1	.251	.333	.400	.733	4	.996
	— San Diego (N.L.)	1B	7	19	0	3	0	0	0	1	1	6	0	...	1-0	.158	.200	.158	.358	0	1.000
2003—	Albuquerque (PCL)		10	24	1	4	0	0	0	1	7	5	0	1	0-0	.167	.355	.167	.522	...	...
2004—	Reading (East.)		112	405	69	116	38	3	18	58	53	95	2	8	2-1	.286	.367	.528	.895	...	...
	— Scran./W.B. (Int'l)		13	36	3	7	1	0	2	4	3	8	0	1	0-0	.194	.256	.389	.645	...	...
2005—	New Hampshire (East.)	DH-1B-P	52	185	18	47	11	1	6	27	28	42	1	2	1-2	.254	.350	.422	.772	1	.990
	— Syracuse (Int'l)	1B-DH	91	351	58	107	24	1	23	87	38	89	3	4	1-0	.305	.373	.575	.948	2	.998
2006—	Syracuse (Int'l)		130	473	72	130	39	2	18	76	80	119	2	10	5-3	.275	.379	.480	.859	10	.989
	— Toronto (A.L.)	DH-1B-OF	12	17	3	4	1	0	1	1	1	10	0	...	0-0	.235	.278	.471	.748	1	.933
	American League totals (1 year)		12	17	3	4	1	0	1	1	1	10	0	0	0-0	.235	.278	.471	.748	1	.933
	National League totals (3 years)		85	236	27	58	8	0	5	32	30	46	1	...	3-0	.246	.331	.343	.674	3	.995
	Major League totals (4 years)		97	253	30	62	9	0	6	33	31	56	1	0	3-0	.245	.328	.352	.679	4	.993

2006 LEFTY-RIGHTY SPLITS

vs.	Avg.	AB	H	2B	3B	HR	RBI	BB	SO	OBP	Slg.	vs.	Avg.	AB	H	2B	3B	HR	RBI	BB	SO	OBP	Slg.
L	.000	1	0	0	0	0	0	1	1	.500	.000	R	.250	16	4	1	0	1	1	0	9	.250	.500

BARMES, CLINT — SS/2B

PERSONAL: Born March 6, 1979, in Vincennes, Ind. ... 6-0/175. ... Bats right, throws right. ... Full name: Clint Harold Barmes. ... High school: Lincoln (Vincennes, Ind.). ... College: Indiana State. **TRANSACTIONS/CAREER NOTES:** Selected by Colorado Rockies in 10th round of 2000 free-agent draft. ... On disabled list (June 6-September 2, 2005); included rehabilitation assignment to Tulsa.
2006 GAMES PLAYED BY POSITION (MLB): SS—125, 2B—4.

B

Year	Team (League)	Pos.	G	AB	R	H	2B	3B	HR	RBI	BB	SO	HBP	GDP	SB-CS	Avg.	OBP	SLG	OPS	E	Avg.
2000—Portland (N'west)	SS-OF		45	181	37	51	6	4	2	16	18	28	5	1	12-9	.282	.361	.392	.753	12	.934
—Asheville (S. Atl.)	2B-SS-3B OF		19	81	11	14	4	0	0	4	10	13	1	3	4-1	.173	.269	.222	.491	2	.977
2001—Asheville (S. Atl.)	SS		74	285	40	74	14	1	5	24	17	37	7	6	21-7	.260	.314	.368	.683	22	.943
—Salem (Carol.)	SS		38	121	17	30	3	3	0	9	15	20	4	5	4-1	.248	.350	.322	.672	13	.934
2002—Carolina (Sou.)	SS		103	438	62	119	23	2	15	60	31	72	9	3	15-11	.272	.329	.436	.765	33	.940
2003—Colo. Springs (PCL)	SS-2B		136	493	63	136	35	1	7	54	22	63	9	9	12-7	.276	.316	.394	.709	29	.951
—Colorado (N.L.)	SS		12	25	2	8	2	0	0	2	0	10	2	0	0-0	.320	.357	.400	.757	2	.958
2004—Colo. Springs (PCL)	SS-2B-DH		125	533	104	175	42	2	16	51	28	61	15	5	20-8	.328	.376	.505	.881	20	.964
—Colorado (N.L.)	2B-SS		20	71	14	20	3	1	2	10	3	10	1	2	0-1	.282	.320	.437	.757	2	.980
2005—Tulsa (Texas)	SS-3B		8	34	6	11	1	0	0	0	1	3	0	2	1-0	.324	.343	.353	.696	1	.957
—Colorado (N.L.)	SS		81	350	55	101	19	1	10	46	16	36	6	4	6-4	.289	.330	.434	.764	17	.958
2006—Colorado (N.L.)	SS-2B		131	478	57	105	26	4	7	56	22	72	9	2	5-4	.220	.264	.335	.598	18	.970
Major League totals (4 years)			244	924	128	234	50	6	19	114	41	128	18	8	11-9	.253	.295	.382	.677	39	.966

2006 LEFTY-RIGHTY SPLITS

vs.	Avg.	AB	H	2B	3B	HR	RBI	BB	SO	OBP	Slg.
L	.267	86	23	7	0	2	14	6	9	.327	.419
R	.209	392	82	19	4	5	42	16	63	.249	.316

BARNWELL, CHRIS — IF

PERSONAL: Born March 1, 1979, in Jacksonville, Fla. ... Bats right, throws right. ... Full name: Christopher E. Barnwell. ... College: Flagler (Fla.). **TRANSACTIONS/CAREER NOTES:** Selected by Milwaukee Brewers organization in 25th round of 2001 free-agent draft.

2006 GAMES PLAYED BY POSITION (MLB): SS—5, 2B—3, 3B—3.

Year	Team (League)	Pos.	G	AB	R	H	2B	3B	HR	RBI	BB	SO	HBP	GDP	SB-CS	Avg.	OBP	SLG	OPS	E	Avg.
2001—Ogden (Pion.)			69	261	49	80	19	5	0	37	7	28	7	2	17-2	.307	.337	.418	.755	...	...
2002—Beloit (Midw.)			91	344	37	78	12	2	1	40	27	47	7	4	13-5	.227	.294	.282	.576	...	...
—High Desert (Calif.)			35	132	19	32	7	0	1	14	8	14	2	2	1-1	.242	.294	.318	.612	...	...
2003—Huntsville (Sou.)			102	313	39	77	7	0	3	25	27	47	9	12	6-6	.246	.322	.297	.619	...	...
2004—Huntsville (Sou.)			138	484	43	119	24	4	6	51	36	76	12	3	11-14	.246	.310	.349	.659	...	...
2005—Huntsville (Sou.)	2B-3B		15	35	6	9	1	1	1	4	1	7	1	0	0-0	.257	.289	.457	.747	1	.962
—Nashville (PCL)	3B-SS-2B P-1B		100	261	30	64	14	1	3	20	18	46	3	6	5-3	.245	.299	.341	.640	16	.949
2006—Nashville (PCL)			106	383	46	115	18	2	4	37	38	60	10	11	16-6	.300	.375	.389	.764	11	.979
—Milwaukee (N.L.)	SS-2B-3B		13	30	2	2	0	0	0	1	1	6	0	0	1-0	.067	.097	.067	.163	2	.947
Major League totals (1 year)			13	30	2	2	0	0	0	1	1	6	0	0	1-0	.067	.097	.067	.163	2	.947

2006 LEFTY-RIGHTY SPLITS

vs.	Avg.	AB	H	2B	3B	HR	RBI	BB	SO	OBP	Slg.
L	.100	10	1	0	0	0	0	0	1	.100	.100
R	.050	20	1	0	0	0	1	1	5	.095	.050

BARRETT, MICHAEL — C

PERSONAL: Born October 22, 1976, in Atlanta. ... 6-3/210. ... Bats right, throws right. ... Full name: Michael Patrick Barrett. ... High school: Pace Academy (Atlanta). **TRANSACTIONS/CAREER NOTES:** Selected by Montreal Expos organization in first round (28th pick overall) of 1995 free-agent draft. ... On disabled list (June 24-July 11, 1999); included rehabilitation assignment to Ottawa. ... On disabled list (July 27-September 10, 2003); included rehabilitation assignment to Edmonton. ... Traded by Expos to Oakland Athletics for P Brett Price (December 15, 2003). ... Traded by Athletics to Chicago Cubs for C Damian Miller (December 16, 2003). ... On suspended list (June 19-30, 2006). ... On disabled list (September 3, 2006-remainder of season). **HONORS:** Named catcher on N.L. Silver Slugger team (2005). **STATISTICAL NOTES:** Career major league grand slams: 3.

2006 GAMES PLAYED BY POSITION (MLB): C—102, DH—1.

Year	Team (League)	Pos.	G	AB	R	H	2B	3B	HR	RBI	BB	SO	HBP	GDP	SB-CS	Avg.	OBP	SLG	OPS	E	Avg.
1995—GC Expos (GCL)	3B-SS		50	183	22	57	13	4	0	19	15	19	0	1	7-6	.311	.362	.426	.788	25	.893
—Vermont (NYP)	SS		3	10	0	1	0	0	0	1	1	1	0	0	0-0	.100	.167	.100	.267	0	1.000
1996—Delmarva (S. Atl.)	C-DH-3B		129	474	57	113	29	4	8	62	18	42	9	9	5-11	.238	.277	.342	.618	15	.978
1997—W.P. Beach (Fla. St.)	C-DH		119	423	52	120	30	0	8	61	36	49	5	11	7-4	.284	.340	.411	.751	13	.982
1998—Harrisburg (East.)	C-3B-DH		120	453	78	145	32	2	19	87	27	43	2	16	7-6	.320	.358	.525	.883	12	.981
—Montreal (N.L.)	3B-C		8	23	3	7	2	0	1	2	3	6	1	0	0-0	.304	.407	.522	.929	3	.912
1999—Montreal (N.L.)	3B-C-SS		126	433	53	127	32	3	8	52	32	39	3	18	0-2	.293	.345	.436	.782	14	.973
—Ottawa (Int'l)	3B		2	7	1	3	0	0	0	2	1	0	0	0	0-1	.429	.500	.429	.929	1	.800
2000—Ottawa (Int'l)	3B-C		31	120	21	43	7	0	2	19	13	10	2	5	1-0	.358	.430	.467	.896	5	.945
—Montreal (N.L.)	3B-C		89	271	28	58	15	1	1	22	23	35	1	7	0-1	.214	.277	.288	.565	15	.949
2001—Montreal (N.L.)	C		132	472	42	118	33	2	6	38	25	54	2	14	2-1	.250	.289	.367	.655	7	.993
2002—Montreal (N.L.)	C-1B		117	376	41	99	20	1	12	49	40	65	1	14	6-3	.263	.332	.418	.749	9	.989
2003—Edmonton (PCL)	C		2	6	2	2	0	0	0	2	0	2	0	0	1-0	.333	.333	.500	.833	0	1.000
—Montreal (N.L.)	C		70	226	33	47	9	2	10	30	21	37	2	6	0-0	.208	.280	.398	.678	1	.998
2004—Chicago (N.L.)	C		134	456	55	131	32	6	16	65	33	64	5	13	1-4	.287	.337	.489	.826	6	.994
2005—Chicago (N.L.)	C-DH		133	424	48	117	32	3	16	61	40	61	7	7	0-3	.276	.345	.479	.824	6	.994
2006—Chicago (N.L.)	C-DH		107	375	54	115	25	3	16	53	33	41	5	12	0-1	.307	.368	.517	.885	5	.994
Major League totals (9 years)			916	3056	357	819	200	21	86	372	250	402	27	91	9-15	.268	.326	.432	.758	66	.989

2006 LEFTY-RIGHTY SPLITS

vs.	Avg.	AB	H	2B	3B	HR	RBI	BB	SO	OBP	Slg.
L	.313	83	26	7	2	6	16	11	7	.396	.663
R	.305	292	89	18	1	10	37	22	34	.359	.476

BARRY, KEVIN — P

PERSONAL: Born August 18, 1978, in Princeton Junction, N.J. ... Throws right, bats right. ... Full name: Kevin Thomas Barry. ... College: Rider. **TRANSACTIONS/CAREER NOTES:** Selected by Atlanta Braves organization in 14th round of 2001 free-agent draft.

CAREER HITTING: 0-for-2 (.000), 0 R, 0 2B, 0 3B, 0 HR, 0 RBI.

Year	Team (League)	W	L	Pct.	ERA	WHIP	G	GS	CG	ShO	Hld.	Sv.-Opp.	IP	H	R	ER	HR	BB-IBB	SO	Avg.
2001—Jamestown (NYP)	1	0	1.000	0.86	1.02	29	0	0	0		12-...	31.1	14	5	3	0	18-0	54	.131
2002—Myrtle Beach (Carol.)	4	2	.667	2.52	1.08	47	0	0	0		26-...	50.0	37	14	14	2	17-1	67	.215
2003—Greenville (Sou.)	4	4	.500	4.95	1.53	51	0	0	0		5-...	56.1	54	36	31	1	32-0	68	.249

Year	Team (League)	W	L	Pct.	ERA	WHIP	G	GS	CG	ShO	Hld.	Sv.-Opp.	IP	H	R	ER	HR	BB-IBB	SO	Avg.
2004—	Greenville (Sou.)	2	1	.667	0.73	1.01	20	0	0	0	...	4-...	24.2	15	2	2	0	10-2	31	.172
	— Richmond (Int'l)	3	3	.500	2.52	1.40	30	0	0	0	...	2-...	35.2	25	15	10	1	25-2	40	.189
2005—	Mississippi (Sou.)	0	0	...	1.23	1.23	8	0	0	0	...	0-0	7.1	3	1	1	0	6-0	7	.120
	— Richmond (Int'l)	5	3	.625	2.85	1.32	32	8	0	0	1	1-5	79.0	60	28	25	8	44-0	73	.209
2006—	Richmond (Int'l)	4	5	.444	3.30	1.29	18	15	0	0	0	0-0	95.1	87	40	35	5	36-2	73	.241
	— Atlanta (N.L.)	1	1	.500	5.61	1.48	19	1	0	0	1	0-1	25.2	24	16	16	2	14-0	19	.253
	Major League totals (1 year)	1	1	.500	5.61	1.48	19	1	0	0	1	0-1	25.2	24	16	16	2	14-0	19	.253

2006 LEFTY-RIGHTY SPLITS

vs.	Avg.	AB	H	2B	3B	HR	RBI	BB	SO	OBP	Slg.	vs.	Avg.	AB	H	2B	3B	HR	RBI	BB	SO	OBP	Slg.
L	.194	36	7	3	0	0	3	8	9	.333	.278	R	.288	59	17	5	2	2	13	6	10	.358	.542

BARTLETT, JASON — SS

PERSONAL: Born October 30, 1979, in Mountain View, Calif. ... 6-0/180. ... Bats right, throws right. ... Full name: Jason Alan Bartlett. ... High school: St. Mary's (Lodi, Calif.). ... College: Oklahoma. **TRANSACTIONS/CAREER NOTES:** Selected by San Diego Padres organization in 13th round of 2001 free-agent draft. ... Traded by Padres to Minnesota Twins for OF Brian Buchanan (July 12, 2002).

2006 GAMES PLAYED BY POSITION (MLB): SS—99.

										BATTING										FIELDING	
Year	Team (League)	Pos.	G	AB	R	H	2B	3B	HR	RBI	BB	SO	HBP	GDP	SB-CS	Avg.	OBP	SLG	OPS	E	Avg.
2001—	Eugene (Northwest)	SS	68	267	49	80	12	4	3	37	28	47	4	6	12-4	.300	.371	.408	.779	17	.946
2002—	Lake Elsinore (Calif.)	SS	75	308	57	77	14	4	1	33	32	53	5	7	24-5	.250	.329	.331	.660	22	.929
	— Fort Myers (Fla. St.)	SS-3B-2B	39	145	24	38	7	0	2	9	17	24	2	1	11-2	.262	.341	.352	.693	7	.949
2003—	New Britain (East.)	SS	139	548	96	162	31	8	8	48	58	67	20	7	41-24	.296	.380	.425	.805	20	.969
2004—	GC Twins (GCL)	SS	5	14	1	5	1	0	0	1	0	3	1	0	0-0	.357	.400	.429	.829	2	.846
	— Rochester (Int'l)	SS-2B-DH	67	269	54	89	15	7	3	29	33	37	7	1	7-3	.331	.415	.472	.873	19	.946
	— Minnesota (A.L.)	SS-2B-DH	8	12	2	1	0	0	0	1	1	1	0	0	2-0	.083	.154	.083	.237	2	.895
2005—	Rochester (Int'l)	SS-DH	61	229	41	76	10	2	5	33	29	34	4	3	2-2	.332	.405	.459	.864	12	.956
	— Minnesota (A.L.)	SS-DH	74	224	33	54	10	1	3	16	21	37	4	6	4-0	.241	.316	.335	.651	7	.979
2006—	Rochester (Int'l)		58	235	42	72	23	3	1	20	10	28	2	1	6-3	.306	.336	.443	.779	8	.968
	— Minnesota (A.L.)	SS	99	333	44	103	18	2	2	32	22	46	11	8	10-5	.309	.367	.393	.760	13	.971
	Major League totals (3 years)		181	569	79	158	28	3	5	49	44	84	15	14	16-5	.278	.342	.364	.706	22	.972

DIVISION SERIES RECORD

Year	Team (League)	Pos.	G	AB	R	H	2B	3B	HR	RBI	BB	SO	HBP	GDP	SB-CS	Avg.	OBP	SLG	OPS	E	Avg.
2006—	Minnesota (A.L.)	SS	3	11	0	3	1	0	0	0	0	2	0	0	0-0	.273	.273	.364	.636	2	.889

2006 LEFTY-RIGHTY SPLITS

vs.	Avg.	AB	H	2B	3B	HR	RBI	BB	SO	OBP	Slg.	vs.	Avg.	AB	H	2B	3B	HR	RBI	BB	SO	OBP	Slg.
L	.314	102	32	5	0	0	9	6	12	.368	.363	R	.307	231	71	13	2	2	23	16	34	.366	.407

BARZILLA, PHIL — P

PERSONAL: Born January 25, 1979, in Houston, Texas. ... Throws left, bats left. ... Full name: Philip Joseph Barzilla. ... College: Rice. **TRANSACTIONS/CAREER NOTES:** Selected by Houston Astros organization in fourth round of 2001 free-agent draft.

CAREER HITTING: 0-for-0 (.000), 0 R, 0 2B, 0 3B, 0 HR, 0 RBI.

Year	Team (League)	W	L	Pct.	ERA	WHIP	G	GS	CG	ShO	Hld.	Sv.-Opp.	IP	H	R	ER	HR	BB-IBB	SO	Avg.
2001—	Pittsfield (NYP)	4	5	.444	4.71	1.54	16	14	0	0	...	0-...	78.1	87	52	41	1	34-0	56	.277
2002—	Lexington (S. Atl.)	6	9	.400	3.26	1.17	43	0	0	0	...	4-...	85.2	66	39	31	2	34-5	62	.214
2003—	Salem (Carol.)	8	3	.727	3.10	1.37	52	0	0	0	...	5-...	93.0	86	39	32	1	41-5	51	.254
2004—	Round Rock (Texas)	3	1	.750	2.54	1.28	17	1	0	0	...	0-...	39.0	33	13	11	2	17-2	31	.226
	— New Orleans (PCL)	1	1	.500	4.28	1.87	27	0	0	0	...	0-...	33.2	42	21	16	4	21-1	22	.294
2005—	Corpus Christi (Texas)	7	7	.500	3.03	1.38	41	14	0	0	7	0-0	113.0	126	49	38	6	30-0	87	.281
	— Round Rock (PCL)	0	0	...			1	0	0	0	...	0-...	1.0	0	1	0	0	0-0	0	.000
2006—	Round Rock (PCL)	8	5	.615	3.85	1.44	25	14	1	1	1	1-1	112.1	114	57	48	5	48-2	80	.262
	— Houston (N.L.)	0	0	...	0.00	3.00	1	0	0	0	...	0-0	0.1	1	0	0	0	0-0	0	.500
	Major League totals (1 year)	0	0	...	0.00	3.00	1	0	0	0	...	0-0	0.1	1	0	0	0	0-0	0	.500

2006 LEFTY-RIGHTY SPLITS

vs.	Avg.	AB	H	2B	3B	HR	RBI	BB	SO	OBP	Slg.	vs.	Avg.	AB	H	2B	3B	HR	RBI	BB	SO	OBP	Slg.
L	.000	0	0	0	0	0	0	0	0	.000	.000	R	.500	2	1	0	0	0	0	0	0	.500	.500

BATISTA, MIGUEL — P

PERSONAL: Born February 19, 1971, in Santo Domingo, Dominican Republic. ... 6-1/197. ... Throws right, bats right. ... Full name: Miguel Jerez Batista. ... Name pronounced: bah-TEESE-tah. ... High school: Nuevo Horizondes (San Pedro de Macoris, D.R.). **TRANSACTIONS/CAREER NOTES:** Signed as a non-drafted free agent by Montreal Expos organization (February 29, 1988). ... Selected by Pittsburgh Pirates from Expos organization in Rule 5 major league draft (December 9, 1991). ... Returned to Expos organization (April 23, 1992). ... Released by Expos (November 18, 1994). ... Signed by Florida Marlins organization (December 9, 1994). ... Claimed on waivers by Chicago Cubs (December 17, 1996). ... Traded by Cubs to Expos for OF Henry Rodriguez (December 12, 1997). ... On disabled list (July 16-August 10, 1999); included rehabilitation assignment to Ottawa. ... Traded by Expos to Kansas City Royals for P Brad Rigby (April 25, 2000). ... Signed as a free agent by Arizona Diamondbacks organization (November 3, 2000). ... On suspended list (May 23-June 2, 2003). ... Signed as a free agent by Toronto Blue Jays (December 18, 2003). ... Traded by Blue Jays with 2B Orlando Hudson to Diamondbacks for 3B Troy Glaus and SS Sergio Santos (December 27, 2005).

CAREER HITTING: 27-for-284 (.095), 19 R, 5 2B, 0 3B, 2 HR, 9 RBI.

Year	Team (League)	W	L	Pct.	ERA	WHIP	G	GS	CG	ShO	Hld.	Sv.-Opp.	IP	H	R	ER	HR	BB-IBB	SO	Avg.
1989—	Dom. Expos (DSL)	1	7	.125	4.24	1.56	13	11	0	0	...	0-...	68.0	56	46	32	...	50-...	60	...
1990—	GC Expos (GCL)	4	3	.571	2.06	1.27	9	6	0	0	...	0-...	39.1	33	16	9	0	17-0	21	.226
	— Rockford (Midwest)	0	1	.000	8.76	1.70	3	2	0	0	...	0-...	12.1	16	13	12	2	5-0	7	.302
1991—	Rockford (Midwest)	11	5	.688	4.04	1.37	23	23	2	1	...	0-...	133.2	126	74	60	1	57-0	90	.245
1992—	Pittsburgh (N.L.)	0	0	...	9.00	3.50	1	0	0	0	0	0-0	2.0	4	2	2	1	3-0	1	.400
	— W.P. Beach (Fla. St.)	7	7	.500	3.79	1.36	24	24	1	0	...	0-...	135.1	130	69	57	3	54-1	92	.251
1993—	Harrisburg (East.)	13	5	.722	4.34	1.60	26	26	0	0	...	0-...	141.0	139	79	68	11	86-0	91	.263
1994—	Harrisburg (East.)	0	1	.000	2.38	1.50	3	3	0	0	...	0-...	11.1	8	3	3	0	9-0	5	.200
1995—	Charlotte (Int'l)	6	12	.333	4.80	1.53	34	18	0	0	...	0-...	116.1	118	79	62	11	60-2	58	.260
1996—	Charlotte (Int'l)	4	3	.571	5.38	1.71	47	2	0	0	...	4-...	77.0	93	57	46	4	39-0	56	.303
	— Florida (N.L.)	0	0	...	5.56	1.41	9	0	0	0	0	0-0	11.1	9	8	7	0	6-2	8	.231
1997—	Iowa (Am. Assoc.)	9	4	.692	4.20	1.37	31	14	2	0	...	0-...	122.0	117	60	57	19	38-1	95	.252
	— Chicago (N.L.)	0	5	.000	5.70	1.65	11	6	0	0	...	0-0	36.1	36	24	23	4	24-2	27	.267

Year	Team (League)	W	L	Pct.	ERA	WHIP	G	GS	CG	ShO	Hld.	Sv.-Opp.	IP	H	R	ER	HR	BB-IBB	SO	Avg.
1998— Montreal (N.L.)		3	5	.375	3.80	1.53	56	13	0	0	3	0-0	135.0	141	66	57	12	65-7	92	.274
1999— Montreal (N.L.)		8	7	.533	4.88	1.51	39	17	2	1	0	1-1	134.2	146	88	73	10	58-2	95	.280
—Ottawa (Int'l)		0	1	.000	2.25	0.89	3	3	0	0	...	0-...	8.0	3	2	2	1	4-0	7	.115
2000— Montreal (N.L.)		0	1	.000	14.04	2.64	4	0	0	0	0	0-2	8.1	19	14	13	2	3-0	7	.452
—Kansas City (A.L.)		2	6	.250	7.74	1.75	14	9	0	0	0	0-0	57.0	66	54	49	17	34-2	30	.292
—Omaha (PCL)		2	2	.500	6.04	1.48	18	1	0	0	...	3-...	28.1	35	20	19	6	7-0	27	.302
2001— Arizona (N.L.)		11	8	.579	3.36	1.24	48	18	0	0	4	0-0	139.1	113	57	52	13	60-2	90	.226
2002— Arizona (N.L.)		8	9	.471	4.29	1.31	36	29	1	0	2	0-0	184.2	172	99	88	12	70-3	112	.245
2003— Arizona (N.L.)		10	9	.526	3.54	1.33	36	26	2	1	0	0-0	193.1	197	85	76	13	60-3	142	.267
2004— Toronto (A.L.)		10	13	.435	4.80	1.52	38	31	2	1	0	5-5	198.2	206	115	106	22	•96-1	104	.273
2005— Toronto (A.L.)		5	8	.385	4.10	1.43	71	0	0	0	0	31-39	74.2	80	39	34	9	27-5	54	.268
2006— Arizona (N.L.)		11	8	.579	4.58	1.53	34	33	3	1	0	0-0	206.1	231	116	105	18	84-5	110	.288
American League totals (3 years)		17	27	.386	5.15	1.54	123	40	2	1	0	36-44	330.1	352	208	189	48	157-8	188	.275
National League totals (10 years)		51	52	.495	4.25	1.43	274	145	8	3	9	1-3	1051.1	1068	559	496	85	434-26	682	.267
Major League totals (12 years)		68	79	.463	4.46	1.46	397	185	10	4	9	37-47	1381.2	1420	767	685	133	591-34	870	.269

DIVISION SERIES RECORD

Year	Team (League)	W	L	Pct.	ERA	WHIP	G	GS	CG	ShO	Hld.	Sv.-Opp.	IP	H	R	ER	HR	BB-IBB	SO	Avg.
2001— Arizona (N.L.)		1	0	1.000	2.70	0.60	2	1	0	0	0	0-0	6.2	3	2	2	1	1-0	4	.136
2002— Arizona (N.L.)		0	1	.000	9.82	2.18	1	1	0	0	0	0-0	3.2	5	4	4	0	3-0	1	.357
Division series totals (2 years)		1	1	.500	5.23	1.16	3	2	0	0	0	0-0	10.1	8	6	6	1	4-0	5	.222

CHAMPIONSHIP SERIES RECORD

Year	Team (League)	W	L	Pct.	ERA	WHIP	G	GS	CG	ShO	Hld.	Sv.-Opp.	IP	H	R	ER	HR	BB-IBB	SO	Avg.
2001— Arizona (N.L.)		0	1	.000	5.14	1.00	2	1	0	0	0	0-0	7.0	5	4	4	2	2-0	3	.185

WORLD SERIES RECORD

Year	Team (League)	W	L	Pct.	ERA	WHIP	G	GS	CG	ShO	Hld.	Sv.-Opp.	IP	H	R	ER	HR	BB-IBB	SO	Avg.
2001— Arizona (N.L.)		0	0	...	0.00	1.25	2	1	0	0	0	0-0	8.0	5	0	0	0	5-0	6	.192

2006 LEFTY-RIGHTY SPLITS

vs.	Avg.	AB	H	2B	3B	HR	RBI	BB	SO	OBP	Slg.	vs.	Avg.	AB	H	2B	3B	HR	RBI	BB	SO	OBP	Slg.
L	.321	383	123	24	6	10	50	55	61	.405	.493	R	.257	420	108	19	1	8	51	29	49	.312	.364

BATISTA, TONY — 3B

PERSONAL: Born December 9, 1973, in Puerto Plata, Dominican Republic. ... 6-0/208. ... Bats right, throws right. ... Full name: Leocadio Francisco Batista. ... Name pronounced: bah-TEESE-tah. **TRANSACTIONS/CAREER NOTES:** Signed as non-drafted free agent by Oakland Athletics organization (February 8, 1991). ... On disabled list (August 27-September 12, 1997); included rehabilitation assignment to Edmonton. ... Selected by Arizona Diamondbacks in first round (27th pick overall) of expansion draft (November 18, 1997). ... Traded by Diamondbacks with P John Frascatore to Toronto Blue Jays for P Dan Plesac (June 12, 1999). ... Claimed on waivers by Baltimore Orioles (June 25, 2001). ... Signed as a free agent by Montreal Expos (January 6, 2004). ... Expos franchise transferred to Washington, D.C., and renamed Washington Nationals for 2005 season (December 3, 2004). ... Signed by Fukuoka Daiei Hawks of the Japan Pacific League (January 9, 2005). ... Signed as a free agent by Minnesota Twins (December 15, 2005). ... Released by Twins (June 19, 2006). **RECORDS:** Shares major league record for most strikeouts, 9-inning game (5, August 31, 2004). **STATISTICAL NOTES:** Career major league grand slams: 9.

2006 GAMES PLAYED BY POSITION (MLB): 3B—50.

Year	Team (League)	Pos.	G	AB	R	H	2B	3B	HR	RBI	BB	SO	HBP	GDP	SB-CS	Avg.	OBP	SLG	OPS	E	Avg.
1991— Dom. Athletics (DSL)			46	166	16	31	5	1	2	15	23	16	...	...	4-...	.187	...	.265	...	8	.960
1992— Ariz. A's (Ariz.)	2B-OF-SS		45	167	32	41	6	2	0	22	15	29	2	4	1-0	.246	.315	.305	.621	8	.960
1993— Ariz. A's (Ariz.)	2B-3B-SS		24	104	21	34	6	2	2	17	6	14	0	1	6-2	.327	.357	.481	.838	3	.967
—Tacoma (PCL)	OF		4	12	1	2	1	0	0	1	1	4	1	0	0-0	.167	.286	.250	.536	0	1.000
1994— Modesto (California)	2B-SS		119	466	91	131	26	3	17	68	54	108	4	10	7-7	.281	.359	.459	.819	30	.949
1995— Huntsville (Sou.)	SS-2B		120	419	55	107	23	1	16	61	29	98	2	8	7-8	.255	.305	.430	.734	29	.949
1996— Edmonton (PCL)	SS		57	205	33	66	17	4	8	40	15	30	2	8	2-1	.322	.372	.561	.933	8	.973
—Oakland (A.L.)	2B-3B-DH-SS		74	238	38	71	10	2	6	25	19	49	1	2	7-3	.298	.350	.433	.783	5	.983
1997— Oakland (A.L.)	SS-3B-2B-DH		68	188	22	38	10	1	4	18	14	31	2	8	2-2	.202	.265	.330	.594	8	.971
—Edmonton (PCL)	SS-DH		33	124	25	39	10	1	3	21	17	18	1	4	2-2	.315	.396	.484	.880	6	.952
1998— Arizona (N.L.)	2B-SS-3B		106	293	46	80	16	1	18	41	18	52	3	7	1-1	.273	.318	.519	.836	6	.982
1999— Arizona (N.L.)	SS		44	144	16	37	5	0	5	21	16	17	2	1	2-0	.257	.335	.396	.731	4	.979
—Toronto (A.L.)	SS		98	375	61	107	25	1	26	79	22	79	4	11	2-0	.285	.328	.565	.893	12	.975
2000— Toronto (A.L.)	3B		154	620	96	189	32	2	41	114	35	121	6	15	5-4	.263	.307	.519	.827	17	.963
2001— Toronto (A.L.)	3B		72	271	29	56	11	1	13	45	13	66	4	2	0-1	.207	.251	.399	.649	10	.953
—Baltimore (A.L.)	DH-3B-SS		84	308	41	82	16	5	12	42	19	47	0	5	5-1	.266	.305	.468	.773	6	.965
2002— Baltimore (A.L.)	3B-DH		161	615	90	150	36	1	31	87	50	107	11	13	5-4	.244	.309	.457	.766	16	.962
2003— Baltimore (A.L.)	3B-DH		161	631	76	148	20	1	26	99	28	102	5	20	4-3	.235	.270	.393	.663	20	.950
2004— Montreal (N.L.)	3B		157	606	76	146	30	2	32	110	26	78	4	14	14-6	.241	.272	.455	.728	19	.954
2005— Fukuoka (Jp. Pac.)	3B		135	559	78	147	29	1	27	90	23	115	4		3-2	.263	.294	.463	.757	13	
2006— Minnesota (A.L.)	3B		50	178	24	42	12	0	5	21	15	27	2	5	0-1	.236	.303	.388	.690	6	.954
American League totals (8 years)			922	3424	477	857	172	14	164	530	215	629	35	83	30-19	.250	.299	.452	.751	100	.965
National League totals (3 years)			307	1043	138	263	51	3	55	172	60	147	9	22	17-7	.252	.294	.465	.759	29	.969
Major League totals (10 years)			1229	4467	615	1120	223	17	219	702	275	776	44	105	47-26	.251	.298	.455	.753	129	.966

ALL-STAR GAME RECORD

	G	AB	R	H	2B	3B	HR	RBI	BB	SO	HBP	GDP	SB-CS	Avg.	OBP	SLG	OPS	E	Avg.
All-Star Game totals (2 years)	2	4	1	1	0	0	0	1	0	0	0	0	0-0	.250	.250	.250	.500	0	1.000

2006 LEFTY-RIGHTY SPLITS

vs.	Avg.	AB	H	2B	3B	HR	RBI	BB	SO	OBP	Slg.	vs.	Avg.	AB	H	2B	3B	HR	RBI	BB	SO	OBP	Slg.
L	.212	52	11	5	0	1	5	3	8	.268	.365	R	.246	126	31	7	0	4	16	12	19	.317	.397

BAUER, RICK — P

PERSONAL: Born January 10, 1977, in Garden Grove, Calif. ... 6-6/223. ... Throws right, bats right. ... Full name: Richard Edward Bauer. ... Name pronounced: BOW-er. ... High school: Centennial (Meridian, Idaho). ... Junior college: Treasure Valley (Ore.) C.C. **TRANSACTIONS/CAREER NOTES:** Selected by Baltimore Orioles organization in fifth round of 1997 free-agent draft. ... On disabled list (June 15-July 3, 2004); included rehabilitation assignments to Bowie and Ottawa. ... Signed as a free agent by Texas Rangers organization (November 9, 2005).
CAREER HITTING: 0-for-0 (.000), 0 R, 0 2B, 0 3B, 0 HR, 0 RBI.

Year Team (League)	W	L	Pct.	ERA	WHIP	G	GS	CG	ShO	Hld.	Sv.-Opp.	IP	H	R	ER	HR	BB-IBB	SO	Avg.
1997— Bluefield (Appal.)	8	3	.727	2.86	1.08	13	13	0	0	...	0-...	72.1	58	31	23	1	20-0	67	.218
— Delmarva (S. Atl.)	0	0	...	0.00	0.50	1	0	0	0	...	1-...	2.0	0	0	0	0	1-0	2	.000
1998— Delmarva (S. Atl.)	5	8	.385	4.73	1.45	22	22	1	1	...	0-...	118.0	127	69	62	11	44-0	81	.285
1999— Frederick (Carolina)	10	9	.526	4.56	1.40	26	26	4	0	...	0-...	152.0	159	85	77	17	54-2	123	.273
2000— Bowie (East.)	6	8	.429	5.30	1.50	26	23	1	0	...	1-...	129.0	154	89	76	16	39-1	87	.293
— Frederick (Carolina)	0	1	.000	5.21	1.37	3	3	0	0	...	0-...	19.0	20	13	11	1	6-0	15	.278
2001— Bowie (East.)	2	6	.250	3.54	1.02	9	9	2	0	...	0-...	61.0	52	27	24	8	10-0	34	.227
— Rochester (Int'l)	10	4	.714	3.89	1.30	19	18	1	1	...	0-...	113.1	119	63	49	10	28-0	89	.263
— Baltimore (A.L.)	0	5	.000	4.64	1.33	6	6	0	0	0	0-0	33.0	35	22	17	7	9-0	16	.265
2002— Baltimore (A.L.)	6	7	.462	3.98	1.43	56	1	0	0	12	1-5	83.2	84	41	37	12	36-4	45	.268
— Rochester (Int'l)	0	1	.000	6.75	1.50	1	1	0	0	...	0-...	4.0	4	4	3	2	2-0	1	.267
2003— Ottawa (Int'l)	3	1	.750	2.45	1.20	7	7	0	0	...	0-...	36.2	31	10	10	1	13-0	21	.235
— Baltimore (A.L.)	0	0	...	4.55	1.34	35	0	0	0	3	0-1	61.1	58	36	31	5	24-3	43	.256
2004— Bowie (East.)	0	0	...	0.00	0.67	1	1	0	0	...	0-...	3.0	2	0	0	0	0-0	1	.200
— Ottawa (Int'l)	3	5	.375	4.00	1.40	11	11	0	0	...	0-...	63.0	69	28	28	3	19-0	42	.285
— Baltimore (A.L.)	2	1	.667	4.70	1.29	23	2	0	0	0	0-1	53.2	49	31	28	4	20-0	37	.238
2005— Baltimore (A.L.)	0	0	...	9.72	2.04	5	0	0	0	0	0-0	8.1	13	9	9	2	4-0	5	.361
— Ottawa (Int'l)	3	8	.273	4.00	1.60	30	10	0	0	7	1-2	74.1	84	38	33	12	35-3	43	.294
2006— Texas (A.L.)	3	1	.750	3.55	1.38	58	1	0	0	7	2-5	71.0	73	31	28	4	25-0	35	.272
Major League totals (6 years)	11	14	.440	4.34	1.38	183	10	0	0	22	3-12	311.0	312	170	150	34	118-7	181	.264

2006 LEFTY-RIGHTY SPLITS

vs.	Avg.	AB	H	2B	3B	HR	RBI	BB	SO	OBP	Slg.	vs.	Avg.	AB	H	2B	3B	HR	RBI	BB	SO	OBP	Slg.
L	.231	104	24	8	1	1	14	11	16	.311	.356	R	.299	164	49	5	1	3	24	14	19	.355	.396

BAUTISTA, DENNY   P

PERSONAL: Born August 23, 1980, in Sanchez, Dominican Republic. ... 6-5/170. ... Throws right, bats right. ... Full name: Denny M. Bautista. **TRANSACTIONS/CAREER NOTES:** Signed as a non-drafted free agent by Florida Marlins organization (April 11, 2000). ... Traded by Marlins with P Don Levinski to Baltimore Orioles for OF/1B Jeff Conine (August 31, 2003). ... Traded by Orioles to Kansas City Royals for P Jason Grimsley (June 21, 2004). ... On disabled list (May 12, 2005-remainder of season). ... On disabled list (April 16-May 8, 2006). ... Traded by Royals with P Jeremy Affeldt to Colorado Rockies for IF Ryan Shealy and P Scott Dohmann (July 31, 2006). **CAREER HITTING:** 0-for-1 (.000), 0 R, 0 2B, 0 3B, 0 HR, 0 RBI.

Year Team (League)	W	L	Pct.	ERA	WHIP	G	GS	CG	ShO	Hld.	Sv.-Opp.	IP	H	R	ER	HR	BB-IBB	SO	Avg.
2000— Dom. Marlins (DSL)	0	1	.000	2.57	1.43	3	3	0	0	0	0-0	14.0	11	6	4	2	9-...	17	...
— GC Marlins (GCL)	6	2	.750	2.43	1.05	11	11	2	0	...	0-...	63.0	49	24	17	1	17-1	58	.209
— Utica (N.Y.-Penn)	0	0	...	3.60	1.20	1	1	0	0	...	0-...	5.0	4	3	2	0	2-0	5	.222
2001— Utica (N.Y.-Penn)	3	1	.750	2.08	0.79	7	7	0	0	...	0-...	39.0	25	16	9	0	6-0	31	.174
— Kane Co. (Midw.)	3	1	.750	4.35	1.45	8	7	0	0	...	0-...	39.1	43	21	19	2	14-0	20	.281
2002— Jupiter (Fla. St.)	4	6	.400	4.99	1.36	19	15	0	0	...	0-...	88.1	80	52	49	6	40-0	79	.242
2003— Jupiter (Fla. St.)	8	4	.667	3.21	1.23	14	14	0	0	...	0-...	84.0	68	32	30	2	35-0	77	.219
— Carolina (Southern)	4	5	.444	3.31	1.50	11	11	0	0	...	0-...	53.1	45	33	22	5	35-0	61	.226
2004— Baltimore (A.L.)	0	0	...	36.00	4.00	2	0	0	0	0	0-0	2.0	6	8	8	1	2-0	1	.545
— Bowie (East.)	3	5	.375	4.74	1.45	14	13	0	0	...	0-...	62.2	58	37	33	5	33-1	72	.243
— Wichita (Texas)	4	3	.571	2.54	1.22	12	12	2	0	...	0-...	81.2	68	32	23	3	32-0	73	.227
— Kansas City (A.L.)	0	4	.000	6.51	1.77	5	5	0	0	0	0-0	27.2	38	20	20	2	11-1	18	.333
2005— Kansas City (A.L.)	2	2	.500	5.80	1.49	7	7	0	0	0	0-0	35.2	36	23	23	2	17-0	23	.259
— Omaha (PCL)	0	1	.000	2.77	1.08	6	6	0	0	...	0-...	13.0	8	4	4	0	6-0	12	.174
2006— Kansas City (A.L.)	0	3	.000	5.66	1.57	8	7	0	0	0	0-0	35.0	38	24	22	5	17-0	22	.277
— Omaha (PCL)	2	5	.286	7.36	1.91	10	10	0	0	0	0-0	44.0	52	38	36	3	32-0	28	.304
— Colo. Springs (PCL)	1	4	.200	4.50	1.72	6	6	0	0	0	0-0	36.0	46	24	18	2	16-0	35	.311
— Colorado (N.L.)	0	1	.000	5.40	1.95	4	1	0	0	0	0-0	6.2	9	10	4	0	4-0	5	.310
American League totals (3 years)	2	8	.200	6.55	1.64	22	19	0	0	0	0-0	100.1	118	75	73	10	47-1	64	.294
National League totals (1 year)	0	1	.000	5.40	1.95	4	1	0	0	0	0-0	6.2	9	10	4	0	4-0	5	.310
Major League totals (3 years)	2	9	.182	6.48	1.66	26	20	0	0	0	0-0	107.0	127	85	77	10	51-1	69	.295

2006 LEFTY-RIGHTY SPLITS

vs.	Avg.	AB	H	2B	3B	HR	RBI	BB	SO	OBP	Slg.	vs.	Avg.	AB	H	2B	3B	HR	RBI	BB	SO	OBP	Slg.
L	.272	81	22	1	1	1	11	7	13	.333	.407	R	.294	85	25	6	0	4	19	14	14	.408	.506

BAUTISTA, JOSE   OF/3B

PERSONAL: Born October 19, 1980, in Santo Domingo, Dominican Republic. ... 6-0/192. ... Bats right, throws right. ... Full name: Jose Antonio Bautista. ... High school: Instituto San Juan Bautista (Santo Domingo, D.R.). ... Junior college: Chipola (Fla.). **TRANSACTIONS/CAREER NOTES:** Selected by Pittsburgh Pirates organization in 20th round of 2000 free-agent draft. ... Selected by Baltimore Orioles from Pirates organization in Rule 5 major league draft (December 15, 2003). ... Claimed on waivers by Tampa Bay Devil Rays (June 3, 2004). ... Traded by Devil Rays to Kansas City Royals for cash (June 28, 2004). ... Traded by Royals to New York Mets for C Justin Huber (July 30, 2004). ... Traded by Mets with IF Ty Wigginton and P Matt Peterson to Pittsburgh Pirates for P Kris Benson and IF Jeff Keppinger (July 30, 2004). ... On bereavement list (May 21-24, 2006). **STATISTICAL NOTES:** Career major league grand slams: 2.
2006 GAMES PLAYED BY POSITION (MLB): OF—85, 3B—33, 2B—3.

Year Team (League)	Pos.	G	AB	R	H	2B	3B	HR	RBI	BB	SO	HBP	GDP	SB-CS	Avg.	OBP	SLG	OPS	E	Avg.
2001— Williamsport. (NYP)	3B-OF	62	220	43	63	10	3	5	30	21	41	6	5	8-1	.286	.364	.427	.792	8	.927
2002— Hickory (S. Atl.)	3B-SS	129	438	72	132	26	3	14	57	67	104	8	12	3-2	.301	.402	.470	.872	24	.918
2003— GC Pirates (GCL)	3B	7	23	5	8	1	0	1	3	4	7	0	0	0-0	.348	.429	.522	.950	1	.929
— Lynchburg (Caro.)	3B-2B	51	165	28	40	14	2	4	20	27	48	3	1	1-5	.242	.359	.424	.783	10	.936
2004— Baltimore (A.L.)	OF-3B-DH	16	11	3	3	0	0	0	0	1	3	0	0	0-0	.273	.333	.273	.606	0	1.000
— Tampa Bay (A.L.)	OF-3B-DH	12	12	1	2	0	0	0	1	3	7	0	0	0-1	.167	.333	.167	.500	1	1.000
— Kansas City (A.L.)	3B-OF	13	25	1	5	1	0	0	1	1	12	0	0	0-0	.200	.231	.240	.471	0	.957
— Pittsburgh (N.L.)	OF	23	40	1	8	2	0	0	2	2	18	0	1	0-0	.200	.238	.250	.488	3	.864
2005— Altoona (East.)	3B-DH	117	445	63	126	27	1	23	90	48	101	10	9	7-3	.283	.364	.503	.868	24	.924
— Indianapolis (Int'l)	3B	13	51	6	13	3	0	1	4	4	10	0	2	1-1	.255	.309	.373	.682	0	1.000
— Pittsburgh (N.L.)	3B	11	28	3	4	1	0	0	1	3	7	0	2	1-0	.143	.226	.179	.404	1	.952
2006— Indianapolis (Int'l)		29	101	12	28	9	0	2	9	14	19	2	3	2-1	.277	.370	.426	.795	1	.984
— Pittsburgh (N.L.)	OF-3B-2B	117	400	58	94	20	3	16	51	46	110	16	12	2-4	.235	.335	.420	.755	12	.970
American League totals (1 year)		41	48	5	10	1	0	0	2	5	22	0	0	0-1	.208	.283	.229	.512	1	.971
National League totals (3 years)		151	468	62	106	23	3	16	52	51	135	16	15	3-4	.226	.321	.391	.712	12	.961
Major League totals (3 years)		192	516	67	116	24	3	16	54	56	157	16	15	3-5	.225	.318	.376	.694	13	.962

B

2006 LEFTY-RIGHTY SPLITS

vs.	Avg.	AB	H	2B	3B	HR	RBI	BB	SO	OBP	Slg.	vs.	Avg.	AB	H	2B	3B	HR	RBI	BB	SO	OBP	Slg.
L	.283	113	32	4	2	7	15	16	29	.404	.540	R	.216	287	62	16	1	9	36	30	81	.306	.373

BAY, JASON — OF

PERSONAL: Born September 20, 1978, in Trail, British Columbia. ... 6-2/200. ... Bats right, throws right. ... Full name: Jason Raymond Bay. ... High school: J. Lloyd Crowe Secondary (Trail, B.C.). ... College: Gonzaga. **TRANSACTIONS/CAREER NOTES:** Selected by Montreal Expos organization in 22nd round of 2000 free-agent draft. ... Traded by Expos with P Jim Serrano to New York Mets for SS Lou Collier (March 27, 2002). ... Traded by Mets with Ps Bobby M. Jones and Josh Reynolds to San Diego Padres for Ps Steve Reed and Jason Middlebrook (July 31, 2002). ... Traded by Padres with P Oliver Perez and a player to be named to Pittsburgh Pirates for OF Brian Giles (August 27, 2003); Pirates acquired P Cory Stewart to complete deal (October 2, 2003). ... On disabled list (March 26-May 7, 2004); included rehabilitation assignment to Nashville.
HONORS: Named N.L. Rookie of the Year by THE SPORTING NEWS (2004). ... Named N.L. Rookie of the Year by Baseball Writers' Association of America (2004). **STATISTICAL NOTES:** Career major league grand slams: 2.
2006 GAMES PLAYED BY POSITION (MLB): OF—157.

Year — Team (League)	Pos.	G	AB	R	H	2B	3B	HR	RBI	BB	SO	HBP	GDP	SB-CS	Avg.	OBP	SLG	OPS	E	Avg.
2000— Vermont (NYP)	OF	35	135	17	41	5	0	2	12	11	25	1	2	17-4	.304	.358	.385	.743	0	1.000
2001— Jupiter (Fla. St.)	OF-2B	38	123	12	24	4	1	1	10	18	26	2	4	10-3	.195	.306	.268	.574	3	.963
— Clinton (Midw.)	OF	87	318	67	115	20	4	13	61	48	62	4	4	15-2	.362	.449	.572	1.021	3	.984
2002— St. Lucie (Fla. St.)	OF	69	261	48	71	12	2	9	54	34	54	5	4	22-2	.272	.363	.437	.800	6	.950
— Binghamton (East.)	OF	34	107	17	31	4	2	4	19	15	23	3	2	13-3	.290	.383	.477	.859	2	.956
— Mobile (Sou.)	OF	23	81	16	25	5	2	4	12	13	22	1	0	4-2	.309	.411	.568	.978	0	1.000
2003— San Diego (N.L.)	OF	3	8	2	2	1	0	1	2	1	1	1	0	0-0	.250	.400	.750	1.150	0	1.000
— Portland (PCL)	OF	91	307	64	93	11	4	20	59	55	71	5	3	23-4	.303	.410	.541	.951	1	.995
— Pittsburgh (N.L.)	OF	27	79	13	23	6	1	3	12	18	28	0	0	3-1	.291	.423	.506	.929	1	.976
2004— Nashville (PCL)	OF	4	10	3	4	2	0	1	3	3	5	0	0	0-0	.400	.538	.900	1.438	0	1.000
— Pittsburgh (N.L.)	OF	120	411	61	116	24	4	26	82	41	129	10	9	4-6	.282	.358	.550	.907	2	.991
2005— Pittsburgh (N.L.)	OF	•162	599	110	183	44	6	32	101	95	142	6	12	21-1	.306	.402	.559	.961	4	.988
2006— Pittsburgh (N.L.)	OF	159	570	101	163	29	3	35	109	102	156	8	15	11-2	.286	.396	.532	.928	3	.991
Major League totals (4 years)		471	1667	287	487	104	14	97	306	257	456	25	36	39-10	.292	.390	.546	.936	10	.989

ALL-STAR GAME RECORD

	G	AB	R	H	2B	3B	HR	RBI	BB	SO	HBP	GDP	SB-CS	Avg.	OBP	SLG	OPS	E	Avg.
All-Star Game totals (1 year)	1	3	0	1	0	0	0	0	0	2	0	0	0-0	.333	.333	.333	.667	0	1.000

2006 LEFTY-RIGHTY SPLITS

vs.	Avg.	AB	H	2B	3B	HR	RBI	BB	SO	OBP	Slg.	vs.	Avg.	AB	H	2B	3B	HR	RBI	BB	SO	OBP	Slg.
L	.304	138	42	8	2	9	30	31	39	.427	.587	R	.280	432	121	21	1	26	79	71	117	.386	.514

BAYLISS, JONAH — P

PERSONAL: Born August 13, 1980, in North Adams, Mass. ... 6-2/210. ... Throws right, bats right. ... Full name: Jonah James Bayliss. ... College: Trinity College. **TRANSACTIONS/CAREER NOTES:** Selected by Kansas City Royals organization in seventh round of 2002 free-agent draft. ... Traded by Royals with a player to be named to Pittsburgh Pirates for P Mark Redman (December 7, 2005); Pirates acquired P Chad Blackwell to complete deal (December 8, 2005).
CAREER HITTING: 0-for-0 (.000), 0 R, 0 2B, 0 3B, 0 HR, 0 RBI.

Year — Team (League)	W	L	Pct.	ERA	WHIP	G	GS	CG	ShO	Hld.	Sv.-Opp.	IP	H	R	ER	HR	BB-IBB	SO	Avg.
2002— Spokane (N'west)	4	8	.333	5.35	1.40	15	15	0	0		0-...	70.2	70	46	42	9	29-0	38	.264
2003— Burlington (Midw.)	7	12	.368	3.86	1.41	26	26	2	1		0-...	140.0	129	78	60	11	69-0	133	.242
2004— Wilmington (Caro.)	6	6	.500	4.93	1.46	24	24	0	0		0-...	111.1	119	70	61	11	44-0	79	.287
2005— Kansas City (A.L.)	0	0	...	4.63	0.94	11	0	0	0		0-0	11.2	7	6	6	2	4-0	10	.167
— Wichita (Texas)	1	2	.333	2.84	1.21	30	0	0	0	1	8-9	57.0	43	19	18	5	26-0	63	.208
2006— Indianapolis (Int'l)	3	3	.500	2.17	1.12	46	0	0	0	1	23-28	58.0	37	15	14	4	28-6	67	.181
— Pittsburgh (N.L.)	1	1	.500	4.30	1.64	11	0	0	0			14.2	13	7	7	1	11-2	15	.241
American League totals (1 year)	0	0	...	4.63	0.94	11	0	0	0		0-0	11.2	7	6	6	2	4-0	10	.167
National League totals (1 year)	1	1	.500	4.30	1.64	11	0	0	0		0-0	14.2	13	7	7	1	11-2	15	.241
Major League totals (2 years)	1	1	.500	4.44	1.33	22	0	0	0		0-0	26.1	20	13	13	3	15-2	25	.208

2006 LEFTY-RIGHTY SPLITS

vs.	Avg.	AB	H	2B	3B	HR	RBI	BB	SO	OBP	Slg.	vs.	Avg.	AB	H	2B	3B	HR	RBI	BB	SO	OBP	Slg.
L	.176	17	3	0	0	0	3	4	3	.333	.176	R	.270	37	10	2	0	1	6	7	12	.391	.405

BEAM, T.J. — P

PERSONAL: Born August 28, 1980, in Scottsdale, Ariz. ... 6-7/215. ... Throws right, bats right. ... Full name: Theodore Lester Beam. ... College: Mississippi. **TRANSACTIONS/CAREER NOTES:** Selected by New York Yankees organization in 10th round of 2003 free-agent draft.
CAREER HITTING: 0-for-1 (.000), 0 R, 0 2B, 0 3B, 0 HR, 0 RBI.

Year — Team (League)	W	L	Pct.	ERA	WHIP	G	GS	CG	ShO	Hld.	Sv.-Opp.	IP	H	R	ER	HR	BB-IBB	SO	Avg.
2003— Staten Is. (N.Y.-Penn.)	2	1	.667	2.70	1.02	9	5	0	0	...	1-...	33.1	25	14	10	4	9-0	31	.200
— Battle Creek (Midw.)	2	1	.667	5.82	1.62	5	5	0	0			21.2	27	16	14	3	8-0	19	.300
2004— Staten Is. (N.Y.-Penn.)	2	4	.333	2.57	1.13	12	12	1	0		0-...	66.2	61	28	19	4	14-0	69	.251
— Battle Creek (Midw.)	2	5	.286	4.35	1.23	11	7	0	0			41.1	34	20	20	8	17-0	54	.227
2005— Tampa (Fla. St.)	1	1	.500	3.12	1.21	12	0	0	0	4	1-1	17.1	14	7	6	2	7-0	27	.215
— Charl. S.C. (S. Atl.)	3	3	.500	1.66	1.06	35	0	0	0	4	2-4	59.2	45	15	11	2	18-0	78	.206
2006— Trenton (East.)	4	0	1.000	0.86	0.90	18	0	0	0	2	3-4	42.0	26	5	4	1	12-0	34	.182
— Columbus (Int'l)	2	0	1.000	1.71	0.92	19	0	0	0	7	1-2	31.2	16	6	6	1	13-0	37	.151
— New York (A.L.)	2	0	1.000	8.50	1.78	20	0	0	0	2	0-1	18.0	26	17	17	5	6-2	12	.338
Major League totals (1 year)	2	0	1.000	8.50	1.78	20	0	0	0		0-1	18.0	26	17	17	5	6-2	12	.338

2006 LEFTY-RIGHTY SPLITS

vs.	Avg.	AB	H	2B	3B	HR	RBI	BB	SO	OBP	Slg.	vs.	Avg.	AB	H	2B	3B	HR	RBI	BB	SO	OBP	Slg.
L	.357	28	10	7	0		2	6	5	.471	.821	R	.327	49	16	5	1		3	9	7	.353	.653

BEAN, COLTER — P

PERSONAL: Born January 16, 1977, in Anniston, Ala. ... 6-6/255. ... Throws right, bats left. ... Full name: Randall Colter Bean. ... College: Auburn. **TRANSACTIONS/CAREER NOTES:** Signed as a non-drafted free agent by New York Yankees organization (May 31, 2000). ... Selected by Boston Red Sox from Yankees organization in Rule 5 major league draft (December 15, 2003); returned to Yankees organization (March 18, 2004).
CAREER HITTING: 0-for-0 (.000), 0 R, 0 2B, 0 3B, 0 HR, 0 RBI.

Year Team (League)	W	L	Pct.	ERA	WHIP	G	GS	CG	ShO	Hld.	Sv.-Opp.	IP	H	R	ER	HR	BB-IBB	SO	Avg.
2000— Staten Is. (N.Y.-Penn.)	0	0	...	4.50	3.00	3	0	0	0	...	0-...	2.0	3	3	1	0	3-1	2	.273
— Greensboro (S. Atl.)	1	0	1.000	4.91	1.25	18	0	0	0	...	0-...	25.2	21	16	14	1	11-0	35	.214
2001— Tampa (Fla. St.)	7	1	.875	1.46	0.91	32	0	0	0	...	2-...	49.1	27	9	8	0	18-2	77	.155
— Norwich (East.)	0	1	.000	9.00	2.00	1	0	0	0	...	0-...	1.0	1	1	1	1	0-0	0	.250
2002— Norwich (East.)	0	2	.000	6.75	1.88	12	0	0	0	...	0-...	10.2	14	8	8	1	6-0	9	.318
— Tampa (Fla. St.)	2	2	.500	1.98	1.01	46	0	0	0	...	9-...	54.2	34	17	12	2	21-2	78	.174
2003— Trenton (East.)	0	0	...	0.00	0.86	3	0	0	0	...	0-...	4.2	2	0	0	0	2-0	9	.125
— Columbus (Int'l)	4	2	.667	2.87	1.16	50	0	0	0	...	4-...	69.0	53	33	22	5	27-2	70	.210
2004— Columbus (Int'l)	9	3	.750	2.29	1.02	53	0	0	0	...	1-...	82.2	61	24	21	3	23-0	109	.198
2005— New York (A.L.)	0	0	...	4.50	1.50	1	0	0	0	0	0-0	2.0	1	1	1	0	2-0	2	.143
— Columbus (Int'l)	4	7	.364	3.01	1.38	65	0	0	0	18	0-2	71.2	60	33	24	5	39-7	82	.226
2006— Columbus (Int'l)	9	2	.818	2.65	1.29	47	6	0	0	3	0-1	88.1	61	26	26	2	53-2	116	.198
— New York (A.L.)	0	0	...	9.00	2.00	2	0	0	0	0	0-0	2.0	2	2	2	0	2-0	1	.333
Major League totals (2 years)	0	0	...	6.75	1.75	3	0	0	0	0	0-0	4.0	3	3	3	0	4-0	3	.231

2006 LEFTY-RIGHTY SPLITS

vs.	Avg.	AB	H	2B	3B	HR	RBI	BB	SO	OBP	Slg.	vs.	Avg.	AB	H	2B	3B	HR	RBI	BB	SO	OBP	Slg.
L	.333	3	1	0	0	0	2	2	0	.500	.333	R	.333	3	1	1	0	0	0	0	1	.500	.667

BECKETT, JOSH — P

PERSONAL: Born May 15, 1980, in Spring, Texas. ... 6-5/222. ... Throws right, bats right. ... Full name: Joshua Patrick Beckett. ... High school: Spring (Texas). **TRANSACTIONS/CAREER NOTES:** Selected by Florida Marlins organization in first round (second pick overall) of 1999 free-agent draft. ... On disabled list (April 29-May 14, June 5-July 16 and August 23-September 11, 2002); included rehabilitation assignments to GCL Marlins and Jupiter. ... On disabled list (May 8-July 1, 2003); included rehabilitation assignments to Jupiter and Carolina. ... On disabled list (May 31-June 17, June 18-July 5 and July 6-30, 2004). ... On disabled list (June 15-30 and July 8-23, 2005). ... Traded by Marlins with P Guillermo Mota and 3B Mike Lowell to Boston Red Sox for SS Hanley Ramirez and Ps Anibal Sanchez, Harvey Garcia and Jesus Delgado (November 24, 2005). **HONORS:** Named Minor League Player of the Year by THE SPORTING NEWS (2001).
CAREER HITTING: 29-for-194 (.149), 13 R, 8 2B, 0 3B, 2 HR, 14 RBI.

Year Team (League)	W	L	Pct.	ERA	WHIP	G	GS	CG	ShO	Hld.	Sv.-Opp.	IP	H	R	ER	HR	BB-IBB	SO	Avg.
2000— Kane Co. (Midw.)	2	3	.400	2.12	1.01	13	12	0	0	...	0-...	59.1	45	18	14	4	15-0	61	.214
2001— Brevard County (Fla. St.)	6	0	1.000	1.23	0.72	13	12	0	0	...	0-...	65.2	32	13	9	0	15-0	101	.145
— Portland (East.)	8	1	.889	1.82	0.93	13	13	0	0	...	0-...	74.1	50	16	15	8	19-0	102	.191
— Florida (N.L.)	2	2	.500	1.50	1.04	4	4	0	0	0	0-0	24.0	14	9	4	3	11-0	24	.161
2002— Florida (N.L.)	6	7	.462	4.10	1.27	23	21	0	0	0	0-0	107.2	93	56	49	13	44-2	113	.232
— GC Marlins (GCL)	0	0	...	4.50	1.50	1	1	0	0	0	0-0	4.0	5	2	2	0	1-0	7	.294
— Jupiter (Fla. St.)	1	0	1.000	0.00	0.83	1	1	0	0	0	0-0	6.0	4	0	0	0	1-0	12	.174
2003— Jupiter (Fla. St.)	0	0	...	0.00	0.70	1	1	0	0	0	0-0	3.0	2	0	0	0	0-0	5	.182
— Carolina (Southern)	0	0	...	4.50	1.00	1	1	0	0	0	0-0	4.0	4	2	2	1	0-0	7	.267
— Florida (N.L.)	9	8	.529	3.04	1.32	24	23	0	0	0	0-0	142.0	132	54	48	9	56-4	152	.246
2004— Florida (N.L.)	9	9	.500	3.79	1.22	26	26	1	1	0	0-0	156.2	137	72	66	16	54-3	152	.235
2005— Florida (N.L.)	15	8	.652	3.38	1.18	29	29	1	1	0	0-0	178.2	153	75	67	14	58-2	166	.234
2006— Boston (A.L.)	16	11	.593	5.01	1.29	33	33	0	0	0	0-0	204.2	191	120	114	36	74-1	158	.245
American League totals (1 year)	16	11	.593	5.01	1.29	33	33	0	0	0	0-0	204.2	191	120	114	36	74-1	158	.245
National League totals (5 years)	41	34	.547	3.46	1.23	106	103	3	2	0	0-0	609.0	529	266	234	55	223-11	607	.234
Major League totals (6 years)	57	45	.559	3.85	1.25	139	136	3	2	0	0-0	813.2	720	386	348	91	297-12	765	.237

DIVISION SERIES RECORD

Year Team (League)	W	L	Pct.	ERA	WHIP	G	GS	CG	ShO	Hld.	Sv.-Opp.	IP	H	R	ER	HR	BB-IBB	SO	Avg.
2003— Florida (N.L.)	0	1	.000	1.29	1.00	1	1	0	0	0	0-0	7.0	2	1	1	0	5-1	9	.087

CHAMPIONSHIP SERIES RECORD

Year Team (League)	W	L	Pct.	ERA	WHIP	G	GS	CG	ShO	Hld.	Sv.-Opp.	IP	H	R	ER	HR	BB-IBB	SO	Avg.
2003— Florida (N.L.)	1	0	1.000	3.26	0.67	3	2	1	0	0	0-0	19.1	11	7	7	3	2-0	19	.162

WORLD SERIES RECORD

Year Team (League)	W	L	Pct.	ERA	WHIP	G	GS	CG	ShO	Hld.	Sv.-Opp.	IP	H	R	ER	HR	BB-IBB	SO	Avg.
2003— Florida (N.L.)	1	1	.500	1.10	0.80	2	2	1	0	0	0-0	16.1	8	2	2	0	5-0	19	.148

2006 LEFTY-RIGHTY SPLITS

vs.	Avg.	AB	H	2B	3B	HR	RBI	BB	SO	OBP	Slg.	vs.	Avg.	AB	H	2B	3B	HR	RBI	BB	SO	OBP	Slg.
L	.251	390	98	21	2	20	60	46	76	.330	.469	R	.238	390	93	23	1	16	49	28	82	.304	.431

BEDARD, ERIK — P

PERSONAL: Born March 6, 1979, in Navan, Ontario. ... 6-1/189. ... Throws left, bats left. ... Full name: Erik Joseph Bedard. ... High school: Garneau (Navan, Ontario). ... Junior college: Norwalk (Conn.) C.C. **TRANSACTIONS/CAREER NOTES:** Selected by Baltimore Orioles organization in sixth round of 1999 free-agent draft. ... On disabled list (March 28-September 1, 2003); included rehabilitation assignment to GCL Orioles. ... On disabled list (May 26-July 18, 2005); included rehabilitation assignments to Bowie and Delmarva.
CAREER HITTING: 0-for-6 (.000), 0 R, 0 2B, 0 3B, 0 HR, 0 RBI.

Year Team (League)	W	L	Pct.	ERA	WHIP	G	GS	CG	ShO	Hld.	Sv.-Opp.	IP	H	R	ER	HR	BB-IBB	SO	Avg.
1999— GC Orioles (GCL)	2	1	.667	1.86	1.14	8	6	0	0	...	0-...	29.0	20	7	6	1	13-0	41	.192
2000— Delmarva (S. Atl.)	9	4	.692	3.57	1.20	29	22	1	1	...	2-...	111.0	98	48	44	2	35-0	131	.233
2001— Frederick (Carolina)	9	2	.818	2.15	0.98	17	17	0	0	...	0-...	96.1	68	27	23	4	26-0	130	.198
— GC Orioles (GCL)	0	1	.000	3.00	1.17	2	2	0	0	0	0-0	6.0	4	2	2	0	3-0	7	.200
2002— Bowie (East.)	6	3	.667	1.97	1.06	13	12	0	0	...	0-...	68.2	43	18	15	0	30-0	66	.176
— Baltimore (A.L.)	0	0	...	13.50	3.00	2	0	0	0	0	0-0	0.2	2	1	1	0	0-0	1	.500
2003— GC Orioles (GCL)	0	0	...	1.13	0.80	3	3	0	0	0	0-0	8.0	4	1	1	0	2-0	11	.154
— Aberdeen (N.Y.-Penn.)	0	0	...	2.35	1.00	2	2	0	0	0	0-0	7.2	7	2	2	0	1-0	13	.233
— Frederick (Carolina)	0	1	.000	7.36	1.60	1	1	0	0	0	0-0	3.2	5	3	3	1	1-0	7	.357
2004— Ottawa (Int'l)	0	0	...	7.20	2.20	2	2	0	0	0	0-0	5.0	8	4	4	1	3-0	3	.348
— Baltimore (A.L.)	6	10	.375	4.59	1.60	27	26	0	0	0	0-0	137.1	149	83	70	13	71-1	121	.270
2005— Bowie (East.)	0	1	.000	9.00	1.50	1	1	0	0	0	0-0	2.0	2	2	2	0	1-0	4	.250
— Delmarva (S. Atl.)	1	0	1.000	0.00	0.80	1	1	0	0	0	0-0	1.0	0	0	0	0	1-0	9	.176
— Baltimore (A.L.)	6	8	.429	4.00	1.38	24	24	0	0	0	0-0	141.2	139	66	63	10	57-1	125	.260
2006— Baltimore (A.L.)	15	11	.577	3.76	1.35	33	33	0	0	0	0-0	196.1	196	92	82	16	69-0	171	.258
Major League totals (4 years)	27	29	.482	4.08	1.43	86	83	0	0	0	0-0	476.0	486	242	216	39	197-2	418	.263

2006 LEFTY-RIGHTY SPLITS

vs.	Avg.	AB	H	2B	3B	HR	RBI	BB	SO	OBP	Slg.	vs.	Avg.	AB	H	2B	3B	HR	RBI	BB	SO	OBP	Slg.
L	.200	150	30	5	0	1	9	22	36	.306	.253	R	.272	610	166	26	3	15	75	47	135	.326	.398

BEIMEL, JOE — P

PERSONAL: Born April 19, 1977, in St. Marys, Pa. ... 6-3/217. ... Throws left, bats left. ... Full name: Joseph Ronald Beimel. ... Name pronounced: BYE-muhl. ... High school: St. Marys Area (Pa.). ... College: Duquesne. **TRANSACTIONS/CAREER NOTES:** Selected by Texas Rangers organization in 26th round of 1996 free-agent draft; did not sign. ... Selected by Pittsburgh Pirates organization in 18th round of 1998 free-agent draft. ... Released by Pirates (March 31, 2004). ... Signed by Minnesota Twins organization (April 11, 2004). ... Signed as a free agent by Tampa Bay Devil Rays organization (November 12, 2004). ... Signed as a free agent by Los Angeles Dodgers organization (January 25, 2006). **MISCELLANEOUS NOTES:** Struck out in only appearance as pinch hitter (2003).
CAREER HITTING: 10-for-42 (.238), 3 R, 1 2B, 0 3B, 0 HR, 1 RBI.

Year	Team (League)	W	L	Pct.	ERA	WHIP	G	GS	CG	ShO	Hld.	Sv.-Opp.	IP	H	R	ER	HR	BB-IBB	SO	Avg.
1998—Erie (N.Y.-Penn)		1	4	.200	6.32	1.66	17	6	0	0	...	0-...	47.0	56	39	33	6	22-0	37	.296
1999—Hickory (S. Atl.)		5	11	.313	4.43	1.45	29	22	0	0	...	0-...	130.0	146	81	64	12	43-0	102	.289
2000—Lynchburg (Caro.)		10	6	.625	3.36	1.28	18	18	2	1	...	0-...	120.2	111	49	45	6	44-1	82	.247
—Altoona (East.)		1	6	.143	4.16	1.48	10	10	1	0	...	0-...	62.2	72	38	29	8	21-0	28	.288
2001—Pittsburgh (N.L.)		7	11	.389	5.23	1.56	42	15	0	0	0	0-0	115.1	131	72	67	12	49-4	58	.290
2002—Pittsburgh (N.L.)		2	5	.286	4.64	1.56	53	8	0	0	5	0-1	85.1	88	49	44	9	45-12	53	.267
2003—Pittsburgh (N.L.)		1	3	.250	5.05	1.64	69	0	0	0	12	0-5	62.1	69	35	35	7	33-6	42	.299
2004—Rochester (Int'l)		2	4	.333	6.97	1.73	49	1	0	0	0	0-0	62.0	83	54	48	12	24-1	44	.322
—Minnesota (A.L.)		0	0	...	43.20	6.00	3	0	0	0	0	0-0	1.2	8	8	8	1	2-0	2	.615
2005—Durham (Int'l)		1	2	.333	3.93	1.50	48	0	0	0	9	0-2	52.2	58	28	23	3	21-1	36	.276
—Tampa Bay (A.L.)		0	0	...	3.27	1.73	7	0	0	0	0	0-0	11.0	15	4	4	1	4-1	3	.319
2006—Las Vegas (PCL)		3	0	1.000	1.38	1.00	10	0	0	0	3	0-0	13.0	9	2	2	0	4-1	9	.209
—Los Angeles (N.L.)		2	1	.667	2.96	1.30	62	0	0	0	10	2-2	70.0	70	26	23	7	21-3	30	.262
American League totals (2 years)		0	0	...	8.53	2.29	10	0	0	0	0	0-0	12.2	23	12	12	2	6-1	5	.383
National League totals (4 years)		12	20	.375	4.57	1.52	226	23	0	0	27	2-8	333.0	358	182	169	35	148-25	183	.280
Major League totals (6 years)		12	20	.375	4.71	1.55	236	23	0	0	27	2-8	345.2	381	194	181	37	154-26	188	.284

2006 LEFTY-RIGHTY SPLITS

vs.	Avg.	AB	H	2B	3B	HR	RBI	BB	SO	OBP	Slg.	vs.	Avg.	AB	H	2B	3B	HR	RBI	BB	SO	OBP	Slg.
L	.234	94	22	5	0	2	8	5	16	.270	.351	R	.277	173	48	14	0	5	21	16	14	.335	.445

BELISLE, MATT — P

PERSONAL: Born June 6, 1980, in Austin, Texas. ... 6-3/195. ... Throws right, bats both. ... Full name: Matthew Thomas Belisle. ... High school: McCallum (Austin, Texas).
TRANSACTIONS/CAREER NOTES: Selected by Atlanta Braves organization in second round of 1998 free-agent draft. ... Traded by Braves to Cincinnati Reds (August 14, 2003), completing deal in which Braves acquired P Kent Mercker for a player to be named (August 12, 2003). ... On disabled list (May 30-June 27 and July 10-August 20, 2006); included rehabilitation assignments to Dayton, Chattanooga and Louisville. **MISCELLANEOUS NOTES:** Appeared in one game as pinch runner (2005).
CAREER HITTING: 1-for-13 (.077), 0 R, 0 2B, 0 3B, 0 HR, 0 RBI.

Year	Team (League)	W	L	Pct.	ERA	WHIP	G	GS	CG	ShO	Hld.	Sv.-Opp.	IP	H	R	ER	HR	BB-IBB	SO	Avg.
1999—Danville (Appal.)		2	5	.286	4.67	1.53	14	14	0	0	...	0-...	71.1	86	50	37	3	23-0	60	.291
2000—Myrtle Beach (Carol.)		3	4	.429	3.43	1.06	12	12	0	0	...	0-...	78.2	72	32	30	5	11-0	71	.246
—Macon (S. Atl.)		9	5	.643	2.37	0.95	15	15	1	0	...	0-...	102.1	79	37	27	7	18-0	97	.216
2001—				Did not play.																
2002—Greenville (Sou.)		5	9	.357	4.35	1.26	26	26	1	0	...	0-...	159.1	162	91	77	18	39-1	123	.261
2003—Greenville (Sou.)		6	8	.429	3.52	1.36	21	21	1	0	...	0-...	125.1	128	59	49	5	42-2	94	.272
—Richmond (Int'l)		1	1	.500	2.25	0.85	3	3	0	0	...	0-...	20.0	17	6	5	1	3-0	10	.230
—Louisville (Int'l)		1	3	.250	3.81	1.38	4	4	0	0	...	0-...	26.0	31	15	11	2	5-0	15	.304
—Cincinnati (N.L.)		1	1	.500	5.19	1.38	6	6	0	0	0	0-1	8.2	10	5	5	1	2-0	6	.303
2004—Louisville (Int'l)		9	11	.450	5.26	1.49	28	28	2	1	...	0-...	162.2	192	104	95	16	51-4	106	.303
2005—Cincinnati (N.L.)		4	8	.333	4.41	1.48	60	5	0	0	8	1-4	85.2	101	49	42	11	26-6	59	.294
2006—Dayton (Midw.)		1	0	1.000	0.00	0.75	2	2	0	0	0	1-1	4.0	3	1	0	0	0-0	3	.200
—Chattanooga (Sou.)		0	0	...	0.00	0.90	2	1	0	0	0	0-0	3.1	3	0	0	0	0-0	4	.231
—Louisville (Int'l)		1	0	1.000	0.00	0.56	8	1	0	0	2	0-0	9.0	4	0	0	0	1-0	9	.129
—Cincinnati (N.L.)		2	0	1.000	3.60	1.55	30	2	0	0	0	0-1	40.0	43	18	16	5	19-1	26	.277
Major League totals (3 years)		7	9	.438	4.22	1.50	96	13	0	0	8	1-6	134.1	154	72	63	17	47-7	91	.290

2006 LEFTY-RIGHTY SPLITS

vs.	Avg.	AB	H	2B	3B	HR	RBI	BB	SO	OBP	Slg.	vs.	Avg.	AB	H	2B	3B	HR	RBI	BB	SO	OBP	Slg.
L	.240	50	12	1	0	2	7	3	9	.309	.380	R	.295	105	31	7	0	3	12	16	17	.387	.448

BELL, DAVID — 3B

PERSONAL: Born September 14, 1972, in Cincinnati. ... 5-10/181. ... Bats right, throws right. ... Full name: David Michael Bell. ... High school: Moeller (Cincinnati). ... Son of Buddy Bell, manager, Kansas City Royals, and third baseman with four major league teams (1972-89); brother of Mike Bell, third baseman with Cincinnati Reds (2000); and grandson of Gus Bell, outfielder with four major league teams (1950-64). **TRANSACTIONS/CAREER NOTES:** Selected by Cleveland Indians organization in seventh round of 1990 free-agent draft. ... Traded by Indians with C Pepe McNeal and P Rick Heiserman to St. Louis Cardinals for P Ken Hill (July 27, 1995); included rehabilitation assignments to Arkansas and Louisville. ... On disabled list (April 29-June 30, 1997); included rehabilitation assignments to Arkansas and Louisville. ... Claimed on waivers by Indians (April 14, 1998). ... Traded by Indians to Seattle Mariners for 2B Joey Cora (August 31, 1998). ... Traded by Mariners to San Francisco Giants for SS Desi Relaford and cash (January 25, 2002). ... Signed as a free agent by Philadelphia Phillies (November 24, 2002). ... On disabled list (July 11-September 23, 2003). ... Traded by Phillies to Milwaukee Brewers for P Wilfrido Laureano (July 28, 2006). **STATISTICAL NOTES:** Hit for the cycle (June 28, 2004). ... Career major league grand slams: 1.
2006 GAMES PLAYED BY POSITION (MLB): 3B—143.

								BATTING										FIELDING	
Year	Team (League)	Pos.	G	AB	R	H	2B	3B	HR	RBI	BB	SO	HBP	GDP	SB-CS	Avg.	OBP	SLG	OPS	E	Avg.
1990—GC Indians (GCL)	3B	30	111	18	29	5	1	0	13	10	8	4	5	1-1	.261	.341	.324	.666	7	.919
—Burlington (Appal.)	3B	12	42	4	7	1	1	0	2	2	5	1	1	2-1	.167	.217	.238	.455	3	.921
1991—Columbus (S. Atl.)	3B	136	491	47	113	24	1	5	63	37	50	5	22	3-2	.230	.287	.314	.601	31	.920
1992—Kinston (Carol.)	3B	123	464	52	117	17	2	6	47	54	66	1	13	2-4	.252	.327	.336	.663	20	.946
1993—Cant./Akr. (Eastern)	3B-2B-SS	129	483	69	141	20	2	9	60	43	54	3	12	3-4	.292	.350	.398	.747	21	.950
1994—Charlotte (Int'l)	3B-SS-2B	134	481	66	141	17	4	18	88	41	54	9	...	2-5	.293	.355	.457	.812	20	.956
1995—Buffalo (A.A.)	3B-SS-2B	70	254	34	69	11	1	8	34	22	37	4	...	0-3	.272	.336	.417	.753	11	.952
—Cleveland (A.L.)	3B	2	2	0	0	0	0	0	0	0	0	0	0	0-0	.000	.000	.000	.000	0	1.000
—Louisville (A.A.)	2B	18	76	9	21	3	1	1	9	2	10	3		4-0	.276	.321	.382	.703	1	.989
—St. Louis (N.L.)	2B-3B	39	144	13	36	7	2	2	19	4	25	2	0	1-2	.250	.278	.368	.646	7	.964
1996—St. Louis (N.L.)	3B-2B-SS	62	145	12	31	6	0	1	9	10	22	1	3	1-1	.214	.268	.276	.543	5	.969
—Louisville (A.A.)	2B-3B-SS	42	136	9	24	5	1	0	7	7	15	0	4	1-2	.176	.217	.228	.445	5	.973
1997—St. Louis (N.L.)	3B-2B	66	142	19	30	7	1	2	12	10	28	0	1	1-0	.211	.261	.310	.571	8	.949
—Arkansas (Texas)	3B-2B	9	32	3	7	2	0	1	3	2	2	0	1	1-0	.219	.265	.375	.640	1	.947

Year Team (League)	Pos.	G	AB	R	H	2B	3B	HR	RBI	BB	SO	HBP	GDP	SB-CS	Avg.	OBP	SLG	OPS	E	Avg.
— Louisville (A.A.) ...2B-3B-DH	SS	6	22	3	5	0	0	1	4	0	6	1	0	0-0	.227	.250	.364	.614	1	.941
1998— St. Louis (N.L.)	3B-2B	4	9	0	2	1	0	0	0	0	3	0	0	0-0	.222	.222	.333	.556	0	1.000
— Cleveland (A.L.) ...2B-3B-1B	SS	107	340	37	89	21	2	10	41	22	54	2	8	0-4	.262	.306	.424	.730	9	.983
— Seattle (A.L.) ...2B-1B-3B	OF	21	80	11	26	8	0	0	8	5	8	0	3	0-0	.325	.365	.425	.790	1	.991
1999— Seattle (A.L.)	2B-1B-SS	157	597	92	160	31	2	21	78	58	90	2	7	7-4	.268	.331	.432	.763	17	.978
2000— Seattle (A.L.) ...3B-2B-1B	DH-SS	133	454	57	112	24	2	11	47	42	66	6	11	2-3	.247	.316	.381	.697	15	.963
2001— Seattle (A.L.) ...3B-2B-SS	1B	135	470	62	122	28	0	15	64	28	59	3	8	2-1	.260	.303	.415	.718	14	.962
2002— San Francisco (N.L.) ...3B-2B-SS	1B	154	552	82	144	29	2	20	73	54	80	9	18	1-2	.261	.333	.429	.762	12	.971
2003— Philadelphia (N.L.)	3B-2B	85	297	32	58	14	0	4	37	41	40	4	7	0-0	.195	.296	.283	.579	8	.968
2004— Philadelphia (N.L.)	3B	143	533	67	155	33	1	18	77	57	75	6	14	1-1	.291	.363	.458	.821	24	.943
2005— Philadelphia (N.L.)	3B	150	557	53	138	31	1	10	61	47	69	5	24	0-1	.248	.310	.361	.671	21	.951
2006— Philadelphia (N.L.)	3B	92	324	39	90	17	2	6	34	32	38	3	11	1-0	.278	.345	.398	.743	14	.945
— Milwaukee (N.L.)	3B	53	180	21	46	10	2	4	29	18	30	1	7	2-1	.256	.323	.400	.723	5	.965
American League totals (5 years)		555	1943	259	509	112	6	57	238	155	277	13	37	11-12	.262	.318	.414	.731	56	.974
National League totals (9 years)		848	2883	328	730	155	12	66	351	273	410	31	86	8-8	.253	.321	.384	.705	104	.957
Major League totals (12 years)		1403	4826	587	1239	267	18	123	589	428	687	44	123	19-20	.257	.320	.396	.716	160	.965

DIVISION SERIES RECORD

Year Team (League)	Pos.	G	AB	R	H	2B	3B	HR	RBI	BB	SO	HBP	GDP	SB-CS	Avg.	OBP	SLG	OPS	E	Avg.
2000— Seattle (A.L.)	3B	3	11	0	4	1	0	0	1	2	2	0	0	0-0	.364	.462	.455	.916	0	1.000
2001— Seattle (A.L.)	3B	5	16	2	5	1	0	1	2	1	6	0	0	0-0	.313	.333	.563	.896	0	1.000
2002— San Francisco (N.L.)	3B	5	16	3	3	0	0	0	1	3	4	0	0	0-0	.188	.316	.188	.503	1	.944
Division series totals (3 years)		13	43	5	12	2	0	1	4	6	12	0	0	0-0	.279	.360	.395	.755	1	.969

CHAMPIONSHIP SERIES RECORD

Year Team (League)	Pos.	G	AB	R	H	2B	3B	HR	RBI	BB	SO	HBP	GDP	SB-CS	Avg.	OBP	SLG	OPS	E	Avg.
2000— Seattle (A.L.)	3B	5	18	0	4	0	0	0	0	0	0	0	0	0-0	.222	.222	.222	.444	0	1.000
2001— Seattle (A.L.)	3B	5	16	1	3	0	0	0	4	0	3	0	0	0-0	.188	.188	.188	.375	1	.923
2002— San Francisco (N.L.)	3B	5	17	4	7	1	0	1	1	2	3	0	0	0-0	.412	.474	.647	1.121	0	1.000
Champ. series totals (3 years)		15	51	5	14	1	0	1	5	2	6	0	0	0-0	.275	.302	.353	.655	1	.974

WORLD SERIES RECORD

Year Team (League)	Pos.	G	AB	R	H	2B	3B	HR	RBI	BB	SO	HBP	GDP	SB-CS	Avg.	OBP	SLG	OPS	E	Avg.
2002— San Francisco (N.L.)	3B	7	23	4	7	0	0	1	4	5	4	1	1	0-1	.304	.448	.435	.883	2	.889

2006 LEFTY-RIGHTY SPLITS

vs.	Avg.	AB	H	2B	3B	HR	RBI	BB	SO	OBP	Slg.	vs.	Avg.	AB	H	2B	3B	HR	RBI	BB	SO	OBP	Slg.
L	.281	121	34	7	2	1	18	9	17	.331	.397	R	.266	383	102	20	2	9	45	41	51	.340	.399

BELL, HEATH   P

PERSONAL: Born September 29, 1977, in Oceanside, Calif. ... 6-2/220. ... Throws right, bats right. ... Full name: Heath Justin Bell. ... High school: Rancho Santiago (Calif.). ... Junior college: Santa Ana (Calif.). **TRANSACTIONS/CAREER NOTES:** Selected by Tampa Bay Devil Rays organization in 69th round of 1997 free-agent draft; did not sign. ... Signed as a non-drafted free agent by New York Mets organization (June 16, 1998).
CAREER HITTING: 0-for-5 (.000), 0 R, 0 2B, 0 3B, 0 HR, 0 RBI.

Year Team (League)	W	L	Pct.	ERA	WHIP	G	GS	CG	ShO	Hld.	Sv.-Opp.	IP	R	ER	HR	BB-IBB	SO	Avg.
1998— Kingsport (Appalachian)	1	0	1.000	2.54	1.11	22	0	0	0	...	8-...	46.0	40	15	13	5	11-0	61	.231
1999— Capital City (SAL)	1	7	.125	2.60	1.03	55	0	0	0	...	25-...	62.1	47	23	18	3	17-0	68	.203
2000— St. Lucie (Fla. St.)	5	1	.833	2.55	1.07	48	0	0	0	...	23-...	60.0	43	19	17	4	21-2	75	.201
2001— Binghamton (East.)	3	1	.750	6.02	1.65	43	0	0	0	...	4-...	61.1	82	44	41	13	19-3	55	.320
2002— Norfolk (Int'l)	3	4	.429	4.26	1.48	22	0	0	0	...	5-...	31.2	38	15	15	2	9-1	28	.302
— Binghamton (East.)	1	0	1.000	1.18	0.74	24	0	0	0	...	6-...	38.0	22	6	5	0	6-0	49	.168
2003— Norfolk (Int'l)	2	3	.400	4.71	1.25	40	0	0	0	...	3-...	49.2	54	26	26	4	8-0	54	.284
2004— Binghamton (East.)	0	0	...	0.00	1.00	1	0	0	0	...	0-...	2.0	2	0	0	0	0-0	0	.250
— Norfolk (Int'l)	3	1	.750	3.23	1.19	45	0	0	0	...	16-...	55.2	42	21	20	4	24-2	69	.210
— New York (N.L.)	0	2	.000	3.33	1.15	17	0	0	0	1	0-1	24.1	22	9	9	5	6-0	27	.253
2005— Norfolk (Int'l)	1	0	1.000	1.69	0.75	13	2	0	0	...	6-6	26.2	15	5	5	1	5-0	29	.167
— New York (N.L.)	1	3	.250	5.59	1.48	42	0	0	0	4	0-0	46.2	56	30	29	3	13-3	43	.298
2006— Norfolk (Int'l)	3	3	.500	1.29	1.00	30	0	0	0	...	12-12	35.0	27	7	5	1	8-1	56	.208
— New York (N.L.)	0	0	...	5.11	1.68	22	0	0	0	...	0-0	37.0	51	25	21	6	11-2	35	.331
Major League totals (3 years)	1	5	.167	4.92	1.47	81	0	0	0	5	0-1	108.0	129	64	59	14	30-5	105	.301

2006 LEFTY-RIGHTY SPLITS

vs.	Avg.	AB	H	2B	3B	HR	RBI	BB	SO	OBP	Slg.	vs.	Avg.	AB	H	2B	3B	HR	RBI	BB	SO	OBP	Slg.
L	.308	65	20	4	0	0	10	8	18	.384	.369	R	.348	89	31	3	0	6	16	3	17	.370	.584

BELLHORN, MARK   2B/3B

PERSONAL: Born August 23, 1974, in Boston, Mass. ... 6-1/205. ... Bats both, throws right. ... Full name: Mark Christian Bellhorn. ... High school: Oviedo (Fla.). ... College: Auburn. **TRANSACTIONS/CAREER NOTES:** Drafted by San Diego Padres organization in 37th round of 1992 free-agent draft; did not sign. ... Selected by Oakland Athletics organization in second round of 1995 free-agent draft. ... Traded by A's to Chicago Cubs for IF Adam Morrissey (November 2, 2001). ... Traded by Cubs to to Colorado Rockies for IF Jose Hernandez (June 20, 2003). ... On disabled list (August 1-23, 2003); included rehabilitation assignment to Colorado Springs. ... Traded by Rockies to Boston Red Sox for a player to be named (December 15, 2003). ... On disabled list (August 2-20, 2004); included rehabilitation assignment to Pawtucket. ... On disabled list (July 18-August 19, 2005); included rehabilitation assignment to Pawtucket. ... Released by Red Sox (August 26, 2005). ... Signed by New York Yankees (August 30, 2005). ... Signed as a free agent by San Diego Padres (December 22, 2005). ... Released by Padres (October 11, 2006). **STATISTICAL NOTES:** Career major league grand slams: 2.
2006 GAMES PLAYED BY POSITION (MLB): 3B—50, 1B—18, 2B—11, DH—2, OF—1.

Year Team (League)	Pos.	G	AB	R	H	2B	3B	HR	RBI	BB	SO	HBP	GDP	SB-CS	Avg.	OBP	SLG	OPS	E	Avg.
1995— Modesto (California)	SS	56	229	35	59	12	0	6	31	27	52	4	9	5-2	.258	.346	.389	.735	21	.927
1996— Huntsville (Sou.) ...2B-SS	3B	131	468	84	117	24	5	10	71	73	124	4	19	19-2	.250	.353	.387	.740	32	.945
1997— Edmonton (PCL) ...2B-SS-3B	DH	70	241	54	79	18	3	11	46	64	59	2	4	6-6	.328	.472	.564	1.037	13	.957

			BATTING																	FIELDING	
Year	Team (League)	Pos.	G	AB	R	H	2B	3B	HR	RBI	BB	SO	HBP	GDP	SB-CS	Avg.	OBP	SLG	OPS	E	Avg.
	—Oakland (A.L.) ...3B-2B-DH-SS	SS	68	224	33	51	9	1	6	19	32	70	0	1	7-1	.228	.324	.357	.681	9	.956
1998—	Edmonton (PCL) ...3B-2B-DH-SS-1B	SS-1B	87	309	57	77	20	4	10	44	62	90	6	8	6-2	.249	.384	.437	.820	11	.965
	—Oakland (A.L.) ...3B-DH-SS-2B	2B	11	12	1	1	1	0	0	1	1	6	0	0	2-0	.083	.313	.167	.479	0	1.000
1999—	Ariz. A's (Ariz.)	2B-DH	12	43	11	10	3	0	0	5	11	9	0	1	0-0	.233	.389	.302	.691	0	1.000
	—Midland (Texas)	2B	17	57	12	17	3	0	2	8	11	13	0	2	1-0	.298	.412	.456	.868	2	.973
2000—	Sacramento (PCL) ...3B-2B-SS-1B	1B	117	436	111	116	17	11	24	73	94	121	5	5	20-5	.266	.399	.521	.920	15	.956
	—Oakland (A.L.) ...2B-2B-SS		9	13	2	2	0	0	0	0	2	6	0	0	0-0	.154	.267	.154	.421	0	1.000
2001—	Sacramento (PCL) ...OF-2B-SS-3B	3B	43	156	30	42	6	0	12	36	22	60	4	0	3-0	.269	.370	.538	.908	2	.985
	—Oakland (A.L.) ...2B-3B-1B-DH-OF	DH-OF	38	74	11	10	1	2	1	4	7	37	0	0	0-0	.135	.210	.243	.453	5	.932
2002—	Chicago (N.L.) ...2B-3B-1B-SS-OF	SS-OF	146	445	86	115	24	4	27	56	76	144	6	6	7-5	.258	.374	.512	.886	11	.977
2003—	Chicago (N.L.)	3B	51	139	15	29	7	1	2	22	29	46	1	2	3-3	.209	.341	.317	.658	6	.938
	—Colo. Springs (PCL)	3B-2B	16	54	11	21	5	1	4	16	11	10	0	0	2-0	.389	.485	.741	1.226	1	.981
	—Colorado (N.L.) ...2B-3B-SS-OF-1B		48	110	12	26	3	0	0	4	21	32	2	1	2-3	.236	.368	.264	.632	3	.974
2004—	Pawtucket (Int'l)	2B	2	6	1	1	1	0	0	0	0	2	0	0	0-0	.167	.167	.333	.500	0	1.000
	—Boston (A.L.) ...2B-3B-DH-SS	SS	138	523	93	138	37	3	17	82	88*	177	5	8	6-1	.264	.373	.444	.817	14	.977
2005—	Boston (A.L.)	2B-SS	85	283	41	61	20	0	7	28	49	109	0	4	3-0	.216	.328	.360	.689	7	.983
	—Pawtucket (Int'l)	2B-DH	16	68	9	12	4	0	2	9	4	24	2	1	0-0	.176	.243	.324	.567	3	.914
	—New York (A.L.)	3B-2B-SS	9	17	2	2	0	0	1	3	2	3	0	0	0-0	.118	.250	.294	.544	1	.958
2006—	San Diego (N.L.) ...3B-1B-2B-DH-OF		115	253	26	48	11	2	8	27	32	90	2	3	0-0	.190	.285	.344	.629	6	.976
American League totals (6 years)			358	1146	183	265	68	6	32	136	184	406	6	14	18-2	.231	.339	.385	.724	36	.973
National League totals (3 years)			360	947	139	218	45	7	37	109	158	312	11	12	12-11	.230	.345	.410	.755	26	.973
Major League totals (9 years)			718	2093	322	483	113	13	69	245	342	718	17	26	30-13	.231	.342	.396	.738	62	.973

DIVISION SERIES RECORD

Year	Team (League)	Pos.	G	AB	R	H	2B	3B	HR	RBI	BB	SO	HBP	GDP	SB-CS	Avg.	OBP	SLG	OPS	E	Avg.
2004—	Boston (A.L.)	2B	3	11	2	1	0	0	0	0	5	4	0	0	0-0	.091	.375	.091	.466	0	1.000
2005—	New York (A.L.)		1	0	0	0	0	0	0	0	0	0	0	0	0-0	...	...	...	...	0	
2006—	San Diego (N.L.)	3B	2	1	0	0	0	0	0	0	0	1	0	0	0-0	.000	.000	.000	.000	0	1.000
Division series totals (3 years)			6	12	2	1	0	0	0	0	5	5	0	0	0-0	.083	.353	.083	.436	0	1.000

CHAMPIONSHIP SERIES RECORD

Year	Team (League)	Pos.	G	AB	R	H	2B	3B	HR	RBI	BB	SO	HBP	GDP	SB-CS	Avg.	OBP	SLG	OPS	E	Avg.
2004—	Boston (A.L.)	2B	7	26	3	5	2	0	2	2	5	11	0	1	0-0	.192	.323	.500	.823	0	1.000

WORLD SERIES RECORD

Year	Team (League)	Pos.	G	AB	R	H	2B	3B	HR	RBI	BB	SO	HBP	GDP	SB-CS	Avg.	OBP	SLG	OPS	E	Avg.
2004—	Boston (A.L.)	2B	4	10	3	3	1	0	1	4	5	2	1	1		.300	.563	.700	1.263	1	.938

2006 LEFTY-RIGHTY SPLITS

vs.	Avg.	AB	H	2B	3B	HR	RBI	BB	SO	OBP	Slg.	vs.	Avg.	AB	H	2B	3B	HR	RBI	BB	SO	OBP	Slg.
L	.224	76	17	4	0	3	10	7	25	.289	.395	R	.175	177	31	7	2	5	17	25	65	.283	.322

BELLIARD, RONNIE — 2B/3B

PERSONAL: Born April 7, 1975, in Bronx, N.Y. ... 5-8/197. ... Bats right, throws right. ... Full name: Ronald Belliard. ... Name pronounced: BELL-ee-yard. ... High school: Central (Miami). ... Cousin of Rafael Belliard, coach, Detroit Tigers, and infielder with two major league teams (1982-98). **TRANSACTIONS/CAREER NOTES:** Selected by Milwaukee Brewers organization in eighth round of 1994 free-agent draft. ... On disabled list (August 8-September 30, 2001). ... Signed as a free agent by Colorado Rockies organization (January 19, 2003). ... On disabled list (June 2-23, 2003); included rehabilitation assignment to Colorado Springs. ... Released by Rockies (November 20, 2003). ... Signed by Cleveland Indians (December 26, 2003). ... Traded by Indians to St. Louis Cardinals for IF Hector Luna (July 30, 2006). **STATISTICAL NOTES:** Career major league grand slams: 1.

2006 GAMES PLAYED BY POSITION (MLB): 2B-145, 3B-1.

			BATTING																	FIELDING	
Year	Team (League)	Pos.	G	AB	R	H	2B	3B	HR	RBI	BB	SO	HBP	GDP	SB-CS	Avg.	OBP	SLG	OPS	E	Avg.
1994—	Ariz. Brewers (Ariz.)	2B-3B-SS	39	143	32	42	7	3	0	27	14	25	3	3	7-0	.294	.366	.385	.751	12	.935
1995—	Beloit (Midw.)	2B-3B	130	461	76	137	28	5	13	76	36	67	7	10	16-12	.297	.356	.464	.821	26	.956
1996—	El Paso (Texas)	2B-DH	109	416	73	116	20	8	3	57	60	51	4	11	26-10	.279	.373	.387	.760	16	.972
1997—	Tucson (PCL)	2B-SS	118	443	80	125	35	4	4	55	61	69	11	13	10-7	.282	.379	.406	.785	26	.959
1998—	Louisville (Int'l)	2B-SS	133	507	114	163	36	7	14	73	69	77	8	8	33-12	.322	.408	.503	.911	14	.979
	—Milwaukee (N.L.)	2B	8	5	1	1	0	0	0	0	0	0	0	0	0-0	.200	.200	.200	.400	0	
1999—	Louisville (Int'l)	2B	29	108	14	26	4	0	1	8	14	13	1	3	12-2	.241	.331	.306	.636	3	.975
	—Milwaukee (N.L.)	2B-3B-SS	124	457	60	135	29	4	8	58	64	59	0	16	4-5	.295	.379	.429	.808	13	.978
2000—	Milwaukee (N.L.)	2B	152	571	83	150	30	9	8	54	82	84	3	12	7-5	.263	.354	.389	.743	*19	.975
2001—	Milwaukee (N.L.)	2B	101	364	69	96	30	3	11	36	35	65	5	5	5-2	.264	.335	.453	.788	5	.990
2002—	Milwaukee (N.L.)	2B-3B	104	289	30	61	13	0	3	26	18	46	1	9	2-3	.211	.257	.287	.544	10	.963
2003—	Colo. Springs (PCL)	2B	6	19	2	5	1	0	0	1	0	1	0	0	0-0	.263	.263	.316	.579	0	1.000
	—Colorado (N.L.)	2B	116	447	73	124	31	2	8	50	49	71	2	7	7-2	.277	.351	.409	.760	15	.973
2004—	Cleveland (A.L.)	2B-DH	152	599	78	169	48	1	12	70	60	98	2	18	3-2	.282	.348	.426	.774	14	.981
2005—	Cleveland (A.L.)	2B	145	536	71	152	36	1	17	78	35	72	1	17	2-2	.284	.325	.450	.774	13	.981
2006—	Cleveland (A.L.)	2B-3B	93	350	43	102	21	0	8	44	21	45	4	20	2-0	.291	.337	.420	.757	8	.981
	—St. Louis (N.L.)	2B	54	194	20	46	9	1	5	23	15	36	1	9	0-3	.237	.295	.371	.666	3	.988
American League totals (3 years)			390	1485	192	423	105	2	37	192	116	215	7	43	7-4	.285	.337	.433	.770	35	.981
National League totals (7 years)			659	2327	336	613	142	19	43	247	263	361	12	58	25-20	.263	.339	.396	.735	65	.978
Major League totals (9 years)			1049	3812	528	1036	247	21	80	439	379	576	19	101	32-24	.272	.338	.411	.749	100	.979

DIVISION SERIES RECORD

Year	Team (League)	Pos.	G	AB	R	H	2B	3B	HR	RBI	BB	SO	HBP	GDP	SB-CS	Avg.	OBP	SLG	OPS	E	Avg.
2006—	St. Louis (N.L.)	2B	4	13	2	6	1	0	0	2	1	0	0	1	1-0	.462	.533	.538	1.072	0	1.000

CHAMPIONSHIP SERIES RECORD

Year Team (League)	Pos.	G	AB	R	H	2B	3B	HR	RBI	BB	SO	HBP	GDP	SB-CS	Avg.	OBP	SLG	OPS	E	Avg.
2006— St. Louis (N.L.)	2B	7	25	0	6	0	0	0	2	2	3	0	0	1-0	.240	.296	.240	.536	2	.939

WORLD SERIES RECORD

Year Team (League)	Pos.	G	AB	R	H	2B	3B	HR	RBI	BB	SO	HBP	GDP	SB-CS	Avg.	OBP	SLG	OPS	E	Avg.
2006— St. Louis (N.L.)	2B	3	12	0	0	0	0	0	0	0	3	0	0	0-0	.000	.000	.000	.000	0	1.000

ALL-STAR GAME RECORD

		G	AB	R	H	2B	3B	HR	RBI	BB	SO	HBP	GDP	SB-CS	Avg.	OBP	SLG	OPS	E	Avg.
All-Star Game totals (1 year)		1	1	0	0	0	0	0	0	0	1	0	0	0-0	.000	.000	.000	.000	0	1.000

2006 LEFTY-RIGHTY SPLITS

vs.	Avg.	AB	H	2B	3B	HR	RBI	BB	SO	OBP	Slg.	vs.	Avg.	AB	H	2B	3B	HR	RBI	BB	SO	OBP	Slg.
L	.220	168	37	11	0	2	15	12	24	.271	.321	R	.295	376	111	19	1	11	52	24	57	.345	.439

BELTRAN, CARLOS — OF

PERSONAL: Born April 24, 1977, in Manati, Puerto Rico. ... 6-1/190. ... Bats both, throws right. ... Full name: Carlos Ivan Beltran. ... Name pronounced: BELL-tron. ... High school: Fernando Callejas (Manati, Puerto Rico). **TRANSACTIONS/CAREER NOTES:** Selected by Kansas City Royals organization in second round of 1995 free-agent draft. ... On disabled list (July 4-September 4, 2000); included rehabilitation assignments to GCL Royals, Wilmington and Omaha. ... On disabled list (March 21-April 18, 2003); included rehabilitation assignment to Wichita. ... Traded by Royals to Houston Astros as part of three-team deal in which Royals received C John Buck and cash from Astros and P Mike Wood and 3B Mark Teahen from Oakland Athletics and A's acquired P Octavio Dotel from Astros (June 24, 2003). ... Signed as a free agent by New York Mets (January 10, 2005). **HONORS:** Named A.L. Rookie Player of the Year by THE SPORTING NEWS (1999). ... Named A.L. Rookie of the Year by Baseball Writers' Association of America (1999). ... Named outfielder on SPORTING NEWS N.L. All-Star team (2006). ... Won N.L. Gold Glove as an outfielder (2006). ... Named outfielder on N.L. Silver Slugger team (2006). **STATISTICAL NOTES:** Career major league grand slams: 7.

2006 GAMES PLAYED BY POSITION (MLB): OF—136, DH—1.

								BATTING											FIELDING	
Year Team (League)	Pos.	G	AB	R	H	2B	3B	HR	RBI	BB	SO	HBP	GDP	SB-CS	Avg.	OBP	SLG	OPS	E	Avg.
1995— GC Royals (GCL)	OF	52	180	29	50	9	0	0	23	13	30	3	1	5-3	.278	.332	.328	.659	2	.977
1996— Lansing (Midw.)	OF	11	42	3	6	2	0	0	0	1	11	0	0	1-0	.143	.163	.190	.353	2	.938
— Spokane (N'west)	OF	59	215	29	58	8	3	7	29	.31	65	0	4	10-2	.270	.359	.433	.791	7	.938
1997— Wilmington (Caro.)	OF	120	419	57	96	15	4	11	46	46	96	4	10	17-7	.229	.311	.363	.673	8	.968
1998— Wilmington (Caro.)	OF	52	192	32	53	14	0	5	32	25	.39	2	2	11-7	.276	.364	.427	.791	2	.983
— Wichita (Texas)	OF	47	182	50	64	13	3	14	44	23	30	1	4	7-1	.352	.427	.687	1.114	4	.960
— Kansas City (A.L.)	OF	14	58	12	16	5	3	0	7	3	12	1	2	3-0	.276	.317	.466	.783	1	.978
1999— Kansas City (A.L.)	OF-DH	156	663	112	194	27	7	22	108	46	123	4	17	27-8	.293	.337	.454	.791	* 12	.972
2000— Kansas City (A.L.)	OF-DH	98	372	49	92	15	4	7	44	35	69	0	12	13-0	.247	.309	.366	.675	4	.975
— GC Royals (GCL)	DH	1	4	3	2	1	0	1	1	1	0	0	0	0-0	.500	.600	1.500	2.100	...	...
— Wilmington (Caro.)	OF	3	13	2	4	0	1	2	6	0	5	0	0	0-0	.308	.308	.923	1.231	0	1.000
— Omaha (PCL)	OF	5	18	4	6	1	0	2	2	3	3	1	0	1-0	.333	.455	.722	1.177	0	1.000
2001— Kansas City (A.L.)	OF-DH	155	617	106	189	32	12	24	101	52	120	5	7	31-1	.306	.362	.514	.876	5	.988
2002— Kansas City (A.L.)	OF-DH	• 162	637	114	174	44	7	29	105	71	135	4	12	35-7	.273	.346	.501	.847	7	.983
2003— Wichita (Texas)	OF-DH	3	9	3	3	2	0	0	1	3	0	0	0	1-0	.333	.455	.556	1.010	0	1.000
— Kansas City (A.L.)	OF-DH	141	521	102	160	14	10	26	100	72	81	2	8	41-4	.307	.389	.522	.911	5	.987
2004— Kansas City (A.L.)	OF	69	266	51	74	19	2	15	51	37	44	2	4	14-3	.278	.367	.534	.901	3	.985
— Houston (N.L.)	OF	90	333	70	86	17	7	23	53	55	57	5	4	28-0	.258	.368	.559	.926	5	.977
2005— New York (N.L.)	OF	151	582	83	155	34	2	16	78	56	96	2	9	17-6	.266	.330	.414	.744	4	.990
2006— New York (N.L.)	OF-DH	140	510	127	140	38	1	41	116	95	99	4	6	18-3	.275	.388	.594	.982	2	.995
American League totals (7 years)		795	3134	546	899	156	45	123	516	316	584	18	62	164-23	.287	.352	.483	.835	39	.982
National League totals (3 years)		381	1425	280	381	89	10	80	247	206	252	11	19	63-9	.267	.360	.512	.873	11	.989
Major League totals (9 years)		1176	4559	826	1280	245	55	203	763	522	836	29	81	227-32	.281	.355	.492	.847	50	.984

DIVISION SERIES RECORD

Year Team (League)	Pos.	G	AB	R	H	2B	3B	HR	RBI	BB	SO	HBP	GDP	SB-CS	Avg.	OBP	SLG	OPS	E	Avg.
2004— Houston (N.L.)	OF	5	22	9	10	2	0	4	9	1	4	1	0	2-0	.455	.500	1.091	1.591	0	1.000
2006— New York (N.L.)	OF	3	9	2	2	0	0	1	5	2	0	0	0	1-0	.222	.500	.222	.722	1	.900
Division series totals (2 years)		8	31	11	12	2	0	5	14	3	4	1	0	3-0	.387	.500	.839	1.339	1	.957

CHAMPIONSHIP SERIES RECORD

Year Team (League)	Pos.	G	AB	R	H	2B	3B	HR	RBI	BB	SO	HBP	GDP	SB-CS	Avg.	OBP	SLG	OPS	E	Avg.
2004— Houston (N.L.)	OF	7	24	12	10	1	0	4	5	8	4	0	0	4-0	.417	.563	.958	1.521	0	1.000
2006— New York (N.L.)	OF	7	27	8	8	1	0	3	4	4	3	0	1	1-0	.296	.387	.667	1.054	0	1.000
Champ. series totals (2 years)		14	51	20	18	2	0	7	9	12	7	0	1	5-0	.353	.476	.804	1.280	0	1.000

ALL-STAR GAME RECORD

		G	AB	R	H	2B	3B	HR	RBI	BB	SO	HBP	GDP	SB-CS	Avg.	OBP	SLG	OPS	E	Avg.
All-Star Game totals (3 years)		3	9	2	4	1	0	0	0	0	1	0	1	1-0	.444	.444	.556	1.000	0	1.000

2006 LEFTY-RIGHTY SPLITS

vs.	Avg.	AB	H	2B	3B	HR	RBI	BB	SO	OBP	Slg.	vs.	Avg.	AB	H	2B	3B	HR	RBI	BB	SO	OBP	Slg.
L	.247	166	41	15	0	8	39	27	25	.352	.482	R	.288	344	99	23	1	33	77	68	74	.405	.648

BELTRE, ADRIAN — 3B

PERSONAL: Born April 7, 1979, in Santo Domingo, Dominican Republic. ... 5-11/220. ... Bats right, throws right. ... Full name: Adrian Perez Beltre. ... Name pronounced: BELL-tray. ... High school: Liceo Maximo Gomez (Santo Domingo, Dominican Republic). **TRANSACTIONS/CAREER NOTES:** Signed as a non-drafted free agent by Los Angeles Dodgers organization (July 7, 1994). ... On disabled list (May 28-June 17, 2000). ... On disabled list (March 23-May 12, 2001); included rehabilitation assignments to Vero Beach and Las Vegas. ... Signed as a free agent by Seattle Mariners (December 17, 2004). **HONORS:** Named third baseman on N.L. Silver Slugger team (2004). **STATISTICAL NOTES:** Career major league grand slams: 7.

2006 GAMES PLAYED BY POSITION (MLB): 3B—155, 2B—1, DH—1.

								BATTING											FIELDING	
Year Team (League)	Pos.	G	AB	R	H	2B	3B	HR	RBI	BB	SO	HBP	GDP	SB-CS	Avg.	OBP	SLG	OPS	E	Avg.
1995— Dom. Dodgers (DSL)	3B	62	218	56	67	15	3	8	40	54	26			2-1	.307	...	.514	...	19	.920
1996— Savannah (S. Atl.)	3B-2B	68	244	48	75	14	3	16	59	35	46	7	7	4-3	.307	.406	.586	.992	19	.912
— San Bern. (Calif.)	3B-DH	63	238	40	62	13	1	10	40	19	44	5	3	3-4	.261	.322	.450	.772	3	.953
1997— Vero Beach (Fla. St.)	3B-OF	123	435	95	138	24	2	26	104	67	66	6	6	25-9	.317	.407	.561	.967	37	.895
1998— San Antonio (Texas)	3B-DH	64	246	49	79	21	2	13	56	39	37	2	3	20-4	.321	.411	.581	.992	17	.910
— Los Angeles (N.L.)	3B-SS	77	195	18	42	9	0	7	22	14	37	3	4	3-1	.215	.278	.369	.648	13	.926
1999— Los Angeles (N.L.)	3B	152	538	84	148	27	5	15	67	61	105	6	4	18-7	.275	.352	.428	.780	• 29	.932

Year	Team (League)	Pos.	G	AB	R	H	2B	3B	HR	RBI	BB	SO	HBP	GDP	SB-CS	Avg.	OBP	SLG	OPS	E	Avg.
								BATTING												FIELDING	
2000—Los Angeles (N.L.)	3B-SS	138	510	71	148	30	2	20	85	56	80	2	13	12-5	.290	.360	.475	.835	23	.944	
2001— Vero Beach (Fla. St.)	3B	3	9	0	4	1	0	0	1	2	1	1	0	0-0	.444	.583	.556	1.139	0	1.000	
— Las Vegas (PCL)	3B	2	5	2	3	1	0	1	2	2	0	0	0	0-0	.600	.714	1.400	2.114	1	.833	
— Los Angeles (N.L.)	3B-SS	126	475	59	126	22	4	13	60	28	82	5	9	13-4	.265	.310	.411	.720	16	.953	
2002—Los Angeles (N.L.)	3B-SS	159	587	70	151	26	5	21	75	37	96	4	17	7-5	.257	.303	.424	.729	20	.954	
2003—Los Angeles (N.L.)	3B-SS	158	559	50	134	30	2	23	80	37	103	5	13	2-2	.240	.290	.424	.714	19	.957	
2004—Los Angeles (N.L.)	3B-SS	156	598	104	200	32	0	*48	121	53	87	2	15	7-2	.334	.388	.629	1.017	10	.978	
2005—Seattle (A.L.)	3B-DH	156	603	69	154	36	1	19	87	38	108	5	15	3-1	.255	.303	.413	.716	14	.967	
2006—Seattle (A.L.)	3B-2B-DH	156	620	88	166	39	4	25	89	47	118	10	15	11-5	.268	.328	.465	.792	15	.968	
American League totals (2 years)		312	1223	157	320	75	5	44	176	85	226	15	30	14-6	.262	.316	.439	.755	29	.968	
National League totals (7 years)		966	3462	456	949	176	18	147	510	286	590	27	75	62-26	.274	.332	.463	.794	130	.951	
Major League totals (9 years)		1278	4685	613	1269	251	23	191	686	371	816	42	105	76-32	.271	.328	.457	.784	159	.956	

DIVISION SERIES RECORD

Year	Team (League)	Pos.	G	AB	R	H	2B	3B	HR	RBI	BB	SO	HBP	GDP	SB-CS	Avg.	OBP	SLG	OPS	E	Avg.
2004—Los Angeles (N.L.)	3B	4	15	1	4	0	0	0	1	0	3	0	0	0-0	.267	.250	.267	.517	0	1.000	

2006 LEFTY-RIGHTY SPLITS

vs.	Avg.	AB	H	2B	3B	HR	RBI	BB	SO	OBP	Slg.	vs.	Avg.	AB	H	2B	3B	HR	RBI	BB	SO	OBP	Slg.
L	.280	132	37	12	0	4	19	13	23	.351	.462	R	.264	488	129	27	4	21	70	34	95	.321	.465

BENITEZ, ARMANDO — P

PERSONAL: Born November 3, 1972, in Ramon Santana, Dominican Republic. ... 6-4/230. ... Throws right, bats right. ... Full name: Armando German Benitez. ... Name pronounced: buh-NEE-tezz. **TRANSACTIONS/CAREER NOTES:** Signed as a non-drafted free agent by Baltimore Orioles organization (April 1, 1990). ... On disabled list (April 20-August 26, 1996); included rehabilitation assignments to Bowie and GCL Orioles. ... On suspended list (May 20-28, 1998). ... Traded by Orioles to New York Mets for C Charles Johnson (December 1, 1998). ... Traded by Mets to New York Yankees for Ps Jason Anderson, Ryan Bicondoa and Anderson Garcia (July 18, 2003). ... Traded by Yankees to Seattle Mariners for P Jeff Nelson (August 6, 2003). ... Signed as a free agent by Florida Marlins (January 6, 2004). ... On disabled list (July 23-August 12, 2004). ... Signed as a free agent by San Francisco Giants (November 30, 2004). ... On disabled list (April 27-August 15, 2005). ... On disabled list (April 2-20, 2006 and September 14, 2006-remainder of season). **HONORS:** Named N.L. co-Reliever of the Year by THE SPORTING NEWS (2001).

CAREER HITTING: 0-for-8 (.000), 0 R, 0 2B, 0 3B, 0 HR, 2 RBI.

Year	Team (League)	W	L	Pct.	ERA	WHIP	G	GS	CG	ShO	Hld.	Sv.-Opp.	IP	H	R	ER	HR	BB-IBB	SO	Avg.
1990—Dom. Orioles/W.S. (DSL)	3	1	.750	2.72	1.37	19	0	0	0	...	8-...	43.0	39	23	13	...	20-...	34	...
1991—GC Orioles (GCL)	3	2	.600	2.72	1.27	14	3	0	0	...	8-...	36.1	35	16	11	2	11-0	33	.252
1992—Bluefield (Appal.)	1	2	.333	4.31	1.85	25	0	0	0	...	5-...	31.1	35	31	15	1	23-0	37	.276
1993—Albany (S. Atl.)	5	1	.833	1.52	0.94	40	0	0	0	...	14-...	53.1	31	10	9	2	19-0	83	.168
—Frederick (Carolina)	3	0	1.000	0.66	0.80	12	0	0	0	...	4-...	13.2	7	1	1	0	4-0	29	.149
1994—Bowie (East.)	8	4	.667	3.14	1.12	53	0	0	0	...	16-...	71.2	41	29	25	6	39-0	106	.160
—Baltimore (A.L.)	0	0	...	0.90	1.20	3	0	0	0	0	0-0	10.0	8	1	1	0	4-0	14	.216
1995—Baltimore (A.L.)	1	5	.167	5.66	1.55	44	0	0	0	6	2-5	47.2	37	33	30	8	37-2	56	.213
—Rochester (Int'l)	2	2	.500	1.25	0.78	17	0	0	0	...	8-...	21.2	10	4	3	2	7-0	37	.135
1996—Baltimore (A.L.)	1	0	1.000	3.77	0.91	18	0	0	0	1	4-5	14.1	7	6	6	2	6-0	20	.143
—Bowie (East.)	0	0	...	4.50	1.17	4	4	0	0	...	0-...	6.0	7	3	3	0	0-0	8	.304
—GC Orioles (GCL)	1	0	1.000	0.00	0.50	1	0	0	0	...	0-...	2.0	1	0	0	0	0-0	5	.143
—Rochester (Int'l)	0	0	...	2.25	1.00	2	0	0	0	...	0-...	4.0	3	1	1	1	1-0	5	.188
1997—Baltimore (A.L.)	4	5	.444	2.45	1.25	71	0	0	0	20	9-14	73.1	49	22	20	7	43-5	106	.191
1998—Baltimore (A.L.)	5	6	.455	3.82	1.27	71	0	0	0	3	22-26	68.1	48	29	29	10	39-2	87	.199
1999—New York (N.L.)	4	3	.571	1.85	1.04	77	0	0	0	17	22-28	78.0	40	17	16	4	41-4	128	.148
2000—New York (N.L.)	4	4	.500	2.61	1.01	76	0	0	0	0	41-46	76.0	39	24	22	10	38-2	106	.148
2001—New York (N.L.)	6	4	.600	3.77	1.30	73	0	0	0	0	43-46	76.1	59	32	32	12	40-6	93	.214
2002—New York (N.L.)	1	0	1.000	2.27	1.05	62	0	0	0	0	33-37	67.1	46	20	17	8	25-0	79	.190
2003—New York (N.L.)	3	3	.500	3.10	1.32	45	0	0	0	0	21-28	49.1	41	18	17	5	24-1	50	.223
—New York (N.L.)	1	1	.500	1.93	1.50	9	0	0	0	0	0-0	9.1	8	4	2	0	6-1	10	.235
—Seattle (A.L.)	0	0	...	3.14	1.47	13	0	0	0	1	0-0	14.1	10	5	5	1	11-1	15	.189
2004—Florida (N.L.)	2	2	.500	1.29	0.82	64	0	0	0	0	•47-51	69.2	36	11	10	6	21-4	62	.152
2005—San Jose (Calif.)	0	0	...	0.00	0.50	2	2	0	0	0	0-0	2.0	0	0	0	0	1-0	0	.000
—San Francisco (N.L.)	2	3	.400	4.50	1.37	30	0	0	0	0	19-23	30.0	25	17	15	5	16-0	23	.229
2006—San Francisco (N.L.)	4	2	.667	3.52	1.57	41	0	0	0	1	17-25	38.1	39	15	15	6	21-2	31	.267
American League totals (6 years)	12	17	.414	3.53	1.32	231	0	0	0	35	37-47	237.1	167	100	93	28	146-11	308	.198
National League totals (8 years)	26	21	.553	2.67	1.14	468	0	0	0	18	243-284	485.0	325	154	144	56	226-19	572	.188
Major League totals (13 years)	38	38	.500	2.95	1.20	699	0	0	0	53	280-331	722.1	492	254	237	84	372-30	880	.191

DIVISION SERIES RECORD

Year	Team (League)	W	L	Pct.	ERA	WHIP	G	GS	CG	ShO	Hld.	Sv.-Opp.	IP	H	R	ER	HR	BB-IBB	SO	Avg.
1996—Baltimore (A.L.)	2	0	1.000	2.25	0.75	3	0	0	0	0	0-1	4.0	1	1	1	1	2-0	6	.083
1997—Baltimore (A.L.)	0	0	...	3.00	1.67	3	0	0	0	2	0-0	3.0	3	1	1	1	2-0	4	.250
1999—New York (N.L.)	0	0	...	0.00	1.29	2	0	0	0	0	0-1	2.1	2	0	0	0	1-1	2	.250
2000—New York (N.L.)	1	0	1.000	6.00	1.67	2	0	0	0	0	0-1	3.0	4	2	2	1	1-1	3	.308
Division series totals (4 years)	3	0	1.000	2.92	1.30	10	0	0	0	2	0-3	12.1	10	4	4	3	6-2	15	.222

CHAMPIONSHIP SERIES RECORD

Year	Team (League)	W	L	Pct.	ERA	WHIP	G	GS	CG	ShO	Hld.	Sv.-Opp.	IP	H	R	ER	HR	BB-IBB	SO	Avg.
1996—Baltimore (A.L.)	0	0	...	7.71	2.14	3	0	0	0	0	1-2	2.1	3	2	2	2	3-1	2	.300
1997—Baltimore (A.L.)	0	2	.000	12.00	2.33	4	0	0	0	0	0-1	3.0	4	4	4	2	4-0	6	.250
1999—New York (N.L.)	0	0	...	1.35	0.75	5	0	0	0	0	1-1	6.2	3	1	1	0	2-0	9	.136
2000—New York (N.L.)	0	0	...	0.00	1.67	3	0	0	0	0	1-1	3.0	3	2	0	0	2-0	2	.231
Champ. series totals (4 years)	0	2	.000	4.20	1.53	15	0	0	0	0	3-5	15.0	12	9	7	4	11-1	19	.211

WORLD SERIES RECORD

Year	Team (League)	W	L	Pct.	ERA	WHIP	G	GS	CG	ShO	Hld.	Sv.-Opp.	IP	H	R	ER	HR	BB-IBB	SO	Avg.
2000—New York (N.L.)	0	0	...	3.00	1.67	3	0	0	0	0	1-2	3.0	3	1	1	0	2-0	2	.250

2006 LEFTY-RIGHTY SPLITS

vs.	Avg.	AB	H	2B	3B	HR	RBI	BB	SO	OBP	Slg.	vs.	Avg.	AB	H	2B	3B	HR	RBI	BB	SO	OBP	Slg.
L	.270	63	17	2	1	2	5	16	14	.413	.429	R	.265	83	22	2	0	4	12	5	17	.300	.434

BENNETT, GARY — C

PERSONAL: Born April 17, 1972, in Waukegan, Ill. ... 6-0/208. ... Bats right, throws right. ... Full name: Gary David Bennett. ... High school: Waukegan East (Ill.). **TRANSACTIONS/CAREER NOTES:** Selected by Philadelphia Phillies organization in 11th round of 1990 free-agent draft. ... Signed as a free agent by Boston Red Sox organization (February 10, 1997). ... Signed as a free agent by Phillies organization (December 27, 1997). ... Traded by Phillies to New York Mets for C Todd Pratt (July 23, 2001). ...

Traded by Mets to Colorado Rockies for a player to be named (August 24, 2001); Mets acquired OF Endy Chavez to complete deal (December 27, 2001). ... Signed as a free agent by San Diego Padres (December 23, 2002). ... On disabled list (April 17-May 23, 2003). ... Signed as a free agent by Milwaukee Brewers organization (December 22, 2003). ... Signed as a free agent by Montreal Expos (November 29, 2004). ... Expos franchise transferred to Washington, D.C., and renamed Washington Nationals for 2005 season (December 3, 2004). ... Signed as a free agent by St. Louis Cardinals (December 3, 2005). **STATISTICAL NOTES:** Career major league grand slams: 1.

2006 GAMES PLAYED BY POSITION (MLB): C—56, 1B—1.

Year — Team (League)	Pos.	G	AB	R	H	2B	3B	HR	RBI	BB	SO	HBP	GDP	SB-CS	Avg.	OBP	SLG	OPS	E	Avg.
1990— Martinsville (App.)	C	16	52	3	14	2	1	0	10	4	15	0	0	0-1	.269	.316	.346	.662	3	.965
1991— Martinsville (App.)	C	41	136	15	32	7	0	1	16	17	26	5	5	0-1	.235	.340	.309	.648	2	.994
1992— Batavia (NY-Penn)	C	47	146	22	30	2	0	0	12	15	27	2	2	2-1	.205	.288	.219	.508	2	.994
1993— Spartanburg (SAL)	C	42	126	18	32	4	1	0	15	12	22	1	2	0-2	.254	.321	.302	.623	2	.992
—Clearwater (Fla. St.)	C	17	55	5	18	0	0	1	6	3	10	1	0	0-1	.327	.373	.382	.755	0	1.000
1994— Clearwater (Fla. St.)	C	19	55	6	13	3	0	0	10	8	6	0	1	0-0	.236	.328	.291	.619	1	.991
—Reading (East.)	C	63	208	13	48	9	0	3	22	14	26	1	6	0-1	.231	.276	.317	.593	4	.995
1995— Reading (East.)	C-DH	86	271	27	64	11	0	4	40	22	36	3	12	0-0	.236	.299	.321	.620	4	.994
—Scran./W.B. (I.L.)	C	7	20	1	3	0	0	0	1	2	2	0	0	0-0	.150	.227	.150	.377	0	1.000
—Philadelphia (N.L.)	PH	1	1	0	0	0	0	0	0	0	1	0	0	0-0	.000	.000	.000	.000	...	...
1996— Scran./W.B. (I.L.)	C	91	286	37	71	15	1	8	37	24	43	3	10	1-0	.248	.310	.392	.702	7	.988
—Philadelphia (N.L.)	C	6	16	0	4	0	0	0	1	2	6	0	0	0-0	.250	.333	.250	.583	0	1.000
1997— Pawtucket (Int'l)	C-1B	71	224	16	48	7	1	4	22	18	39	2	10	1-1	.214	.278	.308	.586	8	.986
1998— Scran./W.B. (I.L.)	C-DH-1B	86	282	33	72	18	0	10	40	25	41	2	6	0-0	.255	.316	.426	.742	1	.998
—Philadelphia (N.L.)	C	9	31	4	9	0	0	0	3	5	5	0	1	0-0	.290	.378	.290	.669	0	1.000
1999— Philadelphia (N.L.)	C	36	88	7	24	4	0	1	21	4	11	0	7	0-0	.273	.298	.352	.650	4	.971
2000— Scran./W.B. (I.L.)	C	92	317	47	97	24	0	12	52	40	44	7	9	1-0	.306	.393	.495	.889	2	.996
—Philadelphia (N.L.)	C	31	74	8	18	5	0	2	5	13	15	2	0	0-0	.243	.371	.392	.763	1	.995
2001— Philadelphia (N.L.)	C	26	75	8	16	3	1	1	6	9	19	0	1	0-0	.213	.294	.320	.614	2	.987
—New York (N.L.)	PH	1	1	0	1	0	0	0	0	0	0	0	0	0-0	1.000	1.000	1.000	2.000	...	...
—Norfolk (Int'l)	C-3B	20	67	7	20	5	0	2	14	4	12	1	0	0-0	.299	.342	.463	.805	0	1.000
—Colorado (N.L.)	C	19	55	7	15	3	0	1	4	3	5	1	0	0-0	.273	.317	.382	.698	0	1.000
2002— Colorado (N.L.)	C	90	291	26	77	10	2	4	26	15	45	6	10	1-3	.265	.314	.354	.668	2	.992
2003— San Diego (N.L.)	C	96	307	26	73	15	0	2	42	24	48	2	8	3-0	.238	.296	.306	.602	2	.996
2004— Milwaukee (N.L.)	C	75	219	18	49	14	0	3	20	22	32	2	9	1-0	.224	.297	.329	.626	3	.993
2005— Wash. (N.L.)	C	68	199	11	44	7	0	1	21	21	37	2	7	0-1	.221	.298	.271	.569	6	.986
2006— St. Louis (N.L.)	C-1B	60	157	13	35	5	0	4	22	11	30	0	3	0-0	.223	.274	.331	.605	3	.988
Major League totals (11 years)		518	1514	128	365	66	3	19	171	129	254	15	46	5-4	.241	.305	.326	.631	25	.991

DIVISION SERIES RECORD

Year — Team (League)	Pos.	G	AB	R	H	2B	3B	HR	RBI	BB	SO	HBP	GDP	SB-CS	Avg.	OBP	SLG	OPS	E	Avg.
2006— St. Louis (N.L.)	C	1	0	0	0	0	0	0	0	0	0	0	0	0-0	...	...	...	...	0	1.000

CHAMPIONSHIP SERIES RECORD

Year — Team (League)	Pos.	G	AB	R	H	2B	3B	HR	RBI	BB	SO	HBP	GDP	SB-CS	Avg.	OBP	SLG	OPS	E	Avg.
2006— St. Louis (N.L.)	C	2	1	0	0	0	0	0	0	1	0	0	0	0-0	.000	.000	.000	.000	0	...

2006 LEFTY-RIGHTY SPLITS

vs.	Avg.	AB	H	2B	3B	HR	RBI	BB	SO	OBP	Slg.	vs.	Avg.	AB	H	2B	3B	HR	RBI	BB	SO	OBP	Slg.
L	.400	35	14	1	0	2	6	4	4	.462	.600	R	.172	122	21	4	0	2	16	7	26	.217	.254

BENOIT, JOAQUIN — P

PERSONAL: Born July 26, 1977, in Santiago, Dominican Republic. ... 6-3/220. ... Throws right, bats right. ... Full name: Joaquin Antonio Benoit. ... Name pronounced: ben-WAH. **TRANSACTIONS/CAREER NOTES:** Signed as a non-drafted free agent by Texas Rangers organization (May 20, 1996). ... On disabled list (June 1-22, 2003); included rehabilitation assignment to Oklahoma. ... On disabled list (August 23-September 7, 2004); included rehabilitation assignment to Frisco. ... On disabled list (March 25-May 2 and June 12-28, 2005); included rehabilitation assignments to Oklahoma and AZL Rangers.

CAREER HITTING: 0-for-9 (.000), 1 R, 0 2B, 0 3B, 0 HR, 0 RBI.

Year — Team (League)	W	L	Pct.	ERA	WHIP	G	GS	CG	ShO	Hld.	Sv.-Opp.	IP	H	R	ER	HR	BB-IBB	SO	Avg.
1996— Dom. Rangers (DSL)	6	5	.545	2.28	1.15	14	13	2	1	...	0-...	75.0	63	26	19	4	23-...	63	...
1997— GC Rangers (GCL)	3	3	.500	2.05	1.16	10	10	1	0	...	0-...	44.0	40	14	10	0	11-0	38	.244
1998— Savannah (S. Atl.)	4	3	.571	3.83	1.21	15	15	1	0	...	0-...	80.0	79	41	34	8	18-0	68	.252
1999— Charlotte (Fla. St.)	7	4	.636	5.31	1.59	22	22	0	0	...	0-...	105.0	117	67	62	5	50-0	83	.283
2000— Tulsa (Texas)	4	4	.500	3.83	1.25	16	16	0	0	...	0-...	82.1	73	40	35	6	30-0	72	.237
2001— Tulsa (Texas)	1	0	1.000	3.32	1.34	4	4	0	0	...	0-...	21.2	23	8	8	1	6-0	23	.264
—Oklahoma (PCL)	9	5	.643	4.19	1.42	24	24	1	1	...	0-...	131.0	113	63	61	14	73-0	142	.234
—Texas (A.L.)	0	0	...	10.80	2.20	1	1	0	0	0	0-...	5.0	8	6	6	3	3-0	4	.364
2002— Oklahoma (PCL)	8	4	.667	3.56	1.13	16	16	0	0	...	0-...	98.2	74	42	39	8	37-0	103	.204
—Texas (A.L.)	4	5	.444	5.31	1.76	17	13	0	0	0	1-1	84.2	91	51	50	6	58-2	59	.272
—Charlotte (Fla. St.)	0	0	...	0.00	0.80	1	1	0	0	...	0-...	5.0	1	0	0	0	3-0	5	.059
2003— Oklahoma (PCL)	2	1	.667	3.82	1.20	6	6	0	0	...	0-...	33.0	28	17	14	3	11-0	31	.231
—Texas (A.L.)	8	5	.615	5.49	1.43	25	17	0	0	0	0-...	105.0	99	67	64	23	51-0	87	.246
2004— Frisco (Texas)	0	0	...	0.00	1.00	1	1	0	0	...	0-...	2.0	0	0	0	0	0-0	6	.000
—Texas (A.L.)	3	5	.375	5.68	1.40	28	15	0	0	0	0-...	103.0	113	67	65	19	31-0	95	.279
2005— Oklahoma (PCL)	0	1	.000	5.40	1.60	3	1	0	0	...	0-...	5.0	4	3	3	1	4-0	2	.235
—Ariz. Rangers (AZL)	0	0	...	0.00	0.50	1	1	0	0	...	0-...	2.0	0	0	0	0	1-0	4	.000
—Texas (A.L.)	4	4	.500	3.72	1.23	32	9	0	0	0	5	0-0	87.0	69	39	36	9	38-0	78	.212
2006— Texas (A.L.)	1	1	.500	4.86	1.33	56	0	0	0	7	0-2	79.2	68	49	43	5	38-4	85	.224
Major League totals (6 years)	20	20	.500	5.12	1.44	159	55	0	0	12	1-3	464.1	448	279	264	65	219-6	408	.250

2006 LEFTY-RIGHTY SPLITS

vs.	Avg.	AB	H	2B	3B	HR	RBI	BB	SO	OBP	Slg.	vs.	Avg.	AB	H	2B	3B	HR	RBI	BB	SO	OBP	Slg.
L	.191	115	22	5	0	3	9	19	34	.306	.296	R	.245	188	46	8	0	2	35	19	51	.319	.319

BENSON, KRIS — P

PERSONAL: Born November 7, 1974, in Superior, Wis. ... 6-4/195. ... Throws right, bats right. ... Full name: Kristin James Benson. ... High school: Spayberry (Marietta, Ga.). ... College: Clemson. **TRANSACTIONS/CAREER NOTES:** Selected by Pittsburgh Pirates organization in first round (first pick overall) of 1996 free-agent draft. ... On disabled list (March 31, 2001-entire season). ... On disabled list (March 22-May 13, 2002); included rehabilitation assignments to Nashville and Altoona. ... On disabled list (July 28, 2003-remainder of season). ... Traded by Pirates with IF Jeff Keppinger to New York Mets for 3B Ty Wigginton, IF Jose Bautista and P Matt Peterson (July 30, 2004). ... On disabled list (April 4-May 5, 2005); included rehabilitation assignment to St. Lucie. ... Traded by Mets to Baltimore Orioles for Ps Jorge Julio and John Maine (January 21, 2006). ... On disabled list (July 26-August 12, 2006). **MISCELLANEOUS NOTES:** Member of 1996 U.S. Olympic baseball team. ... Made an out and struck out in two appearances as pinch hitter (2002).

CAREER HITTING: 41-for-316 (.130), 23 R, 7 2B, 0 3B, 1 HR, 22 RBI.

Year	Team (League)	W	L	Pct.	ERA	WHIP	G	GS	CG	ShO	Hld.	Sv.-Opp.	IP	H	R	ER	HR	BB-IBB	SO	Avg.
1997—	Lynchburg (Caro.)	5	2	.714	2.58	1.04	10	10	0	0	...	0-...	59.1	49	20	17	1	13-0	72	.221
—	Carolina (Southern)	3	5	.375	4.98	1.65	14	14	0	0	...	0-...	68.2	81	49	38	11	32-1	66	.289
1998—	Nashville (PCL)	8	10	.444	5.37	1.36	28	28	1	1	...	0-...	156.0	162	102	93	26	50-5	129	.260
1999—	Pittsburgh (N.L.)	11	14	.440	4.07	1.36	31	31	2	0	0	0-0	196.2	184	105	89	16	83-5	139	.249
2000—	Pittsburgh (N.L.)	10	12	.455	3.85	1.34	32	32	2	1	0	0-0	217.2	206	104	93	24	86-5	184	.249
2001—	Pittsburgh (N.L.)				Did not play.														
2002—	Nashville (PCL)	0	2	.000	1.53	0.91	4	4	0	0	...	0-...	17.2	8	4	3	1	8-0	25	.133
—	Altoona (East.)	1	0	1.000	1.29	0.71	1	1	0	0	...	0-...	7.0	5	1	1	1	0-0	7	.208
—	Pittsburgh (N.L.)	9	6	.600	4.70	1.55	25	25	0	0	0	0-0	130.1	152	76	68	18	50-8	79	.295
2003—	Pittsburgh (N.L.)	5	9	.357	4.97	1.55	18	18	0	0	0	0-0	105.0	127	67	58	14	36-4	68	.295
2004—	Pittsburgh (N.L.)	8	8	.500	4.22	1.37	20	20	0	0	0	0-0	132.1	137	69	62	7	44-5	83	.272
—	New York (N.L.)	4	4	.500	4.50	1.21	11	11	1	1	0	0-0	68.0	65	37	34	8	17-3	51	.244
2005—	St. Lucie (Fla. St.)	0	0	...	0.00	0.00	1	1	0	0	0	0-0	3.0	0	0	0	0	0-0	4	.000
—	New York (N.L.)	10	8	.556	4.13	1.26	30	28	0	0	0	0-0	174.1	171	86	80	24	49-5	95	.253
2006—	Baltimore (A.L.)	11	12	.478	4.82	1.40	30	30	3	0	0	0-0	183.0	199	105	98	33	58-2	88	.287
American League totals (1 year)		11	12	.478	4.82	1.40	30	30	3	0		0-0	183.0	199	105	98	33	58-2	88	.287
National League totals (6 years)		57	61	.483	4.25	1.37	165	165	5	2	0	0-0	1024.1	1042	544	484	111	365-35	699	.263
Major League totals (7 years)		68	73	.482	4.34	1.38	195	195	8	2	0	0-0	1207.1	1241	649	582	144	423-37	787	.267

2006 LEFTY-RIGHTY SPLITS

vs.	Avg.	AB	H	2B	3B	HR	RBI	BB	SO	OBP	Slg.	vs.	Avg.	AB	H	2B	3B	HR	RBI	BB	SO	OBP	Slg.
L	.303	350	106	20	0	21	56	36	42	.370	.540	R	.270	344	93	17	1	12	43	22	46	.313	.430

BERGMANN, JAY — P

PERSONAL: Born September 25, 1981, in Neptune, N.J. ... 6-4/190. ... Throws right, bats right. ... Full name: Jason Chris Bergmann. ... College: Rutgers.
TRANSACTIONS/CAREER NOTES: Selected by Montreal Expos organization in 11th round of 2002 free-agent draft. ... Expos franchise moved to Washington, D.C., and renamed Washington Nationals for 2005 season (December 3, 2004).
CAREER HITTING: 1-for-11 (.091), 2 R, 0 2B, 0 3B, 0 HR, 0 RBI.

Year	Team (League)	W	L	Pct.	ERA	WHIP	G	GS	CG	ShO	Hld.	Sv.-Opp.	IP	H	R	ER	HR	BB-IBB	SO	Avg.
2002—	Vermont (NYP)	7	4	.636	2.89	1.13	14	14	0	0	...	0-...	71.2	48	27	23	4	33-0	57	.194
2003—	Savannah (S. Atl.)	6	11	.353	4.29	1.48	23	22	1	1	...	0-...	109.0	108	57	52	8	53-0	82	.264
2004—	Savannah (S. Atl.)	3	7	.300	4.85	1.55	13	13	0	0	...	0-...	65.0	67	43	35	6	34-0	58	.269
—	Brevard County (Fla. St.)	3	2	.600	1.14	1.20	24	0	0	0	...	8-...	31.2	20	7	4	0	18-3	28	.177
—	Harrisburg (East.)	0	2	.000	9.00	2.25	2	0	0	0	...	0-...	4.0	7	5	4	0	2-1	3	.368
2005—	Harrisburg (East.)	2	0	1.000	1.22	1.16	21	0	0	0	1	5-6	37.0	27	7	5	3	16-1	37	.201
—	New Orleans (PCL)	3	2	.600	3.16	1.05	20	0	0	0	1	2-5	37.0	26	15	13	5	13-1	39	.203
—	Wash. (N.L.)	2	0	1.000	2.75	1.27	15	1	0	0	1	0-0	19.2	14	6	6	1	11-1	21	.200
2006—	New Orleans (PCL)	8	2	.800	3.28	1.23	26	4	0	0	3	4-8	60.1	54	22	22	5	20-2	62	.244
—	Wash. (N.L.)	0	2	.000	6.68	1.67	29	6	0	0	1	0-0	64.2	81	49	48	12	27-6	54	.312
Major League totals (2 years)		2	2	.500	5.76	1.58	44	7	0	0	2	0-0	84.1	95	55	54	13	38-7	75	.288

2006 LEFTY-RIGHTY SPLITS

vs.	Avg.	AB	H	2B	3B	HR	RBI	BB	SO	OBP	Slg.	vs.	Avg.	AB	H	2B	3B	HR	RBI	BB	SO	OBP	Slg.
L	.255	110	28	5	4	4	19	19	21	.359	.509	R	.353	150	53	13	2	7	29	9	33	.404	.607

BERKMAN, LANCE — OF/1B

PERSONAL: Born February 10, 1976, in Waco, Texas. ... 6-1/220. ... Bats both, throws left. ... Full name: William Lance Berkman. ... High school: Canyon (New Braunfels, Texas). ... College: Rice. **TRANSACTIONS/CAREER NOTES:** Selected by Houston Astros organization in first round (16th pick overall) of 1997 free-agent draft. ... On disabled list (March 30-May 6, 2005); included rehabilitation assignment to Round Rock. **HONORS:** Named outfielder on SPORTING NEWS N.L. All-Star team (2006). **STATISTICAL NOTES:** Hit three home runs in one game (April 16, 2002). ... Career major league grand slams: 3.
2006 GAMES PLAYED BY POSITION (MLB): 1B—112, OF—44, DH—3.

									BATTING									FIELDING	
Year	Team (League)	Pos.	G	AB	R	H	2B	3B	HR	RBI	BB	SO	HBP	GDP	SB-CS	Avg.	OBP	SLG	OPS	E	Avg.
1997—	Kissimmee (Fla. St.)	OF-DH	53	184	31	54	10	0	12	35	37	38	2	2	2-1	.293	.417	.543	.961	0	1.000
1998—	Jackson (Texas)	OF-DH	122	425	82	130	34	0	24	89	85	82	4	12	6-4	.306	.424	.555	.979	4	.980
—	New Orleans (PCL)	OF	17	59	14	16	4	0	6	13	12	16	2	1	0-0	.271	.411	.644	1.055	0	1.000
1999—	New Orleans (PCL)	OF-1B	64	226	42	73	20	0	8	49	39	47	0	10	7-1	.323	.419	.518	.937	4	.972
—	Houston (N.L.)	OF-1B	34	93	10	22	2	0	4	15	12	21	0	2	5-1	.237	.321	.387	.708	2	.956
2000—	New Orleans (PCL)	OF-1B	31	112	18	37	4	2	6	27	31	20	1	7	4-4	.330	.479	.563	1.042	3	.982
—	Houston (N.L.)	OF-1B	114	353	76	105	28	1	21	67	56	73	1	6	6-2	.297	.388	.561	.949	6	.968
2001—	Houston (N.L.)	OF	156	577	110	191	* 55	5	34	126	92	121	13	8	7-9	.331	.430	.620	1.051	6	.981
2002—	Houston (N.L.)	OF	158	578	106	169	35	2	42	* 128	107	118	4	10	8-4	.292	.405	.578	.982	7	.977
2003—	Houston (N.L.)	OF	153	538	110	155	35	6	25	93	107	108	9	10	5-3	.288	.412	.515	.927	3	.989
2004—	Houston (N.L.)	OF-1B	160	544	104	172	40	3	30	106	127	101	10	10	9-7	.316	.450	.566	1.016	2	.992
2005—	Round Rock (PCL)	OF	4	14	2	4	1	0	0	1	3	4	0	0	0-0	.286	.412	.357	.769	0	1.000
—	Houston (N.L.)	1B-OF-DH	132	468	76	137	34	1	24	82	91	72	4	18	4-1	.293	.411	.524	.934	8	.991
2006—	Houston (N.L.)	1B-OF-DH	152	536	95	169	29	0	45	136	98	106	4	11	3-2	.315	.420	.621	1.041	9	.992
Major League totals (8 years)			1059	3687	687	1120	258	18	225	753	690	720	45	75	47-29	.304	.416	.567	.983	43	.987

DIVISION SERIES RECORD

Year	Team (League)	Pos.	G	AB	R	H	2B	3B	HR	RBI	BB	SO	HBP	GDP	SB-CS	Avg.	OBP	SLG	OPS	E	Avg.
2001—	Houston (N.L.)	OF	3	12	0	2	0	0	0	0	0	4	0	2	0-0	.167	.167	.167	.333	0	1.000
2004—	Houston (N.L.)	OF	5	22	5	9	1	0	1	3	3	6	0	0	0-1	.409	.480	.591	1.071	1	.800
2005—	Houston (N.L.)	1B-OF	4	14	4	5	1	0	1	5	3	4	1	1	0-0	.357	.500	.643	1.143	0	1.000
Division series totals (3 years)			12	48	9	16	2	0	2	8	6	14	1	3	0-1	.333	.418	.500	.918	1	.977

CHAMPIONSHIP SERIES RECORD

Year	Team (League)	Pos.	G	AB	R	H	2B	3B	HR	RBI	BB	SO	HBP	GDP	SB-CS	Avg.	OBP	SLG	OPS	E	Avg.
2004—	Houston (N.L.)	OF	7	24	7	7	0	0	3	9	4	5	0	0	1-0	.292	.400	.750	1.150	0	1.000
2005—	Houston (N.L.)	1B-OF	6	21	2	6	2	0	1	3	4	3	0	1	0-0	.286	.400	.524	.924	1	1.000
Champ. series totals (2 years)			13	45	9	13	2	0	4	12	8	9	0	1	1-0	.289	.400	.644	1.044	1	1.000

WORLD SERIES RECORD

Year	Team (League)	Pos.	G	AB	R	H	2B	3B	HR	RBI	BB	SO	HBP	GDP	SB-CS	Avg.	OBP	SLG	OPS	E	Avg.
2005—	Houston (N.L.)	OF-1B	4	13	0	5	2	0	0	6	5	5	0	0	1-0	.385	.526	.538	1.065	0	1.000

ALL-STAR GAME RECORD

	G	AB	R	H	2B	3B	HR	RBI	BB	SO	HBP	GDP	SB-CS	Avg.	OBP	SLG	OPS	E	Avg.
All-Star Game totals (4 years)	4	7	0	2	0	0	0	2	1	0	0	0	1-0	.286	.375	.286	.661	0	1.000

2006 LEFTY-RIGHTY SPLITS

vs.	Avg.	AB	H	2B	3B	HR	RBI	BB	SO	OBP	Slg.		vs.	Avg.	AB	H	2B	3B	HR	RBI	BB	SO	OBP	Slg.
L	.266	154	41	8	0	5	27	27	24	.374	.416		R	.335	382	128	21	0	40	109	71	82	.438	.704

BERNERO, ADAM   P

PERSONAL: Born November 28, 1976, in Los Gatos, Calif. ... 6-4/210. ... Throws right, bats right. ... Full name: Adam Gino Bernero. ... Name pronounced: bur-NAIR-o. ... High school: John F. Kennedy (Sacramento, Calif.). ... College: Armstrong Atlantic State (Savannah, Ga.). **TRANSACTIONS/CAREER NOTES:** Selected by Chicago White Sox organization in 24th round of 1994 free-agent draft; did not sign. ... Selected by Colorado Rockies organization in 38th round of 1996 free-agent draft; did not sign. ... Signed as a non-drafted free agent by Detroit Tigers organization (May 21, 1999). ... Traded by Tigers to Colorado Rockies for C Ben Petrick (July 13, 2003). ... On disabled list (April 3-June 30, 2004); included rehabilitation assignments to Tulsa and Colorado Springs. ... Signed by Atlanta Braves organization (January 19, 2005). ... Signed as a free agent by Kansas City Royals organization (November 22, 2005). ... Signed as a free agent by Philadelphia Phillies organization (June 5, 2006). ... Signed as a free agent by Royals organization (July 14, 2006). ... On disabled list (August 17-September 10, 2006). ... Signed as a free agent by Boston Red Sox (October 30, 2006). **MISCELLANEOUS NOTES:** Appeared in one game as pinch runner (2003).

CAREER HITTING: 1-for-16 (.063), 2 R, 0 2B, 0 3B, 0 HR, 0 RBI.

Year — Team (League)	W	L	Pct.	ERA	WHIP	G	GS	CG	ShO	Hld.	Sv.-Opp.	IP	H	R	ER	HR	BB-IBB	SO	Avg.
1999—W. Mich. (Mid.)	8	4	.667	2.54	1.02	15	15	2	1	...	0-...	95.2	75	36	27	8	23-0	80	.210
2000—Jacksonville (Sou.)	2	5	.286	2.79	1.27	10	10	0	0	...	0-...	61.1	54	26	19	6	24-0	46	.237
—Toledo (Int'l)	3	1	.750	2.47	0.93	7	7	1	1	...	0-...	47.1	34	16	13	5	10-0	37	.201
—Detroit (A.L.)	0	1	.000	4.19	1.34	12	4	0	0	1	0-0	34.1	33	18	16	3	13-1	20	.270
2001—Toledo (Int'l)	6	11	.353	5.13	1.61	26	25	1	0	...	0-...	140.1	172	90	80	13	54-0	99	.303
—Detroit (A.L.)	0	0	...	7.30	1.38	5	0	0	0	0	0-0	12.1	13	13	10	4	4-0	8	.260
2002—Toledo (Int'l)	2	2	.500	1.58	1.04	9	9	2	1	...	0-...	57.0	46	13	10	2	13-0	49	.223
—Detroit (A.L.)	4	7	.364	6.20	1.56	28	11	0	0	0	0-0	101.2	128	74	70	17	31-1	69	.309
2003—Detroit (A.L.)	1	12	.077	6.08	1.44	18	17	0	0	0	0-0	100.2	104	68	68	14	41-0	54	.267
—Colorado (N.L.)	0	2	.000	5.23	1.41	31	0	0	0	5	0-2	32.2	33	22	19	5	13-1	26	.266
2004—Tulsa (Texas)	1	0	1.000	0.00	0.50	1	1	0	0	0	0-...	6.0	2	0	0	0	1-1	3	.105
—Colo. Springs (PCL)	3	2	.600	3.17	1.39	9	8	0	0	0	0-...	48.1	57	23	17	0	10-0	48	.294
—Colorado (N.L.)	1	1	.500	5.57	1.64	16	2	0	0	1	0-1	32.1	36	20	20	7	17-2	21	.283
2005—Atlanta (N.L.)	4	3	.571	6.51	1.55	36	0	0	0	4	0-1	47.0	61	35	34	5	12-3	37	.313
—Richmond (Int'l)	5	5	.500	3.40	1.36	10	9	0	0	0	0-0	53.0	57	27	20	6	15-0	41	.274
2006—Omaha (PCL)	5	3	.625	2.84	1.10	16	12	1	0	0	1-1	79.1	64	27	25	5	23-0	47	.225
—Kansas City (A.L.)	1	0	1.000	1.38	1.15	3	0	0	0	0	0-0	13.0	15	2	2	0	0-0	12	.283
—Scran./W.B. (I.L.)	1	1	.500	1.80	0.60	5	5	1	0	0	0-0	25.0	11	5	5	2	4-0	17	.131
—Philadelphia (N.L.)	0	1	.000	36.00	4.50	1	1	0	0	0	0-0	2.0	7	8	8	3	2-0	5	.538
American League totals (5 years)	6	20	.231	5.70	1.46	66	34	0	0	1	0-0	262.0	293	175	166	38	89-2	163	.285
National League totals (4 years)	5	7	.417	6.39	1.59	84	3	0	0	10	0-4	114.0	137	85	81	20	44-6	84	.298
Major League totals (7 years)	11	27	.289	5.91	1.50	150	37	0	0	11	0-4	376.0	430	260	247	58	133-8	247	.289

2006 LEFTY-RIGHTY SPLITS

vs.	Avg.	AB	H	2B	3B	HR	RBI	BB	SO	OBP	Slg.		vs.	Avg.	AB	H	2B	3B	HR	RBI	BB	SO	OBP	Slg.
L	.243	37	9	1	0	3	7	2	11	.282	.514		R	.448	29	13	6	0	3		0	1	.448	.655

BERROA, ANGEL   SS

PERSONAL: Born January 27, 1978, in Santo Domingo, Dominican Republic. ... 6-0/175. ... Bats right, throws right. ... Full name: Angel Maria Berroa. **TRANSACTIONS/CAREER NOTES:** Signed as a non-drafted free agent by Oakland Athletics organization (August 14, 1997). ... Traded by A's with C A.J. Hinch and cash to Kansas City Royals organization as part of three-team deal in which Royals received P Roberto Hernandez from Tampa Devil Rays, A's received P Cory Lidle from Devil Rays and OF Johnny Damon, IF Mark Ellis and player to be named from Royals and Devil Rays received OF Ben Grieve and a player to be named or cash from A's (January 8, 2001). ... On disabled list (April 16-May 1, 2004); included rehabilitation assignment to Wichita. **HONORS:** Named A.L. Rookie of the Year by Baseball Writers' Association of America (2003).

2006 GAMES PLAYED BY POSITION (MLB): SS—131.

Year — Team (League)	Pos.	G	AB	R	H	2B	3B	HR	RBI	BB	SO	HBP	GDP	SB-CS	Avg.	OBP	SLG	OPS	E	Avg.
1998—Dom. Athletics (DSL)		58	196	51	48	7	4	8	37	25	37	...	...	4-...	.245	...	.444	...	...	...
1999—Ariz. A's (Ariz.) ...2B-3B-OF	SS	46	169	42	49	11	4	2	24	16	26	7	1	11-4	.290	.371	.438	.809	18	.925
—Midland (Texas)	SS	4	17	3	1	1	0	0	0	0	2	0	0	0	.059	.059	.118	.176	2	.889
2000—Visalia (Calif.)	SS	129	429	61	119	25	6	10	63	30	70	10	10	11-9	.277	.337	.434	.770	54	.909
2001—Wilmington (Caro.)	SS	51	199	43	63	18	4	6	25	17	55	14	7	10-6	.317	.382	.538	.920	17	.933
—Wichita (Texas)	SS	80	304	63	90	20	4	8	42	9	55	22	6	15-6	.296	.373	.467	.840	13	.965
—Kansas City (A.L.)	SS	15	53	8	16	2	0	0	4	3	10	0	2	2-0	.302	.339	.340	.679	3	.953
2002—Omaha (PCL)	SS	77	297	37	64	11	4	8	35	15	84	11	5	6-4	.215	.277	.360	.637	16	.956
—Kansas City (A.L.)	SS	20	75	8	17	7	1	0	5	7	13	1	1	3-0	.227	.301	.347	.648	4	.964
2003—Kansas City (A.L.)	SS	158	567	92	163	28	7	17	73	29	100	18	13	21-5	.287	.338	.452	.789	24	.968
2004—Wichita (Texas)	SS	11	51	8	16	0	0	3	10	2	8	0	0	3-2	.314	.340	.510	.849	0	1.000
—Kansas City (A.L.)	SS	134	512	72	134	27	6	8	43	23	87	12	10	14-8	.262	.308	.385	.693	28	.955
2005—Kansas City (A.L.)	SS	159	608	68	164	21	5	11	55	18	108	14	13	7-5	.270	.305	.375	.680	25	.965
2006—Kansas City (A.L.)	SS	132	474	45	111	18	1	9	54	14	88	3	21	3-1	.234	.259	.333	.592	18	.969
Major League totals (6 years)		618	2289	293	605	103	20	45	234	94	403	48	60	50-19	.264	.305	.386	.691	102	.964

2006 LEFTY-RIGHTY SPLITS

vs.	Avg.	AB	H	2B	3B	HR	RBI	BB	SO	OBP	Slg.		vs.	Avg.	AB	H	2B	3B	HR	RBI	BB	SO	OBP	Slg.
L	.217	129	28	5	0	4	17	1	25	.223	.349		R	.241	345	83	13	1	5	37	13	63	.272	.328

BETANCOURT, RAFAEL   P

PERSONAL: Born April 29, 1975, in Cumana, Venezuela. ... 6-2/200. ... Throws right, bats right. ... Full name: Rafael Jose Betancourt. ... High school: A.J.S. (Cumana, Venezuela). ... College: Isaac Newton College (Venezuela). **TRANSACTIONS/CAREER NOTES:** Signed as a non-drafted free agent by Boston Red Sox organization (September 6, 1993). ... Played three seasons as an infielder in Red Sox organization (1994-96). ... Contract purchased from Red Sox organization by Yokohama Bay Stars of the Japan Central League (November 18, 1999). ... Signed as a free agent by Red Sox organization (December 13, 2000). ... Signed as a free agent by Cleveland Indians organization (February 6, 2003). ... On disabled list (June 26-July 11, 2004); included rehabilitation assignment to Akron. ... On disabled list (July 3-18, 2005). ... On restricted list (July 8-18, 2005). ... On disabled list (April 20-May 16, 2006); included rehabilitation assignment to Akron.

CAREER HITTING: 0-for-0 (.000), 0 R, 0 2B, 0 3B, 0 HR, 0 RBI.

Year	Team (League)	W	L	Pct.	ERA	WHIP	G	GS	CG	ShO	Hld.	Sv.-Opp.	IP	H	R	ER	HR	BB-IBB	SO	Avg.
1997—	Michigan (Midw.)	0	3	.000	1.95	0.87	27	0	0	0	...	11-...	32.1	26	9	7	2	2-0	52	.213
1998—	GC Red Sox (GCL)	0	2	.000	7.20	1.40	4	3	0	0	...	0-...	5.0	6	5	4	1	1-0	4	.300
	—Sarasota (Fla. St.)	3	1	.750	3.54	1.00	20	0	0	0	...	2-...	28.0	22	12	11	2	6-0	33	.212
	—Trenton (East.)	0	0	...	6.75	1.29	7	0	0	0	...	0-...	9.1	9	7	7	0	3-0	9	.237
1999—	Sarasota (Fla. St.)	0	0	...	0.00	0.86	6	0	0	0	...	4-...	7.0	5	0	0	0	1-0	6	.208
	—Trenton (East.)	6	2	.750	3.62	1.10	39	0	0	0	...	13-...	54.2	50	24	22	7	10-0	57	.248
2000—	Yokohama (Jp. Cn.)	1	2	.333	4.08	1.43	11	4	0	0	...	0-...	28.2	30	16	13	5	11-...	16	...
	—Searex (Kor.)	1	0	1.000	1.17	1.00	20	0	0	0	...	6-...	23.0	17	3	3	0	6-...	29	...
2001—	Trenton (East.)	0	1	.000	5.63	1.29	16	0	0	0	...	4-...	24.0	28	16	15	0	3-0	27	.295
2003—	Akron (East.)	0	0	...	1.39	1.01	31	0	0	0	...	16-...	45.1	33	10	7	0	13-2	75	.195
	—Buffalo (Int'l)	0	0	...	4.05	1.20	4	0	0	0	...	1-...	6.2	6	3	3	1	2-0	6	.240
	—Cleveland (A.L.)	2	2	.500	2.13	1.05	33	0	0	0	4	1-3	38.0	27	11	9	5	13-2	36	.196
2004—	Akron (East.)	0	0	...	0.00	1.00	1	0	0	0	...	0-...	1.0	0	0	0	0	1-0	2	.000
	—Cleveland (A.L.)	5	6	.455	3.92	1.34	68	0	0	0	12	4-11	66.2	71	32	29	7	18-6	76	.268
2005—	Cleveland (A.L.)	4	3	.571	2.79	1.09	54	0	0	0	10	1-3	67.2	57	23	21	5	17-2	73	.224
2006—	Akron (East.)	0	0	...	0.00	1.00	1	1	0	0	0	0-0	1.0	0	0	0	0	1-0	2	...
	—Cleveland (A.L.)	3	4	.429	3.81	1.11	50	0	0	0	7	3-6	56.2	52	25	24	7	11-5	48	.241
	Major League totals (4 years)	14	15	.483	3.26	1.16	205	0	0	0	33	9-23	229.0	207	91	83	24	59-15	233	.237

2006 LEFTY-RIGHTY SPLITS

vs.	Avg.	AB	H	2B	3B	HR	RBI	BB	SO	OBP	Slg.	vs.	Avg.	AB	H	2B	3B	HR	RBI	BB	SO	OBP	Slg.
L	.221	86	19	6	0	1	12	8	17	.281	.326	R	.254	130	33	5	0	6	16	3	31	.271	.431

BETANCOURT, YUNIESKY   SS/2B

PERSONAL: Born January 31, 1982, in Santa Clara, Cuba. ... 5-10/190. ... Bats right, throws right. ... Full name: Yuniesky Betancourt. **TRANSACTIONS/CAREER NOTES:** Signed as a non-drafted free agent by Seattle Mariners organization (January 25, 2005).

2006 GAMES PLAYED BY POSITION (MLB): SS-157.

Year	Team (League)	Pos.	G	AB	R	H	2B	3B	HR	RBI	BB	SO	HBP	GDP	SB-CS	Avg.	OBP	SLG	OPS	E	Avg.
2005—	San Antonio (Texas)	SS-2B	52	227	25	62	10	3	5	20	9	18	1	2	12-7	.273	.301	.410	.711	5	.980
	—Tacoma (PCL)	SS-2B	49	183	13	54	9	6	2	30	6	14	2	3	7-5	.295	.323	.443	.766	3	.989
	—Seattle (A.L.)	SS-2B	60	211	24	54	11	5	1	15	11	24	2	2	1-3	.256	.296	.370	.666	5	.981
2006—	Seattle (A.L.)	SS	157	558	68	161	28	6	8	47	17	54	1	10	11-8	.289	.310	.403	.713	20	.971
	Major League totals (2 years)		217	769	92	215	39	11	9	62	28	78	3	12	12-11	.280	.306	.394	.700	25	.974

2006 LEFTY-RIGHTY SPLITS

vs.	Avg.	AB	H	2B	3B	HR	RBI	BB	SO	OBP	Slg.	vs.	Avg.	AB	H	2B	3B	HR	RBI	BB	SO	OBP	Slg.
L	.240	129	31	7	1	2	8	6	11	.279	.357	R	.303	429	130	21	5	6	39	11	43	.320	.417

BETEMIT, WILSON   3B

PERSONAL: Born July 28, 1980, in Santo Domingo, Dominican Republic. ... 6-3/190. ... Bats both, throws right. ... Name pronounced: BET-a-mitt. ... High school: Juan Bautista Safra (Santo Domingo, Dominican Republic). **TRANSACTIONS/CAREER NOTES:** Signed as a non-drafted free agent by Atlanta Braves organization (July 28, 1996). ... Traded by Braves to Los Angeles Dodgers for P Danys Baez and 3B Willy Aybar (July 28, 2006).

2006 GAMES PLAYED BY POSITION (MLB): 3B—79, SS—18, 2B—10, DH—1.

Year	Team (League)	Pos.	G	AB	R	H	2B	3B	HR	RBI	BB	SO	HBP	GDP	SB-CS	Avg.	OBP	SLG	OPS	E	Avg.
1997—	GC Braves (GCL)	SS	32	113	12	24	6	1	0	15	9	32	0	3	0-0	.212	.270	.283	.554	20	.856
1998—	GC Braves (GCL)	SS	51	173	23	38	8	4	5	16	20	49	0	1	6-5	.220	.301	.399	.699	20	.908
1999—	Danville (Appal.)	SS	67	259	39	83	18	2	5	53	27	63	1	4	6-3	.320	.383	.463	.846	33	.899
2000—	Jamestown (NYP)	SS	69	269	54	89	15	2	5	37	30	37	1	4	3-4	.331	.393	.457	.851	29	.910
2001—	Myrtle Beach (Carol.)	SS	84	318	38	88	20	1	7	43	23	71	1	8	8-5	.277	.324	.412	.736	23	.944
	—Greenville (Sou.)	SS	47	183	22	65	14	0	5	19	12	36	1	4	6-2	.355	.394	.514	.908	9	.954
	—Atlanta (N.L.)	SS	8	3	1	0	0	0	0	0	2	3	0	0	1-0	.000	.400	.000	.400	0	...
2002—	GC Braves (GCL)	SS	7	19	2	5	4	0	0	2	5	2	0	0	1-0	.263	.417	.474	.890	2	.867
	—Richmond (Int'l)	SS	93	343	43	84	17	1	8	34	34	82	1	7	8-5	.245	.312	.370	.683	21	.946
2003—	Richmond (Int'l)	3B-DH-SS	127	478	55	125	23	13	8	65	38	115	0	8	8-5	.262	.315	.414	.729	28	.902
2004—	Richmond (Int'l)	3B	105	356	48	99	24	2	13	59	32	99	0	17	3-3	.278	.336	.466	.802	16	.938
	—Atlanta (N.L.)	SS-3B	22	47	2	8	0	0	0	3	4	16	0	0	0-1	.170	.231	.170	.401	3	.943
2005—	Atlanta (N.L.)	3B-SS-2B	115	246	36	75	12	4	4	20	22	55	0	5	1-3	.305	.359	.435	.794	7	.964
2006—	Atlanta (N.L.)	3B-SS-2B DH	88	199	30	56	16	0	9	29	19	57	0	4	2-1	.281	.344	.497	.842	8	.948
	—Los Angeles (N.L.)	3B	55	174	19	42	7	0	9	24	17	45	0	7	1-0	.241	.306	.437	.742	4	.964
	Major League totals (4 years)		288	669	88	181	35	4	22	76	64	176	0	16	5-5	.271	.332	.433	.765	22	.957

DIVISION SERIES RECORD

Year	Team (League)	Pos.	G	AB	R	H	2B	3B	HR	RBI	BB	SO	HBP	GDP	SB-CS	Avg.	OBP	SLG	OPS	E	Avg.
2004—	Atlanta (N.L.)		1	0	0	0	0	0	0	0	0	0	0	0	0-0	...	...	...	...	0	...
2005—	Atlanta (N.L.)		2	2	0	1	0	0	0	0	0	1	0	0	0-0	.500	.500	.500	1.000	0	...
2006—	Los Angeles (N.L.)	3B	3	8	3	4	1	0	1	1	2	1	0	0	0-0	.500	.600	1.000	1.600	1	.800
	Division series totals (3 years)		6	10	3	5	1	0	1	1	2	2	0	0	0-0	.500	.583	.900	1.483	1	.800

2006 LEFTY-RIGHTY SPLITS

vs.	Avg.	AB	H	2B	3B	HR	RBI	BB	SO	OBP	Slg.	vs.	Avg.	AB	H	2B	3B	HR	RBI	BB	SO	OBP	Slg.
L	.189	74	14	0	0	3	13	6	28	.250	.324	R	.281	299	84	22	0	15	40	30	74	.344	.505

BIGBIE, LARRY   OF

PERSONAL: Born November 4, 1977, in Hobart, Ind. ... 6-4/207. ... Bats left, throws right. ... Full name: Larry Robert Bigbie. ... Name pronounced: BIGG-bee. ... High school: Hobart (Ind.). ... College: Ball State. **TRANSACTIONS/CAREER NOTES:** Selected by Baltimore Orioles organization in first round (21st pick overall) of 1999 free-agent draft; pick received from Texas Rangers as part of compensation for signing of Type A free-agent 1B Rafael Palmeiro. ... On disabled list (May 22-July 27, 2003); included rehabilitation assignments to Ottawa and GCL Orioles. ... On disabled list (August 16-September 1, 2004); included rehabilitation assignment to Frederick. ... On disabled list (May 28-June 13, 2005); included rehabilitation assignment to Ottawa. ... Traded by Orioles to Colorado Rockies for OF Eric Byrnes (July 29, 2005). ... On disabled list (August 23-September 6, 2005); included rehabilitation assignment to Colorado Springs. ... Traded by Rockies with 2B Aaron Miles to St. Louis Cardinals for P Ray King (December 7, 2005). ... On disabled list (March 29-May 8, 2006); included rehabilitation assignment to Memphis. ... On disabled list (June 6, 2006-remainder of season); included rehabilitation assignments to Quad Cities and Springfield.

2006 GAMES PLAYED BY POSITION (MLB): OF—12.

Year Team (League)	Pos.	G	AB	R	H	2B	3B	HR	RBI	BB	SO	HBP	GDP	SB-CS	Avg.	OBP	SLG	OPS	E	Avg.
1999— Bluefield (Appal.)	OF	8	30	3	8	0	0	0	4	3	8	0	1	1-3	.267	.343	.267	.610	0	1.000
— Delmarva (S. Atl.)	OF	43	165	18	46	7	3	2	27	29	42	1	4	3-1	.279	.381	.394	.775	3	.950
2000— Frederick (Carolina)	OF	55	201	33	59	11	0	2	28	23	34	0	3	7-3	.294	.360	.378	.738	3	.975
— Bowie (East.)	OF	31	112	11	27	6	0	0	5	11	28	0	3	3-0	.241	.309	.295	.604	0	1.000
2001— Bowie (East.)	OF	71	262	41	77	13	3	8	33	40	54	1	5	10-7	.294	.386	.458	.844	4	.972
— Baltimore (A.L.)	OF	47	131	15	30	6	0	2	11	17	42	0	2	4-1	.229	.318	.321	.638	0	1.000
— Rochester (Int'l)	OF	10	42	5	13	4	0	1	2	3	8	0	0	1-1	.310	.356	.476	.832	0	1.000
2002— Rochester (Int'l)	.OF	98	348	42	105	23	2	2	35	35	79	1	9	7-3	.302	.363	.397	.760	2	.990
— Baltimore (A.L.)	OF	16	34	1	6	1	0	0	3	1	11	0	1	1-0	.176	.194	.206	.400	0	1.000
2003— GC Orioles (GCL)	OF	2	6	1	2	1	0	0	0	0	1	0	0	0-0	.333	.333	.500	.833	0	1.000
— Ottawa (Int'l)	OF-DH	30	117	23	41	14	4	3	21	14	31	1	1	0-0	.350	.421	.615	1.036	1	.974
— Baltimore (A.L.)	OF	83	287	43	87	15	1	9	31	29	60	0	2	7-1	.303	.365	.456	.821	1	.994
2004— Frederick (Carolina)	OF	1	5	2	2	0	0	2	2	0	1	0	0	0-0	.400	.400	1.600	2.000	0	...
— Baltimore (A.L.)	OF-DH	139	478	76	134	23	1	15	68	45	113	1	7	8-3	.280	.341	.427	.768	2	.993
2005— Ottawa (Int'l)	OF-DH	4	17	3	5	2	0	1	2	0	6	0	1	0-0	.294	.294	.588	.882	0	...
— Baltimore (A.L.)	OF	67	206	22	51	9	1	5	21	21	49	0	2	3-3	.248	.314	.374	.688	0	1.000
— Colo. Springs (PCL)	OF	3	8	4	3	2	1	0	2	2	3	0	0	0-0	.375	.500	.875	1.375	0	1.000
— Colorado (N.L.)	OF	23	66	5	14	1	1	0	2	3	18	1	0	2-0	.212	.257	.258	.515	0	1.000
2006— Memphis (PCL)		11	35	4	5	0	0	0	1	0	7	14	0	2	0-1	.143	.286	.143	.429	0	1.000
— Springfield (Texas)		6	14	3	4	0	0	1	2	5	5	0	1	0-0	.286	.450	.500	.950	0	1.000
— St. Louis (N.L.)	OF	17	25	2	6	1	0	0	1	3	9	0	1	0-0	.240	.321	.280	.601	0	1.000
— Quad Cities (Mid.)		4	14	2	5	0	0	1	2	4	0	1	0	0-0	.357	.438	.357	.795	0	...
American League totals (5 years)		352	1136	157	308	54	3	31	134	113	275	1	14	23-8	.271	.335	.406	.741	3	.996
National League totals (2 years)		40	91	7	20	2	1	0	3	6	27	1	1	2-0	.220	.276	.264	.539	0	1.000
Major League totals (6 years)		392	1227	164	328	56	4	31	137	119	302	2	15	25-8	.267	.331	.395	.726	3	.996

2006 LEFTY-RIGHTY SPLITS

vs.	Avg.	AB	H	2B	3B	HR	RBI	BB	SO	OBP	Slg.	vs.	Avg.	AB	H	2B	3B	HR	RBI	BB	SO	OBP	Slg.
L	.333	3	1	0	0	0	0	0	2	.333	.333	R	.227	22	5	1	0	0	1	3	7	.320	.273

BIGGIO, CRAIG   2B

PERSONAL: Born December 14, 1965, in Smithtown, N.Y. ... 5-11/185. ... Bats right, throws right. ... Full name: Craig Alan Biggio. ... Name pronounced: BIDG-ee-oh. ... High school: Kings Park (N.Y.). ... College: Seton Hall. **TRANSACTIONS/CAREER NOTES:** Selected by Houston Astros organization in first round (22nd pick overall) of 1987 free-agent draft. ... On disabled list (August 2, 2000-remainder of season). **RECORDS:** Shares major league record for grounding into fewest double plays, season; minimum 150 games played (0, 1997). ... Holds major league record for most times hit by pitch, career (282). **HONORS:** Named second baseman on THE SPORTING NEWS N.L. All-Star team (1994-95, 1997-98 and 2001). ... Won N.L. Gold Glove at second base (1994-97). ... Named catcher on N.L. Silver Slugger team (1989). ... Named second baseman on N.L. Silver Slugger team (1994-95, 1997 and 1998). **STATISTICAL NOTES:** Hit for the cycle (April 8, 2002). ... Career major league grand slams: 2.

2006 GAMES PLAYED BY POSITION (MLB): 2B—129, DH—5.

Year Team (League)	Pos.	G	AB	R	H	2B	3B	HR	RBI	BB	SO	HBP	GDP	SB-CS	Avg.	OBP	SLG	OPS	E	Avg.
1987— Asheville (S. Atl.)	C-OF	64	216	59	81	17	2	9	49	39	33	2	5	31-10	.375	.471	.597	1.068	2	.995
1988— Tucson (PCL)	C-OF	77	281	60	90	21	4	3	41	40	39	3	2	19-4	.320	.408	.456	.863	6	.983
— Houston (N.L.)	C	50	123	14	26	6	1	3	5	7	29	0	1	6-1	.211	.254	.350	.603	3	.991
1989— Houston (N.L.)	C-OF	134	443	64	114	21	2	13	60	49	64	6	7	21-3	.257	.336	.402	.738	9	.989
1990— Houston (N.L.)	C-OF	150	555	53	153	24	2	4	42	53	79	3	11	25-11	.276	.342	.348	.689	13	.982
1991— Houston (N.L.)	2B-C-OF	149	546	79	161	23	4	4	46	53	71	2	2	19-6	.295	.358	.374	.747	11	.989
1992— Houston (N.L.)	2B	•162	613	96	170	32	3	6	39	94	95	7	5	38-15	.277	.378	.369	.747	12	.984
1993— Houston (N.L.)	2B	155	610	98	175	41	5	21	64	77	93	10	10	15-17	.287	.373	.474	.847	14	.982
1994— Houston (N.L.)	2B	114	437	88	139	* 44	5	6	56	62	58	8	5	* 39-4	.318	.411	.483	.893	7	.988
1995— Houston (N.L.)	2B	141	553	* 123	167	30	2	22	77	80	85	* 22	6	33-8	.302	.406	.483	.889	10	.986
1996— Houston (N.L.)	2B	•162	605	113	174	24	4	15	75	75	72	* 27	10	-25-7	.288	.386	.415	.801	10	.988
1997— Houston (N.L.)	2B-DH	•162	619	* 146	191	37	8	22	81	84	107	* 34	0	47-10	.309	.415	.501	.916	18	.979
1998— Houston (N.L.)	2B-DH	160	646	123	210	* 51	2	20	88	64	113	23	10	50-8	.325	.403	.503	.906	15	.980
1999— Houston (N.L.)	2B-OF-DH	160	639	123	188	* 56	0	16	73	88	107	11	5	28-14	.294	.386	.457	.843	12	.985
2000— Houston (N.L.)	2B	101	377	67	101	13	5	8	35	61	73	16	10	12-2	.268	.388	.393	.780	6	.987
2001— Houston (N.L.)	2B-DH	155	617	118	180	35	3	20	70	66	100	* 28	11	7-4	.292	.382	.455	.838	11	.984
2002— Houston (N.L.)	2B-OF	145	577	96	146	36	3	15	58	50	111	17	15	16-2	.253	.330	.404	.734	8	.988
2003— Houston (N.L.)	OF	153	628	102	166	44	2	15	62	57	116	* 27	4	8-4	.264	.350	.412	.763	1	.997
2004— Houston (N.L.)	OF-DH	156	633	100	178	47	0	24	63	40	94	15	8	7-2	.281	.337	.469	.806	9	.966
2005— Houston (N.L.)	2B-DH	155	590	94	156	40	1	26	69	37	90	17	10	11-1	.264	.325	.468	.792	16	.976
2006— Houston (N.L.)	2B-DH	145	548	79	135	33	0	21	62	40	84	9	15	3-2	.246	.306	.422	.727	6	.989
Major League totals (19 years)		2709	10359	1776	2930	637	52	281	1125	1137	1641	282	145	410-121	.283	.367	.436	.803	191	.985

DIVISION SERIES RECORD

Year Team (League)	Pos.	G	AB	R	H	2B	3B	HR	RBI	BB	SO	HBP	GDP	SB-CS	Avg.	OBP	SLG	OPS	E	Avg.
1997— Houston (N.L.)	2B	3	12	0	1	0	0	0	0	1	0	0	0	0-0	.083	.154	.083	.237	1	.923
1998— Houston (N.L.)	2B	4	11	3	2	1	0	0	1	4	2	0	0	0-0	.182	.471	.273	.743	1	.950
1999— Houston (N.L.)	2B	4	19	1	2	0	0	0	0	1	5	0	0	0-0	.105	.150	.105	.255	0	1.000
2001— Houston (N.L.)	2B	3	12	0	2	0	0	0	0	0	2	0	0	0-0	.167	.167	.167	.333	0	1.000
2004— Houston (N.L.)	OF	5	20	5	8	2	0	1	4	2	4	0	1	1-0	.400	.455	.650	1.105	0	1.000
2005— Houston (N.L.)	2B	4	19	6	6	4	0	0	1	2	5	0	0	1-0	.316	.364	.526	.890	0	1.000
Division series totals (6 years)		23	93	15	21	7	0	1	6	10	19	2	1	2-0	.226	.311	.333	.645	2	.980

CHAMPIONSHIP SERIES RECORD

Year Team (League)	Pos.	G	AB	R	H	2B	3B	HR	RBI	BB	SO	HBP	GDP	SB-CS	Avg.	OBP	SLG	OPS	E	Avg.
2004— Houston (N.L.)	OF	7	32	3	6	1	0	1	1	0	4	0	0	0-1	.188	.188	.313	.500	0	1.000
2005— Houston (N.L.)	2B	6	24	2	8	0	0	0	3	2	3	0	0	0-0	.333	.385	.333	.718	0	1.000
Champ. series totals (2 years)		13	56	5	14	1	0	1	4	2	7	0	0	0-1	.250	.276	.321	.597	0	1.000

WORLD SERIES RECORD

Year Team (League)	Pos.	G	AB	R	H	2B	3B	HR	RBI	BB	SO	HBP	GDP	SB-CS	Avg.	OBP	SLG	OPS	E	Avg.
2005— Houston (N.L.)	2B	4	18	3	4	1	0	1	1	4	0	0	0	0-0	.222	.263	.278	.541	0	1.000

ALL-STAR GAME RECORD

		G	AB	R	H	2B	3B	HR	RBI	BB	SO	HBP	GDP	SB-CS	Avg.	OBP	SLG	OPS	E	Avg.
All-Star Game totals (7 years)		7	15	2	1	0	0	1	2	0	5	1	0	0-0	.067	.125	.267	.392	1	.957

2006 LEFTY-RIGHTY SPLITS

vs.	Avg.	AB	H	2B	3B	HR	RBI	BB	SO	OBP	Slg.	vs.	Avg.	AB	H	2B	3B	HR	RBI	BB	SO	OBP	Slg.
L	.297	111	33	8	0	6	12	12	16	.373	.532	R	.233	437	102	25	0	15	50	28	68	.288	.394

BILLINGSLEY, CHAD   P

PERSONAL: Born July 29, 1984, in Defiance, Ohio. ... Throws right, bats right. ... Full name: Chad Ryan Billingsley. . **TRANSACTIONS/CAREER NOTES:** Selected by Los Angeles Dodgers organization in first round (24th pick overall) of 2003 free-agent draft.
CAREER HITTING: 2-for-24 (.083), 2 R, 0 2B, 0 3B, 0 HR, 2 RBI.

Year Team (League)	W	L	Pct.	ERA	WHIP	G	GS	CG	ShO	Hld.	Sv.-Opp.	IP	H	R	ER	HR	BB-IBB	SO	Avg.
2003— Ogden (Pion.)	5	4	.556	2.83	1.19	11	11	0	0	...	0-...	54.0	49	24	17	0	15-0	62	.243
2004— Vero Beach (Fla. St.)	7	4	.636	2.35	1.27	18	18	0	0	...	0-...	92.0	68	32	24	6	49-0	111	.208
— Jacksonville (Sou.)	4	0	1.000	2.98	1.28	8	8	0	0	...	0-...	42.1	32	16	14	1	22-0	47	.221
2005— Jacksonville (Sou.)	13	6	.684	3.51	1.14	28	26	2	1	0	0-0	146.0	116	60	57	12	50-0	162	.215
2006— Las Vegas (PCL)	6	3	.667	3.95	1.26	13	13	0	0	0	0-0	70.2	57	32	31	7	32-0	78	.221
— Los Angeles (N.L.)	7	4	.636	3.80	1.67	18	16	0	0	0	0-0	90.0	92	43	38	7	58-3	59	.272
Major League totals (1 year)	7	4	.636	3.80	1.67	18	16	0	0	0	0-0	90.0	92	43	38	7	58-3	59	.272

DIVISION SERIES RECORD

Year Team (League)	W	L	Pct.	ERA	WHIP	G	GS	CG	ShO	Hld.	Sv.-Opp.	IP	H	R	ER	HR	BB-IBB	SO	Avg.
2006— Los Angeles (N.L.)	0	0	...	0.00	0.50	2	0	0	0	0	0-0	2.0	1	0	0	0	0-0	3	.167

2006 LEFTY-RIGHTY SPLITS

vs.	Avg.	AB	H	2B	3B	HR	RBI	BB	SO	OBP	Slg.	vs.	Avg.	AB	H	2B	3B	HR	RBI	BB	SO	OBP	Slg.
L	.328	174	57	6	1	2	20	35	25	.443	.408	R	.213	164	35	9	0	5	14	23	34	.317	.360

BIRKINS, KURT   P

PERSONAL: Born August 11, 1980, in West Hills, Calif. ... Throws left, bats left. ... Full name: Kurt Daniel Birkins. ... Junior College: L.A. Pierce. **TRANSACTIONS/CAREER NOTES:** Selected by Baltimore Orioles in 33rd round of 2000 free-agent draft. ... On disabled list (July 30, 2006-remainder of season); included rehabilitation assignments to Frederick, Aberdeen and Bowie.
CAREER HITTING: 0-for-0 (.000), 0 R, 0 2B, 0 3B, 0 HR, 0 RBI.

Year Team (League)	W	L	Pct.	ERA	WHIP	G	GS	CG	ShO	Hld.	Sv.-Opp.	IP	H	R	ER	HR	BB-IBB	SO	Avg.
2001— GC Orioles (GCL)	2	1	.667	2.05	0.73	5	4	0	0	...	0-...	22.0	13	5	5	2	3-0	24	.167
— Bluefield (Appal.)	4	1	.800	2.92	0.89	6	6	0	0	...	0-...	37.0	28	14	12	2	5-0	42	.206
2002— Delmarva (S. Atl.)	9	7	.563	3.51	1.29	27	25	3	0	...	0-...	143.2	140	66	56	10	46-1	102	.257
2003— Frederick (Carolina)	8	11	.421	4.70	1.52	25	25	0	0	...	0-...	126.1	152	82	66	10	40-0	79	.297
2004— Frederick (Carolina)	5	2	.714	4.50	1.35	27	6	0	0	...	2-...	68.0	70	36	34	9	22-1	55	.269
2005— Bowie (East.)	7	11	.389	3.91	1.36	26	24	0	0	1	0-0	129.0	134	69	56	8	42-0	114	.270
2006— Ottawa (Int'l)	1	3	.250	3.20	1.22	5	5	0	0	0	0-0	25.1	20	10	9	2	11-0	19	.225
— Baltimore (A.L.)	5	2	.714	4.94	1.32	35	0	0	0	4	0-1	31.0	25	19	17	4	16-0	27	.221
— Frederick (Carolina)	0	0	...	0.00	1.00	1	0	0	0	0	0-0	1.0	0	0	0	0	1-0	1	.000
— Aberdeen (N.Y.-Penn.)	1	1	.500	3.38	1.13	2	0	0	0	0	0-1	2.2	3	1	1	0	0-0	2	.273
— Bowie (East.)	0	1	.000	9.00	1.50	2	0	0	0	1	0-0	4.0	5	4	4	2	1-0	5	.313
Major League totals (1 year)	5	2	.714	4.94	1.32	35	0	0	0	4	0-1	31.0	25	19	17	4	16-0	27	.221

2006 LEFTY-RIGHTY SPLITS

vs.	Avg.	AB	H	2B	3B	HR	RBI	BB	SO	OBP	Slg.	vs.	Avg.	AB	H	2B	3B	HR	RBI	BB	SO	OBP	Slg.
L	.212	52	11	3	0	1	5	5	14	.300	.327	R	.230	61	14	1	0	3	7	11	13	.351	.393

BLAKE, CASEY   OF/3B

PERSONAL: Born August 23, 1973, in Des Moines, Iowa. ... 6-2/210. ... Bats right, throws right. ... Full name: William Casey Blake. ... High school: Indianola (Iowa). ... College: Wichita State. **TRANSACTIONS/CAREER NOTES:** Selected by Philadelphia Phillies organization in 11th round of 1992 free-agent draft; did not sign. ... Selected by New York Yankees organization in 45th round of 1995 free-agent draft; did not sign. ... Selected by Toronto Blue Jays organization in seventh round of 1996 free-agent draft. ... Claimed on waivers by Minnesota Twins (May 23, 2000). ... Claimed on waivers by Baltimore Orioles (September 21, 2001). ... Claimed on waivers by Twins (October 12, 2001). ... Released by Twins (October 14, 2002). ... Signed by Cleveland Indians organization (December 18, 2002). ... On disabled list (June 16-July 13 and August 6-25, 2006); included rehabilitation assignments to Akron and Lake County. **STATISTICAL NOTES:** Career major league grand slams: 3.
2006 GAMES PLAYED BY POSITION (MLB): OF—93, 1B—9, DH—8.

Year Team (League)	Pos.	G	AB	R	H	2B	3B	HR	RBI	BB	SO	HBP	GDP	SB-CS	Avg.	OBP	SLG	OPS	E	Avg.
1996— Hagerstown (SAL)	1B-3B-OF	48	172	29	43	13	1	2	18	11	40	7	3	5-3	.250	.318	.372	.690	12	.906
1997— Dunedin (Fla. St.)	3B-SS	129	449	56	107	21	0	7	39	48	91	6	5	19-9	.238	.319	.332	.651	39	.895
1998— Dunedin (Fla. St.)	3B	88	340	62	119	28	3	11	65	30	81	9	5	9-6	.350	.409	.547	.956	16	.939
— Knoxville (Southern)	3B	45	172	41	64	15	4	7	38	22	25	2	6	10-0	.372	.442	.547	1.070	11	.913
1999— Syracuse (Int'l)	3B-DH-SS	110	387	69	95	16	2	22	75	61	82	7	10	9-5	.245	.357	.468	.824	10	.963
— Toronto (A.L.)	3B	14	39	6	10	2	0	1	1	2	7	0	1	0-0	.256	.293	.385	.677	0	1.000
— St. Catharines (NYP)	3B	1	3	0	2	0	0	0	0	1	0	0	0	0-0	.667	.750	.667	1.417	0	1.000
2000— Syracuse (Int'l)	3B-SS	30	106	10	23	6	1	2	7	8	23	3	2	0-3	.217	.291	.349	.640	2	.971
— Salt Lake (PCL)	3B-SS-1B	80	293	59	93	22	2	12	52	39	59	6	4	7-2	.317	.406	.529	.935	14	.934
— Minnesota (A.L.)	3B-1B-DH	7	16	1	3	2	0	0	1	3	7	1	1	0-0	.188	.333	.313	.646	0	1.000
2001— Edmonton (PCL)	3B-1B-2B																			
	SS-OF	94	375	64	116	24	6	10	49	34	66	6	11	14-3	.309	.376	.485	.861	11	.961
— Minnesota (A.L.)	3B-DH-1B	13	22	1	7	1	0	0	2	3	8	0	0	1-0	.318	.400	.364	.764	1	.955
— Baltimore (A.L.)	1B-DH	6	15	2	2	0	0	1	3	1	4	0	0	2-0	.133	.188	.333	.521	1	.967
2002— Edmonton (PCL)	3B-2B-1B																			
	OF	126	482	87	149	25	3	19	58	54	78	6	11	24-9	.309	.383	.492	.874	12	.969
— Minnesota (A.L.)	3B-1B-DH	9	20	2	4	1	0	0	2	2	7	0	0	0-0	.200	.273	.250	.523	2	.920
2003— Cleveland (A.L.)	3B-1B	152	557	80	143	35	0	17	67	38	109	10	11	7-9	.257	.312	.411	.723	19	.965
2004— Cleveland (A.L.)	3B-1B	152	587	93	159	36	3	28	88	68	139	4	19	5-8	.271	.354	.486	.839	26	.940
2005— Cleveland (A.L.)	OF-3B-1B	147	523	72	126	32	1	23	58	43	116	10	9	4-5	.241	.308	.438	.746	10	.971
2006— Akron (East.)		1	3	0	1	0	0	0	0	0	0	0	0	0-0	.333	.333	.667	1.000	0	1.000
— Lake County (S.Atl.)		1	2	1	1	0	0	1	2	0	0	0	0	0-0	.500	.750	2.000	2.750	0	1.000
— Cleveland (A.L.)	OF-1B-DH	109	401	63	113	20	1	19	68	45	93	4	11	6-0	.282	.356	.479	.835	4	.986
Major League totals (8 years)		609	2180	320	567	129	5	89	288	205	490	34	52	25-22	.260	.330	.446	.777	63	.964

2006 LEFTY-RIGHTY SPLITS

vs.	Avg.	AB	H	2B	3B	HR	RBI	BB	SO	OBP	Slg.	vs.	Avg.	AB	H	2B	3B	HR	RBI	BB	SO	OBP	Slg.
L	.272	114	31	3	0	10	24	17	23	.366	.561	R	.286	287	82	17	1	9	44	28	70	.352	.446

BLALOCK, HANK   3B

PERSONAL: Born November 21, 1980, in San Diego. ... 6-1/200. ... Bats left, throws right. ... Full name: Hank Joe Blalock. ... Name pronounced: BLAY-lock. ... High school: Rancho Bernardo (San Diego). **TRANSACTIONS/CAREER NOTES:** Selected by Texas Rangers organization in third round of 1999 free-agent draft. **STATISTICAL NOTES:** Career major league grand slams: 4.
2006 GAMES PLAYED BY POSITION (MLB): 3B—122, DH—29.

Year Team (League)	Pos.	G	AB	R	H	2B	3B	HR	RBI	BB	SO	HBP	GDP	SB-CS	Avg.	OBP	SLG	OPS	E	Avg.
1999— GC Rangers (GCL)	3B	51	191	34	69	17	6	3	38	25	23	1	7	3-2	.361	.428	.560	.988	12	.914
— Savannah (S. Atl.)	3B	7	25	3	6	1	0	1	2	1	3	1	0	0-0	.240	.286	.400	.686	5	.762
2000— Savannah (S. Atl.)	3B	139	512	66	153	32	2	10	77	62	53	5	13	31-8	.299	.373	.428	.801	20	.942
2001— Tulsa (Texas)	3B	68	272	50	89	18	4	11	61	39	38	2	5	3-3	.327	.413	.544	.957	8	.953
— Charlotte (Fla. St.)	3B	63	237	46	90	19	1	7	47	26	31	1	6	7-4	.380	.437	.557	.994	7	.963
2002— Texas (A.L.)	3B	49	147	16	31	8	0	3	17	20	43	1	2	0-0	.211	.306	.327	.632	6	.943
— Oklahoma (PCL)	3B-2B	95	387	63	119	32	1	8	62	34	61	1	9	2-1	.307	.363	.457	.872	16	.938
2003— Texas (A.L.)	3B-2B	143	567	89	170	33	3	29	90	44	97	1	16	2-3	.300	.350	.522	.872	16	.957
2004— Texas (A.L.)	3B	159	624	107	172	38	3	32	110	75	149	6	13	2-2	.276	.355	.500	.855	17	.957
2005— Texas (A.L.)	3B-DH	161	647	80	170	34	0	25	92	51	132	3	16	1-0	.263	.318	.431	.749	11	.973
2006— Texas (A.L.)	3B-DH	152	591	76	157	26	3	16	89	51	98	2	15	1-0	.266	.325	.401	.726	12	.963
Major League totals (5 years)		664	2576	368	700	139	9	105	398	241	519	13	62	6-5	.272	.335	.455	.790	62	.961

ALL-STAR GAME RECORD

	G	AB	R	H	2B	3B	HR	RBI	BB	SO	HBP	GDP	SB-CS	Avg.	OBP	SLG	OPS	E	Avg.
All-Star Game totals (2 years)	2	3	1	1	0	0	1	2	0	0	0		0-0	.333	.333	1.333	1.667	0	...

2006 LEFTY-RIGHTY SPLITS

vs.	Avg.	AB	H	2B	3B	HR	RBI	BB	SO	OBP	Slg.	vs.	Avg.	AB	H	2B	3B	HR	RBI	BB	SO	OBP	Slg.
L	.216	162	35	7	0	3	23	15	27	.281	.315	R	.284	429	122	19	3	13	66	36	71	.342	.434

BLANCO, ANDRES   SS/2B

PERSONAL: Born April 11, 1984, in Carabobo, Venezuela. ... 5-10/155. ... Bats both, throws right. ... Full name: Andres Eloy Blanco. ... Name pronounced: BLAHN-ko. ... High school: El Carmen (Venezuela). **TRANSACTIONS/CAREER NOTES:** Signed as a non-drafted free agent by Kansas City Royals organization (August 2, 2000).
2006 GAMES PLAYED BY POSITION (MLB): SS—25, 2B—7, DH—2.

Year Team (League)	Pos.	G	AB	R	H	2B	3B	HR	RBI	BB	SO	HBP	GDP	SB-CS	Avg.	OBP	SLG	OPS	E	Avg.
2001— Guacara 1 (VSL)		54	188	38	56	0	3	0	16	28	23	...		9-12	.298		.330		22	...
2002— GC Royals (GCL)	SS	52	193	27	48	8	0	0	14	15	29	4	2	16-4	.249	.315	.290	.605	13	.945
— Wilmington (Caro.)	SS	5	13	2	4	1	0	0	0	1	4	0	0	0-0	.308	.357	.385	.742	2	.926
2003— Wilmington (Caro.)	SS	113	394	61	96	11	3	0	25	44	50	8	9	13-7	.244	.330	.287	.617	26	.947
2004— Kansas City (A.L.)	SS	19	60	9	19	2	2	0	5	5	6	1	0	1-2	.317	.379	.417	.795	4	.959
— Wichita (Texas)	SS	93	324	34	80	10	2	0	21	18	44	7	14	7-6	.247	.299	.290	.575	21	.951
2005— High Desert (Calif.)	2B	3	10	0	5	1	0	0	3	0	1	0	0	1-2	.500	.500	.600	1.100	0	1.000
— Ariz. Royals (AZL)	SS-DH	7	25	6	8	1	0	0	3	1	1	1	0	1-2	.320	.370	.600	.970	3	.889
— Wichita (Texas)	SS	9	37	5	7	0	0	0	1	3	7	0	0	0-0	.189	.250	.270	.520	1	1.000
— Omaha (PCL)	SS	35	114	13	29	4	2	1	9	10	23	3	3	2-0	.254	.331	.351	.682	10	.944
— Kansas City (A.L.)	2B-SS	26	79	6	17	0	1	0	5	0	5	1	3	0-1	.215	.220	.241	.460	3	.979
2006— Omaha (PCL)	SS	88	283	30	67	9	4	2	20	21	41	9	7	6-4	.237	.309	.318	.627	21	.956
— Kansas City (A.L.)	SS-2B-DH	33	87	9	21	4	1	0	9	5	14	1	2	0-1	.241	.290	.310	.601	5	.960
Major League totals (3 years)		78	226	24	57	6	4	0	19	10	25	3	5	1-4	.252	.290	.314	.605	12	.967

2006 LEFTY-RIGHTY SPLITS

vs.	Avg.	AB	H	2B	3B	HR	RBI	BB	SO	OBP	Slg.	vs.	Avg.	AB	H	2B	3B	HR	RBI	BB	SO	OBP	Slg.
L	.500	18	9	2	1	0	5	0	4	.500	.722	R	.174	69	12	2	0	0	4	5	10	.240	.203

BLANCO, HENRY   C

PERSONAL: Born August 29, 1971, in Caracas, Venezuela. ... 5-11/220. ... Bats right, throws right. ... Full name: Henry Ramon Blanco. ... Name pronounced: BLAHN-ko. ... High school: Antonio Jose de Sucre (Venezuela). **TRANSACTIONS/CAREER NOTES:** Signed as a non-drafted free agent by Los Angeles Dodgers organization (November 12, 1989). ... On disabled list (March 22-July 29, 1998); included rehabilitation assignment to San Bernardino. ... Signed as a free agent by Colorado Rockies organization (December 18, 1998). ... Traded by Rockies with P Jamey Wright to Milwaukee Brewers as part of three-way deal in which Rockies acquired 3B Jeff Cirillo, P Scott Karl and cash from Brewers, Oakland Athletics acquired P Justin Miller and cash from Rockies and Brewers acquired P Jimmy Haynes from A's (December 13, 1999). ... On disabled list (April 14-May 2, 2000); included rehabilitation assignment to Indianapolis. ... Traded by Brewers to Atlanta Braves for C Paul Bako and P Jose Cabrera (March 20, 2002). ... On disabled list (August 12-27, 2002). ... Signed as a free agent by Minnesota Twins (December 18, 2003). ... Signed as a free agent by Chicago Cubs (December 7, 2004). **STATISTICAL NOTES:** Career major league grand slams: 1.
2006 GAMES PLAYED BY POSITION (MLB): C—69, 1B—6.

Year Team (League)	Pos.	G	AB	R	H	2B	3B	HR	RBI	BB	SO	HBP	GDP	SB-CS	Avg.	OBP	SLG	OPS	E	Avg.
1990— GC Dodgers (GCL)	3B	60	178	23	39	8	0	1	19	26	41	1	6	7-2	.219	.316	.281	.597	11	.941
1991— Vero Beach (Fla. St.)	3B-SS	5	7	0	1	0	0	0	0	2	0	0	0	0-0	.143	.333	.143	.476	0	1.000
— Great Falls (Pio.)	1B-3B	62	216	35	55	7	1	5	28	27	39	1	5	3-6	.255	.336	.366	.702	8	.960
1992— Bakersfield (Calif.)	3B	124	401	42	94	21	2	5	52	51	91	9	10	10-6	.234	.328	.334	.662	14	.959
1993— San Antonio (Texas)	3B-1B-SS	117	374	33	73	19	1	10	42	29	80	4	7	1-3	.195	.266	.332	.591	16	.952
1994— San Antonio (Texas)	3B-1B-P	132	405	36	93	23	2	6	38	53	67	2	12	6-6	.230	.320	.341	.660	21	.924
1995— San Antonio (Texas)	3B-C	88	302	37	77	18	4	12	48	29	48	4	4	1-1	.255	.326	.460	.789	11	.964
— Albuquerque (PCL)	3B-1B-OF	29	97	11	22	4	1	2	13	10	23	0	3	0-0	.227	.294	.351	.644	2	.988
1996— San Antonio (Texas)	C-3B	92	307	39	82	14	1	5	40	28	38	0	8	2-3	.267	.324	.368	.692	13	.979
— Albuquerque (PCL)	C	2	6	1	1	0	0	0	0	0	3	0	0	0-0	.167	.167	.167	.333	0	1.000
1997— Albuquerque (PCL)	C-1B-DH																			
	OF	91	294	38	92	20	1	6	47	37	63	1	7	7-4	.313	.388	.449	.837	3	.996
— Los Angeles (N.L.)	1B-3B	3	5	1	2	0	0	1	1	1	0	0	0	0-0	.400	.400	1.000	1.400	0	1.000
1998— San Bern. (Calif.)	C-DH	7	19	5	6	1	0	2	3	4	6	0	2	1-0	.316	.435	.684	1.119	0	1.000
— Albuquerque (PCL)	C-DH	48	134	19	36	11	0	4	23	22	27	0	5	2-0	.269	.367	.440	.807	4	.985
1999— Colo. Springs (PCL)	C	15	57	8	19	4	0	3	12	1	12	0	1	0-0	.333	.339	.561	.900	1	.990
— Colorado (N.L.)	C-OF	88	263	30	61	12	3	6	28	34	38	1	4	1-1	.232	.320	.369	.689	5	.992
2000— Milwaukee (N.L.)	C	93	284	29	67	24	0	9	31	36	60	0	9	0-3	.236	.318	.394	.712	5	.991
— Indianapolis (Int'l)	DH	1	3	1	1	0	0	0	0	1	0	0	1	0-0	.333	.500	.667	1.167	...	...

B

Year Team (League)	Pos.	G	AB	R	H	2B	3B	HR	RBI	BB	SO	HBP	GDP	SB-CS	Avg.	OBP	SLG	OPS	E	Avg.
2001— Milwaukee (N.L.)	C	104	314	33	66	18	3	6	31	34	72	2	10	3-1	.210	.290	.344	.634	6	.992
2002— Atlanta (N.L.)	C	81	221	17	45	9	1	6	22	20	51	1	5	0-2	.204	.267	.335	.602	3	.993
2003— Atlanta (N.L.)	C	55	151	11	30	8	0	1	13	10	21	1	3	0-0	.199	.252	.272	.523	1	.996
2004— Minnesota (A.L.)	C	114	315	36	65	19	1	10	37	21	56	3	6	0-3	.206	.260	.368	.628	7	.991
2005— Chicago (N.L.)	C	54	161	16	39	6	0	6	25	11	24	0	6	0-0	.242	.287	.391	.679	1	.998
2006— Chicago (N.L.)	C-1B	74	241	23	64	15	2	6	37	14	38	0	8	0-0	.266	.304	.419	.723	1	.998
American League totals (1 year)		114	315	36	65	19	1	10	37	21	56	3	6	0-3	.206	.260	.368	.628	7	.991
National League totals (8 years)		552	1640	160	374	92	9	39	188	159	305	5	45	4-7	.228	.295	.366	.662	22	.994
Major League totals (9 years)		666	1955	196	439	111	10	49	225	180	361	8	53	4-10	.225	.290	.367	.656	29	.993

Year Team (League)	Pos.	G	AB	R	H	2B	3B	HR	RBI	BB	SO	HBP	GDP	SB-CS	Avg.	OBP	SLG	OPS	E	Avg.
				DIVISION	SERIES	RECORD														
2002— Atlanta (N.L.)	C	2	6	0	1	0	0	0	0	0	2	0	0	0-0	.167	.167	.167	.333	0	1.000
2004— Minnesota (A.L.)	C	4	8	1	2	0	0	1	2	0	2	0	1	0-0	.250	.222	.625	.847	1	.957
Division series totals (2 years)		6	14	1	3	0	0	1	2	0	4	0	1	0-0	.214	.200	.429	.629	1	.970

2006 LEFTY-RIGHTY SPLITS

vs.	Avg.	AB	H	2B	3B	HR	RBI	BB	SO	OBP	Slg.	vs.	Avg.	AB	H	2B	3B	HR	RBI	BB	SO	OBP	Slg.
L	.325	80	26	6	0	3	11	4	8	.357	.513	R	.236	161	38	9	2	3	26	10	30	.277	.373

BLANTON, JOE — P

PERSONAL: Born December 11, 1980, in Bowling Green, Ky. — 6-3/225. ... Throws right, bats right. ... Full name: Joseph Matthew Blanton. ... High school: Franklin-Simpson (Franklin, Ky.). ... College: Kentucky. **TRANSACTIONS/CAREER NOTES:** Selected by Oakland Athletics organization in first round (24th pick overall) of 2002 free-agent draft; pick received as compensation for New York Yankees signing Type A free-agent 1B Jason Giambi. ... **CAREER HITTING:** 1-for-5 (.200), 0 R, 0 2B, 0 3B, 0 HR, 0 RBI.

Year Team (League)	W	L	Pct.	ERA	WHIP	G	GS	CG	ShO	Hld.	Sv.-Opp.	IP	H	R	ER	HR	BB-IBB	SO	Avg.
2002— Vancouver (N'west)	1	1	.500	3.14	0.91	4	2	0	0	...	0-...	14.1	11	5	5	0	2-0	15	.216
— Modesto (California)	0	1	.000	7.50	2.33	2	1	0	0	...	0-...	6.0	8	6	5	1	6-0	6	.296
2003— Kane Co. (Midw.)	8	7	.533	2.57	0.97	21	21	0	0	...	0-...	133.0	110	47	38	6	19-0	144	.219
— Midland (Texas)	3	1	.750	1.26	0.79	7	5	1	0	...	1-...	35.2	21	6	5	1	7-0	30	.174
2004— Sacramento (PCL)	11	8	.579	4.19	1.32	28	26	1	0	0	0-0	176.1	199	101	82	13	34-2	143	.284
— Oakland (A.L.)	0	0	...	5.63	1.00	3	0	0	0	0	0-0	8.0	6	5	5	1	2-0	6	.214
2005— Oakland (A.L.)	12	12	.500	3.53	1.22	33	33	2	0	0	0-0	201.1	178	86	79	23	67-3	116	.236
2006— Oakland (A.L.)	16	12	.571	4.82	1.54	32	31	1	0	0	0-0	194.1	241	111	104	17	58-4	107	.309
Major League totals (3 years)	28	24	.538	4.19	1.37	68	64	3	0	0	0-0	403.2	425	202	188	41	127-7	229	.272

Year Team (League)	W	L	Pct.	ERA	WHIP	G	GS	CG	ShO	Hld.	Sv.-Opp.	IP	H	R	ER	HR	BB-IBB	SO	Avg.
					CHAMPIONSHIP	SERIES	RECORD												
2006— Oakland (A.L.)	0	0	...	0.00	1.00	1	0	0	0	0	0-0	2.0	0	0	0	0	2-0	2	.000

2006 LEFTY-RIGHTY SPLITS

vs.	Avg.	AB	H	2B	3B	HR	RBI	BB	SO	OBP	Slg.	vs.	Avg.	AB	H	2B	3B	HR	RBI	BB	SO	OBP	Slg.
L	.314	357	112	17	4	7	41	27	44	.361	.443	R	.304	424	129	33	0	10	55	31	63	.353	.453

BLOOMQUIST, WILLIE — IF/OF

PERSONAL: Born November 27, 1977, in Bremerton, Wash. ... 5-11/185. ... Bats right, throws right. ... Full name: William Paul Bloomquist. ... High school: South Kitsap (Port Orchard, Wash.). ... College: Arizona State. **TRANSACTIONS/CAREER NOTES:** Selected by Seattle Mariners organization in eighth round of 1996 free-agent draft; did not sign. ... Selected by Mariners organization in third round of 1999 free-agent draft. ... On disabled list (May 2-21, 2004); included rehabilitation assignment to Tacoma. ... On disabled list (August 30, 2005-remainder of season). **STATISTICAL NOTES:** Career major league grand slams: 1.
2006 GAMES PLAYED BY POSITION (MLB): OF—59, SS—17, 2B—15, 3B—12, 1B—4, DH—2.

Year Team (League)	Pos.	G	AB	R	H	2B	3B	HR	RBI	BB	SO	HBP	GDP	SB-CS	Avg.	OBP	SLG	OPS	E	Avg.
1999— Everett (N'west)	2B-OF	42	178	35	51	10	3	2	27	22	25	1	1	17-5	.287	.366	.410	.776	7	.954
2000— Lancaster (Calif.)	2B-SS	64	256	63	97	19	6	2	51	37	27	1	3	22-12	.379	.456	.523	.979	12	.961
— Tacoma (PCL)	2B	51	191	17	43	5	1	1	23	7	28	0	3	5-0	.225	.249	.277	.526	3	.987
2001— San Antonio (Texas)	2B-SS	123	491	59	125	23	2	0	28	28	55	1	11	34-9	.255	.294	.310	.603	24	.959
2002— Tacoma (PCL)	SS	104	337	47	91	14	3	2	45	29	44	3	5	20-10	.270	.331	.383	.713	12	.961
— Seattle (A.L.)	OF-2B-DH	12	33	11	15	4	0	0	7	5	2	0	0	3-1	.455	.526	.576	1.102	0	1.000
2003— Seattle (A.L.)	3B-SS-DH	89	196	30	49	7	2	1	14	19	39	1	6	4-1	.250	.317	.321	.638	4	.975
2004— Tacoma (PCL)	OF-2B-1B	3	12	2	5	0	0	1	3	0	2	0	0	1-0	.417	.417	.667	1.083	0	1.000
— Seattle (A.L.)	SS-OF	93	188	27	46	10	0	2	18	10	48	0	2	13-2	.245	.283	.330	.613	10	.956
2005— Seattle (A.L.)	3B-SS-OF	82	249	27	64	11	0	0	22	11	38	1	5	14-1	.257	.289	.333	.622	6	.977
2006— Seattle (A.L.)	OF-DH-2B / 3B-1B-DH / OF-SS-2B	102	251	36	62	6	0	1	15	24	40	4	3	16-3	.247	.320	.299	.619	2	.991
Major League totals (5 years)		378	917	131	236	42	6	4	76	69	167	6	16	50-8	.257	.312	.329	.641	22	.975

2006 LEFTY-RIGHTY SPLITS

vs.	Avg.	AB	H	2B	3B	HR	RBI	BB	SO	OBP	Slg.	vs.	Avg.	AB	H	2B	3B	HR	RBI	BB	SO	OBP	Slg.
L	.253	99	25	2	1	1	5	6	8	.308	.323	R	.243	152	37	4	1	0	10	18	32	.328	.283

BLUM, GEOFF — 2B/3B

PERSONAL: Born April 26, 1973, in Redwood City, Calif. ... 6-3/200. ... Bats both, throws right. ... Full name: Geoffrey Edward Blum. ... Name pronounced: bluhm. ... High school: Chino (Calif.). ... College: California. **TRANSACTIONS/CAREER NOTES:** Selected by Montreal Expos organization in seventh round of 1994 free-agent draft. ... Traded by Expos to Houston Astros for 3B Chris Truby (March 12, 2002). ... Traded by Astros to Tampa Bay Devil Rays for P Brandon Backe (December 14, 2003). ... Released by Devil Rays (November 19, 2004). ... Signed by San Diego Padres (December 8, 2004). ... On disabled list (April 30-May 18, 2005); included rehabilitation assignment to Lake Elsinore. ... Traded by Padres to Chicago White Sox for P Ryan Meaux (July 31, 2005). ... Signed as a free agent by Padres (November 16, 2005).
2006 GAMES PLAYED BY POSITION (MLB): SS—49, 3B—34, 1B—2, 2B—1, OF—1.

Year Team (League)	Pos.	G	AB	R	H	2B	3B	HR	RBI	BB	SO	HBP	GDP	SB-CS	Avg.	OBP	SLG	OPS	E	Avg.
1994— Vermont (NYP)	SS	63	241	48	83	15	1	3	38	33	21	3	4	5-5	.344	.428	.452	.880	15	.948
1995— W.P. Beach (Fla. St.)	2B-3B-SS	125	457	54	120	20	2	1	62	34	61	3	12	6-5	.263	.313	.322	.635	18	.963

B

Year	Team (League)	Pos.	G	AB	R	H	2B	3B	HR	RBI	BB	SO	HBP	GDP	SB-CS	Avg.	OBP	SLG	OPS	E	Avg.
1996— Harrisburg (East.)	2B-SS-1B		120	396	47	95	22	2	1	41	59	51	3	11	6-7	.240	.341	.313	.654	9	.984
1997— Ottawa (Int'l)	2B-3B-SS		118	407	59	101	21	2	3	35	52	73	3	6	14-6	.248	.333	.332	.665	17	.969
1998— Ottawa (Int'l)	2B		8	23	1	4	0	0	0	1	3	6	0	0	0-0	.174	.269	.174	.443	0	1.000
— GC Expos (GCL)	2B		5	18	0	3	1	1	0	1	1	4	0	0	0-0	.167	.211	.333	.544	0	1.000
— Jupiter (Fla. St.)	2B-3B-SS		17	58	13	16	6	0	0	5	13	14	1	0	1-0	.276	.411	.379	.790	2	.976
— Harrisburg (East.)	1B-2B-3B-SS		39	139	25	43	12	3	6	21	17	24	4	3	2-1	.309	.400	.568	.968	2	.986
1999— Ottawa (Int'l)	SS-1B-2B-3B-DH		77	268	43	71	14	1	10	37	37	39	2	5	6-1	.265	.350	.437	.787	12	.965
— Montreal (N.L.)	SS-2B		45	133	21	32	7	2	8	18	17	25	0	3	1-0	.241	.327	.504	.830	10	.929
2000— Montreal (N.L.)	3B-SS-2B-1B		124	343	40	97	20	2	11	45	26	60	3	4	1-4	.283	.335	.449	.784	9	.974
2001— Montreal (N.L.)	3B-OF-2B-1B-SS		148	453	57	107	25	0	9	50	43	94	10	12	9-5	.236	.313	.351	.664	8	.980
2002— Houston (N.L.)	3B-OF-SS-1B-2B		130	368	45	104	20	4	10	52	49	70	1	8	2-0	.283	.367	.440	.807	8	.972
2003— Houston (N.L.)	3B-2B-SS-OF		123	420	51	110	19	0	10	50	20	50	2	15	0-0	.262	.295	.379	.674	7	.975
2004— Tampa Bay (A.L.)	3B-2B-OF-1B-DH-SS		112	339	38	73	21	0	8	35	24	58	0	4	2-3	.215	.266	.348	.614	10	.970
2005— Lake Elsinore (Calif.)	2B-SS		2	8	3	2	0	0	2	5	1	2	0	0	0-0	.250	.333	1.000	1.333	1	.944
— San Diego (N.L.)	3B-2B-SS-1B		78	224	26	54	14	0	5	22	24	28	3	5	3-2	.241	.321	.375	.696	3	.985
— Chicago (A.L.)	1B-3B-SS-2B		31	95	6	19	2	1	1	3	4	15	0	1	0-1	.200	.232	.274	.506	3	.981
2006— San Diego (N.L.)	SS-3B-1B-2B-OF		109	276	27	70	17	1	4	34	17	51	0	5	0-1	.254	.293	.366	.659	6	.978
American League totals (2 years)			143	434	44	92	23	1	9	38	28	73	0	5	2-4	.212	.259	.332	.590	13	.973
National League totals (7 years)			757	2217	267	574	121	10	57	273	196	378	19	52	16-12	.259	.322	.400	.721	51	.974
Major League totals (8 years)			900	2651	311	666	144	11	66	311	224	451	19	57	18-16	.251	.312	.389	.700	64	.974

DIVISION SERIES RECORD

Year	Team (League)	Pos.	G	AB	R	H	2B	3B	HR	RBI	BB	SO	HBP	GDP	SB-CS	Avg.	OBP	SLG	OPS	E	Avg.
2005— Chicago (A.L.)	1B		1	1	0	0	0	0	0	0	0	0	0	0	0-0	.000	.000	.000	.000	0	...
2006— San Diego (N.L.)	SS-3B		4	8	0	1	1	0	0	1	4	1	0	1	0-0	.125	.385	.250	.635	0	1.000
Division series totals (2 years)			5	9	0	1	1	0	0	1	4	1	0	1	0-0	.111	.357	.222	.579	0	1.000

WORLD SERIES RECORD

Year	Team (League)	Pos.	G	AB	R	H	2B	3B	HR	RBI	BB	SO	HBP	GDP	SB-CS	Avg.	OBP	SLG	OPS	E	Avg.
2005— Chicago (A.L.)	2B		1	1	1	1	0	0	1	1	0	0	0	0	0-0	1.000	1.000	4.000	5.000	0	1.000

2006 LEFTY-RIGHTY SPLITS

vs.	Avg.	AB	H	2B	3B	HR	RBI	BB	SO	OBP	Slg.	vs.	Avg.	AB	H	2B	3B	HR	RBI	BB	SO	OBP	Slg.
L	.167	36	6	2	0	0	0	2	10	.211	.222	R	.267	240	64	15	1	4	34	15	41	.305	.388

BOCACHICA, HIRAM — OF

PERSONAL: Born March 4, 1976, in Ponce, Puerto Rico. ... 5-11/180. ... Bats right, throws right. ... Full name: Hiram Colon Bocachica. ... Name pronounced: hear-ram bow-ka-CHEE-ka. ... High school: Rexville (Bayamon, Puerto Rico). **TRANSACTIONS/CAREER NOTES:** Selected by Montreal Expos organization in first round (21st pick overall) of 1994 free-agent draft. ... Traded by Expos with P Carlos Perez and SS Mark Grudzielanek to Los Angeles Dodgers for 2B Wilton Guerrero, P Ted Lilly, OF Peter Bergeron and 1B Jonathan Tucker (July 31, 1998). ... On disabled list (July 9-26, 2001). ... Traded by Dodgers to Detroit Tigers for P Tom Farmer and a player to be named (July 25, 2002); Dodgers acquired P Jason Frasor to complete deal (September 18, 2002). ... Signed as a free agent by Seattle Mariners organization (January 16, 2004). ... Signed as a free agent by Oakland Athletics organization (November 19, 2004).

2006 GAMES PLAYED BY POSITION (MLB): OF—8.

Year	Team (League)	Pos.	G	AB	R	H	2B	3B	HR	RBI	BB	SO	HBP	GDP	SB-CS	Avg.	OBP	SLG	OPS	E	Avg.
1994— GC Expos (GCL)	SS		43	168	31	47	9	0	5	16	15	42	2	1	11-4	.280	.346	.423	.769	23	.896
1995— Albany (S. Atl.)	2B-SS		96	380	65	108	20	10	2	30	52	78	8	4	47-17	.284	.381	.405	.786	58	.881
1996— W.P. Beach (Fla. St.)	DH-SS		71	267	50	90	17	5	2	26	34	47	6	6	21-3	.337	.419	.461	.880	24	.833
— GC Expos (GCL)	DH		9	32	11	8	3	0	0	2	5	3	1	0	2-1	.250	.368	.344	.712		...
1997— Harrisburg (East.)	SS-2B-DH		119	443	82	123	19	3	11	35	41	98	13	3	29-12	.278	.354	.409	.763	32	.909
1998— Harrisburg (East.)	OF-DH		80	296	39	78	18	4	4	27	21	61	11	1	20-8	.264	.334	.392	.726	10	.946
— Ottawa (Int'l)	OF		12	41	5	8	3	1	0	5	6	14	1	1	2-0	.195	.313	.317	.630	0	1.000
— Albuquerque (PCL)	2B		26	101	16	24	7	1	4	16	13	24	6	1	5-3	.238	.358	.446	.804	2	.976
1999— San Antonio (Texas)	2B-DH		123	477	84	139	22	10	11	60	60	71	13	5	30-15	.291	.382	.449	.831	31	.946
2000— Albuquerque (PCL)	2B		124	482	99	155	38	4	23	84	40	100	15	7	10-14	.322	.390	.560	.950	23	.963
— Los Angeles (N.L.)	2B		8	10	2	3	0	0	0	0	0	2	0	0	0-0	.300	.300	.300	.600	0	1.000
2001— Los Angeles (N.L.)	2B-OF-3B		75	133	15	31	11	1	2	9	9	33	1	0	4-1	.233	.287	.376	.663	7	.919
2002— Los Angeles (N.L.)	OF-DH		49	65	12	14	3	0	4	9	5	19	0	1	1-1	.215	.271	.446	.718	1	.960
— Detroit (A.L.)	OF-2B-DH		34	103	14	23	4	0	4	8	5	22	0	2	2-2	.223	.259	.379	.638	2	.969
2003— Detroit (A.L.)	OF		6	22	1	1	1	0	0	0	0	7	0	0	0-0	.045	.045	.091	.136	0	1.000
— Toledo (Int'l)	OF-2B-3B-DH		95	322	48	78	19	3	12	37	24	57	10	5	11-6	.242	.313	.432	.745	11	.954
2004— Tacoma (PCL)	OF-1B-DH		40	136	22	39	5	1	10	25	17	36	8	2	12-3	.287	.393	.559	.951	4	.953
— Seattle (A.L.)	OF-DH		50	90	9	22	5	0	3	6	12	27	1	1	5-4	.244	.337	.400	.737	0	1.000
2005— Ariz. A's (Ariz.)	OF-DH		4	12	1	1	1	0	0	0	0	3	0	0	0-0	.083	.083	.167	.250		...
— Sacramento (PCL)	3B-DH		4	17	2	7	2	0	2	6	1	4	0	0	0-0	.412	.444	.882	1.327	0	1.000
— Oakland (A.L.)	OF-3B-DH		9	19	2	2	0	0	0	0	0	7	0	0	0-0	.105	.105	.105	.211	0	1.000
2006— Stockton (Calif.)			4	14	3	4	2	0	0	2	0	4	2	0	0-1	.286	.375	.429	.804	0	1.000
— Sacramento (PCL)			77	291	61	95	15	3	19	60	43	55	7	7	18-3	.326	.422	.595	1.016	8	.942
— Oakland (A.L.)	OF		8	13	3	3	0	0	0	0	3	4	0	0	1-0	.231	.375	.231	.606	0	1.000
American League totals (5 years)			107	247	29	51	10	0	7	14	20	67	1	3	8-6	.206	.268	.332	.600	2	.988
National League totals (3 years)			132	208	29	48	14	1	6	18	14	54	1	2	5-2	.231	.283	.394	.677	8	.935
Major League totals (7 years)			239	455	58	99	24	1	13	32	34	121	2	5	13-8	.218	.274	.360	.635	10	.965

2006 LEFTY-RIGHTY SPLITS

vs.	Avg.	AB	H	2B	3B	HR	RBI	BB	SO	OBP	Slg.	vs.	Avg.	AB	H	2B	3B	HR	RBI	BB	SO	OBP	Slg.
L	.500	2	1	0	0	0	0	0	2	1	.750	.500	R	.182	11	2	0	0	0	0	0	3	.250	.182

B

BOHN, T.J. — OF

PERSONAL: Born January 17, 1980, in St. Louis Park, Minn. ... 6-5/205. ... Bats right, throws right. ... Full name: Thomas Joseph Bohn Jr.. ... College: Bellevue.
TRANSACTIONS/CAREER NOTES: Selected by Seattle Mariners organization in 30th round of 2002 free-agent draft.
2006 GAMES PLAYED BY POSITION (MLB): OF—18.

									BATTING										FIELDING	
Year Team (League)	Pos.	G	AB	R	H	2B	3B	HR	RBI	BB	SO	HBP	GDP	SB-CS	Avg.	OBP	SLG	OPS	E	Avg.
2002— Everett (N'west)		62	212	28	52	10	0	3	20	29	53	3	4	7-2	.245	.340	.335	.675	1	...
2003— Wisconsin (Midw.)		128	471	75	128	31	2	13	70	70	131	8	5	16-8	.272	.371	.429	.800	6	...
2004— Inland Empire (Calif.)		71	240	46	68	9	3	7	37	44	61	9	4	6-4	.283	.412	.433	.845	2	...
— San Antonio (Texas)		62	220	24	58	9	4	7	29	22	46	3	1	6-1	.264	.336	.436	.772	1	...
2005— San Antonio (Texas)	OF-DH	113	438	67	135	30	2	12	57	35	96	5	8	27-9	.308	.365	.468	.833	8	.985
— Tacoma (PCL)	OF	22	81	15	26	3	0	1	7	2	23	3	5	4-0	.321	.360	.395	.756	2	.983
2006— Tacoma (PCL)		97	378	53	107	20	1	9	43	33	81	4	10	15-3	.283	.345	.413	.758	2	.991
— Ariz. Mariners (Ariz.)		4	16	4	4	3	1	0	1	1	8	0	0	3-0	.250	.294	.563	.857	0	1.000
— Seattle (A.L.)	OF	18	14	2	2	0	0	1	2	2	8	0	0	0-0	.143	.250	.357	.607	1	.875
Major League totals (1 year)		18	14	2	2	0	0	1	2	2	8	0	0	0-0	.143	.250	.357	.607	1	.875

2006 LEFTY-RIGHTY SPLITS

vs.	Avg.	AB	H	2B	3B	HR	RBI	BB	SO	OBP	Slg.	vs.	Avg.	AB	H	2B	3B	HR	RBI	BB	SO	OBP	Slg.
L	.100	10	1	0	0	0	0	1	5	.182	.100	R	.250	4	1	0	0	1	2	1	3	.400	1.000

BONDERMAN, JEREMY — P

PERSONAL: Born October 28, 1982, in Kennewick, Wash. ... 6-2/210. ... Throws right, bats right. ... Full name: Jeremy Allen Bonderman. ... High school: Pasco (Wash.).
TRANSACTIONS/CAREER NOTES: Selected by Oakland Athletics in first round (26th pick overall) of 2001 free-agent draft; pick received as compensation for New York Mets signing free-agent P Kevin Appier. ... Traded by A's to Detroit Tigers (August 22, 2002), completing three-team deal in which Tigers acquired 1B Carlos Pena, P Franklyn German and a player to be named from A's, A's acquired P Ted Lilly, OF John-Ford Griffin and P Jason Arnold from New York Yankees and Yankees acquired P Jeff Weaver from Tigers (July 6, 2002). ... On suspended list (July 25-31, 2005).
CAREER HITTING: 0-for-19 (.000), 0 R, 0 2B, 0 3B, 0 HR, 0 RBI.

Year Team (League)	W	L	Pct.	ERA	WHIP	G	GS	CG	ShO	Hld.	Sv.-Opp.	IP	H	R	ER	HR	BB-IBB	SO	Avg.
2002— Modesto (California)	9	8	.529	3.61	1.27	25	25	1	0	...	0-...	144.2	129	77	58	15	55-11	160	.233
— Lakeland (Fla. St.)	0	1	.000	6.00	1.25	2	2	1	0	...	0-...	12.0	11	8	8	3	4-0	10	.262
2003— Detroit (A.L.)	6	19	.240	5.56	1.55	33	28	0	0	0	0-0	162.0	193	118	100	23	58-2	108	.294
2004— Detroit (A.L.)	11	13	.458	4.89	1.31	33	32	2	•2	0	0-0	184.0	168	101	100	24	73-5	168	.242
2005— Detroit (A.L.)	14	13	.519	4.57	1.35	29	29	4	0	0	0-0	189.0	199	101	96	21	57-0	145	.271
2006— Detroit (A.L.)	14	8	.636	4.08	1.30	34	•34	0	0	0	0-0	214.0	214	104	97	18	64-7	202	.259
Major League totals (4 years)	45	53	.459	4.72	1.37	129	123	6	2	0	0-0	749.0	774	424	393	86	252-14	623	.266

DIVISION SERIES RECORD

Year Team (League)	W	L	Pct.	ERA	WHIP	G	GS	CG	ShO	Hld.	Sv.-Opp.	IP	H	R	ER	HR	BB-IBB	SO	Avg.
2006— Detroit (A.L.)	1	0	1.000	2.16	0.72	1	1	0	0	0	0-0	8.1	5	2	2	0	1-0	4	.167

CHAMPIONSHIP SERIES RECORD

Year Team (League)	W	L	Pct.	ERA	WHIP	G	GS	CG	ShO	Hld.	Sv.-Opp.	IP	H	R	ER	HR	BB-IBB	SO	Avg.
2006— Detroit (A.L.)	0	0	...	4.05	1.20	1	1	0	0	0	0-0	6.2	6	3	3	1	2-0	5	.231

WORLD SERIES RECORD

Year Team (League)	W	L	Pct.	ERA	WHIP	G	GS	CG	ShO	Hld.	Sv.-Opp.	IP	H	R	ER	HR	BB-IBB	SO	Avg.
2006— Detroit (A.L.)	0	0	...	3.38	1.88	1	1	0	0	0	0-0	5.1	6	2	2	0	4-1	4	.300

2006 LEFTY-RIGHTY SPLITS

vs.	Avg.	AB	H	2B	3B	HR	RBI	BB	SO	OBP	Slg.	vs.	Avg.	AB	H	2B	3B	HR	RBI	BB	SO	OBP	Slg.
L	.284	405	115	27	8	11	52	42	88	.350	.472	R	.235	422	99	20	2	7	43	22	114	.275	.341

BONDS, BARRY — OF

PERSONAL: Born July 24, 1964, in Riverside, Calif. ... 6-2/228. ... Bats left, throws left. ... Full name: Barry Lamar Bonds. ... High school: Serra (San Mateo, Calif.). ... College: Arizona State. ... Son of Bobby Bonds, outfielder with eight major league teams (1968-81). **TRANSACTIONS/CAREER NOTES:** Selected by San Francisco Giants organization in second round of June 1982 free-agent draft; did not sign. ... Selected by Pittsburgh Pirates organization in first round (sixth pick overall) of June 1985 free-agent draft. ... On disabled list (June 15-July 4, 1992). ... Signed as a free agent by Giants (December 8, 1992). ... On suspended list (August 14-16, 1998). ... On disabled list (April 18-June 9, 1999). ... On disabled list (April 2-September 12, 2005). **RECORDS:** Holds major league records for most home runs, season (73, 2001); highest slugging percentage, season (.863, 2001); highest on-base percentage, season (.609, 2004); highest on-base plus slugging percentage, season (1.421, 2004); and most bases on balls, season (232, 2004). ... Holds major league record for most bases on balls, career (2,426). **HONORS:** Named Major League Player of the Year by THE SPORTING NEWS (1990, 2001 and 2004). ... Named N.L. Player of the Year by THE SPORTING NEWS (1990 and 1991). ... Named as an outfielder on THE SPORTING NEWS N.L. All-Star team (1990-94, 1996-97 and 2000-04). ... Named N.L. Most Valuable Player by Baseball Writers' Association of America (1990, 1992-93 and 2001-04). ... Won N.L. Gold Glove as outfielder (1990-94 and 1996-98). ... Named outfielder on N.L. Silver Slugger team (1990-94, 1996-97, 2000-04). **STATISTICAL NOTES:** Hit three home runs in one game (August 2, 1994; May 19 and September 9, 2001; and August 27, 2002). ... Career major league grand slams: 11.
2006 GAMES PLAYED BY POSITION (MLB): OF—116, DH—5.

									BATTING										FIELDING	
Year Team (League)	Pos.	G	AB	R	H	2B	3B	HR	RBI	BB	SO	HBP	GDP	SB-CS	Avg.	OBP	SLG	OPS	E	Avg.
1985— Prince Will. (Car.)	OF	71	254	49	76	16	4	13	37	37	52	0	3	15-3	.299	.383	.547	.930	5	.976
1986— Hawaii (PCL)	OF	44	148	30	46	7	2	7	37	33	31	2	1	16-5	.311	.435	.527	.963	2	.983
— Pittsburgh (N.L.)	OF	113	413	72	92	26	3	16	48	65	102	2	4	36-7	.223	.330	.416	.746	5	.983
1987— Pittsburgh (N.L.)	OF	150	551	99	144	34	9	25	59	54	88	3	4	32-10	.261	.329	.492	.821	5	.986
1988— Pittsburgh (N.L.)	OF	144	538	97	152	30	5	24	58	72	82	2	3	17-11	.283	.368	.491	.859	6	.980
1989— Pittsburgh (N.L.)	OF	159	580	96	144	34	6	19	58	93	93	1	9	32-10	.248	.351	.426	.777	6	.984
1990— Pittsburgh (N.L.)		151	519	104	156	32	3	33	114	93	83	3	6	52-13	.301	.406 *	.565	.970	6	.983
1991— Pittsburgh (N.L.)	OF	153	510	95	149	28	5	25	116	107	73	4	8	43-13	.292 *	.410	.514	.924	3	.991
1992— Pittsburgh (N.L.)	OF	140	473	* 109	147	36	5	34	103	* 127	69	5	9	39-8	.311 *	.456 *	.624	1.080	3	.991
1993— San Francisco (N.L.)	OF	159	539	129	181	38	4	* 46	* 123	126	79	2	11	29-12	.336 *	.458 *	.677	1.136	5	.984
1994— San Francisco (N.L.)	OF	112	391	89	122	18	1	37	81	* 74	43	6	3	29-9	.312	.426	.647	1.073	3	.984
1995— San Francisco (N.L.)	OF	* 144	506	109	149	30	7	33	104	* 120	83	5	12	31-10	.294 *	.432	.577	1.009	6	.980
1996— San Francisco (N.L.)	OF	158	517	122	159	27	3	42	129	* 151	76	1	11	40-7	.308	.461	.615	1.076	6	.984
1997— San Francisco (N.L.)	OF	159	532	123	155	26	5	40	101	* 145	87	8	13	37-8	.291	.446	.585	1.031	5	.984
1998— San Francisco (N.L.)	OF	156	552	120	167	44	7	37	122	130	92	8	15	28-12	.303	.438	.609	1.047	6	.984
1999— San Francisco (N.L.)	OF-DH	102	355	91	93	20	2	34	83	73	62	3	6	15-2	.262	.389	.617	1.006	3	.984
2000— San Francisco (N.L.)	OF	143	480	129	147	28	4	49	106	* 117	77	3	6	'11-3	.306	.440	.688	1.127	3	.989

Year	Team (League)	Pos.	G	AB	R	H	2B	3B	HR	RBI	BB	SO	HBP	GDP	SB-CS	Avg.	OBP	SLG	OPS	E	Avg.
															BATTING					FIELDING	
2001—San Francisco (N.L.)		OF-DH	153	476	129	156	32	2	*73	137	*177	93	9	5	13-3	.328	*.515	*.863	1.379	6	.977
2002—San Francisco (N.L.)		OF-DH	143	403	117	149	31	2	46	110	*198	47	9	4	9-2	*.370	*.582	*.799	1.381	8	.968
2003—San Francisco (N.L.)		OF-DH	130	390	111	133	22	1	45	90	*148	58	10	7	7-0	.341	*.529	*.749	1.278	2	.992
2004—San Francisco (N.L.)		OF-DH	147	373	129	135	27	3	45	101	*232	41	9	5	6-1	*.362	*.609	*.812	1.422	4	.983
2005—San Francisco (N.L.)		OF	14	42	8	12	1	0	5	10	9	6	0	0	0-0	.286	.404	.667	1.071	0	1.000
2006—San Francisco (N.L.)		OF-DH	130	367	74	99	23	0	26	77	*115	51	10	9	3-0	.270	.454	.545	.999	3	.985
Major League totals (21 years)			2860	9507	2152	2841	587	77	734	1930	2426	1485	103	152	509-141	.299	.443	.608	1.051	93	.984

DIVISION SERIES RECORD

Year	Team (League)	Pos.	G	AB	R	H	2B	3B	HR	RBI	BB	SO	HBP	GDP	SB-CS	Avg.	OBP	SLG	OPS	E	Avg.
1997—San Francisco (N.L.)		OF	3	12	0	3	2	0	0	2	0	3	0	0	1-0	.250	.231	.417	.647	0	1.000
2000—San Francisco (N.L.)		OF	4	17	2	3	1	1	0	1	3	4	0	0	1-0	.176	.300	.353	.653	0	1.000
2002—San Francisco (N.L.)		OF	5	17	5	5	0	0	3	4	4	1	0	0	0-1	.294	.409	.824	1.233	1	.909
2003—San Francisco (N.L.)		OF	4	9	3	2	1	0	0	2	8	0	0	0	1-0	.222	.556	.333	.889	0	1.000
Division series totals (4 years)			16	55	10	13	4	1	3	9	15	8	0	0	3-1	.236	.384	.509	.893	1	.968

CHAMPIONSHIP SERIES RECORD

Year	Team (League)	Pos.	G	AB	R	H	2B	3B	HR	RBI	BB	SO	HBP	GDP	SB-CS	Avg.	OBP	SLG	OPS	E	Avg.
1990—Pittsburgh (N.L.)		OF	6	18	4	3	0	0	0	1	6	5	0	0	2-0	.167	.375	.167	.542	0	1.000
1991—Pittsburgh (N.L.)		OF	7	27	1	4	1	0	0	0	2	4	0	1	3-0	.148	.207	.185	.392	1	.938
1992—Pittsburgh (N.L.)		OF	7	23	5	6	1	0	1	2	6	4	0	0	1-0	.261	.433	.435	.868	0	1.000
2002—San Francisco (N.L.)		OF	5	11	5	3	0	1	1	6	10	2	0	0	0-0	.273	.591	.727	1.318	0	1.000
Champ. series totals (4 years)			25	79	15	16	2	1	2	9	24	15	1	1	6-0	.203	.390	.329	.720	1	.982

WORLD SERIES RECORD

Year	Team (League)	Pos.	G	AB	R	H	2B	3B	HR	RBI	BB	SO	HBP	GDP	SB-CS	Avg.	OBP	SLG	OPS	E	Avg.
2002—San Francisco (N.L.)		OF	7	17	8	8	2	0	4	6	13	3	0	0	0-0	.471	.700	1.294	1.994	1	.909

ALL-STAR GAME RECORD

			G	AB	R	H	2B	3B	HR	RBI	BB	SO	HBP	GDP	SB-CS	Avg.	OBP	SLG	OPS	E	Avg.
All-Star Game totals (12 years)			12	29	5	6	3	0	2	7	4	5	0	0	1-1	.207	.294	.517	.811	0	1.000

2006 LEFTY-RIGHTY SPLITS

vs.	Avg.	AB	H	2B	3B	HR	RBI	BB	SO	OBP	Slg.
L	.255	106	27	4	0	8	22	33	18	.451	.519
R	.276	261	72	19	0	18	55	82	33	.456	.556

BONSER, BOOF — P

PERSONAL: Born October 14, 1981, in St. Petersburg, Fla. ... 6-4/230. ... Throws right, bats right. ... Full name: Boof Bonser. ... High school: Gibbs (St. Petersburg, Fla.).
TRANSACTIONS/CAREER NOTES: Selected by San Francisco Giants in first round (21st pick overall) of 2000 free-agent draft. ... Traded by Giants with Ps Joe Nathan and Francisco Liriano to Minnesota Twins for C A.J. Pierzynski and cash (November 14, 2003).
CAREER HITTING: 0-for-3 (.000), 1 R, 0 2B, 0 3B, 0 HR, 0 RBI.

Year	Team (League)	W	L	Pct.	ERA	WHIP	G	GS	CG	ShO	Hld.	Sv.-Opp.	IP	H	R	ER	HR	BB-IBB	SO	Avg.
2000—Salem-Keizer (N'west)		1	4	.200	6.00	1.52	10	9	0	0	...	0-...	33.0	21	23	22	2	29-0	41	.188
2001—Hagerstown (SAL)		16	4	.800	2.49	1.13	27	27	0	0	...	0-...	134.0	91	40	37	7	61-2	178	.192
2002—Shreveport (Texas)		1	2	.333	5.55	1.81	5	5	0	0	...	0-...	24.1	30	15	15	3	14-0	23	.316
— San Jose (Calif.)		8	5	.571	2.88	1.24	23	23	0	0	...	0-...	128.1	89	44	41	9	70-0	139	.195
2003—Norwich (East.)		7	10	.412	4.00	1.40	24	24	1	1	...	0-...	135.0	122	80	60	11	67-0	103	.245
— Fresno (PCL)		1	2	.333	3.13	1.09	4	4	0	0	...	0-...	23.0	17	13	8	4	8-0	28	.195
2004—New Britain (East.)		12	9	.571	4.37	1.40	27	27	0	0	...	0-...	154.1	160	89	75	22	56-1	146	.272
— Rochester (Int'l)		1	0	1.000	1.29	0.86	1	1	0	0	...	0-...	7.0	5	1	1	1	1-0	7	.200
2005—Rochester (Int'l)		11	9	.550	3.99	1.31	28	28	0	0	0	0-0	160.1	153	80	71	22	57-0	168	.251
2006—Rochester (Int'l)		6	4	.600	2.81	1.19	14	14	0	0	0	0-0	86.1	68	31	27	8	35-0	83	.211
— Minnesota (A.L.)		7	6	.538	4.22	1.28	18	18	0	0	0	0-0	100.1	104	50	47	18	24-0	84	.267
Major League totals (1 year)		7	6	.538	4.22	1.28	18	18	0	0	0	0-0	100.1	104	50	47	18	24-0	84	.267

DIVISION SERIES RECORD

Year	Team (League)	W	L	Pct.	ERA	WHIP	G	GS	CG	ShO	Hld.	Sv.-Opp.	IP	H	R	ER	HR	BB-IBB	SO	Avg.
2006—Minnesota (A.L.)		0	0	...	3.00	1.33	1	1	0	0	0	0-0	6.0	7	2	2	0	1-0	3	.292

2006 LEFTY-RIGHTY SPLITS

vs.	Avg.	AB	H	2B	3B	HR	RBI	BB	SO	OBP	Slg.
L	.251	183	46	8	1	9	16	14	46	.305	.454
R	.280	207	58	12	0	9	29	10	38	.314	.469

BOOKER, CHRIS — P

PERSONAL: Born December 9, 1976, in Monroeville, Ala. ... 6-3/230. ... Throws right, bats right. ... Full name: Christopher Scott Booker. ... High school: Monroe County (Monroeville, Ala.). **TRANSACTIONS/CAREER NOTES:** Selected by Chicago Cubs organization in 20th round of 1995 free-agent draft. ... Traded by Cubs with P Ben Shaffer to Cincinnati Reds for OF Michael Tucker (July 20, 2001). ... Signed as free agent by Washington Nationals organization (November 3, 2005). ... Selected by Detroit Tigers from Nationals organization in Rule 5 Draft; then traded by Tigers to Philadelphia Phillies for cash (December 8, 2005). ... On disabled list (March 29-May 10, 2006); included rehabilitation assignments to Clearwater and Scranton. ... Claimed on waivers by Kansas City Royals (May 10, 2006). ... On disabled list (May 15-July 9, 2006); included rehabilitation assignments to Omaha and Wichita. ... Returned to Nationals organization via Rule 6 of the Rule 5 draft (July 14, 2006).
CAREER HITTING: 0-for-0 (.000), 0 R, 0 2B, 0 3B, 0 HR, 0 RBI.

Year	Team (League)	W	L	Pct.	ERA	WHIP	G	GS	CG	ShO	Hld.	Sv.-Opp.	IP	H	R	ER	HR	BB-IBB	SO	Avg.
1995—GC Cubs (GCL)		3	2	.600	2.76	1.21	13	7	0	0	...	1-...	43.0	36	22	13	0	16-0	43	.232
1996—Daytona (Fla. St.)		0	0	...	0.00	1.33	1	1	0	0	...	0-...	3.0	1	0	0	0	3-0	2	.125
— Williamsport (NYP)		4	6	.400	5.31	1.77	14	14	0	0	...	0-...	61.0	57	51	36	2	51-1	52	.246
1997—Williamsport (NYP)		1	5	.167	3.35	1.40	24	3	0	0	...	1-...	45.2	39	20	17	2	25-0	60	.234
1998—Rockford (Midwest)		1	2	.333	3.18	1.54	44	1	0	0	...	4-...	65.0	47	32	24	2	53-4	'78	.212
1999—Daytona (Fla. St.)		2	5	.286	3.95	1.49	42	0	0	0	...	6-...	73.0	72	45	32	6	37-1	68	.254
2000—Daytona (Fla. St.)		0	2	.000	2.28	1.41	31	0	0	0	...	10-...	27.2	25	12	7	0	14-1	34	.238
— West Tenn (Sou.)		1	0	1.000	3.68	1.50	14	0	0	0	...	1-...	14.2	10	8	6	1	12-0	21	.189
2001—West Tenn (Sou.)		2	6	.250	4.33	1.44	45	0	0	0	...	1-...	52.0	39	29	25	7	36-2	76	.205
— Chattanooga (Sou.)		2	0	1.000	3.94	1.50	16	0	0	0	...	1-...	16.0	13	7	7	1	11-0	25	.217
2003—Dayton (Midw.)		0	0	...	9.00	1.60	5	0	0	0	...	0-...	5.0	4	5	5	3	4-0	6	.211
— GC Reds (GCL)		0	0	.000	8.49	2.14	12	0	0	0	...	2-...	11.2	17	11	11	1	8-0	11	.327
2004—Chattanooga (Sou.)		2	0	1.000	1.38	1.31	28	0	0	0	...	5-...	39.0	26	6	6	2	25-4	57	.182
— Louisville (Int'l)		0	0	.000	4.50	1.67	7	0	0	0	...	0-...	12.0	10	6	6	2	10-0	9	.213
2005—Louisville (Int'l)		8	4	.667	2.49	1.12	59	0	0	0	1	20-24	65.0	45	20	18	2	28-1	91	.195
— Cincinnati (N.L.)		0	0	...	31.50	5.00	3	0	0	0	0	0-0	2.0	6	8	7	2	4-0	2	.545

Year Team (League)	W	L	Pct.	ERA	WHIP	G	GS	CG	ShO	Hld.	Sv.-Opp.	IP	H	R	ER	HR	BB-IBB	SO	Avg.
2006—Clearwater (Fla. St.)	0	0	...	5.40	0.90	6	0	0	0	3	0-0	10.0	7	6	6	2	2-0	20	.194
—Scran./W.B. (I.L.)	0	0	...	1.29	1.00	6	0	0	0	1	0-1	7.0	4	1	1	1	3-0	7	.174
—Wichita (Texas)	0	0	...	4.15	1.38	4	0	0	0	0	0-0	4.1	6	4	2	0	0-0	5	.300
—Omaha (PCL)	0	0	...	7.71	1.93	4	0	0	0	0	0-0	4.2	6	4	4	2	3-0	6	.375
—Kansas City (A.L.)	0	0	...	54.00	8.00	1	0	0	0	0	0-0	1.0	5	6	6	3	3-0	0	.625
—New Orleans (PCL)	2	2	.500	3.94	1.69	15	0	0	0	3	0-0	16.0	14	7	7	0	13-0	29	.237
—Wash. (N.L.)	0	0	...	3.68	0.82	10	0	0	0	2	0-0	7.1	5	3	3	1	1-0	7	.192
American League totals (1 year)	0	0	...	54.00	8.00	1	0	0	0	0	0-0	1.0	5	6	6	3	3-0	0	.625
National League totals (2 years)	0	0	...	9.64	1.71	13	0	0	0	2	0-0	9.1	11	11	10	3	5-0	9	.297
Major League totals (2 years)	0	0	...	13.94	2.32	14	0	0	0	2	0-0	10.1	16	17	16	6	8-0	9	.356

2006 LEFTY-RIGHTY SPLITS

vs.	Avg.	AB	H	2B	3B	HR	RBI	BB	SO	OBP	Slg.	vs.	Avg.	AB	H	2B	3B	HR	RBI	BB	SO	OBP	Slg.
L	.200	10	2	1	0	0	0	3	3	.385	.300	R	.333	24	8	1	0	4	7	1	4	.360	.875

BOONE, AARON   3B

PERSONAL: Born March 9, 1973, in La Mesa, Calif. ... 6-2/200. ... Bats right, throws right. ... Full name: Aaron John Boone. ... High school: Villa Park (Calif.). ... College: Southern California. ... Son of Bob Boone, catcher with three major league teams (1972-90) and manager of Kansas City Royals (1995-97) and Cincinnati Reds (2001-03); brother of Bret Boone, second baseman with five major league teams (1992-2005); grandson of Ray Boone, infielder with six major league teams (1948-60).
TRANSACTIONS/CAREER NOTES: Selected by California Angels organization in 43rd round of 1991 free-agent draft; did not sign. ... Selected by Cincinnati Reds organization in third round of 1994 free-agent draft. ... On disabled list (July 10, 2000-remainder of season). ... On disabled list (May 15-June 15, August 15-September 1 and September 24, 2001-remainder of season); included rehabilitation assignment to Louisville. ... Traded by Reds to New York Yankees for Ps Brandon Claussen and Charlie Manning and cash (July 31, 2003). ... Released by Yankees (February 26, 2004). ... Signed by Cleveland Indians (June 26, 2004). ... On disabled list (June 26, 2004-remainder of season).
STATISTICAL NOTES: Hit three home runs in one game (August 9, 2002; and May 8, 2003). ... Career major league grand slams: 1.
2006 GAMES PLAYED BY POSITION (MLB): 3B—101, 2B—1, DH—1.

Year Team (League)	Pos.	G	AB	R	H	2B	3B	HR	RBI	BB	SO	HBP	GDP	SB-CS	Avg.	OBP	SLG	OPS	E	FIELDING Avg.
1994—Billings (Pion.)	1B-3B	67	256	48	70	15	5	7	55	36	35	3	7	6-3	.273	.362	.453	.815	18	.924
1995—Chattanooga (Sou.)	3B	23	66	6	15	3	0	0	3	5	12	0	5	2-0	.227	.274	.273	.547	6	.875
—Win.-Salem (Car.)	3B	108	395	61	103	19	1	14	50	43	77	9	4	11-7	.261	.345	.420	.765	21	.940
1996—Chattanooga (Sou.) 3B-SS-DH		136	548	86	158	44	7	17	95	38	77	5	5	21-10	.288	.338	.487	.825	22	.945
1997—Indianapolis (A.A.) 3B-SS-2B		131	476	79	138	30	4	22	75	40	81	1	11	12-4	.290	.344	.508	.853	24	.941
—Cincinnati (N.L.)	3B-2B	16	49	5	12	1	0	0	5	2	5	0	1	1-0	.245	.275	.265	.540	3	.917
1998—Cincinnati (N.L.) 3B-2B-SS		58	181	24	51	13	2	2	28	15	36	5	3	6-1	.282	.350	.409	.759	8	.944
—Indianapolis (Int'l) 3B-2B-SS		87	332	56	80	18	1	7	38	31	71	8	6	17-5	.241	.316	.364	.680	19	.943
1999—Cincinnati (N.L.) 3B-SS		139	472	56	132	26	5	14	72	30	79	8	6	17-6	.280	.330	.445	.775	15	.958
—Indianapolis (Int'l) 3B-2B-SS		11	41	6	14	2	1	0	7	3	4	2	1	2-2	.341	.388	.439	.827	3	.930
2000—Cincinnati (N.L.) 3B-SS		84	291	44	83	18	0	12	43	24	52	10	5	6-1	.285	.356	.471	.826	8	.965
2001—Cincinnati (N.L.)	3B	103	381	54	112	26	2	14	62	29	71	4	6	6-3	.294	.351	.483	.834	19	.936
—Louisville (Int'l)	3B	1	4	0	1	0	0	0	0	0	0	0	0	0-0	.250	.250	.250	.500	0	1.000
2002—Cincinnati (N.L.) 3B-SS		• 162	606	83	146	38	2	26	87	56	111	10	9	32-8	.241	.314	.439	.753	22	.945
2003—Cincinnati (N.L.) 3B-2B-SS		106	403	61	110	19	3	18	65	35	74	5	6	15-3	.273	.339	.469	.808	17	.943
—New York (A.L.)	3B	54	189	31	48	13	0	6	31	11	30	3	7	8-0	.254	.302	.418	.720	6	.961
2004—Cleveland (A.L.)								Did not play.												
2005—Cleveland (A.L.)	3B-DH	143	511	61	124	19	1	16	60	35	92	9	16	9-3	.243	.299	.378	.677	18	.955
2006—Cleveland (A.L.) 3B-2B-DH		104	354	50	89	19	1	7	46	27	62	6	4	5-4	.251	.314	.370	.684	16	.938
American League totals (3 years)		301	1054	142	261	51	2	29	137	73	184	18	27	22-7	.248	.305	.382	.687	40	.951
National League totals (7 years)		668	2383	327	646	141	14	86	362	191	428	46	39	83-22	.271	.334	.450	.785	92	.953
Major League totals (9 years)		969	3437	469	907	192	16	115	499	264	612	64	66	105-29	.264	.325	.429	.755	132	.952

DIVISION SERIES RECORD

Year Team (League)	Pos.	G	AB	R	H	2B	3B	HR	RBI	BB	SO	HBP	GDP	SB-CS	Avg.	OBP	SLG	OPS	E	Avg.
2003—New York (A.L.)	3B	4	15	1	3	1	0	0	2	0	3	0	0	1-0	.200	.200	.267	.467	0	1.000

CHAMPIONSHIP SERIES RECORD

Year Team (League)	Pos.	G	AB	R	H	2B	3B	HR	RBI	BB	SO	HBP	GDP	SB-CS	Avg.	OBP	SLG	OPS	E	Avg.
2003—New York (A.L.)	3B	7	17	2	3	0	0	1	2	1	6	1	0	1-1	.176	.263	.353	.616	2	.857

WORLD SERIES RECORD

Year Team (League)	Pos.	G	AB	R	H	2B	3B	HR	RBI	BB	SO	HBP	GDP	SB-CS	Avg.	OBP	SLG	OPS	E	Avg.
2003—New York (A.L.)	3B	6	21	1	3	0	0	1	2	0	6	0	0	0-0	.143	.136	.286	.422	3	.850

ALL-STAR GAME RECORD

		G	AB	R	H	2B	3B	HR	RBI	BB	SO	HBP	GDP	SB-CS	Avg.	OBP	SLG	OPS	E	Avg.
All-Star Game totals (1 year)		1	1	0	0	0	0	0	0	0	0	0	0	0-0	.000	.000	.000	.000	0	...

2006 LEFTY-RIGHTY SPLITS

vs.	Avg.	AB	H	2B	3B	HR	RBI	BB	SO	OBP	Slg.	vs.	Avg.	AB	H	2B	3B	HR	RBI	BB	SO	OBP	Slg.
L	.280	107	30	6	0	3	13	13	19	.369	.421	R	.239	247	59	13	1	4	33	14	43	.289	.348

BOOTCHECK, CHRIS   P

PERSONAL: Born October 24, 1978, in La Porte, Ind. ... 6-5/200. ... Throws right, bats right. ... Full name: Christopher Brandon Bootcheck. ... High school: La Porte (Ind.). ... College: Auburn. **TRANSACTIONS/CAREER NOTES:** Selected by Anaheim Angels in first round (20th pick overall) of 2000 free-agent draft. ... Angels franchise renamed Los Angeles Angels of Anaheim for 2005 season. ... On disabled list (May 4-22, 2006); included rehabilitation assignment to Salt Lake.
CAREER HITTING: 0-for-0 (.000), 0 R, 0 2B, 0 3B, 0 HR, 0 RBI.

Year Team (League)	W	L	Pct.	ERA	WHIP	G	GS	CG	ShO	Hld.	Sv.-Opp.	IP	H	R	ER	HR	BB-IBB	SO	Avg.
2001—Rancho Cuca. (Calif.)	8	4	.667	3.93	1.23	15	14	1	0	...	0-...	87.0	84	45	38	11	23-0	86	.251
—Arkansas (Texas)	3	3	.500	5.45	1.38	6	6	1	0	...	0-...	36.1	39	25	22	3	11-0	22	.265
2002—Arkansas (Texas)	8	7	.533	4.81	1.42	19	19	3	0	...	0-...	116.0	130	68	62	11	35-0	90	.277
—Salt Lake (PCL)	4	3	.571	3.88	1.38	9	9	1	1	...	0-...	58.0	64	29	25	5	16-0	38	.283
2003—Salt Lake (PCL)	8	9	.471	4.25	1.38	28	26	3	0	...	0-...	171.1	194	103	81	19	43-1	82	.290
—Anaheim (A.L.)	0	1	.000	9.58	2.13	4	1	0	0	...	0-...	10.1	16	13	11	5	6-0	7	.340
2004—Salt Lake (PCL)	11	9	.550	5.12	1.60	28	28	3	1	...	0-...	163.1	202	109	93	22	60-2	105	.306
2005—Los Angeles (A.L.)	0	1	.000	3.38	1.23	5	2	0	0	1	1-1	18.2	19	7	7	1	4-1	8	.257
—Salt Lake (PCL)	7	4	.636	5.42	1.67	21	21	0	0	...	0-0	116.1	144	75	70	13	50-0	90	.312
2006—Salt Lake (PCL)	4	3	.571	6.72	1.80	40	5	0	0	1	1-3	65.2	84	56	49	10	34-0	43	.318
—Los Angeles (A.L.)	0	1	.000	10.45	2.42	7	0	0	0	0	0-0	10.1	16	12	12	3	9-0	7	.364
Major League totals (3 years)	0	3	.000	6.86	1.78	16	3	0	0	1	1-1	39.1	51	32	30	9	19-1	22	.309

2006 LEFTY-RIGHTY SPLITS

vs.	Avg.	AB	H	2B	3B	HR	RBI	BB	SO	OBP	Slg.	vs.	Avg.	AB	H	2B	3B	HR	RBI	BB	SO	OBP	Slg.
L	.250	20	5	0	0	1	3	3	4	.348	.400	R	.458	24	11	4	0	2	10	6	3	.567	.875

BORCHARD, JOE — OF

PERSONAL: Born November 25, 1978, in Panorama City, Calif. ... 6-5/220. ... Bats both, throws right. ... Full name: Joseph Edward Borchard. ... Name pronounced: BORE-churd. ... High school: Camarillo (Calif.). ... College: Stanford. **TRANSACTIONS/CAREER NOTES:** Selected by Baltimore Orioles organization in 20th round of 1997 free-agent draft; did not sign. ... Selected by Chicago White Sox organization in first round (12th pick overall) of 2000 free-agent draft. ... Traded by White Sox to Seattle Mariners for P Matt Thornton (March 20, 2006). ... Claimed on waivers by Florida Marlins (May 3, 2006).

2006 GAMES PLAYED BY POSITION (MLB): OF—66, DH—3, 1B—1.

									BATTING										FIELDING	
Year	Team (League)	Pos.	G	AB	R	H	2B	3B	HR	RBI	BB	SO	HBP	GDP	SB-CS	Avg.	OBP	SLG	OPS	E	Avg.
2000—	Ariz. White Sox (Ariz.)	OF	7	29	3	12	4	0	0	8	4	4	0	0	0-0	.414	.485	.552	1.037	0	1.000
	Win.-Salem (Car.)	OF	14	52	7	15	3	0	2	7	6	9	2	0	0-0	.288	.377	.462	.839	0	1.000
	Birmingham (Sou.)	OF	6	22	3	5	0	1	0	3	3	8	0	1	0-0	.227	.308	.318	.626	1	.875
2001—	Birmingham (Sou.)	OF	133	515	95	152	27	1	27	98	67	158	10	13	5-4	.295	.384	.509	.892	12	.965
2002—	Win.-Salem (Car.)	OF	2	3	1	0	0	0	0	0	6	0	0	0	0-0	.000	.667	.000	.667	0	1.000
	Charlotte (Int'l)	OF	117	438	62	119	35	2	20	59	49	139	4	11	2-4	.272	.349	.498	.847	3	.990
	Chicago (A.L.)	OF	16	36	5	8	0	0	2	5	1	14	0	0	0-0	.222	.243	.389	.632	0	1.000
2003—	Chicago (A.L.)	OF	16	49	5	9	1	0	1	5	5	18	0	0	0-1	.184	.246	.265	.511	0	1.000
	Charlotte (Int'l)	OF	114	435	62	110	20	2	13	53	27	103	8	14	2-4	.253	.307	.398	.705	5	.985
2004—	Charlotte (Int'l)	OF-DH	82	301	44	80	21	0	16	48	30	68	2	7	4-3	.266	.333	.495	.828	4	.980
	Chicago (A.L.)	OF-DH	63	201	26	35	4	1	9	20	19	57	1	4	1-0	.174	.249	.338	.587	3	.972
2005—	Charlotte (Int'l)	OF-DH	134	494	69	130	20	0	29	67	50	143	4	19	6-4	.263	.335	.480	.815	6	.989
	Chicago (A.L.)	DH-OF	7	12	0	5	2	0	0	0	0	4	0	0	0-1	.417	.417	.583	1.000	0	1.000
2006—	Seattle (A.L.)	OF-DH	6	9	3	2	0	0	0	0	0	3	0	0	0-1	.222	.222	.222	.444	0	1.000
	Florida (N.L.)	OF-DH-1B	108	230	30	53	7	1	10	28	28	66	3	5	0-2	.230	.322	.400	.722	2	.982
	American League totals (5 years)		108	307	39	59	7	1	12	30	25	96	1	4	1-3	.192	.253	.339	.592	3	.982
	National League totals (1 year)		108	230	30	53	7	1	10	28	28	66	3	5	0-2	.230	.322	.400	.722	2	.982
	Major League totals (5 years)		216	537	69	112	14	2	22	58	53	162	4	9	1-5	.209	.283	.365	.648	5	.982

2006 LEFTY-RIGHTY SPLITS

vs.	Avg.	AB	H	2B	3B	HR	RBI	BB	SO	OBP	Slg.	vs.	Avg.	AB	H	2B	3B	HR	RBI	BB	SO	OBP	Slg.
L	.148	61	9	2	0	1	3	4	14	.212	.230	R	.258	178	46	5	1	9	25	24	55	.353	.449

BORKOWSKI, DAVE — P

PERSONAL: Born February 7, 1977, in Detroit, Mich. ... 6-1/200. ... Throws right, bats right. ... Full name: David Richard Borkowski. ... Name pronounced: boar-cow-ski. ... High school: Sterling Heights (Mich.). **TRANSACTIONS/CAREER NOTES:** Selected by Detroit Tigers organization in 11th round of 1995 free-agent draft. ... On disabled list (July 7, 2001-remainder of season). ... Released by Tigers (November 5, 2001). ... Re-signed by Tigers organization (November 7, 2001). ... Released by Tigers (April 27, 2003). ... Signed by Baltimore Orioles organization (May 2, 2003). ... Signed as a free agent by Houston Astros organization (December 22, 2005).

CAREER HITTING: 0-for-8 (.000), 0 R, 0 2B, 0 3B, 0 HR, 1 RBI.

Year	Team (League)	W	L	Pct.	ERA	WHIP	G	GS	CG	ShO	Hld.	Sv.-Opp.	IP	H	R	ER	HR	BB-IBB	SO	Avg.
1995—	GC Tigers (GCL)	3	2	.600	2.96	1.03	10	10	1	0	...	0-...	51.2	45	24	17	2	8-0	36	.227
	Lakeland (Fla. St.)	1	0	1.000	0.00	0.60	1	1	0	0	...	0-...	5.0	2	0	0	0	1-0	3	.125
1996—	Fayetteville (SAL)	10	10	.500	3.33	1.19	27	27	5	0	...	0-...	178.1	158	85	66	7	54-0	117	.239
1997—	W. Mich. (Mid.)	15	3	.833	3.46	1.06	25	25	4	2	...	0-...	164.0	143	79	63	15	31-0	104	.228
1998—	Jacksonville (Sou.)	16	7	.696	4.63	1.44	28	28	3	1	...	0-...	178.2	204	99	92	25	54-0	97	.291
1999—	Toledo (Int'l)	6	8	.429	3.50	1.29	19	19	3	0	...	0-...	126.0	119	59	49	16	43-0	94	.251
	Detroit (A.L.)	2	6	.250	6.10	1.64	17	12	0	0	0	0-0	76.2	86	58	52	10	40-0	50	.283
2000—	Toledo (Int'l)	3	1	.750	4.40	1.23	8	8	0	0	0	0-0	47.0	44	27	23	9	14-0	29	.239
	Detroit (A.L.)	0	1	.000	21.94	3.38	2	1	0	0	0	0-0	5.1	11	13	13	2	7-1	1	.423
	GC Tigers (GCL)	0	0	...	2.25	0.88	3	3	0	0	...	0-...	8.0	7	3	2	0	0-0	6	.219
	Lakeland (Fla. St.)	0	1	.000	8.59	2.05	2	2	0	0	...	0-...	7.1	11	7	7	1	4-0	5	.355
2001—	Toledo (Int'l)	1	2	.333	3.54	1.11	18	0	0	0	...	1-...	28.0	22	14	11	1	9-1	22	.214
	Detroit (A.L.)	0	2	.000	6.37	1.62	15	0	0	0	0	0-0	29.2	30	21	21	5	15-3	30	.261
2002—	GC Tigers (GCL)	0	0	...	8.44	1.69	3	2	0	0	...	0-...	5.1	9	5	5	2	0-0	4	.360
	Erie (East.)	0	2	.000	7.56	1.68	2	2	0	0	...	0-...	8.1	12	7	7	0	2-0	6	.343
2003—	Erie (East.)	0	1	.000	3.38	1.50	6	0	0	0	...	0-...	8.0	10	4	3	0	2-2	4	.333
	Bowie (East.)	6	7	.462	3.29	1.20	24	19	2	0	...	0-...	120.1	126	50	44	11	22-1	66	.271
2004—	Ottawa (Int'l)	6	9	.400	4.85	1.46	16	16	0	0	...	0-...	85.1	99	53	46	6	26-0	56	.294
	Baltimore (A.L.)	3	4	.429	5.14	1.43	17	8	0	0	1	0-1	56.0	65	37	32	6	15-1	45	.289
2005—	Ottawa (Int'l)	10	10	.500	4.34	1.40	29	28	1	0	...	0-0	182.2	217	99	88	18	38-3	104	.297
2006—	Round Rock (PCL)	0	1	.000	2.57	1.14	6	0	0	0	0	3-4	7.0	6	2	2	1	2-0	6	.250
	Houston (N.L.)	3	2	.600	4.69	1.31	40	0	0	0	1	0-0	71.0	70	38	37	8	23-7	52	.257
	American League totals (4 years)	5	13	.278	6.33	1.60	51	21	0	0	1	0-1	167.2	192	129	118	23	77-5	126	.287
	National League totals (1 year)	3	2	.600	4.69	1.31	40	0	0	0	1	0-0	71.0	70	38	37	8	23-7	52	.257
	Major League totals (5 years)	8	15	.348	5.84	1.52	91	21	0	0	2	0-1	238.2	262	167	155	31	100-12	178	.278

2006 LEFTY-RIGHTY SPLITS

vs.	Avg.	AB	H	2B	3B	HR	RBI	BB	SO	OBP	Slg.	vs.	Avg.	AB	H	2B	3B	HR	RBI	BB	SO	OBP	Slg.
L	.262	107	28	10	1	3	9	13	20	.339	.458	R	.255	165	42	10	2	5	31	10	32	.295	.430

BOROWSKI, JOE — P

PERSONAL: Born May 4, 1971, in Bayonne, N.J. ... 6-2/225. ... Throws right, bats right. ... Full name: Joseph Thomas Borowski. ... Name pronounced: bor-OW-ski. ... High school: Marist (Bayonne, N.J.). ... College: Rutgers. **TRANSACTIONS/CAREER NOTES:** Selected by Chicago White Sox organization in 32nd round of 1989 free-agent draft. ... Traded by White Sox to Baltimore Orioles for IF Pete Rose II (March 21, 1991). ... Traded by Orioles with P Rachaad Stewart to Atlanta Braves for P Kent Mercker (December 17, 1995). ... Claimed on waivers by New York Yankees (September 15, 1997). ... On disabled list (August 24-September 8, 1998). ... Claimed on waivers by Milwaukee Brewers (December 4, 1998). ... Signed as a free agent by Cincinnati Reds organization (November 9, 1999). ... Released by Reds (April 14, 2000). ... Signed by Newark of independent Atlantic League (2000). ... Signed by Monterrey of the Mexican League (2000). ... Signed by Chicago Cubs organization (December 11, 2000). ... On disabled list (June 5, 2004-remainder of season); included rehabilitation assignment to Iowa. ... On disabled list (March 25-May 20, 2005); included rehabilitation assignment to Iowa. ... Released by Cubs (July 7, 2005). ... Signed by Tampa Bay Devil Rays (July 14, 2005). ... Signed as a free agent by Florida Marlins (January 3, 2006). **MISCELLANEOUS NOTES:** Singled in only appearance as pinch hitter (2002).

CAREER HITTING: 2-for-9 (.222), 1 R, 0 2B, 0 3B, 0 HR, 0 RBI.

Year Team (League)	W	L	Pct.	ERA	WHIP	G	GS	CG	ShO	Hld.	Sv.-Opp.	IP	H	R	ER	HR	BB-IBB	SO	Avg.
1990— GC Whi. Sox (GCL)	2	8	.200	5.58	1.61	12	11	0	0	...	0-...	61.1	74	47	38	3	25-0	67	.289
1991— Kane Co. (Midw.)	7	2	.778	2.56	1.27	49	0	0	0	...	13-...	81.0	60	26	23	2	43-2	76	.207
1992— Frederick (Carolina)	5	6	.455	3.70	1.51	48	0	0	0	...	10-...	80.1	71	40	33	3	50-3	85	.238
1993— Frederick (Carolina)	1	1	.500	3.61	1.57	42	2	0	0	...	11-...	62.1	61	30	25	5	37-0	70	.258
—Bowie (East.)	3	0	1.000	0.00	1.25	9	0	0	0	...	0-...	17.2	11	0	0	0	11-3	17	.180
1994— Bowie (East.)	3	4	.429	1.91	1.21	49	0	0	0	...	14-...	66.0	52	14	14	3	28-3	73	.213
1995—Rochester (Int'l)	1	3	.250	4.04	1.40	28	0	0	0	...	6-...	35.2	32	16	16	3	18-2	32	.256
—Bowie (East.)	2	2	.500	3.92	1.11	16	0	0	0	...	7-...	20.2	16	9	9	2	7-1	32	.211
—Baltimore (A.L.)	0	0	...	1.23	1.23	6	0	0	0	0	0-0	7.1	5	1	1	0	4-0	3	.192
1996—Richmond (Int'l)	1	5	.167	3.71	1.35	34	0	0	0	...	7-...	53.1	42	25	22	4	30-1	40	.226
—Atlanta (N.L.)	2	4	.333	4.85	1.77	22	0	0	0	1	0-0	26.0	33	15	14	4	13-4	15	.324
1997—Atlanta (N.L.)	2	2	.500	3.75	1.79	20	0	0	0	2	0-0	24.0	27	11	10	2	16-4	6	.287
—Richmond (Int'l)	1	2	.333	3.58	1.35	21	0	0	0	...	2-...	37.2	32	16	15	3	19-2	34	.234
—New York (A.L.)	0	1	.000	9.00	3.00	1	0	0	0	0	0-0	2.0	2	2	2	0	4-1	2	.250
1998—Columbus (Int'l)	3	3	.500	2.93	1.43	45	0	0	0	...	4-...	73.2	66	25	24	6	39-1	67	.243
—New York (A.L.)	1	0	1.000	6.52	1.55	8	0	0	0	0	0-0	9.2	11	7	7	0	4-0	7	.289
1999—Louisville (Int'l)	6	2	.750	5.46	1.55	58	0	0	0	...	4-...	89.0	94	59	54	7	44-3	70	.275
2000—Newark (Atl.)	6	3	.667	5.50	1.62	28	0	0	0	...	0-...	37.2	44	23	23	5	17-...	39	
—Monterrey (Mex.)	4	2	.667	3.19	1.16	12	5	0	0	...	1-...	42.1	31	15	15	5	18-...	44	
2001—Iowa (PCL)	8	7	.533	2.62	1.03	39	12	1	1	...	1-...	110.0	87	35	32	10	26-3	131	.216
—Chicago (N.L.)	0	1	.000	32.40	5.40	1	1	0	0	0	0-0	1.2	6	6	6	1	3-0	1	.667
2002—Chicago (N.L.)	4	4	.500	2.73	1.18	73	0	0	0	12	2-6	95.2	84	31	29	10	29-6	97	.239
2003—Chicago (N.L.)	2	2	.500	2.63	1.05	68	0	0	0	1	33-37	68.1	53	23	20	5	19-1	66	.207
2004—Chicago (N.L.)	2	4	.333	8.02	1.97	22	0	0	0	0	9-11	21.1	27	19	19	3	15-2	17	.303
—Iowa (PCL)	0	3	.000	8.22	1.70	7	3	0	0	...	0-...	7.2	9	8	7	1	4-0	2	.290
2005—Iowa (PCL)	0	0	...	2.25	0.75	7	0	0	0	...	0-0	8.0	3	4	2	2	3-0	4	.107
—Chicago (N.L.)	0	0	...	6.55	1.18	11	0	0	0	1	0-0	11.0	12	8	8	5	1-0	11	.261
—Tampa Bay (A.L.)	1	5	.167	3.82	1.05	32	0	0	0	19	0-4	35.1	26	15	15	3	11-1	16	.208
2006—Florida (N.L.)	3	3	.500	3.75	1.38	72	0	0	0	0	36-43	69.2	63	31	29	7	33-7	64	.235
American League totals (4 years)	2	6	.250	4.14	1.23	47	0	0	0	19	0-4	54.1	44	25	25	3	23-2	28	.223
National League totals (8 years)	15	20	.429	3.82	1.37	289	1	0	0	17	80-97	317.2	305	144	135	37	129-24	277	.251
Major League totals (10 years)	17	26	.395	3.87	1.35	336	1	0	0	36	80-101	372.0	349	169	160	40	152-26	305	.247

DIVISION SERIES RECORD

Year Team (League)	W	L	Pct.	ERA	WHIP	G	GS	CG	ShO	Hld.	Sv.-Opp.	IP	H	R	ER	HR	BB-IBB	SO	Avg.
2003—Chicago (N.L.)	0	0	...	0.00	0.50	2	0	0	0	0	1-1	2.0	1	0	0	0	0-0	5	.143

CHAMPIONSHIP SERIES RECORD

Year Team (League)	W	L	Pct.	ERA	WHIP	G	GS	CG	ShO	Hld.	Sv.-Opp.	IP	H	R	ER	HR	BB-IBB	SO	Avg.
2003—Chicago (N.L.)	1	0	1.000	1.59	1.41	3	0	0	0	0	0-1	5.2	5	2	1	0	3-1	1	.227

2006 LEFTY-RIGHTY SPLITS

vs.	Avg.	AB	H	2B	3B	HR	RBI	BB	SO	OBP	Slg.	vs.	Avg.	AB	H	2B	3B	HR	RBI	BB	SO	OBP	Slg.
L	.167	120	20	2	1	3	10	28	35	.324	.275	R	.291	148	43	11	1	4	18	5	29	.323	.459

BOTTS, JASON — OF

PERSONAL: Born July 26, 1980, in Paso Robles, Calif. ... 6-5/250. ... Bats both, throws right. ... Full name: Jason Carl Botts. ... High school: Paso Robles (Calif.). ... Junior college: Glendale (Calif.) C.C. TRANSACTIONS/CAREER NOTES: Selected by Texas Rangers organization in 46th round of 1999 free-agent draft.
2006 GAMES PLAYED BY POSITION (MLB): DH—13, OF—1.

Year Team (League)	Pos.	G	AB	R	H	2B	3B	HR	RBI	BB	SO	HBP	GDP	SB-CS	Avg.	OBP	SLG	OPS	E	Avg.
2000—GC Rangers (GCL)	1B	48	163	36	52	12	0	6	34	26	29	10	5	4-1	.319	.440	.503	.943	4	.991
2001—Savannah (S. Atl.)	1B-OF	114	392	63	121	24	2	9	50	53	88	20	10	13-7	.309	.416	.449	.865	8	.985
—Charlotte (Fla. St.)	OF	4	12	1	2	1	0	0	4	4	0	0	0	0-0	.167	.375	.250	.625	0	1.000
2002—Charlotte (Fla. St.)	OF	116	401	67	102	22	5	9	54	75	99	14	4	7-2	.254	.387	.401	.788	4	.983
2003—Stockton (Calif.)	1B	76	283	58	89	14	2	9	61	45	59	1	8	12-3	.314	.409	.473	.882	16	.977
—Frisco (Texas)	OF-1B	55	194	26	51	11	1	4	27	21	45	3	6	6-1	.263	.341	.392	.733	5	.972
2004—Frisco (Texas)	OF-1B	133	481	85	141	25	3	24	92	77	126	10	18	7-4	.293	.399	.507	.906	19	.992
2005—Oklahoma (PCL)	OF-DH	133	510	93	146	31	7	25	102	67	152	8	13	2-4	.286	.375	.522	.897	14	.948
—Texas (A.L.)	OF-DH	10	27	4	8	0	0	0	3	3	13	0	1	0-0	.296	.367	.296	.663	1	.900
2006—Oklahoma (PCL)		63	220	43	68	19	1	13	39	31	61	4	3	6-0	.309	.398	.582	.980	6	.971
—Frisco (Texas)		5	16	3	2	0	0	0	2	3	3	0	1	0-0	.125	.250	.125	.375	0	1.000
—Texas (A.L.)	DH-OF	20	50	8	11	4	0	1	6	8	18	0	0	0-0	.220	.317	.360	.677	0	1.000
—Ariz. Rangers (AZL)		3	12	1	3	2	0	0	1	2	1	0	0	0-0	.250	.357	.417	.774	0	1.000
Major League totals (2 years)		30	77	12	19	4	0	1	9	11	31	0	1	0-0	.247	.333	.338	.671	1	.909

2006 LEFTY-RIGHTY SPLITS

vs.	Avg.	AB	H	2B	3B	HR	RBI	BB	SO	OBP	Slg.	vs.	Avg.	AB	H	2B	3B	HR	RBI	BB	SO	OBP	Slg.
L	.100	10	1	0	0	0	1	1	4	.167	.100	R	.250	40	10	4	0	1	5	7	14	.354	.425

BOURN, MICHAEL — OF

PERSONAL: Born December 27, 1982, in Houston, Texas. ... Bats left, throws right. ... Full name: Michael Ray Bourn. ... High school: Nimitz (Texas). ... College: Houston.
TRANSACTIONS/CAREER NOTES: Selected by Philadelphia Phillies organization in fourth round of 2003 free-agent draft.
2006 GAMES PLAYED BY POSITION (MLB): OF—15.

Year Team (League)	Pos.	G	AB	R	H	2B	3B	HR	RBI	BB	SO	HBP	GDP	SB-CS	Avg.	OBP	SLG	OPS	E	Avg.
2003—Batavia (NY-Penn)		35	125	12	35	0	1	0	4	23	28	3	2	23-5	.280	.404	.296	.700	2	...
2004—Lakewood (S. Atl.)		109	413	92	131	20	14	5	53	85	88	3	1	57-6	.317	.433	.470	.903	5	...
2005—Reading (East.)	OF-DH	135	544	80	146	18	8	6	44	63	123	3	2	38-12	.268	.348	.364	.712	4	.997
2006—Reading (East.)		80	318	62	87	5	6	4	26	36	67	2	3	30-4	.274	.350	.365	.715	4	.981
—Scran./W.B. (I.L.)		38	152	34	43	5	7	1	15	20	33	1	2	15-1	.283	.368	.428	.795	1	.989
—Philadelphia (N.L.)	OF	17	8	2	1	0	0	0	0	3	0	1	0	1-2	.125	.222	.125	.347	0	1.000
Major League totals (1 year)		17	8	2	1	0	0	0	0	3	0	1	0	1-2	.125	.222	.125	.347	0	1.000

2006 LEFTY-RIGHTY SPLITS

vs.	Avg.	AB	H	2B	3B	HR	RBI	BB	SO	OBP	Slg.	vs.	Avg.	AB	H	2B	3B	HR	RBI	BB	SO	OBP	Slg.
L	.000	1	0	0	0	0	0	0	0	.000	.000	R	.143	7	1	0	0	0	0	1	3	.250	.143

BOWEN, ROB — C

PERSONAL: Born February 24, 1981, in Bedford, Texas. ... 6-3/216. ... Bats both, throws right. ... Full name: Robert McClure Bowen. ... High school: Homestead (Fort Wayne, Ind.). **TRANSACTIONS/CAREER NOTES:** Selected by Minnesota Twins organization in second round of 1999 free-agent draft. ... Claimed on waivers by Detroit Tigers (March 29, 2006). ... Claimed on waivers by San Diego Padres (April 3, 2006). ... On disabled list (May 12-28, 2006); included rehabilitation assignment to Lake Elsinore.

2006 GAMES PLAYED BY POSITION (MLB): C—65, DH—1, 1B—1.

									BATTING									FIELDING	
Year Team (League)	Pos.	G	AB	R	H	2B	3B	HR	RBI	BB	SO	HBP	GDP	SB-CS	Avg.	OBP	SLG	OPS	E	Avg.
1999— GC Twins (GCL)	C	29	77	10	20	4	0	0	11	20	15	0	0	2-2	.260	.400	.312	.712	8	.959
2000— Elizabethton (App.)	C	21	73	17	21	3	0	4	19	11	18	0	0	0-0	.288	.381	.493	.874	3	.983
2001— Quad City (Midw.)	C	106	385	47	98	18	2	18	70	37	112	2	11	4-0	.255	.321	.452	.773	6	.993
2002— Fort Myers (Fla. St.)	C-1B	100	342	52	63	12	1	10	49	38	69	5	12	1-0	.184	.272	.313	.585	12	.981
— Quad City (Midw.)	C	5	21	1	4	1	0	0	2	2	4	0	0	0-0	.190	.261	.238	.499	0	1.000
2003— New Britain (East.)	C	42	134	17	41	13	0	1	16	13	24	2	0	0-0	.306	.376	.425	.801	1	.992
— Rochester (Int'l)	C-DH	30	105	14	27	7	0	6	17	11	25	1	3	0-0	.257	.333	.495	.829	1	.995
— Minnesota (A.L.)	C	7	10	0	1	0	0	0	1	0	4	0	1	0-0	.100	.091	.100	.191	1	.944
2004— Minnesota (A.L.)	C-DH	17	27	1	3	0	0	1	2	4	10	0	1	0-0	.111	.226	.222	.448	1	.985
— New Britain (East.)	C-DH	77	249	28	49	10	0	9	24	31	76	3	3	3-0	.197	.292	.345	.638	8	.985
2005— Rochester (Int'l)	C-DH	87	262	38	70	13	2	6	25	37	68	4	7	0-2	.267	.366	.401	.767	4	.992
2006— Lake Elsinore (Calif.)		2	7	0	1	0	0	0	0	0	2	0	0	0-0	.143	.143	.143	.286	0	1.000
— San Diego (N.L.)	C-1B-DH	94	94	22	23	5	0	3	13	13	26	1	1	0-1	.245	.339	.394	.733	1	.994
American League totals (2 years)		24	37	1	4	0	0	1	3	4	14	0	2	0-0	.108	.190	.189	.380	2	.976
National League totals (1 year)		94	94	22	23	5	0	3	13	13	26	1	1	0-1	.245	.339	.394	.733	1	.994
Major League totals (3 years)		118	131	23	27	5	0	4	16	17	40	1	3	0-1	.206	.298	.336	.634	3	.988

DIVISION SERIES RECORD

Year Team (League)	Pos.	G	AB	R	H	2B	3B	HR	RBI	BB	SO	HBP	GDP	SB-CS	Avg.	OBP	SLG	OPS	E	Avg.
2006— San Diego (N.L.)	C	1	1	0	1	0	0	0	0	0	0	0	0	0-0	1.000	1.000	1.000	2.000	0	1.000

2006 LEFTY-RIGHTY SPLITS

vs.	Avg.	AB	H	2B	3B	HR	RBI	BB	SO	OBP	Slg.	vs.	Avg.	AB	H	2B	3B	HR	RBI	BB	SO	OBP	Slg.
L	.167	18	3	0	0	0	1	5	7	.333	.167	R	.263	76	20	5	0	3	12	8	19	.341	.447

BOWIE, MICAH — P

PERSONAL: Born November 10, 1974, in Webster, Texas. ... 6-4/203. ... Throws left, bats left. ... Full name: Micah Andrew Bowie. ... Name pronounced: BOO-ee. ... High school: Kingwood (Texas). **TRANSACTIONS/CAREER NOTES:** Signed as non-drafted free agent by Atlanta Braves organization (July 15, 1993). ... Traded by Braves with P Ruben Quevedo and a player to be named to Chicago Cubs for P Terry Mulholland and SS Jose Hernandez (July 31, 1999); Cubs acquired P Joey Nation to complete deal (August 24, 1999). ... Released by Cubs (November 27, 2000). ... Signed by Oakland Athletics organization (December 20, 2000). ... On disabled list (May 23, 2003-remainder of season); included rehabilitation assignments to Modesto and Sacramento. ... Released by Athletics (October 13, 2003). ... Signed by Washington Nationals organization (December 23, 2004). ... On disabled list (August 10, 2006-remainder of season).

CAREER HITTING: 3-for-15 (.200), 0 R, 0 2B, 0 3B, 0 HR, 3 RBI.

Year Team (League)	W	L	Pct.	ERA	WHIP	G	GS	CG	ShO	Hld.	Sv.-Opp.	IP	H	R	ER	HR	BB-IBB	SO	Avg.
1994— GC Braves (GCL)	0	3	.000	3.03	1.08	6	5	0	0	...	0-...	29.2	27	14	10	1	5-0	35	.233
— Danville (Appal.)	3	1	.750	3.58	1.26	7	5	0	0	...	0-...	32.2	28	16	13	4	13-1	38	.233
1995— Macon (S. Atl.)	4	1	.800	2.28	0.72	5	5	0	0	...	0-...	27.2	9	8	7	1	11-0	36	.100
— Durham (Carol.)	4	11	.267	3.59	1.38	23	23	1	0	...	0-...	130.1	119	65	52	8	61-3	91	.250
1996— Durham (Carol.)	3	6	.333	3.66	1.33	13	13	0	0	...	0-...	66.1	55	29	27	4	33-0	65	.235
1997— Durham (Carol.)	2	2	.500	3.66	1.42	9	6	0	0	...	0-...	39.1	29	16	16	2	27-0	44	.210
— Greenville (Sou.)	3	2	.600	3.50	1.37	7	7	0	0	...	0-...	43.2	34	19	17	3	26-1	41	.211
1998— Greenville (Sou.)	11	6	.647	3.48	1.20	30	29	1	0*	...	0-...	163.0	132	73	63	12	64-0	160	.221
1999— Richmond (Int'l)	4	4	.500	2.96	1.08	13	13	0	0	...	0-...	73.0	65	24	24	4	14-0	82	.241
— Atlanta (N.L.)	0	1	.000	13.50	3.00	3	0	0	0	0	0-0	4.0	8	6	6	1	4-0	2	.421
— Chicago (N.L.)	2	6	.250	9.96	2.19	11	11	0	0	0	0-0	47.0	73	54	52	8	30-2	39	.358
2000— Iowa (PCL)	1	7	.125	7.94	1.99	9	9	0	0	...	0-...	45.1	59	44	40	9	31-3	35	.321
— West Tenn (Sou.)	7	6	.538	3.45	1.18	18	18	1	1	...	0-...	117.1	91	47	45	6	48-1	106	.216
2001— Sacramento (PCL)	6	8	.429	5.04	1.44	38	10	1	1	...	3-...	116.0	123	68	65	13	44-1	102	.272
2002— Sacramento (PCL)	3	2	.600	3.13	1.17	46	0	0	0	...	4-...	54.2	40	21	19	2	24-2	64	.201
— Oakland (A.L.)	2	0	1.000	1.50	1.67	13	0	0	0	3	0-0	12.0	12	2	2	1	8-1	8	.261
2003— Oakland (A.L.)	0	1	.000	7.56	1.80	6	0	0	0	0	0-0	8.1	13	7	7	1	2-0	4	.361
— Modesto (California)	0	0	...	0.00	0.00	2	2	0	0	...	0-...	2.0	0	0	0	0	1-0	3	.000
— Sacramento (PCL)	0	0	...	0.00	0.80	5	0	0	0	...	2-...	4.0	3	1	0	0	1-0	1	.133
2004—			Did not play.																
2005— GC Nationals (GCL)	1	0	1.000	1.08	1.20	7	2	0	0	0	0-0	8.1	1	1	1	0	1-0	12	.290
— Harrisburg (East.)	1	1	.500	4.41	1.16	10	0	0	0	1	1-2	16.1	16	8	8	1	3-0	19	.254
2006— New Orleans (PCL)	2	0	1.000	3.83	1.35	31	0	0	0	5	1-1	42.1	33	20	18	0	24-0	57	.213
— Wash. (N.L.)	0	1	1.000	0.92	1.50	15	0	0	0	5	0-0	19.2	11	3	3	1	7-0	11	.164
American League totals (2 years)	2	1	.667	3.98	1.72	19	0	0	0	3	0-0	20.1	25	9	9	2	10-1	12	.305
National League totals (2 years)	2	8	.200	7.77	1.88	29	11	0	0	5	0-0	70.2	92	63	61	10	41-2	52	.317
Major League totals (4 years)	4	9	.308	6.92	1.85	48	11	0	0	12	0-0	91.0	117	72	70	12	51-3	64	.315

DIVISION SERIES RECORD

Year Team (League)	W	L	Pct.	ERA	WHIP	G	GS	CG	ShO	Hld.	Sv.-Opp.	IP	H	R	ER	HR	BB-IBB	SO	Avg.
2002— Oakland (A.L.)	0	0	...	0.00	0.00	1	0	0	0	0	0-0	1.1	0	0	0	0	0-0	3	.000

2006 LEFTY-RIGHTY SPLITS

vs.	Avg.	AB	H	2B	3B	HR	RBI	BB	SO	OBP	Slg.	vs.	Avg.	AB	H	2B	3B	HR	RBI	BB	SO	OBP	Slg.
L	.273	22	6	1	0	0	1	1	2	.304	.318	R	.111	45	5	2	0	1	1	6	9	.216	.222

BOYER, BLAINE — P

PERSONAL: Born July 11, 1981, in Atlanta. ... 6-3/215. ... Throws right, bats right. ... Full name: Blaine Thomas Boyer. ... High school: Walton (Marietta, Ga.). **TRANSACTIONS/CAREER NOTES:** Selected by Atlanta Braves organization in third round of 2000 free-agent draft. ... On disabled list (June 24, 2006-remainder of season).

CAREER HITTING: 0-for-0 (.000), 0 R, 0 2B, 0 3B, 0 HR, 0 RBI.

Year Team (League)	W	L	Pct.	ERA	WHIP	G	GS	CG	ShO	Hld.	Sv.-Opp.	IP	H	R	ER	HR	BB-IBB	SO	Avg.
2000— GC Braves (GCL)	1	3	.250	2.51	1.33	11	5	0	0	...	1-...	32.1	24	16	9	0	19-0	27	.200
2001— Danville (Appal.)	4	5	.444	4.32	1.34	13	12	0	0	...	0-...	50.0	48	35	24	4	19-0	57	.250
2002— Macon (S. Atl.)	5	9	.357	3.07	1.29	43	0	0	0	...	1-...	70.1	52	30	24	0	39-3	73	.207

Year	Team (League)	W	L	Pct.	ERA	WHIP	G	GS	CG	ShO	Hld.	Sv.-Opp.	IP	H	R	ER	HR	BB-IBB	SO	Avg.
2003— Rome (S. Atl.)		12	8	.600	3.69	1.49	30	26	1	0	...	0-...	136.2	146	70	56	5	58-0	115	.271
2004— Myrtle Beach (Carol.)		10	10	.500	2.98	1.21	28	28	0	0	...	0-...	154.0	138	63	51	4	49-0	95	.250
2005— Mississippi (Sou.)		2	4	.333	5.03	1.66	14	8	0	0	2	0-0	48.1	62	28	27	4	18-3	40	.321
—Atlanta (N.L.)		4	2	.667	3.11	1.30	43	0	0	0	9	0-2	37.2	32	13	13	1	17-0	33	.234
2006— Atlanta (N.L.)		0	0	...	40.50	7.50	2	0	0	0	1	0-0	0.2	4	3	3	0	1-0	0	.667
Major League totals (2 years)		4	2	.667	3.76	1.41	45	0	0	0	10	0-2	38.1	36	16	16	1	18-0	33	.252

2006 LEFTY-RIGHTY SPLITS

vs.	Avg.	AB	H	2B	3B	HR	RBI	BB	SO	OBP	Slg.	vs.	Avg.	AB	H	2B	3B	HR	RBI	BB	SO	OBP	Slg.
L	.750	4	3	0	0	0	0	1	0	.800	.750	R	.500	2	1	0	0	0	0	2	0	.500	.500

BRADFORD, CHAD — P

PERSONAL: Born September 14, 1974, in Jackson, Miss. ... 6-5/203. ... Throws right, bats right. ... Full name: Chadwick Lee Bradford. ... High school: Byram (Jackson, Miss.). ... College: Southern Mississippi. **TRANSACTIONS/CAREER NOTES:** Selected by Chicago White Sox organization in 34th round of 1994 free-agent draft; did not sign. ... Selected by White Sox organization in 13th round of 1996 free-agent draft. ... Traded by White Sox to Oakland Athletics for a player to be named (December 7, 2000); White Sox acquired C Miguel Olivo to complete deal (December 13, 2000). ... On disabled list (August 8-23, 2004); included rehabilitation assignment to Sacramento. ... On disabled list (March 30-July 13, 2005); included rehabilitation assignments to AZL Athletics, Sacramento and Stockton. ... Traded by Athletics to Boston Red Sox for OF Jay Payton (July 14, 2005). ... Signed as a free agent by New York Mets (December 28, 2005).

CAREER HITTING: 0-for-0 (.000), 0 R, 0 2B, 0 3B, 0 HR, 0 RBI.

Year	Team (League)	W	L	Pct.	ERA	WHIP	G	GS	CG	ShO	Hld.	Sv.-Opp.	IP	H	R	ER	HR	BB-IBB	SO	Avg.
1996— Hickory (S. Atl.)		0	2	.000	0.90	0.93	28	0	0	0	...	18-...	30.0	21	7	3	1	7-1	27	.194
1997— Win.-Salem (Car.)		3	7	.300	3.95	1.39	46	0	0	0	...	15-...	54.2	51	30	24	2	25-5	43	.239
1998— Birmingham (Sou.)		1	1	.500	2.60	1.21	10	0	0	0	...	1-...	17.1	13	6	5	2	8-0	14	.203
—Calgary (PCL)		4	1	.800	1.94	1.20	29	0	0	0	...	0-...	51.0	50	12	11	3	11-2	27	.260
—Chicago (A.L.)		2	1	.667	3.23	1.11	29	0	0	0	9	1-3	30.2	27	16	11	0	7-0	11	.229
1999— Charlotte (Int'l)		9	3	.750	1.94	1.05	47	0	0	0	...	5-...	74.1	63	19	16	2	15-0	56	.231
—Chicago (A.L.)		0	0	...	19.64	3.82	3	0	0	0	0	0-0	3.2	9	8	8	1	5-0	0	.474
2000— Charlotte (Int'l)		2	4	.333	1.51	0.93	55	0	0	0	...	10-...	53.2	38	18	9	2	12-1	42	.200
—Chicago (A.L.)		1	0	1.000	1.98	1.02	12	0	0	0	2	0-0	13.2	13	4	3	0	1-1	9	.255
2001— Sacramento (PCL)		0	0	...	0.38	0.72	12	0	0	0	...	2-...	23.2	15	2	1	0	2-0	24	.181
—Oakland (A.L.)		2	1	.667	2.70	1.28	35	0	0	0	4	1-4	36.2	41	12	11	6	6-0	34	.281
2002— Oakland (A.L.)		4	2	.667	3.11	1.15	75	0	0	0	24	2-5	75.1	73	29	26	2	14-5	56	.253
2003— Oakland (A.L.)		7	4	.636	3.04	1.26	72	0	0	0	23	2-5	77.0	67	28	26	7	30-9	62	.236
2004— Sacramento (PCL)		0	0	...	0.00	0.50	2	0	0	0	...	0-...	2.0	1	0	0	0	0-0	3	.143
—Oakland (A.L.)		5	7	.417	4.42	1.27	68	0	0	0	14	1-4	59.0	51	32	29	5	24-9	34	.234
2005— Ariz. A's (Ariz.)		0	0	...	0.00	1.00	3	3	0	0	0	0-0	3.0	3	0	0	0	0-0	2	.273
—Sacramento (PCL)		0	0	...	6.00	1.33	3	1	0	0	0	0-0	3.0	4	2	2	1	0-0	1	.333
—Stockton (Calif.)		0	0	...	3.86	1.71	3	0	0	0	1	0-0	2.1	3	1	1	0	1-0	1	.300
—Boston (A.L.)		2	1	.667	3.86	1.41	31	0	0	0	8	0-1	23.1	29	10	10	1	4-1	10	.312
2006— New York (N.L.)		4	2	.667	2.90	1.16	70	0	0	0	10	2-3	62.0	59	22	20	1	13-4	45	.254
American League totals (8 years)		23	16	.590	3.49	1.26	325	0	0	0	84	7-22	319.1	310	139	124	22	91-25	216	.255
National League totals (1 year)		4	2	.667	2.90	1.16	70	0	0	0	10	2-3	62.0	59	22	20	1	13-4	45	.254
Major League totals (9 years)		27	18	.600	3.40	1.24	395	0	0	0	94	9-25	381.1	369	161	144	23	104-29	261	.255

DIVISION SERIES RECORD

Year	Team (League)	W	L	Pct.	ERA	WHIP	G	GS	CG	ShO	Hld.	Sv.-Opp.	IP	H	R	ER	HR	BB-IBB	SO	Avg.
2000— Chicago (A.L.)		0	0	...	0.00	3.00	1	0	0	0	0	0-1	0.2	2	0	0	0	0-0	0	.667
2001— Oakland (A.L.)		0	0	...	0.00	0.00	1	0	0	0	0	0-0	1.0	0	0	0	0	0-0	1	.000
2002— Oakland (A.L.)		0	0	...	0.00	0.33	2	0	0	0	0	0-0	3.0	1	0	0	0	0-0	1	.111
2003— Oakland (A.L.)		0	0	...	0.00	1.64	4	0	0	0	0	0-0	3.2	4	0	0	0	2-2	5	.286
2005— Boston (A.L.)		0	0	...	0.00	0.75	2	0	0	0	0	0-0	1.1	1	0	0	0	0-0	1	.200
2006— New York (N.L.)		0	0	...	0.00	6.00	2	0	0	0	0	0-0	0.1	1	0	0	0	1-0	0	.500
Division series totals (6 years)		0	0	...	0.00	1.20	12	0	0	0	0	0-1	10.0	9	0	0	0	3-2	8	.250

CHAMPIONSHIP SERIES RECORD

Year	Team (League)	W	L	Pct.	ERA	WHIP	G	GS	CG	ShO	Hld.	Sv.-Opp.	IP	H	R	ER	HR	BB-IBB	SO	Avg.
2006— New York (N.L.)		0	0	...	0.00	0.56	5	0	0	0	0	0-0	5.1	3	0	0	0	0-0	2	.176

2006 LEFTY-RIGHTY SPLITS

vs.	Avg.	AB	H	2B	3B	HR	RBI	BB	SO	OBP	Slg.	vs.	Avg.	AB	H	2B	3B	HR	RBI	BB	SO	OBP	Slg.
L	.250	60	15	4	0	0	4	6	13	.318	.317	R	.256	172	44	10	0	1	24	7	32	.280	.331

BRADLEY, MILTON — OF

PERSONAL: Born April 15, 1978, in Harbor City, Calif. ... 6-0/205. ... Bats both, throws right. ... Full name: Milton Obelle Bradley. ... High school: Polytechnic (Long Beach, Calif.). **TRANSACTIONS/CAREER NOTES:** Selected by Montreal Expos organization in second round of 1996 free-agent draft. ... Traded by Expos to Cleveland Indians for P Zach Day (July 31, 2001). ... On disabled list (May 2-June 4 and August 14-30, 2002); included rehabilitation assignments to Buffalo and Akron. ... On disabled list (April 23-May 8 and August 15, 2003-remainder of season). ... Traded by Indians to Los Angeles Dodgers for OF Franklin Gutierrez and a player to be named (April 3, 2004); Indians acquired P Andrew Brown to complete deal (May 19, 2004). ... On suspended list (September 29, 2004-remainder of season). ... On disabled list (June 3-July 23; and August 25, 2005-remainder of season); included rehabilitation assignments to Las Vegas. ... Traded by Dodgers with IF Antonio Perez to Oakland Athletics for OF Andre Ethier (December 13, 2005). ... On disabled list (May 7-June 6 and June 20-July 14, 2006); included rehabilitation assignments to Sacramento and Stockton. **STATISTICAL NOTES:** Career major league grand slams: 3.

2006 GAMES PLAYED BY POSITION (MLB): OF—94, DH—1.

Year	Team (League)	Pos.	G	AB	R	H	2B	3B	HR	RBI	BB	SO	HBP	GDP	SB-CS	Avg.	OBP	SLG	OPS	E	Avg.
										BATTING										FIELDING	
1996— GC Expos (GCL)		OF	32	112	18	27	7	1	1	12	13	15	1	2	7-4	.241	.320	.348	.669	3	.949
1997— Vermont (NYP)		OF	50	200	29	60	7	5	3	30	17	34	0	6	7-7	.300	.352	.430	.782	4	.967
—GC Expos (GCL)		OF	9	25	6	5	2	0	1	2	4	4	1	0	2-2	.200	.333	.400	.733	2	.938
1998— Cape Fear (S. Atl.)		OF	75	281	54	85	21	4	6	50	23	57	4	7	13-8	.302	.360	.470	.830	3	.968
—Jupiter (Fla. St.)		OF	67	261	55	75	14	1	5	34	30	42	5	3	17-9	.287	.369	.406	.775	1	.993
1999— Harrisburg (East.)		OF	87	346	62	114	29	5	12	50	33	61	3	5	14-10	.329	.391	.526	.917	5	.971
2000— Ottawa (Int'l)		OF	88	342	58	104	20	1	6	29	45	56	1	5	10-15	.304	.385	.421	.806	3	.987
—Montreal (N.L.)		OF	42	154	20	34	8	1	2	15	14	32	1	3	2-1	.221	.288	.325	.613	2	.979
2001— Montreal (N.L.)		OF	67	220	19	49	16	3	1	19	19	62	1	6	7-4	.223	.288	.336	.624	4	.988
—Ottawa (Int'l)		OF	35	136	21	37	7	2	2	13	23	30	2	...	14-11	.272	.383	.397	.780	3	.966
—Buffalo (Int'l)		OF	30	114	18	29	7	2	2	15	19	31	0	...	9-2	.254	.361	.412	.773	0	1.000
—Cleveland (A.L.)		OF-DH	10	18	3	4	1	0	0	0	3	6	0	1	1-1	.222	.300	.278	.578	1	.929

Year Team (League)	Pos.	G	AB	R	H	2B	3B	HR	RBI	BB	SO	HBP	GDP	SB-CS	Avg.	OBP	SLG	OPS	E	Avg.
																			BATTING	FIELDING
2002—Cleveland (A.L.)	OF-DH	98	325	48	81	18	3	9	38	32	58	0	12	6-3	.249	.317	.406	.723	4	.982
—Buffalo (Int'l)	OF	6	23	3	6	0	0	0	3	3	5	0	0	2-1	.261	.321	.261	.582	0	1.000
—Akron (East.)	OF	3	11	1	3	1	0	0	1	1	1	0	0	0-0	.273	.333	.364	.697	0	1.000
2003—Cleveland (A.L.)	OF-DH	101	377	61	121	34	2	10	56	64	73	5	10	17-7	.321	.421	.501	.923	2	.992
2004—Los Angeles (N.L.)	OF	141	516	72	138	24	0	19	67	71	123	6	12	15-11	.267	.362	.424	.786	8	.977
2005—Las Vegas (PCL)	OF	5	13	2	4	0	0	0	1	1	2	0	0	1-1	.308	.357	.308	.665	0	1.000
—Los Angeles (N.L.)	OF	75	283	49	82	14	1	13	38	25	47	2	6	6-1	.290	.350	.484	.835	2	.989
2006—Sacramento (PCL)		6	24	3	5	0	0	2	6	2	10	1	0	1-0	.208	.296	.458	.755	0	1.000
—Stockton (Calif.)		2	7	1	1	0	0	0	0	1	1	0	0	0-0	.143	.250	.143	.393	0	1.000
—Oakland (A.L.)	OF-DH	96	351	53	97	14	2	14	52	51	65	2	13	10-2	.276	.370	.447	.818	4	.980
American League totals (4 years)		305	1071	165	303	67	7	33	146	149	199	7	36	34-13	.283	.372	.451	.823	11	.984
National League totals (4 years)		325	1173	160	303	62	5	35	139	129	264	10	27	30-17	.258	.336	.409	.745	14	.982
Major League totals (7 years)		630	2244	325	606	129	12	68	285	278	463	17	63	64-30	.270	.354	.429	.783	25	.983

DIVISION SERIES RECORD

Year Team (League)	Pos.	G	AB	R	H	2B	3B	HR	RBI	BB	SO	HBP	GDP	SB-CS	Avg.	OBP	SLG	OPS	E	Avg.
2004—Los Angeles (N.L.)	OF	4	11	1	3	1	0	1	1	5	2	0	1	2-0	.273	.500	.636	1.136	0	1.000
2006—Oakland (A.L.)	OF	3	13	1	1	0	0	1	2	0	1	0	1	0-0	.077	.077	.308	.385	0	1.000
Division series totals (2 years)		7	24	2	4	1	0	2	3	5	3	0	2	2-0	.167	.310	.458	.769	0	1.000

CHAMPIONSHIP SERIES RECORD

Year Team (League)	Pos.	G	AB	R	H	2B	3B	HR	RBI	BB	SO	HBP	GDP	SB-CS	Avg.	OBP	SLG	OPS	E	Avg.
2006—Oakland (A.L.)	OF	4	18	4	9	2	0	2	5	0	2	0	1	0-0	.500	.500	.944	1.444	0	1.000

2006 LEFTY-RIGHTY SPLITS

vs.	Avg.	AB	H	2B	3B	HR	RBI	BB	SO	OBP	Slg.	vs.	Avg.	AB	H	2B	3B	HR	RBI	BB	SO	OBP	Slg.
L	.293	92	27	2	0	6	19	12	15	.375	.511	R	.270	259	70	12	2	8	33	39	50	.369	.425

BRANYAN, RUSSELL — 3B/OF

PERSONAL: Born December 19, 1975, in Warner Robins, Ga. ... 6-3/195. ... Bats left, throws right. ... Full name: Russell Oles Branyan. ... Name pronounced: BRAN-yen. ... High school: Stratford Academy (Warner Robins, Ga.). **TRANSACTIONS/CAREER NOTES:** Selected by Cleveland Indians organization in seventh round of 1994 free-agent draft. ... Traded by Indians to Cincinnati Reds for OF Ben Broussard (June 7, 2002). ... On disabled list (March 18-May 29 and August 13-28, 2003); included rehabilitation assignments to Louisville. ... Signed as a free agent by Atlanta Braves organization (January 21, 2004). ... Traded by Braves to Indians for P Scott Sturkie (April 25, 2004). ... Traded by Indians to Milwaukee Brewers for cash (July 26, 2004). ... On disabled list (June 2-July 4, 2005); included rehabilitation assignment to Nashville. ... Released by Brewers (January 11, 2006). ... Signed by Tampa Bay Devil Rays organization (January 31, 2006). ... Traded by Devil Rays to San Diego Padres for P Evan Meek and cash (August 25, 2006). **STATISTICAL NOTES:** Hit three home runs in one game (August 4, 2002). ... Career major league grand slams: 3.

2006 GAMES PLAYED BY POSITION (MLB): OF—55, 3B—31, 1B—2.

Year Team (League)	Pos.	G	AB	R	H	2B	3B	HR	RBI	BB	SO	HBP	GDP	SB-CS	Avg.	OBP	SLG	OPS	E	Avg.
1994—Burlington (Appal.)	3B	55	171	21	36	10	0	5	13	25	64	4	3	4-2	.211	.323	.357	.680	21	.851
1995—Columbus (S. Atl.)	3B	76	277	46	71	8	6	19	55	27	120	3	6	1-1	.256	.326	.534	.860	26	.856
1996—Columbus (S. Atl.)	3B-DH	130	482	102	129	20	4	40	106	62	166	5	4	7-4	.268	.355	.575	.930	44	.885
1997—Kinston (Carol.)	3B-DH	83	297	59	86	26	2	27	75	52	94	5	9	3-1	.290	.398	.663	1.062	21	.897
—Akron (East.)	3B-DH	41	137	26	32	4	0	12	30	28	56	2	1	0-0	.234	.369	.526	.895	11	.921
1998—Akron (East.)	3B-DH	43	163	35	48	11	3	16	46	35	58	0	2	1-1	.294	.417	.693	1.110	7	.932
—Cleveland (A.L.)	3B	1	4	0	0	0	0	0	0	0	2	0	0	0-0	.000	.000	.000	.000	0	1.000
1999—Buffalo (Int'l)	3B	109	395	51	82	11	1	30	67	52	187	4	5	8-3	.208	.305	.544	.773	23	.921
—Cleveland (A.L.)	3B-DH	11	38	4	8	2	0	1	6	3	19	1	0	0-0	.211	.286	.342	.628	1	.960
2000—Buffalo (Int'l)	3B-OF	64	229	46	56	9	2	21	60	28	93	2	2	1-1	.245	.330	.576	.906	9	.942
—Cleveland (A.L.)	OF-DH-3B	67	193	32	46	7	2	16	38	22	76	4	2	1-1	.238	.327	.544	.871	3	.954
2001—Cleveland (A.L.)	3B-OF-DH	113	315	48	73	16	2	20	54	38	132	3	2	1-1	.232	.316	.486	.802	14	.931
2002—Cleveland (A.L.)	OF-3B-DH	50	161	16	33	4	0	8	17	17	65	0	0	1-2	.205	.278	.379	.657	7	.976
—Cincinnati (N.L.)	OF-1B-3B-DH	84	217	34	53	9	1	16	39	34	86	2	2	3-1	.244	.349	.516	.865	6	.977
2003—Louisville (Int'l)	DH-OF-1B-3B	14	49	5	16	5	0	1	3	9	15	1	0	0-0	.327	.441	.490	.930	1	.968
—Cincinnati (N.L.)	3B-OF-1B-DH	74	176	22	38	12	0	9	26	27	69	1	1	1-0	.216	.322	.438	.759	3	.985
2004—Richmond (Int'l)	OF	11	28	5	5	0	0	1	4	13	11	1	0	1-0	.179	.452	.286	.738	0	1.000
—Buffalo (Int'l)	1B-3B-OF	82	313	58	90	16	2	25	75	42	102	5	5	5-2	.288	.374	.591	.965	6	.987
—Milwaukee (N.L.)	3B-1B	51	158	21	37	11	1	11	27	20	68	2	1	1-0	.234	.324	.525	.849	5	.964
2005—Nashville (PCL)	OF-3B-DH	6	17	4	5	4	0	1	3	3	8	0	0	0-0	.294	.400	.706	1.106	0	1.000
—Milwaukee (N.L.)	3B-1B-OF-DH	85	202	23	52	11	0	12	31	39	80	1	0	1-0	.257	.378	.490	.868	7	.956
2006—Tampa Bay (A.L.)	OF-3B-1B	64	169	23	34	10	0	12	27	19	62	2	1	2-0	.201	.286	.473	.760	6	.948
—San Diego (N.L.)	3B	27	72	14	21	1	0	6	9	15	27	1	0	0-0	.292	.416	.556	.971	3	.933
American League totals (6 years)		306	880	123	194	39	4	57	142	99	356	10	8	4-3	.220	.303	.468	.771	26	.947
National League totals (5 years)		321	825	114	201	44	2	54	132	135	330	6	7	5-1	.244	.352	.498	.850	24	.970
Major League totals (9 years)		627	1705	237	395	83	6	111	274	234	686	16	15	9-4	.232	.327	.483	.810	50	.961

DIVISION SERIES RECORD

Year Team (League)	Pos.	G	AB	R	H	2B	3B	HR	RBI	BB	SO	HBP	GDP	SB-CS	Avg.	OBP	SLG	OPS	E	Avg.
2001—Cleveland (A.L.)	OF	2	3	1	1	0	0	0	0	0	1	0	0	0-0	.333	.333	.667	...	0	...
2006—San Diego (N.L.)	3B	4	13	1	3	1	0	1	3	1	6	0	0	0-0	.231	.286	.462	.747	1	.923
Division series totals (2 years)		6	16	2	4	1	0	1	3	1	6	0	0	0-0	.250	.294	.438	.732	1	.923

2006 LEFTY-RIGHTY SPLITS

vs.	Avg.	AB	H	2B	3B	HR	RBI	BB	SO	OBP	Slg.	vs.	Avg.	AB	H	2B	3B	HR	RBI	BB	SO	OBP	Slg.
L	.220	41	9	1	0	4	6	3	21	.304	.537	R	.230	200	46	10	0	14	30	31	68	.332	.490

BRAUN, RYAN — P

PERSONAL: Born July 29, 1980, in Kitchener, Ontario. ... Throws right, bats right. ... Full name: Ryan Zachary Braun. ... College: UNLV. **TRANSACTIONS/CAREER NOTES:** Selected by Kansas City Royals organization in sixth round of 2003 free-agent draft.
CAREER HITTING: 0-for-0 (.000), 0 R, 0 2B, 0 3B, 0 HR, 0 RBI.

B

Year Team (League)	W	L	Pct.	ERA	WHIP	G	GS	CG	ShO	Hld.	Sv.-Opp.	IP	H	R	ER	HR	BB-IBB	SO	Avg.
2003— Arizona Royals 1 (AZL)	0	0	...	2.95	1.17	18	0	0	0	...	3-...	21.1	15	9	7	0	10-0	25	.185
2004— Wilmington (Caro.)	2	3	.400	2.21	1.28	51	0	0	0	...	23-...	57.0	48	25	14	2	25-4	58	.219
2005— Wichita (Texas)	0	1	.000	17.36	4.71	6	0	0	0	0	0-1	4.2	15	10	9	0	7-0	1	.536
— High Desert (Calif.)	1	0	1.000	4.50	1.25	2	0	0	0	0	0-0	4.0	3	2	2	0	2-0	6	.214
2006— Wichita (Texas)	1	6	.143	2.21	1.13	26	0	0	0	1	10-12	40.2	30	11	10	2	16-3	58	.204
— Omaha (PCL)	0	2	.000	2.16	1.44	17	0	0	0	1	3-3	25.0	23	9	6	0	13-2	22	.247
— Kansas City (A.L.)	0	1	.000	6.75	1.50	9	0	0	0	0	0-2	10.2	13	8	8	2	3-0	6	.317
Major League totals (1 year)	0	1	.000	6.75	1.50	9	0	0	0	0	0-2	10.2	13	8	8	2	3-0	6	.317

2006 LEFTY-RIGHTY SPLITS

vs.	Avg.	AB	H	2B	3B	HR	RBI	BB	SO	OBP	Slg.	vs.	Avg.	AB	H	2B	3B	HR	RBI	BB	SO	OBP	Slg.
L	.357	14	5	1	0	1	2	1	1	.400	.643	R	.296	27	8	3	1	1	5	2	5	.333	.556

BRAY, BILL   P

PERSONAL: Born June 5, 1983, in Virginia Beach, Va. ... Throws left, bats left. ... Full name: William P. Bray. ... College: William & Mary. **TRANSACTIONS/CAREER NOTES:** Selected by Montreal Expos organization in first round (13th pick overall) of 2004 free-agent draft. ... Expos franchise relocated to Washington, D.C., and renamed Washington Nationals for 2005 season (December 3, 2004). ... Traded by Nationals with Ps Gary Majewski and Daryl Thompson, SS Royce Clayton and IF Brendan Harris to Cincinnati Reds for OF Austin Kearns, SS Felipe Lopez and P Ryan Wagner (July 13, 2006).
CAREER HITTING: 0-for-1 (.000), 0 R, 0 2B, 0 HR, 0 RBI.

Year Team (League)	W	L	Pct.	ERA	WHIP	G	GS	CG	ShO	Hld.	Sv.-Opp.	IP	H	R	ER	HR	BB-IBB	SO	Avg.
2004— Brevard County (Fla. St.)	0	2	.000	4.91	1.36	6	0	0	0	0	1-...	7.1	9	5	4	0	1-0	6	.290
2005— Potomac (Carol.)	1	0	1.000	2.13	0.87	8	0	0	0	0	3-4	12.2	8	3	3	1	3-0	18	.170
— Harrisburg (East.)	1	0	1.000	6.35	1.94	3	0	0	0	0	1-1	5.2	10	4	4	1	1-0	6	.385
— New Orleans (PCL)	1	4	.200	5.06	1.50	23	0	0	0	0	2-3	21.1	23	16	12	3	9-0	25	.271
2006— New Orleans (PCL)	4	1	.800	3.98	1.11	21	0	0	0	5	5-6	31.2	26	14	14	5	9-0	45	.217
— Wash. (N.L.)	1	1	.500	3.91	1.43	19	0	0	0	1	0-0	23.0	24	11	10	2	9-2	16	.273
— Cincinnati (N.L.)	2	1	.667	4.23	1.52	29	0	0	0	2	2-3	27.2	33	16	13	3	9-1	23	.292
Major League totals (1 year)	3	2	.600	4.09	1.48	48	0	0	0	3	2-3	50.2	57	27	23	5	18-3	39	.284

2006 LEFTY-RIGHTY SPLITS

vs.	Avg.	AB	H	2B	3B	HR	RBI	BB	SO	OBP	Slg.	vs.	Avg.	AB	H	2B	3B	HR	RBI	BB	SO	OBP	Slg.
L	.333	78	26	4	0	1	10	6	14	.381	.423	R	.252	123	31	9	0	4	22	12	25	.321	.423

BRAZELTON, DEWON   P

PERSONAL: Born June 16, 1980, in Tullahoma, Tenn. ... 6-4/214. ... Throws right, bats right. ... Full name: Dewon Cortez Brazelton. ... Name pronounced: de-wan bra-zel-ton. ... High school: Tullahoma (Tenn.). ... College: Middle Tennessee State. **TRANSACTIONS/CAREER NOTES:** Selected by Tampa Bay Devil Rays organization in first round (third pick overall) of 2001 free-agent draft. ... On suspended list (September 8-11, 2005). ... Traded by Devil Rays to San Diego Padres for 3B Sean Burroughs (December 7, 2005).
CAREER HITTING: 1-for-6 (.167), 0 R, 1 2B, 0 3B, 0 HR, 1 RBI.

Year Team (League)	W	L	Pct.	ERA	WHIP	G	GS	CG	ShO	Hld.	Sv.-Opp.	IP	H	R	ER	HR	BB-IBB	SO	Avg.
2002— Orlando (South.)	5	9	.357	3.33	1.34	26	26	0	1	...	0-...	146.0	129	69	54	7	67-1	109	.241
— Durham (Int'l)	1	0	1.000	0.00	1.20	1	1	0	0	...	0-...	5.0	5	0	0	0	1-0	6	.263
— Tampa Bay (A.L.)	0	1	.000	4.85	1.38	2	2	0	0	...	0-0	13.0	12	7	7	3	6-0	5	.279
2003— Durham (Int'l)	2	2	.500	4.21	1.30	5	5	0	0	...	0-0	25.2	23	14	12	1	11-0	18	.235
— Tampa Bay (A.L.)	1	6	.143	6.89	1.66	10	10	0	0	...	0-0	48.1	57	49	37	9	23-1	24	.292
— Bakersfield (Calif.)	1	5	.167	5.26	1.60	9	9	0	0	...	0-...	49.2	62	33	29	4	19-0	42	.298
— Orlando (South.)	2	0	1.000	2.53	1.50	2	2	0	0	...	0-...	10.2	8	6	3	0	8-0	5	.200
2004— Durham (Int'l)	4	4	.500	4.71	1.53	10	10	0	0	...	0-...	49.2	61	35	26	0	15-0	38	.299
— Tampa Bay (A.L.)	6	8	.429	4.77	1.44	22	21	0	0	...	0-0	120.2	121	71	64	12	53-2	64	.260
2005— Montgom. (Sou.)	0	0	...	0.00	0.67	1	1	0	0	...	0-0	3.0	2	0	0	0	0-0	6	.182
— Durham (Int'l)	2	2	.500	3.72	1.48	5	5	0	0	...	0-0	29.0	29	17	12	3	14-0	26	.252
— Tampa Bay (A.L.)	1	8	.111	7.61	2.07	20	8	0	0	1	0-1	71.0	87	65	60	12	60-3	43	.307
2006— San Diego (N.L.)	0	2	.000	12.00	2.06	9	2	0	0	0	0-0	18.0	28	25	24	6	9-1	9	.354
— Ariz. Padres (Ariz.)	0	0	...	0.00	1.50	1	1	0	0	0	0-0	2.0	1	2	0	0	2-0	2	.125
— Portland (PCL)	5	7	.417	4.53	1.37	17	16	1	1	0	0-0	91.1	100	50	46	15	25-0	53	.281
American League totals (4 years)	8	23	.258	5.98	1.66	54	41	0	0	1	0-1	253.0	277	192	168	36	142-6	136	.281
National League totals (1 year)	0	2	.000	12.00	2.06	9	2	0	0	0	0-0	18.0	28	25	24	6	9-1	9	.354
Major League totals (5 years)	8	25	.242	6.38	1.68	63	43	0	0	1	0-1	271.0	305	217	192	42	151-7	145	.286

2006 LEFTY-RIGHTY SPLITS

vs.	Avg.	AB	H	2B	3B	HR	RBI	BB	SO	OBP	Slg.	vs.	Avg.	AB	H	2B	3B	HR	RBI	BB	SO	OBP	Slg.
L	.361	36	13	0	0	3	9	5	4	.419	.611	R	.349	43	15	4	1	3	13	4	5	.404	.698

BRAZOBAN, YHENCY   P

PERSONAL: Born June 11, 1980, in Santo Domingo, Dominican Republic. ... 6-1/170. ... Throws right, bats right. ... Full name: Yhency Jose Brazoban. **TRANSACTIONS/CAREER NOTES:** Signed as a non-drafted free agent by New York Yankees organization (July 10, 1997). ... Played five seasons as an outfielder in Yankees organization (1998-2002) ... Traded by Yankees with Ps Jeff Weaver and Brandon Wheedon and cash to Los Angeles Dodgers for P Kevin Brown (December 13, 2003). ... On disabled list (April 14, 2006-remainder of season).
CAREER HITTING: 0-for-3 (.000), 0 R, 0 2B, 0 3B, 0 HR, 0 RBI.

Year Team (League)	W	L	Pct.	ERA	WHIP	G	GS	CG	ShO	Hld.	Sv.-Opp.	IP	H	R	ER	HR	BB-IBB	SO	Avg.
2002— GC Yankees (GCL)	0	0	...	4.50	1.17	6	0	0	0	...	0-...	6.0	6	3	3	0	4-0	11	.136
2003— Trenton (East.)	2	2	.500	7.81	1.70	20	0	0	0	...	3-...	27.2	33	25	24	5	14-1	19	.314
— GC Yankees (GCL)	0	0	...	6.00	2.00	3	0	0	0	...	0-...	3.0	5	3	2	0	1-1	5	.385
— Tampa (Fla. St.)	0	2	.000	2.83	1.36	24	0	0	0	...	15-...	28.2	27	13	9	0	12-2	34	.245
2004— Jacksonville (Sou.)	4	4	.500	2.65	1.18	37	0	0	0	...	13-...	51.0	38	18	15	4	22-1	51	.210
— Las Vegas (PCL)	2	0	1.000	2.19	1.22	10	0	0	0	...	1-...	12.1	14	3	3	1	1-0	17	.286
— Los Angeles (N.L.)	6	2	.750	2.48	1.22	31	0	0	0	5	0-0	32.2	25	9	9	2	15-2	27	.219
2005— Los Angeles (N.L.)	4	10	.286	5.33	1.40	74	0	0	0	8	21-27	72.2	70	46	43	11	32-4	61	.258
2006— Los Angeles (N.L.)	0	0	...	5.40	1.80	5	0	0	0	0	0-1	5.0	7	3	3	0	2-0	4	.350
Major League totals (3 years)	10	12	.455	4.49	1.37	110	0	0	0	13	21-28	110.1	102	58	55	13	49-6	92	.252

DIVISION SERIES RECORD

Year Team (League)	W	L	Pct.	ERA	WHIP	G	GS	CG	ShO	Hld.	Sv.-Opp.	IP	H	R	ER	HR	BB-IBB	SO	Avg.
2004— Los Angeles (N.L.)	0	0	...	3.00	1.00	2	0	0	0	...	0-0	3.0	1	1	1	0	2-0	2	.100

2006 LEFTY-RIGHTY SPLITS

vs.	Avg.	AB	H	2B	3B	HR	RBI	BB	SO	OBP	Slg.	vs.	Avg.	AB	H	2B	3B	HR	RBI	BB	SO	OBP	Slg.
L	.333	9	3	1	0	0	0	2	2	.455	.444	R	.364	11	4	1	0	0	5	0	2	.333	.455

BRESLOW, CRAIG   P

PERSONAL: Born August 8, 1980, in New Haven, Conn. ... 6-1/180. ... Throws left, bats left. ... Full name: Craig Andrew Breslow. ... High school: Trumbull (Conn.). ... College: Yale. **TRANSACTIONS/CAREER NOTES:** Selected by Milwaukee Brewers organization in 26th round of 2002 free-agent draft. ... Released by Brewers (July 16, 2004). ... Signed by New Jersey of the independent Northeast league (July 2004). ... Signed as a free agent by San Diego Padres organization (March 3, 2005). ... Signed as a free agent by Boston Red Sox organization (February 1, 2006).
CAREER HITTING: 0-for-1 (.000), 0 R, 0 2B, 0 3B, 0 HR, 0 RBI.

Year	Team (League)	W	L	Pct.	ERA	WHIP	G	GS	CG	ShO	Hld.	Sv.-Opp.	IP	H	R	ER	HR	BB-IBB	SO	Avg.
2002— Ogden (Pion.)		6	2	.750	1.82	1.21	23	0	0	0	...	2-...	54.1	42	15	11	2	24-0	56	.218
2003— Beloit (Midw.)		3	4	.429	5.12	1.40	33	0	0	0	...	2-...	65.0	64	43	37	4	27-0	80	.254
2004— High Desert (Calif.)		1	3	.250	7.19	1.89	23	0	0	0	...	0-...	41.1	54	39	33	5	24-0	41	.305
— New Jersey (Northeast)		3	1	.750	4.10	1.22	19	0	0	0	...	1-...	26.1	19	13	12	2	13-1	37	.204
2005— Mobile (Sou.)		2	1	.667	2.75	1.05	40	0	0	0	9	0-0	52.1	38	16	16	3	17-2	47	.212
— Portland (PCL)		0	1	.000	4.00	1.33	7	0	0	0	1	0-0	9.0	11	4	4	1	1-0	9	.314
— San Diego (N.L.)		0	0		2.20	1.71	14	0	0	0	1	0-0	16.1	15	6	4	1	13-0	14	.238
2006— Pawtucket (Int'l)		7	1	.875	2.69	1.09	39	0	0	0	4	7-11	67.0	49	21	20	3	24-0	77	.200
— Boston (A.L.)		0	2	.000	3.75	1.50	13	0	0	0	3	0-0	12.0	12	5	5	0	6-1	12	.261
American League totals (1 year)		0	2	.000	3.75	1.50	13	0	0	0	3	0-0	12.0	12	5	5	0	6-1	12	.261
National League totals (1 year)		0	0		2.20	1.71	14	0	0	0	1	0-0	16.1	15	6	4	1	13-0	14	.238
Major League totals (2 years)		0	2	.000	2.86	1.62	27	0	0	0	4	0-0	28.1	27	11	9	1	19-1	26	.248

2006 LEFTY-RIGHTY SPLITS

vs.	Avg.	AB	H	2B	3B	HR	RBI	BB	SO	OBP	Slg.	vs.	Avg.	AB	H	2B	3B	HR	RBI	BB	SO	OBP	Slg.
L	.316	19	6	3	0	0	2	1	6	.350	.474	R	.222	27	6	2	0	0	4	5	6	.343	.296

BRITO, EUDE   P

PERSONAL: Born August 19, 1978, in Sabana de la Mar, Dominican Republic. ... 5-11/160. ... Throws left, bats left. ... Full name: Eude Ezequiel Brito. ... High school: Liceo Virginia Pou (Dominican Republic). **TRANSACTIONS/CAREER NOTES:** Signed as a non-drafted free agent by Philadelphia Phillies organization (July 3, 1998).
CAREER HITTING: 1-for-13 (.077), 1 R, 0 2B, 0 3B, 0 HR, 0 RBI.

Year	Team (League)	W	L	Pct.	ERA	WHIP	G	GS	CG	ShO	Hld.	Sv.-Opp.	IP	H	R	ER	HR	BB-IBB	SO	Avg.
1999— GC Phillies (GCL)		0	1	.000	5.02	2.02	12	3	0	0	...	0-...	28.2	39	22	16	0	19-0	23	.336
2000— GC Phillies (GCL)		3	5	.375	2.54	1.15	9	7	0	0	...	0-...	49.2	38	20	14	1	19-0	42	.210
— Batavia (NY-Penn)		1	1	.500	5.40	1.04	4	3	0	0	...	0-...	18.1	16	14	11	0	3-0	11	.225
2001— Lakewood (S. Atl.)		4	3	.571	2.73	0.97	44	0	0	0	...	6-...	69.1	53	28	21	7	14-2	58	.210
2002— Lakewood (S. Atl.)		1	1	.500	2.55	1.13	11	0	0	0	...	1-...	17.2	14	5	5	1	6-0	11	.226
— Clearwater (Fla. St.)		3	3	.500	5.71	1.56	20	0	0	0	...	0-...	34.2	40	22	22	5	14-1	27	.292
2003— Clearwater (Fla. St.)		4	3	.571	3.09	1.32	36	0	0	0	...	6-...	58.1	50	21	20	3	27-1	54	.231
2004— Reading (East.)		8	6	.571	4.42	1.40	43	7	1	0	...	4-...	97.2	95	56	48	10	42-2	84	.256
2005— Scran./W.B. (I.L.)		6	2	.750	4.85	1.38	28	15	0	0	1	0-1	98.1	97	59	53	13	39-0	76	.266
— Philadelphia (N.L.)		1	2	.333	3.68	1.41	6	5	0	0	0	0-0	22.0	20	9	9	2	11-1	15	.250
2006— Scran./W.B. (I.L.)		10	8	.556	3.17	1.16	26	23	2	1	0	1-1	147.2	116	60	52	11	55-0	103	.214
— Philadelphia (N.L.)		1	2	.333	7.36	1.80	5	2	0	0	0	0-0	18.1	21	15	15	2	12-2	9	.296
Major League totals (2 years)		2	4	.333	5.36	1.59	11	7	0	0	0	0-0	40.1	41	24	24	4	23-3	24	.272

2006 LEFTY-RIGHTY SPLITS

vs.	Avg.	AB	H	2B	3B	HR	RBI	BB	SO	OBP	Slg.	vs.	Avg.	AB	H	2B	3B	HR	RBI	BB	SO	OBP	Slg.
L	.238	21	5	2	0	0	5	1	7	.261	.333	R	.320	50	16	6	0	2	11	11	2	.452	.560

BRITTON, CHRIS   P

PERSONAL: Born December 16, 1982, in Hollywood, Fla. ... 6-3/230. ... Throws right, bats right. ... Full name: Christopher Daniel Britton. . **TRANSACTIONS/CAREER NOTES:** Selected by Baltimore Orioles organization in eighth round of 2001 free-agent draft. ... Traded by Orioles to New York Yankees for P Jaret Wright and cash (November 12, 2006).
CAREER HITTING: 0-for-0 (.000), 0 R, 0 2B, 0 3B, 0 HR, 0 RBI.

Year	Team (League)	W	L	Pct.	ERA	WHIP	G	GS	CG	ShO	Hld.	Sv.-Opp.	IP	H	R	ER	HR	BB-IBB	SO	Avg.
2001— GC Orioles (GCL)		2	3	.400	2.76	1.44	12	3	0	0	...	0-...	32.2	35	20	10	3	12-1	20	.265
2002— Bluefield (Appal.)		3	0	1.000	4.54	1.12	9	8	0	0	...	0-...	35.2	30	21	18	5	10-0	27	.227
2003—					Did not play.															
2004— Delmarva (S. Atl.)		9	4	.692	3.75	1.27	27	8	1	0	...	1-...	84.0	76	38	35	11	31-2	80	.239
2005— Frederick (Carolina)		6	0	1.000	1.60	0.89	46	0	0	0	13	6-8	78.2	47	15	14	5	23-0	110	.172
2006— Bowie (East.)		1	0	1.000	2.81	1.25	13	0	0	0	5	2-3	16.0	14	5	5	0	6-1	24	.233
— Baltimore (A.L.)		0	2	.000	3.35	1.17	52	0	0	0	6	1-3	53.2	46	22	20	4	17-3	41	.228
Major League totals (1 year)		0	2	.000	3.35	1.17	52	0	0	0	6	1-3	53.2	46	22	20	4	17-3	41	.228

2006 LEFTY-RIGHTY SPLITS

vs.	Avg.	AB	H	2B	3B	HR	RBI	BB	SO	OBP	Slg.	vs.	Avg.	AB	H	2B	3B	HR	RBI	BB	SO	OBP	Slg.
L	.301	73	22	4	1	0	8	9	15	.378	.384	R	.186	129	24	3	2	4	16	8	26	.232	.333

BROCAIL, DOUG   P

PERSONAL: Born May 16, 1967, in Clearfield, Pa. ... 6-5/235. ... Throws right, bats left. ... Full name: Douglas Keith Brocail. ... Name pronounced: broh-KALE. ... High school: Lamar (Colo.). ... Junior college: Lamar (Colo.) C.C. **TRANSACTIONS/CAREER NOTES:** Selected by San Diego Padres organization in first round (12th pick overall) of January 1986 free-agent draft. ... On disabled list (April 2-June 28, 1994); included rehabilitation assignments to Wichita and Las Vegas. ... Traded by Padres with OFs Phil Plantier and Derek Bell, P Pedro A. Martinez and IF Craig Shipley and SS Ricky Gutierrez to Houston Astros for 3B Ken Caminiti, OF Steve Finley, SS Andujar Cedeno, 1B Roberto Petagine, P Brian Williams and a player to be named (December 28, 1994); Padres acquired P Sean Fesh to complete deal (May 1, 1995). ... On disabled list (May 11-August 15, 1996); included rehabilitation assignments to Jackson and Tucson. ... Traded by Astros with OF Brian L. Hunter, IF Orlando Miller, P Todd Jones and cash to Detroit Tigers with C Brad Ausmus, Ps Jose Lima, C.J. Nitkowski and Trever Miller and 1B Daryle Ward (December 10, 1996). ... On suspended list (June 10-13, 1998). ... On disabled list (August 9-24, 1998). ... On suspended list (April 28-May 1, 2000). ... On disabled list (August 14-September 1 and September 29, 2000-remainder of season). ... Traded by Tigers with C Brad Ausmus and P Nelson Cruz to Astros for C Mitch Meluskey, P Chris Holt and OF Roger Cedeno (December 11, 2000). ... On disabled list (March 31, 2001-entire season); included rehabilitation assignments to New Orleans and Round Rock. ... On disabled list (March 22, 2002-entire season). ... Signed as a free agent by Texas Rangers organization (February 18, 2004). ... On disabled list (May 9-June 7 and July 25-August 9, 2004); included rehabilitation assignments to Oklahoma and Frisco. ... On suspended list (September 26-October 2, 2004). ... Signed as a free agent by Padres (December 16, 2005). ... On disabled list (March 24-July 13, 2006);

included rehabilitation assignment to Lake Elsinore. ... On disabled list (September 20, 2006-remainder of season). **MISCELLANEOUS NOTES:** Appeared in six games as pinch runner (1993). ... Appeared in two games as pinch runner (1994). ... Appeared in one game as pinch runner (1995). ... Appeared in two games as pinch runner (1996).
CAREER HITTING: 11-for-67 (.164), 9 R, 0 2B, 1 3B, 0 HR, 1 RBI.

Year	Team (League)	W	L	Pct.	ERA	WHIP	G	GS	CG	ShO	Hld.	Sv.-Opp.	IP	H	R	ER	HR	BB-IBB	SO	Avg.
1986—	Spokane (N'west)	5	4	.556	3.81	1.62	16	15	0	0		0-...	85.0	85	52	36	4	53-1	77	...
1987—	Char., S.C. (SAL)	2	6	.250	4.09	1.32	19	18	0	0		0-...	92.1	94	51	42	6	28-0	68	.263
1988—	Char., S.C. (SAL)	8	6	.571	2.69	1.23	22	13	5	0		2-...	107.0	107	40	32	3	25-0	107	.257
1989—	Wichita (Texas)	5	9	.357	5.21	1.54	23	22	1	1		0-...	134.2	158	88	78	11	50-4	95	.292
1990—	Wichita (Texas)	2	2	.500	4.33	1.48	12	9	0	0		0-...	52.0	53	30	25	7	24-0	27	.265
1991—	Wichita (Texas)	10	7	.588	3.87	1.30	34	16	3	3		6-...	146.1	147	77	63	15	43-3	108	.259
1992—	Las Vegas (PCL)	10	10	.500	3.97	1.45	29	25	4	0		0-...	172.1	187	82	76	7	63-5	103	.285
—	San Diego (N.L.)	0	0	...	6.43	1.57	3	3	0	0	0	0-0	14.0	17	10	10	2	5-0	15	.298
1993—	Las Vegas (PCL)	4	2	.667	3.68	1.27	10	8	0	0		1-...	51.1	51	26	21	4	14-0	32	.254
—	San Diego (N.L.)	4	13	.235	4.56	1.44	24	24	0	0	0	0-0	128.1	143	75	65	16	42-4	70	.283
1994—	Wichita (Texas)	0	0	...	0.00	1.00	2	0	0	0		0-...	4.0	3	1	0	0	1-0	2	.200
—	Las Vegas (PCL)	0	0	...	7.11	1.82	7	3	0	0		0-...	12.2	21	12	10	1	2-0	8	.357
—	San Diego (N.L.)	0	0	...	5.82	1.53	12	0	0	0	0	0-1	17.0	21	13	11	1	5-3	11	.304
1995—	Houston (N.L.)	6	4	.600	4.19	1.41	36	7	0	0	0	1-1	77.1	87	40	36	10	22-2	39	.280
—	Tucson (PCL)	1	0	1.000	3.86	1.35	3	3	0	0		0-...	16.1	18	9	7	1	4-0	16	.269
1996—	Houston (N.L.)	1	5	.167	4.58	1.53	23	4	0	0	1	0-0	53.0	58	31	27	7	23-1	34	.289
—	Jackson (Texas)	0	0	...	0.00	0.50	2	2	0	0		0-...	4.0	1	0	0	0	1-0	5	.077
—	Tucson (PCL)	0	1	.000	7.36	1.77	5	1	0	0		0-...	7.1	12	6	6	1	1-0	4	.375
1997—	Detroit (A.L.)	3	4	.429	3.23	1.41	61	0	0	0	16	2-9	78.0	74	31	28	10	36-4	60	.256
1998—	Detroit (A.L.)	5	2	.714	2.73	1.04	60	0	0	0	11	0-1	62.2	47	23	19	2	18-3	55	.211
1999—	Detroit (A.L.)	4	4	.500	2.52	1.04	70	0	0	0	23	2-4	82.0	60	23	23	7	25-1	78	.206
2000—	Detroit (A.L.)	5	4	.556	4.09	1.40	49	0	0	0	19	0-5	50.2	57	25	23	5	14-2	41	.285
2001—	New Orleans (PCL)	0	0	...	0.00	1.29	2	0	0	0		0-...	2.1	2	0	0	0	1-0	2	.222
—	Round Rock (Texas)	0	0	...	0.00	0.00	1	1	0	0		0-...	1.0	0	0	0	0	0-0	1	.000
2002—	Houston (N.L.)				Did not play.														
2003—					Did not play.														
2004—	Oklahoma (PCL)	2	0	1.000	4.19	1.14	12	0	0	0		0-...	19.1	20	9	9	1	2-0	19	.263
—	Frisco (Texas)	0	0	...	2.08	0.46	1	1	0	0		0-...	4.1	2	1	1	1	0-0	6	.143
—	Texas (A.L.)	4	1	.800	4.13	1.41	43	0	0	0	4	1-1	52.1	54	29	24	2	20-1	43	.269
2005—	Texas (A.L.)	5	3	.625	5.52	1.69	61	0	0	0	5	1-4	73.1	90	48	45	2	34-3	61	.301
2006—	Lake Elsinore (Calif.)	0	0	...	0.00	0.79	6	2	0	0	3	0-0	6.1	3	1	0	0	2-0	12	.130
—	San Diego (N.L.)	2	2	.500	4.76	1.24	25	0	0	0	0	0-0	28.1	27	16	15	1	8-2	19	.252
	American League totals (6 years)	26	18	.591	3.65	1.33	344	4	0	0	78	6-24	399.0	382	179	162	28	147-14	338	.254
	National League totals (6 years)	13	24	.351	4.64	1.44	123	38	0	0	1	1-2	318.0	353	185	164	37	105-12	188	.282
	Major League totals (12 years)	39	42	.481	4.09	1.38	467	42	0	0	79	7-26	717.0	735	364	326	65	252-26	526	.267

2006 LEFTY-RIGHTY SPLITS

vs.	Avg.	AB	H	2B	3B	HR	RBI	BB	SO	OBP	Slg.	vs.	Avg.	AB	H	2B	3B	HR	RBI	BB	SO	OBP	Slg.
L	.280	50	14	1	0	0	6	6	5	.357	.300	R	.228	57	13	6	0	1	7	2	14	.250	.386

BROUSSARD, BEN   1B/OF

PERSONAL: Born September 24, 1976, in Beaumont, Texas. ... 6-2/220. ... Bats left, throws left. ... Full name: Benjamin Isaac Broussard. ... Name pronounced: brew-SARD. ... High school: Hardin-Jefferson (Sour Lake, Texas). ... College: McNeese State. **TRANSACTIONS/CAREER NOTES:** Selected by Cincinnati Reds organization in second round of 1999 free-agent draft. ... Traded by Reds to Cleveland Indians for 3B Russell Branyan (June 7, 2002). ... On disabled list (March 21-April 6, 2003); included rehabilitation assignment to Buffalo. ... Traded by Indians with cash to Seattle Mariners for OF Shin-Soo Choo and a player to be named to complete deal (July 26, 2006); Indians acquired P Shawn Nottingham to complete deal (August 24, 2006). **STATISTICAL NOTES:** Career major league grand slams: 4.
2006 GAMES PLAYED BY POSITION (MLB): 1B—90, DH—45.

Year	Team (League)	Pos.	G	AB	R	H	2B	3B	HR	RBI	BB	SO	HBP	GDP	SB-CS	Avg.	OBP	SLG	OPS	E	Avg.
1999—	Billings (Pion.)	1B-OF	38	145	39	59	11	2	14	48	34	30	4	0	1-0	.407	.527	.800	1.327	5	.963
—	Clinton (Midw.)	1B-OF	5	20	8	11	4	1	2	6	3	4	0	0	0-0	.550	.609	1.150	1.759	2	.926
—	Chattanooga (Sou.)	1B-OF	35	127	26	27	5	0	8	21	11	41	3	0	1-0	.213	.291	.441	.732	2	.987
2000—	Chattanooga (Sou.)	1B-OF	87	286	64	73	8	4	14	51	72	78	6	4	15-2	.255	.413	.458	.871	10	.958
2001—	Mudville (Calif.)	1B	30	102	14	25	5	0	5	21	16	31	4	2	0-0	.245	.360	.441	.801	2	.992
—	Chattanooga (Sou.)	1B-OF	100	353	81	113	27	0	23	69	61	69	8	5	10-3	.320	.428	.592	1.020	8	.990
2002—	Louisville (Int'l)	1B	57	187	31	51	14	1	11	30	31	50	9	...	4-1	.273	.396	.535	.930	2	.995
—	Buffalo (Int'l)	OF-1B	42	153	30	37	8	0	5	21	24	30	3		0-0	.242	.354	.392	.746	3	.975
—	Cleveland (A.L.)	OF-1B-DH	39	112	10	27	4	0	4	9	7	25	1		0-0	.241	.292	.384	.676	2	.974
2003—	Buffalo (Int'l)	1B-DH	32	120	17	30	2	1	3	15	9	29	1		3-0	.250	.303	.358	.661	2	.990
—	Cleveland (A.L.)	1B	116	386	53	96	21	3	16	55	32	75	5	6	5-2	.249	.312	.443	.755	9	.991
2004—	Cleveland (A.L.)	1B	139	418	57	115	28	5	17	82	52	95	12	4	4-2	.275	.370	.488	.858	6	.994
2005—	Cleveland (A.L.)	1B-DH	142	466	59	119	30	5	19	68	32	98	4	4	2-2	.255	.307	.464	.770	9	.992
2006—	Cleveland (A.L.)	1B	88	268	44	86	14	0	13	46	17	58	1	5	0-1	.321	.361	.519	.880	7	.989
—	Seattle (A.L.)	DH-1B	56	164	17	39	7	0	8	17	9	45	2	3	2-0	.238	.282	.427	.709	2	.976
	Major League totals (5 years)		580	1814	240	482	104	13	77	277	149	396	25	28	13-7	.266	.328	.465	.793	35	.991

2006 LEFTY-RIGHTY SPLITS

vs.	Avg.	AB	H	2B	3B	HR	RBI	BB	SO	OBP	Slg.	vs.	Avg.	AB	H	2B	3B	HR	RBI	BB	SO	OBP	Slg.
L	.177	62	11	2	0	3	8	6	21	.261	.355	R	.308	370	114	19	0	18	55	20	82	.343	.505

BROWER, JIM   P

PERSONAL: Born December 29, 1972, in Edina, Minn. ... 6-3/215. ... Throws right, bats right. ... Full name: James Robert Brower. ... Name pronounced: BROW-er. ... High school: Minnetonka (Minn.). ... College: Minnesota. **TRANSACTIONS/CAREER NOTES:** Selected by Texas Rangers organization in sixth round of 1994 free-agent draft. ... Released by Rangers (April 15, 1998). ... Signed by Cleveland Indians organization (April 18, 1998). ... Traded by Indians with P Robert Pugmire to Cincinnati Reds for C Eddie Taubensee (November 16, 2000). ... Traded by Reds to Montreal Expos for P Bruce Chen (June 14, 2002). ... Traded by Expos with a player to be named to San Francisco Giants for P Livan Hernandez, 3B/C Edwards Guzman and cash (March 24, 2003); Giants acquired P Matt Blank to complete deal (April 30, 2003). ... Released by Giants (June 12, 2005). ... Signed by Atlanta Braves (June 16, 2005). ... Signed as a free agent by Baltimore Orioles (March 28, 2006). ... Released by Orioles (May 8, 2006). ... Signed by San Diego Padres organization (May 12, 2006). ... Traded by Padres to Florida Marlins for P Matt Blank (August 1, 2006). **MISCELLANEOUS NOTES:** Appeared in two games as pinch runner (2001).
CAREER HITTING: 12-for-59 (.203), 9 R, 1 2B, 0 3B, 0 HR, 4 RBI.

Year — Team (League)	W	L	Pct.	ERA	WHIP	G	GS	CG	ShO	Hld.	Sv.-Opp.	IP	H	R	ER	HR	BB-IBB	SO	Avg.
1994— Hudson Valley (NYP)	2	1	.667	3.20	1.02	4	4	1	0	...	0-...	19.2	14	10	7	0	6-0	15	.189
— Char., S.C. (SAL)	7	3	.700	1.72	0.99	12	12	3	2	...	0-...	78.2	52	18	15	2	26-1	84	.186
1995— Charlotte (Fla. St.)	7	10	.412	3.89	1.34	27	27	2	1	...	0-...	173.2	170	93	75	16	62-1	110	.256
1996— Charlotte (Fla. St.)	9	8	.529	3.79	1.30	23	21	2	0	...	0-...	145.0	148	67	61	11	40-0	86	.267
— Tulsa (Texas)	3	2	.600	3.78	1.35	5	5	1	1	...	0-...	33.1	35	16	14	4	10-0	16	.273
1997— Tulsa (Texas)	5	12	.294	5.21	1.41	23	23	1	0	...	0-...	140.0	156	99	81	13	42-1	103	.286
— Okla. City (A.A.)	2	1	.667	7.23	2.04	4	3	0	0	...	0-...	18.2	30	17	15	3	8-0	7	.370
1998— Akron (East.)	13	5	.722	3.01	1.16	23	23	2	2	...	0-...	155.2	142	60	52	9	38-0	91	.246
1999— Buffalo (Int'l)	11	11	.500	4.73	1.39	27	27	0	0	...	0-...	160.0	164	101	84	23	59-6	76	.270
— Cleveland (A.L.)	3	1	.750	4.56	1.44	9	2	0	0	0	0-0	25.2	27	13	13	8	10-1	18	.270
2000— Buffalo (Int'l)	9	4	.692	3.11	1.21	16	15	1	0	...	0-...	101.1	99	41	35	7	24-1	68	.253
— Cleveland (A.L.)	2	3	.400	6.24	1.79	17	11	0	0	0	0-0	62.0	80	45	43	11	31-1	32	.309
2001— Louisville (Int'l)	1	0	1.000	4.09	1.27	2	2	0	0	...	0-...	11.0	12	5	5	1	2-0	11	.273
— Cincinnati (N.L.)	7	10	.412	3.97	1.38	46	10	0	0	2	1-2	129.1	119	65	57	17	60-5	94	.247
2002— Cincinnati (N.L.)	2	0	1.000	3.89	1.22	22	0	0	0	5	0-0	39.1	38	18	17	2	10-1	24	.260
— Montreal (N.L.)	1	2	.333	4.83	1.49	30	0	0	0	6	0-1	41.0	39	22	22	5	22-1	33	.245
2003— San Francisco (N.L.)	8	5	.615	3.96	1.29	51	5	0	0	2	2-3	100.0	90	48	44	8	39-2	65	.249
2004— San Francisco (N.L.)	7	7	.500	3.29	1.35	*89	0	0	0	24	1-5	93.0	90	42	34	6	36-2	63	.259
2005— San Francisco (N.L.)	2	1	.667	6.53	1.81	32	0	0	0	5	1-3	30.1	40	22	22	5	15-0	25	.320
— Richmond (Int'l)	0	1	.000	2.25	0.75	4	0	0	0	0	1-1	4.0	1	1	1	0	2-0	1	.091
— Atlanta (N.L.)	1	2	.333	4.20	1.67	37	0	0	0	7	0-0	30.0	33	14	14	6	17-3	28	.282
2006— Albuquerque (PCL)	0	1	.000	3.93	1.25	15	0	0	0	3	0-0	18.1	20	9	8	3	10-0	13	.282
— Baltimore (A.L.)	0	1	.000	13.86	2.76	12	0	0	0	1	0-1	12.1	21	19	19	1	13-1	9	.389
— San Diego (N.L.)	0	0	...	9.39	1.57	6	0	0	0	0	0-0	7.2	11	8	8	1	1-0	5	.344
— Portland (PCL)	5	2	.714	4.98	1.60	24	0	0	0	2	1-4	34.1	37	21	19	5	18-1	28	.276
American League totals (3 years)	5	5	.500	6.75	1.82	38	13	0	0	1	0-1	100.0	128	77	75	20	54-3	59	.310
National League totals (6 years)	28	27	.509	4.17	1.40	313	15	0	0	46	5-14	470.2	460	239	218	50	200-14	337	.260
Major League totals (8 years)	33	32	.508	4.62	1.48	351	28	0	0	47	5-15	570.2	588	316	293	70	254-17	396	.269

DIVISION SERIES RECORD

Year — Team (League)	W	L	Pct.	ERA	WHIP	G	GS	CG	ShO	Hld.	Sv.-Opp.	IP	H	R	ER	HR	BB-IBB	SO	Avg.
2003— San Francisco (N.L.)	0	0	...	6.00	2.67	2	0	0	0	0	0-0	3.0	5	3	2	0	3-1	3	.357
2005— Atlanta (N.L.)	0	0	...	0.00	0.56	3	0	0	0	0	0-0	5.1	0	0	0	0	3-0	2	.000
Division series totals (2 years)	0	0	...	2.16	1.32	5	0	0	0	0	0-0	8.1	5	3	2	0	6-1	5	.192

2006 LEFTY-RIGHTY SPLITS

vs.	Avg.	AB	H	2B	3B	HR	RBI	BB	SO	OBP	Slg.	vs.	Avg.	AB	H	2B	3B	HR	RBI	BB	SO	OBP	Slg.
L	.342	38	13	1	0	1	14	5	7	.432	.605	R	.396	48	19	5	0	1	10	9	7	.516	.563

BROWN, ADRIAN — OF

PERSONAL: Born February 7, 1974, in McComb, Miss. ... 6-0/200. ... Bats both, throws right. ... Full name: Adrian Demond Brown. ... High school: McComb (Miss.).
TRANSACTIONS/CAREER NOTES: Selected by Pittsburgh Pirates organization in 48th round of 1992 free-agent draft. ... Loaned by Pirates organization to Lethbridge of Pioneer League (June 11-September 19, 1993). ... On disabled list (June 13-July 4 and July 6-August 7, 2000); included rehabilitation assignments to Altoona and Nashville. ... On disabled list (April 17, 2001-remainder of season); included rehabilitation assignments to Altoona, Lynchburg and Williamsport. ... Released by Pirates (October 10, 2002). ... Signed by Tampa Bay Devil Rays organization (November 6, 2002). ... Selected by Boston Red Sox from Devil Rays organization in Rule 5 major league draft (December 16, 2002). ... Offered back to Devil Rays (March 26, 2003); Devil Rays declined offer. ... Signed as a free agent by Kansas City Royals organization (January 21, 2004). ... Signed as a free agent by Texas Rangers organization (November 9, 2005).
2006 GAMES PLAYED BY POSITION (MLB): OF—24.

											BATTING									FIELDING	
Year — Team (League)	Pos.	G	AB	R	H	2B	3B	HR	RBI	BB	SO	HBP	GDP	SB-CS	Avg.	OBP	SLG	OPS	E	Avg.
1992— GC Pirates (GCL)	1B-OF	39	121	11	31	2	2	0	12	0	12	2	3	8-4	.256	.268	.306	.574	1	.985
1993— Lethbridge (Pion.)	OF	69	282	47	75	12	9	3	27	17	34	5	8	22-7	.266	.319	.404	.723	1	.992
1994— Augusta (S. Atl.)	OF	79	308	41	80	17	1	1	18	14	38	0	2	19-12	.260	.292	.331	.623	2	.985
1995— Augusta (S. Atl.)	OF	76	287	64	86	15	4	4	31	33	23	1	2	25-14	.300	.372	.422	.793	7	.950
— Lynchburg (Caro.)	OF	54	215	30	52	5	2	1	14	12	20	1	3	11-6	.242	.284	.298	.582	2	.983
1996— Lynchburg (Caro.)	OF	52	215	39	69	9	3	4	25	14	24	2	1	18-9	.321	.368	.447	.814	2	.981
— Carolina (Southern)	OF	84	341	48	101	11	3	3	25	25	40	1	4	27-11	.296	.345	.372	.718	2	.990
1997— Carolina (Southern)	OF	37	145	29	44	4	4	2	15	18	12	2	1	9-5	.303	.388	.428	.815	3	.956
— Pittsburgh (N.L.)	OF	48	147	17	28	6	0	1	10	13	18	4	3	8-4	.190	.273	.524	1	.987
— Calgary (PCL)	OF	62	248	53	79	10	1	1	19	27	38	0	9	20-4	.319	.383	.379	.762	1	.993
1998— Nashville (PCL)	OF	85	311	58	90	12	5	3	27	28	38	0	7	25-7	.289	.346	.389	.735	5	.977
— Pittsburgh (N.L.)	OF	41	152	20	43	4	1	0	5	9	18	0	3	4-0	.283	.323	.322	.645	2	.977
1999— Pittsburgh (N.L.)	OF	116	226	34	61	5	2	4	17	33	39	1	5	5-3	.270	.364	.363	.727	4	.966
— Nashville (PCL)	OF	17	56	10	18	3	1	0	4	11	8	0	0	6-1	.321	.433	.411	.844	1	.969
2000— Pittsburgh (N.L.)	OF	104	308	64	97	18	3	4	28	29	34	0	1	13-1	.315	.373	.432	.805	4	.976
— Altoona (East.)	OF	2	5	1	0	0	0	0	0	3	1	0	0	0-0	.000	.375	.000	.375	0	1.000
— Nashville (PCL)	OF	8	26	3	6	1	0	0	2	2	4	1	0	3-0	.231	.310	.269	.580	0	1.000
2001— Pittsburgh (N.L.)	OF	8	31	3	6	0	0	1	2	3	3	0	1	2-1	.194	.265	.290	.555	0	1.000
— Altoona (East.)	DH	7	30	7	10	1	1	0	1	1	7	0	0	1-2	.333	.344	.433	.777	...	...
— Lynchburg (Caro.)	DH	4	18	2	6	0	0	0	1	1	3	1	0	2-0	.333	.400	.333	.733	...	...
— Williamsport (NYP)	DH	4	18	4	6	0	1	0	4	1	2	0	0	2-0	.333	.368	.444	.813	...	...
2002— Pittsburgh (N.L.)	OF	91	208	20	45	10	2	1	21	19	34	1	5	10-6	.216	.284	.298	.582	3	.974
— Nashville (PCL)	OF	51	184	36	62	7	1	3	16	23	18	0	3	13-7	.337	.409	.435	.843	2	.975
2003— Pawtucket (Int'l)	OF-DH	122	482	81	136	16	3	5	32	48	81	0	10	34-11	.282	.347	.359	.706	5	.983
— Boston (A.L.)	OF	9	15	2	3	0	0	0	1	1	4	0	0	2-0	.200	.250	.200	.450	0	1.000
2004— Kansas City (A.L.)	OF	5	11	0	3	0	0	0	0	2	0	0	0	0-0	.273	.273	.273	.545	0	1.000
— Omaha (PCL)	OF-DH	114	444	69	118	17	7	7	51	57	74	0	7	28-4	.266	.347	.383	.730	3	.987
2005— Omaha (PCL)	OF	140	553	104	151	28	8	9	49	74	73	4	17	33-7	.273	.361	.401	.763	10	.986
2006— Texas (A.L.)	OF	25	36	6	7	1	0	0	2	2	9	0	2	1-0	.194	.231	.222	.453	1	.971
— Oklahoma (PCL)		36	122	15	36	4	1	1	11	17	18	0	7	11-1	.295	.379	.369	.747	1	.981
American League totals (3 years)		39	62	8	13	1	0	0	3	3	15	0	2	3-0	.210	.242	.226	.468	1	.981
National League totals (6 years)		408	1072	158	280	43	8	11	83	106	146	6	18	42-15	.261	.330	.347	.677	14	.976
Major League totals (9 years)		447	1134	166	293	44	8	11	86	109	161	6	20	45-15	.258	.325	.340	.666	15	.976

DIVISION SERIES RECORD

Year — Team (League)	Pos.	G	AB	R	H	2B	3B	HR	RBI	BB	SO	HBP	GDP	SB-CS	Avg.	OBP	SLG	OPS	E	Avg.
2003— Boston (A.L.)	OF-DH	4	2	0	0	0	0	0	0	0	1	0	0	0-0	.000	.000	.000	.000	0	...

2006 LEFTY-RIGHTY SPLITS

vs.	Avg.	AB	H	2B	3B	HR	RBI	BB	SO	OBP	Slg.	vs.	Avg.	AB	H	2B	3B	HR	RBI	BB	SO	OBP	Slg.
L	.133	15	2	0	0	0	1	0	6	.125	.133	R	.238	21	5	1	0	0	1	2	3	.304	.286

BROWN, ANDREW — P

PERSONAL: Born February 17, 1981, in Chardon, Ohio. ... 6-6/230. ... Throws right, bats right. ... Full name: Andrew Aaron Brown. ... High school: Trinity Christian Academy (Jacksonville). . **TRANSACTIONS/CAREER NOTES:** Selected by Atlanta Braves organization in sixth round of free-agent draft (June 2, 1999). ... Traded by Braves with P Odalis Perez and OF Brian Jordan to Los Angeles Dodgers for OF Gary Sheffield (January 15, 2002). ... Traded by Dodgers to Cleveland Indians (May 19, 2004), completing deal in which Indians traded OF Milton Bradley to Dodgers for OF Franklin Gutierrez and a player to be named (April 3, 2004). ... Traded by Indians with IF Kevin Kouzmanoff to San Diego Padres for 2B Josh Barfield (November 8, 2006).

CAREER HITTING: 0-for-0 (.000), 0 R, 0 2B, 0 3B, 0 HR, 0 RBI.

Year — Team (League)	W	L	Pct.	ERA	WHIP	G	GS	CG	ShO	Hld.	Sv.-Opp.	IP	H	R	ER	HR	BB-IBB	SO	Avg.
1999— GC Braves (GCL)	1	1	.500	2.34	1.32	11	11	0	0	...	0-...	42.1	40	15	11	4	16-0	57	.247
2000—			Did not play.																
2001— Jamestown (NYP)	3	4	.429	3.92	1.26	14	12	0	0	...	0-...	64.1	50	29	28	5	31-0	59	.215
2002— Vero Beach (Fla. St.)	10	10	.500	4.11	1.25	25	24	1	1	...	0-...	127.0	97	63	58	13	62-0	129	.215
2003— Jacksonville (Sou.)	0	0	...	0.00	0.00	1	1	0	0	...	0-...	1.0	0	0	0	0	0-0	1	.000
2004— Jacksonville (Sou.)	1	3	.250	4.02	1.24	8	8	0	0	...	0-...	40.1	36	23	18	5	14-0	58	.235
— Buffalo (Int'l)	1	0	1.000	0.00	1.40	1	1	0	0	...	0-...	5.0	4	0	0	0	3-0	4	.222
— Akron (East.)	3	6	.333	4.66	1.32	17	17	0	0	...	0-...	77.1	66	44	40	7	36-1	67	.234
2005— Buffalo (Int'l)	4	2	.667	3.36	1.02	49	0	0	0	11	4-9	69.2	52	28	26	7	19-0	81	.204
2006— Buffalo (Int'l)	5	4	.556	2.60	1.41	39	0	0	0	3	5-6	62.1	52	21	18	5	36-1	53	.228
— Cleveland (A.L.)	0	0	...	3.60	1.40	9	0	0	0	0	0-0	10.0	6	4	4	0	8-1	7	.171
Major League totals (1 year)	0	0	...	3.60	1.40	9	0	0	0	0	0-0	10.0	6	4	4	0	8-1	7	.171

2006 LEFTY-RIGHTY SPLITS

vs.	Avg.	AB	H	2B	3B	HR	RBI	BB	SO	OBP	Slg.	vs.	Avg.	AB	H	2B	3B	HR	RBI	BB	SO	OBP	Slg.
L	.286	14	4	1	0	0	1	4	5	.444	.357	R	.095	21	2	0	0	0	1	4	2	.269	.095

BROWN, EMIL — OF

PERSONAL: Born December 29, 1974, in Chicago. ... 6-2/193. ... Bats right, throws right. ... Full name: Emil Quincy Brown. ... High school: Harlan (Chicago). ... Junior college: Indian River C.C. (Fla.). **TRANSACTIONS/CAREER NOTES:** Selected by Oakland Athletics organization in sixth round of 1994 free-agent draft. ... Selected by Pittsburgh Pirates organization from A's organization in Rule 5 major league draft (December 9, 1996). ... On disabled list (June 19-July 4, 2000); included rehabilitation assignment to Nashville. ... Traded by Pirates to San Diego Padres for P Shawn Camp and OF Shawn Garrett (July 10, 2001). ... Signed as a free agent by Tampa Bay Devil Rays organization (January 28, 2002). ... Signed as a free agent by Cincinnati Reds organization (November 19, 2002). ... Signed as a free agent by St. Louis Cardinals organization (January 9, 2004). ... Released by Cardinals (May 3, 2004). ... Signed by Campeche of the Mexican League (2004). ... Signed as a free agent by Houston Astros organization (August 12, 2004). ... Signed as a free agent by Kansas City Royals organization (December 16, 2004).

2006 GAMES PLAYED BY POSITION (MLB): OF—134, DH—10.

Year — Team (League)	Pos.	G	AB	R	H	2B	3B	HR	RBI	BB	SO	HBP	GDP	SB-CS	Avg.	OBP	SLG	OPS	E	Avg.
1994— Ariz. A's (Ariz.)	OF-OF	32	86	13	19	1	1	3	12	13	12	4	2	5-1	.221	.350	.360	.710	1	.979
1995— W. Mich. (Mid.)	OF-OF	124	459	63	115	17	3	3	67	52	77	11	17	35-19	.251	.337	.320	.657	8	.957
1996— Modesto (California)	OF-OF	57	211	50	64	10	1	10	47	32	51	6	5	13-5	.303	.406	.502	.908	4	.962
— Scottsdale (Ariz.)	OF	4	15	5	4	3	0	0	2	3	2	...	...	1-1	.267	...	.467	...	0	1.000
— Ariz. A's (Ariz.)	OF	4	15	5	4	3	0	0	2	3	2	1	0	1-1	.267	.421	.467	.888	0	1.000
1997— Pittsburgh (N.L.)	OF	66	95	16	17	2	1	2	6	10	32	...	...	5-1	.179	.257	.284	.541	3	.948
1998— Carolina (Southern)	OF-OF-DH	123	466	89	154	31	2	14	67	50	71	11	12	24-7	.330	.401	.496	.897	6	.972
— Pittsburgh (N.L.)	OF	13	39	2	10	1	0	0	3	1	11	...	...	0-0	.256	.275	.282	.557	0	1.000
1999— Nashville (PCL)	OF-OF-DH	110	430	97	132	20	5	18	60	35	80	7	7	16-5	.307	.366	.502	.868	10	.948
— Pittsburgh (N.L.)	OF	6	14	0	2	1	0	0	0	0	3	0	...	0-0	.143	.143	.214	.357	0	1.000
2000— Nashville (PCL)	OF	70	237	44	74	20	1	5	25	40	44	6	8	26-4	.312	.423	.468	.891	3	.978
— Pittsburgh (N.L.)	OF	50	119	13	26	5	0	3	16	11	34	3	...	3-1	.218	.299	.336	.635	0	1.000
2001— Pittsburgh (N.L.)	OF	61	123	18	25	4	1	3	13	15	42	2	...	10-4	.203	.300	.325	.625	1	.988
— San Diego (N.L.)	OF	13	14	3	1	0	0	0	0	1	7	0	...	2-0	.071	.133	.071	.205	0	1.000
— Portland (PCL)	OF-OF	22	78	10	25	8	2	3	8	6	17	2	2	3-1	.321	.384	.590	.974	1	1.000
2002— Durham (Int'l)	OF-OF	116	422	58	120	24	3	12	58	34	81	10	7	10-2	.284	.347	.441	.788	9	.963
2003— Louisville (Int'l)	OF	97	369	58	109	20	3	12	63	27	76	4	7	18-3	.295	.343	.463	.806	5	.970
2004— Memphis (PCL)	OF	19	57	7	16	3	0	0	4	5	9	1	2	1-1	.281	.349	.333	.682	0	1.000
— Campeche (Mex.)		28	101	23	32	8	0	8	24	15	16	1	1	0-0	.317	.403	.634	1.037	2	.000
— New Orleans (PCL)	OF	26	92	12	31	10	1	2	17	4	20	4	3	4-2	.337	.386	.533	.919	1	.000
2005— Kansas City (A.L.)	OF-DH	150	545	75	156	31	5	17	86	48	108	4	8	10-1	.286	.349	.455	.804	12	.958
2006— Kansas City (A.L.)	OF-DH	147	527	77	151	41	2	15	81	59	95	5	15	6-3	.287	.358	.457	.815	3	.990
American League totals (2 years)		297	1072	152	307	72	7	32	167	107	203	13	29	16-4	.286	.353	.456	.809	15	.975
National League totals (5 years)		209	404	52	81	13	2	8	38	38	129	5	...	20-6	.200	.277	.302	.579	4	.983
Major League totals (7 years)		506	1476	204	388	85	9	40	205	145	332	18	29	36-10	.263	.333	.414	.746	19	.977

2006 LEFTY-RIGHTY SPLITS

vs.	Avg.	AB	H	2B	3B	HR	RBI	BB	SO	OBP	Slg.	vs.	Avg.	AB	H	2B	3B	HR	RBI	BB	SO	OBP	Slg.
L	.236	157	37	10	1	8	27	18	32	.316	.465	R	.308	370	114	31	1	7	54	41	63	.375	.454

BROWN, JEREMY — C

PERSONAL: Born October 25, 1979, in Birmingham, Ala. ... 5-10/210. ... Bats right, throws right. ... Full name: Jeremy Scott Brown. ... College: Alabama.

TRANSACTIONS/CAREER NOTES: Selected by Boston Red Sox organization in 19th round of 2001 free-agent draft; did not sign. ... Selected by Oakland Athletics organization in supplemental round ("sandwich pick" between first and second rounds, 35th pick overall) of 2002 free-agent draft; pick received as compensation for New York Yankees signing Type A free-agent 1B Jason Giambi.

2006 GAMES PLAYED BY POSITION (MLB): DH—4, C—1.

Year — Team (League)	Pos.	G	AB	R	H	2B	3B	HR	RBI	BB	SO	HBP	GDP	SB-CS	Avg.	OBP	SLG	OPS	E	Avg.
2002— Vancouver (N'west)		10	28	7	8	1	0	0	1	10	5	1	1	1-0	.286	.487	.321	.808	...	...
— Visalia (Calif.)		55	187	36	58	14	0	10	40	44	49	2	5	1-1	.310	.444	.545	.989	...	...
2003— Midland (Texas)		66	233	37	64	10	1	5	37	41	38	3	11	3-0	.275	.388	.391	.779	...	...
2004— Midland (Texas)		122	446	59	114	27	0	6	49	71	80	4	20	1-1	.256	.361	.357	.718	...	...
2005— Midland (Texas)	C-1B-DH	115	394	65	103	27	1	20	72	52	88	11	17	0-0	.261	.359	.487	.847	13	.984

Year Team (League)	Pos.	G	AB	R	H	2B	3B	HR	RBI	BB	SO	HBP	GDP	SB-CS	Avg.	OBP	SLG	OPS	E	Avg.
2006—Sacramento (PCL)		77	275	41	70	14	0	13	40	23	60	4	6	0-0	.255	.317	.447	.764		.998
—Oakland (A.L.)	DH-C	5	10	1	3	2	0	0	0	1	1	0	0	0-0	.300	.364	.500	.864	0	1.000
Major League totals (1 year)		5	10	1	3	2	0	0	0	1	1	0	0	0-0	.300	.364	.500	.864	0	1.000

2006 LEFTY-RIGHTY SPLITS

vs.	Avg.	AB	H	2B	3B	HR	RBI	BB	SO	OBP	Slg.	vs.	Avg.	AB	H	2B	3B	HR	RBI	BB	SO	OBP	Slg.
L	.500	2	1	1	0	0	0	0	0	.500	1.000	R	.250	8	2	1	0	0	0	0	1	.333	.375

BROXTON, JONATHAN — P

PERSONAL: Born June 16, 1984, in Augusta, Ga. ... 6-4/240. ... Throws right, bats right. ... Full name: Jonathan Roy Broxton. ... High school: Burke County (Waynesboro, Ga.). **TRANSACTIONS/CAREER NOTES:** Selected by Los Angeles Dodgers organization in second round of 2002 free-agent draft.
CAREER HITTING: 0-for-2 (.000), 0 R, 0 2B, 0 3B, 0 HR, 0 RBI.

Year Team (League)	W	L	Pct.	ERA	WHIP	G	GS	CG	ShO	Hld.	Sv.-Opp.	IP	H	R	ER	HR	BB-IBB	SO	Avg.
2002—Great Falls (Pio.)	2	0	1.000	2.76	1.30	11	6	0	0	...	2-...	29.1	22	9	9	0	16-0	33	.212
2003—South Georgia (S. Atl.)	4	2	.667	3.13	1.31	9	8	0	0	...	0-...	37.1	27	15	13	1	22-0	30	.208
2004—Vero Beach (Fla. St.)	11	6	.647	3.23	1.19	23	23	1	1	...	0-...	128.1	110	49	46	7	43-0	144	.237
2005—Jacksonville (Sou.)	5	3	.625	3.17	1.14	33	13	0	0	2	5-5	96.2	79	36	34	4	31-0	107	.223
—Los Angeles (N.L.)	1	0	1.000	5.93	1.83	14	0	0	0	1	0-1	13.2	13	11	9	0	12-2	22	.245
2006—Las Vegas (PCL)	1	0	1.000	0.00	0.79	11	0	0	0	0	5-5	11.1	6	0	0	0	3-0	18	.154
—Los Angeles (N.L.)	4	1	.800	2.59	1.23	68	0	0	0	12	3-7	76.1	61	25	22	7	33-6	97	.216
Major League totals (2 years)	5	1	.833	3.10	1.32	82	0	0	0	13	3-8	90.0	74	36	31	7	45-8	119	.221

DIVISION SERIES RECORD

Year Team (League)	W	L	Pct.	ERA	WHIP	G	GS	CG	ShO	Hld.	Sv.-Opp.	IP	H	R	ER	HR	BB-IBB	SO	Avg.
2006—Los Angeles (N.L.)	0	1	.000	13.50	3.50	1	0	0	0	0	0-1	2.0	5	3	3	0	2-0	3	.417

2006 LEFTY-RIGHTY SPLITS

vs.	Avg.	AB	H	2B	3B	HR	RBI	BB	SO	OBP	Slg.	vs.	Avg.	AB	H	2B	3B	HR	RBI	BB	SO	OBP	Slg.
L	.244	119	29	6	2	4	14	23	43	.366	.429	R	.196	163	32	6	0	3	14	10	54	.246	.288

BRUNEY, BRIAN — P

PERSONAL: Born February 17, 1982, in Astoria, Ore. ... 6-3/226. ... Throws right, bats right. ... Full name: Brian Anthony Bruney. ... Name pronounced: BREW-nee. ... High school: Warrenton (Ore.). **TRANSACTIONS/CAREER NOTES:** Selected by Arizona Diamondbacks organization in 12th round of 2000 free-agent draft. ... On disabled list (May 27-July 6, 2004); included rehabilitation assignment to Tucson. ... Released by Diamondbacks (May 22, 2006). ... Signed by New York Yankees organization (July 19, 2006).
CAREER HITTING: 0-for-1 (.000), 0 R, 0 2B, 0 3B, 0 HR, 0 RBI.

Year Team (League)	W	L	Pct.	ERA	WHIP	G	GS	CG	ShO	Hld.	Sv.-Opp.	IP	H	R	ER	HR	BB-IBB	SO	Avg.
2000—Ariz. D'backs (Ariz.)	4	1	.800	6.48	2.00	20	2	0	0	...	2-...	25.0	21	23	18	2	29-0	24	.221
2001—South Bend (Mid.)	1	4	.200	4.13	1.32	26	0	0	0	...	8-...	32.2	24	19	15	1	19-2	40	.205
—Yakima (N'west)	1	2	.333	5.14	1.43	15	0	0	0	...	2-...	21.0	19	14	12	2	11-0	28	.226
2002—South Bend (Mid.)	4	3	.571	1.68	1.12	37	0	0	0	...	10-...	48.1	37	15	9	1	17-4	54	.210
—El Paso (Texas)	0	2	.000	2.92	1.22	10	0	0	0	...	0-...	12.1	11	5	4	1	4-1	14	.268
2003—El Paso (Texas)	0	2	.000	2.59	1.34	10	0	0	0	...	14-...	31.1	29	17	9	1	13-2	28	.234
—Tucson (PCL)	3	1	.750	2.81	1.31	32	0	0	0	...	12-...	32.0	24	12	10	0	18-0	32	.207
2004—Tucson (PCL)	2	0	1.000	1.18	1.00	31	0	0	0	...	5-...	38.0	18	8	5	1	20-1	42	.141
—Arizona (N.L.)	3	4	.429	4.31	1.50	30	0	0	0	3	0-1	31.1	20	16	15	2	27-5	34	.189
2005—Tucson (PCL)	1	0	1.000	1.93	1.71	4	0	0	0	0	...	4.2	3	3	1	0	5-0	3	.188
—Arizona (N.L.)	1	3	.250	7.43	1.98	47	0	0	0	4	12-16	46.0	56	39	38	6	35-2	51	.299
2006—Tucson (PCL)	0	1	.000	33.75	5.25	4	0	0	0	0	0-0	2.2	10	12	10	2	4-0	4	.556
—GC Yankees (GCL)	0	0	...	4.91	1.09	3	0	0	0	0	0-0	3.2	1	2	2	0	3-0	5	.091
—Columbus (Int'l)	1	1	.500	3.14	1.26	11	0	0	0	1	3-3	14.1	10	6	5	2	8-0	22	.196
—New York (A.L.)	1	1	.500	0.87	1.40	19	0	0	0	4	0-0	20.2	14	2	2	1	15-0	25	.189
American League totals (1 year)	1	1	.500	0.87	1.40	19	0	0	0	4	0-0	20.2	14	2	2	1	15-0	25	.189
National League totals (2 years)	4	7	.364	6.17	1.78	77	0	0	0	7	12-17	77.1	76	55	53	8	62-7	85	.259
Major League totals (3 years)	5	8	.385	5.05	1.70	96	0	0	0	11	12-17	98.0	90	57	55	9	77-7	110	.245

DIVISION SERIES RECORD

Year Team (League)	W	L	Pct.	ERA	WHIP	G	GS	CG	ShO	Hld.	Sv.-Opp.	IP	H	R	ER	HR	BB-IBB	SO	Avg.
2006—New York (A.L.)	0	0	...	3.38	0.38	3	0	0	0	0	0-0	2.2	1	1	1	1	0-0	4	.125

2006 LEFTY-RIGHTY SPLITS

vs.	Avg.	AB	H	2B	3B	HR	RBI	BB	SO	OBP	Slg.	vs.	Avg.	AB	H	2B	3B	HR	RBI	BB	SO	OBP	Slg.
L	.115	26	3	0	0	0	1	8	9	.343	.115	R	.229	48	11	3	0	1	6	7	16	.327	.354

BRUNTLETT, ERIC — IF/OF

PERSONAL: Born March 29, 1978, in Lafayette, Ind. ... 6-0/190. ... Bats right, throws right. ... Full name: Eric Kevin Bruntlett. ... High school: William Henry Harrison (West Lafayette, Ind.). ... College: Stanford. **TRANSACTIONS/CAREER NOTES:** Selected by Los Angeles Dodgers organization in 72nd round of 1996 free-agent draft; did not sign. ... Selected by Houston Astros in ninth round of 2000 free-agent draft.
2006 GAMES PLAYED BY POSITION (MLB): 2B—23, SS—21, OF—18, 3B—2.

Year Team (League)	Pos.	G	AB	R	H	2B	3B	HR	RBI	BB	SO	HBP	GDP	SB-CS	Avg.	OBP	SLG	OPS	E	Avg.
2000—Martinsville (App.)	SS-OF	50	172	40	47	11	4	1	21	30	22	11	2	14-1	.273	.413	.401	.814	12	.944
2001—Round Rock (Texas)	SS	123	503	84	134	23	3	3	40	50	76	8	7	23-7	.266	.340	.342	.682	23	.956
—New Orleans (PCL)	SS	5	16	3	2	0	0	0	1	2	1	0	1	0-0	.125	.222	.125	.347	0	1.000
2002—Round Rock (Texas)	SS-2B	116	464	81	123	21	2	2	48	56	61	10	17	35-12	.265	.351	.332	.683	19	.966
—New Orleans (PCL)	SS-2B	18	68	9	14	3	0	0	1	10	10	0	3	1-1	.206	.308	.250	.558	6	.941
2003—New Orleans (PCL)	SS-2B-OF	84	324	48	84	10	0	2	27	35	51	3	3	9-4	.259	.332	.309	.641	13	.967
—Houston (N.L.)	SS-2B-OF-3B	31	54	3	14	3	0	1	4	0	10	0	1	0-0	.259	.255	.370	.625	1	.981
2004—New Orleans (PCL)	SS-OF-2B	86	332	50	83	12	4	6	37	35	72	1	10	14-4	.250	.331	.364	.695	12	.970
—Houston (N.L.)	SS-2B-OF	45	52	14	13	2	0	4	8	7	13	0	0	4-0	.250	.328	.519	.847	3	.947
2005—Houston (N.L.)	2B-OF-SS-3B-1B	91	109	19	24	5	2	4	14	10	25	1	4	7-2	.220	.292	.413	.705	2	.982
2006—Round Rock (PCL)		22	73	11	16	3	1	1	7	17	13	2	0	3-2	.219	.380	.329	.709	1	.982
—Houston (N.L.)	2B-SS-OF-3B	73	119	11	33	8	0	0	10	13	21	1	2	3-1	.277	.351	.345	.695	7	.949
Major League totals (4 years)		240	334	47	84	18	2	9	36	30	69	2	7	14-3	.251	.314	.398	.712	13	.964

B

DIVISION SERIES RECORD

Year Team (League)	Pos.	G	AB	R	H	2B	3B	HR	RBI	BB	SO	HBP	GDP	SB-CS	Avg.	OBP	SLG	OPS	E	Avg.
2004— Houston (N.L.)	SS	2	1	0	0	0	0	0	0	1	0	0	0	0-0	.000	.500	.000	.500	0	1.000
2005— Houston (N.L.)	OF-2B-SS	3	6	1	1	0	0	0	0	0	4	0	0	1-0	.167	.167	.167	.333	0	1.000
Division series totals (2 years)		5	7	1	1	0	0	0	0	1	4	0	0	1-0	.143	.250	.143	.393	0	1.000

CHAMPIONSHIP SERIES RECORD

Year Team (League)	Pos.	G	AB	R	H	2B	3B	HR	RBI	BB	SO	HBP	GDP	SB-CS	Avg.	OBP	SLG	OPS	E	Avg.
2004— Houston (N.L.)	SS	4	2	0	0	0	0	0	0	0	0	0	0	0-0	.000	.000	.000	.000	0	...
2005— Houston (N.L.)	2B-SS	5	1	0	0	0	0	0	0	0	1	0	0	0-0	.000	.000	.000	.000	0	1.000
Champ. series totals (2 years)		9	3	0	0	0	0	0	0	0	1	0	0	0-0	.000	.000	.000	.000	0	1.000

WORLD SERIES RECORD

Year Team (League)	Pos.	G	AB	R	H	2B	3B	HR	RBI	BB	SO	HBP	GDP	SB-CS	Avg.	OBP	SLG	OPS	E	Avg.
2005— Houston (N.L.)	2B-OF	2	0	0	0	0	0	0	0	0	0	0	0	0-0	...	...	...	...	0	1.000

2006 LEFTY-RIGHTY SPLITS

vs.	Avg.	AB	H	2B	3B	HR	RBI	BB	SO	OBP	Slg.	vs.	Avg.	AB	H	2B	3B	HR	RBI	BB	SO	OBP	Slg.
L	.350	40	14	3	0	0	5	5	7	.413	.425	R	.241	79	19	5	0	0	5	8	14	.318	.304

BUCHHOLZ, TAYLOR   P

PERSONAL: Born October 13, 1981, in Lower Merion, Pa. ... 6-4/220. ... Throws right, bats right. ... Full name: Taylor Buchholz. . **TRANSACTIONS/CAREER NOTES:** Selected by Philadelphia Phillies organization in sixth round of 2000 free-agent draft ... Traded by Phillies with Ps Brandon Duckworth and Ezequiel Astacio to Houston Astros for P Billy Wagner (November 3, 2003). **MISCELLANEOUS NOTES:** Made an out in only appearance as pinch hitter (2006).
CAREER HITTING: 1-for-30 (.033), 0 R, 0 2B, 0 3B, 0 HR, 0 RBI.

Year Team (League)	W	L	Pct.	ERA	WHIP	G	GS	CG	ShO	Hld.	Sv.-Opp.	IP	H	R	ER	HR	BB-IBB	SO	Avg.
2000— GC Phillies (GCL)	2	3	.400	2.25	1.36	12	7	0	0	...	0-...	44.0	46	22	11	2	14-0	41	.269
2001— Lakewood (S. Atl.)	9	14	.391	3.36	1.26	28	26	5	3	...	0-...	176.2	165	83	66	8	57-0	136	.250
2002— Clearwater (Fla. St.)	10	6	.625	3.29	1.20	23	23	4	2	...	0-...	158.2	140	66	58	11	51-1	129	.233
— Reading (East.)	0	2	.000	7.43	1.52	4	4	0	0	...	0-...	23.0	29	19	19	5	6-0	17	.315
2003— Reading (East.)	9	11	.450	3.55	1.17	25	24	1	0	...	0-...	144.2	136	62	57	14	33-0	114	.249
2004— New Orleans (PCL)	6	7	.462	5.23	1.39	20	17	1	0	...	0-...	98.0	107	60	57	16	29-0	74	.279
2005— Round Rock (PCL)	6	0	1.000	4.81	1.38	20	14	0	0	0	0-0	76.2	79	41	41	14	27-0	45	.275
2006— Round Rock (PCL)	1	3	.250	4.91	1.45	7	7	0	0	0	0-0	44.0	47	27	24	2	17-0	37	.278
— Houston (N.L.)	6	10	.375	5.89	1.25	22	19	1	1	0	0-0	113.0	107	80	74	21	34-4	77	.248
Major League totals (1 year)	6	10	.375	5.89	1.25	22	19	1	1	0	0-0	113.0	107	80	74	21	34-4	77	.248

2006 LEFTY-RIGHTY SPLITS

vs.	Avg.	AB	H	2B	3B	HR	RBI	BB	SO	OBP	Slg.	vs.	Avg.	AB	H	2B	3B	HR	RBI	BB	SO	OBP	Slg.
L	.249	205	51	14	1	11	38	15	34	.296	.488	R	.248	226	56	13	1	10	32	19	43	.310	.447

BUCK, JOHN   C

PERSONAL: Born July 7, 1980, in Kemmerer, Wyo. ... 6-3/210. ... Bats right, throws right. ... Full name: Johnathan R. Buck. ... High school: Taylorsville (Utah). **TRANSACTIONS/CAREER NOTES:** Selected by Houston Astros organization in seventh round of 1998 free-agent draft. ... Traded by Astros with cash to Kansas City Royals as part of three-team deal in which Astros acquired OF Carlos Beltran from Royals, Royals acquired P Mike Wood and 3B Mark Teahen from Oakland Athletics and Athletics acquired P Octavio Dotel from Astros (June 24, 2004). **STATISTICAL NOTES:** Career major league grand slams: 1.
2006 GAMES PLAYED BY POSITION (MLB): C—112.

Year Team (League)	Pos.	G	AB	R	H	2B	3B	HR	RBI	BB	SO	HBP	GDP	SB-CS	Avg.	OBP	SLG	OPS	E	Avg.
1998— GC Astros (GCL)	C	36	126	24	36	9	0	3	15	13	22	2	0	2-2	.286	.362	.429	.790	4	.983
1999— Auburn (NY-Penn)	C	63	233	36	57	17	0	3	29	25	48	5	7	7-1	.245	.328	.356	.685	16	.974
— Michigan (Midw.)	C	4	10	1	1	1	0	0	0	2	3	0	0	0-0	.100	.250	.200	.450	1	1.000
2000— Michigan (Midw.)	C	109	390	57	110	33	0	10	71	55	81	5	8	2-4	.282	.374	.444	.817	15	.982
2001— Lexington (S. Atl.)	C	122	443	72	122	24	1	22	73	37	84	12	8	4-9	.275	.345	.483	.828	6	.995
2002— Round Rock (Texas)	C	120	448	48	118	29	3	12	89	31	93	6	11	2-3	.263	.314	.422	.736	8	.990
2003— New Orleans (PCL)	C	78	274	32	70	18	2	2	39	14	53	4	11	1-0	.255	.301	.358	.659	3	.993
2004— New Orleans (PCL)	C-DH	65	227	31	68	11	0	12	35	21	39	4	13	0-1	.300	.368	.507	.864	11	.971
— Kansas City (A.L.)	C-DH	71	238	36	56	9	0	12	30	15	79	0	6	1-1	.235	.280	.424	.704	3	.992
2005— Kansas City (A.L.)	C	118	401	40	97	21	1	12	47	23	94	3	9	2-2	.242	.287	.389	.676	3	.996
2006— Kansas City (A.L.)	C	114	371	37	91	21	1	11	50	26	84	7	7	0-2	.245	.306	.396	.702	6	.991
Major League totals (3 years)		303	1010	113	244	51	2	35	127	64	257	10	22	3-5	.242	.292	.400	.692	12	.993

2006 LEFTY-RIGHTY SPLITS

vs.	Avg.	AB	H	2B	3B	HR	RBI	BB	SO	OBP	Slg.	vs.	Avg.	AB	H	2B	3B	HR	RBI	BB	SO	OBP	Slg.
L	.246	114	28	4	1	6	14	13	26	.331	.456	R	.245	257	63	17	0	5	36	13	58	.295	.370

BUEHRLE, MARK   P

PERSONAL: Born March 23, 1979, in St. Charles, Mo. ... 6-2/220. ... Throws left, bats left. ... Full name: Mark Anthony Buehrle. ... Name pronounced: BURR-lee. ... High school: Francis Howell North (St. Charles, Mo.). ... Junior college: Jefferson (Hillsboro, Mo.). **TRANSACTIONS/CAREER NOTES:** Selected by Chicago White Sox organization in 38th round of 1998 free-agent draft.
CAREER HITTING: 2-for-25 (.080), 1 R, 0 2B, 0 3B, 0 HR, 1 RBI.

Year Team (League)	W	L	Pct.	ERA	WHIP	G	GS	CG	ShO	Hld.	Sv.-Opp.	IP	H	R	ER	HR	BB-IBB	SO	Avg.
1999— Burlington (Midw.)	7	4	.636	4.10	1.23	20	14	1	1	...	3-...	98.2	105	49	45	8	16-1	91	.271
2000— Birmingham (Sou.)	8	4	.667	2.28	0.94	16	16	1	1	...	0-...	118.2	95	37	30	8	17-0	68	.222
— Chicago (A.L.)	4	1	.800	4.21	1.44	28	3	0	0	3	0-2	51.1	55	27	24	5	19-1	37	.272
2001— Chicago (A.L.)	16	8	.667	3.29	1.07	32	32	4	2	0	0-0	221.1	188	89	81	24	48-2	126	.230
2002— Chicago (A.L.)	19	12	.613	3.58	1.24	34	34	5	2	0	0-0	239.0	236	102	95	25	61-7	134	.260
2003— Chicago (A.L.)	14	14	.500	4.14	1.35	35	35	2	0	0	0-0	230.1	250	124	106	22	61-2	119	.278
2004— Chicago (A.L.)	16	10	.615	3.89	1.26	35	* 35	4	1	0	0-0	* 245.1	219	110	106	33	51-2	165	.271
2005— Chicago (A.L.)	16	8	.667	3.12	1.18	33	33	3	1	0	0-0	* 236.2	* 240	99	82	20	40-4	149	.262
2006— Chicago (A.L.)	12	13	.480	4.99	1.45	32	32	1	0	0	0-0	204.0	• 247	124	113	36	48-5	98	.305
Major League totals (7 years)	97	66	.595	3.83	1.26	229	204	19	6	3	0-2	1428.0	1473	684	607	165	328-23	828	.268

DIVISION SERIES RECORD

Year Team (League)	W	L	Pct.	ERA	WHIP	G	GS	CG	ShO	Hld.	Sv.-Opp.	IP	H	R	ER	HR	BB-IBB	SO	Avg.
2000— Chicago (A.L.)	0	0	...	0.00	6.00	1	0	0	0	0	0-0	0.1	2	0	0	0	0-0	1	.667
2005— Chicago (A.L.)	1	0	1.000	5.14	1.29	1	1	0	0	0	0-0	7.0	8	4	4	0	1-1	2	.276
Division series totals (2 years)	1	0	1.000	4.91	1.50	2	1	0	0	0	0-0	7.1	10	4	4	0	1-1	3	.313

CHAMPIONSHIP SERIES RECORD

Year Team (League)	W	L	Pct.	ERA	WHIP	G	GS	CG	ShO	Hld.	Sv.-Opp.	IP	H	R	ER	HR	BB-IBB	SO	Avg.
2005— Chicago (A.L.)	1	0	1.000	1.00	0.56	1	1	0	0	...	0-0	9.0	5	1	1	1	0-0	4	.167

WORLD SERIES RECORD

Year Team (League)	W	L	Pct.	ERA	WHIP	G	GS	CG	ShO	Hld.	Sv.-Opp.	IP	H	R	ER	HR	BB-IBB	SO	Avg.
2005— Chicago (A.L.)	0	0	...	4.91	0.95	2	1	0	0	...	1-1	7.1	7	4	4	1	0-0	6	.250

ALL-STAR GAME RECORD

Year Team (League)	W	L	Pct.	ERA	WHIP	G	GS	CG	ShO	Hld.	Sv.-Opp.	IP	H	R	ER	HR	BB-IBB	SO	Avg.
All-Star Game totals (2 years)	1	0	1.000	2.25	1.25	2	1	0	0	0	0-0	4.0	5	1	1	0	0-0	5	.313

2006 LEFTY-RIGHTY SPLITS

vs.	Avg.	AB	H	2B	3B	HR	RBI	BB	SO	OBP	Slg.	vs.	Avg.	AB	H	2B	3B	HR	RBI	BB	SO	OBP	Slg.
L	.238	160	38	4	0	8	24	6	23	.282	.413	R	.322	649	209	44	2	28	95	42	75	.362	.525

BULGER, JASON   P

PERSONAL: Born December 6, 1978, in Lawrenceville, Ga. ... 6-4/215. ... Throws right, bats right. ... Full name: Jason Patrick Bulger. ... High school: Snellville (Ga.) Brookwood. ... College: Valdosta State. **TRANSACTIONS/CAREER NOTES:** Selected by Arizona Diamondbacks organization in first round (22nd pick overall) of 2001 free-agent draft. ... Traded by Diamondbacks to Los Angeles Angels of Anaheim for SS Alberto Callaspo (February 28, 2006).

CAREER HITTING: 0-for-0 (.000), 0 R, 0 2B, 0 3B, 0 HR, 0 RBI.

Year Team (League)	W	L	Pct.	ERA	WHIP	G	GS	CG	ShO	Hld.	Sv.-Opp.	IP	H	R	ER	HR	BB-IBB	SO	Avg.
2002— South Bend (Mid.)	4	9	.308	4.94	1.58	20	20	1	0	...	0-...	94.2	111	65	52	5	39-0	84	.291
— Lancaster (Calif.)	1	1	.500	5.40	1.40	2	2	0	0	...	0-...	10.0	11	7	6	0	3-0	12	.289
2003— Lancaster (Calif.)	2	1	.667	6.75	1.62	4	4	0	0	...	0-...	17.1	23	13	13	3	5-0	20	.311
2004— Lancaster (Calif.)	0	1	.000	1.52	1.01	21	0	0	0	...	11-...	23.2	14	4	4	0	10-1	31	.165
— El Paso (Texas)	0	3	.000	3.91	1.70	24	0	0	0	...	8-...	25.1	24	12	11	0	19-2	26	.240
2005— Tucson (PCL)	3	6	.333	3.54	1.38	56	0	0	0	9	4-7	56.0	50	28	22	3	27-1	55	.244
— Arizona (N.L.)	1	0	1.000	5.40	1.90	9	0	0	0	0	0-0	10.0	14	6	6	1	5-1	9	.333
2006— Los Angeles (A.L.)	0	0	...	16.20	2.40	2	0	0	0	0	0-0	1.2	1	3	3	0	3-0	1	.167
— Salt Lake (PCL)	2	2	.500	4.72	1.31	27	0	0	0	3	4-5	34.1	30	19	18	0	15-0	44	.233
American League totals (1 year)	0	0	...	16.20	2.40	2	0	0	0	0	0-0	1.2	1	3	3	0	3-0	1	.167
National League totals (1 year)	1	0	1.000	5.40	1.90	9	0	0	0	0	0-0	10.0	14	6	6	1	5-1	9	.333
Major League totals (2 years)	1	0	1.000	6.94	1.97	11	0	0	0	0	0-0	11.2	15	9	9	1	8-1	10	.313

2006 LEFTY-RIGHTY SPLITS

vs.	Avg.	AB	H	2B	3B	HR	RBI	BB	SO	OBP	Slg.	vs.	Avg.	AB	H	2B	3B	HR	RBI	BB	SO	OBP	Slg.
L	.333	3	1	0	0	0	0	2	0	.600	.333	R	.000	3	0	0	0	0	0	1	1	.250	.000

BULLINGTON, BRYAN   P

PERSONAL: Born September 30, 1980, in Indianapolis, Ind. ... 6-4/222. ... Throws right, bats right. ... Full name: Bryan Paul Bullington. ... College: Ball State. **TRANSACTIONS/CAREER NOTES:** Selected by Pittsburgh Pirates organization in first round (first pick overall) of 2002 free-agent draft. ... On disabled list (March 31, 2006-entire season).

CAREER HITTING: 0-for-0 (.000), 0 R, 0 2B, 0 3B, 0 HR, 0 RBI.

Year Team (League)	W	L	Pct.	ERA	WHIP	G	GS	CG	ShO	Hld.	Sv.-Opp.	IP	H	R	ER	HR	BB-IBB	SO	Avg.
2003— Hickory (S. Atl.)	5	1	.833	1.39	0.79	8	7	0	0	...	0-...	45.1	25	10	7	3	11-0	46	.155
— Lynchburg (Caro.)	8	4	.667	3.05	1.32	17	17	2	1	...	0-...	97.1	101	39	33	5	27-0	67	.270
2004— Altoona (East.)	12	7	.632	4.10	1.43	26	26	0	0	...	0-...	145.0	160	77	66	18	47-1	100	.289
2005— Indianapolis (Int'l)	9	5	.643	3.38	1.19	18	18	1	0	0	0-0	109.1	104	48	41	11	26-1	82	.251
— Pittsburgh (N.L.)	0	0	...	13.50	1.50	1	0	0	0	0	0-0	1.1	1	2	2	0	1-0	1	.250
2006— Pittsburgh (N.L.)				Did not play.															
Major League totals (1 year)	0	0	...	13.50	1.50	1	0	0	0	0	0-0	1.1	1	2	2	0	1-0	1	.250

BURGOS, AMBIORIX   P

PERSONAL: Born April 19, 1984, in Nagua, Dominican Republic. ... 6-3/235. ... Throws right, bats right.... Full name: Ambiorix Burgos.... Name pronounced: am-bee-ORR-ix. ... High school: San Jose de Villa (Nagua, Dominican Republic). **TRANSACTIONS/CAREER NOTES:** Signed as a non-drafted free agent by Kansas City Royals organization (November 14, 2000). ... On disabled list (June 20-July 14, 2005).

CAREER HITTING: 0-for-0 (.000), 0 R, 0 2B, 0 3B, 0 HR, 0 RBI.

Year Team (League)	W	L	Pct.	ERA	WHIP	G	GS	CG	ShO	Hld.	Sv.-Opp.	IP	H	R	ER	HR	BB-IBB	SO	Avg.
2001— Dom. Royals (DSL)	2	5	.286	4.97	1.70	13	11	0	0	...	0-...	50.2	51	36	28	1	35-0	38	.262
2002— Dom. Royals (DSL)	0	9	.000	5.47	1.47	13	12	0	0	...	0-...	51.0	47	42	31	1	28-0	33	.241
2003— Ariz. Royals 1 (AZL)	3	2	.600	4.00	1.47	9	7	0	0	...	0-...	36.0	37	22	16	1	16-0	43	.261
— Burlington (Midw.)	0	1	.000	5.40	1.80	2	2	0	0	...	0-...	5.0	3	3	3	1	6-0	4	.200
2004— Burlington (Midw.)	7	11	.389	4.38	1.38	27	26	0	0	...	0-...	133.2	109	70	65	13	75-1	172	.228
2005— Wichita (Texas)	1	1	.500	4.97	1.26	12	0	0	0	2	1-2	12.2	8	7	7	1	8-0	19	.170
— Kansas City (Texas)	3	5	.375	3.98	1.44	59	0	0	0	11	2-6	63.1	60	29	28	6	31-1	65	.251
2006— Kansas City (A.L.)	4	5	.444	5.52	1.64	68	1	0	0	5	18-30	73.1	83	49	45	16	37-4	72	.288
Major League totals (2 years)	7	10	.412	4.81	1.54	127	1	0	0	16	20-36	136.2	143	78	73	22	68-5	137	.271

2006 LEFTY-RIGHTY SPLITS

vs.	Avg.	AB	H	2B	3B	HR	RBI	BB	SO	OBP	Slg.	vs.	Avg.	AB	H	2B	3B	HR	RBI	BB	SO	OBP	Slg.
L	.345	119	41	5	2	10	30	18	33	.436	.672	R	.249	169	42	6	1	6	27	19	39	.333	.402

BURKE, CHRIS   OF/2B

PERSONAL: Born March 11, 1980, in Louisville, Ky. ... 5-11/180. ... Bats right, throws right. ... Full name: Christopher Allan Burke. ... High school: St. Xavier (Louisville). ... College: Tennessee. **TRANSACTIONS/CAREER NOTES:** Selected by Houston Astros organization in first round (10th pick overall) of 2001 free-agent draft. ... On disabled list (May 7-22, 2006); included rehabilitation assignment to Round Rock.

2006 GAMES PLAYED BY POSITION (MLB): 2B—69, OF—61, SS—8.

Year Team (League)	Pos.	G	AB	R	H	2B	3B	HR	RBI	BB	SO	HBP	GDP	SB-CS	Avg.	OBP	SLG	OPS	E	Avg.
2001— Michigan (Midw.)	SS	56	233	47	70	11	6	3	17	26	31	3	3	21-8	.300	.376	.438	.814	17	.931
2002— Round Rock (Texas)	2B-SS	136	481	66	127	19	8	5	37	39	61	10	8	16-15	.264	.330	.356	.686	23	.965
2003— Round Rock (Texas)	2B-SS-OF	137	549	88	165	23	8	3	41	57	57	14	8	34-10	.301	.379	.388	.767	21	.969
2004— New Orleans (PCL)	2B	123	483	93	152	33	6	16	52	55	76	13	7	37-14	.315	.396	.507	.888	11	.983
— Houston (N.L.)	2B	17	17	2	1	0	0	0	0	3	3	0	0	0-0	.059	.200	.059	.259	0	1.000

B

Year	Team (League)	Pos.	G	AB	R	H	2B	3B	HR	RBI	BB	SO	HBP	GDP	SB-CS	Avg.	OBP	SLG	OPS	E	Avg.
2005—	Round Rock (PCL)	2B-OF	22	90	15	28	6	2	2	11	8	13	2	2	9-0	.311	.380	.489	.869	1	.991
—	Houston (N.L.)	OF-2B	108	318	49	79	19	2	5	26	23	62	6	7	11-6	.248	.309	.368	.676	1	.994
2006—	Round Rock (PCL)		2	8	2	4	1	0	1	2	1	0	0	0	0-0	.500	.556	1.000	1.556	1	.875
—	Houston (N.L.)	2B-OF-SS	123	366	58	101	23	1	9	40	27	77	14	6	11-1	.276	.347	.418	.765	7	.977
Major League totals (3 years)			248	701	109	181	42	3	14	66	53	142	20	13	22-7	.258	.326	.387	.713	8	.984

DIVISION SERIES RECORD

Year	Team (League)	Pos.	G	AB	R	H	2B	3B	HR	RBI	BB	SO	HBP	GDP	SB-CS	Avg.	OBP	SLG	OPS	E	Avg.
2005—	Houston (N.L.)	OF	3	3	1	2	1	0	1	1	1	0	0	0	0-0	.667	.750	2.000	2.750	0	1.000

CHAMPIONSHIP SERIES RECORD

Year	Team (League)	Pos.	G	AB	R	H	2B	3B	HR	RBI	BB	SO	HBP	GDP	SB-CS	Avg.	OBP	SLG	OPS	E	Avg.
2005—	Houston (N.L.)	OF	6	20	5	6	0	1	1	3	3	0	0	0	0-0	.300	.333	.550	.883	0	1.000

WORLD SERIES RECORD

Year	Team (League)	Pos.	G	AB	R	H	2B	3B	HR	RBI	BB	SO	HBP	GDP	SB-CS	Avg.	OBP	SLG	OPS	E	Avg.
2005—	Houston (N.L.)	OF-2B	4	5	1	0	0	0	0	0	2	0	0	0	2-0	.000	.286	.000	.286	0	1.000

2006 LEFTY-RIGHTY SPLITS

vs.	Avg.	AB	H	2B	3B	HR	RBI	BB	SO	OBP	Slg.	vs.	Avg.	AB	H	2B	3B	HR	RBI	BB	SO	OBP	Slg.
L	.327	101	33	6	0	2	8	7	24	.393	.446	R	.257	265	68	17	1	7	32	20	53	.330	.408

BURNETT, A.J.   P

PERSONAL: Born January 3, 1977, in North Little Rock, Ark. ... 6-4/230. ... Throws right, bats right. ... Full name: Allan James Burnett. ... High school: Central Arkansas Christian (North Little Rock). **TRANSACTIONS/CAREER NOTES:** Selected by New York Mets organization in eighth round of 1995 free-agent draft. ... Traded by Mets with P Jesus Sanchez and OF Robert Stratton to Florida Marlins for P Al Leiter and 2B Ralph Milliard (February 6, 1998). ... On disabled list (March 17-July 20, 2000); included rehabilitation assignments to Brevard County and Calgary. ... On disabled list (March 23-May 7, 2001); included rehabilitation assignment to Brevard County. ... On disabled list (August 19-September 14, 2002; and March 21-April 9 and April 26, 2003-remainder of season). ... On disabled list (March 26-June 3, 2004); included rehabilitation assignments to Jupiter and Albuquerque. ... Signed as a free agent by Toronto Blue Jays (December 6, 2005). ... On disabled list (March 31-April 15 and April 22-June 22, 2006); included rehabilitation assignments to Dunedin, Syracuse and New Hampshire. **STATISTICAL NOTES:** Pitched 3-0 no-hit victory against San Diego (May 12, 2001).
CAREER HITTING: 34-for-256 (.133), 12 R, 6 2B, 3 3B, 3 HR, 9 RBI.

Year	Team (League)	W	L	Pct.	ERA	WHIP	G	GS	CG	ShO	Hld.	Sv.-Opp.	IP	H	R	ER	HR	BB-IBB	SO	Avg.
1995—	GC Mets (GCL)	2	3	.400	4.28	1.49	9	8	1	0		0-	33.2	27	16	16	2	23-0	26	.231
1996—	Kingsport (Appalachian)	4	0	1.000	3.88	1.47	12	12	0	0		0-	58.0	31	26	25	0	54-0	68	.171
1997—	GC Mets (GCL)	0	1	.000	3.18	1.41	3	2	0	0		0-	11.1	8	8	4	0	8-0	15	.182
—	Pittsfield (NYP)	3	1	.750	4.70	1.43	20	9	0	0		0-	44.0	28	26	23	3	35-0	48	.188
1998—	Kane Co. (Midw.)	10	4	.714	1.97	1.00	20	20	0	0		0-	119.0	74	27	26	3	45-0	186	.179
1999—	Portland (East.)	6	12	.333	5.52	1.68	26	23	0	0		0-	120.2	132	91	74	15	71-0	121	.281
—	Florida (N.L.)	4	2	.667	3.48	1.50	7	7	0	0		0-	41.1	37	23	16	3	25-2	33	.242
2000—	Brevard County (Fla. St.) ...	0	0	...	3.68	1.36	2	2	0	0		0-	7.1	4	3	3	0	6-0	6	.160
—	Calgary (PCL)	0	0	...	0.00	0.60	1	1	0	0		0-	5.0	0	0	0	0	3-0	6	.000
—	Florida (N.L.)	3	7	.300	4.79	1.50	13	13	0	0		0-0	82.2	80	46	44	8	44-3	57	.259
2001—	Brevard County (Fla. St.) ...	0	0	...	1.93	0.86	2	2	0	0		0-	9.1	4	2	2	0	4-0	10	.129
—	Florida (N.L.)	11	12	.478	4.05	1.32	27	27	2	1		0-0	173.1	145	82	78	20	83-3	128	.231
2002—	Florida (N.L.)	12	9	.571	3.30	1.19	31	29	7	*5		0-1	204.1	153	84	75	12	90-5	203	.209
2003—	Florida (N.L.)	2	0	.000	4.70	1.57	4	4	0	0		0-	23.0	18	13	12	2	18-2	21	.217
2004—	Jupiter (Fla. St.)	0	0	...	0.00	1.00	1	1	0	0		0-	4.0	2	1	0	0	2-0	4	.143
—	Albuquerque (PCL)	0	0	...	10.80	2.70	1	1	0	0		0-	3.1	7	4	4	1	2-0	6	.412
—	Florida (N.L.)	7	6	.538	3.68	1.17	20	19	1	0		0-0	120.0	102	50	49	9	38-0	113	.231
2005—	Florida (N.L.)	12	12	.500	3.44	1.26	32	32	4	2		0-0	209.0	184	97	80	12	79-1	198	.237
2006—	Dunedin (Fla. St.)	0	0	...	3.38	1.38	2	2	0	0		0-	8.0	9	3	3	0	2-0	6	.290
—	Syracuse (Int'l)	1	0	1.000	0.00	0.20	1	1	0	0		0-	5.0	0	0	0	0	1-0	7	
—	New Hampshire (East.)	1	0	1.000	1.50	0.83	1	1	0	0		0-	6.0	2	2	1	1	3-0	9	.105
—	Toronto (A.L.)	10	8	.556	3.98	1.30	21	21	2	1		0-0	135.2	138	67	60	14	39-3	118	.264
American League totals (1 year)		10	8	.556	3.98	1.30	21	21	2	1		0-0	135.2	138	67	60	14	39-3	118	.264
National League totals (7 years)		49	50	.495	3.73	1.28	134	131	14	8		0-1	853.2	719	395	354	66	377-16	753	.230
Major League totals (8 years)		59	58	.504	3.77	1.29	155	152	16	9		0-1	989.1	857	462	414	80	416-19	871	.235

2006 LEFTY-RIGHTY SPLITS

vs.	Avg.	AB	H	2B	3B	HR	RBI	BB	SO	OBP	Slg.	vs.	Avg.	AB	H	2B	3B	HR	RBI	BB	SO	OBP	Slg.
L	.261	280	73	18	0	4	22	27	63	.334	.368	R	.267	243	65	18	0	10	38	12	55	.309	.465

BURNITZ, JEROMY   OF

PERSONAL: Born April 15, 1969, in Westminster, Calif. ... 6-0/210. ... Bats left, throws right. ... Full name: Jeromy Neal Burnitz. ... Name pronounced: ber-NITS. ... High school: Conroe (Texas). ... College: Oklahoma State. **TRANSACTIONS/CAREER NOTES:** Selected by Milwaukee Brewers organization in 24th round of 1987 free-agent draft; did not sign. ... Selected by New York Mets organization in first round (17th pick overall) of 1990 free-agent draft. ... Traded by Mets with P Joe Roa to Cleveland Indians for Ps Paul Byrd, Jerry DiPoto and Dave Mlicki and a player to be named (November 18, 1994). ... Mets acquired 2B Jesus Azuaje to complete deal (December 6, 1994). ... Traded by Indians to Milwaukee Brewers for 3B/1B Kevin Seitzer (August 31, 1996). ... On disabled list (July 18-August 20, 1999). ... Traded by Brewers with P Jeff D'Amico, IF Lou Collier and OF/1B Mark Sweeney to Mets as part of three-team deal in which Brewers acquired P Glendon Rusch and IF Lenny Harris from Mets and OF Alex Ochoa from Rockies, Rockies acquired IFs Todd Zeile, OF Benny Agbayani and cash from Rockies, and Mets acquired 1B/OF Ross Gload and Craig House from Rockies (January 21, 2002). ... On disabled list (April 23-May 23, 2003); included rehabilitation assignment to Binghamton. ... Traded by Mets to Los Angeles Dodgers for IF Victor Diaz and Ps Joselo Diaz and Kole Strayhorn (July 14, 2003). ... Signed as a free agent by Colorado Rockies (January 9, 2004). ... Signed as a free agent by Chicago Cubs (February 2, 2005). ... Signed as a free agent by Pittsburgh Pirates (January 9, 2006). **STATISTICAL NOTES:** Hit three home runs in one game (May 10, 2001 and September 25, 2001). ... Career major league grand slams: 8.
2006 GAMES PLAYED BY POSITION (MLB): OF—84.

Year	Team (League)	Pos.	G	AB	R	H	2B	3B	HR	RBI	BB	SO	HBP	GDP	SB-CS	Avg.	OBP	SLG	OPS	E	Avg.
1990—	Pittsfield (NYP)	OF	51	173	37	52	6	5	6	22	45	39	3	3	12-5	.301	.444	.497	.942	0	1.000
—	St. Lucie (Fla. St.)	OF	11	32	6	5	1	0	0	3	7	12	4	0	1-0	.156	.372	.188	.560	0	1.000
1991—	Williamsport (East.)	OF	135	457	80	103	16	10	31	85	104	127	4	4	31-13	.225	.368	.508	.876	11	.958
1992—	Tidewater (Int'l)	OF	121	445	56	108	21	3	8	40	33	84	3	7	30-7	.243	.298	.357	.655	8	.967
1993—	Norfolk (Int'l)	OF	65	255	33	58	15	3	8	44	25	53	2	6	10-7	.227	.298	.404	.702	1	.993
—	New York (N.L.)	OF	86	263	49	64	10	6	13	38	38	66	1	2	3-6	.243	.339	.475	.814	4	.977
1994—	New York (N.L.)	OF	45	143	26	34	4	0	3	15	23	45	1	1	1-1	.238	.347	.329	.676	2	.970
—	Norfolk (Int'l)	OF-DH	85	314	58	75	15	5	14	49	49	82	1	0	18-6	.239	.340	.452	.792	4	.979

Year	Team (League)	Pos.	G	AB	R	H	2B	3B	HR	RBI	BB	SO	HBP	GDP	SB-CS	Avg.	OBP	SLG	OPS	E	Avg.
1995—Buffalo (A.A.)	OF	128	443	72	126	26	7	19	85	50	83	3	6	13-5	.284	.359	.503	.862	5	.981	
—Cleveland (A.L.)	OF-DH	9	7	4	4	1	0	0	0	0	0	0	0	0-0	.571	.571	.714	1.286	0	1.000	
1996—Cleveland (A.L.)	OF-DH	71	128	30	36	10	0	7	26	25	31	2	3	2-1	.281	.406	.523	.930	0	1.000	
—Milwaukee (A.L.)	OF	23	72	8	17	4	0	2	14	8	16	2	1	2-0	.236	.321	.375	.696	1	.975	
1997—Milwaukee (A.L.)	OF	153	494	85	139	37	8	27	85	75	111	5	8	20-13	.281	.382	.553	.934	7	.975	
1998—Milwaukee (N.L.)	OF	161	609	92	160	28	1	38	125	70	158	4	9	7-4	.263	.339	.499	.838	5	.972	
1999—Milwaukee (N.L.)	OF-DH	130	467	87	126	33	2	33	103	91	124	16	11	7-3	.270	.402	.561	.963	5	.982	
2000—Milwaukee (N.L.)	OF-DH	161	564	91	131	29	2	31	98	99	121	14	12	6-4	.232	.356	.456	.811	7	.979	
2001—Milwaukee (N.L.)	OF	154	562	104	141	32	4	34	100	80	150	5	8	0-4	.251	.347	.504	.851	6	.981	
2002—New York (N.L.)	OF-DH	154	479	65	103	15	0	19	54	58	135	10	11	10-7	.215	.311	.462	.677	9	.966	
2003—Binghamton (East.)	OF	3	13	1	3	0	0	1	3	0	4	0	0	1-0	.231	.231	.462	.692	0	1.000	
—New York (N.L.)	OF	65	234	38	64	18	0	18	45	21	55	4	4	1-4	.274	.344	.581	.925	2	.986	
—Los Angeles (N.L.)	OF	61	230	25	47	4	0	13	32	14	57	1	1	4-0	.204	.252	.391	.643	5	.946	
2004—Colorado (N.L.)	OF-DH	150	540	94	153	30	4	37	110	58	124	5	7	5-6	.283	.356	.559	.916	7	.974	
2005—Chicago (N.L.)	OF	160	605	84	156	31	2	24	87	57	109	3	12	5-4	.258	.322	.435	.757	5	.984	
2006—Pittsburgh (N.L.)	OF	111	313	35	72	12	0	16	49	22	74	5	8	1-1	.230	.289	.422	.711	2	.984	
American League totals (3 years)		256	701	127	196	52	8	36	125	108	158	9	12	24-14	.280	.382	.531	.912	8	.978	
National League totals (11 years)		1438	5009	790	1251	246	21	279	856	631	1218	69	87	50-44	.250	.339	.474	.814	63	.977	
Major League totals (14 years)		1694	5710	917	1447	298	29	315	981	739	1376	78	99	74-58	.253	.345	.481	.826	71	.977	

ALL-STAR GAME RECORD

	G	AB	R	H	2B	3B	HR	RBI	BB	SO	HBP	GDP	SB-CS	Avg.	OBP	SLG	OPS	E	Avg.
All-Star Game totals (1 year)	1	2	1	1	1	0	0	0	0	0	0		0-0	.500	.500	1.000	1.500	0	...

2006 LEFTY-RIGHTY SPLITS

vs.	Avg.	AB	H	2B	3B	HR	RBI	BB	SO	OBP	Slg.	vs.	Avg.	AB	H	2B	3B	HR	RBI	BB	SO	OBP	Slg.
L	.224	58	13	2	0	1	6	3	19	.274	.310	R	.231	255	59	10	0	15	43	19	55	.293	.447

BURNS, MIKE — P

PERSONAL: Born July 14, 1978, in Westminster, Calif. ... 6-1/205. ... Throws right, bats right. ... Full name: Michael John Burns. ... College: UCLA. **TRANSACTIONS/CAREER NOTES:** Selected by Houston Astros organization in 30th round of 2000 free-agent draft. ... Claimed on waivers by Cincinnati Reds (November 16, 2005). ... Traded by Reds to Boston Red Sox for P Tim Bausher and cash (August 28, 2006).
CAREER HITTING: 0-for-0 (.000), 0 R, 0 2B, 0 3B, 0 HR, 0 RBI.

Year	Team (League)	W	L	Pct.	ERA	WHIP	G	GS	CG	ShO	Hld.	Sv.-Opp.	IP	H	R	ER	HR	BB-IBB	SO	Avg.
2000—Martinsville (App.)	2	7	.222	4.52	1.28	12	12	0	0	...	0-...	65.2	75	52	33	12	9-0	51	.281
2001—Michigan (Midw.)	7	7	.500	3.95	1.20	29	21	1	0	...	1-...	132.0	131	67	58	10	27-0	108	.260
2002—Michigan (Midw.)	14	9	.609	2.49	0.97	28	28	3	2	...	0-...	181.0	146	59	50	12	29-1	126	.218
2003—Round Rock (Texas)	2	13	.133	6.13	1.50	38	14	0	0	...	0-...	105.2	129	80	72	15	30-3	89	.297
2004—Round Rock (Texas)	11	3	.786	1.67	0.97	56	0	0	0	...	9-...	80.2	63	18	15	1	15-3	94	.209
2005—Round Rock (PCL)	2	1	.667	2.10	0.87	25	0	0	0	0	13-15	30.0	22	7	7	4	4-0	34	.209
—Houston (N.L.)	0	0	...	4.94	1.19	27	0	0	0	1	0-0	31.0	29	18	17	6	8-1	20	.238
2006—Cincinnati (N.L.)	0	0	...	8.78	2.48	11	0	0	0	1	0-0	13.1	30	13	13	2	3-1	9	.469
—Louisville (Int'l)	6	1	.857	1.75	1.04	40	2	0	0	8	0-2	56.2	47	11	11	3	12-0	52	.226
—Boston (A.L.)	0	0	...	4.70	1.43	7	0	0	0	0	0-0	7.2	10	4	4	0	1-1	7	.323
American League totals (1 year)	0	0	...	4.70	1.43	7	0	0	0	0	0-0	7.2	10	4	4	0	1-1	7	.323
National League totals (2 years)	0	0	...	6.09	1.58	38	0	0	0	2	0-0	44.1	59	31	30	8	11-2	29	.317
Major League totals (2 years)	0	0	...	5.88	1.56	45	0	0	0	2	0-0	52.0	69	35	34	8	12-3	36	.318

2006 LEFTY-RIGHTY SPLITS

vs.	Avg.	AB	H	2B	3B	HR	RBI	BB	SO	OBP	Slg.	vs.	Avg.	AB	H	2B	3B	HR	RBI	BB	SO	OBP	Slg.
L	.303	33	10	3	0	1	5	1	7	.324	.485	R	.484	62	30	7	1	1	15	3	9	.507	.677

BURRELL, PAT — OF

PERSONAL: Born October 10, 1976, in Eureka Springs, Ark. ... 6-4/223. ... Bats right, throws right. ... Full name: Patrick Brian Burrell. ... Name pronounced: BURL. ... High school: Bellarmine Prep (San Jose). ... College: Miami. **TRANSACTIONS/CAREER NOTES:** Selected by Boston Red Sox organization in 43rd round of 1995 free-agent draft; did not sign. ... Selected by Philadelphia Phillies organization in first round (first pick overall) of 1998 free-agent draft. ... On disabled list (August 4-September 3, 2004); included rehabilitation assignment to Reading. **STATISTICAL NOTES:** Career major league grand slams: 5.
2006 GAMES PLAYED BY POSITION (MLB): OF—126, DH—6.

Year	Team (League)	Pos.	G	AB	R	H	2B	3B	HR	RBI	BB	SO	HBP	GDP	SB-CS	Avg.	OBP	SLG	OPS	E	Avg.
1998—Clearwater (Fla. St.)	1B	37	132	29	40	7	1	7	30	27	22	0	3	2-0	.303	.416	.530	.946	1	.995	
1999—Reading (East.)	1B-OF	117	417	84	139	28	6	28	90	79	103	0	13	3-1	.333	.438	.631	1.068	12	.985	
—Scran./W.B. (I.L.)	1B-OF	10	33	4	5	0	0	1	4	4	8	1	0	0-1	.152	.263	.242	.506	0	1.000	
2000—Scran./W.B. (I.L.)	OF-1B	40	143	31	42	15	1	4	25	32	36	0	1	1-1	.294	.420	.497	.917	2	.987	
—Philadelphia (N.L.)	1B-OF-DH	111	408	57	106	27	1	18	79	63	139	1	5	0-0	.260	.359	.463	.822	8	.986	
2001—Philadelphia (N.L.)	OF-DH	155	539	70	139	29	2	27	89	70	162	5	12	2-1	.258	.346	.469	.816	7	.972	
2002—Philadelphia (N.L.)	OF	157	586	96	165	39	2	37	116	89	153	3	16	1-0	.282	.376	.544	.920	6	.979	
2003—Philadelphia (N.L.)	OF-DH	146	522	57	109	31	4	21	64	72	142	4	18	0-0	.209	.309	.404	.713	6	.976	
2004—Reading (East.)	OF	4	15	2	3	0	0	2	4	3	7	0	0	0-0	.200	.333	.600	.933	1	.923	
—Philadelphia (N.L.)	OF	127	448	66	115	17	0	24	84	78	130	2	10	2-0	.257	.365	.455	.821	4	.983	
2005—Philadelphia (N.L.)	OF	154	562	78	158	27	1	32	117	99	160	3	12	0-0	.281	.389	.504	.892	7	.972	
2006—Philadelphia (N.L.)	OF-DH	144	462	80	119	24	1	29	95	98	131	3	11	0-0	.258	.388	.502	.890	3	.986	
Major League totals (7 years)		994	3527	504	911	194	11	188	644	569	1017	21	84	5-1	.258	.362	.479	.842	41	.980	

2006 LEFTY-RIGHTY SPLITS

vs.	Avg.	AB	H	2B	3B	HR	RBI	BB	SO	OBP	Slg.	vs.	Avg.	AB	H	2B	3B	HR	RBI	BB	SO	OBP	Slg.
L	.290	138	40	6	0	11	25	37	38	.440	.572	R	.244	324	79	18	1	18	70	61	93	.365	.472

BURRES, BRIAN — P

PERSONAL: Born April 8, 1981, in Oregon City, Ore. ... 6-1/175. ... Throws left, bats left. ... Full name: Brian James Burres. ... Junior College: Mt. Hood (Ore.). **TRANSACTIONS/CAREER NOTES:** Selected by San Francisco Giants organization in 31st round of 2000 free-agent draft. ... Claimed on waivers by Baltimore Orioles (January 6, 2006).
CAREER HITTING: 0-for-0 (.000), 0 R, 0 2B, 0 3B, 0 HR, 0 RBI.

Year Team (League)	W	L	Pct.	ERA	WHIP	G	GS	CG	ShO	Hld.	Sv.-Opp.	IP	H	R	ER	HR	BB-IBB	SO	Avg.
2001— Salem-Keizer (N'west)	3	1	.750	3.10	1.33	14	6	0	0	...	1-...	40.2	43	20	14	2	11-0	38	.274
2002— Hagerstown (SAL)	5	10	.333	4.75	1.40	32	16	0	0	...	1-...	119.1	114	78	63	15	53-0	119	.252
2003— San Jose (Calif.)	3	3	.500	3.86	1.50	39	0	0	0	...	1-...	60.2	55	33	26	4	36-3	64	.239
2004— San Diego (Calif.)	12	1	.923	2.84	1.17	36	15	0	0	...	0-...	123.2	115	49	39	10	30-0	114	.249
2005— Norwich (East.)	9	6	.600	4.20	1.45	26	24	0	0	1	0-0	128.2	130	66	60	13	57-0	105	.264
2006— Ottawa (Int'l)	10	6	.625	3.76	1.37	26	26	1	1	0	0-0	139.0	133	63	58	14	57-1	110	.255
— Baltimore (A.L.)	0	0	...	2.25	0.88	11	0	0	0	4	0-0	8.0	6	2	2	1	1-0	6	.200
Major League totals (1 year)	0	0	...	2.25	0.88	11	0	0	0	4	0-0	8.0	6	2	2	1	1-0	6	.200

2006 LEFTY-RIGHTY SPLITS

vs.	Avg.	AB	H	2B	3B	HR	RBI	BB	SO	OBP	Slg.	vs.	Avg.	AB	H	2B	3B	HR	RBI	BB	SO	OBP	Slg.
L	.071	14	1	0	0	0	0	0	3	.071	.071	R	.313	16	5	0	0	1	3	1	3	.353	.500

BURROUGHS, SEAN — 3B/2B

PERSONAL: Born September 12, 1980, in Atlanta. ... 6-2/200. ... Bats left, throws right. ... Full name: Sean Patrick Burroughs. ... High school: Wilson (Long Beach, Calif.). ... Son of Jeff Burroughs, outfielder with five major league teams (1970-85). **TRANSACTIONS/CAREER NOTES:** Selected by San Diego Padres organization in first round (ninth pick overall) of 1998 free-agent draft. ... On disabled list (May 29-July 15, 2002); included rehabilitation assignment to Portland. ... Traded by Padres to Tampa Bay Devil Rays for P Dewon Brazelton (December 7, 2005). ... On disabled list (March 30-April 14, 2006). ... Released by Devil Rays (August 15, 2006). **STATISTICAL NOTES:** Career major league pitching: 0-0, 27.0 ERA, 1 G, 1 IP, 4 H, 3 R, 3 ER, 0 BB, 0 SO.

2006 GAMES PLAYED BY POSITION (MLB): 3B—7.

Year Team (League)	Pos.	G	AB	R	H	2B	3B	HR	RBI	BB	SO	HBP	GDP	SB-CS	Avg.	OBP	SLG	OPS	E	Avg.
1999— Rancho Cuca. (Calif.)	3B	6	23	3	10	3	0	1	5	3	3	1	1	0-1	.435	.519	.696	1.214	0	1.000
— Fort Wayne (Midw.)	3B	122	426	65	153	30	3	5	80	74	59	14	10	17-15	.359	.464	.479	.943	37	.898
2000— Mobile (Sou.)	3B	108	392	46	114	29	4	2	42	58	45	3	10	6-8	.291	.383	.401	.783	16	.947
2001— Portland (PCL)	3B	104	394	60	127	28	1	9	55	37	54	4	13	9-2	.322	.386	.467	.853	10	.964
2002— San Diego (N.L.)	3B-2B	63	192	18	52	5	1	1	11	12	30	1	6	2-0	.271	.317	.323	.640	4	.949
— Portland (PCL)	2B-3B	50	179	29	54	16	2	2	23	21	16	3	5	1-0	.302	.380	.447	.827	6	.969
2003— San Diego (N.L.)	3B	146	517	62	148	27	6	7	58	44	75	11	13	7-2	.286	.352	.402	.755	12	.966
2004— San Diego (N.L.)	3B	130	523	76	156	23	3	2	47	31	52	9	6	5-4	.298	.348	.365	.713	14	.957
2005— Portland (PCL)	3B	32	124	21	36	8	0	3	14	9	15	5	5	0-0	.290	.362	.427	.790	4	.949
— San Diego (N.L.)	3B-P-SS	93	284	20	71	7	2	1	17	24	41	5	7	4-0	.250	.318	.299	.618	8	.962
2006— Tampa Bay (A.L.)	3B	8	21	3	4	1	0	0	1	4	7	0	1	1-0	.190	.320	.238	.558	1	.963
— Durham (Int'l)		37	131	8	28	2	0	1	11	9	29	1	5	1-3	.214	.268	.252	.520	8	.922
American League totals (1 year)		8	21	3	4	1	0	0	1	4	7	0	1	1-0	.190	.320	.238	.558	1	.963
National League totals (4 years)		432	1516	176	427	62	12	11	133	111	198	26	32	18-6	.282	.340	.360	.700	42	.960
Major League totals (5 years)		440	1537	179	431	63	12	11	134	115	205	26	33	19-6	.280	.340	.358	.698	43	.960

DIVISION SERIES RECORD

Year Team (League)	Pos.	G	AB	R	H	2B	3B	HR	RBI	BB	SO	HBP	GDP	SB-CS	Avg.	OBP	SLG	OPS	E	Avg.
2005— San Diego (N.L.)		2	1	0	0	0	0	0	0	0	0	0	0	0-0	.000	.000	.000	.000	0	...

2006 LEFTY-RIGHTY SPLITS

vs.	Avg.	AB	H	2B	3B	HR	RBI	BB	SO	OBP	Slg.	vs.	Avg.	AB	H	2B	3B	HR	RBI	BB	SO	OBP	Slg.
L	.000	2	0	0	0	0	0	0	1	1	.333	.000	R	.211	19	4	1	0	0	1	3	6	.318	.263

BUSH, DAVID — P

PERSONAL: Born November 9, 1979, in Pittsburgh. ... 6-2/212. ... Throws right, bats right. ... Full name: David T. Bush. ... High school: Conestoga (Berwyn, Pa.). ... College: Wake Forest. **TRANSACTIONS/CAREER NOTES:** Selected by Tampa Bay Devil Rays organization in fourth round of 2001 free-agent draft; did not sign. ... Selected by Toronto Blue Jays organization in second round of 2002 free-agent draft. ... Traded by Blue Jays with P Zach Jackson and OF Gabe Gross to Milwaukee Brewers for 1B Lyle Overbay and a player to be named (December 7, 2005); Blue Jays acquired P Ty Taubenheim to complete the deal (December 8, 2005).

CAREER HITTING: 11-for-64 (.172), 6 R, 3 2B, 0 3B, 0 HR, 9 RBI.

Year Team (League)	W	L	Pct.	ERA	WHIP	G	GS	CG	ShO	Hld.	Sv.-Opp.	IP	H	R	ER	HR	BB-IBB	SO	Avg.
2002— Auburn (NY-Penn)	1	1	.500	2.82	0.90	18	0	0	0	...	10-...	22.1	13	9	7	1	7-2	39	.159
— Dunedin (Fla. St.)	0	1	.000	2.03	0.90	7	0	0	0	...	0-...	13.1	10	3	3	1	2-0	9	.222
2003— Dunedin (Fla. St.)	7	3	.700	2.81	0.95	14	14	0	0	...	0-...	77.0	64	29	24	6	9-0	75	.223
— New Haven (East.)	7	3	.700	2.78	1.14	14	14	1	0	...	0-...	81.0	73	26	25	4	19-1	73	.239
2004— Syracuse (Int'l)	6	6	.500	4.06	1.28	16	16	2	1	...	0-...	99.2	108	52	45	7	20-1	88	.276
— Toronto (A.L.)	5	4	.556	3.69	1.23	16	16	1	1	0	0-0	97.2	95	47	40	11	25-2	64	.255
2005— Syracuse (Int'l)	2	2	.500	4.42	1.35	9	9	0	0	0	0-0	55.0	65	28	27	6	9-0	40	.298
— Toronto (A.L.)	5	11	.313	4.49	1.25	25	24	2	0	0	0-0	136.1	142	73	68	20	29-3	75	.269
2006— Milwaukee (N.L.)	12	11	.522	4.41	1.14	34	32	3	2	1	0-0	210.0	201	111	103	26	38-2	166	.252
American League totals (2 years)	10	15	.400	4.15	1.24	41	40	3	1	0	0-0	234.0	237	120	108	31	54-5	139	.263
National League totals (1 year)	12	11	.522	4.41	1.14	34	32	3	2	1	0-0	210.0	201	111	103	26	38-2	166	.252
Major League totals (3 years)	22	26	.458	4.28	1.19	75	72	6	3	1	0-0	444.0	438	231	211	57	92-7	305	.258

2006 LEFTY-RIGHTY SPLITS

vs.	Avg.	AB	H	2B	3B	HR	RBI	BB	SO	OBP	Slg.	vs.	Avg.	AB	H	2B	3B	HR	RBI	BB	SO	OBP	Slg.
L	.258	395	102	34	1	11	50	25	96	.304	.433	R	.246	403	99	17	2	15	57	13	70	.294	.409

BYNUM, FREDDIE — OF/2B

PERSONAL: Born March 15, 1980, in Wilson, N.C. ... 6-1/180. ... Bats left, throws right. ... Full name: Freddie Lee Bynum Jr. ... High school: Beddingfield (Wilson, N.C.). ... Junior college: Pitt (Greenville, N.C.) C.C. **TRANSACTIONS/CAREER NOTES:** Selected by Oakland Athletics organization in second round of 2000 free-agent draft. ... Traded by Athletics with P John Rheinecker to Texas Rangers for P Juan Dominguez as part of three-team deal in which Rangers then sent Bynum to Chicago Cubs for P John Koronka and cash (March 31, 2006). ... On disabled list (June 25-August 21, 2006); included rehabilitation assignment to Iowa.

2006 GAMES PLAYED BY POSITION (MLB): OF—22, 2B—15.

Year Team (League)	Pos.	G	AB	R	H	2B	3B	HR	RBI	BB	SO	HBP	GDP	SB-CS	Avg.	OBP	SLG	OPS	E	Avg.
2000— Vancouver (N'west)	SS	72	281	52	72	10	1	1	26	31	58	5	3	22-12	.256	.341	.310	.651	29	.917
2001— Modesto (California)	SS-2B-3B	120	440	59	115	19	7	2	46	41	95	1	8	28-11	.261	.325	.350	.675	41	.922
2002— Visalia (Calif.)	2B-2B	135	539	83	165	26	5	3	56	64	116	7	9	41-21	.306	.385	.390	.775	36	.948
2003— Midland (Texas)	OF-2B	132	510	84	134	18	9	5	58	56	135	8	6	22-8	.263	.344	.363	.707	33	.952
2004— Midland (Texas)	OF-2B	65	265	38	71	13	4	1	22	24	56	2	1	18-7	.268	.332	.358	.690	2	.950
— Sacramento (PCL)	OF-SS-2B	66	258	42	73	11	2	2	26	19	61	3	8	21-4	.283	.339	.364	.703	8	.000

Year	Team (League)	Pos.	G	AB	R	H	2B	3B	HR	RBI	BB	SO	HBP	GDP	SB-CS	Avg.	OBP	SLG	OPS	E	Avg.
												BATTING								FIELDING	
2005— Sacramento (PCL)	OF-SS-2B		102	378	56	105	16	9	2	40	38	83	3	3	23-7	.278	.347	.384	.730	14	.968
—Oakland (A.L.)	2B-OF		7	7	0	2	1	0	0	1	0	3	0	0	0-0	.286	.286	.429	.714	0	1.000
2006— Iowa (PCL)			6	22	3	5	0	0	0	3	1	3	0	0	0-0	.227	.261	.227	.488	0	1.000
—Chicago (N.L.)	OF-2B		71	136	20	35	5	5	4	12	9	44	1	2	8-4	.257	.308	.456	.764	7	.930
American League totals (1 year)			7	7	0	2	1	0	0	1	0	3	0	0	0-0	.286	.286	.429	.714	0	1.000
National League totals (1 year)			71	136	20	35	5	5	4	12	9	44	1	2	8-4	.257	.308	.456	.764	7	.930
Major League totals (2 years)			78	143	20	37	6	5	4	13	9	47	1	2	8-4	.259	.307	.455	.762	7	.933

2006 LEFTY-RIGHTY SPLITS

vs.	Avg.	AB	H	2B	3B	HR	RBI	BB	SO	OBP	Slg.	vs.	Avg.	AB	H	2B	3B	HR	RBI	BB	SO	OBP	Slg.
L	.130	23	3	1	0	0	0	1	12	.200	.174	R	.283	113	32	4	5	4	12	8	32	.331	.513

BYRD, MARLON — OF

PERSONAL: Born August 30, 1977, in Boynton Beach, Fla. ... 6-0/229. ... Bats right, throws right. ... Full name: Marlon Jerrard Byrd. ... High school: Sprayberry (Marietta, Ga.). ... Junior college: Georgia Perimeter. **TRANSACTIONS/CAREER NOTES:** Selected by Philadelphia Phillies organization in 10th round of 1999 free-agent draft. ... On disabled list (April 14-29, 2003); included rehabilitation assignment to Reading. ... On disabled list (April 8-May 3, 2005); included rehabilitation assignment to Scranton/Wilkes Barre. ... Traded by Phillies to Washington Nationals for OF Endy Chavez (May 14, 2005). **STATISTICAL NOTES:** Career major league grand slams: 2.

2006 GAMES PLAYED BY POSITION (MLB): OF—71.

Year	Team (League)	Pos.	G	AB	R	H	2B	3B	HR	RBI	BB	SO	HBP	GDP	SB-CS	Avg.	OBP	SLG	OPS	E	Avg.
												BATTING								FIELDING	
1999— Batavia (NY-Penn)	OF	65	243	40	72	7	6	13	50	28	70	5	3	8-2	.296	.376	.535	.911	7	.926
2000— Piedmont (S. Atl.)	OF	133	515	104	159	29	13	17	93	51	110	10	7	41-5	.309	.379	.515	.893	4	.980
2001— Reading (East.)	OF	137	510	108	161	22	8	28	89	52	93	11	7	32-5	.316	.386	.555	.941	2	.994
2002— Scran./W.B. (I.L.)	OF	136	538	103	160	37	7	15	63	46	98	11	5	15-1	.297	.362	.476	.838	8	.975
—Philadelphia (N.L.)	OF	10	35	2	8	2	0	1	1	1	8	0	0	0-2	.229	.250	.371	.621	0	1.000
2003— Scran./W.B. (I.L.)	OF	1	4	1	3	1	0	0	0	0	1	0	0	0-0	.750	.750	1.000	1.750	0	1.000
—Reading (East.)	OF	3	16	3	5	0	0	0	3	0	3	0	1	0-0	.313	.313	.500	.813	1	.800
—Philadelphia (N.L.)	OF	135	495	86	150	28	4	7	45	44	94	7	8	11-1	.303	.366	.418	.784	5	.984
2004— Scran./W.B. (I.L.)	OF	37	152	13	40	11	1	2	17	10	18	4	5	2-3	.263	.323	.388	.712	2	.980
—Philadelphia (N.L.)	OF	106	346	48	79	13	2	5	33	22	68	7	10	2-2	.228	.287	.321	.608	2	.990
2005— Scran./W.B. (I.L.)	OF	5	19	4	7	1	0	3	5	0	3	0	0	0-0	.368	.368	.895	1.263	6	.824
—Philadelphia (N.L.)	OF	5	13	0	4	0	0	0	0	1	3	1	0	0-0	.308	.400	.308	.708	0	1.000
—New Orleans (PCL)	OF-DH	21	81	19	33	6	0	5	11	9	7	2	6	4-1	.407	.478	.667	1.145	0	1.000
—Wash. (N.L.)	OF-DH	74	216	20	57	15	2	2	26	18	47	1	5	5-1	.264	.318	.380	.698	2	.985
2006— New Orleans (PCL)		46	155	20	42	9	0	7	29	16	31	7	1	3-1	.271	.363	.465	.828	1	.986
—Wash. (N.L.)	OF	78	197	28	44	8	1	5	18	22	47	6	6	3-3	.223	.317	.350	.667	2	.987
Major League totals (5 years)		408	1302	184	342	66	9	20	123	108	267	22	29	21-9	.263	.327	.373	.701	11	.986

2006 LEFTY-RIGHTY SPLITS

vs.	Avg.	AB	H	2B	3B	HR	RBI	BB	SO	OBP	Slg.	vs.	Avg.	AB	H	2B	3B	HR	RBI	BB	SO	OBP	Slg.
L	.188	69	13	1	1	2	4	11	21	.309	.319	R	.242	128	31	7	0	3	14	11	26	.322	.367

BYRD, PAUL — P

PERSONAL: Born December 3, 1970, in Louisville, Ky. ... 6-1/190. ... Throws right, bats right. ... Full name: Paul Gregory Byrd. ... High school: St. Xavier (Louisville, Ky.). ... College: LSU. **TRANSACTIONS/CAREER NOTES:** Selected by Cincinnati Reds organization in 13th round of 1988 free-agent draft; did not sign. ... Selected by Cleveland Indians organization in fourth round of 1991 free-agent draft. ... Traded by Indians with Ps Dave Mlicki and Jerry DiPoto and a player to be named to New York Mets for OF Jeromy Burnitz and P Joe Roa (November 18, 1994); Mets acquired 2B Jesus Azuaje to complete deal (December 6, 1994). ... On disabled list (March 22-June 9, 1996); included rehabilitation assignment to Norfolk. ... Traded by Mets with a player to be named to Atlanta Braves for P Greg McMichael (November 25, 1996); Braves acquired P Andy Zwirchitz to complete deal (May 25, 1997). ... Claimed on waivers by Philadelphia Phillies (August 14, 1998). ... On disabled list (July 27, 2000-remainder of season). ... Traded by Phillies to Kansas City Royals for P Jose Santiago (June 5, 2001). ... On disabled list (September 22, 2001-remainder of season). ... Signed as a free agent by Braves (December 17, 2002). ... On disabled list (March 21, 2003-entire season); included rehabilitation assignment to Greenville. ... On disabled list (March 26-June 19, 2004); included rehabilitation assignments to Greenville and Richmond. ... Signed as a free agent by Anaheim Angels (December 14, 2004). ... Angels franchise renamed Los Angeles Angels of Anaheim for 2005 season. ... Signed as a free agent by Cleveland Indians (December 4, 2005). **MISCELLANEOUS NOTES:** Appeared in one game as pinch runner (2001).

CAREER HITTING: 24-for-149 (.161), 11 R, 0 2B, 0 3B, 0 HR, 10 RBI.

Year	Team (League)	W	L	Pct.	ERA	WHIP	G	GS	CG	ShO	Hld.	Sv.-Opp.	IP	H	R	ER	HR	BB-IBB	SO	Avg.
1991— Kinston (Carol.)	4	3	.571	3.16	1.21	14	11	0	0	...	0-...	62.2	40	27	22	7	36-0	62	.181
1992— Cant./Akr. (Eastern)	14	6	.700	3.01	1.29	24	24	4	0	...	0-...	152.1	122	68	51	4	75-2	118	.216
1993— Charlotte (Int'l)	7	4	.636	3.89	1.36	14	14	1	1	...	0-...	81.0	80	43	35	9	30-0	54	.257
—Cant./Akr. (Eastern)	0	0	...	3.60	1.00	2	1	0	0	...	0-...	10.0	7	4	4	1	3-0	8	.189
1994— Cant./Akr. (Eastern)	5	9	.357	3.81	1.34	21	20	4	1	...	0-...	139.1	135	70	59	10	52-3	106	.255
—Charlotte (Int'l)	2	2	.500	3.93	1.20	9	4	0	0	...	1-...	36.2	33	19	16	5	11-1	15	.250
1995— Norfolk (Int'l)	3	5	.375	2.79	1.06	22	10	1	0	...	6-...	87.0	71	29	27	6	21-0	61	.227
—New York (N.L.)	2	0	1.000	2.05	1.14	17	0	0	0	3	0-0	22.0	18	6	5	1	7-1	26	.222
1996— Norfolk (Int'l)	2	0	1.000	3.52	1.04	5	0	0	0	...	1-...	7.2	4	3	3	0	4-1	8	.148
—New York (N.L.)	1	2	.333	4.24	1.48	38	0	0	0	3	0-2	46.2	48	22	22	7	21-4	31	.265
1997— Atlanta (N.L.)	4	4	.500	5.26	1.42	31	4	0	0	1	0-0	53.0	47	34	31	6	28-4	37	.235
—Richmond (Int'l)	2	1	.667	3.18	0.88	3	3	0	0	...	0-...	17.0	14	6	6	2	1-0	14	.230
1998— Richmond (Int'l)	5	5	.500	3.69	1.25	17	17	2	0	...	0-...	102.1	92	44	42	9	36-2	84	.241
—Atlanta (N.L.)	0	0	...	13.50	2.50	1	0	0	0	0	0-0	2.0	4	3	3	0	1-0	1	.400
—Philadelphia (N.L.)	5	2	.714	2.29	1.05	8	8	2	1	0	0-0	55.0	41	16	14	6	17-1	38	.204
1999— Philadelphia (N.L.)	15	11	.577	4.60	1.38	32	32	1	0	0	0-0	199.2	205	119	102	34	70-2	106	.265
2000— Philadelphia (N.L.)	2	9	.182	6.51	1.49	17	15	0	0	0	0-0	83.0	89	67	60	17	35-2	53	.271
—Scran./W.B. (I.L.)	2	0	1.000	1.73	1.00	3	3	2	0	0	0-0	26.0	20	5	5	1	6-0	10	.215
2001— Clearwater (Fla. St.)	0	3	.000	3.42	1.23	4	4	0	0	...	0-...	23.2	24	10	9	1	5-0	17	.267
—Scran./W.B. (I.L.)	1	3	.250	3.65	1.11	5	5	0	0	...	0-...	37.0	34	18	15	4	7-0	35	.239
—Philadelphia (N.L.)	0	1	.000	8.10	1.40	3	1	0	0	0	0-0	10.0	10	9	9	1	4-0	3	.278
—Kansas City (A.L.)	6	5	.500	4.05	1.41	16	15	1	0	0	0-...	93.1	110	45	42	11	22-1	49	.298
2002— Kansas City (A.L.)	17	11	.607	3.90	1.15	33	33	*7	2	0	0-...	228.1	224	111	99	36	38-1	129	.256
2003— Greenville (Sou.)	0	0	...	8.31	2.10	1	0	0	0	...	0-...	4.1	8	4	4	1	1-0	3	.364
2004— Greenville (Sou.)	1	1	.500	7.11	1.42	3	3	0	0	...	0-...	12.2	13	10	10	2	5-0	11	.271
—Richmond (Int'l)	0	1	.000	7.71	1.07	1	1	0	0	...	0-...	4.2	3	4	4	0	2-0	5	.167
—Atlanta (N.L.)	8	7	.533	3.94	1.24	19	19	0	0	0	0-...	114.1	123	57	50	18	19-0	79	.270

B

Year Team (League)	W	L	Pct.	ERA	WHIP	G	GS	CG	ShO	Hld.	Sv.-Opp.	IP	H	R	ER	HR	BB-IBB	SO	Avg.
2005— Los Angeles (A.L.)	12	11	.522	3.74	1.19	31	31	2	1	0	0-0	204.1	216	95	85	22	28-1	102	.272
2006— Cleveland (A.L.)	10	9	.526	4.88	1.51	31	31	1	0	0	0-0	179.0	232	120	97	26	38-3	88	.308
American League totals (4 years)	45	37	.549	4.12	1.29	111	110	11	3	0	0-0	705.0	782	371	323	95	126-6	368	.280
National League totals (8 years)	37	36	.507	4.55	1.34	166	79	3	1	7	0-2	585.2	585	333	296	90	202-14	374	.258
Major League totals (11 years)	82	73	.529	4.32	1.31	277	189	14	4	7	0-2	1290.2	1367	704	619	185	328-20	742	.270

DIVISION SERIES RECORD

Year Team (League)	W	L	Pct.	ERA	WHIP	G	GS	CG	ShO	Hld.	Sv.-Opp.	IP	H	R	ER	HR	BB-IBB	SO	Avg.
2004— Atlanta (N.L.)	0	1	.000	6.35	1.94	2	0	0	0	0	0-0	5.2	8	4	4	1	3-1	3	.364
2005— Los Angeles (A.L.)	0	0	...	9.82	2.45	1	1	0	0	0	0-0	3.2	7	4	4	1	2-0	2	.389
Division series totals (2 years)	0	1	.000	7.71	2.14	3	1	0	0	0	0-0	9.1	15	8	8	2	5-1	5	.375

CHAMPIONSHIP SERIES RECORD

Year Team (League)	W	L	Pct.	ERA	WHIP	G	GS	CG	ShO	Hld.	Sv.-Opp.	IP	H	R	ER	HR	BB-IBB	SO	Avg.
2005— Los Angeles (A.L.)	1	0	1.000	3.38	1.13	2	0	0	0	0	0-0	10.2	10	4	4	1	2-0	5	.256

ALL-STAR GAME RECORD

Year Team (League)	W	L	Pct.	ERA	WHIP	G	GS	CG	ShO	Hld.	Sv.-Opp.	IP	H	R	ER	HR	BB-IBB	SO	Avg.
All-Star Game totals (1 year)				Did not play															

2006 LEFTY-RIGHTY SPLITS

vs.	Avg.	AB	H	2B	3B	HR	RBI	BB	SO	OBP	Slg.	vs.	Avg.	AB	H	2B	3B	HR	RBI	BB	SO	OBP	Slg.
L	.369	347	128	20	5	12	57	27	23	.413	.559	R	.256	407	104	18	2	14	57	11	65	.282	.413

BYRDAK, TIM — P

PERSONAL: Born October 31, 1973, in Oak Lawn, Ill. ... 5-11/180. ... Throws left, bats left. ... Full name: Timothy Christopher Byrdak. ... Name pronounced: BIRD-ek. ... High school: Oak Forest (Ill.). ... Junior college: South Suburban College (Ill.). ... College: Rice. **TRANSACTIONS/CAREER NOTES:** Selected by Kansas City Royals organization in fifth round of 1994 free-agent draft. ... On disabled list (June 27-August 19, 1996). ... Signed as a free agent by Cleveland Indians organization (December 23, 2000). ... Signed as a free agent by San Diego Padres organization (February 1, 2004). ... Signed as a free agent by Baltimore Orioles organization (June 22, 2004). ... On disabled list (April 19-July 30, 2006); included rehabilitation assignments to Aberdeen, Bowie and Frederick.
CAREER HITTING: 1-for-2 (.500), 1 R, 1 2B, 0 3B, 0 HR, 0 RBI.

Year Team (League)	W	L	Pct.	ERA	WHIP	G	GS	CG	ShO	Hld.	Sv.-Opp.	IP	H	R	ER	HR	BB-IBB	SO	Avg.
1994— Eugene (Northwest)	4	5	.444	3.07	1.09	15	15	0	0	...	0-...	73.1	60	33	25	6	20-0	77	.220
1995— Wilmington (Caro.)	11	5	.688	2.16	0.98	27	26	0	0	...	0-...	166.1	118	46	40	7	45-2	127	.198
1996— Wichita (Texas)	5	7	.417	6.91	1.84	15	15	0	0	...	0-...	84.2	112	73	65	15	44-0	47	.331
1997— Wilmington (Caro.)	4	3	.571	3.51	1.12	22	2	0	0	...	3-...	41.0	34	17	16	3	12-4	47	.228
1998— Wichita (Texas)	3	5	.375	4.15	1.65	34	0	0	0	...	2-...	52.0	58	29	24	3	28-1	37	.284
— Omaha (PCL)	2	1	.667	2.45	1.39	26	0	0	0	...	1-...	36.2	31	13	10	3	20-0	32	.230
— Kansas City (A.L.)	0	0	...	5.40	3.00	3	0	0	0	...	0-...	1.2	5	1	1	1	0-...	1	.556
1999— Omaha (PCL)	3	1	.750	1.81	1.35	33	0	0	0	...	4-...	49.2	39	19	10	0	28-2	51	.219
— Kansas City (A.L.)	0	3	.000	7.66	2.11	33	0	0	0	10	1-...	24.2	32	24	21	5	20-...	17	.308
2000— Omaha (PCL)	6	2	.750	4.44	1.67	34	1	0	0	...	4-...	52.2	59	27	26	5	29-3	47	.286
— Kansas City (A.L.)	0	1	.000	11.37	2.37	12	0	0	0	3	0-...	6.1	11	8	8	3	4-...	8	.367
— Wichita (Texas)	0	0	...	5.40	1.80	4	0	0	0	...	0-...	6.2	9	4	4	1	3-0	1	.346
2001— Buffalo (Int'l)	2	0	1.000	4.67	1.33	4	3	0	0	...	0-...	17.1	18	10	9	1	5-0	17	.265
2002— Kinston (Carol.)	1	0	1.000	4.50	1.75	2	0	0	0	...	0-...	4.0	3	2	2	0	4-0	3	.214
— Akron (East.)	0	0	...	6.23	2.08	9	0	0	0	...	1-...	13.0	16	12	9	0	11-0	8	.308
2003— Joliet (North.)	2	1	.667	2.67	1.22	5	5	0	0	...	0-...	33.2	31	17	10	3	10-0	18	.238
— Gary (North.)	2	4	.333	4.34	1.28	10	10	1	0	...	0-...	66.1	60	33	32	7	25-0	58	.248
2004— Portland (PCL)	3	0	1.000	5.45	1.68	20	2	0	0	...	0-...	38.0	47	28	23	3	17-0	25	.307
— Ottawa (Int'l)	2	1	.667	4.19	1.69	33	1	0	0	...	2-...	34.1	46	20	16	4	12-1	43	.329
2005— Ottawa (Int'l)	3	2	.600	2.09	0.98	37	0	0	0	2	11-14	38.2	23	12	9	4	15-1	44	.170
— Baltimore (A.L.)	0	1	.000	4.05	1.80	41	0	0	0	11	1-1	26.2	27	14	12	1	21-1	31	.255
2006— Aberdeen (N.Y.-Penn.)	0	0	...	9.00	2.00	1	0	0	0	0	0-1	1.0	2	1	1	0	0-0	3	.400
— Frederick (Carolina)	0	0	...	13.50	3.75	1	0	0	0	0	0-0	1.1	4	2	2	0	1-0	5	.500
— Bowie (East.)	0	0	...	2.25	1.50	3	0	0	0	1	0-0	4.0	4	1	1	0	2-0	7	.250
— Baltimore (A.L.)	1	0	1.000	12.86	3.14	16	0	0	0	3	0-0	7.0	14	10	10	2	8-1	2	.438
Major League totals (5 years)	1	5	.167	7.06	2.14	105	0	0	0	27	2-1	66.1	89	57	52	12	53-2	59	.327

2006 LEFTY-RIGHTY SPLITS

vs.	Avg.	AB	H	2B	3B	HR	RBI	BB	SO	OBP	Slg.	vs.	Avg.	AB	H	2B	3B	HR	RBI	BB	SO	OBP	Slg.
L	.381	21	8	4	0	0	5	2	0	.435	.571	R	.545	11	6	2	0	2	6	6	2	.706	1.273

BYRNES, ERIC — OF

PERSONAL: Born February 16, 1976, in Redwood City, Calif. ... 6-2/210. ... Bats right, throws right. ... Full name: Eric James Byrnes. ... Name pronounced: burns. ... High school: St. Francis (Mountain View, Calif.). ... College: UCLA. **TRANSACTIONS/CAREER NOTES:** Selected by Los Angeles Dodgers organization in 38th round of 1994 free-agent draft; did not sign. ... Selected by Houston Astros organization in fourth round of 1997 free-agent draft; did not sign. ... Selected by Oakland Athletics organization in eighth round of 1998 free-agent draft. ... Traded by Athletics with SS Omar Quintanilla to Colorado Rockies for Ps Joe Kennedy and Jay Witasick (July 13, 2005). ... Traded by Rockies to Baltimore Orioles for OF Larry Bigbie (July 29, 2005). ... Signed as a free agent by Arizona Diamondbacks (December 30, 2005). **STATISTICAL NOTES:** Hit for the cycle (June 29, 2003).
2006 GAMES PLAYED BY POSITION (MLB): OF—137.

Year Team (League)	Pos.	G	AB	R	H	2B	3B	HR	RBI	BB	SO	HBP	GDP	SB-CS	Avg.	OBP	SLG	OPS	E	Avg.
1998—S. Oregon (N'west)	OF	42	169	36	53	10	2	7	31	16	16	2	3	6-1	.314	.378	.521	.898	1	.986
—Visalia (Calif.)	OF	29	108	26	46	9	2	4	21	18	15	1	2	11-1	.426	.504	1.161	1.161	3	.952
1999—Modesto (California)	OF	96	365	86	123	28	1	6	66	58	37	9	14	28-8	.337	.433	.468	.901	6	.960
—Midland (Texas)	OF	43	164	25	39	14	0	1	22	17	32	3	5	6-3	.238	.316	.341	.657	5	.923
2000—Midland (Texas)	OF	67	259	49	78	25	2	5	37	43	38	1	5	21-11	.301	.395	.471	.866	2	.983
—Sacramento (PCL)	OF	67	243	55	81	23	1	9	47	31	30	2	3	12-5	.333	.410	.547	.957	2	.980
—Oakland (A.L.)	OF-DH	10	10	5	3	0	0	0	0	0	1	1	0	2-1	.300	.364	.300	.664	0	1.000
2001—Sacramento (PCL)	OF	100	415	81	120	23	2	20	51	33	66	5	10	25-3	.289	.343	.499	.842	5	.973
—Oakland (A.L.)	OF-DH	19	38	9	9	1	0	3	5	4	6	1	0	1-0	.237	.326	.500	.826	1	.933
2002—Sacramento (PCL)	OF	31	119	16	31	7	0	4	16	7	15	0	2	5-1	.261	.302	.420	.722	2	.971
—Oakland (A.L.)	OF-DH	90	94	24	23	4	2	3	11	4	17	3	1	3-0	.245	.291	.426	.717	1	.982
2003—Oakland (A.L.)	OF-DH	121	414	64	109	27	9	12	51	42	71	3	4	10-2	.263	.333	.459	.792	2	.991
2004—Oakland (A.L.)	OF-DH	143	569	91	161	39	3	20	73	46	111	12	11	17-1	.283	.347	.467	.814	3	.989
2005—Oakland (A.L.)	OF-DH	59	192	30	51	15	2	7	24	14	27	7	1	2-2	.266	.336	.474	.810	2	.984

Year Team (League)	Pos.	G	AB	R	H	2B	3B	HR	RBI	BB	SO	HBP	GDP	SB-CS	Avg.	OBP	SLG	OPS	E	Avg.
—Colorado (N.L.)	OF	15	53	2	10	2	0	0	5	7	11	0	1	2-0	.189	.283	.226	.510	...	.976
—Baltimore (A.L.)	OF	52	167	17	32	7	1	3	11	11	33	1	5	3-0	.192	.246	.299	.545	3	.969
2006—Arizona (N.L.)	OF	143	562	82	150	37	3	26	79	34	88	5	12	25-3	.267	.313	.482	.795	1	.997
American League totals (6 years)		494	1484	240	388	93	17	48	175	121	266	27	23	38-6	.261	.326	.444	.771	12	.985
National League totals (2 years)		158	615	84	160	39	3	26	84	41	99	5	13	27-3	.260	.310	.460	.770	2	.994
Major League totals (7 years)		652	2099	324	548	132	20	74	259	162	365	32	36	65-9	.261	.322	.449	.771	14	.988

DIVISION SERIES RECORD

Year Team (League)	Pos.	G	AB	R	H	2B	3B	HR	RBI	BB	SO	HBP	GDP	SB-CS	Avg.	OBP	SLG	OPS	E	Avg.
2001—Oakland (A.L.)		2	2	0	0	0	0	0	0	0	1	0	0	0-0	.000	.000	.000	.000	...	...
2002—Oakland (A.L.)	OF	2	1	0	0	0	0	0	0	0	1	0	0	0-0	.000	.000	.000	.000	0	1.000
2003—Oakland (A.L.)	OF	5	13	2	6	1	0	0	2	0	5	0	0	1-0	.462	.462	.538	1.000	0	1.000
Division series totals (3 years)		9	16	2	6	1	0	0	2	0	7	0	0	1-0	.375	.375	.438	.813	0	1.000

2006 LEFTY-RIGHTY SPLITS

vs.	Avg.	AB	H	2B	3B	HR	RBI	BB	SO	OBP	Slg.	vs.	Avg.	AB	H	2B	3B	HR	RBI	BB	SO	OBP	Slg.
L	.323	161	52	16	1	8	22	14	24	.377	.584	R	.244	401	98	21	2	18	57	20	64	.287	.441

CABRERA, DANIEL   P

PERSONAL: Born May 28, 1981, in San Pedro de Macoris, Dominican Republic. ... 6-7/230. ... Throws right, bats right. ... Full name: Daniel Alberto Cabrera. **TRANSACTIONS/CAREER NOTES:** Signed as a non-drafted free agent by Baltimore Orioles organization (March 15, 1999). ... On disabled list (August 23-September 6, 2005); included rehabilitation assignment to Bowie. ... On disabled list (May 15-June 5, 2006); included rehabilitation assignment to Bowie.
CAREER HITTING: 0-for-6 (.000), 0 R, 0 2B, 0 3B, 0 HR, 0 RBI.

Year Team (League)	W	L	Pct.	ERA	WHIP	G	GS	CG	ShO	Hld.	Sv.-Opp.	IP	H	R	ER	HR	BB-IBB	SO	Avg.
1999—Dom. Orioles (DSL)	2	4	.333	4.71	1.77	14	10	1			0-...	57.1	60	42	30	3	42-...	74	.260
2000—Dom. Orioles (DSL)	8	1	.889	2.52	1.16	12	10	2			0-...	71.1	45	26	20	3	38-...	44	.167
—Dom. Orioles (DSL)	2	4	.333	4.71	1.78	14	10	1			0-...		60	42	30	3	42-...	74	.260
2001—GC Orioles (GCL)	2	3	.400	5.53	1.72	12	7	0	0		0-...	40.2	31	29	25	1	39-2	36	.215
2002—Bluefield (Appal.)	5	2	.714	3.28	1.28	12	12	0	0		0-...	60.1	52	25	22	0	25-0	69	.234
2003—Delmarva (S. Atl.)	5	9	.357	4.24	1.46	26	26	1	0		0-...	125.1	105	74	59	6	78-0	120	.225
2004—Bowie (East.)	0	1	.000	2.63	0.84	5	5	0	0		0-...	27.1	11	10	8	1	12-0	35	.118
—Baltimore (A.L.)	12	8	.600	5.00	1.58	28	27	1	0	0	1-1	147.2	145	85	82	14	89-2	76	.259
2005—Bowie (East.)	1	0	1.000	3.00	1.67	1	1	0	0	0	0-0	6.0	8	3	2	1	2-0	7	.320
—Baltimore (A.L.)	10	13	.435	4.52	1.43	29	29	0	0	0	0-0	161.1	144	92	81	14	87-2	157	.235
2006—Ottawa (Int'l)	3	1	.750	4.07	1.19	4	4	0	0	0	0-0	24.1	20	13	11	1	9-0	27	.220
—Bowie (East.)	0	0	...	0.00	0.25	1	1	0	0	0	0-0	4.0	0	1	0	0	1-0	7	
—Baltimore (A.L.)	9	10	.474	4.74	1.58	26	26	2	1	0	0-0	148.0	130	82	78	11	*104-1	157	.241
Major League totals (3 years)	31	31	.500	4.75	1.53	83	82	3	2	0	1-1	457.0	419	259	241	39	280-5	390	.245

2006 LEFTY-RIGHTY SPLITS

vs.	Avg.	AB	H	2B	3B	HR	RBI	BB	SO	OBP	Slg.	vs.	Avg.	AB	H	2B	3B	HR	RBI	BB	SO	OBP	Slg.
L	.231	273	63	13	1	5	30	49	78	.349	.341	R	.251	267	67	14	1	6	38	55	79	.379	.378

CABRERA, FERNANDO   P

PERSONAL: Born November 16, 1981, in Toja Baja, Puerto Rico. ... 6-4/170. ... Throws right, bats right. ... Full name: Fernando Jose Cabrera. ... High school: Discipulous de Cristo (Toja Baja, Puerto Rico) . **TRANSACTIONS/CAREER NOTES:** Selected by Cleveland Indians organization in 10th round of 1999 free-agent draft. ... On disabled list (April 15-30, 2006); included rehabilitation assignment to Buffalo.
CAREER HITTING: 0-for-0 (.000), 0 R, 0 2B, 0 3B, 0 HR, 0 RBI.

Year Team (League)	W	L	Pct.	ERA	WHIP	G	GS	CG	ShO	Hld.	Sv.-Opp.	IP	H	R	ER	HR	BB-IBB	SO	Avg.
2000—Burlington (Appal.)	3	7	.300	4.61	1.23	13	13	0	0	...	0-...	68.1	64	42	35	4	20-0	50	.252
2001—Columbus (S. Atl.)	5	6	.455	3.61	1.33	20	20	0	0	...	0-...	94.2	89	49	38	7	37-1	96	.242
2002—Kinston (Carol.)	6	8	.429	3.52	1.12	21	21	0	0	...	0-...	110.0	83	48	43	7	40-2	107	.206
—Akron (East.)	1	2	.333	5.33	1.41	7	4	0	0	...	1-...	27.0	26	16	16	1	12-0	29	.252
2003—Akron (East.)	9	4	.692	2.97	1.25	36	15	0	0	...	5-...	109.0	96	41	36	8	40-0	115	.237
2004—Buffalo (Int'l)	4	3	.571	3.79	1.32	45	0	0	0	...	5-...	76.0	57	37	32	9	43-3	93	.208
—Cleveland (A.L.)	0	0	...	3.38	0.75	4	0	0	0	0	0-0	5.1	3	3	2	0	1-0	6	.167
2005—Buffalo (Int'l)	6	1	.857	1.23	0.92	30	0	0	0	3	3-3	51.1	36	8	7	3	11-2	68	.196
—Cleveland (A.L.)	2	1	.667	1.47	1.14	15	0	0	0	1	0-0	30.2	24	7	5	1	11-1	29	.212
2006—Buffalo (Int'l)	1	0	1.000	1.08	1.20	4	0	0	0	1	0-0	8.1	8	1	1	1	2-0	13	.242
—Cleveland (A.L.)	3	3	.500	5.19	1.40	51	0	0	0	6	0-4	60.2	53	36	35	12	32-2	71	.243
Major League totals (3 years)	5	4	.556	3.91	1.28	70	0	0	0	7	0-4	96.2	80	46	42	13	44-3	106	.229

2006 LEFTY-RIGHTY SPLITS

vs.	Avg.	AB	H	2B	3B	HR	RBI	BB	SO	OBP	Slg.	vs.	Avg.	AB	H	2B	3B	HR	RBI	BB	SO	OBP	Slg.
L	.235	81	19	3	0	4	13	19	21	.376	.420	R	.248	137	34	7	1	8	24	13	50	.312	.489

CABRERA, MELKY   OF

PERSONAL: Born August 11, 1984, in Santo Domingo, Dominican Republic. ... 5-11/170. ... Bats both, throws left. ... Full name: Melky Cabrera. . **TRANSACTIONS/CAREER NOTES:** Signed as a nondrafted free agent by New York Yankees organization (November 13, 2001). **STATISTICAL NOTES:** Career major league grand slams: 1.
2006 GAMES PLAYED BY POSITION (MLB): OF—127.

Year Team (League)	Pos.	G	AB	R	H	2B	3B	HR	RBI	BB	SO	HBP	GDP	SB-CS	Avg.	OBP	SLG	OPS	E	Avg.
2002—NY Yankees W (DSL)		60	218	37	73	19	3	2	29	18	23	3	3	7-2	.335	.388	.491	.879	...	...
2003—Staten Is. (N.Y.-Penn.)	OF	67	279	34	79	10	2	2	31	23	36	4	6	13-5	.283	.345	.355	.700	3	.979
2004—Battle Creek (Midw.)	OF	42	171	35	57	16	3	0	16	15	23	0	2	7-2	.333	.383	.462	.845	1	.952
—Tampa (Fla. St.)	OF	85	333	48	96	20	3	8	51	23	59	5	8	3-1	.288	.341	.438	.779	3	.000
2005—New York (A.L.)	OF	6	19	1	4	0	0	0	0	0	5	0	0	0-0	.211	.211	.211	.421	0	1.000
—Columbus (Int'l)	OF-DH	26	101	15	25	3	0	3	17	9	15	0	3	2-0	.248	.309	.366	.675	0	1.000
—Trenton (East.)	OF-DH	106	426	57	117	23	3	10	60	28	72	4	11	11-2	.275	.322	.411	.733	8	.985
2006—Columbus (Int'l)		31	122	19	47	6	2	4	24	10	9	1	6	3-1	.385	.430	.566	.995	2	.967
—New York (A.L.)	OF	130	460	75	129	26	2	7	50	56	59	2	9	12-5	.280	.360	.391	.752	2	.992
Major League totals (2 years)		136	479	76	133	26	2	7	50	56	61	2	9	12-5	.278	.355	.384	.739	2	.993

C

Year	Team (League)	Pos.	G	AB	R	H	2B	3B	HR	RBI	BB	SO	HBP	GDP	SB-CS	Avg.	OBP	SLG	OPS	E	Avg.
														DIVISION SERIES RECORD								
2006— New York (A.L.)		OF	2	3	0	0	0	0	0	0	0	0	0	0	0-0	.000	.000	.000	.000	0	1.000

2006 LEFTY-RIGHTY SPLITS

vs.	Avg.	AB	H	2B	3B	HR	RBI	BB	SO	OBP	Slg.	vs.	Avg.	AB	H	2B	3B	HR	RBI	BB	SO	OBP	Sig.
L	.286	126	36	7	0	1	8	15	13	.359	.365	R	.278	334	93	19	2	6	42	41	46	.361	.401

CABRERA, MIGUEL — 3B

PERSONAL: Born April 18, 1983, in Maracay, Venezuela. ... 6-2/210. ... Bats right, throws right. ... Full name: Jose Miguel Torres Cabrera. **TRANSACTIONS/CAREER NOTES:** Signed as a non-drafted free agent by Florida Marlins organization (July 2, 1999). **HONORS:** Named outfielder on the SPORTING NEWS N.L. All-Star team (2005). ... Named outfielder on N.L. Silver Slugger team (2005). ... Named third baseman on N.L. Silver Slugger team (2006).

2006 GAMES PLAYED BY POSITION (MLB): 3B—157, DH—1.

Year	Team (League)	Pos.	G	AB	R	H	2B	3B	HR	RBI	BB	SO	HBP	GDP	SB-CS	Avg.	OBP	SLG	OPS	E	Avg.
2000— GC Marlins (GCL)		SS	57	219	38	57	10	2	2	22	23	46	6	7	1-0	.260	.344	.352	.696	13	.950
— Utica (N.Y.-Penn)	SS-2B-3B		8	32	3	8	2	0	0	6	2	6	0	0	0-0	.250	.294	.313	.607	4	.902
2001— Kane Co. (Midw.)		SS-3B	110	422	61	113	19	4	7	66	37	76	2	10	3-0	.268	.328	.382	.709	32	.931
2002— Jupiter (Fla. St.)		3B-SS	124	489	77	134	43	1	9	75	38	85	9	19	10-1	.274	.333	.421	.754	17	.941
2003— Carolina (Southern)	3B-OF-DH		69	266	46	97	29	3	10	59	31	49	2	8	9-4	.365	.429	.609	1.038	15	.926
— Florida (N.L.)	OF-3B		87	314	39	84	21	3	12	62	25	84	2	12	0-2	.268	.325	.468	.793	4	.978
2004— Florida (N.L.)	OF-DH		160	603	101	177	31	1	33	112	68	148	6	20	5-2	.294	.366	.512	.879	9	.968
2005— Florida (N.L.)	OF-3B		158	613	106	198	43	2	33	116	64	125	2	20	1-0	.323	.385	.561	.947	7	.975
2006— Florida (N.L.)	3B-DH		158	576	112	195	50	2	26	114	86	108	10	18	9-6	.339	.430	.568	.998	17	.957
Major League totals (4 years)			563	2106	358	654	145	8	104	404	243	465	20	70	15-10	.311	.384	.535	.919	37	.967

DIVISION SERIES RECORD

Year	Team (League)	Pos.	G	AB	R	H	2B	3B	HR	RBI	BB	SO	HBP	GDP	SB-CS	Avg.	OBP	SLG	OPS	E	Avg.
2003— Florida (N.L.)	3B		4	14	1	4	2	0	0	3	1	6	0	0	0-0	.286	.333	.429	.762	1	.900

CHAMPIONSHIP SERIES RECORD

Year	Team (League)	Pos.	G	AB	R	H	2B	3B	HR	RBI	BB	SO	HBP	GDP	SB-CS	Avg.	OBP	SLG	OPS	E	Avg.
2003— Florida (N.L.)	OF-3B-SS		7	30	9	10	0	0	3	6	2	6	1	1	0-0	.333	.394	.633	1.027	0	1.000

WORLD SERIES RECORD

Year	Team (League)	Pos.	G	AB	R	H	2B	3B	HR	RBI	BB	SO	HBP	GDP	SB-CS	Avg.	OBP	SLG	OPS	E	Avg.
2003— Florida (N.L.)	OF		6	24	1	4	0	0	1	3	1	7	0	1	0-0	.167	.200	.292	.492	1	.938

ALL-STAR GAME RECORD

Year	Team (League)	G	AB	R	H	2B	3B	HR	RBI	BB	SO	HBP	GDP	SB-CS	Avg.	OBP	SLG	OPS	E	Avg.
All-Star Game totals (3 years)		3	4	0	0	0	0	0	0	1	0	0		0	.000	.000	.000	.000	0	1.000

2006 LEFTY-RIGHTY SPLITS

vs.	Avg.	AB	H	2B	3B	HR	RBI	BB	SO	OBP	Slg.	vs.	Avg.	AB	H	2B	3B	HR	RBI	BB	SO	OBP	Sig.
L	.321	134	43	14	0	6	28	26	30	.436	.560	R	.344	442	152	36	2	20	86	60	78	.429	.570

CABRERA, ORLANDO — SS

PERSONAL: Born November 2, 1974, in Cartagena, Colombia. ... 5-10/190. ... Bats right, throws right. ... Full name: Orlando Luis Cabrera. ... Name pronounced: kah-BRAY-rah. ... Brother of Jolbert Cabrera, infielder/outfielder, for three major league teams (1998-2004). **TRANSACTIONS/CAREER NOTES:** Signed as a non-drafted free agent by Montreal Expos organization (June 1, 1993). ... On disabled list (August 9, 1999-remainder of season). ... On disabled list (July 15-August 15, 2000); included rehabilitation assignment to Ottawa. ... Traded by Expos to Boston Red Sox as part of four-team deal in which Expos acquired SS Alex S. Gonzalez, P Francis Beltran and IF Brendan Harris from Cubs, Cubs acquired SS Nomar Garciaparra and OF Matt Murton from Red Sox, Red Sox acquired 1B Doug Mientkiewicz from Twins and Twins acquired P Justin Jones from Cubs (July 31, 2004). ... Signed as a free agent by Anaheim Angels (January 12, 2005). ... Angels franchise renamed Los Angeles Angels of Anaheim for 2005 season. ... On disabled list (July 1-16, 2005). **HONORS:** Won N.L. Gold Glove at shortstop (2001).

2006 GAMES PLAYED BY POSITION (MLB): SS—152.

Year	Team (League)	Pos.	G	AB	R	H	2B	3B	HR	RBI	BB	SO	HBP	GDP	SB-CS	Avg.	OBP	SLG	OPS	E	Avg.
1993— Dom. Expos (DSL)			38	122	24	42	6	1	1	17	18	11	...	...	14-...	.344	...	.434	...	2	.982
1994— GC Expos (GCL)	2B-OF-SS		22	73	13	23	4	1	0	11	5	8	0	2	6-0	.315	.359	.397	.756	4	.941
1995— Vermont (NYP)		2B-SS	65	248	37	70	12	5	3	33	16	28	1	3	15-8	.282	.323	.407	.731	17	.950
— W.P. Beach (Fla. St.)		SS	3	5	0	1	0	0	0	0	0	1	0	0	0-0	.200	.200	.200	.400	1	.833
1996— Delmarva (S. Atl.)		2B-SS	134	512	86	129	28	4	14	65	54	63	5	4	51-18	.252	.327	.404	.731	27	.953
1997— W.P. Beach (Fla. St.)	SS-DH-2B		69	279	56	77	19	2	5	26	27	33	0	1	32-12	.276	.340	.412	.752	20	.927
— Harrisburg (East.)		SS-2B	35	133	34	41	13	2	5	20	15	18	0	0	7-2	.308	.378	.549	.927	5	.966
— Ottawa (Int'l)		SS-2B	31	122	17	32	5	2	2	14	7	16	2	0	8-1	.262	.306	.385	.691	3	.979
— Montreal (N.L.)		SS-2B	16	18	4	4	0	0	0	2	1	3	0	1	1-2	.222	.263	.222	.485	1	.963
1998— Ottawa (Int'l)		SS-2B	66	272	31	63	9	4	0	26	28	27	0	8	19-9	.232	.298	.294	.592	12	.963
— Montreal (N.L.)		SS-2B	79	261	44	73	16	5	3	22	18	27	0	6	6-2	.280	.325	.414	.739	7	.978
1999— Montreal (N.L.)		SS	104	382	48	97	23	5	8	39	18	38	3	9	2-2	.254	.293	.403	.696	10	.973
2000— Montreal (N.L.)		SS-2B	125	422	47	100	25	1	13	55	25	28	1	12	4-4	.237	.279	.393	.673	10	.981
— Ottawa (Int'l)		SS	2	6	1	4	0	0	0	0	1	0	0	0	1-0	.667	.750	.667	1.417	0	1.000
2001— Montreal (N.L.)		SS	*162	626	64	173	41	6	14	96	43	54	4	15	19-7	.276	.324	.420	.752	11	.986
2002— Montreal (N.L.)		SS	153	563	64	148	43	1	7	56	48	53	2	16	25-7	.263	.321	.380	.701	*29	.962
2003— Montreal (N.L.)		SS	162	626	95	186	47	2	17	80	52	64	1	24	24-2	.297	.347	.460	.807	18	.975
2004— Montreal (N.L.)		SS	103	390	41	96	19	2	4	31	28	31	2	12	12-3	.246	.298	.336	.634	7	.984
— Boston (A.L.)		SS	58	228	33	67	19	1	6	31	11	23	1	4	4-1	.294	.320	.465	.785	6	.966
2005— Los Angeles (A.L.)		SS	141	540	70	139	28	3	8	57	38	50	3	10	21-2	.257	.309	.365	.674	7	.988
2006— Los Angeles (A.L.)		SS	153	607	95	171	45	1	9	72	51	58	3	12	27-3	.282	.335	.404	.738	16	.975
American League totals (3 years)			352	1375	198	377	92	5	23	160	100	131	7	26	52-6	.274	.322	.399	.721	31	.979
National League totals (8 years)			904	3288	407	877	214	22	66	381	233	298	13	89	93-29	.267	.315	.405	.721	93	.977
Major League totals (10 years)			1256	4663	605	1254	306	27	89	541	333	429	20	115	145-35	.269	.317	.403	.721	124	.978

DIVISION SERIES RECORD

Year	Team (League)	Pos.	G	AB	R	H	2B	3B	HR	RBI	BB	SO	HBP	GDP	SB-CS	Avg.	OBP	SLG	OPS	E	Avg.
2004— Boston (A.L.)		SS	3	13	1	2	1	0	0	3	2	2	0	0	0-0	.154	.267	.231	.497	0	1.000
2005— Los Angeles (A.L.)		SS	5	21	3	5	0	0	1	0	0	1	0	0	0-0	.238	.238	.333	.571	1	.950
Division series totals (2 years)			8	34	4	7	1	0	1	6	2	3	0	0	0-0	.206	.250	.294	.544	1	.964

CHAMPIONSHIP SERIES RECORD

Year Team (League)	Pos.	G	AB	R	H	2B	3B	HR	RBI	BB	SO	HBP	GDP	SB-CS	Avg.	OBP	SLG	OPS	E	Avg.
2004— Boston (A.L.)	SS	7	29	5	11	2	0	5	3	5	0	1	1-0	.379	.424	.448	.873	0	1.000
2005— Los Angeles (A.L.)	SS	5	20	1	4	1	0	1	3	0	2	0	0	0-0	.200	.200	.400	.600	1	.955
Champ. series totals (2 years)		12	49	6	15	3	0	1	8	3	7	0	1	1-0	.306	.340	.429	.768	1	.982

WORLD SERIES RECORD

Year Team (League)	Pos.	G	AB	R	H	2B	3B	HR	RBI	BB	SO	HBP	GDP	SB-CS	Avg.	OBP	SLG	OPS	E	Avg.
2004— Boston (A.L.)	SS	4	17	3	4	1	0	0	3	3	1	1	0	0-0	.235	.381	.294	.675	1	1.000

2006 LEFTY-RIGHTY SPLITS

vs.	Avg.	AB	H	2B	3B	HR	RBI	BB	SO	OBP	Slg.	vs.	Avg.	AB	H	2B	3B	HR	RBI	BB	SO	OBP	Slg.
L	.243	169	41	11	0	1	.14	17	13	.316	.325	R	.297	438	130	34	1	8	58	34	45	.342	.434

CAIN, MATT   P

PERSONAL: Born October 1, 1984, in Dothan, Ala. ... 6-3/231. ... Throws right, bats right. ... Full name: Matthew Thomas Cain. ... High school: Houston (Germantown, Tenn.). **TRANSACTIONS/CAREER NOTES:** Selected by San Francisco Giants organization in first round (25th pick overall) of 2002 free-agent draft.
CAREER HITTING: 9-for-72 (.125), 2 R, 3 2B, 0 3B, 0 HR, 1 RBI.

Year Team (League)	W	L	Pct.	ERA	WHIP	G	GS	CG	ShO	Hld.	Sv.-Opp.	IP	H	R	ER	HR	BB-IBB	SO	Avg.
2002— Ariz. Giants (Ariz.)	0	1	.000	3.72	1.24	8	7	0	0	...	0-...	19.1	13	10	8	1	11-0	20	.197
2003— Hagerstown (SAL)	4	4	.500	2.55	1.09	14	14	0	0	...	0-...	74.0	57	24	21	5	24-0	90	.209
2004— San Jose (Calif.)	7	1	.875	1.86	1.03	13	13	0	0	...	0-...	72.2	58	25	15	5	17-0	89	.216
— Norwich (East.)	6	4	.600	3.35	1.31	15	15	0	0	...	0-...	86.0	73	44	32	7	40-0	72	.236
2005— Fresno (PCL)	10	5	.667	4.39	1.31	26	26	1	0	0	0-0	145.2	118	77	71	22	73-0	176	.218
— San Francisco (N.L.)	2	1	.667	2.33	0.93	7	7	1	0	0	0-0	46.1	24	12	12	4	19-1	30	.151
2006— San Francisco (N.L.)	13	12	.520	4.15	1.28	32	31	1	1	0	0-0	190.2	157	93	88	18	87-1	179	.222
Major League totals (2 years)	15	13	.536	3.80	1.21	39	38	2	1	0	0-0	237.0	181	105	100	22	106-2	209	.209

2006 LEFTY-RIGHTY SPLITS

vs.	Avg.	AB	H	2B	3B	HR	RBI	BB	SO	OBP	Slg.	vs.	Avg.	AB	H	2B	3B	HR	RBI	BB	SO	OBP	Slg.
L	.217	373	81	20	5	10	44	54	93	.318	.378	R	.227	335	76	18	2	8	36	33	86	.300	.364

CAIRO, MIGUEL   IF

PERSONAL: Born May 4, 1974, in Anaco, Venezuela. ... 6-1/208. ... Bats right, throws right. ... Full name: Miguel Jesus Cairo. ... Name pronounced: KYE-row. ... High school: Escuela Anaco (Venezuela). **TRANSACTIONS/CAREER NOTES:** Signed as a non-drafted free agent by Los Angeles Dodgers organization (September 20, 1990). ... Traded by Dodgers with 3B Willis Otanez to Seattle Mariners for 3B Mike Blowers (November 29, 1995). ... Traded by Mariners with P Bill Risley to Toronto Blue Jays for Ps Edwin Hurtado and Paul Menhart (December 18, 1995). ... Traded by Blue Jays to Chicago Cubs for P Jason Stevenson (November 20, 1996). ... Selected by Tampa Bay Devil Rays in first round (eighth pick overall) of expansion draft (November 18, 1997). ... On disabled list (April 24-May 17 and July 26-August 11, 1999); included rehabilitation assignments to Orlando and St. Petersburg. ... Released by Devil Rays (November 27, 2000). ... Signed by Oakland Athletics organization (January 7, 2001). ... Traded by A's to Chicago Cubs for 3B/1B Eric Hinske (March 28, 2001). ... Claimed on waivers by St. Louis Cardinals (August 10, 2001). ... On disabled list (June 19-July 29, 2003); included rehabilitation assignment to Memphis. ... Signed as a free agent by New York Yankees (December 19, 2003). ... Signed as a free agent by New York Mets (January 10, 2005). ... On disabled list (June 15-July 2, 2005); included rehabilitation assignments to GCL Mets and St. Lucie. ... Signed as a free agent by Yankees (January 5, 2006). ... On disabled list (August 6-September 11, 2006). **STATISTICAL NOTES:** Career major league grand slams: 1.
2006 GAMES PLAYED BY POSITION (MLB): 2B—45, 1B—16, SS—14, 3B—8, DH—2, OF—1.

Year Team (League)	Pos.	G	AB	R	H	2B	3B	HR	RBI	BB	SO	HBP	GDP	SB-CS	Avg.	OBP	SLG	OPS	E	Avg.
1991— Dom. Dodgers (DSL)	IF	57	203	16	45	5	1	0	17	0	17	...	...	8-...	.222	...	.256	...	...	...
1992— GC Dodgers (GCL)	3B-SS	21	76	10	23	5	2	0	9	2	6	2	1	3-0	.303	.333	.421	.754	4	.953
— Vero Beach (FSL)	2B-3B	36	125	7	28	0	0	0	7	11	12	0	3	5-3	.224	.285	.224	.509	10	.935
1993— Vero Beach (FSL)	2B-3B-SS	90	346	50	109	10	1	1	23	28	22	7	2	23-16	.315	.378	.358	.736	18	.959
1994— Bakersfield (Calif.)	SS	133	533	76	155	23	4	2	48	34	37	6	9	44-23	.291	.338	.360	.698	28	.958
1995— San Antonio (Texas)	2B-SS-SS	107	435	53	121	20	1	1	41	26	31	5	6	33-16	.278	.323	.336	.659	23	.958
1996— Syracuse (Int'l)	2B-3B-SS	120	465	71	129	14	4	3	48	26	44	8	5	27-9	.277	.323	.344	.667	23	.955
— Toronto (A.L.)	2B	9	27	5	6	2	0	0	1	2	9	1	1	0-0	.222	.300	.296	.596	0	1.000
1997— Iowa (Am. Assoc.)	2B-SS	135	569	82	159	35	4	5	46	24	54	6	6	40-15	.279	.314	.381	.695	20	.969
— Chicago (N.L.)	2B-SS	16	29	7	7	1	0	0	1	2	3	1	0	0-0	.241	.313	.276	.588	0	1.000
1998— Tampa Bay (A.L.)	2B-DH	150	515	49	138	26	5	4	46	24	44	6	9	19-8	.268	.307	.367	.674	16	.978
1999— Tampa Bay (A.L.)	2B-DH	120	465	61	137	15	5	3	36	24	46	7	13	22-7	.295	.335	.368	.703	9	.986
— Orlando (South.)	2B	3	13	1	5	2	0	0	1	1	0	0	0	0-1	.385	.385	.538	.923	0	1.000
— St. Pete. (FSL)	2B	3	13	2	5	0	0	0	1	2	0	0	0	1-1	.385	.429	.385	.813	1	.958
2000— Tampa Bay (A.L.)	2B-DH	119	375	49	98	18	2	1	34	29	34	2	7	28-7	.261	.313	.328	.642	9	.983
2001— Iowa (PCL)	2B-SS-SS	34	123	22	37	7	1	3	14	8	11	1	3	3-4	.301	.348	.447	.796	3	.978
— Chicago (N.L.)	3B-2B-SS	66	123	20	35	3	1	2	9	16	21	0	1	2-1	.285	.364	.374	.738	7	.917
— St. Louis (N.L.)	OF-2B-3B																			
	1B-SS	27	33	5	11	5	0	1	7	2	0	1	0	0-0	.333	.371	.576	.947	1	.929
2002— St. Louis (N.L.)	OF-2B-DH																			
	SS-1B-DH	108	184	28	46	9	2	2	23	13	36	3	6	1-1	.250	.307	.353	.660	4	.963
2003— Memphis (PCL)	2B-DH	3	13	2	3	1	0	0	0	0	3	0	0	0-0	.231	.231	.308	.538	0	1.000
— St. Louis (N.L.)	2B-OF-3B																			
	SS-1B	92	261	41	64	15	2	5	32	13	30	6	6	4-1	.245	.289	.375	.665	6	.972
2004— New York (A.L.)	2B-3B-SS	122	360	48	105	17	5	6	42	18	49	14	7	11-3	.292	.346	.417	.763	8	.984
2005— St. Lucie (Fla. St.)	DH	1	4	0	1	0	0	0	0	0	1	0	0	0-0	.250	.250	.250	.500	0	...
— GC Mets (GCL)	2B-DH	3	13	3	4	1	0	0	0	0	0	0	0	0-0	.308	.308	.385	.692	0	1.000
— New York (N.L.)	2B-1B-3B																			
	OF	100	327	31	82	18	0	2	19	19	31	4	5	13-3	.251	.296	.324	.620	7	.983
2006— New York (A.L.)	2B-1B-SS																			
	3B-DH-OF	81	222	28	53	12	3	0	30	13	31	1	4	13-1	.239	.280	.320	.600	3	.991
American League totals (6 years)		601	1964	240	537	90	20	15	189	110	213	31	41	93-26	.273	.319	.363	.682	45	.984
National League totals (5 years)		409	957	132	245	51	5	12	91	65	123	14	20	20-6	.256	.308	.357	.666	25	.972
Major League totals (11 years)		1010	2921	372	782	141	25	27	280	175	336	45	61	113-32	.268	.316	.361	.676	70	.981

DIVISION SERIES RECORD

Year Team (League)	Pos.	G	AB	R	H	2B	3B	HR	RBI	BB	SO	HBP	GDP	SB-CS	Avg.	OBP	SLG	OPS	E	Avg.
2001— St. Louis (N.L.)	OF	3	5	0	1	0	0	0	0	0	1	0	0	1-0	.200	.200	.200	.400	0	1.000
2002— St. Louis (N.L.)	3B	2	4	2	4	1	0	0	3	0	1	0	1	0-1	1.000	1.000	1.250	2.250	0	1.000
2004— New York (A.L.)	2B	4	14	3	3	1	0	0	1	2	4	1	0	0-0	.214	.313	.286	.598	0	1.000
Division series totals (3 years)		9	23	5	8	2	0	0	4	2	6	1	1	1-1	.348	.423	.435	.858	0	1.000

Year Team (League)	Pos.	G	AB	R	H	2B	3B	HR	RBI	BB	SO	HBP	GDP	SB-CS	Avg.	OBP	SLG	OPS	E	Avg.
2002— St. Louis (N.L.)	3B	3	13	2	5	0	0	1	2	0	2	0	0	0-0	.385	.385	.615	1.000	0	1.000
2004— New York (A.L.)	2B	7	25	4	7	3	0	0	0	2	4	4	0	1-0	.280	.419	.400	.819	0	1.000
Champ. series totals (2 years)		10	38	6	12	3	0	1	2	2	6	4	0	1-0	.316	.409	.474	.883	0	1.000

2006 LEFTY-RIGHTY SPLITS

vs.	Avg.	AB	H	2B	3B	HR	RBI	BB	SO	OBP	Slg.	vs.	Avg.	AB	H	2B	3B	HR	RBI	BB	SO	OBP	Slg.
L	.279	68	19	5	1	0	10	5	8	.333	.382	R	.221	154	34	7	2	0	20	8	23	.256	.292

CALERO, KIKO   P

PERSONAL: Born January 9, 1975, in Santurce, Puerto Rico. ... 6-1/180. ... Throws right, bats right. ... Full name: Enrique Nomar Calero. ... High school: University Gardens (Puerto Rico). ... College: St. Thomas (Fla.). **TRANSACTIONS/CAREER NOTES:** Selected by Kansas City Royals organization in 27th round of 1996 free-agent draft. ... Signed as a free agent by St. Louis Cardinals organization (December 3, 2002). ... On disabled list (August 7-September 4, 2004); included rehabilitation assignments to Memphis. ... Traded by Cardinals with P Danny Haren and C Daric Barton to Oakland Athletics for P Mark Mulder (December 19, 2004). ... On disabled list (May 10-June 5, 2005); included rehabilitation assignment to Sacramento.

CAREER HITTING: 1-for-6 (.167), 1 R, 0 2B, 0 3B, 0 HR, 1 RBI.

Year Team (League)	W	L	Pct.	ERA	WHIP	G	GS	CG	ShO	Hld.	Sv.-Opp.	IP	H	R	ER	HR	BB-IBB	SO	Avg.
1996— Spokane (N'west)	4	2	.667	2.52	1.27	17	11	0	0	...	1-...	75.0	77	34	21	5	18-0	61	.265
1997— Wichita (Texas)	11	9	.550	4.44	1.28	23	22	2	0	...	0-...	127.2	120	78	63	15	44-0	100	.248
1998— Lansing (Midw.)	1	0	1.000	3.78	1.56	4	4	0	0	...	0-...	16.2	19	7	7	1	7-0	10	.284
— Wichita (Texas)	1	0	1.000	9.64	2.07	3	3	0	0	...	0-...	14.0	23	16	15	2	6-0	5	.359
— Wilmington (Caro.)	7	3	.700	2.86	1.28	17	17	0	0	...	0-...	97.2	74	33	31	7	51-1	90	.213
1999— Wichita (Texas)	9	3	.750	4.11	1.55	26	23	1	1	...	1-...	129.1	143	67	59	14	57-3	92	.279
2000— Wichita (Texas)	10	7	.588	3.63	1.35	28	25	0	0	...	0-...	153.2	141	74	62	16	66-0	130	.251
2001— Wichita (Texas)	14	5	.737	3.33	1.29	27	19	0	0	...	0-...	124.1	110	57	46	10	51-1	94	.237
2002— Wichita (Texas)	1	0	1.000	2.25	0.94	5	2	0	0	...	0-...	16.0	10	5	4	2	5-0	15	.172
— Omaha (PCL)	7	7	.500	3.44	1.17	20	18	0	0	...	0-...	125.2	112	52	48	11	35-1	109	.244
2003— St. Louis (N.L.)	1	1	.500	2.82	1.28	26	1	0	0	1	1-4	38.1	29	12	12	5	20-2	51	.212
2004— Memphis (PCL)	0	0	...	2.49	1.22	12	3	0	0	...	1-...	25.1	20	8	7	3	11-2	33	.222
— St. Louis (N.L.)	3	1	.750	2.78	0.82	41	0	0	0	12	2-3	45.1	27	14	14	5	10-1	47	.176
2005— Sacramento (PCL)	0	0	...	9.00	2.00	2	2	0	0	...	0-0	2.0	4	2	2	0	0-0	2	.400
— Oakland (A.L.)	4	1	.800	3.23	1.13	58	0	0	0	12	1-2	55.2	45	20	20	6	18-2	52	.216
2006— Oakland (A.L.)	3	2	.600	3.41	1.28	70	0	0	0	23	2-5	58.0	50	22	22	4	24-3	67	.231
American League totals (2 years)	7	3	.700	3.33	1.21	128	0	0	0	35	3-7	113.2	95	42	42	10	42-5	119	.224
National League totals (2 years)	4	2	.667	2.80	1.03	67	1	0	0	13	3-7	83.2	56	26	26	10	30-3	98	.193
Major League totals (4 years)	11	5	.688	3.10	1.13	195	1	0	0	48	6-14	197.1	151	68	68	20	72-8	217	.211

Year Team (League)	W	L	Pct.	ERA	WHIP	G	GS	CG	ShO	Hld.	Sv.-Opp.	IP	H	R	ER	HR	BB-IBB	SO	Avg.
2004— St. Louis (N.L.)	0	0	...	0.00	0.00	1	0	0	0	0	0-0	1.0	0	0	0	0	0-0	2	.000
2006— Oakland (A.L.)	1	0	1.000	0.00	1.00	1	0	0	0	0	0-0	1.0	1	0	0	0	1-0	1	.000
Division series totals (2 years)	1	0	1.000	0.00	0.50	2	0	0	0	0	0-0	2.0	1	0	0	0	1-0	3	.000

Year Team (League)	W	L	Pct.	ERA	WHIP	G	GS	CG	ShO	Hld.	Sv.-Opp.	IP	H	R	ER	HR	BB-IBB	SO	Avg.
2004— St. Louis (N.L.)	0	0	...	3.86	1.29	5	0	0	0	0	0-1	7.0	8	3	3	1	1-0	7	.296
2006— Oakland (A.L.)	0	0	...	0.00	2.00	3	0	0	0	0	0-0	2.0	3	0	0	0	1-0	1	.333
Champ. series totals (2 years)	0	0	...	3.00	1.44	8	0	0	0	0	0-1	9.0	11	3	3	1	2-0	8	.306

Year Team (League)	W	L	Pct.	ERA	WHIP	G	GS	CG	ShO	Hld.	Sv.-Opp.	IP	H	R	ER	HR	BB-IBB	SO	Avg.
2004— St. Louis (N.L.)	0	0	...	13.50	4.50	2	0	0	0	0	0-0	1.1	2	2	2	0	4-0	0	.400

2006 LEFTY-RIGHTY SPLITS

vs.	Avg.	AB	H	2B	3B	HR	RBI	BB	SO	OBP	Slg.	vs.	Avg.	AB	H	2B	3B	HR	RBI	BB	SO	OBP	Slg.
L	.278	72	20	2	0	2	5	14	25	.395	.389	R	.208	144	30	2	3	2	20	10	42	.258	.306

CALLASPO, ALBERTO   IF

PERSONAL: Born April 19, 1983, in Maracay, Venezuela. ... 5-10/125. ... Bats both, throws right. ... Full name: Alberto Jose Callaspo. ... High school: Inst. De Formacion (Venezuela). **TRANSACTIONS/CAREER NOTES:** Signed as a non-drafted free agent by Anaheim Angels organization (February 16, 2001). ... Angels franchise renamed Los Angeles Angels of Anaheim for 2005 season. ... Traded by Angels to Arizona Diamondbacks for P Jason Bulger (February 28, 2006).

2006 GAMES PLAYED BY POSITION (MLB): SS—4, 2B—3, 3B—2.

Year Team (League)	Pos.	G	AB	R	H	2B	3B	HR	RBI	BB	SO	HBP	GDP	SB-CS	Avg.	OBP	SLG	OPS	E	Avg.
2001— Dominican Angels (DSL) ...		66	275	55	98	11	4	2	39	22	16	2	7	14-13	.356	.403	.447	.850	18	...
2002— Provo (Pion.)		70	299	70	101	16	10	3	60	17	14	2	6	13-4	.338	.374	.488	.862	11	...
2003— Cedar Rap. (Midw.)		133	514	86	168	38	4	2	67	42	28	3	6	20-6	.327	.377	.428	.805	19	...
2004— Arkansas (Texas)		136	550	76	156	29	2	6	48	47	25	0	16	15-14	.284	.338	.376	.714	26	...
2005— Arkansas (Texas)	2B	89	350	53	104	8	0	10	49	28	17	1	4	9-8	.297	.346	.406	.752	7	.983
— Salt Lake (PCL)	2B-DH	50	212	28	67	21	2	1	31	10	13	1	7	2-5	.316	.345	.448	.793	5	.978
2006— Tucson (PCL)		114	490	93	165	24	12	7	68	56	27	2	5	8-5	.337	.404	.478	.882	14	.972
— Arizona (N.L.)	SS-2B-3B	23	42	2	10	1	1	0	6	4	6	0	0	0-1	.238	.298	.310	.607	2	.943
Major League totals (1 year)		23	42	2	10	1	1	0	6	4	6	0	0	0-1	.238	.298	.310	.607	2	.943

2006 LEFTY-RIGHTY SPLITS

vs.	Avg.	AB	H	2B	3B	HR	RBI	BB	SO	OBP	Slg.	vs.	Avg.	AB	H	2B	3B	HR	RBI	BB	SO	OBP	Slg.
L	.278	18	5	0	0	0	1	1	2	.316	.278	R	.208	24	5	1	1	0	5	3	4	.286	.333

CAMERON, MIKE   OF

PERSONAL: Born January 8, 1973, in LaGrange, Ga. ... 6-2/200. ... Bats right, throws right. ... Full name: Michael Terrance Cameron. ... High school: La Grange (Ga.). **TRANSACTIONS/CAREER NOTES:** Selected by Chicago White Sox organization in 18th round of 1991 free-agent draft. ... Traded by White Sox to Cincinnati Reds for 1B/3B Paul Konerko (November 11, 1998). ... Traded by Reds with Ps Brett Tomko and Jake Meyer and IF Antonio Perez to Seattle Mariners for OF Ken Griffey (February 10, 2000). ... Signed as a free agent by New York Mets (December 23, 2003). ... On disabled list (April 8-May 5 and August 12, 2005-remainder of season); included rehabilitation assignment to Norfolk. ... Traded by Mets to San Diego Padres for 1B/OF Xavier Nady (November 18, 2005). ... On disabled list (April 1-23, 2006); included rehabilitation assignment to Lake Elsinore. **RECORDS:** Shares major league record for most home runs, game (4, May 2, 2002). **HONORS:** Won A.L. Gold Glove as outfielder (2001 and 2003). ... Won N.L. Gold Glove as outfielder (2006). **STATISTICAL NOTES:** Hit four home runs in one game (May 2, 2002). ... Career major league grand slams: 4.

2006 GAMES PLAYED BY POSITION (MLB): OF—141.

C

BATTING / FIELDING

Year Team (League)	Pos.	G	AB	R	H	2B	3B	HR	RBI	BB	SO	HBP	GDP	SB-CS	Avg.	OBP	SLG	OPS	E	Avg.
1991— GC Whi. Sox (GCL)	OF	44	136	20	30	3	0	0	11	17	29	4	3	13-2	.221	.325	.243	.567	3	.951
1992— Utica (N.Y.-Penn)	OF	26	87	15	24	1	4	2	12	11	26	0	0	3-7	.276	.354	.448	.802	0	1.000
— South Bend (Mid.)	OF	35	114	19	26	8	1	1	9	10	37	4	0	2-3	.228	.310	.342	.652	3	.957
1993— South Bend (Mid.)	OF	122	411	52	98	14	5	0	30	27	101	6	8	19-10	.238	.292	.297	.589	4	.985
1994— Prince Will. (Car.)	OF	131	468	86	116	15	17	6	48	60	101	8	6	22-10	.248	.343	.391	.734	6	.979
1995— Birmingham (Sou.)	OF	107	350	64	87	20	5	11	60	54	104	6	9	21-12	.249	.355	.429	.784	4	.985
— Chicago (A.L.)	OF	28	38	4	7	2	0	1	2	3	15	0	0	0-0	.184	.244	.316	.560	0	1.000
1996— Birmingham (Sou.)	OF-DH	123	473	120	142	34	12	28	77	71	117	12	5	39-15	.300	.402	.600	1.002	7	.973
— Chicago (A.L.)	OF-DH	11	11	1	1	0	0	0	0	1	3	0	0	0-1	.091	.167	.091	.258	0	1.000
1997— Nashville (A.A.)	OF-DH	30	120	21	33	7	3	6	17	18	31	3	1	4-2	.275	.378	.533	.911	1	.985
— Chicago (A.L.)	OF-DH	116	379	63	98	18	3	14	55	55	105	5	8	23-2	.259	.356	.433	.789	5	.985
1998— Chicago (A.L.)	OF	141	396	53	83	16	5	8	43	37	101	6	6	27-11	.210	.285	.336	.621	4	.988
1999— Cincinnati (N.L.)	OF	146	542	93	139	34	9	21	66	80	145	6	4	38-12	.256	.357	.469	.825	8	.979
2000— Seattle (A.L.)	OF	155	543	96	145	28	4	19	78	78	133	9	10	24-7	.267	.365	.438	.803	6	.985
2001— Seattle (A.L.)	OF-DH	150	540	99	144	30	5	25	110	69	155	10	13	34-5	.267	.353	.480	.832	5	.986
2002— Seattle (A.L.)	OF-DH	158	545	84	130	26	5	25	80	79	176	7	8	31-8	.239	.340	.442	.782	5	.988
2003— Seattle (A.L.)	OF	147	534	74	135	31	5	18	76	70	137	5	13	17-7	.253	.344	.431	.774	4	.992
2004— New York (N.L.)	OF	140	493	76	114	30	1	30	76	57	143	8	5	22-6	.231	.319	.479	.798	8	.978
2005— St. Lucie (Fla. St.)	OF	4	10	3	3	2	0	0	0	3	3	2	0	0-0	.300	.500	.500	1.033	0	1.000
— Norfolk (Int'l)	OF	2	7	2	2	0	1	0	2	3	3	0	0	0-0	.286	.500	.571	1.071	0	1.000
— New York (N.L.)	OF	76	308	47	84	23	2	12	39	29	85	4	5	13-1	.273	.342	.477	.819	6	.963
2006— Lake Elsinore (Calif.)	OF	2	6	1	2	1	0	0	1	1	2	0	0	0-0	.333	.429	.500	.929	0	1.000
— San Diego (N.L.)	OF	141	552	88	148	34	9	22	83	71	142	6	8	25-9	.268	.355	.482	.837	6	.984
American League totals (8 years)		906	2986	474	743	151	27	110	444	392	825	42	58	156-41	.249	.341	.428	.769	30	.988
National League totals (4 years)		503	1895	304	485	121	21	85	264	237	515	24	22	98-28	.256	.344	.477	.821	28	.978
Major League totals (12 years)		1409	4881	778	1228	272	48	195	708	629	1340	66	80	254-69	.252	.342	.447	.789	58	.985

DIVISION SERIES RECORD

Year Team (League)	Pos.	G	AB	R	H	2B	3B	HR	RBI	BB	SO	HBP	GDP	SB-CS	Avg.	OBP	SLG	OPS	E	Avg.
2000— Seattle (A.L.)	OF	3	12	2	3	0	0	0	2	0	1	1	1	1-0	.250	.308	.250	.558	0	1.000
2001— Seattle (A.L.)	OF	5	18	2	4	3	0	1	3	2	7	1	0	0-1	.222	.333	.556	.889	0	1.000
2006— San Diego (N.L.)	OF	4	14	1	2	1	0	0	1	3	7	0	0	1-0	.143	.294	.214	.508	0	1.000
Division series totals (3 years)		12	44	5	9	4	0	1	6	5	14	2	1	2-1	.205	.314	.364	.677	0	1.000

CHAMPIONSHIP SERIES RECORD

Year Team (League)	Pos.	G	AB	R	H	2B	3B	HR	RBI	BB	SO	HBP	GDP	SB-CS	Avg.	OBP	SLG	OPS	E	Avg.
2000— Seattle (A.L.)	OF	6	18	3	2	0	0	0	1	2	7	0	0	1-0	.111	.200	.111	.311	0	1.000
2001— Seattle (A.L.)	OF	5	17	3	3	2	0	0	0	4	4	1	1	0-0	.176	.364	.294	.658	0	1.000
Champ. series totals (2 years)		11	35	6	5	2	0	0	1	6	11	1	1	1-0	.143	.286	.200	.486	0	1.000

ALL-STAR GAME RECORD

	G	AB	R	H	2B	3B	HR	RBI	BB	SO	HBP	GDP	SB-CS	Avg.	OBP	SLG	OPS	E	Avg.
All-Star Game totals (1 year)	1	3	0	1	1	0	0	0	0	1	0	0	0-0	.333	.333	.667	1.000	0	1.000

2006 LEFTY-RIGHTY SPLITS

vs.	Avg.	AB	H	2B	3B	HR	RBI	BB	SO	OBP	Slg.	vs.	Avg.	AB	H	2B	3B	HR	RBI	BB	SO	OBP	Slg.
L	.252	123	31	6	3	4	19	23	30	.362	.447	R	.273	429	117	28	6	18	64	48	112	.353	.492

CAMP, SHAWN — P

PERSONAL: Born November 18, 1975, in Fairfax, Va. ... 6-1/200. ... Throws right, bats right. ... Full name: Shawn Anthony Camp. ... High school: James W. Robinson Jr. Secondary School (Fairfax, Va.). ... College: George Mason. **TRANSACTIONS/CAREER NOTES:** Selected by San Diego Padres organization in 16th round of 1997 free-agent draft. ... Traded by Padres with OF Shawn Gilbert to Pittsburgh Pirates for OF Emil Brown (July 10, 2001). ... Signed as a free agent by Kansas City Royals organization (October 29, 2003). ... Signed as a free agent by Tampa Bay Devil Rays organization (January 17, 2006).
CAREER HITTING: 0-for-0 (.000), 0 R, 0 2B, 0 3B, 0 HR, 0 RBI.

Year Team (League)	W	L	Pct.	ERA	WHIP	G	GS	CG	ShO	Hld.	Sv.-Opp.	IP	H	R	ER	HR	BB-IBB	SO	Avg.
1997— Idaho Falls (Pio.)	2	1	.667	5.51	1.68	30	0	0	0	...	12-...	32.2	41	22	20	3	14-0	41	.311
1998— Clinton (Midw.)	3	5	.375	2.62	1.24	47	0	0	0	...	13-...	55.0	48	19	16	0	20-4	62	.232
1999— Rancho Cuca. (Calif.)	1	5	.167	3.95	1.41	53	0	0	0	...	6-...	66.0	68	37	29	4	25-3	78	.271
2000— Rancho Cuca. (Calif.)	1	0	1.000	1.45	0.80	14	0	0	0	...	10-...	18.2	10	3	3	0	5-0	18	.154
— Mobile (Sou.)	3	3	.500	2.43	1.30	45	0	0	0	...	1-...	59.1	47	23	16	4	30-2	53	.217
2001— Portland (PCL)	1	0	1.000	0.00	0.43	4	1	0	0	...	0-...	7.0	2	0	0	0	1-0	6	.095
— Mobile (Sou.)	6	2	.750	4.44	1.25	35	1	0	0	...	1-...	48.2	46	24	24	2	15-1	55	.261
— Altoona (East.)	4	0	1.000	4.24	1.41	8	3	0	0	...	0-...	23.1	25	14	11	3	8-1	19	.278
— Nashville (PCL)	0	0	...	2.12	1.12	11	0	0	0	...	0-...	17.0	11	4	4	1	8-1	15	.190
2002— Nashville (PCL)	4	1	.800	3.24	1.11	39	0	0	0	...	0-...	58.1	50	22	21	5	15-3	59	.239
2003— Nashville (PCL)	0	1	.000	4.98	1.50	33	1	0	0	...	0-...	43.1	50	26	24	2	15-2	36	.289
— Altoona (East.)	0	2	.000	4.34	1.28	18	4	0	0	...	0-...	29.0	26	14	14	2	11-0	35	.236
2004— Omaha (PCL)	1	1	.500	5.32	1.45	15	0	0	0	...	1-...	22.0	26	14	13	2	6-0	21	.289
— Kansas City (A.L.)	2	2	.500	3.92	1.35	42	0	0	0	...	1-...	66.2	74	37	29	10	16-1	51	.285
2005— Omaha (PCL)	3	6	.333	3.86	1.37	21	7	0	0	1	1-1	67.2	71	36	29	9	22-1	42	.275
— Kansas City (A.L.)	1	4	.200	6.43	1.67	29	0	0	0	...	0-2	49.0	69	40	35	4	13-3	28	.332
2006— Tampa Bay	7	4	.636	4.68	1.49	75	0	0	0	12	4-6	75.0	93	43	39	9	19-3	53	.313
Major League totals (3 years)	10	10	.500	4.86	1.49	146	0	0	0	17	6-11	190.2	236	120	103	23	48-7	132	.308

2006 LEFTY-RIGHTY SPLITS

vs.	Avg.	AB	H	2B	3B	HR	RBI	BB	SO	OBP	Slg.	vs.	Avg.	AB	H	2B	3B	HR	RBI	BB	SO	OBP	Slg.
L	.370	100	37	13	1	2	15	9	10	.432	.580	R	.284	197	56	5	0	7	32	10	43	.330	.416

CAMPBELL, BRETT — P

PERSONAL: Born October 17, 1981, in Atlanta. ... 6-0/170. ... Throws right, bats right. ... Full name: Richard Campbell. ... College: Kennesaw State. **TRANSACTIONS/CAREER NOTES:** Selected by Montreal Expos organization in 34th round of 2004 free-agent draft. ... Expos franchise relocated to Washington, D.C., and renamed Washington Nationals for 2005 season (December 3, 2004).
CAREER HITTING: 0-for-0 (.000), 0 R, 0 2B, 0 3B, 0 HR, 0 RBI.

Year Team (League)	W	L	Pct.	ERA	WHIP	G	GS	CG	ShO	Hld.	Sv.-Opp.	IP	H	R	ER	HR	BB-IBB	SO	Avg.
2004— GC Expos (GCL)	0	1	.000	3.86	1.71	5	0	0	0	...	1-...	7.0	6	3	3	0	6-1	11	.222
— Brevard County (FSL)	1	0	1.000	3.86	1.43	4	0	0	0	...	0-...	7.0	6	3	3	1	4-0	2	.222

C

Year Team (League)	W	L	Pct.	ERA	WHIP	G	GS	CG	ShO	Hld.	Sv.-Opp.	IP	H	R	ER	HR	BB-IBB	SO	Avg.
—Vermont (NYP)	0	1	.000	4.09	1.55	11	0	0	0	...	0-...	22.0	24	14	10	3	10-1	25	.267
2005—Savannah (S. Atl.)	4	2	.667	1.69	0.90	36	0	0	0	1	19-22	48.0	28	10	9	2	15-0	50	.164
—Potomac (Carol.)	0	2	.000	9.60	2.07	12	0	0	0	2	1-3	15.0	21	18	16	3	10-0	13	.328
2006—Harrisburg (East.)	0	3	.000	3.14	1.88	13	0	0	0	0	8-11	14.1	16	6	5	0	11-3	20	.276
—Potomac (Carol.)	3	1	.750	2.38	1.06	19	0	0	0	0	8-10	22.2	22	7	6	3	2-0	27	.253
—New Orleans (PCL)	0	1	.000	3.92	1.21	15	0	0	0	2	0-2	20.2	14	9	9	1	11-1	19	.189
—Wash. (N.L.)	0	0	...	10.38	1.38	4	0	0	0	0	0-0	4.1	4	5	5	1	2-0	4	.250
Major League totals (1 year)	0	0	...	10.38	1.38	4	0	0	0	0	0-0	4.1	4	5	5	1	2-0	4	.250

2006 LEFTY-RIGHTY SPLITS

vs.	Avg.	AB	H	2B	3B	HR	RBI	BB	SO	OBP	Slg.	vs.	Avg.	AB	H	2B	3B	HR	RBI	BB	SO	OBP	Slg.
L	.333	9	3	0	0	1	3	1	1	.400	.667	R	.143	7	1	0	1	0	2	1	3	.333	.429

CAMPILLO, JORGE — P

PERSONAL: Born August 10, 1978, in Tijuana, Mexico. ... 6-1/190. ... Throws right, bats right. ... Full name: Jorge Hidalgo Campillo. . **TRANSACTIONS/CAREER NOTES:** Signed as a free agent by Seattle Mariners organization (March 3, 2005). ... On disabled list (August 3, 2005-remainder of season).
CAREER HITTING: 0-for-0 (.000), 0 R, 0 2B, 0 3B, 0 HR, 0 RBI.

Year Team (League)	W	L	Pct.	ERA	WHIP	G	GS	CG	ShO	Hld.	Sv.-Opp.	IP	H	R	ER	HR	BB-IBB	SO	Avg.
1997—Tigres (Mex.)	1	0	1.000	4.50	1.75	2	0	0	0	...	0-...	4.0	2	2	2	0	5-0	4	.143
1998—Tigres (Mex.)	6	2	.750	5.11	1.91	24	7	1	0	...	0-...	68.2	76	43	39	6	55-3	42	.297
1999—Tigres (Mex.)	1	2	.333	2.90	1.35	32	0	0	0	...	1-...	71.1	50	29	23	3	46-2	41	.200
2000—Tigres (Mex.)	9	7	.563	6.84	1.72	25	17	1	0	...	0-...	98.2	128	79	75	22	42-2	58	.313
2001—Tigres (Mex.)	6	3	.667	3.53	1.52	30	9	0	0	...	2-...	86.2	95	43	34	12	37-4	64	.280
2002—Tigres (Mex.)	5	5	.500	5.53	1.57	25	15	0	0	...	0-...	94.1	111	62	58	14	37-2	64	.292
2003—Tigres (Mex.)	12	5	.706	2.79	1.22	21	21	2	1	...	0-...	119.1	116	47	37	7	30-1	63	.258
2004—Tigres (Mex.)	5	5	.500	5.38	1.50	17	16	1	0	...	0-...	98.2	120	67	59	14	28-2	66	.306
2005—Ariz. Mariners (Ariz.)	0	2	.000	5.73	1.82	4	4	0	0	0	0-0	11.0	18	11	7	0	2-0	10	.391
—Tacoma (PCL)	4	1	.800	2.71	1.22	12	12	0	0	0	0-0	66.1	63	21	20	5	18-0	43	.259
—Seattle (A.L.)	0	0	...	0.00	1.00	2	1	0	0	0	0-0	2.0	1	0	0	0	1-0	1	.125
2006—Ariz. Mariners (Ariz.)	0	0	...	4.15	1.00	6	5	0	0	0	0-0	13.0	13	6	6	0	0-0	15	.277
—San Antonio (Texas)	2	0	1.000	2.53	1.31	2	2	0	0	0	0-0	10.2	12	4	3	0	2-0	3	.293
—Inland Empire (Calif.)	1	1	.500	4.00	1.11	2	2	0	0	0	0-0	9.0	8	4	4	0	2-0	6	.222
—Seattle (A.L.)	0	0	...	15.43	1.71	1	0	0	0	0	0-0	2.1	4	4	4	0	0-0	1	.364
Major League totals (2 years)	0	0	...	8.31	1.38	3	1	0	0	0	0-0	4.1	5	4	4	0	1-0	2	.263

2006 LEFTY-RIGHTY SPLITS

vs.	Avg.	AB	H	2B	3B	HR	RBI	BB	SO	OBP	Slg.	vs.	Avg.	AB	H	2B	3B	HR	RBI	BB	SO	OBP	Slg.
L	.250	4	1	0	0	0	1	0	0	.250	.250	R	.429	7	3	3	0	0	2	0	1	.429	.857

CANNIZARO, ANDY — SS

PERSONAL: Born December 19, 1978, in New Orleans. ... 5-10/170. ... Bats right, throws right. ... Full name: Andrew L. Cannizaro. ... Name pronounced: Can-eh-ZAR-roe. ... College: Tulane. **TRANSACTIONS/CAREER NOTES:** Selected by New York Yankees organization in seventh round of 2001 free-agent draft.
2006 GAMES PLAYED BY POSITION (MLB): SS—10, 2B—2, 3B—2. .

Year Team (League)	Pos.	G	AB	R	H	2B	3B	HR	RBI	BB	SO	HBP	GDP	SB-CS	Avg.	OBP	SLG	OPS	E	Avg.
2001—Staten Is. (N.Y.-Penn)		67	254	38	72	9	2	0	20	22	21	6	15	5-3	.283	.351	.335	.686	...	...
2002—Tampa (Fla. St.)		112	366	52	91	18	1	1	46	38	31	14	14	3-4	.249	.339	.311	.650	...	...
2003—Trenton (East.)		108	369	50	102	23	1	1	39	26	24	9	7	9-4	.276	.337	.352	.689	...	...
2004—Trenton (East.)		85	328	44	103	18	0	3	44	36	31	5	7	7-9	.314	.385	.396	.781	...	...
2005—Trenton (East.)	SS	54	202	28	50	12	0	0	20	11	19	4	4	5-0	.248	.298	.307	.605	7	.969
—Columbus (Int'l)	SS-2B	56	170	22	43	10	2	1	18	17	11	9	11	1-1	.253	.352	.353	.705	6	.971
2006—Columbus (Int'l)		116	416	69	115	32	1	3	32	51	59	10	7	6-5	.276	.367	.380	.746	20	.962
—New York (A.L.)	SS-2B-3B	13	8	5	2	0	0	1	1	1	1	0	1	0-0	.250	.333	.625	.958	1	.909
Major League totals (1 year)		13	8	5	2	0	0	1	1	1	1	0	1	0-0	.250	.333	.625	.958	1	.909

2006 LEFTY-RIGHTY SPLITS

vs.	Avg.	AB	H	2B	3B	HR	RBI	BB	SO	OBP	Slg.	vs.	Avg.	AB	H	2B	3B	HR	RBI	BB	SO	OBP	Slg.
L	1.000	2	2	0	0	1	1	0	0	1.000	2.500	R	.000	6	0	0	0	0	0	1	1	.143	.000

CANO, ROBINSON — 2B

PERSONAL: Born October 22, 1982, in San Pedro de Macoris, Dominican Republic. ... 6-0/170. ... Bats left, throws right. ... Full name: Robinson Jose Cano. . ... Son of Jose Cano, pitcher with Houston Astros (1989). **TRANSACTIONS/CAREER NOTES:** Signed as a non-drafted free agent by New York Yankees organization (January 5, 2001). ... On disabled list (June 27-August 8, 2006); included rehabilitation assignments to GCL Yankees and Trenton. **HONORS:** Named second baseman on SPORTING NEWS A.L. All-Star team (2006). ... Named second baseman on A.L. Silver Slugger team (2006). **STATISTICAL NOTES:** Career major league grand slams: 1.
2006 GAMES PLAYED BY POSITION (MLB): 2B—118, DH—4.

Year Team (League)	Pos.	G	AB	R	H	2B	3B	HR	RBI	BB	SO	HBP	GDP	SB-CS	Avg.	OBP	SLG	OPS	E	Avg.
2001—GC Yankees (GCL)	2B-SS-3B	57	200	37	46	14	2	3	34	28	27	3	4	11-2	.230	.330	.365	.695	11	.959
—Staten Is. (N.Y.-Penn)	3B-SS	2	8	0	2	0	0	0	2	0	2	0	0	0-0	.250	.250	.250	.500	1	.833
2002—Greensboro (S. Atl.)	SS-2B	113	474	67	131	20	9	14	66	29	78	3	8	2-1	.276	.321	.445	.766	37	.935
—Staten Is. (N.Y.-Penn)	3B-SS	22	87	11	24	5	1	1	15	4	8	0	1	6-1	.276	.308	.391	.699	3	.971
2003—Tampa (Fla. St.)	2B	90	366	50	101	16	3	5	50	17	49	4	5	1-1	.276	.313	.377	.690	13	.970
—Trenton (East.)	2B-3B	46	164	21	46	9	1	1	13	9	16	6	6	0-0	.280	.341	.366	.707	5	.977
2004—Trenton (East.)	2B-3B	74	292	43	88	20	8	7	44	24	40	3	4	2-4	.301	.356	.497	.853	12	.864
—Columbus (Int'l)	2B-3B	61	216	22	56	9	2	6	30	18	27	1	7	0-1	.259	.316	.403	.719	4	.000
2005—Columbus (Int'l)	2B-3B-DH	24	108	19	36	8	3	4	24	6	13	0	2	0-0	.333	.368	.574	.942	4	.967
—New York (A.L.)	2B	132	522	78	155	34	4	14	62	16	68	3	16	1-3	.297	.320	.458	.778	17	.974
2006—GC Yankees (GCL)		1	5	0	2	0	0	0	1	0	0	0	0	0-0	.400	.400	.400	.800	0	...
—Trenton (East.)		3	10	1	5	2	0	0	3	0	0	0	0	0-0	.500	.615	.700	1.315	0	1.000
—New York (A.L.)	2B-DH	122	482	62	165	41	1	15	78	18	54	2	19	5-2	.342	.365	.525	.890	9	.984
Major League totals (2 years)		254	1004	140	320	75	5	29	140	34	122	5	35	6-5	.319	.342	.490	.832	26	.979

DIVISION SERIES RECORD

Year Team (League)	Pos.	G	AB	R	H	2B	3B	HR	RBI	BB	SO	HBP	GDP	SB-CS	Avg.	OBP	SLG	OPS	E	Avg.
2005—New York (A.L.)	2B	5	19	3	5	3	0	0	2	2	4	0	0	0-1	.263	.333	.421	.754	2	.941
2006—New York (A.L.)	2B	4	15	0	2	0	0	0	0	0	1	0	0	0-0	.133	.133	.133	.267	0	1.000
Division series totals (2 years)		9	34	3	7	3	0	0	2	2	5	0	0	0-1	.206	.250	.294	.544	2	.962

vs.	Avg.	AB	H	2B	3B	HR	RBI	BB	SO	OBP	Slg.	vs.	Avg.	AB	H	2B	3B	HR	RBI	BB	SO	OBP	Slg.
L	.287	129	37	9	1	0	11	6	15	.328	.372	R	.363	353	128	32	0	15	67	12	39	.378	.581

CANTU, JORGE — 2B/3B

PERSONAL: Born January 30, 1982, in Reynosa, Mexico. ... 6-1/184. ... Bats right, throws right. ... Full name: Jorge Luis Cantu. ... High school: Sharyland (McAllen, Texas).
TRANSACTIONS/CAREER NOTES: Signed as a non-drafted free agent by Tampa Bay Devil Rays organization (July 2, 1998). ... On disabled list (April 27-June 6, 2006); included rehabilitation assignment to Montgomery. **STATISTICAL NOTES:** Career major league grand slams: 1.
2006 GAMES PLAYED BY POSITION (MLB): 2B—103, DH—2.

										BATTING								FIELDING	
Year Team (League)	Pos.	G	AB	R	H	2B	3B	HR	RBI	BB	SO	HBP	GDP	SB-CS	Avg.	OBP	SLG	OPS	E	Avg.
1999—Hudson Valley (NYP)	SS	72	281	33	73	17	2	1	33	20	59	2	8	3-4	.260	.313	.345	.658	25	.928
2000—Char., S.C. (SAL)	SS-2B	46	186	25	56	13	2	2	24	10	39	3	3	3-3	.301	.345	.425	.770	17	.928
—St. Pete. (FSL)	SS	36	130	18	38	5	2	1	14	3	13	1	3	4-2	.292	.313	.385	.698	8	.944
2001—Orlando (South.)	SS	130	512	58	131	26	3	4	45	17	93	8	13	4-9	.256	.287	.342	.629	26	.948
2002—Orlando (South.)	SS-3B-2B	131	512	50	124	31	1	3	43	23	74	4	13	2-6	.242	.278	.324	.602	41	.931
2003—Orlando (South.)	3B-SS-2B	43	158	15	34	10	0	3	17	9	27	1	3	0-3	.215	.259	.335	.594	6	.940
—Durham (Int'l)	SS-3B	60	200	26	59	16	1	4	30	8	21	2	5	2-1	.295	.319	.445	.764	12	.949
2004—Durham (Int'l)	2B-SS-3B																			
	DH	95	368	57	111	33	1	22	80	16	64	4	11	3-0	.302	.335	.576	.904	15	.964
—Tampa Bay (A.L.)	2B-3B-DH																			
	SS	50	173	25	52	20	1	2	17	9	44	2	5	0-0	.301	.341	.462	.803	8	.956
2005—Tampa Bay (A.L.)	2B-3B-DH	150	598	73	171	40	1	28	117	19	83	6	24	1-0	.286	.311	.497	.808	21	.953
2006—Montgom. (Sou.)		8	31	4	6	0	0	2	8	1	9	0	1	0-0	.194	.212	.387	.599	0	1.000
—Tampa Bay (A.L.)	2B-DH	107	413	40	103	18	2	14	62	26	91	3	16	1-1	.249	.295	.404	.699	13	.973
Major League totals (3 years)		307	1184	138	326	78	4	44	196	54	218	11	45	2-1	.275	.310	.459	.769	42	.962

2006 LEFTY-RIGHTY SPLITS

vs.	Avg.	AB	H	2B	3B	HR	RBI	BB	SO	OBP	Slg.	vs.	Avg.	AB	H	2B	3B	HR	RBI	BB	SO	OBP	Slg.
L	.233	116	27	5	1	6	21	4	13	.256	.448	R	.256	297	76	13	1	8	41	22	78	.309	.387

CAPELLAN, JOSE — P

PERSONAL: Born January 13, 1981, in Cotui, Dominican Republic. ... 6-4/235. ... Throws right, bats right. ... Full name: Jose Francisco Capellan. ... Name pronounced: capy-ay-YAN. **TRANSACTIONS/CAREER NOTES:** Signed as a non-drafted free agent by Atlanta Braves organization (August 6, 1998). ... Traded by Braves with a player to be named to Milwaukee Brewers for P Dan Kolb (December 11, 2004); Brewers acquired P Alec Zumwalt to complete deal (December 13, 2004). ... On disabled list (July 25-August 9, 2006); included rehabilitation assignment to Huntsville.
CAREER HITTING: 0-for-4 (.000), 0 R, 0 2B, 0 3B, 0 HR, 0 RBI.

Year Team (League)	W	L	Pct.	ERA	WHIP	G	GS	CG	ShO	Hld.	Sv.-Opp.	IP	H	R	ER	HR	BB-IBB	SO	Avg.
1999—Dom. Braves (DSL)	3	3	.500	3.58	1.36	14	10	0	0		2-...	60.1	54	31	24	1	28-...	46	.242
2000—Dom. Braves (DSL)	3	8	.273	3.69	1.38	14	14	0	0		0-0	68.1	58	45	28	0	36-...	68	.221
2001—Danville (Appal.)	0	0		1.72	1.02	3	3	0	0		0-...	15.2	12	7	3	1	4-0	25	.200
2002—				Did not play.														
2003—GC Braves (GCL)	0	1	.000	2.65	1.53	5	5	0	0		0-...	17.0	18	7	5	0	8-0	17	.277
—Rome (S. Atl.)	1	2	.333	3.80	1.31	14	12	1	0		0-...	47.1	43	23	20	2	19-0	32	.253
2004—Myrtle Beach (Carol.)	5	1	.833	1.94	0.82	8	8	1	1		0-...	46.1	27	11	10	0	11-0	62	.168
—Greenville (Sou.)	5	1	.833	2.50	1.43	9	8	0	0		0-...	50.1	53	15	14	1	19-0	53	.270
—Richmond (Int'l)	4	2	.667	2.51	1.12	7	7	0	0		0-...	43.0	33	13	12	0	15-1	37	.214
—Atlanta (N.L.)	0	1	.000	11.25	2.38	3	2	0	0	0	0-0	8.0	14	10	10	2	5-0	4	.400
2005—Nashville (PCL)	5	3	.625	3.87	1.43	36	12	0	0	6-8		90.2	88	42	39	4	42-2	76	.257
—Milwaukee (N.L.)	1	1	.500	2.87	1.40	17	0	0	0	3	0-0	15.2	17	6	5	1	5-0	14	.293
2006—Huntsville (Sou.)	0	0		0.00	0.00	1	1	0	0	0	0-0	1.0	0	0	0	0	0-0	2	.000
—Milwaukee (N.L.)	4	2	.667	4.40	1.34	61	0	0	0	16	0-2	71.2	65	37	35	11	31-7	58	.244
Major League totals (3 years)	5	4	.556	4.72	1.44	81	2	0	0	19	0-2	95.1	96	53	50	14	41-7	76	.267

2006 LEFTY-RIGHTY SPLITS

vs.	Avg.	AB	H	2B	3B	HR	RBI	BB	SO	OBP	Slg.	vs.	Avg.	AB	H	2B	3B	HR	RBI	BB	SO	OBP	Slg.
L	.248	101	25	6	1	5	12	16	15	.353	.475	R	.242	165	40	11	2	6	26	15	43	.311	.442

CAPPS, MATT — P

PERSONAL: Born September 3, 1983, in Douglasville, Ga. ... 6-3/238. ... Throws right, bats right. ... Full name: Matthew Dicus Capps. . **TRANSACTIONS/CAREER NOTES:** Selected by Pittsburgh Pirates organization in seventh round of 2002 free-agent draft.
CAREER HITTING: 0-for-2 (.000), 1 R, 0 2B, 0 3B, 0 HR, 0 RBI.

Year Team (League)	W	L	Pct.	ERA	WHIP	G	GS	CG	ShO	Hld.	Sv.-Opp.	IP	H	R	ER	HR	BB-IBB	SO	Avg.
2002—GC Pirates (GCL)	1	0	1.000	0.69	1.46	7	0	0	0		1-...	13.0	13	2	1	0	6-0	8	.271
2003—GC Pirates (GCL)	5	1	.833	1.87	0.78	10	10	1	0		0-...	62.2	40	16	13	1	9-0	54	.178
—Lynchburg (Caro.)	0	0		5.40	1.40	1	1	0	0		0-...	5.0	3	3	3	0	4-0	5	.167
2004—Hickory (S. Atl.)	2	3	.400	10.07	2.33	12	0	0	0		0-...	42.0	82	55	47	8	16-0	27	.400
—Will. (NYP)	3	5	.375	4.85	1.35	11	11	0	0		0-...	65.0	84	43	35	7	4-1	33	.312
2005—Hickory (S. Atl.)	3	4	.429	2.52	0.97	35	0	0	0	1	14-20	53.2	47	15	15	0	5-2	39	.239
—Altoona (East.)	0	2	.000	2.70	1.10	17	0	0	0	2	7-9	20.0	21	8	6	2	1-0	26	.250
—Pittsburgh (N.L.)	0	0		4.50	1.25	4	0	0	0	0	0-0	4.0	5	2	2	0	0-0	3	.333
2006—Pittsburgh (N.L.)	9	1	.900	3.79	1.15	85	0	0	0	13	1-10	80.2	81	37	34	12	12-5	56	.266
Major League totals (2 years)	9	1	.900	3.83	1.16	89	0	0	0	13	1-10	84.2	86	39	36	12	12-5	59	.270

2006 LEFTY-RIGHTY SPLITS

vs.	Avg.	AB	H	2B	3B	HR	RBI	BB	SO	OBP	Slg.	vs.	Avg.	AB	H	2B	3B	HR	RBI	BB	SO	OBP	Slg.
L	.250	100	25	5	1	4	12	4	26	.279	.440	R	.275	204	56	12	0	8	38	8	30	.309	.451

CAPUANO, CHRIS — P

PERSONAL: Born August 19, 1978, in Springfield, Mass. ... 6-3/210. ... Throws left, bats left. ... Full name: Christopher Frank Capuano. ... Name pronounced: cap-u-ON-o. ... High school: Cathedral (West Springfield, Mass.). ... College: Duke. **TRANSACTIONS/CAREER NOTES:** Selected by Pittsburgh Pirates organization in 45th round of 1996 free-agent draft; did not sign. ... Selected by Arizona Diamondbacks organization in eighth round of 1999 free-agent draft. ... Traded by Diamondbacks with SS Craig Counsell, 2B Junior Spivey, 1B Lyle Overbay, C Chad Moeller and P Jorge de la Rosa to Milwaukee Brewers for 1B Richie Sexson, P Shane Nance and a player to be named (December 1,

C

2003); Diamondbacks acquired OF Noochie Varner to complete deal (December 15, 2003). ... On disabled list (April 19-May 26, May 27-June 12 and August 25, 2004-remainder of season); included rehabilitation assignments to Beloit, High Desert and Indianapolis. **MISCELLANEOUS NOTES:** Appeared in one game as pinch runner (2006). **CAREER HITTING:** 26-for-177 (.147), 8 R, 6 2B, 0 3B, 0 HR, 14 RBI.

Year	Team (League)	W	L	Pct.	ERA	WHIP	G	GS	CG	ShO	Hld.	Sv.-Opp.	IP	H	R	ER	HR	BB-IBB	SO	Avg.
2000—	South Bend (Mid.)	10	4	.714	2.21	1.11	18	18	0	0	...	0-...	101.2	68	35	25	2	45-0	105	.193
2001—	El Paso (Texas)	10	11	.476	5.31	1.63	28	28	2	2	...	0-...	159.1	184	109	94	13	75-0	167	.290
2002—	Tucson (PCL)	4	1	.800	2.72	1.13	6	6	0	0	...	0-...	36.1	30	12	11	1	11-0	29	.227
2003—	Tucson (PCL)	9	5	.643	3.34	1.23	23	23	0	0	...	0-...	142.2	133	66	53	9	43-2	108	.250
	— Arizona (N.L.)	2	4	.333	4.64	1.15	9	5	0	0	1	0-0	33.0	27	19	17	3	11-1	23	.233
2004—	Beloit (Midw.)	0	0		3.38	1.50	1	1	0	0	...	0-...	2.2	3	1	1	1	1-0	4	.300
	— Indianapolis (Int'l)	0	1	.000	8.31	1.73	2	2	0	0	...	0-...	8.2	10	9	8	1	5-0	9	.294
	— High Desert (Calif.)	0	1	.000	27.00	4.50	1	1	0	0	...	0-...	2.0	6	6	6	1	3-0	2	.600
	— Milwaukee (N.L.)	6	8	.429	4.99	1.45	17	17	0	0	0	0-0	88.1	91	55	49	18	37-1	80	.269
2005—	Milwaukee (N.L.)	18	12	.600	3.99	1.38	35	●35	0	0	0	0-0	219.0	212	105	97	31	91-6	176	.256
2006—	Milwaukee (N.L.)	11	12	.478	4.03	1.25	34	34	3	2	0	0-0	221.1	229	108	99	29	47-4	174	.265
	Major League totals (4 years)	37	36	.507	4.20	1.33	95	91	3	2	1	0-0	561.2	559	287	262	81	186-12	453	.261

2006 LEFTY-RIGHTY SPLITS

vs.	Avg.	AB	H	2B	3B	HR	RBI	BB	SO	OBP	Slg.	vs.	Avg.	AB	H	2B	3B	HR	RBI	BB	SO	OBP	Slg.
L	.273	154	42	7	0	3	20	2	32	.289	.377	R	.264	709	187	59	2	26	87	45	142	.311	.463

CARMONA, FAUSTO   P

PERSONAL: Born December 7, 1983, in Santo Domingo, Dominican Republic. ... 6-4/220. ... Throws right, bats right. ... Full name: Fausto C. Carmona. .
TRANSACTIONS/CAREER NOTES: Signed as a non-drafted free agent by Cleveland Indians organization (December 28, 2000).
CAREER HITTING: 0-for-0 (.000), 0 R, 0 2B, 0 3B, 0 HR, 0 RBI.

Year	Team (League)	W	L	Pct.	ERA	WHIP	G	GS	CG	ShO	Hld.	Sv.-Opp.	IP	H	R	ER	HR	BB-IBB	SO	Avg.
2001—	Dom. Indians (DSL)	4	2	.667	3.11	1.08	14	13	0	0	...	0-...	75.1	69	36	26	0	12-0	47	.254
2002—	Burlington (Appal.)	2	4	.333	3.30	1.30	13	11	0	0	...	1-...	76.1	89	36	28	4	14-0	42	.295
	— Mahoning Valley (N.Y.-Penn.)	0	0		0.00	0.75	3	0	0	0	...	0-...	4.0	2	0	0	0	1-0	0	.182
2003—	Akron (East.)	0	1	.000	4.50	1.33	1	1	0	0	...	0-...	6.0	8	3	3	1	0-0	3	.308
	— Lake County (S.Atl.)	17	4	.810	2.06	0.88	24	24	1	0	...	0-...	148.1	117	48	34	10	14-0	83	.214
2004—	Kinston (Carol.)	5	2	.714	2.83	1.26	12	12	0	0	...	0-...	70.0	68	28	22	6	20-0	57	.251
	— Akron (East.)	4	8	.333	4.97	1.55	15	15	0	0	...	0-...	87.0	114	52	48	3	21-0	57	.329
2005—	Akron (East.)	6	5	.545	4.07	1.32	14	14	0	0	0	0-0	90.2	100	46	41	7	20-0	57	.276
	— Buffalo (Int'l)	7	4	.636	3.25	1.10	13	12	1	0	0	0-0	83.0	76	32	30	10	15-0	49	.244
2006—	Buffalo (Int'l)	1	3	.250	5.53	1.30	6	6	0	0	0	0-0	27.2	28	21	17	2	8-0	28	.264
	— Cleveland (A.L.)	1	10	.091	5.42	1.59	38	7	0	0	10	0-3	74.2	88	46	45	9	31-3	58	.298
	Major League totals (1 year)	1	10	.091	5.42	1.59	38	7	0	0	10	0-3	74.2	88	46	45	9	31-3	58	.298

2006 LEFTY-RIGHTY SPLITS

vs.	Avg.	AB	H	2B	3B	HR	RBI	BB	SO	OBP	Slg.	vs.	Avg.	AB	H	2B	3B	HR	RBI	BB	SO	OBP	Slg.
L	.299	134	40	7	1	4	18	18	18	.377	.455	R	.298	161	48	8	0	5	21	13	40	.372	.441

CARPENTER, CHRIS   P

PERSONAL: Born April 27, 1975, in Exeter, N.H. ... 6-6/230. ... Throws right, bats right. ... Full name: Christopher John Carpenter. ... High school: Trinity (Manchester, N.H.).
TRANSACTIONS/CAREER NOTES: Selected by Toronto Blue Jays organization in first round (15th pick overall) of 1993 free-agent draft. ... On disabled list (June 3-28, 1999); included rehabilitation assignment to St. Catharines. ... On disabled list (April 2-20, April 22-June 21 and August 14, 2002-remainder of season); included rehabilitation assignments to Tennessee and Syracuse. ... Released by Blue Jays (October 9, 2002). ... Signed by St. Louis Cardinals (December 13, 2002). ... On disabled list (March 27, 2003-entire season); included rehabilitation assignments to Palm Beach and Tennessee. ... On disabled list (May 22-June 6, 2006). **HONORS:** Named N.L. Pitcher of the Year by the SPORTING NEWS (2005 and 2006). ... Named N.L. Comeback Player of the Year by THE SPORTING NEWS (2004). ... Named pitcher on the SPORTING NEWS N.L. All-Star team (2005). ... Named N.L. Cy Young Award winner by Baseball Writers' Association of America (2005).
CAREER HITTING: 21-for-221 (.095), 11 R, 2 2B, 0 3B, 0 HR, 5 RBI.

Year	Team (League)	W	L	Pct.	ERA	WHIP	G	GS	CG	ShO	Hld.	Sv.-Opp.	IP	H	R	ER	HR	BB-IBB	SO	Avg.
1994—	Medicine Hat (Pio.)	6	3	.667	2.76	1.36	15	15	0	0	...	0-...	84.2	76	40	26	3	39-0	80	.243
1995—	Dunedin (Fla. St.)	3	5	.375	2.17	1.34	15	15	0	0	...	0-...	99.1	83	29	24	3	50-0	56	.229
	— Knoxville (Southern)	3	7	.300	5.18	1.59	12	12	0	0	...	0-...	64.1	71	47	37	3	31-1	53	.284
1996—	Knoxville (Southern)	7	9	.438	3.94	1.47	28	28	1	0	...	0-...	171.1	161	94	75	13	91-4	150	.250
1997—	Syracuse (Int'l)	4	9	.308	4.50	1.38	19	19	3	2	...	0-...	120.0	113	64	60	16	53-0	97	.257
	— Toronto (A.L.)	3	7	.300	5.09	1.78	14	13	1	1	0	0-0	81.1	108	55	46	7	37-0	55	.325
1998—	Toronto (A.L.)	12	7	.632	4.37	1.36	33	24	1	1	0	0-0	175.0	177	97	85	18	61-1	136	.265
1999—	Toronto (A.L.)	9	8	.529	4.38	1.50	24	24	4	1	0	0-0	150.0	177	81	73	16	48-1	106	.294
	— St. Catharines (NYP)	0	0		4.50	1.50	1	1	0	0	...	0-...	4.0	5	2	2	0	1-0	6	.294
2000—	Toronto (A.L.)	10	12	.455	6.26	1.64	34	27	2	0	0	0-...	175.1	204	*130	*122	30	83-1	113	.290
2001—	Toronto (A.L.)	11	11	.500	4.09	1.41	34	34	3	2	0	0-0	215.2	229	112	98	29	75-5	157	.274
2002—	Tennessee (Sou.)	0	1	.000	8.20	1.82	5	5	0	0	...	0-...	18.2	26	18	17	5	8-0	13	.338
	— Toronto (A.L.)	4	5	.444	5.28	1.58	13	13	1	0	0	0-0	73.1	89	45	43	11	27-0	45	.306
	— Syracuse (Int'l)	0	1	.000	4.50	1.67	1	1	0	0	...	0-...	6.0	8	3	3	1	2-0	6	.320
2003—	Palm Beach (FSL)	0	1	.000	1.29	1.00	4	4	0	0	...	0-...	7.0	6	3	1	0	2-0	5	.222
	— Memphis (PCL)	0	0		5.40	1.60	3	3	0	0	...	0-...	8.1	11	5	5	0	2-0	4	.333
	— Tennessee (Sou.)	0	1	.000	13.50	2.70	1	1	0	0	...	0-...	3.1	7	5	5	0	2-0	2	.438
2004—	St. Louis (N.L.)	15	5	.750	3.46	1.14	28	28	1	0	0	0-0	182.0	169	75	70	24	38-2	152	.245
2005—	St. Louis (N.L.)	21	5	.808	2.83	1.06	33	33	●7	4	0	0-0	241.2	204	82	76	18	51-0	213	.231
2006—	St. Louis (N.L.)	15	8	.652	3.09	1.07	32	32	5	●3	0	0-0	221.2	194	81	76	21	43-3	184	.235
	American League totals (6 years)	49	50	.495	4.83	1.51	152	135	12	5	0	0-0	870.2	984	520	467	111	331-8	612	.287
	National League totals (3 years)	51	18	.739	3.10	1.08	93	93	13	7	0	0-0	645.1	567	238	222	63	132-5	549	.236
	Major League totals (9 years)	100	68	.595	4.09	1.33	245	228	25	12	0	0-0	1516.0	1551	758	689	174	463-13	1161	.266

DIVISION SERIES RECORD

Year	Team (League)	W	L	Pct.	ERA	WHIP	G	GS	CG	ShO	Hld.	Sv.-Opp.	IP	H	R	ER	HR	BB-IBB	SO	Avg.
2005—	St. Louis (N.L.)	1	0	1.000	0.00	1.00	1	1	0	0	...	0-...	6.0	3	0	0	0	3-0	3	.158
2006—	St. Louis (N.L.)	2	0	1.000	2.03	1.20	2	2	0	0	...	0-...	13.1	12	3	3	0	4-0	12	.245
	Division series totals (2 years)	3	0	1.000	1.40	1.14	3	3	0	0	...	0-...	19.1	15	3	3	0	7-0	15	.221

CHAMPIONSHIP SERIES RECORD

Year	Team (League)	W	L	Pct.	ERA	WHIP	G	GS	CG	ShO	Hld.	Sv.-Opp.	IP	H	R	ER	HR	BB-IBB	SO	Avg.
2005—	St. Louis (N.L.)	1	0	1.000	3.00	1.20	2	2	0	0	...	0-...	15.0	14	6	5	2	4-0	9	.255
2006—	St. Louis (N.L.)	0	1	.000	5.73	1.55	2	2	0	0	...	0-...	11.0	13	7	7	3	4-0	5	.302
	Champ. series totals (2 years)	1	1	.500	4.15	1.35	4	4	0	0	...	0-...	26.0	27	13	12	5	8-0	14	.276

C

WORLD SERIES RECORD

Year Team (League)	W	L	Pct.	ERA	WHIP	G	GS	CG	ShO	Hld.	Sv.-Opp.	IP	H	R	ER	HR	BB-IBB	SO	Avg.
2006— St. Louis (N.L.)	1	0	1.000	0.00	0.38	1	1	0	0	0	0-0	8.0	3	0	0	0	0-0	6	.120

ALL-STAR GAME RECORD

	W	L	Pct.	ERA	WHIP	G	GS	CG	ShO	Hld.	Sv.-Opp.	IP	H	R	ER	HR	BB-IBB	SO	Avg.
All-Star Game totals (1 year)	0	0	...	0.00	2.00	1	1	0	0	0	0-0	1.0	2	0	0	0	0-0	0	.500

2006 LEFTY-RIGHTY SPLITS

vs.	Avg.	AB	H	2B	3B	HR	RBI	BB	SO	OBP	Slg.	vs.	Avg.	AB	H	2B	3B	HR	RBI	BB	SO	OBP	Slg.
L	.266	365	97	19	3	10	36	23	83	.314	.416	R	.210	462	97	19	0	11	41	20	101	.252	.323

CARRARA, GIOVANNI — P

PERSONAL: Born March 4, 1968, in Anzoategui, Venezuela. ... 6-2/230. ... Throws right, bats right. ... Full name: Giovanni Jimenez Carrara. ... Name pronounced: ka-RAH-rah. **TRANSACTIONS/CAREER NOTES:** Signed as a non-drafted free agent by Toronto Blue Jays organization (January 23, 1990). ... Claimed on waivers by Cincinnati Reds (July 3, 1996). ... Signed as a free agent by Baltimore Orioles organization (November 12, 1996). ... Released by Orioles (May 14, 1997). ... Signed by Reds organization (May 17, 1997). ... Signed by Seibu Lions of the Japan Pacific League (1998). ... Signed by Reds organization (December 23, 1998). ... Signed as a free agent by Colorado Rockies organization (December 1, 1999). ... On disabled list (August 3-September 4, 2000); included rehabilitation assignment to Colorado Springs. ... Signed as a free agent by Los Angeles Dodgers organization (January 4, 2001). ... On disabled list (August 11-September 1, 2002). ... Released by Dodgers (March 26, 2003). ... Signed by Seattle Mariners (March 28, 2003). ... Signed as a free agent by Cleveland Indians organization (December 19, 2003). ... Released by Indians (March 27, 2004). ... Signed by Chicago Cubs organization (March 28, 2004). ... Released by Cubs (May 31, 2004). ... Signed by Dodgers organization (June 1, 2004). ... Signed as a free agent by Pittsburgh Pirates organization (December 28, 2005). ... Released by Pirates (March 31, 2006). ... Signed by Dodgers (July 4, 2006).

CAREER HITTING: 3-for-31 (.097), 2 R, 0 2B, 0 3B, 0 HR, 0 RBI.

Year Team (League)	W	L	Pct.	ERA	WHIP	G	GS	CG	ShO	Hld.	Sv.-Opp.	IP	H	R	ER	HR	BB-IBB	SO	Avg.
1990— Dom. Blue Jays (DSL)	2	2	.500	2.62	1.35	15	14	4	0	...	0-...	86.0	88	31	25	...	28-...	55	...
1991— St. Catharines (NYP)	5	2	.714	1.71	0.97	15	13	2	2	...	0-...	89.2	66	26	17	5	21-0	83	.200
1992— Dunedin (Fla. St.)	0	1	.000	4.63	1.41	5	4	0	0	...	0-...	23.1	22	13	12	1	11-0	16	.250
— Myrtle Beach (SAL)	11	7	.611	3.14	1.22	22	16	1	0	...	0-...	100.1	86	40	35	12	36-0	100	.231
1993— Dunedin (Fla. St.)	6	11	.353	3.45	1.39	27	24	1	0	...	0-...	140.2	136	69	54	14	59-0	108	.258
1994— Knoxville (Southern)	13	7	.650	3.89	1.32	26	26	1	0	...	0-...	164.1	158	85	71	16	59-0	96	.251
1995— Syracuse (Int'l)	7	7	.500	3.96	1.31	21	21	0	0	...	0-...	131.2	116	72	58	11	56-2	81	.232
— Toronto (A.L.)	2	4	.333	7.21	1.83	12	7	1	0	0	0-0	48.2	64	46	39	10	25-1	27	.322
1996— Toronto (A.L.)	0	1	.000	11.40	2.33	11	0	0	0	0	0-1	15.0	23	19	19	5	12-2	10	.359
— Syracuse (Int'l)	4	4	.500	3.58	1.30	9	6	1	0	...	0-...	37.2	37	16	15	2	12-1	28	.253
— Indianapolis (A.A.)	4	0	1.000	0.76	0.71	8	6	1	1	...	1-...	47.2	25	6	4	2	9-0	45	.152
— Cincinnati (N.L.)	1	0	1.000	5.87	1.91	8	5	0	0	0	0-0	23.0	31	17	15	6	13-1	13	.323
1997— Rochester (Int'l)	4	2	.667	4.44	1.31	8	8	1	0	...	0-...	46.2	45	23	23	4	16-0	48	.259
— Indianapolis (A.A.)	12	5	.706	3.51	1.34	19	18	2	0	...	0-...	120.2	111	50	47	12	51-3	105	.247
— Cincinnati (N.L.)	0	1	.000	7.84	1.94	2	2	0	0	0	0-0	10.1	14	9	9	4	6-1	5	.333
1998— Seibu (Jp. East.)	2	0	1.000	4.50	1.13	4	0	0	0	...	0-...	8.0	8	4	4	...	1-...	8	...
— Seibu (Jp. Pac.)	1	2	.333	4.91	1.47	33	5	0	0	...	1-...	73.1	68	44	40	...	40-...	50	...
1999— Indianapolis (Int'l)	12	7	.632	3.47	1.28	39	21	2	1	...	0-...	158.0	144	68	61	20	58-3	114	.246
2000— Colo. Springs (PCL)	7	2	.778	3.26	1.23	18	15	0	0	...	0-...	96.2	89	39	35	8	30-1	89	.245
— Colorado (N.L.)	0	1	.000	12.83	2.40	8	0	0	0	0	0-1	13.1	21	19	19	5	11-2	15	.356
2001— Las Vegas (PCL)	1	2	.333	3.10	1.24	6	6	0	0	...	0-...	29.0	27	10	10	5	9-0	35	.248
— Los Angeles (N.L.)	6	1	.857	3.16	1.14	47	3	0	0	9	0-3	85.1	73	30	30	12	24-3	70	.231
2002— Los Angeles (N.L.)	6	3	.667	3.28	1.27	63	1	0	0	14	1-6	90.2	83	34	33	14	32-4	56	.243
2003— Seattle (A.L.)	2	0	1.000	6.83	1.86	23	0	0	0	4	0-0	29.0	40	22	22	6	14-0	13	.333
— Tacoma (PCL)	1	1	.500	4.23	1.30	18	0	0	0	...	5-...	27.2	28	14	13	2	9-0	27	.264
2004— Iowa (PCL)	1	2	.333	3.81	1.31	20	0	0	0	...	1-...	28.1	29	12	12	3	8-1	23	.279
— Las Vegas (PCL)	0	1	.000	5.21	1.33	11	0	0	0	...	2-...	14.1	11	4	4	1	8-2	15	.208
— Los Angeles (N.L.)	5	2	.714	2.18	1.23	42	0	0	0	6	2-3	53.2	46	15	13	1	20-3	48	.228
2005— Los Angeles (N.L.)	7	4	.636	3.93	1.36	72	0	0	0	11	0-2	75.2	65	35	33	6	38-5	56	.243
2006— Indianapolis (Int'l)	1	1	.500	0.87	0.87	9	1	0	0	3	0-0	15.0	8	5	5	1	5-1	14	.170
— Las Vegas (PCL)	2	1	.667	4.62	1.38	21	0	0	0	3	4-5	25.1	23	13	13	3	12-0	19	.240
— Los Angeles (N.L.)	4	5	.444	4.62	1.23	25	0	0	0	2	1-2	27.2	27	14	14	5	7-0	25	.250
American League totals (3 years)	4	5	.444	7.77	1.92	46	7	1	0	4	0-1	92.2	127	87	80	21	51-3	50	.332
National League totals (8 years)	25	13	.658	3.94	1.35	267	11	0	0	42	4-17	379.2	360	173	166	53	151-19	288	.251
Major League totals (10 years)	29	18	.617	4.69	1.46	313	18	1	0	46	4-18	472.1	487	260	246	74	202-22	338	.268

DIVISION SERIES RECORD

Year Team (League)	W	L	Pct.	ERA	WHIP	G	GS	CG	ShO	Hld.	Sv.-Opp.	IP	H	R	ER	HR	BB-IBB	SO	Avg.
2004— Los Angeles (N.L.)	0	0	...	9.00	2.50	3	0	0	0	0	0-0	2.0	4	2	2	1	1-0	1	.444

2006 LEFTY-RIGHTY SPLITS

vs.	Avg.	AB	H	2B	3B	HR	RBI	BB	SO	OBP	Slg.	vs.	Avg.	AB	H	2B	3B	HR	RBI	BB	SO	OBP	Slg.
L	.157	51	8	3	1	1	1	4	5	13	.232	.314	R	.333	57	19	3	1	4	14	2	12	.367	.632

CARRASCO, HECTOR — P

PERSONAL: Born October 22, 1969, in San Pedro de Macoris, Dominican Republic. ... 6-2/220. ... Throws right, bats right. ... Full name: Hector Pacheco Pipo Carrasco. ... Name pronounced: kah-RAHS-koh. ... High school: Liceo Mattias Mella (San Pedro de Macoris, Dominican Republic). **TRANSACTIONS/CAREER NOTES:** Signed as a non-drafted free agent by New York Mets organization (March 20, 1988). ... Released by Mets (January 6, 1992). ... Signed by Houston Astros organization (January 21, 1992). ... Traded by Astros with P Brian Griffiths to Florida Marlins for P Tom Edens (November 17, 1992). ... Traded by Marlins to Cincinnati Reds (September 10, 1993), completing deal in which Reds traded P Chris Hammond to Marlins for 3B Gary Scott and a player to be named (March 27, 1993). ... On disabled list (May 12-June 1, 1994). ... Traded by Reds with P Scott Service to Kansas City Royals for OF Jon Nunnally and IF/OF Chris Stynes (July 15, 1997). ... Selected by Arizona Diamondbacks in second round (49th pick overall) of expansion draft (November 18, 1997). ... Claimed on waivers by Minnesota Twins (April 3, 1998). ... On disabled list (April 3-June 25, 1999); included rehabilitation assignments to Fort Myers and Salt Lake. ... Traded by Twins to Boston Red Sox for OF Lew Ford (September 10, 2000). ... Signed as a free agent by Toronto Blue Jays organization (January 9, 2001). ... Released by Blue Jays (March 28, 2001). ... Signed by Twins organization (March 31, 2001). ... Signed as a free agent by Texas Rangers organization (January 18, 2002). ... Signed as a free agent by Baltimore Orioles organization (March 1, 2003). ... Signed by Kintestsu Buffaloes of the Japan Pacific League (February 13, 2004). ... Signed as a free agent by Washington Nationals organization (December 23, 2004). ... Signed as a free agent by Los Angeles Angels of Anaheim (December 2, 2005).

CAREER HITTING: 1-for-26 (.038), 1 R, 0 2B, 0 3B, 0 HR, 0 RBI.

Year Team (League)	W	L	Pct.	ERA	WHIP	G	GS	CG	ShO	Hld.	Sv.-Opp.	IP	H	R	ER	HR	BB-IBB	SO	Avg.
1988— GC Mets (GCL)	0	2	.000	4.17	1.36	14	2	0	0	...	0-...	36.2	37	29	17	0	13-0	21	.248
1989— Kingsport (Appalachian)	1	6	.143	5.74	1.93	12	10	0	0	...	0-...	53.1	69	49	34	6	34-1	55	.314
1990— Kingsport (Appalachian)	0	0	...	4.05	1.35	3	1	0	0	...	0-...	6.2	8	3	3	1	1-0	5	.308
1991— Pittsfield (NYP)	0	1	.000	5.40	1.97	12	1	0	0	...	1-...	23.1	25	17	14	1	21-0	20	.263

Year— Team (League)	W	L	Pct.	ERA	WHIP	G	GS	CG	ShO	Hld.	Sv.-Opp.	IP	H	R	ER	HR	BB-IBB	SO	Avg.
1992— Asheville (S. Atl.)	5	5	.500	2.99	1.44	49	0	0	0	...	8-...	78.1	66	30	26	5	47-6	67	.237
1993— Kane Co. (Midw.)	6	12	.333	4.11	1.54	28	28	0	0	...	0-...	149.0	153	90	68	11	76-6	127	.266
1994— Cincinnati (N.L.)	5	6	.455	2.24	1.28	45	0	0	0	3	6-8	56.1	42	17	14	3	30-1	41	.210
1995— Cincinnati (N.L.)	2	7	.222	4.12	1.51	64	0	0	0	11	5-9	87.1	86	45	40	1	46-5	64	.257
1996— Cincinnati (N.L.)	4	3	.571	3.75	1.39	56	0	0	0	15	0-2	74.1	58	37	31	6	45-5	59	.214
— Indianapolis (A.A.)	0	1	.000	2.14	1.48	13	2	0	0	...	0-...	21.0	18	7	5	1	13-1	17	.222
1997— Indianapolis (A.A.)	0	0	...	6.23	1.85	3	0	0	0	...	1-...	4.1	5	3	3	1	3-0	4	.294
— Cincinnati (N.L.)	1	2	.333	3.68	1.48	38	0	0	0	5	0-0	51.1	51	25	21	3	25-2	46	.250
— Kansas City (A.L.)	1	6	.143	5.45	1.30	28	0	0	0	3	0-2	34.2	29	21	21	4	16-3	30	.227
1998— Minnesota (A.L.)	4	2	.667	4.38	1.72	63	0	0	0	10	1-2	61.2	75	30	30	4	31-1	46	.304
1999— Fort Myers (FSL)	0	0	...	4.50	1.50	1	1	0	0	...	0-...	2.0	2	1	1	0	1-0	1	.286
— Salt Lake (PCL)	1	0	1.000	0.00	0.92	3	0	0	0	...	1-...	4.1	3	0	0	0	1-0	3	.188
— Minnesota (A.L.)	2	3	.400	4.96	1.35	39	0	0	0	7	1-2	49.0	48	29	27	3	18-0	35	.261
2000— Minnesota (A.L.)	4	3	.571	4.25	1.50	61	0	0	0	7	1-5	72.0	75	38	34	6	33-0	57	.271
— Boston (A.L.)	1	1	.500	9.45	3.00	8	1	0	0	1	0-1	6.2	15	8	7	2	5-1	1	.469
2001— Minnesota (A.L.)	4	3	.571	4.64	1.45	56	0	0	0	1	1-2	73.2	77	40	38	8	30-3	70	.277
2002—				Did not play.															
2003— Ottawa (Int'l)	4	2	.667	2.22	1.16	33	0	0	0	...	4-...	44.2	32	11	11	2	20-2	47	.208
— Baltimore (A.L.)	2	6	.250	4.93	1.57	40	0	0	0	8	1-3	38.1	40	22	21	5	20-3	27	.270
2004— Kintetsu (Jp. Pac.)	8	8	.500	5.57	1.46	53	5	0	0	...	5-...	76.0	74	52	47	12	37-...	70	...
2005— New Orleans (PCL)	1	0	1.000	0.00	0.75	6	0	0	0	4-4		8.0	4	1	0	0	2-0	10	.143
— Wash. (N.L.)	5	4	.556	2.04	1.10	64	5	0	0	8	2-4	88.1	59	23	20	6	38-7	75	.193
2006— Los Angeles (A.L.)	7	3	.700	3.41	1.20	56	3	0	0	1	1-2	100.1	93	42	38	10	27-1	72	.244
American League totals (7 years)	25	27	.481	4.46	1.45	351	4	0	0	38	6-19	436.1	452	230	216	42	180-12	344	.270
National League totals (5 years)	17	22	.436	3.17	1.34	267	5	0	0	42	13-23	357.2	296	147	126	19	184-20	285	.225
Major League totals (11 years)	42	49	.462	3.88	1.40	618	9	0	0	80	19-42	794.0	748	377	342	61	364-32	629	.250

CHAMPIONSHIP SERIES RECORD

Year— Team (League)	W	L	Pct.	ERA	WHIP	G	GS	CG	ShO	Hld.	Sv.-Opp.	IP	H	R	ER	HR	BB-IBB	SO	Avg.
1995— Cincinnati (N.L.)	0	0	...	0.00	0.75	1	0	0	0	...	0-...	1.1	1	0	0	...	0-...	3	...

2006 LEFTY-RIGHTY SPLITS

vs.	Avg.	AB	H	2B	3B	HR	RBI	BB	SO	OBP	Slg.	vs.	Avg.	AB	H	2B	3B	HR	RBI	BB	SO	OBP	Slg.
L	.249	173	43	9	1	4	19	13	31	.309	.382	R	.240	208	50	9	1	6	22	14	41	.295	.380

CARROLL, JAMEY — 2B

PERSONAL: Born February 18, 1974, in Evansville, Ind. ... 5-9/170. ... Bats right, throws right. ... Full name: Jamey Blake Carroll. ... High school: Castle (Newburgh, Ind.). ... College: Evansville. **TRANSACTIONS/CAREER NOTES:** Selected by Montreal Expos organization in 14th round of 1996 free-agent draft. ... Expos franchise transferred to Washington, D.C., and renamed Washington Nationals for 2005 season (December 3, 2004). ... Traded by Nationals to Colorado Rockies for cash (February 11, 2006).
2006 GAMES PLAYED BY POSITION (MLB): 2B—109, SS—10, 3B—8.

								BATTING									FIELDING	
Year— Team (League)	Pos.	G	AB	R	H	2B	3B	HR	RBI	BB	SO	HBP	GDP	SB-CS	Avg.	OBP	SLG	OPS	E	Avg.
1996— Vermont (NYP)	SS-2B-3B	54	203	40	56	6	1	0	17	29	25	0	1	16-11	.276	.363	.315	.679	9	.960
1997— W.P. Beach (FSL)	SS-2B	121	407	56	99	19	1	0	38	43	48	4	4	17-11	.243	.319	.295	.614	22	.951
1998— Jupiter (Fla. St.)	2B-SS	55	222	40	58	5	0	0	14	24	26	5	2	11-4	.261	.345	.284	.629	6	.977
— Harrisburg (East.)	2B-SS	75	261	43	66	11	3	0	20	41	29	5	4	11-5	.253	.365	.318	.683	17	.953
1999— Harrisburg (East.)	2B-SS	141	561	78	164	34	5	5	63	48	58	5	13	21-10	.292	.351	.398	.749	14	.979
2000— Ottawa (Int'l)	2B-3B-SS	91	349	53	97	17	2	2	23	33	32	2	9	6-3	.278	.342	.355	.697	13	.967
— Harrisburg (East.)	3B-SS-2B	45	169	23	49	5	3	0	18	12	13	0	5	8-2	.290	.335	.355	.690	6	.960
2001— Ottawa (Int'l)	2B-SS-3B	83	267	26	64	8	2	0	16	18	41	2	8	5-5	.240	.292	.285	.576	9	.972
2002— Harrisburg (East.)	2B	3	9	1	4	0	0	0	1	3	0	0	0	0-0	.444	.583	.444	1.028	0	1.000
— Ottawa (Int'l)	3B-2B-SS	117	421	57	118	19	2	8	49	37	39	3	8	6-10	.280	.342	.392	.734	7	.983
— Montreal (N.L.)	3B-SS-2B	16	71	16	22	5	3	1	6	4	12	0	1	1-0	.310	.347	.507	.854	4	.925
2003— Montreal (N.L.)	3B-SS-2B																			
	DH	105	227	31	59	10	1	0	10	19	39	3	10	5-2	.260	.323	.326	.649	5	.976
2004— Montreal (N.L.)	2B-3B-SS																			
	OF	102	218	36	63	14	2	0	16	32	21	1	3	5-1	.289	.378	.372	.750	3	.988
2005— Wash. (N.L.)	2B-SS-3B	113	303	44	76	8	1	0	22	34	55	5	2	3-4	.251	.333	.284	.617	5	.987
2006— Colorado (N.L.)	2B-SS-3B	136	463	84	139	23	5	5	36	56	66	3	10	10-12	.300	.377	.404	.781	5	.992
Major League totals (5 years)		472	1282	211	359	60	12	7	90	145	193	12	26	24-19	.280	.356	.362	.718	22	.985

2006 LEFTY-RIGHTY SPLITS

vs.	Avg.	AB	H	2B	3B	HR	RBI	BB	SO	OBP	Slg.	vs.	Avg.	AB	H	2B	3B	HR	RBI	BB	SO	OBP	Slg.
L	.359	103	37	4	1	1	7	16	8	.438	.447	R	.283	360	102	19	4	4	29	40	58	.359	.392

CARTER, LANCE — P

PERSONAL: Born December 18, 1974, in Bradenton, Fla. ... 6-1/190. ... Throws right, bats right. ... Full name: Lance David Carter. ... High school: Manatee (Bradenton, Fla.). ... Junior college: Manatee (Fla.) C.C. **TRANSACTIONS/CAREER NOTES:** Selected by Minnesota Twins organization in 41st round of 1993 free-agent draft; did not sign. ... Selected by Kansas City Royals organization in 21st round of 1994 free-agent draft. ... Signed as a free agent by Tampa Bay Devil Rays organization (January 22, 2002). ... On suspended list (June 7-10, 2005). ... Traded by Devil Rays with P Danys Baez to Los Angeles Dodgers for Ps Edwin Jackson and Charles Tiffany (January 14, 2006).
CAREER HITTING: 0-for-0 (.000), 0 R, 0 2B, 0 3B, 0 HR, 0 RBI.

Year— Team (League)	W	L	Pct.	ERA	WHIP	G	GS	CG	ShO	Hld.	Sv.-Opp.	IP	H	R	ER	HR	BB-IBB	SO	Avg.
1994— Eugene (Northwest)	1	0	1.000	5.47	1.56	8	7	0	0	...	0-...	26.1	26	17	16	2	15-0	23	.265
— GC Royals (GCL)	3	0	1.000	0.29	0.71	5	5	0	0	...	0-...	31.0	19	1	1	1	3-0	36	.179
1995— Springfield (Midw.)	9	5	.643	3.99	1.26	27	24	1	1	...	0-...	137.2	151	77	61	14	22-0	118	.276
1996— Wilmington (Caro.)	3	6	.333	6.34	1.50	16	12	0	0	...	0-...	65.1	81	50	46	8	17-2	49	.298
1997—				Did not play.															
1998— Lansing (Midw.)	3	1	.750	0.67	1.07	15	2	0	0	...	2-...	40.1	34	6	3	0	9-1	37	.231
— Wilmington (Caro.)	1	4	.200	3.29	1.23	28	1	0	0	...	5-...	52.0	50	21	19	5	14-1	61	.262
1999— Wichita (Texas)	5	2	.714	0.78	1.09	44	0	0	0	...	13-...	69.2	49	10	6	1	27-5	77	.195
— Kansas City (A.L.)	0	1	.000	5.06	1.13	6	0	0	0	0	0-0	5.1	3	3	3	2	3-0	3	.167
2000— Omaha (PCL)	2	8	.200	4.95	1.39	34	6	0	0	...	5-...	76.1	88	46	42	13	18-1	51	.295
2001—				Did not play.															
2002— Durham (Int'l)	12	2	.857	2.80	0.93	33	18	2	1	...	1-...	132.0	111	43	41	15	12-0	90	.230
— Tampa Bay (A.L.)	2	0	1.000	1.33	0.98	8	0	0	0	0	2-2	20.1	15	3	3	2	5-1	14	.203

Year	Team (League)	W	L	Pct.	ERA	WHIP	G	GS	CG	ShO	Hld.	Sv.-Opp.	IP	H	R	ER	HR	BB-IBB	SO	Avg.
2003—Tampa Bay (A.L.)		7	5	.583	4.33	1.15	62	0	0	0	2	26-33	79.0	72	39	38	12	19-6	47	.242
2004—Tampa Bay (A.L.)		3	3	.500	3.47	1.24	56	0	0	0	7	0-1	80.1	77	32	31	12	23-2	36	.252
2005—Durham (Int'l)		1	5	.167	5.14	1.49	8	7	0	0	0	0-0	35.0	40	24	20	8	12-0	30	.290
—Tampa Bay (A.L.)		1	2	.333	4.89	1.33	39	0	0	0	5	1-4	57.0	61	31	31	9	15-1	22	.279
2006—Las Vegas (PCL)		2	4	.333	3.92	1.29	45	0	0	0	2	13-19	57.1	58	25	25	7	16-1	51	.267
—Los Angeles (N.L.)		0	1	.000	8.49	2.14	10	0	0	0	0	0-1	11.2	17	11	11	1	8-0	5	.347
American League totals (5 years)		13	11	.542	3.94	1.21	171	0	0	0	14	29-40	242.0	228	108	106	37	65-10	122	.249
National League totals (1 year)		0	1	.000	8.49	2.14	10	0	0	0	0	0-1	11.2	17	11	11	1	8-0	5	.347
Major League totals (6 years)		13	12	.520	4.15	1.25	181	0	0	0	14	29-41	253.2	245	119	117	38	73-10	127	.254

2006 LEFTY-RIGHTY SPLITS

vs.	Avg.	AB	H	2B	3B	HR	RBI	BB	SO	OBP	Slg.	vs.	Avg.	AB	H.	2B	3B	HR	RBI	BB	SO	OBP	Slg.
L	.429	21	9	3	0	0	3	2	1	.458	.571	R	.286	28	8	2	0	1	6	6	4	.400	.464

CASEY, SEAN   1B

PERSONAL: Born July 2, 1974, in Willingboro, N.J. ... 6-4/225. ... Bats left, throws right. ... Full name: Sean Thomas Casey. ... High school: Upper St. Clair (Pittsburgh). ... College: Richmond. **TRANSACTIONS/CAREER NOTES:** Selected by Cleveland Indians organization in second round of 1995 free-agent draft. ... Traded by Indians to Cincinnati Reds for P Dave Burba (March 30, 1998). ... On disabled list (April 2-May 5, 1998); included rehabilitation assignment to Indianapolis. ... On disabled list (April 2-19, 2000). ... On disabled list (July 23-August 9 and September 10, 2002-remainder of season); included rehabilitation assignment to Louisville. ... On suspended list (July 2-4, 2003). ... On disabled list (June 28-July 14, 2004). ... Traded by Reds with cash to Pittsburgh Pirates for P Dave Williams (December 8, 2005). ... On disabled list (April 15-May 29, 2006); included rehabilitation assignment to Altoona. ... Traded by Pirates to Detroit Tigers for P Brian Rogers (July 31, 2006).

2006 GAMES PLAYED BY POSITION (MLB): 1B—106.

									BATTING												FIELDING	
Year	Team (League)	Pos.	G	AB	R	H	2B	3B	HR	RBI	BB	SO	HBP	GDP	SB-CS	Avg.	OBP	SLG	OPS	E	Avg.
1995—Watertown (NYP)	1B	55	207	26	68	18	0	2	37	18	21	1	6	3-0	.329	.380	.444	.824	8	.985
1996—Kinston (Carol.)	1B-DH	92	344	62	114	31	3	12	57	36	47	6	5	1-1	.331	.402	.544	.946	6	.991
1997—Akron (East.)	1B-DH	62	241	38	93	19	1	10	66	23	34	5	5	0-1	.386	.448	.598	1.046	5	.988
—Buffalo (A.A.)	DH-1B	20	72	12	26	7	0	5	18	9	11	1	0	0-0	.361	.439	.667	1.106	0	1.000
—Cleveland (A.L.)	1B	6	10	1	2	0	0	0	1	1	2	1	0	0-0	.200	.333	.200	.533	0	1.000
1998—Cincinnati (N.L.)	1B	96	302	44	82	21	1	7	52	43	45	3	11	1-1	.272	.365	.417	.782	4	.994
—Indianapolis (Int'l)	1B-DH	27	95	14	31	8	1	1	13	14	10	1	0	0-0	.326	.418	.463	.881	2	.991
1999—Cincinnati (N.L.)	1B	151	594	103	197	42	3	25	99	61	88	9	15	0-2	.332	.399	.539	.938	6	.995
2000—Cincinnati (N.L.)	1B	133	480	69	151	33	2	20	85	52	80	7	16	1-0	.315	.385	.517	.902	6	.995
2001—Cincinnati (N.L.)	1B-DH	145	533	69	165	40	0	13	89	43	63	9	16	3-1	.310	.369	.458	.827	7	.994
2002—Cincinnati (N.L.)	1B-DH	120	425	56	111	25	0	6	42	43	47	5	11	2-1	.261	.334	.362	.696	7	.993
—Louisville (Int'l)	DH	2	8	2	4	0	0	1	3	1	0	0	0	0-0	.500	.556	.875	1.431	...	...
2003—Cincinnati (N.L.)	1B	147	573	71	167	19	3	14	80	51	58	2	19	4-0	.291	.350	.408	.758	6	.996
2004—Cincinnati (N.L.)	1B-DH	146	571	101	185	44	2	24	99	46	36	10	16	2-0	.324	.381	.534	.915	8	.994
2005—Cincinnati (N.L.)	1B-DH	137	529	75	165	32	0	9	58	48	48	5	* 27	2-0	.312	.371	.423	.795	2	.998
2006—Altoona (East.)		3	11	1	3	0	0	1	2	1	0	1	1	0-0	.273	.333	.545	.879	0	1.000
—Pittsburgh (N.L.)	1B	59	213	30	63	15	0	3	29	23	22	6	7	0-0	.296	.377	.408	.785	0	1.000
—Detroit (A.L.)	1B	53	184	17	45	7	0	5	30	10	21	1	3	0-1	.245	.286	.364	.650	2	.996
American League totals (2 years)		59	194	18	47	7	0	5	31	11	23	2	3	0-1	.242	.288	.356	.644	2	.996
National League totals (9 years)		1134	4220	618	1286	271	11	121	633	410	487	56	138	15-5	.305	.371	.460	.831	46	.995
Major League totals (10 years)		1193	4414	636	1333	278	11	126	664	421	510	58	141	15-6	.302	.368	.456	.823	48	.995

DIVISION SERIES RECORD

Year	Team (League)	Pos.	G	AB	R	H	2B	3B	HR	RBI	BB	SO	HBP	GDP	SB-CS	Avg.	OBP	SLG	OPS	E	Avg.
2006—Detroit (A.L.)	1B	4	17	1	6	3	0	0	2	0	0	0	0	0-0	.353	.353	.529	.882	0	1.000

CHAMPIONSHIP SERIES RECORD

Year	Team (League)	Pos.	G	AB	R	H	2B	3B	HR	RBI	BB	SO	HBP	GDP	SB-CS	Avg.	OBP	SLG	OPS	E	Avg.
2006—Detroit (A.L.)	1B	1	3	0	1	0	0	0	1	0	0	0	0	0-0	.333	.500	.333	.833	0	1.000

WORLD SERIES RECORD

Year	Team (League)	Pos.	G	AB	R	H	2B	3B	HR	RBI	BB	SO	HBP	GDP	SB-CS	Avg.	OBP	SLG	OPS	E	Avg.
2006—Detroit (A.L.)	1B-DH	5	17	2	9	2	0	2	5	2	1	0	0	0-0	.529	.556	1.000	1.556	1	1.000

ALL-STAR GAME RECORD

Year	Team (League)		G	AB	R	H	2B	3B	HR	RBI	BB	SO	HBP	GDP	SB-CS	Avg.	OBP	SLG	OPS		Avg.
All-Star Game totals (2 years)			2	2	0	0	0	0	0	0	1	0	0	...	0-0	.000	.000	.000	.000	0	...

2006 LEFTY-RIGHTY SPLITS

vs.	Avg.	AB	H	2B	3B	HR	RBI	BB	SO	OBP	Slg.	vs.	Avg.	AB	H	2B	3B	HR	RBI	BB	SO	OBP	Slg.
L	.287	108	31	6	0	4	23	4	18	.328	.454	R	.266	289	77	16	0	4	36	29	25	.340	.363

CASILLA, ALEXI   2B/SS

PERSONAL: Born July 20, 1984, in San Cristobal, Dominican Republic. ... Bats both, throws right. ... Full name: Alexi Casilla. ... High school: Enedia Puello Renville (Dominican Republic). **TRANSACTIONS/CAREER NOTES:** Signed as a non-drafted free agent by Anaheim Angels organization (February 21, 2003). ... Franchise renamed Los Angeles of Anaheim for 2005 season. ... Traded by Angels to Minnesota Twins for P J.C. Romero (December 9, 2005).

2006 GAMES PLAYED BY POSITION (MLB): 2B—4, SS—2, DH—2.

									BATTING												FIELDING	
Year	Team (League)	Pos.	G	AB	R	H	2B	3B	HR	RBI	BB	SO	HBP	GDP	SB-CS	Avg.	OBP	SLG	OPS	E	Avg.
2003—Dominican Angels (DSL) ...		33	124	21	37	3	2	0	15	16	14	4	4	28-2	.298	.396	.355	.751	7	...
2004—Cedar Rap. (Midw.)		9	29	6	9	2	1	0	1	5	4	0	0	1-1	.310	.412	.448	.860	6	...
—Ariz. Angels (Ariz.)		45	163	29	42	1	4	0	10	15	10	4	3	24-8	.258	.332	.313	.645	1	...
—Provo (Pion.)		4	12	4	4	1	1	0	4	4	0	1	0	1-0	.333	.529	.583	1.112	2	...
2005—Arkansas (Texas)	SS-DH-2B	7	19	4	4	0	0	0	4	2	3	0	0	1-1	.211	.292	.211	.496	3	.842
—Salt Lake (PCL)	2B-SS	13	39	3	10	0	0	0	3	3	6	0	1	1-1	.256	.310	.256	.566	2	.968
—Cedar Rap. (Midw.)	SS-2B	78	308	62	100	11	3	0	17	29	31	6	6	47-12	.325	.392	.409	.802	15	.961
2006—Fort Myers (FSL)		78	323	56	107	12	6	0	33	30	36	2	8	31-6	.331	.394	.406	.796	16	.958
—New Britain (East.)		45	170	28	50	10	1	1	13	18	20	4	1	19-4	.294	.375	.382	.757	5	.977
—Minnesota (A.L.)	2B-SS-DH	9	4	1	1	0	0	0	0	2	1	0	0	0-0	.250	.500	.250	.750	0	1.000
Major League totals (1 year)		9	4	1	1	0	0	0	0	2	1	0	0	0-0	.250	.500	.250	.750	0	1.000

2006 LEFTY-RIGHTY SPLITS

vs.	Avg.	AB	H	2B	3B	HR	RBI	BB	SO	OBP	Slg.	vs.	Avg.	AB	H	2B	3B	HR	RBI	BB	SO	OBP	Slg.
L	.000	1	0	0	0	0	0	0	0	.000	.000	R	.333	3	1	0	0	0	0	2	1	.600	.333

CASILLA, SANTIAGO   P

PERSONAL: Born June 25, 1980, in Nizao, Dominican Republic. ... 6-0/164. ... Throws right, bats right. ... Full name: Santiago Paulino Casilla. ... Pitched under the name Jairo Garcia prior to 2006. **TRANSACTIONS/CAREER NOTES:** Signed as a non-drafted free agent by Oakland Athletics organization (January 31, 2000). **CAREER HITTING:** 0-for-0 (.000), 0 R, 0 2B, 0 3B, 0 HR, 0 RBI.

Year	Team (League)	W	L	Pct.	ERA	WHIP	G	GS	CG	ShO	Hld.	Sv.-Opp.	IP	H	R	ER	HR	BB-IBB	SO	Avg.
2000—	Dom. Athletics (DSL)	6	2	.750	3.26	1.32	11	10	0	0	...	0-...	47.0	33	24	17	2	29-0	56	...
2001—	Ariz. A's (Ariz.)	4	2	.667	2.85	0.91	12	7	0	0	...	0-...	47.1	37	19	15	2	6-0	50	.214
2002—	Ariz. A's (Ariz.)	2	1	.667	2.44	1.24	13	8	0	0	...	1-...	59.0	56	24	16	5	17-0	66	.258
—	Vancouver (N'west)	0	3	.000	7.30	1.78	3	3	0	0	...	0-...	12.1	15	11	10	1	7-0	16	.300
2003—	Kane Co. (Midw.)	0	1	.000	2.55	1.39	14	9	0	0	...	0-...	42.1	40	14	12	0	19-0	28	.250
2004—	Kane Co. (Midw.)	1	0	1.000	0.30	0.73	25	0	0	0	...	16-...	30.0	16	2	1	0	6-2	49	.154
—	Midland (Texas)	2	0	1.000	1.50	1.39	13	0	0	0	...	2-...	18.0	10	3	3	0	15-0	32	.161
—	Sacramento (PCL)	1	2	.333	3.95	1.39	11	0	0	0	...	1-...	13.2	10	6	6	1	9-1	21	.208
—	Oakland (A.L.)	0	0	...	12.71	2.47	4	0	0	0	0	0-0	5.2	5	8	8	3	9-0	5	.227
2005—	Midland (Texas)	0	0	...	1.08	1.08	10	0	0	0	0	6-7	16.2	9	3	2	1	9-0	30	.153
—	Sacramento (PCL)	3	6	.333	4.47	1.34	44	0	0	0	1	20-25	48.1	45	30	24	6	20-1	73	.239
—	Oakland (A.L.)	0	0	...	3.00	1.00	3	0	0	0	0	0-0	3.0	2	1	1	0	1-0	1	.200
2006—	Oakland (A.L.)	0	0	...	11.57	1.71	2	0	0	0	0	0-0	2.1	2	3	3	0	2-0	2	.250
—	Sacramento (PCL)	2	0	1.000	3.27	1.06	25	0	0	0	3	4-8	33.0	25	13	12	2	10-1	32	.207
Major League totals (3 years)		0	0	...	9.82	1.91	9	0	0	0	0	0-0	11.0	9	12	12	3	12-0	8	.220

2006 LEFTY-RIGHTY SPLITS

vs.	Avg.	AB	H	2B	3B	HR	RBI	BB	SO	OBP	Slg.	vs.	Avg.	AB	H	2B	3B	HR	RBI	BB	SO	OBP	Slg.
L	.400	5	2	1	0	0	1	1	1	.500	.600	R	.000	3	0	0	0	0	0	1	1	.250	.000

CASSIDY, SCOTT   P

PERSONAL: Born October 3, 1975, in Syracuse, N.Y. ... 6-2/175. ... Throws right, bats right. ... Full name: Scott Robert Cassidy. ... High school: Liverpool (N.Y.). ... College: LeMoyne (N.Y.). **TRANSACTIONS/CAREER NOTES:** Signed as a non-drafted free agent by Toronto Blue Jays organization (May 21, 1998). ... Traded by Blue Jays to Boston Red Sox for cash (April 18, 2004). ... Traded by Red Sox to San Diego Padres for OF Adam Hyzdu (July 19, 2005). **CAREER HITTING:** 0-for-2 (.000), 0 R, 0 2B, 0 3B, 0 HR, 0 RBI.

Year	Team (League)	W	L	Pct.	ERA	WHIP	G	GS	CG	ShO	Hld.	Sv.-Opp.	IP	H	R	ER	HR	BB-IBB	SO	Avg.
1998—	Medicine Hat (Pio.)	8	1	.889	2.43	1.05	15	14	0	0	...	0-...	81.1	71	31	22	4	14-0	82	.236
1999—	Hagerstown (SAL)	13	7	.650	3.27	1.06	27	27	1	0	...	0-...	170.2	151	78	62	13	30-0	178	.236
2000—	Dunedin (Fla. St.)	9	3	.750	1.33	0.99	14	13	1	0	...	0-...	88.0	53	15	13	4	34-2	89	.177
—	Tennessee (Sou.)	2	2	.500	5.91	1.48	8	7	0	0	...	0-...	42.2	48	30	28	7	15-0	39	.247
2001—	Tennessee (Sou.)	6	6	.500	3.44	1.09	16	15	4	3	...	0-...	96.2	78	45	37	10	27-0	81	.218
—	Syracuse (Int'l)	3	3	.500	2.71	1.37	11	11	0	0	...	0-...	63.0	60	24	19	6	26-0	48	.247
2002—	Toronto (A.L.)	1	4	.200	5.73	1.27	58	0	0	0	7	0-7	66.0	52	42	42	12	32-3	48	.222
—	Syracuse (Int'l)	1	0	1.000	4.00	0.89	3	2	0	0	...	0-...	9.0	8	4	4	0	0-0	4	.242
2003—	Syracuse (Int'l)	3	4	.429	3.24	1.50	57	0	0	0	...	4-...	80.2	75	31	29	3	46-7	75	.242
2004—	Pawtucket (Int'l)	5	3	.625	3.46	1.36	28	12	0	0	...	1-...	80.2	72	34	31	10	38-0	72	.242
2005—	Boston (A.L.)	0	0	...	40.50	6.00	1	0	0	0	0	0-0	0.2	4	3	3	0	0-0	0	.667
—	Pawtucket (Int'l)	6	3	.667	4.05	1.28	26	3	0	0	3	0-0	60.0	54	31	27	5	23-2	66	.243
—	Portland (PCL)	0	1	.000	1.89	0.89	17	0	0	0	1	11-11	19.0	10	5	4	2	7-1	19	.156
—	San Diego (N.L.)	1	1	.500	6.57	1.46	10	0	0	0	1	0-0	12.1	15	10	9	3	3-0	12	.306
2006—	Portland (PCL)	3	1	.750	2.70	1.35	17	0	0	0	0	9-10	20.0	21	6	6	0	6-2	23	.269
—	San Diego (N.L.)	6	4	.600	2.53	1.36	42	0	0	0	4	0-2	42.2	39	18	12	8	19-2	49	.248
American League totals (2 years)		1	4	.200	6.08	1.32	59	0	0	0	7	0-7	66.2	56	45	45	12	32-3	48	.233
National League totals (2 years)		7	5	.583	3.44	1.38	52	0	0	0	5	0-2	55.0	54	28	21	11	22-2	61	.262
Major League totals (3 years)		8	9	.471	4.88	1.35	111	0	0	0	12	0-9	121.2	110	73	66	23	54-5	109	.247

2006 LEFTY-RIGHTY SPLITS

vs.	Avg.	AB	H	2B	3B	HR	RBI	BB	SO	OBP	Slg.	vs.	Avg.	AB	H	2B	3B	HR	RBI	BB	SO	OBP	Slg.
L	.237	59	14	2	1	2	11	4	16	.286	.407	R	.255	98	25	7	1	6	17	15	33	.357	.531

CASTILLA, VINNY   3B

PERSONAL: Born July 4, 1967, in Oaxaca, Mexico. ... 6-1/205. ... Bats right, throws right. ... Full name: Vinicio Soria Castilla. ... Name pronounced: cas-TEE-yah. ... High school: Instituto Carlos Gracida (Oaxaca, Mexico). ... College: Benito Suarez (Mexico). **TRANSACTIONS/CAREER NOTES:** Contract sold by Saltillo of the Mexican League to Atlanta Braves organization (March 19, 1990). ... Selected by Colorado Rockies in second round (40th pick overall) of expansion draft (November 17, 1992). ... On disabled list (May 20-June 4, 1993). ... Traded by Rockies to Tampa Bay Devil Rays for P Rolando Arrojo and IF Aaron Ledesma (December 13, 1999). ... On disabled list (March 25-April 11, June 14-July 3 and July 30-September 4, 2000); included rehabilitation assignment to Durham. ... Released by Devil Rays (May 10, 2001). ... Signed by Houston Astros (May 15, 2001). ... Signed as a free agent by Braves (December 11, 2001). ... Signed as a free agent by Rockies (December 11, 2003). ... Signed as a free agent by Montreal Expos (November 16, 2004). ... Expos franchise transferred to Washington, D.C., and renamed Washington Nationals for 2005 season (December 3, 2004). ... Traded by Nationals to San Diego Padres for P Brian Lawrence and cash (November 3, 2005). ... Released by Padres (July 19, 2006). ... Signed by Rockies organization (August 14, 2006). **HONORS:** Named third baseman on THE SPORTING NEWS N.L. All-Star team (1995, 1997 and 1998). ... Named third baseman on N.L. Silver Slugger team (1995, 1997 and 1998). **STATISTICAL NOTES:** Hit three home runs in one game (June 5, 1999 and July 28, 2001). ... Career major league grand slams: 4.

2006 GAMES PLAYED BY POSITION (MLB): 3B—70, 1B—7.

Year	Team (League)	Pos.	G	AB	R	H	2B	3B	HR	RBI	BB	SO	HBP	GDP	SB-CS	Avg.	OBP	SLG	OPS	E	Avg.
1987—	Saltillo (Mex.)	3B	13	27	0	5	2	0	0	1	0	5	...	...	0-0	.185	...	.259	...	1	.976
1988—	Salt.-Monc. (Mex.)	SS	50	124	22	30	2	2	5	18	8	29	...	...	1-4	.242	...	.411	...	13	.924
1989—	Saltillo (Mex.)	3B-SS	128	462	70	142	25	13	10	58	33	70	...	...	11-12	.307	...	.483	...	34	.950
1990—	Sumter (S. Atl.)	SS	93	339	47	91	15	2	9	53	28	54	8	8	2-5	.268	.334	.404	.738	23	.952
—	Greenville (Sou.)	SS	46	170	20	40	5	1	4	16	13	23	2	7	4-4	.235	.296	.347	.643	9	.971
1991—	Greenville (Sou.)	SS	66	259	34	70	17	3	7	44	9	35	2	4	0-1	.270	.296	.440	.736	11	.965
—	Richmond (Int'l)	SS	67	240	25	54	7	4	7	36	14	32	3	4	1-1	.225	.271	.375	.646	12	.962
—	Atlanta (N.L.)	SS	12	5	1	1	0	0	0	0	0	2	0	0	0-0	.200	.200	.200	.400	0	1.000
1992—	Richmond (Int'l)	SS	127	449	49	113	29	1	7	44	21	68	4	19	1-2	.252	.288	.367	.655	31	.944
—	Atlanta (N.L.)	3B-SS	9	16	1	4	1	0	0	1	1	4	1	0	0-0	.250	.333	.313	.646	1	.933
1993—	Colorado (N.L.)	SS	105	337	36	86	9	7	9	30	13	45	2	10	2-5	.255	.283	.404	.686	11	.975
1994—	Colorado (N.L.)	SS-2B-3B																			
		1B	52	130	16	43	11	1	3	18	7	23	0	3	2-1	.331	.357	.500	.857	2	.986
—	Colo. Springs (PCL)	3B-2B-SS	22	78	13	19	6	1	1	11	7	11	1	6	0-0	.244	.303	.385	.688	3	.964

Year	Team (League)	Pos.	G	AB	R	H	2B	3B	HR	RBI	BB	SO	HBP	GDP	SB-CS	Avg.	OBP	SLG	OPS	E	Avg.
													BATTING							**FIELDING**	
1995— Colorado (N.L.)		3B-SS	139	527	82	163	34	2	32	90	30	87	4	15	2-8	.309	.347	.564	.911	15	.959
1996— Colorado (N.L.)		3B	160	629	97	191	34	0	40	113	35	88	5	20	7-2	.304	.343	.548	.892	20	.960
1997— Colorado (N.L.)		3B	159	612	94	186	25	2	40	113	44	108	8	17	2-4	.304	.356	.547	.904	21	.954
1998— Colorado (N.L.)		3B-SS	•162	645	108	206	28	4	46	144	40	89	6	24	5-9	.319	.362	.589	.951	13	.970
1999— Colorado (N.L.)		3B	158	615	83	169	24	1	33	102	53	75	1	15	2-3	.275	.331	.478	.809	19	.954
2000— Tampa Bay (A.L.)		3B	85	331	22	73	9	1	6	42	14	41	3	9	1-2	.221	.254	.308	.562	8	.967
— Durham (Int'l)		3B	2	8	1	3	1	0	1	3	0	1	0	0	0-0	.375	.375	.875	1.250	0	1.000
2001— Tampa Bay (A.L.)		3B	24	93	7	20	6	0	2	9	3	22	1	3	0-0	.215	.247	.344	.592	5	.934
— Houston (N.L.)		3B-SS	122	445	62	120	28	1	23	82	32	86	3	19	1-4	.270	.320	.492	.812	12	.963
2002— Atlanta (N.L.)		3B	143	543	56	126	23	2	12	61	22	69	7	22	4-1	.232	.268	.348	.616	6	.982
2003— Atlanta (N.L.)		3B	147	542	65	150	28	3	22	76	26	86	3	22	1-2	.277	.310	.461	.771	19	.955
2004— Colorado (N.L.)		3B	148	583	93	158	43	3	35	•131	51	113	6	22	0-0	.271	.332	.535	.867	6	.987
2005— Wash. (N.L.)		3B	142	494	53	125	36	1	12	66	43	82	7	16	4-2	.253	.319	.403	.722	11	.970
2006— San Diego (N.L.)		3B	72	254	24	59	10	0	4	23	9	46	2	6	0-0	.232	.260	.319	.579	5	.971
— Colo. Springs (PCL)		3B	8	31	6	12	3	0	0	4	2	5	1	0	0-0	.387	.441	.484	.925	2	.913
— Colorado (N.L.)		1B-3B	15	21	2	4	0	0	1	4	0	3	1	2	0-0	.190	.227	.333	.561	0	1.000
American League totals (2 years)			109	424	29	93	15	1	8	51	17	63	4	12	1-2	.219	.253	.316	.569	13	.959
National League totals (15 years)			1745	6398	873	1791	334	27	312	1054	406	1006	56	212	32-41	.280	.325	.487	.812	161	.967
Major League totals (16 years)			1854	6822	902	1884	349	28	320	1105	423	1069	60	224	33-43	.276	.321	.476	.797	174	.967

DIVISION SERIES RECORD

Year	Team (League)	Pos.	G	AB	R	H	2B	3B	HR	RBI	BB	SO	HBP	GDP	SB-CS	Avg.	OBP	SLG	OPS	E	Avg.
1995— Colorado (N.L.)		3B	4	15	3	7	1	0	3	6	0	1	1	1	0-0	.467	.500	1.133	1.633	1	.941
2001— Houston (N.L.)		3B	3	11	1	3	0	0	1	1	0	3	0	1	0-0	.273	.273	.545	.818	0	1.000
2002— Atlanta (N.L.)		3B	5	18	•5	7	0	0	1	4	2	2	0	0	0-0	.389	.450	.556	1.006	0	1.000
2003— Atlanta (N.L.)		3B	5	16	0	4	0	0	0	1	3	6	0	0	0-0	.250	.368	.250	.618	2	.895
Division series totals (4 years)			17	60	9	21	1	0	5	12	5	12	1	2	0-0	.350	.409	.617	1.026	3	.952

ALL-STAR GAME RECORD

			G	AB	R	H	2B	3B	HR	RBI	BB	SO	HBP	GDP	SB-CS	Avg.	OBP	SLG	OPS	E	Avg.
All-Star Game totals (2 years)			2	4	0	0	0	0	0	0	0	1	0	0	0-0	.000	.000	.000	.000	0	1.000

2006 LEFTY-RIGHTY SPLITS

vs.	Avg.	AB	H	2B	3B	HR	RBI	BB	SO	OBP	Slg.	vs.	Avg.	AB	H	2B	3B	HR	RBI	BB	SO	OBP	Slg.
L	.203	74	15	2	0	1	6	3	12	.238	.270	R	.239	201	48	8	0	4	21	6	37	.265	.338

CASTILLO, JOSE — 2B

PERSONAL: Born March 19, 1981, in Las Mercedes, Venezuela. ... 6-1/200. ... Bats right, throws right. ... Name pronounced: cas-TEE-oh. **TRANSACTIONS/CAREER NOTES:** Signed as a non-drafted free agent by Pittsburgh Pirates organization (July 2, 1997). ... On disabled list (April 7-May 5; and August 23, 2005-remainder of season); included rehabilitation assignment to Indianapolis.

2006 GAMES PLAYED BY POSITION (MLB): 2B—145.

Year	Team (League)	Pos.	G	AB	R	H	2B	3B	HR	RBI	BB	SO	HBP	GDP	SB-CS	Avg.	OBP	SLG	OPS	E	Avg.
													BATTING							**FIELDING**	
1998— VSL Pirates (VSL)		SS	55	179	31	52	9	1	1	13	20	30	6	...	23-6	.291	.380	.369	.749	...	...
1999— GC Pirates (GCL)		SS-2B	47	173	27	46	9	0	4	30	11	23	3	4	8-0	.266	.316	.387	.703	18	.923
2000— Hickory (S. Atl.)		SS	125	529	95	158	32	8	16	72	29	107	10	10	16-12	.299	.346	.480	.826	60	.908
2001— Lynchburg (Caro.)		SS	125	485	57	119	20	7	7	49	21	94	9	9	23-10	.245	.288	.359	.647	37	.939
2002— Lynchburg (Caro.)		SS	134	503	82	151	25	2	16	81	49	95	11	18	27-14	.300	.370	.453	.823	33	.951
2003— Altoona (East.)		2B-SS	126	498	68	143	24	6	5	66	40	81	3	18	19-10	.287	.339	.390	.728	23	.963
2004— Pittsburgh (N.L.)		2B-SS	129	383	44	98	15	2	8	39	23	92	1	12	3-2	.256	.298	.368	.666	11	.980
2005— Indianapolis (Int'l)		2B	4	13	2	5	1	0	2	2	1	0	0	0	0-0	.385	.467	.923	1.390	0	1.000
— Pittsburgh (N.L.)		2B	101	370	49	99	16	3	11	53	23	59	0	11	2-3	.268	.307	.416	.724	12	.977
2006— Pittsburgh (N.L.)		2B	148	518	54	131	25	0	14	65	32	98	5	22	6-4	.253	.299	.382	.682	18	.975
Major League totals (3 years)			378	1271	147	328	56	5	33	157	78	249	6	45	11-9	.258	.301	.388	.689	41	.977

2006 LEFTY-RIGHTY SPLITS

vs.	Avg.	AB	H	2B	3B	HR	RBI	BB	SO	OBP	Slg.	vs.	Avg.	AB	H	2B	3B	HR	RBI	BB	SO	OBP	Slg.
L	.259	143	37	7	0	6	20	13	27	.321	.434	R	.251	375	94	18	0	8	45	19	71	.291	.363

CASTILLO, LUIS — 2B

PERSONAL: Born September 12, 1975, in San Pedro de Macoris, Dominican Republic. ... 5-11/190. ... Bats both, throws right. ... Full name: Luis Antonio Castillo. ... Name pronounced: cas-TEE-oh. ... High school: Colegio San Benito Abad (San Pedro de Macoris, Dominican Republic ... College: San Benito Abad (Dominican Republic). **TRANSACTIONS/CAREER NOTES:** Signed as a non-drafted free agent by Florida Marlins organization (August 19, 1992). ... On disabled list (May 7-22, 1997). ... On disabled list (April 16-May 5, 2000); included rehabilitation assignment to Calgary. ... Traded by Marlins to Minnesota Twins for Ps Travis Bowyer and Scott Tyler (December 2, 2005). **HONORS:** Won N.L. Gold Glove at second base (2003-05). **STATISTICAL NOTES:** Career major league grand slams: 1.

2006 GAMES PLAYED BY POSITION (MLB): 2B—142.

Year	Team (League)	Pos.	G	AB	R	H	2B	3B	HR	RBI	BB	SO	HBP	GDP	SB-CS	Avg.	OBP	SLG	OPS	E	Avg.
													BATTING							**FIELDING**	
1993— Dom. Marlins (DSL)		2B	69	266	48	75	7	1	4	31	36	22	...	...	21-...	.282	...	.361	...	20	.943
1994— GC Marlins (GCL)		2B-SS	57	216	49	57	8	0	0	16	37	36	1	1	31-12	.264	.371	.301	.672	9	.972
1995— Kane Co. (Midw.)		2B	89	340	71	111	4	4	0	23	55	50	0	1	41-18	.326	.419	.362	.781	17	.962
1996— Portland (East.)		2B	109	420	83	133	15	7	1	35	66	68	2	2	51-28	.317	.411	.393	.804	14	.975
— Florida (N.L.)		2B	41	164	26	43	2	1	1	8	14	46	0	0	17-4	.262	.320	.305	.625	3	.986
1997— Florida (N.L.)		2B	75	263	27	63	8	0	0	8	27	53	0	6	16-10	.240	.310	.270	.580	9	.971
— Charlotte (Int'l)		2B	37	130	25	46	5	0	0	5	16	22	0	2	8-6	.354	.425	.392	.817	5	.970
1998— Charlotte (Int'l)		2B	100	381	74	109	11	2	0	15	75	68	0	6	41-15	.286	.403	.325	.728	16	.970
— Florida (N.L.)		2B	44	153	21	31	3	2	1	10	20	31	0	3	5-0	.203	.307	.268	.575	7	.970
1999— Florida (N.L.)		2B	128	487	76	147	23	4	0	28	67	85	0	3	50-17	.302	.384	.366	.750	15	.976
2000— Florida (N.L.)		2B	136	539	101	180	17	3	2	17	78	86	0	11	•62-22	.334	.418	.388	.806	11	.983
— Calgary (PCL)		2B	4	13	4	4	1	1	0	4	2	1	0	0	1-0	.308	.471	.538	1.009	1	.944
2001— Florida (N.L.)		2B	134	537	76	141	16	10	2	45	50	90	1	6	33-16	.263	.344	.341	.685	13	.980
2002— Florida (N.L.)		2B	146	606	86	185	18	5	2	39	55	76	2	7	*48-15	.305	.364	.361	.726	-13	.981
2003— Florida (N.L.)		2B	152	595	99	187	19	6	6	39	63	60	2	7	21-19	.314	.381	.397	.778	10	.986
2004— Florida (N.L.)		2B	150	564	91	164	12	7	2	47	75	68	1	15	21-4	.291	.373	.348	.720	6	.991

Year Team (League)	Pos.	G	AB	R	H	2B	3B	HR	RBI	BB	SO	HBP	GDP	SB-CS	Avg.	OBP	SLG	OPS	E	Avg.
2005—Florida (N.L.)	2B	122	439	72	132	12	4	4	30	65	32	1	11	10-7	.301	.391	.374	.765	7	.988
2006—Minnesota (A.L.)	2B	142	584	84	173	22	6	3	49	56	58	1	14	25-11	.296	.358	.370	.728	6	.991
American League totals (1 year)		142	584	84	173	22	6	3	49	56	58	1	14	25-11	.296	.358	.370	.728	6	.991
National League totals (10 years)		1128	4347	675	1273	130	42	20	271	533	629	8	67	281-114	.293	.370	.356	.726	94	.983
Major League totals (11 years)		1270	4931	759	1446	152	48	23	320	589	687	9	81	306-125	.293	.369	.358	.726	100	.983

DIVISION SERIES RECORD

Year Team (League)	Pos.	G	AB	R	H	2B	3B	HR	RBI	BB	SO	HBP	GDP	SB-CS	Avg.	OBP	SLG	OPS	E	Avg.
2003—Florida (N.L.)	2B	4	17	2	5	3	0	0	1	3	3	0	0	0-0	.294	.400	.471	.871	0	1.000
2006—Minnesota (A.L.)	2B	3	11	0	3	0	0	0	0	3	3	0	0	0-1	.273	.429	.273	.701	0	1.000
Division series totals (2 years)		7	28	2	8	3	0	0	1	6	6	0	0	0-1	.286	.412	.393	.805	0	1.000

CHAMPIONSHIP SERIES RECORD

Year Team (League)	Pos.	G	AB	R	H	2B	3B	HR	RBI	BB	SO	HBP	GDP	SB-CS	Avg.	OBP	SLG	OPS	E	Avg.
2003—Florida (N.L.)	2B	7	28	3	6	1	0	0	2	5	2	0	0	2-0	.214	.333	.250	.583	0	1.000

WORLD SERIES RECORD

Year Team (League)	Pos.	G	AB	R	H	2B	3B	HR	RBI	BB	SO	HBP	GDP	SB-CS	Avg.	OBP	SLG	OPS	E	Avg.
2003—Florida (N.L.)	2B	6	26	1	4	0	0	0	1	0	7	0	0	1-1	.154	.154	.154	.308	0	1.000

ALL-STAR GAME RECORD

		G	AB	R	H	2B	3B	HR	RBI	BB	SO	HBP	GDP	SB-CS	Avg.	OBP	SLG	OPS	E	Avg.
All-Star Game totals (3 years)		3	7	1	1	0	0	0	0	0	0	0	0	0-0	.143	.143	.143	.286	0	1.000

2006 LEFTY-RIGHTY SPLITS

vs.	Avg.	AB	H	2B	3B	HR	RBI	BB	SO	OBP	Slg.	vs.	Avg.	AB	H	2B	3B	HR	RBI	BB	SO	OBP	Slg.
L	.256	195	50	10	2	2	12	19	12	.326	.359	R	.316	389	123	12	4	1	37	37	46	.374	.375

CASTRO, BERNIE — 2B

PERSONAL: Born July 14, 1979, in Santo Domingo, Dominican Republic. ... 5-10/160. ... Bats both, throws right. ... Full name: Bernabel Castro. . **TRANSACTIONS/CAREER NOTES:** Signed as a non-drafted free agent by New York Yankees organization (September 25, 1997). ... Traded by Yankees to San Diego Padres for OF Kevin Reese (December 18, 2001). ... Signed as a free agent by Baltimore Orioles organization (March 20, 2005). ... Signed as a free agent by Washington Nationals (October 27, 2005).
2006 GAMES PLAYED BY POSITION (MLB): 2B—29, OF—2.

Year Team (League)	Pos.	G	AB	R	H	2B	3B	HR	RBI	BB	SO	HBP	GDP	SB-CS	Avg.	OBP	SLG	OPS	E	Avg.
1998—Dom. Yankees (DSL)		61	224	78	74	6	4	0	17	37	40	4	4	63-10	.330	.432	.393	.825	...	...
1999—Dom. Yankees (DSL)			Did not play.																	
2000—Dom. Yankees (DSL)		55	210	69	73	9	2	2	13	36	24	4	1	56-15	.348	.450	.438	.888	...	...
— GC Yankees (GCL)	2B	9	34	7	15	4	1	0	6	6	4	0	1	3-1	.441	.525	.618	1.143	2	.867
2001—Greensboro (S. Atl.)	2B	101	389	71	101	15	7	1	36	54	67	1	5	67-20	.260	.350	.342	.692	20	.956
— Staten Is. (N.Y.-Penn)	2B	15	57	6	20	1	0	0	7	11	12	1	0	8-3	.351	.464	.368	.832	1	.984
2002—Mobile (Sou.)	2B	109	419	61	109	13	3	0	32	52	67	3	1	53-20	.260	.345	.305	.650	11	.980
2003—Portland (PCL)	2B	105	425	57	132	17	5	2	24	25	43	1	5	49-13	.311	.349	.388	.737	14	.970
2004—Portland (PCL)	2B-OF	90	308	38	81	8	1	0	20	22	30	0	6	17-9	.263	.310	.295	.605	6	.920
2005—Ottawa (Int'l)	2B-DH	126	502	81	158	21	5	1	36	42	50	0	5	41-6	.315	.364	.382	.746	17	.972
— Baltimore (A.L.)	2B-DH-OF	24	80	14	23	3	1	0	7	9	10	0	0	6-2	.288	.350	.350	.710	4	.925
2006—New Orleans (PCL)		69	268	36	76	5	3	2	25	18	34	0	7	22-2	.284	.329	.347	.676	7	.972
— Wash. (N.L.)	2B-OF	42	110	18	25	1	3	0	10	9	18	0	2	7-2	.227	.286	.291	.577	2	.984
American League totals (1 year)		24	80	14	23	3	1	0	7	9	10	0	0	6-2	.288	.350	.350	.710	4	.925
National League totals (1 year)		42	110	18	25	1	3	0	10	9	18	0	2	7-2	.227	.286	.291	.577	2	.984
Major League totals (2 years)		66	190	32	48	4	4	0	17	18	28	0	2	13-4	.253	.317	.316	.633	6	.966

2006 LEFTY-RIGHTY SPLITS

vs.	Avg.	AB	H	2B	3B	HR	RBI	BB	SO	OBP	Slg.	vs.	Avg.	AB	H	2B	3B	HR	RBI	BB	SO	OBP	Slg.
L	.182	44	8	0	2	0	1	2	11	.217	.273	R	.258	66	17	1	1	0	9	7	7	.329	.303

CASTRO, FABIO — P

PERSONAL: Born January 20, 1985, in Monte Cristi, Dominican Republic. ... 5-8/150. ... Throws left, bats left. ... Full name: Fabio E. Castro. . **TRANSACTIONS/CAREER NOTES:** Signed as a non-drafted free agent by Chicago White Sox organization (December 26, 2001). ... Selected by Kansas City Royals organization from White Sox organizationin Rule 5 major league draft (December 8, 2005). ... Traded by Royals to Texas Rangers for 2B Esteban German (December 8, 2005). ... On disabled list (May 2-June 16, 2006); included rehabilitation assignments to Frisco and Oklahoma. ... Traded by Rangers to Philadelphia Phillies for P Daniel Haigwood and cash (June 29, 2006).
CAREER HITTING: 0-for-2 (.000), 0 R, 0 2B, 0 3B, 0 HR, 0 RBI.

Year Team (League)	W	L	Pct.	ERA	WHIP	G	GS	CG	ShO	Hld.	Sv.-Opp.	IP	H	R	ER	HR	BB-IBB	SO	Avg.
2002—Dom. White Sox (DSL)	10	2	.833	1.95	0.93	25	2	0	0	...	8-...	64.2	37	17	14	3	23-4	89	.159
2003—Bristol (Appal.)	6	2	.750	1.72	1.02	19	0	0	0	...	2-...	47.0	29	14	9	1	19-1	59	.173
— Kannapolis (S. Atl.)	0	2	.000	3.27	1.18	2	2	0	0	...	0-...	11.0	8	5	4	0	5-0	16	.200
2004—Kannapolis (S. Atl.)	4	0	1.000	3.00	1.31	37	0	0	0	...	3-...	51.0	44	20	17	2	23-0	44	.224
— Win.-Salem (Car.)	1	1	.500	2.35	0.52	6	0	0	0	...	0-...	7.2	2	2	2	0	2-0	9	.083
2005—Win.-Salem (Car.)	5	5	.500	2.28	1.20	53	0	0	0	13	6-7	79.0	58	23	20	7	37-0	75	.209
2006—Frisco (Texas)	0	1	.000	1.98	1.61	5	4	0	0	1	0-0	13.2	14	7	3	1	8-0	10	.259
— Oklahoma (PCL)	0	0	...	4.91	1.64	1	1	0	0	...	0-0	3.2	5	2	2	0	1-0	5	.313
— Texas (A.L.)	0	0	...	4.32	1.56	4	0	0	0	...	0-0	8.1	6	5	4	0	7-0	5	.200
— Philadelphia (N.L.)	0	1	.000	1.54	0.77	16	0	0	0	1	1-2	23.1	12	4	4	1	6-0	13	.158
American League totals (1 year)	0	0	...	4.32	1.56	4	0	0	0	...	0-0	8.1	6	5	4	0	7-0	5	.200
National League totals (1 year)	0	1	.000	1.54	0.77	16	0	0	0	1	1-2	23.1	12	4	4	1	6-0	13	.158
Major League totals (1 year)	0	1	.000	2.27	0.98	20	0	0	0	1	1-2	31.2	18	9	8	1	13-0	18	.170

2006 LEFTY-RIGHTY SPLITS

vs.	Avg.	AB	H	2B	3B	HR	RBI	BB	SO	OBP	Slg.	vs.	Avg.	AB	H	2B	3B	HR	RBI	BB	SO	OBP	Slg.
L	.074	27	2	0	0	0	0	3	4	4	.188	.074	R	.203	79	16	5	0	1	7	9	14	.297	.304

CASTRO, JUAN — SS/3B

PERSONAL: Born June 20, 1972, in Los Mochis, Mexico. ... 5-11/195. ... Bats right, throws right. ... Full name: Juan Gabriel Castro. ... Name pronounced: KASS-tro. ... High school: CBTIS 43 (Los Mochis, Mexico). **TRANSACTIONS/CAREER NOTES:** Signed as a non-drafted free agent by Los Angeles Dodgers organization (June 13, 1991). ... On disabled list (June 5-August 1, 1997). ... Traded by Dodgers to Cincinnati Reds for a player to be named and cash (April 1, 2000); Dodgers acquired P Kenny Lutz to complete deal (June 8, 2000). ... On disabled list (March 27-June 1, 2002); included rehabilitation assignment to Louisville. ... On disabled list (March 25-April 14, 2003); included rehabilitation assignment to Louisville. ... On disabled list (June 1-22, 2004); included rehabilitation assignment to Louisville. ... Signed as a free agent by Minnesota Twins (November 23, 2004). ... On disabled list (August 14-September 2, 2005). ... Traded by Twins to Cincinnati Reds for OF Brandon Roberts (June 15, 2006).

2006 GAMES PLAYED BY POSITION (MLB): SS—77, 3B—20, 2B—1.

Year Team (League)	Pos.	G	AB	R	H	2B	3B	HR	RBI	BB	SO	HBP	GDP	SB-CS	Avg.	OBP	SLG	OPS	E	Avg.
1991— Great Falls (Pio.)	2B-SS	60	217	36	60	4	2	1	27	33	31	0	2	7-6	.277	.369	.327	.696	21	.921
1992— Bakersfield (Calif.)	SS	113	446	56	116	15	4	4	42	37	64	1	7	14-11	.260	.314	.339	.652	38	.928
1993— San Antonio (Texas)	2B-SS	118	424	55	117	23	8	7	41	30	40	2	14	12-11	.276	.325	.417	.742	28	.945
1994— San Antonio (Texas)	SS	123	445	55	128	25	4	4	44	31	66	1	9	4-7	.288	.334	.389	.723	29	.951
1995— Albuquerque (PCL)	SS-2B	104	341	51	91	18	4	3	43	20	42	0	11	4-4	.267	.307	.370	.677	14	.973
— Los Angeles (N.L.)	3B-SS	11	4	0	1	0	0	0	0	1	1	0	0	0-0	.250	.400	.250	.650	0	1.000
1996— Albuquerque (PCL)	3B-SS-2B	17	56	12	21	4	2	1	8	6	7	1	0	1-1	.375	.444	.571	1.016	2	.962
— Los Angeles (N.L.)	SS-3B-2B																			
	OF	70	132	16	26	5	3	0	5	10	27	0	3	1-0	.197	.254	.280	.534	3	.979
1997— Los Angeles (N.L.)	SS-2B-3B	40	75	3	11	3	1	0	4	7	20	0	2	0-0	.147	.220	.213	.433	1	.990
— Albuquerque (PCL)	SS-2B	27	101	11	31	5	2	2	11	4	20	0	5	1-0	.307	.327	.455	.782	9	.928
1998— Los Angeles (N.L.)	2B-SS-3B	89	220	25	43	7	0	2	14	15	37	0	5	0-0	.195	.245	.255	.499	10	.965
1999— Albuquerque (PCL)	SS-3B-2B																			
	DH	116	423	52	116	25	4	7	51	34	70	0	14	2-3	.274	.325	.402	.727	19	.956
— Los Angeles (N.L.)	2B-SS	2	1	0	0	0	0	0	0	0	1	0	0	0-0	.000	.000	.000	.000	0	1.000
2000— Louisville (Int'l)	SS-2B-3B	19	60	9	19	5	1	2	10	12	12	0	3	0-1	.317	.425	.533	.958	4	.956
— Cincinnati (N.L.)	SS-2B-3B	82	224	20	54	12	2	4	23	14	33	0	9	0-2	.241	.283	.366	.649	2	.993
2001— Cincinnati (N.L.)	SS-2B-3B																			
	1B	96	242	27	54	10	0	3	13	13	50	0	9	0-0	.223	.261	.302	.562	8	.970
2002— Louisville (Int'l)	SS-2B	5	17	2	3	0	0	0	2	1	3	0	0	0-0	.176	.222	.176	.399	1	.962
— Cincinnati (N.L.)	SS-2B-1B																			
	3B	54	82	5	18	3	0	2	11	7	18	0	0	0-0	.220	.278	.329	.607	3	.971
2003— Louisville (Int'l)	SS	9	32	3	7	0	0	1	5	2	3	0	2	0-1	.219	.257	.313	.570	2	.950
— Cincinnati (N.L.)	2B-3B-SS																			
	1B	113	320	28	81	14	1	9	33	18	58	0	7	2-3	.253	.290	.388	.678	5	.987
2004— Louisville (Int'l)	SS-2B-3B	5	18	1	3	1	0	0	3	1	2	0	0	0-0	.167	.200	.222	.422	1	.955
— Cincinnati (N.L.)	3B-SS-2B																			
	1B	111	299	36	73	21	2	5	26	14	51	0	11	1-0	.244	.277	.378	.655	8	.973
2005— Minnesota (A.L.)	SS-3B-2B	97	272	27	70	18	1	5	33	9	39	0	8	0-1	.257	.279	.386	.665	9	.977
2006— Minnesota (A.L.)	SS-2B	50	156	10	36	5	2	1	14	6	23	0	6	1-1	.231	.258	.308	.565	7	.968
— Cincinnati (N.L.)	SS-3B-2B	54	95	8	27	5	1	2	14	5	13	0	0	0-1	.284	.320	.421	.741	2	.978
American League totals (2 years)		147	428	37	106	23	3	6	47	15	62	0	14	1-2	.248	.271	.357	.629	16	.974
National League totals (11 years)		722	1694	168	388	80	10	27	143	104	309	0	46	4-6	.229	.272	.336	.608	42	.979
Major League totals (12 years)		869	2122	205	494	103	13	33	190	119	371	0	60	5-8	.233	.272	.340	.612	58	.977

DIVISION SERIES RECORD

Year Team (League)	Pos.	G	AB	R	H	2B	3B	HR	RBI	BB	SO	HBP	GDP	SB-CS	Avg.	OBP	SLG	OPS	E	Avg.
1996— Los Angeles (N.L.)	2B	2	5	0	1	1	0	0	1	1	0	0	0	0-0	.200	.333	.400	.733	0	1.000

2006 LEFTY-RIGHTY SPLITS

vs.	Avg.	AB	H	2B	3B	HR	RBI	BB	SO	OBP	Slg.	vs.	Avg.	AB	H	2B	3B	HR	RBI	BB	SO	OBP	Slg.
L	.268	71	19	2	0	2	11	6	10	.321	.380	R	.244	180	44	8	3	1	17	5	26	.265	.339

CASTRO, RAMON A. C

PERSONAL: Born March 1, 1976, in Vega Baja, Puerto Rico. ... 6-3/235. ... Bats right, throws right. ... Full name: Ramon Abraham Castro. ... Name pronounced: RA-mon. ... High school: Lino P. Rivera (Vega Baja, Puerto Rico). **TRANSACTIONS/CAREER NOTES:** Selected by Houston Astros organization in first round (17th pick overall) of 1994 free-agent draft. ... Traded by Astros to Florida Marlins for P Jay Powell and C Scott Makarewicz (July 6, 1998). ... On disabled list (May 17-June 8, 2002; and June 2, 2004-remainder of season). ... Signed as a free agent by New York Mets organization (December 22, 2004). ... On disabled list (May 16-June 2, 2005). ... On disabled list (July 27-September 27, 2006); included rehabilitation assignment to GCL Mets.

2006 GAMES PLAYED BY POSITION (MLB): C—37.

Year Team (League)	Pos.	G	AB	R	H	2B	3B	HR	RBI	BB	SO	HBP	GDP	SB-CS	Avg.	OBP	SLG	OPS	E	Avg.
1994— GC Astros (GCL)	C	37	123	17	34	7	0	3	14	17	14	2	4	5-5	.276	.373	.407	.780	4	.983
1995— Kissimmee (Fla. St.)	C	36	120	6	25	5	0	0	8	6	21	1	1	0-0	.208	.250	.250	.500	7	.967
— Auburn (NY-Penn)	C	63	224	40	67	17	0	9	44	24	27	0	6	0-1	.299	.358	.496	.854	2	.994
1996— Quad City (Midw.)	C	96	314	38	78	15	0	7	43	31	61	2	12	2-0	.248	.317	.363	.680	10	.987
1997— Kissimmee (Fla. St.)	C	115	410	53	115	22	1	8	65	53	73	2	17	1-0	.280	.357	.398	.755	6	.992
1998— Jackson (Texas)	C	48	168	27	43	6	0	8	25	13	31	4	3	0-1	.256	.324	.435	.759	10	.974
— Portland (East.)	C	31	88	9	22	3	0	3	11	8	21	0	3	0-0	.250	.306	.386	.692	5	.946
1999— Calgary (PCL)	C-DH	97	349	43	90	22	0	15	61	24	64	2	11	0-0	.258	.307	.450	.757	7	.989
— Florida (N.L.)	C	24	67	4	12	4	0	2	4	10	14	0	1	0-0	.179	.282	.328	.610	1	.992
2000— Calgary (PCL)	C	67	218	44	73	22	0	14	45	16	38	0	5	0-0	.335	.380	.628	1.009	4	.990
— Florida (N.L.)	C	50	138	10	33	4	0	2	14	16	36	1	1	0-0	.239	.318	.312	.630	6	.980
2001— Florida (N.L.)	C	7	11	0	2	0	0	0	1	1	1	0	0	0-0	.182	.250	.182	.432	0	1.000
— Calgary (PCL)	C	108	390	81	131	33	0	27	90	38	74	1	11	1-1	.336	.393	.628	1.021	7	.989
2002— Florida (N.L.)	C-DH	54	101	11	24	4	0	6	18	14	24	0	4	0-0	.238	.322	.455	.777	0	1.000
2003— Florida (N.L.)	C-DH	40	53	6	15	2	0	5	8	4	11	0	0	0-0	.283	.333	.604	.937	1	.982
2004— Florida (N.L.)	C	32	96	9	13	3	0	3	8	11	30	1	1	0-0	.135	.231	.260	.492	2	.990
2005— New York (N.L.)	C	99	209	26	51	16	0	8	41	25	58	0	7	1-0	.244	.321	.435	.756	3	.993
2006— GC Mets (GCL)		1	3	0	2	0	0	0	0	0	0	0	0	0-0	.667	.667	.667	1.333	0	1.000
— New York (N.L.)	C	40	126	13	30	7	0	4	12	15	40	1	2	0-0	.238	.322	.389	.711	1	.996
Major League totals (8 years)		346	801	79	180	40	0	30	106	96	214	3	16	1-0	.225	.307	.387	.694	14	.991

2006 LEFTY-RIGHTY SPLITS

vs.	Avg.	AB	H	2B	3B	HR	RBI	BB	SO	OBP	Slg.	vs.	Avg.	AB	H	2B	3B	HR	RBI	BB	SO	OBP	Slg.
L	.269	26	7	1	0	1	4	4	7	.367	.423	R	.230	100	23	6	0	3	8	11	33	.310	.380

CATALANOTTO, FRANK OF

PERSONAL: Born April 27, 1974, in Smithtown, N.Y. ... 5-11/195. ... Bats left, throws right. ... Full name: Frank John Catalanotto. ... Name pronounced: ca-tal-a-NAH-tow. ... High school: Smithtown (N.Y.) East. ... College: C.W. Post (Brookville, N.Y.). **TRANSACTIONS/CAREER NOTES:** Selected by Detroit Tigers organization in 10th round of 1992 free-agent draft. ... Selected by Oakland Athletics from Tigers organization in Rule 5 major league draft (December 9, 1996). ... Returned to Tigers organization (March 21, 1997). ... Traded by Tigers with Ps Justin Thompson, Francisco Cordero and Alan Webb, OF Gabe Kapler and C Bill Haselman to Texas Rangers for OF Juan Gonzalez, P Danny Patterson and C Gregg Zaun (November 2, 1999). ... On disabled list (April 22-May 15, 2000); included rehabilitation assignment to Oklahoma. ... On disabled list (May 11-June 28 and August 17, 2002-remainder of season); included rehabilitation assignment to Tulsa. ... Signed as a free agent by Toronto Blue Jays (December 30, 2002). ... On disabled list (May 20-June 8, June 18-July 20 and August 21, 2004-remainder of season). ... On bereavement list (May 24-30, 2005). **STATISTICAL NOTES:** Career major league grand slams: 1.

2006 GAMES PLAYED BY POSITION (MLB): OF—102, DH—20.

Year Team (League)	Pos.	G	AB	R	H	2B	3B	HR	RBI	BB	SO	HBP	GDP	SB-CS	Avg.	OBP	SLG	OPS	E	Avg.
1992— Bristol (Appal.)	2B	21	50	6	10	2	0	0	4	8	8	0	0	0-1	.200	.310	.240	.550	2	.875
1993— Bristol (Appal.)	2B	55	199	37	61	9	5	3	22	15	19	3	3	3-6	.307	.364	.447	.811	10	.957
1994— Fayetteville (SAL)	2B	119	458	72	149	24	8	3	56	37	54	3	4	4-5	.325	.379	.432	.811	15	.973
1995— Jacksonville (Sou.)	2B	134	491	66	111	19	5	8	48	49	56	9	9	13-8	.226	.306	.334	.640	18	.974
1996— Jacksonville (Sou.)	2B	132	497	105	148	34	6	17	67	74	69	11	8	15-14	.298	.398	.493	.891	22	.968
1997— Toledo (Int'l)	2B-3B-OF-DH	134	500	75	150	32	3	16	68	47	80	10	9	12-11	.300	.368	.472	.840	18	.966
— Detroit (A.L.)	2B-DH	13	26	2	8	2	0	0	3	3	7	0	0	0-0	.308	.379	.385	.764	0	1.000
1998— Detroit (A.L.)	2B-DH-1B-3B	89	213	23	60	13	2	6	25	12	39	4	4	3-2	.282	.325	.446	.771	3	.986
— Toledo (Int'l)	1B-2B-3B-DH	28	105	20	35	6	3	4	28	14	21	7	2	0-0	.333	.438	.562	.999	2	.989
1999— Detroit (A.L.)	1B-2B-3B-DH	100	286	41	79	19	0	11	35	15	49	9	5	3-4	.276	.327	.458	.785	5	.986
2000— Texas (A.L.)	2B-DH-1B-OF	103	282	55	82	13	2	10	42	33	36	6	6	6-2	.291	.375	.457	.832	9	.969
— Oklahoma (PCL)	2B-OF	3	11	2	3	0	0	0	1	0	4	1	0	0-0	.273	.333	.273	.606	0	1.000
2001— Texas (A.L.)	OF-2B-1B-DH	133	463	77	153	31	5	11	54	39	55	8	5	15-5	.330	.391	.490	.882	4	.985
2002— Texas (A.L.)	OF-2B-1B	68	212	42	57	16	6	3	23	25	27	8	3	9-5	.269	.364	.443	.808	2	.990
— Tulsa (Texas)	1B-2B-OF	4	16	1	2	0	1	0	3	1	1	1	3	0-0	.125	.222	.250	.472	0	1.000
2003— Toronto (A.L.)	OF-DH-1B	133	489	83	146	34	6	13	59	35	62	6	9	2-2	.299	.351	.472	.823	3	.983
2004— Toronto (A.L.)	OF-DH	75	249	27	73	19	1	1	26	17	33	4	7	1-0	.293	.344	.390	.734	2	.971
2005— Toronto (A.L.)	OF-DH	130	419	56	126	29	5	8	59	37	53	10	9	0-2	.301	.367	.451	.818	0	1.000
2006— Toronto (A.L.)	OF-DH	128	437	56	131	36	2	7	56	52	37	4	11	1-3	.300	.376	.439	.816	1	.994
Major League totals (10 years)		972	3076	462	915	212	29	70	382	268	398	59	62	40-25	.297	.362	.454	.815	29	.985

2006 LEFTY-RIGHTY SPLITS

vs.	Avg.	AB	H	2B	3B	HR	RBI	BB	SO	OBP	Slg.	vs.	Avg.	AB	H	2B	3B	HR	RBI	BB	SO	OBP	Slg.
L	.237	38	9	1	0	1	6	7	6	.348	.342	R	.306	399	122	35	2	6	50	45	31	.379	.449

CEDENO, RONNY — SS

PERSONAL: Born February 2, 1983, in Carabobo, Venezuela. ... 6-0/180. ... Bats right, throws right. ... Full name: Ronny Alexander Cedeno. . **TRANSACTIONS/CAREER NOTES:** Signed as a non-drafted free agent by Chicago Cubs organization (August 27, 1999).

2006 GAMES PLAYED BY POSITION (MLB): SS—134, 2B—15.

Year Team (League)	Pos.	G	AB	R	H	2B	3B	HR	RBI	BB	SO	HBP	GDP	SB-CS	Avg.	OBP	SLG	OPS	E	Avg.
2000— La Pradera (VSL)		51	167	35	48	8	3	3	14	19	37	3	1	13-10	.287	.370	.425	.795		.921
2001— Lansing (Midw.)	SS-2B	17	56	9	11	4	1	1	2	2	18	1	1	0-2	.196	.237	.357	.594	5	.921
— Ariz. Cubs (Ariz.)	SS-2B	52	206	36	72	13	4	1	17	13	32	5	3	17-10	.350	.398	.466	.864	22	.902
2002— Lansing (Midw.)	SS-2B	99	376	44	80	17	4	2	31	22	74	8	6	14-10	.213	.269	.295	.564	26	.946
— Boise (N'west)	SS-2B	29	110	17	24	5	2	0	6	9	25	0	1	8-2	.218	.275	.300	.575	8	.943
2003— Daytona (Fla. St.)	SS-2B	107	380	43	80	18	1	4	36	21	82	4	5	19-6	.211	.257	.295	.552	29	.942
2004— West Tenn (Sou.)	SS	116	384	39	107	19	5	6	48	24	74	8	10	10-10	.279	.328	.401	.729	18	.820
2005— Iowa (PCL)	SS	65	245	42	87	14	1	8	36	20	31	1	9	11-3	.355	.403	.518	.921	12	.961
— Chicago (N.L.)	SS-2B	41	80	13	24	3	0	1	6	5	11	2	4	1-0	.300	.356	.375	.731	1	.986
2006— Chicago (N.L.)	SS-2B	151	534	51	131	18	7	6	41	17	109	3	10	8-8	.245	.271	.339	.610	25	.958
Major League totals (2 years)		192	614	64	155	21	7	7	47	22	120	5	14	9-8	.252	.283	.344	.626	26	.961

2006 LEFTY-RIGHTY SPLITS

vs.	Avg.	AB	H	2B	3B	HR	RBI	BB	SO	OBP	Slg.	vs.	Avg.	AB	H	2B	3B	HR	RBI	BB	SO	OBP	Slg.
L	.230	152	35	3	1	2	13	4	28	.250	.303	R	.251	382	96	15	6	4	28	13	81	.279	.353

CEPICKY, MATT — OF

PERSONAL: Born November 10, 1977, in St. Louis. ... 6-2/215. ... Bats left, throws right. ... Full name: Matthew William Cepicky. ... Name pronounced: suh-PICK-ee. ... High school: Vianney (Kirkwood, Mo.). ... College: Southwest Missouri State. **TRANSACTIONS/CAREER NOTES:** Selected by Montreal Expos organization in fourth round of 1999 free-agent draft. ... Expos franchise transferred to Washington, D.C., and renamed Washington Nationals for 2005 season (December 3, 2004). ... Signed as a free agent by Florida Marlins organization (December 15, 2005). **STATISTICAL NOTES:** Career major league grand slams: 1.

2006 GAMES PLAYED BY POSITION (MLB): OF—6.

Year Team (League)	Pos.	G	AB	R	H	2B	3B	HR	RBI	BB	SO	HBP	GDP	SB-CS	Avg.	OBP	SLG	OPS	E	Avg.
1999— Vermont (NYP)	OF	74	323	50	99	15	5	12	53	20	49	1	6	10-9	.307	.349	.495	.844	1	.986
2000— Jupiter (Fla. St.)	OF	131	536	61	160	32	7	5	88	24	64	2	9	32-13	.299	.328	.412	.740	4	.983
2001— Harrisburg (East.)	OF	122	459	59	121	23	8	15	77	21	97	2	6	5-12	.264	.296	.447	.743	3	.986
2002— Harrisburg (East.)	OF	109	419	54	116	25	2	16	76	33	94	2	14	7-1	.277	.327	.461	.787	2	.988
— Montreal (N.L.)	OF	32	74	7	16	3	0	3	15	4	21	0	0	0-0	.216	.256	.378	.635	0	1.000
2003— Montreal (N.L.)	OF	5	8	0	2	1	0	0	0	0	2	0	0	0-0	.250	.250	.375	.625	0	1.000
— Edmonton (PCL)	OF-DH-1B	122	442	61	133	23	4	7	64	31	82	4	12	7-2	.301	.349	.419	.767	11	.948
2004— Montreal (N.L.)	OF-DH-1B	32	60	4	13	4	0	1	3	1	18	0	1	0-0	.217	.230	.333	.563	0	1.000
— Edmonton (PCL)	OF-DH-1B	82	312	51	84	15	3	15	67	18	75	0	4	2-1	.269	.305	.481	.786	4	.975
2005— Wash. (N.L.)	OF	11	25	1	6	3	0	0	3	1	8	0	1	0-1	.240	.269	.360	.629	0	1.000
— New Orleans (PCL)	OF-DH-2B-3B	99	342	52	92	23	3	14	68	43	85	0	11	1-3	.269	.347	.477	.824	11	.975
2006— Albuquerque (PCL)		107	320	39	85	19	2	7	34	44	66	0	10	2-1	.266	.352	.403	.756	2	.979
— Florida (N.L.)	OF	9	18	0	2	0	0	0	3	1	8	0	0	0-0	.111	.158	.111	.269	0	1.000
Major League totals (5 years)		89	185	12	39	11	0	4	21	7	53	0	2	1-1	.211	.240	.335	.575	0	1.000

C

vs.	Avg.	AB	H	2B	3B	HR	RBI	BB	SO	OBP	Slg.	vs.	Avg.	AB	H	2B	3B	HR	RBI	BB	SO	OBP	Slg.
L	.500	2	1	0	0	0	0	0	1	.500	.500	R	.063	16	1	0	0	0	0	1	3	.118	.063

CHACIN, GUSTAVO　　　　　　　　　　　　P

PERSONAL: Born December 4, 1980, in Maracaibo, Venezuela. ... 5-11/193. ... Throws left, bats left. ... Full name: Gustavo Adolfo Chacin. ... Name pronounced: Shah-SEEN.
TRANSACTIONS/CAREER NOTES: Signed as a non-drafted free agent by Toronto Blue Jays organization (July 3, 1998). ... On disabled list (May 11-30 and June 10-August 23, 2006); included rehabilitation assignments to Syracuse and Dunedin.
CAREER HITTING: 0-for-7 (.000), 1 R, 0 2B, 0 3B, 0 HR, 0 RBI.

Year	Team (League)	W	L	Pct.	ERA	WHIP	G	GS	CG	ShO	Hld.	Sv.-Opp.	IP	H	R	ER	HR	BB-IBB	SO	Avg.
1998—	Dom. Blue Jays (DSL)	3	2	.600	2.70	1.17	9	6	2	2	...	0-...	36.2	28	12	11		15-...	56	...
1999—	Medicine Hat (Pio.)	4	3	.571	3.09	1.42	15	9	0	0	...	1-...	64.0	68	33	22	6	23-0	50	.281
2000—	Dunedin (Fla. St.)	9	5	.643	4.02	1.58	25	21	0	0	...	0-...	127.2	138	69	57	14	64-0	77	.269
	Tennessee (Sou.)	0	2	.000	12.60	3.20	2	2	0	0	...	0-...	5.0	10	7	7	1	6-0	5	.417
2001—	Tennessee (Sou.)	11	8	.579	3.98	1.26	25	23	1	1	...	0-...	140.1	138	66	62	17	39-0	86	.257
2002—	Tennessee (Sou.)	6	5	.545	4.66	1.59	35	13	1	0	...	0-...	119.2	131	73	62	12	59-0	68	.282
2003—	New Haven (East.)	3	4	.429	4.15	1.54	46	2	0	0	...	0-...	69.1	78	39	32	1	29-1	55	.283
2004—	Syracuse (Int'l)	2	0	1.000	2.31	1.63	2	2	0	0	...	0-...	11.2	16	4	3	0	4-0	14	.327
	New Hampshire (East.)	16	2	.889	2.92	1.14	25	25	0	0	...	0-...	141.2	113	53	46	15	49-0	109	.215
	Toronto (A.L.)	1	1	.500	2.57	0.79	2	2	0	0	0	0-0	14.0	8	4	4	0	3-0	6	.167
2005—	Toronto (A.L.)	13	9	.591	3.72	1.39	34	34	0	0	0	0-0	203.0	213	93	84	20	70-3	121	.274
2006—	Syracuse (Int'l)	0	3	.000	10.13	2.34	4	4	0	0	...	0-...	10.2	22	12	12	1	3-0	11	.400
	Dunedin (Fla. St.)	0	0	...	9.64	2.14	1	1	0	0	...	0-...	4.2	6	5	5	0	4-0	5	.300
	Toronto (A.L.)	9	4	.692	5.05	1.47	17	17	0	0	0	0-0	87.1	90	51	49	19	38-2	47	.266
Major League totals (3 years)		23	14	.622	4.05	1.39	53	53	0	0	0	0-0	304.1	311	148	137	39	111-5	174	.268

vs.	Avg.	AB	H	2B	3B	HR	RBI	BB	SO	OBP	Slg.	vs.	Avg.	AB	H	2B	3B	HR	RBI	BB	SO	OBP	Slg.
L	.268	71	19	4	0	7	10	7	12	.350	.620	R	.266	267	71	21	2	12	38	31	35	.351	.494

CHACON, SHAWN　　　　　　　　　　　　P

PERSONAL: Born December 23, 1977, in Anchorage, Alaska. ... 6-3/212. ... Throws right, bats right. ... Full name: Shawn Anthony Chacon. ... Name pronounced: chah-CONE. ... High school: Greeley (Colo.) Central. **TRANSACTIONS/CAREER NOTES:** Selected by Colorado Rockies organization in third round of 1996 free-agent draft. ... On disabled list (May 10-June 6, 2002); included rehabilitation assignment to Colorado Springs. ... On disabled list (June 30-July 19 and August 18, 2003-remainder of season); included rehabilitation assignment to Colorado Springs. ... On disabled list (June 5-July 6, 2005); included rehabilitation assignment to Colorado Springs. ... Traded by Rockies to New York Yankees for Ps Ramon Ramirez and Eduardo Sierra (July 28, 2005). ... On disabled list (May 22-June 11, 2006); included rehabilitation assignment to Trenton. ... Traded by Yankees to Pittsburgh Pirates for OF Craig Wilson (July 31, 2006).
CAREER HITTING: 24-for-163 (.147), 11 R, 4 2B, 0 3B, 1 HR, 10 RBI.

Year	Team (League)	W	L	Pct.	ERA	WHIP	G	GS	CG	ShO	Hld.	Sv.-Opp.	IP	H	R	ER	HR	BB-IBB	SO	Avg.
1996—	Ariz. Rockies (Ariz.)	1	2	.333	1.60	1.08	11	11	1	0	...	0-...	56.1	46	17	10	1	15-0	64	.209
	Portland (N'west)	0	2	.000	6.86	1.68	4	4	0	0	...	0-...	19.2	24	18	15	2	9-0	17	.293
1997—	Asheville (S. Atl.)	11	7	.611	3.89	1.35	28	27	1	0	...	0-...	162.0	155	80	70	13	63-1	149	.252
1998—	Salem (Carol.)	0	4	.000	5.30	1.50	12	12	0	0	...	0-...	56.0	53	35	33	4	31-0	54	.245
1999—	Salem (Carol.)	5	5	.500	4.13	1.43	12	12	0	0	...	0-...	72.0	69	44	33	3	34-0	66	.250
2000—	Carolina (Southern)	10	10	.500	3.16	1.36	27	27	4	3	...	0-...	173.2	151	71	61	10	85-1	172	.236
2001—	Colo. Springs (PCL)	2	0	1.000	2.25	1.04	4	4	0	0	...	0-...	24.0	18	6	6	3	7-0	28	.207
	Colo. (N.L.)	6	10	.375	5.06	1.53	27	27	0	0	0	0-0	160.0	157	96	90	26	87-10	134	.260
2002—	Colorado (N.L.)	5	11	.313	5.73	1.53	21	21	0	0	0	0-0	119.1	122	84	76	25	60-3	67	.264
	Colo. Springs (PCL)	2	0	1.000	4.79	1.60	4	4	0	0	...	0-...	20.2	23	12	11	3	10-0	15	.291
2003—	Colo. Springs (PCL)	0	0	...	6.00	1.70	1	1	0	0	...	0-...	3.0	5	2	2	1	0-0	2	.385
	Colorado (N.L.)	11	8	.579	4.60	1.33	23	23	0	0	0	0-0	137.0	124	73	70	12	58-4	93	.243
2004—	Colorado (N.L.)	1	9	.100	7.11	1.94	66	0	0	0	0	35-44	63.1	71	52	50	12	52-7	52	.282
2005—	Colo. Springs (PCL)	0	2	.000	9.95	1.82	3	3	0	0	...	0-...	12.2	19	14	14	3	4-0	11	.339
	Colo. (N.L.)	1	7	.125	4.09	1.44	13	12	0	0	0	0-0	72.2	69	33	33	7	36-4	39	.260
	New York (A.L.)	7	3	.700	2.85	1.22	14	12	0	0	1	0-0	79.0	66	26	25	7	30-0	40	.225
2006—	Trenton (East.)	0	0	...	5.40	1.20	1	1	0	0	...	0-...	5.0	4	3	3	0	2-0	3	.211
	New York (A.L.)	5	3	.625	7.00	1.79	17	11	0	0	0	0-0	63.0	77	54	49	11	36-2	35	.300
	Pittsburgh (N.L.)	2	3	.400	5.48	1.61	9	9	0	0	0	0-0	46.0	47	32	28	12	27-1	27	.272
American League totals (2 years)		12	6	.667	4.69	1.47	31	23	0	0	1	0-0	142.0	143	80	74	18	66-2	75	.260
National League totals (6 years)		26	48	.351	5.22	1.52	159	92	0	0	0	35-44	598.1	590	370	347	94	320-29	412	.260
Major League totals (6 years)		38	54	.413	5.12	1.51	190	115	0	0	1	35-44	740.1	733	450	421	112	386-31	487	.260

DIVISION SERIES RECORD

Year	Team (League)	W	L	Pct.	ERA	WHIP	G	GS	CG	ShO	Hld.	Sv.-Opp.	IP	H	R	ER	HR	BB-IBB	SO	Avg.
2005—	New York (A.L.)	0	0	...	2.84	0.79	1	1	0	0	0	0-0	6.1	4	2	2	0	1-0	5	.190

vs.	Avg.	AB	H	2B	3B	HR	RBI	BB	SO	OBP	Slg.	vs.	Avg.	AB	H	2B	3B	HR	RBI	BB	SO	OBP	Slg.
L	.305	200	61	17	2	11	41	35	33	.411	.575	R	.274	230	63	15	1	12	33	28	29	.362	.504

CHAVEZ, ENDY　　　　　　　　　　　　OF

PERSONAL: Born February 7, 1978, in Valencia, Venezuela. ... 5-10/189. ... Bats left, throws left. ... Full name: Endy DeJesus Chavez. ... Name pronounced: shah-VEZ. ... High school: Liceo Bataila Carabobo (Venezuela). **TRANSACTIONS/CAREER NOTES:** Signed as a non-drafted free agent by New York Mets organization (April 29, 1996). ... Selected by Kansas City Royals from Mets organization in Rule 5 major league draft (December 11, 2000). ... Returned to Mets organization (March 30, 2001). ... Traded by Mets to Royals for OF Michael Curry (March 30, 2001). ... Claimed on waivers by Detroit Tigers (December 20, 2001). ... Claimed on waivers by Mets (February 1, 2002). ... Claimed on waivers by Montreal Expos (February 22, 2002). ... Expos franchise transferred to Washington, D.C., and renamed Washington Nationals for 2005 season (December 3, 2004). ... Traded by Nationals to Philadelphia Phillies for OF Marlon Byrd (May 14, 2005). ... Signed as a free agent by Mets (December 23, 2005).
2006 GAMES PLAYED BY POSITION (MLB): OF—120.

Year	Team (League)	Pos.	G	AB	R	H	2B	3B	HR	RBI	BB	SO	HBP	GDP	SB-CS	Avg.	OBP	SLG	OPS	E	Avg.
							BATTING													FIELDING	
1996—	Dom. Mets (DSL)	OF	48	164	42	58	11	1	7	29	22	16	...	...	3-...	.354	...	.561	...	3	.963
1997—	GC Mets (GCL)	OF	33	119	26	33	6	3	0	15	20	10	0	2	1-2	.277	.379	.378	.757	2	.967
	Kingsport (Appalachian)	OF	19	73	16	22	4	0	0	4	13	10	0	2	5-2	.301	.407	.356	.763	1	.957
1998—	Kingsport (Appalachian)	OF	33	114	26	33	8	4	0	16	17	17	0	1	10-5	.289	.373	.430	.803	2	.941
1999—	Capital City (SAL)	OF	73	253	40	64	8	1	0	15	34	36	0	3	20-12	.253	.340	.292	.633	5	.967

Year	Team (League)	Pos.	G	AB	R	H	2B	3B	HR	RBI	BB	SO	HBP	GDP	SB-CS	Avg.	OBP	SLG	OPS	E	Avg.
— St. Lucie (Fla. St.)	OF	45	183	33	57	8	3	2	18	22	22	0	5	9-3	.311	.383	.421	.804	2	.980
2000— St. Lucie (Fla. St.)	OF	111	433	84	129	20	2	1	43	47	48	0	3	38-16	.298	.364	.360	.725	5	.980
2001— Wichita (Texas)	OF	43	168	27	50	6	1	1	13	16	13	0	1	11-6	.298	.353	.363	.716	1	.990
— Kansas City (A.L.)	OF	29	77	4	16	2	0	0	5	3	8	0	3	0-2	.208	.238	.234	.471	0	1.000
— Omaha (PCL)	OF	23	104	18	35	6	0	0	4	0	13	0	1	4-3	.337	.333	.394	.728	0	1.000
2002— Ottawa (Int'l)	OF	103	405	67	139	28	5	4	41	33	37	0	8	21-13	.343	.392	.467	.858	4	.985
— Montreal (N.L.)	OF	36	125	20	37	8	5	1	9	5	16	0	0	3-5	.296	.321	.464	.785	1	.989
2003— Montreal (N.L.)	OF	141	483	66	121	25	5	5	47	31	59	0	7	18-7	.251	.294	.354	.648	3	.990
2004— Edmonton (PCL)	OF	14	61	9	21	3	2	0	7	7	7	0	0	5-2	.344	.406	.459	.865	0	1.000
— Montreal (N.L.)	OF	132	502	65	139	20	6	5	34	30	40	1	6	32-7	.277	.318	.371	.688	5	.984
2005— Wash. (N.L.)	OF	7	9	2	2	1	0	0	1	3	1	0	1	0-1	.222	.417	.333	.750	0	1.000
— New Orleans (PCL)	OF	23	87	11	22	4	0	1	4	10	7	0	2	6-1	.253	.330	.333	.663	2	.983
— Philadelphia (N.L.)	OF	91	107	17	23	3	3	0	10	4	13	0	2	2-1	.215	.243	.299	.542	1	1.000
2006— New York (N.L.)	OF	133	353	48	108	22	5	4	42	24	44	0	7	12-3	.306	.348	.431	.779	1	1.000
American League totals (1 year)		29	77	4	16	2	0	0	5	3	8	0	3	0-2	.208	.238	.234	.471	0	1.000
National League totals (5 years)		540	1579	218	430	79	24	15	143	97	173	1	23	67-24	.272	.313	.381	.695	10	.990
Major League totals (6 years)		569	1656	222	446	81	24	15	148	100	181	1	26	67-26	.269	.310	.374	.684	10	.990

DIVISION SERIES RECORD

Year	Team (League)	Pos.	G	AB	R	H	2B	3B	HR	RBI	BB	SO	HBP	GDP	SB-CS	Avg.	OBP	SLG	OPS	E	Avg.
2006— New York (N.L.)	OF	3	8	1	3	0	0	0	0	1	0	0	0	0-0	.375	.375	.375	.750	0	1.000

CHAMPIONSHIP SERIES RECORD

Year	Team (League)	Pos.	G	AB	R	H	2B	3B	HR	RBI	BB	SO	HBP	GDP	SB-CS	Avg.	OBP	SLG	OPS	E	Avg.
2006— New York (N.L.)	OF	7	27	1	5	2	0	0	0	0	1	0	0	0-0	.185	.185	.259	.444	1	1.000

2006 LEFTY-RIGHTY SPLITS

vs.	Avg.	AB	H	2B	3B	HR	RBI	BB	SO	OBP	Slg.	vs.	Avg.	AB	H	2B	3B	HR	RBI	BB	SO	OBP	Slg.
L	.333	78	26	2	0	0	5	3	7	.358	.359	R	.298	275	82	20	5	4	37	21	37	.346	.451

CHAVEZ, ERIC — 3B

PERSONAL: Born December 7, 1977, in Los Angeles. ... 6-1/206. ... Bats left, throws right. ... Full name: Eric Cesar Chavez. ... Name pronounced: shah-VEZ. ... High school: Mount Carmel (San Diego). **TRANSACTIONS/CAREER NOTES:** Selected by Oakland Athletics organization in first round (10th pick overall) of 1996 free-agent draft. ... On disabled list (August 21-September 19, 1999); included rehabilitation assignment to Vancouver. ... On disabled list (June 2-July 9, 2004); included rehabilitation assignment to Sacramento. **HONORS:** Named third baseman on THE SPORTING NEWS A.L. All-Star team (2002). ... Won A.L. Gold Glove at third base (2001-06). ... Named third baseman on A.L. Silver Slugger team (2002). **STATISTICAL NOTES:** Hit for the cycle (June 21, 2000). ... Career major league grand slams: 5.

2006 GAMES PLAYED BY POSITION (MLB): 3B—134, DH—3.

Year	Team (League)	Pos.	G	AB	R	H	2B	3B	HR	RBI	BB	SO	HBP	GDP	SB-CS	Avg.	OBP	SLG	OPS	E	Avg.
1997— Visalia (Calif.)	3B-DH	134	520	67	141	30	3	18	100	37	91	2	20	13-7	.271	.321	.444	.765	32	.917
1998— Huntsville (Sou.)	3B-DH	88	335	66	110	27	1	22	86	42	61	1	6	12-4	.328	.402	.612	1.014	14	.935
— Edmonton (PCL)	3B-DH	47	194	38	63	18	0	11	40	12	32	1	4	2-3	.325	.364	.588	.951	7	.935
— Oakland (A.L.)	3B	16	45	6	14	4	1	0	6	3	5	0	1	1-1	.311	.354	.444	.799	0	1.000
1999— Oakland (A.L.)	3B-DH-SS	115	356	47	88	21	2	13	50	46	56	0	7	1-1	.247	.333	.427	.760	9	.961
2000— Oakland (A.L.)	3B-SS-1B	153	501	89	139	23	4	26	86	62	94	1	9	2-2	.277	.355	.495	.850	18	.951
2001— Oakland (A.L.)	3B-1B-SS / SS	151	552	91	159	43	0	32	114	41	99	4	7	8-2	.288	.338	.540	.878	12	.972
2002— Oakland (A.L.)	3B-DH-OF	153	585	87	161	31	3	34	109	65	119	1	8	8-3	.275	.348	.513	.860	17	.961
2003— Oakland (A.L.)	3B	156	588	94	166	39	5	29	101	62	89	1	14	8-3	.282	.350	.514	.864	14	.971
2004— Sacramento (PCL)	DH-3B	3	13	2	4	1	0	0	0	1	2	0	0	0-0	.308	.357	.385	.742	0	...
— Oakland (A.L.)	3B-OF	125	475	87	131	20	0	29	77	*95	99	3	21	6-3	.276	.397	.501	.898	13	.968
2005— Oakland (A.L.)	3B-DH	160	625	92	168	40	1	27	101	58	129	2	9	6-0	.269	.329	.466	.794	15	.966
2006— Oakland (A.L.)	3B-DH	137	485	74	117	24	2	22	72	84	100	1	19	3-0	.241	.351	.435	.786	5	.987
Major League totals (9 years)		1166	4212	667	1143	245	18	212	716	516	790	13	95	43-15	.271	.350	.489	.839	103	.968

DIVISION SERIES RECORD

Year	Team (League)	Pos.	G	AB	R	H	2B	3B	HR	RBI	BB	SO	HBP	GDP	SB-CS	Avg.	OBP	SLG	OPS	E	Avg.
2000— Oakland (A.L.)	3B	5	21	4	7	3	0	0	4	5	0	1	0	0-0	.333	.333	.476	.810	0	1.000
2001— Oakland (A.L.)	3B	5	21	0	3	1	0	0	0	0	5	0	1	0-0	.143	.143	.190	.333	1	.938
2002— Oakland (A.L.)	3B	5	21	3	8	0	0	1	5	2	1	0	0	0-0	.381	.435	.524	.959	0	1.000
2003— Oakland (A.L.)	3B	5	22	1	1	1	0	0	0	1	3	0	0	1-0	.045	.087	.091	.178	2	.867
2006— Oakland (A.L.)	3B	3	10	2	2	1	0	1	1	2	4	0	0	0-0	.200	.333	.600	.933	0	1.000
Division series totals (5 years)		23	95	10	21	6	0	2	10	5	18	0	2	1-0	.221	.260	.347	.607	3	.955

CHAMPIONSHIP SERIES RECORD

Year	Team (League)	Pos.	G	AB	R	H	2B	3B	HR	RBI	BB	SO	HBP	GDP	SB-CS	Avg.	OBP	SLG	OPS	E	Avg.
2006— Oakland (A.L.)	3B	4	13	1	3	1	0	1	2	2	4	0	0	0-0	.231	.333	.538	.872	1	.933

2006 LEFTY-RIGHTY SPLITS

vs.	Avg.	AB	H	2B	3B	HR	RBI	BB	SO	OBP	Slg.	vs.	Avg.	AB	H	2B	3B	HR	RBI	BB	SO	OBP	Slg.
L	.197	127	25	3	0	5	16	20	29	.311	.339		R	.257	358	92	21	2	17	56	64	71	.364	.469

CHAVEZ, RAUL — C

PERSONAL: Born March 18, 1973, in Valencia, Venezuela. ... 5-11/215. ... Bats right, throws right. ... Full name: Raul Alexander Chavez. **TRANSACTIONS/CAREER NOTES:** Signed as a non-drafted free agent by Houston Astros organization (January 10, 1990). ... Traded by Astros with P Dave Veres to Montreal Expos for 3B Sean Berry (December 20, 1995). ... Traded by Expos to Seattle Mariners for OF Robert Perez (May 8, 1998). ... Signed as a free agent by Astros organization (January 5, 2000). ... Claimed on waivers by Baltimore Orioles (March 31, 2006).

2006 GAMES PLAYED BY POSITION (MLB): C—15.

Year	Team (League)	Pos.	G	AB	R	H	2B	3B	HR	RBI	BB	SO	HBP	GDP	SB-CS	Avg.	OBP	SLG	OPS	E	Avg.
1990— GC Astros (GCL)	2B-3B-SS	48	155	23	50	8	1	0	23	7	12	2	7	5-3	.323	.358	.387	.745	9	.954
1991— Burlington (Midw.)	3B-SS	114	420	54	108	17	0	3	41	25	65	10	13	1-4	.257	.312	.319	.631	41	.914
1992— Asheville (S. Atl.)	C	95	348	37	99	22	1	2	40	16	39	4	11	1-0	.284	.320	.371	.691	13	.976
1993— Osceola (Fla. St.)	C	58	197	13	45	5	1	0	16	8	19	1	12	1-1	.228	.261	.264	.525	5	.986
1994— Jackson (Texas)	C	89	251	17	55	7	0	1	22	17	41	2	5	1-0	.219	.273	.259	.532	9	.986
1995— Jackson (Texas)	C	58	188	16	54	6	0	4	25	8	17	3	7	0-4	.287	.323	.394	.717	5	.987

							BATTING												FIELDING	
Year Team (League)	Pos.	G	AB	R	H	2B	3B	HR	RBI	BB	SO	HBP	GDP	SB-CS	Avg.	OBP	SLG	OPS	E	Avg.
— Tucson (PCL)	C	32	103	14	27	5	0	0	10	8	13	2	7	0-1	.262	.325	.311	.635	5	.980
1996—Ottawa (Int'l)	C	60	198	15	49	10	0	2	24	11	31	1	7	0-2	.247	.290	.328	.619	4	.990
—Montreal (N.L.)	C	3	5	1	1	0	0	0	0	1	1	0	1	1-0	.200	.333	.200	.533	0	1.000
1997—Ottawa (Int'l)	C-DH	92	310	31	76	17	0	4	46	18	42	4	9	1-3	.245	.293	.339	.631	15	.978
—Montreal (N.L.)	C	13	26	0	7	0	0	0	2	0	5	0	1	1-0	.269	.259	.269	.528	0	1.000
1998—Ottawa (Int'l)	C	11	31	2	7	0	0	0	1	5	5	0	1	0-0	.226	.333	.226	.559	0	1.000
—Tacoma (PCL)	C-DH	76	233	27	52	6	0	4	34	22	41	4	7	1-2	.223	.294	.300	.595	6	.990
—Seattle (A.L.)	C	1	1	0	0	0	0	0	0	0	0	0	0	0-0	.000	.000	.000	.000	0	1.000
1999—Tacoma (PCL)	C-DH-1B 2B-3B-SS	102	354	39	95	20	1	3	40	28	63	6	11	1-3	.268	.331	.356	.687	10	.987
2000—New Orleans (PCL)	C	99	303	31	74	13	0	2	36	34	44	4	12	3-0	.244	.325	.307	.632	8	.987
—Houston (N.L.)	C	14	43	3	11	2	0	1	5	3	6	0	5	0-0	.256	.298	.372	.670	1	.986
2001—New Orleans (PCL)	C-1B-3B	85	278	38	84	17	0	8	.40	19	34	7	9	1-1	.302	.361	.450	.810	5	.992
2002—New Orleans (PCL)	C	111	373	24	85	10	0	3	36	21	50	7	11	3-4	.228	.278	.279	.557	7	.991
—Houston (N.L.)	C	2	4	1	1	1	0	0	0	1	0	1	0	0-0	.250	.500	.500	1.000	0	1.000
2003—New Orleans (PCL)	C-3B-DH	101	355	47	97	28	1	6	47	13	43	11	11	0-2	.273	.315	.408	.724	11	.977
—Houston (N.L.)	C	19	37	5	10	1	1	1	4	1	6	0	3	0-0	.270	.289	.432	.722	0	1.000
2004—Houston (N.L.)	C	64	162	9	34	8	0	0	23	10	38	0	9	0-1	.210	.256	.259	.515	4	.991
2005—Round Rock (PCL)	C	34	119	9	30	8	0	0	14	5	24	3	4	0-0	.252	.299	.319	.619	2	.992
—Houston (N.L.)	C	37	99	6	17	3	0	2	6	4	18	1	5	1-0	.172	.210	.263	.472	2	.991
2006—Bowie (East.)		52	196	18	50	10	0	2	21	11	19	0	7	0-0	.255	.290	.337	.627	5	.987
—Baltimore (A.L.)	C	16	28	1	5	0	0	0	0	1	7	0	0	0-0	.179	.207	.179	.385	1	.985
American League totals (2 years)		17	29	1	5	0	0	0	0	1	7	0	0	0-0	.172	.200	.172	.372	1	.986
National League totals (7 years)		152	376	25	81	15	1	4	40	20	74	2	23	3-1	.215	.257	.293	.549	7	.992
Major League totals (9 years)		169	405	26	86	15	1	4	40	21	78	2	23.	3-1	.212	.253	.284	.537	8	.992

DIVISION SERIES RECORD

Year Team (League)	Pos.	G	AB	R	H	2B	3B	HR	RBI	BB	SO	HBP	GDP	SB-CS	Avg.	OBP	SLG	OPS	E	Avg.
2004—Houston (N.L.)	C	2	5	1	3	0	0	1	1	0	0	0	0	0-0	.600	.600	1.200	1.800	1	.941
2005—Houston (N.L.)	C-1B	1	1	0	0	0	0	0	0	1	0	0	0	0-0	.000	.500	.000	.500	0	1.000
Division series totals (2 years)		3	6	1	3	0	0	1	1	1	0	0	0	0-0	.500	.571	1.000	1.571	1	.958

CHAMPIONSHIP SERIES RECORD

Year Team (League)	Pos.	G	AB	R	H	2B	3B	HR	RBI	BB	SO	HBP	GDP	SB-CS	Avg.	OBP	SLG	OPS	E	Avg.
2004—Houston (N.L.)	C	2	4	0	1	0	0	0	0	0	0	0	0	0-0	.250	.250	.250	.500		1.000

2006 LEFTY-RIGHTY SPLITS

vs.	Avg.	AB	H	2B	3B	HR	RBI	BB	SO	OBP	Slg.	vs.	Avg.	AB	H	2B	3B	HR	RBI	BB	SO	OBP	Slg.
L	.000	3	0	0	0	0	0	0	0	.000	.000	R	.200	25	5	0	0	0	0	1	4	.231	.200

CHEN, BRUCE — P

PERSONAL: Born June 19, 1977, in Panama City, Panama. ... 6-1/210. ... Throws left, bats left. ... Full name: Bruce Kastulo Chen. ... High school: Instituto Panamericano (Panama). ... College: Institute of Panama. **TRANSACTIONS/CAREER NOTES:** Signed as a non-drafted free agent by Atlanta Braves organization (July 1, 1993). ... Traded by Braves with P Jimmy Osting to Philadelphia Phillies for P Andy Ashby (July 12, 2000). ... Traded by Phillies with P Adam Walker to New York Mets for Ps Turk Wendell and Dennis Cook (July 27, 2001). ... Traded by Mets with P Dicky Gonzalez, IF Luis Figueroa and a player to be named to Montreal Expos for Ps Scott Strickland and Phil Seibel and OF Matt Watson (April 5, 2002); Expos acquired P Saul Rivera to complete deal (July 14, 2002). ... Traded by Expos to Cincinnati Reds for P Jim Brower (June 14, 2002). ... Released by Reds (March 10, 2003). ... Signed by Houston Astros organization (March 14, 2003). ... Claimed on waivers by Boston Red Sox (May 7, 2003). ... Signed as a free agent by Toronto Blue Jays organization (November 26, 2003). ... Traded by Blue Jays to Baltimore Orioles for future considerations (May 1, 2004).

CAREER HITTING: 15-for-115 (.130), 4 R, 1 2B, 0 3B, 0 HR, 3 RBI.

Year Team (League)	W	L	Pct.	ERA	WHIP	G	GS	CG	ShO	Hld.	Sv.-Opp.	IP	H	R	ER	HR	BB-IBB	SO	Avg.
1994—GC Braves (GCL)	1	4	.200	3.80	1.05	9	7	0	0	...	1-...	42.2	42	21	18	2	3-0	26	.244
1995—Danville (Appal.)	4	4	.500	3.97	1.38	14	13	1	0	...	0-...	70.1	78	42	31	3	19-1	56	.276
1996—Eugene (Northwest)	4	1	.800	2.27	1.04	11	8	0	0	...	0-...	35.2	23	13	9	1	14-0	55	.173
1997—Macon (S. Atl.)	12	7	.632	3.51	1.12	28	28	1	1	...	0-...	146.1	120	67	57	19	44-0	182	.222
1998—Greenville (Sou.)	13	7	.650	3.29	1.11	24	23	1	0	...	0-...	139.1	106	57	51	12	48-0	164	.209
—Richmond (Int'l)	2	1	.667	1.88	1.50	4	4	0	0	...	0-0	24.0	17	5	5	1	19-0	29	.205
—Atlanta (N.L.)	2	0	1.000	3.98	1.57	4	4	0	0	...	0-0	20.1	23	9	9	3	9-1	17	.288
1999—Richmond (Int'l)	6	3	.667	3.81	1.27	14	14	0	0	...	0-0	78.0	73	36	33	10	26-0	90	.251
—Atlanta (N.L.)	2	2	.500	5.47	1.27	16	7	0	0	...	0-0	51.0	38	32	31	11	27-3	45	.208
2000—Atlanta (N.L.)	4	0	1.000	2.50	1.36	22	0	0	0	...	0-0	39.2	35	15	11	4	19-2	32	.232
—Richmond (Int'l)	1	0	1.000	0.00	1.00	1	1	0	0	...	0-0	6.0	5	0	0	0	1-0	6	.238
—Philadelphia (N.L.)	3	4	.429	3.63	1.14	15	15	0	0	...	0-0	94.1	81	39	38	14	27-2	80	.232
2001—Philadelphia (N.L.)	4	5	.444	5.00	1.40	16	16	0	0	...	0-0	86.1	90	53	48	.19	31-4	79	.262
—Reading (East.)	1	0	1.000	0.00	0.50	1	1	0	0	...	0-...	6.0	3	0	0	0	0-0	7	.136
—Scran./W.B. (I.L.)	1	0	1.000	3.86	1.02	3	3	0	0	...	0-...	18.2	14	8	8	2	5-0	14	.212
—New York (N.L.)	3	2	.600	4.68	1.41	11	11	0	0	...	0-0	59.2	56	37	31	10	28-0	47	.255
2002—New York (N.L.)	0	0	...	0.00	1.50	1	0	0	0	...	0-0	0.2	1	0	0	0	0-0	0	.333
—Montreal (N.L.)	2	3	.400	6.99	1.88	15	5	0	0	...	0-0	37.1	47	29	29	9	23-3	43	.303
—Cincinnati (N.L.)	0	2	.000	4.31	1.44	39	1	0	0	4	0-0	39.2	37	24	19	7	20-2	37	.243
2003—Houston (N.L.)	0	0	...	6.00	1.83	11	0	0	0	...	0-0	12.0	14	8	8	2	8-1	8	.311
—Boston (A.L.)	0	1	.000	5.11	1.14	5	2	0	0	...	0-0	12.1	12	8	7	4	2-0	12	.255
—Pawtucket (Int'l)	5	5	.500	4.24	1.10	16	15	1	1	...	1-...	85.0	80	44	40	12	15-1	73	.244
2004—Syracuse (Int'l)	0	1	.000	8.71	2.13	3	3	0	0	...	0-...	10.1	17	12	10	4	5-1	8	.354
—Ottawa (Int'l)	4	3	.571	3.22	1.21	22	17	1	1	...	0-...	95.0	85	41	34	12	30-1	108	.235
—Baltimore (A.L.)	2	1	.667	3.02	1.15	8	7	1	0	...	0-0	47.2	39	19	16	7	16-0	32	.220
2005—Baltimore (A.L.)	13	10	.565	3.83	1.27	34	32	1	0	...	0-0	197.1	197	94	84	33	63-0	133	.248
2006—Baltimore (A.L.)	0	7	.000	6.93	1.74	40	12	0	0	1	0-0	98.2	137	81	76	28	35-3	70	.334
American League totals (4 years)	15	19	.441	4.63	1.38	87	53	2	0	1		356.0	375	202	183	72	116-3	247	.270
National League totals (6 years)	20	18	.526	4.57	1.39	150	59	0	0	5		441.0	422	246	224	79	192-18	388	.251
Major League totals (9 years)	35	37	.486	4.60	1.39	237	112	2	0	6		797.0	797	448	407	151	308-21	635	.260

DIVISION SERIES RECORD

Year Team (League)	W	L	Pct.	ERA	WHIP	G	GS	CG	ShO	Hld.	Sv.-Opp.	IP	H	R	ER	HR	BB-IBB	SO	Avg.
1999—Atlanta (N.L.)	Did not play.																		

CHAMPIONSHIP SERIES RECORD

Year Team (League)	W	L	Pct.	ERA	WHIP	G	GS	CG	ShO	Hld.	Sv.-Opp.	IP	H	R	ER	HR	BB-IBB	SO	Avg.
1999—Atlanta (N.L.)	Did not play.																		

WORLD SERIES RECORD

Year Team (League)	W	L	Pct.	ERA	WHIP	G	GS	CG	ShO	Hld.	Sv.-Opp.	IP	H	R	ER	HR	BB-IBB	SO	Avg.
1999— Atlanta (N.L.)			Did not play.																

2006 LEFTY-RIGHTY SPLITS

vs.	Avg.	AB	H	2B	3B	HR	RBI	BB	SO	OBP	Slg.	vs.	Avg.	AB	H	2B	3B	HR	RBI	BB	SO	OBP	Slg.
L	.328	125	41	5	1	10	26	9	21	.368	.624	R	.337	285	96	15	0	18	44	26	49	.389	.579

CHICK, TRAVIS   P

PERSONAL: Born June 10, 1984, in Irving, Texas. ... 6-3/225. ... Throws right, bats right. ... Full name: Travis Cole Chick. . **TRANSACTIONS/CAREER NOTES:** Selected by Florida Marlins organization in 14th round of 2002 free-agent draft. ... Traded by Marlins to San Diego Padres for P Ismael Valdez (July 31, 2004). ... Traded by Padres with P Justin Germano to Cincinnati Reds for 3B Joe Randa (July 23, 2005). ... Traded by Reds to Seattle Mariners for P Eddie Guardado and cash (July 6, 2006).
CAREER HITTING: 0-for-0 (.000), 0 R, 0 2B, 0 3B, 0 HR, 0 RBI.

Year Team (League)	W	L	Pct.	ERA	WHIP	G	GS	CG	ShO	Hld.	Sv.-Opp.	IP	H	R	ER	HR	BB-IBB	SO	Avg.
2002— GC Marlins (GCL)	3	2	.600	2.76	1.29	12	8	0	0	...	1-...	45.2	40	16	14	1	19-0	39	.227
2003— Jamestown (NYP)	1	2	.333	5.71	1.71	13	10	0	0	...	0-...	52.0	63	41	33	3	26-0	48	.301
2004— Greensboro (S. Atl.)	6	4	.600	4.04	1.16	28	11	0	0	...	0-...	91.1	79	51	41	11	27-0	112	.228
— Fort Wayne (Midw.)	5	0	1.000	2.13	0.97	7	7	0	0	...	0-...	42.1	32	12	10	4	9-0	55	.216
2005— Mobile (Sou.)	2	9	.182	5.27	1.51	19	19	1	0	0	0-0	97.1	107	65	57	12	40-0	92	.279
— Chattanooga (Sou.)	2	2	.500	4.86	1.60	8	8	0	0	0	0-0	46.1	47	25	25	5	27-0	21	.270
2006— Chattanooga (Sou.)	4	5	.444	4.61	1.37	16	16	0	0	0	0-0	84.0	79	45	43	12	36-0	77	.249
— San Antonio (Texas)	4	2	.667	3.19	1.39	11	11	0	0	0	0-0	67.2	57	25	24	3	37-0	44	.230
— Seattle (A.L.)	0	0	...	12.60	3.40	3	0	0	0	0	0-0	5.0	7	7	7	0	10-0	2	.333
Major League totals (1 year)	0	0	...	12.60	3.40	3	0	0	0	0	0-0	5.0	7	7	7	0	10-0	2	.333

2006 LEFTY-RIGHTY SPLITS

vs.	Avg.	AB	H	2B	3B	HR	RBI	BB	SO	OBP	Slg.	vs.	Avg.	AB	H	2B	3B	HR	RBI	BB	SO	OBP	Slg.
L	.500	10	5	1	0	0	1	4	1	.643	.600	R	.182	11	2	1	0	0	3	6	1	.471	.273

CHILDERS, JASON   P

PERSONAL: Born January 13, 1975, in Statesboro, Ga. ... Throws right, bats right. ... Full name: Jason Lee Childers. ... College: Kennesaw State. ... Brother of Matt Childers, pitcher with two major league teams (2002-05). **TRANSACTIONS/CAREER NOTES:** Signed as a non-drafted free agent by Milwaukee Brewers organization (June 14, 1997). ... Traded by Brewers with OF Jason Belcher to Montreal Expos for OF Peter Bergeron and a player to be named (June 6, 2004); Brewers acquired P Saul Rivera to complete deal (June 18, 2004). ... Signed as a free agent by Boston Red Sox organization (January 13, 2005). ... Released by Red Sox (April 2, 2005). ... Signed by Atlanta Braves organization (April 25, 2005). ... Signed as a free agent by Tampa Bay Devil Rays organization (January 11, 2006). ... Released by Devil Rays (June 21, 2006).
CAREER HITTING: 0-for-0 (.000), 0 R, 0 2B, 0 3B, 0 HR, 0 RBI.

Year Team (League)	W	L	Pct.	ERA	WHIP	G	GS	CG	ShO	Hld.	Sv.-Opp.	IP	H	R	ER	HR	BB-IBB	SO	Avg.
1997— Helena (Pion.)	1	1	.500	3.31	1.29	10	0	0	0	...	2-...	16.1	14	9	6	2	7-0	25	.233
1998— Beloit (Midw.)	8	6	.571	1.92	1.08	34	14	1	0	...	0-...	117.0	104	48	25	8	22-2	110	.233
1999— Ogden (Pion.)	0	0	...	1.38	1.00	3	3	0	0	...	0-...	13.0	10	4	2	1	3-0	14	.217
— Stockton (Calif.)	2	8	.200	3.56	1.21	12	12	1	0	...	0-...	73.1	78	39	29	12	11-0	73	.264
2000— Mudville (Calif.)	12	10	.545	3.49	1.23	28	28	0	0	...	0-...	157.1	140	71	61	12	54-0	177	.239
2001— Huntsville (Sou.)	7	6	.538	2.87	1.21	40	2	0	0	...	0-...	87.2	76	32	28	7	30-3	85	.232
2002— Huntsville (Sou.)	1	1	.500	2.10	1.32	11	1	0	0	...	0-...	25.2	22	6	6	1	12-0	22	.244
— Indianapolis (Int'l)	2	3	.400	4.61	1.65	28	2	0	0	...	0-...	52.2	57	31	27	6	30-1	29	.275
2003— Indianapolis (Int'l)	5	4	.556	2.29	1.11	46	0	0	0	...	10-...	63.0	50	22	16	6	20-2	47	.217
2004— Indianapolis (Int'l)	1	0	1.000	1.26	1.01	24	0	0	0	...	15-...	28.2	20	4	4	0	9-0	27	.196
— Edmonton (PCL)	0	3	.000	4.50	1.71	14	0	0	0	...	5-...	14.0	15	8	7	1	9-0	13	.263
2005— Richmond (Int'l)	1	2	.333	2.09	1.34	38	0	0	0	...	16-19	38.2	32	14	9	2	20-0	31	.232
2006— Tampa Bay (A.L.)	0	1	.000	4.70	2.09	5	0	0	0	0	0-0	7.2	12	6	4	1	4-0	5	.343
— Durham (Int'l)	2	3	.400	4.99	1.53	39	0	0	0	3	2-6	52.1	58	34	29	8	22-1	39	.278
Major League totals (1 year)	0	1	.000	4.70	2.09	5	0	0	0	0	0-0	7.2	12	6	4	1	4-0	5	.343

2006 LEFTY-RIGHTY SPLITS

vs.	Avg.	AB	H	2B	3B	HR	RBI	BB	SO	OBP	Slg.	vs.	Avg.	AB	H	2B	3B	HR	RBI	BB	SO	OBP	Slg.
L	.357	14	5	0	1	2	1	2	.400	.571		R	.333	21	7	0	0	0	5	3	3	.400	.333

CHOATE, RANDY   P

PERSONAL: Born September 5, 1975, in San Antonio. ... 6-2/195. ... Throws left, bats left. ... Full name: Randol Doyol Choate. ... Name pronounced: chote. ... High school: Winston Churchill (San Antonio). ... College: Florida State. **TRANSACTIONS/CAREER NOTES:** Selected by New York Yankees organization in fifth round of 1997 free-agent draft. ... Traded by Yankees with 1B Nick Johnson and OF Juan Rivera to Montreal Expos for P Javier Vazquez (December 16, 2003). ... Traded by Expos to Arizona Diamondbacks for P John Patterson (March 27, 2004).
CAREER HITTING: 0-for-5 (.000), 0 R, 0 2B, 0 3B, 0 HR, 0 RBI.

Year Team (League)	W	L	Pct.	ERA	WHIP	G	GS	CG	ShO	Hld.	Sv.-Opp.	IP	H	R	ER	HR	BB-IBB	SO	Avg.
1997— Oneonta (NYP)	5	1	.833	1.73	0.98	10	10	0	0	...	0-...	62.1	49	12	12	1	12-1	61	.216
1998— Tampa (Fla. St.)	1	8	.111	5.27	1.50	13	13	0	0	...	0-...	70.0	83	57	41	6	22-2	55	.290
— Greensboro (S. Atl.)	1	5	.167	3.00	1.36	8	8	1	0	...	0-...	39.0	46	21	13	1	7-0	32	.293
1999— Tampa (Fla. St.)	2	2	.500	4.50	1.50	47	0	0	0	...	1-...	50.0	51	25	25	4	24-5	62	.263
2000— Columbus (Int'l)	2	0	1.000	2.04	1.36	33	0	0	0	...	1-...	35.1	34	8	8	2	14-3	37	.254
— New York (A.L.)	0	1	.000	4.76	1.29	22	0	0	0	2	0-0	17.0	14	10	9	3	8-0	12	.215
2001— New York (A.L.)	3	1	.750	3.35	1.26	37	0	0	0	3	0-0	48.1	34	21	18	0	27-2	35	.202
— Columbus (Int'l)	1	1	.500	2.08	2.31	4	0	0	0	...	0-0	4.1	7	1	1	0	3-0	4	.389
2002— Columbus (Int'l)	3	2	.600	1.72	1.09	31	0	0	0	...	1-0	36.2	25	8	7	0	15-1	32	.189
— New York (A.L.)	0	0	...	6.04	1.48	18	0	0	0	0	0-0	22.1	18	18	15	1	15-0	17	.217
2003— New York (A.L.)	0	0	...	7.36	2.18	5	0	0	0	0	0-0	3.2	7	3	3	0	1-0	5	.467
— Columbus (Int'l)	3	5	.375	3.91	1.40	54	3	0	0	...	1-...	71.1	75	35	31	4	24-3	56	.271
2004— Tucson (PCL)	0	0	...	5.68	1.42	15	0	0	0	...	0-0	12.2	10	8	8	1	8-1	7	.222
— Arizona (N.L.)	2	4	.333	4.62	1.58	74	0	0	0	11	0-2	50.2	52	26	26	1	28-11	49	.267
2005— Arizona (N.L.)	0	0	...	9.00	1.86	8	0	0	0	2	0-0	7.0	8	7	7	0	5-1	4	.276
— Tucson (PCL)	1	1	.500	3.38	1.65	47	0	0	0	5	3-4	40.0	44	22	15	4	22-1	20	.278
2006— Tucson (PCL)	6	0	1.000	2.17	1.07	43	1	0	0	3	8-10	45.2	39	13	11	0	10-1	44	.228
— Arizona (N.L.)	0	1	.000	3.94	1.50	30	0	0	0	5	0-0	16.0	21	9	7	0	3-0	12	.304
American League totals (4 years)	3	2	.600	4.43	1.36	82	0	0	0	5	0-0	91.1	73	52	45	4	51-2	64	.221
National League totals (3 years)	2	5	.286	4.89	1.59	112	0	0	0	18	0-2	73.2	81	42	40	1	36-12	65	.276
Major League totals (7 years)	5	7	.417	4.64	1.46	194	0	0	0	23	0-2	165.0	154	94	85	5	87-14	129	.247

DIVISION SERIES RECORD

Year Team (League)	W	L	Pct.	ERA	WHIP	G	GS	CG	ShO	Hld.	Sv.-Opp.	IP	H	R	ER	HR	BB-IBB	SO	Avg.
2000— New York (A.L.)	0	0	...	6.75	0.75	1	0	0	0	0	0-0	1.1	0	1	1	0	1-0	1	.000
2001— New York (A.L.)		Did not play.																	

CHAMPIONSHIP SERIES RECORD

Year Team (League)	W	L	Pct.	ERA	WHIP	G	GS	CG	ShO	Hld.	Sv.-Opp.	IP	H	R	ER	HR	BB-IBB	SO	Avg.
2000— New York (A.L.)	0	0	...	0.00	0.00	1	0	0	0	0	0-0	0.1	0	0	0	0	0-0	1	.000
2001— New York (A.L.)		Did not play.																	

WORLD SERIES RECORD

Year Team (League)	W	L	Pct.	ERA	WHIP	G	GS	CG	ShO	Hld.	Sv.-Opp.	IP	H	R	ER	HR	BB-IBB	SO	Avg.
2000— New York (A.L.)		Did not play.																	
2001— New York (A.L.)	0	0	...	2.45	2.18	2	0	0	0	0	0-0	3.2	7	4	1	0	1-1	2	.350

2006 LEFTY-RIGHTY SPLITS

vs.	Avg.	AB	H	2B	3B	HR	RBI	BB	SO	OBP	Slg.	vs.	Avg.	AB	H	2B	3B	HR	RBI	BB	SO	OBP	Slg.
L	.294	34	10	3	1	0	3	3	9	.368	.441	R	.314	35	11	2	0	0	3	0	3	.351	.371

CHOI, HEE-SEOP — 1B

PERSONAL: Born March 16, 1979, in Chun-Nam, South Korea. ... 6-5/240. ... Bats left, throws left. ... Full name: Hee-Seop Choi. ... Name pronounced: hee sop choy. ... High school: Kwang-Ju Jae (Kwang-Ju, Korea). ... College: Korea University. **TRANSACTIONS/CAREER NOTES:** Signed as a non-drafted free agent by Chicago Cubs organization (March 8, 1999). ... On disabled list (June 8-30, 2003); included rehabilitation assignment to Iowa. ... Traded by Cubs with P Mike Nannini to Florida Marlins for 1B Derrek Lee (November 25, 2003). ... Traded by Marlins with Ps Brad Penny and Bill Murphy to Los Angeles Dodgers for C Paul Lo Duca, P Guillermo Mota and OF Juan Encarnacion (July 30, 2004). ... Claimed on waivers by Boston Red Sox (March 24, 2006). ... On disabled list (March 29-May 4, 2006); included rehabilitation assignment to Pawtucket. **STATISTICAL NOTES:** Hit three home runs in one game (June 12, 2005). ... Career major league grand slams: 1.

Year Team (League)	Pos.	G	AB	R	H	2B	3B	HR	RBI	BB	SO	HBP	GDP	SB-CS	Avg.	OBP	SLG	OPS	E	Avg.
1999— Lansing (Midw.)	1B	79	290	71	93	18	6	18	70	50	68	2	8	2-1	.321	.422	.610	1.032	18	.976
2000— Daytona (Fla. St.)	1B	96	345	60	102	25	6	15	70	37	78	6	7	4-1	.296	.369	.533	.902	4	.995
— West Tenn (Sou.)	1B	36	122	25	37	9	0	10	25	25	38	0	5	3-1	.303	.419	.623	1.042	1	.997
2001— Iowa (PCL)	1B	77	266	38	61	11	0	13	45	34	67	0	5	5-1	.229	.313	.417	.730	3	.995
2002— Iowa (PCL)	1B	135	478	94	137	24	3	26	97	95	119	6	6	3-2	.287	.406	.513	.919	12	.990
— Chicago (N.L.)	1B	24	50	6	9	1	0	2	4	7	15	0	2	0-0	.180	.281	.320	.601	2	.983
2003— Iowa (PCL)	1B	18	66	12	17	4	1	6	16	9	19	1	2	0-1	.258	.351	.621	.972	0	1.000
— Chicago (N.L.)	1B	80	202	31	44	17	0	8	28	37	71	4	2	1-1	.218	.350	.421	.771	5	.991
2004— Florida (N.L.)	1B	95	281	48	76	16	1	15	40	52	78	3	4	1-0	.270	.388	.495	.882	8	.990
— Los Angeles (N.L.)	1B	31	62	5	10	5	0	0	6	11	18	1	2	0-0	.161	.289	.242	.531	1	.994
2005— Los Angeles (N.L.)	1B	133	320	40	81	15	2	15	42	34	80	8	10	1-3	.253	.336	.453	.789	2	.997
2006— Pawtucket (Int'l)		66	227	35	47	9	1	8	27	47	56	2	7	0-0	.207	.347	.361	.708	5	.988
Major League totals (4 years)		363	915	130	220	54	3	40	120	141	262	16	20	3-4	.240	.349	.437	.786	18	.992

DIVISION SERIES RECORD

Year Team (League)	Pos.	G	AB	R	H	2B	3B	HR	RBI	BB	SO	HBP	GDP	SB-CS	Avg.	OBP	SLG	OPS	E	Avg.
2004— Los Angeles (N.L.)		1	1	0	0	0	0	0	0	0	0	0	0	0-0	.000	.000	.000	.000	0	.000

CHOO, SHIN-SOO — OF

PERSONAL: Born July 13, 1982, in Pusan, South Korea. ... 5-11/178. ... Bats left, throws left. ... Full name: Shin-Soo Choo. ... High school: Pusan (Korea). **TRANSACTIONS/CAREER NOTES:** Signed as a non-drafted free agent by Seattle Mariners organization (August 14, 2000). ... Traded by Mariners with a player to be named to Cleveland Indians for 1B Ben Broussard and cash (July 26, 2006); Indians acquired P Shawn Nottingham to complete the deal (August 24, 2006). **STATISTICAL NOTES:** Career major league grand slams: 1.

2006 GAMES PLAYED BY POSITION (MLB): OF—43, DH—1.

Year Team (League)	Pos.	G	AB	R	H	2B	3B	HR	RBI	BB	SO	HBP	GDP	SB-CS	Avg.	OBP	SLG	OPS	E	Avg.
2001— Ariz. Mariners (Ariz.)	OF	51	199	51	60	10	10	4	35	34	49	9	1	12-4	.302	.420	.513	.933	1	.986
— Wisconsin (Midw.)	OF	3	13	1	6	0	0	0	3	1	3	1	0	2-0	.462	.533	.462	.995	1	.800
2002— Wisconsin (Midw.)	OF	119	420	69	127	24	8	6	48	70	98	13	2	34-21	.302	.417	.440	.857	4	.981
— San Bern. (Calif.)	OF	11	39	14	12	5	1	1	9	9	9	2	0	3-0	.308	.460	.564	1.024	0	1.000
2003— Inland Empire (Calif.)	OF	110	412	62	118	18	13	9	55	44	84	9	8	18-10	.286	.365	.459	.824	4	.980
2004— San Antonio (Texas)	OF	132	517	89	163	17	7	15	84	56	97	2	8	40-8	.315	.382	.462	.844	7	.781
2005— Tacoma (PCL)	OF-DH	115	429	73	121	21	5	11	54	69	97	1	8	20-10	.282	.382	.431	.813	4	.991
— Seattle (A.L.)	OF	10	18	1	1	0	0	0	1	3	4	0	0	0-0	.056	.190	.056	.246	0	1.000
2006— Seattle (A.L.)	OF	4	11	0	1	0	0	0	0	1	4	0	0	0-0	.091	.167	.182	.348	1	.944
— Tacoma (PCL)		94	375	71	121	21	3	13	48	45	73	2	1	26-4	.323	.394	.499	.893	4	.971
— Cleveland (A.L.)	OF-DH	45	146	23	43	11	3	3	22	18	46	1	2	5-3	.295	.373	.473	.846	2	.976
Major League totals (2 years)		59	175	24	45	12	3	3	23	21	54	2	3	5-3	.257	.342	.411	.753	3	.975

2006 LEFTY-RIGHTY SPLITS

vs.	Avg.	AB	H	2B	3B	HR	RBI	BB	SO	OBP	Slg.	vs.	Avg.	AB	H	2B	3B	HR	RBI	BB	SO	OBP	Slg.
L	.278	18	5	0	0	0	1	1	7	.350	.278	R	.281	139	39	12	3	3	21	17	43	.361	.475

CHULK, VINNIE — P

PERSONAL: Born December 19, 1978, in Miami. ... 6-2/185. ... Throws right, bats right. ... Full name: Charles Vincent Chulk. ... High school: Palmetto (Miami). ... College: St. Thomas (Fla.). **TRANSACTIONS/CAREER NOTES:** Selected by Toronto Blue Jays organization in 12th round of 2000 free-agent draft. ... Traded by Blue Jays with 1B/3B Shea Hillenbrand to San Francisco Giants for P Jeremy Accardo (July 22, 2006).

CAREER HITTING: 0-for-1 (.000), 0 R, 0 2B, 0 3B, 0 HR, 0 RBI.

Year Team (League)	W	L	Pct.	ERA	WHIP	G	GS	CG	ShO	Hld.	Sv.-Opp.	IP	H	R	ER	HR	BB-IBB	SO	Avg.
2000— Medicine Hat (Pio.)	2	4	.333	3.80	1.38	14	13	0	0	...	0-...	68.2	75	36	29	5	20-0	51	.277
2001— Dunedin (Fla. St.)	1	2	.333	3.12	1.47	16	1	0	0	...	1-...	34.2	38	16	12	2	13-1	50	.271
— Syracuse (Int'l)	1	0	1.000	1.50	1.50	5	0	0	0	...	0-...	6.0	5	1	1	0	4-0	3	.238
— Tennessee (Sou.)	2	5	.286	3.14	0.98	24	1	0	0	...	2-...	43.0	34	15	15	5	8-1	43	.227
2002— Tennessee (Sou.)	13	5	.722	2.96	1.22	25	24	0	0	...	1-...	152.0	133	55	50	12	53-0	108	.236
— Syracuse (Int'l)	0	1	.000	5.79	2.57	2	1	0	0	...	0-...	4.2	6	6	3	0	6-0	2	.316
2003— Toronto (A.L.)	0	0	...	5.06	1.69	3	0	0	0	...	0-...	5.1	5	3	3	0	3-0	2	.273
— Syracuse (Int'l)	8	10	.444	4.22	1.37	23	21	1	0	...	0-...	119.1	118	70	56	14	46-0	90	.256

Year	Team (League)	W	L	Pct.	ERA	WHIP	G	GS	CG	ShO	Hld.	Sv.-Opp.	IP	H	R	ER	HR	BB-IBB	SO	Avg.
2004—	Toronto (A.L.)	1	3	.250	4.66	1.54	47	0	0	0	13	2-5	56.0	59	30	29	6	27-1	44	.271
—	Syracuse (Int'l)	4	2	.667	2.83	1.33	18	0	0	0	3-...	28.2	27	13	9	5	11-2	26	.235
2005—	Toronto (A.L.)	0	0	.000	3.88	1.31	62	0	0	0	13	0-1	72.0	68	33	31	9	26-3	39	.255
2006—	Toronto (A.L.)	1	0	1.000	5.25	1.42	20	0	0	0	1	0-1	24.0	29	16	14	4	5-0	18	.293
—	San Francisco (N.L.)	0	3	.000	5.24	1.43	28	0	0	0	5	0-1	22.1	17	13	13	2	15-2	25	.210
—	Syracuse (Int'l)	3	2	.600	2.25	1.06	19	0	0	0	1-3	32.0	20	8	8	4	14-1	43	.175
American League totals (4 years)		2	4	.333	4.40	1.42	132	0	0	0	27	2-8	157.1	162	82	77	19	61-4	103	.267
National League totals (1 year)		0	3	.000	5.24	1.43	28	0	0	0	5	0-1	22.1	17	13	13	2	15-2	25	.210
Major League totals (4 years)		2	7	.222	4.51	1.42	160	0	0	0	32	2-9	179.2	179	95	90	21	76-6	128	.261

2006 LEFTY-RIGHTY SPLITS

vs.	Avg.	AB	H	2B	3B	HR	RBI	BB	SO	OBP	Slg.	vs.	Avg.	AB	H	2B	3B	HR	RBI	BB	SO	OBP	Slg.
L	.206	63	13	3	0	1	7	6	14	.271	.302	R	.282	117	33	5	0	5	27	14	29	.370	.453

CHURCH, RYAN — OF

PERSONAL: Born October 14, 1978, in Santa Barbara, Calif. ... 6-1/190. ... Bats left, throws left. ... Full name: Ryan Matthew Church. ... High school: Lompoc (Calif.). ... College: Nevada. **TRANSACTIONS/CAREER NOTES:** Selected by Cleveland Indians organization in 14th round of 2000 free-agent draft. ... Traded by Indians with SS Maicer Izturis to Montreal Expos for P Scott Stewart (January 5, 2004). ... Expos franchise transferred to Washington, D.C., and renamed Washington Nationals for 2005 season (December 3, 2004). ... On disabled list (June 23-July 13 and August 25-September 9, 2005); included rehabilitation assignment to Harrisburg. **STATISTICAL NOTES:** Career major league grand slams: 1.

2006 GAMES PLAYED BY POSITION (MLB): OF—62.

Year	Team (League)	Pos.	G	AB	R	H	2B	3B	HR	RBI	BB	SO	HBP	GDP	SB-CS	Avg.	OBP	SLG	OPS	E	Avg.
2000—	Mahoning Valley (N.Y.-Penn.)	OF	73	272	51	81	16	5	10	65	38	49	8	4	11-4	.298	.396	.504	.899	3	.973
2001—	Columbus (S. Atl.)	OF	101	363	64	104	23	3	17	76	54	79	6	6	4-6	.287	.385	.507	.892	3	.987
—	Kinston (Carol.)	OF	24	83	16	20	7	0	5	15	18	23	1	1	1-0	.241	.379	.506	.885	2	.947
2002—	Kinston (Carol.)	OF	53	181	30	59	12	1	10	30	31	51	4	3	4-4	.326	.433	.569	1.002	3	.965
—	Akron (East.)	OF	71	291	39	86	17	4	12	51	12	58	2	8	1-0	.296	.325	.505	.830	1	.993
2003—	Akron (East.)	OF	99	371	44	97	17	3	13	52	32	64	4	17	4-3	.261	.325	.429	.754	6	.977
2004—	Edmonton (PCL)	OF-DH	98	347	74	120	29	8	17	79	51	62	4	4	0-1	.346	.430	.622	1.041	2	.990
—	Montreal (N.L.)	OF	30	63	6	11	1	0	1	6	7	16	0	3	0-0	.175	.257	.238	.495	0	1.000
2005—	Harrisburg (East.)	OF	4	18	2	5	1	0	0	0	5	0	0	0	0-0	.278	.278	.333	.611	0	1.000
—	Wash. (N.L.)	OF	102	268	41	77	15	3	9	42	24	70	5	6	3-2	.287	.353	.466	.820	0	1.000
2006—	Harrisburg (East.)		5	19	3	4	0	0	2	3	3	5	0	0	1-0	.211	.318	.526	.844	0	1.000
—	New Orleans (PCL)		53	175	29	43	6	0	7	29	25	41	3	5	5-1	.246	.345	.400	.745	3	.970
—	Wash. (N.L.)	OF	71	196	22	54	17	1	10	35	26	60	3	4	6-1	.276	.366	.526	.891	2	.986
Major League totals (3 years)			203	527	69	142	33	4	20	83	57	146	8	13	9-3	.269	.347	.461	.808	2	.994

2006 LEFTY-RIGHTY SPLITS

vs.	Avg.	AB	H	2B	3B	HR	RBI	BB	SO	OBP	Slg.	vs.	Avg.	AB	H	2B	3B	HR	RBI	BB	SO	OBP	Slg.
L	.265	49	13	5	0	1	9	5	17	.321	.429	R	.279	147	41	12	1	9	26	21	43	.380	.558

CINTRON, ALEX — SS/2B

PERSONAL: Born December 17, 1978, in Humacao, Puerto Rico. ... 6-2/199. ... Bats both, throws right. ... Full name: Alexander Cintron. ... Name pronounced: SIN-tron. ... High school: Mech-Tech (Caguas, P.R.). **TRANSACTIONS/CAREER NOTES:** Selected by Arizona Diamondbacks organization in 36th round of 1997 free-agent draft. ... Traded by Diamondbacks to Chicago White Sox for P Jeff Bajenaru (March 8, 2006). **STATISTICAL NOTES:** Career major league grand slams: 1.

2006 GAMES PLAYED BY POSITION (MLB): SS—41, 2B—26, 3B—11, DH—8.

Year	Team (League)	Pos.	G	AB	R	H	2B	3B	HR	RBI	BB	SO	HBP	GDP	SB-CS	Avg.	OBP	SLG	OPS	E	Avg.
1997—	Ariz. D'backs (Ariz.)	SS	43	152	23	30	6	1	0	20	21	32	2	3	1-4	.197	.301	.250	.551	15	.931
—	Lethbridge (Pion.)	SS	1	3	0	1	0	0	0	0	0	1	0	0	0-0	.333	.333	.333	.667	1	.857
1998—	Lethbridge (Pion.)	SS	67	258	41	68	11	4	3	34	20	32	2	8	8-4	.264	.319	.372	.691	27	.921
1999—	High Desert (Calif.)	SS	128	499	78	153	25	4	3	64	19	65	3	14	15-8	.307	.333	.391	.724	28	.950
2000—	El Paso (Texas)	SS	125	522	83	157	30	6	4	59	29	56	2	22	9-9	.301	.336	.404	.740	32	.950
2001—	Tucson (PCL)	SS-2B	107	425	53	124	24	3	3	35	15	42	2	12	9-6	.292	.315	.384	.698	32	.936
—	Arizona (N.L.)	SS	8	7	0	2	0	1	0	0	0	0	0	0	0-0	.286	.286	.571	.857	0	1.000
2002—	Tucson (PCL)	SS-2B	85	351	53	113	22	3	4	26	11	33	2	8	9-5	.322	.345	.436	.781	14	.960
—	Arizona (N.L.)	2B-3B-SS	38	75	11	16	6	0	0	4	12	13	0	2	0-0	.213	.322	.293	.615	1	.989
2003—	Tucson (PCL)	SS-2B	26	107	21	42	11	2	2	21	8	6	0	0	1-0	.393	.435	.589	1.024	4	.970
—	Arizona (N.L.)	SS-3B-2B	117	448	70	142	26	6	13	51	29	33	2	7	2-3	.317	.359	.489	.848	11	.976
2004—	Arizona (N.L.)	SS-3B-2B	154	564	56	148	31	7	4	49	31	59	2	11	3-3	.262	.301	.363	.665	17	.973
2005—	Arizona (N.L.)	SS-3B-2B	122	330	36	90	19	2	8	48	12	33	1	8	1-2	.273	.298	.415	.713	8	.971
2006—	Chicago (A.L.)	SS-2B-3B DH	91	288	35	82	10	3	5	41	10	35	2	10	10-3	.285	.310	.392	.703	8	.972
American League totals (1 year)			91	288	35	82	10	3	5	41	10	35	2	10	10-3	.285	.310	.392	.703	8	.972
National League totals (5 years)			439	1424	173	398	82	16	25	152	84	138	5	28	6-8	.279	.320	.412	.732	37	.974
Major League totals (6 years)			530	1712	208	480	92	19	30	193	94	173	7	38	16-11	.280	.318	.409	.727	45	.974

DIVISION SERIES RECORD

Year	Team (League)	Pos.	G	AB	R	H	2B	3B	HR	RBI	BB	SO	HBP	GDP	SB-CS	Avg.	OBP	SLG	OPS	E	Avg.
2002—	Arizona (N.L.)	3B	2	0	0	0	0	0	0	0	0	0	0	0	0-0	...	...	...	...	0	...

2006 LEFTY-RIGHTY SPLITS

vs.	Avg.	AB	H	2B	3B	HR	RBI	BB	SO	OBP	Slg.	vs.	Avg.	AB	H	2B	3B	HR	RBI	BB	SO	OBP	Slg.
L	.274	62	17	1	0	0	5	3	5	.308	.290	R	.288	226	65	9	3	5	36	7	30	.311	.420

CIRILLO, JEFF — 3B/1B

PERSONAL: Born September 23, 1969, in Pasadena, Calif. ... 6-1/200. ... Bats right, throws right. ... Full name: Jeffrey Howard Cirillo. ... Name pronounced: suh-RILL-oh. ... High school: Providence (Burbank, Calif.). ... College: Southern California. **TRANSACTIONS/CAREER NOTES:** Selected by Chicago Cubs organization in 37th round of 1987 free-agent draft; did not sign. ... Selected by Milwaukee Brewers organization in 11th round of 1991 free-agent draft. ... Traded by Brewers with P Scott Karl and cash to Colorado Rockies as part of three-team deal in which Brewers acquired P Jamey Wright and C Henry Blanco from Rockies and P Jimmy Haynes from Oakland Athletics, and A's acquired P Justin Miller and cash from Rockies (December 13, 1999). ... On disabled list (April 27-May 13, 2001); included rehabilitation assignment to Colorado Springs. ... Traded by Rockies to Seattle Mariners for Ps Jose Paniagua, Denny Stark and Brian Fuentes (December 15, 2001). ... On disabled list (July 24-August 19, 2003); included rehabilitation assignment to AZL Mariners. ... Traded by Mariners with P Brian Sweeney and cash to San Diego Padres for P Kevin Jarvis, IF Dave Hansen, C Wiki

Gonzalez and OF Vince Faison (January 6, 2004). ... On disabled list (April 2-May 11, 2004); included rehabilitation assignment to Portland. ... Released by Padres (August 4, 2004). ... Signed by Brewers organization (February 4, 2005). ... On disabled list (June 25-September 1, 2005); included rehabilitation assignment to Nashville. **STATISTICAL NOTES:** Hit three home runs in one game (June 28, 2000). ... Career major league grand slams: 1.

2006 GAMES PLAYED BY POSITION (MLB): 3B—42, 1B—13, 2B—12, SS—3.

Year Team (League)	Pos.	G	AB	R	H	2B	3B	HR	RBI	BB	SO	HBP	GDP	SB-CS	Avg.	OBP	SLG	OPS	E	Avg.
1991— Helena (Pion.)	3B-OF	70	286	60	100	16	2	10	51	31	28	4	11	3-1	.350	.418	.524	.942	15	.921
1992— Stockton (Calif.)	3B	7	27	2	6	1	0	0	5	2	0	2	2	0-0	.222	.323	.259	.582	0	1.000
— Beloit (Midw.)	2B-3B	126	444	65	135	27	3	9	71	84	85	6	7	21-12	.304	.417	.439	.856	26	.942
1993— El Paso (Texas)	2B-3B	67	249	53	85	16	2	9	41	26	37	5	5	2-3	.341	.410	.530	.940	9	.962
— New Orleans (A.A.)	3B-2B-SS	58	215	31	63	13	2	3	32	29	33	3	7	2-1	.293	.385	.414	.799	5	.974
1994— New Orleans (A.A.)	3B-2B-DH																			
	SS	61	236	45	73	18	2	10	46	28	39	2	9	4-0	.309	.386	.530	.915	8	.963
— Milwaukee (A.L.)	3B-2B	39	126	17	30	9	0	3	12	11	16	2	4	0-1	.238	.309	.381	.690	3	.965
1995— Milwaukee (A.L.)	3B-2B-1B																			
	SS	125	328	57	91	19	4	9	39	47	42	4	8	7-2	.277	.371	.442	.813	15	.958
1996— Milwaukee (A.L.)	3B-DH-1B																			
	2B	158	566	101	184	46	2	16	83	58	69	7	14	4-9	.325	.391	.504	.894	18	.952
1997— Milwaukee (A.L.)	3B-DH	154	580	74	167	46	2	10	82	60	74	14	13	4-3	.288	.367	.426	.793	17	.963
1998— Milwaukee (N.L.)	3B-1B	156	604	97	194	31	1	14	68	79	88	4	* 26	10-4	.321	.402	.445	.847	11	.979
1999— Milwaukee (N.L.)	3B	157	607	98	198	35	1	15	88	75	83	5	15	7-4	.326	.401	.461	.862	15	.967
2000— Colorado (N.L.)	3B	157	598	111	195	53	2	11	115	67	72	6	19	3-4	.326	.392	.477	.869	15	.964
2001— Colorado (N.L.)	3B	138	528	72	165	26	4	17	83	43	63	5	15	12-2	.313	.364	.473	.838	7	.982
— Colo. Springs (PCL)	3B	1	4	2	3	1	0	0	3	1	0	0	0	0-0	.750	.800	1.000	1.800	0	1.000
2002— Seattle (A.L.)	3B-1B	146	485	51	121	20	0	6	54	31	67	9	12	8-4	.249	.302	.328	.629	9	.976
2003— Ariz. Mariners (Ariz.)	DH-3B	6	20	2	6	0	0	0	0	4	1	1	1	0-1	.300	.440	.300	.740	0	1.000
— Inland Empire (Calif.)	3B-DH	5	15	1	3	1	0	0	1	3	1	0	1	0-0	.200	.333	.267	.600	1	.833
— Tacoma (PCL)	3B-DH	5	17	7	6	3	0	2	6	3	3	1	0	0-0	.353	.476	.882	1.359	0	1.000
— Seattle (A.L.)	3B-1B-DH	87	258	24	53	11	0	2	23	24	32	5	6	1-1	.205	.284	.271	.555	4	.978
2004— Portland (PCL)	3B-1B-2B																			
	DH-OF-SS	7	23	3	8	3	0	0	2	5	1	0	1	1-0	.348	.464	.478	.943	1	.960
— San Diego (N.L.)	3B-1B-2B																			
	OF	33	75	12	16	3	0	1	7	5	14	0	0	0-0	.213	.259	.293	.553	2	.979
2005— Nashville (PCL)	3B-DH	9	29	2	7	1	0	0	6	0	5	1	1	0-0	.241	.250	.276	.526	1	.875
— Milwaukee (N.L.)	3B-2B-1B	77	185	29	52	15	0	4	23	23	22	4	3	4-2	.281	.373	.427	.800	5	.954
2006— Milwaukee (N.L.)	3B-1B-2B																			
	SS	112	263	33	84	16	0	3	23	21	33	1	8	1-1	.319	.369	.414	.784	2	.992
American League totals (6 years)		709	2343	324	646	151	11	45	293	231	300	41	57	24-20	.276	.348	.407	.755	66	.964
National League totals (7 years)		830	2860	452	904	179	8	65	407	313	375	25	86	37-17	.316	.384	.452	.837	57	.975
Major League totals (13 years)		1539	5203	776	1550	330	19	110	700	544	675	66	143	61-37	.298	.368	.432	.800	123	.970

ALL-STAR GAME RECORD

	G	AB	R	H	2B	3B	HR	RBI	BB	SO	HBP	GDP	SB-CS	Avg.	OBP	SLG	OPS	E	Avg.
All-Star Game totals (2 years)	2	2	0	0	0	0	0	0	0	1	0	0	0-0	.000	.000	.000	.000	0	1.000

2006 LEFTY-RIGHTY SPLITS

vs.	Avg.	AB	H	2B	3B	HR	RBI	BB	SO	OBP	Slg.	vs.	Avg.	AB	H	2B	3B	HR	RBI	BB	SO	OBP	Slg.
L	.413	75	31	6	0	0	11	6	12	.451	.493	R	.282	188	53	10	0	3	12	15	21	.337	.383

CLARK, BRADY — OF

PERSONAL: Born April 18, 1973, in Portland, Ore. ... 6-2/202. ... Bats right, throws right. ... Full name: Brady William Clark. ... High school: Sunset (Beaverton, Ore.). ... College: San Diego. **TRANSACTIONS/CAREER NOTES:** Signed as a non-drafted free agent by Cincinnati Reds organization (January 13, 1996). ... Released by Reds (April 10, 1996). ... Re-signed by Reds organization (February 15, 1997). ... Traded by Reds to New York Mets (September 9, 2002), completing deal in which Reds traded P Pedro Feliciano, OF Elvin Andujar and two players to be named to Mets for P Shawn Estes (August 15, 2002); Mets acquired OF Raul Gonzalez as part of deal (August 20, 2002). ... Claimed on waivers by Milwaukee Brewers (January 21, 2003). ... On disabled list (March 21-April 15, 2003); included rehabilitation assignment to Indianapolis. ... On disabled list (August 11-26, 2005).

2006 GAMES PLAYED BY POSITION (MLB): OF—119.

Year Team (League)	Pos.	G	AB	R	H	2B	3B	HR	RBI	BB	SO	HBP	GDP	SB-CS	Avg.	OBP	SLG	OPS	E	Avg.
1997— Burlington (Midw.)	OF	126	459	108	149	29	7	11	63	76	71	4	10	31-18	.325	.423	.490	.913	4	.986
1998— Chattanooga (Sou.)	OF	64	222	41	60	13	1	2	16	31	34	4	11	12-4	.270	.370	.365	.735	1	.993
1999— Chattanooga (Sou.)	OF-3B	138	506	103	165	37	4	17	75	89	58	2	6	25-17	.326	.425	.516	.941	5	.981
2000— Louisville (Int'l)	OF	132	487	90	148	41	6	16	79	72	51	9	14	12-8	.304	.397	.511	.908	6	.981
— Cincinnati (N.L.)	OF	11	11	1	3	1	0	0	2	0	2	0	0	0-0	.273	.273	.364	.636	0	1.000
2001— Louisville (Int'l)	OF	49	167	24	44	5	1	2	18	18	17	6	5	6-2	.263	.354	.341	.695	2	.981
— Cincinnati (N.L.)	OF-DH	89	129	22	34	3	0	6	18	22	16	1	6	4-1	.264	.373	.426	.799	1	.981
2002— Cincinnati (N.L.)	OF	51	66	6	10	3	0	0	9	6	9	1	2	1-2	.152	.233	.197	.430	1	.938
— Louisville (Int'l)	OF-3B	25	109	17	33	7	0	1	17	3	9	2	3	0-2	.303	.328	.395	.722	3	.955
— New York (N.L.)	OF	10	12	3	5	1	0	0	1	0	1	0	0	0-0	.417	.462	.500	.962	0	1.000
2003— Indianapolis (Int'l)	OF-DH	9	34	4	9	3	0	0	3	2	6	0	3	1-0	.265	.306	.353	.658	0	1.000
— Milwaukee (N.L.)	OF	128	315	33	86	21	1	6	40	21	40	9	12	13-2	.273	.330	.403	.733	5	.973
2004— Milwaukee (N.L.)	OF	138	353	41	99	18	1	7	46	53	48	9	9	15-8	.280	.385	.397	.782	4	.984
2005— Milwaukee (N.L.)	OF	145	599	94	183	31	1	13	53	47	55	18	13	10-13	.306	.372	.426	.798	2	.995
2006— Milwaukee (N.L.)	OF	138	415	51	109	14	2	4	29	43	60	14	9	3-4	.263	.348	.389	.683	5	.981
Major League totals (7 years)		710	1900	251	529	92	5	36	198	193	232	52	51	46-30	.278	.358	.389	.747	18	.985

2006 LEFTY-RIGHTY SPLITS

vs.	Avg.	AB	H	2B	3B	HR	RBI	BB	SO	OBP	Slg.	vs.	Avg.	AB	H	2B	3B	HR	RBI	BB	SO	OBP	Slg.
L	.273	128	35	5	1	2	11	12	17	.338	.375	R	.258	287	74	9	1	2	18	31	43	.352	.317

CLARK, DOUG — OF

PERSONAL: Born March 5, 1976, in Springfield, Mass. ... 6-2/207. ... Bats left, throws right. ... Full name: Douglas Dwyer Clark. ... College: Massachusetts. **TRANSACTIONS/CAREER NOTES:** Selected by San Francisco Giants organization in seventh round of 1998 free-agent draft. ... Signed as a free agent by Oakland Athletics organization (November 3, 2005).

2006 GAMES PLAYED BY POSITION (MLB): OF—1.

C

Year	Team (League)	Pos.	G	AB	R	H	2B	3B	HR	RBI	BB	SO	HBP	GDP	SB-CS	Avg.	OBP	SLG	OPS	E	Avg.
1998— Salem-Keizer (N'west)	OF		59	227	49	76	8	6	3	41	32	31	3	1	12-8	.335	.422	.463	.885	5	.929
1999— Bakersfield (Calif.)	OF		118	420	67	137	17	2	11	58	59	89	5	5	17-11	.326	.415	.455	.870	9	.956
— Shreveport (Texas)	OF		15	50	6	11	3	0	1	6	4	9	0	2	0-0	.220	.278	.340	.618	0	1.000
2000— Shreveport (Texas)	OF		131	492	68	134	20	7	10	75	43	102	5	13	12-4	.272	.333	.402	.735	8	.965
2001— Shreveport (Texas)	OF		123	414	53	114	16	4	6	51	45	83	3	8	20-5	.275	.348	.377	.725	4	.982
2002— Shreveport (Texas)	OF		44	138	13	36	6	1	2	13	19	35	0	4	5-7	.261	.348	.362	.710	2	.974
— Fresno (PCL)	OF		70	212	24	57	9	1	5	19	15	52	5	5	3-3	.269	.330	.392	.722	2	.982
2003— Fresno (PCL)	OF		13	21	4	5	0	0	0	0	2	3	0	0	0-1	.238	.304	.238	.542	0	1.000
— Norwich (East.)	OF		113	396	47	119	23	4	4	49	45	67	2	9	8-5	.301	.371	.409	.780	0	1.000
2004— Norwich (East.)	OF		140	537	82	157	23	13	10	71	44	103	3	9	33-8	.292	.348	.439	.787	3	.906
2005— Norwich (East.)	OF-DH		127	472	81	149	30	5	13	59	35	87	5	6	29-12	.316	.367	.483	.850	4	.992
— San Francisco (N.L.)			8	5	2	0	0	0	0	0	1	2	0	0	0-0	.000	.167	.000	.167	0	...
2006— Sacramento (PCL)			122	494	93	142	22	2	15	67	57	104	8	10	25-8	.287	.366	.431	.797	2	.992
— Oakland (A.L.)	OF		6	6	0	1	0	0	0	0	0	3	0	0	1-0	.167	.167	.167	.333	0	...
American League totals (1 year)			6	6	0	1	0	0	0	0	0	3	0	0	1-0	.167	.167	.167	.333	0	
National League totals (1 year)			8	5	2	0	0	0	0	0	1	2	0	0	0-0	.000	.167	.000	.167	0	
Major League totals (2 years)			14	11	2	1	0	0	0	0	1	5	0	0	1-0	.091	.167	.091	.258	0	

2006 LEFTY-RIGHTY SPLITS

vs.	Avg.	AB	H	2B	3B	HR	RBI	BB	SO	OBP	Slg.	vs.	Avg.	AB	H	2B	3B	HR	RBI	BB	SO	OBP	Slg.
L	.000	0	0	0	0	0	0	0	0	.000	.000	R	.167	6	1	0	0	0	0	0	3	.167	.167

CLARK, HOWIE — 1F/OF

PERSONAL: Born February 13, 1974, in San Diego... 5-11/180. ... Bats left, throws right. ... Full name: Howard Roddy Clark. ... High school: Huntington Beach (Calif.).
TRANSACTIONS/CAREER NOTES: Selected by Baltimore Orioles organization in 27th round of 1992 free-agent draft. ... Signed by Yucatan of the Mexican League (2001). ... Signed by Chico of independent Western League (August 2001). ... Signed as a free agent by Orioles organization (October 8, 2001). ... Signed as a free agent by Toronto Blue Jays organization (November 5, 2002). ... Signed as a free agent by Pittsburgh Pirates organization (November 18, 2004). ... Signed as a free agent by Orioles organization (December 20, 2005).
2006 GAMES PLAYED BY POSITION (MLB): 3B—1, DH—1.

Year	Team (League)	Pos.	G	AB	R	H	2B	3B	HR	RBI	BB	SO	HBP	GDP	SB-CS	Avg.	OBP	SLG	OPS	E	Avg.
1992— GC Orioles (GCL)	2B-3B-1B	43	138	12	33	7	1	0	6	12	21	2	2	1-2	.239	.309	.304	.614	7	.948
1993— Albany (S. Atl.)	2B	7	17	2	4	0	0	0	1	0	3	0	1	1-0	.235	.235	.235	.471	2	.833
— Bluefield (Appal.)	2B-OF-1B	58	180	29	53	10	1	3	30	26	34	4	4	2-2	.294	.388	.411	.799	10	.900
1994— Albany (S. Atl.)	1B-2B	108	353	56	95	22	7	2	47	51	58	7	7	5-4	.269	.371	.388	.759	14	.978
— Frederick (Carolina)	2B	2	7	1	1	1	0	0	0	0	0	0	1	0-0	.143	.143	.286	.429	0	1.000
1995— High Desert (Calif.)	3B-2B-OF 1B-C-SS	100	329	50	85	20	2	5	40	32	51	4	4	12-6	.258	.329	.377	.706	21	.920
1996— Bowie (East.)	2B-OF-1B 3B-C-SS	127	449	55	122	29	3	4	52	59	54	2	8	2-8	.272	.354	.376	.730	14	.975
1997— Bowie (East.)	3B-2B-1B	105	314	39	90	16	0	9	37	32	38	1	5	2-2	.287	.351	.424	.775	20	.909
1998— Bowie (East.)	OF-1B-2B 3B	88	276	37	79	16	0	9	45	29	42	3	7	1-1	.286	.359	.442	.801	6	.954
— Rochester (Int'l)	1B-2B-3B	30	95	13	22	4	1	3	8	9	11	0	2	1-2	.232	.298	.389	.688	2	.983
1999— Bowie (East.)	2B-1B-OF C	39	126	17	37	6	0	2	12	10	12	3	0	2-0	.294	.360	.389	.749	0	1.000
— Rochester (Int'l)	OF-2B-3B 1B	79	279	33	82	19	4	6	28	34	24	1	8	1-2	.294	.370	.455	.825	2	.988
2000— Bowie (East.)	OF-1B 1B	13	53	11	18	6	0	1	9	3	6	1	1	0-0	.340	.379	.509	.889	0	1.000
— Rochester (Int'l)	2B-OF-3B 1B	54	189	25	54	10	0	3	21	26	14	1	4	3-1	.286	.373	.386	.760	5	.966
2001— Yucatan (Mex.)		121	493	68	164	42	7	5	64	43	47	...	...	5-4	.333	...	.477	...	2	.993
— Chico (West.)		4	15	3	8	1	0	0	2	1	1	...	...	0-...	.533	...	.667	...	...	...
2002— Rochester (Int'l)	OF-1B-2B 3B	108	418	57	129	21	4	7	43	41	28	2	11	3-4	.309	.369	.428	.797	8	.976
— Baltimore (A.L.)	DH-OF-1B	14	53	3	16	5	0	0	4	3	6	2	5	0-0	.302	.362	.396	.758	0	1.000
2003— Syracuse (Int'l)	2B-1B-OF DH-3B	66	252	29	65	14	1	4	30	21	20	3	3	1-0	.258	.316	.369	.685	9	.970
— Toronto (A.L.)	3B-DH-OF 2B-1B-SS	38	70	9	25	3	1	0	7	3	6	2	3	0-1	.357	.400	.429	.829	2	.959
2004— Toronto (A.L.)	OF-1B-DH 2B-3B	40	115	17	25	6	0	3	12	13	15	0	2	0-0	.217	.292	.348	.640	1	.993
— Syracuse (Int'l)	OF-2B-3B 1B-DH	72	256	43	80	14	2	6	32	40	18	3	1	1-0	.313	.407	.453	.860	10	.959
2005— GC Pirates (GCL)	OF-DH-1B 3B	8	27	7	13	3	1	0	4	3	2	0	1	0-0	.481	.533	.667	1.200	1	.950
— Altoona (East.)	DH-OF	31	110	15	41	3	0	2	13	19	5	0	1	2-1	.373	.462	.455	.916	2	.917
2006— Ottawa (Int'l)		86	308	41	81	16	1	3	27	36	28	2	5	2-2	.263	.342	.351	.693	5	.979
— Baltimore (A.L.)	3B-DH	7	7	1	1	0	0	0	0	2	2	0	0	0-0	.143	.333	.143	.476	0	...
Major League totals (4 years)		99	245	30	67	14	1	3	23	21	29	4	10	0-1	.273	.338	.376	.714	3	.986

2006 LEFTY-RIGHTY SPLITS

vs.	Avg.	AB	H	2B	3B	HR	RBI	BB	SO	OBP	Slg.	vs.	Avg.	AB	H	2B	3B	HR	RBI	BB	SO	OBP	Slg.
L	.500	2	1	0	0	0	0	0	1	.500	.500	R	.000	5	0	0	0	0	0	2	1	.286	.000

CLARK, TONY — 1B/DH

PERSONAL: Born June 15, 1972, in Newton, Kan. ... 6-7/245. ... Bats both, throws right. ... Full name: Anthony Christopher Clark. ... High school: Valhalla (El Cajon, Calif.), then Christian (El Cajon, Calif.). ... College: San Diego State. **TRANSACTIONS/CAREER NOTES:** Selected by Detroit Tigers organization in first round (second pick overall) of 1990 free-agent draft. ... On disabled list (May 26-June 10, 1999); included rehabilitation assignment to Toledo. ... On disabled list (May 13-June 12, July 15-September 1 and September 19, 2000-remainder of season); included rehabilitation assignments to Toledo. ... Claimed on waivers by Boston Red Sox (November 20, 2001). ... Signed as a free agent by New York Mets organization (February 20, 2003). ... Signed as a free agent by New York Yankees (January 12, 2004). ... Signed as a free agent by Arizona Diamondbacks (January 26, 2005). ... On disabled list (July 18-August 25, 2006); included rehabilitation assignment to Tucson. **STATISTICAL NOTES:** Hit three home runs in one game (August 28, 2004). ... Career major league grand slams: 2.
2006 GAMES PLAYED BY POSITION (MLB): 1B—53.

Year	Team (League)	Pos.	G	AB	R	H	2B	3B	HR	RBI	BB	SO	HBP	GDP	SB-CS	Avg.	OBP	SLG	OPS	E	Avg.
1990— Bristol (Appal.)	OF	OF	25	73	2	12	2	0	1	8	6	28	1	0	0-0	.164	.238	.233	.470	0	1.000
1991— Niagara Falls (NYP)		Did not play.																			
1992— Niagara Falls (NYP)	OF	27	85	12	26	9	0	5	17	9	34	0	0	1-0	.306	.372	.588	.961	0	1.000
1993— Lakeland (Fla. St.)	OF	36	117	14	31	4	1	1	22	18	32	0	1	0-1	.265	.358	.342	.700	2	.944
1994— Trenton (East.)	DH-1B	107	394	50	110	25	0	21	86	40	113	1	0	0-4	.279	.346	.503	.848	13	.977
— Toledo (Int'l)	1B-DH	25	92	10	24	4	0	2	13	12	25	0	1	2-0	.261	.340	.370	.709	0	1.000
1995— Toledo (Int'l)	1B-DH	110	405	50	98	17	2	14	63	52	129	3	8	0-2	.242	.330	.398	.728	13	.981
— Detroit (A.L.)	1B	27	101	10	24	5	1	3	11	8	30	0	2	0-0	.238	.294	.396	.690	4	.985
1996— Toledo (Int'l)	1B-DH	55	194	42	58	7	1	14	36	31	58	0	3	1-1	.299	.396	.562	.957	3	.993
— Detroit (A.L.)	1B-DH	100	376	56	94	14	0	27	72	29	127	0	7	0-1	.250	.299	.503	.802	6	.993
1997— Detroit (A.L.)	1B-DH	159	580	105	160	28	3	32	117	93	144	3	11	1-3	.276	.376	.500	.876	10	.993
1998— Detroit (A.L.)	1B-DH	157	602	84	175	37	0	34	103	63	128	3	16	3-3	.291	.358	.522	.880	13	.991
1999— Detroit (A.L.)	1B-DH	143	536	74	150	29	0	31	99	64	133	6	14	2-1	.280	.361	.507	.869	10	.992
— Toledo (Int'l)	1B	1	3	0	0	0	0	0	0	0	1	0	0	0-0	.000	.250	.000	.250	0	1.000
2000— Detroit (A.L.)	1B-DH	60	208	32	57	14	0	13	37	24	51	0	10	0-0	.274	.349	.529	.878	4	.993
— Toledo (Int'l)	1B	6	22	1	2	1	0	1	2	1	1	0	0	0-0	.091	.130	.273	.403	0	1.000
2001— Detroit (A.L.)	1B-DH	126	428	67	123	29	3	16	75	62	108	1	14	0-1	.287	.374	.481	.856	3	.996
2002— Boston (A.L.)	1B-DH	90	275	25	57	12	1	3	29	21	57	1	11	0-0	.207	.265	.291	.556	6	.992
2003— St. Lucie (Fla. St.)	1B	4	4	0	1	0	0	0	0	0	0	1	0	0-0	.250	.250	.250	.500	1	1.000
— New York (N.L.)	1B-OF	125	254	29	59	13	0	16	43	24	73	1	8	0-0	.232	.300	.472	.772	4	.992
2004— New York (A.L.)	1B-DH	106	253	37	56	12	0	16	49	26	92	2	6	0-0	.221	.297	.459	.755	4	.994
2005— Arizona (N.L.)	1B-DH	130	349	47	106	22	2	30	87	37	88	1	10	0-0	.304	.366	.636	1.003	2	.997
2006— Tucson (PCL)		2	6	2	2	0	0	1	1	0	1	0	0	0-0	.333	.429	.833	1.262	0	1.000
— Arizona (N.L.)	1B	79	132	13	26	4	0	6	16	13	40	1	2	0-0	.197	.279	.364	.643	2	.993
American League totals (9 years)		968	3359	490	896	180	8	175	592	390	870	16	91	6-9	.267	.343	.481	.825	60	.992
National League totals (3 years)		334	735	89	191	39	2	52	146	74	201	4	23	0-0	.260	.328	.531	.859	8	.995
Major League totals (12 years)		1302	4094	579	1087	219	10	227	738	464	1071	20	114	6-9	.266	.341	.490	.831	68	.993

DIVISION SERIES RECORD

Year	Team (League)	Pos.	G	AB	R	H	2B	3B	HR	RBI	BB	SO	HBP	GDP	SB-CS	Avg.	OBP	SLG	OPS	E	Avg.
2004— New York (A.L.)	1B	1	1	0	0	0	0	0	0	0	0	0	0	0-0	.000	.000	.000	.000	0	1.000

CHAMPIONSHIP SERIES RECORD

Year	Team (League)	Pos.	G	AB	R	H	2B	3B	HR	RBI	BB	SO	HBP	GDP	SB-CS	Avg.	OBP	SLG	OPS	E	Avg.
2004— New York (A.L.)	1B	5	21	0	3	1	0	1	1	0	9	0	0	0-0	.143	.143	.190	.333	1	.976

ALL-STAR GAME RECORD

	G	AB	R	H	2B	3B	HR	RBI	BB	SO	HBP	GDP	SB-CS	Avg.	OBP	SLG	OPS	E	Avg.
All-Star Game totals (1 year)	1	1	0	0	0	0	0	0	0	0	0	0	0-0	.000	.000	.000	...	...

2006 LEFTY-RIGHTY SPLITS

vs.	Avg.	AB	H	2B	3B	HR	RBI	BB	SO	OBP	Slg.	vs.	Avg.	AB	H	2B	3B	HR	RBI	BB	SO	OBP	Slg.
L	.125	24	3	0	0	0	2	5	10	.276	.125	R	.213	108	23	4	0	6	14	8	30	.280	.417

CLAUSSEN, BRANDON — P

PERSONAL: Born May 1, 1979, in Rapid City, S.D. ... 6-1/200. ... Throws left, bats right. ... Full name: Brandon Allen Falker Claussen. ... Name pronounced: CLAW-sin. ... High school: Goddard (Roswell, N.M.). ... Junior college: Howard (Texas). **TRANSACTIONS/CAREER NOTES:** Selected by New York Yankees organization in 34th round of 1998 free-agent draft. ... Traded by Yankees with P Charlie Manning and cash to Cincinnati Reds for 3B Aaron Boone (July 31, 2003). ... On disabled list (June 17, 2006-remainder of season); included rehabilitation assignment to Louisville.

CAREER HITTING: 10-for-99 (.101), 5 R, 0 2B, 0 3B, 0 HR, 2 RBI.

Year	Team (League)	W	L	Pct.	ERA	WHIP	G	GS	CG	ShO	Hld.	Sv.-Opp.	IP	H	R	ER	HR	BB-IBB	SO	Avg.
1999— GC Yankees (GCL)		0	1	.000	3.18	0.79	5	2	0	0	...	0-...	11.1	7	4	4	2	2-0	16	.175
— Staten Is. (N.Y.-Penn)		6	4	.600	3.38	1.14	12	12	1	0	...	0-...	72.0	70	30	27	4	12-2	89	.253
— Greensboro (S. Atl.)		0	1	.000	10.50	1.67	1	1	1	0	...	0-...	6.0	8	7	7	1	2-0	5	.296
2000— Greensboro (S. Atl.)		8	5	.615	4.05	1.38	17	17	1	0	...	0-...	97.2	91	49	44	9	44-0	98	.251
— Tampa (Fla. St.)		2	5	.286	3.10	1.26	9	9	1	0	...	0-...	52.1	49	24	18	1	17-0	44	.245
2001— Tampa (Fla. St.)		5	2	.714	2.73	1.07	8	8	0	0	...	0-...	56.0	47	21	17	2	13-0	69	.224
— Norwich (East.)		9	2	.818	2.13	1.19	21	21	1	0	...	0-...	131.0	101	42	31	6	55-0	151	.210
2002— Columbus (Int'l)		2	8	.200	3.28	1.40	15	15	0	0	...	0-...	93.1	85	47	34	4	46-3	73	.242
2003— Tampa (Fla. St.)		1	0	1.000	1.64	0.86	4	4	0	0	...	0-...	22.0	16	5	4	0	3-0	26	.198
— New York (A.L.)		1	0	1.000	1.42	1.42	1	1	0	0	...	0-0	6.1	8	2	1	1	1-0	5	.296
— Columbus (Int'l)		2	1	.667	2.75	1.03	11	11	1	0	...	0-...	68.2	53	28	21	4	18-0	39	.213
— Louisville (Int'l)		0	1	.000	7.47	1.42	3	3	0	0	...	0-...	15.2	17	13	13	3	6-0	16	.293
2004— Louisville (Int'l)		8	6	.571	4.66	1.45	18	18	0	0	...	0-...	100.1	98	56	52	10	47-0	111	.256
— Cincinnati (N.L.)		2	8	.200	6.14	1.74	14	14	0	0	...	0-...	66.0	80	50	45	9	35-2	45	.299
2005— Cincinnati (N.L.)		10	11	.476	4.21	1.41	29	29	0	0	...	0-...	166.2	178	89	78	24	57-5	121	.273
2006— Louisville (Int'l)		0	2	.000	8.34	1.72	5	5	0	0	...	0-...	22.2	31	21	21	5	8-0	18	.330
— Cincinnati (N.L.)		3	8	.273	6.19	1.57	14	14	0	0	...	0-0	77.0	93	56	53	14	28-1	57	.301
American League totals (1 year)		1	0	1.000	1.42	1.42	1	1	0	0		0-0	6.1	8	2	1	1	1-0	5	.296
National League totals (3 years)		15	27	.357	5.12	1.52	57	57	0	0		0-0	309.2	351	195	176	47	120-8	223	.285
Major League totals (4 years)		16	27	.372	5.04	1.52	58	58	0	0		0-0	316.0	359	197	177	48	121-8	228	.286

2006 LEFTY-RIGHTY SPLITS

vs.	Avg.	AB	H	2B	3B	HR	RBI	BB	SO	OBP	Slg.	vs.	Avg.	AB	H	2B	3B	HR	RBI	BB	SO	OBP	Slg.
L	.164	55	9	4	0	1	6	3	15	.242	.291	R	.331	254	84	18	0	13	42	25	42	.396	.555

CLAYTON, ROYCE — SS

PERSONAL: Born January 2, 1970, in Burbank, Calif. ... 6-0/185. ... Bats right, throws right. ... Full name: Royce Spencer Clayton. ... High school: St. Bernard (Playa del Rey, Calif.). **TRANSACTIONS/CAREER NOTES:** Selected by San Francisco Giants organization in first round (15th pick overall) of 1988 free-agent draft; pick received as compensation for Cincinnati Reds signing Type B free-agent OF Eddie Milner. ... Traded by Giants with a player to be named to St. Louis Cardinals for Ps Allen Watson, Rich DeLucia and Doug Creek (December 14, 1995); Cardinals acquired 2B Chris Wimmer to complete deal (January 16, 1996). ... On disabled list (June 24-July 9, 1998). ... Traded by Cardinals with P Todd Stottlemyre to Texas Rangers for P Darren Oliver, 3B Fernando Tatis and a player to be named (July 31, 1998); Cardinals acquired OF Mark Little to complete deal (August 9, 1998). ... On disabled list (May 1-21, 1999); included rehabilitation assignment to Oklahoma. ... Traded by Rangers to Chicago White Sox for Ps Aaron Myette and Brian Schmack (December 14, 2000). ... Released by White Sox (September 8, 2002). ... Signed by Milwaukee Brewers (December 11, 2002). ... Signed as a free agent by Colorado Rockies organization (January 5, 2004). ... Signed as a free agent by Arizona Diamondbacks (December 21, 2004). ... Signed by Washington Nationals organization (February 2, 2006). ... Traded by Nationals with Ps Gary Majewski, Bill Bray and Daryl Thompson and IF Brendan Harris to Cincinnati Reds for OF Austin Kearns, SS Felipe Lopez and P Ryan Wagner (July 13, 2006). **STATISTICAL NOTES:** Career major league grand slams: 1.

C

2006 GAMES PLAYED BY POSITION (MLB): SS—129.

Year Team (League)	Pos.	G	AB	R	H	2B	3B	HR	RBI	BB	SO	HBP	GDP	SB-CS	Avg.	OBP	SLG	OPS	E	Avg.
									BATTING										FIELDING	
1988— Everett (N'west)	SS	60	212	35	55	4	0	3	29	27	54	3	8	10-4	.259	.348	.321	.669	35	.873
1989— Clinton (Midw.)	SS	104	385	39	91	13	3	0	24	39	101	4	6	28-16	.236	.309	.286	.595	31	.943
— San Jose (Calif.)	SS	28	92	5	11	2	0	0	4	13	27	1	5	10-1	.120	.236	.141	.377	8	.939
1990— San Jose (Calif.)	SS	123	460	80	123	15	10	7	71	68	98	4	13	33-15	.267	.364	.389	.753	37	.938
1991— Shreveport (Texas)	SS	126	485	84	136	22	8	5	68	61	104	3	7	36-10	.280	.361	.390	.751	29	.950
— San Francisco (N.L.)	SS	9	26	0	3	1	0	0	2	1	6	0	1	0-0	.115	.148	.154	.302	3	.880
1992— San Francisco (N.L.)	SS-3B	98	321	31	72	7	4	4	24	26	63	0	11	8-4	.224	.281	.308	.589	11	.973
— Phoenix (PCL)	SS	48	192	30	46	6	2	3	18	17	25	0	8	15-6	.240	.300	.339	.639	7	.971
1993— San Francisco (N.L.)	SS	153	549	54	155	21	5	6	70	38	91	5	16	11-10	.282	.331	.372	.702	27	.963
1994— San Francisco (N.L.)	SS	108	385	38	91	14	6	3	30	30	74	3	7	23-3	.236	.295	.327	.623	14	.973
1995— San Francisco (N.L.)	SS	138	509	56	124	29	3	5	58	38	109	3	9	24-9	.244	.298	.342	.640	20	.969
1996— St. Louis (N.L.)	SS	129	491	64	136	20	4	6	35	33	89	1	13	33-15	.277	.321	.371	.692	15	.972
1997— St. Louis (N.L.)	SS	154	576	75	153	39	5	9	61	33	109	3	19	30-10	.266	.306	.398	.704	19	.973
1998— St. Louis (N.L.)	SS	90	355	59	83	19	1	4	29	40	51	2	10	19-6	.234	.313	.327	.640	13	.970
— Texas (A.L.)	SS	52	186	30	53	12	1	5	24	13	32	1	6	5-5	.285	.330	.441	.771	7	.972
1999— Texas (A.L.)	SS	133	465	69	134	21	5	14	52	39	100	4	6	8-6	.288	.346	.445	.792	* 25	.961
— Oklahoma (PCL)	SS	2	7	1	1	0	0	0	1	3	3	0	0	0-0	.143	.400	.143	.543	0	1.000
2000— Texas (A.L.)	SS	148	513	70	124	21	5	14	54	42	92	3	21	11-7	.242	.301	.384	.685	16	.977
2001— Chicago (A.L.)	SS	135	433	62	114	21	4	9	60	33	72	3	16	10-7	.263	.315	.393	.708	7	.988
2002— Chicago (A.L.)	SS	112	342	51	86	14	2	7	35	20	67	3	7	5-1	.251	.295	.366	.661	5	.989
2003— Milwaukee (N.L.)	SS	146	483	49	110	16	1	11	39	49	92	3	25	5-2	.228	.301	.333	.634	14	.977
2004— Colorado (N.L.)	SS	146	574	95	160	36	4	8	54	48	125	4	13	10-5	.279	.338	.397	.735	9	.986
2005— Arizona (N.L.)	SS	143	522	59	141	28	4	2	44	38	105	1	19	13-3	.270	.320	.351	.670	11	.982
2006— Wash. (N.L.)	SS	87	305	36	82	22	1	0	27	19	53	4	8	8-3	.269	.315	.348	.663	11	.970
— Cincinnati (N.L.)	SS	50	149	13	35	8	0	2	13	11	32	1	3	6-3	.235	.290	.329	.619	7	.958
American League totals (5 years)		580	1939	282	511	89	17	49	225	147	363	14	56	39-26	.264	.317	.403	.720	60	.977
National League totals (12 years)		1451	5245	629	1345	260	38	60	486	404	999	30	152	190-73	.256	.311	.355	.666	174	.973
Major League totals (16 years)		2031	7184	911	1856	349	55	109	711	551	1362	44	208	229-99	.258	.313	.368	.680	234	.974

DIVISION SERIES RECORD

Year Team (League)	Pos.	G	AB	R	H	2B	3B	HR	RBI	BB	SO	HBP	GDP	SB-CS	Avg.	OBP	SLG	OPS	E	Avg.
1996— St. Louis (N.L.)	SS	2	6	1	2	0	0	0	0	3	1	0	0	0-1	.333	.556	.333	.889	0	1.000
1998— Texas (A.L.)	SS	3	9	0	2	0	0	0	0	0	4	0	1	0-0	.222	.222	.222	.444	1	.929
1999— Texas (A.L.)	SS	3	10	0	0	0	0	0	0	0	1	0	0	0-0	.000	.000	.000	.000	0	1.000
Division series totals (3 years)		8	25	1	4	0	0	0	0	3	6	0	1	0-1	.160	.250	.160	.410	1	.973

CHAMPIONSHIP SERIES RECORD

Year Team (League)	Pos.	G	AB	R	H	2B	3B	HR	RBI	BB	SO	HBP	GDP	SB-CS	Avg.	OBP	SLG	OPS	E	Avg.
1996— St. Louis (N.L.)	SS	5	20	4	7	0	0	0	1	1	4	0	0	1-1	.350	.381	.350	.731	2	.913

ALL-STAR GAME RECORD

		G	AB	R	H	2B	3B	HR	RBI	BB	SO	HBP	GDP	SB-CS	Avg.	OBP	SLG	OPS	E	Avg.
		1	1	0	0	0	0	0	0	1	0	0	0	0-0	.000	.000	.000	.000	0	1.000
All-Star Game totals (1 year)																				

2006 LEFTY-RIGHTY SPLITS

vs.	Avg.	AB	H	2B	3B	HR	RBI	BB	SO	OBP	Slg.	vs.	Avg.	AB	H	2B	3B	HR	RBI	BB	SO	OBP	Slg.
L	.303	132	40	5	1	1	16	12	23	.365	.379	R	.239	322	77	25	0	1	24	18	62	.282	.326

CLEMENS, ROGER — P

PERSONAL: Born August 4, 1962, in Dayton, Ohio. ... 6-4/235. ... Throws right, bats right. ... Full name: William Roger Clemens. ... High school: Spring Woods (Houston). ... College: Texas. **TRANSACTIONS/CAREER NOTES:** Selected by New York Mets organization in 12th round of June 1981 free-agent draft; did not sign. ... Selected by Boston Red Sox organization in first round (19th pick overall) of June 1983 free-agent draft. ... On disabled list (July 8-August 3 and August 21, 1985-remainder of season). ... On suspended list (April 26-May 3, 1991). ... On disabled list (June 19-July 16, 1993); included rehabilitation assignment to Pawtucket. ... On disabled list (April 16-June 2, 1995); included rehabilitation assignments to Sarasota and Pawtucket. ... Signed as a free agent by Toronto Blue Jays (December 13, 1996). ... Traded by Blue Jays to New York Yankees for Ps David Wells and Graeme Lloyd and 2B Homer Bush (February 18, 1999). ... On disabled list (April 28-May 21, 1999; and June 15-July 2, 2000). ... On disabled list (July 13-August 7, 2002); included rehabilitation assignments to Tampa and Norwich. ... Signed as a free agent by Houston Astros (January 19, 2004).
RECORDS: Shares major league record for most strikeouts, 9-inning game (20, April 29, 1986; and September 18, 1996). **HONORS:** Named Major League Player of the Year by THE SPORTING NEWS (1986). ... Named A.L. Pitcher of the Year by THE SPORTING NEWS (1986, 1991, 1997, 1998 and 2001). ... Named righthanded pitcher on THE SPORTING NEWS A.L. All-Star team (1986-87, 1991, 1997 and 2001). ... Named A.L. Most Valuable Player by Baseball Writers' Association of America (1986). ... Named A.L. Cy Young Award winner by Baseball Writers' Association of America (1986, 1987, 1991, 1997, 1998 and 2001). ... Named N.L. Cy Young Award winner by Baseball Writers' Association of America (2004). **MISCELLANEOUS NOTES:** Singled in only appearance as pinch hitter (1996).
CAREER HITTING: 30-for-177 (.169), 5 R, 6 2B, 0 3B, 0 HR, 12 RBI.

Year Team (League)	W	L	Pct.	ERA	WHIP	G	GS	CG	ShO	Hld.	Sv.-Opp.	IP	H	R	ER	HR	BB-IBB	SO	Avg.
1983— Winter Haven (FSL)	3	1	.750	1.24	0.76	4	4	3	1	...	0-...	29.0	22	4	4	0	0-0	36	.206
— New Britain (East.)	4	1	.800	1.38	0.83	7	7	1	1	...	0-...	52.0	31	8	8	1	12-0	59	.167
1984— Pawtucket (Int'l)	2	3	.400	1.93	1.14	7	6	3	1	...	0-...	46.2	39	12	10	3	14-0	50	.228
— Boston (A.L.)	9	4	.692	4.32	1.31	21	20	5	1	0	0-0	133.1	146	67	64	13	29-3	126	.271
1985— Boston (A.L.)	7	5	.583	3.29	1.22	15	15	3	1	0	0-0	98.1	83	38	36	5	37-0	74	.228
1986— Boston (A.L.)	* 24	4	* .857	2.48	0.97	33	33	10	1	0	0-0	254.0	179	77	70	21	67-0	238	* .195
1987— Boston (A.L.)	• 20	9	.690	2.97	1.18	36	* 18	* 7	0	0	0-0	281.2	248	100	93	19	83-4	256	.235
1988— Boston (A.L.)	18	12	.600	2.93	1.06	35	35	* 14	* 8	0	0-0	264.0	217	93	86	17	62-4	* 291	.220
1989— Boston (A.L.)	17	11	.607	3.13	1.22	35	35	8	3	0	0-0	253.1	215	101	88	20	93-5	230	.231
1990— Boston (A.L.)	21	6	.778	* 1.93	1.08	31	31	7	* 4	0	0-0	228.1	193	59	49	7	54-3	209	.208
1991— Boston (A.L.)	18	10	.643	* 2.62	1.05	35	* 35	13	* 4	0	0-0	* 271.1	219	93	79	15	65-12	* 241	.221
1992— Boston (A.L.)	18	11	.621	* 2.41	1.07	32	32	11	* 5	0	0-0	246.2	203	80	66	11	62-5	208	.224
1993— Boston (A.L.)	11	14	.440	4.46	1.26	29	29	2	1	0	0-0	191.2	175	99	95	17	67-4	160	.244
— Pawtucket (Int'l)	0	0	...	0.00	1.36	1	1	0	0	0	0-...	3.2	1	0	0	0	4-0	8	.091
1994— Boston (A.L.)	9	7	.563	2.85	1.14	24	24	3	1	0	0-0	170.2	124	62	54	15	71-1	168	* .204
1995— Sarasota (Fla. St.)	0	0	...	0.00	0.50	1	1	0	0	0	0-0	4.0	0	0	0	0	2-0	7	.000
— Pawtucket (Int'l)	0	0	...	0.00	0.80	1	1	0	0	0	0-0	5.0	1	0	0	0	3-0	5	.063
— Boston (A.L.)	10	5	.667	4.18	1.44	23	23	0	0	0	0-0	140.0	141	70	65	15	60-0	132	.259
1996— Boston (A.L.)	10	13	.435	3.63	1.33	34	34	6	2	0	0-0	242.2	216	106	98	19	106-2	* 257	.237
1997— Toronto (A.L.)	* 21	7	.750	* 2.05	1.03	34	34	* 9	• 3	0	0-0	• 264.0	204	65	60	9	68-1	* 292	.213
1998— Toronto (A.L.)	• 20	6	.769	* 2.65	1.10	33	33	5	3	0	0-0	234.2	169	78	69	11	88-0	* 271	* .198
1999— New York (A.L.)	14	10	.583	4.60	1.47	30	30	1	0	0	0-0	187.2	185	101	96	20	90-0	163	.261

Year Team (League)	W	L	Pct.	ERA	WHIP	G	GS	CG	ShO	Hld.	Sv.-Opp.	IP	H	R	ER	HR	BB-IBB	SO	Avg.
2000— New York (A.L.)	13	8	.619	3.70	1.31	32	32	1	0	0	0-0	204.1	184	96	84	26	84-0	188	.236
2001— New York (A.L.)	20	3	* .870	3.51	1.26	33	33	0	0	0	0-0	220.1	205	94	86	19	72-1	213	.246
2002— New York (A.L.)	13	6	.684	4.35	1.31	29	29	0	0	0	0-0	180.0	172	94	87	18	63-6	192	.250
—Tampa (Fla. St.)	1	0	1.000	5.40	1.40	1	1	0	0	0	0-...	5.0	5	3	3	1	2-0	6	.263
—Norwich (East.)	0	1	.000	1.29	0.71	1	1	0	0	0	...	0-...	7.0	5	1	1	0	0-0	7	.200
2003— New York (A.L.)	17	9	.654	3.91	1.21	33	33	1	1	0	0-0	211.2	199	99	92	24	58-1	190	.247
2004— Houston (N.L.)	18	4	.818	2.98	1.16	33	33	0	0	0	0-0	214.1	169	76	71	15	79-5	218	.217
2005— Houston (N.L.)	13	8	.619	* 1.87	1.01	32	32	1	0	0	0-0	211.1	151	51	44	11	62-5	185	* .198
2006— Lexington (S. Atl.)	0	0	...	3.00	1.00	1	1	0	0	0	0-0	3.0	3	1	1	1	0-0	6	.250
—Corpus Christi (Texas)	1	0	1.000	0.00	0.33	1	1	0	0	0	0-0	6.0	2	0	0	0	0-0	11	.105
—Round Rock (PCL)	1	0	1.000	4.76	1.41	1	1	0	0	0	0-0	5.2	5	3	3	0	3-0	5	.227
—Houston (N.L.)	7	6	.538	2.30	1.04	19	19	0	0	0	0-0	113.1	89	34	29	7	29-1	102	.216
American League totals (20 years)	310	160	.660	3.19	1.18	607	606	117	46	0	0-0	4278.2	3677	1672	1517	321	1379-52	4099	.231
National League totals (3 years)	38	18	.679	2.40	1.07	84	84	1	0	0	0-0	539.0	409	161	144	33	170-11	505	.210
Major League totals (23 years)	348	178	.662	3.10	1.17	691	690	118	46	0	0-0	4817.2	4086	1833	1661	354	1549-63	4604	.228

DIVISION SERIES RECORD

Year Team (League)	W	L	Pct.	ERA	WHIP	G	GS	CG	ShO	Hld.	Sv.-Opp.	IP	H	R	ER	HR	BB-IBB	SO	Avg.
1995— Boston (A.L.)	0	0	...	3.86	0.86	1	1	0	0	0		7.0	5	3	3	0	1-0	5	.192
1999— New York (A.L.)	1	0	1.000	0.00	0.71	1	1	0	0	0		7.0	3	0	0	0	2-0	2	.125
2000— New York (A.L.)	0	2	.000	8.18	1.91	2	2	0	0	0		11.0	13	10	10	1	8-1	10	.302
2001— New York (A.L.)	0	1	.000	5.40	1.56	2	2	0	0	0		8.1	9	5	5	1	4-0	6	.265
2002— New York (A.L.)	0	0	...	6.35	1.94	1	1	0	0	0		5.2	8	4	4	1	3-0	5	.348
2003— New York (A.L.)	1	0	1.000	1.29	0.86	1	1	0	0	0		7.0	5	1	1	1	1-0	6	.192
2004— Houston (N.L.)	1	0	1.000	3.00	1.67	2	2	0	0	0		12.0	12	5	4	1	8-0	12	.267
2005— Houston (N.L.)	1	1	.500	5.63	1.25	2	1	0	0	0		8.0	7	5	5	1	3-0	6	.233
Division series totals (8 years)	4	4	.500	4.36	1.39	12	11	0	0	0		66.0	62	33	32	6	30-1	52	.247

CHAMPIONSHIP SERIES RECORD

Year Team (League)	W	L	Pct.	ERA	WHIP	G	GS	CG	ShO	Hld.	Sv.-Opp.	IP	H	R	ER	HR	BB-IBB	SO	Avg.
1986— Boston (A.L.)	1	1	.500	4.37	1.28	3	3	0	0	0	0-0	22.2	22	12	11	1	7-0	17	.244
1988— Boston (A.L.)	0	0	...	3.86	0.86	1	1	0	0	0	0-0	7.0	6	3	3	1	0-0	8	.231
1990— Boston (A.L.)	0	1	.000	3.52	1.57	2	2	0	0	0	0-0	7.2	7	3	3	0	5-0	4	.259
1999— New York (A.L.)	0	1	.000	22.50	4.00	1	1	0	0	0	0-0	2.0	6	5	5	1	2-0	2	.462
2000— New York (A.L.)	1	0	1.000	0.00	0.33	1	1	1	1	0	0-0	9.0	1	0	0	0	2-0	15	.036
2001— New York (A.L.)	0	0	...	1.00	1.00	1	1	0	0	0	0-0	5.0	1	0	0	0	4-0	7	.063
2003— New York (A.L.)	1	0	1.000	5.00	1.44	2	2	0	0	0	0-0	9.0	11	6	5	2	2-0	8	.297
2004— Houston (N.L.)	1	1	.500	4.15	0.92	2	2	0	0	0	0-0	13.0	10	6	6	3	2-0	9	.217
2005— Houston (N.L.)	1	0	1.000	3.00	1.33	1	1	0	0	0	0-0	6.0	6	2	2	0	2-0	1	.286
Champ. series totals (9 years)	5	4	.556	3.87	1.18	14	14	1	1	0	0-0	81.1	70	37	35	8	26-0	71	.230

WORLD SERIES RECORD

Year Team (League)	W	L	Pct.	ERA	WHIP	G	GS	CG	ShO	Hld.	Sv.-Opp.	IP	H	R	ER	HR	BB-IBB	SO	Avg.
1986— Boston (A.L.)	0	0	...	3.18	1.32	2	2	0	0	0	0-0	11.1	9	5	4	0	6-0	11	.225
1999— New York (A.L.)	1	0	1.000	1.17	0.78	1	1	0	0	0	0-0	7.2	4	1	1	0	2-0	4	.154
2000— New York (A.L.)	1	0	1.000	0.00	0.25	1	1	0	0	0	0-0	8.0	2	0	0	0	0-0	9	.074
2001— New York (A.L.)	1	0	1.000	1.35	1.05	2	2	0	0	0	0-0	13.1	10	2	2	0	4-0	19	.204
2003— New York (A.L.)	0	0	...	3.86	1.14	1	1	0	0	0	0-0	7.0	8	3	3	1	0-0	5	.286
2005— Houston (N.L.)	0	0	...	13.50	2.00	1	1	0	0	0	0-0	2.0	4	3	3	1	0-0	1	.400
World series totals (6 years)	3	0	1.000	2.37	0.99	8	8	0	0	0	0-0	49.1	37	14	13	2	12-0	49	.206

ALL-STAR GAME RECORD

	W	L	Pct.	ERA	WHIP	G	GS	CG	ShO	Hld.	Sv.-Opp.	IP	H	R	ER	HR	BB-IBB	SO	Avg.
All-Star Game totals (10 years)	1	1	.500	4.15	0.92	10	3	0	0	0	0-0	13.0	11	9	6	3	1-0	9	.224

2006 LEFTY-RIGHTY SPLITS

vs.	Avg.	AB	H	2B	3B	HR	RBI	BB	SO	OBP	Slg.	vs.	Avg.	AB	H	2B	3B	HR	RBI	BB	SO	OBP	Slg.
L	.254	185	47	11	2	2	13	17	44	.324	.368	R	.185	227	42	8	0	5	18	12	58	.231	.286

CLEMENT, MATT   P

PERSONAL: Born August 12, 1974, in Butler, Pa. ... 6-3/210. ... Throws right, bats right. ... Full name: Matthew Paul Clement. ... Name pronounced: klah-MENT. ... High school: Butler (Pa.). **TRANSACTIONS/CAREER NOTES:** Selected by San Diego Padres organization in third round of 1993 free-agent draft. ... Traded by Padres with OF Eric Owens and P Omar Ortiz to Florida Marlins for OFs Mark Kotsay and Cesar Crespo (March 28, 2001). ... Traded by Marlins with P Antonio Alfonseca to Chicago Cubs for Ps Julian Tavarez, Jose Cueto and Dontrelle Willis and C Ryan Jorgensen (March 27, 2002). ... Signed as a free agent by Boston Red Sox (December 21, 2004). ... On disabled list (June 16, 2006-remainder of season); included rehabilitation assignment to GCL Red Sox. **MISCELLANEOUS NOTES:** Appeared one game as pinch hitter (2001).
CAREER HITTING: 33-for-348 (.095), 22 R, 5 2B, 1 3B, 0 HR, 12 RBI.

Year Team (League)	W	L	Pct.	ERA	WHIP	G	GS	CG	ShO	Hld.	Sv.-Opp.	IP	H	R	ER	HR	BB-IBB	SO	Avg.
1994— Spokane (N'west)	1	1	.500	6.14	2.59	2	2	0	0	...	0-...	7.1	8	7	5	0	11-0	4	.296
—Ariz. Padres (Ariz.)	8	5	.615	4.43	1.22	13	13	0	0	...	0-...	67.0	65	38	33	0	17-0	76	.248
1995— Rancho Cuca. (Calif.)	3	4	.429	4.24	1.92	12	12	0	0	...	0-...	57.1	61	37	27	1	49-0	33	.295
—Idaho Falls (Pio.)	6	3	.667	4.33	1.27	14	14	0	0	...	0-...	81.0	61	53	39	3	42-0	65	.214
1996— Clinton (Midw.)	8	3	.727	2.80	1.22	16	16	1	1	...	0-...	96.1	66	31	30	3	52-0	109	.191
—Rancho Cuca. (Calif.)	4	5	.444	5.59	1.54	11	11	0	0	...	0-...	56.1	61	40	35	8	26-0	75	.280
1997— Rancho Cuca. (Calif.)	6	3	.667	1.60	1.04	14	14	2	1	...	0-...	101.0	74	30	18	3	31-1	109	.202
—Mobile (Sou.)	6	5	.545	2.56	1.31	13	13	1	1	...	0-...	88.0	83	37	25	4	32-0	92	.249
1998— Las Vegas (PCL)	10	9	.526	3.98	1.41	27	27	1	0	...	0-...	171.2	157	94	76	12	85-2	160	.245
—San Diego (N.L.)	2	0	1.000	4.61	1.61	4	2	0	0	0	0-0	13.2	15	8	7	0	7-1	13	.283
1999— San Diego (N.L.)	10	12	.455	4.48	1.53	31	31	0	0	0	0-0	180.2	190	106	90	18	86-2	135	.273
2000— San Diego (N.L.)	13	17	.433	5.14	1.56	34	34	0	0	0	0-0	205.0	194	131	117	22	* 125-4	170	.248
2001— Florida (N.L.)	9	10	.474	5.05	1.52	31	31	0	0	0	0-0	169.1	172	102	95	15	85-2	134	.268
2002— Chicago (N.L.)	12	11	.522	3.60	1.20	32	32	3	2	0	0-0	205.0	162	84	82	18	85-7	215	.215
2003— Chicago (N.L.)	14	12	.538	4.11	1.23	32	32	2	1	0	0-0	201.2	169	100	92	22	79-2	171	.227
2004— Chicago (N.L.)	9	13	.409	3.68	1.28	30	30	0	0	0	0-0	181.0	155	79	74	23	77-4	190	.229
2005— Boston (A.L.)	13	6	.684	4.57	1.36	32	32	1	0	0	0-0	191.0	192	102	97	18	68-1	146	.260
2006— GC Red Sox (GCL)	0	0	...	0.00	1.00	1	1	0	0	0	0-0	1.0	1	0	0	0	0-0	1	.250
—Boston (A.L.)	5	5	.500	6.61	1.76	12	12	0	0	0	0-0	65.1	77	50	48	8	38-0	43	.291
American League totals (2 years)	18	11	.621	5.09	1.46	44	44	1	0	0	0-0	256.1	269	152	145	26	106-1	189	.268
National League totals (7 years)	69	75	.479	4.34	1.38	194	192	5	3	0	0-0	1156.1	1057	610	557	118	544-22	1028	.243
Major League totals (9 years)	87	86	.503	4.47	1.40	238	236	6	3	0	0-0	1412.2	1326	762	702	144	650-23	1217	.248

C

DIVISION SERIES RECORD

Year Team (League)	W	L	Pct.	ERA	WHIP	G	GS	CG	ShO	Hld.	Sv.-Opp.	IP	H	R	ER	HR	BB-IBB	SO	Avg.
2003— Chicago (N.L.)	0	1	.000	7.71	2.57	1	1	0	0	0	0-0	4.2	8	4	4	1	4-0	3	.381
2005— Boston (A.L.)	0	1	.000	21.60	2.10	1	1	0	0	0	0-0	3.1	7	8	8	3	0-0	0	.467
Division series totals (2 years)	0	2	.000	13.50	2.38	2	2	0	0	0	0-0	8.0	15	12	12	4	4-0	3	.417

CHAMPIONSHIP SERIES RECORD

Year Team (League)	W	L	Pct.	ERA	WHIP	G	GS	CG	ShO	Hld.	Sv.-Opp.	IP	H	R	ER	HR	BB-IBB	SO	Avg.
2003— Chicago (N.L.)	1	0	1.000	3.52	0.91	1	1	0	0	0	0-0	7.2	5	3	3	0	2-0	3	.192

ALL-STAR GAME RECORD

	W	L	Pct.	ERA	WHIP	G	GS	CG	ShO	Hld.	Sv.-Opp.	IP	H	R	ER	HR	BB-IBB	SO	Avg.
All-Star Game totals (1 year)	0	0	...	0.00	1.00	1	0	0	0	0	0-0	1.0	0	0	0	0	1-0	1	.000

2006 LEFTY-RIGHTY SPLITS

vs.	Avg.	AB	H	2B	3B	HR	RBI	BB	SO	OBP	Slg.	vs.	Avg.	AB	H	2B	3B	HR	RBI	BB	SO	OBP	Slg.
L	.307	140	43	7	0	5	26	21	12	.401	.464	R	.272	125	34	8	0	3	19	17	31	.381	.408

CLEVLEN, BRENT — OF

PERSONAL: Born October 27, 1983, in Austin, Texas. ... 6-2/190. ... Bats right, throws right. ... Full name: Brent Aaron Clevlen. ..: High school: Westwood (Texas). **TRANSACTIONS/CAREER NOTES:** Selected by Detroit Tigers organization in second round of 2002 free-agent draft.

2006 GAMES PLAYED BY POSITION (MLB): OF—29.

Year Team (League)	Pos.	G	AB	R	H	2B	3B	HR	RBI	BB	SO	HBP	GDP	SB-CS	Avg.	OBP	SLG	OPS	E	Avg.
2002— GC Tigers (GCL)		28	103	14	34	2	3	3	21	8	24	0	0	2-1	.330	.372	.495	.867	3	...
2003— W. Mich. (Mid.)		138	481	67	125	22	7	12	63	72	111	4	16	6-3	.260	.359	.410	.769	10	...
2004— Lakeland (Fla. St.)		117	420	49	94	23	6	6	50	44	127	4	12	2-1	.224	.300	.350	.650	15	...
2005— Lakeland (Fla. St.)	OF	130	494	77	149	28	4	18	102	65	118	5	16	14-5	.302	.387	.484	.871	12	.979
2006— Erie (East.)		109	395	47	91	17	0	11	45	47	138	3	9	6-2	.230	.357	.357	.670	4	.980
— Detroit (A.L.)	OF	31	39	9	11	1	2	3	6	2	15	0	0	0-0	.282	.317	.641	.958	0	1.000
Major League totals (1 year)		31	39	9	11	1	2	3	6	2	15	0	0	0-0	.282	.317	.641	.958	0	1.000

2006 LEFTY-RIGHTY SPLITS

vs.	Avg.	AB	H	2B	3B	HR	RBI	BB	SO	OBP	Slg.	vs.	Avg.	AB	H	2B	3B	HR	RBI	BB	SO	OBP	Slg.
L	.333	24	8	1	2	1	4	1	8	.360	.667	R	.200	15	3	0	0	2	2	1	7	.250	.600

CLOSSER, JD — C

PERSONAL: Born January 15, 1980, in Beech Grove, Ind. ... 5-10/176. ... Bats both, throws right. ... Full name: Jeffrey Darrin Closser. ... High school: Monroe Central (Parker City, Ind.). **TRANSACTIONS/CAREER NOTES:** Selected by Arizona Diamondbacks organization in fifth round of 1998 free-agent draft. ... Traded by Diamondbacks with OF Jack Cust to Colorado Rockies for P Mike Myers (January 7, 2002). ... Claimed on waivers by Milwaukee Brewers (October 13, 2006).

2006 GAMES PLAYED BY POSITION (MLB): C—29.

Year Team (League)	Pos.	G	AB	R	H	2B	3B	HR	RBI	BB	SO	HBP	GDP	SB-CS	Avg.	OBP	SLG	OPS	E	Avg.
1998— Ariz. D'backs (Ariz.)	C-1B	45	150	26	47	13	2	4	21	37	36	2	3	3-2	.313	.453	.507	.959	13	.965
— South Bend (Mid.)	C	4	14	3	3	1	0	0	2	2	7	0	0	0-0	.214	.313	.286	.598	0	1.000
1999— South Bend (Mid.)	C	52	174	29	42	8	0	3	27	34	37	1	3	0-1	.241	.363	.339	.702	12	.951
— Missoula (Pion.)	C	76	275	73	89	22	0	10	54	71	57	2	8	9-3	.324	.458	.513	.970	21	.964
2000— South Bend (Mid.)	C-1B	101	331	54	74	19	1	8	37	60	61	3	7	6-2	.224	.347	.360	.706	12	.979
2001— Lancaster (Calif.)	C-OF	128	468	85	136	26	6	21	87	65	106	2	9	6-7	.291	.377	.506	.883	16	.981
2002— Carolina (Southern)	C	95	315	43	89	27	1	13	62	44	69	0	7	9-3	.283	.369	.498	.868	12	.977
2003— Tulsa (Texas)	C-OF	118	410	62	116	28	5	13	54	47	79	3	10	3-2	.283	.359	.471	.829	18	.976
2004— Colo. Springs (PCL)	C-DH	83	298	53	89	19	1	7	54	41	47	2	3	0-2	.299	.384	.440	.820	10	.983
— Colorado (N.L.)	C	36	113	5	36	6	0	1	10	6	22	2	3	0-0	.319	.364	.398	.762	3	.986
2005— Colorado (N.L.)	C	92	237	31	52	12	2	7	27	32	48	1	9	1-0	.219	.314	.376	.689	8	.982
2006— Colo. Springs (PCL)		70	225	32	67	15	1	8	30	31	38	1	6	8-2	.298	.384	.480	.864	5	.988
— Colorado (N.L.)	C	32	97	10	19	3	1	2	11	12	23	1	1	0-1	.196	.288	.309	.598	2	.989
Major League totals (3 years)		160	447	46	107	21	3	10	48	50	93	4	13	1-1	.239	.320	.367	.687	13	.985

2006 LEFTY-RIGHTY SPLITS

vs.	Avg.	AB	H	2B	3B	HR	RBI	BB	SO	OBP	Slg.	vs.	Avg.	AB	H	2B	3B	HR	RBI	BB	SO	OBP	Slg.
L	.083	12	1	0	0	0	1	2	6	.267	.083	R	.212	85	18	3	1	2	10	10	17	.292	.341

COATS, BUCK — OF

PERSONAL: Born June 9, 1982, in Fort Benning, Ga. ... Bats left, throws right. ... Full name: Buck Coats. . **TRANSACTIONS/CAREER NOTES:** Selected by Chicago Cubs organization in 18th round of 2000 free-agent draft.

2006 GAMES PLAYED BY POSITION (MLB): OF—4.

Year Team (League)	Pos.	G	AB	R	H	2B	3B	HR	RBI	BB	SO	HBP	GDP	SB-CS	Avg.	OBP	SLG	OPS	E	Avg.
2000— Ariz. Cubs (Ariz.)		30	98	20	29	6	3	0	14	12	24	4	1	7-1	.296	.395	.418	.813	3	...
2001— Ariz. Cubs (Ariz.)		33	123	11	32	3	3	1	18	4	19	2	1	3-4	.260	.292	.358	.650	1	...
2002— Lansing (Midw.)		133	501	65	129	21	4	4	47	31	67	4	5	14-3	.257	.303	.339	.642	9	...
2003— Lansing (Midw.)		132	488	64	135	25	7	1	59	64	93	4	13	32-15	.277	.364	.363	.727	51	...
2004— Daytona (Fla. St.)		112	414	64	120	22	4	8	55	32	90	1	6	28-9	.290	.340	.420	.760	56	...
2005— West Tenn (Sou.)	SS-OF	127	439	47	124	32	6	1	49	38	80	2	10	17-5	.282	.340	.390	.729	35	.931
2006— Iowa (PCL)		124	450	60	127	21	0	7	51	38	87	4	9	17-4	.282	.342	.376	.718	9	.970
— Chicago (N.L.)	OF	18	18	2	3	1	0	1	1	0	6	0	1	0-0	.167	.167	.389	.556	0	1.000
Major League totals (1 year)		18	18	2	3	1	0	1	1	0	6	0	1	0-0	.167	.167	.389	.556	0	1.000

2006 LEFTY-RIGHTY SPLITS

vs.	Avg.	AB	H	2B	3B	HR	RBI	BB	SO	OBP	Slg.	vs.	Avg.	AB	H	2B	3B	HR	RBI	BB	SO	OBP	Slg.
L	.000	3	0	0	0	0	0	0	2	.000	.000	R	.200	15	3	1	0	1	1	0	4	.200	.467

COFFEY, TODD — P

PERSONAL: Born September 9, 1980, in Shelby, N.C. ... 6-5/230. ... Throws right, bats right. ... Full name: Justin Todd Coffey. ... High school: Chase (Forest City, N.C.). **TRANSACTIONS/CAREER NOTES:** Selected by Cincinnati Reds organization in 41st round of 1998 free-agent draft. ... On disabled list (June 19-September 27, 2000).

C

CAREER HITTING: 0-for-3 (.000), 0 R, 0 2B, 0 3B, 0 HR, 0 RBI.

Year Team (League)	W	L	Pct.	ERA	WHIP	G	GS	CG	ShO	Hld.	Sv.-Opp.	IP	H	R	ER	HR	BB-IBB	SO	Avg.
1998— Billings (Pion.)	0	0	...	3.00	1.17	3	2	0	0	...	0-...	12.0	13	4	4	1	1-0	8	.302
1999— GC Reds (GCL)	1	1	.500	3.38	1.44	5	2	0	0	...	0-...	16.0	9	12	6	1	14-0	14	.145
2000—				Did not play															
2001— GC Reds (GCL)	0	1	.000	4.26	1.26	3	2	0	0	...	0-...	12.2	11	11	6	1	5-0	15	.234
— Billings (Pion.)	2	2	.500	3.51	1.47	14	2	0	0	...	1-...	33.1	34	21	13	2	15-0	33	.258
2002— Dayton (Midw.)	6	4	.600	3.59	1.28	38	5	0	0	...	2-...	80.1	78	34	32	8	25-5	62	.260
2003— Dayton (Midw.)	3	3	.500	2.25	1.34	39	0	0	0	...	9-...	56.0	61	20	14	1	14-0	53	.289
— Potomac (Carol.)	0	2	.000	1.96	0.83	11	0	0	0	...	2-...	23.0	16	6	5	0	3-0	21	.208
2004— Chattanooga (Sou.)	4	1	.800	2.38	0.88	40	0	0	0	...	20-...	45.1	36	13	12	3	4-1	53	.209
— Louisville (Int'l)	1	0	1.000	5.27	1.24	15	0	0	0	...	4-...	13.2	15	8	8	1	2-0	11	.268
2005— Louisville (Int'l)	0	0	...	5.19	1.15	8	0	0	0	0	3-5	8.2	8	5	5	1	2-1	5	.242
— Cincinnati (N.L.)	4	1	.800	4.50	1.64	57	0	0	0	3	1-2	58.0	84	33	29	5	11-2	26	.344
2006— Cincinnati (N.L.)	6	7	.462	3.58	1.44	81	0	0	0	15	8-12	78.0	85	34	31	7	27-5	60	.274
Major League totals (2 years)	10	8	.556	3.97	1.52	138	0	0	0	18	9-14	136.0	169	67	60	12	38-7	86	.305

2006 LEFTY-RIGHTY SPLITS

vs.	Avg.	AB	H	2B	3B	HR	RBI	BB	SO	OBP	Slg.	vs.	Avg.	AB	H	2B	3B	HR	RBI	BB	SO	OBP	Slg.
L	.347	95	33	6	1	3	10	11	15	.415	.526	R	.242	215	52	10	3	4	24	16	45	.299	.372

COLINA, ALVIN — C

PERSONAL: Born December 26, 1981, in Puerto Cabello, Venezuela. ... Bats right, throws right. ... Full name: Alvin Colina. ... High school: Jose A. Paez (Venezuela). **TRANSACTIONS/CAREER NOTES:** Signed as a non-drafted free agent by Colorado Rockies organization (September 22, 1998).
2006 GAMES PLAYED BY POSITION (MLB): C—1.

Year Team (League)	Pos.	G	AB	R	H	2B	3B	HR	RBI	BB	SO	HBP	GDP	SB-CS	Avg.	OBP	SLG	OPS	E	Avg.
1999— Universidad (VSL)		34	86	10	16	1	0	1	9	21	22	3	5	1-0	.186	.364	.233	.597	...	...
2000— Ariz. Rockies (Ariz.)		35	122	25	43	7	1	4	28	9	26	6	2	2-3	.352	.417	.525	.942	...	...
2001— Tri-City (N'west)		47	164	12	35	10	0	5	17	12	50	4	2	0-2	.213	.283	.366	.649	...	...
2002— Asheville (S. Atl.)		59	212	22	50	8	0	7	36	20	57	4	3	1-0	.236	.312	.373	.685	...	...
2003— Asheville (S. Atl.)		72	256	26	68	20	1	4	23	20	53	4	5	5-4	.266	.329	.398	.727	...	...
2004— Visalia (Calif.)		95	334	43	84	23	0	11	47	24	81	6	8	0-1	.251	.312	.419	.731	...	...
2005— Modesto (California)	C-DH	9	34	2	9	3	0	0	3	3	14	0	0	0-1	.265	.324	.353	.677	1	.984
— Tulsa (Texas)	C-1B-DH	59	207	23	53	5	0	9	35	20	42	4	8	0-2	.256	.330	.411	.741	4	.979
2006— Tulsa (Texas)		92	323	45	82	14	1	12	46	23	77	6	13	3-2	.254	.314	.415	.728	4	.994
— Colorado (N.L.)	C	2	5	0	1	0	0	0	1	0	1	0	0	0-0	.200	.200	.200	.400	0	1.000
Major League totals (1 year)		2	5	0	1	0	0	0	1	0	1	0	0	0-0	.200	.200	.200	.400	0	1.000

2006 LEFTY-RIGHTY SPLITS

vs.	Avg.	AB	H	2B	3B	HR	RBI	BB	SO	OBP	Slg.	vs.	Avg.	AB	H	2B	3B	HR	RBI	BB	SO	OBP	Slg.
L	.250	4	1	0	0	0	1	0	1	.250	.250	R	.000	1	0	0	0	0	0	0	0	.000	.000

COLOME, JESUS — P

PERSONAL: Born December 23, 1977, in San Pedro de Macoris, Dominican Republic. ... 6-4/205. ... Throws right, bats right. ... Full name: Jesus Colome De La Cruz. ... Name pronounced: COL-um-ay. **TRANSACTIONS/CAREER NOTES:** Signed as a nondrafted free agent by Oakland Athletics organization (September 29, 1996). ... Traded by A's with cash to Tampa Bay Devil Rays for Ps Jim Mecir and Todd Belitz (July 28, 2000). ... On disabled list (September 14, 2004-remainder of season). ... On disabled list (June 12-July 22, 2005); included rehabilitation assignment to Montgomery. ... Released by Devil Rays (April 6, 2006). ... Signed by New York Yankees organization (April 15, 2006).

CAREER HITTING: 0-for-1 (.000), 0 R, 0 2B, 0 3B, 0 HR, 0 RBI.

Year Team (League)	W	L	Pct.	ERA	WHIP	G	GS	CG	ShO	Hld.	Sv.-Opp.	IP	H	R	ER	HR	BB-IBB	SO	Avg.
1997— Dom. Athletics (DSL)	9	3	.750	2.70	1.06	18	7	3	0	...	0-...	90.0	73	33	27	...	22-...	55	...
1998— Ariz. A's (Ariz.)	2	5	.286	3.18	1.11	12	11	0	0	...	0-...	56.2	47	27	20	1	16-0	62	.228
1999— Modesto (California)	8	4	.667	3.36	1.44	31	22	0	0	...	1-...	128.2	125	63	48	6	60-2	127	.256
2000— Midland (Texas)	9	4	.692	3.59	1.35	20	20	0	0	...	0-...	110.1	99	62	44	10	50-0	95	.239
— Orlando (South.)	1	2	.333	6.75	1.70	3	3	0	0	...	0-...	14.2	18	12	11	2	7-0	9	.290
2001— Durham (Int'l)	0	3	.000	6.23	1.62	13	0	0	0	...	0-...	17.1	22	13	12	1	6-0	18	.319
— Tampa Bay (A.L.)	2	3	.400	3.33	1.27	30	0	0	0	6	0-0	48.2	37	22	18	8	25-4	31	.208
2002— Tampa Bay (A.L.)	2	7	.222	8.27	2.15	32	0	0	0	3	0-5	41.1	56	41	38	6	33-5	33	.341
— Durham (Int'l)	2	2	.500	2.17	1.07	18	0	0	0	...	1-...	29.0	18	8	7	1	13-0	30	.176
2003— Tampa Bay (A.L.)	3	7	.300	4.50	1.55	54	0	0	0	11	2-8	74.0	69	37	37	9	46-5	69	.247
2004— Durham (Int'l)	2	1	.667	3.52	1.40	18	0	0	0	...	2-...	30.2	27	12	12	0	16-0	17	.243
— Tampa Bay (A.L.)	2	2	.500	3.27	1.11	33	0	0	0	8	3-4	41.1	28	16	15	4	18-1	40	.193
2005— Montgom. (Sou.)	0	0	...	0.00	0.50	3	0	0	0	1	0-0	4.0	2	0	0	0	0-0	3	.143
— Tampa Bay (A.L.)	2	3	.400	4.57	1.59	36	0	0	0	2	0-1	45.1	54	29	23	7	18-3	28	.283
2006— Tampa Bay (A.L.)	0	0	...	27.00	3.00	1	0	0	0	0	0-0	0.1	0	1	1	0	1-0	0	.000
— Trenton (East.)	2	0	1.000	1.93	1.07	3	0	0	0	1	0-0	4.2	2	3	1	1	3-0	2	.125
— Columbus (Int'l)	1	1	.500	3.78	1.50	25	0	0	0	5	0-1	33.1	35	17	14	3	15-0	25	.265
Major League totals (6 years)	11	22	.333	4.73	1.53	186	0	0	0	30	5-18	251.0	244	146	132	34	141-18	201	.255

2006 LEFTY-RIGHTY SPLITS

vs.	Avg.	AB	H	2B	3B	HR	RBI	BB	SO	OBP	Slg.	vs.	Avg.	AB	H	2B	3B	HR	RBI	BB	SO	OBP	Slg.
L	.000	0	0	0	0	0	0	1	0	1.000	.000	R	.000	1	0	0	0	0	0	0	0	.000	.000

COLON, BARTOLO — P

PERSONAL: Born May 24, 1973, in Altamira, Dominican Republic. ... 5-11/250. ... Throws right, bats right. ... Name pronounced: bar-TOE-loh koh-LONE. **TRANSACTIONS/CAREER NOTES:** Signed as a non-drafted free agent by Cleveland Indians organization (June 26, 1993). ... On disabled list (April 16-May 12, 2000); included rehabilitation assignment to Buffalo. ... On suspended list (July 28-August 2, 2001). ... Traded by Indians with future considerations to Montreal Expos for 1B Lee Stevens, SS Brandon Phillips, P Cliff Lee and OF Grady Sizemore (June 27, 2002); Expos acquired P Tim Drew to complete deal (June 28, 2002). ... Traded by Expos with 2B/SS Jorge Nunez to Chicago White Sox for Ps Orlando Hernandez and Rocky Biddle, 3B/OF Jeff Liefer and cash (January 15, 2003). ... On suspended list (May 21-27, 2003). ... Signed as a free agent by Anaheim Angels (December 10, 2003). ... Angels franchise renamed Los Angeles Angels of Anaheim for 2005 season. ... On disabled list (April 19-June 18, 2006 and July 27, 2006-remainder of season); included rehabilitation assignments to Rancho Cucamanga and Salt Lake. **HONORS:** Named A.L. Pitcher of the Year by the SPORTING NEWS (2005). ... Named pitcher on the SPORTING NEWS A.L. All-Star team (2005). ... Named A.L. Cy Young Award winner by Baseball Writers' Association of America (2005).
CAREER HITTING: 10-for-80 (.125), 1 R, 0 2B, 0 3B, 0 HR, 5 RBI.

Year Team (League)	W	L	Pct.	ERA	WHIP	G	GS	CG	ShO	Hld.	Sv.-Opp.	IP	H	R	ER	HR	BB-IBB	SO	Avg.
1993— Santiago (DSL)	6	1	.857	2.59	1.17	11	10	2	1	...	1-...	66.0	44	24	19	...	33-...	48	...
1994— Burlington (Appal.)	7	4	.636	3.14	1.36	12	12	0	0	...	0-...	66.0	46	32	23	3	44-0	84	.192
1995— Kinston (Carol.)	13	3	.813	1.96	1.01	-21	21	0	0	...	0-...	128.2	91	31	28	8	39-0	152	.202
1996— Cant./Akr. (Eastern)	2	2	.500	1.74	1.11	13	12	0	0	...	0-...	62.0	44	17	12	2	25-0	56	.196
— Buffalo (A.A.)	0	0	...	6.00	1.60	8	0	0	0	...	0-...	15.0	16	10	10	2	8-0	19	.271
1997— Cleveland (A.L.)	4	7	.364	5.65	1.62	19	17	1	0	0	0-0	94.0	107	66	59	12	45-1	66	.286
— Buffalo (A.A.)	7	1	.875	2.22	1.20	10	10	1	1	...	0-...	56.2	45	15	14	4	23-0	54	.221
1998— Cleveland (A.L.)	14	9	.609	3.71	1.39	31	31	6	2	0	0-0	204.0	205	91	84	15	79-5	158	.260
1999— Cleveland (A.L.)	18	5	.783	3.95	1.27	32	32	1	1	0	0-0	205.0	185	97	90	24	76-5	161	.242
2000— Cleveland (A.L.)	15	8	.652	3.88	1.39	30	30	2	1	0	0-0	188.0	163	86	81	21	98-4	212	.233
— Buffalo (Int'l)	1	0	1.000	1.80	1.20	1	1	0	0	...	0-...	5.0	6	1	1	0	0-0	4	.286
2001— Cleveland (A.L.)	14	12	.538	4.09	1.39	34	34	1	0	0	0-0	222.1	220	106	101	26	90-2	201	.261
2002— Cleveland (A.L.)	10	4	.714	2.55	1.16	16	16	4	2	0	0-0	116.1	104	37	33	11	31-1	75	.245
— Montreal (N.L.)	10	4	.714	3.31	1.32	17	17	4	1	0	0-0	117.0	115	48	43	9	39-4	74	.259
2003— Chicago (A.L.)	15	13	.536	3.87	1.20	34	34	• 9	0	0	0-0	242.0	223	107	104	30	67-3	173	.248
2004— Anaheim (A.L.) .....:..	18	12	.600	5.01	1.37	34	34	0	0	0	0-0	208.1	215	122	116	38	71-1	158	.265
2005— Los Angeles (A.L.)	* 21	8	.724	3.48	1.16	33	33	0	0	0	0-0	222.2	215	93	86	26	43-0	157	.254
2006— Rancho Cuca. (Calif.)	0	0	...	0.00	0.75	1	1	0	0	0	0-0	4.0	2	0	0	0	1-0	3	.154
— Salt Lake (PCL)	0	1	.000	6.17	1.37	2	2	0	0	0	0-...	11.2	14	8	8	4	-2-0	3	.311
— Los Angeles (A.L.)	1	5	.167	5.11	1.46	10	10	1	1	0	0-0	56.1	71	39	32	11	11-0	31	.306
American League totals (10 years)	130	83	.610	4.02	1.32	273	271	27	7	0	0-0	1759.0	1708	844	786	214	611-22	1392	.255
National League totals (1 year)	10	4	.714	3.31	1.32	17	17	4	1	0	0-0	117.0	115	48	43	9	39-4	74	.259
Major League totals (10 years)	140	87	.617	3.98	1.32	290	288	31	8	0	0-0	1876.0	1823	892	829	223	650-26	1466	.256

DIVISION SERIES RECORD

Year Team (League)	W	L	Pct.	ERA	WHIP	G	GS	CG	ShO	Hld.	Sv.-Opp.	IP	H	R	ER	HR	BB-IBB	SO	Avg.
1997— Cleveland (A.L.)	Did not play.																		
1998— Cleveland (A.L.)	0	0	...	1.59	1.41	1	1	0	0	0	0-0	5.2	5	1	1	1	3-1	3	.250
1999— Cleveland (A.L.)	0	1	.000	9.00	1.67	2	2	0	0	0	0-0	9.0	11	9	9	3	4-0	12	.306
2001— Cleveland (A.L.)	1	1	.500	1.84	1.23	2	2	0	0	0	0-0	14.2	12	3	3	0	6-0	13	.231
2004— Anaheim (A.L.)	0	0	...	4.50	1.67	1	1	0	0	0	0-0	6.0	7	3	3	1	3-0	3	.304
2005— Los Angeles (A.L.)	0	1	.000	4.50	1.50	2	2	0	0	0	0-0	8.0	10	4	4	0	2-0	7	.313
Division series totals (5 years)	1	3	.250	4.15	1.45	8	8	0	0	0	0-0	43.1	45	20	20	5	18-1	38	.276

CHAMPIONSHIP SERIES RECORD

Year Team (League)	W	L	Pct.	ERA	WHIP	G	GS	CG	ShO	Hld.	Sv.-Opp.	IP	H	R	ER	HR	BB-IBB	SO	Avg.
1997— Cleveland (A.L.)	Did not play.																		
1998— Cleveland (A.L.)	1	0	1.000	1.00	0.89	1	1	1	0	0	0-0	9.0	4	1	1	0	4-0	3	.148

WORLD SERIES RECORD

Year Team (League)	W	L	Pct.	ERA	WHIP	G	GS	CG	ShO	Hld.	Sv.-Opp.	IP	H	R	ER	HR	BB-IBB	SO	Avg.
1997— Cleveland (A.L.)	Did not play.																		

ALL-STAR GAME RECORD

	W	L	Pct.	ERA	WHIP	G	GS	CG	ShO	Hld.	Sv.-Opp.	IP	H	R	ER	HR	BB-IBB	SO	Avg.
All-Star Game totals (2 years)	1	0	1.000	13.50	2.00	2	0	0	0	0	0-0	2.0	3	3	3	1	1-0	1	.333

2006 LEFTY-RIGHTY SPLITS

vs.	Avg.	AB	H	2B	3B	HR	RBI	BB	SO	OBP	Slg.	vs.	Avg.	AB	H	2B	3B	HR	RBI	BB	SO	OBP	Slg.
L	.354	113	40	8	0	6	18	7	19	.398	.584	R	.261	119	31	8	0	5	16	4	12	.290	.454

COLON, ROMAN   P

PERSONAL: Born August 13, 1979, in Montecristi, Dominican Republic. ... 6-6/225. ... Throws right, bats right. ... Full name: Roman Benedicto Colon.
TRANSACTIONS/CAREER NOTES: Signed as a non-drafted free agent by Atlanta Braves organization (August 14, 1995). ... Traded by Braves with P Zach Miner to Detroit Tigers for P Kyle Farnsworth (July 31, 2005). ... On disabled list (August 14, 2006-remainder of season).
CAREER HITTING: 0-for-7 (.000), 0 R, 0 2B, 0 3B, 0 HR, 0 RBI.

Year Team (League)	W	L	Pct.	ERA	WHIP	G	GS	CG	ShO	Hld.	Sv.-Opp.	IP	H	R	ER	HR	BB-IBB	SO	Avg.
1996— Dominican Braves (DSL)	5	6	.455	3.52	1.52	14	14	0	0	0	0-0	64.0	59	45	25	0	38-...	39	.229
1997— GC Braves (GCL)	3	4	.429	4.29	1.52	14	12	0	0	...	0-...	63.0	68	47	30	2	28-0	44	.270
1998— Danville (Appal.)	1	7	.125	5.77	1.64	13	13	0	0	...	0-...	73.1	92	59	47	7	28-0	53	.302
1999— Jamestown (NYP)	7	5	.583	4.54	1.32	15	15	1	0	...	0-...	77.1	77	48	39	4	25-0	61	.258
2000—	Did not play.																		
2001— Macon (S. Atl.)	7	7	.500	3.59	1.27	23	21	0	0	...	0-...	128.0	136	69	51	9	26-0	91	.271
2002— Myrtle Beach (Carol.)	9	8	.529	3.53	1.28	26	26	1	0	...	0-...	163.0	170	81	64	8	38-1	94	.269
2003— Greenville (Sou.)	11	3	.786	3.36	1.28	39	12	1	0	...	2-...	107.0	104	48	40	9	33-3	58	.261
2004— Richmond (Int'l)	4	1	.800	3.65	1.27	51	0	0	0	...	0-...	74.0	72	33	30	4	22-1	64	.258
— Greenville (Sou.)	1	0	1.000	0.00	0.33	3	0	0	0	...	0-...	3.0	1	0	0	0	0-0	5	.091
— Atlanta (N.L.)	2	1	.667	3.32	1.37	18	0	0	0	1	0-1	19.0	18	9	7	0	8-1	15	.254
2005— Mississippi (Sou.)	0	0	...	1.17	1.04	2	2	0	0	0	0-0	7.2	6	1	1	0	2-0	7	.222
— Atlanta (N.L.)	1	5	.167	5.28	1.38	23	4	0	0	2	0-0	44.1	47	28	26	10	14-1	30	.272
— Richmond (Int'l)	1	1	.500	1.93	1.21	3	3	0	0	0	0-0	14.0	12	3	3	0	5-0	9	.235
— Detroit (A.L.)	1	1	.500	6.12	1.68	12	3	0	0	0	0-1	25.0	35	17	17	7	7-0	17	.327
2006— Toledo (Int'l)	0	0	...	0.00	0.90	2	2	0	0	0	0-0	6.2	4	5	0	0	2-0	6	.160
— Detroit (A.L.)	2	0	1.000	4.89	1.55	20	1	0	0	3	1-1	38.2	46	21	21	6	14-2	25	.303
American League totals (2 years)	3	1	.750	5.37	1.60	32	4	0	0	3	1-2	63.2	81	38	38	13	21-2	42	.313
National League totals (2 years)	3	6	.333	4.69	1.37	41	4	0	0	3	0-1	63.1	65	37	33	10	22-2	45	.266
Major League totals (3 years)	6	7	.462	5.03	1.49	73	8	0	0	6	1-3	127.0	146	75	71	23	43-4	87	.290

2006 LEFTY-RIGHTY SPLITS

vs.	Avg.	AB	H	2B	3B	HR	RBI	BB	SO	OBP	Slg.	vs.	Avg.	AB	H	2B	3B	HR	RBI	BB	SO	OBP	Slg.
L	.271	59	16	3	2	1	3	6	7	.338	.441	R	.323	93	30	6	0	5	15	8	18	.375	.548

CONDREY, CLAY   P

PERSONAL: Born November 19, 1975, in Beaumont, Texas. ... 6-3/195. ... Throws right, bats right. ... Full name: Clayton Lee Condrey. ... Name pronounced: con-DREE. ... High school: Navasota (Texas). ... College: McNeese State. **TRANSACTIONS/CAREER NOTES:** Selected by New York Yankees organization in 94th round of 1996 free-agent draft; did not sign. ... Signed as non-drafted free agent by San Diego Padres organization (June 29, 1998). ... On disabled list (May 16-July 7, 2003); included rehabilitation assignment to Portland. ... Traded by Padres to Philadelphia Phillies for IF Trino Aguilar (March 29, 2004).
CAREER HITTING: 2-for-18 (.111), 1 R, 0 2B, 0 3B, 0 HR, 0 RBI.

Year Team (League)	W	L	Pct.	ERA	WHIP	G	GS	CG	ShO	Hld.	Sv.-Opp.	IP	H	R	ER	HR	BB-IBB	SO	Avg.
1998— Ariz. Padres (Ariz.)	0	1	.000	3.38	2.06	5	0	0	0	...	0-...	5.1	6	4	2	0	5-1	4	.286
— Idaho Falls (Pio.)	2	1	.667	2.55	1.42	18	0	0	0	...	5-...	24.2	31	12	7	2	4-0	19	.298
1999— Rancho Cuca. (Calif.)	0	0	...	3.68	0.95	6	0	0	0	...	0-...	7.1	4	3	3	1	3-0	9	.154
— Fort Wayne (Midw.)	2	3	.400	3.78	1.24	42	0	0	0	...	20-...	47.2	40	24	20	5	19-4	47	.221
2000— Rancho Cuca. (Calif.)	1	1	.500	3.48	1.21	18	0	0	0	...	4-...	20.2	18	9	8	1	7-0	21	.240
— Mobile (Sou.)	2	2	.500	5.36	1.40	35	0	0	0	...	6-...	43.2	41	27	26	4	20-0	25	.248
2001— Mobile (Sou.)	2	2	.500	4.54	1.43	27	0	0	0	...	12-...	33.2	33	23	17	1	15-4	21	.268
— Portland (PCL)	1	3	.250	4.75	1.43	39	0	0	0	...	2-...	53.0	63	37	28	7	13-1	45	.304
2002— Portland (PCL)	10	4	.714	1.26	1.26	25	23	0	0	...	0-...	133.2	128	55	52	12	40-1	73	.257
— San Diego (N.L.)	1	2	.333	1.69	1.05	9	3	0	0	3	0-0	26.2	20	7	5	1	8-1	16	.217
2003— San Diego (N.L.)	1	2	.333	8.47	1.88	9	6	0	0	...	0-0	34.0	43	32	32	7	21-4	25	.305
— Portland (PCL)	3	3	.500	4.14	1.20	11	11	0	0	...	0-...	63.0	64	34	29	7	12-0	46	.263
2004— Scran./W.B. (I.L.)	9	9	.500	5.46	1.54	27	27	0	0	...	0-...	155.0	205	106	94	23	34-1	70	.323
2005— Scran./W.B. (I.L.)	7	8	.467	4.15	1.42	25	24	0	0	...	0-0	132.1	159	66	61	13	29-0	74	.300
2006— Scran./W.B. (I.L.)	4	2	.667	1.93	1.09	39	0	0	0	10	6-10	51.1	41	12	11	1	15-3	28	.229
— Philadelphia (N.L.)	2	2	.500	3.14	1.53	21	0	0	0	...	0-1	28.2	35	11	10	3	9-2	16	.318
Major League totals (3 years)	4	6	.400	4.74	1.52	39	9	0	0	...	0-1	89.1	98	50	47	11	38-7	57	.286

2006 LEFTY-RIGHTY SPLITS

vs.	Avg.	AB	H	2B	3B	HR	RBI	BB	SO	OBP	Slg.	vs.	Avg.	AB	H	2B	3B	HR	RBI	BB	SO	OBP	Slg.
L	.383	47	18	4	0	2	7	3	9	.412	.596	R	.270	63	17	4	0	1	4	6	7	.333	.381

CONINE, JEFF — OF/1B

PERSONAL: Born June 27, 1966, in Tacoma, Wash. ... 6-1/220. ... Bats right, throws right. ... Full name: Jeffrey Guy Conine. ... Name pronounced: COH-nine. ... High school: Eisenhower (Rialto, Calif.). ... College: UCLA. **TRANSACTIONS/CAREER NOTES:** Selected by Kansas City Royals organization in 58th round of 1987 free-agent draft. ... Selected by Florida Marlins in first round (22nd pick overall) of expansion draft (November 17, 1992). ... Traded by Marlins to Royals for P Blaine Mull (November 20, 1997). ... On disabled list (March 25-May 5 and July 27-August 19, 1998); included rehabilitation assignment to Omaha. ... Traded by Royals to Baltimore Orioles for P Chris Fussell (April 2, 1999). ... On disabled list (June 15-August 7, 2002). ... Traded by Orioles to Marlins for Ps Denny Bautista and Don Levinski (August 31, 2003). ... Signed as a free agent by Orioles (January 4, 2006). ... Traded by Orioles with cash to Philadelphia Phillies for a player to be named (August 27, 2006); Orioles acquired IF Angel Chavez to complete deal (August 30, 2006). **STATISTICAL NOTES:** Career major league grand slams: 8.
2006 GAMES PLAYED BY POSITION (MLB): OF—83, 1B—73, DH—3, 3B—1.

Year Team (League)	Pos.	G	AB	R	H	2B	3B	HR	RBI	BB	SO	HBP	GDP	SB-CS	Avg.	OBP	SLG	OPS	E	Avg.
1988— Baseball City (FSL)	1B-3B	118	415	63	113	23	9	10	59	46	77	0	6	26-12	.272	.342	.443	.785	22	.970
1989— Baseball City (FSL)	1B	113	425	68	116	12	7	14	60	40	91	3	14	32-13	.273	.338	.433	.771	18	.980
1990— Memphis (Sou.)	1B-3B	137	487	89	156	37	8	15	95	94	88	1	10	21-6	.320	.425	.522	.947	22	.983
— Kansas City (A.L.)	1B	9	20	3	5	2	0	0	2	2	5	0	1	0-0	.250	.318	.350	.668	1	.977
1991— Omaha (A.A.)	1B-OF	51	171	23	44	9	1	3	15	26	39	1	3	0-6	.257	.359	.374	.733	7	.984
1992— Omaha (A.A.)	1B-OF	110	397	69	120	24	5	20	72	54	64	2	6	4-5	.302	.383	.539	.922	6	.993
— Kansas City (A.L.)	OF-1B	28	91	10	23	5	2	0	9	8	23	0	1	0-0	.253	.313	.352	.665	0	1.000
1993— Florida (N.L.)	OF-1B	*162	595	75	174	24	3	12	79	52	135	5	14	2-2	.292	.351	.403	.754	2	.995
1994— Florida (N.L.)	OF-1B	115	451	60	144	27	6	18	82	40	92	1	8	1-2	.319	.375	.526	.898	6	.986
1995— Florida (N.L.)	OF-1B	133	483	72	146	26	2	25	105	66	94	1	13	2-0	.302	.379	.520	.899	6	.981
1996— Florida (N.L.)	OF-1B	157	597	84	175	32	2	26	95	62	121	4	17	1-4	.293	.360	.484	.844	8	.985
1997— Florida (N.L.)	OF-1B	151	405	46	98	13	1	17	61	57	89	2	11	2-0	.242	.337	.405	.742	8	.992
1998— Kansas City (A.L.)	OF-1B-DH	93	309	30	79	26	0	8	43	26	68	2	3	3-0	.256	.312	.417	.729	1	.996
— Omaha (PCL)	DH-OF	2	9	0	0	0	0	0	0	0	3	0	0	0-0	.000	.000	.000	.000	0	1.000
1999— Baltimore (A.L.)	1B-DH-OF-3B	139	444	54	129	31	1	13	75	30	40	3	12	0-3	.291	.335	.453	.787	7	.992
2000— Baltimore (A.L.)	3B-1B-DH-OF	119	409	53	116	20	2	13	46	36	53	2	14	4-3	.284	.341	.438	.779	15	.969
2001— Baltimore (A.L.)	1B-OF-3B-DH	139	524	75	163	23	2	14	97	64	75	5	12	12-8	.311	.386	.443	.829	4	.995
2002— Baltimore (A.L.)	1B-DH-OF	116	451	44	123	26	4	15	64	25	66	2	10	8-0	.273	.307	.448	.755	10	.990
2003— Baltimore (A.L.)	1B-OF-3B	124	493	75	143	33	3	15	80	37	60	5	14	5-0	.290	.338	.460	.799	9	.992
— Florida (N.L.)	OF	25	84	13	20	3	0	5	15	13	10	0	2	0-0	.238	.337	.452	.789	0	1.000
2004— Florida (N.L.)	OF-1B	140	521	55	146	35	1	14	83	48	78	2	15	5-5	.280	.340	.432	.772	5	.993
2005— Florida (N.L.)	OF-1B-DH	131	335	42	102	20	2	3	33	38	58	3	12	2-0	.304	.374	.403	.777	7	.981
2006— Baltimore (A.L.)	1B-OF-DH-3B	114	389	43	103	20	0	9	49	35	53	2	12	3-2	.265	.325	.401	.726	3	.994
— Philadelphia (N.L.)	OF	28	100	11	28	6	1	1	17	5	12	2	1	0-0	.280	.327	.390	.717	1	.973
American League totals (9 years)		881	3130	387	884	186	17	87	464	263	443	21	84	35-16	.282	.337	.436	.773	50	.991
National League totals (9 years)		1042	3571	458	1033	186	18	121	570	381	689	20	93	15-13	.289	.357	.453	.810	43	.989
Major League totals (16 years)		1923	6701	845	1917	372	35	208	1034	644	1132	41	177	50-29	.286	.348	.445	.793	93	.990

DIVISION SERIES RECORD

Year Team (League)	Pos.	G	AB	R	H	2B	3B	HR	RBI	BB	SO	HBP	GDP	SB-CS	Avg.	OBP	SLG	OPS	E	Avg.
1997— Florida (N.L.)	1B	3	11	3	4	1	0	0	0	1	0	0	0	0-0	.364	.417	.455	.871	1	.964
2003— Florida (N.L.)	OF	4	15	2	4	0	0	0	2	2	1	0	0	0-0	.267	.353	.267	.620	1	1.000
Division series totals (2 years)		7	26	5	8	1	0	0	2	3	1	0	0	0-0	.308	.379	.346	.725	1	.973

CHAMPIONSHIP SERIES RECORD

Year Team (League)	Pos.	G	AB	R	H	2B	3B	HR	RBI	BB	SO	HBP	GDP	SB-CS	Avg.	OBP	SLG	OPS	E	Avg.
1997— Florida (N.L.)	1B	6	18	1	2	0	0	0	1	1	4	0	1	0-0	.111	.158	.111	.269	0	1.000
2003— Florida (N.L.)	OF	7	24	4	11	1	1	1	3	4	2	0	0	0-0	.458	.500	.708	1.208	1	.875
Champ. series totals (2 years)		13	42	5	13	1	1	1	4	5	6	0	1	0-0	.310	.367	.452	.820	1	.979

WORLD SERIES RECORD

Year Team (League)	Pos.	G	AB	R	H	2B	3B	HR	RBI	BB	SO	HBP	GDP	SB-CS	Avg.	OBP	SLG	OPS	E	Avg.
1997— Florida (N.L.)	1B	6	13	1	3	0	0	0	2	0	1	0	0	0-0	.231	.231	.231	.462	0	1.000
2003— Florida (N.L.)	DH-OF	6	21	4	7	1	0	0	0	3	1	0	0	0-0	.333	.417	.381	.798	0	1.000
World series totals (2 years)		12	34	5	10	1	0	0	2	3	2	0	0	0-0	.294	.351	.324	.675	0	1.000

ALL-STAR GAME RECORD

	G	AB	R	H	2B	3B	HR	RBI	BB	SO	HBP	GDP	SB-CS	Avg.	OBP	SLG	OPS	E	Avg.
All-Star Game totals (1 year)	1	1	1	1	0	0	1	1	0	0	0	0	0-0	1.000	1.000	4.000	5.000	...	...

2006 LEFTY-RIGHTY SPLITS

vs.	Avg.	AB	H	2B	3B	HR	RBI	BB	SO	OBP	Slg.	vs.	Avg.	AB	H	2B	3B	HR	RBI	BB	SO	OBP	Slg.
L	.260	150	39	7	1	4	20	18	23	.337	.400	R	.271	339	92	19	3	6	46	22	42	.320	.398

C

CONTRERAS, JOSE — P

PERSONAL: Born December 6, 1971, in Havana, Cuba. ... 6-4/224. ... Throws right, bats right. ... Full name: Jose Ariel Contreras. **TRANSACTIONS/CAREER NOTES:** Signed as a free agent by New York Yankees (February 6, 2003). ... On disabled list (June 7-August 24, 2003); included rehabilitation assignment to Tampa. ... Traded by Yankees with cash to Chicago White Sox for P Esteban Loaiza (July 31, 2003). ... On disabled list (May 5-21, 2006).

CAREER HITTING: 0-for-18 (.000), 1 R, 0 2B, 0 3B, 0 HR, 0 RBI.

Year Team (League)	W	L	Pct.	ERA	WHIP	G	GS	CG	ShO	Hld.	Sv.-Opp.	IP	H	R	ER	HR	BB-IBB	SO	Avg.
2003— Columbus (Int'l)	2	0	1.000	1.20	0.80	3	3	0	0	...	0-...	15.0	10	2	2	1	2-0	18	.189
— Trenton (East.)	0	0		0.00	1.80	1	1	0	0	...	0-...	1.2	1	0	0	0	2-0	3	.167
— Tampa (Fla. St.)	0	0		4.50	1.75	1	1	0	0	...	0-...	4.0	4	2	2	0	3-0	5	.286
— Staten Is. (N.Y.-Penn)	0	0		0.00	0.29	1	1	0	0	...	0-...	7.0	2	0	0	0	0-0	15	.087
— New York (A.L.)	7	2	.778	3.30	1.15	18	9	0	0	1	0-1	71.0	52	27	26	4	30-1	72	.202
2004— Columbus (Int'l)	2	0	1.000	3.29	1.17	2	2	0	0	...	0-...	13.2	11	5	5	2	5-0	19	.216
— New York (A.L.)	8	5	.615	5.64	1.41	18	18	0	0	0	0-0	95.2	93	66	60	22	42-1	82	.250
— Chicago (A.L.)	5	4	.556	5.30	1.54	13	13	0	0	0	0-0	74.2	73	48	44	9	42-0	68	.256
2005— Chicago (A.L.)	15	7	.682	3.61	1.23	32	32	1	0	0	0-0	204.2	177	91	82	23	75-2	154	.232
2006— Chicago (A.L.)	13	9	.591	4.27	1.27	30	30	1	1	0	0-0	196.0	194	101	93	20	55-4	134	.256
Major League totals (4 years)	**48**	**27**	**.640**	**4.28**	**1.30**	**111**	**102**	**2**	**1**	**1**	**0-1**	**642.0**	**589**	**333**	**305**	**78**	**244-8**	**510**	**.242**

DIVISION SERIES RECORD

Year Team (League)	W	L	Pct.	ERA	WHIP	G	GS	CG	ShO	Hld.	Sv.-Opp.	IP	H	R	ER	HR	BB-IBB	SO	Avg.
2005— Chicago (A.L.)	1	0	1.000	2.35	1.04	1	1	0	0	0	0-0	7.2	8	2	2	0	0-0	6	.258

CHAMPIONSHIP SERIES RECORD

Year Team (League)	W	L	Pct.	ERA	WHIP	G	GS	CG	ShO	Hld.	Sv.-Opp.	IP	H	R	ER	HR	BB-IBB	SO	Avg.
2003— New York (A.L.)	0	1	.000	5.79	1.71	4	0	0	0	2	0-1	4.2	6	3	3	0	2-0	7	.316
2005— Chicago (A.L.)	1	1	.500	3.12	0.81	2	2	1	0	0	0-0	17.1	12	6	6	1	2-0	6	.197
Champ. series totals (2 years)	**1**	**2**	**.333**	**3.68**	**1.00**	**6**	**2**	**1**	**0**	**2**	**0-1**	**22.0**	**18**	**9**	**9**	**1**	**4-0**	**13**	**.225**

WORLD SERIES RECORD

Year Team (League)	W	L	Pct.	ERA	WHIP	G	GS	CG	ShO	Hld.	Sv.-Opp.	IP	H	R	ER	HR	BB-IBB	SO	Avg.
2003— New York (A.L.)	0	1	.000	5.68	1.58	4	0	0	0	0	0-0	6.1	5	4	4	0	5-0	10	.227
2005— Chicago (A.L.)	1	0	1.000	3.86	0.86	1	1	0	0	0	0-0	7.0	6	3	3	1	0-0	2	.240
World series totals (2 years)	**1**	**1**	**.500**	**4.73**	**1.20**	**5**	**1**	**0**	**0**	**0**	**0-0**	**13.1**	**11**	**7**	**7**	**1**	**5-0**	**12**	**.234**

2006 LEFTY-RIGHTY SPLITS

vs.	Avg.	AB	H	2B	3B	HR	RBI	BB	SO	OBP	Slg.	vs.	Avg.	AB	H	2B	3B	HR	RBI	BB	SO	OBP	Slg.
L	.267	326	87	13	3	8	35	38	63	.339	.399	R	.248	432	107	21	4	12	55	17	71	.290	.398

COOK, AARON — P

PERSONAL: Born February 8, 1979, in Ft. Campbell, Ky. ... 6-3/205. ... Throws right, bats right. ... Full name: Aaron Lane Cook. ... High school: Hamilton (Ohio). **TRANSACTIONS/CAREER NOTES:** Selected by Colorado Rockies organization in second round of 1997 free-agent draft. ... On disabled list (August 8, 2004-remainder of season). ... On disabled list (March 30-July 30, 2005); included rehabilitation assignments to Tri-City, Modesto, Tulsa and Colorado Springs.

CAREER HITTING: 18-for-162 (.111), 8 R, 0 2B, 1 3B, 0 HR, 5 RBI.

Year Team (League)	W	L	Pct.	ERA	WHIP	G	GS	CG	ShO	Hld.	Sv.-Opp.	IP	H	R	ER	HR	BB-IBB	SO	Avg.
1997— Ariz. Rockies (Ariz.)	1	3	.250	3.13	1.41	9	8	0	0	...	0-...	46.0	48	27	16	1	17-0	35	.261
1998— Portland (N'west)	5	8	.385	4.88	1.59	15	15	1	0	...	0-...	79.1	87	50	43	8	39-0	38	.275
1999— Asheville (S. Atl.)	4	12	.250	6.44	1.64	25	25	2	0	...	0-...	121.2	157	99	87	17	42-0	73	.310
2000— Asheville (S. Atl.)	10	7	.588	2.96	1.07	21	21	4	2	...	0-...	142.2	130	54	47	10	23-0	118	.241
— Salem (Carol.)	1	6	.143	5.44	1.49	7	7	1	0	...	0-...	43.0	52	33	26	4	12-0	37	.297
2001— Salem (Carol.)	11	11	.500	3.08	1.26	27	27	0	0	...	0-...	155.0	157	73	53	4	38-0	122	.263
2002— Carolina (Southern)	7	2	.778	1.42	0.97	14	14	2	2	...	0-...	95.0	73	24	15	4	19-0	58	.213
— Colo. Springs (PCL)	4	4	.500	3.78	1.32	10	10	1	0	...	0-...	64.1	67	40	27	6	18-0	32	.264
— Colorado (N.L.)	2	1	.667	4.54	1.51	9	5	0	0	1	0-0	35.2	41	18	18	4	13-0	14	.295
2003— Colo. Springs (PCL)	1	1	.500	2.25	0.90	2	2	1	0	...	0-...	16.0	10	4	4	2	4-0	12	.175
— Colorado (N.L.)	4	6	.400	6.02	1.75	43	16	1	0	1	0-0	124.0	160	89	83	8	57-7	43	.317
2004— Colo. Springs (PCL)	3	1	.750	2.74	0.91	7	7	1	1	...	0-...	46.0	34	15	14	1	8-0	25	.206
— Colorado (N.L.)	6	4	.600	4.28	1.56	16	16	1	0	...	0-0	96.2	112	47	46	7	39-5	40	.294
2005— Tri-City (N'west)	0	0		0.00	0.14	2	2	0	0	...	0-...	7.0	1	0	0	0	0-0	5	.043
— Modesto (California)	1	0	1.000	1.80	1.00	1	1	0	0	...	0-0	5.0	5	1	1	0	0-0	5	.263
— Tulsa (Texas)	0	1	.000	17.18	3.00	1	1	0	0	...	0-0	3.2	10	9	7	2	1-0	1	.476
— Colo. Springs (PCL)	1	0	1.000	5.51	1.53	3	3	0	0	...	0-0	16.1	18	10	10	0	7-0	11	.295
— Colorado (N.L.)	7	2	.778	3.67	1.40	13	13	2	0	0	0-0	83.1	101	38	34	8	16-2	24	.301
2006— Colorado (N.L.)	9	15	.375	4.23	1.40	32	32	0	0	0	0-0	212.2	242	107	100	17	55-11	92	.288
Major League totals (5 years)	**28**	**28**	**.500**	**4.58**	**1.51**	**113**	**82**	**4**	**0**	**1**	**0-0**	**552.1**	**656**	**299**	**281**	**44**	**180-25**	**213**	**.298**

2006 LEFTY-RIGHTY SPLITS

vs.	Avg.	AB	H	2B	3B	HR	RBI	BB	SO	OBP	Slg.	vs.	Avg.	AB	H	2B	3B	HR	RBI	BB	SO	OBP	Slg.
L	.314	449	141	31	7	13	51	36	43	.370	.501	R	.258	391	101	12	2	4	42	19	49	.294	.330

CORA, ALEX — SS/2B

PERSONAL: Born October 18, 1975, in Caguas, Puerto Rico. ... 6-0/180. ... Bats left, throws right. ... Full name: Jose Alexander Cora. ... High school: Bautista (Caguas, Puerto Rico). ... College: Miami. ... Brother of Joey Cora, coach, Chicago White Sox, and second baseman with four major league teams (1987-98). **TRANSACTIONS/CAREER NOTES:** Selected by Minnesota Twins organization in 12th round of 1993 free-agent draft; did not sign. ... Selected by Los Angeles Dodgers organization in third round of 1996 free-agent draft. ... On disabled list (March 25-June 27, 1999); included rehabilitation assignment to Albuquerque. ... Signed as a free agent by Cleveland Indians (January 18, 2005). ... Traded by Indians to Boston Red Sox for SS Ramon Vazquez (July 7, 2005).

2006 GAMES PLAYED BY POSITION (MLB): SS—63, 2B—18, 3B—11, DH—2.

Year Team (League)	Pos.	G	AB	R	H	2B	3B	HR	RBI	BB	SO	HBP	GDP	SB-CS	Avg.	OBP	SLG	OPS	E	Avg.
1996— Vero Beach (FSL)	OF-SS	61	214	26	55	5	4	0	26	12	36	3	1	5-5	.257	.306	.318	.623	16	.940
1997— San Antonio (Texas)	SS	127	448	52	105	20	4	3	48	25	60	3	17	12-9	.234	.279	.317	.596	20	.968
1998— Albuquerque (PCL)	2B-SS	81	299	42	79	17	5	5	45	15	38	3	1	10-7	.264	.303	.405	.708	18	.957
— Los Angeles (N.L.)	SS	29	33	1	4	0	1	0	3	2	8	1	0	0-0	.121	.194	.182	.376	2	.965
1999— Albuquerque (PCL)	SS-2B-DH	80	302	51	93	11	7	4	37	12	37	8	0	9-5	.308	.348	.430	.778	12	.968
— Los Angeles (N.L.)	SS-2B	11	30	2	5	1	0	0	3	0	4	1	1	0-0	.167	.194	.200	.394	2	.943
2000— Albuquerque (PCL)	SS	30	110	18	41	8	0	2	20	7	14	2	1	5-3	.373	.417	.500	.917	7	.959
— Los Angeles (N.L.)	SS-2B	109	354	39	84	18	6	4	32	26	53	7	6	4-1	.238	.302	.357	.658	12	.973

Year Team (League)	Pos.	G	AB	R	H	2B	3B	HR	RBI	BB	SO	HBP	GDP	SB-CS	Avg.	OBP	SLG	OPS	E	Avg.
2001— Los Angeles (N.L.)	SS-2B	134	405	38	88	18	3	4	29	31	58	8	16	0-2	.217	.285	.306	.591	20	.962
2002— Los Angeles (N.L.)	SS-2B	115	258	37	75	14	4	5	28	26	38	7	3	7-2	.291	.371	.434	.805	7	.977
2003— Los Angeles (N.L.)	2B-SS	148	477	39	119	24	.3	4	34	16	59	10	5	4-2	.249	.287	.338	.625	15	.979
2004— Los Angeles (N.L.)	2B	138	405	47	107	9	4	10	47	47	41	18	9	3-4	.264	.364	.380	.745	8	.987
2005— Cleveland (A.L.)	SS-2B-OF	49	146	11	30	5	2	1	8	5	18	4	3	6-0	.205	.250	.288	.538	3	.984
— Boston (A.L.)	2B-SS-3B	47	104	14	28	3	2	2	16	6	12	1	3	1-2	.269	.310	.394	.704	5	.969
2006— Boston (A.L.)	SS-2B-3B-DH	96	235	31	56	7	2	1	18	19	29	6	4	6-2	.238	.312	.298	.609	7	.976
American League totals (2 years)		192	485	56	114	15	6	4	42	30	59	11	10	13-4	.235	.293	.315	.608	15	.977
National League totals (7 years)		684	1961	203	482	84	21	27	173	148	261	52	40	18-11	.246	.314	.351	.666	66	.975
Major League totals (9 years)		876	2446	259	596	99	27	31	215	178	320	63	50	31-15	.244	.310	.344	.654	81	.976

DIVISION SERIES RECORD

Year Team (League)	Pos.	G	AB	R	H	2B	3B	HR	RBI	BB	SO	HBP	GDP	SB-CS	Avg.	OBP	SLG	OPS	E	Avg.
2004— Los Angeles (N.L.)	2B	4	15	1	2	0	1	0	1	0	3	1	2	0-0	.133	.188	.267	.454	0	1.000
2005— Boston (A.L.)	SS	1	0	0	0	0	0	0	0	0	0	0	0	0-0	...	...	...	...	0	...
Division series totals (2 years)		5	15	1	2	0	1	0	1	0	3	1	2	0-0	.133	.188	.267	.454	0	1.000

2006 LEFTY-RIGHTY SPLITS

vs.	Avg.	AB	H	2B	3B	HR	RBI	BB	SO	OBP	Slg.	vs.	Avg.	AB	H	2B	3B	HR	RBI	BB	SO	OBP	Slg.
L	.333	39	13	3	0	0	4	1	9	.366	.410	R	.219	196	43	4	2	1	14	18	20	.301	.276

CORCORAN, ROY   P

PERSONAL: Born May 11, 1980, in Baton Rouge, La. ... 5-10/170. ... Throws right, bats right. ... Full name: Roy Elliot Corcoran. ... High school: Silliman Institute (Clinton, La.). ... College: LSU. **TRANSACTIONS/CAREER NOTES:** Signed as a non-drafted free agent by Montreal Expos organization (June 15, 2001). ... Expos franchise relocated to Washington, D.C., and renamed Washington Nationals for 2005 season (December 3, 2004).
CAREER HITTING: 0-for-2 (.000), 0 R, 0 2B, 0 3B, 0 HR, 0 RBI.

Year Team (League)	W	L	Pct.	ERA	WHIP	G	GS	CG	ShO	Hld.	Sv.-Opp.	IP	H	R	ER	HR	BB-IBB	SO	Avg.
2001— Jupiter (Fla. St.)	0	0	...	1.00	1.00	1	0	0	0	...	0-...	2.0	0	0	0	0	2-0	5	.000
— GC Expos (GCL)	2	0	1.000	1.56	0.81	13	0	0	0	...	2-...	17.1	12	4	3	2	2-0	21	.185
2002— Clinton (Midw.)	3	4	.429	4.16	1.33	48	1	0	0	...	11-...	80.0	82	51	37	5	24-1	106	.253
2003— Brevard County (FSL)	5	3	.625	1.91	0.91	28	0	0	0	...	12-...	33.0	19	8	7	1	11-1	35	.171
— Harrisburg (East.)	1	1	.500	0.38	0.89	14	0	0	0	...	3-...	23.2	14	4	1	0	7-1	26	.167
— Edmonton (PCL)	0	0	...	1.23	1.36	5	0	0	0	0	0-...	7.1	7	2	1	0	3-0	2	.250
— Montreal (N.L.)	0	0	...	0.00	0.00	2	0	0	0	0	0-...	2.0	0	0	0	0	0-0	1	.000
2004— Montreal (N.L.)	0	0	...	6.75	2.25	5	0	0	0	0	0-0	5.1	7	4	4	0	5-0	4	.304
— Edmonton (PCL)	6	1	.857	3.05	1.42	30	0	0	0	...	5-...	44.1	39	16	15	0	24-1	35	.245
2005— New Orleans (PCL)	4	4	.500	4.85	1.50	52	1	0	0	6	3-5	68.2	67	51	37	7	36-2	55	.251
2006— New Orleans (PCL)	2	4	.333	2.41	1.46	28	0	0	0	0	11-14	33.2	24	11	9	0	25-2	37	.202
— Harrisburg (East.)	0	2	.000	0.35	0.85	21	0	0	0	0	16-18	26.0	12	6	1	1	10-1	40	.138
— Wash. (N.L.)	0	1	.000	11.12	2.82	6	0	0	0	0	0-1	5.2	12	8	7	1	4-0	6	.414
Major League totals (3 years)	0	1	.000	5.89	2.07	16	0	0	0	0	0-1	18.1	26	14	12	1	12-0	12	.325

2006 LEFTY-RIGHTY SPLITS

vs.	Avg.	AB	H	2B	3B	HR	RBI	BB	SO	OBP	Slg.	vs.	Avg.	AB	H	2B	3B	HR	RBI	BB	SO	OBP	Slg.
L	.625	16	10	0	1	1	6	2	2	.667	.938	R	.154	13	2	0	0	0	4	2	4	.250	.154

CORCORAN, TIM   P

PERSONAL: Born April 15, 1978, in Baton Rouge, La. ... 6-2/205. ... Throws right, bats right. ... Full name: Timothy Hugh Corcoran. ... Junior college: Gulf Coast (Fla.) C.C. **TRANSACTIONS/CAREER NOTES:** Selected by New York Mets organization in 44th round of 1996 free-agent draft. ... Selected by Baltimore Orioles organization from Mets organization in Rule 5 minor league draft (December 11, 2000). ... Selected by Tampa Bay Devil Rays organization from Orioles organization in Rule 5 minor league draft (December 15, 2003).
CAREER HITTING: 0-for-4 (.000), 0 R, 0 2B, 0 3B, 0 HR, 0 RBI.

Year Team (League)	W	L	Pct.	ERA	WHIP	G	GS	CG	ShO	Hld.	Sv.-Opp.	IP	H	R	ER	HR	BB-IBB	SO	Avg.
1997— GC Mets (GCL)	3	0	1.000	3.00	1.48	10	0	0	0	...	3-...	21.0	16	8	7	0	15-0	20	.208
— Kingsport (Appalachian)	2	0	1.000	4.24	1.18	7	0	0	0	...	0-...	17.0	12	10	8	2	8-2	14	.194
1998— St. Lucie (Fla. St.)	0	0	...	8.22	1.57	4	0	0	0	...	0-...	7.2	10	7	7	1	2-0	8	.303
— Columbia (S. Atl.)	2	3	.400	2.61	1.20	20	1	0	0	...	4-...	48.1	43	21	14	4	15-0	38	.236
1999— Columbia (S. Atl.)	0	3	.000	4.44	1.37	40	3	0	0	...	3-...	75.0	62	43	37	5	41-0	89	.225
2000— Columbia (S. Atl.)	3	5	.375	4.05	1.37	31	0	0	0	...	3-...	53.1	46	28	24	7	27-2	58	.231
2001— Frederick (Carolina)	6	5	.545	2.68	1.11	33	0	0	0	...	6-...	50.1	37	16	15	4	19-3	42	.208
— Bowie (East.)	1	0	1.000	0.77	0.60	7	0	0	0	...	0-...	11.2	4	1	1	0	3-0	13	.105
2002— Bowie (East.)	0	5	.000	3.67	1.84	35	0	0	0	...	1-...	49.0	61	31	20	5	29-3	48	.308
2003— Frederick (Carolina)	2	5	.286	5.74	1.79	22	3	0	0	...	0-...	47.0	57	38	30	3	27-2	41	.294
— Bowie (East.)	4	1	.800	4.09	1.27	26	2	0	0	...	3-...	44.0	37	22	20	1	19-2	33	.231
2004— Durham (Int'l.)	3	3	.500	3.91	1.56	33	0	0	0	...	0-...	50.2	46	22	22	4	33-1	40	.242
— Montgom. (Sou.)	0	1	.000	2.76	1.04	6	2	0	0	...	0-...	16.1	14	5	5	2	3-0	12	.255
2005— Durham (Int'l.)	5	1	.833	2.89	1.27	29	0	0	0	2	0-2	56.0	49	22	18	3	22-0	49	.230
— Tampa Bay (A.L.)	0	0	...	5.96	1.37	10	1	0	0	0	0-0	22.2	19	15	15	1	12-0	13	.226
2006— Durham (Int'l.)	5	1	.833	1.91	1.04	19	3	0	0	1	1-3	37.2	30	13	8	0	9-1	32	.219
— Tampa Bay (A.L.)	5	9	.357	4.38	1.55	21	16	0	0	0	0-0	90.1	92	48	44	10	48-3	59	.271
Major League totals (2 years)	5	9	.357	4.70	1.51	31	17	0	0	0	0-0	113.0	111	63	59	11	60-3	72	.262

2006 LEFTY-RIGHTY SPLITS

vs.	Avg.	AB	H	2B	3B	HR	RBI	BB	SO	OBP	Slg.	vs.	Avg.	AB	H	2B	3B	HR	RBI	BB	SO	OBP	Slg.
L	.281	167	47	12	0	6	28	27	27	.384	.461	R	.262	172	45	13	2	4	17	21	32	.345	.430

CORDERO, CHAD   P

PERSONAL: Born March 18, 1982, in Upland, Calif. ... 6-0/198. ... Throws right, bats right. ... Full name: Chad Patrick Cordero. ... High school: Don Lugo (Chino, Calif.). ... College: Cal State Fullerton. **TRANSACTIONS/CAREER NOTES:** Selected by San Diego Padres organization in 26th round of 2000 free-agent draft; did not sign. ... Selected by Montreal Expos organization in first round (20th pick overall) of 2003 free-agent draft. ... Expos franchise transferred to Washington, D.C., and renamed Washington Nationals for 2005 season (December 3, 2004). **HONORS:** Named N.L. Fireman of the Year by the SPORTING NEWS (2005).
CAREER HITTING: 0-for-4 (.000), 0 R, 0 2B, 0 3B, 0 HR, 0 RBI.

C

Year Team (League)	W	L	Pct.	ERA	WHIP	G	GS	CG	ShO	Hld.	Sv.-Opp.	IP	H	R	ER	HR	BB-IBB	SO	Avg.
2003— Brevard County (FSL)	1	1	.500	2.05	1.03	19	0	0	0	...	6-...	26.1	17	8	6	1	10-0	17	.198
— Montreal (N.L.)	1	0	1.000	1.64	0.64	12	0	0	0	1	1-1	11.0	4	2	2	1	3-1	12	.111
2004— Montreal (N.L.)	7	3	.700	2.94	1.34	69	0	0	0	8	14-18	82.2	68	28	27	8	43-4	83	.222
2005— Wash. (N.L.)	2	4	.333	1.82	0.97	74	0	0	0	0	* 47-54	74.1	55	24	15	9	17-2	61	.198
2006— Wash. (N.L.)	7	4	.636	3.19	1.10	68	0	0	0	0	29-33	73.1	59	27	26	13	22-5	69	.215
Major League totals (4 years)	**17**	**11**	**.607**	**2.61**	**1.12**	**223**	**0**	**0**	**0**	**9**	**91-106**	**241.1**	**186**	**81**	**70**	**31**	**85-12**	**225**	**.208**

ALL-STAR GAME RECORD

	W	L	Pct.	ERA	WHIP	G	GS	CG	ShO	Hld.	Sv.-Opp.	IP	H	R	ER	HR	BB-IBB	SO	Avg.
All-Star Game totals (1 year)	0	0	...	0.00	0.00	1	0	0	0	...	0-0	0.1	0	0	0	0	0-0	1	.000

2006 LEFTY-RIGHTY SPLITS

vs.	Avg.	AB	H	2B	3B	HR	RBI	BB	SO	OBP	Slg.	vs.	Avg.	AB	H	2B	3B	HR	RBI	BB	SO	OBP	Slg.
L	.219	128	28	8	1	4	10	14	35	.297	.391	R	.212	146	31	4	1	9	18	8	34	.263	.438

CORDERO, FRANCISCO — P

PERSONAL: Born May 11, 1975, in Santo Domingo, Dominican Republic. ... 6-2/235. ... Throws right, bats right. ... Full name: Francisco Javier Cordero. ... High school: Colegio Luz de Arroyo Hondo (Dominican Republic). **TRANSACTIONS/CAREER NOTES:** Signed as a non-drafted free agent by Detroit Tigers organization (June 18, 1994). ... Traded by Tigers with Ps Justin Thompson and Alan Webb, OF Gabe Kapler, C Bill Haselman and 2B Frank Catalanotto to Texas Rangers for OF Juan Gonzalez, P Danny Patterson and C Gregg Zaun (November 2, 1999). ... On disabled list (March 23-June 19 and June 26, 2001-remainder of season); included rehabilitation assignment to Oklahoma. ... On disabled list (June 25-July 27, 2002); included rehabilitation assignment to Oklahoma. ... Traded by Rangers with OFs Kevin Mench and Laynce Nix and P Julian Cordero to Milwaukee Brewers for OFs Carlos Lee and Nelson Cruz (July 28, 2006).

CAREER HITTING: 0-for-1 (.000), 0 R, 0 2B, 0 3B, 0 HR, 0 RBI.

Year Team (League)	W	L	Pct.	ERA	WHIP	G	GS	CG	ShO	Hld.	Sv.-Opp.	IP	H	R	ER	HR	BB-IBB	SO	Avg.
1994— Dom. Tigers (DSL)	4	3	.571	3.90	1.53	12	12	0	0	...	0-...	60.0	65	47	26	...	27-...	36	...
1995— Fayetteville (SAL)	0	3	.000	6.30	1.90	4	4	0	0	...	0-...	20.0	26	16	14	1	12-0	19	.342
— Jamestown (NYP)	4	7	.364	5.22	1.51	15	14	0	0	...	0-...	88.0	96	62	51	3	37-0	54	.282
1996— Fayetteville (SAL)	0	0		2.57	1.14	2	1	0	0	...	0-...	7.0	2	2	2	0	6-0	7	.095
— Jamestown (NYP)	0	0		0.82	0.64	2	2	0	0	...	0-...	11.0	5	1	1	0	2-0	10	.135
1997— W. Mich. (Mid.)	6	1	.857	0.99	0.94	50	0	0	0	...	35-...	54.1	36	13	6	2	15-2	67	.193
1998— Jacksonville (Sou.)	1	1	.500	4.86	1.68	17	0	0	0	...	8-...	16.2	19	12	9	1	9-0	18	.284
1999— Jacksonville (Sou.)	4	1	.800	1.38	1.09	47	0	0	0	...	27-...	52.1	35	9	8	3	22-0	58	.183
— Detroit (A.L.)	2	2	.500	3.32	1.95	20	0	0	0	6	0-0	19.0	19	7	7	2	18-2	19	.284
2000— Texas (A.L.)	1	2	.333	5.35	1.75	56	0	0	0	4	0-3	77.1	87	51	46	11	48-3	49	.285
— Oklahoma (PCL)	0	0		4.15	2.31	3	0	0	0	...	1-...	4.1	7	3	2	0	3-0	5	.350
2001— Oklahoma (PCL)	0	1	.000	0.59	0.72	12	0	0	0	...	6-...	15.1	8	2	1	0	3-0	20	.148
— Texas (A.L.)	0	1	.000	3.86	2.14	3	0	0	0	1	0-0	2.1	3	1	1	0	2-1	1	.300
2002— Texas (A.L.)	2	0	1.000	1.79	1.01	39	0	0	0	1	10-12	45.1	33	12	9	2	13-1	41	.204
— Oklahoma (PCL)	0	2	.000	5.84	1.78	11	1	0	0	...	2-...	12.1	15	14	8	2	7-1	21	.278
2003— Texas (A.L.)	5	8	.385	2.94	1.31	73	0	0	0	18	15-25	82.2	70	33	27	4	38-6	90	.230
2004— Texas (A.L.)	3	4	.429	2.13	1.28	67	0	0	0	0	49-54	71.2	60	19	17	1	32-2	79	.226
2005— Texas (A.L.)	3	1	.750	3.39	1.32	69	0	0	0	0	37-45	69.0	61	28	26	5	30-2	79	.245
2006— Texas (A.L.)	7	4	.636	4.81	1.34	49	0	0	0	15	6-15	48.2	49	27	26	5	16-1	54	.265
— Milwaukee (N.L.)	3	1	.750	1.69	1.35	28	0	0	0	1	16-18	26.2	20	5	5	2	16-1	30	.213
American League totals (8 years)	**23**	**22**	**.511**	**3.44**	**1.39**	**376**	**0**	**0**	**0**	**45**	**117-154**	**416.0**	**382**	**178**	**159**	**30**	**197-18**	**412**	**.245**
National League totals (1 year)	**3**	**1**	**.750**	**1.69**	**1.35**	**28**	**0**	**0**	**0**	**1**	**16-18**	**26.2**	**20**	**5**	**5**	**2**	**16-1**	**30**	**.213**
Major League totals (8 years)	**26**	**23**	**.531**	**3.33**	**1.39**	**404**	**0**	**0**	**0**	**46**	**133-172**	**442.2**	**402**	**183**	**164**	**32**	**213-19**	**442**	**.243**

2006 LEFTY-RIGHTY SPLITS

vs.	Avg.	AB	H	2B	3B	HR	RBI	BB	SO	OBP	Slg.	vs.	Avg.	AB	H	2B	3B	HR	RBI	BB	SO	OBP	Slg.
L	.286	119	34	6	2	4	19	23	30	.408	.471	R	.219	160	35	6	0	3	20	9	54	.256	.313

COREY, BRYAN — P

PERSONAL: Born October 21, 1973, in Thousand Oaks, Calif. ... 6-0/170. ... Throws right, bats right. ... Full name: Bryan Scott Corey. ... High school: Thousand Oaks (Calif.). ... Junior college: Pierce Junior College (Calif.). **TRANSACTIONS/CAREER NOTES:** Selected by Detroit Tigers organization in 12th round of 1993 free-agent draft. ... Selected by Arizona Diamondbacks in third round (63rd pick overall) of expansion draft (November 18, 1997). ... Claimed on waivers by Tigers (December 4, 1998). ... Signed as a free agent by Oakland Athletics organization (December 3, 1999). ... Signed as a free agent by San Diego Padres organization (November 20, 2000). ... Signed as a free agent by Los Angeles Dodgers organization (January 7, 2002). ... On disabled list (May 29-June 13, 2002). ... Released by Dodgers (October 8, 2002). ... Re-signed by Dodgers organization (December 1, 2002). ... Signed as a free agent by Chicago Cubs organization (November 9, 2003). ... Released by Cubs (May 5, 2004). ... Signed by Florida Marlins organization (November 11, 2004). ... Signed as a free agent by Cubs organization (December 21, 2005). ... Released by Cubs (March 2006). ... Signed by Texas Rangers organization (March 29, 2006). ... Traded by Rangers to Boston Red Sox for P Luis Mendoza (July 30, 2006).

CAREER HITTING: 0-for-0 (.000), 0 R, 0 2B, 0 3B, 0 HR, 0 RBI.

Year Team (League)	W	L	Pct.	ERA	WHIP	G	GS	CG	ShO	Hld.	Sv.-Opp.	IP	H	R	ER	HR	BB-IBB	SO	Avg.
1995— Jamestown (NYP)	2	2	.500	3.86	1.18	29	0	0	0	...	10-...	28.0	21	14	12	2	12-1	41	.206
1996— Fayetteville (SAL)	6	4	.600	1.21	0.82	60	0	0	0	...	34-...	82.0	50	19	11	2	17-3	101	.175
1997— Jacksonville (Sou.)	3	8	.273	4.76	1.40	52	0	0	0	...	9-...	68.0	74	42	36	8	21-3	37	.276
1998— Tucson (PCL)	4	6	.400	5.44	1.60	39	10	0	0	...	2-...	87.2	116	61	53	14	24-0	50	.315
— Arizona (N.L.)	0	0		9.00	2.00	3	0	0	0	...	0-0	4.0	6	4	4	1	2-0	1	.375
1999— Toledo (Int'l)	5	2	.714	2.86	1.40	48	0	0	0	...	0-0	69.1	63	27	22	6	34-4	36	.240
2000— Sacramento (PCL)	8	3	.727	4.24	1.38	47	6	0	0	...	4-...	85.0	88	43	40	11	29-2	55	.273
2001— Portland (PCL)	8	7	.533	4.67	1.46	47	12	0	0	...	6-...	106.0	124	55	55	12	31-3	66	.300
2002— Las Vegas (PCL)	5	4	.556	4.36	1.81	37	0	0	0	...	1-...	53.2	79	·31	26	5	18-1	33	.348
— Los Angeles (N.L.)	0	0		0.00	0.00	1	0	0	0	...	0-0	1.0	0	0	0	0	0-0	0	.000
2003— Las Vegas (PCL)	4	5	.444	2.97	1.35	60	0	0	0	...	3-...	91.0	94	40	30	8	29-2	46	.268
2004— Iowa (PCL)	2	0	1.000	3.38	1.13	10	0	0	0	...	5-...	13.1	10	5	5	1	5-0	13	.208
2005— Albuquerque (PCL)	3	6	.333	7.65	1.63	44	1	0	0	6	0-2	60.0	78	52	51	11	20-0	44	.312
2006— Oklahoma (PCL)	0	0		0.60	0.67	12	0	0	0	1	8-8	15.0	8	1	1	0	2-0	16	.163
— Frisco (Texas)	1	0	1.000	2.08	1.27	13	0	0	0	1	7-8	17.1	16	7	4	0	6-1	19	.242
— Texas (A.L.)	1	1	.500	2.60	1.33	16	0	0	0	0	0-0	17.1	15	5	5	0	8-0	13	.231
— Pawtucket (Int'l)	0	0		7.20	1.80	3	0	0	0	1	0-0	5.0	7	4	4	2	2-0	4	.333
— Boston (A.L.)	1	0	1.000	4.57	1.25	16	0	0	0	3	0-0	21.2	20	11	11	1	7-0	15	.250
American League totals (1 year)	**2**	**1**	**.667**	**3.69**	**1.28**	**32**	**0**	**0**	**0**	**3**	**0-0**	**39.0**	**35**	**16**	**16**	**1**	**15-0**	**28**	**.241**
National League totals (2 years)	**0**	**0**		**7.20**	**1.60**	**4**	**0**	**0**	**0**	**...**	**0-0**	**5.0**	**6**	**4**	**4**	**1**	**2-0**	**1**	**2.000**
Major League totals (3 years)	**2**	**1**	**.667**	**4.09**	**1.32**	**36**	**0**	**0**	**0**	**3**	**0-0**	**44.0**	**41**	**20**	**20**	**2**	**17-0**	**29**	**.277**

2006 LEFTY-RIGHTY SPLITS

vs.	Avg.	AB	H	2B	3B	HR	RBI	BB	SO	OBP	Slg.	vs.	Avg.	AB	H	2B	3B	HR	RBI	BB	SO	OBP	Slg.
L	.225	71	16	4	1	1	7	5	18	.282	.352	R	.257	74	19	7	0	0	11	10	10	.345	.351

CORMIER, LANCE — P

PERSONAL: Born August 19, 1980, in Lafayette, La. ... 6-1/190. ... Throws right, bats right. ... Full name: Lance Robert Cormier. ... Name pronounced: COR-mee-ay. ... High school: Lafayette (La.). ... College: Alabama. **TRANSACTIONS/CAREER NOTES:** Selected by Cincinnati Reds organization in 40th round of 1998 free-agent draft; did not sign. ... Selected by Houston Astros organization in 10th round of 2001 free-agent draft; did not sign. ... Selected by Arizona Diamondbacks organization in fourth round of 2002 free-agent draft. ... Traded by Diamondbacks with P Oscar Villarreal to Atlanta Braves for C Johnny Estrada (December 7, 2005). ... On disabled list (May 3-18, 2006); included rehabilitation assignment to Rome.

CAREER HITTING: 5-for-26 (.192), 1 R, 1 2B, 0 3B, 0 HR, 2 RBI.

Year	Team (League)	W	L	Pct.	ERA	WHIP	G	GS	CG	ShO	Hld.	Sv.-Opp.	IP	H	R	ER	HR	BB-IBB	SO	Avg.
2002—	Yakima (N'west)	0	0	...	27.00	4.00	1	0	0	0	...	0-...	1.0	4	4	3	0	0-0	3	.500
	—South Bend (Mid.)	3	0	1.000	2.93	1.12	11	3	0	0	...	1-...	27.2	29	9	9	1	2-0	17	.259
2003—	Lancaster (Calif.)	6	5	.545	3.82	1.25	15	15	0	0	...	0-...	94.1	102	55	40	6	16-1	59	.280
	—Tucson (PCL)	1	1	.500	2.60	1.12	5	4	0	0	...	0-...	27.2	26	10	8	1	5-0	11	.260
	—El Paso (Texas)	2	3	.400	6.10	1.96	9	8	0	0	...	0-...	41.1	59	33	28	3	22-0	26	.337
2004—	El Paso (Texas)	2	3	.400	2.29	1.32	10	8	0	0	...	0-...	63.0	66	19	16	3	17-0	58	.277
	—Tucson (PCL)	3	3	.500	2.68	1.33	8	8	2	1	...	0-...	50.1	50	17	15	0	17-1	37	.260
	—Arizona (N.L.)	1	4	.200	8.14	1.92	17	5	0	0	2	0-0	45.1	62	42	41	13	25-2	24	.333
2005—	Tucson (PCL)	0	1	.000	14.73	3.00	1	1	0	0	...	0-0	3.2	6	6	6	1	5-0	5	.429
	—Arizona (N.L.)	7	3	.700	5.11	1.63	67	0	0	0	13	0-1	79.1	86	50	45	7	43-5	63	.285
2006—	Richmond (Int'l)	4	3	.571	3.95	1.45	9	9	1	1	0	0-0	54.2	65	26	24	4	14-1	27	.301
	—Rome (S. Atl.)	0	0	...	0.00	0.00	1	0	0	0	0	0-0	1.0	0	0	0	0	0-0	2	...
	—Atlanta (N.L.)	4	5	.444	4.89	1.75	29	9	0	0	2	0-0	73.2	90	44	40	8	39-7	43	.314
	Major League totals (3 years)	12	12	.500	5.72	1.74	113	14	0	0	17	0-1	198.1	238	136	126	28	107-14	130	.307

2006 LEFTY-RIGHTY SPLITS

vs.	Avg.	AB	H	2B	3B	HR	RBI	BB	SO	OBP	Slg.	vs.	Avg.	AB	H	2B	3B	HR	RBI	BB	SO	OBP	Slg.
L	.271	133	36	3	1	4	15	25	21	.389	.398	R	.351	154	54	15	2	4	18	14	22	.400	.552

CORMIER, RHEAL — P

PERSONAL: Born April 23, 1967, in Moncton, New Brunswick. ... 5-10/195. ... Throws left, bats left. ... Full name: Rheal Paul Cormier. ... Name pronounced: ray-AL COR-mee-ay. ... High school: Polyvalente Louis J. Robichaud (New Brunswick, Can. ... Junior college: Rhode Island C.C.. **TRANSACTIONS/CAREER NOTES:** Selected by St. Louis Cardinals organization in sixth round of 1988 free-agent draft. ... On disabled list (August 12-September 7, 1993). ... On disabled list (April 28-May 13 and May 21-August 3, 1994); included rehabilitation assignments to Arkansas and Louisville. ... Traded by Cardinals with OF Mark Whiten to Boston Red Sox for 3B Scott Cooper, P Cory Bailey and a player to be named (April 8, 1995). ... Traded by Red Sox with 1B Ryan McGuire and P Shayne Bennett to Montreal Expos for SS Wil Cordero and P Bryan Eversgerd (Jauary 10, 1996). ... On disabled list (August 26-September 10, 1996). ... Signed as a free agent by Cleveland Indians organization (December 18, 1997). ... Signed as a free agent by Red Sox organization (January 5, 1999). ... On suspended list (May 7-10, 1999). ... Signed as a free agent by Philadelphia Phillies (November 29, 2000). ... On disabled list (August 10-29, 2001); included rehabilitation assignment to Reading. ... Traded by Phillies to Cincinnati Reds for P Justin Germano (July 31, 2006). **MISCELLANEOUS NOTES:** Member of 1988 Canadian Olympic baseball team.

CAREER HITTING: 36-for-192 (.188), 15 R, 4 2B, 1 3B, 0 HR, 12 RBI.

Year	Team (League)	W	L	Pct.	ERA	WHIP	G	GS	CG	ShO	Hld.	Sv.-Opp.	IP	H	R	ER	HR	BB-IBB	SO	Avg.
1989—	St. Pete. (FSL)	12	7	.632	2.23	1.03	26	26	4	1	...	0-...	169.2	141	63	42	9	33-2	122	.225
1990—	Arkansas (Texas)	5	12	.294	5.04	1.34	22	21	3	1	...	0-...	121.1	133	81	68	7	30-2	102	.273
	—Louisville (A.A.)	1	1	.500	2.25	0.88	4	4	0	0	...	0-...	24.0	18	8	6	1	3-0	9	.202
1991—	Louisville (A.A.)	7	9	.438	4.23	1.34	21	21	3	3	...	0-...	127.2	140	64	60	5	31-1	74	.286
	—St. Louis (N.L.)	4	5	.444	4.12	1.21	11	10	2	0	0	0-0	67.2	74	35	31	5	8-1	38	.277
1992—	St. Louis (N.L.)	10	10	.500	3.68	1.22	31	30	3	0	0	0-0	186.0	194	83	76	15	33-2	117	.269
	—Louisville (A.A.)	0	1	.000	6.75	2.00	1	1	0	0	...	0-...	4.0	8	4	3	0	0-0	1	.400
1993—	St. Louis (N.L.)	7	6	.538	4.33	1.31	38	21	1	0	0	0-0	145.1	163	80	70	18	27-3	75	.284
1994—	St. Louis (N.L.)	3	2	.600	5.45	1.18	7	7	0	0	0	0-0	39.2	40	24	24	6	7-0	26	.256
	—Arkansas (Texas)	1	0	1.000	1.93	0.96	2	2	0	0	...	0-...	9.1	9	2	2	0	0-0	11	.257
	—Louisville (A.A.)	1	2	.333	4.50	1.32	3	3	1	0	...	0-...	22.0	21	11	11	3	8-1	13	.250
1995—	Boston (A.L.)	7	5	.583	4.07	1.41	48	12	0	0	9	0-2	115.0	131	60	52	12	31-2	69	.294
1996—	Montreal (N.L.)	7	10	.412	4.17	1.29	33	27	1	1	0	0-0	159.2	165	80	74	16	41-3	100	.270
1997—	Montreal (N.L.)	0	1	.000	33.75	3.75	1	1	0	0	0	0-0	1.1	4	5	5	1	1-0	0	.500
1998—	Akron (East.)	0	0	...	6.52	1.76	3	0	0	0	0	0-...	9.2	15	7	7	3	2-0	6	.366
1999—	Boston (A.L.)	2	0	1.000	3.69	1.25	60	0	0	0	15	0-3	63.1	61	34	26	4	18-2	39	.246
2000—	Boston (A.L.)	3	3	.500	4.61	1.33	64	0	0	0	9	0-2	68.1	74	40	35	7	17-2	43	.275
2001—	Philadelphia (N.L.)	5	6	.455	4.21	1.29	60	0	0	0	12	1-6	51.1	49	26	24	5	17-4	37	.247
	—Reading (East.)	0	0	...	0.00	0.50	1	1	0	0	0	0-...	2.0	0	0	0	0	1-0	2	.000
2002—	Philadelphia (N.L.)	5	6	.455	5.25	1.55	54	0	0	0	9	0-3	60.0	61	38	35	6	32-6	49	.266
2003—	Philadelphia (N.L.)	8	0	1.000	1.70	0.93	65	0	0	0	14	1-4	84.2	54	18	16	4	25-2	67	.182
2004—	Philadelphia (N.L.)	4	5	.444	3.56	1.19	84	0	0	0	28	0-7	81.0	70	32	32	7	26-6	46	.237
2005—	Philadelphia (N.L.)	4	2	.667	5.89	1.52	57	0	0	0	17	0-2	47.1	56	33	31	9	16-1	34	.296
2006—	Philadelphia (N.L.)	2	2	.500	1.59	1.18	43	0	0	0	12	0-4	34.0	27	6	6	2	13-3	13	.225
	—Cincinnati (N.L.)	0	1	.000	4.50	1.79	21	0	0	0	0	0-0	14.0	21	7	7	3	4-0	15	.350
	American League totals (3 years)	12	8	.600	4.12	1.35	172	12	0	0	33	0-7	246.2	266	134	113	23	66-6	151	.276
	National League totals (12 years)	59	56	.513	3.99	1.26	505	96	7	1	94	2-26	972.0	978	467	431	97	250-31	608	.263
	Major League totals (15 years)	71	64	.526	4.02	1.28	677	108	7	1	127	2-33	1218.2	1244	601	544	120	316-37	759	.265

DIVISION SERIES RECORD

Year	Team (League)	W	L	Pct.	ERA	WHIP	G	GS	CG	ShO	Hld.	Sv.-Opp.	IP	H	R	ER	HR	BB-IBB	SO	Avg.
1995—	Boston (A.L.)	0	0	...	13.50	4.50	2	0	0	0	0	0-0	0.2	2	1	1	0	1-0	2	.500
1999—	Boston (A.L.)	0	0	...	0.00	0.75	2	0	0	0	0	0-0	4.0	2	0	0	0	1-0	4	.154
	Division series totals (2 years)	0	0	...	1.93	1.29	4	0	0	0	0	0-0	4.2	4	1	1	0	2-0	6	.235

CHAMPIONSHIP SERIES RECORD

Year	Team (League)	W	L	Pct.	ERA	WHIP	G	GS	CG	ShO	Hld.	Sv.-Opp.	IP	H	R	ER	HR	BB-IBB	SO	Avg.
1999—	Boston (A.L.)	0	0	...	0.00	1.64	2	0	0	0	0	0-0	3.2	3	0	0	0	3-1	4	.200

2006 LEFTY-RIGHTY SPLITS

vs.	Avg.	AB	H	2B	3B	HR	RBI	BB	SO	OBP	Slg.	vs.	Avg.	AB	H	2B	3B	HR	RBI	BB	SO	OBP	Slg.
L	.289	83	24	5	1	4	15	6	9	.344	.518	R	.247	97	24	6	0	1	15	11	10	.336	.340

C

CORPAS, MANUEL   P

PERSONAL: Born December 3, 1982, in Panama City, Panama. ... 6-3/170. ... Throws right, bats right. ... Full name: Manuel Corpas. **TRANSACTIONS/CAREER NOTES:** Signed as a non-drafted free agent by Colorado Rockies organization (August 26, 1999).

CAREER HITTING: 0-for-0 (.000), 0 R, 0 2B, 0 3B, 0 HR, 0 RBI.

Year Team (League)	W	L	Pct.	ERA	WHIP	G	GS	CG	ShO	Hld.	Sv.-Opp.	IP	H	R	ER	HR	BB-IBB	SO	Avg.
2000— Venoco (VSL)	0	1	.000	15.43	2.14	1	0	0	0	...	0-...	2.1	5	4	4	0	0-0	3	.385
2001— Dominican Rockies (DSL)	2	1	.667	2.24	1.30	15	5	0	0	...	2-...	56.1	56	23	14	0	17-0	41	.248
2002— Casper (Pion.)	2	4	.333	5.73	1.67	29	0	0	0	...	2-...	33.0	37	24	21	4	18-3	42	.274
2003— Tri-City (N'west)	5	6	.455	5.79	1.43	15	15	0	0	...	0-...	84.0	98	61	54	7	22-1	47	.292
2004— Asheville (S. Atl.)	2	2	.500	3.05	1.38	43	0	0	0	...	3-...	44.1	48	20	15	3	13-1	52	.267
2005— Modesto (California)	3	2	.600	3.78	1.41	47	0	0	0	12	2-3	69.0	83	33	29	2	14-0	52	.299
2006— Tulsa (Texas)	2	1	.667	0.98	0.71	34	0	0	0	7	19-22	36.2	22	7	4	0	4-1	35	.177
— Colo. Springs (PCL)	0	0	...	1.04	0.81	8	0	0	0	2	0-0	8.2	5	1	1	1	2-0	7	.167
— Colorado (N.L.)	1	2	.333	3.62	1.36	35	0	0	0	7	0-2	32.1	36	13	13	3	8-1	27	.286
Major League totals (1 year)	1	2	.333	3.62	1.36	35	0	0	0	7	0-2	32.1	36	13	13	3	8-1	27	.286

2006 LEFTY-RIGHTY SPLITS

vs.	Avg.	AB	H	2B	3B	HR	RBI	BB	SO	OBP	Slg.	vs.	Avg.	AB	H	2B	3B	HR	RBI	BB	SO	OBP	Slg.
L	.281	64	18	4	1	1	4	2	10	.303	.422	R	.290	62	18	5	0	2	8	6	17	.371	.468

CORREIA, KEVIN   P

PERSONAL: Born August 24, 1980, in San Diego. ... 6-3/200. ... Throws right, bats right. ... Full name: Kevin John Correia. ... Name pronounced: cor-RAY-ah. ... High school: Grossmont (San Diego). ... College: Cal-Poly San Luis Obispo. **TRANSACTIONS/CAREER NOTES:** Selected by St. Louis Cardinals organization in 23rd round of 2001 free-agent draft; did not sign. ... Selected by San Francisco Giants organization in fourth round of 2002 free-agent draft.

CAREER HITTING: 5-for-42 (.119), 3 R, 1 2B, 0 3B, 0 HR, 2 RBI.

Year Team (League)	W	L	Pct.	ERA	WHIP	G	GS	CG	ShO	Hld.	Sv.-Opp.	IP	H	R	ER	HR	BB-IBB	SO	Avg.
2002— Salem-Keizer (N'west)	2	2	.500	4.54	1.35	10	8	0	0	...	0-...	37.2	37	20	19	1	14-0	31	.257
2003— Norwich (East.)	6	6	.500	3.65	1.27	16	14	0	0	...	0-...	86.1	80	38	35	3	30-0	73	.248
— Fresno (PCL)	1	0	1.000	2.84	0.95	3	3	0	0	...	0-...	19.0	16	8	6	3	2-0	23	.222
— San Francisco (N.L.)	3	1	.750	3.66	1.50	10	7	0	0	0	0-0	39.1	41	16	16	6	18-1	28	.275
2004— Fresno (PCL)	3	7	.300	4.53	1.45	29	16	0	0	...	0-...	105.1	118	61	53	12	35-3	70	.284
— San Francisco (N.L.)	0	1	.000	8.05	1.84	12	1	0	0	0	0-0	19.0	25	20	17	3	10-0	14	.333
2005— Fresno (PCL)	3	2	.600	6.07	1.59	31	3	0	0	0	7-7	46.0	50	38	31	6	23-0	35	.273
— San Jose (Calif.)	0	1	.000	2.57	1.43	1	1	0	0	0	0-0	7.0	5	2	2	0	5-0	7	.208
— San Francisco (N.L.)	2	5	.286	4.63	1.58	16	11	0	0	0	0-0	58.1	61	31	30	12	31-2	44	.274
2006— San Francisco (N.L.)	2	0	1.000	3.49	1.23	48	0	0	0	10	0-1	69.2	64	27	27	5	22-0	57	.242
Major League totals (4 years)	7	7	.500	4.35	1.46	86	19	0	0	10	0-1	186.1	191	94	90	26	81-3	143	.268

2006 LEFTY-RIGHTY SPLITS

vs.	Avg.	AB	H	2B	3B	HR	RBI	BB	SO	OBP	Slg.	vs.	Avg.	AB	H	2B	3B	HR	RBI	BB	SO	OBP	Slg.
L	.275	109	30	6	1	2	20	12	19	.339	.404	R	.218	156	34	14	0	3	15	10	38	.276	.365

CORTES, DAVID   P

PERSONAL: Born October 15, 1973, in Mexicali, Mexico. ... 5-11/195. ... Throws right, bats right. ... Full name: David C. Cortes. ... Name pronounced: cor-tez. ... High school: Central Union (Calif.). ... Junior college: Imperial Valley College (Calif.). **TRANSACTIONS/CAREER NOTES:** Signed as a non-drafted free agent by Atlanta Braves organization (July 13, 1996). ... On disabled list (June 4-July 5, 1998). ... Traded by Braves with P Mike Porzio to Colorado Rockies for 1B Greg Colbrunn (July 30, 1998). ... Traded by Rockies to Braves for a player to be named (August 19, 1998); Rockies acquired P Anthony Briggs to complete deal (September 8, 1998). ... On disabled list (April 2, 2000-entire season; and April 5-May 17, 2001). ... Signed as a free agent by Dos Laredos of the Mexican League (April 1, 2002). ... Contract purchased by Arizona Diamondbacks organization (August 24, 2002). ... Released by Diamondbacks (March 29, 2003). ... Signed by Dos Laredos (April 1, 2003). ... Contract purchased by Cleveland Indians organization (July 31, 2003). ... Signed as a free agent by Detroit Tigers organization (December 11, 2003). ... Loaned to Tijuana of the Mexican League (May 22, 2004). ... Released by Tigers (June 15, 2004). ... Signed by Colorado Rockies organization (December 22, 2004).

CAREER HITTING: 0-for-2 (.000), 0 R, 0 2B, 0 3B, 0 HR, 0 RBI.

Year Team (League)	W	L	Pct.	ERA	WHIP	G	GS	CG	ShO	Hld.	Sv.-Opp.	IP	H	R	ER	HR	BB-IBB	SO	Avg.
1996— Eugene (Northwest)	2	1	.667	0.73	0.77	15	0	0	0	...	4-...	24.2	13	2	2	0	6-0	33	.148
1997— Macon (S. Atl.)	3	0	1.000	0.57	0.64	27	0	0	0	...	15-...	31.1	16	3	2	0	4-0	32	.152
— Durham (Carol.)	2	0	1.000	2.33	1.03	19	0	0	0	...	8-...	19.1	15	5	5	1	5-0	16	.214
— Greenville (Sou.)	1	0	1.000	1.80	1.00	3	0	0	0	...	0-...	5.0	4	1	1	1	1-0	7	.211
1998— Richmond (Int'l)	3	3	.500	2.82	1.14	29	0	0	0	...	4-...	44.2	37	15	14	2	14-3	46	.227
— Colo. Springs (PCL)	1	0	1.000	7.71	2.29	6	0	0	0	...	0-...	7.0	14	6	6	0	2-0	5	.400
1999— Richmond (Int'l)	2	3	.400	3.35	1.40	47	0	0	0	...	22-...	45.2	50	19	17	2	14-5	42	.276
— Atlanta (N.L.)	0	0	...	4.91	1.91	4	0	0	0	0	0-0	3.2	3	3	2	0	4-0	2	.214
2000— Atlanta (N.L.)							Did not play.												
2001— Myrtle Beach (Carol.)	0	2	.000	5.91	1.50	9	0	0	0	...	2-...	10.2	11	7	7	2	5-0	9	.256
— Greenville (Sou.)	0	3	.000	8.15	1.70	14	0	0	0	...	0-...	17.2	19	18	16	2	11-2	10	.264
— Macon (S. Atl.)	1	0	1.000	7.11	1.50	10	0	0	0	...	0-...	12.2	14	11	10	1	5-0	8	.259
2002— Tucson (PCL)	0	0	...	0.00	0.75	3	0	0	0	...	0-...	4.0	3	0	0	0	0-0	1	.188
— Dos Laredos (Mex.)	3	1	.750	4.18	1.42	39	0	0	0	...	14-...	47.1	52	22	22	2	15-2	50	.278
2003— Dos Laredos (Mex.)	4	3	.571	2.70	1.43	48	0	0	0	...	18-...	53.1	58	17	16	3	18-1	39	.287
— Cleveland (A.L.)	0	0	...	12.00	2.67	2	0	0	0	0	0-0	3.0	8	5	4	1	0-0	1	.471
— Buffalo (Int'l)	1	0	1.000	2.70	0.60	5	0	0	0	...	1-...	6.2	4	3	2	1	0-0	9	.154
2004— Toledo (Int'l)	1	0	1.000	3.95	1.32	14	0	0	0	...	0-...	13.2	12	6	6	0	6-2	10	.235
— Tijuana (Mex.)	0	1	.000	5.17	1.40	14	0	0	0	...	3-...	15.2	16	10	9	3	6-1	18	.254
2005— Colo. Springs (PCL)	1	0	1.000	4.02	1.40	12	0	0	0	1	1-2	15.2	15	9	7	3	7-0	15	.250
— Colorado (N.L.)	2	0	1.000	4.10	1.14	50	0	0	0	4	2-3	52.2	50	24	24	9	10-2	36	.251
2006— Colo. Springs (PCL)	1	1	.500	4.82	1.66	18	0	0	0	4	2-3	18.2	22	10	10	2	9-1	16	.282
— Colorado (N.L.)	3	1	.750	4.30	1.40	30	0	0	0	3	0-1	29.1	35	14	14	3	6-1	14	.310
American League totals (1 year)	0	0	...	12.00	2.67	2	0	0	0	0	0-0	3.0	8	5	4	1	0-0	1	.471
National League totals (3 years)	5	1	.833	4.20	1.26	84	0	0	0	7	2-4	85.2	88	41	40	12	20-3	52	.270
Major League totals (4 years)	5	1	.833	4.47	1.31	86	0	0	0	7	2-4	88.2	96	46	44	13	20-3	53	.280

2006 LEFTY-RIGHTY SPLITS

vs.	Avg.	AB	H	2B	3B	HR	RBI	BB	SO	OBP	Slg.	vs.	Avg.	AB	H	2B	3B	HR	RBI	BB	SO	OBP	Slg.
L	.279	43	12	1	0	1	7	4	4	.333	.372	R	.329	70	23	3	0	2	9	2	10	.351	.457

COSTA, SHANE   OF

PERSONAL: Born December 12, 1981, in Visalia, Calif. ... 6-0/220. ... Bats left, throws right. ... Full name: Shane Jeremy Costa. ... College: Cal State Fullerton. **TRANSACTIONS/CAREER NOTES:** Selected by Kansas City Royals organization in second round of 2003 free-agent draft. ... On disabled list (April 29-May 19, 2006); included rehabilitation assignment to Wichita.

2006 GAMES PLAYED BY POSITION (MLB): OF—65, DH—1.

										BATTING										FIELDING	
Year	Team (League)	Pos.	G	AB	R	H	2B	3B	HR	RBI	BB	SO	HBP	GDP	SB-CS	Avg.	OBP	SLG	OPS	E	Avg.
2003—	Arizona Royals 2 (AZL)	OF	23	88	22	34	6	4	1	24	6	7	4	2	4-3	.386	.444	.580	1.024	4	.889
—	Wilmington (Caro.)	OF	3	7	1	1	0	0	0	0	2	1	1	0	0-0	.143	.400	.286	.686	0	1.000
2004—	Wilmington (Caro.)	OF	123	451	70	139	20	4	7	59	32	43	11	7	9-4	.308	.364	.417	.781	5	.500
2005—	Kansas City (A.L.)	OF-DH	27	81	13	19	2	0	2	7	5	11	1	3	0-0	.235	.287	.333	.621	0	1.000
—	Wichita (Texas)	OF-DH	75	277	37	78	18	2	8	43	24	23	8	10	5-1	.282	.349	.448	.797	6	.975
—	Omaha (PCL)	OF	4	16	1	3	1	0	0	1	0	1	0	0	0-0	.188	.188	.250	.438	0	1.000
2006—	Omaha (PCL)		52	199	35	68	12	4	10	29	13	25	7	6	4-0	.342	.398	.593	.991	0	1.000
—	Wichita (Texas)		2	8	0	3	0	0	0	1	0	1	0	0	0-0	.375	.375	.375	.750	0	1.000
—	Kansas City (A.L.)	OF-DH	72	237	23	65	20	1	3	23	6	29	5	5	2-0	.274	.304	.405	.709	6	.959
	Major League totals (2 years)		99	318	36	84	22	1	5	30	11	40	6	8	2-0	.264	.300	.387	.686	6	.966

2006 LEFTY-RIGHTY SPLITS

vs.	Avg.	AB	H	2B	3B	HR	RBI	BB	SO	OBP	Slg.	vs.	Avg.	AB	H	2B	3B	HR	RBI	BB	SO	OBP	Slg.
L	.244	41	10	4	0	1	5	1	6	.256	.415	R	.281	196	55	16	1	2	18	5	23	.314	.403

COSTE, CHRIS   C

PERSONAL: Born February 4, 1973, in Fargo, N.D. ... Bats right, throws right. ... Full name: Christopher Robert Coste. ... College: Concordia College (Minn). **TRANSACTIONS/CAREER NOTES:** Signed as a non-drafted free agent by Pittsburgh Pirates organization (January 5, 1999). ... Played pitcher for parts of four seasons (1995, 2002-03 and 2005). ... Released by Pirates (November 13, 1999). ... Signed by Cleveland Indians organization (November 16, 1999). ... Signed as a free agent by Boston Red Sox organization (November 21, 2002). ... Signed as a free agent by Milwaukee Brewers organization (November 12, 2003). ... Signed as a free agent by Philadelphia Phillies organization (October 29, 2004).

2006 GAMES PLAYED BY POSITION (MLB): C—54, 1B—2.

										BATTING										FIELDING	
Year	Team (League)	Pos.	G	AB	R	H	2B	3B	HR	RBI	BB	SO	HBP	GDP	SB-CS	Avg.	OBP	SLG	OPS	E	Avg.
1995—	Brandon (Prairie)		24	94	12	24	7	0	0	13	3	10	0	...	2-1	.255	.278	.330	.608	0	...
1996—	Fargo-Moorhead (North.) ..		81	315	40	99	30	0	6	56	17	56	10	6	2-3	.314	.364	.467	.831	10	...
1997—	Fargo-Moorhead (North.) ..		84	337	45	105	22	0	12	50	23	53	7	10	7-1	.312	.367	.484	.851	12	...
1998—	Fargo-Moorhead (North.) ..		85	326	59	107	17	2	16	55	31	30	3	14	6-3	.328	.390	.485	.875	2	...
1999—	Fargo-Moorhead (North.) ..		85	352	67	118	18	2	16	60	31	42	2	17	4-1	.335	.389	.534	.923	11	...
2000—	Buffalo (Int'l)		31	96	15	29	2	0	4	8	3	12	1	4	0-1	.302	.330	.448	.778	3	...
—	Akron (East.)		65	240	32	80	20	4	2	31	15	33	4	7	1-2	.333	.381	.475	.856	3	...
2001—	Akron (East.)		6	24	1	3	0	0	0	0	1	3	0	0	0-1	.125	.160	.125	.285	1	...
—	Buffalo (Int'l)		75	271	31	78	16	2	7	50	15	50	4	11	0-1	.288	.330	.439	.769	4	...
2002—	Buffalo (Int'l)		124	478	59	152	32	1	8	67	34	54	13	14	0-0	.318	.377	.439	.816	10	...
2003—	GC Red Sox (GCL)		11	30	3	7	2	1	1	6	7	5	0	2	0-0	.233	.378	.467	.845	0	...
—	Pawtucket (Int'l)		29	96	5	18	5	0	1	8	4	18	0	3	0-0	.188	.218	.271	.489	3	...
2004—	Indianapolis (Int'l)		78	262	34	77	21	1	2	26	20	37	5	6	2-3	.294	.353	.405	.758	10	...
2005—	Scran./W.B. (I.L.)	3B-1B-C DH-P	134	506	73	148	26	1	20	89	40	85	9	25	3-4	.292	.351	.466	.817	12	.978
2006—	Scran./W.B. (I.L.)		39	147	12	26	8	0	2	14	9	28	3	2	1-1	.177	.236	.272	.508	0	1.000
—	Philadelphia (N.L.)	C-1B	65	198	25	65	14	0	7	32	10	31	5	6	0-0	.328	.376	.505	.881	4	.988
	Major League totals (1 year)		65	198	25	65	14	0	7	32	10	31	5	6	0-0	.328	.376	.505	.881	4	.988

2006 LEFTY-RIGHTY SPLITS

vs.	Avg.	AB	H	2B	3B	HR	RBI	BB	SO	OBP	Slg.	vs.	Avg.	AB	H	2B	3B	HR	RBI	BB	SO	OBP	Slg.
L	.288	59	17	4	0	3	15	4	16	.333	.508	R	.345	139	48	10	0	4	17	6	15	.393	.504

COTA, HUMBERTO   C

PERSONAL: Born February 7, 1979, in San Luis Rio Colorado, Mexico. ... 6-0/210. ... Bats right, throws right. ... Full name: Humberto Figueroa Cota. ... Name pronounced: KOH-ta. ... High school: Preparatoria Abierta (Mexico). **TRANSACTIONS/CAREER NOTES:** Signed as a non-drafted free agent by Atlanta Braves organization (December 22, 1995). ... Loaned by Braves organization to Mexico City Tigers of the Mexican League (June 23-September 23, 1996). ... Released by Braves (January 27, 1997). ... Signed by Tampa Bay Devil Rays organization (May 22, 1997). ... Traded by Devil Rays with C Joe Oliver to Pittsburgh Pirates for OF Jose Guillen and P Jeff Sparks (July 23, 1999). ... On disabled list (May 28-August 2, 2004); included rehabilitation assignment to Nashville.

2006 GAMES PLAYED BY POSITION (MLB): C—33.

										BATTING										FIELDING	
Year	Team (League)	Pos.	G	AB	R	H	2B	3B	HR	RBI	BB	SO	HBP	GDP	SB-CS	Avg.	OBP	SLG	OPS	E	Avg.
1996—	M.C. Tigers (Mex.)			Did not play.																	
1997—	GC Devil Rays (GCL)	C	44	133	14	32	6	1	2	20	17	27	3	1	3-1	.241	.333	.346	.679	5	.985
—	Hudson Valley (NYP)		3	9	0	2	0	0	0	2	0	1	0	0	0-0	.222	.222	.222	.444	0	1.000
1998—	Princeton (Appal.)	C	67	245	48	76	13	4	15	61	32	59	6	3	4-4	.310	.399	.580	.978	12	.973
1999—	Char., S.C. (SAL)	C-1B	85	336	42	94	21	1	9	61	20	51	2		1-1	.280	.320	.429	.748	7	.986
—	Hickory (S. Atl.)		37	133	28	36	11	2	2	20	21	20	0		3-1	.271	.365	.429	.794	2	.992
2000—	Altoona (East.)	C-1B	112	429	49	112	20	1	8	44	21	80	3	8	6-4	.261	.297	.368	.665	17	.973
2001—	Nashville (PCL)	C	111	377	61	112	22	2	14	72	25	74	8	8	7-2	.297	.351	.477	.829	8	.986
—	Pittsburgh (N.L.)	C	7	9	0	2	0	0	0	1	0	5	0	0	0-0	.222	.222	.222	.444	0	1.000
2002—	Nashville (PCL)	C-1B	118	404	51	108	27	1	9	54	31	106	5	11	5-8	.267	.321	.406	.727	4	.994
—	Pittsburgh (N.L.)	C	7	17	2	5	1	0	0	3	1	4	0	0	0-0	.294	.333	.353	.686	0	1.000
2003—	Pittsburgh (N.L.)	C	10	16	1	4	0	0	0	1	1	5	0	0	0-0	.250	.294	.313	.607	0	1.000
—	Nashville (PCL)	C-DH	62	200	23	41	9	0	8	27	20	59	2	4	2-0	.205	.284	.370	.654	0	1.000
2004—	Nashville (PCL)	C-DH	8	27	4	7	0	0	1	2	3	7	0	3	0-0	.259	.333	.370	.704	0	1.000
—	Pittsburgh (N.L.)	C	36	66	10	15	1	1	5	8	3	20	1	1	0-0	.227	.271	.500	.771	1	.991
2005—	Indianapolis (Int'l)	C	3	11	0	3	0	0	1	0	0	3	0	2	0-0	.273	.273	.273	.545	0	1.000
—	Pittsburgh (N.L.)	C	93	297	29	72	20	1	7	43	17	69	2	8	0-0	.242	.285	.387	.672	4	.992
2006—	Pittsburgh (N.L.)	C	38	100	5	19	1	0	0	5	8	26	0	3	0-0	.190	.248	.200	.448	0	1.000
	Major League totals (6 years)		191	505	47	117	24	2	12	58	30	140	3	12	0-0	.232	.277	.358	.635	5	.994

C

2006 LEFTY-RIGHTY SPLITS

vs.	Avg.	AB	H	2B	3B	HR	RBI	BB	SO	OBP	Slg.		vs.	Avg.	AB	H	2B	3B	HR	RBI	BB	SO	OBP	Slg.
L	.125	24	3	0	0	0	2	4	2	.241	.125		R	.211	76	16	1	0	0	3	4	24	.250	.224

COTTS, NEAL — P

PERSONAL: Born March 25, 1980, in Belleville, Ill. ... 6-2/200. ... Throws left, bats left. ... Full name: Neal James Cotts. ... High school: Lebanon (Ill.). ... College: Illinois State.
TRANSACTIONS/CAREER NOTES: Selected by Oakland Athletics organization in second round of 2001 free-agent draft. ... Traded by Athletics with OF Dayton Holt to Chicago White Sox (December 16, 2002), completing deal in which White Sox traded Ps Keith Foulke and Joe Valentine and C Mark Johnson to Athletics for P Billy Koch and two players to be named (December 3, 2002).
CAREER HITTING: 1-for-1 (1.000), 0 R, 1 2B, 0 3B, 0 HR, 0 RBI.

Year — Team (League)	W	L	Pct.	ERA	WHIP	G	GS	CG	ShO	Hld.	Sv.-Opp.	IP	H	R	ER	HR	BB-IBB	SO	Avg.
2001— Vancouver (N'west)	1	0	1.000	3.09	1.17	9	7	0	0	...	0-...	35.0	28	14	12	2	13-0	44	.215
— Visalia (Calif.)	3	2	.600	2.32	1.35	7	7	0	0	...	0-...	31.0	27	14	8	0	15-0	34	.225
2002— Modesto (California)	12	6	.667	4.12	1.53	28	28	0	0	...	0-...	137.2	123	72	63	5	87-0	178	.239
2003— Chicago (A.L.)	1	1	.500	8.10	2.40	4	4	0	0	...	0-...	13.1	15	12	12	1	17-0	10	.294
— Birmingham (Sou.)	9	7	.563	2.16	1.14	21	21	0	0	...	0-...	108.1	67	32	26	2	56-1	133	.178
2004— Chicago (A.L.)	4	4	.500	5.65	1.39	56	1	0	0	4	0-2	65.1	61	45	41	13	30-2	58	.247
2005— Chicago (A.L.)	4	0	1.000	1.94	1.11	69	0	0	0	13	0-2	60.1	38	15	13	1	29-5	58	.179
2006— Chicago (A.L.)	1	2	.333	5.17	1.63	70	0	0	0	14	1-4	54.0	64	33	31	12	24-6	43	.291
Major League totals (4 years)	**10**	**7**	**.588**	**4.52**	**1.44**	**199**	**5**	**0**	**0**	**31**	**1-8**	**193.0**	**178**	**105**	**97**	**27**	**100-13**	**169**	**.244**

DIVISION SERIES RECORD

Year — Team (League)	W	L	Pct.	ERA	WHIP	G	GS	CG	ShO	Hld.	Sv.-Opp.	IP	H	R	ER	HR	BB-IBB	SO	Avg.
2005— Chicago (A.L.)	0	0	...	0.00	0.00	1	0	0	0	0	0-0	0.1	0	0	0	0	0-0	0	.000

CHAMPIONSHIP SERIES RECORD

Year — Team (League)	W	L	Pct.	ERA	WHIP	G	GS	CG	ShO	Hld.	Sv.-Opp.	IP	H	R	ER	HR	BB-IBB	SO	Avg.
2005— Chicago (A.L.)	0	0	...	0.00	0.00	1	0	0	0	0	0-0	0.2	0	0	0	0	0-0	0	.000

WORLD SERIES RECORD

Year — Team (League)	W	L	Pct.	ERA	WHIP	G	GS	CG	ShO	Hld.	Sv.-Opp.	IP	H	R	ER	HR	BB-IBB	SO	Avg.
2005— Chicago (A.L.)	1	0	1.000	0.00	1.50	4	0	0	0	2	0-0	1.1	1	0	0	0	1-0	2	.200

2006 LEFTY-RIGHTY SPLITS

vs.	Avg.	AB	H	2B	3B	HR	RBI	BB	SO	OBP	Slg.		vs.	Avg.	AB	H	2B	3B	HR	RBI	BB	SO	OBP	Slg.
L	.263	99	26	4	2	5	23	5	29	.318	.495		R	.314	121	38	9	1	7	18	19	14	.404	.579

COUNSELL, CRAIG — SS

PERSONAL: Born August 21, 1970, in South Bend, Ind. ... 6-0/184. ... Bats left, throws right. ... Full name: Craig John Counsell. ... High school: Whitefish Bay (Milwaukee). ... College: Notre Dame. **TRANSACTIONS/CAREER NOTES:** Selected by Colorado Rockies organization in 11th round of 1992 free-agent draft. ... On disabled list (May 1-July 15 and July 18-September 3, 1996). ... Traded by Rockies to Florida Marlins for P Mark Hutton (July 27, 1997). ... On disabled list (August 4, 1998-remainder of season). ... Traded by Marlins to Los Angeles Dodgers for a player to be named (June 15, 1999). ... Marlins acquired P Ryan Moskau to complete deal (July 15, 1999). ... Released by Dodgers (March 15, 2000). ... Signed by Arizona Diamondbacks organization (March 20, 2000). ... On disabled list (August 9, 2002-remainder of season). ... On disabled list (May 7-July 7, 2003); included rehabilitation assignment to Tucson. ... Traded by Diamondbacks with 2B Junior Spivey, 1B Lyle Overbay, C Chad Moeller and Ps Chris Capuano and Jorge de la Rosa to Milwaukee Brewers for 1B Richie Sexson, P Shane Nance and a player to be named (December 1, 2003); Diamondbacks acquired OF Noochie Varner to complete deal (December 15, 2003). ... Signed as a free agent by Diamondbacks (December 21, 2004). ... On disabled list (July 15-August 22, 2006); included rehabilitation assignments to Tucson and Lancaster. **STATISTICAL NOTES:** Career major league grand slams: 2.
2006 GAMES PLAYED BY POSITION (MLB): SS—88, 3B—7, 2B—2.

Year — Team (League)	Pos.	G	AB	R	H	2B	3B	HR	RBI	BB	SO	HBP	GDP	SB-CS	Avg.	OBP	SLG	OPS	FIELDING E	FIELDING Avg.
1992— Bend (N'west)	2B-SS	18	61	11	15	6	1	0	8	9	10	1	2	1-2	.246	.352	.377	.729	2	.967
1993— Central Valley (Cal.)	SS	131	471	79	132	26	3	5	59	95	68	3	8	14-8	.280	.401	.380	.781	35	.944
1994— New Haven (East.)	2B-SS	83	300	47	84	20	1	5	37	37	32	5	6	4-1	.280	.366	.403	.770	27	.931
1995— Colo. Springs (PCL)	SS	118	399	60	112	22	6	5	53	34	47	2	12	10-2	.281	.336	.404	.739	30	.950
— Colorado (N.L.)	SS	3	1	0	0	0	0	0	0	1	0	0	0	0-0	.000	.500	.000	.500	0	1.000
1996— Colo. Springs (PCL)	2B-3B-SS	25	75	17	18	3	0	2	10	24	7	0	2	4-3	.240	.424	.360	.784	4	.961
1997— Colo. Springs (PCL)	2B-SS	96	376	77	126	31	6	5	63	45	38	6	6	12-2	.335	.409	.489	.898	9	.981
— Colorado (N.L.)		1	0	0	0	0	0	0	0	0	0	0	0	0-0	...	...	...	...	0	...
— Florida (N.L.)	2B	51	164	20	49	9	2	1	16	18	17	3	5	1-1	.299	.376	.396	.773	3	.989
1998— Florida (N.L.)	2B	107	335	43	84	19	5	4	40	51	47	4	5	3-0	.251	.356	.373	.729	5	.991
1999— Florida (N.L.)	2B	37	66	4	10	1	0	0	2	5	10	0	1	0-0	.152	.211	.167	.378	1	.980
— Los Angeles (N.L.)	2B-SS	50	108	20	28	6	0	0	9	9	14	0	1	1-0	.259	.311	.315	.626	1	.993
2000— Tucson (PCL)	2B-3B-SS	50	198	45	69	14	3	3	27	22	20	1	1	4-1	.348	.413	.495	.908	4	.981
— Arizona (N.L.)	2B-3B-SS	67	152	23	48	8	1	2	11	20	18	2	4	3-3	.316	.400	.421	.821	6	.957
2001— Arizona (N.L.)	SS-2B-3B																			
	1B	141	458	76	126	22	3	4	38	61	76	2	9	6-8	.275	.359	.362	.721	8	.985
2002— Arizona (N.L.)	3B-SS-2B	112	436	63	123	22	1	2	51	45	52	1	10	7-5	.282	.348	.351	.699	8	.979
2003— Tucson (PCL)	2B-SS-3B	5	23	8	10	2	0	0	2	1	3	0	0	0-0	.435	.458	.522	.980	1	.963
— Arizona (N.L.)	3B-SS-2B																			
	1B	89	303	40	71	6	3	3	21	41	32	2	4	11-4	.234	.328	.304	.631	3	.989
2004— Milwaukee (N.L.)	SS-3B	140	473	59	114	19	5	2	23	59	88	5	5	17-4	.241	.330	.315	.645	9	.983
2005— Arizona (N.L.)	2B-SS	150	578	85	148	34	4	9	42	78	69	8	8	26-7	.256	.350	.375	.726	8	.990
2006— Tucson (PCL)		2	11	2	2	0	0	0	0	1	1	0	0	0-0	.182	.250	.182	.432	0	...
— Lancaster (Calif.)		1	3	1	3	1	0	0	1	0	0	0	0	0-0	1.000	1.000	1.333	2.333	0	...
— Arizona (N.L.)	SS-3B-2B	105	372	56	95	14	4	4	30	31	47	9	1	15-8	.255	.327	.347	.674	9	.980
Major League totals (11 years)		**1053**	**3446**	**489**	**896**	**160**	**28**	**31**	**283**	**419**	**470**	**36**	**53**	**90-40**	**.260**	**.344**	**.350**	**.694**	**61**	**.985**

DIVISION SERIES RECORD

Year — Team (League)	Pos.	G	AB	R	H	2B	3B	HR	RBI	BB	SO	HBP	GDP	SB-CS	Avg.	OBP	SLG	OPS	E	Avg.
1997— Florida (N.L.)	2B	3	5	0	2	1	0	0	1	1	0	0	0	0-0	.400	.500	.600	1.100	1	.875
2001— Arizona (N.L.)	2B	5	16	2	3	0	0	1	3	2	2	0	1	0-0	.188	.278	.375	.653	0	1.000
Division series totals (2 years)		**8**	**21**	**2**	**5**	**1**	**0**	**1**	**4**	**3**	**2**	**0**	**1**	**0-0**	**.238**	**.333**	**.429**	**.762**	**1**	**.963**

CHAMPIONSHIP SERIES RECORD

Year — Team (League)	Pos.	G	AB	R	H	2B	3B	HR	RBI	BB	SO	HBP	GDP	SB-CS	Avg.	OBP	SLG	OPS	E	Avg.
1997— Florida (N.L.)	2B	5	14	0	6	0	0	0	3	2	3	0	0	0-0	.429	.529	.429	.958	1	.941
2001— Arizona (N.L.)	2B-SS	5	21	5	8	3	0	0	4	0	3	0	0	1-0	.381	.381	.524	.905	0	1.000
Champ. series totals (2 years)		**10**	**35**	**5**	**14**	**3**	**0**	**0**	**6**	**3**	**6**	**0**	**0**	**1-0**	**.400**	**.447**	**.486**	**.933**	**1**	**.972**

Year Team (League)	Pos.	G	AB	R	H	2B	3B	HR	RBI	BB	SO	HBP	GDP	SB-CS	Avg.	OBP	SLG	OPS	E	Avg.
1997— Florida (N.L.)	2B	7	22	4	4	1	0	0	2	6	5	0		1-0	.182	.345	.227	.572	1	.971
2001— Arizona (N.L.)	2B	6	24	1	2	0	0	1	1	0	7	1	0	0-0	.083	.120	.208	.328	0	1.000
World series totals (2 years)		13	46	5	6	1	0	1	3	6	12	1	0	1-0	.130	.241	.217	.458	1	.984

2006 LEFTY-RIGHTY SPLITS

vs.	Avg.	AB	H	2B	3B	HR	RBI	BB	SO	OBP	Slg.	vs.	Avg.	AB	H	2B	3B	HR	RBI	BB	SO	OBP	Slg.
L	.256	86	22	1	0	0	8	11	18	.347	.267	R	.255	286	73	13	4	4	22	20	29	.321	.371

CRAIN, JESSE — P

PERSONAL: Born July 5, 1981, in Toronto. ... 6-1/205. ... Throws right, bats right. ... Full name: Jesse Alan Crain. ... High school: Fairview (Colo.). ... College: Houston.
TRANSACTIONS/CAREER NOTES: Selected by Minnesota Twins organization in second round of 2002 free-agent draft.
CAREER HITTING: 0-for-0 (.000), 0 R, 0 2B, 0 3B, 0 HR, 0 RBI.

Year Team (League)	W	L	Pct.	ERA	WHIP	G	GS	CG	ShO	Hld.	Sv.-Opp.	IP	H	R	ER	HR	BB-IBB	SO	Avg.
2002— Elizabethton (App.)	2	1	.667	0.57	0.70	9	0	0	0		2-...	15.2	4	2	1	0	7-3	18	.082
— Quad City (Midw.)	1	1	.500	1.50	0.83	9	0	0	0		1-...	12.0	6	3	2	0	4-0	11	.154
2003— Fort Myers (FSL)	2	1	.667	2.84	0.79	10	0	0	0		0-...	19.0	10	6	6	0	5-0	25	.154
— New Britain (East.)	1	1	.500	0.69	0.59	22	0	0	0		9-...	39.0	13	4	3	0	10-1	56	.099
2004— Rochester (Int'l)	3	1	.750	3.12	1.31	23	0	0	0		10-...	26.0	24	10	9	0	10-1	33	.245
2004— Rochester (Int'l)	3	2	.600	2.49	1.09	41	0	0	0		19-...	50.2	38	20	14	5	17-2	64	.208
— Minnesota (A.L.)	3	0	1.000	2.00	1.07	22	0	0	0	2	0-1	27.0	17	6	6	2	12-1	14	.179
2005— Minnesota (A.L.)	12	5	.706	2.71	1.13	75	0	0	0	11	1-4	79.2	61	28	24	6	29-7	25	.219
2006— Minnesota (A.L.)	4	5	.444	3.52	1.27	68	0	0	0	10	1-4	76.2	79	31	30	6	18-2	60	.262
Major League totals (3 years)	19	10	.655	2.95	1.18	165	0	0	0	23	2-9	183.1	157	65	60	14	59-10	99	.232

Year Team (League)	W	L	Pct.	ERA	WHIP	G	GS	CG	ShO	Hld.	Sv.-Opp.	IP	H	R	ER	HR	BB-IBB	SO	Avg.
2004— Minnesota (A.L.)	0	0	...	0.00	3.00	1	0	0	0	0	0-0	0.1	1	0	0	0	0-0	0	.500
2006— Minnesota (A.L.)	0	0	...	9.00	4.00	2	0	0	0	0	0-0	1.0	3	3	1	1	1-0	1	.429
Division series totals (2 years)	0	0	...	6.75	3.75	3	0	0	0	0	0-0	1.1	4	3	1	1	1-0	1	.444

2006 LEFTY-RIGHTY SPLITS

vs.	Avg.	AB	H	2B	3B	HR	RBI	BB	SO	OBP	Slg.	vs.	Avg.	AB	H	2B	3B	HR	RBI	BB	SO	OBP	Slg.
L	.259	116	30	2	0	3	10	8	21	.304	.353	R	.263	186	49	11	2	3	30	10	39	.307	.392

CRAWFORD, CARL — OF

PERSONAL: Born August 5, 1981, in Houston. ... 6-2/219. ... Bats left, throws left. ... Full name: Carl Demonte Crawford. ... High school: Jefferson Davis (Houston). **TRANSACTIONS/CAREER NOTES:** Selected by Tampa Bay Devil Rays organization in second round of 1999 free-agent draft. ... On suspended list (July 19-22, 2003).
2006 GAMES PLAYED BY POSITION (MLB): OF—148, DH—3.

Year Team (League)	Pos.	G	AB	R	H	2B	3B	HR	RBI	BB	SO	HBP	GDP	SB-CS	Avg.	OBP	SLG	OPS	E	Avg.
1999— Princeton (Appal.)	OF	60	260	62	83	14	4	0	25	13	47	1	5	17-2	.319	.350	.404	.754	8	.934
2000— Char., S.C. (SAL)	OF	135	564	99	170	21	11	6	57	32	102	3	1	55-9	.301	.342	.410	.751	8	.968
2001— Orlando (South.)	OF	132	537	64	147	24	3	4	51	36	90	4	3	36-20	.274	.323	.352	.675	6	.981
2002— Durham (Int'l)	OF	85	353	59	105	17	9	7	52	20	69	2	5	26-8	.297	.335	.456	.791	1	.994
— Tampa Bay (A.L.)	OF	63	259	23	67	11	6	2	30	9	41	3	0	9-5	.259	.290	.371	.661	1	.994
2003— Tampa Bay (A.L.)	OF-DH	151	630	80	177	18	*19	5	54	26	102	1	5	* 55-10	.281	.309	.362	.671	3	.992
2004— Tampa Bay (A.L.)	OF-DH	152	626	104	185	26	* 19	11	55	35	81	1	2	* 59-15	.296	.331	.450	.781	2	.994
2005— Tampa Bay (A.L.)	OF-DH	156	644	101	194	33	15	15	81	27	84	5	11	46-8	.301	.331	.469	.800	2	.995
2006— Tampa Bay (A.L.)	OF-DH	151	600	89	183	20	*16	18	77	37	85	4	8	* 58-9	.305	.348	.482	.830	3	.991
Major League totals (5 years)		673	2759	397	806	108	65	51	297	134	393	14	26	227-47	.292	.326	.434	.760	11	.993

	G	AB	R	H	2B	3B	HR	RBI	BB	SO	HBP	GDP	SB-CS	Avg.	OBP	SLG	OPS	E	Avg.
All-Star Game totals (1 year)	1	2	0	0	0	0	0	0	0	1	0	0	0-0	.000	.000	.000	.000	0	1.000

2006 LEFTY-RIGHTY SPLITS

vs.	Avg.	AB	H	2B	3B	HR	RBI	BB	SO	OBP	Slg.	vs.	Avg.	AB	H	2B	3B	HR	RBI	BB	SO	OBP	Slg.
L	.288	163	47	6	3	4	26	10	31	.341	.436	R	.311	437	136	14	13	14	51	27	54	.351	.499

CREDE, JOE — 3B

PERSONAL: Born April 26, 1978, in Jefferson City, Mo. ... 6-1/200. ... Bats right, throws right. ... Full name: Joseph Crede. ... Name pronounced: CREE-dee. ... High school: Fatima (Westphalia, Mo.). **TRANSACTIONS/CAREER NOTES:** Selected by Chicago White Sox organization in fifth round of 1996 free-agent draft. ... On disabled list (August 26-September 10, 2005). **HONORS:** Named third baseman on SPORTING NEWS A.L. All-Star team (2006). ... Named third baseman on A.L. Silver Slugger team (2006).
STATISTICAL NOTES: Career major league grand slams: 4.
2006 GAMES PLAYED BY POSITION (MLB): 3B—149.

Year Team (League)	Pos.	G	AB	R	H	2B	3B	HR	RBI	BB	SO	HBP	GDP	SB-CS	Avg.	OBP	SLG	OPS	E	Avg.
1996— GC Whi. Sox (GCL)	3B	56	221	30	66	17	1	4	32	9	41	2	8	1-1	.299	.326	.439	.765	25	.857
1997— Hickory (S. Atl.)	3B	113	402	45	109	25	0	5	62	24	83	5	6	3-1	.271	.319	.371	.689	33	.905
1998— Win.-Salem (Car.)	3B	137	492	92	155	32	3	20	88	53	98	12	10	9-7	.315	.387	.514	.902	30	.929
1999— Birmingham (Sou.)	3B	74	291	37	73	14	1	4	42	22	47	1	15	2-6	.251	.303	.347	.650	20	.910
2000— Birmingham (Sou.)	3B	138	533	84	163	35	0	21	94	56	111	15	18	3-4	.306	.384	.490	.874	19	.942
— Chicago (A.L.)	3B-DH	7	14	2	5	1	0	0	3	0	3	0	0	0-0	.357	.333	.429	.762	1	.933
2001— Charlotte (Int'l)	3B	124	463	67	128	34	1	17	65	46	88	7	5	2-1	.276	.349	.464	.813	20	.946
— Chicago (A.L.)	3B	17	50	1	11	1	1	0	7	3	11	1	1	1-0	.220	.273	.280	.553	1	1.000
2002— Charlotte (Int'l)	3B	95	359	57	112	21	0	24	65	26	48	4	8	0-1	.312	.359	.513	.930	15	.944
— Chicago (A.L.)	3B	53	200	28	57	10	0	12	35	8	40	0	1	0-2	.285	.311	.515	.826	8	.938
2003— Chicago (A.L.)	3B	151	536	68	140	31	2	19	75	32	75	6	11	1-1	.261	.308	.433	.741	14	.964
2004— Chicago (A.L.)	3B	144	490	67	117	25	0	21	69	34	81	10	14	1-2	.239	.299	.418	.717	12	.965
2005— Chicago (A.L.)	3B-SS-DH	132	432	54	109	21	0	22	62	25	66	8	7	1-1	.252	.303	.454	.756	10	.972
2006— Chicago (A.L.)	3B	150	544	76	154	31	0	30	94	28	58	7	18	0-2	.283	.323	.506	.828	10	.978
Major League totals (7 years)		654	2266	296	593	120	3	104	345	130	334	32	52	4-8	.262	.308	.455	.763	55	.968

C

Year Team (League)	Pos.	G	AB	R	H	2B	3B	HR	RBI	BB	SO	HBP	GDP	SB-CS	Avg.	OBP	SLG	OPS	E	Avg.
DIVISION SERIES RECORD																				
2005— Chicago (A.L.)	3B	3	9	2	1	0	0	0	1	1	0	0	0	0-0	.111	.200	.111	.311	1	.938
CHAMPIONSHIP SERIES RECORD																				
2005— Chicago (A.L.)	3B	5	19	2	7	2	0	2	7	0	3	0	0	0-1	.368	.350	.789	1.139	0	1.000
WORLD SERIES RECORD																				
2005— Chicago (A.L.)	3B	4	17	2	5	1	0	2	3	1	2	1	0	0-0	.294	.368	.706	1.074	0	1.000

2006 LEFTY-RIGHTY SPLITS

vs.	Avg.	AB	H	2B	3B	HR	RBI	BB	SO	OBP	Slg.	vs.	Avg.	AB	H	2B	3B	HR	RBI	BB	SO	OBP	Slg.
L	.273	183	50	13	0	10	34	17	16	.340	.508	R	.288	361	104	18	0	20	60	11	42	.313	.504

CRISP, COCO — OF

PERSONAL: Born November 1, 1979, in Los Angeles, Calif. ... 6-0/185. ... Bats both, throws right. ... Full name: Covelli Loyce Crisp. ... High school: Inglewood (Los Angeles). ... Junior college: Los Angeles Pierce. **TRANSACTIONS/CAREER NOTES:** Selected by St. Louis Cardinals organization in seventh round of 1999 free-agent draft. ... Traded by Cardinals to Cleveland Indians (August 6, 2002), completing deal in which Cardinals traded 1B Luis Garcia and a player to be named to Indians for P Chuck Finley (July 19, 2002). ... On disabled list (May 18-June 2, 2005). ... Traded by Indians with C Josh Bard and P David Riske to Boston Red Sox for 3B Andy Marte, P Guillermo Mota and C Kelly Shoppach (January 27, 2006). ... On disabled list (April 11-May 28, 2006); included rehabilitation assignment to Pawtucket. **STATISTICAL NOTES:** Career major league grand slams: 1.

2006 GAMES PLAYED BY POSITION (MLB): OF—103.

Year Team (League)	Pos.	G	AB	R	H	2B	3B	HR	RBI	BB	SO	HBP	GDP	SB-CS	Avg.	OBP	SLG	OPS	E	Avg.
1999— Johnson City (App.)	2B	65	229	55	59	5	4	3	22	44	41	2	0	27-5	.258	.379	.354	.733	24	.912
2000— New Jersey (NYP)	OF-2B	36	134	18	32	5	0	0	14	11	22	1	1	25-3	.239	.301	.276	.577	2	.972
— Peoria (Midw.)	OF	27	98	14	27	9	0	0	7	16	15	0	1	7-3	.276	.377	.367	.745	0	1.000
2001— Potomac (Carol.)	OF	139	530	80	162	23	3	11	47	52	64	1	8	39-21	.306	.368	.423	.791	6	.975
2002— New Haven (East.)	OF	89	355	61	107	16	1	9	47	36	56	0	...	26-10	.301	.365	.428	.793	3	.985
— Akron (East.)	OF	7	32	9	13	1	0	1	4	3	3	0	...	4-0	.406	.457	.531	.988	0	1.000
— Cleveland (A.L.)	OF	32	127	16	33	9	2	1	9	11	19	0	0	4-1	.260	.314	.386	.700	1	.988
— Buffalo (Int'l)	OF	4	21	3	5	1	0	0	2	0	2	0	2	1-0	.238	.238	.286	.524	0	1.000
2003— Buffalo (Int'l)	OF	56	225	42	81	19	6	1	24	26	24	5	5	20-8	.360	.434	.511	.945	3	.982
— Cleveland (A.L.)	OF-DH	99	414	55	110	15	6	3	27	23	51	0	4	15-9	.266	.302	.353	.655	1	.995
2004— Cleveland (A.L.)	OF-DH	139	491	78	146	24	2	15	71	36	69	0	8	20-13	.297	.344	.446	.790	4	.986
2005— Cleveland (A.L.)	OF	145	594	86	178	42	4	16	69	44	81	0	7	15-6	.300	.345	.465	.810	5	.985
2006— Pawtucket (Int'l)	OF	1	3	0	1	0	0	0	2	1	0	0	0	0-0	.333	.500	.333	.833	0	1.000
— Boston (A.L.)	OF	105	413	58	109	22	2	8	36	31	67	1	5	22-4	.264	.317	.385	.702	1	.996
Major League totals (5 years)		520	2039	293	576	112	16	43	212	145	287	1	24	76-33	.282	.329	.416	.745	12	.990

2006 LEFTY-RIGHTY SPLITS

vs.	Avg.	AB	H	2B	3B	HR	RBI	BB	SO	OBP	Slg.	vs.	Avg.	AB	H	2B	3B	HR	RBI	BB	SO	OBP	Slg.
L	.277	112	31	10	1	1	9	7	28	.325	.411	R	.259	301	78	12	1	7	27	24	39	.314	.375

CROSBY, BOBBY — SS

PERSONAL: Born January 12, 1980, in Lakewood, Calif. ... 6-3/195. ... Bats right, throws right. ... Full name: Robert Edward Crosby. ... High school: La Quinta (Westminster, Calif.). ... College: Long Beach State. ... Son of Ed Crosby, infielder with three major league teams (1970-76). **TRANSACTIONS/CAREER NOTES:** Selected by Anaheim Angels organization in 34th round of 1998 free-agent draft; did not sign. ... Selected by Oakland Athletics organization in first round (25th pick overall) of 2001 free-agent draft. ... On disabled list (April 7-May 30 and August 31-September 19, 2005); included rehabilitation assignments to Stockton and Sacramento. ... On disabled list (July 31-August 18 and August 22, 2006-remainder of season). **HONORS:** Named A.L. Rookie of the Year by THE SPORTING NEWS (2004). ... Named A.L. Rookie of the Year by Baseball Writers' Association of America (2004).

2006 GAMES PLAYED BY POSITION (MLB): SS—95.

Year Team (League)	Pos.	G	AB	R	H	2B	3B	HR	RBI	BB	SO	HBP	GDP	SB-CS	Avg.	OBP	SLG	OPS	E	Avg.
2001— Modesto (California)	SS	11	38	7	15	5	0	1	3	3	8	0	1	0-0	.395	.439	.605	1.044	4	.889
2002— Modesto (California)	SS	73	280	47	86	17	2	2	38	33	43	7	5	5-0	.307	.393	.404	.796	19	.938
— Midland (Texas)	SS	59	228	31	64	16	0	7	31	19	41	0	9	9-2	.281	.335	.443	.778	13	.952
2003— Sacramento (PCL)	SS-DH	127	465	86	143	32	6	22	90	63	110	7	16	24-4	.308	.395	.544	.939	15	.973
— Oakland (A.L.)	SS-DH	11	12	1	0	0	0	0	0	1	5	1	0	0-0	.000	.143	.000	.143	2	.889
2004— Oakland (A.L.)	SS	151	545	70	130	34	1	22	64	58	141	9	20	7-3	.239	.319	.426	.744	19	.975
2005— Stockton (Calif.)	SS-DH	3	9	1	3	1	0	0	1	2	1	0	0	0-0	.333	.455	.444	.899	0	1.000
— Sacramento (PCL)	SS-DH	3	12	0	1	0	0	0	1	0	0	0	0	0-0	.083	.083	.083	.167	0	1.000
— Oakland (A.L.)	SS	84	333	66	92	25	4	9	38	35	54	1	10	0-0	.276	.346	.456	.802	7	.981
2006— Oakland (A.L.)	SS	96	358	42	82	12	0	9	40	36	76	0	11	8-1	.229	.298	.338	.636	12	.972
Major League totals (4 years)		342	1248	179	304	71	5	40	142	130	276	11	41	15-4	.244	.318	.405	.723	40	.975

2006 LEFTY-RIGHTY SPLITS

vs.	Avg.	AB	H	2B	3B	HR	RBI	BB	SO	OBP	Slg.	vs.	Avg.	AB	H	2B	3B	HR	RBI	BB	SO	OBP	Slg.
L	.185	81	15	6	0	0	5	10	21	.272	.259	R	.242	277	67	6	0	9	35	26	55	.306	.361

CROSBY, BUBBA — OF

PERSONAL: Born August 11, 1976, in Houston. ... 5-11/185. ... Bats left, throws left. ... Full name: Richard Stephen Crosby. ... High school: Bellaire (Texas). ... College: Rice. **TRANSACTIONS/CAREER NOTES:** Selected by Los Angeles Dodgers organization in first round (23rd pick overall) in 1998 free-agent draft. ... Traded by Dodgers with P Scott Proctor to New York Yankees for IF Robin Ventura (July 31, 2003). ... On disabled list (May 19-June 15, 2006); included rehabilitation assignments to Tampa and Columbus. ... Signed as free agent by Cincinnati Reds (November 10, 2006).

2006 GAMES PLAYED BY POSITION (MLB): OF—62, DH—1.

Year Team (League)	Pos.	G	AB	R	H	2B	3B	HR	RBI	BB	SO	HBP	GDP	SB-CS	Avg.	OBP	SLG	OPS	E	Avg.
1998— San Bern. (Calif.)	OF	56	199	25	43	9	2	0	14	17	38	0	3	3-5	.216	.274	.281	.555	1	.990
1999— San Bern. (Calif.)	OF	96	371	53	110	21	3	1	37	42	71	6	6	19-8	.296	.376	.377	.754	5	.975
2000— Vero Beach (FSL)	OF	73	274	50	73	13	8	8	51	31	41	7	9	27-10	.266	.335	.460	.814	4	.969
— San Bern. (Calif.)	OF	3	12	2	3	0	0	0	2	0	4	0	1	1-0	.250	.250	.250	.500	—	—
2001— Las Vegas (PCL)	OF	13	42	5	9	2	1	0	5	1	8	0	1	1-1	.214	.233	.310	.542	0	1.000
— Jacksonville (Sou.)	OF	107	384	68	116	22	5	6	47	37	60	8	7	22-6	.302	.369	.432	.802	3	.985

Year Team (League)	Pos.	G	AB	R	H	2B	3B	HR	RBI	BB	SO	HBP	GDP	SB-CS	Avg.	OBP	SLG	OPS	E	Avg.
															BATTING				**FIELDING**	
2002—Las Vegas (PCL)	OF	73	279	26	73	12	1	9	36	19	47	2	3	3-1	.262	.312	.409	.721	2	.989
— Jacksonville (Sou.)	OF	38	150	14	39	6	2	2	20	11	23	2		7-3	.260	.317	.367	.684	0	1.000
2003—Las Vegas (PCL)	OF-DH	76	277	57	100	24	8	12	57	25	47	3	6	8-0	.361	.410	.635	1.046	1	.991
— Los Angeles (N.L.)	OF	9	12	0	1	0	0	0	1	0	3	0	0	0-0	.083	.083	.083	.167	1	.667
— Columbus (Int'l)	OF	16	63	9	19	2	1	2	8	6	12	1	0	3-0	.302	.366	.460	.827	0	1.000
2004—Columbus (Int'l)	OF-DH	33	116	18	32	5	2	1	15	14	26	4	2	3-3	.276	.365	.379	.744	0	1.000
— New York (A.L.)	OF-DH	55	53	8	8	2	0	2	7	2	13	1	0	2-0	.151	.196	.302	.498	1	.973
2005—Columbus (Int'l)	OF-DH	42	160	18	37	7	1	4	22	12	28	6	2	2-1	.231	.306	.363	.668	2	.989
— New York (A.L.)	OF	76	98	15	27	0	1	1	6	4	14	0	1	4-1	.276	.304	.327	.630	0	1.000
2006—Columbus (Int'l)	OF	22	84	13	20	5	1	2	10	11	16	3	1	7-0	.238	.347	.393	.740	1	1.000
— Tampa (Fla. St.)		3	8	0	1	0	0	0	0	1	2	1	1	0-0	.125	.300	.125	.425	0	1.000
— New York (A.L.)	OF-DH	65	87	9	18	3	1	1	6	4	21	2	0	3-1	.207	.258	.299	.557	0	·1.000
American League totals (3 years)		196	238	32	53	5	2	4	19	10	48	3	1	9-2	.223	.263	.311	.574	1	.995
National League totals (1 year)		9	12	0	1	0	0	0	1	0	3	0	0	0-0	.083	.083	.083	.167	1	.667
Major League totals (4 years)		205	250	32	54	5	2	4	20	10	51	3	1	9-2	.216	.255	.300	.555	2	.989

DIVISION SERIES RECORD

Year Team (League)	Pos.	G	AB	R	H	2B	3B	HR	RBI	BB	SO	HBP	GDP	SB-CS	Avg.	OBP	SLG	OPS	E	Avg.
2004—New York (A.L.)	OF	2	0	0	0	0	0	0	0	0	0	0	0	0-0	...	...	...	...	0	...
2005—New York (A.L.)	OF	3	8	0	2	0	0	0	0	1	0	0	0	1-0	.250	.250	.250	.500	0	1.000
Division series totals (2 years)		5	8	0	2	0	0	0	0	1	0	0	0	1-0	.250	.250	.250	.500	0	1.000

CHAMPIONSHIP SERIES RECORD

Year Team (League)	Pos.	G	AB	R	H	2B	3B	HR	RBI	BB	SO	HBP	GDP	SB-CS	Avg.	OBP	SLG	OPS	E	Avg.
2004—New York (A.L.)	OF	1	0	1	0	0	0	0	0	0	0	0	0	0-0	...	...	...	...	0	...

2006 LEFTY-RIGHTY SPLITS

vs.	Avg.	AB	H	2B	3B	HR	RBI	BB	SO	OBP	Slg.	vs.	Avg.	AB	H	2B	3B	HR	RBI	BB	SO	OBP	Slg.
L	.300	10	3	0	0	0	1	1	2	.364	.300	R	.195	77	15	3	1	1	5	3	19	.244	.299

CRUCETA, FRANCISCO   P

PERSONAL: Born July 4, 1981, in La Vega, Dominican Republic. ... 6-2/180. ... Throws right, bats right. ... Full name: Francisco Alberto Cruceta. **TRANSACTIONS/CAREER NOTES:** Signed as a non-drafted free agent by Los Angeles Dodgers organization (May 20, 1999). ... Traded by Dodgers with Ps Terry Mulholland and Ricardo Rodriguez to Cleveland Indians for P Paul Shuey (July 28, 2002). ... Claimed on waivers by Seattle Mariners (August 26, 2005). ... Claimed on waivers by Texas Rangers (October 11, 2006).

CAREER HITTING: 0-for-0 (.000), 0 R, 0 2B, 0 3B, 0 HR, 0 RBI.

Year Team (League)	W	L	Pct.	ERA	WHIP	G	GS	CG	ShO	Hld.	Sv.-Opp.	IP	H	R	ER	HR	BB-IBB	SO	Avg.
1999—Dom. Dodgers (DSL)	3	2	.600	7.56	1.92	14	1	0	0		0-	25.0	33	34	21	4	15-...	21	...
2000—Dom. Dodgers (DSL)	4	2	.667	3.31	1.41	21	6	0	0		0-	49.0	33	29	18	1	36-...	49	...
2001—Dom. Dodgers (DSL)	0	4	.000	1.50	1.23	11	9	0	0		0-	48.0	35	24	8	1	24-...	47	...
2002—South Georgia (S. Atl.)	8	5	.615	2.80	1.17	20	20	3	2		0-	112.2	98	42	35	7	34-0	111	.231
— Kinston (Carol.)	2	0	1.000	2.50	1.41	7	7	0	0		0-	39.2	31	13	11	2	25-1	37	.217
2003—Akron (East.)	13	9	.591	3.09	1.27	27	25	6	0		0-	163.1	141	70	56	7	66-0	134	.232
2004—Akron (East.)	6	3	.333	5.28	1.38	15	15	1	0		0-	88.2	89	58	52	11	33-0	45	.261
— Buffalo (Int'l)	6	5	.545	3.25	1.37	14	14	1	0		0-	83.0	78	35	30	4	36-0	62	.252
— Cleveland (A.L.)	0	1	.000	9.39	1.83	2	2	0	0		0-0	7.2	10	9	8	1	4-0	9	.303
2005—Buffalo (Int'l)	6	4	.600	4.19	1.51	30	13	1	0		0-0	102.1	123	65	59	16	32-0	92	.297
— Tacoma (PCL)	1	1	.500	5.00	1.56	2	2	0	0		0-0	9.0	11	6	5	3	3-0	10	.297
2006—Tacoma (PCL)	13	9	.591	4.38	1.41	28	28	1	0		0-0	160.1	150	81	78	25	76-3	185	.247
— Seattle (A.L.)	0	0		10.80	2.40	4	1	0	0		0-0	6.2	10	8	8	2	6-0	7	.370
Major League totals (2 years)	0	1	.000	10.05	2.09	6	3	0	0		0-0	14.1	20	17	16	3	10-0	11	.333

2006 LEFTY-RIGHTY SPLITS

vs.	Avg.	AB	H	2B	3B	HR	RBI	BB	SO	OBP	Slg.	vs.	Avg.	AB	H	2B	3B	HR	RBI	BB	SO	OBP	Slg.
L	.200	10	2	1	0	0	2	3	2	.357	.300	R	.471	17	8	2	0	2	7	3	0	.550	.941

CRUZ, JOSE   OF

PERSONAL: Born April 19, 1974, in Arroyo, Puerto Rico. ... 6-0/210. ... Bats both, throws right. ... Full name: Jose Luis Cruz Jr... High school: Bellaire (Houston). ... College: Rice. ... Son of Jose Cruz, coach, Houston Astros, and outfielder with three major league teams (1970-88); nephew of Hector Cruz, outfielder/third baseman with four major league teams (1973, 1975-82); and nephew of Tommy Cruz, outfielder with two major league teams (1973-77). **TRANSACTIONS/CAREER NOTES:** Selected by Atlanta Braves organization in 15th round of 1992 free-agent draft; did not sign. ... Selected by Seattle Mariners organization in first round (third pick overall) of 1995 free-agent draft. ... Traded by Mariners to Toronto Blue Jays for Ps Mike Timlin and Paul Spoljaric (July 31, 1997). ... On disabled list (June 24-July 9, 1999); included rehabilitation assignment to Syracuse. ... On disabled list (May 6-21, 2001; and August 10-September 15, 2002). ... Signed as a free agent by San Francisco Giants (January 28, 2003). ... Signed as a free agent by Tampa Bay Devil Rays (December 17, 2003). ... Traded by Devil Rays to Arizona Diamondbacks for P Casey Fossum (February 6, 2005). ... On disabled list (April 16-May 9, 2005); included rehabilitation assignment to Tucson. ... Traded by Diamondbacks to Boston Red Sox for P Kyle Bono and SS Kenny Perez (July 30, 2005). ... Claimed on waivers by Los Angeles Dodgers (August 9, 2005). ... Released by Dodgers (August 4, 2006). **HONORS:** Won N.L. Gold Glove as outfielder (2003). **STATISTICAL NOTES:** Career major league grand slams: 1.

2006 GAMES PLAYED BY POSITION (MLB): OF—71.

Year Team (League)	Pos.	G	AB	R	H	2B	3B	HR	RBI	BB	SO	HBP	GDP	SB-CS	Avg.	OBP	SLG	OPS	E	Avg.
															BATTING				**FIELDING**	
1995—Everett (N'west)	OF	3	11	6	5	0	0	0	2	3	3	0	0	1-0	.455	.571	.455	1.026	0	1.000
— Riverside (Calif.)	OF	35	144	34	37	7	1	7	29	24	50	0	1	3-1	.257	.359	.465	.824	3	.961
1996—Lancaster (Calif.)	OF-DH	53	203	38	66	17	1	6	43	39	33	0	4	7-1	.325	.423	.507	.931	1	.986
— Port City (Sou.)	OF-DH	47	181	39	51	10	2	3	31	27	38	0	8	5-0	.282	.373	.409	.782	1	.990
— Tacoma (PCL)	OF	22	76	15	18	1	2	6	15	18	12	0	2	1-1	.237	.383	.539	.922	0	1.000
1997—Tacoma (PCL)	OF-DH	50	190	33	51	16	2	6	30	34	44	1	4	3-0	.268	.382	.468	.851	0	1.000
— Seattle (A.L.)	OF	49	183	28	49	12	1	12	34	13	45	0	3	1-0	.268	.315	.541	.856	3	.966
— Toronto (A.L.)	OF	55	212	31	49	9	0	14	34	34	72	0	2	6-2	.231	.316	.462	.778	2	.981
1998—Toronto (A.L.)	OF	105	352	55	89	14	3	11	42	57	99	0	4	11-4	.253	.354	.403	.757	4	.985
— Syracuse (Int'l)	OF	40	141	29	42	14	1	7	23	32	32	0	2	8-4	.298	.425	.560	.986	1	.991
1999—Toronto (A.L.)	OF	106	349	63	84	19	3	14	45	64	91	0	6	14-4	.241	.358	.430	.791	3	.990
— Syracuse (Int'l)	OF-DH	31	103	17	19	3	1	3	14	28	20	0	3	5-0	.184	.356	.320	.676	1	1.000
2000—Toronto (A.L.)	OF	•162	603	91	146	32	5	31	76	71	129	2	11	15-5	.242	.323	.466	.789	5	.993
2001—Toronto (A.L.)	OF-DH	146	577	92	158	34	3	34	88	45	138	1	8	32-5	.274	.326	.530	.857	3	.990

C

Year Team (League)	Pos.	G	AB	R	H	2B	3B	HR	RBI	BB	SO	HBP	GDP	SB-CS	Avg.	OBP	SLG	OPS	FIELDING E	Avg.
2002—Toronto (A.L.)	OF-DH	124	466	64	114	26	5	18	70	51	106	0	8	7-1	.245	.317	.438	.754	2	.992
2003—San Francisco (N.L.)	OF	158	539	90	135	26	1	20	68	102	121	0	14	5-8	.250	.366	.414	.779	2	.994
2004—Tampa Bay (A.L.)	OF	153	545	76	132	25	8	21	78	76	117	2	6	11-6	.242	.333	.433	.766	10	.970
2005—Tucson (PCL)	OF	1	3	1	1	1	0	0	1	0	1	0	0	0-0	.333	.333	.667	1.000	0	1.000
—Arizona (N.L.)	OF	64	202	23	43	9	0	12	28	42	54	0	6	0-1	.213	.347	.436	.783	2	.980
—Boston (A.L.)	OF	4	12	0	3	1	0	0	0	1	4	0	0	0-0	.250	.308	.333	.641	0	1.000
—Los Angeles (N.L.)	OF	47	156	23	47	14	2	6	22	23	43	0	4	0-1	.301	.391	.532	.923	5	.954
2006—Los Angeles (N.L.)	OF	86	223	34	52	16	1	5	17	43	54	0	3	5-1	.233	.353	.381	.734	0	1.000
American League totals (8 years)		904	3299	500	824	174	29	155	467	406	801	5	44	97-27	.250	.331	.461	.792	30	.985
National League totals (3 years)		355	1120	170	277	65	4	43	135	210	272	0	27	10-11	.247	.363	.428	.791	9	.987
Major League totals (10 years)		1259	4419	670	1101	239	33	198	602	616	1073	5	71	107-38	.249	.339	.453	.792	39	.986

DIVISION SERIES RECORD

Year Team (League)	Pos.	G	AB	R	H	2B	3B	HR	RBI	BB	SO	HBP	GDP	SB-CS	Avg.	OBP	SLG	OPS	E	Avg.
2003—San Francisco (N.L.)	OF	4	11	0	0	0	0	0	1	2	4	0	0	0-0	.000	.154	.000	.154	1	.938

2006 LEFTY-RIGHTY SPLITS

vs.	Avg.	AB	H	2B	3B	HR	RBI	BB	SO	OBP	Slg.	vs.	Avg.	AB	H	2B	3B	HR	RBI	BB	SO	OBP	Slg.
L	.313	67	21	8	0	2	6	13	12	.420	.522	R	.199	156	31	8	1	3	11	30	42	.324	.321

CRUZ, JUAN — P

PERSONAL: Born October 15, 1978, in Bonao, Dominican Republic. ... 6-2/165. ... Throws right, bats right. ... Full name: Juan Carlos Cruz. ... High school: Jallaco Bonao (Bonao, Dominican Republic). **TRANSACTIONS/CAREER NOTES:** Signed as a non-drafted free agent by Chicago Cubs organization (July 4, 1997). ... On disabled list (August 10-25, 2002). ... Traded by Cubs with P Steve Smyth to Atlanta Braves for P Andy Pratt and IF Richard Lewis (March 25, 2004). ... Traded by Braves with P Dan Meyer and OF Charles Thomas to Oakland Athletics for P Tim Hudson (December 16, 2004). ... Traded by Athletics to Arizona Diamondbacks for P Brad Halsey (March 26, 2006). ... On disabled list (June 7-July 3, 2006); included rehabilitation assignment to Tucson. **MISCELLANEOUS NOTES:** Appeared in three games as pinch runner (2001).
CAREER HITTING: 8-for-68 (.118), 2 R, 1 2B, 1 3B, 0 HR, 2 RBI.

Year Team (League)	W	L	Pct.	ERA	WHIP	G	GS	CG	ShO	Hld.	Sv.-Opp.	IP	H	R	ER	HR	BB-IBB	SO	Avg.
1998—Ariz. Cubs (Ariz.)	2	4	.333	6.10	1.81	12	6	0	0	...	0-...	41.1	61	48	28	2	14-0	36	.326
1999—Eugene (Northwest)	5	6	.455	5.94	1.62	15	15	0	0	...	0-...	80.1	97	59	53	11	33-0	65	.297
2000—Lansing (Midw.)	5	5	.500	3.28	1.41	17	17	2	1	...	0-...	96.0	75	50	35	6	60-0	106	.215
—Daytona (Fla. St.)	3	0	1.000	3.25	1.08	8	7	1	0	...	0-...	44.1	30	22	16	5	18-0	54	.186
2001—West Tenn (Sou.)	9	6	.600	4.01	1.38	23	23	0	0	...	0-...	121.1	107	56	54	6	60-0	137	.238
—Chicago (N.L.)	3	1	.750	3.22	1.28	8	8	0	0	0	0-0	44.2	40	16	16	4	17-1	39	.244
2002—Chicago (N.L.)	3	11	.214	3.98	1.47	45	9	0	0	3	1-4	97.1	84	56	43	11	59-4	81	.241
2003—Iowa (PCL)	4	0	1.000	1.95	0.90	9	9	0	0	...	0-...	50.2	37	12	11	1	11-0	47	.207
—Chicago (N.L.)	2	7	.222	6.05	1.54	25	6	0	0	1	0-1	61.0	66	44	41	7	28-0	65	.275
2004—Atlanta (N.L.)	6	2	.750	2.75	1.24	50	0	0	0	7	0-0	72.0	59	24	22	7	30-1	70	.224
2005—Sacramento (PCL)	5	1	.833	2.40	1.05	13	13	0	0	...	0-...	75.0	51	23	20	4	28-0	90	.192
—Oakland (A.L.)	0	3	.000	7.44	1.84	28	0	0	0	0	0-0	32.2	38	33	27	5	22-4	34	.290
2006—Tucson (PCL)	0	0	...	2.70	1.50	1	1	0	0	0	0-0	3.1	4	1	1	0	1-0	4	.286
—Arizona (N.L.)	5	6	.455	4.18	1.34	31	15	0	0	0	0-0	94.2	80	45	44	7	47-2	88	.230
American League totals (1 year)	0	3	.000	7.44	1.84	28	0	0	0	0	0-0	32.2	38	33	27	5	22-4	34	.290
National League totals (5 years)	19	27	.413	4.04	1.38	159	38	0	0	6	1-5	369.2	329	185	166	36	181-8	343	.241
Major League totals (6 years)	19	30	.388	4.32	1.42	187	38	0	0	6	1-5	402.1	367	218	193	41	203-12	377	.245

DIVISION SERIES RECORD

Year Team (League)	W	L	Pct.	ERA	WHIP	G	GS	CG	ShO	Hld.	Sv.-Opp.	IP	H	R	ER	HR	BB-IBB	SO	Avg.
2003—Chicago (N.L.)	0	0	...	0.00	1.00	1	0	0	0	0	0-0	1.0	0	0	0	0	1-0	2	.000
2004—Atlanta (N.L.)	0	0	...	9.82	2.73	3	0	0	0	0	0-0	3.2	6	4	4	0	4-0	4	.353
Division series totals (2 years)	0	0	...	7.71	2.36	4	0	0	0	0	0-0	4.2	6	4	4	0	5-0	6	.300

2006 LEFTY-RIGHTY SPLITS

vs.	Avg.	AB	H	2B	3B	HR	RBI	BB	SO	OBP	Slg.	vs.	Avg.	AB	H	2B	3B	HR	RBI	BB	SO	OBP	Slg.
L	.263	167	44	11	0	5	24	23	33	.359	.419	R	.199	181	36	9	2	2	18	24	55	.319	.304

CRUZ, NELSON — OF

PERSONAL: Born July 1, 1980, in Monte Cristi, Dominican Republic. ... 6-3/175. ... Bats right, throws right. ... Full name: Nelson Ramon Cruz. **TRANSACTIONS/CAREER NOTES:** Signed as a non-drafted free agent by New York Mets organization (February 17, 1998). ... Traded by Mets to Oakland Athletics for SS Jorge Velandia (August 30, 2000). ... Traded by Athletics with P Justin Lehr to Milwaukee Brewers for 3B Keith Ginter (December 15, 2004). ... Traded by Brewers with OF Carlos Lee to Texas Rangers for OFs Kevin Mench and Laynce Nix and Ps Francisco Cordero and Julian Cordero (July 28, 2006). **STATISTICAL NOTES:** Career major league grand slams: 1.
2006 GAMES PLAYED BY POSITION (MLB): OF—39.

Year Team (League)	Pos.	G	AB	R	H	2B	3B	HR	RBI	BB	SO	HBP	GDP	SB-CS	Avg.	OBP	SLG	OPS	FIELDING E	Avg.
1998—Dom. Mets (DSL)		30	70	10	19	0	0	1	13	7	21	3	1	6-0	.271	.363	.314	.677	...	...
1999—Dom. Mets 2 (DSL)		36	115	20	32	4	1	1	21	16	27	1	1	14-0	.278	.366	.357	.723	...	...
—Dom. Mets (DSL)		35	90	7	18	4	1	0	11	6	21	1	1	6-1	.200	.255	.267	.522	...	...
2000—Dom. Mets E (DSL)		69	259	60	91	14	4	15	80	33	56	8	5	17-4	.351	.434	.610	1.044	...	...
2001—Ariz. A's (Ariz.)	OF	23	88	11	22	3	1	3	16	4	29	0	1	6-3	.250	.283	.409	.692	0	1.000
2002—Vancouver (N'west)	OF	63	214	23	59	14	0	4	25	9	58	4	2	12-1	.276	.316	.397	.713	4	.961
2003—Kane Co. (Midw.)	OF	119	470	65	112	26	2	20	85	29	128	9	7	10-5	.238	.292	.430	.722	6	.979
2004—Modesto (California)	OF	66	261	54	90	27	1	11	52	24	73	4	2	8-4	.345	.407	.582	.989	3	.842
—Midland (Texas)	OF	67	262	51	82	14	2	14	45	26	69	1	4	8-3	.313	.377	.542	.919	4	.000
—Sacramento (PCL)	OF	4	13	4	3	1	0	1	2	1	7	0	0	0-0	.231	.286	.538	.824	0	...
2005—Huntsville (Sou.)	OF-DH	68	248	45	76	19	0	16	54	31	71	4	7	10-3	.306	.388	.577	.965	8	.967
—Nashville (PCL)	OF-DH	60	208	33	56	13	0	11	27	30	62	8	4	9-4	.269	.382	.490	.872	4	.983
—Milwaukee (N.L.)	OF	8	5	1	1	0	1	0	0	0	2	0	0	0-0	.200	.429	.400	.829	1	1.000
2006—Nashville (PCL)		104	371	68	112	22	1	20	73	42	100	6	6	17-6	.302	.378	.528	.907	8	.960
—Texas (A.L.)	OF	41	130	15	29	3	0	6	22	7	32	0	1	1-0	.223	.261	.385	.645	0	1.000
American League totals (1 year)		41	130	15	29	3	0	6	22	7	32	0	1	1-0	.223	.261	.385	.645	0	1.000
National League totals (1 year)		8	5	1	1	0	1	0	0	0	2	0	0	0-0	.200	.429	.400	.829	1	1.000
Major League totals (2 years)		49	135	16	30	4	0	6	22	9	34	0	1	1-0	.222	.269	.385	.654	1	1.000

2006 LEFTY-RIGHTY SPLITS

vs.	Avg.	AB	H	2B	3B	HR	RBI	BB	SO	OBP	Slg.	vs.	Avg.	AB	H	2B	3B	HR	RBI	BB	SO	OBP	Slg.
L	.217	46	10	1	0	3	11	2	7	.245	.435	R	.226	84	19	2	0	3	11	5	25	.270	.357

C

CUDDYER, MICHAEL — OF

PERSONAL: Born March 27, 1979, in Norfolk, Va. ... 6-2/222. ... Bats right, throws right. ... Full name: Michael Brent Cuddyer. ... Name pronounced: cuh-DIE-er. ... High school: Great Bridge (Chesapeake, Va.). **TRANSACTIONS/CAREER NOTES:** Selected by Minnesota Twins organization in first round (ninth pick overall) of 1997 free-agent draft. ... On disabled list (July 2-17, 2005); included rehabilitation assignment to Rochester. **STATISTICAL NOTES:** Career major league grand slams: 3.

2006 GAMES PLAYED BY POSITION (MLB): OF—143, 1B—6, DH—2.

													BATTING							FIELDING	
Year	Team (League)	Pos.	G	AB	R	H	2B	3B	HR	RBI	BB	SO	HBP	GDP	SB-CS	Avg.	OBP	SLG	OPS	E	Avg.
1998— Fort Wayne (Midw.)		2B-SS	129	497	82	137	37	7	12	81	61	107	10	13	16-7	.276	.364	.451	.814	61	.907
1999— Fort Myers (FSL)		3B	130	466	87	139	24	4	16	82	76	91	10	20	14-4	.298	.403	.470	.873	28	.921
2000— New Britain (East.)		3B	138	490	72	129	30	8	6	61	55	93	12	16	5-4	.263	.351	.394	.745	34	.903
2001— New Britain (East.)		3B-1B-OF	141	509	95	153	36	3	30	87	75	106	6	6	5-9	.301	.395	.560	.955	28	.963
— Minnesota (A.L.)		1B-3B-DH	8	18	1	4	2	0	0	1	2	6	0	1	1-0	.222	.300	.333	.633	1	.975
2002— Edmonton (PCL)		OF-1B-3B	86	330	70	102	16	9	20	53	36	79	3	9	12-7	.309	.379	.594	.973	7	.970
— Minnesota (A.L.)		OF-3B-1B DH	41	112	12	29	4	0	4	13	8	30	1	3	2-0	.259	.311	.429	.740	1	.990
2003— GC Twins (GCL)		DH-OF	2	5	1	4	0	0	1	3	1	0	1	0	0-1	.800	.857	1.400	2.257	0	1.000
— Rochester (Int'l)		OF-2B-DH 3B-1B	53	186	25	57	17	0	3	34	25	49	1	4	5-4	.306	.381	.446	.827	1	.993
— Minnesota (A.L.)		OF-3B-1B DH-2B	35	102	14	25	1	3	4	8	12	19	0	6	1-1	.245	.325	.431	.756	1	.985
2004— Minnesota (A.L.)		2B-3B-OF 1B-DH	115	339	49	89	22	1	12	45	37	74	3	8	5-5	.263	.339	.440	.779	10	.968
2005— Rochester (Int'l)		3B-1B	3	9	1	1	0	0	0	0	3	1	0	0	2-0	.111	.333	.111	.444	0	1.000
— Minnesota (A.L.)		3B-OF-2B 1B	126	422	55	111	25	3	12	42	41	93	3	19	3-4	.263	.330	.422	.752	15	.959
2006— Minnesota (A.L.)		OF-1B-DH	150	557	102	158	41	5	24	109	62	130	10	11	6-0	.284	.362	.504	.867	5	.984
Major League totals (6 years)			475	1550	233	416	98	12	56	218	162	352	17	48	18-10	.268	.342	.455	.797	33	.972

DIVISION SERIES RECORD

Year	Team (League)	Pos.	G	AB	R	H	2B	3B	HR	RBI	BB	SO	HBP	GDP	SB-CS	Avg.	OBP	SLG	OPS	E	Avg.
2002— Minnesota (A.L.)		OF	5	13	1	5	1	0	0	1	3	3	0	0	0-0	.385	.500	.462	.962	0	1.000
2003— Minnesota (A.L.)		DH	1	4	0	1	0	0	0	1	0	3	0	0	0-0	.250	.250	.250	.500	0	...
2004— Minnesota (A.L.)		2B-OF	4	15	1	7	0	0	0	2	0	3	0	0	0-2	.467	.467	.467	.933	0	1.000
2006— Minnesota (A.L.)		OF	3	12	2	3	0	1	1	1	0	2	0	1	0-0	.250	.250	.667	.917	1	.833
Division series totals (4 years)			13	44	4	16	1	1	1	5	3	11	0	1	0-2	.364	.404	.500	.904	1	.973

CHAMPIONSHIP SERIES RECORD

Year	Team (League)	Pos.	G	AB	R	H	2B	3B	HR	RBI	BB	SO	HBP	GDP	SB-CS	Avg.	OBP	SLG	OPS	E	Avg.
2002— Minnesota (A.L.)		OF	3	5	0	1	0	0	0	0	1	1	0	0	0-0	.200	.333	.200	.533	0	1.000

2006 LEFTY-RIGHTY SPLITS

vs.	Avg.	AB	H	2B	3B	HR	RBI	BB	SO	OBP	Slg.		vs.	Avg.	AB	H	2B	3B	HR	RBI	BB	SO	OBP	Slg.
L	.297	195	58	17	1	8	36	24	47	.376	.518		R	.276	362	100	24	4	16	73	38	83	.355	.497

CUST, JACK — OF

PERSONAL: Born January 16, 1979, in Flemington, N.J. ... 6-1/231. ... Bats left, throws right. ... Full name: John Joseph Cust. ... High school: Immaculata (Somerville, N.J.). **TRANSACTIONS/CAREER NOTES:** Selected by Arizona Diamondbacks organization in first round (30th pick overall) of 1997 free-agent draft. ... Traded by Diamondbacks with C JD Closser to Colorado Rockies for P Mike Myers (January 7, 2002). ... Traded by Rockies to Baltimore Orioles for OF/1B Chris Richard (March 11, 2003). ... Signed as a free agent by Oakland Athletics organization (November 15, 2004). ... Signed as a free agent by San Diego Padres organization (December 28, 2005).

2006 GAMES PLAYED BY POSITION (MLB): OF—1.

													BATTING							FIELDING	
Year	Team (League)	Pos.	G	AB	R	H	2B	3B	HR	RBI	BB	SO	HBP	GDP	SB-CS	Avg.	OBP	SLG	OPS	E	Avg.
1997— Ariz. D'backs (Ariz.)		OF	35	121	26	37	11	1	3	33	31	39	0	4	2-0	.306	.447	.488	.935	5	.902
1998— South Bend (Mid.)		OF	16	62	5	15	3	0	0	4	5	20	0	0	0-1	.242	.294	.290	.584	4	.975
— Lethbridge (Pion.)		OF	73	223	75	77	20	2	11	56	86	71	4	3	15-8	.345	.530	.601	1.131	0	1.000
1999— High Desert (Calif.)		OF	125	455	107	152	42	3	32	112	96	145	2	5	1-4	.334	.450	.651	1.100	12	.922
2000— El Paso (Texas)		OF	129	447	100	131	32	6	20	75	117	150	2	10	12-9	.293	.440	.526	.966	11	.944
2001— Tucson (PCL)		OF	135	442	81	123	24	2	27	79	102	160	5	10	6-3	.278	.415	.525	.940	11	.948
— Arizona (N.L.)		OF	3	2	0	1	0	0	0	0	1	0	0	0	0-0	.500	.667	.500	1.167	0	...
2002— Colo. Springs (PCL)		OF	105	359	74	95	24	0	23	55	83	121	5	5	6-3	.265	.407	.524	.930	6	.961
— Colorado (N.L.)		OF	35	65	8	11	2	0	1	8	12	32	0	3	0-1	.169	.295	.246	.541	1	.960
2003— Ottawa (Int'l)		OF-DH	97	333	55	95	18	1	9	58	80	94	0	9	5-2	.285	.422	.426	.848	3	.978
— Baltimore (A.L.)		DH-OF	27	73	7	19	7	0	4	11	10	25	1	0	0-0	.260	.357	.521	.878	0	1.000
2004— Baltimore (A.L.)			1	1	0	0	0	0	0	0	0	1	0	0	0-0	.000	.000	.000	.000	0	...
— Ottawa (Int'l)		DH-OF	102	344	55	81	15	1	17	55	65	127	2	6	4-0	.235	.358	.433	.791	2	.966
2005— Sacramento (PCL)		OF-DH	134	479	95	123	28	1	19	73	115	153	3	14	2-4	.257	.402	.438	.840	8	.971
2006— Portland (PCL)		OF-DH	138	441	97	129	23	0	30	77	143	124	4	10	0-3	.293	.460	.549	1.016	5	.974
— San Diego (N.L.)		OF	4	3	1	1	0	0	0	0	0	1	0	0	0-0	.333	.333	.333	.667	0	...
American League totals (2 years)			28	74	7	19	7	0	4	11	10	26	1	0	0-0	.257	.353	.514	.866	0	1.000
National League totals (3 years)			42	70	9	13	2	0	1	8	13	33	0	3	0-1	.186	.310	.257	.567	1	.960
Major League totals (5 years)			70	144	16	32	9	0	5	19	23	59	1	3	0-1	.222	.331	.389	.720	1	.964

2006 LEFTY-RIGHTY SPLITS

vs.	Avg.	AB	H	2B	3B	HR	RBI	BB	SO	OBP	Slg.		vs.	Avg.	AB	H	2B	3B	HR	RBI	BB	SO	OBP	Slg.
L	.000	0	0	0	0	0	0	0	0	.000	.000		R	.333	3	1	0	0	0	0	0	1	.333	.333

DAIGLE, CASEY — P

PERSONAL: Born April 4, 1981, in Lake Charles, La. ... 6-5/217. ... Throws right, bats right. ... Full name: Sean Casey Daigle. ... High school: Sulphur (La.). **TRANSACTIONS/CAREER NOTES:** Selected by Arizona Diamondbacks organization in suplemental round ("sandwich pick" between first and second rounds, 31st pick overall) of 1999 free-agent draft; pick received as compensation for Los Angeles Dodgers signing Type A free-agent OF Devon White. **MISCELLANEOUS NOTES:** Struck out in only appearance as pinch hitter (2004).

CAREER HITTING: 2-for-18 (.111), 2 R, 2 2B, 0 3B, 0 HR, 0 RBI.

Year	Team (League)	W	L	Pct.	ERA	WHIP	G	GS	CG	ShO	Hld.	Sv.-Opp.	IP	H	R	ER	HR	BB-IBB	SO	Avg.
2000— Missoula (Pion.)		3	5	.375	4.90	1.72	15	15	0	0	0	0-..	82.2	88	57	45	4	54-0	56	.271

D

Year — Team (League)	W	L	Pct.	ERA	WHIP	G	GS	CG	ShO	Hld.	Sv.-Opp.	IP	H	R	ER	HR	BB-IBB	SO	Avg.
2001— South Bend (Mid.)	10	10	.500	4.12	1.43	28	27	2	1	...	0-...	164.0	180	100	75	11	55-0	85	.279
2002— Lancaster (Calif.)	4	10	.286	5.09	1.47	21	21	0	0	...	0-...	122.0	137	82	69	19	42-0	85	.285
— El Paso (Texas)	3	2	.600	3.25	1.24	7	7	2	0	...	0-...	44.1	46	19	16	5	9-0	29	.275
2003— El Paso (Texas)	11	11	.500	4.59	1.53	29	27	1	0	...	0-...	176.1	219	108	90	9	51-1	115	.304
2004— Arizona (N.L.)	2	3	.400	7.16	1.84	10	10	0	0	0	0-0	49.0	63	41	39	9	27-3	17	.320
— Tucson (PCL)	4	9	.308	6.88	1.77	18	15	0	0	0	0-0	100.2	154	85	77	21	24-0	51	.348
2005— Tennessee (Sou.)	9	3	.750	2.67	1.45	58	2	0	0	3	19-23	64.0	75	24	19	3	18-4	50	.290
2006— Tucson (PCL)	3	5	.375	4.69	1.60	42	0	0	0	6	4-11	48.0	60	31	25	6	17-0	41	.302
— Arizona (N.L.)	0	0	...	3.65	1.62	10	0 *	0	0	2	0-0	12.1	14	5	5	1	6-0	7	.311
Major League totals (2 years)	2	3	.400	6.46	1.79	20	10	0	0	2	0-0	61.1	77	46	44	10	33-3	24	.318

2006 LEFTY-RIGHTY SPLITS

vs.	Avg.	AB	H	2B	3B	HR	RBI	BB	SO	OBP	Slg.	vs.	Avg.	AB	H	2B	3B	HR	RBI	BB	SO	OBP	Slg.
L	.375	24	9	1	0	1	4	1	3	.385	.542	R	.238	21	5	0	0	1	5	4	.385	.238

DAMON, JOHNNY — OF

PERSONAL: Born November 5, 1973, in Fort Riley, Kan. ... 6-2/190. ... Bats left, throws left. ... Full name: Johnny David Damon. ... Name pronounced: DAY-mun. ... High school: Dr. Phillips (Orlando). **TRANSACTIONS/CAREER NOTES:** Selected by Kansas City Royals organization in supplemental round ("sandwich pick" between first and second round, 35th pick overall) of 1992 free-agent draft; pick received as part of compensation for San Diego Padres signing Type A free-agent IF Kurt Stillwell. ... On suspended list (September 5-7, 1997). ... Traded by Royals with IF Mark Ellis and a player to be named to Oakland Athletics as part of three-team deal in which Royals acquired P Roberto Hernandez and A's acquired P Cory Lidle from Tampa Bay Devil Rays, Royals acquired C A.J. Hinch, IF Angel Berroa and cash from A's and Devil Rays acquired OF Ben Grieve and cash from A's (January 8, 2001). ... Signed as a free agent by Boston Red Sox (December 21, 2001). ... Signed as a free agent by New York Yankees (January 3, 2006). **RECORDS:** Shares major league record for most doubles, game (4, July 18, 2000). **HONORS:** Named outfielder on the SPORTING NEWS A.L. All-Star team (2005). **STATISTICAL NOTES:** Career major league grand slams: 6.
2006 GAMES PLAYED BY POSITION (MLB): OF—131, DH—16, 1B—1.

										BATTING							FIELDING	
Year — Team (League)	Pos.	G	AB	R	H	2B	3B	HR	RBI	BB	SO	HBP	GDP	SB-CS	Avg.	OBP	SLG	OPS	E	Avg.
1992— GC Royals (GCL)	OF	50	192	58	67	12	9	4	24	31	21	4	1	33-6	.349	.449	.568	1.017	1	.988
— Baseball City (FSL)	OF	1	1	0	0	0	0	0	0	0	0	0	0	0-0	.000	.000	.000	.000	0	...
1993— Rockford (Midwest)	OF	127	511	82	148	25	13	5	50	52	83	6	4	59-18	.290	.360	.419	.779	6	.977
1994— Wilmington (Caro.)	OF	119	472	96	149	25	13	6	75	62	55	8	4	44-9	.316	.399	.462	.861	3	.989
1995— Wichita (Texas)	OF-DH	111	423	83	145	15	9	16	54	67	35	2	3	26-15	.343	.434	.534	.968	5	.984
— Kansas City (A.L.)	OF	47	188	32	53	11	5	3	23	12	22	1	2	7-0	.282	.324	.441	.765	1	.991
1996— Kansas City (A.L.)	OF-DH	145	517	61	140	22	5	6	50	31	64	3	4	25-5	.271	.313	.368	.680	6	.983
1997— Kansas City (A.L.)	OF-DH	146	472	70	130	12	8	8	48	42	70	3	3	16-10	.275	.338	.386	.723	4	.988
1998— Kansas City (A.L.)	OF	161	642	104	178	30	10	18	66	58	84	4	4	26-12	.277	.339	.439	.779	4	.990
1999— Kansas City (A.L.)	OF-DH	145	583	101	179	39	9	14	77	67	50	3	13	36-6	.307	.379	.477	.856	4	.987
2000— Kansas City (A.L.)	OF-DH	159	655	* 136	214	42	10	16	88	65	60	1	7	* 46-9	.327	.382	.495	.877	5	.986
2001— Oakland (A.L.)	OF	155	644	108	165	34	4	9	49	61	70	5	7	27-12	.256	.324	.363	.687	3	.991
2002— Boston (A.L.)	OF-DH	154	623	118	178	34	* 11	14	63	65	70	6	4	31-6	.286	.356	.443	.799	1	.997
2003— Boston (A.L.)	OF-DH	145	608	103	166	32	6	12	67	68	74	2	5	30-6	.273	.345	.405	.750	1	.997
2004— Boston (A.L.)	OF-DH	150	621	123	189	35	6	20	94	76	71	2	8	19-8	.304	.380	.477	.857	5	.986
2005— Boston (A.L.)	OF-DH	148	624	117	197	35	6	10	75	53	69	2	5	18-1	.316	.366	.439	.805	4	.985
2006— New York (A.L.)	OF-DH-1B	149	593	115	169	35	6	24	80	67	85	4	4	25-10	.285	.359	.482	.841	3	.990
Major League totals (12 years)		1704	6770	1188	1958	361	85	154	780	665	789	36	66	306-85	.289	.353	.436	.789	43	.989

DIVISION SERIES RECORD

Year — Team (League)	Pos.	G	AB	R	H	2B	3B	HR	RBI	BB	SO	HBP	GDP	SB-CS	Avg.	OBP	SLG	OPS	E	Avg.
2001— Oakland (A.L.)	OF	5	22	3	9	2	1	0	1	1	0	0		2-0	.409	.435	.591	1.026	0	1.000
2003— Boston (A.L.)	OF	5	19	2	6	2	0	1	3	2	1	1	1	2-0	.316	.409	.579	.988	0	1.000
2004— Boston (A.L.)	OF	3	15	4	7	1	0	0	0	1	2	0		3-0	.467	.500	.533	1.033	0	1.000
2005— Boston (A.L.)	OF	3	13	2	3	1	0	0	0	1	4	0	1	0-0	.231	.286	.308	.594	0	1.000
2006— New York (A.L.)	OF	4	17	3	4	0	0	1	3	1	2	0		0-0	.235	.278	.412	.690	0	1.000
Division series totals (5 years)		20	86	14	29	6	1	2	6	6	10	1	2	7-0	.337	.387	.500	.887	0	1.000

CHAMPIONSHIP SERIES RECORD

Year — Team (League)	Pos.	G	AB	R	H	2B	3B	HR	RBI	BB	SO	HBP	GDP	SB-CS	Avg.	OBP	SLG	OPS	E	Avg.
2003— Boston (A.L.)	OF	5	20	1	4	1	0	1	3	3	3	0	1	1-0	.200	.304	.250	.554	0	1.000
2004— Boston (A.L.)	OF	7	35	5	6	0	0	2	7	2	8	0		2-1	.171	.216	.343	.559	0	1.000
Champ. series totals (2 years)		12	55	6	10	1	0	3	10	5	11	0	2	3-1	.182	.250	.309	.559	0	1.000

WORLD SERIES RECORD

Year — Team (League)	Pos.	G	AB	R	H	2B	3B	HR	RBI	BB	SO	HBP	GDP	SB-CS	Avg.	OBP	SLG	OPS	E	Avg.
2004— Boston (A.L.)	OF	4	21	4	6	2	1	1	2	0	1	0	1	0-0	.286	.286	.619	.905	0	1.000

ALL-STAR GAME RECORD

		G	AB	R	H	2B	3B	HR	RBI	BB	SO	HBP	GDP	SB-CS	Avg.	OBP	SLG	OPS	E	Avg.
All-Star Game totals (2 years)		2	5	2	2	0	0	0	0	0	0	0		1-0	.400	.400	.400	.800	0	1.000

2006 LEFTY-RIGHTY SPLITS

vs.	Avg.	AB	H	2B	3B	HR	RBI	BB	SO	OBP	Slg.	vs.	Avg.	AB	H	2B	3B	HR	RBI	BB	SO	OBP	Slg.
L	.297	165	49	6	2	6	27	25	22	.395	.467	R	.280	428	120	29	3	18	53	42	63	.344	.488

DAVANON, JEFF — OF

PERSONAL: Born December 8, 1973, in San Diego. ... 6-0/200. ... Bats both, throws right. ... Full name: Jeffrey Graham DaVanon. ... Name pronounced: duh-VAN-un. ... High school: Bellaire (Texas). ... College: San Diego State. ... Son of Jerry DaVanon, infielder with five major league teams (1969-77). **TRANSACTIONS/CAREER NOTES:** Selected by Oakland Athletics organization in 26th round of 1995 free-agent draft. ... Traded by A's with P Elvin Nina and OF Nathan Haynes to Anaheim Angels for P Omar Olivares and 2B Randy Velarde (July 29, 1999). ... On disabled list (March 20, 2000-entire season). ... On disabled list (July 24-August 10, 2004); included rehabilitation assignment to Salt Lake. ... Angels franchise renamed Los Angeles Angels of Anaheim for 2005 season. ... Signed as free agent by Arizona Diamondbacks (February 7, 2006). ... On disabled list (August 6, 2006-remainder of season). **STATISTICAL NOTES:** Hit for the cycle (August 25, 2004).
2006 GAMES PLAYED BY POSITION (MLB): OF—58, DH—3.

										BATTING							FIELDING	
Year — Team (League)	Pos.	G	AB	R	H	2B	3B	HR	RBI	BB	SO	HBP	GDP	SB-CS	Avg.	OBP	SLG	OPS	E	Avg.
1995— S. Oregon (N'west)	OF	57	167	29	42	6	2	1	17	34	49	0	1	6-5	.252	.376	.329	.706	8	.864
1996— W. Mich. (Mid.)	1B-2B-OF	89	289	43	70	13	4	2	33	49	66	1	6	5-7	.242	.353	.336	.689	2	.976
1997— Visalia (Calif.)	OF	119	408	70	104	17	3	6	38	81	101	0	7	23-14	.255	.377	.355	.732	10	.948
1998— Modesto (California)	OF	84	301	66	101	17	4	5	60	59	69	1	4	33-10	.336	.439	.468	.907	13	.902

Year Team (League)	Pos.	G	AB	R	H	2B	3B	HR	RBI	BATTING BB	SO	HBP	GDP	SB-CS	Avg.	OBP	SLG	OPS	FIELDING E	Avg.
1999— Midland (Texas)	OF-DH	100	374	87	128	29	11	11	60	53	68	4	6	18-10	.342	.424	.567	.991	7	.960
— Edmonton (PCL)	OF-DH	34	132	35	43	8	3	6	19	20	27	1	1	11-4	.326	.416	.568	.984	0	1.000
— Anaheim (A.L.)	OF-DH	7	20	4	4	0	1	1	4	2	7	0	0	0-1	.200	.273	.450	.723	0	1.000
2000— Anaheim (A.L.)			Did not play.																	
2001— Salt Lake (PCL)	OF	69	256	46	80	19	8	10	48	32	57	3	4	8-3	.313	.390	.566	.956	1	.992
— Anaheim (A.L.)	OF-DH	40	88	7	17	2	1	5	9	11	29	0	1	1-3	.193	.280	.409	.689	1	.980
2002— Anaheim (A.L.)	OF-DH	16	30	3	5	3	0	1	4	2	6	0	0	1-0	.167	.219	.367	.585	0	1.000
— Salt Lake (PCL)	OF	25	100	21	33	10	1	5	18	17	24	1	1	5-3	.330	.429	.600	1.029	2	.962
— Ariz. Angels (Ariz.)	OF	5	15	5	10	6	1	0	4	5	2	0	0	2-0	.667	.714	1.200	1.914	0	1.000
2003— Salt Lake (PCL)	OF-DH	16	60	11	18	4	1	2	14	9	9	1	1	4-1	.300	.400	.500	.900	2	.933
— Anaheim (A.L.)	OF-DH	123	330	56	93	16	1	12	43	42	59	1	6	17-5	.282	.360	.445	.805	4	.983
2004— Salt Lake (PCL)	OF	3	8	4	5	0	0	1	1	2	0	0	0	1-1	.625	.700	1.000	1.700	0	1.000
— Anaheim (A.L.)	OF-DH	108	285	41	79	11	4	7	34	46	54	0	2	18-3	.277	.372	.418	.790	1	.993
2005— Los Angeles (A.L.)	OF-DH	108	225	42	52	10	1	2	15	39	44	2	6	11-6	.231	.347	.351	.658	1	.991
2006— Arizona (N.L.)	OF-DH	87	221	38	64	12	4	5	35	31	42	0	6	10-4	.290	.371	.448	.819	2	.979
American League totals (6 years)		402	978	153	250	42	8	28	109	142	199	3	15	48-18	.256	.348	.401	.749	7	.987
National League totals (1 year)		87	221	38	64	12	4	5	35	31	42	0	6	10-4	.290	.371	.448	.819	2	.979
Major League totals (7 years)		489	1199	191	314	54	12	33	144	173	241	3	21	58-22	.262	.352	.410	.762	9	.986

DIVISION SERIES RECORD

Year Team (League)	Pos.	G	AB	R	H	2B	3B	HR	RBI	BB	SO	HBP	GDP	SB-CS	Avg.	OBP	SLG	OPS	E	Avg.
2004— Anaheim (A.L.)	OF	3	10	1	2	0	0	0	0	2	1	0	0	0-1	.200	.333	.200	.533	0	1.000
2005— Los Angeles (A.L.)	DH	1	0	1	0	0	0	0	0	0	0	0	0	0-0	...	...	...	...	0	...
Division series totals (2 years)		4	10	2	2	0	0	0	0	2	1	0	0	0-1	.200	.333	.200	.533	0	1.000

CHAMPIONSHIP SERIES RECORD

Year Team (League)	Pos.	G	AB	R	H	2B	3B	HR	RBI	BB	SO	HBP	GDP	SB-CS	Avg.	OBP	SLG	OPS	E	Avg.
2005— Los Angeles (A.L.)	DH	3	1	0	0	0	0	0	0	0	0	0	0	0-0	.000	.000	.000	.000	0	...

2006 LEFTY-RIGHTY SPLITS

vs.	Avg.	AB	H	2B	3B	HR	RBI	BB	SO	OBP	Slg.	vs.	Avg.	AB	H	2B	3B	HR	RBI	BB	SO	OBP	Slg.
L	.205	39	8	1	2	0	0	3	7	12	.319	.231	R	.308	182	56	11	4	5	32	24	30	.383	.495

DAVIES, KYLE   P

PERSONAL: Born September 9, 1983, in Decatur, Ga. ... 6-2/205. ... Throws right, bats right. ... Full name: Hiram Kyle Davies. ... High school: Stockbridge (Ga.). **TRANSACTIONS/CAREER NOTES:** Selected by Atlanta Braves organization in fourth round of 2001 free-agent draft. ... On disabled list (May 17-September 1, 2006); included rehabilitation assignments to Mississippi and Richmond.
CAREER HITTING: 4-for-38 (.105), 1 R, 0 2B, 0 3B, 1 HR, 5 RBI.

Year Team (League)	W	L	Pct.	ERA	WHIP	G	GS	CG	ShO	Hld.	Sv.-Opp.	IP	H	R	ER	HR	BB-IBB	SO	Avg.
2001— GC Braves (GCL)	4	2	.667	2.25	0.98	12	9	1	1	...	0-...	56.0	47	17	14	2	8-0	53	.224
— Macon (S. Atl.)	1	0	1.000	0.00	0.53	1	1	0	0	...	0-...	5.2	2	0	0	0	1-0	7	.105
2002— Macon (S. Atl.)	0	1	.000	6.00	1.67	2	1	0	0	...	0-...	6.0	6	4	4	1	4-0	4	.273
— Danville (Appal.)	5	3	.625	3.50	1.38	14	14	0	0	...	0-...	69.1	73	39	27	4	23-0	62	.263
2003— Rome (S. Atl.)	8	8	.500	2.89	1.24	27	27	1	0	...	0-...	146.1	128	52	47	9	53-0	148	.238
2004— Myrtle Beach (Carol.)	9	2	.818	2.63	1.15	14	14	0	0	...	0-...	75.1	55	24	22	3	32-0	95	.208
— Greenville (Sou.)	4	0	1.000	2.32	1.00	11	10	0	0	...	0-...	62.0	40	18	16	9	22-0	73	.191
— Richmond (Int'l)	0	1	.000	9.00	1.60	1	1	0	0	...	0-...	5.0	5	5	5	0	3-0	4	.294
2005— Richmond (Int'l)	5	2	.714	3.44	1.36	13	13	0	0	0	0-0	73.1	66	28	28	8	34-2	62	.245
— Atlanta (N.L.)	7	6	.538	4.93	1.68	21	14	0	0	2	0-1	87.2	98	51	48	8	49-5	62	.280
2006— Mississippi (Sou.)	1	1	.500	4.50	1.14	4	4	0	0	0	0-0	14.0	11	8	7	1	5-0	9	.216
— Richmond (Int'l)	2	0	1.000	0.60	0.67	2	2	0	0	0	0-0	15.0	7	1	1	0	3-0	8	.140
— Atlanta (N.L.)	3	7	.300	8.38	1.94	14	14	1	0	0	0-0	63.0	90	60	59	14	33-0	51	.332
Major League totals (2 years)	10	13	.435	6.38	1.79	35	28	1	0	2	0-1	151.0	188	111	107	22	82-5	113	.303

2006 LEFTY-RIGHTY SPLITS

vs.	Avg.	AB	H	2B	3B	HR	RBI	BB	SO	OBP	Slg.	vs.	Avg.	AB	H	2B	3B	HR	RBI	BB	SO	OBP	Slg.
L	.333	144	48	7	2	9	33	21	28	.417	.597	R	.331	127	42	12	0	5	19	12	23	.397	.543

DAVIS, DOUG   P

PERSONAL: Born September 21, 1975, in Sacramento, Calif. ... 6-4/213. ... Throws left, bats right. ... Full name: Douglas P. Davis. ... High school: Northgate (Walnut Creek, Calif.). ... Junior college: San Francisco City College. **TRANSACTIONS/CAREER NOTES:** Selected by Los Angeles Dodgers organization in 31st round of 1993 free-agent draft; did not sign. ... Selected by Texas Rangers organization in 10th round of 1996 free-agent draft. ... Claimed on waivers by Toronto Blue Jays (April 30, 2003). ... Signed as a free agent by Milwaukee Brewers organization (July 14, 2003).
CAREER HITTING: 16-for-226 (.071), 7 R, 3 2B, 1 3B, 0 HR, 5 RBI.

Year Team (League)	W	L	Pct.	ERA	WHIP	G	GS	CG	ShO	Hld.	Sv.-Opp.	IP	H	R	ER	HR	BB-IBB	SO	Avg.
1996— GC Rangers (GCL)	3	1	.750	1.90	1.27	8	7	0	0	...	0-...	42.2	28	13	9	0	26-1	49	.193
1997— GC Rangers (GCL)	3	1	.750	1.71	1.38	4	4	0	0	...	0-...	21.0	14	5	4	0	15-0	27	.200
— Charlotte (Fla. St.)	5	3	.625	3.10	1.26	9	8	1	0	...	0-...	49.1	29	19	17	2	33-1	52	.175
1998— Charlotte (Fla. St.)	11	7	.611	3.24	1.31	27	27	1	1	...	0-...	155.1	129	69	56	7	74-0	173	.225
1999— Tulsa (Texas)	4	4	.500	2.42	1.21	12	12	1	0	...	0-...	74.1	65	26	20	9	25-0	79	.235
— Oklahoma (PCL)	7	0	1.000	3.00	1.38	13	11	0	0	...	0-...	78.0	77	27	26	4	31-0	74	.263
— Texas (A.L.)	0	0	...	33.75	4.50	2	0	0	0	0	0-0	2.2	12	10	10	3	0-0	3	.600
2000— Oklahoma (PCL)	8	3	.727	2.84	1.38	12	12	2	0	...	0-...	69.2	62	32	22	8	34-1	53	.248
— Texas (A.L.)	7	6	.538	5.38	1.69	30	13	1	0	2	0-3	98.2	109	61	59	14	58-3	66	.288
2001— Texas (A.L.)	11	10	.524	4.45	1.55	30	30	1	0	0	0-0	186.0	220	103	92	14	69-1	115	.295
— Oklahoma (PCL)	2	0	1.000	2.87	0.89	2	2	0	0	0	0-0	15.2	10	5	5	1	4-0	14	.189
2002— Texas (A.L.)	3	5	.375	4.98	1.49	10	10	1	0	1	0-0	59.2	67	36	33	7	22-0	28	.290
— Oklahoma (PCL)	4	3	.571	4.99	1.32	9	9	0	0	0	0-0	61.1	70	38	34	7	11-0	48	.290
2003— Oklahoma (PCL)	3	0	1.000	3.25	1.10	4	4	0	0	0	0-0	27.2	29	10	10	3	1-0	18	.271
— Texas (A.L.)	0	0	...	12.00	2.67	1	1	0	0	0	0-0	3.0	4	4	4	2	4-0	2	.308
— Toronto (A.L.)	4	6	.400	5.00	1.78	12	11	0	0	0	0-0	54.0	70	33	30	6	26-1	25	.318
— Huntsville (Sou.)	1	0	1.000	3.00	1.30	1	1	0	0	0	0-0	6.0	5	2	2	0	2-0	7	.227
— Indianapolis (Int'l)	1	2	.333	4.15	1.20	5	5	0	0	0	0-0	34.2	33	16	16	2	10-0	19	.250
— Milwaukee (N.L.)	3	2	.600	2.58	1.34	8	8	0	0	0	0-0	52.1	49	18	15	8	21-0	35	.247
2004— Milwaukee (N.L.)	12	12	.500	3.39	1.31	34	34	0	0	0	0-0	207.1	192	84	78	14	79-3	166	.247

Year Team (League)	W	L	Pct.	ERA	WHIP	G	GS	CG	ShO	Hld.	Sv.-Opp.	IP	H	R	ER	HR	BB-IBB	SO	Avg.
2005— Milwaukee (N.L.)	11	11	.500	3.84	1.30	35	•35	2	1	0	0-0	222.2	196	103	95	26	93-5	208	.235
2006— Milwaukee (N.L.)	11	11	.500	4.91	1.51	34	34	1	1	0	0-0	203.1	206	118	111	19	102-1	159	.266
American League totals (5 years)	25	27	.481	5.08	1.64	85	65	3	1	2	0-3	404.0	482	247	228	46	179-5	239	.300
National League totals (4 years)	37	36	.507	3.92	1.37	111	111	4	2	0	0-0	685.2	643	323	299	67	295-9	568	.249
Major League totals (8 years)	62	63	.496	4.35	1.47	196	176	7	3	2	0-3	1089.2	1125	570	527	113	474-14	807	.268

2006 LEFTY-RIGHTY SPLITS

vs.	Avg.	AB	H	2B	3B	HR	RBI	BB	SO	OBP	Slg.	vs.	Avg.	AB	H	2B	3B	HR	RBI	BB	SO	OBP	Slg.
L	.307	189	58	13	1	4	30	16	44	.359	.450	R	.253	584	148	29	3	15	79	86	115	.351	.390

DAVIS, JASON P

PERSONAL: Born May 8, 1980, in Chattanooga, Tenn. ... 6-6/210. ... Throws right, bats right. ... Full name: Jason Thomas Davis. ... High school: Charleston (Tenn.). ... College: Cleveland State. **TRANSACTIONS/CAREER NOTES:** Selected by Cleveland Indians organization in 21st round of 1999 free-agent draft. **MISCELLANEOUS NOTES:** Appeared in one game as pinch runner (2003).

CAREER HITTING: 1-for-9 (.111), 1 R, 0 2B, 0 3B, 1 HR, 1 RBI.

Year Team (League)	W	L	Pct.	ERA	WHIP	G	GS	CG	ShO	Hld.	Sv.-Opp.	IP	H	R	ER	HR	BB-IBB	SO	Avg.
2000— Burlington (Appal.)	4	4	.500	4.40	1.42	10	10	0	0	...	0-...	45.0	48	27	22	5	16-0	35	.276
2001— Columbus (S. Atl.)	14	6	.700	2.70	1.24	27	27	1	1	...	0-...	160.0	147	72	48	9	51-1	115	.243
2002— Kinston (Carol.)	3	6	.333	4.15	1.38	17	17	1	1	...	0-...	99.2	107	64	46	7	31-2	68	.272
— Akron (East.)	6	2	.750	3.51	1.34	10	10	0	0	...	0-...	59.0	63	26	23	2	16-0	45	.278
— Cleveland (A.L.)	1	0	1.000	1.84	1.09	3	2	0	0	0	0-0	14.2	12	3	3	1	4-0	11	.218
2003— Cleveland (A.L.)	8	11	.421	4.68	1.32	27	27	1	0	0	0-0	165.1	172	101	86	25	47-4	85	.273
2004— Buffalo (Int'l)	3	2	.600	3.00	1.31	9	9	0	0	...	0-...	54.0	53	26	18	4	18-1	39	.261
— Cleveland (A.L.)	2	7	.222	5.51	1.74	26	19	0	0	1	0-0	114.1	148	81	70	13	51-1	72	.311
2005— Cleveland (A.L.)	4	2	.667	4.69	1.59	11	4	0	0	0	0-0	40.1	44	22	21	4	20-0	32	.282
— Buffalo (Int'l)	8	5	.615	4.61	1.39	16	16	1	0	0	0-0	95.2	106	65	49	9	27-0	77	.283
2006— Buffalo (Int'l)	0	0	.000	0.54	0.66	11	0	0	0	0	4-5	16.2	8	2	1	0	3-1	15	.138
— Cleveland (A.L.)	3	2	.600	3.74	1.46	39	0	0	0	6	1-3	55.1	67	28	23	4	14-2	37	.302
Major League totals (5 years)	18	22	.450	4.68	1.48	106	52	1	0	7	1-3	390.0	443	235	203	44	136-7	237	.288

2006 LEFTY-RIGHTY SPLITS

vs.	Avg.	AB	H	2B	3B	HR	RBI	BB	SO	OBP	Slg.	vs.	Avg.	AB	H	2B	3B	HR	RBI	BB	SO	OBP	Slg.
L	.316	79	25	6	1	0	13	7	8	.364	.418	R	.294	143	42	8	1	1	24	7	29	.335	.385

DAVIS, RAJAI OF

PERSONAL: Born October 19, 1980, in Norwich, Conn. ... 5-11/190. ... Bats right, throws right. ... Full name: Rajai Lavae Davis. ... Name pronounced: RAHJ-ay. ... High school: New London (Conn.). ... College: Connecticut-Avery Point. **TRANSACTIONS/CAREER NOTES:** Selected by Pittsburgh Pirates organization in 38th round of 2001 free-agent draft.

2006 GAMES PLAYED BY POSITION (MLB): OF—1.

Year Team (League)	Pos.	G	AB	R	H	2B	3B	HR	RBI	BB	SO	HBP	GDP	SB-CS	Avg.	OBP	SLG	OPS	E	Avg.
2001— Williamsport. (NYP)		6	12	1	1	0	0	0	0	2	4	0	0	0-1	.083	.214	.083	.297	0	...
— GC Pirates (GCL)		26	84	19	22	1	0	0	4	13	26	1	0	11-3	.262	.364	.274	.638	1	...
2002— GC Pirates (GCL)		58	224	38	86	16	5	4	35	20	25	3	3	24-6	.384	.436	.554	.990	3	...
— Williamsport. (NYP)		1	4	0	0	0	0	0	0	0	1	0	0	0-0	.000	.000	.000	.000	0	...
— Hickory (S. Atl.)		6	14	4	6	0	0	0	3	6	2	1	0	2-2	.429	.619	.429	1.048	0	...
2003— Hickory (S. Atl.)		125	478	84	146	21	7	6	54	55	65	6	7	40-13	.305	.383	.416	.799	7	...
2004— Lynchburg (Caro.)		127	509	91	160	27	7	5	38	59	60	2	4	57-15	.314	.388	.424	.812	9	...
2005— Altoona (East.)	OF-DH	123	499	82	140	22	5	4	34	43	76	12	6	45-9	.281	.351	.369	.720	20	.966
2006— Indianapolis (Int'l)		100	385	53	109	17	1	2	21	27	59	3	3	45-13	.283	.335	.348	.683	2	.991
— Pittsburgh (N.L.)	OF	20	14	1	2	1	0	0	0	2	3	0	0	1-3	.143	.250	.214	.464	0	...
Major League totals (1 year)		20	14	1	2	1	0	0	0	2	3	0	0	1-3	.143	.250	.214	.464	0	...

2006 LEFTY-RIGHTY SPLITS

vs.	Avg.	AB	H	2B	3B	HR	RBI	BB	SO	OBP	Slg.	vs.	Avg.	AB	H	2B	3B	HR	RBI	BB	SO	OBP	Slg.
L	.000	2	0	0	0	0	0	0	0	.000	.000	R	.167	12	2	1	0	0	0	2	3	.286	.250

DAY, ZACH P

PERSONAL: Born June 15, 1978, in Cincinnati. ... 6-4/216. ... Throws right, bats right. ... Full name: Stephen Zachary Day. ... High school: La Salle (Cincinnati). ... College: Cincinnati. **TRANSACTIONS/CAREER NOTES:** Selected by New York Yankees organization in fifth round of 1996 free-agent draft. ... Traded by Yankees to Cleveland Indians with P Jake Westbrook (July 24, 2000), completing deal in which Indians traded OF David Justice to Yankees for OF Ricky Ledee and two players to be named (June 29, 2000). ... Traded by Indians to Montreal Expos for OF Milton Bradley (July 31, 2001). ... On disabled list (May 29-July 26, 2003); included rehabilitation assignments to GCL Expos and Brevard County. ... On disabled list (July 6-22 and August 2, 2004-remainder of season). ... Expos franchise transferred to Washington, D.C., and renamed Washington Nationals for 2005 season (December 3, 2004). ... On disabled list (May 31-July 13, 2005); included rehabilitation assignment to Harrisburg. ... Traded by Nationals with OF J.J. Davis to Colorado Rockies for OF Preston Wilson and cash (July 13, 2005). ... On disabled list (September 21, 2005-remainder of season). ... Claimed on waivers by Nationals (April 26, 2006). ... On disabled list (May 23, 2006-remainder of season). ... Released by Nationals (October 3, 2006).

CAREER HITTING: 6-for-105 (.057), 5 R, 0 2B, 0 3B, 1 HR, 3 RBI.

Year Team (League)	W	L	Pct.	ERA	WHIP	G	GS	CG	ShO	Hld.	Sv.-Opp.	IP	H	R	ER	HR	BB-IBB	SO	Avg.
1996— GC Yankees (GCL)	5	2	.714	5.61	1.31	7	5	0	0	...	0-...	33.2	41	26	21	3	3-0	23	.311
1997— Oneonta (NYP)	7	2	.778	2.15	1.14	14	14	0	0	...	0-...	92.0	82	26	22	2	23-0	92	.240
1998— Tampa (Fla. St.)	5	8	.385	5.49	1.74	18	17	0	0	...	0-...	100.0	142	89	61	5	32-4	69	.326
— Greensboro (S. Atl.)	1	2	.333	2.75	1.14	7	6	1	0	...	0-...	36.0	35	22	11	1	6-0	30	.245
1999— GC Yankees (GCL)	1	1	.500	3.78	1.44	5	4	0	0	...	0-...	16.2	20	10	7	1	4-0	17	.290
— Greensboro (S. Atl.)	0	1	.000	2.25	1.88	2	2	0	0	...	0-...	8.0	14	11	2	0	1-0	4	.359
2000— Greensboro (S. Atl.)	9	3	.750	1.90	1.21	13	13	1	1	...	0-...	85.1	72	29	18	6	31-0	101	.232
— Tampa (Fla. St.)	2	4	.333	4.19	1.40	7	7	0	0	...	0-...	34.1	33	22	16	2	15-1	36	.246
— Akron (East.)	4	2	.667	3.52	1.28	8	8	0	0	...	0-...	46.0	38	20	18	1	21-0	43	.232
2001— Akron (East.)	9	10	.474	3.10	1.23	22	22	2	0	...	0-...	136.2	123	57	47	8	45-1	94	.237
— Buffalo (Int'l)	1	0	1.000	1.50	0.67	1	1	0	0	...	0-...	6.0	3	1	1	0	1-0	4	.143
— Ottawa (Int'l)	2	2	.500	7.43	1.73	6	5	0	0	...	0-...	26.2	38	23	22	2	11-0	16	.349
2002— Ottawa (Int'l)	5	6	.455	3.50	1.21	17	16	1	0	...	0-...	90.0	77	38	35	5	32-0	68	.231
— Montreal (N.L.)	4	1	.800	3.62	1.15	19	2	0	0	2	1-2	37.1	28	18	15	3	15-2	25	.207
2003— GC Expos (GCL)	0	0	...	3.86	1.70	1	1	0	0	...	0-...	2.1	3	1	1	0	1-0	3	.300

Year	Team (League)	W	L	Pct.	ERA	WHIP	G	GS	CG	ShO	Hld.	Sv.-Opp.	IP	H	R	ER	HR	BB-IBB	SO	Avg.
	— Brevard County (FSL)	0	0	...	1.69	0.80	1	1	0	0	...	0-...	5.1	3	1	1	0	1-0	3	.167
	— Montreal (N.L.)	9	8	.529	4.18	1.45	23	23	1	1	0	0-0	131.1	132	64	61	8	59-3	61	.262
2004	— Montreal (N.L.)	5	10	.333	3.93	1.39	19	19	1	1	0	0-0	116.2	117	53	51	13	45-7	61	.265
2005	— Wash. (N.L.)	1	2	.333	6.75	1.83	12	5	0	0	0	0-0	36.0	41	29	27	4	25-3	16	.289
	— Harrisburg (East.)	1	0	1.000	2.77	1.15	3	3	0	0	0	0-0	13.0	14	4	4	1	1-0	10	.286
	— Colo. Springs (PCL)	2	3	.400	5.89	1.66	7	7	0	0	0	0-0	36.2	46	29	24	4	15-0	17	.305
	— Colorado (N.L.)	0	1	.000	7.15	2.38	5	3	0	0	0	0-1	11.1	20	11	9	2	7-1	7	.385
2006	— Colorado (N.L.)	1	2	.333	10.80	2.40	3	3	0	0	0	0-0	13.1	22	17	16	3	10-1	5	.373
	— Wash. (N.L.)	1	3	.250	4.73	1.50	5	5	0	0	0	0-0	26.2	29	15	14	2	11-1	13	.276
	Major League totals (5 years)	21	27	.438	4.66	1.51	86	60	2	2	2	1-3	372.2	389	207	193	35	172-18	189	.270

2006 LEFTY-RIGHTY SPLITS

vs.	Avg.	AB	H	2B	3B	HR	RBI	BB	SO	OBP	Slg.
L	.348	69	24	2	0	2	11	11	5	.444	.464
R	.284	95	27	3	1	3	14	10	14	.361	.432

DECASTER, YURENDELL — 3B

PERSONAL: Born September 26, 1979, in Curacao, Netherlands Antilles. ... 6-1/203. ... Bats right, throws right. ... Full name: Yurendell Eithel DeCaster.
TRANSACTIONS/CAREER NOTES: Signed as a non-drafted free agent by Tampa Bay Devil Rays (August 2, 1996). ... Selected by Pittsburgh Pirates organization from Devil Rays organization in Rule 5 minor league draft (December 11, 2000).
2006 GAMES PLAYED BY POSITION (MLB): DH—1.

Year	Team (League)	Pos.	G	AB	R	H	2B	3B	HR	RBI	BB	SO	HBP	GDP	SB-CS	Avg.	OBP	SLG	OPS	FIELDING E	Avg.
1997	— Dom. Devil Rays (DSL)		68	243	27	58	8	1	5	31	29	44	2	...	4-5	.239	.320	.342	.662	6	...
1998	— GC Devil Rays (GCL)		56	174	25	41	4	3	2	17	19	48	2	...	10-4	.236	.315	.328	.643	11	...
1999	— Princeton (Appal.)		48	183	37	47	12	0	11	36	20	65	6	...	4-2	.257	.346	.503	.849	17	...
2000	— Charl. SC (SAL)		69	242	34	58	21	0	7	28	16	89	6	...	4-1	.240	.299	.413	.712	15	...
2001	— Lynchburg (Carol.)		13	48	1	5	2	0	0	4	3	16	0	...	0-0	.104	.157	.146	.303	2	...
	— Hickory (SAL)		97	341	66	99	17	4	19	74	35	83	8	...	4-4	.290	.365	.531	.896	21	...
2002	— Lynchburg (Carol.)		125	432	54	109	25	3	15	62	30	102	8	...	1-2	.252	.309	.428	.737	32	...
2003	— Lynchburg (Carol.)		97	330	50	76	24	1	13	56	22	86	4	...	3-2	.230	.283	.427	.710	9	...
2004	— Altoona (East.)		97	330	54	92	18	1	15	42	22	78	5	...	4-2	.279	.331	.476	.807	17	...
2005	— Indianapolis (Int'l.)	OF-3B-1B-2B	122	415	60	116	31	4	11	61	37	103	6	...	7-5	.280	.346	.453	.799	11	...
2006	— Indianapolis (Int'l.)		119	421	47	115	22	3	11	51	35	100	2	16	7-7	.273	.330	.418	.748	21	.962
	— Pittsburgh (N.L.)	DH	3	2	0	0	0	0	0	0	0	2	0	0	0-0	.000	.000	.000	.000	0	...
	Major League totals (1 year)		3	2	0	0	0	0	0	0	0	2	0	0	0-0	.000	.000	.000	.000	0	...

2006 LEFTY-RIGHTY SPLITS

vs.	Avg.	AB	H	2B	3B	HR	RBI	BB	SO	OBP	Slg.
L	.000									.000	.000
R	.000	2							2	.000	.000

DEJEAN, MIKE — P

PERSONAL: Born September 28, 1970, in Baton Rouge, La. ... 6-2/219. ... Throws right, bats right. ... Full name: Michel Dwain DeJean. ... Name pronounced: DAY-zhan. ... High school: Walker (La.). ... College: Livingston University (Ala.). **TRANSACTIONS/CAREER NOTES:** Selected by New York Yankees organization in 24th round of 1992 free-agent draft. ... Traded by Yankees with a player to be named to Colorado Rockies for C Joe Girardi (November 20, 1995); Rockies acquired P Steve Shoemaker to complete deal (December 6, 1995). ... On disabled list (July 18-August 8, 1997); included rehabilitation assignment to New Haven. ... On disabled list (September 2, 1998-remainder of season). ... On disabled list (August 14-September 1, 1999); included rehabilitation assignment to Colorado Springs. ... On disabled list (March 29-April 28 and July 25-August 15, 2000); included rehabilitation assignment to Colorado Springs. ... Traded by Rockies with P Mark Leiter and 2B/SS Elvis Pena to Milwaukee Brewers for Ps Juan Acevedo and Kane Davis and IF Jose Flores (April 4, 2001). ... Traded by Milwaukee Brewers to St. Louis Cardinals for two players to be named (August 22, 2003); Brewers acquired Ps Mike Crudale (August 27, 2003) and John Novinsky (September 10, 2003) to complete deal. ... Signed as a free agent by Baltimore Orioles (January 8, 2004). ... Traded by Orioles to New York Mets for OF Karim Garcia (July 19, 2004). ... On disabled list (August 30, 2004-remainder of season). ... Released by Mets (June 20, 2005). ... Signed by Colorado Rockies (July 7, 2005). ... On disabled list (April 8, 2006-remainder of season).
CAREER HITTING: 1-for-17 (.059), 0 R, 1 2B, 0 3B, 0 HR, 0 RBI.

Year	Team (League)	W	L	Pct.	ERA	WHIP	G	GS	CG	ShO	Hld.	Sv.-Opp.	IP	H	R	ER	HR	BB-IBB	SO	Avg.
1992	— Oneonta (NYP)	0	0	...	0.44	0.73	20	0	0	0	...	16-...	20.2	12	3	1	1	3-0	20	.160
1993	— Greensboro (S. Atl.)	2	3	.400	5.00	1.67	20	0	0	0	...	9-...	18.0	22	12	10	1	8-2	16	.286
1994	— Tampa (Fla. St.)	0	2	.000	2.38	1.53	34	0	0	0	...	16-...	34.0	39	15	9	1	13-0	22	.283
	— Albany (East.)	0	2	.000	4.38	1.50	16	0	0	0	...	4-...	24.2	22	14	12	1	15-3	13	.250
1995	— Norwich (East.)	5	5	.500	2.99	1.17	59	0	0	0	...	20-...	78.1	58	29	26	5	34-2	57	.208
1996	— Colo. Springs (PCL)	0	2	.000	5.13	1.81	30	0	0	0	...	1-...	40.1	52	24	23	3	21-3	31	.319
	— New Haven (East.)	0	0	...	3.22	1.25	16	0	0	0	...	11-...	22.1	20	9	8	2	8-0	12	.247
1997	— Colo. Springs (PCL)	0	1	.000	5.40	2.40	10	0	0	0	...	4-...	10.0	17	6	6	0	7-1	9	.405
	— Colorado (N.L.)	5	0	1.000	3.99	1.45	55	0	0	0	13	2-4	67.2	74	34	30	4	24-2	38	.280
	— New Haven (East.)	0	1	.000	6.00	1.67	2	0	0	0	...	0-...	3.0	3	2	2	0	2-0	2	.273
1998	— Colorado (N.L.)	3	1	.750	3.03	1.37	59	1	0	0	11	2-3	74.1	78	29	25	4	24-1	27	.285
1999	— Colorado (N.L.)	2	4	.333	8.41	1.89	56	0	0	0	9	0-4	61.0	83	61	57	13	32-8	31	.335
	— Colo. Springs (PCL)	0	0	...	0.00	1.00	1	0	0	0	...	0-...	1.0	1	0	0	0	0-0	0	.333
2000	— Colo. Springs (PCL)	1	0	1.000	2.51	1.33	12	0	0	0	...	5-...	14.1	15	4	4	0	4-0	12	.273
	— Colorado (N.L.)	4	4	.500	4.89	1.58	54	0	0	0	7	0-4	53.1	54	31	29	4	30-6	34	.269
2001	— Milwaukee (N.L.)	4	2	.667	2.77	1.35	75	0	0	0	8	2-4	84.1	75	31	26	4	39-7	68	.236
2002	— Milwaukee (N.L.)	1	5	.167	3.12	1.40	68	0	0	0	...	27-30	75.0	66	28	26	7	39-8	65	.237
2003	— Milwaukee (N.L.)	4	7	.364	4.87	1.48	58	0	0	0	...	18-26	64.2	69	38	35	12	27-7	58	.271
	— St. Louis (N.L.)	1	1	.500	4.00	1.61	18	0	0	0	5	1-1	18.0	17	8	8	1	12-0	13	.262
2004	— Baltimore (A.L.)	0	5	.000	6.13	1.94	37	0	0	0	1	0-0	39.2	49	29	27	4	28-6	36	.308
	— New York (N.L.)	0	0	...	1.69	1.22	17	0	0	0	2	0-0	21.1	21	5	4	0	5-2	24	.256
2005	— New York (N.L.)	3	1	.750	6.31	2.10	28	0	0	0	2	0-0	25.2	36	19	18	3	18-2	17	.327
	— Colorado (N.L.)	2	3	.400	3.19	1.04	38	0	0	0	18	0-3	36.2	26	14	13	0	12-1	35	.195
2006	— Colorado (N.L.)	1	0	1.000	0.00	1.80	2	0	0	0	...	0-0	1.2	1	0	0	0	2-0	0	.167
	American League totals (1 year)	0	5	.000	6.13	1.94	37	0	0	0	1	0-0	39.2	49	29	27	4	28-6	36	.308
	National League totals (10 years)	30	28	.517	4.18	1.48	528	1	0	0	81	52-79	583.2	600	298	271	57	264-44	410	.268
	Major League totals (10 years)	30	33	.476	4.30	1.51	565	1	0	0	82	52-79	623.1	649	327	298	59	292-50	446	.271

2006 LEFTY-RIGHTY SPLITS

vs.	Avg.	AB	H	2B	3B	HR	RBI	BB	SO	OBP	Slg.
L	.000	2	0	0	0	0	0	1	0	.333	.000
R	.250	4	1	0	0	0	0	1	0	.400	.250

D

DEJESUS, DAVID — OF

PERSONAL: Born December 20, 1979, in Brooklyn, N.Y. ... 6-0/175. ... Bats left, throws left. ... Full name: David Christopher DeJesus. ... High school: Manalapan (N.J.). ... College: Rutgers. **TRANSACTIONS/CAREER NOTES:** Selected by New York Mets organization in 43rd round of 1997 free-agent draft; did not sign. ... Selected by Kansas City Royals organization in fourth round of 2000 free-agent draft. ... On disabled list (April 21-May 29, 2006); included rehabilitation assignment to Omaha.

2006 GAMES PLAYED BY POSITION (MLB): OF—119.

										BATTING											FIELDING	
Year	Team (League)	Pos.	G	AB	R	H	2B	3B	HR	RBI	BB	SO	HBP	GDP	SB-CS	Avg.	OBP	SLG	OPS		E	Avg.
2001—	....			Did not play.																		
2002—	Wilmington (Caro.)	OF	87	334	69	99	22	6	4	41	48	42	13	8	15-6	.296	.400	.434	.834		1	.994
—	Wichita (Texas)	OF	25	79	7	20	5	2	2	15	8	10	5	3	3-1	.253	.347	.443	.790		1	.976
2003—	Wichita (Texas)	OF	17	71	14	24	4	0	2	10	9	8	2	3	1-3	.338	.422	.479	.901		1	.980
—	Omaha (PCL)	OF-DH	59	215	49	64	16	3	5	23	34	30	9	9	8-4	.298	.412	.470	.881		0	1.000
—	Kansas City (A.L.)	OF	12	7	0	2	0	1	0	0	1	2	1	0	0-0	.286	.444	.571	1.016		0	1.000
2004—	Omaha (PCL)	OF	50	197	38	62	14	4	6	16	21	30	7	5	7-6	.315	.400	.518	.918		1	.991
—	Kansas City (A.L.)	OF	96	363	58	104	15	3	7	39	33	53	9	6	8-11	.287	.360	.402	.763		4	.984
2005—	Kansas City (A.L.)	OF	122	461	69	135	31	6	9	56	42	76	9	6	5-5	.293	.359	.445	.804		4	.987
2006—	Omaha (PCL)	OF	3	13	0	5	0	0	0	2	0	2	0	1	0-0	.385	.385	.385	.769		0	1.000
—	Kansas City (A.L.)	OF	119	491	83	145	36	7	8	56	43	70	12	10	6-3	.295	.364	.446	.810		3	.990
Major League totals (4 years)			349	1322	210	386	82	17	24	151	119	201	31	22	19-19	.292	.362	.434	.796		11	.987

2006 LEFTY-RIGHTY SPLITS

vs.	Avg.	AB	H	2B	3B	HR	RBI	BB	SO	OBP	Slg.	vs.	Avg.	AB	H	2B	3B	HR	RBI	BB	SO	OBP	Slg.
L	.307	140	43	16	3	3	14	16	16	.384	.529	R	.291	351	102	20	4	5	42	27	54	.355	.413

DE LA ROSA, JORGE — P

PERSONAL: Born April 5, 1981, in Monterrey, Mexico. ... 6-1/190. ... Throws left, bats left. ... Full name: Jorge Alberto de la Rosa. **TRANSACTIONS/CAREER NOTES:** Signed as a non-drafted free agent by Arizona Diamondbacks organization (March 20, 1998). ... Contract sold by Diamondbacks organization to Monterrey of the Mexican League (April 2, 2000). ... Contract purchased by Boston Red Sox organization from Monterrey (February 22, 2001). ... Traded with Ps Casey Fossum and Brandon Lyon and OF Mike Goss to Diamondbacks for P Curt Schilling (November 28, 2003). ... Traded by Diamondbacks with SS Craig Counsell, 2B Junior Spivey, 1B Lyle Overbay, C Chad Moeller and P Chris Capuano to Milwaukee Brewers for 1B Richie Sexson, P Shane Nance and a player to be named (December 1, 2003); Diamondbacks acquired OF Noochie Varner to complete deal (December 15, 2003). ... On disabled list (June 10-July 25, 2006); included rehabilitation assignment to Huntsville. ... Traded by Brewers to Kansas City Royals for IF Tony Graffanino (July 25, 2006).

CAREER HITTING: 0-for-11 (.000), 0 R, 0 2B, 0 3B, 0 HR, 0 RBI.

Year	Team (League)	W	L	Pct.	ERA	WHIP	G	GS	CG	ShO	Hld.	Sv.-Opp.	IP	H	R	ER	HR	BB-IBB	SO	Avg.
1999—	High Desert (Calif.)	0	0	...	0.00	1.00	2	0	0	0	...	0-...	3.0	1	0	0	0	2-0	3	.100
—	Ariz. D'backs (Ariz.)	0	0	...	3.21	1.07	8	0	0	0	...	2-...	14.0	12	5	5	1	3-0	17	.226
—	Missoula (Pion.)	0	1	.000	7.98	2.11	13	0	0	0	...	2-...	14.2	22	17	13	2	9-0	14	.333
2000—	Monterrey (Mex.)	3	2	.600	6.28	1.81	37	0	0	0	...	1-...	38.2	38	27	27	2	32-...	50	...
2001—	Sarasota (Fla. St.)	0	1	.000	1.21	0.84	12	0	0	0	...	2-...	29.2	13	7	4	0	12-0	27	.127
—	Trenton (East.)	1	3	.250	5.84	2.05	29	0	0	0	...	0-...	37.0	56	35	24	4	20-1	27	.348
2002—	Sarasota (Fla. St.)	7	7	.500	3.65	1.30	23	23	1	1	...	0-...	120.2	105	53	49	10	52-1	95	.231
—	Trenton (East.)	1	2	.333	5.50	1.44	4	4	0	0	...	0-...	18.0	17	12	11	0	9-0	15	.239
2003—	Portland (East.)	6	3	.667	2.80	1.23	22	20	0	0	...	0-...	99.2	87	39	31	6	36-0	102	.236
—	Pawtucket (Int'l)	1	2	.333	3.75	1.63	5	5	0	0	...	0-...	24.0	27	14	10	0	12-0	17	.278
2004—	Indianapolis (Int'l)	5	6	.455	4.52	1.35	20	20	0	0	...	0-...	85.2	80	45	43	9	36-1	86	.249
—	Milwaukee (N.L.)	0	3	.000	6.35	1.90	5	5	0	0	0	0-0	22.2	29	20	16	1	14-0	5	.309
2005—	Milwaukee (N.L.)	2	2	.500	4.46	2.03	38	0	0	0	5	0-2	42.1	48	23	21	1	38-4	42	.289
2006—	Milwaukee (N.L.)	2	2	.500	8.60	1.78	18	3	0	0	1	0-0	30.1	32	30	29	4	22-1	31	.269
—	Huntsville (Sou.)	3	1	.750	2.40	1.13	6	6	0	0	0	0-0	30.0	31	12	8	1	3-0	23	.277
—	Kansas City (A.L.)	3	4	.429	5.18	1.66	10	10	0	0	0	0-0	48.2	49	29	28	10	32-0	36	.263
American League totals (1 year)		3	4	.429	5.18	1.66	10	10	0	0	0	0-0	48.2	49	29	28	10	32-0	36	.263
National League totals (3 years)		4	7	.364	6.23	1.92	61	8	0	0	6	0-2	95.1	109	73	66	6	74-5	78	.288
Major League totals (3 years)		7	11	.389	5.88	1.83	71	18	0	0	6	0-2	144.0	158	102	94	16	106-5	114	.280

2006 LEFTY-RIGHTY SPLITS

vs.	Avg.	AB	H	2B	3B	HR	RBI	BB	SO	OBP	Slg.	vs.	Avg.	AB	H	2B	3B	HR	RBI	BB	SO	OBP	Slg.
L	.250	60	15	2	0	4	14	13	9	.387	.483	R	.269	245	66	12	0	10	23	41	58	.372	.441

DE LA ROSA, TOMAS — SS

PERSONAL: Born January 28, 1978, in La Victoria, Dominican Republic. ... 5-10/165. ... Bats right, throws right. ... Full name: Tomas Agramonte de la Rosa. ... High school: Licey Padre Garcia (La Victoria, Dominican Republic). **TRANSACTIONS/CAREER NOTES:** Signed as a non-drafted free agent by Montreal Expos organization (July 12, 1995). ... Claimed on waivers by Pittsburgh Pirates (April 15, 2002). ... Signed by Nashua of the independent Atlantic League (2005). ... Signed as a free agent by Colorado Rockies organization (May 27, 2005). ... Signed as a free agent by San Francisco Giants organization (December 21, 2005).

2006 GAMES PLAYED BY POSITION (MLB): SS—8, 2B—2, 3B—2.

										BATTING											FIELDING	
Year	Team (League)	Pos.	G	AB	R	H	2B	3B	HR	RBI	BB	SO	HBP	GDP	SB-CS	Avg.	OBP	SLG	OPS		E	Avg.
1996—	GC Expos (GCL)	SS	54	187	35	47	7	1	0	21	22	25	...	...	8-...	.251		.299	...		26	.914
—	Vermont (NYP)	SS	3	8	1	2	0	0	0	1	0	3	...	...	0-...	.250		.250	...		1	.833
1997—	W.P. Beach (FSL)	SS	4	9	1	2	0	0	0	0	2	3	...	...	2-...	.222		.222	...		1	.917
—	Vermont (NYP)	SS	69	271	46	72	14	6	2	40	32	47	...	...	19-...	.266		.384	...		21	.932
1998—	Jupiter (Fla. St.)	SS	117	390	56	98	22	1	3	43	37	61	...	...	27-...	.251		.336	...		30	.952
1999—	Harrisburg (East.)	SS	135	467	70	122	23	3	6	43	42	64	...	...	28-...	.261		.360	...		34	.946
2000—	Ottawa (Int'l)	SS	103	340	27	69	10	1	1	36	31	43	...	...	10-3	.203		.247	...		16	.964
—	Montreal (N.L.)	SS-DH	32	66	7	19	3	1	2	7	9	11	1	...	2-1	.288	.365	.455	.819		2	.980
2001—	Ottawa (Int'l)	SS	121	420	56	100	24	0	7	30	40	63	...	...	12-9	.238		.345	...		20	.965
—	Montreal (N.L.)		1	1	0	0	0	0	0	0	0	0	...	...	0-0	.000	.000	.000	.000		0	...
2002—	Ottawa (Int'l)	3B-SS	2	3	0	0	0	0	0	0	2	0	...	...	1-0	.000	.400	.000	.400		0	1.000
—	Nashville (PCL)	SS-2B-3B	105	348	38	78	17	2	3	33	24	52	4	...	9-5	.224	.279	.310	.589		16	.964
2003—	Nashville (PCL)		101	263	33	65	12	1	4	30	25	38	3	...	6-2	.247	.318	.346	.664		15	...
2004—	Nashville (PCL)		63	173	22	48	6	2	7	29	16	34	0	...	3-0	.277	.333	.457	.790		14	...
—	Altoona (East.)		8	18	3	6	1	0	1	4	1	2	0	...	1-1	.333	.368	.556	.924		3	...
2005—	Nashua (Atl.)		22	81	12	18	6	0	1	8	9	15	3	...	3-1	.222	.319	.333	.652		2	...
—	Colo. Springs (PCL)	SS-3B-2B	89	311	44	91	18	1	6	48	29	39	1	11	9-4	.293	.350	.415	.765		11	.969

– 118 –

Year	Team (League)	Pos.	G	AB	R	H	2B	3B	HR	RBI	BB	SO	HBP	GDP	SB-CS	Avg.	OBP	SLG	OPS	E	Avg.
2006—Ariz. Giants (Ariz.)			7	27	4	11	1	0	0	2	1	2	1	0	2-0	.407	.433	.444	.878	2	.947
— Fresno (PCL)			79	300	43	88	21	2	8	43	23	45	5	10	8-5	.293	.352	.457	.808	14	.960
— San Francisco (N.L.)	SS-2B-3B		16	16	1	5	0	0	0	1	1	3	0	0	0-0	.313	.353	.313	.665	1	.941
Major League totals (3 years)			49	83	8	24	3	1	2	10	8	14	1	0	2-1	.289	.359	.422	.780	3	.974

2006 LEFTY-RIGHTY SPLITS

vs.	Avg.	AB	H	2B	3B	HR	RBI	BB	SO	OBP	Slg.	vs.	Avg.	AB	H	2B	3B	HR	RBI	BB	SO	OBP	Slg.
L	.250	4	1	0	0	0	0	1	0	.400	.250	R	.333	12	4	0	0	0	1	0	3	.333	.333

DELCARMEN, MANNY — P

PERSONAL: Born February 16, 1982, in Boston, Mass. ... 6-3/195. ... Throws right, bats right. ... Full name: Manuel Delcarmen. . **TRANSACTIONS/CAREER NOTES:** Selected by Boston Red Sox organization in second round of 2000 free-agent draft.
CAREER HITTING: 0-for-0 (.000), 0 R, 0 2B, 0 3B, 0 HR, 0 RBI.

Year	Team (League)	W	L	Pct.	ERA	WHIP	G	GS	CG	ShO	Hld.	Sv.-Opp.	IP	H	R	ER	HR	BB-IBB	SO	Avg.
2001—GC Red Sox (GCL)		4	2	.667	2.54	1.17	11	8	0	0	...	1-...	46.0	35	16	13	0	19-0	62	.211
2002—Augusta (S. Atl.)		7	8	.467	4.10	1.32	26	24	0	0	...	0-...	136.0	124	77	62	15	56-0	136	.242
2003—Sarasota (Fla. St.)		1	1	.500	3.13	1.00	4	3	0	0	...	0-...	23.0	16	9	8	1	7-0	16	.200
2004—Sarasota (Fla. St.)		3	6	.333	4.68	1.42	19	18	0	0	...	0-...	73.0	84	43	38	10	20-1	76	.301
2005—Portland (East.)		4	4	.500	3.23	1.31	31	0	0	0		3-6	39.0	31	23	14	3	20-1	49	.212
—Pawtucket (Int'l)		3	1	.750	1.29	1.43	15	0	0	0	2	2-3	21.0	17	3	3	0	13-1	23	.218
—Boston (A.L.)		0	0		3.00	1.67	10	0	0	0	0	0-0	9.0	8	3	3	0	7-0	9	.242
2006—Pawtucket (Int'l)		0	1	.000	2.12	0.88	10	0	0	0	0	0-0	17.0	9	4	4	0	6-0	19	.155
—Boston (A.L.)		2	0	1.000	5.06	1.59	50	0	0	0	14	0-4	53.1	68	32	30	2	17-2	45	.309
Major League totals (2 years)		2	0	1.000	4.76	1.60	60	0	0	0	14	0-4	62.1	76	35	33	2	24-2	54	.300

2006 LEFTY-RIGHTY SPLITS

vs.	Avg.	AB	H	2B	3B	HR	RBI	BB	SO	OBP	Slg.	vs.	Avg.	AB	H	2B	3B	HR	RBI	BB	SO	OBP	Slg.
L	.319	94	30	6	3	1	23	12	15	.398	.479	R	.302	126	38	3	2	1	17	5	30	.333	.381

DELGADO, CARLOS — 1B

PERSONAL: Born June 25, 1972, in Aguadilla, Puerto Rico. ... 6-3/230. ... Bats left, throws right. ... Full name: Carlos Juan Delgado. ... Name pronounced: del-GAH-doh. ... High school: Jose de Diego (Aguadilla, Puerto Rico). **TRANSACTIONS/CAREER NOTES:** Signed as a non-drafted free agent by Toronto Blue Jays organization (October 9, 1988). ... On disabled list (March 15-April 24, 1998); included rehabilitation assignments to Dunedin and Syracuse. ... On disabled list (August 9-25, 2002). ... On disabled list (May 30-July 6, 2004); included rehabilitation assignments to Dunedin and Syracuse. ... Signed as a free agent by Florida Marlins (January 27, 2005). ... On disabled list (July 28-August 13, 2005). ... Traded by Marlins with cash to New York Mets for 1B Mike Jacobs, P Yusmeiro Petit and IF Grant Psomas (November 24, 2005). **RECORDS:** Shares major league record for home runs, game (4, September 25, 2003). **HONORS:** Named Major League Player of the Year by THE SPORTING NEWS (2000). ... Named first baseman on THE SPORTING NEWS A.L. All-Star team (2000 and 2003). ... Named first baseman on A.L. Silver Slugger team (1999, 2000 and 2003). **STATISTICAL NOTES:** Hit four home runs in one game (September 25, 2003). ... Hit three home runs in one game (August 4, 1998; August 6, 1999; April 4, 2001; and April 20, 2001). ... Career major league grand slams: 11.

2006 GAMES PLAYED BY POSITION (MLB): 1B—141, DH—1.

Year	Team (League)	Pos.	G	AB	R	H	2B	3B	HR	RBI	BB	SO	HBP	GDP	SB-CS	Avg.	OBP	SLG	OPS	E	Avg.
1989—St. Catharines (NYP)	C	31	89	9	16	5	0	0	11	23	39	0	4	0-0	.180	.345	.236	.581	2	.974
1990—St. Catharines (NYP)	C	67	228	30	64	13	0	6	39	35	65	5	2	2-7	.281	.382	.417	.799	7	.987
1991—Myrtle Beach (SAL)	C	132	441	72	126	18	2	18	70	75	97	8	7	9-10	.286	.396	.458	.854	19	.976
—Syracuse (Int'l)	C	3	0	0	0	0	0	0	0	0	2	0	0	0-0	.000	.000	.000	.000	0	1.000
1992—Dunedin (Fla. St.)	C	133	485	83	157	30	2	30	100	59	91	6	8	2-5	.324	.402	.579	.982	11	.986
1993—Knoxville (Southern)	C	140	468	91	142	28	0	25	102	102	98	6	11	10-3	.303	.430	.524	.954	14	.983
—Toronto (A.L.)	C-DH	2	1	0	0	0	0	0	0	0	1	0	0	0-0	.000	.500	.000	.500	0	1.000
1994—Toronto (A.L.)	OF-C	43	130	17	28	2	0	9	24	25	46	3	5	1-1	.215	.352	.438	.791	2	.967
—Syracuse (Int'l)	DH-C-1B	85	307	52	98	11	0	19	58	42	58	3	1	1-0	.319	.404	.541	.945	7	.974
1995—Toronto (A.L.)	OF-DH-1B	37	91	7	15	3	0	3	11	6	26	0	1	0-0	.165	.212	.297	.509	0	1.000
—Syracuse (Int'l)	1B-OF	91	333	59	106	23	4	22	74	45	78	5	8	0-4	.318	.403	.610	1.013	4	.995
1996—Toronto (A.L.)	DH-1B	138	488	68	132	28	2	25	92	58	139	9	13	0-0	.270	.353	.490	.843	4	.983
1997—Toronto (A.L.)	1B-DH	153	519	79	136	42	3	30	91	64	133	8	6	0-3	.262	.350	.528	.878	12	.988
1998—Dunedin (Fla. St.)	1B-DH	4	16	4	5	1	0	2	7	2	4	0	1	0-0	.313	.389	.750	1.139	0	1.000
—Syracuse (Int'l)	1B	2	7	4	4	2	0	1	6	2	0	0	0	0-0	.571	.667	1.286	1.952	0	1.000
—Toronto (A.L.)	1B-DH	142	530	94	155	43	1	38	115	73	139	11	8	3-0	.292	.385	.592	.978	4	.992
1999—Toronto (A.L.)	1B-DH	152	573	113	156	39	0	44	134	86	141	15	11	1-1	.272	.377	.571	.948	*14	.990
2000—Toronto (A.L.)	1B	•162	569	115	196	*57	1	41	137	123	104	•15	12	0-1	.344	.470	.664	1.134	13	.991
2001—Toronto (A.L.)	1B	•162	574	102	160	31	1	39	102	111	136	16	9	3-0	.279	.408	.540	.948	9	.994
2002—Toronto (A.L.)	1B-DH	143	505	103	140	34	2	33	108	102	126	13	8	1-0	.277	.406	.549	.955	12	.991
2003—Toronto (A.L.)	1B-DH	161	570	117	172	38	1	42	*145	109	137	19	9	0-0	.302	.426	.593	1.019	10	.993
2004—Dunedin (Fla. St.)	1B	2	8	1	2	0	0	1	2	1	0	0	0	0-0	.250	.250	.625	.875	0	1.000
—Syracuse (Int'l)	1B	2	9	2	5	2	0	1	4	0	0	0	0	0-0	.556	.556	1.111	1.667	0	1.000
—Toronto (A.L.)	1B-DH	128	458	74	123	26	0	32	99	69	115	13	11	0-1	.269	.372	.535	.907	5	.996
2005—Florida (N.L.)	1B-DH	144	521	81	157	41	3	33	115	72	121	17	16	0-0	.301	.399	.582	.981	14	.989
2006—New York (N.L.)	1B-DH	144	524	89	139	30	2	38	114	74	120	10	12	0-0	.265	.361	.548	.909	8	.994
American League totals (12 years)		1423	5008	889	1413	343	11	336	1058	827	1242	122	93	9-7	.282	.392	.556	.949	91	.992
National League totals (2 years)		288	1045	170	296	71	5	71	229	146	241	27	28	0-0	.283	.380	.565	.945	22	.991
Major League totals (14 years)		1711	6053	1059	1709	414	16	407	1287	973	1483	149	121	9-7	.282	.390	.556	.948	113	.992

DIVISION SERIES RECORD

Year	Team (League)	Pos.	G	AB	R	H	2B	3B	HR	RBI	BB	SO	HBP	GDP	SB-CS	Avg.	OBP	SLG	OPS	E	Avg.
2006—New York (N.L.)	1B	3	14	3	6	0	0	1	2	0	0	0	0	0-0	.429	.429	.643	1.071	0	1.000

CHAMPIONSHIP SERIES RECORD

Year	Team (League)	Pos.	G	AB	R	H	2B	3B	HR	RBI	BB	SO	HBP	GDP	SB-CS	Avg.	OBP	SLG	OPS	E	Avg.
2006—New York (N.L.)	1B	7	23	5	7	3	0	3	9	6	3	0	0	0-0	.304	.448	.826	1.274	3	.958

ALL-STAR GAME RECORD

	G	AB	R	H	2B	3B	HR	RBI	BB	SO	HBP	GDP	SB-CS	Avg.	OBP	SLG	OPS	E	Avg.
All-Star Game totals (2 years)	2	4	0	2	1	0	0	1	0	1	0	0	0-0	.500	.500	.750	1.250	0	1.000

2006 LEFTY-RIGHTY SPLITS

vs.	Avg.	AB	H	2B	3B	HR	RBI	BB	SO	OBP	Slg.	vs.	Avg.	AB	H	2B	3B	HR	RBI	BB	SO	OBP	Slg.
L	.226	159	36	9	2	7	33	16	44	.311	.440	R	.282	365	103	21	0	31	81	58	76	.382	.595

D

DELLUCCI, DAVID — OF

PERSONAL: Born October 31, 1973, in Baton Rouge, La. ... 5-11/190. ... Bats left, throws left. ... Full name: David Michael Dellucci. ... Name pronounced: duh-LOO-chee. ... High school: Catholic (Baton Rouge, La.). ... College: Mississippi. **TRANSACTIONS/CAREER NOTES:** Selected by Minnesota Twins in 11th round of 1994 free-agent draft; did not sign. ... Selected by Baltimore Orioles organization in 10th round of 1995 free-agent draft. ... Selected by Arizona Diamondbacks in second round (45th pick overall) of expansion draft (November 18, 1997). ... On disabled list (July 25, 1999-remainder of season). ... On disabled list (May 3-24, 2002); included rehabilitation assignment to Tucson. ... Traded by Diamondbacks with P Bret Prinz and C Jon-Mark Sprowl to New York Yankees for OF Raul Mondesi (July 29, 2003). ... On disabled list (June 2-17, 2003). ... On disabled list (August 28-September 27, 2003). ... Signed as a free agent by Texas Rangers (December 23, 2003). ... Traded by Rangers to Philadelphia Phillies for 3B Jake Blalock and RHP Robinson Tejeda (April 1, 2006). **STATISTICAL NOTES:** Career major league grand slams: 3.

2006 GAMES PLAYED BY POSITION (MLB): OF—67, DH—2.

Year Team (League)	Pos.	G	AB	R	H	2B	3B	HR	RBI	BB	SO	HBP	GDP	SB-CS	Avg.	OBP	SLG	OPS	E	Avg.
1995—Bluefield (Appal.)	OF	20	69	11	23	5	1	2	12	6	7	1	1	3-1	.333	.390	.522	.911	2	.846
—Frederick (Carolina)	OF	28	96	16	27	3	0	1	10	12	10	3	3	1-2	.281	.378	.344	.722	1	.966
1996—Frederick (Carolina)	OF	59	185	33	60	11	1	4	28	38	34	0	2	5-6	.324	.438	.459	.897	3	.972
—Bowie (East.)	OF	66	251	27	73	14	1	2	33	28	56	1	4	2-7	.291	.363	.378	.741	3	.979
1997—Bowie (East.)	OF-DH	107	385	71	126	29	3	20	55	58	69	5	6	11-4	.327	.421	.574	.995	1	.994
—Baltimore (A.L.)	OF-DH	17	27	3	6	1	0	1	3	4	7	1	2	0-0	.222	.344	.370	.714	0	1.000
1998—Tucson (PCL)	OF	17	72	17	22	4	3	1	11	5	8	0	2	4-0	.306	.346	.486	.832	0	1.000
—Arizona (N.L.)	OF	124	416	43	108	19 * 12		5	51	33	103	3	6	3-5	.260	.318	.399	.717	3	.987
1999—Arizona (N.L.)	OF-DH	63	109	27	43	7	1	1	15	11	24	3	3	2-0	.395	.463	.505	.968	0	1.000
2000—Arizona (N.L.)	OF	34	50	2	15	3	0	0	2	4	9	0	1	0-2	.300	.352	.360	.712	0	1.000
—Tucson (PCL)	OF	33	122	16	28	6	3	3	9	13	15	0	0	4-0	.230	.301	.402	.703	2	.966
—Ariz. D'backs (Ariz.)	OF	2	6	0	2	1	0	0	2	0	1	0	0	0-0	.333	.333	.500	.833	0	...
—South Bend (Mid.)	OF	2	5	3	1	1	0	0	1	2	0	0	0	0-0	.200	.375	.400	.775	0	1.000
2001—Arizona (N.L.)	OF	115	217	28	60	10	2	10	40	22	52	2	2	2-1	.277	.349	.479	.828	1	.989
2002—Arizona (N.L.)	OF-DH	97	229	34	56	11	2	7	29	28	55	1	7	2-4	.245	.326	.402	.727	3	.967
—Tucson (PCL)	OF	4	15	2	2	1	0	0	1	2	4	0	0	0-0	.133	.235	.200	.435	0	1.000
2003—Arizona (N.L.)	OF	70	165	18	40	11	3	2	19	19	45	3	4	9-0	.242	.328	.382	.710	2	.976
—New York (A.L.)	OF	21	51	8	9	1	0	1	4	4	13	2	2	3-0	.176	.263	.255	.518	0	1.000
2004—Texas (A.L.)	OF-DH	107	331	59	80	13	1	17	61	47	88	5	4	9-4	.242	.342	.441	.783	2	.989
2005—Texas (A.L.)	DH-OF	128	435	97	109	17	5	29	65	76	121	5	7	5-3	.251	.367	.513	.879	3	.970
2006—Philadelphia (N.L.)	OF-DH	132	264	41	77	14	5	13	39	28	62	6	1	1-3	.292	.369	.530	.899	1	.990
American League totals (4 years)		273	844	167	204	32	6	48	133	131	229	13	15	17-7	.242	.350	.464	.815	5	.985
National League totals (7 years)		635	1450	193	399	75	25	38	195	145	350	18	24	19-15	.275	.346	.440	.786	10	.985
Major League totals (10 years)		908	2294	360	603	107	31	86	328	276	579	31	39	36-22	.263	.348	.449	.797	15	.985

DIVISION SERIES RECORD

Year Team (League)	Pos.	G	AB	R	H	2B	3B	HR	RBI	BB	SO	HBP	GDP	SB-CS	Avg.	OBP	SLG	OPS	E	Avg.
2001—Arizona (N.L.)		2	0	0	0	0	0	0	0	0	0	0	0	0-0	...	...	...	...		...
2002—Arizona (N.L.)	OF	3	7	1	2	0	0	1	2	0	1	0	0	0-0	.286	.286	.714	1.000	0	1.000
2003—New York (A.L.)	DH	1	0	0	0	0	0	0	0	0	0	0	0	0-0	...	...	...	...	0	...
Division series totals (3 years)		6	7	1	2	0	0	1	2	0	1	0	0	0-0	.286	.286	.714	1.000	0	1.000

CHAMPIONSHIP SERIES RECORD

Year Team (League)	Pos.	G	AB	R	H	2B	3B	HR	RBI	BB	SO	HBP	GDP	SB-CS	Avg.	OBP	SLG	OPS	E	Avg.
2001—Arizona (N.L.)		2	2	1	1	0	0	0	0	0	0	0	0	0-0	.500	.500	.500	1.000	...	...
2003—New York (A.L.)	DH-OF	3	3	2	1	0	0	0	0	0	1	1	0	1-0	.333	.500	.333	.833	0	...
Champ. series totals (2 years)		5	5	3	2	0	0	0	0	0	1	1	0	1-0	.400	.500	.400	.900	0	...

WORLD SERIES RECORD

Year Team (League)	Pos.	G	AB	R	H	2B	3B	HR	RBI	BB	SO	HBP	GDP	SB-CS	Avg.	OBP	SLG	OPS	E	Avg.
2001—Arizona (N.L.)	OF	2	2	0	1	0	0	0	0	0	0	0	0	0-0	.500	.500	.500	1.000	0	1.000
2003—New York (A.L.)	OF-DH	4	2	1	0	0	0	0	0	0	0	0	0	0-0	.000	.000	.000	.000	0	1.000
World series totals (2 years)		6	4	1	1	0	0	0	0	0	0	0	0	0-0	.250	.250	.250	.500	0	1.000

2006 LEFTY-RIGHTY SPLITS

vs.	Avg.	AB	H	2B	3B	HR	RBI	BB	SO	OBP	Slg.	vs.	Avg.	AB	H	2B	3B	HR	RBI	BB	SO	OBP	Slg.
L	.200	20	4	1	0	2	4	3	5	.292	.550	R	.299	244	73	13	5	11	35	25	57	.375	.529

DEMARIA, CHRIS — P

PERSONAL: Born September 28, 1980, in Torrance, Calif. ... 6-3/210. ... Throws right, bats both. ... Full name: Christopher Neil Demaria. ... College: Long Beach State. **TRANSACTIONS/CAREER NOTES:** Selected by Pittsburgh Pirates organization in 17th round of 2002 free-agent draft. ... Selected by Kansas City Royals organization from Pirates organization in Rule 5 minor league draft (December 13, 2004). ... Traded by Royals to Milwaukee Brewers for P Justin Barnes (December 21, 2005). **CAREER HITTING:** 0-for-0 (.000), 0 R, 0 2B, 0 3B, 0 HR, 0 RBI.

Year Team (League)	W	L	Pct.	ERA	WHIP	G	GS	CG	ShO	Hld.	Sv.-Opp.	IP	H	R	ER	HR	BB-IBB	SO	Avg.
2002—Williamsport. (NYP)	1	1	.500	4.35	1.23	16	0	0	0	...	1-...	31.0	34	20	15	6	4-1	15	.272
2003—Williamsport. (NYP)	6	3	.667	2.68	0.98	25	1	0	0	...	3-...	47.0	36	15	14	3	10-1	48	.209
2004—Hickory (S. Atl.)	8	3	.727	2.94	1.03	40	0	0	0	...	10-...	79.2	62	29	26	5	20-2	101	.209
2005—High Desert (Calif.)	4	2	.667	2.23	1.10	48	0	0	0	0	19-24	60.2	57	19	15	8	10-1	73	.247
—Wichita (Texas)	0	1	.000	1.76	0.91	10	0	0	0	...	1-2	15.1	12	3	3	3	2-0	19	.218
—Kansas City (A.L.)	1	0	1.000	9.00	2.11	8	0	0	0	...	0-0	9.0	14	10	9	3	5-0	11	.359
2006—Nashville (PCL)	4	0	1.000	2.96	1.26	38	0	0	0	7	1-2	51.2	48	20	17	4	17-0	50	.242
—Milwaukee (N.L.)	0	1	.000	5.93	1.39	10	0	0	0	0	0-0	13.2	10	11	9	4	9-0	11	.200
American League totals (1 year)	1	0	1.000	9.00	2.11	8	0	0	0	...	0-0	9.0	14	10	9	3	5-0	11	.359
National League totals (1 year)	0	1	.000	5.93	1.39	10	0	0	0	0	0-0	13.2	10	11	9	4	9-0	11	.200
Major League totals (2 years)	1	1	.500	7.15	1.68	18	0	0	0	0	0-0	22.2	24	21	18	7	14-0	22	.270

2006 LEFTY-RIGHTY SPLITS

vs.	Avg.	AB	H	2B	3B	HR	RBI	BB	SO	OBP	Slg.	vs.	Avg.	AB	H	2B	3B	HR	RBI	BB	SO	OBP	Slg.
L	.263	19	5	2	0	3	6	5	5	.417	.842	R	.161	31	5	1	0	1	4	4	6	.297	.290

DEMPSTER, RYAN — P

PERSONAL: Born May 3, 1977, in Sechelt, British Columbia. ... 6-2/215. ... Throws right, bats right. ... Full name: Ryan Scott Dempster. ... High school: Elphinstone (Gibsons, B.C.). **TRANSACTIONS/CAREER NOTES:** Selected by Texas Rangers organization in third round of 1995 free-agent draft. ... Traded by Rangers with a player to be named to Florida Marlins for P John Burkett (August 8, 1996); Marlins acquired P Rick Helling to complete deal (September 3, 1996). ... Traded by Marlins to Cincinnati

Reds for OF Juan Encarnacion, OF/2B Wilton Guerrero and P Ryan Snare (July 11, 2002). ... On disabled list (May 23-June 7 and July 29, 2003-remainder of season); included rehabilitation assignment to Louisville. ... Released by Reds (November 4, 2003). ... Signed by Chicago Cubs (January 21, 2004). ... On disabled list (March 26-August 1, 2004); included rehabilitation assignments to Lansing and Iowa. **MISCELLANEOUS NOTES:** Appeared in one game as pinch runner (1999). ... Appeared in two games as pinch runner (2002). ... Scored a run in two appearances as pinch runner (2003).

CAREER HITTING: 24-for-313 (.077), 12 R, 5 2B, 1 3B, 0 HR, 7 RBI.

Year Team (League)	W	L	Pct.	ERA	WHIP	G	GS	CG	ShO	Hld.	Sv.-Opp.	IP	H	R	ER	HR	BB-IBB	SO	Avg.
1995— GC Rangers (GCL)	3	1	.750	2.36	1.49	8	6	1	0	...	0-...	34.1	34	21	9	1	17-0	37	.254
— Hudson Valley (NYP)	1	0	1.000	3.18	1.41	1	1	0	0	...	0-...	5.2	7	2	2	0	1-0	6	.318
1996— Char. S.C. (SAL)	7	11	.389	3.30	1.23	23	23	2	0	...	0-...	144.1	120	71	53	13	58-1	141	.229
— Kane Co. (Midw.)	2	1	.667	2.73	1.37	4	4	1	1	...	0-...	26.1	18	10	8	0	18-0	16	.202
1997— Brevard County (FSL)	10	9	.526	4.90	1.43	28	26	2	1	...	0-...	165.1	190	100	90	19	46-1	131	.290
1998— Portland (East.)	4	3	.571	3.22	1.10	7	7	0	0	...	0-...	44.2	34	20	16	8	15-0	33	.214
— Florida (N.L.)	1	5	.167	7.08	2.01	14	11	0	0	0	0-1	54.2	72	47	43	6	38-1	35	.336
— Charlotte (Int'l)	3	1	.750	3.27	1.36	5	5	1	0	...	0-...	33.0	33	14	12	4	12-1	24	.270
1999— Calgary (PCL)	1	1	.500	4.99	1.30	5	5	0	0	...	0-...	30.2	30	17	17	6	10-1	29	.252
— Florida (N.L.)	7	8	.467	4.71	1.63	25	25	0	0	0	0-0	147.0	146	77	77	21	93-2	126	.262
2000— Florida (N.L.)	14	10	.583	3.66	1.36	33	33	2	1	0	0-0	226.1	210	102	92	30	97-7	209	.243
2001— Florida (N.L.)	15	12	.556	4.94	1.56	34	34	2	1	0	0-0	211.1	218	123	116	21	* 112-5	171	.269
2002— Florida (N.L.)	5	8	.385	4.79	1.50	18	18	3	0	0	0-0	120.1	126	66	64	12	55-1	87	.281
— Cincinnati (N.L.)	5	5	.500	6.19	1.58	15	15	1	0	0	0-0	88.2	102	61	§ 61	16	38-1	66	.293
2003— Louisville (Int'l)	1	1	.500	3.29	1.20	2	2	1	0	...	0-...	13.2	13	5	5	1	3-0	9	.255
— Cincinnati (N.L.)	3	7	.300	6.54	1.76	22	20	0	0	0	0-0	115.2	134	89	84	14	70-4	84	.293
2004— Lansing (Midw.)	0	0	...	1.96	1.20	5	5	0	0	...	0-...	18.1	20	5	4	0	2-0	21	.270
— Iowa (PCL)	1	1	.500	3.86	1.38	6	4	0	0	...	0-...	21.0	19	9	9	1	10-0	20	.244
— Chicago (N.L.)	1	1	.500	3.92	1.40	23	0	0	0	3	2-2	20.2	16	9	9	1	13-0	18	.208
2005— Chicago (N.L.)	5	3	.625	3.13	1.43	63	6	0	0	0	33-35	92.0	83	35	32	4	49-7	89	.242
2006— Chicago (N.L.)	1	9	.100	4.80	1.51	74	0	0	0	0	24-33	75.0	77	47	40	5	36-3	67	.262
Major League totals (9 years)	57	68	.456	4.83	1.55	321	162	8	2	5	59-71	1151.2	1184	656	618	130	601-31	952	.268

ALL-STAR GAME RECORD

	W	L	Pct.	ERA	WHIP	G	GS	CG	ShO	Hld.	Sv.-Opp.	IP	H	R	ER	HR	BB-IBB	SO	Avg.
All-Star totals (1 year)	Did not play																		

2006 LEFTY-RIGHTY SPLITS

vs.	Avg.	AB	H	2B	3B	HR	RBI	BB	SO	OBP	Slg.	vs.	Avg.	AB	H	2B	3B	HR	RBI	BB	SO	OBP	Slg.
L	.310	126	39	7	2	3	17	19	33	.395	.444	R	.226	168	38	5	0	3	23	17	34	.305	.310

DENORFIA, CHRIS   OF

PERSONAL: Born July 15, 1980, in Bristol, Conn. ... 6-1/185. ... Bats right, throws right. ... Full name: Christopher Anthony Denorfia. ... College: Wheaton College. **TRANSACTIONS/CAREER NOTES:** Selected by Cincinnati Reds organization in 19th round of 2002 free-agent draft.

2006 GAMES PLAYED BY POSITION (MLB): OF—37.

										BATTING							FIELDING	
Year Team (League)	Pos.	G	AB	R	H	2B	3B	HR	RBI	BB	SO	HBP	GDP	SB-CS	Avg.	OBP	SLG	OPS	E	Avg.
2002— GC Reds (GCL)	OF	57	200	38	68	9	2	0	19	31	23	0	8	18-8	.340	.425	.405	.830	4	.966
— Chattanooga (Sou.)	OF	3	7	0	3	2	1	0	0	2	1	0	0	0-0	.429	.556	1.000	1.556	0	1.000
— Dayton (Midw.)	OF	3	10	2	0	0	0	0	0	0	3	0	1	0-0	.000	.000	.000	.000	0	1.000
2003— Potomac (Carol.)	OF	128	470	60	111	10	5	4	39	54	106	3	10	20-7	.236	.317	.304	.621	9	.982
2004— Potomac (Carol.)	OF	75	269	52	84	18	4	11	51	48	66	1	3	10-6	.312	.416	.532	.948	4	.846
— Chattanooga (Sou.)	OF	61	221	30	55	10	2	6	27	30	42	1	1	5-2	.249	.340	.394	.734	2	.000
2005— Chattanooga (Sou.)	OF	46	188	40	62	17	3	7	26	17	38	2	1	4-3	.330	.391	.564	.955	4	.979
— Louisville (Int'l)	OF	91	323	50	100	12	6	13	61	41	54	4	7	8-3	.310	.391	.505	.895	0	1.000
— Cincinnati (N.L.)	OF	18	38	8	10	3	0	1	2	6	9	0	1	0-0	.263	.364	.421	.785	1	.962
2006— Louisville (Int'l)		83	312	46	109	19	1	7	45	34	41	1	12	15-1	.349	.409	.484	.893	2	.989
— Cincinnati (N.L.)	OF	49	106	14	30	6	0	1	7	11	21	1	1	1-1	.283	.356	.368	.724	0	1.000
Major League totals (2 years)		67	144	22	40	9	0	2	9	17	30	1	2	2-1	.278	.358	.382	.740	1	.988

2006 LEFTY-RIGHTY SPLITS

vs.	Avg.	AB	H	2B	3B	HR	RBI	BB	SO	OBP	Slg.	vs.	Avg.	AB	H	2B	3B	HR	RBI	BB	SO	OBP	Slg.
L	.317	41	13	3	0	0	5	6	4	.378	.390	R	.262	65	17	3	0	1	2	7	15	.342	.354

DEROSA, MARK   IF/OF

PERSONAL: Born February 26, 1975, in Passaic, N.J. ... 6-1/205. ... Bats right, throws right. ... Full name: Mark Thomas DeRosa. ... High school: Bergen Catholic (Oradell, N.J.). ... College: Pennsylvania. **TRANSACTIONS/CAREER NOTES:** Selected by Atlanta Braves organization in seventh round of 1996 free-agent draft. ... On disabled list (May 18-July 17, 2002); included rehabilitation assignments to Richmond and Myrtle Beach. ... Signed as a free agent by Texas Rangers organization (January 19, 2005). ... On disabled list (April 15-30, 2006); included rehabilitation assignment to Oklahoma. **STATISTICAL NOTES:** Career major league grand slams: 1.

2006 GAMES PLAYED BY POSITION (MLB): OF—64, 3B—40, 2B—26, SS—7, DH—3, 1B—1.

										BATTING							FIELDING	
Year Team (League)	Pos.	G	AB	R	H	2B	3B	HR	RBI	BB	SO	HBP	GDP	SB-CS	Avg.	OBP	SLG	OPS	E	Avg.
1996— Eugene (Northwest)	SS	70	255	43	66	13	1	2	28	38	48	5	10	3-4	.259	.363	.341	.705	24	.921
1997— Durham (Carol.)	SS	92	346	51	93	11	3	8	37	25	73	10	12	6-5	.269	.332	.387	.720	21	.948
1998— Greenville (Sou.)	SS	125	461	67	123	26	2	8	49	60	57	5	18	7-13	.267	.356	.384	.740	20	.964
— Atlanta (N.L.)	SS	5	3	2	1	0	0	0	0	0	1	0	0	0-0	.333	.333	.333	.667	0	1.000
1999— Richmond (Int'l)	SS-DH	105	364	41	99	16	2	1	40	21	49	5	5	7-6	.272	.317	.335	.652	9	.951
— Atlanta (N.L.)	SS	7	8	0	0	0	0	0	0	0	2	0	0	0-0	.000	.000	.000	.000	0	1.000
2000— Richmond (Int'l)	SS-2B-3B	101	370	62	108	22	3	3	35	38	36	3	13	13-4	.292	.359	.392	.751	19	.958
— Atlanta (N.L.)	SS	22	13	9	4	1	0	0	3	2	1	0	0	0-0	.308	.400	.385	.785	0	1.000
2001— Richmond (Int'l)	SS-3B-2B	49	186	31	55	11	2	2	17	17	22	1	6	7-3	.296	.351	.425	.776	4	.978
— Atlanta (N.L.)	SS-2B-DH																			
	3B-OF	66	164	27	47	8	0	2	20	12	19	5	3	2-1	.287	.350	.390	.740	7	.966
2002— Atlanta (N.L.)	2B-SS-OF																			
	3B	72	212	24	63	9	2	5	23	12	24	3	5	2-3	.297	.339	.429	.768	6	.976
— Richmond (Int'l)	2B-SS	16	55	9	14	3	0	0	6	5	2	2	4	2-0	.255	.339	.309	.648	3	.952
— Myrtle Beach (Carol.)	2B	2	8	0	1	0	0	0	1	1	0	0	0	0-0	.125	.000	.125	.125	1	.889
2003— Atlanta (N.L.)	2B-3B-SS																			
	DH-OF-1B	103	266	40	70	14	0	6	22	16	49	5	6	1-0	.263	.316	.383	.699	6	.976
2004— Atlanta (N.L.)	3B-SS-2B																			
	OF	118	309	33	74	16	0	4	31	23	53	3	6	1-3	.239	.293	.320	.614	12	.942

Year	Team (League)	Pos.	G	AB	R	H	2B	3B	HR	RBI	BB	SO	HBP	GDP	SB-CS	Avg.	OBP	SLG	OPS	E	Avg.
2005—Texas (A.L.)	OF-2B-SS 3B-DH-1B		66	148	26	36	5	0	8	20	16	35	2	5	1-0	.243	.325	.439	.764	3	.980
2006—Oklahoma (PCL)			3	12	2	6	1	0	0	0	0	1	0	0	0-0	.500	.500	.583	1.083	0	1.000
—Texas (A.L.)	OF-3B-2B SS-DH-1B		136	520	78	154	40	2	13	74	44	102	6	13	4-4	.296	.357	.456	.812	5	.988
American League totals (2 years)			202	668	104	190	45	2	21	94	60	137	8	18	5-4	.284	.350	.452	.802	8	.986
National League totals (7 years)			393	975	135	259	48	2	17	99	65	149	16	20	6-7	.266	.318	.371	.690	31	.967
Major League totals (9 years)			595	1643	239	449	93	4	38	193	125	286	24	38	11-11	.273	.331	.404	.735	39	.974

DIVISION SERIES RECORD

Year	Team (League)	Pos.	G	AB	R	H	2B	3B	HR	RBI	BB	SO	HBP	GDP	SB-CS	Avg.	OBP	SLG	OPS	E	Avg.
2001—Atlanta (N.L.)	SS		1	1	0	1	0	0	0	0	0	0	0	0	0-0	1.000	1.000	1.000	2.000	0	1.000
2002—Atlanta (N.L.)	2B		4	7	2	3	1	1	0	3	1	1	0	0	0-0	.429	.500	.857	1.357	0	1.000
2003—Atlanta (N.L.)	2B-3B		4	7	1	3	2	0	0	2	1	2	0	0	0-0	.429	.500	.714	1.214	0	1.000
Division series totals (3 years)			9	15	3	7	3	1	0	5	2	3	0	0	0-0	.467	.529	.800	1.329	0	1.000

CHAMPIONSHIP SERIES RECORD

Year	Team (League)	Pos.	G	AB	R	H	2B	3B	HR	RBI	BB	SO	HBP	GDP	SB-CS	Avg.	OBP	SLG	OPS	E	Avg.
2001—Atlanta (N.L.)	SS		4	4	0	0	0	0	0	0	0	0	0	0	0-0	.000	.000	.000	.000	0	1.000

2006 LEFTY-RIGHTY SPLITS

vs.	Avg.	AB	H	2B	3B	HR	RBI	BB	SO	OBP	Slg.	vs.	Avg.	AB	H	2B	3B	HR	RBI	BB	SO	OBP	Slg.
L	.342	146	50	15	0	7	27	13	27	.394	.589	R	.278	374	104	25	2	6	47	31	75	.342	.404

DESSENS, ELMER P

PERSONAL: Born January 13, 1971, in Hermosillo, Mexico. ... 5-10/198. ... Throws right, bats right. ... Full name: Elmer Dessens Jusaino. ... Name pronounced: duh-SENZ. ... High school: Carrera Technica (Hermosillo, Mexico). **TRANSACTIONS/CAREER NOTES:** Signed as a non-drafted free agent by Pittsburgh Pirates organization (January 27, 1993). ... Loaned by Pirates organization to Mexico City Red Devils of the Mexican League for 1993 and 1994 seasons; returned to Pirates organization for 1995 season. ... Loaned by Pirates organization to Red Devils (May 7, 1996). ... Returned to Pirates organization (June 21, 1996). ... On disabled list (July 31-September 10, 1996); included rehabilitation assignment to Carolina. ... Loaned by Pirates to Red Devils (March 27-September 5, 1997). ... On disabled list (April 8-24, 1998); included rehabilitation assignment to Nashville. ... Contract purchased by Yomiuri Giants of the Japan Central League (March 31, 1999). ... Signed as a free agent by Cincinnati Reds organization (December 15, 1999). ... On disabled list (August 2-27, 2002). ... Traded by Reds with cash to Arizona Diamondbacks as part of four-team deal in which Reds acquired SS Felipe Lopez from Toronto Blue Jays, Blue Jays acquired a player to be named from Oakland Athletics and Athletics acquired 1B Erubiel Durazo from Diamondbacks (December 15, 2002; Blue Jays acquired P Jason Arnold to complete deal (December 16, 2002). ... Traded by Diamondbacks to Los Angeles Dodgers for OF Jereme Milons (August 19, 2004). ... On disabled list (April 24-June 15, 2005); included rehabilitation assignment to Las Vegas. ... Signed as a free agent by Kansas City Royals (December 8, 2005). ... Traded by Royals to Dodgers for Ps Odalis Perez, Blake Johnson and Julio Pimentel and cash (July 25, 2006). ... On disabled list (August 3-18, 2006); included rehabilitation assignment to Las Vegas. **MISCELLANEOUS NOTES:** Struck out in only appearance as pinch hitter (2001). ... Scored a run in only appearance as pinch runner (2002). ... Had a sacrifice hit and struck out in two appearances as pinch hitter (2003).
CAREER HITTING: 39-for-234 (.167), 12 R, 4 2B, 1 3B, 0 HR, 16 RBI.

Year	Team (League)	W	L	Pct.	ERA	WHIP	G	GS	CG	ShO	Hld.	Sv.-Opp.	IP	H	R	ER	HR	BB-IBB	SO	Avg.
1993—M.C. R. Dev. (Mex.)	3	1	.750	2.35	1.17	14	0	0	0	...	2-...	30.2	31	8	8	2	5-...	16	...
1994—M.C. R. Dev. (Mex.)	11	4	.733	2.04	1.20	37	15	4	1	...	3-...	127.2	121	37	29	5	32-...	51	...
1995—Carolina (Southern)	15	8	.652	2.49	1.26	27	27	1	0	...	0-...	152.0	170	62	42	10	21-3	68	.284
1996—Calgary (PCL)	2	2	.500	3.15	1.60	6	6	0	0	...	0-...	34.1	40	14	12	5	15-1	15	.305
—M.C. R. Dev. (Mex.)	7	0	1.000	1.26	1.08	7	7	1	0	...	0-...	50.0	44	12	7	1	10-...	17	...
—Pittsburgh (N.L.)	0	2	.000	8.28	1.76	15	3	0	0	3	0-0	25.0	40	23	23	2	4-0	13	.385
—Carolina (Southern)	0	1	.000	5.40	1.63	5	1	0	0	...	0-...	11.2	15	8	7	1	4-0	7	.300
1997—M.C. R. Dev. (Mex.)	16	5	.762	3.56	1.30	26	25	3	1	...	0-...	159.1	156	73	63	1	51-...	61	...
—Pittsburgh (N.L.)	0	0	...	0.00	0.60	3	0	0	0	0	0-0	3.1	2	0	0	0	0-0	2	.167
1998—Pittsburgh (N.L.)	2	6	.250	5.67	1.54	43	5	0	0	6	0-1	74.2	90	50	47	10	25-2	43	.300
—Nashville (PCL)	3	1	.750	3.30	1.27	6	5	0	0	...	0-...	30.0	32	12	11	2	6-1	13	.274
1999—Yomiuri (Jp. East.)	4	3	.571	2.08	0.96	15	14	3	...	...	0-...	95.0	67	26	22	...	24-...	58	...
—Yomiuri (Jp. Cen.)	0	1	.000	3.86	1.71	8	0	0	0	...	0-...	16.1	24	7	7	...	4-...	6	...
2000—Louisville (Int'l)	2	1	1.000	3.18	1.37	4	4	0	0	...	0-...	22.2	24	10	8	1	7-0	14	.270
—Cincinnati (N.L.)	11	5	.688	4.28	1.45	40	16	1	0	1	1-1	147.1	170	73	70	10	43-7	85	.296
2001—Cincinnati (N.L.)	10	14	.417	4.48	1.38	34	34	1	1	0	0-0	205.0	221	103	102	32	56-1	128	.279
2002—Cincinnati (N.L.)	7	8	.467	3.03	1.25	30	30	0	0	0	0-0	178.0	173	70	60	24	49-8	93	.257
2003—Arizona (N.L.)	8	8	.500	5.07	1.53	34	30	0	0	0	0-0	175.2	212	107	99	22	57-6	113	.299
2004—Arizona (N.L.)	1	6	.143	4.75	1.52	38	9	0	0	4	2-4	85.1	107	54	45	11	23-4	55	.301
—Los Angeles (N.L.)	1	0	1.000	3.20	1.22	12	1	0	0	0	0-1	19.2	16	7	7	4	8-0	18	.216
2005—Las Vegas (PCL)	0	0	...	3.38	1.00	3	3	0	0	0	0-0	8.0	6	3	3	1	2-0	6	.214
—Los Angeles (N.L.)	1	2	.333	3.56	1.25	28	7	0	0	1	0-0	65.2	63	30	26	6	19-2	37	.249
2006—Kansas City (A.L.)	5	7	.417	4.50	1.41	43	0	0	0	12	2-7	54.0	63	31	27	4	13-6	36	.292
—Las Vegas (PCL)	0	1	.000	13.50	4.50	1	0	0	0	0	0-1	0.2	2	1	1	1	1-0	0	.400
—Los Angeles (N.L.)	0	1	.000	4.70	1.39	19	0	0	0	6	0-0	23.0	23	12	12	4	9-2	16	.258
American League totals (1 year)	5	7	.417	4.50	1.41	43	0	0	0	12	2-7	54.0	63	31	27	4	13-6	36	.292
National League totals (10 years)	41	52	.441	4.41	1.41	296	135	2	1	21	3-7	1002.2	1117	529	491	125	293-32	603	.284
Major League totals (10 years)	46	59	.438	4.41	1.41	339	135	2	1	33	5-14	1056.2	1180	560	518	129	306-38	639	.284

DIVISION SERIES RECORD

Year	Team (League)	W	L	Pct.	ERA	WHIP	G	GS	CG	ShO	Hld.	Sv.-Opp.	IP	H	R	ER	HR	BB-IBB	SO	Avg.
2004—Los Angeles (N.L.)	0	0	...	6.75	0.75	1	0	0	0	0	0-0	1.1	1	1	1	1	0-0	1	.200

2006 LEFTY-RIGHTY SPLITS

vs.	Avg.	AB	H	2B	3B	HR	RBI	BB	SO	OBP	Slg.	vs.	Avg.	AB	H	2B	3B	HR	RBI	BB	SO	OBP	Slg.
L	.267	120	32	5	1	1	18	12	18	.331	.350	R	.292	185	54	5	1	7	28	10	34	.332	.443

DEVINE, JOEY P

PERSONAL: Born September 19, 1983, in Junction City, Kan. ... 5-11/195. ... Throws right, bats right. ... Full name: Joseph Devine. ... College: North Carolina State. **TRANSACTIONS/CAREER NOTES:** Selected by Atlanta Braves organization in first round (27th pick overall) of 2005 free-agent draft.
CAREER HITTING: 0-for-1 (.000), 0 R, 0 2B, 0 3B, 0 HR, 0 RBI.

Year	Team (League)	W	L	Pct.	ERA	WHIP	G	GS	CG	ShO	Hld.	Sv.-Opp.	IP	H	R	ER	HR	BB-IBB	SO	Avg.
2005—Myrtle Beach (Carol.)	0	0	...	0.00	0.60	4	0	0	0	0	1-1	5.0	0	0	0	0	3-0	7	.000
—Mississippi (Sou.)	1	1	.500	2.70	1.55	18	0	0	0	0	5-6	20.0	19	13	6	2	12-1	28	.250
—Richmond (Int'l)	0	0	...	18.00	4.00	1	0	0	0	0	0-1	1.0	3	2	2	0	1-0	1	.600

Year	Team (League)	W	L	Pct.	ERA	WHIP	G	GS	CG	ShO	Hld.	Sv.-Opp.	IP	H	R	ER	HR	BB-IBB	SO	Avg.
—	Atlanta (N.L.)	0	1	.000	12.60	2.20	5	0	0	0	1	0-0	5.0	6	7	7	2	5-1	3	.286
2006—	Richmond (Int'l)	0	0	...	...	...	1	0	0	0	0	0-0	0.0	1	1	1	0	1-0	0	1.000
—	Myrtle Beach (Carol.)	1	3	.250	5.89	1.31	13	2	0	0	0	0-1	18.1	13	12	12	1	11-1	28	.203
—	Mississippi (Sou.)	2	0	1.000	0.82	0.55	6	0	0	0	0	0-0	11.0	2	1	1	1	4-0	20	.065
—	Atlanta (N.L.)	0	0	...	9.95	2.68	10	0	0	0	0	0-1	6.1	8	7	7	1	9-1	10	.308
	Major League totals (2 years)	0	1	.000	11.12	2.47	15	0	0	0	0	0-1	11.1	14	14	14	3	14-2	13	.298

DIVISION SERIES RECORD

Year	Team (League)	W	L	Pct.	ERA	WHIP	G	GS	CG	ShO	Hld.	Sv.-Opp.	IP	H	R	ER	HR	BB-IBB	SO	Avg.
2005—	Atlanta (N.L.)	0	1	.000	10.80	2.40	3	0	0	0	0	0-0	1.2	3	2	2	1	1-1	3	.375

2006 LEFTY-RIGHTY SPLITS

vs.	Avg.	AB	H	2B	3B	HR	RBI	BB	SO	OBP	Slg.	vs.	Avg.	AB	H	2B	3B	HR	RBI	BB	SO	OBP	Slg.
L	.333	12	4	0	0	0	4	5	6	.529	.333	R	.286	14	4	1	0	1	5	4	4	.474	.571

DIAZ, EINAR — C

PERSONAL: Born December 28, 1972, in Chiriqui, Panama. ... 5-10/200. ... Bats right, throws right. ... Full name: Einar Antonio Diaz. ... Name pronounced: AY-een-ar.

TRANSACTIONS/CAREER NOTES: Signed as a non-drafted free agent by Cleveland Indians organization (October 5, 1990). ... On disabled list (August 23-September 30, 2002); included rehabilitation assignment to Mahoning Valley. ... Traded by Indians with P Ryan Drese to Texas Rangers for 1B Travis Hafner and P Aaron Myette (December 6, 2002). ... Traded by Rangers with P Justin Echols and cash to Montreal Expos for IF Josh McKinley and P Chris Young (April 3, 2004). ... Signed as a free agent by St. Louis Cardinals (December 14, 2004). ... Signed as a free agent by Indians organization (December 23, 2005).

2006 GAMES PLAYED BY POSITION (MLB): C—1.

										BATTING										FIELDING	
Year	Team (League)	Pos.	G	AB	R	H	2B	3B	HR	RBI	BB	SO	HBP	GDP	SB-CS	Avg.	OBP	SLG	OPS	E	Avg.
1991—Dom. Inds. (DSL)			62	239	35	67	6	3	1	29	14	5			10-...	.280		.343			...
1992—Burlington (Appal.)	3B-SS		52	178	19	37	3	0	1	14	20	9	3	4	2-3	.208	.296	.242	.537	7	.959
1993—Burlington (Appal.)	3B-C		60	231	40	69	15	3	5	33	8	7	4	5	7-3	.299	.328	.455	.782	10	.974
— Columbus (S. Atl.)	C		1	5	0	0	0	0	0	0	0	1	0	1	0-0	.000	.000	.000	.000	0	1.000
1994—Columbus (S. Atl.)	3B-C		120	491	67	137	23	2	16	71	17	34	21	18	4-4	.279	.330	.432	.762	9	.991
1995—Kinston (Carol.)	C-3B-DH		104	373	46	98	21	0	6	43	12	29	8	6	3-6	.263	.297	.367	.665	7	.991
1996—Cant./Akr. (Eastern)	C-3B		104	395	47	111	26	2	3	35	12	22	9	11	3-2	.281	.317	.380	.696	15	.983
— Cleveland (A.L.)	C		4	1	0	0	0	0	0	0	0	0	0	0	0-0	.000	.000	.000	.000	0	1.000
1997—Buffalo (A.A.)	C-3B		109	336	40	86	18	2	3	31	18	34	5	12	2-6	.256	.302	.348	.650	19	.974
— Cleveland (A.L.)	C		5	7	1	1	1	0	0	1	0	2	0	0	0-0	.143	.143	.286	.429	1	.955
1998—Buffalo (Int'l)	C		115	415	62	130	21	3	8	63	21	33	6	3	3-3	.313	.354	.436	.790	12	.986
— Cleveland (A.L.)	C		17	48	8	11	1	0	2	9	1	3	0	2	0-0	.229	.286	.375	.661	3	.973
1999—Cleveland (A.L.)	C		119	392	43	110	21	1	3	32	23	41	5	10	11-4	.281	.328	.362	.690	10	.988
2000—Cleveland (A.L.)	C-3B		75	250	29	68	14	2	4	25	11	29	8	7	4-2	.272	.323	.392	.715	4	.994
2001—Cleveland (A.L.)	C-2B		134	437	54	121	34	1	4	56	17	44	16	11	1-2	.277	.328	.387	.714	8	.992
2002†—Cleveland (A.L.)	C		102	320	34	66	19	0	2	16	17	27	6	13	0-1	.206	.258	.284	.542	8	.989
— Mahoning Valley (NYP)			3	13	2	5	2	0	0	5	0	1	1		0-0	.385	.429	.538	.967	0	1.000
2003—Texas (A.L.)	C		101	334	30	86	14	1	4	35	9	32	10	12	3-1	.257	.294	.341	.635	8	.989
2004—Montreal (N.L.)	C-3B		55	139	9	31	6	1	1	11	11	10	4	6	2-0	.223	.293	.302	.595	1	.990
2005—St. Louis (N.L.)	C-1B		58	130	14	27	6	0	1	17	5	12	2	8	0-0	.208	.248	.277	.525	1	.995
2006—Buffalo (Int'l)			64	220	22	48	13	0	3	29	14	23	1	9	0-1	.218	.267	.318	.585	5	.989
— Las Vegas (PCL)			2	7	0	3	0	0	0	0	0	0	0		0-0	.429	.429	.714	1.143	0	1.000
— Los Angeles (N.L.)	C		3	3	0	2	0	0	0	0	0	0	0	0	0-0	.667	.667	.667	1.333	0	...
American League totals (8 years)			557	1789	199	463	104	5	19	174	80	177	47	55	19-10	.259	.306	.354	.661	42	.990
National League totals (3 years)			116	272	23	60	12	1	2	28	16	22	6	14	2-0	.221	.276	.294	.570	4	.992
Major League totals (11 years)			673	2061	222	523	116	6	21	202	96	199	53	69	21-10	.254	.302	.346	.649	46	.990

DIVISION SERIES RECORD

Year	Team (League)	Pos.	G	AB	R	H	2B	3B	HR	RBI	BB	SO	HBP	GDP	SB-CS	Avg.	OBP	SLG	OPS	E	Avg.
1998—Cleveland (A.L.)		Did not play.																			
1999—Cleveland (A.L.)	C	2	1	0	0	0	0	0	0	0	0	0	0	0-0	.000	.000	.000	.000	0	1.000
2001—Cleveland (A.L.)	C	5	16	3	5	0	0	0	2	2	1	0	0	0-0	.313	.389	.313	.701	1	.982
Division series totals (2 years)		7	17	3	5	0	0	0	2	2	1	0	0	0-0	.294	.368	.294	.663	1	.983

CHAMPIONSHIP SERIES RECORD

Year	Team (League)	Pos.	G	AB	R	H	2B	3B	HR	RBI	BB	SO	HBP	GDP	SB-CS	Avg.	OBP	SLG	OPS	E	Avg.
1998—Cleveland (A.L.)	C	4	0	0	0	0	0	0	0	0	0	0	0	0-0	.000	.000	.000	.000	0	1.000

2006 LEFTY-RIGHTY SPLITS

vs.	Avg.	AB	H	2B	3B	HR	RBI	BB	SO	OBP	Slg.	vs.	Avg.	AB	H	2B	3B	HR	RBI	BB	SO	OBP	Slg.
L	.000	1	0	0	0	0	0	0	0	.000	.000	R	1.000	2	2	0	0	0	0	0	0	1.000	1.000

DIAZ, JOSE — P

PERSONAL: Born April 13, 1980, in San Pedro de Macoris, Dominican Republic. ... 175. ... Throws right, bats right. ... Full name: Joselo Soriano Diaz. .

TRANSACTIONS/CAREER NOTES: Signed as non-drafted free agent by Los Angeles Dodgers organization (August 24, 1996). ... Played five seasons as a catcher and infielder in the Dodgers organization (1997-2001). ... Traded by Dodgers with P Kole Strayhorn and IF/OF Victor Diaz to New York Mets for OF Jeromy Burnitz and cash (July 14, 2003). ... Traded by Mets with P Scott Kazmir to Tampa Bay Devil Rays for Ps Victor Zambrano and Bartolome Fortunato (July 30, 2004). ... Claimed on waivers by Cleveland Indians (June 7, 2005). ... Signed as free agent by Texas Rangers organization (January 2, 2006). ... Traded by Rangers to Kansas City Royals for OF Matt Stairs (July 31, 2006).

CAREER HITTING: 0-for-0 (.000), 0 R, 0 2B, 0 3B, 0 HR, 0 RBI.

Year	Team (League)	W	L	Pct.	ERA	WHIP	G	GS	CG	ShO	Hld.	Sv.-Opp.	IP	H	R	ER	HR	BB-IBB	SO	Avg.
1999—Dom. Dodgers (DSL)		Did not play.																		
2001—Great Falls (Pio.)	0	0	...	0.00	0.00	1	0	0	0		0-...	1.0	0	0	0	0	0-0	2	.000
2002—South Georgia (S. Atl.)	3	1	.750	4.21	1.52	19	0	0	0		1-...	25.2	14	12	12	1	25-0	33	.163
2003—Vero Beach (FSL)	5	2	.714	3.50	1.41	15	11	0	0		1-...	61.2	39	25	24	2	48-1	69	.181
— Jacksonville (Sou.)	1	0	1.000	0.00	1.04	5	0	0	0		1-...	7.2	5	1	0	0	3-0	7	.185
— St. Lucie (Fla. St.)	2	2	.500	2.97	1.35	11	2	0	0		1-...	30.1	16	12	10	0	25-0	41	.162
2004—Binghamton (East.)	4	7	.364	5.18	1.55	21	19	1	0		0-...	83.1	59	53	48	3	70-0	90	.208
— Montgom. (Sou.)	1	3	.250	5.40	1.77	6	6	0	0		0-...	30.0	26	19	18	4	27-0	37	.245
2005—Montgom. (Sou.)	2	2	.500	9.13	1.77	18	0	0	0	1	0-2	23.2	22	24	24	2	20-0	22	.247
— Akron (East.)	0	0	...	0.00	0.51	8	0	0	0	1	1-1	15.2	5	1	0	0	3-0	19	.100
— Buffalo (Int'l)	1	2	.333	3.89	1.53	20	0	0	0		2-4	34.2	27	19	15	4	26-0	44	.221

D

Year Team (League)	W	L	Pct.	ERA	WHIP	G	GS	CG	ShO	Hld.	Sv.-Opp.	IP	H	R	ER	HR	BB-IBB	SO	Avg.
2006—Frisco (Texas)	2	0	1.000	1.29	1.29	8	4	0	0	0	0-0	28.0	16	5	4	0	20-0	29	.174
—Oklahoma (PCL)	0	0	...	3.28	1.40	28	1	0	0	4	4-4	35.2	28	14	13	2	22-0	46	.215
—Omaha (PCL)	2	3	.400	5.40	1.58	13	0	0	0	2	0-4	18.1	14	13	11	3	15-2	16	.219
—Kansas City (A.L.)	0	0	...	10.80	2.70	4	0	0	0	0	0-0	6.2	10	8	8	2	8-0	3	.345
Major League totals (1 year)	0	0	...	10.80	2.70	4	0	0	0	0	0-0	6.2	10	8	8	2	8-0	3	.345

2006 LEFTY-RIGHTY SPLITS

vs.	Avg.	AB	H	2B	3B	HR	RBI	BB	SO	OBP	Slg.	vs.	Avg.	AB	H	2B	3B	HR	RBI	BB	SO	OBP	Slg.
L	.333	12	4	0	0	1	6	4	1	.500	.583	R	.353	17	6	1	0	1	3	4	2	.500	.588

DIAZ, MATT — OF

PERSONAL: Born March 3, 1978, in Portland, Ore. ... 6-1/206. ... Bats right, throws right. ... Full name: Matthew Edward Diaz. ... High school: Sante Fe (Fla.). ... College: Florida State. **TRANSACTIONS/CAREER NOTES:** Selected by Tampa Bay Devil Rays organization in 17th round of 1999 free-agent draft. ... On disabled list (June 11-July 18, 2005); included rehabilitation assignments to AZL Royals and Wichita. ... Claimed on waivers by Baltimore Orioles (February 18, 2005). ... Refused to report and became a free agent (February 22, 2005). ... Signed as a free agent by Kansas City Royals organization (February 24, 2005). ... Traded by Royals to Atlanta Braves for P Ricardo Rodriguez (December 20, 2005).

2006 GAMES PLAYED BY POSITION (MLB): OF—99.

Year Team (League)	Pos.	G	AB	R	H	2B	3B	HR	RBI	BB	SO	HBP	GDP	SB-CS	Avg.	OBP	SLG	OPS	E	Avg.
1999—Hudson Valley (NYP)	OF	54	208	22	51	15	2	1	20	6	43	6	5	6-2	.245	.284	.351	.635	3	.972
2000—St. Pete. (FSL)	OF	106	392	37	106	21	3	6	53	11	54	11	21	2-3	.270	.305	.385	.691	10	.957
2001—Bakersfield (Calif.)	OF	131	524	79	172	40	2	17	81	24	73	14	11	11-5	.328	.370	.510	.880	10	.961
2002—Orlando (South.)	OF-1B	122	449	71	123	28	1	10	50	34	72	10	11	31-9	.274	.337	.408	.744	3	.987
2003—Orlando (South.)	OF	60	227	32	87	21	0	5	41	19	24	8	7	9-5	.383	.444	.542	.985	1	.994
—Tampa Bay (A.L.)	DH-OF	4	9	2	1	0	0	0	0	1	3	0	0	0-0	.111	.200	.111	.311	1	.857
—Durham (Int'l)	OF-DH	67	253	35	83	18	3	8	45	16	45	8	8	6-2	.328	.382	.518	.900	1	.993
2004—Durham (Int'l)	OF-DH	134	503	81	167	47	5	21	93	26	96	13	9	15-4	.332	.377	.571	.947	7	.974
—Tampa Bay (A.L.)	DH-OF	10	21	3	4	1	1	1	3	1	6	2	0	0-0	.190	.292	.476	.768	0	1.000
2005—Arizona Royals (AZL)	OF-DH	3	13	2	6	2	0	0	2	0	2	0	1	0-1	.462	.462	.615	1.077	0	1.000
—Wichita (Texas)	OF-DH	7	26	6	7	0	0	1	6	3	5	0	1	1-0	.269	.333	.385	.718	0	1.000
—Omaha (PCL)	OF	65	259	48	96	22	4	14	56	12	49	5	14	10-3	.371	.408	.649	1.057	8	.969
—Kansas City (A.L.)	OF-DH	34	89	7	25	4	2	1	9	4	15	2	3	0-1	.281	.323	.404	.727	2	.950
2006—Atlanta (N.L.)	OF	124	297	37	97	15	4	7	32	11	49	9	5	5-5	.327	.364	.475	.839	4	.977
American League totals (3 years)		48	119	12	30	5	3	2	12	6	24	4	3	0-1	.252	.308	.395	.703	3	.948
National League totals (1 year)		124	297	37	97	15	4	7	32	11	49	9	5	5-5	.327	.364	.475	.839	4	.977
Major League totals (4 years)		172	416	49	127	20	7	9	44	17	73	13	12	5-6	.305	.348	.452	.800	7	.970

2006 LEFTY-RIGHTY SPLITS

vs.	Avg.	AB	H	2B	3B	HR	RBI	BB	SO	OBP	Slg.	vs.	Avg.	AB	H	2B	3B	HR	RBI	BB	SO	OBP	Slg.
L	.295	146	43	5	3	5	16	4	23	.327	.473	R	.358	151	54	10	1	2	16	7	26	.400	.477

DIAZ, VICTOR — OF

PERSONAL: Born December 10, 1981, in Santo Domingo, Dominican Republic. ... 6-0/200. ... Bats right, throws right. ... Full name: Victor Israel Diaz. ... High school: Roberto Clemente (Chicago). ... Junior college: Grayson County (Texas). **TRANSACTIONS/CAREER NOTES:** Selected by Los Angeles Dodgers organization in 37th round of 2000 free-agent draft. ... Traded by Dodgers with Ps Kole Strayhorn and Jose Diaz to New York Mets for OF Jeromy Burnitz and cash (July 14, 2003). ... Traded by Mets to Texas Rangers for C Mike Nickeas (August 30, 2006).

2006 GAMES PLAYED BY POSITION (MLB): OF—4.

Year Team (League)	Pos.	G	AB	R	H	2B	3B	HR	RBI	BB	SO	HBP	GDP	SB-CS	Avg.	OBP	SLG	OPS	E	Avg.
2001—GC Dodgers (GCL)	2B-3B	53	195	36	69	22	2	3	31	16	23	6	3	6-3	.354	.414	.533	.947	12	.949
2002—South Georgia (S. Atl.)	3B-2B-1B	91	349	64	122	26	2	10	58	27	69	10	4	20-6	.350	.407	.521	.928	23	.903
—Jacksonville (Sou.)	1B-3B-2B	42	152	22	32	7	0	4	24	7	42	3	3	7-5	.211	.258	.336	.593	3	.989
2003—Jacksonville (Sou.)	2B	85	316	42	92	20	2	10	55	27	60	6	10	8-10	.291	.353	.462	.815	14	.962
—Binghamton (East.)	2B	45	175	29	62	11	0	6	23	8	32	1	3	7-5	.354	.382	.520	.902	6	.968
2004—Norfolk (Int'l)	OF-DH	141	528	81	154	31	1	24	94	31	133	5	12	6-8	.292	.332	.491	.816	9	.969
—New York (N.L.)	OF	15	51	8	15	3	0	3	8	1	15	1	3	0-0	.294	.321	.529	.850	2	.935
2005—Norfolk (Int'l)	1B-OF	42	170	30	51	11	0	10	34	14	47	0	6	6-2	.300	.353	.541	.894	2	.994
—New York (N.L.)	OF	89	280	41	72	17	3	12	38	30	82	1	13	6-2	.257	.329	.468	.797	3	.981
2006—New York (N.L.)	OF	6	11	0	2	1	0	0	2	0	5	0	0	0-0	.182	.182	.273	.455	1	.800
—Norfolk (Int'l)		103	379	30	85	16	0	8	38	25	99	3	13	5-5	.224	.276	.330	.606	6	.963
—Oklahoma (PCL)		3	13	1	5	0	0	0	2	1	6	0	0	0-0	.385	.400	.385	.785	1	.500
Major League totals (3 years)		110	342	49	89	21	3	15	48	31	102	2	16	6-2	.260	.324	.471	.794	6	.952

2006 LEFTY-RIGHTY SPLITS

vs.	Avg.	AB	H	2B	3B	HR	RBI	BB	SO	OBP	Slg.	vs.	Avg.	AB	H	2B	3B	HR	RBI	BB	SO	OBP	Slg.
L	.143	7	1	0	0	0	0	0	3	.143	.143	R	.250	4	1	1	0	0	2	0	2	.250	.500

DICKEY, R.A. — P

PERSONAL: Born October 29, 1974, in Nashville. ... 6-3/220. ... Throws right, bats right. ... Full name: Robert Alan Dickey. ... High school: Montgomery Bell Academy (Nashville). ... College: Tennessee. **TRANSACTIONS/CAREER NOTES:** Selected by Detroit Tigers organization in 10th round of 1993 free-agent draft; did not sign. ... Selected by Texas Rangers organization in first round (18th pick overall) of 1996 free-agent draft. ... On disabled list (June 25-July 19 and July 30-August 23, 2004); included rehabilitation assignment to Frisco. ... On disabled list (April 13-May 25, 2005); included rehabilitation assignment to Oklahoma. **RECORDS:** Shares major league record for home runs allowed, game (6, April 6, 2006). **MISCELLANEOUS NOTES:** Member of 1996 U.S. Olympic baseball team. **CAREER HITTING:** 1-for-1 (1.000), 0 R, 0 2B, 0 3B, 0 HR, 0 RBI.

Year Team (League)	W	L	Pct.	ERA	WHIP	G	GS	CG	ShO	Hld.	Sv.-Opp.	IP	H	R	ER	HR	BB-IBB	SO	Avg.
1997—Charlotte (Fla. St.)	1	4	.200	6.94	1.80	8	6	0	0	...	0-...	35.0	51	32	27	8	12-1	32	.340
1998—Charlotte (Fla. St.)	1	5	.167	3.30	1.33	57	0	0	0	...	38-...	60.0	58	31	22	9	22-3	53	.249
1999—Tulsa (Texas)	6	7	.462	4.55	1.53	35	11	0	0	...	10-...	95.0	105	60	48	13	40-1	59	.282
—Oklahoma (PCL)	2	2	.500	4.37	1.32	6	2	0	0	...	...	22.2	23	12	11	1	7-1	17	.261
2000—Oklahoma (PCL)	8	9	.471	4.49	1.47	30	23	2	0	...	1-...	158.1	167	83	79	13	65-1	85	.281
2001—Oklahoma (PCL)	11	7	.611	3.75	1.28	24	24	3	0	...	...	163.0	164	77	68	14	45-1	120	.262
—Texas (A.L.)	0	1	.000	6.75	1.67	4	0	0	0	0	0-0	12.0	13	9	9	3	7-1	4	.283
2002—Oklahoma (PCL)	8	7	.533	4.09	1.45	37	19	1	0	...	0-...	154.0	176	81	70	8	47-5	109	.295

Year Team (League)	W	L	Pct.	ERA	WHIP	G	GS	CG	ShO	Hld.	Sv.-Opp.	IP	H	R	ER	HR	BB-IBB	SO	Avg.
2003— Oklahoma (PCL)	1	1	.500	1.20	1.10	3	2	0	0	...	0-...	15.0	14	3	2	1	3-0	4	.259
— Texas (A.L.)	9	8	.529	5.09	1.48	38	13	1	1	3	1-1	116.2	135	68	66	16	38-5	94	.292
2004— Frisco (Texas)	1	1	.500	1.98	1.24	4	4	0	0	...	0-...	13.2	16	5	3	0	1-0	9	.286
— Texas (A.L.)	6	7	.462	5.61	1.62	25	15	0	0	0	1-1	104.1	136	77	65	17	33-1	57	.311
2005— Oklahoma (PCL)	10	6	.625	5.99	1.57	19	17	1	0	0	0-0	121.2	152	88	81	12	39-0	81	.308
— Texas (A.L.)	1	2	.333	6.67	1.55	9	4	0	0	0	0-0	29.2	29	23	22	4	17-0	15	.254
2006— Oklahoma (PCL)	9	8	.529	4.92	1.37	22	19	3	0	0	1-1	131.2	134	80	72	17	46-0	61	.272
— Texas (A.L.)	0	1	.000	18.90	2.70	1	1	0	0	0	0-0	3.1	8	7	7	6	1-0	1	.471
Major League totals (5 years)	16	19	.457	5.72	1.57	77	33	1	1	3	2-2	266.0	321	184	169	46	96-7	171	.298

2006 LEFTY-RIGHTY SPLITS

vs.	Avg.	AB	H	2B	3B	HR	RBI	BB	SO	OBP	Slg.	vs.	Avg.	AB	H	2B	3B	HR	RBI	BB	SO	OBP	Slg.
L	.000	1	0	0	0	0	0	0	0	.000	.000	R	.500	16	8	0	0	6	7	1	1	.529	1.625

DIFELICE, MIKE — C

PERSONAL: Born May 28, 1969, in Philadelphia. ... 6-2/205. ... Bats right, throws right. ... Full name: Michael William DiFelice. ... Name pronounced: DEE-fah-lease. ... High school: Bearden (Knoxville, Tenn.). ... College: Tennessee. **TRANSACTIONS/CAREER NOTES:** Selected by St. Louis Cardinals organization in 11th round of 1991 free-agent draft. ... Selected by Tampa Bay Devil Rays in first round (20th pick overall) of expansion draft (November 18, 1997). ... Traded by Devil Rays with P Albie Lopez to Arizona Diamondbacks for OF Jason Conti and P Nick Bierbrodt (July 25, 2001). ... Released by Diamondbacks (September 4, 2001). ... Signed by Cardinals (November 20, 2001). ... Signed as a free agent by Kansas City Royals (January 9, 2003). ... On suspended list (September 4-6, 2003). ... Signed as a free agent by Detroit Tigers (December 18, 2003). ... Traded by Tigers to Chicago Cubs for a player to be named (August 31, 2004). ... Signed as a free agent by Florida Marlins organization (December 18, 2004). ... Released by Marlins (March 27, 2005). ... Signed by New York Mets organization (March 31, 2005). ... Signed by Washington Nationals organization (December 13, 2005). ... Signed as a free agent by Mets organization (May 30, 2006).

2006 GAMES PLAYED BY POSITION (MLB): C—15.

Year Team (League)	Pos.	G	AB	R	H	2B	3B	HR	RBI	BB	SO	HBP	GDP	SB-CS	Avg.	OBP	SLG	OPS	FIELDING E	Avg.
1991— Hamilton (NYP)	C	43	157	10	33	5	0	4	15	9	40	1	3	1-5	.210	.257	.318	.576	9	.974
1992— Hamilton (NYP)	1B-C	18	58	11	20	3	0	2	9	4	7	1	0	2-0	.345	.397	.500	.897	5	.969
— St. Pete. (FSL)	C	17	53	0	12	3	0	0	4	3	11	0	3	0-0	.226	.259	.283	.542	2	.977
1993— Springfield (Midw.)	C	8	20	5	7	1	0	0	3	2	3	1	0	0-1	.350	.435	.400	.835	0	1.000
— St. Pete. (FSL)	C	30	97	5	22	2	0	0	8	11	13	1	4	0-0	.227	.306	.247	.554	7	.964
1994— Arkansas (Texas)	C	71	200	19	50	11	2	2	15	12	48	2	9	0-1	.250	.296	.355	.651	6	.987
1995— Arkansas (Texas)	C	62	176	14	47	10	1	1	24	23	29	3	13	0-2	.267	.360	.352	.712	6	.984
— Louisville (A.A.)	C	21	63	8	17	4	0	0	3	5	11	0	4	0-0	.270	.324	.333	.657	2	.984
1996— Louisville (A.A.)	C	79	246	25	70	13	0	9	33	20	43	1	15	0-3	.285	.338	.447	.785	6	.984
— St. Louis (N.L.)	C	4	7	0	2	1	0	0	2	0	1	0	0	0-0	.286	.286	.429	.714	0	1.000
1997— Arkansas (Texas)	C	1	3	0	1	1	0	0	0	1	0	0	0	0-0	.333	.500	.667	1.167	0	1.000
— St. Louis (N.L.)	C-1B	93	260	16	62	10	1	4	30	19	61	3	11	1-1	.238	.297	.331	.628	6	.991
— Louisville (A.A.)	C	1	4	1	1	0	0	1	1	0	1	0	0	0-0	.250	.250	1.250	1.250	0	1.000
1998— Tampa Bay (A.L.)	C	84	248	17	57	12	3	3	23	15	56	1	12	0-0	.230	.274	.339	.613	4	.993
1999— Tampa Bay (A.L.)	C	51	179	21	55	11	0	6	27	8	23	1	3	0-0	.307	.346	.469	.815	5	.987
2000— Tampa Bay (A.L.)	C	60	204	23	49	13	1	6	19	12	40	0	8	0-0	.240	.280	.402	.682	8	.985
2001— Tampa Bay (A.L.)	C	48	149	13	31	5	1	2	9	8	39	3	3	1-1	.208	.259	.295	.555	6	.982
— Arizona (N.L.)	C	12	21	1	1	0	0	0	1	0	10	1	0	0-0	.048	.091	.048	.139	1	.982
— Tucson (PCL)	C-1B	7	26	6	9	0	0	1	2	3	6	0	2	0-0	.346	.414	.462	.875	3	.940
2002— St. Louis (N.L.)	C	70	174	17	40	11	0	4	19	17	42	1	4	0-0	.230	.297	.362	.660	3	.991
2003— Kansas City (A.L.)	C-DH	62	189	29	48	16	1	3	25	9	30	4	6	1-0	.254	.299	.397	.696	2	.994
2004— Detroit (A.L.)	C-DH	13	22	3	3	0	1	0	2	2	3	0	3	0-0	.136	.240	.227	.467	0	1.000
— Toledo (Int'l)	C-DH	64	237	20	64	14	0	5	36	14	37	1	7	1-0	.270	.311	.392	.703	4	.990
— Chicago (N.L.)	C	4	3	0	0	0	0	0	0	0	2	0	0	0-0	.000	.000	.000	.000	0	1.000
2005— Norfolk (Int'l)	C-DH	81	300	31	74	17	0	14	52	36	72	5	13	1-2	.247	.337	.443	.781	4	.993
— New York (N.L.)	C	11	17	0	2	0	0	0	0	2	5	0	1	0-0	.118	.211	.118	.328	1	.976
2006— Binghamton (East.)		39	112	9	31	7	0	1	19	15	24	4	2	0-0	.277	.373	.366	.739	3	.989
— Norfolk (Int'l)		1	2	1	0	0	0	0	0	1	0	0	0	0-0	.000	.333	.000	.333	0	1.000
— New York (N.L.)	C	15	25	3	2	1	0	0	1	5	10	0	0	0-0	.080	.233	.120	.353	2	.974
American League totals (6 years)		318	991	106	243	57	7	20	105	55	191	11	33	2-1	.245	.290	.377	.667	25	.988
National League totals (7 years)		209	507	37	109	23	1	8	53	43	130	5	16	1-1	.215	.281	.312	.592	13	.989
Major League totals (11 years)		527	1498	143	352	80	8	28	158	98	321	16	49	3-2	.235	.287	.355	.642	38	.988

CHAMPIONSHIP SERIES RECORD

Year Team (League)	Pos.	G	AB	R	H	2B	3B	HR	RBI	BB	SO	HBP	GDP	SB-CS	Avg.	OBP	SLG	OPS	E	Avg.
2002— St. Louis (N.L.)		1	1	0	0	0	0	0	0	0	0	0	0	0-0	.000	.000	.000	.000	...	...

2006 LEFTY-RIGHTY SPLITS

vs.	Avg.	AB	H	2B	3B	HR	RBI	BB	SO	OBP	Slg.	vs.	Avg.	AB	H	2B	3B	HR	RBI	BB	SO	OBP	Slg.
L	.143	7	1	1	0	0	0	0	1	.250	.286	R	.056	18	1	0	0	0	1	4	6	.227	.056

DINARDO, LENNY — P

PERSONAL: Born September 19, 1979, in Miami. ... 6-4/195. ... Throws left, bats left. ... Full name: Leonard Edward DiNardo. ... High school: Santa Fe (Alachua, Fla.). ... College: Stetson. **TRANSACTIONS/CAREER NOTES:** Selected by Boston Red Sox organization in 10th round of 1998 free-agent draft; did not sign. ... Selected by New York Mets organization in third round of 2001 free-agent draft. ... Selected by Red Sox from Mets organization in Rule 5 major league draft (December 15, 2003). ... On disabled list (April 4-19 and July 5-September 16, 2004); included rehabilitation assignments to GCL Red Sox, Sarasota, Portland and Pawtucket. ... On disabled list (May 24-August 31, 2006); included rehabilitation assignments to Pawtucket, GCL Red Sox and Portland (Maine).

CAREER HITTING: 0-for-1 (.000), 0 R, 0 2B, 0 3B, 0 HR, 0 RBI.

Year Team (League)	W	L	Pct.	ERA	WHIP	G	GS	CG	ShO	Hld.	Sv.-Opp.	IP	H	R	ER	HR	BB-IBB	SO	Avg.
2001— Brook. (N.Y.-Penn.)	1	2	.333	2.00	1.19	9	5	0	0	...	0-...	36.0	26	10	8	0	17-0	40	.200
2002— Capital City (SAL)	5	5	.500	4.35	1.60	24	19	0	0	...	0-...	101.1	106	60	49	3	56-1	103	.274
2003— Binghamton (East.)	1	3	.250	3.60	1.20	7	7	1	0	...	0-...	40.0	35	19	16	3	13-0	36	.236
— St. Lucie (Fla. St.)	3	3	.273	2.01	0.92	19	13	1	0	...	1-...	85.0	64	27	19	1	14-0	93	.211
2004— Sarasota (Fla. St.)	0	0	...	0.00	0.67	1	1	0	0	...	0-...	3.0	2	0	0	0	0-0	2	.182
— Pawtucket (Int'l)	0	0	...	0.00	1.00	1	1	0	0	...	0-...	3.0	3	0	0	0	0-0	4	.273
— Boston (A.L.)	0	0	...	4.23	1.66	22	0	0	0	...	0-0	27.2	34	17	13	1	12-1	21	.298
— Portland (East.)	0	0	1.000	9.53	1.59	3	0	0	0	...	0-...	3.0	8	6	6	0	1-0	4	.333
2005— Pawtucket (Int'l)	6	3	.667	3.15	1.33	23	22	0	0	...	0-0	108.2	109	51	38	7	35-0	93	.265

D

Year	Team (League)	W	L	Pct.	ERA	WHIP	G	GS	CG	ShO	Hld.	Sv.-Opp.	IP	H	R	ER	HR	BB-IBB	SO	Avg.
	—Boston (A.L.)	0	1	.000	1.84	1.23	8	1	0	0	0	0-0	14.2	13	6	3	1	5-1	15	.236
2006	—GC Red Sox (GCL)	0	0		0.00	0.43	2	2	0	0	0	0-0	4.2	2	1	0	0	0-0	4	.118
	—Portland (East.)	0	1	.000	31.50	4.50	1	1	0	0	0	0-0	2.0	7	7	7	2	2-0	2	.583
	—Pawtucket (Int'l)	0	0		12.00	2.00	2	2	0	0	0	0-0	3.0	5	4	4	1	1-0	2	.357
	—Boston (A.L.)	1	2	.333	7.85	2.08	13	6	0	0	1	0-0	39.0	61	35	34	6	20-1	17	.363
	Major League totals (3 years)	1	3	.250	5.53	1.78	43	7	0	0	1	0-0	81.1	108	58	50	8	37-3	53	.320

2006 LEFTY-RIGHTY SPLITS

vs.	Avg.	AB	H	2B	3B	HR	RBI	BB	SO	OBP	Slg.	vs.	Avg.	AB	H	2B	3B	HR	RBI	BB	SO	OBP	Slg.
L	.375	48	18	3	1	1	8	1	5	.392	.542	R	.358	120	43	11	0	5	20	19	12	.446	.575

DINGMAN, CRAIG   P

PERSONAL: Born March 12, 1974, in Wichita, Kan. ... 6-4/215. ... Throws right, bats right. ... Full name: Craig Allen Dingman. ... High school: North (Wichita, Kan.). ... Junior college: Hutchinson (Kan.) C.C. **TRANSACTIONS/CAREER NOTES:** Selected by New York Yankees organization in 36th round of 1993 free-agent draft. ... Traded by Yankees to Colorado Rockies for a player to be named (March 29, 2001); Yankees acquired P Jorge DePaula to complete deal (April 20, 2001). ... On disabled list (April 9-24, 2001); included rehabilitation assignment to Colorado Springs. ... Signed as a free agent by Cincinnati Reds organization (December 21, 2001). ... Traded by Reds to Yankees for cash (June 6, 2002). ... Signed as a free agent by Yucatan of the Mexican League (March 1, 2003). ... Signed by Cancun of the Mexican League (May 29, 2003). ... Contract purchased by Chicago Cubs organization from Cancun (July 22, 2003). ... Signed as a free agent by Detroit Tigers organization (December 19, 2003). ... On disabled list (April 1, 2006-entire season).

CAREER HITTING: 0-for-0 (.000), 0 R, 0 2B, 0 3B, 0 HR, 0 RBI.

Year	Team (League)	W	L	Pct.	ERA	WHIP	G	GS	CG	ShO	Hld.	Sv.-Opp.	IP	H	R	ER	HR	BB-IBB	SO	Avg.
1994	—GC Yankees (GCL)	0	5	.000	3.38	1.16	17	1	0	0	...	1-...	32.0	27	17	12	0	10-0	51	.239
1995	—							Did not play.												
1996	—Oneonta (NYP)	0	2	.000	2.04	0.74	20	0	0	0	...	9-...	35.1	17	11	8	0	9-0	52	.136
1997	—Greensboro (S. Atl.)	2	0	1.000	1.91	0.94	30	0	0	0	...	19-...	33.0	19	7	7	0	12-0	41	.165
	—Tampa (Fla. St.)	0	4	.000	5.24	1.30	19	0	0	0	...	6-...	22.1	15	14	13	2	14-2	26	.195
1998	—Tampa (Fla. St.)	5	4	.556	2.93	1.23	50	0	0	0	...	7-...	70.2	48	29	23	8	39-9	95	.194
1999	—Norwich (East.)	8	6	.571	1.57	0.91	55	0	0	0	...	9-...	74.1	56	16	13	2	12-2	90	.206
2000	—Columbus (Int'l)	6	1	.857	3.05	1.09	47	2	0	0	...	1-...	73.2	60	31	25	5	20-2	65	.220
	—New York (A.L.)	0	0		6.55	1.91	10	0	0	0	...	0-...	11.0	18	8	8	1	3-0	8	.375
2001	—Colo. Springs (PCL)	3	5	.375	3.75	1.38	46	0	0	0	...	7-...	48.0	57	28	20	4	9-1	55	.294
	—Colorado (N.L.)	0	0		13.50	1.91	7	0	0	0	0	1-1	7.1	11	11	11	4	3-2	2	.355
2002	—Louisville (Int'l)	0	1	.000	4.15	1.27	22	0	0	0	...	0-...	26.0	20	12	12	3	13-0	26	.215
	—Columbus (Int'l)	0	0		13.50	5.25	2	0	0	0	...	0-...	1.1	6	6	2	0	1-1	2	.545
2003	—West Tenn (Sou.)	0	1	.000	6.00	1.80	4	0	0	0	...	0-...	6.0	6	4	4	2	5-1	5	.273
	—Iowa (PCL)	1	0	1.000	2.00	1.20	11	0	0	0	...	0-...	18.0	14	4	4	0	7-0	12	.667
2004	—Toledo (Int'l)	1	2	.333	4.56	1.44	21	0	0	0	...	0-...	25.2	26	14	13	4	11-2	31	.260
	—Detroit (A.L.)	2	2	.500	6.75	1.88	24	0	0	0	0	0-2	29.1	33	22	22	3	22-3	16	.295
2005	—Toledo (Int'l)	2	1	.667	2.81	1.15	35	0	0	0	7	4-6	48.0	42	18	15	3	13-0	67	.230
	—Detroit (A.L.)	2	3	.400	3.66	1.22	34	0	0	0	4	4-5	32.0	30	14	13	5	9-0	24	.259
2006	—Detroit (A.L.)							Did not play.												
	American League totals (3 years)	4	5	.444	5.35	1.59	68	0	0	0	4	4-7	72.1	81	44	43	9	34-3	48	.293
	National League totals (1 year)	0	0		13.50	1.91	7	0	0	0	0	1-1	7.1	11	11	11	4	3-2	2	.355
	Major League totals (4 years)	4	5	.444	6.10	1.62	75	0	0	0	4	5-8	79.2	92	55	54	13	37-5	50	.300

DOBBS, GREG   OF/3B

PERSONAL: Born July 2, 1978, in Los Angeles. ... 6-1/205. ... Bats left, throws right. ... Full name: Gregory Stuart Dobbs. ... High school: Canyon Springs (Calif.). ... Junior college: Riverside (Calif.) C.C. ... College: Oklahoma. **TRANSACTIONS/CAREER NOTES:** Selected by Seattle Mariners organization in 52nd round of 1996 free-agent draft; did not sign. ... Selected by Houston Astros organizti on in 10th round of 1999 free-agent draft; did not sign. ... Signed as a non-drafted free agent by Seattle Mariners organization (May 28, 2001). **STATISTICAL NOTES:** Hit home run in first major league at-bat (September 8, 2004).

2006 GAMES PLAYED BY POSITION (MLB): DH—5, 1B—3, OF—3, 3B—2.

										BATTING										FIELDING	
Year	Team (League)	Pos.	G	AB	R	H	2B	3B	HR	RBI	BB	SO	HBP	GDP	SB-CS	Avg.	OBP	SLG	OPS	E	Avg.
2001	—Everett (N'west)	1B-OF-3B	65	249	37	80	17	2	6	41	30	39	2	2	5-3	.321	.396	.478	.874	12	.972
	—San Bern. (Calif.)	OF	3	13	2	5	1	0	1	3	0	4	0	0	0-0	.385	.357	.692	1.049	0	1.000
2002	—Wisconsin (Midw.)	3B	86	320	43	88	16	2	10	48	31	50	1	6	13-3	.275	.338	.431	.769	23	.902
	—San Antonio (Texas)	OF-1B	27	96	13	35	2	0	5	15	9	17	1	2	1-3	.365	.425	.542	.966	2	.964
2003	—San Antonio (Texas)	3B	2	6	0	2	0	0	0	0	0	1	0	0	0-0	.333	.333	.667	1.000	1	1.000
2004	—San Antonio (Texas)	3B	51	203	25	66	14	4	5	34	11	23	5	5	5-4	.325	.373	.507	.866	10	.918
	—Tacoma (PCL)	3B-DH	67	255	28	69	9	2	8	31	5	36	1	10	4-3	.271	.286	.416	.699	13	.931
	—Seattle (A.L.)	3B-DH	18	53	4	12	1	0	1	9	1	14	1	0	0-0	.226	.250	.302	.552	2	.929
2005	—Tacoma (PCL)	1B-3B-DH-OF	50	190	27	61	9	0	3	22	14	22	1	4	5-2	.321	.367	.416	.783	8	.977
	—Seattle (A.L.)	DH-1B-OF-3B	59	142	8	35	7	1	1	20	9	25	0	4	1-0	.246	.288	.331	.619	0	1.000
2006	—Tacoma (PCL)	1B-3B-DH	99	379	60	119	19	3	9	55	37	58	2	10	14-5	.314	.375	.451	.826	0	.993
	—Seattle (A.L.)	DH-1B-OF-3B	23	27	4	10	3	1	0	3	0	4	1	0	0-1	.370	.393	.556	.948	0	1.000
	Major League totals (3 years)		100	222	16	57	11	2	2	32	10	43	2	4	1-1	.257	.291	.351	.642	2	.978

2006 LEFTY-RIGHTY SPLITS

vs.	Avg.	AB	H	2B	3B	HR	RBI	BB	SO	OBP	Slg.	vs.	Avg.	AB	H	2B	3B	HR	RBI	BB	SO	OBP	Slg.
L	.000	1	0	0	0	0	0	0	1	.000	.000	R	.385	26	10	3	1	0	3	0	3	.407	.577

DOHMANN, SCOTT   P

PERSONAL: Born February 13, 1978, in New Orleans, La. ... 6-1/181. ... Throws right, bats right. ... Full name: Christopher Scott Dohmann. ... High school: St. Thomas More Catholic (Lafayette, La.). ... College: Louisiana-Lafayette. **TRANSACTIONS/CAREER NOTES:** Selected by Colorado Rockies in sixth round of 2000 free-agent draft. ... On disabled list (March 28-18, 2006); included rehabilitation assignments to Modesto and Colorado Springs. ... Traded by Rockies with IF Ryan Shealy to Kansas City Royals for Ps Denny Bautista and Jeremy Affeldt (July 31, 2006).

CAREER HITTING: 0-for-3 (.000), 0 R, 0 2B, 0 3B, 0 HR, 0 RBI.

Year	Team (League)	W	L	Pct.	ERA	WHIP	G	GS	CG	ShO	Hld.	Sv.-Opp.	IP	H	R	ER	HR	BB-IBB	SO	Avg.
2000	—Portland (N'west)	2	1	.667	0.78	0.83	5	4	0	0		0-...	23.0	14	3	2	0	5-0	23	.177

D

Year	Team (League)	W	L	Pct.	ERA	WHIP	G	GS	CG	ShO	Hld.	Sv.-Opp.	IP	H	R	ER	HR	BB-IBB	SO	Avg.
— Asheville (S. Atl.)	1	5	.167	6.06	1.56	7	7	0	0	...	0-...	32.2	43	24	22	3	8-0	36	.319
2001— Asheville (S. Atl.)	11	13	.458	4.32	1.14	28	28	3	1	...	0-...	173.0	165	88	83	27	33-5	154	.251
2002— Salem (Carol.)	13	5	.722	4.23	1.19	28	28	0	0	...	0-...	170.1	149	85	80	22	53-0	131	.233
2003— Tulsa (Texas)	9	4	.692	4.13	1.31	50	4	0	0	...	4-...	93.2	94	47	43	11	29-2	102	.259
2004— Colo. Springs (PCL)	1	0	1.000	1.64	1.32	18	0	0	0	...	2-...	22.0	22	5	4	1	7-1	31	.250
— Colorado (N.L.)	0	3	.000	4.11	1.30	41	0	0	0	4	0-4	46.0	41	22	21	8	19-0	49	.236
2005— Colo. Springs (PCL)	2	1	.667	4.38	1.46	34	0	0	0	5	1-3	39.0	41	19	19	5	16-1	53	.266
— Colorado (N.L.)	2	1	.667	6.10	1.68	32	0	0	0	7	0-3	31.0	33	21	21	6	19-1	35	.266
2006— Modesto (California)	0	1	.000	2.25	1.00	3	3	0	0	...	0-0	4.0	2	1	1	0	2-0	5	.154
— Colorado (N.L.)	1	1	.500	6.20	1.66	27	0	0	0	3	1-2	24.2	26	18	17	4	15-2	22	.277
— Colo. Springs (PCL)	0	0	...	2.53	0.66	10	0	0	0	3	1-2	10.2	6	3	3	* 2	1-0	12	.158
— Kansas City (A.L.)	1	3	.250	7.99	2.15	21	0	0	0	3	0-1	23.2	33	21	21	5	18-5	22	.347
American League totals (1 year)	1	3	.250	7.99	2.15	21	0	0	0	3	0-1	23.2	33	21	21	5	18-5	22	.347
National League totals (3 years)	3	5	.375	5.22	1.50	100	0	0	0	14	1-9	101.2	100	61	59	18	53-3	106	.255
Major League totals (3 years)	4	8	.333	5.74	1.63	121	0	0	0	17	1-10	125.1	133	82	80	23	71-8	128	.273

2006 LEFTY-RIGHTY SPLITS

vs.	Avg.	AB	H	2B	3B	HR	RBI	BB	SO	OBP	Slg.	vs.	Avg.	AB	H	2B	3B	HR	RBI	BB	SO	OBP	Slg.
L	.357	56	20	1	0	7	15	18	13	.514	.750	R	.293	133	39	9	2	2	20	15	31	.382	.436

DONNELLY, BRENDAN — P

PERSONAL: Born July 4, 1971, in Washington, D.C. ... 6-3/240. ... Throws right, bats right. ... Full name: Brendan Kevin Donnelly. ... High school: Sandia (Albuquerque, N.M.). ... Junior college: New Mexico J.C. ... College: Mesa State (Colo.). **TRANSACTIONS/CAREER NOTES:** Selected by Chicago White Sox organization in 27th round of 1992 free-agent draft. ... Released by White Sox (April 16, 1993). ... Signed by Chicago Cubs organization (June 16, 1993). ... Released by Cubs (March 29, 1994). ... Signed by Ohio Valley of the independent Frontier League (July 1994). ... Signed by Cincinnati Reds organization (March 4, 1995). ... Released by Reds (April 3, 1999). ... Signed by Nashua of independent Atlantic League (May 1999). ... Contract purchased by Tampa Bay Devil Rays organization from Nashua (May 15, 1999). ... Released by Devil Rays (August 12, 1999). ... Signed by Pittsburgh Pirates organization (August 18, 1999). ... Released by Pirates (August 25, 1999). ... Signed by Toronto Blue Jays organization (August 26, 1999). ... Released by Blue Jays (July 28, 2000). ... Signed by Cubs organization (August 10, 2000). ... Signed as a free agent by Anaheim Angels organization (January 9, 2001). ... On disabled list (March 26-June 17, 2004); included rehabilitation assignments to Rancho Cucamonga and Salt Lake. ... Angels franchise renamed Los Angeles Angels of Anaheim for 2005 season. ... On suspended list (July 1-9, 2005 and September 11-15, 2006).

CAREER HITTING: 0-for-1 (.000), 0 R, 0 2B, 0 3B, 0 HR, 0 RBI.

Year	Team (League)	W	L	Pct.	ERA	WHIP	G	GS	CG	ShO	Hld.	Sv.-Opp.	IP	H	R	ER	HR	BB-IBB	SO	Avg.
1992— GC Whi. Sox (GCL)	0	3	.000	3.67	1.49	9	7	0	0	...	1-...	41.2	41	25	17	0	21-0	31	.256
1993— Geneva (NY-Penn)	4	0	1.000	6.28	1.58	21	3	0	0	...	1-...	43.0	39	34	30	4	29-0	29	.242
1994— Ohio Valley (Fron.)	1	1	.500	2.57	1.21	10	0	0	0	...	0-...	14.0	13	5	4	1	4-0	20	.250
1995— Char., W.Va. (SAL)	1	1	.500	1.19	0.69	24	0	0	0	...	12-...	30.1	14	4	4	0	7-1	33	.139
— Win.-Salem (Car.)	1	2	.333	1.02	0.96	23	0	0	0	...	2-...	35.1	20	6	4	1	14-2	32	.167
— Indianapolis (A.A.)	1	1	.500	23.63	3.38	3	0	0	0	...	0-...	2.2	7	8	7	2	2-0	1	.500
1996— Chattanooga (Sou.)	1	2	.333	5.52	1.50	22	0	0	0	...	2-...	29.1	27	21	18	4	17-2	22	.237
1997— Chattanooga (Sou.)	6	4	.600	3.27	1.31	62	0	0	0	...	6-...	82.2	71	43	30	8	37-4	64	.228
1998— Chattanooga (Sou.)	2	5	.286	2.98	1.48	38	0	0	0	...	13-...	45.1	43	16	15	4	24-5	47	.247
— Indianapolis (Int'l)	4	1	.800	2.65	1.21	19	1	0	0	...	0-...	37.1	29	16	11	3	16-3	39	.212
1999— Nashua (Atl.)			...	3.00	1.33	3	0	0	0	...	0-...	3.0	1	1	1		3-...	4	
— Durham (Int'l)	5	5	.500	3.05	1.15	37	1	0	0	...	0-...	62.0	53	23	21	5	18-1	61	.240
— Altoona (East.)	0	0	...	7.71	2.57	2	0	0	0	...	1-...	2.1	4	2	2	0	2-0	5	.571
— Syracuse (Int'l)	0	1	.000	2.89	1.29	5	0	0	0	...	0-...	9.1	8	4	3	1	4-1	9	.242
2000— Syracuse (Int'l)	4	6	.400	5.48	1.73	37	0	0	0	...	0-...	42.2	47	34	26	5	27-2	34	.278
— Iowa (PCL)	0	3	.000	7.56	1.86	9	0	0	0	...	1-...	16.2	25	19	14	3	6-1	14	.338
2001— Arkansas (Texas)	4	1	.800	2.48	1.17	27	0	0	0	...	12-...	29.0	21	8	8	2	13-1	37	.200
— Salt Lake (PCL)	5	1	.833	2.40	1.11	29	0	0	0	...	1-...	41.1	38	11	11	4	8-0	50	.245
2002— Salt Lake (PCL)	4	0	1.000	3.48	1.13	25	0	0	0	...	6-...	33.2	27	13	13	5	11-0	42	.213
— Anaheim (A.L.)	1	1	.500	2.17	1.03	46	0	0	0	13	1-3	49.2	32	13	12	2	19-3	54	.184
2003— Anaheim (A.L.)	2	2	.500	1.58	1.07	63	0	0	0	* 29	3-5	74.0	55	14	13	2	24-1	79	.200
2004— Rancho Cuca. (Calif.)	0	0	...	0.00	1.33	2	0	0	0	...	0-...	3.0	3	0	0	0	1-0	5	.250
— Salt Lake (PCL)	0	0	...	7.71	1.71	3	0	0	0	...	0-...	2.1	2	2	2	0	2-0	6	.250
— Anaheim (A.L.)	5	2	.714	3.00	1.17	40	0	0	0	5	0-...	42.0	34	14	14	5	15-0	56	.224
2005— Los Angeles (A.L.)	9	3	.750	3.72	1.21	65	0	0	0	16	0-5	65.1	60	30	27	4	19-3	53	.244
2006— Los Angeles (A.L.)	6	0	1.000	3.94	1.34	62	0	0	0	11	0-1	64.0	58	32	28	8	28-3	53	.240
Major League totals (5 years)	23	8	.742	2.87	1.17	276	0	0	0	74	4-14	295.0	239	103	94	26	105-10	295	.219

DIVISION SERIES RECORD

Year	Team (League)	W	L	Pct.	ERA	WHIP	G	GS	CG	ShO	Hld.	Sv.-Opp.	IP	H	R	ER	HR	BB-IBB	SO	Avg.
2002— Anaheim (A.L.)	0	0	...	13.50	2.00	3	0	0	0	1	0-0	2.0	3	3	3	2	1-0	2	.333
2004— Anaheim (A.L.)	0	0	...	10.80	1.50	2	0	0	0	0	0-0	3.1	3	4	4	0	2-2	5	.231
2005— Los Angeles (A.L.)	0	0	...	27.00	9.00	1	0	0	0	0	0-0	0.1	2	2	1	0	1-0	0	.667
Division series totals (3 years)	0	0	...	12.71	2.12	6	0	0	0	1	0-0	5.2	8	9	8	2	4-2	7	.320

CHAMPIONSHIP SERIES RECORD

Year	Team (League)	W	L	Pct.	ERA	WHIP	G	GS	CG	ShO	Hld.	Sv.-Opp.	IP	H	R	ER	HR	BB-IBB	SO	Avg.
2002— Anaheim (A.L.)	0	0	...	8.10	0.90	3	0	0	0	2	0-0	3.1	3	3	3	0	0-0	5	.231
2005— Los Angeles (A.L.)	0	0	...	0.00	0.90	3	0	0	0	0	0-0	3.1	2	0	0	0	1-0	5	.182
Champ. series totals (2 years)	0	0	...	4.05	0.90	6	0	0	0	2	0-0	6.2	5	3	3	0	1-0	10	.208

WORLD SERIES RECORD

Year	Team (League)	W	L	Pct.	ERA	WHIP	G	GS	CG	ShO	Hld.	Sv.-Opp.	IP	H	R	ER	HR	BB-IBB	SO	Avg.
2002— Anaheim (A.L.)	1	0	1.000	0.00	0.65	5	0	0	0	1	0-0	7.2	1	0	0	0	4-0	6	.042

ALL-STAR GAME RECORD

Year	Team (League)	W	L	Pct.	ERA	WHIP	G	GS	CG	ShO	Hld.	Sv.-Opp.	IP	H	R	ER	HR	BB-IBB	SO	Avg.
All-Star Game totals (1 year)	1	0	1.000	0.00	0.00	1	0	0	0	0	0-0	1.0	0	0	0	0	0-0	1	.000

2006 LEFTY-RIGHTY SPLITS

vs.	Avg.	AB	H	2B	3B	HR	RBI	BB	SO	OBP	Slg.	vs.	Avg.	AB	H	2B	3B	HR	RBI	BB	SO	OBP	Slg.
L	.290	100	29	0	2	4	12	19	21	.415	.450	R	.204	142	29	5	0	4	17	9	32	.255	.324

DORTA, MELVIN — 3B

PERSONAL: Born January 15, 1982, in Valencia, Venezuela. ... Bats right, throws right. ... Full name: Melvin A. Dorta.
TRANSACTIONS/CAREER NOTES: Signed as a non-drafted free agent by Boston Red Sox organization (September 15, 1998). ... Traded by Red Sox to Montreal Expos for cash (January 5, 2004). ... Expos franchise relocated to Washington, D.C., and renamed Washington Nationals for 2005 season (December 3, 2004).

2006 GAMES PLAYED BY POSITION (MLB): 3B—3, SS—3.

Year Team (League)	Pos.	G	AB	R	H	2B	3B	HR	RBI	BB	SO	HBP	GDP	SB-CS	Avg.	OBP	SLG	OPS	E	Avg.
1999—Cagua (VSL)		48	146	23	31	9	0	1	15	31	30	4	6	7-0	.212	.363	.295	.658	...	...
2000—San Joaquin (VSL)		25	73	16	24	2	0	1	15	12	10	4	3	6-4	.329	.440	.397	.837	...	...
2001—GC Red Sox (GCL)		21	76	19	31	6	0	2	8	11	5	1	0	7-3	.408	.489	.566	1.055	1	...
—Augusta (S. Atl.)		36	135	19	36	4	1	0	18	8	16	3	2	6-5	.267	.320	.311	.631	3	...
2002—Sarasota (Fla. St.)		99	378	46	97	8	1	0	31	49	54	3	7	9-10	.257	.342	.283	.625	16	...
2003—Sarasota (Fla. St.)		93	324	36	70	7	1	0	27	28	46	7	9	20-9	.216	.288	.244	.532	14	...
2004—Harrisburg (East.)	OF-SS-2B	72	226	20	59	11	2	0	22	15	24	2	6	12-4	.261	.310	.327	.637	11	...
2005—Harrisburg (East.)	1B-DH-3B	121	408	56	103	16	0	11	50	35	46	3	6	22-13	.252	.314	.373	.687	11	.978
2006—Harrisburg (East.)		108	404	54	104	15	3	5	30	30	34	0	6	33-10	.257	.307	.347	.653	8	.972
—New Orleans (PCL)		8	30	6	13	1	0	1	3	1	2	0	1	3-2	.433	.438	.567	1.004	1	.971
—Wash. (N.L.)	3B-SS	15	19	3	4	1	0	0	0	1	2	0	0	0-2	.211	.250	.263	.513	1	.929
Major League totals (1 year)		15	19	3	4	1	0	0	0	1	2	0	0	0-2	.211	.250	.263	.513	1	.929

2006 LEFTY-RIGHTY SPLITS

vs.	Avg.	AB	H	2B	3B	HR	RBI	BB	SO	OBP	Slg.	vs.	Avg.	AB	H	2B	3B	HR	RBI	BB	SO	OBP	Sig.
L	.333	6	2	1	0	0	0	1	1	.429	.500	R	.154	13	2	0	0	0	0	0	1	.154	.1

DOTEL, OCTAVIO — P

PERSONAL: Born November 25, 1973, in Santo Domingo, Dominican Republic. ... 6-0/210. ... Throws right, bats right. ... Full name: Octavio Eduardo Dotel. ... Name pronounced: Oc-TAH-vee-oh dough-TEL. ... High school: Liceo Eansino Afuera (Dominican Republic). **TRANSACTIONS/CAREER NOTES:** Signed as a non-drafted free agent by New York Mets organization (March 20, 1993). ... Traded by Mets with OF Roger Cedeno and P Kyle Kessel to Houston Astros for P Mike Hampton and OF Derek Bell (December 23, 1999). ... Traded by Astros to Oakland Athletics as part of three-team deal in which Astros acquired OF Carlos Beltran and cash from Kansas City Royals and Royals acquired C John Buck and cash from Astros and P Mike Wood and 3B Mark Teahen from Athletics (June 24, 2004). ... On disabled list (May 20, 2005-remainder of season). ... Signed as a free agent by New York Yankees (January 4, 2006). ... On disabled list (April 1-August 16, 2006); included rehabilitation assignments to Columbus, Tampa, Trenton, Staten Island and GCL Yankees. **STATISTICAL NOTES:** Pitched one inning, combining with Roy Oswalt (one inning), Peter Munro (2 2/3 innings), Kirk Saarloos (1 1/3 innings), Brad Lidge (two innings) and Billy Wagner (one inning) on 8-0 no-hitter against New York Yankees (June 11, 2003).

CAREER HITTING: 5-for-74 (.068), 3 R, 0 2B, 0 3B, 0 HR, 1 RBI.

Year Team (League)	W	L	Pct.	ERA	WHIP	G	GS	CG	ShO	Hld.	Sv.-Opp.	IP	H	R	ER	HR	BB-IBB	SO	Avg.
1993—Dom. Mets (DSL)	6	2	.750	4.10	1.42	15	11	0	0	...	0-...	59.1	46	30	27	...	38-...	48	...
1994—Dom. Mets (DSL)	5	0	1.000	4.32	1.41	15	14	1	0	...	0-...	81.1	84	53	39	...	31-...	95	...
1995—GC Mets (GCL)	7	4	.636	2.18	0.87	13	12	2	0	...	0-...	74.1	48	23	18	0	17-1	86	.178
—St. Lucie (Fla. St.)	1	0	1.000	5.63	1.75	3	0	0	0	...	0-...	8.0	10	5	5	1	4-0	9	.323
1996—Capital City (SAL)	11	3	.786	3.59	1.20	22	19	0	0	...	0-...	115.1	89	49	46	7	49-0	142	.212
1997—St. Lucie (Fla. St.)	5	2	.714	2.52	1.34	9	8	1	1	...	0-...	50.0	44	18	14	2	23-0	39	.235
—Binghamton (East.)	3	4	.429	5.98	1.87	12	12	0	0	...	0-...	55.2	66	50	37	5	38-1	40	.293
—GC Mets (GCL)	0	0	...	0.96	1.18	3	2	0	0	...	1-...	9.1	9	1	1	0	2-0	7	.250
1998—Binghamton (East.)	4	2	.667	1.97	0.95	10	10	2	1	...	0-...	68.2	41	19	15	4	24-1	82	.175
—Norfolk (Int'l)	8	6	.571	3.45	1.26	17	16	1	0	...	0-...	99.0	82	47	38	9	43-1	118	.221
1999—Norfolk (Int'l)	5	2	.714	3.84	1.22	13	13	1	0	...	0-...	70.1	52	33	30	9	34-1	90	.204
—New York (N.L.)	8	3	.727	5.38	1.38	19	14	0	0	0	0-0	85.1	69	52	51	12	49-1	85	.226
2000—Houston (N.L.)	3	7	.300	5.40	1.50	50	16	0	0	0	16-23	125.0	127	80	75	26	61-3	142	.265
2001—Houston (N.L.)	7	5	.583	2.66	1.20	61	4	0	0	14	2-4	105.0	79	35	31	5	47-2	145	.205
2002—Houston (N.L.)	6	4	.600	1.85	0.87	83	0	0	0	31	6-10	97.1	58	21	20	7	27-2	118	.173
2003—Houston (N.L.)	6	4	.600	2.48	0.97	76	0	0	0	* 33	4-6	87.0	53	25	24	9	31-2	97	.172
2004—Houston (N.L.)	0	4	.000	3.12	1.21	32	0	0	0	0	14-17	34.2	27	15	12	4	15-4	50	.213
—Oakland (A.L.)	6	4	.750	4.09	1.16	45	0	0	0	0	22-28	50.2	41	23	23	9	18-3	72	.220
2005—Oakland (A.L.)	1	2	.333	3.52	1.37	15	0	0	0	0	7-11	15.1	10	6	6	2	11-2	16	.185
2006—GC Yankees (GCL)	0	0	...	0.00	0.33	3	3	0	0	1	0-0	3.0	0	0	0	0	1-0	6	...
—Tampa (Fla. St.)	0	0	...	0.00	0.50	2	1	0	0	0	0-0	2.0	1	0	0	0	0-0	2	.143
—Staten Is. (N.Y.-Penn)	0	0	...	0.00	2.00	1	0	0	0	1	0-0	1.0	2	0	0	0	0-0	1	.500
—Trenton (East.)	0	0	...	0.00	0.50	2	0	0	0	1	0-0	2.0	1	0	0	0	0-0	3	.167
—Columbus (Int'l)	0	0	...	3.38	1.13	5	0	0	0	1	0-0	5.1	6	2	2	1	0-0	8	.286
—New York (A.L.)	0	0	...	10.80	2.90	14	0	0	0	1	0-0	10.0	18	13	12	2	11-1	7	.383
American League totals (3 years)	7	4	.636	4.86	1.43	74	0	0	0	1	29-39	76.0	69	42	41	13	40-6	95	.240
National League totals (6 years)	30	27	.526	3.59	1.20	321	34	0	0	78	42-60	534.1	413	228	213	63	230-14	637	.213
Major League totals (8 years)	37	31	.544	3.75	1.23	395	34	0	0	79	71-99	610.1	482	270	254	76	270-20	732	.216

DIVISION SERIES RECORD

Year Team (League)	W	L	Pct.	ERA	WHIP	G	GS	CG	ShO	Hld.	Sv.-Opp.	IP	H	R	ER	HR	BB-IBB	SO	Avg.
1999—New York (N.L.)	0	0	...	54.00	9.00	1	0	0	0	0	0-0	0.1	2	2	2	0	2-0	0	.500
2001—Houston (N.L.)	0	0	...	5.40	1.50	2	0	0	0	0	0-0	3.1	5	2	2	1	0-0	5	.333
Division series totals (2 years)	0	0	...	9.82	2.18	3	0	0	0	0	0-0	3.2	6	4	4	1	2-0	5	.353

CHAMPIONSHIP SERIES RECORD

Year Team (League)	W	L	Pct.	ERA	WHIP	G	GS	CG	ShO	Hld.	Sv.-Opp.	IP	H	R	ER	HR	BB-IBB	SO	Avg.
1999—New York (N.L.)	1	0	1.000	3.00	2.00	1	0	0	0	0	0-0	3.0	4	1	1	0	2-1	5	.333

2006 LEFTY-RIGHTY SPLITS

vs.	Avg.	AB	H	2B	3B	HR	RBI	BB	SO	OBP	Slg.	vs.	Avg.	AB	H	2B	3B	HR	RBI	BB	SO	OBP	Sig.
L	.333	18	6	1	0	0	5	3	1	.429	.389	R	.414	29	12	3	1	2	8	8	6	.526	.793

DOUMIT, RYAN — C/1B

PERSONAL: Born April 3, 1981, in Moses Lake, Wash. ... 6-0/200. ... Bats both, throws right. ... Full name: Ryan Matthew Doumit. . **TRANSACTIONS/CAREER NOTES:** Selected by Pittsburgh Pirates organization in second round of 1999 free-agent draft. ... On disabled list (April 16-May 3 and June 5-August 23, 2006); included rehabilitation assignments to Indianapolis, GCL Pirates and Altoona.

2006 GAMES PLAYED BY POSITION (MLB): 1B—28, C—11, DH—3.

Year Team (League)	Pos.	G	AB	R	H	2B	3B	HR	RBI	BB	SO	HBP	GDP	SB-CS	Avg.	OBP	SLG	OPS	E	Avg.
1999—GC Pirates (GCL)	C	29	85	17	24	5	0	1	7	15	14	4	0	4-2	.282	.410	.376	.786	2	.975
2000—Will. (NYP)	C	66	246	25	77	15	5	2	40	23	33	4	7	2-2	.313	.371	.439	.810	6	.985
2001—Hickory (S. Atl.)	C	39	148	14	40	6	0	2	14	10	32	4	2	2-1	.270	.333	.351	.684	3	.984
—GC Pirates (GCL)	C	7	17	2	4	2	0	0	3	2	0	0	0	0-0	.235	.316	.353	.669	1	.944

Year Team (League)	Pos.	G	AB	R	H	2B	3B	HR	RBI	BB	SO	HBP	GDP	SB-CS	Avg.	OBP	SLG	OPS	FIELDING E	Avg.
—Altoona (East.)	C	2	4	0	1	0	0	0	2	1	1	0	0	0-0	.250	.400	.250	.650	0	1.000
2002—Hickory (S. Atl.)	C-C	68	258	46	83	14	1	6	47	18	40	8	6	3-5	.322	.377	.453	.830	7	.968
2003—Lynchburg (Caro.)	C	127	458	75	126	38	1	11	77	45	79	13	7	4-0	.275	.351	.434	.785	9	.985
2004—Altoona (East.)	C	67	221	31	58	20	0	10	34	21	49	8	4	0-1	.262	.343	.489	.832	3	.983
2005—Indianapolis (Int'l)	C-DH-OF	51	165	41	57	11	0	12	35	16	36	5	3	1-3	.345	.415	.630	1.045	4	.984
—Pittsburgh (N.L.)	C-DH-OF	75	231	25	59	13	1	6	35	11	48	13	5	2-1	.255	.324	.398	.722	8	.975
2006—Indianapolis (Int'l)		6	22	3	7	1	1	0	7	2	4	0	1	0-0	.318	.375	.455	.830	0	1.000
—GC Pirates (GCL)		5	14	1	0	0	0	0	0	1	4	1	0	0-0	.000	.125	.000	.125	1	.971
—Altoona (East.)		4	15	4	5	3	0	0	4	0	1	2	0	0-0	.333	.412	.533	.945	0	1.000
—Pittsburgh (N.L.)	1B-C-DH	61	149	15	31	9	0	6	17	15	42	11	3	0-0	.208	.322	.389	.711	4	.987
Major League totals (2 years)		136	380	40	90	22	1	12	52	26	90	24	8	2-1	.237	.323	.395	.718	12	.981

2006 LEFTY-RIGHTY SPLITS

vs.	Avg.	AB	H	2B	3B	HR	RBI	BB	SO	OBP	Slg.	vs.	Avg.	AB	H	2B	3B	HR	RBI	BB	SO	OBP	Slg.
L	.208	24	5	1	0	0	0	3	6	.406	.250	R	.208	125	26	8	0	6	17	12	36	.303	.416

DOWNS, SCOTT — P

PERSONAL: Born March 17, 1976, in Louisville, Ky. ... 6-2/190. ... Throws left, bats left. ... Full name: Scott Jeremy Downs. ... High school: Pleasure Ridge Park (Louisville, Ky.). ... College: Kentucky. **TRANSACTIONS/CAREER NOTES:** Selected by Atlanta Braves organization in 12th round of 1994 free-agent draft; did not sign. ... Selected by Chicago Cubs organization in third round of 1997 free-agent draft. ... Traded by Cubs to Minnesota Twins (November 3, 1998), completing deal in which Twins traded P Mike Morgan to Cubs for cash and a player to be named (August 25, 1998). ... Traded by Twins with P Rick Aguilera to Cubs for Ps Kyle Lohse and Jason Ryan (May 21, 1999). ... Traded by Cubs to Montreal Expos for OF Rondell White (July 31, 2000). ... On disabled list (August 9, 2000-remainder of season; and March 23, 2001-entire season). ... On disabled list (March 27-June 10, 2002); included rehabilitation assignments to Brevard County and Ottawa. ... Released by Expos (November 23, 2004). ... Signed by Toronto Blue Jays organization (December 16, 2004). ... On bereavement list (April 29-May 2, 2006).

CAREER HITTING: 3-for-44 (.068), 3 R, 0 2B, 0 3B, 0 HR, 1 RBI.

Year Team (League)	W	L	Pct.	ERA	WHIP	G	GS	CG	ShO	Hld.	Sv.-Opp.	IP	H	R	ER	HR	BB-IBB	SO	Avg.
1997—Will. (NYP)	0	2	.000	2.74	0.96	5	5	0	0	...	0-...	23.0	15	11	7	0	7-0	28	.181
—Rockford (Midwest)	3	0	1.000	1.25	0.69	5	5	0	0	...	0-...	36.0	17	5	5	1	8-0	43	.144
1998—Daytona (Fla. St.)	8	9	.471	3.90	1.45	27	27	2	0	...	0-...	161.2	179	83	70	12	55-0	117	.280
1999—New Britain (East.)	0	0	...	8.69	2.19	6	3	0	0	...	0-...	19.2	33	21	19	5	10-1	22	.375
—Fort Myers (FSL)	0	1	.000	0.00	1.34	2	2	0	0	...	0-...	9.2	7	3	0	0	6-0	9	.184
—Daytona (Fla. St.)	5	0	1.000	1.88	1.08	7	7	1	1	...	0-...	48.0	41	12	10	2	11-0	41	.237
—West Tenn (Sou.)	8	1	.889	1.35	1.05	13	12	1	0	...	0-...	80.0	56	13	12	2	28-0	101	.194
2000—Chicago (N.L.)	4	3	.571	5.17	1.64	18	18	0	0	0	0-0	94.0	117	59	54	13	37-1	63	.310
—Montreal (N.L.)	0	0	...	9.00	2.67	1	1	0	0	0	0-0	3.0	5	3	3	0	3-0	0	.385
2001—Montreal (N.L.)						Did not play.													
2002—Brevard County (FSL)	0	0	...	3.00	1.00	7	0	0	0	0	1-...	9.0	7	3	3	0	2-0	7	.206
—Ottawa (Int'l)	2	1	.667	5.79	1.46	17	0	0	0	0	0-...	23.1	31	21	15	6	3-0	15	.320
2003—Montreal (N.L.)	0	1	.000	15.00	2.67	1	1	0	0	0	0-0	3.0	5	5	5	2	3-2	4	.357
—Edmonton (PCL)	8	9	.471	4.29	1.30	21	21	3	0	...	0-...	121.2	119	67	58	13	39-0	54	.263
2004—Edmonton (PCL)	10	6	.625	3.53	1.25	22	22	2	2	...	0-...	135.1	143	57	53	16	26-0	67	.274
—Montreal (N.L.)	3	6	.333	5.14	1.62	12	12	1	1	0	0-0	63.0	79	47	36	9	23-2	38	.310
2005—Syracuse (Int'l)	2	3	.400	4.81	1.22	7	7	0	0	0	0-0	39.1	45	21	21	5	3-0	35	.285
—Toronto (A.L.)	4	3	.571	4.31	1.35	26	13	0	0	0	0-0	94.0	93	49	45	12	34-0	75	.253
2006—Toronto (A.L.)	6	2	.750	4.09	1.34	59	5	0	0	6	1-4	77.0	73	38	35	9	30-6	61	.249
American League totals (2 years)	10	5	.667	4.21	1.35	85	18	0	0	6	1-4	171.0	166	87	80	21	64-6	136	.252
National League totals (3 years)	7	10	.412	5.41	1.67	32	32	1	1	0	0-0	163.0	206	114	98	24	66-5	105	.312
Major League totals (5 years)	17	15	.531	4.80	1.50	117	50	1	1	6	1-4	334.0	372	201	178	45	130-11	241	.282

2006 LEFTY-RIGHTY SPLITS

vs.	Avg.	AB	H	2B	3B	HR	RBI	BB	SO	OBP	Slg.	vs.	Avg.	AB	H	2B	3B	HR	RBI	BB	SO	OBP	Slg.
L	.232	95	22	8	0	2	11	8	23	.298	.379	R	.258	198	51	13	0	7	23	22	38	.333	.429

DRESE, RYAN — P

PERSONAL: Born April 5, 1976, in San Francisco. ... 6-3/235. ... Throws right, bats right. ... Full name: Ryan Thomas Drese. ... Name pronounced: drees. ... High school: Bishop O'Dowd (Oakland). ... College: California. **TRANSACTIONS/CAREER NOTES:** Selected by Oakland Athletics organization in fifth round of 1994 free-agent draft; did not sign. ... Selected by Athletics organization in 14th round of 1997 free-agent draft; did not sign. ... Selected by Cleveland Indians organization in fifth round of 1998 free-agent draft. ... Traded by Indians with C Einar Diaz to Texas Rangers for 1B Travis Hafner and P Aaron Myette (December 6, 2002). ... Claimed on waivers by Washington Nationals (June 10, 2005). ... On disabled list (August 24, 2005-remainder of season). ... On disabled list (March 27-April 9, 2006); included rehabilitation assignment to Harrisburg. ... On disabled list (April 15, 2006-remainder of season). ... Released by Nationals (October 3, 2006). **MISCELLANEOUS NOTES:** Appeared in one game as pinch runner (2005).

CAREER HITTING: 3-for-25 (.120), 1 R, 1 2B, 0 3B, 0 HR, 0 RBI.

Year Team (League)	W	L	Pct.	ERA	WHIP	G	GS	CG	ShO	Hld.	Sv.-Opp.	IP	H	R	ER	HR	BB-IBB	SO	Avg.
1998—Watertown (NYP)	2	5	.286	4.07	1.29	9	9	0	0	...	0-...	42.0	40	21	19	1	14-0	40	.250
1999—Kinston (Carol.)	5	4	.556	4.93	1.41	15	15	1	0	...	0-...	69.1	46	47	38	2	52-0	81	.189
—Mahoning Valley (N.Y.-Penn.)	0	2	.000	2.65	0.88	5	5	0	0	...	0-...	17.0	8	6	5	1	7-0	26	.143
—Columbus (S. Atl.)	0	2	.000	4.50	1.08	2	2	0	0	...	0-...	12.0	9	6	6	2	4-0	15	.200
2000—Kinston (Carol.)	0	1	.000	3.86	1.29	1	1	0	0	...	0-...	2.1	2	1	1	0	1-0	4	.286
2001—Akron (East.)	5	7	.417	3.35	1.08	14	13	1	1	...	0-...	86.0	64	34	32	4	29-0	73	.215
—Buffalo (Int'l)	5	1	.833	4.01	1.27	11	10	0	0	...	0-...	60.2	60	28	27	7	17-0	52	.262
—Cleveland (A.L.)	1	2	.333	3.44	1.28	9	4	0	0	0	0-0	36.2	32	15	14	2	15-2	24	.242
2002—Cleveland (A.L.)	10	9	.526	6.55	1.73	26	26	1	0	0	0-0	137.1	176	104	100	15	62-1	102	.317
—Buffalo (Int'l)	1	0	1.000	1.64	0.91	3	3	0	0	...	0-...	22.0	16	4	4	1	4-0	16	.200
2003—Frisco (Texas)	1	1	.500	4.00	1.10	2	2	0	0	...	0-...	9.0	10	4	4	1	0-0	8	.278
—Oklahoma (PCL)	8	6	.571	4.65	1.50	20	20	0	0	...	0-...	122.0	143	70	63	8	39-1	68	.300
—Texas (A.L.)	2	4	.333	6.85	1.85	11	8	0	0	1	0-0	46.0	61	42	35	8	24-1	26	.314
2004—Oklahoma (PCL)	1	0	1.000	1.80	1.20	1	1	0	0	...	0-...	5.0	6	1	1	1	0-0	3	.300
—Texas (A.L.)	14	10	.583	4.20	1.40	34	33	2	0	0	0-0	207.2	233	104	97	16	58-6	98	.285
2005—Texas (A.L.)	4	6	.400	6.46	1.72	12	12	1	0	0	0-0	69.2	96	52	50	8	24-1	20	.334
—Wash. (N.L.)	3	6	.333	4.98	1.47	11	11	0	0	0	0-0	59.2	66	38	33	3	22-1	26	.283
2006—Wash. (N.L.)	0	2	.000	5.19	1.96	2	2	0	0	0	0-0	8.2	9	8	5	0	8-0	5	.290
—Harrisburg (East.)	0	2	.000	3.86	1.82	3	3	0	0	...	0-...	9.1	11	7	4	1	6-1	4	.306
American League totals (5 years)	31	31	.500	5.36	1.57	92	83	4	0	1	0-0	497.1	598	317	296	46	183-11	270	.301
National League totals (2 years)	3	8	.273	5.00	1.54	13	13	0	0	0	0-0	68.1	75	46	38	3	30-1	31	.284
Major League totals (6 years)	34	39	.466	5.31	1.57	105	96	4	0	1	0-0	565.2	673	363	334	49	213-12	301	.299

D

vs.	Avg.	AB	H	2B	3B	HR	RBI	BB	SO	OBP	Slg.	vs.	Avg.	AB	H	2B	3B	HR	RBI	BB	SO	OBP	Slg.
L	.250	8	2	0	0	0	2	0	3	.250	.250	R	.304	23	7	3	0	0	5	8	2	.484	.435

DREW, J.D.　　　　　　　　　　　OF

PERSONAL: Born November 20, 1975, in Valdosta, Ga. ... 6-1/200. ... Bats left, throws right. ... Full name: David Jonathan Drew. ... High school: Lowndes County (Hahira, Ga.). ... College: Florida State. ... Brother of Tim Drew, pitcher with three teams (2000-04); and brother of Stephen Drew, shortstop, Arizona Diamondbacks. **TRANSAC-TIONS/CAREER NOTES:** Selected by San Francisco Giants organization in 20th round of 1994 free-agent draft; did not sign. ... Selected by Philadelphia Phillies organization in first round (second pick overall) of 1997 free-agent draft; did not sign. ... Signed by St. Paul of the independent Northern League (1997). ... Selected by St. Louis Cardinals organization in first round (fifth pick overall) of 1998 free-agent draft. ... On disabled list (May 16-June 17, 1999); included rehabilitation assignment to Memphis. ... On disabled list (July 8-27, 2000). ... On disabled list (June 18-July 31, 2001); included rehabilitation assignment to Peoria. ... On disabled list (June 28-July 13, 2002). ... On disabled list (March 21-April 20 and August 9-September 1, 2003); included rehabilitation assignment to Palm Beach. ... Traded by Cardinals with OF/C Eli Marrero to Atlanta Braves for Ps Jason Marquis, Ray King and Adam Wainwright (December 14, 2003). ... Signed as a free agent by Los Angeles Dodgers (January 11, 2005). ... On disabled list (July 4, 2005-remainder of season). **HONORS:** Named College Player of the Year by THE SPORTING NEWS (1997). ... Named outfielder on THE SPORTING NEWS N.L. All-Star team (2004). **STATISTICAL NOTES:** Career major league grand slams: 3.

2006 GAMES PLAYED BY POSITION (MLB): OF—135, DH—4.

Year	Team (League)	Pos.	G	AB	R	H	2B	3B	HR	RBI	BB	SO	HBP	GDP	SB-CS	Avg.	OBP	SLG	OPS	E	Avg.
1997—St. Paul (North.)		OF	44	170	51	58	6	1	18	50	30	40	2	1	5-3	.341	.443	.706	1.149	...	...
1998—St. Paul (North.)		OF	30	114	27	44	11	2	9	33	21	32	6	2	8-1	.386	.504	.754	1.258	...	...
—Arkansas (Texas)		OF	19	67	18	22	3	1	5	11	13	15	1	0	2-1	.328	.444	.627	1.071	1	.980
—Memphis (PCL)		OF	26	79	15	25	8	1	2	13	22	18	1	1	1-3	.316	.471	.519	.990	2	.964
—St. Louis (N.L.)		OF	14	36	9	15	3	1	5	13	4	10	0	4	0-0	.417	.463	.972	1.436	0	1.000
1999—St. Louis (N.L.)		OF	104	368	72	89	16	6	13	39	50	77	6	4	19-3	.242	.340	.424	.763	7	.972
—Memphis (PCL)		OF	25	87	11	26	5	1	2	15	8	20	2	0	6-1	.299	.371	.448	.819	0	1.000
2000—St. Louis (N.L.)		OF	135	407	73	120	17	2	18	57	67	99	6	3	17-9	.295	.401	.479	.880	9	.966
2001—St. Louis (N.L.)		OF	109	375	80	121	18	5	27	73	57	75	4	6	13-3	.323	.414	.613	1.027	6	.973
—Peoria (Midw.)		OF	3	11	3	6	2	0	0	0	1	0	0	1	0-0	.545	.583	.727	1.311	0	1.000
2002—St. Louis (N.L.)		OF	135	424	61	107	19	1	18	56	57	104	8	4	8-2	.252	.349	.429	.778	3	.987
2003—Palm Beach (FSL)		OF-DH	8	19	4	7	0	0	1	3	7	4	1	0	0-0	.368	.556	.526	1.082	0	1.000
—Atlanta (N.L.)		OF	100	287	60	83	13	3	15	42	36	48	3	6	2-2	.289	.374	.512	.886	1	.994
2004—Atlanta (N.L.)		OF-DH	145	518	118	158	28	4	31	93	118	116	5	7	12-3	.305	.436	.570	1.006	3	.990
2005—Los Angeles (N.L.)		OF	72	252	48	72	12	1	15	36	51	50	5	3	1-1	.286	.412	.520	.931	2	.987
2006—Los Angeles (N.L.)		OF-DH	146	494	84	140	34	6	20	100	89	106	4	4	2-3	.283	.393	.498	.891	5	.983
Major League totals (9 years)			960	3161	605	905	160	33	162	509	529	685	41	41	74-26	.286	.393	.512	.904	36	.981

DIVISION SERIES RECORD

Year	Team (League)	Pos.	G	AB	R	H	2B	3B	HR	RBI	BB	SO	HBP	GDP	SB-CS	Avg.	OBP	SLG	OPS	E	Avg.
2000—St. Louis (N.L.)		OF	2	6	1	1	0	0	0	0	2	1	0	0	2-0	.167	.375	.167	.542	0	1.000
2001—St. Louis (N.L.)		OF	5	13	1	2	0	0	1	2	3	1	0	0	0-0	.154	.313	.385	.697	0	1.000
2002—St. Louis (N.L.)		OF	2	9	1	2	0	0	1	1	1	2	0	0	0-0	.222	.300	.556	.856	0	1.000
2004—Atlanta (N.L.)		OF	5	20	1	4	0	0	0	1	4	7	0	0	1-1	.200	.333	.200	.533	1	.889
2006—Los Angeles (N.L.)		OF	3	13	1	2	0	0	0	0	0	3	0	0	0-0	.154	.154	.154	.308	0	1.000
Division series totals (5 years)			17	61	5	11	0	0	2	4	10	14	0	0	3-1	.180	.296	.279	.574	1	.970

CHAMPIONSHIP SERIES RECORD

Year	Team (League)	Pos.	G	AB	R	H	2B	3B	HR	RBI	BB	SO	HBP	GDP	SB-CS	Avg.	OBP	SLG	OPS	E	Avg.
2000—St. Louis (N.L.)		OF	5	12	2	4	1	0	0	0	3	0	0	0	0-0	.333	.333	.417	.750	0	1.000
2002—St. Louis (N.L.)		OF	5	13	1	5	0	0	1	1	2	0	1	0	0-0	.385	.429	.615	1.044	0	1.000
Champ. series totals (2 years)			10	25	3	9	1	0	1	2	1	5	0	1	0-0	.360	.385	.520	.905	0	1.000

2006 LEFTY-RIGHTY SPLITS

vs.	Avg.	AB	H	2B	3B	HR	RBI	BB	SO	OBP	Slg.	vs.	Avg.	AB	H	2B	3B	HR	RBI	BB	SO	OBP	Slg.
L	.244	119	29	5	1	3	25	18	30	.338	.378	R	.296	375	111	29	5	17	75	71	76	.410	.536

DREW, STEPHEN　　　　　　　　　　SS

PERSONAL: Born March 16, 1983, in Hahira, Ga. ... 6-1/195. ... Bats left, throws right. ... Full name: Stephen O. Drew. ... College: Florida State. ... Brother of J.D. Drew, outfielder with Los Angeles Dodgers in 2006; and brother of Tim Drew, pitcher with three teams (2000-2004). **TRANSACTIONS/CAREER NOTES:** Signed by Camden of independent Northern League (2005). ... Selected by Arizona Diamondbacks organization in first round (15th pick overall) of 2004 free-agent draft.

2006 GAMES PLAYED BY POSITION (MLB): SS—56.

Year	Team (League)	Pos.	G	AB	R	H	2B	3B	HR	RBI	BB	SO	HBP	GDP	SB-CS	Avg.	OBP	SLG	OPS	E	Avg.
2005—Camden (Atl.)			19	82	17	35	8	3	4	18	8	18	1	...	0-0	.427	.484	.744	1.227	8	...
—Lancaster (Calif.)		SS-DH	38	149	33	58	16	3	10	39	26	25	2	1	1-1	.389	.486	.738	1.224	8	.950
—Tennessee (Sou.)		SS	27	101	11	22	5	0	4	13	12	24	0	1	2-3	.218	.301	.386	.687	8	.935
2006—Tucson (PCL)			83	342	55	97	16	3	13	51	33	50	0	7	3-3	.284	.340	.462	.802	15	.955
—Arizona (N.L.)		SS	59	209	27	66	13	7	5	23	14	50	0	2	2-0	.316	.357	.517	.874	5	.978
Major League totals (1 year)			59	209	27	66	13	7	5	23	14	50	0	2	2-0	.316	.357	.517	.874	5	.978

2006 LEFTY-RIGHTY SPLITS

vs.	Avg.	AB	H	2B	3B	HR	RBI	BB	SO	OBP	Slg.	vs.	Avg.	AB	H	2B	3B	HR	RBI	BB	SO	OBP	Slg.
L	.350	40	14	3	2	1	3	3	17	.395	.600	R	.308	169	52	10	5	4	20	11	33	.348	.497

DUBOSE, ERIC　　　　　　　　　　P

PERSONAL: Born May 15, 1976, in Bradenton, Fla. ... 6-3/216. ... Throws left, bats left. ... Full name: Eric Ladell DuBose. ... Name pronounced: dew-BOWES. ... High school: Patrician Academy (Butler, Ala.). ... College: Mississippi State. **TRANSACTIONS/CAREER NOTES:** Selected by Los Angeles Dodgers organization in sixth round of 1994 free-agent draft; did not sign. ... Selected by Oakland Athletics organization in first round (21st pick overall) of 1997 free-agent draft; pick received as compensation for Baltimore Orioles signing Type A free-agent SS Mike Bordick. ... Claimed on waivers by Cleveland Indians (September 8, 2000). ... Claimed on waivers by Detroit Tigers (September 22, 2000). ... Released by Tigers (March 31, 2001). ... Signed by Baltimore Orioles organization (February 4, 2002). ... On disabled list (June 20, 2004-remainder of season).

CAREER HITTING: 0-for-2 (.000), 0 R, 0 2B, 0 3B, 0 HR, 0 RBI.

Year	Team (League)	W	L	Pct.	ERA	WHIP	G	GS	CG	ShO	Hld.	Sv.-Opp.	IP	H	R	ER	HR	BB-IBB	SO	Avg.
1997—S. Oregon (N'west)		1	0	1.000	0.00	1.10	3	1	0	0		0-...	10.0	5	0	0	0	6-0	15	.152
—Visalia (Calif.)		1	3	.250	7.04	1.85	10	9	0	0		0-...	38.1	43	34	30	4	28-0	39	.270
1998—Visalia (Calif.)		6	1	.857	3.38	1.13	17	10	0	0		1-...	72.0	56	34	27	5	25-0	85	.212
—Huntsville (Sou.)		7	6	.538	2.70	1.44	14	14	1	1		0-...	83.1	86	37	25	2	34-1	66	.273

D

Year	Team (League)	W	L	Pct.	ERA	WHIP	G	GS	CG	ShO	Hld.	Sv.-Opp.	IP	H	R	ER	HR	BB-IBB	SO	Avg.
1999— Midland (Texas)		4	2	.667	5.49	1.73	21	14	0	0	...	1-...	77.0	89	57	47	10	44-1	68	.293
2000— Midland (Texas)		5	1	.833	4.13	1.52	18	0	0	0	...	0-...	28.1	25	16	13	1	18-2	20	.227
— Visalia (Calif.)		0	1	.000	1.69	1.22	5	0	0	0	...	1-...	10.2	8	2	2	0	5-1	12	.200
2001—					Did not play.															
2002— Rochester (Int'l)		0	0	...	27.00	9.00	1	0	0	0	...	0-...	0.1	1	2	1	0	2-0	0	.333
— Bowie (East.)		5	3	.625	2.51	1.04	41	0	0	0	...	3-...	64.2	46	21	18	2	21-0	66	.198
— Baltimore (A.L.)		0	0	...	3.00	1.33	4	0	0	0	0	0-0	6.0	7	2	2	1	1-0	4	.304
2003— Ottawa (Int'l)		9	5	.643	3.39	1.30	19	19	0	0	...	0-...	114.0	112	49	43	7	34-2	107	.261
— Baltimore (A.L.)		3	6	.333	3.79	1.15	17	10	1	0	1	0-1	73.2	60	33	31	6	25-2	44	.222
2004— Baltimore (A.L.)		4	6	.400	6.39	1.61	14	14	0	0	0	0-0	74.2	76	55	53	12	44-0	48	.263
2005— Ottawa (Int'l)		0	1	.000	11.42	2.08	2	2	0	0	...	0-0	8.2	17	13	11	5	1-0	7	.395
— Bowie (East.)		8	10	.444	3.25	1.16	21	20	0	0	...	0-...	122.0	113	52	44	10	29-0	114	.247
— Baltimore (A.L.)		2	3	.400	5.52	1.60	15	3	0	0	3	0-0	29.1	28	21	18	4	19-0	17	.243
2006— Baltimore (A.L.)		0	0	...	9.64	2.79	2	0	0	0	0	0-0	4.2	10	5	5	2	3-0	2	.500
— Ottawa (Int'l)		3	4	.429	5.54	1.72	8	8	0	0	...	0-...	39.0	44	26	24	3	23-1	30	.293
— Bowie (East.)		7	1	.875	3.11	1.24	20	11	2	2	0	0-1	84.0	70	33	29	7	34-1	67	.230
Major League totals (5 years)		**9**	**15**	**.375**	**5.21**	**1.45**	**52**	**27**	**1**	**0**	**4**	**0-1**	**188.1**	**181**	**116**	**109**	**25**	**92-2**	**115**	**.252**

2006 LEFTY-RIGHTY SPLITS

vs.	Avg.	AB	H	2B	3B	HR	RBI	BB	SO	OBP	Slg.	vs.	Avg.	AB	H	2B	3B	HR	RBI	BB	SO	OBP	Slg.
L	.400	5	2	0	0	1	3	1	1	.500	1.000	R	.533	15	8	1	0	1	3	2	1	.588	.800

DUCHSCHERER, JUSTIN   P

PERSONAL: Born November 19, 1977, in Aberdeen, S.D. ... 6-3/190. ... Throws right, bats right. ... Full name: Justin Craig Duchscherer. ... Name pronounced: DUKE-sher. ... High school: Coronado (Lubbock, Texas). **TRANSACTIONS/CAREER NOTES:** Selected by Boston Red Sox organization in eighth round of 1996 free-agent draft. ... Traded by Red Sox to Texas Rangers for C Doug Mirabelli (June 12, 2001). ... Traded by Rangers to Oakland Athletics for P Luis Vizcaino (March 18, 2002). ... On disabled list (May 13-June 23, 2006); included rehabilitation assignment to Sacramento.

CAREER HITTING: 0-for-0 (.000), 0 R, 0 2B, 0 3B, 0 HR, 0 RBI.

Year	Team (League)	W	L	Pct.	ERA	WHIP	G	GS	CG	ShO	Hld.	Sv.-Opp.	IP	H	R	ER	HR	BB-IBB	SO	Avg.
1996— GC Red Sox (GCL)		0	2	.000	3.13	1.21	13	8	0	0	...	1-...	54.2	52	26	19	0	14-0	45	.249
1997— GC Red Sox (GCL)		2	3	.400	1.81	1.14	10	8	0	0	...	0-...	44.2	34	18	9	0	17-0	59	.204
— Michigan (Midw.)		1	1	.500	5.63	1.50	4	4	0	0	...	0-...	24.0	26	17	15	1	10-0	19	.274
1998— Michigan (Midw.)		7	12	.368	4.79	1.49	30	26	0	0	...	0-...	142.2	166	87	76	9	47-3	106	.298
1999— Augusta (S. Atl.)		4	0	1.000	0.22	0.71	6	6	0	0	...	0-...	41.0	21	1	1	0	8-0	39	.148
— Sarasota (Fla. St.)		7	7	.500	4.49	1.17	20	18	0	0	...	0-...	112.1	101	62	56	14	30-0	105	.237
2000— Trenton (East.)		7	9	.438	3.39	1.18	24	24	2	2	...	0-...	143.1	134	59	54	7	35-1	126	.246
2001— Trenton (East.)		6	3	.667	2.44	0.86	12	12	1	1	...	0-...	73.2	49	25	20	4	14-1	69	.179
— Tulsa (Texas)		4	0	1.000	2.08	1.13	6	6	1	0	...	0-...	43.1	39	14	10	3	10-0	55	.242
— Texas (A.L.)		1	1	.500	12.27	1.91	5	2	0	0	0	0-0	14.2	24	20	20	5	4-0	11	.353
— Oklahoma (PCL)		3	3	.500	2.84	1.14	7	7	1	1	...	0-...	50.2	48	20	16	6	10-0	52	.255
2002— Sacramento (PCL)		2	4	.333	5.57	1.43	14	11	0	0	...	0-...	63.0	73	45	39	7	17-0	52	.283
2003— Sacramento (PCL)		14	2	.875	3.25	1.10	24	23	0	0	...	0-...	155.0	151	59	56	12	18-0	117	.254
— Oakland (A.L.)		1	1	.500	3.31	1.22	4	3	0	0	0	0-0	16.1	17	7	6	1	3-0	15	.262
2004— Oakland (A.L.)		7	6	.538	3.27	1.21	53	0	0	0	6	0-2	96.1	85	37	35	13	32-6	59	.241
2005— Oakland (A.L.)		7	4	.636	2.21	1.00	65	0	0	0	10	5-7	85.2	67	25	21	7	19-3	85	.215
2006— Sacramento (PCL)		0	0	...	0.00	1.00	2	1	0	0	0	0-0	2.0	2	0	0	0	0-0	1	.286
— Oakland (A.L.)		2	1	.667	2.91	1.10	53	0	0	0	17	9-11	55.2	52	18	18	4	9-0	51	.244
Major League totals (5 years)		**18**	**13**	**.581**	**3.35**	**1.16**	**180**	**5**	**0**	**0**	**33**	**14-20**	**268.2**	**245**	**107**	**100**	**30**	**67-9**	**221**	**.243**

DIVISION SERIES RECORD

Year	Team (League)	W	L	Pct.	ERA	WHIP	G	GS	CG	ShO	Hld.	Sv.-Opp.	IP	H	R	ER	HR	BB-IBB	SO	Avg.
2006— Oakland (A.L.)		0	0	...	2.25	0.25	2	0	0	0	2	0-0	4.0	1	1	1	1	0-0	4	.077

2006 LEFTY-RIGHTY SPLITS

vs.	Avg.	AB	H	2B	3B	HR	RBI	BB	SO	OBP	Slg.	vs.	Avg.	AB	H	2B	3B	HR	RBI	BB	SO	OBP	Slg.
L	.248	101	25	4	0	1	4	5	27	.283	.317	R	.241	112	27	2	0	3	10	4	24	.274	.339

DUCKWORTH, BRANDON   P

PERSONAL: Born January 23, 1976, in Salt Lake City. ... 6-2/190. ... Throws right, bats right. ... Full name: Brandon J. Duckworth. ... High school: Kearns (Utah). ... College: Cal State Fullerton. **TRANSACTIONS/CAREER NOTES:** Selected by Toronto Blue Jays organization in 30th round of 1995 free-agent draft; did not sign. ... Selected by Arizona Diamondbacks organization in 61st round of 1996 free-agent draft; did not sign. ... Signed as a non-drafted free agent by Philadelphia Phillies organization (August 13, 1997). ... On disabled list (March 21-April 20, 2003); included rehabilitation assignments to Clearwater and Reading. ... Traded by Phillies with Ps Taylor Buchholz and Ezequiel Astacio to Houston Astros for P Billy Wagner (November 3, 2003). ... Signed as a free agent by Pittsburgh Pirates organization (January 5, 2006). ... Traded by Pirates to Kansas City Royals for cash (June 11, 2006). ... On disabled list (July 31, 2006-remainder of season).

CAREER HITTING: 24-for-112 (.214), 8 R, 4 2B, 0 3B, 0 HR, 8 RBI.

Year	Team (League)	W	L	Pct.	ERA	WHIP	G	GS	CG	ShO	Hld.	Sv.-Opp.	IP	H	R	ER	HR	BB-IBB	SO	Avg.
1998— Piedmont (S. Atl.)		9	8	.529	2.80	0.95	21	21	5	3	...	0-...	147.2	116	58	46	10	24-0	119	.215
— Clearwater (FSL)		6	2	.750	3.74	1.62	9	9	1	1	...	0-...	53.0	64	25	22	2	22-0	46	.306
1999— Clearwater (FSL)		11	5	.688	4.84	1.55	27	17	0	0	...	1-...	132.0	164	84	71	13	40-0	101	.301
2000— Reading (East.)		13	7	.650	3.16	1.19	27	27	1	0	...	0-...	165.0	145	70	58	17	52-0	178	.233
2001— Scran./W.B. (I.L.)		13	2	.867	2.63	1.07	22	20	2	1	...	0-...	147.0	122	46	43	14	36-2	150	.228
— Philadelphia (N.L.)		3	2	.600	3.52	1.25	11	11	0	0	0	0-0	69.0	57	29	27	2	29-5	40	.234
2002— Philadelphia (N.L.)		8	9	.471	5.41	1.45	30	29	0	0	0	0-0	163.0	167	103	98	26	69-5	167	.261
2003— Clearwater (FSL)		0	0	...	1.00	0.60	2	2	0	0	...	0-...	9.0	3	1	1	1	2-0	11	.100
— Reading (East.)		0	0	...	4.50	0.50	1	1	0	0	...	0-...	2.0	1	1	1	0	0-0	2	.143
— Scran./W.B. (I.L.)		2	1	.667	3.38	1.30	3	3	0	0	...	0-...	18.2	21	11	7	3	4-0	14	.280
— Philadelphia (N.L.)		4	7	.364	4.94	1.53	24	18	0	0	0	0-0	93.0	98	58	51	12	44-3	68	.272
2004— New Orleans (PCL)		5	5	.500	5.53	1.56	14	13	0	0	...	0-...	70.0	81	44	43	10	28-1	63	.286
— Houston (N.L.)		1	2	.333	6.86	1.73	19	6	0	0	0	0-0	39.1	55	30	30	11	13-3	23	.337
2005— Round Rock (PCL)		8	6	.571	4.62	1.52	20	20	0	0	...	0-...	115.0	138	68	59	17	37-2	89	.301
— Houston (N.L.)		0	1	.000	11.02	1.90	7	2	0	0	0	0-0	16.1	24	20	20	4	7-1	10	.348
2006— Indianapolis (Int'l)		8	3	.727	2.42	1.21	12	12	0	0	...	0-...	74.1	67	23	20	4	23-1	57	.242
— Kansas City (A.L.)		1	5	.167	6.11	1.88	10	8	0	0	0	0-0	45.2	62	36	31	3	24-4	27	.332
American League totals (1 year)		**1**	**5**	**.167**	**6.11**	**1.88**	**10**	**8**	**0**	**0**	**0**	**0-0**	**45.2**	**62**	**36**	**31**	**3**	**24-4**	**27**	**.332**
National League totals (5 years)		**16**	**21**	**.432**	**5.34**	**1.48**	**91**	**66**	**0**	**0**	**0**	**0-0**	**380.2**	**401**	**240**	**226**	**55**	**162-17**	**308**	**.272**
Major League totals (6 years)		**17**	**26**	**.395**	**5.43**	**1.52**	**101**	**74**	**0**	**0**	**0**	**0-0**	**426.1**	**463**	**276**	**257**	**58**	**186-21**	**335**	**.279**

D

2006 LEFTY-RIGHTY SPLITS

vs.	Avg.	AB	H	2B	3B	HR	RBI	BB	SO	OBP	Slg.	vs.	Avg.	AB	H	2B	3B	HR	RBI	BB	SO	OBP	Slg.
L	.232	69	16	2	0	0	10	12	14	.341	.261	R	.390	118	46	14	0	3	20	12	13	.451	.585

DUFFY, CHRIS — OF

PERSONAL: Born April 20, 1980, in Brattleboro, Vt. ... 5-10/180. ... Bats left, throws left. ... Full name: Christopher Ellis Duffy. ... College: Arizona State.
TRANSACTIONS/CAREER NOTES: Selected by Pittsburgh Pirates in eighth round of 2001 free-agent draft. ... On disabled list (August 28, 2005-remainder of season).
2006 GAMES PLAYED BY POSITION (MLB): OF—77.

									BATTING								FIELDING	
Year Team (League)	Pos.	G	AB	R	H	2B	3B	HR	RBI	BB	SO	HBP	GDP	SB-CS	Avg.	OBP	SLG	OPS	E	Avg.
2001—Williamsport (NYP)	OF	64	221	50	70	12	4	1	24	33	33	17	0	30-5	.317	.440	.421	.861	1	.992
2002—Lynchburg (Caro.)	OF	132	539	85	162	27	5	10	52	33	101	12	1	22-7	.301	.353	.425	.778	3	.989
2003—Altoona (East.)	OF	137	494	84	135	23	6	1	42	44	78	20	7	34-12	.273	.355	.350	.705	4	.987
2004—Altoona (East.)	OF	113	453	84	140	23	6	8	41	33	77	17	4	30-8	.309	.378	.439	.817	2	.962
2005—Indianapolis (Int'l)	OF	78	308	55	95	13	7	7	31	16	57	10	4	17-9	.308	.358	.464	.822	4	.989
—Pittsburgh (N.L.)	OF	39	126	22	43	4	2	1	9	7	22	2	1	2-2	.341	.385	.429	.814	1	.988
2006—Indianapolis (Int'l)		26	106	18	37	7	2	2	19	10	13	2	2	13-3	.349	.415	.509	.925	2	.970
—Pittsburgh (N.L.)	OF	84	314	46	80	14	3	2	18	19	71	10	1	26-1	.255	.317	.338	.654	3	.983
Major League totals (2 years)		123	440	68	123	18	5	3	27	26	93	12	2	28-3	.280	.336	.364	.700	4	.984

2006 LEFTY-RIGHTY SPLITS

vs.	Avg.	AB	H	2B	3B	HR	RBI	BB	SO	OBP	Slg.	vs.	Avg.	AB	H	2B	3B	HR	RBI	BB	SO	OBP	Slg.
L	.229	83	19	2	0	2	6	5	21	.286	.325	R	.264	231	61	12	3	0	12	14	50	.328	.342

DUKE, ZACH — P

PERSONAL: Born April 19, 1983, in Clifton, Texas. ... 6-2/212. ... Throws left, bats left. ... Full name: Zachary Thomas Duke. . **TRANSACTIONS/CAREER NOTES:** Selected by Pittsburgh Pirates organization in 20th round of 2001 free-agent draft. ... On disabled list (August 27-September 16, 2005).
CAREER HITTING: 17-for-96 (.177), 3 R, 3 2B, 0 3B, 0 HR, 8 RBI.

Year Team (League)	W	L	Pct.	ERA	WHIP	G	GS	CG	ShO	Hld.	Sv.-Opp.	IP	H	R	ER	HR	BB-IBB	SO	Avg.
2002—GC Pirates (GCL)	8	1	.889	1.95	0.93	11	11	1	1	...	0-...	60.0	38	15	13	2	18-0	48	.185
2003—Hickory (S. Atl.)	8	7	.533	3.11	1.20	26	26	1	1	...	0-...	141.2	124	66	49	7	46-0	113	.237
2004—Lynchburg (Caro.)	10	5	.667	1.39	0.96	17	17	1	0	...	0-...	97.0	73	24	15	3	20-1	106	.210
—Altoona (East.)	5	1	.833	1.58	0.99	9	9	0	0	...	0-...	51.1	41	11	9	2	10-0	36	.236
2005—Indianapolis (Int'l)	12	3	.800	2.92	1.21	16	16	1	0	0	0-0	108.0	108	39	35	8	23-1	66	.267
—Pittsburgh (N.L.)	8	2	.800	1.81	1.20	14	14	0	0	0	0-0	84.2	79	20	17	3	23-2	58	.253
2006—Pittsburgh (N.L.)	10	15	.400	4.47	1.50	34	34	2	1	0	0-0	215.1	255	116	107	17	68-6	117	.302
Major League totals (2 years)	18	17	.514	3.72	1.42	48	48	2	1	0	0-0	300.0	334	136	124	20	91-8	175	.289

2006 LEFTY-RIGHTY SPLITS

vs.	Avg.	AB	H	2B	3B	HR	RBI	BB	SO	OBP	Slg.	vs.	Avg.	AB	H	2B	3B	HR	RBI	BB	SO	OBP	Slg.
L	.264	144	38	6	0	2	13	12	30	.338	.347	R	.310	699	217	54	3	15	87	56	87	.362	.461

DUNCAN, CHRIS — OF/1B

PERSONAL: Born May 5, 1981, in Tucson, Ariz. ... 6-5/210. ... Bats left, throws right. ... Full name: Christopher Edward Duncan. ... High school: Canyon del Oro (Tucson, Ariz.). ... Son of Dave Duncan, coach with St. Louis Cardinals; and catcher with four major league teams (1964-76). **TRANSACTIONS/CAREER NOTES:** Selected by St. Louis Cardinals organization in supplemental round ("sandwich" pick, 46th pick overall) of 1999 free-agent draft; pick received as compensation for Baltimore Orioles signing 2B Delino DeShields.
2006 GAMES PLAYED BY POSITION (MLB): OF—70, 1B—11, DH—1.

									BATTING								FIELDING	
Year Team (League)	Pos.	G	AB	R	H	2B	3B	HR	RBI	BB	SO	HBP	GDP	SB-CS	Avg.	OBP	SLG	OPS	E	Avg.
1999—Johnson City (App.)	1B	55	201	23	43	8	1	6	34	25	62	1	4	3-1	.214	.300	.353	.653	12	.977
2000—Peoria (Midw.)	1B	122	450	52	115	34	0	8	57	36	111	6	11	1-2	.256	.318	.384	.702	35	.962
2001—Potomac (Carol.)	1B	49	168	12	30	6	0	3	16	10	47	1	5	4-4	.179	.229	.268	.497	9	.982
—Peoria (Midw.)	1B	80	297	44	91	23	2	13	59	36	55	3	10	13-3	.306	.386	.529	.915	21	.973
2002—Peoria (Midw.)	1B	129	487	58	132	25	4	16	75	44	118	7	8	5-5	.271	.337	.437	.774	19	.982
2003—Palm Beach (FSL)	1B	121	425	26	108	20	0	2	42	44	115	1	12	4-4	.254	.322	.315	.637	14	.987
—Tennessee (Sou.)	OF	10	25	1	5	1	0	1	3	0	6	0	1	0-0	.200	.200	.360	.560	1	.889
2004—Tennessee (Sou.)	OF	120	387	57	112	23	0	16	65	64	94	3	6	8-4	.289	.393	.473	.866	8	.994
2005—Memphis (PCL)	1B-OF-DH	128	431	57	114	21	2	21	73	63	104	2	14	1-3	.265	.358	.469	.827	21	.977
—St. Louis (N.L.)	1B-OF	9	10	2	2	1	0	1	3	0	5	0	1	0-0	.200	.200	.800	.800	0	1.000
2006—Memphis (PCL)		52	181	23	49	11	0	7	31	25	53	0	5	1-2	.271	.359	.448	.807	4	.935
—St. Louis (N.L.)	OF-1B-DH	90	280	60	82	11	3	22	43	30	69	2	4	0-0	.293	.363	.589	.952	6	.965
Major League totals (2 years)		99	290	62	84	12	3	23	46	30	74	2	5	0-0	.290	.358	.590	.948	6	.965

DIVISION SERIES RECORD

Year Team (League)	Pos.	G	AB	R	H	2B	3B	HR	RBI	BB	SO	HBP	GDP	SB-CS	Avg.	OBP	SLG	OPS	E	Avg.
2006—St. Louis (N.L.)	OF	2	6	1	1	0	0	0	0	2	2	0	0	0-0	.167	.375	.167	.542	1	.667

CHAMPIONSHIP SERIES RECORD

Year Team (League)	Pos.	G	AB	R	H	2B	3B	HR	RBI	BB	SO	HBP	GDP	SB-CS	Avg.	OBP	SLG	OPS	E	Avg.
2006—St. Louis (N.L.)	OF	5	8	1	1	0	0	1	1	0	2	0	1	0-0	.125	.125	.500	.625	0	1.000

WORLD SERIES RECORD

Year Team (League)	Pos.	G	AB	R	H	2B	3B	HR	RBI	BB	SO	HBP	GDP	SB-CS	Avg.	OBP	SLG	OPS	E	Avg.
2006—St. Louis (N.L.)	OF-DH	3	8	1	1	1	0	1	0	1	2	0	0	0-0	.125	.300	.250	.550	1	.667

2006 LEFTY-RIGHTY SPLITS

vs.	Avg.	AB	H	2B	3B	HR	RBI	BB	SO	OBP	Slg.	vs.	Avg.	AB	H	2B	3B	HR	RBI	BB	SO	OBP	Slg.
L	.170	47	8	1	0	2	3	3	14	.220	.319	R	.318	233	74	10	3	20	40	27	55	.390	.644

DUNN, ADAM — OF/1B

PERSONAL: Born November 9, 1979, in Houston. ... 6-6/240. ... Bats left, throws right. ... Full name: Adam Troy Dunn. ... High school: New Caney (Texas). **TRANSACTIONS/CAREER NOTES:** Selected by Cincinnati Reds organization in second round of 1998 free-agent draft. ... On suspended list (June 20-22, 2003). ... On disabled list (August 16, 2003-remainder of season). **RECORDS:** Holds major league record for most strikeouts, season (195, 2004). ... Shares major league record for most strikeouts, 9-inning game (5, August 20, 2002). **STATISTICAL NOTES:** Career major league grand slams: 6.
2006 GAMES PLAYED BY POSITION (MLB): OF—156, 1B—2, DH—1.

D

Year	Team (League)	Pos.	G	AB	R	H	2B	3B	HR	RBI	BB	SO	HBP	GDP	SB-CS	Avg.	OBP	SLG	OPS	E	Avg.
1998—Billings (Pion.)		OF	34	125	26	36	3	1	4	13	22	33	3	3	4-2	.288	.404	.424	.828	6	.860
1999—Rockford (Midwest)		OF	93	313	62	96	16	2	11	44	46	64	10	6	21-9	.307	.409	.476	.885	8	.918
2000—Dayton (Midw.)		OF	122	420	101	118	29	1	16	79	100	101	12	10	24-5	.281	.428	.469	.897	9	.958
2001—Chattanooga (Sou.)		OF	39	140	30	48	9	0	12	31	24	31	3	1	6-3	.343	.449	.664	1.113	3	.961
—Louisville (Int'l)		OF	55	210	44	69	13	0	20	53	38	51	5	1	5-1	.329	.441	.676	1.117	5	.954
—Cincinnati (N.L.)		OF	66	244	54	64	18	1	19	43	38	74	4	4	4-2	.262	.371	.578	.949	2	.986
2002—Cincinnati (N.L.)		OF-1B-DH	158	535	84	133	28	2	26	71	128	170	9	8	19-9	.249	.400	.454	.854	15	.975
2003—Cincinnati (N.L.)		OF-1B-DH	116	381	70	82	12	1	27	57	74	126	10	4	8-2	.215	.354	.465	.819	11	.965
2004—Cincinnati (N.L.)		OF-1B-DH	161	568	105	151	34	0	46	102	108 *	195	5	8	6-1	.266	.388	.569	.956	8	.977
2005—Cincinnati (N.L.)		OF-1B	160	543	107	134	35	2	40	101	114 *	168	12	6	4-2	.247	.387	.540	.927	9	.983
2006—Cincinnati (N.L.)		OF-1B-DH	160	561	99	131	24	0	40	92	112 *	194	6	8	7-0	.234	.365	.490	.855	13	.959
Major League totals (6 years)			821	2832	519	695	151	6	198	466	574	927	46	38	48-16	.245	.380	.513	.892	58	.974

ALL-STAR GAME RECORD

	G	AB	R	H	2B	3B	HR	RBI	BB	SO	HBP	GDP	SB-CS	Avg.	OBP	SLG	OPS	E	Avg.
All-Star Game totals (1 year)	1	1	0	0	0	0	0	0	1	0	0	0	0-0	.000	.500	.000	.500	0	...

2006 LEFTY-RIGHTY SPLITS

vs.	Avg.	AB	H	2B	3B	HR	RBI	BB	SO	OBP	Slg.	vs.	Avg.	AB	H	2B	3B	HR	RBI	BB	SO	OBP	Slg.
L	.270	185	50	10	0	11	26	34	64	.393	.503	R	.215	376	81	14	0	29	66	78	130	.352	.484

DUNN, SCOTT — P

PERSONAL: Born May 23, 1978, in San Antonio. ... 6-3/200. ... Throws right, bats right. ... Full name: Scott Allen Dunn. ... High school: Winston Churchill (San Antonio). ... College: Texas. **TRANSACTIONS/CAREER NOTES:** Selected by Florida Marlins organization in 26th round of 1996 free-agent draft; did not sign. ... Selected by Cincinnati Reds organization in 10th round of 1999 free-agent draft. ... Traded by Reds to Chicago White Sox for IF D'Angelo Jimenez (July 6, 2003). ... Traded by White Sox with Ps Gary Glover and Tim Bittner to Anaheim Angels for Ps Scott Schoeneweis and Doug Nickle (July 30, 2003). ... Angels franchise renamed Los Angeles Angels of Anaheim for 2005 season. ... Claimed on waivers by Tampa Bay Devil Rays (April 5, 2006).

CAREER HITTING: 0-for-0 (.000), 0 R, 0 2B, 0 3B, 0 HR, 0 RBI.

Year	Team (League)	W	L	Pct.	ERA	WHIP	G	GS	CG	ShO	Hld.	Sv.-Opp.	IP	H	R	ER	HR	BB-IBB	SO	Avg.
1999—Billings (Pion.)		1	3	.250	4.31	1.51	9	8	0	0	...	0-...	39.2	36	24	19	3	24-0	36	.240
2000—Clinton (Midw.)		11	3	.786	3.96	1.44	26	26	2	1	...	0-...	147.2	123	78	65	9	89-1	159	.228
2001—Mudville (Calif.)		5	3	.625	2.11	1.27	10	10	1	1	...	0-...	59.2	45	17	14	2	31-0	73	.208
—Chattanooga (Sou.)		7	2	.778	4.12	1.70	17	17	0	0	...	0-...	98.1	96	51	45	10	71-0	87	.262
2002—Chattanooga (Sou.)		5	7	.417	3.92	1.39	37	12	0	0	...	1-...	110.1	99	57	48	10	54-3	114	.245
2003—Chattanooga (Sou.)		3	2	.600	3.79	1.17	31	0	0	0	...	8-...	40.1	31	21	17	3	16-2	54	.211
—Birmingham (Sou.)		3	1	.750	1.69	1.22	8	0	0	0	...	1-...	10.2	8	2	2	0	5-2	14	.216
—Arkansas (Texas)		1	0	1.000	0.00	0.40	3	0	0	0	...	0-...	5.0	2	0	0	0	0-0	7	.125
—Salt Lake (PCL)		0	0	...	11.74	2.48	6	0	0	0	...	0-...	7.2	9	10	10	1	10-0	11	.273
2004—Salt Lake (PCL)		10	4	.714	3.21	1.43	46	6	0	0	...	1-...	89.2	72	36	32	6	56-0	84	.224
—Anaheim (A.L.)		0	0	...	9.00	2.67	3	0	0	0	...	0-...	3.0	7	3	3	0	1-0	2	.438
2005—Salt Lake (PCL)		5	7	.417	3.82	1.35	47	6	0	0	3	9-11	92.0	83	44	39	7	41-1	98	.242
2006—Durham (Int'l)		4	2	.667	2.73	1.29	38	0	0	0	6	0-...	66.0	57	21	20	2	28-0	70	.228
—Tampa Bay (A.L.)		1	0	1.000	11.74	2.74	7	0	0	0	0	0-1	7.2	17	10	10	2	4-0	4	.436
Major League totals (2 years)		1	0	1.000	10.97	2.72	10	0	0	0	0	0-1	10.2	24	13	13	2	5-0	6	.436

2006 LEFTY-RIGHTY SPLITS

vs.	Avg.	AB	H	2B	3B	HR	RBI	BB	SO	OBP	Slg.	vs.	Avg.	AB	H	2B	3B	HR	RBI	BB	SO	OBP	Slg.
L	.438	16	7	2	0	0	0	2	3	.550	.563	R	.435	23	10	4	0	2	10	2	1	.480	.870

DURBIN, CHAD — P

PERSONAL: Born December 3, 1977, in Spring Valley, Ill. ... 6-2/200. ... Throws right, bats both. ... Full name: Chad Griffin Durbin. ... High school: Woodlawn (Shreveport, La.). **TRANSACTIONS/CAREER NOTES:** Selected by Kansas City Royals organization in third round of 1996 free-agent draft. ... Signed as a free agent by Cleveland Indians organization (February 17, 2003). ... Claimed on waivers by Arizona Diamondbacks (August 31, 2004). ... Claimed on waivers by Washington Nationals organization (January 10, 2005). ... Signed as a free agent by Detroit Tigers organization (November 14, 2005).

CAREER HITTING: 0-for-2 (.000), 0 R, 0 2B, 0 3B, 0 HR, 0 RBI.

Year	Team (League)	W	L	Pct.	ERA	WHIP	G	GS	CG	ShO	Hld.	Sv.-Opp.	IP	H	R	ER	HR	BB-IBB	SO	Avg.
1996—GC Royals (GCL)		3	2	.600	4.26	1.33	11	8	1	1	...	0-...	44.1	34	22	21	3	25-0	43	.213
1997—Lansing (Midw.)		5	8	.385	4.79	1.45	26	26	0	0	...	0-...	144.2	157	85	77	15	53-0	116	.277
1998—Wilmington (Caro.)		10	7	.588	2.93	1.25	26	26	0	0	...	0-...	147.2	126	57	48	10	59-3	162	.231
1999—Wichita (Texas)		8	10	.444	4.64	1.29	28	27	1	1	...	0-...	157.0	154	88	81	20	49-1	122	.258
—Kansas City (A.L.)		0	0	...	0.00	0.86	1	0	0	0	0	0-0	2.1	1	0	0	0	1-0	3	.125
2000—Kansas City (A.L.)		2	5	.286	8.21	1.85	16	16	0	0	0	0-0	72.1	91	71	66	14	43-1	37	.301
—Omaha (PCL)		4	4	.500	4.46	1.33	12	12	0	0	0	0-0	72.2	75	37	36	10	22-0	53	.269
2001—Omaha (PCL)		2	2	.500	3.33	1.04	5	5	0	0	0	0-0	27.0	22	11	10	4	6-0	35	.216
—Kansas City (A.L.)		9	16	.360	4.93	1.45	29	29	2	0	0	0-0	179.0	201	109	98	26	58-0	95	.288
2002—Kansas City (A.L.)		0	1	.000	11.88	2.04	2	2	0	0	0	0-0	8.1	13	11	11	3	4-0	5	.342
—Omaha (PCL)		0	1	.000	10.80	2.40	1	1	0	0	0	0-0	1.2	4	2	2	0	0-0	2	.444
—GC Royals (GCL)		0	0	...	0.00	0.83	3	3	0	0	0	0-0	6.0	4	0	0	0	1-0	5	.200
—Wichita (Texas)		0	0	...	5.06	1.69	3	1	0	0	0	0-0	5.1	5	4	3	1	3-0	8	.238
2003—Mahoning Valley (N.Y.-Penn.)		1	1	.500	2.25	1.00	2	2	0	0	0	0-...	12.0	9	4	3	1	3-0	8	.220
—Akron (East.)		2	0	1.000	1.50	0.70	3	3	0	0	0	0-...	12.0	7	2	2	1	1-0	11	.163
—Buffalo (Int'l)		3	6	.333	4.60	1.10	10	10	0	0	0	0-...	58.2	51	30	30	9	16-0	64	.233
—Cleveland (A.L.)		0	1	.000	7.27	2.42	3	1	0	0	0	0-0	8.2	18	12	7	2	3-0	8	.429
2004—Buffalo (Int'l)		3	3	.500	3.46	1.37	9	9	0	0	0	0-0	52.0	55	22	20	7	16-0	40	.271
—Cleveland (A.L.)		5	6	.455	6.66	1.69	17	8	1	0	0	0-0	51.1	63	40	38	10	24-3	38	.301
—Arizona (N.L.)		1	1	.500	8.68	2.14	7	1	0	0	0	0-0	9.1	9	10	9	1	11-0	10	.237
2005—New Orleans (PCL)		4	5	.444	5.77	1.47	26	20	0	0	0	0-0	115.1	121	78	74	24	48-3	99	.271
2006—Toledo (Int'l)		11	8	.579	3.11	1.16	28	28	2	2	0	0-0	185.0	169	72	64	17	46-1	149	.242
—Detroit (A.L.)		0	0	...	1.50	1.00	3	0	0	0	0	0-0	6.0	6	1	1	1	1-0	2	.250
American League totals (7 years)		16	29	.356	6.06	1.60	71	56	3	0	0	0-0	328.0	393	244	221	56	133-4	189	.298
National League totals (1 year)		1	1	.500	8.68	2.14	7	0	0	0	0	0-0	9.1	9	10	9	1	11-0	10	.237
Major League totals (7 years)		17	30	.362	6.14	1.62	78	56	3	0	0	0-0	337.1	402	254	230	57	144-4	199	.296

2006 LEFTY-RIGHTY SPLITS

vs.	Avg.	AB	H	2B	3B	HR	RBI	BB	SO	OBP	Slg.	vs.	Avg.	AB	H	2B	3B	HR	RBI	BB	SO	OBP	Slg.
L	.286	7	2	0	0	0	0	0	1	.286	.286	R	.235	17	4	1	0	1	2	0	2	.235	.471

D

DURHAM, RAY — 2B

PERSONAL: Born November 30, 1971, in Charlotte, N.C. ... 5-8/196. ... Bats both, throws right. ... High school: Harding (Charlotte). **TRANSACTIONS/CAREER NOTES:** Selected by Chicago White Sox organization in fifth round of 1990 free-agent draft. ... Traded by White Sox to Oakland Athletics for P Jon Adkins (July 25, 2002). ... Signed as a free agent by San Francisco Giants (December 7, 2002). ... On disabled list (May 11-26 and August 7-September 1, 2003). ... On disabled list (April 28-May 13 and May 23-June 15, 2004); included rehabilitation assignments to Fresno and San Jose. ... On disabled list (April 28-May 12, 2006). **STATISTICAL NOTES:** Career major league grand slams: 4.

2006 GAMES PLAYED BY POSITION (MLB): 2B—133.

									BATTING										FIELDING	
Year Team (League)	Pos.	G	AB	R	H	2B	3B	HR	RBI	BB	SO	HBP	GDP	SB-CS	Avg.	OBP	SLG	OPS	E	Avg.
1990—GC Whi. Sox (GCL)	2B-SS	35	116	18	32	3	3	0	13	15	36	4	0	23-9	.276	.375	.353	.728	15	.907
1991—Utica (N.Y.-Penn)	2B	39	142	29	36	2	7	0	17	25	44	2	0	12-1	.254	.371	.366	.737	12	.928
—GC Whi. Sox (GCL)	2B	6	23	3	7	1	0	0	4	3	5	0	0	5-1	.304	.385	.348	.732	0	1.000
1992—Sarasota (Fla. St.)	2B	57	202	37	55	6	3	0	7	32	36	10	2	28-8	.272	.398	.332	.729	10	.945
—GC Whi. Sox (GCL)	2B	5	13	3	7	2	0	0	2	3	1	0	1	1-0	.538	.625	.692	1.317	0	1.000
1993—Birmingham (Sou.)	2B	137	528	83	143	22	10	3	37	42	100	14	5	39-25	.271	.338	.367	.705	30	.945
1994—Nashville (A.A.)	2B	133	527	89	156	33	4	16	66	46	91	12	5	34-11	.296	.363	.495	.859	19	.973
1995—Chicago (A.L.)	2B-DH	125	471	68	121	27	6	7	51	31	83	6	8	18-5	.257	.309	.384	.693	15	.973
1996—Chicago (A.L.)	2B-DH	156	557	79	153	33	5	10	65	58	95	10	6	30-4	.275	.350	.406	.755	11	.984
1997—Chicago (A.L.)	2B-DH	155	634	106	172	27	5	11	53	61	96	6	14	33-16	.271	.337	.382	.719	* 18	.974
1998—Chicago (A.L.)	2B	158	635	126	181	35	8	19	67	73	105	6	3	36-9	.285	.363	.455	.818	18	.976
1999—Chicago (A.L.)	2B-DH	153	612	109	181	30	8	13	60	73	105	4	9	34-11	.296	.373	.435	.808	19	.974
2000—Chicago (A.L.)	2B	151	614	121	172	35	9	17	75	75	105	7	13	25-13	.280	.361	.450	.810	15	.980
2001—Chicago (A.L.)	2B-DH	152	611	104	163	42	10	20	65	64	110	4	10	23-10	.267	.337	.466	.804	10	.986
2002—Chicago (A.L.)	2B	96	345	71	103	20	2	9	48	49	59	5	13	20-5	.299	.390	.446	.836	15	.968
—Oakland (A.L.)	DH-2B	54	219	43	60	14	4	6	22	24	34	2	2	6-2	.274	.350	.457	.806	2	.967
2003—San Francisco (N.L.)	2B	110	410	61	117	30	5	8	33	50	82	3	4	7-7	.285	.366	.441	.807	5	.990
2004—San Jose (Calif.)	2B	1	3	0	1	0	0	0	0	0	0	0	0	0-0	.333	.333	.333	.667	0	1.000
—Fresno (PCL)	2B	5	14	4	8	0	1	1	5	2	2	1	0	0-1	.571	.647	.929	1.576	2	.944
—San Francisco (N.L.)	2B	120	471	95	133	28	8	17	65	57	60	6	6	10-4	.282	.364	.484	.848	16	.972
2005—San Francisco (N.L.)	2B-OF	142	497	67	144	33	0	12	62	48	59	7	19	6-3	.290	.356	.429	.785	11	.982
2006—San Francisco (N.L.)	2B	137	498	79	146	30	7	26	93	51	61	2	17	7-2	.293	.360	.538	.898	11	.982
American League totals (8 years)		1200	4698	827	1306	263	57	112	506	508	792	50	80	225-75	.278	.352	.430	.782	123	.977
National League totals (4 years)		509	1876	302	540	121	20	63	253	206	262	18	46	30-16	.288	.361	.474	.836	43	.981
Major League totals (12 years)		1709	6574	1129	1846	384	77	175	759	714	1054	68	126	255-91	.281	.354	.443	.797	166	.978

DIVISION SERIES RECORD

									BATTING											
Year Team (League)	Pos.	G	AB	R	H	2B	3B	HR	RBI	BB	SO	HBP	GDP	SB-CS	Avg.	OBP	SLG	OPS	E	Avg.
2000—Chicago (A.L.)	2B	3	10	2	2	1	0	1	3	3	0	0	2	0-0	.200	.385	.600	.985	0	1.000
2002—Oakland (A.L.)	DH	5	21	7	7	3	0	2	2	2	4	1	0	0-0	.333	.417	.762	1.179	0	...
2003—San Francisco (N.L.)	2B	4	17	2	4	0	0	0	1	1	5	1	0	1-0	.235	.316	.235	.551	0	1.000
Division series totals (3 years)		12	48	11	13	4	0	3	6	12	2	1	2	1-0	.271	.375	.542	.917	0	1.000

ALL-STAR GAME RECORD

								BATTING										
	G	AB	R	H	2B	3B	HR	RBI	BB	SO	HBP	GDP	SB-CS	Avg.	OBP	SLG	OPS	E	Avg.
All-Star Game totals (2 years)	2	3	2	2	0	0	1	0	0	0	0	.667	.667	.667	1.333	0	1.000

2006 LEFTY-RIGHTY SPLITS

vs.	Avg.	AB	H	2B	3B	HR	RBI	BB	SO	OBP	Slg.	vs.	Avg.	AB	H	2B	3B	HR	RBI	BB	SO	OBP	Slg.
L	.341	123	42	9	1	9	21	15	11	.413	.650	R	.277	375	104	21	6	17	72	36	50	.342	.501

DYE, JERMAINE — OF

PERSONAL: Born January 28, 1974, in Vacaville, Calif. ... 6-5/220. ... Bats right, throws right. ... Full name: Jermaine Terrell Dye. ... Name pronounced: ger-MAIN. ... High school: Will C. Wood (Vacaville, Calif.). ... Junior college: Cosumnes River (Calif.). **TRANSACTIONS/CAREER NOTES:** Selected by Atlanta Braves organization in 17th round of 1993 free-agent draft. ... Traded by Braves with P Jamie Walker to Kansas City Royals for OF Michael Tucker and IF Keith Lockhart (March 27, 1997). ... On disabled list (April 17-May 3 and July 10-August 13, 1997); included rehabilitation assignments to Omaha. ... On disabled list (March 23-May 8 and September 1, 1998-remainder of season); included rehabilitation assignment to Omaha. ... Traded by Royals to Colorado Rockies for SS Neifi Perez (July 25, 2001). ... Traded by Rockies to Oakland Athletics for OF Mario Encarnacion, 2B/SS Jose Ortiz and P Todd Belitz (July 25, 2001). ... On disabled list (March 22-April 26, 2002); included rehabilitation assignments to Sacramento and Modesto. ... On disabled list (April 25-May 30 and July 7-September 1, 2003); included rehabilitation assignments to Sacramento. ... Signed as a free agent by Chicago White Sox (December 9, 2004). **HONORS:** Won A.L. Gold Glove as outfielder (2000). ... Named outfielder on SPORTING NEWS A.L. All-Star team (2006). ... Named outfielder on A.L. Silver Slugger team (2006). **STATISTICAL NOTES:** Hit home run in first major league at-bat (May 17, 1996). ... Career major league grand slams: 5.

2006 GAMES PLAYED BY POSITION (MLB): OF—146.

									BATTING										FIELDING	
Year Team (League)	Pos.	G	AB	R	H	2B	3B	HR	RBI	BB	SO	HBP	GDP	SB-CS	Avg.	OBP	SLG	OPS	E	Avg.
1993—GC Braves (GCL)	3B-OF	31	124	17	43	14	0	0	27	5	13	5	5	5-0	.347	.393	.460	.852	3	.948
—Danville (Appal.)	OF	25	94	6	26	6	1	2	12	8	10	0	2	19-1	.277	.327	.426	.752	2	.963
1994—Macon (S. Atl.)	OF	135	506	73	151	41	1	15	98	33	82	8	10	19-10	.298	.346	.472	.818	9	.969
1995—Greenville (Sou.)	OF	104	403	50	115	26	4	15	71	27	74	1	9	4-8	.285	.329	.481	.810	5	.981
1996—Richmond (Int'l)	OF	36	142	25	33	7	1	6	19	5	25	1	3	3-0	.232	.264	.423	.686	4	.955
—Atlanta (N.L.)	OF	98	292	32	82	16	0	12	37	8	67	3	11	1-4	.281	.304	.459	.763	8	.950
1997—Kansas City (A.L.)	OF	75	263	26	62	14	0	7	22	17	51	1	6	2-1	.236	.284	.369	.653	6	.966
—Omaha (A.A.)	OF-DH	39	144	21	44	6	0	10	25	9	25	1	3	0-2	.306	.348	.556	.904	0	1.000
1998—Omaha (PCL)	OF-1B-DH	41	157	29	47	6	0	12	35	19	29	1	8	7-0	.299	.374	.567	.941	1	.992
—Kansas City (A.L.)	OF	60	214	24	50	5	1	5	23	11	46	1	4	2-2	.234	.270	.336	.606	2	.987
1999—Kansas City (A.L.)	OF-DH	158	608	96	179	44	8	27	119	58	119	1	17	2-3	.294	.354	.526	.880	6	.984
2000—Kansas City (A.L.)	OF-DH	157	601	107	193	41	2	33	118	69	99	3	12	0-1	.321	.390	.561	.951	7	.976
2001—Kansas City (A.L.)	OF-DH	97	367	50	100	14	0	13	47	30	68	6	2	7-1	.272	.333	.417	.749	3	.984
—Oakland (A.L.)	OF	61	232	41	69	17	1	13	59	27	44	1	6	2-0	.297	.366	.547	.913	3	.971
2002—Sacramento (PCL)	DH	4	16	3	3	2	0	0	2	2	0	0	1	0-0	.188	.278	.313	.590	...	...
—Modesto (California)	OF	2	8	1	4	3	0	0	2	0	0	0	0	0-0	.500	.500	.875	1.375	0	1.000
—Oakland (A.L.)	OF-DH	131	488	74	123	27	1	24	86	52	108	10	15	2-0	.252	.333	.459	.792	5	.972
2003—Sacramento (PCL)	DH-OF	13	49	9	14	2	0	2	9	11	11	0	1	0-0	.286	.417	.449	.866	0	1.000
—Oakland (A.L.)	OF	65	221	28	38	6	0	4	20	25	42	3	11	1-0	.172	.261	.253	.514	0	1.000
2004—Oakland (A.L.)	OF-DH	137	532	87	141	29	4	23	80	49	128	4	16	4-2	.265	.329	.464	.793	2	.992
2005—Chicago (A.L.)	OF-1B-SS DH	145	529	74	145	29	4	31	86	39	99	9	15	11-4	.274	.333	.512	.846	8	.972

D

Year Team (League)	Pos.	G	AB	R	H	2B	3B	HR	RBI	BB	SO	HBP	GDP	SB-CS	Avg.	OBP	SLG	OPS	E	Avg.
2006— Chicago (A.L.)	OF	146	539	103	170	27	3	44	120	59	118	6	15	7-3	.315	.385	.622	1.006	6	.981
American League totals (10 years)		1232	4594	710	1270	253	22	224	780	436	922	45	123	40-17	.276	.342	.487	.829	48	.980
National League totals (1 year)		98	292	32	82	16	0	12	37	8	67	3	11	1-4	.281	.304	.459	.763	8	.950
Major League totals (11 years)		1330	4886	742	1352	269	22	236	817	444	989	48	134	41-21	.277	.339	.486	.825	56	.979

DIVISION SERIES RECORD

Year Team (League)	Pos.	G	AB	R	H	2B	3B	HR	RBI	BB	SO	HBP	GDP	SB-CS	Avg.	OBP	SLG	OPS	E	Avg.
1996— Atlanta (N.L.)	OF	3	11	1	2	0	0	1	1	0	6	0	0	1-0	.182	.182	.455	.636	0	1.000
2001— Oakland (A.L.)	OF	4	13	0	3	2	0	0	0	2	2	0	0	0-0	.231	.333	.385	.718	0	1.000
2002— Oakland (A.L.)	OF	5	20	3	8	2	0	1	1	5	0	0	0	0-0	.400	.480	.650	1.079	0	1.000
2003— Oakland (A.L.)	OF	4	13	2	3	0	0	1	3	0	2	1	0	0-0	.231	.286	.462	.747	0	1.000
2005— Chicago (A.L.)	OF	3	10	1	2	0	0	0	0	1	1	0	0	0-0	.200	.333	.200	.533	0	1.000
Division series totals (5 years)		19	67	7	18	4	0	3	5	4	17	2	0	1-0	.269	.329	.463	.791	0	1.000

CHAMPIONSHIP SERIES RECORD

Year Team (League)	Pos.	G	AB	R	H	2B	3B	HR	RBI	BB	SO	HBP	GDP	SB-CS	Avg.	OBP	SLG	OPS	E	Avg.
1996— Atlanta (N.L.)	OF	7	28	2	6	1	0	0	4	1	7	0	0	0-1	.214	.226	.250	.476	0	1.000
2005— Chicago (A.L.)	OF	5	19	3	5	2	0	0	3	3	3	0	0	1-0	.263	.364	.368	.732	0	1.000
Champ. series totals (2 years)		12	47	5	11	3	0	0	7	4	10	0	0	1-1	.234	.283	.298	.581	0	1.000

WORLD SERIES RECORD

Year Team (League)	Pos.	G	AB	R	H	2B	3B	HR	RBI	BB	SO	HBP	GDP	SB-CS	Avg.	OBP	SLG	OPS	E	Avg.
1996— Atlanta (N.L.)	OF	5	17	0	2	0	0	0	1	1	1	0	0	0-0	.118	.167	.118	.284	1	.938
2005— Chicago (A.L.)	OF	4	16	3	7	1	0	1	3	2	1	1	1	0-0	.438	.526	.688	1.214	0	1.000
World series totals (2 years)		9	33	3	9	1	0	1	4	3	1	1	1	0-0	.273	.351	.394	.745	1	.955

ALL-STAR GAME RECORD

	G	AB	R	H	2B	3B	HR	RBI	BB	SO	HBP	GDP	SB-CS	Avg.	OBP	SLG	OPS	E	Avg.
All-Star Game totals (2 years)	2	3	1	0	0	0	0	0	1	1	0	0	0-0	.000	.250	.000	.250	0	1.000

2006 LEFTY-RIGHTY SPLITS

vs.	Avg.	AB	H	2B	3B	HR	RBI	BB	SO	OBP	Slg.	vs.	Avg.	AB	H	2B	3B	HR	RBI	BB	SO	OBP	Slg.
L	.337	172	58	8	0	15	35	29	35	.429	.645	R	.305	367	112	19	3	29	85	30	83	.362	.610

EASLEY, DAMION — SS/3B

PERSONAL: Born November 11, 1969, in New York. ... 5-11/190. ... Bats right, throws right. ... Full name: Jacinto Damion Easley. ... High school: Lakewood (Calif.). ... Junior college: Long Beach (Calif.) City College. **TRANSACTIONS/CAREER NOTES:** Selected by California Angels organization in 30th round of 1988 free-agent draft. ... On disabled list (June 19-July 4 and July 28, 1993-remainder of season; and May 30-June 17, 1994). ... On disabled list (April 1-May 10, 1996); included rehabilitation assignment to Vancouver. ... Traded by Angels to Detroit Tigers for P Greg Gohr (July 31, 1996). ... On disabled list (April 10-25 and May 9-June 2, 2000); included rehabilitation assignments to Toledo. ... On disabled list (April 17-June 1, 2002) included rehabilitation assignment to Toledo. ... Released by Tigers (March 28, 2003). ... Signed by Tampa Bay Devil Rays (April 2, 2003). ... Released by Devil Rays (June 4, 2003). ... Signed by Florida Marlins organization (January 8, 2004). ... Signed as a free agent by Arizona Diamondbacks (December 12, 2005). **RECORDS:** Shares major league record for most times hit by pitch, game (3, May 31, 1999; and July 16, 2002). **HONORS:** Named second baseman on A.L. Silver Slugger team (1998). **STATISTICAL NOTES:** Hit three home runs in one game (June 3, 2006). ... Hit for the cycle (June 8, 2001). ... Career major league grand slams: 1.

2006 GAMES PLAYED BY POSITION (MLB): SS—27, 3B—20, 2B—9, 1B—3, DH—1, OF—1.

Year Team (League)	Pos.	G	AB	R	H	2B	3B	HR	RBI	BB	SO	HBP	GDP	SB-CS	Avg.	OBP	SLG	OPS	E	Avg.
1989— Bend (N'west)	2B	36	131	34	39	5	1	4	21	25	21	4	1	9-4	.298	.425	.443	.868	22	.863
1990— Quad City (Midw.)	SS	103	365	59	100	19	3	10	56	41	60	8	8	25-8	.274	.358	.425	.783	41	.893
1991— Midland (Texas)	SS	127	452	73	115	24	5	6	57	58	67	7	12	23-9	.254	.347	.369	.716	47	.924
1992— Edmonton (PCL)	SS-3B	108	429	61	124	18	3	3	44	31	44	5	13	26-10	.289	.340	.366	.706	30	.943
— California (A.L.)	3B-SS	47	151	14	39	5	0	1	12	8	26	3	2	9-5	.258	.307	.311	.618	5	.964
1993— California (A.L.)	2B-3B-DH	73	230	33	72	13	2	2	22	28	35	3	5	6-6	.313	.392	.413	.805	6	.978
1994— California (A.L.)	3B-2B	88	316	41	68	16	1	6	30	29	48	4	8	4-5	.215	.288	.329	.617	7	.977
1995— California (A.L.)	2B-SS	114	357	35	77	14	2	4	35	32	47	6	11	5-2	.216	.288	.300	.588	10	.979
1996— Vancouver (PCL)	SS-2B-3B	12	48	13	15	2	1	2	8	9	6	1	0	4-1	.313	.424	.521	.945	2	.958
— Midland (Texas)	3B-SS	4	14	1	6	2	0	0	2	0	0	0	0	1-0	.429	.429	.571	1.000	1	.944
— California (A.L.)	SS-2B-3B DH-OF	28	45	4	7	1	0	2	7	6	12	0	0	0-0	.156	.255	.311	.566	3	.954
— Detroit (A.L.)	2B-SS-3B DH	21	67	10	23	1	0	2	10	4	13	1	0	3-1	.343	.384	.448	.831	3	.958
1997— Detroit (A.L.)	2B-SS-DH	151	527	97	139	37	3	22	72	68	102	16	18	28-13	.264	.362	.471	.833	12	.982
1998— Detroit (A.L.)	2B-SS-DH	153	594	84	161	38	2	27	100	39	112	16	8	15-5	.271	.332	.478	.810	12	.985
1999— Detroit (A.L.)	2B-SS	151	549	83	146	30	1	20	65	51	124	19	15	11-3	.266	.346	.434	.779	8	.990
2000— Detroit (A.L.)	2B	126	464	76	120	27	2	14	58	55	79	11	11	13-4	.259	.350	.416	.766	6	.990
— Toledo (Int'l)	2B	4	13	3	3	1	0	1	4	4	2	2	0	0-0	.231	.474	.538	1.012	0	1.000
2001— Detroit (A.L.)	2B	154	585	77	146	29	1	11	65	52	90	10	10	10-5	.250	.323	.376	.699	14	.982
2002— Detroit (A.L.)	2B-DH	85	304	29	68	14	1	8	30	27	43	11	4	1-3	.224	.307	.355	.663	9	.980
— Toledo (Int'l)	2B	8	26	5	3	1	0	0	1	5	0	1	1	0-2	.115	.281	.154	.435	2	.949
2003— Tampa Bay (A.L.)	3B-DH-2B	36	107	8	20	3	1	2	18	10	19	0	3	0-0	.187	.202	.262	.464	4	.935
2004— Florida (N.L.)	2B-1B-SS 3B-OF-DH	98	223	26	53	20	1	9	43	24	36	8	6	4-1	.238	.331	.457	.788	7	.974
2005— Florida (N.L.)	2B-SS-3B	102	267	37	64	19	1	9	30	26	47	4	6	4-1	.240	.312	.419	.732	9	.973
2006— Arizona (N.L.)	SS-3B-2B 1B-OF-DH	90	189	24	44	6	1	9	28	21	30	5	4	1-1	.233	.323	.418	.741	5	.967
American League totals (12 years)		1227	4296	591	1086	226	22	120	513	401	749	103	95	105-52	.253	.329	.399	.729	99	.982
National League totals (3 years)		290	679	87	161	45	3	27	101	71	113	17	16	9-3	.237	.321	.432	.753	21	.972
Major League totals (15 years)		1517	4975	678	1247	271	25	147	614	472	862	120	111	114-55	.251	.328	.404	.732	120	.981

ALL-STAR GAME RECORD

	G	AB	R	H	2B	3B	HR	RBI	BB	SO	HBP	GDP	SB-CS	Avg.	OBP	SLG	OPS	E	Avg.
All-Star Game totals (1 year)	1	1	1	1	0	0	0	0	0	0	0	0	0-0	1.000	1.000	1.000	2.000	0	...

2006 LEFTY-RIGHTY SPLITS

vs.	Avg.	AB	H	2B	3B	HR	RBI	BB	SO	OBP	Slg.	vs.	Avg.	AB	H	2B	3B	HR	RBI	BB	SO	OBP	Slg.
L	.245	106	26	5	1	4	13	13	17	.339	.425	R	.217	83	18	1	0	5	15	8	13	.301	.410

E

EATON, ADAM — P

PERSONAL: Born November 23, 1977, in Seattle. ... 6-2/196. ... Throws right, bats right. ... Full name: Adam Thomas Eaton. ... High school: Snohomish (Wash.). **TRANSACTIONS/CAREER NOTES:** Selected by Philadelphia Phillies organization in first round (11th pick overall) of 1996 free-agent draft. ... Traded by Phillies with Ps Carlton Loewer and Steve Montgomery to San Diego Padres for P Andy Ashby (November 10, 1999). ... On disabled list (July 6, 2001-remainder of season). ... On disabled list (March 27-September 1, 2002); included rehabilitation assignments to Lake Elsinore and Portland. ... On disabled list (May 5-20, 2003). ... On disabled list (June 22-August 1 and August 5-26, 2005); included rehabilitation assignments to Lake Elsinore and Portland. ... Traded by Padres with P Akinori Otsuka and C Billy Killian to Texas Rangers for 1B Adrian Gonzalez, OF Termel Sledge and P Chris Young (January 4, 2006). ... On disabled list (April 1-July 25, 2006); included rehabilitation assignments to Oklahoma and Frisco.
MISCELLANEOUS NOTES: Appeared in one game as pinch runner (2000). ... Made an out in only appearance as pinch hitter and appeared in five games as pinch runner (2001). ... Singled, doubled, had a sacrifice hit and struck out three times in six appearances as pinch hitter and appeared in two games as pinch runner (2003). ... Recorded one RBI, received a base on balls, had two sacrifice hits and struck out once in five appearances as pinch hitter (2004). ... Singled in both appearances as pinch hitter (2005).
CAREER HITTING: 48-for-251 (.191), 24 R, 13 2B, 1 3B, 2 HR, 19 RBI.

Year — Team (League)	W	L	Pct.	ERA	WHIP	G	GS	CG	ShO	Hld.	Sv.-Opp.	IP	H	R	ER	HR	BB-IBB	SO	Avg.
1997— Piedmont (S. Atl.)	5	6	.455	4.16	1.56	14	14	0	0	...	0-...	71.1	81	38	33	2	30-0	57	.287
1998— Clearwater (FSL)	9	8	.529	4.44	1.51	24	23	1	0	...	0-...	131.2	152	68	65	9	47-1	89	.293
1999— Clearwater (FSL)	5	5	.500	3.91	1.52	13	13	0	0	...	0-...	69.0	81	39	30	2	24-0	50	.293
— Reading (East.)	5	4	.556	2.92	1.14	12	12	2	0	...	0-...	77.0	60	30	25	9	28-1	67	.214
— Scran./W.B. (I.L.)	1	1	.500	3.00	1.10	3	3	0	0	...	0-...	21.0	17	10	7	1	6-0	10	.224
2000— Mobile (Sou.)	4	1	.800	2.68	1.14	10	10	1	1	..	0-...	57.0	47	20	17	3	18-0	58	.219
— San Diego (N.L.)	7	4	.636	4.13	1.44	22	22	0	0	0	0-0	135.0	134	63	62	14	61-3	90	.260
2001— San Diego (N.L.)	8	5	.615	4.32	1.27	17	17	2	0	0	0-0	116.2	108	61	56	20	40-3	109	.241
2002— Lake Elsinore (Calif.)	0	0	...	2.70	0.98	3	3	0	0	0	0-...	13.1	10	7	4	0	3-0	19	.204
— Portland (PCL)	1	1	.500	2.92	0.97	2	2	0	0	0	0-...	12.1	9	9	4	3	3-0	6	.200
— San Diego (N.L.)	1	1	.500	5.40	1.35	6	6	0	0	0	0-0	33.1	28	20	20	5	17-0	25	.235
2003— San Diego (N.L.)	9	12	.429	4.08	1.32	31	31	1	0	0	0-0	183.0	173	91	83	20	68-6	146	.251
2004— San Diego (N.L.)	11	14	.440	4.61	1.28	33	33	0	0	0	0-0	199.1	204	113	102	28	52-3	153	.266
2005— Lake Elsinore (Calif.)	0	0	...	0.00	1.00	1	1	0	0	0	0-0	3.0	1	0	0	0	0-0	2	.111
— Portland (PCL)	0	0	...	5.63	1.50	2	2	0	0	0	0-0	8.0	11	5	5	3	2-0	4	.344
— San Diego (N.L.)	11	5	.688	4.27	1.43	24	22	0	0	0	0-0	128.2	140	70	61	14	44-6	100	.275
2006— Frisco (Texas)	0	0	...	1.42	1.26	2	2	0	0	0	0-0	6.1	7	1	1	0	1-0	5	.269
— Oklahoma (PCL)	0	0	...	1.50	0.83	2	2	0	0	0	0-0	6.0	3	1	1	0	2-0	8	.136
— Texas (A.L.)	7	4	.636	5.12	1.57	13	13	0	0	0	0-0	65.0	78	38	37	11	24-0	43	.299
American League totals (1 year)	7	4	.636	5.12	1.57	13	13	0	0	0	0-0	65.0	78	38	37	11	24-0	43	.299
National League totals (6 years)	47	41	.534	4.34	1.34	133	131	3	0	0	0-0	796.0	787	418	384	101	282-21	623	.257
Major League totals (7 years)	54	45	.545	4.40	1.36	146	144	3	0	0	0-0	861.0	865	456	421	112	306-21	666	.260

2006 LEFTY-RIGHTY SPLITS

vs.	Avg.	AB	H	2B	3B	HR	RBI	BB	SO	OBP	Slg.	vs.	Avg.	AB	H	2B	3B	HR	RBI	BB	SO	OBP	Slg.
L	.320	125	40	8	1	8	19	13	19	.393	.592	R	.279	136	38	5	0	3	18	11	24	.340	.382

ECKSTEIN, DAVID — SS

E

PERSONAL: Born January 20, 1975, in Sanford, Fla. ... 5-7/165. ... Bats right, throws right. ... Full name: David Mark Eckstein. ... Name pronounced: ECK-styne. ... High school: Seminole (Sanford, Fla.). ... College: Florida. **TRANSACTIONS/CAREER NOTES:** Selected by Boston Red Sox organization in 19th round of 1997 free-agent draft. ... Claimed on waivers by Anaheim Angels (August 16, 2000). ... On disabled list (August 18-September 9, 2003). ... Signed as a free agent by St. Louis Cardinals (December 23, 2004). ... On disabled list (August 19-September 15, 2006). **STATISTICAL NOTES:** Career major league grand slams: 4.
2006 GAMES PLAYED BY POSITION (MLB): SS—120.

Year — Team (League)	Pos.	G	AB	R	H	2B	3B	HR	RBI	BB	SO	HBP	GDP	SB-CS	Avg.	OBP	SLG	OPS	E	Avg.
1997— Lowell (NY-Penn)	2B	68	249	43	75	11	4	4	39	33	29	12	2	21-5	.301	.407	.426	.832	9	.971
1998— Sarasota (Fla. St.)	2B-SS	135	503	99	154	29	4	3	58	87	51	22	8	45-16	.306	.428	.398	.826	8	.986
1999— Trenton (East.)	2B	131	483	109	151	22	5	6	52	89	48	25	6	32-13	.313	.440	.416	.856	9	.985
2000— Pawtucket (Int'l)	2B-SS	119	422	77	104	20	0	1	31	60	45	20	8	11-8	.246	.364	.301	.665	4	.992
— Edmonton (PCL)	2B	15	52	17	18	8	0	3	9	9	1	5	0	5-3	.346	.485	.673	1.158	0	1.000
2001— Anaheim (A.L.)	SS-2B-DH	153	582	82	166	26	2	4	41	43	60	* 21	11	29-4	.285	.355	.357	.712	18	.969
2002— Anaheim (A.L.)	SS-DH	152	608	107	178	22	6	8	63	45	44	* 27	7	21-13	.293	.363	.388	.752	14	.977
2003— Anaheim (A.L.)	SS-DH	120	452	59	114	22	1	3	31	36	45	15	9	16-5	.252	.325	.325	.651	8	.984
2004— Anaheim (A.L.)	SS-DH	142	566	92	156	24	1	2	35	42	49	13	11	16-5	.276	.339	.332	.671	6	.988
2005— St. Louis (N.L.)	SS	158	630	90	185	26	7	8	61	58	44	13	13	11-8	.294	.363	.395	.758	15	.981
2006— St. Louis (N.L.)	SS	123	500	68	146	18	1	2	23	31	41	15	7	7-6	.292	.350	.344	.694	6	.989
American League totals (4 years)		567	2208	340	614	94	10	17	170	166	198	76	38	82-27	.278	.347	.353	.700	46	.979
National League totals (2 years)		281	1130	158	331	44	8	10	84	89	85	28	20	18-14	.293	.357	.373	.730	21	.984
Major League totals (6 years)		848	3338	498	945	138	18	27	254	255	283	104	58	100-41	.283	.351	.359	.710	67	.981

DIVISION SERIES RECORD

Year — Team (League)	Pos.	G	AB	R	H	2B	3B	HR	RBI	BB	SO	HBP	GDP	SB-CS	Avg.	OBP	SLG	OPS	E	Avg.
2002— Anaheim (A.L.)	SS	4	18	2	5	0	0	0	1	0	0	1	0	1-0	.278	.316	.278	.594	0	1.000
2004— Anaheim (A.L.)	SS	3	12	2	4	0	0	0	0	0	1	0	0	0-0	.333	.333	.333	.667	1	.917
2005— St. Louis (N.L.)	SS	3	13	3	5	0	0	1	4	1	1.	0	0	0-0	.385	.429	.615	1.044	1	.895
2006— St. Louis (N.L.)	SS	4	15	1	2	0	0	0	1	1	0	1	2	1-0	.133	.188	.133	.321	1	1.000
Division series totals (4 years)		14	58	8	16	0	0	1	6	1	2	2	2	2-0	.276	.311	.328	.639	3	.952

CHAMPIONSHIP SERIES RECORD

Year — Team (League)	Pos.	G	AB	R	H	2B	3B	HR	RBI	BB	SO	HBP	GDP	SB-CS	Avg.	OBP	SLG	OPS	E	Avg.
2002— Anaheim (A.L.)	SS	5	21	1	6	0	0	0	2	0	2	1	0	0-0	.286	.318	.286	.604	1	.944
2005— St. Louis (N.L.)	SS	6	20	5	4	0	0	0	2	3	2	2	0	1-1	.200	.346	.200	.546	1	.964
2006— St. Louis (N.L.)	SS	7	26	3	6	1	0	1	1	4	2	0	0	3-0	.231	.375	.385	.760	1	1.000
Champ. series totals (3 years)		18	67	9	16	1	0	1	5	7	4	5	0	4-1	.239	.350	.299	.649	2	.977

WORLD SERIES RECORD

Year — Team (League)	Pos.	G	AB	R	H	2B	3B	HR	RBI	BB	SO	HBP	GDP	SB-CS	Avg.	OBP	SLG	OPS	E	Avg.
2002— Anaheim (A.L.)	SS	7	29	6	9	0	0	0	3	2	0	0	0	1-0	.310	.364	.310	.674	0	1.000
2006— St. Louis (N.L.)	SS	5	22	3	8	3	0	0	4	1	1	0	1	0-0	.364	.391	.500	.891	0	1.000
World series totals (2 years)		12	51	9	17	3	0	0	7	3	1	0	1	1-0	.333	.375	.392	.767	0	1.000

ALL-STAR GAME RECORD

	G	AB	R	H	2B	3B	HR	RBI	BB	SO	HBP	GDP	SB-CS	Avg.	OBP	SLG	OPS	E	Avg.
All-Star Game totals (2 years)	2	3	0	0	0	0	0	0	1	0	0	0	0-0	.000	.000	.000	.000	0	1.000

2006 LEFTY-RIGHTY SPLITS

vs.	Avg.	AB	H	2B	3B	HR	RBI	BB	SO	OBP	Slg.	vs.	Avg.	AB	H	2B	3B	HR	RBI	BB	SO	OBP	Slg.
L	.280	161	45	5	.1	0	12	12	12	.352	.323	R	.298	339	101	13	0	2	11	19	29	.349	.354

EDMONDS, JIM — OF

PERSONAL: Born June 27, 1970, in Fullerton, Calif. ... 6-1/212. ... Bats left, throws left. ... Full name: James Patrick Edmonds. ... Name pronounced: ED-munds. ... High school: Diamond Bar (Calif.). **TRANSACTIONS/CAREER NOTES:** Selected by California Angels organization in seventh round of 1988 free-agent draft. ... On disabled list (May 26-June 10 and June 12-July 18, 1996); included rehabilitation assignment to Lake Elsinore. ... Angels franchise renamed Anaheim Angels for 1997 season. ... On disabled list (August 1-16, 1997). ... On disabled list (March 30-August 2, 1999); included rehabilitation assignment to Lake Elsinore. ... Traded by Angels to St. Louis Cardinals for 2B Adam Kennedy and P Kent Bottenfield (March 23, 2000). ... On disabled list (June 1-16, 2002). **HONORS:** Named outfielder on THE SPORTING NEWS A.L. All-Star team (1995). ... Named outfielder on THE SPORTING NEWS N.L. All-Star team (2004). ... Won A.L. Gold Glove as outfielder (1997-98). ... Won N.L. Gold Glove as outfielder (2000-05). ... Named outfielder on N.L. Silver Slugger team (2004). **STATISTICAL NOTES:** Career major league grand slams: 6.

2006 GAMES PLAYED BY POSITION (MLB): OF—99, 1B—6.

										BATTING									FIELDING	
Year Team (League)	Pos.	G	AB	R	H	2B	3B	HR	RBI	BB	SO	HBP	GDP	SB-CS	Avg.	OBP	SLG	OPS	E	Avg.
1988— Bend (N'west)	OF	35	122	23	27	4	0	0	13	20	44	0	2	4-0	.221	.329	.254	.583	1	.984
1989— Quad City (Midw.)	OF	31	92	11	24	4	0	1	4	7	34	0	3	1-0	.261	.313	.337	.650	3	.942
1990— Palm Springs (Calif.)	OF	91	314	36	92	18	6	3	56	27	75	2	10	5-2	.293	.351	.417	.768	10	.954
1991— Palm Springs (Calif.)	OF	60	187	28	55	15	1	2	27	40	57	0	2	2-2	.294	.417	.417	.834	0	1.000
1992— Midland (Texas)	OF	70	246	42	77	15	2	8	32	41	83	1	8	3-4	.313	.413	.488	.901	5	.967
—Edmonton (PCL)	OF	50	194	37	58	15	2	6	36	14	55	0	2	3-1	.299	.343	.490	.833	1	.988
1993— Vancouver (PCL)	OF	95	356	59	112	28	4	9	74	41	81	0	5	6-8	.315	.382	.492	.873	3	.983
—California (A.L.)	OF	18	61	5	15	4	1	0	4	2	16	0	1	0-2	.246	.270	.344	.614	1	.981
1994— California (A.L.)	OF-1B	94	289	35	79	13	1	5	37	30	72	1	3	4-2	.273	.343	.377	.720	3	.991
1995— California (A.L.)	OF	141	558	120	162	30	4	33	107	51	130	5	10	1-4	.290	.352	.536	.888	1	.998
1996— California (A.L.)	OF-DH	114	431	73	131	28	3	27	66	46	101	4	8	4-0	.304	.375	.571	.946	1	.997
—Lake Elsinore (Calif.)	OF	5	15	4	6	2	0	1	4	1	1	1	0	0-0	.400	.471	.733	1.204	0	1.000
1997— Anaheim (A.L.)	OF-1B-DH	133	502	82	146	27	0	26	80	60	80	4	5	5-7	.291	.368	.500	.868	5	.988
1998— Anaheim (A.L.)	OF	154	599	115	184	42	1	25	91	57	114	1	16	7-5	.307	.368	.506	.874	5	.988
1999— Lake Elsinore (Calif.)	DH	5	19	4	8	2	0	0	3	4	2	0	0	2-0	.421	.522	.526	1.048	0	...
—Anaheim (A.L.)	OF-DH-1B	55	204	34	51	17	2	5	23	28	45	0	3	5-4	.250	.339	.426	.766	1	.993
2000— St. Louis (N.L.)	OF-1B	152	525	129	155	25	0	42	108	103	167	6	5	10-3	.295	.411	.583	.994	4	.990
2001— St. Louis (N.L.)	OF-1B	150	500	95	152	38	1	30	110	93	136	4	8	5-5	.304	.410	.564	.974	6	.983
2002— St. Louis (N.L.)	OF	144	476	96	148	31	2	28	83	86	134	8	9	4-3	.311	.420	.561	.981	5	.986
2003— St. Louis (N.L.)	OF-DH	137	447	89	123	32	2	39	89	77	127	4	11	1-3	.275	.385	.617	1.002	5	.986
2004— St. Louis (N.L.)	OF-1B-DH	153	498	102	150	38	3	42	111	101	150	5	4	8-3	.301	.418	.643	1.061	4	.988
2005— St. Louis (N.L.)	OF	142	467	88	123	37	1	29	89	91	139	4	6	5-5	.263	.385	.533	.918	2	.994
2006— St. Louis (N.L.)	OF-1B	110	350	52	90	18	0	19	70	53	101	0	11	4-0	.257	.350	.471	.822	3	.989
American League totals (7 years)		709	2644	464	768	161	12	121	408	274	558	15	49	26-24	.290	.359	.498	.856	17	.992
National League totals (7 years)		988	3263	651	941	219	9	229	660	604	954	31	54	37-22	.288	.400	.572	.971	29	.988
Major League totals (14 years)		1697	5907	1115	1709	380	21	350	1068	878	1512	46	103	63-46	.289	.382	.539	.921	46	.990

DIVISION SERIES RECORD

										BATTING									FIELDING	
Year Team (League)	Pos.	G	AB	R	H	2B	3B	HR	RBI	BB	SO	HBP	GDP	SB-CS	Avg.	OBP	SLG	OPS	E	Avg.
2000— St. Louis (N.L.)	OF	3	14	5	8	4	0	2	7	1	2	0	0	1-0	.571	.600	1.286	1.886	0	1.000
2001— St. Louis (N.L.)	OF	5	17	3	4	1	0	2	3	3	6	0	0	0-0	.235	.350	.647	.997	0	1.000
2002— St. Louis (N.L.)	OF	3	11	1	3	0	0	1	2	2	4	0	0	0-1	.273	.385	.545	.930	0	1.000
2004— St. Louis (N.L.)	OF	4	15	1	4	0	0	1	2	1	9	0	0	0-1	.267	.313	.467	.779	0	1.000
2005— St. Louis (N.L.)	OF	3	11	5	4	2	0	1	1	2	2	0	0	0-0	.364	.462	.818	1.280	0	1.000
2006— St. Louis (N.L.)	OF	4	13	2	4	0	0	0	2	2	3	1	0	0-0	.308	.438	.308	.745	0	1.000
Division series totals (6 years)		22	81	17	27	7	0	7	17	11	26	1	0	1-2	.333	.419	.679	1.098	0	1.000

CHAMPIONSHIP SERIES RECORD

										BATTING									FIELDING	
Year Team (League)	Pos.	G	AB	R	H	2B	3B	HR	RBI	BB	SO	HBP	GDP	SB-CS	Avg.	OBP	SLG	OPS	E	Avg.
2000— St. Louis (N.L.)	OF	5	22	1	5	1	0	1	5	1	9	0	0	0-0	.227	.261	.409	.670	1	.933
2002— St. Louis (N.L.)	OF	5	20	2	8	2	0	1	4	2	5	0	0	0-0	.400	.455	.650	1.105	0	1.000
2004— St. Louis (N.L.)	OF	7	24	2	7	2	0	2	7	2	6	1	0	0-0	.292	.357	.625	.982	1	.952
2005— St. Louis (N.L.)	OF	6	19	2	4	0	0	0	0	5	5	0	1	1-0	.211	.375	.263	.638	1	.923
2006— St. Louis (N.L.)	OF	7	22	5	5	0	0	2	4	5	5	0	0	0-0	.227	.370	.500	.870	0	1.000
Champ. series totals (5 years)		30	107	12	29	6	0	6	20	15	30	1	1	1-0	.271	.363	.495	.858	3	.964

WORLD SERIES RECORD

										BATTING									FIELDING	
Year Team (League)	Pos.	G	AB	R	H	2B	3B	HR	RBI	BB	SO	HBP	GDP	SB-CS	Avg.	OBP	SLG	OPS	E	Avg.
2004— St. Louis (N.L.)	OF	4	15	2	1	0	0	0	0	1	6	0	0	0-0	.067	.125	.067	.192	0	1.000
2006— St. Louis (N.L.)	OF	5	17	1	4	2	0	0	4	3	8	0	0	0-0	.235	.350	.353	.703	0	1.000
World series totals (2 years)		9	32	3	5	2	0	0	4	4	14	0	0	0-0	.156	.250	.219	.469	0	1.000

ALL-STAR GAME RECORD

								BATTING									
Year Team (League)		G	AB	R	H	2B	3B	HR	RBI	BB	SO	HBP	GDP	SB-CS	Avg.	OBP	SLG	OPS	E	Avg.
All-Star Game totals (4 years)		4	6	0	2	0	0	0	0	1	2	0	0	0-0	.333	.429	.333	.762	0	1.000

2006 LEFTY-RIGHTY SPLITS

vs.	Avg.	AB	H	2B	3B	HR	RBI	BB	SO	OBP	Slg.	vs.	Avg.	AB	H	2B	3B	HR	RBI	BB	SO	OBP	Slg.
L	.156	96	15	3	0	3	12	6	32	.198	.281	R	.295	254	75	15	0	16	58	47	69	.404	.543

EDWARDS, MIKE — 3B/OF

PERSONAL: Born November 24, 1976, in Goshen, N.Y. ... 6-1/185. ... Bats right, throws right. ... Full name: Michael Donald Edwards. ... High school: Mechanicsburg, Pa. **TRANSACTIONS/CAREER NOTES:** Selected by Cleveland Indians organization in ninth round of 1995 free-agent draft. ... Signed as a free agent by Cincinnati Reds organization (November 8, 2001). ... Signed as a free agent by Oakland Athletics organization (November 8, 2002). ... Signed as a free agent by Los Angeles Dodgers organization (November 20, 2004). ... Signed as a free agent by Pittsburgh Pirates organization (December 30, 2005).

2006 GAMES PLAYED BY POSITION (MLB): 3B—3.

										BATTING									FIELDING	
Year Team (League)	Pos.	G	AB	R	H	2B	3B	HR	RBI	BB	SO	HBP	GDP	SB-CS	Avg.	OBP	SLG	OPS	E	Avg.
1995— Burlington (Appal.)	SS	43	130	20	22	2	0	0	5	17	35	2	2	5-2	.169	.275	.185	.460	18	.897
1996— Burlington (Appal.)	SS-3B	58	206	31	58	13	1	1	17	37	26	3	4	5-4	.282	.394	.369	.763	13	.901
1997— Burlington (Appal.) 3B-SS-1B OF		60	236	50	68	16	2	4	41	38	53	1	2	10-5	.288	.386	.424	.810	21	.903

E

Year Team (League)	Pos.	G	AB	R	H	2B	3B	HR	RBI	BB	SO	HBP	GDP	SB-CS	Avg.	OBP	SLG	OPS	E	Avg.
									BATTING										FIELDING	
1998— Columbus (S. Atl.)	3B-1B	124	497	82	146	34	4	8	81	66	95	3	13	16-6	.294	.379	.427	.806	31	.910
1999— Kinston (Carol.)	3B	133	456	76	132	25	4	16	89	93	117	9	12	8-3	.289	.413	.467	.880	28	.910
2000— Akron (East.)	3B-1B	136	481	72	142	25	2	11	63	68	86	5	9	7-3	.295	.386	.424	.810	20	.943
2001— Mahoning Valley (N.Y.-Penn.)	3B	20	71	19	26	5	0	6	24	12	7	1	0	0-1	.366	.464	.690	1.154	1	.960
— Akron (East.)	1B-3B	29	111	21	37	7	3	6	24	13	26	0	3	0-0	.333	.403	.613	1.016	4	.978
— Buffalo (Int'l)	1B	3	9	1	2	0	0	0	1	1	3	0	1	0-0	.222	.300	.222	.522	0	1.000
2002— Chattanooga (Sou.)	OF-1B-3B	119	424	57	130	19	2	11	60	41	57	10	19	9-11	.307	.377	.439	.816	10	.981
— Louisville (Int'l)	OF-1B-P	15	57	7	23	5	1	2	8	6	9	0	1	0-0	.404	.460	.632	1.092	1	.976
2003— Sacrámento (PCL)	OF-DH																			
	3B-SS	125	436	78	130	23	4	14	95	60	78	6	17	5-2	.298	.387	.466	.853	3	.984
— Oakland (A.L.)	DH-OF	4	4	0	1	0	0	0	0	2	1	0	0	0-0	.250	.500	.250	.750	0	...
2004— Sacramento (PCL)	OF-3B-SS	140	551	91	158	41	0	13	81	76	100	13	14	11-2	.287	.384	.432	.816	24	.657
2005— Las Vegas (PCL)	OF-1B-3B																			
	DH	32	118	18	33	6		4	21	11	21	3	4	3-1	.280	.353	.432	.786	1	.994
— Los Angeles (N.L.)	3B-OF-DH																			
	SS	88	239	23	59	9	2	3	15	16	34	2	6	1-1	.247	.300	.339	.639	7	.950
2006— Indianapolis (Int'l)		92	325	40	84	21	3	3	29	27	48	4	9	5-4	.258	.320	.369	.690	2	.990
— Pittsburgh (N.L.)	3B	14	16	1	3	0	0	0	0	1	5	0	1	0-0	.188	.235	.188	.423	0	1.000
American League totals (1 year)		4	4	0	1	0	0	0	0	2	1	0	0	0-0	.250	.500	.250	.750	0	...
National League totals (2 years)		102	255	24	62	9	2	3	15	17	39	2	7	1-1	.243	.296	.329	.625	7	.952
Major League totals (3 years)		106	259	24	63	9	2	3	15	19	40	2	7	1-1	.243	.300	.328	.628	7	.952

2006 LEFTY-RIGHTY SPLITS

vs.	Avg.	AB	H	2B	3B	HR	RBI	BB	SO	OBP	Slg.	vs.	Avg.	AB	H	2B	3B	HR	RBI	BB	SO	OBP	Slg.
L	.000	2	0	0	0	0	0	1	0	.333	.000	R	.214	14	3	0	0	0	0	0	5	.214	.214

EISCHEN, JOEY — P

PERSONAL: Born May 25, 1970, in West Covina, Calif. ... 6-0/214. ... Throws left, bats left. ... Full name: Joseph Raymond Eischen. ... Name pronounced: EYE-shen. ... High school: West Covina (Calif.). ... Junior college: Pasadena (Calif.) City College. **TRANSACTIONS/CAREER NOTES:** Selected by Chicago White Sox organization in fifth round of 1988 free-agent draft; did not sign. ... Selected by Texas Rangers in fourth round of 1989 free-agent draft. ... Traded by Rangers with P Jonathan Hurst and a player to be named to Montreal Expos for P Dennis Boyd (July 21, 1991); Expos acquired P Travis Buckley to complete deal (September 1, 1991). ... Traded by Expos with OF Roberto Kelly to Los Angeles Dodgers for P Henry Rodriguez and IF Jeff Treadway (May 23, 1995). ... Traded by Dodgers with P John Cummings to Detroit Tigers for OF Chad Curtis (July 31, 1996). ... Traded by Tigers with P Cam Smith to San Diego Padres for C Brian Johnson and P Willie Blair (December 17, 1996). ... Traded by Padres to Cincinnati Reds for a player to be named (March 16, 1997); Padres acquired IF Ray Brown to complete deal (March 19, 1997). ... On disabled list (March 25-April 26 and April 29-July 18, 1997); included rehabilitation assignment to Indianapolis. ... Signed as a free agent by New York Yankees organization (February 3, 1998). ... Released by Yankees (March 11, 1998). ... Signed by Reds (March 19, 1998). ... Released by Reds (March 12, 1999). ... Signed by Arizona Diamondbacks organization (March 18, 1999). ... Released by Diamondbacks (July 1, 1999). ... Signed by Adirondack of independent Northern League (1999). ... Signed as a free agent by Cleveland Indians organization (December 23, 1999). ... Released by Indians (April 29, 2000). ... Signed by Adirondack (2000). ... Signed as a free agent by Expos organization (July 12, 2000). ... On disabled list (March 26-August 2, 2004); included rehabilitation assignments to GCL Expos and Brevard County. ... Expos franchise transferred to Washington, D.C., and renamed Washington Nationals for 2005 season (December 3, 2004). ... On disabled list (May 2-July 1, 2005). ... On disabled list (May 31, 2006-remainder of season). ... Released by Nationals (October 3, 2006). **MISCELLANEOUS NOTES:** Made an out in only appearance as pinch hitter (2002). ... Singled and struck out in two appearances as pinch hitter and scored in one appearance as pinch runner (2003). ... Singled and scored a run in only appearance as pinch hitter (2004). ... Struck out in only appearance as pinch hitter (2005). ... Had a sacrifice hit and struck out in two appearances as pinch hitter (2006).

CAREER HITTING: 5-for-28 (.179), 4 R, 1 2B, 0 3B, 0 HR, 0 RBI.

Year Team (League)	W	L	Pct.	ERA	WHIP	G	GS	CG	ShO	Hld.	Sv.-Opp.	IP	H	R	ER	HR	BB-IBB	SO	Avg.
1989— Butte (Pion.)	3	7	.300	5.30	1.67	12	12	0	0	...	0-...	52.2	50	45	31	4	38-0	57	.246
1990— Gastonia (S. Atl.)	3	7	.300	2.70	1.24	17	14	0	0	...	0-...	73.1	51	36	22	0	40-0	69	.195
1991— Charlotte (Fla. St.)	4	10	.286	3.41	1.42	18	18	1	0	...	0-...	108.1	99	59	41	5	55-1	80	.249
— W.P. Beach (FSL)	4	2	.667	5.17	1.54	8	8	1	0	...	0-...	38.1	35	27	22	3	24-0	26	.238
1992— W.P. Beach (FSL)	9	8	.529	3.08	1.24	27	26	3	2	...	0-...	169.2	128	68	58	5	83-2	167	.211
1993— Harrisburg (East.)	14	4	.778	3.62	1.53	20	20	0	0	...	0-...	119.1	122	62	48	11	60-0	110	.265
— Ottawa (Int'l)	2	2	.500	3.54	1.20	6	6	0	0	...	0-...	40.2	34	18	16	3	15-0	29	.230
1994— Ottawa (Int'l)	2	6	.250	4.94	1.52	48	2	0	0	...	2-...	62.0	54	38	34	7	40-4	57	.238
— Montreal (N.L.)	0	0	...	54.00	6.00	1	0	0	0	0	0-0	0.2	4	4	4	0	0-0	1	.667
1995— Ottawa (Int'l)	2	1	.667	1.72	1.09	11	0	0	0	...	0-...	15.2	9	4	3	0	8-1	13	.173
— Los Angeles (N.L.)	0	0	...	3.10	1.48	17	0	0	0	1	0-0	20.1	19	9	7	1	11-1	15	.232
— Albuquerque (PCL)	3	0	1.000	0.00	0.67	13	0	0	0	...	2-...	16.1	8	0	0	0	3-0	14	.145
1996— Los Angeles (N.L.)	0	1	.000	4.78	1.57	28	0	0	0	1	0-0	43.1	48	25	23	4	20-4	36	.282
— Detroit (A.L.)	1	1	.500	3.24	1.64	24	0	0	0	1	0-2	25.0	27	11	9	3	14-3	15	.284
1997— Indianapolis (A.A.)	1	0	1.000	1.27	1.27	26	5	0	0	...	2-...	42.2	41	7	6	1	13-1	26	.261
— Cincinnati (N.L.)	0	0	...	6.75	2.25	1	0	0	0	0	0-0	1.1	2	2	1	0	1-0	2	.333
1998— Indianapolis (Int'l)	2	5	.286	4.54	1.39	61	0	0	0	...	2-...	73.1	73	42	37	9	29-3	60	.258
1999— Tucson (PCL)	1	3	.250	9.07	2.14	27	1	0	0	...	1-...	41.2	63	47	42	7	26-3	36	.350
— Adirondack (North.)	4	2	.667	3.75	1.31	7	7	1	0	...	0-...	48.0	52	22	20	1	11-...	49	...
2000— Buffalo (Int'l)	0	0	...	40.50	6.00	1	0	0	0	...	0-...	0.2	4	3	3	0	0-0	0	.667
— Adirondack (North.)	7	1	.875	1.80	1.22	10	10	0	0	...	0-...	65.0	55	25	13	...	24-...	57	...
— Ottawa (Int'l)	0	4	.000	3.64	1.30	10	9	0	0	...	0-...	59.1	55	31	24	8	22-0	34	.250
2001— Ottawa (Int'l)	2	3	.400	2.24	1.01	34	1	0	0	...	7-...	52.1	42	16	13	6	11-0	54	.220
— Montreal (N.L.)	0	1	.000	4.85	1.52	24	0	0	0	2	0-2	29.2	29	17	16	4	16-1	19	.257
2002— Ottawa (Int'l)	1	0	1.000	0.00	0.79	11	0	0	0	...	4-...	14.0	8	4	0	0	3-0	15	.167
— Montreal (N.L.)	6	1	.857	1.34	1.14	59	0	0	0	11	2-3	53.2	43	11	8	1	18-5	51	.224
2003— Montreal (N.L.)	2	2	.500	3.06	1.32	70	0	0	0	15	1-4	53.0	57	27	18	7	13-1	40	.282
2004— GC Expos (GCL)	0	0	...	0.00	0.00	1	0	0	0	...	0-...	1.0	0	0	0	0	0-0	2	.000
— Brevard County (FSL)	0	0	...	0.00	1.00	4	0	0	0	...	0-...	6.0	5	4	0	0	1-0	7	.217
— Montreal (N.L.)	0	1	.000	3.93	1.31	21	0	0	0	2	0-1	18.1	16	10	8	2	8-2	17	.232
2005— New Orleans (PCL)	0	0	...	1.35	1.05	6	4	0	0	1	0-0	6.2	4	1	1	0	3-0	6	.167
— Wash. (N.L.)	2	1	.667	3.22	1.46	57	0	0	0	8	0-1	36.1	34	14	13	1	19-7	30	.252
2006— Wash. (N.L.)	0	1	.000	8.59	2.52	22	0	0	0	...	0-...	14.2	18	18	14	2	19-5	18	.295
American League totals (1 year)	1	1	.500	3.24	1.64	24	0	0	0	1	0-2	25.0	27	11	9	3	14-3	15	.284
National League totals (10 years)	10	8	.556	3.71	1.46	300	0	0	0	40	3-12	271.1	270	137	112	22	125-26	229	.261
Major League totals (10 years)	11	9	.550	3.67	1.47	324	0	0	0	41	3-14	296.1	297	148	121	25	139-29	244	.263

2006 LEFTY-RIGHTY SPLITS

vs.	Avg.	AB	H	2B	3B	HR	RBI	BB	SO	OBP	Slg.	vs.	Avg.	AB	H	2B	3B	HR	RBI	BB	SO	OBP	Slg.
L	.087	23	2	1	0	1	5	6	9	.267	.261	R	.421	38	16	2	0	1	15	13	9	.566	.553

E

ELARTON, SCOTT — P

PERSONAL: Born February 23, 1976, in Lamar, Colo. ... 6-8/240. ... Throws right, bats right. ... Full name: Vincent Scott Elarton. ... High school: Lamar (Colo.). **TRANSACTIONS/CAREER NOTES:** Selected by Houston Astros organization in first round (25th pick overall) of 1994 free-agent draft. ... On disabled list (March 29-April 23, 2000); included rehabilitation assignments to New Orleans and Round Rock. ... On disabled list (July 17-September 4, 2001). ... Traded by Astros with a player to be named to Colorado Rockies for P Pedro Astacio and cash (July 31, 2001); Rockies acquired C Garrett Gentry to complete deal (September 27, 2001). ... On disabled list (July 31-September 4, 2001); included rehabilitation assignment to Colorado Springs. ... On disabled list (March 8, 2002-entire season). ... On disabled list (March 26-April 30, 2003); included rehabilitation assignment to Colorado Springs. ... Released by Rockies (May 20, 2004). ... Signed by Cleveland Indians organization (May 25, 2004). ... Signed as a free agent by Kansas City Royals (December 16, 2005). ... On disabled list (July 18, 2006-remainder of season). **MISCELLANEOUS NOTES:** Appeared in one game as outfielder with no chances (1999).

CAREER HITTING: 23-for-165 (.139), 13 R, 3 2B, 0 3B, 0 HR, 3 RBI.

Year	Team (League)	W	L	Pct.	ERA	WHIP	G	GS	CG	ShO	Hld.	Sv.-Opp.	IP	H	R	ER	HR	BB-IBB	SO	Avg.
1994—	GC Astros (GCL)	4	0	1.000	0.00	0.50	5	5	0	0	...	0-...	28.0	9	0	0	0	5-0	28	.103
	— Quad City (Midw.)	4	1	.800	3.29	1.10	9	9	0	0	...	0-...	54.2	42	23	20	4	18-0	42	.213
1995—	Quad City (Midw.)	13	7	.650	4.45	1.47	26	26	0	0	...	0-...	149.2	149	86	74	12	71-2	112	.259
1996—	Kissimmee (Fla. St.)	12	7	.632	2.92	1.21	27	27	3	0	...	0-...	172.1	154	67	56	13	54-0	130	.241
1997—	Jackson (Texas)	7	4	.636	3.24	1.13	20	20	2	0	...	0-...	133.1	103	57	48	6	47-3	141	.210
	— New Orleans (A.A.)	4	4	.500	5.33	1.26	9	9	0	0	...	0-...	54.0	51	36	32	4	17-1	50	.249
1998—	New Orleans (PCL)	9	4	.692	4.01	1.22	14	14	2	1	...	0-...	92.0	71	42	41	6	41-3	100	.212
	— Houston (N.L.)	2	1	.667	3.32	1.05	28	2	0	0	2	2-3	57.0	40	21	21	7	20-0	56	.196
1999—	Houston (N.L.)	9	5	.643	3.48	1.24	42	15	0	0	5	1-4	124.0	111	55	48	8	43-0	121	.238
2000—	New Orleans (PCL)	1	0	1.000	0.75	0.58	2	2	0	0	...	0-...	12.0	3	1	1	0	4-0	12	.081
	— Round Rock (Texas)	1	0	1.000	2.84	1.11	1	1	0	0	...	0-...	6.1	7	2	2	1	0-0	7	.280
	— Houston (N.L.)	17	7	.708	4.81	1.46	30	30	2	0	0	0-0	192.2	198	117	103	29	84-1	131	.263
2001—	Houston (N.L.)	4	8	.333	7.14	1.60	20	20	0	0	0	0-0	109.2	126	88	87	26	49-1	76	.290
	— Colo. Springs (PCL)	0	1	.000	7.04	1.83	2	2	0	0	...	0-...	7.2	14	6	6	2	0-0	8	.378
	— Colorado (N.L.)	0	2	.000	6.65	1.30	4	4	0	0	0	0-0	23.0	20	17	17	8	10-1	11	.233
2002—	Colorado (N.L.)								Did not play.											
2003—	Colo. Springs (PCL)	6	4	.429	5.31	1.60	20	20	0	0	0	0-...	118.2	146	81	70	15	39-1	92	.298
	— Colorado (N.L.)	4	4	.500	6.27	1.80	11	10	0	0	0	0-0	51.2	73	46	36	13	20-3	20	.329
2004—	Colorado (N.L.)	0	6	.000	9.80	1.86	8	8	0	0	0	0-0	41.1	57	45	45	8	20-1	23	.328
	— Buffalo (Int'l)	1	1	.500	3.15	1.20	3	3	1	1	...	0-...	20.0	19	7	7	1	5-0	10	.250
	— Cleveland (A.L.)	3	5	.375	4.53	1.27	21	21	1	1	0	0-0	117.1	107	62	59	25	42-2	80	.240
2005—	Cleveland (A.L.)	11	9	.550	4.61	1.30	31	31	1	0	0	0-0	181.2	189	100	93	32	48-1	103	.267
2006—	Kansas City (A.L.)	4	9	.308	5.34	1.47	20	20	0	0	0	0-0	114.2	117	73	68	26	52-1	49	.267
	American League totals (3 years)	18	23	.439	4.79	1.34	72	72	2	1	0	0-0	413.2	413	235	220	83	142-4	232	.260
	National League totals (6 years)	36	33	.522	5.36	1.45	143	89	2	0	7	3-7	599.1	625	389	357	97	246-7	438	.267
	Major League totals (8 years)	54	56	.491	5.13	1.41	215	161	4	1	7	3-7	1013.0	1038	624	577	180	388-11	670	.264

DIVISION SERIES RECORD

Year	Team (League)	W	L	Pct.	ERA	WHIP	G	GS	CG	ShO	Hld.	Sv.-Opp.	IP	H	R	ER	HR	BB-IBB	SO	Avg.
1998—	Houston (N.L.)	0	1	.000	4.50	1.00	1	0	0	0	0	0-0	2.0	1	1	1	0	1-0	3	.167
1999—	Houston (N.L.)	0	0	...	3.86	2.14	2	0	0	0	0	0-0	2.1	4	1	1	0	1-0	3	.400
	Division series totals (2 years)	0	1	.000	4.15	1.62	3	0	0	0	0	0-0	4.1	5	2	2	0	2-0	6	.313

2006 LEFTY-RIGHTY SPLITS

vs.	Avg.	AB	H	2B	3B	HR	RBI	BB	SO	OBP	Slg.	vs.	Avg.	AB	H	2B	3B	HR	RBI	BB	SO	OBP	Slg.
L	.253	194	49	10	0	12	24	32	17	.360	.490	R	.278	245	68	17	1	14	37	20	32	.343	.527

ELLIS, MARK — 2B

PERSONAL: Born June 6, 1977, in Rapid City, S.D. ... 5-11/180. ... Bats right, throws right. ... Full name: Mark William Ellis. ... High school: Stevens (Rapid City, S.D.). ... College: Florida. **TRANSACTIONS/CAREER NOTES:** Selected by Kansas City Royals organization in ninth round of 1999 free-agent draft. ... Traded by Royals with OF Johnny Damon and cash to Oakland Athletics as part of three-team deal in which Royals acquired P Roberto Hernandez from Tampa Bay Devil Rays, A's acquired P Cory Lidle from Devil Rays, Royals acquired C A.J. Hinch, IF Angel Berroa and cash from A's and Devil Rays received OF Ben Grieve and cash from A's (January 8, 2001). ... On disabled list (March 26, 2004-entire season). ... On disabled list (June 1-June 30, 2006); included rehabilitation assignment to Sacramento. **STATISTICAL NOTES:** Career major league grand slams: 1.

2006 GAMES PLAYED BY POSITION (MLB): 2B—123, 1B—1.

Year	Team (League)	Pos.	G	AB	R	H	2B	3B	HR	RBI	BB	SO	HBP	GDP	SB-CS	Avg.	OBP	SLG	OPS	E	Avg.
1999—	Spokane (N'west)	SS	71	281	67	92	14	0	7	47	47	40	3	1	21-7	.327	.424	.452	.876	16	.958
2000—	Wilmington (Caro.)	2B-SS	132	484	83	146	27	4	6	62	78	72	7	11	25-7	.302	.404	.411	.815	31	.954
	— Wichita (Texas)	2B	7	22	4	7	1	0	0	4	5	5	0	0	1-0	.318	.444	.364	.808	0	1.000
2001—	Sacramento (PCL)	SS	132	472	71	129	38	0	10	53	54	78	5	13	21-7	.273	.351	.417	.768	19	.968
2002—	Sacramento (PCL)	SS	21	84	14	25	10	1	0	5	6	13	4	1	4-0	.298	.372	.440	.813	3	.974
	— Oakland (A.L.)	2B-SS-3B DH	98	345	58	94	16	4	6	35	44	54	4	3	4-2	.272	.359	.394	.753	11	.976
2003—	Oakland (A.L.)	2B	154	553	78	137	31	5	9	52	48	94	7	7	6-2	.248	.313	.371	.684	14	.982
2004—								Did not play.													
2005—	Oakland (A.L.)	2B-SS-1B DH	122	434	76	137	21	5	13	52	44	51	4	10	1-3	.316	.384	.477	.861	6	.989
2006—	Sacramento (PCL)		4	12	1	2	0	0	0	2	4	2	0	0	0-0	.167	.375	.167	.542	0	1.000
	— Oakland (A.L.)	2B-1B	124	441	64	110	25	1	11	52	40	76	8	13	4-0	.249	.319	.385	.704	2	.997
	Major League totals (4 years)		498	1773	276	478	93	15	39	191	176	275	23	33	15-7	.270	.341	.405	.746	33	.987

DIVISION SERIES RECORD

Year	Team (League)	Pos.	G	AB	R	H	2B	3B	HR	RBI	BB	SO	HBP	GDP	SB-CS	Avg.	OBP	SLG	OPS	E	Avg.
2002—	Oakland (A.L.)	2B	5	19	1	7	2	0	1	4	1	2	0	0	0-0	.368	.400	.632	1.032	1	.960
2003—	Oakland (A.L.)	2B	5	17	2	2	0	0	0	0	4	7	1	0	0-0	.118	.318	.118	.436	1	.964
2006—	Oakland (A.L.)	2B	2	7	0	2	0	0	0	0	0	2	0	0	0-0	.286	.286	.571	1.000	0	1.000
	Division series totals (3 years)		12	43	3	11	2	0	1	4	5	11	1	0	0-0	.256	.347	.372	.719	2	.969

2006 LEFTY-RIGHTY SPLITS

vs.	Avg.	AB	H	2B	3B	HR	RBI	BB	SO	OBP	Slg.	vs.	Avg.	AB	H	2B	3B	HR	RBI	BB	SO	OBP	Slg.
L	.278	90	25	5	0	2	11	18	12	.402	.400	R	.242	351	85	20	1	9	41	22	64	.294	.382

ELLISON, JASON — OF

PERSONAL: Born April 4, 1978, in Quincy, Calif. ... 5-10/180. ... Bats right, throws right. ... Full name: Jason Jerome Ellison. ... High school: South Kitsap High (Port Orchar, Wash.). ... College: Lewis-Clark State (Lewiston, Idaho). **TRANSACTIONS/CAREER NOTES:** Selected by San Francisco Giants organization in 22nd round of 2000 free-agent draft.

E

2006 GAMES PLAYED BY POSITION (MLB): OF—64.

Year Team (League)	Pos.	G	AB	R	H	2B	3B	HR	RBI	BB	SO	HBP	GDP	SB-CS	Avg.	OBP	SLG	OPS	E	Avg.
										BATTING									FIELDING	
2000—Salem-Keizer (N'west)	OF	74	300	67	90	15	2	0	28	29	45	7	1	13-7	.300	.374	.363	.737	4	.976
2001—Hagerstown (SAL)	OF	130	494	95	144	38	3	8	55	71	68	10	6	19-15	.291	.388	.429	.817	5	.984
2002—San Jose (Calif.)	OF	81	322	40	87	13	0	5	40	25	37	2	10	9-9	.270	.325	.357	.682	4	.980
—Fresno (PCL)	OF	49	196	31	61	8	1	3	8	21	28	4	4	16-3	.311	.389	.408	.797	1	.992
2003—San Francisco (N.L.)	OF	7	10	1	1	0	0	0	0	0	1	0	0	0-0	.100	.100	.100	.200	0	1.000
—Fresno (PCL)	OF-DH	119	461	74	136	22	4	6	39	39	52	6	7	21-13	.295	.356	.399	.755	9	.974
2004—Fresno (PCL)	OF	125	505	90	159	32	7	9	40	40	66	3	8	27-12	.315	.368	.459	.827	6	.983
—San Francisco (N.L.)	OF	13	4	4	2	0	0	1	3	0	1	0	0	2-0	.500	.500	1.250	1.750	0	1.000
2005—Fresno (PCL)	OF	8	38	5	9	2	0	0	3	2	9	1	0	0-0	.237	.293	.289	.582	0	1.000
—San Francisco (N.L.)	OF	131	352	49	93	18	2	4	24	24	44	3	7	14-6	.264	.316	.361	.677	8	.968
2006—Fresno (PCL)		46	192	41	78	18	2	1	18	14	20	3	3	7-4	.406	.452	.536	.989	0	1.000
—San Francisco (N.L.)	OF	84	81	14	18	5	1	2	4	5	14	1	3	2-2	.222	.273	.383	.655	2	.960
Major League totals (4 years)		235	447	68	114	23	3	7	31	29	60	4	10	18-8	.255	.305	.367	.672	10	.967

2006 LEFTY-RIGHTY SPLITS

vs.	Avg.	AB	H	2B	3B	HR	RBI	BB	SO	OBP	Slg.	vs.	Avg.	AB	H	2B	3B	HR	RBI	BB	SO	OBP	Slg.
L	.269	26	7	0	1	1	3	2	2	.333	.462	R	.200	55	11	5	0	1	1	3	12	.241	.345

EMBREE, ALAN — P

PERSONAL: Born January 23, 1970, in The Dalles, Ore. ... 6-2/190. ... Throws left, bats left. ... Full name: Alan Duane Embree. ... Name pronounced: EMM-bree. ... High school: Prairie (Vancouver, Wash.). **TRANSACTIONS/CAREER NOTES:** Selected by Cleveland Indians organization in fifth round of 1989 free-agent draft. ... On disabled list (April 1-June 2 and June 2, 1993-remainder of season); included rehabilitation assignment to Canton/Akron. ... On disabled list (August 1-September 7, 1996); included rehabilitation assignment to Buffalo. ... Traded by Indians with OF Kenny Lofton to Atlanta Braves for OFs Marquis Grissom and David Justice (March 25, 1997). ... Traded by Braves to Arizona Diamondbacks for P Russ Springer (June 23, 1998). ... Traded by Giants to Chicago White Sox for P Derek Hasselhoff (June 29, 2001). ... Signed as a free agent by San Diego Padres (January 3, 2002). ... Traded by Padres with P Andy Shibilo to Boston Red Sox for Ps Brad Baker and Dan Giese (June 26, 2002). ... On disabled list (July 14-29, 2002). ... On disabled list (April 9-29, 2003); included rehabilitation assignment to Sarasota. ... Released by Red Sox (July 27, 2005). ... Signed by New York Yankees (July 30, 2005). ... Signed as free agent by San Diego Padres organization (January 12, 2006). ... On disabled list (July 2-17, 2006).

CAREER HITTING: 0-for-3 (.000), 0 R, 0 2B, 0 3B, 0 HR, 0 RBI.

Year Team (League)	W	L	Pct.	ERA	WHIP	G	GS	CG	ShO	Hld.	Sv.-Opp.	IP	H	R	ER	HR	BB-IBB	SO	Avg.
1990—Burlington (Appal.)	4	4	.500	2.64	1.43	15	15	0	0	...	0-...	81.2	87	36	24	3	30-0	58	.274
1991—Columbus (S. Atl.)	10	8	.556	3.59	1.31	27	26	3	1	...	0-...	155.1	126	80	62	4	77-1	137	.224
1992—Kinston (Carol.)	10	5	.667	3.30	1.20	15	15	1	0	...	0-...	101.0	89	48	37	10	32-0	115	.234
—Cant./Akr. (Eastern)	7	2	.778	2.28	1.13	12	12	0	0	...	0-...	79.0	61	24	20	2	28-1	56	.216
—Cleveland (A.L.)	0	2	.000	7.00	1.50	4	4	0	0	0	0-0	18.0	19	14	14	3	8-0	12	.271
1993—Cant./Akr. (Eastern)	0	0	...	3.38	1.13	1	1	0	0	...	0-...	5.1	3	2	2	0	3-0	4	.176
1994—Cant./Akr. (Eastern)	9	16	.360	5.50	1.57	30	27	2	1	...	0-...	157.0	183	106	96	15	64-3	81	.294
1995—Buffalo (A.A.)	3	4	.429	0.89	1.23	30	0	0	0	...	5-...	40.2	31	10	4	0	19-2	56	.211
—Cleveland (A.L.)	3	2	.600	5.11	1.58	23	0	0	0	6	1-1	24.2	23	16	14	2	16-0	23	.253
1996—Cleveland (A.L.)	1	1	.500	6.39	1.65	24	0	0	0	...	0-0	31.0	30	26	22	10	21-3	33	.259
—Buffalo (A.A.)	4	1	.800	3.93	1.17	20	0	0	0	...	5-...	34.1	26	16	15	1	14-0	46	.210
1997—Atlanta (N.L.)	3	1	.750	2.54	1.22	66	0	0	0	16	0-0	46.0	36	13	13	1	20-2	45	.221
1998—Atlanta (N.L.)	1	0	1.000	4.34	1.77	20	0	0	0	6	0-1	18.2	23	14	9	2	10-0	19	.307
—Arizona (N.L.)	3	2	.600	4.11	1.31	35	0	0	0	6	1-2	35.0	33	18	16	5	13-0	24	.248
1999—San Francisco (N.L.)	3	2	.600	3.38	1.16	68	0	0	0	22	0-3	58.2	42	22	22	6	26-2	53	.200
2000—San Francisco (N.L.)	3	5	.375	4.95	1.45	63	0	0	0	9	2-5	60.0	62	34	33	4	25-2	49	.274
2001—San Francisco (N.L.)	0	2	.000	11.25	2.20	22	0	0	0	1	0-1	20.0	34	26	25	7	10-2	15	.374
—Fresno (PCL)	1	0	1.000	1.13	0.75	7	0	0	0	...	1-...	8.0	5	3	1	0	1-0	6	.179
—Chicago (A.L.)	1	2	.333	5.03	1.12	39	0	0	0	9	0-2	34.0	31	21	19	7	7-0	34	.242
2002—San Diego (N.L.)	3	4	.429	1.26	1.12	36	0	0	0	10	0-2	28.2	23	7	4	2	9-2	38	.211
—Boston (A.L.)	1	2	.333	2.97	1.05	32	0	0	0	8	2-5	33.1	24	12	11	4	11-1	43	.203
2003—Sarasota (Fla. St.)	0	0	...	13.50	3.00	1	1	0	0	...	0-...	0.2	2	1	1	0	0-0	2	.500
—Boston (A.L.)	4	1	.800	4.25	1.18	65	0	0	0	14	1-2	55.0	49	26	26	5	16-3	45	.244
2004—Boston (A.L.)	2	2	.500	4.13	1.15	71	0	0	0	20	0-1	52.1	49	28	24	7	11-1	37	.244
2005—Boston (A.L.)	1	4	.200	7.65	1.41	43	0	0	0	4	1-3	37.2	42	33	32	8	11-2	30	.284
—New York (A.L.)	1	1	.500	7.53	1.60	24	0	0	0	6	0-0	14.1	20	14	12	2	3-1	8	.328
2006—San Diego (N.L.)	4	3	.571	3.27	1.24	73	0	0	0	16	0-0	52.1	50	21	19	4	15-2	53	.249
American League totals (8 years)	14	17	.452	5.21	1.30	325	4	0	0	68	5-14	300.1	287	190	174	48	104-11	265	.253
National League totals (7 years)	20	19	.513	3.97	1.35	383	0	0	0	85	3-14	319.1	303	155	141	31	128-12	306	.251
Major League totals (13 years)	34	36	.486	4.58	1.33	708	4	0	0	153	8-28	619.2	590	345	315	79	232-23	571	.252

DIVISION SERIES RECORD

Year Team (League)	W	L	Pct.	ERA	WHIP	G	GS	CG	ShO	Hld.	Sv.-Opp.	IP	H	R	ER	HR	BB-IBB	SO	Avg.
1996—Cleveland (A.L.)	0	0	...	9.00	0.00	3	0	0	0	1	0-0	1.0	0	1	1	0	0-0	1	.000
2000—San Francisco (N.L.)	0	0	...	0.00	0.00	2	0	0	0	1	0-0	1.2	0	0	0	0	0-0	0	.000
2003—Boston (A.L.)	0	0	...	0.00	0.50	3	0	0	0	1	0-1	2.0	1	0	0	0	1-0	0	.143
2004—Boston (A.L.)	0	0	...	0.00	1.00	2	0	0	0	0	0-0	1.0	0	0	0	0	1-0	0	.000
2006—San Diego (N.L.)	0	0	...	0.00	0.00	1	0	0	0	1	0-0	0.1	0	0	0	0	0-0	1	.000
Division series totals (5 years)	0	0	...	1.50	0.33	11	0	0	0	4	0-1	6.0	1	1	1	0	1-0	2	.056

CHAMPIONSHIP SERIES RECORD

Year Team (League)	W	L	Pct.	ERA	WHIP	G	GS	CG	ShO	Hld.	Sv.-Opp.	IP	H	R	ER	HR	BB-IBB	SO	Avg.
1995—Cleveland (A.L.)	0	0	...	0.00	0.00	1	0	0	0	0	0-0	0.1	0	0	0	0	0-0	1	.000
1997—Atlanta (N.L.)	0	0	...	0.00	1.00	1	0	0	0	0	0-0	1.0	1	0	0	0	1-0	1	.000
2003—Boston (A.L.)	1	0	1.000	0.00	0.64	5	0	0	0	0	0-0	4.2	3	0	0	0	0-0	1	.214
2004—Boston (A.L.)	0	0	...	3.86	2.14	6	0	0	0	0	0-0	4.2	9	2	2	0	1-1	2	.409
Champ. series totals (4 years)	1	0	1.000	1.69	1.31	13	0	0	0	0	0-0	10.2	12	2	2	0	2-1	5	.308

WORLD SERIES RECORD

Year Team (League)	W	L	Pct.	ERA	WHIP	G	GS	CG	ShO	Hld.	Sv.-Opp.	IP	H	R	ER	HR	BB-IBB	SO	Avg.
1995—Cleveland (A.L.)	0	0	...	2.70	1.20	4	0	0	0	0	0-0	3.1	2	1	1	0	2-1	2	.182
2004—Boston (A.L.)	0	0	...	0.00	0.60	3	0	0	0	1	0-0	1.2	1	1	0	0	0-1	4	.167
World series totals (2 years)	0	0	...	1.80	1.00	7	0	0	0	1	0-0	5.0	3	2	1	0	2-1	6	.176

2006 LEFTY-RIGHTY SPLITS

vs.	Avg.	AB	H	2B	3B	HR	RBI	BB	SO	OBP	Slg.	vs.	Avg.	AB	H	2B	3B	HR	RBI	BB	SO	OBP	Slg.
L	.240	104	25	5	1	1	11	7	25	.288	.337	R	.258	97	25	4	1	3	18	8	28	.306	.412

E

ENCARNACION, EDWIN — 3B

PERSONAL: Born January 7, 1983, in La Romana, Dominican Republic. ... 6-1/195. ... Bats right, throws right. ... Full name: Edwin Encarnacion. . **TRANSACTIONS/CAREER NOTES:** Selected by Texas Rangers organization in ninth round of 2000 free-agent draft. ... Traded by Rangers to with OF Ruben Mateo to Cincinnati Reds for P Rob Bell (June 15, 2001). ... On disabled list (June 9-July 6, 2006); included rehabilitation assignment to Louisville. **STATISTICAL NOTES:** Career major league grand slams: 1.

2006 GAMES PLAYED BY POSITION (MLB): 3B—111, 1B—2.

Year	Team (League)	Pos.	G	AB	R	H	2B	3B	HR	RBI	BB	SO	HBP	GDP	SB-CS	Avg.	OBP	SLG	OPS	E	Avg.
2000—	GC Rangers (GCL)	3B	51	177	31	55	6	3	0	36	21	27	1	7	3-1	.311	.381	.379	.760	11	.927
2001—	Savannah (S. Atl.)	3B	45	170	23	52	9	2	4	25	12	34	2	5	3-3	.306	.355	.453	.808	12	.891
—	Dayton (Midw.)	3B-SS	9	37	2	6	2	0	1	6	1	5	0	1	0-1	.162	.184	.297	.481	1	.962
—	Billings (Pion.)	3B	52	211	27	55	8	2	5	26	15	29	0	6	8-1	.261	.307	.389	.696	23	.863
2002—	Dayton (Midw.)	3B-SS	136	518	80	146	32	4	17	73	40	108	7	15	25-7	.282	.338	.458	.796	40	.900
2003—	Chattanooga (Sou.)	3B	67	254	40	69	13	1	5	36	22	44	3	3	8-3	.272	.331	.390	.721	23	.890
—	Potomac (Carol.)	3B	58	215	40	69	15	1	6	29	24	32	1	2	7-1	.321	.387	.484	.871	17	.879
2004—	Chattanooga (Sou.)	3B	120	469	73	132	35	1	13	76	53	79	0	5	17-3	.281	.352	.443	.795	25	.924
2005—	Louisville (Int'l)	3B	78	290	44	91	23	0	15	54	33	53	4	8	7-2	.314	.388	.548	.936	19	.917
—	Cincinnati (N.L.)	3B	69	211	25	49	16	0	9	31	20	60	3	8	3-0	.232	.308	.436	.744	10	.944
2006—	Louisville (Int'l)	3B	10	36	6	11	3	0	1	1	2	11	0	1	0-0	.306	.342	.472	.814	1	.968
—	Cincinnati (N.L.)	3B-1B	117	406	60	112	33	1	15	72	41	78	13	9	6-3	.276	.359	.473	.831	25	.918
	Major League totals (2 years)		186	617	85	161	49	1	24	103	61	138	16	17	9-3	.261	.341	.460	.802	35	.928

2006 LEFTY-RIGHTY SPLITS

vs.	Avg.	AB	H	2B	3B	HR	RBI	BB	SO	OBP	Slg.	vs.	Avg.	AB	H	2B	3B	HR	RBI	BB	SO	OBP	Slg.
L	.248	113	28	9	0	5	24	18	23	.368	.460	R	.287	293	84	24	1	10	48	23	55	.355	.478

ENCARNACION, JUAN — OF

PERSONAL: Born March 8, 1976, in Las Matas de Farfan, Dominican Republic. ... 6-3/215. ... Bats right, throws right. ... Full name: Juan de Dios Encarnacion. ... Name pronounced: en-car-NAH-see-own. ... High school: Liceo Mercedes Maria Mateo (Las Matas de Faran, Dominican Republic). **TRANSACTIONS/CAREER NOTES:** Signed as a non-drafted free agent by Detroit Tigers organization (December 27, 1992). ... On disabled list (March 20-April 29, 1998); included rehabilitation assignment to Lakeland. ... On suspended list (May 27-29, 2000). ... Traded by Tigers with P Luis Pineda to Cincinnati Reds for OF Dmitri Young (December 11, 2001). ... Traded by Reds with OF/2B Wilton Guerrero and P Ryan Snare to Florida Marlins for P Ryan Dempster (July 11, 2002). ... Traded by Marlins to Los Angeles Dodgers for OF Travis Ezi (December 13, 2003). ... On disabled list (July 4-19, 2004). ... Traded by Dodgers with C Paul Lo Duca and P Guillermo Mota to Marlins for Ps Brad Penny and Bill Murphy and 1B Hee-Seop Choi (July 30, 2004). ... Signed as a free agent by St. Louis Cardinals (January 10, 2006). **STATISTICAL NOTES:** Career major league grand slams: 3.

2006 GAMES PLAYED BY POSITION (MLB): OF—148.

Year	Team (League)	Pos.	G	AB	R	H	2B	3B	HR	RBI	BB	SO	HBP	GDP	SB-CS	Avg.	OBP	SLG	OPS	E	Avg.
1993—	Dom. Tigers (DSL)	OF	72	251	36	63	13	4	13	49	15	65	...	5	6-	.251	...	.490	...	17	.879
1994—	Bristol (Appal.)	OF	54	197	16	49	7	1	4	31	13	54	5	2	9-2	.249	.310	.355	.666	3	.968
—	Fayetteville (SAL)	OF	24	83	6	16	1	1	1	4	8	36	1	2	1-1	.193	.272	.265	.537	2	.920
—	Lakeland (Fla. St.)	OF	3	6	1	2	0	0	0	0	0	3	1	0	0-0	.333	.429	.333	.762	0	...
1995—	Fayetteville (SAL)	OF	124	457	62	129	31	7	16	72	30	113	8	10	30-6	.282	.336	.486	.822	7	.956
1996—	Lakeland (Fla. St.)	OF	131	499	54	120	31	2	15	58	24	104	12	10	11-5	.240	.290	.401	.691	6	.976
1997—	Jacksonville (Sou.)	OF-DH	131	493	91	159	31	4	26	90	43	86	19	8	17-3	.323	.394	.560	.954	3	.987
—	Detroit (A.L.)	OF	11	33	3	7	1	1	1	5	3	12	1	1	3-1	.212	.316	.394	.710	0	1.000
1998—	Lakeland (Fla. St.)	OF	4	16	4	4	0	1	0	4	2	4	1	0	4-0	.250	.368	.375	.743	0	1.000
—	Toledo (Int'l)	OF-DH	92	356	55	102	17	3	8	41	29	85	10	9	24-4	.287	.353	.419	.772	5	.973
—	Detroit (A.L.)	OF-DH	40	164	30	54	9	4	7	21	7	31	1	2	7-4	.329	.354	.561	.915	1	.985
1999—	Detroit (A.L.)	OF	132	509	62	130	30	6	19	74	14	113	4	9	33-12	.255	.287	.450	.736	9	.968
2000—	Detroit (A.L.)	OF	141	547	75	158	25	6	14	72	29	90	7	15	16-4	.289	.330	.433	.764	5	.987
2001—	Detroit (A.L.)	OF-DH	120	417	52	101	19	7	12	52	25	93	6	9	9-5	.242	.292	.408	.700	6	.977
2002—	Cincinnati (N.L.)	OF	83	321	43	89	11	2	16	51	26	63	1	7	9-4	.277	.330	.474	.804	5	.977
—	Florida (N.L.)	OF	69	263	34	69	11	3	8	34	20	51	3	5	12-5	.262	.317	.418	.735	1	.993
2003—	Florida (N.L.)	OF	156	601	80	162	37	6	19	94	37	82	4	17	19-8	.270	.313	.446	.759	0	1.000
2004—	Los Angeles (N.L.)	OF	86	324	42	76	18	1	13	43	21	53	4	9	3-3	.235	.289	.417	.705	4	.976
—	Florida (N.L.)	OF	49	160	21	38	12	1	3	19	17	33	3	2	2-1	.238	.320	.381	.702	2	.980
2005—	Florida (N.L.)	OF	141	506	59	145	27	3	16	76	41	104	6	5	6-5	.287	.349	.447	.795	4	.983
2006—	St. Louis (N.L.)	OF	153	557	74	155	25	5	19	79	30	86	4	11	6-5	.278	.317	.443	.760	6	.978
	American League totals (5 years)		444	1670	222	450	84	24	53	224	78	339	25	36	68-26	.269	.310	.444	.753	21	.979
	National League totals (5 years)		737	2732	353	734	141	21	94	396	192	471	28	66	57-31	.269	.321	.439	.759	22	.985
	Major League totals (10 years)		1181	4402	575	1184	225	45	147	620	270	810	53	105	125-57	.269	.316	.441	.757	43	.983

DIVISION SERIES RECORD

Year	Team (League)	Pos.	G	AB	R	H	2B	3B	HR	RBI	BB	SO	HBP	GDP	SB-CS	Avg.	OBP	SLG	OPS	E	Avg.
2003—	Florida (N.L.)	OF	4	15	1	2	0	0	1	1	2	3	0	1	0-0	.133	.235	.333	.569	0	1.000
2006—	St. Louis (N.L.)	OF	4	14	1	4	0	1	0	2	1	2	0	0	0-1	.286	.313	.429	.741	0	1.000
	Division series totals (2 years)		8	29	2	6	0	1	1	3	3	5	0	1	0-1	.207	.273	.379	.652	0	1.000

CHAMPIONSHIP SERIES RECORD

Year	Team (League)	Pos.	G	AB	R	H	2B	3B	HR	RBI	BB	SO	HBP	GDP	SB-CS	Avg.	OBP	SLG	OPS	E	Avg.
2003—	Florida (N.L.)	OF	5	12	1	3	1	0	1	1	0	4	0	1	0-0	.250	.250	.583	.833	0	1.000
2006—	St. Louis (N.L.)	OF	6	22	1	4	0	1	0	2	3	5	1	2	0-0	.182	.280	.273	.553	0	1.000
	Champ. series totals (2 years)		11	34	2	7	1	1	1	3	3	9	1	3	0-0	.206	.270	.382	.653	0	1.000

WORLD SERIES RECORD

Year	Team (League)	Pos.	G	AB	R	H	2B	3B	HR	RBI	BB	SO	HBP	GDP	SB-CS	Avg.	OBP	SLG	OPS	E	Avg.
2003—	Florida (N.L.)	OF	6	11	1	2	0	0	0	1	1	5	0	0	0-0	.182	.231	.182	.413	0	1.000
2006—	St. Louis (N.L.)	OF	3	8	0	0	0	0	0	1	1	2	0	0	0-0	.000	.111	.000	.111	1	.750
	World series totals (2 years)		9	19	1	2	0	0	0	2	2	7	0	0	0-0	.105	.182	.105	.287	1	.929

2006 LEFTY-RIGHTY SPLITS

vs.	Avg.	AB	H	2B	3B	HR	RBI	BB	SO	OBP	Slg.	vs.	Avg.	AB	H	2B	3B	HR	RBI	BB	SO	OBP	Slg.
L	.316	177	56	8	1	7	28	8	22	.346	.492	R	.261	380	99	17	4	12	51	22	64	.303	.421

ENSBERG, MORGAN — 3B

PERSONAL: Born August 26, 1975, in Hermosa Beach, Calif. ... 6-2/210. ... Bats right, throws right. ... Full name: Morgan Paul Ensberg. ... High school: Redondo Union (Redondo Beach, Calif.). ... College: Southern California. **TRANSACTIONS/CAREER NOTES:** Selected by Seattle Mariners organization in 61st round of 1994 free-agent draft; did not sign. ... Selected by Houston Astros organization in ninth round of 1998 free-agent draft. ... On disabled list (July 14-August 1, 2006); included rehabilitation assignment to Round Rock. **HONORS:** Named third baseman on the SPORTING NEWS N.L. All-Star team (2005). ... Named third baseman on N.L. Silver Slugger team (2005). **STATISTICAL NOTES:** Hit three home runs in one game (May 15, 2005). ... Career major league grand slams: 3.

Year Team (League)	Pos.	G	AB	R	H	2B	3B	HR	RBI	BB	SO	HBP	GDP	SB-CS	Avg.	OBP	SLG	OPS	E	Avg.
1998— Auburn (NY-Penn)	3B-SS	59	196	39	45	10	1	5	31	46	51	6	5	15-3	.230	.388	.367	.755	11	.927
1999— Kissimmee (Fla. St.)	1B-3B-SS	123	427	72	102	25	2	15	69	68	90	9	9	17-6	.239	.353	.412	.765	35	.900
2000— Round Rock (Texas)	3B	137	483	95	145	34	0	28	90	92	107	8	15	9-12	.300	.416	.545	.960	24	.942
—Houston (N.L.)	3B	4	7	0	2	0	0	0	0	0	0	1	0	0-0	.286	.286	.286	.571	1	.667
2001— New Orleans (PCL)	3B-SS	87	316	65	98	20	0	23	61	45	60	3	12	6-3	.310	.397	.592	.989	17	.929
2002— Houston (N.L.)	3B	49	132	14	32	7	2	3	19	18	25	3	8	2-0	.242	.346	.394	.740	8	.924
—New Orleans (PCL)	3B-1B	83	292	50	84	12	3	7	37	50	56	7	9	9-5	.288	.401	.421	.822	19	.926
2003— Houston (N.L.)	3B-DH	127	385	69	112	15	1	25	60	48	60	6	10	7-2	.291	.377	.530	.907	9	.967
2004— Houston (N.L.)	3B-SS	131	411	51	113	20	3	10	66	36	46	0	17	6-4	.275	.330	.411	.742	13	.949
2005— Houston (N.L.)	3B	150	526	86	149	30	3	36	101	85	119	8	12	6-7	.283	.388	.557	.945	15	.964
2006— Round Rock (PCL)		3	12	2	6	2	0	2	7	3	1	0	1	0-0	.500	.600	1.167	1.767	4	.692
—Houston (N.L.)	3B	127	387	67	91	17	1	23	58	101	96	4	3	1-4	.235	.396	.463	.858	12	.963
Major League totals (6 years)		588	1848	287	499	89	10	97	304	288	347	21	50	22-17	.270	.372	.486	.859	58	.958

DIVISION SERIES RECORD

Year Team (League)	Pos.	G	AB	R	H	2B	3B	HR	RBI	BB	SO	HBP	GDP	SB-CS	Avg.	OBP	SLG	OPS	E	Avg.
2004— Houston (N.L.)	3B	5	19	1	7	2	0	0	5	3	1	0	1	0-1	.368	.455	.474	.928	0	1.000
2005— Houston (N.L.)	3B	4	18	2	5	2	0	0	7	2	3	0	1	0-0	.278	.350	.389	.739	1	.941
Division series totals (2 years)		9	37	3	12	4	0	0	12	5	4	0	2	0-1	.324	.405	.432	.837	1	.960

CHAMPIONSHIP SERIES RECORD

Year Team (League)	Pos.	G	AB	R	H	2B	3B	HR	RBI	BB	SO	HBP	GDP	SB-CS	Avg.	OBP	SLG	OPS	E	Avg.
2004— Houston (N.L.)	3B	7	22	2	3	0	0	1	2	1	3	2	1	0-1	.136	.240	.273	.513	0	1.000
2005— Houston (N.L.)	3B	6	21	1	5	1	0	0	2	2	2	0	1	0-0	.238	.292	.286	.577	1	.941
Champ. series totals (2 years)		13	43	3	8	1	0	1	4	3	5	2	2	0-1	.186	.265	.279	.544	1	.968

WORLD SERIES RECORD

Year Team (League)	Pos.	G	AB	R	H	2B	3B	HR	RBI	BB	SO	HBP	GDP	SB-CS	Avg.	OBP	SLG	OPS	E	Avg.
2005— Houston (N.L.)	3B	4	18	2	2	0	0	1	2	1	7	0	1	0-0	.111	.158	.278	.436	1	.938

ALL-STAR GAME RECORD

	G	AB	R	H	2B	3B	HR	RBI	BB	SO	HBP	GDP	SB-CS	Avg.	OBP	SLG	OPS	E	Avg.
All-Star Game totals (1 year)	1	2	0	0	0	0	0	0	0	1	0	0	0-0	.000	.000	.000	.000	1	1.000

2006 LEFTY-RIGHTY SPLITS

vs.	Avg.	AB	H	2B	3B	HR	RBI	BB	SO	OBP	Slg.	vs.	Avg.	AB	H	2B	3B	HR	RBI	BB	SO	OBP	Slg.
L	.245	94	23	2	0	9	19	38	23	.463	.553	R	.232	293	68	15	1	14	39	63	73	.370	.433

ERICKSON, SCOTT — P

PERSONAL: Born February 2, 1968, in Long Beach, Calif. ... 6-4/230. ... Throws right, bats right. ... Full name: Scott Gavin Erickson. ... High school: Homestead (Cupertino, Calif.). ... Junior college: San Jose City College. ... College: Arizona. **TRANSACTIONS/CAREER NOTES:** Selected by New York Mets organization in 36th round of June 1986 free-agent draft; did not sign. ... Selected by Houston Astros organization in 34th round of 1987 free-agent draft; did not sign. ... Selected by Toronto Blue Jays organization in 44th round of 1988 free-agent draft; did not sign. ... Selected by Minnesota Twins organization in fourth round of 1989 free-agent draft. ... On disabled list (June 30-July 15, 1991, April 3-18, 1993, and May 15-31, 1994). ... Traded by Twins to Baltimore Orioles for P Scott Klingenbeck and a player to be named (July 7, 1995); Twins acquired OF Kimera Bartee to complete deal (September 18, 1995). ... On disabled list (March 28-May 4 and July 28, 2000-remainder of season); included rehabilitation assignments to Frederick and Bowie. ... On disabled list (April 1, 2001-entire season; and March 28, 2003-entire season). ... Signed as a free agent by Mets organization (February 5, 2004). ... On disabled list (April 4-June 30, 2004); included rehabilitation assignments to St. Lucie and Norfolk. ... Traded by Mets to Texas Rangers for a player to be named (July 31, 2004); Mets acquired IF Josh Hoffpauir to complete deal (September 17, 2004). ... Signed as a free agent by Los Angeles Dodgers organization (January 25, 2005). ... Signed as free agent by New York Yankees organization (February 16, 2006). ... Released by Yankees (June 19, 2006). **STATISTICAL NOTES:** Pitched 6-0 no-hit victory against Milwaukee (April 27, 1994). **MISCELLANEOUS NOTES:** Appeared in one game as pinch runner (2000).
CAREER HITTING: 4-for-35 (.114), 4 R, 1 2B, 0 3B, 0 HR, 1 RBI.

Year Team (League)	W	L	Pct.	ERA	WHIP	G	GS	CG	ShO	Hld.	Sv.-Opp.	IP	H	R	ER	HR	BB-IBB	SO	Avg.
1989— Visalia (Calif.)	3	4	.429	2.97	1.28	12	12	2	0	...	0-...	78.2	79	29	26	3	22-0	59	.265
1990— Orlando (South.)	8	3	.727	3.03	0.98	15	15	3	1	...	0-...	101.0	75	38	34	3	24-0	69	.205
—Minnesota (A.L.)	8	4	.667	2.87	1.41	19	17	1	0	0	0-0	113.0	108	49	36	9	51-4	53	.256
1991— Minnesota (A.L.)	•20	8	.714	3.18	1.27	32	32	5	3	0	0-0	204.0	189	80	72	13	71-3	108	.248
1992— Minnesota (A.L.)	13	12	.520	3.40	1.32	32	32	5	3	0	0-0	212.0	197	86	80	18	83-3	101	.252
1993— Minnesota (A.L.)	8	*19	.296	5.19	1.54	34	34	1	0	0	0-0	218.2	*266	*138	126	17	71-1	116	.305
1994— Minnesota (A.L.)	8	11	.421	5.44	1.61	23	23	2	1	0	0-0	144.0	173	95	87	15	59-0	104	.299
1995— Minnesota (A.L.)	4	6	.400	5.95	1.53	15	15	0	0	0	0-0	87.2	102	61	58	11	32-0	45	.291
—Baltimore (A.L.)	9	4	.692	3.89	1.34	17	16	7	2	0	0-0	108.2	111	47	47	7	35-0	61	.273
1996— Baltimore (A.L.)	13	12	.520	5.02	1.48	34	34	6	0	0	0-0	222.1	262	137	124	21	66-4	100	.297
1997— Baltimore (A.L.)	16	7	.696	3.69	1.26	34	33	3	2	0	0-0	221.2	218	100	91	16	61-5	131	.257
1998— Baltimore (A.L.)	16	13	.552	4.01	1.40	36	*36	*11	2	0	0-0	251.1	*284	125	112	23	69-4	186	.281
1999— Baltimore (A.L.)	15	12	.556	4.81	1.49	34	34	6	*3	0	0-0	230.1	244	127	123	27	*99-4	106	.280
2000— Frederick (Carolina)	0	0	...	2.70	0.60	1	1	0	0	...	0-...	6.2	3	2	2	0	1-0	5	.130
—Bowie (East.)	0	0	...	0.00	0.57	1	1	0	0	...	0-...	7.0	4	0	0	0	0-0	5	.160
—Baltimore (A.L.)	5	8	.385	7.87	1.89	16	16	1	0	0	0-0	92.2	127	81	81	14	48-0	41	.331
2001— Baltimore (A.L.)								Did not play.											
2002— Baltimore (A.L.)	5	12	.294	5.55	1.62	29	28	3	1	0	0-0	160.2	192	109	99	20	68-2	74	.303
2003— Baltimore (A.L.)								Did not play.											
2004— St. Lucie (Fla. St.)	1	0	1.000	0.00	0.86	2	2	0	0	...	0-...	7.0	6	0	0	0	0-0	5	.222
—Norfolk (Int'l)	3	3	.500	4.50	1.31	8	8	0	0	...	0-...	52.0	56	30	26	5	12-0	30	.279
—New York (N.L.)	0	1	.000	7.88	2.38	2	2	0	0	0	0-0	8.0	15	9	7	1	4-0	3	.395
—Texas (A.L.)	1	3	.250	6.16	2.05	4	4	0	0	0	0-0	19.0	23	13	13	2	16-0	6	.307
—Oklahoma (PCL)	0	1	.000	9.82	2.36	2	2	0	0	...	0-...	11.0	17	13	12	1	9-0	11	.370
2005— Los Angeles (N.L.)	1	4	.200	6.02	1.57	19	6	0	0	0	0-0	55.1	62	37	37	12	25-0	15	.288
—Las Vegas (PCL)	2	4	.333	7.20	1.70	7	7	0	0	0	0-0	40.0	47	34	32	6	21-0	26	.294
2006— Columbus (Int'l)	1	2	.333	4.24	1.29	12	0	0	0	1		17.0	11	10	8	1	11-0	11	.180
—	0	0	...	7.94	1.76	9	0	0	0	0	0-0	11.1	13	10	10	1	7-2	2	.283
American League totals (14 years)	141	131	.518	4.54	1.46	368	354	51	17	2	0-0	2297.1	2509	1260	1159	215	836-32	1234	.281
National League totals (2 years)	1	5	.167	6.25	1.67	21	10	0	0	0	0-0	63.1	77	46	44	13	29-0	18	.304
Major League totals (15 years)	142	136	.511	4.59	1.46	389	364	51	17	2	0-0	2360.2	2586	1306	1203	228	865-32	1252	.282

DIVISION SERIES RECORD

Year Team (League)	W	L	Pct.	ERA	WHIP	G	GS	CG	ShO	Hld.	Sv.-Opp.	IP	H	R	ER	HR	BB-IBB	SO	Avg.
1996— Baltimore (A.L.)	0	0	...	4.05	1.20	1	1	0	0	0	0-0	6.2	6	3	3	1	2-0	6	.240
1997— Baltimore (A.L.)	1	0	1.000	4.05	1.35	1	1	0	0	0	0-0	6.2	7	3	3	0	2-0	6	.269
Division series totals (2 years)	1	0	1.000	4.05	1.28	2	2	0	0	0	0-0	13.1	13	6	6	1	4-0	12	.254

E

CHAMPIONSHIP SERIES RECORD

Year Team (League)	W	L	Pct.	ERA	WHIP	G	GS	CG	ShO	Hld.	Sv.-Opp.	IP	H	R	ER	HR	BB-IBB	SO	Avg.
1991— Minnesota (A.L.)	0	0	...	4.50	2.00	1	1	0	0	0	0-0	4.0	3	2	2	1	5-0	2	.214
1996— Baltimore (A.L.)	0	1	.000	2.38	1.59	2	2	0	0	0	0-0	11.1	14	9	3	3	4-0	8	.286
1997— Baltimore (A.L.)	1	0	1.000	4.26	1.26	2	2	0	0	0	0-0	12.2	15	7	6	2	1-0	6	.300
Champ. series totals (3 years)	1	1	.500	3.54	1.50	5	5	0	0	0	0-0	28.0	32	18	11	6	10-0	16	.283

WORLD SERIES RECORD

Year Team (League)	W	L	Pct.	ERA	WHIP	G	GS	CG	ShO	Hld.	Sv.-Opp.	IP	H	R	ER	HR	BB-IBB	SO	Avg.
1991— Minnesota (A.L.)	0	0	...	5.06	1.31	2	2	0	0	0	0-0	10.2	10	7	6	3	4-0	5	.233

2006 LEFTY-RIGHTY SPLITS

vs.	Avg.	AB	H	2B	3B	HR	RBI	BB	SO	OBP	Slg.	vs.	Avg.	AB	H	2B	3B	HR	RBI	BB	SO	OBP	Slg.
L	.333	21	7	0	0	0	5	4	1	.440	.333	R	.240	25	6	2	0	2	5	3	1	.387	.560

ERSTAD, DARIN   OF/1B

PERSONAL: Born June 4, 1974, in Jamestown, N.D. ... 6-2/210. ... Bats left, throws left. ... Full name: Darin Charles Erstad. ... Name pronounced: ER-stad. ... High school: Jamestown (N.D.). ... College: Nebraska. **TRANSACTIONS/CAREER NOTES:** Selected by New York Mets organization in 13th round of 1992 free-agent draft; did not sign. ... Selected by California Angels organization in first round (first pick overall) of 1995 free-agent draft. ... Angels franchise renamed Anaheim Angels for 1997 season. ... On disabled list (August 4-19, 1998; and August 11-26, 1999). ... On disabled list (April 20-June 9 and August 7, 2003-remainder of season); included rehabilitation assignment to Salt Lake. ... On disabled list (May 9-June 14, 2004); included rehabilitation assignment to Salt Lake. ... Angels franchise renamed Los Angeles Angels of Anaheim for 2005 season. ... On disabled list (May 8-June 12 and June 23-September 1, 2006); included rehabilitation assignments to Rancho Cucamonga and Salt Lake. **HONORS:** Named outfielder on THE SPORTING NEWS A.L. All-Star team (2000). ... Won A.L. Gold Glove as outfielder (2000 and 2002). ... Won A.L. Gold Glove at first base (2004). ... Named outfielder on A.L. Silver Slugger team (2000). **STATISTICAL NOTES:** Career major league grand slams: 1.

2006 GAMES PLAYED BY POSITION (MLB): OF—27, 1B—13.

								BATTING										FIELDING	
Year Team (League)	Pos.	G	AB	R	H	2B	3B	HR	RBI	BB	SO	HBP	GDP	SB-CS	Avg.	OBP	SLG	OPS	E	Avg.
1995— Ariz. Angels (Ariz.)	OF	4	18	2	10	1	0	0	1	1	1	0	0	1-0	.556	.579	.611	1.190	0	1.000
— Lake Elsinore (Calif.)	OF	25	113	24	41	7	2	5	24	6	22	0	2	3-0	.363	.392	.593	.985	1	.985
1996— Vancouver (PCL) OF-1B-DH		85	351	63	107	22	5	6	41	44	53	3	5	11-6	.305	.385	.447	.832	1	.995
— California (A.L.)	OF	57	208	34	59	5	1	4	20	17	29	0	3	3-3	.284	.333	.375	.708	3	.976
1997— Anaheim (A.L.) 1B-DH-OF		139	539	99	161	34	4	16	77	51	86	4	5	23-8	.299	.360	.466	.826	11	.990
1998— Anaheim (A.L.) OF-1B-DH		133	537	84	159	39	3	19	82	43	77	6	2	20-6	.296	.353	.466	.839	3	.995
1999— Anaheim (A.L.) 1B-OF-DH		142	585	84	148	22	5	13	53	47	101	1	16	13-7	.253	.308	.374	.683	1	.999
2000— Anaheim (A.L.) OF-DH-1B		157	*676	121	*240	39	6	25	100	64	82	1	8	28-8	.355	.409	.541	.951	3	.992
2001— Anaheim (A.L.) OF-1B-DH		157	631	89	163	35	1	9	63	62	113	10	8	24-10	.258	.331	.360	.691	1	.998
2002— Anaheim (A.L.) OF-1B-DH		150	625	99	177	28	4	10	73	27	67	2	9	23-3	.283	.313	.389	.702	1	.998
2003— Salt Lake (PCL)	OF	7	27	6	11	0	0	0	4	2	1	0	0	1-0	.407	.448	.407	.856	0	1.000
— Anaheim (A.L.)	OF	67	258	35	65	7	1	4	17	18	40	4	8	9-1	.252	.309	.333	.642	0	1.000
2004— Salt Lake (PCL)	1B	4	16	2	2	0	0	0	3	1	1	0	0	0-0	.125	.176	.125	.301	1	.963
— Anaheim (A.L.)	1B	125	495	79	146	29	1	7	69	37	74	4	9	16-1	.295	.346	.400	.746	4	.996
2005— Los Angeles (A.L.) 1B-DH		153	609	86	166	33	3	7	66	47	109	1	8	10-3	.273	.325	.371	.696	4	.997
2006— Salt Lake (PCL)		7	30	0	3	0	0	0	3	1	2	0		1-0	.100	.129	.100	.229	0	1.000
— Rancho Cuca. (Calif.)		7	14	4	3	0	0	0	0	1	2	0	0	0-0	.214	.389	.214	.603	0	1.000
— Los Angeles (A.L.)	OF-1B	40	95	8	21	8	1	0	5	6	18	2	2	1-1	.221	.279	.326	.605	0	1.000
Major League totals (11 years)		1320	5258	818	1505	279	30	114	625	419	796	35	78	170-51	.286	.341	.416	.756	31	.995

DIVISION SERIES RECORD

Year Team (League)	Pos.	G	AB	R	H	2B	3B	HR	RBI	BB	SO	HBP	GDP	SB-CS	Avg.	OBP	SLG	OPS	E	Avg.
2002— Anaheim (A.L.)	OF	4	19	4	8	2	0	0	2	0	1	0	1	1-0	.421	.421	.526	.947	0	1.000
2004— Anaheim (A.L.)	1B	3	10	2	5	1	0	1	2	3	1	1	0	0-0	.500	.643	.900	1.543	0	1.000
2005— Los Angeles (A.L.)	1B	5	20	1	6	2	0	0	3	0	6	0	1	0-0	.300	.300	.400	.700	0	1.000
Division series totals (3 years)		12	49	7	19	5	0	1	7	3	8	1	3	1-0	.388	.434	.551	.985	0	1.000

CHAMPIONSHIP SERIES RECORD

Year Team (League)	Pos.	G	AB	R	H	2B	3B	HR	RBI	BB	SO	HBP	GDP	SB-CS	Avg.	OBP	SLG	OPS	E	Avg.
2002— Anaheim (A.L.)	OF	5	22	4	8	0	0	1	2	0	3	0	0	1-0	.364	.364	.500	.864	0	1.000
2005— Los Angeles (A.L.)	1B	5	17	1	4	1	0	0	0	1	2	0	0	1-0	.235	.278	.294	.572	0	1.000
Champ. series totals (2 years)		10	39	5	12	1	0	1	2	1	5	0	0	2-0	.308	.325	.410	.735	0	1.000

WORLD SERIES RECORD

Year Team (League)	Pos.	G	AB	R	H	2B	3B	HR	RBI	BB	SO	HBP	GDP	SB-CS	Avg.	OBP	SLG	OPS	E	Avg.
2002— Anaheim (A.L.)	OF	7	30	6	9	3	0	1	3	1	4	0	0	1-0	.300	.313	.500	.813	1	.955

ALL-STAR GAME RECORD

		G	AB	R	H	2B	3B	HR	RBI	BB	SO	HBP	GDP	SB-CS	Avg.	OBP	SLG	OPS	E	Avg.
All-Star Game totals (2 years)		2	4	1	0	0	0	0	1	0	0	0	0	0-0	.000	.000	.000	.000	0	1.000

2006 LEFTY-RIGHTY SPLITS

vs.	Avg.	AB	H	2B	3B	HR	RBI	BB	SO	OBP	Slg.	vs.	Avg.	AB	H	2B	3B	HR	RBI	BB	SO	OBP	Slg.
L	.192	26	5	2	1	0	1	3	6	.300	.346	R	.232	69	16	6	0	0	4	3	12	.270	.319

ESCOBAR, ALEX   OF

PERSONAL: Born September 6, 1978, in Valencia, Venezuela. ... 6-1/190. ... Bats right, throws right. ... Full name: Alexander Jose Escobar. ... Name pronounced: ess-COE-bar. ... High school: El Santuario (Valencia, Venezuela). **TRANSACTIONS/CAREER NOTES:** Signed as a non-drafted free agent by New York Mets organization (July 1, 1995). ... Traded by Mets with OF Matt Lawton, P Jerrod Riggan and two players to be named to Cleveland Indians for 2B Roberto Alomar, P Mike Bacsik and OF Danny Peoples (December 11, 2001); Indians acquired P Billy Traber and 1B Earl Snyder to complete deal (December 13, 2001). ... On disabled list (March 30, 2002-entire season). ... Claimed on waivers by Chicago White Sox (August 17, 2004). ... On disabled list (August 17, 2004-remainder of season). ... Traded by White Sox to Washington Nationals for OF Jerry Owens (February 13, 2005). ... On disabled list (March 24, 2005-entire season). ... On disabled list (May 23-July 6, 2006); included rehabilitation assignments to GCL Nationals and Harrisburg. ... On disabled list (August 25, 2006-remainder of season).

2006 GAMES PLAYED BY POSITION (MLB): OF—23.

								BATTING										FIELDING	
Year Team (League)	Pos.	G	AB	R	H	2B	3B	HR	RBI	BB	SO	HBP	GDP	SB-CS	Avg.	OBP	SLG	OPS	E	Avg.
1996— GC Mets (GCL)	OF-SS	24	75	15	27	4	0	0	10	4	9	3	0	7-1	.360	.410	.413	.823	3	.936
1997— Kingsport (Appalachian) ...	OF	10	36	6	7	3	0	0	3	3	8	0	3	1-0	.194	.250	.278	.528	2	.905
— GC Mets (GCL)	OF	26	73	12	18	4	1	1	11	10	17	1	1	0-0	.247	.341	.370	.711	1	.966
1998— Capital City (SAL)	OF	112	416	90	129	23	5	27	91	54	133	5	1	49-7	.310	.393	.584	.977	12	.941
1999— GC Mets (GCL)	OF	2	8	1	3	2	0	0	1	1	2	0	0	0-0	.375	.444	.625	1.069	0	1.000

E

Year Team (League)	Pos.	G	AB	R	H	2B	3B	HR	RBI	BB	SO	HBP	GDP	SB-CS	Avg.	OBP	SLG	OPS	E	Avg.
—St. Lucie (Fla. St.)	OF	1	3	1	2	0	0	1	3	1	1	0	0	1-1	.667	.600	1.667	2.267	0	1.000
2000—Binghamton (East.)	OF	122	437	79	126	25	7	16	67	57	114	7	8	24-5	.288	.375	.487	.863	5	.983
2001—Norfolk (Int'l)	OF	111	397	55	106	21	4	12	52	35	146	3	10	18-3	.267	.327	.431	.758	5	.980
—New York (N.L.)	OF	18	50	3	10	1	0	3	8	3	19	0	1	1-0	.200	.245	.400	.645	2	.935
2002—Cleveland (A.L.)						Did not play.														
2003—Buffalo (Int'l) ....a	OF-DH	118	439	63	110	21	2	24	78	24	133	7	11	8-3	.251	.296	.472	.768	5	.975
—Cleveland (A.L.)	OF	28	99	16	27	2	0	5	14	7	33	1	0	1-0	.273	.324	.444	.769	2	.969
2004—Cleveland (A.L.)	OF-DH	46	152	20	32	8	2	1	12	23	42	1	1	1-1	.211	.318	.309	.627	1	.991
—Buffalo (Int'l)	OF-DH	16	63	10	18	5	0	4	10	4	15	2	0	0-1	.286	.348	.556	.903	0	1.000
2005—Wash. (N.L.)						Did not play.														
2006—Harrisburg (East.)		35	122	21	38	11	0	5	26	20	23	8	2	2-2	.311	.440	.525	.965	2	.972
—GC Nationals (GCL)		3	7	1	1	0	0	0	1	2	1	0	0	0-0	.143	.333	.143	.476	0	1.000
—Wash. (N.L.)	OF	33	87	14	31	3	2	4	18	8	18	0	3	2-0	.356	.394	.575	.969	1	.984
American League totals (2 years)		74	251	36	59	10	2	6	26	30	75	2	1	2-1	.235	.320	.363	.683	3	.983
National League totals (2 years)		51	137	17	41	4	2	7	26	11	37	0	4	3-0	.299	.342	.511	.853	3	.968
Major League totals (4 years)		125	388	53	100	14	4	13	52	41	112	2	5	5-1	.258	.328	.415	.743	6	.978

2006 LEFTY-RIGHTY SPLITS

vs.	Avg.	AB	H	2B	3B	HR	RBI	BB	SO	OBP	Slg.	vs.	Avg.	AB	H	2B	3B	HR	RBI	BB	SO	OBP	Slg.
L	.400	30	12	1	1	3	10	2	8	.417	.800	R	.333	57	19	2	1	1	8	5	10	.381	.456

ESCOBAR, KELVIM — P

PERSONAL: Born April 11, 1976, in La Guaria, Venezuela. ... 6-1/210. ... Throws right, bats right. ... Full name: Kelvim Jose Escobar. ... Name pronounced: kel-VEEM ESS-koh-bar. **TRANSACTIONS/CAREER NOTES:** Signed as a non-drafted free agent by Toronto Blue Jays organization (July 9, 1992). ... On disabled list (April 16-May 6, 1998); included rehabilitation assignment to Syracuse. ... Signed as a free agent by Anaheim Angels (November 24, 2003). ... Angels franchise renamed Los Angeles Angels of Anaheim for 2005 season. ... On disabled list (May 12-28 and June 9-September 6, 2005); included rehabilitation assignment to Salt Lake. ... On disabled list (July 7-22, 2006).

CAREER HITTING: 1-for-21 (.048), 1 R, 0 2B, 0 3B, 0 HR, 1 RBI.

Year Team (League)	W	L	Pct.	ERA	WHIP	G	GS	CG	ShO	Hld.	Sv.-Opp.	IP	H	R	ER	HR	BB-IBB	SO	Avg.
1993—Dom. Blue. Jays (DSL)	2	1	.667	4.13	1.81	8	7	0	0	...	0-...	32.2	34	17	15	...	25-...	31	...
1994—GC Jays (GCL)	4	4	.500	2.35	1.14	11	10	1	0	...	1-...	65.0	56	23	17	0	18-0	64	.237
1995—Dom. Blue. Jays (DSL)	0	1	.000	1.72	1.21	3	2	0	0	...	0-...	15.2	14	3	3		5-...	20	...
—Medicine Hat (Pio.)	3	3	.500	5.71	1.43	14	14	1	1	...	0-...	69.1	66	47	44	6	33-0	75	.253
1996—Dunedin (Fla. St.)	9	5	.643	2.69	1.21	18	18	1	0	...	0-...	110.1	101	44	33	5	33-0	113	.240
—Knoxville (Southern)	3	4	.429	5.33	1.57	10	10	0	0	...	0-...	54.0	61	36	32	7	24-0	44	.288
1997—Dunedin (Fla. St.)	0	1	.000	3.75	1.58	3	2	0	0	...	0-...	12.0	16	9	5	0	3-0	16	.327
—Knoxville (Southern)	2	1	.667	3.70	1.48	5	5	0	0	...	0-...	24.1	20	13	10	1	16-0	31	.222
—Toronto (A.L.)	3	2	.600	2.90	1.52	27	0	0	0	1	14-17	31.0	28	12	10	1	19-2	36	.237
1998—Toronto (A.L.)	7	3	.700	3.73	1.34	22	10	0	0	5	0-1	79.2	72	37	33	5	35-0	72	.238
—Syracuse (Int'l)	2	2	.500	3.77	1.81	13	10	0	0	...	1-...	59.2	51	26	25	7	24-0	64	.229
1999—Toronto (A.L.)	14	11	.560	5.69	1.63	33	30	1	0	0	0-0	174.0	203	118	110	19	81-2	129	.293
2000—Toronto (A.L.)	10	15	.400	5.35	1.51	43	24	3	1	3	2-3	180.0	186	118	107	26	85-3	142	.267
2001—Toronto (A.L.)	6	8	.429	3.50	1.15	59	11	1	1	13	0-0	126.0	93	51	49	8	52-5	121	.204
2002—Toronto (A.L.)	5	7	.417	4.27	1.53	76	0	0	0		38-46	78.0	75	39	37	10	44-6	85	.246
2003—Toronto (A.L.)	13	9	.591	4.29	1.48	41	26	1	0	0	4-5	180.1	189	94	86	15	78-3	159	.270
2004—Anaheim (A.L.)	11	12	.478	3.93	1.29	33	33	0	0	0	0-0	208.1	192	91	91	21	76-2	191	.244
2005—Rancho Cuca. (Calif.)	0	0	...	0.00	1.00	1	1	0	0	0	0-0	3.0	1	0	0	0	2-0	7	.100
—Salt Lake (PCL)	1	0	1.000	2.51	1.53	4	4	0	0	0	0-0	14.1	14	4	4	2	8-0	22	.250
—Los Angeles (A.L.)	3	2	.600	3.02	1.11	16	7	0	0	2	1-1	59.2	45	21	20	4	21-1	63	.207
2006—Los Angeles (A.L.)	11	14	.440	3.61	1.28	30	30	1	0	0	0-0	189.1	192	93	76	17	50-2	147	.264
Major League totals (10 years)	83	83	.500	4.26	1.39	380	171	7	3	24	59-73	1306.1	1275	674	619	126	541-26	1145	.255

DIVISION SERIES RECORD

Year Team (League)	W	L	Pct.	ERA	WHIP	G	GS	CG	ShO	Hld.	Sv.-Opp.	IP	H	R	ER	HR	BB-IBB	SO	Avg.
2004—Anaheim (A.L.)	0	0	...	8.10	3.00	1	1	0	0	0	0-0	3.1	5	5	3	0	5-1	4	.333
2005—Los Angeles (A.L.)	1	0	1.000	1.29	1.00	4	0	0	0	2	0-0	7.0	2	1	1	1	5-0	5	.091
Division series totals (2 years)	1	0	1.000	3.48	1.65	5	1	0	0	2	0-0	10.1	7	6	4	1	10-1	9	.189

CHAMPIONSHIP SERIES RECORD

Year Team (League)	W	L	Pct.	ERA	WHIP	G	GS	CG	ShO	Hld.	Sv.-Opp.	IP	H	R	ER	HR	BB-IBB	SO	Avg.
2005—Los Angeles (A.L.)	0	2	.000	2.08	1.38	2	0	0	0	0	0-1	4.1	4	3	1	1	2-0	10	.222

2006 LEFTY-RIGHTY SPLITS

vs.	Avg.	AB	H	2B	3B	HR	RBI	BB	SO	OBP	Slg.	vs.	Avg.	AB	H	2B	3B	HR	RBI	BB	SO	OBP	Slg.
L	.258	345	89	13	2		15	50	30	60	.320	.438	R	.270	381	103	25	0		28	20	87	.309	.352

ESTES, SHAWN — P

PERSONAL: Born February 18, 1973, in San Bernardino, Calif. ... 6-2/200. ... Throws left, bats right. ... Full name: Aaron Shawn Estes. ... Name pronounced: ES-tus. ... High school: Douglas (Minden, Nev.). **TRANSACTIONS/CAREER NOTES:** Selected by Seattle Mariners organization in first round (11th pick overall) of 1991 free-agent draft. ... Traded by Mariners with IF Wilson Delgado to San Francisco Giants for P Salomon Torres (May 21, 1995). ... On disabled list (March 23-April 6, 1997). ... On disabled list (July 11-September 4, 1998); included rehabilitation assignments to Bakersfield and Fresno. ... On disabled list (March 29-April 17, 2000); included rehabilitation assignments to Fresno and San Jose. ... On disabled list (May 9-24 and August 23, 2001-remainder of season). ... Traded by Mets with cash to Cincinnati Reds for P Pedro Feliciano, OF Elvin Andujar and two players to be named (August 15, 2002); Mets acquired OF Raul Gonzalez (August 20, 2002) and OF Brady Clark (September 9, 2002) to complete deal. ... Signed as a free agent by Chicago Cubs (December 20, 2002). ... Signed as a free agent by Colorado Rockies organization (January 23, 2004). ... Signed as a free agent by Arizona Diamondbacks (January 12, 2005). ... On disabled list (July 7-September 9, 2005); included rehabilitation assignment to Tucson. ... Signed as free agent by San Diego Padres (January 11, 2006). ... On disabled list (April 6, 2006-remainder of season). **STATISTICAL NOTES:** Career major league grand slams: 1. **MISCELLANEOUS NOTES:** Appeared in four games as pinch runner (1996). ... Appeared in four games as pinch runner (1997). ... Scored two runs in two games as pinch runner (1998). ... Struck out in both appearances as pinch hitter and scored two runs in eight appearances as pinch runner (1999). ... Appeared in two games as pinch runner (2000). ... Appeared in one game as pinch runner (2002). ... Had a sacrifice hit in only appearance as pinch hitter (2003). ... Scored a run in two appearances as pinch runner (2004).

CAREER HITTING: 77-for-489 (.157), 49 R, 14 2B, 2 3B, 4 HR, 28 RBI.

Year Team (League)	W	L	Pct.	ERA	WHIP	G	GS	CG	ShO	Hld.	Sv.-Opp.	IP	H	R	ER	HR	BB-IBB	SO	Avg.
1991—Bellingham (N'west)	1	3	.250	6.88	2.41	9	9	0	0	...	0-...	34.0	27	33	26	2	55-0	35	.218
1992—Bellingham (N'west)	3	3	.500	4.32	1.68	15	15	0	0	...	0-...	77.0	84	55	37	6	45-0	77	.279
1993—Appleton (Midwest)	5	9	.357	7.24	1.92	19	18	0	0	...	0-...	83.1	108	75	67	12	52-1	65	.305

E

Year Team (League)	W	L	Pct.	ERA	WHIP	G	GS	CG	ShO	Hld.	Sv.-Opp.	IP	H	R	ER	HR	BB-IBB	SO	Avg.
1994—Ariz. Mariners (Ariz.)	0	3	.000	3.15	1.10	5	5	0	0	...	0-...	20.0	16	9	7	0	6-0	31	.205
—Appleton (Midwest)	0	2	.000	4.58	1.83	5	4	0	0	...	0-...	19.2	19	13	10	1	17-0	28	.271
1995—Wisconsin (Midw.)	0	0	...	0.90	1.00	2	2	0	0	...	0-...	10.0	5	1	1	0	5-0	11	.156
—Burlington (Midw.)	0	0	...	4.11	1.63	4	4	0	0	...	0-...	15.1	13	8	7	2	12-0	22	.224
—San Jose (Calif.)	5	2	.714	2.17	0.99	9	8	0	0	...	0-...	49.2	32	13	12	1	17-0	61	.188
—Shreveport (Texas)	2	0	1.000	2.01	1.07	4	4	0	0	...	0-...	22.1	14	5	5	1	10-0	18	.184
—San Francisco (N.L.)	0	3	.000	6.75	1.21	3	3	0	0	...	0-0	17.1	16	14	13	2	5-0	14	.229
1996—Phoenix (PCL)	9	3	.750	3.43	1.18	18	18	0	0	...	0-0	110.1	92	43	42	7	38-1	95	.228
—San Francisco (N.L.)	3	5	.375	3.60	1.46	11	11	0	0	0	0-0	70.0	63	30	28	3	39-3	60	.243
1997—San Francisco (N.L.)	19	5	.792	3.18	1.30	32	32	3	2	0	0-0	201.0	162	80	71	12	* 100-2	181	.223
1998—San Francisco (N.L.)	7	12	.368	5.06	1.54	25	25	1	0	0	0-0	149.1	150	89	84	14	80-6	136	.269
—Bakersfield (Calif.)	0	0	...	0.00	0.92	1	1	0	0	...	0-...	4.1	3	0	0	0	1-0	5	.188
—Fresno (PCL)	1	0	1.000	1.80	1.20	1	1	0	0	...	0-...	5.0	3	1	1	1	3-0	6	.188
1999—San Francisco (N.L.)	11	11	.500	4.92	1.58	32	32	1	1	0	0-0	203.0	209	121	111	21	112-2	159	.268
2000—Fresno (PCL)	0	1	.000	9.00	2.33	1	1	0	0	...	0-...	3.0	5	3	3	2	2-0	2	.294
—San Jose (Calif.)	1	0	1.000	0.00	0.43	1	1	0	0	...	0-...	7.0	2	0	0	0	1-0	11	.095
—San Francisco (N.L.)	15	6	.714	4.26	1.59	30	30	4	2	0	0-0	190.1	194	99	90	11	108-1	136	.275
2001—San Francisco (N.L.)	9	8	.529	4.02	1.43	27	27	0	0	0	0-0	159.0	151	78	71	11	77-7	109	.253
2002—New York (N.L.)	4	9	.308	4.55	1.50	23	23	1	1	0	0-0	132.2	133	70	67	12	66-9	92	.267
—Cincinnati (N.L.)	1	3	.250	7.71	1.96	6	6	0	0	0	0-0	28.0	38	24	24	1	17-0	17	.345
2003—Chicago (N.L.)	8	11	.421	5.73	1.74	29	29	1	1	0	0-0	152.1	182	113	97	20	83-1	103	.305
2004—Colorado (N.L.)	15	8	.652	5.84	1.62	34	34	1	0	0	0-0	202.0	223	* 133	* 131	30	105-5	117	.291
2005—Tucson (PCL)	0	0	...	1.64	0.82	2	2	0	0	0	0-0	11.0	5	2	2	1	4-0	9	.132
—Arizona (N.L.)	7	8	.467	4.80	1.43	21	21	2	0	0	0-0	123.2	132	70	66	15	45-0	63	.280
2006—San Diego (N.L.)	0	1	.000	4.50	1.33	1	1	0	0	0	0-0	6.0	5	3	3	0	3-0	4	.217
Major League totals (12 years)	99	90	.524	4.71	1.53	274	273	14	8	0	0-0	1634.2	*1658	924	856	152	840-36	1191	.269

DIVISION SERIES RECORD

Year Team (League)	W	L	Pct.	ERA	WHIP	G	GS	CG	ShO	Hld.	Sv.-Opp.	IP	H	R	ER	HR	BB-IBB	SO	Avg.
1997—San Francisco (N.L.)	0	0	...	15.00	3.00	1	1	0	0	0	0-0	3.0	5	5	5	1	4-0	3	.357
2000—San Francisco (N.L.)	0	0	...	6.00	2.00	1	1	0	0	0	0-0	3.0	3	2	2	0	3-0	3	.250
Division series totals (2 years)	0	0	...	10.50	2.50	2	2	0	0	0	0-0	6.0	8	7	7	1	7-0	6	.308

ALL-STAR GAME RECORD

	W	L	Pct.	ERA	WHIP	G	GS	CG	ShO	Hld.	Sv.-Opp.	IP	H	R	ER	HR	BB-IBB	SO	Avg.
All-Star Game totals (1 year)	0	1	.000	18.00	2.00	1	0	0	0	0	0-0	1.0	1	2	2	1	1-0	1	.250

2006 LEFTY-RIGHTY SPLITS

vs.	Avg.	AB	H	2B	3B	HR	RBI	BB	SO	OBP	Slg.	vs.	Avg.	AB	H	2B	3B	HR	RBI	BB	SO	OBP	Slg.
L	.000	0	0	0	0	0	0	1	0	.667	.000	R	.227	22	5	0	0	0	2	2	4	.292	.227

ESTRADA, JOHNNY — C

PERSONAL: Born June 27, 1976, in Hayward, Calif. ... 5-11/210. ... Bats both, throws right. ... Full name: Johnny P. Estrada. ... High school: Roosevelt (Fresno, Calif.). ... Junior college: College of the Sequoias (Calif.). **TRANSACTIONS/CAREER NOTES:** Selected by Houston Astros organization in 71st round of 1994 free-agent draft; did not sign. ... Selected by Philadelphia Phillies organization in 17th round of 1997 free-agent draft. ... Traded by Phillies to Atlanta Braves for P Kevin Millwood (December 20, 2002). ... On suspended list (July 27-29, 2005). ... On disabled list (August 7-22, 2005). ... Traded by Braves to Arizona Diamondbacks for Ps Oscar Villarreal and Lance Cormier (December 7, 2005). **HONORS:** Named catcher on THE SPORTING NEWS N.L. All-Star team (2004). ... Named catcher on N.L. Silver Slugger team (2004).

2006 GAMES PLAYED BY POSITION (MLB): C—108.

Year Team (League)	Pos.	G	AB	R	H	2B	3B	HR	RBI	BB	SO	HBP	GDP	SB-CS	Avg.	OBP	SLG	OPS	E (FIELDING)	Avg. (FIELDING)
1997—Batavia (NY-Penn)	1B-C	58	223	28	70	17	2	6	43	9	15	1	9	0-0	.314	.336	.489	.825	1	1.000
1998—Piedmont (S. Atl.)	C	77	303	33	94	14	2	7	44	6	19	5	11	0-1	.310	.331	.439	.770	6	.990
—Clearwater (FSL)	C	37	117	8	26	8	0	0	13	5	7	0	2	0-0	.222	.250	.291	.541	5	.979
1999—Clearwater (FSL)	C	98	346	35	96	15	0	9	52	14	26	2	12	1-0	.277	.303	.399	.702	5	.990
2000—Reading (East.)	C	95	356	42	105	18	0	12	42	10	20	4	8	1-0	.295	.322	.447	.768	7	.990
2001—Scran./W.B. (I.L.)	C	32	131	13	38	13	0	6	16	5	6	1	5	0-0	.290	.319	.389	.708	0	1.000
—Philadelphia (N.L.)	C	89	298	26	68	15	0	8	37	16	32	4	15	0-0	.228	.273	.359	.632	4	.993
2002—Scran./W.B. (I.L.)	C	118	434	49	121	27	0	11	67	26	53	5	19	1-0	.279	.322	.417	.739	4	.995
—Philadelphia (N.L.)	C	10	17	0	2	1	0	0	2	2	2	0	0	0-0	.118	.211	.176	.387	0	1.000
2003—Richmond (Int'l)	C-DH	106	354	40	116	29	0	10	66	30	20	12	11	0-0	.328	.393	.494	.887	4	.994
—Atlanta (N.L.)	C	16	36	2	11	0	0	0	2	0	3	3	1	0-0	.306	.359	.306	.665	0	1.000
2004—Atlanta (N.L.)	C	134	462	56	145	36	0	9	76	39	66	11	18	0-0	.314	.378	.450	.828	9	.989
2005—Atlanta (N.L.)	C	105	357	31	93	26	0	4	39	20	38	3	13	0-0	.261	.303	.367	.670	2	.997
2006—Arizona (N.L.)	C	115	414	43	125	26	0	11	71	13	40	7	17	0-0	.302	.328	.444	.772	3	.996
Major League totals (6 years)		469	1584	158	444	104	0	32	227	90	181	28	64	0-0	.280	.327	.407	.733	18	.994

DIVISION SERIES RECORD

Year Team (League)	Pos.	G	AB	R	H	2B	3B	HR	RBI	BB	SO	HBP	GDP	SB-CS	Avg.	OBP	SLG	OPS	E	Avg.
2004—Atlanta (N.L.)	C	5	17	3	6	0	0	2	4	3	3	0	0	0-0	.353	.429	.706	1.134	0	1.000
2005—Atlanta (N.L.)	C	1	4	0	1	0	0	0	1	0	2	0	0	0-0	.250	.250	.250	.500	0	1.000
Division series totals (2 years)		6	21	3	7	0	0	2	5	3	5	0	0	0-0	.333	.400	.619	1.019	0	1.000

ALL-STAR GAME RECORD

	G	AB	R	H	2B	3B	HR	RBI	BB	SO	HBP	GDP	SB-CS	Avg.	OBP	SLG	OPS	E	Avg.
All-Star Game totals (1 year)	1	2	0	0	0	0	0	0	0	1	0	0	0-0	.000	.000	.000	.000	0	1.000

2006 LEFTY-RIGHTY SPLITS

vs.	Avg.	AB	H	2B	3B	HR	RBI	BB	SO	OBP	Slg.	vs.	Avg.	AB	H	2B	3B	HR	RBI	BB	SO	OBP	Slg.
L	.296	98	29	2	0	3	17	4	9	.317	.408	R	.304	316	96	24	0	8	54	9	31	.331	.456

ETHERTON, SETH — P

PERSONAL: Born October 17, 1976, in Laguna Beach, Calif. ... 6-1/200. ... Throws right, bats right. ... Full name: Seth Michael Etherton. ... High school: Dana Hills (Dana Point, Calif.). ... College: Southern California. **TRANSACTIONS/CAREER NOTES:** Selected by Florida Marlins organization in 16th round of 1994 free-agent draft; did not sign. ... Selected by St. Louis Cardinals organization in ninth-round of 1997 free-agent draft; did not sign. ... Selected by Anaheim Angels organization in first round (18th pick overall) of 1998 free-agent draft. ... On disabled list (August 5, 2000-remainder of season). ... Traded by Angels to Cincinnati Reds for SS Wilmy Caceres (December 10, 2000). ... On disabled list (March 22, 2001-entire season). ... On disabled list (March 21-July 11 and July 23, 2002-remainder of season); included rehabilitation assignments to Dayton, Chattanooga and Louisville. ... Claimed on waivers by New York Yankees (July 11, 2002). ... Waiver claim voided by commissioner's office (July 23, 2002). ...

E

Signed as a free agent by Oakland Athletics (November 1, 2004). ... Signed as a free agent by Kansas City Royals organization (November 22, 2005). ... Selected by San Diego Padres organization from Royals organization in Rule 5 major league draft (December 8, 2005). ... Traded by Padres to Royals for cash (May 27, 2006).
CAREER HITTING: 1-for-9 (.111), 1 R, 0 2B, 0 3B, 0 HR, 0 RBI.

Year	Team (League)	W	L	Pct.	ERA	WHIP	G	GS	CG	ShO	Hld.	Sv.-Opp.	IP	H	R	ER	HR	BB-IBB	SO	Avg.
1998— Midland (Texas)		1	5	.167	6.14	1.43	9	7	1	0	...	0-...	48.1	57	36	33	9	12-0	35	.295
1999— Erie (East.)		10	10	.500	3.27	1.17	24	24	4	1	...	0-...	167.2	153	72	61	14	43-0	153	.241
— Edmonton (PCL)		0	2	.000	5.48	1.45	4	4	0	0	...	0-...	21.1	25	13	13	7	6-0	19	.291
2000— Edmonton (PCL)		3	2	.600	4.01	1.35	9	9	0	0	...	0-...	58.1	60	30	26	6	19-0	50	.264
— Anaheim (A.L.)		5	1	.833	5.52	1.49	11	11	0	0	...	0-0	60.1	68	38	37	16	22-0	32	.278
2001— Cincinnati (N.L.)				Did not play.																
2002— Dayton (Midw.)		0	0	...	0.00	1.00	1	1	0	0	...	0-...	1.0	1	0	0	0	0-0	2	.250
— Chattanooga (Sou.)		0	1	.000	0.96	0.75	3	3	0	0	...	0-...	9.1	5	1	1	0	2-0	4	.167
— Louisville (Int'l)		0	1	.000	8.22	1.76	5	5	0	0	...	0-...	15.1	21	16	14	4	6-0	10	.328
— Norwich (East.)		0	0	...	0.00	1.00	1	1	0	0	...	0-...	2.0	1	1	0	0	1-0	2	.143
2003— Louisville (Int'l)		7	7	.500	4.31	1.38	21	21	2	1	...	0-...	123.1	144	62	59	11	26-1	69	.297
— Cincinnati (N.L.)		2	4	.333	6.90	1.80	7	7	0	0	0	0-0	30.0	39	23	23	4	15-1	17	.322
2004— Chattanooga (Sou.)		4	1	.800	1.98	0.98	7	7	0	0	...	0-...	41.0	31	12	9	2	9-0	46	.204
— Louisville (Int'l)		5	6	.455	3.47	1.24	19	19	3	1	...	0-...	111.2	107	45	43	13	32-1	110	.252
2005— Oakland (A.L.)		1	1	.500	6.62	1.19	3	3	0	0	0	0-0	17.2	16	13	13	4	5-0	10	.235
— Sacramento (PCL)		7	7	.500	2.72	1.09	20	19	0	0	0	0-0	112.1	93	44	34	11	30-1	99	.220
2006— Portland (PCL)		2	2	.500	4.38	1.26	9	9	0	0	0	0-0	49.1	48	25	24	8	14-0	49	.253
— Kansas City (A.L.)		1	1	.500	9.39	2.09	2	2	0	0	0	0-0	7.2	10	9	8	3	6-0	4	.313
— Omaha (PCL)		1	4	.200	6.49	1.62	10	6	0	0	0	0-0	34.2	43	25	25	11	13-0	29	.307
American League totals (3 years)		7	3	.700	6.09	1.48	16	16	0	0	0	0-0	85.2	94	60	58	23	33-0	46	.272
National League totals (1 year)		2	4	.333	6.90	1.80	7	7	0	0	0	0-0	30.0	39	23	23	4	15-1	17	.322
Major League totals (4 years)		9	7	.563	6.30	1.56	23	23	0	0	0	0-0	115.2	133	83	81	27	48-1	63	.285

2006 LEFTY-RIGHTY SPLITS

vs.	Avg.	AB	H	2B	3B	HR	RBI	BB	SO	OBP	Slg.	vs.	Avg.	AB	H	2B	3B	HR	RBI	BB	SO	OBP	Slg.
L	.231	13	3	1	0	0	2	4	4	.389	.308	R	.368	19	7	1	0	3	7	2	0	.409	.895

ETHIER, ANDRE — OF

PERSONAL: Born April 10, 1982, in Phoenix, Ariz. ... 6-3/195. ... Bats left, throws right. ... Full name: Andre Everett Ethier. ... High school: St. Mary's (Phoenix). ... College: Arizona State. **TRANSACTIONS/CAREER NOTES:** Selected by Oakland Athletics organization in second round of 2003 free-agent draft. ... Traded by A's to Los Angeles Dodgers for OF Milton Bradley and IF Antonio Perez (December 13, 2005).
2006 GAMES PLAYED BY POSITION (MLB): OF-109.

Year	Team (League)	Pos.	G	AB	R	H	2B	3B	HR	RBI	BB	SO	HBP	GDP	SB-CS	Avg.	OBP	SLG	OPS	E	Avg.
								BATTING												**FIELDING**	
2003— Vancouver (N'west)			10	41	7	16	4	1	1	7	3	3	1	3	2-1	.390	.444	.610	1.054	0	...
— Kane Co. (Midw.)			40	162	23	44	10	0	0	11	19	25	2	4	2-2	.272	.355	.333	.688	3	...
2004— Modesto (California)			99	419	72	131	23	5	7	53	45	64	4	12	2-5	.313	.383	.442	.825	8	...
2005— Midland (Texas)		OF-DH	131	505	104	161	30	3	18	80	48	93	11	18	1-4	.319	.385	.497	.882	5	.990
— Sacramento (PCL)		OF	4	15	0	4	1	0	0	2	2	3	0	0	0-0	.267	.353	.333	.686	2	.800
2006— Las Vegas (PCL)			25	86	15	30	4	3	1	12	14	16	2	1	2-1	.349	.447	.500	.947	1	.977
— Los Angeles (N.L.)		OF	126	396	50	122	20	7	11	55	34	77	5	11	5-5	.308	.365	.477	.842	6	.968
Major League totals (1 year)			126	396	50	122	20	7	11	.55	34	77	5	11	5-5	.308	.365	.477	.842	6	.968

DIVISION SERIES RECORD

Year	Team (League)	Pos.	G	AB	R	H	2B	3B	HR	RBI	BB	SO	HBP	GDP	SB-CS	Avg.	OBP	SLG	OPS	E	Avg.
2006— Los Angeles (N.L.)		OF	2	1	0	0	0	0	0	0	0	0	0	0	0-0	.000	.000	.000	.000	0	...

2006 LEFTY-RIGHTY SPLITS

vs.	Avg.	AB	H	2B	3B	HR	RBI	BB	SO	OBP	Slg.	vs.	Avg.	AB	H	2B	3B	HR	RBI	BB	SO	OBP	Slg.
L	.351	77	27	2	2	1	11	3	13	.378	.468	R	.298	319	95	18	5	10	44	31	64	.362	.480

EVELAND, DANA — P

PERSONAL: Born October 29, 1983, in Olympia, Wash. ... 6-1/220. ... Throws left, bats left. ... Full name: Dana J. Eveland. ... Junior college: Hill Junior College. **TRANSACTIONS/CAREER NOTES:** Selected by Milwaukee Brewers organization in 16th round of 2002 free-agent draft.
CAREER HITTING: 0-for-8 (.000), 0 R, 0 2B, 0 3B, 0 HR, 0 RBI.

Year	Team (League)	W	L	Pct.	ERA	WHIP	G	GS	CG	ShO	Hld.	Sv.-Opp.	IP	H	R	ER	HR	BB-IBB	SO	Avg.
2003— Helena (Pion.)		2	1	.667	2.08	1.46	19	0	0	0	...	14-...	26.0	30	9	6	1	8-1	41	.286
2004— Beloit (Midw.)		9	6	.600	2.84	1.13	22	16	1	0	...	2-...	117.1	108	48	37	8	24-0	119	.244
— Huntsville (Sou.)		0	2	.000	2.28	1.14	4	4	0	0	...	0-...	23.2	23	9	6	0	4-0	14	.261
2005— Huntsville (Sou.)		10	4	.714	2.72	1.23	18	18	0	0	0	0-0	109.0	96	42	33	4	38-1	98	.237
— Milwaukee (N.L.)		1	1	.500	5.97	1.83	27	0	0	0	7	1-2	31.2	40	21	21	2	18-3	23	.317
2006— Nashville (PCL)		6	5	.545	2.74	1.07	20	19	0	0	0	0-1	105.0	71	40	32	4	41-1	110	.191
— Milwaukee (N.L.)		0	3	.000	8.13	1.99	9	5	0	0	0	0-1	27.2	39	25	25	4	16-2	32	.331
Major League totals (2 years)		1	4	.200	6.98	1.90	36	5	0	0	7	1-3	59.1	79	46	46	6	34-5	55	.324

2006 LEFTY-RIGHTY SPLITS

vs.	Avg.	AB	H	2B	3B	HR	RBI	BB	SO	OBP	Slg.	vs.	Avg.	AB	H	2B	3B	HR	RBI	BB	SO	OBP	Slg.
L	.421	38	16	5	0	2	12	5	13	.500	.711	R	.288	80	23	3	0	2	11	19	19	.396	.400

EVERETT, ADAM — SS

PERSONAL: Born February 5, 1977, in Austell, Ga. ... 6-0/170. ... Bats right, throws right. ... Full name: Jeffrey Adam Everett. ... High school: Harrison (Kennesaw, Ga.). ... College: South Carolina. **TRANSACTIONS/CAREER NOTES:** Selected by Chicago Cubs organization in fourth round of 1995 free-agent draft; did not sign. ... Selected by Boston Red Sox organization in first round (12th pick overall) of 1998 free-agent draft. ... Traded by Red Sox with P Greg Miller to Houston Astros for OF Carl Everett (December 14, 1999). ... On disabled list (August 7-September 29, 2004). **STATISTICAL NOTES:** Career major league grand slams: 1. **MISCELLANEOUS NOTES:** Member of 2000 U.S. Olympic baseball team.
2006 GAMES PLAYED BY POSITION (MLB): SS-149.

Year	Team (League)	Pos.	G	AB	R	H	2B	3B	HR	RBI	BB	SO	HBP	GDP	SB-CS	Avg.	OBP	SLG	OPS	E	Avg.
								BATTING												**FIELDING**	
1998— Lowell (NY-Penn)		SS	21	71	11	21	6	2	0	9	11	13	3	2	2-1	.296	.407	.437	.844	9	.918
1999— Trenton (East.)		SS	98	338	56	89	11	0	10	44	41	64	10	3	21-5	.263	.356	.385	.741	18	.959
2000— New Orleans (PCL)		SS	126	453	82	111	25	2	5	37	75	100	11	6	13-4	.245	.363	.342	.705	25	.959

Year Team (League)	Pos.	G	AB	R	H	2B	3B	HR	RBI	BB	SO	HBP	GDP	SB-CS	Avg.	OBP	SLG	OPS	E	Avg.
2001—New Orleans (PCL)	SS	114	441	69	110	20	8	5	40	39	74	16	4	24-5	.249	.330	.365	.695	24	.956
—Houston (N.L.)	SS	9	3	1	0	0	0	0	0	0	1	0	0	1-0	.000	.000	.000	.000	2	.667
2002—Houston (N.L.)	SS	40	88	11	17	3	0	0	4	12	19	1	1	3-0	.193	.297	.227	.524	5	.962
—New Orleans (PCL)	SS	88	345	51	95	16	7	2	25	24	59	6	3	12-3	.275	.331	.380	.710	7	.984
2003—New Orleans (PCL)	SS-2B	25	100	23	25	6	1	1	9	7	16	1	1	3-1	.250	.306	.360	.666	2	.982
—Houston (N.L.)	SS	128	387	51	99	18	3	8	51	28	66	9	7	8-1	.256	.320	.380	.700	17	.970
2004—Houston (N.L.)	SS	104	384	66	105	15	2	8	31	17	56	9	4	13-2	.273	.317	.385	.703	10	.977
2005—Houston (N.L.)	SS	152	549	58	136	27	2	11	54	24	103	8	5	21-7	.248	.290	.364	.654	14	.978
2006—Houston (N.L.)	SS	150	514	52	123	28	6	6	59	34	71	4	5	9-6	.239	.290	.352	.642	7	.990
Major League totals (6 years)		583	1925	239	480	91	13	33	199	117	316	31	22	55-16	.249	.301	.362	.663	55	.978

DIVISION SERIES RECORD

Year Team (League)	Pos.	G	AB	R	H	2B	3B	HR	RBI	BB	SO	HBP	GDP	SB-CS	Avg.	OBP	SLG	OPS	E	Avg.
2004—Houston (N.L.)	SS	2	0	0	0	0	0	0	0	0	0	0	0	0-0	...	...	...	...	0	...
2005—Houston (N.L.)	SS	4	14	1	3	0	0	0	1	1	1	0	1	0-0	.214	.250	.214	.464	1	.944
Division series totals (2 years)		6	14	1	3	0	0	0	1	1	1	0	1	0-0	.214	.250	.214	.464	1	.944

CHAMPIONSHIP SERIES RECORD

Year Team (League)	Pos.	G	AB	R	H	2B	3B	HR	RBI	BB	SO	HBP	GDP	SB-CS	Avg.	OBP	SLG	OPS	E	Avg.
2004—Houston (N.L.)	SS	3	1	0	0	0	0	0	0	0	0	0	0	0-0	.000	.000	.000	.000	1	1.000
2005—Houston (N.L.)	SS	6	23	2	7	1	1	0	2	0	4	0	0	0-0	.304	.304	.435	.739	1	.963
Champ. series totals (2 years)		9	24	2	7	1	1	0	2	0	4	0	0	0-0	.292	.292	.417	.708	1	.964

WORLD SERIES RECORD

Year Team (League)	Pos.	G	AB	R	H	2B	3B	HR	RBI	BB	SO	HBP	GDP	SB-CS	Avg.	OBP	SLG	OPS	E	Avg.
2005—Houston (N.L.)	SS	4	15	2	1	0	0	0	0	4	0	1	0	0-1	.067	.125	.067	.192	1	.962

2006 LEFTY-RIGHTY SPLITS

vs.	Avg.	AB	H	2B	3B	HR	RBI	BB	SO	OBP	Slg.	vs.	Avg.	AB	H	2B	3B	HR	RBI	BB	SO	OBP	Slg.
L	.250	100	25	6	3	1	15	13	6	.333	.400	R	.237	414	98	22	3	5	44	21	65	.278	.341

EVERETT, CARL — OF/DH

PERSONAL: Born June 3, 1971, in Tampa, Fla. ... 6-0/215. ... Bats both, throws right. ... Full name: Carl Edward Everett. ... High school: Hillsborough (Tampa). **TRANSACTIONS/CAREER NOTES:** Selected by New York Yankees organization in first round (10th pick overall) of 1990 free-agent draft. ... Selected by Florida Marlins in second round (27th pick overall) of expansion draft (November 17, 1992). ... On disabled list (July 23-August 10, 1994). ... Traded by Marlins to New York Mets for 2B Quilvio Veras (November 29, 1994). ... On disabled list (April 12-27, 1996). ... Traded by Mets to Houston Astros for P John Hudek (December 22, 1997). ... On disabled list (July 16-August 6, 1999). ... Traded by Astros to Boston Red Sox for SS Adam Everett and P Greg Miller (December 14, 1999). ... On suspended list (July 24-August 5, 2000; and March 29-30, 2001). ... On disabled list (June 22-July 28, 2001); included rehabilitation assignments to Sarasota and GCL Red Sox. ... Traded by Red Sox to Texas Rangers for P Darren Oliver (December 13, 2001). ... On disabled list (May 5-21 and June 3-July 2, 2002); included rehabilitation assignment to Charlotte. ... Traded by Rangers to Chicago White Sox for three players to be named (July 1, 2003); Rangers acquired Ps Frank Francisco and Josh Rupe and OF Anthony Webster to complete deal (July 24, 2003). ... Signed as a free agent by Montreal Expos (December 19, 2003). ... On disabled list (April 15-May 17 and May 30-June 16, 2004); included rehabilitation assignment to Brevard County. ... Traded by Expos to White Sox for Ps Jon Rauch and Gary Majewski (July 18, 2004). ... Signed as a free agent by Seattle Mariners (January 4, 2006). ... Released by Mariners (August 3, 2006). **STATISTICAL NOTES:** Career major league grand slams: 8.

2006 GAMES PLAYED BY POSITION (MLB): DH—80, OF—2.

Year Team (League)	Pos.	G	AB	R	H	2B	3B	HR	RBI	BB	SO	HBP	GDP	SB-CS	Avg.	OBP	SLG	OPS	E	Avg.
1990—GC Yankees (GCL)	OF	48	185	28	48	8	5	1	14	15	38	6	1	15-2	.259	.333	.373	.706	5	.932
1991—Greensboro (S. Atl.)	OF	123	468	96	127	18	0	4	40	57	122	23	1	28-19	.271	.376	.335	.711	7	.974
1992—Fort Laud. (FSL)	OF	46	183	30	42	8	2	2	9	12	40	4	1	11-3	.230	.291	.328	.619	3	.975
—Prince Will. (Car.)	OF	6	22	7	7	0	0	4	9	5	7	0	0	1-0	.318	.444	.864	1.308	0	1.000
1993—High Desert (Calif.)	OF	59	253	48	73	12	6	10	52	22	73	6	3	24-9	.289	.358	.502	.860	2	.985
—Florida (N.L.)	OF	11	19	0	2	0	0	0	1	1	9	0	0	1-0	.105	.150	.105	.255	1	.857
—Edmonton (PCL)	OF	35	136	28	42	13	4	6	16	19	45	2	1	12-1	.309	.401	.596	.997	2	.976
1994—Edmonton (PCL)	OF-DH	78	321	63	108	17	2	11	47	19	65	4	7	16-13	.336	.380	.505	.884	2	.989
—Florida (N.L.)	OF	16	51	7	11	1	0	2	6	3	15	0	0	4-0	.216	.259	.353	.612	0	1.000
1995—New York (N.L.)	OF	79	289	48	75	13	1	12	54	39	67	2	11	2-5	.260	.352	.436	.788	3	.981
—Norfolk (Int'l)	OF-DH-SS	67	260	52	78	16	4	6	35	20	47	4	2	12-6	.300	.358	.462	.819	0	1.000
1996—New York (N.L.)	OF	101	192	29	46	8	1	1	16	21	53	4	4	6-0	.240	.326	.307	.633	7	.935
1997—New York (N.L.)	OF	142	443	58	110	28	3	14	57	32	102	7	3	17-9	.248	.308	.420	.728	4	.971
1998—Houston (N.L.)	OF	133	467	72	138	34	4	15	76	44	102	3	11	14-12	.296	.359	.482	.840	4	.987
1999—Houston (N.L.)	OF-DH	123	464	86	151	33	3	25	108	50	94	11	5	27-7	.325	.398	.571	.969	6	.978
2000—Boston (A.L.)	OF-DH	137	496	82	149	32	4	34	108	52	113	8	4	11-4	.300	.373	.587	.959	6	.980
2001—Boston (A.L.)	OF-DH	102	409	61	105	24	4	14	58	27	104	13	3	9-2	.257	.323	.438	.761	5	.974
—Sarasota (Fla. St.)	DH	2	7	0	3	0	0	0	0	2	0	0	0	0-0	.429	.556	.429	.984	...	...
—GC Red Sox (GCL)	OF	3	10	2	2	0	0	2	2	1	3	0	0	0-0	.200	.273	.800	1.073	0	1.000
2002—Texas (A.L.)	OF-DH	105	374	47	100	16	0	16	62	33	77	6	7	2-3	.267	.333	.439	.772	5	.969
—Charlotte (Fla. St.)	OF	1	4	1	2	0	1	0	1	0	1	0	0	0-0	.500	.500	1.000	1.500	0	1.000
2003—Texas (A.L.)	OF-DH	74	270	53	74	13	3	18	51	31	48	5	2	4-1	.274	.356	.544	.900	2	.986
—Chicago (A.L.)	OF-DH	73	256	40	77	14	0	10	41	22	36	10	5	4-3	.301	.377	.473	.850	2	.987
2004—Brevard County (FSL)	OF-DH	5	15	2	6	1	0	0	3	2	3	0	0	0-0	.400	.444	.467	.911	0	1.000
—Montreal (N.L.)	OF-DH	39	127	8	32	10	0	2	14	8	19	5	8	1-0	.252	.319	.378	.697	3	.955
—Chicago (A.L.)	DH-OF	43	154	21	41	7	1	5	21	8	26	5	3	1-0	.266	.320	.422	.742	0	1.000
2005—Chicago (A.L.)	DH-OF	135	490	58	123	17	2	23	87	42	99	5	11	4-5	.251	.311	.435	.745	0	1.000
2006—Seattle (A.L.)	DH-OF	92	308	37	70	8	0	11	33	29	57	3	6	1-3	.227	.297	.360	.658	0	1.000
American League totals (7 years)		761	2757	399	739	131	14	131	461	244	560	55	41	36-21	.268	.337	.468	.805	20	.980
National League totals (8 years)		644	2052	308	565	127	12	71	331	198	461	32	42	71-33	.275	.346	.453	.799	31	.974
Major League totals (14 years)		1405	4809	707	1304	258	26	202	792	442	1021	87	83	107-54	.271	.341	.462	.802	51	.977

DIVISION SERIES RECORD

Year Team (League)	Pos.	G	AB	R	H	2B	3B	HR	RBI	BB	SO	HBP	GDP	SB-CS	Avg.	OBP	SLG	OPS	E	Avg.
1998—Houston (N.L.)	OF	4	13	1	2	0	0	0	0	0	4	0	1	0-0	.154	.154	.154	.308	0	1.000
1999—Houston (N.L.)	OF	4	15	2	2	0	0	0	1	2	8	1	0	1-0	.133	.263	.133	.396	0	1.000
2005—Chicago (A.L.)	DH	3	11	2	3	0	0	0	0	0	0	1	1	0-0	.273	.333	.273	.606	0	...
Division series totals (3 years)		11	39	5	7	0	0	0	1	2	12	2	2	1-0	.179	.250	.179	.429	0	1.000

E

Year Team (League)	Pos.	G	AB	R	H	2B	3B	HR	RBI	BB	SO	HBP	GDP	SB-CS	Avg.	OBP	SLG	OPS	E	Avg.
						CHAMPIONSHIP SERIES RECORD														
2005—Chicago (A.L.)	DH	5	20	2	5	0	0	0	3	1	4	0	0	0-0	.250	.286	.250	.536	0	...

Year Team (League)	Pos.	G	AB	R	H	2B	3B	HR	RBI	BB	SO	HBP	GDP	SB-CS	Avg.	OBP	SLG	OPS	E	Avg.
						WORLD SERIES RECORD														
2005—Chicago (A.L.)	DH	4	9	1	4	0	0	0	0	0	2	0	0	0-1	.444	.444	.444	.889	0	...

	Pos.	G	AB	R	H	2B	3B	HR	RBI	BB	SO	HBP	GDP	SB-CS	Avg.	OBP	SLG	OPS	E	Avg.
						ALL-STAR GAME RECORD														
All-Star Game totals (2 years)		2	3	0	0	0	0	0	1	1	0	0	0	0-0	.000	.250	.000	.250	0	1.000

2006 LEFTY-RIGHTY SPLITS

vs.	Avg.	AB	H	2B	3B	HR	RBI	BB	SO	OBP	Slg.	vs.	Avg.	AB	H	2B	3B	HR	RBI	BB	SO	OBP	Slg.
L	.186	70	13	1	0	2	5	5	18	.269	.286	R	.239	238	57	7	0	9	28	24	39	.306	.382

EYRE, SCOTT   P

PERSONAL: Born May 30, 1972, in Inglewood, Calif. ... 6-1/210. ... Throws left, bats left. ... Full name: Scott Alan Eyre. ... Name pronounced: AIR. ... High school: Cyprus (Magna, Utah). ... Junior college: Southern Idaho. ... Brother of Willie Eyre, pitcher, Minnesota Twins. **TRANSACTIONS/CAREER NOTES:** Selected by Texas Rangers organization in ninth round of 1991 free-agent draft. ... Traded by Rangers to Chicago White Sox for SS Esteban Beltre (March 28, 1994). ... On disabled list (August 31-September 26, 1999); included rehabilitation assignment to Charlotte. ... Traded by White Sox to Toronto Blue Jays for P Gary Glover (November 7, 2000). ... Claimed on waivers by San Francisco Giants (August 8, 2002). ... On disabled list (March 27-April 22, 2004); included rehabilitation assignment to Fresno. ... Signed as a free agent by Chicago Cubs (November 16, 2005). ... On disabled list (August 16-September 1, 2006).

CAREER HITTING: 2-for-12 (.167), 0 R, 0 2B, 0 3B, 0 HR, 0 RBI.

Year Team (League)	W	L	Pct.	ERA	WHIP	G	GS	CG	ShO	Hld.	Sv.-Opp.	IP	H	R	ER	HR	BB-IBB	SO	Avg.
1992—Butte (Pion.)	7	3	.700	2.90	1.36	15	14	2	1	...	0-...	80.2	71	30	26	6	39-0	94	.241
1993—Char., S.C. (SAL)	11	7	.611	3.45	1.21	26	26	0	0	...	0-...	143.2	115	74	55	6	59-1	154	.220
1994—South Bend (Mid.)	8	4	.667	3.47	1.30	19	18	2	0	...	0-...	111.2	108	56	43	7	37-0	111	.248
1995—GC Whi. Sox (GCL)	0	2	.000	2.30	1.02	9	9	0	0	...	0-...	27.1	16	7	7	0	12-0	40	.174
1996—Birmingham (Sou.)	12	7	.632	4.38	1.57	27	27	0	0	...	0-...	158.1	170	90	77	12	79-3	137	.277
1997—Birmingham (Sou.)	13	5	.722	3.84	1.30	22	22	0	0	...	0-...	126.2	110	61	54	14	55-2	127	.231
—Chicago (A.L.)	4	4	.500	5.04	1.53	11	11	0	0	0	0-...	60.2	62	36	34	11	31-1	36	.267
1998—Chicago (A.L.)	3	8	.273	5.38	1.66	33	11	0	0	0	0-...	107.0	114	78	64	24	64-0	73	.271
1999—Charlotte (Int'l)	6	4	.600	3.82	1.43	12	11	0	0	...	0-...	68.1	75	32	29	3	23-1	63	.284
—Chicago (A.L.)	1	1	.500	7.56	2.12	21	0	0	0	1	0-...	25.0	38	22	21	6	15-2	17	.339
2000—Chicago (A.L.)	1	1	.500	6.63	2.16	13	1	0	0	0	0-...	19.0	29	15	14	3	12-0	16	.372
—Charlotte (Int'l)	3	2	.600	3.00	1.10	47	0	0	0	...	12-...	48.0	33	18	16	1	20-3	46	.200
2001—Syracuse (Int'l)	4	6	.400	3.18	1.17	62	2	0	0	...	0-...	79.1	67	30	28	8	26-4	96	.224
—Toronto (A.L.)	1	2	.333	3.45	1.40	17	0	0	0	3	2-3	15.2	15	6	6	1	7-2	16	.263
2002—Toronto (A.L.)	2	4	.333	4.97	1.55	49	3	0	0	12	0-1	63.1	69	37	35	4	29-7	51	.278
—San Francisco (N.L.)	0	0	...	1.59	1.59	21	0	0	0	2	0-0	11.1	11	4	2	0	7-1	7	.256
2003—San Francisco (N.L.)	2	1	.667	3.32	1.51	74	0	0	0	20	1-3	57.0	60	23	21	4	26-0	35	.268
2004—Fresno (PCL)	0	0	...	0.00	1.67	3	0	0	0	...	0-...	3.0	3	0	0	0	2-0	1	.250
—San Francisco (N.L.)	2	2	.500	4.10	1.33	83	0	0	0	23	1-5	52.2	43	26	24	8	27-3	49	.219
2005—San Francisco (N.L.)	2	2	.500	2.63	1.08	86	0	0	0	•32	0-2	68.1	48	21	20	3	26-0	65	.200
2006—Chicago (N.L.)	1	3	.250	3.38	1.48	74	0	0	0	18	0-3	61.1	61	25	23	11	30-4	73	.265
American League totals (6 years)	12	20	.375	5.39	1.67	144	32	0	0	16	2-4	290.2	327	194	174	49	158-12	209	.285
National League totals (5 years)	7	8	.467	3.23	1.35	338	0	0	0	99	2-13	250.2	223	99	90	26	116-8	229	.239
Major League totals (10 years)	19	28	.404	4.39	1.52	482	32	0	0	115	4-17	541.1	550	293	264	75	274-20	438	.264

Year Team (League)	W	L	Pct.	ERA	WHIP	G	GS	CG	ShO	Hld.	Sv.-Opp.	IP	H	R	ER	HR	BB-IBB	SO	Avg.
							DIVISION SERIES RECORD												
2002—San Francisco (N.L.)	0	0	...	0.00	0.75	3	0	0	0	1	0-0	1.1	1	0	0	0	0-0	1	.200
2003—San Francisco (N.L.)	0	0	...	0.00	0.00	1	0	0	0	0	0-0	0.1	0	0	0	0	0-0	0	.000
Division series totals (2 years)	0	0	...	0.00	0.60	4	0	0	0	1	0-0	1.2	1	0	0	0	0-0	1	.167

Year Team (League)	W	L	Pct.	ERA	WHIP	G	GS	CG	ShO	Hld.	Sv.-Opp.	IP	H	R	ER	HR	BB-IBB	SO	Avg.
							CHAMPIONSHIP SERIES RECORD												
2002—San Francisco (N.L.)	0	0	...	0.00	1.20	1	0	0	0	0	0-0	1.2	2	0	0	0		0	.286

Year Team (League)	W	L	Pct.	ERA	WHIP	G	GS	CG	ShO	Hld.	Sv.-Opp.	IP	H	R	ER	HR	BB-IBB	SO	Avg.
							WORLD SERIES RECORD												
2002—San Francisco (N.L.)	0	0	...	0.00	2.00	3	0	0	0	0	0-0	3.0	5	1	0	0	1-1	2	.385

2006 LEFTY-RIGHTY SPLITS

vs.	Avg.	AB	H	2B	3B	HR	RBI	BB	SO	OBP	Slg.	vs.	Avg.	AB	H	2B	3B	HR	RBI	BB	SO	OBP	Slg.
L	.273	88	24	3	0	6	16	12	32	.353	.511	R	.261	142	37	6	1	5	16	18	41	.340	.423

EYRE, WILLIE   P

PERSONAL: Born July 21, 1978, in Fountain Valley, Calif. ... 6-1/200. ... Throws right, bats right. ... Full name: William Mays Eyre. ... Junior college: College of Eastern Utah. ... Brother of Scott Eyre, pitcher, Chicago Cubs. **TRANSACTIONS/CAREER NOTES:** Selected by Minnesota Twins organization in 23rd round of 1999 free-agent draft.

CAREER HITTING: 0-for-1 (.000), 0 R, 0 2B, 0 3B, 0 HR, 0 RBI.

Year Team (League)	W	L	Pct.	ERA	WHIP	G	GS	CG	ShO	Hld.	Sv.-Opp.	IP	H	R	ER	HR	BB-IBB	SO	Avg.
1999—Elizabethton (App.)	6	3	.667	4.53	1.63	16	10	1	0	...	0-...	57.2	60	38	29	4	34-0	59	.261
—Quad City (Midw.)	1	0	1.000	4.26	1.11	2	2	0	0	...	0-...	12.2	8	6	6	0	6-0	10	.186
2000—Quad City (Midw.)	5	7	.417	4.61	1.61	26	18	1	1	...	0-...	99.2	104	64	51	9	56-0	81	.266
2001—Quad City (Midw.)	3	0	1.000	2.42	0.94	17	0	0	0	...	4-...	22.1	19	6	6	1	2-0	21	.226
—Fort Myers (FSL)	2	5	.286	2.52	1.35	32	0	0	0	...	1-...	64.1	54	27	18	2	33-2	51	.232
2002—Fort Myers (FSL)	4	1	.800	2.41	1.22	19	0	0	0	...	2-...	33.2	28	9	9	0	13-1	25	.233
—New Britain (East.)	6	4	.600	3.24	1.22	28	0	0	0	...	2-...	50.0	40	21	18	1	21-0	43	.220
2003—Rochester (Int'l)	0	2	.000	6.00	1.92	6	5	0	0	...	0-...	24.0	30	18	16	2	16-0	23	.309
—New Britain (East.)	6	5	.545	3.46	1.36	29	14	1	1	...	0-...	96.1	93	42	37	6	38-4	66	.253
2004—Rochester (Int'l)	6	7	.462	3.64	1.35	36	21	1	1	...	0-...	136.0	131	60	55	13	53-1	91	.264
2005—Rochester (Int'l)	10	3	.769	2.72	1.29	56	0	0	0	10	7-10	82.2	79	30	25	3	28-0	74	.253
2006—Minnesota (A.L.)	1	0	1.000	5.31	1.63	42	0	0	0	...	0-0	59.1	75	36	35	8	22-4	26	.309
Major League totals (1 year)	1	0	1.000	5.31	1.63	42	0	0	0	...	0-0	59.1	75	36	35	8	22-4	26	.309

2006 LEFTY-RIGHTY SPLITS

vs.	Avg.	AB	H	2B	3B	HR	RBI	BB	SO	OBP	Slg.	vs.	Avg.	AB	H	2B	3B	HR	RBI	BB	SO	OBP	Slg.
L	.379	103	39	9	1	5	19	14	6	.458	.631	R	.257	140	36	10	0	3	14	8	20	.312	.393

E

FAHEY, BRANDON　　　　　　　　　　IF

PERSONAL: Born January 18, 1981, in Dallas, Texas. ... 6-2/185. ... Bats left, throws right. ... Full name: Brandon W. Fahey. ... College: Texas. ... Son of Bill Fahey, catcher with three major league teams (1971-72, 1974-78, 1979-83). **TRANSACTIONS/CAREER NOTES:** Selected by Baltimore Orioles organization in 12th round of 2002 free-agent draft.

2006 GAMES PLAYED BY POSITION (MLB): OF—54, SS—17, 2B—13, 3B—1, DH—1.

										BATTING									FIELDING	
Year	Team (League)	Pos.	G	AB	R	H	2B	3B	HR	RBI	BB	SO	HBP	GDP	SB-CS	Avg.	OBP	SLG	OPS	E	Avg.
2002— Aberdeen (N.Y.-Penn.)			63	253	31	71	10	6	0	15	20	34	1	4	5-8	.281	.333	.368	.701	...	...
2003— Frederick (Carolina)			107	365	41	85	11	3	1	22	22	56	2	7	4-2	.233	.279	.288	.567	...	...
2004— Frederick (Carolina)			62	181	20	49	7	0	3	19	22	20	2	3	3-3	.271	.354	.359	.713	...	...
— Bowie (East.)			63	208	20	49	7	1	1	15	17	27	0	5	3-1	.236	.293	.293	.586	...	...
2005— Bowie (East.)		SS	139	502	63	146	21	4	3	47	44	71	4	12	17-8	.291	.349	.367	.715	25	.962
2006— Ottawa (Int'l)			20	68	8	19	1	1	0	3	10	5	4	1	4-3	.279	.402	.324	.726	6	.948
— Baltimore (A.L.)	OF-SS-2B 3B-DH		91	251	36	59	8	2	2	23	23	48	3	2	3-3	.235	.307	.307	.614	8	.963
Major League totals (1 year)			91	251	36	59	8	2	2	23	23	48	3	2	3-3	.235	.307	.307	.614	8	.963

2006 LEFTY-RIGHTY SPLITS

vs.	Avg.	AB	H	2B	3B	HR	RBI	BB	SO	OBP	Slg.	vs.	Avg.	AB	H	2B	3B	HR	RBI	BB	SO	OBP	Slg.
L	.190	42	8	1	0	0	2	4	13	.277	.214	R	.244	209	51	7	2	2	21	19	35	.313	.325

FALKENBORG, BRIAN　　　　　　　　　　P

PERSONAL: Born January 18, 1978, in Newport Beach, Calif. ... 6-6/190. ... Throws right, bats right. ... Full name: Brian Thomas Falkenborg. ... High school: Redmond (Wash.). **TRANSACTIONS/CAREER NOTES:** Selected by Baltimore Orioles organization in second round of 1996 free-agent draft. ... On disabled list (March 23, 2000-entire season). ... Released by Orioles (December 19, 2000). ... Signed by Seattle Mariners organization (January 24, 2001). ... Signed as a free agent by Los Angeles Dodgers organization (November 10, 2003). ... On disabled list (April 5-24, 2004); included rehabilitation assignment to Las Vegas. ... Signed as a free agent by San Diego Padres organization (January 18, 2005). ... Signed as a free agent by St. Louis Cardinals organization (August 6, 2005).

CAREER HITTING: 0-for-3 (.000), 1 R, 0 2B, 0 3B, 0 HR, 0 RBI.

Year	Team (League)	W	L	Pct.	ERA	WHIP	G	GS	CG	ShO	Hld.	Sv.-Opp.	IP	H	R	ER	HR	BB-IBB	SO	Avg.
1996— GC Orioles (GCL)		0	3	.000	2.57	1.04	8	6	0	0	...	0-...	28.0	21	13	8	1	8-0	36	.196
— High Desert (Calif.)		0	0	...	0.00	1.00	1	0	0	0	...	0-...	1.0	1	0	0	0	0-0	1	.333
1997— Delmarva (S. Atl.)		7	9	.438	4.46	1.32	25	25	0	0	...	0-...	127.0	122	73	63	6	46-2	107	.253
— Bowie (East.)		0	1	.000	16.20	3.60	1	1	0	0	...	0-...	1.2	3	3	3	0	3-0	0	.375
1998— Frederick (Carolina)		5	5	.500	4.50	1.29	15	14	1	1	...	0-...	78.0	83	42	39	6	18-0	70	.267
1999— Bowie (East.)		3	6	.333	3.78	1.36	16	16	0	0	...	0-...	83.1	77	40	35	11	36-0	77	.242
— GC Orioles (GCL)		1	0	1.000	2.00	1.00	3	2	0	0	...	0-...	9.0	6	2	2	0	3-0	11	.176
— Baltimore (A.L.)		0	0	...	0.00	1.33	1	0	0	0	0	0-...	3.0	2	0	0	0	2-0	1	.200
2000— Baltimore (A.L.)		Did not play.																		
2001— San Antonio (Texas)		5	6	.455	5.45	1.58	12	12	2	1	...	0-...	66.0	80	47	40	9	24-0	56	.305
— Tacoma (PCL)		2	4	.333	4.47	1.41	8	8	0	0	...	0-...	48.1	50	25	24	6	18-0	27	.273
2002— Tacoma (PCL)		4	4	.500	2.74	1.30	9	9	0	0	...	0-...	49.1	51	22	15	3	13-0	42	.267
2003— Tacoma (PCL)		4	2	.667	2.94	1.20	17	14	0	0	...	0-...	79.2	66	28	26	7	26-0	62	.221
2004— Los Angeles (N.L.)		1	0	1.000	7.53	1.95	6	0	0	0	...	0-0	14.1	19	14	12	2	9-0	11	.322
— Las Vegas (PCL)		4	6	.400	6.17	1.45	18	16	0	0	...	1-...	89.0	104	66	61	17	25-0	87	.286
2005— San Diego (N.L.)		0	0	...	8.18	2.00	10	0	0	0	...	0-...	11.0	17	11	10	2	5-1	10	.347
— Portland (PCL)		3	4	.429	5.25	1.56	28	0	0	0	3	1-2	36.0	35	25	21	2	21-1	26	.257
— Memphis (PCL)		1	0	1.000	1.69	0.94	13	0	0	0	5	5-5	16.0	10	3	3	1	5-0	14	.182
2006— St. Louis (N.L.)		0	1	.000	2.84	0.79	5	0	0	0	1	0-0	6.1	5	2	2	0	0-0	5	.217
— Memphis (PCL)		4	5	.444	4.18	1.28	47	0	0	0	9	16-21	51.2	51	29	24	6	15-0	53	.259
American League totals (1 year)		0	0	...	0.00	1.33	1	0	0	0	0	0-...	3.0	2	0	0	0	2-0	1	.200
National League totals (3 years)		1	1	.500	6.82	1.74	21	0	0	0	1	0-0	31.2	41	27	24	4	14-1	26	.313
Major League totals (4 years)		1	1	.500	6.23	1.70	23	0	0	0	1	0-0	34.2	43	27	24	4	16-1	27	.305

2006 LEFTY-RIGHTY SPLITS

vs.	Avg.	AB	H	2B	3B	HR	RBI	BB	SO	OBP	Slg.	vs.	Avg.	AB	H	2B	3B	HR	RBI	BB	SO	OBP	Slg.
L	.250	8	2	0	0	0	2	0	3	.250	.250	R	.200	15	3	1	0	0	0	0	2	.250	.267

FARNSWORTH, KYLE　　　　　　　　　　P

PERSONAL: Born April 14, 1976, in Wichita, Kan. ... 6-4/240. ... Throws right, bats right. ... Full name: Kyle Lynn Farnsworth. ... High school: Milton (Alpharetta, Ga.). ... Junior college: Abraham Baldwin (Tifton, Ga.). **TRANSACTIONS/CAREER NOTES:** Selected by Chicago Cubs organization in 47th round of 1994 free-agent draft. ... On disabled list (April 10-June 4, 2002); included rehabilitation assignment to Iowa. ... On suspended list (June 26-28, 2003). ... On disabled list (August 28-September 12, 2004). ... Traded by Cubs to Detroit Tigers for P Roberto Novoa, OF Bo Flowers and SS Scott Moore (February 9, 2005). ... Traded by Tigers to Atlanta Braves for Ps Roman Colon and Zach Miner (July 31, 2005). ... On suspended list (August 9-14, 2005). ... Signed as a free agent by New York Yankees (December 2, 2005).

CAREER HITTING: 4-for-54 (.074), 3 R, 1 2B, 0 3B, 0 HR, 3 RBI.

Year	Team (League)	W	L	Pct.	ERA	WHIP	G	GS	CG	ShO	Hld.	Sv.-Opp.	IP	H	R	ER	HR	BB-IBB	SO	Avg.
1995— GC Cubs (GCL)		3	2	.600	0.87	1.06	16	0	0	0	...	1-...	31.0	22	8	3	0	11-0	18	.214
1996— Rockford (Midwest)		9	6	.600	3.70	1.40	20	20	1	0	...	0-...	112.0	122	62	46	7	35-0	82	.274
1997— Daytona (Fla. St.)		10	10	.500	4.09	1.44	27	27	2	0	...	0-...	156.1	178	91	71	13	47-1	105	.286
1998— West Tenn (Sou.)		8	2	.800	2.77	1.12	13	13	0	0	...	0-...	81.1	70	32	25	6	21-0	73	.231
— Iowa (PCL)		5	9	.357	6.93	1.61	18	18	0	0	...	0-...	102.2	129	88	79	18	36-0	79	.309
1999— Iowa (PCL)		2	2	.500	3.20	1.19	6	6	0	0	...	0-...	39.1	38	16	14	5	9-0	29	.262
— Chicago (N.L.)		5	9	.357	5.05	1.48	27	21	1	1	...	0-0	130.0	140	80	73	28	52-1	70	.271
2000— Chicago (N.L.)		2	9	.182	6.43	1.82	46	5	0	0	6	1-6	77.0	90	58	55	14	50-8	74	.291
— Iowa (PCL)		0	2	.000	3.20	1.66	22	0	0	0	...	9-...	25.1	24	10	9	1	18-2	22	.250
2001— Chicago (N.L.)		4	6	.400	2.74	1.15	76	0	0	0	24	2-3	82.0	65	26	25	8	29-2	107	.213
2002— Chicago (N.L.)		4	6	.400	7.33	1.65	45	0	0	0	6	1-7	46.2	53	47	38	9	24-7	46	.293
— Iowa (PCL)		0	1	.000	6.00	1.00	2	0	0	0	...	0-...	3.0	2	2	2	1	0-0	2	.273
2003— Chicago (N.L.)		3	2	.600	3.30	1.17	77	0	0	0	19	0-3	76.1	53	31	28	6	36-1	92	.196
2004— Chicago (N.L.)		4	5	.444	4.73	1.50	72	0	0	0	18	6-6	66.2	67	39	35	10	33-1	78	.260
2005— Detroit (A.L.)		1	1	.500	2.32	1.15	46	0	0	0	15	6-8	42.2	29	12	11	1	20-0	55	.192
— Atlanta (N.L.)		0	0	...	1.98	0.80	26	0	0	0	4	10-10	27.1	15	6	6	4	7-0	32	.161
2006— Charlotte (Int'l)		7	3	.700	4.71	1.33	48	0	0	0	19	14-19	49.2	57	27	26	6	8-1	40	.286
— New York (A.L.)		3	6	.333	4.36	1.36	72	0	0	0	19	6-10	66.0	62	34	32	8	28-3	75	.243
American League totals (2 years)		4	7	.364	3.56	1.28	118	0	0	0	34	12-18	108.2	91	46	43	9	48-3	130	.224
National League totals (7 years)		22	37	.373	4.62	1.41	369	26	1	1	77	14-33	506.0	483	287	260	79	231-20	499	.250
Major League totals (8 years)		26	44	.371	4.44	1.39	487	26	1	1	111	26-51	614.2	574	333	303	88	279-23	629	.245

DIVISION SERIES RECORD

Year Team (League)	W	L	Pct.	ERA	WHIP	G	GS	CG	ShO	Hld.	Sv.-Opp.	IP	H	R	ER	HR	BB-IBB	SO	Avg.
2003— Chicago (N.L.)	0	0	...	0.00	0.75	3	0	0	0	1	0-0	2.2	1	0	0	0	1-0	2	.111
2005— Atlanta (N.L.)	0	0	...	9.00	1.00	2	0	0	0	0	0-0	3.0	2	3	3	2	1-0	4	.182
2006— New York (A.L.)	0	0	...	0.00	1.00	2	0	0	0	1	0-0	2.0	1	0	0	0	1-0	1	.143
Division series totals (3 years)	0	0	...	3.52	0.91	7	0	0	0	2	0-0	7.2	4	3	3	2	3-0	7	.148

CHAMPIONSHIP SERIES RECORD

Year Team (League)	W	L	Pct.	ERA	WHIP	G	GS	CG	ShO	Hld.	Sv.-Opp.	IP	H	R	ER	HR	BB-IBB	SO	Avg.
2003— Chicago (N.L.)	0	0	...	10.13	1.50	5	0	0	0	0	0-0	5.1	6	6	6	0	2-2	7	.300

2006 LEFTY-RIGHTY SPLITS

vs.	Avg.	AB	H	2B	3B	HR	RBI	BB	SO	OBP	Slg.	vs.	Avg.	AB	H	2B	3B	HR	RBI	BB	SO	OBP	Slg.
L	.215	107	23	6	0	3	11	6	42	.263	.355	R	.264	148	39	4	0	5	25	22	33	.355	.392

FASANO, SAL   C

PERSONAL: Born August 10, 1971, in Chicago. ... 6-2/254. ... Bats right, throws right. ... Full name: Salvatore Frank Fasano. ... Name pronounced: fuh-SAH-noh. ... High school: Hoffman Estates (Ill.). ... College: Evansville. **TRANSACTIONS/CAREER NOTES:** Selected by Kansas City Royals organization in 37th round of 1993 free-agent draft. ... On disabled list (April 20-May 9 and August 30, 1998-remainder of season); included rehabilitation assignment to Omaha. ... Traded by Royals to Oakland Athletics for cash (March 30, 2000). ... Contract purchased by Royals from A's (May 22, 2001). ... Traded by Royals with P Mac Suzuki to Colorado Rockies for C Brent Mayne (June 24, 2001). ... Signed as a free agent by Tampa Bay Devil Rays organization (January 28, 2002). ... Released by Devil Rays (June 1, 2002). ... Signed by Milwaukee Brewers organization (June 6, 2002). ... Traded by Brewers with OF Alex Ochoa to Anaheim Angels for C Jorge Fabregas and two players to be named (July 31, 2002); Brewers acquired IF Johnny Raburn (August 14, 2002) and P Pedro Liriano (September 20, 2002) to complete deal. ... Released by Angels (November 5, 2002). ... Signed by New York Yankees organization (January 14, 2004). ... Signed as a free agent by Baltimore Orioles organization (December 20, 2004). ... Signed as a free agent by Philadelphia Phillies (December 1, 2005). ... On disabled list (July 4-22, 2006); included rehabilitation assignments to Clearwater and Reading. ... Traded by Phillies to New York Yankees for IF Hector Made (July 26, 2006). **STATISTICAL NOTES:** Career major league grand slams: 1.

2006 GAMES PLAYED BY POSITION (MLB): C—77, DH—1.

Year Team (League)	Pos.	G	AB	R	H	2B	3B	HR	RBI	BB	SO	HBP	GDP	SB-CS	Avg.	OBP	SLG	OPS	E	Avg.
1993— Eugene (Northwest)	C	49	176	25	47	11	1	10	36	19	49	6	1	4-3	.267	.355	.511	.866	1	.997
1994— Rockford (Midwest)	1B-C	97	345	61	97	16	1	25	81	33	66	16	10	8-3	.281	.366	.551	.917	12	.981
— Wilmington (Caro.)	1B-C	23	90	15	29	7	0	7	32	13	24	0	3	0-0	.322	.408	.633	1.041	4	.957
1995— Wilmington (Caro.)	1B-C	23	88	12	20	2	1	2	7	5	16	1	4	0-0	.227	.277	.341	.618	0	1.000
— Wichita (Texas)	1B-C-C	87	317	60	92	19	2	20	66	27	61	16	8	3-6	.290	.373	.552	.925	14	.979
1996— Kansas City (A.L.)	C	51	143	20	29	2	0	6	19	14	25	2	.	1-1	.203	.283	.343	.626	5	.984
— Omaha (A.A.)	C-1B-3B	29	104	12	24	4	0	4	15	6	21	1	3	0-1	.231	.277	.385	.662	4	.982
1997— Omaha (A.A.)	C-DH	49	152	17	25	7	0	4	14	12	53	5	1	0-0	.164	.247	.289	.536	4	.988
— Kansas City (A.L.)	C-DH	13	38	4	8	2	0	1	1	1	12	0		0-0	.211	.231	.342	.573	1	.982
— Wichita (Texas)	C-1B	40	131	27	31	5	0	13	27	20	35	7	2	0-2	.237	.360	.573	.933	4	.984
1998— Kansas City (A.L.)	C-1B-3B	74	216	21	49	10	0	8	31	10	56	16		1-0	.227	.307	.384	.692	2	.996
— Omaha (PCL)	C	4	14	1	3	1	0	1	2	1	4	0	1	0-1	.214	.267	.500	.767	0	1.000
1999— Omaha (PCL)	C-DH-1B	88	280	63	77	15	0	21	49	42	69	26	7	4-2	.275	.415	.554	.969	12	.984
— Kansas City (A.L.)	C	23	60	11	14	2	0	5	16	7	17	7		0-1	.233	.373	.517	.890	0	1.000
2000— Oakland (A.L.)	C	52	126	21	27	6	0	7	19	14	47	3		0-0	.214	.306	.429	.734	5	.981
2001— Oakland (A.L.)	C-DH	11	21	2	1	0	0	0	0	1	12	1		0-0	.048	.130	.048	.178	2	.952
— Kansas City (A.L.)	C	3	1	0	0	0	0	0	0	0	0	0		0-0	.000	.000	.000	.000	0	1.000
— Omaha (PCL)	C-1B	13	46	6	11	1	0	2	7	4	11	5	1	0-0	.239	.364	.391	.755	3	.966
— Colo. Springs (PCL)	C	26	82	16	25	4	0	7	23	9	26	4	4	0-0	.305	.396	.610	1.006	3	.984
— Colorado (N.L.)	C	25	63	10	16	5	0	3	9	4	19	3		0-0	.254	.329	.476	.805	3	.982
2002— Durham (Int'l)	C	31	101	11	26	6	0	6	9	12	29	9	1	0-1	.257	.385	.495	.880	4	.984
— Indianapolis (Int'l)	C-1B	34	97	5	20	9	0	1	11	3	24	6	2	0-0	.206	.271	.330	.601	3	.984
— Salt Lake (PCL)	C	22	76	13	21	3	0	5	10	7	24	2	0	1-0	.276	.349	.513	.862	4	.978
— Anaheim (A.L.)	C	2	1	0	0	0	0	0	0	0	1	0		0-0	.000	.000	.000	.000	0	1.000
2003—		Did not play																		
2004— Columbus (Int'l)	C	76	236	21	54	15	1	10	34	10	45	6	6	0-0	.229	.273	.428	.701	4	.993
2005— Ottawa (Int'l)	C-1B-DH	14	45	6	12	3	0	4	12	2	15	2	1	0-0	.267	.327	.600	.927	1	.986
— Baltimore (A.L.)	C-DH-1B	64	160	25	40	3	0	11	20	9	41	5	5	0-0	.250	.310	.475	.785	4	.987
2006— Philadelphia (N.L.)	C	50	140	9	34	8	0	4	10	5	47	3	4	0-1	.243	.284	.386	.669	3	.990
— Clearwater (FSL)		4	12	0	1	0	0	0	1	0	1	0	1	0-0	.083	.083	.083	.167	0	1.000
— Reading (East.)		1	3	0	0	0	0	0	0	0	0	0		0-0	.000	.000	.000	.000	0	1.000
— New York (A.L.)	C-DH	28	49	3	7	4	0	1	5	2	14	3	1	0-0	.143	.222	.286	.508	1	.991
American League totals (9 years)		321	815	107	175	29	0	39	111	58	225	37	6	2-2	.215	.295	.394	.689	20	.988
National League totals (2 years)		75	203	19	50	13	0	7	19	9	66	6	4	0-1	.246	.298	.414	.712	6	.987
Major league totals (9 years)		396	1018	126	225	42	0	46	130	67	291	43	10	2-3	.221	.296	.398	.694	26	.988

DIVISION SERIES RECORD

Year Team (League)	Pos.	G	AB	R	H	2B	3B	HR	RBI	BB	SO	HBP	GDP	SB-CS	Avg.	OBP	SLG	OPS	E	Avg.
2000— Oakland (A.L.)	C	1	0	0	0	0	0	0	0	0	0	0		0-0	...	...	...	...	0	1.000

2006 LEFTY-RIGHTY SPLITS

vs.	Avg.	AB	H	2B	3B	HR	RBI	BB	SO	OBP	Slg.	vs.	Avg.	AB	H	2B	3B	HR	RBI	BB	SO	OBP	Slg.
L	.241	54	13	4	0	1	5	4	17	.317	.370	R	.207	135	28	8	0	4	10	3	44	.246	.356

FASSERO, JEFF   P

PERSONAL: Born January 5, 1963, in Springfield, Ill. ... 6-1/200. ... Throws left, bats left. ... Full name: Jeffrey Joseph Fassero. ... Name pronounced: fuh-SAIR-oh. ... High school: Griffin (Springfield, Ill.). ... College: Mississippi. **TRANSACTIONS/CAREER NOTES:** Selected by St. Louis Cardinals organization in 22nd round of June 1984 free-agent draft. ... Selected by Chicago White Sox organization from Cardinals organization in Rule 5 minor league draft (December 5, 1989). ... Released by White Sox (April 3, 1990). ... Signed by Cleveland Indians organization (April 9, 1990). ... Signed as a free agent by Montreal Expos organization (January 3, 1991). ... On disabled list (July 24-August 11, 1994). ... Traded by Expos with P Alex Pacheco to Seattle Mariners for C Chris Widger and Ps Trey Moore and Matt Wagner (October 29, 1996). ... On disabled list (March 22-April 12, 1998). ... Traded by Mariners to Texas Rangers for a player to be named (August 27, 1999); Mariners acquired OF Adrian Myers to complete deal (September 22, 1999). ... Signed as a free agent by Boston Red Sox (December 22, 1999). ... On disabled list (June 19-July 5, 2000). ... Signed as a free agent by Chicago Cubs (December 8, 2000). ... Traded by Cubs with cash to Cardinals for two players to be named (August 24, 2002); Cubs acquired Ps Jason Karnuth and Jared Blasdell to complete deal (September 24, 2002). ... On suspended list (May 2-4, 2003). ... Signed as a free agent by Colorado Rockies organization (January 13, 2004). ... Released by Rockies (September 24, 2004). ... Signed by Arizona Diamondbacks (September 29, 2004). ... Signed as a free agent by San Francisco Giants organization (December 14, 2004). ... Released by Giants (May 10, 2006).

CAREER HITTING: 23-for-276 (.083), 21 R, 2 2B, 1 3B, 0 HR, 6 RBI.

F

Year	Team (League)	W	L	Pct.	ERA	WHIP	G	GS	CG	ShO	Hld.	Sv.-Opp.	IP	H	R	ER	HR	BB-IBB	SO	Avg.
1984— Johnson City (App.)		4	7	.364	4.59	1.56	13	11	2	0	...	1-...	66.2	65	42	34	2	39-0	59	.261
1985— Springfield (Midw.)		4	8	.333	4.01	1.43	29	15	1	0	...	1-...	119.0	125	78	53	11	45-3	65	.262
1986— St. Pete. (FSL)		13	7	.650	2.45	1.20	26	•26	6	1	...	0-...	176.0	156	63	48	5	56-4	112	.239
1987— Arkansas (Texas)		10	7	.588	4.10	1.55	28	27	2	1	...	0-...	151.1	168	90	69	16	67-7	118	.283
1988— Arkansas (Texas)		5	5	.500	3.58	1.77	70	1	0	0	...	17-...	78.0	97	48	31	1	41-13	72	.301
1989— Louisville (A.A.)		3	10	.231	5.22	1.63	22	19	0	0	...	0-...	112.0	136	79	65	13	47-1	73	.302
— Arkansas (Texas)		4	1	.800	1.64	1.00	6	6	2	1	...	0-...	44.0	32	11	8	1	12-0	38	.200
1990— Cant./Akr. (Eastern)		5	4	.556	2.80	1.40	61	0	0	0	...	6-...	64.1	66	24	20	5	24-6	61	.263
1991— Indianapolis (A.A.)		3	0	1.000	1.47	0.98	18	0	0	0	...	4-...	18.1	11	3	3	1	7-3	12	.177
— Montreal (N.L.)		2	5	.286	2.44	1.01	51	0	0	0	7	8-11	55.1	39	17	15	1	17-1	42	.196
1992— Montreal (N.L.)		8	7	.533	2.84	1.34	70	0	0	0	12	1-7	85.2	81	35	27	1	34-6	63	.249
1993— Montreal (N.L.)		12	5	.706	2.29	1.16	56	15	1	0	6	1-3	149.2	119	50	38	7	54-0	140	.216
1994— Montreal (N.L.)		8	6	.571	2.99	1.15	21	21	1	0	0	0-0	138.2	119	54	46	13	40-4	119	.229
1995— Montreal (N.L.)		13	14	.481	4.33	1.49	30	30	1	0	0	0-0	189.0	207	102	91	15	74-3	164	.283
1996— Montreal (N.L.)		15	11	.577	3.30	1.17	34	34	5	1	0	0-0	231.2	217	95	85	20	55-3	222	.244
1997— Seattle (A.L.)		16	9	.640	3.61	1.32	35	•35	2	1	0	0-0	234.1	226	108	94	21	84-6	189	.249
1998— Seattle (A.L.)		13	12	.520	3.97	1.29	32	32	7	0	0	0-0	224.2	223	115	99	33	66-2	176	.259
1999— Seattle (A.L.)		4	14	.222	7.38	1.88	30	24	0	0	2	0-0	139.0	188	123	114	34	73-3	101	.321
— Texas (A.L.)		1	0	1.000	5.71	1.73	7	3	0	0	0	0-0	17.1	20	12	11	1	10-0	13	.286
2000— Boston (A.L.)		8	8	.500	4.78	1.56	38	23	0	0	5	0-0	130.0	153	72	69	16	50-2	97	.296
2001— Chicago (N.L.)		4	4	.500	3.42	1.21	82	0	0	0	25	12-17	73.2	66	31	28	6	23-5	79	.235
2002— Chicago (N.L.)		5	6	.455	6.18	1.71	57	0	0	0	6	0-1	51.0	65	37	35	5	22-5	44	.313
— St. Louis (N.L.)		3	0	1.000	3.00	1.17	16	0	0	0	7	0-2	18.0	16	6	6	4	5-0	12	.232
2003— St. Louis (N.L.)		1	7	.125	5.68	1.64	62	6	0	0	11	3-6	77.2	93	51	49	17	34-4	55	.296
2004— Colorado (N.L.)		3	8	.273	5.51	1.62	40	12	0	0	2	0-0	111.0	136	73	68	9	44-5	59	.306
— Arizona (N.L.)		0	0	...	0.00	0.00	1	0	0	0	0	0-0	0.0	0	0	0	0	0-0	1	1.000
2005— San Francisco (N.L.)		4	7	.364	4.05	1.35	48	6	0	0	2	0-2	91.0	92	48	41	7	31-1	60	.268
2006— San Francisco (N.L.)		1	1	.500	7.80	2.07	10	1	0	0	0	0-0	15.0	23	13	13	4	8-0	7	.365
American League totals (4 years)		42	43	.494	4.67	1.47	142	117	9	1	7	0-0	745.1	810	430	387	105	283-13	576	.276
National League totals (12 years)		79	81	.494	3.79	1.33	578	125	8	1	78	25-49	1288.1	1273	612	542	109	441-37	1067	.258
Major League totals (16 years)		121	124	.494	4.11	1.38	720	242	17	2	85	25-49	2033.2	2083	1042	929	214	724-50	1643	.264

DIVISION SERIES RECORD

Year	Team (League)	W	L	Pct.	ERA	WHIP	G	GS	CG	ShO	Hld.	Sv.-Opp.	IP	H	R	ER	HR	BB-IBB	SO	Avg.
1997— Seattle (A.L.)		1	0	1.000	1.13	0.88	1	1	0	0	0	0-0	8.0	3	1	1	0	4-0	3	.120
1999— Texas (A.L.)		0	0	...	9.00	3.00	1	0	0	0	0	0-0	1.0	2	1	1	0	1-0	1	.400
2002— St. Louis (N.L.)		2	0	1.000	0.00	1.13	3	0	0	0	0	0-0	2.2	3	0	0	0	0-0	2	.300
Division series totals (3 years)		3	0	1.000	1.54	1.11	5	1	0	0	0	0-0	11.2	8	2	2	0	5-0	6	.200

CHAMPIONSHIP SERIES RECORD

Year	Team (League)	W	L	Pct.	ERA	WHIP	G	GS	CG	ShO	Hld.	Sv.-Opp.	IP	H	R	ER	HR	BB-IBB	SO	Avg.
2002— St. Louis (N.L.)		0	0	...	0.00	0.00	1	0	0	0	0	0-0	0.2	0	0	0	0	0-0	1	.000

2006 LEFTY-RIGHTY SPLITS

vs.	Avg.	AB	H	2B	3B	HR	RBI	BB	SO	OBP	Slg.	vs.	Avg.	AB	H	2B	3B	HR	RBI	BB	SO	OBP	Slg.
L	.333	21	7	2	0	1	4	4	3	.440	.571	R	.381	42	16	1	1	3	9	4	4	.426	.667

FEIERABEND, RYAN — P

PERSONAL: Born August 22, 1985, in Cleveland, Ohio. ... Throws left, bats left. ... Full name: Ryan R. Feierabend. **TRANSACTIONS/CAREER NOTES:** Selected by Seattle Mariners organization in third round of 2003 free-agent draft.
CAREER HITTING: 0-for-0 (.000), 0 R, 0 2B, 0 3B, 0 HR, 0 RBI.

Year	Team (League)	W	L	Pct.	ERA	WHIP	G	GS	CG	ShO	Hld.	Sv.-Opp.	IP	H	R	ER	HR	BB-IBB	SO	Avg.
2003— Ariz. Mariners (Ariz.)		2	3	.400	2.61	1.40	6	5	0	0	...	1-...	20.2	23	11	6	0	6-0	12	.288
2004— Wisconsin (Midw.)		9	7	.563	3.63	1.25	26	26	1	1	...	0-...	161.0	158	78	65	17	44-0	106	.263
2005— Inland Empire (Calif.)		8	7	.533	3.88	1.57	29	29	0	0	0	0-0	150.2	186	80	65	16	51-0	122	.310
2006— San Antonio (Texas)		9	12	.429	4.28	1.37	28	28	0	0	0	0-0	153.2	156	87	73	16	55-1	127	.267
— Seattle (A.L.)		0	1	.000	3.71	1.29	4	2	0	0	0	0-0	17.0	15	7	7	3	7-0	11	.231
Major League totals (1 year)		0	1	.000	3.71	1.29	4	2	0	0	0	0-0	17.0	15	7	7	3	7-0	11	.231

2006 LEFTY-RIGHTY SPLITS

vs.	Avg.	AB	H	2B	3B	HR	RBI	BB	SO	OBP	Slg.	vs.	Avg.	AB	H	2B	3B	HR	RBI	BB	SO	OBP	Slg.
L	.231	13	3	1	0	0	1	0	1	.231	.308	R	.231	52	12	2	0	3	6	7	10	.322	.442

FELDMAN, SCOTT — P

PERSONAL: Born February 7, 1983, in Kailua, Hawaii. ... 6-5/210. ... Throws right, bats left. ... Full name: Scott Wayne Feldman. ... Junior college: San Mateo (Calif.). **TRANS-ACTIONS/CAREER NOTES:** Selected by Texas Rangers organization in 30th round of 2003 free-agent draft. ... On suspended list (September 8-15, 2006).
CAREER HITTING: 0-for-0 (.000), 0 R, 0 2B, 0 3B, 0 HR, 0 RBI.

Year	Team (League)	W	L	Pct.	ERA	WHIP	G	GS	CG	ShO	Hld.	Sv.-Opp.	IP	H	R	ER	HR	BB-IBB	SO	Avg.
2003— Arizona Rangers (AZL)		1	1	.500	4.26	0.79	0	0	0	0	...	0-...	6.1	4	6	3	0	1-0	7	.138
2004— Arizona Rangers (AZL)		0	0	...	0.00	0.43	4	3	0	0	...	0-...	7.0	2	0	0	0	1-0	5	.091
2005— Bakersfield (Calif.)		0	0	...	0.00	0.78	6	0	0	0	3	3-3	9.0	5	2	0	0	2-0	11	.152
— Frisco (Texas)		1	2	.333	2.36	1.08	46	0	0	0	14	14-20	61.0	43	18	16	3	23-8	41	.202
— Texas (A.L.)		0	1	.000	0.96	1.18	8	0	0	0	1	0-0	9.1	9	1	1	0	2-1	4	.257
2006— Oklahoma (PCL)		2	2	.500	1.98	1.06	23	0	0	0	2	4-6	27.1	20	9	6	2	9-0	24	.206
— Texas (A.L.)		0	2	.000	3.92	1.26	36	0	0	0	7	0-1	41.1	42	19	18	4	10-0	30	.266
Major League totals (2 years)		0	3	.000	3.38	1.24	44	0	0	0	8	0-1	50.2	51	20	19	4	12-1	34	.264

2006 LEFTY-RIGHTY SPLITS

vs.	Avg.	AB	H	2B	3B	HR	RBI	BB	SO	OBP	Slg.	vs.	Avg.	AB	H	2B	3B	HR	RBI	BB	SO	OBP	Slg.
L	.280	50	14	2	0	0	7	3	13	.357	.440	R	.259	108	28	3	0	2	14	7	17	.308	.343

FELICIANO, PEDRO — P

PERSONAL: Born August 25, 1976, in Rio Piedras, Puerto Rico. ... 5-10/185. ... Throws left, bats left. ... Full name: Pedro Juan Feliciano. ... High school: Jose S. Alegria (Dorado, Puerto Rico). **TRANSACTIONS/CAREER NOTES:** Selected by Los Angeles Dodgers organization in 31st round of 1995 free-agent draft. ... Signed as a free agent by Cincinnati Reds organization (November 19, 2001). ... Traded by Reds with OF Elvin Andujar and two players to be named to New York Mets for P Shawn Estes and cash (August 15, 2002); Mets acquired OF Raul Gonzalez (August 20, 2002) and OF Brady Clark (September 9, 2002) to complete deal. ... Claimed on waivers by Detroit Tigers

F

(October 11, 2002). ... Released by Tigers (December 16, 2002). ... Signed by Mets organization (January 13, 2003). ... Released by Mets (January 18, 2005). ... Signed by Fukuoka Daiei Hawks of the Japan Pacific League (January 21, 2005). ... Signed as a free agent by Mets organization (December 19, 2005).

CAREER HITTING: 0-for-6 (.000), 0 R, 0 2B, 0 3B, 0 HR, 0 RBI.

Year	Team (League)	W	L	Pct.	ERA	WHIP	G	GS	CG	ShO	Hld.	Sv.-Opp.	IP	H	R	ER	HR	BB-IBB	SO	Avg.
1995— Great Falls (Pio.)		0	0	...	13.50	2.85	6	0	0	0	...	0-...	6.2	12	12	10	0	7-1	9	.333
1996— Great Falls (Pio.)		2	3	.400	5.71	1.85	22	1	0	0	...	3-...	41.0	50	36	26	1	26-2	39	.291
1997— Savannah (S. Atl.)		3	7	.300	2.64	1.22	36	9	1	0	...	4-...	105.2	90	45	31	11	39-0	94	.230
— Vero Beach (FSL)		0	0	...	4.50	1.50	1	0	0	0	...	0-...	2.0	3	1	1	1	0-0	1	.429
1998— Vero Beach (FSL)		2	5	.286	4.61	1.43	22	10	0	0	...	2-...	68.1	68	44	35	8	30-1	51	.255
1999—	Did not play.																			
2000— Vero Beach (FSL)		4	5	.444	3.82	1.63	25	2	0	0	...	0-...	61.1	76	31	26	4	24-1	48	.303
— San Antonio (Texas)		0	0	...	1.93	1.18	9	0	0	0	...	2-...	9.1	7	2	2	0	4-1	11	.226
— Albuquerque (PCL)		0	0	...	18.00	4.00	1	0	0	0	...	0-...	1.0	3	3	2	2	1-0	2	.375
2001— Jacksonville (Sou.)		5	4	.556	1.94	0.86	54	0	0	0	...	17-...	60.1	41	14	13	3	11-1	55	.194
— Las Vegas (PCL)		0	1	.000	7.27	2.42	6	0	0	0	...	0-...	8.2	16	11	7	2	5-1	5	.390
2002— Chattanooga (Sou.)		2	1	.667	2.56	1.14	28	0	0	0	...	4-...	38.2	33	14	11	1	11-1	26	.230
— Louisville (Int'l)		1	1	.500	3.04	1.46	20	0	0	0	...	0-...	26.2	35	10	9	3	4-0	19	.327
— Norfolk (Int'l)		0	0	...	7.00	1.67	5	0	0	0	...	2-...	9.0	14	7	7	1	1-0	11	.359
— New York (N.L.)		0	0	...	7.50	1.67	6	0	0	0	0	0-0	6.0	9	5	5	0	1-0	4	.360
2003— Norfolk (Int'l)		3	2	.600	3.97	1.10	15	0	0	0	0	1-...	22.2	20	10	10	3	6-1	18	.238
— New York (N.L.)		0	0	...	3.35	1.51	23	0	0	0	0	0-0	48.1	52	21	18	5	21-3	43	.269
2004— Norfolk (Int'l)		4	3	.571	5.30	1.40	32	0	0	0	...	2-...	35.2	35	25	21	4	15-1	25	.259
— New York (N.L.)		1	1	.500	5.40	1.42	22	0	0	0	2	0-0	18.1	14	12	11	2	12-0	14	.209
2005— Fukuoka (Jp. Pac.)		3	2	.600	3.89	1.16	37	0	0	0	...	4-...	37.0	30	17	16	5	13-...	36	...
2006— Norfolk (Int'l)		0	0	...	6.23	1.15	3	0	0	0	...	0-...	4.1	4	3	3	1	1-0	5	.250
— New York (N.L.)		7	2	.778	2.09	1.26	64	0	0	0	10	0-3	60.1	56	15	14	4	20-1	54	.248
Major League totals (4 years)		**8**	**3**	**.727**	**3.25**	**1.39**	**115**	**0**	**0**	**0**	**12**	**0-3**	**133.0**	**131**	**53**	**48**	**11**	**54-4**	**115**	**.256**

DIVISION SERIES RECORD

Year	Team (League)	W	L	Pct.	ERA	WHIP	G	GS	CG	ShO	Hld.	Sv.-Opp.	IP	H	R	ER	HR	BB-IBB	SO	Avg.
2006— New York (N.L.)		1	0	1.000	0.00	1.20	3	0	0	0	0	0-0	1.2	0	0	0	0	2-0	2	.000

CHAMPIONSHIP SERIES RECORD

Year	Team (League)	W	L	Pct.	ERA	WHIP	G	GS	CG	ShO	Hld.	Sv.-Opp.	IP	H	R	ER	HR	BB-IBB	SO	Avg.
2006— New York (N.L.)		0	0	...	3.00	0.67	3	0	0	0	1	0-0	3.0	2	1	1	1	0-0	1	.182

2006 LEFTY-RIGHTY SPLITS

vs.	Avg.	AB	H	2B	3B	HR	RBI	BB	SO	OBP	Slg.	vs.	Avg.	AB	H	2B	3B	HR	RBI	BB	SO	OBP	Slg.
L	.231	117	27	4	0	2	11	5	44	.272	.316	R	.266	109	29	3	0	2	10	15	10	.354	.349

FELIZ, PEDRO — 3B

PERSONAL: Born April 27, 1975, in Azua, Dominican Republic. ... 6-1/205. ... Bats right, throws right. ... Full name: Pedro Julio Feliz. ... High school: Los Toros (Azua, Dominican Republic). **TRANSACTIONS/CAREER NOTES:** Signed as a non-drafted free agent by San Francisco Giants organization (February 7, 1994). **STATISTICAL NOTES:** Career major league grand slams: 4.

2006 GAMES PLAYED BY POSITION (MLB): 3B—159, OF—3, SS—2.

Year	Team (League)	Pos.	G	AB	R	H	2B	3B	HR	RBI	BB	SO	HBP	GDP	SB-CS	Avg.	OBP	SLG	OPS	E	Avg.
1994— Ariz. Giants (Ariz.)		3B	38	119	7	23	0	0	0	3	2	20		3	2-3	.193	.220	.193	.413	5	.953
1995— Bellingham (N'west)		1B-3B	43	113	14	31	2	1	0	16	7	33	0	2	1-1	.274	.311	.310	.621	2	.971
1996— Burlington (Midw.)		1B-3B	93	321	36	85	12	2	5	36	18	65	1	11	5-2	.265	.303	.361	.665	17	.937
1997— Bakersfield (Calif.)		3B	135	515	59	140	25	4	14	56	23	90	7	15	5-7	.272	.310	.417	.728	23	.950
1998— Shreveport (Texas)		3B	100	364	39	96	23	2	12	50	9	62	2	15	0-1	.264	.282	.437	.719	22	.926
— Fresno (PCL)		3B	3	7	1	3	1	0	1	3	1	0	0	1	0-0	.429	.500	1.000	1.500	0	1.000
1999— Shreveport (Texas)		3B	131	491	52	124	24	6	13	77	19	90	3	18	4-2	.253	.282	.405	.687	17	.934
2000— Fresno (PCL)		3B-SS	128	503	85	150	34	2	33	105	30	94	2	18	1-1	.298	.337	.571	.908	24	.939
— San Francisco (N.L.)		3B	8	7	1	2	0	0	0	0	0	1	0	0	0-0	.286	.286	.286	.571	0	...
2001— San Francisco (N.L.)		3B-DH	94	220	23	50	9	1	7	22	10	50	2	5	2-1	.227	.264	.373	.637	12	.908
2002— San Francisco (N.L.)		3B-OF-SS	67	146	14	37	4	1	2	13	6	27	0	2	0-0	.253	.281	.336	.617	3	.966
2003— San Francisco (N.L.)		3B-OF-1B	95	235	31	58	9	3	16	48	10	53	1	7	2-2	.247	.278	.515	.793	4	.982
2004— San Francisco (N.L.)		1B-3B-SS																			
		OF	144	503	72	139	33	3	22	84	23	85	0	18	5-2	.276	.305	.485	.790	13	.983
2005— San Francisco (N.L.)		3B-OF-1B	156	569	69	142	30	4	20	81	38	102	1	20	0-2	.250	.295	.422	.717	10	.976
2006— San Francisco (N.L.)		3B-OF-SS	160	603	75	147	35	5	22	98	33	112	1	18	1-1	.244	.281	.428	.709	21	.956
Major League totals (7 years)			**724**	**2283**	**285**	**575**	**120**	**17**	**89**	**346**	**120**	**430**	**5**	**70**	**10-8**	**.252**	**.288**	**.436**	**.724**	**63**	**.970**

DIVISION SERIES RECORD

Year	Team (League)	Pos.	G	AB	R	H	2B	3B	HR	RBI	BB	SO	HBP	GDP	SB-CS	Avg.	OBP	SLG	OPS	E	Avg.
2002— San Francisco (N.L.)			1	1	0	0	0	0	0	0	0	0	0	0	0-0	.000	.000	.000	.000		...
2003— San Francisco (N.L.)			3	3	1	2	0	1	0	1	0	1	0	0	0-0	.667	.667	1.333	2.000	0	...
Division series totals (2 years)			**4**	**4**	**1**	**2**	**0**	**1**	**0**	**1**	**0**	**2**	**0**	**0**	**0-0**	**.500**	**.500**	**1.000**	**1.500**	**0**	**...**

CHAMPIONSHIP SERIES RECORD

Year	Team (League)	Pos.	G	AB	R	H	2B	3B	HR	RBI	BB	SO	HBP	GDP	SB-CS	Avg.	OBP	SLG	OPS	E	Avg.
2002— San Francisco (N.L.)			1	1	0	0	0	0	0	0	0	0	0	0	0-0	.000	.000	.000	.000		...

WORLD SERIES RECORD

Year	Team (League)	Pos.	G	AB	R	H	2B	3B	HR	RBI	BB	SO	HBP	GDP	SB-CS	Avg.	OBP	SLG	OPS	E	Avg.
2002— San Francisco (N.L.)		DH	3	5	0	0	0	0	0	0	0	2	0	0	0-0	.000	.000	.000	.000		...

2006 LEFTY-RIGHTY SPLITS

vs.	Avg.	AB	H	2B	3B	HR	RBI	BB	SO	OBP	Slg.	vs.	Avg.	AB	H	2B	3B	HR	RBI	BB	SO	OBP	Slg.
L	.212	132	28	7	2	3	19	10	23	.269	.364	R	.253	471	119	28	3	19	79	23	89	.285	.446

FERNANDEZ, JARED — P

PERSONAL: Born February 2, 1972, in Salt Lake City. ... 6-1/235. ... Throws right, bats right. ... Full name: Jared Wade Fernandez. ... High school: Kearns (Utah). ... College: Fresno State. **TRANSACTIONS/CAREER NOTES:** Signed as a non-drafted free agent by Boston Red Sox organization (June 23, 1994). ... Signed as a free agent by Cincinnati Reds organization (December 15, 2000). ... Released by Reds (December 15, 2002). ... Signed by Houston Astros organization (December 20, 2002). ... Signed as a free agent by Reds organization (December 17, 2004). ... Released by Reds (July 7, 2005). ... Signed by Philadelphia Phillies organization (August 1, 2005). ... Signed as a free agent by Milwaukee Brewers organization (November 23, 2005).

F

CAREER HITTING: 2-for-21 (.095), 3 R, 0 2B, 0 3B, 0 HR, 1 RBI.

Year	Team (League)	W	L	Pct.	ERA	WHIP	G	GS	CG	ShO	Hld.	Sv.-Opp.	IP	H	R	ER	HR	BB-IBB	SO	Avg.
1994—	Utica (N.Y.-Penn)	1	1	.500	3.60	1.70	21	1	0	0	...	4-...	30.0	43	18	12	4	8-2	24	.316
1995—	Utica (N.Y.-Penn)	3	2	.600	1.89	1.03	5	5	1	0	...	0-...	38.0	30	11	8	2	9-1	23	.219
	—Trenton (East.)	5	4	.556	3.90	1.37	11	10	1	0	...	0-...	67.0	64	32	29	4	28-1	40	.253
1996—	Trenton (East.)	9	9	.500	5.08	1.50	30	29	3	0	...	0-...	179.0	185	•115	101	19	83-5	94	.268
1997—	Trenton (East.)	4	6	.400	5.41	1.68	21	16	1	0	...	0-...	121.1	138	90	73	12	66-0	73	.282
	—Pawtucket (Int'l)	0	3	.000	5.79	1.71	11	11	0	0	...	0-...	60.2	76	45	39	7	28-1	33	.311
1998—	Trenton (East.)	3	7	.300	5.25	1.55	36	7	0	0	...	1-...	118.1	132	80	69	8	51-3	70	.286
	—Pawtucket (Int'l)	1	1	.500	4.74	1.34	5	2	0	0	...	0-...	24.2	26	16	13	5	7-0	15	.274
1999—	Trenton (East.)	3	0	1.000	3.38	1.39	7	0	0	0	...	0-...	18.2	18	9	7	4	8-0	10	.250
	—Pawtucket (Int'l)	12	9	.571	4.25	1.29	27	20	3	0	...	0-...	163.0	172	88	77	20	39-0	76	.273
2000—	Pawtucket (Int'l)	10	4	.714	3.02	1.23	31	9	2	0	...	4-...	113.1	103	51	38	10	36-0	65	.248
2001—	Louisville (Int'l)	10	9	.526	4.13	1.39	33	28	4	1	...	0-...	196.1	218	105	90	24	54-0	118	.281
	—Cincinnati (N.L.)	0	1	.000	4.38	1.54	5	2	0	0	0	0-0	12.1	13	9	6	1	6-0	5	.265
2002—	Louisville (Int'l)	12	5	.706	3.93	1.42	26	18	1	0	...	1-...	128.1	151	63	56	14	31-1	80	.298
	—Cincinnati (N.L.)	1	3	.250	4.44	1.64	14	8	0	0	0	0-0	50.2	59	31	25	5	24-1	36	.294
2003—	New Orleans (PCL)	7	10	.412	3.81	1.30	26	23	0	0	...	0-...	156.0	164	73	66	16	37-1	51	.270
	—Houston (N.L.)	3	3	.500	3.90	1.28	12	6	0	0	0	0-0	38.1	37	17	17	2	12-2	19	.259
2004—	Houston (N.L.)	0	0	...	54.00	11.00	2	1	0	0	0	0-0	1.0	6	6	6	0	5-0	0	.750
	—New Orleans (PCL)	7	11	.389	4.77	1.30	35	28	3	0	...	0-...	196.1	209	120	104	27	46-2	98	.272
2005—	Louisville (Int'l)	5	5	.500	4.38	1.33	13	13	0	0	...	0-...	84.1	86	45	41	8	26-0	51	.270
	—Scran./W.B. (I.L.)	4	2	.667	2.66	1.33	7	7	0	0	...	0-...	40.2	40	18	12	4	14-0	30	.255
2006—	Nashville (PCL)	6	4	.600	3.27	1.27	24	15	4	2	0	3-4	129.1	141	64	47	9	23-1	76	.274
	—Milwaukee (N.L.)	0	0	...	9.95	1.89	4	0	0	0	0	0-0	6.1	11	7	7	2	1-0	1	.367
	Major League totals (5 years)	4	7	.364	5.05	1.60	37	17	0	0	0	0-0	108.2	126	70	61	10	48-3	61	.292

2006 LEFTY-RIGHTY SPLITS

vs.	Avg.	AB	H	2B	3B	HR	RBI	BB	SO	OBP	Slg.	vs.	Avg.	AB	H	2B	3B	HR	RBI	BB	SO	OBP	Slg.
L	.467	15	7	1	1	2	5	1	1	.500	1.067	R	.267	15	4	2	0	0	4	0	0	.267	.400

FICK, ROBERT — 1B/C

PERSONAL: Born March 15, 1974, in Torrance, Calif. ... 6-1/205. ... Bats left, throws right. ... Full name: Robert Charles Fick. ... High school: Newbury Park (Calif.). ... College: Cal State Northridge. **TRANSACTIONS/CAREER NOTES:** Selected by Oakland Athletics organization in 45th round of 1992 free-agent draft; did not sign. ... Selected by Detroit Tigers organization in 43rd round of 1995 free-agent draft; did not sign. ... Selected by Tigers organization in fifth round of 1996 free-agent draft. ... On disabled list (March 31-September 7, 1999); included rehabilitation assignments to GCL Tigers, West Michigan and Toledo. ... On suspended list (May 23-26, 2000). ... On disabled list (July 6-September 1, 2000); included rehabilitation assignment to Toledo. ... On suspended list (September 22-27, 2001). ... Signed as a free agent by Atlanta Braves organization (January 6, 2003). ... On disabled list (April 13-29, 2003). ... Released by Braves (November 5, 2003). ... Signed by Tampa Bay Devil Rays (January 9, 2004). ... Released by Devil Rays (August 13, 2004). ... Signed by San Diego Padres organization (August 19, 2004). ... Signed as a free agent by Washington Nationals (December 13, 2005). ... On disabled list (March 27-May 13 and August 1-25, 2006); included rehabilitation assignments to Harrisburg and New Orleans. **STATISTICAL NOTES:** Career major league grand slams: 3.

2006 GAMES PLAYED BY POSITION (MLB): C—26, 1B—13, OF—6.

Year	Team (League)	Pos.	G	AB	R	H	2B	3B	HR	RBI	BB	SO	HBP	GDP	SB-CS	Avg.	OBP	SLG	OPS	E	Avg.
1996—	Jamestown (NYP)	C	43	133	18	33	6	0	1	14	12	25	0	4	3-1	.248	.306	.316	.622	3	.982
1997—	W. Mich. (Mid.)	1B-3B-C	122	463	100	158	50	3	16	90	75	74	1	10	13-4	.341	.429	.566	.994	12	.989
1998—	Jacksonville (Sou.)	1B-C-OF	130	515	101	164	•47	6	18	114	71	83	6	8	8-4	.318	.401	.538	.939	9	.985
	—Detroit (A.L.)	C-DH-1B	7	22	6	8	1	0	3	7	2	7	0	1	1-0	.364	.417	.818	1.235	1	.966
1999—	GC Tigers (GCL)	1B-C-DH	3	9	2	3	1	0	0	2	0	0	0	0	1-0	.333	.455	.444	.899	0	1.000
	—W. Mich. (Mid.)	1B-C-DH	3	11	2	3	0	0	0	0	2	0	0	0	1-0	.273	.385	.273	.657	2	.913
	—Toledo (Int'l)	1B-C-DH																			
		3B	14	48	11	15	0	1	2	8	8	5	1	0	1-0	.313	.414	.479	.893	5	.944
	—Detroit (A.L.)	DH-C	15	41	6	9	0	0	3	10	7	6	0	1	1-0	.220	.327	.439	.766	0	1.000
2000—	Detroit (A.L.)	1B-C-DH	66	163	18	41	7	2	3	22	22	39	1	4	2-1	.252	.340	.374	.715	5	.983
	—Toledo (Int'l)	1B	17	68	5	10	0	0	1	7	6	13	2	0	1-0	.147	.234	.265	.498	0	1.000
2001—	Detroit (A.L.)	C-1B-DH																			
		OF	124	401	62	109	21	2	19	61	39	62	4	10	0-3	.272	.339	.476	.816	7	.989
2002—	Detroit (A.L.)	OF-DH	148	556	66	150	36	2	17	63	46	90	7	17	0-1	.270	.331	.433	.764	*12	.963
2003—	Atlanta (N.L.)	1B	126	409	52	110	26	1	11	80	42	47	2	9	1-0	.269	.335	.418	.753	14	.987
2004—	Tampa Bay (A.L.)	DH-OF-1B																			
		C	76	214	12	43	5	2	6	26	20	32	2	2	0-0	.201	.273	.327	.600	3	.977
	—Portland (PCL)	1B-C	12	50	8	19	4	0	2	6	2	11	0	0	0-0	.380	.404	.580	.984	1	.990
	—San Diego (N.L.)	1B	13	12	2	2	0	0	0	0	2	4	1	0	0-0	.167	.333	.167	.500	1	1.000
2005—	Portland (PCL)	1B-C	10	32	5	12	1	0	3	11	10	3	1	1	0-0	.375	.523	.688	1.210	1	.989
	—San Diego (N.L.)	1B-C-DH																			
		DH-3B	93	230	25	61	10	2	3	30	26	33	1	4	0-2	.265	.340	.365	.705	6	.986
2006—	New Orleans (PCL)		2	7	0	1	0	0	0	0	1	2	0	0	1-0	.143	.250	.143	.393	0	1.000
	—Harrisburg (East.)		16	57	11	16	1	0	1	4	8	8	0	1	2-1	.281	.369	.351	.720	1	.986
	—Wash. (N.L.)	C-1B-OF	60	128	14	34	4	0	2	9	10	24	1	4	1-1	.266	.324	.344	.667	1	.994
	American League totals (6 years)		436	1397	170	360	70	8	51	189	136	236	14	35	4-5	.258	.327	.429	.755	28	.981
	National League totals (4 years)		292	779	93	207	40	3	16	119	80	108	5	17	2-3	.266	.334	.386	.721	21	.988
	Major League totals (9 years)		728	2176	263	567	110	11	67	308	216	344	19	52	6-8	.261	.329	.414	.743	49	.984

DIVISION SERIES RECORD

Year	Team (League)	Pos.	G	AB	R	H	2B	3B	HR	RBI	BB	SO	HBP	GDP	SB-CS	Avg.	OBP	SLG	OPS	E	Avg.
2003—	Atlanta (N.L.)	1B	4	11	0	0	0	0	0	0	1	2	0	1	0-0	.000	.083	.000	.083	0	1.000
2005—	San Diego (N.L.)	1B	2	5	0	1	0	0	0	0	1	0	0	0	0-0	.200	.333	.200	.533	0	1.000
	Division series totals (2 years)		6	16	0	1	0	0	0	0	2	2	0	1	0-0	.063	.167	.063	.229	0	1.000

ALL-STAR GAME RECORD

			G	AB	R	H	2B	3B	HR	RBI	BB	SO	HBP	GDP	SB-CS	Avg.	OBP	SLG	OPS	E	Avg.
	All-Star Game totals (1 year)		1	2	1	1	0	0	0	0	0	0	0	0	1-0	.500	.500	.500	1.000	0	1.000

2006 LEFTY-RIGHTY SPLITS

vs.	Avg.	AB	H	2B	3B	HR	RBI	BB	SO	OBP	Slg.	vs.	Avg.	AB	H	2B	3B	HR	RBI	BB	SO	OBP	Slg.
L	.273	44	12	1	0	0	2	2	9	.319	.295	R	.262	84	22	3	0	2	8	8	15	.326	.369

FIELD, NATE — P

PERSONAL: Born December 11, 1975, in Denver. ... 6-2/200. ... Throws right, bats right. ... Full name: Nathan Patrick Field. ... High school: Heritage (Littleton, Colo.). ... College: Fort Hays State (Kan.). **TRANSACTIONS/CAREER NOTES:** Signed as a non-drafted free agent by Montreal Expos organization (June 11, 1998). ... Released by Expos (March 29, 2000). ... Signed by Sioux City of independent Norther League (2000). ... Contract purchased by Kansas City Royals organization from Sioux City (June 29, 2000). ... Claimed on waivers by New York Yankees (June 12, 2002). ... Signed as a free agent by Royals organization (January 6, 2003). ... On disabled list (August 11, 2004-remainder of season). ... Signed as a free agent by Colorado Rockies organization (November 8, 2005).

CAREER HITTING: 0-for-0 (.000), 0 R, 0 2B, 0 3B, 0 HR, 0 RBI.

Year Team (League)	W	L	Pct.	ERA	WHIP	G	GS	CG	ShO	Hld.	Sv.-Opp.	IP	H	R	ER	HR	BB-IBB	SO	Avg.
1998— Vermont (NYP)	3	1	.750	3.09	1.23	25	0	0	0	...	2-...	35.0	32	16	12	1	11-0	39	.237
1999— Cape Fear (S. Atl.)	4	8	.333	5.40	1.49	42	0	0	0	...	2-...	65.0	75	49	39	8	22-2	55	.282
— Ottawa (Int'l)	0	0	...	3.00	2.67	2	0	0	0	...	0-...	3.0	4	1	1	0	4-0	4	.333
2000— Sioux City (Nor.)	3	0	1.000	1.93	1.37	11	0	0	0	...	0-...	23.1	17	10	5	...	15-...	19	...
— Char., W.Va. (SAL)	1	2	.333	2.23	1.18	17	0	0	0	...	0-...	36.1	28	10	9	2	15-0	31	.215
2001— Wichita (Texas)	4	2	.667	1.48	1.08	52	0	0	0	...	19-...	73.0	61	16	12	3	18-3	67	.222
2002— Omaha (PCL)	0	1	.000	3.31	1.84	18	0	0	0	...	7-...	16.1	22	10	6	0	8-0	13	.326
— Kansas City (A.L.)	0	0	...	9.00	2.20	5	0	0	0	0	0-0	5.0	8	5	5	2	3-1	3	.364
— Columbus (Int'l)	2	1	.667	6.75	1.73	21	2	0	0	...	0-...	38.2	46	30	29	6	21-1	25	.305
2003— Wichita (Texas)	1	0	1.000	3.60	1.40	15	0	0	0	...	3-...	20.0	20	9	8	2	8-1	20	.256
— Omaha (PCL)	2	2	.500	3.18	0.80	19	0	0	0	...	4-...	22.2	15	8	8	4	4-0	17	.188
— Kansas City (A.L.)	1	1	.500	4.15	1.52	19	0	0	0	2	0-0	21.2	19	10	10	3	14-1	19	.235
2004— Kansas City (A.L.)	2	3	.400	4.26	1.33	43	0	0	0	2	3-5	44.1	40	25	21	5	19-2	30	.243
2005— Kansas City (A.L.)	0	0	...	9.45	2.70	7	0	0	0	1	0-0	6.2	13	7	7	1	5-2	4	.433
— Omaha (PCL)	1	0	1.000	4.91	1.82	16	0	0	0	2	0-0	22.0	26	12	12	1	14-1	24	.295
2006— Colo. Springs (PCL)	3	3	.500	4.74	1.46	49	0	0	0	0	25-30	49.1	63	28	26	7	9-0	55	.313
— Colorado (N.L.)	1	1	.500	4.00	1.56	14	0	0	0	4	0-1	9.0	9	4	4	2	5-1	14	.257
American League totals (4 years)	3	4	.429	4.98	1.56	74	0	0	0	5	3-5	77.2	80	47	43	11	41-6	56	.266
National League totals (1 year)	1	1	.500	4.00	1.56	14	0	0	0	4	0-1	9.0	9	4	4	2	5-1	14	.257
Major League totals (5 years)	4	5	.444	4.88	1.56	88	0	0	0	9	3-6	86.2	89	51	47	13	46-7	70	.266

2006 LEFTY-RIGHTY SPLITS

vs.	Avg.	AB	H	2B	3B	HR	RBI	BB	SO	OBP	Slg.	vs.	Avg.	AB	H	2B	3B	HR	RBI	BB	SO	OBP	Slg.
L	.417	12	5	2	0	2	4	4	2	.563	1.083	R	.174	23	4	1	1	0	11	1	12	.208	.304

FIELDER, PRINCE — 1B

PERSONAL: Born May 9, 1984, in Ontario, Calif. ... 6-0/260. ... Bats left, throws right. ... Full name: Prince Semien Fielder. ... Son of Cecil Fielder, 1B/DH with five major league teams (1985-1998). **TRANSACTIONS/CAREER NOTES:** Selected by Milwaukee Brewers organization in first round (seventh pick overall) of 2002 free-agent draft.

2006 GAMES PLAYED BY POSITION (MLB): 1B—152, DH—1.

Year Team (League)	Pos.	G	AB	R	H	2B	3B	HR	RBI	BB	SO	HBP	GDP	SB-CS	Avg.	OBP	SLG	OPS	E	Avg.
2002— Ogden (Pion.)		41	146	35	57	12	0	10	40	37	27	8	2	3-4	.390	.531	.678	1.209	8	.974
— Beloit (Midw.)		32	112	15	27	7	0	3	11	10	27	3	1	0-0	.241	.320	.384	.704	7	.973
2003— Beloit (Midw.)		137	502	81	157	22	2	27	112	71	80	15	14	2-1	.313	.409	.526	.935	18	.984
2004— Huntsville (Sou.)		135	497	70	135	29	1	23	78	65	93	11	11	11-7	.272	.366	.473	.839	15	.994
2005— Nashville (PCL)	1B-DH	103	378	68	110	21	0	28	86	54	93	7	12	8-5	.291	.388	.569	.957	12	.985
— Milwaukee (N.L.)	1B-DH	39	59	2	17	4	0	2	10	2	17	0	0	0-0	.288	.306	.458	.764	0	1.000
2006— Milwaukee (N.L.)	1B-DH	157	569	82	154	35	1	.28	81	59	125	12	17	7-2	.271	.347	.483	.831	11	.992
Major League totals (2 years)		196	628	84	171	39	1	30	91	61	142	12	17	7-2	.272	.344	.481	.825	11	.992

2006 LEFTY-RIGHTY SPLITS

vs.	Avg.	AB	H	2B	3B	HR	RBI	BB	SO	OBP	Slg.	vs.	Avg.	AB	H	2B	3B	HR	RBI	BB	SO	OBP	Slg.
L	.247	166	41	9	0	11	31	11	49	.319	.500	R	.280	403	113	26	1	17	50	48	76	.359	.476

FIELDS, JOSH — 3B/OF

PERSONAL: Born December 14, 1982, in Ada, Okla. ... Bats right, throws right. ... Full name: Joshua Dean Fields. ... College: Oklahoma State. **TRANSACTIONS/CAREER NOTES:** Selected by Chicago White Sox organization in first round (18th pick overall) of 2004 free-agent draft. **STATISTICAL NOTES:** Hit home run in first major league at-bat (September 18, 2006).

2006 GAMES PLAYED BY POSITION (MLB): 3B—6, DH—2, OF—1.

Year Team (League)	Pos.	G	AB	R	H	2B	3B	HR	RBI	BB	SO	HBP	GDP	SB-CS	Avg.	OBP	SLG	OPS	E	Avg.
2004— Win.-Salem (Car.)		66	256	36	73	12	4	7	39	18	74	2	2	0-0	.285	.333	.445	.778	12	...
2005— Birmingham (Sou.)	3B-1B-DH	134	477	76	120	27	4	16	79	55	142	13	4	7-6	.252	.341	.409	.750	25	.932
2006— Charlotte (Int'l)		124	462	85	141	32	4	19	70	54	136	3	8	28-5	.305	.379	.515	.894	16	.944
— Chicago (A.L.)	3B-DH-OF	11	20	4	3	2	0	1	2	5	8	0	0	0-0	.150	.320	.400	.720	0	1.000
Major League totals (1 year)		11	20	4	3	2	0	1	2	5	8	0	0	0-0	.150	.320	.400	.720	0	1.000

2006 LEFTY-RIGHTY SPLITS

vs.	Avg.	AB	H	2B	3B	HR	RBI	BB	SO	OBP	Slg.	vs.	Avg.	AB	H	2B	3B	HR	RBI	BB	SO	OBP	Slg.
L	.167	6	1	0	0	1	2	1	3	.286	.667	R	.143	14	2	2	0	0	0	4	5	.333	.286

FIGGINS, CHONE — 3B/OF

PERSONAL: Born January 22, 1978, in Leary, Ga. ... 5-8/160. ... Bats both, throws right. ... Full name: Desmond DeChone Figgins. ... Name pronounced: shawn. ... High school: Brandon (Fla.). **TRANSACTIONS/CAREER NOTES:** Selected by Colorado Rockies organization in fourth round of 1997 free-agent draft. ... Traded by Rockies to Anaheim Angels for OF Kimera Bartee (July 13, 2001). ... Angels franchise renamed Los Angeles Angels of Anaheim for 2005 season. **STATISTICAL NOTES:** Career major league grand slams: 1.

2006 GAMES PLAYED BY POSITION (MLB): OF—112, 3B—34, 2B—9, DH—6, SS—2.

Year Team (League)	Pos.	G	AB	R	H	2B	3B	HR	RBI	BB	SO	HBP	GDP	SB-CS	Avg.	OBP	SLG	OPS	E	Avg.
1997— Ariz. Rockies (Ariz.)	SS	54	214	41	60	5	6	1	23	35	51	3	2	30-12	.280	.386	.374	.760	40	.865
1998— Portland (N'west)	SS	69	269	41	76	9	3	1	26	24	56	2	3	25-4	.283	.345	.349	.694	16	.947
1999— Salem (Carol.)	SS	123	444	65	106	12	3	0	22	41	86	3	5	27-13	.239	.306	.279	.585	45	.925
2000— Salem (Carol.)	2B	134	522	92	145	26	14	3	48	67	107	1	7	37-19	.278	.358	.398	.756	28	.955
2001— Carolina (Southern)	2B-SS	86	332	41	73	14	5	2	25	40	73	2	0	27-8	.220	.306	.310	.616	16	.963

F

Year	Team (League)	Pos.	G	AB	R	H	2B	3B	HR	RBI	BB	SO	HBP	GDP	SB-CS	Avg.	OBP	SLG	OPS	E	Avg.
	—Arkansas (Texas)	2B-SS-3B	39	138	21	37	12	2	0	12	14	26	0	0	7-2	.268	.329	.384	.713	10	.945
2002	—Salt Lake (PCL)	2B-SS	125	511	100	156	25	18	7	62	53	83	0	0	39-8	.305	.364	.466	.830	23	.964
	—Anaheim (A.L.)	2B	15	12	6	2	1	0	0	1	0	5	0	1	2-1	.167	.167	.250	.417	1	.941
2003	—Salt Lake (PCL) 2B-SS-SS	3B	68	285	55	89	14	15	4	30	29	36	3	4	16-6	.312	.379	.509	.888	17	.949
	—Anaheim (A.L.) OF-2B-SS	DH	71	240	34	71	9	4	0	27	20	38	0	1	13-7	.296	.345	.367	.711	3	.985
2004	—Anaheim (A.L.) 3B-OF-2B	SS-DH	148	577	83	171	22	17	5	60	49	94	0	6	34-13	.296	.350	.419	.770	15	.964
2005	—Los Angeles (A.L.) OF-3B-2B	DH-SS	158	642	113	186	25	10	8	57	64	101	0	* 62-17	.290	.352	.397	.749	10	.979
2006	—Los Angeles (A.L.) OF-3B-2B	DH-SS	155	604	93	161	23	8	9	62	65	100	2	6	52-16	.267	.336	.376	.712	16	.959
	Major League totals (5 years)		547	2075	329	591	80	39	22	207	198	338	2	23	163-54	.285	.345	.393	.738	45	.970

DIVISION SERIES RECORD

Year	Team (League)	Pos.	G	AB	R	H	2B	3B	HR	RBI	BB	SO	HBP	GDP	SB-CS	Avg.	OBP	SLG	OPS	E	Avg.
2002	—Anaheim (A.L.)	DH	1	0	1	0	0	0	0	0	0	0	0	0	1-0	...	...	...	...		...
2004	—Anaheim (A.L.)	2B-3B	3	14	0	2	0	0	0	0	0	5	1	0	1-0	.143	.200	.143	.343	2	.875
2005	—Los Angeles (A.L.)	3B-OF	5	21	2	3	1	1	0	2	1	8	0	1	0-1	.143	.182	.286	.468	0	1.000
	Division series totals (3 years)		9	35	3	5	1	1	0	2	1	13	1	1	2-1	.143	.189	.229	.418	2	.923

CHAMPIONSHIP SERIES RECORD

Year	Team (League)	Pos.	G	AB	R	H	2B	3B	HR	RBI	BB	SO	HBP	GDP	SB-CS	Avg.	OBP	SLG	OPS	E	Avg.
2002	—Anaheim (A.L.)		3	1	2	1	0	0	0	0	0	0	0	0	0-0	1.000	1.000	1.000	2.000		...
2005	—Los Angeles (A.L.)	3B-OF	5	17	1	2	1	0	0	1	1	3	0	0	1-0	.118	.167	.176	.343	1	.917
	Champ. series totals (2 years)		8	18	3	3	1	0	0	1	1	3	0	0	1-0	.167	.211	.222	.433	1	.917

WORLD SERIES RECORD

Year	Team (League)	Pos.	G	AB	R	H	2B	3B	HR	RBI	BB	SO	HBP	GDP	SB-CS	Avg.	OBP	SLG	OPS	E	Avg.
2002	—Anaheim (A.L.)		2	0	1	0	0	0	0	0	0	0	0	0	0-0	...	...	...	...		...

2006 LEFTY-RIGHTY SPLITS

vs.	Avg.	AB	H	2B	3B	HR	RBI	BB	SO	OBP	Slg.	vs.	Avg.	AB	H	2B	3B	HR	RBI	BB	SO	OBP	Slg.
L	.233	172	40	8	1	3	12	19	38	.307	.343	R	.280	432	121	15	7	6	50	46	62	.348	.389

FIGUEROA, LUIS   SS/2B

PERSONAL: Born February 16, 1974, in Bayamon, Puerto Rico. ... 5-9/150. ... Bats both, throws right. ... Full name: Luis R. Figueroa. ... High school: Berkshire (Homestead, Fla.). **TRANSACTIONS/CAREER NOTES:** Signed as non-drafted free agent by Pittsburgh Pirates organization (March 31, 1997). ... Claimed on waivers by New York Mets (August 15, 2001). ... Traded by Mets with P Bruce Chen and a player to be named to Montreal Expos for Ps Scott Strickland and Phil Seibel and OF Matt Watson (April 5, 2002); Expos acquired P Saul Rivera to complete deal (July 14, 2002). ... Signed as a free agent by Milwaukee Brewers organization (January 8, 2004). ... Signed as a free agent by Boston Red Sox organization (January 21, 2005). ... Signed as a free agent by Toronto Blue Jays organization (November 14, 2005).

2006 GAMES PLAYED BY POSITION (MLB): 2B—5, SS—2.

Year	Team (League)	Pos.	G	AB	R	H	2B	3B	HR	RBI	BB	SO	HBP	GDP	SB-CS	Avg.	OBP	SLG	OPS	E	Avg.
1997	—Augusta (S. Atl.)	2B-SS	71	248	38	56	8	0	0	21	35	29	1	2	22-6	.226	.322	.258	.580	19	.941
	—Lynchburg (Caro.)	2B	26	89	12	25	5	0	0	2	7	6	0	5	1-2	.281	.333	.337	.670	1	.990
1998	—Carolina (Southern)	2B-SS	117	350	54	87	9	3	0	24	71	46	2	12	6-5	.249	.376	.291	.667	27	.954
1999	—Altoona (East.)	2B-SS	131	418	61	110	15	5	3	50	52	44	3	7	9-9	.263	.347	.344	.691	28	.957
2000	—Altoona (East.)	SS	94	342	45	97	10	4	1	28	37	32	2	8	14-5	.284	.356	.345	.701	26	.948
	—Nashville (PCL) 2B-3B-SS		23	64	6	16	1	0	3	8	1	8	0	2	2-1	.250	.262	.406	.668	5	.915
2001	—Nashville (PCL) SS-2B-2B		92	347	45	104	11	1	4	29	31	26	1	8	8-5	.300	.357	.372	.729	19	.960
	—Pittsburgh (N.L.)	2B	4	2	0	0	0	0	0	0	0	0	0	...	0-0	.000	.000	.000	.000	0	1.000
	—Norfolk (Int'l)	SS-2B	17	58	7	15	3	1	1	5	5	6	0	1	0-0	.259	.317	.397	.714	2	.975
2002	—Norfolk (Int'l)	SS	2	4	0	0	0	0	0	0	0	0	0	0	0-0	.000	.000	.000	.000	0	1.000
	—Brevard County (FSL)	SS	15	61	8	16	1	1	0	8	5	2	1	3	2-4	.262	.328	.311	.640	6	.918
	—Ottawa (Int'l)	SS	27	82	6	12	1	1	1	9	3	14	1	2	0-2	.146	.186	.220	.406	3	.975
	—Harrisburg (East.)	SS	66	250	47	68	17	3	1	30	25	16	2	5	6-7	.272	.341	.376	.717	6	.981
2003	—Edmonton (PCL)		126	480	66	152	30	2	2	44	36	31	3	12	7-7	.317	.364	.400	.764	...	...
2004	—Indianapolis (Int'l)		116	383	44	104	14	0	5	48	24	24	1	6	5-6	.272	.314	.347	.661	...	...
2005	—Pawtucket (Int'l) SS-3B-2B		109	402	58	116	22	1	4	48	29	28	1	10	2-6	.289	.334	.400	.735	18	.956
2006	—Syracuse (Int'l)		93	377	39	104	22	3	6	38	24	35	2	9	11-9	.276	.318	.398	.716	12	.962
	—Toronto (A.L.) 2B-SS		8	9	1	1	1	0	0	0	0	2	0	0	0-0	.111	.111	.222	.333	1	.929
	American League totals (1 year)		8	9	1	1	1	0	0	0	0	2	0	0	0-0	.111	.111	.222	.333	1	.929
	National League totals (1 year)		4	2	0	0	0	0	0	0	0	0	0	...	0-0	.000	.000	.000	.000	0	1.000
	Major League totals (2 years)		12	11	1	1	1	0	0	0	0	2	0	0	0-0	.091	.091	.182	.273	1	.947

2006 LEFTY-RIGHTY SPLITS

vs.	Avg.	AB	H	2B	3B	HR	RBI	BB	SO	OBP	Slg.	vs.	Avg.	AB	H	2B	3B	HR	RBI	BB	SO	OBP	Slg.
L	.000	2	0	0	0	0	0	0	1	.000	.000	R	.143	7	1	1	0	0	0	0	1	.143	.286

FINLEY, STEVE   OF

PERSONAL: Born March 12, 1965, in Union City, Tenn. ... 6-2/195. ... Bats left, throws left. ... Full name: Steven Allen Finley. ... High school: Paducah (Ky.) Tilghman. ... College: Southern Illinois. **TRANSACTIONS/CAREER NOTES:** Selected by Atlanta Braves organization in 11th round of June 1986 free-agent draft; did not sign. ... Selected by Baltimore Orioles organization in 13th round of 1987 free-agent draft. ... On disabled list (April 4-22 and July 29-September 1, 1989); included rehabilitation assignment to Hagerstown. ... Traded by Orioles with Ps Pete Harnisch and Curt Schilling to Houston Astros for 1B Glenn Davis (January 10, 1991). ... On disabled list (April 25-May 14, 1993). ... On disabled list (June 13-July 3, 1994); included rehabilitation assignment to Jackson. ... Traded by Astros with 3B Ken Caminiti, SS Andujar Cedeno, 1B Roberto Petagine, P Brian Williams and a player to be named to San Diego Padres for OFs Phil Plantier and Derek Bell, Ps Pedro Martinez and Doug Brocail, IF Craig Shipley and SS Ricky Gutierrez (December 28, 1994); Padres acquired P Sean Fesh to complete deal (May 1, 1995). ... On disabled list (April 20-May 6, 1997); included rehabilitation assignment to Rancho Cucamonga. ... Signed as a free agent by Arizona Diamondbacks (December 18, 1998). ... Traded by Diamondbacks with C Brent Mayne to Los Angeles Dodgers for C Koyie Hill, P Bill Murphy and OF Reggie Abercrombie (July 31, 2004). ... Signed as a free agent by Anaheim Angels (December 10, 2004). ... Angels franchise renamed Los Angeles Angels of Anaheim prior to 2005 season. ... On disabled list (June 20-July 14, 2005); included rehabilitation assignment to Rancho Cucamonga. ... Traded by Angels to San Francisco Giants for 3B Edgardo Alfonzo (December 21, 2005). **HONORS:** Won N.L. Gold Glove as outfielder (1995, 1996, 1999, 2000 and 2004). **STATISTICAL NOTES:** Hit three home runs in one game (May 19 and June 23, 1997; September 8, 1999; and April 28, 2004). ... Career major league grand slams: 10. ... Career major league pitching: 0-0, 0.00 ERA, 1 G, 1.0 IP, 0 H, 0 ER, 1 BB, 0 SO.

F

Year Team (League)	Pos.	G	AB	R	H	2B	3B	HR	RBI	BB	SO	HBP	GDP	SB-CS	Avg.	OBP	SLG	OPS	E	Avg.
1987— Newark (NY-Penn)	OF	54	222	40	65	13	2	3	33	22	24	2	4	26-5	.293	.359	.410	.769	4	.970
— Hagerstown (Car.)	OF	15	65	9	22	3	2	1	5	1	6	0	2	7-2	.338	.348	.492	.841	0	1.000
1988— Hagerstown (Car.)	OF	8	28	2	6	2	0	0	3	4	3	0	2	4-0	.214	.313	.286	.598	0	1.000
— Charlotte (Sou.)	OF	10	40	7	12	4	2	1	6	4	3	1	1	2-0	.300	.378	.575	.953	0	1.000
— Rochester (Int'l)	OF	120	456	61	143	19	7	5	54	28	55	0	4	20-11	.314	.352	.419	.771	12	.962
1989— Baltimore (A.L.)	DH-OF	81	217	35	54	5	2	2	25	15	30	1	3	17-3	.249	.298	.318	.616	2	.986
— Rochester (Int'l)	OF	7	25	2	4	0	0	0	2	1	5	0	0	3-0	.160	.192	.160	.352	0	1.000
— Hagerstown (East.)	OF	11	48	11	20	3	1	0	7	4	3	0	0	4-0	.417	.453	.521	.974	3	.925
1990— Baltimore (A.L.)	DH-OF	142	464	46	119	16	4	3	37	32	53	2	8	22-9	.256	.304	.328	.632	7	.977
1991— Houston (N.L.)	OF	159	596	84	170	28	10	8	54	42	65	2	8	34-18	.285	.331	.406	.737	5	.985
1992— Houston (N.L.)	OF	• 162	607	84	177	29	13	5	55	58	63	3	10	44-9	.292	.355	.407	.762	3	.993
1993— Houston (N.L.)	OF	142	545	69	145	15	* 13	8	44	28	65	3	8	19-6	.266	.304	.385	.689	4	.988
1994— Houston (N.L.)	OF	94	373	64	103	16	5	11	33	28	52	2	3	13-7	.276	.329	.434	.764	4	.982
— Jackson (Texas)	OF-DH	5	13	3	4	0	0	0	0	4	0	0	0	1-0	.308	.471	.308	.778	0	1.000
1995— San Diego (N.L.)	OF	139	562	104	167	23	8	10	44	59	62	3	8	36-12	.297	.366	.420	.786	7	.977
1996— San Diego (N.L.)	OF	161	655	126	195	45	9	30	95	56	87	4	20	22-8	.298	.354	.531	.885	7	.982
1997— San Diego (N.L.)	OF	143	560	101	146	26	5	28	92	43	92	3	10	15-3	.261	.313	.475	.788	4	.989
— Mobile (Sou.)	DH	1	4	1	2	0	0	1	2	1	2	0	0	0-0	.500	.600	1.250	1.850	...	...
— Rancho Cuca. (Calif.)	DH-OF	4	14	3	4	0	0	2	3	3	2	1	0	1-0	.286	.444	.714	1.159	0	...
1998— San Diego (N.L.)	OF	159	619	92	154	40	6	14	67	45	103	3	9	12-3	.249	.301	.401	.702	7	.981
1999— Arizona (N.L.)	OF-DH	156	590	100	156	32	10	34	103	63	94	3	4	8-4	.264	.336	.525	.861	2	.995
2000— Arizona (N.L.)	OF-DH	152	539	100	151	27	5	35	96	65	87	8	9	12-6	.280	.361	.544	.904	3	.992
2001— Arizona (N.L.)	OF-P	140	495	66	136	27	4	14	73	47	67	1	8	11-7	.275	.337	.430	.767	2	.994
2002— Arizona (N.L.)	OF	150	505	82	145	24	4	25	89	65	73	3	10	16-4	.287	.370	.499	.869	2	.994
2003— Arizona (N.L.)	OF	147	516	82	148	24	• 10	22	70	57	94	6	9	15-8	.287	.363	.500	.863	5	.982
2004— Arizona (N.L.)	OF-DH	104	404	61	111	16	1	23	48	40	52	1	9	8-4	.275	.338	.490	.828	2	.991
— Los Angeles (N.L.)	OF	58	224	31	59	12	0	13	46	21	30	0	5	1-3	.263	.324	.491	.815	1	.993
2005— Rancho Cuca. (Calif.)	DH	1	4	2	2	1	0	0	1	0	0	0	0	0-0	.500	.600	.750	1.350	0	...
— Los Angeles (A.L.)	OF-DH	112	406	41	90	20	3	12	54	26	71	3	6	8-4	.222	.271	.374	.645	4	.985
2006— San Francisco (N.L.)	OF	139	426	66	105	21	12	6	40	46	55	2	6	7-0	.246	.320	.394	.714	1	.997
American League totals (3 years)		335	1087	122	263	41	9	17	116	73	154	6	17	47-16	.242	.291	.343	.634	13	.982
National League totals (15 years)		2205	8216	1312	2268	405	115	286	1049	763	1141	47	133	273-102	.276	.339	.458	.796	59	.988
Major League totals (18 years)		2540	9303	1434	2531	446	124	303	1165	836	1295	53	150	320-118	.272	.333	.444	.777	72	.988

DIVISION SERIES RECORD

Year Team (League)	Pos.	G	AB	R	H	2B	3B	HR	RBI	BB	SO	HBP	GDP	SB-CS	Avg.	OBP	SLG	OPS	E	Avg.
1996— San Diego (N.L.)	OF	3	12	0	1	0	0	0	1	0	4	1	0	1-0	.083	.154	.083	.237	0	1.000
1998— San Diego (N.L.)	OF	4	10	2	1	1	0	0	1	1	4	0	0	0-0	.100	.182	.200	.382	0	1.000
1999— Arizona (N.L.)	OF	4	13	0	5	1	0	0	5	3	1	0	1	0-0	.385	.500	.462	.962	0	1.000
2001— Arizona (N.L.)	OF	5	19	1	8	1	0	0	2	0	2	0	0	0-0	.421	.421	.474	.895	0	1.000
2002— Arizona (N.L.)	OF	3	9	1	2	0	0	0	1	2	2	0	0	1-0	.222	.333	.222	.556	0	1.000
2004— Los Angeles (N.L.)	OF	4	16	0	2	1	0	0	2	1	0	0	0	0-0	.125	.176	.188	.364	0	1.000
2005— Los Angeles (A.L.)	OF	5	11	2	1	1	0	0	1	1	4	0	0	0-0	.091	.167	.182	.348	0	1.000
Division series totals (7 years)		28	90	6	20	5	0	0	13	8	17	1	1	2-0	.222	.290	.278	.568	0	1.000

CHAMPIONSHIP SERIES RECORD

Year Team (League)	Pos.	G	AB	R	H	2B	3B	HR	RBI	BB	SO	HBP	GDP	SB-CS	Avg.	OBP	SLG	OPS	E	Avg.
1998— San Diego (N.L.)	OF	6	21	3	7	1	0	0	2	6	2	0	0	1-0	.333	.481	.381	.862	0	1.000
2001— Arizona (N.L.)	OF	5	14	1	4	1	0	0	4	3	1	0	1	1-0	.286	.412	.357	.769	0	1.000
2005— Los Angeles (A.L.)	OF	3	9	1	2	0	0	0	0	0	2	0	1	0-0	.222	.222	.222	.444	0	1.000
Champ. series totals (3 years)		14	44	5	13	2	0	0	6	9	5	0	2	2-0	.295	.415	.341	.756	0	1.000

WORLD SERIES RECORD

Year Team (League)	Pos.	G	AB	R	H	2B	3B	HR	RBI	BB	SO	HBP	GDP	SB-CS	Avg.	OBP	SLG	OPS	E	Avg.
1998— San Diego (N.L.)	OF	3	12	0	1	1	0	0	0	0	2	0	0	1-0	.083	.083	.167	.250	0	1.000
2001— Arizona (N.L.)	OF	7	19	5	7	0	0	1	2	4	5	0	0	0-1	.368	.478	.526	1.005	0	1.000
World series totals (2 years)		10	31	5	8	1	0	1	2	4	7	0	0	1-1	.258	.343	.387	.730	0	1.000

ALL-STAR GAME RECORD

		G	AB	R	H	2B	3B	HR	RBI	BB	SO	HBP	GDP	SB-CS	Avg.	OBP	SLG	OPS	E	Avg.
All-Star Game totals (2 years)		2	2	0	1	0	0	0	1	0	1	0	0	0-0	.500	.500	.500	1.000	0	1.000

2006 LEFTY-RIGHTY SPLITS

vs.	Avg.	AB	H	2B	3B	HR	RBI	BB	SO	OBP	Slg.	vs.	Avg.	AB	H	2B	3B	HR	RBI	BB	SO	OBP	Slg.
L	.255	98	25	4	4	0	9	6	14	.308	.378	R	.244	328	80	17	8	6	31	40	41	.323	.399

FIORENTINO, JEFF — OF

PERSONAL: Born April 14, 1983, in Pembroke Pines, Fla. ... 6-1/188. ... Bats left, throws right. ... Full name: Jeffrey Philip Fiorentino. ... College: Florida Atlantic. **TRANSACTIONS/CAREER NOTES:** Selected by Baltimore Orioles organization in third round of 2004 free-agent draft.

2006 GAMES PLAYED BY POSITION (MLB): OF—17, DH—2.

Year Team (League)	Pos.	G	AB	R	H	2B	3B	HR	RBI	BB	SO	HBP	GDP	SB-CS	Avg.	OBP	SLG	OPS	E	Avg.
2004— Aberdeen (N.Y.-Penn.)	OF-SS-C	14	46	9	16	7	1	2	12	9	4	2	0	3-1	.348	.474	.674	1.148	1	.909
— Delmarva (S. Atl.)	OF	49	179	40	54	15	2	10	36	20	50	3	1	2-2	.302	.379	.575	.954	5	.000
2005— Baltimore (A.L.)	OF	13	44	7	11	2	0	1	5	2	10	0	0	1-0	.250	.277	.364	.640	0	1.000
— Frederick (Carolina)	OF	103	413	70	118	18	4	22	66	34	90	4	5	12-6	.286	.346	.508	.854	12	.968
2006— Bowie (East.)	OF	104	385	63	106	14	0	13	62	53	58	3	7	9-3	.275	.365	.413	.778	3	.983
— Baltimore (A.L.)	OF-DH	19	39	8	10	2	0	0	7	7	3	1	1	2-0	.256	.375	.308	.683	0	1.000
Major League totals (2 years)		32	83	15	21	4	0	1	12	9	13	1	1	2-0	.253	.326	.337	.664	0	1.000

2006 LEFTY-RIGHTY SPLITS

vs.	Avg.	AB	H	2B	3B	HR	RBI	BB	SO	OBP	Slg.	vs.	Avg.	AB	H	2B	3B	HR	RBI	BB	SO	OBP	Slg.
L	.182	11	2	0	0	0	2	0	1	.182	.182	R	.286	28	8	2	0	0	5	7	2	.432	.357

F

FLORES, RANDY — P

PERSONAL: Born July 31, 1975, in Bellflower, Calif. ... 6-0/180. ... Throws left, bats left. ... Full name: Randy Alan Flores. ... High school: El Rancho (Pico Rivera, Calif.). ... College: Southern California. ... Brother of Ron Flores, pitcher, Oakland Athletics **TRANSACTIONS/CAREER NOTES:** Selected by St. Louis Cardinals organization in 21st round of 1996 free-agent draft; did not sign. ... Selected by New York Yankees organization in ninth round of 1997 free-agent draft. ... Traded by Yankees with P Rosman Garcia to Texas Rangers (October 11, 2001), completing deal in which Rangers traded 2B Randy Velarde to Yankees for two players to be named (August 31, 2001). ... Claimed on waivers by Colorado Rockies (July 18, 2002). ... Signed as a free agent by Cardinals organization (November 21, 2003). ... On disabled list (June 24-July 9, 2005); included rehabilitation assignment to Memphis.
CAREER HITTING: 0-for-7 (.000), 0 R, 0 2B, 0 3B, 0 HR, 0 RBI.

Year	Team (League)	W	L	Pct.	ERA	WHIP	G	GS	CG	ShO	Hld.	Sv.-Opp.	IP	H	R	ER	HR	BB-IBB	SO	Avg.
1997—	Oneonta (NYP)	4	4	.500	3.25	1.17	13	13	2	1	...	0-...	74.2	64	32	27	3	23-1	70	.229
1998—	Tampa (Fla. St.)	1	2	.333	6.46	1.86	5	5	0	0	...	0-...	23.2	28	23	17	2	16-2	15	.298
—	Greensboro (S. Atl.)	12	7	.632	2.62	1.16	21	20	2	1	...	0-...	130.2	119	48	38	6	33-0	139	.243
1999—	Tampa (Fla. St.)	11	4	.733	2.87	1.16	21	20	1	1	...	0-...	135.0	118	56	43	4	38-0	99	.235
—	Norwich (East.)	0	1	.000	6.48	1.72	4	4	0	0	...	0-...	25.0	32	20	18	0	11-1	19	.302
2000—	Norwich (East.)	10	9	.526	2.94	1.39	31	20	3	0	...	1-...	141.0	138	64	46	8	58-1	97	.259
—	Columbus (Int'l)	1	2	.333	7.33	2.14	4	4	0	0	...	0-...	23.1	43	21	19	2	7-0	16	.391
2001—	Columbus (Int'l)	0	1	.000	4.76	1.24	3	0	0	0	...	0-...	5.2	5	4	3	2	2-0	4	.238
—	Norwich (East.)	14	6	.700	2.78	1.38	25	25	3	2	...	0-...	158.2	156	64	49	13	63-0	115	.258
2002—	Oklahoma (PCL)	1	1	.500	5.75	1.33	15	0	0	0	...	1-...	20.1	22	13	13	1	5-1	16	.268
—	Texas (A.L.)	0	0	...	4.50	1.58	20	0	0	0	2	1-2	12.0	11	7	6	2	8-2	7	.268
—	Colo. Springs (PCL)	2	2	.500	3.28	1.51	7	7	0	0	...	0-...	35.2	36	15	13	1	18-0	27	.269
—	Colorado (N.L.)	0	2	.000	9.53	2.18	8	2	0	0	0	0-0	17.0	29	19	18	5	8-1	7	.382
2003—	Colo. Springs (PCL)	10	8	.556	4.98	1.60	28	24	0	0	...	0-...	142.2	156	89	79	16	67-4	116	.279
2004—	Memphis (PCL)	5	7	.417	3.82	1.31	36	15	1	1	...	2-...	122.2	115	60	52	10	46-1	99	.251
—	St. Louis (N.L.)	1	0	1.000	1.93	1.14	9	1	0	0	0	0-0	14.0	13	3	3	0	3-1	7	.265
2005—	Memphis (PCL)	1	0	1.000	6.43	1.14	6	0	0	0	1	0-1	7.0	8	6	5	1	0-0	6	.296
—	St. Louis (N.L.)	3	1	.750	3.46	1.20	50	0	0	0	11	1-3	41.2	37	22	16	5	13-0	43	.240
2006—	St. Louis (N.L.)	1	1	.500	5.62	1.70	65	0	0	0	18	0-1	41.2	49	29	26	5	22-3	40	.290
	American League totals (1 year)	0	0	...	4.50	1.58	20	0	0	0	2	1-2	12.0	11	7	6	2	8-2	7	.268
	National League totals (4 years)	5	4	.556	4.96	1.52	132	3	0	0	29	1-4	114.1	128	73	63	15	46-5	97	.286
	Major League totals (4 years)	5	4	.556	4.92	1.53	152	3	0	0	31	2-6	126.1	139	80	69	17	54-7	104	.284

DIVISION SERIES RECORD

Year	Team (League)	W	L	Pct.	ERA	WHIP	G	GS	CG	ShO	Hld.	Sv.-Opp.	IP	H	R	ER	HR	BB-IBB	SO	Avg.
2005—	St. Louis (N.L.)	0	0	...	4.50	1.00	3	0	0	0	1	0-0	2.0	2	1	1	1	0-0	3	.250
2006—	St. Louis (N.L.)	0	0	...	0.00	3.00	2	0	0	0	1	0-0	1.0	2	0	0	0	1-0	1	.400
	Division series totals (2 years)	0	0	...	3.00	1.67	5	0	0	0	2	0-0	3.0	4	1	1	1	1-0	4	.308

CHAMPIONSHIP SERIES RECORD

Year	Team (League)	W	L	Pct.	ERA	WHIP	G	GS	CG	ShO	Hld.	Sv.-Opp.	IP	H	R	ER	HR	BB-IBB	SO	Avg.
2005—	St. Louis (N.L.)	0	0	...	0.00	0.75	2	0	0	0	1	0-0	1.1	0	0	0	0	1-0	0	.000
2006—	St. Louis (N.L.)	1	0	1.000	0.00	0.55	4	0	0	0	1	0-0	3.2	2	0	0	0	0-0	3	.154
	Champ. series totals (2 years)	1	0	1.000	0.00	0.60	6	0	0	0	1	0-0	5.0	2	0	0	0	1-0	3	.125

WORLD SERIES RECORD

Year	Team (League)	W	L	Pct.	ERA	WHIP	G	GS	CG	ShO	Hld.	Sv.-Opp.	IP	H	R	ER	HR	BB-IBB	SO	Avg.
2006—	St. Louis (N.L.)	0	0	...	0.00	1.00	1	0	0	0	0	0-0	1.0	1	0	0	0	0-0	0	.333

2006 LEFTY-RIGHTY SPLITS

vs.	Avg.	AB	H	2B	3B	HR	RBI	BB	SO	OBP	Slg.	vs.	Avg.	AB	H	2B	3B	HR	RBI	BB	SO	OBP	Slg.
L	.258	93	24	3	0	2	15	10	23	.337	.355	R	.329	76	25	5	2	3	15	12	17	.416	.566

FLORES, RON — P

PERSONAL: Born August 9, 1979, in Whittier, Calif. ... 5-11/190. ... Throws left, bats left. ... Full name: Ronald Joel Flores. ... College: Southern California. ... Brother of Randy Flores, pitcher, St. Louis Cardinals. **TRANSACTIONS/CAREER NOTES:** Selected by Oakland Athletics organization in 29th round of 2000 free-agent draft.
CAREER HITTING: 0-for-1 (.000), 0 R, 0 2B, 0 3B, 0 HR, 0 RBI.

Year	Team (League)	W	L	Pct.	ERA	WHIP	G	GS	CG	ShO	Hld.	Sv.-Opp.	IP	H	R	ER	HR	BB-IBB	SO	Avg.
2000—	Vancouver (N'west)	1	1	.500	5.11	1.62	13	0	0	0	...	0-...	12.1	16	10	7	2	4-0	10	.296
2001—	Modesto (California)	5	2	.714	2.86	1.24	47	0	0	0	...	6-...	66.0	53	24	21	4	29-7	71	.217
2002—	Visalia (Calif.)	8	6	.571	3.25	1.32	53	0	0	0	...	11-...	80.1	90	41	29	7	16-2	92	.281
2003—	Midland (Texas)	3	2	.600	2.88	0.99	39	0	0	0	...	6-...	59.1	44	19	19	6	15-3	66	.204
—	Sacramento (PCL)	2	0	1.000	6.59	1.39	12	0	0	0	...	0-...	13.2	16	10	10	0	3-1	10	.302
2004—	Sacramento (PCL)	4	3	.571	3.83	1.46	55	0	0	0	...	1-...	54.0	60	27	23	5	19-4	55	.271
2005—	Sacramento (PCL)	5	3	.625	2.39	1.26	52	0	0	0	12	3-7	60.1	46	18	16	5	30-6	66	.213
—	Oakland (A.L.)	0	0	...	1.04	0.92	11	0	0	0	1	0-0	8.2	8	1	1	1	6-0	6	.235
2006—	Sacramento (PCL)	5	5	.500	6.48	1.56	26	0	0	0	3	2-3	25.0	25	20	18	0	14-1	27	.260
—	Oakland (A.L.)	1	2	.333	3.34	1.28	25	0	0	0	1	1-1	29.2	28	11	11	3	10-2	20	.255
	Major League totals (2 years)	1	2	.333	2.82	1.20	36	0	0	0	2	1-1	38.1	36	12	12	4	10-2	26	.250

2006 LEFTY-RIGHTY SPLITS

vs.	Avg.	AB	H	2B	3B	HR	RBI	BB	SO	OBP	Slg.	vs.	Avg.	AB	H	2B	3B	HR	RBI	BB	SO	OBP	Slg.
L	.323	31	10	1	0	1	7	2	11	.364	.452	R	.228	79	18	7	1	2	11	8	9	.292	.418

FLOYD, CLIFF — OF

PERSONAL: Born December 5, 1972, in Chicago. ... 6-4/230. ... Bats left, throws right. ... Full name: Cornelius Clifford Floyd. ... High school: Thornwood (South Holland, Ill.). **TRANSACTIONS/CAREER NOTES:** Selected by Montreal Expos organization in first round (14th pick overall) of 1991 free-agent draft. ... On disabled list (May 16-September 11, 1995). ... Traded by Expos to Florida Marlins for OF Joe Orsulak and P Dustin Hermanson (March 26, 1997). ... On disabled list (May 9-24 and June 21-September 1, 1997); included rehabilitation assignment to Charlotte. ... On disabled list (March 30-April 27 and June 20-September 7, 1999); included rehabilitation assignment to Calgary. ... On disabled list (July 29-August 29, 2000). ... Traded by Marlins with P Claudio Vargas, OF/2B Wilton Guerrero, a player to be named and cash considerations to Expos for Ps Carl Pavano, Graeme Lloyd and Justin Wayne and IF Mike Mordecai (July 11, 2002); Expos acquired P Don Levinski to complete deal (August 5, 2002). ... Traded by Expos to Boston Red Sox for Ps Seung Song and Sun-Woo Kim (July 30, 2002). ... Signed as a free agent by New York Mets (December 20, 2002). ... On disabled list (August 19, 2003-remainder of season). ... On disabled list (April 12-May 13, 2004); included rehabilitation assignment to St. Lucie. ... On disabled list (June 7-30 and August 9-September 2, 2006); included rehabilitation assignments to GCL Mets, St. Lucie and Brooklyn. **HONORS:** Named Minor League Player of the Year by THE SPORTING NEWS (1993). **STATISTICAL NOTES:** Career major league grand slams: 6.
2006 GAMES PLAYED BY POSITION (MLB): OF—92.

F

Year	Team (League)	Pos.	G	AB	R	H	2B	3B	HR	RBI	BB	SO	HBP	GDP	SB-CS	Avg.	OBP	SLG	OPS	E	Avg.
																			BATTING	FIELDING	
1991—GC Expos (GCL)	1B	56	214	35	56	9	3	6	30	19	37	5	3	13-3	.262	.335	.416	.751	15	.970
1992—Albany (S. Atl.)	1B-OF	134	516	83	157	24	16	16	97	45	75	4	4	32-11	.304	.368	.506	.874	17	.964
—W.P. Beach (FSL)	OF	1	4	0	0	0	0	0	0	1	0	1	0	0-0	.000	.000	.000	.000	0	1.000
1993—Harrisburg (East.)	1B-OF	101	380	82	125	17	4	•26	101	54	71	5	5	31-10	.329	.417	.600	1.017	19	.969
—Ottawa (Int'l)	1B	32	125	12	30	2	2	2	18	16	34	1	1	2-2	.240	.329	.336	.665	5	.983
—Montreal (N.L.)	1B	10	31	3	7	0	0	1	2	0	9	0	0	0-0	.226	.226	.323	.548	0	1.000
1994—Montreal (N.L.)	1B-OF	100	334	43	94	19	4	4	41	24	63	3	3	10-3	.281	.332	.398	.731	6	.990
1995—Montreal (N.L.)	1B-OF	29	69	6	9	1	0	1	8	7	22	1	1	3-0	.130	.221	.188	.409	3	.981
1996—Ottawa (Int'l)	OF-3B-DH	20	76	7	23	3	1	1	8	7	20	1	0	2-2	.303	.369	.408	.777	2	.951
—Montreal (N.L.)	OF-1B	117	227	29	55	15	4	6	26	30	52	5	3	7-1	.242	.340	.423	.763	5	.957
1997—Florida (N.L.)	OF-1B	61	137	23	32	9	1	6	19	24	33	2	3	6-2	.234	.354	.445	.799	3	.971
—Charlotte (Int'l)	OF	39	131	27	48	10	0	9	33	10	29	1	3	7-2	.366	.415	.649	1.064	1	.988
1998—Florida (N.L.)	OF-DH	153	588	85	166	45	3	22	90	47	112	3	10	27-14	.282	.337	.481	.818	7	.974
1999—Florida (N.L.)	OF-DH	69	251	37	76	19	1	11	49	30	47	2	8	5-6	.303	.379	.518	.897	6	.952
—Calgary (PCL)	OF	9	31	6	12	1	0	3	8	2	8	0	0	0-1	.387	.424	.710	1.134	0	1.000
2000—Florida (N.L.)	OF-DH	121	420	75	126	30	0	22	91	50	82	8	4	24-3	.300	.378	.529	.906	9	.951
2001—Florida (N.L.)	OF-DH	149	555	123	176	44	4	31	103	59	101	10	9	18-3	.317	.390	.578	.968	8	.972
2002—Florida (N.L.)	OF-DH	84	296	49	85	20	0	18	57	58	68	7	0	10-5	.287	.414	.537	.952	3	.983
—Montreal (N.L.)	OF	15	53	7	11	2	0	3	4	3	10	1	0	1-0	.208	.263	.415	.678	1	.941
—Boston (A.L.)	OF-DH	47	171	30	54	21	0	7	18	15	28	2	6	4-0	.316	.374	.561	.935	1	.977
2003—New York (N.L.)	OF-DH	108	365	57	106	25	2	18	68	51	66	3	10	3-0	.290	.376	.518	.894	3	.971
2004—St. Lucie (Fla. St.)	OF	1	4	2	2	0	0	0	1	0	2	0	0	0-0	.500	.500	.500	1.000	0	1.000
—New York (N.L.)	OF-DH	113	396	55	103	26	0	18	63	47	103	11	8	11-4	.260	.352	.462	.814	2	.988*
2005—New York (N.L.)	OF	150	550	85	150	22	2	34	98	63	98	11	5	12-2	.273	.358	.505	.863	2	.993
2006—St. Lucie (Fla. St.)		3	10	2	4	0	0	2	4	1	3	0	0	0-0	.400	.455	1.000	1.455	1	.750
—GC Mets (GCL)		2	6	2	3	0	0	1	4	1	0	0	0	0-0	.500	.571	1.000	1.571	0	—
—Brooklyn (N.Y.-Penn.)		1	2	0	0	0	0	0	0	1	1	0	0	0-0	.000	.333	.000	.333	0	1.000
—New York (N.L.)	OF	97	332	45	81	19	1	11	44	29	58	12	5	6-0	.244	.324	.407	.731	2	.987
American League totals (1 year)		47	171	30	54	21	0	7	18	15	28	2	6	4-0	.316	.374	.561	.935	1	.977
National League totals (14 years)		1376	4604	722	1277	296	22	206	763	522	924	79	69	143-43	.277	.358	.485	.843	62	.979
Major League totals (14 years)		1423	4775	752	1331	317	22	213	781	537	952	81	75	147-43	.279	.359	.488	.847	63	.979

DIVISION SERIES RECORD

Year	Team (League)	Pos.	G	AB	R	H	2B	3B	HR	RBI	BB	SO	HBP	GDP	SB-CS	Avg.	OBP	SLG	OPS	E	Avg.
1997—Florida (N.L.)		Did not play.																			
2006—New York (N.L.)	OF	3	9	3	4	0	0	1	2	1	2	0	0	0-0	.444	.500	.778	1.278	0	1.000

CHAMPIONSHIP SERIES RECORD

Year	Team (League)	Pos.	G	AB	R	H	2B	3B	HR	RBI	BB	SO	HBP	GDP	SB-CS	Avg.	OBP	SLG	OPS	E	Avg.
1997—Florida (N.L.)		Did not play.																			
2006—New York (N.L.)	OF	3	3	0	0	0	0	0	0	0	1	0	0	0-0	.000	.000	.000	.000	0	1.000

WORLD SERIES RECORD

Year	Team (League)	Pos.	G	AB	R	H	2B	3B	HR	RBI	BB	SO	HBP	GDP	SB-CS	Avg.	OBP	SLG	OPS	E	Avg.
1997—Florida (N.L.)	DH	4	2	1	0	0	0	0	0	1	1	0	0	0-0	.000	.333	.000	.333	...	...

ALL-STAR GAME RECORD

		G	AB	R	H	2B	3B	HR	RBI	BB	SO	HBP	GDP	SB-CS	Avg.	OBP	SLG	OPS	E	Avg.
All-Star Game totals (1 year)		1	2	0	0	0	0	0	0	0	0	0	0	0-0	.000	.000	.000	...		

2006 LEFTY-RIGHTY SPLITS

vs.	Avg.	AB	H	2B	3B	HR	RBI	BB	SO	OBP	Slg.	vs.	Avg.	AB	H	2B	3B	HR	RBI	BB	SO	OBP	Slg.
L	.179	84	15	6	0	3	16	7	13	.274	.357	R	.266	248	66	13	1	8	28	22	45	.342	.423

FLOYD, GAVIN   P

PERSONAL: Born January 27, 1983, in Annapolis, Md. ... 6-4/212. ... Throws right, bats right. ... Full name: Gavin Christopher Floyd. ... High school: Mount St. Joseph (Baltimore). **TRANSACTIONS/CAREER NOTES:** Selected by Philadelphia Phillies organization in first round (fourth pick overall) of 2001 free-agent draft.
CAREER HITTING: 2-for-42 (.048), 0 R, 0 2B, 0 3B, 0 HR, 0 RBI.

Year	Team (League)	W	L	Pct.	ERA	WHIP	G	GS	CG	ShO	Hld.	Sv.-Opp.	IP	H	R	ER	HR	BB-IBB	SO	Avg.
2002—Lakewood (S. Atl.)	11	10	.524	2.77	1.10	27	27	3	0	...	0-...	166.0	119	59	51	13	64-0	140	.200
2003—Clearwater (FSL)	7	8	.467	3.00	1.25	24	20	1	1	...	0-...	138.0	128	61	46	9	45-0	115	.247
2004—Reading (East.)	6	6	.500	2.57	1.17	20	20	2	1	...	0-...	119.0	93	39	34	5	46-1	94	.212
—Scran./W.B. (I.L.)	1	3	.250	4.99	1.57	5	5	0	0	...	0-...	30.2	39	20	17	4	9-0	18	.312
—Philadelphia (N.L.)	2	0	1.000	3.49	1.45	6	4	0	0	...	0-0	28.1	25	11	11	1	16-0	24	.240
2005—Scran./W.B. (I.L.)	6	9	.400	6.16	1.61	24	23	0	0	...	0-0	137.1	155	103	94	11	66-1	97	.290
—Philadelphia (N.L.)	1	2	.333	10.04	1.77	7	4	0	0	...	0-0	26.0	30	31	29	5	16-2	17	.283
2006—Philadelphia (N.L.)	4	3	.571	7.29	1.88	11	11	1	1	...	0-0	54.1	70	48	44	14	32-3	34	.315
—Scran./W.B. (I.L.)	7	4	.636	4.23	1.35	17	17	2	0	...	0-0	115.0	117	57	54	9	38-0	85	.267
Major League totals (3 years)	7	5	.583	6.96	1.74	24	19	1	1	...	0-0	108.2	125	90	84	20	64-5	75	.289

2006 LEFTY-RIGHTY SPLITS

vs.	Avg.	AB	H	2B	3B	HR	RBI	BB	SO	OBP	Slg.	vs.	Avg.	AB	H	2B	3B	HR	RBI	BB	SO	OBP	Slg.
L	.306	98	30	10	1	6	19	20	11	.417	.612	R	.323	124	40	9	0	8	21	12	23	.387	.589

FOGG, JOSH   P

PERSONAL: Born December 13, 1976, in Lynn, Mass. ... 6-0/203. ... Throws right, bats right. ... Full name: Joshua Smith Fogg. ... High school: Cadinal Gibbons (Fort Lauderdale, Fla.). ... College: Florida. **TRANSACTIONS/CAREER NOTES:** Selected by Chicago White Sox organization in third round of 1998 free-agent draft. ... Traded by White Sox with Ps Kip Wells and Sean Lowe to Pittsburgh Pirates for P Todd Ritchie and C Lee Evans (December 13, 2001). ... On disabled list (April 21-May 26, 2003); included rehabilitation assignment to Nashville. ... Signed as a free agent by Colorado Rockies (February 10, 2006). **MISCELLANEOUS NOTES:** Scored a run in only appearance as pinch runner (2002). ... Had a sacrifice hit and struck out in two appearances as pinch hitter (2006).
CAREER HITTING: 29-for-251 (.116), 15 R, 3 2B, 0 3B, 0 HR, 10 RBI.

Year	Team (League)	W	L	Pct.	ERA	WHIP	G	GS	CG	ShO	Hld.	Sv.-Opp.	IP	H	R	ER	HR	BB-IBB	SO	Avg.
1998—Ariz. White Sox (Ariz.)	1	0	1.000	0.00	0.25	2	0	0	0	...	0-...	4.0	0	0	0	0	1-0	5	.000
—Hickory (S. Atl.)	1	3	.250	2.18	1.19	8	8	0	0	...	0-...	41.1	36	17	10	4	13-0	29	.228
—Win.-Salem (Car.)	0	1	.000	0.00	2.00	1	0	0	0	...	0-...	1.0	2	2	0	0	0-0	2	.333
1999—Win.-Salem (Car.)	10	5	.667	2.96	1.22	17	17	1	1	...	0-...	103.1	93	44	34	3	33-0	109	.235
—Birmingham (Sou.)	3	2	.600	5.89	1.53	10	10	0	0	...	0-...	55.0	66	37	36	8	18-0	40	.296

F

Year Team (League)	W	L	Pct.	ERA	WHIP	G	GS	CG	ShO	Hld.	Sv.-Opp.	IP	H	R	ER	HR	BB-IBB	SO	Avg.
2000— Birmingham (Sou.)	11	7	.611	2.57	1.22	27	27	2	0		0-...	192.1	190	68	55	7	44-2	136	.261
2001— Charlotte (Int'l)	4	7	.364	4.79	1.39	40	16	0	0		4-...	114.2	129	68	61	19	30-1	89	.283
—Chicago (A.L.)	0	0	...	2.03	0.98	11	0	0	0	2	0-0	13.1	10	3	3	0	3-1	17	.208
2002— Pittsburgh (N.L.)	12	12	.500	4.35	1.38	33	33	0	0	0	0-0	194.1	199	102	94	28	69-12	113	.267
2003— Nashville (PCL)	0	1	.000	5.40	1.30	2	2	0	0	0	0-...	10.0	12	6	6	1	1-0	7	.324
—Pittsburgh (N.L.)	10	9	.526	5.26	1.45	26	26	1	0	0	0-0	142.0	166	90	83	22	40-0	71	.293
2004— Pittsburgh (N.L.)	11	10	.524	4.64	1.45	32	32	0	0	0	0-0	178.1	193	98	92	17	66-8	82	.283
2005— Pittsburgh (N.L.)	6	11	.353	5.05	1.47	34	28	0	0	0	0-0	169.1	196	106	95	27	53-11	85	.291
2006— Colorado (N.L.)	11	9	.550	5.49	1.55	31	31	1	1	0	0-0	172.0	206	115	105	24	60-13	93	.300
American League totals (1 year)	0	0	...	2.03	0.98	11	0	0	0	2	0-0	13.1	10	3	3	0	3-1	17	.208
National League totals (5 years)	50	51	.495	4.93	1.46	156	150	2	1	0	0-0	856.0	960	511	469	118	288-44	444	.286
Major League totals (6 years)	50	51	.495	4.89	1.45	167	150	2	1	2	0-0	869.1	970	514	472	118	291-45	461	.285

2006 LEFTY-RIGHTY SPLITS

vs.	Avg.	AB	H	2B	3B	HR	RBI	BB	SO	OBP	Slg.	vs.	Avg.	AB	H	2B	3B	HR	RBI	BB	SO	OBP	Slg.
L	.309	330	102	24	5	11	49	43	37	.389	.512	R	.291	357	104	24	5	13	49	17	56	.329	.496

FORD, LEW — OF

PERSONAL: Born August 12, 1976, in Port Neches, Texas. ... 6-0/195. ... Bats right, throws right. ... Full name: Jon Lewis Ford. ... High school: Port Neches-Groves (Texarkana, Texas). ... College: Dallas Baptist. **TRANSACTIONS/CAREER NOTES:** Selected by Boston Red Sox organization in 12th round of 1999 free-agent draft. ... Traded by Red Sox to Minnesota Twins for P Hector Carrasco (September 10, 2000). ... On disabled list (July 14-September 2, 2003); included rehabilitation assignment to Rochester. ... On disabled list (July 14-August 11, 2006); included rehabilitation assignment to Rochester.

2006 GAMES PLAYED BY POSITION (MLB): OF—92, DH—5.

						BATTING												FIELDING	
Year Team (League)	Pos.	G	AB	R	H	2B	3B	HR	RBI	BB	SO	HBP	GDP	SB-CS	Avg.	OBP	SLG	OPS	E	Avg.
1999— Lowell (NY-Penn)	OF	62	250	48	70	17	4	7	34	19	35	5	6	15-2	.280	.339	.464	.803	1	.993
2000— Augusta (S. Atl.)	OF	126	514	122	162	35	11	9	74	52	83	12	12	52-4	.315	.390	.479	.868	2	.994
2001— Fort Myers (FSL)	OF	67	265	42	79	15	2	2	24	21	30	12	3	19-9	.298	.373	.392	.766	1	.993
—New Britain (East.)	OF	62	252	30	55	9	3	7	25	20	35	6	4	5-5	.218	.289	.361	.650	3	.974
2002— New Britain (East.)	OF	93	373	81	116	27	2	15	51	49	47	8	5	17-5	.311	.401	.515	.916	3	.986
—Edmonton (PCL)	OF	47	193	40	64	11	2	5	24	13	21	6	2	11-1	.332	.390	.487	.877	5	.964
2003— Rochester (Int'l)	OF-DH	53	211	33	64	18	2	3	31	10	28	8	1	4-5	.303	.357	.450	.807	1	.990
—Minnesota (A.L.)	OF-DH	34	73	16	24	7	1	3	15	8	9	1	1	2-0	.329	.402	.575	.978	3	.923
2004— Rochester (Int'l)	OF	1	5	0	1	0	0	0	0	0	1	0	0	0-0	.200	.200	.200	.400	0	1.000
—Minnesota (A.L.)	OF-DH	154	569	89	170	31	4	15	72	67	75	13	15	20-2	.299	.381	.446	.827	4	.986
2005— Minnesota (A.L.)	OF-DH	147	522	70	138	30	4	7	53	45	85	16	9	13-6	.264	.338	.377	.716	6	.972
2006— Rochester (Int'l)	OF	8	29	5	8	2	0	0	2	6	5	3	0	0-1	.276	.447	.345	.792	0	1.000
—Minnesota (A.L.)	OF-DH	104	234	40	53	6	1	4	18	16	43	4	5	9-1	.226	.287	.312	.599	2	.986
Major League totals (4 years)		439	1398	215	385	74	10	29	158	136	212	34	30	44-9	.275	.351	.405	.756	15	.978

DIVISION SERIES RECORD

Year Team (League)	Pos.	G	AB	R	H	2B	3B	HR	RBI	BB	SO	HBP	GDP	SB-CS	Avg.	OBP	SLG	OPS	E	Avg.
2003— Minnesota (A.L.)		1	1	0	0	0	0	0	0	0	0	1	0	0-0	.000	.000	.000	.000	0	...
2004— Minnesota (A.L.)	DH-OF	3	11	1	3	1	0	0	2	2	2	0		1-1	.273	.385	.364	.748	0	1.000
2006— Minnesota (A.L.)		1	0	0	0	0	0	0	0	0	0	0		0-0	...				0	...
Division series totals (3 years)		5	12	1	3	1	0	0	2	0	3	2	0	1-1	.250	.357	.333	.690	0	1.000

2006 LEFTY-RIGHTY SPLITS

vs.	Avg.	AB	H	2B	3B	HR	RBI	BB	SO	OBP	Slg.	vs.	Avg.	AB	H	2B	3B	HR	RBI	BB	SO	OBP	Slg.
L	.206	102	21	3	0	4	8	4	16	.250	.353	R	.242	132	32	3	1	0	10	12	27	.315	.280

FORTUNATO, BARTOLOME — P

PERSONAL: Born August 24, 1974, in Santo Domingo, Dominican Republic. ... 6-1/180. ... Throws right, bats right. ... Full name: Bartolome Araujo Fortunato. **TRANSACTIONS/CAREER NOTES:** Signed as a non-drafted free agent by Tampa Bay Devil Rays (August 15, 1996). ... Played three seasons as an outfielder in Devil Rays organization (1996-99). ... Traded by Devil Rays with P Victor Zambrano to New York Mets for Ps Scott Kazmir and Jose Diaz (July 30, 2004). ... On disabled list (April 4, 2005-remainder of season). ... On disabled list (May 12, 2006-remainder of season). ... Released by Mets (May 19, 2006).

CAREER HITTING: 0-for-0 (.000), 0 R, 0 2B, 0 3B, 0 HR, 0 RBI.

Year Team (League)	W	L	Pct.	ERA	WHIP	G	GS	CG	ShO	Hld.	Sv.-Opp.	IP	H	R	ER	HR	BB-IBB	SO	Avg.
1999— Dom. Marlins (DSL)	7	0	1.000	2.57	1.43	13	5	1	1	...	1-...	49.0	38	18	14	3	32-...	44	...
2000— Princeton (Appal.)	3	4	.429	4.63	1.61	17	5	0	0	...	1-...	46.2	56	31	24	4	19-0	51	.284
2001— Hudson Valley (NYP)	2	5	.286	5.13	1.66	16	9	0	0	...	0-...	59.2	70	35	34	3	29-0	53	.299
2002— Bakersfield (Calif.)	2	4	.333	4.01	1.37	25	5	0	0	...	0-...	60.2	58	31	27	3	25-0	85	.251
—Durham (Int'l)	1	0	1.000	4.15	1.85	2	0	0	0	...	0-...	4.1	6	3	2	1	2-0	0	.333
—Orlando (South.)	3	0	1.000	2.10	1.05	10	2	0	0	...	0-...	25.2	16	7	6	2	11-1	34	.180
2003— Durham (Int'l)	1	2	.333	3.32	1.20	5	4	0	0	...	0-...	21.2	15	11	8	3	11-0	20	.192
—Orlando (South.)	4	2	.667	3.06	1.28	35	1	0	0	...	1-...	53.0	48	25	18	4	20-1	63	.242
2004— Tampa Bay (A.L.)	0	0	...	3.68	1.64	3	0	0	0		0-0	7.1	10	3	3	1	2-0	5	.357
—Durham (Int'l)	4	3	.571	2.42	1.10	34	0	0	0	...	9-...	44.2	28	14	12	4	21-1	54	.183
—Norfolk (Int'l)	0	0	...	3.38	1.31	6	0	0	0	...	0-...	5.1	4	2	2	0	3-0	5	.211
—New York (N.L.)	1	0	1.000	3.86	1.45	15	0	0	0		1-2	18.2	14	8	8	2	13-0	20	.203
2005—			Did not play.																
2006— Norfolk (Int'l)	1	0	1.000	2.70	0.96	11	0	0	0	...	0-0	16.2	12	6	5	0	4-0	21	.197
—New York (N.L.)	1	0	1.000	27.00	3.00	2	0	0	0		0-0	3.0	7	9	9	2	2-0	0	.467
American League totals (1 year)	0	0	...	3.68	1.64	3	0	0	0		0-0	7.1	10	3	3	1	2-0	5	.357
National League totals (2 years)	2	0	1.000	7.06	1.66	17	0	0	0		1-2	21.2	21	17	17	4	15-0	20	.250
Major League totals (2 years)	2	0	1.000	6.21	1.66	20	0	0	0		1-2	29.0	31	20	20	5	17-0	25	.277

2006 LEFTY-RIGHTY SPLITS

vs.	Avg.	AB	H	2B	3B	HR	RBI	BB	SO	OBP	Slg.	vs.	Avg.	AB	H	2B	3B	HR	RBI	BB	SO	OBP	Slg.
L	.667	6	4	1	0	1	2	2	0	.750	1.333	R	.333	9	3	1	0	1	4	0	0	.400	.778

FOSSUM, CASEY — P

PERSONAL: Born January 9, 1978, in Cherry Hill, N.J. ... 6-1/160. ... Throws left, bats left. ... Full name: Casey Paul Fossum. ... High school: Midway (Waco, Texas). ... College: Texas A&M. **TRANSACTIONS/CAREER NOTES:** Selected by Arizona Diamondbacks organization in sixth round of 1996 free-agent draft; did not sign. ... Selected by

F

Boston Red Sox organization in the supplemental round ("sandwich pick" between first and second round, 48th pick overall), of 1999 free-agent draft; pick received as part of compensation for Diamondbacks signing Type A free agent P Greg Swindell. ... On disabled list (June 8-July 17, 2003); included rehabilitation assignment to Portland. ... Traded by Red Sox with Ps Brandon Lyon and Jorge de la Rosa and a player to be named to Arizona Diamondbacks for P Curt Schilling (November 28, 2003); Diamondbacks acquired OF Michael Goss to complete deal (December 15, 2004). ... On disabled list (March 26-May 14, 2004); included rehabilitation assignments to El Paso and Tucson. ... Traded by Diamondbacks to Tampa Bay Devil Rays for OF Jose Cruz (February 6, 2005). ... On disabled list (May 25-June 9, 2006). **MISCELLANEOUS NOTES:** Appeared in one game as pinch runner (2003). ... Scored a run in two appearances as pinch runner (2004).

CAREER HITTING: 4-for-46 (.087), 3 R, 0 2B, 0 3B, 0 HR, 0 RBI.

Year— Team (League)	W	L	Pct.	ERA	WHIP	G	GS	CG	ShO	Hld.	Sv.-Opp.	IP	H	R	ER	HR	BB-IBB	SO	Avg.
1999— Lowell (NY-Penn)	0	1	.000	1.26	0.77	5	5	0	0	...	0-...	14.1	6	2	2	1	5-0	16	.122
2000— Sarasota (Fla. St.)	9	10	.474	3.44	1.23	27	27	3	3	...	0-...	149.1	147	71	57	7	36-0	143	.257
2001— Trenton (East.)	3	7	.300	2.83	1.10	20	20	0	0	...	0-...	117.2	102	47	37	5	28-0	130	.231
— Boston (A.L.)	3	2	.600	4.87	1.44	13	7	0	0	0	0-0	44.1	44	26	24	4	20-1	26	.259
2002— Boston (A.L.)	5	4	.556	3.46	1.34	43	12	0	0	3	1-1	106.2	113	56	41	12	30-0	101	.268
— Pawtucket (Int'l)	0	3	.000	3.96	1.60	5	3	1	0	...	0-...	25.0	34	15	11	1	6-0	28	.337
2003— Portland (East.)	0	1	.000	6.75	2.00	3	2	0	0	...	0-...	4.0	5	3	3	1	3-0	7	.294
— Pawtucket (Int'l)	1	0	1.000	3.46	1.20	5	4	0	0	...	1-...	13.0	11	5	5	1	5-0	14	.234
— Boston (A.L.)	6	5	.545	5.47	1.47	19	14	0	0	0	1-1	79.0	82	55	48	9	34-0	63	.270
2004— El Paso (Texas)	0	0	...	2.08	1.38	2	2	0	0	...	0-...	4.1	3	1	1	0	3-0	5	.188
— Tucson (PCL)	2	0	1.000	0.60	0.93	3	3	0	0	...	0-...	15.0	11	2	1	0	3-0	16	.196
— Arizona (N.L.)	4	15	.211	6.65	1.65	27	27	0	0	0	0-0	142.0	171	111	105	31	63-5	117	.302
2005— Tampa Bay (A.L.)	8	12	.400	4.92	1.41	36	25	0	0	0	0-1	162.2	170	100	89	21	60-3	128	.266
2006— Tampa Bay (A.L.)	6	6	.500	5.33	1.53	25	25	0	0	0	0-0	130.0	136	89	77	18	63-3	88	.265
American League totals (5 years)	28	29	.491	4.80	1.44	136	83	0	0	3	2-3	522.2	545	326	279	64	207-7	406	.266
National League totals (1 year)	4	15	.211	6.65	1.65	27	27	0	0	0	0-0	142.0	171	111	105	31	63-5	117	.302
Major League totals (6 years)	32	44	.421	5.20	1.48	163	110	0	0	3	2-3	664.2	716	437	384	95	270-12	523	.274

2006 LEFTY-RIGHTY SPLITS

vs.	Avg.	AB	H	2B	3B	HR	RBI	BB	SO	OBP	Slg.	vs.	Avg.	AB	H	2B	3B	HR	RBI	BB	SO	OBP	Slg.
L	.271	85	23	5	0	3	14	17	17	.410	.435	R	.263	429	113	22	2	15	62	46	71	.345	.429

FOSTER, JOHN — P

PERSONAL: Born May 17, 1978, in Stockton, Calif. ... 6-0/200. ... Throws left, bats left. ... Full name: John Norman Foster. ... College: Lewis-Clark State (Lewiston, Idaho).
TRANSACTIONS/CAREER NOTES: Selected by Atlanta Braves organization in 25th round of 1999 free-agent draft. ... On disabled list (August 18, 2002-remainder of season); included rehabilitation assignment to Richmond. ... Traded by Braves with 3B Wes Helms to Milwaukee Brewers for P Ray King (December 16, 2002). ... Selected by Chicago Cubs organization from Brewers organization in Rule 5 minor league draft (December 15, 2003). ... Signed as a free agent by Atlanta Braves organization (March 10, 2005). ... On disabled list (April 1, 2006-entire season). ... Released by Braves (October 10, 2006).

CAREER HITTING: 0-for-0 (.000), 0 R, 0 2B, 0 3B, 0 HR, 0 RBI.

Year— Team (League)	W	L	Pct.	ERA	WHIP	G	GS	CG	ShO	Hld.	Sv.-Opp.	IP	H	R	ER	HR	BB-IBB	SO	Avg.
1999— Danville (Appal.)	4	1	.800	1.38	0.87	18	0	0	0	...	1-...	39.0	28	10	6	0	6-0	36	.207
2000— Myrtle Beach (Carol.)	2	1	.667	1.85	1.27	38	0	0	0	...	3-...	48.2	48	13	10	2	14-4	46	.264
2001— Greenville (Sou.)	8	7	.533	3.01	1.51	50	0	0	0	...	7-...	68.2	71	30	23	6	33-7	63	.280
2002— Richmond (Int'l)	8	4	.667	4.21	1.53	55	0	0	0	...	8-...	62.0	67	30	29	5	28-8	48	.276
— Atlanta (N.L.)	1	0	1.000	10.80	2.40	5	0	0	0	0	0-0	5.0	6	6	6	3	6-0	6	.286
2003— Milwaukee (N.L.)	1	0	1.000	4.71	1.81	23	0	0	0	3	0-2	21.0	30	11	11	5	8-2	16	.341
— Indianapolis (Int'l)	2	2	.500	3.70	1.38	27	0	0	0	...	0-...	41.1	44	21	17	4	13-1	37	.272
2005— Richmond (Int'l)	0	0	...	1.59	0.53	3	0	0	0	...	1-1	5.2	2	1	1	0	1-0	5	.105
— Atlanta (N.L.)	4	2	.667	4.15	1.33	62	0	0	0	12	1-2	34.2	27	17	16	3	19-0	32	.213
2006— Atlanta (N.L.)					Did not play.														
Major League totals (3 years)	7	2	.778	4.90	1.58	90	0	0	0	15	1-4	60.2	63	34	33	11	33-2	54	.267

DIVISION SERIES RECORD

Year— Team (League)	W	L	Pct.	ERA	WHIP	G	GS	CG	ShO	Hld.	Sv.-Opp.	IP	H	R	ER	HR	BB-IBB	SO	Avg.
2005— Atlanta (N.L.)	0	0	...	54.00	12.00	2	0	0	0	0	0-0	0.1	2	2	2	0	2-1	1	.667

FOULKE, KEITH — P

PERSONAL: Born October 19, 1972, in Rapid City, S.D. ... 6-0/210. ... Throws right, bats right. ... Full name: Keith Charles Foulke. ... Name pronounced: FOLK. ... High school: Hargrove (Huffman, Texas). ... College: Lewis-Clark State (Lewiston, Idaho). **TRANSACTIONS/CAREER NOTES:** Selected by Detroit Tigers organization in 14th round of 1993 free-agent draft; did not sign. ... Selected by San Francisco Giants organization in ninth round of 1994 free-agent draft. ... Traded by Giants with SS Mike Caruso, OF Brian Manning and Ps Lorenzo Barcelo, Bob Howry and Ken Vining to Chicago White Sox for Ps Wilson Alvarez, Danny Darwin and Roberto Hernandez (July 31, 1997). ... On disabled list (August 28, 1998-remainder of season). ... On suspended list (May 5-7, 2000). ... Traded by White Sox with C Mark Johnson, P Joe Valentine and cash to Oakland Athletics for P Billy Koch and two players to be named (December 3, 2002); White Sox acquired P Neal Cotts and OF Daylon Holt to complete deal (December 16, 2002). ... Signed as a free agent by Boston Red Sox (January 7, 2004). ... On disabled list (July 6-September 1, 2005); included rehabilitation assignment to Lowell. ... On disabled list (June 13-August 18, 2006); included rehabilitation assignments to Lowell and Pawtucket. **HONORS:** Named A.L. Reliever of the Year by THE SPORTING NEWS (2003).

CAREER HITTING: 2-for-16 (.125), 0 R, 0 2B, 0 3B, 0 HR, 0 RBI.

Year— Team (League)	W	L	Pct.	ERA	WHIP	G	GS	CG	ShO	Hld.	Sv.-Opp.	IP	H	R	ER	HR	BB-IBB	SO	Avg.
1994— Everett (N'west)	2	0	1.000	0.93	1.03	4	4	0	0	...	0-...	19.1	17	4	2	0	3-0	22	.233
1995— San Jose (Calif.)	13	6	.684	3.50	1.12	28	26	2	1	...	0-...	177.1	166	85	69	16	32-0	168	.247
1996— Shreveport (Texas)	12	7	.632	2.76	1.01	27	27	4	2	...	0-...	182.2	149	61	56	16	35-0	129	.225
1997— Phoenix (PCL)	5	4	.556	4.50	1.24	12	12	0	0	...	0-...	76.0	79	38	38	11	15-0	54	.270
— San Francisco (N.L.)	1	5	.167	8.26	1.75	11	8	0	0	0	0-1	44.2	60	41	41	9	18-1	33	.324
— Nashville (A.A.)	0	0	...	5.79	1.71	1	1	0	0	...	0-...	4.2	8	3	3	1	0-0	4	.400
— Chicago (A.L.)	3	0	1.000	3.45	1.15	16	0	0	0	5	3-5	28.2	28	11	11	4	5-1	21	.255
1998— Chicago (A.L.)	3	2	.600	4.13	1.09	54	0	0	0	13	1-2	65.1	51	31	30	9	20-3	57	.213
1999— Chicago (A.L.)	3	3	.500	2.22	0.88	67	0	0	0	22	9-13	105.1	72	28	26	11	21-4	123	.188
2000— Chicago (A.L.)	3	1	.750	2.97	1.00	72	0	0	0	3	34-39	88.0	66	31	29	9	22-2	91	.207
2001— Chicago (A.L.)	4	9	.308	2.33	0.98	72	0	0	0	0	42-45	81.0	57	21	21	3	22-1	75	.207
2002— Chicago (A.L.)	2	4	.333	2.90	1.00	65	0	0	0	8	11-14	77.2	65	26	25	7	13-2	58	.225
2003— Oakland (A.L.)	9	1	.900	2.08	0.89	72	0	0	0	*	43-48	86.2	57	21	20	10	20-2	88	.184
2004— Boston (A.L.)	5	3	.625	2.17	0.94	72	0	0	0	0	32-39	83.0	63	22	20	8	15-5	79	.206
2005— Lowell (NY-Penn)	0	0	...	7.36	2.45	3	0	0	0	0	0-0	3.2	8	4	3	0	1-0	5	.421
— Boston (A.L.)	5	5	.500	5.91	1.55	43	0	0	0	1	15-19	45.2	53	30	30	8	18-1	34	.287
2006— Pawtucket (Int'l)	0	1	.000	1.80	1.60	4	2	0	0	0	0-0	5.0	4	1	1	0	4-0	5	.235
— Lowell (NY-Penn)	0	0	...	0.00	0.00	1	1	0	0	0	0-0	1.0	0	0	0	0	0-0	1	...
— Boston (A.L.)	3	1	.750	4.35	1.19	44	0	0	0	14	0-0	49.2	52	24	24	9	7-0	36	.271
American League totals (10 years)	40	29	.580	2.99	1.02	577	0	0	0	66	190-224	711.0	564	245	236	78	163-21	662	.215
National League totals (1 year)	1	5	.167	8.26	1.75	11	8	0	0	0	0-1	44.2	60	41	41	9	18-1	33	.324
Major League totals (10 years)	41	34	.547	3.30	1.07	588	8	0	0	66	190-225	755.2	624	286	277	87	181-22	695	.223

F

DIVISION SERIES RECORD

Year	Team (League)	W	L	Pct.	ERA	WHIP	G	GS	CG	ShO	Hld.	Sv.-Opp.	IP	H	R	ER	HR	BB-IBB	SO	Avg.
2000—	Chicago (A.L.)	0	1	.000	11.57	2.57	2	0	0	0	0	0-0	2.1	4	3	3	2	2-0	2	.400
2003—	Oakland (A.L.)	0	1	.000	3.60	1.20	3	0	0	0	0	0-1	5.0	4	2	2	0	2-1	3	.211
2004—	Boston (A.L.)	0	0	...	0.00	1.00	2	0	0	0	0	1-1	3.0	2	0	0	0	1-1	5	.182
	Division series totals (3 years)	0	2	.000	4.35	1.45	7	0	0	0	0	1-2	10.1	10	5	5	2	5-2	10	.250

CHAMPIONSHIP SERIES RECORD

Year	Team (League)	W	L	Pct.	ERA	WHIP	G	GS	CG	ShO	Hld.	Sv.-Opp.	IP	H	R	ER	HR	BB-IBB	SO	Avg.
2004—	Boston (A.L.)	0	0	...	0.00	1.17	5	0	0	0	0	1-1	6.0	1	0	0	0	6-0	6	.053

WORLD SERIES RECORD

Year	Team (League)	W	L	Pct.	ERA	WHIP	G	GS	CG	ShO	Hld.	Sv.-Opp.	IP	H	R	ER	HR	BB-IBB	SO	Avg.
2004—	Boston (A.L.)	1	0	1.000	1.80	1.00	4	0	0	0	0	1-2	5.0	4	1	1	1	1-1	8	.200

ALL-STAR GAME RECORD

		W	L	Pct.	ERA	WHIP	G	GS	CG	ShO	Hld.	Sv.-Opp.	IP	H	R	ER	HR	BB-IBB	SO	Avg.
	All-Star Game totals (1 year)	0	0	...	0.00	0.00	1	0	0	0	0	1-1	1.0	0	0	0	0	0-0	0	.000

2006 LEFTY-RIGHTY SPLITS

vs.	Avg.	AB	H	2B	3B	HR	RBI	BB	SO	OBP	Slg.	vs.	Avg.	AB	H	2B	3B	HR	RBI	BB	SO	OBP	Slg.
L	.301	103	31	9	0	6	15	3	18	.324	.563	R	.236	89	21	6	0	3	11	4	18	.268	.404

FRANCIS, JEFF — P

PERSONAL: Born January 8, 1981, in Vancouver. ... 6-5/200. ... Throws left, bats left. ... Full name: Jeffrey William Francis. ... High school: North Delta Senior (Delta, B.C.). ... College: British Columbia. **TRANSACTIONS/CAREER NOTES:** Selected by Colorado Rockies organization in first round (ninth pick overall) of 2002 free-agent draft.
CAREER HITTING: 13-for-129 (.101), 11 R, 2 2B, 0 3B, 0 HR, 10 RBI.

Year	Team (League)	W	L	Pct.	ERA	WHIP	G	GS	CG	ShO	Hld.	Sv.-Opp.	IP	H	R	ER	HR	BB-IBB	SO	Avg.
2002—	Tri-Cities (NWL)	0	0	...	0.00	0.84	4	3	0	0	...	0-...	10.2	5	0	0	0	4-0	16	.143
—	Asheville (S. Atl.)	0	0	...	1.80	1.00	4	4	0	0	...	0-...	20.0	16	6	4	2	4-0	23	.232
2003—	Visalia (Calif.)	12	9	.571	3.47	1.12	27	27	2	2	...	0-...	160.2	135	66	62	8	45-1	153	.229
2004—	Tulsa (Texas)	13	1	.929	1.98	0.84	17	17	1	1	...	0-...	113.2	73	26	25	9	22-0	147	.180
—	Colo. Springs (PCL)	3	2	.600	2.85	1.02	7	7	0	0	...	0-...	41.0	35	16	13	3	7-0	49	.230
—	Colorado (N.L.)	3	2	.600	5.15	1.50	7	7	0	0	0	0-0	36.2	42	22	21	8	13-1	32	.286
2005—	Colorado (N.L.)	14	12	.538	5.68	1.62	33	33	0	0	0	0-0	183.2	228	119	116	26	70-5	128	.311
2006—	Colorado (N.L.)	13	11	.542	4.16	1.29	32	32	1	1	0	0-0	199.0	187	101	92	18	69-15	117	.250
	Major League totals (3 years)	30	25	.545	4.91	1.45	72	72	1	1	0	0-0	419.1	457	242	229	52	152-21	277	.281

2006 LEFTY-RIGHTY SPLITS

vs.	Avg.	AB	H	2B	3B	HR	RBI	BB	SO	OBP	Slg.	vs.	Avg.	AB	H	2B	3B	HR	RBI	BB	SO	OBP	Slg.
L	.241	145	35	6	2	2	14	8	24	.313	.352	R	.252	602	152	40	5	16	71	61	93	.324	.415

FRANCISCO, FRANK — P

PERSONAL: Born September 11, 1979, in Santo Domingo, Dominican Republic. ... 6-2/180. ... Throws right, bats right. ... Full name: Franklin Francisco.
TRANSACTIONS/CAREER NOTES: Signed as a non-drafted free agent by Boston Red Sox organization (December 15, 1996). ... Traded by Red Sox with P Byeong Hak An to Chicago White Sox for P Bob Howry (July 31, 2002). ... Traded by White Sox with OF Anthony Webster and P Josh Rupe to Texas Rangers (July 24, 2003), completing deal in which White Sox acquired OF Carl Everett for three players to be named (July 1, 2003). ... On suspended list (September 18, 2004-remainder of season). ... On disabled list (March 25, 2005-entire season); included rehabilitation assignments to Oklahoma and Frisco. ... On disabled list (March 31-June 19, 2006); included rehabilitation assignment to Frisco.
CAREER HITTING: 0-for-0 (.000), 0 R, 0 2B, 0 3B, 0 HR, 0 RBI.

Year	Team (League)	W	L	Pct.	ERA	WHIP	G	GS	CG	ShO	Hld.	Sv.-Opp.	IP	H	R	ER	HR	BB-IBB	SO	Avg.
1997—					Did not play.															
1998—	Dominican Red Sox (DSL)	0	5	.000	10.31	2.50	16	13	0	0	...	0-...	48.0	44	66	55	4	76-0	53	...
1999—	GC Red Sox (GCL)	2	4	.333	4.56	1.74	12	7	0	0	...	0-...	53.1	58	39	27	3	35-0	48	.275
2000—	GC Red Sox (GCL)	0	0	...	18.00	4.00	1	0	0	0	...	0-...	1.0	2	3	2	0	2-0	1	.400
2001—	Augusta (S. Atl.)	4	3	.571	2.91	1.03	37	0	0	0	...	2-...	68.0	40	25	22	3	30-0	90	.168
2002—	Trenton (East.)	2	2	.500	5.63	1.63	9	0	0	0	...	0-...	16.0	10	13	10	0	16-1	18	.172
—	Sarasota (Fla. St.)	1	5	.167	2.55	1.13	16	0	0	0	...	0-...	53.0	33	19	15	1	27-0	58	.185
—	Win.-Salem (Car.)	0	4	.000	8.06	1.91	6	6	0	0	...	0-...	25.2	31	23	23	3	18-0	25	.310
2003—	Win.-Salem (Car.)	7	3	.700	3.56	1.21	16	16	1	1	...	0-...	78.1	59	40	31	7	36-0	67	.207
—	Frisco (Texas)	2	3	.400	8.41	1.73	7	6	0	0	...	0-...	35.1	43	33	33	5	18-1	22	.305
2004—	Frisco (Texas)	1	3	.250	2.55	0.96	15	0	0	0	...	6-...	17.2	7	6	5	1	10-1	30	.119
—	Texas (A.L.)	5	1	.833	3.33	1.25	45	0	0	0	10	0-3	51.1	36	19	19	4	28-2	60	.198
2005—	Oklahoma (PCL)	0	0	...	3.00	1.33	2	0	0	0	0	1-1	3.0	2	1	1	0	2-0	4	.200
—	Frisco (Texas)	0	1	.000	8.10	1.80	4	3	0	0	0	0-0	3.1	4	6	3	0	2-0	3	.333
2006—	Frisco (Texas)	0	0	...	1.84	0.95	13	0	0	0	0	0-1	14.2	10	3	3	1	4-0	22	.189
—	Spokane (N'west)	0	0	...	0.00	0.75	4	0	0	0	1	0-0	4.0	3	0	0	0	0-0	6	.200
—	Texas (A.L.)	0	1	.000	4.91	1.36	8	0	0	0	2	0-0	7.1	8	4	4	2	2-0	6	.267
	Major League totals (2 years)	5	2	.714	3.53	1.26	53	0	0	0	12	0-3	58.2	44	23	23	6	30-2	66	.208

2006 LEFTY-RIGHTY SPLITS

vs.	Avg.	AB	H	2B	3B	HR	RBI	BB	SO	OBP	Slg.	vs.	Avg.	AB	H	2B	3B	HR	RBI	BB	SO	OBP	Slg.
L	.000	12	0	0	0	0	0	1	2	.077	.000	R	.444	18	8	1	0	2	2	1	4	.474	.833

FRANCO, JULIO — 1B

PERSONAL: Born August 23, 1958, in San Pedro de Macoris, Dominican Republic. ... 6-1/188. ... Bats right, throws right. ... Full name: Julio Cesar Franco. ... High school: Divine Providence (San Pedro de Macoris, Dominican Republic). **TRANSACTIONS/CAREER NOTES:** Signed as a non-drafted free agent by Philadelphia Phillies organization (June 23, 1978). ... Traded by Phillies with 2B Manny Trillo, OF George Vukovich, P Jay Baller and C Jerry Willard to Cleveland Indians for OF Von Hayes (December 9, 1982). ... On disabled list (July 13-August 8, 1987). ... Traded by Indians to Texas Rangers for 1B Pete O'Brien, OF Oddibe McDowell and 2B Jerry Browne (December 6, 1988). ... On disabled list (March 28-April 19, May 4-June 1 and July 9, 1992-remainder of season). ... Signed as a free agent by Chicago White Sox (December 15, 1993). ... Signed by Chiba Lotte Marines of the Japan Pacific League (December 28, 1994). ... Signed as a free agent by Indians (December 7, 1995). ... On disabled list (July 7-25 and August 4-30, 1996). ... Released by Indians (August 13, 1997). ... Signed by Milwaukee Brewers (August 13, 1997). ... Signed by Chiba (1998). ... Signed as a free agent by Tampa Bay Devil Rays organization (February 19, 1999). ... Loaned by Devil Rays organization to Mexico City Tigers of the Mexican League (March 29-September 18, 1999). ... Signed by Samsung of the Korean League (2000). ... Signed as a free agent by Devil Rays (March 8, 2001). ... Loaned by Devil Rays to Tigers (March 12, 2001). ... Contract purchased by Atlanta Braves organization from Mexico City Tigers (August 31, 2001). ... On disabled list (August 17-September 1, 2003). ... Signed as a free agent by New York Mets (December 9, 2005). **HONORS:** Named second baseman on THE SPORTING NEWS A.L. All-Star team (1989-91). ... Named second baseman on A.L. Silver Slugger team (1988-91). ... Named designated hitter on A.L. Silver Slugger team (1994). **STATISTICAL NOTES:** Career major league grand slams: 8.

2006 GAMES PLAYED BY POSITION (MLB): 1B—27, 3B—3, DH—3.

Year Team (League)	Pos.	G	AB	R	H	2B	3B	HR	RBI	BB	SO	HBP	GDP	SB-CS	Avg.	OBP	SLG	OPS	E	Avg.
1978— Butte (Pion.)	SS	47	141	34	43	5	2	3	28	17	30	1	...	4-3	.305	.381	.433	.814	25	.781
1979— Cen. Oregon (NWL)	SS	•71	299	57	98	15	5	•10	45	24	59	3	...	22-9	.328	.381	.512	.893	31	.921
1980— Peninsula (Caro.)	SS	•140	555	105	178	25	6	11	99	33	66	8	...	44-12	.321	.361	.447	.808	42	.934
1981— Reading (East.)	SS	139	532	70	160	17	3	8	74	52	60	5	...	27-14	.301	.365	.389	.754	30	.958
1982— Okla. City (A.A.)	3B-SS	120	463	80	139	19	5	21	66	39	56	3	...	33-11	.300	.357	.499	.856	42	.930
—Philadelphia (N.L.)	3B-SS	16	29	3	8	1	0	0	3	2	4	0	1	0-2	.276	.323	.310	.633	0	1.000
1983— Cleveland (A.L.)	SS	149	560	68	153	24	8	8	80	27	50	2	21	32-12	.273	.306	.388	.693	28	.961
1984— Cleveland (A.L.)	DH-SS	160	*658	82	188	22	5	3	79	43	68	6	23	19-10	.286	.331	.348	.679	*36	.955
1985— Cleveland (A.L.)	2B-DH-SS	160	636	97	183	33	4	6	90	54	74	4	26	13-9	.288	.343	.381	.723	36	.950
1986— Cleveland (A.L.)		149	599	80	183	30	5	10	74	32	66	0	*28	10-7	.306	.338	.422	.760	19	.972
1987— Cleveland (A.L.)	2B-DH-SS	128	495	86	158	24	3	8	52	57	56	3	23	32-9	.319	.389	.428	.818	18	.964
1988— Cleveland (A.L.)	2B-DH	152	613	88	186	23	6	10	54	56	72	2	17	25-11	.303	.361	.409	.771	14	.982
1989— Texas (A.L.)		150	548	80	173	31	5	13	92	66	69	1	*27	21-3	.316	.386	.462	.848	13	.980
1990— Texas (A.L.)	2B-DH	157	582	96	172	27	1	11	69	82	83	2	12	31-10	.296	.383	.402	.785	•19	.979
1991— Texas (A.L.)		146	589	108	201	27	3	15	78	65	78	3	13	36-9	*.341	.408	.474	.882	14	.979
1992— Texas (A.L.)	DH-2B-OF	35	107	19	25	7	0	2	8	15	17	0	3	1-1	.234	.328	.355	.683	3	.927
1993— Texas (A.L.)	DH	144	532	85	154	31	3	14	84	62	95	1	16	9-3	.289	.360	.438	.798	...	...
1994— Chicago (A.L.)	DH-1B	112	433	72	138	19	2	20	98	62	75	5	14	8-1	.319	.406	.510	.916	3	.969
1995— Chiba Lotte (Jap. Pac.)	1B	127	474	60	145	25	3	10	58	...	...	...	...	11-...	.306	...	.435	...	...	...
1996— Cleveland (A.L.)	1B-DH	112	432	72	139	20	1	14	76	61	82	3	14	8-8	.322	.407	.470	.877	9	.990
1997— Cleveland (A.L.)	DH-2B-1B	•78	289	46	82	13	1	3	25	38	75	0	13	8-5	.284	.367	.367	.734	3	.983
—Milwaukee (N.L.)	DH-1B	42	141	22	34	3	0	4	19	31	41	1	4	7-1	.241	.373	.348	.720	1	.992
1998— Chiba Lotte (Jap. Pac.)		131	487	78	141	27	2	18	77	...	...	...	...	7-...	.290	...	.464	...	...	...
1999— Tigres (Mex.)	1B	93	326	90	138	22	6	14	77	80	44	...	...	9-1	.423	...	.656	...	2	.993
—Tampa Bay (A.L.)	1B	1	1	0	0	0	0	0	0	0	0	0	0	0-0	.000	.000	.000	.000	0	1.000
2000— Samsung (Kor.)		132	477	...	156	...	...	22	110	...	...	...	0	0-...	.327	...	.465	...	...	...
2001— Tigres (Mex.)	1B-DH-OF	110	407	90	178	34	5	18	90	50	56	...	...	15-6	.437	...	.678	...	5	.991
—Atlanta (N.L.)	1B	25	90	13	27	4	0	3	11	10	20	1	3	0-0	.300	.376	.444	.821	1	.995
2002— Atlanta (N.L.)	1B-DH	125	338	51	96	13	1	6	30	39	75	1	13	5-1	.284	.357	.382	.739	8	.990
2003— Atlanta (N.L.)	1B	103	197	28	58	12	2	5	31	25	43	0	8	0-1	.294	.372	.452	.824	1	.995
2004— Atlanta (N.L.)	1B-DH	125	320	37	99	18	3	6	57	36	68	1	10	4-2	.309	.378	.441	.818	2	.997
2005— Atlanta (N.L.)	1B-DH	108	233	30	64	12	1	9	42	27	57	1	10	4-0	.275	.348	.451	.799	5	.990
2006— New York (N.L.)	1B-3B-DH	95	165	14	45	10	0	2	26	13	49	1	11	6-1	.273	.330	.370	.699	1	.995
American League totals (15 years)		1875	7215	1101	2169	334	47	141	978	751	1002	33	254	260-99	.301	.366	.419	.785	216	.972
National League totals (7 years)		597	1372	176	397	70	7	31	200	152	316	5	56	19-7	.289	.360	.418	.778	18	.994
Major League totals (22 years)		2472	8587	1277	2566	404	54	172	1178	903	1318	38	310	279-106	.299	.365	.419	.784	234	.978

DIVISION SERIES RECORD

Year Team (League)	Pos.	G	AB	R	H	2B	3B	HR	RBI	BB	SO	HBP	GDP	SB-CS	Avg.	OBP	SLG	OPS	E	Avg.
1996— Cleveland (A.L.)	1B-DH	4	15	1	2	0	0	0	1	1	6	0	0	0-0	.133	.176	.133	.310	0	1.000
2001— Atlanta (N.L.)	1B	3	13	3	4	0	0	1	1	0	1	0	0	0-1	.308	.308	.538	.846	0	1.000
2002— Atlanta (N.L.)	1B	5	22	2	4	0	0	0	1	2	3	0	1	1-0	.182	.250	.182	.432	0	1.000
2003— Atlanta (N.L.)	1B	4	8	1	4	1	0	0	0	2	2	0	0	0-0	.500	.600	.625	1.225	0	1.000
2004— Atlanta (N.L.)	1B	3	4	0	0	0	0	0	0	0	1	0	0	0-0	.000	.000	.000	.000	0	1.000
2005— Atlanta (N.L.)	1B	3	9	0	2	0	0	0	0	1	3	0	0	0-0	.222	.300	.222	.522	0	1.000
2006— New York (N.L.)		2	2	0	0	0	0	0	1	0	1	0	0	0-0	.000	.000	.000	.000	0	...
Division series totals (7 years)		24	73	7	16	1	0	1	4	6	17	0	1	1-1	.219	.275	.274	.549	0	1.000

CHAMPIONSHIP SERIES RECORD

Year Team (League)	Pos.	G	AB	R	H	2B	3B	HR	RBI	BB	SO	HBP	GDP	SB-CS	Avg.	OBP	SLG	OPS	E	Avg.
2001— Atlanta (N.L.)	1B	5	23	2	6	0	0	1	2	0	2	0	0	0-0	.261	.261	.391	.652	0	1.000
2006— New York (N.L.)		2	2	0	0	0	0	0	0	0	2	0	0	0-0	.000	.000	.000	.000	0	...
Champ. series totals (2 years)		7	25	2	6	0	0	1	2	0	4	0	0	0-0	.240	.240	.360	.600	0	1.000

ALL-STAR GAME RECORD

	G	AB	R	H	2B	3B	HR	RBI	BB	SO	HBP	GDP	SB-CS	Avg.	OBP	SLG	OPS	E	Avg.
All-Star Game totals (2 years)	2	6	0	2	1	0	0	2	0	0	0	0	0-0	.333	.333	.500	.833	0	1.000

2006 LEFTY-RIGHTY SPLITS

vs.	Avg.	AB	H	2B	3B	HR	RBI	BB	SO	OBP	Slg.	vs.	Avg.	AB	H	2B	3B	HR	RBI	BB	SO	OBP	Slg.
L	.227	66	15	3	0	0	8	5	25	.282	.273	R	.303	99	30	7	0	2	18	8	24	.361	.434

FRANCOEUR, JEFF — OF

PERSONAL: Born January 8, 1984, in Atlanta. ... 6-4/220. ... Bats right, throws right. ... Full name: Jeffrey Braden Francoeur. ... High school: Parkview (Lilburn, Ga.). **TRANSACTIONS/CAREER NOTES:** Selected by Atlanta Braves organization in first round (23rd pick overall) of 2002 free-agent draft. **STATISTICAL NOTES:** Career major league grand slams: 1.

2006 GAMES PLAYED BY POSITION (MLB): OF—162.

Year Team (League)	Pos.	G	AB	R	H	2B	3B	HR	RBI	BB	SO	HBP	GDP	SB-CS	Avg.	OBP	SLG	OPS	E	Avg.
2002— Danville (Appal.)	OF	38	147	31	48	12	1	8	31	15	34	3	2	8-5	.327	.395	.585	.980	1	.990
2003— Rome (S. Atl.)	OF	134	524	78	147	26	9	14	68	30	68	7	21	14-6	.281	.325	.445	.770	4	.986
2004— Myrtle Beach (Carol.)	OF	88	334	56	98	26	0	15	52	22	70	7	5	10-6	.293	.346	.506	.852	4	.765
—Greenville (Sou.)	OF	18	76	8	15	2	0	3	9	0	14	0	0	1-0	.197	.197	.342	.539	1	.000
2005— Mississippi (Sou.)	OF	84	335	40	92	28	2	13	62	21	76	5	7	13-4	.275	.322	.487	.808	6	.981
—Atlanta (N.L.)	OF	70	257	41	77	20	1	14	45	11	58	4	4	3-2	.300	.336	.549	.884	5	.966
2006— Atlanta (N.L.)	OF	•162	651	83	169	24	6	29	103	23	132	9	15	1-6	.260	.293	.449	.742	9	.973
Major League totals (2 years)		232	908	124	246	44	7	43	148	34	190	13	19	4-8	.271	.305	.477	.782	14	.971

DIVISION SERIES RECORD

Year Team (League)	Pos.	G	AB	R	H	2B	3B	HR	RBI	BB	SO	HBP	GDP	SB-CS	Avg.	OBP	SLG	OPS	E	Avg.
2005— Atlanta (N.L.)	OF	4	17	2	4	1	1	0	1	2	4	1	1	0-0	.235	.350	.412	.762	0	1.000

2006 LEFTY-RIGHTY SPLITS

vs.	Avg.	AB	H	2B	3B	HR	RBI	BB	SO	OBP	Slg.	vs.	Avg.	AB	H	2B	3B	HR	RBI	BB	SO	OBP	Slg.
L	.292	168	49	9	1	9	25	10	29	.335	.518	R	.248	483	120	15	5	20	78	13	103	.278	.424

FRANDSEN, KEVIN — 2B/SS

PERSONAL: Born May 24, 1982, in San Jose, Calif. ... Bats right, throws right. ... Full name: Kevin Vincent Frandsen. ... High school: Bellarmine Prep (San Jose). ... College: San Jose State. **TRANSACTIONS/CAREER NOTES:** Selected by San Francisco Giants organization in 12th round of 2004 free-agent draft. ... On disabled list (August 18-September 2, 2006).

2006 GAMES PLAYED BY POSITION (MLB): 2B—28, SS—3.

Year	Team (League)	Pos.	G	AB	R	H	2B	3B	HR	RBI	BB	SO	HBP	GDP	SB-CS	Avg.	OBP	SLG	OPS	E	Avg.
2004—Salem-Keizer (N'west)		25	98	22	29	5	0	3	14	9	9	3	...	0-1	.296	.369	.439	.808	6	...
2005—San Jose (Calif.)	2B-SS	75	291	57	102	22	3	2	40	26	22	15	12	13-11	.351	.429	.467	.897	8	.976
—Norwich (East.)	2B-SS-3B	33	129	22	37	8	0	2	20	4	14	6	3	7-3	.287	.336	.395	.731	1	.994
—Fresno (PCL)	2B	20	94	18	33	10	1	2	16	2	5	2	6	1-1	.351	.378	.543	.920	6	.940
2006—San Jose (Calif.)		2	7	1	3	0	0	0	1	0	0	2	0	0-0	.429	.556	.429	.984	0	1.000
—Fresno (PCL)		71	293	46	89	25	3	3	30	12	30	14	9	7-4	.304	.358	.440	.799	11	.966
—San Francisco (N.L.)	2B-SS	41	93	12	20	4	0	2	7	3	14	6	3	0-1	.215	.284	.323	.607	3	.969
Major League totals (1 year)		41	93	12	20	4	0	2	7	3	14	6	3	0-1	.215	.284	.323	.607	3	.969

2006 LEFTY-RIGHTY SPLITS

vs.	Avg.	AB	H	2B	3B	HR	RBI	BB	SO	OBP	Slg.	vs.	Avg.	AB	H	2B	3B	HR	RBI	BB	SO	OBP	Slg.
L	.200	10	2	0	0	1	3	0	1	.200	.500	R	.217	83	18	4	0	1	4	3	13	.293	.301

FRANKLIN, RYAN — P

PERSONAL: Born March 5, 1973, in Fort Smith, Ark. ... 6-3/180. ... Throws right, bats right. ... Full name: Ryan Ray Franklin. ... High school: Spiro (Okla.). ... Junior college: Seminole (Okla.). **TRANSACTIONS/CAREER NOTES:** Selected by Toronto Blue Jays organization in 25th round of 1991 free-agent draft; did not sign. ... Selected by Seattle Mariners organization in 23rd round of 1992 free-agent draft. ... On disabled list (June 28-July 15, 2002); included rehabilitation assignment to Everett. ... On restricted list (August 2-12, 2005). ... Signed as a free agent by Philadelphia Phillies (January 13, 2006). ... Traded by Phillies to Cincinnati Reds for a player to be named (August 7, 2006); Phillies acquired P Zac Stott to complete deal (August 8, 2006). **MISCELLANEOUS NOTES:** Member of 2000 U.S. Olympic baseball team.

CAREER HITTING: 1-for-15 (.067), 1 R, 0 2B, 0 3B, 0 HR, 0 RBI.

Year	Team (League)	W	L	Pct.	ERA	WHIP	G	GS	CG	ShO	Hld.	Sv.-Opp.	IP	H	R	ER	HR	BB-IBB	SO	Avg.
1993—Bellingham (N'west)	5	3	.625	2.92	1.34	15	14	1	1	...	0-...	74.0	72	38	24	2	27-0	55	.250
1994—Appleton (Midwest)	9	6	.600	3.13	1.08	18	18	5	1	...	0-...	118.0	105	60	41	6	23-0	102	.234
—Riverside (Calif.)	4	2	.667	3.06	1.12	8	8	1	1	...	0-...	61.2	61	26	21	5	8-0	35	.249
—Calgary (PCL)	0	0	...	7.94	1.76	1	1	0	0	...	0-...	5.2	9	6	5	2	1-0	2	.333
1995—Port City (Sou.)	6	10	.375	4.32	1.34	31	20	1	1	...	0-...	146.0	153	84	70	13	43-4	102	.274
1996—Port City (Sou.)	6	12	.333	4.01	1.23	28	27	2	0	...	0-...	182.0	186	99	81	23	37-0	127	.265
1997—Memphis (Sou.)	4	2	.667	3.03	0.99	11	8	2	2	...	0-...	59.1	45	22	20	4	14-1	49	.208
—Tacoma (PCL)	5	5	.500	4.18	1.34	14	14	0	0	...	0-...	90.1	97	48	42	11	24-1	59	.281
1998—Tacoma (PCL)	5	6	.455	4.51	1.41	34	16	1	0	...	1-...	127.2	148	75	64	18	32-2	90	.292
1999—Tacoma (PCL)	6	9	.400	4.71	1.29	29	19	2	1	...	2-...	135.2	142	81	71	17	33-1	94	.270
—Seattle (A.L.)	0	0	...	4.76	1.59	6	0	0	0	1	0-0	11.1	10	6	6	2	8-1	6	.238
2000—Tacoma (PCL)	11	5	.688	3.90	1.11	31	22	4	0	...	0-...	164.0	147	85	71	28	35-1	142	.240
2001—Seattle (A.L.)	5	1	.833	3.56	1.28	38	0	0	0	5	0-1	78.1	76	32	31	13	24-4	60	.250
—Tacoma (PCL)	0	0	...	0.00	0.55	1	0	0	0	...	0-...	3.0	2	0	0	0	0-0	3	.167
2002—Seattle (A.L.)	7	5	.583	4.02	1.17	41	12	0	0	3	0-0	118.2	117	62	53	14	22-1	65	.255
—Everett (N'west)	0	0	...	0.00	0.75	1	1	0	0	...	0-...	2.2	2	1	0	0	0-0	1	.200
2003—Seattle (A.L.)	11	13	.458	3.57	1.23	32	32	2	1	0	0-0	212.0	199	93	84	•34	61-3	99	.251
2004—Seattle (A.L.)	4	16	.200	4.90	1.42	32	32	2	1	0	0-0	200.1	224	116	109	33	61-1	104	.285
2005—Seattle (A.L.)	8	15	.348	5.10	1.44	32	30	2	1	0	0-0	190.2	212	110	108	28	62-4	93	.280
2006—Philadelphia (N.L.)	1	5	.167	4.58	1.43	46	0	0	0	8	0-1	53.0	59	28	27	10	17-4	25	.280
—Cincinnati (N.L.)	5	2	.714	4.44	1.77	20	0	0	0	0	0-2	24.1	27	14	12	3	16-6	18	.297
American League totals (6 years)	35	50	.412	4.34	1.33	181	106	6	3	9	0-2	811.1	838	419	391	124	238-14	427	.267
National League totals (1 year)	6	7	.462	4.54	1.54	66	0	0	0	8	0-3	77.1	86	42	39	13	33-10	43	.285
Major League totals (7 years)	41	57	.418	4.34	1.34	247	106	6	3	17	0-5	888.2	924	461	430	137	271-24	470	.268

2006 LEFTY-RIGHTY SPLITS

vs.	Avg.	AB	H	2B	3B	HR	RBI	BB	SO	OBP	Slg.	vs.	Avg.	AB	H	2B	3B	HR	RBI	BB	SO	OBP	Slg.
L	.265	98	26	8	2	2	6	19	13	.390	.449	R	.294	204	60	14	1	11	35	14	30	.345	.534

FRANKLIN, WAYNE — P

PERSONAL: Born March 9, 1974, in Wilmington, Del. ... 6-2/204. ... Throws left, bats left. ... Full name: Gary Wayne Franklin. ... High school: Northeast (Md.). ... College: Maryland-Baltimore County. **TRANSACTIONS/CAREER NOTES:** Selected by Los Angeles Dodgers organization in 36th round of 1995 free-agent draft. ... Selected by Houston Astros organization from Dodgers organization in Rule 5 minor league draft (December 14, 1998). ... Traded by Astros to Milwaukee Brewers (September 3, 2002), as part of deal in which Brewers traded IF Mark Loretta to Astros for two players to be named (August 31, 2002); Brewers acquired 2B Keith Ginter to complete deal (September 5, 2002). ... Traded by Brewers with P Leo Estrella to San Francisco Giants for Ps Carlos Villanueva and Glenn Woolard (March 30, 2004). ... On disabled list (July 29-August 18, 2004); included rehabilitation assignment to Fresno. ... Released by Giants (March 30, 2005). ... Signed by New York Yankees organization (April 4, 2005). ... Signed as a free agent by Tampa Bay Devil Rays organization (January 15, 2006). ... Traded by Devil Rays to Atlanta Braves for cash (March 28, 2006).

CAREER HITTING: 11-for-70 (.157), 3 R, 1 2B, 0 3B, 0 HR, 5 RBI.

Year	Team (League)	W	L	Pct.	ERA	WHIP	G	GS	CG	ShO	Hld.	Sv.-Opp.	IP	H	R	ER	HR	BB-IBB	SO	Avg.
1996—Yakima (N'west)	1	0	1.000	2.52	1.76	20	0	0	0	...	1-...	25.0	32	10	7	2	12-3	22	.311
1997—Savannah (S. Atl.)	5	3	.625	3.18	1.39	28	7	1	0	...	2-...	82.0	79	41	29	10	35-0	58	.246
—San Bern. (Calif.)	0	0	...	0.00	1.00	1	0	0	0	...	0-...	2.0	2	0	0	0	0-0	1	.286
1998—Vero Beach (FSL)	9	3	.750	3.53	1.23	48	0	0	0	...	10-...	86.2	81	43	34	7	26-0	78	.243
1999—Kissimmee (Fla. St.)	3	0	1.000	1.53	0.96	12	0	0	0	...	1-...	17.2	11	4	3	0	6-0	22	.180
—Jackson (Texas)	3	1	.750	1.61	0.93	46	0	0	0	...	20-...	50.1	31	11	9	3	16-3	40	.178
2000—New Orleans (PCL)	3	3	.500	3.63	1.57	48	0	0	0	...	4-...	44.2	51	29	18	4	19-3	37	.279
—Houston (N.L.)	0	0	...	5.48	1.69	25	0	0	0	...	0-0	21.1	24	14	13	2	12-1	21	.282
2001—Houston (N.L.)	0	0	...	6.75	2.17	11	0	0	0	1	0-0	12.0	17	9	9	4	9-0	9	.333
—New Orleans (PCL)	2	1	.667	3.81	1.31	41	0	0	0	...	0-...	49.2	47	28	21	6	18-2	51	.244
2002—Milwaukee (N.L.)	13	9	.591	3.12	1.18	29	27	1	0	...	0-...	179.0	153	68	62	14	59-2	141	.235
—Milwaukee (N.L.)	2	1	.667	2.63	1.38	4	4	0	0	...	0-0	24.0	16	8	7	1	17-1	17	.184
2003—Milwaukee (N.L.)	10	13	.435	5.50	1.52	36	34	1	0	...	0-0	194.2	201	*129	•119	*36	94-2	116	.268
2004—Fresno (PCL)	0	2	.000	3.86	1.07	3	3	0	0	...	0-0	9.1	6	4	4	0	4-0	11	.182
—San Francisco (N.L.)	2	1	.667	6.39	1.52	43	2	0	0	...	0-1	50.2	55	37	36	11	22-2	40	.281
2005—Columbus (Int'l)	2	3	.400	3.61	1.11	46	0	0	0	11	1-1	42.1	36	18	17	4	11-1	50	.231

F

Year Team (League)	W	L	Pct.	ERA	WHIP	G	GS	CG	ShO	Hld.	Sv.-Opp.	IP	H	R	ER	HR	BB-IBB	SO	Avg.
— New York (A.L.)	0	1	.000	6.39	1.50	13	0	0	0	3	0-3	12.2	11	12	9	1	8-0	10	.239
2006— Richmond (Int'l)	2	3	.400	2.36	1.05	35	1	0	0	11	4-4	53.1	39	15	14	2	17-2	52	.202
— Atlanta (N.L.)	0	0	...	7.04	1.83	11	0	0	0	1	0-0	7.2	8	6	6	2	6-2	3	.296
American League totals (1 year)	0	1	.000	6.39	1.50	13	0	0	0	3	0-3	12.2	11	12	9	1	8-0	10	.239
National League totals (6 years)	14	15	.483	5.51	1.55	130	40	1	1	15	0-1	310.1	321	203	190	56	160-8	206	.269
Major League totals (7 years)	14	16	.467	5.54	1.55	143	40	1	1	18	0-4	323.0	332	215	199	57	168-8	216	.268

2006 LEFTY-RIGHTY SPLITS

vs.	Avg.	AB	H	2B	3B	HR	RBI	BB	SO	OBP	Slg.
L	.308	13	4	1	0	1	2	2	2	.375	.615
R	.286	14	4	1	0	1	2	4	1	.421	.571

FRASOR, JASON — P

PERSONAL: Born August 9, 1977, in Chicago. ... 5-10/170. ... Throws right, bats right. ... Full name: Jason Andrew Frasor. ... High school: Oak Forest (Ill.). ... College: Southern Illinois. **TRANSACTIONS/CAREER NOTES:** Selected by Detroit Tigers organization in 33rd round of 1999 free-agent draft. ... Traded by Tigers to Los Angeles Dodgers (September 18, 2002), completing deal in which Tigers acquired OF Hiram Bocachica for P Tom Farmer and a player to be named (July 25, 2002). ... Traded by Dodgers to Toronto Blue Jays for OF Jayson Werth (March 29, 2004).

CAREER HITTING: 0-for-0 (.000), 0 R, 0 2B, 0 3B, 0 HR, 0 RBI.

Year Team (League)	W	L	Pct.	ERA	WHIP	G	GS	CG	ShO	Hld.	Sv.-Opp.	IP	H	R	ER	HR	BB-IBB	SO	Avg.
1999—Oneonta (NYP)	3	3	.500	1.69	0.99	12	11	0	0	...	0-...	58.2	36	16	11	3	22-0	69	.176
—W. Mich. (Mid.)	2	1	.667	2.63	1.08	4	4	1	1	...	0-...	24.0	17	10	7	2	9-0	33	.198
2000—W. Mich. (Mid.)	5	3	.625	3.28	1.18	14	14	0	0	...	0-...	71.1	55	32	26	2	29-0	65	.208
2002—Lakeland (Fla. St.)	5	6	.455	3.54	1.35	24	24	0	0	...	0-...	117.0	112	54	46	10	46-1	87	.257
2003—Vero Beach (FSL)	1	0	1.000	1.85	0.82	15	0	0	0	...	6-...	24.1	16	7	5	0	4-0	36	.182
—Jacksonville (Sou.)	1	0	1.000	2.95	1.28	35	0	0	0	...	17-...	36.2	33	14	12	2	14-0	50	.241
2004—Syracuse (Int'l)	0	0	...	2.25	1.50	3	0	0	0	...	0-...	4.0	1	1	1	0	5-0	6	.077
—Toronto (A.L.)	4	6	.400	4.08	1.46	63	0	0	0	8	17-19	68.1	64	31	31	4	36-3	54	.251
2005—Toronto (A.L.)	3	5	.375	3.25	1.27	67	0	0	0	15	1-3	74.2	67	31	27	8	28-2	62	.247
2006—Syracuse (Int'l)	3	1	.750	3.98	1.67	18	0	0	0	3	1-2	20.1	21	10	9	1	13-0	33	.266
—Toronto (A.L.)	3	2	.600	4.32	1.28	51	0	0	0	12	0-1	50.0	47	24	24	8	17-1	51	.244
Major League totals (3 years)	10	13	.435	3.82	1.34	181	0	0	0 ·	35	18-23	193.0	178	86	82	20	81-6	167	.248

2006 LEFTY-RIGHTY SPLITS

vs.	Avg.	AB	H	2B	3B	HR	RBI	BB	SO	OBP	Slg.
L	.211	71	15	3	0	3	10	7	21	.282	.380
R	.262	122	32	3	0	5	22	10	30	.321	.410

FREEL, RYAN — OF/IF

PERSONAL: Born March 8, 1976, in Jacksonville. ... 5-10/180. ... Bats right, throws right. ... Full name: Ryan Paul Freel. ... High school: Englewood (Jacksonville). ... Junior college: Tallahassee (Fla.). **TRANSACTIONS/CAREER NOTES:** Selected by St. Louis Cardinals organization in 14th round of 1994 free-agent draft. ... Selected by Toronto Blue Jays organization in 10th round of 1995 free-agent draft. ... Signed as a free agent by Tampa Bay Devil Rays organization (November 8, 2001). ... Signed as a free agent by Cincinnati Reds organization (November 19, 2002). ... On disabled list (May 29-July 4, 2003). ... On disabled list (June 19-July 20 and August 16-September 5, 2005); included rehabilitation assignment to Chattanooga.

2006 GAMES PLAYED BY POSITION (MLB): OF—105, 2B—13, 3B—13.

Year Team (League)	Pos.	G	AB	R	H	2B	3B	HR	RBI	BB	SO	HBP	GDP	SB-CS	Avg.	OBP	SLG	OPS	E	Avg.
1995—St. Catharines (NYP)	2B	65	243	30	68	10	5	3	29	22	49	7	3	12-7	.280	.350	.399	.749	19	.940
1996—Dunedin (Fla. St.)	2B-3B	104	381	64	97	23	3	4	41	33	76	5	4	19-15	.255	.321	.362	.683	20	.959
1997—Knoxville (Southern)	SS	33	94	18	19	1	1	0	4	19	13	2	3	5-3	.202	.348	.234	.582	13	.913
—Dunedin (Fla. St.)	2B-3B-OF SS	61	181	42	51	8	2	3	17	46	28	9	3	24-5	.282	.447	.398	.845	18	.910
1998—Knoxville (Southern)	2B-OF-SS	66	252	47	72	17	3	4	36	33	32	1	3	18-9	.286	.366	.425	.790	3	.982
—Syracuse (Int'l)	2B-OF	37	118	19	27	4	0	2	12	26	16	4	3	9-4	.229	.377	.314	.691	3	.962
1999—Knoxville (Southern)	OF	11	46	9	13	5	1	1	9	8	4	0	0	4-2	.283	.382	.500	.882	0	1.000
—Syracuse (Int'l)	OF-SS	20	77	15	23	3	2	1	11	8	13	4	3	10-3	.299	.393	.429	.822	1	.976
2000—Dunedin (Fla. St.)	OF-2B	4	18	7	9	1	0	3	6	0	1	0	0	0-0	.500	.500	1.056	1.556	0	1.000
—Tennessee (Sou.)	OF-2B	12	44	11	13	3	1	0	8	8	6	1	3	2-3	.295	.400	.409	.809	0	1.000
—Syracuse (Int'l)	2B-OF-3B SS	80	283	62	81	14	5	10	30	35	44	9	3	30-7	.286	.380	.477	.857	9	.957
2001—Toronto (A.L.)	2B-OF	9	22	1	6	1	0	0	3	1	4	1	0	2-1	.273	.333	.318	.652	1	.969
—Syracuse (Int'l)	OF-2B-3B SS	85	319	60	83	21	3	5	33	42	42	7	4	22-9	.260	.357	.392	.749	9	.959
2002—Durham (Int'l)	2B-OF	119	448	65	117	27	4	8	48	38	51	14	10	37-10	.261	.337	.393	.730	7	.981
2003—Louisville (Int'l)	2B-OF-3B DH	54	215	38	59	11	1	3	12	21	32	0	2	25-6	.274	.336	.377	.713	2	.990
—Cincinnati (N.L.)	OF-3B-2B	43	137	23	39	6	1	4	12	9	13	4	2	9-4	.285	.344	.431	.775	1	.990
2004—Cincinnati (N.L.)	OF-3B-2B	143	505	74	140	21	8	3	28	67	88	12	7	37-10	.277	.375	.368	.743	15	.963
2005—Chattanooga (Sou.)	2B-OF-3B	5	17	3	3	0	0	0	1	3	5	0	1	0-1	.176	.286	.176	.462	0	1.000
—Cincinnati (N.L.)	OF-2B-3B	103	369	69	100	19	3	4	21	51	59	8	9	36-10	.271	.371	.371	.743	8	.978
2006—Cincinnati (N.L.)	OF-2B-3B	132	454	67	123	30	2	8	27	57	98	9	5	37-11	.271	.363	.399	.762	6	.982
American League totals (1 year)		9	22	1	6	1	0	0	3	1	4	1	0	2-1	.273	.333	.318	.652	1	.969
National League totals (4 years)		421	1465	233	402	76	14	19	88	184	258	33	23	119-35	.274	.368	.384	.752	30	.975
Major League totals (5 years)		430	1487	234	408	77	14	19	91	185	262	34	23	121-36	.274	.367	.383	.751	31	.975

2006 LEFTY-RIGHTY SPLITS

vs.	Avg.	AB	H	2B	3B	HR	RBI	BB	SO	OBP	Slg.
L	.303	109	33	7	1	1		23	16	.424	.413
R	.261	345	90	23	1	7	22	34	82	.343	.394

FREEMAN, CHOO — OF

PERSONAL: Born October 20, 1979, in Pine Bluff, Ark. ... 6-2/200. ... Bats right, throws right. ... Full name: Raphael Freeman. ... High school: Dallas Christian. **TRANSACTIONS/CAREER NOTES:** Selected by Colorado Rockies organization in supplemental round ("sandwich pick" between first and second rounds, 36th pick overall) of 1998 free-agent draft; pick received as part of compensation for Atlanta Braves signing Type A free-agent 1B Andres Galarraga.

2006 GAMES PLAYED BY POSITION (MLB): OF—51.

F

Year Team (League)	Pos.	G	AB	R	H	2B	3B	HR	RBI	BB	SO	HBP	GDP	SB-CS	Avg.	OBP	SLG	OPS	E	Avg.
1998— Ariz. Rockies (Ariz.)	OF	40	147	35	47	3	6	1	24	15	25	4	2	14-1	.320	.391	.442	.833	6	.880
1999— Asheville (S. Atl.)	OF	131	485	82	133	22	4	14	66	39	132	7	3	16-4	.274	.336	.423	.759	6	.975
2000— Salem (Carol.)	OF	127	429	73	114	18	7	5	54	37	104	4	7	16-8	.266	.326	.375	.702	8	.965
2001— Salem (Carol.)	OF	132	517	63	124	16	5	8	42	31	108	9	8	19-7	.240	.292	.337	.628	5	.979
2002— Carolina (Southern)	OF	124	430	81	125	18	6	12	64	64	101	15	15	15-13	.291	.400	.444	.844	6	.977
2003— Colo. Springs (PCL)	OF	103	327	44	83	9	4	7	36	23	71	7	7	2-8	.254	.315	.370	.685	12	.936
2004— Colo. Springs (PCL)	OF-DH	103	360	58	107	21	7	10	50	26	84	6	11	7-3	.297	.350	.478	.818	4	.983
— Colorado (N.L.)	OF	45	90	15	17	3	2	1	11	14	21	0	5	1-1	.189	.298	.300	.598	1	.986
2005— Colo. Springs (PCL)	OF	97	354	46	99	10	6	10	59	29	78	2	13	4-3	.280	.334	.427	.761	4	.989
— Colorado (N.L.)	OF	18	22	6	6	1	1	0	0	0	5	0	0	0-0	.273	.273	.409	.682	0	1.000
2006— Colorado (N.L.)	OF	88	173	24	41	6	3	2	18	14	42	1	1	5-6	.237	.298	.341	.639	1	.991
Major League totals (3 years)		151	285	45	64	10	6	3	29	28	68	1	6	6-7	.225	.296	.333	.630	2	.990

2006 LEFTY-RIGHTY SPLITS

vs.	Avg.	AB	H	2B	3B	HR	RBI	BB	SO	OBP	Slg.	vs.	Avg.	AB	H	2B	3B	HR	RBI	BB	SO	OBP	Slg.
L	.276	76	21	2	2	1	6	8	12	.353	.395	R	.206	97	20	4	1	1	12	6	30	.252	.299

FRUTO, EMILIANO — P

PERSONAL: Born June 6, 1984, in Cartagena, Colombia. ... 6-3/170. ... Throws right, bats right. ... Full name: Emiliano Fruto. **TRANSACTIONS/CAREER NOTES:** Signed as a non-drafted free agent by Seattle Mariners organization (July 2, 2000).
CAREER HITTING: 0-for-0 (.000), 0 R, 0 2B, 0 3B, 0 HR, 0 RBI.

Year Team (League)	W	L	Pct.	ERA	WHIP	G	GS	CG	ShO	Hld.	Sv.-Opp.	IP	H	R	ER	HR	BB-IBB	SO	Avg.
2001— Ariz. Mariners (Ariz.)	5	3	.625	5.84	1.54	12	12	0	0	...	0-...	61.2	73	45	40	3	22-0	51	.291
2002— Wisconsin (Midw.)	6	6	.500	3.55	1.40	33	13	0	0	...	1-...	111.2	101	57	44	6	55-1	99	.239
2003— Tacoma (PCL)	1	0	1.000	0.00	0.75	1	0	0	0	...	0-...	4.0	1	0	0	0	2-0	2	.083
— Inland Empire (Calif.)	7	8	.467	3.78	1.50	42	4	0	0	...	7-...	78.2	80	43	33	5	38-5	83	.267
2004— San Antonio (Texas)	3	3	.500	5.66	1.67	43	1	0	0	...	1-...	68.1	77	47	43	6	37-0	56	.277
2005— San Antonio (Texas)	2	3	.400	2.57	1.17	40	0	0	0	2	12-15	66.2	56	22	19	6	22-0	63	.231
— Tacoma (PCL)	1	2	.333	13.09	2.00	9	0	0	0	2	0-2	11.0	11	17	16	1	11-0	12	.268
2006— Tacoma (PCL)	1	3	.250	3.18	1.19	28	0	0	0	1	10-12	45.1	33	23	16	1	21-0	55	.204
— Seattle (A.L.)	2	2	.500	5.50	1.61	23	0	0	0	1	1-2	36.0	34	24	22	4	24-1	34	.246
Major League totals (1 year)	2	2	.500	5.50	1.61	23	0	0	0	1	1-2	36.0	34	24	22	4	24-1	34	.246

2006 LEFTY-RIGHTY SPLITS

vs.	Avg.	AB	H	2B	3B	HR	RBI	BB	SO	OBP	Slg.	vs.	Avg.	AB	H	2B	3B	HR	RBI	BB	SO	OBP	Slg.
L	.267	45	12	2	0	0	5	10	9	.393	.311	R	.237	93	22	4	0	4	18	14	25	.349	.409

FUENTES, BRIAN — P

PERSONAL: Born August 9, 1975, in Merced, Calif. ... 6-4/220. ... Throws left, bats left. ... Full name: Brian Christopher Fuentes. ... Name pronounced: foo-WHEN-tayz. ... High school: Merced (Calif.). ... Junior college: Merced (Calif.). **TRANSACTIONS/CAREER NOTES:** Selected by Seattle Mariners organization in 25th round of 1995 free-agent draft. ... Traded by Mariners with Ps Jose Paniagua and Denny Stark to Colorado Rockies for 3B Jeff Cirillo (December 15, 2001). ... On disabled list (June 7-August 15, 2004); included rehabilitation assignment to Colorado Springs.
CAREER HITTING: 0-for-1 (.000), 0 R, 0 2B, 0 3B, 0 HR, 0 RBI.

Year Team (League)	W	L	Pct.	ERA	WHIP	G	GS	CG	ShO	Hld.	Sv.-Opp.	IP	H	R	ER	HR	BB-IBB	SO	Avg.
1996— Everett (N'west)	0	1	.000	4.39	1.35	13	2	0	0	0	0-...	26.2	23	14	13	2	13-0	26	.230
1997— Wisconsin (Midw.)	6	7	.462	3.56	1.21	22	22	0	0	0	0-...	118.2	84	52	47	6	59-0	153	.203
1998— Lancaster (Calif.)	7	7	.500	4.17	1.70	24	22	0	0	0	0-...	118.2	121	73	55	8	81-0	137	.273
1999— New Haven (East.)	3	3	.500	4.95	1.65	15	14	0	0	0	0-...	60.0	53	36	33	5	46-0	66	.255
2000— New Haven (East.)	7	12	.368	4.51	1.41	26	26	1	0	0	0-...	139.2	127	80	70	7	70-0	152	.246
2001— Tacoma (PCL)	3	2	.600	2.94	1.15	35	0	0	0	6	6-...	52.0	35	19	17	4	25-0	70	.206
— Seattle (A.L.)	1	1	.500	4.63	1.42	10	0	0	0	1	0-1	11.2	6	6	6	2	8-0	10	.171
2002— Colo. Springs (PCL)	3	3	.500	3.70	1.56	41	0	0	0	1	1-...	48.2	44	25	20	2	32-1	61	.246
— Colorado (N.L.)	2	0	1.000	4.73	1.43	31	0	0	0	0	0-0	26.2	25	14	14	4	13-0	38	.250
2003— Colorado (N.L.)	3	3	.500	2.75	1.30	75	0	0	0	19	4-6	75.1	64	24	23	7	34-2	82	.231
2004— Colo. Springs (PCL)	0	0	...	0.00	0.80	5	5	0	0	0	0-...	5.0	1	0	0	0	3-0	6	.063
— Colorado (N.L.)	2	4	.333	5.64	1.46	47	0	0	0	13	0-1	44.2	46	30	28	5	19-6	48	.269
2005— Colorado (N.L.)	2	5	.286	2.91	1.25	78	0	0	0	6	31-34	74.1	59	25	24	6	34-4	91	.218
2006— Colorado (N.L.)	3	4	.429	3.44	1.16	66	0	0	0	0	30-36	65.1	50	25	25	8	26-4	73	.209
American League totals (1 year)	1	1	.500	4.63	1.42	10	0	0	0	1	0-1	11.2	6	6	6	2	8-0	10	.171
National League totals (5 years)	12	16	.429	3.58	1.29	297	0	0	0	38	65-77	286.1	244	118	114	30	126-16	332	.231
Major League totals (6 years)	13	17	.433	3.62	1.29	307	0	0	0	39	65-78	298.0	250	124	120	32	134-16	342	.229

ALL-STAR GAME RECORD

	W	L	Pct.	ERA	WHIP	G	GS	CG	ShO	Hld.	Sv.-Opp.	IP	H	R	ER	HR	BB-IBB	SO	Avg.
All-Star Game totals (1 year)	0	0	...	0.00	0.00	1	0	0	0	...	0-0	1.0	0	0	0	0	0-0	1	.000

2006 LEFTY-RIGHTY SPLITS

vs.	Avg.	AB	H	2B	3B	HR	RBI	BB	SO	OBP	Slg.	vs.	Avg.	AB	H	2B	3B	HR	RBI	BB	SO	OBP	Slg.
L	.186	59	11	0	0	0	4	9	28	.250	.390	R	.217	180	39	13	1	4	15	22	45	.317	.367

FULCHINO, JEFF — P

PERSONAL: Born November 26, 1979, in Titusville, Fla. ... Throws right, bats right. ... Full name: Jeffrey P. Fulchino. ... College: Connecticut. **TRANSACTIONS/CAREER NOTES:** Selected by Florida Marlins organization in eighth round of 2001 free-agent draft.
CAREER HITTING: 0-for-0 (.000), 0 R, 0 2B, 0 3B, 0 HR, 0 RBI.

Year Team (League)	W	L	Pct.	ERA	WHIP	G	GS	CG	ShO	Hld.	Sv.-Opp.	IP	H	R	ER	HR	BB-IBB	SO	Avg.
2001— Utica (N.Y.-Penn)	3	8	.273	3.56	1.30	14	13	0	0	0	0-...	60.2	48	34	24	2	31-0	33	.211
2002— Kane Co. (Midw.)	5	5	.500	3.87	1.24	24	22	0	0	0	0-...	132.2	114	67	57	7	51-0	94	.231
2003— Greensboro (S. Atl.)	1	2	.333	4.01	1.42	5	4	0	0	0	0-...	24.2	28	14	11	1	7-0	16	.277
— Jupiter (Fla. St.)	2	4	.333	4.04	1.38	17	16	1	0	0	0-...	78.0	76	41	35	1	32-0	47	.258
2004— Jupiter (Fla. St.)	2	2	.500	2.72	1.28	8	8	0	0	0	0-...	43.0	39	17	13	1	16-0	26	.262
— Carolina (Southern)	5	5	.545	4.47	1.43	17	17	0	0	0	0-...	90.2	93	45	45	5	37-3	84	.271
2005— Albuquerque (PCL)	11	7	.611	5.06	1.61	29	29	0	0	0	0-0	153.0	179	102	86	21	67-0	101	.297
2006— Florida (N.L.)	0	0	...	0.00	3.00	1	0	0	0	0	0-0	0.1	0	0	0	0	1-0	0	.000
— (PCL)	6	10	.375	4.50	1.43	25	24	0	0	0	0-0	140.0	144	82	70	12	56-0	109	.271
Major League totals (1 year)	0	0	...	0.00	3.00	1	0	0	0	0	0-0	0.1	0	0	0	0	1-0	0	.000

F

vs.	Avg.	AB	H	2B	3B	HR	RBI	BB	SO	OBP	Slg.	vs.	Avg.	AB	H	2B	3B	HR	RBI	BB	SO	OBP	Slg.
L	.000	0	0	0	0	0	0	0	0	.000	.000	R	.000	1	0	0	0	0	0	1	0	.500	.000

FULTZ, AARON   P

PERSONAL: Born September 4, 1973, in Memphis. ... 6-0/205. ... Throws left, bats left. ... Full name: Richard Aaron Fultz. ... High school: Munford (Tenn.). ... Junior college: North Florida. ... College: North Florida JC. **TRANSACTIONS/CAREER NOTES:** Selected by San Francisco Giants organization in sixth round of 1992 free-agent draft. ... Traded by Giants with SS Andres Duncan and P Greg Brummett to Minnesota Twins for P Jim Deshaies (August 28, 1993). ... Released by Twins (April 1, 1996). ... Signed by Giants organization (April 4, 1996). ... Signed as a free agent by Texas Rangers (December 31, 2002). ... On disabled list (June 23-July 11, 2003); included rehabilitation assignments to Oklahoma and Frisco. ... Signed as a free agent by Twins organization (January 11, 2004). ... Claimed on waivers by Philadelphia Phillies (October 14, 2004).
CAREER HITTING: 5-for-19 (.263), 2 R, 0 2B, 0 3B, 0 HR, 0 RBI.

Year	Team (League)	W	L	Pct.	ERA	WHIP	G	GS	CG	ShO	Hld.	Sv.-Opp.	IP	H	R	ER	HR	BB-IBB	SO	Avg.
1992—	Ariz. Giants (Ariz.)	3	2	.600	2.13	1.24	14	14	0	0	...	0-...	67.2	51	24	16	0	33-0	72	.213
1993—	Clinton (Midw.)	14	8	.636	3.41	1.32	26	25	2	1	...	0-...	148.0	132	63	56	8	64-2	144	.239
	— Fort Wayne (Midw.)	0	0	...	9.00	2.50	1	1	0	0	...	0-...	4.0	10	4	4	0	0-0	3	.476
1994—	Fort Myers (FSL)	9	10	.474	4.33	1.50	28	28	3	0	...	0-...	168.1	193	95	81	9	60-5	132	.289
1995—	New Britain (East.)	0	2	.000	6.60	1.33	3	3	0	0	...	0-...	15.0	11	12	11	1	9-0	12	.208
	— Fort Myers (FSL)	3	6	.333	3.25	1.28	21	21	2	2	...	0-...	122.0	115	52	44	10	41-1	127	.250
1996—	San Jose (Calif.)	9	5	.643	3.96	1.48	36	12	0	0	...	1-...	104.2	101	52	46	• 7	54-2	103	.262
1997—	Shreveport (Texas)	6	3	.667	2.83	1.20	49	0	0	0	...	1-...	70.0	65	30	22	4	19-0	60	.247
1998—	Shreveport (Texas)	5	7	.417	3.77	1.40	54	0	0	0	...	15-...	62.0	58	40	26	4	29-10	61	.252
	— Fresno (PCL)	0	0	...	5.06	1.50	10	0	0	0	...	0-...	16.0	22	10	9	2	2-1	13	.333
1999—	Fresno (PCL)	9	8	.529	4.98	1.40	37	20	1	0	...	0-...	137.1	141	87	76	32	51-1	151	.266
2000—	San Francisco (N.L.)	5	2	.714	4.67	1.37	58	0	0	0	7	1-3	69.1	67	38	36	8	28-0	62	.263
2001—	San Francisco (N.L.)	3	1	.750	4.56	1.28	66	0	0	0	12	1-2	71.0	70	40	36	9	21-3	67	.259
2002—	San Francisco (N.L.)	2	2	.500	4.79	1.60	43	0	0	0	4	0-1	41.1	47	22	22	4	19-3	31	.294
	— Fresno (PCL)	1	3	.250	3.18	1.28	17	0	0	0	...	4-...	22.2	18	8	8	1	11-2	22	.222
2003—	Oklahoma (PCL)	0	0	...	27.00	3.00	1	0	0	0	...	0-...	1.0	2	3	3	2	1-0	1	.400
	— Frisco (Texas)	0	0	...	9.00	2.00	1	0	0	0	...	0-...	1.0	2	1	1	0	0-0	0	.333
	— Texas (A.L.)	1	3	.250	5.21	1.51	64	0	0	0	19	0-0	67.1	75	43	39	9	27-7	53	.287
2004—	Rochester (Int'l)	0	0	...	0.00	1.32	7	0	0	0	...	0-...	8.1	6	1	0	0	5-0	5	.194
	— Minnesota (A.L.)	3	3	.500	5.04	1.46	55	0	0	0	5	1-4	50.0	50	28	28	5	23-2	37	.267
2005—	Philadelphia (N.L.)	4	0	1.000	2.24	0.97	62	0	0	0	2	0-1	72.1	47	21	18	6	23-2	54	.186
2006—	Philadelphia (N.L.)	3	1	.750	4.54	1.51	66	1	0	0	9	0-2	71.1	80	39	36	7	28-8	62	.288
	American League totals (2 years)	4	6	.400	5.14	1.49	119	0	0	0	24	1-4	117.1	125	71	67	14	50-9	90	.279
	National League totals (5 years)	17	6	.739	4.09	1.32	295	1	0	0	34	2-9	325.1	311	160	148	34	119-16	276	.256
	Major League totals (7 years)	21	12	.636	4.37	1.37	414	1	0	0	58	3-13	442.2	436	231	215	48	169-25	366	.262

DIVISION SERIES RECORD

Year	Team (League)	W	L	Pct.	ERA	WHIP	G	GS	CG	ShO	Hld.	Sv.-Opp.	IP	H	R	ER	HR	BB-IBB	SO	Avg.
2000—	San Francisco (N.L.)	0	1	.000	6.75	2.25	1	0	0	0	0	0-0	1.1	3	1	1	1	0-0	0	.500
2002—	San Francisco (N.L.)	0	0	...			2	0	0	0	0	0-0	0.0	2	1	1	0	0-0	0	1.000
	Division series totals (2 years)	0	1	.000	13.50	3.75	3	0	0	0	0	0-0	1.1	5	2	2	1	0-0	0	.625

CHAMPIONSHIP SERIES RECORD

Year	Team (League)	W	L	Pct.	ERA	WHIP	G	GS	CG	ShO	Hld.	Sv.-Opp.	IP	H	R	ER	HR	BB-IBB	SO	Avg.
2002—	San Francisco (N.L.)	0	0	...	0.00	0.00	1	0	0	0	0	0-0	0.1	0	0	0	0	0-0	0	.000

WORLD SERIES RECORD

Year	Team (League)	W	L	Pct.	ERA	WHIP	G	GS	CG	ShO	Hld.	Sv.-Opp.	IP	H	R	ER	HR	BB-IBB	SO	Avg.
2002—	San Francisco (N.L.)	0	0	...	3.86	2.14	2	0	0	0	0	0-1	2.1	4	1	1	0	1-0	0	.400

vs.	Avg.	AB	H	2B	3B	HR	RBI	BB	SO	OBP	Slg.	vs.	Avg.	AB	H	2B	3B	HR	RBI	BB	SO	OBP	Slg.
L	.277	94	26	5	1	0	24	6	27	.317	.351	R	.293	184	54	15	3	7	34	22	35	.367	.522

FURCAL, RAFAEL   SS

PERSONAL: Born August 24, 1978, in Loma de Cabrera, Dominican Republic. ... 5-10/165. ... Bats both, throws right. ... Full name: Rafael Antoni Furcal. ... Name pronounced: fur-CALL. ... High school: Jose Cabrera (Loma De Cabrera, Dominican Republic). **TRANSACTIONS/CAREER NOTES:** Signed as a free agent by Atlanta Braves organization (November 9, 1996). ... On disabled list (June 13-29, 2000; and July 7, 2001-remainder of season). ... Signed as a free agent by Los Angeles Dodgers (December 7, 2005). **RECORDS:** Shares major league record for most triples, game (3, April 21, 2002). **HONORS:** Named N.L. Rookie Player of the Year by THE SPORTING NEWS (2000). ... Named N.L. Rookie of the Year by Baseball Writers' Association of America (2000).
2006 GAMES PLAYED BY POSITION (MLB): SS—156.

Year	Team (League)	Pos.	G	AB	R	H	2B	3B	HR	RBI	BB	SO	HBP	GDP	SB-CS	Avg.	OBP	SLG	OPS	E	Avg.
1997—	GC Braves (GCL)	2B-OF	50	190	31	49	5	4	1	9	20	21	2	1	15-2	.258	.335	.342	.677	10	.961
1998—	Danville (Appal.)	2B	66	268	56	88	15	4	0	23	36	29	3	2	60-15	.328	.412	.414	.827	14	.965
1999—	Macon (S. Atl.)	SS	83	335	73	113	15	1	1	29	41	36	5	4	73-22	.337	.417	.397	.814	30	.912
	— Myrtle Beach (Carol.)	SS	43	184	32	54	9	3	0	12	14	42	0	4	23-8	.293	.343	.375	.718	4	.975
2000—	Greenville (Sou.)	SS	3	10	1	2	0	1	0	3	1	0	0	0	0-0	.200	.273	.500	.773	1	.889
	— Atlanta (N.L.)	SS-2B	131	455	87	134	20	4	4	37	73	80	3	2	40-14	.295	.394	.382	.776	24	.958
2001—	Atlanta (N.L.)	SS	79	324	39	89	19	0	4	30	24	56	1	5	22-6	.275	.321	.370	.692	11	.970
2002—	Atlanta (N.L.)	SS-2B	154	636	95	175	31	8	8	47	43	114	3	8	27-15	.275	.323	.387	.710	27	.964
2003—	Atlanta (N.L.)	SS	156	664	130	194	35	* 10	15	61	60	76	3	1	25-2	.292	.352	.443	.794	31	.959
2004—	Atlanta (N.L.)	SS-2B	143	563	103	157	14	6	14	59	58	71	1	9	29-6	.279	.345	.414	.758	24	.962
2005—	Atlanta (N.L.)	SS	154	616	100	175	31	11	12	58	62	78	1	11	46-10	.284	.348	.429	.777	15	.981
2006—	Los Angeles (N.L.)	SS	159	654	113	196	32	9	15	63	73	98	1	7	37-13	.300	.369	.445	.814	27	.966
	Major League totals (7 years)		976	3912	667	1120	192	47	72	355	393	573	13	43	226-66	.286	.351	.415	.766	159	.966

DIVISION SERIES RECORD

Year	Team (League)	Pos.	G	AB	R	H	2B	3B	HR	RBI	BB	SO	HBP	GDP	SB-CS	Avg.	OBP	SLG	OPS	E	Avg.
2000—	Atlanta (N.L.)	2B-SS	3	11	2	1	0	0	0	0	3	0	0	1	1-1	.091	.286	.091	.377	1	.933
2002—	Atlanta (N.L.)	SS	5	24	2	6	1	1	0	2	0	5	0	0	1-1	.250	.250	.375	.625	0	1.000
2003—	Atlanta (N.L.)	SS	5	19	3	4	0	0	0	0	3	5	0	0	1-0	.211	.318	.211	.529	1	.968
2004—	Atlanta (N.L.)	SS	5	21	3	8	0	1	2	4	3	3	1	0	3-0	.381	.480	.762	1.242	0	1.000
2005—	Atlanta (N.L.)	SS	4	20	1	3	0	0	0	0	3	2	0	0	3-0	.150	.261	.150	.411	0	1.000
2006—	Los Angeles (N.L.)	SS	3	11	1	2	0	0	0	1	0	2	0	0	0-0	.182	.357	.182	.539	0	1.000
	Division series totals (6 years)		25	106	· 14	24	1	2	2	7	15	17	1	1	11-2	.226	.328	.330	.658	2	.985

	G	AB	R	H	2B	3B	HR	RBI	BB	SO	HBP	GDP	SB-CS	Avg.	OBP	SLG	OPS	E	Avg.
All-Star Game totals (1 year)	1	3	1	1	0	0	0	0	0	1	0	0	0-0	.333	.333	.333	.667	1	.500

2006 LEFTY-RIGHTY SPLITS

vs.	Avg.	AB	H	2B	3B	HR	RBI	BB	SO	OBP	Slg.	vs.	Avg.	AB	H	2B	3B	HR	RBI	BB	SO	OBP	Slg.
L	.324	142	46	10	3	5	19	15	13	.386	.542	R	.293	512	150	22	6	10	44	58	85	.365	.418

GABBARD, KASON   P

PERSONAL: Born April 8, 1982, in Oxford, Ohio. ... Throws left, bats left. ... Full name: Kason R. Gabbard. ... Junior College: Indian River CC. **TRANSACTIONS/CAREER NOTES:** Selected by Boston Red Sox organization in 29th round of 2000 free-agent draft.
CAREER HITTING: 0-for-0 (.000), 0 R, 0 2B, 0 3B, 0 HR, 0 RBI.

Year	Team (League)	W	L	Pct.	ERA	WHIP	G	GS	CG	ShO	Hld.	Sv.-Opp.	IP	H	R	ER	HR	BB-IBB	SO	Avg.
2001— GC Red Sox (GCL)		0	1	.000	5.65	1.40	6	6	0	0		0-...	14.1	11	11	9	1	9-0	17	.208
2002— Augusta (S. Atl.)		0	4	.000	1.89	1.00	7	7	0	0		0-...	38.0	31	14	8	0	7-0	31	.221
2003— Sarasota (Fla. St.)		0	1	.000	10.29	2.29	2	2	0	0		0-...	7.0	13	8	8	0	3-0	4	.464
2004— Sarasota (Fla. St.)		3	2	.600	2.70	1.36	10	7	0	0		1-...	43.1	43	17	13	2	16-1	30	.256
— Portland (East.)		3	6	.333	6.28	1.64	14	14	0	0			53.0	61	42	37	5	26-0	35	.290
2005— Portland (East.)		9	11	.450	4.61	1.45	27	25	0	0	0	0-0	132.2	128	80	68	10	65-0	96	.255
2006— Portland (East.)		9	2	.818	2.57	1.03	13	13	1	0	0	0-0	73.2	51	26	21	4	25-0	68	.192
— Pawtucket (Int'l)		1	7	.125	5.23	1.49	9	8	0	0	0	0-0	51.2	51	31	30	8	26-0	48	.268
— Boston (A.L.)		1	3	.250	3.51	1.56	7	4	0	0	0	0-0	25.2	24	11	10	0	16-0	15	.255
Major League totals (1 year)		1	3	.250	3.51	1.56	7	4	0	0	0	0-0	25.2	24	11	10	0	16-0	15	.255

2006 LEFTY-RIGHTY SPLITS

vs.	Avg.	AB	H	2B	3B	HR	RBI	BB	SO	OBP	Slg.	vs.	Avg.	AB	H	2B	3B	HR	RBI	BB	SO	OBP	Slg.
L	.250	20	5	0	0	0	3	6	8	.423	.250	R	.257	74	19	5	0	0	3	10	7	.345	.324

GAGNE, ERIC   P

PERSONAL: Born January 7, 1976, in Montreal. ... 6-2/235. ... Throws right, bats right. ... Full name: Eric Serge Gagne. ... Name pronounced: gahn-yay. ... High school: Polyvalente Edouard Montpetit (Montreal). ... Junior college: Seminole (Okla.). **TRANSACTIONS/CAREER NOTES:** Selected by Chicago White Sox organization in 30th round of 1994 free-agent draft; did not sign. ... Signed as a non-drafted free agent by Los Angeles Dodgers organization (July 26, 1995). ... On disabled list (April 2-May 14, 2005); included rehabilitation assignment to Las Vegas. ... On disabled list (June 15, 2005-remainder of season). ... On disabled list (April 1-May 30, 2006); included rehabilitation assignment to Las Vegas. ... On suspended list (May 30-June 1, 2006). ... On disabled list (June 13, 2006-remainder of season). **HONORS:** Named N.L. Pitcher of the Year by THE SPORTING NEWS (2003). ... Named N.L. Reliever of the Year by THE SPORTING NEWS (2003 and 2004). ... Named righthanded pitcher on THE SPORTING NEWS N.L. All-Star team (2003). ... Named N.L. Cy Young Award winner by Baseball Writers' Association of America (2003).
CAREER HITTING: 12-for-86 (.140), 5 R, 2 2B, 1 3B, 1 HR, 3 RBI.

Year	Team (League)	W	L	Pct.	ERA	WHIP	G	GS	CG	ShO	Hld.	Sv.-Opp.	IP	H	R	ER	HR	BB-IBB	SO	Avg.
1996— Savannah (S. Atl.)		7	6	.538	3.28	1.19	23	21	1	1		0-...	115.1	94	48	42	11	43-1	131	.221
1997—					Did not play.															
1998— Vero Beach (FSL)		9	7	.563	3.74	1.19	25	25	3	1		0-...	139.2	118	69	58	16	48-0	144	.225
1999— San Antonio (Texas)		12	4	.750	2.63	1.11	26	26	0	0		0-...	167.2	122	55	49	17	64-0	185	.201
— Los Angeles (N.L.)		1	1	.500	2.10	1.10	5	5	0	0	0	0-0	30.0	18	8	7	3	15-0	30	.175
2000— Albuquerque (PCL)		5	1	.833	3.88	1.28	9	9	0	0	0	0-0	55.2	56	30	24	8	15-0	59	.260
— Los Angeles (N.L.)		4	6	.400	5.15	1.64	20	19	0	0	0	0-0	101.1	106	62	58	20	60-1	79	.270
2001— Los Angeles (N.L.)		6	7	.462	4.75	1.25	33	24	0	0	0	0-0	151.2	144	90	80	24	46-1	130	.251
— Las Vegas (PCL)		3	0	1.000	1.52	0.97	4	4	0	0		0-...	23.2	15	4	4	2	8-0	31	.195
2002— Los Angeles (N.L.)		4	1	.800	1.97	0.86	77	0	0	0	1	52-56	82.1	55	18	18	6	16-4	114	.189
2003— Los Angeles (N.L.)		2	3	.400	1.20	0.69	77	0	0	0		* 55-55	82.1	37	12	11	2	20-2	137	.133
2004— Los Angeles (N.L.)		7	3	.700	2.19	0.91	70	0	0	0	0	45-47	82.1	53	24	20	5	22-3	114	.181
2005— Las Vegas (PCL)		0	0		0.00	0.00	2	0	0	0	1	0-0	1.0	0	0	0	0	0-0	0	.000
— Los Angeles (N.L.)		1	0	1.000	2.70	0.98	14	0	0	0	0	8-8	13.1	10	4	4	2	3-0	22	.200
2006— Las Vegas (PCL)		0	0		0.00	0.50	2	0	0	0	0	2-2	2.0	1	0	0	0	0-0	3	.143
— Los Angeles (N.L.)		0	0		0.00	0.50	2	0	0	0	0	1-1	2.0	1	0	0	0	1-0	3	.000
Major League totals (8 years)		25	21	.543	3.27	1.11	298	48	0	0	1	161-167	545.1	423	218	198	62	183-11	629	.213

Year	Team (League)	W	L	Pct.	ERA	WHIP	G	GS	CG	ShO	Hld.	Sv.-Opp.	IP	H	R	ER	HR	BB-IBB	SO	Avg.
2004— Los Angeles (N.L.)		0	0		0.00	0.67	2	0	0	0		0-0	3.0	1	0	0	0	1-0	3	.111

	W	L	Pct.	ERA	WHIP	G	GS	CG	ShO	Hld.	Sv.-Opp.	IP	H	R	ER	HR	BB-IBB	SO	Avg.
All-Star Game totals (3 years)	0	1	.000	12.00	2.00	3	0	0	0		0-0	3.0	5	4	4	2	1-0	4	.357

2006 LEFTY-RIGHTY SPLITS

vs.	Avg.	AB	H	2B	3B	HR	RBI	BB	SO	OBP	Slg.	vs.	Avg.	AB	H	2B	3B	HR	RBI	BB	SO	OBP	Slg.
L	.000	3	0	0	0	0	0	0	2	.000	.000	R	.000	3	0	0	0	0	0	1	1	.400	.000

GALL, JOHN   OF

PERSONAL: Born April 2, 1978, in Stanford, Calif. ... 6-0/195. ... Bats right, throws right. ... Full name: John Christopher Gall. ... College: Stanford. **TRANSACTIONS/CAREER NOTES:** Selected by St. Louis Cardinals organization in 11th round of 2000 free-agent draft. ... Released by Cardinals (July 17, 2006).
2006 GAMES PLAYED BY POSITION (MLB): OF—2, 1B—1.

Year	Team (League)	Pos.	G	AB	R	H	2B	3B	HR	RBI	BB	SO	HBP	GDP	SB-CS	Avg.	OBP	SLG	OPS	E	Avg.
2000— New Jersey (NYP)	1B-3B	71	259	28	62	10	0	2	27	25	37	1	7	16-5	.239	.304	.301	.605	10	.983
2001— Peoria (Midw.)	1B	57	205	27	62	23	0	4	44	16	18	4	3	0-3	.302	.353	.473	.826	3	.993
— Potomac (Carol.)	1B-3B	84	319	44	101	25	0	4	33	24	40	3	9	5-6	.317	.369	.433	.802	11	.978
2002— New Haven (East.)	1B-3B-OF	135	526	82	166	45	3	20	81	38	75	2	26	4-1	.316	.362	.527	.889	16	.984
2003— Memphis (PCL)	OF-1B-3B	123	461	62	144	24	1	16	73	39	56	2	13	5-2	.312	.368	.473	.841	7	.993
— Tennessee (Sou.)	OF-1B	12	52	6	17	1	0	3	12	3	4	0	0	0-1	.327	.357	.519	.876	0	1.000
2004— Memphis (PCL)	OF-1B-3B	135	506	77	148	34	0	22	84	48	68	1	19	1-1	.292	.350	.490	.840	5	.986
2005— Memphis (PCL)	OF-1B-DH																			
	3B	114	374	61	101	22	0	13	64	45	42	1	12	9-2	.270	.345	.433	.778	9	.981
— St. Louis (N.L.)	OF	22	37	5	10	3	0	2	10	1	9	0	0	0-0	.270	.282	.514	.796	0	1.000
2006— St. Louis (N.L.)	OF-1B	8	12	1	3	0	0	0	3	0	4	0	0	0-0	.250	.250	.250	.500	0	1.000
— Memphis (PCL)		82	289	31	83	13	0	6	34	28	36	6	8	3-4	.287	.361	.408	.769	8	.976
Major League totals (2 years)		30	49	6	13	3	0	2	13	1	13	0	0	0-0	.265	.275	.449	.723	0	1.000

G

Year	Team (League)	Pos.	G	AB	R	H	2B	3B	HR	RBI	BB	SO	HBP	GDP	SB-CS	Avg.	OBP	SLG	OPS	E	Avg.
2005— St. Louis (N.L.)			1	1	0	0	0	0	0	0	0	0	0	0	0-0	.000	.000	.000	.000	0	...

2006 LEFTY-RIGHTY SPLITS

vs.	Avg.	AB	H	2B	3B	HR	RBI	BB	SO	OBP	Slg.		vs.	Avg.	AB	H	2B	3B	HR	RBI	BB	SO	OBP	Slg.
L	.333	6	2	0	0	0	1	0	2	.333	.333		R	.167	6	1	0	0	0	0	0	3	.167	.167

GALLO, MIKE — P

PERSONAL: Born April 2, 1977, in Long Beach, Calif. ... 6-0/175. ... Throws left, bats left. ... Full name: Michael Dwain Gallo. ... High school: Millikan (Calif.). ... College: Long Beach State. **TRANSACTIONS/CAREER NOTES:** Selected by Houston Astros organization in fifth round of 1999 free-agent draft.
CAREER HITTING: 0-for-4 (.000), 0 R, 0 2B, 0 3B, 0 HR, 0 RBI.

Year	Team (League)	W	L	Pct.	ERA	WHIP	G	GS	CG	ShO	Hld.	Sv.-Opp.	IP	H	R	ER	HR	BB-IBB	SO	Avg.
1999— Auburn (NY-Penn)	1	0	1.000	1.23	1.36	3	3	0	0	...	0-...	14.2	13	4	2	0	7-0	11	.232
— Michigan (Midw.)	2	3	.400	5.85	1.65	12	12	0	0	...	0-...	60.0	76	47	39	6	23-0	32	.315
2000— Michigan (Midw.)	8	3	.727	4.86	1.44	24	13	0	0	...	0-...	90.2	104	58	49	6	27-1	56	.285
2001— Michigan (Midw.)	9	2	.818	3.84	1.21	44	0	0	0	...	4-...	84.1	83	38	36	4	19-1	67	.252
2002— Lexington (S. Atl.)	4	4	.500	1.83	1.08	42	2	0	0	...	8-...	88.1	69	29	18	6	26-4	93	.211
— Round Rock (Texas)	0	0	...	6.75	0.75	1	0	0	0	...	0-...	1.1	1	1	1	1	0-0	0	.200
2003— Round Rock (Texas)	1	1	.500	1.37	1.17	17	0	0	0	...	2-...	19.2	17	3	3	1	6-2	22	.246
— New Orleans (PCL)	3	0	1.000	2.08	0.92	16	0	0	0	...	0-...	17.1	13	4	4	0	3-0	11	.217
— Houston (N.L.)	1	0	1.000	3.00	1.27	32	0	0	0	6	0-1	30.0	28	10	10	3	10-2	16	.267
2004— New Orleans (PCL)	0	0	...	0.00	0.50	3	0	0	0	...	1-...	4.0	0	0	0	0	2-0	4	.000
— Houston (N.L.)	2	0	1.000	4.74	1.52	69	0	0	0	4	0-1	49.1	55	27	26	12	20-7	34	.284
2005— Round Rock (PCL)	4	2	.667	3.64	1.40	37	1	0	0	4	0-2	54.1	56	29	22	2	20-4	33	.271
— Houston (N.L.)	0	1	...	2.66	1.38	36	0	0	0	8	0-2	20.1	18	6	6	1	10-2	12	.250
2006— Round Rock (PCL)	2	0	1.000	5.63	1.55	33	0	0	0	7	0-1	40.0	46	25	25	4	16-2	25	.283
— Houston (N.L.)	1	2	.333	6.06	2.14	23	0	0	0	0	0-1	16.1	28	11	11	3	7-1	7	.400
Major League totals (4 years)	**4**	**3**	**.571**	**4.11**	**1.52**	**160**	**0**	**0**	**0**	**18**	**0-5**	**116.0**	**129**	**54**	**53**	**19**	**47-12**	**69**	**.293**

DIVISION SERIES RECORD

Year	Team (League)	W	L	Pct.	ERA	WHIP	G	GS	CG	ShO	Hld.	Sv.-Opp.	IP	H	R	ER	HR	BB-IBB	SO	Avg.
2004— Houston (N.L.)	0	0	...	4.50	2.00	3	0	0	0	0	0-0	2.0	3	1	1	0	1-0	4	.333
2005— Houston (N.L.)	0	0	...	0.00	1.20	3	0	0	0	1	0-0	1.2	1	0	0	0	1-1	0	.200
Division series totals (2 years)	**0**	**0**	**...**	**2.45**	**1.64**	**6**	**0**	**0**	**0**	**1**	**0-0**	**3.2**	**4**	**1**	**1**	**0**	**2-1**	**4**	**.286**

CHAMPIONSHIP SERIES RECORD

Year	Team (League)	W	L	Pct.	ERA	WHIP	G	GS	CG	ShO	Hld.	Sv.-Opp.	IP	H	R	ER	HR	BB-IBB	SO	Avg.
2005— Houston (N.L.)	0	0	...	0.00	0.00	2	0	0	0	1	0-0	0.2	0	0	0	0	0-0	0	.000

WORLD SERIES RECORD

Year	Team (League)	W	L	Pct.	ERA	WHIP	G	GS	CG	ShO	Hld.	Sv.-Opp.	IP	H	R	ER	HR	BB-IBB	SO	Avg.
2005— Houston (N.L.)	0	0	...	0.00	0.00	2	0	0	0	0	0-0	1.0	0	0	0	0	0-0	0	.000

2006 LEFTY-RIGHTY SPLITS

vs.	Avg.	AB	H	2B	3B	HR	RBI	BB	SO	OBP	Slg.		vs.	Avg.	AB	H	2B	3B	HR	RBI	BB	SO	OBP	Slg.
L	.360	25	9	1	0	0	3	1	3	.370	.400		R	.422	45	19	3	0	3	7	6	4	.509	.689

GARCIA, FREDDY — P

PERSONAL: Born June 10, 1976, in Caracas, Venezuela. ... 6-4/240. ... Throws right, bats right. ... Full name: Freddy Antonio Garcia. **TRANSACTIONS/CAREER NOTES:** Signed as a non-drafted free agent by Houston Astros organization (October 21, 1993). ... Traded by Astros with SS Carlos Guillen and a player to be named to Seattle Mariners for P Randy Johnson (July 31, 1998); Mariners acquired P John Halama to complete deal (October 1, 1998). ... On disabled list (April 22-July 7, 2000); included rehabilitation assignments to Tacoma and Everett. ... Traded by Mariners with C Ben Davis to Chicago White Sox for C Miguel Olivo, OF Jeremy Reed and SS Michael Morse (June 27, 2004). **MISCELLANEOUS NOTES:** Struck out in only appearance as pinch hitter (1999).
CAREER HITTING: 8-for-41 (.195), 0 R, 1 2B, 0 3B, 0 HR, 2 RBI.

Year	Team (League)	W	L	Pct.	ERA	WHIP	G	GS	CG	ShO	Hld.	Sv.-Opp.	IP	H	R	ER	HR	BB-IBB	SO	Avg.
1994— Dom. Astros (DSL)	4	6	.400	5.29	1.39	16	15	0	0	...	0-...	85.0	80	61	50	...	38-...	68	...
1995— GC Astros (GCL)	6	3	.667	4.47	1.27	11	11	0	0	...	0-...	58.1	60	32	29	2	14-0	58	.261
1996— Quad City (Midw.)	5	4	.556	3.12	1.38	13	13	0	0	...	0-...	60.2	57	27	21	3	27-0	50	.247
1997— Kissimmee (Fla. St.)	10	8	.556	2.56	1.20	27	27	5	2	...	0-...	179.0	165	63	51	6	49-3	131	.242
1998— Jackson (Texas)	6	7	.462	3.24	1.27	19	19	2	0	...	0-...	119.1	94	48	43	8	58-0	115	.215
— New Orleans (PCL)	1	0	1.000	3.14	1.05	2	2	0	0	...	0-...	14.1	14	5	5	2	1-0	13	.255
— Tacoma (PCL)	3	1	.750	3.86	1.32	5	5	0	0	...	0-...	32.2	30	14	14	6	13-0	30	.246
1999— Seattle (A.L.)	17	8	.680	4.07	1.47	33	33	2	1	0	0-0	201.1	205	96	91	18	90-4	170	.263
2000— Seattle (A.L.)	9	5	.643	3.91	1.42	21	20	0	0	0	0-0	124.1	112	62	54	16	64-4	79	.241
— Everett (N'west)	0	0	...	4.50	1.30	2	2	0	0	0	0-...	10.0	11	5	5	1	2-0	15	.262
— Tacoma (PCL)	1	0	1.000	2.57	1.00	1	1	0	0	0	0-...	7.0	5	2	2	2	2-0	11	.208
2001— Seattle (A.L.)	18	6	.750	* 3.05	1.12	34	34	4	3	0	0-0	* 238.2	199	88	81	16	69-6	163	* .225
2002— Seattle (A.L.)	16	10	.615	4.39	1.30	34	34	1	0	0	0-0	223.2	227	110	109	30	66-3	181	.260
2003— Seattle (A.L.)	12	14	.462	4.51	1.33	33	33	1	0	0	0-0	201.1	196	109	101	31	71-2	144	.255
2004— Seattle (A.L.)	4	7	.364	3.20	1.20	15	15	1	0	0	0-0	107.0	96	39	38	8	32-1	82	.236
— Chicago (A.L.)	9	4	.692	4.46	1.24	16	16	0	0	0	0-0	103.0	96	53	51	14	32-2	102	.247
2005— Chicago (A.L.)	14	8	.636	3.87	1.25	33	33	2	0	0	0-0	228.0	225	102	98	26	60-2	146	.259
2006— Chicago (A.L.)	17	9	.654	4.53	1.28	33	33	1	0	0	0-0	216.1	228	116	109	32	48-3	135	.267
Major League totals (8 years)	**116**	**71**	**.620**	**4.01**	**1.29**	**252**	**251**	**12**	**4**	**0**	**0-0**	**1643.2**	**1584**	**775**	**732**	**191**	**529-27**	**1202**	**.252**

DIVISION SERIES RECORD

Year	Team (League)	W	L	Pct.	ERA	WHIP	G	GS	CG	ShO	Hld.	Sv.-Opp.	IP	H	R	ER	HR	BB-IBB	SO	Avg.
2000— Seattle (A.L.)	0	0	...	10.80	2.70	1	1	0	0	0	0-0	3.1	6	4	4	1	3-0	2	.375
2001— Seattle (A.L.)	1	1	.500	3.86	1.37	2	2	0	0	0	0-0	11.2	13	6	5	1	3-0	13	.277
2005— Chicago (A.L.)	1	0	1.000	5.40	1.80	1	1	0	0	0	0-0	5.0	5	3	3	3	4-0	1	.278
Division series totals (3 years)	**2**	**1**	**.667**	**5.40**	**1.70**	**4**	**4**	**0**	**0**	**0**	**0-0**	**20.0**	**24**	**13**	**12**	**5**	**10-0**	**16**	**.296**

CHAMPIONSHIP SERIES RECORD

Year	Team (League)	W	L	Pct.	ERA	WHIP	G	GS	CG	ShO	Hld.	Sv.-Opp.	IP	H	R	ER	HR	BB-IBB	SO	Avg.
2000— Seattle (A.L.)	2	0	1.000	1.54	1.20	2	2	0	0	0	0-0	11.2	10	2	2	0	4-0	11	.227
2001— Seattle (A.L.)	0	1	.000	3.68	1.50	1	1	0	0	0	0-0	7.1	7	3	3	0	4-0	6	.292
2005— Chicago (A.L.)	1	0	1.000	2.00	0.78	1	1	1	0	0	0-0	9.0	6	2	2	0	1-0	5	.188
Champ. series totals (3 years)	**3**	**1**	**.750**	**2.25**	**1.14**	**4**	**4**	**1**	**0**	**0**	**0-0**	**28.0**	**23**	**7**	**7**	**0**	**9-0**	**22**	**.230**

G

WORLD SERIES RECORD

Year	Team (League)	W	L	Pct.	ERA	WHIP	G	GS	CG	ShO	Hld.	Sv.-Opp.	IP	H	R	ER	HR	BB-IBB	SO	Avg.
2005—	Chicago (A.L.)	1	0	1.000	0.00	1.00	1	1	0	0	...	0-0	7.0	4	0	0	0	3-1	7	.174

ALL-STAR GAME RECORD

		W	L	Pct.	ERA	WHIP	G	GS	CG	ShO	Hld.	Sv.-Opp.	IP	H	R	ER	HR	BB-IBB	SO	Avg.
	All-Star Game totals (2 years)	1	0	1.000	0.00	0.67	2	0	0	0	...	0-0	3.0	2	0	0	0	0-0	3	.182

2006 LEFTY-RIGHTY SPLITS

vs.	Avg.	AB	H	2B	3B	HR	RBI	BB	SO	OBP	Slg.	vs.	Avg.	AB	H	2B	3B	HR	RBI	BB	SO	OBP	Slg.
L	.262	397	104	18	3	9	41	27	62	.309	.390	R	.271	458	124	28	2	23	63	21	73	.308	.491

GARCIA, JOSE — P

PERSONAL: Born January 7, 1985, in De Jabon, Dominican Republic. ... 5-11/165. ... Throws right, bats right. ... Full name: Jose Luis Garcia. **TRANSACTIONS/CAREER NOTES:** Signed as a non-drafted free agent by Florida Marlins organization (July 3, 2001).
CAREER HITTING: 1-for-2 (.500), 0 R, 0 2B, 0 3B, 0 HR, 0 RBI.

Year	Team (League)	W	L	Pct.	ERA	WHIP	G	GS	CG	ShO	Hld.	Sv.-Opp.	IP	H	R	ER	HR	BB-IBB	SO	Avg.
2002—	Dom. Marlins (DSL)	3	2	.600	1.16	0.98	15	1	0	0	...	3-...	38.2	25	18	5	0	13-2	42	.179
2003—	Dom. Marlins (DSL)	2	6	.250	2.83	1.31	12	12	2	0	...	0-...	70.0	78	37	22	3	14-1	87	.284
2004—	Dom. Marlins (DSL)	5	3	.625	1.43	0.77	14	10	0	0	...	0-...	69.0	43	16	11	2	10-0	84	.176
2005—	Greensboro (S. Atl.)	3	0	1.000	1.27	0.53	5	4	0	0	...	0-0	28.1	11	5	4	1	4-0	39	.115
—	GC Marlins (GCL)	0	0	...	0.00	1.00	1	1	0	0	...	0-0	2.0	1	0	0	0	1-0	3	.167
—	Jupiter (Fla. St.)	0	0	...	18.00	2.00	1	1	0	0	...	0-0	2.0	2	4	4	0	2-0	0	.286
2006—	Jupiter (Fla. St.)	6	2	.750	1.87	0.99	12	11	1	0	...	0-0	77.0	60	31	16	3	16-0	69	.210
—	Albuquerque (PCL)	0	1	.000	11.25	2.25	1	1	0	0	...	0-0	4.0	5	5	5	0	4-1	5	.294
—	Carolina (Southern)	6	7	.462	3.40	1.22	14	14	0	0	...	0-0	84.2	78	37	32	10	25-2	87	.242
—	Florida (N.L.)	0	0	...	4.91	1.36	5	0	0	0	...	0-0	11.0	10	6	6	1	5-0	8	.233
Major League totals (1 year)		0	0	...	4.91	1.36	5	0	0	0	...	0-0	11.0	10	6	6	1	5-0	8	.233

2006 LEFTY-RIGHTY SPLITS

vs.	Avg.	AB	H	2B	3B	HR	RBI	BB	SO	OBP	Slg.	vs.	Avg.	AB	H	2B	3B	HR	RBI	BB	SO	OBP	Slg.
L	.267	30	8	2	0	1	4	3	4	.333	.433	R	.154	13	2	1	0	0	1	2	4	.267	.231

GARCIAPARRA, NOMAR — 1B

PERSONAL: Born July 23, 1973, in Whittier, Calif. ... 6-0/190. ... Bats right, throws right. ... Full name: Anthony Nomar Garciaparra. ... Name pronounced: no-mar GARCIA-par-uh. ... High school: St. John Bosco (Bellflower, Calif.). ... College: Georgia Tech. **TRANSACTIONS/CAREER NOTES:** Selected by Milwaukee Brewers organization in fifth round of 1991 free-agent draft; did not sign. ... Selected by Boston Red Sox organization in first round (12th pick overall) of 1994 free-agent draft. ... On disabled list (May 9-28, 1998; and May 12-27, 2000). ... On disabled list (March 21-July 29 and August 27, 2001-remainder of season); included rehabilitation assignment to Pawtucket. ... On disabled list (March 26-June 9, 2004); included rehabilitation assignment to Pawtucket. ... Traded by Red Sox with OF Matt Murton to Chicago Cubs as part of four-team deal in which Red Sox acquired SS Orlando Cabrera from Expos and 1B Doug Mientkiewicz from Twins, Expos acquired SS Alex S. Gonzalez, P Francis Beltran and IF Brendan Harris from Cubs, and Twins acquired P Justin Jones from Cubs (July 31, 2004). ... On disabled list (April 21-August 5, 2005); included rehabilitation assignments to AZL Cubs, Peoria and West Tennessee. ... Signed as a free agent by Los Angeles Dodgers (December 19, 2005). ... On disabled list (April 3-22, 2006); included rehabilitation assignment to Las Vegas. ... On disabled list (July 25-August 9, 2006). **HONORS:** Named A.L. Rookie Player of the Year by THE SPORTING NEWS (1997). ... Named N.L. Comeback Player of the Year by the SPORTING NEWS (2006). ... Named shortstop on THE SPORTING NEWS A.L. All-Star team (1997 and 1999). ... Named A.L. Rookie of the Year by Baseball Writers' Association of America (1997). ... Named shortstop on A.L. Silver Slugger team (1997). **STATISTICAL NOTES:** Hit three home runs in one game (May 10, 1999; and July 23, 2002). ... Career major league grand slams: 7. **MISCELLANEOUS NOTES:** Member of 1992 U.S. Olympic baseball team.
2006 GAMES PLAYED BY POSITION (MLB): 1B—118.

								BATTING										FIELDING	
Year	Team (League)	Pos.	G	AB	R	H	2B	3B	HR	RBI	BB	SO	HBP	GDP	SB-CS	Avg.	OBP	SLG	OPS	E	Avg.
---	---	---	---	---	---	---	---	---	---	---	---	---	---	---	---	---	---	---	---	---	---
1994—	Sarasota (Fla. St.)	SS	28	105	20	31	8	1	1	16	10	6	1	2	5-2	.295	.356	.419	.775	3	.974
1995—	Trenton (East.)	SS	125	513	77	137	20	8	8	47	50	42	8	10	35-12	.267	.338	.384	.722	23	.963
1996—	Pawtucket (Int'l)	SS	43	172	40	59	15	2	16	46	14	21	1	6	3-1	.343	.387	.733	1.120	5	.973
—	GC Red Sox (GCL)	SS	5	14	4	4	2	1	0	5	1	0	1	1	0-0	.286	.375	.571	.946	1	.950
—	Boston (A.L.)	SS-2B-DH	24	87	11	21	2	3	4	16	4	14	0	0	5-0	.241	.272	.471	.743	1	.989
1997—	Boston (A.L.)	SS	153	* 684	122	* 209	44	* 11	30	98	35	92	6	9	22-9	.306	.342	.534	.875	21	.971
1998—	Boston (A.L.)	SS	143	604	111	195	37	8	35	122	33	62	8	20	12-6	.323	.362	.584	.946	25	.962
1999—	Boston (A.L.)	SS	135	532	103	190	42	4	27	104	51	39	8	11	14-3	* .357	.418	.603	1.022	17	.972
2000—	Boston (A.L.)	SS-DH	140	529	104	197	51	3	21	96	61	50	2	8	5-2	* .372	.434	.599	1.033	18	.971
2001—	Pawtucket (Int'l)	SS	4	16	3	7	2	0	1	4	1	2	1	0	0-0	.438	.500	.750	1.250	1	.941
—	Boston (A.L.)	SS	21	83	13	24	3	0	4	8	7	9	1	1	0-1	.289	.352	.470	.822	3	.968
2002—	Boston (A.L.)	SS	156	635	101	197	• 56	5	24	120	41	63	6	17	5-2	.310	.352	.528	.880	* 25	.965
2003—	Boston (A.L.)	SS	156	658	120	198	37	13	28	105	39	61	11	10	19-5	.301	.345	.524	.870	20	.971
2004—	Pawtucket (Int'l)	SS	6	21	1	5	1	0	1	3	1	3	0	0	0-0	.238	.273	.429	.701	0	1.000
—	Boston (A.L.)	SS-DH	38	156	24	50	7	3	5	21	8	16	4	4	2-0	.321	.367	.500	.867	6	.957
—	Chicago (N.L.)	SS	43	165	28	49	14	0	4	20	16	14	2	6	2-1	.297	.364	.455	.819	3	.982
2005—	Ariz. Cubs (Ariz.)	SS	2	5	0	1	0	0	0	0	0	1	0	0	0-0	.200	.200	.200	.400	0	1.000
—	Peoria (Midw.)	SS	2	5	-1	1	0	0	0	2	0	0	0	0	0-0	.200	.429	.200	.629	0	1.000
—	West Tenn (Sou.)	SS	4	13	2	3	0	0	0	1	1	1	1	0	0-0	.231	.333	.231	.564	1	.933
—	Chicago (N.L.)	3B-SS	62	230	28	65	12	0	9	30	12	24	2	6	0-0	.283	.320	.452	.772	12	.937
2006—	Las Vegas (PCL)	SS	2	8	3	4	2	0	0	1	0	0	0	0	0-0	.500	.500	.750	1.250	0	1.000
—	Los Angeles (N.L.)	1B	122	469	82	142	31	2	20	93	42	30	8	15	3-0	.303	.367	.505	.872	4	.996
American League totals (9 years)			966	3968	709	1281	279	50	178	690	279	406	46	80	84-28	.323	.367	.553	.923	136	.969
National League totals (3 years)			227	864	138	256	57	2	33	143	70	68	12	27	5-1	.296	.354	.481	.836	19	.987
Major League totals (11 years)			1193	4832	847	1537	336	52	211	833	349	474	58	107	89-29	.318	.367	.540	.907	155	.973

DIVISION SERIES RECORD

Year	Team (League)	Pos.	G	AB	R	H	2B	3B	HR	RBI	BB	SO	HBP	GDP	SB-CS	Avg.	OBP	SLG	OPS	E	Avg.
1998—	Boston (A.L.)	SS	4	15	1	5	0	0	3	11	1	0	0	1	0-0	.333	.333	1.000	1.333	0	1.000
1999—	Boston (A.L.)	SS	4	12	6	5	2	0	2	4	3	3	1	0	0-0	.417	.563	1.083	1.646	0	1.000
2003—	Boston (A.L.)	SS	5	20	2	6	3	0	0	0	3	3	0	0	1-0	.300	.391	.350	.741	1	.958
2006—	Los Angeles (N.L.)	1B	3	9	0	2	1	0	0	2	0	1	0	0	0-0	.222	.222	.333	.556	0	1.000
Division series totals (4 years)			16	56	12	18	5	0	5	17	7	6	1	2	1-0	.321	.394	.679	1.073	1	.983

CHAMPIONSHIP SERIES RECORD

Year	Team (League)	Pos.	G	AB	R	H	2B	3B	HR	RBI	BB	SO	HBP	GDP	SB-CS	Avg.	OBP	SLG	OPS	E	Avg.
1999—	Boston (A.L.)	SS	5	20	2	8	2	0	2	5	2	2	0	0	1-0	.400	.455	.800	1.255	4	.833
2003—	Boston (A.L.)	SS	7	29	2	7	0	1	0	1	2	8	0	1	0-0	.241	.290	.310	.601	1	.966
Champ. series totals (2 years)			12	49	4	15	2	1	2	6	4	10	0	1	1-0	.306	.358	.510	.869	5	.906

G

ALL-STAR GAME RECORD

	G	AB	R	H	2B	3B	HR	RBI	BB	SO	HBP	GDP	SB-CS	Avg.	OBP	SLG	OPS	E	Avg.
All-Star Game totals (5 years)	5	7	1	1	0	0	0	0	0	0	0	0	0-0	.143	.143	.143	.286	2	.778

2006 LEFTY-RIGHTY SPLITS

vs.	Avg.	AB	H	2B	3B	HR	RBI	BB	SO	OBP	Slg.	vs.	Avg.	AB	H	2B	3B	HR	RBI	BB	SO	OBP	Slg.
L	.341	85	29	7	0	5	16	11	8	.420	.600	R	.294	384	113	24	2	15	77	31	22	.355	.484

GARKO, RYAN — 1B/C

PERSONAL: Born January 2, 1981, in Pittsburgh, Pa. ... 6-2/225. ... Bats right, throws right. ... Full name: Ryan F. Garko. ... College: Stanford. **TRANSACTIONS/CAREER NOTES:** Selected by Cleveland Indians organization in third round of 2003 free-agent draft.

2006 GAMES PLAYED BY POSITION (MLB): 1B—45, DH—2.

							BATTING												FIELDING		
Year Team (League)	Pos.	G	AB	R	H	2B	3B	HR	RBI	BB	SO	HBP	GDP	SB-CS	Avg.	OBP	SLG	OPS	E	Avg.
2003— Mahoning Valley (N.Y.-Penn.)	C	45	165	23	45	8	1	4	16	12	19	4	5	1-1	.273	.337	.406	.743	5	.982
2004— Kinston (Carol.)	1B-C	65	238	44	78	17	1	16	57	26	34	15	6	4-1	.328	.425	.609	1.034	3	.995
— Akron (East.)	C-1B	43	172	29	57	15	0	6	38	14	28	6	3	1-0	.331	.397	.523	.920	4	.991
— Buffalo (Int'l)	1B-C	5	20	2	7	1	0	0	4	2	3	0	0	0-0	.350	.391	.400	.791	0	1.000
2005— Buffalo (Int'l)	1B-C-DH	127	452	75	137	25	3	19	77	44	92	18	11	1-3	.303	.384	.498	.882	8	.992
— Cleveland (A.L.)	DH	1	1	0	0	0	0	0	0	0	1	0	0	0-0	.000	.000	.000	.000	0	...
2006— Buffalo (Int'l)		103	364	43	90	18	0	15	59	45	67	19	9	4-5	.247	.352	.420	.773	6	.993
— Cleveland (A.L.)	1B-DH	50	185	28	54	12	0	7	45	14	37	7	5	0-0	.292	.359	.470	.829	6	.986
Major League totals (2 years)		51	186	28	54	12	0	7	45	14	38	7	5	0-0	.290	.357	.468	.825	6	.986

2006 LEFTY-RIGHTY SPLITS

vs.	Avg.	AB	H	2B	3B	HR	RBI	BB	SO	OBP	Slg.	vs.	Avg.	AB	H	2B	3B	HR	RBI	BB	SO	OBP	Slg.
L	.333	39	13	2	0	2	9	5	4	.400	.538	R	.281	146	41	10	0	5	36	9	33	.348	.452

GARLAND, JON — P

PERSONAL: Born September 27, 1979, in Valencia, Calif. ... 6-6/210. ... Throws right, bats right. ... Full name: Jon Steven Garland. ... High school: John F. Kennedy (Granada Hills, Calif.). **TRANSACTIONS/CAREER NOTES:** Selected by Chicago Cubs organization in first round (10th pick overall) of 1997 free-agent draft. ... Traded by Cubs to Chicago White Sox for P Matt Karchner (July 29, 1998). ... On disabled list (August 19-September 3, 2000); included rehabilitation assignment to Birmingham.

CAREER HITTING: 3-for-17 (.176), 2 R, 0 2B, 0 3B, 1 HR, 3 RBI.

Year Team (League)	W	L	Pct.	ERA	WHIP	G	GS	CG	ShO	Hld.	Sv.-Opp.	IP	H	R	ER	HR	BB-IBB	SO	Avg.
1997— Ariz. Cubs (Ariz.)	3	2	.600	2.70	1.18	10	7	0	0	...	0-...	40.0	37	14	12	3	10-0	39	.247
1998— Rockford (Midwest)	4	7	.364	5.03	1.57	19	19	1	0	...	0-...	107.1	124	69	60	11	45-0	70	.301
— Hickory (S. Atl.)	1	4	.200	5.40	1.84	5	5	0	0	...	0-...	26.2	36	20	16	2	13-0	19	.333
1999— Win.-Salem (Car.)	5	7	.417	3.33	1.24	19	19	2	1	...	0-...	119.0	109	57	44	7	39-2	84	.244
— Birmingham (Sou.)	3	1	.750	4.38	1.46	7	7	0	0	...	0-...	39.0	39	22	19	4	18-0	27	.258
2000— Charlotte (Int'l)	9	2	.818	2.26	1.26	16	16	2	1	...	0-...	103.2	99	28	26	3	32-2	63	.251
— Chicago (A.L.)	4	8	.333	6.46	1.75	15	13	0	0	1	0-0	69.2	82	55	50	10	40-0	42	.292
— Birmingham (Sou.)	0	0	...	0.00	0.83	1	1	0	0	...	0-...	6.0	4	0	0	0	1-0	10	.200
2001— Charlotte (Int'l)	0	3	.000	2.73	1.27	5	5	1	0	...	0-...	33.0	31	10	10	1	11-1	26	.261
— Chicago (A.L.)	6	7	.462	3.69	1.52	35	16	0	0	2	1-1	117.0	123	59	48	16	55-2	61	.277
2002— Chicago (A.L.)	12	12	.500	4.58	1.41	33	33	1	0	0	0-0	192.2	188	109	98	23	83-1	112	.258
2003— Chicago (A.L.)	12	13	.480	4.51	1.37	32	32	0	0	0	0-0	191.2	188	103	96	28	74-1	108	.261
2004— Chicago (A.L.)	12	11	.522	4.89	1.38	34	33	1	0	0	0-0	217.0	223	125	118	34	76-2	113	.269
2005— Chicago (A.L.)	18	10	.643	3.50	1.17	32	32	3	3	0	0-0	221.0	212	93	86	26	47-3	115	.255
2006— Chicago (A.L.)	18	7	.720	4.51	1.36	33	32	1	1	0	0-0	211.1	247	112	106	26	41-4	112	.294
Major League totals (7 years)	82	68	.547	4.44	1.38	214	191	6	5	3	1-1	1220.1	1263	656	602	163	416-13	663	.270

CHAMPIONSHIP SERIES RECORD

Year Team (League)	W	L	Pct.	ERA	WHIP	G	GS	CG	ShO	Hld.	Sv.-Opp.	IP	H	R	ER	HR	BB-IBB	SO	Avg.
2005— Chicago (A.L.)	1	0	1.000	2.00	0.56	1	1	1	0	0	0-0	9.0	4	2	2	1	1-0	7	.138

WORLD SERIES RECORD

Year Team (League)	W	L	Pct.	ERA	WHIP	G	GS	CG	ShO	Hld.	Sv.-Opp.	IP	H	R	ER	HR	BB-IBB	SO	Avg.
2005— Chicago (A.L.)	0	0	...	2.57	1.29	1	1	0	0	0	0-0	7.0	7	4	2	1	2-0	4	.292

ALL-STAR GAME RECORD

Year Team (League)	W	L	Pct.	ERA	WHIP	G	GS	CG	ShO	Hld.	Sv.-Opp.	IP	H	R	ER	HR	BB-IBB	SO	Avg.
All-Star Game totals (1 year)	0	0	...	0.00	2.00	1	0	0	0	0	0-0	1.0	0	0	0	0	2-0	0	.000

2006 LEFTY-RIGHTY SPLITS

vs.	Avg.	AB	H	2B	3B	HR	RBI	BB	SO	OBP	Slg.	vs.	Avg.	AB	H	2B	3B	HR	RBI	BB	SO	OBP	Slg.
L	.290	359	104	17	4	10	39	19	50	.328	.443	R	.297	481	143	34	1	16	61	22	62	.329	.472

GARZA, MATT — P

PERSONAL: Born November 11, 1983, in Selma, Calif. ... Throws right, bats right. ... Full name: Matthew Scott Garza. ... College: Fresno State. **TRANSACTIONS/CAREER NOTES:** Selected by Minnesota Twins organization in first round (25th pick overall) of 2005 free-agent draft.

CAREER HITTING: 0-for-0 (.000), 0 R, 0 2B, 0 3B, 0 HR, 0 RBI.

Year Team (League)	W	L	Pct.	ERA	WHIP	G	GS	CG	ShO	Hld.	Sv.-Opp.	IP	H	R	ER	HR	BB-IBB	SO	Avg.
2005— Elizabethton (App.)	1	1	.500	3.66	1.02	4	4	0	0	0	0-0	19.2	14	10	8	3	6-0	25	.200
— Beloit (Midw.)	3	3	.500	3.54	1.21	10	10	0	0	0	0-0	56.0	53	24	22	5	15-0	64	.251
2006— New Britain (East.)	6	2	.750	2.51	0.94	10	10	0	0	0	0-0	57.1	40	22	16	2	14-0	68	.190
— Rochester (Int'l)	3	1	.750	1.85	0.79	5	5	2	1	0	0-0	34.0	20	7	7	1	7-0	33	.174
— Fort Myers (FSL)	5	1	.833	1.42	0.86	8	8	0	0	0	0-0	44.1	27	13	7	3	11-0	53	.169
— Minnesota (A.L.)	3	6	.333	5.76	1.70	10	9	0	0	0	0-0	50.0	62	33	32	6	23-0	38	.301
Major League totals (1 year)	3	6	.333	5.76	1.70	10	9	0	0	0	0-0	50.0	62	33	32	6	23-0	38	.301

2006 LEFTY-RIGHTY SPLITS

vs.	Avg.	AB	H	2B	3B	HR	RBI	BB	SO	OBP	Slg.	vs.	Avg.	AB	H	2B	3B	HR	RBI	BB	SO	OBP	Slg.
L	.245	102	25	7	0	1	14	13	21	.325	.343	R	.356	104	37	7	2	5	18	10	17	.409	.606

GASSNER, DAVE — P

PERSONAL: Born December 14, 1978, in Hortonville, Wis. ... 6-2/190. ... Throws left, bats right. ... Full name: David K. Gassner. ... College: Purdue.
TRANSACTIONS/CAREER NOTES: Selected by Toronto Blue Jays organization in 24th round of 2001 free-agent draft. ... Traded by Blue Jays to Minnesota Twins (December

G

15, 2003); completed trade in which Twins traded OF Bobby Kielty to Blue Jays for OF Shannon Stewart and a player to be named (July 16, 2003). ... On disabled list (March 29-August 2, 2006); included rehabilitation assignments to GCL Twins and Fort Myers.

CAREER HITTING: 0-for-0 (.000), 0 R, 0 2B, 0 3B, 0 HR, 0 RBI.

Year Team (League)	W	L	Pct.	ERA	WHIP	G	GS	CG	ShO	Hld.	Sv.-Opp.	IP	H	R	ER	HR	BB-IBB	SO	Avg.
2001— Char., W.Va. (SAL)	4	4	.500	3.03	1.12	13	11	1	0	...	0-...	74.1	72	30	25	3	11-0	51	.247
2002— Dunedin (Fla. St.)	11	6	.647	3.44	1.15	23	21	2	1	...	0-...	146.2	143	64	56	17	26-1	104	.255
— Syracuse (Int'l)	0	1	.000	5.40	1.80	1	1	0	0	...	0-...	5.0	7	3	3	0	2-0	1	.333
— Tennessee (Sou.)	1	2	.333	2.49	1.14	4	4	0	0	...	0-...	25.1	22	8	7	1	7-1	14	.232
2003— New Haven (East.)	10	4	.714	2.79	1.15	35	19	1	0	...	1-...	145.1	139	54	45	10	28-1	92	.253
— Syracuse (Int'l)	1	0	1.000	1.80	1.20	1	1	0	0	...	0-...	5.0	5	1	1	0	1-0	4	.250
2004— Rochester (Int'l)	16	8	.667	3.41	1.18	28	28	0	0	...	0-...	174.1	175	72	66	16	30-1	93	.265
2005— Minnesota (A.L.)	1	0	1.000	5.87	1.30	2	2	0	0	0	0-0	7.2	9	7	5	1	1-0	2	.281
— Rochester (Int'l)	8	8	.500	4.95	1.47	22	20	2	0	0	0-0	116.1	138	65	64	18	33-0	64	.302
2006— Fort Myers (FSL)	0	1	.000	3.75	1.08	3	3	0	0	0	0-0	12.0	11	5	5	1	2-0	5	.239
— Rochester (Int'l)	2	0	1.000	4.73	1.43	6	5	0	0	0	0-0	26.2	29	15	14	2	9-0	14	.293
— GC Twins (GCL)	0	0	...	3.60	0.80	2	2	0	0	0	0-0	5.0	4	3	2	0	0-0	4	.235
Major League totals (1 year)	**1**	**0**	**1.000**	**5.87**	**1.30**	**2**	**2**	**0**	**0**	**0**	**0-0**	**7.2**	**9**	**7**	**5**	**1**	**1-0**	**2**	**.281**

GATHRIGHT, JOEY   OF

PERSONAL: Born April 27, 1981, in Hattiesburg, Miss. ... 5-10/170. ... Bats left, throws right. ... Full name: Joey Renard Gathright. ... High school: Bonnabel (Kenner, La.).
TRANSACTIONS/CAREER NOTES: Selected by Tampa Bay Devil Rays organization in 32nd round of 2001 free-agent draft. ... Traded by Devil Rays with 2B Fernando Cortez to Kansas City Royals for P J.P. Howell (June 20, 2006).
2006 GAMES PLAYED BY POSITION (MLB): OF—130, DH—1.

Year Team (League)	Pos.	G	AB	R	H	2B	3B	HR	RBI	BB	SO	HBP	GDP	SB-CS	Avg.	OBP	SLG	OPS	E	FIELDING Avg.
2002— Char., S.C. (SAL)	OF	59	208	30	55	1	0	0	14	21	36	10	1	22-7	.264	.360	.269	.629	1	.992
2003— Bakersfield (Calif.)	OF	89	340	65	110	6	3	0	23	41	54	6	3	57-13	.324	.406	.359	.765	3	.981
— Orlando (South.)	OF	22	85	12	32	1	0	0	5	5	15	2	0	12-3	.376	.419	.388	.808	1	.983
2004— Montgom. (Sou.)	OF-DH	32	126	23	43	5	1	0	8	11	30	1	1	10-6	.341	.399	.397	.795	1	.985
— Tampa Bay (A.L.)	OF-DH	19	52	11	13	0	0	0	1	2	14	3	2	6-1	.250	.316	.250	.566	0	1.000
— Durham (Int'l)	OF	60	236	34	77	9	1	0	8	19	46	3	5	33-13	.326	.384	.373	.749	4	.968
2005— Durham (Int'l)	OF-DH	58	226	46	69	10	5	1	18	29	47	2	0	31-8	.305	.388	.407	.795	14	.948
— Tampa Bay (A.L.)	OF-DH	76	203	29	56	7	3	0	13	10	39	2	5	20-5	.276	.316	.340	.656	3	.984
2006— Tampa Bay (A.L.)	OF	55	154	25	31	6	0	0	13	20	30	3	1	12-3	.201	.305	.240	.545	1	.994
— Durham (Int'l)		10	31	5	8	2	0	0	1	6	3	2	0	6-2	.258	.410	.323	.733	0	1.000
— Kansas City (A.L.)	OF-DH	79	229	34	60	3	1	0	28	22	45	4	2	10-6	.262	.332	.328	.660	2	.990
Major League totals (3 years)		**229**	**638**	**99**	**160**	**19**	**6**	**1**	**55**	**54**	**128**	**12**	**10**	**48-15**	**.251**	**.319**	**.304**	**.623**	**6**	**.989**

2006 LEFTY-RIGHTY SPLITS

vs.	Avg.	AB	H	2B	3B	HR	RBI	BB	SO	OBP	Slg.	vs.	Avg.	AB	H	2B	3B	HR	RBI	BB	SO	OBP	Slg.
L	.232	82	19	1	1	0	8	9	16	.344	.268	R	.239	301	72	11	2	1	33	33	59	.315	.299

GAUDIN, CHAD   P

PERSONAL: Born March 24, 1983, in New Orleans. ... 5-11/165. ... Throws right, bats right. ... Full name: Chad Edward Gaudin. ... High school: Crescent City (Calif.).
TRANSACTIONS/CAREER NOTES: Selected by Tampa Bay Devil Rays organization in 34th round of 2001 free-agent draft. ... Traded by Devil Rays to Toronto Blue Jays for C Kevin Cash (December 12, 2004). ... Traded by Blue Jays to Oakland Athletics for a player to be named (December 4, 2005); Blue Jays acquired OF Dustin Majewski to complete deal (December 8, 2005). **MISCELLANEOUS NOTES:** Appeared in two games as pinch runner (2004).
CAREER HITTING: 0-for-1 (.000), 0 R, 0 2B, 0 3B, 0 HR, 0 RBI.

Year Team (League)	W	L	Pct.	ERA	WHIP	G	GS	CG	ShO	Hld.	Sv.-Opp.	IP	H	R	ER	HR	BB-IBB	SO	Avg.
2002— Char., S.C. (SAL)	4	6	.400	2.26	1.20	26	17	0	0	...	1-...	119.1	106	43	30	5	37-0	106	.244
2003— Bakersfield (Calif.)	5	3	.625	2.13	1.07	14	14	1	0	...	0-...	80.1	63	23	19	2	23-0	70	.214
— Orlando (South.)	2	0	1.000	0.47	0.58	3	3	1	1	...	0-...	19.0	8	1	1	0	3-0	23	.131
— Tampa Bay (A.L.)	2	0	1.000	3.60	1.33	15	3	0	0	0	0-0	40.0	37	18	16	4	16-0	23	.240
2004— Durham (Int'l)	1	3	.250	4.72	1.36	17	7	0	0	...	2-...	47.2	48	26	25	8	17-0	52	.264
— Tampa Bay (A.L.)	1	2	.333	4.85	1.76	26	4	0	0	5	0-1	42.2	59	27	23	4	16-4	30	.337
2005— Toronto (A.L.)	1	3	.250	13.15	2.85	5	3	0	0	0	0-0	13.0	31	19	19	6	6-0	12	.470
— Syracuse (Int'l)	9	8	.529	3.35	1.16	23	23	2	2	0	0-0	150.1	140	61	56	12	35-1	113	.251
2006— Sacramento (PCL)	3	0	1.000	0.37	0.90	4	4	0	0	0	0-0	24.1	14	6	1	0	8-0	26	.173
— Oakland (A.L.)	4	2	.667	3.09	1.45	55	2	0	0	11	2-3	64.0	51	24	22	3	42-2	36	.222
Major League totals (4 years)	**8**	**7**	**.533**	**4.51**	**1.62**	**101**	**10**	**0**	**0**	**16**	**2-4**	**159.2**	**178**	**88**	**80**	**17**	**80-6**	**101**	**.285**

CHAMPIONSHIP SERIES RECORD

Year Team (League)	W	L	Pct.	ERA	WHIP	G	GS	CG	ShO	Hld.	Sv.-Opp.	IP	H	R	ER	HR	BB-IBB	SO	Avg.
2006— Oakland (A.L.)	0	0	...	0.00	1.50	3	0	0	0	0	0-0	3.1	2	0	0	0	3-1	1	.182

2006 LEFTY-RIGHTY SPLITS

vs.	Avg.	AB	H	2B	3B	HR	RBI	BB	SO	OBP	Slg.	vs.	Avg.	AB	H	2B	3B	HR	RBI	BB	SO	OBP	Slg.
L	.253	91	23	4	3	2	7	19	7	.382	.429	R	.201	139	28	6	0	1	13	23	29	.313	.266

GEARY, GEOFF   P

PERSONAL: Born August 26, 1976, in Buffalo, N.Y. ... 6-0/167. ... Throws right, bats right. ... Full name: Geoffrey Michael Geary. ... High school: Grossmont (El Cajon, Calif.). ... College: Oklahoma. **TRANSACTIONS/CAREER NOTES:** Selected by Milwaukee Brewers organization in 41st round of 1997 free-agent draft; did not sign. ... Selected by Philadelphia Phillies organization in 15th round of 1998 free-agent draft. ... On disabled list (July 9-July 24, 2005); included rehabilitation assignment to Reading.
CAREER HITTING: 2-for-12 (.167), 2 R, 1 2B, 0 3B, 0 HR, 1 RBI.

Year Team (League)	W	L	Pct.	ERA	WHIP	G	GS	CG	ShO	Hld.	Sv.-Opp.	IP	H	R	ER	HR	BB-IBB	SO	Avg.
1998— Batavia (NY-Penn)	9	1	.900	1.60	0.97	16	15	1	1	...	0-...	95.1	78	20	17	6	14-0	101	.222
1999— Clearwater (FSL)	10	5	.667	3.95	1.48	24	19	2	0	...	0-...	139.0	175	77	61	11	31-1	75	.310
2000— Reading (East.)	7	6	.538	4.11	1.26	22	22	1	0	...	0-...	129.1	141	66	59	15	22-0	112	.272
2001— Reading (East.)	9	7	.563	3.61	1.09	29	13	0	0	...	2-...	112.1	101	48	45	14	21-3	88	.245
— Scran./W.B. (I.L.)	0	3	.000	6.95	1.86	7	3	0	0	...	0-...	22.0	35	17	17	2	6-1	21	.376
2002— Scran./W.B. (I.L.)	4	2	.667	3.03	1.39	38	8	0	0	...	1-...	101.0	108	46	34	9	32-1	82	.277
2003— Scran./W.B. (I.L.)	9	4	.692	2.16	0.98	46	3	0	0	...	5-...	87.2	73	26	21	3	13-1	80	.229
— Philadelphia (N.L.)	0	0	...	4.50	1.83	5	0	0	0	0	0-0	6.0	8	3	3	0	3-0	5	.333
2004— Scran./W.B. (I.L.)	1	2	.333	2.31	1.41	21	0	0	0	...	10-...	23.1	20	7	6	1	13-4	23	.235

G

Year Team (League)	W	L	Pct.	ERA	WHIP	G	GS	CG	ShO	Hld.	Sv.-Opp.	IP	H	R	ER	HR	BB-IBB	SO	Avg.
— Philadelphia (N.L.)	1	0	1.000	5.44	1.52	33	0	0	0	0	0-0	44.2	52	29	27	8	16-3	30	.292
2005—Scran./W.B. (I.L.)	1	2	.333	2.70	1.02	10	0	0	0	1	1-2	16.2	15	5	5	0	2-0	14	.238
—Reading (East.)	0	0	...	0.00	0.00	1	0	0	0	0	0-0	2.0	0	0	0	0	0-0	2	.000
—Philadelphia (N.L.)	2	1	.667	3.72	1.29	40	0	0	0	3	0-1	58.0	54	29	24	5	21-4	42	.248
2006—Philadelphia (N.L.)	7	1	.875	2.96	1.35	81	0	0	0	15	1-4	91.1	103	34	30	6	20-4	60	.287
Major League totals (4 years)	10	2	.833	3.78	1.39	159	0	0	0	18	1-5	200.0	217	95	84	19	60-11	135	.279

2006 LEFTY-RIGHTY SPLITS

vs.	Avg.	AB	H	2B	3B	HR	RBI	BB	SO	OBP	Slg.	vs.	Avg.	AB	H	2B	3B	HR	RBI	BB	SO	OBP	Slg.
L	.348	138	48	8	1	5	17	10	23	.396	.529	R	.249	221	55	5	1	1	16	10	37	.295	.294

GERMAN, ESTEBAN — IF/OF

PERSONAL: Born January 26, 1978, in Santo Domingo, Dominican Republic. ... 5-9/165. ... Bats right, throws right. ... Full name: Esteban German Guridi. ... Name pronounced: her-MAHN. **TRANSACTIONS/CAREER NOTES:** Traded by Rangers to Kansas City Royals for P Fabio Castro (December 8, 2005). ... Signed as a non-drafted free agent by Oakland Athletics organization (July 4, 1996). ... On disabled list (July 4-31, 2004); included rehabilitation assignment to Sacramento. ... Signed as a free agent by Texas Rangers organization (November 19, 2004). ... Traded by Rangers to Kansas City Royals for P Fabio Castro (December 8, 2005).
2006 GAMES PLAYED BY POSITION (MLB): 2B—26, DH—25, OF—25, 3B—24, SS—1, 1B—1.

Year Team (League)	Pos.	G	AB	R	H	2B	3B	HR	RBI	BB	SO	HBP	GDP	SB-CS	Avg.	OBP	SLG	OPS	E	Avg.
1997—Dom. Athletics (DSL)		69	249	69	79	17	1	2	29	73	30	...	...	58-...	.317	...	.418	...		
1998—Dom. Athletics (DSL)		10	32	9	10	1	1	0	4	7	2	...	...	1-...	.313	...	.406	...		
—Ariz. A's (Ariz.)	2B	55	202	52	62	3	10	2	28	33	43	4	1	40-8	.307	.413	.451	.863	13	.940
1999—Modesto (California)	2B	128	501	107	156	16	12	4	52	102	128	5	3	40-16	.311	.428	.415	.843	38	.932
2000—Midland (Texas)	2B	24	75	13	16	1	0	1	6	18	21	2	1	5-3	.213	.379	.267	.646	5	.951
—Visalia (Calif.)	2B-SS	109	428	82	113	14	10	2	35	61	86	5	4	78-8	.264	.361	.357	.718	25	.954
2001—Midland (Texas)	2B	92	335	79	95	20	3	6	30	63	66	12	6	31-11	.284	.415	.415	.830	16	.963
—Sacramento (PCL)	2B	38	150	40	56	8	0	4	14	18	20	6	4	17-2	.373	.457	.507	.964	7	.962
2002—Sacramento (PCL)	2B	121	458	72	126	16	4	2	43	78	66	8	7	26-14	.275	.390	.341	.730	8	.986
—Oakland (A.L.)	2B	9	35	4	7	0	0	0	0	4	11	1	0	1-0	.200	.300	.200	.500	1	.978
2003—Sacramento (PCL)	2B	115	467	86	143	20	8	3	51	56	64	2	17	32-8	.306	.379	.403	.781	13	.976
—Oakland (A.L.)	2B	5	4	0	1	0	0	0	1	0	1	0	1	0-0	.250	.250	.250	.500	0	1.000
2004—Sacramento (PCL)	2B-SS-DH	55	231	33	76	8	4	2	29	19	28	3	6	18-2	.329	.380	.424	.804	9	.961
—Oakland (A.L.)	3B-2B-DH	31	60	9	15	1	1	0	7	4	13	0	1	0-1	.250	.297	.300	.597	2	.967
2005—Oklahoma (PCL)	3B-SS-DH-2B-OF	117	489	103	153	27	6	5	68	65	74	7	20	43-6	.313	.400	.423	.823	15	.954
—Texas (A.L.)	2B-3B-DH	5	4	3	3	1	0	0	1	0	2	0	0	0-0	.750	.750	1.000	1.750	1	.917
2006—Kansas City (A.L.)	2B-OF-DH-3B-1B-SS	106	279	44	91	18	5	3	34	40	49	6	8	7-3	.326	.422	.459	.880	8	.956
Major League totals (5 years)		156	382	60	117	20	6	3	43	48	75	7	10	10-4	.306	.394	.414	.807	12	.962

2006 LEFTY-RIGHTY SPLITS

vs.	Avg.	AB	H	2B	3B	HR	RBI	BB	SO	OBP	Slg.	vs.	Avg.	AB	H	2B	3B	HR	RBI	BB	SO	OBP	Slg.
L	.347	118	41	7	3	1	15	17	20	.430	.483	R	.311	161	50	11	2	2	19	23	29	.416	.441

GERMAN, FRANKLYN — P

PERSONAL: Born January 20, 1980, in San Cristobal, Dominican Republic. ... 6-7/270. ... Throws right, bats right. ... Full name: Franklyn Miguel German. ... Name pronounced: her-MAHN. **TRANSACTIONS/CAREER NOTES:** Signed as a non-drafted free agent by Oakland Athletics organization (July 2, 1996). ... Traded by A's with 1B Carlos Pena and a player to be named to Detroit Tigers as part of three-team deal in which New York Yankees acquired P Jeff Weaver from Tigers and A's acquired Ps Ted Lilly and Jason Arnold and OF John-Ford Griffin from Yankees (July 6, 2002); Tigers acquired P Jeremy Bonderman to complete deal (August 22, 2002).
CAREER HITTING: 0-for-1 (.000), 0 R, 0 2B, 0 3B, 0 HR, 0 RBI.

Year Team (League)	W	L	Pct.	ERA	WHIP	G	GS	CG	ShO	Hld.	Sv.-Opp.	IP	H	R	ER	HR	BB-IBB	SO	Avg.
1997—Dom. Athletics (DSL)	8	3	.727	2.33	1.09	13	13	5	...	...	0-...	89.0	66	33	23	...	31-...	80	...
1998—Ariz. A's (Ariz.)	2	1	.667	6.13	1.60	14	12	0	0	...	0-...	54.1	69	43	37	5	18-0	48	.317
1999—S. Oregon (N'west)	3	5	.375	5.99	1.82	15	15	0	0	...	0-...	73.2	89	52	49	10	45-1	58	.306
2000—Modesto (California)	5	5	.500	5.50	1.74	17	14	0	0	...	0-...	72.0	88	55	44	4	37-0	52	.307
—Vancouver (N'west)	1	0	1.000	1.77	1.13	9	2	0	0	...	0-...	20.1	13	4	4	0	10-0	20	.173
2001—Visalia (Calif.)	2	4	.333	3.98	1.55	53	0	0	0	...	19-...	63.1	67	34	28	7	31-1	93	.262
2002—Midland (Texas)	1	1	.500	3.05	1.33	37	0	0	0	...	16-...	41.1	28	14	14	0	27-2	59	.194
—Toledo (Int'l)	1	1	.500	1.59	0.97	23	0	0	0	...	13-...	22.2	15	4	4	0	7-0	31	.158
—Detroit (A.L.)	1	0	1.000	0.00	0.75	7	0	0	0	1	1-1	6.2	3	0	0	0	2-1	6	.150
2003—Toledo (Int'l)	1	4	.200	2.45	1.00	24	0	0	0	...	4-...	29.1	21	9	8	2	9-1	32	.212
—Detroit (A.L.)	2	4	.333	6.04	2.06	45	0	0	0	...	5-7	44.2	47	32	30	5	45-3	41	.273
2004—Toledo (Int'l)	3	5	.375	4.59	1.45	49	0	0	0	...	27-...	49.0	46	25	25	6	25-2	60	.246
—Detroit (A.L.)	1	0	1.000	7.36	1.91	16	0	0	0	...	0-1	14.2	17	15	12	4	11-1	8	.279
2005—Detroit (A.L.)	4	0	1.000	3.66	1.64	58	0	0	0	4	1-3	59.0	63	26	24	7	34-4	38	.284
2006—Florida (N.L.)	0	0	...	3.00	1.75	12	0	0	0	0	0-1	12.0	7	4	4	1	14-2	6	.171
American League totals (4 years)	8	4	.667	4.75	1.78	126	0	0	0	10	7-12	125.0	130	73	66	16	92-9	93	.274
National League totals (1 year)	0	0	...	3.00	1.75	12	0	0	0	0	0-1	12.0	7	4	4	1	14-2	6	.171
Major League totals (5 years)	8	4	.667	4.60	1.77	138	0	0	0	11	7-13	137.0	137	77	70	17	106-11	99	.266

2006 LEFTY-RIGHTY SPLITS

vs.	Avg.	AB	H	2B	3B	HR	RBI	BB	SO	OBP	Slg.	vs.	Avg.	AB	H	2B	3B	HR	RBI	BB	SO	OBP	Slg.
L	.235	17	4	1	0	1	2	10	1	.519	.471	R	.125	24	3	1	0	0	3	4	5	.276	.167

GERMANO, JUSTIN — P

PERSONAL: Born August 6, 1982, in Pasadena, Calif. ... 6-1/190. ... Throws right, bats right. ... Full name: Justin William Germano. ... High school: Claremont (Calif.). **TRANSACTIONS/CAREER NOTES:** Selected by San Diego Padres organization in 13th round of 2000 free-agent draft. ... Traded by Padres to Cincinnati Reds for 3B Joe Randa (July 23, 2005). ... Traded by Reds to Philadelphia Phillies for P Rheal Cormier (July 31, 2006).
CAREER HITTING: 0-for-9 (.000), 0 R, 0 2B, 0 3B, 0 HR, 0 RBI.

Year Team (League)	W	L	Pct.	ERA	WHIP	G	GS	CG	ShO	Hld.	Sv.-Opp.	IP	H	R	ER	HR	BB-IBB	SO	Avg.
2000—Ariz. Padres (Ariz.)	5	5	.500	4.59	1.11	17	8	0	0	...	1-...	66.2	65	36	34	4	9-0	67	.249
2001—Fort Wayne (Midw.)	2	6	.250	4.98	1.48	13	13	0	0	...	0-...	65.0	80	47	36	7	16-1	55	.302
—Eugene (Northwest)	6	5	.545	3.49	1.10	13	13	2	0	...	0-...	80.0	77	35	31	5	11-0	74	.246

G

Year	Team (League)	W	L	Pct.	ERA	WHIP	G	GS	CG	ShO	Hld.	Sv.-Opp.	IP	H	R	ER	HR	BB-IBB	SO	Avg.
2002— Fort Wayne (Midw.)		12	5	.706	3.18	1.19	24	24	1	0	...	0-...	155.2	166	63	55	14	19-2	119	.269
— Lake Elsinore (Calif.)		2	0	1.000	0.95	0.89	3	3	0	0	...	0-...	19.0	12	3	2	1	5-0	18	.174
2003— Lake Elsinore (Calif.)		9	5	.643	4.23	1.37	19	19	1	0	...	0-...	110.2	127	61	52	4	25-1	78	.287
— Mobile (Sou.)		2	5	.286	4.34	1.26	9	9	1	0	...	0-...	58.0	60	34	28	6	13-3	44	.268
2004— Mobile (Sou.)		2	1	.667	2.51	1.18	5	5	0	0	...	0-...	32.1	31	11	9	3	7-0	20	.258
— Portland (PCL)		9	5	.643	3.38	1.13	20	20	2	2	...	0-...	122.2	113	48	46	12	25-0	98	.241
— San Diego (N.L.)		1	2	.333	8.86	2.11	7	5	0	0	...	0-0	21.1	31	24	21	2	14-0	16	.341
2005— Portland (PCL)		7	6	.538	3.70	1.28	19	19	1	1	0	0-0	112.0	111	56	46	13	32-1	100	.259
— Louisville (Int'l)		3	2	.600	4.01	1.36	8	8	0	0	0	0-0	49.1	62	27	22	7	5-0	38	.313
2006— Scran./W.B. (I.L.)		2	0	1.000	2.82	1.10	6	6	0	0	0	0-0	38.1	40	13	12	2	2-0	25	.265
— Louisville (Int'l)		8	6	.571	3.69	1.25	19	19	0	0	0	0-0	117.0	124	53	48	11	22-0	67	.279
— Cincinnati (N.L.)		0	1	.000	5.40	1.65	2	1	0	0	0	0-0	6.2	8	4	4	1	3-1	5	.296
Major League totals (2 years)		1	3	.250	8.04	2.00	9	6	0	0	0	0-0	28.0	39	28	25	3	17-1	24	.331

2006 LEFTY-RIGHTY SPLITS

vs.	Avg.	AB	H	2B	3B	HR	RBI	BB	SO	OBP	Slg.	vs.	Avg.	AB	H	2B	3B	HR	RBI	BB	SO	OBP	Slg.
L	.000	6	0	0	0	0	0	2	2	.250	.000	R	.381	21	8	1	0	1	4	1	6	.435	.571

GIAMBI, JASON — 1B/DH

PERSONAL: Born January 8, 1971, in West Covina, Calif. ... 6-3/230. ... Bats left, throws right. ... Full name: Jason Gilbert Giambi. ... Name pronounced: gee-OM-bee. ... High school: South Hills (West Covina, Calif.). ... College: Long Beach State. ... Brother of Jeremy Giambi, first baseman/outfielder with four major league teams (1998-2003). **TRANSACTIONS/CAREER NOTES:** Selected by Milwaukee Brewers organization in 43rd round of 1989 free-agent draft; did not sign. ... Selected by Oakland Athletics organization in second round of 1992 free-agent draft. ... Signed as a free agent by New York Yankees (December 18, 2001). ... On disabled list (May 22-June 6 and July 26-September 14, 2004); included rehabilitation assignments to Tampa and Columbus. **HONORS:** Named A.L. Comeback Player of the Year by the SPORTING NEWS (2005). ... Named first baseman on THE SPORTING NEWS A.L. All-Star team (2002). ... Named A.L. Most Valuable Player by Baseball Writers' Association of America (2000). ... Named first baseman on A.L. Silver Slugger team (2001 and 2002). **STATISTICAL NOTES:** Career major league grand slams: 11. **MISCELLANEOUS NOTES:** Member of 1992 U.S. Olympic baseball team.

2006 GAMES PLAYED BY POSITION (MLB): DH—70, 1B—68.

Year	Team (League)	Pos.	G	AB	R	H	2B	3B	HR	RBI	BB	SO	HBP	GDP	SB-CS	Avg.	OBP	SLG	OPS	E	Avg.
1992— S. Oregon (N'west)		3B	13	41	9	13	3	0	3	13	9	6	0	0	1-1	.317	.440	.610	1.050	1	.962
1993— Modesto (California)		3B	89	313	72	91	16	2	12	60	73	47	10	12	2-3	.291	.436	.470	.906	19	.911
1994— Huntsville (Sou.)		1B-3B	56	193	31	43	9	0	6	30	27	31	2	8	0-0	.223	.319	.363	.681	11	.945
— Tacoma (PCL)		3B-SS	52	176	28	56	20	4	4	38	25	32	0	1	1-0	.318	.388	.500	.888	8	.949
1995— Edmonton (PCL)		3B-DH-1B	55	190	34	65	26	1	3	41	34	26	2	4	0-0	.342	.444	.537	.978	9	.938
— Oakland (A.L.)		3B-1B-DH	54	176	27	45	7	0	6	25	28	31	3	4	2-1	.256	.364	.398	.761	4	.984
1996— Oakland (A.L.)		DH	140	536	84	156	40	1	20	79	51	95	5	15	0-1	.291	.355	.481	.836	11	.982
1997— Oakland (A.L.)		OF-1B-DH	142	519	66	152	41	2	20	81	55	89	6	11	0-1	.293	.362	.495	.857	7	.987
1998— Oakland (A.L.)		1B-DH	153	562	92	166	28	0	27	110	81	102	5	16	2-2	.295	.384	.489	.873	*14	.990
1999— Oakland (A.L.)		1B-DH-3B	158	575	115	181	36	1	33	123	105	106	7	11	1-1	.315	.422	.553	.975	7	.995
2000— Oakland (A.L.)		1B-DH	152	510	108	170	29	1	43	137	*137	96	9	9	2-0	.333	*.476	.647	1.123	6	.995
2001— Oakland (A.L.)		1B-DH	154	520	109	178	*47	2	38	120	*129	83	13	17	2-0	.342	*.477	*.660	1.137	11	.992
2002— New York (A.L.)		1B-DH	155	560	120	176	34	1	41	122	109	112	15	18	2-2	.314	.435	.598	1.034	4	.995
2003— New York (A.L.)		1B-DH	156	535	97	134	25	0	41	*107	*129	140	*21	9	2-1	.250	.412	.527	.939	4	.995
2004— Tampa (Fla. St.)		1B	2	6	0	1	0	0	0	1	1	0	0	0	0-0	.167	.286	.167	.452	0	1.000
— New York (A.L.)		1B-DH	80	264	33	55	9	0	12	40	47	62	8	5	0-0	.208	.342	.379	.720	4	.990
2005— New York (A.L.)		1B-DH	139	417	74	113	14	0	32	87	*108	109	19	7	0-0	.271	*.440	.535	.975	7	.988
2006— New York (A.L.)		DH-1B	139	446	92	113	25	0	37	113	110	106	16	10	2-0	.253	.413	.558	.971	7	.985
Major League totals (12 years)			1622	5620	1017	1639	335	8	350	1144	1089	1131	127	132	15-10	.292	.413	.541	.954	86	.991

DIVISION SERIES RECORD

Year	Team (League)	Pos.	G	AB	R	H	2B	3B	HR	RBI	BB	SO	HBP	GDP	SB-CS	Avg.	OBP	SLG	OPS	E	Avg.
2000— Oakland (A.L.)		1B	5	14	2	4	0	0	0	1	7	2	0	0	1-0	.286	.500	.286	.786	1	.976
2001— Oakland (A.L.)		1B	5	17	2	6	0	0	1	4	4	2	0	1	0-0	.353	.455	.529	.984	1	.982
2002— New York (A.L.)		1B-DH	4	14	5	5	0	0	1	3	4	1	1	1	0-0	.357	.556	.571	1.098	0	1.000
2003— New York (A.L.)		DH	4	16	1	4	2	0	0	2	5	5	0	0	0-0	.250	.333	.375	.708	0	...
2005— New York (A.L.)		1B-DH	5	19	1	8	3	0	1	2	3	4	0	0	0-0	.421	.500	.579	1.079	0	1.000
2006— New York (A.L.)		DH-1B	3	8	1	1	0	0	1	2	2	3	2	0	1-0	.125	.417	.500	.917	0	1.000
Division series totals (6 years)			26	88	12	28	5	0	3	14	22	17	3	2	2-0	.318	.461	.477	.938	2	.987

CHAMPIONSHIP SERIES RECORD

Year	Team (League)	Pos.	G	AB	R	H	2B	3B	HR	RBI	BB	SO	HBP	GDP	SB-CS	Avg.	OBP	SLG	OPS	E	Avg.
2003— New York (A.L.)		DH	7	26	4	6	0	0	3	3	4	7	0	0	0-0	.231	.333	.577	.910	0	...

WORLD SERIES RECORD

Year	Team (League)	Pos.	G	AB	R	H	2B	3B	HR	RBI	BB	SO	HBP	GDP	SB-CS	Avg.	OBP	SLG	OPS	E	Avg.
2003— New York (A.L.)		DH-1B	6	17	2	4	1	0	1	1	4	3	1	1	0-0	.235	.409	.471	.880	0	1.000

ALL-STAR GAME RECORD

Year	Team (League)		G	AB	R	H	2B	3B	HR	RBI	BB	SO	HBP	GDP	SB-CS	Avg.	OBP	SLG	OPS	E	Avg.
All-Star Game totals (5 years)			5	8	4	3	0	0	1	1	1	3	0	0	0-0	.375	.444	.750	1.194	0	1.000

2006 LEFTY-RIGHTY SPLITS

vs.	Avg.	AB	H	2B	3B	HR	RBI	BB	SO	OBP	Slg.	vs.	Avg.	AB	H	2B	3B	HR	RBI	BB	SO	OBP	Slg.
L	.213	127	27	6	0	9	32	21	36	.356	.472	R	.270	319	86	19	0	28	81	89	70	.434	.592

GIBBONS, JAY — OF/1B

PERSONAL: Born March 2, 1977, in Rochester, Mich. ... 6-0/197. ... Bats left, throws left. ... Full name: Jay Jonathon Gibbons. ... High school: Mayfair (Lakewood, Calif.). ... College: Cal State Los Angeles. **TRANSACTIONS/CAREER NOTES:** Selected by Toronto Blue Jays organization in 14th round of 1998 free-agent draft. ... Selected by Baltimore Orioles from Blue Jays organization in Rule 5 major league draft (December 11, 2000). ... On disabled list (August 5, 2001-remainder of season). ... On disabled list (May 26-June 14 and June 29-August 10, 2004); included rehabilitation assignments to Frederick and Bowie. ... On disabled list (May 28-June 12 and June 14-July 29, 2006); included rehabilitation assignments to Bowie and Frederick. **STATISTICAL NOTES:** Career major league grand slams: 2.

2006 GAMES PLAYED BY POSITION (MLB): DH—46, OF—44.

Year	Team (League)	Pos.	G	AB	R	H	2B	3B	HR	RBI	BB	SO	HBP	GDP	SB-CS	Avg.	OBP	SLG	OPS	E	Avg.
1998— Medicine Hat (Pio.)		1B	73	290	66	115	29	1	19	98	37	25	3	7	2-1	.397	.457	.700	1.157	6	.983

G

Year Team (League)	Pos.	G	AB	R	H	2B	3B	HR	RBI	BB	SO	HBP	GDP	SB-CS	Avg.	OBP	SLG	OPS	E	Avg.
1999— Hagerstown (SAL)	1B-OF	71	292	53	89	20	2	16	69	32	56	1	12	3-0	.305	.370	.551	.921	6	.975
— Dunedin (Fla. St.)	1B	60	212	34	66	14	0	9	39	25	38	0	4	2-1	.311	.382	.505	.887	5	.991
2000— Tennessee (Sou.)	1B-OF	132	474	85	152	38	1	19	75	61	67	10	10	3-1	.321	.404	.525	.929	8	.991
2001— Baltimore (A.L.)	DH-OF-1B	73	225	27	53	10	0	15	36	17	39	4	7	0-1	.236	.301	.480	.781	0	1.000
2002— Baltimore (A.L.)	OF-1B-DH	136	490	71	121	29	1	28	69	45	66	2	9	1-3	.247	.311	.482	.792	2	.995
2003— Baltimore (A.L.)	OF-1B-DH	160	625	80	173	39	2	23	100	49	89	3	12	0-1	.277	.330	.456	.786	6	.985
2004— Frederick (Carolina)	OF-DH	3	11	2	2	1	0	1	5	2	2	0	0	0-0	.182	.308	.545	.853	0	...
— Bowie (East.)	OF-DH	5	15	3	1	0	0	0	1	2	2	0	1	0-0	.067	.167	.067	.233	0	1.000
— Baltimore (A.L.)	OF-DH-1B	97	346	36	85	14	1	10	47	29	64	1	11	1-1	.246	.303	.379	.682	3	.988
2005— Baltimore (A.L.)	OF-DH-1B	139	488	72	135	33	3	26	79	28	56	1	15	0-0	.277	.317	.516	.833	3	.991
2006— Frederick (Carolina)		2	8	1	0	0	0	0	0	0	4	0	0	0-0	.000	.000	.000	.000	0	...
— Bowie (East.)		3	10	2	4	0	0	0	1	1	1	0	1	0-0	.400	.455	.600	1.055	0	...
— Baltimore (A.L.)	DH-OF	90	343	34	95	23	0	13	46	32	48	2	12	0-0	.277	.341	.458	.799	2	.980
Major League totals (6 years)		695	2517	320	662	148	7	115	377	200	362	13	66	2-6	.263	.319	.464	.783	16	.990

2006 LEFTY-RIGHTY SPLITS

vs.	Avg.	AB	H	2B	3B	HR	RBI	BB	SO	OBP	Slg.	vs.	Avg.	AB	H	2B	3B	HR	RBI	BB	SO	OBP	Slg.
L	.258	62	16	3	0	2	7	2	12	.277	.403	R	.281	281	79	20	0	11	39	30	36	.355	.470

GILES, BRIAN — OF

PERSONAL: Born January 20, 1971, in El Cajon, Cálif. ... 5-10/205. ... Bats left, throws left. ... Full name: Brian Stephen Giles. ... Name pronounced: JYLES. ... High school: Granite Hills (El Cajon, Calif.). ... Brother of Marcus Giles, second baseman, Atlanta Braves. **TRANSACTIONS/CAREER NOTES:** Selected by Cleveland Indians organization in 17th round of 1989 free-agent draft. ... On disabled list (June 1-July 7, 1998); included rehabilitation assignment to Buffalo. ... Traded by Indians to Pittsburgh Pirates for P Ricardo Rincon (November 18, 1998). ... On disabled list (April 11-May 7, 2003). ... Traded by Pirates to San Diego Padres for P Oliver Perez, OF Jason Bay and a player to be named (August 26, 2003); Padres acquired P Cory Stewart to complete deal (October 2, 2003). **STATISTICAL NOTES:** Career major league grand slams: 5.

2006 GAMES PLAYED BY POSITION (MLB): OF—158.

Year Team (League)	Pos.	G	AB	R	H	2B	3B	HR	RBI	BB	SO	HBP	GDP	SB-CS	Avg.	OBP	SLG	OPS	E	Avg.
1989— Burlington (Appal.)	OF	36	129	18	40	7	0	0	20	11	19	1	0	6-3	.310	.366	.364	.731	1	.982
1990— Watertown (NYP)	OF	70	246	44	71	15	2	1	23	48	23	0	3	11-8	.289	.403	.378	.781	1	.991
1991— Kinston (Carol.)	OF	125	394	71	122	14	0	4	47	68	70	2	5	19-7	.310	.411	.376	.787	5	.975
1992— Cant./Akr. (Eastern)	OF	23	74	6	16	4	0	0	3	10	10	0	4	3-1	.216	.310	.270	.580	0	1.000
— Kinston (Carol.)	OF	42	140	28	37	5	1	3	18	30	21	1	5	3-5	.264	.398	.379	.776	1	.987
1993— Cant./Akr. (Eastern)	OF	123	425	64	139	17	6	6	64	57	43	4	9	18-12	.327	.409	.438	.847	5	.974
1994— Charlotte (Int'l)	OF	128	434	74	136	18	3	16	58	55	61	2	5	8-5	.313	.390	.479	.869	4	.985
1995— Buffalo (A.A.)	OF-DH	123	413	67	128	18	8	15	67	54	40	8	9	7-3	.310	.395	.501	.896	5	.981
— Cleveland (A.L.)	OF-DH	6	9	6	5	0	0	1	3	0	1	0	0	0-0	.556	.556	.889	1.444	0	1.000
1996— Buffalo (A.A.)	OF	83	318	65	100	17	6	20	64	42	29	2	4	1-0	.314	.395	.594	.989	3	.986
— Cleveland (A.L.)	DH-OF	51	121	26	43	14	1	5	27	19	13	0	6	3-0	.355	.434	.612	1.045	0	1.000
1997— Cleveland (A.L.)	OF-DH	130	377	62	101	15	3	17	61	63	50	1	10	13-3	.268	.368	.459	.827	6	.972
1998— Cleveland (A.L.)	OF-DH	112	350	56	94	19	0	16	66	73	75	3	7	10-5	.269	.396	.460	.856	5	.978
— Buffalo (Int'l)	OF-DH	13	46	5	11	2	0	2	7	6	8	0	2	0-0	.239	.327	.413	.740	1	.947
1999— Pittsburgh (N.L.)	OF-DH	141	521	109	164	33	3	39	115	95	80	3	14	6-2	.315	.418	.614	1.032	3	.990
2000— Pittsburgh (N.L.)	OF	156	559	111	176	37	7	35	123	114	69	7	15	6-0	.315	.432	.594	1.026	6	.982
2001— Pittsburgh (N.L.)	OF	160	576	116	178	37	7	37	95	90	67	4	10	13-6	.309	.404	.590	.994	10	.969
2002— Pittsburgh (N.L.)	OF	153	497	95	148	37	5	38	103	135	74	7	10	15-6	.298	.450	.622	1.072	7	.973
2003— Pittsburgh (N.L.)	OF	105	388	70	116	30	4	16	70	85	48	6	8	0-3	.299	.430	.521	.951	2	.992
— San Diego (N.L.)	OF	29	104	33	31	4	2	4	18	20	10	2	4	4-0	.298	.414	.490	.904	2	.966
2004— San Diego (N.L.)	OF	159	609	97	173	33	7	23	94	89	80	4	12	10-3	.284	.374	.475	.849	7	.979
2005— San Diego (N.L.)	OF	158	545	92	164	38	8	15	83	* 119	64	2	14	13-5	.301	.423	.483	.905	4	.988
2006— San Diego (N.L.)	OF	158	604	87	159	37	1	14	83	104	60	5	18	9-4	.263	.374	.397	.771	7	.978
American League totals (4 years)		299	857	150	243	48	4	39	157	155	139	4	23	26-8	.284	.391	.485	.876	11	.976
National League totals (8 years)		1219	4403	800	1309	286	44	221	784	851	552	40	105	76-29	.297	.412	.533	.944	48	.981
Major League totals (12 years)		1518	5260	950	1552	334	48	260	941	1006	691	44	128	102-37	.295	.408	.525	.933	59	.980

DIVISION SERIES RECORD

Year Team (League)	Pos.	G	AB	R	H	2B	3B	HR	RBI	BB	SO	HBP	GDP	SB-CS	Avg.	OBP	SLG	OPS	E	Avg.
1996— Cleveland (A.L.)		1	1	0	0	0	0	0	0	0	1	0	0	0-0	.000	.000	.000	.000	...	...
1997— Cleveland (A.L.)	OF	3	7	0	1	0	0	0	0	0	1	0	0	0-0	.143	.143	.143	.286	0	1.000
1998— Cleveland (A.L.)	DH-OF	3	10	1	2	1	0	0	0	1	4	1	0	0-0	.200	.333	.300	.633	0	1.000
2005— San Diego (N.L.)	OF	3	13	0	3	0	0	0	1	1	2	0	1	1-0	.231	.286	.231	.516	0	1.000
2006— San Diego (N.L.)	OF	4	14	1	4	1	0	0	1	2	3	0	1	0-0	.286	.353	.357	.710	0	1.000
Division series totals (5 years)		14	45	2	10	2	0	0	2	4	11	1	2	1-0	.222	.294	.267	.561	0	1.000

CHAMPIONSHIP SERIES RECORD

Year Team (League)	Pos.	G	AB	R	H	2B	3B	HR	RBI	BB	SO	HBP	GDP	SB-CS	Avg.	OBP	SLG	OPS	E	Avg.
1997— Cleveland (A.L.)	OF	6	16	1	3	3	0	0	0	2	6	0	0	0-0	.188	.278	.375	.653	0	1.000
1998— Cleveland (A.L.)	OF	4	12	0	1	0	0	0	0	1	3	0	0	0-0	.083	.154	.083	.237	1	.875
Champ. series totals (2 years)		10	28	1	4	3	0	0	0	3	9	0	0	0-0	.143	.226	.250	.476	1	.941

WORLD SERIES RECORD

Year Team (League)	Pos.	G	AB	R	H	2B	3B	HR	RBI	BB	SO	HBP	GDP	SB-CS	Avg.	OBP	SLG	OPS	E	Avg.
1997— Cleveland (A.L.)	OF	5	4	1	2	1	0	0	0	2	4	1	0	0-1	.500	.750	.750	1.500	0	1.000

ALL-STAR GAME RECORD

		G	AB	R	H	2B	3B	HR	RBI	BB	SO	HBP	GDP	SB-CS	Avg.	OBP	SLG	OPS	E	Avg.
		2	3	0	0	0	0	0	0	0	1	0	0	0-0	.000	.000	.000	.000	0	...
All-Star Game totals (2 years)																				

2006 LEFTY-RIGHTY SPLITS

vs.	Avg.	AB	H	2B	3B	HR	RBI	BB	SO	OBP	Slg.	vs.	Avg.	AB	H	2B	3B	HR	RBI	BB	SO	OBP	Slg.
L	.217	175	38	8	1	2	13	23	14	.315	.309	R	.282	429	121	29	0	12	70	81	46	.397	.434

GILES, MARCUS — 2B

PERSONAL: Born May 18, 1978, in San Diego. ... 5-8/180. ... Bats right, throws right. ... Full name: Marcus William Giles. ... Name pronounced: JYLES. ... High school: Granite Hills (Calif.). ... Junior college: Grossmont (Calif.). ... Brother of Brian Giles, outfielder, San Diego Padres. **TRANSACTIONS/CAREER NOTES:** Selected by Atlanta Braves organization in 53rd round of 1996 free-agent draft. ... On disabled list (May 29-July 16, 2002); included rehabilitation assignment to Richmond. ... On disabled

G

list (May 16-July 15, 2004); included rehabilitation assignments to Rome and Myrtle Beach. **RECORDS:** Shares major league record for most doubles, game (4, July 27, 2003). **HONORS:** Named second baseman on THE SPORTING NEWS N.L. All-Star team (2003). **STATISTICAL NOTES:** Career major league grand slams: 2.

2006 GAMES PLAYED BY POSITION (MLB): 2B—134.

Year	Team (League)	Pos.	G	AB	R	H	2B	3B	HR	RBI	BB	SO	HBP	GDP	SB-CS	Avg.	OBP	SLG	OPS	E	Avg.
1997—Danville (Appal.)		2B	55	207	53	72	13	8	45	32	47	3	4	5-2	.348	.437	.556	.992	7	.962
1998—Macon (S. Atl.)		2B	135	505	111	166	38	3	37	108	85	103	10	15	12-5	.329	.433	.636	1.068	25	.954
1999—Myrtle Beach (Carol.)		2B	126	497	80	162	40	7	13	73	54	89	4	9	9-6	.326	.393	.513	.906	8	.985
2000—Greenville (Sou.)		2B	132	458	73	133	28	2	17	62	72	71	2	11	25-5	.290	.388	.472	.860	18	.973
2001—Richmond (Int'l)	2B-SS-3B	OF	67	252	48	84	19	1	6	44	22	48	2	4	13-5	.333	.387	.488	.875	8	.975
—Atlanta (N.L.)		2B	68	244	36	64	10	2	9	31	28	37	0	8	2-5	.262	.338	.430	.769	6	.978
2002—Atlanta (N.L.)		2B-3B	68	213	27	49	10	1	8	23	25	41	2	5	1-1	.230	.315	.399	.714	8	.972
—Richmond (Int'l)		2B-3B	31	115	25	37	6	0	3	16	13	15	0	1	3-0	.322	.385	.452	.837	3	.970
2003—Atlanta (N.L.)		2B	145	551	101	174	49	2	21	69	59	80	11	7	14-4	.316	.390	.526	.917	14	.982
2004—Rome (S. Atl.)		DH	1	2	0	0	0	0	0	0	0	2	0	0	0-0	.000	.500	.000	.500	0	...
—Myrtle Beach (Carol.)		2B-DH	4	13	1	1	1	0	0	2	1	4	0	0	0-0	.077	.133	.154	.287	0	1.000
—Atlanta (N.L.)		2B	102	379	61	118	22	2	8	48	36	70	9	6	17-4	.311	.378	.443	.821	12	.975
2005—Atlanta (N.L.)		2B-3B	152	577	104	168	45	4	15	63	64	108	5	13	16-3	.291	.365	.461	.826	12	.984
2006—Atlanta (N.L.)		2B	141	550	87	144	32	2	11	60	62	105	6	12	10-5	.262	.341	.387	.729	11	.983
Major League totals (6 years)			676	2514	416	717	168	13	72	294	274	441	33	51	60-22	.285	.361	.448	.809	63	.980

DIVISION SERIES RECORD

Year	Team (League)	Pos.	G	AB	R	H	2B	3B	HR	RBI	BB	SO	HBP	GDP	SB-CS	Avg.	OBP	SLG	OPS	E	Avg.
2001—Atlanta (N.L.)		2B	3	12	1	3	1	0	1	1	0	3	0	0	0-0	.250	.250	.333	.583	0	1.000
2002—Atlanta (N.L.)			3	2	0	1	0	0	0	0	1	0	0	0	0-0	.500	.500	.500	1.000	0	...
2003—Atlanta (N.L.)		2B	5	14	3	5	0	0	1	3	2	2	0	0	0-0	.357	.412	.571	.983	1	.955
2004—Atlanta (N.L.)		2B	5	24	1	3	0	0	0	1	0	6	0	0	1-0	.125	.125	.125	.250	0	1.000
2005—Atlanta (N.L.)		2B	4	20	5	4	1	0	0	0	2	5	1	0	0-0	.200	.304	.250	.554	0	1.000
Division series totals (5 years)			20	72	11	16	2	0	4	5	4	16	1	0	1-0	.222	.269	.292	.561	1	.990

CHAMPIONSHIP SERIES RECORD

Year	Team (League)	Pos.	G	AB	R	H	2B	3B	HR	RBI	BB	SO	HBP	GDP	SB-CS	Avg.	OBP	SLG	OPS	E	Avg.
2001—Atlanta (N.L.)		2B	5	20	4	4	1	0	1	4	3	4	0	1	0-0	.200	.304	.400	.704	2	.917

2006 LEFTY-RIGHTY SPLITS

vs.	Avg.	AB	H	2B	3B	HR	RBI	BB	SO	OBP	Slg.	vs.	Avg.	AB	H	2B	3B	HR	RBI	BB	SO	OBP	Slg.
L	.229	144	33	6	1	3	13	12	26	.296	.347	R	.273	406	111	26	1	8	47	50	79	.357	.401

GIMENEZ, HECTOR — C

PERSONAL: Born September 28, 1982, in San Felipe, Venezuela. ... 5-10/180. ... Bats both, throws right. ... Full name: Hector C. Gimenez. . **TRANSACTIONS/CAREER NOTES:** Signed as a non-drafted free agent by Houston Astros organization (July 2, 1999).

Year	Team (League)	Pos.	G	AB	R	H	2B	3B	HR	RBI	BB	SO	HBP	GDP	SB-CS	Avg.	OBP	SLG	OPS	E	Avg.
2000—Venoco (VSL)			34	91	9	27	8	0	1	13	12	21	3	0	0-4	.297	.396	.418	.814	...	...
2001—Venoco (VSL)			42	144	27	40	12	3	5	34	26	30	0	0	4-2	.278	.388	.507	.895	...	...
2002—Lexington (S. Atl.)			85	297	41	78	16	1	11	42	25	78	0	4	2-3	.263	.320	.434	.754	5	...
2003—Salem (Carol.)			109	381	41	94	17	1	7	54	29	75	4	7	2-0	.247	.304	.352	.656	6	...
2004—Round Rock (Texas)			97	331	38	81	16	3	6	46	18	64	2	3	2-0	.245	.284	.366	.650	8	...
2005—Corpus Christi (Texas)		C-DH-1B	121	454	47	124	19	1	12	58	32	88	2	4	2-3	.273	.322	.399	.720	8	.991
2006—Round Rock (PCL)			76	275	31	75	8	0	8	37	24	42	1	3	2-3	.273	.331	.389	.720	5	.990
—Houston (N.L.)			2	2	0	0	0	0	0	0	0	1	0	0	0-0	.000	.000	.000	.000	0	...
Major League totals (1 year)			2	2	0	0	0	0	0	0	0	1	0	0	0-0	.000	.000	.000	.000	0	...

2006 LEFTY-RIGHTY SPLITS

vs.	Avg.	AB	H	2B	3B	HR	RBI	BB	SO	OBP	Slg.	vs.	Avg.	AB	H	2B	3B	HR	RBI	BB	SO	OBP	Slg.
L	.000	1	0	0	0	0	0	0	0	.000	.000	R	.000	1	0	0	0	0	0	0	1	.000	.000

GLAUS, TROY — 3B

PERSONAL: Born August 3, 1976, in Tarzana, Calif. ... 6-5/240. ... Bats right, throws right. ... Full name: Troy Edward Glaus. ... Name pronounced: gloss. ... High school: Carlsbad (Calif.). ... College: UCLA. **TRANSACTIONS/CAREER NOTES:** Selected by San Diego Padres organization in second round of 1994 free-agent draft; did not sign. ... Selected by Anaheim Angels organization in first round (third pick overall) of 1997 free-agent draft. ... On disabled list (July 22-August 11, 2003); included rehabilitation assignment to Rancho Cucamonga. ... On disabled list (May 12-August 29, 2004); included rehabilitation assignment to Rancho Cucamonga. ... Signed as a free agent by Arizona Diamondbacks (December 9, 2004). ... Traded by Diamondbacks with SS Sergio Santos to Toronto Blue Jays for P Miguel Batista and 2B Orlando Hudson (December 27, 2005). **HONORS:** Named third baseman on THE SPORTING NEWS A.L. All-Star team (2001). ... Named third baseman on A.L. Silver Slugger team (2000 and 2001). **STATISTICAL NOTES:** Hit three home runs in one game (September 15, 2002). ... Career major league grand slams: 3. **MISCELLANEOUS NOTES:** Member of 1996 U.S. Olympic baseball team.

2006 GAMES PLAYED BY POSITION (MLB): 3B—145, SS—8, DH—4.

Year	Team (League)	Pos.	G	AB	R	H	2B	3B	HR	RBI	BB	SO	HBP	GDP	SB-CS	Avg.	OBP	SLG	OPS	E	Avg.
1998—Midland (Texas)		3B	50	188	51	58	11	2	19	51	39	41	2	4	4-2	.309	.430	.691	1.122	11	.925
—Vancouver (PCL)		3B	59	219	33	67	16	0	16	42	21	55	3	1	3-2	.306	.374	.598	.973	13	.932
—Anaheim (A.L.)		3B	48	165	19	36	9	0	1	23	15	51	0	3	1-0	.218	.280	.291	.571	7	.941
1999—Anaheim (A.L.)		3B-DH	154	551	85	132	29	0	29	79	71	143	6	9	5-1	.240	.331	.450	.781	19	.954
2000—Anaheim (A.L.)		3B-SS-DH	159	563	120	160	37	4	*47	102	112	163	2	14	14-11	.284	.404	.604	1.008	33	.934
2001—Anaheim (A.L.)		3B-DH-SS	161	588	100	147	38	2	41	108	107	158	6	16	10-3	.250	.367	.531	.898	19	.954
2002—Anaheim (A.L.)		3B-SS	156	569	99	142	24	1	30	111	88	144	6	12	10-3	.250	.352	.453	.805	20	.950
2003—Anaheim (A.L.)		3B-DH	91	319	53	79	17	2	16	50	46	73	1	8	7-2	.248	.343	.464	.807	16	.923
—Rancho Cuca. (Calif.)		DH	2	6	1	2	0	0	0	1	3	2	0	0	0-0	.333	.556	.333	.889	0	...
2004—Rancho Cuca. (Calif.)		DH	5	15	4	3	0	0	2	4	6	5	0	0	0-0	.200	.429	.600	1.029	0	...
—Anaheim (A.L.)		DH-3B	58	207	47	52	11	1	18	42	31	52	3	6	2-3	.251	.355	.575	.930	2	.950
2005—Arizona (N.L.)		3B	149	538	78	139	29	1	37	97	84	145	6	7	4-2	.258	.363	.522	.885	24	.946
2006—Toronto (A.L.)		3B-SS-DH	153	540	105	136	27	0	38	104	86	134	3	25	3-2	.252	.355	.513	.868	14	.965
American League totals (8 years)			980	3502	628	884	192	7	220	619	556	918	27	93	52-25	.252	.357	.500	.856	130	.948
National League totals (1 year)			149	538	78	139	29	1	37	97	84	145	6	7	4-2	.258	.363	.522	.885	24	.946
Major League totals (9 years)			1129	4040	706	1023	221	8	257	716	640	1063	34	100	56-27	.253	.357	.503	.860	154	.948

G

DIVISION SERIES RECORD

Year Team (League)	Pos.	G	AB	R	H	2B	3B	HR	RBI	BB	SO	HBP	GDP	SB-CS	Avg.	OBP	SLG	OPS	E	Avg.
2002—Anaheim (A.L.)	3B	4	16	4	5	0	0	3	3	1	3	1	0	0-0	.313	.389	.875	1.264	1	.929
2004—Anaheim (A.L.)	DH	3	11	3	4	2	0	2	3	2	4	0	0	0-0	.364	.462	1.091	1.552	0	...
Division series totals (2 years)		7	27	7	9	2	0	5	6	3	7	1	0	0-0	.333	.419	.963	1.382	1	.929

CHAMPIONSHIP SERIES RECORD

Year Team (League)	Pos.	G	AB	R	H	2B	3B	HR	RBI	BB	SO	HBP	GDP	SB-CS	Avg.	OBP	SLG	OPS	E	Avg.
2002—Anaheim (A.L.)	3B	5	19	4	6	0	1	1	4	2	5	0	0	0-0	.316	.381	.579	.960	0	1.000

WORLD SERIES RECORD

Year Team (League)	Pos.	G	AB	R	H	2B	3B	HR	RBI	BB	SO	HBP	GDP	SB-CS	Avg.	OBP	SLG	OPS	E	Avg.
2002—Anaheim (A.L.)	3B	7	26	7	10	3	0	3	8	4	6	0	1	0-0	.385	.467	.846	1.313	1	.938

ALL-STAR GAME RECORD

		G	AB	R	H	2B	3B	HR	RBI	BB	SO	HBP	GDP	SB-CS	Avg.	OBP	SLG	OPS	E	Avg.
All-Star Game totals (4 years)		4	7	1	1	0	0	0	0	0	2	0	1	0-0	.143	.143	.286	.429	0	1.000

2006 LEFTY-RIGHTY SPLITS

vs.	Avg.	AB	H	2B	3B	HR	RBI	BB	SO	OBP	Slg.	vs.	Avg.	AB	H	2B	3B	HR	RBI	BB	SO	OBP	Slg.
L	.292	137	40	11	0	12	31	29	29	.413	.635	R	.238	403	96	16	0	26	73	57	105	.334	.471

GLAVINE, TOM   P

PERSONAL: Born March 25, 1966, in Concord, Mass. ... 6-0/185. ... Throws left, bats left. ... Full name: Thomas Michael Glavine. ... Name pronounced: GLA-vin. ... High school: Billerica (Mass.). ... Brother of Mike Glavine, first baseman with New York Mets (2003). **TRANSACTIONS/CAREER NOTES:** Selected by Atlanta Braves organization in second round of June 1984 free-agent draft. ... Signed as a free agent by New York Mets (December 5, 2002). **HONORS:** Named N.L. Pitcher of the Year by THE SPORTING NEWS (1991 and 2000). ... Named lefthanded pitcher on THE SPORTING NEWS N.L. All-Star Team (1991-92, 1998 and 2000). ... Named N.L. Cy Young Award winner by Baseball Writers' Association of America (1991 and 1998). ... Named pitcher on N.L. Silver Slugger team (1991, 1995-96 and 1998). **MISCELLANEOUS NOTES:** Selected by Los Angeles Kings in fourth round (69th pick overall) of 1984 NHL entry draft. ... Appeared in eight games as pinch runner (1988). ... Appeared in one game as pinch runner (1989). ... Appeared in one game as pinch runner (1990). ... Received a base on balls and scored once in one game as pinch hitter and appeared in one game as pinch runner (1991). ... Singled and struck out in two appearances as pinch hitter (1992). ... Struck out in only appearance as pinch hitter (1994). ... Singled, struck out and made an out in three appearances as pinch hitter (1996). ... Had a sacrifice hit in only appearance as pinch hitter (1999). ... Made outs in both appearances as pinch hitter (2000). ... Made an out in only appearance as pinch hitter (2002). ... Made an out in only appearance as pinch hitter (2003). ... Received a base on balls and made an out in two appearances as pinch hitter (2004).

CAREER HITTING: 232-for-1248 (.186), 88 R, 24 2B, 2 3B, 1 HR, 85 RBI.

Year Team (League)	W	L	Pct.	ERA	WHIP	G	GS	CG	ShO	Hld.	Sv.-Opp.	IP	H	R	ER	HR	BB-IBB	SO	Avg.
1984—GC Braves (GCL)	2	3	.400	3.34	1.30	8	7	0	0	...	0-...	32.1	29	17	12	0	13-0	34	.236
1985—Sumter (S. Atl.)	9	6	.600	2.35	1.11	26	26	2	1	...	0-...	168.2	114	58	44	6	73-0	174	.193
1986—Greenville (Sou.)	11	6	.647	3.41	1.37	22	22	2	1	...	0-...	145.1	129	62	55	14	70-3	114	.237
—Richmond (Int'l)	1	5	.167	5.63	1.68	7	7	1	1	...	0-...	40.0	40	29	25	4	27-0	12	.260
1987—Richmond (Int'l)	6	12	.333	3.35	1.32	22	22	* 4	1	...	0-...	150.1	142	70	56	15	56-3	91	.248
—Atlanta (N.L.)	2	4	.333	5.54	1.75	9	9	0	0		0-0	50.1	55	34	31	5	33-4	20	.279
1988—Atlanta (N.L.)	7	* 17	.292	4.56	1.35	34	34	1	0		0-0	195.1	201	111	99	12	63-7	84	.270
1989—Atlanta (N.L.)	14	8	.636	3.68	1.14	29	29	6	4		0-0	186.0	172	88	76	20	40-3	90	.243
1990—Atlanta (N.L.)	10	12	.455	4.28	1.45	33	33	1	0		0-0	214.1	232	111	102	18	78-10	129	.281
1991—Atlanta (N.L.)	* 20	11	.645	2.55	1.09	34	34	* 9	1		0-0	246.2	201	83	70	·17	69-6	192	.222
1992—Atlanta (N.L.)	* 20	8	.714	2.76	1.19	33	33	7	* 5		0-0	225.0	197	81	69	6	70-7	129	.235
1993—Atlanta (N.L.)	* 22	6	.786	3.20	1.36	36	* 36	4	2		0-0	239.1	236	91	85	16	90-7	120	.259
1994—Atlanta (N.L.)	13	9	.591	3.97	1.47	25	25	2	0		0-0	165.1	173	76	73	10	70-10	140	.268
1995—Atlanta (N.L.)	16	7	.696	3.08	1.25	29	29	3	1		0-0	198.2	182	76	68	9	66-0	127	.246
1996—Atlanta (N.L.)	15	10	.600	2.98	1.30	36	* 36	1	0		0-0	235.1	222	91	78	14	85-7	181	.249
1997—Atlanta (N.L.)	14	7	.667	2.96	1.15	33	33	5	2		0-0	240.0	197	86	79	20	79-9	152	.226
1998—Atlanta (N.L.)	* 20	6	.769	2.47	1.20	33	33	4	3		0-0	229.1	202	67	63	13	74-2	157	.238
1999—Atlanta (N.L.)	14	11	.560	4.12	1.46	35	35	2	0		0-0	234.0	* 259	115	107	18	83-14	138	.287
2000—Atlanta (N.L.)	* 21	9	.700	3.40	1.19	35	* 35	4	2		0-0	241.0	222	101	91	24	65-6	152	.244
2001—Atlanta (N.L.)	16	7	.696	3.57	1.41	35	* 35	1	1		0-0	219.1	213	92	87	24	97-10	116	.261
2002—Atlanta (N.L.)	18	11	.621	2.96	1.28	36	* 36	2	1		0-0	224.2	210	85	74	21	78-8	127	.252
2003—New York (N.L.)	9	14	.391	4.52	1.48	32	32	0	0		0-0	183.1	205	94	92	21	66-7	82	.288
2004—New York (N.L.)	11	14	.440	3.60	1.29	33	33	1	1		0-0	212.1	204	94	85	20	70-10	109	.252
2005—New York (N.L.)	13	13	.500	3.53	1.36	33	33	2	1		0-0	211.1	227	88	83	12	61-5	105	.279
2006—New York (N.L.)	15	7	.682	3.82	1.33	32	32	0	0		0-0	198.0	202	94	84	22	62-7	131	.267
Major League totals (20 years)	290	191	.603	3.46	1.30	635	635	55	24	0	0-0	4149.2	4012	1758	1596	322	1399-139	2481	.256

DIVISION SERIES RECORD

Year Team (League)	W	L	Pct.	ERA	WHIP	G	GS	CG	ShO	Hld.	Sv.-Opp.	IP	H	R	ER	HR	BB-IBB	SO	Avg.
1995—Atlanta (N.L.)	0	0	...	2.57	0.86	1	1	0	0	0	0-0	7.0	5	3	2	1	1-0	3	.185
1996—Atlanta (N.L.)	1	0	1.000	1.35	1.20	1	1	0	0	0	0-0	6.2	5	1	1	0	3-0	7	.217
1997—Atlanta (N.L.)	1	0	1.000	4.50	1.67	1	1	0	0	0	0-0	6.0	5	3	3	0	5-0	4	.217
1998—Atlanta (N.L.)	0	0	...	1.29	0.57	1	1	0	0	0	0-0	7.0	3	1	1	0	1-0	6	.136
1999—Atlanta (N.L.)	0	0	...	3.00	1.33	1	1	0	0	0	0-0	6.0	5	2	2	0	3-0	6	.238
2000—Atlanta (N.L.)	0	1	.000	27.00	3.00	1	1	0	0	0	0-0	2.1	6	7	7	2	1-0	2	.500
2001—Atlanta (N.L.)	1	0	1.000	0.00	1.00	1	1	0	0	0	0-0	8.0	6	0	0	0	2-0	3	.222
2002—Atlanta (N.L.)	0	2	.000	15.26	3.13	2	2	0	0	0	0-0	7.2	17	13	13	1	7-3	4	.459
2006—New York (N.L.)	1	0	1.000	0.00	1.00	1	1	0	0	0	0-0	6.0	4	0	0	0	2-0	2	.182
Division series totals (9 years)	4	3	.571	4.61	1.43	10	10	0	0	0	0-0	56.2	56	30	29	4	25-3	39	.262

CHAMPIONSHIP SERIES RECORD

Year Team (League)	W	L	Pct.	ERA	WHIP	G	GS	CG	ShO	Hld.	Sv.-Opp.	IP	H	R	ER	HR	BB-IBB	SO	Avg.
1991—Atlanta (N.L.)	0	2	.000	3.21	1.29	2	2	0	0	0	0-0	14.0	12	5	5	1	6-2	11	.226
1992—Atlanta (N.L.)	0	2	.000	12.27	2.18	2	2	0	0	0	0-0	7.1	13	11	10	3	3-1	2	.382
1993—Atlanta (N.L.)	1	0	1.000	2.57	0.86	2	2	0	0	0	0-0	7.0	6	2	2	1	0-0	5	.222
1995—Atlanta (N.L.)	0	0	...	1.29	1.29	1	1	0	0	0	0-0	7.0	7	1	1	0	2-1	5	.292
1996—Atlanta (N.L.)	1	1	.500	2.08	0.77	2	2	0	0	0	0-0	13.0	10	3	3	2	0-0	9	.217
1997—Atlanta (N.L.)	1	1	.500	5.40	1.80	2	2	0	0	0	0-0	13.1	13	8	8	0	11-3	9	.271
1998—Atlanta (N.L.)	0	2	.000	2.31	1.89	2	2	0	0	0	0-0	11.2	11	3	3	0	10-0	8	.283
1999—Atlanta (N.L.)	1	0	1.000	0.00	1.14	1	1	0	0	0	0-0	7.0	7	0	0	0	1-0	8	.280
2001—Atlanta (N.L.)	1	1	.500	1.50	1.25	2	2	0	0	0	0-0	12.0	11	3	2	1	5-0	5	.217
2006—New York (N.L.)	1	1	.500	2.45	1.45	2	2	0	0	0	0-0	11.0	11	3	3	1	5-1	4	.268
Champ. series totals (10 years)	6	10	.375	3.22	1.39	17	17	0	0	0	0-0	103.1	102	43	37	9	42-8	66	.260

G

Year Team (League)	W	L	Pct.	ERA	WHIP	G	GS	CG	ShO	Hld.	Sv.-Opp.	IP	H	R	ER	HR	BB-IBB	SO	Avg.
WORLD SERIES RECORD																			
1991— Atlanta (N.L.)	1	1	.500	2.70	1.13	2	2	1	0	0	0-0	13.1	8	6	4	2	7-0	8	.174
1992— Atlanta (N.L.)	1	1	.500	1.59	0.82	2	2	2	0	0	0-0	17.0	10	3	3	2	4-0	8	.175
1995— Atlanta (N.L.)	2	0	1.000	1.29	0.71	2	2	0	0	0	0-0	14.0	4	2	2	1	6-0	11	.087
1996— Atlanta (N.L.)	0	1	.000	1.29	1.00	1	1	0	0	0	0-0	7.0	4	2	1	0	3-0	8	.174
1999— Atlanta (N.L.)	0	0	...	5.14	1.00	1	1	0	0	0	0-0	7.0	7	5	4	3	0-0	3	.250
World series totals (5 years)	4	3	.571	2.16	0.91	8	8	3	0	0	0-0	58.1	33	18	14	8	20-0	38	.165
ALL-STAR GAME RECORD																			
	W	L	Pct.	ERA	WHIP	G	GS	CG	ShO	Hld.	Sv.-Opp.	IP	H	R	ER	HR	BB-IBB	SO	Avg.
All-Star Game totals (6 years)	0	1	.000	10.13	2.50	6	2	0	0	0	0-0	8.0	16	9	9	0	4-0	7	.421

2006 LEFTY-RIGHTY SPLITS

vs.	Avg.	AB	H	2B	3B	HR	RBI	BB	SO	OBP	Slg.	vs.	Avg.	AB	H	2B	3B	HR	RBI	BB	SO	OBP	Slg.
L	.200	170	34	9	0	3	12	13	40	.273	.306	R	.287	586	168	35	3	19	68	49	91	.340	.454

GLOAD, ROSS   1B/OF

PERSONAL: Born April 5, 1976, in Brooklyn, N.Y. ... 6-0/185. ... Bats left, throws left. ... Full name: Ross Peter Gload. ... High school: East Hampton (N.Y.). ... College: South Florida. **TRANSACTIONS/CAREER NOTES:** Selected by Florida Marlins organization in 13th round of 1997 free-agent draft. ... Traded by Marlins with P David Noyce to Chicago Cubs for OF Henry Rodriguez (July 31, 2000). ... Claimed on waivers by Colorado Rockies (September 12, 2001). ... Traded by Rockies with P Craig House to New York Mets as part of three-team deal in which Rockies acquired 1B/3B Todd Zeile, OF Benny Agbayani and cash from Mets, Mets acquired P Jeff D'Amico, OF Jeromy Burnitz, IF Lou Collier, OF/1B Mark Sweeney and cash from Milwaukee Brewers, and Brewers acquired P Glendon Rusch and IF Lenny Harris from Mets and OF Alex Ochoa from Rockies (January 21, 2002). ... Traded by Mets to Rockies for cash (January 27, 2002). ... Traded by Rockies to Chicago White Sox for P Wade Parrish (March 27, 2003). ... On disabled list (April 25-July 17, 2005); included rehabilitation assignment to Charlotte. **STATISTICAL NOTES:** Career major league grand slams: 1.

2006 GAMES PLAYED BY POSITION (MLB): 1B—49, OF—19, DH—1.

Year Team (League)	Pos.	G	AB	R	H	2B	3B	HR	RBI	BB	SO	HBP	GDP	SB-CS	Avg.	OBP	SLG	OPS	E	Avg.
1997— Utica (N.Y.-Penn)	1B	68	245	28	64	15	2	3	43	28	57	2	5	1-1	.261	.336	.376	.711	16	.973
1998— Kane Co. (Midw.)	1B	132	501	77	157	41	3	12	92	58	84	3	13	7-6	.313	.386	.479	.865	14	.989
1999— Brevard County (FSL)	1B	133	490	80	146	26	3	10	74	53	76	5	8	3-1	.298	.369	.424	.793	9	.993
2000— Portland (East.)	OF-1B	100	401	60	114	28	4	16	65	29	53	2	4	4-1	.284	.333	.494	.826	7	.986
— Iowa (PCL)	OF	28	104	24	42	10	2	14	39	9	13	1	2	1-1	.404	.452	.942	1.394	4	.917
— Chicago (N.L.)	OF-1B	18	31	4	6	0	1	1	3	3	10	0	1	0-0	.194	.257	.355	.612	0	1.000
2001— Iowa (PCL)	OF-1B	133	475	70	141	32	10	15	93	35	88	3	8	9-7	.297	.344	.501	.845	3	.994
2002— Colo. Springs (PCL)	1B-OF	104	469	69	139	28	6	16	71	18	59	1	4	9-4	.314	.338	.514	.852	11	.987
— Colorado (N.L.)	1B-OF	26	31	4	8	1	0	1	4	3	7	0	0	0-0	.258	.324	.387	.711	0	1.000
2003— Charlotte (Int'l)	1B-OF	133	508	72	160	40	6	18	70	29	60	1	12	6-3	.315	.349	.524	.873	4	.991
2004— Chicago (A.L.) 1B-OF-DH		110	234	28	75	16	0	7	44	20	37	2	11	0-3	.321	.375	.479	.853	3	.990
2005— Charlotte (Int'l)	1B-DH-OF	60	236	45	86	22	1	15	46	22	37	1	2	0-1	.364	.416	.657	1.073	2	.995
— Chicago (A.L.)	1B-OF	28	42	2	7	2	0	0	5	2	9	1	0	0-0	.167	.205	.214	.419	1	.988
2006— Chicago (A.L.) 1B-OF-DH		77	156	22	51	8	2	3	18	6	15	1	3	6-0	.327	.354	.462	.815	4	.987
American League totals (3 years)		215	432	52	133	26	2	10	67	28	61	3	15	6-3	.308	.351	.447	.798	8	.988
National League totals (2 years)		44	62	8	14	1	1	2	7	6	17	0	1	0-0	.226	.290	.371	.661	0	1.000
Major League totals (5 years)		259	494	60	147	27	3	12	74	34	78	3	16	6-3	.298	.343	.437	.781	8	.989

2006 LEFTY-RIGHTY SPLITS

vs.	Avg.	AB	H	2B	3B	HR	RBI	BB	SO	OBP	Slg.	vs.	Avg.	AB	H	2B	3B	HR	RBI	BB	SO	OBP	Slg.
L	.308	39	12	1	1	1	5	2	5	.341	.462	R	.333	117	39	7	1	2	13	4	10	.358	.462

GOBBLE, JIMMY   P

PERSONAL: Born July 19, 1981, in Bristol, Tenn. ... 6-3/190. ... Throws left, bats left. ... Full name: Billy James Gobble. ... High school: John S. Battle (Bristol, Va.). **TRANS-ACTIONS/CAREER NOTES:** Selected by Kansas City Royals organization in supplemental round ("sandwich" pick between first and second rounds, 43rd pick overall) of 1999 free-agent draft; Royals received pick as compensation for Detroit Tigers signing Type A free-agent 3B Dean Palmer. **CAREER HITTING:** 0-for-2 (.000), 0 R, 0 2B, 0 3B, 0 HR, 0 RBI.

Year Team (League)	W	L	Pct.	ERA	WHIP	G	GS	CG	ShO	Hld.	Sv.-Opp.	IP	H	R	ER	HR	BB-IBB	SO	Avg.
1999— GC Royals (GCL)	0	0	...	2.70	1.65	4	1	0	0		0-...	6.2	6	3	2	0	5-0	8	.222
2000— Char., W.Va. (SAL)	12	10	.545	3.66	1.23	25	25	3	2		0-...	145.0	144	75	59	10	34-0	115	.256
2001— Wilmington (Caro.)	10	6	.625	2.55	1.03	27	27	0	0		0-...	162.1	134	58	46	8	33-3	154	.226
2002— Wichita (Texas)	5	7	.417	3.38	1.30	13	13	0	0		0-...	69.1	71	29	26	3	19-2	52	.267
2003— Wichita (Texas)	12	8	.600	3.19	1.27	22	22	2	1		0-...	132.2	128	57	47	11	40-1	100	.254
— Kansas City (A.L.)	4	5	.444	4.61	1.35	9	7	0	0	0	0-0	52.2	56	32	27	8	15-0	31	.271
2004— Omaha (PCL)	3	1	.750	4.58	1.63	4	4	0	0		0-0	19.2	25	20	10	5	7-0	15	.298
— Kansas City (A.L.)	9	8	.529	5.35	1.35	25	24	0	0	0	0-0	148.0	157	94	88	24	43-0	49	.270
2005— Omaha (PCL)	2	7	.222	6.63	1.68	12	12	0	0		0-0	58.1	76	48	43	8	21-0	45	.314
— Kansas City (A.L.)	1	1	.500	5.70	1.75	28	5	0	0		0-0	53.2	64	34	34	9	30-4	38	.299
2006— Kansas City (A.L.)	4	6	.400	5.14	1.48	60	6	0	0	11	2-4	84.0	95	51	48	12	29-1	80	.282
Major League totals (4 years)	18	20	.474	5.24	1.45	122	43	1	0	15	2-4	338.1	372	211	197	53	117-5	198	.278

2006 LEFTY-RIGHTY SPLITS

vs.	Avg.	AB	H	2B	3B	HR	RBI	BB	SO	OBP	Slg.	vs.	Avg.	AB	H	2B	3B	HR	RBI	BB	SO	OBP	Slg.
L	.255	102	26	6	1	6	23	3	36	.276	.510	R	.294	235	69	19	0	6	29	26	44	.366	.451

GOMES, JONNY   OF/DH

PERSONAL: Born November 22, 1980, in San Francisco. ... 6-1/205. ... Bats right, throws right. ... Full name: Jonny Johnson Gomes. ... High school: Casa Grande (Petaluma, Calif.). ... Junior college: Santa Rosa (Calif.). **TRANSACTIONS/CAREER NOTES:** Selected by Tampa Bay Devil Rays organization in 18th round of 2001 free-agent draft. ... On disabled list (August 22, 2006-remainder of season). **RECORDS:** Shares major league record for most times hit by pitch, game (3, August 15, 2005). **STATISTI-CAL NOTES:** Hit three home runs in one game (July 30, 2005). ... Career major league grand slams: 1.

2006 GAMES PLAYED BY POSITION (MLB): DH—101, OF—8.

Year Team (League)	Pos.	G	AB	R	H	2B	3B	HR	RBI	BB	SO	HBP	GDP	SB-CS	Avg.	OBP	SLG	OPS	E	Avg.
2001— Princeton (Appal.)	OF	62	206	58	60	11	2	16	44	33	73	26	1	15-4	.291	.442	.597	1.039	7	.936
2002— Bakersfield (Calif.)	OF	134	446	102	124	24	9	30	72	91	173	31	4	15-3	.278	.432	.574	1.006	7	.961
2003— Orlando (South.)	OF-DH	120	442	68	110	28	3	17	56	53	148	16	5	23-2	.249	.348	.441	.789	4	.977
— Durham (Int'l)	OF-DH	5	19	2	6	1	0	1	2	5	2	0	0	0-0	.316	.435	.526	.961	0	1.000

Year	Team (League)	Pos.	G	AB	R	H	2B	3B	HR	RBI	BB	SO	HBP	GDP	SB-CS	Avg.	OBP	SLG	OPS	E	Avg.
— Tampa Bay (A.L.)	DH	8	15	1	2	1	0	0	0	0	6	1	0	0-0	.133	.188	.200	.388	0	...
2004— Tampa Bay (A.L.)	DH	5	14	0	1	0	0	0	1	1	6	0	0	0-0	.071	.133	.071	.205	0	...
— Durham (Int'l)	OF-DH	114	389	73	100	27	1	26	78	51	136	22	6	8-5	.257	.368	.532	.900	7	.962
2005— Durham (Int'l)	OF	45	162	34	52	13	0	14	46	30	44	8	2	7-1	.321	.446	.660	1.106	8	.948
— Tampa Bay (A.L.)	OF-DH	101	348	61	98	13	6	21	54	39	113	14	6	9-5	.282	.372	.534	.906	4	.963
2006— Tampa Bay (A.L.)	DH-OF	117	385	53	83	21	1	20	59	61	116	6	0	1-5	.216	.325	.431	.757	0	1.000
Major League totals (4 years)		231	762	115	184	35	7	41	114	101	241	21	16	10-10	.241	.341	.467	.808	4	.969

2006 LEFTY-RIGHTY SPLITS

vs.	Avg.	AB	H	2B	3B	HR	RBI	BB	SO	OBP	Slg.	vs.	Avg.	AB	H	2B	3B	HR	RBI	BB	SO	OBP	Slg.
L	.297	101	30	9	1	7	22	24	24	.438	.614	R	.187	284	53	12	0	13	37	37	92	.282	.366

GOMEZ, ALEXIS — OF

PERSONAL: Born August 8, 1978, in Loma de Cabrera, Dominican Republic. ... 6-2/180. ... Bats left, throws left. ... Full name: Alexis De Jesus Gomez. ... High school: Liceo General Jose Cabrera (Loma de Cabrera, Dominican Republic). **TRANSACTIONS/CAREER NOTES:** Signed as a non-drafted free agent by Kansas City Royals organization (February 21, 1997). ... Claimed on waivers by Detroit Tigers (October 1, 2004).
2006 GAMES PLAYED BY POSITION (MLB): OF—52, DH—7.

Year	Team (League)	Pos.	G	AB	R	H	2B	3B	HR	RBI	BB	SO	HBP	GDP	SB-CS	Avg.	OBP	SLG	OPS	E	Avg.
1997— Dom. Royals (DSL)		64	248	51	87	12	9	0	42	33	52	...	...	9-...	.351	...	.472	...	...	...
1998— Dom. Royals (DSL)		67	233	51	66	11	3	1	34	50	46	...	...	17-...	.283	...	.369	...	...	...
1999— GC Royals (GCL)	OF	56	214	44	59	12	1	5	31	32	48	1	1	13-5	.276	.371	.411	.782	2	.986
2000— Wilmington (Caro.)	OF	121	461	63	117	13	4	1	33	45	121	2	8	21-10	.254	.322	.306	.628	14	.950
2001— Wilmington (Caro.)	OF	48	169	29	51	8	2	1	9	11	43	1	4	7-3	.302	.348	.391	.739	5	.957
— Wichita (Texas)	OF	83	342	55	96	15	6	4	34	27	70	4	4	16-10	.281	.337	.395	.732	6	.971
2002— Wichita (Texas)	OF	114	461	72	136	21	8	14	75	45	84	3	9	36-24	.295	.359	.466	.825	9	.967
— Kansas City (A.L.)	OF	5	10	0	2	0	0	0	0	2	0	0	0	0-0	.200	.200	.200	.400	1	1.000
2003— Omaha (PCL)	OF	121	457	49	123	23	8	8	58	26	92	1	12	4-5	.269	.307	.407	.714	9	.970
2004— Omaha (PCL)	OF	109	383	45	96	17	8	7	34	19	96	1	11	8-6	.251	.285	.392	.677	6	.971
— Kansas City (A.L.)	OF-DH	13	29	1	8	1	0	0	4	2	8	0	1	0-0	.276	.323	.310	.633	1	.955
2005— Detroit (A.L.)	OF	9	16	2	3	0	0	0	1	2	2	0	0	0-0	.188	.278	.188	.465	0	1.000
— Toledo (Int'l)	OF-DH	114	424	51	130	28	6	7	55	27	91	2	7	21-7	.307	.348	.450	.798	12	.968
2006— Toledo (Int'l)	OF	58	226	36	65	18	3	11	36	18	48	2	6	8-4	.288	.343	.540	.883	5	.961
— Detroit (A.L.)	OF-DH	62	103	17	28	5	2	1	6	6	21	1		4-0	.272	.318	.388	.707	1	.988
Major League totals (4 years)		89	158	20	41	6	2	1	11	10	33	1	2	4-0	.259	.308	.342	.649	1	.988

CHAMPIONSHIP SERIES RECORD

Year	Team (League)	Pos.	G	AB	R	H	2B	3B	HR	RBI	BB	SO	HBP	GDP	SB-CS	Avg.	OBP	SLG	OPS	E	Avg.
2006— Detroit (A.L.)	DH	3	9	1	4	0	0	1	4	0	2	0	0	0-0	.444	.444	.778	1.222	0	...

WORLD SERIES RECORD

Year	Team (League)	Pos.	G	AB	R	H	2B	3B	HR	RBI	BB	SO	HBP	GDP	SB-CS	Avg.	OBP	SLG	OPS	E	Avg.
2006— Detroit (A.L.)		3	3	0	0	0	0	0	0	0	1	0	0	0-0	.000	.000	.000	.000		

2006 LEFTY-RIGHTY SPLITS

vs.	Avg.	AB	H	2B	3B	HR	RBI	BB	SO	OBP	Slg.	vs.	Avg.	AB	H	2B	3B	HR	RBI	BB	SO	OBP	Slg.
L	.188	16	3	1	0	0	1	0	3	.188	.250	R	.287	87	25	4	2	1	5	6	18	.340	.414

GOMEZ, CHRIS — IF

PERSONAL: Born June 16, 1971, in Los Angeles, Calif. ... 6-1/188. ... Bats right, throws right. ... Full name: Christopher Cory Gomez. ... High school: Lakewood (Calif.). ... College: Long Beach State. **TRANSACTIONS/CAREER NOTES:** Selected by California Angels organization in 37th round of 1989 free-agent draft; did not sign. ... Selected by Detroit Tigers organization in third round of 1992 free-agent draft. ... Traded by Tigers with C John Flaherty to San Diego Padres for C Brad Ausmus, SS Andujar Cedeno and P Russ Spear (June 18, 1996). ... On disabled list (June 2-July 31, 1999); included rehabilitation assignment to Las Vegas. ... Released by Padres (June 22, 2001). ... Signed by Tampa Bay Devil Rays organization (June 27, 2001). ... Released by Devil Rays (September 30, 2002). ... Signed by Minnesota Twins organization (January 2, 2003). ... On disabled list (June 7-July 5, 2003). ... Signed as a free agent by Toronto Blue Jays (January 7, 2004). ... Signed as a free agent by Baltimore Orioles organization (December 8, 2004). ... Selected by Philadelphia Phillies organization from Orioles organization in Rule 5 minor league draft (December 13, 2004). ... Traded by Phillies to Baltimore Orioles for cash (December 20, 2004). ... On disabled list (May 11-July 11, 2006); included rehabilitation assignments to Aberdeen and Bowie. **STATISTICAL NOTES:** Career major league grand slams: 1.
2006 GAMES PLAYED BY POSITION (MLB): 1B—27, 2B—15, SS—6, 3B—5, DH—2.

Year	Team (League)	Pos.	G	AB	R	H	2B	3B	HR	RBI	BB	SO	HBP	GDP	SB-CS	Avg.	OBP	SLG	OPS	E	Avg.
1992— London (East.)	SS	64	220	20	59	13	2	1	19	20	34	3	11	1-3	.268	.337	.359	.697	14	.951
1993— Toledo (Int'l)	SS	87	277	29	68	12	2	0	20	23	37	3	4	6-2	.245	.308	.303	.611	16	.961
— Detroit (A.L.)	SS-2B-DH	46	128	11	32	7	1	0	11	9	17	1	2	2-2	.250	.304	.320	.625	5	.974
1994— Detroit (A.L.)	SS-2B	84	296	32	76	19	0	8	53	33	64	3	8	5-3	.257	.336	.402	.738	8	.978
1995— Detroit (A.L.)	SS-2B	123	431	49	96	20	2	11	50	41	96	3	13	4-1	.223	.292	.355	.647	15	.974
1996— Detroit (A.L.)	SS	48	128	21	31	5	0	1	16	18	20	1	5	1-1	.242	.340	.305	.645	6	.970
— San Diego (N.L.)	SS	89	328	32	86	16	1	3	29	39	64	6	11	2-2	.262	.349	.345	.694	13	.967
1997— San Diego (N.L.)	SS	150	522	62	132	19	2	5	54	53	114	5	16	5-8	.253	.326	.326	.652	15	.978
1998— San Diego (N.L.)	SS	145	449	55	120	32	3	4	39	51	87	5	11	1-3	.267	.346	.379	.725	12	.980
1999— San Diego (N.L.)	SS	76	234	20	59	8	1	1	15	27	49	1	6	1-2	.252	.331	.308	.638	12	.961
— Las Vegas (PCL)	SS	10	27	3	9	1	0	0	4	2	5	1		0-0	.333	.400	.370	.770	2	.933
2000— San Diego (N.L.)	SS-2B	33	54	4	12	0	0	0	3	7	5	0	1	0-0	.222	.306	.222	.529	5	.933
2001— San Diego (N.L.)	SS-2B	40	112	6	21	3	0	0	7	9	14	0	5	1-0	.188	.244	.214	.458	6	.948
— Portland (PCL)	SS-2B	11	40	5	12	3	0	1	5	2	4	0	1	1-0	.300	.333	.450	.783	2	.959
— Durham (Int'l)	SS	23	93	16	28	5	1	4	17	11	5	0	5	1-1	.301	.375	.505	.880	2	.978
— Tampa Bay (A.L.)	SS	58	189	31	57	16	0	8	36	8	24	2	4	3-0	.302	.332	.513	.845	7	.968
2002— Tampa Bay (A.L.)	SS	130	461	51	122	31	3	10	46	21	58	7	8	1-3	.265	.305	.410	.715	12	.980
2003— Minnesota (A.L.)	2B-3B-SS / DH	58	175	14	44	9	1	1	15	7	13	0	10	2-1	.251	.279	.354	.633	3	.982
2004— Toronto (A.L.)	SS-1B-3B / DH-2B	109	341	41	96	11	1	3	37	28	41	2	4	3-2	.282	.337	.346	.683	12	.974
2005— Baltimore (A.L.)	1B-2B-3B / SS-DH	89	219	27	61	11	0	1	18	27	17	1	14	2-1	.279	.359	.342	.701	5	.987

G

Year	Team (League)	Pos.	G	AB	R	H	2B	3B	HR	RBI	BB	SO	HBP	GDP	SB-CS	Avg.	OBP	SLG	OPS	E	Avg.
2006—Aberdeen (N.Y.-Penn.)			1	3	0	1	0	0	0	1	0	1	0	0	0-0	.333	.333	.333	.667	0	1.000
—Bowie (East.)			4	16	4	4	1	0	0	1	1	3	0	1	0-0	.250	.294	.313	.607	0	1.000
—Baltimore (A.L.)	1B-2B-SS 3B-DH		55	132	14	45	7	0	2	17	7	11	3	7	1-2	.341	.387	.439	.827	3	.986
American League totals (10 years)			800	2500	291	660	136	10	45	299	199	361	23	75	24-16	.264	.322	.380	.703	76	.978
National League totals (6 years)			533	1699	179	430	78	7	13	147	186	333	17	50	10-15	.253	.331	.330	.661	63	.971
Major League totals (14 years)			1333	4199	470	1090	214	17	58	446	385	694	40	125	34-31	.260	.326	.360	.686	139	.975

DIVISION SERIES RECORD

Year	Team (League)	Pos.	G	AB	R	H	2B	3B	HR	RBI	BB	SO	HBP	GDP	SB-CS	Avg.	OBP	SLG	OPS	E	Avg.
1996—San Diego (N.L.)	SS		3	12	0	2	0	0	0	1	0	4	0	0	0-0	.167	.167	.167	.333	0	1.000
1998—San Diego (N.L.)	SS		4	11	1	3	0	0	0	0	4	1	0	0	0-0	.273	.467	.273	.739	1	.938
2003—Minnesota (A.L.)	2B		1	0	0	0	0	0	0	0	0	0	0	0	0-0	...	...	...	...	0	...
Division series totals (3 years)			8	23	1	5	0	0	0	1	4	5	0	0	0-0	.217	.333	.217	.551	1	.966

CHAMPIONSHIP SERIES RECORD

Year	Team (League)	Pos.	G	AB	R	H	2B	3B	HR	RBI	BB	SO	HBP	GDP	SB-CS	Avg.	OBP	SLG	OPS	E	Avg.
1998—San Diego (N.L.)	SS		6	20	2	3	1	0	0	0	2	5	0	3	0-0	.150	.227	.200	.427	1	.950

WORLD SERIES RECORD

Year	Team (League)	Pos.	G	AB	R	H	2B	3B	HR	RBI	BB	SO	HBP	GDP	SB-CS	Avg.	OBP	SLG	OPS	E	Avg.
1998—San Diego (N.L.)	SS		4	11	2	4	0	1	0	1	1	0	0	0	0-0	.364	.417	.545	.962	0	1.000

2006 LEFTY-RIGHTY SPLITS

vs.	Avg.	AB	H	2B	3B	HR	RBI	BB	SO	OBP	Slg.	vs.	Avg.	AB	H	2B	3B	HR	RBI	BB	SO	OBP	Slg.
L	.333	48	16	2	0	1	3	5	3	.396	.438	R	.345	84	29	5	0	1	14	2	8	.382	.440

GONZALEZ, ADRIAN   1B

PERSONAL: Born May 8, 1982, in San Diego. ... 6-2/220. ... Bats left, throws left. ... High school: Eastlake High (Chula Vista, Calif.). **TRANSACTIONS/CAREER NOTES:** Selected by Florida Marlins organization in first round (first pick overall) of 2000 draft. ... Traded by Marlins with P Ryan Snare and OF Will Smith to Texas Rangers for P Ugueth Urbina (July 11, 2003). ... Traded by Rangers with OF Terrmel Sledge and P Chris Young to San Diego Padres for Ps Adam Eaton and Akinori Otsuka and C Billy Killian (January 4, 2006).

2006 GAMES PLAYED BY POSITION (MLB): 1B—155.

Year	Team (League)	Pos.	G	AB	R	H	2B	3B	HR	RBI	BB	SO	HBP	GDP	SB-CS	Avg.	OBP	SLG	OPS	E	Avg.
2000—GC Marlins (GCL)	1B	53	193	24	57	10	1	0	30	32	35	2	6	0-0	.295	.397	.358	.755	7	.986
—Utica (N.Y.-Penn)	1B	8	29	7	9	3	0	0	3	7	6	0	0	0-0	.310	.444	.414	.858	2	.976
2001—Kane Co. (Midw.)	1B	127	516	86	161	37	1	17	103	57	83	5	17	5-5	.312	.382	.486	.868	14	.988
2002—Portland (East.)	1B	138	508	70	135	34	1	17	96	54	112	8	13	6-3	.266	.344	.437	.781	16	.987
2003—Albuquerque (PCL)	1B	39	139	17	30	5	1	1	18	14	25	0	6	1-0	.216	.286	.288	.573	1	.997
—Carolina (Southern)	1B	36	137	15	42	9	1	1	16	14	25	1	6	1-1	.307	.368	.409	.777	4	.987
—Frisco (Texas)	1B	45	173	16	49	6	2	3	17	11	27	1	6	0-0	.283	.326	.393	.719	7	.983
2004—Oklahoma (PCL)	1B	123	457	61	139	28	3	12	88	39	73	6	11	1-1	.304	.364	.457	.813	6	.995
—Texas (A.L.)	1B-DH	16	42	7	10	3	0	1	7	2	6	0	0	0-0	.238	.273	.381	.654	1	.990
2005—Oklahoma (PCL)	1B-DH	84	328	61	111	17	1	18	65	32	44	4	13	0-0	.338	.399	.561	.960	5	.994
—Texas (A.L.) DH-1B-OF	43	150	17	34	7	1	6	17	10	37	0	3	0-1	.227	.272	.407	.678	3	.969
2006—San Diego (N.L.)	1B	156	570	83	173	38	1	24	82	52	113	3	• 24	0-1	.304	.362	.500	.862	7	.995
American League totals (2 years)		59	192	24	44	10	1	7	24	12	43	0	3	0-0	.229	.272	.401	.673	4	.980
National League totals (1 year)		156	570	83	173	38	1	24	82	52	113	3	24	0-0	.304	.362	.500	.862	7	.995
Major League totals (3 years)		215	762	107	217	48	2	31	106	64	156	3	27	0-1	.285	.340	.475	.815	11	.993

DIVISION SERIES RECORD

Year	Team (League)	Pos.	G	AB	R	H	2B	3B	HR	RBI	BB	SO	HBP	GDP	SB-CS	Avg.	OBP	SLG	OPS	E	Avg.
2006—San Diego (N.L.)	1B	4	14	2	5	0	0	0	0	3	3	0	0	0-0	.357	.471	.357	.828	0	1.000

2006 LEFTY-RIGHTY SPLITS

vs.	Avg.	AB	H	2B	3B	HR	RBI	BB	SO	OBP	Slg.	vs.	Avg.	AB	H	2B	3B	HR	RBI	BB	SO	OBP	Slg.
L	.312	141	44	10	0	5	20	5	33	.345	.489	R	.301	429	129	28	1	19	62	47	80	.367	.503

GONZALEZ, ALEX L.   SS

PERSONAL: Born February 15, 1977, in Cagua, Venezuela. ... 6-0/202. ... Bats right, throws right. ... Full name: Alexander Luis Gonzalez. ... High school: Liceo Ramon Bastidas (Venezuela). **TRANSACTIONS/CAREER NOTES:** Signed as a non-drafted free agent by Florida Marlins organization (April 18, 1994). ... On disabled list (July 28-September 1, 2000); included rehabilitation assignment to Brevard County. ... On disabled list (May 19, 2002-remainder of season); included rehabilitation assignment to GCL Marlins. ... On suspended list (June 3-5, 2004) ... Signed as free agent by Boston Red Sox (February 6, 2006). ... On disabled list (August 19-September 3, 2006); included rehabilitation assignment to Pawtucket. **STATISTICAL NOTES:** Career major league grand slams: 1.

2006 GAMES PLAYED BY POSITION (MLB): SS—111.

Year	Team (League)	Pos.	G	AB	R	H	2B	3B	HR	RBI	BB	SO	HBP	GDP	SB-CS	Avg.	OBP	SLG	OPS	E	Avg.
1994—Dom. Marlins (DSL)	SS	54	239	30	54	7	3	3	31	15	36	...		4-...	.226	...	.318	...	34	.914
1995—Brevard County (FSL)	SS	17	59	6	12	2	1	0	8	1	14	1	2	1-1	.203	.230	.271	.501	8	.906
—GC Marlins (GCL)	SS	53	187	30	55	7	4	2	30	19	27	2	2	11-2	.294	.358	.406	.765	17	.932
1996—GC Marlins (GCL)	SS	10	41	6	16	3	0	0	6	2	4	0	1	1-0	.390	.419	.463	.882	5	.898
—Kane Co. (Midw.)	SS	4	10	2	2	0	0	0	2	2	4	1	1	0-0	.200	.385	.200	.585	0	1.000
—Portland (East.)	SS	11	34	4	8	0	1	0	1	2	10	1	2	0-0	.235	.294	.294	.591	7	.887
1997—Portland (East.)	SS	133	449	69	114	16	4	19	65	27	83	7	7	4-7	.254	.305	.434	.739	37	.943
1998—Charlotte (Int'l)	SS	108	422	71	117	20	10	10	51	28	80	6	6	4-7	.277	.330	.443	.773	20	.960
—Florida (N.L.)	SS	25	86	11	13	0	3	7	9	30	1	2	0-0	.151	.240	.279	.519	2	.978
1999—Florida (N.L.)	SS	136	560	81	155	28	8	14	59	15	113	12	13	3-5	.277	.308	.430	.739	27	.955
2000—Florida (N.L.)	SS	109	385	35	77	17	4	7	42	13	77	2	7	7-1	.200	.229	.319	.548	19	.957
—Brevard County (FSL)	SS	4	17	1	2	0	0	0	2	1	3	0	0	1-0	.118	.167	.118	.284	0	1.000
2001—Florida (N.L.)	SS-C	145	515	57	129	36	1	9	48	30	107	10	13	2-2	.250	.303	.377	.680	26	.960
2002—Florida (N.L.)	SS	42	151	15	34	7	1	2	18	12	32	4	2	3-1	.225	.290	.325	.620	3	.984
—GC Marlins (GCL)	SS	5	12	0	2	1	0	0	1	0	5	0	0	0-0	.167	.154	.250	.404	1	.923
2003—Florida (N.L.)	SS	150	528	52	135	33	6	18	77	33	106	13	8	0-4	.256	.313	.443	.756	16	.976
2004—Florida (N.L.)	SS	159	561	67	130	30	4	23	79	27	126	4	17	3-1	.232	.270	.419	.689	16	.976
2005—Florida (N.L.)	SS	130	435	45	115	30	0	5	45	31	81	5	11	5-3	.264	.319	.368	.686	16	.974

Year Team (League)	Pos.	G	AB	R	H	2B	3B	HR	RBI	BB	SO	HBP	GDP	SB-CS	Avg.	OBP	SLG	OPS	E	Avg.
														BATTING					**FIELDING**
2006— Pawtucket (Int'l)		1	3	0	1	0	0	0	0	0	1	1	0	0-0	.333	.500	.333	.833	0	1.000
— Boston (A.L.)	SS	111	388	48	99	24	2	9	50	22	67	5	6	1-0	.255	.299	.397	.695	7	.985
American League totals (1 year)		111	388	48	99	24	2	9	50	22	67	5	6	1-0	.255	.299	.397	.695	7	.985
National League totals (8 years)		896	3221	363	788	183	23	81	375	170	672	51	73	23-17	.245	.291	.391	.682	125	.968
Major League totals (9 years)		1007	3609	411	887	207	25	90	425	192	739	56	79	24-17	.246	.292	.392	.684	132	.970

DIVISION SERIES RECORD

Year Team (League)	Pos.	G	AB	R	H	2B	3B	HR	RBI	BB	SO	HBP	GDP	SB-CS	Avg.	OBP	SLG	OPS	E	Avg.
2003— Florida (N.L.)	SS	4	16	2	1	0	0	0	0	1	3	0	1	0-0	.063	.118	.063	.180	1	.929

CHAMPIONSHIP SERIES RECORD

Year Team (League)	Pos.	G	AB	R	H	2B	3B	HR	RBI	BB	SO	HBP	GDP	SB-CS	Avg.	OBP	SLG	OPS	E	Avg.
2003— Florida (N.L.)	SS	7	24	1	3	2	0	0	4	0	6	0	0	0-0	.125	.125	.208	.333	1	.970

WORLD SERIES RECORD

Year Team (League)	Pos.	G	AB	R	H	2B	3B	HR	RBI	BB	SO	HBP	GDP	SB-CS	Avg.	OBP	SLG	OPS	E	Avg.
2003— Florida (N.L.)	SS	6	22	3	6	2	0	1	2	0	7	0	1	0-1	.273	.273	.500	.773	0	1.000

ALL-STAR GAME RECORD

		G	AB	R	H	2B	3B	HR	RBI	BB	SO	HBP	GDP	SB-CS	Avg.	OBP	SLG	OPS	E	Avg.
All-Star Game totals (1 year)		1	1	0	0	0	0	0	0	0	0	0	0	0-0	.000	.000	.000	.000	0	1.000

2006 LEFTY-RIGHTY SPLITS

vs.	Avg.	AB	H	2B	3B	HR	RBI	BB	SO	OBP	Slg.	vs.	Avg.	AB	H	2B	3B	HR	RBI	BB	SO	OBP	Slg.
L	.278	126	35	8	0	3	18	10	26	.333	.413	R	.244	262	64	16	2	6	32	12	41	.282	.389

GONZALEZ, ALEX S.   IF/OF

PERSONAL: Born April 8, 1973, in Miami. ... 6-0/200. ... Bats right, throws right. ... Full name: Alexander Scott Gonzalez. ... High school: Miami Killian.

TRANSACTIONS/CAREER NOTES: Selected by Toronto Blue Jays organization in 14th round of 1991 free-agent draft. ... On disabled list (April 29-May 27, 1994); included rehabilitation assignment to Syracuse. ... On disabled list (August 13-September 14, 1997; and May 17, 1999-remainder of season). ... On disabled list (July 7-22, 2000); included rehabilitation assignment to Syracuse. ... Traded by Blue Jays to Chicago Cubs for P Felix Heredia and a player to be named (December 10, 2001); Blue Jays acquired IF James Deschaine to complete deal (December 13, 2001). ... On disabled list (May 10-25, 2002). ... On disabled list (May 6-July 19, 2004); included rehabilitation assignment to Iowa. ... Traded by Cubs with P Francis Beltran and IF Brendan Harris to Montreal Expos as part of four-team deal in which Cubs acquired SS Nomar Garciaparra and OF Matt Murton from Red Sox, Red Sox acquired SS Orlando Cabrera from Expos and 1B Doug Mientkiewicz from Twins, and Twins acquired P Justin Jones from Cubs (July 31, 2004). ... Traded by Expos to San Diego Padres for cash (September 16, 2004). ... Signed as a free agent by Tampa Bay Devil Rays (January 7, 2005). ... On disabled list (July 1-16, 2005). ... On voluntary retired list (May 21-November 9, 2006). **RECORDS:** Shares major league record for most strikeouts, extra-inning game (6, September 9, 1998, 13 innings).

2006 GAMES PLAYED BY POSITION (MLB): SS—3, 1B—3, 3B—2, OF—1.

Year Team (League)	Pos.	G	AB	R	H	2B	3B	HR	RBI	BB	SO	HBP	GDP	SB-CS	Avg.	OBP	SLG	OPS	E	Avg.
														BATTING					**FIELDING**
1991— GC Jays (GCL)	SS	53	191	29	40	5	4	0	10	12	41	3	1	7-2	.209	.267	.277	.544	21	.915
1992— Myrtle Beach (SAL)	SS	134	535	83	145	22	9	10	62	38	119	3	9	26-14	.271	.322	.402	.724	48	.932
1993— Knoxville (Southern)	SS	142	561	93	162	29	7	16	69	39	110	6	9	38-13	.289	.339	.451	.790	30	.956
1994— Toronto (A.L.)	SS	15	53	7	8	3	1	0	1	4	17	1	2	3-0	.151	.224	.245	.469	6	.918
— Syracuse (Int'l)	SS-DH	110	437	69	124	22	4	12	57	53	92	1	9	23-6	.284	.361	.435	.796	31	.943
1995— Toronto (A.L.)	SS-3B-DH	111	367	51	89	19	4	10	42	44	114	1	7	4-4	.243	.322	.398	.720	19	.954
1996— Toronto (A.L.)	SS	147	527	64	124	30	5	14	64	45	127	5	12	16-6	.235	.300	.391	.691	21	.973
1997— Toronto (A.L.)	SS	.126	426	46	102	23	2	12	35	34	94	5	9	15-6	.239	.302	.387	.689	8	.986
1998— Toronto (A.L.)	SS	158	568	70	136	28	1	13	51	28	121	6	13	21-6	.239	.281	.361	.642	17	.976
1999— Toronto (A.L.)	SS-DH	38	154	22	45	13	0	2	12	16	23	3	4	4-2	.292	.370	.416	.786	4	.980
2000— Toronto (A.L.)	SS	141	527	68	133	31	2	15	69	43	113	4	14	4-4	.252	.313	.404	.717	16	.975
— Syracuse (Int'l)	SS	1	5	0	0	0	0	0	0	0	2	0	0	0-0	.000	.000	.000	.000	0	1.000
2001— Toronto (A.L.)	SS	154	636	79	161	25	5	17	76	43	149	7	16	18-11	.253	.303	.388	.692	10	.987
2002— Chicago (N.L.)	SS	142	513	58	127	27	5	18	61	46	136	3	11	5-3	.248	.312	.425	.737	21	.965
2003— Chicago (N.L.)	SS	152	536	71	122	37	0	20	59	47	123	6	17	3-3	.228	.295	.409	.704	10	.984
2004— Iowa (PCL)	SS	8	24	7	8	3	0	0	4	4	7	0	1	1-0	.333	.429	.458	.887	0	1.000
— Chicago (N.L.)	SS	37	129	15	28	10	0	3	8	4	26	0	6	1-1	.217	.241	.364	.605	5	.967
— Montreal (N.L.)	SS	35	133	19	32	7	0	4	16	8	32	1	1	1-1	.241	.289	.383	.672	6	.960
— San Diego (N.L.)	SS	11	23	2	4	1	1	0	3	2	6	0	0	0-0	.174	.240	.304	.544	0	1.000
2005— Tampa Bay (A.L.)	3B-SS	109	349	47	94	20	1	9	42	26	74	3	13	2-1	.269	.323	.410	.733	16	.944
2006— Philadelphia (N.L.)	1B-SS-3B OF	20	36	4	4	0	0	1	2	1	10	0	3	0-0	.111	.158	.111	.269	1	.966
American League totals (9 years)		999	3607	454	892	192	21	92	388	283	832	35	90	87-40	.247	.306	.389	.695	117	.973
National League totals (4 years)		397	1370	169	317	82	6	45	148	109	333	10	38	10-8	.231	.292	.399	.690	43	.973
Major League totals (13 years)		1396	4977	623	1209	274	27	137	536	392	1165	45	128	97-48	.243	.302	.391	.694	160	.973

DIVISION SERIES RECORD

Year Team (League)	Pos.	G	AB	R	H	2B	3B	HR	RBI	BB	SO	HBP	GDP	SB-CS	Avg.	OBP	SLG	OPS	E	Avg.
2003— Chicago (N.L.)	SS	5	12	1	3	0	0	1	1	2	3	0	0	0-1	.250	.357	.500	.857	0	1.000

CHAMPIONSHIP SERIES RECORD

Year Team (League)	Pos.	G	AB	R	H	2B	3B	HR	RBI	BB	SO	HBP	GDP	SB-CS	Avg.	OBP	SLG	OPS	E	Avg.
2003— Chicago (N.L.)	SS	7	28	5	8	2	0	3	7	2	7	0	0	0-0	.286	.333	.679	1.012	1	.968

2006 LEFTY-RIGHTY SPLITS

vs.	Avg.	AB	H	2B	3B	HR	RBI	BB	SO	OBP	Slg.	vs.	Avg.	AB	H	2B	3B	HR	RBI	BB	SO	OBP	Slg.
L	.130	23	3	0	0	0	1	2	7	.200	.130	R	.077	13	1	0	0	0	0	0	3	.077	.077

GONZALEZ, EDGAR   P

PERSONAL: Born February 23, 1983, in Monterrey, Mexico. ... 6-0/215. ... Throws right, bats right. ... Full name: Edgar Gerardo Gonzalez. **TRANSACTIONS/CAREER NOTES:** Signed as a non-drafted free agent by Arizona Diamondbacks organization (April 18, 2000). ... On suspended list for 2000 and 2001 seasons.

CAREER HITTING: 4-for-30 (.133), 1 R, 0 2B, 0 3B, 0 HR, 0 RBI.

Year Team (League)	W	L	Pct.	ERA	WHIP	G	GS	CG	ShO	Hld.	Sv.-Opp.	IP	H	R	ER	HR	BB-IBB	SO	Avg.
2002— South Bend (Mid.)	11	8	.579	2.91	1.16	23	23	4	2	...	0-...	151.1	141	66	49	4	34-0	110	.246
— Lancaster (Calif.)	3	0	1.000	0.78	1.17	4	4	0	0	...	0-...	23.0	24	7	2	1	3-0	21	.264
2003— El Paso (Texas)	2	2	.500	3.50	1.42	6	6	0	0	...	0-...	36.0	40	18	14	1	11-0	30	.282
— Tucson (PCL)	8	7	.533	3.75	1.19	20	19	1	0	...	0-...	129.2	126	65	54	4	28-0	69	.255
— Arizona (N.L.)	2	1	.667	4.91	1.91	2	2	0	0	...	0-1	18.1	28	10	10	3	7-2	14	.368

G

Year Team (League)	W	L	Pct.	ERA	WHIP	G	GS	CG	ShO	Hld.	Sv.-Opp.	IP	H	R	ER	HR	BB-IBB	SO	Avg.
2004—Tucson (PCL)	5	5	.500	4.88	1.32	15	15	1	1		0-...	94.0	89	52	51	15	25-0	66	.277
—Arizona (N.L.)	0	9	.000	9.32	1.94	10	10	0	0	0	0-0	46.1	72	49	48	15	18-4	31	.362
2005—Arizona (N.L.)	0	0	...	99.99	12.00	1	0	0	0	0	0-0	0.1	2	4	4	1	2-0	1	.667
—Tucson (PCL)	11	6	.647	4.37	1.34	28	24	0	0	0	0-0	167.0	185	94	81	20	38-0	116	.283
2006—Tucson (PCL)	3	8	.273	3.90	1.22	24	24	3	1	0	0-0	138.1	142	69	60	11	27-0	107	.268
—Arizona (N.L.)	3	4	.429	4.22	1.27	11	5	0	0	1	0-0	42.2	45	20	20	7	9-0	28	.273
Major League totals (4 years)	5	14	.263	6.85	1.70	31	17	0	0	1	0-1	107.2	147	83	82	26	36-6	74	.332

2006 LEFTY-RIGHTY SPLITS

vs.	Avg.	AB	H	2B	3B	HR	RBI	BB	SO	OBP	Slg.	vs.	Avg.	AB	H	2B	3B	HR	RBI	BB	SO	OBP	Slg.
L	.259	85	22	5	0	5	10	7	12	.312	.494	R	.288	80	23	9	1	2	10	2	16	.329	.500

GONZALEZ, ENRIQUE — P

PERSONAL: Born August 6, 1982, in Bolivar, Venezuela. ... 5-10/195. ... Throws right, bats right. ... Full name: Enrique Cesar Gonzalez. . **TRANSACTIONS/CAREER NOTES:** Signed as a non-drafted free agent by Arizona Diamondbacks organization (October 30, 1998). **MISCELLANEOUS NOTES:** Made an out in only appearance as pinch hitter (2006).

CAREER HITTING: 9-for-32 (.281), 3 R, 1 2B, 0 3B, 0 HR, 3 RBI.

Year Team (League)	W	L	Pct.	ERA	WHIP	G	GS	CG	ShO	Hld.	Sv.-Opp.	IP	H	R	ER	HR	BB-IBB	SO	Avg.
1999—Dom. D'backs (DSL)	7	3	.700	1.64	0.92	12	11	1	0		0-...	71.0	41	21	13	0	24-0	82	.169
2000—Ariz. D'backs (Ariz.)	1	0	1.000	1.53	1.58	11	0	0	0		1-...	17.2	16	13	3	0	12-0	17	.239
—Tucson (PCL)	1	0	1.000	0.00	0.50	1	0	0	0		0-...	4.0	1	0	0	0	1-0	1	.091
2001—South Bend (Mid.)	4	12	.250	4.01	1.34	26	26	1	0		0-...	146.0	142	81	65	9	53-0	92	.257
2002—Lancaster (Calif.)	1	4	.200	12.27	2.62	5	5	0	0		0-...	18.1	34	27	25	3	14-0	11	.410
—Yakima (N'west)	5	2	.714	2.45	1.15	11	11	0	0		0-...	66.0	53	27	18	2	23-0	57	.219
—South Bend (Mid.)	1	2	.333	3.74	1.48	4	4	0	0		0-...	21.2	23	16	9	1	9-0	20	.271
2003—South Bend (Mid.)	4	3	.571	2.13	1.21	55	0	0	0		3-...	72.0	58	22	17	5	29-3	63	.218
2004—Lancaster (Calif.)	13	6	.684	3.22	1.21	42	17	0	0		0-...	142.1	128	64	51	13	44-0	110	.242
2005—Tennessee (Sou.)	11	8	.579	3.46	1.31	27	27	2	2	0	0-0	161.1	160	76	62	8	52-0	146	.264
2006—Tucson (PCL)	4	3	.571	2.24	1.24	10	10	0	0	0'	0-0	60.1	61	22	15	2	14-0	35	.263
—Arizona (N.L.)	3	7	.300	5.67	1.39	22	18	0	0	0	0-0	106.1	114	71	67	14	34-0	66	.275
Major League totals (1 year)	3	7	.300	5.67	1.39	22	18	0	0	0	0-0	106.1	114	71	67	14	34-0	66	.275

2006 LEFTY-RIGHTY SPLITS

vs.	Avg.	AB	H	2B	3B	HR	RBI	BB	SO	OBP	Slg.	vs.	Avg.	AB	H	2B	3B	HR	RBI	BB	SO	OBP	Slg.
L	.288	184 -	53	7	1	4	37	18	22	.350	.402	R	.265	230	61	10	2	10	32	16	44	.321	.457

GONZALEZ, GEREMI — P

PERSONAL: Born January 8, 1975, in Maracaibo, Venezuela. ... 6-0/220. ... Throws right, bats right. ... Full name: Geremis Segundo Gonzalez. ... High school: Colegro La Chinita (Maracaibo). **TRANSACTIONS/CAREER NOTES:** Signed as a non-drafted free agent by Chicago Cubs organization (October 21, 1991). ... On disabled list (July 25, 1998-remainder of season). ... On disabled list (April 1, 1999-entire season); included rehabilitation assignments to Daytona, West Tenn and Iowa. ... On disabled list (March 28, 2000-entire season); included rehabilitation assignments to AZL Cubs and Lansing. ... Released by Cubs (March 13, 2001). ... Signed by Texas Rangers organization (December 18, 2001). ... Signed as a free agent by Tampa Bay Devil Rays organization (November 21, 2002). ... Released by Devil Rays (November 19, 2004). ... Signed by Boston Red Sox organization (February 1, 2005). ... Signed as free agent by New York Mets organization (January 24, 2006). ... Traded by Mets to Milwaukee Brewers for P Mike Adams (May 26, 2006). ... Released by Brewers (October 12, 2006). ... Signed by Toronto Blue Jays organization (November 10, 2006). **MISCELLANEOUS NOTES:** Appeared in one game as pinch runner (1998).

CAREER HITTING: 10-for-86 (.116), 2 R, 1 2B, 0 3B, 0 HR, 3 RBI.

Year Team (League)	W	L	Pct.	ERA	WHIP	G	GS	CG	ShO	Hld.	Sv.-Opp.	IP	H	R	ER	HR	BB-IBB	SO	Avg.
1992—Ariz. Cubs (Ariz.)	0	5	.000	7.80	1.93	14	7	0	0		0-...	45.0	65	59	39	0	22-0	39	.325
1993—Huntington (Appal.)	3	9	.250	6.25	1.77	12	12	1	0		0-...	67.2	82	59	47	6	38-0	42	.300
1994—Peoria (Midw.)	1	7	.125	5.55	1.65	13	13	1	0		0-...	71.1	86	53	44	4	32-0	39	.306
—Will. (NYP)	4	6	.400	4.24	1.39	16	12	1	1		1-...	80.2	83	46	38	6	29-0	64	.266
1995—Rockford (Midwest)	4	4	.500	5.10	1.39	12	12	1	0		0-...	65.1	63	43	37	4	28-0	36	.247
—Daytona (Fla. St.)	5	1	.833	1.22	1.06	19	2	0	0		4-...	44.1	34	15	6	0	13-1	30	.211
1996—Orlando (South.)	6	3	.667	3.34	1.27	17	14	0	0		0-...	97.0	95	39	36	6	28-1	85	.250
1997—Iowa (Am. Assoc.)	2	2	.500	3.48	1.10	10	10	1	1		0-...	62.0	47	27	24	8	21-0	58	.209
—Chicago (N.L.)	11	9	.550	4.25	1.35	23	23	1	1	0	0-...	144.0	126	73	68	16	69-5	93	.236
1998—Chicago (N.L.)	7	7	.500	5.32	1.50	20	20	1	1	0	0-...	110.0	124	72	65	13	41-5	70	.281
1999—Daytona (Fla. St.)	0	0	...	0.00	0.43	2	2	0	0		0-...	4.2	2	0	0	0	0-0	4	.125
—West Tenn (Sou.)	0	0	...	1.74	1.55	3	3	0	0		0-...	10.1	7	2	2	0	9-0	12	.200
—Iowa (PCL)	0	1	.000	4.50	1.60	3	3	0	0		0-...	10.0	10	8	5	1	6-0	10	.270
2000—Ariz. Cubs (Ariz.)	0	1	.000	2.70	1.00	4	4	0	0		0-...	10.0	8	3	3	0	2-0	15	.211
—Lansing (Midw.)	0	0	...	0.00	0.00	1	1	0	0		0-...	0.2	0	0	0	0	0-0	2	.000
2001—			Did not play.																
2002—Oklahoma (PCL)	6	5	.545	3.33	1.36	46	5	0	0		14-...	92.0	86	40	34	8	39-5	93	.249
2003—Durham (Int'l)	1	0	1.000	2.53	0.90	7	6	0	0		0-...	32.0	24	11	9	2	6-0	33	.202
—Tampa Bay (A.L.)	6	11	.353	3.91	1.28	25	25	0	0	0	0-0	156.1	131	71	68	18	69-1	97	.228
2004—Tampa Bay (A.L.)	0	5	.000	6.97	1.83	11	8	0	0	0	0-0	50.1	72	42	39	9	20-0	22	.346
—Durham (Int'l)	4	2	.667	3.90	1.20	19	8	0	0		1-...	57.2	50	27	25	7	19-0	44	.233
2005—Pawtucket (Int'l)	5	2	.714	2.61	1.12	11	11	0	0		0-...	69.0	63	20	20	8	14-0	62	.245
—Boston (A.L.)	2	1	.667	6.11	1.43	28	3	0	0	1	0-0	56.0	64	39	38	7	16-2	28	.288
2006—Norfolk (Int'l)	1	2	.333	3.03	1.12	6	6	0	0		0-...	35.2	31	14	12	1	9-0	30	.230
—New York (N.L.)	0	0	...	7.71	1.93	3	3	0	0	0	0-0	14.0	21	12	12	4	6-1	8	.362
—Milwaukee (N.L.)	4	2	.667	5.14	1.60	21	1	0	0	0	0-1	42.0	50	31	24	6	17-1	36	.298
American League totals (3 years)	8	17	.320	4.97	1.42	64	36	0	0	1	0-0	262.2	267	152	145	34	105-3	147	.266
National League totals (3 years)	22	18	.550	4.91	1.46	67	47	2	2	0	0-1	310.0	321	188	169	39	133-12	207	.267
Major League totals (6 years)	30	35	.462	4.93	1.44	131	83	2	2	1	0-1	572.2	588	340	314	73	238-15	354	.267

DIVISION SERIES RECORD

Year Team (League)	W	L	Pct.	ERA	WHIP	G	GS	CG	ShO	Hld.	Sv.-Opp.	IP	H	R	ER	HR	BB-IBB	SO	Avg.
2005—Boston (A.L.)	0	0	...	15.43	1.29	1	0	0	0	0	0-0	2.1	2	4	4	1	1-0	0	.222

2006 LEFTY-RIGHTY SPLITS

vs.	Avg.	AB	H	2B	3B	HR	RBI	BB	SO	OBP	Slg.	vs.	Avg.	AB	H	2B	3B	HR	RBI	BB	SO	OBP	Slg.
L	.442	86	38	9	2	5	22	6	11	.473	.767	R	.236	140	33	9	0	5	21	17	33	.323	.407

G

GONZALEZ, LUIS — OF

PERSONAL: Born September 3, 1967, in Tampa. ... 6-2/200. ... Bats left, throws right. ... Full name: Luis Emilio Gonzalez. ... High school: Jefferson (Tampa). ... College: South Alabama. **TRANSACTIONS/CAREER NOTES:** Selected by Houston Astros organization in fourth round of 1988 free-agent draft. ... On disabled list (August 29-September 13, 1991; and July 21-August 5, 1992). ... Traded by Astros with C Scott Servais to Chicago Cubs for C Rick Wilkins (June 28, 1995). ... Signed as a free agent by Astros (December 19, 1996). ... Signed as a free agent by Detroit Tigers (December 9, 1997). ... Traded by Tigers to Arizona Diamondbacks for OF Karim Garcia (December 28, 1998). ... On disabled list (August 2, 2004-remainder of season). ... On bereavement list (June 25-29, 2005). **HONORS:** Named outfielder on THE SPORTING NEWS N.L. All-Star team (2001). ... Named outfielder on N.L. Silver Slugger team (2001). **STATISTICAL NOTES:** Hit for the cycle (July 5, 2000). ... Hit three home runs in one game (June 8, 2001; and May 10, 2004). ... Career major league grand slams: 3.

2006 GAMES PLAYED BY POSITION (MLB): OF—150, DH—1.

											BATTING								FIELDING	
Year	Team (League)	Pos.	G	AB	R	H	2B	3B	HR	RBI	BB	SO	HBP	GDP	SB-CS	Avg.	OBP	SLG	OPS	E	Avg.
1988—	Asheville (S. Atl.)	3B	31	115	13	29	7	1	2	14	12	17	2	4	2-2	.252	.333	.383	.716	6	.931
—	Auburn (NY-Penn)	1B-3B-SS	39	157	32	49	10	3	5	27	12	19	1	1	2-0	.312	.354	.510	.864	13	.902
1989—	Osceola (Fla. St.)	DH	86	287	46	82	16	7	6	38	37	49	4	3	2-1	.286	.370	.453	.823	...	...
1990—	Columbus (Southern)	1B-3B	138	495	86	131	30	6	24	89	54	100	6	6	27-9	.265	.337	.495	.832	23	.980
—	Houston (N.L.)	1B-3B	12	21	1	4	2	0	0	0	2	5	0	0	0-0	.190	.261	.286	.547	0	1.000
1991—	Houston (N.L.)	OF	137	473	51	120	28	9	13	69	40	101	8	9	10-7	.254	.320	.433	.753	5	.984
1992—	Houston (N.L.)	OF	122	387	40	94	19	3	10	55	24	52	2	6	7-7	.243	.289	.385	.674	2	.993
—	Tucson (PCL)	OF	13	44	11	19	4	2	1	9	5	7	1	0	4-1	.432	.490	.682	1.172	1	.963
1993—	Houston (N.L.)	OF	154	540	82	162	34	3	15	72	47	83	10	9	20-9	.300	.361	.457	.818	8	.978
1994—	Houston (N.L.)	OF	112	392	57	107	29	4	8	67	49	57	3	10	15-13	.273	.353	.429	.782	2	.991
1995—	Houston (N.L.)	OF	56	209	35	54	10	4	6	35	18	30	3	8	1-3	.258	.322	.431	.753	2	.980
—	Chicago (N.L.)	OF	77	262	34	76	19	4	7	34	39	33	3	8	5-5	.290	.384	.473	.858	4	.978
1996—	Chicago (N.L.)	OF-1B	146	483	70	131	30	4	15	79	61	49	4	13	9-6	.271	.354	.443	.797	5	.988
1997—	Houston (N.L.)	OF-1B	152	550	78	142	31	2	10	68	71	67	5	12	10-7	.258	.345	.376	.722	5	.988
1998—	Detroit (A.L.)	OF-DH	154	547	84	146	35	5	23	71	57	62	8	9	12-7	.267	.340	.475	.816	3	.988
1999—	Arizona (N.L.)	OF-DH	153	614	112	*206	45	4	26	111	66	63	7	13	9-5	.336	.403	.549	.952	5	.983
2000—	Arizona (N.L.)	OF	•162	618	106	192	47	2	31	114	78	85	12	12	2-4	.311	.392	.544	.935	3	.990
2001—	Arizona (N.L.)	OF	•162	609	128	198	36	7	57	142	100	83	14	14	1-1	.325	.429	.688	1.117	0	1.000
2002—	Arizona (N.L.)	OF	148	524	90	151	19	3	28	103	97	76	5	14	9-2	.288	.400	.496	.896	4	.985
2003—	Arizona (N.L.)	OF	156	579	92	176	46	4	26	104	94	67	3	19	5-3	.304	.402	.532	.934	3	.989
2004—	Arizona (N.L.)	OF-DH	105	379	69	98	28	5	17	48	68	58	2	9	2-2	.259	.373	.493	.866	6	.965
2005—	Arizona (N.L.)	OF	155	579	90	157	37	0	24	79	78	90	11	14	4-1	.271	.366	.459	.825	3	.989
2006—	Arizona (N.L.)	OF-DH	153	586	93	159	52	2	15	73	69	58	7	14	0-1	.271	.352	.444	.795	1	.996
	American League totals (1 year)		154	547	84	146	35	5	23	71	57	62	8	9	12-7	.267	.340	.475	.816	3	.988
	National League totals (16 years)		2162	7805	1228	2227	512	60	308	1253	1001	1057	99	182	109-76	.285	.370	.485	.855	56	.986
	Major League totals (17 years)		2316	8352	1312	2373	547	65	331	1324	1058	1119	107	191	121-83	.284	.368	.484	.852	59	.986

DIVISION SERIES RECORD

											BATTING								FIELDING	
Year	Team (League)	Pos.	G	AB	R	H	2B	3B	HR	RBI	BB	SO	HBP	GDP	SB-CS	Avg.	OBP	SLG	OPS	E	Avg.
1997—	Houston (N.L.)	OF	3	12	0	4	0	0	0	0	0	1	0	0	0-0	.333	.333	.333	.667	1	.933
1999—	Arizona (N.L.)	OF	4	10	3	2	1	0	1	2	5	1	0	0	0-0	.200	.500	.600	1.100	0	1.000
2001—	Arizona (N.L.)	OF	5	19	1	5	0	0	1	5	2	4	0	0	0-0	.263	.333	.421	.754	0	1.000
	Division series totals (3 years)		12	41	4	11	1	0	2	7	6	1	0	0	0-0	.268	.388	.439	.827	1	.958

CHAMPIONSHIP SERIES RECORD

											BATTING								FIELDING	
Year	Team (League)	Pos.	G	AB	R	H	2B	3B	HR	RBI	BB	SO	HBP	GDP	SB-CS	Avg.	OBP	SLG	OPS	E	Avg.
2001—	Arizona (N.L.)	OF	5	19	4	4	0	0	1	4	3	3	1	0	0-0	.211	.348	.368	.716	0	1.000

WORLD SERIES RECORD

											BATTING								FIELDING	
Year	Team (League)	Pos.	G	AB	R	H	2B	3B	HR	RBI	BB	SO	HBP	GDP	SB-CS	Avg.	OBP	SLG	OPS	E	Avg.
2001—	Arizona (N.L.)	OF	7	27	4	7	2	0	1	5	1	11	2	1	0-0	.259	.333	.444	.778	0	1.000

ALL-STAR GAME RECORD

									BATTING								
	G	AB	R	H	2B	3B	HR	RBI	BB	SO	HBP	GDP	SB-CS	Avg.	OBP	SLG	OPS	E	Avg.
All-Star Game totals (5 years)	5	7	1	4	2	0	0	0	0	0	0	0	0-0	.571	.571	.857	1.429	0

2006 LEFTY-RIGHTY SPLITS

vs.	Avg.	AB	H	2B	3B	HR	RBI	BB	SO	OBP	Slg.		vs.	Avg.	AB	H	2B	3B	HR	RBI	BB	SO	OBP	Slg.
L	.259	174	45	15	1	3	16	16	19	.332	.408		R	.277	412	114	37	1	12	57	53	39	.360	.459

GONZALEZ, LUIS A. — 2B

PERSONAL: Born June 26, 1979, in Maracay, Venezuela. ... 5-11/170. ... Bats right, throws right. ... Full name: Luis Alberto Gonzalez. **TRANSACTIONS/CAREER NOTES:** Signed as a non-drafted free agent by Cleveland Indians organization (July 5, 1996). ... Selected by Colorado Rockies from Indians organization in Rule 5 major league draft (December 15, 2003). ... On disabled list (May 27-June 11, 2006); included rehabilitation assignment to Asheville and Colorado Springs.

2006 GAMES PLAYED BY POSITION (MLB): 2B—32, 1B—7, OF—7, 3B—3.

											BATTING								FIELDING	
Year	Team (League)	Pos.	G	AB	R	H	2B	3B	HR	RBI	BB	SO	HBP	GDP	SB-CS	Avg.	OBP	SLG	OPS	E	Avg.
1997—	Maracay 1 (VSL)	2B-SS-3B	52	105	17	38	7	1	1	19	17	10	0	1	7-0	.362	.433	.476	.909	...	...
1998—	Columbus (S. Atl.)	SS	101	320	48	87	14	1	3	32	28	63	8	5	10-3	.272	.345	.350	.695	28	.940
1999—	Kinston (Carol.)		1	1	0	0	0	0	0	0	0	0	0	0	0-0	.000	.000	.000	.000	...	...
—	Columbus (S. Atl.)	SS-3B-2B	83	299	41	88	18	2	7	50	26	40	5	5	6-5	.294	.355	.438	.793	21	.931
2000—	Kinston (Carol.)	2B-SS	79	284	32	70	11	0	2	33	21	54	6	6	6-6	.246	.310	.306	.616	12	.961
2001—	Kinston (Carol.)	3B-2B-SS	52	183	31	59	14	0	5	19	14	36	8	1	3-5	.322	.391	.481	.872	9	.945
—	Akron (East.)	2B-SS-3B	52	199	41	60	12	2	5	17	7	26	2	3	2-3	.302	.329	.457	.786	3	.987
2002—	Buffalo (Int'l)	2B	8	19	0	2	0	0	0	1	1	4	1	1	0-0	.105	.190	.105	.296	1	.967
—	Akron (East.)	OF-1B	73	263	42	70	10	3	6	24	12	37	5	6	4-0	.266	.304	.395	.700	8	.962
2003—	Akron (East.)	1B-2B-3B-SS																			
		3B-SS	116	431	72	137	22	4	7	62	46	41	6	17	1-0	.318	.385	.436	.821	9	.985
2004—	Colorado (N.L.)	2B-3B-SS																			
		SS-DH	102	322	42	94	17	2	12	40	15	67	4	5	1-5	.292	.330	.469	.799	2	.993
2005—	Colorado (N.L.)	2B-SS-3B																			
		1B-OF	128	404	51	118	25	0	9	44	20	63	6	7	3-4	.292	.333	.421	.753	4	.991
2006—	Colo. Springs (PCL)		27	97	15	26	4	2	2	10	6	11	6	10	1-0	.268	.345	.412	.758	1	.991
—	Colorado (N.L.)	2B-1B-OF																			
		3B	61	149	7	36	9	1	2	14	4	27	2	3	1-1	.242	.269	.356	.625	2	.989
	Major League totals (3 years)		291	875	100	248	51	3	23	98	39	157	12	15	5-10	.283	.321	.427	.749	8	.991

G

vs.	Avg.	AB	H	2B	3B	HR	RBI	BB	SO	OBP	Slg.	vs.	Avg.	AB	H	2B	3B	HR	RBI	BB	SO	OBP	Slg.
L	.219	32	7	3	0	1	4	1	9	.235	.406	R	.248	117	29	6	1	1	10	3	18	.279	.342

GONZALEZ, MIKE P

PERSONAL: Born May 23, 1978, in Corpus Christi, Texas. ... 6-2/205. ... Throws left, bats right. ... Full name: Michael Vela Gonzalez. ... High school: Harvest Christian Academy (Pasadena, Texas). ... Junior college: San Jacinto (Texas). **TRANSACTIONS/CAREER NOTES:** Selected by Pittsburgh Pirates organization in 17th round of 1996 free-agent draft; did not sign. ... Selected by Pittsburgh Pirates organization in 30th round of 1997 free-agent draft. ... Traded by Pirates with P Scott Sauerbeck to Boston Red Sox for Ps Brandon Lyon and Anastacio Martinez (July 22, 2003). ... Traded by Red Sox with IF Freddy Sanchez to Pirates for Ps Jeff Suppan, Brandon Lyon and Anastacio Martinez (July 31, 2003). ... On disabled list (June 23-August 16, 2005); included rehabilitation assignment to Indianapolis. ... On disabled list (August 25, 2006-remainder of season).

CAREER HITTING: 1-for-2 (.500), 0 R, 1 2B, 0 3B, 0 HR, 2 RBI.

Year	Team (League)	W	L	Pct.	ERA	WHIP	G	GS	CG	ShO	Hld.	Sv.-Opp.	IP	H	R	ER	HR	BB-IBB	SO	Avg.
1997— GC Pirates (GCL)		2	0	1.000	2.48	1.00	7	3	0	0	...	0-...	29.0	21	9	8	0	8-0	33	.200
— Augusta (S. Atl.)		1	1	.500	1.86	0.98	4	3	0	0	...	0-...	19.1	11	5	4	1	8-0	22	.164
1998— Lynchburg (Caro.)		0	3	.000	6.67	1.87	7	7	0	0	...	0-...	28.1	40	21	21	5	13-0	22	.351
— Augusta (S. Atl.)		4	2	.667	2.84	1.36	11	9	0	0	...	0-...	50.2	43	24	16	2	26-0	72	.231
1999— Lynchburg (Caro.)		10	4	.714	4.02	1.44	20	20	0	0	...	0-...	112.0	98	55	50	10	63-0	119	.240
— Altoona (East.)		2	3	.400	8.10	1.99	7	5	0	0	...	0-...	26.2	34	25	24	4	19-0	31	.312
2000— GC Pirates (GCL)		1	0	1.000	4.50	2.00	2	1	0	0	...	0-...	6.0	8	6	3	1	4-0	7	.267
— Lynchburg (Caro.)		4	3	.571	4.66	1.63	12	10	0	0	...	0-...	56.0	57	34	29	6	34-0	53	.269
2001— Lynchburg (Caro.)		2	2	.500	2.93	1.14	14	2	0	0	...	0-...	30.2	28	14	10	3	7-1	32	.241
— Altoona (East.)		5	4	.556	3.71	1.34	14	14	1	1	...	0-...	87.1	81	38	36	5	36-0	66	.251
2002— GC Pirates (GCL)		2	0	1.000	0.00	0.60	2	2	0	0	...	0-...	13.1	5	1	0	0	3-0	14	.114
— Altoona (East.)		8	4	.667	3.80	1.45	16	16	0	0	...	0-...	85.1	77	38	36	4	47-2	82	.244
2003— Lynchburg (Caro.)		0	1	.000	5.14	1.71	5	0	0	0	...	0-...	7.0	7	9	4	0	5-0	9	.269
— Pawtucket (Int'l)		0	0	...	1.23	0.82	5	0	0	0	...	1-...	7.1	4	1	1	1	2-0	10	.154
— Nashville (PCL)		0	0	...	0.00	1.80	2	0	0	0	...	1-...	1.2	2	0	0	0	1-0	2	.286
— Altoona (East.)		0	0	...	4.50	1.30	7	0	0	0	...	2-...	10.0	9	5	5	0	4-1	10	.231
— Pittsburgh (N.L.)		0	1	.000	7.56	1.56	16	0	0	0	3	0-0	8.1	7	7	7	4	6-0	6	.233
2004— Nashville (PCL)		2	0	1.000	0.90	0.95	14	0	0	0	...	2-...	20.0	12	2	2	0	6-0	35	.185
— Pittsburgh (N.L.)		3	1	.750	1.25	0.88	47	0	0	0	13	1-4	43.1	32	7	6	2	6-0	55	.201
2005— Indianapolis (Int'l)		0	0	...	0.00	0.00	2	0	0	0	0	0-0	3.1	0	0	0	0	0-0	5	.000
— Pittsburgh (N.L.)		1	3	.250	2.70	1.32	51	0	0	0	15	3-3	50.0	35	15	15	2	31-2	58	.197
2006— Pittsburgh (N.L.)		3	4	.429	2.17	1.35	54	0	0	0	3	24-24	54.0	42	13	13	1	31-2	64	.213
Major League totals (4 years)		7	9	.438	2.37	1.22	168	0	0	0	34	28-31	155.2	116	42	41	9	74-4	183	.206

2006 LEFTY-RIGHTY SPLITS

vs.	Avg.	AB	H	2B	3B	HR	RBI	BB	SO	OBP	Slg.	vs.	Avg.	AB	H	2B	3B	HR	RBI	BB	SO	OBP	Slg.
L	.163	43	7	1	0	1	4	5	16	.265	.256	R	.227	154	35	5	0	0	10	26	48	.341	.260

GONZALEZ, WIKI C

PERSONAL: Born May 17, 1974, in Aragua, Venezuela. ... 5-11/203. ... Bats right, throws right. ... Full name: Wiklenman Vicente Gonzalez. ... Name pronounced: WICK-ee. **TRANSACTIONS/CAREER NOTES:** Signed as non-drafted free agent by Pittsburgh Pirates organization (February 12, 1992). ... Selected by San Diego Padres organization from Pirates organization in Rule 5 minor league draft (December 9, 1996). ... On disabled list (June 3-July 3, 2001); included rehabilitation assignment to Lake Elsinore. ... On disabled list (April 5-May 15 and July 18-August 24, 2002); included rehabilitation assignment to Lake Elsinore. ... Traded by Padres with P Kevin Jarvis, IF Dave Hansen and OF Vince Faison To Seattle Mariners for IF Jeff Cirillo, P Brian Sweeney and cash (January 6, 2004). ... On disabled list (May 15-July 1, 2005); included rehabilitation assignment to Tacoma. ... Signed as a free agent by Washington Nationals organization (December 13, 2005). **STATISTICAL NOTES:** Career major league pitching: 0-0, 0.00 ERA, 1 G, 1 IP, 0 H, 0 R, 0 ER, 1 BB, 0 SO.

2006 GAMES PLAYED BY POSITION (MLB): C—12.

										BATTING										FIELDING	
Year	Team (League)	Pos.	G	AB	R	H	2B	3B	HR	RBI	BB	SO	HBP	GDP	SB-CS	Avg.	OBP	SLG	OPS	E	Avg.
1992— Dom. Pirates (DSL)			63	190	20	48	6	1	3	33	22	12	4	6	4-1	.253	.338	.342	.680	9	.969
1993— Dom. Pirates (DSL)		C-IF	69	244	48	73	10	3	7	47	40	15	9	8	24-8	.299	.412	.451	.863	8	.986
1994— GC Pirates (GCL)		1B-C-P	41	143	25	48	8	2	4	26	13	13	3	3	2-3	.336	.400	.503	.903	12	.962
1995— Augusta (S. Atl.)		C	84	278	41	67	17	0	3	36	26	32	2	7	5-4	.241	.305	.335	.640	6	.985
1996— Augusta (S. Atl.)		C	118	419	52	106	21	3	4	62	58	41	7	14	4-6	.253	.350	.346	.696	23	.976
1997— Rancho Cuca. (Calif.)		C	33	110	18	33	9	1	5	26	7	25	0	1	1-1	.300	.339	.536	.875	2	.985
— Mobile (Sou.)		C	47	143	15	39	7	1	4	25	10	12	2	5	1-1	.273	.327	.420	.747	3	.989
1998— Rancho Cuca. (Calif.)		C	75	292	51	84	24	2	10	59	26	54	2	6	0-0	.288	.346	.486	.832	3	.993
— Mobile (Sou.)		C	22	67	20	26	9	0	4	26	14	4	2	1	0-0	.388	.494	.701	1.195	0	1.000
1999— Mobile (Sou.)		C-DH	61	225	38	76	16	2	10	49	29	28	7	8	0-0	.338	.424	.560	.984	7	.982
— Las Vegas (PCL)		C-DH	24	92	13	25	6	0	6	12	5	10	3	3	0-0	.272	.330	.533	.863	3	.984
— San Diego (N.L.)		C	30	83	7	21	2	1	3	12	1	8	1	5	0-0	.253	.271	.410	.680	1	.992
2000— San Diego (N.L.)		C	95	284	25	66	15	1	5	30	30	31	3	5	1-2	.232	.311	.345	.656	5	.991
2001— San Diego (N.L.)		C-DH	64	160	16	44	9	0	8	27	11	28	4	3	2-0	.275	.335	.463	.798	3	.989
— Lake Elsinore (Calif.)		C	4	13	1	2	0	0	0	1	2	4	0	0	0-0	.154	.250	.154	.404	1	.973
2002— San Diego (N.L.)		C	56	164	16	36	8	1	1	20	27	24	1	10	0-0	.220	.330	.299	.629	6	.985
— Lake Elsinore (Calif.)		C	19	53	10	18	8	0	1	6	12	3	4	2	0-0	.340	.486	.547	1.033	2	.993
2003— San Diego (N.L.)		C-P	24	65	11	13	5	0	0	10	5	13	1	3	0-0	.200	.264	.277	.541	1	.993
— Portland (PCL)		C-DH	44	149	17	42	8	1	4	20	21	12	3	5	0-0	.282	.379	.430	.809	4	.987
2004— Tacoma (PCL)		C	13	52	9	16	5	0	5	14	2	5	0	1	0-0	.308	.333	.692	1.025	1	.991
2005— Seattle (A.L.)		C	14	45	7	12	5	0	0	2	3	3	0	0	0-0	.267	.298	.378	.676	0	1.000
— Tacoma (PCL)		C-DH	47	176	25	55	10	1	5	28	16	13	2	2	1-0	.313	.374	.466	.840	2	.993
2006— New Orleans (PCL)			26	84	9	25	4	0	4	16	9	9	4	3	1-0	.298	.384	.488	.872	2	.991
— Wash. (N.L.)		C	12	35	3	8	0	0	0	2	2	5	0	0	0-0	.229	.263	.229	.492	2	.972
American League totals (1 year)			14	45	7	12	5	0	0	2	3	3	0	0	0-0	.267	.298	.378	.676	0	1.000
National League totals (6 years)			281	791	68	188	36	3	17	101	76	109	10	26	3-2	.238	.310	.355	.666	18	.989
Major League totals (7 years)			295	836	75	200	41	3	17	103	78	112	10	27	3-2	.239	.310	.356	.666	18	.989

2006 LEFTY-RIGHTY SPLITS

vs.	Avg.	AB	H	2B	3B	HR	RBI	BB	SO	OBP	Slg.	vs.	Avg.	AB	H	2B	3B	HR	RBI	BB	SO	OBP	Slg.
L	.222	9	2	0	0	0	0	1	1	2	.300	.222	R	.231	26	6	0	0	0	1	1	3	.250	.231

G

GORDON, TOM — P

PERSONAL: Born November 18, 1967, in Sebring, Fla. ... 5-10/190. ... Throws right, bats right. ... Full name: Thomas Gordon. ... High school: Avon Park (Fla.). **TRANSACTIONS/CAREER NOTES:** Selected by Kansas City Royals organization in sixth round of June 1986 free-agent draft. ... On disabled list (August 12-September 1, 1992; and May 8-24, 1995). ... Signed as a free agent by Boston Red Sox (December 21, 1995). ... On disabled list (April 18-May 10 and June 12-September 27, 1999); included rehabilitation assignments to Trenton and Augusta. ... On disabled list (April 2, 2000-entire season). ... Signed as a free agent by Chicago Cubs (December 14, 2000). ... On disabled list (March 23-May 1, 2001); included rehabilitation assignments to Daytona and Iowa. ... On disabled list (March 28-July 2, 2002); included rehabilitation assignments to Daytona and Iowa. ... Traded by Cubs to Houston Astros for P Russ Rohlicek and two players to be named (August 22, 2002); Cubs acquired Ps Travis Anderson and Mike Nannini to complete deal (September 11, 2002). ... Signed as a free agent by Chicago White Sox (January 20, 2003). ... Signed as a free agent by New York Yankees (December 16, 2003). ... Signed as a free agent by Philadelphia Phillies (December 3, 2005). ... On disabled list (August 13-September 3, 2006); included rehabilitation assignment to Clearwater. **HONORS:** Named A.L. Rookie Pitcher of the Year by THE SPORTING NEWS (1989). **MISCELLANEOUS NOTES:** Appeared in one game as pinch runner (1991). ... Appeared in one game as pinch runner (1995).

CAREER HITTING: 0-for-2 (.000), 0 R, 0 2B, 0 3B, 0 HR, 0 RBI.

Year	Team (League)	W	L	Pct.	ERA	WHIP	G	GS	CG	ShO	Hld.	Sv.-Opp.	IP	H	R	ER	HR	BB-IBB	SO	Avg.
1986—	GC Royals (GCL)	3	1	.750	1.02	1.23	9	7	2	1	...	0-...	44.0	31	12	5	0	23-1	47	.194
—	Omaha (A.A.)	0	0	...	47.25	6.00	1	0	0	0	...	0-...	1.1	6	7	7	0	2-0	3	.600
1987—	Eugene (Northwest)	9	0	1.000	2.86	1.31	15	13	0	0	...	1-...	72.1	48	33	23	2	47-0	91	.183
—	Fort Myers (FSL)	1	0	1.000	2.63	1.61	3	3	0	0	...	0-...	13.2	5	4	4	0	17-0	11	.122
1988—	Appleton (Midwest)	7	5	.583	2.06	0.95	17	17	5	1	...	0-...	118.0	69	30	27	3	43-1	172	.163
—	Memphis (Sou.)	6	0	1.000	0.38	0.70	6	6	2	2	...	0-...	47.1	16	3	2	1	17-0	62	.103
—	Omaha (A.A.)	3	0	1.000	1.33	1.28	3	3	0	0	...	0-...	20.1	11	3	3	0	15-0	29	.157
—	Kansas City (A.L.)	0	2	.000	5.17	1.47	5	2	0	0	2	0-0	15.2	16	9	9	1	7-0	18	.267
1989—	Kansas City (A.L.)	17	9	.654	3.64	1.28	49	16	1	1	3	1-7	163.0	122	67	66	10	86-4	153	.210
1990—	Kansas City (A.L.)	12	11	.522	3.73	1.49	32	32	6	1	0	0-0	195.1	192	99	81	17	99-1	175	.258
1991—	Kansas City (A.L.)	9	14	.391	3.87	1.37	45	14	1	0	4	1-4	158.0	129	76	68	16	87-6	167	.221
1992—	Kansas City (A.L.)	6	10	.375	4.59	1.45	40	11	0	0	0	0-2	117.2	116	67	60	9	55-4	98	.258
1993—	Kansas City (A.L.)	12	6	.667	3.58	1.30	48	14	2	0	2	1-6	155.2	125	65	62	11	77-5	143	.223
1994—	Kansas City (A.L.)	11	7	.611	4.35	1.44	24	24	0	0	0	0-0	155.1	136	79	75	14	87-3	126	.237
1995—	Kansas City (A.L.)	12	12	.500	4.43	1.55	31	31	2	1	0	0-0	189.0	204	110	93	12	89-4	119	.279
1996—	Boston (A.L.)	12	9	.571	5.59	1.64	34	34	4	1	0	0-0	215.2	249	134	134	28	105-5	171	.284
1997—	Boston (A.L.)	6	10	.375	3.74	1.28	42	25	2	1	0	11-13	182.2	155	85	76	10	78-1	159	.226
1998—	Boston (A.L.)	7	4	.636	2.72	1.01	73	0	0	0	0	*46-47	79.1	55	24	24	2	25-1	78	.191
1999—	Boston (A.L.)	0	0	...	5.60	1.64	21	0	0	0	1	11-13	17.2	17	11	11	2	12-2	24	.246
2000—	Boston (A.L.)					Did not play.														
2001—	Daytona (Fla. St.)	0	0	...	0.00	0.00	2	2	0	0	...	0-...	2.0	0	0	0	0	0-0	3	.000
—	Iowa (PCL)	0	0	...	0.00	1.00	2	0	0	0	...	0-...	2.0	1	0	0	0	1-0	2	.167
—	Chicago (N.L.)	1	2	.333	3.38	1.06	47	0	0	0	0	27-31	45.1	32	18	17	4	16-1	67	.188
2002—	Daytona (Fla. St.)	0	0	...	3.38	1.13	2	2	0	0	...	0-...	2.2	1	1	1	0	2-0	3	.100
—	Iowa (PCL)	0	0	...	16.20	2.40	2	0	0	0	...	1-...	1.2	4	3	3	0	3-0	0	.167
—	Chicago (N.L.)	1	1	.500	3.42	1.56	19	0	0	0	2	0-0	23.2	27	12	9	1	10-1	31	.293
—	Houston (N.L.)	0	2	.000	3.32	1.11	15	0	0	0	4	0-0	19.0	15	7	7	2	6-2	17	.217
2003—	Chicago (A.L.)	7	6	.538	3.16	1.19	66	0	0	0	7	12-17	74.0	57	29	26	4	31-3	91	.213
2004—	New York (A.L.)	9	4	.692	2.21	0.88	80	0	0	0	* 36	4-10	89.2	56	23	22	5	23-5	96	.180
2005—	New York (A.L.)	5	4	.556	2.57	1.09	79	0	0	0	• 33	2-9	80.2	59	25	23	8	29-4	69	.203
2006—	Clearwater (FSL)	0	0	...	0.00	0.50	2	0	0	0	0	0-0	4.0	1	0	0	0	1-0	5	.083
—	Philadelphia (N.L.)	3	4	.429	3.34	1.26	59	0	0	0	0	34-39	59.1	53	23	22	9	22-4	68	.233
American League totals (15 years)		125	110	.532	3.95	1.36	669	203	18	4	88	89-128	1889.1	1688	912	830	150	890-48	1687	.239
National League totals (3 years)		5	9	.357	3.36	1.23	140	0	0	0	6	61-70	147.1	127	60	55	16	54-8	183	.228
Major League totals (18 years)		130	119	.522	3.91	1.35	809	203	18	4	94	150-198	2036.2	1815	972	885	166	944-56	1870	.238

DIVISION SERIES RECORD

Year	Team (League)	W	L	Pct.	ERA	WHIP	G	GS	CG	ShO	Hld.	Sv.-Opp.	IP	H	R	ER	HR	BB-IBB	SO	Avg.
1998—	Boston (A.L.)	0	1	.000	9.00	2.67	2	0	0	0	0	0-1	3.0	4	3	3	0	4-0	1	.333
1999—	Boston (A.L.)	0	0	...	4.50	1.00	2	0	0	0	0	0-0	2.0	1	1	1	1	1-0	3	.143
2004—	New York (A.L.)	0	0	...	4.91	0.55	3	0	0	0	1	0-0	3.2	2	2	2	0	0-0	3	.143
2005—	New York (A.L.)	0	0	...	3.86	0.86	3	0	0	0	0	0-0	2.1	2	2	1	0	0-0	2	.200
Division series totals (4 years)		0	1	.000	5.73	1.27	10	0	0	0	1	0-1	11.0	9	8	7	1	5-0	9	.209

CHAMPIONSHIP SERIES RECORD

Year	Team (League)	W	L	Pct.	ERA	WHIP	G	GS	CG	ShO	Hld.	Sv.-Opp.	IP	H	R	ER	HR	BB-IBB	SO	Avg.
1999—	Boston (A.L.)	0	0	...	13.50	2.00	3	0	0	0	0	0-0	2.0	3	3	3	2	1-0	3	.333
2004—	New York (A.L.)	0	0	...	8.10	1.80	6	0	0	0	3	0-0	6.2	10	6	6	2	2-0	3	.357
Champ. series totals (2 years)		0	0	...	9.35	1.85	9	0	0	0	3	0-0	8.2	13	9	9	4	3-0	6	.351

ALL-STAR GAME RECORD

	W	L	Pct.	ERA	WHIP	G	GS	ShO	Hld.	Sv.-Opp.	IP	H	R	ER	HR	BB-IBB	SO	Avg.
All-Star Game totals (3 years)	0	0	...	7.71	2.14	3	0	0	1	0-0	2.1	4	2	2	0	1-0	1	.400

2006 LEFTY-RIGHTY SPLITS

vs.	Avg.	AB	H	2B	3B	HR	RBI	BB	SO	OBP	Slg.	vs.	Avg.	AB	H	2B	3B	HR	RBI	BB	SO	OBP	Slg.
L	.185	108	20	2	1	3	11	11	42	.258	.306	R	.277	119	33	6	0	6	18	11	26	.344	.479

GORZELANNY, TOM — P

PERSONAL: Born July 12, 1982, in Evergreen Park, Ill. ... 6-2/207. ... Throws left, bats left. ... Full name: Thomas Stephen Gorzelanny. ... Name pronounced: gore-zah-LAWN-ee. ... Junior College: Triton (Ill.). **TRANSACTIONS/CAREER NOTES:** Selected by Pittsburgh Pirates organization in second round of 2003 free-agent draft. ... On disabled list (August 18-September 16, 2006).

CAREER HITTING: 0-for-20 (.000), 0 R, 0 2B, 0 3B, 0 HR, 1 RBI.

Year	Team (League)	W	L	Pct.	ERA	WHIP	G	GS	CG	ShO	Hld.	Sv.-Opp.	IP	H	R	ER	HR	BB-IBB	SO	Avg.
2003—	Will. (NYP)	1	2	.333	1.78	1.09	8	8	0	0	...	0-...	30.1	23	6	6	1	10-0	22	.215
2004—	Hickory (S. Atl.)	7	2	.778	2.23	1.04	16	15	1	0	...	0-...	93.0	63	30	23	9	34-0	106	.194
—	Lynchburg (Caro.)	3	5	.375	4.85	1.31	10	10	0	0	...	0-...	55.2	54	31	30	6	19-0	61	.255
2005—	Altoona (East.)	8	5	.615	3.26	1.23	23	23	1	1	0	0-0	129.2	114	50	47	6	46-1	124	.236
—	Pittsburgh (N.L.)	0	1	.000	12.00	2.17	3	1	0	0	0	0-0	6.0	10	8	8	1	3-0	3	.357
2006—	Indianapolis (Int'l)	6	5	.545	2.35	0.94	16	16	0	0	0	0-0	99.2	67	28	26	4	27-1	94	.194
—	Pittsburgh (N.L.)	2	5	.286	3.79	1.31	11	11	0	0	0	0-0	61.2	50	29	26	3	31-2	40	.226
Major League totals (2 years)		2	6	.250	4.52	1.39	14	12	0	0	0	0-0	67.2	60	37	34	4	34-2	43	.241

2006 LEFTY-RIGHTY SPLITS

vs.	Avg.	AB	H	2B	3B	HR	RBI	BB	SO	OBP	Slg.	vs.	Avg.	AB	H	2B	3B	HR	RBI	BB	SO	OBP	Slg.
L	.239	46	11	4	0	1	7	3	8	.314	.413	R	.223	175	39	8	0	2	18	28	32	.330	.303

G

GOSLING, MIKE — P

PERSONAL: Born September 23, 1980, in Madison, Wis. ... 6-0/210. ... Throws left, bats left. ... Full name: Michael Frederick Gosling. ... High school: East (Salt Lake City). ... College: Stanford. **TRANSACTIONS/CAREER NOTES:** Selected by Minnesota Twins organization in 14th round of 1998 free-agent draft; did not sign. ... Selected by Arizona Diamondbacks organization in second round of 2001 free-agent draft. ... Claimed on waivers by Cincinnati Reds (February 10, 2006).

CAREER HITTING: 0-for-12 (.000), 0 R, 0 2B, 0 3B, 0 HR, 0 RBI.

Year Team (League)	W	L	Pct.	ERA	WHIP	G	GS	CG	ShO	Hld.	Sv.-Opp.	IP	H	R	ER	HR	BB-IBB	SO	Avg.
2002— El Paso (Texas)	14	5	.737	3.13	1.27	27	27	2	2	...	0-...	166.2	149	66	58	7	62-4	115	.238
2003— Tucson (PCL)	9	12	.429	5.61	1.80	26	26	0	0	...	0-...	136.1	190	106	85	13	56-0	89	.330
2004— Tucson (PCL)	9	5	.643	5.82	1.66	24	21	0	0	...	0-...	128.1	160	101	83	16	53-0	67	.305
— Arizona (N.L.)	1	1	.500	4.62	1.54	26	4	0	0	0	0-0	25.1	26	13	13	5	13-1	14	.274
2005— Arizona (N.L.)	0	3	.000	4.45	1.82	13	5	0	0	0	0-0	32.1	40	20	16	2	19-2	14	.301
— Tucson (PCL)	4	6	.400	5.95	1.72	18	17	0	0	0	0-0	92.1	129	70	61	11	30-0	76	.328
2006— Cincinnati (N.L.)	0	0	...	13.50	1.50	1	0	0	0	0	0-0	1.1	1	2	2	1	1-0	1	.200
— Louisville (Int'l)	6	8	.429	4.58	1.45	23	22	0	0	0	0-0	118.0	118	68	60	12	53-0	100	.263
Major League totals (3 years)	**1**	**4**	**.200**	**4.73**	**1.69**	**20**	**9**	**0**	**0**	**0**	**0-0**	**59.0**	**67**	**35**	**31**	**8**	**33-3**	**29**	**.288**

2006 LEFTY-RIGHTY SPLITS

vs.	Avg.	AB	H	2B	3B	HR	RBI	BB	SO	OBP	Slg.	vs.	Avg.	AB	H	2B	3B	HR	RBI	BB	SO	OBP	Slg.
L	.000	1	0	0	0	0	1	1	0	.667	.000	R	.250	4	1	0	0	1	1	0	0	.250	1.000

GRABOW, JOHN — P

PERSONAL: Born November 4, 1978, in Arcadia, Calif. ... 6-2/210. ... Throws left, bats left. ... Full name: John William Grabow. ... Name pronounced: GRAY-bo. ... High school: San Gabriel (Calif.). **TRANSACTIONS/CAREER NOTES:** Selected by Pittsburgh Pirates organization in third round of 1997 free-agent draft.

CAREER HITTING: 0-for-2 (.000), 0 R, 0 2B, 0 3B, 0 HR, 0 RBI.

Year Team (League)	W	L	Pct.	ERA	WHIP	G	GS	CG	ShO	Hld.	Sv.-Opp.	IP	H	R	ER	HR	BB-IBB	SO	Avg.
1997— GC Pirates (GCL)	2	7	.222	4.57	1.57	11	8	0	0	...	0-...	45.1	57	32	23	0	14-0	28	.305
1998— Augusta (S. Atl.)	6	3	.667	5.78	1.65	17	16	0	0	...	0-...	71.2	84	59	46	7	34-0	67	.294
1999— Hickory (S. Atl.)	9	10	.474	3.80	1.18	26	26	0	0	...	0-...	156.1	152	82	66	16	32-0	164	.249
2000— Altoona (East.)	8	7	.533	4.33	1.44	24	24	1	0	...	0-...	145.1	145	81	70	10	65-0	109	.259
2001— GC Pirates (GCL)	0	1	.000	3.75	1.25	6	6	0	0	...	0-...	12.0	11	6	5	1	4-0	9	.244
— Lynchburg (Caro.)	1	3	.250	6.38	1.85	7	7	0	0	...	0-...	36.2	42	30	26	3	26-0	35	.294
— Altoona (East.)	2	5	.286	3.38	1.36	10	10	0	0	...	0-...	50.2	30	23	19	1	39-0	42	.175
2002— Altoona (East.)	8	13	.381	5.47	1.56	28	27	1	1	...	0-...	146.1	181	94	89	10	47-0	97	.308
2003— Altoona (East.)	6	1	.857	3.36	1.28	24	9	0	0	'	1-...	83.0	87	34	31	9	19-2	73	.281
— Nashville (PCL)	0	2	.000	4.74	1.54	17	0	0	0	...	0-...	24.2	31	17	13	0	7-2	26	.298
— Pittsburgh (N.L.)	0	0	...	3.60	1.20	5	0	0	0	0	0-0	5.0	6	3	2	0	0-0	9	.273
2004— Pittsburgh (N.L.)	2	5	.286	5.11	1.77	68	0	0	0	11	1-7	61.2	81	39	35	8	28-7	64	.323
2005— Pittsburgh (N.L.)	2	3	.400	4.85	1.37	63	0	0	0	14	0-1	52.0	46	31	28	6	25-2	42	.238
2006— Pittsburgh (N.L.)	4	2	.667	4.13	1.41	72	0	0	0	11	0-2	69.2	68	34	32	7	30-3	66	.260
Major League totals (4 years)	**8**	**10**	**.444**	**4.64**	**1.51**	**208**	**0**	**0**	**0**	**36**	**1-10**	**188.1**	**201**	**107**	**97**	**21**	**83-12**	**181**	**.276**

2006 LEFTY-RIGHTY SPLITS

vs.	Avg.	AB	H	2B	3B	HR	RBI	BB	SO	OBP	Slg.	vs.	Avg.	AB	H	2B	3B	HR	RBI	BB	SO	OBP	Slg.
L	.275	91	25	5	0	2	10	6	30	.337	.396	R	.251	171	43	10	2	5	20	24	36	.340	.421

GRAFFANINO, TONY — 2B

PERSONAL: Born June 6, 1972, in Amityville, N.Y. ... 6-1/190. ... Bats right, throws right. ... Full name: Anthony Joseph Graffanino. ... Name pronounced: graf-a-NEEN-oh. ... High school: East Islip (Islip Terrace, N.Y.). **TRANSACTIONS/CAREER NOTES:** Selected by Atlanta Braves organization in 10th round of 1990 free-agent draft. ... Released by Braves (April 2, 1999). ... Signed by Tampa Bay Devil Rays organization (April 9, 1999). ... Traded by Devil Rays to Chicago White Sox for P Tanyon Sturtze (May 31, 2000). ... On disabled list (August 26-September 30, 2002). ... Signed as a free agent by Kansas City Royals (December 16, 2003). ... On disabled list (May 1-28 and August 1, 2004-remainder of season; included rehabilitation assignment to Omaha. ... Traded by Royals to Boston Red Sox for P Juan Cedeno and OF Chip Ambres (July 19, 2005). ... Claimed on waivers by Royals (March 28, 2006). ... Traded by Royals to Milwaukee Brewers for P Jorge De la Rosa (July 31, 2006). **STATISTICAL NOTES:** Career major league grand slams: 1.

2006 GAMES PLAYED BY POSITION (MLB): 2B—67, 3B—27, 1B—16, SS—13, DH—6.

Year Team (League)	Pos.	G	AB	R	H	2B	3B	HR	RBI	BB	SO	HBP	GDP	SB-CS	Avg.	OBP	SLG	OPS	E	Avg.
1990— Pulaski (Appalachian)	SS	42	131	23	27	5	1	0	11	26	17	2	3	6-3	.206	.344	.260	.603	24	.873
1991— Idaho Falls (Pio.)	SS	66	274	53	95	16	4	4	56	27	37	3	3	19-4	.347	.408	.478	.887	29	.912
1992— Macon (S. Atl.)	2B	112	400	50	96	15	5	10	31	50	84	8	6	19-9	.240	.333	.378	.711	17	.961
1993— Durham (Carol.)	2B	123	459	78	126	30	5	15	69	45	78	4	10	24-11	.275	.342	.460	.801	15	.968
1994— Greenville (Sou.)	2B-DH	124	440	66	132	28	3	7	52	50	53	2	8	29-7	.300	.372	.425	.797	14	.976
1995— Richmond (Int'l)	2B	50	179	20	34	6	0	4	17	15	49	1	4	2-2	.190	.254	.291	.544	4	.983
1996— Richmond (Int'l)	2B	96	353	57	100	29	2	7	33	34	72	3	3	11-7	.283	.350	.436	.787	10	.977
— Atlanta (N.L.)	2B	22	46	7	8	1	1	0	2	4	13	1	0	0-0	.174	.250	.239	.489	2	.969
1997— Atlanta (N.L.)	2B-3B-SS	1B	104	186	33	48	9	1	8	20	26	46	1	3	6-4	.258	.344	.446	.790	5	.982
1998— Atlanta (N.L.)	2B-SS-3B	105	289	32	61	14	1	5	22	24	68	2	7	1-4	.211	.275	.318	.594	11	.971
1999— Durham (Int'l)	2B-DH-3B	87	345	66	108	25	6	9	58	37	46	3	9	16-9	.313	.379	.499	.878	1	.998
— Tampa Bay (A.L.)	DH	39	130	20	41	9	4	2	19	9	22	1	1	3-2	.315	.364	.492	.857	5	.973
2000— Tampa Bay (A.L.)	2B-3B-SS	13	20	8	6	1	0	0	1	1	2	1	1	0-0	.300	.364	.350	.714	0	1.000
— Durham (Int'l)	SS-2B-1B	3B	10	35	9	10	3	0	2	6	7	8	0	0	2-0	.286	.405	.543	.948	0	1.000
— Chicago (A.L.)	SS-2B-3B	DH	57	148	25	40	5	1	6	16	21	36	1	7	7-4	.270	.363	.358	.721	6	.968
2001— Chicago (A.L.)	3B-2B-SS	DH-OF-1B	74	145	23	44	9	2	15	16	29	1	4	4-1	.303	.370	.407	.777	7	.957
2002— Chicago (A.L.)	SS-2B-3B	70	229	35	60	12	4	6	31	22	38	2	2	2-1	.262	.329	.428	.757	10	.953
2003— Chicago (A.L.)	DH-1B	2B-DH	90	250	51	65	15	3	7	23	24	37	3	1	8-0	.260	.331	.428	.759	6	.972
2004— Omaha (PCL)	2B-DH	4	14	2	3	0	0	1	2	5	5	0	0	0-0	.214	.353	.429	.782	0	1.000
— Kansas City (A.L.)	2B	75	278	37	73	11	0	3	26	27	34	3	5	10-2	.263	.332	.335	.667	5	.988
2005— Kansas City (A.L.)	1B-2B-3B	SS-DH	59	191	29	57	5	3	3	18	22	28	2	6	3-1	.298	.377	.393	.769	7	.974

G

Year	Team (League)	Pos.	G	AB	R	H	2B	3B	HR	RBI	BB	SO	HBP	GDP	SB-CS	Avg.	OBP	SLG	OPS	E	Avg.
																BATTING				FIELDING	
— Boston (A.L.)	2B	51	188	39	60	12	1	4	20	9	23	2	8	4-1	.319	.355	.457	.812	3	.987
2006—Kansas City (A.L.)	3B-1B-2B SS-DH	69	220	34	59	16	0	5	32	25	31	1	4	3-4	.268	.346	.409	.755	5	.980
— Milwaukee (N.L.)	2B-SS	60	236	34	66	17	3	2	27	20	37	4	6	2-0	.280	.345	.403	.747	3	.988
American League totals (8 years)		597	1799	301	505	95	15	34	201	176	273	17	33	44-16	.281	.349	.407	.756	56	.975
National League totals (4 years)		291	757	106	183	41	6	15	71	74	164	8	16	9-8	.242	.313	.371	.684	21	.978
Major League totals (11 years)		888	2556	407	688	136	21	49	272	250	437	25	49	53-24	.269	.338	.396	.734	77	.976

DIVISION SERIES RECORD

Year	Team (League)	Pos.	G	AB	R	H	2B	3B	HR	RBI	BB	SO	HBP	GDP	SB-CS	Avg.	OBP	SLG	OPS	E	Avg.
1997—Atlanta (N.L.)	2B	3	3	0	0	0	0	0	0	2	1	0	0	0-0	.000	.400	.000	.400	0	1.000
1998—Atlanta (N.L.)		1	0	0	0	0	0	0	0	0	0	0	0	0-0	...	...	...	...		
2000—Chicago (A.L.)	3B	1	0	0	0	0	0	0	0	0	0	0	0	0-0	...	...	...	...	0	1.000
2005—Boston (A.L.)	2B	3	12	0	3	2	0	0	0	0	2	0	0	0-0	.250	.250	.417	.667	1	.950
Division series totals (4 years)		8	15	0	3	2	0	0	0	2	3	0	0	0-0	.200	.294	.333	.627	1	.964

CHAMPIONSHIP SERIES RECORD

Year	Team (League)	Pos.	G	AB	R	H	2B	3B	HR	RBI	BB	SO	HBP	GDP	SB-CS	Avg.	OBP	SLG	OPS	E	Avg.
1997—Atlanta (N.L.)	2B	3	8	1	2	1	0	0	0	3	0	1	0	0-0	.250	.250	.375	.625	0	1.000
1998—Atlanta (N.L.)	2B	4	3	2	1	1	0	0	1	2	1	0	0	0-0	.333	.600	.667	1.267	0	1.000
Champ. series totals (2 years)		7	11	3	3	2	0	0	1	2	4	0	1	0-0	.273	.385	.455	.839	0	1.000

2006 LEFTY-RIGHTY SPLITS

vs.	Avg.	AB	H	2B	3B	HR	RBI	BB	SO	OBP	Slg.	vs.	Avg.	AB	H	2B	3B	HR	RBI	BB	SO	OBP	Slg.
L	.275	142	39	10	0	4	17	12	20	.331	.430	R	.274	314	86	23	3	3	42	33	48	.351	.395

GRANDERSON, CURTIS   OF

PERSONAL: Born March 16, 1981, in Blue Island, Ill. ... 6-1/185. ... Bats left, throws right. ... High school: Thornton Fractional South (Lansing, Ill.). ... College: Illinois-Chicago. **TRANSACTIONS/CAREER NOTES:** Selected by Detroit Tigers organization in third round of 2002 free-agent draft.
2006 GAMES PLAYED BY POSITION (MLB): OF—157.

Year	Team (League)	Pos.	G	AB	R	H	2B	3B	HR	RBI	BB	SO	HBP	GDP	SB-CS	Avg.	OBP	SLG	OPS	E	Avg.
																BATTING				FIELDING	
2002—Oneonta (NYP)	OF	52	212	45	73	15	4	3	34	20	35	7	1	9-2	.344	.417	.495	.912	1	.989
2003—Lakeland (Fla. St.)	OF	127	476	71	136	29	10	11	51	49	91	12	5	10-7	.286	.365	.458	.823	3	.984
2004—Erie (East.)	OF	123	462	89	139	19	8	21	94	80	95	4	2	14-8	.301	.405	.513	.918	3	.991
—Detroit (A.L.)	OF	9	25	2	6	1	1	0	0	3	8	0	1	0-0	.240	.321	.360	.681	0	1.000
2005—Toledo (Int'l)	OF-DH	111	445	79	129	29	13	15	65	48	129	3	7	22-6	.290	.359	.515	.874	8	.985
—Detroit (A.L.)	OF	47	162	18	44	6	3	8	20	10	43	0	2	1-1	.272	.314	.494	.808	0	1.000
2006—Detroit (A.L.)	OF	159	596	90	155	31	9	19	68	66 *	174	4	4	8-5	.260	.335	.438	.773	1	.997
Major League totals (3 years)		215	783	110	205	38	13	27	88	79	225	4	7	9-6	.262	.330	.447	.777	1	.998

DIVISION SERIES RECORD

Year	Team (League)	Pos.	G	AB	R	H	2B	3B	HR	RBI	BB	SO	HBP	GDP	SB-CS	Avg.	OBP	SLG	OPS	E	Avg.
2006—Detroit (A.L.)	OF	4	17	3	5	0	1	2	5	0	1	0	0	1-0	.294	.278	.765	1.042	0	1.000

CHAMPIONSHIP SERIES RECORD

Year	Team (League)	Pos.	G	AB	R	H	2B	3B	HR	RBI	BB	SO	HBP	GDP	SB-CS	Avg.	OBP	SLG	OPS	E	Avg.
2006—Detroit (A.L.)	OF	4	15	4	5	2	0	1	2	4	2	0	0	1-0	.333	.474	.667	1.140	0	1.000

WORLD SERIES RECORD

Year	Team (League)	Pos.	G	AB	R	H	2B	3B	HR	RBI	BB	SO	HBP	GDP	SB-CS	Avg.	OBP	SLG	OPS	E	Avg.
2006—Detroit (A.L.)	OF	5	21	1	2	1	0	0	1	1	7	0	1	0-0	.095	.136	.143	.279	0	1.000

2006 LEFTY-RIGHTY SPLITS

vs.	Avg.	AB	H	2B	3B	HR	RBI	BB	SO	OBP	Slg.	vs.	Avg.	AB	H	2B	3B	HR	RBI	BB	SO	OBP	Slg.
L	.218	147	32	8		4	16	10	49	.277	.395	R	.274	449	123	23	6	15	52	56	125	.353	.452

GRAVES, DANNY   P

PERSONAL: Born August 7, 1973, in Saigon, Vietnam. ... 6-0/185. ... Throws right, bats right. ... Full name: Daniel Peter Graves. ... High school: Brandon (Fla.). ... College: Miami. **TRANSACTIONS/CAREER NOTES:** Selected by Cleveland Indians organization in fourth round of 1994 free-agent draft. ... Traded by Indians with Ps Jim Crowell and Scott Winchester and IF Damian Jackson to Cincinnati Reds for P John Smiley and IF Jeff Branson (July 31, 1997). ... On disabled list (August 19-September 3, 2004). ... Released by Reds (June 2, 2005). ... Signed by New York Mets (June 11, 2005). ... Signed as a free agent by Indians organization (December 19, 2005). **MISCELLANEOUS NOTES:** Scored a run in only appearance as pinch runner (2002). ... Appeared in one game as pinch runner (2003).
CAREER HITTING: 8-for-76 (.105), 5 R, 0 2B, 0 3B, 2 HR, 3 RBI.

Year	Team (League)	W	L	Pct.	ERA	WHIP	G	GS	CG	ShO	Hld.	Sv.-Opp.	IP	H	R	ER	HR	BB-IBB	SO	Avg.
1995—Kinston (Carol.)	3	1	.750	0.82	0.95	38	0	0	0	...	21-...	44.0	30	11	4	0	12-2	46	.183
—Cant./Akr. (Eastern)	1	0	1.000	0.00	0.51	17	0	0	0	...	10-...	23.1	10	1	0	0	2-0	11	.133
—Buffalo (A.A.)	0	0	...	3.00	2.00	3	0	0	0	...	0-...	3.0	5	4	1	0	1-0	2	.333
1996—Buffalo (A.A.)	4	3	.571	1.48	1.03	43	0	0	0	...	19-...	79.0	57	14	13	1	24-2	46	.208
—Cleveland (A.L.)	2	0	1.000	4.55	1.31	15	0	0	0	0	0-1	29.2	29	18	15	2	10-0	22	.246
1997—Buffalo (A.A.)	2	3	.400	4.19	1.30	19	3	0	0	...	0-0	43.0	45	21	20	3	11-0	21	.276
—Cleveland (A.L.)	0	0	...	4.76	2.12	5	0	0	0	0	0-0	11.1	15	8	6	2	9-0	4	.326
—Indianapolis (A.A.)	1	0	1.000	3.09	1.03	11	0	0	0	...	5-...	11.2	7	4	4	0	5-0	5	.184
—Cincinnati (N.L.)	0	0	...	6.14	2.52	10	0	0	0	1	0-...	14.2	26	14	10	0	11-1	7	.413
1998—Indianapolis (Int'l)	1	0	1.000	1.93	1.29	13	0	0	0	...	0-...	14.0	15	3	3	0	8-0	11	.273
—Cincinnati (N.L.)	2	1	.667	3.32	1.28	62	0	0	0	6	8-8	81.1	76	31	30	6	28-4	44	.252
1999—Cincinnati (N.L.)	8	7	.533	3.08	1.25	75	0	0	0	...	27-36	111.0	90	42	38	10	49-4	69	.227
2000—Cincinnati (N.L.)	10	5	.667	2.56	1.35	66	0	0	0	...	30-35	91.1	81	31	26	8	42-7	53	.243
2001—Cincinnati (N.L.)	6	5	.545	4.15	1.26	66	0	0	0	...	32-39	80.1	83	41	37	7	18-6	49	.268
2002—Cincinnati (N.L.)	7	3	.700	3.19	1.26	68	4	0	0	...	32-39	98.2	99	37	35	7	25-9	58	.264
2003—Cincinnati (N.L.)	4	15	.211	5.33	1.45	30	26	2	1	...	2-2	169.0	204	108	100	30	41-6	60	.298
2004—Cincinnati (N.L.)	1	6	.143	3.95	1.32	68	0	0	0	...	41-50	68.1	77	39	30	12	13-6	40	.282
2005—Cincinnati (N.L.)	1	1	.500	7.36	2.29	20	0	0	0	...	10-12	18.1	30	18	15	4	12-3	8	.357
—Norfolk (Int'l)	0	1	.000	18.00	3.67	5	0	0	0	...	0-0	6.0	15	12	12	2	7-0	4	.484
—New York (N.L.)	0	0	...	5.75	1.82	20	0	0	0	...	0-0	20.1	29	11	13	4	8-1	12	.337
2006—Buffalo (Int'l)	1	1	.500	4.01	1.32	33	1	0	0	8	1-2	51.2	55	26	23	5	13-2	21	.278
—Cleveland (A.L.)	2	1	.667	5.79	1.64	13	0	0	0	...	0-1	14.0	18	12	9	3	5-1	3	.305
American League totals (3 years)	4	1	.800	4.91	1.56	33	0	0	0	0	0-2	55.0	62	38	30	7	24-1	29	.278
National League totals (9 years)	39	43	.476	3.99	1.38	485	30	2	1	8	182-221	753.1	795	378	334	89	247-47	400	.274
Major League totals (11 years)	43	44	.494	4.05	1.40	518	30	2	1	8	182-223	808.1	857	416	364	96	271-48	429	.274

					ALL-STAR GAME RECORD															
	W	L	Pct.	ERA	WHIP	G	GS	CG	ShO	Hld.	Sv.-Opp.		IP	H	R	ER	HR	BB-IBB	SO	Avg.
All-Star Game totals (1 year)	0	0	...	0.00	1.00	1	0	0	0	0	0-0		1.0	1	0	0	0	0-0	1	.250

2006 LEFTY-RIGHTY SPLITS

vs.	Avg.	AB	H	2B	3B	HR	RBI	BB	SO	OBP	Slg.	vs.	Avg.	AB	H	2B	3B	HR	RBI	BB	SO	OBP	Slg.
L	.348	23	8	1	0	0		3	1	.423	.478	R	.278	36	10	1	0	0	3	13	2	2	.308	.556

GREEN, ANDY — 3B/2B

PERSONAL: Born July 7, 1977, in Lexington, Ky. ... 5-9/180. ... Bats right, throws right. ... Full name: Andrew Mulligan Green. ... High school: Lexington (Ky.) Christian Academy. ... College: Kentucky. **TRANSACTIONS/CAREER NOTES:** Selected by Arizona Diamondbacks organization in 24th round of 2000 free-agent draft. ... On disabled list (August 3-September 1, 2006); included rehabilitation assignment to Tucson.

2006 GAMES PLAYED BY POSITION (MLB): 3B—7, OF—7, 2B—6, SS—2, DH—1.

							BATTING											FIELDING	
Year Team (League)	Pos.	G	AB	R	H	2B	3B	HR	RBI	BB	SO	HBP	GDP	SB-CS	Avg.	OBP	SLG	OPS	E	Avg.
2000— South Bend (Mid.)	2B	3	9	1	0	0	0	0	0	0	2	1	0	0-0	.000	.182	.000	.182	0	1.000
—Missoula (Pion.)	2B-3B	23	83	10	19	2	1	0	16	12	9	2	1	8-3	.229	.324	.277	.601	5	.949
2001— South Bend (Mid.)	2B	128	477	76	143	18	6	5	59	59	50	7	7	51-15	.300	.379	.394	.773	16	.973
2002—Tucson (PCL)	2B	27	99	13	22	8	0	1	13	9	17	1	2	2-1	.222	.294	.333	.627	2	.980
—Lancaster (Calif.)	2B	102	401	74	124	36	4	6	50	60	59	5		15-10	.309	.401	.464	.865	10	.979
2003—El Paso (Texas)	2B-SS-OF																			
	3B	126	490	70	148	38	2	2	51	38	51	13	6	17-9	.302	.366	.400	.766	21	.962
2004—Tucson (PCL)	3B-2B-SS																			
	OF-DH	77	309	56	101	31	3	9	45	34	45	3	3	10-4	.327	.394	.534	.923	11	.961
—Arizona (N.L.)	3B-2B-OF	46	109	13	22	2	1	1	4	5	17	1	2	1-1	.202	.241	.266	.507	5	.946
2005—Tucson (PCL)	2B-OF-3B																			
	DH-SS	135	530	125	182	46	13	19	80	68	82	6	9	9-6	.343	.422	.587	1.009	13	.976
—Arizona (N.L.)	2B-SS-OF	17	31	5	7	1	0	0	2	7	3	0	1	0-0	.226	.359	.258	.617	0	1.000
2006—Tucson (PCL)	3B-OF-2B	18	75	10	18	3	0	1	6	4	14	1	0	0-0	.240	.288	.320	.608	1	.983
—Arizona (N.L.)	SS-DH	73	86	15	16	4	0	1	6	13	20	0	0	1-0	.186	.293	.267	.560	1	.968
Major League totals (3 years)		136	226	33	45	7	1	2	12	25	40	1	3	2-1	.199	.280	.265	.545	6	.961

2006 LEFTY-RIGHTY SPLITS

vs.	Avg.	AB	H	2B	3B	HR	RBI	BB	SO	OBP	Slg.	vs.	Avg.	AB	H	2B	3B	HR	RBI	BB	SO	OBP	Slg.
L	.171	35	6	1	0	1	3	7	6	.310	.286	R	.196	51	10	3	0	0	3	6	14	.281	.255

GREEN, NICK — 2B/SS

PERSONAL: Born September 10, 1978, in Pensacola, Fla. ... 6-0/178. ... Bats right, throws right. ... Full name: Nicholas Anthony Green. ... High school: Duluth (Ga.). ... Junior college: Georgia Perimeter. ... College: Georgia Perimeter JC. **TRANSACTIONS/CAREER NOTES:** Selected by Atlanta Braves organization in 32nd round of 1998 free-agent draft. ... On disabled list (March 22-April 24, 2002). ... Traded by Braves to Tampa Bay Devil Rays for P Jorge Sosa (March 31, 2005). ... Traded by Devil Rays to New York Yankees for cash (May 24, 2006).

2006 GAMES PLAYED BY POSITION (MLB): 2B—23, SS—20, 3B—17, DH—2, 1B—1, OF—1.

							BATTING											FIELDING	
Year Team (League)	Pos.	G	AB	R	H	2B	3B	HR	RBI	BB	SO	HBP	GDP	SB-CS	Avg.	OBP	SLG	OPS	E	Avg.
1999—Jamestown (NYP)	2B	73	273	52	81	15	6	11	41	26	66	4	4	14-4	.297	.363	.473	.835	15	.955
—Macon (S. Atl.)	2B	3	10	1	2	0	0	1	3	0	4	0	0	1-0	.200	.200	.500	.700	0	1.000
2000—Macon (S. Atl.)	SS-2B	91	339	47	83	19	4	11	43	22	75	5	4	10-4	.245	.296	.422	.718	37	.911
—Myrtle Beach (Carol.)	SS-2B	27	91	13	22	6	0	1	6	10	23	3	0	3-2	.242	.337	.341	.677	9	.890
2001—Richmond (Int'l)	2B	2	5	0	1	0	0	0	1	0	3	0	0	0-0	.200	.200	.200	.400	1	.833
—Myrtle Beach (Carol.)	2B-SS	80	297	49	79	18	1	10	42	32	66	7	2	9-2	.266	.348	.434	.782	13	.958
2002—Greenville (Sou.)	2B-SS	94	355	49	85	16	2	15	50	36	92	8	9	2-5	.239	.321	.423	.743	14	.962
2003—Richmond (Int'l)	2B-SS	124	399	40	99	26	1	11	51	26	79	7	7	7-5	.248	.303	.401	.704	20	.961
2004—Richmond (Int'l)	2B-3B	22	77	8	29	4	1	0	11	6	9	4	2	0-3	.377	.443	.455	.871	3	.969
—Atlanta (N.L.)	2B-3B-OF	95	264	40	72	15	3	6	26	12	63	4	2	1-2	.273	.312	.386	.698	8	.977
2005—Tampa Bay (A.L.)	2B-3B-DH																			
	OF	111	318	53	76	15	2	5	29	33	86	11	5	3-1	.239	.329	.346	.675	7	.981
2006—Tampa Bay (A.L.)	SS-2B-OF																			
	DH	17	39	4	3	0	0	0	0	6	11	0	2	0-3	.077	.200	.077	.277	0	1.000
—Durham (Int'l)		10	42	2	10	0	0	1	2	0	14	1	0	0-0	.238	.256	.310	.565	1	.963
—Columbus (Int'l)		14	48	3	10	4	0	0	4	1	13	1	0	1-0	.208	.316	.292	.607	5	.907
—New York (A.L.)	2B-3B-SS																			
	1B-DH	46	75	8	18	5	0	2	4	5	29	1	0	1-1	.240	.296	.387	.683	5	.958
American League totals (2 years)		174	432	65	97	20	2	7	33	44	126	12	7	4-5	.225	.312	.329	.640	12	.978
National League totals (1 year)		95	264	40	72	15	3	6	26	12	63	4	2	1-2	.273	.312	.386	.698	8	.977
Major League totals (3 years)		269	696	105	169	35	5	10	59	56	189	16	7	5-7	.243	.312	.351	.662	20	.977

							DIVISION SERIES RECORD												
Year Team (League)	Pos.	G	AB	R	H	2B	3B	HR	RBI	BB	SO	HBP	GDP	SB-CS	Avg.	OBP	SLG	OPS	E	Avg.
2004—Atlanta (N.L.)		2	0	0	0	0	0	0	0	0	0	0	0	0-0	...	...	...	...	0	...

2006 LEFTY-RIGHTY SPLITS

vs.	Avg.	AB	H	2B	3B	HR	RBI	BB	SO	OBP	Slg.	vs.	Avg.	AB	H	2B	3B	HR	RBI	BB	SO	OBP	Slg.
L	.150	40	6	1	0	0	0	3	11	.227	.175	R	.203	74	15	4	0	2	4	8	29	.280	.338

GREEN, SEAN — P

PERSONAL: Born April 20, 1979, in Louisville, Ky. ... Throws right, bats right. ... Full name: Sean William Green. ... College: Louisville. **TRANSACTIONS/CAREER NOTES:** Selected by Colorado Rockies organization in 12th round of 2000 free-agent draft. ... Traded by Rockies to Seattle Mariners for P Aaron Taylor (December 20, 2004). ... On disabled list (July 3-29, 2006 and September 8, 2006-remainder of season).

CAREER HITTING: 0-for-0 (.000), 0 R, 0 2B, 0 3B, 0 HR, 0 RBI.

Year Team (League)	W	L	Pct.	ERA	WHIP	G	GS	CG	ShO	Hld.	Sv.-Opp.	IP	H	R	ER	HR	BB-IBB	SO	Avg.
2000—Portland (N'west)	1	4	.200	8.48	2.23	22	0	0	0	...	0-...	28.2	45	32	27	0	19-2	17	.352
2001—Asheville (S. Atl.)	3	4	.429	5.90	1.62	43	0	0	0	...	0-...	58.0	66	43	38	4	28-1	37	.282
2002—Salem (Carol.)	2	5	.286	3.90	1.84	52	0	0	0	...	2-...	67.0	92	41	29	5	31-8	26	.332
2003—Visalia (Calif.)	3	4	.429	4.84	1.60	46	0	0	0	...	0-...	80.0	90	54	43	2	38-2	56	.281

G

Year—Team (League)	W	L	Pct.	ERA	WHIP	G	GS	CG	ShO	Hld.	Sv.-Opp.	IP	H	R	ER	HR	BB-IBB	SO	Avg.
2004—Tulsa (Texas)	4	3	.571	3.03	1.19	52	0	0	0	...	2-...	77.1	63	32	26	5	29-1	50	.215
2005—San Antonio (Texas)	0	1	.000	2.96	1.03	21	0	0	0	...	14-16	24.1	17	11	8	1	8-0	18	.189
—Tacoma (PCL)	4	2	.667	3.65	1.40	33	0	0	0	6	1-1	49.1	40	23	20	1	29-0	44	.221
2006—Tacoma (PCL)	4	1	.800	2.25	1.21	15	0	0	0	1	5-7	24.0	18	6	6	0	11-1	12	.225
—Seattle (A.L.)	0	0	...	4.50	1.47	24	0	0	0	3	0-1	32.0	34	16	16	2	13-1	15	.279
Major League totals (1 year)	0	0	...	4.50	1.47	24	0	0	0	3	0-1	32.0	34	16	16	2	13-1	15	.279

2006 LEFTY-RIGHTY SPLITS

vs.	Avg.	AB	H	2B	3B	HR	RBI	BB	SO	OBP	Slg.	vs.	Avg.	AB	H	2B	3B	HR	RBI	BB	SO	OBP	Slg.
L	.190	42	3	1	0	1	4	9	10	.346	.333	R	.325	80	26	5	0	1	10	4	5	.360	.425

GREEN, SHAWN — OF

PERSONAL: Born November 10, 1972, in Des Plaines, Ill. ... 6-4/200. ... Bats left, throws left. ... Full name: Shawn David Green. ... High school: Tustin (Calif.). **TRANSACTIONS/CAREER NOTES:** Selected by Toronto Blue Jays organization in first round (16th pick overall) of 1991 free-agent draft; pick received as compensation for San Francisco Giants signing Type A free-agent P Bud Black. ... Traded by Blue Jays with 2B Jorge Nunez to Los Angeles Dodgers for OF Raul Mondesi and P Pedro Borbon (November 8, 1999). ... Traded by Dodgers with cash to Arizona Diamondbacks for C Dioner Navarro and Ps William Juarez, Danny Muegge and Beltran Perez (January 11, 2005). ... Traded by Diamondbacks with cash to New York Mets for P Evan MacLane (August 22, 2006). **RECORDS:** Shares major league records for most home runs, game (4, May 23, 2002). **HONORS:** Named as outfielder on THE SPORTING NEWS A.L. All-Star team (1999). ... Won A.L. Gold Glove as outfielder (1999). **STATISTICAL NOTES:** Hit four home runs in one game (May 23, 2002). ... Hit three home runs in one game (August 15, 2001). ... Career major league grand slams: 9.

2006 GAMES PLAYED BY POSITION (MLB): OF-131, 1B—13, DH—1.

							BATTING										FIELDING	
Year—Team (League)	Pos.	G	AB	R	H	2B	3B	HR	RBI	BB	SO	HBP	GDP	SB-CS	Avg.	OBP	SLG	OPS	E	Avg.
1992—Dunedin (Fla. St.)	OF	114	417	44	114	21	3	1	49	28	66	4	9	22-9	.273	.319	.345	.665	5	.974
1993—Knoxville (Southern)	OF	99	360	40	102	14	2	4	34	26	72	5	6	4-9	.283	.339	.367	.706	8	.956
—Toronto (A.L.)	OF-DH	3	6	0	0	0	0	0	0	0	1	0	0	0-0	.000	.000	.000	.000	0	1.000
1994—Syracuse (Int'l)	OF-DH	109	433	82	149	27	3	13	61	40	54	4	5	19-7	.344	.401	.510	.912	1	.996
—Toronto (A.L.)	OF	14	33	1	3	1	0	0	1	1	8	0	1	1-0	.091	.118	.121	.239	0	1.000
1995—Toronto (A.L.)	OF	121	379	52	109	31	4	15	54	20	68	3	4	1-2	.288	.326	.509	.835	6	.973
1996—Toronto (A.L.)	OF-DH	132	422	52	118	32	3	11	45	33	75	8	9	5-1	.280	.342	.448	.790	2	.992
1997—Toronto (A.L.)	OF-DH	135	429	57	123	22	4	16	53	36	99	1	4	14-3	.287	.340	.494	.809	3	.984
1998—Toronto (A.L.)	OF	138	630	106	175	33	4	35	100	50	142	5	6	35-12	.278	.334	.510	.844	7	.979
1999—Toronto (A.L.)	OF	153	614	134	190	*45	0	42	123	66	117	11	13	20-7	.309	.384	.588	.972	1	.997
2000—Los Angeles (N.L.)	OF	•162	610	98	164	44	4	24	99	90	121	8	18	24-5	.269	.367	.472	.839	6	.980
2001—Los Angeles (N.L.)	OF-1B	161	619	121	184	31	4	49	125	72	107	5	10	20-4	.297	.372	.598	.970	6	.982
2002—Los Angeles (N.L.)	OF-DH	158	582	110	166	31	1	42	114	93	112	5	26	8-5	.285	.385	.558	.944	2	.994
2003—Los Angeles (N.L.)	OF-DH	160	611	84	171	49	2	19	85	68	112	6	18	6-2	.280	.355	.460	.814	5	.982
2004—Los Angeles (N.L.)	1B-OF-DH	157	590	92	157	28	1	28	86	71	114	8	17	5-2	.266	.352	.459	.811	7	.993
2005—Arizona (N.L.)	OF	158	581	87	166	37	4	22	73	62	95	5	19	8-4	.286	.355	.477	.832	0	1.000
2006—Arizona (N.L.)	OF-1B-DH	115	417	59	118	22	3	11	51	37	64	6	9	4-4	.283	.348	.429	.778	2	.993
—New York (N.L.)	OF-1B	34	113	14	29	9	0	4	15	8	18	4	8	0-0	.257	.325	.442	.768	3	.951
American League totals (7 years)		716	2513	402	718	164	15	119	376	206	510	28	37	76-25	.286	.344	.505	.849	19	.986
National League totals (7 years)		1105	4123	665	1155	251	19	199	648	501	743	47	124	75-26	.280	.362	.495	.857	31	.989
Major League totals (14 years)		1821	6636	1067	1873	415	34	318	1024	707	1253	75	161	151-51	.282	.355	.499	.854	50	.988

DIVISION SERIES RECORD

Year—Team (League)	Pos.	G	AB	R	H	2B	3B	HR	RBI	BB	SO	HBP	GDP	SB-CS	Avg.	OBP	SLG	OPS	E	Avg.
2004—Los Angeles (N.L.)	1B	4	16	3	4	0	0	3	3	3	0	0	0	0-0	.250	.250	.813	1.063	0	1.000
2006—New York (N.L.)	OF	2	9	1	3	2	0	0	2	2	0	0	1	0-0	.333	.333	.556	.889	0	1.000
Division series totals (2 years)		6	25	4	7	2	0	3	5	5	0	0	1	0-0	.280	.280	.720	1.000	0	1.000

CHAMPIONSHIP SERIES RECORD

Year—Team (League)	Pos.	G	AB	R	H	2B	3B	HR	RBI	BB	SO	HBP	GDP	SB-CS	Avg.	OBP	SLG	OPS	E	Avg.
2006—New York (N.L.)	OF	7	23	2	7	1	0	0	2	4	3	1	0	1-0	.304	.429	.348	.776	0	1.000

ALL-STAR GAME RECORD

		G	AB	R	H	2B	3B	HR	RBI	BB	SO	HBP	GDP	SB-CS	Avg.	OBP	SLG	OPS	E	Avg.
All-Star Game totals (2 years)		2	4	0	2	0	0	0	0	0	1	0	0	1-0	.500	.500	.500	1.000	0	1.000

2006 LEFTY-RIGHTY SPLITS

vs.	Avg.	AB	H	2B	3B	HR	RBI	BB	SO	OBP	Slg.	vs.	Avg.	AB	H	2B	3B	HR	RBI	BB	SO	OBP	Slg.
L	.267	165	44	11	1	6	23	15	33	.344	.455	R	.282	365	103	20	2	9	43	30	49	.343	.422

GREENE, KHALIL — SS

PERSONAL: Born October 21, 1979, in Butler, Pa. ... 5-11/210. ... Bats right, throws right. ... Full name: Khalil Thabit Greene. ... High school: Key West (Fla.). ... College: Clemson. **TRANSACTIONS/CAREER NOTES:** Selected by Chicago Cubs organization in 14th round of 2001 free-agent draft; did not sign. ... Selected by San Diego Padres organization in first round (13th pick overall) of 2002 free-agent draft. ... On disabled list (April 18-May 9 and August 15-30, 2005); included rehabilitation assignment to Lake Elsinore. ... On disabled list (August 18-September 3, 2006). **STATISTICAL NOTES:** Career major league grand slams: 1.

2006 GAMES PLAYED BY POSITION (MLB): SS—113.

							BATTING									FIELDING	
Year—Team (League)	Pos.	G	AB	R	H	2B	3B	HR	RBI	BB	SO	HBP	GDP	SB-CS	Avg.	OBP	SLG	OPS	E	Avg.
2002—Eugene (Northwest)	SS	10	37	5	10	1	0	0	6	5	6	3	1	0-0	.270	.400	.297	.697	3	.900
—Lake Elsinore (Calif.)	SS-2B-3B	46	183	33	58	9	1	9	32	12	33	4	7	0-0	.317	.368	.525	.893	9	.947
2003—Mobile (Sou.)	SS-DH	59	229	20	63	17	2	3	20	16	55	2	7	2-3	.275	.327	.406	.733	9	.949
—Portland (PCL)	SS	76	319	42	92	19	0	10	47	20	52	11	3	5-4	.288	.346	.442	.788	11	.967
—San Diego (N.L.)	SS	20	65	8	14	4	1	2	6	4	19	1	3	0-1	.215	.271	.400	.671	3	.963
2004—San Diego (N.L.)	SS	139	484	67	132	31	4	15	65	53	94	8	9	4-2	.273	.349	.446	.795	20	.965
2005—Lake Elsinore (Calif.)	SS	4	12	4	6	1	0	0	3	2	1	1	0	0-0	.500	.600	.583	1.183	0	1.000
—San Diego (N.L.)	SS	121	436	51	109	30	2	15	70	25	93	6	9	4-2	.250	.296	.431	.727	14	.971
2006—San Diego (N.L.)	SS	121	412	56	101	26	2	15	56	39	87	7	15	5-1	.245	.320	.427	.747	9	.980
Major League totals (4 years)		401	1397	182	356	91	9	47	196	121	293	22	35	14-4	.255	.321	.434	.754	46	.971

DIVISION SERIES RECORD

Year—Team (League)	Pos.	G	AB	R	H	2B	3B	HR	RBI	BB	SO	HBP	GDP	SB-CS	Avg.	OBP	SLG	OPS	E	Avg.
2005—San Diego (N.L.)	SS	3	10	2	4	2	0	1	1	1	2	0	0	0-0	.400	.417	.600	1.017	2	.905
2006—San Diego (N.L.)	SS	3	4	0	0	0	0	0	0	0	2	0	0	0-0	.000	.000	.000	.000	0	1.000
Division series totals (2 years)		6	14	2	4	2	0	1	1	1	4	0	0	0-0	.286	.313	.429	.741	2	.920

G

2006 LEFTY-RIGHTY SPLITS

vs.	Avg.	AB	H	2B	3B	HR	RBI	BB	SO	OBP	Slg.	vs.	Avg.	AB	H	2B	3B	HR	RBI	BB	SO	OBP	Slg.
L	.271	96	26	8	0	3	11	14	15	.372	.448	R	.237	316	75	18	2	12	44	25	72	.303	.421

GREENE, TODD   C/DH

PERSONAL: Born May 8, 1971, in Augusta, Ga. ... 5-10/208. ... Bats right, throws right. ... Full name: Todd Anthony Greene. ... High school: Evans (Ga.). ... College: Georgia Southern. **TRANSACTIONS/CAREER NOTES:** Selected by Atlanta Braves organization in 27th round of 1989 free-agent draft; did not sign. ... Selected by California Angels organization in 12th round of 1993 free-agent draft. ... Angels franchise renamed Anaheim Angels for 1997 season. ... On disabled list (August 20, 1997-remainder of season). ... On disabled list (March 19-August 5, 1998); included rehabilitation assignments to Lake Elsinore and Vancouver. ... On suspended list (May 13-16, 1999). ... Released by Angels (March 29, 2000). ... Signed by Toronto Blue Jays organization (April 10, 2000); included rehabilitation assignment to Dunedin. ... Released by Blue Jays (March 28, 2001). ... Signed by New York Yankees organization (April 5, 2001). ... Released by Yankees (March 26, 2002). ... Signed by Los Angeles Dodgers organization (April 2, 2002). ... Released by Dodgers (May 15, 2002). ... Signed by Texas Rangers (May 16, 2002). ... On disabled list (April 30-May 15, 2003); included rehabilitation assignment to Frisco. ... Signed as a free agent by Colorado Rockies organization (December 22, 2003). ... On disabled list (August 8-September 1, 2004); included rehabilitation assignment to Colorado Springs. ... On disabled list (June 6-August 17, 2005); included rehabilitation assignment to Colorado Springs. ... Signed as a free agent by San Diego Padres organization (December 30, 2005).... Released by Padres (February 3, 2006). ... Signed by San Francisco Giants organization (February 7, 2006). **STATISTICAL NOTES:** Career major league grand slams: 1.
2006 GAMES PLAYED BY POSITION (MLB): C—42, 1B—5, DH—1.

								BATTING										FIELDING	
Year	Team (League)	Pos.	G	AB	R	H	2B	3B	HR	RBI	BB	SO	HBP	GDP	SB-CS	Avg.	OBP	SLG	OPS	E	Avg.
1993— Boise (N'west)	OF	76	305	55	82	15	3	15	71	34	44	9	3	4-3	.269	.356	.485	.841	3	.979
1994— Lake Elsinore (Calif.)	1B-C-OF	133	524	98	158	39	2	35	124	64	96	4	12	10-3	.302	.378	.584	.962	15	.979
1995— Midland (Texas)	C-DH	82	318	59	104	19	1	26	57	17	55	5	6	3-5	.327	.365	.638	1.004	3	.992
— Vancouver (PCL)	C-DH	43	168	28	42	3	1	14	35	11	36	4	3	1-0	.250	.308	.530	.838	1	.995
1996— Vancouver (PCL)	C-DH	60	223	27	68	18	0	5	33	16	36	1	6	0-2	.305	.347	.453	.800	3	.988
— California (A.L.)	C-DH	29	79	9	15	1	0	2	9	4	11	1	4	2-0	.190	.238	.278	.517	0	1.000
1997— Anaheim (A.L.)	C-DH	34	124	24	36	6	0	9	24	7	25	0	1	2-0	.290	.328	.556	.885	0	1.000
— Vancouver (PCL)	C-DH-1B																			
	OF	64	260	51	92	22	0	25	75	20	31	5	6	5-1	.354	.408	.727	1.135	3	.992
1998— Lake Elsinore (Calif.)	DH-1B	12	44	9	10	2	0	1	6	4	7	0	1	1-0	.227	.286	.341	.627	2	.833
— Vancouver (PCL)	DH-1B-C																			
	OF	30	108	16	30	12	0	7	20	12	17	3	2	1-0	.278	.360	.583	.943	1	.990
— Anaheim (A.L.)	OF-DH-1B	29	71	3	18	4	0	1	7	2	20	0	0	0-0	.254	.274	.352	.626	0	1.000
1999— Anaheim (A.L.)	DH-OF-C	97	321	36	78	20	0	14	42	17	63	3	8	1-4	.243	.275	.436	.711	2	.980
— Edmonton (PCL)	DH-OF	19	74	10	18	6	0	5	14	0	12	1	4	0-0	.243	.253	.527	.780	0	1.000
2000— Syracuse (Int'l)	OF-C	24	91	14	27	3	0	7	14	6	16	0	3	0-0	.297	.337	.560	.897	1	.970
— Toronto (A.L.)	DH-C-OF	34	85	11	20	2	0	5	10	5	18	0	4	0-0	.235	.278	.435	.713	0	1.000
— Dunedin (Fla. St.)	OF	5	20	2	4	1	0	1	4	2	4	1	0	0-0	.200	.304	.400	.704	0	1.000
2001— Columbus (Int'l)	C-OF	34	131	16	33	8	0	6	17	4	19	1	3	3-2	.252	.279	.450	.730	4	.982
— New York (A.L.)	C-OF	35	96	9	20	4	0	1	11	3	21	1	3	0-0	.208	.240	.281	.521	0	1.000
2002— Las Vegas (PCL)	C-1B-OF	32	125	27	44	12	0	11	44	3	22	1	...	0-0	.352	.373	.712	1.085	2	.989
— Texas (A.L.)	1B-C-DH																			
	OF	42	112	15	30	5	0	10	19	2	23	1	4	0-0	.268	.282	.580	.862	3	.985
— Oklahoma (PCL)	C-OF-1B	39	152	21	46	9	0	6	29	9	27	1		2-0	.303	.339	.480	.820	2	.991
2003— Frisco (Texas)	C-1B	3	9	3	3	0	0	2	4	2	2	0	1	0-0	.333	.455	1.000	1.455	0	1.000
— Texas (A.L.)	C-DH-1B	62	205	25	47	10	1	10	20	2	47	2	2	0-0	.229	.243	.434	.677	4	.988
2004— Colo. Springs (PCL)	C-1B	4	12	2	4	1	0	1	4	1	3	0	0	0-0	.333	.385	.667	1.051	0	1.000
— Colorado (N.L.)	C	75	195	23	55	14	0	10	35	13	38	0	9	0-0	.282	.325	.508	.833	3	.989
2005— Colo. Springs (PCL)	C	11	33	4	13	0	0	3	8	1	3	0	2	0-0	.394	.412	.667	1.078	1	.980
— Colorado (N.L.)	C	38	126	10	32	4	0	7	23	7	21	1	5	0-0	.254	.299	.452	.751	4	.975
2006— San Francisco (N.L.)	C-1B-DH	61	159	16	46	12	2	2	17	10	45	1	5	0-0	.289	.335	.428	.763	1	.995
American League totals (8 years)		362	1093	132	264	52	1	52	142	37	228	8	26	5-4	.242	.270	.434	.704	9	.992
National League totals (3 years)		174	480	49	133	30	2	19	75	30	104	2	14	0-0	.277	.322	.467	.788	8	.988
Major League totals (11 years)		536	1573	181	397	82	3	71	217	67	332	10	40	5-4	.252	.286	.444	.730	17	.991

DIVISION SERIES RECORD

Year	Team (League)	Pos.	G	AB	R	H	2B	3B	HR	RBI	BB	SO	HBP	GDP	SB-CS	Avg.	OBP	SLG	OPS	E	Avg.
2001— New York (A.L.)			Did not play.																		

CHAMPIONSHIP SERIES RECORD

Year	Team (League)	Pos.	G	AB	R	H	2B	3B	HR	RBI	BB	SO	HBP	GDP	SB-CS	Avg.	OBP	SLG	OPS	E	Avg.
2001— New York (A.L.)		C	1	1	0	0	0	0	0	0	0	0	0	0	0-0	.000	.000	.000	.000	0	1.000

WORLD SERIES RECORD

Year	Team (League)	Pos.	G	AB	R	H	2B	3B	HR	RBI	BB	SO	HBP	GDP	SB-CS	Avg.	OBP	SLG	OPS	E	Avg.
2001— New York (A.L.)		C	1	2	1	1	1	0	0	0	0	0	0	1	0-0	.500	.500	1.000	1.500	0	1.000

2006 LEFTY-RIGHTY SPLITS

vs.	Avg.	AB	H	2B	3B	HR	RBI	BB	SO	OBP	Slg.	vs.	Avg.	AB	H	2B	3B	HR	RBI	BB	SO	OBP	Slg.
L	.250	36	9	3	1	1	6	2	8	.289	.472	R	.301	123	37	9	1	1	11	8	37	.348	.415

GREGG, KEVIN   P

PERSONAL: Born June 20, 1978, in Corvallis, Ore. ... 6-6/220. ... Throws right, bats right. ... Full name: Kevin Marschall Gregg. ... High school: Corvallis (Ore.). **TRANSACTIONS/CAREER NOTES:** Selected by Oakland Athletics organization in 15th round of 1996 free-agent draft. ... Signed as a free agent by Anaheim Angels organization (November 19, 2002). ... Angels franchise renamed Los Angeles Angels of Anaheim for 2005 season. ... On suspended list (August 18-25, 2006).
CAREER HITTING: 0-for-3 (.000), 0 R, 0 2B, 0 3B, 0 HR, 0 RBI.

Year	Team (League)	W	L	Pct.	ERA	WHIP	G	GS	CG	ShO	Hld.	Sv.-Opp.	IP	H	R	ER	HR	BB-IBB	SO	Avg.
1996— Ariz. A's (Ariz.)	3	3	.500	3.10	1.25	11	9	0	0	...	0-...	40.2	30	14	14	1	21-0	48	.208
1997— Visalia (Calif.)	6	8	.429	5.70	1.65	25	24	0	0	...	0-...	115.1	116	81	73	8	74-0	136	.258
1998— Modesto (California)	8	7	.533	3.81	1.49	30	24	0	0	...	1-...	144.0	139	72	61	7	76-2	141	.254
1999— Visalia (Calif.)	4	4	.500	3.80	1.30	13	11	1	1	...	1-...	64.0	60	34	27	3	23-0	48	.249
— Midland (Texas)	4	7	.364	3.74	1.16	16	16	2	0	...	0-...	91.1	75	45	38	7	31-1	66	.221
— Vancouver (PCL)	1	0	1.000	3.60	1.60	1	1	0	0	...	0-...	5.0	6	2	2	0	2-0	4	.316
2000— Midland (Texas)	5	14	.263	6.40	1.73	28	27	0	0	...	0-...	140.2	171	120	100	18	73-0	97	.304
2001— Midland (Texas)	5	5	.500	4.54	1.57	44	1	0	0	...	1-...	81.1	88	48	41	5	40-4	72	.274
2002— Midland (Texas)	3	3	.500	4.30	1.30	11	4	0	0	...	0-...	37.2	31	20	18	3	18-0	45	.221
— Visalia (Calif.)	2	1	.667	2.08	0.98	3	3	0	0	...	0-...	17.1	8	5	4	0	9-0	11	.140
— Sacramento (PCL)	2	5	.286	7.52	1.79	16	8	0	0	...	0-...	58.2	82	56	49	7	23-0	45	.332

G

Year Team (League)	W	L	Pct.	ERA	WHIP	G	GS	CG	ShO	Hld.	Sv.-Opp.	IP	H	R	ER	HR	BB-IBB	SO	Avg.
2003— Arkansas (Texas)	4	3	.571	3.53	1.19	15	11	2	0	...	0-...	66.1	60	29	26	2	19-0	60	.241
— Salt Lake (PCL)	7	4	.636	4.03	1.18	15	15	0	0	...	0-...	91.2	90	47	41	10	18-0	75	.256
— Anaheim (A.L.)	2	0	1.000	3.28	1.05	5	3	0	0	0	0-0	24.2	18	9	9	3	8-0	14	.205
2004— Anaheim (A.L.)	5	2	.714	4.21	1.30	55	0	0	0	3	1-2	87.2	86	43	41	6	28-3	84	.255
2005— Salt Lake (PCL)	3	1	.750	3.89	1.33	7	6	0	0	0	0-0	34.2	36	15	15	2	10-0	36	.273
— Los Angeles (A.L.)	1	2	.333	5.04	1.54	33	2	0	0	1	0-1	64.1	70	37	36	8	29-2	52	.273
2006— Salt Lake (PCL)	1	0	1.000	0.00	0.90	3	2	0	0	1	0-0	10.0	5	0	0	0	4-0	8	.152
— Los Angeles (A.L.)	3	4	.429	4.14	1.39	32	3	0	0	0	0-0	78.1	88	41	36	10	21-0	71	.280
Major League totals (4 years)	11	8	.579	4.31	1.36	125	8	0	0	4	1-3	255.0	262	130	122	27	86-5	221	.263

DIVISION SERIES RECORD

Year Team (League)	W	L	Pct.	ERA	WHIP	G	GS	CG	ShO	Hld.	Sv.-Opp.	IP	H	R	ER	HR	BB-IBB	SO	Avg.
2004— Anaheim (A.L.)	0	0	...	0.00	2.00	1	0	0	0	0	0-0	2.0	3	0	0	0	1-0	1	.333

CHAMPIONSHIP SERIES RECORD

Year Team (League)	W	L	Pct.	ERA	WHIP	G	GS	CG	ShO	Hld.	Sv.-Opp.	IP	H	R	ER	HR	BB-IBB	SO	Avg.
2005— Los Angeles (A.L.)	0	0	...	0.00	1.00	1	0	0	0	0	0-0	2.0	1	0	0	0	1-0	3	.143

2006 LEFTY-RIGHTY SPLITS

vs.	Avg.	AB	H	2B	3B	HR	RBI	BB	SO	OBP	Slg.	vs.	Avg.	AB	H	2B	3B	HR	RBI	BB	SO	OBP	Slg.
L	.298	131	39	5	2	5	20	13	34	.359	.481	R	.268	183	49	7	0	5	22	8	37	.303	.388

GREINKE, ZACK — P

PERSONAL: Born October 21, 1983, in Orlando. ... 6-2/200. ... Throws right, bats right. ... Full name: Donald Zackary Greinke. ... Name pronounced: GRAIN-key. ... High school: Apopka (Fla.). **TRANSACTIONS/CAREER NOTES:** Selected by Kansas City Royals organization in first round (sixth pick overall) of 2002 free-agent draft. ... On disabled list (April 1-June 21, 2006); included rehabilitation assignment to Wichita. **HONORS:** Named Minor League Player of the Year by THE SPORTING NEWS (2003).
CAREER HITTING: 1-for-4 (.250), 1 R, 0 2B, 0 3B, 1 HR, 1 RBI.

Year Team (League)	W	L	Pct.	ERA	WHIP	G	GS	CG	ShO	Hld.	Sv.-Opp.	IP	H	R	ER	HR	BB-IBB	SO	Avg.
2002— GC Royals (GCL)	0	0	...	1.93	1.29	3	3	0	0	0	0-...	4.2	3	1	1	0	3-0	4	.200
— Spokane (N'west)	0	0	...	7.71	1.93	2	2	0	0	0	0-...	4.2	9	4	4	0	0-0	5	.391
— Wilmington (Caro.)	0	0	...	0.00	0.50	1	0	0	0	0	0-...	2.0	1	0	0	0	0-0	0	.167
2003— Wilmington (Caro.)	11	1	.917	1.14	0.79	14	14	3	1	0	0-...	87.0	56	16	11	5	13-0	78	.178
— Wichita (Texas)	4	3	.571	3.23	1.19	9	9	0	0	0	0-...	53.0	58	20	19	5	5-2	34	.286
2004— Omaha (PCL)	1	1	.500	2.51	1.08	6	6	0	0	0	0-...	28.2	25	8	8	2	6-0	23	.225
— Kansas City (A.L.)	8	11	.421	3.97	1.17	24	24	0	0	0	0-0	145.0	143	64	64	26	26-3	100	.256
2005— Kansas City (A.L.)	5	* 17	.227	5.80	1.56	33	33	2	0	0	0-0	183.0	233	125	118	23	53-0	114	.309
2006— Wichita (Texas)	8	3	.727	4.34	1.16	18	17	1	0	0	0-...	105.2	96	53	51	12	27-0	94	.280
— Kansas City (A.L.)	1	0	1.000	4.26	1.58	3	0	0	0	0	0-0	6.1	7	3	3	1	3-2	5	.280
Major League totals (3 years)	14	28	.333	4.98	1.39	60	57	2	0	0	0-0	334.1	383	192	185	50	82-5	219	.286

2006 LEFTY-RIGHTY SPLITS

vs.	Avg.	AB	H	2B	3B	HR	RBI	BB	SO	OBP	Slg.	vs.	Avg.	AB	H	2B	3B	HR	RBI	BB	SO	OBP	Slg.
L	.400	10	4	0	0	0	1	2	2	.500	.400	R	.200	15	3	0	0	1	2	1	3	.250	.400

GRIFFEY, KEN — OF

PERSONAL: Born November 21, 1969, in Donora, Pa. ... 6-3/205. ... Bats left, throws left. ... Full name: George Kenneth Griffey Jr.. ... High school: Moeller (Cincinnati). ... Son of Ken Griffey, special consultant to general manager, Cincinnati Reds, and outfielder with four major league teams (1973-91). **TRANSACTIONS/CAREER NOTES:** Selected by Seattle Mariners organization in first round (first pick overall) of 1987 free-agent draft. ... On disabled list (July 24-August 20, 1989; and June 9-25, 1992). ... On disabled list (May 27-August 15, 1995); included rehabilitation assignment to Tacoma. ... On disabled list (June 20-July 13, 1996). ... Traded by Mariners to Cincinnati Reds for Ps Brett Tomko and Jake Meyer, OF Mike Cameron and IF Antonio Perez (February 10, 2000). ... On disabled list (April 29-June 15, 2001; and April 7-May 24 and June 24-July 22, 2002). ... On disabled list (April 6-May 13 and July 18, 2003-remainder of season). ... On disabled list (July 11-August 3 and August 12, 2004-remainder of season). ... On disabled list (April 17-May 11, 2006). **HONORS:** Named Major League Player of the Year by THE SPORTING NEWS (1997). ... Named N.L. Comeback Player of the Year by the SPORTING NEWS (2005). ... Named as an outfielder on THE SPORTING NEWS A.L. All-Star team (1991, 1993-94, 1996-99). ... Named as an outfielder on the SPORTING NEWS N.L. All-Star team (2005). ... Named A.L. Most Valuable Player by Baseball Writers' Association of America (1997). ... Won A.L. Gold Glove as outfielder (1990-99). ... Named outfielder on A.L. Silver Slugger team (1991, 1993-94, 1996-99). **STATISTICAL NOTES:** Hit three home runs in one game (May 24, 1996 and April 25, 1997). ... Career major league grand slams: 15.
2006 GAMES PLAYED BY POSITION (MLB): OF—100, DH—3.

Year Team (League)	Pos.	G	AB	R	H	2B	3B	HR	RBI	BB	SO	HBP	GDP	SB-CS	Avg.	OBP	SLG	OPS	E	Avg.
1987— Bellingham (N'west)	OF	54	182	43	57	9	1	14	40	44	42	0	2	13-6	.313	.445	.604	1.049	1	.992
1988— San Bern. (Calif.)	OF	58	219	50	74	13	3	11	42	34	39	1	3	32-9	.338	.431	.575	1.007	2	.987
— Vermont (East.)	OF	17	61	10	17	5	1	2	10	5	12	2	3	4-2	.279	.353	.492	.845	1	.977
1989— Seattle (A.L.)	DH-OF	127	455	61	120	23	0	16	61	44	83	2	4	16-7	.264	.329	.420	.748	10	.969
1990— Seattle (A.L.)	OF	155	597	91	179	28	7	22	80	63	81	2	12	16-11	.300	.366	.481	.847	5	.980
1991— Seattle (A.L.)	DH-OF	154	548	76	179	42	1	22	100	71	82	1	10	18-6	.327	.399	.527	.926	4	.989
1992— Seattle (A.L.)	OF-DH	142	565	83	174	39	4	27	103	44	67	5	15	10-5	.308	.361	.535	.896	1	.990
1993— Seattle (A.L.) OF-DH-1B	156	582	113	180	38	3	45	109	96	91	9	14	17-9	.309	.408	.617	1.025	3	.991
1994— Seattle (A.L.)	OF-DH	111	433	94	140	24	4	* 40	90	56	73	9	11-3	.323	.402	.674	1.076	4	.983
1995— Seattle (A.L.)	OF-DH	72	260	52	67	7	0	17	42	52	53	0	4	4-2	.258	.379	.481	.860	2	.990
— Tacoma (PCL)	DH	1	3	0	0	0	0	0	0	0	1	0	...	0-0	.000	.000	.000	.000	...	...
1996— Seattle (A.L.)	OF-DH	140	545	125	165	26	2	49	140	78	104	7	7	16-1	.303	.392	.628	1.020	4	.990
1997— Seattle (A.L.)	OF-DH	157	608	* 125	185	34	3	* 56	* 147	76	121	8	12	15-4	.304	.382	* .646	1.028	6	.985
1998— Seattle (A.L.) OF-DH-1B	161	633	120	180	33	3	* 56	146	76	121	7	14	20-5	.284	.365	.611	.977	5	.988
1999— Seattle (A.L.)	OF-DH	160	606	123	173	26	3	* 48	134	91	108	7	8	24-7	.285	.384	.576	.960	9	.978
2000— Cincinnati (N.L.)	OF	145	520	100	141	22	3	40	118	94	117	9	7	6-4	.271	.387	.556	.942	5	.987
2001— Cincinnati (N.L.)	OF-DH	111	364	57	104	20	2	22	65	44	72	4	8	2-0	.286	.365	.533	.898	3	.985
2002— Cincinnati (N.L.)	OF	70	197	17	52	8	0	8	23	28	39	3	6	1-2	.264	.358	.426	.784	3	.971
2003— Cincinnati (N.L.)	OF-DH	53	166	34	41	12	1	13	26	27	44	6	3	1-0	.247	.370	.566	.936	1	.989
2004— Cincinnati (N.L.)	OF-DH	83	300	49	76	18	0	20	60	44	67	2	8	1-0	.253	.351	.513	.864	1	.994
2005— Cincinnati (N.L.)	OF-DH	128	491	85	148	30	0	35	92	54	93	3	9	0-1	.301	.369	.576	.946	3	.990
2006— Cincinnati (N.L.)	OF-DH	109	428	62	108	19	0	27	72	39	78	2	13	0-0	.252	.316	.486	.802	5	.979
American League totals (11 years)		1535	5832	1063	1742	320	30	398	1152	747	984	47	109	167-60	.299	.380	.569	.948	55	.986
National League totals (7 years)		699	2466	404	670	129	6	165	456	330	510	29	54	11-7	.272	.361	.530	.890	21	.986
Major League totals (18 years)		2234	8298	1467	2412	449	36	563	1608	1077	1494	76	163	178-67	.291	.374	.557	.931	76	.986

G

Year	Team (League)	Pos.	G	AB	R	H	2B	3B	HR	RBI	BB	SO	HBP	GDP	SB-CS	Avg.	OBP	SLG	OPS	E	Avg.
							DIVISION SERIES RECORD															
1995—	Seattle (A.L.)	OF	5	23	9	9	0	0	5	7	2	4	1	0	1-0	.391	.444	1.043	1.488	0	1.000
1997—	Seattle (A.L.)	OF	4	15	0	2	0	0	0	2	1	3	0	0	2-0	.133	.188	.133	.321	0	1.000
	Division series totals (2 years)		9	38	9	11	0	0	5	9	3	7	1	0	3-0	.289	.349	.684	1.033	0	1.000

Year	Team (League)	Pos.	G	AB	R	H	2B	3B	HR	RBI	BB	SO	HBP	GDP	SB-CS	Avg.	OBP	SLG	OPS	E	Avg.
							CHAMPIONSHIP SERIES RECORD															
1995—	Seattle (A.L.)	OF	6	21	2	7	2	0	1	2	4	4	0	0	2-1	.333	.440	.571	1.011	1	.929

			G	AB	R	H	2B	3B	HR	RBI	BB	SO	HBP	GDP	SB-CS	Avg.	OBP	SLG	OPS	E	Avg.
							ALL-STAR GAME RECORD															
	All-Star Game totals (8 years)		8	23	4	10	2	0	1	5	2	4	0	0	1-0	.435	.480	.652	1.132	1	.900

2006 LEFTY-RIGHTY SPLITS

vs.	Avg.	AB	H	2B	3B	HR	RBI	BB	SO	OBP	Slg.	vs.	Avg.	AB	H	2B	3B	HR	RBI	BB	SO	OBP	Slg.
L	.204	147	30	4	0	9	29	9	27	.256	.415	R	.278	281	78	15	0	18	43	30	51	.346	.523

GRILLI, JASON — P

PERSONAL: Born November 11, 1976, in Royal Oak, Mich. ... 6-4/185. ... Throws right, bats right. ... Full name: Jason Michael Grilli. ... High school: C.W. Baker (Baldwinsville, N.Y.). ... College: Seton Hall. ... Son of Steve Grilli, pitcher with two major league teams (1975-79). **TRANSACTIONS/CAREER NOTES:** Selected by New York Yankees organization in 24th round of 1994 free-agent draft; did not sign. ... Selected by San Francisco Giants organization in first round (fourth pick overall) of 1997 free-agent draft. ... Traded by Giants with P Nate Bump to Florida Marlins for P Livan Hernandez (July 24, 1999). ... Selected by Chicago White Sox from Marlins organization in Rule 5 major league draft (December 15, 2003). ... Released by White Sox (Feburary 3, 2005). ... Signed by Detroit Tigers organization (February 9, 2005).
CAREER HITTING: 3-for-9 (.333), 1 R, 0 2B, 0 3B, 1 HR, 3 RBI.

Year	Team (League)	W	L	Pct.	ERA	WHIP	G	GS	CG	ShO	Hld.	Sv.-Opp.	IP	H	R	ER	HR	BB-IBB	SO	Avg.
1998—	Shreveport (Texas)	7	10	.412	3.79	1.22	21	21	3	0	...	0-...	123.1	113	60	52	11	37-0	100	.245
	Fresno (PCL)	2	3	.400	5.14	1.60	8	8	0	0	...	0-...	42.0	49	30	24	7	18-0	37	.290
1999—	Fresno (PCL)	7	5	.583	5.54	1.62	19	19	1	0	...	0-...	100.2	124	69	62	22	39-0	76	.302
	Calgary (PCL)	1	5	.167	7.68	1.93	8	8	0	0	...	0-...	41.0	56	48	35	7	23-0	27	.316
2000—	Calgary (PCL)	1	4	.200	7.19	1.96	8	8	0	0	...	0-...	41.1	58	37	33	4	23-0	21	.335
	Florida (N.L.)	1	0	1.000	5.40	1.95	1	1	0	0	...	0-0	6.2	11	4	4	0	2-0	3	.379
2001—	Florida (N.L.)	2	2	.500	6.08	1.54	6	5	0	0	...	0-0	26.2	30	18	18	6	11-0	17	.297
	Calgary (PCL)	1	2	.333	4.02	1.40	8	8	0	0	...	0-0	47.0	48	26	21	4	20-0	35	.256
	GC Marlins (GCL)	0	0	...	0.00	0.50	2	2	0	0	...	0-0	4.0	2	0	0	0	0-0	6	.143
	Brevard County (FSL)	2	0	1.000	1.98	1.24	3	3	0	0	...	0-0	13.2	12	4	3	0	5-0	14	.231
	Portland (East.)	0	1	.000	2.25	0.75	1	1	0	0	...	0-0	4.0	3	1	1	0	0-0	3	.200
2002—	Calgary (PCL)	0	1	.000	1.59	1.06	1	1	0	0	...	0-0	5.2	3	1	1	0	3-0	8	.158
2003—	Jupiter (Fla. St.)	4	2	.667	2.53	1.03	7	7	0	0	...	0-0	42.2	38	13	12	1	6-...	30	.236
	Albuquerque (PCL)	6	2	.750	3.38	1.41	12	12	0	0	...	0-0	66.2	64	30	25	3	30-...	38	.260
2004—	Charlotte (Int'l)	9	9	.500	4.83	1.45	25	25	1	0	...	0-0	152.2	163	95	82	22	58-0	101	.276
	Chicago (A.L.)	2	3	.400	7.40	1.60	8	8	1	0	0	0-0	45.0	52	38	37	11	20-0	26	.294
2005—	Toledo (Int'l)	12	9	.571	4.09	1.36	28	28	3	2	0	0-0	167.1	170	89	76	21	58-0	120	.263
	Detroit (A.L.)	1	1	.500	3.38	1.25	3	2	0	0	0	0-0	16.0	16	6	6	0	5-0	5	.255
2006—	Detroit (A.L.)	2	3	.400	4.21	1.39	51	0	0	0	1	0-0	62.0	61	31	29	6	25-3	31	.261
	American League totals (3 years)	5	7	.417	5.27	1.45	62	10	1	0	1	0-0	123.0	127	75	72	18	51-3	62	.273
	National League totals (2 years)	3	2	.600	5.94	1.62	7	6	0	0	0	0-0	33.1	41	22	22	6	13-0	20	.315
	Major League totals (5 years)	8	9	.471	5.41	1.48	69	16	1	0	1	0-0	156.1	168	97	94	24	64-3	82	.282

Year	Team (League)	W	L	Pct.	ERA	WHIP	G	GS	CG	ShO	Hld.	Sv.-Opp.	IP	H	R	ER	HR	BB-IBB	SO	Avg.
						DIVISION SERIES RECORD														
2006—	Detroit (A.L.)	0	0	...	0.00	0.00	1	0	0	0	0	0-0	0.1	0	0	0	0	0-0	0	.000

Year	Team (League)	W	L	Pct.	ERA	WHIP	G	GS	CG	ShO	Hld.	Sv.-Opp.	IP	H	R	ER	HR	BB-IBB	SO	Avg.
						CHAMPIONSHIP SERIES RECORD														
2006—	Detroit (A.L.)	0	0	...	0.00	4.00	2	0	0	0	1	0-0	1.0	1	0	0	0	3-0	1	.333

Year	Team (League)	W	L	Pct.	ERA	WHIP	G	GS	CG	ShO	Hld.	Sv.-Opp.	IP	H	R	ER	HR	BB-IBB	SO	Avg.
						WORLD SERIES RECORD														
2006—	Detroit (A.L.)	0	0	...	0.00	0.60	2	0	0	0	0	0-0	1.2	1	0	0	0	1-1	0	.000

2006 LEFTY-RIGHTY SPLITS

vs.	Avg.	AB	H	2B	3B	HR	RBI	BB	SO	OBP	Slg.	vs.	Avg.	AB	H	2B	3B	HR	RBI	BB	SO	OBP	Slg.
L	.292	65	19	6	3	0	9	10	11	.382	.477	R	.249	169	42	6	0	6	25	15	20	.323	.391

GRIMSLEY, JASON — P

PERSONAL: Born August 7, 1967, in Cleveland, Texas. ... 6-3/205. ... Throws right, bats right. ... Full name: Jason Alan Grimsley. ... High school: Tarkington (Cleveland, Texas). **TRANSACTIONS/CAREER NOTES:** Selected by Philadelphia Phillies organization in 10th round of June 1985 free-agent draft. ... On disabled list (June 6-August 22, 1991); included rehabilitation assignments to Scranton/Wilkes-Barre. ... Traded by Phillies to Houston Astros for P Curt Schilling (April 2, 1992). ... On disabled list (May 14-June 14, 1992). ... Released by Astros (March 30, 1993). ... Signed by Cleveland Indians organization (April 7, 1993). ... Traded by Indians with P Pep Harris to California Angels for P Brian Anderson (February 15, 1996). ... Signed as a free agent by Detroit Tigers organization (January 17, 1997). ... Released by Tigers (March 20, 1997). ... Signed by Milwaukee Brewers (April 3, 1997). ... Traded by Brewers to Kansas City Royals for P Jamie Brewington (July 29, 1997). ... Signed as a free agent by Indians organization (January 8, 1998). ... Signed as a free agent by New York Yankees organization (January 26, 1999). ... On suspended list (August 11-15, 1999). ... Released by Yankees (November 20, 2000). ... Signed by Royals (January 19, 2001). ... On disabled list (June 4-22, 2002); included rehabilitation assignment to Wichita. ... Traded by Royals to Baltimore Orioles for P Denny Bautista (June 17, 2004). ... On disabled list (April 1-July 14 and August 19-September 2, 2005); included rehabilitation assignment to Bowie. ... Signed as a free agent by Arizona Diamondbacks (December 13, 2005). ... Released by Diamondbacks (June 7, 2006). **MISCELLANEOUS NOTES:** Appeared in one game as pinch runner with Philadelphia (1990).
CAREER HITTING: 4-for-43 (.093), 4 R, 0 2B, 0 3B, 0 HR, 2 RBI.

Year	Team (League)	W	L	Pct.	ERA	WHIP	G	GS	CG	ShO	Hld.	Sv.-Opp.	IP	H	R	ER	HR	BB-IBB	SO	Avg.
1985—	Bend (N'west)	0	1	.000	13.50	3.26	6	1	0	0	...	0-...	11.1	12	21	17	0	25-0	10	...
1986—	Utica (N.Y.-Penn)	1	10	.091	6.40	2.16	14	14	3	0	...	0-...	64.2	63	61	46	3	77-0	46	.251
1987—	Spartanburg (SAL)	7	4	.636	3.16	1.28	23	9	3	0	...	0-...	88.1	59	48	31	4	54-2	98	.190
1988—	Clearwater (FSL)	4	7	.364	3.73	1.15	16	15	2	0	...	0-...	101.1	80	48	42	2	37-1	90	.217
	Reading (East.)	1	3	.250	7.17	1.55	5	4	0	0	...	0-...	21.1	20	19	17	1	13-1	14	.247
1989—	Reading (East.)	11	8	.579	2.98	1.34	26	26	8	2	...	0-...	172.0	121	65	57	13	109-4	134	.202
	Philadelphia (N.L.)	1	3	.250	5.89	2.07	4	4	0	0	...	0-...	18.1	19	13	12	2	19-1	7	.268
1990—	Scran./W.B. (I.L.)	8	5	.615	3.93	1.47	22	22	0	0	...	0-...	128.1	111	68	56	7	78-1	99	.236
	Philadelphia (N.L.)	3	2	.600	3.30	1.57	11	11	0	0	...	0-0	57.1	47	21	21	4	43-0	41	.227
1991—	Philadelphia (N.L.)	1	7	.125	4.87	1.56	12	11	0	0	...	0-0	61.0	54	34	33	4	41-3	42	.242

G

Year	Team (League)	W	L	Pct.	ERA	WHIP	G	GS	CG	ShO	Hld.	Sv.-Opp.	IP	H	R	ER	HR	BB-IBB	SO	Avg.
—	Scran./W.B. (I.L.)	2	3	.400	4.35	1.65	9	9	0	0	...	0-...	51.2	48	28	25	3	37-2	43	.254
1992—	Tucson (PCL)	8	7	.533	5.05	1.66	26	20	0	0	...	0-...	124.2	152	79	70	4	55-0	90	.308
1993—	Charlotte (Int'l)	6	6	.500	3.39	1.38	28	19	3	1	...	0-...	135.1	138	64	51	10	49-1	102	.263
—	Cleveland (A.L.)	3	4	.429	5.31	1.70	10	6	0	0	...	0-0	42.1	52	26	25	3	20-1	27	.302
1994—	Charlotte (Int'l)	7	0	1.000	3.42	1.06	10	10	2	0	...	0-...	71.0	58	36	27	10	17-0	60	.218
—	Cleveland (A.L.)	5	2	.714	4.57	1.51	14	13	1	0	0	0-0	82.2	91	47	42	7	34-1	59	.283
1995—	Cleveland (A.L.)	0	0	...	6.09	2.03	15	2	0	0	0	1-1	34.0	37	24	23	4	32-1	25	.289
—	Buffalo (A.A.)	5	3	.625	2.91	1.18	10	10	2	0	...	0-...	68.0	61	26	22	4	19-0	40	.236
1996—	Vancouver (PCL)	2	0	1.000	1.20	0.73	2	2	1	0	...	0-...	15.0	8	2	2	0	3-0	11	.163
—	California (A.L.)	5	7	.417	6.84	1.72	35	20	2	1	0	0-...	130.1	150	110	99	14	74-5	82	.286
1997—	Tucson (PCL)	5	10	.333	5.70	1.63	36	10	0	0	...	4-...	85.1	96	70	54	6	43-2	65	.293
—	Omaha (A.A.)	1	5	.167	6.68	2.10	7	6	0	0	...	0-...	31.0	36	26	23	3	29-0	22	.293
1998—	Buffalo (Int'l)	6	3	.667	3.76	1.50	52	0	0	0	...	0-...	88.2	76	40	37	10	57-3	68	.234
1999—	New York (A.L.)	7	2	.778	3.60	1.41	55	0	0	0	8	1-4	75.0	66	39	30	7	40-5	49	.231
2000—	New York (A.L.)	3	2	.600	5.04	1.47	63	4	0	0	4	1-4	96.1	100	58	54	10	42-1	53	.268
2001—	Kansas City (A.L.)	1	5	.167	3.02	1.23	73	0	0	0	26	0-7	80.1	71	32	27	8	28-5	61	.242
2002—	Kansas City (A.L.)	4	7	.364	3.91	1.42	70	0	0	0	13	1-3	71.1	64	32	31	4	37-8	59	.236
—	Wichita (Texas)	0	0	...	9.00	2.00	1	1	0	0	...	0-...	1.0	1	1	1	0	1-0	0	.250
2003—	Kansas City (A.L.)	2	6	.250	5.16	1.65	76	0	0	0	28	0-7	75.0	88	47	43	6	36-5	58	.299
2004—	Kansas City (A.L.)	3	3	.500	3.38	1.46	32	0	0	0	5	0-3	26.2	24	11	10	1	15-3	18	.238
—	Baltimore (A.L.)	2	4	.333	4.21	1.57	41	0	0	0	12	0-6	36.1	37	25	17	3	20-3	21	.261
2005—	Bowie (East.)	2	0	1.000	1.13	1.00	8	2	0	0	...	0-0	8.0	4	1	1	0	4-1	4	.143
—	Baltimore (A.L.)	1	2	.333	5.73	1.50	22	0	0	0	3	0-3	22.0	24	15	14	5	9-2	10	.289
2006—	Arizona (N.L.)	1	2	.333	4.88	1.37	19	0	0	0	0	0-0	27.2	30	15	15	4	8-2	10	.280
American League totals (11 years)		36	44	.450	4.84	1.54	506	45	3	1	100	4-38	772.1	804	466	415	72	387-40	522	.269
National League totals (4 years)		6	14	.300	4.44	1.59	46	27	0	0	0	0-0	164.1	150	83	81	11	111-6	100	.247
Major League totals (15 years)		42	58	.420	4.77	1.55	552	72	3	1	100	4-38	936.2	954	549	496	83	498-46	622	.265

DIVISION SERIES RECORD

Year	Team (League)	W	L	Pct.	ERA	WHIP	G	GS	CG	ShO	Hld.	Sv.-Opp.	IP	H	R	ER	HR	BB-IBB	SO	Avg.
1999—	New York (A.L.)			Did not play.																
2000—	New York (A.L.)			Did not play.																

CHAMPIONSHIP SERIES RECORD

Year	Team (League)	W	L	Pct.	ERA	WHIP	G	GS	CG	ShO	Hld.	Sv.-Opp.	IP	H	R	ER	HR	BB-IBB	SO	Avg.
1999—	New York (A.L.)			Did not play.																
2000—	New York (A.L.)	0	0	...	0.00	5.00	2	0	0	0	0	0-0	1.0	2	0	0	0	3-0	1	.400

WORLD SERIES RECORD

Year	Team (League)	W	L	Pct.	ERA	WHIP	G	GS	CG	ShO	Hld.	Sv.-Opp.	IP	H	R	ER	HR	BB-IBB	SO	Avg.
1999—	New York (A.L.)	0	0	...	0.00	1.71	1	0	0	0	0	0-0	2.1	2	0	0	0	2-0	0	.250
2000—	New York (A.L.)			Did not play.																

2006 LEFTY-RIGHTY SPLITS

vs.	Avg.	AB	H	2B	3B	HR	RBI	BB	SO	OBP	Slg.	vs.	Avg.	AB	H	2B	3B	HR	RBI	BB	SO	OBP	Slg.
L	.271	48	13	1	0	0	7	5	3	.340	.292	R	.288	59	17	4	0	4	13	3	7	.323	.559

GROSS, GABE — OF

PERSONAL: Born October 21, 1979, in Baltimore. ... 6-3/209. ... Bats left, throws right. ... Full name: Gabriel Jordan Gross. ... High school: Northview (Dothan, Ala.). ... College: Auburn. **TRANSACTIONS/CAREER NOTES:** Selected by Toronto Blue Jays organization in first round (15th pick overall) of 2001 free-agent draft. ... Traded by Blue Jays with Ps Zach Jackson and Dave Bush to Milwaukee Brewers for 1B Lyle Overbay and a player to be named (December 7, 2005); Blue Jays acquired P Ty Taubenheim to complete the deal (December 8, 2005). **STATISTICAL NOTES:** Career major league grand slams: 1.

2006 GAMES PLAYED BY POSITION (MLB): OF—59.

							BATTING										FIELDING	
Year	Team (League)	Pos.	G	AB	R	H	2B	3B	HR	RBI	BB	SO	HBP	GDP	SB-CS	Avg.	OBP	SLG	OPS	E	Avg.
2001—	Dunedin (Fla. St.)	OF	35	126	23	38	9	2	4	15	26	29	2	2	4-2	.302	.426	.500	.926	5	.930
—	Tennessee (Sou.)	OF	11	41	8	10	1	0	3	11	6	12	3	1	0-1	.244	.373	.488	.860	1	1.000
2002—	Tennessee (Sou.)	OF	112	403	57	96	17	5	10	54	53	71	5	4	8-2	.238	.333	.380	.712	2	.991
2003—	New Haven (East.)	OF	84	310	52	99	23	3	7	51	52	53	5	9	3-2	.319	.423	.484	.903	3	.980
—	Syracuse (Int'l)	OF	53	182	22	48	16	2	5	23	31	56	3	2	1-1	.264	.380	.456	.836	2	.985
2004—	Syracuse (Int'l)	DH-OF	103	377	52	111	29	2	9	54	53	81	1	8	4-5	.294	.381	.454	.833	3	.957
—	Toronto (A.L.)	OF-DH	44	129	18	27	4	0	3	16	19	31	0	1	2-2	.209	.311	.310	.621	0	1.000
2005—	Syracuse (Int'l)	OF-DH	102	390	64	116	29	4	6	46	52	83	2	5	14-2	.297	.380	.438	.819	8	.981
—	Toronto (A.L.)	OF-DH	40	92	11	23	4	1	1	7	10	21	0	0	1-1	.250	.324	.348	.671	1	.981
2006—	Milwaukee (N.L.)	OF	117	208	42	57	15	0	9	38	36	60	2	3	1-0	.274	.382	.476	.857	2	.984
American League totals (2 years)			84	221	29	50	8	1	4	23	29	52	0	1	3-3	.226	.316	.326	.642	1	.992
National League totals (1 year)			117	208	42	57	15	0	9	38	36	60	2	3	1-0	.274	.382	.476	.857	2	.984
Major League totals (3 years)			201	429	71	107	23	1	13	61	65	112	2	4	4-3	.249	.349	.399	.747	3	.989

2006 LEFTY-RIGHTY SPLITS

vs.	Avg.	AB	H	2B	3B	HR	RBI	BB	SO	OBP	Slg.	vs.	Avg.	AB	H	2B	3B	HR	RBI	BB	SO	OBP	Slg.
L	.095	21	2	2	0	0	0	0	3	10	.208	.190	R	.294	187	55	13	0	9	38	33	50	.400	.508

GRUDZIELANEK, MARK — 2B

PERSONAL: Born June 30, 1970, in Milwaukee. ... 6-1/190. ... Bats right, throws right. ... Full name: Mark James Grudzielanek. ... Name pronounced: grud-zuh-LAN-nick. ... High school: J.M. Hanks (El Paso, Texas). ... Junior college: Trinidad State (Colo.). **TRANSACTIONS/CAREER NOTES:** Selected by New York Mets organization in 17th round of 1989 free-agent draft; did not sign. ... Selected by Montreal Expos organization in 11th round of 1991 free-agent draft. ... Traded by Expos with P Carlos Perez and OF Hiram Bocachica to Los Angeles Dodgers for 2B Wilton Guerrero, P Ted Lilly, OF Peter Bergeron and 1B Jonathan Tucker (July 31, 1998). ... On disabled list (June 12-July 6, 1999); included rehabilitation assignment to San Bernardino. ... On disabled list (June 12-28, 2001). ... Traded by Dodgers with 1B Eric Karros and cash to Chicago Cubs for C Todd Hundley and OF Chad Hermansen (December 4, 2002). ... On disabled list (August 3-September 2, 2003); included rehabilitation assignment to Iowa. ... On disabled list (April 10-June 19, 2004); included rehabilitation assignment to Iowa. ... Signed as a free agent by St. Louis Cardinals (January 6, 2005). ... Signed as a free agent by Kansas City Royals (December 16, 2005). **HONORS:** Won A.L. Gold Glove at second base (2006). **STATISTICAL NOTES:** Hit for the cycle (April 27, 2005). ... Career major league grand slams: 1.

2006 GAMES PLAYED BY POSITION (MLB): 2B—132, SS—4.

G

Year Team (League)	Pos.	G	AB	R	H	2B	3B	HR	RBI	BB	SO	HBP	GDP	SB-CS	Avg.	OBP	SLG	OPS	E	Avg.
									BATTING										FIELDING	
1991—Jamestown (NYP)	SS	72	275	44	72	9	3	2	32	18	43	3	6	14-4	.262	.311	.338	.649	23	.933
1992—Rockford (Midwest)	SS	128	496	64	122	12	5	5	54	22	59	5	10	25-4	.246	.285	.321	.605	41	.919
1993—W.P. Beach (FSL)	2B-3B-OF-SS	86	300	41	80	11	6	1	34	14	42	7	6	17-10	.267	.315	.353	.668	13	.949
1994—Harrisburg (East.)	3B-SS	122	488	92	157	37	3	11	66	43	66	8	15	32-10	.322	.382	.477	.860	23	.958
1995—Montreal (N.L.)	SS-3B-2B	78	269	27	66	12	2	1	20	14	47	7	7	8-3	.245	.300	.316	.616	10	.967
—Ottawa (Int'l)	SS	49	181	26	54	9	1	1	22	10	17	4	6	12-1	.298	.342	.376	.717	14	.939
1996—Montreal (N.L.)	SS	153	657	99	201	34	4	6	49	26	83	9	10	33-7	.306	.340	.397	.737	27	.959
1997—Montreal (N.L.)	SS	156	*649	76	177	*54	3	4	51	23	76	10	13	25-9	.273	.307	.384	.690	*32	.955
1998—Montreal (N.L.)	SS	105	396	51	109	15	1	8	41	21	50	9	11	11-5	.275	.323	.379	.702	23	.950
—Los Angeles (N.L.)	SS	51	193	11	51	6	0	2	21	5	23	2	7	7-0	.264	.286	.326	.612	§10	.962
1999—Los Angeles (N.L.)	SS	123	488	72	159	23	5	7	46	31	65	10	13	6-6	.326	.376	.436	.812	13	.973
—San Bern. (Calif.)	SS	4	16	2	4	0	0	0	0	0	1	0	1	0-2	.250	.250	.250	.500	0	1.000
2000—Los Angeles (N.L.)	2B-SS	148	617	101	172	35	6	7	49	45	81	9	16	12-3	.279	.335	.389	.724	17	.976
2001—Los Angeles (N.L.)	2B	133	539	83	146	21	3	13	55	28	83	11	9	4-4	.271	.317	.393	.711	10	.984
2002—Los Angeles (N.L.)	2B-DH	150	536	56	145	23	0	9	50	22	89	3	17	4-1	.271	.301	.364	.665	7	.989
2003—Iowa (PCL)	2B-DH	2	10	1	5	0	0	0	1	1	1	0	0	0-0	.500	.545	.500	1.045	0	1.000
—Chicago (N.L.)	2B	121	481	73	151	38	1	3	38	30	64	11	12	6-2	.314	.366	.416	.782	8	.986
2004—Iowa (PCL)	2B-DH	8	28	6	7	3	0	2	4	0	4	0	1	0-0	.250	.250	.571	.821	0	1.000
—Chicago (N.L.)	2B	81	257	32	79	12	1	6	23	15	32	1	7	1-1	.307	.347	.432	.779	5	.985
2005—St. Louis (N.L.)	2B	137	528	64	155	30	3	8	59	26	81	7	14	8-6	.294	.334	.407	.741	7	.990
2006—Kansas City (A.L.)	2B-SS	134	548	85	163	32	4	7	52	28	69	2	12	3-2	.297	.331	.409	.740	4	.994
American League totals (1 year)		134	548	85	163	32	4	7	52	28	69	2	12	3-2	.297	.331	.409	.740	4	.994
National League totals (11 years)		1436	5610	745	1611	303	29	74	502	286	774	89	136	125-47	.287	.330	.391	.721	169	.974
Major League totals (12 years)		1570	6158	830	1774	335	33	81	554	314	843	91	148	128-49	.288	.330	.393	.723	173	.976

DIVISION SERIES RECORD

Year Team (League)	Pos.	G	AB	R	H	2B	3B	HR	RBI	BB	SO	HBP	GDP	SB-CS	Avg.	OBP	SLG	OPS	E	Avg.
2003—Chicago (N.L.)	2B	5	20	2	3	0	0	0	0	3	4	0	1	0-0	.150	.261	.150	.411	0	1.000
2005—St. Louis (N.L.)	2B	3	13	2	2	0	0	0	0	0	1	0	0	0-0	.154	.154	.154	.308	0	1.000
Division series totals (2 years)		8	33	4	5	0	0	0	0	3	5	0	2	0-0	.152	.222	.152	.374	0	1.000

CHAMPIONSHIP SERIES RECORD

Year Team (League)	Pos.	G	AB	R	H	2B	3B	HR	RBI	BB	SO	HBP	GDP	SB-CS	Avg.	OBP	SLG	OPS	E	Avg.
2003—Chicago (N.L.)	2B	7	30	2	6	1	1	0	3	0	5	0	0	0-0	.200	.200	.300	.500	2	.956
2005—St. Louis (N.L.)	2B	6	22	2	5	0	0	0	2	0	3	1	0	0-0	.227	.261	.227	.488	0	1.000
Champ. series totals (2 years)		13	52	4	11	1	1	0	5	0	8	1	0	0-0	.212	.226	.269	.496	2	.972

ALL-STAR GAME RECORD

	G	AB	R	H	2B	3B	HR	RBI	BB	SO	HBP	GDP	SB-CS	Avg.	OBP	SLG	OPS	E	Avg.
All-Star Game totals (1 year)	1	1	0	0	0	0	0	0	0	0	0	0	0-0	.000	.000	.000	.000	0	...

2006 LEFTY-RIGHTY SPLITS

vs.	Avg.	AB	H	2B	3B	HR	RBI	BB	SO	OBP	Slg.	vs.	Avg.	AB	H	2B	3B	HR	RBI	BB	SO	OBP	Slg.
L	.277	148	41	6	1	2	15	9	25	.316	.372	R	.305	400	122	26	3	5	37	19	44	.336	.423

GRYBOSKI, KEVIN — P

PERSONAL: Born November 15, 1973, in Wilkes-Barre, Pa. ... 6-5/225. ... Throws right, bats right. ... Full name: Kevin John Gryboski. ... Name pronounced: gri-BOS-ski. ... High school: Bishop Hoban (Wilkes-Barre, Pa.). ... College: Wilkes University (Pa.). **TRANSACTIONS/CAREER NOTES:** Selected by Cincinnati Reds organization in 16th round of 1994 free-agent draft; did not sign. ... Selected by Seattle Mariners organization in 16th round of 1995 free-agent draft. ... Traded by Mariners to Atlanta Braves for P Elvis Perez (January 18, 2002). ... On disabled list (July 24-August 20, 2002); included rehabilitation assignment to Macon. ... On disabled list (August 28-September 20, 2003). ... On disabled list (May 7-22, 2005); included rehabilitation assignment to Rome. ... Traded by Braves to Texas Rangers for P Matt Lorenzo (July 21, 2005). ... Signed as a free agent by Washington Nationals organization (February 20, 2006).

CAREER HITTING: 0-for-1 (.000), 0 R, 0 2B, 0 3B, 0 HR, 0 RBI.

Year Team (League)	W	L	Pct.	ERA	WHIP	G	GS	CG	ShO	Hld.	Sv.-Opp.	IP	H	R	ER	HR	BB-IBB	SO	Avg.
1995—Everett (N'west)	1	5	.167	3.50	1.25	25	0	0	0	...	2-...	36.0	27	18	14	2	18-2	25	.206
1996—Wisconsin (Midw.)	10	5	.667	4.74	1.50	32	21	3	0	...	1-...	138.2	146	90	73	7	62-2	100	.270
1997—Lancaster (Calif.)	0	7	.000	9.89	2.06	21	15	0	0	...	0-...	67.1	113	82	74	13	26-0	41	.383
1998—Lancaster (Calif.)	5	5	.500	2.65	1.25	37	3	0	0	...	8-...	85.0	75	35	25	4	31-1	73	.240
—Orlando (South.)	0	0	...	9.00	1.80	2	0	0	0	...	0-...	5.0	8	5	5	1	1-0	4	.364
1999—New Haven (East.)	2	5	.286	2.89	1.40	47	0	0	0	...	10-...	62.1	67	27	20	5	20-4	41	.283
2000—New Haven (East.)	2	2	.500	2.50	1.28	16	0	0	0	...	9-...	18.0	15	5	5	0	8-1	20	.221
—Tacoma (PCL)	2	2	.500	4.83	1.66	31	0	0	0	...	2-...	41.0	45	23	22	3	23-4	35	.288
2001—Tacoma (PCL)	2	5	.286	3.90	1.38	58	0	0	0	...	22-...	60.0	64	29	26	8	19-2	50	.277
2002—Richmond (Int'l)	1	0	1.000	1.29	1.14	7	0	0	0	...	3-...	7.0	7	1	1	0	1-0	5	.250
—Atlanta (N.L.)	2	1	.667	3.48	1.68	57	0	0	0	11	0-2	51.2	50	20	20	6	37-5	33	.256
—Macon (S. Atl.)	0	0	...	0.00	1.00	2	1	0	0	...	0-...	2.0	1	0	0	0	1-0	2	.143
2003—Atlanta (N.L.)	6	4	.600	3.86	1.51	64	0	0	0	12	0-4	44.1	44	22	19	3	23-6	32	.272
2004—Atlanta (N.L.)	3	2	.600	2.84	1.52	69	0	0	0	16	2-4	50.2	54	22	16	2	23-4	24	.280
2005—Rome (S. Atl.)	0	0	...	0.00	1.00	1	1	0	0	0	0-0	1.0	1	0	0	0	0-0	0	.250
—Atlanta (N.L.)	0	0	...	2.95	1.69	31	0	0	0	2	0-2	21.1	24	10	7	0	12-3	8	.300
—Texas (A.L.)	1	1	.500	11.17	2.59	11	0	0	0	3	0-0	9.2	17	15	12	1	8-2	2	.378
—Oklahoma (PCL)	0	2	.000	5.23	1.94	9	0	0	0	2	0-1	10.1	14	7	6	2	6-1	5	.326
2006—New Orleans (PCL)	4	6	.400	3.71	1.53	52	0	0	0	5	7-13	60.2	67	31	25	4	26-3	43	.284
—Wash. (N.L.)	0	0	...	14.29	2.82	6	0	0	0	0	0-1	5.2	14	11	9	3	2-0	4	.452
American League totals (1 year)	1	1	.500	11.17	2.59	11	0	0	0	3	0-0	9.2	17	15	12	1	8-2	2	.378
National League totals (5 years)	11	7	.611	3.68	1.63	227	0	0	0	41	2-13	173.2	186	85	71	14	97-18	101	.281
Major League totals (5 years)	12	8	.600	4.07	1.68	238	0	0	0	44	2-13	183.1	203	100	83	15	105-20	103	.288

DIVISION SERIES RECORD

Year Team (League)	W	L	Pct.	ERA	WHIP	G	GS	CG	ShO	Hld.	Sv.-Opp.	IP	H	R	ER	HR	BB-IBB	SO	Avg.
2002—Atlanta (N.L.)	0	0	...	0.00	1.09	3	0	0	0	0	0-0	3.2	2	0	0	0	2-1	3	.154
2003—Atlanta (N.L.)	0	0	...	3.00	1.33	5	0	0	0	2	0-0	3.0	2	1	1	0	2-1	4	.222
2004—Atlanta (N.L.)	0	0	...	2.08	0.92	5	0	0	0	0	0-0	4.1	3	1	1	0	1-0	3	.200
Division series totals (3 years)	0	0	...	1.64	1.09	13	0	0	0	2	0-0	11.0	7	2	2	0	5-2	10	.189

2006 LEFTY-RIGHTY SPLITS

vs.	Avg.	AB	H	2B	3B	HR	RBI	BB	SO	OBP	Slg.	vs.	Avg.	AB	H	2B	3B	HR	RBI	BB	SO	OBP	Slg.
L	.500	16	8	1	0	2	6	1	1	.529	.938	R	.400	15	6	0	0	1	5	1	3	.471	.600

G

GUARDADO, EDDIE — P

PERSONAL: Born October 2, 1970, in Stockton, Calif. ... 6-0/205. ... Throws left, bats right. ... Full name: Edward Adrian Guardado. ... Name pronounced: gwar-DAH-doe. ... High school: Franklin (Stockton, Calif.). ... Junior college: San Joaquin Delta (Calif.). **TRANSACTIONS/CAREER NOTES:** Selected by Minnesota Twins organization in 21st round of 1990 free-agent draft. ... On disabled list (May 22-June 28, 1999); included rehabilitation assignment to New Britain. ... On disabled list (June 5-20, 2001). ... Signed as a free agent by Seattle Mariners (December 16, 2003). ... On dsabled list (August 1, 2004-remainder of season). ... Traded by Mariners with cash to Cincinnati Reds for P Travis Chick (July 6, 2006). ... On disabled list (August 20, 2006-remainder of season).

CAREER HITTING: 0-for-1 (.000), 0 R, 0 2B, 0 3B, 0 HR, 0 RBI.

Year Team (League)	W	L	Pct.	ERA	WHIP	G	GS	CG	ShO	Hld.	Sv.-Opp.	IP	H	R	ER	HR	BB-IBB	SO	Avg.
1991—Elizabethton (App.)	8	4	.667	1.86	1.07	14	13	3	1	...	0-...	92.0	67	30	19	5	31-0	106	.199
1992—Kenosha (Midw.)	5	10	.333	4.37	1.35	18	18	2	1	...	0-...	101.0	106	57	49	5	30-0	103	.274
—Visalia (Calif.)	7	0	1.000	1.64	1.16	7	7	1	1	...	0-...	49.1	47	13	9	1	10-0	39	.258
1993—Nashville (Southern)	4	0	1.000	1.24	0.96	10	10	2	2	...	0-...	65.1	53	10	9	1	10-0	57	.221
—Minnesota (A.L.)	3	8	.273	6.18	1.68	19	16	0	0	0	0-0	94.2	123	-68	65	13	36-2	46	.319
1994—Salt Lake (PCL)	12	7	.632	4.83	1.47	24	24	2	0	...	0-...	151.0	171	90	81	23	51-0	87	.290
—Minnesota (A.L.)	0	2	.000	8.47	1.76	4	4	0	0	0	0-0	17.0	26	16	16	3	4-0	8	.351
1995—Minnesota (A.L.)	4	9	.308	5.12	1.58	51	5	0	0	5	2-5	91.1	99	54	52	13	45-2	71	.280
1996—Minnesota (A.L.)	6	5	.545	5.25	1.28	•83	0	0	0	18	4-7	73.2	61	45	43	12	33-4	74	.228
1997—Minnesota (A.L.)	0	4	.000	3.91	1.35	69	0	0	0	13	1-1	46.0	45	23	20	7	17-2	54	.251
1998—Minnesota (A.L.)	3	1	.750	4.52	1.43	79	0	0	0	16	0-4	65.2	66	34	33	10	28-6	53	.265
1999—Minnesota (A.L.)	2	5	.286	4.50	1.29	63	0	0	0	15	2-4	48.0	37	24	24	6	25-4	50	.222
—New Britain (East.)	0	0	...	1.93	0.64	3	0	0	0	0	0-...	4.2	3	1	1	0	0-0	5	.176
2000—Minnesota (A.L.)	7	4	.636	3.94	1.30	70	0	0	0	8	9-11	61.2	55	27	27	14	25-3	52	.238
2001—Minnesota (A.L.)	7	1	.875	3.51	1.05	67	0	0	0	14	12-14	66.2	47	27	26	5	23-4	67	.197
2002—Minnesota (A.L.)	1	3	.250	2.93	1.05	68	0	0	0	0	* 45-*51	67.2	53	22	22	8	18-2	70	.215
2003—Minnesota (A.L.)	3	5	.375	2.89	0.98	66	0	0	0	0	41-45	65.1	50	22	21	7	14-2	60	.207
2004—Seattle (A.L.)	2	2	.500	2.78	0.99	41	0	0	0	0	18-25	45.1	31	14	14	8	14-0	45	.194
2005—Seattle (A.L.)	2	3	.400	2.72	1.19	58	0	0	0	0	36-41	56.1	52	23	17	7	15-3	48	.239
2006—Seattle (A.L.)	1	3	.250	5.48	1.74	28	0	0	0	0	5-8	23.0	29	14	14	8	11-1	22	.309
—Cincinnati (N.L.)	0	0	...	1.29	1.21	15	0	0	0	0	8-10	14.0	15	5	2	2	2-1	17	.278
American League totals (14 years)	41	55	.427	4.31	1.32	766	25	0	0	91	175-216	822.1	774	413	394	122	308-35	720	.249
National League totals (1 year)	0	0	...	1.29	1.21	15	0	0	0	0	8-10	14.0	15	5	2	2	2-1	17	.278
Major League totals (14 years)	41	55	.427	4.26	1.31	781	25	0	0	91	183-226	836.1	789	418	396	124	310-36	737	.250

DIVISION SERIES RECORD

Year Team (League)	W	L	Pct.	ERA	WHIP	G	GS	CG	ShO	Hld.	Sv.-Opp.	IP	H	R	ER	HR	BB-IBB	SO	Avg.
2002—Minnesota (A.L.)	0	0	...	13.50	3.00	2	0	0	0	0	1-1	2.0	5	3	3	1	1-0	1	.455
2003—Minnesota (A.L.)	0	0	...	9.00	2.50	2	0	0	0	0	1-1	2.0	5	2	2	1	0-0	2	.455
Division series totals (2 years)	0	0	...	11.25	2.75	4	0	0	0	0	2-2	4.0	10	5	5	2	1-0	3	.455

CHAMPIONSHIP SERIES RECORD

Year Team (League)	W	L	Pct.	ERA	WHIP	G	GS	CG	ShO	Hld.	Sv.-Opp.	IP	H	R	ER	HR	BB-IBB	SO	Avg.
2002—Minnesota (A.L.)	0	0	...	0.00	1.00	1	0	0	0	0	1-1	1.0	1	0	0	0	1-0	2	.000

ALL-STAR GAME RECORD

	W	L	Pct.	ERA	WHIP	G	GS	CG	ShO	Hld.	Sv.-Opp.	IP	H	R	ER	HR	BB-IBB	SO	Avg.
All-Star Game totals (2 years)	0	0	...	9.00	2.00	2	0	0	0	0	0-0	1.0	2	1	1	0	0-0	2	.400

2006 LEFTY-RIGHTY SPLITS

vs.	Avg.	AB	H	2B	3B	HR	RBI	BB	SO	OBP	Slg.	vs.	Avg.	AB	H	2B	3B	HR	RBI	BB	SO	OBP	Slg.
L	.239	46	11	3	0	1	4	1	12	.271	.370	R	.324	102	33	5	0	9	19	12	27	.391	.637

GUERRERO, VLADIMIR — OF

PERSONAL: Born February 9, 1976, in Nizao Bani, Dominican Republic. ... 6-3/225. ... Bats right, throws right. ... Full name: Vladimir Alvino Guerrero. ... Name pronounced: guh-RAR-oh. ... Brother of Wilton Guerrero, infielder/outfielder with four major league teams (1996-2004). **TRANSACTIONS/CAREER NOTES:** Signed as a non-drafted free agent by Montreal Expos organization (March 1, 1993). ... On disabled list (March 30-May 2, June 5-21 and July 12-27, 1997); included rehabilitation assignment to West Palm Beach. ... On suspended list (March 30-April 3, 2003). ... On disabled list (June 5-July 21, 2003); included rehabilitation assignment to Brevard County. ... Signed as a free agent by Anaheim Angels (January 14, 2004). ... Angels franchise renamed Los Angeles Angels of Anaheim for 2005 season. ... On disabled list (May 22-June 10, 2005). **HONORS:** Named Minor League Player of the Year by THE SPORTING NEWS (1996). ... Named outfielder on THE SPORTING NEWS N.L. All-Star team (1999, 2000 and 2002). ... Named outfielder on THE SPORTING NEWS A.L. All-Star team (2004 and 2005). ... Named A.L. Most Valuable Player by Baseball Writers' Association of America (2004). ... Named outfielder on N.L. Silver Slugger team (2000 and 2002). ... Named outfielder on A.L. Silver Slugger team (2004-06). **STATISTICAL NOTES:** Hit for the cycle (September 14, 2003). ... Career major league grand slams: 4.

2006 GAMES PLAYED BY POSITION (MLB): OF—126, DH—30.

Year Team (League)	Pos.	G	AB	R	H	2B	3B	HR	RBI	BB	SO	HBP	GDP	SB-CS	Avg.	OBP	SLG	OPS	E	Avg.
1993—Dom. Expos (DSL)	P	34	105	19	35	4	0	1	14	8	13	...	...	4-...	.333	...	.400	...	5	.943
1994—Dom. Expos (DSL)	OF	25	92	34	39	11	0	12	35	21	6	...	...	5-...	.424	...	.935	...	2	.957
—GC Expos (GCL)	OF	37	137	24	43	13	3	5	25	11	18	2	0	0-7	.314	.366	.562	.928	1	.986
1995—Albany (S. Atl.)	OF	110	421	77	140	21	10	16	63	30	45	7	8	12-7	.333	.383	.544	.927	11	.953
1996—W.P. Beach (FSL)	OF	20	80	16	29	8	0	5	18	3	10	1	1	2-2	.363	.388	.650	1.038	3	.917
—Harrisburg (East.)	OF	118	417	84	150	32	8	19	78	51	42	9	8	17-10	.360	.438	.612	1.050	8	.961
—Montreal (N.L.)	OF	9	27	2	5	0	0	1	1	2	3	0	1	0-0	.185	.185	.296	.481	0	1.000
1997—W.P. Beach (FSL)	OF	3	10	0	4	2	0	0	2	1	0	0	1	1-0	.400	.455	.600	1.055	0	1.000
—Montreal (N.L.)	OF	90	325	44	98	22	2	11	40	19	39	7	11	3-4	.302	.350	.483	.833	* 12	.929
1998—Montreal (N.L.)	OF	159	623	108	202	37	7	38	109	42	95	7	15	11-9	.324	.371	.589	.960	* 17	.951
1999—Montreal (N.L.)	OF	160	610	102	193	37	5	42	131	55	62	7	18	14-7	.316	.378	.600	.978	* 19	.948
2000—Montreal (N.L.)	OF-DH	154	571	101	197	28	11	44	123	58	74	8	15	9-10	.345	.410	.664	1.074	* 10	.969
2001—Montreal (N.L.)	OF	159	599	107	184	45	4	34	108	60	88	9	* 24	37-16	.307	.377	.566	.943	12	.965
2002—Montreal (N.L.)	OF	161	614	106	* 206	37	2	39	111	84	70	6	20	40-* 20	.336	.417	.593	1.010	* 10	.969
2003—Brevard County (FSL)	OF-DH	3	6	2	3	0	0	1	1	0	1	0	0	0-0	.500	.571	1.000	1.571	0	1.000
—Montreal (N.L.)	OF	112	394	71	130	20	3	25	79	63	53	6	18	9-5	.330	.426	.586	1.012	7	.970
2004—Anaheim (A.L.)	OF-DH	156	612	* 124	206	39	2	39	126	52	74	8	19	15-3	.337	.391	.598	.989	9	.973
2005—Los Angeles (A.L.)	OF-DH	141	520	95	165	29	2	32	108	61	48	8	16	13-1	.317	.394	.565	.959	3	.988
2006—Los Angeles (A.L.)	OF-DH	156	607	92	200	34	1	33	116	50	68	4	16	15-5	.329	.382	.552	.934	11	.959
American League totals (3 years)		453	1739	311	571	102	5	104	350	163	190	20	51	43-9	.328	.389	.572	.961	23	.973
National League totals (8 years)		1004	3763	641	1215	226	34	234	702	381	484	50	122	123-71	.323	.390	.588	.978	87	.959
Major League totals (11 years)		1457	5502	952	1786	328	39	338	1052	544	674	70	173	166-80	.325	.390	.583	.972	110	.963

G

DIVISION SERIES RECORD

Year Team (League)	Pos.	G	AB	R	H	2B	3B	HR	RBI	BB	SO	HBP	GDP	SB-CS	Avg.	OBP	SLG	OPS	E	Avg.
2004— Anaheim (A.L.)	OF	3	12	1	2	0	0	1	6	2	4	0	0	0-0	.167	.286	.417	.702	0	1.000
2005— Los Angeles (A.L.)	OF	5	18	5	6	0	0	0	0	2	2	1	0	1-1	.333	.429	.333	.762	0	1.000
Division series totals (2 years)		8	30	6	8	0	0	1	6	4	6	1	0	1-1	.267	.371	.367	.738	0	1.000

CHAMPIONSHIP SERIES RECORD

Year Team (League)	Pos.	G	AB	R	H	2B	3B	HR	RBI	BB	SO	HBP	GDP	SB-CS	Avg.	OBP	SLG	OPS	E	Avg.
2005— Los Angeles (A.L.)	OF-DH	5	20	0	1	0	0	0	1	0	1	0	2	0-0	.050	.050	.050	.100	1	.923

ALL-STAR GAME RECORD

		G	AB	R	H	2B	3B	HR	RBI	BB	SO	HBP	GDP	SB-CS	Avg.	OBP	SLG	OPS	E	Avg.
All-Star Game totals (7 years)		7	15	3	5	0	0	1	1	0	1	0	0	0-0	.333	.333	.533	.867	0	1.000

2006 LEFTY-RIGHTY SPLITS

vs.	Avg.	AB	H	2B	3B	HR	RBI	BB	SO	OBP	Slg.	vs.	Avg.	AB	H	2B	3B	HR	RBI	BB	SO	OBP	Slg.
L	.401	147	59	12	0	10	31	24	16	.483	.687	R	.307	460	141	22	1	23	85	26	52	.347	.509

GUERRIER, MATT — P

PERSONAL: Born August 2, 1978, in Cleveland. ... 6-3/185. ... Throws right, bats right. ... Full name: Matthew Olson Guerrier. ... Name pronounced: GER-air. ... High school: Shaker Heights (Ohio). ... College: Kent State. **TRANSACTIONS/CAREER NOTES:** Selected by Kansas City Royals organization in 33rd round of 1996 free-agent draft; did not sign. ... Selected by Chicago White Sox organization in 10th round of 1999 free-agent draft. ... Traded by White Sox to Pittsburgh Pirates for P Damaso Marte and IF Edwin Yan (March 27, 2002). ... Claimed on waivers by Minnesota Twins (November 20, 2003). ... On disabled list (June 9-August 1, 2006); included rehabilitation assignment to New Britain.

CAREER HITTING: 0-for-2 (.000), 0 R, 0 2B, 0 3B, 0 HR, 0 RBI.

Year Team (League)	W	L	Pct.	ERA	WHIP	G	GS	CG	ShO	Hld.	Sv.-Opp.	IP	H	R	ER	HR	BB-IBB	SO	Avg.
1999— Bristol (Appal.)	5	0	1.000	1.05	1.25	21	0	0	0	...	10-...	25.2	18	9	3	1	14-2	37	.196
— Win.-Salem (Car.)	0	0	...	5.40	0.90	4	0	0	0	...	2-...	3.1	3	2	2	0	0-0	5	.214
2000— Win.-Salem (Car.)	0	3	.000	1.30	1.07	30	0	0	0	...	19-...	34.2	25	13	5	0	12-0	35	.194
— Birmingham (Sou.)	3	1	.750	2.70	1.24	23	0	0	0	...	7-...	23.1	17	9	7	1	12-1	19	.207
2001— Birmingham (Sou.)	11	3	.786	3.10	1.19	15	15	1	1	...	0-...	98.2	85	42	34	8	32-1	75	.237
— Charlotte (Int'l)	7	1	.875	3.54	1.14	12	12	3	0	...	0-...	81.1	75	33	32	7	18-0	43	.250
2002— Nashville (PCL)	7	12	.368	4.59	1.28	27	26	2	1	...	0-...	157.0	154	88	80	20	47-3	130	.253
2003— Nashville (PCL)	4	6	.400	4.53	1.20	20	19	0	0	...	0-...	105.1	108	56	53	15	18-1	78	.262
2004— Rochester (Int'l)	5	10	.333	3.19	1.11	24	23	0	0	...	0-...	144.0	135	65	51	15	25-0	97	.248
— Minnesota (A.L.)	0	1	.000	5.68	1.47	9	2	0	0	0	0-0	19.0	22	13	12	5	6-0	11	.293
2005— Minnesota (A.L.)	0	3	.000	3.39	1.33	43	0	0	0	1	0-0	71.2	71	29	27	6	24-5	46	.259
2006— New Britain (East.)	2	0	1.000	1.04	0.69	4	0	0	0	0	0-0	8.2	3	1	1	0	3-0	10	.111
— Minnesota (A.L.)	1	0	1.000	3.36	1.42	39	1	0	0	2	1-1	69.2	78	29	26	9	21-0	37	.287
Major League totals (3 years)	1	4	.200	3.65	1.38	91	3	0	0	3	1-1	160.1	171	71	65	20	51-5	94	.275

DIVISION SERIES RECORD

Year Team (League)	W	L	Pct.	ERA	WHIP	G	GS	CG	ShO	Hld.	Sv.-Opp.	IP	H	R	ER	HR	BB-IBB	SO	Avg.
2006— Minnesota (A.L.)	0	0	...	0.00	0.00	1	0	0	0	0	0-0	1.0	0	0	0	0	0-0	0	.000

2006 LEFTY-RIGHTY SPLITS

vs.	Avg.	AB	H	2B	3B	HR	RBI	BB	SO	OBP	Slg.	vs.	Avg.	AB	H	2B	3B	HR	RBI	BB	SO	OBP	Slg.
L	.333	108	36	7	1	3	14	12	16	.400	.500	R	.256	164	42	2	0	6	16	9	21	.288	.378

GUIEL, AARON — OF

PERSONAL: Born October 5, 1972, in Vancouver. ... 5-10/200. ... Bats left, throws right. ... Full name: Aaron Colin Guiel. ... Name pronounced: GUY-el. ... High school: Woodlands Senior (B.C.). ... Junior college: Kwantlen (B.C.). **TRANSACTIONS/CAREER NOTES:** Selected by California Angels organization in 21st round of 1992 free-agent draft. ... Traded by Angels to San Diego Padres for C Angelo Encarnacion (August 25, 1997). ... Signed as a free agent by Oakland Athletics organization (March 18, 2000). ... Released by A's (March 30, 2000). ... Signed by Oaxaca of the Mexican League (April 2000). ... Signed by Kansas City Royals organization (June 13, 2000). ... On disabled list (May 13-July 17, 2004); included rehabilitation assignments to AZL Royals and Omaha. ... Claimed on waivers by New York Yankees (July 5, 2006).

2006 GAMES PLAYED BY POSITION (MLB): OF—41, 1B—15, DH—4.

Year Team (League)	Pos.	G	AB	R	H	2B	3B	HR	RBI	BB	SO	HBP	GDP	SB-CS	Avg.	OBP	SLG	OPS	E	Avg.
1993— Boise (N'west)	2B-OF	35	104	24	31	6	4	2	12	26	21	4	1	3-0	.298	.455	.490	.946	12	.874
1994— Cedar Rap. (Midw.)	2B	127	454	84	122	30	1	18	82	64	93	6	7	21-7	.269	.364	.458	.822	32	.944
1995— Lake Elsinore (Calif.)	2B	113	409	73	110	25	7	5	58	69	96	7	7	7-6	.269	.380	.416	.796	22	.958
1996— Midland (Texas)	3B-2B-OF	129	439	72	118	29	7	10	48	56	71	10	6	11-7	.269	.364	.435	.799	28	.933
1997— Midland (Texas)	OF-3B-2B	116	419	91	138	37	7	22	85	59	94	18	9	14-10	.329	.431	.609	1.039	8	.953
— Mobile (Sou.)	OF	8	26	9	10	2	0	1	5	4	1	0	1	1-0	.385	.500	.577	1.077	1	1.000
1998— Las Vegas (PCL)	OF-3B	60	183	33	57	15	4	5	31	28	51	4	4	5-1	.311	.410	.519	.929	4	.947
— Ariz. Padres (Ariz.)	OF	8	16	8	8	3	1	1	6	5	5	3	0	1-1	.500	.667	1.000	1.667	0	1.000
1999— Las Vegas (PCL)	OF	84	257	46	63	25	2	12	39	44	86	5	6	5-4	.245	.362	.498	.861	5	.944
2000— Oaxaca (Mex.)		56	192	55	70	11	1	22	62	52	35			7-5	.365	...	.776	...	4	...
— Omaha (PCL)	OF	73	258	47	74	15	2	13	40	35	54	8	3	6-0	.287	.389	.512	.900	6	.977
2001— Omaha (PCL)	OF	121	442	78	118	27	3	21	73	51	92	13	12	6-4	.267	.355	.484	.840	6	.973
2002— Omaha (PCL)	OF	61	215	44	76	11	1	9	50	29	34	8	4	8-1	.353	.443	.540	.983	3	.977
— Kansas City (A.L.)	OF-DH	70	240	30	56	13	0	4	38	19	61	4	3	1-5	.233	.296	.338	.633	6	.952
2003— Omaha (PCL)	OF	52	190	38	53	9	2	8	30	33	43	9	3	3-0	.279	.408	.474	.881	5	.962
— Kansas City (A.L.)	OF-DH	99	354	63	98	30	0	15	52	27	63	13	3	3-5	.277	.346	.489	.835	3	.985
2004— Royals (Ariz.)	DH	4	17	3	8	1	0	2	5	0	2	1	0	0-0	.471	.500	.882	1.382	0	1.000
— Wichita (Texas)	OF	6	20	7	5	0	0	0	4	8	6	3	0	2-0	.250	.516	.250	.766	1	.933
— Omaha (PCL)	OF-DH	30	116	29	36	6	0	10	30	21	33	6	1	0-2	.310	.438	.621	1.058	1	.980
— Kansas City (A.L.)	OF-DH	42	135	15	21	4	0	5	13	17	42	3	3	1-1	.156	.263	.296	.559	3	.966
2005— Omaha (PCL)	OF-DH	128	496	94	137	32	4	30	95	64	103	15	14	6-3	.276	.371	.538	.909	4	.993
— Kansas City (A.L.)	OF-DH	33	109	18	32	6	0	4	9	6	21	5	1	3-0	.294	.355	.450	.805	1	.985
2006— Kansas City (A.L.)	OF-DH	19	50	9	11	3	0	3	7	7	11	2	1	0-0	.220	.339	.460	.799	0	1.000
— Omaha (PCL)		52	177	32	44	14	1	11	32	35	45	8	0	0-0	.249	.388	.525	.914	2	.983
— Columbus (Int'l)		16	50	10	13	2	1	2	8	6	10	3	0	0-0	.260	.387	.460	.847	0	1.000
— New York (A.L.)	OF-1B-DH	44	82	16	21	3	0	2	7	13	20	3	2	2-1	.256	.357	.439	.776	0	1.000
Major League totals (5 years)		307	970	151	239	58	0	35	128	83	218	30	15	8-12	.246	.322	.414	.736	13	.979

2006 LEFTY-RIGHTY SPLITS

vs.	Avg.	AB	H	2B	3B	HR	RBI	BB	SO	OBP	Slg.	vs.	Avg.	AB	H	2B	3B	HR	RBI	BB	SO	OBP	Slg.
L	.174	23	4	1	0	1	3	1	7	.208	.348	R	.257	109	28	5	0	6	15	13	24	.362	.468

G

GUILLEN, CARLOS — SS/1B

PERSONAL: Born September 30, 1975, in Maracay, Venezuela. ... 6-1/204. ... Bats both, throws right. ... Full name: Carlos Alfonso Guillen. ... Name pronounced: GHEE-yen. **TRANSACTIONS/CAREER NOTES:** Signed as a non-drafted free agent by Houston Astros organization (September 19, 1992). ... Traded by Astros with P Freddy Garcia and a player to be named to Seattle Mariners for P Randy Johnson (July 31, 1998); Mariners acquired P John Halama to complete deal (October 1, 1998). ... On disabled list (April 7, 1999-remainder of season). ... On disabled list (April 13-28, 2000); included rehabilitation assignment to Tacoma. ... On disabled list (July 29-August 23, 2003); included rehabilitation assignment to Tacoma. ... Traded by Mariners to Detroit Tigers for IFs Ramon Santiago and Juan Gonzalez (January 8, 2004). ... On disabled list (June 11-26 and August 17-September 23, 2005). **STATISTICAL NOTES:** Hit for the cycle (August 1, 2006). ... Career major league grand slams: 1.
2006 GAMES PLAYED BY POSITION (MLB): SS—145, 1B—8, DH—4.

									BATTING										FIELDING	
Year Team (League)	Pos.	G	AB	R	H	2B	3B	HR	RBI	BB	SO	HBP	GDP	SB-CS	Avg.	OBP	SLG	OPS		E	Avg.
1993— Dom. Astros (DSL)	IF	18	56	12	14	4	2	0	8	8	12			0-...	.250		.393	...		2	.956
1994—		Did not play.																			
1995— GC Astros (GCL)	DH	30	105	17	31	4	2	2	15	9	17	1	0	17-1	.295	.350	.429	.779		...	...
1996— Quad City (Midw.)	SS	29	112	23	37	7	1	3	17	16	25	0	1	13-6	.330	.405	.491	.896		9	.929
1997— Jackson (Texas)	SS-DH	115	390	47	99	16	1	10	39	38	78	2	9	6-5	.254	.322	.377	.699		35	.932
— New Orleans (A.A.)	SS	3	13	3	4	1	0	0	0	0	4	0	0	0-0	.308	.308	.385	.692		0	1.000
1998— New Orleans (PCL)	SS	100	374	67	109	18	4	12	51	31	61	5	...	3-4	.291	.350	.457	.807		26	.943
— Tacoma (PCL)	2B	24	92	8	21	1	1	1	4	9	17	0	...	1-2	.228	.297	.293	.591		2	.982
— Seattle (A.L.)	2B	10	39	9	13	1	1	0	5	3	9	0	0	2-0	.333	.381	.410	.791		0	1.000
1999— Seattle (A.L.)	SS-2B	5	19	2	3	0	0	1	3	1	6	0	1	0-0	.158	.200	.316	.516		1	.964
2000— Seattle (A.L.)	3B-SS	90	288	45	74	15	2	7	42	28	53	2	6	1-3	.257	.324	.396	.720		21	.921
— Tacoma (PCL)	3B-SS	24	87	19	26	4	1	2	11	12	17	1	3	4-1	.299	.386	.437	.823		6	.926
2001— Seattle (A.L.)	SS-DH	140	456	72	118	21	4	5	53	53	89	1	9	4-1	.259	.333	.355	.689		10	.980
2002— Seattle (A.L.)	SS-DH	134	475	73	124	24	6	9	56	46	91	1	8	4-5	.261	.326	.394	.719		18	.966
2003— Tacoma (PCL)	3B-DH	4	14	2	5	1	0	2	4	0	1	1	2	0-0	.357	.400	.857	1.257		0	1.000
— Seattle (A.L.)	SS-3B-DH	109	388	63	107	19	3	7	52	52	64	1	12	4-4	.276	.359	.394	.753		14	.963
2004— Detroit (A.L.)	SS	136	522	97	166	37	10	20	97	52	87	2	12	12-5	.318	.379	.542	.921		17	.974
2005— Detroit (A.L.)	SS-DH	87	334	48	107	15	4	5	23	24	45	2	9	2-3	.320	.368	.434	.803		7	.978
2006— Detroit (A.L.)	SS-1B-DH	153	543	100	174	41	5	19	85	71	87	4	16	20-9	.320	.400	.519	.920		28	.958
Major League totals (9 years)		864	3064	509	886	173	35	73	416	330	531	13	73	49-30	.289	.358	.440	.798		116	.966

DIVISION SERIES RECORD

									BATTING												
Year Team (League)	Pos.	G	AB	R	H	2B	3B	HR	RBI	BB	SO	HBP	GDP	SB-CS	Avg.	OBP	SLG	OPS		E	Avg.
2000— Seattle (A.L.)		1	1	0	1	0	0	0	1	0	0	0	0	0-0	1.000	1.000	1.000	2.000		...	...
2001— Seattle (A.L.)		Did not play.																			
2006— Detroit (A.L.)	SS	4	14	3	8	3	0	1	2	2	1	0	0	0-0	.571	.625	1.000	1.625		0	1.000
Division series totals (2 years)		5	15	3	9	3	0	1	3	2	1	0	0	0-0	.600	.647	1.000	1.647		0	1.000

CHAMPIONSHIP SERIES RECORD

									BATTING												
Year Team (League)	Pos.	G	AB	R	H	2B	3B	HR	RBI	BB	SO	HBP	GDP	SB-CS	Avg.	OBP	SLG	OPS		E	Avg.
2000— Seattle (A.L.)	3B	2	5	1	1	0	1	2	2	2	0	0	0-1		.200	.429	.800	1.229		0	1.000
2001— Seattle (A.L.)	SS	3	8	1	2	1	0	0	0	1	0	0	0-0		.250	.250	.250	.500		0	1.000
2006— Detroit (A.L.)	1B-SS	4	16	1	3	1	0	0	0	1	4	0	2	0-0	.188	.235	.250	.485		1	.972
Champ. series totals (3 years)		9	29	3	6	1	0	1	2	3	7	0	2	0-1	.207	.281	.345	.626		1	.980

WORLD SERIES RECORD

									BATTING												
Year Team (League)	Pos.	G	AB	R	H	2B	3B	HR	RBI	BB	SO	HBP	GDP	SB-CS	Avg.	OBP	SLG	OPS		E	Avg.
2006— Detroit (A.L.)	SS-1B	5	17	2	6	1	0	2	3	4	0	0		1-0	.353	.450	.529	.979		0	1.000

2006 LEFTY-RIGHTY SPLITS

vs.	Avg.	AB	H	2B	3B	HR	RBI	BB	SO	OBP	Slg.	vs.	Avg.	AB	H	2B	3B	HR	RBI	BB	SO	OBP	Slg.
L	.291	148	43	10	1	5	13	13	22	.354	.473	R	.332	395	131	31	4	14	72	58	65	.417	.537

GUILLEN, JOSE — OF

PERSONAL: Born May 17, 1976, in San Cristobal, Dominican Republic. ... 5-11/190. ... Bats right, throws right. ... Full name: Jose Manuel Guillen. ... Name pronounced: GHEE-yen. **TRANSACTIONS/CAREER NOTES:** Signed as a non-drafted free agent by Pittsburgh Pirates organization (August 19, 1992). ... Traded by Pirates with P Jeff Sparks to Tampa Bay Devil Rays for Cs Joe Oliver and Humberto Cota (July 23, 1999). ... On disabled list (March 28-April 12, 2000). ... On disabled list (May 17-June 24 and June 25-July 30, 2001); included rehabilitation assignments to Durham. ... Released by Devil Rays (November 27, 2001). ... Signed by Arizona Diamondbacks (December 18, 2001). ... Released by Diamondbacks (July 22, 2002). ... Signed by Colorado Rockies organization (July 29, 2002). ... Released by Rockies (August 1, 2002). ... Signed by Cincinnati Reds organization (August 20, 2002). ... Released by Reds (March 12, 2003). ... Re-signed by Reds organization (March 13, 2003). ... Traded by Reds to Oakland Athletics for Ps Aaron Harang, Joe Valentine and Jeff Bruksch (July 30, 2003). ... On suspended list (September 4-6, 2003). ... Signed as a free agent by Anaheim Angels (December 20, 2003). ... On Anaheim suspended list (September 26, 2004-remainder of season). ... Traded by Angels to Montreal Expos for OF Juan Rivera and SS Maicer Izturis (November 19, 2004). ... Expos franchise transferred to Washington, D.C., and renamed Washington Nationals for 2005 season (December 3, 2004). ... On suspended list (September 24-25, 2005). ... On disabled list (May 26-10, 2006); included rehabilitation assignment to Potomac. ... On disabled list (July 20, 2006-remainder of season). **STATISTICAL NOTES:** Career major league grand slams: 3.
2006 GAMES PLAYED BY POSITION (MLB): OF—68.

									BATTING										FIELDING	
Year Team (League)	Pos.	G	AB	R	H	2B	3B	HR	RBI	BB	SO	HBP	GDP	SB-CS	Avg.	OBP	SLG	OPS		E	Avg.
1993— Dom. Pirates (DSL)	OF	63	234	39	53	3	4	11	41	21	55		...	10-...	.227	...	.415	...		7	.947
1994— GC Pirates (GCL)	OF	30	110	17	29	4	1	4	11	7	15	6	0	2-1	.264	.341	.427	.769		2	.970
1995— Erie (N.Y.-Penn)	OF	66	258	41	81	17	1	12	46	10	44	12	5	1-5	.314	.367	.527	.894		13	.900
— Augusta (S. Atl.)	OF	10	34	6	8	1	1	2	6	2	9	2	0	0-0	.235	.316	.500	.816		0	1.000
1996— Lynchburg (Caro.)	OF-DH	136	528	78	170	30	0	21	94	20	73	13	16	24-13	.322	.357	.498	.855		13	.949
1997— Pittsburgh (N.L.)	OF	143	498	58	133	20	5	14	70	17	88	8	16	1-2	.267	.300	.412	.712		9	.963
1998— Pittsburgh (N.L.)	OF	153	573	60	153	38	2	14	84	21	100	6	7	3-5	.267	.298	.414	.712		10	.968
1999— Pittsburgh (N.L.)	OF	40	120	18	32	6	0	1	18	10	21	0	7	1-0	.267	.321	.342	.662		3	.952
— Nashville (PCL)	OF-DH	35	132	28	44	10	0	5	22	8	21	2	4	0-1	.333	.378	.523	.900		4	.939
— Durham (Int'l)	OF	9	34	8	13	1	0	3	12	7	7	0	2	0-1	.382	.476	.676	1.153		0	1.000
— Tampa Bay (A.L.)	OF	47	168	24	41	10	0	4	13	10	36	7	0	0-0	.244	.312	.339	.651		3	.966
2000— Durham (Int'l)	OF	19	78	20	33	8	2	9	31	8	11	1	2	0-1	.423	.477	.923	1.400		3	.912
— Tampa Bay (A.L.)	OF	105	316	40	80	16	5	10	41	18	65	13	6	3-1	.253	.320	.430	.750		4	.978
2001— Tampa Bay (A.L.)	OF-DH	41	135	14	37	5	0	3	11	6	26	3	2	2-3	.274	.317	.378	.695		3	.969
— Durham (Int'l)	OF	33	119	18	35	9	0	7	29	3	28	0	3	0-0	.294	.306	.546	.853		1	.982
2002— Arizona (N.L.)	OF-DH	54	131	13	30	4	0	4	15	7	25	2	7	3-4	.229	.277	.351	.628		0	1.000
— Colo. Springs (PCL)	OF	5	17	2	7	3	0	1	2	1	1	0	0	0-0	.412	.474	.588	1.062		0	1.000
— Louisville (Int'l)	OF	8	29	4	9	4	0	2	8	5	5	0	1	0-0	.310	.310	.655	.966		0	1.000

G

Year Team (League)	Pos.	G	AB	R	H	2B	3B	HR	RBI	BB	SO	HBP	GDP	SB-CS	Avg.	OBP	SLG	OPS	E	Avg.
—Cincinnati (N.L.)	OF	31	109	12	27	3	0	4	16	7	18	1	6	1-1	.248	.299	.385	.684	1	.979
2003—Louisville (Int'l)	OF	4	15	4	5	1	0	0	3	1	3	0	1	1-0	.333	.353	.400	.753	0	1.000
—Cincinnati (N.L.)	OF	91	315	52	106	21	1	23	63	17	63	9	8	1-3	.337	.385	.629	1.013	8	.957
—Oakland (A.L.)	OF-DH	45	170	25	45	7	1	8	23	7	32	5	8	0-0	.265	.311	.459	.770	4	.942
2004—Anaheim (A.L.)	OF-DH	148	565	88	166	28	3	27	104	37	92	15	14	5-4	.294	.352	.497	.849	6	.979
2005—Wash. (N.L.)	OF-DH	148	551	81	156	32	2	24	76	31	102	•19	14	1-1	.283	.338	.479	.817	7	.978
2006—Potomac (Carol.)		3	6	2	3	0	0	2	3	1	0	0	1	0-0	.500	.571	1.500	2.071	0	1.000
—Wash. (N.L.)	OF	69	241	28	52	15	1	9	40	15	48	7	8	1-0	.216	.276	.398	.674	2	.988
American League totals (5 years)		386	1354	191	369	66	9	50	192	78	251	43	39	10-8	.273	.331	.445	.776	20	.972
National League totals (7 years)		729	2538	322	689	139	11	93	382	125	465	52	73	12-16	.271	.316	.445	.761	40	.971
Major League totals (10 years)		1115	3892	513	1058	205	20	143	574	203	716	95	112	22-24	.272	.321	.445	.766	60	.972

DIVISION SERIES RECORD

Year Team (League)	Pos.	G	AB	R	H	2B	3B	HR	RBI	BB	SO	HBP	GDP	SB-CS	Avg.	OBP	SLG	OPS	E	Avg.
2003—Oakland (A.L.)	OF	4	11	1	5	1	0	0	1	3	2	0	0	0-0	.455	.571	.545	1.117	0	1.000

2006 LEFTY-RIGHTY SPLITS

vs.	Avg.	AB	H	2B	3B	HR	RBI	BB	SO	OBP	Slg.	vs.	Avg.	AB	H	2B	3B	HR	RBI	BB	SO	OBP	Slg.
L	.200	60	12	4	0	3	10	5	10	.269	.417	R	.221	181	40	11	1	6	30	10	38	.279	.392

GUTHRIE, JEREMY P

PERSONAL: Born April 8, 1979, in Roseburg, Ore. ... 6-1/200. ... Throws right, bats right. ... Full name: Jeremy Shane Guthrie. ... High school: Ashland (Ore.). ... College: Stanford. **TRANSACTIONS/CAREER NOTES:** Selected by New York Mets organization in 15th round of 1997 free-agent draft; did not sign. ... Selected by Pittsburgh Pirates organization in third round of 2001 free-agent draft; did not sign. ... Selected by Cleveland Indians organization in first round (22nd pick overall) of 2002 free-agent draft.
CAREER HITTING: 0-for-0 (.000), 0 R, 0 2B, 0 3B, 0 HR, 0 RBI.

Year Team (League)	W	L	Pct.	ERA	WHIP	G	GS	CG	ShO	Hld.	Sv.-Opp.	IP	H	R	ER	HR	BB-IBB	SO	Avg.
2003—Akron (East.)	6	2	.750	1.44	0.93	10	9	2	2	...	0-...	62.2	44	11	10	0	14-0	35	.196
—Buffalo (Int'l)	4	9	.308	6.52	1.64	18	18	1	0	...	0-...	96.2	129	75	70	15	30-1	62	.321
2004—Buffalo (Int'l)	1	2	.333	7.91	2.12	4	4	0	0	...	0-...	19.1	23	19	17	0	18-0	10	.303
—Akron (East.)	8	8	.500	4.21	1.43	23	21	1	0	...	0-...	130.1	145	76	61	16	42-0	94	.277
—Cleveland (A.L.)	0	0	...	4.63	1.29	6	0	0	0	0	0-0	11.2	9	6	6	1	6-0	7	.214
2005—Cleveland (A.L.)	0	0	...	6.00	1.83	1	0	0	0	0	0-0	6.0	9	4	4	2	2-0	3	.360
—Buffalo (Int'l)	12	10	.545	5.08	1.47	25	25	1	0	...	0-...	136.1	152	88	77	15	49-0	100	.286
2006—Buffalo (Int'l)	9	5	.643	3.14	1.23	21	20	2	0	...	0-...	123.1	104	50	43	6	48-0	88	.229
—Cleveland (A.L.)	0	0	...	6.98	2.02	9	1	0	0	0	0-0	19.1	24	15	15	2	15-1	14	.316
Major League totals (3 years)	0	0	...	6.08	1.76	16	1	0	0	0	0-0	37.0	42	25	25	5	23-1	24	.294

2006 LEFTY-RIGHTY SPLITS

vs.	Avg.	AB	H	2B	3B	HR	RBI	BB	SO	OBP	Slg.	vs.	Avg.	AB	H	2B	3B	HR	RBI	BB	SO	OBP	Slg.
L	.394	33	13	5	0	0	6	11	5	.545	.545	R	.256	43	11	3	0	2	9	4	9	.347	.465

GUTIERREZ, FRANKLIN OF

PERSONAL: Born February 21, 1983, in Caricuao, Venezuela. ... 6-2/180. ... Bats right, throws right. ... Full name: Franklin Rafael Gutierrez. ... **TRANSACTIONS/CAREER NOTES:** Signed as a non-drafted free agent by Los Angeles Dodgers organization (November 18, 2000). ... Traded by Dodgers with player to be named to Cleveland Indians for OF Milton Bradley (April 4, 2004); Indians acquired P Andrew Brown to complete deal (May 19, 2004).
2006 GAMES PLAYED BY POSITION (MLB): OF—42.

Year Team (League)	Pos.	G	AB	R	H	2B	3B	HR	RBI	BB	SO	HBP	GDP	SB-CS	Avg.	OBP	SLG	OPS	E	Avg.
2001—GC Dodgers (GCL)	OF	56	234	38	63	16	0	4	30	16	39	4	1	9-3	.269	.324	.389	.713	2	.980
2002—South Georgia (S. Atl.)	OF	92	361	61	102	18	4	12	45	31	88	6	5	13-4	.283	.344	.454	.798	3	.986
—Las Vegas (PCL)	OF	2	10	2	3	2	0	0	2	1	4	0	1	0-0	.300	.364	.500	.864	0	1.000
2003—Vero Beach (FSL)	OF	110	425	65	120	28	5	20	68	39	111	3	9	17-5	.282	.345	.513	.858	4	.984
—Jacksonville (Sou.)	OF	18	67	12	21	3	2	4	12	7	20	1	1	3-3	.313	.387	.597	.984	1	1.000
2004—Akron (East.)	OF	70	262	38	79	24	2	5	35	23	77	9	4	6-3	.302	.372	.466	.838	3	.927
—Buffalo (Int'l)		7	27	4	4	1	0	1	3	1	11	0	0	0-0	.148	.179	.296	.475		
2005—Akron (East.)	OF-DH	95	383	70	100	25	2	11	42	30	77	7	7	14-4	.261	.322	.423	.745	2	.995
—Buffalo (Int'l)	OF	19	67	10	17	6	2	0	7	6	13	1	1	2-2	.254	.320	.403	.723	0	1.000
—Cleveland (A.L.)	DH-OF	7	1	2	0	0	0	0	0	1	0	0	0	0-0	.000	.500	.000	.500	0	1.000
2006—Buffalo (Int'l)		90	349	63	97	27	0	9	38	49	84	5	2	13-8	.278	.373	.433	.806	1	.995
—Cleveland (A.L.)	OF	43	136	21	37	9	0	1	8	3	28	0	4	0-0	.272	.288	.360	.648	3	.966
Major League totals (2 years)		50	137	23	37	9	0	1	8	4	28	0	4	0-0	.270	.291	.358	.648	3	.967

2006 LEFTY-RIGHTY SPLITS

vs.	Avg.	AB	H	2B	3B	HR	RBI	BB	SO	OBP	Slg.	vs.	Avg.	AB	H	2B	3B	HR	RBI	BB	SO	OBP	Slg.
L	.262	42	11	2	0	1	4	1	5	.279	.381	R	.277	94	26	7	0	0	4	2	23	.292	.351

GUZMAN, ANGEL P

PERSONAL: Born December 14, 1981, in Caracas, Venezuela. ... 6-3/190. ... Throws right, bats right. ... Full name: Angel Moises Guzman. . **TRANSACTIONS/CAREER NOTES:** Signed as a non-drafted free agent by Chicago Cubs organization (November 12, 1999).
CAREER HITTING: 2-for-12 (.167), 0 R, 1 2B, 0 3B, 0 HR, 2 RBI.

Year Team (League)	W	L	Pct.	ERA	WHIP	G	GS	CG	ShO	Hld.	Sv.-Opp.	IP	H	R	ER	HR	BB-IBB	SO	Avg.
2000—La Pradera (VSL)	1	1	.500	1.93	0.89	7	6	0	0	...	0-...	32.2	24	13	7	0	5-0	25	.197
2001—Boise (N'west)	9	1	.900	2.23	1.13	14	14	0	0	...	0-...	76.2	68	27	19	2	19-0	63	.233
2002—Lansing (Midw.)	5	2	.714	1.89	0.94	9	9	1	0	...	0-...	62.0	42	18	13	3	16-0	49	.186
—Daytona (Fla. St.)	6	2	.750	2.39	1.40	16	15	1	0	...	0-...	94.0	99	34	25	2	33-1	74	.268
2003—West Tenn (Sou.)	3	3	.500	2.81	1.22	15	15	0	0	...	0-...	89.2	83	30	28	8	26-0	87	.249
2004—Daytona (Fla. St.)	3	1	.750	4.20	0.90	7	7	0	0	...	0-...	30.0	27	15	14	2	10-0	40	.235
—West Tenn (Sou.)	0	3	.000	5.60	1.36	4	4	0	0	...	0-...	17.2	20	11	11	2	4-0	13	.299
2005—Ariz. Cubs (Ariz.)	0	0	...	1.50	0.92	4	4	0	0	0	0-0	12.0	10	3	2	0	1-0	17	.217
—Peoria (Midw.)	0	1	.000	4.26	1.58	2	2	0	0	0	0-0	6.1	10	5	3	1	0-0	7	.345
2006—Iowa (PCL)	4	4	.500	4.04	1.27	15	15	0	0	0	0-0	75.2	72	37	34	5	24-0	77	.252
—Chicago (N.L.)	0	6	.000	7.39	1.88	15	10	0	0	0	0-0	56.0	68	48	46	9	37-1	60	.308
Major League totals (1 year)	0	6	.000	7.39	1.88	15	10	0	0	0	0-0	56.0	68	48	46	9	37-1	60	.308

2006 LEFTY-RIGHTY SPLITS

vs.	Avg.	AB	H	2B	3B	HR	RBI	BB	SO	OBP	Slg.	vs.	Avg.	AB	H	2B	3B	HR	RBI	BB	SO	OBP	Slg.
L	.305	82	25	5	1	5	12	19	20	.453	.573	R	.309	139	43	8	1	4	26	18	40	.391	.468

GUZMAN, CRISTIAN — SS

PERSONAL: Born March 21, 1978, in Santo Domingo, Dominican Republic. ... 6-0/205. ... Bats both, throws right. ... Full name: Christian Antonio Guzman. ... Name pronounced: GOOZ-mahn. **TRANSACTIONS/CAREER NOTES:** Signed as a non-drafted free agent by New York Yankees organization (August 24, 1994). ... Traded by Yankees with Ps Eric Milton and Danny Mota, OF Brian Buchanan and cash to Minnesota Twins for 2B Chuck Knoblauch (February 6, 1998). ... On disabled list (May 27-June 11, 1999). ... On suspended list (September 10-13, 1999). ... On disabled list (July 13-August 17, 2001); included rehabilitation assignment to GCL Twins. ... Signed as a free agent by Montreal Expos (November 16, 2004). ... Expos franchise transferred to Washington, D.C., and renamed Washington Nationals for 2005 season (December 3, 2004). ... On disabled list (March 27, 2006-entire season). **STATISTICAL NOTES:** Career major league grand slams: 1.

							BATTING											FIELDING	
Year	Team (League)	Pos.	G	AB	R	H	2B	3B	HR	RBI	BB	SO	HBP	GDP	SB-CS	Avg.	OBP	SLG	OPS	E	Avg.
1995— Dom. Yankees (DSL)		SS	46	160	24	43	6	5	3	20	12	23	...	...	11-...	.269		.425		13	.935
1996— GC Yankees (GCL)		SS	42	170	37	50	8	2	1	21	10	31	3	2	7-6	.294	.341	.382	.723	20	.890
1997— Greensboro (S. Atl.)		SS	124	495	68	135	21	4	4	52	17	105	10	3	23-12	.273	.309	.356	.665	37	.936
— Tampa (Fla. St.)		SS	4	14	4	4	0	0	0	1	1	1	0	0	0-1	.286	.333	.286	.619	2	.889
1998— New Britain (East.)		SS	140	566	68	157	29	5	1	40	21	111	1	13	23-14	.277	.304	.352	.655	32	.952
1999— Minnesota (A.L.)		SS	131	420	47	95	12	3	1	26	22	90	3	5	9-7	.226	.267	.276	.543	24	.959
2000— Minnesota (A.L.)		SS-DH	156	631	89	156	25 *	20	8	54	46	101	2	5	28-10	.247	.299	.388	.687	22	.959
2001— Minnesota (A.L.)		SS	118	493	80	149	28 *	14	10	51	21	78	5	6	25-8	.302	.337	.477	.814 *	21	.959
— GC Twins (GCL)		SS	5	16	4	4	0	1	0	0	2	4	1	1	0-1	.250	.368	.375	.743	0	1.000
2002— Minnesota (A.L.)		SS-DH	148	623	80	170	31	6	9	59	17	79	2	12	12-13	.273	.292	.385	.677	12	.981
2003— Minnesota (A.L.)		SS	143	534	78	143	15 *	14	3	53	30	79	5	4	18-9	.268	.311	.365	.676	11	.980
2004— Minnesota (A.L.)		SS	145	576	84	158	31	4	8	46	30	64	1	15	10-5	.274	.309	.384	.693	12	.980
2005— Wash. (N.L.)		SS	142	456	39	100	19	6	4	31	25	76	1	12	7-4	.219	.260	.314	.574	15	.973
2006— Wash. (N.L.)					Did not play.																
American League totals (6 years)			841	3277	458	871	142	61	39	289	166	491	18	47	102-52	.266	.303	.382	.685	102	.972
National League totals (1 year)			142	456	39	100	19	6	4	31	25	76	1	12	7-4	.219	.260	.314	.574	15	.973
Major League totals (7 years)			983	3733	497	971	161	67	43	320	191	567	19	59	109-56	.260	.298	.374	.671	117	.972

DIVISION SERIES RECORD

Year	Team (League)	Pos.	G	AB	R	H	2B	3B	HR	RBI	BB	SO	HBP	GDP	SB-CS	Avg.	OBP	SLG	OPS	E	Avg.
2002— Minnesota (A.L.)		SS	5	21	5	6	2	0	1	2	2	4	0	0	2-0	.286	.348	.524	.872	1	.923
2003— Minnesota (A.L.)		SS	4	13	1	2	0	0	0	0	1	2	0	0	0-0	.154	.214	.154	.368	0	1.000
2004— Minnesota (A.L.)		SS	4	15	2	5	0	0	0	0	2	3	0	0	1-0	.333	.412	.333	.745	1	.964
Division series totals (3 years)			13	49	8	13	2	0	1	2	5	9	0	0	3-0	.265	.333	.367	.701	2	.966

CHAMPIONSHIP SERIES RECORD

Year	Team (League)	Pos.	G	AB	R	H	2B	3B	HR	RBI	BB	SO	HBP	GDP	SB-CS	Avg.	OBP	SLG	OPS	E	Avg.
2002— Minnesota (A.L.)		SS	5	18	1	3	0	0	0	0	0	3	1	0	0-0	.167	.211	.222	.433	1	.962

ALL-STAR GAME RECORD

			G	AB	R	H	2B	3B	HR	RBI	BB	SO	HBP	GDP	SB-CS	Avg.	OBP	SLG	OPS	E	Avg.
All-Star Game totals (1 year)			1	1	0	0	0	0	0	0	0	1	0	0	0-0	.000	.000	.000	.000	0	...

GUZMAN, FREDDY — OF

PERSONAL: Born January 20, 1981, in Santo Domingo, Dominican Republic. ... 5-10/165. ... Bats both, throws right. ... Full name: Freddy Antonio Guzman. **TRANSACTIONS/CAREER NOTES:** Signed as a non-drafted free agent by San Diego Padres organization (April 17, 2000). ... On disabled list (March 28, 2005-entire season). ... Traded by Padres with RHP Cesar Rojas to Texas Rangers for RHP John Hudgins and OF Vince Sinisi (May 11, 2006).
2006 GAMES PLAYED BY POSITION (MLB): OF—4, DH—1.

							BATTING											FIELDING	
Year	Team (League)	Pos.	G	AB	R	H	2B	3B	HR	RBI	BB	SO	HBP	GDP	SB-CS	Avg.	OBP	SLG	OPS	E	Avg.
2000— Dominican Padres (DSL)			49	167	38	35	6	1	1	10	46	38	2	...	24-12	.210	.386	.275	.661	...	...
2001— Idaho Falls (Pio.)		2B	12	46	11	16	4	1	0	5	2	10	1	1	5-0	.348	.388	.478	.866	4	.932
2002— Lake Elsinore (Calif.)		OF-2B-3B	21	81	13	21	3	0	1	6	8	12	0	1	14-4	.259	.326	.333	.659	7	.865
— Fort Wayne (Midw.)		OF	47	190	35	53	7	5	0	18	18	37	0	3	39-7	.279	.341	.368	.710	6	.950
— Eugene (Northwest)		OF	21	80	14	18	2	1	0	8	7	15	2	0	16-1	.225	.293	.275	.568	3	.921
2003— Lake Elsinore (Calif.)		OF	70	281	64	80	12	3	2	22	40	60	2	1	49-10	.285	.375	.370	.745	5	.962
— Mobile (Sou.)		OF	46	177	30	48	5	2	1	11	26	34	1	0	38-7	.271	.368	.339	.707	2	.984
— Portland (PCL)		OF	2	10	1	3	0	0	0	0	1	0	0	0	3-0	.300	.300	.300	.600	0	1.000
2004— Mobile (Sou.)		OF-DH	35	138	21	39	5	2	1	7	16	28	1	2	17-5	.283	.359	.370	.724	1 *	.989
— Portland (PCL)		OF	66	264	48	77	12	4	1	19	30	46	1	1	48-5	.292	.365	.379	.742	3	.983
— San Diego (N.L.)		OF	20	76	8	16	3	0	0	5	3	13	1	0	5-2	.211	.250	.250	.500	2	.960
2005—					Did not play.																
2006— Portland (PCL)			30	124	15	34	7	2	2	14	14	19	0	3	11-3	.274	.348	.411	.759	2	.977
— Oklahoma (PCL)			69	252	45	71	9	2	1	14	36	36	2	4	31-9	.282	.375	.345	.720	1	.993
— Texas (A.L.)		OF-DH	9	7	1	2	0	0	0	0	1	1	1	0	0-0	.286	.444	.286	.730	0	1.000
American League totals (1 year)			9	7	1	2	0	0	0	0	1	1	1	0	0-0	.286	.444	.286	.730	0	1.000
National League totals (1 year)			20	76	8	16	3	0	0	5	3	13	1	0	5-2	.211	.250	.250	.500	2	.960
Major League totals (2 years)			29	83	9	18	3	0	0	5	4	14	2	0	5-2	.217	.270	.253	.523	2	.964

2006 LEFTY-RIGHTY SPLITS

vs.	Avg.	AB	H	2B	3B	HR	RBI	BB	SO	OBP	Slg.	vs.	Avg.	AB	H	2B	3B	HR	RBI	BB	SO	OBP	Slg.
L	.500	4	2	0	0	0	0	1	0	.600	.500	R	.000	3	0	0	0	0	0	0	1	.250	.000

GUZMAN, JOEL — IF

PERSONAL: Born November 24, 1984, in Quisqueya, Dominican Republic. ... 6-6/225. ... Bats right, throws right. ... Full name: Irvin Joel Vigo Guzman. **TRANSACTIONS/CAREER NOTES:** Signed as a non-drafted free agent by Los Angeles Dodgers organization (July 2, 2001). ... Traded by Dodgers with OF Sergio Pedroza to Tampa Bay Devil Rays for SS Julio Lugo (July 31, 2006).
2006 GAMES PLAYED BY POSITION (MLB): 3B—6, 1B—1, OF—1.

							BATTING											FIELDING	
Year	Team (League)	Pos.	G	AB	R	H	2B	3B	HR	RBI	BB	SO	HBP	GDP	SB-CS	Avg.	OBP	SLG	OPS	E	Avg.
2002— GC Dodgers (GCL)			10	33	4	7	2	0	0	2	5	8	0	0	1-0	.212	.316	.273	.589	...	...
— Great Falls (Pio.)			43	151	19	38	8	2	3	27	18	54	0	4	5-3	.252	.331	.391	.722	...	...
2003— South Georgia (S. Atl.)			58	217	33	51	13	0	8	29	9	62	0	4	4-4	.235	.263	.406	.669	...	...
— Vero Beach (FSL)			62	240	30	59	13	1	5	24	11	60	0	7	0-4	.246	.279	.371	.650	...	...

G

Year	Team (League)	Pos.	G	AB	R	H	2B	3B	HR	RBI	BB	SO	HBP	GDP	SB-CS	Avg.	OBP	SLG	OPS	E	Avg.
2004— Vero Beach (FSL)			87	329	52	101	22	8	14	51	21	78	2	8	8-5	.307	.349	.550	.899	...	...
— Jacksonville (Sou.)			46	182	25	51	11	3	9	35	13	44	1	4	1-2	.280	.325	.522	.847	...	...
2005— Jacksonville (Sou.)	SS-3B-DH		122	442	63	127	31	2	16	75	42	128	5	10	7-3	.287	.351	.475	.826	29	.930
2006— Los Angeles (N.L.)	3B-1B-OF		8	19	2	4	0	0	0	3	3	2	1	3	0-0	.211	.348	.211	.558	0	1.000
— Las Vegas (PCL)			85	317	44	94	16	2	11	55	26	72	4	11	9-5	.297	.353	.464	.817	6	.980
— Durham (Int'l)			25	88	7	17	5	0	4	9	4	23	0	5	0-0	.193	.228	.386	.615	5	.896
Major League totals (1 year)			8	19	2	4	0	0	0	3	3	2	1	3	0-0	.211	.348	.211	.558	0	1.000

2006 LEFTY-RIGHTY SPLITS

vs.	Avg.	AB	H	2B	3B	HR	RBI	BB	SO	OBP	Slg.	vs.	Avg.	AB	H	2B	3B	HR	RBI	BB	SO	OBP	Slg.
L	.143	7	1	0	0	0	1	1	1	.250	.143	R	.250	12	3	0	0	0	2	2	2	.400	.250

GWYNN, TONY — OF

PERSONAL: Born October 4, 1982, in Long Beach, Calif. ... 6-0/185. ... Bats left, throws right. ... Full name: Anthony Keith Gwynn Jr.. ... College: San Diego State. ... Son of Tony Gwynn, outfielder, San Diego Padres (1982-2001); and nephew of Chris Gwynn, outfielder/first baseman with three major league teams (1987-96).
TRANSACTIONS/CAREER NOTES: Selected by Milwaukee Brewers organization in second round of 2003 free-agent draft.
2006 GAMES PLAYED BY POSITION (MLB): OF—19.

Year	Team (League)	Pos.	G	AB	R	H	2B	3B	HR	RBI	BB	SO	HBP	GDP	SB-CS	Avg.	OBP	SLG	OPS	E	Avg.
2003— Beloit (Midw.)			61	236	35	66	8	0	1	33	32	31	2	3	14-2	.280	.364	.326	.690	2	...
2004— Huntsville (Sou.)			138	534	74	130	20	5	2	37	53	95	6	4	34-16	.243	.318	.311	.629	9	...
2005— Huntsville (Sou.)	OF		133	509	83	138	21	5	1	41	76	75	5	11	34-15	.271	.370	.338	.708	10	.984
2006— Nashville (PCL)			112	447	73	134	21	5	4	42	42	84	2	7	30-11	.300	.360	.396	.756	5	.981
— Milwaukee (N.L.)	OF		32	77	5	20	2	1	0	4	2	15	0	2	3-1	.260	.275	.312	.587	0	1.000
Major League totals (1 year)			32	77	5	20	2	1	0	4	2	15	0	2	3-1	.260	.275	.312	.587	0	1.000

2006 LEFTY-RIGHTY SPLITS

vs.	Avg.	AB	H	2B	3B	HR	RBI	BB	SO	OBP	Slg.	vs.	Avg.	AB	H	2B	3B	HR	RBI	BB	SO	OBP	Slg.
L	.167	6	1	0	0	0	0	0	3	.167	.167	R	.268	71	19	2	1	0	4	2	12	.284	.324

HAEGER, CHARLIE — P

PERSONAL: Born September 19, 1983, in Livonia, Mich. ... 6-1/205. ... Throws right, bats right. ... Full name: Charles Wallis Haeger. . **TRANSACTIONS/CAREER NOTES:** Selected by Chicago White Sox organization in 25th round of 2001 free-agent draft. ... On voluntary retired list for entire 2003 season.
CAREER HITTING: 0-for-0 (.000), 0 R, 0 2B, 0 3B, 0 HR, 0 RBI.

Year	Team (League)	W	L	Pct.	ERA	WHIP	G	GS	CG	ShO	Hld.	Sv.-Opp.	IP	H	R	ER	HR	BB-IBB	SO	Avg.
2001— Ariz. White Sox (Ariz.)	0	3	.000	6.39	1.97	13	4	0	0	...	0-...	31.0	44	29	22	2	17-0	17	.336
2002— Ariz. White Sox (Ariz.)	1	4	.200	4.17	1.44	25	0	0	0"	...	6-...	41.0	46	25	19	2	13-2	24	.295
2003—		Did not play																	
2004— Bristol (Appal.)	1	6	.143	5.18	1.60	10	10	0	0	...	0-...	57.1	70	41	33	6	22-1	23	.303
— Kannapolis (S. Atl.)	1	3	.250	2.01	1.37	5	5	0	0	...	0-...	31.1	31	17	7	0	12-0	21	.270
2005— Win.-Salem (Car.)	8	2	.800	3.20	1.49	14	13	0	0	0	0-0	81.2	82	33	29	3	40-0	64	.267
— Birmingham (Sou.)	6	3	.667	3.78	1.51	13	13	3	2	0	0-0	85.2	84	43	36	1	45-0	48	.263
2006— Charlotte (Int'l)	14	6	.700	3.07	1.30	26	25	2	0	0	0-0	170.0	143	71	58	9	78-3	130	.231
— Chicago (A.L.)	1	1	.500	3.44	1.36	7	1	0	0	0	1-1	18.1	12	10	7	0	13-0	19	.182
Major League totals (1 year)	1	1	.500	3.44	1.36	7	1	0	0	0.	1-1	18.1	12	10	7	0	13-0	19	.182

2006 LEFTY-RIGHTY SPLITS

vs.	Avg.	AB	H	2B	3B	HR	RBI	BB	SO	OBP	Slg.	vs.	Avg.	AB	H	2B	3B	HR	RBI	BB	SO	OBP	Slg.
L	.133	15	2	1	0	0	4	4	5	.316	.200	R	.196	51	10	0	1	0	7	9	14	.317	.235

HAFNER, TRAVIS — DH/1B

PERSONAL: Born June 3, 1977, in Jamestown, N.D. ... 6-3/240. ... Bats left, throws right. ... Full name: Travis Lee Hafner. ... Name pronounced: HAF-ner. ... High school: Sykeston (N.D.). ... Junior college: Cowley County (Kan.) Community College.. **TRANSACTIONS/CAREER NOTES:** Selected by Texas Rangers organization in 31st round of 1996 free-agent draft. ... Traded by Rangers with P Aaron Myette to Cleveland Indians for C Einar Diaz and P Ryan Drese (December 6, 2002). ... On disabled list (May 10-26, 2003); included rehabilitation assignment to Buffalo. ... On disabled list (July 26-August 4, 2005); included rehabilitation assignment to Akron. **STATISTICAL NOTES:** Hit for the cycle (August 14, 2003). ... Hit three home runs in one game (July 20, 2004). ... Career major league grand slams: 8.
2006 GAMES PLAYED BY POSITION (MLB): DH—122, 1B—4.

Year	Team (League)	Pos.	G	AB	R	H	2B	3B	HR	RBI	BB	SO	HBP	GDP	SB-CS	Avg.	OBP	SLG	OPS	E	Avg.
1997— GC Rangers (GCL)	1B-OF		55	189	38	54	14	0	5	24	24	45	3	3	7-2	.286	.375	.439	.814	3	.991
1998— Savannah (S. Atl.)	1B-3B-OF		123	405	62	96	15	4	16	84	68	139	6	8	7-3	.237	.351	.412	.764	12	.980
1999— Savannah (S. Atl.)	1B-3B		134	480	94	140	30	4	28	111	67	151	11	11	5-4	.292	.387	.546	.933	15	.984
2000— Charlotte (Fla. St.)	1B-3B		122	436	90	151	34	1	22	109	67	86	18	9	0-4	.346	.447	.580	1.027	13	.978
2001— Tulsa (Texas)	1B		88	323	59	91	25	0	14	74	59	82	4	10	3-1	.282	.396	.545	.941	5	.993
2002— Oklahoma (PCL)	1B		110	401	79	137	22	1	21	77	79	76	12	9	2-1	.342	.463	.559	1.022	4	.993
— Texas (A.L.)	DH-1B		23	62	6	15	4	1	1	6	8	15	0	0	0-1	.242	.329	.387	.716	1	.909
2003— Buffalo (Int'l)	1B-DH		29	100	15	27	4	0	2	10	25	26	1	2	2-1	.270	.421	.370	.791	3	.986
— Cleveland (A.L.)	DH-1B		91	291	35	74	19	3	14	40	22	81	10	7	2-1	.254	.327	.485	.812	6	.985
2004— Cleveland (A.L.)	DH-1B		140	482	96	150	41	4	28	109	68	111	• 17	11	3-2	.311	.410	.583	.993	0	1.000
2005— Akron (East.)	DH		3	9	0	0	0	0	0	0	1	0	0	0-0	.000	.000	.000	.182	0	...
— Cleveland (A.L.)	DH-1B		137	486	94	148	42	0	33	108	79	123	9	9	0-0	.305	.408	.595	1.003	0	1.000
2006— Cleveland (A.L.)	DH-1B		129	454	100	140	31	4	42	117	100	111	9	10	0-0	.308	.439 *	.659*	1.097	0	1.000
Major League totals (5 years)			520	1775	331	527	137	8	118	380	277	441	43	37	5-4	.297	.402	.583	.984	7	.987

2006 LEFTY-RIGHTY SPLITS

vs.	Avg.	AB	H	2B	3B	HR	RBI	BB	SO	OBP	Slg.	vs.	Avg.	AB	H	2B	3B	HR	RBI	BB	SO	OBP	Slg.
L	.321	184	59	12	1	16	46	38	47	.442	.658	R	.300	270	81	19	0	26	71	62	64	.436	.659

HAIRSTON, JERRY — OF/IF

PERSONAL: Born May 29, 1976, in Naperville, Ill. ... 5-10/183. ... Bats right, throws right. ... Full name: Jerry Wayne Hairston Jr.. ... High school: Naperville (Ill.) North. ... College: Southern Illinois. ... Son of Jerry Hairston, outfielder with two major league teams (1973-77 and 1981-89); brother of Scott Hairston, second baseman, Arizona

H

Diamondbacks; nephew of John Hairston, catcher/outfielder with Chicago Cubs (1969); grandson of Sam Hairston, catcher with Chicago White Sox (1951). **TRANSAC-TIONS/CAREER NOTES:** Selected by Baltimore Orioles organization in 42nd round of 1995 free-agent draft; did not sign. ... Selected by Orioles organization in 11th round of 1997 free-agent draft. ... On disabled list (May 21-September 4, 2003); included rehabilitation assignment to Bowie and Aberdeen. ... On disabled list (March 26-May 11 and August 18, 2004-remainder of season); included rehabilitation assignment to Bowie. ... Traded by Orioles with 2B Mike Fontenot and P David Crouthers to Chicago Cubs for OF Sammy Sosa and cash (February 2, 2005). ... On disabled list (August 4-19, 2005); included rehabilitation assignment to Iowa. ... Traded by Cubs to Texas Rangers for 1B Phil Nevin and cash (May 31, 2006). **STATISTICAL NOTES:** Career major league grand slams: 1.

2006 GAMES PLAYED BY POSITION (MLB): OF—60, 2B—25, SS—3, DH—3, 3B—1, 1B—1.

									BATTING										FIELDING	
Year	Team (League)	Pos.	G	AB	R	H	2B	3B	HR	RBI	BB	SO	HBP	GDP	SB-CS	Avg.	OBP	SLG	OPS	E	Avg.
1997— Bluefield (Appal.)		SS	59	221	44	73	13	4	2	36	21	29	10	4	13-9	.330	.409	.452	.862	14	.949
1998— Frederick (Carolina)		2B-SS	80	293	56	83	22	3	5	33	28	32	12	4	13-7	.283	.366	.430	.796	24	.943
— Bowie (East.)		2B-SS	55	221	42	72	12	3	5	37	20	25	5	5	6-4	.326	.393	.475	.868	5	.980
— Baltimore (A.L.)		2B	6	7	2	0	0	0	0	0	0	1	0	0	0-0	.000	.000	.000	.000	2	.750
1999— Rochester (Int'l)		2B-SS	107	413	65	120	24	5	7	48	30	50	19	9	19-10	.291	.363	.424	.787	16	.968
— Baltimore (A.L.)		2B	50	175	26	47	12	1	4	17	11	24	3	2	9-4	.269	.323	.417	.740	0	1.000
2000— Baltimore (A.L.)		2B	49	180	27	46	5	0	5	19	21	22	6	8	8-5	.256	.353	.367	.719	5	.981
— Rochester (Int'l)		2B-SS	58	201	43	59	15	1	4	21	29	32	5	2	6-4	.294	.392	.438	.830	11	.963
— GC Orioles (GCL)		2B	4	10	3	3	2	0	0	3	3	2	2	0	4-0	.300	.500	.500	1.000	0	1.000
— Frederick (Carolina)		2B	2	8	1	3	2	0	0	1	1	0	0	0	0-0	.375	.444	.625	1.069	0	1.000
2001— Baltimore (A.L.)		2B	159	532	63	124	25	5	8	47	44	73	13	12	29-11	.233	.305	.344	.649	19	.976
2002— Baltimore (A.L.)		2B	122	426	55	114	25	3	5	32	34	55	7	5	21-6	.268	.329	.376	.705	11	.982
2003— Bowie (East.)		2B-DH	6	20	4	6	1	0	1	2	1	4	2	0	0-0	.300	.391	.500	.891	1	.941
— Aberdeen (N.Y.-Penn.)		2B-DH	2	3	2	1	0	0	0	0	3	0	0	0	0-0	.333	.667	.333	1.000	0	1.000
— Baltimore (A.L.)		2B-DH	58	218	25	59	12	2	2	21	23	25	6	8	14-5	.271	.353	.372	.725	5	.980
2004— Bowie (East.)		2B	5	13	0	2	1	0	0	2	0	5	0	0	2-0	.154	.313	.231	.543	1	.929
— Baltimore (A.L.)		OF-DH-2B																			
		3B	86	287	43	87	19	1	2	24	29	29	8	3	13-8	.303	.378	.397	.775	2	.988
2005— Iowa (PCL)		2B-OF-DH	5	22	3	7	0	1	0	2	0	3	2	0	3-0	.318	.360	.409	.769	0	1.000
— Chicago (N.L.)		OF-2B-SS	114	380	51	99	25	2	4	30	31	46	12	5	8-9	.261	.336	.368	.704	7	.977
2006— Chicago (N.L.)		2B-OF-1B	38	82	8	17	3	0	0	4	4	14	1	1	3-0	.207	.253	.244	.497	0	1.000
— Texas (A.L.)		OF-SS-DH																			
		2B-3B	63	88	17	18	3	1	0	6	9	20	1	4	2-2	.205	.286	.261	.547	1	.987
American League totals (8 years)			593	1913	258	495	101	13	26	166	171	249	44	42	96-41	.259	.331	.366	.697	45	.982
National League totals (2 years)			152	462	59	116	28	2	4	34	35	60	13	6	11-9	.251	.322	.346	.668	7	.982
Major League totals (9 years)			745	2375	317	611	129	15	30	200	206	309	57	48	107-50	.257	.330	.362	.692	52	.982

2006 LEFTY-RIGHTY SPLITS

vs.	Avg.	AB	H	2B	3B	HR	RBI	BB	SO	OBP	Slg.		vs.	Avg.	AB	H	2B	3B	HR	RBI	BB	SO	OBP	Slg.
L	.153	72	11	1	0	0	4	7	16	.228	.167		R	.245	98	24	5	1	0	6	6	18	.302	.316

HAIRSTON, SCOTT   OF

PERSONAL: Born May 25, 1980, in Fort Worth, Texas. ... 6-0/188. ... Bats right, throws right. ... Full name: Scott Alexander Hairston. ... High school: Canyon del Oro (Tucson, Ariz.). ... Junior college: Central Arizona. ... Son of Jerry Hairston, outfielder with two major league teams (1973-77 and 1981-89); brother of Jerry Hairston Jr., infielder/outfielder, Texas Rangers; nephew of John Hairston, catcher/outfielder with Cubs (1969); grandson of Sam Hairston, catcher with Chicago White Sox (1951). **TRANSACTIONS/CAREER NOTES:** Selected by Chicago White Sox organization in 18th round of 1999 free-agent draft; did not sign. ... Selected by Arizona Diamondbacks in third round of 2001 free-agent draft. ... On disabled list (September 2, 2005-remainder of season). ... On disabled list (June 21-July 29, 2006); included rehabilitation assignment to Tucson.

2006 GAMES PLAYED BY POSITION (MLB): OF—5.

									BATTING										FIELDING	
Year	Team (League)	Pos.	G	AB	R	H	2B	3B	HR	RBI	BB	SO	HBP	GDP	SB-CS	Avg.	OBP	SLG	OPS	E	Avg.
2001— Missoula (Pion.)		2B	74	291	81	101	16	6	14	65	38	50	7	5	2-2	.347	.432	.588	1.020	20	.935
2002— South Bend (Mid.)		2B-3B	109	394	79	131	35	4	16	72	58	74	10	11	9-3	.332	.426	.563	.990	28	.944
— Lancaster (Calif.)		2B-3B	18	79	20	32	11	1	6	26	6	16	0	4	1-0	.405	.442	.797	1.239	2	.952
2003— El Paso (Texas)		2B	88	337	53	93	21	7	10	47	30	80	6	10	6-2	.276	.345	.469	.814	15	.960
— Tucson (PCL)			1	0	0	0	0	0	0	1	0	0	0	0	0-0	.000	...	...	...	...	...
2004— Tucson (PCL)		2B-OF-DH	28	115	29	36	8	3	5	20	11	21	1	1	0-3	.313	.375	.565	.935	6	.940
— Arizona (N.L.)		2B-OF	101	339	39	84	15	6	13	29	21	88	1	4	3-3	.248	.293	.442	.735	11	.972
2005— Arizona (N.L.)		OF-DH	15	20	0	2	1	0	0	0	0	6	0	1	0-0	.100	.100	.150	.250	0	1.000
— Tucson (PCL)		OF-DH-2B	58	209	45	65	8	3	16	40	21	40	5	4	3-0	.311	.384	.608	.992	4	.979
2006— Tucson (PCL)			98	381	83	123	22	1	26	81	52	78	4	3	3-0	.323	.407	.591	.997	3	.980
— Arizona (N.L.)		OF	9	15	2	6	2	0	2	4	1	5	0	1	0-0	.400	.438	.533	.971	0	1.000
Major League totals (3 years)			125	374	41	92	18	6	13	31	22	99	1	6	3-3	.246	.289	.430	.719	11	.975

2006 LEFTY-RIGHTY SPLITS

vs.	Avg.	AB	H	2B	3B	HR	RBI	BB	SO	OBP	Slg.		vs.	Avg.	AB	H	2B	3B	HR	RBI	BB	SO	OBP	Slg.
L	.375	8	3	2	0	0	2	1	1	.444	.625		R	.429	7	3	0	0	0	0	0	4	.429	.429

HALAMA, JOHN   P

PERSONAL: Born February 22, 1972, in Brooklyn, N.Y. ... 6-5/215. ... Throws left, bats left. ... Full name: John Thadeuz Halama. ... Name pronounced: ha-LA-ma. ... High school: Bishop Ford (Brooklyn, N.Y.). ... College: St. Francis (N.Y.). **TRANSACTIONS/CAREER NOTES:** Selected by Houston Astros organization in 23rd round of 1994 free-agent draft. ... Traded by Astros to Seattle Mariners (October 1, 1998), completing deal in which Mariners traded P Randy Johnson to Astros for SS Carlos Guillen, P Freddy Garcia and a player to be named (July 31, 1998). ... Signed as a free agent by Oakland Athletics (January 17, 2003). ... Signed as a free agent by Tampa Bay Devil Rays (November 14, 2003). ... Signed as a free agent by Boston Red Sox (December 17, 2004). ... Released by Red Sox (August 2, 2005). ... Signed by Washington Nationals organization (August 5, 2005). ... Released by Nationals (October 3, 2005). ... Signed by Baltimore Orioles organization (February 8, 2006). ... Released by Orioles (June 21, 2006).

CAREER HITTING: 3-for-26 (.115), 2 R, 1 2B, 0 3B, 0 HR, 0 RBI.

Year	Team (League)	W	L	Pct.	ERA	WHIP	G	GS	CG	ShO	Hld.	Sv.-Opp.	IP	H	R	ER	HR	BB-IBB	SO	Avg.
1994— Auburn (NY-Penn)		4	1	.800	1.29	0.82	6	3	0	0	...	1-...	28.0	18	5	4	1	5-0	27	.180
— Quad City (Midw.)		3	4	.429	4.56	1.58	9	9	1	1	...	0-...	51.1	63	31	26	2	18-1	37	.317
1995— Quad City (Midw.)		1	2	.333	2.02	1.12	55	0	0	0	...	2-...	62.1	48	16	14	7	22-1	56	.225
1996— Jackson (Texas)		9	10	.474	3.21	1.29	27	27	0	0	...	0-...	162.2	151	77	58	10	59-0	110	.248
1997— New Orleans (A.A.)		13	3	.813	2.58	1.06	26	24	1	0	...	0-...	171.0	150	57	49	9	32-1	126	.238
1998— Houston (N.L.)		1	1	.500	5.85	1.55	6	6	0	0	...	0-0	32.1	37	21	21	0	13-0	21	.296
— New Orleans (PCL)		12	3	.800	3.13	1.11	17	17	4	1	...	0-...	121.0	118	48	43	11	16-1	86	.255

H

Year Team (League)	W	L	Pct.	ERA	WHIP	G	GS	CG	ShO	Hld.	Sv.-Opp.	IP	H	R	ER	HR	BB-IBB	SO	Avg.
1999—Seattle (A.L.)	11	10	.524	4.22	1.39	38	24	1	1	1	0-0	179.0	193	88	84	20	56-3	105	.282
2000—Seattle (A.L.)	14	9	.609	5.08	1.57	30	30	1	1	0	0-0	166.2	206	108	94	19	56-0	87	.308
2001—Seattle (A.L.)	10	7	.588	4.73	1.43	31	11	0	0	1	0-0	110.1	132	69	58	18	26-0	50	.296
— Tacoma (PCL)	2	0	1.000	0.47	0.47	3	3	1	1	...	0-...	19.0	9	2	1	1	0-0	22	.138
2002—Seattle (A.L.)	6	5	.545	3.56	1.44	31	10	0	0	0	0-0	101.0	112	45	40	9	33-5	70	.281
— Tacoma (PCL)	0	1	.000	6.14	1.36	2	2	0	0	...	0-...	14.2	19	11	10	0	1-1	9	.322
2003—Oakland (A.L.)	3	5	.375	4.22	1.41	35	13	0	0	3	0-0	108.2	117	68	51	18	36-2	51	.268
2004—Tampa Bay (A.L.)	7	6	.538	4.70	1.36	34	14	0	0	0	0-0	118.2	134	68	62	17	27-3	59	.284
2005—Boston (A.L.)	1	1	.500	6.18	1.49	30	1	0	0	0	0-0	43.2	56	33	30	5	9-3	26	.299
— New Orleans (PCL)	1	0	1.000	1.13	0.75	2	2	0	0	0	0-0	8.0	6	2	1	0	0-0	1	.194
— Wash. (N.L.)	0	3	.000	4.64	1.45	10	3	0	0	0	0-0	21.1	23	11	11	1	8-0	11	.277
2006—Baltimore (A.L.)	3	1	.750	6.14	1.74	17	1	0	0	0	0-1	29.1	38	20	20	6	13-2	12	.325
American League totals (8 years)	55	44	.556	4.61	1.45	246	110	2	2	5	0-1	857.1	988	499	439	112	256-18	460	.290
National League totals (2 years)	1	4	.200	5.37	1.51	16	9	0	0	0	0-0	53.2	60	32	32	1	21-0	32	.288
Major League totals (9 years)	56	48	.538	4.65	1.45	262	119	2	2	5	0-1	911.0	1048	531	471	113	277-18	492	.290

DIVISION SERIES RECORD

Year Team (League)	W	L	Pct.	ERA	WHIP	G	GS	CG	ShO	Hld.	Sv.-Opp.	IP	H	R	ER	HR	BB-IBB	SO	Avg.
2000—Seattle (A.L.)	Did not play.																		
2001—Seattle (A.L.)	0	0	...	0.00	1.00	2	0	0	0	0	0-0	3.0	3	0	0	0	0-0	3	.300

CHAMPIONSHIP SERIES RECORD

Year Team (League)	W	L	Pct.	ERA	WHIP	G	GS	CG	ShO	Hld.	Sv.-Opp.	IP	H	R	ER	HR	BB-IBB	SO	Avg.
2000—Seattle (A.L.)	0	0	...	2.89	1.61	2	2	0	0	0	0-0	9.1	10	3	3	0	5-0	3	.278
2001—Seattle (A.L.)	0	0	...	13.50	1.50	2	0	0	0	0	0-0	2.0	3	3	3	0	0-0	5	.333
Champ. series totals (2 years)	0	0	...	4.76	1.59	4	2	0	0	0	0-0	11.1	13	6	6	0	5-0	3	.289

2006 LEFTY-RIGHTY SPLITS

vs.	Avg.	AB	H	2B	3B	HR	RBI	BB	SO	OBP	Slg.	vs.	Avg.	AB	H	2B	3B	HR	RBI	BB	SO	OBP	Slg.
L	.304	46	14	2	1	0	4	5	5	.373	.391	R	.338	71	24	3	0	6	20	8	7	.400	.634

HALL, BILL — IF/OF

PERSONAL: Born December 28, 1979, in Nettleton, Miss. ... 6-0/195. ... Bats right, throws right. ... Full name: William Hall. ... High school: Nettleton (Miss.). **TRANSACTIONS/CAREER NOTES:** Selected by Milwaukee Brewers organization in sixth round of 1998 free-agent draft.
2006 GAMES PLAYED BY POSITION (MLB): SS—127, 3B—11, OF—7, 2B—4.

Year Team (League)	Pos.	G	AB	R	H	2B	3B	HR	RBI	BB	SO	HBP	GDP	SB-CS	Avg.	OBP	SLG	OPS	E	Avg.
1998—Helena (Pion.)	SS	29	85	11	15	3	0	0	5	9	27	1	2	5-5	.176	.263	.212	.475	16	.876
1999—Ogden (Pion.)	SS	69	280	41	81	15	2	6	31	15	61	2	6	19-8	.289	.329	.421	.750	38	.894
2000—Beloit (Midw.)	SS	130	470	57	123	30	6	3	41	18	127	1	12	10-11	.262	.287	.370	.658	40	.939
2001—High Desert (Calif.)	SS	89	346	61	105	21	6	15	51	22	78	3	3	18-9	.303	.348	.529	.876	30	.929
— Huntsville (Sou.)	SS	41	160	14	41	8	1	3	14	5	46	0	5	5-3	.256	.279	.375	.654	15	.925
2002—Indianapolis (Int'l)	SS	134	465	35	106	20	1	4	31	25	105	4	12	17-10	.228	.272	.301	.573	41	.934
— Milwaukee (N.L.)	SS-3B	19	36	3	7	1	1	1	3	3	13	0	1	0-1	.194	.256	.361	.618	2	.951
2003—Indianapolis (Int'l)	2B-SS-OF	89	354	57	100	25	2	5	32	27	79	1	7	10-11	.282	.335	.407	.742	19	.957
— Milwaukee (N.L.)	2B-SS-3B	52	142	23	37	9	2	5	20	7	28	1	5	1-2	.261	.298	.458	.756	9	.948
2004—Milwaukee (N.L.)	2B-SS-3B	126	390	43	93	20	3	9	53	20	119	1	4	12-6	.238	.276	.374	.650	19	.956
2005—Milwaukee (N.L.)	SS-3B-2B	146	501	69	146	39	6	17	62	39	103	1	11	18-6	.291	.342	.495	.837	16	.967
2006—Milwaukee (N.L.)	SS-3B-OF-2B	148	537	101	145	39	4	35	85	63	162	1	12	8-9	.270	.345	.553	.899	19	.966
Major League totals (5 years)		491	1606	239	428	108	16	67	225	132	425	4	33	39-24	.267	.322	.479	.801	65	.961

2006 LEFTY-RIGHTY SPLITS

vs.	Avg.	AB	H	2B	3B	HR	RBI	BB	SO	OBP	Slg.	vs.	Avg.	AB	H	2B	3B	HR	RBI	BB	SO	OBP	Slg.
L	.300	120	36	6	0	12	25	26	39	.422	.650	R	.261	417	109	33	4	23	60	37	123	.321	.525

HALL, TOBY — C

PERSONAL: Born October 21, 1975, in Tacoma, Wash. ... 6-3/240. ... Bats right, throws right. ... Full name: Toby Jason Hall. ... High school: El Dorado (Placentia, Calif.). ... College: UNLV. **TRANSACTIONS/CAREER NOTES:** Selected by San Francisco Giants organization in 24th round of 1995 free-agent draft; did not sign. ... Selected by Tampa Bay Devil Rays organization in ninth round of 1997 free-agent draft. ... Traded by Devil Rays with P Mark Hendrickson and cash to Los Angeles Dodgers for C Dioner Navarro, P Jae Seo and a player to be named (June 27, 2006). **STATISTICAL NOTES:** Career major league grand slams: 1.
2006 GAMES PLAYED BY POSITION (MLB): C—82, DH—2, 3B—1.

Year Team (League)	Pos.	G	AB	R	H	2B	3B	HR	RBI	BB	SO	HBP	GDP	SB-CS	Avg.	OBP	SLG	OPS	E	Avg.
1997—Hudson Valley (NYP)	C	55	200	25	50	3	0	1	27	13	33	1	3	0-0	.250	.295	.280	.575	3	.989
1998—Char., S.C. (SAL)	C	105	377	59	121	25	1	6	50	39	32	5	15	3-7	.321	.386	.440	.827	18	.979
1999—Orlando (South.)	C	46	173	20	44	7	0	9	34	4	10	1	7	1-1	.254	.269	.451	.720	4	.986
— St. Pete. (FSL)	C	56	212	24	63	13	1	4	36	17	9	2	7	0-2	.297	.350	.425	.775	4	.980
2000—Orlando (South.)	C	68	271	37	93	14	0	9	50	17	24	1	6	3-2	.343	.387	.494	.872	7	.984
— Durham (Int'l)	C	47	184	21	56	10	0	7	35	3	19	2	9	0-0	.304	.314	.500	.814	2	.993
— Tampa Bay (A.L.)	C	4	12	1	2	0	0	1	1	1	0	0	0	0-0	.167	.231	.417	.647	0	1.000
2001—Durham (Int'l)	C	94	373	59	125	28	1	19	72	29	22	3	15	1-3	.335	.385	.568	.953	6	.987
— Tampa Bay (A.L.)	C	49	188	28	56	16	0	4	30	4	16	3	5	2-2	.298	.321	.447	.768	5	.986
2002—Tampa Bay (A.L.)	C	85	330	37	85	19	1	6	42	17	27	1	14	0-1	.258	.295	.376	.669	6	.989
— Durham (Int'l)	C	22	92	13	32	4	0	2	20	3	10	4	3	0-0	.348	.382	.457	.839	1	.993
2003—Tampa Bay (A.L.)	C	130	463	50	117	23	0	12	47	23	40	7	14	0-1	.253	.295	.380	.675	9	.988
2004—Tampa Bay (A.L.)	C	119	404	35	103	21	0	8	60	24	51	5	20	0-2	.255	.300	.366	.666	6	.992
2005—Tampa Bay (A.L.)	C-1B	135	432	28	124	20	0	5	48	16	39	5	15	0-0	.287	.315	.368	.683	9	.989
2006—Tampa Bay (A.L.)	C-DH-3B	64	221	15	51	13	0	8	23	8	21	2	9	0-2	.231	.261	.398	.659	4	.991
— Los Angeles (N.L.)	C	21	57	2	21	4	0	0	8	2	5	0	2	0-0	.368	.383	.439	.822	1	.989
American League totals (7 years)		586	2050	194	538	112	1	44	251	93	180	23	76	2-8	.262	.298	.382	.681	38	.989
National League totals (1 year)		21	57	2	21	4	0	0	8	2	5	0	2	0-0	.368	.383	.439	.822	1	.989
Major League totals (7 years)		607	2107	196	559	116	1	44	259	95	185	23	78	2-8	.265	.301	.384	.685	39	.989

2006 LEFTY-RIGHTY SPLITS

vs.	Avg.	AB	H	2B	3B	HR	RBI	BB	SO	OBP	Slg.	vs.	Avg.	AB	H	2B	3B	HR	RBI	BB	SO	OBP	Slg.
L	.292	72	21	6	0	3	12	4	6	.333	.500	R	.248	206	51	11	0	5	19	6	16	.269	.374

H

HALLADAY, ROY   P

PERSONAL: Born May 14, 1977, in Denver. ... 6-6/230. ... Throws right, bats right. ... Full name: Harry Leroy Halladay. ... Name pronounced: HAL-uh-day. ... High school: Arvada (Colo.) West. **TRANSACTIONS/CAREER NOTES:** Selected by Toronto Blue Jays organization in first round (17th pick overall) of 1995 free-agent draft. ... On disabled list (May 28-June 12 and July 17-September 21, 2004; and July 9, 2005-remainder of season). **HONORS:** Named A.L. Pitcher of the Year by THE SPORTING NEWS (2003). ... Named righthanded pitcher on THE SPORTING NEWS A.L. All-Star team (2003). ... Named A.L. Cy Young Award winner by Baseball Writers' Association of America (2003).

CAREER HITTING: 1-for-29 (.034), 2 R, 0 2B, 0 3B, 0 HR, 0 RBI.

Year — Team (League)	W	L	Pct.	ERA	WHIP	G	GS	CG	ShO	Hld.	Sv.-Opp.	IP	H	R	ER	HR	BB-IBB	SO	Avg.
1995— GC Jays (GCL)	3	5	.375	3.40	1.01	10	8	0	0	...	0-...	50.1	35	25	19	4	16-0	48	.190
1996— Dunedin (Fla. St.)	15	7	.682	2.73	1.24	27	27	2	2	...	0-...	164.2	158	75	50	7	46-0	109	.251
1997— Knoxville (Southern)	2	3	.400	5.40	1.55	7	7	0	0	...	0-...	36.2	46	26	22	4	11-0	30	.305
— Syracuse (Int'l)	7	10	.412	4.58	1.47	22	22	2	2	...	0-...	125.2	132	74	64	13	53-1	64	.276
1998— Syracuse (Int'l)	9	5	.643	3.79	1.38	21	21	1	1	...	0-...	116.1	107	52	49	11	53-3	71	.246
— Toronto (A.L.)	1	0	1.000	1.93	0.79	2	2	1	0	0	0-0	14.0	9	4	3	2	2-0	13	.176
1999— Toronto (A.L.)	8	7	.533	3.92	1.57	36	18	1	1	2	1-1	149.1	156	76	65	19	79-1	82	.273
2000— Toronto (A.L.)	4	7	.364	10.64	2.20	19	13	0	0	0	0-0	67.2	107	87	80	14	42-0	44	.357
— Syracuse (Int'l)	2	3	.400	5.50	1.44	11	11	3	0	...	0-...	73.2	85	46	45	10	21-0	38	.294
2001— Dunedin (Fla. St.)	0	1	.000	3.97	1.37	13	0	0	0	...	2-...	22.2	28	12	10	1	3-0	15	.304
— Tennessee (Sou.)	2	1	.667	2.12	0.91	5	5	3	0	...	0-...	34.0	25	9	8	2	6-0	29	.202
— Syracuse (Int'l)	1	0	1.000	3.21	0.86	2	2	0	0	...	0-...	14.0	12	5	5	2	0-0	13	.222
— Toronto (A.L.)	5	3	.625	3.16	1.16	17	16	1	1	0	0-0	105.1	97	41	37	3	25-0	96	.241
2002— Toronto (A.L.)	19	7	.731	2.93	1.19	34	34	2	1	0	0-0	* 239.1	223	93	78	10	62-6	168	.244
2003— Toronto (A.L.)	* 22	7	.759	3.25	1.07	36	* 36	• 9	• 2	0	0-0	* 266.0	* 253	111	96	26	32-1	204	.251
2004— Toronto (A.L.)	8	8	.500	4.20	1.35	21	21	1	1	0	0-0	133.0	140	66	62	13	39-1	95	.272
2005— Toronto (A.L.)	12	4	.750	2.41	0.96	19	19	* 5	2	0	0-0	141.2	118	39	38	11	18-2	108	.225
2006— Toronto (A.L.)	16	5	.762	3.19	1.10	32	32	4	0	0	0-0	220.0	208	82	78	19	34-5	132	.251
Major League totals (9 years)	* 95	48	.664	3.62	1.23	216	191	24	8	2	1-1	1336.1	1311	599	537	117	333-16	942	.255

ALL-STAR GAME RECORD

	W	L	Pct.	ERA	WHIP	G	GS	CG	ShO	Hld.	Sv.-Opp.	IP	H	R	ER	HR	BB-IBB	SO	Avg.
All-Star Game totals (2 years)	0	0	...	12.00	2.00	2	0	0	0	0	0-0	3.0	6	4	4	1	0-0	2	.462

2006 LEFTY-RIGHTY SPLITS

vs.	Avg.	AB	H	2B	3B	HR	RBI	BB	SO	OBP	Slg.	vs.	Avg.	AB	H	2B	3B	HR	RBI	BB	SO	OBP	Slg.
L	.259	394	102	21	2	9	38	13	56	.288	.391	R	.244	435	106	14	3	10	40	21	76	.279	.359

HALSEY, BRAD   P

PERSONAL: Born February 14, 1981, in Houston. ... 6-1/180. ... Throws left, bats left. ... Full name: Bradford Alexander Halsey. ... High school: Westfield (Houston). ... Junior college: Hill College (Hillsboro, Texas). ... College: Texas. **TRANSACTIONS/CAREER NOTES:** Selected by New York Yankees organization in 19th round of 2000 free-agent draft; did not sign. ... Selected by New York Yankees organization in eighth round of 2002 free-agent draft. ... Traded by Yankees with P Javier Vazquez, C Dioner Navarro and cash to Arizona Diamondbacks for P Randy Johnson (January 11, 2005). ... On suspended list (April 5-7, 2005). ... Traded by Diamondbacks to Oakland Athletics for P Juan Cruz (March 26, 2006).

CAREER HITTING: 4-for-50 (.080), 2 R, 0 2B, 0 3B, 0 HR, 2 RBI.

Year — Team (League)	W	L	Pct.	ERA	WHIP	G	GS	CG	ShO	Hld.	Sv.-Opp.	IP	H	R	ER	HR	BB-IBB	SO	Avg.
2002— Staten Is. (N.Y.-Penn)	6	1	.857	1.93	1.00	11	10	0	0	...	0-...	56.0	39	15	12	0	17-0	53	.195
2003— Tampa (Fla. St.)	10	4	.714	3.43	1.31	14	13	1	0	...	0-...	84.0	96	36	32	3	14-0	56	.287
— Trenton (East.)	7	5	.583	4.93	1.59	15	15	0	0	...	0-...	91.1	123	51	50	4	22-0	78	.325
2004— Columbus (Int'l)	11	4	.733	2.63	1.15	24	23	3	2	...	0-...	144.0	128	46	42	8	37-0	109	.237
— New York (A.L.)	1	3	.250	6.47	1.72	8	7	0	0	0	0-0	32.0	41	26	23	4	14-0	25	.306
2005— Arizona (N.L.)	8	12	.400	4.61	1.44	28	26	0	0	0	0-0	160.0	191	101	82	20	39-3	82	.300
2006— Sacramento (PCL)	1	0	1.000	0.96	0.54	2	2	0	0	0	0-0	9.1	4	1	1	0	1-0	3	.129
— Oakland (A.L.)	5	4	.556	4.67	1.63	52	7	0	0	8	0-0	94.1	108	53	49	11	46-7	53	.288
American League totals (2 years)	6	7	.462	5.13	1.65	60	14	0	0	8	0-0	126.1	149	79	72	15	60-7	78	.293
National League totals (1 year)	8	12	.400	4.61	1.44	28	26	0	0	0	0-0	160.0	191	101	82	20	39-3	82	.300
Major League totals (3 years)	14	19	.424	4.84	1.53	88	40	0	0	8	0-0	286.1	340	180	154	35	99-10	160	.297

2006 LEFTY-RIGHTY SPLITS

vs.	Avg.	AB	H	2B	3B	HR	RBI	BB	SO	OBP	Slg.	vs.	Avg.	AB	H	2B	3B	HR	RBI	BB	SO	OBP	Slg.
L	.317	104	33	7	1	4	15	14	16	.405	.519	R	.277	271	75	11	0	7	37	32	37	.358	.395

HAMELS, COLE   P

PERSONAL: Born December 27, 1983, in San Diego, Calif. ... Throws left, bats left. ... Full name: Colbert Richard Hamels. . **TRANSACTIONS/CAREER NOTES:** Selected by Philadelphia Phillies organization in first round (17th pick overall) of 2002 free-agent draft. ... On disabled list (May 19-June 6, 2006); included rehabilitation assignment to Lakewood.

CAREER HITTING: 5-for-44 (.114), 4 R, 0 2B, 0 3B, 0 HR, 3 RBI.

Year — Team (League)	W	L	Pct.	ERA	WHIP	G	GS	CG	ShO	Hld.	Sv.-Opp.	IP	H	R	ER	HR	BB-IBB	SO	Avg.
2003— Lakewood (S. Atl.)	6	1	.857	0.84	0.76	13	13	1	1	...	0-...	74.2	32	8	7	0	25-0	115	.136
— Clearwater (FSL)	0	2	.000	2.73	1.63	5	5	0	0	...	0-...	26.1	29	9	8	0	14-0	32	.299
2004— Clearwater (FSL)	1	0	1.000	1.13	0.88	4	4	0	0	...	0-...	16.0	10	2	2	0	4-0	24	.192
2005— Clearwater (FSL)	2	0	1.000	2.25	0.88	3	3	0	0	0	0-0	16.0	7	5	4	0	7-0	18	.137
— Reading (East.)	2	0	1.000	2.37	1.16	3	3	0	0	0	0-0	19.0	10	6	5	2	12-0	19	.159
2006— Scran./W.B. (I.L.)	2	0	1.000	0.39	0.48	3	3	1	1	0	0-0	23.0	10	1	1	0	1-0	36	.130
— Lakewood (S. Atl.)	0	0	...	1.59	0.88	1	1	0	0	0	0-0	5.2	3	1	1	1	2-0	3	.158
— Clearwater (FSL)	1	1	.500	1.77	1.23	4	4	0	0	0	0-0	20.1	16	8	4	0	9-0	29	.205
— Philadelphia (N.L.)	9	8	.529	4.08	1.25	23	23	0	0	0	0-0	132.1	117	66	60	19	48-4	145	.237
Major League totals (1 year)	9	8	.529	4.08	1.25	23	23	0	0	0	0-0	132.1	117	66	60	19	48-4	145	.237

2006 LEFTY-RIGHTY SPLITS

vs.	Avg.	AB	H	2B	3B	HR	RBI	BB	SO	OBP	Slg.	vs.	Avg.	AB	H	2B	3B	HR	RBI	BB	SO	OBP	Slg.
L	.207	92	19	6	0	4	10	9	28	.277	.402	R	.244	401	98	20	5	15	53	39	117	.310	.431

H

HAMMEL, JASON   P

PERSONAL: Born September 2, 1982, in Greenville, S.C. ... 6-6/200. ... Throws right, bats right. ... Full name: Jason Aaron Hammel. ... Junior college: Treasure Valley C.C. **TRANSACTIONS/CAREER NOTES:** Selected by Tampa Bay Devil Rays organization in 10th round of 2002 free-agent draft.

CAREER HITTING: 0-for-0 (.000), 0 R, 0 2B, 0 3B, 0 HR, 0 RBI.

Year	Team (League)	W	L	Pct.	ERA	WHIP	G	GS	CG	ShO	Hld.	Sv.-Opp.	IP	H	R	ER	HR	BB-IBB	SO	Avg.
2002—	Princeton (Appal.)	0	0	...	0.00	1.31	2	0	0	0	...	1-...	5.1	7	0	0	0	0-0	5	.318
	— Hudson Valley (NYP)	1	5	.167	5.23	1.65	13	10	0	0	...	1-...	51.2	71	41	30	0	14-0	38	.314
2003—	Char., S.C. (SAL)	6	2	.750	3.40	1.27	14	12	1	0	...	0-...	76.2	70	32	29	2	27-1	50	.246
2004—	Char., S.C. (SAL)	4	7	.364	3.23	1.28	18	18	0	0	...	0-...	94.2	94	54	34	7	27-0	88	.257
	— Bakersfield (Calif.)	6	2	.750	1.89	1.01	11	11	0	0	...	0-...	71.1	52	18	15	4	20-0	65	.211
2005—	Montgom. (Sou.)	8	2	.800	2.66	1.09	12	12	3	0	0	0-0	81.1	70	26	24	5	19-0	76	.235
	— Durham (Int'l)	3	2	.600	4.12	1.54	10	10	0	0	0	0-0	54.2	57	31	25	8	27-0	48	.264
2006—	Durham (Int'l)	5	9	.357	4.23	1.32	24	24	1	0	0	0-0	127.2	133	71	60	11	36-0	117	.270
	— Tampa Bay (A.L.)	0	6	.000	7.77	1.86	9	9	0	0	0	0-0	44.0	61	38	38	7	21-0	32	.333
Major League totals (1 year)		0	6	.000	7.77	1.86	9	9	0	0	0	0-0	44.0	61	38	38	7	21-0	32	.333

2006 LEFTY-RIGHTY SPLITS

vs.	Avg.	AB	H	2B	3B	HR	RBI	BB	SO	OBP	Slg.	vs.	Avg.	AB	H	2B	3B	HR	RBI	BB	SO	OBP	Slg.
L	.372	86	32	6	1	5	22	12	16	.444	.640	R	.299	97	29	9	1	2	14	9	16	.358	.474

HAMMOCK, ROBBY   IF/C

PERSONAL: Born May 13, 1977, in Macon, Ga. ... 5-10/187. ... Bats right, throws right. ... Full name: Robert Wade Hammock. ... Name pronounced: HAM-uk. ... High school: South Cobb (Dacula, Ga.). ... College: Georgia. **TRANSACTIONS/CAREER NOTES:** Selected by Florida Marlins organization in 66th round of 1995 free-agent draft; did not sign. ... Selected by Tampa Bay Devil Rays organization in 89th round of 1997 free-agent draft; did not sign. ... Selected by Arizona Diamondbacks organization in 23rd round of 1998 free-agent draft. ... On disabled list (April 1-20 and July 16-September 7, 2004); included rehabilitation assignments to Tucson and Lancaster. ... Released by Diamondbacks (February 4, 2005). ... Re-signed by Diamondbacks organization (April 11, 2005).

2006 GAMES PLAYED BY POSITION (MLB): 1B—1.

Year	Team (League)	Pos.	G	AB	R	H	2B	3B	HR	RBI	BB	SO	HBP	GDP	SB-CS	Avg.	OBP	SLG	OPS	E	Avg.
1998—	Lethbridge (Pion.)	C-3B	62	227	46	65	14	2	10	56	28	34	2	3	5-4	.286	.367	.498	.865	4	.990
1999—	High Desert (Calif.)	C-OF-3B	114	379	80	126	20	7	9	72	47	63	2	8	3-6	.332	.403	.493	.897	18	.975
2000—	High Desert (Calif.)	C-1B	40	136	25	48	15	1	3	23	27	24	1	5	3-3	.353	.455	.544	.999	11	.962
	— El Paso (Texas)	C-3B-OF	45	140	22	35	5	1	1	15	11	25	1	1	1-2	.250	.305	.321	.627	2	.990
2001—	South Bend (Mid.)	C-OF	34	125	16	31	3	2	2	14	14	21	0	2	5-6	.248	.324	.352	.676	2	.988
		C*	26	74	6	12	5	0	0	4	7	18	0	1	2-2	.162	.235	-.230	.464	5	.948
	— Lancaster (Calif.)	OF-C-3B																			
		1B-2B	0	45	190	33	88	11	3	4	7	1	4	2	42-3	.733	.463	6.000	4.163	7	.966
2002—	El Paso (Texas)	OF-C-3B	122	441	68	128	28	4	11	73	43	68	8	14	5-4	.290	.358	.447	.805	8	.986
2003—	Tucson (PCL)	C-OF-1B																			
		3B	33	116	14	31	6	2	2	17	11	24	0	2	1-0	.267	.321	.405	.726	5	.972
	— Arizona (N.L.)	C-OF-3B																			
		DH	65	195	30	55	10	2	6	28	17	44	2	5	3-2	.282	.343	.477	.820	7	.980
2004—	Tucson (PCL)	C-DH	8	21	1	6	1	0	0	4	2	1	0	0	2-0	.286	.333	.333	.667	1	.968
	— Lancaster (Calif.)	C-DH	2	9	2	6	1	0	1	3	1	1	0	0	0-0	.667	.700	.889	1.589	0	1.000
	— Arizona (N.L.)	C-OF-3B	62	195	22	47	16	2	4	18	13	39	0	9	3-3	.241	.287	.405	.692	2	.994
2005—	Tucson (PCL)	OF	3	11	0	4	0	0	0	3	0	1	0	0	0-0	.364	.333	.364	.697	0	1.000
2006—	Tucson (PCL)	C-DH	103	369	57	107	21	1	20	65	24	59	7	11	2-2	.290	.342	.515	.856	4	.993
	— Arizona (N.L.)	1B	1	2	1	1	1	0	0	0	0	0	0	0	0-0	.500	.500	1.000	1.500	0	1.000
Major League totals (3 years)			128	392	53	103	27	4	12	46	30	83	2	14	6-5	.263	.316	.444	.760	4	.987

2006 LEFTY-RIGHTY SPLITS

vs.	Avg.	AB	H	2B	3B	HR	RBI	BB	SO	OBP	Slg.	vs.	Avg.	AB	H	2B	3B	HR	RBI	BB	SO	OBP	Slg.
L	.000	0	0	0	0	0	0	0	0	.000	.000	R	.500	2	1	1	0	0	0	0	0	.500	1.000

HAMMOND, CHRIS   P

PERSONAL: Born January 21, 1966, in Atlanta. ... 6-1/210. ... Throws left, bats left. ... Full name: Chris Andrew Hammond. ... High school: Vestavia Hills (Birmingham, Ala.). ... Junior college: Gulf Coast (Fla.) Community College. ... Brother of Steve Hammond, outfielder with Kansas City Royals (1982). **TRANSACTIONS/CAREER NOTES:** Selected by Cincinnati Reds organization in sixth round of January 1986 free-agent draft. ... On disabled list (July 27-September 1, 1991). ... Traded to Florida Marlins for 3B Gary Scott and a player to be named (March 27, 1993); Reds acquired P Hector Carrasco to complete deal (September 10, 1993). ... On disabled list (June 11-August 3, 1994); included rehabilitation assignments to Portland and Brevard County. ... On disabled list (April 16-May 13 and August 3-19, 1995); included rehabilitation assignments to Brevard County and Charlotte. ... On disabled list (June 9-July 14, 1996); included rehabilitation assignments to Brevard County and Charlotte. ... Signed as a free agent by Boston Red Sox (December 17, 1996). ... On disabled list (June 30, 1997-remainder of season). ... Signed as a free agent by Kansas City Royals organization (January 12, 1998). ... Released by Royals (March 23, 1998). ... Signed by Marlins organization (March 27, 1998). ... Released by Marlins (June 2, 1998). ... Signed by Cleveland Indians organization (March 30, 2001). ... Released by Indians (July 3, 2001). ... Signed by Atlanta Braves organization (July 3, 2001). ... On suspended list (September 13-16, 2002). ... Signed as a free agent by New York Yankees (December 12, 2002). ... Traded by Yankees to Oakland Athletics for P Eduardo Sierra and SS J.T. Stotts (December 18, 2003). ... On disabled list (June 12-July 27, 2004); included rehabilitation assignment to Sacramento. ... Signed as a free agent by San Diego Padres (January 17, 2005). ... On disabled list (July 20-August 8, 2005). ... Signed as a free agent by Cincinnati Reds (December 20, 2005). ... Released by Reds (July 7, 2006). **STATISTICAL NOTES:** Career major league grand slams: 1. **MISCELLANEOUS NOTES:** Appeared in two games as pinch runner (1992). ... Struck out in only appearance as pinch hitter (1993).

CAREER HITTING: 48-for-238 (.202), 30 R, 7 2B, 1 3B, 4 HR, 14 RBI.

Year	Team (League)	W	L	Pct.	ERA	WHIP	G	GS	CG	ShO	Hld.	Sv.-Opp.	IP	H	R	ER	HR	BB-IBB	SO	Avg.
1986—	GC Reds (GCL)	3	2	.600	2.81	1.06	7	7	1	0	...	0-...	41.2	27	21	13	0	17-1	53	.172
	— Tampa (Fla. St.)	0	2	.000	3.32	1.75	5	5	0	0	...	0-...	21.2	25	8	8	0	13-1	15	.291
1987—	Tampa (Fla. St.)	11	11	.500	3.55	1.38	25	24	6	0	...	0-...	170.0	174	81	67	10	60-1	126	.258
1988—	Chattanooga (Sou.)	16	5	.762	1.72	1.12	26	26	4	2	...	0-...	182.2	127	48	35	2	77-3	127	.193
1989—	Nashville (A.A.)	11	7	.611	3.38	1.53	24	24	1	0	...	0-...	157.1	144	69	59	7	96-1	142	.245
1990—	Nashville (A.A.)	15	1	.938	2.17	1.21	24	24	5	3	...	0-...	149.0	118	43	36	7	63-1	149	.219
	— Cincinnati (N.L.)	0	2	.000	6.35	2.21	3	3	0	0	...	0-...	11.1	13	9	8	2	12-1	4	.302
1991—	Cincinnati (N.L.)	7	7	.500	4.06	1.40	20	18	0	0	...	0-...	99.2	92	51	45	4	48-3	50	.250
1992—	Cincinnati (N.L.)	7	10	.412	4.21	1.38	28	26	0	0	...	0-...	147.1	149	75	69	13	55-6	79	.266
1993—	Florida (N.L.)	11	12	.478	4.66	1.43	32	32	1	0	...	0-...	191.0	207	106	99	18	66-2	108	.277
1994—	Florida (N.L.)	4	4	.500	3.07	1.39	13	13	1	1	...	0-...	73.1	79	30	25	5	23-1	40	.281
	— Portland (East.)	0	0	...	0.00	0.00	1	1	0	0	...	0-...	2.0	0	0	0	0	0-0	1	.000
	— Brevard County (FSL)	0	0	...	1.23	0.95	2	2	0	0	...	0-...	7.1	4	3	1	0	3-0	5	.160
1995—	Charlotte (Int'l)	0	0	...	0.00	1.25	1	1	0	0	...	0-...	4.0	3	1	0	0	2-0	3	.176
	— Florida (N.L.)	9	6	.600	3.80	1.27	25	24	3	2	0	0-0	161.0	157	73	68	17	47-2	126	.256
1996—	Florida (N.L.)	5	8	.385	6.56	1.62	38	9	0	0	...	5-...	81.0	104	65	59	14	27-3	50	.315

Year Team (League)	W	L	Pct.	ERA	WHIP	G	GS	CG	ShO	Hld.	Sv.-Opp.	IP	H	R	ER	HR	BB-IBB	SO	Avg.
— Brevard County (FSL)	0	0	...	0.00	0.75	1	1	0	0	...	0-...	4.0	3	0	0	0	0-0	8	.214
— Charlotte (Int'l)	1	0	1.000	7.20	1.00	1	1	0	0	...	0-...	5.0	5	4	4	0	0-0	3	.250
1997— Boston (A.L.)	3	4	.429	5.92	1.65	29	8	0	0	4	1-2	65.1	81	45	43	5	27-4	48	.310
1998— Charlotte (Int'l)	1	3	.250	4.82	1.75	5	5	0	0	...	0-...	28.0	35	17	15	2	14-2	22	.315
— Florida (N.L.)	0	2	.000	6.59	2.05	3	3	0	0	0	0-0	13.2	20	11	10	3	8-0	8	.357
1999—	Did not play.																		
2000—	Did not play.																		
2001— Buffalo (Int'l)	7	3	.700	3.31	1.41	28	4	0	0	...	0-...	51.2	53	22	19	5	20-1	54	.261
— Richmond (Int'l)	3	1	.750	2.35	1.17	21	0	0	0	...	1-...	30.2	32	9	8	0	4-0	29	.281
2002— Atlanta (N.L.)	7	2	.778	0.95	1.11	63	0	0	0	17	0-2	76.0	53	15	8	1	31-9	63	.195
2003— New York (A.L.)	3	2	.600	2.86	1.21	62	0	0	0	17	1-4	63.0	65	23	20	5	11-0	45	.270
2004— Sacramento (PCL)	0	0	...	0.00	1.50	3	3	0	0	...	0-...	4.0	6	0	0	0	0-0	5	.353
— Oakland (A.L.)	4	1	.800	2.68	1.29	41	0	0	0	3	1-3	53.2	56	21	16	4	13-1	34	.277
2005— San Diego (N.L.)	5	1	.833	3.84	1.11	55	0	0	0	6	0-3	58.2	51	25	25	9	14-0	34	.270
2006— Cincinnati (N.L.)	1	1	.500	6.91	1.43	29	0	0	0	6	0-2	28.2	36	23	22	5	5-0	23	.303
American League totals (3 years)	10	7	.588	3.91	1.39	132	8	0	0	24	3-9	182.0	202	89	79	14	51-5	127	.287
National League totals (11 years)	56	55	.505	4.19	1.38	309	128	5	3	34	0-7	941.2	961	483	438	91	336-27	585	.266
Major League totals (14 years)	66	62	.516	4.14	1.38	441	136	5	3	58	3-16	1123.2	1163	572	517	105	387-32	712	.269

DIVISION SERIES RECORD

Year Team (League)	W	L	Pct.	ERA	WHIP	G	GS	CG	ShO	Hld.	Sv.-Opp.	IP	H	R	ER	HR	BB-IBB	SO	Avg.
2002— Atlanta (N.L.)	0	0	...	6.75	1.88	3	0	0	0	0	0-0	2.2	2	2	2	0	3-1	2	.200

WORLD SERIES RECORD

Year Team (League)	W	L	Pct.	ERA	WHIP	G	GS	CG	ShO	Hld.	Sv.-Opp.	IP	H	R	ER	HR	BB-IBB	SO	Avg.
2003— New York (A.L.)	0	0	...	0.00	1.00	1	0	0	0	0	0-0	2.0	2	2	0	0	0-0	0	.250

2006 LEFTY-RIGHTY SPLITS

vs.	Avg.	AB	H	2B	3B	HR	RBI	BB	SO	OBP	Slg.	vs.	Avg.	AB	H	2B	3B	HR	RBI	BB	SO	OBP	Slg.
L	.286	49	14	1	0	3	9	0	10	.286	.490	R	.314	70	22	5	0	2	8	5	13	.360	.471

HAMPSON, JUSTIN   P

PERSONAL: Born May 24, 1980, in Belleville, Ill. ... Throws left, bats left. ... Full name: Justin Michael Hampson. ... Junior college: Belleville (Ill.). **TRANSACTIONS/CAREER NOTES:** Selected by Colorado Rockies organization in 28th round of 1999 free-agent draft. ... Claimed on waivers by San Diego Padres (October 12, 2006).
CAREER HITTING: 0-for-3 (.000), 2 R, 0 2B, 0 3B, 0 HR, 0 RBI.

Year Team (League)	W	L	Pct.	ERA	WHIP	G	GS	CG	ShO	Hld.	Sv.-Opp.	IP	H	R	ER	HR	BB-IBB	SO	Avg.
2000— Portland (N'west)	1	8	.111	3.54	1.47	14	13	0	0	...	0-...	68.2	74	43	27	5	27-0	44	.271
2001— Tri-City (N'west)	4	6	.400	4.52	1.31	15	15	0	0	...	0-...	81.2	84	55	41	5	23-0	63	.266
2002— Asheville (S. Atl.)	9	8	.529	3.83	1.34	27	27	1	0	...	0-...	164.1	162	87	70	12	58-1	123	.261
2003— Tulsa (Texas)	0	1	.000	13.50	2.75	1	1	0	0	...	0-...	4.0	8	6	6	0	3-0		.421
— Visalia (Calif.)	14	7	.667	3.68	1.28	26	26	1	0	...	0-...	159.0	153	73	65	12	51-1	150	.252
2004— Tulsa (Texas)	10	9	.526	3.49	1.40	27	27	1	0	...	0-...	170.1	176	82	66	22	63-0	104	.287
2005— Colo. Springs (PCL)	5	13	.278	5.99	1.65	27	26	1	0	0	0-0	144.1	167	109	96	18	71-0	93	.287
2006— Colo. Springs (PCL)	8	4	.667	3.33	1.32	31	13	0	0	3	0-0	121.2	121	57	45	10	39-1	95	.264
— Colorado (N.L.)	1	0	1.000	7.50	2.00	5	1	0	0	0	0-1	12.0	19	10	10	3	5-0	9	.352
Major League totals (1 year)	1	0	1.000	7.50	2.00	5	1	0	0	0	0-1	12.0	19	10	10	3	5-0	9	.352

2006 LEFTY-RIGHTY SPLITS

vs.	Avg.	AB	H	2B	3B	HR	RBI	BB	SO	OBP	Slg.	vs.	Avg.	AB	H	2B	3B	HR	RBI	BB	SO	OBP	Slg.
L	.364	11	4	2	0	0	4	1	4	.462	.545	R	.349	43	15	3	0	3	9	4	5	.404	.721

HAMPTON, MIKE   P

PERSONAL: Born September 9, 1972, in Brooksville, Fla. ... 5-10/195. ... Throws left, bats right. ... Full name: Michael William Hampton. ... High school: Crystal River (Fla.).
TRANSACTIONS/CAREER NOTES: Selected by Seattle Mariners organization in sixth round of 1990 free-agent draft. ... Traded by Mariners with OF Mike Felder to Houston Astros for OF Eric Anthony (December 10, 1993). ... On disabled list (May 15-June 13, 1995; June 16-July 4, 1998). ... Traded by Astros with OF Derek Bell to New York Mets for OF Roger Cedeno and Ps Octavio Dotel and Kyle Kessel (December 23, 1999). ... Signed as a free agent by Colorado Rockies (December 9, 2000). ... On suspended list (October 3-8, 2001). ... Traded by Rockies with OF Juan Pierre and cash to Florida Marlins for C Charles Johnson, P Vic Darensbourg, OF Preston Wilson and 2B Pablo Ozuna (November 16, 2002). ... Traded by Marlins with cash to Atlanta Braves for Ps Tim Spooneybarger and Ryan Baker (November 18, 2002). ... On disabled list (March 28-April 19, 2003). ... On disabled list (May 16-31, June 5-July 17, July 27-August 14 and August 24-September 11, 2005); included rehabilitation assignments to Richmond and GCL Braves. ... On disabled list (April 1, 2006-entire season). **HONORS:** Named N.L. Pitcher of the Year by THE SPORTING NEWS (1999). ... Named lefthanded pitcher on THE SPORTING NEWS N.L. All-Star team (1999). ... Won N.L. Gold Glove at pitcher (2003). ... Named pitcher on N.L. Silver Slugger team (2000-03). **MISCELLANEOUS NOTES:** Appeared in two games as pinch runner (1996). ... Scored run in only appearance as pinch runner (2000). ... Struck out in only appearance as pinch hitter (2000). ... Appeared in eight games as pinch runner (2001). ... Appeared in three games as pinch hitter (2001). ... Singled, scored a run and struck out twice in four appearances as pinch hitter and scored a run in two appearances as pinch runner (2002). ... Had a sacrifice hit in only appearance as pinch hitter (2003). ... Made an out and struck out twice in three appearances as pinch hitter and scored two runs in four appearances as pinch runner (2004).
CAREER HITTING: 161-for-664 (.242), 88 R, 19 2B, 5 3B, 15 HR, 68 RBI.

Year Team (League)	W	L	Pct.	ERA	WHIP	G	GS	CG	ShO	Hld.	Sv.-Opp.	IP	H	R	ER	HR	BB-IBB	SO	Avg.
1990— Ariz. Mariners (Ariz.)	7	2	.778	2.66	1.43	14	13	0	0	...	0-...	64.1	52	32	19	0	40-0	59	.213
1991— San Bern. (Calif.)	1	7	.125	5.25	1.60	18	15	1	1	...	0-...	73.2	71	58	43	3	47-1	65	.249
— Bellingham (N'west)	5	2	.714	1.58	1.02	9	9	0	0	...	0-...	57.0	32	15	10	0	26-0	65	.162
1992— San Bern. (Calif.)	13	8	.619	3.12	1.35	25	25	6	2	...	0-...	170.0	163	75	59	8	66-1	132	.255
— Jacksonville (Sou.)	0	1	.000	4.35	1.35	2	2	1	0	...	0-...	10.1	13	5	5	0	1-0	6	.317
1993— Seattle (A.L.)	1	3	.250	9.53	2.65	13	3	0	0	2	1-1	17.0	28	20	18	3	17-3	8	.368
— Jacksonville (Sou.)	6	4	.600	3.71	1.19	15	14	1	0	...	0-...	87.1	71	43	36	3	33-1	84	.225
1994— Houston (N.L.)	2	1	.667	3.70	1.50	44	0	0	0	10	0-1	41.1	46	19	17	4	16-1	24	.282
1995— Houston (N.L.)	9	8	.529	3.35	1.26	24	24	0	0	0	0-0	150.2	141	73	56	13	49-3	115	.247
1996— Houston (N.L.)	10	10	.500	3.59	1.40	27	27	2	1	0	0-0	160.1	175	79	64	12	49-1	101	.280
1997— Houston (N.L.)	15	10	.600	3.83	1.32	34	34	7	2	0	0-0	223.0	217	105	95	16	77-2	139	.257
1998— Houston (N.L.)	11	7	.611	3.36	1.46	32	32	1	1	0	0-0	211.2	227	92	79	18	81-1	137	.278
1999— Houston (N.L.)	* 22	4	* .846	2.90	1.28	34	34	3	2	0	0-0	239.0	206	86	77	12	101-2	177	.241
2000— New York (N.L.)	15	10	.600	3.14	1.35	33	33	3	1	0	0-0	217.2	194	89	76	10	99-5	151	.241
2001— Colorado (N.L.)	14	13	.519	5.41	1.58	32	32	2	1	0	0-0	203.0	236	138	122	31	89-5	122	.296
2002— Colorado (N.L.)	7	15	.318	6.15	1.79	30	30	0	0	0	0-0	178.2	228	* 135	122	24	91-4	74	.313
2003— Atlanta (N.L.)	14	8	.636	3.84	1.39	31	31	1	0	0	0-0	190.0	186	91	81	14	78-4	110	.255
2004— Atlanta (N.L.)	13	8	.591	4.28	1.53	29	29	1	0	0	0-0	172.1	198	86	82	15	65-3	87	.290

H

Year Team (League)	W	L	Pct.	ERA	WHIP	G	GS	CG	ShO	Hld.	Sv.-Opp.	IP	H	R	ER	HR	BB-IBB	SO	Avg.
2005— Richmond (Int'l)	0	0	...	2.25	1.00	1	1	0	0	0	0-0	4.0	4	1	1	0	0-0	3	.250
—GC Braves (GCL)	0	0	...	0.00	1.20	1	1	0	0	0	0-0	5.0	6	0	0	0	0-0	4	.300
—Atlanta (N.L.)	5	3	.625	3.50	1.33	12	12	1	1	0	0-0	69.1	74	28	27	5	18-0	27	.281
2006— Atlanta (N.L.)		Did not play.																	
American League totals (1 year)	1	3	.250	9.53	2.65	13	3	0	0	2	1-1	17.0	28	20	18	3	17-3	8	.368
National League totals (12 years)	137	98	.583	3.93	1.43	362	318	21	9	10	0-1	2057.0	2128	1021	898	174	809-33	1264	.270
Major League totals (13 years)	138	101	.577	3.97	1.44	375	321	21	9	12	1-2	2074.0	2156	1041	916	177	826-36	1272	.271

DIVISION SERIES RECORD

Year Team (League)	W	L	Pct.	ERA	WHIP	G	GS	CG	ShO	Hld.	Sv.-Opp.	IP	H	R	ER	HR	BB-IBB	SO	Avg.
1997— Houston (N.L.)	0	1	.000	11.57	2.14	1	1	0	0	0	0-0	4.2	2	6	6	1	8-0	2	.125
1998— Houston (N.L.)	0	0	...	1.50	0.50	1	1	0	0	0	0-0	6.0	2	1	1	0	1-0	2	.111
1999— Houston (N.L.)	0	0	...	3.86	1.00	1	1	0	0	0	0-0	7.0	6	3	3	1	1-0	9	.231
2000— New York (N.L.)	0	1	.000	8.44	1.69	1	1	0	0	0	0-0	5.1	6	5	5	1	3-1	2	.273
2003— Atlanta (N.L.)	0	1	.000	4.26	1.34	2	2	0	0	0	0-0	12.2	11	6	6	2	6-0	16	.224
2004— Atlanta (N.L.)	0	0	...	2.45	1.09	2	1	0	0	0	0-0	7.1	4	2	2	2	4-0	6	.174
Division series totals (6 years)	0	3	.000	4.81	1.26	8	7	0	0	0	0-0	43.0	31	23	23	7	23-1	37	.201

CHAMPIONSHIP SERIES RECORD

Year Team (League)	W	L	Pct.	ERA	WHIP	G	GS	CG	ShO	Hld.	Sv.-Opp.	IP	H	R	ER	HR	BB-IBB	SO	Avg.
2000— New York (N.L.)	2	0	1.000	0.00	0.81	2	2	1	1	0	0-0	16.0	9	0	0	0	4-0	12	.158

WORLD SERIES RECORD

Year Team (League)	W	L	Pct.	ERA	WHIP	G	GS	CG	ShO	Hld.	Sv.-Opp.	IP	H	R	ER	HR	BB-IBB	SO	Avg.
2000— New York (N.L.)	0	1	.000	6.00	2.17	1	1	0	0	0	0-0	6.0	8	4	4	1	5-1	4	.320

ALL-STAR GAME RECORD

Year Team (League)	W	L	Pct.	ERA	WHIP	G	GS	CG	ShO	Hld.	Sv.-Opp.	IP	H	R	ER	HR	BB-IBB	SO	Avg.
All-Star Game totals (2 years)	0	0	...	0.00	0.60	2	0	0	0	0	0-0	1.2	1	1	0	0	0-0	0	.143

HAMULACK, TIM — P

PERSONAL: Born November 14, 1976, in Ithaca, N.Y. ... 6-4/220. ... Throws left, bats left. ... Full name: Timothy William Alexander Hamulack. ... Junior college: Montgomery (Md.) C.C. **TRANSACTIONS/CAREER NOTES:** Selected by Houston Astros organization in 32nd round of 1995 free-agent draft. ... Selected by Kansas City Royals organization from Astros organization in Rule 5 minor league draft (December 11, 2000). ...Traded by Royals to Florida Marlins for cash (December 12, 2000). ... Signed as a free agent by Seattle Mariners organization (November 4, 2002). ... Signed as a free agent by Boston Red Sox (November 19, 2003). ... Signed as a free agent by New York Mets organization (February 1, 2005). ... Traded by Mets with P Jae Seo to Los Angeles Dodgers for Ps Duaner Sanchez and Steve Schmoll (January 4, 2006).
CAREER HITTING: 0-for-1 (.000), 0 R, 0 2B, 0 3B, 0 RBI.

Year Team (League)	W	L	Pct.	ERA	WHIP	G	GS	CG	ShO	Hld.	Sv.-Opp.	IP	H	R	ER	HR	BB-IBB	SO	Avg.
1996— GC Astros (GCL)	4	1	.800	2.33	1.33	22	0	0	0		2-...	27.0	23	9	7	1	13-1	24	.230
1997— GC Astros (GCL)	1	1	.500	4.20	1.64	23	0	0	0		9-...	45.0	56	31	21	3	18-0	38	.311
1998— Quad City (Midw.)	0	2	.000	3.24	1.44	52	0	0	0		0-...	58.1	58	23	21	3	26-3	52	.265
1999— Michigan (Midw.)	3	0	1.000	3.04	1.28	25	0	0	0		0-...	26.2	23	9	9	0	11-0	32	.235
2000— Kissimmee (Fla. St.)	3	1	.750	4.98	1.57	41	0	0	0		1-...	56.0	67	37	31	3	21-1	54	.296
2001— Brevard County (FSL)	2	4	.333	3.15	1.46	40	0	0	0		1-...	71.1	83	42	25	3	21-1	39	.287
2002— Portland (East.)	8	4	.667	2.88	1.31	38	1	0	0		6-...	78.0	73	32	25	6	29-5	53	.252
2003— Tacoma (PCL)	1	0	1.000	3.86	1.71	10	0	0	0		1-...	14.0	16	6	6	1	8-0	12	.302
—San Antonio (Texas)	0	1	.000	2.09	0.99	40	0	0	0		1-...	47.1	32	13	11	0	15-2	54	.192
2004— Pawtucket (Int'l)	7	4	.636	6.98	2.12	35	0	0	0		0-...	29.2	44	26	23	4	19-2	25	.336
—Portland (East.)	2	0	1.000	3.52	1.50	7	0	0	0		0-...	15.1	16	6	6	0	7-0	16	.258
2005— Binghamton (East.)	2	2	.500	1.26	0.91	21	0	0	0	1	6-7	28.2	20	7	4	0	6-1	27	.187
—Norfolk (Int'l)	3	1	.750	1.02	0.82	28	0	0	0	4	6-8	35.1	20	5	4	1	9-1	34	.167
—New York (N.L.)	0	0	...	23.14	3.43	6	0	0	0	1	0-0	2.1	7	6	6	3	1-1	2	.583
2006— Las Vegas (PCL)	0	1	.000	1.42	1.47	28	0	0	0	2	3-4	38.0	30	9	6	1	26-0	44	.222
—Los Angeles (N.L.)	0	3	.000	6.35	1.71	33	0	0	0	4	0-0	34.0	36	28	24	7	22-1	34	.265
Major League totals (2 years)	0	3	.000	7.43	1.82	39	0	0	0	5	0-0	36.1	43	34	30	10	23-2	36	.291

2006 LEFTY-RIGHTY SPLITS

vs.	Avg.	AB	H	2B	3B	HR	RBI	BB	SO	OBP	Slg.	vs.	Avg.	AB	H	2B	3B	HR	RBI	BB	SO	OBP	Slg.
L	.302	43	13	4	0	4	14	8	16	.434	.674	R	.247	93	23	4	0	3	14	14	18	.346	.387

HANCOCK, JOSH — P

PERSONAL: Born April 11, 1978, in Cleveland, Miss. ... 6-3/205. ... Throws right, bats right. ... Full name: Joshua Morgan Hancock. ... High school: Vestavia Hills (Ala.). ... College: Auburn. **TRANSACTIONS/CAREER NOTES:** Selected by Milwaukee Brewers organization in fourth round of 1996 free-agent draft; did not sign. ... Selected by Boston Red Sox organization in fifth round of 1998 free-agent draft. ... Traded by Red Sox to Philadelphia Phillies for 1B/OF Jeremy Giambi (December 15, 2002). ... Traded by Phillies with SS Anderson Machado to Cincinnati Reds for P Todd Jones (July 30, 2004). ... On disabled list (April 2-September 1, 2005); included rehabilitation assignment to Louisville. ... Released by Reds (January 12, 2006). ... Signed by St. Louis Cardinals organization (February 22, 2006).
CAREER HITTING: 2-for-23 (.087), 1 R, 0 2B, 0 3B, 0 HR, 1 RBI.

Year Team (League)	W	L	Pct.	ERA	WHIP	G	GS	CG	ShO	Hld.	Sv.-Opp.	IP	H	R	ER	HR	BB-IBB	SO	Avg.
1998— GC Red Sox (GCL)	1	1	.500	3.38	0.90	5	1	0	0		0-...	13.1	9	5	5	1	3-0	21	.196
—Lowell (NY-Penn)	0	1	.000	2.25	2.25	1	1	0	0		0-...	4.0	5	2	1	0	4-0	4	.333
1999— Augusta (S. Atl.)	6	8	.429	3.80	1.43	25	25	0	0		0-...	139.2	154	79	59	12	46-0	106	.279
2000— Sarasota (Fla. St.)	5	10	.333	4.45	1.40	26	24	1	0		0-...	143.2	164	89	71	9	37-0	95	.286
2001— Trenton (East.)	8	6	.571	3.65	1.34	24	24	0	0		0-...	130.2	138	60	53	8	37-0	119	.273
2002— Trenton (East.)	3	4	.429	3.61	1.18	15	14	2	0		1-...	84.2	82	40	34	9	18-0	69	.250
—Pawtucket (Int'l)	4	2	.667	3.45	1.47	8	8	0	0		0-...	44.1	39	20	17	2	26-0	29	.235
—Boston (A.L.)	0	1	.000	3.68	0.95	3	1	0	0		0-0	7.1	5	3	3	1	2-0	6	.200
2003— Scran./W.B. (I.L.)	10	9	.526	3.86	1.20	28	27	2	2		0-0	165.2	147	78	71	14	46-1	122	.238
—Philadelphia (N.L.)	0	0	...	3.00	0.67	2	0	0	0		0-0	3.0	2	1	1	0	0-0	4	.182
2004— Scran./W.B. (I.L.)	8	7	.533	4.01	1.19	18	18	1	0		0-0	107.2	107	52	48	10	21-1	65	.263
—Philadelphia (N.L.)	0	1	.000	9.00	1.78	4	2	0	0		0-0	9.0	13	9	9	3	3-0	5	.333
—Cincinnati (N.L.)	5	1	.833	4.45	1.55	12	9	0	0		0-0	54.2	60	34	27	14	25-2	31	.273
2005— Louisville (Int'l)	1	2	.333	5.93	1.73	11	6	0	0		0-0	44.0	59	33	29	5	17-0	38	.328
—Cincinnati (N.L.)	1	0	1.000	1.93	0.86	11	0	0	0		0-0	14.0	11	4	3	1	1-0	5	.208
2006— St. Louis (N.L.)	3	3	.500	4.09	1.21	62	0	0	0		1-3	77.0	70	37	35	9	23-2	50	.241
American League totals (1 year)	0	1	.000	3.68	0.95	3	1	0	0		0-0	7.1	5	3	3	1	2-0	6	.200
National League totals (4 years)	9	5	.643	4.28	1.32	91	11	0	0		1-3	157.2	156	85	75	27	52-4	95	.254
Major League totals (5 years)	9	6	.600	4.25	1.30	94	12	0	0	5	1-3	165.0	161	88	78	28	54-4	101	.252

H

DIVISION SERIES RECORD

Year Team (League)	W	L	Pct.	ERA	WHIP	G	GS	CG	ShO	Hld.	Sv.-Opp.	IP	H	R	ER	HR	BB-IBB	SO	Avg.
2006— St. Louis (N.L.)	0	0	...	0.00	1.80	1	0	0	0	...	0-0	1.2	1	0	0	0	2-0	1	.167

CHAMPIONSHIP SERIES RECORD

Year Team (League)	W	L	Pct.	ERA	WHIP	G	GS	CG	ShO	Hld.	Sv.-Opp.	IP	H	R	ER	HR	BB-IBB	SO	Avg.
2006— St. Louis (N.L.)	0	0	...	99.99	21.00	2	0	0	0	...	0-0	0.1	4	6	6	0	3-0	1	.800

2006 LEFTY-RIGHTY SPLITS

vs.	Avg.	AB	H	2B	3B	HR	RBI	BB	SO	OBP	Slg.	vs.	Avg.	AB	H	2B	3B	HR	RBI	BB	SO	OBP	Slg.
L	.239	117	28	10	1	4	20	8	15	.286	.444	R	.241	174	42	11	1	5	25	15	35	.301	.402

HANNAHAN, JACK — 1B/3B

PERSONAL: Born March 4, 1980, in St. Paul, Minn. ... Bats left, throws right. ... Full name: John Joseph Hannahan. ... College: Minnesota. **TRANSACTIONS/CAREER NOTES:** Selected by Detroit Tigers organization in third round of 2001 free-agent draft.
2006 GAMES PLAYED BY POSITION (MLB): DH—1, 1B—1.

Year Team (League)	Pos.	G	AB	R	H	2B	3B	HR	RBI	BB	SO	HBP	GDP	SB-CS	Avg.	OBP	SLG	OPS	E	FIELDING Avg.
2001— Oneonta (NYP)		14	55	11	16	4	1	0	8	5	7	0	2	2-1	.291	.333	.400	.733	2	...
— W. Mich. (Mid.)		46	170	24	54	11	0	1	27	26	39	1	5	4-2	.318	.409	.400	.809	9	...
2002— Lakeland (Fla. St.)		66	246	28	67	11	1	6	42	36	44	1	2	9-3	.272	.362	.398	.760	12	...
— Erie (East.)		65	226	17	54	12	1	3	20	21	50	2	7	2-1	.239	.309	.341	.650	9	...
2003— Erie (East.)		135	471	64	121	18	0	9	45	48	78	3	13	2-0	.257	.328	.352	.680	34	...
2004— Erie (East.)		108	374	48	102	21	1	8	39	53	60	2	9	7-3	.273	.365	.398	.763	15	...
2005— Erie (East.)	3B-DH	7	22	1	3	0	0	0	1	4	8	0	0	0-0	.136	.269	.136	.406	1	.967
— Toledo (Int'l)	3B-DH-1B																			
	2B	68	238	31	64	15	0	4	28	25	58	3	5	6-3	.269	.342	.382	.724	9	.955
2006— Toledo (Int'l)		119	415	59	117	27	0	9	62	61	114	8	5	9-6	.282	.379	.412	.791	16	.972
— Detroit (A.L.)	1B-DH	3	9	0	0	0	0	0	1	1	0	0	0	0-0	.000	.100	.000	.100	0	1.000
Major League totals (1 year)		3	9	0	0	0	0	0	1	1	0	0	0	0-0	.000	.100	.000	.100	0	1.000

2006 LEFTY-RIGHTY SPLITS

vs.	Avg.	AB	H	2B	3B	HR	RBI	BB	SO	OBP	Slg.	vs.	Avg.	AB	H	2B	3B	HR	RBI	BB	SO	OBP	Slg.
L	.000	1	0	0	0	0	0	0	0	.000	.000	R	.000	8	0	0	0	0	1	1	0	.111	.000

HANSACK, DEVERN — P

PERSONAL: Born February 5, 1978, in Pearl Lagoon, Nicaragua. ... 6-2/180. ... Throws right, bats right. ... Full name: Devern M. Hansack. .
TRANSACTIONS/CAREER NOTES: Signed as a non-drafted free agent by Houston Astros organization (October 21, 1999). ... Released by Astros (March 29, 2004). ... Signed by Boston Red Sox organization (December 9, 2005).
CAREER HITTING: 0-for-0 (.000), 0 R, 0 2B, 0 3B, 0 HR, 0 RBI.

Year Team (League)	W	L	Pct.	ERA	WHIP	G	GS	CG	ShO	Hld.	Sv.-Opp.	IP	H	R	ER	HR	BB-IBB	SO	Avg.
2000— Venoco (VSL)	1	2	.333	2.67	0.74	8	4	1	0	...	2-...	27.0	14	9	8	0	6-0	20	.154
2001— Venoco (VSL)	2	3	.400	4.98	1.43	13	0	0	0	...	2-...	21.2	23	14	12	0	8-0	13	...
2002— Tri-City (N.Y.-Penn.)	3	4	.429	3.60	1.22	12	10	0	0	...	0-...	50.0	44	21	20	6	17-0	37	.240
2003— Lexington (S. Atl.)	10	6	.625	4.52	1.44	22	16	0	0	...	0-...	91.2	100	53	46	10	32-0	76	.279
2004—	Did not play																		
2005—	Did not play																		
2006— Portland (East.)	8	7	.533	3.26	1.19	31	18	0	0	...	1-1	132.1	122	55	48	14	36-4	124	.242
— Boston (A.L.)	1	1	.500	2.70	0.70	2	2	1	1	0	0-0	10.0	6	3	3	2	1-0	8	.171
Major League totals (1 year)	1	1	.500	2.70	0.70	2	2	1	1	0	0-0	10.0	6	3	3	2	1-0	8	.171

2006 LEFTY-RIGHTY SPLITS

vs.	Avg.	AB	H	2B	3B	HR	RBI	BB	SO	OBP	Slg.	vs.	Avg.	AB	H	2B	3B	HR	RBI	BB	SO	OBP	Slg.
L	.235	17	4	1	0	1	1	0	3	.235	.471	R	.111	18	2	0	0	1	1	1	5	.158	.278

HANSEN, CRAIG — P

PERSONAL: Born November 15, 1983, in Glen Cove, N.Y. ... 6-6/210. ... Throws right, bats right. ... Full name: Craig R. Hansen. ... College: St. John's.
TRANSACTIONS/CAREER NOTES: Selected by the Boston Red Sox organization in the first round (26th pick overall) of 2005 free-agent draft.
CAREER HITTING: 0-for-0 (.000), 0 R, 0 2B, 0 3B, 0 HR, 0 RBI.

Year Team (League)	W	L	Pct.	ERA	WHIP	G	GS	CG	ShO	Hld.	Sv.-Opp.	IP	H	R	ER	HR	BB-IBB	SO	Avg.
2005— GC Red Sox (GCL)	1	0	1.000	0.00	0.67	2	1	0	0	0	0-0	3.0	2	0	0	0	0-0	4	.182
— Portland (East.)	0	0	...	0.00	1.03	8	0	0	0	0	1-1	9.2	9	0	0	0	1-0	10	.243
— Boston (A.L.)	0	0	...	6.00	2.33	4	0	0	0	0	0-1	3.0	6	2	2	1	1-0	3	.429
2006— Pawtucket (Int'l)	1	2	.333	2.75	1.39	14	4	0	0	2	0-0	36.0	31	14	11	0	19-0	26	.238
— Portland (East.)	1	0	1.000	0.82	0.73	5	0	0	0	1	0-0	11.0	4	1	1	0	4-0	12	.105
— Boston (A.L.)	2	2	.500	6.63	1.61	38	0	0	0	8	0-2	38.0	46	32	28	5	15-0	30	.305
Major League totals (2 years)	2	2	.500	6.59	1.66	42	0	0	0	8	0-3	41.0	52	34	30	6	16-0	33	.315

2006 LEFTY-RIGHTY SPLITS

vs.	Avg.	AB	H	2B	3B	HR	RBI	BB	SO	OBP	Slg.	vs.	Avg.	AB	H	2B	3B	HR	RBI	BB	SO	OBP	Slg.
L	.344	64	22	5	0	3	12	3	10	.371	.563	R	.276	87	24	5	0	2	12	12	20	.379	.402

HARANG, AARON — P

PERSONAL: Born May 9, 1978, in San Diego. ... 6-7/240. ... Throws right, bats right. ... Full name: Aaron Michael Harang. ... Name pronounced: ha-RANG. ... High school: Patrick Henry (San Diego). ... College: San Diego State. **TRANSACTIONS/CAREER NOTES:** Selected by Boston Red Sox organization in 22nd round of 1996 free-agent draft; did not sign. ... Selected by Texas Rangers organization in sixth round of 1999 free-agent draft. ... Traded by Rangers with P Ryan Cullen to Oakland Athletics for 2B Randy Velarde (December 12, 2000). ... Traded by Athletics with Ps Joe Valentine and Jeff Bruksch to Cincinnati Reds for OF Jose Guillen (July 30, 2003). ... On disabled list (June 2-26, 2004); included rehabilitation assignment to Louisville.
CAREER HITTING: 15-for-226 (.066), 3 R, 1 2B, 0 3B, 0 HR, 5 RBI.

Year Team (League)	W	L	Pct.	ERA	WHIP	G	GS	CG	ShO	Hld.	Sv.-Opp.	IP	H	R	ER	HR	BB-IBB	SO	Avg.
1999— Pulaski (Appalachian)	9	2	.818	2.30	1.03	15	10	1	1	...	1-...	78.1	64	22	20	5	17-1	87	.226
2000— Charlotte (Fla. St.)	13	5	.722	3.32	1.13	28	27	3	2	...	0-...	157.0	128	68	58	10	50-0	136	.220
2001— Midland (Texas)	10	8	.556	4.14	1.40	27	27	0	0	...	0-...	150.0	173	81	69	9	37-1	112	.285
2002— Midland (Texas)	2	0	1.000	1.08	1.14	3	3	0	0	...	0-...	16.2	12	3	2	0	7-0	21	.218

H

Year Team (League)	W	L	Pct.	ERA	WHIP	G	GS	CG	ShO	Hld.	Sv.-Opp.	IP	H	R	ER	HR	BB-IBB	SO	Avg.
—Sacramento (PCL)	3	3	.500	3.26	1.29	8	8	0	0	...	0-...	38.2	41	17	14	0	9-0	39	.301
—Oakland (A.L.)	5	4	.556	4.83	1.57	16	15	0	0	0	0-0	78.1	78	44	42	7	45-2	64	.261
2003—Oakland (A.L.)	1	3	.250	5.34	1.65	7	6	0	0	0	0-0	30.1	41	19	18	5	9-0	16	.331
—Sacramento (PCL)	8	2	.800	2.71	1.10	12	12	0	0	0	0-...	69.2	62	24	21	5	17-0	60	.234
—Louisville (Int'l)	0	1	.000	15.00	2.30	1	1	0	0	...	0-...	3.0	5	5	5	1	2-0	4	.357
—Cincinnati (N.L.)	4	3	.571	5.28	1.26	9	9	0	0	0	0-0	46.0	48	28	27	6	10-0	26	.271
2004—Louisville (Int'l)	0	1	.000	12.00	4.00	1	1	0	0	...	0-...	3.0	9	8	4	1	3-0	3	.529
—Cincinnati (N.L.)	10	9	.526	4.86	1.43	28	28	1	1	0	0-0	161.0	177	90	87	26	53-5	125	.280
2005—Cincinnati (N.L.)	11	13	.458	3.83	1.27	32	32	1	0	0	0-0	211.2	217	93	90	22	51-3	163	.267
2006—Cincinnati (N.L.)	• 16	11	.593	3.76	1.27	36	•35	* 6	2	0	0-0	234.1	242	109	98	28	56-8	* 216	.269
American League totals (2 years)	6	7	.462	4.97	1.59	23	21	0	0	0	0-0	108.2	119	63	60	12	54-2	80	.281
National League totals (4 years)	41	36	.532	4.16	1.31	105	104	8	3	0	0-0	653.0	684	320	302	82	170-16	530	.271
Major League totals (5 years)	47	43	.522	4.28	1.35	128	125	8	3	.0	0-0	761.2	803	383	362	94	224-18	610	.273

2006 LEFTY-RIGHTY SPLITS

vs.	Avg.	AB	H	2B	3B	HR	RBI	BB	SO	OBP	Slg.	vs.	Avg.	AB	H	2B	3B	HR	RBI	BB	SO	OBP	Slg.
L	.267	374	100	25	5	10	39	27	107	.318	.441	R	.270	526	142	29	0	18	59	29	109	.313	.428

HARDEN, RICH — P

PERSONAL: Born November 30, 1981, in Victoria, British Columbia. ... 6-1/180. ... Throws right, bats left. ... Full name: James Richard Harden. ... High school: Claremont Secondary (Victoria, B.C.). ... Junior college: Central Arizona.. **TRANSACTIONS/CAREER NOTES:** Selected by Seattle Mariners organization in 38th round of 1999 free-agent draft; did not sign. ... Selected by Oakland Athletics organization in 17th round of 2000 free-agent draft. ... On disabled list (May 15-June 21, 2005); included rehabilitation assignment to Sacramento. ... On disabled list (April 28-June 4 and June 8-September 21, 2006); included rehabilitation assignment to Sacramento.

CAREER HITTING: 0-for-5 (.000), 0 R, 0 2B, 0 3B, 0 HR, 0 RBI.

Year Team (League)	W	L	Pct.	ERA	WHIP	G	GS	CG	ShO	Hld.	Sv.-Opp.	IP	H	R	ER	HR	BB-IBB	SO	Avg.
2001—Vancouver (N'west)	2	4	.333	3.39	1.14	18	14	0	0	...	0-...	74.1	47	29	28	3	38-0	100	.179
2002—Visalia (Calif.)	4	3	.571	2.93	1.08	12	12	1	0	...	0-...	67.2	49	27	22	4	24-0	85	.201
—Midland (Texas)	8	3	.727	2.95	1.39	16	16	1	0	...	0-...	85.1	67	33	28	2	52-1	102	.217
2003—Midland (Texas)	2	0	1.000	0.00	0.00	2	2	0	0	...	0-...	13.0	5	0	0	0	0-0	17	.000
—Sacramento (PCL)	9	4	.692	3.15	1.21	16	14	0	0	...	0-...	88.2	72	34	31	6	35-0	91	.226
—Oakland (A.L.)	5	4	.556	4.46	1.50	15	13	0	0	0	0-0	74.2	72	38	37	5	40-1	67	.259
2004—Oakland (A.L.)	0	0	...	5.40	1.80	1	1	0	0	0	0-0	5.0	6	3	3	0	3-0	6	.300
—Oakland (A.L.)	11	7	.611	3.99	1.33	31	31	0	0	0	0-0	189.2	171	90	84	16	81-6	167	.242
2005—Sacramento (PCL)	0	0	...	0.00	0.33	1	1	0	0	0	0-0	3.0	1	0	0	0	0-0	7	.100
—Oakland (A.L.)	10	5	.667	2.53	1.06	22	22	1	0	1	0-0	128.0	93	42	36	7	43-0	121	.201
2006—Sacramento (PCL)	0	0	...	0.00	0.50	1	1	0	0	0	0-0	2.0	1	0	0	0	0-0	3	.125
—Oakland (A.L.)	4	0	1.000	4.24	1.22	9	9	0	0	0	0-0	46.2	31	22	22	5	26-0	49	.191
Major League totals (4 years)	30	16	.652	3.67	1.27	77	77	0	0	0	0-0	439.0	367	192	179	33	190-7	404	.228

DIVISION SERIES RECORD

Year Team (League)	W	L	Pct.	ERA	WHIP	G	GS	CG	ShO	Hld.	Sv.-Opp.	IP	H	R	ER	HR	BB-IBB	SO	Avg.
2003—Oakland (A.L.)	1	1	.500	13.50	3.00	1	1	0	0	0	0-0	1.1	2	2	2	1	2-1	1	.333

CHAMPIONSHIP SERIES RECORD

Year Team (League)	W	L	Pct.	ERA	WHIP	G	GS	CG	ShO	Hld.	Sv.-Opp.	IP	H	R	ER	HR	BB-IBB	SO	Avg.
2006—Oakland (A.L.)	0	1	.000	4.76	1.76	1	1	0	0	0	0-0	5.2	5	3	3	1	5-0	4	.238

2006 LEFTY-RIGHTY SPLITS

vs.	Avg.	AB	H	2B	3B	HR	RBI	BB	SO	OBP	Slg.	vs.	Avg.	AB	H	2B	3B	HR	RBI	BB	SO	OBP	Slg.
L	.176	91	16	2	0	3	9	15	25	.287	.297	R	.211	71	15	3	0	2	8	11	24	.325	.338

HARDY, J.J. — SS

PERSONAL: Born August 19, 1982, in Tucson, Ariz. ... 6-2/181. ... Bats right, throws right. ... Full name: James Jerry Hardy. . **TRANSACTIONS/CAREER NOTES:** Selected by Milwaukee Brewers in second round of 2001 free-agent draft. ... On disabled list (May 17, 2006-remainder of season). **STATISTICAL NOTES:** Career major league grand slams: 1.

2006 GAMES PLAYED BY POSITION (MLB): SS—32.

						BATTING										FIELDING		
Year Team (League)	Pos.	G	AB	R	H	2B	3B	HR	RBI	BB	SO	HBP	GDP	SB-CS	Avg.	OBP	SLG	OPS	E	Avg.
2001—Ariz. Brewers (Ariz.)	SS	5	20	6	5	2	1	0	1	1	2	0	0	0-0	.250	.286	.450	.736	2	.931
—Ogden (Pion.)	SS	35	125	20	31	5	0	2	15	15	12	0	1	1-2	.248	.326	.336	.662	9	.948
2002—High Desert (Calif.)	SS	84	335	53	98	19	1	6	48	19	38	1	3	9-3	.293	.327	.409	.736	11	.973
—Huntsville (Sou.)	SS	38	145	34	33	7	0	1	13	9	19	0	4	1-2	.228	.269	.297	.566	10	.948
2003—Huntsville (Sou.)	SS	114	416	67	116	26	0	12	62	58	54	3	11	6-4	.279	.368	.428	.796	15	.970
2004—Indianapolis (Int'l)	SS	26	101	17	28	10	0	4	20	9	8	0	1	0-0	.277	.330	.495	.825	5	.925
2005—Milwaukee (N.L.)	SS	124	372	46	92	22	1	9	50	44	48	1	10	0-0	.247	.327	.384	.711	10	.975
2006—Milwaukee (N.L.)	SS	35	128	13	31	5	0	5	14	10	23	0	4	1-1	.242	.295	.398	.693	2	.986
Major League totals (2 years)		159	500	59	123	27	1	14	64	54	71	1	14	1-1	.246	.319	.388	.707	12	.978

2006 LEFTY-RIGHTY SPLITS

vs.	Avg.	AB	H	2B	3B	HR	RBI	BB	SO	OBP	Slg.	vs.	Avg.	AB	H	2B	3B	HR	RBI	BB	SO	OBP	Slg.
L	.294	34	10	1	0	3	6	4	6	.368	.588	R	.223	94	21	4	0	2	8	6	17	.267	.330

HAREN, DANNY — P

PERSONAL: Born September 17, 1980, in Monterey Park, Calif. ... 6-5/220. ... Throws right, bats right. ... Full name: Daniel John Haren. ... High school: Bishop (La Puente, Calif.). ... College: Pepperdine. **TRANSACTIONS/CAREER NOTES:** Selected by St. Louis Cardinals organization in second round of 2001 free-agent draft. ... Traded by Cardinals with P Kiko Calero and C Daric Barton to Oakland Athletics for P Mark Mulder (December 19, 2004). **MISCELLANEOUS NOTES:** Appeared in one game as pinch runner (2003).

CAREER HITTING: 4-for-49 (.082), 1 R, 3 2B, 0 3B, 0 HR, 3 RBI.

Year Team (League)	W	L	Pct.	ERA	WHIP	G	GS	CG	ShO	Hld.	Sv.-Opp.	IP	H	R	ER	HR	BB-IBB	SO	Avg.
2001—New Jersey (NYP)	3	3	.500	3.10	1.05	12	8	0	0	...	1-...	52.1	47	22	18	6	8-0	57	.239
2002—Peoria (Midw.)	7	3	.700	1.95	0.99	14	14	1	0	...	0-...	101.2	89	32	22	6	12-0	89	.234
—Potomac (Carol.)	3	6	.333	3.62	1.18	14	14	1	0	...	0-...	92.0	90	43	37	8	19-2	82	.252
2003—Tennessee (Sou.)	6	0	1.000	0.82	0.76	8	8	0	0	...	0-...	55.0	36	8	5	2	6-0	49	.181
—Memphis (PCL)	2	1	.667	4.93	1.27	8	8	0	0	...	0-...	45.2	50	25	25	1	8-1	35	.272
—St. Louis (N.L.)	3	7	.300	5.08	1.46	14	14	0	0	0	0-0	72.2	84	44	41	9	22-0	43	.293

H

Year Team (League)	W	L	Pct.	ERA	WHIP	G	GS	CG	ShO	Hld.	Sv.-Opp.	IP	H	R	ER	HR	BB-IBB	SO	Avg.
2004—Memphis (PCL)	11	4	.733	4.15	1.33	21	21	0	0	...	0-...	128.0	137	60	59	19	33-1	150	.276
—St. Louis (N.L.)	3	3	.500	4.50	1.35	14	5	0	0	0	0-0	46.0	45	23	23	4	17-2	32	.265
2005—Oakland (A.L.)	14	12	.538	3.73	1.22	34	34	3	0	0	0-0	217.0	212	101	90	26	53-5	163	.255
2006—Oakland (A.L.)	14	13	.519	4.12	1.21	34	•34	2	0	0	0-0	223.0	224	109	102	31	45-6	176	.258
American League totals (2 years)	28	25	.528	3.93	1.21	68	68	5	0	0	0-0	440.0	436	210	192	57	98-11	339	.257
National League totals (2 years)	6	10	.375	4.85	1.42	28	19	0	0	0	0-0	118.2	129	67	64	13	39-2	75	.282
Major League totals (4 years)	34	35	.493	4.12	1.26	96	87	5	0	0	0-0	558.2	565	277	256	70	137-13	414	.262

DIVISION SERIES RECORD

Year Team (League)	W	L	Pct.	ERA	WHIP	G	GS	CG	ShO	Hld.	Sv.-Opp.	IP	H	R	ER	HR	BB-IBB	SO	Avg.
2004—St. Louis (N.L.)	1	0	1.000	0.00	1.00	1	0	0	0	0	0-0	2.0	1	0	0	0	1-0	3	.143
2006—Oakland (A.L.)	1	0	1.000	3.00	1.67	1	1	0	0	0	0-0	6.0	9	2	2	1	1-0	2	.375
Division series totals (2 years)	2	0	1.000	2.25	1.50	2	1	0	0	0	0-0	8.0	10	2	2	1	2-0	5	.323

CHAMPIONSHIP SERIES RECORD

Year Team (League)	W	L	Pct.	ERA	WHIP	G	GS	CG	ShO	Hld.	Sv.-Opp.	IP	H	R	ER	HR	BB-IBB	SO	Avg.
2004—St. Louis (N.L.)	0	0	...	10.80	1.80	2	0	0	0	0	0-0	1.2	3	2	2	1	0-0	2	.375
2006—Oakland (A.L.)	0	0	...	5.40	1.80	1	1	0	0	0	0-0	5.0	7	3	3	1	2-0	7	.333
Champ. series totals (2 years)	0	0	...	6.75	1.80	3	1	0	0	0	0-0	6.2	10	5	5	2	2-0	9	.345

WORLD SERIES RECORD

Year Team (League)	W	L	Pct.	ERA	WHIP	G	GS	CG	ShO	Hld.	Sv.-Opp.	IP	H	R	ER	HR	BB-IBB	SO	Avg.
2004—St. Louis (N.L.)	0	0	...	0.00	1.50	2	0	0	0	0	0-0	4.2	4	0	0	0	3-0	2	.222

2006 LEFTY-RIGHTY SPLITS

vs.	Avg.	AB	H	2B	3B	HR	RBI	BB	SO	OBP	Slg.	vs.	Avg.	AB	H	2B	3B	HR	RBI	BB	SO	OBP	Slg.
L	.246	407	100	21	3	14	45	28	82	.296	.415	R	.268	462	124	22	3	17	54	17	94	.305	.439

HARPER, BRANDON — C

PERSONAL: Born April 29, 1976, in Odessa, Texas. ... Bats right, throws right. ... Full name: Brandon S. Harper. ... College: Dallas Baptist. **TRANSACTIONS/CAREER NOTES:** Selected by Florida Marlins organization in fourth round of 1997 free-agent draft. ... Signed as a free agent by Detroit Tigers organization (February 9, 2004). ... Signed as a free agent by Washington Nationals organization (December 13, 2005).

2006 GAMES PLAYED BY POSITION (MLB): C—14.

Year Team (League)	Pos.	G	AB	R	H	2B	3B	HR	RBI	BB	SO	HBP	GDP	SB-CS	Avg.	OBP	SLG	OPS	E	Avg.
1997—GC Marlins (GCL)		2	6	0	0	0	0	0	1	0	1	0	1	0-0	.000	.000	.000	.000	0	...
—Utica (N.Y.-Penn)		47	152	27	39	7	2	2	22	19	32	1	9	1-1	.257	.339	.368	.707	9	...
1998—Kane Co. (Midw.)		113	412	34	95	22	2	4	50	42	64	4	16	1-3	.231	.305	.323	.628	17	...
1999—Brevard County (FSL)		81	280	35	75	9	0	4	40	30	31	3	4	1-1	.268	.342	.343	.685	8	...
2000—GC Marlins (GCL)		8	27	8	8	1	0	0	2	7	4	0	0	0-0	.296	.441	.333	.774	0	...
—Portland (East.)		37	125	15	26	3	0	5	17	12	23	1	4	0-0	.208	.283	.352	.635	4	...
2001—Brevard County (FSL)		29	101	14	24	6	0	2	16	12	14	2	4	0-1	.238	.330	.356	.686	4	...
—Portland (East.)		76	247	21	59	13	0	3	24	27	52	5	7	0-0	.239	.323	.328	.651	2	...
2002—	Did not play																			
2003—Carolina (Southern)		67	195	18	47	12	0	2	20	24	34	2	6	2-0	.241	.327	.333	.660	3	...
2004—Toledo (Int'l)		21	58	10	11	0	0	3	7	6	10	3	2	0-1	.190	.294	.345	.639	3	...
—Erie (East.)		48	166	26	48	12	0	9	29	16	31	6	2	2-1	.289	.372	.524	.896	6	...
2005—Toledo (Int'l)	C-DH-OF-1B	81	252	33	62	14	1	6	34	28	36	7	8	4-0	.246	.334	.381	.715	2	.997
2006—New Orleans (PCL)		43	120	18	35	10	0	2	11	15	21	6	0	3-1	.292	.394	.425	.819	2	.993
—Wash. (N.L.)	C	18	41	6	12	3	0	2	6	4	4	1	1	0-0	.293	.362	.512	.874	1	.987
Major League totals (1 year)		18	41	6	12	3	0	2	6	4	4	1	1	0-0	.293	.362	.512	.874	1	.987

2006 LEFTY-RIGHTY SPLITS

vs.	Avg.	AB	H	2B	3B	HR	RBI	BB	SO	OBP	Slg.	vs.	Avg.	AB	H	2B	3B	HR	RBI	BB	SO	OBP	Slg.
L	.258	31	8	2	0	2	6	3	4	.333	.516	R	.400	10	4	1	0	0	0	1	0	.455	.500

HARPER, TRAVIS — P

PERSONAL: Born May 21, 1976, in Harrisonburg, Va. ... 6-4/192. ... Throws right, bats left. ... Full name: Travis Boyd Harper. ... High school: Circleville (W. Va.). ... College: James Madison (Va.). **TRANSACTIONS/CAREER NOTES:** Selected by New York Mets organization in 14th round of 1994 free-agent draft; did not sign. ... Selected by Boston Red Sox organization in third round of 1997 free-agent draft. ... Contract with Red Sox voided due to pre-existing injury (October 29, 1997). ... Signed by Tampa Bay Devil Rays organization (June 29, 1998). ... On disabled list (August 3, 2006-remainder of season).

CAREER HITTING: 0-for-1 (.000), 0 R, 0 2B, 0 3B, 0 HR, 0 RBI.

Year Team (League)	W	L	Pct.	ERA	WHIP	G	GS	CG	ShO	Hld.	Sv.-Opp.	IP	H	R	ER	HR	BB-IBB	SO	Avg.
1998—Hudson Valley (NYP)	6	2	.750	1.92	1.03	13	10	0	0	...	0-...	56.1	38	14	12	2	20-0	81	.192
1999—St. Pete. (FSL)	5	4	.556	3.43	1.29	14	14	0	0	...	0-...	81.1	82	36	31	4	23-0	79	.265
—Orlando (South.)	6	3	.667	5.38	1.38	14	14	1	1	...	0-...	72.0	73	45	43	10	26-0	68	.263
2000—St. Pete. (FSL)	3	1	.750	2.63	1.17	9	9	0	0	...	0-...	51.1	49	19	15	1	11-0	33	.255
—Durham (Int'l)	7	4	.636	4.24	1.19	17	17	0	0	...	0-...	104.0	98	53	49	15	26-1	48	.246
—Tampa Bay (A.L.)	1	2	.333	4.78	1.41	6	5	1	1	...	0-0	32.0	30	17	17	5	15-0	14	.244
2001—Tampa Bay (A.L.)	0	2	.000	7.71	2.57	2	2	0	0	...	0-0	7.0	15	11	6	5	3-0	2	.455
—Durham (Int'l)	12	6	.667	3.70	1.14	25	25	1	1	...	0-...	155.2	140	70	64	25	38-0	115	.241
2002—Tampa Bay (A.L.)	1	2	.333	6.98	1.76	4	4	0	0	...	0-...	19.1	31	15	15	5	3-0	17	.289
—Durham (Int'l)	5	9	.357	5.46	1.49	37	7	0	0	...	1-2	85.2	101	54	52	14	27-3	60	.289
2003—Tampa Bay (A.L.)	4	8	.333	3.77	1.26	61	0	0	0	15	1-6	93.0	86	45	39	9	31-8	64	.252
2004—Durham (Int'l)	1	0	1.000	3.52	1.30	2	1	0	0	...	0-...	7.2	10	3	3	1	0-0	4	.294
—Tampa Bay (A.L.)	6	2	.750	3.89	1.17	52	0	0	0	9	0-1	78.2	69	37	34	8	23-3	59	.234
2005—Tampa Bay (A.L.)	4	6	.400	6.75	1.53	52	0	0	0	11	0-3	73.1	88	57	55	14	24-9	40	.304
2006—Tampa Bay (A.L.)	2	0	1.000	4.93	1.79	30	0	0	0	5	0-2	42.0	62	27	23	6	13-1	32	.348
Major League totals (7 years)	22	29	.431	4.94	1.43	240	14	1	1	43	2-14	411.2	451	248	226	61	136-24	271	.280

2006 LEFTY-RIGHTY SPLITS

vs.	Avg.	AB	H	2B	3B	HR	RBI	BB	SO	OBP	Slg.	vs.	Avg.	AB	H	2B	3B	HR	RBI	BB	SO	OBP	Slg.
L	.400	60	24	6	0	3	10	4	12	.438	.650	R	.322	118	38	9	1	3	20	9	20	.377	.492

H

HARRIS, BRENDAN — IF

PERSONAL: Born August 26, 1980, in Albany, N.Y. ... 6-1/200. ... Bats right, throws right. ... Full name: Brendan Michael Harris. ... High school: Queensbury (N.Y.). ... College: William & Mary. **TRANSACTIONS/CAREER NOTES:** Selected by Chicago Cubs organization in fifth round of 2001 free-agent draft. ... Traded by Cubs with SS Alex S. Gonzalez and P Francis Beltran to Montreal Expos as part of four-team deal in which Cubs acquired SS Nomar Garciaparra and OF Matt Murton from Boston Red Sox, Red Sox acquired SS Orlando Cabrera from Expos and 1B Doug Mientkiewicz from Twins, and Twins acquired P Justin Jones from Cubs (July 31, 2004). ... Expos franchise transferred to Washington, D.C., and renamed Washington Nationals for 2005 season (December 3, 2004). ... Traded by Nationals with Ps Gary Majewski, Bill Bray and Daryl Thompson and SS Royce Clayton to Cincinnati Reds for OF Austin Kearns, SS Felipe Lopez and P Ryan Wagner (July 13, 2006).

2006 GAMES PLAYED BY POSITION (MLB): 2B—7, SS—5, 3B—3.

Year	Team (League)	Pos.	G	AB	R	H	2B	3B	HR	RBI	BB	SO	HBP	GDP	SB-CS	Avg.	OBP	SLG	OPS	E	Avg.
2001—	Lansing (Midw.)	2B-3B-SS	32	113	25	31	5	1	4	22	17	26	2	4	5-1	.274	.370	.442	.813	4	.966
2002—	Daytona (Fla. St.)	3B-2B	110	425	82	140	35	6	13	54	43	57	4	7	16-4	.329	.395	.532	.926	16	.965
—	West Tenn (Sou.)	3B-2B	13	53	8	17	4	1	2	11	2	5	0	1	1-1	.321	.345	.547	.893	0	1.000
2003—	West Tenn (Sou.)	3B-2B-SS	120	435	56	122	34	7	5	52	51	72	8	10	6-7	.280	.364	.425	.789	17	.939
2004—	Chicago (N.L.)	3B	3	9	0	2	1	0	0	1	1	1	0	0	0-0	.222	.300	.333	.633	1	.889
—	Iowa (PCL)	2B-SS-3B																			
		DH	69	254	48	79	21	1	11	35	16	40	1	8	0-2	.311	.353	.531	.882	5	.983
—	Edmonton (PCL)	3B	35	130	20	35	6	0	6	24	10	21	1	4	0-0	.269	.317	.454	.811	5	.943
—	Montreal (N.L.)	2B-3B	20	50	4	8	2	0	1	2	2	11	1	0	0-0	.160	.208	.260	.468	2	.952
2005—	Wash. (N.L.)	2B-3B	4	9	1	3	1	0	1	3	0	0	1	2	0-0	.333	.400	.778	1.178	0	1.000
—	New Orleans (PCL)	2B-3B-OF	127*	470	67	127	22	4	13	81	40	77	3	12	9-5	.270	.329	.417	.746	15	.972
2006—	New Orleans (PCL)		59	219	37	62	14	0	5	32	26	56	9	5	3-2	.283	.379	.416	.794	9	.956
—	Wash. (N.L.)	SS-2B-3B	17	32	3	8	2	0	0	2	3	3	1	1	0-0	.250	.333	.313	.646	1	.964
—	Louisville (Int'l)		43	148	22	48	14	1	5	28	14	29	1	4	2-0	.324	.384	.534	.918	5	.958
—	Cincinnati (N.L.)	2B	8	10	2	2	0	0	1	1	1	4	0	1	0-0	.200	.273	.500	.773	0	1.000
Major League totals (3 years)			52	110	10	23	6	0	3	9	7	19	3	4	0-0	.209	.275	.345	.620	4	.959

2006 LEFTY-RIGHTY SPLITS

vs.	Avg.	AB	H	2B	3B	HR	RBI	BB	SO	OBP	Slg.	vs.	Avg.	AB	H	2B	3B	HR	RBI	BB	SO	OBP	Slg.
L	.313	16	5	1	0	1	2	3	3	.421	.563	R	.192	26	5	1	0	0	1	1	4	.250	.231

HARRIS, JEFF — P

PERSONAL: Born July 4, 1974, in Alameda, Calif. ... 6-1/190. ... Throws right, bats right. ... Full name: Jeffrey Austin Harris. ... College: San Francisco. **TRANSACTIONS/CAREER NOTES:** Selected by Minnesota Twins organization in 28th round of 1995 free-agent draft. ... Released by Twins (January 11, 2001). ... Signed by Chico of the independent Western league (May 2002). ... Signed by Quebec of the independent Northeast league (May 2003). ... Signed by Aguascalientes of the Mexican league (April 2004). ... Signed by Quebec (May 2004). ... Signed as a free agent by Seattle Mariners organization (June 4, 2004). ... Released by Mariners (July 14, 2006).

CAREER HITTING: 0-for-0 (.000), 0 R, 0 2B, 0 3B, 0 HR, 0 RBI.

Year	Team (League)	W	L	Pct.	ERA	WHIP	G	GS	CG	ShO	Hld.	Sv.-Opp.	IP	H	R	ER	HR	BB-IBB	SO	Avg.
1995—	Elizabethton (App.)	1	3	.250	3.82	1.67	21	0	0	0	...	0-...	33.0	42	15	14	2	13-1	27	.309
1996—	Fort Wayne (Midw.)	8	3	.727	3.11	1.37	42	0	0	0	...	3-...	89.2	90	35	31	4	33-1	85	.266
1997—	Fort Myers (FSL)	2	4	.333	2.14	1.07	24	0	0	0	...	1-...	42.0	30	11	10	4	15-2	32	.207
—	New Britain (East.)	2	1	.667	2.34	1.09	28	0	0	0	...	3-...	42.1	30	15	11	2	16-0	44	.199
1998—	New Britain (East.)	1	0	1.000	1.66	0.68	26	0	0	0	...	5-...	38.0	21	7	7	3	5-0	40	.160
—	Salt Lake (PCL)	8	0	1.000	5.91	1.78	25	0	0	0	...	3-...	32.0	38	24	21	4	19-4	24	.309
1999—	Salt Lake (PCL)	4	3	.571	6.90	1.91	36	0	0	0	...	0-...	45.2	61	38	35	7	26-1	20	.332
—	New Britain (East.)	3	1	.750	1.48	1.44	20	0	0	0	...	0-...	24.1	21	5	4	0	14-2	12	.239
2000—	New Britain (East.)	2	0	1.000	4.82	1.61	24	0	0	0	...	0-...	28.0	35	17	15	5	10-0	28	.313
2001—	Chico (West.)	11	7	.611	3.94	1.46	21	20	2	0	...	0-...	130.1	144	78	57	11	46-3	99	.277
2002—	Chico (West.)	9	5	.643	2.85	1.11	20	19	3	1	...	0-...	135.2	120	64	43	11	31-2	109	.232
2003—	Quebec (Northeast)	9	4	.692	2.51	1.00	18	18	3	2	...	0-...	129.1	107	42	36	6	22-0	119	.226
2004—	Aguascal. (Mex.)	0	0	...	6.23	2.08	5	0	0	0	...	2-...	4.1	3	3	3	0	6-0	2	.200
—	Tacoma (PCL)	5	3	.625	4.34	1.15	26	8	1	1	...	1-...	74.2	60	37	36	6	26-0	53	.223
—	Quebec (Northeast)	0	0	...	0.75	1.08	2	2	0	0	...	0-...	12.0	9	1	1	0	4-1	12	.214
2005—	San Antonio (Texas)	5	0	1.000	0.96	1.20	11	2	0	0	...	0-1	34.1	25	9	8	4	8-1	31	.200
—	Tacoma (PCL)	5	2	.714	2.78	0.99	16	9	0	0	2	1-1	68.0	50	22	21	8	17-0	56	.207
—	Seattle (A.L.)	2	5	.286	4.19	1.27	11	8	0	0	0	0-0	53.2	48	27	25	9	20-2	25	.238
2006—	Ariz. Mariners (Ariz.)	0	0	...	0.00	1.00	4	2	0	0	0	0-0	6.0	6	0	0	0	0-0	6	.250
—	Tacoma (PCL)	0	3	.000	5.52	1.61	15	4	0	0	3	0-0	31.0	43	22	19	6	7-0	13	.319
—	Seattle (A.L.)	0	0	...	5.40	0.90	3	0	0	0	0	0-0	3.1	3	2	2	0	0-0	1	.250
Major League totals (2 years)		2	5	.286	4.26	1.25	14	8	0	0	0	0-0	57.0	51	29	27	9	20-2	26	.238

2006 LEFTY-RIGHTY SPLITS

vs.	Avg.	AB	H	2B	3B	HR	RBI	BB	SO	OBP	Slg.	vs.	Avg.	AB	H	2B	3B	HR	RBI	BB	SO	OBP	Slg.
L	.000	4	0	0	0	0	0	0	0	.000	.000	R	.375	8	3	1	0	0	0	0	1	.375	.500

HARRIS, WILLIE — OF/2B

PERSONAL: Born June 22, 1978, in Cairo, Ga. ... 5-9/170. ... Bats left, throws right. ... Full name: William Charles Harris. ... High school: Cairo (Ga.). ... College: Kennesaw State. ... Nephew of Ernest Riles, infielder with five major league teams (1985-1993). **TRANSACTIONS/CAREER NOTES:** Selected by Pittsburgh Pirates organization in 28th round of 1996 free-agent draft; did not sign. ... Selected by Baltimore Orioles organization in 24th round of 1999 free-agent draft. ... Traded by Orioles to Chicago White Sox for OF Chris Singleton (January 29, 2002). ... On disabled list (May 22-June 16, 2003); included rehabilitation assignment to Charlotte.

2006 GAMES PLAYED BY POSITION (MLB): OF—36, 2B—1.

Year	Team (League)	Pos.	G	AB	R	H	2B	3B	HR	RBI	BB	SO	HBP	GDP	SB-CS	Avg.	OBP	SLG	OPS	E	Avg.
1999—	Bluefield (Appal.)	2B	5	22	3	6	1	0	0	3	4	2	0	1	1-0	.273	.370	.318	.689	1	.966
—	Delmarva (S. Atl.)	2B-OF	66	272	42	72	13	3	2	32	20	41	1	4	11-11	.265	.313	.357	.670	11	.965
2000—	Delmarva (S. Atl.)	2B-OF-SS	133	474	106	150	27	10	6	60	89	89	9	3	38-15	.316	.396	.411	.807	19	.968
2001—	Bowie (East.)	2B-OF	133	525	83	160	27	4	9	49	46	71	5	6	54-16	.305	.364	.423	.787	14	.974
—	Baltimore (A.L.)	OF	9	24	3	3	1	0	0	0	0	7	0	0	0-0	.125	.125	.167	.292	0	1.000
2002—	Charlotte (Int'l)	2B-OF	89	360	54	102	16	5	5	33	33	61	2	4	32-14	.283	.345	.397	.742	6	.986
—	Chicago (A.L.)	2B-OF	49	163	14	38	4	0	2	12	9	21	0	3	8-0	.233	.270	.294	.565	3	.986
2003—	Charlotte (Int'l)	2B-OF	28	100	23	38	6	1	6	13	17	20	0	0	9-3	.380	.470	.640	1.110	0	1.000
—	Chicago (A.L.)	OF-2B	79	137	19	28	3	1	0	5	10	28	0	4	12-2	.204	.259	.241	.499	2	.984
2004—	Chicago (A.L.)	2B-OF-DH	129	409	68	107	15	4	2	27	51	79	1	4	19-7	.262	.343	.323	.665	5	.989

Year	Team (League)	Pos.	G	AB	R	H	2B	3B	HR	RBI	BB	SO	HBP	GDP	SB-CS	Avg.	OBP	SLG	OPS	E	Avg.
2005— Charlotte (Int'l)	2B	28	109	21	29	11	1	1	10	16	27	0	0	10-2	.266	.360	.413	.773	3	.977
— Chicago (A.L.)	2B-DH-SS	56	121	17	31	2	1	1	8	13	25	1	1	10-3	.256	.333	.314	.647	2	.986
2006— Pawtucket (Int'l)		60	218	32	48	6	1	8	17	29	56	3	4	11-3	.220	.319	.367	.686	9	.953
— Boston (A.L.)	OF-2B	47	45	17	7	2	0	0	4	4	11	2	0	6-3	.156	.250	.200	.450	1	1.000
Major League totals (6 years)		369	899	138	214	27	4	5	53	87	171	4	9	55-15	.238	.306	.294	.600	12	.988

DIVISION SERIES RECORD

Year	Team (League)	Pos.	G	AB	R	H	2B	3B	HR	RBI	BB	SO	HBP	GDP	SB-CS	Avg.	OBP	SLG	OPS	E	Avg.
2005— Chicago (A.L.)	2B	1	1	0	1	0	0	0	1	0	0	0	0	0-0	1.000	1.000	1.000	2.000	0	1.000

WORLD SERIES RECORD

Year	Team (League)	Pos.	G	AB	R	H	2B	3B	HR	RBI	BB	SO	HBP	GDP	SB-CS	Avg.	OBP	SLG	OPS	E	Avg.
2005— Chicago (A.L.)	2B	2	1	1	1	0	0	0	0	0	0	0	0	1-0	1.000	1.000	1.000	2.000	0	1.000

2006 LEFTY-RIGHTY SPLITS

vs.	Avg.	AB	H	2B	3B	HR	RBI	BB	SO	OBP	Slg.	vs.	Avg.	AB	H	2B	3B	HR	RBI	BB	SO	OBP	Slg.
L	.250	8	2	1	0	0	0	0	0	.250	.375	R	.135	37	5	1	0	0	1	4	11	.250	.162

HART, COREY — OF

PERSONAL: Born March 24, 1982, in Bowling Green, Ky. ... 6-6/200. ... Bats right, throws right. ... Full name: Jon Corey Hart. ... High school: Greenwood (Bowling Green, Ky.). **TRANSACTIONS/CAREER NOTES:** Selected by Milwaukee Brewers organization in 11th round of 2000 free-agent draft.
2006 GAMES PLAYED BY POSITION (MLB): OF—61, 1B—2.

Year	Team (League)	Pos.	G	AB	R	H	2B	3B	HR	RBI	BB	SO	HBP	GDP	SB-CS	Avg.	OBP	SLG	OPS	E	Avg.
2000— Ogden (Pion.)	1B	57	216	32	62	9	1	2	30	13	27	2	6	6-0	.287	.332	.366	.698	11	.978
2001— Ogden (Pion.)	1B-OF	69	262	53	89	18	1	11	62	26	47	2	4	14-1	.340	.395	.542	.937	9	.985
2002— High Desert (Calif.)	3B-1B	100	393	76	113	26	10	22	84	37	101	5	3	24-11	.288	.356	.573	.928	22	.959
— Huntsville (Sou.)	3B-1B	28	94	16	25	3	0	2	15	7	16	4	1	3-2	.266	.340	.362	.701	10	.906
2003— Huntsville (Sou.)	3B-OF	130	493	70	149	40	1	13	94	28	101	5	7	25-8	.302	.340	.467	.807	32	.897
2004— Milwaukee (N.L.)		1	1	0	0	0	0	0	0	0	1	0	0	0-0	.000	.000	.000	.000	0	
— Indianapolis (Int'l)	OF-DH-1B	121	440	68	124	29	8	15	67	42	92	3	6	17-7	.282	.344	.486	.823	9	.954
2005— Nashville (PCL)	OF-DH-1B	113	429	85	132	29	9	17	69	48	88	3	11	31-7	.308	.377	.536	.913	6	.986
— Milwaukee (N.L.)	OF	21	57	9	11	2	1	2	7	6	11	0	6	2-0	.193	.270	.368	.638	1	.966
2006— Nashville (PCL)		26	100	19	32	10	1	4	21	12	25	1	1	11-2	.320	.391	.560	.951	1	.985
— Milwaukee (N.L.)	OF-1B	87	237	32	67	13	2	9	33	17	58	0	7	5-8	.283	.328	.468	.796	2	.983
Major League totals (3 years)		109	295	41	78	15	3	11	40	23	70	0	13	7-8	.264	.316	.447	.763	3	.979

2006 LEFTY-RIGHTY SPLITS

vs.	Avg.	AB	H	2B	3B	HR	RBI	BB	SO	OBP	Slg.	vs.	Avg.	AB	H	2B	3B	HR	RBI	BB	SO	OBP	Slg.
L	.304	79	24	3	0	3	15	7	16	.352	.456	R	.272	158	43	10	2	6	18	10	42	.315	.475

HARVILLE, CHAD — P

PERSONAL: Born September 16, 1976, in Selmer, Tenn. ... 5-9/185. ... Throws right, bats right. ... Full name: Chad Ashley Harville. ... High school: Hardin County (Savannah, Tenn.). ... College: Memphis. **TRANSACTIONS/CAREER NOTES:** Selected by Oakland Athletics organization in second round of 1997 free-agent draft. ... On disabled list (March 31-June 9, 2001); included rehabilitation assignments to Visalia and Modesto. ... Traded by A's to Houston Astros for RHP Kirk Saarloos (April 17, 2004). ... On disabled list (May 6-31, 2004); included rehabilitation assignment to Round Rock. ... Claimed on waivers by Boston Red Sox (August 29, 2005). ... Signed as a free agent by Tampa Bay Devil Rays (November 22, 2005).
CAREER HITTING: 0-for-2 (.000), 0 R, 0 2B, 0 3B, 0 HR, 0 RBI.

Year	Team (League)	W	L	Pct.	ERA	WHIP	G	GS	CG	ShO	Hld.	Sv.-Opp.	IP	H	R	ER	HR	BB-IBB	SO	Avg.
1997— S. Oregon (N'west)	1	0	1.000	0.00	1.20	3	0	0	0	...	0-...	5.0	3	0	0	0	3-0	6	.176
— Visalia (Calif.)	0	0	...	5.79	2.04	14	0	0	0	...	0-...	18.2	25	14	12	2	13-1	24	.325
1998— Visalia (Calif.)	4	3	.571	3.00	1.30	24	7	0	0	...	4-...	69.0	59	25	23	0	31-0	76	.230
— Huntsville (Sou.)	0	0	...	2.45	1.30	12	0	0	0	...	8-...	14.2	6	4	4	0	13-1	24	.122
1999— Midland (Texas)	2	0	1.000	2.01	0.99	17	0	0	0	...	7-...	22.1	13	6	5	1	9-0	35	.165
— Vancouver (PCL)	1	0	1.000	1.75	1.36	22	0	0	0	...	11-...	25.2	24	5	5	1	10-1	36	.240
— Oakland (A.L.)	0	2	.000	6.91	1.95	15	0	0	0	0	0-0	14.1	18	11	11	2	10-1	15	.310
2000— Sacramento (PCL)	5	3	.625	4.50	1.38	53	0	0	0	...	9-...	64.0	53	35	32	8	35-0	77	.222
2001— Modesto (California)	0	0	...	3.00	0.67	2	1	0	0	...	0-...	3.0	2	1	1	0	0-0	3	.182
— Visalia (Calif.)	0	0	...	0.00	1.00	1	1	0	0	...	0-...	3.0	3	0	0	0	0-0	3	.250
— Sacramento (PCL)	5	2	.714	3.98	1.16	33	0	0	0	...	8-...	40.2	35	20	18	5	12-0	55	.233
— Oakland (A.L.)	0	0	...	0.00	0.67	3	0	0	0	1	0-0	3.0	2	0	0	0	0-0	2	.182
2002— Sacramento (PCL)	1	2	.333	5.40	1.50	24	0	0	0	...	0-...	30.0	32	19	18	5	13-1	26	.274
2003— Sacramento (PCL)	3	5	.375	2.05	1.10	48	0	0	0	...	18-...	57.0	42	16	13	5	21-2	57	.200
— Oakland (A.L.)	1	0	1.000	5.82	1.94	21	0	0	0	0	1-1	21.2	25	15	14	3	17-1	15	.294
2004— Oakland (A.L.)	0	0	...	3.38	1.13	3	0	0	0	1	0-0	2.2	2	1	1	0	1-0	0	.200
— Round Rock (Texas)	0	0	...	0.00	0.67	2	2	0	0	...	0-...	3.0	0	0	0	0	2-0	2	.000
— Houston (N.L.)	3	2	.600	4.75	1.51	56	0	0	0	3	0-4	53.0	54	35	28	8	26-2	46	.260
2005— Houston (N.L.)	0	2	.000	4.46	1.57	37	0	0	0	2	0-1	38.1	36	21	19	7	24-1	33	.254
— Boston (A.L.)	0	1	.000	6.43	1.43	9	0	0	0	0	0-0	7.0	7	5	5	1	3-0	3	.269
2006— Durham (Int'l)	0	0	...	3.00	1.53	11	0	0	0	1	1-3	15.0	15	5	5	0	8-2	9	.263
— Tampa Bay (A.L.)	0	2	.000	5.93	1.61	32	0	0	0	2	1-2	41.0	44	27	27	5	22-2	30	.277
American League totals (6 years)	1	5	.167	5.82	1.68	82	0	0	0	4	2-3	89.2	98	59	58	11	53-4	68	.281
National League totals (2 years)	3	4	.429	4.63	1.53	93	0	0	0	5	0-5	91.1	90	56	47	15	50-3	79	.257
Major League totals (6 years)	4	9	.308	5.22	1.61	175	0	0	0	9	2-8	181.0	188	115	105	26	103-7	147	.269

DIVISION SERIES RECORD

Year	Team (League)	W	L	Pct.	ERA	WHIP	G	GS	CG	ShO	Hld.	Sv.-Opp.	IP	H	R	ER	HR	BB-IBB	SO	Avg.
2004— Houston (N.L.)	0	0	...	0.00	0.00	3	0	0	0	0	0-0	0.2	0	0	0	0	0-0	0	.000

CHAMPIONSHIP SERIES RECORD

Year	Team (League)	W	L	Pct.	ERA	WHIP	G	GS	CG	ShO	Hld.	Sv.-Opp.	IP	H	R	ER	HR	BB-IBB	SO	Avg.
2004— Houston (N.L.)	0	0	...	13.50	3.00	3	0	0	0	0	0-0	1.1	3	2	2	0	1-0	3	.429

2006 LEFTY-RIGHTY SPLITS

vs.	Avg.	AB	H	2B	3B	HR	RBI	BB	SO	OBP	Slg.	vs.	Avg.	AB	H	2B	3B	HR	RBI	BB	SO	OBP	Slg.
L	.284	67	19	3	0	3	9	9	12	.368	.463	R	.272	92	25	2	0	2	23	13	18	.358	.359

H

HATTEBERG, SCOTT — 1B

PERSONAL: Born December 14, 1969, in Salem, Ore. ... 6-1/210. ... Bats left, throws right. ... Full name: Scott Allen Hatteberg. ... Name pronounced: HATT-eh-berg. ... High school: Eisenhower (Yakima, Wash.). ... College: Washington State. **TRANSACTIONS/CAREER NOTES:** Selected by Philadelphia Phillies organization in 12th round of 1988 free-agent draft; did not sign. ... Selected by Boston Red Sox organization in supplemental round ("sandwich pick" between first and second round, 43rd pick overall) of 1991 free-agent draft; pick received as part of compensation for Kansas City Royals signing Type A free-agent P Mike Boddicker. ... On disabled list (April 15-May 7 and May 17-August 16, 1999); included rehabilitation assignments to Pawtucket, GCL Red Sox and Sarasota. ... Traded by Red Sox to Colorado Rockies for 2B Pokey Reese (December 19, 2001). ... Signed as a free agent by Oakland Athletics (January 2, 2002). ... Signed as a free agent by Cincinnati Reds (February 14, 2006). **STATISTICAL NOTES:** Career major league grand slams: 4.

2006 GAMES PLAYED BY POSITION (MLB): 1B—131.

Year	Team (League)	Pos.	G	AB	R	H	2B	3B	HR	RBI	BB	SO	HBP	GDP	SB-CS	Avg.	OBP	SLG	OPS	E	Avg.
1991— Winter Haven (FSL)		C	56	191	21	53	7	3	1	25	22	22	0	6	1-2	.277	.349	.361	.710	5	.983
— Lynchburg (Caro.)		C	8	25	4	5	1	0	0	2	7	6	0	0	0-0	.200	.375	.240	.615	0	1.000
1992— New Britain (East.)		C	103	297	28	69	13	2	1	30	41	49	2	6	1-3	.232	.327	.300	.626	11	.979
1993— New Britain (East.)		C	68	227	35	63	10	2	7	28	42	38	1	6	1-3	.278	.393	.432	.824	10	.978
— Pawtucket (Int'l)		C	18	53	6	10	0	0	1	2	6	12	1	5	0-0	.189	.283	.245	.529	5	.964
1994— New Britain (East.)		C	20	68	6	18	4	1	1	9	7	9	0	2	0-2	.265	.329	.397	.726	1	.993
— Pawtucket (Int'l)		C	78	238	26	56	14	0	7	19	32	49	3	14	2-1	.235	.332	.382	.714	7	.986
1995— Pawtucket (Int'l)		C-DH	85	251	36	68	15	1	7	27	40	39	4	8	0-0	.271	.376	.422	.798	4	.984
— Boston (A.L.)		C	2	2	1	1	0	0	0	0	0	0	0	1	0-0	.500	.500	.500	1.000	0	1.000
1996— Pawtucket (Int'l)		C-DH	90	287	52	77	16	0	12	49	58	66	2	6	1-1	.268	.391	.449	.841	6	.990
— Boston (A.L.)		C	10	11	3	2	1	0	0	0	3	2	0	2	0-0	.182	.357	.273	.630	0	1.000
1997— Boston (A.L.)		C-DH	114	350	46	97	23	1	10	44	40	70	2	11	0-1	.277	.354	.434	.788	11	.983
1998— Boston (A.L.)		C	112	359	46	99	23	1	12	43	43	58	5	11	0-0	.276	.359	.446	.804	5	.993
1999— Boston (A.L.)		C-DH	30	80	12	22	5	0	1	11	18	14	1	2	0-0	.275	.410	.375	.785	1	.993
— Pawtucket (Int'l)		C-DH	10	34	3	6	2	0	0	4	4	6	0	2	0-0	.176	.263	.235	.498	1	1.000
— GC Red Sox (GCL)		C-DH	6	15	4	6	2	0	1	6	7	1	0	1	0-0	.400	.591	.733	1.324	0	1.000
— Sarasota (Fla. St.)		C	1	1	0	1	0	0	0	1	0	0	0	0	0-0	1.000	1.000	1.000	2.000	1	1.000
2000— Boston (A.L.)		C-DH-3B	92	230	21	61	15	0	8	36	38	39	0	8	0-0	.265	.367	.435	.801	6	.981
2001— Boston (A.L.)		C-DH	94	278	34	68	19	0	3	25	33	26	4	7	1-1	.245	.332	.345	.677	4	.992
2002— Oakland (A.L.)		1B-DH	136	492	58	138	22	4	15	61	68	56	6	8	0-0	.280	.374	.433	.807	5	.994
2003— Oakland (A.L.)		1B-DH	147	541	63	137	34	0	12	61	66	53	9	14	0-1	.253	.342	.383	.725	10	.992
2004— Oakland (A.L.)		1B-DH	152	550	87	156	30	4	15	82	72	46	5	10	0-0	.284	.367	.420	.787	10	.993
2005— Oakland (A.L.)		DH-1B	134	464	52	119	19	0	7	59	51	54	4	22	0-1	.256	.334	.343	.677	7	.985
2006— Cincinnati (N.L.)		1B	141	456	62	132	28	0	13	51	74	41	3	13	2-2	.289	.389	.436	.826	4	.996
American League totals (11 years)			1023	3357	423	900	191	6	83	422	432	420	36	96	1-5	.268	.356	.403	.758	59	.991
National League totals (1 year)			141	456	62	132	28	0	13	51	74	41	3	13	2-2	.289	.389	.436	.826	4	.996
Major League totals (12 years)			1164	3813	485	1032	219	6	96	473	506	461	39	109	3-7	.271	.360	.407	.766	63	.992

DIVISION SERIES RECORD

Year	Team (League)	Pos.	G	AB	R	H	2B	3B	HR	RBI	BB	SO	HBP	GDP	SB-CS	Avg.	OBP	SLG	OPS	E	Avg.
1998— Boston (A.L.)		C	3	9	0	1	0	0	0	0	3	1	0	0	0-0	.111	.333	.111	.444	0	1.000
1999— Boston (A.L.)		C	1	1	0	1	0	0	0	1	0	0	0	0	0-0	1.000	1.000	1.000	2.000	0	1.000
2002— Oakland (A.L.)		1B	5	14	5	7	2	0	1	3	3	0	0	0	0-0	.500	.588	.857	1.445	1	.973
2003— Oakland (A.L.)		1B	5	17	3	3	0	0	0	0	5	3	0	0	0-0	.176	.364	.176	.540	0	1.000
Division series totals (4 years)			14	41	9	12	2	0	1	4	11	4	0	0	0-0	.293	.442	.415	.857	1	.990

CHAMPIONSHIP SERIES RECORD

Year	Team (League)	Pos.	G	AB	R	H	2B	3B	HR	RBI	BB	SO	HBP	GDP	SB-CS	Avg.	OBP	SLG	OPS	E	Avg.
1999— Boston (A.L.)		C	3	1	0	0	0	0	0	0	1	0	0	0	0-0	.000	.000	.000	.000	0	...

2006 LEFTY-RIGHTY SPLITS

vs.	Avg.	AB	H	2B	3B	HR	RBI	BB	SO	OBP	Slg.	vs.	Avg.	AB	H	2B	3B	HR	RBI	BB	SO	OBP	Slg.
L	.231	78	18	6	0	1	9	10	13	.333	.346	R	.302	378	114	22	0	12	42	64	28	.401	.455

HATTIG, JOHN — IF

PERSONAL: Born February 27, 1980, in Tamuning, Guam. ... 6-2/215. ... Bats both, throws right. ... Full name: John Duane Hattig. **TRANSACTIONS/CAREER NOTES:** Selected by Boston Red Sox organization in 25th round of 1998 free-agent draft. ... Traded by Red Sox to Toronto Blue Jays for P Terry Adams (July 24, 2004).

2006 GAMES PLAYED BY POSITION (MLB): 3B—10.

Year	Team (League)	Pos.	G	AB	R	H	2B	3B	HR	RBI	BB	SO	HBP	GDP	SB-CS	Avg.	OBP	SLG	OPS	E	Avg.
1999— GC Red Sox (GCL)			50	163	28	44	7	3	1	17	16	20	1	8	1-1	.270	.333	.368	.701	...	...
2000— Lowell (NY-Penn)			61	242	30	70	8	1	0	28	20	43	0	1	1-1	.289	.342	.331	.673	...	...
2001— Lowell (NY-Penn)			11	45	4	5	0	1	1	5	3	7	1	6	1-0	.111	.184	.222	.406	...	...
— Augusta (S. Atl.)			50	179	25	51	9	1	1	23	22	42	3	3	4-1	.285	.371	.363	.734	...	...
2002— Sarasota (Fla. St.)			24	85	6	21	6	0	0	6	7	16	0	2	0-0	.247	.301	.318	.619	...	...
— Augusta (S. Atl.)			93	347	46	98	20	4	7	56	52	73	2	13	1-2	.282	.377	.401	.778	...	...
2003— Sarasota (Fla. St.)			114	400	51	118	29	2	6	70	59	70	2	15	9-7	.295	.385	.423	.808	...	...
— Portland (East.)			8	32	3	7	2	0	0	1	2	11	0	2	0-0	.219	.265	.281	.546	...	...
2004— Portland (East.)			75	264	53	78	21	1	12	35	47	68	6	8	3-3	.295	.411	.519	.930	...	...
— New Hampshire (East.)			40	142	24	42	7	0	10	30	12	41	2	0	0-1	.296	.352	.556	.908	...	...
2005— Dunedin (Fla. St.)		3B-DH	11	44	8	17	3	0	5	3	7	0	2	0-0	.386	.417	.455	.871	3	.909
— Syracuse (Int'l)		3B-DH	26	95	15	30	7	0	1	10	10	16	1	5	0-0	.316	.387	.421	.808	0	1.000
2006— Syracuse (Int'l)			103	373	48	103	30	1	4	36	35	108	2	9	0-0	.276	.341	.394	.736	14	.960
— Toronto (A.L.)		3B	13	24	2	8	1	0	0	3	5	8	0	1	0-0	.333	.448	.375	.823	0	1.000
Major League totals (1 year)			13	24	2	8	1	0	0	3	5	8	0	1	0-0	.333	.448	.375	.823	0	1.000

2006 LEFTY-RIGHTY SPLITS

vs.	Avg.	AB	H	2B	3B	HR	RBI	BB	SO	OBP	Slg.	vs.	Avg.	AB	H	2B	3B	HR	RBI	BB	SO	OBP	Slg.
L	.000	3	0	0	0	0	0	1	.1	.250	.000	R	.381	21	8	1	0	0	3	4	7	.480	.429*

HAWKINS, LATROY — P

PERSONAL: Born December 21, 1972, in Gary, Ind. ... 6-5/215. ... Throws right, bats right. ... Full name: LaTroy Hawkins. ... High school: West Side (Gary, Ind.). **TRANSACTIONS/CAREER NOTES:** Selected by Minnesota Twins organization in seventh round of 1991 free-agent draft. ... Signed as a free agent by Chicago Cubs (December 3, 2003). ... On suspended list (August 13-17, 2004). ... Traded by Cubs to San Francisco Giants for Ps Jerome Williams and David Aardsma (May 28, 2005). ... On disabled list

(June 17-July 4, 2005); included rehabilitation assignment to Fresno. ... Traded by Giants to Baltimore Orioles for P Steve Kline (December 6, 2005). ... On bereavement list (July 30-August 4, 2006).

CAREER HITTING: 0-for-5 (.000), 0 R, 0 2B, 0 3B, 0 HR, 0 RBI.

Year Team (League)	W	L	Pct.	ERA	WHIP	G	GS	CG	ShO	Hld.	Sv.-Opp.	IP	H	R	ER	HR	BB-IBB	SO	Avg.
1991— GC Twins (GCL)	4	3	.571	4.75	1.60	11	11	0	0	...	0-...	55.0	62	34	29	2	26-0	47	.281
1992— GC Twins (GCL)	3	2	.600	3.22	1.27	6	6	1	0	...	0-...	36.1	36	19	13	1	10-0	35	.243
— Elizabethton (App.)	0	1	.000	3.38	1.20	5	5	1	0	...	0-...	26.2	21	12	10	2	11-0	36	.202
1993— Fort Wayne (Midw.)	15	5	.750	2.06	0.96	26	23	4	3	...	0-...	157.1	110	53	36	5	41-0	179	.195
1994— Fort Myers (FSL)	4	0	1.000	2.33	0.98	6	6	1	1	...	0-...	38.2	32	10	10	1	6-0	36	.224
— Nashville (Southern)	9	2	.818	2.33	1.06	11	11	1	0	...	0-...	73.1	50	23	19	2	28-0	43	.191
— Salt Lake (PCL)	5	4	.556	4.08	1.53	12	12	1	0	...	0-...	81.2	92	42	37	8	33-0	37	.296
1995— Minnesota (A.L.)	2	3	.400	8.67	1.89	6	6	1	0	0	0-0	27.0	39	29	26	3	12-0	9	.335
— Salt Lake (PCL)	9	7	.563	3.55	1.32	22	22	4	1	0	0-0	144.1	150	63	57	7	40-1	74	.271
1996— Minnesota (A.L.)	1	1	.500	8.20	1.94	7	6	0	0	0	0-0	26.1	42	24	24	8	9-0	24	.372
— Salt Lake (PCL)	9	8	.529	3.92	1.23	20	20	4	1	...	0-...	137.2	138	66	60	11	31-3	99	.263
1997— Salt Lake (PCL)	9	4	.692	5.45	1.53	14	13	2	1	...	0-...	76.0	100	53	46	4	16-1	53	.311
— Minnesota (A.L.)	6	12	.333	5.84	1.75	20	20	1	0	0	0-0	103.1	134	71	67	19	47-0	58	.317
1998— Minnesota (A.L.)	7	14	.333	5.25	1.51	33	33	0	0	0	0-0	190.1	227	126	111	27	61-1	105	.299
1999— Minnesota (A.L.)	10	14	.417	6.66	1.71	33	33	0	0	0	0-0	174.1	238	* 136	* 129	29	60-2	103	.323
2000— Minnesota (A.L.)	2	5	.286	3.39	1.33	66	0	0	0	7	14-14	87.2	85	34	33	7	32-1	59	.256
2001— Minnesota (A.L.)	1	5	.167	5.96	1.91	62	0	0	0	9	28-37	51.1	59	34	34	3	39-3	36	.291
2002— Minnesota (A.L.)	6	0	1.000	2.13	0.97	65	0	0	0	13	0-3	80.1	63	23	19	5	15-1	63	.219
2003— Minnesota (A.L.)	9	3	.750	1.86	1.09	74	0	0	0	28	2-8	77.1	69	20	16	4	15-1	75	.239
2004— Chicago (N.L.)	5	4	.556	2.63	1.05	77	0	0	0	4	25-34	82.0	72	27	24	10	14-5	69	.233
2005— Chicago (N.L.)	1	4	.200	3.32	1.32	21	0	0	0	1	4-8	19.0	18	9	7	4	7-0	13	.250
— Fresno (PCL)	0	0	...	0.00	1.00	2	0	0	0	1	0-0	2.0	2	0	0	0	0-0	1	.250
— San Francisco (N.L.)	1	4	.200	4.10	1.53	45	0	0	0	15	2-7	37.1	40	18	17	3	17-3	30	.272
2006— Baltimore (A.L.)	3	2	.600	4.48	1.46	60	0	0	0	16	0-4	60.1	73	30	30	4	15-3	27	.300
American League totals (10 years)	47	59	.443	5.01	1.52	426	98	2	0	65	44-66	878.1	1029	527	489	109	305-12	559	.294
National League totals (2 years)	7	12	.368	3.12	1.21	143	0	0	0	19	31-49	138.1	130	54	48	17	38-8	112	.246
Major League totals (12 years)	54	71	.432	4.75	1.48	569	98	2	0	84	75-115	1016.2	1159	581	537	126	343-20	671	.287

DIVISION SERIES RECORD

Year Team (League)	W	L	Pct.	ERA	WHIP	G	GS	CG	ShO	Hld.	Sv.-Opp.	IP	H	R	ER	HR	BB-IBB	SO	Avg.
2002— Minnesota (A.L.)	0	0	...	0.00	0.00	3	0	0	0	1	0-0	2.1	0	0	0	0	0-0	5	.000
2003— Minnesota (A.L.)	1	0	1.000	6.00	1.67	3	0	0	0	1	0-0	3.0	5	3	2	0	0-0	5	.357
Division series totals (2 years)	1	0	1.000	3.38	0.94	6	0	0	0	2	0-0	5.1	5	3	2	0	0-0	10	.238

CHAMPIONSHIP SERIES RECORD

Year Team (League)	W	L	Pct.	ERA	WHIP	G	GS	CG	ShO	Hld.	Sv.-Opp.	IP	H	R	ER	HR	BB-IBB	SO	Avg.
2002— Minnesota (A.L.)	0	0	...	20.25	3.75	4	0	0	0	0	0-0	1.1	4	3	3	0	1-0	1	.571

2006 LEFTY-RIGHTY SPLITS

vs.	Avg.	AB	H	2B	3B	HR	RBI	BB	SO	OBP	Slg.	vs.	Avg.	AB	H	2B	3B	HR	RBI	BB	SO	OBP	Slg.
L	.323	99	32	8	2	2	12	10	12	.385	.505	R	.285	144	41	5	1	2	15	5	15	.305	.375

HAWPE, BRAD — OF

PERSONAL: Born June 22, 1979, in Fort Worth, Texas. ... 6-3/200. ... Bats left, throws left. ... Full name: Bradley Bonte Hawpe. ... High school: Boswell (Fort Worth, Texas). ... College: LSU. **TRANSACTIONS/CAREER NOTES:** Selected by Toronto Blue Jays organization in 46th round of 1997 free-agent draft; did not sign. ... Selected by Colorado Rockies organization in 11th round of 2000 free-agent draft. ... On disabled list (July 15-September 2, 2005); included rehabilitation assignment to Colorado Springs.
2006 GAMES PLAYED BY POSITION (MLB): OF—145.

Year Team (League)	Pos.	G	AB	R	H	2B	3B	HR	RBI	BB	SO	HBP	GDP	SB-CS	Avg.	OBP	SLG	OPS	E	Avg.
2000— Portland (N'west)	OF-1B	62	205	38	59	19	2	7	29	40	51	2	1	2-0	.288	.398	.502	.900	5	.983
2001— Asheville (S. Atl.)	OF-1B	111	393	78	105	22	3	22	72	59	113	6	8	7-4	.267	.363	.506	.870	11	.981
2002— Salem (Carol.)	1B	122	450	87	156	38	2	22	97	81	84	2	7	1-1	.347	.447	.587	1.033	8	.994
2003— Tulsa (Texas)	OF-1B	93	346	52	96	27	0	17	68	31	84	1	5	1-3	.277	.338	.503	.841	6	.976
2004— Colo. Springs (PCL)	OF-DH	92	345	62	111	19	1	31	86	36	91	1	10	3-2	.322	.384	.652	1.035	3	.984
— Colorado (N.L.)	OF	42	105	12	26	3	2	3	9	11	34	1	4	1-1	.248	.322	.400	.722	1	.982
2005— Colo. Springs (PCL)	OF-DH	7	28	7	13	3	0	3	11	6	7	0	2	0-0	.464	.559	.893	1.452	0	1.000
— Colorado (N.L.)	OF	101	305	38	80	10	3	9	47	43	70	0	5	2-2	.262	.350	.403	.754	3	.981
2006— Colorado (N.L.)	OF	150	499	67	146	33	6	22	84	74	123	0	8	5-5	.293	.383	.515	.898	4	.987
Major League totals (3 years)		293	909	117	252	46	11	34	140	128	227	1	17	8-8	.277	.365	.464	.829	8	.985

2006 LEFTY-RIGHTY SPLITS

vs.	Avg.	AB	H	2B	3B	HR	RBI	BB	SO	OBP	Slg.	vs.	Avg.	AB	H	2B	3B	HR	RBI	BB	SO	OBP	Slg.
L	.232	69	16	3	1	3	10	7	25	.303	.435	R	.302	430	130	30	5	19	74	67	98	.395	.528

HEILMAN, AARON — P

PERSONAL: Born November 12, 1978, in Logansport, Ind. ... 6-5/220. ... Throws right, bats right. ... Full name: Aaron Michael Heilman. ... High school: Logansport (Ind.). ... College: Notre Dame. **TRANSACTIONS/CAREER NOTES:** Selected by New York Yankees organization in 55th round of 1997 free-agent draft; did not sign. ... Selected by Minnesota Twins organization in supplemental round ("sandwich" pick between first and second rounds, 31st pick overall) of 2000 free-agent draft; did not sign; pick received as part of compensation for Baltimore Orioles signing Type A free-agent P Mike Trombley. ... Selected by New York Mets organization in first round (18th pick overall) of 2001 free-agent draft.
CAREER HITTING: 1-for-43 (.023), 1 R, 0 2B, 0 3B, 0 HR, 1 RBI.

Year Team (League)	W	L	Pct.	ERA	WHIP	G	GS	CG	ShO	Hld.	Sv.-Opp.	IP	H	R	ER	HR	BB-IBB	SO	Avg.
2001— St. Lucie (Fla. St.)	0	1	.000	2.35	1.02	7	7	0	0	...	0-...	38.1	26	11	10	0	13-0	39	.190
2002— Binghamton (East.)	4	4	.500	3.82	1.17	17	17	0	0	...	0-...	96.2	85	43	41	7	28-2	97	.237
— Norfolk (Int'l)	2	3	.400	3.28	1.18	10	7	0	0	...	0-...	49.1	42	18	18	3	16-1	35	.240
2003— Norfolk (Int'l)	6	4	.600	3.24	1.39	16	16	0	0	...	0-...	94.1	99	37	34	5	32-0	71	.274
— New York (N.L.)	2	7	.222	6.75	1.84	14	13	0	0	0	0-0	65.1	79	53	49	13	41-2	51	.300
2004— Norfolk (Int'l)	7	10	.412	4.33	1.46	26	26	1	0	...	0-...	151.2	156	88	73	15	66-0	123	.264
— New York (N.L.)	1	3	.250	5.46	1.43	5	5	0	0	0	0-0	28.0	27	17	17	4	13-0	22	.257
2005— New York (N.L.)	5	3	.625	3.17	1.15	53	7	1	1	5	5-6	108.0	87	40	38	6	37-4	106	.223
2006— New York (N.L.)	4	5	.444	3.62	1.16	74	0	0	0	5	0-5	87.0	73	37	35	5	28-2	73	.231
Major League totals (4 years)	12	18	.400	4.34	1.34	146	25	1	1	32	5-11	288.1	266	147	139	28	119-8	252	.247

H

DIVISION SERIES RECORD

Year — Team (League)	W	L	Pct.	ERA	WHIP	G	GS	CG	ShO	Hld.	Sv.-Opp.	IP	H	R	ER	HR	BB-IBB	SO	Avg.
2006— New York (N.L.)	0	0	...	3.00	1.00	3	0	0	0		0-0	3.0	3	1	1	1	0-0	1	.250

CHAMPIONSHIP SERIES RECORD

Year — Team (League)	W	L	Pct.	ERA	WHIP	G	GS	CG	ShO	Hld.	Sv.-Opp.	IP	H	R	ER	HR	BB-IBB	SO	Avg.
2006— New York (N.L.)	0	1	.000	4.15	1.15	3	0	0	0		0-0	4.1	4	2	2	1	1-1	5	.235

2006 LEFTY-RIGHTY SPLITS

vs.	Avg.	AB	H	2B	3B	HR	RBI	BB	SO	OBP	Slg.	vs.	Avg.	AB	H	2B	3B	HR	RBI	BB	SO	OBP	Slg.
L	.231	147	34	4	2	2	14	22	35	.337	.327	R	.231	169	39	9	0	3	26	6	38	.260	.337

HEINTZ, CHRIS — C

PERSONAL: Born August 6, 1974, in Syosset, N.Y. ... 6-1/210. ... Bats right, throws right. ... Full name: Christopher John Heintz. ... High school: Countryside (Fla.) Clearwater. ... College: South Florida. **TRANSACTIONS/CAREER NOTES:** Selected by Chicago White Sox organization in 19th round of 1996 free-agent draft. ... Released by White Sox (January 8, 2002). ... Signed by St. Louis Cardinals organization (January 25, 2002). ... Signed as a free agent by Pittsburgh Pirates organization (December 2, 2002). ... Signed as a free agent by Minnesota Twins organization (November 21, 2003).

2006 GAMES PLAYED BY POSITION (MLB): C—2.

									BATTING										FIELDING	
Year — Team (League)	Pos.	G	AB	R	H	2B	3B	HR	RBI	BB	SO	HBP	GDP	SB-CS	Avg.	OBP	SLG	OPS	E	Avg.
1996— Bristol (Appal.)	1B	8	29	7	10	7	0	2	8	4	2	0	0	1-1	.345	.424	.793	1.217	4	.939
— South Bend (Mid.)	3B-1B	64	230	25	61	12	1	1	22	23	46	3	3	1-1	.265	.339	.339	.678	14	.943
1997— Hickory (S. Atl.)	1B-C	107	388	57	110	28	1	2	54	28	57	9	6	1-3	.284	.342	.376	.718	10	.990
1998— Win.-Salem (Car.)	1B-C-3B	130	508	66	147	21	4	8	79	31	87	5	17	10-8	.289	.331	.394	.725	18	.984
1999— Win.-Salem (Car.)	1B-C-3B	118	417	55	122	33	2	7	60	40	72	4	7	6-3	.293	.359	.432	.791	16	.982
2000— Birmingham (Sou.)	C-3B	73	239	27	64	15	1	2	34	21	33	0	2	4-1	.268	.320	.364	.684	8	.984
2001— Birmingham (Sou.)	C-3B	37	119	14	28	8	0	2	8	10	23	2	2	0-2	.235	.303	.353	.656	4	.982
— Charlotte (Int'l)		3	10	1	1	1	0	0	1	0	3	0	0	0-0	.100	.091	.200	.291	0	1.000
2002— New Haven (East.)	C-1B-3B	105	373	40	117	29	1	7	45	19	61	2	13	1-0	.314	.349	.453	.802	8	.986
2003— Altoona (East.)	C	78	271	28	70	12	4	2	26	19	24	3	6	0-0	.258	.313	.354	.667	5	.991
2004— Rochester (Int'l)	C	86	294	33	82	14	0	8	45	16	40	3	6	0-2	.279	.318	.408	.726	5	.991
2005— Rochester (Int'l)	DH-C-3B	89	329	38	100	18	2	8	58	22	61	0	16	0-0	.304	.343	.444	.786	5	.981
— Minnesota (A.L.)	C	8	25	1	5	3	0	0	2	1	6	0	1	0-0	.200	.231	.320	.551	0	1.000
2006— Rochester (Int'l)		100	374	46	107	22	0	3	39	21	63	0	5	0-4	.286	.323	.369	.692	11	.974
— Minnesota (A.L.)	C	2	1	0	0	0	0	0	0	0	0	0	0	0-0	.000	.000	.000	.000	0	...
Major League totals (2 years)		10	26	1	5	3	0	0	2	1	6	0	1	0-0	.192	.222	.308	.530	0	1.000

2006 LEFTY-RIGHTY SPLITS

vs.	Avg.	AB	H	2B	3B	HR	RBI	BB	SO	OBP	Slg.	vs.	Avg.	AB	H	2B	3B	HR	RBI	BB	SO	OBP	Slg.
L	.000	0	0	0	0	0	0	0	0	.000	.000	R	.000	1	0	0	0	0	0	0	0	.000	.000

HELLING, RICK — P

PERSONAL: Born December 15, 1970, in Devils Lake, N.D. ... 6-3/241. ... Throws right, bats right. ... Full name: Ricky Allen Helling. ... High school: Lakota (Fargo, N.D.), then Shanley (Fargo, N.D.). ... College: Stanford. **TRANSACTIONS/CAREER NOTES:** Selected by New York Mets organization in 50th round of 1990 free-agent draft; did not sign. ... Selected by Texas Rangers organization in first round (22nd pick overall) of 1992 free-agent draft. ... Traded by Rangers to Florida Marlins (September 3, 1996), completing deal in which Marlins traded P John Burkett to Rangers for P Ryan Dempster and a player to be named (August 8, 1996). ... Traded by Marlins to Rangers for P Ed Vosberg (August 12, 1997). ... Signed as a free agent by Arizona Diamondbacks (January 19, 2002). ... On Arizona disabled list (July 16-August 7, 2002); included rehabilitation assignment to Tucson. ... Signed as a free agent by Baltimore Orioles organization (February 11, 2003). ... Released by Orioles (August 18, 2003). ... Signed by Marlins (August 22, 2003). ... Signed as a free agent by Minnesota Twins organization (January 13, 2004). ... Signed as a free agent by Rangers organization (June 8, 2004). ... Released by Rangers (July 16, 2004). ... Signed by Milwaukee Brewers organization (January 13, 2005). ... On disabled list (April 16-June 20, 2006); included rehabilitation assignment to Nashville. **MISCELLANEOUS NOTES:** Member of 1992 U.S. Olympic baseball team.

CAREER HITTING: 6-for-104 (.058), 4 R, 1 2B, 0 3B, 0 HR, 1 RBI.

Year — Team (League)	W	L	Pct.	ERA	WHIP	G	GS	CG	ShO	Hld.	Sv.-Opp.	IP	H	R	ER	HR	BB-IBB	SO	Avg.
1992— Charlotte (Fla. St.)	1	1	.500	2.29	0.86	3	3	0	0		0-...	19.2	13	5	5	1	4-0	20	.181
1993— Tulsa (Texas)	12	8	.600	3.60	1.11	26	26	2	2		0-...	177.1	150	76	71	14	46-1	188	.227
— Okla. City (A.A.)	1	1	.500	1.64	0.73	2	2	1	0		0-...	11.0	5	3	2	0	3-0	17	.135
1994— Texas (A.L.)	3	2	.600	5.88	1.54	9	9	1	1	0	0-0	52.0	62	34	34	14	18-0	25	.295
— Okla. City (A.A.)	4	12	.250	5.78	1.48	20	20	2	0		0-...	132.1	153	93	85	17	43-2	85	.294
1995— Texas (A.L.)	0	2	.000	6.57	2.03	3	3	0	0	0	0-0	12.1	17	11	9	2	8-0	5	.340
— Okla. City (A.A.)	4	8	.333	5.33	1.58	20	20	2	0		0-...	109.2	132	73	65	13	41-1	80	.304
1996— Okla. City (A.A.)	12	4	.750	2.96	1.16	23	22	2	1		0-...	140.0	124	54	46	10	38-1	157	.238
— Texas (A.L.)	1	2	.333	7.52	1.57	6	2	0	0	1	0-0	20.1	23	17	17	7	9-0	16	.280
— Florida (N.L.)	2	1	.667	1.95	0.76	5	4	0	0	0	0-0	27.2	14	6	6	2	7-0	26	.143
1997— Florida (N.L.)	2	6	.250	4.38	1.43	31	6	0	0	6	0-1	76.0	61	38	37	12	48-2	53	.232
— Texas (A.L.)	3	3	.500	4.58	1.24	10	8	0	0	0	0-0	55.0	47	29	28	5	21-0	46	.235
1998— Texas (A.L.)	• 20	7	.741	4.41	1.33	33	33	4	2	0	0-0	216.1	209	109	106	27	78-6	164	.253
1999— Texas (A.L.)	13	11	.542	4.84	1.43	35	* 35	3	0	0	0-0	219.1	228	127	118	* 41	85-5	131	.272
2000— Texas (A.L.)	16	13	.552	4.48	1.43	35	• 35	0	0	0	0-0	217.0	212	122	108	29	99-2	146	.252
2001— Texas (A.L.)	12	11	.522	5.17	1.48	34	34	2	1	0	0-0	215.2	* 256	* 134	* 124	* 38	63-2	154	.297
2002— Arizona (N.L.)	10	12	.455	4.51	1.30	30	30	0	0	0	0-0	175.2	180	94	88	31	48-6	120	.264
— Tucson (PCL)	1	0	1.000	1.29	0.71	1	1	0	0		0-...	7.0	4	1	1	0	1-0	7	.167
2003— Baltimore (A.L.)	7	8	.467	5.71	1.41	24	24	0	0	0	0-0	138.2	156	90	88	30	40-0	86	.286
— Florida (N.L.)	1	0	1.000	0.55	0.98	11	0	0	0	1	0-0	16.1	11	1	1	1	5-0	12	.193
2004— New Britain (East.)	1	2	.333	4.94	1.32	5	5	0	0		0-...	31.0	30	18	17	5	11-0	21	.261
— Rochester (Int'l)	1	0	1.000	0.00	0.71	1	1	1	1		0-...	7.0	4	0	0	0	1-0	2	.167
— Oklahoma (PCL)	1	4	.200	9.00	2.26	6	6	0	0		0-...	31.0	59	35	31	8	11-0	20	.440
2005— Nashville (PCL)	9	3	.750	4.13	1.36	21	21	0	0	0	0-0	130.2	128	74	60	12	50-1	105	.256
— Milwaukee (N.L.)	3	1	.750	2.39	1.16	15	7	0	0	2	0-0	49.0	39	13	13	2	18-1	42	.219
2006— Nashville (PCL)	1	0	1.000	3.75	0.92	2	2	0	0	0	0-0	12.0	9	5	5	0	2-0	6	.205
— Milwaukee (N.L.)	0	2	.000	4.11	1.14	20	2	0	0	0	0-1	35.0	25	17	16	6	15-0	32	.202
American League totals (9 years)	75	59	.560	4.96	1.42	189	183	10	4	1	0-0	1146.2	1210	673	632	193	421-15	773	.272
National League totals (6 years)	18	22	.450	3.82	1.24	112	51	0	0	11	0-2	379.2	330	169	161	54	141-9	285	.236
Major League totals (12 years)	93	81	.534	4.68	1.38	301	234	10	4	12	0-2	1526.1	1540	842	793	247	562-24	1058	.263

DIVISION SERIES RECORD

Year — Team (League)	W	L	Pct.	ERA	WHIP	G	GS	CG	ShO	Hld.	Sv.-Opp.	IP	H	R	ER	HR	BB-IBB	SO	Avg.
1998— Texas (A.L.)	0	1	.000	4.50	1.50	1	1	0	0	...	0-0	6.0	8	3	3	2	1-0	9	...

H

Year Team (League)	W	L	Pct.	ERA	WHIP	G	GS	CG	ShO	Hld.	Sv.-Opp.	IP	H	R	ER	HR	BB-IBB	SO	Avg.
1999— Texas (A.L.)	0	1	.000	2.84	0.95	1	1	0	0	...	0-0	6.1	5	2	2	0	1-0	8	...
2002— Arizona (N.L.)	0	0	...	0.00	0.25	2	0	0	0	0	0-0	4.0	1	0	0	0	0-0	2	.077
2003— Florida (N.L.)	0	1	.000	27.00	12.00	1	0	0	0	0	0-0	0.1	2	1	1	0	2-1	0	.667
Division series totals (4 years)	0	2	.000	3.24	1.20	5	2	0	0	0	0-0	16.2	16	6	6	2	4-1	19	1.000

CHAMPIONSHIP SERIES RECORD

Year Team (League)	W	L	Pct.	ERA	WHIP	G	GS	CG	ShO	Hld.	Sv.-Opp.	IP	H	R	ER	HR	BB-IBB	SO	Avg.
2003— Florida (N.L.)	0	0	...	6.35	1.94	2	0	0	0	0	0-0	5.2	7	5	4	2	4-1	5	.304

WORLD SERIES RECORD

Year Team (League)	W	L	Pct.	ERA	WHIP	G	GS	CG	ShO	Hld.	Sv.-Opp.	IP	H	R	ER	HR	BB-IBB	SO	Avg.
2003— Florida (N.L.)	0	0	...	6.75	0.75	1	0	0	0	0	0-0	2.2	2	2	2	1	0-0	2	.200

2006 LEFTY-RIGHTY SPLITS

vs.	Avg.	AB	H	2B	3B	HR	RBI	BB	SO	OBP	Slg.	vs.	Avg.	AB	H	2B	3B	HR	RBI	BB	SO	OBP	Slg.
L	.250	48	12	8	0	2	8	9	11	.362	.542	R	.171	76	13	3	0	4	10	6	21	.229	.368

HELMS, WES — 3B/1B

PERSONAL: Born May 12, 1976, in Gastonia, N.C. ... 6-4/231. ... Bats right, throws right. ... Full name: Wesley Ray Helms. ... High school: Ashbrook (Gastonia, N.C.). **TRANSACTIONS/CAREER NOTES:** Selected by Atlanta Braves organization in 10th round of 1994 free-agent draft. ... On disabled list (April 3-July 15 and September 5, 1999-remainder of season); included rehabilitation assignment to GCL Braves. ... On disabled list (August 10-September 10, 2002). ... Traded by Braves with P John Foster to Milwaukee Brewers for P Ray King (December 16, 2002). ... On disabled list (August 7-22, 2003); included rehabilitation assignment to Indianapolis. ... On disabled list (May 19-June 28, 2004); included rehabilitation assignment to Indianapolis. ... Signed as a free agent by Florida Marlins (January 3, 2006). **STATISTICAL NOTES:** Career major league grand slams: 3.

2006 GAMES PLAYED BY POSITION (MLB): 1B—88, 3B—24, OF—1.

Year Team (League)	Pos.	G	AB	R	H	2B	3B	HR	RBI	BB	SO	HBP	GDP	SB-CS	Avg.	OBP	SLG	OPS	E	Avg.
1994— GC Braves (GCL)	3B	56	184	22	49	15	1	4	29	22	36	4	3	6-1	.266	.355	.424	.779	20	.875
1995— Macon (S. Atl.)	3B	136	539	89	149	32	1	11	85	50	107	10	8	2-2	.276	.347	.401	.748	40	.900
1996— Durham (Carol.)	3B	67	258	40	83	19	2	13	54	12	51	7	7	1-1	.322	.367	.562	.929	15	.920
— Greenville (Sou.)	3B	64	231	24	59	13	2	4	22	13	48	4	6	2-1	.255	.306	.381	.687	12	.924
1997— Richmond (Int'l)	3B	32	110	11	21	4	0	3	15	10	34	5	4	1-1	.191	.286	.309	.595	9	.902
— Greenville (Sou.)	3B	86	314	50	93	14	1	11	44	33	50	6	14	3-4	.296	.371	.452	.823	11	.950
1998— Richmond (Int'l)	3B-DH	125	451	56	124	27	1	13	75	35	103	13	11	6-2	.275	.342	.426	.768	15	.952
— Atlanta (N.L.)	3B	7	13	2	4	1	0	1	2	0	4	0	0	0-0	.308	.308	.615	.923	1	.750
1999— GC Braves (GCL)	DH-1B	9	33	1	15	3	0	0	10	5	4	1	0	0-1	.455	.538	.515	1.054	0	1.000
— Greenville (Sou.)	1B	30	113	15	34	6	0	8	26	7	34	1	3	1-0	.301	.347	.566	.913	4	.984
2000— Richmond (Int'l)	3B	136	539	74	155	27	7	20	88	27	92	6	10	0-6	.288	.325	.475	.800	23	.933
— Atlanta (N.L.)	3B	6	5	0	1	0	0	0	0	0	2	0	0	0-0	.200	.200	.200	.400	1	.833
2001— Atlanta (N.L.)	1B-3B-OF	100	216	28	48	10	3	10	36	21	56	1	3	1-1	.222	.293	.435	.728	4	.992
2002— Atlanta (N.L.)	1B-3B-OF	85	210	20	51	16	0	6	22	11	57	3	5	1-1	.243	.283	.405	.687	5	.986
2003— Indianapolis (Int'l)	3B	2	5	0	2	0	0	0	2	1	1	0	0	0-0	.400	.500	.400	.900	0	1.000
— Milwaukee (N.L.)	3B	134	476	56	124	21	0	23	67	43	131	10	10	0-1	.261	.330	.450	.780	19	.945
2004— Indianapolis (Int'l)	3B-DH	6	19	4	6	1	0	0	1	3	4	0	0	0-0	.316	.409	.368	.778	2	.857
— Milwaukee (N.L.)	3B-1B	92	274	24	72	13	1	4	28	24	60	5	10	0-0	.263	.331	.361	.692	18	.925
2005— Milwaukee (N.L.)	3B-1B-DH	95	168	18	50	13	1	4	24	14	30	3	7	0-1	.298	.356	.458	.815	3	.982
2006— Florida (N.L.)	1B-3B-OF	140	240	30	79	15	3	10	47	21	55	6	7	0-4	.329	.390	.575	.965	2	.995
Major League totals (8 years)		659	1602	178	429	93	10	58	226	134	395	28	42	2-9	.268	.331	.447	.777	53	.974

DIVISION SERIES RECORD

Year Team (League)	Pos.	G	AB	R	H	2B	3B	HR	RBI	BB	SO	HBP	GDP	SB-CS	Avg.	OBP	SLG	OPS	E	Avg.
2002— Atlanta (N.L.)	1B	1	0	0	0	0	0	0	0	0	0	0	0	0-0	...	...	...	...	0	...

2006 LEFTY-RIGHTY SPLITS

vs.	Avg.	AB	H	2B	3B	HR	RBI	BB	SO	OBP	Slg.	vs.	Avg.	AB	H	2B	3B	HR	RBI	BB	SO	OBP	Slg.
L	.336	107	36	9	2	3	22	13	29	.414	.505	R	.323	133	43	10	5	7	25	8	26	.368	.632

HELTON, TODD — 1B

PERSONAL: Born August 20, 1973, in Knoxville, Tenn. ... 6-2/204. ... Bats left, throws left. ... Full name: Todd Lynn Helton. ... High school: Knoxville (Tenn.) Central. ... **College:** Tennessee. **TRANSACTIONS/CAREER NOTES:** Selected by San Diego Padres organization in second round of 1992 free-agent draft; did not sign. ... Selected by Colorado Rockies organization in first round (eighth pick overall) of 1995 free-agent draft. ... On disabled list (July 26-August 10, 2005); included rehabilitation assignment to Colorado Springs. ... On disabled list (April 20-May 5, 2006); included rehabilitation assignment to Colorado Springs. **HONORS:** Named N.L. Rookie Player of the Year by THE SPORTING NEWS (1998). ... Named first baseman on THE SPORTING NEWS N.L. All-Star team (2000-03). ... Won N.L. Gold Glove at first base (2001, 2002 and 2004). ... Named first baseman on N.L. Silver Slugger team (2000-03). **STATISTICAL NOTES:** Hit for the cycle (June 19, 1999). ... Hit three home runs in one game (May 1, 2000; and May 29, 2003). ... Career major league grand slams: 4.

2006 GAMES PLAYED BY POSITION (MLB): 1B—145.

Year Team (League)	Pos.	G	AB	R	H	2B	3B	HR	RBI	BB	SO	HBP	GDP	SB-CS	Avg.	OBP	SLG	OPS	E	Avg.
1995— Asheville (S. Atl.)	1B-DH	54	201	24	51	11	1	1	15	25	32	1	7	1-1	.254	.339	.333	.673	4	.990
1996— New Haven (East.)	1B-DH	93	319	46	106	24	2	7	51	51	37	1	8	2-5	.332	.425	.486	.911	5	.994
— Colo. Springs (PCL)	1B-OF	21	71	13	25	4	1	2	13	11	12	0	3	0-0	.352	.439	.521	.960	2	.988
1997— Colo. Springs (PCL)	1B-OF-DH	99	392	87	138	31	2	16	88	61	68	0	10	3-1	.352	.434	.564	.997	9	.987
— Colorado (N.L.)	OF-1B	35	93	13	26	2	1	5	11	8	11	0	1	0-1	.280	.337	.484	.821	0	1.000
1998— Colorado (N.L.)	1B	152	530	78	167	37	1	25	97	53	54	6	15	3-3	.315	.380	.530	.911	9	.995
1999— Colorado (N.L.)	1B	159	578	114	185	39	5	35	113	68	77	6	14	7-6	.320	.395	.587	.981	9	.993
2000— Colorado (N.L.)	1B	160	580	138	* 216	* 59	2	42	* 147	103	61	4	12	5-3	* .372	* .463	* .698	1.162	7	.995
2001— Colorado (N.L.)	1B	159	587	132	197	54	2	49	146	98	104	5	14	7-5	.336	.432	.685	1.116	2	.999
2002— Colorado (N.L.)	1B	156	553	107	182	39	4	30	109	99	91	5	14	5-1	.329	.429	.577	1.006	7	.995
2003— Colorado (N.L.)	1B	160	583	135	209	49	5	33	117	111	72	2	19	0-4	.358	.458	.630	1.088	11	.993
2004— Colorado (N.L.)	1B	154	547	115	190	49	2	32	96	127	72	3	12	3-0	.347	.469	.620	1.088	4	.997
2005— Colo. Springs (PCL)	1B	2	5	1	3	2	0	1	1	1	1	0	0	0-0	.600	.714	1.000	1.714	0	1.000
— Colorado (N.L.)	1B	144	509	92	163	45	2	20	79	106	80	9	14	3-0	.320	* .445	.534	.979	5	.996
2006— Colo. Springs (PCL)	1B	2	6	0	2	0	0	0	0	1	1	0	0	0-0	.333	.429	.333	.762	0	1.000
— Colorado (N.L.)	1B	145	546	94	165	40	5	15	81	91	64	6	10	3-2	.302	.404	.476	.880	4	.997
Major League totals (10 years)		1424	5106	1018	1700	413	29	286	996	864	686	46	121	36-25	.333	.430	.593	1.023	56	.996

				ALL-STAR GAME RECORD																
	G	AB	R	H	2B	3B	HR	RBI	BB	SO	HBP	GDP	SB-CS	Avg.	OBP	SLG	OPS	E	Avg.
All-Star Game totals (5 years)	5	9	2	2	0	0	1	3	0	2	0	0	0-0	.222	.222	.556	.778	0	1.000

2006 LEFTY-RIGHTY SPLITS

vs.	Avg.	AB	H	2B	3B	HR	RBI	BB	SO	OBP	Slg.	vs.	Avg.	AB	H	2B	3B	HR	RBI	BB	SO	OBP	Slg.
L	.326	132	43	8	0	2	24	14	19	.392	.432	R	.295	414	122	32	5	13	57	77	45	.407	.490

HENDRICKSON, BEN — P

PERSONAL: Born February 4, 1981, in St. Cloud, Minn. ... 6-4/190. ... Throws right, bats right. ... Full name: Benjamin J. Hendrickson. ... High school: Jefferson (Bloomington, Minn.). **TRANSACTIONS/CAREER NOTES:** Selected by Milwaukee Brewers organization in 10th round of 1999 free-agent draft.
CAREER HITTING: 2-for-19 (.105), 0 R, 0 2B, 0 3B, 0 HR, 0 RBI.

Year	Team (League)	W	L	Pct.	ERA	WHIP	G	GS	CG	ShO	Hld.	Sv.-Opp.	IP	H	R	ER	HR	BB-IBB	SO	Avg.
2000—	Ogden (Pion.)	4	3	.571	5.68	1.56	13	7	0	0	...	1-...	50.2	50	37	32	7	29-0	48	.245
2001—	Beloit (Midw.)	8	9	.471	2.84	1.46	25	25	1	0	...	0-...	133.1	122	58	42	3	72-0	133	.246
2002—	High Desert (Calif.)	5	5	.500	2.55	1.25	14	14	0	0	...	0-...	81.1	61	31	23	3	41-0	70	.209
—	Huntsville (Sou.)	4	2	.667	2.97	1.32	13	13	0	0	...	0-...	69.2	57	31	23	2	35-0	50	.231
2003—	Huntsville (Sou.)	7	6	.538	3.45	1.40	17	16	0	0	...	0-...	78.1	82	35	30	6	28-0	56	.278
2004—	Indianapolis (Int'l)	11	3	.786	2.02	1.12	21	21	2	2	...	0-...	125.0	114	32	28	6	26-0	93	.246
—	Milwaukee (N.L.)	1	8	.111	6.22	1.68	10	9	0	0	0	0-0	46.1	58	33	32	6	20-1	29	.310
2005—	Nashville (PCL)	6	12	.333	4.97	1.50	28	27	1	0	0	0-0	155.2	176	100	86	17	58-2	122	.292
2006—	Nashville (PCL)	9	8	.529	3.36	1.20	23	23	1	0	0	0-0	139.1	121	60	52	9	46-0	97	.241
—	Milwaukee (N.L.)	0	2	.000	12.00	2.50	4	3	0	0	0	0-0	12.0	21	17	16	0	9-0	8	.382
Major League totals (2 years)		1	10	.091	7.41	1.85	14	12	0	0	0	0-0	58.1	79	50	48	6	29-1	37	.326

2006 LEFTY-RIGHTY SPLITS

vs.	Avg.	AB	H	2B	3B	HR	RBI	BB	SO	OBP	Slg.	vs.	Avg.	AB	H	2B	3B	HR	RBI	BB	SO	OBP	Slg.
L	.571	21	12	4	0	0	8	6	2	.643	.762	R	.265	34	9	2	0	0	8	3	6	.324	.324

HENDRICKSON, MARK — P

PERSONAL: Born June 23, 1974, in Mount Vernon, Wash. ... 6-9/230. ... Throws left, bats left. ... Full name: Mark Allan Hendrickson. ... High school: Mount Vernon (Wash.). ... College: Washington State. **TRANSACTIONS/CAREER NOTES:** Selected by Atlanta Braves organization in 12th round of 1992 free-agent draft; did not sign. ... Selected by San Diego Padres organization in 21st round of 1993 free-agent draft; did not sign. ... Selected by Braves organization in 32nd round of 1994 free-agent draft; did not sign. ... Selected by Detroit Tigers organization in 16th round of 1995 free-agent draft; did not sign. ... Selected by Texas Rangers organization in 19th round of 1996 free-agent draft; did not sign. ... Selected by Toronto Blue Jays organization in 20th round of 1997 free-agent draft. ... Traded by Blue Jays to Tampa Bay Devil Rays as part of three-team deal in which Blue Jays acquired P Justin Speier from Colorado Rockies and Rockies acquired P Joe Kennedy from Devil Rays and a player to be named from Blue Jays (December 14, 2003); Rockies acquired P Sandy Nin to complete deal (December 15, 2003). ... On disabled list (April 7-25, 2006). ... Traded by Devil Rays with C Toby Hall and cash to Los Angeles Dodgers for C Dioner Navarro, P Jae Seo and a player to be named (June 27, 2006). **MISCELLANEOUS NOTES:** Drafted by Philadelphia 76ers in second round (31st pick overall) of 1996 NBA draft. ... Played for four NBA teams (1997-2000).
CAREER HITTING: 3-for-35 (.086), 3 R, 0 2B, 0 3B, 1 HR, 1 RBI.

Year	Team (League)	W	L	Pct.	ERA	WHIP	G	GS	CG	ShO	Hld.	Sv.-Opp.	IP	H	R	ER	HR	BB-IBB	SO	Avg.
1998—	Dunedin (Fla. St.)	4	3	.571	2.37	1.42	16	5	0	0	...	1-...	49.1	44	16	13	2	26-1	38	.249
1999—	Knoxville (Southern)	2	7	.222	6.63	1.69	12	11	0	0	...	0-...	55.2	73	46	41	4	21-0	39	.319
2000—	Dunedin (Fla. St.)	2	2	.500	5.61	1.79	12	12	1	0	...	0-...	51.1	63	34	32	7	29-0	38	.315
—	Tennessee (Sou.)	3	1	.750	3.63	1.11	6	6	0	0	...	0-...	39.2	32	17	16	5	12-0	29	.216
2001—	Syracuse (Int'l)	2	9	.182	4.66	1.34	38	6	0	0	...	0-...	73.1	80	43	38	13	18-1	33	.274
2002—	Syracuse (Int'l)	7	5	.583	3.52	1.22	19	14	0	0	...	0-...	92.0	90	38	36	12	22-0	68	.254
—	Toronto (A.L.)	3	0	1.000	2.45	1.01	16	4	0	0	1	0-1	36.2	25	11	10	1	12-3	21	.202
2003—	Syracuse (Int'l)	0	0	...	4.50	1.50	1	1	0	0	...	0-...	6.0	8	4	3	1	1-0	5	.333
—	Dunedin (Fla. St.)	1	0	1.000	1.59	1.60	1	1	0	0	...	0-...	5.2	5	2	1	0	4-0	3	.227
—	Toronto (A.L.)	9	9	.500	5.51	1.58	30	30	1	1	0	0-0	158.1	207	111	97	24	40-3	76	.317
2004—	Tampa Bay (A.L.)	10	15	.400	4.81	1.40	32	30	2	0	0	0-0	183.1	211	113	98	21	46-5	87	.285
2005—	Tampa Bay (A.L.)	11	8	.579	5.90	1.55	31	31	1	0	0	0-0	178.1	227	126	117	24	49-1	89	.311
2006—	Tampa Bay (A.L.)	4	8	.333	3.81	1.28	13	13	1	1	0	0-0	89.2	81	42	38	10	34-0	51	.241
—	Los Angeles (N.L.)	2	7	.222	4.68	1.60	18	12	0	0	1	0-0	75.0	92	45	39	7	28-0	48	.299
American League totals (5 years)		37	40	.481	5.01	1.44	122	108	5	2	1	0-1	646.1	751	403	360	80	181-12	324	.291
National League totals (1 year)		2	7	.222	4.68	1.60	18	12	0	0	1	0-0	75.0	92	45	39	7	28-0	48	.299
Major League totals (5 years)		39	47	.453	4.98	1.46	140	120	5	2	2	0-1	721.1	843	448	399	87	209-12	372	.291

					DIVISION SERIES RECORD															
Year	Team (League)	W	L	Pct.	ERA	WHIP	G	GS	CG	ShO	Hld.	Sv.-Opp.	IP	H	R	ER	HR	BB-IBB	SO	Avg.
2006—	Los Angeles (N.L.)	0	0	...	0.00	0.75	3	0	0	0	0	0-0	2.2	1	0	0	0	1-0	1	.125

2006 LEFTY-RIGHTY SPLITS

vs.	Avg.	AB	H	2B	3B	HR	RBI	BB	SO	OBP	Slg.	vs.	Avg.	AB	H	2B	3B	HR	RBI	BB	SO	OBP	Slg.
L	.287	129	37	6	0	2	14	16	25	.370	.380	R	.264	515	136	25	0	15	62	46	74	.326	.400

HENN, SEAN — P

PERSONAL: Born April 23, 1981, in Fort Worth, Texas. ... 6-4/215. ... Throws left, bats right. ... Full name: Sean Michael Henn. ... Junior college: McLennan (Texas) C.C. **TRANSACTIONS/CAREER NOTES:** Selected by New York Yankees organization in 26th round of 2000 free-agent draft.
CAREER HITTING: 0-for-0 (.000), 0 R, 0 2B, 0 3B, 0 HR, 0 RBI.

Year	Team (League)	W	L	Pct.	ERA	WHIP	G	GS	CG	ShO	Hld.	Sv.-Opp.	IP	H	R	ER	HR	BB-IBB	SO	Avg.
2001—	Staten Is. (N.Y.-Penn)	3	1	.750	3.00	0.98	9	8	0	0	...	1-...	42.0	26	15	14	3	15-0	49	.178
2003—	Tampa (Fla. St.)	4	3	.571	3.61	1.47	16	16	0	0	...	0-...	72.1	69	31	29	3	37-0	52	.259
—	GC Yankees (GCL)	1	1	.500	2.25	1.00	2	1	0	0	...	0-...	8.0	5	3	2	1	3-0	10	.167
2004—	Trenton (East.)	6	8	.429	4.41	1.44	27	27	0	0	...	0-...	163.1	173	94	80	11	63-2	118	.280
2005—	Trenton (East.)	2	1	.667	0.71	0.99	4	4	0	0	0	0-0	25.1	16	2	2	1	9-0	21	.188
—	New York (A.L.)	0	3	.000	11.12	2.56	5	3	0	0	0	0-0	11.1	18	16	14	3	11-0	3	.360
—	Columbus (Int'l)	5	5	.500	3.23	1.23	16	16	1	1	0	0-0	86.1	79	37	31	5	27-1	64	.254
2006—	Columbus (Int'l)	3	1	.750	4.01	1.50	18	6	0	0	0	1	42.2	44	19	19	1	20-0	33	.275
—	New York (A.L.)	0	1	.000	4.82	1.71	4	1	0	0	0	0-0	9.1	11	5	5	2	5-0	7	.297
Major League totals (2 years)		0	4	.000	8.27	2.18	7	4	0	0	0	0-0	20.2	29	21	19	5	16-0	10	.333

2006 LEFTY-RIGHTY SPLITS

vs.	Avg.	AB	H	2B	3B	HR	RBI	BB	SO	OBP	Slg.	vs.	Avg.	AB	H	2B	3B	HR	RBI	BB	SO	OBP	Slg.
L	.357	14	5	0	0	1	1	0	1	.357	.571	R	.261	23	6	2	0	1	2	5	6	.400	.478

H

HENNESSEY, BRAD — P

PERSONAL: Born February 7, 1980, in Toledo, Ohio. ... 6-2/185. ... Throws right, bats right. ... Full name: Brad Martin Hennessey. ... High school: Whitmer (Toldeo). ... College: Youngstown State. **TRANSACTIONS/CAREER NOTES:** Selected by San Francisco Giants organization in first round (21st pick overall) of 2001 free-agent draft. **MISCELLANEOUS NOTES:** Had a sacrifice hit in only appearance as pinch hitter and appeared in one game as pinch runner (2006).
CAREER HITTING: 18-for-79 (.228), 5 R, 2 2B, 0 3B, 2 HR, 7 RBI.

Year Team (League)	W	L	Pct.	ERA	WHIP	G	GS	CG	ShO	Hld.	Sv.-Opp.	IP	H	R	ER	HR	BB-IBB	SO	Avg.
2001— Salem-Keizer (N'west)	1	0	1.000	2.38	1.15	9	9	0	0	...	0-...	34.0	28	9	9	1	11-0	22	.224
2002—		Did not play.																	
2003— Hagerstown (SAL)	3	9	.250	4.20	1.36	15	15	1	0	...	0-...	79.1	81	49	37	6	27-0	44	.265
2004— Norwich (East.)	5	5	.500	3.56	1.39	18	18	0	0	...	0-...	101.0	106	42	40	8	34-0	55	.272
— Fresno (PCL)	4	1	.800	2.02	1.15	5	5	0	0	...	0-...	35.2	26	8	8	2	15-0	16	.202
— San Francisco (N.L.)	2	2	.500	4.98	1.66	7	7	0	0	0	0-0	34.1	42	24	19	2	15-1	25	.294
2005— Fresno (PCL)	4	2	.667	5.19	1.43	11	11	0	0	0	0-0	67.2	75	40	39	7	22-1	46	.279
— San Francisco (N.L.)	5	8	.385	4.64	1.51	21	21	0	0	0	0-0	118.1	127	63	61	15	52-3	64	.276
2006— Fresno (PCL)	0	1	.000	2.53	1.13	2	2	0	0	0	0-0	10.2	11	9	3	1	1-0	7	.250
— San Francisco (N.L.)	5	6	.455	4.26	1.35	34	12	0	0	2	1-1	99.1	92	53	47	12	42-1	42	.251
Major League totals (3 years)	**12**	**16**	**.429**	**4.54**	**1.47**	**62**	**40**	**0**	**0**	**2**	**1-1**	**252.0**	**261**	**140**	**127**	**29**	**109-5**	**131**	**.269**

2006 LEFTY-RIGHTY SPLITS

vs.	Avg.	AB	H	2B	3B	HR	RBI	BB	SO	OBP	Slg.	vs.	Avg.	AB	H	2B	3B	HR	RBI	BB	SO	OBP	Slg.
L	.230	148	34	9	2	5	20	23	16	.335	.419	R	.265	219	58	12	0	7	30	19	26	.347	.416

HENSLEY, CLAY — P

PERSONAL: Born August 31, 1979, in Tomball, Texas. ... 5-11/190. ... Throws right, bats right. ... Full name: Clayton Allen Hensley. ... High school: Dearland (Texas). ... College: Lamar. **TRANSACTIONS/CAREER NOTES:** Selected by San Francisco Giants organization in eighth round of 2002 free-agent draft. ... Traded by Giants with a player to be named or cash to San Diego Padres for RHP Matt Herges (July 13, 2003); Padres acquired P R.D. Spiehs to complete deal (July 27, 2003). **RECORDS:** Shares major league record for most strikeouts as a batter, 9-inning game (5, May 14, 2006). **MISCELLANEOUS NOTES:** Appeared in two games as pinch runner (2006).
CAREER HITTING: 5-for-54 (.093), 2 R, 2 2B, 0 3B, 2 RBI.

Year Team (League)	W	L	Pct.	ERA	WHIP	G	GS	CG	ShO	Hld.	Sv.-Opp.	IP	H	R	ER	HR	BB-IBB	SO	Avg.
2002— Salem-Keizer (N'west)	7	0	1.000	2.53	1.19	15	15	1	0	...	0-...	81.2	72	31	23	3	25-0	84	.235
2003— Hagerstown (SAL)	4	3	.571	3.18	1.12	12	12	3	2	...	0-...	68.0	56	26	24	4	20-0	74	.223
— San Jose (Calif.)	2	3	.400	5.83	1.60	5	5	0	0	...	0-...	29.1	38	20	19	4	9-0	25	.336
— Lake Elsinore (Calif.)	3	4	.429	3.45	1.44	8	8	0	0	...	0-...	44.1	50	24	17	0	14-0	40	.286
2004— Mobile (Sou.)	11	10	.524	4.30	1.35	27	27	2	1	0	0-...	159.0	167	84	76	14	48-2	125	.281
2005— Portland (PCL)	2	2	.500	2.99	0.94	15	14	0	0	0	0-0	90.1	63	31	30	8	22-0	71	.197
— San Diego (N.L.)	1	1	.500	1.70	1.05	24	1	0	0	2	0-0	47.2	33	12	9	0	17-2	28	.195
2006— San Diego (N.L.)	11	12	.478	3.71	1.34	37	29	1	1	1	0-1	187.0	174	82	77	15	76-7	122	.250
Major League totals (2 years)	**12**	**13**	**.480**	**3.30**	**1.28**	**61**	**30**	**1**	**1**	**3**	**0-1**	**234.2**	**207**	**94**	**86**	**15**	**93-9**	**150**	**.240**

DIVISION SERIES RECORD

Year Team (League)	W	L	Pct.	ERA	WHIP	G	GS	CG	ShO	Hld.	Sv.-Opp.	IP	H	R	ER	HR	BB-IBB	SO	Avg.
2005— San Diego (N.L.)	0	0	...	3.86	1.50	3	0	0	0	0	0-0	4.2	4	2	2	0	3-0	1	.235
2006— San Diego (N.L.)	0	0	...	0.00	1.13	2	0	0	0	0	0-0	2.2	2	0	0	0	1-0	0	.200
Division series totals (2 years)	**0**	**0**	**...**	**2.45**	**1.36**	**5**	**0**	**0**	**0**	**0**	**0-0**	**7.1**	**6**	**2**	**2**	**0**	**4-0**	**1**	**.222**

2006 LEFTY-RIGHTY SPLITS

vs.	Avg.	AB	H	2B	3B	HR	RBI	BB	SO	OBP	Slg.	vs.	Avg.	AB	H	2B	3B	HR	RBI	BB	SO	OBP	Slg.
L	.263	327	86	20	2	4	29	36	59	.337	.373	R	.239	368	88	17	1	11	48	40	63	.316	.380

HERGES, MATT — P

PERSONAL: Born April 1, 1970, in Champaign, Ill. ... 6-0/200. ... Throws right, bats left. ... Full name: Matthew Tyler Herges. ... Name pronounced: hur-JISS. ... High school: Centennial (Champaign, Ill.). ... College: Illinois State. **TRANSACTIONS/CAREER NOTES:** Signed as a non-drafted free agent by Los Angeles Dodgers organization (June 13, 1992). ... Traded by Dodgers with IF Jorge Nunez to Montreal Expos for P Guillermo Mota and OF Wilkin Ruan (March 24, 2002). ... Traded by Expos to Pittsburgh Pirates for Ps Chris Young and Jon Searles (December 20, 2002). ... Released by Pirates (March 26, 2003). ... Signed by San Diego Padres organization (April 11, 2003). ... Traded by Padres to San Francisco Giants for P Clay Hensley and a player to be named (July 13, 2003); Padres acquired P R.D. Spiehs to complete the deal (July 28, 2003). ... Traded by Giants to Arizona Diamondbacks for OF Doug Devore (June 3, 2005). ... Signed as a free agent by Florida Marlins (February 1, 2006).
CAREER HITTING: 6-for-27 (.222), 0 R, 0 2B, 0 3B, 0 HR, 1 RBI.

Year Team (League)	W	L	Pct.	ERA	WHIP	G	GS	CG	ShO	Hld.	Sv.-Opp.	IP	H	R	ER	HR	BB-IBB	SO	Avg.
1992— Yakima (N'west)	2	3	.400	3.22	1.28	27	0	0	0	...	9-...	44.2	33	21	16	2	24-1	57	.199
1993— Bakersfield (Calif.)	2	6	.250	3.69	1.39	51	0	0	0	...	2-...	90.1	70	49	37	6	56-6	84	.214
1994— Vero Beach (FSL)	8	9	.471	3.32	1.33	48	3	1	0	...	3-...	111.0	115	45	41	8	33-3	61	.268
1995— San Antonio (Texas)	0	3	.000	4.88	1.81	19	0	0	0	...	8-...	27.2	34	16	15	2	16-1	18	.306
— San Bern. (Calif.)	5	2	.714	3.66	1.41	22	2	0	0	...	1-...	51.2	58	29	21	3	15-0	35	.275
1996— San Antonio (Texas)	3	2	.600	2.71	1.34	30	6	0	0	...	3-...	83.0	83	38	25	3	28-0	45	.261
— Albuquerque (PCL)	4	1	.800	2.60	1.36	10	4	2	1	...	0-...	34.2	33	11	10	2	14-0	15	.270
1997— Albuquerque (PCL)	0	8	.000	8.89	1.72	31	12	0	0	...	0-...	85.0	120	92	84	13	46-1	61	.340
— San Antonio (Texas)	0	1	.000	8.80	2.09	4	3	0	0	...	0-...	15.1	22	15	15	2	10-0	12	.355
1998— Albuquerque (PCL)	3	5	.375	5.71	1.72	34	8	0	0	...	0-...	88.1	115	64	56	9	37-1	75	.325
— San Antonio (Texas)	0	0	...	0.83	0.83	3	0	0	0	...	0-...	6.0	3	0	0	0	2-0	3	.158
1999— Albuquerque (PCL)	8	3	.727	4.73	1.39	21	21	0	0	...	0-...	131.1	135	82	69	17	47-0	88	.272
— Los Angeles (N.L.)	0	2	.000	4.07	1.32	17	0	0	0	1	0-2	24.1	24	13	11	5	8-0	18	.255
2000— Los Angeles (N.L.)	11	3	.786	3.17	1.41	59	4	0	0	4	1-3	110.2	100	43	39	7	40-5	75	.249
2001— Los Angeles (N.L.)	9	8	.529	3.44	1.44	75	0	0	0	15	1-8	99.1	97	39	38	8	46-12	76	.259
2002— Montreal (N.L.)	2	5	.286	4.04	1.64	62	0	0	0	9	6-14	64.2	80	33	29	10	26-8	50	.305
2003— Portland (PCL)	0	0	...	1.80	0.60	4	0	0	0	...	0-...	5.0	1	1	1	0	2-0	5	.063
— San Diego (N.L.)	2	2	.500	2.86	1.36	40	0	0	0	4	3-5	44.0	40	16	14	2	20-2	40	.244
— San Francisco (N.L.)	1	0	1.000	2.31	1.06	22	0	0	0	3	0-1	35.0	28	11	9	1	9-0	28	.219
2004— San Francisco (N.L.)	5	1	.444	5.23	1.70	70	0	0	0	5	23-31	65.1	90	44	38	8	21-4	39	.338
2005— San Francisco (N.L.)	1	1	.500	4.71	1.43	21	0	0	0	3	0-0	21.0	23	11	11	2	7-1	6	.288
— Arizona (N.L.)	0	0	...	13.50	2.13	7	0	0	0	0	0-0	8.0	12	12	12	4	5-0	3	.343
— Tucson (PCL)	1	2	.333	3.14	1.64	26	0	0	0	0	0-0	28.2	39	13	10	3	8-0	29	.339
2006— Florida (N.L.)	2	3	.400	4.31	1.72	66	0	0	0	9	0-4	71.0	94	42	34	5	28-5	36	.321
Major League totals (8 years)	**32**	**29**	**.525**	**3.89**	**1.47**	**444**	**4**	**0**	**0**	**55**	**34-68**	**543.1**	**588**	**264**	**235**	**52**	**210-37**	**371**	**.280**

H

DIVISION SERIES RECORD

Year Team (League)	W	L	Pct.	ERA	WHIP	G	GS	CG	ShO	Hld.	Sv.-Opp.	IP	H	R	ER	HR	BB-IBB	SO	Avg.
2003— San Francisco (N.L.)	0	0	...	0.00	0.69	3	0	0	0	0	0-0	4.1	1	0	0	0	2-0	5	.083

2006 LEFTY-RIGHTY SPLITS

vs.	Avg.	AB	H	2B	3B	HR	RBI	BB	SO	OBP	Slg.	vs.	Avg.	AB	H	2B	3B	HR	RBI	BB	SO	OBP	Slg.
L	.300	140	42	12	0	2	19	11	19	.359	.429	R	.340	153	52	8	1	3	35	17	17	.407	.464

HERMANSON, DUSTIN — P

PERSONAL: Born December 21, 1972, in Springfield, Ohio. ... 6-2/200. ... Throws right, bats right. ... Full name: Dustin Michael Hermanson. ... High school: Kenton Ridge (Springfield, Ohio). ... College: Kent State. **TRANSACTIONS/CAREER NOTES:** Selected by Pittsburgh Pirates organization in 39th round of 1991 free-agent draft; did not sign. ... Selected by San Diego Padres organization in first round (third pick overall) of 1994 free-agent draft. ... Traded by Padres to Florida Marlins for 2B Quilvio Veras (November 21, 1996). ... Traded by Marlins with OF Joe Orsulak to Montreal Expos for OF/1B Cliff Floyd (March 27, 1997). ... On disabled list (May 15-30, 1998). ... Traded by Expos with P Steve Kline to St. Louis Cardinals for 3B Fernando Tatis and P Britt Reames (December 14, 2000). ... Traded by Cardinals to Boston Red Sox for OF Rick Asadoorian and 1B Garcia and Dustin Brisson (December 15, 2001). ... On disabled list (April 4-July 20 and July 21-August 22, 2002); included rehabilitation assignments to Pawtucket and GCL Red Sox. ... Signed as a free agent by Cardinals (January 20, 2003). ... Released by Cardinals (June 26, 2003). ... Signed by San Francisco Giants organization (July 11, 2003). ... On disabled list (August 24-September 9, 2003). ... On disabled list (April 21-May 8, 2004). ... Signed as a free agent by Chicago White Sox (December 8, 2004). ... On suspended list (April 5-7, 2005). ... On disabled list (April 1-September 5, 2006); included rehabilitation assignment to Charlotte. **STATISTICAL NOTES:** Hit home run in first major league at-bat (April 16, 1997). **MISCELLANEOUS NOTES:** Appeared in one game as pinch runner (2001).

CAREER HITTING: 30-for-322 (.093), 14 R, 5 2B, 0 3B, 2 HR, 10 RBI.

Year Team (League)	W	L	Pct.	ERA	WHIP	G	GS	CG	ShO	Hld.	Sv.-Opp.	IP	H	R	ER	HR	BB-IBB	SO	Avg.
1994— Wichita (Texas)	1	0	1.000	0.43	0.90	16	0	0	0	...	8-...	21.0	13	1	1	0	6-2	30	.176
— Las Vegas (PCL)	0	0	...	6.14	1.50	7	0	0	0	...	3-...	7.1	6	5	5	1	5-0	6	.222
1995— Las Vegas (PCL)	0	1	.000	3.50	1.78	31	0	0	0	...	11-...	36.0	35	23	14	5	29-0	42	.245
— San Diego (N.L.)	3	1	.750	6.82	1.80	26	0	0	0	1	0-0	31.2	35	26	24	8	22-1	19	.280
1996— Las Vegas (PCL)	1	4	.200	3.13	1.48	42	0	0	0	...	21-...	46.0	41	20	16	3	27-7	54	.229
— San Diego (N.L.)	1	0	1.000	8.56	1.61	8	0	0	0	0	0-0	13.2	16	15	13	3	4-0	11	.340
1997— Montreal (N.L.)	8	8	.500	3.69	1.26	32	28	1	1	0	0-0	158.1	134	68	65	15	66-2	136	.234
1998— Montreal (N.L.)	14	11	.560	3.13	1.17	32	30	1	0	1	0-0	187.0	163	80	65	21	56-3	154	.234
1999— Montreal (N.L.)	9	14	.391	4.20	1.36	34	34	0	0	0	0-0	216.1	225	110	101	20	69-4	145	.271
2000— Montreal (N.L.)	12	14	.462	4.77	1.52	38	30	2	1	1	4-7	198.0	226	128	105	26	75-5	94	.290
2001— St. Louis (N.L.)	14	13	.519	4.45	1.39	33	33	0	0	0	0-0	192.1	195	106	95	34	73-3	123	.264
2002— Boston (A.L.)	1	1	.500	7.77	1.91	12	1	0	0	2	0-1	22.0	35	19	19	3	7-0	13	.354
— Pawtucket (Int'l)	0	1	.000	2.63	1.17	5	3	0	0	...	0-...	13.2	9	5	4	0	7-0	11	.191
— GC Red Sox (GCL)	0	0	...	9.00	2.50	1	1	0	0	...	0-...	2.0	5	3	2	0	0-0	1	.500
2003— St. Louis (N.L.)	1	2	.333	5.46	1.65	23	0	0	0	1	1-6	29.2	35	18	18	4	14-2	12	.315
— Fresno (PCL)	0	1	.000	4.85	1.20	4	4	0	0	...	0-...	26.0	29	16	14	2	3-1	17	.290
— San Francisco (N.L.)	2	1	.667	3.00	1.15	9	6	0	0	0	0-0	39.0	35	14	13	5	10-2	27	.238
2004— San Francisco (N.L.)	6	9	.400	4.53	1.36	47	18	0	0	1	17-20	131.0	132	71	66	15	46-5	102	.262
2005— Chicago (A.L.)	2	4	.333	2.04	1.10	57	0	0	0	5	34-39	57.1	46	17	13	4	17-4	33	.222
2006— Charlotte (Int'l)	0	1	.000	3.29	1.10	14	0	0	0	5	0-0	13.2	8	5	5	1	7-0	16	.174
— Chicago (A.L.)	0	0	...	4.05	1.05	6	0	0	0	0	0-0	6.2	6	3	3	2	1-1	5	.240
American League totals (3 years)	3	5	.375	3.66	1.30	75	1	0	0	7	34-40	86.0	87	39	35	9	25-5	51	.263
National League totals (9 years)	70	73	.490	4.25	1.36	282	179	4	2	5	22-33	1197.0	1198	636	565	151	435-27	823	.263
Major League totals (12 years)	73	78	.483	4.21	1.36	357	180	4	2	12	56-73	1283.0	1285	675	600	160	460-32	874	.263

DIVISION SERIES RECORD

Year Team (League)	W	L	Pct.	ERA	WHIP	G	GS	CG	ShO	Hld.	Sv.-Opp.	IP	H	R	ER	HR	BB-IBB	SO	Avg.
2001— St. Louis (N.L.)	0	0	...	0.00	0.00	1	0	0	0	0	0-0	3.0	0	0	0	0	0-0	0	.000
2003— San Francisco (N.L.)	0	0	...	0.00	2.00	1	0	0	0	0	0-0	1.0	1	0	0	0	1-0	0	.250
Division series totals (2 years)	0	0	...	0.00	0.50	2	0	0	0	0	0-0	4.0	1	0	0	0	1-0	0	.077

WORLD SERIES RECORD

Year Team (League)	W	L	Pct.	ERA	WHIP	G	GS	CG	ShO	Hld.	Sv.-Opp.	IP	H	R	ER	HR	BB-IBB	SO	Avg.
2005— Chicago (A.L.)	0	0	...	0.00	3.00	1	0	0	0	0	0-1	0.1	1	0	0	0	0-0	1	.500

2006 LEFTY-RIGHTY SPLITS

vs.	Avg.	AB	H	2B	3B	HR	RBI	BB	SO	OBP	Slg.	vs.	Avg.	AB	H	2B	3B	HR	RBI	BB	SO	OBP	Slg.
L	.167	12	2	1	0	1	1	0	2	.167	.500	R	.308	13	4	2	0	1	4	1	3	.400	.692

HERMIDA, JEREMY — OF

PERSONAL: Born January 30, 1984, in Marietta, Ga. ... 6-4/200. ... Bats left, throws right. ... Full name: Jeremy Ryan Hermida. ... High school: Wheeler (Marietta, Ga.). ... **TRANSACTIONS/CAREER NOTES:** Selected by Florida Marlins organization in first round (11th pick overall) of 2002 free-agent draft. ... On disabled list (April 17-May 22, 2006); included rehabilitation assignment to Jupiter. **STATISTICAL NOTES:** Hit grand slam home run in first major league at-bat (August 31, 2005). ... Career major league grand slams: 1.

2006 GAMES PLAYED BY POSITION (MLB): OF—89.

Year Team (League)	Pos.	G	AB	R	H	2B	3B	HR	RBI	BB	SO	HBP	GDP	SB-CS	Avg.	OBP	SLG	OPS	E	Avg.
2002— GC Marlins (GCL)	OF	38	134	15	30	7	3	0	14	15	25	3	3	5-0	.224	.316	.321	.637	2	.950
— Jamestown (NYP)	OF	13	47	8	15	2	1	0	7	7	10	0	0	1-3	.319	.407	.404	.811	1	.947
2003— Greensboro (S. Atl.)	OF	133	468	73	133	23	5	6	49	80	100	2	3	28-2	.284	.387	.393	.780	8	.964
— Albuquerque (PCL)	OF	1	3	0	0	0	0	0	0	0	3	0	0	0-0	.000	.000	.000	.000	0	1.000
2004— Jupiter (Fla. St.)	OF	91	340	53	101	17	1	10	50	42	73	5	3	10-3	.297	.377	.441	.818	9	.500
2005— Carolina (Southern)	OF-DH	118	386	77	113	29	2	18	63	111	89	7	8	23-2	.293	.457	.518	.975	8	.982
— Florida (N.L.)	OF	23	41	9	12	2	0	4	11	6	12	0	1	2-0	.293	.383	.634	1.017	0	1.000
2006— Jupiter (Fla. St.)		6	17	3	3	1	0	0	2	3	7	0	0	0-0	.176	.300	.235	.535	0	1.000
— Florida (N.L.)	OF	99	307	37	77	19	1	5	28	33	70	5	6	4-1	.251	.332	.368	.700	8	.957
Major League totals (2 years)		122	348	46	89	21	1	9	39	39	82	5	7	6-1	.256	.338	.399	.738	8	.961

2006 LEFTY-RIGHTY SPLITS

vs.	Avg.	AB	H	2B	3B	HR	RBI	BB	SO	OBP	Slg.	vs.	Avg.	AB	H	2B	3B	HR	RBI	BB	SO	OBP	Slg.
L	.219	73	16	2	0	1	2	7	18	.321	.288	R	.261	234	61	17	1	4	26	26	52	.336	.393

HERNANDEZ, ANDERSON — 2B

PERSONAL: Born October 30, 1982, in Santo Domingo, Dominican Republic. ... 5-9/168. ... Bats both, throws right. ... Full name: Anderson Hernandez. ... High school: Don Jose Fe-alegria (Santo Domingo, Dominican Republic). **TRANSACTIONS/CAREER NOTES:** Signed as a non-drafted free agent by Detroit Tigers organization (April 23, 2001).

H

... Traded by Tigers to New York Mets for C Vance Wilson (January 6, 2005). ... On disabled list (April 20-May 22, 2006); included rehabilitation assignments to St. Lucie and Norfolk.

2006 GAMES PLAYED BY POSITION (MLB): 2B—13, SS—10.

Year Team (League)	Pos.	G	AB	R	H	2B	3B	HR	RBI	BB	SO	HBP	GDP	SB-CS	Avg.	OBP	SLG	OPS	E	Avg.
2001— GC Tigers (GCL)	SS-3B	55	216	37	57	5	11	0	18	13	38	0	0	34-8	.264	.303	.389	.692	21	.914
— Lakeland (Fla. St.)	SS	7	21	2	4	0	1	0	1	0	8	0	0	0-0	.190	.190	.286	.476	3	.917
2002— Lakeland (Fla. St.)	SS	123	410	52	106	13	7	2	42	33	102	0	2	16-14	.259	.310	.339	.649	27	.953
2003— Lakeland (Fla. St.)	SS	106	380	47	87	11	4	2	28	27	69	0	10	15-7	.229	.278	.295	.573	26	.947
2004— Lakeland (Fla. St.)	SS	32	122	20	36	4	3	0	11	6	26	0	0	7-0	.295	.326	.377	.703	3	.857
— Erie (East.)	SS	101	394	65	108	19	3	5	29	26	89	5	5	17-6	.274	.326	.376	.702	16	.000
2005— Binghamton (East.)	SS-2B-DH	66	273	46	89	14	1	7	24	14	58	1	0	11-9	.326	.360	.462	.821	14	.946
— Norfolk (Int'l)	2B-SS	66	261	34	79	6	4	2	30	22	46	1	2	24-9	.303	.354	.379	.733	9	.971
— New York (N.L.)	2B-SS	6	18	1	1	0	0	0	0	1	4	0	0	0-1	.056	.105	.056	.161	1	.964
2006— St. Lucie (Fla. St.)		2	9	0	1	0	0	0	0	0	1	0	0	0-0	.111	.111	.111	.222	1	.923
— Norfolk (Int'l)		102	414	44	103	11	4	0	23	21	70	0	4	15-5	.249	.285	.295	.580	14	.973
— New York (N.L.)	2B-SS	25	66	4	10	1	1	0	3	1	12	0	3	0-0	.152	.164	.242	.407	0	1.000
Major League totals (2 years)		31	84	5	11	1	1	0	3	2	16	0	3	0-1	.131	.151	.202	.354	1	.989

CHAMPIONSHIP SERIES RECORD

Year Team (League)	Pos.	G	AB	R	H	2B	3B	HR	RBI	BB	SO	HBP	GDP	SB-CS	Avg.	OBP	SLG	OPS	E	Avg.
2006— New York (N.L.)		2	1	0	0	0	0	0	0	0	1	0	0	0-0	.000	.000	.000	.000	0	...

2006 LEFTY-RIGHTY SPLITS

vs.	Avg.	AB	H	2B	3B	HR	RBI	BB	SO	OBP	Slg.	vs.	Avg.	AB	H	2B	3B	HR	RBI	BB	SO	OBP	Slg.
L	.211	19	4	0	0	1	1	1	2	.250	.368	R	.128	47	6	1	1	0	2	0	10	.128	.191

HERNANDEZ, FELIX   P

PERSONAL: Born April 8, 1986, in Valencia, Venezuela. ... 6-3/225. ... Throws right, bats right. ... Full name: Felix Abraham Hernandez. **TRANSACTIONS/CAREER NOTES:** Signed as a non-drafted free agent by Seattle Mariners organization (July 4, 2002).

CAREER HITTING: 0-for-4 (.000), 0 R, 0 2B, 0 3B, 0 HR, 0 RBI.

Year Team (League)	W	L	Pct.	ERA	WHIP	G	GS	CG	ShO	Hld.	Sv.-Opp.	IP	H	R	ER	HR	BB-IBB	SO	Avg.
2003— Everett (N'west)	7	2	.778	2.29	1.22	11	7	0	0		0-...	55.0	43	17	14	2	24-0	73	.218
— Wisconsin (Midw.)	0	0		1.93	0.86	2	2	0	0		0-...	14.0	9	4	3	1	3-0	18	.176
2004— Inland Empire (Calif.)	9	3	.750	2.74	1.21	16	15	0	0		0-...	92.0	85	31	28	5	26-0	114	.248
— San Antonio (Texas)	5	1	.833	3.30	1.19	10	10	1	1		0-...	57.1	47	23	21	3	21-0	58	.230
2005— Tacoma (PCL)	9	4	.692	2.25	1.25	19	14	1	0	2	0-0	88.0	62	24	22	3	48-0	100	.196
— Seattle (A.L.)	4	4	.500	2.67	1.00	12	12	0	0	0	0-0	84.1	61	26	25	5	23-0	77	.203
2006— Seattle (A.L.)	12	14	.462	4.52	1.34	31	31	2	1	0	0-0	191.0	195	105	96	23	60-2	176	.262
Major League totals (2 years)	16	18	.471	3.96	1.23	43	43	2	1	0	0-0	275.1	256	131	121	28	83-2	253	.245

2006 LEFTY-RIGHTY SPLITS

vs.	Avg.	AB	H	2B	3B	HR	RBI	BB	SO	OBP	Slg.	vs.	Avg.	AB	H	2B	3B	HR	RBI	BB	SO	OBP	Slg.
L	.281	388	109	21	1	18	65	34	91	.340	.479	R	.241	357	86	15	1	5	31	26	85	.300	.331

HERNANDEZ, JOSE   IF/OF

PERSONAL: Born July 14, 1969, in Vega Alta, Puerto Rico. ... 6-1/190. ... Bats right, throws right. ... Full name: Jose Antonio Hernandez. ... Name pronounced: her-NAN-dezz. ... High school: Maestro Ladi (Vega Alta, Puerto Rico). ... College: Interamericana University (Puerto Rico). **TRANSACTIONS/CAREER NOTES:** Signed as a non-drafted free agent by Texas Rangers organization (January 13, 1987). ... Claimed on waivers by Cleveland Indians (April 3, 1992). ... Traded by Indians to Chicago Cubs for P Heathcliff Slocumb (June 1, 1993). ... Traded by Cubs with P Terry Mulholland to Atlanta Braves for Ps Micah Bowie and Ruben Quevedo and a player to be named (July 31, 1999); Cubs acquired P Joey Nation to complete deal (August 24, 1999). ... Signed as a free agent by Milwaukee Brewers (December 16, 1999). ... On disabled list (August 10-September 1, 2000); included rehabilitation assignment to Indianapolis. ... Signed as a free agent by Colorado Rockies (January 24, 2003). ... Traded by Rockies to Chicago Cubs for IF Mark Bellhorn (June 20, 2003). ... Traded by Cubs with P Matt Bruback and a player to be named to Pittsburgh Pirates for 3B Aramis Ramirez, OF Kenny Lofton and cash (July 23, 2003); Pirates acquired IF Bobby Hill to complete deal (August 15, 2003). ... Released by Pirates (October 1, 2003). ... Signed by Los Angeles Dodgers organization (January 27, 2004). ... Signed as a free agent by Cleveland Indians (December 14, 2004). ... Signed as a free agent by Pirates organization (January 27, 2006). ... Traded by Pirates to Philadelphia Phillies for cash (August 22, 2006). **STATISTICAL NOTES:** Career major league grand slams: 5.

2006 GAMES PLAYED BY POSITION (MLB): 1B—19, OF—12, 3B—11, SS—11, 2B—3.

Year Team (League)	Pos.	G	AB	R	H	2B	3B	HR	RBI	BB	SO	HBP	GDP	SB-CS	Avg.	OBP	SLG	OPS	E	Avg.
1987— GC Rangers (GCL)	SS	24	52	5	9	1	1	0	2	9	25	1	1	2-1	.173	.306	.231	.537	5	.932
1988— GC Rangers (GCL)	3B-2B-SS																			
	1B-OF	55	162	19	26	7	1	1	13	12	36	0	5	4-1	.160	.217	.235	.452	8	.958
1989— Gastonia (S. Atl.)	2B-3B-OF																			
	SS	91	215	35	47	7	6	1	16	33	67	0	3	9-2	.219	.323	.321	.644	17	.941
1990— Charlotte (Fla. St.)	OF-SS	121	388	43	99	14	7	1	44	50	122	4	8	11-8	.255	.345	.335	.680	25	.943
1991— Tulsa (Texas)	SS	91	301	36	72	17	4	1	20	26	75	1	6	4-3	.239	.298	.332	.630	15	.968
— Okla. City (A.A.)	SS	14	46	6	14	1	1	1	3	4	10	0	1	0-0	.304	.353	.435	.788	3	.962
— Texas (A.L.)	3B-SS	45	98	8	18	2	1	0	4	3	31	0	2	0-1	.184	.208	.224	.432	4	.976
1992— Cant./Akr. (Eastern)	SS	130	404	56	103	16	4	3	46	37	108	5	5	7-2	.255	.315	.337	.652	40	.932
— Cleveland (A.L.)	SS	3	4	0	0	0	0	0	0	0	2	0	0	0-0	.000	.000	.000	.000	1	.857
1993— Cant./Akr. (Eastern)	SS-3B	45	150	19	30	6	0	2	17	10	39	0	3	9-2	.200	.250	.280	.530	7	.968
— Orlando (South.)	SS	71	263	42	80	8	3	8	33	20	60	0	5	8-4	.304	.352	.449	.801	14	.961
— Iowa (Am. Assoc.)	SS	6	24	3	6	1	0	0	3	0	2	1	1	0-0	.250	.280	.292	.572	1	.976
1994— Chicago (N.L.)	3B-SS-2B																			
	OF	56	132	18	32	2	3	1	9	8	29	1	4	2-2	.242	.291	.326	.617	4	.971
1995— Chicago (N.L.)	SS-3B-2B	93	245	37	60	11	4	13	40	13	69	0	8	1-0	.245	.281	.482	.762	9	.971
1996— Chicago (N.L.)	SS-3B-2B																			
	OF	131	331	52	80	14	1	10	41	24	97	1	10	4-0	.242	.293	.381	.674	20	.952
1997— Chicago (N.L.)	3B-SS-2B																			
	OF-1B-DH	121	183	33	50	8	5	7	26	14	42	0	5	2-5	.273	.323	.486	.810	8	.955
1998— Chicago (N.L.)	3B-OF-SS																			
	1B-2B	149	488	76	124	23	7	23	75	40	140	1	12	4-6	.254	.311	.471	.782	13	.970
1999— Chicago (N.L.)	SS-OF-1B	99	342	57	93	12	2	15	43	40	101	5	5	7-2	.272	.357	.450	.807	11	.973
— Atlanta (N.L.)	SS-1B-OF	48	166	22	42	8	0	4	19	12	44	0	5	4-1	.253	.302	.373	.675	6	.966
2000— Milwaukee (N.L.)	3B-SS-OF	124	446	51	109	22	1	11	59	41	125	6	12	3-7	.244	.315	.372	.687	19	.955

H

Year	Team (League)	Pos.	G	AB	R	H	2B	3B	HR	RBI	BB	SO	HBP	GDP	SB-CS	Avg.	OBP	SLG	OPS	E	Avg.
— Indianapolis (Int'l)	3B	2	9	2	3	0	0	2	3	1	3	0	0	0-0	.333	.400	1.000	1.400	0	1.000
2001— Milwaukee (N.L.)	SS-OF	152	542	67	135	26	2	25	78	39 *	185	2	9	5-4	.249	.300	.443	.743	18	.972
2002— Milwaukee (N.L.)	SS	152	525	72	151	24	2	.24	73	52 *	188	4	19	3-5	.288	.356	.478	.834	19	.973
2003— Colorado (N.L.)	SS-1B	69	257	33	61	6	1	8	27	27	95	0	6	1-1	.237	.308	.362	.670	5	.984
— Chicago (N.L.)	3B-SS-OF																			
	2B	23	69	6	13	3	1	2	9	3	26	0	1	0-0	.188	.222	.348	.570	1	.977
— Pittsburgh (N.L.)	3B	58	193	19	43	9	1	3	21	16	56	1	9	1-0	.223	.282	.326	.608	8	.955
2004— Los Angeles (N.L.)	2B-SS-3B																			
	OF-1B	95	211	32	61	12	1	13	29	26	61	1	3	3-1	.289	.370	.540	.910	5	.981
2005— Cleveland (A.L.)	1B-3B-OF																			
	2B-SS-DH	84	234	28	54	7	0	6	31	14	60	2	11	1-3	.231	.277	.338	.614	2	.995
2006— Pittsburgh (N.L.)	1B-OF-SS																			
	3B-2B	67	120	8	32	7	1	2	12	11	29	0	1	0-0	.267	.328	.350	.678	1	.994
— Philadelphia (N.L.)	3B-SS-OF																			
	1B	18	32	4	8	0	1	7		1	11	0	1	0-0	.250	.273	.406	.679	0	1.000
American League totals (3 years)		132	336	36	72	9	1	6	35	17	93	2	13	1-4	.214	.254	.301	.555	7	.989
National League totals (12 years)		1455	4282	587	1094	184	32	162	568	367	1298	22	112	40-34	.255	.316	.427	.743	147	.970
Major League totals (15 years)		1587	4618	623	1166	193	33	168	603	384	1391	24	125	41-38	.252	.312	.418	.729	154	.972

DIVISION SERIES RECORD

Year	Team (League)	Pos.	G	AB	R	H	2B	3B	HR	RBI	BB	SO	HBP	GDP	SB-CS	Avg.	OBP	SLG	OPS	E	Avg.
1998— Chicago (N.L.)	SS	2	7	1	2	0	0	0	0	0	2	0	0	0-0	.286	.286	.286	.571	2	.750
1999— Atlanta (N.L.)	SS	4	11	1	1	0	0	0	0	1	3	0	1	1-0	.091	.167	.091	.258	1	.938
2004— Los Angeles (N.L.)		1	0	0	0	0	0	0	0	1	0	0	0	0-0	...	1.000	...	1.000	0	...
Division series totals (3 years)		7	18	2	3	0	0	0	0	2	5	0	1	1-0	.167	.250	.167	.417	3	.875

CHAMPIONSHIP SERIES RECORD

Year	Team (League)	Pos.	G	AB	R	H	2B	3B	HR	RBI	BB	SO	HBP	GDP	SB-CS	Avg.	OBP	SLG	OPS	E	Avg.
1999— Atlanta (N.L.)		2	2	0	1	0	0	0	0	1	0	0	0	0-0	.500	.500	.500	1.000	...	...

WORLD SERIES RECORD

Year	Team (League)	Pos.	G	AB	R	H	2B	3B	HR	RBI	BB	SO	HBP	GDP	SB-CS	Avg.	OBP	SLG	OPS	E	Avg.
1999— Atlanta (N.L.)	DH-SS	2	5	0	1	1	0	0	2	0	2	0	0	1-0	.200	.200	.400	.600	0	1.000

ALL-STAR GAME RECORD

			G	AB	R	H	2B	3B	HR	RBI	BB	SO	HBP	GDP	SB-CS	Avg.	OBP	SLG	OPS	E	Avg.
All-Star Game totals (1 year)			1	3	0	0	0	0	0	0	0	2	0	0	0-0	.000	.000	.000	.000	0	1.000

2006 LEFTY-RIGHTY SPLITS

vs.	Avg.	AB	H	2B	3B	HR	RBI	BB	SO	OBP	Slg.	vs.	Avg.	AB	H	2B	3B	HR	RBI	BB	SO	OBP	Slg.
L	.290	62	18	2	0	2	12	5	17	.343	.419	R	.244	90	22	2	1	1	7	7	23	.299	.322

HERNANDEZ, LIVAN — P

PERSONAL: Born February 20, 1975, in Villa Clara, Cuba. ... 6-2/245. ... Throws right, bats right. ... Full name: Eisler Livan Hernandez. ... Name pronounced: lee-VAHN. ... Half-brother of Orlando Hernandez, pitcher with Arizona Diamondbacks and New York Mets in 2006. **TRANSACTIONS/CAREER NOTES:** Signed as a non-drafted free agent by Florida Marlins oorganization (January 13, 1996). ... Traded by Marlins to San Francisco Giants for Ps Jason Grilli and P Nate Bump (July 24, 1999). ... Traded by Giants with 3B/C Edwards Guzman and cash to Montreal Expos for P Jim Brower and a player to be named (March 24, 2003); Giants acquired P Matt Blank to complete deal (April 30, 2003). ... Expos franchise transferred to Washington, D.C., and renamed Washington Nationals for 2005 season (December 3, 2004). ... Traded by Nationals with cash to Arizona Diamondbacks for Ps Garrett Mock and Matthew Chico (August 7, 2006). **HONORS:** Named pitcher on N.L. Silver Slugger team (2004). **MISCELLANEOUS NOTES:** Made an out and struck out in two appearances as pinch hitter (1998). ... Struck out in only appearance as pinch hitter (1999). ... Struck out in only appearance as pinch hitter (2000). ... Appeared one game as pinch hitter (2001). ... Had a sacrifice hit and made two outs in three appearances as pinch hitter (2002). ... Had a sacrifice hit in only appearance as pinch hitter (2004). ... Singled, drove in a run and struck out in three appearances as pinch hitter (2006).
CAREER HITTING: 167-for-714 (.234), 48 R, 33 2B, 2 3B, 8 HR, 68 RBI.

Year	Team (League)	W	L	Pct.	ERA	WHIP	G	GS	CG	ShO	Hld.	Sv.-Opp.	IP	H	R	ER	HR	BB-IBB	SO	Avg.
1996—Charlotte (Int'l)	2	4	.333	5.14	1.94	10	10	0	0	...	0-...	49.0	61	32	28	3	34-1	45	.308
— Portland (East.)	9	2	.818	4.34	1.23	15	15	0	0	...	0-...	93.1	81	48	45	14	34-1	95	.238
— Florida (N.L.)	0	0	...	0.00	1.67	1	0	0	0	0.	0-0	3.0	3	0	0	0	2-0	2	.273
1997—Charlotte (Int'l)	5	3	.625	3.98	1.40	14	14	0	0	...	0-...	81.1	76	39	36	7	38-2	58	.247
— Florida (N.L.)	9	3	.750	3.18	1.24	17	17	0	0	0	0-0	96.1	81	39	34	5	38-1	72	.229
— Portland (East.)	0	0	...	2.25	2.25	1	1	0	0	...	0-...	4.0	2	1	1	0	7-0	2	.154
1998—Florida (N.L.)	10	12	.455	4.72	1.57	33	33	9	0	...	0-0	234.1 *	265	133	123	37	104-8	162	.289
1999—Florida (N.L.)	5	9	.357	4.76	1.59	20	20	2	0	0	0-0	136.0	161	78	72	17	55-3	97	.294
— San Francisco (N.L.)	3	3	.500	4.38	1.37	10	10	0	0	0	0-0	63.2	66	32	31	6	21-2	47	.267
2000—San Francisco (N.L.)	17	11	.607	3.75	1.36	33	33	3	0	...	0-0	240.0	254 *	114	100	22	73-3	165	.273
2001—San Francisco (N.L.)	13	15	.464	5.24	1.55	34	34	2	0	...	0-0	226.2	266 *	143 *	132	24	85-7	138	.297
2002—San Francisco (N.L.)	12	• 16	.429	4.38	1.41	33	33	5	3	0	0-0	216.0	233	113	105	19	71-5	134	.283
2003—Montreal (N.L.)	15	10	.600	3.20	1.21	33	33	* 8	0	0	0-0	* 233.1	225	92	83	27	57-3	178	.253
2004—Montreal (N.L.)	11	15	.423	3.60	1.24	35	• 35	* 9	2	0	0-0	* 255.0	234	105	102	26	83-9	186	.248
2005—Wash. (N.L.)	15	10	.600	3.98	1.43	35	• 35	2	0	0	0-0	* 246.1	268 *	116	109	25	84-14	147	.284
2006—Wash. (N.L.)	9	8	.529	5.34	1.55	24	24	0	0	0	0-0	146.2	176	94	87	22	52-4	89	.298
— Arizona (N.L.)	4	5	.444	3.76	1.38	10	10	0	0	0	0-0	69.1	70	31	29	7	26-2	39	.266
Major League totals (11 years)	123	117	.513	4.18	1.41	318	317	42	7	0	0-0	2166.2	2302	1090	1007	237	751-61	1456	.275

DIVISION SERIES RECORD

Year	Team (League)	W	L	Pct.	ERA	WHIP	G	GS	CG	ShO	Hld.	Sv.-Opp.	IP	H	R	ER	HR	BB-IBB	SO	Avg.
1997—Florida (N.L.)	0	0	...	2.25	0.75	1	1	0	0	0	0-0	4.0	3	1	1	0	0-0	3	.200
2000—San Francisco (N.L.)	1	0	1.000	1.17	1.30	1	1	1	0	0	0-0	7.2	5	1	1	0	5-0	5	.185
2002—San Francisco (N.L.)	1	0	1.000	3.24	1.20	1	1	0	0	0	0-0	8.1	8	3	3	0	2-0	6	.250
Division series totals (3 years)	2	0	1.000	2.25	1.15	3	3	1	0	0	0-0	20.0	16	5	5	0	7-0	14	.216

CHAMPIONSHIP SERIES RECORD

Year	Team (League)	W	L	Pct.	ERA	WHIP	G	GS	CG	ShO	Hld.	Sv.-Opp.	IP	H	R	ER	HR	BB-IBB	SO	Avg.
1997—Florida (N.L.)	2	0	1.000	0.84	0.66	2	1	1	0	0	0-0	10.2	5	1	1	1	2-0	16	.143
2002—San Francisco (N.L.)	0	0	...	2.84	1.58	1	1	0	0	0	0-0	6.1	9	2	2	0	1-0	0	.360
Champ. series totals (2 years)	2	0	1.000	1.59	1.00	3	2	1	0	0	0-0	17.0	14	3	3	1	3-0	16	.233

WORLD SERIES RECORD

Year	Team (League)	W	L	Pct.	ERA	WHIP	G	GS	CG	ShO	Hld.	Sv.-Opp.	IP	H	R	ER	HR	BB-IBB	SO	Avg.
1997—Florida (N.L.)	2	0	1.000	5.27	1.83	2	2	0	0	0	0-0	13.2	15	9	8	3	10-0	7	.283
2002—San Francisco (N.L.)	0	2	.000	14.29	3.18	2	2	0	0	0	0-0	5.2	9	10	9	0	9-3	4	.360
World series totals (2 years)	2	2	.500	7.91	2.22	4	4	0	0	0	0-0	19.1	24	19	17	3	19-3	11	.308

H

ALL-STAR GAME RECORD

	W	L	Pct.	ERA	WHIP	G	GS	CG	ShO	Hld.	Sv.-Opp.	IP	H	R	ER	HR	BB-IBB	SO	Avg.
All-Star Game totals (1 year)	0	0	...	18.00	3.00	1	0	0	0	0	0-0	1.0	2	2	2	0	1-0	0	.500

2006 LEFTY-RIGHTY SPLITS

vs.	Avg.	AB	H	2B	3B	HR	RBI	BB	SO	OBP	Slg.	vs.	Avg.	AB	H	2B	3B	HR	RBI	BB	SO	OBP	Slg.
L	.302	427	129	17	4	15	55	46	58	.370	.466	R	.275	426	117	22	4	14	66	32	70	.325	.444

HERNANDEZ, ORLANDO   P

PERSONAL: Born October 11, 1969, in Havana, Cuba. ... 6-2/220. ... Throws right, bats right. ... Full name: Orlando P. Hernandez. ... Name pronounced: her-NAN-dezz. ... Half-brother of Livan Hernandez, pitcher, Arizona Diamondbacks. **TRANSACTIONS/CAREER NOTES:** Signed as a free agent by New York Yankees (March 23, 1998). ... On disabled list (July 18-August 6, 2000); included rehabilitation assignment to Tampa. ... On disabled list (June 1-August 21, 2001); included rehabilitation assignments to Tampa and Staten Island. ... On disabled list (May 16-June 27, 2002); included rehabilitation assignment to Columbus. ... On suspended list (July 21-28, 2002). ... Traded by Yankees to Chicago White Sox for Ps Antonio Osuna and Delvis Lantigua (January 15, 2003). ... Traded by White Sox with P Rocky Biddle, 3B/OF Jeff Liefer and cash to Montreal Expos for P Bartolo Colon and 2B/SS Jorge Nunez (January 15, 2003). ... On disabled list (March 21, 2003-entire season); included rehabilitation assignment to Brevard County. ... Signed as a free agent by Yankees (March 12, 2004). ... On disabled list (March 19-July 11, 2004); included rehabilitation assignments to Tampa and Columbus. ... Signed as a free agent by White Sox (January 3, 2005). ... On disabled list (May 22-June 3 and June 20-July 18, 2005). ... Traded by White Sox with P Luis Vizcaino and OF Chris Young to Arizona Diamondbacks for P Javier Vazquez and cash (December 20, 2005). ... Traded by Diamondbacks to New York Mets for P Jorge Julio (May 24, 2006).

CAREER HITTING: 10-for-68 (.147), 5 R, 1 2B, 1 3B, 0 HR, 2 RBI.

Year Team (League)	W	L	Pct.	ERA	WHIP	G	GS	CG	ShO	Hld.	Sv.-Opp.	IP	H	R	ER	HR	BB-IBB	SO	Avg.
1998— Tampa (Fla. St.)	1	1	.500	1.00	0.67	2	2	0	0	...	0-...	9.0	3	2	1	0	4-0	15	.100
—Columbus (Int'l)	6	0	1.000	3.83	1.37	7	7	0	0	...	0-...	42.1	41	19	18	2	17-0	59	.261
—New York (A.L.)	12	4	.750	3.13	1.17	21	21	3	1	0	0-0	141.0	113	53	49	11	52-1	131	.222
1999—New York (A.L.)	17	9	.654	4.12	1.28	33	33	2	1	0	0-0	214.1	187	108	98	24	87-2	157	.233
2000—New York (A.L.)	12	13	.480	4.51	1.21	29	29	3	0	0	0-0	195.2	186	104	98	34	51-2	141	.247
—Tampa (Fla. St.)	0	0	...	0.00	0.50	1	0	0	0	...	0-...	4.0	1	0	0	0	1-0	5	.067
2001—New York (A.L.)	4	7	.364	4.85	1.39	17	16	0	0	0	0-0	94.2	90	51	51	19	42-1	77	.248
—Tampa (Fla. St.)	0	0	...	0.00	1.00	2	2	0	0	0	0-...	7.0	6	2	0	0	1-0	8	.214
—Staten Is. (N.Y.-Penn)	1	0	1.000	0.00	0.50	1	1	0	0	0	0-...	6.0	2	0	0	0	1-0	11	.100
2002—New York (A.L.)	8	5	.615	3.64	1.14	24	22	0	0	1	1-1	146.0	131	63	59	17	36-2	113	.236
—Columbus (Int'l)	1	0	1.000	1.59	1.41	1	1	0	0	0	0-...	5.2	7	2	1	0	1-0	5	.280
2003—Brevard County (FSL)	0	1	.000	10.80	1.80	2	2	0	0	0	0-...	5.0	5	6	6	0	4-0	7	.250
2004—Tampa (Fla. St.)	1	0	1.000	1.50	0.83	3	3	0	0	0	0-0	12.0	3	4	2	0	7-0	11	.079
—Columbus (Int'l)	2	1	.667	5.60	1.13	3	3	0	0	0	0-...	17.2	17	11	11	3	3-0	16	.243
—New York (A.L.)	8	2	.800	3.30	1.29	15	15	0	0	0	0-0	84.2	73	31	31	9	36-0	84	.230
2005—Charlotte (Int'l)	0	0	...	2.25	1.00	1	1	0	0	0	0-0	4.0	4	1	1	0	0-0	2	.267
—Chicago (A.L.)	9	9	.500	5.12	1.46	24	22	0	0	1	1-1	128.1	137	77	73	18	50-1	91	.275
2006—Arizona (N.L.)	2	4	.333	6.11	1.58	11	11	0	0	0	0-0	45.2	52	32	31	8	20-3	52	.292
—New York (N.L.)	9	7	.563	4.09	1.23	20	20	1	0	0	0-0	116.2	103	58	53	14	41-2	112	.236
American League totals (7 years)	70	49	.588	4.11	1.27	163	158	8	2	2	2-2	1004.2	917	487	459	132	354-9	794	.242
National League totals (1 year)	11	11	.500	4.66	1.33	29	29	1	0	0	0-0	162.1	155	90	84	22	61-5	164	.252
Major League totals (8 years)	81	60	.574	4.19	1.27	192	187	9	2	2	2-2	1167.0	1072	577	543	154	415-14	958	.243

DIVISION SERIES RECORD

Year Team (League)	W	L	Pct.	ERA	WHIP	G	GS	CG	ShO	Hld.	Sv.-Opp.	IP	H	R	ER	HR	BB-IBB	SO	Avg.
1998—New York (A.L.)				Did not play.															
1999—New York (A.L.)	1	0	1.000	0.00	1.00	1	1	0	0	0	0-0	8.0	2	0	0	0	6-0	4	.083
2000—New York (A.L.)	1	0	1.000	2.45	1.36	2	1	0	0	1	0-0	7.1	5	2	2	1	5-0	5	.200
2001—New York (A.L.)	1	0	1.000	3.18	1.76	1	1	0	0	0	0-0	5.2	8	2	2	0	2-0	5	.333
2002—New York (A.L.)	0	1	.000	2.84	0.79	2	0	0	0	0	0-0	6.1	5	2	2	2	0-0	7	.208
2005—Chicago (A.L.)	0	0	...	0.00	0.33	1	0	0	0	1	0-0	3.0	1	0	0	0	0-0	4	.100
Division series totals (5 years)	3	1	.750	1.78	1.12	7	3	0	0	2	0-0	30.1	21	6	6	3	13-0	25	.196

CHAMPIONSHIP SERIES RECORD

Year Team (League)	W	L	Pct.	ERA	WHIP	G	GS	CG	ShO	Hld.	Sv.-Opp.	IP	H	R	ER	HR	BB-IBB	SO	Avg.
1998—New York (A.L.)	1	0	1.000	0.00	0.71	1	1	0	0	0	0-0	7.0	3	0	0	0	2-0	6	.125
1999—New York (A.L.)	1	0	1.000	1.80	1.20	2	2	0	0	0	0-0	15.0	12	4	3	1	6-0	13	.207
2000—New York (A.L.)	2	0	1.000	4.20	1.40	2	2	0	0	0	0-0	15.0	13	7	7	2	8-2	14	.241
2001—New York (A.L.)	0	1	.000	7.20	2.00	1	1	0	0	0	0-0	5.0	5	5	4	1	5-0	7	.250
2004—New York (A.L.)	0	0	...	5.40	1.60	1	1	0	0	0	0-0	5.0	3	3	3	0	5-0	6	.167
Champ. series totals (5 years)	4	1	.800	3.26	1.32	7	7	0	0	0	0-0	47.0	36	19	17	4	26-2	46	.207

WORLD SERIES RECORD

Year Team (League)	W	L	Pct.	ERA	WHIP	G	GS	CG	ShO	Hld.	Sv.-Opp.	IP	H	R	ER	HR	BB-IBB	SO	Avg.
1998—New York (A.L.)	1	0	1.000	1.29	1.29	1	1	0	0	0	0-0	7.0	6	1	1	0	3-0	7	.222
1999—New York (A.L.)	1	0	1.000	1.29	0.43	1	1	0	0	0	0-0	7.0	1	1	1	0	3-0	10	.048
2000—New York (A.L.)	0	1	.000	4.91	1.64	1	1	0	0	0	0-0	7.1	9	4	4	1	3-0	12	.300
2001—New York (A.L.)	0	0	...	1.42	1.26	1	0	0	0	0	0-0	6.1	4	1	1	0	4-0	5	.222
2005—Chicago (A.L.)	0	0	...	0.00	4.00	1	0	0	0	0	0-0	1.0	0	0	0	0	4-1	2	.000
World series totals (5 years)	2	1	.667	2.20	1.26	5	4	0	0	0	0-0	28.2	20	7	7	3	16-1	36	.202

2006 LEFTY-RIGHTY SPLITS

vs.	Avg.	AB	H	2B	3B	HR	RBI	BB	SO	OBP	Slg.	vs.	Avg.	AB	H	2B	3B	HR	RBI	BB	SO	OBP	Slg.
L	.300	327	98	25	4	15	55	36	54	.375	.538	R	.199	287	57	15	2	7	26	25	110	.276	.338

HERNANDEZ, RAMON   C

PERSONAL: Born May 20, 1976, in Caracas, Venezuela. ... 6-0/210. ... Bats right, throws right. ... Full name: Ramon Jose Hernandez. **TRANSACTIONS/CAREER NOTES:** Signed as a non-drafted free agent by Oakland Athletics organization (February 18, 1994). ... On disabled list (July 26-August 27, 1999); included rehabilitation assignment to Vancouver. ... Traded by Athletics with OF Terrence Long to San Diego Padres for OF Mark Kotsay (November 26, 2003). ... On disabled list (June 21-July 26, 2004); included rehabilitation assignment to Portland. ... On disabled list (June 22-July 7 and July 29-September 2, 2005). ... Signed as a free agent by Baltimore Orioles (December 13, 2005). **STATISTICAL NOTES:** Career major league grand slams: 4.

2006 GAMES PLAYED BY POSITION (MLB): C—135, DH—6, 1B—2.

							BATTING										FIELDING	
Year Team (League)	Pos.	G	AB	R	H	2B	3B	HR	RBI	BB	SO	HBP	GDP	SB-CS	Avg.	OBP	SLG	OPS	E	Avg.
1994—Dom. Athletics (DSL)	C	42	134	24	33	2	0	2	18	18	10	...		1-5	.246	...	.306	...	2	.991
1995—Ariz. A's (Ariz.)	1B-3B-C	48	143	37	52	9	6	4	37	39	16	8	3	6-2	.364	.510	.594	1.105	12	.972

Year	Team (League)	Pos.	G	AB	R	H	2B	3B	HR	RBI	BB	SO	HBP	GDP	SB-CS	Avg.	OBP	SLG	OPS	E	Avg.
1996—	W. Mich. (Mid.)	C-DH-1B	123	447	62	114	26	2	12	68	69	62	4	22	2-3	.255	.355	.403	.758	20	.980
1997—	Visalia (Calif.)	C-DH-1B	86	332	57	120	21	2	15	85	35	47	9	5	2-4	.361	.427	.572	.999	16	.976
—	Huntsville (Sou.)	C-DH-1B																			
		3B	44	161	27	31	3	0	4	24	18	23	3	8	0-0	.193	.281	.286	.567	1	.997
1998—	Huntsville (Sou.)	DH-C-1B	127	479	83	142	24	1	15	98	57	61	19	15	4-5	.296	.389	.445	.833	11	.981
1999—	Vancouver (PCL)	C-3B-1B	77	291	38	76	11	3	13	55	23	37	7	13	1-2	.261	.326	.454	.780	5	.987
—	Oakland (A.L.)	C	40	136	13	38	7	0	3	21	18	11	1	5	1-0	.279	.363	.397	.760	6	.980
2000—	Oakland (A.L.)	C	143	419	52	101	19	0	14	62	38	64	7	14	1-0	.241	.311	.387	.698	* 13	.984
2001—	Oakland (A.L.)	C-1B	136	453	55	115	25	0	15	60	37	68	6	10	1-1	.254	.316	.408	.724	12	.988
2002—	Oakland (A.L.)	C	136	403	51	94	20	0	7	42	43	64	5	11	0-0	.233	.313	.335	.648	11	.992
2003—	Oakland (A.L.)	C	140	483	70	132	24	1	21	78	33	79	12	14	0-0	.273	.331	.458	.789	8	.991
2004—	Portland (PCL)	C	7	19	2	6	1	0	0	6	2	3	0	1	0-0	.316	.381	.368	.749	2	.938
—	San Diego (N.L.)	C	111	384	45	106	23	0	18	63	35	45	5	16	1-0	.276	.341	.477	.818	6	.992
2005—	San Diego (N.L.)	C	99	369	36	107	19	2	12	58	18	40	1	14	1-0	.290	.322	.450	.772	8	.988
2006—	Baltimore (A.L.)	C-DH-1B	144	501	66	138	29	2	23	91	43	79	11	13	1-0	.275	.343	.479	.822	13	.985
	American League totals (6 years)		739	2395	307	618	124	3	83	354	212	365	42	67	4-1	.258	.326	.416	.742	59	.988
	National League totals (2 years)		210	753	81	213	42	2	30	121	53	85	6	30	2-0	.283	.332	.463	.796	14	.991
	Major League totals (8 years)		949	3148	388	831	166	5	113	475	265	450	48	97	6-1	.264	.328	.428	.755	73	.988

DIVISION SERIES RECORD

Year	Team (League)	Pos.	G	AB	R	H	2B	3B	HR	RBI	BB	SO	HBP	GDP	SB-CS	Avg.	OBP	SLG	OPS	E	Avg.
2000—	Oakland (A.L.)	C	5	16	3	6	2	0	0	3	0	3	1	0	0-0	.375	.412	.500	.912	1	.974
2001—	Oakland (A.L.)	C	5	10	0	0	0	0	0	0	1	4	1	0	0-0	.000	.167	.000	.167	0	1.000
2002—	Oakland (A.L.)	C	5	17	0	1	0	0	0	0	1	4	0	1	0-0	.059	.059	.059	.118	0	1.000
2003—	Oakland (A.L.)	C	4	15	1	3	0	0	0	2	2	1	1	0	0-0	.200	.333	.200	.533	1	.974
2005—	San Diego (N.L.)	C	3	11	2	5	0	0	1	1	2	1	0	1	0-0	.455	.538	.727	1.266	0	1.000
	Division series totals (5 years)		22	69	6	15	2	0	1	6	6	13	3	2	0-0	.217	.299	.290	.589	2	.987

ALL-STAR GAME RECORD

			G	AB	R	H	2B	3B	HR	RBI	BB	SO	HBP	GDP	SB-CS	Avg.	OBP	SLG	OPS	E	Avg.
	All-Star Game totals (1 year)		1	1	0	0	0	0	0	0	0	0	0	0	0-0	.000	.000	.000	.000	0	1.000

2006 LEFTY-RIGHTY SPLITS

vs.	Avg.	AB	H	2B	3B	HR	RBI	BB	SO	OBP	Slg.	vs.	Avg.	AB	H	2B	3B	HR	RBI	BB	SO	OBP	Slg.
L	.291	127	37	7	0	10	30	19	16	.393	.583	R	.270	374	101	22	2	13	61	24	63	.324	.444

HERNANDEZ, ROBERTO   P

PERSONAL: Born November 11, 1964, in Santurce, Puerto Rico. ... 6-4/250. ... Throws right, bats right. ... Full name: Roberto Manuel Hernandez.. ... High school: New Hampton (N.H.) Prep. ... College: South Carolina-Aiken. **TRANSACTIONS/CAREER NOTES:** Selected by California Angels organization in first round (16th pick overall) of June 1986 free-agent draft; pick received as compensation for Baltimore Orioles signing Type A free-agent OF/IF Juan Beniquez. ... Traded by Angels with OF Mark Doran to Chicago White Sox for OF Mark Davis (August 2, 1989). ... Traded by White Sox with Ps Wilson Alvarez and Danny Darwin to San Francisco Giants for SS Mike Caruso, OF Brian Manning and Ps Lorenzo Barcelo, Keith Foulke, Bob Howry and Ken Vining (July 31, 1997). ... Signed as a free agent by Tampa Bay Devil Rays (November 18, 1997). ... Traded by Devil Rays to Kansas City Royals as part of three-team deal in which Devil Rays acquired OF Ben Grieve and cash from Oakland Athletics, A's acquired P Cory Lidle from Devil Rays and OF Johnny Damon, IF Mark Ellis and cash from Royals and Royals acquired C A.J. Hinch, IF Angel Berroa and cash from A's (January 8, 2001). ... On disabled list (March 22-May 2, 2002); included rehabilitation assignment to Omaha. ... Signed as a free agent by Atlanta Braves (January 22, 2003). ... On disabled list (June 12-27 and August 13-September 2, 2003); included rehabilitation assignment to Richmond. ... Signed as a free agent by Philadelphia Phillies (December 18, 2003). ... On disabled list (May 5-20, 2004). ... Signed as a free agent by New York Mets organization (January 18, 2005). ... Signed as a free agent by Pittsburgh Pirates (December 15, 2005). ... Traded by Pirates with P Oliver Perez to New York Mets for OF Xavier Nady (July 31, 2006).

CAREER HITTING: 1-for-2 (.500), 0 R, 0 2B, 0 3B, 0 HR, 0 RBI.

Year	Team (League)	W	L	Pct.	ERA	WHIP	G	GS	CG	ShO	Hld.	Sv.-Opp.	IP	H	R	ER	HR	BB-IBB	SO	Avg.
1986—	Salem (N'west)	2	2	.500	4.58	1.48	10	10	0	0	...	0-...	55.0	57	37	28	3	42-1	38	
1987—	Quad City (Midw.)	2	3	.400	6.86	1.71	7	6	0	0	...	1-...	21.0	24	21	16	2	12-0	21	.273
1988—	Quad City (Midw.)	9	10	.474	3.17	1.24	24	24	6	1	...	0-...	164.2	157	70	58	8	48-0	114	.248
—	Midland (Texas)	0	2	.000	6.57	1.95	3	3	0	0	...	0-...	12.1	16	13	9	0	8-0	7	.320
1989—	Midland (Texas)	2	7	.222	6.89	1.94	12	12	0	0	...	0-...	64.0	94	57	49	4	30-0	42	.352
—	Palm Springs (Calif.)	1	4	.200	4.64	1.52	7	7	0	0	...	0-...	42.2	49	27	22	2	16-0	33	.295
—	South Bend (Mid.)	1	1	.500	3.33	1.07	4	4	0	0	...	0-...	24.1	19	9	9	1	7-0	17	.221
1990—	Birmingham (Sou.)	8	5	.615	3.67	1.35	17	17	1	0	...	0-...	108.0	103	53	44	6	43-2	62	.251
—	Vancouver (PCL)	3	5	.375	2.84	1.25	11	11	3	1	...	0-...	79.1	73	33	25	4	26-0	49	.247
1991—	Vancouver (PCL)	4	1	.800	3.22	1.43	7	7	0	0	...	0-...	44.2	41	17	16	2	23-0	40	.241
—	GC Whi. Sox (GCL)	0	0	...	0.00	0.33	1	1	0	0	...	0-...	6.0	2	0	0	0	0-0	7	.111
—	Birmingham (Sou.)	2	1	.667	1.99	0.75	4	4	0	0	...	0-...	22.2	11	5	5	2	6-0	25	.145
—	Chicago (A.L.)	1	0	1.000	7.80	1.67	9	3	0	0	0	0-0	15.0	18	15	13	1	7-0	6	.290
1992—	Chicago (A.L.)	7	3	.700	1.65	0.92	43	0	0	0	6	12-16	71.0	45	15	13	4	20-1	68	.180
—	Vancouver (PCL)	3	3	.500	2.61	1.16	9	0	0	0	...	2-...	20.2	13	9	6	0	11-1	23	.176
1993—	Chicago (A.L.)	3	4	.429	2.29	1.09	70	0	0	0	...	38-44	78.2	66	21	20	6	20-1	71	.228
1994—	Chicago (A.L.)	4	4	.500	4.91	1.32	45	0	0	0	...	14-20	47.2	44	29	26	4	19-1	50	.238
1995—	Chicago (A.L.)	3	7	.300	3.92	1.53	60	0	0	0	...	32-42	59.2	63	30	26	9	28-4	84	.266
1996—	Chicago (A.L.)	6	5	.545	1.91	1.22	72	0	0	0	...	38-46	84.2	65	21	18	2	38-5	85	.208
1997—	Chicago (A.L.)	5	1	.833	2.44	1.29	46	0	0	0	...	27-31	48.0	38	15	13	5	24-4	47	.216
—	San Francisco (N.L.)	5	2	.714	2.48	1.32	28	0	0	0	9	4-8	32.2	29	9	9	2	14-1	35	.238
1998—	Tampa Bay (A.L.)	2	6	.250	4.04	1.30	67	0	0	0	...	26-35	71.1	55	33	32	5	41-4	55	.212
1999—	Tampa Bay (A.L.)	2	3	.400	3.07	1.38	72	0	0	0	...	43-47	73.1	68	27	25	1	33-1	69	.245
2000—	Tampa Bay (A.L.)	4	7	.364	3.19	1.35	68	0	0	0	...	32-40	73.1	76	33	26	9	23-1	61	.272
2001—	Kansas City (A.L.)	5	6	.455	4.12	1.40	63	0	0	0	...	28-34	67.2	69	34	31	7	26-3	46	.266
2002—	Omaha (PCL)	0	0	...	0.00	1.50	2	0	0	0	...	0-...	2.0	0	1	0	0	3-0	3	.000
—	Kansas City (A.L.)	1	4	.250	4.33	1.42	62	0	0	0	...	26-33	52.0	62	29	25	6	12-2	39	.300
2003—	Richmond (Int'l)	1	1	.500	9.45	2.20	6	0	0	0	...	0-...	6.2	11	9	7	0	4-0	10	.333
—	Atlanta (N.L.)	5	3	.625	4.35	1.73	66	0	0	0	19	0-4	60.0	61	36	29	10	49-7	45	.263
2004—	Philadelphia (N.L.)	3	5	.375	4.76	1.68	63	0	0	0	14	0-4	56.2	66	39	30	6	29-3	44	.297
2005—	New York (N.L.)	8	6	.571	2.58	1.22	67	0	0	0	18	4-10	69.2	57	20	20	5	28-4	61	.228
2006—	Pittsburgh (N.L.)	0	3	.000	2.93	1.63	46	0	0	0	3	2-5	43.0	46	24	14	3	24-7	33	.264
—	New York (N.L.)	0	0	...	3.48	1.11	22	0	0	0	3	0-0	20.2	15	8	8	2	8-1	15	.208
	American League totals (12 years)	43	49	.467	3.25	1.29	668	3	0	0	7	316-388	742.1	669	302	268	60	291-27	681	.239
	National League totals (5 years)	21	19	.525	3.50	1.49	292	0	0	0	67	10-31	282.2	274	136	110	31	146-23	233	.256
	Major League totals (16 years)	64	68	.485	3.32	1.35	960	3	0	0	74	326-419	1025.0	943	438	378	91	437-50	914	.244

H

Year	Team (League)	W	L	Pct.	ERA	WHIP	G	GS	CG	ShO	Hld.	Sv.-Opp.	IP	H	R	ER	HR	BB-IBB	SO	Avg.
	DIVISION SERIES RECORD																			
1997—	San Francisco (N.L.)	0	1	.000	20.25	6.00	3	0	0	0	0	0-0	1.1	5	3	3	0	3-1	1	.625
2003—	Atlanta (N.L.)	0	0	...	0.00	1.00	1	0	0	0	0	0-0	1.0	1	0	0	0	0-0	0	.333
	Division series totals (2 years)	0	1	.000	11.57	3.86	4	0	0	0	0	0-0	2.1	6	3	3	0	3-1	1	.545
	CHAMPIONSHIP SERIES RECORD																			
1993—	Chicago (A.L.)	0	0	...	0.00	1.00	4	0	0	0	0	1-1	4.0	4	0	0	0	0-0	1	.267
2006—	New York (N.L.)	0	0	...	0.00	0.86	3	0	0	0	0		2.1	0	0	0	0	2-1	0	.000
	Champ. series totals (2 years)	0	0	...	0.00	0.95	7	0	0	0	0	1-1	6.1	4	0	0	0	2-1	1	.182
	ALL-STAR GAME RECORD																			
	All-Star Game totals (2 years)	0	0	...	0.00	0.50	2	0	0	0	0	0-0	2.0	1	0	0	0	0-0	0	.143

2006 LEFTY-RIGHTY SPLITS

vs.	Avg.	AB	H	2B	3B	HR	RBI	BB	SO	OBP	Slg.	vs.	Avg.	AB	H	2B	3B	HR	RBI	BB	SO	OBP	Slg.
L	.290	100	29	7	0	3	12	19	20	.405	.450	R	.219	146	32	3	2	2	18	12	29	.283	.308

HERNANDEZ, RUNELVYS — P

PERSONAL: Born April 27, 1978, in Santo Domingo, Dominican Republic. ... 6-1/205. ... Throws right, bats right. ... Full name: Runelvys Antonio Hernandez. **TRANSACTIONS/CAREER NOTES:** Signed as a non-drafted free agent by Kansas City Royals organization (December 16, 1997). ... On disabled list (May 17-July 11 and August 17, 2003-remainder of season); included rehabilitation assignments to Omaha and Wichita. ... On disabled list (March 26, 2004-entire season; and August 22-September 6, 2005). ... On suspended list (September 6-17, 2005).
CAREER HITTING: 0-for-5 (.000), 0 R, 0 2B, 0 3B, 0 HR, 0 RBI.

Year	Team (League)	W	L	Pct.	ERA	WHIP	G	GS	CG	ShO	Hld.	Sv.-Opp.	IP	H	R	ER	HR	BB-IBB	SO	Avg.
1998—	Dom. Royals (DSL)	0	2	.000	5.34	1.88	19	2	0	0		0-...	32.0	31	26	19		29-...	27	...
	Kansas City (DSL)	0	2	.000	5.29	1.86	19	2	0	0		0-...	32.1	31	26	19	0	29-0	27	.263
1999—	Dom. Royals (DSL)	2	2	.500	3.09	1.25	16	2	0	0		5-...	32.0	23	19	11		17-...	36	...
	Kansas City (DSL)	2	2	.500	3.06	1.24	16	2	0	0		5-...	32.1	23	19	11	0	17-0	36	.192
2000—	Dom. Royals (DSL)	7	3	.700	2.25	1.04	14	10	0	0		1-...	72.0	57	25	18		18-...	70	...
	Kansas City (DSL)	7	3	.700	2.25	1.04	14	10	0	0		1-...	72.0	57	25	18	0	18-0	70	.210
2001—	Burlington (Midw.)	7	5	.583	3.40	1.22	17	17	0	0		0-...	100.2	94	46	38	5	29-0	100	.241
2002—	Wilmington (Caro.)	1	1	.500	3.75	1.08	2	2	0	0		0-...	12.0	12	6	5	0	1-0	9	.273
	Wichita (Texas)	8	3	.727	2.71	1.13	16	14	2	0		0-...	106.1	96	38	32	3	24-1	86	.249
	Kansas City (A.L.)	4	4	.500	4.36	1.36	12	12	0	0	0	0-0	74.1	79	36	36	8	22-0	45	.273
2003—	Omaha (PCL)	1	0	1.000	1.80	1.00	1	1	0	0		0-...	5.0	3	1	1	0	2-0	5	.176
	Wichita (Texas)	0	2	.000	3.86	1.50	2	2	0	0		0-...	9.1	9	4	4	0	5-0	5	.257
	Kansas City (A.L.)	7	5	.583	4.61	1.35	16	16	0	0	0	0-0	91.2	87	51	47	9	37-0	48	.249
2004—	Kansas City (A.L.)					Did not play														
2005—	Kansas City (A.L.)	8	14	.364	5.52	1.52	29	29	0	0	0	0-0	159.2	172	101	98	18	70-0	88	.277
2006—	Omaha (PCL)	5	6	.455	4.59	1.42	12	11	1	0	0	0-0	64.2	65	35	33	6	27-1	43	.261
	Kansas City (A.L.)	6	10	.375	6.48	1.76	21	21	1	1	0	0-0	109.2	145	87	79	22	48-0	50	.327
	Major League totals (4 years)	25	33	.431	5.38	1.52	78	78	1	1	0	0-0	435.1	483	275	260	57	177-0	231	.284

2006 LEFTY-RIGHTY SPLITS

vs.	Avg.	AB	H	2B	3B	HR	RBI	BB	SO	OBP	Slg.	vs.	Avg.	AB	H	2B	3B	HR	RBI	BB	SO	OBP	Slg.
L	.325	191	62	12	0	12	42	26	20	.397	.576	R	.329	252	83	10	0	10	38	22	30	.391	.488

HILL, AARON — SS/2B

PERSONAL: Born March 21, 1982, in Visalia, Calif. ... 5-11/195. ... Bats right, throws right. ... Full name: Aaron Walter Hill. ... College: LSU. **TRANSACTIONS/CAREER NOTES:** Selected by Toronto Blue Jays organization in first round (13th pick overall) of 2003 free-agent draft.
2006 GAMES PLAYED BY POSITION (MLB): 2B—112, SS—63, DH—1.

Year	Team (League)	Pos.	G	AB	R	H	2B	3B	HR	RBI	BB	SO	HBP	GDP	SB-CS	Avg.	OBP	SLG	OPS	E	Avg.
2003—	Auburn (NY-Penn)	SS	33	122	22	44	4	0	4	34	16	20	6	2	1-1	.361	.446	.492	.938	8	.934
	Dunedin (Fla. St.)	SS	32	119	26	34	7	0	0	11	11	10	1	3	1-0	.286	.343	.345	.688	8	.930
2004—	New Hampshire (East.)	SS	135	480	78	134	26	2	11	80	63	61	11	12	3-2	.279	.368	.410	.778	24	.724
2005—	Syracuse (Int'l)	SS	38	156	22	47	11	0	5	18	4	17	6	6	2-0	.301	.339	.468	.807	10	.945
	Toronto (A.L.)	3B-DH-2B	105	361	49	99	25	3	3	40	34	41	5	5	2-1	.274	.342	.385	.727	6	.978
2006—	Toronto (A.L.)	2B-SS-DH	155	546	70	159	28	3	6	50	42	66	9	15	5-2	.291	.349	.386	.735	19	.974
	Major League totals (2 years)		260	907	119	258	53	6	9	90	76	107	14	20	7-3	.284	.346	.386	.732	25	.975

2006 LEFTY-RIGHTY SPLITS

vs.	Avg.	AB	H	2B	3B	HR	RBI	BB	SO	OBP	Slg.	vs.	Avg.	AB	H	2B	3B	HR	RBI	BB	SO	OBP	Slg.
L	.298	161	48	6	0	3	10	16	20	.362	.391	R	.288	385	111	22	3	3	40	26	46	.344	.384

HILL, RICH — P

PERSONAL: Born March 11, 1980, in Boston. ... 6-5/205. ... Throws left, bats left. ... Full name: Richard Joseph Hill. ... High school: Milton (Miss.) ... College: Michigan.
TRANSACTIONS/CAREER NOTES: Selected by Chicago Cubs organization in fourth round of 2002 free-agent draft.
CAREER HITTING: 5-for-36 (.139), 1 R, 1 2B, 0 3B, 0 HR, 0 RBI.

Year	Team (League)	W	L	Pct.	ERA	WHIP	G	GS	CG	ShO	Hld.	Sv.-Opp.	IP	H	R	ER	HR	BB-IBB	SO	Avg.
2002—	Boise (N'west)	0	2	.000	8.36	2.07	6	5	0	0	...	0-...	14.0	15	19	13	0	14-0	12	.268
2003—	Lansing (Midw.)	0	1	.000	2.76	1.70	5	4	0	0	...	0-...	29.1	14	12	9	0	36-0	50	.141
	Boise (N'west)	1	6	.143	4.35	1.30	14	14	0	0	...	0-...	68.1	57	40	33	5	32-0	99	.233
2004—	Daytona (Fla. St.)	7	6	.538	4.03	1.46	28	19	0	0	...	0-...	109.1	88	64	49	9	72-0	136	.221
2005—	West Tenn (Sou.)	4	3	.571	3.28	1.09	10	10	0	0	0	0-0	57.2	42	22	21	9	21-0	90	.200
	Peoria (Midw.)	1	0	1.000	1.13	0.63	1	1	0	0	0	0-0	8.0	5	2	1	0	0-0	12	.179
	Iowa (PCL)	6	1	.857	3.60	1.03	11	10	0	0	0	0-0	65.0	53	28	26	11	14-0	92	.218
	Chicago (N.L.)	0	2	.000	9.13	1.77	10	4	0	0	0	0-0	23.2	25	24	24	3	17-1	21	.260
2006—	Iowa (PCL)	7	1	.875	1.80	0.83	15	15	0	0	0	0-0	100.0	62	22	20	6	21-0	135	.179
	Chicago (N.L.)	6	7	.462	4.17	1.23	17	16	2	1	0	0-0	99.1	83	51	46	16	39-1	90	.227
	Major League totals (2 years)	6	9	.400	5.12	1.33	27	20	2	1	0	0-0	123.0	108	75	70	19	56-2	111	.234

H

2006 LEFTY-RIGHTY SPLITS

vs.	Avg.	AB	H	2B	3B	HR	RBI	BB	SO	OBP	Slg.	vs.	Avg.	AB	H	2B	3B	HR	RBI	BB	SO	OBP	Slg.
L	.262	61	16	3	1	2	3	9	17	.357	.443	R	.220	304	67	18	0	14	42	30	73	.292	.418

HILL, SHAWN — P

PERSONAL: Born April 28, 1981, in Mississauga, Ontario. ... 6-2/185. ... Throws right, bats right. ... Full name: Shawn Richard Hill. ... High school: Bishop Reding (Milton, Ontario). **TRANSACTIONS/CAREER NOTES:** Selected by San Diego Padres organization in 33rd round of 1999 free-agent draft; did not sign. ... Selected by Montreal Expos organization in sixth round of 2000 free-agent draft. ... Expos franchise transferred to Washington, D.C., and renamed Washington Nationals for 2005 season (December 3, 2004). ... On disabled list (July 1, 2006-remainder of season); included rehabilitation assignment to Harrisburg.

CAREER HITTING: 1-for-8 (.125), 1 R, 0 2B, 0 3B, 0 HR, 0 RBI.

Year	Team (League)	W	L	Pct.	ERA	WHIP	G	GS	CG	ShO	Hld.	Sv.-Opp.	IP	H	R	ER	HR	BB-IBB	SO	Avg.
2000— GC Expos (GCL)		1	3	.250	4.81	1.44	7	7	0	0	...	0-...	24.1	25	17	13	0	10-0	20	.250
2001— Vermont (NYP)		2	2	.500	2.27	0.84	7	7	0	0	...	0-...	35.2	22	12	9	0	8-0	23	.172
2002— Clinton (Midw.)		12	7	.632	3.44	1.25	25	25	0	0	...	0-...	146.2	149	75	56	7	35-2	99	.261
2003— Brevard County (FSL)		9	4	.692	2.56	1.14	22	21	2	1	...	0-...	126.2	118	47	36	3	26-0	66	.248
— Harrisburg (East.)		3	1	.750	3.54	1.67	4	4	0	0	...	0-...	20.1	23	12	8	0	11-1	12	.280
2004— Montreal (N.L.)		1	2	.333	16.00	2.67	3	3	0	0	0	0-0	9.0	17	16	16	1	7-0	10	.415
— Harrisburg (East.)		5	7	.417	3.39	1.25	17	17	2	0	0	0-0	87.2	90	39	33	4	20-0	53	.272
2005—	Did not play.																			
2006— New Orleans (PCL)		0	0	...	3.60	1.60	1	1	0	0	0	0-0	5.0	6	2	2	0	2-0	2	.286
— Wash. (N.L.)		1	3	.250	4.66	1.50	6	6	0	0	0	0-0	36.2	43	20	19	2	12-2	16	.297
— Harrisburg (East.)		3	3	.500	2.68	1.01	10	10	0	0	0	0-0	50.1	46	20	15	2	5-0	32	.237
Major League totals (2 years)		2	5	.286	6.90	1.73	9	9	0	0	0	0-0	45.2	60	36	35	3	19-2	26	.323

2006 LEFTY-RIGHTY SPLITS

vs.	Avg.	AB	H	2B	3B	HR	RBI	BB	SO	OBP	Slg.	vs.	Avg.	AB	H	2B	3B	HR	RBI	BB	SO	OBP	Slg.
L	.324	74	24	7	1	2	12	7	7	.386	.527	R	.268	71	19	2	1	0	4	5	9	.333	.324

HILLENBRAND, SHEA — 1B/3B

PERSONAL: Born July 27, 1975, in Mesa, Ariz. ... 6-1/211. ... Bats right, throws right. ... Full name: Shea Matthew Hillenbrand. ... Name pronounced: SHAY. ... High school: Mountain View (Mesa, Ariz.). ... Junior college: Mesa (Ariz.) Community College. ... College: Mesa (AZ) CC. **TRANSACTIONS/CAREER NOTES:** Selected by Boston Red Sox organization in 10th round of 1996 free-agent draft. ... On disabled list (August 31, 1999-remainder of season). ... Traded by Red Sox to Arizona Diamondbacks for P Byung-Hyun Kim (May 29, 2003). ... On disabled list (June 9-29, 2003); included rehabilitation assignment to Tucson. ... Traded by Diamondbacks to Toronto Blue Jays for P Adam Peterson (January 12, 2005). ... Traded by Blue Jays with P Vinnie Chulk to San Francisco Giants for P Jeremy Accardo (July 22, 2006). **STATISTICAL NOTES:** Hit three home runs in one game (July 7, 2003). ... Career major league grand slams: 1.

2006 GAMES PLAYED BY POSITION (MLB): 1B—77, DH—44, 3B—25.

Year	Team (League)	Pos.	G	AB	R	H	2B	3B	HR	RBI	BB	SO	HBP	GDP	SB-CS	Avg.	OBP	SLG	OPS	E	Avg.
1996— Lowell (NY-Penn)	1B-3B-SS	72	279	33	88	18	2	2	38	18	32	8	6	4-3	.315	.371	.416	.787	33	.938
1997— Michigan (Midw.)	1B-3B	64	224	28	65	13	3	3	39	9	20	1	2	1-3	.290	.315	.415	.730	8	.950
— Sarasota (Fla. St.)	1B-3B	57	220	25	65	12	0	2	28	7	29	2	4	9-8	.295	.320	.377	.698	20	.926
1998— Michigan (Midw.)	1B-3B-C	129	498	80	174	33	4	19	93	19	49	10	11	13-7	.349	.383	.546	.929	14	.982
1999— Trenton (East.)	C	69	282	41	73	15	0	7	36	14	27	3	6	6-5	.259	.298	.387	.685	5	.987
2000— Trenton (East.)	1B-3B	135	529	77	171	35	3	11	79	19	39	8	15	3-3	.323	.355	.463	.818	15	.979
2001— Boston (A.L.)	3B-1B-DH	139	468	52	123	20	2	12	49	13	61	7	12	3-4	.263	.291	.391	.682	18	.950
2002— Boston (A.L.)	3B	156	634	94	186	43	4	18	83	25	95	12	18	4-2	.293	.330	.459	.789 *	23	.943
2003— Boston (A.L.)	3B-1B-DH	49	185	20	56	17	0	3	38	7	24	4	9	1-0	.303	.335	.443	.778	3	.989
— Tucson (PCL)	1B-3B	3	10	0	3	1	0	0	1	0	1	0	0	0-0	.300	.300	.400	.700	0	1.000
— Arizona (N.L.)	1B-3B	85	330	40	88	18	1	17	59	17	44	2	13	0-0	.267	.302	.482	.784	12	.978
2004— Arizona (N.L.)	1B-3B	148	562	68	174	36	3	15	80	24	49	12	18	2-0	.310	.348	.464	.812	16	.987
2005— Toronto (A.L.)	1B-3B-DH	152	594	91	173	36	2	18	82	26	79 *	22	41	5-1	.291	.343	.449	.792	12	.985
2006— Toronto (A.L.)	DH-1B-3B	81	296	40	89	15	1	12	39	14	40	6	15	1-2	.301	.342	.480	.821	7	.961
— San Francisco (N.L.)	1B-3B	60	234	33	58	12	0	9	29	7	40	3	7	0-0	.248	.275	.415	.690	2	.996
American League totals (5 years)		577	2177	297	627	131	9	63	291	85	301	51	75	14-9	.288	.327	.443	.770	63	.969
National League totals (3 years)		293	1126	141	320	66	4	41	168	48	133	17	38	2-0	.284	.320	.459	.779	30	.987
Major League totals (6 years)		870	3303	438	947	197	13	104	459	133	434	68	113	16-9	.287	.325	.449	.773	93	.978

ALL-STAR GAME RECORD

	G	AB	R	H	2B	3B	HR	RBI	BB	SO	HBP	GDP	SB-CS	Avg.	OBP	SLG	OPS	E	Avg.
All-Star Game totals (2 years)	2	2	0	0	0	0	0	0	0	1	0	0	0-0	.000	.000	.000	.000	0	1.000

2006 LEFTY-RIGHTY SPLITS

vs.	Avg.	AB	H	2B	3B	HR	RBI	BB	SO	OBP	Slg.	vs.	Avg.	AB	H	2B	3B	HR	RBI	BB	SO	OBP	Slg.
L	.338	139	47	9	0	4	18	9	18	.373	.489	R	.256	391	100	18	1	17	50	12	62	.291	.437

HINSKE, ERIC — OF/3B

PERSONAL: Born August 5, 1977, in Menasha, Wis. ... 6-2/235. ... Bats left, throws right. ... Full name: Eric Scott Hinske. ... Name pronounced: hin-SKEE. ... High school: Menasha (Wis.). ... College: Arkansas. **TRANSACTIONS/CAREER NOTES:** Selected by Chicago Cubs organization in 17th round of 1998 free-agent draft. ... Traded by Cubs to Oakland Athletics for 2B Miguel Cairo (March 28, 2001). ... Traded by Athletics with P Justin Miller to Toronto Blue Jays for P Billy Koch (December 7, 2001). ... On disabled list (May 24-June 26, 2003); included rehabilitation assignment to Syracuse. ... Traded by Blue Jays with cash to Boston Red Sox for a player to be named (August 17, 2006). **HONORS:** Named A.L. Rookie Player of the Year by THE SPORTING NEWS (2002). ... Named A.L. Rookie of the Year by Baseball Writers' Association of America (2002). **STATISTICAL NOTES:** Career major league grand slams: 1.

2006 GAMES PLAYED BY POSITION (MLB): OF—45, DH—21, 1B—16, 3B—10.

Year	Team (League)	Pos.	G	AB	R	H	2B	3B	HR	RBI	BB	SO	HBP	GDP	SB-CS	Avg.	OBP	SLG	OPS	E	Avg.
1998— Will. (NYP)	1B	68	248	46	74	20	0	9	57	35	61	2	2	19-3	.298	.384	.488	.872	2	.997
— Rockford (Midwest)	1B	6	20	8	9	4	0	1	4	5	6	0	0	1-0	.450	.538	.800	1.338	0	1.000
1999— Daytona (Fla. St.)	1B-3B-OF	130	445	76	132	28	6	19	79	62	90	5	5	16-10	.297	.385	.515	.900	22	.965
— Iowa (PCL)	1B-3B	4	15	3	4	0	1	1	2	1	4	0	0	0-0	.267	.313	.600	.913	1	.952
2000— West Tenn (Sou.)	1B-3B-OF	131	436	76	113	20	9	20	73	78	133	3	7	14-5	.259	.373	.486	.859	28	.916
2001— Sacramento (PCL)	3B-1B	121	436	71	123	27	1	25	79	54	113	10	6	20-7	.282	.373	.521	.893	17	.941
2002— Toronto (A.L.)	3B	151	566	99	158	38	2	24	84	77	138	6	12	13-1	.279	.365	.481	.845	20	.946
2003— Syracuse (Int'l)	3B	2	8	2	4	1	0	1	2	0	0	0	0	0-0	.500	.500	1.000	1.500	0	1.000
— Toronto (A.L.)	3B	124	449	74	109	45	3	12	63	59	104	1	11	12-2	.243	.329	.437	.765	22	.930

H

Year Team (League)	Pos.	G	AB	R	H	2B	3B	HR	RBI	BB	SO	HBP	GDP	SB-CS	Avg.	OBP	SLG	OPS	E	Avg.
2004— Toronto (A.L.)	3B-DH	155	570	66	140	23	3	15	69	54	109	4	14	12-8	.246	.312	.375	.688	8	.978
2005— Toronto (A.L.)	1B-DH	147	477	79	125	31	2	15	68	46	121	8	8	8-4	.262	.333	.430	.763	7	.993
2006— Toronto (A.L.)	OF-DH-3B																			
	1B	78	197	35	52	9	2	12	29	27	49	0	6	1-1	.264	.353	.513	.865	0	1.000
— Boston (A.L.)	OF-1B-DH	31	80	8	23	8	0	1	5	8	30	0	2	1-1	.288	.352	.425	.777	1	.991
Major League totals (5 years)		686	2339	361	607	154	12	79	318	271	551	15	53	47-17	.260	.337	.437	.774	58	.973

2006 LEFTY-RIGHTY SPLITS

vs.	Avg.	AB	H	2B	3B	HR	RBI	BB	SO	OBP	Slg.	vs.	Avg.	AB	H	2B	3B	HR	RBI	BB	SO	OBP	Slg.
L	.167	48	8	3	0	1	4	8	16	.286	.292	R	.293	229	67	14	2	12	30	27	63	.367	.528

HIRSH, JASON   P

PERSONAL: Born February 20, 1982, in Santa Monica, Calif. ... 6-8/250. ... Throws right, bats right. ... Full name: Jason Michael Hirsh. ... College: Cal Lutheran. **TRANSAC-TIONS/CAREER NOTES:** Selected by Houston Astros organization in second round of 2003 free-agent draft.
CAREER HITTING: 0-for-15 (.000), 0 R, 0 2B, 0 3B, 0 HR, 0 RBI.

Year Team (League)	W	L	Pct.	ERA	WHIP	G	GS	CG	ShO	Hld.	Sv.-Opp.	IP	H	R	ER	HR	BB-IBB	SO	Avg.
2003— Tri-City (N.Y.-Penn.)	3	1	.750	1.95	0.90	10	8	0	0	...	0-...	32.1	22	10	7	0	7-0	33	.190
2004— Salem (Carol.)	11	7	.611	4.01	1.42	26	23	0	0	...	0-...	130.1	128	66	58	8	57-0	96	.269
2005— Corpus Christi (Texas)	13	8	.619	2.87	1.04	29	29	1	1	0	0-...	172.1	137	63	55	12	42-0	165	.218
2006— Round Rock (PCL)	13	2	.867	2.10	1.06	23	23	1	1	0	0-0	137.1	94	37	32	5	51-0	118	.193
— Houston (N.L.)	3	4	.429	6.04	1.57	9	9	0	0	0	0-0	44.2	48	32	30	11	22-2	29	.267
Major League totals (1 year)	3	4	.429	6.04	1.57	9	9	0	0	0	0-0	44.2	48	32	30	11	22-2	29	.267

2006 LEFTY-RIGHTY SPLITS

vs.	Avg.	AB	H	2B	3B	HR	RBI	BB	SO	OBP	Slg.	vs.	Avg.	AB	H	2B	3B	HR	RBI	BB	SO	OBP	Slg.
L	.211	71	15	3	0	4	7	16	16	.360	.423	R	.303	109	33	5	0	7	17	6	13	.350	.541

HOEY, JAMES   P

PERSONAL: Born December 30, 1982, in Trenton, N.J. ... Throws right, bats right. ... Full name: James U. Hoey. ... College: Rider. **TRANSACTIONS/CAREER NOTES:** Selected by Baltimore Orioles organization in 13th round of 2003 free-agent draft.
CAREER HITTING: 0-for-0 (.000), 0 R, 0 2B, 0 3B, 0 HR, 0 RBI.

Year Team (League)	W	L	Pct.	ERA	WHIP	G	GS	CG	ShO	Hld.	Sv.-Opp.	IP	H	R	ER	HR	BB-IBB	SO	Avg.
2003— Bluefield (Appal.)	2	3	.400	2.79	1.24	11	8	0	0	...	0-...	42.0	33	19	13	3	19-0	20	.219
2004— Aberdeen (N.Y.-Penn.)	0	1	.000	9.45	1.95	2	2	0	0	...	0-...	6.2	12	8	7	1	1-0	6	.375
2005— Aberdeen (N.Y.-Penn.)	1	1	.500	4.80	1.40	9	0	0	0	2	0-...	15.0	11	10	8	1	10-0	15	.216
2006— Delmarva (S. Atl.)	2	1	.667	2.54	0.95	27	0	0	0	0	18-22	28.1	17	8	8	2	10-2	46	.175
— Frederick (Carolina)	0	0	...	0.64	1.29	14	0	0	0	0	11-11	14.0	13	3	1	0	5-0	16	.228
— Bowie (East.)	0	0	...	4.00	1.33	8	0	0	0	0	4-5	9.0	9	5	4	1	3-0	11	.243
— Baltimore (A.L.)	0	1	.000	10.24	1.97	12	0	0	0	4	0-1	9.2	14	11	11	1	5-0	6	.359
Major League totals (1 year)	0	1	.000	10.24	1.97	12	0	0	0	4	0-1	9.2	14	11	11	1	5-0	6	.359

2006 LEFTY-RIGHTY SPLITS

vs.	Avg.	AB	H	2B	3B	HR	RBI	BB	SO	OBP	Slg.	vs.	Avg.	AB	H	2B	3B	HR	RBI	BB	SO	OBP	Slg.
L	.375	16	6	3	1	1	8	3	1	.500	.875	R	.348	23	8	1	0	0	5	2	5	.385	.391

HOFFMAN, TREVOR   P

PERSONAL: Born October 13, 1967, in Bellflower, Calif. ... 6-0/215. ... Throws right, bats right. ... Full name: Trevor William Hoffman. ... High school: Savanna (Anaheim). ... College: Arizona. ... Brother of Glenn Hoffman, coach, Los Angeles Dodgers and infielder with three major league teams (1980-87 and 1989). **TRANSACTIONS/CAREER NOTES:** Selected by Cincinnati Reds organization in 11th round of 1989 free-agent draft. ... Played two seasons as a shortstop in Reds organization (1989-90). ... Selected by Florida Marlins in first round (eighth pick overall) of expansion draft (November 17, 1992). ... Traded by Marlins with Ps Jose Martinez and Andres Berumen to San Diego Padres for 3B Gary Sheffield and P Rich Rodriguez (June 24, 1993). ... On disabled list (March 25-September 2, 2003); included rehabilitation assignment to Lake Elsinore. **RECORDS:** Holds major league record for most saves, career (482). **HONORS:** Named N.L. Fireman of the Year by the SPORTING NEWS (1996, 1998 and 2006).
CAREER HITTING: 4-for-33 (.121), 1 R, 2 2B, 0 3B, 0 HR, 5 RBI.

Year Team (League)	W	L	Pct.	ERA	WHIP	G	GS	CG	ShO	Hld.	Sv.-Opp.	IP	H	R	ER	HR	BB-IBB	SO	Avg.
1991— Cedar Rap. (Midw.)	1	1	.500	1.87	1.04	27	0	0	0	...	12-...	33.2	22	8	7	0	13-0	52	.188
— Chattanooga (Sou.)	1	0	1.000	1.93	1.21	14	0	0	0	...	8-...	14.0	10	4	3	0	7-0	23	.192
1992— Chattanooga (Sou.)	3	0	1.000	1.52	1.11	6	6	0	0	...	0-...	29.2	22	6	5	1	11-1	31	.212
— Nashville (A.A.)	4	6	.400	4.27	1.36	42	5	0	0	...	6-...	65.1	57	32	31	6	32-3	63	.234
1993— Florida (N.L.)	2	2	.500	3.28	1.21	28	0	0	0	8	2-3	35.2	24	13	13	5	19-7	26	.185
— San Diego (N.L.)	2	4	.333	4.31	1.40	39	0	0	0	7	3-5	54.1	56	30	26	6	20-6	53	.264
1994— San Diego (N.L.)	4	4	.500	2.57	1.05	47	0	0	0	1	20-23	56.0	39	16	16	4	20-6	68	.193
1995— San Diego (N.L.)	7	4	.636	3.88	1.16	55	0	0	0	0	31-38	53.1	48	25	23	10	14-3	52	.235
1996— San Diego (N.L.)	9	5	.643	2.25	0.92	70	0	0	0	0	42-49	88.0	50	23	22	6	31-5	111	.161
1997— San Diego (N.L.)	6	4	.600	2.66	1.02	70	0	0	0	0	37-44	81.1	59	25	24	9	24-4	111	.200
1998— San Diego (N.L.)	4	2	.667	1.48	0.85	66	0	0	0	0	* 53-54	73.0	41	12	12	2	21-2	86	.155
1999— San Diego (N.L.)	2	3	.400	2.14	0.94	64	0	0	0	0	40-43	67.1	48	23	16	5	15-2	73	.197
2000— San Diego (N.L.)	4	7	.364	2.99	1.00	70	0	0	0	0	43-*50	72.1	61	29	24	7	11-4	85	.224
2001— San Diego (N.L.)	3	4	.429	3.43	1.14	62	0	0	0	0	43-46	60.1	48	25	23	10	21-2	63	.216
2002— San Diego (N.L.)	2	5	.286	2.73	1.18	61	0	0	0	0	38-41	59.1	52	20	18	2	18-2	69	.234
2003— Lake Elsinore (Calif.)	0	0	...	0.00	0.70	3	0	0	0	0	0-...	3.0	2	0	0	0	0-0	4	.182
— San Diego (N.L.)	0	0	...	2.00	1.11	9	0	0	0	0	0-0	9.0	7	2	2	1	3-0	11	.212
2004— San Diego (N.L.)	3	3	.500	2.30	0.91	55	0	0	0	0	41-45	54.2	42	14	14	5	8-1	53	.211
2005— San Diego (N.L.)	1	6	.143	2.97	1.11	60	0	0	0	0	43-46	57.2	52	23	19	3	12-1	54	.235
2006— San Diego (N.L.)	0	2	.000	2.14	0.97	65	0	0	0	0	* 46-* 51	63.0	48	16	15	6	13-1	50	.205
Major League totals (14 years)	49	55	.471	2.71	1.04	821	0	0	0	16	482-538	885.1	675	296	267	80	250-46	965	.208

DIVISION SERIES RECORD

Year Team (League)	W	L	Pct.	ERA	WHIP	G	GS	CG	ShO	Hld.	Sv.-Opp.	IP	H	R	ER	HR	BB-IBB	SO	Avg.
1996— San Diego (N.L.)	0	1	.000	10.80	2.40	2	0	0	0	0	0-0	1.2	3	2	2	1	1-0	2	.375
1998— San Diego (N.L.)	0	0	...	0.00	1.33	4	0	0	0	0	2-2	3.0	3	1	0	0	1-1	4	.250
2005— San Diego (N.L.)	0	0	...	0.00	1.00	1	0	0	0	0	0-0	1.0	1	0	0	0	0-0	0	.250
2006— San Diego (N.L.)	0	0	...	0.00	0.00	1	0	0	0	0	1-1	1.0	0	0	0	0	0-0	1	.000
Division series totals (4 years)	0	1	.000	2.70	1.35	8	0	0	0	0	3-3	6.2	7	3	2	1	2-1	7	.259

H

Year Team (League)	W	L	Pct.	ERA	WHIP	G	GS	CG	ShO	Hld.	Sv.-Opp.	IP	H	R	ER	HR	BB-IBB	SO	Avg.
1998— San Diego (N.L.)	1	0	1.000	2.08	0.92	3	0	0	0	0	1-2	4.1	2	1	1	0	2-0	7	.143

WORLD SERIES RECORD

Year Team (League)	W	L	Pct.	ERA	WHIP	G	GS	CG	ShO	Hld.	Sv.-Opp.	IP	H	R	ER	HR	BB-IBB	SO	Avg.
1998— San Diego (N.L.)	0	1	.000	9.00	1.50	1	0	0	0	0	0-1	2.0	2	2	2	1	1-0	0	.250

ALL-STAR GAME RECORD

	W	L	Pct.	ERA	WHIP	G	GS	CG	ShO	Hld.	Sv.-Opp.	IP	H	R	ER	HR	BB-IBB	SO	Avg.
All-Star Game totals (5 years)	0	1	.000	12.46	1.85	5	0	0	0	0	0-1	4.1	8	6	6	1	0-0	5	.381

2006 LEFTY-RIGHTY SPLITS

vs.	Avg.	AB	H	2B	3B	HR	RBI	BB	SO	OBP	Slg.	vs.	Avg.	AB	H	2B	3B	HR	RBI	BB	SO	OBP	Slg.
L	.194	103	20	5	0	2	6	10	24	.272	.301	R	.214	131	28	3	0	4	9	3	26	.231	.328

HOLLANDSWORTH, TODD — OF

PERSONAL: Born April 20, 1973, in Dayton, Ohio. ... 6-2/215. ... Bats left, throws left. ... Full name: Todd Mathew Hollandsworth. ... Name pronounced: HAHL-enz-worth. ... High school: Newport (Bellevue, Wash.). **TRANSACTIONS/CAREER NOTES:** Selected by Los Angeles Dodgers organization in third round of 1991 free-agent draft; pick received as part of compensation for Kansas City Royals signing Type B free-agent OF/DH Kirk Gibson. ... On disabled list (May 3-July 7 and August 9-September 12, 1995); included rehabilitation assignments to San Bernardino and Albuquerque. ... On disabled list (August 1-16 and August 17-September 6, 1997); included rehabilitation assignment to San Bernardino. ... On disabled list (June 5, 1998-remainder of season). ... On disabled list (April 3-23 and June 4-19, 1999); included rehabilitation assignments to San Bernardino. ... Traded by Dodgers with OF Kevin Gibbs and P Randey Dorame to Colorado Rockies for OF Tom Goodwin and cash (July 31, 2000). ... On disabled list (May 12, 2001-remainder of season). ... Traded by Rockies with P Dennys Reyes to Texas Rangers for OF Gabe Kapler and 2B Jason Romano (July 31, 2002). ... On disabled list (August 4-20, 2002). ... Signed as a free agent by Florida Marlins (January 8, 2003). ... On disabled list (August 14-September 1, 2003). ... Signed as a free agent by Chicago Cubs (December 18, 2003). ... On disabled list (June 28, 2004-remainder of season). ... Traded by Cubs to Atlanta Braves for Ps Todd Blackford and Angelo Burrows (August 29, 2005). ... Claimed on waivers by Cincinnati Reds (August 9, 2006). ... Signed as free agent by Cleveland Indians organization (January 9, 2006). **HONORS:** Named N.L. Rookie of the Year by Baseball Writers' Association of America (1996). **STATISTICAL NOTES:** Hit three home runs in one game (April 15, 2001). ... Career major league grand slams: 2.

2006 GAMES PLAYED BY POSITION (MLB): OF—64, DH—1.

					BATTING														FIELDING	
Year Team (League)	Pos.	G	AB	R	H	2B	3B	HR	RBI	BB	SO	HBP	GDP	SB-CS	Avg.	OBP	SLG	OPS	E	Avg.
1991— GC Dodgers (GCL)	OF	6	16	1	5	0	0	0	0	0	6	0	1	0-0	.313	.313	.313	.625	0	1.000
— Yakima (N'west)	OF	56	203	34	48	5	1	8	33	27	57	4	2	11-1	.236	.338	.389	.727	7	.939
1992— Bakersfield (Calif.)	OF	119	430	70	111	23	5	13	58	50	113	3	6	27-13	.258	.338	.426	.764	6	.975
1993— San Antonio (Texas)	OF	126	474	57	119	24	9	17	63	29	101	5	7	24-12	.251	.298	.447	.746	12	.956
1994— Albuquerque (PCL)	OF	132	505	80	144	31	5	19	91	46	96	0	15	15-9	.285	.343	.479	.822	13	.949
1995— Los Angeles (N.L.)	OF	41	103	16	24	2	0	5	13	10	29	1	1	2-1	.233	.304	.398	.702	4	.938
— San Bern. (Calif.)	OF	1	2	0	1	0	0	0	0	0	0	0	0	0-1	.500	.500	.500	1.000	0	...
— Albuquerque (PCL)	OF	10	38	9	9	2	0	2	4	6	8	1	1	1-0	.237	.356	.447	.803	1	1.000
1996— Los Angeles (N.L.)	OF	149	478	64	139	26	4	12	59	41	93	2	2	21-6	.291	.348	.437	.785	5	.978
1997— Los Angeles (N.L.)	OF	106	296	39	73	20	2	4	31	17	60	0	8	5-5	.247	.286	.368	.654	5	.984
— Albuquerque (PCL)	OF	13	56	13	24	4	3	1	14	4	4	0	0	2-3	.429	.467	.661	1.127	0	1.000
— San Bern. (Calif.)	OF	2	8	1	2	0	1	0	2	1	2	0	0	0-0	.250	.333	.500	.833	0	1.000
1998— Los Angeles (N.L.)	OF	55	175	23	47	6	4	3	20	9	42	1	2	4-3	.269	.308	.400	.708	4	.957
1999— San Bern. (Calif.)	OF	4	13	3	5	0	0	0	3	2	4	1	1	0-1	.385	.500	.538	1.038	0	1.000
— Los Angeles (N.L.)	OF-1B	92	261	39	74	12	2	9	32	24	61	1	2	5-2	.284	.345	.448	.793	3	.987
2000— Los Angeles (N.L.)	OF	81	261	42	61	12	0	8	24	30	61	1	4	11-4	.234	.314	.372	.686	1	.987
— Colorado (N.L.)	OF	56	167	39	54	8	0	11	23	11	38	0	4	7-3	.323	.365	.569	.934	1	.988
2001— Colorado (N.L.)	OF	33	117	21	43	15	1	6	19	8	20	0	1	5-0	.368	.408	.667	1.075	1	.981
2002— Colorado (N.L.)	OF	95	298	39	88	21	1	11	48	26	71	1	7	7-8	.295	.352	.483	.835	4	.973
— Texas (A.L.)	OF	39	132	16	34	6	0	5	19	14	27	0	0	1-0	.258	.327	.417	.743	0	1.000
2003— Florida (N.L.)	OF-DH	93	228	32	58	23	3	3	20	22	55	0	2	2-3	.254	.317	.421	.739	2	.983
2004— Chicago (N.L.)	OF-1B-DH	57	148	28	47	6	2	8	22	17	26	1	2	1-1	.318	.392	.547	.939	1	.988
2005— Chicago (N.L.)	OF-1B	107	268	23	68	17	2	5	35	18	53	1	4	4-4	.254	.301	.388	.689	2	.981
— Atlanta (N.L.)	OF-1B	24	35	3	6	0	0	1	1	5	13	0	1	0-1	.171	.275	.257	.532	0	1.000
2006— Cleveland (A.L.)	OF-DH	56	156	21	37	12	1	6	27	4	33	0	2	0-1	.237	.253	.442	.695	2	.976
— Cincinnati (N.L.)	OF	34	68	6	18	6	0	1	8	6	19	0	1	0-1	.265	.324	.397	.721	0	1.000
American League totals (2 years)		95	288	37	71	18	1	11	46	18	60	0	2	1-1	.247	.288	.431	.719	2	.986
National League totals (12 years)		1023	2903	414	800	174	21	87	355	244	641	9	42	74-42	.276	.332	.440	.772	32	.980
Major League totals (12 years)		1118	3191	451	871	192	22	98	401	262	701	9	44	75-43	.273	.328	.439	.767	34	.980

DIVISION SERIES RECORD

Year Team (League)	Pos.	G	AB	R	H	2B	3B	HR	RBI	BB	SO	HBP	GDP	SB-CS	Avg.	OBP	SLG	OPS	E	Avg.
1995— Los Angeles (N.L.)	OF	2	2	0	0	0	0	0	0	0	0	0	0	0-0	.000	.000	.000	.000	0	...
1996— Los Angeles (N.L.)	OF	3	12	1	4	3	0	0	1	0	3	0	0	0-0	.333	.333	.583	.917	0	1.000
2003— Florida (N.L.)		3	3	1	1	0	0	0	0	0	2	0	0	0-0	.333	.333	.333	.667	0	...
Division series totals (3 years)		8	17	2	5	3	0	0	1	0	5	0	0	0-0	.294	.294	.471	.765	0	1.000

CHAMPIONSHIP SERIES RECORD

Year Team (League)	Pos.	G	AB	R	H	2B	3B	HR	RBI	BB	SO	HBP	GDP	SB-CS	Avg.	OBP	SLG	OPS	E	Avg.
2003— Florida (N.L.)		4	3	2	3	1	0	0	0	0	0	0	0	0-0	1.000	1.000	1.333	2.333	0	...

WORLD SERIES RECORD

Year Team (League)	Pos.	G	AB	R	H	2B	3B	HR	RBI	BB	SO	HBP	GDP	SB-CS	Avg.	OBP	SLG	OPS	E	Avg.
2003— Florida (N.L.)		2	2	0	0	0	0	0	0	0	0	0	0	0-0	.000	.000	.000	.000	0	...

2006 LEFTY-RIGHTY SPLITS

vs.	Avg.	AB	H	2B	3B	HR	RBI	BB	SO	OBP	Slg.	vs.	Avg.	AB	H	2B	3B	HR	RBI	BB	SO	OBP	Slg.
L	.174	23	4	1	0	0	4	1	10	.200	.217	R	.254	201	51	17	1	7	31	9	42	.284	.453

HOLLIDAY, MATT — OF

PERSONAL: Born January 15, 1980, in Stillwater, Okla. ... 6-4/235. ... Bats right, throws right. ... Full name: Matthew Thomas Holliday. ... High school: Stillwater (Okla.). **TRANSACTIONS/CAREER NOTES:** Selected by Colorado Rockies organization in seventh round of 1998 free-agent draft. ... On disabled list (June 9-July 19, 2005); included rehabilitation assignment to Tulsa. **HONORS:** Named outfielder on N.L. Silver Slugger team (2006). **STATISTICAL NOTES:** Career major league grand slams: 2.

2006 GAMES PLAYED BY POSITION (MLB): OF—153, DH—1.

					BATTING														FIELDING	
Year Team (League)	Pos.	G	AB	R	H	2B	3B	HR	RBI	BB	SO	HBP	GDP	SB-CS	Avg.	OBP	SLG	OPS	E	Avg.
1998— Ariz. Rockies (Ariz.)	3B	32	117	20	40	4	1	5	23	15	21	2	0	2-1	.342	.413	.521	.934	10	.851
1999— Asheville (S. Atl.)	3B	121	444	76	117	28	0	16	64	53	116	9	8	10-3	.264	.350	.435	.785	37	.871

H

Year	Team (League)	Pos.	G	AB	R	H	2B	3B	HR	RBI	BB	SO	HBP	GDP	SB-CS	Avg.	OBP	SLG	OPS	E	Avg.
2000— Salem (Carol.)		3B	123	460	64	126	28	2	7	72	43	74	2	12	11-5	.274	.335	.389	.724	32	.893
2001— Salem (Carol.)		OF	72	255	36	70	16	1	11	52	33	42	3	10	11-3	.275	.358	.475	.833	1	1.000
2002— Carolina (Southern)		OF	130	463	79	128	19	2	10	64	67	102	7	14	16-2	.276	.375	.391	.766	7	.961
2003— Tulsa (Texas)		OF	135	522	65	132	28	5	12	72	43	74	6	9	15-9	.253	.313	.395	.708	2	.991
2004— Colo. Springs (PCL)		OF	6	22	8	8	5	0	2	4	5	6	0	1	2-0	.364	.481	.864	1.345	0	1.000
— Colorado (N.L.)		OF	121	400	65	116	31	3	14	57	31	86	6	9	3-3	.290	.349	.488	.837	7	.963
2005— Tulsa (Texas)		OF	7	26	6	14	3	0	1	6	1	3	0	0	1-0	.538	.536	.769	1.305	0	1.000
— Colorado (N.L.)		OF	125	479	68	147	24	7	19	87	36	79	7	11	14-3	.307	.361	.505	.866	7	.972
2006— Colorado (N.L.)		OF-DH	155	602	119	196	45	5	34	114	47	110	15	22	10-5	.326	.387	.586	.973	6	.979
Major League totals (3 years)			401	1481	252	459	100	15	67	258	114	275	28	42	27-11	.310	.368	.533	.902	20	.972

ALL-STAR GAME RECORD

		G	AB	R	H	2B	3B	HR	RBI	BB	SO	HBP	GDP	SB-CS	Avg.	OBP	SLG	OPS	E	Avg.
All-Star Game totals (1 year)		1	3	0	0	0	0	0	0	0	0	0	0	0-0	.000	.000	.000	.000	0	1.000

2006 LEFTY-RIGHTY SPLITS

vs.	Avg.	AB	H	2B	3B	HR	RBI	BB	SO	OBP	Slg.	vs.	Avg.	AB	H	2B	3B	HR	RBI	BB	SO	OBP	Slg.
L	.327	107	35	11	2	4	17	13	19	.405	.579	R	.325	495	161	34	3	30	97	34	91	.383	.588

HOLLINS, DAMON — OF

PERSONAL: Born June 12, 1974, in Fairfield, Calif. ... 5-11/180. ... Bats right, throws left. ... Full name: Damon Jamall Hollins. ... High school: Vallejo (Calif.). **TRANSACTIONS/CAREER NOTES:** Selected by Atlanta Braves organization in fourth round of 1992 free-agent draft. ... Traded by Braves to Los Angeles Dodgers for 2B Jose Pimentel (September 9, 1998). ... Released by Dodgers (November 22, 1998). ... Signed by Cincinnati Reds organization (December 15, 1998). ... Signed as a free agent by Milwaukee Brewers organization (December 1, 1999). ... Signed as a free agent by Minnesota Twins organization (February 23, 2001). ... Traded by Twins to Braves for future considerations (July 26, 2001). ... On disabled list (August 31, 2003-remainder of season). ... Signed as a free agent by Tampa Bay Devil Rays organization (November 12, 2004).

2006 GAMES PLAYED BY POSITION (MLB): OF—115, DH—3.

Year	Team (League)	Pos.	G	AB	R	H	2B	3B	HR	RBI	BB	SO	HBP	GDP	SB-CS	Avg.	OBP	SLG	OPS	E	Avg.
1992— GC Braves (GCL)		OF	49	179	35	41	12	1	1	15	30	22	2	3	15-2	.229	.346	.324	.670	1	.989
1993— Danville (Appal.)		OF	62	240	37	77	15	2	7	51	19	30	1	5	10-2	.321	.369	.488	.856	6	.946
1994— Durham (Carol.)		OF	131	485	76	131	28	0	23	88	45	115	4	9	12-7	.270	.335	.470	.805	13	.957
1995— Greenville (Sou.)		OF	129	466	64	115	26	2	18	77	44	120	4	7	6-6	.247	.313	.427	.741	8	.978
1996— Richmond (Int'l)		OF	42	146	16	29	9	0	0	8	16	37	0	2	2-3	.199	.278	.260	.538	3	.976
1997— Richmond (Int'l)		OF-DH	134	498	73	132	31	3	20	63	45	84	3	18	7-2	.265	.329	.460	.789	8	.977
1998— Richmond (Int'l)		OF-DH	119	436	61	115	26	3	13	48	45	90	0	16	10-2	.264	.330	.427	.757	5	.980
— Atlanta (N.L.)		OF	3	6	0	1	0	0	0	0	0	1	0	0	0-0	.167	.167	.167	.333	0	1.000
— Los Angeles (N.L.)		OF	5	9	1	2	0	0	0	0	0	2	0	0	0-1	.222	.222	.222	.444	0	1.000
1999— Indianapolis (Int'l)		OF	106	328	58	86	19	0	9	43	31	44	1	13	11-2	.262	.328	.402	.730	4	.983
2000— Indianapolis (Int'l)		OF	87	287	33	82	16	3	2	32	21	35	1	5	5-3	.286	.334	.383	.718	0	1.000
2001— Edmonton (PCL)		OF	69	232	29	64	8	2	6	30	22	44	2	8	3-3	.276	.342	.405	.748	5	.954
— Richmond (Int'l)		OF	43	160	27	42	10	2	5	24	14	34	0	7	2-2	.263	.318	.444	.762	2	.981
2002— Richmond (Int'l)		OF	128	498	66	139	34	1	12	59	35	77	1	18	10-2	.279	.326	.424	.750	4	.988
2003— Richmond (Int'l)		OF	91	307	39	84	23	4	11	45	22	62	2	10	7-2	.274	.324	.482	.806	4	.981
2004— Atlanta (N.L.)		OF	7	22	3	8	2	0	0	0	0	4	0	0	0-0	.364	.364	.455	.818	0	1.000
— Richmond (Int'l)		OF-DH	109	356	50	107	26	2	20	67	24	57	0	9	5-3	.301	.341	.553	.895	7	.967
2005— Durham (Int'l)		OF-DH	22	81	11	24	5	0	2	17	15	17	2	3	3-2	.296	.414	.432	.846	0	1.000
— Tampa Bay (A.L.)		OF	120	342	44	85	17	1	13	46	23	63	1	8	8-1	.249	.296	.418	.714	6	.977
2006— Tampa Bay (A.L.)		OF-DH	121	333	37	76	20	0	15	33	19	64	0	4	3-3	.228	.269	.423	.693	4	.982
American League totals (2 years)			241	675	81	161	37	1	28	79	42	127	1	12	11-4	.239	.283	.421	.704	10	.980
National League totals (2 years)			15	37	4	11	2	0	0	7	0	7	0	0	0-1	.297	.297	.351	.649	0	1.000
Major League totals (4 years)			256	712	85	172	39	1	28	86	42	134	1	12	11-5	.242	.284	.417	.701	10	.980

2006 LEFTY-RIGHTY SPLITS

vs.	Avg.	AB	H	2B	3B	HR	RBI	BB	SO	OBP	Slg.	vs.	Avg.	AB	H	2B	3B	HR	RBI	BB	SO	OBP	Slg.
L	.240	129	31	8	0	9	18	8	32	.283	.512	R	.221	204	45	12	0	6	15	11	32	.260	.368

HOLTZ, MIKE — P

PERSONAL: Born October 10, 1972, in Arlington, Va. ... 5-9/185. ... Throws left, bats left. ... Full name: Michael James Holtz. ... High school: Central Cambria (Ebensburg, Pa.). ... College: Clemson. **TRANSACTIONS/CAREER NOTES:** Selected by California Angels organization in 17th round of 1994 free-agent draft. ... Angels franchise renamed Anaheim Angels for 1997 season. ... On suspended list (June 18-20, 1998). ... On disabled list (August 25-September 10, 1999). ... On disabled list (May 11-30, 2001); included rehabilitation assignment to Rancho Cucamonga. ... Signed as a free agent by Oakland Athletics (January 2, 2002). ... Released by A's (June 5, 2002). ... Signed by San Diego Padres (July 2, 2002). ... Released by Padres (October 2, 2002). ... Signed by Pittsburgh Pirates organization (January 24, 2003). ... Signed as a free agent by Tampa Bay Devil Rays organization (January 13, 2004). ... Signed by Yokohama BayStars of the Japan Central League (January 18, 2005). ... Signed as free agent by Boston Red Sox organization (February 1, 2006). ... On disabled list (May 19-June 16, 2006); included rehabilitation assignment to Pawtucket. ... Released by Red Sox (June 26, 2006).

CAREER HITTING: 0-for-3 (.000), 0 R, 0 2B, 0 3B, 0 HR, 0 RBI.

Year	Team (League)	W	L	Pct.	ERA	WHIP	G	GS	CG	ShO	Hld.	Sv.-Opp.	IP	H	R	ER	HR	BB-IBB	SO	Avg.
1994— Boise (N'west)		0	0	...	0.51	0.94	22	0	0	0	...	11-...	35.0	22	4	2	0	11-2	59	.171
1995— Lake Elsinore (Calif.)		4	4	.500	2.29	1.13	56	0	0	0	...	3-...	82.2	70	26	21	7	23-3	101	.230
1996— Midland (Texas)		1	2	.333	4.17	1.49	33	0	0	0	...	2-...	41.0	52	34	19	6	9-1	41	.295
— California (A.L.)		3	3	.500	2.45	1.36	30	0	0	0	...	0-0	29.1	21	11	8	1	19-2	31	.204
1997— Anaheim (A.L.)		3	4	.429	3.32	1.22	66	0	0	0	...	2-8	43.1	38	21	16	7	15-4	40	.228
1998— Anaheim (A.L.)		2	2	.500	4.75	1.75	53	0	0	0	...	1-2	30.1	38	16	16	0	15-1	29	.322
— Vancouver (PCL)		0	0	...	1.74	1.55	10	0	0	0	...	0-...	10.1	10	4	2	1	6-0	18	.244
1999— Anaheim (A.L.)		2	3	.400	8.06	1.84	28	0	0	0	1	0-0	22.1	26	20	20	3	15-1	17	.295
— Edmonton (PCL)		2	1	.667	2.30	1.13	20	0	0	0	...	1-...	27.1	20	7	7	4	11-1	39	.202
2000— Edmonton (PCL)		0	1	.000	10.80	1.20	6	0	0	0	...	0-...	5.0	5	6	6	1	1-0	1	.250
— Anaheim (A.L.)		3	4	.429	5.05	1.34	61	0	0	0	10	0-0	41.0	37	26	23	4	18-2	40	.248
2001— Anaheim (A.L.)		1	2	.333	4.86	1.49	63	0	0	0	15	0-1	37.0	40	24	20	5	15-4	38	.274
— Rancho Cuca. (Calif.)		0	0	...	9.00	2.00	2	0	0	0	...	0-...	2.0	3	2	2	1	1-0	3	.375
2002— Oakland (A.L.)		0	0	...	6.43	2.36	16	0	0	0	1	0-1	14.0	24	11	10	3	9-0	7	.358
— San Diego (N.L.)		2	2	.500	4.71	1.86	33	0	0	0	...	0-3	21.0	18	14	11	2	21-3	19	.237
— Portland (PCL)		0	0	...	4.26	0.95	7	0	0	0	...	0-...	6.1	3	3	3	0	3-0	3	.136
2003— Nashville (PCL)		3	2	.600	4.91	1.45	45	0	0	0	...	0-...	44.0	45	25	24	4	19-3	49	.266

H

Year — Team (League)	W	L	Pct.	ERA	WHIP	G	GS	CG	ShO	Hld.	Sv.-Opp.	IP	H	R	ER	HR	BB-IBB	SO	Avg.
2004— Durham (Int'l)	1	2	.333	3.80	1.06	17	0	0	0	...	0-...	23.2	17	10	10	4	8-0	27	.198
2005— Yokohama. (Jp. Cn.)	0	1	.000	4.38	1.46	44	0	0	0	...	0-...	24.2	26	16	12	4	10-...	22	...
2006— Boston (A.L.)	0	0	...	16.20	4.20	3	0	0	0	1	0-0	1.2	3	3	3	0	4-0	2	.429
— Pawtucket (Int'l)	0	0	...	1.93	0.91	14	0	0	0	0	3-4	18.2	10	4	4	2	7-0	29	.154
American League totals (8 years)	14	18	.438	4.77	1.54	320	0	0	0	28	3-12	219.0	227	132	116	23	110-14	204	.497
National League totals (1 year)	2	2	.500	4.71	1.86	33	0	0	0	4	0-3	21.0	18	14	11	2	21-3	19	.237
Major League totals (8 years)	16	20	.444	4.76	1.57	353	0	0	0	32	3-15	240.0	245	146	127	25	131-17	223	.460

2006 LEFTY-RIGHTY SPLITS

vs.	Avg.	AB	H	2B	3B	HR	RBI	BB	SO	OBP	Slg.	vs.	Avg.	AB	H	2B	3B	HR	RBI	BB	SO	OBP	Slg.
L	.333	3	1	0	0	0	1	1	0	.600	.333	R	.500	4	2	1	0	2	3	2	.714	1.250

HOOPER, KEVIN — IF

PERSONAL: Born December 7, 1976, in Lawrence, Kan. ... 5-10/160. ... Bats right, throws right. ... Full name: Kevin J. Hooper. ... College: Wichita State. **TRANSACTIONS/CAREER NOTES:** Selected by Florida Marlins organization in eighth round of free-agent draft (June 2, 1999). ... Claimed on waivers by New York Yankees (May 26, 2004). ... Released by Yankees (August 6, 2004). ... Signed by Kansas City Royals organization (August 13, 2004). ... Signed as a free agent by Detroit Tigers organization (November 19, 2004).

2006 GAMES PLAYED BY POSITION (MLB): 2B—3, 3B—2, DH—1.

Year — Team (League)	Pos.	G	AB	R	H	2B	3B	HR	RBI	BB	SO	HBP	GDP	SB-CS	Avg.	OBP	SLG	OPS	E	Avg.
1999— Utica (N.Y.-Penn)	2B	73	289	52	81	18	6	0	22	39	35	4	2	14-8	.280	.370	.384	.754	4	.989
2000— Kane Co. (Midw.)	2B	123	457	73	114	25	6	3	38	73	83	6	6	17-2	.249	.359	.350	.709	13	.978
2001— Kane Co. (Midw.)	2B	17	65	11	19	2	0	0	4	11	13	0	0	3-1	.292	.390	.323	.713	4	.957
— Portland (East.)	2B	117	468	70	144	19	6	2	39	59	78	7	8	24-12	.308	.392	.387	.779	7	.986
2002— Calgary (PCL)	2B-SS	117	452	70	130	21	3	2	38	34	51	4	7	17-10	.288	.341	.361	.702	12	.977
2003— Albuquerque (PCL)	2B-SS	130	493	77	131	9	4	1	54	35	62	0	5	25-9	.266	.325	.306	.631	11	.982
2004— Albuquerque (PCL)	2B-SS	39	155	21	43	3	2	0	17	14	24	0	1	6-5	.277	.335	.323	.658	3	.971
— Columbus (Int'l)	2B-SS-P	29	87	6	17	1	0	0	4	5	11	0	1	3-1	.195	.239	.207	.446	2	.000
— Omaha (PCL)	2B-SS	27	92	12	15	2	0	0	4	9	14	1	1	2-2	.163	.245	.185	.430	3	.000
2005— Detroit (A.L.)	OF-SS-2B	6	5	0	1	0	0	0	0	0	1	0	0	0-0	.200	.200	.200	.400	1	.900
— Toledo (Int'l)	2B-SS-OF 3B-DH-P-C 1B	85	313	41	75	13	2	1	27	22	37	2	4	16-4	.240	.291	.304	.595	9	.976
2006— Toledo (Int'l)		121	504	66	139	15	4	1	29	23	71	3	4	24-12	.276	.309	.327	.636	13	.977
— Detroit (A.L.)	2B-3B-DH	8	3	1	0	0	0	0	0	1	1	0	0	0-0	.000	.250	.000	.250	0	1.000
Major League totals (2 years)		14	8	1	1	0	0	0	0	1	2	0	0	0-0	.125	.222	.125	.347	1	.933

2006 LEFTY-RIGHTY SPLITS

vs.	Avg.	AB	H	2B	3B	HR	RBI	BB	SO	OBP	Slg.	vs.	Avg.	AB	H	2B	3B	HR	RBI	BB	SO	OBP	Slg.
L	.000	0	0	0	0	0	0	0	0	.000	.000	R	.000	3	0	0	0	0	0	1	1	.250	.000

HOOVER, PAUL — C/IF

PERSONAL: Born April 14, 1976, in Columbus, Ohio. ... 6-1/211. ... Bats right, throws right. ... Full name: Paul Chester Hoover. ... High school: Steubenville (Ohio). ... College: Kent State. **TRANSACTIONS/CAREER NOTES:** Selected by Houston Astros organization in 64th round of 1994 free-agent draft; did not sign. ... Selected by Tampa Bay Devil Rays organization in 23rd round of 1997 free-agent draft. ... Signed as a free agent by Florida Marlins organization (November 14, 2002). ... Signed as a free agent by Montreal Expos organization (February 6, 2004). ... Released by Expos (August 11, 2004). ... Signed by Devil Rays organization (August 14, 2004). ... Signed as a free agent by Marlins organization (January 12, 2006).

2006 GAMES PLAYED BY POSITION (MLB): C—3.

Year — Team (League)	Pos.	G	AB	R	H	2B	3B	HR	RBI	BB	SO	HBP	GDP	SB-CS	Avg.	OBP	SLG	OPS	E	Avg.
1997— Princeton (Appal.)	SS	66	251	55	76	16	4	4	37	20	37	6	3	7-4	.303	.363	.446	.809	33	.904
1998— Char., S.C. (SAL)	1B-3B-C SS	40	124	24	36	10	1	3	19	22	29	5	0	2-1	.290	.417	.460	.877	8	.969
— Hudson Valley (NYP)	3B-C	73	269	51	76	20	1	4	37	39	44	11	5	26-3	.283	.388	.409	.797	5	.990
1999— St. Pete. (FSL)	1B-3B-C	118	408	66	111	13	6	8	54	54	81	16	13	23-7	.272	.376	.392	.768	5	.992
2000— Orlando (South.)	C	106	360	54	90	20	4	3	44	67	66	13	5	9-8	.250	.382	.353	.735	18	.961
— Durham (Int'l)	3B-C-OF	4	10	0	3	0	0	0	0	0	5	1	0	1-0	.300	.364	.300	.664	0	1.000
2001— Durham (Int'l)	C-3B-OF 1B-SS-2B	89	293	37	63	18	4	3	21	11	66	7	7	5-3	.215	.260	.334	.594	6	.987
— Tampa Bay (A.L.)	C	3	4	1	1	0	0	0	0	1	0	0	0	0-0	.250	.250	.250	.500	1	1.000
2002— Durham (Int'l)	C-1B-3B OF	69	227	27	50	12	3	5	20	18	67	3	2	3-3	.220	.285	.366	.651	5	.989
— Tampa Bay (A.L.)	C	5	17	1	3	0	0	0	2	0	5	0	...	0-0	.176	.176	.176	.353	0	1.000
2003— Albuquerque (PCL)		81	256	35	69	22	2	5	20	18	62	2	7	10-3	.270	.321	.430	.751	...	...
2004— Edmonton (PCL)		69	194	27	56	14	1	1	20	20	46	3	5	4-0	.289	.361	.387	.748	...	...
— Durham (Int'l)		16	54	9	16	1	0	1	8	4	15	1	2	0-0	.296	.350	.370	.720	...	...
2005— Durham (Int'l)	2B-OF-3B C-1B	79	257	32	60	17	1	5	26	25	56	5	7	5-1	.233	.314	.366	.679	10	.974
2006— Albuquerque (PCL)		92	302	38	84	21	1	6	41	33	71	3	8	3-2	.278	.351	.414	.765	12	.981
— Florida (N.L.)	C	4	5	0	2	0	0	0	1	0	0	0	0	0-0	.400	.400	.400	.800	1	.875
American League totals (2 years)		8	21	2	4	0	0	0	2	0	6	0	0	0-0	.190	.190	.190	.381	0	1.000
National League totals (1 year)		4	5	0	2	0	0	0	1	0	0	0	0	0-0	.400	.400	.400	.800	1	.875
Major League totals (3 years)		12	26	2	6	0	0	0	3	0	6	0	0	0-0	.231	.231	.231	.462	1	.966

2006 LEFTY-RIGHTY SPLITS

vs.	Avg.	AB	H	2B	3B	HR	RBI	BB	SO	OBP	Slg.	vs.	Avg.	AB	H	2B	3B	HR	RBI	BB	SO	OBP	Slg.
L	.400	5	2	0	0	0	1	0	0	.400	.400	R	.000	0	0	0	0	0	0	0	0	.000	.000

HOPPER, NORRIS — OF

PERSONAL: Born March 24, 1979, in Shelby, N.C. ... Bats right, throws right. ... Full name: Norris Hopper. ... High school: Shelby (N.C.) **TRANSACTIONS/CAREER NOTES:** Selected by Kansas City Royals organization in eighth round of 1998 free-agent draft. ... Signed as a free agent by Cincinnati Reds organization (January 7, 2005).

2006 GAMES PLAYED BY POSITION (MLB): OF—15.

H

Year Team (League)	Pos.	G	AB	R	H	2B	3B	HR	RBI	BB	SO	HBP	GDP	SB-CS	Avg.	OBP	SLG	OPS	E	Avg.
1998— GC Royals (GCL)		40	133	19	41	2	1	0	11	13	12	0	1	11-2	.308	.365	.338	.703	14	...
1999— GC Royals (GCL)		46	179	33	46	3	2	0	13	19	20	0	2	22-6	.257	.322	.296	.618	4	...
— Char., W.Va. (SAL)		5	22	3	11	0	2	0	2	0	1	0	0	1-0	.500	.500	.682	1.182	2	...
2000— Char., W.Va. (SAL)		116	454	70	127	20	6	0	29	51	55	4	10	24-10	.280	.350	.350	.707	.14	...
2001— Wilmington (Caro.)		110	389	38	96	6	2	1	38	32	60	5	15	16-4	.247	.312	.280	.592	6	...
2002— Wilmington (Caro.)		125	514	78	140	12	3	1	46	31	55	8	15	22-9	.272	.323	.313	.636	4	...
2003— Wichita (Texas)		115	424	56	127	14	2	0	40	27	58	4	10	24-10	.300	.346	.342	.688	5	...
2004— Wichita (Texas)		98	363	48	101	5	3	0	40	33	44	5	10	17-7	.278	.345	.309	.654	1	...
2005— Chattanooga (Sou.)	OF-2B	116	451	70	140	15	4	1	37	27	38	4	12	25-7	.310	.354	.368	.722	12	.973
2006— Chattanooga (Sou.)		13	46	7	13	2	1	0	10	6	3	0	0	3-0	.283	.365	.370	.735	1	.962
— Louisville (Int'l)		98	383	47	133	11	3	0	26	20	25	0	7	25-7	.347	.378	.392	.769	3	.985
— Cincinnati (N.L.)	OF	21	39	6	14	1	0	1	5	6	4	0	1	2-2	.359	.435	.462	.896	0	1.000
Major League totals (1 year)		21	39	6	14	1	0	1	5	6	4	0	1	2-2	.359	.435	.462	.896	0	1.000

2006 LEFTY-RIGHTY SPLITS

vs.	Avg.	AB	H	2B	3B	HR	RBI	BB	SO	OBP	Slg.	vs.	Avg.	AB	H	2B	3B	HR	RBI	BB	SO	OBP	Slg.
L	.571	21	12	1	0	1	3	3	1	.600	.762	R	.111	18	2	0	0	0	2	3	3	.238	.111

HOUSE, J.R.   C/1B

PERSONAL: Born November 11, 1979, in Charleston, W.Va. ... 6-0/215. ... Bats right, throws right. ... Full name: James Rodger House. ... High school: Seabreeze (Daytona Beach, Fla.). **TRANSACTIONS/CAREER NOTES:** Selected by Pittsburgh Pirates organization in fifth round of 1999 free-agent draft. ... Released by Pirates (March 8, 2005). ... Signed by Houston Astros organization (January 25, 2006).

2006 GAMES PLAYED BY POSITION (MLB): C—3, 1B—2.

Year Team (League)	Pos.	G	AB	R	H	2B	3B	HR	RBI	BB	SO	HBP	GDP	SB-CS	Avg.	OBP	SLG	OPS	E	Avg.
1999— GC Pirates (GCL)	1B-C-3B	33	113	13	37	9	3	5	23	11	28	2	...	1-0	.327	.394	.593	.987	3	.987
— Will. (NYP)	C-1B	26	100	11	30	6	0	1	13	9	21	0	2	0-1	.300	.358	.390	.748	3	.985
— Hickory (S. Atl.)	3B	4	11	1	3	0	0	0	0	0	3	0	0	0-0	.273	.273	.273	.545	0	...
2000— Hickory (S. Atl.)	C-1B	110	420	78	146	29	1	23	90	46	91	6	7	1-2	.348	.414	.586	1.000	8	.990
2001— Altoona (East.)	C-1B	112	426	51	110	25	1	11	56	37	103	5	12	1-1	.258	.323	.399	.722	7	.991
2002— GC Pirates (GCL)	C-1B	5	16	3	5	2	0	1	2	3	1	0	0	0-0	.313	.421	.625	1.046	0	1.000
— Altoona (East.)	C	30	91	9	24	6	0	2	11	13	21	0	4	0-0	.264	.349	.396	.745	1	.994
2003— GC Pirates (GCL)	DH-C	20	65	16	26	9	0	4	23	12	5	1	...	0-0	.400	.476	.723	1.199	1	.984
— Altoona (East.)	C-DH	20	63	12	21	6	0	2	11	5	11	0	4	0-0	.333	.382	.524	.906	1	.983
— Pittsburgh (N.L.)		1	1	0	1	0	0	0	0	0	0	0	0	0-0	1.000	1.000	1.000	2.000	1	...
2004— Nashville (PCL)	C-1B-OF																			
	DH	92	309	38	89	21	1	15	49	23	72	4	6	1-1	.288	.344	.508	.852	4	.993
— Pittsburgh (N.L.)	C	5	9	1	1	1	0	0	0	0	2	0	1	0-0	.111	.111	.222	.333	1	1.000
2005—		Did not play.																		
2006— Round Rock (PCL)		31	114	25	47	15	0	5	36	9	15	1	4	0-0	.412	.445	.675	1.121	3	.987
— Corpus Christi (Texas)		97	379	58	123	23	2	10	69	32	44	4	9	2-2	.325	.376	.475	.851	7	.992
— Houston (N.L.)	C-1B	4	9	0	0	0	0	0	0	0	2	0	1	0-0	.000	.000	.000	.000	0	1.000
Major League totals (3 years)		10	19	1	2	1	0	0	0	0	4	0	2	0-0	.105	.105	.158	.263	0	1.000

2006 LEFTY-RIGHTY SPLITS

vs.	Avg.	AB	H	2B	3B	HR	RBI	BB	SO	OBP	Slg.	vs.	Avg.	AB	H	2B	3B	HR	RBI	BB	SO	OBP	Slg.
L	.000	7	0	0	0	0	0	0	1	.000	.000	R	.000	2	0	0	0	0	0	0	1	.000	.000

HOWARD, RYAN   1B

PERSONAL: Born November 19, 1979, in St. Louis. ... 6-4/230. ... Bats left, throws left. ... Full name: Ryan James Howard. ... High school: Lafayette (St. Louis). ... College: Southwest Missouri State. **TRANSACTIONS/CAREER NOTES:** Selected by Philadelphia Phillies in fifth round of 2001 free-agent draft. **HONORS:** Named N.L. Rookie of the Year by Baseball Writers' Association of America (2005). ... Named Major League Player of the Year by SPORTING NEWS (2006). ... Named first baseman on SPORTING NEWS N.L. All-Star team (2006). ... Named N.L. Most Valuable Player by Baseball Writers' Association of America (2006). ... Named first baseman on N.L. Silver Slugger team (2006). **STATISTICAL NOTES:** Hit three home runs in one game (September 3, 2006). ... Career major league grand slams: 3.

2006 GAMES PLAYED BY POSITION (MLB): 1B—159.

Year Team (League)	Pos.	G	AB	R	H	2B	3B	HR	RBI	BB	SO	HBP	GDP	SB-CS	Avg.	OBP	SLG	OPS	E	Avg.
2001— Batavia (NY-Penn)	1B	48	169	26	46	7	3	6	35	30	55	2	1	0-0	.272	.384	.456	.840	5	.987
2002— Lakewood (S. Atl.)	1B	135	493	56	138	20	6	19	87	66	145	5	9	5-4	.280	.367	.460	.828	17	.985
2003— Clearwater (FSL)	1B	130	490	67	149	32	1	23	82	50	151	8	12	0-0	.304	.374	.514	.889	10	.991
2004— Reading (East.)	1B-DH	102	374	73	111	18	1	37	102	46	129	10	2	1-2	.297	.386	.647	1.033	7	.992
— Scran./W.B. (I.L.)	1B	29	111	21	30	10	0	9	29	14	37	2	4	0-0	.270	.362	.604	.966	6	.977
— Philadelphia (N.L.)	1B	19	39	5	11	5	0	2	5	2	13	1	2	0-0	.282	.333	.564	.897	0	1.000
2005— Scran./W.B. (I.L.)	1B-DH	61	210	38	78	19	0	16	54	39	66	3	3	0-0	.371	.467	.690	1.157	8	.986
— Philadelphia (N.L.)	1B	88	312	52	90	17	2	22	63	33	100	1	6	0-1	.288	.356	.567	.924	5	.993
2006— Philadelphia (N.L.)	1B	159	581	104	182	25	1	*58	*149	108	181	9	7	0-0	.313	.425	.659	1.084	14	.991
Major League totals (3 years)		266	932	161	283	47	3	82	217	143	294	11	15	0-1	.304	.399	.624	1.024	19	.992

ALL-STAR GAME RECORD

		G	AB	R	H	2B	3B	HR	RBI	BB	SO	HBP	GDP	SB-CS	Avg.	OBP	SLG	OPS	E	Avg.
All-Star Game totals (1 year)		1	1	0	0	0	0	0	0	0	0	0	0	0-0	.000	.000	.000	.000	0	1.000

2006 LEFTY-RIGHTY SPLITS

vs.	Avg.	AB	H	2B	3B	HR	RBI	BB	SO	OBP	Slg.	vs.	Avg.	AB	H	2B	3B	HR	RBI	BB	SO	OBP	Slg.
L	.279	197	55	5	1	16	45	22	76	.364	.558	R	.331	384	127	20	0	42	104	86	105	.453	.711

HOWELL, J.P.   P

PERSONAL: Born April 25, 1983, in Modesto, Calif. ... 6-0/175. ... Throws left, bats left. ... Full name: James Phillip Howell. ... High school: Jesuit (Carmichael, Calif.). ... College: Texas. **TRANSACTIONS/CAREER NOTES:** Selected by Kansas City Royals organization in first round (31st pick overall) of 2004 free-agent draft ... Traded by Royals to Tampa Bay Devil Rays for OF Joey Gathright and 2B Fernando Cortez (June 20, 2006).

CAREER HITTING: 0-for-3 (.000), 0 R, 0 2B, 0 3B, 0 HR, 0 RBI.

Year Team (League)	W	L	Pct.	ERA	WHIP	G	GS	CG	ShO	Hld.	Sv.-Opp.	IP	H	R	ER	HR	BB-IBB	SO	Avg.
2004— Idaho Falls (Pio.)	3	1	.750	2.77	1.08	6	4	0	0	0-...		26.0	16	9	8	1	12-0	38	.190

H

Year	Team (League)	W	L	Pct.	ERA	WHIP	G	GS	CG	ShO	Hld.	Sv.-Opp.	IP	H	R	ER	HR	BB-IBB	SO	Avg.
2005—High Desert (Calif.)	3	1	.750	1.96	1.24	8	8	0	0	0	0-0	46.0	33	16	10	0	24-0	48	.202
—Wichita (Texas)	2	0	1.000	2.50	0.94	3	3	0	0	0	0-0	18.0	12	5	5	2	5-0	23	.188
—Omaha (PCL)	3	1	.750	4.06	1.57	7	7	0	0	0	0-0	37.2	40	19	17	1	19-0	29	.286
—Kansas City (A.L.)	3	5	.375	6.19	1.54	15	15	0	0	0	0-0	72.2	73	55	50	7	39-0	54	.264
2006—Omaha (PCL)	3	2	.600	4.75	1.47	8	8	0	0	0	0-0	36.0	39	19	19	3	14-0	33	.287
—Durham (Int'l)	5	3	.625	2.62	1.24	10	10	0	0	0	0-0	55.0	53	18	16	2	15-0	49	.260
—Tampa Bay (A.L.)	1	3	.250	5.10	1.56	8	8	0	0	0	0-0	42.1	52	25	24	4	14-0	33	.310
Major League totals (2 years)	4	8	.333	5.79	1.55	23	23	0	0	0	0-0	115.0	125	80	74	13	53-0	87	.281

2006 LEFTY-RIGHTY SPLITS

vs.	Avg.	AB	H	2B	3B	HR	RBI	BB	SO	OBP	Slg.	vs.	Avg.	AB	H	2B	3B	HR	RBI	BB	SO	OBP	Slg.
L	.400	40	16	3	0		3	2	6	.429	.550	R	.281	128	36	4	1	3	16	12	27	.352	.398

HOWRY, BOB — P

PERSONAL: Born August 4, 1973, in Phoenix. ... 6-5/220. ... Throws right, bats left. ... Full name: Bobby Dean Howry. ... Name pronounced: HOW-ree. ... High school: Deer Valley (Phoenix). ... College: McNeese State. **TRANSACTIONS/CAREER NOTES:** Selected by San Francisco Giants organization in fifth round of 1994 free-agent draft. ... Traded by Giants with SS Mike Caruso, OF Brian Manning and Ps Keith Foulke, Lorenzo Barcelo and Ken Vining to Chicago White Sox for Ps Wilson Alvarez, Danny Darwin and Roberto Hernandez (July 31, 1997). ... On suspended list (April 28-May 30, 2000). ... Traded by White Sox to Boston Red Sox for Ps Frank Francisco and Byeong An (July 31, 2002). ... On disabled list (August 22, 2003-remainder of season). ... Released by Red Sox (October 24, 2003). ... Signed by Cleveland Indians organization (December 17, 2003). ... Signed as a free agent by Chicago Cubs (November 29, 2005).
CAREER HITTING: 1-for-2 (.500), 0 R, 0 2B, 0 3B, 0 HR, 0 RBI.

Year	Team (League)	W	L	Pct.	ERA	WHIP	G	GS	CG	ShO	Hld.	Sv.-Opp.	IP	H	R	ER	HR	BB-IBB	SO	Avg.
1994—Everett (N'west)	0	4	.000	4.74	2.05	5	5	0	0	...	0-...	19.0	29	15	10	3	10-2	16	.341
1995—Clinton (Midw.)	1	3	.250	4.20	1.56	9	8	0	0	...	0-...	49.1	61	29	23	1	16-0	22	.316
—San Jose (Calif.)	12	10	.545	3.54	1.36	27	25	1	0	...	0-...	165.1	171	79	65	6	54-0	107	.277
1996—Shreveport (Texas)	12	10	.545	4.65	1.40	27	27	0	0	...	0-...	156.2	163	90	81	17	56-3	57	.269
1997—Shreveport (Texas)	6	3	.667	4.91	1.44	48	0	0	0	...	22-...	55.0	58	35	30	6	21-0	43	.270
—Birmingham (Sou.)	0	0	...	2.84	1.50	12	0	0	0*	...	0-...	12.2	16	4	4	1	3-0	3	.314
1998—Calgary (PCL)	1	2	.333	3.41	1.11	23	0	0	0	...	5-...	31.2	25	12	12	2	10-3	22	.216
—Chicago (A.L.)	0	3	.000	3.15	1.03	44	0	0	0	19	9-11	54.1	37	20	19	7	19-2	51	.194
1999—Chicago (A.L.)	5	3	.625	3.59	1.42	69	0	0	0	1	28-34	67.2	58	34	27	8	38-3	80	.229
2000—Chicago (A.L.)	2	4	.333	3.17	1.17	65	0	0	0	14	7-12	71.0	54	26	25	6	29-2	60	.216
2001—Chicago (A.L.)	4	5	.444	4.69	1.46	69	0	0	0	21	5-11	78.2	85	41	41	11	30-9	64	.279
2002—Chicago (A.L.)	2	2	.500	3.91	1.22	47	0	0	0	10	0-0	50.2	45	22	22	7	17-2	31	.245
—Boston (A.L.)	1	3	.250	5.00	1.44	20	0	0	0	5	0-1	18.0	22	15	10	2	4-2	14	.306
2003—Boston (A.L.)	0	0	...	12.46	3.23	4	0	0	0	0	0-1	4.1	11	6	6	1	3-1	4	.478
—Pawtucket (Int'l)	2	0	1.000	1.06	0.90	13	0	0	0	...	0-...	17.0	14	2	2	1	1-0	10	.215
2004—Buffalo (Int'l)	1	1	.500	5.19	1.08	18	0	0	0	...	0-...	26.0	22	15	15	0	6-0	24	.222
—Cleveland (A.L.)	4	2	.667	2.74	1.15	37	0	0	0	8	0-2	42.2	37	14	13	5	12-0	39	.228
2005—Cleveland (A.L.)	7	4	.636	2.47	0.89	79	0	0	0	29	3-5	73.0	49	23	20	4	16-1	48	.191
2006—Chicago (N.L.)	4	5	.444	3.17	1.13	84	0	0	0	21	5-9	76.2	70	28	27	8	17-4	71	.245
American League totals (8 years)	25	26	.490	3.58	1.23	434	0	0	0	107	52-77	460.1	398	201	183	51	168-22	391	.235
National League totals (1 year)	4	5	.444	3.17	1.13	84	0	0	0	21	5-9	76.2	70	28	27	8	17-4	71	.245
Major League totals (9 years)	29	31	.483	3.52	1.22	518	0	0	0	128	57-86	537.0	468	229	210	59	185-26	462	.236

DIVISION SERIES RECORD

Year	Team (League)	W	L	Pct.	ERA	WHIP	G	GS	CG	ShO	Hld.	Sv.-Opp.	IP	H	R	ER	HR	BB-IBB	SO	Avg.
2000—Chicago (A.L.)	0	0	...	3.38	1.50	2	0	0	0	1	0-0	2.2	2	1	1	0	2-0	4	.222

2006 LEFTY-RIGHTY SPLITS

vs.	Avg.	AB	H	2B	3B	HR	RBI	BB	SO	OBP	Slg.	vs.	Avg.	AB	H	2B	3B	HR	RBI	BB	SO	OBP	Slg.
L	.247	89	22	3	0	3	6	8	23	.309	.382	R	.244	197	48	7	1	5	30	9	48	.283	.365

HUBER, JON — P

PERSONAL: Born July 7, 1981, in Sacramento, Calif. ... Throws right, bats right. ... Full name: Jonathon Lloyd Huber. ... High school: Nokomis (Ill.). ... College: Southern Illinois-Edwardsville. **TRANSACTIONS/CAREER NOTES:** Selected by San Diego Padres organization in fifth round of 2000 free-agent draft. ... Traded by Padres to Seattle Mariners for 1B/3B Dave Hansen (July 30, 2004).
CAREER HITTING: 0-for-0 (.000), 0 R, 0 2B, 0 3B, 0 HR, 0 RBI.

Year	Team (League)	W	L	Pct.	ERA	WHIP	G	GS	CG	ShO	Hld.	Sv.-Opp.	IP	H	R	ER	HR	BB-IBB	SO	Avg.
2000—Ariz. Padres (Ariz.)	1	4	.200	6.60	1.91	14	10	0	0	...	0-...	45.0	54	49	33	1	32-0	39	.293
2001—Idaho Falls (Pio.)	5	9	.357	6.04	1.71	15	15	0	0	...	0-...	73.0	77	61	49	7	48-0	75	.274
2002—Fort Wayne (Midw.)	8	12	.400	5.12	1.55	28	26	2	0	...	0-...	146.0	168	99	83	7	59-0	86	.292
2003—Fort Wayne (Midw.)	1	1	.500	3.76	1.10	7	7	0	0	...	0-...	38.1	31	18	16	2	11-0	34	.226
—Lake Elsinore (Calif.)	3	5	.375	5.18	1.74	12	11	0	0	...	0-...	57.1	69	41	33	2	31-1	43	.300
2004—Lake Elsinore (Calif.)	8	6	.571	3.70	1.41	20	20	0	0	...	0-...	107.0	107	53	44	9	44-0	100	.262
—Inland Empire (Calif.)	4	1	.800	6.12	1.73	7	5	0	0	...	0-...	32.1	42	24	22	4	14-0	38	.302
2005—San Antonio (Texas)	7	8	.467	4.74	1.41	26	26	1	1	0	0-0	148.0	159	87	78	11	49-0	112	.276
2006—San Antonio (Texas)	0	3	.000	4.88	1.42	21	0	0	0	0	11-12	24.0	30	13	13	0	4-1	19	.316
—Tacoma (PCL)	3	1	.750	2.61	1.35	29	0	0	0	0	12-13	41.1	46	14	12	3	10-0	38	.280
—Seattle (A.L.)	2	1	.667	1.08	0.96	16	0	0	0	6	0-0	16.2	10	3	2	0	6-1	11	.172
Major League totals (1 year)	2	1	.667	1.08	0.96	16	0	0	0	6	0-0	16.2	10	3	2	0	6-1	11	.172

2006 LEFTY-RIGHTY SPLITS

vs.	Avg.	AB	H	2B	3B	HR	RBI	BB	SO	OBP	Slg.	vs.	Avg.	AB	H	2B	3B	HR	RBI	BB	SO	OBP	Slg.
L	.067	15	1	0	0	0	0	1	4	.125	.067	R	.209	43	9	1	0	0	5	5	7	.292	.279

HUBER, JUSTIN — 1B

PERSONAL: Born July 1, 1982, in Melbourne, Australia. ... 6-2/200. ... Bats right, throws right. ... Full name: Justin Patrick Huber. ... Junior college: Beacon Hill (Victoria, Australia) C.C. **TRANSACTIONS/CAREER NOTES:** Signed as a non-drafted free agent by New York Mets organization (July 26, 2000). ... Traded by Mets to Kansas City Royals for IF Jose Bautista (July 30, 2004).
2006 GAMES PLAYED BY POSITION (MLB): DH—4.

H

							BATTING												FIELDING	
Year	Team (League)	Pos.	G	AB	R	H	2B	3B	HR	RBI	BB	SO	HBP	GDP	SB-CS	Avg.	OBP	SLG	OPS	E	Avg.
2001—St. Lucie (Fla. St.)	C-OF	2	6	0	0	0	0	0	0	0	2	0	0	0-0	.000	.000	.000	.000	0	1.000

Year	Team (League)	Pos.	G	AB	R	H	2B	3B	HR	RBI	BB	SO	HBP	GDP	SB-CS	Avg.	OBP	SLG	OPS	E	Avg.
	—Kingsport (Appalachian)	C	47	159	24	50	11	1	7	31	17	42	13	4	4-2	.314	.415	.528	.943	8	.981
	—Brook. (N.Y.-Penn.)	C	3	9	0	0	0	0	0	0	0	4	0	1	0-0	.000	.000	.000	.000	0	1.000
2002	—Columbia (S. Atl.)	C	95	330	49	96	22	2	11	78	45	81	23	5	1-2	.291	.408	.470	.878	8	.989
	—St. Lucie (Fla. St.)	C-OF	28	100	15	27	2	1	3	15	11	18	6	3	0-0	.270	.370	.400	.770	3	.983
2003	—St. Lucie (Fla. St.)	C-OF	50	183	26	52	15	0	9	36	17	30	9	9	1-1	.284	.370	.514	.884	5	.982
	—Binghamton (East.)	C-1B	55	193	16	51	13	0	6	36	19	54	7	4	0-2	.264	.350	.425	.775	6	.979
2004	—St. Lucie (Fla. St.)	C-OF	14	49	10	12	2	0	2	8	5	8	1	0	1-0	.245	.327	.408	.735	0	1.000
	—Binghamton (East.)	C-1B	70	236	44	64	16	1	11	33	46	57	12	5	2-2	.271	.414	.487	.901	5	.991
	—Norfolk (Int'l)	C	5	16	3	5	2	0	0	3	3	3	0	0	0-0	.313	.421	.438	.859	0	1.000
2005	—Wichita (Texas)	1B-DH	88	335	68	115	23	3	16	74	51	70	5	11	7-3	.343	.432	.570	1.002	12	.981
	—Omaha (PCL)	1B-DH	32	113	19	31	6	1	7	23	16	33	2	3	3-0	.274	.374	.531	.905	3	.990
	—Kansas City (A.L.)	1B-DH	25	78	6	17	3	0	0	6	5	20	1	1	0-0	.218	.271	.256	.527	3	.978
2006	—Omaha (PCL)		100	352	47	98	22	2	15	44	40	94	4	11	2-2	.278	.358	.480	.838	8	.980
	—Kansas City (A.L.)	DH	5	10	1	2	1	0	0	1	1	4	0	0	1-0	.200	.273	.300	.573	0	—
	Major League totals (2 years)		30	88	7	19	4	0	0	7	6	24	1	1	1-0	.216	.271	.261	.532	3	.978

2006 LEFTY-RIGHTY SPLITS

vs.	Avg.	AB	H	2B	3B	HR	RBI	BB	SO	OBP	Slg.	vs.	Avg.	AB	H	2B	3B	HR	RBI	BB	SO	OBP	Slg.
L	.125	8	1	0	0	0	1	3	.222	.125		R	.500	2	1	1	0	0	1	0	1	.500	1.000

HUCKABY, KEN   C

PERSONAL: Born January 27, 1971, in San Leandro, Calif. ... 6-1/210. ... Bats right, throws right. ... Full name: Kenneth Paul Huckaby. ... Name pronounced: HUCK-a-be. ... High school: Manteca (Calif.). ... Junior college: San Joaquin Delta (Calif.). **TRANSACTIONS/CAREER NOTES:** Selected by Los Angeles Dodgers organization in 22nd round of 1991 free-agent draft. ... Signed as a free agent by Seattle Mariners organization (December 3, 1997). ... Released by Mariners (June 13, 1998). ... Signed by New York Yankees organization (June 28, 1998). ... Signed as a free agent by Arizona Diamondbacks organization (January 22, 1999). ... Released by Diamondbacks (October 29, 2001). ... Signed by Toronto Blue Jays organization (February 10, 2002). ... Signed as a free agent by Texas Rangers organization (November 13, 2003). ... Claimed on waivers by Baltimore Orioles (July 6, 2004). ... Signed as a free agent by Rangers organization (August 17, 2004). ... Signed as a free agent by Blue Jays organization (January 10, 2005). ... Signed as a free agent by Boston Red Sox organization (December 11, 2005).

2006 GAMES PLAYED BY POSITION (MLB): C—8.

Year	Team (League)	Pos.	G	AB	R	H	2B	3B	HR	RBI	BB	SO	HBP	GDP	SB-CS	Avg.	OBP	SLG	OPS	E	Avg.
1991	—Great Falls (Pio.)	C	57	213	39	55	16	0	3	37	17	38	4	4	3-2	.258	.321	.376	.696	12	.977
1992	—Vero Beach (FSL)	C	73	261	14	63	9	0	0	21	7	42	1	5	1-1	.241	.262	.276	.538	9	.982
1993	—Vero Beach (FSL)	C	79	281	22	75	14	1	4	41	11	35	2	3	2-1	.267	.297	.367	.664	12	.980
	—San Antonio (Texas)	C	28	82	4	18	1	0	0	5	2	7	2	0	0-0	.220	.253	.232	.485	4	.978
1994	—San Antonio (Texas)	C	11	41	3	11	1	0	1	9	1	1	0	1	1-0	.268	.286	.366	.652	6	.931
	—Bakersfield (Calif.)	C	77	270	29	81	18	1	2	30	10	37	2	7	2-3	.300	.329	.396	.725	10	.986
1995	—Albuquerque (PCL)	1B-C	89	278	30	90	16	2	1	40	12	26	4	16	3-1	.324	.359	.406	.766	16	.973
1996	—Albuquerque (PCL)	C	103	287	37	79	16	2	3	41	17	35	2	10	0-0	.275	.319	.376	.696	6	.990
1997	—Albuquerque (PCL)	C-DH	69	201	14	40	5	1	0	18	9	36	0	5	0-0	.199	.231	.234	.465	10	.975
1998	—Tacoma (PCL)	1B-C	16	49	4	11	2	0	0	1	5	6	0	2	0-0	.224	.296	.265	.562	0	1.000
	—Columbus (Int'l)	C	36	101	13	21	3	1	1	10	11	14	0	3	0-2	.208	.286	.287	.573	5	.978
1999	—Tucson (PCL)	C-3B-1B																			
		DH	107	355	44	107	20	1	2	42	13	33	2	11	0-0	.301	.325	.380	.706	10	.987
2000	—Tucson (PCL)	C-3B-OF																			
		1B	76	243	31	67	11	1	4	33	10	30	2	10	2-2	.276	.306	.379	.685	8	.982
2001	—El Paso (Texas)	1B-C	30	104	14	36	4	0	2	14	3	16	3	3	0-0	.346	.368	.442	.811	4	.983
	—Tucson (PCL)	C-1B-3B																			
		2B	78	262	31	76	15	1	2	34	7	62	2	3	1-3	.290	.313	.378	.690	14	.972
	—Arizona (N.L.)	C	1	1	0	0	0	0	0	0	0	1	0	0	0-0	.000	.000	.000	.000	0	1.000
2002	—Syracuse (Int'l)	C-1B	21	81	7	22	2	0	0	9	2	15	0	6	0-2	.272	.286	.296	.582	3	.981
	—Toronto (A.L.)	C	88	273	29	67	6	1	3	22	9	44	0	10	0-0	.245	.270	.308	.577	6	.989
2003	—Toronto (A.L.)	C	5	11	1	2	1	0	0	2	0	2	0	0	0-0	.182	.182	.273	.455	0	1.000
	—Syracuse (Int'l)	C-1B-3B																			
		3B	75	267	24	78	14	0	3	25	15	30	0	11	1-1	.292	.326	.378	.705	7	.987
2004	—Oklahoma (PCL)	C-1B	35	127	18	35	8	1	2	20	9	18	0	6	0-0	.276	.317	.402	.718	3	.988
	—Texas (A.L.)	C	16	38	3	5	2	0	0	0	5	12	0	1	0-0	.132	.233	.184	.417	2	.978
	—Baltimore (A.L.)	C	8	12	1	2	1	0	0	0	0	0	0	0	0-0	.167	.167	.250	.417	0	1.000
2005	—Syracuse (Int'l)	C-1B	15	56	3	15	1	0	1	3	1	13	0	1	0-0	.268	.281	.339	.620	1	.991
	—Toronto (A.L.)	C	35	87	8	18	4	0	0	6	5	19	0	4	0-0	.207	.250	.253	.503	2	.987
2006	—Pawtucket (Int'l)		88	288	18	63	10	0	2	23	9	72	0	9	4-0	.219	.239	.274	.514	9	.984
	—Boston (A.L.)	C	8	5	0	1	0	0	0	0	0	1	0	0	0-0	.200	.200	.200	.400	0	1.000
	American League totals (5 years)		160	426	42	95	14	1	3	31	19	77	0	16	0-0	.223	.256	.282	.538	10	.988
	National League totals (1 year)		1	1	0	0	0	0	0	0	0	1	0	0	0-0	.000	.000	.000	.000	0	1.000
	Major League totals (6 years)		161	427	42	95	14	1	3	31	19	78	0	16	0-0	.222	.256	.281	.537	10	.988

2006 LEFTY-RIGHTY SPLITS

vs.	Avg.	AB	H	2B	3B	HR	RBI	BB	SO	OBP	Slg.	vs.	Avg.	AB	H	2B	3B	HR	RBI	BB	SO	OBP	Slg.
L	.000	1	0	0	0	0	0	0	0	.000	.000		R	.250	4	1	0	0	0	0	0	1	.250	.250

HUDSON, LUKE   P

PERSONAL: Born May 2, 1977, in Fountain Valley, Calif. ... 6-3/195. ... Throws right, bats right. ... Full name: Luke Stephen Hudson. ... High school: Fountain Valley (Calif.). ... College: Tennessee. **TRANSACTIONS/CAREER NOTES:** Selected by Baltimore Orioles organization in fifth round of 1995 draft; did not sign. ... Selected by Colorado Rockies organization in fourth round of 1998 free-agent draft. ... Traded by Rockies with P Gabe White to Cincinnati Reds for 2B Pokey Reese and P Dennys Reyes (December 18, 2001). ... On disabled list (April 2-June 9, 2005); included rehabilitation assignment to Chattanooga. ... Signed as a free agent by Kansas City Royals organization (March 13, 2006). **MISCELLANEOUS NOTES:** Scored a run in two reappearances as pinch runner (2005).

CAREER HITTING: 10-for-41 (.244), 8 R, 2 2B, 0 3B, 0 HR, 5 RBI.

Year	Team (League)	W	L	Pct.	ERA	WHIP	G	GS	CG	ShO	Hld.	Sv.-Opp.	IP	H	R	ER	HR	BB-IBB	SO	Avg.
1998	—Portland (N'west)	3	6	.333	4.74	1.49	15	15	0	0	...	0-...	79.2	68	46	42	8	51-0	82	.226
1999	—Asheville (S. Atl.)	6	5	.545	4.30	1.28	21	20	1	0	...	0-...	88.0	89	47	42	10	24-0	96	.265
2000	—Salem (Carol.)	5	8	.385	3.27	1.23	19	19	2	2	...	0-...	110.0	101	47	40	9	34-0	80	.246
2001	—Carolina (Southern)	7	12	.368	4.20	1.38	29	28	1	0	...	0-...	165.0	159	90	77	19	68-0	145	.250
2002	—Louisville (Int'l)	5	9	.357	4.51	1.35	30	17	0	0	...	3-...	117.2	102	64	59	6	57-1	129	.233

H

Year	Team (League)	W	L	Pct.	ERA	WHIP	G	GS	CG	ShO	Hld.	Sv.-Opp.	IP	H	R	ER	HR	BB-IBB	SO	Avg.
	— Cincinnati (N.L.)	0	0	...	4.50	1.83	3	0	0	0	1	0-0	6.0	5	5	3	1	6-0	7	.227
2003—			Did not play.																	
2004—	Chattanooga (Sou.)	7	7	.500	3.32	1.11	16	16	0	0	...	0-...	86.2	71	35	32	9	25-1	91	.225
	— Louisville (Int'l)	2	1	.667	2.84	1.05	3	3	0	0	...	0-...	19.0	15	8	6	2	5-0	17	.214
	— Cincinnati (N.L.)	4	2	.667	2.42	1.26	9	9	0	0		0-0	48.1	36	16	13	3	25-1	38	.208
2005—	Chattanooga (Sou.)	0	1	.000	5.40	1.05	1	1	0	0		0-0	6.2	6	4	4	2	1-0	7	.231
	— Cincinnati (N.L.)	6	9	.400	6.38	1.57	19	16	0	0		0-0	84.2	83	62	60	14	50-2	53	.268
2006—	Omaha (PCL)	2	0	1.000	2.80	1.05	13	2	0	0	2	1-1	35.1	30	14	11	0	7-1	21	.226
	— Kansas City (A.L.)	7	6	.538	5.12	1.44	26	15	0	0	1	0-1	102.0	109	62	58	7	38-1	64	.276
American League totals (1 year)		7	6	.538	5.12	1.44	26	15	0	0		0-1	102.0	109	62	58	7	38-1	64	.276
National League totals (3 years)		10	11	.476	4.92	1.47	31	25	0	0		0-0	139.0	124	83	76	18	81-3	98	.246
Major League totals (4 years)		17	17	.500	5.00	1.46	57	40	0	0	2	0-1	241.0	233	145	134	25	119-4	162	.259

2006 LEFTY-RIGHTY SPLITS

vs.	Avg.	AB	H	2B	3B	HR	RBI	BB	SO	OBP	Slg.	vs.	Avg.	AB	H	2B	3B	HR	RBI	BB	SO	OBP	Slg.
L	.258	190	49	12	2	2	22	19	29	.330	.374	R	.293	205	60	9	2	5	26	19	35	.355	.429

HUDSON, ORLANDO — 2B

PERSONAL: Born December 12, 1977, in Darlington, S.C. ... 6-0/185. ... Bats both, throws right. ... Full name: Orlando Thill Hudson. ... High school: Darlington (S.C.). ... College: Spartanburg Methodist (S.C.). **TRANSACTIONS/CAREER NOTES:** Selected by Toronto Blue Jays organization in 33rd round of 1996 free-agent draft; did not sign. ... Selected by Blue Jays organization in 43rd round of 1997 free-agent draft. ... On disabled list (May 24-June 16, 2004). ... Traded by Blue Jays with P Miguel Batista to Arizona Diamondbacks for 3B Troy Glaus and SS Sergio Santos (December 27, 2005). **HONORS:** Won A.L. Gold Glove at second base (2005). ... Won N.L. Gold Glove at second base (2006). **STATISTICAL NOTES:** Career major league grand slams: 1.

2006 GAMES PLAYED BY POSITION (MLB): 2B—157.

											BATTING									FIELDING	
Year	Team (League)	Pos.	G	AB	R	H	2B	3B	HR	RBI	BB	SO	HBP	GDP	SB-CS	Avg.	OBP	SLG	OPS	E	Avg.
1998—	Medicine Hat (Pio.)	2B	65	242	50	71	18	1	8	42	22	36	7	3	6-5	.293	.366	.475	.842	13	.959
1999—	Hagerstown (SAL)	2B-3B-OF	132	513	66	137	36	6	7	74	42	85	2	10	8-6	.267	.322	.402	.724	21	.946
2000—	Dunedin (Fla. St.)	2B-3B-SS	96	358	54	102	16	2	7	48	37	42	2	15	9-5	.285	.354	.399	.754	19	.941
	— Tennessee (Sou.)	3B	39	134	17	32	4	3	2	15	15	18	2	3	3-2	.239	.320	.358	.678	11	.921
2001—	Tennessee (Sou.)	2B-3B	84	306	51	94	22	8	4	52	37	42	3	12	8-3	.307	.385	.471	.856	8	.979
	— Syracuse (Int'l)	2B-3B	55	194	31	59	14	3	4	27	23	34	2	1	11-3	.304	.378	.469	.847	4	.986
2002—	Syracuse (Int'l)	2B	100	417	63	127	27	3	10	37	35	54	4	14	8-5	.305	.363	.456	.819	10	.982
	— Toronto (A.L.)	2B	54	192	20	53	10	5	4	23	11	27	2	6	0-1	.276	.319	.443	.762	4	.986
2003—	Toronto (A.L.)	2B	142	474	54	127	21	6	9	57	39	87	5	13	5-4	.268	.328	.395	.723	12	.984
2004—	Toronto (A.L.)	2B	135	489	73	132	32	7	12	58	51	98	4	12	7-3	.270	.341	.438	.779	12	.984
2005—	Toronto (A.L.)	2B	131	461	62	125	25	5	10	63	30	65	3	10	7-1	.271	.315	.412	.728	6	.991
2006—	Arizona (N.L.)	2B	157	579	87	166	34	9	15	67	61	78	2	17	9-6	.287	.354	.454	.809	13	.984
American League totals (4 years)			462	1616	209	437	88	23	35	201	131	277	14	41	19-9	.270	.328	.418	.746	34	.986
National League totals (1 year)			157	579	87	166	34	9	15	67	61	78	2	17	9-6	.287	.354	.454	.809	13	.984
Major League totals (5 years)			619	2195	296	603	122	32	50	268	192	355	16	58	28-15	.275	.335	.428	.762	47	.986

2006 LEFTY-RIGHTY SPLITS

vs.	Avg.	AB	H	2B	3B	HR	RBI	BB	SO	OBP	Slg.	vs.	Avg.	AB	H	2B	3B	HR	RBI	BB	SO	OBP	Slg.
L	.338	142	48	10	3	3	19	16	10	.398	.514	R	.270	437	118	24	6	12	48	45	68	.340	.435

HUDSON, TIM — P

PERSONAL: Born July 14, 1975, in Columbus, Ga. ... 6-1/164. ... Throws right, bats right. ... Full name: Timothy Adam Hudson. ... High school: Glenwood (Phenix City, Ala.). ... College: Auburn. **TRANSACTIONS/CAREER NOTES:** Selected by Oakland Athletics organization in 35th round of 1994 free-agent draft; did not sign. ... Selected by Athletics organization in sixth round of 1997 free-agent draft. ... On disabled list (June 23-August 7, 2004); included rehabilitation assignment to Sacramento. ... Traded by A's to Atlanta Braves for Ps Juan Cruz and Dan Meyer and OF Charles Thomas (December 16, 2004). ... On disabled list (June 16-July 16, 2005). **HONORS:** Named A.L. Rookie Pitcher of the Year by THE SPORTING NEWS (1999). **MISCELLANEOUS NOTES:** Appeared in three games as pinch runner (1999). ... Appeared in one game as pinch runner (2000). ... Appeared in one game as pinch runner (2001).

CAREER HITTING: 18-for-154 (.117), 8 R, 4 2B, 1 3B, 0 HR, 10 RBI.

Year	Team (League)	W	L	Pct.	ERA	WHIP	G	GS	CG	ShO	Hld.	Sv.-Opp.	IP	H	R	ER	HR	BB-IBB	SO	Avg.
1997—	S. Oregon (N'west)	3	1	.750	2.51	0.94	8	4	0	0	...	0-...	28.2	12	8	8	0	15-2	37	.128
1998—	Modesto (California)	4	0	1.000	1.67	0.98	8	5	0	0	...	0-...	37.2	19	10	7	0	18-0	48	.148
	— Huntsville (Sou.)	10	9	.526	4.54	1.54	22	22	2	0	...	0-...	134.2	136	84	68	13	71-2	104	.270
1999—	Midland (Texas)	3	0	1.000	0.50	0.67	3	3	0	0	...	0-...	18.0	9	1	1	0	3-0	18	.153
	— Vancouver (PCL)	4	0	1.000	2.20	1.20	8	8	0	0	...	0-...	49.0	38	16	12	2	21-0	61	.212
	— Oakland (A.L.)	11	2	.846	3.23	1.34	21	21	1	0	...	0-0	136.1	121	56	49	8	62-2	132	.237
2000—	Oakland (A.L.)	•20	6	.769	4.14	1.24	32	32	2	2	0	0-0	202.1	169	100	93	24	82-5	169	.227
2001—	Oakland (A.L.)	18	9	.667	3.37	1.22	35	•35	3	0	0	0-0	235.0	216	100	88	20	71-5	181	.245
2002—	Oakland (A.L.)	15	9	.625	2.98	1.25	34	34	4	2	0	0-0	238.1	237	87	79	19	62-9	152	.263
2003—	Oakland (A.L.)	16	7	.696	2.70	1.08	34	34	3	•2	0	0-0	240.0	197	84	72	15	61-9	162	.223
2004—	Sacramento (PCL)	0	0	...	6.00	1.33	1	1	0	0	...	0-...	3.0	2	2	2	0	2-0	3	.167
	— Oakland (A.L.)	12	6	.667	3.53	1.26	27	27	3	•2	0	0-0	188.2	194	82	74	8	44-3	103	.267
2005—	Atlanta (N.L.)	14	9	.609	3.52	1.35	29	29	2	1	0	0-0	192.0	194	79	75	20	65-15	115	.265
2006—	Atlanta (N.L.)	13	12	.520	4.86	1.44	35	•35	2	1	0	0-0	218.1	235	129	118	25	79-10	141	.273
American League totals (6 years)		92	39	.702	3.30	1.22	183	183	16	8	0	0-0	1240.0	1134	509	455	94	382-33	899	.244
National League totals (2 years)		27	21	.563	4.23	1.40	64	64	4	2	0	0-0	410.1	429	208	193	45	144-15	256	.269
Major League totals (8 years)		119	60	.665	3.53	1.27	247	247	20	9	0	0-0	1651.0	1563	717	648	139	526-48	1155	.250

DIVISION SERIES RECORD

Year	Team (League)	W	L	Pct.	ERA	WHIP	G	GS	CG	ShO	Hld.	Sv.-Opp.	IP	H	R	ER	HR	BB-IBB	SO	Avg.
2000—	Oakland (A.L.)	0	1	.000	3.38	1.25	1	1	1	0	0	0-0	8.0	6	4	3	0	4-0	5	.194
2001—	Oakland (A.L.)	1	0	1.000	0.93	0.93	2	1	1	0	0	0-0	9.2	8	1	1	1	1-0	5	.222
2002—	Oakland (A.L.)	0	1	.000	6.23	1.96	2	2	0	0	0	0-0	8.2	13	11	6	2	4-0	8	.333
2003—	Oakland (A.L.)	0	0	...	3.52	1.43	2	2	0	0	0	0-0	7.2	10	3	3	2	1-0	8	.323
2005—	Atlanta (N.L.)	0	1	.000	5.27	1.39	2	2	0	0	0	0-0	13.2	13	8	8	0	6-1	6	.283
Division series totals (5 years)		1	3	.250	3.97	1.38	9	8	2	0	0	0-0	47.2	50	27	21	5	16-1	32	.273

ALL-STAR GAME RECORD

	W	L	Pct.	ERA	WHIP	G	GS	CG	ShO	Hld.	Sv.-Opp.	IP	H	R	ER	HR	BB-IBB	SO	Avg.
All-Star Game totals (1 year)	0	0	...	0.00	0.00	1	0	0	0	0	0-0	1.0	0	0	0	0	0-0	1	.000

H

2006 LEFTY-RIGHTY SPLITS

vs.	Avg.	AB	H	2B	3B	HR	RBI	BB	SO	OBP	Slg.	vs.	Avg.	AB	H	2B	3B	HR	RBI	BB	SO	OBP	Slg.
L	.281	434	122	23	9	17	74	44	58	.353	.493	R	.265	426	113	23	0	8	43	35	83	.325	.376

HUFF, AUBREY — OF/3B

PERSONAL: Born December 20, 1976, in Marion, Ohio. ... 6-4/231. ... Bats left, throws right. ... Full name: Aubrey Lewis Huff. ... High school: Brewer (Fort Worth, Texas). ... College: Miami. **TRANSACTIONS/CAREER NOTES:** Selected by Tampa Bay Devil Rays organization in fifth round of 1998 free-agent draft. ... On disabled list (April 14-May 5, 2006); included rehabilitation assignment to Visalia. ... Traded by Devil Rays with cash to Houston Astros for P Mitch Talbot and IF Ben Zobrist (July 12, 2006). **STATISTICAL NOTES:** Career major league grand slams: 2.

2006 GAMES PLAYED BY POSITION (MLB): 3B—90, OF—37, DH—3, 1B—3.

Year Team (League)	Pos.	G	AB	R	H	2B	3B	HR	RBI	BB	SO	HBP	GDP	SB-CS	Avg.	OBP	SLG	OPS	E	Avg.
															BATTING				FIELDING	
1998— Char., S.C. (SAL)	3B	69	265	38	85	19	1	13	54	24	40	0	5	3-1	.321	.371	.547	.918	8	.957
1999— Orlando (South.)	3B	133	491	85	148	40	3	22	78	64	77	4	14	2-3	.301	.385	.530	.915	29	.927
2000— Durham (Int'l)	3B-1B	108	408	73	129	36	3	20	76	51	72	2	15	2-3	.316	.394	.566	.960	21	.915
— Tampa Bay (A.L.)	3B	39	122	12	35	7	0	4	14	5	18	1	6	0-0	.287	.318	.443	.760	5	.939
2001— Durham (Int'l)	3B	17	66	14	19	6	0	3	10	5	7	0	3	0-0	.288	.338	.515	.853	4	.929
— Tampa Bay (A.L.)	3B-DH-1B	111	411	42	102	25	1	8	45	23	72	0	18	1-3	.248	.288	.372	.660	20	.940
2002— Durham (Int'l)	1B	32	126	18	41	9	0	3	20	12	13	1	4	0-0	.325	.386	.468	.854	0	1.000
— Tampa Bay (A.L.)	DH-1B-3B	113	454	67	142	25	0	23	59	37	55	1	17	4-1	.313	.364	.520	.884	8	.981
2003— Tampa Bay (A.L.)	OF-DH-1B 3B	162	636	91	198	47	3	34	107	53	80	8	19	2-3	.311	.367	.555	.922	9	.977
2004— Tampa Bay (A.L.)	3B-1B-DH OF	157	600	92	178	27	2	29	104	56	74	6	9	5-1	.297	.360	.493	.853	13	.975
2005— Tampa Bay (A.L.)	OF-DH-1B 3B	154	575	70	150	26	2	22	92	49	88	5	12	8-7	.261	.321	.428	.749	3	.992
2006— Visalia (Calif.)		2	8	2	2	1	0	0	1	1	2	0	0	0-0	.250	.333	.375	.708	0	1.000
— Tampa Bay (A.L.)	3B-DH	63	230	26	65	15	1	8	28	24	25	0	4	0-0	.283	.348	.461	.809	3	.980
— Houston (N.L.)	OF-3B-1B	68	224	31	56	10	1	13	38	26	39	7	7	0-0	.250	.341	.478	.819	4	.968
American League totals (7 years)		799	3028	400	870	172	9	128	449	247	412	21	85	20-15	.287	.343	.477	.819	61	.973
National League totals (1 year)		68	224	31	56	10	1	13	38	26	39	7	7	0-0	.250	.341	.478	.819	4	.968
Major League totals (7 years)		867	3252	431	926	182	10	141	487	273	451	28	92	20-15	.285	.342	.477	.819	65	.973

2006 LEFTY-RIGHTY SPLITS

vs.	Avg.	AB	H	2B	3B	HR	RBI	BB	SO	OBP	Slg.	vs.	Avg.	AB	H	2B	3B	HR	RBI	BB	SO	OBP	Slg.
L	.233	120	28	6	0	4	16	11	15	.303	.383	R	.278	334	93	19	2	17	50	39	49	.358	.500

HUGHES, TRAVIS — P

PERSONAL: Born May 25, 1978, in Newton, Kan. ... 6-5/240. ... Throws right, bats right. ... Full name: Travis Wade Hughes. ... High school: Elwood (Kan.). ... Junior college: Cowley County (Kan.) Community College.. **TRANSACTIONS/CAREER NOTES:** Selected by Texas Rangers organization in 19th round of 1997 free-agent draft. ... Claimed on waivers by Washington Nationals (April 7, 2005).

CAREER HITTING: 1-for-1 (1.000), 0 R, 0 2B, 0 3B, 0 HR, 0 RBI.

Year Team (League)	W	L	Pct.	ERA	WHIP	G	GS	CG	ShO	Hld.	Sv.-Opp.	IP	H	R	ER	HR	BB-IBB	SO	Avg.
1998— Pulaski (Appalachian)	2	6	.250	3.89	1.32	22	3	0	0	...	2-...	41.2	30	25	18	2	25-1	48	.189
1999— Savannah (S. Atl.)	11	7	.611	2.81	1.15	30	23	1	0	...	2-...	157.0	127	60	49	9	54-0	150	.221
2000— Charlotte (Fla. St.)	9	9	.500	4.42	1.39	39	14	1	0	...	9-...	126.1	122	76	62	9	54-3	96	.254
2001— Tulsa (Texas)	5	7	.417	4.64	1.56	47	5	0	0	...	8-...	87.1	91	52	45	8	45-2	86	.270
2002— Tulsa (Texas)	9	7	.563	3.52	1.54	26	26	1	1	...	0-...	143.1	139	68	56	11	82-0	137	.255
2003— Oklahoma (PCL)	1	3	.250	5.46	1.84	11	11	0	0	...	0-...	57.2	79	41	35	4	27-0	36	.329
— Frisco (Texas)	4	8	.333	4.99	1.45	24	10	1	1	...	0-...	74.0	81	47	41	6	26-1	58	.277
2004— Frisco (Texas)	3	6	.333	3.70	1.52	40	0	0	0	...	7-...	63.1	63	34	26	4	33-7	68	.256
— Oklahoma (PCL)	1	2	.333	5.26	1.17	13	0	0	0	...	0-...	25.2	21	15	15	2	9-0	24	.221
— Texas (A.L.)	0	0	...	13.50	4.50	2	0	0	0	0	0-0	1.1	4	2	2	0	2-0	4	.500
2005— New Orleans (PCL)	2	5	.286	3.02	1.21	52	0	0	0	9	13-17	59.2	47	25	20	3	25-1	73	.214
— Wash. (N.L.)	1	1	.500	5.54	2.00	14	0	0	0	0	0-1	13.0	18	8	8	4	8-1	8	.333
2006— New Orleans (PCL)	2	6	.250	2.32	1.24	51	0	0	0	7	4-8	73.2	50	30	19	3	41-4	87	.192
— Wash. (N.L.)	0	0	...	6.35	1.68	8	0	0	0	0	0-0	11.1	13	8	8	2	6-1	4	.310
American League totals (1 year)	0	0	...	13.50	4.50	2	0	0	0	0	0-0	1.1	4	2	2	0	2-0	4	.500
National League totals (2 years)	1	1	.500	5.92	1.85	22	0	0	0	0	0-1	24.1	31	16	16	6	14-2	12	.323
Major League totals (3 years)	1	1	.500	6.31	1.99	24	0	0	0	0	0-1	25.2	35	18	18	6	16-2	16	.337

2006 LEFTY-RIGHTY SPLITS

vs.	Avg.	AB	H	2B	3B	HR	RBI	BB	SO	OBP	Slg.	vs.	Avg.	AB	H	2B	3B	HR	RBI	BB	SO	OBP	Slg.
L	.182	22	4	1	0	1	4	5	1	.345	.364	R	.450	20	9	2	0	1	5	1	3	.522	.700

HUMBER, PHILIP — P

PERSONAL: Born December 21, 1982, in Nacogdoches, Texas. ... 6-4/210. ... Throws right, bats right. ... Full name: Philip Gregory Humber. ... College: Rice. **TRANSACTIONS/CAREER NOTES:** Selected by New York Mets organization in first round (third pick overall) of 2004 free-agent draft.

CAREER HITTING: 0-for-0 (.000), 0 R, 0 2B, 0 3B, 0 HR, 0 RBI.

Year Team (League)	W	L	Pct.	ERA	WHIP	G	GS	CG	ShO	Hld.	Sv.-Opp.	IP	H	R	ER	HR	BB-IBB	SO	Avg.
2005— St. Lucie (Fla. St.)	2	6	.250	4.99	1.31	14	14	0	0	0	0-0	70.1	74	41	39	6	18-0	65	.273
— Binghamton (East.)	0	1	.000	6.75	1.50	1	1	0	0	0	0-0	4.0	4	3	3	0	2-0	2	.250
2006— Binghamton (East.)	2	2	.500	2.88	1.02	6	6	0	0	0	0-0	34.1	25	12	11	4	10-0	36	.195
— GC Mets (GCL)	0	0	...	6.75	2.00	1	1	0	0	0	0-0	4.0	7	3	3	0	1-0	7	.389
— St. Lucie (Fla. St.)	3	1	.750	2.37	0.87	7	7	0	0	0	0-0	38.0	24	12	10	4	9-0	36	.178
— New York (N.L.)	0	0	...	0.00	0.50	2	0	0	0	0	0-0	2.0	0	0	0	0	1-0	2	.000
Major League totals (1 year)	0	0	...	0.00	0.50	2	0	0	0	0	0-0	2.0	0	0	0	0	1-0	2	.000

2006 LEFTY-RIGHTY SPLITS

vs.	Avg.	AB	H	2B	3B	HR	RBI	BB	SO	OBP	Slg.	vs.	Avg.	AB	H	2B	3B	HR	RBI	BB	SO	OBP	Slg.
L	.000	4	0	0	0	0	0	1	2	.200	.000	R	.000	2	0	0	0	0	0	0	0	.000	.000

H

HUNTER, TORII   OF

PERSONAL: Born July 18, 1975, in Pine Bluff, Ark. ... 6-2/211. ... Bats right, throws right. ... Full name: Torii Kedar Hunter. ... High school: Pine Bluff (Ark.). **TRANSACTIONS/CAREER NOTES:** Selected by Minnesota Twins organization in first round (20th pick overall) of 1993 free-agent draft; pick recieved as part of compensation for Cincinnati Reds signing Type A free-agent P John Smiley. ... On disabled list (April 6-21, 2001; April 7-25, 2004; and July 30, 2005-remainder of season). ... On suspended list (July 20-23, 2002). ... On disabled list (July 16-31, 2006). **HONORS:** Named outfielder on THE SPORTING NEWS A.L. All-Star team (2002). ... Won A.L. Gold Glove as outfielder (2001-06). **STATISTICAL NOTES:** Career major league grand slams: 6.
2006 GAMES PLAYED BY POSITION (MLB): OF—143, DH—4.

Year	Team (League)	Pos.	G	AB	R	H	2B	3B	HR	RBI	BB	SO	HBP	GDP	SB-CS	Avg.	OBP	SLG	OPS	E	Avg.
1993—GC Twins (GCL)		OF	28	100	6	19	3	0	0	8	4	23	9	1	4-2	.190	.283	.220	.503	6	.895
1994—Fort Wayne (Midw.)		OF	91	335	57	98	17	1	10	50	25	80	10	5	8-10	.293	.358	.439	.796	7	.971
1995—Fort Myers (FSL)		OF	113	391	64	96	15	2	7	36	38	77	12	8	7-4	.246	.330	.348	.678	7	.973
1996—Fort Myers (FSL)		OF	4	16	1	3	0	0	0	1	2	5	0	0	1-1	.188	.278	.188	.465	0	1.000
—New Britain (East.)		OF	99	342	49	90	20	3	7	33	28	60	7	7	7-7	.263	.331	.401	.731	4	.982
1997—New Britain (East.)		OF-DH	127	471	57	109	22	2	8	56	47	94	3	6	8-8	.231	.305	.338	.642	7	.974
—Minnesota (A.L.)			1	0	0	0	0	0	0	0	0	0	0	0	0-0	...	...	...	...	...	...
1998—New Britain (East.)		OF	82	308	42	87	24	3	6	33	19	64	4	2	11-9	.282	.329	.438	.768	2	.989
—Minnesota (A.L.)		OF	6	17	0	4	1	0	0	2	2	6	0	1	0-1	.235	.316	.294	.610	0	1.000
—Salt Lake (PCL)		OF-DH	26	92	15	31	7	0	4	20	1	13	1	3	2-2	.337	.347	.543	.891	2	.966
1999—Minnesota (A.L.)		OF	135	384	52	98	17	2	9	35	26	72	6	9	10-6	.255	.309	.380	.689	1	.997
2000—Minnesota (A.L.)		OF	99	336	44	94	14	7	5	44	18	68	2	13	4-3	.280	.318	.408	.726	3	.989
—Salt Lake (PCL)			55	209	58	77	17	2	18	61	11	28	3	4	11-3	.368	.403	.727	1.130	3	.973
2001—Minnesota (A.L.)		OF	148	564	82	147	32	5	27	92	29	125	8	12	9-6	.261	.306	.479	.784	4	.992
2002—Minnesota (A.L.)		OF-DH	148	561	89	162	37	4	29	94	35	118	5	17	23-8	.289	.334	.524	.859	3	.992
2003—Minnesota (A.L.)		OF-DH	154	581	83	145	31	4	26	102	50	106	5	15	6-7	.250	.312	.451	.762	4	.991
2004—Minnesota (A.L.)		OF-DH	138	520	79	141	37	0	23	81	40	101	7	23	24-7	.271	.330	.475	.805	4	.988
2005—Minnesota (A.L.)		OF-DH	98	372	63	100	14	1	14	56	34	65	6	8	23-7	.269	.337	.452	.788	3	.987
2006—Minnesota (A.L.)		OF-DH	147	557	86	155	21	2	31	98	45	108	5	19	12-6	.278	.336	.490	.826	4	.989
Major League totals (10 years)			1074	3892	578	1046	214	25	164	604	279	769	44	117	108-51	.269	.323	.463	.786	26	.991

DIVISION SERIES RECORD

Year	Team (League)	Pos.	G	AB	R	H	2B	3B	HR	RBI	BB	SO	HBP	GDP	SB-CS	Avg.	OBP	SLG	OPS	E	Avg.
2002—Minnesota (A.L.)		OF	5	20	4	6	4	0	0	2	1	4	0	0	0-0	.300	.333	.500	.833	0	1.000
2003—Minnesota (A.L.)		OF	4	14	3	6	0	1	1	2	2	0	0	0	0-0	.429	.500	.786	1.286	0	1.000
2004—Minnesota (A.L.)		OF	4	17	5	6	1	0	1	2	1	1	0	0	2-0	.353	.368	.588	.957	0	1.000
2006—Minnesota (A.L.)		OF	3	11	1	3	1	0	0	2	0	1	0	0	0-0	.273	.273	.636	.909	0	1.000
Division series totals (4 years)			16	62	13	21	6	1	3	8	4	8	0	0	2-0	.339	.373	.613	.986	0	1.000

CHAMPIONSHIP SERIES RECORD

Year	Team (League)	Pos.	G	AB	R	H	2B	3B	HR	RBI	BB	SO	HBP	GDP	SB-CS	Avg.	OBP	SLG	OPS	E	Avg.
2002—Minnesota (A.L.)		OF	5	18	2	3	2	0	0	0	1	3	0	2	0-0	.167	.211	.278	.488	0	1.000

ALL-STAR GAME RECORD

	G	AB	R	H	2B	3B	HR	RBI	BB	SO	HBP	GDP	SB-CS	Avg.	OBP	SLG	OPS	E	Avg.
All-Star Game totals (1 year)	1	2	0	0	0	0	0	0	0	0	0	0	0-0	.000	.000	.000	.000	0	1.000

2006 LEFTY-RIGHTY SPLITS

vs.	Avg.	AB	H	2B	3B	HR	RBI	BB	SO	OBP	Slg.	vs.	Avg.	AB	H	2B	3B	HR	RBI	BB	SO	OBP	Slg.
L	.319	160	51	9	1	8	29	18	31	.381	.538	R	.262	397	104	12	1	23	69	27	77	.316	.471

HYZDU, ADAM   OF

PERSONAL: Born December 6, 1971, in San Jose, Calif. ... 6-2/220. ... Bats right, throws right. ... Full name: Adam David Hyzdu. ... Name pronounced: HIGHS-doo. ... High school: Moeller (Cincinnati). **TRANSACTIONS/CAREER NOTES:** Selected by San Francisco Giants organization in first round (15th pick overall) of 1990 free-agent draft; pick received as compensation for Houston Astros signing Type B free-agent IF Ken Oberkfell. ... Selected by Cincinnati Reds from Giants organization in Rule 5 major league draft (December 13, 1993). ... Released by Reds (March 23, 1996). ... Signed by Boston Red Sox organization (April 26, 1996). ... Signed as a free agent by Arizona Diamondbacks organization (January 2, 1998). ... Loaned by Diamondbacks organization to Monterrey of the Mexican League (April 7-May 17, 1998). ... On disabled list (June 30-August 23, 1998). ... Signed as a free agent by Red Sox organization (January 5, 1999). ... Released by Red Sox (May 5, 1999). ... Signed by Pittsburgh Pirates organization (May 10, 1999). ... Signed as a free agent by Red Sox organization (November 10, 2003). ... Traded by Red Sox to San Diego Padres for P Blaine Neal (March 22, 2005). ... Traded by Padres to Red Sox for P Scott Cassidy (July 19, 2005). ... Released by Red Sox (October 15, 2005). ... Signed by Texas Rangers organization (November 3, 2005). **STATISTICAL NOTES:** Career major league grand slams: 3.
2006 GAMES PLAYED BY POSITION (MLB): DH—1, OF—1.

Year	Team (League)	Pos.	G	AB	R	H	2B	3B	HR	RBI	BB	SO	HBP	GDP	SB-CS	Avg.	OBP	SLG	OPS	E	Avg.
1990—Everett (N'west)		OF	69	253	31	62	16	1	6	34	28	78	2	4	2-4	.245	.319	.387	.707	5	.963
1991—Clinton (Midw.)		OF	124	410	47	96	13	5	5	50	64	131	3	10	4-5	.234	.340	.327	.667	9	.955
1992—San Jose (Calif.)		OF	128	457	60	127	25	5	9	60	55	134	1	6	10-5	.278	.351	.414	.765	5	.976
1993—San Jose (Calif.)		OF	44	165	35	48	11	3	13	38	29	53	0	1	1-1	.291	.393	.630	1.023	3	.963
—Shreveport (Texas)		OF	86	302	30	61	17	0	6	25	20	82	1	5	0-5	.202	.253	.318	.571	4	.973
1994—Chattanooga (Sou.)		OF-1B-DH	38	133	17	35	10	0	3	9	8	21	1	1	0-2	.263	.310	.406	.716	4	.949
—Win.-Salem (Car.)		OF-DH	55	210	30	58	11	1	15	39	18	33	2	3	1-5	.276	.336	.552	.889	4	.945
—Indianapolis (A.A.)		OF	12	25	3	3	2	0	0	3	1	5	0	0	0-0	.120	.143	.200	.343	1	.917
1995—Chattanooga (Sou.)		OF	102	312	55	82	14	1	13	48	45	56	4	4	3-2	.263	.362	.439	.801	1	.995
1996—Trenton (East.)		OF-DH-C	109	374	71	126	24	3	25	80	56	75	2	7	1-8	.337	.424	.618	1.042	3	.980
1997—Pawtucket (Int'l)		OF-DH	119	413	77	114	21	1	23	84	72	113	4	6	10-6	.276	.387	.499	.886	4	.978
1998—Monterrey (Mex.)		OF	29	110	20	36	3	0	5	22	14	17	...	...	7-1	.327	...	.491	...	0	1.000
—Tucson (PCL)		OF-DH-P	34	100	21	34	7	1	4	14	15	23	0	0	0-1	.340	.419	.550	.969	1	.974
—Pawtucket (Int'l)		OF	12	35	4	8	1	0	1	6	4	13	0	1	0-0	.229	.308	.314	.622	0	1.000
1999—Altoona (East.)		OF-1B-3B																			
		DH	91	345	64	109	26	2	24	78	40	62	3	2	8-4	.316	.392	.612	1.003	11	.965
—Nashville (PCL)		OF	14	44	6	11	1	0	3	5	3	11	0	2	0-0	.250	.313	.614	.926	0	1.000
2000—Altoona (East.)		OF-1B	142	514	96	149	39	2	31	106	94	102	8	6	3-7	.290	.405	.554	.960	1	.996
—Pittsburgh (N.L.)		OF	12	18	2	7	2	0	1	4	4	0	0	0	0-0	.389	.389	.667	1.056	0	1.000
2001—Nashville (PCL)		OF-1B-3B	69	261	38	76	17	2	11	39	17	68	0	3	1-3	.291	.332	.498	.830	1	.994
—Pittsburgh (N.L.)		OF-1B	51	72	7	15	1	0	5	9	4	18	1	1	0-1	.208	.260	.431	.690	1	1.000
2002—Nashville (PCL)		OF-1B	65	243	39	59	11	0	16	50	29	59	0	1	1-2	.243	.318	.436	.754	3	.980
—Pittsburgh (N.L.)		OF-1B	59	155	24	36	6	0	11	34	21	44	1	1	0-0	.232	.324	.484	.808	0	1.000

Year Team (League)	Pos.	G	AB	R	H	2B	3B	HR	RBI	BB	SO	HBP	GDP	SB-CS	Avg.	OBP	SLG	OPS	E	Avg.
2003—Pittsburgh (N.L.)	OF	51	63	16	13	5	0	1	8	10	21	1	2	0-0	.206	.320	.333	.653	0	1.000
—Nashville (PCL)	OF-1B	40	135	22	38	10	1	6	18	18	28	1	2	2-2	.281	.365	.504	.869	2	.981
2004—Pawtucket (Int'l)	OF-DH	129	465	92	140	33	2	29	79	84	106	7	12	8-4	.301	.413	.568	.980	6	.976
—Boston (A.L.)	OF-DH	17	10	3	3	2	0	1	2	1	2	0	0	0-0	.300	.364	.800	1.164	0	1.000
2005—San Diego (N.L.)	OF	17	20	1	3	1	0	0	4	3	4	0	1	1-0	.150	.250	.200	.450	0	1.000
—Portland (PCL)	OF	62	207	38	57	9	1	11	32	47	61	1	5	2-5	.275	.410	.488	.898	2	.993
—Pawtucket (Int'l)	OF-DH	31	118	17	30	7	0	4	25	16	32	0	2	0-1	.254	.343	.415	.759	0	1.000
—Boston (A.L.)	OF	12	16	1	4	1	0	0	0	2	3	0	0	0-0	.250	.333	.313	.646	1	.909
2006—Oklahoma (PCL)		128	439	64	119	25	4	19	80	74	102	1	8	7-4	.271	.370	.476	.846	1	.996
—Texas (A.L.)	OF-DH	2	4	0	1	0	0	0	0	0	2	0	0	0-0	.250	.250	.250	.500	0	1.000
American League totals (3 years)		31	30	4	8	3	0	1	2	3	7	0	0	0-0	.267	.333	.467	.800	1	.950
National League totals (5 years)		190	328	50	74	15	0	18	59	38	91	3	5	1-1	.226	.308	.436	.744	0	1.000
Major League totals (7 years)		221	358	54	82	18	0	19	61	41	98	3	5	1-1	.229	.310	.439	.749	1	.995

DIVISION SERIES RECORD

Year Team (League)	Pos.	G	AB	R	H	2B	3B	HR	RBI	BB	SO	HBP	GDP	SB-CS	Avg.	OBP	SLG	OPS	E	Avg.
2005—Boston (A.L.)	OF	1	0	0	0	0	0	0	0	0	0	0	0	0-0	...	...	...	...	0	1.000

2006 LEFTY-RIGHTY SPLITS

vs.	Avg.	AB	H	2B	3B	HR	RBI	BB	SO	OBP	Slg.	vs.	Avg.	AB	H	2B	3B	HR	RBI	BB	SO	OBP	Slg.
L	.000	2	0	0	0	0	0	0	1	.000	.000	R	.500	2	1	0	0	0	0	0	1	.500	.500

IANNETTA, CHRIS — C

PERSONAL: Born April 8, 1983, in Providence, R.I. ... Bats right, throws right. ... Full name: Christopher Domenic Iannetta. ... Name pronounced: eye-a-NET-ah. ... High school: St. Raphael Academy (Pawtucket, R.I.). ... College: North Carolina. **TRANSACTIONS/CAREER NOTES:** Selected by Colorado Rockies organization in fourth round of 2004 free-agent draft.

2006 GAMES PLAYED BY POSITION (MLB): C—21.

Year Team (League)	Pos.	G	AB	R	H	2B	3B	HR	RBI	BB	SO	HBP	GDP	SB-CS	Avg.	OBP	SLG	OPS	E	Avg.
2004—Asheville (S. Atl.)		36	121	23	38	5	1	5	17	27	29	4	3	0-1	.314	.454	.496	.950	...	...
2005—Modesto (California)	C-DH	74	261	51	72	17	3	11	58	45	61	2	9	1-2	.276	.381	.490	.872	6	.989
—Tulsa (Texas)	C-DH	19	60	7	14	3	1	2	11	8	15	1	5	0-0	.233	.329	.417	.745	2	.980
2006—Tulsa (Texas)		44	156	38	50	10	2	11	26	24	26	3	3	1-0	.321	.418	.622	1.040	3	.990
—Colo. Springs (PCL)		47	151	23	53	12	1	3	22	24	29	3	9	0-0	.351	.447	.503	.950	2	.992
—Colorado (N.L.)	C	21	77	12	20	4	0	2	10	13	17	1	1	0-1*	.260	.370	.390	.759	0	1.000
Major League totals (1 year)		21	77	12	20	4	0	2	10	13	17	1	1	0-1	.260	.370	.390	.759	0	1.000

2006 LEFTY-RIGHTY SPLITS

vs.	Avg.	AB	H	2B	3B	HR	RBI	BB	SO	OBP	Slg.	vs.	Avg.	AB	H	2B	3B	HR	RBI	BB	SO	OBP	Slg.
L	.231	13	3	1	0	1	3	6	2	.474	.538	R	.266	64	17	3	0	1	7	7	15	.342	.359

IBANEZ, RAUL — OF

PERSONAL: Born June 2, 1972, in New York. ... 6-2/200. ... Bats left, throws right. ... Full name: Raul Javier Ibanez. ... Name pronounced: ee-BON-yez. ... High school: Sunset (Miami). ... Junior college: Miami-Dade Community College South. **TRANSACTIONS/CAREER NOTES:** Selected by Seattle Mariners organization in 36th round of 1992 free-agent draft. ... On disabled list (March 30-June 29, 1998); included rehabilitation assignment to Tacoma. ... On disabled list (May 18-June 3, 1999); included rehabilitation assignment to Tacoma. ... On disabled list (August 7-22, 2000); included rehabilitation assignment to Tacoma. ... Signed as a free agent by Kansas City Royals organization (January 22, 2001). ... Signed as a free agent by Mariners (November 19, 2003). ... On disabled list (June 3-July 10, 2004); included rehabilitation assignment to Tacoma. **STATISTICAL NOTES:** Career major league grand slams: 3.

2006 GAMES PLAYED BY POSITION (MLB): OF—157, DH—1.

Year Team (League)	Pos.	G	AB	R	H	2B	3B	HR	RBI	BB	SO	HBP	GDP	SB-CS	Avg.	OBP	SLG	OPS	E	Avg.
1992—Ariz. Mariners (Ariz.)	1B-C-OF	33	120	25	37	8	2	1	16	9	18	2	3	1-2	.308	.366	.433	.800	4	.931
1993—Appleton (Midwest)	1B-C-OF	52	157	26	43	9	0	5	21	24	31	1	2	0-2	.274	.370	.427	.796	2	.980
—Bellingham (N'west)	C	43	134	16	38	5	2	0	15	21	23	0	0	0-3	.284	.378	.351	.729	1	.993
1994—Appleton (Midwest)	1B-C-OF	91	327	55	102	30	3	7	59	32	37	2	3	10-5	.312	.375	.486	.861	10	.971
1995—Riverside (Calif.)	1B-C	95	361	59	120	23	9	20	108	41	49	2	7	4-3	.332	.395	.612	1.007	12	.977
1996—Tacoma (PCL)	OF-1B-DH	111	405	59	115	20	3	11	47	44	56	2	4	7-7	.284	.353	.430	.783	11	.951
—Port City (Sou.)	OF-DH-1B																			
	C	19	76	12	28	8	1	1	13	8	7	0	1	3-2	.368	.424	.539	.963	4	.905
—Seattle (A.L.)	DH	4	5	0	0	0	0	0	0	0	1	1	0	0-0	.000	.167	.000	.167	0	...
1997—Tacoma (PCL)	OF	111	438	84	133	30	5	15	84	32	75	1	12	7-5	.304	.349	.498	.847	5	.976
—Seattle (A.L.)	OF-DH	11	26	3	4	1	1	1	4	0	6	0	0	0-0	.154	.154	.346	.500	1	1.000
1998—Tacoma (PCL)	OF-1B-DH	52	190	24	41	8	1	6	25	24	47	0	3	1-1	.216	.301	.363	.664	1	.988
—Seattle (A.L.)	OF-1B-DH	37	98	12	25	7	1	2	12	5	27	0	4	0-0	.255	.291	.408	.699	1	.991
1999—Seattle (A.L.)	OF-1B-C																			
	DH	87	209	23	54	7	0	9	27	17	32	0	4	5-1	.258	.313	.421	.734	3	.988
—Tacoma (PCL)	OF-1B-DH	8	31	6	11	1	0	3	5	1	7	0	0	1-0	.355	.375	.677	1.052	0	1.000
2000—Seattle (A.L.)	OF-DH-1B	92	140	21	32	8	0	2	15	14	25	1	2	2-0	.229	.301	.329	.630	2	.980
—Tacoma (PCL)	OF	10	40	3	10	4	0	0	6	1	7	0	0	0-0	.250	.268	.350	.618	0	1.000
2001—Kansas City (A.L.)	OF-DH-1B																			
	3B	104	279	44	78	11	5	13	54	32	51	0	6	0-2	.280	.353	.495	.847	5	.962
—Omaha (PCL)	OF-SS	8	27	3	4	1	0	2	5	1	10	0	0	0-0	.148	.179	.407	.586	1	.857
2002—Kansas City (A.L.)	OF-1B-DH	137	497	70	146	37	6	24	103	40	76	2	11	5-3	.294	.345	.537	.883	3	.994
2003—Kansas City (A.L.)	OF-1B-DH	157	608	95	179	33	5	18	90	49	81	3	10	8-4	.294	.345	.454	.799	4	.991
2004—Tacoma (PCL)	DH-OF	4	17	2	4	1	0	0	1	0	4	0	0	0-0	.235	.235	.294	.529	0	1.000
—Seattle (A.L.)		123	481	67	146	31	1	16	62	36	72	3	10	1-2	.304	.353	.472	.825	5	.984
2005—Seattle (A.L.)	DH-OF-1B	• 162	614	92	172	32	2	20	89	71	99	2	12	9-4	.280	.355	.436	.792	2	.986
2006—Seattle (A.L.)	OF-DH	159	626	103	181	33	5	33	123	65	115	1	13	2-4	.289	.353	.516	.869	2	.994
Major League totals (11 years)		1073	3583	530	1017	199	26	138	579	329	580	13	71	32-20	.284	.344	.469	.813	27	.988

DIVISION SERIES RECORD

Year Team (League)	Pos.	G	AB	R	H	2B	3B	HR	RBI	BB	SO	HBP	GDP	SB-CS	Avg.	OBP	SLG	OPS	E	Avg.
2000—Seattle (A.L.)	OF	3	8	2	3	0	0	0	0	0	0	0	0	0-0	.375	.375	.375	.750	0	1.000

CHAMPIONSHIP SERIES RECORD

Year Team (League)	Pos.	G	AB	R	H	2B	3B	HR	RBI	BB	SO	HBP	GDP	SB-CS	Avg.	OBP	SLG	OPS	E	Avg.
2000— Seattle (A.L.)	OF	6	9	0	0	0	0	0	0	2	0	0		0-0	.000	.000	.000	.000	0	1.000

2006 LEFTY-RIGHTY SPLITS

vs.	Avg.	AB	H	2B	3B	HR	RBI	BB	SO	OBP	Slg.		vs.	Avg.	AB	H	2B	3B	HR	RBI	BB	SO	OBP	Slg.
L	.243	185	45	10	0	4	36	16	43	.301	.362		R	.308	441	136	23	5	29	87	49	72	.375	.580

IGUCHI, TADAHITO — 2B

PERSONAL: Born December 4, 1974, in Tokyo, Japan. ... 5-10/185. ... Bats right, throws right. ... Full name: Tadahito Iguchi. ... Name pronounced: ta-da-HEAT-o ig-GOO-chee. ... College: Aoyama Gakuin. **TRANSACTIONS/CAREER NOTES:** Signed as a free agent by Chicago White Sox (January 27, 2005). **STATISTICAL NOTES:** Career major league grand slams: 2.
2006 GAMES PLAYED BY POSITION (MLB): 2B—136, DH—1.

									BATTING										FIELDING	
Year Team (League)	Pos.	G	AB	R	H	2B	3B	HR	RBI	BB	SO	HBP	GDP	SB-CS	Avg.	OBP	SLG	OPS	E	Avg.
1997— Fukuoka (Jp. Pac.)	SS	76	217	31	44	6	3	8	23	24	67	8	...	3-3	.203	.304	.369	.673	3	.989
1998— Fukuoka (Jp. Pac.)	SS	135	421	58	93	18	4	21	66	28	121	8	...	12-6	.221	.280	.432	.712	10	.983
1999— Fukuoka (Jp. Pac.)	SS	116	370	38	83	15	1	14	47	38	113	9	...	14-7	.224	.310	.384	.693	15	.968
2000— Fukuoka (Jp. Pac.)	SS	54	162	21	40	9	2	7	23	15	29	2	...	5-2	.247	.317	.457	.773	8	.959
2001— Fukuoka (Jp. Pac.)	2B	140	552	104	144	26	3	30	97	61	117	12	...	44-9	.261	.346	.475	.821	5	.994
2002— Fukuoka (Jp. Pac.)	2B	114	428	64	111	14	1	18	53	27	84	10	...	21-7	.259	.317	.423	.740	6	.990
2003— Fukuoka (Jp. Pac.)	2B	135	515	112	175	37	1	27	109	81	81	14	...	42-6	.340	.438	.573	1.011	10	.986
2004— Fukuoka (Jp. Pac.)	2B	124	510	96	170	34	2	24	89	47	90	9	...	18-5	.333	.394	.549	.943	6	.991
2005— Chicago (A.L.)	2B	135	511	74	142	25	6	15	71	47	114	6	16	15-5	.278	.342	.438	.780	14	.978
2006— Chicago (A.L.)	2B-DH	138	555	97	156	24	0	18	67	59	110	3	7	11-5	.281	.352	.422	.774	8	.988
Major League totals (2 years)		273	1066	171	298	49	6	33	138	106	224	9	23	26-10	.280	.347	.430	.777	22	.983

DIVISION SERIES RECORD

Year Team (League)	Pos.	G	AB	R	H	2B	3B	HR	RBI	BB	SO	HBP	GDP	SB-CS	Avg.	OBP	SLG	OPS	E	Avg.
2005— Chicago (A.L.)	2B	3	12	1	3	0	0	1	4	0	3	0	0	0-0	.250	.250	.500	.750	0	1.000

CHAMPIONSHIP SERIES RECORD

Year Team (League)	Pos.	G	AB	R	H	2B	3B	HR	RBI	BB	SO	HBP	GDP	SB-CS	Avg.	OBP	SLG	OPS	E	Avg.
2005— Chicago (A.L.)	2B	5	17	4	3	1	0	0	1	1	6	3	0	0-1	.176	.333	.235	.569	0	1.000

WORLD SERIES RECORD

Year Team (League)	Pos.	G	AB	R	H	2B	3B	HR	RBI	BB	SO	HBP	GDP	SB-CS	Avg.	OBP	SLG	OPS	E	Avg.
2005— Chicago (A.L.)	2B	4	18	2	3	0	0	0	1	1	3	0	1	0-0	.167	.211	.167	.377	0	1.000

2006 LEFTY-RIGHTY SPLITS

vs.	Avg.	AB	H	2B	3B	HR	RBI	BB	SO	OBP	Slg.		vs.	Avg.	AB	H	2B	3B	HR	RBI	BB	SO	OBP	Slg.
L	.252	206	52	11	0	6	19	26	42	.335	.393		R	.298	349	104	13	0	12	48	33	68	.363	.438

INFANTE, OMAR — IF

PERSONAL: Born December 26, 1981, in Puerto la Cruz, Venezuela. ... 6-0/176. ... Bats right, throws right. ... Full name: Omar Rafael Infante. ... Name pronounced: in-fahn-TAY. **TRANSACTIONS/CAREER NOTES:** Signed as a non-drafted free agent by Detroit Tigers organization (April 28, 1999).
2006 GAMES PLAYED BY POSITION (MLB): 2B—37, DH—17, SS—10, 3B—7, OF—4.

									BATTING										FIELDING	
Year Team (League)	Pos.	G	AB	R	H	2B	3B	HR	RBI	BB	SO	HBP	GDP	SB-CS	Avg.	OBP	SLG	OPS	E	Avg.
1999— GC Tigers (GCL)	SS	25	97	11	26	4	0	0	7	4	11	0	1	4-0	.268	.294	.309	.603	8	.932
2000— W. Mich. (Mid.)	SS	12	48	7	11	0	0	0	5	5	7	2	2	1-0	.229	.327	.229	.556	1	.983
— Lakeland (Fla. St.)	SS	79	259	35	71	11	0	2	24	20	29	1	4	11-5	.274	.324	.340	.664	19	.951
2001— Erie (East.)	SS	132	540	86	163	21	4	2	62	46	87	2	9	27-12	.302	.355	.367	.721	27	.955
2002— Toledo (Int'l)	SS	120	436	49	117	16	8	4	51	28	49	0	5	19-15	.268	.309	.369	.678	26	.959
— Detroit (A.L.)	SS-2B	18	72	4	24	3	0	1	6	3	10	0	0	0-1	.333	.360	.417	.777	5	.945
2003— Toledo (Int'l)	SS	64	224	28	50	10	0	2	18	22	32	3	3	22-4	.223	.299	.295	.593	18	.942
— Detroit (A.L.)	SS-3B-2B	69	221	24	49	6	1	0	8	18	37	0	1	6-3	.222	.278	.258	.536	14	.961
2004— Detroit (A.L.)	2B-SS-3B OF	142	503	69	133	27	9	16	55	40	112	1	4	13-7	.264	.317	.449	.766	16	.974
2005— Detroit (A.L.)	2B-SS	121	406	36	90	28	2	6	43	16	73	2	6	8-0	.222	.254	.367	.621	10	.983
2006— Detroit (A.L.)	2B-DH-SS 3B-OF	78	224	35	62	11	4	4	25	14	45	3		3-2	.277	.325	.415	.740	5	.977
Major League totals (5 years)		428	1426	168	358	75	16	30	137	91	277	6	15	30-13	.251	.297	.389	.686	50	.973

CHAMPIONSHIP SERIES RECORD

Year Team (League)	Pos.	G	AB	R	H	2B	3B	HR	RBI	BB	SO	HBP	GDP	SB-CS	Avg.	OBP	SLG	OPS	E	Avg.
2006— Detroit (A.L.)	DH	1	2	0	1	0	0	0	0	1	1	0	0	1-0	.500	.667	.500	1.167	0	...

WORLD SERIES RECORD

Year Team (League)	Pos.	G	AB	R	H	2B	3B	HR	RBI	BB	SO	HBP	GDP	SB-CS	Avg.	OBP	SLG	OPS	E	Avg.
2006— Detroit (A.L.)		1	1	0	0	0	0	0	0	0	0	0	0	0-0	.000	.000	.000	.000	0	...

2006 LEFTY-RIGHTY SPLITS

vs.	Avg.	AB	H	2B	3B	HR	RBI	BB	SO	OBP	Slg.		vs.	Avg.	AB	H	2B	3B	HR	RBI	BB	SO	OBP	Slg.
L	.286	70	20	3	0	2	5	3	14	.333	.414		R	.273	154	42	8	4	2	20	11	31	.321	.416

INGE, BRANDON — 3B/C

PERSONAL: Born May 19, 1977, in Lynchburg, Va. ... 5-11/195. ... Bats right, throws right. ... Full name: Charles Brandon Inge. ... Name pronounced: inj. ... High school: Brookville (Lynchburg, Va.). ... College: Virginia Commonwealth. **TRANSACTIONS/CAREER NOTES:** Selected by Detroit Tigers organization in second round of 1998 free-agent draft. ... On disabled list (June 25-August 6, 2001); included rehabilitation assignments to GCL Tigers, West Michigan and Toledo. ... On disabled list (May 12-May 27, 2002); included rehabilitation assignment to Toledo. ... On disabled list (June 26-July 15, 2004). **STATISTICAL NOTES:** Career major league grand slams: 3.
2006 GAMES PLAYED BY POSITION (MLB): 3B—159.

									BATTING										FIELDING	
Year Team (League)	Pos.	G	AB	R	H	2B	3B	HR	RBI	BB	SO	HBP	GDP	SB-CS	Avg.	OBP	SLG	OPS	E	Avg.
1998— Jamestown (NYP)	C	51	191	24	44	10	1	8	29	17	53	6	4	8-8	.230	.312	.419	.730	8	.981
1999— W. Mich. (Mid.)	C	100	352	54	86	25	2	9	46	39	87	3	7	15-3	.244	.320	.403	.723	8	.990
2000— Jacksonville (Sou.)	C-OF	78	298	39	77	25	1	6	53	26	73	0	10	10-3	.258	.313	.409	.722	5	.990
— Toledo (Int'l)	C	55	190	24	42	9	3	5	20	15	51	1		2-1	.221	.280	.379	.659	3	.991

Year Team (League)	Pos.	G	AB	R	H	2B	3B	HR	RBI	BB	SO	HBP	GDP	SB-CS	Avg.	OBP	SLG	OPS	E	Avg.
												BATTING							**FIELDING**	
2001—Detroit (A.L.)	C	79	189	13	34	11	0	0	15	9	41	0	2	1-4	.180	.215	.238	.453	4	.989
—GC Tigers (GCL)	C	3	10	1	1	0	0	1	2	2	2	0	0	0-0	.100	.250	.400	.650	0	1.000
—W. Mich. (Mid.)	C	4	16	3	3	1	0	0	2	2	5	1	0	0-0	.188	.316	.250	.566	0	1.000
—Toledo (Int'l)	C	27	90	11	26	11	1	2	15	7	24	1	2	1-0	.289	.337	.500	.837	2	.989
2002—Toledo (Int'l)	C	21	65	10	17	2	4	3	13	11	16	2	2	1-3	.262	.380	.554	.934	4	.978
—Detroit (A.L.)	C-DH	95	321	27	65	15	3	7	24	24	101	4	7	1-3	.202	.266	.333	.599	1	.998
2003—Toledo (Int'l)	C-DH	39	142	15	39	9	0	5	15	11	23	0	6	3-1	.275	.327	.444	.770	0	1.000
—Detroit (A.L.)	C	104	330	32	67	15	3	8	30	24	79	5	8	4-4	.203	.265	.339	.605	2	.996
2004—Detroit (A.L.)	3B-C-OF	131	408	43	117	15	7	13	64	32	72	4	4	5-4	.287	.340	.453	.794	16	.966
2005—Detroit (A.L.)	3B-OF	160	616	75	161	31	9	16	72	63	140	3	14	7-6	.261	.330	.419	.749	23	.957
2006—Detroit (A.L.)	3B	159	542	83	137	29	2	27	83	43	128	7	12	7-4	.253	.313	.463	.776	22	.960
Major League totals (6 years)		728	2406	273	581	116	24	71	288	195	561	23	47	25-25	.241	.302	.398	.700	68	.978

DIVISION SERIES RECORD

Year Team (League)	Pos.	G	AB	R	H	2B	3B	HR	RBI	BB	SO	HBP	GDP	SB-CS	Avg.	OBP	SLG	OPS	E	Avg.
2006—Detroit (A.L.)	3B	4	15	1	2	0	0	0	0	0	6	0	0	0-0	.133	.133	.133	.267	0	1.000

CHAMPIONSHIP SERIES RECORD

Year Team (League)	Pos.	G	AB	R	H	2B	3B	HR	RBI	BB	SO	HBP	GDP	SB-CS	Avg.	OBP	SLG	OPS	E	Avg.
2006—Detroit (A.L.)	3B	4	12	3	4	1	0	1	3	3	3	0	0	0-0	.333	.438	.667	1.104	0	1.000

WORLD SERIES RECORD

Year Team (League)	Pos.	G	AB	R	H	2B	3B	HR	RBI	BB	SO	HBP	GDP	SB-CS	Avg.	OBP	SLG	OPS	E	Avg.
2006—Detroit (A.L.)	3B	5	17	0	6	2	0	0	1	0	6	0	1	0-0	.353	.389	.471	.859	3	.824

2006 LEFTY-RIGHTY SPLITS

vs.	Avg.	AB	H	2B	3B	HR	RBI	BB	SO	OBP	Slg.	vs.	Avg.	AB	H	2B	3B	HR	RBI	BB	SO	OBP	Slg.
L	.243	140	34	7	1	6	25	11	38	.301	.436	R	.256	402	103	22	1	21	58	32	90	.318	.473

INGLETT, JOE — 2B/OF

PERSONAL: Born June 29, 1978, in Sacramento, Calif. ... Bats left, throws right. ... Full name: Joseph S. Inglett. ... College: Nevada. **TRANSACTIONS/CAREER NOTES:** Selected by Cleveland Indians organization in eighth round of 2000 free-agent draft.
2006 GAMES PLAYED BY POSITION (MLB): 2B—53, OF—9, SS—1, DH—1.

Year Team (League)	Pos.	G	AB	R	H	2B	3B	HR	RBI	BB	SO	HBP	GDP	SB-CS	Avg.	OBP	SLG	OPS	E	Avg.
2000—Mahoning Valley (N.Y.-Penn.)		56	202	37	58	12	4	2	37	31	30	5	1	4-5	.287	.395	.416	.811	8	...
2001—Columbus (S. Atl.)		62	237	34	71	9	2	2	33	24	22	0	7	5-3	.300	.361	.380	.741	11	...
2002—Columbus (S. Atl.)		60	235	44	73	18	5	2	46	28	25	4	5	5-3	.311	.389	.455	.844	13	...
—Kinston (Carol.)		66	238	24	67	12	0	0	29	29	38	2	3	5-2	.282	.362	.332	.694	8	...
2003—Kinston (Carol.)		28	85	21	28	10	1	0	15	20	14	1	2	1-0	.329	.454	.477	.925	2	...
—Akron (East.)		71	276	41	78	16	1	4	25	37	36	6	8	1-2	.283	.377	.391	.768	10	...
2004—Akron (East.)		66	266	49	85	19	7	1	20	31	28	1	1	3-5	.320	.393	.455	.848	11	...
2005—Buffalo (Int'l)	2B-OF-SS	95	327	57	108	20	9	2	40	17	41	9	7	13-6	.330	.376	.465	.841	10	.977
2006—Akron (East.)		18	64	20	33	9	0	3	9	11	4	0	0	7-3	.516	.587	.797	1.384	2	.973
—Buffalo (Int'l)		40	157	21	47	7	2	1	13	13	24	2	6	3-2	.299	.358	.389	.747	4	.973
—Cleveland (A.L.)	2B-OF-SS DH	64	201	26	57	8	3	2	21	14	39	1	1	5-1	.284	.332	.383	.715	4	.986
Major League totals (1 year)		64	201	26	57	8	3	2	21	14	39	1	1	5-1	.284	.332	.383	.715	4	.986

2006 LEFTY-RIGHTY SPLITS

vs.	Avg.	AB	H	2B	3B	HR	RBI	BB	SO	OBP	Slg.	vs.	Avg.	AB	H	2B	3B	HR	RBI	BB	SO	OBP	Slg.
L	.217	23	5	1	0	0	0	2	5	.280	.261	R	.292	178	52	7	3	2	21	12	34	.339	.399

ISHIKAWA, TRAVIS — IF

PERSONAL: Born September 24, 1983, in Seattle. ... 6-3/200. ... Bats left, throws left. ... Full name: Travis Takashi Ishikawa. ... High school: Federal Way (Wash.) **TRANSACTIONS/CAREER NOTES:** Selected by San Francisco Giants organization in 21st round of 2002 free-agent draft.
2006 GAMES PLAYED BY POSITION (MLB): 1B—10.

Year Team (League)	Pos.	G	AB	R	H	2B	3B	HR	RBI	BB	SO	HBP	GDP	SB-CS	Avg.	OBP	SLG	OPS	E	Avg.
2002—Ariz. Giants (Ariz.)		19	68	10	19	4	2	1	10	7	20	2	...	7-0	.279	.364	.441	.805	1	...
—Salem-Keizer (N'west.)		23	88	14	27	2	1	1	17	5	22	1	...	1-1	.307	.347	.386	.733	4	...
2003—Hagerstown (SAL.)		57	194	20	40	5	0	3	22	33	69	3	...	3-4	.206	.329	.278	.607	5	...
—Salem-Keizer (N'west.)		66	248	53	63	17	4	3	31	44	77	5	...	0-0	.254	.376	.391	.767	11	...
2004—Hagerstown (SAL.)		97	355	59	91	19	2	15	54	45	110	11	...	10-5	.256	.357	.448	.805	5	...
—San Jose (Calif.)		16	56	10	13	7	0	1	10	10	16	1	...	0-0	.232	.353	.411	.764	0	...
2005—San Jose (Calif.)	1B	127	432	87	122	28	7	22	79	70	129	7	1	1-4	.282	.387	.532	.920	8	.993
2006—Connecticut (East.)		86	298	33	69	13	4	10	42	35	88	3	4	0-0	.232	.316	.403	.718	5	.993
—San Francisco (N.L.)	1B	12	24	1	7	3	1	0	4	1	6	0	1	0-0	.292	.320	.500	.820	0	1.000
Major League totals (1 year)		12	24	1	7	3	1	0	4	1	6	0	1	0-0	.292	.320	.500	.820	0	1.000

2006 LEFTY-RIGHTY SPLITS

vs.	Avg.	AB	H	2B	3B	HR	RBI	BB	SO	OBP	Slg.	vs.	Avg.	AB	H	2B	3B	HR	RBI	BB	SO	OBP	Slg.
L	.400	5	2	1	0	0	2	1	0	.500	.600	R	.263	19	5	2	1	0	2	0	6	.263	.474

ISRINGHAUSEN, JASON — P

PERSONAL: Born September 7, 1972, in Brighton, Ill. ... 6-3/230. ... Throws right, bats right. ... Full name: Jason Derek Isringhausen. ... Name pronounced: IS-ring-how-zin. ... High school: Southwestern (Brighton, Ill.). ... Junior college: Lewis & Clark (Ill.) Community College.. **TRANSACTIONS/CAREER NOTES:** Selected by New York Mets organization in 44th round of 1991 free-agent draft. ... On disabled list (August 13-September 1, 1996). ... On disabled list (March 24-August 27, 1997); included rehabilitation assignments to Norfolk, GCL Mets and St. Lucie. ... On disabled list (March 21, 1998-entire season). ... Traded by Mets with P Greg McMichael to Oakland Athletics for P Billy Taylor (July 31, 1999). ... Signed as a free agent by St. Louis Cardinals (December 11, 2001). ... On disabled list (March 21-June 10, 2003); included rehabilitation assignment to Tennessee. ... On disabled list (April 27-May 13, 2005).
CAREER HITTING: 21-for-102 (.206), 11 R, 4 2B, 1 3B, 2 HR, 16 RBI.

Year Team (League)	W	L	Pct.	ERA	WHIP	G	GS	CG	ShO	Hld.	Sv.-Opp.	IP	H	R	ER	HR	BB-IBB	SO	Avg.
1992—GC Mets (GCL)	2	4	.333	4.34	1.48	6	6	0	0	...	0-...	29.0	26	19	14	0	17-1	25	.230
—Kingsport (Appalachian)	4	1	.800	3.25	1.22	7	6	1	0	...	0-...	36.0	32	22	13	2	12-1	24	.222

Year	Team (League)	W	L	Pct.	ERA	WHIP	G	GS	CG	ShO	Hld.	Sv.-Opp.	IP	H	R	ER	HR	BB-IBB	SO	Avg.
1993— Pittsfield (NYP)		7	4	.636	3.29	1.06	15	15	2	0	...	0-...	90.1	68	45	33	7	28-0	104	.204
1994— St. Lucie (Fla. St.)		6	4	.600	2.23	1.02	14	14	6	3	...	0-...	101.0	76	31	25	2	27-2	59	.211
— Binghamton (East.)		5	4	.556	3.02	1.09	14	14	2	0	...	0-...	92.1	87	35	31	6	23-0	69	.234
1995— Binghamton (East.)		2	1	.667	2.85	0.93	6	6	1	0	...	0-...	41.0	26	15	13	1	12-0	59	.174
— Norfolk (Int'l)		9	1	.900	1.55	1.01	12	12	3	3	...	0-...	87.0	64	17	15	2	24-0	75	.203
— New York (N.L.)		9	2	.818	2.81	1.28	14	14	1	0	0	0-0	93.0	88	29	29	6	31-2	55	.254
1996— New York (N.L.)		6	14	.300	4.77	1.53	27	27	2	1	0	0-0	171.2	190	103	91	13	73-5	114	.284
1997— Norfolk (Int'l)		0	2	.000	4.05	1.40	3	3	0	0	...	0-...	20.0	20	10	9	4	8-0	17	.267
— GC Mets (GCL)		1	0	1.000	1.93	0.64	1	0	0	0	...	0-...	4.2	2	1	1	0	1-0	7	.125
— St. Lucie (Fla. St.)		1	0	1.000	0.00	1.08	2	2	0	0	...	0-...	12.0	8	1	0	0	5-0	15	.190
— New York (N.L.)		2	2	.500	7.58	2.09	6	6	0	0	0	0-0	29.2	40	27	25	3	22-0	25	.336
1998— New York (N.L.)		Did not play.																		
1999— Norfolk (Int'l)		3	1	.750	2.29	1.04	12	8	0	0	0	0-...	51.0	33	18	13	4	20-0	51	.182
— New York (N.L.)		1	3	.250	6.41	1.65	13	5	0	0	0	1-1	39.1	43	29	28	7	22-2	31	.279
— Oakland (A.L.)		0	1	.000	2.13	1.30	20	0	0	0	0	8-8	25.1	21	6	6	2	12-2	20	.223
2000— Oakland (A.L.)		6	4	.600	3.78	1.43	66	0	0	0	0	33-40	69.0	67	34	29	6	32-5	57	.252
2001— Oakland (A.L.)		4	3	.571	2.65	1.08	65	0	0	0	0	34-43	71.1	54	24	21	5	23-5	74	.203
2002— St. Louis (N.L.)		3	2	.600	2.48	0.98	60	0	0	0	0	32-37	65.1	46	22	18	0	18-1	68	.199
2003— Tennessee (Sou.)		0	0	...	0.00	0.50	2	2	0	0	0	0-...	2.0	1	0	0	0	0-0	3	.143
— St. Louis (N.L.)		0	1	.000	2.36	1.17	40	0	0	0	1	22-25	42.0	31	14	11	2	18-1	41	.200
2004— St. Louis (N.L.)		4	2	.667	2.87	1.04	74	0	0	0	0	• 47-54	75.1	55	27	24	5	23-4	71	.199
2005— St. Louis (N.L.)		1	2	.333	2.14	1.19	63	0	0	0	1	39-43	59.0	43	14	14	4	27-5	51	.202
2006— St. Louis (N.L.)		4	8	.333	3.55	1.46	59	0	0	0	0	33-43	58.1	47	25	23	10	38-3	52	.222
American League totals (3 years)		10	8	.556	3.04	1.26	151	0	0	0	0	75-91	165.2	142	64	56	13	67-12	151	.227
National League totals (9 years)		30	36	.455	3.74	1.35	356	52	3	1	2	174-203	633.2	583	290	263	50	272-23	508	.245
Major League totals (11 years)		40	44	.476	3.59	1.33	507	52	3	1	2	249-294	799.1	725	354	319	63	339-35	659	.242

DIVISION SERIES RECORD

Year	Team (League)	W	L	Pct.	ERA	WHIP	G	GS	CG	ShO	Hld.	Sv.-Opp.	IP	H	R	ER	HR	BB-IBB	SO	Avg.
2000— Oakland (A.L.)		0	0	...	0.00	0.50	2	0	0	0	0	1-1	2.0	1	0	0	0	0-0	3	.143
2001— Oakland (A.L.)		0	0	...	0.00	1.00	2	0	0	0	0'	2-2	2.0	1	0	0	0	1-0	3	.143
2002— St. Louis (N.L.)		0	0	...	0.00	0.00	2	0	0	0	0	2-2	2.0	0	0	0	0	0-0	1	.000
2004— St. Louis (N.L.)		0	0	...	4.50	1.50	2	0	0	0	0	0-0	2.0	1	1	1	1	2-0	2	.143
2005— St. Louis (N.L.)		0	0	...	3.00	2.00	3	0	0	0	0	1-1	3.0	5	1	1	0	1-0	4	.357
Division series totals (5 years)		0	0	...	1.64	1.09	11	0	0	0	0	6-6	11.0	8	2	2	1	4-0	13	.195

CHAMPIONSHIP SERIES RECORD

Year	Team (League)	W	L	Pct.	ERA	WHIP	G	GS	CG	ShO	Hld.	Sv.-Opp.	IP	H	R	ER	HR	BB-IBB	SO	Avg.
2002— St. Louis (N.L.)		0	0	...	4.50	2.00	2	0	0	0	0	1-1	2.0	1	1	1	0	3-2	3	.167
2004— St. Louis (N.L.)		0	1	.000	4.70	1.04	6	0	0	0	0	3-4	7.2	4	4	4	1	4-2	3	.154
2005— St. Louis (N.L.)		1	0	1.000	0.00	0.75	3	0	0	0	0	1-1	4.0	3	0	0	0	0-0	2	.214
Champ. series totals (3 years)		1	1	.500	3.29	1.10	11	0	0	0	0	5-6	13.2	8	6	5	1	7-4	8	.174

WORLD SERIES RECORD

Year	Team (League)	W	L	Pct.	ERA	WHIP	G	GS	CG	ShO	Hld.	Sv.-Opp.	IP	H	R	ER	HR	BB-IBB	SO	Avg.
2004— St. Louis (N.L.)		0	0	...	0.00	1.00	1	0	0	0	0	0-0	2.0	1	0	0	0	1-0	1	.143

ALL-STAR GAME RECORD

	W	L	Pct.	ERA	WHIP	G	GS	CG	ShO	Hld.	Sv.-Opp.	IP	H	R	ER	HR	BB-IBB	SO	Avg.
All-Star Game totals (1 year)	0	0	...	9.00	3.00	1	0	0	0	0	0-0	1.0	2	1	1	0	1-0	1	.400

2006 LEFTY-RIGHTY SPLITS

vs.	Avg.	AB	H	2B	3B	HR	RBI	BB	SO	OBP	Slg.	vs.	Avg.	AB	H	2B	3B	HR	RBI	BB	SO	OBP	Slg.
L	.270	89	24	4	0	4	13	19	22	.404	.449	R	.187	123	23	3	0	6	19	19	30	.299	.358

IZTURIS, CESAR — 3B/SS

PERSONAL: Born February 10, 1980, in Barquisimeto, Venezuela. ... 5-9/175. ... Bats both, throws right. ... Full name: Cesar David Izturis. ... Name pronounced: IS-tur-is. ... Brother of Maicer Izturis, infielder, Los Angeles Angels of Anaheim. **TRANSACTIONS/CAREER NOTES:** Signed as a non-drafted free agent by Toronto Blue Jays organization (July 11, 1996). ... Traded by Blue Jays with P Paul Quantrill to Los Angeles Dodgers for Ps Luke Prokopec and Chad Ricketts (December 13, 2001). ... On disabled list (July 1-15 and August 28, 2005-remainder of season). ... On disabled list (March 30-June 20, 2006); included rehabilitation assignment to Las Vegas. ... Traded by Dodgers to Chicago Cubs for P Greg Maddux (July 31, 2006). ... On disabled list (August 22-September 6, 2006). **HONORS:** Won N.L. Gold Glove at shortstop (2004).

2006 GAMES PLAYED BY POSITION (MLB): 3B—28, SS—23, 2B—1.

Year	Team (League)	Pos.	G	AB	R	H	2B	3B	HR	RBI	BB	SO	HBP	GDP	SB-CS	Avg.	OBP	SLG	OPS	FIELDING E	Avg.
1997— St. Catharines (NYP)		2B-SS	70	231	32	44	3	0	1	11	15	27	1	3	6-3	.190	.241	.216	.457	16	.951
1998— Hagerstown (SAL)		2B-3B-SS	130	413	56	108	13	1	1	38	20	43	2	5	20-9	.262	.297	.305	.603	29	.952
1999— Dunedin (Fla. St.)		2B-3B-SS	131	536	77	165	28	12	3	77	22	58	6	9	32-16	.308	.337	.422	.758	21	.969
2000— Syracuse (Int'l)		SS	132	435	54	95	16	5	0	27	20	44	1	5	21-11	.218	.253	.278	.531	12	.981
2001— Syracuse (Int'l)		SS-2B	87	342	32	100	16	3	2	35	10	22	1	4	24-9	.292	.310	.374	.684	16	.962
— Toronto (A.L.)		2B-SS	46	134	19	36	6	2	2	9	2	15	0	0	8-1	.269	.279	.388	.667	3	.985
2002— Los Angeles (N.L.)		SS-2B-DH	135	439	43	102	24	2	1	31	14	39	0	12	7-7	.232	.253	.303	.556	10	.979
2003— Los Angeles (N.L.)		SS	158	558	47	140	21	6	1	40	25	70	0	8	10-5	.251	.282	.315	.597	16	.977
2004— Los Angeles (N.L.)		SS	159	670	90	193	32	9	4	62	43	70	0	6	25-9	.288	.330	.381	.710	10	.985
2005— Los Angeles (N.L.)		SS	106	444	48	114	19	2	2	31	25	51	4	11	8-8	.257	.302	.322	.624	11	.977
2006— Las Vegas (PCL)			15	59	9	16	3	0	0	3	10	3	0	1	0-0	.271	.371	.322	.693	1	.981
— Los Angeles (N.L.)		3B-SS-2B	32	119	10	30	7	1	1	12	7	6	2	1	1-3	.252	.302	.353	.655	4	.963
— Chicago (N.L.)		SS	22	73	4	17	2	0	0	6	5	8	0	3	0-1	.233	.282	.260	.542	2	.975
American League totals (1 year)			46	134	19	36	6	2	2	9	2	15	0	0	8-1	.269	.279	.388	.667	3	.985
National League totals (5 years)			612	2303	242	596	105	20	9	182	119	244	6	41	51-33	.259	.295	.333	.629	53	.979
Major League totals (6 years)			658	2437	261	632	111	22	11	191	121	259	6	41	59-34	.259	.295	.336	.631	56	.979

DIVISION SERIES RECORD

Year	Team (League)	Pos.	G	AB	R	H	2B	3B	HR	RBI	BB	SO	HBP	GDP	SB-CS	Avg.	OBP	SLG	OPS	E	Avg.
2004— Los Angeles (N.L.)		SS	4	17	1	3	1	0	0	0	1	2	0	0	0-0	.176	.222	.235	.458	0	1.000

2006 LEFTY-RIGHTY SPLITS

vs.	Avg.	AB	H	2B	3B	HR	RBI	BB	SO	OBP	Slg.	vs.	Avg.	AB	H	2B	3B	HR	RBI	BB	SO	OBP	Slg.
L	.206	34	7	1	0	0	4	2	5	.270	.235	R	.253	158	40	8	1	1	14	10	9	.300	.335

IZTURIS, MAICER — IF

PERSONAL: Born September 12, 1980, in Barquisimeto, Venezuela. ... 5-8/155. ... Bats both, throws right. ... Full name: Maicer E. Izturis. ... Brother of Cesar Izturis, shortstop, Chicago Cubs. **TRANSACTIONS/CAREER NOTES:** Signed as a non-drafted free agent by Cleveland Indians organization (April 1, 1998). ... Traded by Indians with OF Ryan Church to Montreal Expos for P Scott Stewart (January 5, 2004). ... Traded by Expos with OF Juan Rivera to Anaheim Angels for OF Jose Guillen (November 23, 2004). ... Angels franchise renamed Los Angeles Angels of Anaheim for 2005 season. ... On disabled list (April 27-June 18, 2005); included rehabilitation assignment to Salt Lake. ... On disabled list (April 24-June 9, 2006); included rehabilitation assignment to Salt Lake.

2006 GAMES PLAYED BY POSITION (MLB): 3B—87, SS—10, 2B—4, DH—2.

Year Team (League)	Pos.	G	AB	R	H	2B	3B	HR	RBI	BB	SO	HBP	GDP	SB-CS	Avg.	OBP	SLG	OPS	E	Avg.
1998— Burlington (Appal.)	SS	55	217	33	63	8	2	2	33	17	32	0	4	16-6	.290	.342	.373	.715	20	.929
1999— Columbus (S. Atl.)	SS	57	220	46	66	5	3	4	23	20	28	1	2	14-2	.300	.357	.405	.761	12	.939
2000— Columbus (S. Atl.)	SS	10	29	4	8	1	0	0	1	3	3	0	1	0-0	.276	.344	.310	.654	2	.846
2001— Kinston (Carol.)	2B	114	433	47	104	16	6	1	39	31	81	8	8	32-9	.240	.300	.312	.612	17	.959
2002— Kinston (Carol.)	2B	58	233	28	61	13	1	1	30	24	26	1	2	24-6	.262	.332	.339	.671	8	.967
— Akron (East.)	2B	67	253	34	70	12	7	0	32	17	28	3	10	8-4	.277	.326	.379	.706	11	.961
2003— Akron (East.)	2B-SS	53	218	31	61	11	5	1	20	24	23	1	4	14-6	.280	.351	.390	.741	12	.946
— Buffalo (Int'l)	SS-2B	85	301	43	79	16	4	2	29	24	28	1	14	14-6	.262	.317	.362	.679	13	.967
2004— Edmonton (PCL)	SS-2B-DH	99	376	65	127	19	2	3	36	57	30	4	12	14-12	.338	.428	.423	.846	12	.969
— Montreal (N.L.)	SS-2B	32	107	10	22	5	2	1	4	10	20	2	1	4-0	.206	.286	.318	.603	8	.948
2005— Salt Lake (PCL)	SS-3B-DH	28	31	10	14	4	0	0	2	7	4	0	2	4-2	.452	.553	.581	1.133	0	1.000
— Los Angeles (A.L.)	OF	77	191	18	47	8	4	1	15	17	21	0	5	9-3	.246	.306	.346	.652	10	.950
2006— Salt Lake (PCL)	3B-SS-2B	9	36	5	11	5	1	0	5	5	5	0	0	1-0	.306	.372	.500	.872	2	.938
— Los Angeles (A.L.)	3B-SS-2B DH	104	352	64	103	21	3	5	44	38	35	3	7	14-6	.293	.365	.412	.777	14	.941
American League totals (2 years)		181	543	82	150	29	7	6	59	55	56	3	12	23-9	.276	.345	.389	.734	24	.945
National League totals (1 year)		32	107	10	22	5	2	1	4	10	20	2	1	4-0	.206	.286	.318	.603	8	.948
Major League totals (3 years)		213	650	92	172	34	9	7	63	65	76	5	13	27-9	.265	.335	.377	.712	32	.946

CHAMPIONSHIP SERIES RECORD

Year Team (League)	Pos.	G	AB	R	H	2B	3B	HR	RBI	BB	SO	HBP	GDP	SB-CS	Avg.	OBP	SLG	OPS	E	Avg.
2005— Los Angeles (A.L.)	SS	1	0	0	0	0	0	0	0	0	0	0	0	0-0	...	...	...	...	0	...

2006 LEFTY-RIGHTY SPLITS

vs.	Avg.	AB	H	2B	3B	HR	RBI	BB	SO	OBP	Slg.	vs.	Avg.	AB	H	2B	3B	HR	RBI	BB	SO	OBP	Slg.
L	.247	85	21	7	0	0	12	11	5	.333	.329	R	.307	267	82	14	3	5	32	27	30	.376	.438

JACKSON, CONOR — 1B

PERSONAL: Born May 7, 1982, in Austin, Texas. ... 6-2/225. ... Bats right, throws right. ... Full name: Conor S. Jackson. ... High school: El Camino Real (Woodland Hills, Calif.) ... College: California. **TRANSACTIONS/CAREER NOTES:** Selected by Arizona Diamondbacks organization in first round (19th pick overall) of 2003 free-agent draft.

2006 GAMES PLAYED BY POSITION (MLB): 1B—129, DH—1.

Year Team (League)	Pos.	G	AB	R	H	2B	3B	HR	RBI	BB	SO	HBP	GDP	SB-CS	Avg.	OBP	SLG	OPS	E	Avg.
2003— Yakima (N'west)	OF	68	257	44	82	35	1	6	60	36	41	5	7	3-0	.319	.410	.533	.943	0	1.000
2004— Lancaster (Pion.)	OF	67	258	64	89	19	2	11	54	45	36	3	3	4-3	.345	.438	.562	1.000	...	...
— El Paso (Texas)	OF-3B	60	226	33	68	13	2	6	37	24	36	2	4	3-3	.301	.367	.456	.823	3	.000
2005— Tucson (PCL)	1B-OF-DH	93	333	66	118	38	2	8	73	69	32	0	8	3-2	.354	.457	.553	1.010	11	.985
— Arizona (N.L.)	1B-OF	40	85	8	17	3	0	2	8	12	11	1	6	0-0	.200	.303	.306	.609	5	.973
2006— Arizona (N.L.)	1B-DH	140	485	75	141	26	1	15	79	54	73	9	18	1-0	.291	.368	.441	.809	12	.990
Major League totals (2 years)		180	570	83	158	29	1	17	87	66	84	10	24	1-0	.277	.358	.421	.779	17	.988

2006 LEFTY-RIGHTY SPLITS

vs.	Avg.	AB	H	2B	3B	HR	RBI	BB	SO	OBP	Slg.	vs.	Avg.	AB	H	2B	3B	HR	RBI	BB	SO	OBP	Slg.
L	.296	162	48	7	0	5	20	21	27	.378	.432	R	.288	323	93	19	1	10	59	33	46	.362	.446

JACKSON, DAMIAN — 2B/OF

PERSONAL: Born August 16, 1973, in Los Angeles. ... 5-11/185. ... Bats right, throws right. ... Full name: Damian Jacques Jackson. ... High school: Ygnacio Valley (Concord, Calif.). ... Junior college: Laney (Calif.). **TRANSACTIONS/CAREER NOTES:** Selected by Cleveland Indians organization in 44th round of 1991 free-agent draft. ... Traded by Indians with Ps Danny Graves, Jim Crowell and Scott Winchester to Cincinnati Reds for P John Smiley and IF Jeff Branson (July 31, 1997). ... Traded by Reds with OF Reggie Sanders and P Josh Harris to San Diego Padres for OF Greg Vaughn and OF/1B Mark Sweeney (February 2, 1999). ... On disabled list (May 13-June 22, 2001); included rehabilitation assignment to Portland. ... Traded by Padres with C Matt Walbeck to Detroit Tigers for C Javier Cardona and OF Rich Gomez (March 24, 2002). ... On disabled list (April 7-22, 2002). ... Released by Tigers (November 20, 2002). ... Signed by Boston Red Sox (December 18, 2002). ... Signed as a free agent by Colorado Rockies organization (January 5, 2004). ... Released by Rockies (March 28, 2004). ... Signed by Chicago Cubs organization (April 1, 2004). ... Traded by Cubs to Kansas City Royals for IF Gookie Dawkins (May 31, 2004). ... Signed as a free agent by Padres organization (November 17, 2004). ... Signed as a free agent by Washington Nationals (October 27, 2005). ... On disabled list (July 9-24, 2006). ... Released by Nationals (August 25, 2006). **STATISTICAL NOTES:** Career major league grand slams: 2.

2006 GAMES PLAYED BY POSITION (MLB): OF—26, SS—16, 2B—11, 3B—6.

Year Team (League)	Pos.	G	AB	R	H	2B	3B	HR	RBI	BB	SO	HBP	GDP	SB-CS	Avg.	OBP	SLG	OPS	E	Avg.
1992— Burlington (Appal.)	SS	62	226	32	56	12	1	0	23	32	31	6	1	29-5	.248	.352	.310	.662	23	.933
1993— Columbus (S. Atl.)	SS	108	350	70	94	19	3	6	45	41	61	5	1	26-7	.269	.353	.391	.744	52	.908
1994— Cant./Akr. (Eastern)	OF-SS	138	531	85	143	29	5	5	60	60	121	5	8	37-16	.269	.346	.371	.717	54	.927
1995— Cant./Akr. (Eastern)	SS	131	484	67	120	20	2	3	34	65	103	9	6	40-22	.248	.348	.316	.664	36	.939
1996— Buffalo (A.A.)	SS	133	452	77	116	15	1	12	49	48	78	7	7	24-7	.257	.333	.374	.707	29	.954
— Cleveland (A.L.)	SS	5	10	2	3	2	0	0	1	1	4	0	0	0-0	.300	.364	.500	.864	0	1.000
1997— Buffalo (A.A.)	SS-2B-OF	73	266	51	78	12	0	4	13	37	45	3	...	20-8	.293	.383	.383	.767	23	.942
— Cleveland (A.L.)	SS-2B	8	9	2	1	0	0	0	0	0	1	1	0	1-0	.111	.200	.111	.311	0	1.000
— Indianapolis (A.A.)	2B-SS	19	71	12	19	6	1	0	7	10	17	1	...	4-1	.268	.361	.380	.742	5	.948
— Cincinnati (N.L.)	SS-2B	12	27	6	6	2	1	1	2	4	7	0	0	1-1	.222	.323	.481	.804	1	.971
1998— Cincinnati (N.L.)	SS	13	38	4	12	5	0	0	7	6	4	0	1	2-0	.316	.400	.447	.847	1	.976
— Indianapolis (Int'l)	SS-OF	131	517	102	135	36	10	6	49	62	125	10	2	25-10	.261	.349	.404	.753	44	.938
1999— San Diego (N.L.)	SS-2B-OF	133	388	56	87	20	2	9	39	53	105	3	2	34-10	.224	.320	.356	.676	26	.948
2000— San Diego (N.L.)	SS-2B-OF	138	470	68	120	27	6	6	37	62	108	3	7	28-6	.255	.345	.377	.721	25	.960

Year Team (League)	Pos.	G	AB	R	H	2B	3B	HR	RBI	BB	SO	HBP	GDP	SB-CS	Avg.	OBP	SLG	OPS	E	Avg.
2001— San Diego (N.L.) 2B-SS-OF		122	440	67	106	21	6	4	38	44	128	6	6	23-6	.241	.316	.343	.660	8	.986
— Portland (PCL)	SS	3	10	4	3	3	0	0	0	3	1	0	0	0-1	.300	.462	.600	1.062	0	1.000
2002— Detroit (A.L.) 2B-OF-SS/DH-3B		81	245	31	63	20	1	1	25	21	36	3	3	12-3	.257	.320	.359	.679	8	.972
2003— Boston (A.L.) 2B-OF-SS/DH-3B-1B		109	161	34	42	7	0	1	13	8	28	0	4	16-8	.261	.294	.323	.617	9	.951
2004— Iowa (PCL) SS-OF-2B		28	97	18	27	6	5	3	13	11	20	0	0	3-1	.278	.352	.536	.888	1	.990
— Chicago (N.L.)	2B	7	15	1	1	0	0	1	1	3	6	0	0	0-0	.067	.222	.267	.489	1	.957
— Kansas City (A.L.) OF-DH-2B/SS		14	15	1	2	2	0	0	2	1	6	0	0	0-0	.133	.188	.267	.454	0	1.000
— Omaha (PCL) SS-2B		48	169	46	52	13	1	8	27	30	36	6	3	12-2	.308	.425	.538	.964	9	.961
2005— Portland (PCL) SS-3B-OF/2B-DH		14	51	14	18	4	1	3	10	13	9	0	0	1-1	.353	.477	.647	1.124	3	.939
— San Diego (N.L.) OF-2B-SS/3B		118	275	44	70	9	0	5	23	30	45	4	4	15-2	.255	.335	.342	.677	3	.970
2006— Wash. (N.L.) OF-SS-2B/3B		67	116	16	23	6	1	4	10	12	39	4	1	1-3	.198	.295	.371	.666	10	.907
American League totals (5 years)		217	440	70	111	31	1	2	41	31	75	4	7	29-11	.252	.305	.341	.646	17	.966
National League totals (8 years)		610	1769	262	425	90	16	30	157	214	442	20	21	104-28	.240	.327	.360	.687	81	.963
Major League totals (11 years)		827	2209	332	536	121	17	32	198	245	517	24	28	133-39	.243	.323	.356	.679	98	.964

DIVISION SERIES RECORD

Year Team (League)	Pos.	G	AB	R	H	2B	3B	HR	RBI	BB	SO	HBP	GDP	SB-CS	Avg.	OBP	SLG	OPS	E	Avg.
2003— Boston (A.L.)	2B	4	5	0	0	0	0	0	0	0	2	0	0	0-0	.000	.000	.000	.000	0	1.000
2005— San Diego (N.L.)	OF	3	3	1	2	0	0	0	0	0	1	1	0	1-0	.667	.750	.667	1.417	0	1.000
Division series totals (2 years)		7	8	1	2	0	0	0	0	0	3	1	0	1-0	.250	.333	.250	.583	0	1.000

CHAMPIONSHIP SERIES RECORD

Year Team (League)	Pos.	G	AB	R	H	2B	3B	HR	RBI	BB	SO	HBP	GDP	SB-CS	Avg.	OBP	SLG	OPS	E	Avg.
2003— Boston (A.L.)	2B	5	3	1	1	0	0	0	1	0	1	0	0	0-1	.333	.333	.333	.667	1	.857

2006 LEFTY-RIGHTY SPLITS

vs.	Avg.	AB	H	2B	3B	HR	RBI	BB	SO	OBP	Slg.	vs.	Avg.	AB	H	2B	3B	HR	RBI	BB	SO	OBP	Slg.
L	.233	43	10	2	0	2	4	9	13	.365	.419	R	.178	73	13	4	1	2	6	3	26	.250	.342

JACKSON, EDWIN — P

PERSONAL: Born September 9, 1983, in Neu-Ulm, West Germany. ... 6-3/190. ... Throws right, bats right. ... Full name: Edwin Jackson Jr.. ... High school: Shaw (Columbus, Ga.). **TRANSACTIONS/CAREER NOTES:** Selected by Los Angeles Dodgers organization in sixth round of 2001 free-agent draft. ... On disabled list (July 9-September 7, 2004); included rehabilitation assignment to Las Vegas. ... Traded by Dodgers with P Charles Tiffany to Tampa Bay Devil Rays for Ps Danys Baez and Lance Carter (January 14, 2006). **MISCELLANEOUS NOTES:** Appeared in three games as pinch runner (2005).
CAREER HITTING: 3-for-20 (.150), 0 R, 0 2B, 0 3B, 0 HR, 2 RBI.

Year Team (League)	W	L	Pct.	ERA	WHIP	G	GS	CG	ShO	Hld.	Sv.-Opp.	IP	H	R	ER	HR	BB-IBB	SO	Avg.
2001— GC Dodgers (GCL)	2	1	.667	2.45	1.50	12	2	0	0	...	0-...	22.0	14	12	6	1	19-0	23	.173
2002— South Georgia (S. Atl.)	5	2	.714	1.98	1.07	19	19	0	0	...	0-...	104.2	79	34	23	2	33-0	85	.206
2003— Jacksonville (Sou.)	7	7	.500	3.70	1.17	27	27	0	0	...	0-...	148.1	121	68	61	9	53-0	157	.220
— Los Angeles (N.L.)	2	1	.667	2.45	1.27	4	3	0	0	0	0-0	22.0	17	6	6	2	11-1	19	.221
2004— Las Vegas (PCL)	6	4	.600	5.86	1.60	19	19	0	0	0	0-0	90.2	90	65	59	4	55-1	70	.265
— Los Angeles (N.L.)	2	1	.667	7.30	1.70	8	5	0	0	0	0-0	24.2	31	20	20	7	11-1	16	.307
2005— Las Vegas (PCL)	3	7	.300	8.62	2.04	12	11	1	0	0	0-0	55.1	76	61	53	13	37-2	33	.328
— Jacksonville (Sou.)	6	4	.600	3.48	1.13	11	11	0	0	0	0-0	62.0	52	31	24	7	18-0	44	.224
— Los Angeles (N.L.)	2	2	.500	6.28	1.67	.7	6	0	0	0	0-0	28.2	31	22	20	2	17-0	13	.272
2006— Durham (Int'l)	3	7	.300	5.55	1.63	22	13	0	0	0	5-6	73.0	84	55	45	7	35-0	66	.288
— Tampa Bay (A.L.)	0	0	...	5.45	1.84	23	1	0	0	0	0-0	36.1	42	27	22	2	25-0	27	.292
American League totals (1 year)	0	0	...	5.45	1.84	23	1	0	0	0	0-0	36.1	42	27	22	2	25-0	27	.292
National League totals (3 years)	6	4	.600	5.50	1.57	19	14	0	0	0	0-0	75.1	79	48	46	11	39-2	48	.271
Major League totals (4 years)	6	4	.600	5.48	1.66	42	15	0	0	0	0-0	111.2	121	75	68	13	64-2	75	.278

2006 LEFTY-RIGHTY SPLITS

vs.	Avg.	AB	H	2B	3B	HR	RBI	BB	SO	OBP	Slg.	vs.	Avg.	AB	H	2B	3B	HR	RBI	BB	SO	OBP	Slg.
L	.233	60	14	5	1	0	12	14	13	.382	.350	R	.333	84	28	5	1	2	16	11	14	.406	.488

JACKSON, ZACH — P

PERSONAL: Born May 13, 1983, in Greensburg, Pa. ... Throws left, bats left. ... Full name: Zachary Thomas Jackson. ... High school: Seneca Valley (Cranberry Township, Pa.). ... College: Texas A&M. **TRANSACTIONS/CAREER NOTES:** Selected by Toronto Blue Jays organization in supplemental round ("sandwich pick" between first and second rounds, 32nd pick overall) of 2004 draft; pick received as part of compensation for Anaheim Angels signing Type A free-agent P Kelvim Escobar. ... Traded by Blue Jays to Milwaukee Brewers for P Ty Taubeheim (December 8, 2005), completing deal in which Brewers traded 1B Lyle Overbay and a player to be named to Blue Jays for P David Bush, OF Gabe Gross and a player to be named (December 7, 2005).
CAREER HITTING: 1-for-9 (.111), 1 R, 0 2B, 0 3B, 0 HR, 0 RBI.

Year Team (League)	W	L	Pct.	ERA	WHIP	G	GS	CG	ShO	Hld.	Sv.-Opp.	IP	H	R	ER	HR	BB-IBB	SO	Avg.
2004— Auburn (NY-Penn)	0	0	...	5.40	1.73	4	4	0	0	...	0-...	15.0	20	9	9	1	6-0	11	.323
2005— Dunedin (Fla. St.)	8	1	.889	2.88	1.04	10	10	0	0	0	0-0	59.1	56	25	19	3	6-0	48	.247
— New Hampshire (East.)	4	3	.571	4.00	1.28	9	9	0	0	0	0-0	54.0	57	27	24	3	12-0	43	.277
— Syracuse (Int'l)	4	4	.500	5.13	1.73	9	9	0	0	0	0-0	47.1	61	33	27	3	21-0	33	.323
2006— Nashville (PCL)	4	6	.400	4.12	1.40	18	18	1	0	0	0-0	107.0	106	55	49	11	44-0	58	.262
— Milwaukee (N.L.)	2	2	.500	5.40	1.62	8	7	0	0	0	0-0	38.1	48	26	23	6	14-0	22	.304
Major League totals (1 year)	2	2	.500	5.40	1.62	8	7	0	0	0	0-0	38.1	48	26	23	6	14-0	22	.304

2006 LEFTY-RIGHTY SPLITS

vs.	Avg.	AB	H	2B	3B	HR	RBI	BB	SO	OBP	Slg.	vs.	Avg.	AB	H	2B	3B	HR	RBI	BB	SO	OBP	Slg.
L	.333	39	13	2	0	2	6	3	1	.409	.538	R	.294	119	35	8	1	4	17	11	21	.361	.479

JACOBS, MIKE — IF

PERSONAL: Born October 30, 1980, in Chula Vista, Calif. ... 6-2/180. ... Bats left, throws right. ... Full name: Michael James Jacobs. ... High school: Hilltop (Calif.). ... Junior college: Grossmont (Calif.). **TRANSACTIONS/CAREER NOTES:** Selected by New York Mets organization in 38th round of 1999 free-agent draft. ... Traded by Mets with P

Yusmeiro Petit and IF Grant Psomas to Florida Marlins for 1B Carlos Delgado and cash (November 24, 2005). **STATISTICAL NOTES:** Hit home run in first major league at-bat (August 21, 2005).
2006 GAMES PLAYED BY POSITION (MLB): 1B—124, DH—1.

Year	Team (League)	Pos.	G	AB	R	H	2B	3B	HR	RBI	BB	SO	HBP	GDP	SB-CS	Avg.	OBP	SLG	OPS	E	FIELDING Avg.
1999—	GC Mets (GCL)	C-1B	44	147	18	49	12	0	4	30	14	30	1	3	2-0	.333	.383	.497	.880	7	.960
2000—	Columbia (S. Atl.)	C	18	56	1	12	5	0	0	8	6	19	0	2	1-1	.214	.290	.304	.594	2	.989
—	Kingsport (Appalachian)	C	59	204	28	55	15	4	7	40	33	62	1	3	6-3	.270	.371	.485	.856	8	.973
2001—	Brook. N.Y.-Penn. (N.Y.-Penn.)	C	19	66	12	19	5	0	1	15	6	11	3	1	1-1	.288	.364	.409	.773	3	.977
—	Columbia (S. Atl.)	C	46	180	18	50	13	0	2	26	13	46	1	4	0-1	.278	.328	.383	.711	4	.988
2002—	St. Lucie (Fla. St.)	C-1B	118	467	62	117	26	1	11	64	25	95	4	11	2-3	.251	.291	.383	.672	8	.984
2003—	Binghamton (East.)	1B-C-OF	119	407	56	134	36	1	17	81	28	87	7	11	0-3	.329	.376	.548	.924	7	.987
2004—	Norfolk (Int'l)	C-1B-SS	27	96	8	17	3	0	2	6	9	30	0	1	0-0	.177	.245	.271	.516	1	.992
2005—	Binghamton (East.)	1B-C-DH																			
—		OF	117	433	66	139	37	2	25	93	35	94	7	11	1-2	.321	.376	.589	.965	14	.983
—	New York (N.L.)	1B	30	100	19	31	7	0	11	23	10	22	1	5	0-0	.310	.375	.710	1.085	4	.984
2006—	Florida (N.L.)	1B-DH	136	469	54	123	37	1	20	77	45	105	1	16	3-0	.262	.325	.473	.798	7	.993
	Major League totals (2 years)		166	569	73	154	44	1	31	100	55	127	2	21	3-0	.271	.334	.515	.849	11	.991

2006 LEFTY-RIGHTY SPLITS

vs.	Avg.	AB	H	2B	3B	HR	RBI	BB	SO	OBP	Slg.		vs.	Avg.	AB	H	2B	3B	HR	RBI	BB	SO	OBP	Slg.
L	.182	88	16	4	0	2	11	5	26	.234	.295		R	.281	381	107	33	1	18	66	40	79	.345	.514

JAMES, CHUCK — P

PERSONAL: Born November 9, 1981, in Atlanta, Ga. ... 6-0/170. ... Throws left, bats left. ... Full name: Charles H. James. ... College: Chattahoochie Valley.
TRANSACTIONS/CAREER NOTES: Selected by Atlanta Braves organization in 20th round of 2002 free-agent draft. ... On disabled list (May 6-June 7, 2006); included rehabilitation assignments to Rome and Richmond.
CAREER HITTING: 2-for-36 (.056), 2 R, 0 2B, 0 3B, 0 HR, 1 RBI.

Year	Team (League)	W	L	Pct.	ERA	WHIP	G	GS	CG	ShO	Hld.	Sv.-Opp.	IP	H	R	ER	HR	BB-IBB	SO	Avg.
2003—	Danville (Appal.)	2	1	.667	1.25	0.89	11	11	0	0	...	0-...	50.1	26	9	7	1	19-0	68	.151
2004—	Rome (S. Atl.)	10	5	.667	2.25	1.06	26	22	1	0	...	0-...	132.0	92	41	33	6	48-1	156	.203
2005—	Myrtle Beach (Carol.)	3	3	.500	1.08	0.67	7	7	0	0	...	0-0	41.2	20	6	5	1	8-0	59	.139
—	Mississippi (Sou.)	9	1	.900	2.09	0.93	16	16	0	0	...	0-0	86.0	62	25	20	4	18-0	104	.199
—	Richmond (Int'l)	1	3	.250	3.48	0.92	6	6	0	0	...	0-0	33.2	21	13	13	4	10-0	30	.176
—	Atlanta (N.L.)	0	0	...	1.59	1.24	2	0	0	0	...	0-0	5.2	4	1	1	0	3-0	5	.200
2006—	Rome (S. Atl.)	0	0	...	0.00	0.00	1	1	0	0	...	0-0	1.0	0	0	0	0	0-0	1	...
—	Richmond (Int'l)	1	0	1.000	2.67	1.07	7	6	0	0	...	0-0	33.2	30	10	10	3	6-0	25	.236
—	Atlanta (N.L.)	11	4	*.733	3.78	1.24	25	18	0	0	...	0-0	119.0	101	54	50	20	47-2	91	.232
	Major League totals (2 years)	11	4	.733	3.68	1.24	27	18	0	0	...	0-0	124.2	105	55	51	20	50-2	96	.231

2006 LEFTY-RIGHTY SPLITS

vs.	Avg.	AB	H	2B	3B	HR	RBI	BB	SO	OBP	Slg.		vs.	Avg.	AB	H	2B	3B	HR	RBI	BB	SO	OBP	Slg.
L	.297	91	27	6	1	3	7	12	20	.381	.484		R	.215	344	74	15	1	17	43	35	71	.292	.413

JANSSEN, CASEY — P

PERSONAL: Born September 17, 1981, in Orange, Calif. ... Throws right, bats right. ... Full name: Robert Casey Janssen. ... High school: Fountain Valley (Calif.). ... College: UCLA. **TRANSACTIONS/CAREER NOTES:** Selected by Toronto Blue Jays organization in fourth round of 2004 free-agent draft.
CAREER HITTING: 0-for-1 (.000), 0 R, 0 2B, 0 3B, 0 HR, 0 RBI.

Year	Team (League)	W	L	Pct.	ERA	WHIP	G	GS	CG	ShO	Hld.	Sv.-Opp.	IP	H	R	ER	HR	BB-IBB	SO	Avg.
2004—	Auburn (NY-Penn)	3	1	.750	3.48	1.10	10	10	0	0	...	0-...	51.2	47	21	20	2	10-0	45	.240
2005—	Lansing (Midw.)	4	0	1.000	1.37	0.67	7	7	0	0	...	0-0	46.0	27	8	7	0	4-0	38	.174
—	Dunedin (Fla. St.)	6	1	.857	2.26	0.97	10	10	0	0	...	0-0	59.2	46	16	15	2	12-0	51	.216
—	New Hampshire (East.)	3	3	.500	2.93	1.23	9	9	0	0	...	0-0	43.0	49	20	14	3	4-0	47	.288
2006—	Toronto (A.L.)	6	10	.375	5.07	1.32	19	17	0	0	...	0-0	94.0	103	58	53	12	21-3	44	.275
—	Syracuse (Int'l)	1	5	.167	4.85	1.29	9	9	0	0	...	0-0	42.2	47	23	23	3	8-0	32	.283
	Major League totals (1 year)	6	10	.375	5.07	1.32	19	17	0	0	...	0-0	94.0	103	58	53	12	21-3	44	.275

2006 LEFTY-RIGHTY SPLITS

vs.	Avg.	AB	H	2B	3B	HR	RBI	BB	SO	OBP	Slg.		vs.	Avg.	AB	H	2B	3B	HR	RBI	BB	SO	OBP	Slg.
L	.292	168	49	10	1	5	20	14	16	.351	.452		R	.261	207	54	10	1	7	29	7	28	.300	.420

JARVIS, KEVIN — P

PERSONAL: Born August 1, 1969, in Lexington, Ky. ... 6-2/200. ... Throws right, bats right. ... Full name: Kevin Thomas Jarvis. ... High school: Tates Creek (Lexington, Ky.). ... College: Wake Forest. **TRANSACTIONS/CAREER NOTES:** Selected by Cincinnati Reds organization in 21st round of 1991 free-agent draft. ... Claimed on waivers by Detroit Tigers (May 2, 1997). ... Claimed on waivers by Minnesota Twins (May 9, 1997). ... Claimed on waivers by Tigers (June 17, 1997). ... On disabled list (June 25-July 14, 1997); included rehabilitation assignment to Toledo. ... Released by Tigers (December 12, 1997). ... Signed by Chunichi Dragons of the Japan Central League (January 23, 1998). ... Signed as a free agent by Reds organization (August 27, 1998). ... Released by Reds (September 9, 1998). ... Signed by Oakland Athletics organization (January 4, 1999). ... On disabled list (April 19-June 4, 1999); included rehabilitation assignment to Modesto. ... Signed as a free agent by Colorado Rockies organization (December 1, 1999). ... On disabled list (July 28-September 1, 2000); included rehabilitation assignment to Colorado Springs. ... Signed as a free agent by San Diego Padres (January 5, 2001). ... On disabled list (April 18-May 5, May 13-June 27 and July 12, 2002-remainder of season); included rehabilitation assignments to Mobile and Lake Elsinore. ... On disabled list (March 26, 2003-June 13, 2003); included rehabilitation assignment to Lake Elsinore. ... Traded by Padres with IF Dave Hansen, C Wiki Gonzalez and OF Vince Faison to Seattle Mariners for IF Jeff Cirillo and RHP Brian Sweeney (January 6, 2004). ... Released by Mariners (May 4, 2004). ... Signed by Rockies organization (May 10, 2004). ... Released by Rockies (July 2, 2004). ... Signed by Pittsburgh Pirates organization (July 8, 2004). ... Signed as a free agent by St. Louis Cardinals organization (February 16, 2005). ... Signed as free agent by Arizona Diamondbacks organization (December 10, 2005). ... Traded by Diamondbacks to Boston Red Sox for a player to be named (August 31, 2006). **MISCELLANEOUS NOTES:** Appeared in one game as pinch runner (2000). ... Appeared in two games as pinch hitter (2001). ... Appeared in one game as pinch runner (2003).
CAREER HITTING: 30-for-188 (.160), 19 R, 6 2B, 0 3B, 1 HR, 14 RBI.

Year	Team (League)	W	L	Pct.	ERA	WHIP	G	GS	CG	ShO	Hld.	Sv.-Opp.	IP	H	R	ER	HR	BB-IBB	SO	Avg.
1991—	Princeton (Appal.)	5	6	.455	2.42		13	13	4	1	...	0-...	85.2	73	34	23	6	29-3	79	.220
1992—	Cedar Rap. (Midw.)	0	0	...	0.00	1.00	1	0	0	0	...	0-...	1.0	1	0	0	0	0-0	0	.333
—	Char., W.Va. (SAL)	6	8	.429	3.11	1.20	28	18	2	1	...	0-...	133.0	123	59	46	3	37-1	131	.244
1993—	Win.-Salem (Car.)	7	7	.533	3.41	1.25	21	20	2	1	...	0-...	145.0	133	68	55	13	48-2	101	.241
—	Chattanooga (Sou.)	3	1	.750	1.69	0.99	7	3	2	0	...	0-...	37.1	26	7	7	1	11-0	18	.203
1994—	Cincinnati (N.L.)	1	1	.500	7.13	1.53	6	3	0	0	...	0-0	17.2	22	14	14	4	5-0	10	.301

Year	Team (League)	W	L	Pct.	ERA	WHIP	G	GS	CG	ShO	Hld.	Sv.-Opp.	IP	H	R	ER	HR	BB-IBB	SO	Avg.
	— Indianapolis (A.A.)	10	2	.833	3.54	1.28	21	20	2	0	...	0-...	132.1	136	55	52	13	34-2	90	.261
1995—	Indianapolis (A.A.)	4	2	.667	4.45	1.32	10	10	2	1	...	0-...	60.2	62	33	30	2	18-1	37	.256
	— Cincinnati (N.L.)	3	4	.429	5.70	1.56	19	11	1	1	0	0-0	79.0	91	56	50	13	32-2	33	.292
1996—	Indianapolis (A.A.)	4	3	.571	5.06	1.34	8	8	0	0	...	0-...	42.2	45	27	24	3	12-0	32	.263
	— Cincinnati (N.L.)	8	9	.471	5.98	1.62	24	20	2	1	0	0-0	120.1	152	93	80	17	43-5	63	.305
1997—	Cincinnati (N.L.)	0	1	.000	10.13	2.10	9	0	0	0	0	1-1	13.1	21	16	15	4	7-0	12	.344
	— Minnesota (A.L.)	0	0	...	12.46	2.38	6	2	0	0	0	0-0	13.0	23	18	18	4	8-0	9	.371
	— Detroit (A.L.)	0	3	.000	5.40	1.66	17	3	0	0	0	0-0	41.2	55	28	25	9	14-0	27	.318
	— Toledo (Int'l)	0	1	.000	6.75	1.38	2	2	0	0	...	0-...	8.0	7	6	6	0	4-0	5	.226
1998—	Chunichi (Jp. Cn.)	1	2	.333	4.41	1.41	4	3	0	0	...	0-...	16.1	18	8	8	...	5-...	7	...
	— Indianapolis (Int'l)	1	0	1.000	9.00	1.57	2	2	0	0	0	0-...	7.0	10	7	7	3	1-0	5	.323
1999—	Oakland (A.L.)	0	1	.000	11.57	2.43	4	1	0	0	0	0-0	14.0	28	19	18	6	6-0	11	.418
	— Modesto (California)	0	0	...	1.29	0.71	2	2	0	0	0	0-...	7.0	4	1	1	0	1-0	10	.167
	— Vancouver (PCL)	10	2	.833	3.41	1.32	17	16	2	1	0	0-...	103.0	110	47	39	14	26-0	64	.270
2000—	Colo. Springs (PCL)	3	2	.600	0.69	0.79	7	7	0	0	0	0-...	39.0	18	6	3	1	13-0	18	.138
	— Colorado (N.L.)	3	4	.429	5.95	1.49	24	19	0	0	0	0-0	115.0	138	83	76	26	33-3	60	.300
2001—	San Diego (N.L.)	12	11	.522	4.79	1.23	32	32	1	1	0	0-0	193.1	189	107	103	* 37	49-4	133	.254
2002—	San Diego (N.L.)	2	4	.333	4.37	1.31	7	7	0	0	0	0-0	35.0	36	19	17	5	10-1	24	.269
	— Mobile (Sou.)	0	0	...	0.00	0.67	1	1	0	0	0	0-...	3.0	2	0	0	0	0-0	3	.182
	— Lake Elsinore (Calif.)	1	0	1.000	0.00	0.60	1	1	0	0	0	0-...	5.0	2	0	0	0	1-0	1	.133
2003—	Lake Elsinore (Calif.)	2	1	.667	4.09	1.00	3	3	0	0	0	0-...	22.0	18	11	10	1	4-0	19	.222
	— San Diego (N.L.)	4	8	.333	5.87	1.58	16	16	0	0	0	0-0	92.0	113	65	60	15	32-5	49	.304
2004—	Seattle (A.L.)	1	0	1.000	8.31	1.92	8	0	0	0	0	0-0	13.0	20	12	12	4	5-0	7	.345
	— Colo. Springs (PCL)	0	4	.000	5.79	1.45	6	6	1	0	0	0-0	37.1	44	34	24	12	10-0	25	.293
	— Colorado (N.L.)	0	0	...	27.00	5.00	2	0	0	0	0	0-0	2.0	6	6	6	1	4-2	0	.600
	— Nashville (PCL)	2	5	.286	4.11	1.60	11	11	1	0	0	0-...	65.2	93	31	30	3	12-1	46	.338
2005—	St. Louis (N.L.)	0	1	.000	13.50	1.80	4	0	0	0	0	0-1	3.1	3	5	5	1	3-0	2	.250
	— Memphis (PCL)	11	6	.647	3.38	1.29	26	25	1	0	1	0-0	157.0	164	63	59	19	39-1	112	.272
2006—	Arizona (N.L.)	0	1	.000	11.91	2.03	5	1	0	0	0	0-0	11.1	18	15	15	2	5-0	6	.360
	— Tucson (PCL)	3	6	.333	3.44	1.17	15	13	0	0	0	0-0	83.2	76	40	32	7	22-0	58	.240
	— Boston (A.L.)	0	1	.000	4.86	1.68	4	3	0	0	0	0-0	16.2	22	12	9	1	6-1	7	.324
	American League totals (4 years)	1	5	.167	7.51	1.90	39	9	0	0	0	0-0	98.1	148	89	82	24	39-1	61	.346
	National League totals (11 years)	33	44	.429	5.82	1.48	148	109	4	3	0	1-2	682.1	789	479	441	125	223-22	392	.289
	Major League totals (12 years)	34	49	.410	6.03	1.54	187	118	4	3	0	1-2	780.2	937	568	523	149	262-23	453	.297

2006 LEFTY-RIGHTY SPLITS

vs.	Avg.	AB	H	2B	3B	HR	RBI	BB	SO	OBP	Slg.	vs.	Avg.	AB	H	2B	3B	HR	RBI	BB	SO	OBP	Slg.
L	.327	52	17	7	0	1	11	6	6	.410	.519	R	.348	66	23	7	2	2	16	5	7	.384	.606

JENKINS, GEOFF — OF

PERSONAL: Born July 21, 1974, in Olympia, Wash. ... 6-1/212. ... Bats left, throws right. ... Full name: Geoff Scott Jenkins. ... High school: Cordova Senior (Rancho Cordova, Calif.). ... College: Southern California. **TRANSACTIONS/CAREER NOTES:** Selected by Milwaukee Brewers organization in first round (ninth pick overall) of 1995 free-agent draft. ... On disabled list (May 7-29, 2000). ... On disabled list (May 2-19 and July 29-August 28, 2001); included rehabilitation assignment to Beloit. ... On disabled list (June 18, 2002-remainder of season). ... On disabled list (March 21-April 9 and August 29, 2003-remainder of season); included rehabilitation assignment to Huntsville. **RECORDS:** Shares major league record for most strikeouts, extra-inning game (6, June 8, 2004, 17 innings). **STATISTICAL NOTES:** Hit three home runs in one game (April 28, 2001; and May 21, 2003). ... Career major league grand slams: 3.

2006 GAMES PLAYED BY POSITION (MLB): OF—133.

									BATTING								FIELDING	
Year	Team (League)	Pos.	G	AB	R	H	2B	3B	HR	RBI	BB	SO	HBP	GDP	SB-CS	Avg.	OBP	SLG	OPS	E	Avg.
1995—	Helena (Pion.)	OF	7	28	2	9	0	1	0	9	3	11	0	0	0-2	.321	.375	.393	.768	0	1.000
	— Stockton (Calif.)	OF	13	47	13	12	2	0	3	12	10	12	0	0	2-0	.255	.373	.489	.862	2	.895
	— El Paso (Texas)	OF	22	79	12	22	4	2	1	13	8	23	0	1	3-1	.278	.341	.418	.759	7	.857
1996—	El Paso (Texas)	DH	22	77	17	22	5	4	1	11	12	21	2	2	1-2	.286	.391	.494	.885	...	...
	— Stockton (Calif.)	DH-OF	37	138	27	48	8	4	3	25	20	32	3	3	3-3	.348	.433	.529	.962	0	1.000
1997—	Tucson (PCL)	OF-SS	93	347	44	82	24	3	10	56	33	87	3	7	0-2	.236	.308	.409	.717	5	.961
1998—	Louisville (Int'l)	OF	55	215	38	71	10	4	9	52	14	39	5	6	1-1	.330	.381	.512	.893	2	.979
	— Milwaukee (N.L.)	OF	84	262	33	60	12	1	9	28	20	61	2	7	1-3	.229	.288	.386	.673	4	.968
1999—	Milwaukee (N.L.)	OF	135	447	70	140	43	3	21	82	35	87	7	10	5-1	.313	.371	.564	.935	7	.974
2000—	Milwaukee (N.L.)	OF	135	512	100	155	36	4	34	94	33	135	15	9	11-1	.303	.360	.588	.948	7	.975
2001—	Milwaukee (N.L.)	OF	105	397	60	105	21	1	20	63	36	120	8	11	4-2	.264	.334	.474	.808	3	.986
	— Beloit (Midw.)	OF	1	3	1	1	1	0	0	1	1	1	0	0	0-0	.333	.500	.667	1.167	0	...
2002—	Milwaukee (N.L.)	OF	67	243	35	59	17	1	10	29	22	60	4	1	1-2	.243	.320	.444	.764	1	.992
2003—	Huntsville (Sou.)	OF	6	20	4	5	2	0	2	3	1	7	0	0	1-0	.250	.286	.550	.836	0	1.000
	— Milwaukee (N.L.)	OF-DH	124	487	81	144	30	2	28	95	58	120	6	12	0-0	.296	.375	.538	.913	0	1.000
2004—	Milwaukee (N.L.)	OF	157	617	88	163	36	6	27	93	46	152	12	19	3-1	.264	.325	.473	.798	1	.996
2005—	Milwaukee (N.L.)	OF-DH	148	538	87	157	42	1	25	86	56	138	• 19	13	0-0	.292	.375	.513	.888	5	.984
2006—	Milwaukee (N.L.)	OF	147	484	62	131	26	1	17	70	56	129	11	9	4-1	.271	.357	.434	.791	6	.977
	Major League totals (9 years)		1102	3987	616	1114	263	20	191	640	362	1002	86	98	29-11	.279	.350	.499	.849	34	.984

2006 LEFTY-RIGHTY SPLITS

vs.	Avg.	AB	H	2B	3B	HR	RBI	BB	SO	OBP	Slg.	vs.	Avg.	AB	H	2B	3B	HR	RBI	BB	SO	OBP	Slg.
L	.133	98	13	2	0	2	7	12	43	.265	.214	R	.306	386	118	24	1	15	63	44	86	.381	.490

JENKS, BOBBY — P

PERSONAL: Born March 14, 1981, in Mission Hills, Calif. ... 6-3/270. ... Throws right, bats right. ... Full name: Robert Scott Jenks. ... High school: Inglemoor (Bathell, Wash.). **TRANSACTIONS/CAREER NOTES:** Selected by Anaheim Angels organization in fifth round of free-agent draft (June 5, 2000). ... Claimed on waivers by Chicago White Sox (December 17, 2004).

CAREER HITTING: 0-for-0 (.000), 0 R, 0 2B, 0 3B, 0 HR, 0 RBI.

Year	Team (League)	W	L	Pct.	ERA	WHIP	G	GS	CG	ShO	Hld.	Sv.-Opp.	IP	H	R	ER	HR	BB-IBB	SO	Avg.
2000—	Butte (Pion.)	1	7	.125	7.86	1.99	14	12	0	0	...	0-...	52.2	61	57	46	2	44-0	42	.290
2001—	Cedar Rap. (Midw.) ...	3	7	.300	5.27	1.56	21	21	0	0	...	0-...	99.0	90	74	58	10	64-0	98	.245
	— Arkansas (Texas)	1	0	1.000	3.60	1.30	2	2	0	0	...	0-...	10.0	8	5	4	0	5-0	10	.200
2002—	Arkansas (Texas)	3	6	.333	4.66	1.60	10	10	1	0	...	0-...	58.0	49	34	30	2	44-0	58	.234
	— Rancho Cuca. (Calif.)	3	5	.375	4.82	1.47	11	10	1	1	...	0-:..	65.1	50	42	35	4	46-0	64	.212

Year Team (League)	W	L	Pct.	ERA	WHIP	G	GS	CG	ShO	Hld.	Sv.-Opp.	IP	H	R	ER	HR	BB-IBB	SO	Avg.
2003—Arkansas (Texas)	7	2	.778	2.17	1.29	16	16	0	0	...	0-...	83.0	56	23	20	2	51-0	103	.191
—Ariz. Angels (Ariz.)	0	0	...	0.00	0.50	1	1	0	0	...	0-...	4.0	2	0	0	0	0-0	5	.154
2004—Salt Lake (PCL)	0	1	.000	8.76	2.03	3	3	0	0	...	0-...	12.1	19	15	12	1	6-0	13	.358
—Ariz. Angels (Ariz.)	0	0	...	8.10	1.50	1	1	0	0	...	0-...	3.1	2	3	3	0	3-0	5	.182
—Rancho Cuca. (Calif.)	0	1	.000	19.64	3.27	1	1	0	0	...	0-...	3.2	5	8	8	0	7-0	3	.385
2005—Birmingham (Sou.)	1	2	.333	2.85	1.32	35	0	0	0	1	19-21	41.0	34	17	13	1	20-1	48	.224
—Chicago (A.L.)	1	1	.500	2.75	1.25	32	0	0	0	3	6-8	39.1	34	15	12	3	15-3	50	.225
2006—Chicago (A.L.)	3	4	.429	4.00	1.39	67	0	0	0	0	41-45	69.2	66	32	31	5	31-10	80	.253
Major League totals (2 years)	4	5	.444	3.55	1.34	99	0	0	0	3	47-53	109.0	100	47	43	8	46-13	130	.243

DIVISION SERIES RECORD

Year Team (League)	W	L	Pct.	ERA	WHIP	G	GS	CG	ShO	Hld.	Sv.-Opp.	IP	H	R	ER	HR	BB-IBB	SO	Avg.
2005—Chicago (A.L.)	0	0	...	0.00	0.67	2	0	0	0	...	2-2	3.0	1	0	0	0	1-0	1	.100

WORLD SERIES RECORD

Year Team (League)	W	L	Pct.	ERA	WHIP	G	GS	CG	ShO	Hld.	Sv.-Opp.	IP	H	R	ER	HR	BB-IBB	SO	Avg.
2005—Chicago (A.L.)	0	0	...	3.60	1.00	4	0	0	0	0	2-3	5.0	3	2	2	0	2-0	7	.176

2006 LEFTY-RIGHTY SPLITS

vs.	Avg.	AB	H	2B	3B	HR	RBI	BB	SO	OBP	Slg.	vs.	Avg.	AB	H	2B	3B	HR	RBI	BB	SO	OBP	Slg.
L	.227	97	22	4	0	0	9	14	26	.319	.268	R	.268	164	44	10	0	5	23	17	54	.344	.421

JENNINGS, JASON — P

PERSONAL: Born July 17, 1978, in Dallas, Texas. ... 6-2/245. ... Throws right, bats left. ... Full name: Jason Ryan Jennings. ... High school: Dr. Ralph H. Poteet (Mesquite, Texas). ... College: Baylor. **TRANSACTIONS/CAREER NOTES:** Selected by Arizona Diamondbacks organization in 54th round of 1996 free-agent draft; did not sign. ... Selected by Colorado Rockies organization in first round (16th pick overall) of 1999 free-agent draft. ... On disabled list (July 21, 2005-remainder of season). **HONORS:** Named N.L. Rookie Pitcher of the Year by THE SPORTING NEWS (2002). ... Named N.L. Rookie of the Year by Baseball Writers' Association of America (2002). **STATISTICAL NOTES:** Pitched shutout in first major league game (August 23, 2001). **MISCELLANEOUS NOTES:** Singled in only appearance as pinch hitter (2003). ... Singled twice in four appearances as pinch hitter (2005). ... Made outs in both appearances as pinch hitter (2006).
CAREER HITTING: 66-for-302 (.219), 17 R, 14 2B, 0 3B, 2 HR, 25 RBI.

Year Team (League)	W	L	Pct.	ERA	WHIP	G	GS	CG	ShO	Hld.	Sv.-Opp.	IP	H	R	ER	HR	BB-IBB	SO	Avg.
1999—Portland (N'west)	1	0	1.000	1.00	0.78	2	2	0	0	...	0-...	9.0	5	1	1	0	2-0	11	.161
—Asheville (S. Atl.)	2	2	.500	3.70	1.08	12	12	0	0	...	0-...	58.1	55	27	24	3	8-0	69	.247
2000—Salem (Carol.)	7	10	.412	3.47	1.18	22	22	3	1	...	0-...	150.1	136	66	58	6	42-0	133	.234
—Carolina (Southern)	1	3	.250	3.44	1.17	6	6	0	0	...	0-...	36.2	32	19	14	4	11-0	33	.234
2001—Carolina (Southern)	2	0	1.000	2.88	1.32	4	4	0	0	...	0-...	25.0	25	9	8	1	8-0	24	.258
—Colo. Springs (PCL)	7	8	.467	4.72	1.41	22	22	4	0	...	0-...	131.2	145	80	69	9	41-0	110	.281
—Colorado (N.L.)	4	1	.800	4.58	1.55	7	7	1	1	0	0-0	39.1	42	21	20	2	19-0	26	.276
2002—Colorado (N.L.)	16	8	.667	4.52	1.46	32	32	0	0	0	0-0	185.1	201	102	93	26	70-2	127	.280
2003—Colorado (N.L.)	12	13	.480	5.11	1.65	32	32	1	0	0	0-0	181.1	212	115	103	20	88-7	119	.299
2004—Colorado (N.L.)	11	12	.478	5.51	1.70	33	33	0	0	0	0-0	201.0	*241	125	123	27	101-14	133	.299
2005—Colorado (N.L.)	6	9	.400	5.02	1.57	20	20	1	0	0	0-0	122.0	130	73	68	11	62-4	75	.274
2006—Colorado (N.L.)	9	13	.409	3.78	1.37	32	32	3	2	0	0-0	212.0	206	94	89	17	85-7	142	.258
Major League totals (6 years)	58	56	.509	4.74	1.55	156	156	6	3	0	0-0	941.0	1032	530	496	103	425-34	622	.282

2006 LEFTY-RIGHTY SPLITS

vs.	Avg.	AB	H	2B	3B	HR	RBI	BB	SO	OBP	Slg.	vs.	Avg.	AB	H	2B	3B	HR	RBI	BB	SO	OBP	Slg.
L	.254	378	96	18	7	6	32	62	66	.356	.386	R	.261	422	110	18	1	11	53	23	76	.302	.386

JETER, DEREK — SS

PERSONAL: Born June 26, 1974, in Pequannock, N.J. ... 6-3/195. ... Bats right, throws right. ... Full name: Derek Sanderson Jeter. ... Name pronounced: JEE-ter. ... High school: Central (Kalamazoo, Mich.). **TRANSACTIONS/CAREER NOTES:** Selected by New York Yankees organization in first round (sixth pick overall) of 1992 free-agent draft. ... On disabled list (June 3-19, 1998); included rehabilitation assignment to Columbus. ... On disabled list (May 12-27, 2000); included rehabilitation assignment to Tampa. ... On disabled list (March 23-April 7, 2001). ... On disabled list (April 1-May 13, 2003); included rehabilitation assignment to Trenton. **HONORS:** Named Minor League Player of the Year by THE SPORTING NEWS (1994). ... Named A.L. Rookie Player of the Year by THE SPORTING NEWS (1996). ... Named A.L. Rookie of the Year by Baseball Writers' Association of America (1996). ... Won A.L. Gold Glove at shortstop (2004-06). ... Named shortstop on SPORTING NEWS A.L. All-Star team (2006). ... Named shortstop on A.L. Silver Slugger team (2006). **STATISTICAL NOTES:** Career major league grand slams: 1.
2006 GAMES PLAYED BY POSITION (MLB): SS—150, DH—5.

Year Team (League)	Pos.	G	AB	R	H	2B	3B	HR	RBI	BB	SO	HBP	GDP	SB-CS	Avg.	OBP	SLG	OPS	E	Avg.
1992—GC Yankees (GCL)	SS	47	173	19	35	10	0	3	25	19	36	5	4	2-2	.202	.296	.312	.609	12	.943
—Greensboro (S. Atl.)	SS	11	37	4	9	0	0	1	4	7	16	1	0	0-1	.243	.378	.324	.702	9	.813
1993—Greensboro (S. Atl.)	SS	128	515	85	152	14	11	5	71	56	95	11	9	18-9	.295	.374	.394	.768	56	.889
1994—Tampa (Fla. St.)	SS	69	292	61	96	13	8	0	39	23	30	3	4	28-2	.329	.380	.428	.808	12	.961
—Alb./Colon. (East.)	SS	34	122	17	46	7	2	2	13	15	16	1	3	12-2	.377	.446	.516	.962	6	.961
—Columbus (Int'l)	SS	35	126	25	44	7	1	3	16	20	15	1	6	10-4	.349	.439	.492	.931	7	.955
1995—Columbus (Int'l)	SS	123	486	96	154	27	9	2	45	61	56	4	9	20-12	.317	.394	.422	.816	29	.953
—New York (A.L.)	SS	15	48	5	12	4	1	0	7	3	11	0	0	0-0	.250	.294	.375	.669	2	.962
1996—New York (A.L.)	SS	157	582	104	183	25	6	10	78	48	102	9	13	14-7	.314	.370	.430	.800	22	.969
1997—New York (A.L.)	SS	159	654	116	190	31	7	10	70	74	125	10	14	23-12	.291	.370	.405	.775	18	.975
1998—New York (A.L.)	SS	149	626	*127	203	25	8	19	84	57	119	5	14	30-6	.324	.384	.481	.864	9	.986
—Columbus (Int'l)	SS	1	5	2	2	0	0	0	0	0	2	0	0	0-0	.400	.400	.800	1.200	1	.875
1999—New York (A.L.)	SS	158	627	134	*219	37	9	24	102	91	116	12	14	19-8	.349	.438	.552	.989	14	.978
2000—New York (A.L.)	SS	148	593	119	201	31	4	15	73	68	99	12	14	22-4	.339	.416	.481	.896	24	.961
—Tampa (Fla. St.)	SS	1	3	2	2	1	0	0	0	0	0	0	0	0-0	.667	.667	1.000	1.667	0	1.000
2001—New York (A.L.)	SS	150	614	110	191	35	3	21	74	56	99	10	14	27-3	.311	.377	.480	.858	15	.974
2002—New York (A.L.)	SS-DH	157	644	124	191	26	0	18	75	73	114	7	14	32-3	.297	.373	.421	.794	14	.977
2003—Trenton (East.)	SS	5	18	2	8	1	1	0	5	3	4	1	0	0-0	.444	.545	.611	1.157	1	.957
—New York (A.L.)	SS	119	482	87	156	25	3	10	52	43	88	13	10	11-5	.324	.393	.450	.844	14	.968
2004—New York (A.L.)	SS	154	643	111	188	44	1	23	78	46	99	14	14	23-4	.292	.352	.471	.823	13	.981
2005—New York (A.L.)	SS-DH	159	654	122	202	25	5	19	70	77	117	11	15	14-5	.309	.389	.450	.839	15	.979
2006—New York (A.L.)	SS-DH	154	623	118	214	39	3	14	97	69	102	12	15	34-5	.343	.417	.483	.900	15	.975
Major League totals (12 years)		1679	6790	1277	2150	347	50	183	860	705	1191	115	150	249-62	.317	.388	.463	.852	175	.975

J

DIVISION SERIES RECORD

Year Team (League)	Pos.	G	AB	R	H	2B	3B	HR	RBI	BB	SO	HBP	GDP	SB-CS	Avg.	OBP	SLG	OPS	E	Avg.
1996— New York (A.L.)	SS	4	17	2	7	1	0	0	1	0	2	0	0	0-0	.412	.412	.471	.882	1	.947
1997— New York (A.L.)	SS	5	21	6	7	1	0	2	2	3	5	0	0	1-0	.333	.417	.667	1.083	0	1.000
1998— New York (A.L.)	SS	3	9	0	1	0	0	0	0	2	2	0	0	0-0	.111	.273	.111	.384	0	1.000
1999— New York (A.L.)	SS	3	11	3	5	1	1	0	0	2	3	0	0	0-0	.455	.538	.727	1.266	0	1.000
2000— New York (A.L.)	SS	5	19	1	4	0	0	0	2	2	3	1	0	0-1	.211	.318	.211	.529	0	1.000
2001— New York (A.L.)	SS	5	18	2	8	1	0	0	1	1	0	1	0	0-1	.444	.476	.500	.976	1	1.000
2002— New York (A.L.)	SS	4	16	6	8	0	0	1	2	3	2	3	0	1-0	.500	.526	.875	1.401	1	.944
2003— New York (A.L.)	SS	4	14	2	6	0	0	1	1	4	2	0	0	1-0	.429	.556	.643	1.198	1	.923
2004— New York (A.L.)	SS	4	19	3	6	1	0	1	4	1	4	0	1	1-0	.316	.350	.526	.876	1	.960
2005— New York (A.L.)	SS	5	21	4	7	0	0	2	5	1	5	0	0	1-0	.333	.348	.619	.967	0	1.000
2006— New York (A.L.)	SS	4	16	4	8	4	0	1	1	1	2	0	1	0-1	.500	.529	.938	1.467	1	.947
Division series totals (11 years)		46	181	33	67	9	1	9	20	19	31	2	2	4-3	.370	.429	.580	1.009	5	.975

CHAMPIONSHIP SERIES RECORD

Year Team (League)	Pos.	G	AB	R	H	2B	3B	HR	RBI	BB	SO	HBP	GDP	SB-CS	Avg.	OBP	SLG	OPS	E	Avg.
1996— New York (A.L.)	SS	5	24	5	10	2	0	1	1	0	5	0	0	2-0	.417	.417	.625	1.042	0	1.000
1998— New York (A.L.)	SS	6	25	3	5	1	1	0	2	2	5	0	0	3-0	.200	.259	.320	.579	0	1.000
1999— New York (A.L.)	SS	5	20	3	7	0	1	0	1	3	2	3	0	1-0	.350	.409	.550	.959	2	.909
2000— New York (A.L.)	SS	6	22	6	7	0	0	2	5	4	7	0	0	1-0	.318	.464	.591	1.055	0	1.000
2001— New York (A.L.)	SS	5	17	0	2	1	0	0	2	2	2	0	0	1-0	.118	.200	.118	.318	0	1.000
2003— New York (A.L.)	SS	7	30	3	7	2	0	1	2	2	4	0	0	1-0	.233	.281	.400	.681	1	.956
2004— New York (A.L.)	SS	7	30	5	6	1	0	0	5	6	2	0	1	0-0	.200	.333	.233	.567	2	.956
Champ. series totals (7 years)		41	168	25	44	7	1	5	20	20	28	0	1	8-0	.262	.339	.405	.743	4	.979

WORLD SERIES RECORD

Year Team (League)	Pos.	G	AB	R	H	2B	3B	HR	RBI	BB	SO	HBP	GDP	SB-CS	Avg.	OBP	SLG	OPS	E	Avg.
1996— New York (A.L.)	SS	6	20	5	5	0	0	0	1	4	6	1	1	1-0	.250	.400	.250	.650	0	.949
1998— New York (A.L.)	SS	4	17	4	6	0	0	0	1	3	3	0	1	0-0	.353	.450	.353	.803	0	1.000
1999— New York (A.L.)	SS	4	17	4	6	1	0	0	3	1	3	0	0	3-1	.353	.389	.412	.801	0	1.000
2000— New York (A.L.)	SS	5	22	6	9	2	1	2	2	3	8	0	0	0-0	.409	.480	.864	1.344	0	1.000
2001— New York (A.L.)	SS	7	27	3	4	0	0	1	1	0	6	1	1	0-0	.148	.179	.259	.438	1	1.000
2003— New York (A.L.)	SS	6	26	5	9	3	0	0	2	1	7	1	2	0-0	.346	.393	.462	.854	1	.969
World series totals (6 years)		32	129	27	39	6	1	3	8	12	33	3	4	4-1	.302	.375	.434	.809	3	.980

ALL-STAR GAME RECORD

	G	AB	R	H	2B	3B	HR	RBI	BB	SO	HBP	GDP	SB-CS	Avg.	OBP	SLG	OPS	E	Avg.
All-Star Game totals (7 years)	7	13	3	7	1	0	1	3	0	5	0		0-0	.538	.538	.846	1.385	0	1.000

2006 LEFTY-RIGHTY SPLITS

vs.	Avg.	AB	H	2B	3B	HR	RBI	BB	SO	OBP	Slg.	vs.	Avg.	AB	H	2B	3B	HR	RBI	BB	SO	OBP	Slg.
L	.390	159	62	12	1	4	22	18	25	.458	.553	R	.328	464	152	27	2	10	75	51	77	.403	.459

JIMENEZ, CESAR   P

PERSONAL: Born November 12, 1984, in Cunana, Venezuela. ... 5-11/180. ... Throws left, bats left. ... Full name: Cesar Enrique Jimenez. **TRANSACTIONS/CAREER NOTES:** Signed as a non-drafted free agent by Seattle Mariners organization (July 2, 2001).
CAREER HITTING: 0-for-0 (.000), 0 R, 0 2B, 0 3B, 0 HR, 0 RBI.

Year Team (League)	W	L	Pct.	ERA	WHIP	G	GS	CG	ShO	Hld.	Sv.-Opp.	IP	H	R	ER	HR	BB-IBB	SO	Avg.
2002—Aguirre (VSL)	7	1	.875	0.83	0.75	11	11	2	1		0-...	65.1	37	6	6	0	12-0	67	.167
— Ariz. Mariners (Ariz.)	0	0	...	3.38	1.13	1	0	0	0		0-...	2.2	3	2	1	0	0-0	3	.300
— Everett (N'west)	2	1	.667	2.70	0.85	8	0	0	0		1-...	20.0	12	7	6	2	5-0	25	.174
2003—Wisconsin (Midw.)	8	11	.421	2.94	1.43	28	20	0	0		0-...	125.2	134	61	41	7	46-2	76	.273
2004—Inland Empire (Calif.)	6	7	.462	2.29	1.15	43	2	0	0	6	6-...	86.1	80	28	22	3	19-0	81	.241
2005—Tacoma (PCL)	0	0	...	9.39	1.30	4	0	0	0	0	0-0	7.2	9	8	8	5	1-0	9	.290
— San Antonio (Texas)	3	5	.375	2.62	1.28	45	1	0	0	10	4-7	68.2	64	21	20	3	24-0	54	.250
2006—Tacoma (PCL)	5	10	.333	4.36	1.51	24	19	1	1	1	3-3	107.1	107	54	52	8	55-1	66	.266
— San Antonio (Texas)	0	2	.000	2.76	0.92	3	3	0	0	0	0-0	16.1	10	5	5	0	5-0	10	.179
— Seattle (A.L.)	0	0	...	14.73	2.32	4	1	0	0	0	0-0	7.1	13	12	12	4	4-0	3	.382
Major League totals (1 year)	0	0	...	14.73	2.32	4	1	0	0	0	0-0	7.1	13	12	12	4	4-0	3	.382

2006 LEFTY-RIGHTY SPLITS

vs.	Avg.	AB	H	2B	3B	HR	RBI	BB	SO	OBP	Slg.	vs.	Avg.	AB	H	2B	3B	HR	RBI	BB	SO	OBP	Slg.
L	.167	6	1	0	0	1	3	2	1	.375	.667	R	.429	28	12	4	0	3	10	2	2	.467	.893

JIMENEZ, D'ANGELO   2B

PERSONAL: Born December 21, 1977, in Santo Domingo, Dominican Republic. ... 6-0/195. ... Bats both, throws right. ... Name pronounced: he-MEN-ez.
TRANSACTIONS/CAREER NOTES: Signed as a non-drafted free agent by New York Yankees organization (August 1, 1994). ... On disabled list (March 23-August 24, 2000); included rehabilitation assignments to GCL Yankees, Tampa and Columbus. ... Traded by Yankees to San Diego Padres for P Jay Witasick (June 23, 2001). ... Traded by Padres to Chicago White Sox for OF Alex Fernandez and C Humberto Quintero (July 12, 2002). ... Traded by White Sox to Cincinnati Reds for P Scott Dunn (July 6, 2003). ... Signed as a free agent by Texas Rangers organization (December 16, 2005). ... Released by Rangers (June 14, 2006). ... Signed by Oakland Athletics organization (June 23, 2006). ... Released by Athletics (October 23, 2006). **STATISTICAL NOTES:** Career major league pitching: 0-0, 0.00 ERA, 1 G, 1.1 IP, 0 H, 0 R, 0 ER, 0 BB, 0 SO.
2006 GAMES PLAYED BY POSITION (MLB): 2B—18, 3B—5, SS—3.

Year Team (League)	Pos.	G	AB	R	H	2B	3B	HR	RBI	BB	SO	HBP	GDP	SB-CS	Avg.	OBP	SLG	OPS	E	Avg.
1995— GC Yankees (GCL)	SS	57	214	41	60	14	8	2	28	23	31	1	4	6-3	.280	.347	.449	.796	21	.927
1996— Greensboro (S. Atl.)	SS	138	537	68	131	25	5	6	48	56	113	3	7	15-17	.244	.317	.343	.660	50	.922
1997— Tampa (Fla. St.)	SS	94	352	52	99	14	6	6	48	50	50	2	3	8-14	.281	.368	.406	.775	21	.953
— Columbus (Int'l)	SS	2	7	1	1	0	0	0	1	0	1	0	1	0-0	.143	.125	.143	.268	2	.833
1998— Norwich (East.)	SS	40	152	21	41	6	2	2	21	25	26	2	3	5-5	.270	.378	.375	.753	12	.938
— Columbus (Int'l)	2B-SS	91	344	55	88	19	4	8	51	46	67	1	7	6-6	.256	.341	.404	.745	26	.946
1999— Columbus (Int'l)	SS-3B-2B	126	526	97	172	32	5	15	88	59	75	1	8	26-14	.327	.392	.492	.884	26	.957
— New York (A.L.)	3B-2B	7	20	3	8	2	0	0	4	3	4	0	0	0-0	.400	.478	.500	.978	0	1.000
2000— GC Yankees (GCL)	2B-SS	4	10	2	1	0	0	0	0	5	1	0	0	0-0	.100	.400	.100	.500	2	.900
— Tampa (Fla. St.)	SS-2B	12	41	8	8	1	1	1	2	8	7	0	1	0-0	.195	.320	.341	.661	7	.875
— Columbus (Int'l)	2B-3B-SS	21	73	11	17	3	1	1	5	6	12	1	2	2-0	.233	.309	.342	.651	4	.944
2001— Columbus (Int'l)	2B-SS-3B	56	214	33	56	11	1	5	19	24	31	1	0	5-6	.262	.333	.393	.726	7	.965

Year	Team (League)	Pos.	G	AB	R	H	2B	3B	HR	RBI	BB	SO	HBP	GDP	SB-CS	Avg.	OBP	SLG	OPS	E	Avg.
—San Diego (N.L.)	SS	86	308	45	85	19	0	3	33	39	68	0	9	2-3	.276	.355	.367	.722	21	.948
2002—San Diego (N.L.)	2B-3B-P	87	321	39	77	11	4	3	33	34	63	0	10	4-2	.240	.311	.327	.638	12	.968
—Charlotte (Int'l)	SS	42	157	24	44	11	1	6	18	24	14	0	2	6-2	.280	.372	.478	.849	6	.966
—Chicago (A.L.)	2B-SS-3B	27	108	22	31	4	3	1	11	16	10	1	1	2-1	.287	.384	.407	.791	2	.985
2003—Chicago (A.L.)	2B-3B	73	271	35	69	11	5	7	26	32	46	0	3	4-3	.255	.332	.410	.742	9	.970
—Cincinnati (N.L.)	2B-3B	73	290	34	84	13	2	7	31	34	43	2	4	7-4	.290	.365	.421	.785	4	.990
2004—Cincinnati (N.L.)	2B-SS	152	563	76	152	28	3	12	67	82	99	2	15	13-7	.270	.364	.394	.758	7	.990
2005—Cincinnati (N.L.)	2B	35	105	14	24	7	0	0	5	14	23	0	1	2-1	.229	.319	.295	.615	2	.983
—Chattanooga (Sou.)	SS-DH-2B	90	327	55	91	20	0	9	45	69	34	0	4	16-4	.278	.401	.422	.823	8	.978
2006—Sacramento (PCL)	2B	35	125	30	38	8	1	4	23	24	14	0	3	2-4	.304	.413	.480	.893	6	.957
—Texas (A.L.)	2B-3B	20	57	7	12	3	0	1	8	10	6	0	2	0-0	.211	.328	.316	.644	4	.944
—Oakland (A.L.)	3B-SS-2B	8	14	1	1	0	0	0	0	6	7	0	1	0-0	.071	.350	.071	.421	1	.938
American League totals (4 years)		135	470	68	121	20	8	9	49	67	73	1	7	6-4	.257	.351	.391	.742	16	.970
National League totals (5 years)		433	1587	208	422	78	9	25	169	203	296	4	39	28-17	.266	.349	.374	.723	46	.977
Major League totals (7 years)		568	2057	276	543	98	17	34	218	270	369	5	46	34-21	.264	.349	.378	.727	62	.975

DIVISION SERIES RECORD

Year	Team (League)	Pos.	G	AB	R	H	2B	3B	HR	RBI	BB	SO	HBP	GDP	SB-CS	Avg.	OBP	SLG	OPS	E	Avg.
2006—Oakland (A.L.)	2B	2	4	0	0	0	0	0	0	0	1	0	0	0-0	.000	.000	.000	.000	0	1.000

CHAMPIONSHIP SERIES RECORD

Year	Team (League)	Pos.	G	AB	R	H	2B	3B	HR	RBI	BB	SO	HBP	GDP	SB-CS	Avg.	OBP	SLG	OPS	E	Avg.
2006—Oakland (A.L.)	2B	4	12	0	2	0	0	0	0	0	1	0	0	0-0	.167	.167	.167	.333	2	.917

2006 LEFTY-RIGHTY SPLITS

vs.	Avg.	AB	H	2B	3B	HR	RBI	BB	SO	OBP	Slg.	vs.	Avg.	AB	H	2B	3B	HR	RBI	BB	SO	OBP	Slg.
L	.188	16	3	1	0	0	4	3	1	.316	.250	R	.182	55	10	2	0	1	4	13	12	.338	.273

JIMENEZ, UBALDO — P

PERSONAL: Born January 22, 1984, in Nagua, Dominican Republic. ... 6-4/200. ... Throws right, bats right. ... Full name: Ubaldo Jimenez. **TRANSACTIONS/CAREER NOTES:** Signed as a non-drafted free agent by Colorado Rockies organization (April 25, 2001).
CAREER HITTING: 1-for-3 (.333), 1 R, 0 2B, 0 3B, 0 HR, 0 RBI.

Year	Team (League)	W	L	Pct.	ERA	WHIP	G	GS	CG	ShO	Hld.	Sv.-Opp.	IP	H	R	ER	HR	BB-IBB	SO	Avg.
2001—Dominican Rockies (DSL)	2	5	.286	4.88	1.77	13	13	0	0	...	0-...	48.0	41	36	26	1	44-0	36	.225
2002—Casper (Pion.)	3	5	.375	6.53	1.63	14	14	0	0	...	0-...	62.0	72	46	45	6	29-1	65	.288
—Dominican Rockies (DSL)	2	0	1.000	0.00	0.87	3	3	0	0	...	0-...	18.1	10	1	0	0	6-0	25	.152
2003—Asheville (S. Atl.)	10	6	.625	3.46	1.28	27	27	0	0	...	0-...	153.2	129	67	59	11	67-0	138	.230
—Visalia (Calif.)	1	0	1.000	0.00	0.80	1	0	0	0	...	0-...	5.0	3	0	0	0	1-0	7	.176
2004—Visalia (Calif.)	4	1	.800	2.23	0.92	9	9	1	0	...	0-...	44.1	29	15	11	1	12-0	61	.184
2005—Modesto (California)	5	3	.625	3.98	1.40	14	14	0	0	...	0-0	72.1	61	35	32	5	40-0	78	.232
—Tulsa (Texas)	2	5	.286	5.43	1.41	12	11	0	0	...	0-0	63.0	58	40	38	12	31-0	53	.243
2006—Colo. Springs (PCL)	5	2	.714	5.06	1.49	13	13	0	0	...	0-0	78.1	74	49	44	7	43-1	64	.252
—Tulsa (Texas)	9	2	.818	2.45	1.21	13	13	1	1	0	0-0	73.1	49	21	20	2	40-1	86	.194
—Colorado (N.L.)	0	0	...	3.52	1.04	2	1	0	0	0	0-0	7.2	5	4	3	1	3-0	3	.185
Major League totals (1 year)	0	0	...	3.52	1.04	2	1	0	0	0	0-0	7.2	5	4	3	1	3-0	3	.185

2006 LEFTY-RIGHTY SPLITS

vs.	Avg.	AB	H	2B	3B	HR	RBI	BB	SO	OBP	Slg.	vs.	Avg.	AB	H	2B	3B	HR	RBI	BB	SO	OBP	Slg.
L	.182	11	2	0	0	0	0	1	1	.250	.182	R	.188	16	3	0	0	1	2	2	2	.278	.375

JIMERSON, CHARLTON — OF

PERSONAL: Born September 22, 1979, in San Leandro, Calif. ... 6-3/210. ... Bats right, throws right. ... Full name: Charlton Maxwell Jimerson. ... High school: Mt. Eden (Calif.). ... College: Miami. **TRANSACTIONS/CAREER NOTES:** Selected by Houston Astros organization in fifth round of 2001 free-agent draft. **STATISTICAL NOTES:** Hit home run in first major league at-bat (September 4, 2006).
2006 GAMES PLAYED BY POSITION (MLB): OF—9.

Year	Team (League)	Pos.	G	AB	R	H	2B	3B	HR	RBI	BB	SO	HBP	GDP	SB-CS	Avg.	OBP	SLG	OPS	E	Avg.
2001—Pittsfield (NYP)	OF	51	197	35	46	12	1	9	31	18	79	2	4	15-4	.234	.304	.442	.746	7	.903
2002—Lexington (S. Atl.)	OF	125	439	65	100	22	4	14	57	36	168	7	7	34-9	.228	.295	.392	.687	8	.970
2003—Salem (Carol.)	OF	97	336	53	89	19	3	12	55	25	109	2	4	27-4	.265	.317	.446	.763	3	.985
2004—Round Rock (Texas)	OF	131	488	78	116	22	5	18	53	31	163	5	8	39-6	.238	.290	.414	.704	6	.857
2005—Corpus Christi (Texas)	OF-DH	115	425	67	110	24	3	16	44	29	145	8	0	27-10	.259	.317	.442	.759	14	.971
—Round Rock (PCL)	OF	7	23	1	7	1	0	0	1	0	7	0	0	3-0	.304	.292	.348	.639	2	.950
—Houston (N.L.)	OF	1	0	0	0	0	0	0	0	0	0	0	0	0-0	...	...	...	...	0	...
2006—Round Rock (PCL)		123	470	56	116	27	6	18	45	23	183	4	2	28-8	.247	.287	.445	.732	4	.986
—Houston (N.L.)	OF	17	6	2	2	0	0	1	1	0	3	0	0	2-0	.333	.333	.833	1.167	0	1.000
Major League totals (2 years)		18	6	2	2	0	0	1	1	0	3	0	0	2-0	.333	.333	.833	1.167	0	1.000

2006 LEFTY-RIGHTY SPLITS

vs.	Avg.	AB	H	2B	3B	HR	RBI	BB	SO	OBP	Slg.	vs.	Avg.	AB	H	2B	3B	HR	RBI	BB	SO	OBP	Slg.
L	.667	3	2	0	0	1	0	1		.667	1.667	R	.000	3	0	0	0	0	0	0	2	.000	.000

JOHJIMA, KENJI — C

PERSONAL: Born June 8, 1976, in Nagasaki, Japan. ... 6-0/200. ... Bats right, throws right. ... Full name: Kenji Johjima. **TRANSACTIONS/CAREER NOTES:** Signed as a free agent by Seattle Mariners (November 21, 2005).
2006 GAMES PLAYED BY POSITION (MLB): C—144.

Year	Team (League)	Pos.	G	AB	R	H	2B	3B	HR	RBI	BB	SO	HBP	GDP	SB-CS	Avg.	OBP	SLG	OPS	E	Avg.
1995—Fukuoka (Jp. Pac.)	C	12	12	2	2	0	0	0	1	1	4	0	...	0-0	.167	.231	.167	.397	1	.955
1996—Fukuoka (Jp. Pac.)	C	17	58	5	14	2	0	4	9	3	9	1	...	1-0	.241	.290	.483	.773	0	1.000
1997—Fukuoka (Jp. Pac.)	C-1B	120	432	49	133	24	2	15	68	22	62	5	...	6-2	.308	.343	.477	.820	8	.991
1998—Fukuoka (Jp. Pac.)	C	122	395	53	99	19	0	16	58	27	67	8	...	5-2	.251	.309	.420	.729	8	...
1999—Fukuoka (Jp. Pac.)	C	135	493	65	151	33	1	17	77	31	61	8	...	6-2	.306	.356	.481	.837	9	...
2000—Fukuoka (Jp. Pac.)	C	84	303	38	94	22	2	9	50	27	48	6	...	10-2	.310	.377	.485	.862	3	...
2001—Fukuoka (Jp. Pac.)	C	140	534	63	138	18	0	31	95	31	55	6	...	9-4	.258	.305	.466	.772	6	...

Year Team (League)	Pos.	G	AB	R	H	2B	3B	HR	RBI	BB	SO	HBP	GDP	SB-CS	Avg.	OBP	SLG	OPS	E	Avg.
2002—Fukuoka (Jp. Pac.)	C	115	416	60	122	18	0	25	74	30	41	8	...	8-7	.293	.348	.517	.865	3	...
2003—Fukuoka (Jp. Pac.)	C	140	551	101	182	39	2	34	119	53	50	15	...	9-4	.330	.399	.593	.993	7	...
2004—Fukuoka (Jp. Pac.)	C	116	426	91	144	25	1	36	91	49	45	22	...	6-5	.338	.432	.655	1.087	4	...
2005—Fukuoka (Jp. Pac.)	C	116	411	70	127	22	4	24	57	33	32	16	...	3-4	.309	.381	.557	.938	3	...
2006—Seattle (A.L.)	C	144	506	61	147	25	1	18	76	20	46	13	15	3-1	.291	.332	.451	.783	7	.993
Major League totals (1 year)		144	506	61	147	25	1	18	76	20	46	13	15	3-1	.291	.332	.451	.783	7	.993

2006 LEFTY-RIGHTY SPLITS

vs.	Avg.	AB	H	2B	3B	HR	RBI	BB	SO	OBP	Slg.	vs.	Avg.	AB	H	2B	3B	HR	RBI	BB	SO	OBP	Slg.
L	.263	114	30	7	0	0	9	5	10	.315	.325	R	.298	392	117	18	1	18	67	15	36	.337	.487

JOHNSON, BEN — OF

PERSONAL: Born June 18, 1981, in Memphis, Tenn. ... 6-1/200. ... Bats right, throws right. ... Full name: Benjamin Joseph Johnson. ... High school: Germantown (Ten.).
TRANSACTIONS/CAREER NOTES: Selected by St. Louis Cardinals organization in fourth round of 1999 free-agent draft. ... Traded by Cardinals with RHP Heathcliff Slocumb to San Diego Padres for C Carlos Hernandez and IF Nate Tebbs (July 31, 2000). ... On disabled list (July 5-August 1, 2006); included rehabilitation assignment to Portland.
2006 GAMES PLAYED BY POSITION (MLB): OF—43.

Year Team (League)	Pos.	G	AB	R	H	2B	3B	HR	RBI	BB	SO	HBP	GDP	SB-CS	Avg.	OBP	SLG	OPS	E	Avg.
1999—Johnson City (App.)	OF	57	203	38	67	9	1	10	51	29	57	5	0	14-6	.330	.423	.532	.955	2	.978
2000—Peoria (Midw.)	OF	93	330	58	80	22	1	13	46	53	78	5	8	17-6	.242	.353	.433	.786	6	.962
—Fort Wayne (Midw.)	OF	29	109	11	21	6	2	3	13	7	25	3	5	0-3	.193	.261	.367	.628	0	1.000
2001—Lake Elsinore (Calif.)	OF	136	503	79	139	35	6	12	63	54	141	11	15	22-7	.276	.358	.441	.799	12	.948
2002—Mobile (Sou.)	OF	131	456	58	110	23	4	10	55	65	127	3	9	11-9	.241	.337	.375	.712	9	.965
2003—Mobile (Sou.)	OF	44	127	8	23	5	0	1	7	10	36	2	0	0-1	.181	.252	.244	.496	1	.984
—Lake Elsinore (Calif.)	OF	52	184	30	49	9	0	8	29	20	49	5	5	6-1	.266	.354	.446	.800	4	.969
2004—Mobile (Sou.)	OF	136	475	80	119	28	6	23	85	55	136	7	0	5-6	.251	.334	.480	.814	9	.775
2005—Portland (PCL)	OF	107	414	79	129	27	0	25	83	51	88	6	7	6-1	.312	.394	.558	.952	8	.981
2006—Portland (PCL)	OF	31	75	10	16	8	1	3	13	11	23	0	4	0-2	.213	.310	.467	.777	2	.962
—Portland (PCL)		51	198	35	52	11	1	7	22	23	55	3	3	7-1	.263	.344	.434	.778	2	.983
—San Diego (N.L.)	OF	58	120	19	30	5	2	4	12	14	36	1	3	3-0	.250	.333	.425	.758	0	1.000
Major League totals (2 years)		89	195	29	46	13	3	7	25	25	59	1	7	3-2	.236	.324	.441	.765	2	.986

DIVISION SERIES RECORD

Year Team (League)	Pos.	G	AB	R	H	2B	3B	HR	RBI	BB	SO	HBP	GDP	SB-CS	Avg.	OBP	SLG	OPS	E	Avg.
2005—San Diego (N.L.)	OF	2	2	0	0	0	0	0	0	0	2	0	0	0-0	.000	.000	.000	.000	0	...

2006 LEFTY-RIGHTY SPLITS

vs.	Avg.	AB	H	2B	3B	HR	RBI	BB	SO	OBP	Slg.	vs.	Avg.	AB	H	2B	3B	HR	RBI	BB	SO	OBP	Slg.
L	.275	51	14	2	1	2	5	8	13	.383	.471	R	.232	69	16	3	1	2	7	6	23	.293	.391

JOHNSON, DAN — 1B

PERSONAL: Born August 10, 1979, in Coon Rapids, Minn. ... 6-2/220. ... Bats left, throws right. ... Full name: Daniel Ryan Johnson. ...High school: Blaine (Minn.) ... College: Nebraska. **TRANSACTIONS/CAREER NOTES:** Selected by Oakland Athletics organization in seventh round of 2001 free-agent draft. **STATISTICAL NOTES:** Career major league grand slams: 2.
2006 GAMES PLAYED BY POSITION (MLB): 1B—85, DH—2.

Year Team (League)	Pos.	G	AB	R	H	2B	3B	HR	RBI	BB	SO	HBP	GDP	SB-CS	Avg.	OBP	SLG	OPS	E	Avg.
2001—Vancouver (N'west)	1B	69	247	36	70	15	2	11	41	27	63	2	6	0-0	.283	.354	.494	.848	12	.975
2002—Modesto (California)	1B	126	426	56	125	23	1	21	85	57	87	0	8	4-1	.293	.371	.500	.871	7	.990
2003—Midland (Texas)	1B-OF	139	538	90	156	26	4	27	114	68	82	2	14	7-4	.290	.365	.504	.869	8	.992
—Sacramento (PCL)	1B-OF	1	4	0	1	0	0	0	0	0	0	0	0	0-0	.250	.250	.500	.750	0	1.000
2004—Sacramento (PCL)	1B-OF	142	536	95	160	29	5	29	111	89	93	9	15	0-1	.299	.403	.534	.937	12	.993
2005—Sacramento (PCL) 1B-OF-DH		47	182	36	59	17	0	8	41	32	24	1	1	0-1	.324	.424	.549	.973	4	.990
—Oakland (A.L.)	1B-DH	109	375	54	103	21	0	15	58	50	52	1	11	0-1	.275	.355	.451	.806	6	.994
2006—Sacramento (PCL)		46	172	34	54	13	1	7	44	32	27	3	6	0-1	.314	.426	.523	.949	4	.989
—Oakland (A.L.)	1B-DH	91	286	30	67	13	1	9	37	40	45	0	6	0-0	.234	.323	.381	.704	4	.995
Major League totals (2 years)		200	661	84	170	34	1	24	95	90	97	1	17	0-1	.257	.341	.421	.762	10	.994

2006 LEFTY-RIGHTY SPLITS

vs.	Avg.	AB	H	2B	3B	HR	RBI	BB	SO	OBP	Slg.	vs.	Avg.	AB	H	2B	3B	HR	RBI	BB	SO	OBP	Slg.
L	.217	46	10	3	0	0	4	3	15	.260	.283	R	.238	240	57	10	1	9	33	37	30	.335	.400

JOHNSON, JASON — P

PERSONAL: Born October 27, 1973, in Santa Barbara, Calif. ... 6-6/217. ... Throws right, bats right. ... Full name: Jason Michael Johnson. ... High school: Conner (Hebron, Ky.). **TRANSACTIONS/CAREER NOTES:** Signed as a non-drafted free agent by Pittsburgh Pirates organization (July 21, 1992). ... Selected by Tampa Bay Devil Rays in first round (14th pick overall) of expansion draft (November 18, 1997). ... On disabled list (July 4, 1998-remainder of season). ... Traded by Devil Rays to Baltimore Orioles for OF Danny Clyburn and a player to be named (March 29, 1999); Devil Rays acquired SS Bolivar Voquez to complete deal (April 22, 1999). ... On disabled list (April 25-June 7 and July 23-August 9, 2002); included rehabilitation assignment to Bowie. ... Signed as a free agent by Detroit Tigers (December 30, 2003). ... Signed as a free agent by Cleveland Indians (January 3, 2004). ... Traded by Indians with cash to Boston Red Sox for a player to be named or cash (June 21, 2006). ... Released by Red Sox (August 28, 2006). ... Signed by Cincinnati Reds organization (August 30, 2006).
CAREER HITTING: 3-for-25 (.120), 2 R, 0 2B, 0 3B, 1 HR, 1 RBI.

Year Team (League)	W	L	Pct.	ERA	WHIP	G	GS	CG	ShO	Hld.	Sv.-Opp.	IP	H	R	ER	HR	BB-IBB	SO	Avg.
1992—GC Pirates (GCL)	2	0	1.000	3.68	1.64	5	0	0	0	...	0-...	7.1	6	3	3	0	6-0	3	.240
1993—GC Pirates (GCL) ....^	1	4	.200	2.33	1.15	9	9	0	0	...	0-...	54.0	48	22	14	0	14-0	39	.239
—Welland (NYP)	1	5	.167	4.63	1.20	6	6	1	0	...	0-...	35.0	33	24	18	0	9-0	19	.243
1994—Augusta (S. Atl.)	2	12	.143	4.03	1.47	20	19	1	0	...	0-...	102.2	119	67	46	5	32-0	69	.285
1995—Augusta (S. Atl.)	3	5	.375	4.36	1.38	11	11	1	0	...	0-...	53.2	57	32	26	2	17-0	42	.271
—Lynchburg (Caro.)	1	4	.200	4.91	1.42	10	10	0	0	...	0-...	55.0	58	37	30	9	20-0	41	.275
1996—Lynchburg (Caro.)	1	4	.200	6.50	1.53	15	5	0	0	...	0-...	44.1	56	37	32	6	12-0	27	.303
—Augusta (S. Atl.)	4	4	.500	3.11	1.27	14	14	1	1	...	0-...	84.0	82	40	29	8	28-3	36	.256
1997—Lynchburg (Caro.)	8	4	.667	3.71	1.29	17	17	0	0	...	0-...	99.1	98	43	41	4	30-1	92	.266
—Carolina (Southern)	3	3	.500	4.08	1.26	9	9	1	0	...	0-...	57.1	56	31	26	6	16-0	63	.249
—Pittsburgh (N.L.)	0	0	...	6.00	1.83	3	0	0	0	...	0-0	6.0	10	4	4	2	1-0	3	.400

Year Team (League)	W	L	Pct.	ERA	WHIP	G	GS	CG	ShO	Hld.	Sv.-Opp.	IP	H	R	ER	HR	BB-IBB	SO	Avg.
1998— Durham (Int'l)	1	0	1.000	2.92	0.65	2	2	0	0	...	0-...	12.1	6	4	4	2	2-0	14	.143
— Tampa Bay (A.L.)	2	5	.286	5.70	1.68	13	13	0	0	0	0-0	60.0	74	38	38	9	27-0	36	.306
1999— Rochester (Int'l)	4	2	.667	3.65	1.40	8	8	0	0	...	0-...	44.1	35	19	18	6	27-0	47	.212
— Baltimore (A.L.)	8	7	.533	5.46	1.52	22	21	0	0	0	0-0	115.1	120	74	70	16	55-0	71	.267
2000— Rochester (Int'l)	3	1	.750	1.47	0.96	8	8	1	1	...	0-...	55.0	32	12	9	2	21-0	56	.170
— Baltimore (A.L.)	1	10	.091	7.02	1.67	25	13	0	0	0	2	0-0	107.2	119	95	84	21	61-2	79	.278
2001— Baltimore (A.L.)	10	12	.455	4.09	1.38	32	32	2	0	0	0-0	196.0	194	109	89	28	77-3	114	.257
2002— Baltimore (A.L.)	5	14	.263	4.59	1.39	22	22	1	0	0	0-0	131.1	141	68	67	19	41-2	97	.276
— Bowie (East.)	1	0	1.000	0.00	1.00	1	1	0	0	...	0-...	5.0	4	0	0	0	1-0	6	.211
2003— Baltimore (A.L.)	10	10	.500	4.18	1.56	32	32	0	0	0	0-0	189.2	216	100	88	22	80-8	118	.283
2004— Detroit (A.L.)	8	15	.348	5.13	1.43	33	33	2	1	0	0-0	196.2	222	121	112	22	60-3	125	.284
2005— Detroit (A.L.)	8	13	.381	4.54	1.34	33	33	1	0	0	0-0	210.0	233	117	106	23	49-4	93	.285
2006— Cleveland (A.L.)	3	8	.273	5.96	1.69	14	14	0	0	0	0-0	77.0	108	55	51	10	22-0	32	.341
— Boston (A.L.)	0	4	.000	7.36	1.84	6	6	0	0	0	0-0	29.1	41	26	24	3	13-0	18	.333
— Pawtucket (Int'l)	2	0	1.000	3.32	1.11	3	3	1	0	...	0-...	19.0	15	7	7	1	6-0	12	.217
— Wilmington (Caro.)	1	0	1.000	5.14	1.43	1	1	0	0	0	0-0	7.0	10	4	4	0	0-0	1	.333
— Louisville (Int'l)	0	1	.000	9.00	1.40	1	1	0	0	...	0-...	5.0	6	6	5	1	1-0	2	.273
— Cincinnati (N.L.)	0	0	...	3.12	1.27	4	0	0	0	0	0-0	8.2	11	5	3	1	0-0	4	.297
American League totals (9 years)	55	98	.359	5.00	1.49	232	219	6	1	2	0-0	1313.0	1468	803	729	173	485-22	783	.283
National League totals (2 years)	0	0	...	4.30	1.50	7	0	0	0	0	0-0	14.2	21	9	7	3	1-0	7	.339
Major League totals (10 years)	55	98	.359	4.99	1.49	239	219	6	1	2	0-0	1327.2	1489	812	736	176	486-22	790	.284

2006 LEFTY-RIGHTY SPLITS

vs.	Avg.	AB	H	2B	3B	HR	RBI	BB	SO	OBP	Slg.	vs.	Avg.	AB	H	2B	3B	HR	RBI	BB	SO	OBP	Slg.
L	.380	221	84	19	3	7	37	15	23	.416	.588	R	.297	256	76	12	0	7	37	20	31	.351	.426

JOHNSON, JIM — P

PERSONAL: Born June 27, 1983, in Johnson City, N.Y. ... 6-5/225. ... Throws right, bats right. ... Full name: James Robert Johnson. ... High school: Union-Endicott (Endicott, N.Y.). **TRANSACTIONS/CAREER NOTES:** Selected by Baltimore Orioles organization in fifth round of 2001 free-agent draft.
CAREER HITTING: 0-for-0 (.000), 0 R, 0 2B, 0 3B, 0 HR, 0 RBI.

Year Team (League)	W	L	Pct.	ERA	WHIP	G	GS	CG	ShO	Hld.	Sv.-Opp.	IP	H	R	ER	HR	BB-IBB	SO	Avg.
2001— GC Orioles (GCL)	0	1	.000	3.86	1.29	7	4	0	0	...	0-...	18.2	17	10	8	3	7-1	19	.239
2002— Bluefield (Appal.)	4	2	.667	4.37	1.22	11	9	0	0	...	0-...	55.2	52	36	27	5	16-2	36	.250
2003— Bluefield (Appal.)	3	2	.600	3.68	1.56	11	11	0	0	...	0-...	51.1	62	24	21	2	18-0	46	.291
2004— Delmarva (S. Atl.)	8	7	.533	3.29	1.19	20	17	0	0	...	0-...	106.2	97	44	39	9	30-1	93	.246
2005— Bowie (East.)	0	0	...	0.00	0.71	1	1	0	0	0	0-0	7.0	3	0	0	0	2-0	6	.136
— Frederick (Carolina)	12	9	.571	3.49	1.27	28	27	2	0	0	1-1	159.2	139	77	62	11	64-0	168	.231
2006— Baltimore (A.L.)	0	1	.000	24.00	4.00	1	1	0	0	0	0-0	3.0	9	8	8	1	3-0	0	.563
— Bowie (East.)	13	6	.684	4.44	1.42	27	26	0	0	0	0-0	156.0	165	80	77	13	57-0	124	.274
Major League totals (1 year)	0	1	.000	24.00	4.00	1	1	0	0	0	0-0	3.0	9	8	8	1	3-0	0	.563

2006 LEFTY-RIGHTY SPLITS

vs.	Avg.	AB	H	2B	3B	HR	RBI	BB	SO	OBP	Slg.	vs.	Avg.	AB	H	2B	3B	HR	RBI	BB	SO	OBP	Slg.
L	.375	8	3	0	0	0	2	1	0	.500	.375	R	.750	8	6	3	0	1	6	2	0	.727	1.500

JOHNSON, JOSH — P

PERSONAL: Born January 31, 1984, in Minneapolis, Minn. ... 6-7/240. ... Throws right, bats left. ... Full name: Joshua Michael Johnson. ... High school: Jenks (Okla.).
TRANSACTIONS/CAREER NOTES: Selected by Florida Marlins organization in fourth round of 2002 free-agent draft.
CAREER HITTING: 5-for-46 (.109), 2 R, 2 2B, 0 3B, 0 HR, 3 RBI.

Year Team (League)	W	L	Pct.	ERA	WHIP	G	GS	CG	ShO	Hld.	Sv.-Opp.	IP	H	R	ER	HR	BB-IBB	SO	Avg.
2002— GC Marlins (GCL)	2	0	1.000	0.60	0.73	4	3	0	0	...	0-...	15.0	8	3	1	0	3-0	11	.154
— Jamestown (NYP)	0	2	.000	12.38	2.75	2	2	0	0	...	0-...	8.0	15	15	11	0	7-0	5	.385
2003— Greensboro (S. Atl.)	4	7	.364	3.61	1.19	17	17	0	0	...	0-...	82.1	69	44	33	5	29-0	59	.223
2004— Jupiter (Fla. St.)	5	12	.294	3.38	1.50	23	22	1	0	...	0-...	114.1	124	63	43	4	47-1	103	.285
2005— Carolina (Southern)	12	4	.750	3.87	1.35	26	26	1	0	0	0-0	139.2	139	67	60	4	50-4	113	.261
— Florida (N.L.)	0	0	...	3.65	1.70	4	1	0	0	0	0-0	12.1	11	5	5	0	10-0	10	.256
2006— Florida (N.L.)	12	7	.632	3.10	1.30	31	24	0	0	0	0-1	157.0	136	63	54	14	68-6	133	.236
Major League totals (2 years)	12	7	.632	3.14	1.33	35	25	0	0	0	0-1	169.1	147	68	59	14	78-6	143	.237

2006 LEFTY-RIGHTY SPLITS

vs.	Avg.	AB	H	2B	3B	HR	RBI	BB	SO	OBP	Slg.	vs.	Avg.	AB	H	2B	3B	HR	RBI	BB	SO	OBP	Slg.
L	.246	276	68	8	2	7	30	35	59	.338	.366	R	.227	300	68	16	3	7	32	33	74	.305	.370

JOHNSON, KELLY — OF

PERSONAL: Born February 22, 1982, in Austin, Texas. ... 6-1/205. ... Bats left, throws right. ... Full name: Kelly Andrew Johnson. **TRANSACTIONS/CAREER NOTES:** Selected by Atlanta Braves organization in supplemental round ("sandwich" pick between first and second rounds, 38th pick overall) of 2000 free-agent draft; Braves received pick as compensation for Milwaukee Brewers signing Type-A free agent Jose Hernandez. ... On disabled list (April 1, 2006-entire season). **STATISTICAL NOTES:** Career major league grand slams: 1.

Year Team (League)	Pos.	G	AB	R	H	2B	3B	HR	RBI	BB	SO	HBP	GDP	SB-CS	Avg.	OBP	SLG	OPS	E	Avg.
														BATTING					FIELDING	
2000— GC Braves (GCL)	SS	53	193	27	52	12	3	4	29	24	45	0	4	6-1	.269	.349	.425	.774	17	.896
2001— Macon (S. Atl.)	SS	124	415	75	120	22	1	23	66	71	111	10	0	25-6	.289	.404	.513	.917	45	.905
2002— Myrtle Beach (Carol.)	SS-3B	126	482	62	123	21	5	12	49	51	105	1	5	12-15	.255	.325	.394	.719	24	.953
2003— Greenville (Sou.)	OF-3B-2B	98	334	46	92	22	5	6	45	35	81	0	4	10-3	.275	.340	.425	.765	16	.959
— GC Braves (GCL)	SS	6	26	10	10	1	1	1	3	3	-4	1	2	1-1	.385	.467	.615	1.082	0	1.000
2004— Greenville (Sou.)	OF-3B-2B	135	479	70	135	35	3	16	50	49	102	3	5	9-9	.282	.350	.468	.818	11	.686
2005— Richmond (Int'l)	OF-3B-SS	44	155	35	48	13	3	8	22	34	22	2	3	2-1	.310	.438	.581	1.018	5	.974
— Atlanta (N.L.)	OF-DH	87	290	46	70	12	3	9	40	40	75	1	11	2-1	.241	.334	.397	.731	0	1.000
2006— Rome (S. Atl.)		5	19	5	9	2	1	1	3	4	3	1	0	2-2	.474	.583	.842	1.425	0	1.000
— Richmond (Int'l)		10	39	3	13	4	0	1	7	6	6	1	0	1-0	.333	.426	.513	.938	0	1.000
Major League totals (1 year)		87	290	46	70	12	3	9	40	40	75	1	11	2-1	.241	.334	.397	.731	0	1.000

DIVISION SERIES RECORD

Year Team (League)	Pos.	G	AB	R	H	2B	3B	HR	RBI	BB	SO	HBP	GDP	SB-CS	Avg.	OBP	SLG	OPS	E	Avg.
2005— Atlanta (N.L.)		4	2	0	0	0	0	0	0	1	0	0	0	0-0	.000	.333	.000	.333	0	

JOHNSON, NICK — 1B

PERSONAL: Born September 19, 1978, in Sacramento. ... 6-3/224. ... Bats left, throws left. ... Full name: Nicholas Robert Johnson. ... High school: McClatchy (Sacramento). ... Nephew of Larry Bowa, coach, New York Yankees, shortstop with three major league teams (1970-85) and manager of San Diego Padres (1987-88) and Philadelphia Phillies (2001-04). **TRANSACTIONS/CAREER NOTES:** Selected by New York Yankees organization in third round of 1996 free-agent draft. ... On disabled list (March 25, 2000-entire season). ... On disabled list (August 8-September 3, 2002); included rehabilitation assignment to Columbus. ... On disabled list (May 16-July 25, 2003); included rehabilitation assignment to Columbus. ... Traded by Yankees with OF Juan Rivera and P Randy Choate to Montreal Expos for P Javier Vazquez (December 16, 2003). ... On disabled list (March 31-May 28 and August 21, 2004-remainder of season); included rehabilitation assignments to Brevard County and Edmonton. ... Expos franchise transferred to Washington, D.C., and renamed Washington Nationals for 2005 season (December 3, 2004). ... On disabled list (July 4-26, 2005); included rehabilitation assignment to New Orleans. **STATISTICAL NOTES:** Career major league grand slams: 2.

2006 GAMES PLAYED BY POSITION (MLB): 1B—147.

									BATTING											FIELDING	
Year Team (League)	Pos.	G	AB	R	H	2B	3B	HR	RBI	BB	SO	HBP	GDP	SB-CS	Avg.	OBP	SLG	OPS		E	Avg.
1996— GC Yankees (GCL)	1B	47	157	31	45	11	1	2	33	30	35	9	5	0-0	.287	.422	.408	.830		3	.991
1997—Greensboro (S. Atl.)	1B	127	433	77	118	23	1	16	75	76	99	18	5	16-3	.273	.398	.441	.839		16	.987
1998—Tampa (Fla. St.)	1B	92	303	69	96	14	1	17	58	68	76	19	5	1-4	.317	.466	.538	1.004		12	.986
1999—Norwich (East.)	1B	132	420	114	145	33	5	14	87	123	88	37	9	8-6	.345	.525	.548	1.073		20	.983
2000—New York (A.L.)					Did not play.																
2001—Columbus (Int'l)	1B	110	359	68	92	20	0	18	49	81	105	14	6	9-2	.256	.407	.462	.870		10	.989
—New York (A.L.)	1B-DH	23	67	6	13	2	0	2	8	7	15	4	3	0-0	.194	.308	.313	.621		0	1.000
2002—New York (A.L.)	1B-DH-OF	129	378	56	92	15	0	15	58	48	98	12	11	1-3	.243	.347	.402	.749		7	.988
—Columbus (Int'l)	1B	3	11	1	1	0	0	0	0	1	4	0	1	0-0	.091	.167	.091	.258		0	1.000
2003—Columbus (Int'l)	1B-DH	3	10	1	5	2	0	1	3	2	2	0	0	0-0	.500	.583	1.000	1.583		1	.952
—Trenton (East.)	1B	4	12	3	5	1	0	0	1	5	0	1	1	0-0	.417	.611	.500	1.111		0	1.000
—New York (A.L.)	1B-DH	96	324	60	92	19	0	14	47	70	57	8	9	5-2	.284	.422	.472	.894		5	.991
2004—Brevard County (FSL)	1B	6	21	3	4	0	0	1	5	4	6	0	1	0-0	.190	.320	.333	.653		0	1.000
—Edmonton (PCL)	1B	3	9	2	2	1	0	0	0	4	3	0	1	0-0	.222	.462	.333	.795		0	1.000
—Montreal (N.L.)	1B	73	251	35	63	16	0	7	33	40	58	3	5	6-3	.251	.359	.398	.758		4	.994
2005—New Orleans (PCL)	1B	3	6	0	0	0	0	0	0	1	2	0	0	0-0	.000	.143	.000	.143		0	1.000
—Wash. (N.L.)	1B	131	453	66	131	35	3	15	74	80	87	12	15	3-8	.289	.408	.479	.887		5	.996
2006—Wash. (N.L.)	1B	147	500	100	145	46	0	23	77	110	99	13	12	10-3	.290	.428	.520	.948		15	.988
American League totals (3 years)		248	769	122	197	36	0	31	113	125	170	24	23	6-5	.256	.376	.424	.800		12	.990
National League totals (3 years)		351	1204	201	339	97	3	45	184	230	244	28	32	19-14	.282	.407	.479	.886		24	.992
Major League totals (6 years)		599	1973	323	536	133	3	76	297	355	414	52	55	25-19	.272	.395	.458	.853		36	.992

DIVISION SERIES RECORD

Year Team (League)	Pos.	G	AB	R	H	2B	3B	HR	RBI	BB	SO	HBP	GDP	SB-CS	Avg.	OBP	SLG	OPS	E	Avg.
2002—New York (A.L.)	DH-1B	3	11	1	2	0	0	0	1	1	5	0	0	0-0	.182	.308	.182	.432	0	1.000
2003—New York (A.L.)	1B	4	13	2	1	1	0	0	2	3	2	1	0	0-0	.077	.294	.154	.448	0	1.000
Division series totals (2 years)		7	24	3	3	1	0	0	3	4	7	1	0	0-0	.125	.276	.167	.443	0	1.000

CHAMPIONSHIP SERIES RECORD

Year Team (League)	Pos.	G	AB	R	H	2B	3B	HR	RBI	BB	SO	HBP	GDP	SB-CS	Avg.	OBP	SLG	OPS	E	Avg.
2003—New York (A.L.)	1B	7	26	4	6	1	0	1	3	2	4	0	1	0-0	.231	.286	.385	.670	0	1.000

WORLD SERIES RECORD

Year Team (League)	Pos.	G	AB	R	H	2B	3B	HR	RBI	BB	SO	HBP	GDP	SB-CS	Avg.	OBP	SLG	OPS	E	Avg.
2003—New York (A.L.)	1B	6	17	3	5	1	0	0	0	2	3	0	1	0-0	.294	.368	.353	.721	0	1.000

2006 LEFTY-RIGHTY SPLITS

vs.	Avg.	AB	H	2B	3B	HR	RBI	BB	SO	OBP	Slg.	vs.	Avg.	AB	H	2B	3B	HR	RBI	BB	SO	OBP	Slg.
L	.303	142	43	13	0	5	24	31	30	.438	.500	R	.285	358	102	33	0	18	53	79	69	.424	.528

JOHNSON, RANDY — P

PERSONAL: Born September 10, 1963, in Walnut Creek, Calif. ... 6-10/231. ... Throws left, bats right. ... Full name: Randall David Johnson. ... High school: Livermore (Calif.). ... College: Southern California. **TRANSACTIONS/CAREER NOTES:** Selected by Atlanta Braves organization in third round of June 1982 free-agent draft; did not sign. ... Selected by Montreal Expos organization in second round of June 1985 free-agent draft. ... Traded by Expos with Ps Brian Holman and Gene Harris to Seattle Mariners for P Mark Langston and a player to be named (May 25, 1989); Expos acquired P Mike Campbell to complete deal (July 31, 1989). ... On disabled list (June 11-27, 1992). ... On disabled list (May 15-August 6 and August 27, 1996-remainder of season); included rehabilitation assignment to Everett. ... On suspended list (April 24-27, 1998). ... Traded by Mariners to Houston Astros for SS Carlos Guillen, P Freddy Garcia and a player to be named (July 31, 1998); Mariners acquired P John Halama to complete deal (October 1, 1998). ... Signed as a free agent by Arizona Diamondbacks (December 10, 1998). ... On disabled list (April 12-27 and April 28-July 20, 2003); included rehabilitation assignment to Lancaster. ... Traded by Diamondbacks to New York Yankees for Ps Javier Vazquez and Brad Halsey, C Dioner Navarro and cash (January 11, 2005). ... On suspended list (June 20-26, 2006). **HONORS:** Named A.L. Pitcher of the Year by THE SPORTING NEWS (1995). ... Named lefthanded pitcher on THE SPORTING NEWS A.L. All-Star team (1995 and 1997). ... Named lefthanded pitcher on THE SPORTING NEWS N.L. All-Star team (2001 and 2002). ... Named A.L. Cy Young Award winner by Baseball Writers' Association of America (1995). ... Named N.L. Cy Young Award winner by Baseball Writers' Association of America (1999, 2000, 2001 and 2002). **STATISTICAL NOTES:** Pitched 2-0 no-hit victory against Detroit (June 2, 1990). ... Struck out 20 batters in one game (May 8, 2001). ... Pitched 2-0 perfect game against Atlanta (May 18, 2004). **MISCELLANEOUS NOTES:** Appeared in one game as outfielder with no chances (1993).

CAREER HITTING: 68-for-534 (.127), 17 R, 13 2B, 0 3B, 1 HR, 35 RBI.

Year Team (League)	W	L	Pct.	ERA	WHIP	G	GS	CG	ShO	Hld.	Sv.-Opp.	IP	H	R	ER	HR	BB-IBB	SO	Avg.
1985—Jamestown (NYP)	0	3	.000	5.93	1.94	8	8	0	0	...	0-...	27.1	29	22	18	2	24-0	21	.287
1986—W.P. Beach (FSL)	8	7	.533	3.16	1.53	26	26	2	1	...	0-...	119.2	89	49	42	3	94-0	133	.211
1987—Jacksonville (Sou.)	11	8	.579	3.73	1.63	25	24	0	0	...	0-...	140.0	100	63	58	10	128-0	163	.204
1988—Indianapolis (A.A.)	8	7	.533	3.26	1.39	20	19	0	0	.	0-...	113.1	85	52	41	6	72-0	111	.209
—Montreal (N.L.)	3	0	1.000	2.42	1.15	4	4	1	0	0	0-0	26.0	23	8	7	3	7-0	25	.225
1989—Montreal (N.L.)	0	4	.000	6.67	1.85	7	6	0	0	0	0-0	29.2	29	25	22	2	26-1	26	.264
—Indianapolis (A.A.)	1	1	.500	2.00	1.22	3	3	0	0	.	0-0	18.0	13	5	4	0	9-0	17	.194
—Seattle (A.L.)	7	9	.438	4.40	1.44	22	22	2	0	0	0-0	131.0	118	75	64	11	70-1	104	.244
1990—Seattle (A.L.)	14	11	.560	3.65	1.34	33	33	5	2	0	0-0	219.2	174	103	89	26	* 120-2	194	.216
1991—Seattle (A.L.)	13	10	.565	3.98	1.50	33	33	2	1	0	0-0	201.1	151	96	89	15	* 152-0	228	.213
1992—Seattle (A.L.)	12	14	.462	3.77	1.42	31	31	6	2	0	0-0	210.1	154	104	88	13	* 144-1	* 241	.206
1993—Seattle (A.L.)	19	8	.704	3.24	1.11	35	34	10	3	0	1-1	255.1	185	97	92	22	99-1	* 308	.203
1994—Seattle (A.L.)	13	6	.684	3.19	1.19	23	23	* 9	* 4	0	0-0	172.0	132	65	61	14	72-2	* 204	.216
1995—Seattle (A.L.)	18	2	* .900	* 2.48	1.05	30	30	6	3	0	0-0	214.1	159	65	59	12	65-1	* 294	* .201
1996—Seattle (A.L.)	5	0	1.000	3.67	1.19	14	8	0	0	0	1-2	61.1	48	27	25	8	25-0	85	.211
—Everett (N'west)	0	0	...	0.00	0.00	1	1	0	0	...	0-...	2.0	0	0	0	0	0-0	5	.000
1997—Seattle (A.L.)	20	4	* .833	2.28	1.05	30	29	5	2	0	0-0	213.0	147	60	54	20	77-2	291	* .194
1998—Seattle (A.L.)	9	10	.474	4.33	1.29	23	23	6	2	0	0-0	160.0	146	90	77	19	60-0	213	.240

J

Year Team (League)	W	L	Pct.	ERA	WHIP	G	GS	CG	ShO	Hld.	Sv.-Opp.	IP	H	R	ER	HR	BB-IBB	SO	Avg.
— Houston (N.L.)	10	1	.909	1.28	0.98	11	11	4	4	0	0-0	84.1	57	12	12	4	26-1	116	.191
1999— Arizona (N.L.)	17	9	.654	* 2.48	1.02	35	• 35	* 12	2	0	0-0	* 271.2	207	86	75	30	70-3	* 364	.208
2000— Arizona (N.L.)	19	7	* .731	2.64	1.12	35	• 35	8	• 3	0	0-0	248.2	202	89	73	23	76-1	* 347	.224
2001— Arizona (N.L.)	21	6	.778	* 2.49	1.01	35	34	3	2	0	0-0	249.2	181	74	69	19	71-2	* 372	.203
2002— Arizona (N.L.)	* 24	5	* .828	* 2.32	1.03	35	35	* 8	4	0	0-0	* 260.0	197	78	67	26	71-1	* 334	* .208
2003— Tucson (PCL)	0	0	...	0.00	0.00	1	1	0	0	...	0-...	4.0	0	0	0	0	0-0	4	.000
— El Paso (Texas)	0	0	...	0.00	1.00	1	1	0	0	...	0-...	4.0	3	2	0	0	1-0	5	.231
— Lancaster (Calif.)	0	1	.000	6.00	1.80	1	1	0	0	...	0-...	6.0	11	5	4	1	0-0	6	.367
— Arizona (N.L.)	6	8	.429	4.26	1.33	18	18	1	1	0	0-0	114.0	125	61	54	16	27-3	125	.280
2004— Arizona (N.L.)	16	14	.533	2.60	0.90	• 35	35	4	2	0	0-0	245.2	177	88	71	18	44-1	* 290	.197
2005— New York (A.L.)	17	8	.680	3.79	1.13	34	34	4	0	0	0-0	225.2	207	102	95	32	47-2	211	.243
2006— New York (A.L.)	17	11	.607	5.00	1.24	33	33	2	0	0	0-0	205.0	194	125	114	28	60-1	172	.250
American League totals (12 years)	164	93	.638	3.60	1.24	341	333	57	19	0	2-3	2269.0	1815	1009	907	220	991-13	2545	.219
National League totals (9 years)	116	54	.682	2.65	1.06	215	213	41	18	0	0-0	1529.2	1198	521	450	141	418-13	1999	.215
Major League totals (19 years)	280	147	.656	3.22	1.16	556	546	98	37	0	2-3	3798.2	3013	1530	1357	361	1409-26	4544	.217

DIVISION SERIES RECORD

Year Team (League)	W	L	Pct.	ERA	WHIP	G	GS	CG	ShO	Hld.	Sv.-Opp.	IP	H	R	ER	HR	BB-IBB	SO	Avg.
1995— Seattle (A.L.)	2	0	1.000	2.70	1.10	2	1	0	0	0	0-0	10.0	5	3	3	1	6-1	16	.156
1997— Seattle (A.L.)	0	2	.000	5.54	1.54	2	2	1	0	0	0-0	13.0	14	8	8	3	6-0	16	.286
1998— Houston (N.L.)	0	2	.000	1.93	1.00	2	2	1	0	0	0-0	14.0	12	4	3	2	2-0	17	.226
1999— Arizona (N.L.)	0	1	.000	7.56	1.32	1	1	0	0	0	0-0	8.1	8	7	7	2	3-0	11	.250
2001— Arizona (N.L.)	0	1	.000	3.38	1.00	1	1	0	0	0	0-0	8.0	6	3	3	1	2-0	9	.222
2002— Arizona (N.L.)	0	1	.000	7.50	2.00	1	1	0	0	0	0-0	6.0	10	6	5	2	2-1	4	.370
2005— New York (A.L.)	0	0	...	6.14	1.77	2	1	0	0	0	0-0	7.1	12	5	5	2	1-0	4	.375
2006— New York (A.L.)	0	1	.000	7.94	1.76	1	1	0	0	0	0-0	5.2	8	5	5	0	2-0	4	.348
Division series totals (8 years)	2	8	.200	4.85	1.37	12	10	1	0	0	0-0	72.1	75	41	39	13	24-2	81	.273

CHAMPIONSHIP SERIES RECORD

Year Team (League)	W	L	Pct.	ERA	WHIP	G	GS	CG	ShO	Hld.	Sv.-Opp.	IP	H	R	ER	HR	BB-IBB	SO	Avg.
1995— Seattle (A.L.)	0	1	.000	2.35	0.91	2	2	0	0	0	0-0	15.1	12	6	4	1	2-0	13	.211
2001— Arizona (N.L.)	2	0	1.000	1.13	0.81	2	2	1	1	0	0-0	16.0	10	2	2	1	3-0	19	.169
Champ. series totals (2 years)	2	1	.667	1.72	0.86	4	4	1	1	0	0-0	31.1	22	8	6	2	5-0	32	.190

WORLD SERIES RECORD

Year Team (League)	W	L	Pct.	ERA	WHIP	G	GS	CG	ShO	Hld.	Sv.-Opp.	IP	H	R	ER	HR	BB-IBB	SO	Avg.
2001— Arizona (N.L.)	3	0	1.000	1.04	0.69	3	2	1	1	0	0-0	17.1	9	2	2	0	3-0	19	.150

ALL-STAR GAME RECORD

	W	L	Pct.	ERA	WHIP	G	GS	CG	ShO	Hld.	Sv.-Opp.	IP	H	R	ER	HR	BB-IBB	SO	Avg.
All-Star Game totals (8 years)	0	0	...	0.75	0.75	8	4	0	0	0	0-0	12.0	7	1	1	1	2-0	12	.171

2006 LEFTY-RIGHTY SPLITS

vs.	Avg.	AB	H	2B	3B	HR	RBI	BB	SO	OBP	Slg.	vs.	Avg.	AB	H	2B	3B	HR	RBI	BB	SO	OBP	Slg.
L	.194	108	21	3	2	1	8	5	32	.252	.287	R	.259	669	173	36	1	27	106	55	140	.318	.436

JOHNSON, REED — OF

PERSONAL: Born December 8, 1976, in Riverside, Calif. ... 5-10/180. ... Bats right, throws right. ... Full name: Reed Cameron Johnson. ... High school: Temecula Valley (Temecula, Calif.). ... College: Cal State Fullerton. **TRANSACTIONS/CAREER NOTES:** Selected by Toronto Blue Jays organization in 17th round of 1999 free-agent draft.
RECORDS: Shares major league record for most times hit by pitch, game (3, April 16, 2005). **STATISTICAL NOTES:** Career major league grand slams: 1.
2006 GAMES PLAYED BY POSITION (MLB): OF—133, DH—1.

Year Team (League)	Pos.	G	AB	R	H	2B	3B	HR	RBI	BB	SO	HBP	GDP	SB-CS	Avg.	OBP	SLG	OPS	E	Avg.
1999— St. Catharines (NYP)	OF	60	191	24	46	8	2	2	23	24	31	2	4	5-5	.241	.326	.335	.661	3	.976
2000— Hagerstown (SAL)	OF	95	324	66	94	24	5	8	70	62	49	14	9	14-2	.290	.422	.469	.891	1	.995
— Dunedin (Fla. St.)	OF	36	133	26	42	9	2	4	28	14	27	11	1	3-2	.316	.416	.504	.920	2	.975
2001— Tennessee (Sou.)	OF	136	554	104	174	29	4	13	74	45	79	18	11	42-12	.314	.383	.451	.834	4	.983
2002— Dunedin (Fla. St.)	OF	8	33	7	9	3	0	0	6	3	3	2	0	0-1	.273	.368	.364	.732	1	1.000
— Syracuse (Int'l)	OF	44	159	27	37	8	3	2	10	12	23	8	1	1-4	.233	.317	.358	.675	1	.991
2003— Syracuse (Int'l)	OF	26	101	14	33	4	1	2	16	3	13	5	2	3-1	.327	.369	.446	.815	0	1.000
— Toronto (A.L.)	OF-DH	114	412	79	121	21	2	10	52	20	67	20	10	5-3	.294	.353	.427	.780	4	.977
2004— Toronto (A.L.)	OF-DH	141	537	68	145	25	2	10	61	28	98	12	17	6-3	.270	.320	.380	.699	3	.989
2005— Toronto (A.L.)	OF	142	398	55	107	21	6	8	58	22	82	16	8	5-6	.269	.332	.412	.744	2	.990
2006— Toronto (A.L.)	OF-DH	134	461	86	147	34	2	12	49	33	81	* 21	9	8-2	.319	.390	.479	.869	1	.996
Major League totals (4 years)		531	1808	288	520	101	12	40	220	103	328	69	44	24-14	.288	.348	.423	.771	10	.989

2006 LEFTY-RIGHTY SPLITS

vs.	Avg.	AB	H	2B	3B	HR	RBI	BB	SO	OBP	Slg.	vs.	Avg.	AB	H	2B	3B	HR	RBI	BB	SO	OBP	Slg.
L	.323	164	53	9	1	3	13	15	23	.422	.445	R	.316	297	94	25	1	9	36	18	58	.370	.498

JOHNSON, TYLER — P

PERSONAL: Born June 7, 1981, in Columbia, Mo. ... 6-2/180. ... Throws left, bats both. ... Full name: Tyler James Johnson. ... Junior college: Moorpark.
TRANSACTIONS/CAREER NOTES: Selected by St. Louis Cardinals organization in 34th round of 2000 free-agent draft. ... Selected by Oakland Athletics organization from Cardinals in Rule 5 major league draft (December 13, 2004). ... Returned by Athletics to Cardinals (February 22, 2005).
CAREER HITTING: 0-for-1 (.000), 0 R, 0 2B, 0 3B, 0 HR, 0 RBI.

Year Team (League)	W	L	Pct.	ERA	WHIP	G	GS	CG	ShO	Hld.	Sv.-Opp.	IP	H	R	ER	HR	BB-IBB	SO	Avg.
2002— Peoria (Mid.)	15	3	.833	2.00	1.14	22	18	0	0	...	0-...	121.1	96	35	27	7	42-1	132	.218
2003— Palm Beach (FSL)	5	5	.500	3.08	1.48	22	10	0	0	...	0-...	79.0	79	29	27	2	38-2	81	.262
— Tennessee (South.)	1	0	1.000	1.65	1.13	20	0	0	0	...	0-...	27.1	16	7	5	1	15-1	39	.168
2004— Tennessee (South.)	2	2	.500	4.79	1.51	53	0	0	0	...	4-...	56.1	48	32	30	4	37-1	77	.221
2005— Memphis (PCL)	2	1	.667	4.27	1.31	57	0	0	0	13	7-9	59.0	51	31	28	6	26-2	77	.232
— St. Louis (N.L.)	0	0	...	0.00	2.25	5	0	0	0	1	0-1	2.2	3	0	0	0	3-0	4	.300
2006— Memphis (PCL)	0	0	...	8.64	1.92	8	0	0	0	2	0-1	8.1	12	8	8	1	4-3	8	.316
— St. Louis (N.L.)	2	4	.333	4.95	1.54	56	0	0	0	11	0-2	36.1	33	21	20	5	23-2	37	.244
Major League totals (2 years)	2	4	.333	4.62	1.59	61	0	0	0	12	0-3	39.0	36	21	20	5	26-2	41	.248

DIVISION SERIES RECORD

Year Team (League)	W	L	Pct.	ERA	WHIP	G	GS	CG	ShO	Hld.	Sv.-Opp.	IP	H	R	ER	HR	BB-IBB	SO	Avg.
2006— St. Louis (N.L.)	0	0	...	0.00	1.13	4	0	0	0	3	0-0	2.2	2	0	0	0	1-0	6	.200

CHAMPIONSHIP SERIES RECORD

Year Team (League)	W	L	Pct.	ERA	WHIP	G	GS	CG	ShO	Hld.	Sv.-Opp.	IP	H	R	ER	HR	BB-IBB	SO	Avg.
2006— St. Louis (N.L.)	0	0	...	2.45	0.82	4	0	0	0	1	0-0	3.2	2	1	1	0	1-0	5	.143

Year	Team (League)	W	L	Pct.	ERA	WHIP	G	GS	CG	ShO	Hld.	Sv.-Opp.	IP	H	R	ER	HR	BB-IBB	SO	Avg.
2006—St. Louis (N.L.)		0	0	...	0.00	0.00	2	0	0	0	0	0-0	1.0	0	0	0	0	0-0	1	.000

2006 LEFTY-RIGHTY SPLITS

vs.	Avg.	AB	H	2B	3B	HR	RBI	BB	SO	OBP	Slg.	vs.	Avg.	AB	H	2B	3B	HR	RBI	BB	SO	OBP	Slg.
L	.221	77	17	2	2	3	19	10	24	.322	.416	R	.276	58	16	2	0	2	11	13	13	.425	.414

JONES, ADAM — OF

PERSONAL: Born August 1, 1985, in San Diego, Calif. ... Bats right, throws right. ... Full name: Adam LaMarque Jones....High school: Morse (San Diego). **TRANSACTIONS/CAREER NOTES:** Selected by Seattle Mariners organization in first round (37 pick overall) of 2003 free-agent draft.

2006 GAMES PLAYED BY POSITION (MLB): OF—26, DH—1.

Year	Team (League)	Pos.	G	AB	R	H	2B	3B	HR	RBI	BB	SO	HBP	GDP	SB-CS	Avg.	OBP	SLG	OPS	E	Avg.
2003—Ariz. Mariners (Ariz.)			28	109	18	31	5	1	0	8	5	19	10	1	5-1	.284	.368	.349	.717	...	...
—Everett (N'west)			3	13	2	6	1	0	0	4	1	3	0	1	0-0	.462	.467	.538	1.005	...	...
2004—Wisconsin (Midw.)			130	510	76	136	23	7	11	72	33	124	5	13	8-4	.267	.314	.404	.718	...	...
2005—Inland Empire (Calif.)	SS-DH		68	271	43	80	20	5	8	46	29	64	8	4	4-5	.295	.374	.494	.868	22	.935
—San Antonio (Texas)	SS-OF		63	228	33	68	10	3	7	20	22	48	3	4	9-4	.298	.365	.461	.825	12	.959
2006—Tacoma (PCL)			96	380	69	109	19	4	16	62	28	78	6	12	13-4	.287	.348	.829	8	.966
—Seattle (A.L.)	OF-DH		32	74	6	16	4	0	1	8	2	22	0	3	3-1	.216	.237	.311	.548	3	.960
Major League totals (1 year)			32	74	6	16	4	0	1	8	2	22	0	3	3-1	.216	.237	.311	.548	3	.960

2006 LEFTY-RIGHTY SPLITS

vs.	Avg.	AB	H	2B	3B	HR	RBI	BB	SO	OBP	Slg.	vs.	Avg.	AB	H	2B	3B	HR	RBI	BB	SO	OBP	Slg.
L	.235	17	4	0	0	0	0	1	6	.278	.235	R	.211	57	12	4	0	1	8	1	16	.224	.333

JONES, ANDRUW — OF

PERSONAL: Born April 23, 1977, in Willemstad, Curacao. ... 6-1/210. ... Bats right, throws right. ... Full name: Andruw Rudolf Jones. ... High school: St. Paulus (Willemstad, Curacao). **TRANSACTIONS/CAREER NOTES:** Signed as a non-drafted free agent by Atlanta Braves organization (July 1, 1993). **HONORS:** Named Major League Player of the Year by the SPORTING NEWS (2005). ... Named outfielder on the SPORTING NEWS N.L. All-Star team (2005 and 2006). ... Won N.L. Gold Glove as outfielder (1998-2006). ... Named outfielder on N.L. Silver Slugger team (2005). **STATISTICAL NOTES:** Hit three home runs in one game (September 25, 2002). ... Career major league grand slams: 4.

2006 GAMES PLAYED BY POSITION (MLB): OF—153, DH—2.

Year	Team (League)	Pos.	G	AB	R	H	2B	3B	HR	RBI	BB	SO	HBP	GDP	SB-CS	Avg.	OBP	SLG	OPS	E	Avg.
1994—GC Braves (GCL)	OF		27	95	22	21	5	1	2	10	16	19	2	3	5-2	.221	.345	.358	.703	3	.968
—Danville (Appal.)	OF		36	143	20	48	9	2	1	16	9	25	3	0	16-9	.336	.385	.448	.832	2	.977
1995—Macon (S. Atl.)	OF		139	537	104	149	41	5	25	100	70	122	16	9	56-11	.277	.372	.512	.884	4	.988
1996—Durham (Carol.)	OF		66	243	65	76	14	3	17	43	42	54	3	5	16-4	.313	.419	.605	1.024	1	.963
—Greenville (Sou.)	OF		38	157	39	58	10	1	12	37	17	34	1	3	12-4	.369	.432	.675	1.107	1	.993
—Richmond (Int'l)	OF		12	45	11	17	3	1	5	12	1	9	0	0	2-2	.378	.391	.822	1.214	1	.972
—Atlanta (N.L.)	OF		31	106	11	23	7	1	5	13	7	29	0	1	3-0	.217	.265	.443	.709	2	.975
1997—Atlanta (N.L.)	OF		153	399	60	92	18	1	18	70	56	107	4	11	20-11	.231	.329	.416	.745	7	.977
1998—Atlanta (N.L.)	OF		159	582	89	158	33	8	31	90	40	129	4	10	27-4	.271	.321	.515	.836	2	.995
1999—Atlanta (N.L.)	OF •		162	592	97	163	35	5	26	84	76	103	9	12	24-12	.275	.365	.483	.848	10	.981
2000—Atlanta (N.L.)	OF		161	* 656	122	199	36	6	36	104	59	100	9	12	21-6	.303	.366	.541	.907	2	.996
2001—Atlanta (N.L.)	OF		161	625	104	157	25	2	34	104	56	142	3	10	11-4	.251	.312	.461	.772	6	.987
2002—Atlanta (N.L.)	OF-DH		154	560	91	148	34	0	35	94	83	135	10	14	8-3	.264	.366	.513	.878	3	.993
2003—Atlanta (N.L.)	OF		156	595	101	165	28	2	36	116	53	125	5	18	4-3	.277	.338	.513	.851	3	.993
2004—Atlanta (N.L.)	OF		154	570	85	149	34	4	29	91	71	147	3	24	6-6	.261	.345	.488	.833	3	.993
2005—Atlanta (N.L.)	OF		160	586	95	154	24	3	* 51	* 128	64	112	15	19	5-3	.263	.347	.575	.922	2	.995
2006—Atlanta (N.L.)	OF-DH		156	565	107	148	29	0	41	129	82	127	13	13	4-1	.262	.363	.531	.894	2	.995
Major League totals (11 years)			1607	5836	962	1556	303	32	342	1023	647	1256	75	144	133-53	.267	.345	.505	.850	42	.990

DIVISION SERIES RECORD

Year	Team (League)	Pos.	G	AB	R	H	2B	3B	HR	RBI	BB	SO	HBP	GDP	SB-CS	Avg.	OBP	SLG	OPS	E	Avg.
1996—Atlanta (N.L.)	OF		3	0	0	0	0	0	0	0	1	0	0	0	0-0	...	1.000	...	1.000	0	1.000
1997—Atlanta (N.L.)	OF		3	5	1	0	0	0	0	1	1	1	0	0	0-0	.000	.167	.000	.167	0	1.000
1998—Atlanta (N.L.)	OF		3	9	2	0	0	0	0	0	3	1	0	0	2-0	.000	.231	.000	.231	0	1.000
1999—Atlanta (N.L.)	OF		4	18	1	4	1	0	0	2	1	3	0	0	0-0	.222	.263	.278	.541	0	1.000
2000—Atlanta (N.L.)	OF		3	9	3	1	0	0	1	1	4	1	0	1	0-1	.111	.385	.444	.829	0	1.000
2001—Atlanta (N.L.)	OF		3	12	2	6	1	0	0	1	0	3	0	0	0-0	.500	.500	.750	1.250	0	1.000
2002—Atlanta (N.L.)	OF		5	19	4	6	1	0	1	5	2	3	0	0	0-0	.316	.381	.368	.749	1	1.000
2003—Atlanta (N.L.)	OF		5	17	1	1	0	0	0	1	4	7	0	0	0-0	.059	.238	.059	.297	1	.900
2004—Atlanta (N.L.)	OF		5	19	4	10	2	0	2	5	2	3	1	0	1-0	.526	.571	.947	1.519	0	1.000
2005—Atlanta (N.L.)	OF		4	17	5	8	3	0	1	5	2	3	1	1	0-0	.471	.524	.824	1.347	0	1.000
Division series totals (10 years)			38	125	23	36	7	0	5	19	20	26	1	3	3-1	.288	.385	.464	.849	1	.990

CHAMPIONSHIP SERIES RECORD

Year	Team (League)	Pos.	G	AB	R	H	2B	3B	HR	RBI	BB	SO	HBP	GDP	SB-CS	Avg.	OBP	SLG	OPS	E	Avg.
1996—Atlanta (N.L.)	OF		5	9	3	2	0	0	1	3	3	2	0	0	0-0	.222	.417	.556	.972	0	1.000
1997—Atlanta (N.L.)	OF		5	9	0	4	0	0	0	1	1	1	0	0	0-0	.444	.500	.444	.944	0	1.000
1998—Atlanta (N.L.)	OF		6	22	3	6	0	0	1	2	1	4	0	0	1-1	.273	.292	.409	.701	0	1.000
1999—Atlanta (N.L.)	OF		6	23	5	5	0	0	0	1	3	3	0	0	0-1	.217	.333	.217	.551	0	1.000
2001—Atlanta (N.L.)	OF		5	17	4	3	0	0	1	1	1	5	0	0	0-0	.176	.222	.353	.575	0	1.000
Champ. series totals (5 years)			27	80	15	20	0	0	3	8	10	15	0	0	1-2	.250	.330	.363	.692	0	1.000

WORLD SERIES RECORD

Year	Team (League)	Pos.	G	AB	R	H	2B	3B	HR	RBI	BB	SO	HBP	GDP	SB-CS	Avg.	OBP	SLG	OPS	E	Avg.
1996—Atlanta (N.L.)	OF		6	20	4	8	0	0	2	6	3	6	1	0	1-2	.400	.500	.750	1.250	0	1.000
1999—Atlanta (N.L.)	OF		4	13	1	1	0	0	0	0	1	3	0	1	0-0	.077	.143	.077	.220	0	1.000
World series totals (2 years)			10	33	5	9	1	0	2	6	4	9	1	1	1-2	.273	.368	.485	.853	0	1.000

ALL-STAR GAME RECORD

			G	AB	R	H	2B	3B	HR	RBI	BB	SO	HBP	GDP	SB-CS	Avg.	OBP	SLG	OPS	E	Avg.
All-Star Game totals (4 years)			4	8	4	4	1	0	2	6	1	0	0	0	0-0	.500	.556	1.375	1.931	0	1.000

J

vs.	Avg.	AB	H	2B	3B	HR	RBI	BB	SO	OBP	Slg.	vs.	Avg.	AB	H	2B	3B	HR	RBI	BB	SO	OBP	Slg.
L	.260	127	33	6	0	10	21	23	29	.390	.543	R	.263	438	115	23	0	31	108	59	98	.355	.527

JONES, CHIPPER — 3B

PERSONAL: Born April 24, 1972, in DeLand, Fla. ... 6-4/210. ... Bats both, throws right. ... Full name: Larry Wayne Jones. ... High school: The Bolles School (Jacksonville).
TRANSACTIONS/CAREER NOTES: Selected by Atlanta Braves organization in first round (first pick overall) of 1990 free-agent draft. ... On disabled list (March 20, 1994-entire season; and March 22-April 16, 1996). ... On disabled list (April 19-May 8, 2004); included rehabilitation assignment to Rome. ... On disabled list (June 6-July 18, 2005); included rehabilitation assignment to Rome. ... On disabled list (April 10-25, 2006). ... On disabled list (July 30-August 13, 2006); included rehabilitation assignment to Mississippi. ... On disabled list (September 4-19, 2006). **HONORS:** Named N.L. Rookie Player of the Year by THE SPORTING NEWS (1995). ... Named third baseman on THE SPORTING NEWS N.L. All-Star team (1999-2001). ... Named N.L. Most Valuable Player by Baseball Writers' Association of America (1999). ... Named third baseman on N.L. Silver Slugger team (2000). **STATISTICAL NOTES:** Hit three home runs in one game (August 14, 2006). ... Career major league grand slams: 6.
2006 GAMES PLAYED BY POSITION (MLB): 3B—105, DH—2.

Year Team (League)	Pos.	G	AB	R	H	2B	3B	HR	RBI	BB	SO	HBP	GDP	SB-CS	Avg.	OBP	SLG	OPS	E	Avg.
1990— GC Braves (GCL)	SS	44	140	20	32	1	1	1	18	14	25	6	3	5-3	.229	.321	.271	.592	18	.919
1991— Macon (S. Atl.)	SS	136	473	104	154	24	11	15	98	69	70	3	6	40-11	.326	.407	.518	.925	56	.919
1992— Durham (Carol.)	SS	70	264	43	73	22	1	4	31	31	34	2	5	10-8	.277	.353	.413	.766	14	.956
— Greenville (Sou.)	SS	67	266	43	92	17	11	9	42	11	32	0	5	14-1	.346	.367	.594	.961	18	.945
1993— Richmond (Int'l)	SS	139	536	97	174	31	12	13	89	57	70	1	8	23-7	.325	.387	.500	.887	43	.931
— Atlanta (N.L.)	SS	8	3	2	2	1	0	0	0	1	1	0	0	0-0	.667	.750	1.000	1.750	0	1.000
1994— Atlanta (N.L.)							Did not play.													
1995— Atlanta (N.L.)	3B-OF	140	524	87	139	22	3	23	86	73	99	0	10	8-4	.265	.353	.450	.803	25	.935
1996— Atlanta (N.L.)	3B-SS-OF	157	598	114	185	32	5	30	110	87	88	0	14	14-1	.309	.393	.530	.923	17	.958
1997— Atlanta (N.L.)	3B-OF	157	597	100	176	41	3	21	111	76	88	0	19	20-5	.295	.371	.479	.850	15	.956
1998— Atlanta (N.L.)	3B	160	601	123	188	29	5	34	107	96	93	1	17	16-6	.313	.404	.547	.951	12	.971
1999— Atlanta (N.L.)	3B-SS	157	567	116	181	41	1	45	110	126	94	2	20	25-3	.319	.441	.633	1.074	17	.951
2000— Atlanta (N.L.)	3B-SS	156	579	118	180	38	1	36	111	95	64	2	14	14-7	.311	.404	.566	.970	25	.941
2001— Atlanta (N.L.)	3B-OF-DH	159	572	113	189	33	5	38	102	98	82	2	13	9-10	.330	.427	.605	1.032	18	.947
2002— Atlanta (N.L.)	OF	158	548	90	179	35	1	26	100	107	89	2	18	8-2	.327	.435	.537	.972	7	.975
2003— Atlanta (N.L.)	OF-DH	153	555	103	169	33	2	27	106	94	83	1	10	2-2	.305	.402	.517	.920	7	.968
2004— Rome (S. Atl.)	OF	1	4	0	0	0	0	0	0	0	0	0	0	0-0	.000	.000	.000	.000	0	1.000
— Atlanta (N.L.)	3B-OF-DH	137	472	69	117	20	1	30	96	84	96	4	14	2-0	.248	.362	.485	.847	6	.978
2005— Rome (S. Atl.)	3B-DH	3	6	1	3	0	0	0	2	3	1	0	1	0-0	.500	.667	.500	1.167	1	.833
— Atlanta (N.L.)	3B	109	358	66	106	30	0	21	72	72	56	0	9	5-1	.296	.412	.556	.968	5	.980
2006— Mississippi (Sou.)		2	6	1	1	0	0	0	0	0	2	0	0	0-0	.167	.167	.167	.333	1	.857
— Atlanta (N.L.)	3B-DH	110	411	87	133	28	3	26	86	61	73	1	12	6-1	.324	.409	.596	1.005	18	.936
Major League totals (13 years)		1761	6385	1188	1944	383	30	357	1197	1070	1006	15	170	129-42	.304	.402	.542	.943	172	.957

DIVISION SERIES RECORD

Year Team (League)	Pos.	G	AB	R	H	2B	3B	HR	RBI	BB	SO	HBP	GDP	SB-CS	Avg.	OBP	SLG	OPS	E	Avg.
1995— Atlanta (N.L.)	3B	4	18	4	7	2	0	2	4	2	2	0	2	0-0	.389	.450	.833	1.283	0	1.000
1996— Atlanta (N.L.)	3B	3	9	2	2	0	0	1	2	3	4	0	0	1-1	.222	.417	.556	.972	0	1.000
1997— Atlanta (N.L.)	3B	3	8	3	4	0	0	1	2	3	2	0	1	1-0	.500	.583	.875	1.458	1	.833
1998— Atlanta (N.L.)	3B	3	10	2	2	0	0	0	1	4	3	0	0	0-0	.200	.429	.200	.629	0	1.000
1999— Atlanta (N.L.)	3B	4	13	2	3	0	0	1	5	2	0	1	0	0-0	.231	.421	.231	.652	1	.875
2000— Atlanta (N.L.)	3B	3	12	2	4	1	0	0	1	1	4	0	0	0-0	.333	.385	.417	.801	2	.800
2001— Atlanta (N.L.)	3B	3	9	2	4	0	0	2	5	3	1	0	0	0-1	.444	.583	1.111	1.694	0	1.000
2002— Atlanta (N.L.)	OF	5	17	3	5	0	0	0	2	5	2	0	1	0-0	.294	.455	.294	.749	0	1.000
2003— Atlanta (N.L.)	OF	5	18	3	3	0	0	2	6	3	4	0	1	0-0	.167	.286	.500	.786	0	1.000
2004— Atlanta (N.L.)	3B	5	20	4	4	0	0	0	0	3	2	0	1	0-0	.200	.304	.200	.504	0	1.000
2005— Atlanta (N.L.)	3B	4	17	3	3	2	0	1	2	4	4	0	1	0-0	.176	.333	.471	.804	0	1.000
Division series totals (11 years)		42	151	30	41	5	0	9	26	36	30	0	7	2-2	.272	.407	.483	.891	4	.952

CHAMPIONSHIP SERIES RECORD

Year Team (League)	Pos.	G	AB	R	H	2B	3B	HR	RBI	BB	SO	HBP	GDP	SB-CS	Avg.	OBP	SLG	OPS	E	Avg.
1995— Atlanta (N.L.)	3B	4	16	3	7	0	0	1	3	3	1	0	0	1-0	.438	.526	.625	1.151	0	1.000
1996— Atlanta (N.L.)	3B	7	25	6	11	2	0	0	4	3	1	0	0	1-0	.440	.483	.520	1.003	1	.923
1997— Atlanta (N.L.)	3B	6	24	5	7	1	0	2	4	2	3	0	0	0-0	.292	.346	.583	.929	0	1.000
1998— Atlanta (N.L.)	3B	6	24	2	5	1	0	0	1	4	5	0	2	0-0	.208	.321	.250	.571	0	1.000
1999— Atlanta (N.L.)	3B	6	19	3	5	2	0	1	1	9	7	1	0	3-0	.263	.517	.368	.886	2	.867
2001— Atlanta (N.L.)	3B	5	19	1	5	1	0	0	2	3	6	0	0	0-0	.263	.364	.316	.679	1	.923
Champ. series totals (6 years)		34	127	20	40	7	0	3	15	24	23	1	2	5-0	.315	.425	.441	.866	4	.950

WORLD SERIES RECORD

Year Team (League)	Pos.	G	AB	R	H	2B	3B	HR	RBI	BB	SO	HBP	GDP	SB-CS	Avg.	OBP	SLG	OPS	E	Avg.
1995— Atlanta (N.L.)	3B	6	21	3	6	3	0	0	1	4	3	0	0	0-0	.286	.385	.429	.813	1	.947
1996— Atlanta (N.L.)	3B-SS	6	21	3	6	3	0	0	3	4	2	0	1	1-0	.286	.385	.429	.813	0	1.000
1999— Atlanta (N.L.)	3B	4	13	2	3	0	0	1	2	4	2	0	0	0-1	.231	.412	.462	.873	0	1.000
World series totals (3 years)		16	55	8	15	6	0	1	6	12	7	0	1	1-1	.273	.391	.436	.828	1	.972

ALL-STAR GAME RECORD

		G	AB	R	H	2B	3B	HR	RBI	BB	SO	HBP	GDP	SB-CS	Avg.	OBP	SLG	OPS	E	Avg.
All-Star Game totals (5 years)		5	10	3	4	0	0	1	1	1	0	1		0-0	.400	.455	.700	1.155	0	1.000

2006 LEFTY-RIGHTY SPLITS

vs.	Avg.	AB	H	2B	3B	HR	RBI	BB	SO	OBP	Slg.	vs.	Avg.	AB	H	2B	3B	HR	RBI	BB	SO	OBP	Slg.
L	.293	92	27	4	2	6	22	3	17	.309	.576	R	.332	319	106	24	1	20	64	58	56	.434	.602

JONES, GREG — P

PERSONAL: Born November 15, 1976, in Clearwater, Fla. ... 6-2/195. ... Throws right, bats right. ... Full name: Greg Alan Jones. ... High school: Seminole (Fla.) ... College: Pasco Hernando (Fla.) **TRANSACTIONS/CAREER NOTES:** Selected by Anaheim Angels organization in 42nd round of 1996 free-agent draft. ... On disabled list (March 26-June 7, 2004); included rehabilitation assignment to Salt Lake. ... Angels franchise renamed Los Angeles Angels of Anaheim for 2005 season.
CAREER HITTING: 0-for-0 (.000), 0 R, 0 2B, 0 3B, 0 HR, 0 RBI.

Year Team (League)	W	L	Pct.	ERA	WHIP	G	GS	CG	ShO	Hld.	Sv.-Opp.	IP	H	R	ER	HR	BB-IBB	SO	Avg.
1997— Boise (N'west)	2	2	.500	3.62	1.45	21	4	0	0	...	2-...	37.1	35	19	15	1	19-1	39	.243
1998— Boise (N'west)	0	2	.000	4.93	1.44	22	0	0	0	...	1-...	34.2	37	22	19	3	13-0	28	.278

Year—Team (League)	W	L	Pct.	ERA	WHIP	G	GS	CG	ShO	Hld.	Sv.-Opp.	IP	H	R	ER	HR	BB-IBB	SO	Avg.
1999—Cedar Rap. (Midw.)	2	4	.333	3.83	1.25	34	0	0	0	...	13-...	40.0	37	18	17	5	13-2	41	.247
2000—Lake Elsinore (Calif.)	0	0	...	4.08	1.64	16	0	0	0	...	3-...	17.2	19	9	8	0	10-3	12	.284
—Erie (East.)	0	2	.000	5.40	1.53	11	0	0	0	...	2-...	15.0	19	9	9	1	4-0	7	.306
—Edmonton (PCL)	2	2	.500	7.65	2.13	25	0	0	0	...	1-...	42.1	57	42	36	5	33-1	21	.324
2001—Rancho Cuca. (Calif.)	1	3	.250	4.23	1.30	6	6	0	0	...	0-...	27.2	25	15	13	2	11-0	27	.238
—Ariz. Angels (Ariz.)	0	0	...	0.00	2.50	2	2	0	0	...	0-...	2.0	3	0	0	0	2-0	2	.375
2002—Salt Lake (PCL)	7	4	.636	4.31	1.44	39	0	0	0	...	2-...	62.2	68	35	30	5	22-0	55	.273
2003—Salt Lake (PCL)	2	3	.400	4.40	0.96	33	0	0	0	...	4-...	47.0	36	24	23	4	9-0	56	.207
—Anaheim (A.L.)	0	0	...	4.88	1.55	18	0	0	0	2	0-0	27.2	29	15	15	3	14-0	28	.261
2004—Arkansas (Texas)	0	1	.000	2.70	0.90	3	0	0	0	0	0-0	3.1	2	1	1	0	1-0	2	.167
—Salt Lake (PCL)	1	4	.200	5.74	1.54	36	0	0	0	0	3-...	53.1	63	38	34	11	19-0	43	.283
2005—Salt Lake (PCL)	1	2	.333	3.20	1.03	23	0	0	0	0	10-12	25.1	20	9	9	3	6-0	25	.218
—Los Angeles (A.L.)	0	0	...	6.75	1.69	6	0	0	0	0	0-0	5.1	7	4	4	2	2-0	6	.318
2006—Salt Lake (PCL)	5	6	.455	4.25	1.29	47	0	0	0	2	17-24	55.0	52	28	26	7	19-2	45	.252
—Los Angeles (A.L.)	0	0	...	6.00	1.67	5	0	0	0	0	0-0	6.0	8	5	4	1	2-0	1	.348
Major League totals (3 years)	0	0	...	5.31	1.59	29	0	0	0	2	0-0	39.0	44	24	23	6	18-0	35	.282

2006 LEFTY-RIGHTY SPLITS

vs.	Avg.	AB	H	2B	3B	HR	RBI	BB	SO	OBP	Slg.	vs.	Avg.	AB	H	2B	3B	HR	RBI	BB	SO	OBP	Slg.
L	.000	5	0	0	0	0	2	0	0	.222	.000	R	.444	18	8	1	1	1	3	0	1	.421	.778

JONES, JACQUE — OF

PERSONAL: Born April 25, 1975, in San Diego. ... 5-10/195. ... Bats left, throws left. ... Full name: Jacque Dewayne Jones. ... High school: San Diego High. ... College: Southern California. **TRANSACTIONS/CAREER NOTES:** Selected by Kansas City Royals organization in 31st round of 1993 free-agent draft; did not sign. ... Selected by Minnesota Twins organization in second round of 1996 free-agent draft. ... On disabled list (July 1-17, 2003). ... Signed as a free agent by Chicago Cubs (January 10, 2006). **STATISTICAL NOTES:** Career major league grand slams: 2. **MISCELLANEOUS NOTES:** Member of 1996 U.S. Olympic baseball team.

2006 GAMES PLAYED BY POSITION (MLB): OF—143.

Year—Team (League)	Pos.	G	AB	R	H	2B	3B	HR	RBI	BB	SO	HBP	GDP	SB-CS	Avg.	OBP	SLG	OPS	FIELDING E	Avg.
1996—Fort Myers (FSL)	OF	1	3	0	2	1	0	0	1	0	0	0	0	0-1	.667	.667	1.000	1.667	0	...
1997—Fort Myers (FSL)	OF	131	539	84	160	33	6	15	82	33	110	3	9	24-12	.297	.340	.464	.804	7	.979
1998—New Britain (East.)	OF-DH	134	518	78	155	39	3	21	85	37	134	4	4	18-11	.299	.349	.508	.856	10	.968
1999—Salt Lake (PCL)	OF	52	198	32	59	13	2	4	26	9	36	0	5	9-2	.298	.325	.444	.770	2	.987
—Minnesota (A.L.)	OF	95	322	54	93	24	2	9	44	17	63	4	7	3-4	.289	.329	.460	.789	5	.980
2000—Minnesota (A.L.)	OF	154	523	66	149	26	5	19	76	26	111	0	17	7-5	.285	.319	.463	.781	2	.994
2001—Minnesota (A.L.)	OF-DH	149	475	57	131	25	0	14	49	39	92	3	10	12-9	.276	.335	.417	.751	5	.983
2002—Minnesota (A.L.)	OF-DH	149	577	96	173	37	2	27	85	37	129	2	6-7	.300	.341	.511	.852	5	.986
2003—Minnesota (A.L.)	OF-DH	136	517	76	157	33	1	16	69	21	105	4	10	13-1	.304	.333	.464	.797	5	.977
2004—Minnesota (A.L.)	OF-DH	151	555	69	141	22	1	24	80	40	117	10	12	13-10	.254	.315	.427	.742	2	.994
2005—Minnesota (A.L.)	OF-DH	142	523	74	130	22	4	23	73	51	120	5	17	13-4	.249	.319	.438	.757	4	.994
2006—Chicago (N.L.)	OF	149	533	73	152	31	1	27	81	35	116	5	17	9-1	.285	.334	.499	.833	7	.976
American League totals (7 years)		976	3492	492	974	189	15	132	476	231	737	28	81	67-40	.279	.327	.455	.782	28	.986
National League totals (1 year)		149	533	73	152	31	1	27	81	35	116	5	17	9-1	.285	.334	.499	.833	7	.976
Major League totals (8 years)		1125	4025	565	1126	220	16	159	557	266	853	33	98	76-41	.280	.328	.461	.789	35	.985

DIVISION SERIES RECORD

Year—Team (League)	Pos.	G	AB	R	H	2B	3B	HR	RBI	BB	SO	HBP	GDP	SB-CS	Avg.	OBP	SLG	OPS	E	Avg.
2002—Minnesota (A.L.)	OF	5	20	3	5	3	0	0	1	1	8	1	1	0-0	.250	.318	.400	.718	1	.952
2003—Minnesota (A.L.)	OF	4	16	0	2	0	0	0	0	0	5	0	0	0-0	.125	.125	.125	.250	0	1.000
2004—Minnesota (A.L.)	OF	4	20	3	6	1	0	2	2	0	6	0	2	0-1	.300	.300	.650	.950	0	1.000
Division series totals (3 years)		13	56	6	13	4	0	2	3	1	19	1	3	0-1	.232	.259	.411	.669	1	.972

CHAMPIONSHIP SERIES RECORD

Year—Team (League)	Pos.	G	AB	R	H	2B	3B	HR	RBI	BB	SO	HBP	GDP	SB-CS	Avg.	OBP	SLG	OPS	E	Avg.
2002—Minnesota (A.L.)	OF	5	20	0	2	1	0	0	2	0	4	0	0	0-0	.100	.095	.150	.245	0	1.000

2006 LEFTY-RIGHTY SPLITS

vs.	Avg.	AB	H	2B	3B	HR	RBI	BB	SO	OBP	Slg.	vs.	Avg.	AB	H	2B	3B	HR	RBI	BB	SO	OBP	Slg.
L	.234	137	32	7	0	6	22	2	33	.261	.416	R	.303	396	120	24	1	21	59	33	83	.358	.528

JONES, TODD — P

PERSONAL: Born April 24, 1968, in Marietta, Ga. ... 6-3/230. ... Throws right, bats left. ... Full name: Todd Barton Jones. ... High school: Osborne (Ga.). ... College: Jacksonville (Ala.) State. **TRANSACTIONS/CAREER NOTES:** Selected by New York Mets organization in 41st round of June 1986 free-agent draft; did not sign. ... Selected by Houston Astros organization in supplemental round ("sandwich pick" between first and second rounds, 27th pick overall) of 1989 free-agent draft; pick received as part of compensation for Texas Rangers signing Type A free-agent P Nolan Ryan. ... On suspended list (September 14-16, 1993). ... On disabled list (July 19-August 12 and August 18-September 12, 1996); included rehabilitation assignment to Tucson. ... Traded by Astros with OF Brian Hunter, IF Orlando Miller, P Doug Brocail and cash to Detroit Tigers for C Brad Ausmus, Ps Jose Lima, C.J. Nitkowski and Trever Miller and 1B Daryle Ward (December 10, 1996). ... Traded by Tigers to Minnesota Twins for P Mark Redman (July 28, 2001). ... Signed as a free agent by Colorado Rockies (January 15, 2002). ... Released by Rockies (June 30, 2003). ... Signed by Boston Red Sox (July 2, 2003). ... Signed as a free agent by Tampa Bay Devil Rays organization (January 11, 2004). ... Released by Devil Rays (March 24, 2004). ... Signed by Cincinnati Reds organization (March 25, 2004). ... Traded by Reds with OF Brad Correll to Philadelphia Phillies for P Josh Hancock and SS Anderson Machado (July 30, 2004). ... Signed as a free agent by Florida Marlins (December 13, 2004). ... Signed as a free agent by Tigers (December 8, 2005). ... On disabled list (April 3-21, 2006). **HONORS:** Named A.L. Fireman of the Year by THE SPORTING NEWS (2000).

CAREER HITTING: 4-for-19 (.211), 1 R, 1 2B, 0 3B, 0 HR, 0 RBI.

Year—Team (League)	W	L	Pct.	ERA	WHIP	G	GS	CG	ShO	Hld.	Sv.-Opp.	IP	H	R	ER	HR	BB-IBB	SO	Avg.
1989—Auburn (NY-Penn)	2	3	.400	5.44	1.79	11	9	1	0	...	0-...	49.2	47	39	30	2	42-1	71	.240
1990—Osceola (Fla. St.)	12	10	.545	3.51	1.54	27	27	1	0	...	0-...	151.1	124	81	59	2	109-1	106	.223
1991—Osceola (Fla. St.)	4	4	.500	4.35	1.44	14	14	0	0	...	0-...	72.1	69	38	35	2	35-0	51	.256
—Jackson (Texas)	4	3	.571	4.88	1.63	10	10	0	0	...	0-...	55.1	51	37	30	2	39-1	37	.241
1992—Jackson (Texas)	3	7	.300	3.14	1.45	61	0	0	0	...	25-...	66.0	52	28	23	3	44-3	60	.213
—Tucson (PCL)	0	1	.000	4.50	2.75	3	0	0	0	...	0-...	4.0	1	2	2	0	10-1	4	.077
1993—Tucson (PCL)	4	2	.667	4.44	1.64	41	0	0	0	...	12-...	48.2	49	26	24	5	31-2	45	.265
—Houston (N.L.)	1	2	.333	3.13	1.15	27	0	0	0	6	2-4	37.1	28	14	13	4	15-2	25	.214
1994—Houston (N.L.)	5	2	.714	2.72	1.07	48	0	0	0	8	5-9	72.2	52	23	22	3	26-4	63	.202
1995—Houston (N.L.)	6	5	.545	3.07	1.41	68	0	0	0	8	15-20	99.2	89	38	34	8	52-17	96	.237
1996—Houston (N.L.)	6	3	.667	4.40	1.62	51	0	0	0	0	17-23	57.1	61	30	28	5	32-6	44	.274
—Tucson (PCL)	0	0	...	0.00	1.50	1	0	0	0	0	0-...	2.0	1	1	0	0	2-0	5	.200

J

Year Team (League)	W	L	Pct.	ERA	WHIP	G	GS	CG	ShO	Hld.	Sv.-Opp.	IP	H	R	ER	HR	BB-IBB	SO	Avg.
1997— Detroit (A.L.)	5	4	.556	3.09	1.36	68	0	0	0	5	31-36	70.0	60	29	24	3	35-2	70	.231
1998— Detroit (A.L.)	1	4	.200	4.97	1.48	65	0	0	0	0	28-32	63.1	58	38	35	7	36-4	57	.249
1999— Detroit (A.L.)	4	4	.500	3.80	1.49	65	0	0	0	0	30-35	66.1	64	30	28	7	35-1	64	.259
2000— Detroit (A.L.)	2	4	.333	3.52	1.44	67	0	0	0	0	• 42-46	64.0	67	28	25	6	25-1	67	.276
2001— Detroit (A.L.)	4	5	.444	4.62	1.68	45	0	0	0	3	11-17	48.2	60	31	25	6	22-1	39	.303
—Minnesota (A.L.)	1	0	1.000	3.26	1.76	24	0	0	0	7	2-4	19.1	27	8	7	3	7-0	15	.333
2002— Colorado (N.L.)	1	4	.200	4.70	1.36	79	0	0	0	30	1-3	82.1	84	43	43	10	28-3	73	.269
2003— Colorado (N.L.)	1	4	.200	8.24	2.01	33	1	0	0	3	0-5	39.1	61	39	36	8	18-0	28	.361
—Boston (A.L.)	2	1	.667	5.52	1.53	26	0	0	0	1	0-0	29.1	32	19	18	2	13-2	31	.269
2004— Cincinnati (N.L.)	8	2	.800	3.79	1.30	51	0	0	0	22	1-6	57.0	49	25	24	4	25-2	37	.243
—Philadelphia (N.L.)	3	3	.500	4.97	1.70	27	0	0	0	5	1-2	25.1	35	14	14	3	8-3	22	.330
2005— Florida (N.L.)	1	5	.167	2.10	1.03	68	0	0	0	1	40-45	73.0	61	19	17	2	14-2	62	.230
2006— Detroit (A.L.)	2	6	.250	3.94	1.27	62	0	0	0	0	37-43	64.0	70	31	28	4	11-3	28	.276
American League totals (7 years)	21	28	.429	4.02	1.46	422	0	0	0	16	181-213	425.0	438	214	190	38	184-14	371	.268
National League totals (8 years)	32	30	.516	3.82	1.36	452	1	0	0	84	82-116	544.0	520	245	231	47	218-39	450	.255
Major League totals (14 years)	53	58	.477	3.91	1.40	874	1	0	0	100	263-329	969.0	958	459	421	85	402-53	821	.261

DIVISION SERIES RECORD

Year Team (League)	W	L	Pct.	ERA	WHIP	G	GS	CG	ShO	Hld.	Sv.-Opp.	IP	H	R	ER	HR	BB-IBB	SO	Avg.
2006— Detroit (A.L.)	0	0	...	0.00	0.50	2	0	0	0	0	1-1	2.0	1	0	0	0	0-0	2	.143

CHAMPIONSHIP SERIES RECORD

Year Team (League)	W	L	Pct.	ERA	WHIP	G	GS	CG	ShO	Hld.	Sv.-Opp.	IP	H	R	ER	HR	BB-IBB	SO	Avg.
2003— Boston (A.L.)	0	0	...	0.00	6.00	1	0	0	0	0	0-0	0.1	1	0	0	0	1-0	1	.500
2006— Detroit (A.L.)	0	0	...	0.00	1.33	3	0	0	0	0	2-2	3.0	3	0	0	0	1-0	2	.250
Champ. series totals (2 years)	0	0	...	0.00	1.80	4	0	0	0	0	2-2	3.1	4	0	0	0	2-0	3	.286

WORLD SERIES RECORD

Year Team (League)	W	L	Pct.	ERA	WHIP	G	GS	CG	ShO	Hld.	Sv.-Opp.	IP	H	R	ER	HR	BB-IBB	SO	Avg.
2006— Detroit (A.L.)	0	0	...	0.00	1.80	2	0	0	0	0	1-1	1.2	3	1	0	0	0-0	1	.333

ALL-STAR GAME RECORD

	W	L	Pct.	ERA	WHIP	G	GS	CG	ShO	Hld.	Sv.-Opp.	IP	H	R	ER	HR	BB-IBB	SO	Avg.
All-Star Game totals (1 year)	0	0	...	0.00	0.00	1	0	0	0	1	0-0	1.0	0	0	0	0	0-0	1	.000

2006 LEFTY-RIGHTY SPLITS

vs.	Avg.	AB	H	2B	3B	HR	RBI	BB	SO	OBP	Slg.	vs.	Avg.	AB	H	2B	3B	HR	RBI	BB	SO	OBP	Slg.
L	.264	106	28	1	1	1	14	7	14	.313	.321	R	.284	148	42	6	3	3	16	4	14	.312	.426

JORDAN, BRIAN — OF/1B

PERSONAL: Born March 29, 1967, in Baltimore. ... 6-1/225. ... Bats right, throws right. ... Full name: Brian O'Neal Jordan. ... High school: Milford (Baltimore). ... College: Richmond. **TRANSACTIONS/CAREER NOTES:** Selected by Cleveland Indians organization in 20th round of June 1985 free-agent draft; did not sign. ... Selected by St. Louis Cardinals organization in supplemental round ("sandwich pick" between first and second rounds, 30th pick overall) of 1988 free-agent draft; pick received as part of compensation for New York Yankees signing Type A free-agent 1B/OF Jack Clark. ... On temporarily inactive list (July 3, 1991-remainder of season). ... On disabled list (May 23-June 22, 1992); included rehabilitation assignment to Louisville. ... On disabled list (July 10, 1994-remainder of season; and March 31-April 15, 1996). ... On disabled list (May 6-June 13, June 26-August 10 and August 25, 1997-remainder of season); included rehabilitation assignment to Louisville. ... Signed as a free agent by Atlanta Braves (November 23, 1998). ... On disabled list (April 4-19, 2000). ... Traded by Braves with Ps Odalis Perez and Andrew Brown to Los Angeles Dodgers for OF Gary Sheffield (January 15, 2002). ... On disabled list (August 17-September 1, 2002; and June 25, 2003-remainder of season). ... Signed as a free agent by Texas Rangers (January 8, 2004). ... On disabled list (March 27-April 27 and May 24-July 23, 2004); included rehabilitation assignments to Frisco and Oklahoma. ... Signed as a free agent by Braves (January 19, 2005). ... On disabled list (July 7-September 1, 2005); included rehabilitation assignment to Rome. ... On disabled list (June 18-September 1, 2006); included rehabilitation assignments to Rome and Richmond. **STATISTICAL NOTES:** Career major league grand slams: 7. **MISCELLANEOUS NOTES:** Played in NFL with Atlanta Falcons (1989-91).

2006 GAMES PLAYED BY POSITION (MLB): 1B—25, OF—6.

Year Team (League)	Pos.	G	AB	R	H	2B	3B	HR	RBI	BB	SO	HBP	GDP	SB-CS	Avg.	OBP	SLG	OPS	E	Avg.
1988— Hamilton (NYP)	OF	19	71	12	22	3	1	4	12	6	15	3	0	3-3	.310	.388	.549	.937	1	.971
1989— St. Pete. (FSL)	OF	11	43	7	15	4	1	2	11	0	8	2	1	0-2	.349	.378	.628	1.006	0	1.000
1990— Arkansas (Texas)	OF	16	50	4	8	1	0	0	0	0	11	1	1	0-0	.160	.176	.180	.356	2	.933
—St. Pete. (FSL)	OF	9	30	3	5	0	1	0	1	2	11	0	0	0-2	.167	.219	.233	.452	0	1.000
1991— Louisville (A.A.)	OF	61	212	35	56	11	4	4	24	17	41	8	5	10-4	.264	.342	.410	.752	2	.987
1992— St. Louis (N.L.)	OF	55	193	17	40	9	4	5	22	10	48	1	6	7-2	.207	.250	.373	.623	1	.991
—Louisville (A.A.)	OF	43	155	23	45	3	1	4	16	8	21	4	1	13-2	.290	.337	.400	.737	1	.989
1993— St. Louis (N.L.)	OF	67	223	33	69	10	6	10	44	12	35	4	6	6-6	.309	.351	.543	.894	4	.973
—Louisville (A.A.)	OF	38	144	24	54	13	2	5	35	16	17	3	4	9-4	.375	.442	.597	1.040	1	1.000
1994— St. Louis (N.L.)	OF-1B	53	178	14	46	8	2	5	15	16	40	1	6	4-3	.258	.320	.410	.730	1	.991
1995— St. Louis (N.L.)	OF	131	490	83	145	20	4	22	81	22	79	11	5	24-9	.296	.339	.488	.827	1	.996
1996— St. Louis (N.L.)	OF-1B	140	513	82	159	36	1	17	104	29	84	7	6	22-5	.310	.349	.483	.833	2	.994
1997— St. Louis (N.L.)	OF	47	145	17	34	5	0	0	10	10	21	6	4	6-1	.234	.311	.269	.580	0	1.000
—Louisville (A.A.)	OF-DH	6	20	1	3	0	0	0	2	1	2	1	0	0-1	.150	.227	.150	.377	0	1.000
1998— St. Louis (N.L.)	OF-DH-3B	150	564	100	178	34	7	25	91	40	66	9	18	17-5	.316	.368	.534	.902	9	.970
1999— Atlanta (N.L.)	OF	153	576	100	163	28	4	23	115	51	81	9	9	13-8	.283	.346	.465	.811	3	.990
2000— Atlanta (N.L.)	OF-DH	133	489	71	129	26	0	17	77	38	80	5	12	10-2	.264	.320	.421	.742	3	.990
2001— Atlanta (N.L.)	OF-DH	148	560	82	165	32	3	25	97	31	88	6	18	3-2	.295	.334	.496	.830	3	.991
2002— Los Angeles (N.L.)	OF-DH	128	471	65	134	27	3	18	80	34	86	6	10	2-2	.285	.338	.469	.807	4	.982
2003— Los Angeles (N.L.)	OF-DH	66	224	28	67	9	0	6	28	23	30	4	3	1-1	.299	.372	.420	.791	1	.990
2004— Frisco (Texas)	OF-DH	6	19	1	3	1	0	0	0	0	6	0	0	0-0	.158	.158	.211	.368	0	1.000
—Oklahoma (PCL)	OF-DH	7	26	3	10	2	0	0	8	3	3	1	0	1-0	.385	.467	.462	.928	0	1.000
—Texas (A.L.)	OF-DH	61	212	27	47	13	1	5	23	16	35	1	7	2-2	.222	.275	.363	.638	1	.990
2005— Rome (S. Atl.)	DH-OF	5	16	5	8	1	0	1	7	2	2	0	0	1-0	.500	.500	.750	1.250	0	1.000
—Atlanta (N.L.)	OF	76	231	25	57	8	2	3	24	14	46	3	5	2-0	.247	.295	.338	.632	0	1.000
2006— Rome (S. Atl.)		1	1	0	0	0	0	0	0	3	0	0	0	0-0	.000	.750	.000	.750	0	...
—Richmond (Int'l)		4	15	3	5	1	0	2	4	1	7	0	0	0-0	.333	.375	.800	1.175	0	...
—Atlanta (N.L.)	1B-OF	48	91	11	21	2	0	3	10	7	23	1	3	0-0	.231	.287	.352	.639	2	.987
American League totals (1 year)		61	212	27	47	13	1	5	23	16	35	1	7	2-2	.222	.275	.363	.638	1	.990
National League totals (14 years)		1395	4948	728	1407	254	36	179	798	337	807	73	111	117-46	.284	.336	.459	.795	34	.988
Major League totals (15 years)		1456	5160	755	1454	267	37	184	821	353	842	74	118	119-48	.282	.333	.455	.788	35	.988

DIVISION SERIES RECORD

Year Team (League)	Pos.	G	AB	R	H	2B	3B	HR	RBI	BB	SO	HBP	GDP	SB-CS	Avg.	OBP	SLG	OPS	E	Avg.
1996— St. Louis (N.L.)	OF	3	12	4	4	0	0	1	3	1	3	0	0	1-0	.333	.385	.583	.968	0	1.000
1999— Atlanta (N.L.)	OF	4	17	2	8	1	0	1	7	1	2	0	0	0-1	.471	.474	.706	1.180	0	1.000
2000— Atlanta (N.L.)	OF	3	11	1	4	1	0	0	4	1	1	0	0	0-0	.364	.417	.455	.871	0	1.000
2001— Atlanta (N.L.)	OF	3	11	1	2	0	0	1	2	0	5	0	0	0-1	.182	.167	.455	.621	0	1.000
2005— Atlanta (N.L.)	OF	3	5	0	1	1	0	0	0	0	0	0	1	0-0	.200	.200	.400	.600	0	1.000
Division series totals (5 years)		16	56	8	19	3	0	3	16	3	11	0	1	1-2	.339	.361	.554	.914	0	1.000

CHAMPIONSHIP SERIES RECORD

Year Team (League)	Pos.	G	AB	R	H	2B	3B	HR	RBI	BB	SO	HBP	GDP	SB-CS	Avg.	OBP	SLG	OPS	E	Avg.
1996— St. Louis (N.L.)	OF	7	25	3	6	1	1	1	2	1	3	0	1	0-0	.240	.269	.480	.749	0	1.000
1999— Atlanta (N.L.)	OF	6	25	3	5	0	0	2	5	3	5	1	0	0-0	.200	.310	.440	.750	0	1.000
2001— Atlanta (N.L.)	OF	5	21	1	4	2	0	0	3	0	6	0	1	0-0	.190	.190	.286	.476	0	1.000
Champ. series totals (3 years)		18	71	7	15	3	1	3	10	4	14	1	2		.211	.263	.408	.672	0	1.000

WORLD SERIES RECORD

Year Team (League)	Pos.	G	AB	R	H	2B	3B	HR	RBI	BB	SO	HBP	GDP	SB-CS	Avg.	OBP	SLG	OPS	E	Avg.
1999— Atlanta (N.L.)	OF	4	13	1	1	0	0	0	1	4	2	0	1	0-0	.077	.294	.077	.371	1	.889

ALL-STAR GAME RECORD

		G	AB	R	H	2B	3B	HR	RBI	BB	SO	HBP	GDP	SB-CS	Avg.	OBP	SLG	OPS	E	Avg.
All-Star Game totals (1 year)		1	1	0	1	0	0	0	0	0	0	0	0	0-1	1.000	1.000	1.000	2.000	0	...

2006 LEFTY-RIGHTY SPLITS

vs.	Avg.	AB	H	2B	3B	HR	RBI	BB	SO	OBP	Slg.	vs.	Avg.	AB	H	2B	3B	HR	RBI	BB	SO	OBP	Slg.
L	.180	50	9	0	0	0	5	5	9	.246	.180	R	.293	41	12	2	0	3	5	2	14	.341	.561

JULIO, JORGE — P

PERSONAL: Born March 3, 1979, in Caracas, Venezuela. ... 6-1/232. ... Throws right, bats right. ... Full name: Jorge Dandys Julio. ... Name pronounced: HOR-hay HOO-lee-oh. ... High school: Fundacion Bolivariana (Caracas, Venezuela). **TRANSACTIONS/CAREER NOTES:** Signed as a non-drafted free agent by Montreal Expos organization (February 14, 1996). ... Traded by Expos to Baltimore Orioles for 3B Ryan Minor (December 22, 2000). ... On suspended list (September 24-28, 2004). ... Traded by Orioles with P John Maine to New York Mets for P Kris Benson (January 21, 2006). ... Traded by Mets to Arizona Diamondbacks for P Orlando Hernandez (May 24, 2006).
CAREER HITTING: 0-for-1 (.000), 0 R, 0 2B, 0 3B, 0 HR, 0 RBI.

Year Team (League)	W	L	Pct.	ERA	WHIP	G	GS	CG	ShO	Hld.	Sv.-Opp.	IP	H	R	ER	HR	BB-IBB	SO	Avg.
1996— Dom. Expos (DSL)	1	1	.500	6.06	1.47	10	0	0	0	...	0-...	16.1	13	12	11		11-...	21	...
1997— GC Expos (GCL)	5	6	.455	3.58	1.41	15	8	0	0	...	1-...	55.1	57	25	22	0	21-0	42	.256
— W.P. Beach (FSL)	0	0	...			1	0	0	0	...	0-...	0.0	2	1	1	0	0-0	0	1.000
1998— Vermont (NYP)	3	1	.750	2.57	1.07	7	7	0	0	...	0-...	42.0	30	12	12	1	15-0	52	.196
— Cape Fear (S. Atl.)	2	2	.500	5.68	1.42	6	6	0	0	...	0-...	31.2	33	20	20	4	12-0	20	.275
1999— Jupiter (Fla. St.)	4	8	.333	3.92	1.31	23	22	0	0	...	0-...	114.2	116	62	50	6	34-0	80	.260
2000— Jupiter (Fla. St.)	2	10	.167	5.90	1.61	21	15	0	0	...	1-...	79.1	93	60	52	4	35-0	67	.292
2001— Bowie (East.)	0	0	...	0.73	0.57	12	0	0	0	...	7-...	12.1	5	1	1	0	2-1	14	.125
— Baltimore (A.L.)	1	1	.500	3.80	1.59	18	0	0	0	3	0-1	21.1	25	13	9	2	9-0	22	.287
— Rochester (Int'l)	1	2	.333	3.74	1.34	34	0	0	0	...	12-...	43.1	39	27	18	4	19-3	48	.232
2002— Baltimore (A.L.)	5	6	.455	1.99	1.21	67	0	0	0	1	25-31	69.0	55	22	15	5	27-3	55	.213
2003— Baltimore (A.L.)	0	7	.000	4.38	1.52	64	0	0	0	2	36-44	61.2	60	36	30	10	34-4	52	.256
2004— Baltimore (A.L.)	2	5	.286	4.57	1.42	65	0	0	0	2	22-26	69.0	59	35	35	11	39-4	70	.228
2005— Baltimore (A.L.)	3	5	.375	5.90	1.40	67	0	0	0	12	0-1	71.2	76	50	47	14	24-4	58	.269
2006— New York (N.L.)	1	2	.333	5.06	1.45	18	0	0	0	1	1-1	21.1	21	15	12	4	10-1	33	.247
— Arizona (N.L.)	1	2	.333	3.83	1.25	44	0	0	0	1	15-19	44.2	31	20	19	6	25-1	55	.190
American League totals (5 years)	11	24	.314	4.20	1.40	281	0	0	0	20	83-104	291.2	275	156	136	42	133-15	257	.245
National League totals (1 year)	2	4	.333	4.23	1.32	62	0	0	0	1	16-20	66.0	52	35	31	10	35-2	88	.210
Major league totals (6 years)	13	28	.317	4.20	1.38	343	0	0	0	21	99-124	357.2	327	191	167	52	168-17	345	.239

2006 LEFTY-RIGHTY SPLITS

vs.	Avg.	AB	H	2B	3B	HR	RBI	BB	SO	OBP	Slg.	vs.	Avg.	AB	H	2B	3B	HR	RBI	BB	SO	OBP	Slg.
L	.185	124	23	5	0	6	12	17	38	.284	.371	R	.234	124	29	7	2	4	18	18	50	.336	.419

KAPLER, GABE — OF

PERSONAL: Born August 31, 1975, in Hollywood, Calif. ... 6-2/200. ... Bats right, throws right. ... Full name: Gabriel Stefan Kapler. ... Name pronounced: CAP-ler. ... High school: Taft (Woodland Hills, Calif.). ... Junior college: Moorpark (Calif.). . **TRANSACTIONS/CAREER NOTES:** Selected by Detroit Tigers organization in 57th round of 1995 free-agent draft. ... Traded by Tigers with Ps Justin Thompson, Francisco Cordero and Alan Webb, C Bill Haselman and 2B Frank Catalanotto to Texas Rangers for OF Juan Gonzalez, P Danny Patterson and C Gregg Zaun (November 2, 1999). ... On disabled list (May 4-June 9, 2000); included rehabilitation assignments to Oklahoma and Tulsa. ... On disabled list (March 23-April 22, 2001); included rehabilitation assignment to Tulsa. ... On disabled list (June 24-July 16, 2002); included rehabilitation assignment to Oklahoma. ... Traded by Rangers with 2B Jason Romano to Colorado Rockies for OF Todd Hollandsworth and P Dennys Reyes (July 31, 2002). ... Released by Rockies (June 20, 2003). ... Signed by Boston Red Sox organization (June 26, 2003). ... Granted free agency (October 28, 2004). ... Signed by Yomiuri Giants of the Japan Central league (November 22, 2004). ... Signed as free agent by Boston Red Sox (July 15, 2005). ... On disabled list (July 15-30, 2005); included rehabilitation assignments to Lowell and Pawtucket. ... Released by Red Sox (November 18, 2005). ... Re-signed by Red Sox (February 1, 2006). **HONORS:** Named Minor League Player of the Year by THE SPORTING NEWS (1998). **STATISTICAL NOTES:** Career major league grand slams: 1.
2006 GAMES PLAYED BY POSITION (MLB): OF—68, DH—1.

Year Team (League)	Pos.	G	AB	R	H	2B	3B	HR	RBI	BB	SO	HBP	GDP	SB-CS	Avg.	OBP	SLG	OPS	E	Avg.
1995— Jamestown (NYP)	OF	63	236	38	68	19	4	4	34	23	37	2	4	1-2	.288	.351	.453	.804	9	.926
1996— Fayetteville (SAL)	3B-OF	138	524	81	157	45	0	26	99	62	73	7	6	14-4	.300	.378	.534	.912	7	.968
1997— Lakeland (Fla. St.)	OF	137	519	87	153	40	6	19	87	54	68	5	8	8-6	.295	.361	.505	.865	6	.978
1998— Jacksonville (Sou.)	1B-OF	139	547	113	176	47	6	28	146	66	93	5	6	6-4	.322	.393	.583	.976	5	.984
— Detroit (A.L.)	OF-DH	7	25	3	5	0	1	0	1	1	4	0	0	2-0	.200	.231	.280	.511	0	1.000
1999— Detroit (A.L.)	OF-DH	130	416	60	102	22	4	18	49	42	74	2	7	11-5	.245	.315	.447	.762	6	.981
— Toledo (Int'l)	OF	14	54	11	17	6	2	3	14	9	10	0	0	0-1	.315	.406	.667	1.067	0	1.000
2000— Texas (A.L.)	OF	116	444	59	134	32	6	14	66	42	57	0	12	8-4	.302	.360	.473	.833	• 10	.969
— Oklahoma (PCL)	OF	3	9	3	3	0	0	0	3	2	0	0	0	0-0	.333	.500	.333	.833	0	1.000
— Tulsa (Texas)	OF	3	12	3	7	0	0	1	4	1	2	0	0	0-0	.583	.615	.833	1.449	0	1.000
2001— Tulsa (Texas)	OF	5	15	2	5	1	0	0	6	1	0	0	0	0-1	.333	.524	.400	.924	0	1.000
— Texas (A.L.)	OF-DH	134	483	77	129	29	1	17	72	61	70	3	10	23-6	.267	.348	.437	.785	1	.997
2002— Texas (A.L.)	OF-1B-DH	72	196	25	51	12	1	0	17	8	30	0	1	5-2	.260	.285	.332	.617	3	.977
— Oklahoma (PCL)	OF	5	17	6	8	2	0	1	5	2	0	0	0	1-0	.471	.550	.765	1.315	0	1.000

Year	Team (League)	Pos.	G	AB	R	H	2B	3B	HR	RBI	BB	SO	HBP	GDP	SB-CS	Avg.	OBP	SLG	OPS	E	Avg.
																	BATTING			FIELDING	
— Colorado (N.L.)	OF	40	119	12	37	4	3	2	17	8	23	1	2	6-2	.311	.359	.445	.805	0	1.000
2003— Colorado (N.L.)	OF	39	67	10	15	2	0	0	4	8	18	0	3	2-0	.224	.307	.254	.560	1	.970
— Colo. Springs (PCL)	OF	13	35	5	6	2	1	0	2	8	10	1	0	4-0	.171	.333	.286	.619	1	.955
— Lowell (NY-Penn)	OF	1	3	2	2	0	0	0	1	0	0	1	0	1-0	.667	.750	.667	1.417	0	...
— Portland (East.)	1B-OF	1	3	1	1	1	0	0	0	0	1	0	0	0-0	.333	.333	.667	1.000	0	1.000
— Boston (A.L.)	OF-1B-DH	68	158	29	46	11	1	4	23	14	23	0	5	4-2	.291	.349	.449	.798	6	.934
2004— Boston (A.L.)	OF-DH	136	290	51	79	14	1	6	33	15	49	2	5	5-4	.272	.311	.390	.700	4	.978
2005— Lowell (NY-Penn)		2	8	1	1	0	0	0	0	1	3	0	0	0-0	.125	.222	.125	.347	0	...
— Pawtucket (Int'l)		6	22	7	14	3	1	2	6	0	3	0	0	0-0	.636	.636	1.136	1.773	0	1.000
— Boston (A.L.)	OF	36	97	15	24	7	0	1	9	3	15	2	1	1-0	.247	.282	.351	.632	0	1.000
2006— Portland (East.)		3	10	2	4	3	1	0	2	1	2	0	0	0-0	.400	.455	.900	1.355	0	1.000
— Pawtucket (Int'l)		4	15	0	3	1	0	0	2	1	4	0	0	0-0	.200	.250	.267	.517	0	...
— Boston (A.L.)	OF-DH	72	130	21	33	7	0	2	12	14	35	1	1	1-1	.254	.340	.354	.694	0	1.000
American League totals (9 years)		771	2239	340	603	134	10	62	281	200	337	12	48	60-24	.269	.340	.421	.751	30	.981
National League totals (2 years)		79	186	22	52	6	3	2	21	16	41	1	5	8-2	.280	.340	.376	.716	1	.990
Major League totals (9 years)		850	2425	362	655	140	13	64	302	216	378	13	53	68-26	.270	.331	.418	.748	31	.981

DIVISION SERIES RECORD

Year	Team (League)	Pos.	G	AB	R	H	2B	3B	HR	RBI	BB	SO	HBP	GDP	SB-CS	Avg.	OBP	SLG	OPS	E	Avg.
2003— Boston (A.L.)	OF-DH	4	9	0	0	0	0	0	0	0	3	0	1	0-0	.000	.000	.000	.000	0	1.000
2004— Boston (A.L.)	OF	2	5	2	1	0	0	0	0	0	0	0	0	0-0	.200	.200	.200	.400	0	1.000
Division series totals (2 years)		6	14	2	1	0	0	0	0	0	3	0	1	0-0	.071	.071	.071	.143	0	1.000

CHAMPIONSHIP SERIES RECORD

Year	Team (League)	Pos.	G	AB	R	H	2B	3B	HR	RBI	BB	SO	HBP	GDP	SB-CS	Avg.	OBP	SLG	OPS	E	Avg.
2003— Boston (A.L.)	OF-DH	3	8	0	1	0	0	0	0	0	0	0	0	0-1	.125	.125	.125	.250	0	1.000
2004— Boston (A.L.)	OF	2	3	0	1	0	0	0	0	0	0	0	0	0-0	.333	.333	.333	.667	0	1.000
Champ. series totals (2 years)		5	11	0	2	0	0	0	0	0	0	0	0	0-1	.182	.182	.182	.364	0	1.000

WORLD SERIES RECORD

Year	Team (League)	Pos.	G	AB	R	H	2B	3B	HR	RBI	BB	SO	HBP	GDP	SB-CS	Avg.	OBP	SLG	OPS	E	Avg.
2004— Boston (A.L.)	OF	4	2	0	0	0	0	0	0	0	1	0	0	0-0	.000	.000	.000	.000	0	1.000

2006 LEFTY-RIGHTY SPLITS

vs.	Avg.	AB	H	2B	3B	HR	RBI	BB	SO	OBP	Slg.	vs.	Avg.	AB	H	2B	3B	HR	RBI	BB	SO	OBP	Slg.
L	.265	68	18	5	0	1	1	8	7	.367	.382	R	.242	62	15	2	0	1	11	6	8	.309	.323

KARSAY, STEVE   P

PERSONAL: Born March 24, 1972, in Flushing, N.Y. ... 6-3/210. ... Throws right, bats right. ... Full name: Stefan Andrew Karsay. ... Name pronounced: CAR-say. ... High school: Christ the King (Queens, N.Y.). **TRANSACTIONS/CAREER NOTES:** Selected by Toronto Blue Jays organization in first round (22nd pick overall) of 1990 free-agent draft. ... Traded by Blue Jays with a player to be named to Oakland Athletics for OF Rickey Henderson (July 31, 1993); A's acquired OF Jose Herrera to complete deal (August 6, 1993). ... On disabled list (April 26, 1994-remainder of season; April 24, 1995-entire season; and August 6, 1997-remainder of season). ... Traded by A's to Cleveland Indians for P Mike Fetters (December 8, 1997). ... On disabled list (July 2-26 and August 25-September 22, 1999). ... Traded by Indians with P Steve Reed to Atlanta Braves for P John Rocker and 3B Troy Cameron (June 22, 2001). ... Signed as a free agent by New York Yankees (December 7, 2001). ... On disabled list (March 21, 2003-entire season). ... On disabled list (March 12-September 1, 2004); included rehabilitation assignments to Staten Island, Trenton and Columbus. ... Released by Yankees (May 12, 2005). ... Signed by Texas Rangers organization (May 15, 2005). ... Signed as a free agent by Indians organization (December 19, 2005). ... Signed as a free agent by Oakland Athletics (May 16, 2006). ... On voluntary retired list (June 18-November 10, 2006). **MISCELLANEOUS NOTES:** Appeared in one game as pinch runner (1997).
CAREER HITTING: 0-for-4 (.000), 1 R, 0 2B, 0 3B, 0 HR, 0 RBI.

Year	Team (League)	W	L	Pct.	ERA	WHIP	G	GS	CG	ShO	Hld.	Sv.-Opp.	IP	H	R	ER	HR	BB-IBB	SO	Avg.
1990— St. Catharines (NYP)	1	1	.500	0.79	1.01	5	5	0	0	...	0-...	22.2	11	4	2	0	12-0	25	.141
1991— Myrtle Beach (SAL)	4	9	.308	3.58	1.30	20	20	1	0	...	0-...	110.2	96	58	44	7	48-0	100	.240
1992— Dunedin (Fla. St.)	6	3	.667	2.73	0.99	16	16	3	2	...	0-...	85.2	56	32	26	6	29-0	87	.187
1993— Knoxville (Southern)	8	4	.667	3.38	1.25	19	18	1	0	...	0-...	104.0	98	42	39	9	32-1	100	.251
— Huntsville (Sou.)	0	0	...	5.14	1.14	2	2	0	0	...	0-...	14.0	13	8	8	2	3-0	22	.255
— Oakland (A.L.)	3	3	.500	4.04	1.33	8	8	0	0	...	0-0	49.0	49	23	22	4	16-1	33	.258
1994— Oakland (A.L.)	1	1	.500	2.57	1.21	8	8	0	0	...	0-0	28.0	26	8	8	1	8-0	15	.252
1995— Oakland (A.L.)							Did not play.													
1996— Modesto (California)	0	1	.000	2.65	1.06	14	14	0	0	...	0-...	34.0	35	16	10	2	1-0	31	.255
1997— Oakland (A.L.)	3	12	.200	5.77	1.61	24	24	0	0	0	0-0	132.2	166	92	85	20	47-3	92	.304
1998— Buffalo (Int'l)	6	4	.600	3.76	1.32	16	14	0	0	...	0-0	79.0	89	39	33	5	15-0	63	.276
— Cleveland (A.L.)	0	2	.000	5.92	1.52	11	1	0	0	...	0-0	24.1	31	16	16	3	6-1	13	.310
1999— Cleveland (A.L.)	10	2	.833	2.97	1.28	50	2	0	0	9	1-3	78.2	71	29	26	6	30-3	68	.247
2000— Cleveland (A.L.)	5	9	.357	3.76	1.36	72	0	0	0	11	20-29	76.2	79	33	32	5	25-4	66	.266
2001— Cleveland (A.L.)	0	1	.000	1.25	0.85	31	0	0	0	8	1-1	43.1	29	6	6	1	8-2	44	.188
— Atlanta (N.L.)	3	4	.429	3.43	1.37	43	0	0	0	4	7-11	44.2	44	21	17	4	17-8	39	.265
2002— New York (A.L.)	6	4	.600	3.26	1.32	78	0	0	0	14	12-16	88.1	87	33	32	7	30-14	65	.258
2003— New York (A.L.)							Did not play.													
2004— Trenton (East.)	1	0	1.000	7.50	1.67	4	0	0	0	...	0-...	6.0	6	5	5	0	4-0	7	.273
— Staten Is. (N.Y.-Penn)	0	0	...	0.00	0.67	3	0	0	0	...	0-...	3.0	1	0	0	0	1-0	1	.100
— Columbus (Int'l)	0	0	...	5.56	1.59	11	0	0	0	...	0-...	11.1	12	10	7	0	6-0	8	.255
— New York (A.L.)	0	0	...	2.70	1.05	7	0	0	0	...	0-0	6.2	5	3	2	2	2-0	4	.217
2005— New York (A.L.)	0	0	...	6.00	2.00	6	0	0	0	...	0-0	6.0	10	5	4	0	2-1	5	.385
— Oklahoma (PCL)	0	1	.000	13.50	3.00	4	0	0	0	1	0-0	4.0	11	9	6	0	1-0	5	.458
— Frisco (Texas)	1	2	.333	3.64	1.18	19	0	0	0	3	0-2	29.2	29	18	12	2	6-2	30	.248
— Texas (A.L.)	0	1	.000	7.47	1.98	14	0	0	0	2	0-0	15.2	26	14	13	2	5-0	9	.366
2006— Buffalo (Int'l)	1	1	.500	2.00	0.72	8	0	0	0	2	0-0	18.0	12	6	4	2	1-0	14	.188
— Oakland (A.L.)	1	0	1.000	5.79	1.71	9	0	0	0	0	0-0	9.1	13	6	6	4	3-1	5	.351
American League totals (11 years)	29	35	.453	4.06	1.39	314	40	1	0	48	34-49	558.2	592	268	252	55	182-30	419	.273
National League totals (1 year)	3	4	.429	3.43	1.37	43	0	0	0	4	7-11	44.2	44	21	17	4	17-8	39	.265
Major League totals (11 years)	32	39	.451	4.01	1.38	357	40	1	0	52	41-60	603.1	636	289	269	59	199-38	458	.272

DIVISION SERIES RECORD

Year	Team (League)	W	L	Pct.	ERA	WHIP	G	GS	CG	ShO	Hld.	Sv.-Opp.	IP	H	R	ER	HR	BB-IBB	SO	Avg.
1999— Cleveland (A.L.)	0	0	...	9.00	2.00	2	0	0	0	0	0-0	3.0	5	3	3	1	1-0	3	.357
2001— Atlanta (N.L.)	0	0	...	0.00	0.00	1	0	0	0	0	0-0	1.0	0	0	0	0	0-0	1	.000
2002— New York (A.L.)	1	0	1.000	6.75	1.13	4	0	0	0	0	0-0	2.2	3	2	2	1	0-0	1	.273
Division series totals (3 years)	1	0	1.000	6.75	1.35	7	0	0	0	0	0-0	6.2	8	5	5	2	1-0	5	.286

Year Team (League)	W	L	Pct.	ERA	WHIP	G	GS	CG	ShO	Hld.	Sv.-Opp.	IP	H	R	ER	HR	BB-IBB	SO	Avg.
2001— Atlanta (N.L.)	0	0	...	2.08	0.92	4	0	0	0	0	0-0	4.1	3	1	1	0	1-1	6	.176

2006 LEFTY-RIGHTY SPLITS

vs.	Avg.	AB	H	2B	3B	HR	RBI	BB	SO	OBP	Slg.	vs.	Avg.	AB	H	2B	3B	HR	RBI	BB	SO	OBP	Slg.
L	.444	18	8	1	0	2	6	1	2	.450	.833	R	.263	19	5	1	0	2	2	2	3	.364	.684

KARSTENS, JEFF   P

PERSONAL: Born September 24, 1982, in San Diego. ... 6-3/185. ... Throws right, bats right. ... Full name: Jeffrey Wayne Karstens. ... High school: Mount Miguel (Spring Valley). ... College: Texas Tech. **TRANSACTIONS/CAREER NOTES:** Selected by New York Yankees organization in 19th round of 2003 free-agent draft.

CAREER HITTING: 0-for-0 (.000), 0 R, 0 2B, 0 3B, 0 HR, 0 RBI.

Year Team (League)	W	L	Pct.	ERA	WHIP	G	GS	CG	ShO	Hld.	Sv.-Opp.	IP	H	R	ER	HR	BB-IBB	SO	Avg.
2003— Staten Is. (N.Y.-Penn)	4	2	.667	2.54	1.17	14	10	0	0	...	0-...	67.1	63	22	19	2	16-1	53	.256
2004— Tampa (Fla. St.)	6	9	.400	4.02	1.31	24	24	1	1	...	0-...	138.2	151	70	62	11	31-3	116	.284
2005— Trenton (East.)	12	11	.522	4.15	1.38	28	27	0	0	0	0-0	169.0	192	91	78	16	42-0	147	.285
2006— Trenton (East.)	6	0	1.000	2.31	0.92	11	11	0	0	0	0-0	74.0	54	20	19	4	14-1	67	.198
— Columbus (Int'l)	5	5	.500	4.28	1.49	14	14	0	0	0	0-0	73.2	80	42	35	9	30-1	48	.275
— New York (A.L.)	2	1	.667	3.80	1.20	8	6	0	0	0	0-0	42.2	40	20	18	6	11-2	16	.242
Major League totals (1 year)	2	1	.667	3.80	1.20	8	6	0	0	0	0-0	42.2	40	20	18	6	11-2	16	.242

2006 LEFTY-RIGHTY SPLITS

vs.	Avg.	AB	H	2B	3B	HR	RBI	BB	SO	OBP	Slg.	vs.	Avg.	AB	H	2B	3B	HR	RBI	BB	SO	OBP	Slg.
L	.253	79	20	3	0	1	4	6	10	.306	.329	R	.233	86	20	6	1	5	14	5	6	.277	.500

KAZMIR, SCOTT   P

PERSONAL: Born January 24, 1984, in Houston. ... 6-0/170. ... Throws left, bats left. ... Full name: Scott Edward Kazmir. ... High school: Cypress Falls (Houston). **TRANSACTIONS/CAREER NOTES:** Selected by New York Mets organization in first round (15th pick overall) of 2002 free-agent draft. ... Traded by Mets with P Jose Diaz to Tampa Bay Devil Rays for Ps Victor Zambrano and Bartolome Fortunato (July 30, 2004). ... On disabled list (July 24-August 8, 2006). ... On disabled list (August 23, 2006-remainder of season).

CAREER HITTING: 0-for-4 (.000), 0 R, 0 2B, 0 3B, 0 HR, 0 RBI.

Year Team (League)	W	L	Pct.	ERA	WHIP	G	GS	CG	ShO	Hld.	Sv.-Opp.	IP	H	R	ER	HR	BB-IBB	SO	Avg.
2002— Brook. N.Y.-Penn. (N.Y.-Penn.)	0	1	.000	0.50	0.67	5	5	0	0	...	0-...	18.0	5	2	1	0	7-0	34	.089
2003— Capital City (SAL)	4	4	.500	2.36	1.02	18	18	0	0	...	0-...	76.1	50	26	20	6	28-0	105	.185
— St. Lucie (Fla. St.)	1	2	.333	3.27	1.36	7	7	0	0	...	0-...	33.0	29	15	12	0	16-0	40	.240
2004— St. Lucie (Fla. St.)	1	1	.333	3.42	1.42	11	11	0	0	...	0-...	50.0	49	20	19	3	22-0	51	.257
— Binghamton (East.)	2	1	.667	1.73	0.96	4	4	0	0	...	0-...	26.0	16	6	5	0	9-0	29	.188
— Montgom. (Sou.)	1	2	.333	1.44	1.00	4	4	0	0	...	0-...	25.0	14	7	4	0	11-0	24	.171
— Tampa Bay (A.L.)	2	3	.400	5.67	1.62	8	7	0	0	0	0-0	33.1	33	22	21	4	21-0	41	.256
2005— Tampa Bay (A.L.)	10	9	.526	3.77	1.46	32	32	0	0	0	0-0	186.0	172	90	78	12	*100-3	174	.248
2006— Tampa Bay (A.L.)	10	8	.556	3.24	1.27	24	24	1	1	0	0-0	144.2	132	59	52	15	52-3	163	.240
Major League totals (3 years)	22	20	.524	3.73	1.40	64	63	1	1	0	0-0	364.0	337	171	151	31	173-6	378	.245

	W	L	Pct.	ERA	WHIP	G	GS	CG	ShO	Hld.	Sv.-Opp.	IP	H	R	ER	HR	BB-IBB	SO	Avg.
All-Star Game totals (1 year)	0	0	...	0.00	0.00	1	0	0	0	...	0-0	1.0	0	0	0	0	0-0	0	.000

2006 LEFTY-RIGHTY SPLITS

vs.	Avg.	AB	H	2B	3B	HR	RBI	BB	SO	OBP	Slg.	vs.	Avg.	AB	H	2B	3B	HR	RBI	BB	SO	OBP	Slg.
L	.227	97	22	2	2	2	12	8	24	.283	.340	R	.242	454	110	28	3	13	42	44	139	.310	.403

KEARNS, AUSTIN   OF

PERSONAL: Born May 20, 1980, in Lexington, Ky. ... 6-3/220. ... Bats right, throws right. ... Full name: Austin Ryan Kearns. ... High school: Lafayette (Lexington, Ky.). **TRANSACTIONS/CAREER NOTES:** Selected by Cincinnati Reds organization in first round (seventh pick overall) of 1998 free-agent draft. ... On disabled list (August 27, 2002-remainder of season). ... On disabled list (July 9, 2003-remainder of season); included rehabilitation assignment to Chattanooga. ... On disabled list (April 27-May 19 and June 2-August 24, 2004); included rehabilitation assignments to Louisville. ... Traded by Reds with SS Felipe Lopez and P Ryan Wagner to Washington Nationals for Ps Gary Majewski, Bill Bray and Daryl Thompson, SS Royce Clayton and IF Brendan Harris (July 13, 2006). **STATISTICAL NOTES:** Career major league grand slams: 1.

2006 GAMES PLAYED BY POSITION (MLB): OF—145.

Year Team (League)	Pos.	G	AB	R	H	2B	3B	HR	RBI	BB	SO	HBP	GDP	SB-CS	Avg.	OBP	SLG	OPS	E	Avg.
1998— Billings (Pion.)	OF	30	108	17	34	9	0	1	14	23	22	1	4	1-1	.315	.433	.426	.859	4	.905
1999— Rockford (Midwest)	OF	124	426	72	110	36	5	13	48	50	120	9	4	21-8	.258	.346	.458	.804	13	.939
2000— Dayton (Midw.)	OF	136	484	110	148	37	2	27	104	90	93	7	14	18-5	.306	.415	.558	.973	12	.955
2001— Chattanooga (Sou.)	OF	59	205	30	55	11	2	6	36	26	43	6	4	7-5	.268	.364	.429	.793	2	.979
— GC Reds (GCL)	OF	6	17	2	3	2	0	0	2	4	7	0	0	0-0	.176	.227	.294	.521	0	1.000
2002— Chattanooga (Sou.)	OF	12	41	10	11	2	0	5	13	9	9	3	0	1-0	.268	.434	.683	1.117	0	1.000
— Cincinnati (N.L.)	OF	107	372	66	117	24	3	13	56	54	81	6	11	6-3	.315	.407	.500	.907	6	.983
— Louisville (Int'l)	OF	1	4	3	3	2	0	0	2	1	0	0	0	0-0	.750	.800	1.250	2.050	0	1.000
2003— Cincinnati (N.L.)	OF	82	292	39	77	11	0	15	58	41	68	5	7	5-2	.264	.364	.455	.819	2	.990
— Chattanooga (Sou.)	OF	3	5	2	1	0	0	0	1	2	2	1	0	0-0	.200	.500	.200	.700	0	1.000
2004— Louisville (Int'l)	OF-DH	25	83	19	28	7	1	2	15	19	16	2	3	3-1	.337	.471	.518	.989	3	.949
— Cincinnati (N.L.)	OF	64	217	28	50	14	2	9	32	28	71	1	8	2-1	.230	.321	.419	.740	3	.975
2005— Louisville (Int'l)	OF-DH	28	111	24	38	15	1	7	21	11	30	1	9	0-0	.342	.407	.685	1.091	0	1.000
— Cincinnati (N.L.)	OF	112	387	62	93	26	1	18	67	48	107	8	8	0-0	.240	.333	.452	.785	3	.988
2006— Cincinnati (N.L.)	OF	87	325	53	89	21	1	16	50	35	85	6	14	7-1	.274	.351	.492	.843	2	.991
— Wash. (N.L.)	OF	63	212	33	53	12	1	8	36	41	50	4	4	2-3	.250	.381	.429	.810	5	.968
Major League totals (5 years)		515	1805	281	479	104	8	79	299	247	462	30	52	22-10	.265	.361	.463	.824	19	.984

2006 LEFTY-RIGHTY SPLITS

vs.	Avg.	AB	H	2B	3B	HR	RBI	BB	SO	OBP	Slg.	vs.	Avg.	AB	H	2B	3B	HR	RBI	BB	SO	OBP	Slg.
L	.336	152	51	14	0	9	33	27	33	.434	.605	R	.236	385	91	19	2	15	53	49	102	.334	.413

KEISLER, RANDY   P

PERSONAL: Born February 24, 1976, in Richards, Texas. ... 6-3/190. ... Throws left, bats left. ... Full name: Randy Dean Keisler. ... Name pronounced: keyz-lur. ... High school: Navasota (Texas), then Palmer (Texas). ... College: Louisiana State. **TRANSACTIONS/CAREER NOTES:** Selected by Cleveland Indians organization in 40th round of

K

1995 free-agent draft; did not sign. ... Selected by Indians organization in 57th round of 1996 free-agent draft; did not sign. ... Selected by New York Yankees organization in second round of 1998 free-agent draft. ... On disabled list (March 31, 2002-entire season). ... Released by Yankees (February 5, 2003). ... Signed by San Diego Padres organization (February 16, 2003). ... Signed as a free agent by Texas Rangers organization (June 16, 2003). ... Released by Rangers (July 14, 2003). ... Signed by Houston Astros organization (July 17, 2003). ... Signed as a free agent by New York Mets organization (March 5, 2004). ... Signed as a free agent by Cincinnati Reds organization (November 12, 2004). ... On disabled list (June 26-July 15, 2005); included rehabilitation assignment to Louisville. ... Released by Reds (December 7, 2005). ... Signed as a free agent by Oakland Athletics organization (January 5, 2006). ... On bereavement list (May 15-18, 2006). **MISCELLANEOUS NOTES:** Appeared in one game as pinch runner (2003).

CAREER HITTING: 4-for-19 (.211), 3 R, 2 2B, 0 3B, 1 HR, 2 RBI.

Year — Team (League)	W	L	Pct.	ERA	WHIP	G	GS	CG	ShO	Hld.	Sv.-Opp.	IP	H	R	ER	HR	BB-IBB	SO	Avg.
1998— Oneonta (NYP)	1	1	.500	7.45	2.17	6	2	0	0	...	1-...	9.2	14	10	8	0	7-1	11	.341
1999— Greensboro (S. Atl.)	1	1	.500	2.38	0.97	4	4	0	0	...	0-...	22.2	12	6	6	1	10-0	42	.150
— Tampa (Fla. St.)	10	3	.769	3.30	1.19	15	15	1	0	...	0-...	90.0	67	43	33	2	40-0	77	.204
— Norwich (East.)	3	4	.429	4.57	1.43	8	8	0	0	...	0-...	43.1	45	24	22	2	17-0	33	.273
2000— Norwich (East.)	6	2	.750	2.60	1.33	11	11	1	0	...	0-...	72.2	63	29	21	4	34-1	70	.227
— Columbus (Int'l)	8	3	.727	3.02	1.29	17	17	1	1	...	0-...	113.1	104	44	38	9	42-1	86	.244
— New York (A.L.)	1	0	1.000	11.81	2.25	4	1	0	0	0	0-0	10.2	16	14	14	1	8-0	6	.364
2001— Columbus (Int'l)	5	7	.417	5.18	1.54	18	18	3	1	...	0-...	97.1	111	67	56	10	39-0	88	.280
— New York (A.L.)	1	2	.333	6.22	1.70	10	10	0	0	0	0-0	50.2	52	36	35	12	34-0	36	.259
2002— New York (A.L.)		Did not play.																	
2003— Portland (PCL)	5	1	.833	2.61	1.09	8	6	0	0	...	0-...	41.1	33	12	12	6	12-0	24	.216
— San Diego (N.L.)	0	0	.000	12.00	2.33	2	2	0	0	0	0-0	6.0	7	9	8	3	7-0	5	.292
— Oklahoma (PCL)	0	2	.000	8.53	2.05	5	2	0	0	...	0-...	12.2	21	13	12	2	5-0	9	.389
— New Orleans (PCL)	2	3	.400	4.28	1.53	9	9	0	0	...	0-...	48.1	53	24	23	3	21-2	27	.267
2004— Norfolk (Int'l)	6	7	.462	3.81	1.46	22	21	1	0	...	0-...	130.0	145	72	55	13	45-1	110	.284
— St. Lucie (Fla. St.)	1	0	1.000	0.00	0.82	1	0	0	0	...	0-...	3.2	3	0	0	0	0-0	1	.214
2005— Louisville (Int'l)	5	2	.714	2.88	1.19	12	7	0	0	0	2-3	56.1	54	19	18	6	13-0	46	.250
— Cincinnati (N.L.)	2	1	.667	6.27	1.64	24	4	0	0	0	0-0	56.0	64	45	39	10	28-2	43	.277
2006— Oakland (A.L.)	0	0		4.50	1.60	11	0	0	0	1	0-0	10.0	14	5	5	3	2-1	5	.350
— Sacramento (PCL)	9	5	.643	3.83	1.49	25	16	0	0	1	0-1	103.1	107	53	44	2	47-3	82	.268
American League totals (3 years)	2	2	.500	6.81	1.77	25	11	0	0	1	0-0	71.1	82	55	54	16	44-1	47	.288
National League totals (2 years)	2	2	.500	6.82	1.71	26	6	0	0	0	0-0	62.0	71	54	47	13	35-2	48	.278
Major League totals (5 years)	4	4	.500	6.82	1.74	51	17	0	0	1	0-0	133.1	153	109	101	29	79-3	95	.283

2006 LEFTY-RIGHTY SPLITS

vs.	Avg.	AB	H	2B	3B	HR	RBI	BB	SO	OBP	Slg.	vs.	Avg.	AB	H	2B	3B	HR	RBI	BB	SO	OBP	Slg.
L	.353	17	6	2	0	0	4	1	3	.389	.471	R	.348	23	8	3	0	3	4	1	2	.375	.870

KEMP, MATT — OF

PERSONAL: Born September 23, 1984, in Midwest City, Okla. ... Bats right, throws right. ... Full name: Matthew Ryan Kemp. ... High school: Midwest City (Okla.). **TRANS-ACTIONS/CAREER NOTES:** Selected by Los Angeles Dodgers organization in sixth round of 2003 free-agent draft.

2006 GAMES PLAYED BY POSITION (MLB): OF—46.

Year — Team (League)	Pos.	G	AB	R	H	2B	3B	HR	RBI	BB	SO	HBP	GDP	SB-CS	Avg.	OBP	SLG	OPS	E (FIELDING)	Avg.
2003— GC Dodgers (GCL)		43	159	11	43	5	2	1	17	7	25	0	1	2-1	.270	.298	.346	.644	...	...
2004— Columbus (S. Atl.)		111	423	67	122	22	8	17	66	24	100	5	10	8-7	.288	.330	.499	.829	...	...
— Vero Beach (FSL)		11	37	5	13	5	0	1	9	4	12	0	0	2-1	.351	.405	.568	.973	...	...
2005— Vero Beach (FSL)	OF-DH	109	418	76	128	21	4	27	90	25	92	5	8	23-6	.306	.349	.569	.918	10	.976
2006— Jacksonville (Sou.)		48	199	38	65	15	2	7	34	20	38	5	10	11-2	.327	.402	.528	.929	2	.981
— Las Vegas (PCL)		44	182	37	67	14	6	3	36	17	26	2	4	14-3	.368	.428	.560	.988	1	.990
— Los Angeles (N.L.)	OF	52	154	30	39	7	1	7	23	9	53	0	1	6-0	.253	.289	.448	.737	5	.929
Major League totals (1 year)		52	154	30	39	7	1	7	23	9	53	0	1	6-0	.253	.289	.448	.737	5	.929

2006 LEFTY-RIGHTY SPLITS

vs.	Avg.	AB	H	2B	3B	HR	RBI	BB	SO	OBP	Slg.	vs.	Avg.	AB	H	2B	3B	HR	RBI	BB	SO	OBP	Slg.
L	.229	48	11	3	1	0	2	1	18	.245	.333	R	.264	106	28	4	0	7	21	8	35	.308	.500

KENDALL, JASON — C

PERSONAL: Born June 26, 1974, in San Diego. ... 6-0/195. ... Bats right, throws right. ... Full name: Jason Daniel Kendall. ... High school: Torrance (Calif.). ... Son of Fred Kendall, coach, Kansas City Royals, and catcher/first baseman with three major league teams (1969-80). **TRANSACTIONS/CAREER NOTES:** Selected by Pittsburgh Pirates organization in first round (23rd pick overall) of 1992 free-agent draft. ... On suspended list (July 21-23, 1998). ... On disabled list (July 5, 1999-remainder of season). ... On suspended list (September 19-20, 2001; July 29-August 1, 2003; and September 17-20, 2004). ... Traded by Pirates with cash to Oakland Athletics for Ps Mark Redman and Arthur Rhodes (November 24, 2004). ... On suspended list (May 9-13, 2006). **HONORS:** Named N.L. Rookie Player of the Year by THE SPORTING NEWS (1996). **STATISTICAL NOTES:** Hit for the cycle (May 19, 2000). ... Career major league grand slams: 1.

2006 GAMES PLAYED BY POSITION (MLB): C—141, DH—1.

Year — Team (League)	Pos.	G	AB	R	H	2B	3B	HR	RBI	BB	SO	HBP	GDP	SB-CS	Avg.	OBP	SLG	OPS	E (FIELDING)	Avg.
1992— GC Pirates (GCL)	C	33	111	7	29	2	0	0	10	8	9	2	3	2-2	.261	.317	.279	.596	5	.978
1993— Augusta (S. Atl.)	C	102	366	43	101	17	4	1	40	22	30	7	17	8-5	.276	.325	.352	.677	20	.964
1994— Salem (Carol.)	C	101	371	68	118	19	2	7	66	47	21	13	15	14-3	.318	.406	.437	.843	9	.980
— Carolina (Southern)	C	13	47	6	11	2	0	0	6	2	3	0	0	0-0	.234	.294	.277	.571	2	.969
1995— Carolina (Southern)	C	117	429	87	140	26	1	8	71	56	22	14	10	10-7	.326	.414	.448	.862	8	.989
1996— Pittsburgh (N.L.)	C	130	414	54	124	23	5	3	42	35	30	15	7	5-2	.300	.372	.401	.773	* 18	.989
1997— Pittsburgh (N.L.)	C	144	486	71	143	36	4	8	49	49	53	31	11	18-6	.294	.391	.434	.825	11	.990
1998— Pittsburgh (N.L.)	C	149	535	95	175	36	3	12	75	51	51	* 31	6	26-5	.327	.411	.473	.884	9	.992
1999— Pittsburgh (N.L.)	C	78	280	61	93	20	3	8	41	38	32	12	8	22-3	.332	.428	.511	.939	7	.990
2000— Pittsburgh (N.L.)	C	152	579	112	185	33	6	14	58	79	79	15	13	22-12	.320	.412	.470	.882	10	.991
2001— Pittsburgh (N.L.)	C-OF	157	606	84	161	22	2	10	53	44	48	18	13-14	266	.335	.358	.693	17	.980
2002— Pittsburgh (N.L.)	C	145	545	59	154	25	3	3	44	49	29	9	11	15-8	.283	.350	.356	.706	9	.990
2003— Pittsburgh (N.L.)	C	150	587	84	191	29	3	6	58	44	40	25	9	8-7	.325	.399	.416	.815	10	.989
2004— Pittsburgh (N.L.)	C	147	574	86	183	30	0	3	51	60	41	19	12	11-8	.319	.399	.390	.789	10	.991
2005— Oakland (A.L.)	C-DH	150	601	70	163	28	1	0	53	50	39	20	• 26	8-3	.271	.345	.321	.666	7	.993
2006— Oakland (A.L.)	C-DH	143	552	76	163	23	0	1	53	53	54	12	19	11-5	.295	.367	.342	.709	5	.995
American League totals (2 years)		293	1153	146	326	51	1	1	103	103	93	32	45	19-8	.283	.355	.331	.686	12	.994
National League totals (9 years)		1252	4606	706	1409	256	29	67	471	454	403	177	95	140-65	.306	.387	.418	.805	101	.988
Major League totals (11 years)		1545	5759	852	1735	307	30	68	574	557	496	209	140	159-73	.301	.381	.400	.781	113	.989

Year	Team (League)	Pos.	G	AB	R	H	2B	3B	HR	RBI	BB	SO	HBP	GDP	SB-CS	Avg.	OBP	SLG	OPS	E	Avg.
2006— Oakland (A.L.)		C	3	14	1	3	1	0	0	1	0	4	0	0	0-0	.214	.214	.286	.500	1	.929

Year	Team (League)	Pos.	G	AB	R	H	2B	3B	HR	RBI	BB	SO	HBP	GDP	SB-CS	Avg.	OBP	SLG	OPS	E	Avg.
2006— Oakland (A.L.)		C	4	17	0	5	0	0	0	2	2	0	0	0	0-0	.294	.368	.294	.663	0	1.000

			G	AB	R	H	2B	3B	HR	RBI	BB	SO	HBP	GDP	SB-CS	Avg.	OBP	SLG	OPS	E	Avg.
All-Star Game totals (3 years)			3	3	0	1	0	0	0	0	0	1	0	0	0-0	.333	.333	.333	.667	0	1.000

2006 LEFTY-RIGHTY SPLITS

vs.	Avg.	AB	H	2B	3B	HR	RBI	BB	SO	OBP	Slg.	vs.	Avg.	AB	H	2B	3B	HR	RBI	BB	SO	OBP	Slg.
L	.331	124	41	10	0	0	17	18	8	.421	.411	R	.285	428	122	13	0	1	33	35	46	.350	.322

KENDRICK, HOWIE — 2B

PERSONAL: Born July 12, 1983, in Jacksonville, Fla. ... 5-10/195. ... Bats right, throws right. ... Full name: Howard Joseph Kendrick III. ... Junior college: St. John's River C.C. **TRANSACTIONS/CAREER NOTES:** Selected by Anaheim Angels organization in 10th round of 2002 free-agent draft. ... Angels franchise renamed Los Angeles Angels of Anaheim for 2005 season.

2006 GAMES PLAYED BY POSITION (MLB): 1B—44, 2B—28, DH—2, 3B—1.

Year	Team (League)	Pos.	G	AB	R	H	2B	3B	HR	RBI	BB	SO	HBP	GDP	SB-CS	Avg.	OBP	SLG	OPS	E	Avg.
2002— Ariz. Angels (Ariz.)			42	157	24	50	6	4	0	13	7	11	6	2	12-6	.318	.368	.408	.776	...	...
2003— Provo (Pion.)			63	234	65	86	20	3	3	36	24	28	6	5	8-3	.368	.434	.517	.951	...	...
2004— Ariz. Angels (Ariz.)			3	12	1	3	1	0	0	0	1	0	0	0	2-0	.250	.308	.333	.641	...	...
— Cedar Rap. (Midw.)			75	313	66	115	24	6	10	49	12	41	6	2	15-6	.367	.398	.578	.976	...	...
2005— Rancho Cuca. (Calif.)		2B-DH	63	279	69	107	23	6	12	47	14	42	7	5	13-4	.384	.421	.638	1.059	8	.973
— Arkansas (Texas)		2B	46	190	35	65	20	2	7	42	6	20	7	7	12-4	.342	.382	.579	.961	6	.974
2006— Salt Lake (PCL)			69	290	57	107	25	6	13	62	12	48	8	2	11-3	.369	.408	.631	1.039	5	.984
— Los Angeles (A.L.) 1B-2B-DH																					
		3B	72	267	25	76	21	1	4	30	9	44	4	5	6-0	.285	.314	.416	.730	2	.996
Major League totals (1 year)			72	267	25	76	21	1	4	30	9	44	4	5	6-0	.285	.314	.416	.730	2	.996

2006 LEFTY-RIGHTY SPLITS

vs.	Avg.	AB	H	2B	3B	HR	RBI	BB	SO	OBP	Slg.	vs.	Avg.	AB	H	2B	3B	HR	RBI	BB	SO	OBP	Slg.
L	.264	91	24	8	1	1	10	3	11	.299	.407	R	.295	176	52	13	0	3	20	6	33	.323	.420

KENNEDY, ADAM — 2B

PERSONAL: Born January 10, 1976, in Riverside, Calif. ... 6-1/185. ... Bats left, throws right. ... Full name: Adam Thomas Kennedy. ... High school: J.W. North (Riverside, Calif.). ... College: Cal State Northridge. **TRANSACTIONS/CAREER NOTES:** Selected by St. Louis Cardinals organization in first round (20th pick overall) of 1997 free-agent draft. ... Traded by Cardinals with P Kent Bottenfield to Anaheim Angels for OF Jim Edmonds (March 23, 2000). ... On disabled list (March 23-April 13, 2001); included rehabilitation assignment to Rancho Cucamonga. ... On disabled list (April 7-22, 2003); included rehabilitation assignment to Rancho Cucamonga. ... Angels franchise renamed Los Angeles Angels of Anaheim for 2005 season. ... On disabled list (March 25-May 2, 2005). ... On suspended list (August 17-21, 2006). **STATISTICAL NOTES:** Career major league grand slams: 1.

2006 GAMES PLAYED BY POSITION (MLB): 2B—133, DH—2.

Year	Team (League)	Pos.	G	AB	R	H	2B	3B	HR	RBI	BB	SO	HBP	GDP	SB-CS	Avg.	OBP	SLG	OPS	E	Avg.
1997— New Jersey (NYP)		SS	29	114	20	39	6	3	0	19	13	10	2	3	9-1	.342	.412	.447	.860	7	.951
— Prince Will. (Car.)		SS	35	154	24	48	9	3	1	27	6	17	2	3	4-3	.312	.346	.429	.774	10	.939
1998— Prince Will. (Car.)		2B-SS	17	69	9	18	6	0	0	7	5	12	0	1	5-2	.261	.307	.348	.654	5	.938
— Arkansas (Texas)		2B-SS	52	205	35	57	11	2	6	24	8	21	2	4	6-2	.278	.307	.439	.746	15	.940
— Memphis (PCL)		2B-SS	74	305	36	93	22	7	4	41	12	42	1	3	15-4	.305	.331	.462	.794	10	.972
1999— Memphis (PCL) 2B-SS-OF																					
		3B-2B	91	367	69	120	22	4	10	63	29	36	4	7	20-6	.327	.378	.490	.868	18	.953
— St. Louis (N.L.)		2B	33	102	12	26	10	1	1	16	3	8	2	1	0-1	.255	.284	.402	.686	4	.971
2000— Anaheim (A.L.)		2B	156	598	82	159	33	11	9	72	28	73	3	10	22-8	.266	.300	.403	.703	19	.976
2001— Rancho Cuca. (Calif.)		2B	3	8	3	3	2	0	0	1	2	1	1	0	3-0	.375	.545	.625	1.170	0	1.000
— Anaheim (A.L.)		2B	137	478	48	129	25	3	6	40	27	71	11	7	12-7	.270	.318	.372	.690	10	.984
2002— Anaheim (A.L.) 2B-DH-OF			144	474	65	148	32	6	7	52	19	80	7	5	17-4	.312	.345	.449	.795	11	.983
2003— Rancho Cuca. (Calif.)		2B	3	11	3	3	1	0	1	1	0	2	1	0	0-0	.273	.333	.636	.970	1	.923
— Anaheim (A.L.)		2B-DH	143	449	71	121	17	1	13	49	45	73	9	7	22-9	.269	.344	.399	.743	6	.990
2004— Anaheim (A.L.)		2B	144	468	70	130	20	5	10	48	41	92	13	10	15-5	.278	.351	.406	.757	12	.982
2005— Salt Lake (PCL)		2B-DH	4	17	4	7	1	0	0	4	2	2	1	0	2-0	.412	.450	.471	.921	0	1.000
— Rancho Cuca. (Calif.)		2B-DH	2	5	1	2	0	0	0	1	1	1	0	0	1-1	.400	.500	.400	.900	0	1.000
— Los Angeles (A.L.)		2B	129	416	49	125	23	0	4	37	29	64	7	5	19-4	.300	.354	.370	.724	5	.991
2006— Los Angeles (A.L.)		2B-DH	139	451	50	123	26	6	4	55	39	72	5	15	16-10	.273	.334	.384	.718	9	.984
American League totals (7 years)			992	3334	435	935	176	32	51	353	228	525	55	59	123-47	.280	.334	.398	.732	72	.984
National League totals (1 year)			33	102	12	26	10	1	1	16	3	8	2	1	0-1	.255	.284	.402	.686	4	.971
Major League totals (8 years)			1025	3436	447	961	186	33	52	369	231	533	57	60	123-48	.280	.332	.398	.731	76	.983

Year	Team (League)	Pos.	G	AB	R	H	2B	3B	HR	RBI	BB	SO	HBP	GDP	SB-CS	Avg.	OBP	SLG	OPS	E	Avg.
2002— Anaheim (A.L.)		2B	4	8	4	4	1	0	1	3	1	2	0	0	1-0	.500	.455	1.000	1.455	0	1.000
2005— Los Angeles (A.L.)		2B	5	17	0	4	0	1	0	2	0	3	0	0	0-2	.235	.235	.353	.588	0	1.000
Division series totals (2 years)			9	25	4	8	1	1	1	5	1	5	0	0	1-2	.320	.321	.560	.881	0	1.000

Year	Team (League)	Pos.	G	AB	R	H	2B	3B	HR	RBI	BB	SO	HBP	GDP	SB-CS	Avg.	OBP	SLG	OPS	E	Avg.
2002— Anaheim (A.L.)		2B	4	14	5	5	0	0	3	5	0	2	0	0	1-0	.357	.357	1.000	1.357	0	1.000
2005— Los Angeles (A.L.)		2B	5	14	3	4	0	0	0	1	0	1	0	1	0-0	.286	.286	.286	.571	1	.952
Champ. series totals (2 years)			9	28	8	9	0	0	3	6	0	3	0	1	1-0	.321	.321	.643	.964	1	.977

Year	Team (League)	Pos.	G	AB	R	H	2B	3B	HR	RBI	BB	SO	HBP	GDP	SB-CS	Avg.	OBP	SLG	OPS	E	Avg.
2002— Anaheim (A.L.)		2B	7	25	1	7	2	0	2	2	0	7	1	0	0-0	.280	.308	.360	.668	0	1.000

2006 LEFTY-RIGHTY SPLITS

vs.	Avg.	AB	H	2B	3B	HR	RBI	BB	SO	OBP	Slg.	vs.	Avg.	AB	H	2B	3B	HR	RBI	BB	SO	OBP	Slg.
L	.193	83	16	3	2	0	6	5	18	.256	.277	R	.291	368	107	23	4	4	49	34	54	.351	.408

KENNEDY, JOE — P

PERSONAL: Born May 24, 1979, in La Mesa, Calif. ... 6-4/237. ... Throws left, bats right. ... Full name: Joseph Darley Kennedy. ... High school: El Cajon Valley (El Cajon, Calif.). ... Junior college: Grossmont (Calif.. **TRANSACTIONS/CAREER NOTES:** Selected by Tampa Bay Devil Rays organization in eighth round of 1998 free-agent draft. ... On suspended list (July 12-19, 2002). ... On disabled list (June 1-July 9, 2003); included rehabilitation assignments to Orlando and Durham. ... Traded by Devil Rays to Colorado Rockies as part of three-team deal in which Devil Rays acquired P Mark Hendrickson from Blue Jays, Blue Jays acquired P Justin Speier from Rockies and Rockies acquired a player to be named from Blue Jays (December 14, 2003); Rockies acquired P Sandy Nin to complete deal (December 15, 2003). ... On disabled list (July 3-August 10, 2004); included rehabilitation assignment to Colorado Springs. ... On suspended list (September 19-25, 2004). ... Traded by Rockies with P Jay Witasick to Oakland Athletics for OF Eric Byrnes and SS Omar Quintanilla (July 13, 2005). ... On disabled list (May 21-August 14, 2006); included rehabilitation assignment to Sacramento.

CAREER HITTING: 15-for-88 (.170), 5 R, 1 2B, 1 3B, 0 HR, 6 RBI.

Year	Team (League)	W	L	Pct.	ERA	WHIP	G	GS	CG	ShO	Hld.	Sv.-Opp.	IP	H	R	ER	HR	BB-IBB	SO	Avg.
1998—	Princeton (Appal.)	6	4	.600	3.74	1.37	13	13	0	0	...	0-...	67.1	66	37	28	5	26-0	44	.264
1999—	Hudson Valley (NYP)	6	5	.545	2.65	1.09	16	16	1	1	...	0-...	95.0	78	33	28	2	26-0	101	.227
2000—	Char., S.C. (SAL)	11	6	.647	3.30	1.11	22	22	3	2	...	0-...	136.1	122	59	50	6	29-1	142	.242
2001—	Orlando (South.)	4	0	1.000	0.19	0.68	7	7	0	0	...	0-...	47.0	29	3	1	0	3-0	52	.178
—	Durham (Int'l)	2	0	1.000	2.42	1.19	4	4	0	0	...	0-...	26.0	22	8	7	2	9-0	23	.227
—	Tampa Bay (A.L.)	7	8	.467	4.44	1.33	20	20	0	0	...	0-0	117.2	122	63	58	16	34-0	75	.269
2002—	Tampa Bay (A.L.)	8	11	.421	4.53	1.32	30	30	5	1	0	0-0	196.2	204	114	99	23	55-0	109	.269
2003—	Orlando (South.)	0	0	...	8.10	2.10	1	1	0	0	...	0-...	3.1	6	3	3	0	1-0	3	.400
—	Durham (Int'l)	1	0	1.000	1.42	0.90	1	1	0	0	...	0-...	6.1	6	1	1	0	0-0	4	.250
—	Tampa Bay (A.L.)	3	12	.200	6.13	1.60	32	22	1	1	1	1-2	133.2	167	101	91	19	47-1	77	.303
2004—	Colo. Springs (PCL)	1	1	.500	7.11	1.50	3	2	0	0	...	0-...	12.2	17	11	10	1	2-0	12	.321
—	Colorado (N.L.)	9	7	.563	3.66	1.42	27	27	1	0	0	0-...	162.1	163	68	66	17	67-12	117	.265
2005—	Colorado (N.L.)	4	8	.333	7.04	1.87	16	16	0	0	0	0-...	92.0	128	81	72	12	44-4	52	.334
—	Oakland (A.L.)	4	5	.444	4.45	1.38	19	8	0	0	0	0-2	60.2	64	33	30	8	20-2	45	.267
2006—	Sacramento (PCL)	0	0	...	0.00	0.75	3	1	0	0	0	0-1	4.0	2	0	0	0	1-0	2	.154
—	Oakland (A.L.)	4	1	.800	2.31	1.34	39	0	0	0	14	1-3	35.0	34	10	9	1	13-3	29	.254
American League totals (5 years)		26	37	.413	4.75	1.40	140	80	6	2	15	2-7	543.2	591	321	287	67	169-6	338	.276
National League totals (2 years)		13	15	.464	4.88	1.58	43	43	1	0	0	0-...	254.1	291	149	138	29	111-16	169	.292
Major League totals (6 years)		39	52	.429	4.79	1.46	183	123	7	2	15	2-7	798.0	882	470	425	96	280-22	507	.281

CHAMPIONSHIP SERIES RECORD

Year	Team (League)	W	L	Pct.	ERA	WHIP	G	GS	CG	ShO	Hld.	Sv.-Opp.	IP	H	R	ER	HR	BB-IBB	SO	Avg.
2006—	Oakland (A.L.)	0	0	...	0.00	1.09	4	0	0	0	0	0-0	3.2	2	0	0	0	2-1	2	.143

2006 LEFTY-RIGHTY SPLITS

vs.	Avg.	AB	H	2B	3B	HR	RBI	BB	SO	OBP	Slg.	vs.	Avg.	AB	H	2B	3B	HR	RBI	BB	SO	OBP	Slg.
L	.326	43	14	2	2	0	3	3	12	.370	.465	R	.220	91	20	2	0	1	5	10	17	.304	.275

KENSING, LOGAN — P

PERSONAL: Born July 3, 1982, in San Antonio. ... 6-1/185. ... Throws right, bats right. ... Full name: Logan French Kensing. ... High school: Boerne (Texas). ... College: Texas A&M. **TRANSACTIONS/CAREER NOTES:** Selected by Florida Marlins organization in second round of 2003 free-agent draft. ... On disabled list (June 17, 2005-remainder of season). ... On disabled list (August 7, 2006-remainder of season). **MISCELLANEOUS NOTES:** Appeared in one game as pinch runner (2006).

CAREER HITTING: 0-for-3 (.000), 0 R, 0 2B, 0 3B, 0 HR, 0 RBI.

Year	Team (League)	W	L	Pct.	ERA	WHIP	G	GS	CG	ShO	Hld.	Sv.-Opp.	IP	H	R	ER	HR	BB-IBB	SO	Avg.
2003—	Jamestown (NYP)	2	4	.333	5.73	1.64	8	6	0	0	...	0-...	33.0	48	23	21	1	6-0	20	.333
—	Greensboro (S. Atl.)	0	2	.000	4.50	1.15	4	4	0	0	...	0-...	20.0	18	10	10	2	5-0	11	.243
2004—	Jupiter (Fla. St.)	6	7	.462	2.96	1.21	23	23	1	0	...	0-...	127.2	120	53	42	5	35-1	100	.251
—	Florida (N.L.)	0	3	.000	9.88	2.05	5	3	0	0	0	0-0	13.2	19	15	15	5	9-0	7	.345
2005—	Carolina (Southern)	4	1	.800	3.18	1.24	7	7	0	0	0	0-0	39.2	35	16	14	4	14-0	33	.229
—	Florida (N.L.)	0	0	...	11.12	2.47	3	0	0	0	1	0-0	5.2	11	7	7	2	3-0	4	.407
2006—	Albuquerque (PCL)	1	1	.500	3.00	0.89	13	0	0	0	3	2-4	18.0	11	6	6	2	5-0	18	.180
—	Florida (N.L.)	1	3	.250	4.54	1.30	37	0	0	0	14	1-7	37.2	30	19	19	6	19-2	45	.221
Major League totals (3 years)		1	6	.143	6.47	1.60	45	3	0	0	15	1-7	57.0	60	41	41	13	31-2	56	.275

2006 LEFTY-RIGHTY SPLITS

vs.	Avg.	AB	H	2B	3B	HR	RBI	BB	SO	OBP	Slg.	vs.	Avg.	AB	H	2B	3B	HR	RBI	BB	SO	OBP	Slg.
L	.218	55	12	4	0	4	9	11	15	.358	.509	R	.222	81	18	3	1	2	9	8	30	.308	.358

KENT, JEFF — 2B

PERSONAL: Born March 7, 1968, in Bellflower, Calif. ... 6-1/210. ... Bats right, throws right. ... Full name: Jeffrey Frank Kent. ... High school: Edison (Huntington Beach, Calif.). ... College: California. **TRANSACTIONS/CAREER NOTES:** Selected by Toronto Blue Jays organization in 20th round of 1989 free-agent draft. ... Traded by Blue Jays with a player to be named to New York Mets for P David Cone (August 27, 1992); Mets acquired OF Ryan Thompson to complete deal (September 1, 1992). ... On disabled list (July 6-21, 1995). ... Traded by New York Mets with IF Jose Vizcaino to Cleveland Indians for 2B Carlos Baerga and IF Alvaro Espinoza (July 29, 1996). ... Traded by Indians with IF Jose Vizcaino, P Julian Tavarez and a player to be named to San Francisco Giants for 3B Matt Williams and a player to be named (November 13, 1996); Indians traded P Joe Roa to Giants for OF Trenidad Hubbard to complete deal (December 16, 1996). ... On suspended list (August 22-25, 1997). ... On disabled list (June 10-July 10, 1998; August 3-21, 1999; and March 21-April 6, 2002). ... Signed as a free agent by Houston Astros (December 18, 2002). ... On disabled list (June 19-July 16, 2003); included rehabilitation assignment to Round Rock. ... On suspended list (August 6-9, 2003; and September 24-26, 2004). ... Signed as a free agent by Los Angeles Dodgers (December 9, 2004). ... On disabled list (May 30-June 13 and July 18-August 7, 2006). **RECORDS:** Holds major league record for most home runs by a second baseman, career (306). **HONORS:** Named second baseman on THE SPORTING NEWS N.L. All-Star team (2000, 2002 and 2005). ... Named N.L. Most Valuable Player by Baseball Writers' Association of America (2000). ... Named second baseman on N.L. Silver Slugger team (2000-02 and 2005). **STATISTICAL NOTES:** Hit for the cycle (May 3, 1999). ... Career major league grand slams: 13.

2006 GAMES PLAYED BY POSITION (MLB): 2B—108, 1B—9.

Year	Team (League)	Pos.	G	AB	R	H	2B	3B	HR	RBI	BB	SO	HBP	GDP	SB-CS	Avg.	OBP	SLG	OPS	E	Avg.
1989—	St. Catharines (NYP)	3B-SS	73	268	34	60	14	1	13	37	33	81	6	2	5-1	.224	.318	.429	.747	29	.906
1990—	Dunedin (Fla. St.)	2B	132	447	72	124	32	2	16	60	53	98	6	4	17-7	.277	.360	.465	.825	15	.978
1991—	Knoxville (Southern)	2B	139	445	68	114	34	1	2	61	80	104	10	3	25-6	.256	.379	.351	.730	29	.957
1992—	Toronto (A.L.)	3B-2B-1B	65	192	36	46	13	1	8	35	20	47	6	3	2-1	.240	.324	.443	.767	11	.941
—	New York (N.L.)	2B-3B-SS	37	113	16	27	8	1	3	15	7	29	1	2	0-2	.239	.289	.407	.696	3	.981
1993—	New York (N.L.)	2B-3B-SS	140	496	65	134	24	0	21	80	30	88	8	11	4-4	.270	.320	.446	.765	22	.965
1994—	New York (N.L.)	2B	107	415	53	121	24	5	14	68	23	84	10	7	1-4	.292	.341	.475	.816 •	14	.976
1995—	New York (N.L.)	2B	125	472	65	131	22	3	20	65	29	89	8	9	3-3	.278	.327	.464	.791	10	.984
1996—	New York (N.L.)	2B	89	335	45	97	20	1	9	39	21	56	1	7	4-3	.290	.331	.436	.766	21	.925
—	Cleveland (A.L.)	1B-2B-3B																			
		DH	39	102	16	27	7	0	3	16	10	22	1	1	2-1	.265	.328	.422	.749	1	.994

K

Year	Team (League)	Pos.	G	AB	R	H	2B	3B	HR	RBI	BB	SO	HBP	GDP	SB-CS	Avg.	OBP	SLG	OPS	E	Avg.
																				FIELDING	
1997—San Francisco (N.L.)	2B-1B	155	580	90	145	38	2	29	121	48	133	13	14	11-3	.250	.316	.472	.789	16	.981	
1998—San Francisco (N.L.)	2B-1B	137	526	94	156	37	3	31	128	48	110	9	16	9-4	.297	.359	.555	.914	20	.972	
1999—San Francisco (N.L.)	2B-1B	138	511	86	148	40	2	23	101	61	112	5	12	13-6	.290	.366	.511	.877	10	.984	
2000—San Francisco (N.L.)	2B-1B	159	587	114	196	41	7	33	125	90	107	9	17	12-9	.334	.424	.596	1.021	12	.985	
2001—San Francisco (N.L.)	2B-1B	159	607	84	181	49	6	22	106	65	96	11	11	7-6	.298	.369	.507	.877	11	.987	
2002—San Francisco (N.L.)	2B-1B	152	623	102	195	42	2	37	108	52	101	4	20	5-1	.313	.368	.565	.933	16	.979	
2003—Round Rock (Texas)	2B-DH	3	10	1	3	0	0	1	6	1	1	0	1	0-1	.300	.333	.600	.933	1	.875	
—Houston (N.L.)	2B	130	505	77	150	39	1	22	93	39	85	5	13	6-2	.297	.351	.509	.860	11	.983	
2004—Houston (N.L.)	2B-DH	145	540	96	156	34	8	27	107	49	96	6	23	7-3	.289	.348	.531	.880	7	.989	
2005—Los Angeles (N.L.)	2B-1B	149	553	100	160	36	0	29	105	72	85	8	19	6-2	.289	.377	.512	.889	18	.978	
2006—Los Angeles (N.L.)	2B-1B	115	407	61	119	27	3	14	68	55	69	8	9	1-2	.292	.385	.477	.861	8	.986	
American League totals (2 years)		104	294	52	73	20	1	11	51	30	69	7	4	4-2	.248	.325	.435	.761	12	.966	
National League totals (15 years)		1937	7270	1148	2116	481	44	334	1329	689	1340	106	190	89-54	.291	.357	.507	.864	199	.979	
Major League totals (15 years)		2041	7564	1200	2189	501	45	345	1380	719	1409	113	194	93-56	.289	.356	.504	.860	211	.979	

DIVISION SERIES RECORD

Year	Team (League)	Pos.	G	AB	R	H	2B	3B	HR	RBI	BB	SO	HBP	GDP	SB-CS	Avg.	OBP	SLG	OPS	E	Avg.
1996—Cleveland (A.L.)	1B-2B-3B	4	8	2	1	0	0	0	0	0	0	0	0	0-0	.125	.125	.250	.375	0	1.000
1997—San Francisco (N.L.)	1B	3	10	2	3	0	0	2	2	2	1	0	0	0-0	.300	.417	.900	1.317	0	1.000
2000—San Francisco (N.L.)	1B-2B	4	16	3	6	1	0	0	1	1	3	0	0	1-0	.375	.412	.438	.849	0	1.000
2002—San Francisco (N.L.)	2B	5	19	1	5	2	0	1	2	7	1	0	0	0-0	.263	.364	.368	.732	1	.960
2004—Houston (N.L.)	2B	5	22	3	5	3	0	0	3	2	5	0	2	0-0	.227	.292	.364	.655	0	1.000
2006—Los Angeles (N.L.)	2B-1B	3	13	2	8	1	0	1	2	0	1	0	0	0-0	.615	.615	.923	1.538	1	.909
Division series totals (6 years)		24	88	13	28	8	0	3	9	7	17	1	2	1-0	.318	.375	.511	.886	2	.984

CHAMPIONSHIP SERIES RECORD

Year	Team (League)	Pos.	G	AB	R	H	2B	3B	HR	RBI	BB	SO	HBP	GDP	SB-CS	Avg.	OBP	SLG	OPS	E	Avg.
2002—San Francisco (N.L.)	2B	5	19	3	5	0	0	0	2	4	1	1	0	0-0	.263	.364	.263	.627	0	1.000
2004—Houston (N.L.)	2B	7	25	3	6	2	0	3	7	3	5	2	0	0-0	.240	.367	.680	1.047	0	1.000
Champ. series totals (2 years)		12	44	6	11	2	0	3	7	5	9	3	1	0-0	.250	.365	.500	.865	0	1.000

WORLD SERIES RECORD

Year	Team (League)	Pos.	G	AB	R	H	2B	3B	HR	RBI	BB	SO	HBP	GDP	SB-CS	Avg.	OBP	SLG	OPS	E	Avg.
2002—San Francisco (N.L.)	2B	7	29	6	8	1	0	3	7	1	7	0	0	0-0	.276	.290	.621	.911	0	1.000

ALL-STAR GAME RECORD

	G	AB	R	H	2B	3B	HR	RBI	BB	SO	HBP	GDP	SB-CS	Avg.	OBP	SLG	OPS	E	Avg.
All-Star Game totals (5 years)	5	8	2	2	1	0	0	0	1	1	0	1	0-0	.250	.333	.375	.708	2	.882

2006 LEFTY-RIGHTY SPLITS

vs.	Avg.	AB	H	2B	3B	HR	RBI	BB	SO	OBP	Slg.	vs.	Avg.	AB	H	2B	3B	HR	RBI	BB	SO	OBP	Slg.
L	.347	98	34	6	0	6	16	17	16	.444	.592	R	.275	309	85	21	3	8	52	38	53	.365	.440

KEPPEL, BOBBY   P

PERSONAL: Born June 11, 1982, in St. Louis, Mo. ... Throws right, bats right. ... Full name: Robert Griffin Keppel. **TRANSACTIONS/CAREER NOTES:** Selected by New York Mets organization in supplemental round ("sandwich pick" between first and second rounds, 36th pick overall) of 2000 free-agent draft; pick received as part of compensation for Seattle Mariners signing Type A free-agent 1B John Olerud. ... Released by Mets (May 19, 2005). ... Signed by Kansas City Royals organization (August 23, 2005).
CAREER HITTING: 0-for-2 (.000), 0 R, 0 2B, 0 3B, 0 HR, 0 RBI.

Year	Team (League)	W	L	Pct.	ERA	WHIP	G	GS	CG	ShO	Hld.	Sv.-Opp.	IP	H	R	ER	HR	BB-IBB	SO	Avg.
2000—Kingsport (Appalachian)		1	2	.333	6.83	1.52	8	6	0	0	...	0-...	29.0	31	22	22	1	13-0	29	.261
2001—Columbia (S. Atl.)		6	7	.462	3.11	1.15	26	20	1	0	...	0-...	124.1	118	58	43	6	25-1	87	.249
2002—St. Lucie (Fla. St.)		9	7	.563	4.32	1.35	27	26	0	0	...	0-...	152.0	162	83	73	13	43-0	109	.277
2003—Brook. (N.Y.-Penn.)		2	0	1.000	2.51	0.84	3	3	0	0	...	0-...	14.1	10	5	4	0	2-0	13	.189
—Binghamton (East.)		7	4	.636	3.04	1.26	18	17	2	2	...	0-...	94.2	92	36	32	6	27-0	46	.264
2004—St. Lucie (Fla. St.)		1	1	.500	0.90	0.90	2	2	0	0	...	0-...	10.0	7	2	1	0	2-0	6	.206
—Norfolk (Int'l)		3	7	.300	4.71	1.42	17	16	1	0	...	0-...	93.2	111	51	49	8	22-1	42	.311
2005—Norfolk (Int'l)		2	1	.667	3.29	1.10	5	5	0	0		0-0	27.1	24	11	10	0	6-0	19	.238
2006—Omaha (PCL)		6	7	.462	5.67	1.57	25	14	0	0	1	1-3	98.1	126	73	62	12	28-1	43	.318
—Kansas City (A.L.)		0	4	.000	5.50	1.75	8	6	0	0		0-0	34.1	45	21	21	6	15-2	20	.326
Major League totals (1 year)		0	4	.000	5.50	1.75	8	6	0	0		0-0	34.1	45	21	21	6	15-2	20	.326

2006 LEFTY-RIGHTY SPLITS

vs.	Avg.	AB	H	2B	3B	HR	RBI	BB	SO	OBP	Slg.	vs.	Avg.	AB	H	2B	3B	HR	RBI	BB	SO	OBP	Slg.
L	.394	66	26	5	0	5	16	6	5	.432	.697	R	.264	72	19	3	0	1	3	9	15	.354	.347

KEPPINGER, JEFF   2B

PERSONAL: Born April 21, 1980, in Miami. ... 6-0/180. ... Bats right, throws right. ... Full name: Jeffrey Scott Keppinger. ... High school: Parkview (Lilburn, Ga.). ... College: Georgia. **TRANSACTIONS/CAREER NOTES:** Selected by Pittsburgh Pirates organization in fourth round of 2001 free-agent draft. ... Traded by Pirates with P Kris Benson to New York Mets for 3B Ty Wigginton, IF Jose Bautista and P Matt Peterson (July 30, 2004). ... On disabled list (September 9, 2005-remainder of season). ... Traded by Mets to Kansas City Royals for IF Ruben Gotay (July 19, 2006).
2006 GAMES PLAYED BY POSITION (MLB): 3B—12, 1B—4, DH—3, 2B—1, OF—1.

Year	Team (League)	Pos.	G	AB	R	H	2B	3B	HR	RBI	BB	SO	HBP	GDP	SB-CS	Avg.	OBP	SLG	OPS	E	Avg.
																				FIELDING	
2002—Hickory (S. Atl.)	2B	126	478	75	132	23	4	10	73	47	33	6	13	6-2	.276	.344	.404	.748	10	.981
2003—Lynchburg (Caro.)	2B-3B-1B	92	342	55	111	21	2	3	51	23	28	1	10	3-2	.325	.365	.424	.789	11	.972
2004—Altoona (East.)	2B-DH	81	315	44	106	17	2	1	33	27	15	0	11	10-5	.337	.387	.413	.792	6	.982
—Binghamton (East.)	2B-3B-DH	14	47	14	17	3	1	0	5	6	2	0	2	2-1	.362	.426	.468	.894	1	.981
—Norfolk (Int'l)	2B-DH	6	19	1	6	1	0	0	2	4	2	1	2	0-0	.316	.458	.368	.803	0	1.000
—New York (N.L.)	2B	33	116	9	33	2	0	0	9	6	7	0	6	2-1	.284	.317	.379	.696	2	.987
2005—Norfolk (Int'l)	2B-3B-SS	64	255	40	86	15	3	3	29	16	13	1	7	5-1	.337	.377	.455	.832	4	.987
2006—Norfolk (Int'l)	2B	87	323	36	97	19	2	2	26	28	21	0	7	0-4	.300	.353	.359	.712	5	.979
—Omaha (PCL)	2B	32	127	21	45	6	1	2	17	12	9	0	5	0-0	.354	.407	.465	.872	2	.986
—Kansas City (A.L.)	3B-1B-DH 2B-OF	22	60	11	16	4	0	2	8	5	6	0	2	0-0	.267	.323	.400	.723	2	.976
American League totals (1 year)		22	60	11	16	4	0	2	8	5	6	0	2	0-0	.267	.323	.400	.723	2	.976
National League totals (1 year)		33	116	9	33	2	0	0	9	6	7	0	6	2-1	.284	.317	.379	.696	2	.987
Major League totals (2 years)		55	176	20	49	6	0	2	17	11	13	0	8	2-1	.278	.319	.386	.706	4	.983

K

2006 LEFTY-RIGHTY SPLITS

vs.	Avg.	AB	H	2B	3B	HR	RBI	BB	SO	OBP	Slg.	vs.	Avg.	AB	H	2B	3B	HR	RBI	BB	SO	OBP	Slg.
L	.222	27	6	2	0	1	2	3	4	.300	.407	R	.303	33	10	0	0	1	6	2	2	.343	.394

KIELTY, BOBBY   OF

PERSONAL: Born August 5, 1976, in Fontana, Calif. ... 6-1/225. ... Bats both, throws right. ... Full name: Robert Michael Kielty. ... Name pronounced: kell-tee. ... High school: Canyon Springs (Moreno Valley, Calif.). ... College: Mississippi. **TRANSACTIONS/CAREER NOTES:** Signed as a non-drafted free agent by Minnesota Twins organization (February 16, 1999). ... Traded by Twins to Toronto Blue Jays for OF Shannon Stewart and a player to be named (July 16, 2003); Twins acquired P Dave Gassner to complete deal (December 16, 2003). ... Traded by Blue Jays with cash to Oakland Athletics for P Ted Lilly (November 18, 2003). **STATISTICAL NOTES:** Career major league grand slams: 1.

2006 GAMES PLAYED BY POSITION (MLB): OF—73, DH—3.

											BATTING									FIELDING	
Year Team (League)	Pos.	G	AB	R	H	2B	3B	HR	RBI	BB	SO	HBP	GDP	SB-CS	Avg.	OBP	SLG	OPS	E	Avg.
1999—Quad City (Midw.)	OF	69	245	52	72	13	1	13	43	43	56	3	7	12-3	.294	.401	.514	.916	3	.977
2000—New Britain (East.)	OF	129	451	79	118	30	3	14	65	98	109	5	16	6-4	.262	.396	.435	.831	3	.988
—Salt Lake (PCL)	OF	9	33	8	8	4	0	0	2	7	10	0	0	0-0	.242	.375	.364	.739	1	.957
2001—Edmonton (PCL)	OF	94	341	58	98	25	2	12	50	53	76	6	11	5-0	.287	.391	.478	.869	2	.991
—Minnesota (A.L.)	OF-DH	37	104	8	26	8	0	2	14	8	25	1	2	3-0	.250	.297	.385	.681	3	.956
2002—Edmonton (PCL)	OF	2	7	0	3	1	0	0	1	1	1	0	1	0-0	.429	.500	.571	1.071	0	1.000
—Minnesota (A.L.)	OF-DH-1B	112	289	49	84	14	3	12	46	52	66	5	4	4-1	.291	.405	.484	.890	0	1.000
2003—Minnesota (A.L.)	OF-DH	75	238	40	60	13	0	9	32	42	56	3	6	6-2	.252	.370	.420	.790	2	.972
—Toronto (A.L.)	OF-1B	62	189	31	44	13	1	4	25	29	36	4	6	2-1	.233	.342	.376	.718	1	.991
2004—Oakland (A.L.)	OF-DH	83	238	29	51	14	1	7	31	35	47	3	5	1-0	.214	.321	.370	.691	1	.990
2005—Oakland (A.L.)	OF-DH	116	377	55	99	20	0	10	57	50	67	2	14	3-2	.263	.350	.395	.746	3	.983
2006—Sacramento (PCL)		10	36	5	8	0	0	1	4	7	12	0	2	0-0	.222	.349	.306	.654	1	.960
—Oakland (A.L.)	OF-DH	81	270	35	73	20	1	8	36	22	49	2	9	2-0	.270	.329	.441	.770	1	.993
Major League totals (6 years)		566	1705	247	437	102	6	52	241	238	346	20	45	21-6	.256	.351	.415	.766	11	.987

DIVISION SERIES RECORD

Year Team (League)	Pos.	G	AB	R	H	2B	3B	HR	RBI	BB	SO	HBP	GDP	SB-CS	Avg.	OBP	SLG	OPS	E	Avg.
2002—Minnesota (A.L.)	OF-DH	3	4	0	0	0	0	0	0	1	0	0	0	0-0	.000	.000	.000	.000	0	1.000

CHAMPIONSHIP SERIES RECORD

Year Team (League)	Pos.	G	AB	R	H	2B	3B	HR	RBI	BB	SO	HBP	GDP	SB-CS	Avg.	OBP	SLG	OPS	E	Avg.
2002—Minnesota (A.L.)	DH-OF	4	3	0	0	0	0	0	1	1	2	0	0	0-0	.000	.250	.000	.250	0	...
2006—Oakland (A.L.)		2	2	0	0	0	0	0	0	0	0	0	1	0-0	.000	.000	.000	.000	0	...
Champ. series totals (2 years)		6	5	0	0	0	0	0	1	1	2	0	1	0-0	.000	.167	.000	.167	0	...

2006 LEFTY-RIGHTY SPLITS

vs.	Avg.	AB	H	2B	3B	HR	RBI	BB	SO	OBP	Slg.	vs.	Avg.	AB	H	2B	3B	HR	RBI	BB	SO	OBP	Slg.
L	.325	117	38	12	0	7	20	6	16	.358	.607	R	.229	153	35	8	1	1	16	16	33	.308	.314

KIM, BYUNG-HYUN   P

PERSONAL: Born January 19, 1979, in Gwangju, South Korea. ... 5-9/180. ... Throws right, bats right. ... Name pronounced: bee-yung hee-yun. ... High school: Kwang-ju (Korea). ... College: Sungkyunkwan (South Korea). **TRANSACTIONS/CAREER NOTES:** Signed as a non-drafted free agent by Arizona Diamondbacks organization (February 19, 1999). ... On disabled list (July 28-September 7, 2000). ... On disabled list (April 30-May 27, 2003); included rehabilitation assignment to Tucson. ... Traded by Diamondbacks to Boston Red Sox for IF Shea Hillenbrand (May 30, 2003). ... On disabled list (March 26-April 29, 2004); included rehabilitation assignment to Sarasota. ... Traded by Red Sox to Colorado Rockies for P Christopher Narveson and C Charles Johnson (March 30, 2005). ... On disabled list (April 2-30, 2006); included rehabilitation assignment to Colorado Springs.... Traded by Rockies to Cincinnati Reds for future considerations (September 5, 2006). **MISCELLANEOUS NOTES:** Member of Korean National Team (1997-98).

CAREER HITTING: 17-for-120 (.142), 4 R, 2 2B, 0 3B, 0 HR, 9 RBI.

Year Team (League)	W	L	Pct.	ERA	WHIP	G	GS	CG	ShO	Hld.	Sv.-Opp.	IP	H	R	ER	HR	BB-IBB	SO	Avg.
1999—El Paso (Texas)	2	0	1.000	2.11	0.70	10	0	0	0	...	0-...	21.1	6	5	5	0	9-0	32	.092
—Tucson (PCL)	4	0	1.000	2.40	1.20	11	3	0	0	...	1-...	30.0	21	9	8	2	15-1	40	.196
—Arizona (N.L.)	1	2	.333	4.61	1.46	25	0	0	0	3	1-4	27.1	20	15	14	2	20-2	31	.211
—Ariz. D'backs (Ariz.)	0	0	...	0.00	1.00	1	1	0	0	...	0-...	2.0	1	0	0	0	1-0	2	.167
2000—Arizona (N.L.)	6	6	.500	4.46	1.39	61	1	0	0	5	14-20	70.2	52	39	35	9	46-5	111	.200
—Tucson (PCL)	0	0	...	0.00	0.60	2	2	0	0	...	0-...	8.1	1	0	0	0	4-0	13	.042
2001—Arizona (N.L.)	5	6	.455	2.94	1.04	78	0	0	0	11	19-23	98.0	58	32	32	10	44-3	113	.173
2002—Arizona (N.L.)	8	3	.727	2.04	1.07	72	0	0	0	0	36-42	84.0	64	20	19	5	26-2	92	.208
2003—Tucson (PCL)	1	1	.500	2.55	1.00	3	3	0	0	...	0-...	17.2	17	5	5	2	1-0	8	.270
—Boston (A.L.)	8	5	.615	3.18	1.11	49	5	0	0	1	16-19	79.1	70	38	28	6	18-3	69	.230
2004—Sarasota (Fla. St.)	0	0	...	0.00	0.00	1	1	0	0	...	0-...	2.0	0	0	0	0	0-0	2	.000
—Pawtucket (Int'l)	2	6	.250	5.34	1.37	22	19	0	0	...	0-...	60.2	71	43	36	6	12-0	39	.289
—Boston (A.L.)	2	1	.667	6.23	1.38	7	3	0	0	0	0-0	17.1	17	15	12	1	7-1	6	.258
2005—Colorado (N.L.)	5	12	.294	4.86	1.53	40	22	0	0	1	0-2	148.0	156	82	80	17	71-8	115	.275
2006—Colo. Springs (PCL)	0	1	.000	6.23	1.69	3	3	0	0	0	0-0	13.0	18	11	9	0	4-0	11	.310
—Colorado (N.L.)	8	12	.400	5.57	1.55	27	27	0	0	0	0-0	155.0	179	103	96	18	61-8	129	.295
American League totals (2 years)	10	6	.625	3.72	1.16	56	8	0	0	1	16-19	96.2	87	53	40	7	25-4	75	.235
National League totals (7 years)	34	46	.425	4.21	1.35	310	57	0	0	20	70-91	626.0	563	308	293	67	283-28	624	.242
Major League totals (8 years)	44	52	.458	4.15	1.33	366	65	0	0	21	86-110	722.2	650	361	333	74	308-32	699	.241

DIVISION SERIES RECORD

Year Team (League)	W	L	Pct.	ERA	WHIP	G	GS	CG	ShO	Hld.	Sv.-Opp.	IP	H	R	ER	HR	BB-IBB	SO	Avg.
2001—Arizona (N.L.)	0	0	...	0.00	2.25	1	0	0	0	0	1-1	1.1	1	0	0	0	2-0	1	.250
2002—Arizona (N.L.)	0	0	...	18.00	5.00	1	0	0	0	0	0-0	1.0	2	2	2	0	3-1	0	.400
2003—Boston (A.L.)	0	0	...	13.50	1.50	1	0	0	0	1	0-0	0.2	0	1	1	0	1-0	1	.000
Division series totals (3 years)	0	0	...	9.00	3.00	3	0	0	0	1	1-1	3.0	3	3	3	0	6-1	2	.273

CHAMPIONSHIP SERIES RECORD

Year Team (League)	W	L	Pct.	ERA	WHIP	G	GS	CG	ShO	Hld.	Sv.-Opp.	IP	H	R	ER	HR	BB-IBB	SO	Avg.
2001—Arizona (N.L.)	0	0	...	0.00	0.20	3	0	0	0	2	2-2	5.0	0	0	0	0	1-0	3	.000

WORLD SERIES RECORD

Year Team (League)	W	L	Pct.	ERA	WHIP	G	GS	CG	ShO	Hld.	Sv.-Opp.	IP	H	R	ER	HR	BB-IBB	SO	Avg.
2001—Arizona (N.L.)	0	1	.000	13.50	2.10	2	0	0	0	0	0-2	3.1	6	5	5	3	1-0	6	.375

ALL-STAR GAME RECORD

	W	L	Pct.	ERA	WHIP	G	GS	CG	ShO	Hld.	Sv.-Opp.	IP	H	R	ER	HR	BB-IBB	SO	Avg.
All-Star Game totals (1 year)	0	0	...	54.00	9.00	1	0	0	0	0	0-0	0.1	3	2	2	0	0-0	0	.750

2006 LEFTY-RIGHTY SPLITS

vs.	Avg.	AB	H	2B	3B	HR	RBI	BB	SO	OBP	Slg.	vs.	Avg.	AB	H	2B	3B	HR	RBI	BB	SO	OBP	Slg.
L	.325	305	99	21	2	13	49	43	51	.414	.534	R	.265	302	80	19	2	5	41	18	78	.310	.391

KIM, SUN-WOO — P

PERSONAL: Born September 4, 1977, in Inchon, South Korea. ... 6-1/185. ... Throws right, bats right. ... Full name: Sun-Woo Kim. ... College: Korea University. **TRANSACTIONS/CAREER NOTES:** Signed as a non-drafted free agent by Boston Red Sox organization (November 21, 1997). ... Traded by Red Sox with P Seung Song and a player to be named to Montreal Expos for OF Cliff Floyd (July 30, 2002). ... Expos franchise transferred to Washington, D.C., and renamed Washington Nationals for 2005 season (December 3, 2004). ... Claimed on waivers by Colorado Rockies (August 5, 2005). ... On disabled list (April 18-May 23, 2006); included rehabilitation assignment to Colorado Springs.

CAREER HITTING: 11-for-60 (.183), 5 R, 3 2B, 0 3B, 0 HR, 8 RBI.

Year	Team (League)	W	L	Pct.	ERA	WHIP	G	GS	CG	ShO	Hld.	Sv.-Opp.	IP	H	R	ER	HR	BB-IBB	SO	Avg.
1998—Sarasota (Fla. St.)		12	8	.600	4.82	1.30	26	24	5	0	...	0-...	153.0	159	88	82	18	40-1	132	.264
1999—Trenton (East.)		9	8	.529	4.89	1.37	26	26	1	1	...	0-...	149.0	160	86	81	16	44-2	130	.275
2000—Pawtucket (Int'l)		11	7	.611	6.03	1.58	26	25	0	0	...	0-...	134.1	170	98	90	17	42-1	116	.309
2001—Pawtucket (Int'l)		6	7	.462	5.36	1.35	19	14	0	0	...	0-...	89.0	93	55	53	10	27-1	79	.272
—Boston (A.L.)		0	2	.000	5.83	1.80	20	2	0	0	1	0-0	41.2	54	27	27	1	21-5	27	.312
2002—Pawtucket (Int'l)		4	2	.667	3.18	1.10	8	8	1	0	...	0-...	45.1	34	18	16	4	16-0	37	.206
—Boston (A.L.)		2	0	1.000	7.45	1.41	15	2	0	0	2	0-0	29.0	34	24	24	5	7-0	18	.288
—Ottawa (Int'l)		3	0	1.000	1.24	1.03	7	7	1	1	...	0-0	43.2	29	11	6	2	16-0	28	.195
—Montreal (N.L.)		1	0	1.000	0.89	1.23	4	3	0	0	0	0-0	20.1	18	2	2	0	7-2	11	.250
2003—Montreal (N.L.)		0	1	.000	8.36	2.29	4	2	0	0	0	0-0	14.0	24	13	13	6	8-0	5	.407
—Edmonton (PCL)		10	8	.556	5.03	1.50	22	22	3	2	...	0-...	132.1	147	83	74	18	53-1	83	.281
2004—Montreal (N.L.)		4	6	.400	4.58	1.47	43	17	0	0	2	0-0	135.2	145	80	69	17	55-11	87	.275
2005—New Orleans (PCL)		4	2	.667	2.76	1.24	9	9	0	0	...	0-...	49.0	46	23	15	4	15-0	38	.249
—Wash. (N.L.)		1	2	.333	6.14	1.67	12	2	0	0	0	0-0	29.1	41	20	20	3	8-2	17	.336
—Colorado (N.L.)		5	1	.833	4.22	1.29	12	8	1	1	0	0-0	53.1	56	26	25	7	13-0	38	.268
2006—Colorado (N.L.)		0	0	...	19.29	3.57	6	0	0	0	0	0-0	7.0	17	15	15	2	8-0	4	.500
—Colo. Springs (PCL)		8	6	.571	5.05	1.48	21	21	0	0	...	0-...	124.2	149	77	70	14	36-0	71	.305
—Cincinnati (N.L.)		0	1	.000	5.40	1.05	2	1	0	0	0	0-0	6.2	7	4	4	3	0-0	4	.259
American League totals (2 years)		2	2	.500	6.50	1.64	35	4	0	0	3	0-0	70.2	88	51	51	6	28-5	45	.302
National League totals (5 years)		11	11	.500	5.00	1.53	83	34	1	1	2	0-0	266.1	308	160	148	38	99-15	166	.293
Major League totals (6 years)		13	13	.500	5.31	1.55	118	38	1	1	5	0-0	337.0	396	211	199	44	127-20	211	.295

2006 LEFTY-RIGHTY SPLITS

vs.	Avg.	AB	H	2B	3B	HR	RBI	BB	SO	OBP	Slg.	vs.	Avg.	AB	H	2B	3B	HR	RBI	BB	SO	OBP	Slg.
L	.471	34	16	2	0	3	9	2	4	.487	.794	R	.296	27	8	3	0	2	9	6	4	.412	.630

KING, RAY — P

PERSONAL: Born January 15, 1974, in Chicago. ... 6-1/242. ... Throws left, bats left. ... Full name: Raymond Keith King. ... High school: Ripley (Tenn.). ... College: Lambuth (Tenn.). **TRANSACTIONS/CAREER NOTES:** Selected by Cincinnati Reds organization in eighth round of 1995 free-agent draft. ... Loaned by Reds organization to Atlanta Braves organization (March 22-June 11, 1996). ... Traded by Reds to Braves (June 11, 1996), completing deal in which Braves traded OF Mike Kelly to Reds for P Chad Fox and a player to be named (January 9, 1996). ... Traded by Braves to Chicago Cubs for P Jon Ratliff (January 20, 1998). ... Traded by Cubs to Milwaukee Brewers for P Doug Johnston (April 14, 2000). ... On disabled list (April 4-19, 2002); included rehabilitation assignment to Indianapolis. ... Traded by Brewers to Braves for 3B Wes Helms and P John Foster (December 16, 2002). ... Traded by Braves with Ps Jason Marquis and Adam Wainwright to St. Louis Cardinals for OF J.D. Drew and C/OF Eli Marrero (December 14, 2003). ... Traded by Cardinals to Colorado Rockies for OF Larry Bigbie and 2B Aaron Miles (December 7, 2005).

CAREER HITTING: 0-for-6 (.000), 0 R, 0 2B, 0 3B, 0 HR, 0 RBI.

Year	Team (League)	W	L	Pct.	ERA	WHIP	G	GS	CG	ShO	Hld.	Sv.-Opp.	IP	H	R	ER	HR	BB-IBB	SO	Avg.
1995—Billings (Pion.)		3	0	1.000	1.67	1.07	28	0	0	0	...	5-...	43.0	31	11	8	1	15-3	43	.204
1996—Macon (S. Atl.)		3	5	.375	2.80	1.17	18	10	1	0	...	0-...	70.2	63	34	22	4	20-0	63	.237
—Durham (Carol.)		3	6	.333	4.46	1.44	14	14	2	0	...	0-...	82.2	104	54	41	3	15-2	52	.308
1997—Greenville (Sou.)		5	5	.500	6.85	1.66	12	9	0	0	...	0-...	65.2	85	53	50	9	24-2	42	.304
—Durham (Carol.)		6	9	.400	5.40	1.60	24	6	0	0	...	3-...	71.2	89	54	43	6	26-4	60	.300
1998—West Tenn (Sou.)		1	2	.333	2.43	1.11	25	0	0	0	...	3-...	29.2	23	9	8	1	10-0	26	.213
1999—Iowa (PCL)		1	3	.250	5.01	1.58	37	0	0	0	...	1-...	32.1	36	20	18	4	15-1	26	.283
—Iowa (PCL)		4	4	.500	1.88	1.23	37	0	0	0	...	2-...	43.0	31	11	9	1	22-3	41	.200
—Chicago (N.L.)		0	0	...	5.91	1.97	10	0	0	0	2	0-0	10.2	11	8	7	2	10-0	5	.289
2000—Iowa (PCL)		1	0	1.000	0.00	0.75	1	0	0	0	...	0-0	1.1	1	0	0	0	0-0	1	.200
—Indianapolis (Int'l)		0	3	.000	3.51	1.48	29	0	0	0	...	1-...	25.2	26	15	10	1	12-0	20	.271
—Milwaukee (N.L.)		3	2	.600	1.26	0.98	36	0	0	0	5	0-1	28.2	18	7	4	1	10-1	19	.180
2001—Milwaukee (N.L.)		0	4	.000	3.60	1.35	82	0	0	0	18	1-4	55.0	49	22	22	5	25-7	49	.241
2002—Milwaukee (N.L.)		3	2	.600	3.05	1.31	76	0	0	0	15	0-1	65.0	61	24	24	4	24-6	50	.255
—Indianapolis (Int'l)		0	0	...	0.00	2.00	1	1	0	0	...	0-0	1.0	1	0	0	0	1-0	1	.333
2003—Atlanta (N.L.)		3	4	.429	3.51	1.24	80	0	0	0	18	0-0	59.0	46	30	23	3	27-2	43	.213
2004—St. Louis (N.L.)		5	2	.714	2.61	1.08	86	0	0	0	31	0-1	62.0	43	19	18	1	24-0	40	.197
2005—St. Louis (N.L.)		4	4	.500	3.38	1.55	77	0	0	0	16	0-6	40.0	46	17	15	4	16-0	23	.293
2006—Colorado (N.L.)		1	4	.200	4.43	1.70	67	0	0	0	15	1-2	44.2	56	26	22	6	20-0	23	.327
Major League totals (8 years)		19	22	.463	3.28	1.33	514	0	0	0	2-16		365.0	330	153	133	27	156-16	252	.246

DIVISION SERIES RECORD

Year	Team (League)	W	L	Pct.	ERA	WHIP	G	GS	CG	ShO	Hld.	Sv.-Opp.	IP	H	R	ER	HR	BB-IBB	SO	Avg.
2003—Atlanta (N.L.)		0	0	...	0.00	2.00	4	0	0	0	1	0-0	1.0	1	0	0	0	1-0	0	.500
2004—St. Louis (N.L.)		0	0	...	0.00	0.00	3	0	0	0	1	0-0	2.1	0	0	0	0	0-0	1	.000
Division series totals (2 years)		0	0	...	0.00	0.60	7	0	0	0	2	0-0	3.1	1	0	0	0	1-0	1	.111

CHAMPIONSHIP SERIES RECORD

Year	Team (League)	W	L	Pct.	ERA	WHIP	G	GS	CG	ShO	Hld.	Sv.-Opp.	IP	H	R	ER	HR	BB-IBB	SO	Avg.
2004—St. Louis (N.L.)		0	0	...	10.80	2.40	4	0	0	0	1	0-0	1.2	4	2	2	2	0-0	1	.500

WORLD SERIES RECORD

Year	Team (League)	W	L	Pct.	ERA	WHIP	G	GS	CG	ShO	Hld.	Sv.-Opp.	IP	H	R	ER	HR	BB-IBB	SO	Avg.
2004—St. Louis (N.L.)		0	0	...	0.00	0.75	3	0	0	0	0	0-0	2.2	1	0	0	0	1-0	1	.125

2006 LEFTY-RIGHTY SPLITS

vs.	Avg.	AB	H	2B	3B	HR	RBI	BB	SO	OBP	Slg.	vs.	Avg.	AB	H	2B	3B	HR	RBI	BB	SO	OBP	Slg.
L	.303	76	23	5	2	3	13	7	14	.365	.539	R	.347	95	33	3	0	3	21	13	9	.423	.474

K

KINNEY, JOSH   P

PERSONAL: Born March 31, 1979, in Coudersport, Pa. ... Throws right, bats right. ... Full name: Josh T. Kinney. ... College: Quincy. **TRANSACTIONS/CAREER NOTES:** Contract purchased by St. Louis Cardinals organization from River City of the independent Frontier League (June 15, 2001).
CAREER HITTING: 0-for-0 (.000), 0 R, 0 2B, 0 3B, 0 HR, 0 RBI.

Year — Team (League)	W	L	Pct.	ERA	WHIP	G	GS	CG	ShO	Hld.	Sv.-Opp.	IP	H	R	ER	HR	BB-IBB	SO	Avg.
2001— River City (Fron.)	1	0	1.000	1.71	1.19	3	3	0	0	...	0-...	21.0	18	7	4	1	7-0	18	.237
— New Jersey (NYP)	2	0	1.000	0.00	0.35	3	0	0	0	...	0-...	5.2	2	0	0	0	0-0	5	.111
— Peoria (Midw.)	1	4	.200	4.39	1.51	27	0	0	0	...	0-...	41.0	47	24	20	1	15-0	35	.287
2002— Potomac (Carol.)	1	3	.250	2.29	1.36	44	0	0	0	...	7-...	55.0	52	21	14	2	23-1	42	.248
2003— Palm Beach (FSL)	3	0	1.000	1.52	1.16	31	0	0	0	...	3-...	41.1	38	7	7	0	10-4	35	.248
— Tennessee (Sou.)	2	1	.667	0.68	0.78	29	0	0	0	...	2-...	39.2	19	4	3	2	12-0	48	.142
2004— Palm Beach (FSL)	0	1	.000	4.32	1.68	7	0	0	0	...	0-...	8.1	8	6	4	1	6-2	12	.216
— Tennessee (Sou.)	3	8	.273	5.50	1.81	50	0	0	0	...	4-...	55.2	67	40	34	6	34-6	48	.288
2005— Memphis (PCL)	1	2	.333	7.36	2.30	26	0	0	0	6	0-3	25.2	40	21	21	4	19-0	25	.354
— Springfield (Texas)	5	2	.714	1.29	0.95	32	0	0	0	4	11-14	42.0	28	9	6	2	12-0	42	.185
2006— Memphis (PCL)	2	2	.500	1.52	1.06	51	0	0	0	12	3-9	71.0	46	16	12	2	29-4	76	.186
— St. Louis (N.L.)	0	0	...	3.24	1.00	21	0	0	0	2	0-0	25.0	17	9	9	3	8-0	22	.189
Major League totals (1 year)	0	0	...	3.24	1.00	21	0	0	0	2	0-0	25.0	17	9	9	3	8-0	22	.189

DIVISION SERIES RECORD

Year — Team (League)	W	L	Pct.	ERA	WHIP	G	GS	CG	ShO	Hld.	Sv.-Opp.	IP	H	R	ER	HR	BB-IBB	SO	Avg.
2006— St. Louis (N.L.)	0	0	...	0.00	0.50	2	0	0	0	2	0-0	2.0	0	0	0	0	1-0	1	.000

CHAMPIONSHIP SERIES RECORD

Year — Team (League)	W	L	Pct.	ERA	WHIP	G	GS	CG	ShO	Hld.	Sv.-Opp.	IP	H	R	ER	HR	BB-IBB	SO	Avg.
2006— St. Louis (N.L.)	1	0	1.000	0.00	1.20	3	0	0	0	1	0-0	3.1	3	0	0	0	1-0	4	.250

WORLD SERIES RECORD

Year — Team (League)	W	L	Pct.	ERA	WHIP	G	GS	CG	ShO	Hld.	Sv.-Opp.	IP	H	R	ER	HR	BB-IBB	SO	Avg.
2006— St. Louis (N.L.)	0	0	...	0.00	2.00	2	0	0	0	0	0-0	1.0	0	0	0	0	2-0	1	.000

2006 LEFTY-RIGHTY SPLITS

vs.	Avg.	AB	H	2B	3B	HR	RBI	BB	SO	OBP	Slg.	vs.	Avg.	AB	H	2B	3B	HR	RBI	BB	SO	OBP	Slg.
L	.162	37	6	1	0	2	3	6	10	.279	.351	R	.208	53	11	2	0	1	2	2	12	.250	.302

KINSLER, IAN   2B

PERSONAL: Born June 22, 1982, in Tucson, Ariz. ... 6-0/175. ... Bats right, throws right. ... Full name: Ian M. Kinsler. ... Junior college: Central Arizona. ... College: Arizona State, then Missouri. **TRANSACTIONS/CAREER NOTES:** Selected by Texas Rangers organization in 17th round of 2003 free-agent draft. ... On disabled list (April 12-May 25, 2006); included rehabilitation assignment to Oklahoma.
2006 GAMES PLAYED BY POSITION (MLB): 2B—119.

Year — Team (League)	Pos.	G	AB	R	H	2B	3B	HR	RBI	BB	SO	HBP	GDP	SB-CS	Avg.	OBP	SLG	OPS	E	Avg.
2003— Spokane (N'west)		51	188	32	52	10	6	1	15	20	34	4	5	11-3	.277	.352	.410	.762	...	...
2004— Clinton (Midw.)		59	224	52	90	30	1	11	52	25	36	3	7	16-5	.402	.465	.692	1.157	...	...
— Frisco (Texas)		71	277	51	83	21	1	9	46	32	47	15	5	7-4	.300	.400	.480	.880	...	...
2005— Oklahoma (PCL)	2B-SS-3B DH	131	530	102	145	28	2	23	94	53	89	9	21	19-5	.274	.348	.464	.812	21	.971
2006— Oklahoma (PCL)		10	39	7	10	3	0	2	6	2	5	0	1	1-1	.256	.293	.487	.780	2	.963
— Texas (A.L.)	2B	120	423	65	121	27	1	14	55	40	64	3	12	11-4	.286	.347	.454	.801	18	.973
Major League totals (1 year)		120	423	65	121	27	1	14	55	40	64	3	12	11-4	.286	.347	.454	.801	18	.973

2006 LEFTY-RIGHTY SPLITS

vs.	Avg.	AB	H	2B	3B	HR	RBI	BB	SO	OBP	Slg.	vs.	Avg.	AB	H	2B	3B	HR	RBI	BB	SO	OBP	Slg.
L	.271	118	32	8	0	5	18	9	11	.315	.466	R	.292	305	89	19	1	9	37	31	53	.359	.449

KLESKO, RYAN   OF/1B

PERSONAL: Born June 12, 1971, in Westminster, Calif. ... 6-3/220. ... Bats left, throws left. ... Full name: Ryan Anthony Klesko. ... High school: Westminster (Calif.). **TRANS-ACTIONS/CAREER NOTES:** Selected by Atlanta Braves organization in fifth round of 1989 free-agent draft. ... On disabled list (May 3-18, 1995); included rehabilitation assignment to Greenville. ... Traded by Braves with 2B Bret Boone and P Jason Shiell to San Diego Padres for 2B Quilvio Veras, 1B Wally Joyner and OF Reggie Sanders (December 22, 1999). ... On disabled list (September 1, 2003-remainder of season; and May 27-June 16, 2004). ... On disabled list (April 1-September 20, 2006); included rehabilitation assignment to Lake Elsinore. **STATISTICAL NOTES:** Career major league grand slams: 9.

Year — Team (League)	Pos.	G	AB	R	H	2B	3B	HR	RBI	BB	SO	HBP	GDP	SB-CS	Avg.	OBP	SLG	OPS	E	Avg.
1989— GC Braves (GCL)	DH	17	57	14	23	5	4	1	16	6	6	0	2	4-3	.404	.453	.684	1.137	...	...
— Sumter (S. Atl.)	1B	25	90	17	26	6	0	1	12	11	14	0	5	1-0	.289	.363	.389	.752	4	.979
1990— Sumter (S. Atl.)	1B	63	231	41	85	15	1	10	38	31	30	1	6	13-1	.368	.437	.571	1.008	14	.978
— Durham (Carol.)	1B	77	292	40	80	16	1	7	47	32	53	2	8	10-5	.274	.343	.408	.751	8	.976
1991— Greenville (Sou.)	1B	126	419	64	122	22	3	14	67	75	60	4	5	14-17	.291	.404	.458	.862	17	.985
1992— Richmond (Int'l)	1B	123	418	63	105	22	2	17	59	41	72	4	14	3-5	.251	.323	.435	.758	11	.989
— Atlanta (N.L.)	1B	13	14	0	0	0	0	0	1	0	5	1	0	0-0	.000	.067	.000	.067	1	1.000
1993— Richmond (Int'l)	1B-OF	98	343	59	94	14	2	22	74	47	69	2	8	4-3	.274	.361	.519	.880	12	.981
— Atlanta (N.L.)	1B-OF	22	17	3	6	1	0	2	5	3	4	0	0	0-0	.353	.450	.765	1.215	0	1.000
1994— Atlanta (N.L.)	OF-1B	92	245	42	68	13	3	17	47	26	48	1	8	1-0	.278	.344	.563	.907	7	.929
1995— Atlanta (N.L.)	OF-1B	107	329	48	102	25	2	23	70	47	72	2	6	5-4	.310	.396	.608	1.004	8	.944
— Greenville (Sou.)	DH-OF	4	13	1	3	0	0	1	4	2	1	0	1	0-0	.231	.333	.462	.795	0	1.000
1996— Atlanta (N.L.)	OF-1B	153	528	90	149	21	4	34	93	68	129	2	10	6-3	.282	.364	.530	.894	5	.977
1997— Atlanta (N.L.)	OF-1B	143	467	67	122	23	4	24	84	48	130	4	12	4-4	.261	.334	.490	.824	6	.977
1998— Atlanta (N.L.)	OF-1B	129	427	69	117	29	1	18	70	56	66	3	9	5-3	.274	.359	.473	.832	2	.990
1999— Atlanta (N.L.)	1B-OF-DH	133	404	55	120	28	2	21	80	53	69	6	2	5-2	.297	.376	.532	.908	6	.990
2000— San Diego (N.L.)	1B-OF	145	494	88	140	33	2	26	92	91	81	4	10	23-7	.283	.393	.516	.909	9	.992
2001— San Diego (N.L.)	1B	146	538	105	154	34	6	30	113	88	89	3	16	23-4	.286	.384	.539	.923	11	.991
2002— San Diego (N.L.)	1B-OF-DH	146	540	90	162	39	1	29	95	76	86	4	7	6-2	.300	.388	.537	.925	7	.993
2003— San Diego (N.L.)	1B-DH	121	397	47	100	18	0	21	67	65	83	3	11	2-5	.252	.354	.456	.810	6	.994
2004— San Diego (N.L.)	OF-DH-1B	127	402	58	117	32	2	9	66	73	67	1	8	3-2	.291	.399	.448	.847	4	.986
2005— San Diego (N.L.)	OF-DH-1B	137	443	61	110	19	1	18	58	75	80	1	6	3-4	.248	.358	.418	.775	4	.982
2006— Lake Elsinore (Calif.)		8	22	2	6	0	0	0	1	5	5	0	1	0-0	.273	.407	.364	.771	0	1.000
— San Diego (N.L.)		6	4	0	3	0	0	0	2	2	0	0	0	0-0	.750	.833	1.000	1.833	0	...
Major League totals (15 years)		1620	5249	823	1470	316	30	272	943	771	1009	28	111	86-40	.280	.372	.507	.879	75	.988

K

DIVISION SERIES RECORD

Year Team (League)	Pos.	G	AB	R	H	2B	3B	HR	RBI	BB	SO	HBP	GDP	SB-CS	Avg.	OBP	SLG	OPS	E	Avg.
1995— Atlanta (N.L.)	OF	4	15	5	7	1	0	0	1	0	3	0	1	0-0	.467	.467	.533	1.000	0	1.000
1996— Atlanta (N.L.)	OF	3	8	1	1	0	0	1	1	3	4	0	0	1-0	.125	.364	.500	.864	1	.667
1997— Atlanta (N.L.)	OF	3	8	2	2	1	0	1	1	0	2	0	1	0-0	.250	.250	.750	1.000	1	.750
1998— Atlanta (N.L.)	OF	3	11	1	3	0	0	1	4	0	3	0	0	0-0	.273	.273	.545	.818	0	1.000
1999— Atlanta (N.L.)	1B	4	12	3	4	0	0	0	1	1	4	0	0	0-0	.333	.385	.333	.718	0	1.000
2005— San Diego (N.L.)	OF	3	10	1	2	0	0	0	0	2	4	0	0	0-0	.200	.333	.200	.533	0	1.000
2006— San Diego (N.L.)		3	3	0	2	1	0	0	0	0	0	0	0	0-0	.667	.667	1.000	1.667	0	...
Division series totals (7 years)		23	67	13	21	3	0	3	8	6	20	0	2	1-0	.313	.370	.493	.862	2	.953

CHAMPIONSHIP SERIES RECORD

Year Team (League)	Pos.	G	AB	R	H	2B	3B	HR	RBI	BB	SO	HBP	GDP	SB-CS	Avg.	OBP	SLG	OPS	E	Avg.
1995— Atlanta (N.L.)	OF	4	7	0	0	0	0	0	3	4	0	0	0	0-1	.000	.300	.000	.300	0	1.000
1996— Atlanta (N.L.)	OF	6	16	1	4	0	0	1	3	2	6	0	1	0-0	.250	.333	.438	.771	0	1.000
1997— Atlanta (N.L.)	OF	5	17	2	4	0	0	2	4	2	3	0	0	0-0	.235	.316	.588	.904	0	1.000
1998— Atlanta (N.L.)	OF	5	12	2	1	0	0	0	1	6	3	0	0	0-0	.083	.389	.083	.472	1	.750
1999— Atlanta (N.L.)	1B	4	8	1	1	0	0	1	1	2	1	0	0	0-0	.125	.300	.500	.800	2	.935
Champ. series totals (5 years)		24	60	6	10	0	0	4	9	15	17	0	1	0-1	.167	.333	.367	.700	3	.944

WORLD SERIES RECORD

Year Team (League)	Pos.	G	AB	R	H	2B	3B	HR	RBI	BB	SO	HBP	GDP	SB-CS	Avg.	OBP	SLG	OPS	E	Avg.
1995— Atlanta (N.L.)	DH-OF	6	16	4	5	0	0	3	4	3	4	0	0	0-0	.313	.421	.875	1.296	0	1.000
1996— Atlanta (N.L.)	1B-DH-OF	5	10	2	1	0	0	0	1	2	4	0	0	0-0	.100	.250	.100	.350	1	.500
1999— Atlanta (N.L.)	1B	4	12	0	2	0	0	0	0	0	1	0	0	0-0	.167	.167	.167	.333	0	1.000
World series totals (3 years)		15	38	6.	8	0	0	3	5	5	9	0	0	0-0	.211	.302	.447	.750	1	.958

ALL-STAR GAME RECORD

		G	AB	R	H	2B	3B	HR	RBI	BB	SO	HBP	GDP	SB-CS	Avg.	OBP	SLG	OPS	E	Avg.
All-Star Game totals (1 year)		1	1	0	0	0	0	0	1	0	1	0	0	0-0	.000	.000	.000	.000	0	1.000

2006 LEFTY-RIGHTY SPLITS

vs.	Avg.	AB	H	2B	3B	HR	RBI	BB	SO	OBP	Slg.	vs.	Avg.	AB	H	2B	3B	HR	RBI	BB	SO	OBP	Slg.
L	1.000	1	1	0	0	0	1	0	0	1.000	2.000	R	.667	3	2	0	0	0	1	2	0	.800	.667

KLINE, STEVE   P

PERSONAL: Born August 22, 1972, in Sunbury, Pa. ... 6-1/215. ... Throws left, bats both. ... Full name: Steven James Kline. ... High school: Lewisburg (Pa.). ... College: West Virginia. **TRANSACTIONS/CAREER NOTES:** Selected by Cleveland Indians organization in eighth round of 1993 free-agent draft. ... Traded by Indians to Montreal Expos for P Jeff Juden (July 31, 1997). ... On disabled list (April 11-27, 1999). ... Traded by Expos with P Dustin Hermanson to St. Louis Cardinals for 3B Fernando Tatis and P Britt Reames (December 14, 2000). ... On disabled list (April 29-May 31, 2002); included rehabilitation assignments to Peoria and New Haven. ... On disabled list (August 28-September 29, 2004). ... Signed as a free agent by Baltimore Orioles (December 20, 2004). ... On suspended list (July 22-26, 2005). ... Traded by Orioles to San Francisco Giants for P LaTroy Hawkins (December 6, 2005).

CAREER HITTING: 2-for-13 (.154), 1 R, 1 2B, 0 3B, 0 HR, 2 RBI.

Year Team (League)	W	L	Pct.	ERA	WHIP	G	GS	CG	ShO	Hld.	Sv.-Opp.	IP	H	R	ER	HR	BB-IBB	SO	Avg.
1993— Burlington (Appal.)	1	1	.500	4.91	1.77	2	1	0	0		0-...	7.1	11	4	4	0	2-1	4	.355
— Watertown (NYP)	5	4	.556	3.19	1.13	13	13	2	1		0-...	79.0	77	36	28	3	12-0	45	.248
1994— Columbus (S. Atl.)	18	5	.783	3.01	1.14	28	28	3	1		0-...	185.2	175	67	62	14	36-0	174	.251
1995— Cant./Akr. (Eastern)	2	3	.400	2.42	1.30	14	14	0	0		0-...	89.1	86	34	24	6	30-3	45	.252
1996— Cant./Akr. (Eastern)	8	12	.400	5.46	1.52	25	24	0	0		0-...	146.2	168	98	89	16	55-2	107	.288
1997— Cleveland (A.L.)	3	1	.750	5.81	2.09	20	1	0	0	4	0-2	26.1	42	19	17	6	13-1	17	.365
— Buffalo (A.A.)	3	3	.500	4.03	1.29	20	4	0	0		1-...	51.1	53	26	23	4	13-1	41	.265
— Montreal (N.L.)	1	3	.250	6.15	1.56	26	0	0	0	1	0-1	26.1	31	18	18	4	10-3	20	.307
1998— Ottawa (Int'l)	0	0	...	0.00	0.38	2	0	0	0		0-...	2.2	1	0	0	0	0-0	1	.125
— Montreal (N.L.)	3	6	.333	2.76	1.44	78	0	0	0	18	1-2	71.2	62	25	22	4	41-7	56	.228
1999— Montreal (N.L.)	7	4	.636	3.75	1.28	82	0	0	0	16	0-2	69.2	56	32	29	8	33-6	69	.218
2000— Montreal (N.L.)	1	5	.167	3.50	1.40	83	0	0	0	12	14-18	82.1	88	36	32	8	27-2	64	.278
2001— St. Louis (N.L.)	3	3	.500	1.80	1.09	89	0	0	0	17	9-10	75.0	53	16	15	3	29-7	54	.203
2002— St. Louis (N.L.)	2	1	.667	3.39	1.29	66	0	0	0	21	6-8	58.1	54	23	22	3	21-2	41	.251
— Peoria (Midw.)	0	0	...	0.00	0.86	2	1	0	0		0-...	2.1	1	0	0	0	1-0	5	.111
— New Haven (East.)	0	0	...	0.00	0.50	1	1	0	0		0-...	2.0	0	0	0	0	1-0	2	.000
2003— St. Louis (N.L.)	5	5	.500	3.82	1.35	78	0	0	0	18	3-7	63.2	56	29	27	5	30-5	31	.237
2004— St. Louis (N.L.)	2	2	.500	1.79	1.07	67	0	0	0	15	3-4	50.1	37	12	10	3	17-4	35	.209
2005— Baltimore (A.L.)	2	4	.333	4.28	1.46	67	0	0	0	9	0-3	61.0	59	34	29	11	30-5	36	.257
2006— San Francisco (N.L.)	4	3	.571	3.66	1.53	72	0	0	0	18	1-1	51.2	53	24	21	3	26-3	33	.275
American League totals (2 years)	5	5	.500	4.74	1.65	87	1	0	0	13	0-5	87.1	101	53	46	17	43-6	53	.293
National League totals (9 years)	28	32	.467	3.21	1.32	641	0	0	0	136	37-53	549.0	490	215	196	41	234-39	423	.242
Major League totals (10 years)	33	37	.471	3.42	1.36	728	1	0	0	149	37-58	636.1	591	268	242	58	277-45	476	.249

DIVISION SERIES RECORD

Year Team (League)	W	L	Pct.	ERA	WHIP	G	GS	CG	ShO	Hld.	Sv.-Opp.	IP	H	R	ER	HR	BB-IBB	SO	Avg.
2001— St. Louis (N.L.)	0	1	.000	2.08	1.38	4	0	0	0	0	2-2	4.1	4	1	1	0	2-1	0	.308
2002— St. Louis (N.L.)	0	0	...	0.00	1.50	2	0	0	0	2	0-0	1.1	1	0	0	0	1-0	0	.200
2004— St. Louis (N.L.)	0	0	...	0.00	0.00	2	0	0	0	0	0-0	1.1	0	0	0	0	0-0	0	.000
Division series totals (3 years)	0	1	.000	1.29	1.14	8	0	0	0	2	2-2	7.0	5	1	1	0	3-1	0	.227

CHAMPIONSHIP SERIES RECORD

Year Team (League)	W	L	Pct.	ERA	WHIP	G	GS	CG	ShO	Hld.	Sv.-Opp.	IP	H	R	ER	HR	BB-IBB	SO	Avg.
2002— St. Louis (N.L.)	0	0	...	0.00	0.86	4	0	0	0	1	0-0	2.1	2	0	0	0	0-0	1	.250
2004— St. Louis (N.L.)	0	0	...	0.00	1.00	1	0	0	0	0	0-0	0.0	2	0	0	0	0-0	0	1.000
Champ. series totals (2 years)	0	0	...	0.00	1.71	5	0	0	0	1	0-0	2.1	4	0	0	0	0-0	1	.400

2006 LEFTY-RIGHTY SPLITS

vs.	Avg.	AB	H	2B	3B	HR	RBI	BB	SO	OBP	Slg.	vs.	Avg.	AB	H	2B	3B	HR	RBI	BB	SO	OBP	Slg.
L	.261	92	24	3	2	0	15	10	22	.340	.337	R	.287	101	29	7	0	3	17	16	11	.381	.446

KNOEDLER, JUSTIN   C

PERSONAL: Born July 17, 1980, in Springfield, Ill. ... 6-2/210. ... Bats right, throws right. ... Full name: Justin Joseph Knoedler. ... High school: Springfield (Ill.). ... Junior college: Lincoln Land C.C. (Springfield, Ill.). ... College: Miami (Ohio). **TRANSACTIONS/CAREER NOTES:** Selected by St. Louis Cardinals organization in 41st round of 1998 free-agent draft; did not sign. ... Selected by San Francisco Giants organization in 13th round of 2000 free-agent draft; did not sign. ... Selected by Giants organization in fifth round of 2001 free-agent draft.

K

Year	Team (League)	Pos.	G	AB	R	H	2B	3B	HR	RBI	BB	SO	HBP	GDP	SB-CS	Avg.	OBP	SLG	OPS	E	Avg.
																		BATTING			**FIELDING**
2002— Hagerstown (SAL)	C	86	280	32	72	16	2	5	33	37	56	4	8	6-5	.257	.349	.382	.731	15	.977
2003— San Jose (Calif.)	C	101	354	48	91	25	2	10	43	35	78	3	5	13-3	.257	.326	.424	.749	9	.989
2004— Norwich (East.)	C-DH-OF	115	409	64	112	28	3	9	47	32	98	8	7	5-3	.274	.335	.423	.758	7	.991
— San Francisco (N.L.)	C	1	1	0	0	0	0	0	0	0	0	0	0	0-0	.000	.000	.000	.000	0	1.000
2005— Norwich (East.)	C	4	10	2	3	0	0	0	0	2	0	0	0	2-1	.300	.417	.300	.717	0	1.000
— Lakeland (Fla. St.) OF-DH-1B	40	89	18	25	6	0	0	9	16	21	0	1	3-1	.281	.387	.348	.735	8	.915
— Fresno (PCL)	C-DH	85	287	35	78	19	1	4	32	26	61	7	2	5-5	.272	.345	.387	.731	4	.994
— Erie (East.)	OF-1B	32	79	10	18	6	0	1	8	10	26	1	1	1-0	.228	.322	.342	.664	0	1.000
— San Francisco (N.L.)	C	8	10	0	1	0	0	0	1	1	1	0	0	0-0	.100	.182	.100	.282	0	1.000
2006— San Francisco (N.L.)	C	5	7	0	1	0	0	0	0	0	1	0	0	0-0	.143	.143	.143	.286	0	1.000
— Fresno (PCL)	C	71	233	32	59	13	4	4	27	22	58	1	4	4-0	.253	.319	.395	.714		
— Connecticut (East.)	C	21	71	7	15	6	0	1	8	4	24			1-1	.211	.263	.338	.601		
Major League totals (3 years)		14	18	0	2	0	0	0	0	2	1	0	0	0-0	.111	.158	.111	.269	0	1.000

2006 LEFTY-RIGHTY SPLITS

vs.	Avg.	AB	H	2B	3B	HR	RBI	BB	SO	OBP	Slg.	vs.	Avg.	AB	H	2B	3B	HR	RBI	BB	SO	OBP	Slg.
L	.000	1	0	0	0	0	0	0	0	.000	.000	R	.167	6	1	0	0	0	0	0	1	.167	.167

KNOTT, JON   OF

PERSONAL: Born August 4, 1978, in Manassas, Va. ... 6-3/220. ... Bats right, throws right. ... Full name: Jonathan David Knott. ... High school: Venice (Fla.). ... College: Mississippi State. **TRANSACTIONS/CAREER NOTES:** Signed as a non-drafted free agent by San Diego Padres organization (September 21, 2001).

Year	Team (League)	Pos.	G	AB	R	H	2B	3B	HR	RBI	BB	SO	HBP	GDP	SB-CS	Avg.	OBP	SLG	OPS	E	Avg.
																		BATTING			**FIELDING**
2002— Fort Wayne (Midw.)	OF-1B	37	126	19	42	12	3	3	18	17	33	1	1	2-1	.333	.411	.548	.959	3	.959
— Lake Elsinore (Calif.) ...1B-OF-3B	93	367	55	125	33	8	8	73	46	68	3	7	5-4	.341	.414	.540	.954	9	.981
2003— Mobile (Sou.)	OF-1B	127	432	83	109	32	0	27	82	82	117	17	1	5-3	.252	.387	.514	.901	11	.980
— Portland (PCL)	1B	7	26	5	9	1	0	1	5	4	3	0	1	0-0	.346	.433	.500	.933	0	1.000
2004— San Diego (N.L.)	OF	9	14	1	3	2	0	0	1	1	5	0	0	0-0	.214	.267	.357	.624	0	1.000
— Portland (PCL) OF-DH-1B	113	435	79	126	22	3	26	85	58	110	7	12	5-3	.290	.376	.533	.901	2	.989
2005— Portland (PCL) OF-1B-DH	134	503	81	126	34	4	25	78	55	112	11	17	1-0	.250	.333	.483	.816	13	.980
2006— Portland (PCL)		136	479	80	134	32	6	32	113	52	103	6	22	3-3	.280	.353	.572	.925	9	.988
— San Diego (N.L.)		3	3	0	0	0	0	0	0	0	1	0	0	0-0	.000	.000	.000	.000	0	...
Major League totals (2 years)		12	17	1	3	2	0	0	1	1	6	0	0	0-0	.176	.222	.294	.516	0	1.000

2006 LEFTY-RIGHTY SPLITS

vs.	Avg.	AB	H	2B	3B	HR	RBI	BB	SO	OBP	Slg.	vs.	Avg.	AB	H	2B	3B	HR	RBI	BB	SO	OBP	Slg.
L	.000	3	0	0	0	0	0	0	1	.000	.000	R	.000	0	0	0	0	0	0	0	0	.000	.000

KOLB, DAN   P

PERSONAL: Born March 29, 1975, in Sterling, Ill. ... 6-4/240. ... Throws right, bats right. ... Full name: Daniel Lee Kolb. ... High school: Walnut (Ill.). ... College: Illinois State. **TRANSACTIONS/CAREER NOTES:** Selected by Minnesota Twins organization in 17th round of 1993 free-agent draft; did not sign. ... Selected by Texas Rangers organization in sixth round of 1995 free-agent draft. ... On disabled list (October 3, 1999-remainder of season; and May 29, 2000-remainder of season). ... On disabled list (March 23-July 11, 2001); included rehabilitation assignments to Charlotte and Tulsa. ... On disabled list (March 28-July 16, 2002); included rehabilitation assignments to Charlotte and Tulsa. ... Released by Rangers (March 26, 2003). ... Signed by Milwaukee Brewers organization (April 2, 2003). ... Traded by Brewers to Atlanta Braves for P Jose Capellan and a player to be named (December 11, 2004); Brewers acquired P Alec Zumwalt to complete deal (December 13, 2004). ... Traded by Braves to Brewers for P Wes Obermueller (December 7, 2005).

CAREER HITTING: 0-for-1 (.000), 0 R, 0 2B, 0 3B, 0 HR, 0 RBI.

Year	Team (League)	W	L	Pct.	ERA	WHIP	G	GS	CG	ShO	Hld.	Sv.-Opp.	IP	H	R	ER	HR	BB-IBB	SO	Avg.
1995— GC Rangers (GCL)	1	7	.125	2.21	1.25	12	11	0	0	...	0-...	53.0	38	22	13	0	28-0	46	.204
1996— Char., S.C. (SAL)	8	6	.571	2.57	1.11	20	20	4	2	...	0-...	126.0	80	50	36	5	60-2	127	.181
— Charlotte (Fla. St.)	2	2	.500	4.26	1.37	6	6	0	0	...	0-...	38.0	38	18	18	1	14-0	28	.260
— Tulsa (Texas)	1	0	1.000	0.77	1.11	2	2	0	0	...	0-...	11.2	5	1	1	0	8-0	7	.139
1997— Charlotte (Fla. St.)	4	10	.286	4.87	1.56	24	23	3	0	...	0-...	133.0	146	91	72	10	62-1	83	.282
— Tulsa (Texas)	0	2	.000	4.76	1.59	2	2	0	0	...	0-...	11.1	7	7	6	1	11-0	6	.179
1998— Tulsa (Texas)	12	11	.522	4.82	1.62	28	28	2	0	...	0-...	162.1	187	104	87	11	76-1	83	.293
— Oklahoma (PCL)	0	0	...	0.00	2.00	1	0	0	0	...	0-...	1.0	1	0	0	0	1-0	0	.250
1999— Tulsa (Texas)	1	2	.333	2.79	1.45	7	7	1	1	...	0-...	38.2	38	16	12	0	18-0	32	.260
— Oklahoma (PCL)	5	3	.625	5.10	1.68	11	8	0	0	...	0-...	60.0	74	35	34	4	27-0	21	.320
— Texas (A.L.)	2	1	.667	4.65	1.55	16	0	0	0	0	0-0	31.0	33	18	16	2	15-0	15	.268
2000— Oklahoma (PCL)	4	1	.800	0.98	1.04	13	0	0	0	...	0-...	18.1	11	6	2	0	8-1	18	.175
— Texas (A.L.)	0	0	...	67.50	10.50	1	0	0	0	0	0-...	0.2	5	5	5	0	2-0	0	.833
2001— Charlotte (Fla. St.)	1	2	.333	3.86	1.23	7	3	0	0	...	0-...	18.2	21	8	8	1	2-0	16	.276
— Tulsa (Texas)	1	0	1.000	0.00	0.50	1	0	0	0	...	0-...	2.0	0	0	0	0	1-0	0	.000
— Oklahoma (PCL)	0	1	.000	1.42	0.89	12	0	0	0	...	3-...	19.0	13	3	3	1	4-0	21	.188
— Texas (A.L.)	0	0	...	4.70	1.63	17	0	0	0	7	0-...	15.1	15	8	8	2	10-1	15	.259
2002— Charlotte (Fla. St.)	1	0	1.000	1.50	1.50	4	0	0	0	...	0-...	6.0	5	1	1	0	4-0	2	.227
— Tulsa (Texas)	0	1	.000	2.16	1.44	5	1	0	0	...	0-...	8.1	9	2	2	0	3-0	4	.290
— Texas (A.L.)	3	6	.333	4.22	1.53	34	0	0	0	2	1-4	32.0	27	17	15	1	22-2	20	.227
2003— Indianapolis (Int'l)	0	1	.000	1.37	1.00	26	0	0	0	...	4-...	39.1	26	10	6	1	13-0	46	.183
— Milwaukee (N.L.)	1	2	.333	1.96	1.28	37	0	0	0	4	21-23	41.1	34	10	9	2	19-3	39	.221
2004— Milwaukee (N.L.)	0	4	.000	2.98	1.13	64	0	0	0	6	39-44	57.1	50	22	19	3	15-1	21	.234
2005— Atlanta (N.L.)	3	8	.273	5.93	1.86	65	0	0	0	6	11-18	57.2	78	39	38	5	29-5	39	.329
2006— Milwaukee (N.L.)	2	2	.500	4.84	1.51	53	0	0	0	6	1-3	48.1	53	28	26	4	20-1	26	.282
American League totals (4 years)	5	7	.417	5.01	1.63	68	0	0	0	9	1-4	79.0	80	48	44	5	49-3	50	.261
National League totals (4 years)	6	16	.273	4.05	1.46	219	0	0	0	17	72-88	204.2	215	99	92	14	83-10	125	.271
Major League totals (8 years)	11	23	.324	4.31	1.51	287	0	0	0	26	73-92	283.2	295	147	136	19	132-13	175	.268

ALL-STAR GAME RECORD

	W	L	Pct.	ERA	WHIP	G	GS	CG	ShO	Hld.	Sv.-Opp.	IP	H	R	ER	HR	BB-IBB	SO	Avg.
All-Star Game totals (1 year)	0	0	...	0.00	1.00	1	0	0	0	0	0-0	1.0	1	0	0	0	0-0	0	.250

2006 LEFTY-RIGHTY SPLITS

vs.	Avg.	AB	H	2B	3B	HR	RBI	BB	SO	OBP	Slg.	vs.	Avg.	AB	H	2B	3B	HR	RBI	BB	SO	OBP	Slg.
L	.323	65	21	4	0	1	13	7	7	.387	.431	R	.260	123	32	4	2	3	20	13	19	.328	.398

KOMINE, SHANE — P

PERSONAL: Born October 18, 1980, in Honolulu, Hawaii. ... 5-9/175. ... Throws right, bats right. ... Full name: Shane Kenji Komine. ...High school: Kalani (Honolulu, Hawaii). ... College: Nebraska. **TRANSACTIONS/CAREER NOTES:** Selected by St. Louis Cardinals organization in 19th round of 2001 free-agent draft; did not sign. ... Selected by Oakland Athletics organization in ninth round of 2002 free-agent draft.

CAREER HITTING: 0-for-0 (.000), 0 R, 0 2B, 0 3B, 0 HR, 0 RBI.

Year Team (League)	W	L	Pct.	ERA	WHIP	G	GS	CG	ShO	Hld.	Sv.-Opp.	IP	H	R	ER	HR	BB-IBB	SO	Avg.
2002— Visalia (Calif.)	1	3	.250	5.96	1.68	18	0	0	0	...	0-...	25.2	23	20	17	2	20-3	22	.240
2003— Kane Co. (Midw.)	6	0	1.000	1.82	0.99	8	8	1	1	...	0-...	54.1	45	12	11	1	9-0	50	.223
—Midland (Texas)	4	6	.400	3.75	1.34	19	18	1	1	...	0-...	103.1	108	51	43	6	30-2	75	.271
2004— Midland (Texas)	4	5	.444	4.77	1.39	17	17	0	0	...	0-...	94.1	103	56	50	10	28-0	65	.281
2005— Ariz. A's (Ariz.)	0	1	.000	9.72	2.04	4	4	0	0	0	0-0	8.1	10	10	9	0	7-0	11	.294
—Stockton (Calif.)	0	0	...	4.15	1.50	2	2	0	0	0	0-0	8.2	10	4	4	0	3-0	11	.294
—Midland (Texas)	2	1	.667	3.16	1.09	5	5	0	0	0	0-0	31.1	27	12	11	5	7-0	33	.235
2006— Sacramento (PCL)	11	8	.579	4.05	1.31	24	22	1	1	1	0-0	140.0	145	67	63	13	38-2	116	.267
—Oakland (A.L.)	0	0	...	5.00	2.00	2	2	0	0	0	0-0	9.0	10	5	5	3	8-1	1	.270
Major League totals (1 year)	**0**	**0**	...	**5.00**	**2.00**	**2**	**2**	**0**	**0**	**0**	**0-0**	**9.0**	**10**	**5**	**5**	**3**	**8-1**	**1**	**.270**

2006 LEFTY-RIGHTY SPLITS

vs.	Avg.	AB	H	2B	3B	HR	RBI	BB	SO	OBP	Slg.	vs.	Avg.	AB	H	2B	3B	HR	RBI	BB	SO	OBP	Slg.
L	.250	12	3	0	0	0	0	6	1	.500	.250	R	.280	25	7	1	0	3	5	2	0	.333	.680

KONERKO, PAUL — 1B

PERSONAL: Born March 5, 1976, in Providence, R.I. ... 6-2/215. ... Bats right, throws right. ... Full name: Paul Henry Konerko. ... Name pronounced: kone-err-coe. ... High school: Chaparral (Scottsdale, Ariz.). **TRANSACTIONS/CAREER NOTES:** Selected by Los Angeles Dodgers organization in first round (13th pick overall) of 1994 free-agent draft. ... Traded by Dodgers with P Dennys Reyes to Cincinnati Reds for P Jeff Shaw (July 4, 1998). ... Traded by Reds to Chicago White Sox for OF Mike Cameron (November 11, 1998). **HONORS:** Named A.L. Comeback Player of the Year by THE SPORTING NEWS (2004). ... Named first baseman on THE SPORTING NEWS A.L. All-Star team (2004). **STATISTICAL NOTES:** Career major league grand slams: 6.

2006 GAMES PLAYED BY POSITION (MLB): 1B—140, DH—12.

Year Team (League)	Pos.	G	AB	R	H	2B	3B	HR	RBI	BB	SO	HBP	GDP	SB-CS	Avg.	OBP	SLG	OPS	E	Avg.
1994— Yakima (N'west)	C-DH	67	257	25	74	15	2	6	58	36	52	6	6	1-0	.288	.379	.432	.811	5	.984
1995— San Bern. (Calif.)	C-DH	118	448	7	124	21	1	19	77	59	88	4	12	3-1	.277	.362	.455	.817	11	.985
1996— San Antonio (Texas)	1B-DH	133	470	78	141	23	2	29	86	72	85	8	7	1-3	.300	.397	.543	.939	14	.989
—Albuquerque (PCL)	1B	4	14	2	6	0	0	1	2	1	2	0	0	0-1	.429	.467	.643	1.110	0	1.000
1997— Albuquerque (PCL)	3B-1B-DH																			
	2B	130	483	97	156	31	1	37	127	64	61	8	16	2-3	.323	.407	.621	1.028	24	.952
—Los Angeles (N.L.)	1B-3B	6	7	0	1	0	0	0	0	1	2	0	1	0-0	.143	.250	.143	.393	0	1.000
1998— Los Angeles (N.L.)	1B-3B-OF	49	144	14	31	1	0	4	16	10	30	2	5	0-1	.215	.272	.306	.578	2	.991
—Albuquerque (PCL)	OF-1B-3B	24	87	16	33	10	0	6	26	11	12	0	3	0-0	.379	.436	.701	1.137	3	.955
—Cincinnati (N.L.)	3B-1B-OF	26	73	7	16	3	0	3	13	6	10	1	5	0-0	.219	.284	.384	.668	0	1.000
—Indianapolis (Int'l)	3B	39	150	25	49	8	0	8	39	19	18	2	8	1-0	.327	.402	.540	.942	4	.957
1999— Chicago (A.L.)	1B-DH-3B	142	513	71	151	31	4	24	81	45	68	2	19	1-0	.294	.352	.511	.862	4	.995
2000— Chicago (A.L.)	1B-3B-DH	143	524	84	156	31	1	21	97	47	72	10	22	1-0	.298	.363	.481	.844	11	.990
2001— Chicago (A.L.)	1B-DH	156	582	92	164	35	0	32	99	54	89	9	17	1-0	.282	.354	.507	.856	8	.994
2002— Chicago (A.L.)	1B-DH	151	570	81	173	30	0	27	104	44	72	9	17	0-0	.304	.359	.498	.857	8	.993
2003— Chicago (A.L.)	1B-DH	137	444	49	104	19	0	18	65	43	50	4	* 28	0-0	.234	.305	.399	.704	2	.998
2004— Chicago (A.L.)	1B-DH	155	563	84	156	22	0	41	117	69	107	6	23	1-0	.277	.359	.535	.894	6	.995
2005— Chicago (A.L.)	1B-DH	158	575	98	163	24	0	40	100	81	109	5	9	0-0	.283	.375	.534	.909	5	.996
2006— Chicago (A.L.)	1B-DH	152	566	97	177	30	0	35	113	60	104	8	25	1-0	.313	.381	.551	.932	6	.995
American League totals (8 years)		1194	4337	656	1244	222	5	238	776	443	671	53	160	5-0	.287	.357	.505	.862	50	.995
National League totals (2 years)		81	224	21	48	4	0	7	29	17	42	3	11	0-1	.214	.275	.326	.601	2	.993
Major League totals (10 years)		1275	4561	677	1292	226	5	245	805	460	713	56	171	5-1	.283	.353	.496	.849	52	.995

DIVISION SERIES RECORD

Year Team (League)	Pos.	G	AB	R	H	2B	3B	HR	RBI	BB	SO	HBP	GDP	SB-CS	Avg.	OBP	SLG	OPS	E	Avg.
2000— Chicago (A.L.)	1B	3	9	1	0	0	0	0	0	1	1	0	1	0-0	.000	.100	.000	.100	0	1.000
2005— Chicago (A.L.)	1B	3	12	3	3	0	0	2	4	0	1	0	1	0-0	.250	.250	.750	1.000	0	1.000
Division series totals (2 years)		6	21	4	3	0	0	2	4	1	2	0	1	0-0	.143	.182	.429	.610	0	1.000

CHAMPIONSHIP SERIES RECORD

Year Team (League)	Pos.	G	AB	R	H	2B	3B	HR	RBI	BB	SO	HBP	GDP	SB-CS	Avg.	OBP	SLG	OPS	E	Avg.
2005— Chicago (A.L.)	1B	5	21	2	6	1	0	2	7	1	4	0	0	0-0	.286	.318	.619	.937	0	1.000

WORLD SERIES RECORD

Year Team (League)	Pos.	G	AB	R	H	2B	3B	HR	RBI	BB	SO	HBP	GDP	SB-CS	Avg.	OBP	SLG	OPS	E	Avg.
2005— Chicago (A.L.)	1B	4	16	1	4	0	0	1	4	2	3	1	1	0-0	.250	.368	.500	.868	0	1.000

ALL-STAR GAME RECORD

		G	AB	R	H	2B	3B	HR	RBI	BB	SO	HBP	GDP	SB-CS	Avg.	OBP	SLG	OPS	E	Avg.
All-Star Game totals (3 years)		3	5	0	4	2	0	1	2	0	1	0	0	0-0	.800	.800	1.200	2.000	0	1.000

2006 LEFTY-RIGHTY SPLITS

vs.	Avg.	AB	H	2B	3B	HR	RBI	BB	SO	OBP	Slg.	vs.	Avg.	AB	H	2B	3B	HR	RBI	BB	SO	OBP	Slg.
L	.318	195	62	11	0	14	38	22	36	.394	.590	R	.310	371	115	19	0	21	75	38	68	.374	.531

KOPLOVE, MIKE — P

PERSONAL: Born August 30, 1976, in Philadelphia. ... 5-10/178. ... Throws right, bats right. ... Full name: Michael Paul Koplove. ... Name pronounced: COP-luv. ... High school: Chestnut Hill Academy (Philadelphia). ... College: Delaware. **TRANSACTIONS/CAREER NOTES:** Selected by Arizona Diamondbacks organization in 29th round of 1998 free-agent draft. ... On disabled list (May 28-June 13 and June 19, 2003-remainder of season); included rehabilitation assignment to Tucson.

CAREER HITTING: 0-for-5 (.000), 0 R, 0 2B, 0 3B, 0 HR, 0 RBI.

Year Team (League)	W	L	Pct.	ERA	WHIP	G	GS	CG	ShO	Hld.	Sv.-Opp.	IP	H	R	ER	HR	BB-IBB	SO	Avg.
1998— Ariz. D'backs (Ariz.)	0	0	...	9.00	1.50	2	0	0	0	0	0-...	4.0	4	4	4	0	2-0	5	.250
—Lethbridge (Pion.)	1	2	.333	3.54	0.93	12	1	0	0	0	2-...	28.0	23	12	11	2	3-0	22	.217
1999— South Bend (Mid.)	5	2	.714	2.04	1.18	45	45	0	0	0	7-...	84.0	70	23	19	5	29-0	98	.227
2000— High Desert (Calif.)	2	0	1.000	1.42	0.95	20	0	0	0	0	8-...	25.1	14	4	4	0	10-0	31	.163

K

Year Team (League)	W	L	Pct.	ERA	WHIP	G	GS	CG	ShO	Hld.	Sv.-Opp.	IP	H	R	ER	HR	BB-IBB	SO	Avg.
—El Paso (Texas)	4	3	.571	4.46	1.41	35	0	0	0	...	6-...	40.1	38	28	20	2	19-1	47	.225
2001—El Paso (Texas)	3	2	.600	2.66	1.43	34	0	0	0	...	4-...	44.0	44	18	13	3	19-3	43	.263
—Tucson (PCL)	4	1	.800	2.82	1.21	17	0	0	0	...	9-...	22.1	17	7	7	1	10-1	22	.207
—Arizona (N.L.)	0	1	.000	3.60	1.70	9	0	0	0	1	0-0	10.0	8	7	4	1	9-1	14	.211
2002—Tucson (PCL)	1	2	.333	1.17	0.82	23	0	0	0	...	3-...	30.2	21	5	4	1	4-0	31	.196
—Arizona (N.L.)	6	1	.857	3.36	1.14	55	0	0	0	10	0-0	61.2	47	24	23	2	23-4	46	.213
2003—Arizona (N.L.)	3	0	1.000	2.15	1.09	31	0	0	0	5	0-1	37.2	31	11	9	3	10-1	27	.225
—Tucson (PCL)	0	1	.000	13.50	2.60	3	0	0	0	...	1-...	2.2	4	4	4	1	3-0	2	.333
2004—Arizona (N.L.)	4	4	.500	4.05	1.42	76	0	0	0	19	2-8	86.2	86	42	39	7	37-10	55	.269
2005—Arizona (N.L.)	2	1	.667	5.07	1.37	44	0	0	0	9	0-2	49.2	48	31	28	6	20-3	28	.257
—Tucson (PCL)	0	2	.000	13.00	2.11	9	0	0	0	...	0-1	9.0	12	13	13	1	7-0	6	.316
2006—Tucson (PCL)	5	0	1.000	3.60	1.34	48	0	0	0	11	0-0	65.0	63	31	26	4	24-1	49	.260
—Arizona (N.L.)	0	0	...	3.00	2.33	2	0	0	0	0	0-0	3.0	5	1	1	0	2-0	1	.417
Major League totals (6 years)	15	7	.682	3.76	1.31	217	0	0	0	44	2-11	248.2	225	116	104	19	101-19	171	.246

DIVISION SERIES RECORD

Year Team (League)	W	L	Pct.	ERA	WHIP	G	GS	CG	ShO	Hld.	Sv.-Opp.	IP	H	R	ER	HR	BB-IBB	SO	Avg.
2002—Arizona (N.L.)	0	1	.000	6.75	1.50	1	0	0	0	...	0-0	1.1	2	1	1	0	0-0	1	.400

2006 LEFTY-RIGHTY SPLITS

vs.	Avg.	AB	H	2B	3B	HR	RBI	BB	SO	OBP	Slg.	vs.	Avg.	AB	H	2B	3B	HR	RBI	BB	SO	OBP	Slg.
L	.250	4	1	1	0	0	0	2	1	.500	.500	R	.500	8	4	1	0	0	1	0	0	.500	.625

KORONKA, JOHN — P

PERSONAL: Born July 3, 1980, in Clearwater, Fla. ... 6-1/180. ... Throws left, bats left. ... Full name: John Vincent Koronka. ... Name pronounced: CORE-on-kuh. **TRANSACTIONS/CAREER NOTES:** Selected by Cincinnati Reds organization in 12th round of free-agent draft (June 2, 1998). ... Selected by Texas Rangers from Reds organization in Rule 5 major league draft (December 16, 2002). ... Returned to Reds (March 21, 2003). ... Traded by Cincinnati Reds to Chicago Cubs for P Phil Norton (August 25, 2003). ... Traded by Cubs with a player to be named for SS Freddie Bynum as part of a three-team trade that sent Bynum and P John Rheinecker to Texas Rangers for P Juan Dominguez (March 31, 2006).

CAREER HITTING: 0-for-10 (.000), 0 R, 0 2B, 0 3B, 0 HR, 0 RBI.

Year Team (League)	W	L	Pct.	ERA	WHIP	G	GS	CG	ShO	Hld.	Sv.-Opp.	IP	H	R	ER	HR	BB-IBB	SO	Avg.
1998—Billings (Pion.)	0	3	.000	8.04	2.33	12	3	0	0	...	0-...	31.1	47	43	28	2	26-0	36	.326
1999—GC Reds (GCL)	3	3	.500	1.69	1.04	7	7	0	0	...	0-...	37.1	25	11	7	1	14-0	27	.194
—Billings (Pion.)	2	3	.400	5.58	1.44	7	7	0	0	...	0-...	40.1	41	26	25	1	17-0	34	.301
2000—Clinton (Midw.)	4	13	.235	4.33	1.55	20	18	4	0	...	0-...	104.0	123	65	50	7	38-2	74	.301
2001—Dayton (Midw.)	3	1	.750	0.75	1.29	5	5	0	0	...	0-...	24.0	23	12	2	0	8-0	25	.264
—Mudville California (Calif.)	5	2	.714	4.94	1.65	12	12	0	0	...	0-...	71.0	78	44	39	10	39-0	66	.281
—Chattanooga (Sou.)	1	5	.167	5.73	1.64	9	9	0	0	...	0-...	55.0	62	37	35	7	28-0	44	.286
2002—Stockton (Calif.)	11	0	1.000	3.07	1.28	12	12	0	0	...	0-...	73.1	59	36	25	4	35-0	69	.214
—Chattanooga (Sou.)	2	8	.200	4.99	1.68	16	15	0	0	...	0-...	95.2	109	56	53	10	52-1	69	.298
2003—Chattanooga (Sou.)	7	13	.350	4.39	1.52	25	25	0	0	...	0-...	155.2	177	88	76	8	60-1	115	.298
—West Tenn (Sou.)	0	0	...	0.00	0.57	1	1	0	0	...	0-...	7.0	3	0	0	0	1-0	3	.136
2004—Iowa (PCL)	12	9	.571	4.34	1.49	29	23	2	2	...	0-...	153.1	164	86	74	19	65-3	116	.281
2005—Chicago (N.L.)	1	2	.333	7.47	1.72	4	3	0	0	0	0-0	15.2	19	13	13	2	8-0	10	.284
—Iowa (PCL)	9	11	.450	4.24	1.35	23	21	0	0	...	0-...	136.0	135	65	64	12	48-0	96	.265
2006—Oklahoma (PCL)	0	1	.000	4.12	1.32	3	3	0	0	...	0-...	19.2	19	9	9	2	7-0	17	.260
—Texas (A.L.)	7	7	.500	5.69	1.54	23	23	0	0	...	0-0	125.0	145	80	79	17	47-2	61	.294
American League totals (1 year)	7	7	.500	5.69	1.54	23	23	0	0	...	0-0	125.0	145	80	79	17	47-2	61	.294
National League totals (1 year)	1	2	.333	7.47	1.72	4	3	0	0	0	0-0	15.2	19	13	13	2	8-0	10	.284
Major League totals (2 years)	8	9	.471	5.89	1.56	27	26	0	0	0	0-0	140.2	164	93	92	19	55-2	71	.292

2006 LEFTY-RIGHTY SPLITS

vs.	Avg.	AB	H	2B	3B	HR	RBI	BB	SO	OBP	Slg.	vs.	Avg.	AB	H	2B	3B	HR	RBI	BB	SO	OBP	Slg.
L	.274	124	34	5	0	7	25	7	12	.319	.484	R	.300	370	111	24	3	10	52	40	49	.368	.462

KOSKIE, COREY — 3B

PERSONAL: Born June 28, 1973, in Anola, Manitoba. ... 6-3/219. ... Bats left, throws right. ... Full name: Cordel Leonard Koskie. ... Name pronounced: KOSS-key. ... High school: Springfield Collegiate (Oakbank, Man.). ... College: University of Manitoba. **TRANSACTIONS/CAREER NOTES:** Selected by Minnesota Twins organization in 26th round of 1994 free-agent draft. ... On disabled list (May 8-24, 2002; July 12-August 4, 2003; and May 12-27, 2004). ... Signed as a free agent by Toronto Blue Jays (December 14, 2004). ... On disabled list (May 20-July 26, 2005); included rehabilitation assignment to Syracuse. ... Traded by Blue Jays to Milwaukee Brewers for P Brian Wolfe (January 6, 2006). ... On disabled list (July 15, 2006-remainder of season). **RECORDS:** Shares major league record for most times hit by pitch, game (3, July 27, 2004). **STATISTICAL NOTES:** Career major league grand slams: 2.

2006 GAMES PLAYED BY POSITION (MLB): 3B—70.

Year Team (League)	Pos.	G	AB	R	H	2B	3B	HR	RBI	BB	SO	HBP	GDP	SB-CS	Avg.	OBP	SLG	OPS	E	Avg.
1994—Elizabethton (App.)	3B	34	107	13	25	2	1	3	10	18	27	2	3	0-0	.234	.354	.355	.709	4	.930
1995—Fort Wayne (Midw.)	3B	123	462	64	143	37	5	16	78	38	79	9	10	2-4	.310	.370	.515	.885	36	.900
1996—Fort Myers (FSL)	3B	95	338	43	88	19	4	9	55	40	76	1	4	1-1	.260	.338	.420	.758	19	.926
1997—New Britain (East.)	3B-DH	131	437	88	125	26	6	23	79	90	106	7	13	9-5	.286	.414	.531	.945	22	.933
1998—Salt Lake (PCL)	3B-DH	135	505	91	152	32	5	26	105	51	104	8	17	15-7	.301	.368	.539	.906	23	.935
—Minnesota (A.L.)	3B	11	29	2	4	0	0	1	2	2	10	0	0	0-0	.138	.194	.241	.435	1	.941
1999—Minnesota (A.L.)	3B-OF-DH	117	342	42	106	21	0	11	58	40	72	5	6	4-4	.310	.387	.468	.855	8	.962
2000—Minnesota (A.L.)	3B-DH	146	474	79	142	32	4	9	65	77	104	4	11	5-4	.300	.400	.441	.841	12	.964
2001—Minnesota (A.L.)	3B-DH	153	562	100	155	37	2	26	103	68	118	12	16	27-6	.276	.362	.488	.850	15	.964
2002—Minnesota (A.L.)	3B-DH	140	490	71	131	37	3	15	69	72	127	9	14	10-11	.267	.368	.447	.815	12	.969
2003—Minnesota (A.L.)	3B	131	469	76	137	29	2	14	69	77	113	7	5	11-5	.292	.393	.452	.845	9	.973
2004—Minnesota (A.L.)	3B-DH	118	422	68	106	24	2	25	71	49	103	12	6	9-3	.251	.342	.495	.837	11	.963
2005—Syracuse (Int'l)	3B-DH	7	25	1	6	2	0	0	2	3	6	2	1	0-0	.240	.367	.320	.687	0	1.000
—Toronto (A.L.)	3B-DH	97	354	49	88	20	0	11	36	44	90	4	10	4-1	.249	.337	.398	.735	7	.968
2006—Milwaukee (N.L.)	3B	76	257	29	67	23	0	12	33	29	58	3	7	1-2	.261	.343	.490	.833	7	.967
American League totals (8 years)		913	3142	487	869	200	13	112	473	429	737	53	68	70-34	.277	.369	.455	.825	75	.966
National League totals (1 year)		76	257	29	67	23	0	12	33	29	58	3	7	1-2	.261	.343	.490	.833	7	.967
Major League totals (9 years)		989	3399	516	936	223	13	124	506	458	795	56	75	71-36	.275	.367	.458	.825	82	.966

DIVISION SERIES RECORD

Year Team (League)	Pos.	G	AB	R	H	2B	3B	HR	RBI	BB	SO	HBP	GDP	SB-CS	Avg.	OBP	SLG	OPS	E	Avg.
2002—Minnesota (A.L.)	3B	5	21	3	3	0	1	1	5	2	6	1	0	0-0	.143	.250	.381	.631	1	.923
2003—Minnesota (A.L.)	3B	4	15	0	3	1	0	0	0	0	5	0	0	0-1	.200	.200	.267	.467	0	1.000
2004—Minnesota (A.L.)	3B	4	13	2	4	1	0	2	2	3	2	0	0	0-0	.308	.474	.385	.858	0	1.000
Division series totals (3 years)		13	49	5	10	2	1	3	7	5	13	1	0	0-1	.204	.310	.347	.657	1	.963

K

CHAMPIONSHIP SERIES RECORD

Year Team (League)	Pos.	G	AB	R	H	2B	3B	HR	RBI	BB	SO	HBP	GDP	SB-CS	Avg.	OBP	SLG	OPS	E	Avg.
2002—Minnesota (A.L.)	3B	5	18	3	5	2	0	0	2	2	8	0	0	0-0	.278	.350	.389	.739	0	1.000

2006 LEFTY-RIGHTY SPLITS

vs.	Avg.	AB	H	2B	3B	HR	RBI	BB	SO	OBP	Slg.	vs.	Avg.	AB	H	2B	3B	HR	RBI	BB	SO	OBP	Slg.
L	.263	57	15	5	0	1	5	2	14	.288	.404	R	.260	200	52	18	0	11	28	27	44	.357	.515

KOTCHMAN, CASEY   1B

PERSONAL: Born February 22, 1983, in St. Petersburg, Fla. ... 6-3/210. ... Bats left, throws left. ... Full name: Casey John Kotchman. ... High school: Seminole (Fla.). **TRANSACTIONS/CAREER NOTES:** Selected by Anaheim Angels organization in first round (13th pick overall) of 2001 free-agent draft. ... Angels franchise renamed Los Angeles Angels of Anaheim for 2005 season. ... On disabled list (May 24, 2006-remainder of season); included rehabilitation assignment to Salt Lake. **STATISTICAL NOTES:** Career major league grand slams: 1.

2006 GAMES PLAYED BY POSITION (MLB): 1B—26.

								BATTING											FIELDING	
Year Team (League)	Pos.	G	AB	R	H	2B	3B	HR	RBI	BB	SO	HBP	GDP	SB-CS	Avg.	OBP	SLG	OPS	E	Avg.
2001—Ariz. Angels (Ariz.)	1B	4	15	5	9	1	0	1	5	3	2	0	0	0-0	.600	.632	.867	1.498	1	.974
—Provo (Pion.)	1B	7	22	6	11	3	0	0	7	2	0	0	0	0-0	.500	.542	.636	1.178	0	1.000
2002—Cedar Rap. (Midw.)	1B	81	288	42	81	30	1	5	50	48	37	6	7	2-1	.281	.390	.444	.835	5	.992
2003—Ariz. Angels (Ariz.)	1B	7	27	5	9	1	0	2	6	2	3	0	1	0-0	.333	.379	.593	.972	0	1.000
—Rancho Cuca. (Calif.)	1B	57	206	42	72	12	0	8	28	30	16	6	4	2-0	.350	.441	.524	.965	5	.988
2004—Arkansas (Texas)	1B-DH	28	114	19	42	11	0	3	18	10	7	5	6	0-0	.368	.438	.544	.960	0	1.000
—Salt Lake (PCL)	1B-DH	49	199	32	74	22	0	5	38	14	25	5	9	0-0	.372	.423	.558	.967	3	.992
—Anaheim (A.L.)	1B-DH	38	116	7	26	6	0	0	15	5	11	4	3	3-0	.224	.289	.276	.565	3	.988
2005—Salt Lake (PCL)	1B	94	363	62	105	23	1	10	58	43	40	7	15	0-2	.289	.372	.441	.812	4	.995
—Los Angeles (A.L.)	1B-DH	47	126	16	35	5	0	7	22	15	18	0	3	1-1	.278	.352	.484	.836	0	1.000
2006—Los Angeles (A.L.)	1B	29	79	6	12	2	0	1	6	7	13	0	2	0-0	.152	.221	.215	.436	0	1.000
—Salt Lake (PCL)		3	7	0	0	0	0	0	1	1	1	0	1	0-0	.000	.125	.000	.125	1	.857
Major League totals (3 years)		114	321	29	73	13	0	8	43	29	42	4	8	4-2	.227	.298	.343	.640	3	.995

DIVISION SERIES RECORD

Year Team (League)	Pos.	G	AB	R	H	2B	3B	HR	RBI	BB	SO	HBP	GDP	SB-CS	Avg.	OBP	SLG	OPS	E	Avg.
2004—Anaheim (A.L.)		2	1	0	0	0	0	0	0	0	0	0	0	0-0	.000	.000	.000	.000	0	...
2005—Los Angeles (A.L.)	DH	2	2	0	0	0	0	0	0	0	0	0	0	0-0	.000	.000	.000	.000	0	...
Division series totals (2 years)		4	3	0	0	0	0	0	0	0	0	0	0	0-0	.000	.000	.000	.000	0	...

CHAMPIONSHIP SERIES RECORD

Year Team (League)	Pos.	G	AB	R	H	2B	3B	HR	RBI	BB	SO	HBP	GDP	SB-CS	Avg.	OBP	SLG	OPS	E	Avg.
2005—Los Angeles (A.L.)	DH	2	7	0	2	1	0	0	1	1	1	0	0	0-0	.286	.375	.429	.804	0	...

2006 LEFTY-RIGHTY SPLITS

vs.	Avg.	AB	H	2B	3B	HR	RBI	BB	SO	OBP	Slg.	vs.	Avg.	AB	H	2B	3B	HR	RBI	BB	SO	OBP	Slg.
L	.214	14	3	0	0	0	2	1	1	.267	.214	R	.138	65	9	2	0	1	4	6	12	.211	.215

KOTSAY, MARK   OF

PERSONAL: Born December 2, 1975, in Whittier, Calif. ... 6-0/201. ... Bats left, throws left. ... Full name: Mark Steven Kotsay. ... Name pronounced: KAH-tsay. ... High school: Santa Fe Springs (Calif.). ... College: Cal State Fullerton. **TRANSACTIONS/CAREER NOTES:** Selected by Florida Marlins organization in first round (ninth pick overall) of 1996 free-agent draft. ... Traded by Marlins with OF Cesar Crespo to San Diego Padres for OF Eric Owens and Ps Matt Clement and Omar Ortiz (March 28, 2001). ... On disabled list (April 16-May 1, 2001; and May 19-June 5, 2003). ... Traded by Padres to Oakland Athletics for C Ramon Hernandez and OF Terrence Long (November 26, 2003). **STATISTICAL NOTES:** Career major league grand slams: 3. **MISCELLANEOUS NOTES:** Member of 1996 U.S. Olympic baseball team.

2006 GAMES PLAYED BY POSITION (MLB): OF—127, 1B—4, DH—1.

								BATTING											FIELDING	
Year Team (League)	Pos.	G	AB	R	H	2B	3B	HR	RBI	BB	SO	HBP	GDP	SB-CS	Avg.	OBP	SLG	OPS	E	Avg.
1996—Kane Co. (Midw.)	OF	17	60	16	17	5	0	2	8	16	8	1	3	3-0	.283	.436	.467	.903	0	1.000
1997—Portland (East.)	OF-DH	114	438	103	134	27	2	20	77	75	65	0	16	17-5	.306	.405	.514	.919	2	.992
—Florida (N.L.)	OF	14	52	5	10	1	1	0	4	4	7	0	1	3-0	.192	.250	.250	.500	1	1.000
1998—Florida (N.L.)	OF-1B	154	578	72	161	25	7	11	68	34	61	1	17	10-5	.279	.318	.403	.721	6	.984
1999—Florida (N.L.)	OF-1B	148	495	57	134	23	9	8	50	29	50	0	11	7-6	.271	.306	.402	.708	5	.987
2000—Florida (N.L.)	OF-1B	152	530	87	158	31	5	12	57	42	46	0	17	19-9	.298	.347	.443	.791	3	.990
2001—San Diego (N.L.)	OF	119	406	67	118	29	1	10	58	49	58	2	11	13-5	.291	.366	.441	.807	4	.986
2002—San Diego (N.L.)	OF	153	578	82	169	27	4	17	61	59	89	3	10	11-9	.292	.359	.452	.810	4	.989
2003—San Diego (N.L.)	OF	128	482	64	128	28	4	7	38	56	82	1	8	6-3	.266	.343	.384	.726	3	.991
2004—Oakland (A.L.)	OF-DH	148	606	78	190	37	3	15	63	55	70	2	6	8-5	.314	.370	.459	.829	4	.984
2005—Oakland (A.L.)	OF-DH	139	582	75	163	35	1	15	82	40	51	1	13	5-5	.280	.325	.421	.746	4	.987
2006—Oakland (A.L.)	OF-1B-DH	129	502	57	138	29	3	7	59	44	55	2	18	6-3	.275	.332	.386	.719	4	.987
American League totals (3 years)		416	1690	210	491	101	7	37	204	139	176	5	37	19-13	.291	.343	.424	.768	14	.986
National League totals (7 years)		868	3121	434	878	164	34	65	336	272	393	7	75	69-37	.281	.338	.418	.756	25	.988
Major League totals (10 years)		1284	4811	644	1369	265	41	102	540	411	569	12	112	88-50	.285	.340	.420	.760	39	.987

DIVISION SERIES RECORD

Year Team (League)	Pos.	G	AB	R	H	2B	3B	HR	RBI	BB	SO	HBP	GDP	SB-CS	Avg.	OBP	SLG	OPS	E	Avg.
2006—Oakland (A.L.)	OF	3	14	2	2	0	0	1	2	0	2	0	1	0-0	.143	.143	.357	.500	0	1.000

CHAMPIONSHIP SERIES RECORD

Year Team (League)	Pos.	G	AB	R	H	2B	3B	HR	RBI	BB	SO	HBP	GDP	SB-CS	Avg.	OBP	SLG	OPS	E	Avg.
2006—Oakland (A.L.)	OF	4	16	3	4	2	0	0	0	2	3	0	2	0-0	.250	.333	.375	.708	0	1.000

2006 LEFTY-RIGHTY SPLITS

vs.	Avg.	AB	H	2B	3B	HR	RBI	BB	SO	OBP	Slg.	vs.	Avg.	AB	H	2B	3B	HR	RBI	BB	SO	OBP	Slg.
L	.265	117	31	6	1	3	14	5	17	.293	.410	R	.278	385	107	23	2	4	45	39	38	.343	.379

KOUZMANOFF, KEVIN   3B

PERSONAL: Born July 25, 1981, in Newport Beach, Calif. ... Bats right, throws right. ... Full name: Kevin Kouzmanoff. ... High school: Evergreen (Colo.). ... College: Nevada. **TRANSACTIONS/CAREER NOTES:** Selected by Cleveland Indians organization in sixth round of 2003 free-agent draft. ... Traded by Indians with P Andrew Brown to San Diego Padres for 2B Josh Barfield (November 8, 2006). **STATISTICAL NOTES:** Hit a grand slam home run in first major league at-bat (September 2, 2006).

2006 GAMES PLAYED BY POSITION (MLB): DH—14, 3B—2.

Year	Team (League)	Pos.	G	AB	R	H	2B	3B	HR	RBI	BB	SO	HBP	GDP	SB-CS	Avg.	OBP	SLG	OPS	E	Avg.
2003—Mahoning Valley (N.Y.-Penn.)		54	206	31	56	8	1	8	33	21	36	3	6	2-1	.272	.342	.437	.779	...	...
2004—Akron (East.)		7	24	3	5	1	1	1	6	2	5	0	2	0-0	.208	.259	.458	.717	...	...
—Lake County (S.Atl.)		123	473	74	156	35	5	16	87	44	75	9	17	5-4	.330	.394	.526	.920	...	...
2005—Mahoning Valley (N.Y.-Penn.)	3B	3	7	0	1	0	0	0	0	1	2	0	0	0-0	.143	.250	.143	.393	2	.750
—Kinston (Carol.)	3B-DH	68	254	47	86	20	4	12	58	24	51	5	6	3-1	.339	.401	.591	.991	12	.925
2006—Buffalo (Int'l)		27	102	22	36	9	0	7	20	10	12	1	1	2-1	.353	.409	.647	1.056	5	.960
—Akron (East.)		67	244	46	95	19	1	15	55	23	34	6	5	2-3	.389	.449	.660	1.109	10	.938
—Cleveland (A.L.)	DH-3B	16	56	4	12	2	0	3	11	5	12	0	3	0-0	.214	.279	.411	.689	1	.857
Major League totals (1 year)		16	56	4	12	2	0	3	11	5	12	0	3	0-0	.214	.279	.411	.689	1	.857

2006 LEFTY-RIGHTY SPLITS

vs.	Avg.	AB	H	2B	3B	HR	RBI	BB	SO	OBP	Slg.	vs.	Avg.	AB	H	2B	3B	HR	RBI	BB	SO	OBP	Slg.
L	.167	12	2	0	0	0	0	0	5	.167	.167	R	.227	44	10	2	0	3	11	5	7	.306	.477

KUBEL, JASON — OF

PERSONAL: Born May 25, 1982, in Belle Fourche, S.D. ... 5-11/200. ... Bats left, throws right. ... Full name: Jason James Kubel. ... High school: Highland (Calif.). **TRANSACTIONS/CAREER NOTES:** Selected by Minnesota Twins organization in 12th round of 2000 free-agent draft. ... On disabled list (March 15, 2005-entire season). **STATISTICAL NOTES:** Career major league grand slams: 1.

2006 GAMES PLAYED BY POSITION (MLB): OF—37, DH—30.

Year	Team (League)	Pos.	G	AB	R	H	2B	3B	HR	RBI	BB	SO	HBP	GDP	SB-CS	Avg.	OBP	SLG	OPS	E	Avg.
2000—GC Twins (GCL)	OF	23	78	17	22	3	2	0	13	10	9	1	1	0-0	.282	.367	.372	.738	0	1.000
2001—GC Twins (GCL)	OF	37	124	14	41	10	4	1	30	19	14	2	3	3-2	.331	.422	.500	.922	1	.980
2002—Quad City (Midw.)	OF	115	424	60	136	26	4	17	69	41	48	1	11	3-5	.321	.380	.521	.901	3	.982
2003—Fort Myers (FSL)	OF	116	420	56	125	20	4	5	82	48	54	1	11	4-6	.298	.361	.400	.761	2	.991
2004—New Britain (East.)	OF-DH	37	138	25	52	14	4	6	29	19	19	1	3	0-2	.377	.453	.667	1.116	3	.961
—Rochester (Int'l)	OF-DH	90	350	71	120	28	0	16	71	34	40	1	2	16-3	.343	.398	.560	.957	2	.990
—Minnesota (A.L.)	OF-DH	23	60	10	18	2	0	2	7	6	9	0	0	1-1	.300	.358	.433	.792	0	1.000
2005—Minnesota (A.L.)		Did not play.																			
2006—Rochester (Int'l)		30	120	18	34	7	2	4	22	12	23	0	5	2-0	.283	.343	.475	.818	0	1.000
—Minnesota (A.L.)	OF-DH	73	220	23	53	8	0	8	26	12	45	0	13	2-0	.241	.279	.386	.665	2	.953
Major League totals (2 years)		96	280	33	71	10	0	10	33	18	54	0	13	3-1	.254	.297	.396	.693	2	.966

DIVISION SERIES RECORD

Year	Team (League)	Pos.	G	AB	R	H	2B	3B	HR	RBI	BB	SO	HBP	GDP	SB-CS	Avg.	OBP	SLG	OPS	E	Avg.
2004—Minnesota (A.L.)	DH	2	7	0	1	1	0	0	0	0	2	0	0	0-0	.143	.143	.286	.429	0	...

2006 LEFTY-RIGHTY SPLITS

vs.	Avg.	AB	H	2B	3B	HR	RBI	BB	SO	OBP	Slg.	vs.	Avg.	AB	H	2B	3B	HR	RBI	BB	SO	OBP	Slg.
L	.243	37	9	0	0	2	7	2	9	.282	.405	R	.240	183	44	8	0	6	19	10	36	.278	.383

KUO, HONG-CHIH — P

PERSONAL: Born July 23, 1981, in Tainan City, Taiwan. ... 6-0/200. ... Throws left, bats left. ... Full name: Hong-Chih Kuo. **TRANSACTIONS/CAREER NOTES:** Signed as a non-drafted free agent by Los Angeles Dodgers organization (June 19, 1999).

CAREER HITTING: 1-for-8 (.125), 1 R, 1 2B, 0 3B, 0 HR, 0 RBI.

Year	Team (League)	W	L	Pct.	ERA	WHIP	G	GS	CG	ShO	Hld.	Sv.-Opp.	IP	H	R	ER	HR	BB-IBB	SO	Avg.
2000—San Bern. (Calif.)	0	0	...	0.00	0.00	1	1	0	0	...	0-...	3.0	0	0	0	0	0-0	7	.000
2001—GC Dodgers (GCL)	0	0	...	2.33	0.88	7	6	0	0	...	0-...	19.1	13	5	5	0	4-0	21	.186
2002—GC Dodgers (GCL)	0	0	...	4.50	0.83	3	3	0	0	...	0-...	6.0	4	3	3	0	1-0	9	.200
—Vero Beach (FSL)	0	1	.000	6.75	1.63	4	4	0	0	...	0-...	8.0	11	6	6	0	2-0	8	.324
2003—	Did not play.																		
2004—Columbus (S. Atl.)	1	0	1.000	4.50	2.00	3	0	0	0	...	0-...	6.0	8	3	3	0	4-0	10	.308
2005—Vero Beach (FSL)	1	1	.500	2.08	1.12	11	3	0	0	4	0-0	26.0	19	7	6	2	10-0	42	.202
—Jacksonville (Sou.)	1	1	.500	1.91	1.16	17	0	0	0	4	3-4	28.1	22	7	6	1	11-1	44	.210
—Los Angeles (N.L.)	0	1	.000	6.75	1.88	9	0	0	0	3	0-1	5.1	5	4	4	1	5-1	10	.238
2006—Las Vegas (PCL)	4	3	.571	3.06	1.40	23	9	0	0	2	1-1	53.0	52	24	18	5	22-1	63	.260
—Los Angeles (N.L.)	1	5	.167	4.22	1.46	28	5	0	0	2	0-0	59.2	54	30	28	3	33-5	71	.244
Major League totals (2 years)	1	6	.143	4.43	1.49	37	5	0	0	5	0-1	65.0	59	34	32	4	38-6	81	.244

DIVISION SERIES RECORD

Year	Team (League)	W	L	Pct.	ERA	WHIP	G	GS	CG	ShO	Hld.	Sv.-Opp.	IP	H	R	ER	HR	BB-IBB	SO	Avg.
2006—Los Angeles (N.L.)	0	1	.000	4.15	1.38	1	1	0	0	0	0-0	4.1	4	2	2	0	2-1	4	.250

2006 LEFTY-RIGHTY SPLITS

vs.	Avg.	AB	H	2B	3B	HR	RBI	BB	SO	OBP	Slg.	vs.	Avg.	AB	H	2B	3B	HR	RBI	BB	SO	OBP	Slg.
L	.241	54	13	4	0	1	4	9	20	.349	.315	R	.246	167	41	10	1	3	20	24	51	.342	.371

LACKEY, JOHN — P

PERSONAL: Born October 23, 1978, in Abilene, Texas. ... 6-6/235. ... Throws right, bats right. ... Full name: John Derran Lackey. ... High school: Abilene (Texas). ... Junior college: Grayson County (Texas). **TRANSACTIONS/CAREER NOTES:** Selected by Anaheim Angels organization in second round of 1999 free-agent draft. ... On suspended list (June 22-27, 2004). ... Angels franchise renamed Los Angeles Angels of Anaheim for 2005 season.

CAREER HITTING: 0-for-14 (.000), 0 R, 0 2B, 0 3B, 0 HR, 0 RBI.

Year	Team (League)	W	L	Pct.	ERA	WHIP	G	GS	CG	ShO	Hld.	Sv.-Opp.	IP	H	R	ER	HR	BB-IBB	SO	Avg.
1999—Boise (N'west)	6	2	.750	4.98	1.61	15	15	1	0	...	0-...	81.1	81	59	45	7	50-1	77	.264
2000—Cedar Rap. (Midw.)	3	5	.600	2.08	0.82	5	5	0	0	...	0-...	30.1	20	7	7	1	5-0	21	.185
—Lake Elsinore (Calif.)	6	6	.500	3.40	1.35	15	15	2	•1	...	0-...	100.2	94	56	38	9	42-0	74	.249
—Erie (East.)	6	1	.857	3.30	1.17	8	8	2	0	...	0-...	57.1	58	23	21	6	9-0	43	.260
2001—Arkansas (Texas)	9	7	.563	3.46	1.06	18	18	3	2	...	0-...	127.1	106	55	49	11	29-0	94	.227
—Salt Lake (PCL)	3	4	.429	6.71	1.58	10	10	1	0	...	0-...	57.2	75	44	43	5	16-0	42	.312
2002—Salt Lake (PCL)	4	1	.800	2.57	1.15	16	16	2	1	...	0-...	101.2	89	35	29	8	28-0	82	.235
—Anaheim (A.L.)	9	4	.692	3.66	1.35	18	18	1	0	0	0-0	108.1	113	52	44	10	33-0	69	.267
2003—Anaheim (A.L.)	10	16	.385	4.63	1.42	33	33	2	•2	0	0-0	204.0	223	117	105	31	66-4	151	.278
2004—Anaheim (A.L.)	14	13	.519	4.67	1.39	33	32	1	0	0	0-0	198.1	215	108	103	22	60-4	144	.278
2005—Los Angeles (A.L.)	14	5	.737	3.44	1.33	33	33	1	0	0	0-0	209.0	208	85	80	13	71-3	199	.258

Year Team (League)	W	L	Pct.	ERA	WHIP	G	GS	CG	ShO	Hld.	Sv.-Opp.	IP	H	R	ER	HR	BB-IBB	SO	Avg.
2006— Los Angeles (A.L.)	13	11	.542	3.56	1.26	33	33	3	•2	0	0-0	217.2	203	98	86	14	72-4	190	.246
Major League totals (5 years)	60	49	.550	4.01	1.35	150	149	8	5	0	0-0	937.1	962	460	418	90	302-15	753	.265

DIVISION SERIES RECORD

Year Team (League)	W	L	Pct.	ERA	WHIP	G	GS	CG	ShO	Hld.	Sv.-Opp.	IP	H	R	ER	HR	BB-IBB	SO	Avg.
2002— Anaheim (A.L.)	0	0	...	0.00	1.33	1	0	0	0	0	0-0	3.0	3	0	0	0	1-0	3	.250
2005— Los Angeles (A.L.)	0	0	...	2.38	1.41	2	2	0	0	0	0-0	11.1	7	3	3	0	9-0	9	.179
Division series totals (2 years)	0	0	...	1.88	1.40	3	2	0	0	0	0-0	14.1	10	3	3	0	10-0	12	.196

CHAMPIONSHIP SERIES RECORD

Year Team (League)	W	L	Pct.	ERA	WHIP	G	GS	CG	ShO	Hld.	Sv.-Opp.	IP	H	R	ER	HR	BB-IBB	SO	Avg.
2002— Anaheim (A.L.)	1	0	1.000	0.00	0.43	1	1	0	0	0	0-0	7.0	3	0	0	0	0-0	7	.130
2005— Los Angeles (A.L.)	0	1	.000	9.00	1.80	1	1	0	0	0	0-0	5.0	8	5	5	1	1-0	3	.381
Champ. series totals (2 years)	1	1	.500	3.75	1.00	2	2	0	0	0	0-0	12.0	11	5	5	1	1-0	10	.250

WORLD SERIES RECORD

Year Team (League)	W	L	Pct.	ERA	WHIP	G	GS	CG	ShO	Hld.	Sv.-Opp.	IP	H	R	ER	HR	BB-IBB	SO	Avg.
2002— Anaheim (A.L.)	1	0	1.000	4.38	1.62	3	2	0	0	0	0-0	12.1	15	6	6	0	5-4	7	.319

2006 LEFTY-RIGHTY SPLITS

vs.	Avg.	AB	H	2B	3B	HR	RBI	BB	SO	OBP	Slg.	vs.	Avg.	AB	H	2B	3B	HR	RBI	BB	SO	OBP	Slg.
L	.263	392	103	22	1	5	39	47	79	.347	.362	R	.231	433	100	26	1	9	55	25	111	.277	.358

LAIRD, GERALD   C

PERSONAL: Born November 13, 1979, in Westminster, Calif. ... 6-2/220. ... Bats right, throws right. ... Full name: Gerald Lee Laird. ... High school: La Quinta (Westminster,Calif.). ... Junior college: Cypress (Calif.). **TRANSACTIONS/CAREER NOTES:** Selected by Oakland Athletics organization in second round of 1998 free-agent draft. ... Traded by A's with P Mario Ramos, 1B Jason Hart and OF Ryan Ludwick to Texas Rangers for P Mike Venafro and 1B Carlos Pena (January 14, 2002). ... On disabled list (May 21-July 23, 2004); included rehabilitation assignment to Oklahoma.

2006 GAMES PLAYED BY POSITION (MLB): C—71, DH—1, OF—1.

Year Team (League)	Pos.	G	AB	R	H	2B	3B	HR	RBI	BB	SO	HBP	GDP	SB-CS	Avg.	OBP	SLG	OPS	E	Avg.
1999— S. Oregon (N'west)	C	60	228	45	65	7	2	2	39	28	43	2	4	10-5	.285	.361	.360	.721	11	.972
2000— Ariz. A's (Ariz.)	C	14	50	10	15	2	1	0	9	6	7	1	3	2-0	.300	.379	.380	.759	0	1.000
— Visalia (Calif.)	C	33	103	14	25	3	0	0	13	14	27	1	3	7-2	.243	.333	.272	.605	8	.969
2001— Modesto (California)	C-OF-1B																			
	2B-3B-SS	119	443	71	113	13	5	5	46	48	101	10	9	10-9	.255	.337	.341	.678	18	.976
2002— Tulsa (Texas)	C-OF	123	442	70	122	21	4	11	67	45	95	5	14	8-6	.276	.343	.416	.759	8	.988
2003— Oklahoma (PCL)	C-DH	99	338	50	88	20	5	9	42	37	61	7	7	9-3	.260	.344	.429	.773	11	.983
— Texas (A.L.)	C	19	44	9	12	2	1	1	4	5	11	1	2	0-0	.273	.360	.432	.792	1	.986
2004— Oklahoma (PCL)	C-DH	6	22	2	4	2	0	0	2	2	8	0	1	1-0	.182	.250	.273	.523	1	.955
— Texas (A.L.)	C	49	147	20	33	6	0	1	16	12	35	2	5	0-1	.224	.287	.286	.572	5	.983
2005— Arizona Rangers (AZL)	C-DH	8	26	4	5	2	2	0	3	2	1	1	1	1-0	.192	.276	.423	.699	0	1.000
— Oklahoma (PCL)	C-DH	75	281	51	87	12	4	17	55	28	61	5	5	12-2	.310	.380	.562	.942	6	.988
— Texas (A.L.)	C-OF	13	40	7	9	2	0	1	4	2	7	0	1	0-0	.225	.262	.350	.612	3	.957
2006— Texas (A.L.)	C-OF-DH	78	243	46	72	20	1	7	22	12	54	2	7	3-1	.296	.332	.473	.805	6	.986
Major League totals (4 years)		159	474	82	126	30	2	10	46	31	107	5	15	3-2	.266	.315	.401	.715	15	.983

2006 LEFTY-RIGHTY SPLITS

vs.	Avg.	AB	H	2B	3B	HR	RBI	BB	SO	OBP	Slg.	vs.	Avg.	AB	H	2B	3B	HR	RBI	BB	SO	OBP	Slg.
L	.400	85	34	8	0	3	9	2	13	.414	.600	R	.241	158	38	12	1	4	13	10	41	.291	.405

LAKER, TIM   C

PERSONAL: Born November 27, 1969, in Encino, Calif. ... 6-3/225. ... Bats right, throws right. ... Full name: Timothy John Laker. ... High school: Simi Valley (Calif.). ... Junior college: Oxnard (Calif.). **TRANSACTIONS/CAREER NOTES:** Selected by Kansas City Royals organization in 49th round of 1987 free-agent draft; did not sign. ... Selected by Montreal Expos organization in sixth round of 1988 free-agent draft. ... On disabled list (March 29, 1996-entire season). ... Claimed on waivers by Baltimore Orioles (March 25, 1997). ... Signed as a free agent by Tampa Bay Devil Rays (December 19, 1997). ... Released by Devil Rays (June 26, 1998). ... Signed by Pittsburgh Pirates organization (July 9, 1998). ... Released by Pirates (December 18, 1998). ... Signed by Los Angeles Dodgers organization (January 11, 1999). ... Traded by Dodgers to Pirates for a player to be named (March 26, 1999); Dodgers acquired P Jay Ryan to complete the deal (June 1, 2001). ... Signed as a free agent by Cleveland Indians organization (December 20, 2000). ... Signed as a free agent by Devil Rays organization (December 16, 2004). ... Signed as a free agent by Cleveland Indians organization (December 16, 2005).
STATISTICAL NOTES: Career major league pitching: 0-0, 0.00 ERA, 2 G, 2.0 IP, 2 H, 0 R, 0 ER, 2 BB, 1 SO.

2006 GAMES PLAYED BY POSITION (MLB): C—4.

Year Team (League)	Pos.	G	AB	R	H	2B	3B	HR	RBI	BB	SO	HBP	GDP	SB-CS	Avg.	OBP	SLG	OPS	E	Avg.
1988— Jamestown (NYP)	C-OF	47	152	14	34	9	0	0	17	8	30	0	4	2-1	.224	.261	.283	.544	2	.992
1989— Rockford (Midwest)	C	14	48	4	11	1	1	0	4	3	6	0	1	1-0	.229	.275	.292	.566	4	.960
— Jamestown (NYP)	C	58	216	25	48	9	1	2	24	16	40	2	4	8-4	.222	.278	.301	.579	8	.984
1990— Rockford (Midwest)	C-OF	120	425	46	94	18	3	7	57	32	83	1	9	7-2	.221	.273	.327	.600	18	.981
— W.P. Beach (FSL)	C	2	3	0	0	0	0	0	0	0	1	0	0	0-0	.000	.000	.000	.000	0	1.000
1991— W.P. Beach (FSL)	C	100	333	35	77	15	2	5	33	22	51	2	9	10-1	.231	.280	.333	.613	14	.979
— Harrisburg (East.)	C	11	35	4	10	1	0	1	5	2	5	1	1	0-1	.286	.342	.400	.742	3	.959
1992— Harrisburg (East.)	C	117	409	55	99	19	3	15	68	39	89	5	10	3-1	.242	.312	.413	.725	14	.980
— Montreal (N.L.)	C	28	46	8	10	3	0	0	4	2	14	0	1	1-1	.217	.250	.283	.533	1	.991
1993— Montreal (N.L.)	C	43	86	3	17	2	1	0	7	2	16	1	2	2-0	.198	.222	.244	.466	2	.987
— Ottawa (Int'l)	C-1B	56	204	26	47	10	0	4	23	21	41	1	10	3-2	.230	.304	.338	.642	11	.972
1994— Ottawa (Int'l)	C-DH	118	424	68	131	32	2	12	71	47	96	3	10	11-6	.309	.381	.479	.860	•11	.985
1995— Montreal (N.L.)	C	64	141	17	33	8	1	3	20	14	38	1	5	0-1	.234	.306	.369	.675	7	.977
1996— Montreal (N.L.)	C		Did not play.																	
1997— Rochester (Int'l)	DH-C	79	290	45	75	11	•11	37	34	49	5	4	1-2	.259	.342	.417	.760	6	.980
— Baltimore (A.L.)	C	7	14	0	0	0	0	0	1	2	9	0	0	0-0	.000	.118	.000	.118	1	.966
1998— Durham (Int'l)	C-DH	40	134	36	32	7	0	11	26	28	32	1	4	1-1	.239	.372	.537	.909	2	.991
— Tampa Bay (A.L.)	C-DH	3	5	1	1	0	0	0	1	1	0	0	0	0-1	.200	.333	.200	.533	0	1.000
— Nashville (PCL)	C-1B-DH	44	152	30	54	16	1	11	34	•21	26	3	6	1-0	.355	.441	.691	1.131	4	.987
— Pittsburgh (N.L.)	1B-C	14	24	2	9	1	0	1	2	1	3	0	1	0-0	.375	.385	.542	.926	0	1.000
1999— Nashville (PCL)	C-1B-DH																			
	3B	112	405	48	109	29	3	12	65	29	68	4	10	3-0	.269	.322	.444	.766	15	.981
— Pittsburgh (N.L.)	C	6	9	0	3	0	0	0	1	0	1	0	0	0-0	.333	.333	.333	.667	0	1.000

L

Year Team (League)	Pos.	G	AB	R	H	2B	3B	HR	RBI	BB	SO	HBP	GDP	SB-CS	Avg.	OBP	SLG	OPS	E	Avg.
2000— Nashville (PCL)	C-1B-3B	121	421	70	104	28	4	19	75	54	73	1	9	5-0	.247	.329	.468	.796	12	.984
2001— Buffalo (Int'l)	C-1B	86	320	45	79	13	0	20	57	28	53	4	10	2-1	.247	.314	.475	.789	6	.990
— Cleveland (A.L.)	C	16	33	5	6	0	0	1	5	6	8	0	1	0-0	.182	.308	.273	.580	1	.988
2002— Columbus (S. Atl.)	C	11	38	5	11	1	0	2	13	10	6	1	0	0-0	.289	.440	.474	.914	0	1.000
— Buffalo (Int'l)	C-1B	62	216	23	49	10	0	4	28	21	52	3	9	2-0	.227	.303	.329	.632	3	.992
2003— Cleveland (A.L.)	C-DH	52	162	17	39	11	0	3	21	9	38	0	4	2-2	.241	.281	.364	.645	5	.983
2004— Cleveland (A.L.)	C-P	44	117	12	25	2	0	3	17	7	28	1	5	0-0	.214	.262	.308	.570	4	.985
2005— Tampa Bay (A.L.)	C	1	1	0	0	0	0	0	0	0	1	0	0	0-0	.000	.000	.000	.000	0	1.000
— Durham (Int'l)	C-DH-P	89	327	48	74	19	0	11	44	37	80	2	12	0-0	.226	.305	.385	.691	6	.987
2006— Cleveland (A.L.)	C	4	13	1	4	1	0	0	2	0	4	0	0	0-0	.308	.308	.385	.692	0	1.000
— Buffalo (Int'l)		54	188	24	39	14	0	0	12	13	50	2	5	0-0	.207	.265	.282	.547	6	.984
American League totals (7 years)		127	345	36	75	14	0	7	46	25	89	1	10	2-3	.217	.271	.319	.590	11	.984
National League totals (5 years)		155	306	30	72	14	2	4	33	19	73	2	9	3-2	.235	.282	.333	.615	10	.984
Major League totals (11 years)		282	651	66	147	28	2	11	79	44	162	3	19	5-5	.226	.276	.326	.602	21	.984

2006 LEFTY-RIGHTY SPLITS

vs.	Avg.	AB	H	2B	3B	HR	RBI	BB	SO	OBP	Slg.	vs.	Avg.	AB	H	2B	3B	HR	RBI	BB	SO	OBP	Slg.
L	.400	5	2	1	0	0	2	0	3	.400	.600	R	.250	8	2	0	0	0	0	0	1	.250	.250

LAMB, MIKE — 3B/OF

PERSONAL: Born August 9, 1975, in West Covina, Calif. ... 6-1/190. ... Bats left, throws right. ... Full name: Michael Robert Lamb. ... High school: Bishop Amat (La Puente, Calif.). ... College: Cal State Fullerton. **TRANSACTIONS/CAREER NOTES:** Selected by Minnesota Twins organization in 31st round of 1996 free-agent draft; did not sign. ... Selected by Texas Rangers organization in seventh round of 1997 free-agent draft. ... Traded by Rangers to New York Yankees for P Jose Garcia (February 5, 2004). ... Traded by Yankees to Houston Astros for P Juan DeLeon (March 25, 2004). **STATISTICAL NOTES:** Career major league grand slams: 1.

2006 GAMES PLAYED BY POSITION (MLB): 1B—68, 3B—36, 2B—2.

Year Team (League)	Pos.	G	AB	R	H	2B	3B	HR	RBI	BB	SO	HBP	GDP	SB-CS	Avg.	OBP	SLG	OPS	E	Avg.
1997— Pulaski (Appalachian)	3B	60	233	59	78	19	3	9	47	31	18	4	5	7-2	.335	.412	.558	.970	25	.862
1998— Charlotte (Fla. St.)	1B-3B	135	536	83	162	35	3	9	93	45	63	4	10	18-7	.302	.356	.429	.785	31	.933
1999— Tulsa (Texas)	3B-C	137	544	98	176	51	5	21	100	53	65	7	11	4-3	.324	.386	.551	.937	28	.930
— Oklahoma (PCL)	3B	2	2	0	1	0	0	0	0	1	0	1	0	0-1	.500	.750	.500	1.250	0	...
2000— Oklahoma (PCL)	3B	14	55	8	14	5	1	2	5	5	6	0	5	2-1	.255	.317	.491	.808	7	.806
— Texas (A.L.)	3B-DH	138	493	65	137	25	2	6	47	34	60	4	10	0-2	.278	.328	.373	.702	• 33	.913
2001— Oklahoma (PCL)	3B	69	273	35	81	19	3	8	40	13	31	3	8	0-2	.297	.331	.476	.807	15	.908
— Texas (A.L.)	3B	76	284	42	87	18	0	4	35	14	27	5	6	2-1	.306	.348	.412	.760	18	.914
2002— Oklahoma (PCL)	C-3B	6	28	3	11	1	0	0	4	1	4	0	1	0-0	.393	.414	.429	.842	3	.893
— Texas (A.L.) 1B-DH-OF	3B-C-2B	115	314	54	89	13	0	9	33	33	48	3	7	0-0	.283	.354	.411	.765	9	.980
2003— Texas (A.L.)	DH-1B-OF																			
	3B	28	38	3	5	0	0	0	2	2	7	1	1	1-0	.132	.190	.132	.322	0	1.000
— Oklahoma (PCL) 3B-1B-DH	73	274	45	79	19	4	9	46	42	45	2	4	1-1	.288	.383	.485	.869	11	.953
2004— Houston (N.L.) 3B-1B-2B																				
	DH	112	278	38	80	14	3	14	58	31	63	0	4	1-1	.288	.356	.511	.867	14	.947
2005— Houston (N.L.)	1B-3B-OF																			
	DH	125	322	41	76	13	5	12	53	22	65	1	10	1-1	.236	.284	.419	.703	6	.989
2006— Houston (N.L.)	1B-3B-2B	126	381	70	117	25	3	12	45	35	55	0	10	2-4	.307	.361	.475	.836	11	.982
American League totals (4 years)		357	1129	164	318	56	2	19	117	83	142	13	24	3-3	.282	.336	.385	.721	60	.943
National League totals (3 years)		363	981	149	273	49	11	38	156	88	183	1	24	4-6	.278	.335	.467	.801	31	.978
Major League totals (7 years)		720	2110	313	591	105	13	57	273	171	325	14	48	7-9	.280	.335	.423	.758	91	.963

DIVISION SERIES RECORD

Year Team (League)	Pos.	G	AB	R	H	2B	3B	HR	RBI	BB	SO	HBP	GDP	SB-CS	Avg.	OBP	SLG	OPS	E	Avg.
2004— Houston (N.L.)		4	3	0	0	0	0	0	1	0	0	0	0	0-0	.000	.000	.000	.000	0	...
2005— Houston (N.L.)	1B	2	6	1	3	0	0	1	1	2	0	0	0	0-0	.500	.625	1.000	1.625	0	1.000
Division series totals (2 years)		6	9	1	3	0	0	1	2	2	0	0	0	0-0	.333	.417	.667	1.083	0	1.000

CHAMPIONSHIP SERIES RECORD

Year Team (League)	Pos.	G	AB	R	H	2B	3B	HR	RBI	BB	SO	HBP	GDP	SB-CS	Avg.	OBP	SLG	OPS	E	Avg.
2004— Houston (N.L.)	3B	2	5	2	2	0	0	2	2	1	1	0	1	0-0	.400	.500	1.600	2.100	0	1.000
2005— Houston (N.L.)	1B	4	16	3	3	1	0	1	2	0	3	0	0	0-0	.188	.188	.438	.625	1	.975
Champ. series totals (2 years)		6	21	5	5	1	0	3	4	1	4	0	1	0-0	.238	.273	.714	.987	1	.977

WORLD SERIES RECORD

Year Team (League)	Pos.	G	AB	R	H	2B	3B	HR	RBI	BB	SO	HBP	GDP	SB-CS	Avg.	OBP	SLG	OPS	E	Avg.
2005— Houston (N.L.)	1B	4	10	1	2	1	0	1	1	2	3	0	0	0-0	.200	.333	.600	.933	0	1.000

2006 LEFTY-RIGHTY SPLITS

vs.	Avg.	AB	H	2B	3B	HR	RBI	BB	SO	OBP	Slg.	vs.	Avg.	AB	H	2B	3B	HR	RBI	BB	SO	OBP	Slg.
L	.211	57	12	3	1	1	7	3	14	.250	.351	R	.324	324	105	19	2	11	38	32	41	.380	.497

LANE, JASON — OF

PERSONAL: Born December 22, 1976, in Santa Rosa, Calif. ... 6-2/220. ... Bats right, throws left. ... Full name: Jason Dean Lane. ... High school: Santa Rosa (Calif.). ... College: Southern California. **TRANSACTIONS/CAREER NOTES:** Selected by Houston Astros organization in sixth round of 1999 free-agent draft. **STATISTICAL NOTES:** Career major league grand slams: 1.

2006 GAMES PLAYED BY POSITION (MLB): OF—98, 1B—1.

Year Team (League)	Pos.	G	AB	R	H	2B	3B	HR	RBI	BB	SO	HBP	GDP	SB-CS	Avg.	OBP	SLG	OPS	E	Avg.
1999— Auburn (NY-Penn)	1B-P	74	283	46	79	18	5	13	59	38	46	3	2	6-4	.279	.366	.516	.882	9	.986
2000— Michigan (Midw.)	1B-OF	133	511	98	153	38	0	23	• 104	62	91	8	9	20-7	.299	.375	.509	.884	6	.986
2001— Round Rock (Texas)	OF	137	526	103	166	36	2	38	124	61	98	21	6	14-2	.316	.407	.608	1.016	2	.992
2002— New Orleans (PCL)	OF-1B	111	426	65	116	36	2	15	83	31	90	7	6	13-3	.272	.328	.472	.799	2	.993
— Houston (N.L.)	OF	44	69	12	20	3	1	4	10	10	12	0	0	1-1	.290	.375	.536	.911	1	.980
2003— New Orleans (PCL) OF-1B-DH	71	248	37	74	17	0	7	39	30	26	3	6	2-1	.298	.374	.452	.826	4	.976
— Houston (N.L.)	OF	18	27	5	8	2	0	4	10	0	2	0	0	0-0	.296	.296	.815	1.111	0	1.000
2004— Houston (N.L.)	OF-1B	107	136	21	37	10	2	4	19	16	33	1	2	1-0	.272	.348	.463	.812	2	.974

Year Team (League)	Pos.	G	AB	R	H	2B	3B	HR	RBI	BB	SO	HBP	GDP	SB-CS	Avg.	OBP	SLG	OPS	E	Avg.
														BATTING					**FIELDING**	
2005— Houston (N.L.)	OF	145	517	65	138	34	4	26	78	32	105	1	10	6-2	.267	.316	.499	.815	6	.976
2006— Round Rock (PCL)		12	46	7	12	2	0	1	11	5	16	1		1-0	.261	.327	.370	.697	0	1.000
— Houston (N.L.)	OF-1B	112	288	44	58	10	0	15	45	49	75	2	6	1-2	.201	.318	.392	.710	0	1.000
Major League totals (5 years)		426	1037	147	261	59	7	53	162	107	227	10	18	9-5	.252	.324	.475	.800	9	.984

DIVISION SERIES RECORD

Year Team (League)	Pos.	G	AB	R	H	2B	3B	HR	RBI	BB	SO	HBP	GDP	SB-CS	Avg.	OBP	SLG	OPS	E	Avg.
2004— Houston (N.L.)	OF	5	5	2	3	0	0	1	2	0	1	0		0-0	.600	.600	1.200	1.800	0	1.000
2005— Houston (N.L.)	OF	4	17	1	4	1	0	0	3	1	3	1	1	0-0	.235	.300	.294	.594	0	1.000
Division series totals (2 years)		9	22	3	7	1	0	1	5	1	4	1	1	0-0	.318	.360	.500	.860	0	1.000

CHAMPIONSHIP SERIES RECORD

Year Team (League)	Pos.	G	AB	R	H	2B	3B	HR	RBI	BB	SO	HBP	GDP	SB-CS	Avg.	OBP	SLG	OPS	E	Avg.
2004— Houston (N.L.)	OF	2	1	0	0	0	0	0	0	0	0	0		0-0	.000	.000	.000	.000	0	1.000
2005— Houston (N.L.)	OF	6	21	3	5	0	0	2	3	2	4	1	0	0-0	.238	.333	.524	.857	0	1.000
Champ. series totals (2 years)		8	22	3	5	0	0	2	3	2	4	1	0	0-0	.227	.320	.500	.820	0	1.000

WORLD SERIES RECORD

Year Team (League)	Pos.	G	AB	R	H	2B	3B	HR	RBI	BB	SO	HBP	GDP	SB-CS	Avg.	OBP	SLG	OPS	E	Avg.
2005— Houston (N.L.)	OF	4	18	1	4	1	0	1	2	1	5	0	1	1-0	.222	.263	.444	.708	0	1.000

2006 LEFTY-RIGHTY SPLITS

vs.	Avg.	AB	H	2B	3B	HR	RBI	BB	SO	OBP	Slg.	vs.	Avg.	AB	H	2B	3B	HR	RBI	BB	SO	OBP	Slg.
L	.198	96	19	4	0	6	20	22	25	.344	.427	R	.203	192	39	6	0	9	25	27	50	.303	.375

LANGERHANS, RYAN — OF

PERSONAL: Born February 20, 1980, in San Antonio. ... 6-3/195. ... Bats left, throws left. ... Full name: Ryan David Langerhans. ... Name pronounced: lahn-ger-hahns. ... High school: Round Rock (Texas). **TRANSACTIONS/CAREER NOTES:** Selected by Atlanta Braves organization in third round of 1998 free-agent draft.

2006 GAMES PLAYED BY POSITION (MLB): OF—119.

Year Team (League)	Pos.	G	AB	R	H	2B	3B	HR	RBI	BB	SO	HBP	GDP	SB-CS	Avg.	OBP	SLG	OPS	E	Avg.
														BATTING					**FIELDING**	
1998— GC Braves (GCL)	OF-OF	43	148	15	41	10	4	2	19	19	38	0	0	2-5	.277	.357	.439	.796	2	.975
1999— Macon (S. Atl.)	OF-OF	121	448	66	120	30	1	9	49	52	99	7	8	19-11	.268	.352	.400	.752	5	.976
2000— Myrtle Beach (Carol.)	OF-OF	116	392	55	83	14	7	6	37	32	104	9	3	25-11	.212	.286	.329	.615	6	.961
2001— Myrtle Beach (Carol.)	OF-OF	125	450	66	129	30	3	7	48	55	104	8	6	22-13	.287	.374	.413	.787	7	.972
2002— Greenville (Sou.)	OF-OF	109	391	57	98	23	2	9	62	68	83	6	9	10-5	.251	.366	.389	.755	2	.992
— Atlanta (N.L.)	OF	1	1	0	0	0	0	0	0	0	0	0	0	0-0	.000	.000	.000	.000	0	...
2003— Greenville (Sou.)	OF-OF	94	336	42	85	23	2	6	38	46	85	3	6	10-10	.253	.348	.387	.735	2	.991
— Richmond (Int'l)	OF-OF	38	132	13	37	10	2	4	11	11	29	1	2	2-1	.280	.338	.477	.815	4	.949
— Atlanta (N.L.)	OF	16	15	2	4	0	0	0	0	0	6	0	1	0-0	.267	.267	.267	.533	0	1.000
2004— Richmond (Int'l)	OF	135	456	103	136	34	3	20	72	70	113	6	6	5-9	.298	.397	.518	.915	3	.933
2005— Atlanta (N.L.)	OF	128	326	48	87	22	3	8	42	37	75	5	2	0-2	.267	.348	.426	.774	1	.995
2006— Atlanta (N.L.)	OF	131	315	46	76	16	3	7	28	50	91	3	9	1-2	.241	.350	.378	.727	1	.995
Major League totals (4 years)		276	657	96	167	38	6	15	70	87	172	8	12	1-4	.254	.347	.399	.745	2	.995

DIVISION SERIES RECORD

Year Team (League)	Pos.	G	AB	R	H	2B	3B	HR	RBI	BB	SO	HBP	GDP	SB-CS	Avg.	OBP	SLG	OPS	E	Avg.
2005— Atlanta (N.L.)	OF	4	12	1	4	1	0	0	0	3	3	1	0	0-0	.333	.500	.417	.917	0	1.000

2006 LEFTY-RIGHTY SPLITS

vs.	Avg.	AB	H	2B	3B	HR	RBI	BB	SO	OBP	Slg.	vs.	Avg.	AB	H	2B	3B	HR	RBI	BB	SO	OBP	Slg.
L	.308	39	12	1	0	0	6	6	11	.400	.333	R	.232	276	64	15	3	7	22	44	80	.343	.384

LARA, JUAN — P

PERSONAL: Born January 26, 1981, in Azua, Dominican Republic. ... Throws left, bats right. ... Full name: Juan Lara. **TRANSACTIONS/CAREER NOTES:** Signed as a non-drafted free agent by Cleveland Indians organization (May 22, 1999).

CAREER HITTING: 0-for-0 (.000), 0 R, 0 2B, 0 3B, 0 HR, 0 RBI.

Year Team (League)	W	L	Pct.	ERA	WHIP	G	GS	CG	ShO	Hld.	Sv.-Opp.	IP	H	R	ER	HR	BB-IBB	SO	Avg.
1999— Dominican Indians (DSL)	1	0	1.000	4.05	1.65	4	0	0	0	...	0-...	6.2	7	3	3	1	4-0	3	.280
2000— Dominican Indians (DSL)	4	1	.800	3.31	1.34	12	10	0	0	...	1-...	54.1	58	29	20	1	15-0	51	.269
2001— Dominican Indians (DSL)	3	5	.375	1.80	1.03	13	12	0	0	...	0-...	65.0	57	28	13	0	10-0	49	.230
2002— Burlington (Appal.)	2	6	.250	4.98	1.46	14	14	0	0	...	0-...	65.0	67	42	36	4	28-0	50	.275
2003— Lake County (S.Atl.)	4	4	.200	5.00	1.71	16	3	0	0	...	1-...	45.0	51	31	25	7	26-0	37	.279
— Mahoning Valley (N.Y.-Penn.)	3	3	.500	3.50	1.17	12	12	0	0	...	0-...	61.2	54	29	24	4	18-1	54	.235
2004— Kinston (Carol.)	4	3	.571	5.66	1.71	35	8	0	0	...	1-...	84.1	106	60	53	6	38-1	74	.308
2005— Kinston (Carol.)	0	1	.000	4.04	1.30	26	0	0	0	0	0-0	42.1	40	22	19	4	15-0	46	.244
— Akron (East.)	1	2	.333	4.56	1.73	18	0	0	0	3	5-7	23.2	27	15	12	1	14-0	16	.290
2006— Buffalo (Int'l)	1	1	.500	3.00	1.33	13	0	0	0	1	1-2	15.0	17	6	5	1	3-0	15	.279
— Akron (East.)	4	2	.667	2.70	1.14	40	0	0	0	8	7-9	46.2	32	14	14	2	21-1	48	.189
— Cleveland (A.L.)	0	0	...	1.80	1.00	9	0	0	0	0	0-1	5.0	4	2	1	0	1-0	2	.222
Major League totals (1 year)	0	0	...	1.80	1.00	9	0	0	0	0	0-1	5.0	4	2	1	0	1-0	2	.222

2006 LEFTY-RIGHTY SPLITS

vs.	Avg.	AB	H	2B	3B	HR	RBI	BB	SO	OBP	Slg.	vs.	Avg.	AB	H	2B	3B	HR	RBI	BB	SO	OBP	Slg.
L	.091	11	1	0	0	0	0	1	1	.167	.091	R	.429	7	3	0	0	0	2	0	1	.429	.429

LAROCHE, ADAM — 1B

PERSONAL: Born November 6, 1979, in Orange County, Calif. ... 6-3/180. ... Bats left, throws left. ... Full name: David Adam LaRoche. ... High school: Fort Scott (Kan.). ... Junior college: Fort Scott (Kan.), then Seminole (Okla.). ... Son of Dave LaRoche, pitcher for five major league clubs (1970-83). **TRANSACTIONS/CAREER NOTES:** Selected by Florida Marlins organization in 18th round of 1998 free-agent draft; did not sign. ... Selected by Marlins organization in 42nd round of 1999 free-agent draft; did not sign. ... Selected by Atlanta Braves organization in 29th round of 2000 free-agent draft. ... On disabled list (May 29-July 2, 2004); included rehabilitation assignment to Richmond. **RECORDS:** Shares major league record for most doubles, game (4, May 15, 2004). **STATISTICAL NOTES:** Career major league grand slams: 2.

2006 GAMES PLAYED BY POSITION (MLB): 1B—142.

Year Team (League)	Pos.	G	AB	R	H	2B	3B	HR	RBI	BB	SO	HBP	GDP	SB-CS	Avg.	OBP	SLG	OPS	E	Avg.
														BATTING					**FIELDING**	
2000— Danville (Appal.)	1B	56	201	38	62	13	3	7	45	24	46	2	2	4-1	.308	.381	.507	.888	2	.994
2001— Myrtle Beach (Carol.)	1B-OF-P	126	471	49	118	31	0	7	47	30	108	9	13	10-8	.251	.305	.361	.666	8	.993

Year Team (League)	Pos.	G	AB	R	H	2B	3B	HR	RBI	BB	SO	HBP	GDP	SB-CS	Avg.	OBP	SLG	OPS	E	Avg.
											BATTING								**FIELDING**	
2002— Myrtle Beach (Carol.)	1B	69	250	30	84	17	0	9	53	27	37	4	3	0-2	.336	.406	.512	.918	5	.991
— Greenville (Sou.)	1B	45	173	17	50	9	0	4	19	19	38	1	6	1-1	.289	.363	.410	.773	1	.998
2003— Greenville (Sou.)	1B-P	61	219	42	62	12	1	12	37	34	53	3	6	1-2	.283	.381	.511	.892	2	.996
— Richmond (Int'l)	1B	72	264	33	78	21	0	8	35	27	58	3	6	1-2	.295	.360	.466	.826	4	.993
2004— Richmond (Int'l)	1B	4	11	1	2	0	0	1	2	1	0	0	2	0-0	.182	.250	.455	.705	0	1.000
— Atlanta (N.L.)	1B	110	324	45	90	27	1	13	45	27	78	1	10	0-0	.278	.333	.488	.821	5	.994
2005— Atlanta (N.L.)	1B	141	451	53	117	28	0	20	78	39	87	4	15	0-2	.259	.320	.455	.775	7	.994
2006— Atlanta (N.L.)	1B	149	492	89	140	38	1	32	90	55	128	2	9	0-2	.285	.354	.561	.915	5	.996
Major League totals (3 years)		400	1267	187	347	93	2	65	213	121	293	7	34	0-4	.274	.337	.504	.841	17	.995

DIVISION SERIES RECORD

Year Team (League)	Pos.	G	AB	R	H	2B	3B	HR	RBI	BB	SO	HBP	GDP	SB-CS	Avg.	OBP	SLG	OPS	E	Avg.
2004— Atlanta (N.L.)	1B	5	17	1	4	1	0	1	4	2	5	0	1	0-0	.235	.316	.471	.786	0	1.000
2005— Atlanta (N.L.)	1B	3	8	2	4	1	0	1	6	3	1	0	0	0-0	.500	.636	1.000	1.636	0	1.000
Division series totals (2 years)		8	25	3	8	2	0	2	10	5	6	0	1	0-0	.320	.433	.640	1.073	0	1.000

2006 LEFTY-RIGHTY SPLITS

vs.	Avg.	AB	H	2B	3B	HR	RBI	BB	SO	OBP	Slg.	vs.	Avg.	AB	H	2B	3B	HR	RBI	BB	SO	OBP	Slg.
L	.241	112	27	6	0	7	20	11	36	.315	.482	R	.297	380	113	32	1	25	70	44	92	.366	.584

LARUE, JASON — C

PERSONAL: Born March 19, 1974, in Houston. ... 5-11/200. ... Bats right, throws right. ... Full name: Michael Jason LaRue. ... Name pronounced: la-ROO. ... High school: Spring Valley (Spring Branch, Texas). ... College: Dallas Baptist. **TRANSACTIONS/CAREER NOTES:** Selected by Cincinnati Reds organization in fifth round of 1995 free-agent draft. ... On disabled list (September 23, 2002-remainder of season). ... On disabled list (April 29-May 14, 2004); included rehabilitation assignment to Louisville. ... On bereavement list (June 12-15, 2005). ... On disabled list (April 1-18, 2006); included rehabilitation assignments to Sarasota and Louisville. **STATISTICAL NOTES:** Career major league grand slams: 4.

2006 GAMES PLAYED BY POSITION (MLB): C—63.

Year Team (League)	Pos.	G	AB	R	H	2B	3B	HR	RBI	BB	SO	HBP	GDP	SB-CS	Avg.	OBP	SLG	OPS	E	Avg.
											BATTING								**FIELDING**	
1995— Billings (Pion.)	C	52	183	35	50	8	1	5	31	16	28	12	2	3-5	.273	.366	.410	.776	8	.980
1996— Char., W.Va. (SAL)	1B-C	37	123	17	26	8	0	2	14	11	28	2	2	3-0	.211	.287	.325	.612	6	.979
1997— Char., W.Va. (SAL)	1B-3B-C-OF	132	473	78	149	50	3	8	81	47	90	5	8	14-4	.315	.377	.484	.861	19	.977
1998— Chattanooga (Sou.)	1B-3B-C	105	386	71	141	39	8	14	82	40	60	10	13	4-3	.365	.429	.617	1.046	10	.985
— Indianapolis (Int'l)	C	15	51	5	12	4	0	0	5	4	8	0	2	0-1	.235	.286	.314	.599	0	1.000
1999— Indianapolis (Int'l)	C-DH	70	263	42	66	12	2	12	37	15	52	4	13	0-3	.251	.299	.449	.748	7	.984
— Cincinnati (N.L.)	C	36	90	12	19	7	0	3	10	11	32	2	4	4-1	.211	.311	.389	.700	2	.990
2000— Louisville (Int'l)	C	82	307	54	78	22	1	14	48	22	52	8	4	3-2	.254	.320	.469	.790	8	.984
— Cincinnati (N.L.)	C-3B-OF	31	98	12	23	3	0	5	12	5	19	4	1	0-0	.235	.299	.418	.717	2	.991
2001— Cincinnati (N.L.)	1B	121	364	39	86	21	2	12	43	27	106	9	11	3-3	.236	.303	.404	.707	7	.990
2002— Cincinnati (N.L.)	C	113	353	42	88	17	1	12	52	27	117	13	13	1-2	.249	.324	.405	.729	4	.994
2003— Cincinnati (N.L.)	C-1B-OF	118	379	52	87	23	1	16	50	33	111	20	9	3-3	.230	.321	.422	.743	11	.985
2004— Louisville (Int'l)	C	3	10	3	1	0	0	1	4	1	3	1	0	0-0	.100	.214	.400	.614	1	.917
— Cincinnati (N.L.)	C-DH-OF	114	390	46	98	24	2	14	55	26	108	24	7	0-2	.251	.334	.431	.765	8	.989
2005— Cincinnati (N.L.)	C-OF	110	361	38	94	27	1	14	60	41	101	13	8	0-0	.260	.355	.452	.806	5	.993
2006— Sarasota (Fla. St.)		3	12	1	2	0	0	0	1	1	3	0	1	0-0	.167	.231	.167	.397	0	1.000
— Louisville (Int'l)		2	8	1	2	1	0	0	0	0	1	0	0	0-0	.250	.250	.375	.625	0	1.000
— Cincinnati (N.L.)	C	72	191	22	37	5	0	8	21	27	51	8	3	1-0	.194	.317	.346	.663	2	.995
Major League totals (8 years)		715	2226	263	532	127	6	84	303	197	645	93	56	12-11	.239	.325	.415	.740	41	.990

2006 LEFTY-RIGHTY SPLITS

vs.	Avg.	AB	H	2B	3B	HR	RBI	BB	SO	OBP	Slg.	vs.	Avg.	AB	H	2B	3B	HR	RBI	BB	SO	OBP	Slg.
L	.235	51	12	2	0	2	3	5	14	.328	.392	R	.179	140	25	3	0	6	18	22	37	.314	.329

LAWRENCE, BRIAN — P

PERSONAL: Born May 14, 1976, in Fort Collins, Colo. ... 6-0/197. ... Throws right, bats right. ... Full name: Brian Michael Lawrence. ... High school: Carthage (Texas). ... College: Northwestern State (La.). **TRANSACTIONS/CAREER NOTES:** Selected by San Diego Padres organization in 17th round of 1998 free-agent draft. ... Traded by Padres with cash to Washington Nationals for 3B Vinny Castilla (November 3, 2005). ... On disabled list (March 27, 2006-entire season). ... Released by Nationals (October 3, 2006). **MISCELLANEOUS NOTES:** Grounded out in only appearance as pinch hitter and appeared in one game as pinch runner (2004).

CAREER HITTING: 35-for-277 (.126), 15 R, 7 2B, 0 3B, 1 HR, 17 RBI.

Year Team (League)	W	L	Pct.	ERA	WHIP	G	GS	CG	ShO	Hld.	Sv.-Opp.	IP	H	R	ER	HR	BB-IBB	SO	Avg.
1998— Idaho Falls (Pio.)	3	0	1.000	2.45	1.23	4	4	2	•1	...	0-...	22.0	22	7	6	1	5-0	21	.262
— Clinton (Midw.)	5	3	.625	2.80	1.00	12	12	2	0	...	0-...	80.1	67	34	25	6	13-0	79	.221
1999— Rancho Cuca. (Calif.)	12	8	.600	3.39	1.19	27	27	4	3	...	0-...	175.1	178	72	66	6	30-1	166	.265
2000— Mobile (Sou.)	7	6	.538	2.42	1.00	21	21	0	0	...	0-...	126.2	99	40	34	6	28-0	119	.217
— Las Vegas (PCL)	4	0	1.000	1.93	1.18	8	8	0	0	...	0-...	46.2	48	13	10	6	7-0	46	.264
2001— Portland (PCL)	1	3	.250	3.80	1.31	9	8	0	0	...	1-...	45.0	42	22	19	3	17-2	42	.239
— San Diego (N.L.)	5	5	.500	3.45	1.23	27	15	1	0	0	0-0	114.2	107	53	44	10	34-5	84	.244
2002— San Diego (N.L.)	12	12	.500	3.69	1.34	35	31	2	2	1	0-0	210.0	230	97	86	16	52-6	149	.281
2003— San Diego (N.L.)	10	15	.400	4.19	1.25	33	33	1	0	0	0-0	210.2	206	106	98	27	57-8	116	.258
2004— San Diego (N.L.)	15	14	.517	4.12	1.38	34	34	2	1	0	0-0	203.0	226	101	93	26	55-7	121	.287
2005— San Diego (N.L.)	7	15	.318	4.83	1.37	33	33	1	0	0	0-0	195.2	211	106	105	18	57-7	109	.273
2006— Wash. (N.L.)	Did not play.																		
Major League totals (5 years)	49	61	.445	4.10	1.32	162	146	7	3	1	0-0	934.0	980	463	426	97	255-33	579	.271

DIVISION SERIES RECORD

Year Team (League)	W	L	Pct.	ERA	WHIP	G	GS	CG	ShO	Hld.	Sv.-Opp.	IP	H	R	ER	HR	BB-IBB	SO	Avg.
2005— San Diego (N.L.)	0	0	...	0.00	0.43	2	0	0	0	0	0-0	2.1	1	0	0	0	0-0	2	.125

LAWTON, MATT — OF

PERSONAL: Born November 3, 1971, in Gulfport, Miss. ... 5-10/195. ... Bats left, throws right. ... Full name: Matthew Lawton III. ... Name pronounced: LAW-ton. ... High school: Harrison Central (Gulfport, Miss.). ... Junior college: Mississippi Gulf Coast C.C. ... Brother of Marcus Lawton, outfielder with New York Yankees (1989); and cousin of Fred Lewis, pitcher, San Francisco Giants. **TRANSACTIONS/CAREER NOTES:** Selected by Minnesota Twins organization in 13th round of 1991 free-agent draft. ... On disabled list (June 9-July 18, 1999); included rehabilitation assignments to Fort Myers and GCL Twins. ... Traded by Twins to New York Mets for P Rick Reed (July 30, 2001). ... Traded by Mets with OF Alex Escobar, P Jerrod Riggan and two players to be named to Cleveland Indians for 2B Roberto Alomar, P Mike Bacsik and OF Danny Peoples (December 11, 2001); Indians acquired P Billy Traber and 1B Earl Snyder to complete deal (December 13, 2001). ... On disabled list (July 12-July 27 and September 4, 2002-remainder of season); included rehabilitation assignment to Akron. ... On disabled list (July 12-August 18 and September 6, 2003-remainder of season); included rehabilitation assignments to Akron. ... Traded by Indians with cash to Pittsburgh Pirates for P Arthur Rhodes and cash (December 11, 2004). ... Traded by Pirates to Chicago Cubs for OF Jody Gerut (July 31, 2005). ... Traded by Cubs to New York Yankees for P Justin Berg (August 27, 2005). ... Signed as free agent by Seattle Mariners (January 11, 2006). ... On restricted list (April 2-12, 2006). ... Released by Mariners (May 30, 2006). **STATISTICAL NOTES:** Career major league grand slams: 4.

2006 GAMES PLAYED BY POSITION (MLB): OF—7, DH—2.

Year	Team (League)	Pos.	G	AB	R	H	2B	3B	HR	RBI	BB	SO	HBP	GDP	SB-CS	Avg.	OBP	SLG	OPS	E	Avg.
																				FIELDING	
												BATTING									
1992—	GC Twins (GCL)	2B	53	173	39	45	8	3	2	26	27	27	9	2	20-1	.260	.375	.376	.751	12	.958
1993—	Fort Wayne (Midw.)	OF	111	340	50	97	21	3	9	38	65	42	8	8	23-15	.285	.410	.444	.854	3	.959
1994—	Fort Myers (FSL)	OF	122	446	79	134	30	1	7	51	80	64	2	7	42-19	.300	.407	.419	.826	6	.971
1995—	New Britain (East.)	OF-DH	114	412	75	111	19	5	13	54	56	70	12	8	26-9	.269	.371	.434	.805	2	.991
—	Minnesota (A.L.)	OF-DH	21	60	11	19	4	1	1	12	7	11	3	1	1-1	.317	.414	.467	.881	1	.972
1996—	Minnesota (A.L.)	OF-DH	79	252	34	65	7	1	6	42	28	28	4	6	4-4	.258	.339	.365	.704	3	.985
—	Salt Lake (PCL)	OF-DH	53	212	40	63	16	1	7	33	26	34	3	2	2-4	.297	.379	.481	.860	6	.936
1997—	Minnesota (A.L.)	OF	142	460	74	114	29	3	14	60	76	81	10	7	7-4	.248	.366	.415	.781	7	.976
1998—	Minnesota (A.L.)	OF	152	557	91	155	36	6	21	77	86	64	15	10	16-8	.278	.387	.478	.864	4	.990
1999—	Minnesota (A.L.)	OF-DH	118	406	58	105	18	0	7	54	57	42	6	11	26-4	.259	.355	.355	.708	4	.982
—	Fort Myers (FSL)	OF	4	14	3	8	1	0	0	2	3	1	0	0	1-0	.571	.647	.643	1.290	0	1.000
—	GC Twins (GCL)	OF	1	4	0	1	0	0	0	1	0	2	0	0	0-0	.250	.250	.250	.500	0	1.000
2000—	Minnesota (A.L.)	OF-DH	156	561	84	171	44	2	13	88	91	63	7	10	23-7	.305	.405	.460	.865	5	.983
2001—	Minnesota (A.L.)	OF-DH	103	376	71	110	25	0	10	51	63	46	3	14	19-6	.293	.396	.439	.835	4	.980
—	New York (N.L.)	OF	48	183	24	45	11	1	3	13	22	34	8	2	10-2	.246	.352	.366	.718	0	1.000
2002—	Cleveland (A.L.)	OF-DH	114	416	71	98	19	2	15	57	59	34	8	13	8-9	.236	.342	.399	.741	6	.975
—	Akron (East.)	OF	3	10	1	0	0	0	0	0	0	3	1	0	0-0	.000	.231	.000	.231	0	1.000
2003—	Akron (East.)	DH	3	19	1	1	0	0	0	1	2	6	0	1	0-0	.053	.143	.053	.195	0	...
—	Cleveland (A.L.)	OF-DH	99	374	57	93	19	0	15	53	47	47	7	7	10-3	.249	.343	.420	.762	1	.993
2004—	Cleveland (A.L.)	OF-DH	150	591	109	164	25	4	20	70	74	84	11	21	23-9	.278	.366	.421	.788	4	.986
2005—	Pittsburgh (N.L.)	OF	101	374	53	102	28	1	10	44	58	61	9	7	16-9	.273	.380	.433	.813	1	.995
—	Chicago (N.L.)	OF	19	78	8	19	2	0	1	5	4	8	1	3	1-0	.244	.289	.308	.597	1	.971
—	New York (A.L.)	OF	21	48	6	6	0	0	2	4	7	4	1	0	1-0	.125	.263	.250	.513	1	.969
2006—	Seattle (A.L.)	OF-DH	11	27	5	7	0	0	0	1	2	2	0	0	0-0	.259	.310	.259	.570	0	1.000
	American League totals (12 years)		1166	4128	671	1107	226	15	124	569	597	510	76	101	138-55	.268	.369	.420	.789	40	.983
	National League totals (2 years)		168	635	85	166	41	2	14	62	84	103	18	12	27-11	.261	.362	.398	.760	2	.994
	Major League totals (12 years)		1334	4763	756	1273	267	17	138	631	681	613	94	113	165-66	.267	.368	.417	.785	42	.984

ALL-STAR GAME RECORD

		G	AB	R	H	2B	3B	HR	RBI	BB	SO	HBP	GDP	SB-CS	Avg.	OBP	SLG	OPS	E	Avg.
	All-Star Game totals (2 years)	2	4	1	2	0	0	0	1	0	1	0	0	1-0	.500	.500	.500	1.000	0	...

2006 LEFTY-RIGHTY SPLITS

vs.	Avg.	AB	H	2B	3B	HR	RBI	BB	SO	OBP	Slg.	vs.	Avg.	AB	H	2B	3B	HR	RBI	BB	SO	OBP	Slg.
L	1.000	1	1	0	0	0	1	0	0	1.000	1.000	R	.231	26	6	0	0	0	0	2	2	.286	.231

LEAGUE, BRANDON — P

PERSONAL: Born March 16, 1983, in Honolulu. ... 6-3/192. ... Throws right, bats right. ... Full name: Brandon Paul League. ... High school: Saint Louis (Honolulu). **TRANSACTIONS/CAREER NOTES:** Selected by Toronto Blue Jays organization in second round of 2001 free-agent draft.

CAREER HITTING: 0-for-0 (.000), 0 R, 0 2B, 0 3B, 0 HR, 0 RBI.

Year	Team (League)	W	L	Pct.	ERA	WHIP	G	GS	CG	ShO	Hld.	Sv.-Opp.	IP	H	R	ER	HR	BB-IBB	SO	Avg.
2001—	Medicine Hat (Pio.)	2	2	.500	4.66	1.22	9	9	0	0		0-...	38.2	36	23	20	3	11-1	38	.245
2002—	Auburn (NY-Penn)	7	2	.778	3.15	1.20	16	16	0	0		0-...	85.2	80	42	30	2	23-0	72	.248
2003—	Char., W.Va. (SAL)	2	3	.400	1.91	1.08	12	12	0	0		0-...	70.2	58	15	15	1	18-0	61	.230
—	Dunedin (Fla. St.)	4	3	.571	4.75	1.45	13	12	0	0		0-...	66.1	76	40	35	3	20-0	34	.288
2004—	New Hampshire (East.)	6	4	.600	3.38	1.28	41	10	0	0		2-...	104.0	92	44	39	3	41-1	90	.240
—	Toronto (A.L.)	1	0	1.000	0.00	0.86	3	0	0	0	1	0-0	4.2	3	0	0	0	1-0	2	.176
2005—	Syracuse (Int'l)	4	4	.500	5.71	1.52	19	10	0	0	1	0-1	63.0	78	44	40	7	18-0	35	.306
—	Toronto (A.L.)	1	0	1.000	6.56	1.74	20	0	0	0	1	0-0	35.2	42	27	26	8	20-1	17	.302
2006—	Syracuse (Int'l)	3	2	.600	2.14	1.32	31	1	0	0	1	8-10	54.2	57	19	13	0	15-1	43	.273
—	Toronto (A.L.)	1	2	.333	2.53	1.01	33	0	0	0	12	1-4	42.2	34	17	12	3	9-2	29	.214
	Major totals (3 years)	3	2	.600	4.12	1.31	56	0	0	0	14	1-4	83.0	79	44	38	11	30-3	48	.251

2006 LEFTY-RIGHTY SPLITS

vs.	Avg.	AB	H	2B	3B	HR	RBI	BB	SO	OBP	Slg.	vs.	Avg.	AB	H	2B	3B	HR	RBI	BB	SO	OBP	Slg.
L	.276	58	16	2	0	1	8	3	9	.323	.362	R	.178	101	18	0	0	2	7	6	20	.239	.238

LECROY, MATTHEW — C

PERSONAL: Born December 13, 1975, in Belton, S.C. ... 6-2/225. ... Bats right, throws right. ... Full name: Matthew Hanks LeCroy. ... Name pronounced: LEE-croy. ... High school: Belton-Honea Path (S.C.). ... College: Clemson. **TRANSACTIONS/CAREER NOTES:** Selected by New York Mets organization in supplemental round ("sandwich" pick between second and third rounds, 63rd pick overall) of 1994 free-agent draft; did not sign; pick received as compensation for Atlanta Braves signing Type C free-agent C Charlie O'Brien. ... Selected by Minnesota Twins organization in supplemental round ("sandwich pick" between first and second rounds, 50th pick overall) of 1997 free-agent draft; pick received as compensation for failure to sign 1996 first-round pick Travis Lee. ... On disabled list (April 8-May 11, 2004). ... Signed as a free agent by Washington Nationals (February 8, 2006). ... Released by Nationals (July 20, 2006). **STATISTICAL NOTES:** Career major league grand slams: 1. **MISCELLANEOUS NOTES:** Member of 1996 U.S. Olympic baseball team.

2006 GAMES PLAYED BY POSITION (MLB): C—13, 1B—6, DH—2.

Year	Team (League)	Pos.	G	AB	R	H	2B	3B	HR	RBI	BB	SO	HBP	GDP	SB-CS	Avg.	OBP	SLG	OPS	E	Avg.
																				FIELDING	
													BATTING									
1998—	Fort Wayne (Midw.)	C	64	225	33	62	17	1	9	40	34	45	8	9	0-0	.276	.387	.480	.867	1	.997
—	Fort Myers (FSL)	C	51	200	32	61	9	1	12	51	21	35	4	6	2-1	.305	.372	.540	.912	3	.991
—	Salt Lake (PCL)	C	3	13	2	4	1	0	2	4	0	7	0	0	0-0	.308	.308	.846	1.154	0	1.000
1999—	Fort Myers (FSL)	C	89	333	54	93	20	1	20	69	42	51	3	10	0-0	.279	.364	.526	.890	8	.983
—	Salt Lake (PCL)	C	29	119	23	36	4	1	10	30	5	22	1	8	0-1	.303	.331	.605	.936	0	1.000
2000—	Minnesota (A.L.)	C-1B-DH	56	167	18	29	10	0	5	17	17	38	2	6	0-0	.174	.254	.383	.577	4	.989

L

Year	Team (League)	Pos.	G	AB	R	H	2B	3B	HR	RBI	BB	SO	HBP	GDP	SB-CS	Avg.	OBP	SLG	OPS	E	Avg.
	—New Britain (East.)	C	54	195	33	55	12	1	10	38	29	34	6	8	0-0	.282	.391	.508	.899	10	.970
	—Salt Lake (PCL)	C-1B	16	65	15	20	5	0	5	15	4	11	0	4	0-0	.308	.348	.615	.963	0	1.000
2001	—Edmonton (PCL)	C-1B	101	396	53	130	17	0	20	80	36	95	6	8	0-2	.328	.390	.523	.913	5	.980
	—Minnesota (A.L.)	DH-C-1B	15	40	6	17	5	0	3	12	0	8	1	0	0-1	.425	.429	.775	1.204	0	1.000
2002	—Edmonton (PCL)	C-1B	46	174	36	61	7	1	12	50	17	34	4	1	2-0	.351	.412	.609	1.021	1	.993
	—Minnesota (A.L.)	DH-1B-C	63	181	19	47	11	1	7	27	13	38	0	5	0-2	.260	.306	.448	.754	1	.984
2003	—Minnesota (A.L.)	DH-C-1B	107	345	39	99	19	0	17	64	25	82	4	8	0-1	.287	.342	.490	.832	3	.985
2004	—Minnesota (A.L.)	DH-C-1B	88	264	25	71	14	0	9	39	16	60	5	7	0-0	.269	.321	.424	.745	5	.983
2005	—Minnesota (A.L.)	DH-1B-C	101	304	33	79	5	0	17	50	41	85	4	7	0-0	.260	.354	.444	.798	3	.986
2006	—Wash. (N.L.)	C-1B-DH	39	67	5	16	3	0	2	9	11	17	1	2	0-0	.239	.350	.373	.723	3	.964
	—New Orleans (PCL)		5	15	0	4	1	0	0	2	0	4	0	1	0-0	.267	.267	.333	.600	0	1.000
	American League totals (6 years)		430	1301	140	342	64	1	58	209	112	311	16	33	0-4	.263	.327	.447	.774	16	.986
	National League totals (1 year)		39	67	5	16	3	0	2	9	11	17	1	2	0-0	.239	.350	.373	.723	3	.964
	Major League totals (7 years)		469	1368	145	358	67	1	60	218	123	328	17	35	0-4	.262	.328	.444	.772	19	.984

DIVISION SERIES RECORD

Year	Team (League)	Pos.	G	AB	R	H	2B	3B	HR	RBI	BB	SO	HBP	GDP	SB-CS	Avg.	OBP	SLG	OPS	E	Avg.
2002	—Minnesota (A.L.)	DH	3	9	1	4	0	0	0	1	0	3	0	1	0-0	.444	.444	.444	.889	0	...
2003	—Minnesota (A.L.)	DH	3	11	1	1	0	0	0	0	1	4	0	0	0-0	.091	.167	.091	.258	0	...
2004	—Minnesota (A.L.)	1B-C	3	3	0	1	0	0	0	0	1	1	0	0	0-0	.333	.500	.333	.833	0	1.000
	Division series totals (3 years)		9	23	2	6	0	0	0	1	2	8	0	1	0-0	.261	.320	.261	.581	0	1.000

CHAMPIONSHIP SERIES RECORD

Year	Team (League)	Pos.	G	AB	R	H	2B	3B	HR	RBI	BB	SO	HBP	GDP	SB-CS	Avg.	OBP	SLG	OPS	E	Avg.
2002	—Minnesota (A.L.)	DH	1	3	0	1	0	0	0	0	0	1	0	0	0-0	.333	.333	.333	.667	0	...

2006 LEFTY-RIGHTY SPLITS

vs.	Avg.	AB	H	2B	3B	HR	RBI	BB	SO	OBP	Slg.	vs.	Avg.	AB	H	2B	3B	HR	RBI	BB	SO	OBP	Slg.
L	.229	35	8	1	0	1	5	8	10	.386	.343	R	.250	32	8	2	0	1	4	3	7	.306	.406

LEDEE, RICKY   OF

PERSONAL: Born November 22, 1973, in Ponce, Puerto Rico. ... 6-1/216. ... Bats left, throws left. ... Full name: Ricardo Alberto Ledee. ... Name pronounced: la-DAY. ... High school: Colonel Nuestra Sonora de Valvanera (Coano, Puerto.Rico). **TRANSACTIONS/CAREER NOTES:** Selected by New York Yankees organization in 16th round of 1990 free-agent draft. ... Traded by Yankees with two players to be named to Cleveland Indians for OF David Justice (June 29, 2000); Indians acquired P Jake Westbrook and P Zach Day to complete deal (July 24, 2000). ... Traded by Indians to Texas Rangers for 1B/DH David Segui (July 28, 2000). ... On disabled list (March 23-June 13, 2001); included rehabilitation assignment to Oklahoma. ... Signed as a free agent by Philadelphia Phillies (January 29, 2002). ... On disabled list (June 23-July 8, 2004). ... Traded by Phillies with P Alfredo Simon to San Francisco Giants for P Felix Rodriguez (July 30, 2004). ... Signed as a free agent by Los Angeles Dodgers (December 7, 2004). ... On disabled list (June 7-July 8, 2005). ... On disabled list (May 2-July 14, 2006); included rehabilitation assignment to Jacksonville. ... Claimed on waivers by New York Mets (August 8, 2006). **STATISTICAL NOTES:** Career major league grand slams: 2.
2006 GAMES PLAYED BY POSITION (MLB): OF—13.

Year	Team (League)	Pos.	G	AB	R	H	2B	3B	HR	RBI	BB	SO	HBP	GDP	SB-CS	Avg.	OBP	SLG	OPS	E	Avg.
1990	—GC Yankees (GCL)	OF	19	37	5	4	2	0	0	1	6	18	0	1	2-0	.108	.233	.162	.395	0	1.000
1991	—GC Yankees (GCL)	OF	47	165	22	44	6	2	0	18	22	40	0	3	3-1	.267	.351	.327	.678	6	.934
1992	—GC Yankees (GCL)	OF	52	179	25	41	9	2	2	23	24	47	1	2	1-4	.229	.322	.335	.657	2	.971
1993	—Oneonta (NYP)	OF	52	192	32	49	7	6	8	20	25	46	2	2	7-5	.255	.347	.479	.826	3	.969
1994	—Greensboro (S. Atl.)	OF	134	484	87	121	23	9	22	71	91	126	4	7	10-11	.250	.369	.471	.840	5	.973
1995	—Greensboro (S. Atl.)	OF	89	335	65	90	16	6	14	49	51	66	2	3	10-4	.269	.368	.478	.845	3	.982
1996	—Norwich (East.)	OF	39	137	27	50	11	1	8	37	16	25	1	4	2-2	.365	.421	.635	1.056	1	.975
	—Columbus (Int'l)	OF	96	358	79	101	22	6	21	64	44	95	1	4	6-3	.282	.360	.553	.914	5	.952
1997	—Columbus (Int'l)	OF-DH	43	170	38	52	12	1	10	39	21	49	1	5	4-0	.306	.385	.565	.950	2	.966
	—GC Yankees (GCL)	DH-OF	7	21	3	7	1	0	0	2	2	4	1	1	0-0	.333	.417	.381	.798	0	1.000
1998	—Columbus (Int'l)	OF-DH	96	360	70	102	21	1	19	41	54	108	4	7	7-2	.283	.378	.506	.884	4	.971
	—New York (A.L.)	OF	42	79	13	19	5	2	1	12	7	29	0	1	3-1	.241	.299	.392	.691	1	.981
1999	—New York (A.L.)	OF-DH	88	250	45	69	13	5	9	40	28	73	0	2	4-3	.276	.346	.476	.822	9	.942
	—Columbus (Int'l)	OF	30	115	18	29	7	1	4	15	17	29	0	1	4-2	.252	.346	.435	.781	3	.953
2000	—New York (A.L.)	OF-DH	62	191	23	46	11	1	7	31	26	39	1	7	7-3	.241	.332	.419	.751	2	.979
	—Cleveland (A.L.)	OF	17	63	13	14	2	1	2	8	8	9	0	3	0-0	.222	.310	.381	.691	0	1.000
	—Texas (A.L.)	OF	58	213	23	50	6	3	4	38	25	50	1	7	6-3	.235	.317	.347	.664	3	.977
2001	—Oklahoma (PCL)	OF	4	16	4	8	1	0	1	3	1	1	0	1	0-0	.500	.529	.750	1.279	0	1.000
	—Texas (A.L.)	OF	78	242	33	56	21	1	2	36	23	58	3	3	3-3	.231	.303	.351	.654	4	.977
2002	—Philadelphia (N.L.)	OF	96	203	33	46	13	1	8	23	35	50	1	3	1-2	.227	.342	.419	.760	0	1.000
2003	—Philadelphia (N.L.)	OF-DH	121	255	37	63	15	2	13	46	34	59	0	4	0-0	.247	.334	.475	.809	0	1.000
2004	—Philadelphia (N.L.)	OF-DH	73	123	19	35	7	0	7	26	22	27	0	5	2-0	.285	.393	.512	.905	0	1.000
	—San Francisco (N.L.)	OF	31	53	6	6	2	0	0	4	5	20	1	1	1-0	.113	.200	.151	.351	1	.960
2005	—Los Angeles (N.L.)	OF	102	237	31	66	16	1	7	39	20	55	3	5	0-0	.278	.335	.443	.778	2	.975
2006	—Jacksonville (Sou.)		3	10	0	1	0	0	0	1	0	4	0	0	0-0	.100	.250	.100	.350	1	1.000
	—Los Angeles (N.L.)	OF	43	53	4	13	5	0	1	8	2	10	0	3	1-0	.245	.273	.396	.669	0	1.000
	—Norfolk (Int'l)		4	12	1	1	0	0	0	1	0	2	0	0	0-0	.083	.083	.083	.167	0	1.000
	—New York (N.L.)	OF	27	32	4	3	1	0	1	4	4	6	0	0	0-0	.094	.194	.219	.413	0	1.000
	American League totals (4 years)		345	1038	150	254	58	13	25	165	117	258	5	23	23-13	.245	.322	.398	.720	18	.971
	National League totals (5 years)		493	956	134	232	59	4	37	147	122	227	5	21	5-2	.243	.329	.429	.758	3	.992
	Major League totals (9 years)		838	1994	284	486	117	17	62	312	239	485	10	44	28-15	.244	.325	.413	.738	21	.979

DIVISION SERIES RECORD

Year	Team (League)	Pos.	G	AB	R	H	2B	3B	HR	RBI	BB	SO	HBP	GDP	SB-CS	Avg.	OBP	SLG	OPS	E	Avg.
1998	—New York (A.L.)		Did not play.																		
1999	—New York (A.L.)	OF	3	11	1	3	2	0	0	2	1	5	0	0	0-0	.273	.333	.455	.788	0	1.000

CHAMPIONSHIP SERIES RECORD

Year	Team (League)	Pos.	G	AB	R	H	2B	3B	HR	RBI	BB	SO	HBP	GDP	SB-CS	Avg.	OBP	SLG	OPS	E	Avg.
1998	—New York (A.L.)	DH-OF	3	5	0	0	0	0	0	0	0	0	0	0	0-0	.000	.000	.000	.000	0	1.000
1999	—New York (A.L.)	DH-OF	3	8	0	2	0	0	1	4	1	4	0	0	0-1	.250	.333	.625	.958	1	.750
	Champ. series totals (2 years)		6	13	0	2	0	0	1	4	1	4	0	0	0-1	.154	.214	.385	.599	1	.857

Year	Team (League)	Pos.	G	AB	R	H	2B	3B	HR	RBI	BB	SO	HBP	GDP	SB-CS	Avg.	OBP	SLG	OPS	E	Avg.
1998— New York (A.L.)		OF	4	10	1	6	3	0	0	4	2	1	0	0	0-1	.600	.615	.900	1.515	0	1.000
1999— New York (A.L.)		OF	3	10	0	2	1	0	0	1	1	4	0	0	0-0	.200	.273	.300	.573	0	1.000
World series totals (2 years)			7	20	1	8	4	0	0	5	3	5	0	0	0-1	.400	.458	.600	1.058	0	1.000

2006 LEFTY-RIGHTY SPLITS

vs.	Avg.	AB	H	2B	3B	HR	RBI	BB	SO	OBP	Slg.	vs.	Avg.	AB	H	2B	3B	HR	RBI	BB	SO	OBP	Slg.
L	.111	9	1	0	0	0	1	0	3	.111	.111	R	.197	76	15	6	0	2	8	6	13	.256	.355

LEDEZMA, WILFREDO — P

PERSONAL: Born January 21, 1981, in Guarico, Venezuela. ... 6-4/212. ... Throws left, bats left. ... Full name: Wilfredo Jose Ledezma. ... Name pronounced: la-DEZ-ma. ... College: Ciudad Jardin University. **TRANSACTIONS/CAREER NOTES:** Signed as a non-drafted free agent by Boston Red Sox organization (April 3, 1998). ... Selected by Detroit Tigers from Red Sox organization in Rule 5 major league draft (December 16, 2002).
CAREER HITTING: 0-for-0 (.000), 0 R, 0 2B, 0 3B, 0 HR, 0 RBI.

Year	Team (League)	W	L	Pct.	ERA	WHIP	G	GS	CG	ShO	Hld.	Sv.-Opp.	IP	H	R	ER	HR	BB-IBB	SO	Avg.
1999— GC Red Sox (GCL)		5	1	.833	3.30	1.24	13	6	0	0	...	1-...	57.1	51	28	21	2	20-0	52	.233
2000— Augusta (S. Atl.)		2	4	.333	5.13	1.65	14	14	0	0	...	0-...	52.2	51	33	30	3	36-0	60	.254
2001—	Did not play.																			
2002— Augusta (S. Atl.)		2	2	.500	3.80	1.31	5	5	0	0	...	0-...	23.2	23	10	10	0	8-0	38	.250
— GC Red Sox (GCL)		0	0	...	6.00	1.33	1	0	0	0	...	0-...	3.0	4	2	2	0	0-0	3	.308
2003— Detroit (A.L.)		3	7	.300	5.79	1.60	34	8	0	0	1	0-1	84.0	99	55	54	12	35-3	49	.297
2004— Erie (East.)		10	3	.769	2.42	1.07	17	16	2	1	...	0-...	111.2	95	36	30	8	24-0	98	.228
— Detroit (A.L.)		4	3	.571	4.39	1.37	15	8	0	0	0	0-1	53.1	55	28	26	3	18-0	29	.272
2005— Detroit (A.L.)		2	4	.333	7.07	1.71	10	10	0	0	0	0-0	49.2	61	46	39	10	24-0	30	.303
— Toledo (Int'l)		5	3	.625	5.29	1.55	11	10	0	0	0	0-0	51.0	52	30	30	3	27-0	44	.260
2006— Toledo (Int'l)		4	3	.571	2.52	1.16	12	12	0	0	0	0-0	71.1	60	22	20	6	23-1	66	.235
— Detroit (A.L.)		3	3	.500	3.58	1.38	24	7	0	0	2	0-1	60.1	60	28	24	5	23-0	39	.254
Major League totals (4 years)		12	17	.414	5.20	1.52	83	33	0	0	3	0-3	247.1	275	157	143	30	100-3	147	.283

CHAMPIONSHIP SERIES RECORD

Year	Team (League)	W	L	Pct.	ERA	WHIP	G	GS	CG	ShO	Hld.	Sv.-Opp.	IP	H	R	ER	HR	BB-IBB	SO	Avg.
2006— Detroit (A.L.)		1	0	1.000	3.38	1.13	2	0	0	0	0	0-0	2.2	2	1	1	1	1-0	1	.200

WORLD SERIES RECORD

Year	Team (League)	W	L	Pct.	ERA	WHIP	G	GS	CG	ShO	Hld.	Sv.-Opp.	IP	H	R	ER	HR	BB-IBB	SO	Avg.
2006— Detroit (A.L.)		0	0	...	0.00	1.50	1	0	0	0	0	0-0	1.1	2	0	0	0	0-0	1	.333

2006 LEFTY-RIGHTY SPLITS

vs.	Avg.	AB	H	2B	3B	HR	RBI	BB	SO	OBP	Slg.	vs.	Avg.	AB	H	2B	3B	HR	RBI	BB	SO	OBP	Slg.
L	.241	79	19	3	1	0	12	4	14	.286	.304	R	.261	157	41	8	1	5	16	19	25	.343	.420

LEE, CARLOS — OF

PERSONAL: Born June 20, 1976, in Aguadulce, Panama. ... 6-2/240. ... Bats right, throws right. ... Full name: Carlos Noriel Lee. ... High school: Rodolfo Chiari (Panama). **TRANSACTIONS/CAREER NOTES:** Signed as a non-drafted free agent by Chicago White Sox organization (February 8, 1994). ... On suspended list (April 28-May 1, 2000). ... Traded by White Sox to Milwaukee Brewers for OF Scott Podsednik, P Luis Vizcaino and a player to be named (December 13, 2004); White Sox acquired 1B Travis Hinton to complete the deal (January 10, 2005). ... Traded by Brewers with OF Nelson Cruz to Texas Rangers for OFs Kevin Mench and Laynce Nix and Ps Francisco Cordero and Julian Cordero (July 28, 2006). **HONORS:** Named outfielder on N.L. Silver Slugger team (2005). **STATISTICAL NOTES:** Hit home run in first major league at-bat (May 7, 1999). ... Career major league grand slams: 9.
2006 GAMES PLAYED BY POSITION (MLB): OF—149, DH—12.

Year	Team (League)	Pos.	G	AB	R	H	2B	3B	HR	RBI	BB	SO	HBP	GDP	SB-CS	Avg.	OBP	SLG	OPS	E	Avg.
1994— GC Whi. Sox (GCL)		3B	29	56	6	7	1	0	0	1	4	8	0	1	0-1	.125	.183	.143	.326	2	.959
1995— Hickory (S. Atl.)		3B	63	218	18	54	9	1	4	30	8	34	1	7	1-5	.248	.278	.353	.631	19	.848
— Bristol (Appal.)		1B-3B	67	269	43	93	17	1	7	45	8	34	2	6	17-7	.346	.365	.494	.860	18	.914
1996— Hickory (S. Atl.)		1B-3B	109	480	65	150	23	6	8	70	23	50	0	15	18-13	.313	.337	.435	.772	32	.923
1997— Win.-Salem (Car.)		3B-DH	139	546	81	173	50	4	17	82	36	65	2	12	11-5	.317	.357	.516	.874	34	.906
1998— Birmingham (Sou.)		3B-DH	138	549	77	166	33	2	21	106	39	55	2	32	11-5	.302	.350	.485	.834	35	.902
1999— Charlotte (Int'l)	3B-OF-1B	25	94	16	33	5	0	4	20	8	14	1	3	2-1	.351	.396	.532	.928	4	.951
— Chicago (A.L.)	OF-DH-1B	127	492	66	144	32	2	16	84	13	72	4	11	4-2	.293	.312	.463	.775	5	.979
2000— Chicago (A.L.)		OF-DH	152	572	107	172	29	2	24	92	38	94	3	17	13-4	.301	.345	.484	.829	3	.990
2001— Chicago (A.L.)		OF-DH	150	558	75	150	33	3	24	84	38	85	6	15	17-7	.269	.321	.468	.789	6	.969
2002— Chicago (A.L.)		OF-DH	140	492	82	130	26	2	26	80	75	73	2	5	1-4	.264	.359	.484	.843	1	.996
2003— Chicago (A.L.)		OF-DH	158	623	100	181	35	1	31	113	37	91	4	10	18-4	.291	.331	.499	.830	7	.978
2004— Chicago (A.L.)		OF-DH	153	591	103	180	37	0	31	99	54	86	7	10	11-5	.305	.366	.525	.891	0	1.000
2005— Milwaukee (N.L.)		OF	162	618	85	164	41	6	32	114	57	87	2	8	13-4	.265	.324	.487	.811	6	.981
2006— Milwaukee (N.L.)		OF-DH	102	388	60	111	18	0	28	81	38	39	2	13	12-2	.286	.347	.549	.896	4	.974
— Texas (A.L.)		OF-DH	59	236	42	76	19	1	9	35	20	26	0	9	7-0	.322	.369	.525	.895	2	.976
American League totals (7 years)			939	3564	575	1033	211	11	161	587	275	527	26	87	71-26	.290	.342	.491	.833	26	.985
National League totals (2 years)			264	1006	145	275	59	6	60	195	95	126	4	21	25-6	.273	.333	.511	.844	10	.979
Major League totals (8 years)			1203	4570	720	1308	270	11	221	782	370	653	30	108	96-32	.286	.340	.495	.835	36	.984

DIVISION SERIES RECORD

Year	Team (League)	Pos.	G	AB	R	H	2B	3B	HR	RBI	BB	SO	HBP	GDP	SB-CS	Avg.	OBP	SLG	OPS	E	Avg.
2000— Chicago (A.L.)		OF	3	11	0	1	0	0	0	1	0	2	0	0	0-0	.091	.083	.182	.265	0	1.000

ALL-STAR GAME RECORD

			G	AB	R	H	2B	3B	HR	RBI	BB	SO	HBP	GDP	SB-CS	Avg.	OBP	SLG	OPS	E	Avg.
All-Star Game totals (2 years)			2	4	0	0	0	0	0	0	1	0	0	0		.000	.000	.000	.000	0	...

2006 LEFTY-RIGHTY SPLITS

vs.	Avg.	AB	H	2B	3B	HR	RBI	BB	SO	OBP	Slg.	vs.	Avg.	AB	H	2B	3B	HR	RBI	BB	SO	OBP	Slg.
L	.313	147	46	6	1	6	20	11	14	.354	.490	R	.296	477	141	31	0	31	96	47	51	.356	.556

LEE, CLIFF — P

PERSONAL: Born August 30, 1978, in Benton, Ark. ... 6-3/190. ... Throws left, bats left. ... Full name: Clifton Phifer Lee. ... High school: Benton (Ark.). ... College: Arkansas.
TRANSACTIONS/CAREER NOTES: Selected by Montreal Expos organization in fourth round of 2000 free-agent draft. ... Traded by Expos with 1B Lee Stevens, SS Brandon

Phillips and OF Grady Sizemore to Cleveland Indians for P Bartolo Colon and future considerations (June 27, 2002); Expos acquired P Tim Drew to complete deal (June 28, 2002). ... On disabled list (March 29-May 30, 2003); included rehabilitation assignment to Kinston. ... On suspended list (June 24-July 1, 2004).

CAREER HITTING: 2-for-17 (.118), 0 R, 0 2B, 0 3B, 0 HR, 0 RBI.

Year	Team (League)	W	L	Pct.	ERA	WHIP	G	GS	CG	ShO	Hld.	Sv.-Opp.	IP	H	R	ER	HR	BB-IBB	SO	Avg.
2000—	Cape Fear (S. Atl.)	1	4	.200	5.24	1.93	11	11	0	0	...	0-...	44.2	50	39	26	1	36-0	63	.281
2001—	Jupiter (Fla. St.)	6	7	.462	2.79	1.13	21	20	0	0	...	0-...	109.2	78	43	34	13	46-0	129	.199
2002—	Harrisburg (East.)	7	2	.778	3.23	0.97	15	15	0	0	...	0-...	86.1	61	31	31	12	23-0	105	.197
	—Akron (East.)	2	1	.667	5.40	1.26	3	3	0	0	...	0-...	16.2	11	11	10	1	10-0	18	.180
	—Buffalo (Int'l)	3	2	.600	3.77	1.35	8	8	0	0	...	0-...	43.0	36	18	18	7	22-0	30	.229
	—Cleveland (A.L.)	0	1	.000	1.74	1.35	2	2	0	0	0	0-0	10.1	6	2	2	0	8-1	6	.171
2003—	Kinston (Carol.)	0	0	...	0.00	0.70	1	1	0	0	...	0-...	4.1	0	1	0	0	3-0	4	.000
	—Akron (East.)	1	0	1.000	1.50	0.90	2	2	0	0	...	0-...	12.0	7	2	2	1	4-0	13	.167
	—Buffalo (Int'l)	6	1	.857	3.27	1.50	11	11	0	0	...	0-...	63.1	62	24	23	4	31-0	61	.261
	—Cleveland (A.L.)	3	3	.500	3.61	1.17	9	9	0	0	0	0-0	52.1	41	28	21	7	20-1	44	.220
2004—	Cleveland (A.L.)	14	8	.636	5.43	1.50	33	33	#0	0	0	0-0	179.0	188	113	108	30	81-1	161	.268
2005—	Cleveland (A.L.)	18	5	* .783	3.79	1.22	32	32	1	0	0	0-0	202.0	194	91	85	22	52-1	143	.251
2006—	Cleveland (A.L.)	14	11	.560	4.40	1.41	33	33	1	0	0	0-0	200.2	224	114	98	29	58-3	129	.278
	Major League totals (5 years)	49	28	.636	4.39	1.35	109	109	2	0	0	0-0	644.1	653	348	314	88	219-7	483	.261

2006 LEFTY-RIGHTY SPLITS

vs.	Avg.	AB	H	2B	3B	HR	RBI	BB	SO	OBP	Slg.	vs.	Avg.	AB	H	2B	3B	HR	RBI	BB	SO	OBP	Slg.
L	.261	176	46	11	0	6	21	7	25	.302	.426	R	.282	631	178	36	1	23	80	51	104	.338	.452

LEE, DERREK — 1B

PERSONAL: Born September 6, 1975, in Sacramento. ... 6-5/245. ... Bats right, throws right. ... Full name: Derrek Leon Lee. ... High school: El Camino (Sacramento). ... Nephew of Leron Lee, outfielder with four major league teams (1969-76). **TRANSACTIONS/CAREER NOTES:** Selected by San Diego Padres in first round (14th pick overall) of 1993 free-agent draft. ... Traded by Padres with Ps Rafael Medina and Steve Hoff to Florida Marlins for P Kevin Brown (December 15, 1997). ... Traded by Marlins to Chicago Cubs for 1B Hee Seop Choi and P Mike Nannini (November 25, 2003). ... On disabled list (April 20-June 25, 2006); included rehabilitation assignment to Iowa. ... On disabled list (July 24-August 28, 2006). **HONORS:** Won N.L. Gold Glove at first base (2003 and 2005). ... Named first baseman on N.L. Silver Slugger team (2005). **STATISTICAL NOTES:** Career major league grand slams: 7.

2006 GAMES PLAYED BY POSITION (MLB): 1B—47, DH—1.

Year	Team (League)	Pos.	G	AB	R	H	2B	3B	HR	RBI	BB	SO	HBP	GDP	SB-CS	Avg.	OBP	SLG	OPS	E	Avg.
1993—	Ariz. Padres (Ariz.)	1B	15	52	11	17	1	1	2	5	6	7	0	1	4-0	.327	.397	.500	.897	2	.985
	—Rancho Cuca. (Calif.)	1B-DH	20	73	13	20	5	1	1	10	10	20	1	0	0-2	.274	.369	.411	.780	5	.960
1994—	Rancho Cuca. (Calif.)	1B	126	442	66	118	19	2	8	53	42	95	7	11	18-14	.267	.336	.373	.709	4	.988
1995—	Rancho Cuca. (Calif.)	1B	128	502	82	151	25	2	23	95	49	130	7	8	14-7	.301	.366	.496	.862	18	.983
	—Memphis (Sou.)	1B	2	9	0	1	0	0	0	1	0	2	0	0	0-0	.111	.111	.111	.222	0	1.000
1996—	Memphis (Sou.)	1B-3B-DH	134	500	98	140	39	2	34	104	65	170	2	8	13-6	.280	.360	.570	.930	11	.991
1997—	Las Vegas (PCL)	1B	125	472	86	153	29	2	13	64	60	116	0	9	17-3	.324	.399	.477	.876	9	.992
	—San Diego (N.L.)	1B	22	54	-9	14	3	0	1	4	9	24	0	1	0-0	.259	.365	.370	.735	0	1.000
1998—	Florida (N.L.)	1B	141	454	62	106	29	1	17	74	47	120	10	12	5-2	.233	.318	.414	.732	8	.993
1999—	Florida (N.L.)	1B	70	218	21	45	9	1	5	20	17	70	0	3	2-1	.206	.263	.326	.588	3	.994
	—Calgary (PCL)	1B-DH	89	339	60	96	20	1	19	73	30	90	4	7	3-4	.283	.345	.516	.861	14	.983
2000—	Florida (N.L.)	1B	158	477	70	134	18	3	28	70	63	123	4	14	0-3	.281	.368	.507	.875	8	.993
2001—	Florida (N.L.)	1B	158	561	83	158	37	4	21	75	50	126	8	18	4-2	.282	.346	.474	.820	8	.994
2002—	Florida (N.L.)	1B	* 162	581	95	157	35	7	27	86	98	164	5	14	19-9	.270	.378	.494	.872	12	.992
2003—	Florida (N.L.)	1B	155	539	91	146	31	2	31	92	88	131	10	9	21-8	.271	.379	.508	.888	5	.996
2004—	Chicago (N.L.)	1B	161	605	90	168	39	1	32	98	68	128	8	14	12-5	.278	.356	.504	.860	6	.996
2005—	Chicago (N.L.)	1B	158	594	120	* 199	* 50	3	46	107	85	109	5	12	15-3	* .335	.418	* .662	* 1.080	6	.996
2006—	Iowa (PCL)		1	4	0	1	0	0	0	1	0	0	0	0	0-0	.250	.250	.250	.500	0	1.000
	—Chicago (N.L.)	1B-DH	50	175	30	50	9	0	8	30	25	41	0	11	8-4	.286	.368	.474	.842	5	.988
	Major League totals (10 years)		1235	4258	671	1177	260	22	216	656	550	1036	50	108	86-37	.276	.363	.500	.863	61	.994

DIVISION SERIES RECORD

Year	Team (League)	Pos.	G	AB	R	H	2B	3B	HR	RBI	BB	SO	HBP	GDP	SB-CS	Avg.	OBP	SLG	OPS	E	Avg.
2003—	Florida (N.L.)	1B	4	16	2	4	1	0	0	2	1	2	2	0	1-0	.250	.368	.313	.681	0	1.000

CHAMPIONSHIP SERIES RECORD

Year	Team (League)	Pos.	G	AB	R	H	2B	3B	HR	RBI	BB	SO	HBP	GDP	SB-CS	Avg.	OBP	SLG	OPS	E	Avg.
2003—	Florida (N.L.)	1B	7	32	2	6	2	0	1	4	1	8	1	2	1-0	.188	.235	.344	.579	0	1.000

WORLD SERIES RECORD

Year	Team (League)	Pos.	G	AB	R	H	2B	3B	HR	RBI	BB	SO	HBP	GDP	SB-CS	Avg.	OBP	SLG	OPS	E	Avg.
2003—	Florida (N.L.)	1B	6	24	2	5	0	0	0	2	1	7	0	1	0-0	.208	.240	.208	.448	1	.977

ALL-STAR GAME RECORD

			G	AB	R	H	2B	3B	HR	RBI	BB	SO	HBP	GDP	SB-CS	Avg.	OBP	SLG	OPS	E	Avg.
	All-Star Game totals (1 year)		1	3	0	1	1	0	0	0	0	1	0	0	0-0	.333	.333	.667	1.000	0	1.000

2006 LEFTY-RIGHTY SPLITS

vs.	Avg.	AB	H	2B	3B	HR	RBI	BB	SO	OBP	Slg.	vs.	Avg.	AB	H	2B	3B	HR	RBI	BB	SO	OBP	Slg.
L	.292	48	14	4	0	0	3	7	8	.382	.375	R	.283	127	36	5	0	8	27	18	33	.362	.512

LEE, TRAVIS — 1B

PERSONAL: Born May 26, 1975, in San Diego. ... 6-3/225. ... Bats left, throws left. ... Full name: Travis Reynolds Lee. ... High school: Olympia (Wash.). ... College: San Diego State. **TRANSACTIONS/CAREER NOTES:** Selected by Minnesota Twins organization in first round (second pick overall) of 1996 free-agent draft. ... Signed as a free agent by Arizona Diamondbacks organization (October 15, 1996). ... Loaned by Diamondbacks organization to Milwaukee Brewers organization (June 5, 1997-remainder of season). ... On disabled list (July 25-August 9, 1998; and August 16-September 9, 1999). ... On disabled list (May 25-June 9, 2000); included rehabilitation assignment to El Paso. ... Traded by Diamondbacks with Ps Vicente Padilla, Omar Daal and Nelson Figueroa to Philadelphia Phillies for P Curt Schilling (July 26, 2000). ... Signed as a free agent by Tampa Bay Devil Rays (February 6, 2003). ... On disabled list (April 14-29, 2003). ... Signed as a free agent by New York Yankees (March 2, 2004). ... On disabled list (March 29-April 17 and May 1, 2004-remainder of season); included rehabilitation assignment to Tampa. ... Signed as a free agent by Devil Rays (February 4, 2005). ... On disabled list (May 2-20, 2005). ... Released by Devil Rays (September 10, 2006). **STATISTICAL NOTES:** Career major league grand slams: 3. **MISCELLANEOUS NOTES:** Member of 1996 U.S. Olympic baseball team.

2006 GAMES PLAYED BY POSITION (MLB): 1B—112.

Year	Team (League)	Pos.	G	AB	R	H	2B	3B	HR	RBI	BB	SO	HBP	GDP	SB-CS	Avg.	OBP	SLG	OPS	E	Avg.
1997—	High Desert (Calif.)	1B-DH	61	226	63	82	18	1	18	63	47	36	3	8	5-1	.363	.473	.690	1.163	1	.998

Year	Team (League)	Pos.	G	AB	R	H	2B	3B	HR	RBI	BB	SO	HBP	GDP	SB-CS	Avg.	OBP	SLG	OPS	E	Avg.
—	Tucson (PCL)	1B-DH-OF	59	227	42	68	16	2	14	46	31	46	2	10	2-0	.300	.387	.573	.960	3	.993
1998	Arizona (N.L.)	1B	146	562	71	151	20	2	22	72	67	123	0	13	8-1	.269	.346	.429	.775	3	.998
1999	Arizona (N.L.)	1B-OF	120	375	57	89	16	2	9	50	58	50	0	10	17-3	.237	.337	.363	.700	3	.997
2000	Arizona (N.L.)	OF-1B	72	224	34	52	13	0	8	40	25	46	0	6	5-1	.232	.308	.397	.705	4	.983
—	El Paso (Texas)	1B-OF	3	10	0	2	0	0	0	0	2	1	0	1	0-0	.200	.333	.200	.533	0	1.000
—	Tucson (PCL)	1B-OF	7	30	4	11	4	0	0	3	1	6	0	1	1-0	.367	.387	.500	.887	0	1.000
—	Philadelphia (N.L.)	1B-OF	56	180	19	43	11	1	1	14	40	33	2	6	3-0	.239	.381	.328	.709	1	1.000
2001	Philadelphia (N.L.)	1B	157	555	75	143	34	2	20	90	71	109	4	15	3-4	.258	.341	.434	.775	6	.996
2002	Philadelphia (N.L.)	1B	153	536	55	142	26	2	13	70	54	104	0	12	5-3	.265	.331	.394	.725	6	.996
2003	Tampa Bay (A.L.)	1B-DH	145	542	75	149	37	3	19	70	64	97	0	13	6-2	.275	.348	.459	.807	3	.998
2004	Tampa (Fla. St.)	1B	3	12	2	3	1	0	0	3	1	4	0	1	0-0	.250	.308	.333	.641	0	1.000
—	New York (N.L.)	1B	7	19	1	2	1	0	0	2	1	3	0	2	0-0	.105	.150	.158	.308	0	1.000
2005	Tampa Bay (A.L.)	1B	129	404	54	110	22	2	12	49	35	66	1	7	7-4	.272	.331	.426	.757	4	.996
2006	Tampa Bay (A.L.)	1B	114	343	35	77	11	2	11	31	42	73	2	8	5-2	.224	.312	.364	.676	2	.998
American League totals (4 years)			395	1308	165	338	71	7	42	152	142	239	3	30	18-8	.258	.331	.420	.750	9	.997
National League totals (5 years)			704	2432	311	620	120	9	73	336	315	465	6	62	41-12	.255	.340	.402	.741	22	.996
Major League totals (9 years)			1099	3740	476	958	191	16	115	488	457	704	9	92	59-20	.256	.337	.408	.745	31	.996

2006 LEFTY-RIGHTY SPLITS

vs.	Avg.	AB	H	2B	3B	HR	RBI	BB	SO	OBP	Slg.	vs.	Avg.	AB	H	2B	3B	HR	RBI	BB	SO	OBP	Slg.
L	.226	93	21	2	0	7	13	6	21	.273	.473	R	.224	250	56	9	2	4	18	36	52	.325	.324

LEHR, JUSTIN — P

PERSONAL: Born August 3, 1977, in Orange, Calif. ... 6-1/200. ... Throws right, bats right. ... Full name: Charles Larry Lehr. ... High school: West Covina (Calif.). ... College: Southern California. **TRANSACTIONS/CAREER NOTES:** Selected by Detroit Tigers organization in 15th round of 1995 free-agent draft; did not sign. ... Selected by Anaheim Angels organization in 10th round of 1998 free-agent draft; did not sign. ... Selected by Oakland Athletics organization in eighth round of 1999 free-agent draft. ... Traded by Athletics with OF Nelson Cruz to Milwaukee Brewers for 3B Keith Ginter (December 15, 2004).

CAREER HITTING: 0-for-3 (.000), 0 R, 0 2B, 0 3B, 0 HR, 0 RBI.

Year	Team (League)	W	L	Pct.	ERA	WHIP	G	GS	CG	ShO	Hld.	Sv.-Opp.	IP	H	R	ER	HR	BB-IBB	SO	Avg.
1999	S. Oregon (N'west)	2	6	.250	5.95	1.87	14	4	0	0	...	0-...	42.1	62	36	28	3	17-3	40	.341
2000	Sacramento (PCL)	0	0	...	11.25	2.50	1	1	0	0	...	0-...	4.0	7	5	5	1	3-0	3	.389
—	Modesto (California)	13	6	.684	3.19	1.18	29	25	0	0	...	0-...	175.0	161	71	62	10	46-1	138	.249
2001	Midland (Texas)	11	12	.478	5.45	1.60	29	27	0	0	...	0-...	155.1	206	107	94	20	43-1	103	.318
2002	Midland (Texas)	8	3	.727	4.05	1.49	58	0	0	0	...	4-...	80.0	88	39	36	7	31-10	59	.290
2003	Sacramento (PCL)	3	2	.600	3.72	1.35	53	0	0	0	...	4-...	75.0	74	34	31	3	27-3	64	.259
2004	Sacramento (PCL)	4	2	.667	2.65	1.26	32	0	0	0	...	13-...	37.1	37	14	11	1	10-0	40	.250
—	Oakland (A.L.)	1	1	.500	5.23	1.50	27	0	0	0	5	0-1	32.2	35	19	19	3	14-2	16	.280
2005	Nashville (PCL)	7	7	.500	3.99	1.52	27	11	0	0	1	1-1	88.0	102	49	39	8	32-2	68	.290
—	Milwaukee (N.L.)	1	1	.500	3.89	1.44	23	0	0	0	3	0-1	34.2	32	19	15	4	18-2	23	.242
2006	Nashville (PCL)	4	7	.364	3.94	1.35	19	17	0	0	0	0-0	112.0	120	53	49	15	31-1	90	.278
—	Milwaukee (N.L.)	2	1	.667	8.62	1.98	16	0	0	0	0	0-0	15.2	24	16	15	2	7-1	12	.369
American League totals (1 year)		1	1	.500	5.23	1.50	27	0	0	0	5	0-1	32.2	35	19	19	3	14-2	16	.280
National League totals (2 years)		3	2	.600	5.36	1.61	39	0	0	0	3	0-1	50.1	56	35	30	6	25-3	35	.284
Major League totals (3 years)		4	3	.571	5.31	1.57	66	0	0	0	8	0-2	83.0	91	54	49	9	39-5	51	.283

2006 LEFTY-RIGHTY SPLITS

vs.	Avg.	AB	H	2B	3B	HR	RBI	BB	SO	OBP	Slg.	vs.	Avg.	AB	H	2B	3B	HR	RBI	BB	SO	OBP	Slg.
L	.323	31	10	1	0	1	6	1	6	.333	.452	R	.412	34	14	4	2	1	15	6	6	.512	.735

LEONE, JUSTIN — 3B

PERSONAL: Born March 9, 1977, in Las Vegas, Nev. ... 6-1/190. ... Bats right, throws right. ... Full name: Justin Paul Leone. ... High school: Bonanza (Las Vegas). ... College: St. Martin's. **TRANSACTIONS/CAREER NOTES:** Selected by Seattle Mariners organization in 13th round of 1999 free-agent draft. ... On disabled list (August 18, 2004-remainder of season). ... Signed as a free agent by San Diego Padres organization (November 6, 2005).

Year	Team (League)	Pos.	G	AB	R	H	2B	3B	HR	RBI	BB	SO	HBP	GDP	SB-CS	Avg.	OBP	SLG	OPS	E	Avg.
1999	Everett (N'west)	3B-SS	62	205	34	54	14	2	6	35	32	49	2	5	5-3	.263	.361	.439	.800	18	.911
2000	Wisconsin (Midw.)	3B-SS-OF																			
		2B	115	374	77	100	32	3	18	63	79	107	11	3	9-2	.267	.407	.513	.920	26	.912
2001	San Bern. (Calif.)	3B-OF	130	485	70	113	27	4	22	69	57	158	5	8	4-3	.233	.318	.441	.759	27	.927
2002	San Bern. (Calif.)	3B-OF-SS	98	358	64	89	20	5	18	58	57	98	5	9	6-0	.249	.358	.483	.841	24	.919
2003	San Antonio (Texas)	3B-SS-1B																			
		2B	135	455	103	131	38	7	21	92	92	104	3	7	20-6	.288	.405	.541	.946	21	.947
2004	Tacoma (PCL)	3B-OF-SS																			
		DH	68	253	56	68	10	5	21	51	26	82	4	4	5-6	.269	.344	.597	.931	15	.924
—	Seattle (A.L.)	3B-SS-DH	31	102	15	22	5	0	6	13	9	32	3	0	1-0	.216	.298	.441	.739	9	.895
2005	Tacoma (PCL)	3B-OF-SS	87	313	51	76	19	2	7	38	51	93	2	14	5-2	.243	.351	.383	.734	24	.915
2006	San Diego (N.L.)		1	1	0	0	0	0	0	0	0	0	0	0	0-0	.000	.000	.000	.000	0	...
—	Portland (PCL)		124	453	66	118	20	0	20	73	61	106	6	18	4-4	.260	.353	.437	.790	20	.951
American League totals (1 year)			31	102	15	22	5	0	6	13	9	32	3	0	1-0	.216	.298	.441	.739	9	.895
National League totals (1 year)			1	1	0	0	0	0	0	0	0	0	0	0	0-0	.000	.000	.000	.000	0	...
Major League totals (2 years)			32	103	15	22	5	0	6	13	9	32	3	0	1-0	.214	.296	.437	.733	9	.895

2006 LEFTY-RIGHTY SPLITS

vs.	Avg.	AB	H	2B	3B	HR	RBI	BB	SO	OBP	Slg.	vs.	Avg.	AB	H	2B	3B	HR	RBI	BB	SO	OBP	Slg.
L	.000	0	0	0	0	0	0	0	0	.000	.000	R	.000	1	0	0	0	0	0	0	0	.000	.000

LEREW, ANTHONY — P

PERSONAL: Born October 28, 1982, in Carlisle, Pa. ... 6-3/220. ... Throws right, bats left. ... Full name: Anthony Allen Lerew. **TRANSACTIONS/CAREER NOTES:** Selected by Atlanta Braves organization in 11th round of 2001 free-agent draft.

CAREER HITTING: 0-for-0 (.000), 0 R, 0 2B, 0 3B, 0 HR, 0 RBI.

Year	Team (League)	W	L	Pct.	ERA	WHIP	G	GS	CG	ShO	Hld.	Sv.-Opp.	IP	H	R	ER	HR	BB-IBB	SO	Avg.
2001	GC Braves (GCL)	1	2	.333	2.92	1.16	12	7	0	0	...	0-...	49.1	43	25	16	3	14-0	40	.228

L

Year Team (League)	W	L	Pct.	ERA	WHIP	G	GS	CG	ShO	Hld.	Sv.-Opp.	IP	H	R	ER	HR	BB-IBB	SO	Avg.
2002— Danville (Appal.)	8	3	.727	1.73	1.02	14	14	0	0	...	0-...	83.0	60	23	16	2	25-0	75	.205
2003— Rome (S. Atl.)	7	6	.538	2.38	1.08	25	25	0	0	...	0-...	143.2	112	45	38	7	43-2	127	.215
2004— Myrtle Beach (Carol.)	8	9	.471	3.75	1.33	27	27	0	0	...	0-...	144.0	145	75	60	12	46-0	125	.271
2005— Mississippi (Sou.)	6	2	.750	3.93	1.35	14	14	1	0	0	0-0	75.2	70	34	33	6	32-1	64	.246
— Richmond (Int'l)	4	4	.500	3.48	1.19	13	13	0	0	0	0-0	72.1	63	34	28	9	23-0	53	.232
— Atlanta (N.L.)	0	0	...	5.63	1.75	7	0	0	0	0	0-1	8.0	9	5	5	1	5-2	5	.290
2006— Mississippi (Sou.)	4	2	.667	2.03	1.15	9	8	0	0	0	0-0	48.2	43	18	11	1	13-0	37	.234
— Richmond (Int'l)	3	5	.375	7.48	1.80	16	15	1	0	0	0-0	71.0	92	63	59	12	36-0	69	.315
— Atlanta (N.L.)	0	0	...	22.50	4.00	1	0	0	0	0	0-0	2.0	5	5	5	0	3-0	1	.455
Major League totals (2 years)	0	0	...	9.00	2.20	8	0	0	0	0	0-1	10.0	14	10	10	1	8-2	6	.333

2006 LEFTY-RIGHTY SPLITS

vs.	Avg.	AB	H	2B	3B	HR	RBI	BB	SO	OBP	Slg.	vs.	Avg.	AB	H	2B	3B	HR	RBI	BB	SO	OBP	Slg.
L	.200	5	1	1	0	0	0	1	0	.333	.400	R	.667	6	4	0	0	0	5	2	1	.778	.667

LESTER, JON — P

PERSONAL: Born January 7, 1984, in Tacoma, Wash. ... 6-2/190. ... Throws left, bats left. ... Full name: Jonathan T. Lester. **TRANSACTIONS/CAREER NOTES:** Selected by Boston Red Sox in second round of 2002 free-agent draft. ... On disabled list (August 24, 2006-remainder of season).

CAREER HITTING: 0-for-4 (.000), 0 R, 0 2B, 0 3B, 0 HR, 0 RBI.

Year Team (League)	W	L	Pct.	ERA	WHIP	G	GS	CG	ShO	Hld.	Sv.-Opp.	IP	H	R	ER	HR	BB-IBB	SO	Avg.
2002— GC Red Sox (GCL)	0	1	.000	13.50	9.00	1	1	0	0	...	0-...	0.2	5	6	1	0	1-0	1	.714
2003— Augusta (S. Atl.)	6	9	.400	3.65	1.38	24	24	0	0	...	0-...	106.0	102	54	43	7	44-0	71	.262
2004— GC Red Sox (GCL)	0	0	...	0.00	2.00	1	1	0	0	...	0-...	1.0	0	0	0	0	2-0	1	.000
— Sarasota (Fla. St.)	7	6	.538	4.28	1.32	21	20	0	0	...	0-...	90.1	82	46	43	2	37-0	97	.245
2005— Portland (East.)	11	6	.647	2.61	1.15	26	26	3	1	0	0-0	148.1	114	52	43	10	57-0	163	.215
2006— Pawtucket (Int'l)	3	4	.429	2.70	1.46	11	11	0	0	0	0-0	46.2	43	17	14	5	25-0	43	.240
— Boston (A.L.)	7	2	.778	4.76	1.65	15	15	0	0	0	0-0	81.1	91	43	43	7	43-1	60	.294
Major League totals (1 year)	7	2	.778	4.76	1.65	15	15	0	0	0	0-0	81.1	91	43	43	7	43-1	60	.294

2006 LEFTY-RIGHTY SPLITS

vs.	Avg.	AB	H	2B	3B	HR	RBI	BB	SO	OBP	Slg.	vs.	Avg.	AB	H	2B	3B	HR	RBI	BB	SO	OBP	Slg.
L	.397	58	23	6	1	3	11	4	8	.431	.690	R	.271	251	68	14	0	4	30	39	52	.370	.375

LEWIS, COLBY — P

PERSONAL: Born August 2, 1979, in Bakersfield, Calif. ... 6-4/230. ... Throws right, bats right. ... Full name: Colby Preston Lewis. ... High school: North (Bakersfield, Calif.). ... Junior college: Bakersfield (Calif.). **TRANSACTIONS/CAREER NOTES:** Selected by Texas Rangers organization in supplemental round ("sandwich pick") between first and second rounds, 38th pick overall) of 1999 free-agent draft; pick received as part of compensation for Arizona Diamondbacks signing Type A free-agent P Todd Stottlemyre. ... On disabled list (April 18, 2004-remainder of season). ... Claimed on waivers by Detroit Tigers (October 8, 2004). ... On disabled list (April 2, 2005-entire season). ... Signed as free agent by Washington Nationals organization (November 6, 2006).

CAREER HITTING: 0-for-1 (.000), 0 R, 0 2B, 0 3B, 0 HR, 0 RBI.

Year Team (League)	W	L	Pct.	ERA	WHIP	G	GS	CG	ShO	Hld.	Sv.-Opp.	IP	H	R	ER	HR	BB-IBB	SO	Avg.
1999— Pulaski (Appalachian)	7	3	.700	1.95	1.13	14	11	1	1	...	0-...	64.2	46	24	14	3	27-0	84	.189
2000— Charlotte (Fla. St.)	11	10	.524	4.07	1.31	28	27	3	1	...	0-...	163.2	169	83	74	11	45-0	153	.270
2001— Charlotte (Fla. St.)	1	0	1.000	0.00	0.00	1	0	0	0	...	0-...	4.1	0	0	0	0	0-0	8	.000
— Tulsa (Texas)	10	10	.500	4.50	1.36	25	25	1	0	...	0-...	156.0	150	85	78	15	62-2	162	.253
2002— Texas (A.L.)	1	3	.250	6.29	1.98	15	4	0	0	1	0-2	34.1	42	26	24	4	26-2	28	.304
— Oklahoma (PCL)	5	6	.455	3.63	1.20	20	20	0	0	...	0-...	106.2	100	49	43	4	28-0	99	.245
2003— Oklahoma (PCL)	5	1	.833	3.02	1.20	7	7	0	0	...	0-...	47.2	36	16	16	6	19-0	43	.208
— Texas (A.L.)	10	9	.526	7.30	1.83	26	26	0	0	0	0-0	127.0	163	104	103	23	70-1	88	.317
2004— Texas (A.L.)	1	1	.500	4.11	1.70	3	3	0	0	0	0-0	15.1	13	7	7	1	13-0	11	.228
2005—			Did not play.																
2006— Toledo (Int'l)	6	7	.462	3.96	1.29	24	24	0	0	0	0-0	147.2	154	70	65	13	36-0	104	.271
— Detroit (A.L.)	0	0	...	3.00	3.00	2	0	0	0	0	0-0	3.0	8	1	1	1	1-0	5	.471
Major League totals (4 years)	12	13	.480	6.76	1.87	46	33	0	0	1	0-2	179.2	226	138	135	29	110-3	132	.311

2006 LEFTY-RIGHTY SPLITS

vs.	Avg.	AB	H	2B	3B	HR	RBI	BB	SO	OBP	Slg.	vs.	Avg.	AB	H	2B	3B	HR	RBI	BB	SO	OBP	Slg.
L	.429	7	3	1	0	0	0	0	2	.429	.571	R	.500	10	5	1	0	1	4	1	3	.545	.900

LEWIS, FRED — OF

PERSONAL: Born December 9, 1980, in Hattiesburg, Miss. ... 6-2/190. ... Bats left, throws right. ... Full name: Frederick Deshaun Lewis. ... College: Southern University. ... Cousin of Matt Lawton, outfielder with seven teams (1992-2006); and cousin of Marcus Lawton, outfielder with New York Yankees (1989). **TRANSACTIONS/CAREER NOTES:** Selected by Montreal Expos organization in 20th round of 2000 free-agent draft; did not sign. ... Selected by San Francisco Giants organization in second round of 2002 free-agent draft.

2006 GAMES PLAYED BY POSITION (MLB): OF—6.

Year Team (League)	Pos.	G	AB	R	H	2B	3B	HR	RBI	BB	SO	HBP	GDP	SB-CS	Avg.	OBP	SLG	OPS	E	Avg.
2002— Salem-Keizer (N'west)		58	239	43	77	9	3	1	23	26	58	3		9-6	.322	.396	.397	.793	4	...
2003— Hagerstown (SAL)		114	420	61	105	17	8	1	27	68	112	6		30-15	.250	.361	.336	.697	3	...
2004— San Jose (Calif.)		115	439	88	132	20	11	8	57	84	109	12		33-14	.301	.424	.451	.875	8	...
— Fresno (PCL)		6	23	3	7	1	0	1	2	5	5	0		1-1	.304	.429	.478	.907	1	...
2005— Norwich (East.)	OF-DH	137	512	79	140	28	7	7	47	69	124	5	9	30-13	.273	.361	.396	.757	28	.948
2006— Fresno (PCL)		120	439	85	121	20	11	12	56	68	105	4	13	18-8	.276	.375	.453	.828	5	.976
— San Francisco (N.L.)	OF	13	11	5	5	1	0	0	2	0	3	0	0	0-0	.455	.455	.545	1.000	1	.889
Major League totals (1 year)		13	11	5	5	1	0	0	2	0	3	0	0	0-0	.455	.455	.545	1.000	1	.889

2006 LEFTY-RIGHTY SPLITS

vs.	Avg.	AB	H	2B	3B	HR	RBI	BB	SO	OBP	Slg.	vs.	Avg.	AB	H	2B	3B	HR	RBI	BB	SO	OBP	Slg.
L	.500	2	1	1	0	0	1	0	0	.500	1.000	R	.444	9	4	0	0	0	1	0	3	.444	.444

LIDGE, BRAD — P

PERSONAL: Born December 23, 1976, in Sacramento. ... 6-5/210. ... Throws right, bats right. ... Full name: Bradley Thomas Lidge. ... High school: Cherry Creek (Englewood, Colo.). ... College: Notre Dame. **TRANSACTIONS/CAREER NOTES:** Selected by San Francisco Giants organization in 42nd round of 1995 free-agent draft; did not sign. ...

Selected by Houston Astros organization in first round (17th pick overall) of 1998 free-agent draft; pick received as part of compensation for Colorado Rockies signing Type A free-agent P Darryl Kile. **STATISTICAL NOTES:** Pitched two innings, combining with Roy Oswalt (one inning), Peter Munro (2 2/3 innings), Kirk Saarloos (1 1/3 innings), Octavio Dotel (one inning) and Billy Wagner (one inning) on 8-0 no-hitter against New York Yankees (June 11, 2003).

CAREER HITTING: 2-for-7 (.286), 0 R, 1 2B, 0 3B, 0 HR, 2 RBI.

Year	Team (League)	W	L	Pct.	ERA	WHIP	G	GS	CG	ShO	Hld.	Sv.-Opp.	IP	H	R	ER	HR	BB-IBB	SO	Avg.
1998—	Quad City (Midw.)	0	1	.000	3.27	1.36	4	4	0	0	...	0-...	11.0	10	5	4	0	5-0	6	.227
1999—	Kissimmee (Fla. St.)	0	2	.000	3.38	1.13	6	6	0	0	...	0-...	21.1	13	8	8	0	11-0	19	.183
2000—	Kissimmee (Fla. St.)	2	1	.667	2.81	1.03	8	8	0	0	...	0-...	41.2	28	14	13	3	15-0	46	.190
2001—	Round Rock (Texas)	2	0	1.000	1.73	1.08	5	5	0	0	...	0-...	26.0	21	5	5	1	7-0	42	.219
2002—	Round Rock (Texas)	1	1	.500	2.45	1.09	5	0	0	0	...	0-...	11.0	9	4	3	0	3-0	18	.220
—	Houston (N.L.)	1	0	1.000	6.23	2.42	6	1	0	0	0	0-0	8.2	12	6	6	0	9-1	12	.333
—	New Orleans (PCL)	5	5	.500	3.39	1.16	24	19	0	0	...	0-...	111.2	83	47	42	9	47-0	110	.206
2003—	Houston (N.L.)	6	3	.667	3.60	1.20	78	0	0•	0	28	1-6	85.0	60	36	34	6	42-7	97	.202
2004—	Houston (N.L.)	6	5	.545	1.90	0.92	80	0	0	0	17	29-33	94.2	57	21	20	8	30-5	157	.174
2005—	Houston (N.L.)	4	4	.500	2.29	1.15	70	0	0	0	0	42-46	70.2	58	21	18	5	23-1	103	.223
2006—	Houston (N.L.)	1	5	.167	5.28	1.40	78	0	0	0	6	32-38	75.0	69	47	44	10	36-4	104	.238
Major League totals (5 years)		18	17	.514	3.29	1.19	312	1	0	0	51	104-123	334.0	256	131	122	29	140-18	473	.211

DIVISION SERIES RECORD

Year	Team (League)	W	L	Pct.	ERA	WHIP	G	GS	CG	ShO	Hld.	Sv.-Opp.	IP	H	R	ER	HR	BB-IBB	SO	Avg.
2004—	Houston (N.L.)	0	0	...	2.08	1.15	3	0	0	0	0	1-2	4.1	4	1	1	0	1-0	6	.286
2005—	Houston (N.L.)	0	0	...	0.00	1.50	3	0	0	0	0	0-0	4.0	2	0	0	0	4-0	5	.143
Division series totals (2 years)		0	0	...	1.08	1.32	6	0	0	0	0	1-2	8.1	6	1	1	0	5-0	11	.214

CHAMPIONSHIP SERIES RECORD

Year	Team (League)	W	L	Pct.	ERA	WHIP	G	GS	CG	ShO	Hld.	Sv.-Opp.	IP	H	R	ER	HR	BB-IBB	SO	Avg.
2004—	Houston (N.L.)	1	0	1.000	0.38	0.38	4	0	0	0	0	2-2	8.0	1	0	0	0	2-0	14	.040
2005—	Houston (N.L.)	0	1	.000	7.20	1.60	4	0	0	0	0	3-4	5.0	6	4	4	1	2-0	7	.300
Champ. series totals (2 years)		1	1	.500	2.77	0.85	8	0	0	0	0	5-6	13.0	7	4	4	1	4-0	21	.156

WORLD SERIES RECORD

Year	Team (League)	W	L	Pct.	ERA	WHIP	G	GS	CG	ShO	Hld.	Sv.-Opp.	IP	H	R	ER	HR	BB-IBB	SO	Avg.
2005—	Houston (N.L.)	0	2	.000	4.91	1.09	3	0	0	0	0	0-0	3.2	4	2	2	1	0-0	6	.286

ALL-STAR GAME RECORD

Year	Team (League)	W	L	Pct.	ERA	WHIP	G	GS	CG	ShO	Hld.	Sv.-Opp.	IP	H	R	ER	HR	BB-IBB	SO	Avg.
All-Star Game totals (1 year)		0	0	...	0.00	0.00	1	0	0	0	0	0-0	1.0	0	0	0	0	0-0	3	.000

2006 LEFTY-RIGHTY SPLITS

vs.	Avg.	AB	H	2B	3B	HR	RBI	BB	SO	OBP	Slg.	vs.	Avg.	AB	H	2B	3B	HR	RBI	BB	SO	OBP	Slg.
L	.286	126	36	7	2	4	18	22	42	.400	.468	R	.201	164	33	5	1	6	24	14	62	.277	.354

IN MEMORIAM—CORY LIDLE

PERSONAL: Born March 22, 1972, in Hollywood, Calif. ... 5-11/192. ... Throws right, bats right. ... Full name: Cory Fulton Lidle. ... Died October 11, 2006. ... High school: South Hills (Covina, Calif.). **TRANSACTIONS/CAREER NOTES:** Signed as a non-drafted free agent by Minnesota Twins organization (August 25, 1990). ... Released by Twins (April 1, 1993). ... Signed by Pocatello of the Pioneer League (May 28, 1993). ... Contract sold by Pocatello to Milwaukee Brewers organization (September 17, 1993). ... Traded by Brewers to New York Mets for C Kelly Stinnett (January 17, 1996). ... Selected by Arizona Diamondbacks in first round (13th pick overall) of expansion draft (November 18, 1997). ... On disabled list (March 31, 1998-entire season); included rehabilitation assignments to High Desert and Tucson. ... Claimed on waivers by Tampa Bay Devil Rays (October 7, 1998). ... On disabled list (March 23-September 18, 1999); included rehabilitation assignments to St. Petersburg and Durham. ... On suspended list (September 5-8, 2000). ... Traded by Devil Rays to Oakland Athletics as part of three-team deal in which Devil Rays acquired OF Ben Grieve and cash from A's, Kansas City Royals acquired P Roberto Hernandez from Devil Rays and C A.J. Hinch, IF Angel Berroa and cash from A's and A's received OF Johnny Damon, IF Mark Ellis and cash from Royals (January 8, 2001). ... On disabled list (May 13-30, 2002); included rehabilitation assignment to Sacramento. ... Traded by A's to Toronto Blue Jays for IF Michael Rouse and P Christopher Mowday (November 16, 2002). ... On disabled list (August 5-25, 2003); included rehabilitation assignment to Syracuse. ... Signed as a free agent by Cincinnati Reds (January 6, 2004). ... Traded by Reds to Philadelphia Phillies for OF Javon Moran, P Joe Wilson and a player to be named or cash (August 9, 2004); Reds acquired P Elizardo Ramirez to complete deal (August 11, 2004). ... On disabled list (August 25-September 9, 2005). ... Traded by Phillies with OF Bobby Abreu to New York Yankees for SS C.J. Henry, Ps Matt Smith and Carlos Monastrios, and C Jesus Sanchez (July 30, 2006). ... On bereavement list (August 17-20, 2006). **STATISTICAL NOTES:** Pitched 10-0 one-hit, complete-game victory against Texas (July 19, 2002). ... Pitched 6-0 one-hit, complete-game victory against Cleveland (August 21, 2002).

CAREER HITTING: 22-for-170 (.129), 10 R, 4 2B, 1 3B, 1 HR, 8 RBI.

Year	Team (League)	W	L	Pct.	ERA	WHIP	G	GS	CG	ShO	Hld.	Sv.-Opp.	IP	H	R	ER	HR	BB-IBB	SO	Avg.
1991—	GC Twins (GCL)	1	1	.500	5.79	1.07	4	0	0	0	...	0-...	4.2	5	3	3	0	0-0	5	.263
1992—	Elizabethton (App.)	2	1	.667	3.71	1.40	19	2	0	0	...	6-...	43.2	40	29	18	2	21-0	32	.240
1993—	Pocatello (Pion.)	•8	4	.667	4.13	1.48	17	16	3	0	...	1-...	106.2	104	59	49	6	54-0	91	.261
1994—	Stockton (Calif.)	1	2	.333	4.43	1.71	25	1	0	0	...	4-...	42.2	60	32	21	2	13-1	38	.323
—	Beloit (Midw.)	3	4	.429	2.61	1.10	13	9	1	1	...	0-...	69.0	65	24	20	4	11-0	62	.245
1995—	El Paso (Texas)	5	4	.556	3.36	1.48	45	9	0	0	...	2-...	109.2	126	52	41	6	36-3	78	.292
1996—	Binghamton (East.)	14	10	.583	3.31	1.23	27	27	6	1	...	0-...	190.1	186	78	70	13	49-4	141	.259
1997—	Norfolk (Int'l)	4	2	.667	3.64	1.33	7	7	1	0	...	0-...	42.0	46	20	17	1	10-0	34	.279
—	New York (N.L.)	7	2	.778	3.53	1.30	54	2	0	0	9	2-3	81.2	86	38	32	7	20-4	54	.274
1998—	High Desert (Calif.)	0	0	...	0.00	1.50	1	1	0	0	...	0-...	2.2	2	1	0	0	2-0	6	.182
—	Tucson (PCL)	0	0	...	0.00	0.86	1	1	0	0	...	0-...	4.2	2	0	0	0	2-0	2	.125
1999—	St. Pete. (FSL)	0	0	...	0.00	0.80	2	2	0	0	...	0-...	5.0	2	0	0	0	2-0	1	.118
—	Durham (Int'l)	0	0	...	4.76	1.76	3	2	0	0	...	0-...	5.2	8	3	3	0	1-0	6	.360
—	Tampa Bay (A.L.)	1	0	1.000	7.20	2.00	5	1	0	0	0	0-0	5.0	8	4	4	0	2-0	2	.364
2000—	Durham (Int'l)	6	2	.750	2.52	1.20	9	9	0	0	...	0-...	50.0	52	15	14	3	8-0	44	.267
—	Tampa Bay (A.L.)	4	6	.400	5.03	1.48	31	11	0	0	2	0-0	96.2	114	61	54	13	29-3	62	.294
2001—	Sacramento (PCL)	1	0	1.000	3.00	1.50	1	1	0	0	...	0-...	6.0	6	2	2	0	3-0	2	.261
—	Oakland (A.L.)	13	6	.684	3.59	1.15	29	29	1	0	...	0-0	188.0	170	84	75	23	47-7	118	.242
2002—	Oakland (A.L.)	8	10	.444	3.89	1.20	31	30	2	2	0	0-0	192.0	191	90	83	17	39-3	111	.258
—	Sacramento (PCL)	0	0	...	2.25	1.25	1	1	0	0	...	0-...	4.0	2	1	1	0	3-0	3	.167
2003—	Syracuse (Int'l)	0	0	...	0.00	1.20	1	1	0	0	...	0-...	4.0	3	0	0	0	1-0	2	.313
—	Toronto (A.L.)	12	15	.444	5.75	1.43	31	31	2	0	0	0-0	192.2	216	*133	•123	24	60-3	112	.282
2004—	Cincinnati (N.L.)	7	10	.412	5.32	1.44	24	24	3	1	0	0-0	149.0	170	95	88	24	44-4	93	.288
—	Philadelphia (N.L.)	5	2	.714	3.90	1.14	10	10	2	§2	0	0-0	62.1	54	28	27	3	17-1	33	.236
2005—	Philadelphia (N.L.)	13	11	.542	4.53	1.35	31	31	0	0	0	0-0	184.2	210	105	93	18	40-5	.121	98	.289
2006—	Philadelphia (N.L.)	8	7	.533	4.74	1.36	21	21	0	0	0	0-0	125.1	132	74	66	19	39-3	98	.271
—	New York (A.L.)	4	3	.571	5.16	1.50	10	9	0	0	0	0-0	45.1	49	26	26	11	19-1	32	.272
American League totals (6 years)		42	40	.512	4.56	1.31	137	111	5	2	2	0-0	719.2	748	398	365	88	196-17	439	.267
National League totals (4 years)		40	32	.556	4.57	1.35	140	88	6	3	9	2-3	603.0	652	340	306	71	160-17	399	.278
Major League totals (9 years)		82	72	.532	4.57	1.33	277	199	11	5	11	2-3	1322.2	1400	738	671	159	356-34	838	.272

							DIVISION SERIES RECORD												
Year Team (League)	W	L	Pct.	ERA	WHIP	G	GS	CG	ShO	Hld.	Sv.-Opp.	IP	H	R	ER	HR	BB-IBB	SO	Avg.
2001— Oakland (A.L.)	0	1	.000	10.80	2.40	1	1	0	0	0	0-0	3.1	5	6	4	0	3-0	0	.357
2002— Oakland (A.L.)	0	0	...	9.00	2.00	1	0	0	0	0	0-0	1.0	2	1	1	0	0-0	0	.400
2006— New York (A.L.)	0	0	...	20.25	3.00	1	0	0	0	0	0-0	1.1	4	3	3	0	0-0	1	.500
Division series totals (3 years)	0	1	.000	12.71	2.47	3	1	0	0	0	0-0	5.2	11	10	8	0	3-0	1	.407

2006 LEFTY-RIGHTY SPLITS

vs.	Avg.	AB	H	2B	3B	HR	RBI	BB	SO	OBP	Slg.	vs.	Avg.	AB	H	2B	3B	HR	RBI	BB	SO	OBP	Slg.
L	.290	307	89	26	2	15	42	30	50	.360	.534	R	.256	360	92	16	1	15	48	28	80	.319	.431

LIEBER, JON — P

PERSONAL: Born April 2, 1970, in Council Bluffs, Iowa. ... 6-2/230. ... Throws right, bats left. ... Full name: Jonathan Ray Lieber. ... Name pronounced: LEE-ber. ... High school: Abraham Lincoln (Council Bluffs, Iowa.). ... Junior college: Iowa Western Community College-Council Bluffs. ... College: South Alabama. **TRANSACTIONS/CAREER NOTES:** Selected by Chicago Cubs organization in ninth round of 1991 free-agent draft; did not sign. ... Selected by Kansas City Royals organization in second round of 1992 free-agent draft; pick received as part of compensation for New York Yankees signing Type A free-agent OF Danny Tartabull. ... Traded by Royals with P Dan Miceli to Pittsburgh Pirates for P Stan Belinda (July 31, 1993). ... On disabled list (August 21-September 15, 1998). ... Traded by Pirates to Chicago Cubs for OF Brant Brown (December 14, 1998). ... On disabled list (April 21-May 8, 1999; and August 2, 2002-remainder of season). ... Signed as a free agent by New York Yankees (February 4, 2003). ... On disabled list (March 21, 2003-entire season); included rehabilitation assignments to Tampa and GCL Yankees. ... On disabled list (March 19-May 1, 2004); included rehabilitation assignment to Tampa. ... Signed as a free agent by Philadelphia Phillies (December 8, 2004). ... On disabled list (May 30-July 7, 2006); included rehabilitation assignments to GCL Phillies and Clearwater. **MISCELLANEOUS NOTES:** Walked in only appearance as pinch hitter (2000). ... Struck out in only appearance as pinch hitter (2001). ... Struck out in only appearance as pinch hitter (2006). **CAREER HITTING:** 84-for-590 (.142), 34 R, 17 2B, 0 3B, 0 HR, 24 RBI.

Year Team (League)	W	L	Pct.	ERA	WHIP	G	GS	CG	ShO	Hld.	Sv.-Opp.	IP	H	R	ER	HR	BB-IBB	SO	Avg.
1992— Eugene (Northwest)	3	0	1.000	1.16	0.90	5	5	0	0	...	0-...	31.0	26	6	4	1	2-0	23	.226
— Baseball City (FSL)	3	3	.500	4.65	1.71	7	6	0	0	...	0-...	31.0	45	20	16	2	8-0	19	.344
1993— Wilmington (Caro.)	9	3	.750	2.67	1.17	17	16	2	0	...	0-...	114.2	125	47	34	4	9-1	89	.275
— Memphis (Sou.)	2	1	.667	6.86	1.81	4	4	0	0	...	0-...	21.0	32	16	16	4	6-0	17	.340
— Carolina (Southern)	4	2	.667	3.97	1.44	6	6	0	0	...	0-...	34.0	39	15	15	3	10-0	28	.298
1994— Carolina (Southern)	2	0	1.000	1.29	0.71	3	3	1	1	...	0-...	21.0	13	4	3	0	2-0	21	.171
— Buffalo (A.A.)	1	1	.500	1.69	0.80	3	3	0	0	...	0-...	21.1	16	4	4	1	1-0	21	.208
— Pittsburgh (N.L.)	6	7	.462	3.73	1.30	17	17	1	0	...	0-0	108.2	116	62	45	12	25-3	71	.271
1995— Pittsburgh (N.L.)	4	7	.364	6.32	1.61	21	12	0	0	3	0-1	72.2	103	56	51	7	14-0	45	.346
— Calgary (PCL)	1	5	.167	7.01	1.83	14	14	0	0	...	0-...	77.0	122	69	60	6	19-0	34	.354
1996— Pittsburgh (N.L.)	9	5	.643	3.99	1.30	51	15	0	0	9	1-4	142.0	156	70	63	19	28-2	94	.279
1997— Pittsburgh (N.L.)	11	14	.440	4.49	1.30	33	32	1	0	0	0-0	188.1	193	102	94	23	51-8	160	.263
1998— Pittsburgh (N.L.)	8	14	.364	4.11	1.30	29	28	2	0	0	1-1	171.0	182	93	78	23	40-4	138	.269
1999— Chicago (N.L.)	10	11	.476	4.07	1.34	31	31	3	0	0	0-0	203.1	226	107	92	28	46-6	186	.279
2000— Chicago (N.L.)	12	11	.522	4.41	1.20	35	•35	6	1	0	0-0	*251.0	248	130	123	36	54-3	192	.257
2001— Chicago (N.L.)	20	6	.769	3.80	1.15	34	34	5	1	0	0-0	232.1	226	104	98	25	41-4	148	.255
2002— Chicago (N.L.)	6	8	.429	3.70	1.17	21	21	3	0	0	0-0	141.0	153	64	58	15	12-2	87	.277
2003— GC Yankees (GCL)	0	0	...	4.50	1.30	2	2	0	0	...	0-...	6.0	8	3	3	0	0-0	6	.308
— Tampa (Fla. St.)	0	0	...	13.50	2.50	1	1	0	0	...	0-...	2.0	5	3	3	0	0-0	4	.455
2004— Tampa (Fla. St.)	1	0	1.000	0.00	0.29	1	1	0	0	...	0-...	7.0	2	0	0	0	0-0	4	.083
— New York (A.L.)	14	8	.636	4.33	1.32	27	27	0	0	0	0-0	176.2	216	95	85	20	18-2	102	.301
2005— Philadelphia (N.L.)	17	13	.567	4.20	1.21	35	•35	1	0	0	0-0	218.1	223	107	102	33	41-6	149	.263
2006— Clearwater (FSL)	0	2	.000	7.15	1.68	2	2	0	0	...	0-...	11.1	19	10	9	1	0-0	6	.380
— GC Phillies (GCL)	0	0	...	3.00	1.33	1	1	0	0	...	0-...	3.0	4	1	1	0	0-0	1	.308
— Philadelphia (N.L.)	9	11	.450	4.93	1.31	27	27	2	1	0	0-0	168.0	196	100	92	27	24-3	100	.291
American League totals (1 year)	14	8	.636	4.33	1.32	27	27	0	0	0	0-0	176.2	216	95	85	20	18-2	102	.301
National League totals (11 years)	112	107	.511	4.25	1.26	334	287	24	4	12	2-6	1896.2	2022	995	896	248	376-41	1370	.272
Major League totals (12 years)	126	115	.523	4.26	1.27	361	314	24	4	12	2-6	2073.1	2238	1090	981	268	394-43	1472	.275

						DIVISION SERIES RECORD												
Year Team (League)	W	L	Pct.	ERA	WHIP	G	GS	CG	ShO	Hld.	Sv.-Opp.	IP	H	R	ER	HR	BB-IBB	SO	Avg.
2004— New York (A.L.)	0	0	...	4.05	1.20	1	1	0	0	0	0-0	6.2	7	3	3	0	1-0	4	.292

						CHAMPIONSHIP SERIES RECORD												
Year Team (League)	W	L	Pct.	ERA	WHIP	G	GS	CG	ShO	Hld.	Sv.-Opp.	IP	H	R	ER	HR	BB-IBB	SO	Avg.
2004— New York (A.L.)	1	1	.500	3.14	0.91	2	2	0	0	0	0-0	14.1	12	5	5	1	1-0	5	.231

						ALL-STAR GAME RECORD												
	W	L	Pct.	ERA	WHIP	G	GS	CG	ShO	Hld.	Sv.-Opp.	IP	H	R	ER	HR	BB-IBB	SO	Avg.
All-Star Game totals (1 year)	0	0	...	18.00	3.00	1	0	0	0	0	0-0	1.0	3	2	2	2	0-0	1	.500

2006 LEFTY-RIGHTY SPLITS

vs.	Avg.	AB	H	2B	3B	HR	RBI	BB	SO	OBP	Slg.	vs.	Avg.	AB	H	2B	3B	HR	RBI	BB	SO	OBP	Slg.
L	.304	339	103	17	2	16	47	15	40	.334	.507	R	.278	335	93	17	2	11	40	9	60	.304	.439

LIEBERTHAL, MIKE — C

PERSONAL: Born January 18, 1972, in Glendale, Calif. ... 6-0/190. ... Bats right, throws right. ... Full name: Michael Scott Lieberthal. ... Name pronounced: LEE-ber-thal. ... High school: Westlake (Westlake Village, Calif.). **TRANSACTIONS/CAREER NOTES:** Selected by Philadelphia Phillies organization in first round (third pick overall) of 1990 free-agent draft. ... On disabled list (August 22, 1996-remainder of season; July 24-September 2, 1998; July 18-August 4 and September 11, 2000-remainder of season; May 13, 2001-remainder of season). ... On disabled list (May 5-29 and June 10-July 14, 2006); included rehabilitation assignments to Reading and Scranton-Wilkes Barre. **HONORS:** Won N.L. Gold Glove at catcher (1999). ... Named N.L. Comeback Player of the Year by THE SPORTING NEWS (2002). **STATISTICAL NOTES:** Hit three home runs in one game (August 10, 2002). ... Career major league grand slams: 4.

2006 GAMES PLAYED BY POSITION (MLB): C—60.

								BATTING											FIELDING		
Year Team (League)	Pos.	G	AB	R	H	2B	3B	HR	RBI	BB	SO	HBP	GDP	SB-CS	Avg.	OBP	SLG	OPS	E	Avg.
1990— Martinsville (App.)	C	49	184	26	42	9	0	4	22	11	40	2	3	2-0	.228	.279	.342	.622	5	.990
1991— Spartanburg (SAL)	C	72	243	34	74	17	0	0	31	23	25	5	4	1-2	.305	.372	.374	.747	10	.984
— Clearwater (FSL)	C	16	52	7	15	2	0	0	7	3	12	1	2	0-0	.288	.333	.327	.660	1	.993
1992— Reading (East.)	C	86	309	30	88	16	1	2	37	19	26	10	15	4-1	.285	.342	.362	.705	7	.988
— Scran./W.B. (I.L.)	C	16	45	4	9	1	0	0	4	2	5	1	2	0-0	.200	.245	.222	.467	1	.989
1993— Scran./W.B. (I.L.)	C	112	382	35	100	17	0	7	40	24	32	6	15	2-0	.262	.313	.361	.674	•11	.983
1994— Scran./W.B. (I.L.)	C-DH	84	296	23	69	16	0	1	32	21	29	2	7	1-1	.233	.286	.297	.583	9	.983
— Philadelphia (N.L.)	C	24	79	6	21	3	1	1	5	3	5	1	4	0-0	.266	.301	.367	.668	4	.969

Year	Team (League)	Pos.	G	AB	R	H	2B	3B	HR	RBI	BB	SO	HBP	GDP	SB-CS	Avg.	OBP	SLG	OPS	E	Avg.
1995—Philadelphia (N.L.)		C	16	47	1	12	2	0	0	4	5	5	0	1	0-0	.255	.327	.298	.625	1	.991
—Scran./W.B. (I.L.)		C-DH-3B	85	278	44	78	20	2	6	42	44	26	9	14	1-4	.281	.388	.432	.819	5	.991
1996—Philadelphia (N.L.)		C	50	166	21	42	8	0	7	23	10	30	2	4	0-0	.253	.297	.428	.724	3	.990
1997—Philadelphia (N.L.)		C-DH	134	455	59	112	27	1	20	77	44	76	4	10	3-4	.246	.314	.442	.755	12	.988
1998—Philadelphia (N.L.)		C	86	313	39	80	15	3	8	45	17	44	7	4	2-1	.256	.304	.399	.703	8	.988
1999—Philadelphia (N.L.)		C	145	510	84	153	33	1	31	96	44	86	11	15	0-0	.300	.363	.551	.914	3	.997
2000—Philadelphia (N.L.)		C	108	389	55	108	30	0	15	71	40	53	6	12	2-0	.278	.352	.470	.822	5	.994
2001—Philadelphia (N.L.)		C	34	121	21	28	8	0	2	11	12	21	3	2	0-0	.231	.316	.347	.663	2	.992
2002—Philadelphia (N.L.)		C	130	476	46	133	29	2	15	52	38	58	14	16	0-1	.279	.349	.443	.792	6	.993
2003—Philadelphia (N.L.)		C	131	508	68	159	30	1	13	81	38	59	12	14	0-0	.313	.373	.453	.825	9	.990
2004—Philadelphia (N.L.)		C	131	476	58	129	31	1	17	61	37	69	11	19	1-1	.271	.335	.447	.783	6	.993
2005—Philadelphia (N.L.)		C	118	392	48	103	25	0	12	47	35	35	11	6	0-0	.263	.336	.418	.755	6	.993
2006—Scran./W.B. (I.L.)			2	6	3	4	1	0	0	2	0	1	0	0	0-0	.667	.714	.833	1.548	1	1.000
—Reading (East.)			2	6	0	1	0	0	0	0	0	0	0	0	0-0	.167	.167	.167	.333	0	1.000
—Philadelphia (N.L.)		C	67	209	22	57	14	0	9	36	8	19	6	5	0-0	.273	.316	.469	.784	4	.991
Major League totals (13 years)			1174	4141	528	1137	255	10	150	609	331	560	88	112	8-7	.275	.338	.450	.788	69	.992

ALL-STAR GAME RECORD

		G	AB	R	H	2B	3B	HR	RBI	BB	SO	HBP	GDP	SB-CS	Avg.	OBP	SLG	OPS	E	Avg.
All-Star Game totals (2 years)		2	3	1	1	0	0	0	0	0	0	1	0-0		.333	.333	.333	.667	0	1.000

2006 LEFTY-RIGHTY SPLITS

vs.	Avg.	AB	H	2B	3B	HR	RBI	BB	SO	OBP	Slg.	vs.	Avg.	AB	H	2B	3B	HR	RBI	BB	SO	OBP	Slg.
L	.286	42	12	1	0	2	8	2	3	.311	.452	R	.269	167	45	13	0	7	28	6	16	.317	.473

LILLY, TED · P

PERSONAL: Born January 4, 1976, in Lomita, Calif. ... 6-1/190. ... Throws left, bats left. ... Full name: Theodore Roosevelt Lilly. ... Name pronounced: LILL-ee. ... High school: Yosemite (Oakhurst, Calif.). ... Junior college: Fresno City (Calif.). **TRANSACTIONS/CAREER NOTES:** Selected by Los Angeles Dodgers organization in 23rd round of 1996 free-agent draft. ... Traded by Dodgers with 2B Wilton Guerrero, OF Peter Bergeron and 1B Jonathan Tucker to Montreal Expos for P Carlos Perez, SS Mark Grudzielanek and IF Hiram Bocachica (July 31, 1998). ... Traded by Expos to New York Yankees (March 17, 2000), as part of deal in which Yankees traded P Hideki Irabu to Expos for P Jake Westbrook and two players to be named (December 29, 1999); Yankees acquired P Christian Parker to complete deal (March 22, 2000). ... On disabled list (April 2-May 23, 2000); included rehabilitation assignments to Tampa and Columbus. ... On suspended list (August 11-17, 2001). ... Traded by Yankees with OF John-Ford Griffin and P Jason Arnold to Oakland Athletics as part of three-team deal in which Tigers acquired 1B Carlos Pena, P Franklyn German and a player to be named from A's and Yankees acquired P Jeff Weaver from Tigers (July 5, 2002); Tigers acquired P Jeremy Bonderman to complete deal (August 22, 2002). ... On disabled list (July 23-September 10, 2002). ... Traded by Athletics to Toronto Blue Jays for OF Bobby Kielty and cash (November 18, 2003). ... On disabled list (March 25-April 10 and July 30-September 6, 2005); included rehabilitation assignment to Syracuse.

CAREER HITTING: 1-for-23 (.043), 0 R, 0 2B, 0 3B, 0 HR, 0 RBI.

Year	Team (League)	W	L	Pct.	ERA	WHIP	G	GS	CG	ShO	Hld.	Sv.-Opp.	IP	H	R	ER	HR	BB-IBB	SO	Avg.
1996—Yakima (N'west)		4	0	1.000	0.84	0.73	13	8	0	0	...	0-...	53.2	25	9	5	0	14-1	75	.135
1997—San Bern. (Calif.) .:.......		7	8	.467	2.81	1.10	23	21	2	1	...	0-...	134.2	116	52	42	9	32-0	158	.234
1998—San Antonio (Texas)		8	4	.667	3.30	1.35	17	17	0	0	...	0-...	111.2	114	50	41	8	37-0	96	.266
—Albuquerque (PCL)		1	3	.250	4.94	1.55	5	5	0	0	...	0-...	31.0	39	20	17	3	9-0	25	.310
—Ottawa (Int'l)		2	2	.500	4.85	1.64	7	7	0	0	...	0-...	39.0	45	28	21	8	19-0	49	.280
1999—Ottawa (Int'l)		8	5	.615	3.84	1.11	16	16	0	0	...	0-...	89.0	81	40	38	12	23-0	78	.241
—Montreal (N.L.)		0	1	.000	7.61	1.65	9	3	0	0	0	0-0	23.2	30	20	20	7	9-0	28	.309
2000—Tampa (Fla. St.)		0	0	...	1.35	0.90	1	1	0	0	...	0-...	6.2	5	3	1	0	1-0	6	.192
—Columbus (Int'l)		8	11	.421	4.19	1.49	22	22	3	1	...	0-...	137.1	157	77	64	14	48-0	127	.287
—New York (A.L.)		0	0	...	5.63	1.63	7	0	0	0	0	0-0	8.0	8	6	5	1	5-0	11	.235
2001—Columbus (Int'l)		0	0	...	2.84	0.95	5	5	0	0	...	0-...	25.1	16	10	8	2	8-0	30	.176
—New York (A.L.)		5	6	.455	5.37	1.42	26	21	0	0	0	0-0	120.2	126	81	72	20	51-1	112	.267
2002—New York (A.L.)		3	6	.333	3.40	1.06	16	11	2	1	0	0-0	76.2	57	31	29	10	24-3	59	.202
—Oakland (A.L.)		2	1	.667	4.63	1.29	6	5	0	0	0	0-0	23.1	23	12	12	5	7-0	18	.253
2003—Oakland (A.L.)		12	10	.545	4.34	1.33	32	31	0	0	0	0-0	178.1	179	92	86	24	58-3	147	.255
2004—Toronto (A.L.)		12	10	.545	4.06	1.32	32	32	2	1	0	0-0	197.1	171	92	89	26	89-2	168	.230
2005—Syracuse (Int'l)		0	1	.000	3.12	1.15	2	2	0	0	...	0-...	8.2	5	4	3	1	5-0	9	.172
—Toronto (A.L.)		10	11	.476	5.56	1.53	25	25	0	0	0	0-0	126.1	135	79	78	23	58-1	96	.272
2006—Toronto (A.L.)		15	13	.536	4.31	1.43	32	32	0	0	0	0-0	181.2	179	98	87	28	81-6	160	.254
American League totals (7 years)		59	57	.509	4.52	1.37	176	157	4	2	0	0-0	912.1	878	491	458	137	373-16	771	.249
National League totals (1 year)		0	1	.000	7.61	1.65	9	3	0	0	0	0-0	23.2	30	20	20	7	9-0	28	.309
Major League totals (8 years)		59	58	.504	4.60	1.38	185	160	4	2	0	0-0	936.0	908	511	478	144	382-16	799	.250

DIVISION SERIES RECORD

Year	Team (League)	W	L	Pct.	ERA	WHIP	G	GS	CG	ShO	Hld.	Sv.-Opp.	IP	H	R	ER	HR	BB-IBB	SO	Avg.
2002—Oakland (A.L.)		0	1	.000	13.50	2.75	2	0	0	0	0	0-1	4.0	10	6	6	1	1-0	3	.476
2003—Oakland (A.L.)		0	0	...	0.00	0.44	2	1	0	0	0	0-0	9.0	2	1	0	0	2-0	7	.065
Division series totals (2 years)		0	1	.000	4.15	1.15	4	1	0	0	0	0-1	13.0	12	7	6	1	3-0	10	.231

ALL-STAR GAME RECORD

		W	L	Pct.	ERA	WHIP	G	GS	CG	ShO	Hld.	Sv.-Opp.	IP	H	R	ER	HR	BB-IBB	SO	Avg.
All-Star Game totals (1 year)		0	0	...	0.00	2.00	1	0	0	0	0	0-0	1.0	2	0	0	0	0-0	1	.400

2006 LEFTY-RIGHTY SPLITS

vs.	Avg.	AB	H	2B	3B	HR	RBI	BB	SO	OBP	Slg.	vs.	Avg.	AB	H	2B	3B	HR	RBI	BB	SO	OBP	Slg.
L	.202	124	25	4	0	1	6	13	22	.281	.258	R	.265	582	154	33	2	27	72	68	138	.344	.467

LIMA, JOSE · P

PERSONAL: Born September 30, 1972, in Santiago, Dominican Republic. ... 6-2/205. ... Throws right, bats right. ... Full name: Jose Desiderio Lima. ... Name pronounced: LEE-mah. ... High school: Escuela Primaria Las Charcas (Santiago, Dominican . **TRANSACTIONS/CAREER NOTES:** Signed as a non-drafted free agent by Detroit Tigers organization (July 5, 1989). ... Traded by Tigers with C Brad Ausmus, Ps C.J. Nitkowski and Trever Miller and 1B Daryle Ward to Houston Astros for OF Brian Hunter, IF Orlando Miller, Ps Doug Brocail and Todd Jones and cash (December 10, 1996). ... On suspended list (May 9-15, 2001). ... Traded by Astros to Detroit Tigers for P Dave Mlicki (June 23, 2001). ... Released by Tigers (September 7, 2002). ... Contract purchased by Kansas City Royals from Newark of the independent Atlantic League (June 4, 2003). ... On disabled list (August 2-18 and August 24-September 18, 2003). ... Signed as a free agent by Los Angeles Dodgers organization (January 27, 2004). ... Signed as a free agent by Royals (December 25, 2004). ... Signed as a free agent by New York Mets organization (February 14, 2006). **HONORS:** Named righthanded pitcher on THE SPORTING NEWS N.L. All-Star team (1999). **MISCELLANEOUS NOTES:** Appeared in one game as third baseman with no chances (1999). ... Appeared in two games as pinch runner (2004).

CAREER HITTING: 38-for-292 (.130), 18 R, 4 2B, 0 3B, 0 HR, 10 RBI.

Year Team (League)	W	L	Pct.	ERA	WHIP	G	GS	CG	ShO	Hld.	Sv.-Opp.	IP	H	R	ER	HR	BB-IBB	SO	Avg.
1990— Bristol (Appal.)	3	8	.273	5.02	1.47	14	12	1	0	…	1-...	75.1	89	49	42	9	22-3	64	.299
1991— Lakeland (Fla. St.)	0	1	.000	10.38	2.08	4	1	0	0	…	0-...	8.2	16	10	10	1	2-0	5	.421
— Fayetteville (SAL)	1	3	.250	4.97	1.34	18	7	0	0	…	0-...	58.0	53	38	32	4	25-0	60	.241
1992— Lakeland (Fla. St.)	5	11	.313	3.16	1.01	25	25	5	2	…	0-...	151.0	132	57	53	14	21-2	137	.237
1993— London (East.)	8	•13	.381	4.07	1.24	27	27	2	0	…	0-...	177.0	160	96	80	19	59-4	138	.238
1994— Toledo (Int'l)	7	9	.438	3.60	1.21	23	22	3	2	…	0-...	142.1	124	70	57	16	48-1	117	.235
— Detroit (A.L.)	0	1	.000	13.50	2.10	3	1	0	0	0	0-0	6.2	11	10	10	2	3-1	7	.355
1995— Lakeland (Fla. St.)	3	1	.750	2.57	1.10	4	4	0	0	…	0-...	21.0	23	11	6	2	0-0	20	.271
— Toledo (Int'l)	5	3	.625	3.01	1.11	11	11	1	0	…	0-...	74.2	69	26	25	9	14-2	40	.247
— Detroit (A.L.)	3	9	.250	6.11	1.40	15	15	0	0	0	0-0	73.2	85	52	50	10	18-4	37	.288
1996— Toledo (Int'l)	5	4	.556	6.78	1.52	12	12	0	0	…	0-...	72.2	87	48	46	13	22-4	59	.296
— Detroit (A.L.)	5	6	.455	5.70	1.50	39	4	0	0	0	3-7	75.0	79	45	44	9	16-2	63	.271
1997— Houston (N.L.)	1	6	.143	5.28	1.27	52	1	0	0	3	2-2	75.0	79	45	44	9	16-2	63	.271
1998— Houston (N.L.)	16	8	.667	3.70	1.12	33	33	3	1	0	0-0	233.1	229	100	96	34	32-1	169	.256
1999— Houston (N.L.)	21	10	.677	3.58	1.22	35	•35	3	0	0	0-0	246.1	256	108	98	20	44-2	187	.265
2000— Houston (N.L.)	7	16	.304	6.65	1.62	33	33	0	0	0	0-0	196.1	251	* 152	* 145	* 48	68-3	124	.313
2001— Houston (N.L.)	1	2	.333	7.30	1.75	14	9	0	0	0	0-0	53.0	77	44	43	12	16-1	41	.350
— Detroit (A.L.)	5	10	.333	4.71	1.26	18	18	2	0	0	0-0	112.2	120	66	59	23	22-2	43	.274
2002— Detroit (A.L.)	4	6	.400	7.77	1.57	20	12	0	0	0	0-0	68.1	86	60	59	12	21-0	33	.314
2003— Newark (Atl.)	6	1	.857	2.33	0.91	8	8	2	0	0	0-...	54.0	44	20	14	4	5-...	52	…
— Kansas City (A.L.)	8	3	.727	4.91	1.45	14	14	0	0	0	0-0	73.1	80	40	40	7	26-0	32	.280
2004— Los Angeles (N.L.)	13	5	.722	4.07	1.24	36	24	0	0	1	0-0	170.1	178	81	77	33	34-6	93	.271
2005— Kansas City (A.L.)	5	16	.238	6.99	1.66	32	32	1	0	0	0-0	168.2	219	140	131	31	61-1	81	.314
2006— Norfolk (Int'l)	7	8	.467	3.92	1.14	25	22	0	0	0	0-0	140.0	140	64	61	15	20-0	88	.264
— New York (N.L.)	0	4	.000	9.87	2.02	4	4	0	0	0	0-0	17.1	25	22	19	3	10-0	12	.329
American League totals (7 years)	30	51	.370	6.17	1.49	141	96	3	0	6	3-7	576.0	688	416	395	98	173-12	291	.297
National League totals (7 years)	59	51	.536	4.74	1.33	207	139	6	1	4	2-2	991.2	1095	556	522	169	220-15	689	.280
Major League totals (13 years)	89	102	.466	5.26	1.39	348	235	9	1	10	5-9	1567.2	1783	972	917	267	393-27	980	.287

DIVISION SERIES RECORD

Year Team (League)	W	L	Pct.	ERA	WHIP	G	GS	CG	ShO	Hld.	Sv.-Opp.	IP	H	R	ER	HR	BB-IBB	SO	Avg.
1997— Houston (N.L.)	0	0	…	0.00	1.00	1	0	0	0	0	0-0	1.0	0	0	0	0	1-0	1	.000
1998— Houston (N.L.)		Did not play.																	
1999— Houston (N.L.)	0	1	.000	5.40	1.65	1	1	0	0	0	0-0	6.2	9	4	4	0	2-2	4	.333
2004— Los Angeles (N.L.)	1	0	1.000	0.00	0.67	1	1	1	1	0	0-0	9.0	5	0	0	0	1-0	4	.161
Division series totals (3 years)	1	1	.500	2.16	1.08	3	2	1	1	0	0-0	16.2	14	4	4	0	4-2	9	.233

ALL-STAR GAME RECORD

Year Team (League)	W	L	Pct.	ERA	WHIP	G	GS	CG	ShO	Hld.	Sv.-Opp.	IP	H	R	ER	HR	BB-IBB	SO	Avg.
All-Star Game totals (1 year)	0	0	…	0.00	1.00	1	0	0	0	0	0-0	1.0	1	0	0	0	0-0	0	.250

2006 LEFTY-RIGHTY SPLITS

vs.	Avg.	AB	H	2B	3B	HR	RBI	BB	SO	OBP	Slg.	vs.	Avg.	AB	H	2B	3B	HR	RBI	BB	SO	OBP	Slg.
L	.412	34	14	4	0	2	12	6	4	.488	.706	R	.262	42	11	0	1	1	7	4	8	.354	.381

LIND, ADAM — OF

PERSONAL: Born July 17, 1983, in Anderson, Ind. ... Bats left, throws left. ... Full name: Adam A. Lind. ... College: South Alabama. **TRANSACTIONS/CAREER NOTES:** Selected by Toronto Blue Jays organization in third round of 2004 free-agent draft.

2006 GAMES PLAYED BY POSITION (MLB): DH—15, OF—2.

Year Team (League)	Pos.	G	AB	R	H	2B	3B	HR	RBI	BB	SO	HBP	GDP	SB-CS	Avg.	OBP	SLG	OPS	E	Avg.
2004— Auburn (NY-Penn)		70	266	43	83	23	0	7	50	24	36	2	7	1-0	.312	.371	.477	.848	…	…
2005— Dunedin (Fla. St.)	OF-DH	126	495	80	155	42	4	12	84	49	77	4	12	2-1	.313	.375	.487	.862	12	.962
2006— New Hampshire (East.)		91	348	43	108	24	0	19	71	25	87	2	5	2-1	.310	.357	.543	.900	2	.985
— Syracuse (Int'l)		34	109	20	43	7	0	5	18	23	18	2	1	1-0	.394	.496	.596	1.093	1	.988
— Toronto (A.L.)	DH-OF	18	60	8	22	8	0	2	8	5	12	0	0	0-0	.367	.415	.600	1.015	0	1.000
Major League totals (1 year)		18	60	8	22	8	0	2	8	5	-12	0	0	0-0	.367	.415	.600	1.015	0	1.000

2006 LEFTY-RIGHTY SPLITS

vs.	Avg.	AB	H	2B	3B	HR	RBI	BB	SO	OBP	Slg.	vs.	Avg.	AB	H	2B	3B	HR	RBI	BB	SO	OBP	Slg.
L	.444	9	4	1	0	0	2	2	0	.545	.556	R	.353	51	18	7	0	2	6	3	12	.389	.608

LINDEN, TODD — OF

PERSONAL: Born June 30, 1980, in Edmonds, Wash. ... 6-3/210. ... Bats both, throws right. ... Full name: Todd Anthony Linden. ... High school: Central Kitsap (Silverdale, Wash.). ... College: Louisiana State. **TRANSACTIONS/CAREER NOTES:** Selected by San Francisco Giants in supplemental round ("sandwich pick" between first and second rounds, 41st pick overall) of 2001 free-agent draft; pick received as part of compensation for Cleveland Indians signing Type A free-agent OF Ellis Burks.

2006 GAMES PLAYED BY POSITION (MLB): OF—47.

Year Team (League)	Pos.	G	AB	R	H	2B	3B	HR	RBI	BB	SO	HBP	GDP	SB-CS	Avg.	OBP	SLG	OPS	E	Avg.
2002— Shreveport (Texas)	OF	111	392	64	123	26	2	12	52	61	101	12	12	9-5	.314	.419	.482	.901	3	.987
— Fresno (PCL)	OF	29	100	18	25	2	1	3	10	20	35	1	2	2-0	.250	.380	.380	.760	1	1.000
2003— Fresno (PCL)	OF-DH	125	471	75	131	24	3	11	56	40	105	17	9	14-4	.278	.356	.412	.768	4	.985
— San Francisco (N.L.)	OF	18	38	2	8	1	0	1	6	1	8	0	2	0-0	.211	.231	.395	.547	1	.929
2004— Fresno (PCL)	OF-DH	130	489	93	127	28	2	23	75	63	149	7	9	8-6	.260	.349	.466	.816	7	.976
— San Francisco (N.L.)	OF	16	32	6	5	1	0	0	1	5	7	1	0	0-0	.156	.289	.188	.477	0	1.000
2005— Fresno (PCL)	OF-DH	95	340	81	109	25	4	30	80	62	97	10	11	6-2	.321	.437	.662	1.120	8	.977
— San Francisco (N.L.)	OF	60	171	20	37	8	0	4	13	10	54	5	5	3-0	.216	.280	.333	.613	2	.983
2006— Fresno (PCL)		52	187	31	52	11	3	5	23	29	44	4	3	5-0	.278	.385	.449	.834	2	.982
— San Francisco (N.L.)	OF	61	77	15	21	4	2	2	5	9	20	1	2	1-0	.273	.356	.455	.811	0	1.000
Major League totals (4 years)		155	318	43	71	14	2	7	25	25	89	7	9	4-0	.223	.294	.346	.640	3	.983

2006 LEFTY-RIGHTY SPLITS

vs.	Avg.	AB	H	2B	3B	HR	RBI	BB	SO	OBP	Slg.	vs.	Avg.	AB	H	2B	3B	HR	RBI	BB	SO	OBP	Slg.
L	.208	24	5	0	1	0	1	2	3	7	.321	.333	R	.302	53	16	4	2	1	3	6	13	.373	.509

LINEBRINK, SCOTT   P

PERSONAL: Born August 4, 1976, in Austin, Texas. ... 6-3/208. ... Throws right, bats right. ... Full name: Scott Cameron Linebrink. ... High school: McNeil (Austin, Texas). ... College: Texas State. **TRANSACTIONS/CAREER NOTES:** Selected by San Francisco Giants organization in second round of 1997 free-agent draft. ... Traded by Giants to Houston Astros for P Doug Henry (July 30, 2000). ... On disabled list (May 20-June 17, 2002); included rehabilitation assignments by New Orleans and Round Rock. ... Claimed on waivers by San Diego Padres (May 29, 2003).
CAREER HITTING: 4-for-17 (.235), 0 R, 1 2B, 0 3B, 0 HR, 0 RBI.

Year	Team (League)	W	L	Pct.	ERA	WHIP	G	GS	CG	ShO	Hld.	Sv.-Opp.	IP	H	R	ER	HR	BB-IBB	SO	Avg.
1997—	Salem-Keizer (N'west)	0	0	...	4.50	1.30	3	3	0	0	...	0-...	10.0	7	5	5	1	6-0	6	.194
—	San Jose (Calif.)	2	1	.667	3.18	1.38	6	6	0	0	...	0-...	28.1	29	11	10	2	10-0	40	.264
1998—	Shreveport (Texas)	10	8	.556	5.02	1.41	21	21	0	0	...	0-...	113.0	101	66	63	12	58-1	128	.243
1999—	Shreveport (Texas)	1	8	.111	6.44	1.43	10	10	0	0	...	0-...	43.1	48	31	31	7	14-0	33	.279
2000—	Fresno (PCL)	1	4	.200	5.23	1.06	28	7	0	0	...	4-...	62.0	54	42	36	10	12-0	49	.225
—	San Francisco (N.L.)	0	0	...	11.57	3.86	3	0	0	0	0	0-0	2.1	7	3	3	1	2-0	0	.500
—	Houston (N.L.)	0	0	...	4.66	1.76	8	0	0	0	0	0-0	9.2	11	5	5	3	6-0	6	.289
—	New Orleans (PCL)	2	0	1.000	1.80	1.47	11	0	0	0	...	1-...	15.0	15	4	3	0	7-0	22	.259
2001—	Houston (N.L.)	0	0	...	2.61	1.16	9	0	0	0	0	0-0	10.1	6	4	3	0	6-0	9	.176
—	New Orleans (PCL)	7	6	.538	3.50	1.06	50	0	0	0	...	8-...	72.0	52	28	28	4	24-6	72	.204
2002—	Houston (N.L.)	0	0	...	7.03	1.81	22	0	0	0	1	0-0	24.1	31	21	19	2	13-4	24	.298
—	New Orleans (PCL)	1	1	.500	6.00	1.87	13	0	0	0	...	0-...	15.0	17	11	10	1	11-3	16	.293
—	Round Rock (Texas)	0	0	...	0.00	2.00	2	2	0	0	...	0-...	2.0	2	0	0	0	2-0	1	.286
2003—	New Orleans (PCL)	0	2	.000	2.70	1.30	2	2	0	0	...	0-...	10.0	8	3	3	1	5-0	6	.222
—	Houston (N.L.)	1	1	.500	4.26	1.64	9	6	0	0	0	0-0	31.2	38	15	15	4	14-1	17	.317
—	San Diego (N.L.)	2	1	.667	2.82	1.27	43	0	0	0	6	0-0	60.2	55	22	19	5	22-3	51	.244
2004—	San Diego (N.L.)	7	3	.700	2.14	1.04	73	0	0	0	28	0-5	84.0	61	22	20	8	26-2	83	.209
2005—	San Diego (N.L.)	8	1	.889	1.83	1.06	73	0	0	0	26	1-6	73.2	55	17	15	4	23-4	70	.209
2006—	San Diego (N.L.)	7	4	.636	3.57	1.22	73	0	0	0	36	2-11	75.2	70	31	30	9	22-3	68	.243
Major League totals (7 years)		25	10	.714	3.12	1.26	313	6	0	0	97	3-22	372.1	334	140	129	36	134-17	328	.242

DIVISION SERIES RECORD

Year	Team (League)	W	L	Pct.	ERA	WHIP	G	GS	CG	ShO	Hld.	Sv.-Opp.	IP	H	R	ER	HR	BB-IBB	SO	Avg.
2005—	San Diego (N.L.)	0	0	...	0.00	2.00	1	0	0	0	1	0-0	1.0	2	0	0	0	0-0	1	.400
2006—	San Diego (N.L.)	0	0	...	6.75	1.50	2	0	0	0	1	0-0	1.1	1	1	1	1	1-0	0	.250
Division series totals (2 years)		0	0	...	3.86	1.71	3	0	0	0	1	0-0	2.1	3	1	1	1	1-0	1	.333

2006 LEFTY-RIGHTY SPLITS

vs.	Avg.	AB	H	2B	3B	HR	RBI	BB	SO	OBP	Slg.	vs.	Avg.	AB	H	2B	3B	HR	RBI	BB	SO	OBP	Slg.
L	.204	162	33	4	1	4	11	13	38	.263	.315	R	.294	126	37	5	1	5	17	9	30	.341	.468

LIRIANO, FRANCISCO   P

PERSONAL: Born October 26, 1983, in San Cristobal, Dominican Republic. ... 6-2/185. ... Throws left, bats left. ... Full name: Francisco Casillas Liriano. ... College: None. **TRANSACTIONS/CAREER NOTES:** Signed as a nondrafted free agent by San Francisco Giants organization (September 9, 2000). ... Traded by Giants with Ps Boof Bonser and Joe Nathan to Minnesota Twins for C A.J. Pierzynski and cash (November 14, 2003). ... On disabled list (August 8-September 11, 2006).
CAREER HITTING: 1-for-5 (.200), 0 R, 0 2B, 0 3B, 0 HR, 1 RBI.

Year	Team (League)	W	L	Pct.	ERA	WHIP	G	GS	CG	ShO	Hld.	Sv.-Opp.	IP	H	R	ER	HR	BB-IBB	SO	Avg.
2001—	Ariz. Giants (Ariz.)	5	4	.556	3.63	1.21	13	12	0	0	...	0-...	62.0	51	26	25	3	24-0	67	.232
—	Salem-Keizer (N'west)	0	0	...	5.00	0.89	2	2	0	0	...	0-...	9.0	7	5	5	2	1-0	12	.206
2002—	Hagerstown (SAL)	3	6	.333	3.49	1.15	16	16	0	0*	...	0-...	80.0	61	45	31	6	31-0	85	.210
2003—	San Jose (Calif.)	0	1	.000	54.00	10.50	1	1	0	0	...	0-...	0.2	5	4	4	0	2-0	0	.714
—	Ariz. Giants (Ariz.)	0	1	.000	4.32	1.32	4	4	0	0	...	0-...	8.1	5	4	4	1	6-0	9	.192
2004—	Fort Myers (FSL)	6	7	.462	4.00	1.38	21	21	0	0	...	0-...	117.0	118	56	52	6	43-2	125	.269
—	New Britain (East.)	3	2	.600	3.18	1.56	7	7	0	0	...	0-...	39.2	45	14	14	4	17-0	49	.287
2005—	New Britain (East.)	3	5	.375	3.64	1.25	13	13	0	0	0	0-0	76.2	70	36	31	6	26-0	92	.242
—	Rochester (Int'l)	9	2	.818	1.78	0.88	14	14	0	0	0	0-0	91.0	56	25	18	4	24-0	112	.177
—	Minnesota (A.L.)	1	2	.333	5.70	1.10	6	4	0	0	0	0-0	23.2	19	15	15	4	7-0	33	.221
2006—	Minnesota (A.L.)	12	3	*.800	2.16	1.00	28	16	0	0	1	1-1	121.0	89	31	29	9	32-0	144	.205
Major League totals (2 years)		13	5	.722	2.74	1.02	34	20	0	0	1	1-1	144.2	108	46	44	13	39-0	177	.208

2006 LEFTY-RIGHTY SPLITS

vs.	Avg.	AB	H	2B	3B	HR	RBI	BB	SO	OBP	Slg.	vs.	Avg.	AB	H	2B	3B	HR	RBI	BB	SO	OBP	Slg.
L	.202	84	17	1	0	1	4	7	26	.264	.250	R	.206	350	72	16	0	8	27	25	118	.259	.320

LITTLETON, WES   P

PERSONAL: Born September 2, 1982, in Hayward, Calif. ... 6-3/200. ... Throws right, bats right. ... Full name: Wes Avi Littleton. ... College: Cal State Fullerton. **TRANSACTIONS/CAREER NOTES:** Selected by Texas Rangers organization in fourth round of 2003 free-agent draft.
CAREER HITTING: 0-for-0 (.000), 0 R, 0 2B, 0 3B, 0 HR, 0 RBI.

Year	Team (League)	W	L	Pct.	ERA	WHIP	G	GS	CG	ShO	Hld.	Sv.-Opp.	IP	H	R	ER	HR	BB-IBB	SO	Avg.
2003—	Spokane (N'west)	6	0	1.000	1.56	0.85	12	8	0	0	...	0-...	52.0	36	9	9	2	8-0	47	.198
2004—	Stockton (Calif.)	8	10	.444	4.15	1.38	30	23	0	0	...	0-...	141.0	139	76	65	7	56-0	72	.273
2005—	Frisco (Texas)	2	3	.400	3.97	1.43	48	0	0	0	...	3-5	81.2	93	37	36	9	24-0	71	.293
2006—	Oklahoma (PCL)	4	1	.800	2.16	1.14	13	0	0	0	2	2-2	16.2	14	4	4	3	5-0	15	.233
—	Frisco (Texas)	3	0	1.000	0.66	0.73	17	0	0	0	2	3-4	27.1	13	3	2	1	7-0	25	.137
—	Texas (A.L.)	2	1	.667	1.73	0.99	33	0	0	0	7	1-1	36.1	23	7	7	2	13-0	17	.189
Major League totals (1 year)		2	1	.667	1.73	0.99	33	0	0	0	7	.1-1	36.1	23	7	7	2	13-0	17	.189

2006 LEFTY-RIGHTY SPLITS

vs.	Avg.	AB	H	2B	3B	HR	RBI	BB	SO	OBP	Slg.	vs.	Avg.	AB	H	2B	3B	HR	RBI	BB	SO	OBP	Slg.
L	.256	39	10	1	1	1	5	6	4	.375	.410	R	.157	83	13	0	0	1	3	7	13	.222	.193

LIVINGSTON, BOBBY   P

PERSONAL: Born September 3, 1982, in St. Louis, Mo. ... 6-3/195. ... Throws left, bats left. ... Full name: Robert James Livingston. **TRANSACTIONS/CAREER NOTES:** Selected by Seattle Mariners organization in fourth round of 2001 free-agent draft.
CAREER HITTING: 0-for-0 (.000), 0 R, 0 2B, 0 3B, 0 HR, 0 RBI.

Year	Team (League)	W	L	Pct.	ERA	WHIP	G	GS	CG	ShO	Hld.	Sv.-Opp.	IP	H	R	ER	HR	BB-IBB	SO	Avg.
2002—	Everett (N'west)	6	5	.545	3.02	1.17	15	14	0	0	...	0-...	80.1	80	33	27	2	14-0	76	.255

Year	Team (League)	W	L	Pct.	ERA	WHIP	G	GS	CG	ShO	Hld.	Sv.-Opp.	IP	H	R	ER	HR	BB-IBB	SO	Avg.
2003—Wisconsin (Midw.)		15	7	.682	2.73	1.15	26	26	1	0	...	0-...	178.0	176	72	54	10	28-0	105	.259
2004—Inland Empire (Calif.)		12	6	.667	3.57	1.16	28	27	1	1	...	0-...	186.2	187	90	74	15	30-0	141	.262
2005—San Antonio (Texas)		8	4	.667	2.86	1.12	18	18	0	0	0	0-0	116.1	103	45	37	7	27-0	78	.242
—Tacoma (PCL)		6	2	.750	4.70	1.32	10	10	0	0	0	0-0	51.2	53	31	27	2	15-0	41	.260
2006—Tacoma (PCL)		8	11	.421	4.59	1.49	23	22	0	0	0	0-0	135.1	165	74	69	18	36-2	69	.308
—Seattle (A.L.)		0	0	...	18.00	3.00	3	0	0	0	0	0-0	5.0	9	10	10	2	6-1	3	.375
Major League totals (1 year)		0	0	...	18.00	3.00	3	0	0	0	0	0-0	5.0	9	10	10	2	6-1	3	.375

2006 LEFTY-RIGHTY SPLITS

vs.	Avg.	AB	H	2B	3B	HR	RBI	BB	SO	OBP	Slg.	vs.	Avg.	AB	H	2B	3B	HR	RBI	BB	SO	OBP	Slg.
L	.364	11	4	0	0	0	3	1	2	.500	.364	R	.385	13	5	1	0	2	7	5	1	.556	.923

LOAIZA, ESTEBAN   P

PERSONAL: Born December 31, 1971, in Tijuana, Mexico. ... 6-3/215. ... Throws right, bats right. ... Full name: Esteban Antonio Veyna Loaiza. ... Name pronounced: ess-TAY-bahn low-EYE-zah. ... High school: Mar Vista (Imperial Beach, Calif.). **TRANSACTIONS/CAREER NOTES:** Signed as a non-drafted free agent by Pittsburgh Pirates organization (March 21, 1991). ... Loaned by Pirates organization to Mexico City Red Devils of the Mexican League (May 7-28, 1993; and June 19-August 14, 1996). ... Traded by Pirates to Texas Rangers for P Todd Van Poppel and 2B Warren Morris (July 17, 1998). ... On disabled list (May 12-July 5, 1999); included rehabilitation assignment to Oklahoma City. ... Traded by Rangers to Toronto Blue Jays for P Darwin Cubillan and 2B/SS Michael Young (July 19, 2000). ... On disabled list (March 22-May 14, 2002); included rehabilitation assignments to Dunedin, Syracuse and Tennessee. ... Signed as a free agent by Chicago White Sox organization (January 27, 2003). ... Traded by White Sox to New York Yankees for P Jose Contreras and cash (July 31, 2004). ... Signed as a free agent by Washington Nationals (January 19, 2005). ... Signed as a free agent by Oakland Athletics (November 28, 2005). ... On disabled list (April 29-June 8, 2006); included rehabilitation assignment to Sacramento. **MISCELLANEOUS NOTES:** Made an out in only appearance as pinch hitter (1995). ... Had a sacrifice hit in only appearance as pinch hitter (1996).
CAREER HITTING: 43-for-258 (.167), 15 R, 4 2B, 1 3B, 0 HR, 15 RBI.

Year	Team (League)	W	L	Pct.	ERA	WHIP	G	GS	CG	ShO	Hld.	Sv.-Opp.	IP	H	R	ER	HR	BB-IBB	SO	Avg.
1991—GC Pirates (GCL)		5	1	.833	2.26	1.20	11	11	1	•1	...	0-...	51.2	48	17	13	0	14-0	41	.241
1992—Augusta (S. Atl.)		10	8	.556	3.89	1.35	26	25	3	0	...	0-...	143.1	134	72	62	7	60-0	123	.249
1993—Salem (Carol.)		6	7	.462	3.39	1.31	17	17	3	0	...	0-...	109.0	113	53	41	7	30-0	61	.268
—M.C. R. Dev. (Mex.)		1	1	.500	5.18	1.48	4	3	0	0	...	0-...	24.1	32	18	14	...	4-...	15	...
—Carolina (Southern)		2	1	.667	3.77	1.19	7	7	1	0	...	0-...	43.0	39	18	18	5	12-1	40	.241
1994—Carolina (Southern)		10	5	.667	3.79	1.29	24	24	3	0	...	0-...	154.1	169	69	65	15	30-0	115	.280
1995—Pittsburgh (N.L.)		8	9	.471	5.16	1.51	32	•31	1	0	0	0-0	172.2	205	*115	*99	21	55-3	85	.300
1996—Calgary (PCL)		3	4	.429	4.02	1.24	12	11	1	1	...	0-...	69.1	61	34	31	5	25-2	38	.243
—Pittsburgh (N.L.)		2	3	.400	4.96	1.59	10	10	1	0	0	0-0	52.2	65	32	29	11	19-2	32	.308
—M.C. R. Dev. (Mex.)		2	0	1.000	2.43	1.26	5	5	0	0	...	0-...	33.1	28	12	9	...	14-...	16	...
1997—Pittsburgh (N.L.)		11	11	.500	4.13	1.38	33	32	1	0	0	0-0	196.1	214	99	90	17	56-9	122	.279
1998—Pittsburgh (N.L.)		6	5	.545	4.52	1.37	21	14	0	0	0	0-1	91.2	96	50	46	13	30-1	53	.275
—Texas (A.L.)		3	6	.333	5.90	1.58	14	14	1	0	0	0-0	79.1	103	57	52	15	22-3	55	.316
1999—Texas (A.L.)		9	5	.643	4.56	1.40	30	15	0	0	0	0-0	120.1	128	65	61	10	40-2	77	.275
—Oklahoma (PCL)		0	0	...	0.00	1.38	2	2	0	0	0	0-...	4.1	3	0	0	0	3-0	6	.188
2000—Texas (A.L.)		5	6	.455	5.37	1.53	20	17	0	0	0	1-1	107.1	133	67	64	21	31-1	75	.302
—Toronto (A.L.)		5	7	.417	3.62	1.32	14	14	1	0	0	0-0	92.0	95	45	37	8	26-0	62	.270
2001—Toronto (A.L.)		11	11	.500	5.02	1.48	36	30	1	1	0	0-0	190.0	239	113	106	27	40-1	110	.307
2002—Toronto (A.L.)		9	10	.474	5.71	1.52	25	25	3	1	0	0-0	151.1	192	102	96	18	38-3	87	.309
—Dunedin (Fla. St.)		0	0	...	0.00	0.80	2	2	0	0	0	0-...	5.0	2	0	0	0	2-0	2	.125
—Syracuse (Int'l)		0	0	...	2.08	0.92	1	1	0	0	0	0-...	4.1	4	1	1	0	0-0	4	.222
—Tennessee (Sou.)		2	0	1.000	1.88	0.77	2	2	0	0	0	0-...	14.1	10	3	3	0	1-0	13	.208
2003—Chicago (A.L.)		21	9	.700	2.90	1.11	34	34	1	0	0	0-0	226.1	196	75	73	17	56-2	*207	.233
2004—Chicago (A.L.)		9	5	.643	4.86	1.43	21	21	2	1	0	0-0	140.2	156	81	76	23	45-3	83	.283
—New York (A.L.)		1	2	.333	8.50	2.06	10	6	0	0	0	0-0	42.1	61	43	40	7	26-2	34	.337
2005—Wash. (N.L.)		12	10	.545	3.77	1.30	34	34	0	0	0	0-0	217.0	227	93	91	18	55-3	173	.270
2006—Sacramento (PCL)		1	1	.500	5.87	1.70	2	1	0	0	0	0-0	7.2	11	5	5	0	2-0	4	.344
—Oakland (A.L.)		11	9	.550	4.89	1.42	26	26	2	1	0	0-0	154.2	179	92	84	17	40-3	97	.288
American League totals (8 years)		84	70	.545	4.75	1.42	230	202	11	5	0	1-1	1304.1	1482	740	689	165	364-20	887	.286
National League totals (5 years)		39	38	.506	4.37	1.40	130	121	3	1	0	0-1	730.1	807	389	355	80	215-18	465	.283
Major League totals (12 years)		123	108	.532	4.62	1.41	360	323	14	6	0	1-2	2034.2	2289	1129	1044	245	579-38	1352	.285

DIVISION SERIES RECORD

Year	Team (League)	W	L	Pct.	ERA	WHIP	G	GS	CG	ShO	Hld.	Sv.-Opp.	IP	H	R	ER	HR	BB-IBB	SO	Avg.
1998—Texas (A.L.)	Did not play.																			
1999—Texas (A.L.)		0	1	.000	3.86	0.86	1	1	0	0	0	0-0	7.0	5	3	3	1	1-0	4	.192
2004—New York (A.L.)		0	0	...	0.00	2.00	1	0	0	0	0	0-0	2.0	4	0	0	0	0-0	0	.500
2006—Oakland (A.L.)		0	0	...	3.60	1.60	1	1	0	0	0	0-0	5.0	8	2	2	2	0-0	2	.348
Division series totals (3 years)		0	1	.000	3.21	1.29	3	2	0	0	0	0-0	14.0	17	5	5	3	1-0	6	.298

CHAMPIONSHIP SERIES RECORD

Year	Team (League)	W	L	Pct.	ERA	WHIP	G	GS	CG	ShO	Hld.	Sv.-Opp.	IP	H	R	ER	HR	BB-IBB	SO	Avg.
2004—New York (A.L.)		0	1	.000	1.42	1.26	2	0	0	0	0	0-0	6.1	5	1	1	0	3-0	5	.217
2006—Oakland (A.L.)		0	1	.000	10.50	1.67	1	1	0	0	0	0-0	6.0	9	7	7	1	1-0	5	.375
Champ. series totals (2 years)		0	2	.000	5.84	1.46	3	1	0	0	0	0-0	12.1	14	8	8	1	4-0	10	.298

ALL-STAR GAME RECORD

Year	Team (League)	W	L	Pct.	ERA	WHIP	G	GS	CG	ShO	Hld.	Sv.-Opp.	IP	H	R	ER	HR	BB-IBB	SO	Avg.
All-Star Game totals (2 years)		0	0	...	0.00	1.00	2	1	0	0	0	...	3.0	2	0	0	0	1-0	1	.182

2006 LEFTY-RIGHTY SPLITS

vs.	Avg.	AB	H	2B	3B	HR	RBI	BB	SO	OBP	Slg.	vs.	Avg.	AB	H	2B	3B	HR	RBI	BB	SO	OBP	Slg.
L	.319	270	86	20	4	9	36	22	45	.369	.522	R	.265	351	93	17		8	47	18	52	.303	.382

LO DUCA, PAUL   C

PERSONAL: Born April 12, 1972, in Brooklyn, N.Y. ... 5-10/185. ... Bats right, throws right. ... Full name: Paul Anthony Lo Duca. ... Name pronounced: low-DUKE-uh. ... High school: Apollo (Phoenix). ... College: Arizona State. **TRANSACTIONS/CAREER NOTES:** Selected by Los Angeles Dodgers organization in 25th round of 1993 free-agent draft. ... On disabled list (April 29-May 21, 2001); included rehabilitation assignment to Las Vegas. ... Traded by Dodgers with P Guillermo Mota and OF Juan Encarnacion to Florida Marlins for Ps Brad Penny and Bill Murphy and 1B Hee Seop Choi (July 30, 2004). ... Traded by Marlins to New York Mets for two players to be named (December 4, 2005); Marlins acquired OF Dante Brinkley and P Gaby Hernandez to complete deal (December 9, 2005). **HONORS:** Named catcher on the SPORTING NEWS N.L. All-Star team (2005). **STATISTICAL NOTES:** Career major league grand slams: 1.
2006 GAMES PLAYED BY POSITION (MLB): C—118, DH—3.

Year	Team (League)	Pos.	G	AB	R	H	2B	3B	HR	RBI	BB	SO	HBP	GDP	SB-CS	Avg.	OBP	SLG	OPS	E	Avg.
1993—Vero Beach (FSL)		C	39	134	17	42	6	0	0	13	13	22	2	2	0-0	.313	.380	.358	.738	2	.992
1994—Bakersfield (Calif.)		1B-C	123	455	65	144	32	1	6	68	52	49	3	5	16-9	.316	.387	.431	.818	5	.993
1995—San Antonio (Texas)		1B-3B-C	61	199	27	49	8	0	1	8	26	25	2	12	5-5	.246	.339	.302	.641	11	.973
1996—Vero Beach (FSL)		1B-3B-C	124	439	54	134	22	0	3	66	70	38	2	14	8-2	.305	.400	.376	.776	18	.980
1997—San Antonio (Texas)		1B-C	105	385	63	126	28	2	7	69	46	27	3	17	16-8	.327	.399	.465	.864	7	.990
1998—Albuquerque (PCL)		1B-3B-C	126	451	69	144	30	3	8	58	59	40	5	20	19-7	.319	.399	.452	.852	17	.980
—Los Angeles (N.L.)		C	6	14	2	4	1	0	0	1	0	1	0	0	0-0	.286	.286	.357	.643	0	1.000
1999—Los Angeles (N.L.)		C	36	95	11	22	1	0	3	11	10	9	2	3	1-2	.232	.312	.337	.649	2	.990
—Albuquerque (PCL)		C-1B-DH	26	76	17	28	9	0	1	8	10	1	6	0	1-1	.368	.478	.526	1.005	4	.978
2000—Albuquerque (PCL)		C-OF-1B																			
		3B-2B	78	279	47	98	27	3	4	54	33	14	2	13	8-5	.351	.421	.513	.933	9	.979
—Los Angeles (N.L.)		C-OF-3B	34	65	6	16	2	0	2	8	6	8	0	2	0-2	.246	.301	.369	.671	1	.993
2001—Los Angeles (N.L.)		C-1B-OF																			
		DH	125	460	71	147	38	0	25	90	39	30	6	11	2-4	.320	.374	.543	.917	9	.990
—Las Vegas (PCL)		C-1B	3	9	3	3	2	0	0	3	1	0	0	0	0-0	.333	.400	.556	.956	1	.950
2002—Los Angeles (N.L.)		C-1B-OF	149	580	74	163	38	1	10	64	34	31	10	20	3-1	.281	.330	.402	.731	9	.992
2003—Los Angeles (N.L.)		C-1B-OF	147	568	64	155	34	2	7	52	44	54	10	21	0-2	.273	.335	.377	.712	16	.988
2004—Los Angeles (N.L.)		C-OF-1B	91	349	41	105	18	1	10	49	22	27	6	15	2-4	.301	.351	.444	.795	3	.995
—Florida (N.L.)		C	52	186	27	48	11	1	3	31	14	22	3	7	2-1	.258	.314	.376	.690	1	.997
2005—Florida (N.L.)		C	132	445	45	126	23	1	6	57	34	31	4	16	4-3	.283	.334	.380	.714	8	.991
2006—New York (N.L.)		C-DH	124	512	80	163	39	1	5	49	24	38	6	15	3-0	.318	.355	.428	.783	11	.987
Major League totals (9 years)			896	3274	421	949	195	7	71	412	227	251	47	110	17-19	.290	.341	.419	.760	60	.991

DIVISION SERIES RECORD

Year	Team (League)	Pos.	G	AB	R	H	2B	3B	HR	RBI	BB	SO	HBP	GDP	SB-CS	Avg.	OBP	SLG	OPS	E	Avg.
2006—New York (N.L.)		C	3	11	2	5	1	0	0	3	1	1	1	0	0-0	.455	.500	.545	1.045	0	1.000

CHAMPIONSHIP SERIES RECORD

Year	Team (League)	Pos.	G	AB	R	H	2B	3B	HR	RBI	BB	SO	HBP	GDP	SB-CS	Avg.	OBP	SLG	OPS	E	Avg.
2006—New York (N.L.)		C	7	29	3	6	1	0	0	3	2	2	0	0	0-0	.207	.258	.241	.499	1	.972

ALL-STAR GAME RECORD

			G	AB	R	H	2B	3B	HR	RBI	BB	SO	HBP	GDP	SB-CS	Avg.	OBP	SLG	OPS	E	Avg.
All-Star Game totals (4 years)			4	6	0	1	0	0	0	0	0	0	0	2	0-0	.167	.167	.167	.333	0	1.000

2006 LEFTY-RIGHTY SPLITS

vs.	Avg.	AB	H	2B	3B	HR	RBI	BB	SO	OBP	Slg.	vs.	Avg.	AB	H	2B	3B	HR	RBI	BB	SO	OBP	Slg.
L	.336	152	51	13	0	2	16	9	10	.373	.461	R	.311	360	112	26	1	3	33	15	28	.347	.414

LOE, KAMERON   P

PERSONAL: Born September 10, 1981, in Simi Valley, Calif. ... 6-8/225. ... Throws right, bats right. ... Full name: Kameron David Loe. ... High school: Granada Hills (Chatworth, Calif.). ... College: Cal State Northridge. **TRANSACTIONS/CAREER NOTES:** Selected by Philadelphia Phillies organization in 39th round of 1999 free-agent draft; did not sign. ... Selected by Texas Rangers organization in 20th round of 2002 free-agent draft. ... On disabled list (June 20-August 3, 2006); included rehabilitation assignments to Frisco and Oklahoma.
CAREER HITTING: 0-for-0 (.000), 0 R, 0 2B, 0 3B, 0 HR, 0 RBI.

Year	Team (League)	W	L	Pct.	ERA	WHIP	G	GS	CG	ShO	Hld.	Sv.-Opp.	IP	H	R	ER	HR	BB-IBB	SO	Avg.
2002—Pulaski (Appalachian)		4	4	.500	4.47	1.39	14	11	0	0	...	1-...	58.1	64	34	29	3	17-0	55	.271
2003—Clinton (Midw.)		4	3	.571	1.95	1.00	23	11	0	0	...	2-...	97.0	78	34	21	3	19-0	94	.217
—Stockton (Calif.)		3	0	1.000	0.96	0.85	9	4	0	0	...	1-...	37.2	26	7	4	1	6-0	31	.183
2004—Frisco (Texas)		7	7	.500	3.10	1.33	19	19	0	0	...	0-...	113.1	122	42	39	5	29-3	97	.280
—Oklahoma (PCL)		5	2	.714	3.27	1.24	8	8	0	0	...	0-...	52.1	52	20	19	6	13-0	42	.265
—Texas (A.L.)		0	0	...	5.40	1.80	2	1	0	0	0	0-0	6.2	6	5	4	0	6-0	3	.273
2005—Oklahoma (PCL)		2	1	.667	5.08	1.48	5	5	0	0	0	0-0	28.1	32	17	16	5	10-1	23	.281
—Texas (A.L.)		9	6	.600	3.42	1.30	48	8	0	0	4	1-4	92.0	89	43	35	7	31-6	45	.252
2006—Oklahoma (PCL)		1	2	.333	9.13	1.99	13	3	0	0	0	1-3	22.2	32	24	23	3	13-0	21	.327
—Texas (A.L.)		3	6	.333	5.86	1.62	15	15	1	1	0	0-0	78.1	105	54	51	10	22-0	34	.317
—Frisco (Texas)		0	1	.000	5.14	1.71	2	2	0	0	0	0-0	7.0	8	5	4	1	4-0	4	.286
Major League totals (3 years)		12	12	.500	4.58	1.46	65	24	1	1	4	1-4	177.0	200	102	90	17	59-6	82	.283

2006 LEFTY-RIGHTY SPLITS

vs.	Avg.	AB	H	2B	3B	HR	RBI	BB	SO	OBP	Slg.	vs.	Avg.	AB	H	2B	3B	HR	RBI	BB	SO	OBP	Slg.
L	.313	166	52	11	3	4	21	10	12	.354	.488	R	.321	165	53	9	0	6	28	12	22	.363	.485

LOEWEN, ADAM   P

PERSONAL: Born April 9, 1984, in Surrey, British Columbia. ... 6-5/220. ... Throws left, bats left. ... Full name: Adam A. Loewen. ... Junior college: Chipola (Fla.) **TRANSACTIONS/CAREER NOTES:** Selected by Baltimore Orioles organization in first round (fourth pick overall) of 2002 free-agent draft.
CAREER HITTING: 0-for-2 (.000), 0 R, 0 2B, 0 3B, 0 HR, 0 RBI.

Year	Team (League)	W	L	Pct.	ERA	WHIP	G	GS	CG	ShO	Hld.	Sv.-Opp.	IP	H	R	ER	HR	BB-IBB	SO	Avg.
2003—Aberdeen (N.Y.-Penn.)		0	2	.000	2.70	0.94	7	7	0	0	...	0-...	23.1	13	7	7	0	9-0	25	.167
2004—Delmarva (S. Atl.)		4	5	.444	4.11	1.58	20	19	1	0	...	0-...	85.1	77	47	39	3	58-0	82	.250
—Frederick (Carolina)		0	2	.000	6.75	2.00	2	2	1	0	...	0-...	8.0	7	6	6	2	9-0	3	.259
2005—Frederick (Carolina)		10	8	.556	4.12	1.52	28	27	1	0	0	0-0	142.0	130	77	65	8	86-0	146	.245
2006—Ottawa (Int'l)		2	0	1.000	1.27	0.61	3	3	0	0	0	0-0	21.1	10	3	3	0	3-0	21	.143
—Bowie (East.)		4	2	.667	2.72	1.45	9	8	0	0	0	0-0	49.2	46	17	15	3	26-0	55	.250
—Baltimore (A.L.)		6	6	.500	5.37	1.54	22	19	0	0	1	0-0	112.1	111	72	67	8	62-0	98	.259
Major League totals (1 year)		6	6	.500	5.37	1.54	22	19	0	0	1	0-0	112.1	111	72	67	8	62-0	98	.259

2006 LEFTY-RIGHTY SPLITS

vs.	Avg.	AB	H	2B	3B	HR	RBI	BB	SO	OBP	Slg.	vs.	Avg.	AB	H	2B	3B	HR	RBI	BB	SO	OBP	Slg.
L	.277	94	26	4	0	1	13	18	26	.393	.351	R	.254	335	85	16	1	7	47	44	72	.350	.370

LOFTON, KENNY   OF

PERSONAL: Born May 31, 1967, in East Chicago, Ind. ... 6-0/180. ... Bats left, throws left. ... Full name: Kenneth Lofton. ... High school: Washington (East Chicago, Ind.). ... College: Arizona. **TRANSACTIONS/CAREER NOTES:** Selected by Houston Astros organization in 17th round of 1988 free-agent draft. ... Traded by Astros with IF Dave Rohde to Cleveland Indians for P Willie Blair and C Eddie Taubensee (December 10, 1991). ... On disabled list (July 17-August 1, 1995). ... Traded by Indians with P Alan Embree to

L

Atlanta Braves for OFs Marquis Grissom and David Justice (March 25, 1997). ... On disabled list (June 18-July 5 and July 6-28, 1997). ... Signed as a free agent by Indians (December 8, 1997). ... On disabled list (July 28-August 14 and August 17-September 1, 1999; April 30-May 12, 2000; and May 16-June 1, 2001). ... Signed as a free agent by Chicago White Sox (February 1, 2002). ... Traded by White Sox to San Francisco Giants for Ps Felix Diaz and Ryan Meaux (July 28, 2002). ... Signed as a free agent by Pittsburgh Pirates (March 14, 2003). ... Traded by Pirates with 3B Aramis Ramirez to Chicago Cubs for IF Jose Hernandez, P Matt Bruback and a player to be named (July 23, 2003); Pirates acquired IF Bobby Hill to complete deal (August 15, 2003). ... Signed as a free agent by New York Yankees (January 6, 2004). ... On disabled list (April 17-May 2 and May 28-June 12, 2004); included rehabilitation assignments to Tampa and Trenton. ... Traded by Yankees with cash to Philadelphia Phillies for P Felix Rodriguez (December 3, 2004). ... Signed as a free agent by Los Angeles Dodgers (December 20, 2005). ... On disabled list (March 29-April 14, 2006). **HONORS:** Won A.L. Gold Glove as outfielder (1993-96). **STATISTICAL NOTES:** Career major league grand slams: 2.

2006 GAMES PLAYED BY POSITION (MLB): OF—120, DH—2.

Year Team (League)	Pos.	G	AB	R	H	2B	3B	HR	RBI	BB	SO	HBP	GDP	SB-CS	Avg.	OBP	SLG	OPS	E	Avg.
															BATTING				**FIELDING**	
1988— Auburn (NY-Penn)	OF	48	187	23	40	6	1	1	14	19	51	0	3	26-4	.214	.286	.273	.559	4	.961
1989— Auburn (NY-Penn)	OF	34	110	21	29	3	1	0	8	14	30	0	1	26-5	.264	.336	.309	.645	8	.837
— Asheville (S. Atl.)	OF	22	82	14	27	2	0	1	9	12	10	1	1	14-6	.329	.421	.390	.811	2	.951
1990— Osceola (Fla. St.)	OF	124	481	98	159	15	5	2	35	61	77	3	4	62-16	.331	.407	.395	.802	7	.974
1991— Tucson (PCL)	OF	130	545	93	168	19	17	2	50	52	95	0	2	40-23	.308	.367	.417	.784	9	.974
— Houston (N.L.)	OF	20	74	9	15	1	0	0	0	5	19	0	0	2-1	.203	.253	.216	.469	1	.977
1992— Cleveland (A.L.)	OF	148	576	96	164	15	8	5	42	68	54	2	7	* 66-12	.285	.362	.365	.726	8	.982
1993— Cleveland (A.L.)	OF	148	569	116	185	28	8	1	42	81	83	1	8	* 70-14	.325	.408	.408	.815	• 9	.979
1994— Cleveland (A.L.)	OF	112	459	105	* 160	32	9	12	57	52	56	2	5	* 60-12	.349	.412	.536	.948	2	.993
1995— Cleveland (A.L.)	OF-DH	118	481	93	149	22	* 13	7	53	49	49	1	6	* 54-15	.310	.362	.453	.815	• 8	.970
1996— Cleveland (A.L.)	OF	154	* 662	132	210	35	4	14	67	61	82	0	7	* 75-17	.317	.372	.446	.817	10	.975
1997— Atlanta (N.L.)	OF	122	493	90	164	20	6	5	48	64	83	2	10	27-20	.333	.409	.428	.837	5	.983
1998— Cleveland (A.L.)	OF	154	600	101	169	31	6	12	64	87	80	2	7	54-10	.282	.371	.413	.785	• 8	.978
1999— Cleveland (A.L.)	OF-DH	120	465	110	140	28	6	7	39	79	84	6	6	25-6	.301	.405	.432	.838	3	.989
2000— Cleveland (A.L.)	OF-DH	137	543	107	151	23	5	15	73	79	72	4	11	30-7	.278	.369	.422	.791	4	.989
2001— Cleveland (A.L.)	OF	133	517	91	135	21	4	14	66	47	69	2	8	16-8	.261	.322	.398	.721	6	.981
2002— Chicago (A.L.)	OF	93	352	68	91	20	6	8	42	49	51	0	0	22-8	.259	.348	.418	.766	0	1.000
— San Francisco (N.L.)	OF	46	180	30	48	10	3	3	9	23	22	1	1	7-3	.267	.353	.406	.759	0	1.000
2003— Pittsburgh (N.L.)	OF	84	339	58	94	19	4	9	26	28	29	2	2	18-5	.277	.333	.437	.770	0	1.000
— Chicago (N.L.)	OF	56	208	39	68	13	4	3	20	18	22	2	4	12-4	.327	.381	.471	.852	3	.974
2004— Trenton (East.)	OF	4	14	0	3	1	0	0	2	1	3	0	0	0-0	.214	.267	.286	.552	0	1.000
— New York (A.L.)	OF-DH	83	276	51	76	10	7	3	18	31	27	1	4	7-3	.275	.346	.395	.741	2	.989
2005— Philadelphia (N.L.)	OF-DH	110	367	67	123	15	5	2	36	32	41	2	3	22-3	.335	.392	.420	.811	4	.981
2006— Los Angeles (N.L.)	OF-DH	129	469	79	141	15	12	3	41	45	42	0	16	32-5	.301	.360	.403	.763	3	.988
American League totals (11 years)		1400	5500	1070	1630	265	76	98	563	674	707	21	69	479-112	.296	.372	.426	.798	60	.983
National League totals (6 years)		567	2130	372	653	93	34	25	180	215	258	9	36	120-41	.307	.371	.417	.788	16	.987
Major League totals (16 years)		1967	7630	1442	2283	358	110	123	743	889	965	30	105	599-153	.299	.372	.423	.795	76	.984

DIVISION SERIES RECORD

Year Team (League)	Pos.	G	AB	R	H	2B	3B	HR	RBI	BB	SO	HBP	GDP	SB-CS	Avg.	OBP	SLG	OPS	E	Avg.
1995— Cleveland (A.L.)	OF	3	13	1	2	0	0	0	0	1	3	1	0	0-0	.154	.267	.154	.421	2	.818
1996— Cleveland (A.L.)	OF	4	18	3	3	0	0	0	1	2	3	0	0	5-0	.167	.250	.167	.417	0	1.000
1997— Atlanta (N.L.)	OF	3	13	2	2	1	0	0	0	1	2	0	1	0-1	.154	.214	.231	.445	0	1.000
1998— Cleveland (A.L.)	OF	4	16	5	6	1	0	2	4	1	1	0	0	2-0	.375	.412	.813	1.224	1	1.000
1999— Cleveland (A.L.)	OF	5	16	5	2	1	0	0	1	5	1	0	0	2-0	.125	.333	.188	.521	1	.933
2001— Cleveland (A.L.)	OF	5	19	2	2	0	0	1	3	3	5	0	0	0-0	.105	.217	.263	.481	0	1.000
2002— San Francisco (N.L.)	OF	5	20	5	7	1	0	0	2	2	3	0	0	1-0	.350	.391	.400	.791	0	1.000
2003— Chicago (N.L.)	OF	5	21	3	6	1	0	0	1	2	2	0	1	3-1	.286	.348	.333	.681	0	1.000
2004— New York (A.L.)	DH	1	4	0	1	0	0	0	0	1	0	0	0	0-0	.250	.250	.250	.500	0	...
2006— Los Angeles (N.L.)	OF	3	13	0	1	0	0	0	0	0	4	0	0	0-0	.077	.077	.077	.154	0	1.000
Division series totals (10 years)		38	153	26	32	5	0	3	13	17	30	1	3	13-2	.209	.289	.301	.590	3	.966

CHAMPIONSHIP SERIES RECORD

Year Team (League)	Pos.	G	AB	R	H	2B	3B	HR	RBI	BB	SO	HBP	GDP	SB-CS	Avg.	OBP	SLG	OPS	E	Avg.
1995— Cleveland (A.L.)	OF	6	24	4	11	0	2	0	3	4	6	0	0	5-0	.458	.517	.625	1.142	0	1.000
1997— Atlanta (N.L.)	OF	6	27	3	5	0	0	1	1	1	7	0	1	1-1	.185	.214	.259	.474	2	.833
1998— Cleveland (A.L.)	OF	6	27	2	5	1	0	1	3	1	7	0	0	1-0	.185	.214	.333	.548	1	.889
2002— San Francisco (N.L.)	OF	5	21	4	5	0	0	1	2	2	4	1	0	1-0	.238	.333	.381	.714	0	1.000
2003— Chicago (N.L.)	OF	7	31	8	10	1	0	0	2	3	4	0	0	1-0	.323	.382	.355	.737	0	1.000
2004— New York (A.L.)	DH	3	10	1	3	0	1	0	2	2	3	0	0	1-0	.300	.417	.600	1.017	0	...
Champ. series totals (6 years)		33	140	22	39	2	3	3	13	13	31	1	1	10-1	.279	.342	.400	.742	3	.962

WORLD SERIES RECORD

Year Team (League)	Pos.	G	AB	R	H	2B	3B	HR	RBI	BB	SO	HBP	GDP	SB-CS	Avg.	OBP	SLG	OPS	E	Avg.
1995— Cleveland (A.L.)	OF	6	25	6	5	1	0	0	0	3	1	0	0	6-1	.200	.286	.240	.526	0	1.000
2002— San Francisco (N.L.)	OF	7	31	7	9	1	1	0	2	2	0	0	0	3-0	.290	.333	.387	.720	1	.962
World series totals (2 years)		13	56	13	14	2	1	0	2	5	3	0	0	9-1	.250	.311	.321	.633	1	.974

ALL-STAR GAME RECORD

	G	AB	R	H	2B	3B	HR	RBI	BB	SO	HBP	GDP	SB-CS	Avg.	OBP	SLG	OPS	E	Avg.
All-Star Game totals (5 years)	5	14	1	5	0	0	2	1	3	0	0		5-0	.357	.400	.357	.757	0	1.000

2006 LEFTY-RIGHTY SPLITS

vs.	Avg.	AB	H	2B	3B	HR	RBI	BB	SO	OBP	Slg.	vs.	Avg.	AB	H	2B	3B	HR	RBI	BB	SO	OBP	Slg.
L	.214	84	18	2	0	1	6	7	13	.275	.274	R	.319	385	123	13	12	2	35	38	29	.379	.431

LOGAN, BOONE   P

PERSONAL: Born August 13, 1984, in San Antonio, Texas. ... Throws left, bats right. ... Full name: Boone Logan. ... Junior college: Temple (Texas). **TRANSACTIONS/CAREER NOTES:** Selected by Chicago White Sox organization in 20th round of 2002 free-agent draft.

CAREER HITTING: 0-for-0 (.000), 0 R, 0 2B, 0 3B, 0 HR, 0 RBI.

Year Team (League)	W	L	Pct.	ERA	WHIP	G	GS	CG	ShO	Hld.	Sv.-Opp.	IP	H	R	ER	HR	BB-IBB	SO	Avg.
2003— Great Falls (Pio.)	3	3	.500	6.58	1.60	16	14	0	0	...	0-...	67.0	76	60	49	4	31-0	48	.279
2004— Great Falls (Pio.)	3	7	.300	5.60	1.63	18	9	0	0	...	1-...	64.1	74	48	40	7	31-0	48	.288
2005— Great Falls (Pio.)	1	1	.500	3.31	1.08	21	0	0	0	3	2-3	35.1	34	15	13	1	4-0	29	.258
— Win.-Salem (Car.)	0	0	...	5.06	2.06	4	0	0	0	...	0-0	5.1	7	3	3	2	4-0	5	.318
2006— Charlotte (Int'l.)	3	1	.750	3.38	1.10	38	0	0	0	3	11-14	42.2	35	18	16	1	* 12-3	57	.222
— Chicago (A.L.)	0	0	...	8.31	2.08	21	0	0	0	2	1-2	17.1	21	18	16	2	15-2	15	.288
Major League totals (1 year)	0	0	...	8.31	2.08	21	0	0	0	2	1-2	17.1	21	18	16	2	15-2	15	.288

L

2006 LEFTY-RIGHTY SPLITS

vs.	Avg.	AB	H	2B	3B	HR	RBI	BB	SO	OBP	Slg.	vs.	Avg.	AB	H	2B	3B	HR	RBI	BB	SO	OBP	Slg.
L	.357	28	10	0	0	1	9	6	6	.486	.464	R	.244	45	11	5	0	1	12	9	9	.386	.422

LOGAN, NOOK — OF

PERSONAL: Born November 28, 1979, in Natchez, Miss. ... 6-2/180. ... Bats both, throws right. ... Full name: Exavier Prente Logan. ... High school: Natchez (Miss.). ... Junior college: Copiah-Lincoln C.C. **TRANSACTIONS/CAREER NOTES:** Selected by New York Yankees organization in 40th round of 1998 free-agent draft; did not sign. ... Selected by Detroit Tigers organization in third round of 2000 free-agent draft. ... Traded by Tigers to Washington Nationals for a player to be named or cash (September 1, 2006).

2006 GAMES PLAYED BY POSITION (MLB): OF—26.

Year Team (League)	Pos.	G	AB	R	H	2B	3B	HR	RBI	BB	SO	HBP	GDP	SB-CS	Avg.	OBP	SLG	OPS	E	Avg.
2000— GC Tigers (GCL)	SS	43	136	29	38	2	2	0	14	31	36	1	1	20-3	.279	.412	.324	.735	21	.887
—Lakeland (Fla. St.)	SS	11	42	4	14	1	0	0	3	2	13	0	0	2-1	.333	.364	.357	.721	7	.860
2001— W. Mich. (Mid.)	OF	128	522	82	137	19	8	1	27	53	129	2	3	67-19	.262	.330	.335	.666	9	.968
2002— Lakeland (Fla. St.)	OF	124	506	75	136	14	7	2	26	40	111	0	2	55-16	.269	.321	.336	.657	10	.970
2003— Erie (East.)	OF	136	514	71	129	16	7	4	38	51	103	1	5	37-13	.251	.316	.333	.649	3	.991
2004— Toledo (Int'l)	OF	105	426	67	112	14	9	2	27	23	95	3	3	38-11	.263	.303	.352	.650	5	.979
— Detroit (A.L.)	OF	47	133	12	37	5	2	0	10	13	24	0	1	8-2	.278	.340	.346	.686	2	.984
2005— Detroit (A.L.)	OF-DH	129	322	47	83	12	5	1	17	21	52	1	5	23-6	.258	.305	.335	.641	6	.979
2006— Erie (East.)		20	77	14	19	2	1	0	2	11	23	0	1	9-3	.247	.341	.299	.640	2	.953
— Toledo (Int'l)		19	65	9	12	2	1	0	4	9	18	0	0	3-2	.185	.284	.246	.530	0	1.000
— Wash. (N.L.)	OF	27	90	13	27	3	1	1	8	6	20	0	0	2-1	.300	.337	.389	.726	1	.983
American League totals (2 years)		176	455	59	120	17	7	1	27	34	76	1	6	31-8	.264	.316	.338	.654	8	.981
National League totals (1 year)		27	90	13	27	3	1	1	8	6	20	0	0	2-1	.300	.337	.389	.726	1	.983
Major League totals (3 years)		203	545	72	147	20	8	2	35	40	96	1	6	33-9	.270	.319	.347	.666	9	.981

2006 LEFTY-RIGHTY SPLITS

vs.	Avg.	AB	H	2B	3B	HR	RBI	BB	SO	OBP	Slg.	vs.	Avg.	AB	H	2B	3B	HR	RBI	BB	SO	OBP	Slg.
L	.350	20	7	2	1	1	3	3	2	3	.409	.700	R	.286	70	20	1	0	0	5	4	17	.316	.300

LOHSE, KYLE — P

PERSONAL: Born October 4, 1978, in Chico, Calif. ... 6-2/201. ... Throws right, bats right. ... Full name: Kyle Matthew Lohse. ... Name pronounced: lowshe. ... High school: Hamilton Union (Hamilton City, Calif.). ... Junior college: Butte (Calif.). **TRANSACTIONS/CAREER NOTES:** Selected by Chicago Cubs organization in 29th round of 1996 free-agent draft. ... Traded by Cubs with P Jason Ryan to Minnesota Twins for Ps Rick Aguilera and Scott Downs (May 21, 1999). ... Traded by Twins to Cincinnati Reds for P Zach Ward (July 31, 2006).

CAREER HITTING: 8-for-43 (.186), 2 R, 2 2B, 0 3B, 0 HR, 4 RBI.

Year Team (League)	W	L	Pct.	ERA	WHIP	G	GS	CG	ShO	Hld.	Sv.-Opp.	IP	H	R	ER	HR	BB-IBB	SO	Avg.
1997— Ariz. Cubs (Ariz.)	2	2	.500	3.02	1.43	12	11	0	0		0-...	47.2	46	22	16	0	22-0	49	.249
1998— Rockford (Midwest)	13	8	.619	3.22	1.19	28	26	3	1		0-...	170.2	158	76	61	8	45-1	121	.246
1999— Daytona (Fla. St.)	5	3	.625	2.89	1.21	9	9	1	1		0-...	53.0	48	21	17	4	16-0	41	.242
— Fort Myers (FSL)	2	3	.400	5.18	1.34	7	7	0	0		0-...	41.2	47	28	24	5	9-0	33	.292
— New Britain (East.)	3	4	.429	5.89	1.56	11	11	1	0		0-...	70.1	87	49	46	9	23-0	41	.315
2000— New Britain (East.)	3	18	.143	6.04	1.50	28	28	0	0		0-...	167.0	196	123	112	23	55-0	124	.291
2001— Edmonton (PCL)	4	2	.667	3.12	1.29	8	8	1	1		0-...	49.0	50	21	17	3	13-0	48	.262
— Minnesota (A.L.)	4	7	.364	5.68	1.45	19	16	0	0	0	0-0	90.1	102	60	57	16	29-0	64	.284
2002— Minnesota (A.L.)	13	8	.619	4.23	1.39	32	31	1	1	0	0-1	180.2	181	92	85	26	70-2	124	.259
2003— Minnesota (A.L.)	14	11	.560	4.61	1.27	33	33	2	1	0	0-0	201.0	211	107	103	28	45-1	130	.268
2004— Minnesota (A.L.)	9	13	.409	5.34	1.63	35	34	0	0	0	0-0	194.0	240	128	115	28	76-5	111	.305
2005— Minnesota (A.L.)	9	13	.409	4.18	1.43	31	30	0	0	0	0-0	178.2	211	85	83	22	44-5	86	.299
2006— Rochester (Int'l)	2	1	.667	1.50	0.88	4	4	2	0		0-0	24.0	15	6	4	1	6-0	12	.176
— Minnesota (A.L.)	2	5	.286	7.07	1.65	22	8	0	0	0	0-0	63.2	80	50	50	8	25-2	46	.308
— Cincinnati (N.L.)	3	5	.375	4.57	1.41	12	11	0	0	0	0-0	63.0	70	33	32	7	19-2	51	.287
American League totals (6 years)	51	57	.472	4.88	1.45	172	152	4	3	0	0-1	908.1	1025	522	493	128	289-15	561	.285
National League totals (1 year)	3	5	.375	4.57	1.41	12	11	0	0	0	0-0	63.0	70	33	32	7	19-2	51	.287
Major League totals (6 years)	54	62	.466	4.86	1.44	184	163	4	3	0	0-1	971.1	1095	555	525	135	308-17	612	.285

DIVISION SERIES RECORD

Year Team (League)	W	L	Pct.	ERA	WHIP	G	GS	CG	ShO	Hld.	Sv.-Opp.	IP	H	R	ER	HR	BB-IBB	SO	Avg.
2002— Minnesota (A.L.)	0	0	...	0.00	0.50	2	0	0	0	0	0-0	4.0	2	0	0	0	0-0	5	.143
2003— Minnesota (A.L.)	0	1	.000	5.40	1.60	1	1	0	0	0	0-0	5.0	6	3	3	1	2-0	5	.286
2004— Minnesota (A.L.)	0	1	.000	4.50	0.50	1	1	0	0	0	0-0	2.0	1	1	1	0	0-0	3	.143
Division series totals (3 years)	0	2	.000	3.27	1.00	4	2	0	0	0	0-0	11.0	9	4	4	1	2-0	13	.214

CHAMPIONSHIP SERIES RECORD

Year Team (League)	W	L	Pct.	ERA	WHIP	G	GS	CG	ShO	Hld.	Sv.-Opp.	IP	H	R	ER	HR	BB-IBB	SO	Avg.
2002— Minnesota (A.L.)	0	0	...	0.00	0.00	1	0	0	0	0	0-0	1.0	0	0	0	0	0-0	1	.000

2006 LEFTY-RIGHTY SPLITS

vs.	Avg.	AB	H	2B	3B	HR	RBI	BB	SO	OBP	Slg.	vs.	Avg.	AB	H	2B	3B	HR	RBI	BB	SO	OBP	Slg.
L	.288	215	62	13	0	4	26	20	40	.353	.405	R	.304	289	88	16	0	11	53	24	57	.362	.474

LOMBARD, GEORGE — OF

PERSONAL: Born September 14, 1975, in Atlanta. ... 6-0/215. ... Bats left, throws right. ... Full name: George Paul Lombard. ... High school: Lovett (Atlanta). **TRANSACTIONS/CAREER NOTES:** Selected by Atlanta Braves organization in second round of 1994 free-agent draft. ... On disabled list (March 28, 2001-entire season); included rehabilitation assignments to Richmond. ... On disabled list (March 22-June 19, 2002); included rehabilitation assignments to Greenville and Richmond. ... Traded by Braves to Detroit Tigers for P Kris Keller (June 19, 2002). ... Claimed on waivers by Tampa Bay Devil Rays (March 28, 2003). ... Signed as a free agent by Boston Red Sox organization (March 7, 2004). ... Signed as a free agent by Washington Nationals organization (February 2, 2006).

2006 GAMES PLAYED BY POSITION (MLB): OF—8.

Year Team (League)	Pos.	G	AB	R	H	2B	3B	HR	RBI	BB	SO	HBP	GDP	SB-CS	Avg.	OBP	SLG	OPS	E	Avg.
1994— GC Braves (GCL)	OF	40	129	10	18	2	0	0	5	18	47	3	1	10-4	.140	.260	.155	.415	2	.944
1995— Macon (S. Atl.)	OF	49	180	32	37	6	1	3	16	27	44	5	4	16-4	.206	.325	.300	.625	4	.958
— Eugene (Northwest)	OF	68	262	38	66	5	3	5	19	23	91	6	4	35-13	.252	.323	.351	.674	3	.963
1996— Macon (S. Atl.)	OF-DH	116	444	76	109	16	8	15	51	36	122	7	4	24-17	.245	.311	.419	.730	7	.971

Year Team (League)	Pos.	G	AB	R	H	2B	3B	HR	RBI	BB	SO	HBP	GDP	SB-CS	Avg.	OBP	SLG	OPS	E	Avg.
1997— Durham (Carol.)	OF-DH	131	462	65	122	25	7	14	72	66	145	9	4	35-7	.264	.365	.439	.805	9	.968
1998— Greenville (Sou.)	OF	122	422	84	130	25	4	22	65	71	140	5	2	35-5	.308	.410	.543	.953	10	.947
— Atlanta (N.L.)	OF	6	6	2	2	0	0	1	1	0	1	0	0	1-0	.333	.333	.833	1.167	0	1.000
1999— Richmond (Int'l)	OF	74	233	25	48	11	3	7	29	35	98	3	2	21-6	.206	.317	.369	.686	3	.974
— Atlanta (N.L.)	OF	6	6	1	2	0	0	0	0	1	2	0	0	0-0	.333	.429	.333	.762	0	1.000
2000— Richmond (Int'l)	OF	112	424	72	117	25	7	10	48	55	130	6	3	32-9	.276	.365	.439	.803	6	.972
— Atlanta (N.L.)	OF	27	39	8	4	0	0	0	2	1	14	1	2	4-0	.103	.146	.103	.249	0	1.000
2001— Richmond (Int'l)	OF	13	44	7	14	2	1	4	8	6	14	2	1	3-2	.318	.423	.682	1.105	0	1.000
2002— Greenville (Sou.)	OF	8	25	4	7	0	0	3	5	5	6	1	0	2-0	.280	.419	.640	1.059	0	1.000
— Richmond (Int'l)	OF	11	39	10	12	4	1	1	5	5	12	1	0	2-0	.308	.400	.538	.938	0	1.000
— Detroit (A.L.)	OF-DH	72	241	34	58	11	3	5	13	20	78	1	0	13-2	.241	.300	.373	.674	3	.982
2003— Tampa Bay (A.L.)	OF	13	37	8	8	1	0	1	4	0	6	1	0	1-0	.216	.237	.324	.561	1	.964
— Durham (Int'l)	OF-DH	112	438	57	117	25	4	17	64	45	143	6	6	23-6	.267	.342	.459	.801	3	.989
2004— Portland (East.)		16	63	11	24	3	3	2	11	7	8	1	0	7-0	.381	.444	.619	1.063	...	...
— Pawtucket (Int'l)		55	192	38	53	8	3	3	23	20	33	9	1	16-3	.276	.371	.396	.767	...	...
2005— Pawtucket (Int'l)	OF-DH	131	496	90	130	28	8	20	65	67	159	9	2	23-5	.262	.357	.472	.829	2	.996
2006— GC Nationals (GCL)		6	17	1	3	1	0	0	1	6	3	1	0	1-0	.176	.417	.235	.652	0	1.000
— New Orleans (PCL)		62	189	35	57	10	1	10	24	23	49	5	1	18-2	.302	.392	.524	.916	1	.989
— Wash. (N.L.)	OF	20	21	2	3	0	0	1	1	5	10	0	0	2-0	.143	.308	.286	.593	1	.933
American League totals (2 years)		85	278	42	66	12	3	6	17	20	84	2	0	14-2	.237	.292	.367	.659	4	.979
National League totals (4 years)		59	72	13	11	0	0	2	4	7	27	1	2	9-0	.153	.238	.236	.474	1	.974
Major League totals (6 years)		144	350	55	77	12	3	8	21	27	111	3	2	23-2	.220	.281	.340	.621	5	.978

2006 LEFTY-RIGHTY SPLITS

vs.	Avg.	AB	H	2B	3B	HR	RBI	BB	SO	OBP	Slg.	vs.	Avg.	AB	H	2B	3B	HR	RBI	BB	SO	OBP	Slg.
L	.000	9	0	0	0	0	0	1	5	.100	.000	R	.250	12	3	0	0	1	1	4	5	.438	.500

LONEY, JAMES   IF

PERSONAL: Born May 7, 1984, in Houston, Texas. ... 6-3/200. ... Bats left, throws left. ... Full name: James Anthony Loney. **TRANSACTIONS/CAREER NOTES:** Selected by Los Angeles Dodgers organization in first round (19th overall pick) of 2002 free-agent draft. **STATISTICAL NOTES:** Career major league grand slams: 1.

2006 GAMES PLAYED BY POSITION (MLB): 1B—39, OF—2.

Year Team (League)	Pos.	G	AB	R	H	2B	3B	HR	RBI	BB	SO	HBP	GDP	SB-CS	Avg.	OBP	SLG	OPS	E	Avg.
2002— Great Falls (Pio.)		47	170	33	63	22	3	5	30	25	18	2	4	5-4	.371	.457	.624	1.081	5	...
— Vero Beach (FSL)		17	67	6	20	6	0	0	5	6	10	0	2	0-0	.299	.356	.388	.744	0	...
2003— Vero Beach (FSL)		125	468	64	129	31	3	7	46	43	80	1	13	9-4	.276	.337	.400	.737	7	...
2004— Jacksonville (Sou.)		104	395	39	94	19	2	4	35	42	75	3	7	5-5	.238	.314	.327	.641	11	...
2005— Jacksonville (Sou.)	1B-OF-DH	138	504	74	143	31	2	11	65	59	87	2	13	1-4	.284	.357	.419	.776	7	.993
2006— Las Vegas (PCL)		98	366	64	139	33	2	8	67	32	34	2	11	9-5	.380	.426	.546	.973	12	.984
— Los Angeles (N.L.)	1B-OF	48	102	20	29	6	5	4	18	8	10	1	8	1-0	.284	.342	.559	.901	1	.996
Major League totals (1 year)		48	102	20	29	6	5	4	18	8	10	1	8	1-0	.284	.342	.559	.901	1	.996

DIVISION SERIES RECORD

Year Team (League)	Pos.	G	AB	R	H	2B	3B	HR	RBI	BB	SO	HBP	GDP	SB-CS	Avg.	OBP	SLG	OPS	E	Avg.
2006— Los Angeles (N.L.)	1B	1	4	0	3	0	0	0	3	1	0	0	1	0-0	.750	.800	.750	1.550	1	.909

2006 LEFTY-RIGHTY SPLITS

vs.	Avg.	AB	H	2B	3B	HR	RBI	BB	SO	OBP	Slg.	vs.	Avg.	AB	H	2B	3B	HR	RBI	BB	SO	OBP	Slg.
L	.350	20	7	1	1	0	4	0	2	.350	.500	R	.268	82	22	5	4	4	14	8	8	.341	.573

LONG, TERRENCE   OF

PERSONAL: Born February 29, 1976, in Montgomery, Ala. ... 6-1/200. ... Bats left, throws left. ... Full name: Terrence Deon Long. ... High school: Stanhope Elmore (Millbrook, Ala.). **TRANSACTIONS/CAREER NOTES:** Selected by New York Mets organization in first round (20th pick overall) of 1994 free-agent draft; pick received as compensation for Baltimore Orioles signing Type A free-agent P Sid Fernandez. ... Traded by Mets with P Leo Vasquez to Oakland Athletics for P Kenny Rogers (July 23, 1999). ... On suspended list (September 9-12, 2003). ... Traded by A's with C Ramon Hernandez to San Diego Padres for OF Mark Kotsay (November 26, 2003). ... Traded by Padres with P Dennis Tankersley and cash to Kansas City Royals for Ps Darrell May and Ryan Bukvich (November 8, 2004). ... Signed as a free agent by Cincinnati Reds organization (March 27, 2006). ... Released by Reds (May 5, 2006). ... Signed by New York Yankees organization (May 19, 2006). **STATISTICAL NOTES:** Career major league grand slams: 1.

2006 GAMES PLAYED BY POSITION (MLB): OF—10, DH—1.

Year Team (League)	Pos.	G	AB	R	H	2B	3B	HR	RBI	BB	SO	HBP	GDP	SB-CS	Avg.	OBP	SLG	OPS	E	Avg.
1994— Kingsport (Appalachian)	1B-OF	60	215	39	50	9	2	12	39	32	52	4	2	9-3	.233	.340	.460	.800	5	.980
1995— Capital City (SAL)	OF	55	178	27	35	1	2	2	13	28	43	1	3	8-5	.197	.309	.258	.568	5	.937
— Pittsfield (NYP)	OF	51	187	24	48	9	4	4	31	18	36	1	2	11-4	.257	.324	.412	.735	1	.958
1996— Capital City (SAL)	DH-OF	123	473	66	136	26	9	12	78	36	120	5	9	32-7	.288	.342	.457	.798	5	.981
1997— St. Lucie (Fla. St.)	OF-DH	126	470	52	118	29	7	8	61	40	102	2	6	24-8	.251	.310	.394	.704	7	.972
1998— Binghamton (East.)	OF-DH	130	455	69	135	20	10	16	58	62	105	2	8	23-11	.297	.380	.490	.871	10	.958
1999— Norfolk (Int'l)	OF	78	304	41	99	20	4	7	47	23	41	1	6	14-6	.326	.374	.487	.861	4	.980
— New York (N.L.)		3	3	0	0	0	0	0	0	0	2	0	0	0-0	.000	.000	.000	.000	...	...
— Vancouver (PCL)	OF	40	154	16	38	6	2	2	21	10	29	1	4	7-5	.247	.297	.351	.648	4	.961
2000— Sacramento (PCL)	OF	15	60	11	24	6	0	3	15	4	4	0	2	0-3	.400	.431	.650	1.081	3	.903
— Oakland (A.L.)	OF	138	584	104	168	34	4	18	80	43	77	1	18	5-0	.288	.336	.452	.788	•10	.971
2001— Oakland (A.L.)	OF	•162	629	90	178	37	4	12	85	52	103	0	17	9-3	.283	.335	.412	.747	7	.980
2002— Oakland (A.L.)	OF	•162	587	71	141	32	4	16	67	48	96	2	17	3-6	.240	.298	.390	.689	8	.980
2003— Oakland (A.L.)	OF-DH	140	486	64	119	22	2	14	61	31	67	3	9	4-1	.245	.293	.385	.678	4	.986
2004— San Diego (N.L.)	OF-DH	136	288	31	85	19	4	3	28	19	51	1	13	3-2	.295	.335	.420	.756	2	.986
2005— Kansas City (A.L.)	OF-DH	137	455	62	127	21	3	6	53	30	56	0	15	3-3	.279	.321	.378	.699	3	.986
2006— Louisville (Int'l)		15	48	2	11	3	0	0	6	2	10	0	1	0-0	.229	.260	.292	.552	1	.960
— Columbus (Int'l)		69	260	29	72	13	1	10	38	19	53	1	5	0-0	.277	.329	.450	.779	1	.984
— New York (A.L.)	OF-DH	12	36	6	6	1	0	0	2	4	8	0	0	0-0	.167	.250	.194	.444	1	.958
American League totals (6 years)		751	2777	397	739	147	17	66	348	208	407	6	76	24-13	.266	.317	.403	.719	33	.980
National League totals (2 years)		139	291	31	85	19	4	3	28	19	53	1	14	3-2	.292	.332	.416	.748	2	.986
Major League totals (8 years)		890	3068	428	824	166	21	69	376	227	460	7	90	27-15	.269	.318	.404	.722	35	.980

DIVISION SERIES RECORD

Year	Team (League)	Pos.	G	AB	R	H	2B	3B	HR	RBI	BB	SO	HBP	GDP	SB-CS	Avg.	OBP	SLG	OPS	E	Avg.
2000—	Oakland (A.L.)	OF	5	19	2	3	0	0	1	1	3	2	0	2	0-0	.158	.273	.316	.589	1	.923
2001—	Oakland (A.L.)	OF	5	18	3	7	3	0	2	3	1	2	0	0	0-0	.389	.421	.889	1.310	0	1.000
2002—	Oakland (A.L.)	OF	5	18	1	3	0	0	1	1	1	2	0	0	0-0	.167	.211	.333	.544	0	1.000
2003—	Oakland (A.L.)	OF	4	8	0	2	0	0	0	0	1	3	0	0	0-0	.250	.333	.250	.583	0	1.000
Division series totals (4 years)			19	63	6	15	3	0	4	5	6	9	0	2	0-0	.238	.304	.476	.781	1	.974

2006 LEFTY-RIGHTY SPLITS

vs.	Avg.	AB	H	2B	3B	HR	RBI	BB	SO	OBP	Slg.	vs.	Avg.	AB	H	2B	3B	HR	RBI	BB	SO	OBP	Slg.
L	.143	7	1	1	0	0	0	1	5	.250	.286	R	.172	29	5	0	0	0	2	3	3	.250	.172

LOOPER, BRADEN — P

PERSONAL: Born October 28, 1974, in Weatherford, Okla. ... 6-3/220. ... Throws right, bats right. ... Full name: Braden LaVern Looper. ... High school: Mangum (Okla.). ... College: Wichita State. **TRANSACTIONS/CAREER NOTES:** Selected by St. Louis Cardinals organization in first round (third pick overall) of 1996 free-agent draft. ... Traded by Cardinals with P Armando Almanza and SS Pablo Ozuna to Florida Marlins for SS Edgar Renteria (December 14, 1998). ... Signed as a free agent by New York Mets (January 8, 2004). ... Signed as a free agent by Cardinals (December 15, 2005). **MISCELLANEOUS NOTES:** Member of 1996 U.S. Olympic baseball team.

CAREER HITTING: 2-for-10 (.200), 1 R, 1 2B, 0 3B, 0 HR, 0 RBI.

Year	Team (League)	W	L	Pct.	ERA	WHIP	G	GS	CG	ShO	Hld.	Sv.-Opp.	IP	H	R	ER	HR	BB-IBB	SO	Avg.
1997—	Prince Will. (Car.)	3	6	.333	4.48	1.49	12	12	0	0	...	0-...	64.1	71	38	32	6	25-0	58	.276
—	Arkansas (Texas)	1	4	.200	5.91	1.45	19	0	0	0	...	5-...	21.1	24	14	14	2	7-2	20	.286
1998—	St. Louis (N.L.)	0	1	.000	5.40	1.80	4	0	0	0	0	0-2	3.1	5	4	2	1	1-0	4	.357
• —	Memphis (PCL)	2	3	.400	3.10	1.38	40	0	0	0	...	20-...	40.2	43	16	14	3	13-1	43	.270
1999—	Florida (N.L.)	3	3	.500	3.80	1.53	72	0	0	0	8	0-4	83.0	96	43	35	7	31-6	50	.293
2000—	Florida (N.L.)	5	1	.833	4.41	1.59	73	0	0	0	18	2-5	67.1	71	41	33	3	36-6	29	.268
2001—	Florida (N.L.)	3	3	.500	3.55	1.31	71	0	0	0	16	3-6	71.0	63	28	28	8	30-3	52	.242
2002—	Florida (N.L.)	2	5	.286	3.14	1.17	78	0	0	0	16	13-16	86.0	73	31	30	8	28-3	55	.230
2003—	Florida (N.L.)	6	4	.600	3.68	1.38	74	0	0	0	0	28-34	80.2	82	34	33	4	29-1	56	.264
2004—	New York (N.L.)	2	5	.286	2.70	1.22	71	0	0	0	0	29-34	83.1	86	28	25	5	16-3	60	.266
2005—	New York (N.L.)	4	7	.364	3.94	1.47	60	0	0	0	0	28-36	59.1	65	31	26	7	22-3	27	.271
2006—	St. Louis (N.L.)	9	3	.750	3.56	1.31	69	0	0	0	15	0-2	73.1	76	30	29	3	20-5	41	.277
Major League totals (9 years)		34	32	.515	3.57	1.37	572	0	0	0	73	103-139	607.1	617	270	241	46	213-30	374	.265

DIVISION SERIES RECORD

Year	Team (League)	W	L	Pct.	ERA	WHIP	G	GS	CG	ShO	Hld.	Sv.-Opp.	IP	H	R	ER	HR	BB-IBB	SO	Avg.
2003—	Florida (N.L.)	1	0	1.000	0.00	1.80	2	0	0	0	1	0-0	1.2	1	1	0	0	2-1	0	.167
2006—	St. Louis (N.L.)	0	0	...	0.00	0.60	1	0	0	0	0	0-0	1.2	1	0	0	0	0-0	0	.200
Division series totals (2 years)		1	0	1.000	0.00	1.20	3	0	0	0	1	0-0	3.1	2	1	0	0	2-1	0	.182

CHAMPIONSHIP SERIES RECORD

Year	Team (League)	W	L	Pct.	ERA	WHIP	G	GS	CG	ShO	Hld.	Sv.-Opp.	IP	H	R	ER	HR	BB-IBB	SO	Avg.
2003—	Florida (N.L.)	0	0	...	0.00	1.20	2	0	0	0	0	1-1	1.2	1	0	0	0	1-1	1	.167
2006—	St. Louis (N.L.)	0	0	...	5.79	1.50	3	0	0	0	0	0-0	4.2	7	3	3	1	0-0	1	.350
Champ. series totals (2 years)		0	0	...	4.26	1.42	5	0	0	0	0	1-1	6.1	8	3	3	1	1-1	2	.308

WORLD SERIES RECORD

Year	Team (League)	W	L	Pct.	ERA	WHIP	G	GS	CG	ShO	Hld.	Sv.-Opp.	IP	H	R	ER	HR	BB-IBB	SO	Avg.
2003—	Florida (N.L.)	1	0	1.000	9.82	1.64	4	0	0	0	0	0-0	3.2	6	4	4	2	0-0	4	.353
2006—	St. Louis (N.L.)	0	0	...	3.86	0.43	3	0	0	0	1	0-0	2.1	1	1	1	0	0-0	1	.111
World series totals (2 years)		1	0	1.000	7.50	1.17	7	0	0	0	1	0-0	6.0	7	5	5	2	0-0	5	.269

2006 LEFTY-RIGHTY SPLITS

vs.	Avg.	AB	H	2B	3B	HR	RBI	BB	SO	OBP	Slg.	vs.	Avg.	AB	H	2B	3B	HR	RBI	BB	SO	OBP	Slg.
L	.287	94	27	8	0	1	12	14	15	.373	.404	R	.272	180	49	9	0	2	18	6	26	.298	.356

LOPEZ, FELIPE — SS

PERSONAL: Born May 12, 1980, in Bayamon, Puerto Rico. ... 6-1/185. ... Bats both, throws right. ... Full name: Felipe Lopez Jr. ... High school: Lake Brantley (Altamonte Springs, Fla.). **TRANSACTIONS/CAREER NOTES:** Selected by Toronto Blue Jays organization in first round (eighth pick overall) of 1998 free-agent draft. ... Traded by Blue Jays to Cincinnati Reds as part of four-team deal in which Blue Jays acquired a player to be named from Oakland Athletics, A's acquired 1B Erubiel Durazo from Arizona Diamondbacks and Diamondbacks acquired P Elmer Dessens and cash from Reds (December 15, 2002); Blue Jays acquired P Jason Arnold to complete deal (December 16, 2002). ... Traded by Reds with OF Austin Kearns and P Ryan Wagner to Washington Nationals for Ps Gary Majewski, Bill Bray and Daryl Thompson, SS Royce Clayton and IF Brendan Harris (July 13, 2006). **HONORS:** Named shortstop on the SPORTING NEWS N.L. All-Star team (2005). ... Named shortstop on N.L. Silver Slugger team (2005). **STATISTICAL NOTES:** Career major league grand slams: 2.

2006 GAMES PLAYED BY POSITION (MLB): SS—155.

							BATTING													FIELDING	
Year	Team (League)	Pos.	G	AB	R	H	2B	3B	HR	RBI	BB	SO	HBP	GDP	SB-CS	Avg.	OBP	SLG	OPS	E	Avg.
1998—	St. Catharines (NYP)	SS	19	83	14	31	5	2	1	11	3	14	0	1	4-2	.373	.395	.518	.913	9	.895
—	Dunedin (Fla. St.)	SS	4	13	3	5	0	1	1	1	0	3	0	1	0-0	.385	.385	.769	1.154	4	.692
1999—	Hagerstown (SAL)	SS	134	537	87	149	27	4	14	80	61	157	3	7	21-14	.277	.351	.421	.772	22	.960
2000—	Tennessee (Sou.)	SS	127	463	52	119	18	4	9	41	31	110	1	6	12-11	.257	.303	.371	.675	44	.923
2001—	Tennessee (Sou.)	SS-2B	19	72	12	16	2	1	2	4	9	23	0	1	4-4	.222	.309	.361	.670	8	.904
—	Syracuse (Int'l)	SS-2B-3B	89	358	65	100	19	7	16	44	30	94	3	5	13-5	.279	.337	.506	.842	19	.950
—	Toronto (A.L.)	3B-SS	49	177	21	46	5	4	5	23	12	39	0	2	4-3	.260	.304	.418	.722	9	.938
2002—	Toronto (A.L.)	SS-3B-DH	85	282	35	64	15	3	8	34	23	90	1	4	5-4	.227	.287	.387	.673	8	.975
—	Syracuse (Int'l)	SS	43	173	35	55	11	2	3	16	29	37	1	3	13-0	.318	.419	.457	.875	16	.934
2003—	Cincinnati (N.L.)	SS-3B-2B	59	197	28	42	7	2	2	13	28	59	1	2	8-5	.213	.313	.299	.612	16	.928
—	Louisville (Int'l)	SS-2B	35	143	22	40	11	0	2	18	12	38	0	0	2-5	.280	.333	.399	.732	9	.940
2004—	Louisville (Int'l)	SS-2B-3B	75	293	50	80	11	3	9	43	25	71	2	2	2-2	.273	.329	.423	.752	13	.956
—	Cincinnati (N.L.)	SS-3B-2B	79	264	35	64	18	2	7	31	25	81	3	1	1-1	.242	.314	.405	.719	15	.949
2005—	Cincinnati (N.L.)	SS-2B-3B	148	580	97	169	34	5	23	85	57	111	1	8	15-7	.291	.352	.486	.838	17	.971
2006—	Cincinnati (N.L.)	SS	85	343	55	92	14	1	9	30	47	66	0	6	23-6	.268	.355	.394	.749	14	.959
—	Wash. (N.L.)	SS	71	274	43	77	13	2	2	22	34	60	2	3	21-6	.281	.362	.365	.727	14	.947
American League totals (2 years)			134	459	56	110	20	7	13	57	35	129	1	6	9-7	.240	.293	.399	.692	17	.964
National League totals (4 years)			442	1658	258	444	86	12	43	181	191	377	7	20	68-25	.268	.344	.412	.756	76	.955
Major League totals (6 years)			576	2117	314	554	106	19	56	238	226	506	8	26	77-32	.262	.333	.409	.742	93	.957

ALL-STAR GAME RECORD	G	AB	R	H	2B	3B	HR	RBI	BB	SO	HBP	GDP	SB-CS	Avg.	OBP	SLG	OPS	E	Avg.
All-Star Game totals (1 year)	1	1	0	1	0	0	0	0	0	0	0	0	0	1.000	1.000	1.000	2.000	0	...

2006 LEFTY-RIGHTY SPLITS

vs.	Avg.	AB	H	2B	3B	HR	RBI	BB	SO	OBP	Slg.	vs.	Avg.	AB	H	2B	3B	HR	RBI	BB	SO	OBP	Slg.
L	.246	175	43	8	0	2	20	18	49	.315	.326	R	.285	442	126	19	3	9	32	63	77	.375	.403

LOPEZ, JAVIER — P

PERSONAL: Born July 11, 1977, in San Juan, Puerto Rico. ... 6-4/200. ... Throws left, bats left. ... Full name: Javier Alfonso Lopez. ... High school: Robinson (Fairfax, Va.). ... College: Virginia. **TRANSACTIONS/CAREER NOTES:** Selected by Arizona Diamondbacks organization in fourth round of 1998 free-agent draft. ... Selected by Boston Red Sox from Diamondbacks organization in Rule 5 major league draft (December 16, 2002). ... Traded by Red Sox to Colorado Rockies for future considerations (March 18, 2003); Red Sox acquired P Ryan Cameron to complete deal (March 29, 2003). ... Claimed on waivers by Diamondbacks (April 14, 2005). ... Signed as a free agent by Chicago White Sox organization (January 9, 2006). ... Traded by White Sox to Red Sox for P David Riske (June 15, 2006).

CAREER HITTING: 1-for-7 (.143), 1 R, 0 2B, 0 3B, 0 HR, 1 RBI.

Year	Team (League)	W	L	Pct.	ERA	WHIP	G	GS	CG	ShO	Hld.	Sv.-Opp.	IP	H	R	ER	HR	BB-IBB	SO	Avg.
1998—	South Bend (Mid.)	2	4	.333	6.55	2.05	16	9	0	0	—	0-...	44.0	60	36	32	2	30-0	31	.328
1999—	South Bend (Mid.)	4	6	.400	6.00	1.67	20	20	0	0	—	0-...	99.0	122	74	66	9	43-0	70	.300
2000—	High Desert (Calif.)	4	8	.333	5.22	1.53	30	21	0	0	—	2-...	136.1	152	87	79	14	57-0	98	.288
2001—	Lancaster (Calif.)	1	3	.250	2.63	1.46	17	0	0	0	—	1-...	24.0	30	9	7	2	5-0	18	.313
—	El Paso (Texas)	1	0	1.000	7.43	1.95	22	1	0	0	—	0-...	40.0	64	39	33	6	14-2	21	.370
2002—	El Paso (Texas)	2	2	.500	2.72	1.08	61	0	0	0	—	6-...	46.1	34	16	14	3	16-1	47	.204
2003—	Colorado (N.L.)	4	1	.800	3.70	1.20	75	0	0	0	15	1-2	58.1	58	25	24	5	12-2	40	.258
2004—	Colo. Springs (PCL)	0	1	.000	4.00	1.33	8	0	0	0	—	...	9.0	10	4	4	2	2-0	9	.294
—	Colorado (N.L.)	1	2	.333	7.52	1.75	64	0	0	0	12	0-1	40.2	45	34	34	1	26-4	20	.287
2005—	Colorado (N.L.)	0	0	...	22.50	3.50	3	0	0	0	0	0-1	2.0	7	5	5	0	4-1	1	.538
—	Arizona (N.L.)	1	1	.500	9.42	2.09	29	0	0	0	6	2-3	14.1	19	15	15	2	11-3	11	.311
—	Tucson (PCL)	0	1	.000	2.22	1.19	27	0	0	0	2	2-2	24.1	17	7	6	0	12-1	16	.213
2006—	Pawtucket (Int'l)	0	0	...	4.86	1.68	13	0	0	0	4-5		16.2	20	10	9	1	8-1	12	.299
—	Charlotte (Int'l)	2	1	.667	0.55	1.03	26	0	0	0	3	12-12	33.0	28	2	2	1	6-0	26	.235
—	Boston (A.L.)	1	0	1.000	2.70	1.38	27	0	0	0	6	1-1	16.2	13	10	5	1	10-1	11	.232
American League totals (1 year)		1	0	1.000	2.70	1.38	27	0	0	0	6	1-1	16.2	13	10	5	1	10-1	11	.232
National League totals (3 years)		6	4	.600	6.09	1.54	171	0	0	0	33	3-7	115.1	129	79	78	8	49-9	72	.283
Major League totals (4 years)		7	4	.636	5.66	1.52	198	0	0	0	39	4-8	132.0	142	89	83	9	59-10	83	.277

2006 LEFTY-RIGHTY SPLITS

vs.	Avg.	AB	H	2B	3B	HR	RBI	BB	SO	OBP	Slg.	vs.	Avg.	AB	H	2B	3B	HR	RBI	BB	SO	OBP	Slg.
L	.250	32	8	1	0	0	6	6	7	.385	.281	R	.208	24	5	2	0	1	10	4	4	.333	.417

LOPEZ, JAVY — C

PERSONAL: Born November 5, 1970, in Ponce, Puerto Rico. ... 6-3/224. ... Bats right, throws right. ... Full name: Javier Torres Lopez. ... Name pronounced: HAH-vee. ... High school: Academia Cristo Rey (Urb la Ramble Ponce, Puerto Rico). **TRANSACTIONS/CAREER NOTES:** Signed as a non-drafted free agent by Atlanta Braves organization (November 6, 1987). ... On disabled list (July 6-22, 1997; June 21-July 15 and July 25, 1999-remainder of season; and August 1-16, 2002). ... Signed as a free agent by Baltimore Orioles (January 6, 2004). ... On disabled list (May 25-July 25, 2005); included rehabilitation assignment to Bowie. ... On disabled list (April 28-May 13, 2006); included rehabilitation assignment to Bowie. ... Traded by Orioles to Boston Red Sox for a player to be named (August 4, 2006); Orioles acquired OF Adam Stern to complete deal (October 3, 2006). ... Released by Red Sox (September 8, 2006). **HONORS:** Named N.L. Comeback Player of the Year by THE SPORTING NEWS (2003). ... Named catcher on THE SPORTING NEWS N.L. All-Star team (2003). ... Named catcher on N.L. Silver Slugger team (2003). **STATISTICAL NOTES:** Career major league grand slams: 7.

2006 GAMES PLAYED BY POSITION (MLB): DH—53, C—38.

								BATTING									FIELDING		
Year	Team (League)	Pos.	G	AB	R	H	2B	3B	HR	RBI	BB	SO	HBP	GDP	SB-CS	Avg.	OBP	SLG	OPS	E	Avg.
1988—	GC Braves (GCL)	C	31	94	8	18	4	0	1	9	3	19	0	0	1-0	.191	.214	.266	.480	7	.958
1989—	Pulaski (Appalachian)	C	51	153	27	40	8	1	3	27	5	35	1	8	3-2	.261	.284	.386	.670	5	.983
1990—	Burlington (Midw.)	C	116	422	48	112	17	3	11	55	14	84	5	10	0-2	.265	.297	.398	.695	11	.986
1991—	Durham (Carol.)	C	113	384	43	94	14	2	11	51	25	88	3	10	10-3	.245	.294	.378	.672	6	.991
1992—	Greenville (Sou.)	C	115	442	63	142	28	3	16	60	24	47	5	8	7-3	.321	.362	.507	.868	8	.990
—	Atlanta (N.L.)	C	9	16	3	6	2	0	0	2	0	1	0	0	0-0	.375	.375	.500	.875	0	1.000
1993—	Richmond (Int'l)	C	100	380	56	116	23	2	17	74	12	53	6	8	1-6	.305	.334	.511	.845	10	.987
—	Atlanta (N.L.)	C	8	16	1	6	1	1	1	2	0	2	1	0	0-0	.375	.375	.750	1.162	1	.975
1994—	Atlanta (N.L.)	C	80	277	27	68	9	0	13	35	17	61	5	12	0-2	.245	.299	.419	.718	3	.995
1995—	Atlanta (N.L.)	C	100	333	37	105	11	4	14	51	14	57	2	13	0-1	.315	.344	.499	.842	8	.988
1996—	Atlanta (N.L.)	C	138	489	56	138	19	1	23	69	28	84	3	17	1-6	.282	.322	.466	.788	6	.994
1997—	Atlanta (N.L.)	C	123	414	52	122	28	1	23	68	40	82	5	9	1-1	.295	.361	.534	.895	6	.993
1998—	Atlanta (N.L.)	C-DH	133	489	73	139	21	1	34	106	30	85	6	22	5-3	.284	.328	.545	.868	5	.995
1999—	Atlanta (N.L.)	C-DH	65	246	34	78	18	1	11	45	20	41	3	6	0-3	.317	.375	.533	.908	4	.991
2000—	Atlanta (N.L.)	C	134	481	60	138	21	1	24	89	35	80	4	20	0-0	.287	.337	.484	.822	6	.993
2001—	Atlanta (N.L.)	C	128	438	45	117	16	1	17	66	28	82	10	12	1-0	.267	.322	.425	.747	10	.989
2002—	Atlanta (N.L.)	C	109	347	31	81	15	0	11	52	26	63	8	15	0-1	.233	.299	.372	.670	10	.986
2003—	Atlanta (N.L.)	C-DH	129	457	89	150	29	3	43	109	33	90	4	10	0-1	.328	.378	.687	1.065	5	.994
2004—	Baltimore (A.L.)	C-DH	150	579	83	183	33	3	23	86	47	97	6	16	0-0	.316	.370	.503	.873	5	.994
2005—	Bowie (East.)	C-DH	4	15	1	6	1	0	0	3	0	3	0	0	0-0	.400	.375	.467	.842	0	1.000
—	Baltimore (A.L.)	C-DH-1B	103	395	47	110	24	1	15	49	19	68	7	10	0-1	.278	.322	.458	.780	3	.994
2006—	Bowie (East.)		2	7	1	2	1	0	1	1	1	2	0	0	0-0	.286	.375	.857	1.232	0	...
—	Baltimore (A.L.)	DH-C	76	279	30	74	15	1	8	31	18	60	2	5	0-0	.265	.314	.412	.727	0	1.000
—	Boston (A.L.)	C	18	63	6	12	5	0	0	4	2	16	0	5	0-0	.190	.215	.270	.485	1	.990
American League totals (3 years)			347	1316	166	379	77	5	46	170	86	241	15	36	0-1	.288	.337	.459	.796	9	.995
National League totals (12 years)			1156	4003	508	1148	190	14	214	694	271	728	51	136	8-18	.287	.337	.502	.839	64	.992
Major League totals (15 years)			1503	5319	674	1527	267	19	260	864	357	969	66	172	8-19	.287	.337	.491	.828	73	.992

DIVISION SERIES RECORD																			
Year	Team (League)	Pos.	G	AB	R	H	2B	3B	HR	RBI	BB	SO	HBP	GDP	SB-CS	Avg.	OBP	SLG	OPS	E	Avg.
1995—	Atlanta (N.L.)	C	3	9	0	4	0	0	0	0	0	3	0	0	0-1	.444	.400	.444	.844	0	1.000
1996—	Atlanta (N.L.)	C	2	7	1	2	1	0	0	1	1	0	0	0	1-0	.286	.375	.714	1.089	1	.958
1997—	Atlanta (N.L.)	C	2	7	3	2	2	0	0	1	1	0	0	0	0-0	.286	.444	.571	1.016	0	1.000
1998—	Atlanta (N.L.)	C	2	7	1	2	2	0	0	1	1	1	0	0	0-0	.286	.375	.714	1.089	0	1.000

L

Year Team (League)	Pos.	G	AB	R	H	2B	3B	HR	RBI	BB	SO	HBP	GDP	SB-CS	Avg.	OBP	SLG	OPS	E	Avg.
2000—Atlanta (N.L.)	C	3	11	0	1	0	0	0	0	0	1	0	0	0-1	.091	.091	.091	.182	0	1.000
2002—Atlanta (N.L.)	C	4	15	4	5	1	0	2	4	1	3	0	1	0-0	.333	.375	.800	1.175	0	1.000
2003—Atlanta (N.L.)	C	5	21	1	7	2	0	0	0	0	6	0	0	0-0	.333	.333	.429	.762	1	.977
Division series totals (7 years)		21	77	10	23	5	0	4	10	5	15	0	1	1-2	.299	.337	.519	.857	2	.989

CHAMPIONSHIP SERIES RECORD

Year Team (League)	Pos.	G	AB	R	H	2B	3B	HR	RBI	BB	SO	HBP	GDP	SB-CS	Avg.	OBP	SLG	OPS	E	Avg.
1992—Atlanta (N.L.)	C	1	1	0	0	0	0	0	0	0	0	0	0	0-0	.000	.000	.000	.000	0	1.000
1995—Atlanta (N.L.)	C	3	14	2	5	1	0	1	3	0	1	0	0	0-0	.357	.357	.643	1.000	0	1.000
1996—Atlanta (N.L.)	C	7	24	8	13	5	0	2	6	3	1	1	0	1-0	.542	.607	1.000	1.607	0	1.000
1997—Atlanta (N.L.)	C	5	17	0	1	1	0	0	2	1	7	0	0	0-0	.059	.100	.118	.218	0	1.000
1998—Atlanta (N.L.)	C	6	20	2	6	0	0	1	1	0	7	0	1	0-0	.300	.300	.450	.750	1	.978
2001—Atlanta (N.L.)	C	5	14	1	2	0	0	1	2	1	4	0	1	0-0	.143	.200	.357	.557	1	.957
Champ. series totals (6 years)		27	90	13	27	7	0	5	14	5	20	1	2	1-0	.300	.337	.544	.881	2	.990

WORLD SERIES RECORD

Year Team (League)	Pos.	G	AB	R	H	2B	3B	HR	RBI	BB	SO	HBP	GDP	SB-CS	Avg.	OBP	SLG	OPS	E	Avg.
1992—Atlanta (N.L.)		Did not play.																		
1995—Atlanta (N.L.)	C	6	17	1	3	2	0	1	3	1	1	1	1	0-0	.176	.263	.471	.734	0	1.000
1996—Atlanta (N.L.)	C	6	21	3	4	0	0	0	1	3	4	0	2	0-0	.190	.280	.190	.470	0	1.000
World series totals (2 years)		12	38	4	7	2	0	1	4	4	5	1	3	0-0	.184	.273	.316	.589	0	1.000

ALL-STAR GAME RECORD

	G	AB	R	H	2B	3B	HR	RBI	BB	SO	HBP	GDP	SB-CS	Avg.	OBP	SLG	OPS	E	Avg.
All-Star Game totals (3 years)	3	4	1	1	0	0	1	1	0	1	0	0	0-0	.250	.250	1.000	1.250	0	1.000

2006 LEFTY-RIGHTY SPLITS

vs.	Avg.	AB	H	2B	3B	HR	RBI	BB	SO	OBP	Slg.	vs.	Avg.	AB	H	2B	3B	HR	RBI	BB	SO	OBP	Slg.
L	.270	89	24	4	1	2	11	3	26	.293	.404	R	.245	253	62	16	0	6	24	17	50	.298	.379

LOPEZ, JOSE — SS

PERSONAL: Born November 24, 1983, in Anzoategui, Venezuela. ... 6-2/170. ... Bats right, throws right. ... Full name: Jose Celestino Lopez. ... High school: Unidad Educativa Cas Puerta Barcelona (Venezuela). **TRANSACTIONS/CAREER NOTES:** Signed as a non-drafted free agent by Seattle Mariners organization (July 2, 2000).

2006 GAMES PLAYED BY POSITION (MLB): 2B—150.

Year Team (League)	Pos.	G	AB	R	H	2B	3B	HR	RBI	BB	SO	HBP	GDP	SB-CS	Avg.	OBP	SLG	OPS	E	Avg.
2001—Everett (N'west)	SS-2B	70	289	42	74	15	0	2	20	13	44	10	3	13-6	.256	.309	.329	.638	17	.950
2002—San Bern. (Calif.)	SS-2B	123	522	82	169	39	5	8	60	27	45	5	8	31-13	.324	.360	.464	.824	31	.939
2003—San Antonio (Texas)	SS-2B-3B	132	538	82	139	35	2	13	69	27	56	10	12	18-8	.258	.303	.403	.706	28	.954
2004—Ariz. Mariners (Ariz.)	3B-SS-2B	4	12	3	2	1	0	0	1	2	1	0	1	1-0	.167	.267	.250	.517	1	.933
—Tacoma (PCL)	SS-3B-2B DH	74	275	40	81	19	0	13	39	16	30	6	2	6-2	.295	.342	.505	.834	20	.934
—Seattle (A.L.)	SS-3B	57	207	28	48	13	0	5	22	8	31	1	1	0-1	.232	.263	.367	.630	10	.956
2005—Tacoma (PCL)	2B	44	182	29	58	19	0	5	31	8	25	2	6	2-3	.319	.354	.505	.860	6	.972
—Seattle (A.L.)	2B-3B	54	190	18	47	19	0	2	25	6	25	4	5	4-2	.247	.282	.379	.661	7	.976
2006—Seattle (A.L.)	2B	151	603	78	170	28	8	10	79	26	80	9	17	5-2	.282	.319	.405	.723	16	.978
Major League totals (3 years)		262	1000	124	265	60	8	17	126	40	136	14	23	9-5	.265	.300	.392	.692	33	.973

ALL-STAR GAME RECORD

	G	AB	R	H	2B	3B	HR	RBI	BB	SO	HBP	GDP	SB-CS	Avg.	OBP	SLG	OPS	E	Avg.
All-Star Game totals (1 year)	1	0	1	0	0	0	0	0	0	0	0	0	0-0	...	...	...	...	1	.500

2006 LEFTY-RIGHTY SPLITS

vs.	Avg.	AB	H	2B	3B	HR	RBI	BB	SO	OBP	Slg.	vs.	Avg.	AB	H	2B	3B	HR	RBI	BB	SO	OBP	Slg.
L	.331	151	50	7	1	4	23	8	15	.370	.470	R	.265	452	120	21	7	6	56	18	65	.301	.383

LOPEZ, RODRIGO — P

PERSONAL: Born December 14, 1975, in Tlalnepantla, Mexico. ... 6-1/190. ... Throws right, bats right. ... Full name: Rodrigo Munoz Lopez. ... Name pronounced: rod-REE-go. **TRANSACTIONS/CAREER NOTES:** Contract sold by Aguila of the Mexican League to San Diego Padres organization (March 21, 1995). ... Loaned by Padres to Mexico City Red Devils of the Mexican League (March 13-August 19, 1998). ... Signed as a free agent by Baltimore Orioles organization (February 4, 2002). ... On disabled list (May 2-June 15, 2003); included rehabilitation assignment to Bowie. **HONORS:** Named A.L. Rookie Pitcher of the Year by THE SPORTING NEWS (2002).

CAREER HITTING: 1-for-20 (.050), 1 R, 0 2B, 0 3B, 0 HR, 0 RBI.

Year Team (League)	W	L	Pct.	ERA	WHIP	G	GS	CG	ShO	Hld.	Sv.-Opp.	IP	H	R	ER	HR	BB-IBB	SO	Avg.
1993—Aguila (Mex.)	0	0	...	36.00	6.00	2	0	0	0	...	0-...	1.0	3	4	4	0	3-...	0	...
1994—Aguila (Mex.)	0	0	...	4.97	1.42	10	0	0	0	...	0-...	12.2	15	7	7	2	3-...	5	...
1995—Ariz. Padres (Ariz.)	1	1	.500	5.45	1.59	11	7	0	0	...	1-...	34.2	41	29	21	0	14-0	33	.287
1996—Poza Rica (Mex.)	1	1	.500	3.54	1.52	7	3	0	0	...	1-...	20.1	15	8	8	2	16-...	22	...
—Idaho Falls (Pio.)	4	4	.500	5.70	1.55	15	14	0	0	...	1-...	71.0	76	52	45	3	34-0	72	.283
1997—Clinton (Midw.)	6	8	.429	3.18	1.19	37	14	2	0	...	9-...	121.2	103	49	43	6	42-1	123	.228
1998—M.C. R. Dev. (Mex.)	10	6	.625	3.35	1.49	26	26	1	0	...	0-...	163.2	165	73	61	9	79-...	95	...
—Mobile (Sou.)	3	0	1.000	1.40	0.97	4	4	2	1	...	0-...	25.2	21	11	4	1	4-0	20	.219
1999—Mobile (Sou.)	10	8	.556	4.41	1.45	28	28	2	1	...	0-...	169.1	187	91	83	14	58-3	138	.286
2000—Las Vegas (PCL)	8	7	.533	4.69	1.54	20	20	1	0	...	0-...	109.1	123	66	57	9	45-1	100	.289
—San Diego (N.L.)	0	3	.000	8.76	2.15	6	6	0	0	...	0-...	24.2	40	24	24	5	13-0	17	.377
2001—Lake Elsinore (Calif.)	0	1	.000	0.69	1.46	9	0	0	0	...	0-...	13.0	15	7	1	1	4-0	9	.278
—Portland (PCL)	2	2	.500	3.44	1.15	11	8	0	0	...	0-...	52.1	45	22	20	7	15-0	37	.230
2002—Baltimore (A.L.)	15	9	.625	3.57	1.19	33	28	1	0	...	0-...	196.2	172	83	78	23	62-4	136	.234
2003—Bowie (East.)	1	0	1.000	0.00	0.50	1	1	0	0	...	0-...	6.1	3	0	0	0	0-0	13	.143
—Baltimore (A.L.)	7	10	.412	5.82	1.57	26	26	3	1	0	0-0	147.0	188	101	95	24	43-6	103	.313
2004—Baltimore (A.L.)	14	9	.609	3.59	1.28	37	23	1	1	4	0-1	170.2	164	71	68	21	54-2	121	.252
2005—Baltimore (A.L.)	15	12	.556	4.90	1.41	35	•35	0	0	0	0-0	209.1	232	126	114	28	63-1	118	.276
2006—Baltimore (A.L.)	9	*18	.333	5.90	1.55	36	29	0	0	0	0-0	189.0	234	129	*124	32	59-2	136	.302
American League totals (5 years)	60	58	.508	4.72	1.39	167	141	5	2	4	0-1	912.2	990	510	479	128	281-15	614	.275
National League totals (1 year)	0	3	.000	8.76	2.15	6	6	0	0	0	0-0	24.2	40	24	24	5	13-0	17	.377
Major League totals (6 years)	60	61	.496	4.83	1.41	173	147	5	2	4	0-1	937.1	1030	534	503	133	294-15	631	.278

2006 LEFTY-RIGHTY SPLITS

vs.	Avg.	AB	H	2B	3B	HR	RBI	BB	SO	OBP	Slg.	vs.	Avg.	AB	H	2B	3B	HR	RBI	BB	SO	OBP	Slg.
L	.308	389	120	20	1	15	49	32	65	.363	.481	R	.296	385	114	29	3	17	64	27	71	.342	.519

LORETTA, MARK — 2B

PERSONAL: Born August 14, 1971, in Santa Monica, Calif. ... 6-0/186. ... Bats right, throws right. ... Full name: Mark David Loretta. ... High school: St. Francis (La Canada, Calif.). ... College: Northwestern. **TRANSACTIONS/CAREER NOTES:** Selected by Milwaukee Brewers organization in seventh round of 1993 free-agent draft. ... On disabled list (June 3-August 16, 2000); included rehabilitation assignment to Indianapolis. ... On disabled list (March 27-May 19, 2001); included rehabilitation assignment to Indianapolis. ... Traded by Brewers to Houston Astros from two players to be named (August 31, 2002); Brewers acquired P Wayne Franklin (September 3, 2002) and 2B Keith Ginter (September 5, 2002) to complete deal. ... Signed as a free agent by San Diego Padres (December 16, 2002). ... On disabled list (May 24-July 18, 2005); included rehabilitation assignment to Portland. ... Traded by Padres to Boston Red Sox for C Doug Mirabelli (December 7, 2005). **HONORS:** Named second baseman on THE SPORTING NEWS N.L. All-Star team (2004). ... Named second baseman on N.L. Silver Slugger team (2004). **STATISTICAL NOTES:** Career major league grand slams: 1. ... Career major league pitching: 0-0, 0.00 ERA, 1 G, 1.0 IP, 1 H, 0 R, 0 ER, 1 BB, 2 SO.
2006 GAMES PLAYED BY POSITION (MLB): 2B—138, 1B—11, DH—6.

Year	Team (League)	Pos.	G	AB	R	H	2B	3B	HR	RBI	BB	SO	HBP	GDP	SB-CS	Avg.	OBP	SLG	OPS	E	Avg.
1993—Helena (Pion.)		SS	6	28	5	9	1	0	1	8	1	4	1	1	0-0	.321	.367	.464	.831	0	1.000
—Stockton (Calif.)		3B-SS	53	201	36	73	4	1	4	31	22	17	2	6	8-2	.363	.427	.453	.880	15	.943
1994—El Paso (Texas)		P	77	302	50	95	13	6	0	38	27	33	2	12	8-5	.315	.369	.397	.766	11	.973
—New Orleans (A.A.)		2B-SS	43	138	16	29	7	0	1	14	12	13	3	2	2-1	.210	.282	.283	.565	11	.945
1995—New Orleans (A.A.)	SS-3B-2B	DH	127	479	48	137	22	5	7	79	34	47	9	12	8-9	.286	.340	.397	.737	25	.959
—Milwaukee (A.L.)		SS-2B-DH	19	50	13	13	3	0	1	3	4	7	1	1	1-1	.260	.327	.380	.707	1	.984
1996—New Orleans (A.A.)		SS	19	71	10	18	5	1	0	11	9	8	2	1	1-1	.254	.345	.352	.697	5	.948
—Milwaukee (A.L.)		2B-3B-SS	73	154	20	43	3	0	1	13	14	15	0	7	2-1	.279	.339	.318	.657	2	.989
1997—Milwaukee (A.L.)		2B-SS-1B 3B	132	418	56	120	17	5	5	47	47	60	2	15	5-5	.287	.354	.388	.742	15	.976
1998—Milwaukee (N.L.)		1B-SS-3B 2B-OF	140	434	55	137	29	0	6	54	42	47	7	14	9-6	.316	.382	.424	.806	6	.991
1999—Milwaukee (N.L.)		SS-1B-2B 3B	153	587	93	170	34	5	5	67	52	59	10	14	4-1	.290	.354	.390	.744	13	.986
2000—Milwaukee (N.L.)		SS-2B	91	352	49	99	21	1	7	40	37	38	1	9	0-3	.281	.350	.406	.757	2	.995
—Indianapolis (Int'l)		SS	10	25	6	6	1	0	0	5	2	4	1	1	0-0	.240	.310	.280	.590	0	1.000
2001—Indianapolis (Int'l)		SS-2B	8	31	4	3	0	0	0	1	2	4	0	1	0-0	.097	.152	.097	.248	3	.850
—Milwaukee (N.L.)		2B-3B-SS DH-P	102	384	40	111	14	2	2	29	28	46	7	6	1-2	.289	.346	.352	.698	8	.978
2002—Milwaukee (N.L.)		3B-SS-1B 2B-DH	86	217	23	58	14	0	2	19	23	32	5	6	0-0	.267	.350	.359	.709	3	.982
—Houston (N.L.)		3B-SS-2B	21	66	10	28	4	0	2	8	9	5	0	1	1-1	.424	.481	.576	1.056	2	.964
2003—San Diego (N.L.)		2B-SS	154	589	74	185	28	4	13	72	54	62	3	17	5-4	.314	.372	.441	.814	7	.990
2004—San Diego (N.L.)		2B	154	620	108	208	47	2	16	76	58	45	9	10	5-3	.335	.391	.495	.886	10	.987
2005—Portland (PCL)		2B-DH	3	10	0	1	0	0	0	0	2	1	0	1	0-0	.100	.250	.100	.350	0	1.000
—San Diego (N.L.)		2B-3B	105	404	54	113	16	1	3	38	45	34	8	11	8-4	.280	.360	.347	.707	6	.987
2006—San Diego (A.L.)		2B-1B-DH	155	635	75	181	33	0	5	59	49	63	12	16	4-1	.285	.345	.361	.706	4	.994
American League totals (4 years)			379	1257	164	357	56	5	12	122	114	145	15	39	12-8	.284	.347	.365	.712	22	.986
National League totals (8 years)			1006	3653	506	1109	207	15	56	403	348	368	50	88	33-24	.304	.368	.414	.783	57	.987
Major League totals (12 years)			1385	4910	670	1466	263	20	68	525	462	513	65	127	45-32	.299	.363	.402	.765	79	.987

DIVISION SERIES RECORD

Year	Team (League)	Pos.	G	AB	R	H	2B	3B	HR	RBI	BB	SO	HBP	GDP	SB-CS	Avg.	OBP	SLG	OPS	E	Avg.
2005—San Diego (N.L.)		2B	3	15	0	4	0	0	0	0	0	0	0	1	0-0	.267	.267	.267	.533	0	1.000

ALL-STAR GAME RECORD

			G	AB	R	H	2B	3B	HR	RBI	BB	SO	HBP	GDP	SB-CS	Avg.	OBP	SLG	OPS	E	Avg.
All-Star Game totals (2 years)			2	4	0	1	0	0	0	0	0	0	0	0	0-0	.250	.250	.250	.500	0	1.000

2006 LEFTY-RIGHTY SPLITS

vs.	Avg.	AB	H	2B	3B	HR	RBI	BB	SO	OBP	Slg.	vs.	Avg.	AB	H	2B	3B	HR	RBI	BB	SO	OBP	Slg.
L	.274	186	51	10	0	4	14	22	17	.355	.392	R	.290	449	130	23	0	1	45	27	46	.341	.347

LOWE, DEREK — P

PERSONAL: Born June 1, 1973, in Dearborn, Mich. ... 6-6/210. ... Throws right, bats right. ... Full name: Derek Christopher Lowe. ... High school: Edsel Ford (Dearborn, Mich.). **TRANSACTIONS/CAREER NOTES:** Selected by Seattle Mariners organization in eighth round of 1991 free-agent draft. ... Traded by Mariners with C Jason Varitek to Boston Red Sox for P Heathcliff Slocumb (July 31, 1997). ... On suspended list (September 15-20, 2002). ... Signed as a free agent by Los Angeles Dodgers (January 12, 2005). **HONORS:** Named righthanded pitcher on THE SPORTING NEWS A.L. All-Star team (2002). **STATISTICAL NOTES:** Pitched 10-0 no-hit victory against Tampa Bay (April 27, 2002). **MISCELLANEOUS NOTES:** Struck out in only appearance as pinch hitter (2000).
CAREER HITTING: 18-for-149 (.121), 8 R, 5 2B, 0 3B, 0 HR, 8 RBI.

Year	Team (League)	W	L	Pct.	ERA	WHIP	G	GS	CG	ShO	Hld.	Sv.-Opp.	IP	H	R	ER	HR	BB-IBB	SO	Avg.
1991—Ariz. Mariners (Ariz.)	5	3	.625	2.41	1.11	12	12	0	0	...	0-...	71.0	58	26	19	2	21-0	60	.217
1992—Bellingham (N'west)	7	3	.700	2.42	1.06	14	13	2	•1	...	0-...	85.2	69	34	23	2	27-0	66	.216
1993—Riverside (Calif.)	12	9	.571	5.26	1.62	27	26	3	2	...	0-...	154.0	189	104	90	9	60-0	80	.304
1994—Jacksonville (Sou.)	7	10	.412	4.94	1.50	26	26	2	0	...	0-...	151.1	177	92	83	7	50-1	75	.291
1995—Ariz. Mariners (Ariz.)	1	0	1.000	0.93	0.72	2	2	0	0	...	0-...	9.2	5	1	1	0	2-0	11	.152
—Port City (Sou.)	1	6	.143	6.08	1.73	10	10	1	0	...	0-...	53.1	70	41	36	8	22-1	30	.327
1996—Port City (Sou.)	5	3	.625	3.05	1.12	10	10	0	0	...	0-...	65.0	56	27	22	7	17-0	33	.235
—Tacoma (PCL)	6	9	.400	4.54	1.48	17	16	1	1	...	0-...	105.0	118	64	53	7	37-1	54	.285
1997—Tacoma (PCL)	3	4	.429	3.45	1.27	10	9	1	0	...	0-...	57.1	53	26	22	3	20-0	49	.242
—Seattle (A.L.)	2	4	.333	6.96	1.49	12	9	0	0	0	0-0	53.0	59	43	41	11	20-2	39	.282
—Pawtucket (Int'l)	4	0	1.000	2.37	1.12	6	5	0	0	...	0-...	30.1	23	8	8	3	11-0	21	.213
—Boston (A.L.)	0	2	.000	3.38	1.13	8	0	0	0	1	0-2	16.0	15	6	6	0	3-1	13	.268
1998—Boston (A.L.)	3	9	.250	4.02	1.37	63	10	0	0	12	4-9	123.0	126	65	55	5	42-5	77	.267
1999—Boston (A.L.)	6	3	.667	2.63	1.00	74	0	0	0	22	15-20	109.1	84	35	32	7	25-1	80	.208
2000—Boston (A.L.)	4	4	.500	2.56	1.23	74	0	0	0	0	•42-47	91.1	90	27	26	8	22-5	79	.257
2001—Boston (A.L.)	5	10	.333	3.53	1.44	67	3	0	0	0	24-30	91.2	103	39	36	7	29-9	82	.283
2002—Boston (A.L.)	21	8	.724	2.58	0.97	32	32	1	1	0	0-0	219.2	166	65	63	12	48-0	127	.211
2003—Boston (A.L.)	17	7	.708	4.47	1.42	33	33	1	0	0	0-0	203.1	216	113	101	17	72-4	110	.272
2004—Boston (A.L.)	14	12	.538	5.42	1.61	33	33	0	0	0	0-0	182.2	224	•138	110	15	71-2	105	.299
2005—Los Angeles (N.L.)	12	15	.444	3.61	1.25	35	•35	2	2	0	0-0	222.0	223	113	89	28	55-1	146	.260
2006—Los Angeles (N.L.)	•16	8	.667	3.63	1.27	35	34	1	0	0	0-0	218.0	221	97	88	14	55-2	123	.262
American League totals (8 years)	72	59	.550	3.88	1.30	396	120	2	1	39	85-108	1090.0	1083	531	470	80	332-29	712	.259
National League totals (2 years)	28	23	.549	3.62	1.26	70	69	3	2	0	0-0	440.0	444	210	177	42	110-3	269	.261
Major League totals (10 years)	100	82	.549	3.81	1.29	466	189	5	3	39	85-108	1530.0	1527	741	647	122	442-32	981	.259

DIVISION SERIES RECORD

Year Team (League)	W	L	Pct.	ERA	WHIP	G	GS	CG	ShO	Hld.	Sv.-Opp.	IP	H	R	ER	HR	BB-IBB	SO	Avg.
1998—Boston (A.L.)	0	0	...	2.08	0.92	2	0	0	0	0	0-0	4.1	3	1	1	0	1-1	2	.200
1999—Boston (A.L.)	1	1	.500	4.32	0.84	3	0	0	0	0	0-0	8.1	6	7	4	2	1-0	7	.188
2003—Boston (A.L.)	0	1	.000	0.93	1.45	3	1	0	0	0	1-1	9.2	7	2	1	0	7-2	6	.200
2004—Boston (A.L.)	1	0	1.000	0.00	2.00	1	0	0	0	0	0-0	1.0	1	0	0	0	1-0	0	.333
2006—Los Angeles (N.L.)	0	0	...	6.75	1.50	1	1	0	0	0	0-0	5.1	6	4	4	2	2-1	6	.273
Division series totals (5 years)	2	2	.500	3.14	1.22	10	2	0	0	1	1-1	28.2	23	14	10	4	12-4	21	.215

CHAMPIONSHIP SERIES RECORD

Year Team (League)	W	L	Pct.	ERA	WHIP	G	GS	CG	ShO	Hld.	Sv.-Opp.	IP	H	R	ER	HR	BB-IBB	SO	Avg.
1999—Boston (A.L.)	0	0	...	1.42	1.26	3	0	0	0	0	0-1	6.1	6	3	1	0	2-0	7	.231
2003—Boston (A.L.)	0	2	.000	6.43	1.50	2	2	0	0	0	0-0	14.0	14	10	10	1	7-1	5	.255
2004—Boston (A.L.)	1	0	1.000	3.18	0.71	2	2	0	0	0	0-0	11.1	7	4	4	1	1-0	6	.175
Champ. series totals (3 years)	1	2	.333	4.26	1.17	7	4	0	0	0	0-1	31.2	27	17	15	2	10-1	18	.223

WORLD SERIES RECORD

Year Team (League)	W	L	Pct.	ERA	WHIP	G	GS	CG	ShO	Hld.	Sv.-Opp.	IP	H	R	ER	HR	BB-IBB	SO	Avg.
2004—Boston (A.L.)	1	0	1.000	0.00	0.57	1	1	0	0	0	0-0	7.0	3	0	0	0	1-0	4	.130

ALL-STAR GAME RECORD

	W	L	Pct.	ERA	WHIP	G	GS	CG	ShO	Hld.	Sv.-Opp.	IP	H	R	ER	HR	BB-IBB	SO	Avg.
All-Star Game totals (2 years)	0	0	...	3.00	0.67	2	1	0	1	1	0-0	3.0	2	1	1	0	0-0	0	.182

2006 LEFTY-RIGHTY SPLITS

vs.	Avg.	AB	H	2B	3B	HR	RBI	BB	SO	OBP	Slg.	vs.	Avg.	AB	H	2B	3B	HR	RBI	BB	SO	OBP	Slg.
L	.270	404	109	17	2	10	47	41	48	.341	.396	R	.255	440	112	20	0	4	35	14	75	.280	.327

LOWE, MARK — P

PERSONAL: Born June 7, 1983, in Houston, Texas. ... Throws right, bats right. ... Full name: Mark C. Lowe. ... College: Texas-Arlington. **TRANSACTIONS/CAREER NOTES:** Selected by Seattle Mariners organization in fifth round of 2004 free-agent draft.
CAREER HITTING: 0-for-0 (.000), 0 R, 0 2B, 0 3B, 0 HR, 0 RBI.

Year Team (League)	W	L	Pct.	ERA	WHIP	G	GS	CG	ShO	Hld.	Sv.-Opp.	IP	H	R	ER	HR	BB-IBB	SO	Avg.
2004—Everett (N'west)	1	2	.333	4.93	1.46	18	3	0	0	...	7-...	38.1	42	22	21	4	14-0	38	.276
2005—Wisconsin (Midw.)	6	6	.500	5.47	1.50	22	22	0	0	0	0-0	103.2	107	72	63	12	49-0	72	.264
2006—Inland Empire (Calif.)	1	0	1.000	1.84	0.85	13	2	0	0	0	2-2	29.1	14	10	6	0	11-1	46	.132
—San Antonio (Texas)	0	2	.000	2.16	1.02	11	0	0	0	0	4-6	16.2	14	4	4	1	3-0	14	.233
—Seattle (A.L.)	1	0	1.000	1.93	1.13	15	0	0	0	6	0-0	18.2	12	4	4	1	9-1	20	.190
Major League totals (1 year)	1	0	1.000	1.93	1.13	15	0	0	0	6	0-0	18.2	12	4	4	1	9-1	20	.190

2006 LEFTY-RIGHTY SPLITS

vs.	Avg.	AB	H	2B	3B	HR	RBI	BB	SO	OBP	Slg.	vs.	Avg.	AB	H	2B	3B	HR	RBI	BB	SO	OBP	Slg.
L	.167	24	4	0	0	1	2	3	9	.310	.292	R	.205	39	8	3	0	0	4	6	11	.311	.282

LOWELL, MIKE — 3B

PERSONAL: Born February 24, 1974, in San Juan, Puerto Rico. ... 6-3/210. ... Bats right, throws right. ... Full name: Michael Averett Lowell. ... High school: Coral Gables (Fla.). ... College: Florida International. **TRANSACTIONS/CAREER NOTES:** Selected by New York Yankees organization in 20th round of 1995 free-agent draft. ... Traded by Yankees to Florida Marlins for Ps Ed Yarnall, Mark Johnson and Todd Noel (February 1, 1999). ... On disabled list (March 26-May 29, 1999); included rehabilitation assignment to Calgary. ... On disabled list (May 13-29, 2000; and August 31-September 28, 2003). ... Traded by Marlins with Ps Josh Beckett and Guillermo Mota to Boston Red Sox for SS Hanley Ramirez and Ps Anibal Sanchez, Harvey Garcia and Jesus Delgado (November 24, 2005). **HONORS:** Won N.L. Gold Glove at third base (2005). ... Named third baseman on N.L. Silver Slugger team (2003). **STATISTICAL NOTES:** Hit three home runs in one game (April 21, 2004). ... Career major league grand slams: 5.
2006 GAMES PLAYED BY POSITION (MLB): 3B—153.

Year Team (League)	Pos.	G	AB	R	H	2B	3B	HR	RBI	BB	SO	HBP	GDP	SB-CS	Avg.	OBP	SLG	OPS	E	Avg.
1995—Oneonta (NYP)	3B	72	281	36	73	18	0	1	27	23	34	3	5	3-1	.260	.316	.335	.651	24	.911
1996—Greensboro (S. Atl.)	3B-SS	113	433	58	122	33	0	8	64	46	43	4	7	10-3	.282	.355	.413	.768	32	.925
—Tampa (Fla. St.)	3B	24	78	8	22	5	0	0	11	3	13	0	2	1-1	.282	.298	.346	.644	3	.954
1997—Norwich (East.)	3B-SS	78	285	60	98	17	0	15	47	48	30	4	11	2-1	.344	.439	.561	1.000	15	.927
—Columbus (Int'l)	3B-SS	57	210	36	58	13	1	15	45	23	34	3	6	2-4	.276	.347	.562	.909	4	.954
1998—Columbus (Int'l)	1B-3B-SS	126	510	79	155	34	3	26	99	37	85	6	10	4-0	.304	.355	.535	.890	21	.950
—New York (A.L.)	3B-DH	8	15	1	4	0	0	0	0	0	1	0	0	0-0	.267	.267	.267	.533	1	1.000
1999—Calgary (PCL)	3B	24	83	11	26	3	0	2	9	8	19	0	0	0-0	.313	.374	.422	.795	4	.939
—Florida (N.L.)	3B	97	308	32	78	15	0	12	47	26	69	5	8	0-0	.253	.317	.419	.736	4	.981
2000—Florida (N.L.)	3B	140	508	73	137	38	0	22	91	54	75	9	4	4-0	.270	.344	.474	.818	12	.968
2001—Florida (N.L.)	3B	146	531	65	156	37	0	18	100	43	79	10	9	1-2	.283	.340	.448	.789	9	.976
2002—Florida (N.L.)	3B	160	597	88	165	44	0	24	92	65	92	4	16	4-3	.276	.346	.471	.816	14	.969
2003—Florida (N.L.)	3B-DH	130	492	76	136	27	1	32	105	56	78	3	14	3-1	.276	.350	.530	.881	9	.973
2004—Florida (N.L.)	3B-DH	158	598	87	175	44	1	27	85	64	77	6	17	5-1	.293	.365	.505	.870	7	.982
2005—Florida (N.L.)	3B-2B	150	500	56	118	36	1	8	58	46	58	2	14	4-0	.236	.298	.360	.658	7	.982
2006—Boston (A.L.)	3B	153	573	79	163	47	1	20	80	47	61	4	22	2-2	.284	.339	.475	.814	6	.987
American League totals (2 years)		161	588	80	167	47	1	20	80	47	62	4	22	2-2	.284	.337	.469	.807	6	.987
National League totals (7 years)		981	3554	477	965	241	3	143	578	354	528	39	82	21-7	.272	.339	.462	.801	62	.975
Major League totals (9 years)		1142	4142	557	1132	288	4	163	658	401	590	43	104	23-9	.273	.339	.463	.802	68	.977

DIVISION SERIES RECORD

Year Team (League)	Pos.	G	AB	R	H	2B	3B	HR	RBI	BB	SO	HBP	GDP	SB-CS	Avg.	OBP	SLG	OPS	E	Avg.
2003—Florida (N.L.)	3B	2	3	0	0	0	0	0	0	0	1	0	0	0-0	.000	.000	.000	.000	0	1.000

CHAMPIONSHIP SERIES RECORD

Year Team (League)	Pos.	G	AB	R	H	2B	3B	HR	RBI	BB	SO	HBP	GDP	SB-CS	Avg.	OBP	SLG	OPS	E	Avg.
2003—Florida (N.L.)	3B	7	20	5	4	0	0	2	3	3	4	0	0	0-0	.200	.304	.500	.804	0	1.000

WORLD SERIES RECORD

Year Team (League)	Pos.	G	AB	R	H	2B	3B	HR	RBI	BB	SO	HBP	GDP	SB-CS	Avg.	OBP	SLG	OPS	E	Avg.
2003—Florida (N.L.)	3B	6	23	1	5	1	0	0	2	2	3	0	0	0-0	.217	.280	.261	.541	0	1.000

ALL-STAR GAME RECORD

		G	AB	R	H	2B	3B	HR	RBI	BB	SO	HBP	GDP	SB-CS	Avg.	OBP	SLG	OPS	E	Avg.
All-Star Game totals (3 years)		3	6	1	3	1	0	0	4	0	0	0	0	0-0	.500	.500	.667	1.167	0	1.000

2006 LEFTY-RIGHTY SPLITS

vs.	Avg.	AB	H	2B	3B	HR	RBI	BB	SO	OBP	Slg.	vs.	Avg.	AB	H	2B	3B	HR	RBI	BB	SO	OBP	Slg.
L	.241	166	40	11	0	4	18	17	22	.316	.380	R	.302	407	123	36	1	16	62	30	39	.349	.514

L

LOWRY, NOAH   P

PERSONAL: Born October 10, 1980, in Ventura, Calif. ... 6-2/210. ... Throws left, bats right. ... Full name: Noah Ryan Lowry. ... High school: Nordhoff (Ojai, Calif.). ... College: Pepperdine. **TRANSACTIONS/CAREER NOTES:** Selected by Texas Rangers organization in 19th round of 1999 free-agent draft; did not sign. ... Selected by San Francisco Giants organization in first round (30th pick overall) of 2001 free-agent draft. ... On disabled list (April 7-May 8, 2006); included rehabilitation assignments to San Jose and Fresno. **MISCELLANEOUS NOTES:** Lined out in only appearance as pinch hitter (2005). ... Appeared in two games as pinch runner (2006).
CAREER HITTING: 30-for-140 (.214), 11 R, 8 2B, 0 3B, 1 HR, 9 RBI.

Year	Team (League)	W	L	Pct.	ERA	WHIP	G	GS	CG	ShO	Hld.	Sv.-Opp.	IP	H	R	ER	HR	BB-IBB	SO	Avg.
2001—	Salem-Keizer (N'west)	1	1	.500	3.60	1.36	8	7	0	0	...	0-...	25.0	26	15	10	2	8-0	28	.265
2002—	San Jose (Calif.)	6	5	.545	2.15	0.99	15	12	0	0	...	0-...	58.2	38	21	14	4	20-0	62	.186
2003—	Norwich (East.)	9	6	.600	4.72	1.47	23	23	2	0	...	0-...	118.1	127	66	62	7	47-0	97	.285
	—Fresno (PCL)	1	0	1.000	2.37	1.11	4	4	0	0	...	0-...	19.0	15	5	5	0	6-0	13	.227
	—San Francisco (N.L.)	0	0	...	0.00	0.47	4	0	0	0	0	0-0	6.1	1	0	0	0	2-0	5	.048
2004—	Fresno (PCL)	7	5	.583	4.13	1.41	17	17	1	1	...	0-...	89.1	98	53	41	9	28-0	73	.278
	—San Francisco (N.L.)	6	0	1.000	3.82	1.29	16	14	2	1	0	0-0	92.0	91	41	39	10	28-1	72	.262
2005—	San Francisco (N.L.)	13	13	.500	3.78	1.31	33	33	0	0	0	0-0	204.2	193	92	86	21	76-1	172	.249
2006—	Fresno (PCL)	0	0	...	4.50	1.00	1	1	0	0	0	0-0	6.0	5	3	3	1	1-0	6	.208
	—San Jose (Calif.)	0	0	...	0.00	1.29	1	1	0	0	0	0-0	4.2	5	0	0	0	1-0	9	.277
	—San Francisco (N.L.)	7	10	.412	4.74	1.39	27	27	1	1	0	0-0	159.1	166	89	84	21	56-2	84	.273
	Major League totals (4 years)	26	23	.531	4.07	1.33	80	74	3	2	0	0-0	462.1	451	222	209	52	162-4	333	.257

2006 LEFTY-RIGHTY SPLITS

vs.	Avg.	AB	H	2B	3B	HR	RBI	BB	SO	OBP	Slg.	vs.	Avg.	AB	H	2B	3B	HR	RBI	BB	SO	OBP	Slg.
L	.312	125	39	11	3	4	15	16	18	.407	.544	R	.262	484	127	23	3	17	60	40	66	.317	.428

LUGO, JULIO   SS

PERSONAL: Born November 16, 1975, in Barahona, Dominican Republic. ... 6-1/170. ... Bats right, throws right. ... Full name: Julio Cesar Lugo. ... Name pronounced: LOU-go. ... Junior college: Connors State (Okla.). ... Brother of Ruddy Lugo, pitcher, Tampa Bay Devil Rays. **TRANSACTIONS/CAREER NOTES:** Selected by Houston Astros organization in 43rd round of 1994 free-agent draft. ... On disabled list (August 13, 2002-remainder of season). ... Released by Astros (May 9, 2003). ... Signed by Tampa Bay Devil Rays (May 15, 2003). ... On disabled list (April 6-May 5, 2006). ... Traded by Devil Rays to Los Angeles Dodgers for OF Sergio Pedroza and SS Joel Guzman (July 31, 2006).
STATISTICAL NOTES: Career major league grand slams: 2.
2006 GAMES PLAYED BY POSITION (MLB): SS—81, 2B—29, 3B—16, OF—3.

Year	Team (League)	Pos.	G	AB	R	H	2B	3B	HR	RBI	BB	SO	HBP	GDP	SB-CS	Avg.	OBP	SLG	OPS	E	Avg.
																			FIELDING		
1995—	Auburn (NY-Penn)	2B-OF-SS	59	230	36	67	6	3	1	16	26	31	2	7	17-7	.291	.368	.357	.725	12	.944
1996—	Quad City (Midw.)	2B-3B-SS	101	393	60	116	18	2	10	50	32	75	3	7	24-11	.295	.350	.427	.777	29	.938
1997—	Kissimmee (Fla. St.)	2B-SS	125	505	89	135	22	14	7	61	46	99	2	8	35-8	.267	.329	.408	.736	41	.938
1998—	Kissimmee (Fla. St.)	SS	128	509	81	154	20	14	7	62	49	72	4	13	51-18	.303	.367	.438	.805	42	.921
1999—	Jackson (Texas)	SS-2B	116	445	77	142	24	5	10	42	44	53	3	6	25-11	.319	.381	.463	.844	29	.946
2000—	New Orleans (PCL)	2B-SS	24	101	22	33	4	3	1	12	11	20	0	2	12-7	.327	.393	.475	.868	4	.964
	—Houston (N.L.)	SS-2B-OF	116	420	78	119	22	5	10	40	37	93	4	9	22-9	.283	.346	.431	.777	17	.963
2001—	Houston (N.L.)	SS-OF-2B	140	513	93	135	20	3	10	37	46	116	5	7	12-11	.263	.326	.372	.698	23	.964
2002—	Houston (N.L.)	SS	88	322	45	84	15	1	8	35	28	74	2	6	9-3	.261	.322	.388	.710	8	.965
2003—	Houston (N.L.)	SS	22	65	6	16	3	0	0	2	9	12	0	2	2-1	.246	.338	.292	.630	3	.966
	—Tampa Bay (A.L.)	SS	117	433	58	119	13	4	15	53	35	88	4	5	10-3	.275	.333	.427	.760	17	.970
2004—	Tampa Bay (A.L.)	SS-2B-DH	157	581	83	160	41	4	7	75	54	106	5	8	21-5	.275	.338	.396	.734	26	.968
2005—	Tampa Bay (A.L.)	SS	158	616	89	182	36	6	6	57	61	72	6	5	39-11	.295	.362	.403	.765	24	.968
2006—	Tampa Bay (A.L.)	SS	73	289	53	89	17	1	12	27	27	47	3	7	18-4	.308	.373	.498	.871	14	.957
	—Los Angeles (N.L.)	2B-3B-SS																			
		OF	49	146	16	32	5	1	0	12	19	29	1	2	6-5	.219	.278	.267	.545	5	.969
	American League totals (4 years)		505	1919	283	550	107	15	40	212	177	313	18	25	88-23	.287	.350	.421	.770	81	.966
	National League totals (5 years)		415	1466	238	386	65	10	28	124	132	324	12	26	51-29	.263	.327	.379	.705	55	.967
	Major League totals (7 years)		920	3385	521	936	172	25	68	336	309	637	30	51	139-52	.277	.340	.402	.742	136	.966

DIVISION SERIES RECORD

Year	Team (League)	Pos.	G	AB	R	H	2B	3B	HR	RBI	BB	SO	HBP	GDP	SB-CS	Avg.	OBP	SLG	OPS	E	Avg.
2001—	Houston (N.L.)	SS	3	8	1	0	0	0	0	0	0	2	0	1	0-0	.000	.000	.000	.000	3	.786
2006—	Los Angeles (N.L.)	2B-3B	2	4	0	1	1	0	0	0	1	1	0	0	0-0	.250	.400	.500	.900	0	1.000
	Division series totals (2 years)		5	12	1	1	1	0	0	0	1	3	0	1	0-0	.083	.154	.167	.321	3	.842

2006 LEFTY-RIGHTY SPLITS

vs.	Avg.	AB	H	2B	3B	HR	RBI	BB	SO	OBP	Slg.	vs.	Avg.	AB	H	2B	3B	HR	RBI	BB	SO	OBP	Slg.
L	.263	118	31	4	0	4	11	9	11	.318	.398	R	.284	317	90	18	2	8	26	30	65	.349	.429

LUGO, RUDDY   P

PERSONAL: Born May 22, 1980, in Barahona, Dominican Republic. ... Throws right, bats right. ... Full name: Ruddy Joraider Lugo. ... College: None. ... Brother of Julio Lugo, shortstop, Los Angeles Dodgers. **TRANSACTIONS/CAREER NOTES:** Selected by Milwaukee Brewers organization in third round of 1999 free-agent draft. ... Traded by Brewers to Los Angeles Dodgers (June 1, 2001), completing deal in which Dodgers traded OF Devon White to Brewers for OF Marquis Grissom and a player to be named (February 25, 2001). ... Traded by Dodgers to Houston Astros for 1B/OF Daryle Ward (January 25, 2003). ... Signed as a free agent by Florida Marlins organization (April 2, 2004). ... Signed as a free agent by Tampa Bay Devil Rays organization (April 20, 2005). ... On disabled list (June 21-July 14, 2006); included rehabilitation assignment to Visalia.
CAREER HITTING: 0-for-0 (.000), 0 R, 0 2B, 0 3B, 0 HR, 0 RBI.

Year	Team (League)	W	L	Pct.	ERA	WHIP	G	GS	CG	ShO	Hld.	Sv.-Opp.	IP	H	R	ER	HR	BB-IBB	SO	Avg.
1999—	Ogden (Pion.)	1	2	.333	7.88	1.96	6	6	0	0	...	0-...	24.0	35	23	21	2	12-0	26	.340
2000—	Ogden (Pion.)	5	5	.500	3.44	1.46	16	16	1	0	...	0-...	91.2	82	48	35	7	52-1	88	.253
2001—	Beloit (Midw.)	1	0	1.000	0.60	1.07	10	0	0	0	...	5-...	15.0	10	1	1	0	6-0	20	.192
	—Wilmington (S. Atl.)	0	2	.000	3.77	1.35	16	0	0	0	...	2-...	31.0	29	14	13	2	13-0	23	.259
2002—	Vero Beach (FSL)	8	2	.800	2.38	1.08	22	9	1	1	...	1-...	87.0	68	28	23	5	26-0	77	.217
	—Jacksonville (Sou.)	3	1	.750	4.05	1.41	11	2	0	0	...	1-...	33.1	34	15	15	3	13-5	23	.274
2003—	Round Rock (Texas)	4	15	.211	6.01	1.57	41	15	1	0	...	1-...	118.1	133	93	79	12	53-5	112	.284
2004—	Carolina (Southern)	0	0	.000	4.91	1.70	8	1	0	0	...	0-...	14.2	16	10	8	3	9-0	6	.281
	—Jupiter (Fla. St.)	1	7	.125	5.22	1.44	31	0	0	0	...	11-...	39.2	42	31	23	4	15-4	33	.261
2005—	Visalia (Calif.)	0	0	...	13.50	4.00	1	0	0	0	...	0-0	2.0	7	4	3	0	1-0	1	.583
	—Montgom. (Sou.)	1	1	.500	1.12	1.19	26	0	0	0	4	2-2	40.1	25	12	5	1	23-0	48	.169
2006—	Visalia (Calif.)	0	0	...	6.75	2.00	4	0	0	0	0	1-2	4.0	16	3	3	0	2-0	5	.316
	—Tampa Bay (A.L.)	2	4	.333	3.81	1.32	64	0	0	0	8	0-0	85.0	75	39	36	4	37-0	48	.240
	Major League totals (1 year)	2	4	.333	3.81	1.32	64	0	0	0	8	0-0	85.0	75	39	36	4	37-0	48	.240

vs.	Avg.	AB	H	2B	3B	HR	RBI	BB	SO	OBP	Slg.	vs.	Avg.	AB	H	2B	3B	HR	RBI	BB	SO	OBP	Slg.
L	.213	150	32	6	1	0	18	13	27	.282	.267	R	.264	163	43	9	2	4	23	24	21	.359	.417

LUNA, HECTOR — SS/2B

PERSONAL: Born February 1, 1980, in Montecristi, Dominican Republic. ... 6-1/170. ... Bats right, throws right. ... Full name: Hector R. Luna. **TRANSACTIONS/CAREER NOTES:** Signed as a non-drafted free agent by Cleveland Indians organization (February 2, 1999). ... Selected by Tampa Bay Devil Rays from Indians organization in Rule 5 major league draft (December 16, 2002); returned to Indians organization (April 2, 2003). ... Selected by St. Louis Cardinals from Indians organization in Rule 5 major league draft (December 15, 2003). ... Traded by Cardinals to Indians for 2B Ronnie Belliard (July 30, 2006).

2006 GAMES PLAYED BY POSITION (MLB): 2B—61, SS—24, OF—19, 1B—6, 3B—4, DH—3.

										BATTING										FIELDING	
Year	Team (League)	Pos.	G	AB	R	H	2B	3B	HR	RBI	BB	SO	HBP	GDP	SB-CS	Avg.	OBP	SLG	OPS	E	Avg.
1999— Dom. Inds. (DSL)			61	234	44	60	13	2	1	24	27	36	5	9	29-5	.256	.345	.342	.687	...	...
2000— Burlington (Appal.)		SS	55	201	25	41	5	0	1	15	27	35	3	4	19-4	.204	.306	.244	.550	26	.900
— Mahoning Valley (N.Y.-Penn.)		SS	5	19	2	6	2	0	0	4	1	3	0	0	0-0	.316	.350	.421	.771	2	.875
2001— Columbus (S. Atl.)		SS	66	241	36	64	8	3	3	23	23	48	5	2	15-4	.266	.339	.361	.700	22	.933
2002— Kinston (Carol.)		SS	128	468	67	129	15	6	11	51	39	79	3	7	32-11	.276	.334	.404	.738	32	.947
2003— Akron (East.)		SS-2B	127	462	87	137	19	2	2	38	48	64	5	10	17-5	.297	.368	.359	.727	35	.936
2004— St. Louis (N.L.)		SS-2B-3B																			
		OF	83	173	25	43	7	2	3	22	13	37	2	2	6-3	.249	.304	.364	.668	7	.962
2005— Memphis (PCL)		2B-SS	57	223	24	50	13	1	3	21	20	38	2	2	11-4	.224	.294	.332	.626	5	.980
— St. Louis (N.L.)		OF-2B-3B																			
		SS	64	137	26	39	10	2	1	18	9	25	4	4	10-2	.285	.344	.409	.753	5	.967
2006— St. Louis (N.L.)		2B-OF-SS																			
		1B-3B-DH	76	223	27	65	14	1	4	21	21	34	1	3	5-3	.291	.355	.417	.772	5	.980
— Cleveland (A.L.)		2B-SS-3B																			
		DH-OF	37	127	14	35	7	1	2	17	6	26	0	4	0-1	.276	.306	.394	.700	5	.965
American League totals (1 year)			37	127	14	35	7	1	2	17	6	26	0	4	0-1	.276	.306	.394	.700	5	.965
National League totals (3 years)			223	533	78	147	31	5	8	61	43	96	7	9	21-8	.276	.336	.398	.733	17	.971
Major League totals (3 years)			260	660	92	182	38	6	10	78	49	122	7	13	21-9	.276	.330	.397	.727	22	.970

CHAMPIONSHIP SERIES RECORD

Year	Team (League)	Pos.	G	AB	R	H	2B	3B	HR	RBI	BB	SO	HBP	GDP	SB-CS	Avg.	OBP	SLG	OPS	E	Avg.
2004— St. Louis (N.L.)		2B-SS	2	4	0	0	0	0	0	0	0	2	0	0	0-0	.000	.000	.000	.000	0	1.000
2005— St. Louis (N.L.)		3B	2	4	0	0	0	0	0	0	0	2	0	0	0-0	.000	.000	.000	.000	2	.600
Champ. series totals (2 years)			4	8	0	0	0	0	0	0	0	4	0	0	0-0	.000	.000	.000	.000	2	.833

WORLD SERIES RECORD

Year	Team (League)	Pos.	G	AB	R	H	2B	3B	HR	RBI	BB	SO	HBP	GDP	SB-CS	Avg.	OBP	SLG	OPS	E	Avg.
2004— St. Louis (N.L.)		2B	1	1	0	0	0	0	0	0	1	0	0	0	0-0	.000	.500	.000	.500	0	...

2006 LEFTY-RIGHTY SPLITS

vs.	Avg.	AB	H	2B	3B	HR	RBI	BB	SO	OBP	Slg.	vs.	Avg.	AB	H	2B	3B	HR	RBI	BB	SO	OBP	Slg.
L	.315	162	51	10	0	2	16	11	23	.358	.414	R	.261	188	49	11	2	4	22	16	37	.320	.404

LYON, BRANDON — P

PERSONAL: Born August 10, 1979, in Salt Lake City. ... 6-1/185. ... Throws right, bats right. ... Full name: Brandon James Lyon. ... Name pronounced: lion. ... High school: Taylorsville (Salt Lake City). ... Junior college: Dixie College (Utah). **TRANSACTIONS/CAREER NOTES:** Selected by New York Mets organization in 37th round of 1997 free-agent draft; did not sign. ... Selected by Toronto Blue Jays organization in 14th round of 1999 free-agent draft. ... Claimed on waivers by Boston Red Sox (October 9, 2002). ... On disabled list (July 24-September 1, 2003); included rehabilitation assignment to Pawtucket. ... Traded by Red Sox with P Anastacio Martinez to Pittsburgh Pirates for Ps Scott Sauerbeck and Mike Gonzalez (July 22, 2003). ... Traded by Pirates with Ps Jeff Suppan and Anastacio Martinez to Red Sox for IF Freddy Sanchez, P Mike Gonzalez and cash (July 31, 2003). ... Traded by Red Sox with Ps Casey Fossum and Jorge de la Rosa and OF Mike Goss to Arizona Diamondbacks for P Curt Schilling (November 28, 2003). ... On disabled list (April 3, 2004-entire season). ... On disabled list (April 13-August 13, 2005); included rehabilitation assignment to Tucson.

CAREER HITTING: 0-for-0 (.000), 1 R, 0 2B, 0 3B, 0 HR, 0 RBI.

Year	Team (League)	W	L	Pct.	ERA	WHIP	G	GS	CG	ShO	Hld.	Sv.-Opp.	IP	H	R	ER	HR	BB-IBB	SO	Avg.
2000— Queens (N.Y.-Penn.)		5	3	.625	2.39	0.81	15	13	0	0		0-...	60.1	43	20	16	1	6-0	55	.197
2001— Tennessee (Sou.)		5	0	1.000	3.68	1.13	9	9	0	0		0-...	58.2	57	25	24	7	9-0	45	.252
— Syracuse (Int'l)		5	3	.625	3.69	1.14	11	11	2	1		0-...	68.1	68	33	28	7	10-0	53	.257
— Toronto (A.L.)		5	4	.556	4.29	1.24	11	11	0	0	0	0-0	63.0	63	31	30	6	15-0	35	.266
2002— Toronto (A.L.)		1	4	.200	6.53	1.56	15	10	0	0		0-1	62.0	78	47	45	14	19-2	35	.308
— Syracuse (Int'l)		4	9	.308	5.11	1.56	14	14	0	0		0-...	75.2	99	54	43	4	19-0	35	.315
2003— Pawtucket (Int'l)		0	0	...	3.24	1.08	5	0	0	0		0-...	8.1	7	3	3	1	2-0	7	.219
— Boston (A.L.)		4	6	.400	4.12	1.56	49	0	0	0	2	9-12	59.0	73	33	27	6	19-5	50	.296
2004— Tucson (PCL)		2	3	.400	15.12	2.28	6	3	0	0		0-...	8.1	15	14	14	3	4-0	4	.366
2005— Tucson (PCL)		0	1	.000	5.40	1.00	5	0	0	0		0-...	5.0	5	3	3	0	1-0	4	.250
— Arizona (N.L.)		0	2	.000	6.44	1.84	32	0	0	0		14-15	29.1	44	25	21	6	10-2	17	.341
2006— Arizona (N.L.)		2	4	.333	3.89	1.30	68	0	0	0	23	0-7	69.1	68	32	30	7	22-7	46	.258
American League totals (3 years)		10	14	.417	4.99	1.45	75	21	0	0	2	9-13	184.0	214	111	102	26	53-7	115	.290
National League totals (2 years)		2	6	.250	4.65	1.46	100	0	0	0	24	14-22	98.2	112	57	51	13	32-9	63	.285
Major League totals (5 years)		12	20	.375	4.87	1.45	175	21	0	0	26	23-35	282.2	326	168	153	39	85-16	178	.288

2006 LEFTY-RIGHTY SPLITS

vs.	Avg.	AB	H	2B	3B	HR	RBI	BB	SO	OBP	Slg.	vs.	Avg.	AB	H	2B	3B	HR	RBI	BB	SO	OBP	Slg.
L	.244	123	30	8	0	4	17	13	26	.314	.407	R	.270	141	38	16	2	3	21	9	20	.307	.475

MABEUS, CHRIS — P

PERSONAL: Born February 11, 1979, in Peoria, Ill. ... 6-3/210. ... Throws right, bats right. ... Full name: Christopher Eugene Mabeus. ... College: Lewis-Clark (Id.) State. **TRANSACTIONS/CAREER NOTES:** Selected by Boston Red Sox organization in 37th round of 1999 free-agent draft; did not sign. ... Selected by Oakland Athletics organization in 13th round of 2001 free-agent draft. ... Selected by Texas Rangers in Rule 5 major league draft (December 15, 2003). ... Returned to Athletics organization (March 25, 2004). ... Claimed on waivers by Milwaukee Brewers (May 16, 2006).

CAREER HITTING: 0-for-0 (.000), 0 R, 0 2B, 0 3B, 0 HR, 0 RBI.

Year	Team (League)	W	L	Pct.	ERA	WHIP	G	GS	CG	ShO	Hld.	Sv.-Opp.	IP	H	R	ER	HR	BB-IBB	SO	Avg.
2001— Vancouver (N'west)		2	5	.286	4.50	1.50	20	8	0	0		2-...	62.0	75	34	31	3	18-0	28	.300
2002— Modesto (California)		3	1	.750	4.04	1.52	37	1	0	0		1-...	84.2	97	39	38	3	32-4	69	.290
2003— Modesto (California)		2	0	1.000	1.52	1.06	18	0	0	0		2-...	23.2	19	6	4	1	6-0	30	.207

M

Year	Team (League)	W	L	Pct.	ERA	WHIP	G	GS	CG	ShO	Hld.	Sv.-Opp.	IP	H	R	ER	HR	BB-IBB	SO	Avg.
— Midland (Texas)		1	3	.250	3.52	1.20	32	0	0	0	...	13-...	38.1	37	20	15	1	9-2	40	.255
2004— Midland (Texas)		4	0	1.000	1.99	1.10	20	0	0	0	...	11-...	22.2	23	5	5	0	2-1	27	.253
— Sacramento (PCL)		7	2	.778	3.00	1.12	38	0	0	0	...	4-...	51.0	45	18	17	6	12-1	61	.227
2005— Sacramento (PCL)		9	2	.818	4.21	1.37	42	0	0	0	8	1-6	62.0	61	31	29	4	24-0	72	.256
2006— Huntsville (Sou.)		1	2	.333	6.04	1.84	18	1	0	0	3	0-0	22.1	21	15	15	1	20-2	15	.256
— Sacramento (PCL)		0	1	.000	4.58	1.32	12	0	0	0	1	0-1	19.2	16	11	10	1	10-1	20	.219
— Milwaukee (N.L.)		0	0	...	21.60	4.20	1	0	0	0	0	0-0	1.2	4	4	4	1	3-0	2	.444
— Nashville (PCL)		1	0	1.000	5.68	1.89	6	0	0	0	0	0-0	6.1	7	8	4	1	5-0	6	.280
Major League totals (1 year)		0	0	...	21.60	4.20	1	0	0	0	0	0-0	1.2	4	4	4	1	3-0	2	.444

2006 LEFTY-RIGHTY SPLITS

vs.	Avg.	AB	H	2B	3B	HR	RBI	BB	SO	OBP	Slg.	vs.	Avg.	AB	H	2B	3B	HR	RBI	BB	SO	OBP	Slg.
L	.000	1	0	0	0	0	0	1	1	.500	.000	R	.500	8	4	2	0	1	4	2	1	.600	1.125

MABRY, JOHN — OF/3B

PERSONAL: Born October 17, 1970, in Wilmington, Del. ... 6-4/210. ... Bats left, throws right. ... Full name: John Steven Mabry. ... Name pronounced: MAY-bree. ... High school: Bohemia Manor (Chesapeake City, Md.). ... College: West Chester (Pa.). **TRANSACTIONS/CAREER NOTES:** Selected by St. Louis Cardinals organization in sixth round of 1991 free-agent draft. ... On disabled list (August 20-September 24, 1997). ... Signed as a free agent by Seattle Mariners (December 30, 1998). ... On disabled list (August 14, 1999-remainder of season). ... On disabled list (April 22-May 12, 2000); included rehabilitation assignment to Tacoma. ... Traded by Mariners with P Tom Davey to San Diego Padres for OF Al Martin (July 31, 2000). ... Signed as a free agent by Cardinals organization (January 5, 2001). ... Traded by Cardinals to Florida Marlins for cash (April 9, 2001). ... On disabled list (April 16-May 20, 2001); included rehabilitation assignment to Brevard County. ... Signed as a free agent by Philadelphia Phillies organization (January 28, 2002). ... Traded by Phillies to Oakland Athletics for 1B/OF Jeremy Giambi (May 22, 2002). ... Signed as a free agent by Mariners (January 15, 2003). ... On disabled list (May 28-June 20, 2003); included rehabilitation assignment to Tacoma. ... Signed as a free agent by Cardinals (December 7, 2004). ... Signed as a free agent by Chicago Cubs (December 7, 2005). **STATISTICAL NOTES:** Hit for the cycle (May 18, 1996). ... Career major league grand slams: 1. ... Career major league pitching: 0-0, 63.00 ERA, 2 G, 1.0 IP, 6 H, 7 R, 7 ER, 4 BB, 0 SO.

2006 GAMES PLAYED BY POSITION (MLB): 1B—51, OF—11, 3B—2, DH—2.

											BATTING									FIELDING	
Year	Team (League)	Pos.	G	AB	R	H	2B	3B	HR	RBI	BB	SO	HBP	GDP	SB-CS	Avg.	OBP	SLG	OPS	E	Avg.
1991— Hamilton (NYP)		OF	49	187	25	58	11	0	1	31	17	18	2	6	9-3	.310	.370	.385	.755	5	.943
— Savannah (S. Atl.)		OF	22	86	10	20	6	1	0	8	7	12	0	2	1-0	.233	.284	.326	.610	1	.974
1992— Springfield (Midw.)		OF	115	438	63	115	13	6	11	57	24	39	0	12	2-8	.263	.300	.395	.695	6	.969
1993— Arkansas (Texas)		OF	136	528	68	153	32	2	16	72	27	68	4	17	7-15	.290	.326	.449	.775	3	.989
— Louisville (A.A.)		OF	4	7	0	1	0	0	0	1	0	1	0	1	0-0	.143	.143	.143	.286	0	1.000
1994— Louisville (A.A.)		OF	122	477	76	125	30	1	15	68	32	67	3	14	2-6	.262	.311	.423	.735	2	.992
— St. Louis (N.L.)		OF	6	23	2	7	3	0	0	3	2	4	0	0	0-0	.304	.360	.435	.795	0	1.000
1995— St. Louis (N.L.)		1B-OF	129	388	35	119	21	1	5	41	24	45	2	6	0-3	.307	.347	.405	.752	4	.994
— Louisville (A.A.)		OF	4	12	0	1	0	0	0	0	0	0	0	0	0-0	.083	.083	.083	.167	1	.889
1996— St. Louis (N.L.)		1B	151	543	63	161	30	2	13	74	37	84	3	21	3-2	.297	.342	.431	.773	8	.994
1997— St. Louis (N.L.)		OF-1B-3B	116	388	40	110	19	0	5	36	39	77	3	11	0-1	.284	.352	.371	.723	1	.998
1998— St. Louis (N.L.)		OF-3B-1B	142	377	41	94	22	0	9	46	30	76	1	6	0-2	.249	.305	.379	.684	9	.968
1999— Seattle (A.L.)		OF-3B-1B-DH	87	262	34	64	14	0	9	33	20	60	0	6	2-1	.244	.297	.401	.698	10	.964
2000— Seattle (A.L.)		3B-OF-DH-1B-P		103	18	25	5	0	1	9	10	31	2	1	0-1	.243	.322	.320	.642	4	.934
— Tacoma (PCL)		1B-3B	4	14	1	3	1	0	0	1	0	4	0	0	0-0	.214	.214	.286	.500	1	.800
— San Diego (N.L.)		OF-1B	48	123	17	28	8	0	7	25	5	38	0	3	0-0	.228	.256	.463	.719	1	.983
2001— St. Louis (N.L.)		OF-1B	5	7	0	0	0	0	0	0	0	3	0	0	0-0	.000	.000	.000	.000	0	1.000
— Florida (N.L.)		OF-1B-DH	82	147	14	32	7	0	6	20	13	44	5	6	1-0	.218	.299	.388	.687	2	.964
— Brevard County (FSL)		OF	4	13	0	2	0	0	0	4	2	1	0	0	0-0	.154	.250	.154	.404	0	1.000
2002— Philadelphia (N.L.)		1B-OF	21	21	1	6	0	0	0	3	1	5	0	0	0-0	.286	.304	.286	.590	0	1.000
— Oakland (A.L.)		OF-1B	89	193	27	53	13	1	11	40	14	37	1	7	1-1	.275	.322	.523	.846	2	.992
2003— Tacoma (PCL)		DH	3	11	1	4	0	0	0	2	1	0	0	0	0-0	.364	.462	.364	.825	0	...
— Seattle (A.L.)		OF-1B-DH	64	104	12	22	6	0	3	16	15	21	3	3	0-0	.212	.328	.356	.684	1	.987
2004— Memphis (PCL)		1B-OF-3B	39	136	27	46	7	0	12	35	17	29	2	3	0-0	.338	.406	.654	1.061	2	.991
— St. Louis (N.L.)		OF-3B-1B	87	240	32	71	11	0	13	40	26	63	0	1	0-1	.296	.363	.504	.867	6	.972
2005— St. Louis (N.L.)		OF-3B-1B	112	246	26	59	15	1	8	32	20	63	0	6	0-0	.240	.295	.407	.701	3	.980
2006— Chicago (N.L.)		1B-OF-3B-DH	107	210	16	43	8	1	5	25	23	57	1	5	0-0	.205	.283	.324	.607	2	.994
American League totals (4 years)			288	662	91	164	38	1	24	96	59	149	6	17	3-3	.248	.313	.417	.730	17	.974
National League totals (11 years)			1006	2713	287	730	144	5	71	345	220	558	16	70	4-9	.269	.325	.404	.729	36	.990
Major League totals (13 years)			1294	3375	378	894	182	6	95	441	279	707	22	87	7-12	.265	.323	.407	.729	53	.988

DIVISION SERIES RECORD

Year	Team (League)	Pos.	G	AB	R	H	2B	3B	HR	RBI	BB	SO	HBP	GDP	SB-CS	Avg.	OBP	SLG	OPS	E	Avg.
1996— St. Louis (N.L.)		1B	3	10	1	3	0	1	0	1	1	1	0	0	0-0	.300	.364	.500	.864	0	1.000
2002— Oakland (A.L.)		1B-OF	2	2	0	0	0	0	0	0	0	1	0	0	0-0	.000	.000	.000	.000	0	1.000
2004— St. Louis (N.L.)			1	1	0	0	0	0	0	0	0	1	0	0	0-0	.000	.000	.000	.000	0	...
2005— St. Louis (N.L.)		OF	2	2	0	1	0	0	0	0	1	0	0	0	0-0	.500	.500	.500	1.000	0	1.000
Division series totals (4 years)			8	15	1	4	0	1	0	1	1	3	0	0	0-0	.267	.313	.400	.713	0	1.000

CHAMPIONSHIP SERIES RECORD

Year	Team (League)	Pos.	G	AB	R	H	2B	3B	HR	RBI	BB	SO	HBP	GDP	SB-CS	Avg.	OBP	SLG	OPS	E	Avg.
1996— St. Louis (N.L.)		1B-OF	7	23	1	6	0	0	0	0	0	6	1	0	0-0	.261	.292	.261	.553	0	1.000
2004— St. Louis (N.L.)		OF	4	6	0	1	0	0	0	1	0	3	0	0	0-0	.167	.167	.167	.333	0	1.000
2005— St. Louis (N.L.)		OF-3B	5	8	1	1	1	0	0	1	0	3	0	0	0-0	.125	.125	.250	.375	0	1.000
Champ. series totals (3 years)			16	37	2	8	1	0	0	2	0	12	1	0	0-0	.216	.237	.243	.480	0	1.000

WORLD SERIES RECORD

Year	Team (League)	Pos.	G	AB	R	H	2B	3B	HR	RBI	BB	SO	HBP	GDP	SB-CS	Avg.	OBP	SLG	OPS	E	Avg.
2004— St. Louis (N.L.)		OF	2	4	0	0	0	0	0	0	0	2	0	0	0-0	.000	.000	.000	.000	0	1.000

2006 LEFTY-RIGHTY SPLITS

vs.	Avg.	AB	H	2B	3B	HR	RBI	BB	SO	OBP	Slg.	vs.	Avg.	AB	H	2B	3B	HR	RBI	BB	SO	OBP	Slg.
L	.316	19	6	1	0	1	7	3	7	.409	.526	R	.194	191	37	7	1	4	18	20	50	.270	.304

M

MACDOUGAL, MIKE P

PERSONAL: Born March 5, 1977, in Las Vegas. ... 6-4/195. ... Throws right, bats both. ... Full name: Robert Meiklejohn MacDougal. ... High school: Mesa (Ariz.). ... College: Wake Forest. **TRANSACTIONS/CAREER NOTES:** Selected by Baltimore Orioles organization in 22nd round of 1996 free-agent draft; did not sign. ... Selected by Orioles organization in 17th round of 1998 free-agent draft; did not sign. ... Selected by Kansas City Royals organization in first round (25th pick overall) of 1999 free-agent draft; pick received as part of compensation for Boston Red Sox signing Type A free-agent 2B Jose Offerman. ... On disabled list (March 26-April 24, 2004); included rehabilitation assignment to Wichita. ... On disabled list (April 1-July 13, 2006); included rehabilitation assignments to Wichita and Omaha. ... Traded by Royals to Chicago White Sox for Ps Tyler Lumsden and Daniel Cortes (July 24, 2006).

CAREER HITTING: 0-for-0 (.000), 0 R, 0 2B, 0 3B, 0 HR, 0 RBI.

Year Team (League)	W	L	Pct.	ERA	WHIP	G	GS	CG	ShO	Hld.	Sv.-Opp.	IP	H	R	ER	HR	BB-IBB	SO	Avg.
1999—Spokane (N'west)	2	2	.500	4.47	1.29	11	11	0	0	...	0-...	46.1	43	25	23	3	17-0	57	.251
2000—Wilmington (Caro.)	9	7	.563	3.92	1.32	26	25	0	0	...	1-...	144.2	115	79	63	5	76-0	129	.219
—Wichita (Texas)	0	1	.000	7.71	1.97	2	2	0	0	...	0-...	11.2	16	10	10	0	7-0	9	.356
2001—Omaha (PCL)	8	8	.500	4.68	1.52	28	27	1	0	...	0-...	144.1	144	90	75	13	76-0	110	.259
—Kansas City (A.L.)	1	1	.500	4.70	1.43	3	3	0	0	0	0-0	15.1	18	10	8	2	4-0	7	.290
2002—Omaha (PCL)	3	5	.375	5.60	2.02	12	10	0	0	...	0-...	53.0	52	42	33	4	55-0	30	.265
—Wichita (Texas)	1	1	.500	3.06	1.98	4	4	1	0	...	0-...	17.2	11	12	6	1	24-0	14	.193
—GC Royals (GCL)	0	0	...	3.00	1.00	1	1	0	0	...	0-...	3.0	3	1	1	0	0-0	3	.273
—Wilmington (Caro.)	0	1	.000	1.08	0.96	5	0	0	0	...	2-...	8.1	3	4	1	1	5-0	10	.107
—Kansas City (A.L.)	0	1	.000	5.00	1.33	6	0	0	0	0	0-0	9.0	5	5	5	0	7-1	10	.161
2003—Kansas City (A.L.)	3	5	.375	4.08	1.50	68	0	0	0	1	27-35	64.0	64	36	29	4	32-0	57	.267
2004—Omaha (PCL)	0	1	.000	5.65	1.60	14	0	0	0	...	2-...	14.1	12	9	9	1	11-0	8	.222
—Wichita (Texas)	1	0	1.000	1.47	1.53	17	2	0	0	...	1-...	18.1	14	7	3	0	14-0	13	.209
—Kansas City (A.L.)	1	1	.500	5.56	2.21	13	0	0	0	0	1-3	11.1	16	8	7	2	9-0	14	.314
2005—Kansas City (A.L.)	5	6	.455	3.33	1.32	68	0	0	0	0	21-25	70.1	69	32	26	6	24-2	72	.257
2006—Omaha (PCL)	0	1	.000	4.70	1.17	8	4	0	0	1	1-1	7.2	4	4	4	0	0-0	6	.160
—Wichita (Texas)	0	0	...	0.00	0.00	1	1	0	0	0	0-0	1.0	0	0	0	0	0-0	1	...
—Kansas City (A.L.)	0	0	...	0.00	0.50	4	0	0	0	0	1-1	4.0	2	0	0	0	0-0	2	.154
—Chicago (A.L.)	1	1	.500	1.80	1.00	25	0	0	0	11	0-1	25.0	19	5	5	1	6-0	19	.213
Major League totals (6 years)	11	15	.423	3.62	1.38	187	3	0	0	12	50-65	199.0	193	96	80	15	82-3	181	.256

2006 LEFTY-RIGHTY SPLITS

vs.	Avg.	AB	H	2B	3B	HR	RBI	BB	SO	OBP	Slg.	vs.	Avg.	AB	H	2B	3B	HR	RBI	BB	SO	OBP	Slg.
L	.281	32	9	3	0	1	3	1	4	.303	.469	R	.171	70	12	0	0	0	4	5	17	.237	.171

MACKOWIAK, ROB 3B/OF

PERSONAL: Born June 20, 1976, in Oak Lawn, Ill. ... 5-10/195. ... Bats left, throws right. ... Full name: Robert William Mackowiak. ... Name pronounced: mah-KOH-vee-ak. ... High school: Oak Lawn (Ill.), then Lake Central (Schererville). ... Junior college: South Suburban (Ill.). **TRANSACTIONS/CAREER NOTES:** Selected by Cincinnati Reds organization in 30th round of 1995 free-agent draft; did not sign. ... Selected by Pittsburgh Pirates organization in 53rd round of 1996 free-agent draft. ... On disabled list (July 20-August 18, 2001); included rehabilitation assignment to Nashville. ... Traded by Pirates to Chicago White Sox for P Damaso Marte (December 13, 2005). **STATISTICAL NOTES:** Career major league grand slams: 2.

2006 GAMES PLAYED BY POSITION (MLB): OF—96, 3B—6, DH—2.

Year Team (League)	Pos.	G	AB	R	H	2B	3B	HR	RBI	BB	SO	HBP	GDP	SB-CS	Avg.	OBP	SLG	OPS	E	Avg.
1996—GC Pirates (GCL)	OF-SS	27	86	8	23	6	1	0	14	13	11	1	3	3-1	.267	.366	.360	.727	10	.796
1997—Erie (N.Y.-Penn)	1B-3B-C, OF-P	61	203	26	58	14	2	1	25	21	47	7	5	1-7	.286	.371	.389	.760	6	.949
1998—Augusta (S. Atl.)	1B-OF	25	70	16	17	4	0	1	8	13	19	1	2	4-2	.243	.369	.343	.712	2	.941
—Lynchburg (Caro.)	2B-3B-OF	86	292	30	80	24	6	3	31	17	65	4	4	6-3	.274	.321	.428	.749	18	.916
1999—Lynchburg (Caro.)	2B-OF	74	263	51	80	7	4	7	30	18	57	6	5	9-3	.304	.362	.441	.803	1	.996
—Altoona (East.)	1B-OF	53	195	21	51	15	3	3	27	8	34	7	6	0-2	.262	.308	.415	.724	8	.971
2000—Altoona (East.)	2B-3B-OF, SS	134	526	82	156	33	4	13	87	22	96	9	8	18-5	.297	.332	.449	.780	17	.965
2001—Nashville (PCL)	OF-2B-3B	32	118	14	31	5	0	4	14	7	39	0	0	1-1	.263	.302	.407	.708	7	.940
—Pittsburgh (N.L.)	OF-2B-3B, 1B	83	214	30	57	15	2	4	21	15	52	3	3	4-3	.266	.319	.411	.730	6	.965
2002—Pittsburgh (N.L.)	OF-3B-2B	136	385	57	94	22	0	16	48	42	120	7	0	9-3	.244	.328	.426	.754	6	.974
2003—Nashville (PCL)	1B-3B-2B, OF	59	217	21	50	11	1	2	23	18	51	0	3	7-3	.230	.286	.318	.604	9	.978
—Pittsburgh (N.L.)	OF-3B-2B	77	174	20	47	4	4	6	19	15	53	4	1	6-0	.270	.342	.443	.785	2	.983
2004—Pittsburgh (N.L.)	OF-3B-1B	155	491	65	121	22	6	17	75	50	114	6	3	13-4	.246	.319	.420	.739	9	.968
2005—Pittsburgh (N.L.)	3B-OF-2B, 1B	142	463	57	126	21	3	9	58	43	100	3	7	8-4	.272	.337	.389	.726	12	.968
2006—Chicago (A.L.)	OF-3B-DH	112	255	31	74	12	1	5	23	28	59	3	1	5-2	.290	.365	.404	.769	4	.975
American League totals (1 year)		112	255	31	74	12	1	5	23	28	59	3	1	5-2	.290	.365	.404	.769	4	.975
National League totals (5 years)		593	1727	229	445	84	15	52	221	165	439	23	14	40-14	.258	.328	.414	.742	35	.970
Major League totals (6 years)		705	1982	260	519	96	16	57	244	193	498	26	15	45-16	.262	.333	.413	.746	39	.971

2006 LEFTY-RIGHTY SPLITS

vs.	Avg.	AB	H	2B	3B	HR	RBI	BB	SO	OBP	Slg.	vs.	Avg.	AB	H	2B	3B	HR	RBI	BB	SO	OBP	Slg.
L	.222	54	12	0	0	0	6	3	13	.288	.222	R	.308	201	62	12	1	5	17	25	46	.384	.453

MADDUX, GREG P

PERSONAL: Born April 14, 1966, in San Angelo, Texas. ... 6-0/185. ... Throws right, bats right. ... Full name: Gregory Alan Maddux. ... Name pronounced: MADD-ucks. ... High school: Valley (Las Vegas). ... Brother of Mike Maddux, coach, Milwaukee Brewers, and pitcher with nine major league teams (1986-2000). **TRANSACTIONS/CAREER NOTES:** Selected by Chicago Cubs organization in second round of June 1984 free-agent draft. ... Signed as a free agent by Atlanta Braves (December 9, 1992). ... On disabled list (March 23-April 12, 2002). ... Signed as a free agent by Cubs (March 23, 2004). ... Traded by Cubs to Los Angeles Dodgers for IF Cesar Izturis (July 31, 2006). **HONORS:** Named N.L. Pitcher of the Year by THE SPORTING NEWS (1992-95). ... Named righthanded pitcher on THE SPORTING NEWS N.L. All-Star team (1992-95 and 2000). ... Named N.L. Cy Young Award winner by Baseball Writers' Association of America (1992-95). ... Won N.L. Gold Glove at pitcher (1990-2002 and 2004-06). **MISCELLANEOUS NOTES:** Appeared in three games as pinch runner (1988). ... Singled and scored and struck out in two appearances as pinch hitter (1991). ... Made an out in only appearance as pinch hitter (2001). ... Had a sacrifice hit in only appearance as pinch hitter (2002). ... Had a sacrifice hit in only appearance as pinch hitter (2003). ... Had a sacrifice hit in only appearance as pinch hitter (2004). **CAREER HITTING:** 257-for-1474 (.174), 100 R, 33 2B, 2 3B, 5 HR, 81 RBI.

Year Team (League)	W	L	Pct.	ERA	WHIP	G	GS	CG	ShO	Hld.	Sv.-Opp.	IP	H	R	ER	HR	BB-IBB	SO	Avg.
1984— Pikeville (Appal.)	6	2	.750	2.63	1.21	14	12	2	2	...	0-...	85.2	63	35	25	2	41-2	62	.205
1985— Peoria (Midw.)	13	9	.591	3.19	1.23	27	27	6	0	...	0-...	186.0	176	86	66	9	52-0	125	.245
1986— Pittsfield (East.)	4	3	.571	2.73	1.02	8	8	4	2	...	0-...	62.2	49	22	19	1	15-0	35	.214
— Iowa (Am. Assoc.)	10	1	.909	3.02	1.22	18	18	5	2	...	0-...	128.1	127	49	43	3	30-3	65	.259
— Chicago (N.L.)	2	4	.333	5.52	1.77	6	5	1	0	0	0-0	31.0	44	20	19	3	11-2	20	.336
. 1987— Chicago (N.L.)	6	14	.300	5.61	1.64	30	27	1	1	0	0-0	155.2	181	111	97	17	74-13	101	.294
— Iowa (Am. Assoc.)	3	0	1.000	0.98	1.05	4	4	2	2	...	0-...	27.2	17	3	3	1	12-0	22	.179
1988— Chicago (N.L.)	18	8	.692	3.18	1.25	34	34	9	3	...	0-0	249.0	230	97	88	13	81-16	140	.244
1989— Chicago (N.L.)	19	12	.613	2.95	1.28	35	35	7	1	0	0-0	238.1	222	90	78	13	82-13	135	.249
1990— Chicago (N.L.)	15	15	.500	3.46	1.32	35	• 35	8	2	0	0-0	237.0	* 242	* 116	91	11	71-10	144	.265
1991— Chicago (N.L.)	15	11	.577	3.35	1.13	37	* 37	7	2	0	0-0	* 263.0	232	113	98	18	66-9	198	.237
1992— Chicago (N.L.)	• 20	11	.645	2.18	1.01	35	• 35	9	4	0	0-0	* 268.0	201	68	65	7	70-7	199	.210
1993— Atlanta (N.L.)	20	10	.667	* 2.36	1.05	36	• 36	* 8	1	0	0-0	* 267.0	228	85	70	14	52-7	197	.232
1994— Atlanta (N.L.)	* 16	6	.727	* 1.56	0.90	25	25	* 10	• 3	0	0-0	* 202.0	150	44	35	4	31-3	156	* .207
1995— Atlanta (N.L.)	* 19	2	*.905	*1.63	0.81	28	28	* 10	• 3	0	0-0	• 209.2	147	39	38	8	23-3	181	.197
1996— Atlanta (N.L.)	15	11	.577	2.72	1.03	35	35	5	1	0	0-0	245.0	225	85	74	11	28-11	172	.241
1997— Atlanta (N.L.)	19	4	* .826	2.20	0.95	33	33	5	2	0	0-0	232.2	200	58	57	9	20-6	177	.226
1998— Atlanta (N.L.)	18	9	.667	* 2.22	0.98	34	34	9	* 5	0	0-0	251.0	201	75	62	13	45-10	204	.220
1999— Atlanta (N.L.)	19	9	.679	3.57	1.34	33	33	4	0	0	0-0	219.1	258	103	87	16	37-8	136	.294
2000— Atlanta (N.L.)	19	9	.679	3.00	1.07	35	• 35	6	• 3	0	0-0	249.1	225	91	83	19	42-12	190	.238
2001— Atlanta (N.L.)	17	11	.607	3.05	1.06	34	34	3	• 3	0	0-0	233.0	220	86	79	20	27-10	173	.253
2002— Atlanta (N.L.)	16	6	.727	2.62	1.20	34	34	0	0	0	0-0	199.1	194	67	58	14	45-7	118	.257
2003— Atlanta (N.L.)	16	11	.593	3.96	1.18	36	* 36	1	0	0	0-0	218.1	225	112	96	24	33-7	124	.268
2004— Chicago (N.L.)	16	11	.593	4.02	1.18	33	33	2	1	0	0-0	212.2	218	103	95	35	33-4	151	.269
2005— Chicago (N.L.)	13	15	.464	4.24	1.22	35	• 35	3	0	0	0-0	225.0	239	112	106	29	36-4	136	.275
2006— Chicago (N.L.)	9	11	.450	4.69	1.29	22	22	0	0	0	0-0	136.1	153	78	71	14	23-3	81	.284
— Los Angeles (N.L.)	6	3	.667	3.30	1.09	12	12	0	0	0	0-0	73.2	66	31	27	6	14-4	36	.244
Major League totals (21 years)	333	203	.621	3.07	1.14	677	673	108	35	0	0-0	4616.1	4301	1784	1574	318	944-169	3169	.248

DIVISION SERIES RECORD

Year Team (League)	W	L	Pct.	ERA	WHIP	G	GS	CG	ShO	Hld.	Sv.-Opp.	IP	H	R	ER	HR	BB-IBB	SO	Avg.
1995— Atlanta (N.L.)	1	0	1.000	4.50	1.50	2	2	0	0	0	0-0	14.0	19	7	7	3	2-1	7	.365
1996— Atlanta (N.L.)	1	0	1.000	0.00	0.43	1	1	0	0	0	0-0	7.0	3	2	0	0	0-0	7	.125
1997— Atlanta (N.L.)	1	0	1.000	1.00	0.89	1	1	1	0	0	0-0	9.0	7	1	1	0	1-0	6	.219
1998— Atlanta (N.L.)	1	0	1.000	2.57	1.00	1	1	0	0	0	0-0	7.0	7	2	2	0	0-0	4	.250
1999— Atlanta (N.L.)	0	1	.000	2.57	2.14	1	1	0	0	0	0-0	7.0	10	2	2	1	5-2	5	.370
2000— Atlanta (N.L.)	0	1	.000	11.25	3.00	1	1	0	0	0	0-0	4.0	9	7	5	1	3-2	2	.429
2001— Atlanta (N.L.)	0	0	...	3.00	1.17	1	1	0	0	0	0-0	6.0	6	4	3	0	3-0	5	.190
2002— Atlanta (N.L.)	1	0	1.000	3.00	1.00	1	1	0	0	0	0-0	6.0	5	2	2	1	1-1	3	.238
2003— Atlanta (N.L.)	0	1	.000	3.00	1.17	1	1	0	0	0	0-0	6.0	6	2	2	0	1-0	1	.240
2006— Los Angeles (N.L.)	0	0	...	9.00	2.25	1	1	0	0	0	0-0	4.0	7	4	4	0	2-1	0	.389
Division series totals (10 years)	5	3	.625	3.47	1.36	12	11	1	0	0	0-0	70.0	77	32	27	7	18-7	40	.286

CHAMPIONSHIP SERIES RECORD

Year Team (League)	W	L	Pct.	ERA	WHIP	G	GS	CG	ShO	Hld.	Sv.-Opp.	IP	H	R	ER	HR	BB-IBB	SO	Avg.
1989— Chicago (N.L.)	0	1	.000	13.50	2.32	2	2	0	0	0	0-0	7.1	13	12	11	2	4-2	5	.382
1993— Atlanta (N.L.)	1	1	.500	4.97	1.42	2	2	0	0	0	0-0	12.2	11	8	7	2	7-1	11	.224
1995— Atlanta (N.L.)	1	0	1.000	1.13	1.13	1	1	0	0	0	0-0	8.0	7	1	1	0	2-0	4	.226
1996— Atlanta (N.L.)	1	1	.500	2.51	1.19	2	2	0	0	0	0-0	14.1	15	9	4	1	2-1	10	.263
1997— Atlanta (N.L.)	0	2	.000	1.38	1.00	2	2	0	0	0	0-0	13.0	9	7	2	0	4-1	16	.191
1998— Atlanta (N.L.)	0	1	.000	3.00	1.33	1	1	0	0	0	1-1	6.0	5	2	2	0	3-1	4	.217
1999— Atlanta (N.L.)	1	0	1.000	1.93	0.93	2	2	0	0	0	0-0	14.0	12	3	3	1	1-0	7	.222
2001— Atlanta (N.L.)	0	2	.000	5.40	1.60	2	2	0	0	0	0-0	10.0	14	8	6	0	2-1	7	.311
Champ. series totals (8 years)	4	8	.333	3.80	1.30	15	14	0	0	0	1-1	85.1	86	50	36	6	25-7	64	.253

WORLD SERIES RECORD

Year Team (League)	W	L	Pct.	ERA	WHIP	G	GS	CG	ShO	Hld.	Sv.-Opp.	IP	H	R	ER	HR	BB-IBB	SO	Avg.
1995— Atlanta (N.L.)	1	1	.500	2.25	0.75	2	2	1	0	0	0-0	16.0	9	6	4	1	3-1	8	.158
1996— Atlanta (N.L.)	1	1	.500	1.72	0.96	2	2	0	0	0	0-0	15.2	14	3	3	0	1-0	5	.246
1999— Atlanta (N.L.)	0	1	.000	2.57	1.14	1	1	0	0	0	0-0	7.0	5	4	2	0	3-0	5	.208
World series totals (3 years)	2	3	.400	2.09	0.91	5	5	1	0	0	0-0	38.2	28	13	9	1	7-1	18	.203

ALL-STAR GAME RECORD

	W	L	Pct.	ERA	WHIP	G	GS	CG	ShO	Hld.	Sv.-Opp.	IP	H	R	ER	HR	BB-IBB	SO	Avg.
All-Star Game totals (4 years)	0	0	...	3.24	1.20	4	3	0	0	0	0-0	8.1	9	3	3	2	1-0	3	.281

2006 LEFTY-RIGHTY SPLITS

vs.	Avg.	AB	H	2B	3B	HR	RBI	BB	SO	OBP	Slg.	vs.	Avg.	AB	H	2B	3B	HR	RBI	BB	SO	OBP	Slg.
L	.254	366	93	21	2	11	44	21	52	.293	.413	R	.284	443	126	32	3	9	55	16	65	.307	.431

MADSON, RYAN — P

PERSONAL: Born August 28, 1980, in Long Beach, Calif. ... 6-6/190. ... Throws right, bats left. ... Full name: Ryan Michael Madson. ... High school: Valley View High (Moreno County, Calif.). **TRANSACTIONS/CAREER NOTES:** Selected by Philadelphia Phillies organization in ninth round of 1998 free-agent draft. ... On disabled list (July 26-September 3, 2004); included rehabilitation assignment to Reading.

CAREER HITTING: 6-for-42 (.143), 3 R, 1 2B, 0 3B, 0 HR, 2 RBI.

Year Team (League)	W	L	Pct.	ERA	WHIP	G	GS	CG	ShO	Hld.	Sv.-Opp.	IP	H	R	ER	HR	BB-IBB	SO	Avg.
1998— Martinsville (App.)	3	3	.500	4.83	1.43	12	10	0	0	...	0-...	54.0	57	38	29	5	20-0	52	.265
1999— Batavia (NY-Penn)	5	5	.500	4.72	1.40	15	15	0	0	...	0-...	87.2	80	51	46	5	43-0	75	.247
2000— Piedmont (S. Atl.)	14	5	.737	2.59	1.16	21	21	2	1	...	0-...	135.2	113	50	39	5	45-0	123	.225
2001— Clearwater (FSL)	9	9	.500	3.90	1.58	22	21	1	0	...	0-...	117.2	137	68	51	4	49-1	101	.291
2002— Reading (East.)	16	4	.800	3.20	1.18	26	26	1	0	...	0-...	171.1	150	68	61	11	53-0	132	.242
2003— Clearwater (FSL)	0	0	...	5.63	1.63	2	2	0	0	...	0-...	8.0	11	5	5	0	2-0	9	.324
— Scran./W.B. (I.L.)	12	8	.600	3.50	1.27	26	26	0	0	...	0-...	157.0	157	70	61	9	42-2	138	.262
— Philadelphia (N.L.)	0	0	...	0.00	0.00	1	0	0	0	0	0-0	2.0	0	0	0	0	0-0	0	.000
2004— Reading (East.)	0	0	...	4.50	2.50	2	1	0	0	...	0-...	2.0	3	2	1	0	1-0	1	.375
— Philadelphia (N.L.)	9	3	.750	2.34	1.13	52	1	0	0	7	1-2	77.0	68	23	20	6	19-4	55	.242
2005— Philadelphia (N.L.)	5	5	.545	4.14	1.25	78	0	0	0	• 32	0-7	87.0	84	44	40	11	25-6	79	.259
2006— Philadelphia (N.L.)	11	9	.550	5.69	1.68	50	17	0	0	6	2-4	134.1,	176	92	85	20	50-4	99	.321
Major League totals (4 years)	26	17	.605	4.35	1.41	181	18	0	0	45	3-13	300.1	328	159	145	37	94-14	233	.282

M

vs.	Avg.	AB	H	2B	3B	HR	RBI	BB	SO	OBP	Slg.	vs.	Avg.	AB	H	2B	3B	HR	RBI	BB	SO	OBP	Slg.
L	.306	268	82	20	3	11	37	28	48	.380	.526	R	.336	280	94	19	1	9	39	22	51	.392	.507

MAHAY, RON — P

PERSONAL: Born June 28, 1971, in Crestwood, Ill. ... 6-2/185. ... Throws left, bats left. ... Full name: Ronald Matthew Mahay. ... Name pronounced: MAY-hay. ... High school: Alan B. Shepard (Palos Heights, Ill.). ... Junior college: South Suburban (Ill.). **TRANSACTIONS/CAREER NOTES:** Selected by Boston Red Sox organization in 18th round of 1991 free-agent draft. ... Played outfield in Red Sox organization (1991-95) ... Claimed on waivers by Oakland Athletics (March 30, 1999). ... Traded by A's to Florida Marlins for cash (May 11, 2000). ... Signed as a free agent by San Diego Padres organization (November 20, 2000). ... Released by Padres (May 15, 2001). ... Signed by Chicago Cubs organization (May 19, 2001). ... On disabled list (May 24-June 13, 2002); included rehabilitation assignment to Iowa. ... Released by Cubs (September 30, 2002). ... Signed by Texas Rangers (November 13, 2002). ... On disabled list (June 8-24, 2005); included rehabilitation assignment to Oklahoma. **MISCELLANEOUS NOTES:** Appeared in one game as pinch runner (2000). ... Grounded out in only appearance as pinch hitter (2004). ... Appeared in one game as pinch runner (2005).

CAREER HITTING: 6-for-27 (.222), 3 R, 3 2B, 0 3B, 1 HR, 3 RBI.

Year	Team (League)	W	L	Pct.	ERA	WHIP	G	GS	CG	ShO	Hld.	Sv.-Opp.	IP	H	R	ER	HR	BB-IBB	SO	Avg.
1996—	Sarasota (Fla. St.)	2	2	.500	3.82	1.36	31	4	0	0	...	2-...	70.2	61	33	30	5	35-0	68	.236
	—Trenton (East.)	0	1	.000	29.45	4.91	1	1	0	0	...	0-...	3.2	12	13	12	1	6-0	0	.522
1997—	Trenton (East.)	3	3	.500	3.10	1.03	17	4	0	0	...	5-...	40.2	29	16	14	0	13-0	47	.193
	—Pawtucket (Int'l)	1	0	1.000	0.00	0.86	2	0	0	0	...	0-...	4.2	3	0	0	0	1-0	6	.176
	—Boston (A.L.)	3	0	1.000	2.52	1.20	28	0	0	0	6	0-2	25.0	19	7	7	3	11-0	22	.204
1998—	Pawtucket (Int'l)	3	1	.750	4.17	1.37	23	1	0	0	...	3-...	41.0	37	20	19	8	19-2	41	.234
	—Boston (A.L.)	1	1	.500	3.46	1.58	29	0	0	0	7	1-2	26.0	26	16	10	2	15-1	14	.263
1999—	Vancouver (PCL)	7	2	.778	4.29	1.50	32	15	0	0	...	0-...	107.0	116	57	51	12	45-0	73	.280
	—Oakland (A.L.)	2	0	1.000	1.86	0.57	6	1	0	0	0	1-1	19.1	8	4	4	2	3-0	15	.123
2000—	Oakland (A.L.)	0	0	...	9.00	2.19	5	2	0	0	0	0-0	16.0	26	18	16	4	9-0	5	.366
	—Florida (N.L.)	1	0	1.000	6.04	1.86	18	0	0	0	2	0-0	25.1	31	17	17	6	16-1	27	.310
	—Calgary (PCL)	0	1	.000	4.85	1.08	8	0	0	0	...	0-...	13.0	7	7	7	1	7-1	15	.175
2001—	Portland (PCL)	1	2	.333	3.78	1.48	14	0	0	0	...	0-...	16.2	13	9	7	2	5-0	18	.210
	—Iowa (PCL)	3	1	.750	2.31	0.84	36	0	0	0	...	14-...	46.2	29	12	12	5	10-1	52	.182
	—Chicago (N.L.)	0	0	...	2.61	1.40	17	0	0	0	2	0-0	20.2	14	6	6	4	15-1	24	.197
2002—	Iowa (PCL)	3	1	.750	1.93	1.01	39	1	0	0	...	2-...	46.2	32	11	10	3	15-1	50	.189
	—Chicago (N.L.)	2	0	1.000	8.59	1.43	11	0	0	0	0	0-0	14.2	13	14	14	6	8-0	14	.228
2003—	Oklahoma (PCL)	4	2	.667	4.22	1.10	26	0	0	0	...	3-...	42.2	36	21	20	5	10-0	51	.224
	—Texas (A.L.)	3	3	.500	3.18	1.17	35	0	0	0	9	0-3	45.1	33	19	16	3	20-7	38	.195
2004—	Texas (A.L.)	3	0	1.000	2.55	1.33	60	0	0	0	14	0-2	67.0	60	23	19	5	29-5	54	.235
2005—	Oklahoma (PCL)	0	0	...	0.00	0.82	3	0	0	0	1	0-0	3.2	2	0	0	0	1-0	5	.167
	—Texas (A.L.)	0	0	.000	6.81	1.77	30	0	0	0	6	1-1	35.2	47	28	27	8	16-1	30	.313
	—Frisco (Texas)	1	3	.250	7.78	1.68	5	5	0	0	0	0-0	19.2	24	19	17	3	9-0	20	.300
2006—	Oklahoma (PCL)	0	1	.000	1.42	0.79	5	0	0	0	1	2-2	6.1	5	4	1	0	0-0	11	.227
	—Texas (A.L.)	1	3	.250	3.95	1.44	62	0	0	0	9	0-1	57.0	54	30	25	7	28-2	56	.250
American League totals (8 years)		13	10	.565	3.83	1.39	255	3	0	0	51	3-12	291.1	273	145	124	34	131-16	234	.244
National League totals (3 years)		3	0	1.000	5.49	1.60	46	0	0	0	4	0-0	60.2	58	37	37	16	39-2	65	.254
Major League totals (10 years)		16	10	.615	4.12	1.42	301	3	0	0	55	3-12	352.0	331	182	161	50	170-18	299	.246

vs.	Avg.	AB	H	2B	3B	HR	RBI	BB	SO	OBP	Slg.	vs.	Avg.	AB	H	2B	3B	HR	RBI	BB	SO	OBP	Slg.
L	.240	96	23	7	1	4	20	14	21	.336	.458	R	.258	120	31	3	1	3	13	14	29	.333	.375

MAHOLM, PAUL — P

PERSONAL: Born June 25, 1982, in Greenwood, Miss. ... 6-2/225. ... Throws left, bats left. ... Full name: Paul G. Maholm. ... College: Mississippi State. **TRANSACTIONS/CAREER NOTES:** Selected by Pittsburgh Pirates organization in first round (eighth pick overall) of 2003 free-agent draft.

CAREER HITTING: 8-for-70 (.114), 4 R, 0 2B, 0 3B, 0 HR, 2 RBI.

Year	Team (League)	W	L	Pct.	ERA	WHIP	G	GS	CG	ShO	Hld.	Sv.-Opp.	IP	H	R	ER	HR	BB-IBB	SO	Avg.
2003—	Will. (NYP)	2	1	.667	1.83	1.02	8	8	0	0	...	0-...	34.1	25	11	7	1	10-0	32	.197
2004—	Lynchburg (Caro.)	1	3	.250	1.84	1.23	8	8	0	0	...	0-...	44.0	39	11	9	2	15-0	28	.245
	—GC Pirates (GCL)	0	0	...	2.25	1.50	1	0	0	0	...	0-...	4.0	5	1	1	0	1-0	2	.294
	—Hickory (S. Atl.)	0	2	.000	9.49	2.19	3	3	0	0	...	0-...	12.1	17	14	13	2	10-0	12	.354
2005—	Altoona (East.)	6	2	.750	3.20	1.21	16	16	0	0	0	0-0	81.2	73	32	29	5	26-2	75	.243
	—Indianapolis (Int'l)	1	1	.500	3.53	1.46	6	6	0	0	0	0-0	35.2	40	19	14	2	12-0	21	.286
	—Pittsburgh (N.L.)	3	1	.750	2.18	1.16	6	6	0	0	0	0-0	41.1	31	10	10	2	17-0	26	.209
2006—	Pittsburgh (N.L.)	8	10	.444	4.76	1.61	30	30	0	0	0	0-0	176.0	202	98	93	19	81-6	117	.295
Major League totals (2 years)		11	11	.500	4.27	1.52	36	36	0	0	0	0-0	217.1	233	108	103	21	98-6	143	.280

vs.	Avg.	AB	H	2B	3B	HR	RBI	BB	SO	OBP	Slg.	vs.	Avg.	AB	H	2B	3B	HR	RBI	BB	SO	OBP	Slg.
L	.233	150	35	8	0	1	9	20	43	.345	.307	R	.313	534	167	32	3	18	79	61	74	.387	.485

MAIER, MITCH — OF

PERSONAL: Born June 30, 1982, in Petoskey, Mich. ... Bats left, throws right. ... Full name: Mitchell William Maier. ... College: Toledo. **TRANSACTIONS/CAREER NOTES:** Selected by Kansas City Royals organization in first round (30th pick overall) of 2003 free-agent draft.

2006 GAMES PLAYED BY POSITION (MLB): OF—4, DH—1.

Year	Team (League)	Pos.	G	AB	R	H	2B	3B	HR	RBI	BB	SO	HBP	GDP	SB-CS	Avg.	OBP	SLG	OPS	E	Avg.
2003—	Arizona Royals 1 (AZL)		51	203	41	71	14	6	2	45	18	25	2	4	7-3	.350	.403	.507	.910	...	...
2004—	Burlington (Midw.)		82	317	41	95	24	3	4	36	27	51	0	3	34-10	.300	.354	.432	.786	...	...
	—Wilmington (Caro.)		51	174	25	46	9	2	3	17	15	29	2	3	9-2	.264	.326	.391	.717	...	...
2005—	High Desert (Calif.)	OF-DH	50	211	42	71	26	1	8	32	12	43	1	6	6-1	.336	.370	.583	.953	6	.971
	—Wichita (Texas)	OF-3B-DH	80	322	55	82	21	5	7	49	15	47	2	4	10-3	.255	.289	.416	.706	7	.984
2006—	Wichita (Texas)		138	543	95	166	35	7	14	92	41	96	7	8	13-12	.306	.357	.473	.830	7	.980
	—Kansas City (A.L.)	OF-DH	5	13	3	2	0	0	0	0	2	4	0	1	0-0	.154	.267	.154	.421	1	.800
Major League totals (1 year)			5	13	3	2	0	0	0	0	2	4	0	1	0-0	.154	.267	.154	.421	1	.800

vs.	Avg.	AB	H	2B	3B	HR	RBI	BB	SO	OBP	Slg.	vs.	Avg.	AB	H	2B	3B	HR	RBI	BB	SO	OBP	Slg.
L	.000	5	0	0	0	0	0	1	2	.167	.000	R	.250	8	2	0	0	0	0	1	2	.333	.250

M

MAINE, JOHN — P

PERSONAL: Born May 8, 1981, in Fredericksburg, Va. ... 6-4/193. ... Throws right, bats right. ... Full name: John K. Maine. ... High school: North Stafford (Va.). ... College: Charlotte. **TRANSACTIONS/CAREER NOTES:** Selected by Baltimore Orioles organization in sixth round of 2002 free-agent draft. ... Traded by Orioles with P Jorge Julio to New York Mets for P Kris Benson (January 21, 2006). ... On disabled list (May 6-June 12, 2006); included rehabilitation assignments to St. Lucie and Norfolk.
CAREER HITTING: 1-for-28 (.036), 3 R, 1 2B, 0 3B, 0 HR, 0 RBI.

Year Team (League)	W	L	Pct.	ERA	WHIP	G	GS	CG	ShO	Hld.	Sv.-Opp.	IP	H	R	ER	HR	BB-IBB	SO	Avg.
2002— Aberdeen (N.Y.-Penn.)	1	1	.500	1.74	0.87	4	2	0	0	...	0-...	10.1	6	2	2	0	3-0	21	.154
—Delmarva (S. Atl.)	1	1	.500	1.36	0.76	6	5	0	0	...	0-...	33.0	21	8	5	0	4-0	39	.178
2003—Delmarva (S. Atl.)	7	3	.700	1.53	0.80	14	14	1	0	...	0-...	76.1	43	16	13	1	18-0	108	.165
—Frederick (Carolina)	6	1	.857	3.07	0.97	12	12	1	1	...	0-...	70.1	48	27	24	5	20-0	77	.190
2004—Bowie (East.)	4	0	1.000	2.25	0.82	5	5	0	0	...	0-...	28.0	16	8	7	1	7-0	34	.160
—Baltimore (A.L.)	0	1	.000	9.82	2.73	1	1	0	0	0	0-0	3.2	7	4	4	1	3-0	1	.438
—Ottawa (Int'l)	5	7	.417	3.91	1.46	22	22	0	0	...	0-0	119.2	123	59	52	12	52-0	105	.266
2005—Ottawa (Int'l)	6	11	.353	4.56	1.32	23	23	1	1	0	0-0	128.1	128	72	65	13	42-0	111	.257
—Baltimore (A.L.)	2	3	.400	6.30	1.58	10	8	0	0	0	0-0	40.0	39	30	28	8	24-0	24	.257
2006—St. Lucie (Fla. St.)	1	0	1.000	0.00	1.00	1	1	0	0	0	0-0	5.0	3	0	0	0	2-0	7	.167
—Norfolk (Int'l)	3	5	.375	3.49	1.32	10	10	0	0	0	0-0	56.2	55	25	22	2	20-0	48	.253
—New York (N.L.)	6	5	.545	3.60	1.13	16	15	1	0	0	0-0	90.0	69	40	36	15	33-1	71	.212
American League totals (2 years)	2	4	.333	6.60	1.67	11	9	0	0	0	0-0	43.2	46	34	32	9	27-0	25	.266
National League totals (1 year)	6	5	.545	3.60	1.13	16	15	1	0	0	0-0	90.0	69	40	36	15	33-1	71	.212
Major League totals (3 years)	8	9	.471	4.58	1.31	27	24	1	0	0	0-0	133.2	115	74	68	24	60-1	96	.230

DIVISION SERIES RECORD

Year Team (League)	W	L	Pct.	ERA	WHIP	G	GS	CG	ShO	Hld.	Sv.-Opp.	IP	H	R	ER	HR	BB-IBB	SO	Avg.
2006— New York (N.L.)	0	0	...	2.08	1.85	1	1	0	0	0	0-0	4.1	6	1	1	0	2-1	5	.375

CHAMPIONSHIP SERIES RECORD

Year Team (League)	W	L	Pct.	ERA	WHIP	G	GS	CG	ShO	Hld.	Sv.-Opp.	IP	H	R	ER	HR	BB-IBB	SO	Avg.
2006— New York (N.L.)	1	0	1.000	2.89	1.39	2	2	0	0	0	0-0	9.1	4	4	3	1	9-1	8	.121

2006 LEFTY-RIGHTY SPLITS

vs.	Avg.	AB	H	2B	3B	HR	RBI	BB	SO	OBP	Slg.	vs.	Avg.	AB	H	2B	3B	HR	RBI	BB	SO	OBP	Slg.
L	.231	169	39	7	0	6	11	23	34	.323	.379	R	.191	157	30	9	0	9	23	10	37	.247	.420

MAJEWSKI, GARY — P

PERSONAL: Born February 26, 1980, in Houston. ... 6-1/215. ... Throws right, bats right. ... Full name: Gary Wayne Majewski. ... Name pronounced: my-EV-ski. ... High school: St. Pius X (Houston). **TRANSACTIONS/CAREER NOTES:** Selected by Chicago White Sox organization in second round of 1998 free-agent draft. ... Traded by White Sox with Ps Andre Simpson and Orlando Rodriguez to Los Angeles Dodgers for Ps Antonio Osuna and Carlos Ortega (March 22, 2001). ... Traded by Dodgers with P Onan Masaoka and OF Jeff Barry to White Sox for P James Baldwin (July 26, 2001). ... Selected by Toronto Blue Jays from White Sox organization in Rule 5 major league draft (December 16, 2002). ... Returned to White Sox (March 17, 2003). ... Traded by White Sox with P Jon Rauch to Montreal Expos for OF Carl Everett (July 18, 2004). ... Expos franchise transferred to Washington, D.C., and renamed Washington Nationals for 2005 season (December 3, 2004). ... Traded by Nationals with Ps Bill Bray and Daryl Thompson, SS Royce Clayton and IF Brendan Harris to Cincinnati Reds for OF Austin Kearns, SS Felipe Lopez and P Ryan Wagner (July 13, 2006). ... On disabled list (August 7-September 1, 2006); included rehabilitation assignment to Louisville. **MISCELLANEOUS NOTES:** Struck out in only appearance as pinch hitter (2005).
CAREER HITTING: 0-for-11 (.000), 0 R, 0 2B, 0 3B, 0 HR, 0 RBI.

Year Team (League)	W	L	Pct.	ERA	WHIP	G	GS	CG	ShO	Hld.	Sv.-Opp.	IP	H	R	ER	HR	BB-IBB	SO	Avg.
1999— Bristol (Appal.)	7	1	.875	3.05	1.36	13	13	1	1	...	0-...	76.2	67	34	26	4	37-0	91	.243
—Burlington (Midw.)	0	0	...	37.80	4.50	2	0	0	0	...	0-...	3.1	11	14	14	3	4-0	1	.524
2000—Burlington (Midw.)	6	7	.462	3.07	1.12	22	22	3	3	...	0-...	134.2	83	53	46	8	68-0	137	.182
—Win.-Salem (Car.)	2	4	.333	5.11	1.32	6	6	0	0	...	0-...	37.0	32	21	21	1	17-0	24	.239
2001—Vero Beach (FSL)	4	5	.444	6.24	1.85	23	13	0	0	...	1-...	75.0	103	57	52	9	36-0	41	.340
—Win.-Salem (Car.)	4	2	.667	2.93	1.21	9	6	1	0	...	0-...	43.0	42	15	14	3	10-0	31	.266
2002—Birmingham (Sou.)	5	3	.625	2.65	1.27	57	1	0	0	...	3-...	74.2	61	31	22	3	34-2	75	.221
2003—Charlotte (Int'l)	6	4	.600	3.96	1.25	42	1	0	0	...	4-...	72.2	62	33	32	3	29-2	72	.231
2004—Charlotte (Int'l)	3	3	.500	3.19	1.09	35	0	0	0	...	14-...	42.1	30	16	15	2	16-0	41	.208
—Edmonton (PCL)	1	2	.333	3.86	1.59	15	0	0	0	...	1-...	16.1	18	8	7	0	8-1	17	.295
—Montreal (N.L.)	0	1	.000	3.86	1.57	16	0	0	0	0	1-2	21.0	28	15	9	2	5-1	12	.326
2005—New Orleans (PCL)	0	0	...	4.26	1.42	3	0	0	0	1	0-1	6.1	7	3	3	0	2-0	2	.292
—Wash. (N.L.)	4	4	.500	2.93	1.36	79	0	0	0	24	1-5	86.0	80	32	28	2	37-6	50	.248
2006—Wash. (N.L.)	3	2	.600	3.58	1.34	46	0	0	0	6	0-5	55.1	49	24	22	4	25-1	34	.233
—Louisville (Int'l)	0	0	...	0.00	1.36	4	1	0	0	0	0-0	3.2	4	2	0	0	1-0	3	.267
—Cincinnati (N.L.)	1	2	.333	8.40	2.27	19	0	0	0	2	0-2	15.0	30	14	14	1	4-2	9	.435
Major League totals (3 years)	8	9	.471	3.70	1.45	160	0	0	0	32	2-14	177.1	187	85	73	9	71-10	105	.272

2006 LEFTY-RIGHTY SPLITS

vs.	Avg.	AB	H	2B	3B	HR	RBI	BB	SO	OBP	Slg.	vs.	Avg.	AB	H	2B	3B	HR	RBI	BB	SO	OBP	Slg.
L	.290	107	31	6	0	2	21	9	22	.345	.402	R	.279	172	48	14	3	3	18	20	21	.362	.448

MALDONADO, CARLOS — C

PERSONAL: Born January 3, 1979, in Marcaibo, Venezuela. ... 6-2/185. ... Bats right, throws right. ... Full name: Carlos Luis Maldonado. ... High school: Instituto Perez Bonalde (Marcaibo, Venezuela). **TRANSACTIONS/CAREER NOTES:** Signed as non-drafted free agent by Seattle Mariners organization (September 7, 1995). ... Traded by Mariners to Houston Astros for IF Carlos Hernandez (March 21, 2000). ... Signed as a free agent by Chicago White Sox organization (January 12, 2003). ... Signed as a free agent by Pittsburgh Pirates organization (November 5, 2004).
2006 GAMES PLAYED BY POSITION (MLB): C—8.

Year Team (League)	Pos.	G	AB	R	H	2B	3B	HR	RBI	BB	SO	HBP	GDP	SB-CS	Avg.	OBP	SLG	OPS	E	Avg.
1996— Ariz. Mariners (Ariz.)	C	29	100	10	22	0	0	2	18	6	10	1	7	0-1	.220	.261	.280	.541	2	.990
1997— Wisconsin (Midw.)	C	97	316	15	60	8	2	0	25	17	33	3	8	2-3	.190	.236	.228	.464	11	.989
1998— Wisconsin (Midw.)	C	7	23	4	4	0	0	1	1	2	1	0	1	0-0	.174	.240	.174	.414	1	.990
—Everett (N'west)	C	42	150	19	43	10	0	5	24	10	17	2	5	1-0	.287	.335	.453	.788	5	.984
—Tacoma (PCL)	C	3	9	0	0	0	0	0	0	0	1	0	0	0-0	.000	.000	.000	.000	1	.933
1999— Wisconsin (Midw.)	C	92	302	35	93	13	0	6	33	43	32	0	10	4-6	.308	.392	.351	.743	5	.994
2000— Round Rock (Texas)	C	116	423	46	114	24	2	5	52	35	71	5	15	5-4	.270	.328	.371	.699	12	.988
2001— Round Rock (Texas)	C	76	262	29	75	14	0	4	33	27	55	3	11	1-2	.286	.356	.385	.741	5	.992
2002— New Orleans (PCL)	C	12	29	1	5	0	0	1	7	0	6	0	1	0-0	.172	.200	.172	.372	0	1.000
—Round Rock (Texas)	C-1B	47	123	13	31	8	0	4	20	22	23	0	4	0-0	.252	.356	.415	.770	3	.979

Year Team (League)	Pos.	G	AB	R	H	2B	3B	HR	RBI	BB	SO	HBP	GDP	SB-CS	Avg.	OBP	SLG	OPS	E	Avg.
2003— Birmingham (Sou.)		120	408	50	107	24	1	6	63	43	50	6	13	1-1	.262	.335	.370	.705	...	...
2004— Birmingham (Sou.)		108	388	48	103	30	1	12	68	52	81	3	10	0-3	.265	.353	.441	.794	...	...
2005— Altoona (East.)	C-DH	82	278	27	70	14	0	7	34	35	63	2	10	0-1	.252	.339	.378	.716	11	.982
2006— Indianapolis (Int'l)		103	336	37	95	18	0	6	47	36	67	3	11	2-0	.283	.354	.390	.743	3	.996
— Altoona (East.)		5	18	1	5	2	0	0	0	0	6	0	0	0-0	.278	.278	.389	.667	0	1.000
— Pittsburgh (N.L.)	C	8	19	0	2	0	0	0	0	1	10	0	0	1-0	.105	.150	.105	.255	1	.968
Major League totals (1 year)		8	19	0	2	0	0	0	0	1	10	0	0	1-0	.105	.150	.105	.255	1	.968

2006 LEFTY-RIGHTY SPLITS

vs.	Avg.	AB	H	2B	3B	HR	RBI	BB	SO	OBP	Slg.	vs.	Avg.	AB	H	2B	3B	HR	RBI	BB	SO	OBP	Slg.
L	.000	0	0	0	0	0	0	0	0	.000	.000	R	.105	19	2	0	0	0	0	1	10	.150	.105

MANON, JULIO — P

PERSONAL: Born June 10, 1973, in Guerra, Dominican Republic. ... 6-0/200. ... Throws right, bats right. ... Full name: Julio Alberto Manon. ... Name pronounced: mah-YON. ... High school: Andres Abelino. **TRANSACTIONS/CAREER NOTES:** Signed as non-drafted free agent by St. Louis Cardinals organization (April 16, 1992). ... Loaned by Cardinals to Huntington of the Appalachian League (June 13-September 7, 1995). ... Released by Cardinals (March 26, 1996). ... Signed by Tampa Bay Devil Rays organization (March 18, 1997). ... Loaned by Devil Rays to Orlando of the Seattle Mariners organization (June 4-July 31, 1998). ... Released by Devil Rays (August 4, 1999). ... Signed by St. Paul of the independent Northern League (August 1999). ... Signed as a free agent by Milwaukee Brewers organization (December 17, 1999). ... Released by Brewers (March 28, 2000). ... Signed by Montreal Expos organization (June 20, 2000). ... Released by Expos (December 12, 2003). ... Played with Kia Tigers and Samsung Lions of the Korean League (2004-05). ... Signed as a free agent by Baltimore Orioles organization (December 22, 2005).

CAREER HITTING: 0-for-1 (.000), 0 R, 0 2B, 0 3B, 0 HR, 0 RBI.

Year Team (League)	W	L	Pct.	ERA	WHIP	G	GS	CG	ShO	Hld.	Sv.-Opp.	IP	H	R	ER	HR	BB-IBB	SO	Avg.
1992— Dom. Tigers-Cardinals (DSL)	0	5	.000	7.58	2.54	20	6	1	0	...	1-...	59.1	85	88	50	2	66-0	40	.333
1993— Ariz. Cardinals (Ariz.)	2	3	.400	5.13	1.68	15	4	0	0	...	0-...	33.1	44	21	19	2	12-0	22	.324
1994— Johnson City (App.)	1	2	.333	8.31	1.85	5	0	0	0	...	1-...	8.2	11	8	8	2	5-0	7	.289
— Ariz. Cardinals (Ariz.)	0	1	.000	5.06	1.31	14	0	0	0	...	1-...	16.0	20	9	9	0	1-0	18	.294
1995— Huntington (Appal.)	3	4	.429	3.65	1.42	16	8	2	0	...	1-...	74.0	75	34	30	4	30-0	77	.264
1997— Char., S.C. (SAL)	3	5	.375	4.47	1.32	27	9	0	0	...	0-...	88.2	95	53	44	8	22-1	98	.265
1998— Orlando (South.)	0	2	.000	6.10	1.50	13	0	0	0	...	1-...	20.2	22	19	14	3	9-0	22	.256
— St. Pete. (FSL)	5	5	.500	3.72	1.08	38	0	0	0	...	1-...	55.2	41	25	23	7	19-1	73	.207
1999— St. Paul (North.)	1	1	.500	2.21	1.23	4	3	0	0	0	0-0	20.1	18	9	5	0	7-0	21	.234
— Orlando (South.)	3	3	.500	5.10	1.54	30	5	0	0	...	0-...	67.0	80	43	38	9	23-0	53	.289
2000— GC Expos (GCL)	2	0	1.000	0.87	0.58	4	0	0	0	...	1-...	10.1	4	1	1	0	2-0	10	.129
— Harrisburg (East.)	2	1	.667	5.17	1.28	14	4	0	0	...	1-...	31.1	32	19	18	7	8-0	25	.260
2001— Harrisburg (East.)	4	3	.571	3.12	1.27	10	7	0	0	...	1-...	52.0	50	20	18	6	16-0	44	.265
— Ottawa (Int'l)	1	4	.200	3.11	1.25	15	14	0	0	...	0-...	84.0	71	31	29	11	34-0	67	.234
2002— Harrisburg (East.)	5	1	.833	3.00	1.05	6	6	0	0	...	1-...	39.0	37	13	13	3	4-0	51	.245
— Ottawa (Int'l)	8	6	.571	3.50	1.22	28	13	2	1	...	2-...	105.1	83	42	41	8	45-0	81	.217
2003— Montreal (N.L.)	1	2	.333	4.13	1.52	23	0	0	0	6	1-1	28.1	26	13	-13	3	17-1	15	.252
— Edmonton (PCL)	3	1	.750	2.14	1.20	35	0	0	0	...	14-...	42.0	33	12	10	4	19-1	48	.205
2004— KIA (Korea)			...																
2005— Samsung (Korea)			....																
2006— Ottawa (Int'l)	0	2	.000	2.13	1.09	47	0	0	0	0	30-33	50.2	35	13	12	4	20-4	61	.198
— Baltimore (A.L.)	0	1	.000	5.40	1.95	22	0	0	0	2	0-1	20.0	23	13	12	5	16-1	22	.274
American League totals (1 year)	0	1	.000	5.40	1.95	22	0	0	0	2	0-1	20.0	23	13	12	5	16-1	22	.274
National League totals (1 year)	1	2	.333	4.13	1.52	23	0	0	0	6	1-1	28.1	26	13	13	3	17-1	15	.252
Major League totals (2 years)	1	3	.250	4.66	1.70	45	0	0	0	8	1-2	48.1	49	26	25	8	33-2	37	.262

2006 LEFTY-RIGHTY SPLITS

vs.	Avg.	AB	H	2B	3B	HR	RBI	BB	SO	OBP	Slg.	vs.	Avg.	AB	H	2B	3B	HR	RBI	BB	SO	OBP	Slg.
L	.364	33	12	3	0	2	7	7	9	.475	.636	R	.216	51	11	1	1	3	8	9	13	.355	.451

MARCUM, SHAWN — P

PERSONAL: Born December 14, 1981, in Kansas City, Mo. ... 6-0/180. ... Throws right, bats right. ... Full name: Shawn M. Marcum. ... College: SW Missouri State. **TRANSACTIONS/CAREER NOTES:** Selected by Toronto Blue Jays organization in third round of 2003 free-agent draft.

CAREER HITTING: 0-for-0 (.000), 0 R, 0 2B, 0 3B, 0 HR, 0 RBI.

Year Team (League)	W	L	Pct.	ERA	WHIP	G	GS	CG	ShO	Hld.	Sv.-Opp.	IP	H	R	ER	HR	BB-IBB	SO	Avg.
2003— Auburn (NY-Penn)	1	0	1.000	1.32	0.65	21	0	0	0	...	8-...	34.0	15	6	5	1	7-0	47	.129
2004— Char., W.Va. (SAL)	7	4	.636	3.19	1.01	13	13	1	1	...	0-...	79.0	64	32	28	7	16-0	83	.217
— Dunedin (Fla. St.)	3	2	.600	3.12	1.13	12	12	0	0	...	0-...	69.1	74	30	24	6	4-0	72	.279
2005— New Hampshire (East.)	7	1	.875	2.53	1.01	9	9	1	1	0	0-...	53.1	44	15	15	5	10-0	40	.229
— Syracuse (Int'l)	6	4	.600	4.95	1.25	18	18	0	0	0	0-0	103.2	112	59	57	17	18-2	90	.271
— Toronto (A.L.)	0	0	.000	0.00	1.25	5	0	0	0	0	0-0	8.0	6	0	0	0	4-0	4	.214
2006— Syracuse (Int'l)	4	0	1.000	3.42	1.08	18	5	0	0	1	0-0	52.2	48	20	20	6	9-0	60	.241
— Toronto (A.L.)	3	4	.429	5.06	1.60	21	14	0	0	0	0-0	78.1	87	44	44	14	38-3	65	.279
Major League totals (2 years)	3	4	.429	4.59	1.56	26	14	0	0	0	0-0	86.1	93	44	44	14	42-3	69	.274

2006 LEFTY-RIGHTY SPLITS

vs.	Avg.	AB	H	2B	3B	HR	RBI	BB	SO	OBP	Slg.	vs.	Avg.	AB	H	2B	3B	HR	RBI	BB	SO	OBP	Slg.
L	.303	152	46	10	2	7	19	22	23	.390	.533	R	.256	160	41	10	0	7	24	16	42	.335	.450

MARKAKIS, NICK — OF

PERSONAL: Born November 17, 1983, in Woodstock, Ga. ... 6-2/185. ... Bats left, throws left. ... Full name: Nicholas Markakis. ... Junior college: Young Harris (Ga.). **TRANSACTIONS/CAREER NOTES:** Selected by Baltimore Orioles organization in first round (seventh pick overall) of 2003 free-agent draft. **STATISTICAL NOTES:** Hit three home runs in one game (August 22, 2006).

2006 GAMES PLAYED BY POSITION (MLB): OF—145, DH—1.

Year Team (League)	Pos.	G	AB	R	H	2B	3B	HR	RBI	BB	SO	HBP	GDP	SB-CS	Avg.	OBP	SLG	OPS	E	Avg.
2003— Aberdeen (N.Y.-Penn.)		59	205	22	58	14	3	1	28	30	33	1	6	13-5	.283	.372	.395	.767	...	...
2004— Delmarva (S. Atl.)		96	355	57	106	22	3	11	64	42	66	2	6	12-3	.299	.371	.470	.841	...	...
2005— Frederick (Carolina)	OF-DH	91	350	59	105	25	1	12	62	43	65	4	6	2-1	.300	.379	.480	.859	10	.971

M

Year Team (League)	Pos.	G	AB	R	H	2B	3B	HR	RBI	BB	SO	HBP	GDP	SB-CS	Avg.	OBP	SLG	OPS	FIELDING E	Avg.
— Bowie (East.)	OF	33	124	19	42	16	2	3	30	18	30	0	5	0-1	.339	.420	.573	.992	0	1.000
2006— Baltimore (A.L.)	OF-DH	147	491	72	143	25	2	16	62	43	72	3	15	2-0	.291	.351	.448	.799	2	.994
Major League totals (1 year)		147	491	72	143	25	2	16	62	43	72	3	15	2-0	.291	.351	.448	.799	2	.994

2006 LEFTY-RIGHTY SPLITS

vs.	Avg.	AB	H	2B	3B	HR	RBI	BB	SO	OBP	Sig.	vs.	Avg.	AB	H	2B	3B	HR	RBI	BB	SO	OBP	Sig.
L	.286	119	34	8	0	1	12	8	22	.333	.378	R	.293	372	109	17	2	15	50	35	50	.356	.470

MARMOL, CARLOS — P

PERSONAL: Born October 14, 1982, in Bonao, Dominican Republic. ... 6-2/180. ... Throws right, bats right. ... Full name: Carlos Agustin Marmol. **TRANSACTIONS/CAREER NOTES:** Signed as non-drafted free agent by Chicago Cubs organization (July 3, 1999). ... Played three seasons as an outfielder and catcher in Cubs organization (2000-02). ... On disabled list (August 19-September 4, 2006); included rehabilitation assignment to Iowa. **MISCELLANEOUS NOTES:** Struck out in only appearance as pinch hitter (2006).
CAREER HITTING: 6-for-23 (.261), 3 R, 1 2B, 0 3B, 1 HR, 1 RBI.

Year Team (League)	W	L	Pct.	ERA	WHIP	G	GS	CG	ShO	Hld.	Sv.-Opp.	IP	H	R	ER	HR	BB-IBB	SO	Avg.
2002— Ariz. Cubs (Ariz.)	0	0	...	0.00	2.00	1	0	0	0	...	0-...	1.0	1	0	0	0	1-0	1	.250
2003— Ariz. Cubs (Ariz.)	3	5	.375	4.19	1.46	14	9	0	0	...	0-...	62.1	54	38	29	5	37-0	74	.225
2004— Lansing (Midw.)	14	8	.636	3.20	1.19	26	24	0	0	...	0-...	154.2	131	64	55	15	53-0	154	.237
2005— Daytona (Fla. St.)	6	2	.750	2.99	1.34	13	13	0	0	0	0-0	72.1	60	30	24	7	37-0	71	.227
— West Tenn (Sou.)	3	4	.429	3.65	1.35	14	14	0	0	0	0-0	81.1	70	33	33	10	40-0	70	.239
2006— Iowa (PCL)	0	0	...	9.00	1.67	2	0	0	0	1	0-0	3.0	4	3	3	0	1-0	1	.333
— West Tenn (Sou.)	3	2	.600	2.33	1.16	11	11	0	0	0	0-0	58.0	42	18	15	1	25-0	67	.207
— Chicago (N.L.)	5	7	.417	6.08	1.69	19	13	0	0	0	0-0	77.0	71	54	52	14	59-2	59	.250
Major League totals (1 year)	5	7	.417	6.08	1.69	19	13	0	0	0	0-0	77.0	71	54	52	14	59-2	59	.250

2006 LEFTY-RIGHTY SPLITS

vs.	Avg.	AB	H	2B	3B	HR	RBI	BB	SO	OBP	Sig.	vs.	Avg.	AB	H	2B	3B	HR	RBI	BB	SO	OBP	Sig.
L	.229	105	24	3	3	8	23	21	17	.362	.562	R	.263	179	47	13	0	6	24	38	42	.400	.436

MAROTH, MIKE — P

PERSONAL: Born August 17, 1977, in Orlando. ... 6-0/190. ... Throws left, bats left. ... Full name: Michael Warren Maroth. ... Name pronounced: mah-ROTH. ... High school: William R. Boone (Orlando). ... College: Central Florida. **TRANSACTIONS/CAREER NOTES:** Selected by Boston Red Sox organization in third round of 1998 free-agent draft. ... Traded by Red Sox to Detroit Tigers for P Bryce Florie (July 31, 1999). ... On disabled list (May 26-September 6, 2006); included rehabilitation assignment to Toledo. **MISCELLANEOUS NOTES:** Struck out in only appearance as pinch hitter (2005).
CAREER HITTING: 4-for-16 (.250), 1 R, 0 2B, 0 3B, 0 HR, 2 RBI.

Year Team (League)	W	L	Pct.	ERA	WHIP	G	GS	CG	ShO	Hld.	Sv.-Opp.	IP	H	R	ER	HR	BB-IBB	SO	Avg.
1998— GC Red Sox (GCL)	1	1	.500	0.00	0.87	4	2	0	0	...	0-...	12.2	9	3	0	0	2-0	14	.191
— Lowell (NY-Penn)	2	3	.400	2.90	1.13	6	6	0	0	...	0-...	31.0	22	13	10	1	13-0	34	.200
1999— Sarasota (Fla. St.)	11	6	.647	4.04	1.43	20	19	0	0	...	0-...	111.1	124	65	50	8	35-1	64	...
— Lakeland (Fla. St.)	2	1	.667	3.24	1.50	3	3	0	0	...	0-...	16.2	18	7	6	1	7-0	11	...
— Jacksonville (Sou.)	1	2	.333	4.79	1.65	4	4	0	0	...	0-...	20.2	27	15	11	2	7-0	10	.310
2000— Jacksonville (Sou.)	9	14	.391	3.94	1.42	27	26	2	1	...	0-...	164.1	176	79	72	14	58-0	85	.289
2001— Toledo (Int'l)	7	10	.412	4.65	1.58	24	23	0	0	...	0-...	131.2	158	80	68	11	50-1	63	.302
2002— Toledo (Int'l)	8	1	.889	2.82	1.02	11	11	1	0	...	0-...	73.1	53	25	23	7	22-0	51	.201
— Detroit (A.L.)	6	10	.375	4.48	1.34	21	21	0	0	0	0-0	128.2	136	68	64	7	36-1	58	.276
2003— Detroit (A.L.)	9	*21	.300	5.73	1.45	33	33	1	0	0	0-0	193.1	231	133	* 123	* 34	50-2	87	.299
2004— Detroit (A.L.)	11	13	.458	4.31	1.40	33	33	2	1	0	0-0	217.0	244	112	104	25	59-1	108	.288
2005— Detroit (A.L.)	14	14	.500	4.74	1.37	34	34	0	0	0	0-0	209.0	235	123	110	30	51-1	115	.288
2006— Toledo (Int'l)	3	0	1.000	4.50	1.10	4	4	0	0	0	0-0	20.0	18	10	10	4	4-1	21	.243
— Detroit (A.L.)	5	2	.714	4.19	1.49	13	9	0	0	0	0-0	53.2	64	26	25	11	16-1	24	.295
Major League totals (5 years)	45	60	.429	4.78	1.40	134	130	3	1	0	0-0	801.2	910	460	426	107	212-6	392	.289

2006 LEFTY-RIGHTY SPLITS

vs.	Avg.	AB	H	2B	3B	HR	RBI	BB	SO	OBP	Sig.	vs.	Avg.	AB	H	2B	3B	HR	RBI	BB	SO	OBP	Sig.
L	.250	52	13	0	0	3	6	6	6	.328	.423	R	.309	165	51	12	2	8	17	10	18	.352	.552

MARQUIS, JASON — P

PERSONAL: Born August 21, 1978, in Manhasset, N.Y. ... 6-1/210. ... Throws right, bats right. ... Full name: Jason Scott Marquis. ... Name pronounced: mar-KEE. ... High school: Tottenville (Staten Island, N.Y.). **TRANSACTIONS/CAREER NOTES:** Selected by Atlanta Braves organization in supplemental round ("sandwich" pick between first and second rounds, 35th pick overall) of 1996 free-agent draft; pick received as compensation for Braves' failure to sign 1995 first-round pick P Chad Hutchinson. ... On disabled list (April 22-May 12, 2002). ... Traded with Ps Ray King and Adam Wainwright to St. Louis Cardinals for OF J.D. Drew and C/OF Eli Marrero (December 14, 2003). **HONORS:** Named pitcher on N.L. Silver Slugger team (2005). **MISCELLANEOUS NOTES:** Appeared in two games as pinch runner (2001). ... Grounded out and struck out in two appearances as pinch hitter and scored three runs in six appearances as pinch runner (2002). ... Scored a run in three appearances as pinch runner (2004). ... Was 3-for-9 with two strikeouts in nine appearances as pinch hitter and scored a run in two appearances as pinch runner (2005). ... Was 3-for-10 with three runs scored, a double, a triple, a base on balls, two sacrifice hits and two strikeouts in 13 appearances as pinch hitter (2006).
CAREER HITTING: 69-for-310 (.223), 33 R, 19 2B, 2 3B, 2 HR, 26 RBI.

Year Team (League)	W	L	Pct.	ERA	WHIP	G	GS	CG	ShO	Hld.	Sv.-Opp.	IP	H	R	ER	HR	BB-IBB	SO	Avg.
1996— Danville (Appal.)	1	1	.500	4.63	1.59	7	4	0	0	...	0-...	23.1	30	18	12	0	7-0	24	.286
1997— Macon (S. Atl.)	14	10	.583	4.38	1.49	28	28	0	0	...	0-...	141.2	156	78	69	10	55-1	121	.278
1998— Danville (Carol.)	2	13	.143	4.87	1.40	22	22	1	0	...	0-...	114.2	120	65	62	3	41-0	135	.269
1999— Myrtle Beach (Carol.)	3	0	1.000	0.28	1.22	6	6	0	0	...	0-...	32.0	22	2	1	0	17-0	41	.191
— Greenville (Sou.)	3	4	.429	4.58	1.47	12	12	1	0	...	0-...	55.0	52	33	28	7	29-0	35	.241
2000— Greenville (Sou.)	4	2	.667	3.57	1.34	11	11	0	0	...	0-...	68.0	68	35	27	10	23-0	49	.262
— Atlanta (N.L.)	1	0	1.000	5.01	1.50	15	0	0	0	1	0-1	23.1	23	16	13	4	12-1	17	.261
— Richmond (Int'l)	0	3	.000	9.00	1.95	6	6	0	0	...	0-...	20.0	26	21	20	2	13-0	18	.321
2001— Atlanta (N.L.)	5	6	.455	3.48	1.33	38	16	0	0	2	0-0	129.1	113	62	50	14	59-4	98	.234
2002— Atlanta (N.L.)	8	9	.471	5.04	1.54	22	22	0	0	0	0-0	114.1	127	66	64	19	49-3	84	.283
— Richmond (Int'l)	0	1	.000	3.60	1.20	1	1	0	0	...	0-...	5.0	5	2	2	0	1-0	6	.263
2003— Richmond (Int'l)	8	4	.667	3.35	1.40	15	15	3	1	...	0-...	94.0	93	40	35	5	34-0	75	.256
— Atlanta (N.L.)	0	0	...	5.53	1.50	21	2	0	0	0	1-1	40.2	43	27	25	3	18-2	19	.270
2004— St. Louis (N.L.)	15	7	.682	3.71	1.42	32	32	1	0	0	0-0	201.1	215	90	83	26	70-1	138	.275
2005— St. Louis (N.L.)	13	14	.481	4.13	1.33	33	32	0	0	0	0-0	207.0	206	110	95	29	69-2	100	.262
2006— St. Louis (N.L.)	14	•16	.467	6.02	1.52	33	33	0	0	0	0-0	194.1	221	*136	*130	*35	75-2	96	.289
Major League totals (7 years)	56	52	.519	4.55	1.43	194	137	3	1	3	1-4	910.1	948	507	460	130	352-15	552	.270

DIVISION SERIES RECORD

Year	Team (League)	W	L	Pct.	ERA	WHIP	G	GS	CG	ShO	Hld.	Sv.-Opp.	IP	H	R	ER	HR	BB-IBB	SO	Avg.
2001—	Atlanta (N.L.)	Did not play.																		
2004—	St. Louis (N.L.)	0	0	...	8.10	2.40	1	1	0	0	0	0-0	3.1	4	3	3	3	4-0	0	.308

CHAMPIONSHIP SERIES RECORD

Year	Team (League)	W	L	Pct.	ERA	WHIP	G	GS	CG	ShO	Hld.	Sv.-Opp.	IP	H	R	ER	HR	BB-IBB	SO	Avg.
2001—	Atlanta (N.L.)	0	0	...	0.00	2.00	2	0	0	0	0	0-0	2.0	2	4	0	1	2-0	3	.222
2004—	St. Louis (N.L.)	0	0	...	6.75	1.75	1	1	0	0	0	0-0	4.0	5	3	3	0	2-0	2	.294
2005—	St. Louis (N.L.)	0	1	.000	3.38	1.69	3	0	0	0	0	0-0	5.1	6	3	2	0	3-0	4	.316
Champ. series totals (3 years)		0	1	.000	3.97	1.76	6	1	0	0	0	0-0	11.1	13	10	5	1	7-0	9	.289

WORLD SERIES RECORD

Year	Team (League)	W	L	Pct.	ERA	WHIP	G	GS	CG	ShO	Hld.	Sv.-Opp.	IP	H	R	ER	HR	BB-IBB	SO	Avg.
2004—	St. Louis (N.L.)	0	1	.000	3.86	1.86	2	1	0	0	0	0-0	7.0	6	3	3	1	7-1	4	.231

2006 LEFTY-RIGHTY SPLITS

vs.	Avg.	AB	H	2B	3B	HR	RBI	BB	SO	OBP	Slg.	vs.	Avg.	AB	H	2B	3B	HR	RBI	BB	SO	OBP	Slg.
L	.288	365	105	22	5	15	57	40	46	.363	.499	R	.291	399	116	21	5	20	70	35	50	.364	.519

MARRERO, ELI — OF/C

PERSONAL: Born November 17, 1973, in Havana, Cuba. ... 6-1/180. ... Bats right, throws right. ... Full name: Elieser Marrero. ... Name pronounced: muh-RARE-ro. ... High school: Coral Gables (Fla.). **TRANSACTIONS/CAREER NOTES:** Selected by St. Louis Cardinals organization in third round of 1993 free-agent draft. ... On disabled list (March 22-April 13, 1998). ... On disabled list (July 2-September 1, 2000); included rehabilitation assignment to Memphis. ... On disabled list (May 12-September 1, 2003); included rehabilitation assignment to Memphis. ... Traded with OF J.D. Drew to Atlanta Braves for Ps Jason Marquis, Ray King and Adam Wainwright (December 14, 2003). ... On disabled list (March 29-April 14 and April 25-May 29, 2004); included rehabilitation assignments to Greenville and Richmond. ... Traded by Braves to Kansas City Royals for P Luis Vasquez (December 16, 2004). ... Traded by Royals with cash to Baltimore Orioles for 2B Pete Maestrales (June 8, 2005). ... On disabled list (July 27, 2005-remainder of season). ... Signed as free agent by Colorado Rockies organization (January 9, 2006). ... Traded by Rockies to New York Mets for 2B Kaz Matsui (June 9, 2006). ... Released by Mets (August 15, 2006). **STATISTICAL NOTES:** Career major league grand slams: 3.

2006 GAMES PLAYED BY POSITION (MLB): OF—13, 1B—8, C—7, 3B—1.

			BATTING																FIELDING	
Year	Team (League)	Pos.	G	AB	R	H	2B	3B	HR	RBI	BB	SO	HBP	GDP	SB-CS	Avg.	OBP	SLG	OPS	E	Avg.
1993—	Johnson City (App.)	C	18	61	10	22	8	0	2	14	12	9	1	0	2-2	.361	.467	.590	1.057	1	.994
1994—	Savannah (S. Atl.)	C	116	421	71	110	16	3	21	79	39	92	5	6	5-4	.261	.328	.463	.791	15	.984
1995—	St. Pete. (FSL)	C	107	383	43	81	16	1	10	55	23	55	1	10	9-4	.211	.254	.337	.590	10	.984
1996—	Arkansas (Texas)	C-DH	116	374	65	101	17	3	19	65	32	55	6	7	9-6	.270	.336	.484	.820	3	.996
1997—	Louisville (A.A.)	C-DH	112	395	60	108	21	7	20	68	25	53	3	8	4-4	.273	.318	.514	.832	7	.991
—	St. Louis (N.L.)	C	17	45	4	11	2	0	2	7	2	13	0	1	4-0	.244	.271	.422	.693	3	.969
1998—	St. Louis (N.L.)	C-1B	83	254	28	62	18	1	4	20	28	42	0	5	6-2	.244	.318	.370	.688	4	.991
—	Memphis (PCL)	C-DH	32	130	22	31	5	0	7	21	13	23	0	3	5-4	.238	.306	.438	.744	2	.991
1999—	St. Louis (N.L.)	C-1B	114	317	32	61	13	1	6	34	18	56	1	14	11-2	.192	.236	.297	.533	7	.988
2000—	St. Louis (N.L.)	C-1B	53	102	21	23	3	1	5	17	9	16	3	3	5-0	.225	.302	.422	.723	0	1.000
—	Memphis (PCL)	C	6	15	1	1	0	0	0	0	0	2	0	1	0-0	.067	.067	.067	.133	0	1.000
2001—	St. Louis (N.L.)	C-OF-1B	86	203	37	54	11	3	6	23	15	36	0	4	6-3	.266	.312	.438	.751	7	.983
2002—	St. Louis (N.L.)	OF-C-1B	131	397	63	104	19	1	18	66	40	72	0	5	14-2	.262	.327	.451	.777	7	.981
2003—	Memphis (PCL)	OF-DH	5	12	2	3	1	0	1	1	1	0	1	1	0-0	.250	.357	.583	.940	0	1.000
—	St. Louis (N.L.)	OF-C-1B	41	107	10	24	4	2	2	20	7	18	0	0	0-1	.224	.267	.355	.622	1	.989
2004—	Greenville (Sou.)	OF	3	12	3	5	1	0	2	5	2	6	0	1	0-0	.417	.500	1.000	1.500	0	1.000
—	Richmond (Int'l)	OF	6	24	1	5	2	0	0	3	1	3	0	0	0-0	.208	.240	.292	.532	0	1.000
—	Atlanta (N.L.)	OF	90	250	37	80	18	1	10	40	23	50	1	4	4-1	.320	.374	.520	.894	1	.992
2005—	Kansas City (A.L.)	OF-1B-DH	32	88	11	14	4	0	4	9	7	18	1	2	1-0	.159	.222	.341	.563	2	.981
—	Baltimore (A.L.)	OF	22	50	8	11	3	2	3	10	4	20	0	1	0-0	.220	.268	.540	.808	1	.966
2006—	Colorado (N.L.)	1B-OF-C	30	60	7	13	3	0	4	10	11	16	1	1	3-0	.217	.347	.467	.814	1	.989
—	New York (N.L.)	OF-C-1B 3B	25	33	4	6	1	0	2	5	4	15	1	0	2-0	.182	.282	.394	.676	1	.933
American League totals (1 year)			54	138	19	25	7	2	7	19	11	38	1	3	1-0	.181	.239	.413	.652	3	.978
National League totals (9 years)			670	1768	243	438	92	10	59	242	157	334	7	37	55-11	.248	.308	.411	.719	32	.987
Major League totals (10 years)			724	1906	262	463	99	12	66	261	168	372	8	40	56-11	.243	.303	.411	.714	35	.987

DIVISION SERIES RECORD

Year	Team (League)	Pos.	G	AB	R	H	2B	3B	HR	RBI	BB	SO	HBP	GDP	SB-CS	Avg.	OBP	SLG	OPS	E	Avg.
2000—	St. Louis (N.L.)		Did not play.																		
2001—	St. Louis (N.L.)	C	3	7	0	0	0	0	0	0	0	0	0	0	0-0	.000	.000	.000	.000	0	1.000
2002—	St. Louis (N.L.)	OF	2	6	0	0	0	0	0	1	0	1	0	0	0-0	.000	.000	.000	.000	0	1.000
2004—	Atlanta (N.L.)	OF	3	5	0	1	0	0	0	0	0	2	0	0	0-0	.200	.200	.200	.400	0	...
Division series totals (3 years)			8	18	0	1	0	0	0	1	0	3	0	0	0-0	.056	.053	.056	.108	0	1.000

CHAMPIONSHIP SERIES RECORD

Year	Team (League)	Pos.	G	AB	R	H	2B	3B	HR	RBI	BB	SO	HBP	GDP	SB-CS	Avg.	OBP	SLG	OPS	E	Avg.
2000—	St. Louis (N.L.)	C	4	4	0	0	0	0	0	1	0	1	0	0	0-0	.000	.000	.000	.000	0	1.000
2002—	St. Louis (N.L.)	OF	4	16	1	3	1	0	1	1	1	1	0	0	0-0	.188	.235	.438	.673	0	1.000
Champ. series totals (2 years)			8	20	1	3	1	0	1	2	1	2	0	0	0-0	.150	.190	.350	.540	0	1.000

2006 LEFTY-RIGHTY SPLITS

vs.	Avg.	AB	H	2B	3B	HR	RBI	BB	SO	OBP	Slg.	vs.	Avg.	AB	H	2B	3B	HR	RBI	BB	SO	OBP	Slg.
L	.138	29	4	0	0	1	2	8	9	.342	.241	R	.234	64	15	4	0	5	13	7	22	.315	.531

MARSHALL, SEAN — P

PERSONAL: Born August 30, 1982, in Richmond, Va. ... 6-6/195. ... Throws left, bats left. ... Full name: Sean Christopher Marshall. ... College: Virginia Commonwealth. **TRANSACTIONS/CAREER NOTES:** Selected by Chicago Cubs in sixth round of 2003 free-agent draft. ... On disabled list (July 23-September 1, 2006); included rehabilitation assignment to Iowa.

CAREER HITTING: 5-for-40 (.125), 3 R, 0 2B, 0 3B, 1 HR, 2 RBI.

Year	Team (League)	W	L	Pct.	ERA	WHIP	G	GS	CG	ShO	Hld.	Sv.-Opp.	IP	H	R	ER	HR	BB-IBB	SO	Avg.
2003—	Boise (N'west)	5	6	.455	2.57	1.21	14	14	0	0	...	0-...	73.2	66	31	21	1	23-0	88	.237
—	Lansing (Midw.)	1	0	1.000	0.00	0.71	1	1	0	0	...	0-...	7.0	5	1	0	0	0-0	11	.192
2004—	Lansing (Midw.)	2	0	1.000	1.11	0.68	7	7	1	1	...	0-...	48.2	29	7	6	1	4-0	51	.172
—	West Tenn (Sou.)	2	2	.500	5.90	1.66	6	6	0	0	...	0-...	29.0	36	20	19	2	12-0	23	.319
2005—	Daytona (Fla. St.)	4	4	.500	2.74	1.29	12	12	1	0	0	0-0	69.0	63	24	21	7	26-0	61	.246

Year	Team (League)	W	L	Pct.	ERA	WHIP	G	GS	CG	ShO	Hld.	Sv.-Opp.	IP	H	R	ER	HR	BB-IBB	SO	Avg.
— West Tenn (Sou.)		0	1	.000	2.52	0.84	4	4	0	0	0	0-0	25.0	16	7	7	1	5-0	24	.180
2006— Iowa (PCL)		0	2	.000	3.32	1.43	4	4	0	0	0	0-0	21.2	17	10	8	1	14-0	21	.221
— Chicago (N.L.)		6	9	.400	5.59	1.52	24	24	0	0	0	0-0	125.2	132	85	78	20	59-3	77	.270
Major League totals (1 year)		6	9	.400	5.59	1.52	24	24	0	0	0	0-0	125.2	132	85	78	20	59-3	77	.270

2006 LEFTY-RIGHTY SPLITS

vs.	Avg.	AB	H	2B	3B	HR	RBI	BB	SO	OBP	Slg.	vs.	Avg.	AB	H	2B	3B	HR	RBI	BB	SO	OBP	Slg.
L	.256	78	20	0	1	6	17	10	16	.363	.513	R	.273	411	112	21	1	14	57	49	61	.355	.431

MARTE, ANDY   3B

PERSONAL: Born October 21, 1983, in Villa Tapia, Dominican Republic. ... 6-1/185. ... Bats right, throws right. ... Full name: Andy M. Marte. **TRANSACTIONS/CAREER NOTES:** Signed as a non-drafted free agent by Atlanta Braves organization (September 12, 2000). ... Traded by Braves to Boston Red Sox for SS Edgar Renteria (December 8, 2005). ... Traded by Red Sox with P Guillermo Mota and C Kelly Shoppach to Cleveland Indians for OF Coco Crisp, C Josh Bard and P David Riske (January 27, 2006). **STATISTICAL NOTES:** Career major league grand slams: 1. **2006 GAMES PLAYED BY POSITION (MLB):** 3B—50.

Year	Team (League)	Pos.	G	AB	R	H	2B	3B	HR	RBI	BB	SO	HBP	GDP	SB-CS	Avg.	OBP	SLG	OPS	E	Avg.
2001— Danville (Appal.)	3B-2B	37	125	12	25	6	0	1	12	20	45	0	3	3-0	.200	.306	.272	.578	6	.936
2002— Macon (S. Atl.)	3B	126	488	69	137	32	4	21	105	41	114	6	6	2-1	.281	.339	.492	.831	27	.917
2003— Myrtle Beach (Carol.)	3B	130	463	69	132	35	1	16	63	67	109	2	13	5-2	.285	.372	.469	.841	28	.911
2004— Greenville (Sou.)	3B	107	387	52	104	28	1	23	68	58	105	2	8	1-1	.269	.364	.525	.889	17	.717
— GC Braves (GCL)	2B-3B	3	15	4	7	4	0	1	6	2	2	0	0	0-0	.467	.529	.933	1.462	0	1.000
2005— Richmond (Int'l)	3B	109	389	51	107	26	2	20	74	64	83	0	8	0-3	.275	.372	.506	.878	15	.950
— Atlanta (N.L.)	3B	24	57	3	8	2	1	0	4	7	13	0	2	0-1	.140	.227	.211	.438	3	.857
2006— Buffalo (Int'l)		96	357	49	93	23	0	15	46	34	81	0	11	1-0	.261	.322	.451	.773	19	.935
— Cleveland (A.L.)	3B	50	164	20	37	15	1	5	23	13	38	1	3	0-0	.226	.287	.421	.707	6	.962
American League totals (1 year)		50	164	20	37	15	1	5	23	13	38	1	3	0-0	.226	.287	.421	.707	6	.962
National League totals (1 year)		24	57	3	8	2	1	0	4	7	13	0	2	0-1	.140	.227	.211	.438	3	.857
Major League totals (2 years)		74	221	23	45	17	2	5	27	20	51	1	5	0-1	.204	.270	.367	.637	9	.949

2006 LEFTY-RIGHTY SPLITS

vs.	Avg.	AB	H	2B	3B	HR	RBI	BB	SO	OBP	Slg.	vs.	Avg.	AB	H	2B	3B	HR	RBI	BB	SO	OBP	Slg.
L	.227	44	10	5	0	2	6	4	7	.292	.477	R	.225	120	27	10	1	3	17	9	31	.285	.400

MARTE, DAMASO   P

PERSONAL: Born February 14, 1975, in Santo Domingo, Dominican Republic. ... 6-2/200. ... Throws left, bats left. ... Full name: Damaso Savinon Marte. ... Name pronounced: da-muh-so mar-TAY. **TRANSACTIONS/CAREER NOTES:** Signed as a non-drafted free agent by Seattle Mariners organization (October 28, 1992). ... Signed as a free agent by New York Yankees organization (November 16, 2000). ... Traded by Yankees to Pittsburgh Pirates for IF Enrique Wilson (June 13, 2001). ... Traded by Pirates with IF Edwin Yan to Chicago White Sox for P Matt Guerrier (March 27, 2002). ... On disabled list (June 30-July 14, 2005); included rehabilitation assignment to Charlotte. ... Traded by White Sox to Pirates for IF/OF Rob Mackowiak (December 13, 2005). **CAREER HITTING:** 0-for-7 (.000), 0 R, 0 2B, 0 3B, 0 HR, 0 RBI.

Year	Team (League)	W	L	Pct.	ERA	WHIP	G	GS	CG	ShO	Hld.	Sv.-Opp.	IP	H	R	ER	HR	BB-IBB	SO	Avg.
1993— Dom. Mariners (DSL)	2	5	.286	6.55	1.99	17	15	2	0	...	0-...	56.1	62	48	41	...	50-...	29	
1994— Dom. Mariners (DSL)	7	0	1.000	3.86	1.55	17	13	0	0	...	0-...	65.1	53	41	28	...	48-...	80	
1995— Everett (N'west)	2	2	.500	2.21	0.95	11	11	5	0	...	0-...	36.2	25	11	9	2	10-0	39	.195
1996— Wisconsin (Midw.)	8	6	.571	4.49	1.47	26	26	2	1	...	0-...	142.1	134	82	71	8	75-5	115	.248
1997— Lancaster (Calif.)	8	8	.500	4.13	1.48	25	25	2	1	...	0-...	139.1	144	75	64	15	62-1	127	.272
1998— Orlando (South.)	7	6	.538	5.27	1.51	22	20	0	0	...	0-...	121.1	136	82	71	14	47-0	99	.281
1999— Tacoma (PCL)	3	3	.500	5.13	1.62	31	11	0	0	...	0-...	73.2	79	43	42	13	40-1	59	.271
— Seattle (A.L.)	0	1	.000	9.35	2.54	5	0	0	0	0	0-0	8.2	16	9	9	3	6-0	3	.390
2000— Ariz. Mariners (Ariz.)	0	0	...	0.00	0.20	2	2	0	0	...	0-...	5.0	1	0	0	0	0-0	6	.063
— New Haven (East.)	0	0	...	1.59	1.41	4	0	0	0	...	0-...	5.2	6	1	1	0	2-0	4	.286
2001— Norwich (East.)	3	1	.750	3.50	1.00	23	0	0	0	...	1-...	36.0	29	16	14	3	7-0	36	.215
— Nashville (PCL)	0	0	...	3.38	0.56	4	0	0	0	...	0-...	5.1	3	2	2	2	0-0	4	.167
— Pittsburgh (N.L.)	0	1	.000	4.71	1.27	23	0	0	0	...	0-...	36.1	34	21	19	5	12-3	39	.250
2002— Chicago (A.L.)	1	1	.500	2.83	1.03	68	0	0	0	14	10-12	60.1	44	19	19	5	18-2	72	.204
2003— Chicago (A.L.)	4	2	.667	1.58	1.05	71	0	0	0	14	11-18	79.2	50	16	14	3	34-6	87	.185
2004— Chicago (A.L.)	6	5	.545	3.42	1.22	74	0	0	0	21	6-12	73.2	56	28	28	10	34-4	68	.217
2005— Charlotte (Int'l)	0	0	...	5.40	3.00	1	0	0	0	0	0-0	1.2	4	1	1	0	1-0	2	.400
— Chicago (A.L.)	3	4	.429	3.77	1.72	66	0	0	0	22	4-8	45.1	45	21	19	5	33-4	54	.256
2006— Pittsburgh (N.L.)	1	7	.125	3.70	1.41	75	0	0	0	13	0-4	58.1	51	30	24	5	31-6	63	.244
American League totals (5 years)	14	13	.519	2.99	1.26	284	0	0	0	71	31-50	267.2	211	93	89	26	125-16	284	.219
National League totals (2 years)	1	8	.111	4.09	1.35	98	0	0	0	13	0-4	94.2	85	51	43	10	43-9	102	.246
Major League totals (7 years)	15	21	.417	3.28	1.28	382	0	0	0	84	31-54	362.1	296	144	132	36	168-25	386	.226

DIVISION SERIES RECORD

Year	Team (League)	W	L	Pct.	ERA	WHIP	G	GS	CG	ShO	Hld.	Sv.-Opp.	IP	H	R	ER	HR	BB-IBB	SO	Avg.
2005— Chicago (A.L.)	0	0	...	...	...	1	0	0	0	0	0-0	0.0	1	0	0	0	2-0	0	1.000

WORLD SERIES RECORD

Year	Team (League)	W	L	Pct.	ERA	WHIP	G	GS	CG	ShO	Hld.	Sv.-Opp.	IP	H	R	ER	HR	BB-IBB	SO	Avg.
2005— Chicago (A.L.)	1	0	1.000	0.00	1.20	1	0	0	0	0	0-0	1.2	0	0	0	0	2-0	3	.000

2006 LEFTY-RIGHTY SPLITS

vs.	Avg.	AB	H	2B	3B	HR	RBI	BB	SO	OBP	Slg.	vs.	Avg.	AB	H	2B	3B	HR	RBI	BB	SO	OBP	Slg.
L	.225	89	20	2	0	2	12	8	33	.300	.315	R	.258	120	31	6	1	3	18	23	30	.381	.400

MARTIN, RUSSELL   C

PERSONAL: Born February 15, 1983, in East York, Ontario. ... 5-11/200. ... Bats right, throws right. ... Full name: Russell Nathan Martin Jr.. ... Junior college: Chipola (Fla.). **TRANSACTIONS/CAREER NOTES:** Selected by Los Angeles Dodgers organization in 17th round of 2002 free-agent draft. **2006 GAMES PLAYED BY POSITION (MLB):** C—117, DH—1.

Year	Team (League)	Pos.	G	AB	R	H	2B	3B	HR	RBI	BB	SO	HBP	GDP	SB-CS	Avg.	OBP	SLG	OPS	E	Avg.
2002— GC Dodgers (GCL)		41	126	22	36	3	3	0	10	23	18	4	4	7-1	.286	.412	.357	.769	9	

M

Year Team (League)	Pos.	G	AB	R	H	2B	3B	HR	RBI	BB	SO	HBP	GDP	SB-CS	Avg.	OBP	SLG	OPS	E	Avg.
								BATTING											**FIELDING**	
2003— South Georgia (S. Atl.)		25	98	15	28	4	1	3	14	9	11	0	1	5-2	.286	.343	.439	.782	5	...
—Ogden (Pion.)		52	188	25	51	13	0	6	36	26	26	4	6	3-1	.271	.368	.436	.804	13	...
2004— Vero Beach (FSL)		122	416	74	104	24	1	15	64	72	54	10	10	9-5	.250	.368	.421	.789	10	...
2005— Jacksonville (Sou.)	C-DH-OF	129	409	83	127	17	1	9	61	78	69	10	14	15-7	.311	.430	.423	.853	12	.989
2006— Las Vegas (PCL)		23	74	14	22	9	0	0	9	13	11	0	1	0-2	.297	.389	.419	.808	2	.991
—Los Angeles (N.L.)	C-DH	121	415	65	117	26	4	10	65	45	57	4	17	10-5	.282	.355	.436	.792	6	.993
Major League totals (1 year)		121	415	65	117	26	4	10	65	45	57	4	17	10-5	.282	.355	.436	.792	6	.993

DIVISION SERIES RECORD

Year Team (League)	Pos.	G	AB	R	H	2B	3B	HR	RBI	BB	SO	HBP	GDP	SB-CS	Avg.	OBP	SLG	OPS	E	Avg.
2006— Los Angeles (N.L.)	C	3	12	2	4	0	0	0	0	1	2	0	0	0-0	.333	.385	.333	.718	0	1.000

2006 LEFTY-RIGHTY SPLITS

vs.	Avg.	AB	H	2B	3B	HR	RBI	BB	SO	OBP	Slg.	vs.	Avg.	AB	H	2B	3B	HR	RBI	BB	SO	OBP	Slg.
L	.366	71	26	5	0	2	16	11	6	.451	.521	R	.265	344	91	21	4	8	49	34	51	.335	.419

MARTIN, TOM — P

PERSONAL: Born May 21, 1970, in Charleston, S.C. ... 6-1/206. ... Throws left, bats left. ... Full name: Thomas Edgar Martin. ... High school: Bay (Panama City, Fla.). **TRANSACTIONS/CAREER NOTES:** Selected by Baltimore Orioles organization in sixth round of 1988 free-agent draft. ... Traded by Orioles with 3B Craig Worthington to San Diego Padres for P Jim Lewis and OF Steve Martin (February 17, 1992). ... Selected by Atlanta Braves organization from Padres organization in Rule 5 minor league draft (December 13, 1993). ... Loaned by Braves organization to Mexico City Tigers of the Mexican League (May 1-7, 1995). ... Released by Braves (January 25, 1996). ... Signed by Houston Astros organization (February 21, 1996). ... On disabled list (May 30-June 15, 1997). ... Selected by Arizona Diamondbacks in second round (29th pick overall) of expansion draft (November 18, 1997). ... Traded by Diamondbacks with 3B Travis Fryman and cash to Cleveland Indians for 3B Matt Williams (December 1, 1997). ... On disabled list (April 30-May 18 and August 31-September 19, 1998); included rehabilitation assignments to Buffalo. ... On disabled list (April 4-August 9, 1999); included rehabilitation assignment to Akron. ... On disabled list (June 13-August 4, 2000); included rehabilitation assignment to Buffalo. ... Traded by Indians to New York Mets for C Javier Ochoa (January 11, 2001). ... On disabled list (May 13-August 16, 2001); included rehabilitation assignments to Brooklyn and Norfolk. ... Released by Mets (October 11, 2001). ... Signed by Tampa Bay Devil Rays organization (January 28, 2002). ... On disabled list (April 23-September 30, 2002). ... Released by Devil Rays (September 30, 2002). ... Signed by Los Angeles Dodgers organization (February 26, 2003). ... Traded by Dodgers to Braves for P Matt Merricks (July 31, 2004). ... Released by Braves (April 15, 2005). ... Signed by Astros organization (April 22, 2005). ... Signed as a free agent by Colorado Rockies organization (January 18, 2006).

CAREER HITTING: 0-for-11 (.000). 0 R, 0 2B, 0 3B, 0 HR, 0 RBI.

Year Team (League)	W	L	Pct.	ERA	WHIP	G	GS	CG	ShO	Hld.	Sv.-Opp.	IP	H	R	ER	HR	BB-IBB	SO	Avg.
1989— Bluefield (Appal.)	3	3	.500	4.62	1.56	8	8	0	0	...	0-...	39.0	36	28	20	3	25-0	31	.242
—Erie (N.Y.-Penn)	0	5	.000	6.64	1.65	7	7	0	0	...	0-...	40.2	42	39	30	2	25-0	44	.259
1990— Wausau (Midw.)	2	3	.400	2.48	1.45	9	9	0	0	...	0-...	40.0	31	25	11	1	27-0	45	.209
1991— Kane Co. (Midw.)	4	10	.286	3.64	1.49	38	10	0	0	...	6-...	99.0	92	50	40	4	56-3	106	.247
1992— High Desert (Calif.)	0	2	.000	9.37	2.39	11	0	0	0	...	0-...	16.1	23	19	17	4	16-0	10	.333
—Waterloo (Midw.)	2	6	.250	4.25	1.53	39	2	0	0	...	3-...	55.0	62	38	26	3	22-4	57	.287
1993— Rancho Cuca. (Calif.)	1	4	.200	5.61	1.87	47	1	0	0	...	0-...	59.1	72	41	37	4	39-2	53	.305
1994— Greenville (Sou.)	5	6	.455	4.62	1.47	36	6	0	0	...	0-...	74.0	82	40	38	6	27-3	51	.288
1995— Richmond (Int'l)	0	0	...	9.00	2.22	7	0	0	0	...	0-...	9.0	10	9	9	4	10-2	3	.286
—M.C. Tigers (Mex.)	0	1	.000	27.00	4.50	1	1	0	0	...	0-...	1.1	5	5	4	0	1-...	0	...
1996— Tucson (PCL)	0	0	...	0.00	1.33	5	0	0	0	...	0-...	6.0	6	0	0	0	2-2	1	.261
—Jackson (Texas)	6	2	.750	3.24	1.51	57	0	0	0	...	3-...	75.0	71	35	27	8	42-4	58	.250
1997— Houston (N.L.)	5	3	.625	2.09	1.34	55	0	0	0	7	2-3	56.0	52	13	13	2	23-2	36	.254
1998— Cleveland (A.L.)	1	1	.500	12.89	2.80	14	0	0	0	3	0-0	14.2	29	21	21	3	12-0	9	.408
—Buffalo (Int'l)	3	1	.750	1.00	1.64	41	0	0	0	...	0-...	36.0	46	25	24	4	13-0	35	.309
1999— Akron (East.)	0	0	...	1.00	0.78	3	3	0	0	...	0-...	9.0	4	1	1	0	3-0	9	.138
—Cleveland (A.L.)	0	1	.000	8.68	1.71	6	0	0	0	0	0-0	9.1	13	9	9	2	3-1	8	.325
—Buffalo (Int'l)	1	0	1.000	3.00	1.00	5	0	0	0	...	0-...	6.0	5	2	2	1	1-0	6	.208
2000— Cleveland (A.L.)	1	0	1.000	4.05	1.41	31	0	0	0	0	0-0	33.1	32	16	15	3	15-2	21	.254
—Buffalo (Int'l)	0	1	.000	3.60	1.30	9	3	0	0	...	0-...	10.0	12	4	4	1	1-0	4	.300
2001— Norfolk (Int'l)	2	1	.667	6.26	1.78	23	0	0	0	...	1-...	23.0	31	17	16	4	10-0	24	.330
—New York (N.L.)	1	0	1.000	10.06	1.94	14	0	0	0	1	0-0	17.0	23	22	19	4	10-2	12	.319
—Brook.. (N.Y.-Penn.)	0	0	...	0.00	2.00	1	1	0	0	...	0-...	1.0	2	0	0	0	0-0	0	.500
2002— Durham (Int'l)-	0	0	...	0.00	1.20	4	0	0	0	...	2-...	3.1	3	0	0	0	1-0	6	.231
—Tampa Bay (A.L.)	0	0	...	16.20	3.60	2	0	0	0	0	0-0	1.2	5	3	3	0	1-0	1	.500
2003— Los Angeles (N.L.)	1	2	.333	3.53	1.18	80	0	0	0	28	0-1	51.0	36	21	20	6	24-4	51	.198
2004— Los Angeles (N.L.)	0	1	.000	4.13	1.62	47	0	0	0	5	1-1	28.1	32	13	13	3	14-1	18	.291
—Atlanta (N.L.)	0	1	.000	3.71	1.29	29	0	0	0	7	0-3	17.0	17	7	7	4	5-2	12	.270
2005— Atlanta (N.L.)	0	0	...	19.29	3.43	4	0	0	0	0	0-0	2.1	6	5	5	1	2-0	0	.500
—Round Rock (PCL)	0	0	...	3.62	1.68	20	0	0	0	...	5-7	27.1	33	11	11	4	13-2	13	.308
2006— Colorado (N.L.)	2	0	1.000	5.07	1.44	68	0	0	0	11	0-1	60.1	62	37	34	4	25-5	46	.264
American League totals (4 years)	2	2	.500	7.32	1.86	53	0	0	0	3	0-0	59.0	79	49	48	8	31-3	39	.320
National League totals (6 years)	9	7	.563	4.31	1.43	297	0	0	0	59	3-9	232.0	228	118	111	24	103-16	175	.259
Major League totals (10 years)	11	9	.550	4.92	1.52	350	0	0	0	62	3-9	291.0	307	167	159	32	134-19	214	.273

DIVISION SERIES RECORD

Year Team (League)	W	L	Pct.	ERA	WHIP	G	GS	CG	ShO	Hld.	Sv.-Opp.	IP	H	R	ER	HR	BB-IBB	SO	Avg.
1997— Houston (N.L.)	0	0	...	0.00	3.00	2	0	0	0	0	0-0	0.2	1	1	0	0	1-0	1	.333
2004— Atlanta (N.L.)	0	0	...	54.00	15.00	2	0	0	0	0	0-0	0.1	4	2	2	0	1-0	1	1.000
Division series totals (2 years)	0	0	...	18.00	7.00	4	0	0	0	0	0-0	1.0	5	3	2	0	2-0	1	.714

2006 LEFTY-RIGHTY SPLITS

vs.	Avg.	AB	H	2B	3B	HR	RBI	BB	SO	OBP	Slg.	vs.	Avg.	AB	H	2B	3B	HR	RBI	BB	SO	OBP	Slg.
L	.268	97	26	7	2	3	20	10	24	.355	.474	R	.261	138	36	9	2	1	19	15	22	.335	.377

MARTINEZ, CARLOS — P

PERSONAL: Born May 26, 1982, in Villa Vazquez, Dominican Republic. ... 6-1/170. ... Throws right, bats right. ... Full name: Carlos M. Martinez. **TRANSACTIONS/CAREER NOTES:** Signed as a non-drafted free agent by Florida Marlins organization (August 8, 2000).

CAREER HITTING: 0-for-0 (.000). 0 R, 0 2B, 0 3B, 0 HR, 0 RBI.

Year Team (League)	W	L	Pct.	ERA	WHIP	G	GS	CG	ShO	Hld.	Sv.-Opp.	IP	H	R	ER	HR	BB-IBB	SO	Avg.
2001— Dom. Marlins (DSL)	4	7	.363	4.50	1.42	15	14	0	0	...	0-...	74.0	87	56	37	2	18-...	35	.279
2002— GC Marlins (GCL)	1	2	.333	1.11	0.99	22	0	0	0	...	7-...	32.1	26	8	4	1	6-...	23	.217
2003— Dom. Marlins (DSL)	0	2	.000	3.18	1.32	10	0	0	0	...	1-...	11.1	12	8	4	0	3-...	7	.267
—GC Marlins (GCL)	1	0	1.000	0.00	0.32	6	0	0	0	...	1-...	6.1	1	0	0	0	1-...	7	.053

M

Year	Team (League)	W	L	Pct.	ERA	WHIP	G	GS	CG	ShO	Hld.	Sv.-Opp.	IP	H	R	ER	HR	BB-IBB	SO	Avg.
	— Jamestown (NYP)	0	1	.000	5.40	1.80	1	0	0	0	...	0-...	1.2	2	1	1	0	1-...	4	.250
	— Greensboro (SAL)	0	3	.000	2.95	1.20	15	0	0	0	...	1-...	18.1	18	7	6	1	4-...	15	.250
2004	— Greensboro (SAL)	2	3	.400	3.17	1.14	40	0	0	0	...	6-...	48.1	43	21	17	8	12-...	37	.226
2005	— Jupiter	4	5	.444	3.12	1.22	47	0	0	0	...	22-...	60.2	52	25	21	5	22-...	65	...
	— Albuquerque	0	0	.000	9.00	2.00	2	0	0	0	...	0-...	2.0	4	2	2	1	0-...	0	...
	— Carolina	0	0	.000	9.00	2.00	1	0	0	0	...	1-...	1.0	1	1	1	0	1-...	1	...
2006	— Jupiter	0	0	.000	0.00	0.50	2	1	0	0	0	0-...	2.0	0	0	0	0	1-0	0	.000
	— Florida (N.L.)	0	1	.000	1.74	1.45	12	0	0	0	0	5	10.1	9	2	2	0	6-0	11	.250
	Major League totals (1 year)	0	1	.000	1.74	1.45	12	0	0	0	0	5	0-0	10.1	9	2	2	0	6-0	11	.250

2006 LEFTY-RIGHTY SPLITS

vs.	Avg.	AB	H	2B	3B	HR	RBI	BB	SO	OBP	Slg.	vs.	Avg.	AB	H	2B	3B	HR	RBI	BB	SO	OBP	Slg.
L	.250	12	3	0	0	0	1	4	3	.412	.250	R	.250	24	6	1	0	0	2	2	8	.296	.292

MARTINEZ, PEDRO — P

PERSONAL: Born October 25, 1971, in Manoguayabo, Dominican Republic. ... 5-11/180. ... Throws right, bats right. ... Full name: Pedro Jaime Martinez. ... Brother of Ramon J. Martinez, pitcher with three major league teams (1988-2001). **TRANSACTIONS/CAREER NOTES:** Signed as a non-drafted free agent by Los Angeles Dodgers organization (June 18, 1988). ... Traded by Dodgers to Montreal Expos for 2B Delino DeShields (November 19, 1993). ... On suspended list (April 1-9, 1997). ... Traded by Expos to Boston Red Sox for P Carl Pavano and a player to be named (November 18, 1997); Expos acquired P Tony Armas to complete deal (December 18, 1997). ... On disabled list (July 19-August 3, 1999; June 29-July 13, 2000; June 27-August 26 and September 8, 2001-remainder of season; and May 16-June 11, 2003). ... Signed as a free agent by New York Mets (December 17, 2004). ... On disabled list (June July 6-28, 2006). ... On disabled list (August 15-September 15, 2006). **RECORDS:** Holds major league record for lowest WHIP (walks and hits to innings pitched), season (0.74, 2000). **HONORS:** Named Minor League Player of the Year by THE SPORTING NEWS (1991). ... Named N.L. Pitcher of the Year by THE SPORTING NEWS (1997). ... Named A.L. Pitcher of the Year by THE SPORTING NEWS (1999 and 2000). ... Named righthanded pitcher on THE SPORTING NEWS A.L. All-Star team (1997). ... Named righthanded pitcher on THE SPORTING NEWS A.L. All-Star team (1998, 1999 and 2000). ... Named N.L. Cy Young Award winner by Baseball Writers' Association of America (1997). ... Named A.L. Cy Young Award winner by Baseball Writers' Association of America (1999 and 2000). **STATISTICAL NOTES:** Pitched nine perfect innings against San Diego, before being relieved after yielding leadoff double in 10th inning (June 3, 1995). **MISCELLANEOUS NOTES:** Listed as starting third baseman in one game; did not play in the field (1993).

CAREER HITTING: 35-for-372 (.094), 18 R, 4 2B, 2 3B, 0 HR, 13 RBI.

Year	Team (League)	W	L	Pct.	ERA	WHIP	G	GS	CG	ShO	Hld.	Sv.-Opp.	IP	H	R	ER	HR	BB-IBB	SO	Avg.
1988	— Dom. Dodgers (DSL)	5	1	.833	3.10	1.24	8	7	1	0	...	0-...	49.1	45	25	17	...	16-...	28	...
1989	— Dom. Dodgers (DSL)	7	2	.778	2.73	0.98	13	7	2	3	...	1-...	85.2	59	30	26	...	25-...	63	...
1990	— Great Falls (Pio.)	8	3	.727	3.62	1.48	14	14	0	0	...	0-...	77.0	74	39	31	5	40-1	82	.253
1991	— Bakersfield (Calif.)	8	0	1.000	2.05	0.98	10	10	0	0	...	0-...	61.1	41	17	14	3	19-0	83	.189
	— San Antonio (Texas)	7	5	.583	1.76	1.15	12	12	4	3	...	0-...	76.2	57	21	15	1	31-1	74	.210
	— Albuquerque (PCL)	3	3	.500	3.66	1.12	6	6	0	0	...	0-...	39.1	28	17	16	3	16-0	35	.201
1992	— Albuquerque (PCL)	7	6	.538	3.81	1.28	20	20	3	1	...	0-...	125.1	104	57	53	10	57-0	124	.229
	— Los Angeles (N.L.)	0	1	.000	2.25	0.88	2	1	0	0	0	0-0	8.0	6	2	2	0	1-0	8	.214
1993	— Albuquerque (PCL)	0	0	...	3.00	0.67	1	1	0	0	...	0-...	3.0	1	1	1	0	1-0	4	.100
	— Los Angeles (N.L.)	10	5	.667	2.61	1.24	65	2	0	0	14	2-3	107.0	76	34	31	5	57-4	119	.211
1994	— Montreal (N.L.)	11	5	.688	3.42	1.11	24	23	1	1	0	1-1	144.2	115	58	55	11	45-3	142	.220
1995	— Montreal (N.L.)	14	10	.583	3.51	1.15	30	30	2	2	0	0-0	194.2	158	79	76	21	66-1	174	.227
1996	— Montreal (N.L.)	13	10	.565	3.70	1.20	33	33	4	1	0	0-0	216.2	189	100	89	19	70-3	222	.232
1997	— Montreal (N.L.)	17	8	.680	*1.90	0.93	31	31	* 13	4	0	0-0	241.1	158	65	51	16	67-5	305	*.184
1998	— Boston (A.L.)	19	7	.731	2.89	1.09	33	33	3	2	0	0-0	233.2	188	82	75	26	67-3	251	.217
1999	— Boston (A.L.)	* 23	4	*.852	*2.07	0.92	31	29	5	1	0	0-0	213.1	160	56	49	9	37-1	* 313	*.205
2000	— Boston (A.L.)	18	6	.750	*1.74	0.74	29	29	7	* 4	0	0-0	217.0	128	44	42	17	32-0	* 284	*.167
2001	— Boston (A.L.)	7	3	.700	2.39	0.93	18	18	1	0	0	0-0	116.2	84	33	31	5	25-0	163	.199
2002	— Boston (A.L.)	20	4	*.833	*2.26	0.92	30	30	2	0	0	0-0	199.1	144	62	50	13	40-1	* 239	*.198
2003	— Boston (A.L.)	14	4	.778	*2.22	1.04	29	29	3	0	0	0-0	186.2	147	52	46	7	47-0	206	*.215
2004	— Boston (A.L.)	16	9	.640	3.90	1.17	33	33	1	1	0	0-0	217.0	193	99	94	26	61-0	227	.232
2005	— New York (N.L.)	15	8	.652	2.82	0.95	31	31	4	1	0	0-0	217.0	159	69	68	19	47-3	208	.204
2006	— New York (N.L.)	9	8	.529	4.48	1.11	23	23	0	0	0	0-0	132.2	108	72	66	19	39-2	137	.220
	American League totals (7 years)	117	37	.760	2.52	0.98	203	201	22	8	0	0-0	1383.2	1044	428	387	103	309-5	1683	.206
	National League totals (8 years)	89	55	.618	3.12	1.08	239	174	24	9	14	3-4	1262.0	969	479	438	110	392-21	1315	.212
	Major League totals (15 years)	206	92	.691	2.81	1.03	442	375	46	17	14	3-4	2645.2	2013	907	825	213	701-26	2998	.209

DIVISION SERIES RECORD

Year	Team (League)	W	L	Pct.	ERA	WHIP	G	GS	CG	ShO	Hld.	Sv.-Opp.	IP	H	R	ER	HR	BB-IBB	SO	Avg.
1998	— Boston (A.L.)	1	0	1.000	3.86	0.86	1	1	0	0	0	0-0	7.0	6	3	3	2	0-0	8	.222
1999	— Boston (A.L.)	1	0	1.000	0.00	0.70	2	1	0	0	0	0-0	10.0	3	0	0	0	4-0	11	.091
2003	— Boston (A.L.)	1	0	1.000	3.86	1.29	2	2	0	0	0	0-0	14.0	13	6	6	0	5-0	9	.250
2004	— Boston (A.L.)	1	0	1.000	3.86	1.14	1	1	0	0	0	0-0	7.0	6	3	3	0	2-0	6	.240
	Division series totals (4 years)	4	0	1.000	2.84	1.03	6	5	0	0	0	0-0	38.0	28	12	12	2	11-0	34	.204

CHAMPIONSHIP SERIES RECORD

Year	Team (League)	W	L	Pct.	ERA	WHIP	G	GS	CG	ShO	Hld.	Sv.-Opp.	IP	H	R	ER	HR	BB-IBB	SO	Avg.
1999	— Boston (A.L.)	1	0	1.000	0.00	0.57	1	1	0	0	0	0-0	7.0	2	0	0	0	2-0	12	.087
2003	— Boston (A.L.)	0	1	.000	5.65	1.26	2	2	0	0	0	0-0	14.1	16	9	9	3	2-0	14	.276
2004	— Boston (A.L.)	0	1	.000	6.23	1.77	3	2	0	0	0	0-0	13.0	14	9	9	2	9-0	14	.269
	Champ. series totals (3 years)	1	2	.333	4.72	1.31	6	5	0	0	0	0-0	34.1	32	18	18	5	13-0	40	.241

WORLD SERIES RECORD

Year	Team (League)	W	L	Pct.	ERA	WHIP	G	GS	CG	ShO	Hld.	Sv.-Opp.	IP	H	R	ER	HR	BB-IBB	SO	Avg.
2004	— Boston (A.L.)	1	0	1.000	0.00	0.71	1	1	0	0	0	0-0	7.0	3	0	0	0	2-0	6	.136

ALL-STAR GAME RECORD

	Year Team (League)	W	L	Pct.	ERA	WHIP	G	GS	CG	ShO	Hld.	Sv.-Opp.	IP	H	R	ER	HR	BB-IBB	SO	Avg.
	All-Star Game totals (3 years)	1	0	1.000	0.00	0.50	3	1	0	0	0	0-0	4.0	2	0	0	0	0-0	8	.143

2006 LEFTY-RIGHTY SPLITS

vs.	Avg.	AB	H	2B	3B	HR	RBI	BB	SO	OBP	Slg.	vs.	Avg.	AB	H	2B	3B	HR	RBI	BB	SO	OBP	Slg.
L	.231	234	54	7	0	6	26	25	59	.308	.338	R	.211	256	54	14	1	13	39	14	78	.270	.426

MARTINEZ, RAMON — IF

PERSONAL: Born October 10, 1972, in Philadelphia. ... 6-1/190. ... Bats right, throws right. ... Full name: Ramon E. Martinez. ... High school: Escuela Superior Catholica (Bayamon, Puerto Rico). ... Junior college: Vernon (Texas). **TRANSACTIONS/CAREER NOTES:** Signed as a non-drafted free agent by Kansas City Royals organization (January 15, 1993). ... Traded by Royals to San Francisco Giants (December 9, 1996), completing deal in which Giants traded P Jamie Brewington to Royals for a player to be named (November 26, 1996). ... On disabled list (August 21-September 5, 1999; and June 1-16, 2002). ... Signed as a free agent by Chicago Cubs (January 2, 2003). ...

On disabled list (September 16, 2004-remainder of season). ... Signed as a free agent by Detroit Tigers (January 4, 2005). ... On disabled list (April 9-29, 2005). ... Traded by Tigers with P Ugueth Urbina to Philadelphia Phillies for SS Placido Polanco (June 8, 2005). ... Signed as a free agent by Los Angeles Dodgers organization (January 31, 2006). **STATISTICAL NOTES:** Career major league grand slams: 1.

2006 GAMES PLAYED BY POSITION (MLB): 2B—39, 3B—20, SS—12, 1B—1, OF—1.

Year Team (League)	Pos.	G	AB	R	H	2B	3B	HR	RBI	BB	SO	HBP	GDP	SB-CS	Avg.	OBP	SLG	OPS	E	Avg.
1993— GC Royals (GCL)	2B	37	97	16	23	5	0	0	9	8	6	2	5	3-0	.237	.303	.289	.591	5	.973
— Wilmington (Caro.)	2B-SS	24	75	8	19	4	0	0	6	11	9	1	2	1-4	.253	.352	.307	.659	6	.954
1994— Wilmington (Caro.)	2B	90	325	40	87	13	2	2	35	35	25	4	14	6-3	.268	.341	.338	.680	16	.964
— Rockford (Midwest)	2B	6	18	3	5	0	0	0	3	4	2	0	1	1-0	.278	.409	.278	.687	1	.955
1995— Wichita (Texas)	2B-SS	103	393	58	108	20	2	3	51	42	50	4	11	11-8	.275	.344	.359	.703	9	.982
1996— Omaha (A.A.)	2B	85	320	35	81	12	3	6	41	21	34	3	6	3-2	.253	.305	.366	.671	12	.969
— Wichita (Texas)	2B	26	93	16	32	4	1	1	8	7	8	0	4	4-1	.344	.390	.441	.831	6	.956
1997— Shreveport (Texas)	SS	105	404	72	129	32	4	5	54	40	48	3	6	4-5	.319	.382	.455	.838	18	.968
— Phoenix (PCL)	2B-SS	18	57	6	16	2	0	1	7	5	9	0	1	1-0	.281	.333	.368	.702	3	.959
1998— Fresno (PCL)	2B-SS	98	364	58	114	21	2	14	59	38	42	2	11	0-3	.313	.375	.497	.872	10	.980
— San Francisco (N.L.)	2B	19	19	4	6	1	0	0	0	4	2	0	0	0-0	.316	.435	.368	.803	0	1.000
1999— San Francisco (N.L.)	2B-SS-3B																			
	DH	61	144	21	38	6	0	5	19	14	17	0	2	1-2	.264	.327	.410	.737	6	.966
— Fresno (PCL)	SS-DH-3B	29	114	13	37	7	1	2	17	10	17	0	2	2-0	.325	.376	.456	.832	5	.951
2000— San Francisco (N.L.)	SS-2B-1B																			
	3B	88	189	30	57	13	2	6	25	15	22	1	6	3-2	.302	.354	.487	.841	1	.995
2001— San Francisco (N.L.)	3B-2B-1B	128	391	48	99	18	3	5	37	38	52	5	11	1-2	.253	.323	.353	.676	8	.980
2002— San Francisco (N.L.)	SS-2B-1B																			
	OF-3B	72	181	26	49	10	2	4	25	14	26	4	1	2-0	.271	.335	.414	.749	6	.965
2003— Chicago (N.L.)	2B-3B-SS																			
	1B	108	293	30	83	16	1	6	34	24	50	2	8	0-1	.283	.333	.375	.709	10	.966
2004— Chicago (N.L.)	SS-3B-2B	102	260	22	64	15	1	3	30	26	40	1	5	1-0	.246	.313	.346	.659	9	.970
2005— Toledo (Int'l)	SS-2B	3	15	4	11	0	0	0	1	1	0	0	0	0-0	.733	.750	.733	1.483	0	1.000
— Detroit (A.L.)	SS-2B-1B																			
	3B	19	56	4	15	1	0	0	5	3	4	0	1	0-0	.268	.300	.286	.586	4	.944
— Philadelphia (N.L.)	1B-3B-SS																			
	2B	33	56	7	16	2	0	1	9	3	7	1	1	0-0	.286	.317	.375	.692	1	.989
2006— Los Angeles (N.L.)	2B-3B-SS																			
	1B-OF	82	176	20	49	7	1	2	24	15	20	1	9	0-0	.278	.339	.364	.702	2	.990
American League totals (1 year)		19	56	4	15	1	0	0	5	3	4	0	1	0-0	.268	.300	.286	.586	4	.944
National League totals (9 years)		693	1709	208	461	88	10	29	203	153	236	15	43	8-7	.270	.331	.384	.715	45	.976
Major League totals (9 years)		712	1765	212	476	89	10	29	208	156	240	15	44	8-7	.270	.330	.381	.711	49	.975

DIVISION SERIES RECORD

Year Team (League)	Pos.	G	AB	R	H	2B	3B	HR	RBI	BB	SO	HBP	GDP	SB-CS	Avg.	OBP	SLG	OPS	E	Avg.
2000— San Francisco (N.L.)	2B-SS	2	6	0	2	0	0	0	0	0	2	0	0	0-0	.333	.333	.333	.667	0	1.000
2002— San Francisco (N.L.)		1	0	0	0	0	0	0	0	1	0	0	0	0-0	.000	1.000	...	1.000	0	...
2003— Chicago (N.L.)	SS	2	4	0	0	0	0	0	0	0	2	0	0	0-0	.000	.000	.000	.000	0	1.000
2006— Los Angeles (N.L.)		3	3	0	1	0	0	0	1	0	1	0	0	0-0	.333	.333	.667	1.000	0	1.000
Division series totals (4 years)		8	13	0	3	1	0	0	1	1	5	0	0	0-0	.231	.286	.308	.593	0	1.000

CHAMPIONSHIP SERIES RECORD

Year Team (League)	Pos.	G	AB	R	H	2B	3B	HR	RBI	BB	SO	HBP	GDP	SB-CS	Avg.	OBP	SLG	OPS	E	Avg.
2002— San Francisco (N.L.)	SS	2	1	0	0	0	0	0	1	0	1	0	0	0-0	.000	.000	.000	.000	0	1.000
2003— Chicago (N.L.)	SS-2B	4	4	0	0	0	0	0	0	0	1	0	0	0-0	.000	.000	.000	.000	0	1.000
Champ. series totals (2 years)		6	5	0	0	0	0	0	1	0	2	0	0	0-0	.000	.000	.000	.000	0	1.000

WORLD SERIES RECORD

Year Team (League)	Pos.	G	AB	R	H	2B	3B	HR	RBI	BB	SO	HBP	GDP	SB-CS	Avg.	OBP	SLG	OPS	E	Avg.
2002— San Francisco (N.L.)		2	2	0	0	0	0	0	0	0	2	0	0	0-0	.000	.000	.000	.000	0	...

2006 LEFTY-RIGHTY SPLITS

vs.	Avg.	AB	H	2B	3B	HR	RBI	BB	SO	OBP	Slg.	vs.	Avg.	AB	H	2B	3B	HR	RBI	BB	SO	OBP	Slg.
L	.289	38	11	2	0	0	5	4	8	.357	.342	R	.275	138	38	5	1	2	19	11	12	.333	.370

MARTINEZ, VICTOR   C

PERSONAL: Born December 23, 1978, in Ciudad Bolivar, Venezuela. ... 6-2/190. ... Bats both, throws right. ... Full name: Victor Jesus Martinez. **TRANSACTIONS/CAREER NOTES:** Signed as a non-drafted free agent by Cleveland Indians organization (July 15, 1996). ... On disabled list (August 9-September 2, 2003); included rehabilitation assignment to Akron. **HONORS:** Named catcher on A.L. Silver Slugger team (2004). **STATISTICAL NOTES:** Hit three home runs in one game (July 16, 2004).

2006 GAMES PLAYED BY POSITION (MLB): C—133, 1B—22, DH—3.

Year Team (League)	Pos.	G	AB	R	H	2B	3B	HR	RBI	BB	SO	HBP	GDP	SB-CS	Avg.	OBP	SLG	OPS	E	Avg.
1997— Maracay 1 (VSL)		53	122	21	42	12	0	0	26	32	11	...	...	6-...	.344	...	.443	...	...	...
1998— Guacara 2 (VSL)		55	160	28	43	13	0	1	27	32	14	...	...	8-...	.269	...	.369	...	...	...
1999— Mahoning Valley (N.Y.-Penn.)	C	64	235	37	65	9	0	4	36	27	31	1	4	0-1	.277	.346	.366	.712	8	.984
2000— Kinston (Carol.)	C	26	83	9	18	7	0	0	8	11	5	1	3	1-1	.217	.313	.301	.614	5	.980
— Columbus (S. Atl.)	C	21	70	11	26	9	1	2	12	11	6	1	1	0-0	.371	.452	.614	1.067	2	.988
2001— Kinston (Carol.)	C	114	420	59	138	33	2	10	57	39	60	8	12	3-3	.329	.394	.488	.882	16	.985
2002— Akron (East.)	C	121	443	84	149	40	2	22	85	58	62	8	10	3-3	.336	.417	.576	.993	10	.988
— Cleveland (A.L.)	C-DH	12	32	2	9	1	0	1	5	3	2	0	1	0-0	.281	.333	.406	.740	1	.983
2003— Buffalo (Int'l)	C-1B-DH	73	274	42	90	19	0	7	45	26	32	8	14	3-5	.328	.395	.474	.869	4	.993
— Akron (East.)	DH-C	3	12	1	4	2	0	0	2	0	1	0	1	0-0	.333	.333	.500	.833	0	1.000
— Cleveland (A.L.)	C-DH	49	159	15	46	4	0	1	16	13	21	1	8	1-1	.289	.345	.333	.678	1	.996
2004— Cleveland (A.L.)	C-DH	141	520	77	147	38	1	23	108	60	69	5	16	0-1	.283	.359	.492	.851	6	.994
2005— Cleveland (A.L.)	C-DH	147	547	73	167	33	0	20	80	63	78	5	16	0-1	.305	.378	.475	.853	5	.995
2006— Cleveland (A.L.)	C-1B-DH	153	572	82	181	37	0	16	93	71	78	3	27	0-0	.316	.391	.465	.856	8	.992
Major League totals (5 years)		502	1830	249	550	113	1	61	302	210	248	14	68	1-3	.301	.373	.463	.836	21	.993

ALL-STAR GAME RECORD

		G	AB	R	H	2B	3B	HR	RBI	BB	SO	HBP	GDP	SB-CS	Avg.	OBP	SLG	OPS	E	Avg.
All-Star Game totals (1 year)		1	1	0	0	0	0	0	0	0	0	0	0	0-0	.000	.000	.000	.000	0	1.000

M

vs.	Avg.	AB	H	2B	3B	HR	RBI	BB	SO	OBP	Slg.	vs.	Avg.	AB	H	2B	3B	HR	RBI	BB	SO	OBP	Slg.
L	.290	214	62	12	0	6	28	28	28	.373	.430	R	.332	358	119	25	0	10	65	43	50	.402	.486

MASSET, NICK   P

PERSONAL: Born May 17, 1982, in St. Petersburg, Fla. ... Throws right, bats right. ... Full name: Nicholas A. Masset. **TRANSACTIONS/CAREER NOTES:** Selected by Texas Rangers organization in eighth round of 2000 free-agent draft.
CAREER HITTING: 0-for-0 (.000), 0 R, 0 2B, 0 3B, 0 HR, 0 RBI.

Year	Team (League)	W	L	Pct.	ERA	WHIP	G	GS	CG	ShO	Hld.	Sv.-Opp.	IP	H	R	ER	HR	BB-IBB	SO	Avg.
2001—	GC Rangers (GCL)	0	6	.000	4.35	1.32	15	14	0	0	...	0-...	31.0	34	21	15	2	7-0	32	.281
2002—	Savannah (S. Atl.)	5	8	.385	4.56	1.46	33	16	0	0	...	0-...	120.1	129	75	61	11	47-1	93	.276
2003—	Clinton (Midw.)	7	7	.500	4.08	1.51	30	20	0	0	...	2-...	123.2	144	75	56	7	43-0	63	.292
2004—	Stockton (Calif.)	6	5	.545	3.51	1.17	16	11	0	0	...	0-...	77.0	71	38	30	6	19-0	43	.242
—	Frisco (Texas)	1	0	1.000	1.80	1.20	2	1	0	0	...	0-...	10.0	8	2	2	0	4-0	8	.267
2005—	Frisco (Texas)	7	12	.368	6.18	1.64	29	27	1	0	0	0-0	157.1	197	124	108	19	61-0	105	.313
2006—	Oklahoma (PCL)	4	5	.444	4.81	1.59	24	7	1	0	2	3-3	67.1	79	48	36	4	28-1	65	.293
—	Frisco (Texas)	2	2	.500	2.06	1.21	8	8	0	0	0	0-0	48.0	38	16	11	0	20-0	40	.213
—	Texas (A.L.)	0	0	...	4.15	1.27	8	0	0	0	0	0-0	8.2	9	4	4	0	2-0	4	.300
	Major League totals (1 year)	0	0	...	4.15	1.27	8	0	0	0	0	0-0	8.2	9	4	4	0	2-0	4	.300

2006 LEFTY-RIGHTY SPLITS

vs.	Avg.	AB	H	2B	3B	HR	RBI	BB	SO	OBP	Slg.	vs.	Avg.	AB	H	2B	3B	HR	RBI	BB	SO	OBP	Slg.
L	.250	16	4	1	1	0	2	1	2	.350	.438	R	.357	14	5	1	0	0	2	1	2	.375	.429

MASTNY, TOM   P

PERSONAL: Born February 4, 1981, in East Bontang, Indonesia. ... Throws right, bats right. ... Full name: Thomas Mastny. ... College: Furman. **TRANSACTIONS/CAREER NOTES:** Selected by Toronto Blue Jays organization in 11th round of 2003 free-agent draft. ... Traded by Blue Jays to Cleveland Indians (December 14, 2004), completing deal in which Indians traded IF John McDonald to Blue Jays for a player to be named (December 2, 2004).
CAREER HITTING: 0-for-0 (.000), 0 R, 0 2B, 0 3B, 0 HR, 0 RBI.

Year	Team (League)	W	L	Pct.	ERA	WHIP	G	GS	CG	ShO	Hld.	Sv.-Opp.	IP	H	R	ER	HR	BB-IBB	SO	Avg.
2003—	Auburn (NY-Penn)	8	0	1.000	2.26	1.07	14	14	0	0	...	0-...	63.2	56	19	16	1	12-0	68	.237
2004—	Char., W.Va. (SAL)	10	3	.769	2.17	1.10	27	27	0	0	...	0-...	149.0	123	44	36	4	41-0	141	.230
2005—	Kinston (Carol.)	7	3	.700	2.35	1.18	29	11	0	0	2	2-2	88.0	78	28	23	4	26-0	94	.237
—	Akron (East.)	1	1	.500	2.18	1.11	5	3	0	0	1	0-0	20.2	18	7	5	0	5-0	18	.225
2006—	Akron (East.)	0	1	.000	1.09	0.93	12	1	0	0	4	1-2	24.2	15	5	3	0	8-1	30	.169
—	Buffalo (Int'l)	2	1	.667	2.61	1.08	24	0	0	0	2	0-0	38.0	25	11	11	0	16-2	46	.184
—	Cleveland (A.L.)	0	1	.000	5.51	1.53	15	0	0	0	0	5-7	16.1	17	10	10	1	8-1	14	.279
	Major League totals (1 year)	0	1	.000	5.51	1.53	15	0	0	0	0	5-7	16.1	17	10	10	1	8-1	14	.279

2006 LEFTY-RIGHTY SPLITS

vs.	Avg.	AB	H	2B	3B	HR	RBI	BB	SO	OBP	Slg.	vs.	Avg.	AB	H	2B	3B	HR	RBI	BB	SO	OBP	Slg.
L	.273	22	6	0	0	0	1	6	5	4	.393	.409	R	.282	39	11	2	0	0	4	3	10	.341	.333

MATEO, HENRY   2B

PERSONAL: Born October 14, 1976, in Santo Domingo, Dominican Republic. ... 6-0/176. ... Bats both, throws right. ... Full name: Henry Antonio Valera Mateo. ... Name pronounced: mah-TAY-oh. ... High school: Centro Estudios Libres (Santurce, Puerto Rico). **TRANSACTIONS/CAREER NOTES:** Selected by Montreal Expos organization in second round of 1995 free-agent draft. ... Expos franchise transferred to Washington, D.C., and renamed Washington Nationals for 2005 season (December 3, 2004). ... On disabled list (March 16-May 9 and May 15-August 5, 2005); included rehabilitation assignments to Potomac, Harrisburg and New Orleans.
2006 GAMES PLAYED BY POSITION (MLB): SS—3, 3B—2, OF—1.

							BATTING												FIELDING	
Year	Team (League)	Pos.	G	AB	R	H	2B	3B	HR	RBI	BB	SO	HBP	GDP	SB-CS	Avg.	OBP	SLG	OPS	E	Avg.
1995—GC Expos (GCL)	2B-SS	38	122	11	18	0	0	0	6	14	47	5	2	2-7	.148	.261	.148	.408	9	.951
1996—GC Expos (GCL)	2B	14	44	8	11	3	0	0	3	5	11	3	0	5-1	.250	.365	.318	.684	7	.901
1997—Vermont (NYP)	2B	67	228	32	56	9	3	1	31	30	44	7	4	21-11	.246	.348	.325	.673	14	.956
1998—Cape Fear (S. Atl.)	2B	114	416	72	115	20	5	4	41	40	111	13	5	22-16	.276	.355	.377	.733	15	.971
—Jupiter (Fla. St.)	2B	12	43	11	12	3	1	0	6	2	6	2	0	3-0	.279	.333	.395	.729	0	1.000
1999—Jupiter (Fla. St.)	2B	118	447	69	116	27	7	4	58	44	112	10	4	32-16	.260	.335	.378	.713	17	.962
2000—Harrisburg (East.)	2B	140	530	91	152	25	11	5	63	58	97	6	4	48-16	.287	.362	.404	.766	24	.962
2001—Ottawa (Int'l)	2B	118	500	71	134	14	12	5	43	33	89	7	2	47-14	.268	.322	.374	.696	22	.963
—Montreal (N.L.)	2B	5	9	1	3	1	0	0	0	0	1	0	0	0-0	.333	.333	.444	.778	1	.818
2002—Ottawa (Int'l)	2B-SS	74	285	35	73	10	6	5	25	18	53	3	6	15-6	.256	.306	.386	.692	12	.970
—Montreal (N.L.)	2B-SS	22	23	1	4	1	0	0	2	2	6	0	0	2-0	.174	.240	.261	.501	1	.950
2003—Montreal (N.L.)	2B-OF-DH																			
	SS	100	154	29	37	3	1	0	7	11	38	3	0	11-1	.240	.304	.273	.576	4	.973
2004—GC Expos (GCL)	2B	5	14	7	4	2	0	0	2	6	2	2	0	4-0	.286	.545	.429	.974	0	1.000
—Edmonton (PCL)	2B-DH	30	119	23	36	8	3	0	9	8	16	2	5	10-1	.303	.354	.420	.774	8	.937
—Montreal (N.L.)	2B-OF	40	44	3	12	2	0	0	0	1	9	0	1	2-3	.273	.289	.318	.607	4	.882
2005—Wash. (N.L.)	2B	1	1	0	0	0	0	0	0	0	0	0	0	0-0	.000	.000	.000	.000	1	1.000
—Potomac (Carol.)	2B-DH	13	50	13	14	5	1	0	9	3	10	3	1	2-0	.280	.357	.600	.957	1	.974
—New Orleans (PCL)	2B	9	31	2	9	0	0	0	3	3	7	0	0	3-1	.290	.353	.290	.643	0	1.000
—Harrisburg (East.)	2B-DH	32	122	13	20	5	1	0	6	16	27	0	3	11-5	.164	.261	.221	.482	4	.972
2006—New Orleans (PCL)		113	433	55	110	21	6	2	35	38	78	4	10	33-11	.254	.318	.344	.662	11	.973
—Wash. (N.L.)	SS-3B-OF	22	26	5	4	2	0	1	3	2	3	0	1	0-0	.154	.214	.346	.560	1	.889
Major League totals (6 years)		190	257	39	60	8	2	1	10	17	57	3	2	15-4	.233	.289	.292	.581	12	.946

2006 LEFTY-RIGHTY SPLITS

vs.	Avg.	AB	H	2B	3B	HR	RBI	BB	SO	OBP	Slg.	vs.	Avg.	AB	H	2B	3B	HR	RBI	BB	SO	OBP	Slg.
L	.214	14	3	1	0	1	3	2	0	.313	.500	R	.083	12	1	1	0	0	0	0	3	.083	.167

MATEO, JUAN   P

PERSONAL: Born December 17, 1982, in Bani, Dominican Republic. ... 6-2/180. ... Throws right, bats right. ... Full name: Juan Manuel Mateo. **TRANSACTIONS/CAREER NOTES:** Signed as a non-drafted free agent by Chicago Cubs organization (July 3, 2001). ... Selected by St. Louis Cardinals from Cubs organization in Rule 5 major league draft (December 8, 2005); returned to Cubs (March 26, 2006). **MISCELLANEOUS NOTES:** Scored a run in only appearance as pinch runner (2006).

M

CAREER HITTING: 0-for-12 (.000), 1 R, 0 2B, 0 3B, 0 HR, 0 RBI.

Year	Team (League)	W	L	Pct.	ERA	WHIP	G	GS	CG	ShO	Hld.	Sv.-Opp.	IP	H	R	ER	HR	BB-IBB	SO	Avg.
2002—	Dominican Cubs (DSL)	3	0	1.000	3.18	1.20	11	4	0	0	...	3-...	28.1	24	15	10	1	10-0	22	.214
2003—	Ariz. Cubs (Ariz.)	4	1	.800	4.46	1.54	18	0	0	0	...	2-...	36.1	42	25	18	2	14-0	35	.288
2004—	Lansing (Midw.)	4	1	.800	3.28	1.08	53	1	0	0	...	9-...	74.0	61	28	27	3	19-1	60	.216
2005—	Daytona (Fla. St.)	10	5	.667	1.15	1.15	32	16	1	1	2	2-5	109.1	99	47	39	9	27-0	123	.240
2006—	West Tenn (Sou.)	7	4	.636	2.82	1.12	18	17	0	0	0	0-0	92.2	78	32	29	6	26-0	70	.229
—	Chicago (N.L.)	1	3	.250	5.32	1.62	11	10	0	0	0	0-0	45.2	51	31	27	6	23-1	35	.288
	Major League totals (1 year)	1	3	.250	5.32	1.62	11	10	0	0	0	0-0	45.2	51	31	27	6	23-1	35	.288

2006 LEFTY-RIGHTY SPLITS

vs.	Avg.	AB	H	2B	3B	HR	RBI	BB	SO	OBP	Slg.	vs.	Avg.	AB	H	2B	3B	HR	RBI	BB	SO	OBP	Slg.
L	.277	65	18	8	0	1	11	10	16	.377	.446	R	.295	112	33	3	2	5	18	13	19	.375	.491

MATEO, JULIO   P

PERSONAL: Born August 2, 1977, in Bani, Dominican Republic. ... 6-0/177. ... Throws right, bats right. ... Full name: Julio Cesar Mateo. ... Name pronounced: mah-TAY-oh.
TRANSACTIONS/CAREER NOTES: Signed as a non-drafted free agent by Seattle Mariners organization (May 15, 1996). ... On disabled list (July 29-September 16, 2004; and April 30-May 20, 2006).
CAREER HITTING: 0-for-0 (.000), 0 R, 0 2B, 0 3B, 0 HR, 0 RBI.

Year	Team (League)	W	L	Pct.	ERA	WHIP	G	GS	CG	ShO	Hld.	Sv.-Opp.	IP	H	R	ER	HR	BB-IBB	SO	Avg.
1996—	Dom. Mariners (DSL)	4	2	.667	1.74	1.18	14	5	2	1	...	1-...	51.2	42	14	10		19-...	23	...
1997—	Ariz. Mariners (Ariz.)	3	1	.750	3.30	1.13	13	6	0	0	...	1-...	60.0	45	32	22	1	23-0	54	.205
1998—	Lancaster (Calif.)	0	0	...	6.75	1.50	1	0	0	0	...	0-...	1.1	1	1	1	1	1-0	1	.250
—	Everett (N'west)	3	3	.500	4.70	1.49	28	0	0	0	...	4-...	38.1	40	25	20	6	17-1	37	.274
1999—	Wisconsin (Midw.)	1	3	.250	4.34	1.34	20	0	0	0	...	4-...	29.0	31	18	14	2	8-2	27	.261
2000—	Wisconsin (Midw.)	4	8	.333	4.19	1.25	36	1	0	0	...	4-...	68.2	63	38	32	12	23-1	73	.241
2001—	San Bern. (Calif.)	5	4	.556	2.86	1.12	56	0	0	0	...	26-...	66.0	58	28	21	5	16-5	79	.230
2002—	San Antonio (Texas)	1	0	1.000	0.52	0.58	12	0	0	0	...	0-...	17.1	7	3	1	2	3-0	18	.121
—	Tacoma (PCL)	4	2	.667	4.06	1.48	20	0	0	0	...	6-...	31.0	39	15	14	2	7-1	23	.317
—	Seattle (A.L.)	0	0	...	4.29	1.52	12	0	0	0	2	0-0	21.0	20	10	10	2	12-0	15	.247
2003—	Seattle (A.L.)	4	0	1.000	3.15	0.96	50	0	0	0	2	1-1	85.2	69	32	30	14	13-1	71	.220
2004—	Seattle (A.L.)	1	2	.333	4.68	1.25	45	0	0	0	6	1-4	57.2	56	30	30	11	16-3	43	.251
2005—	Seattle (A.L.)	3	6	.333	3.06	1.09	55	0	0	0	8	0-2	88.1	79	32	30	12	17-6	52	.237
2006—	Seattle (A.L.)	9	4	.692	4.19	1.57	48	0	0	0	7	0-3	53.2	62	27	25	6	22-8	31	.297
	Major League totals (5 years)	17	12	.586	3.67	1.19	210	0	0	0	25	2-10	306.1	286	131	125	45	80-18	212	.247

2006 LEFTY-RIGHTY SPLITS

vs.	Avg.	AB	H	2B	3B	HR	RBI	BB	SO	OBP	Slg.	vs.	Avg.	AB	H	2B	3B	HR	RBI	BB	SO	OBP	Slg.
L	.394	71	28	4	1	2	14	12	14	.482	.563	R	.246	138	34	7	1	4	24	10	17	.299	.399

MATHENY, MIKE   C

PERSONAL: Born September 22, 1970, in Reynoldsburg, Ohio. ... 6-3/220. ... Bats right, throws right. ... Full name: Michael Scott Matheny. ... Name pronounced: ma-THEE-nee. ... High school: Reynoldsburg (Ohio). ... College: Michigan. **TRANSACTIONS/CAREER NOTES:** Selected by Toronto Blue Jays organization in 31st round of 1988 free-agent draft; did not sign. ... Selected by Milwaukee Brewers organization in eighth round of 1991 free-agent draft. ... On suspended list (June 20-23, 1996). ... On disabled list (June 15-July 12, 1998); included rehabilitation assignment to Beloit. ... Signed as a free agent by Blue Jays (December 23, 1998). ... Released by Blue Jays (November 16, 1999). ... Signed by St. Louis Cardinals (December 15, 1999). ... On suspended list (September 26-28, 2003). ... On disabled list (June 3-18, 2004). ... Signed as a free agent by San Francisco Giants (December 13, 2004). ... On bereavement list (August 1-4, 2005). ... On disabled list (June 2, 2006-remainder of season). **HONORS:** Won N.L. Gold Glove at catcher (2000, 2003-05). **STATISTICAL NOTES:** Career major league grand slams: 3.
2006 GAMES PLAYED BY POSITION (MLB): C—46.

								BATTING										FIELDING	
Year	Team (League)	Pos.	G	AB	R	H	2B	3B	HR	RBI	BB	SO	HBP	GDP	SB-CS	Avg.	OBP	SLG	OPS	E	Avg.
1991—	Helena (Pion.)	C	64	253	35	72	14	0	2	34	19	52	6	10	2-4	.285	.348	.364	.711	5	.991
1992—	Stockton (Calif.)	C	106	333	42	73	13	2	6	46	35	81	3	11	2-2	.219	.297	.324	.621	8	.989
1993—	El Paso (Texas)	C	107	339	39	86	21	2	2	28	17	73	2	6	1-4	.254	.292	.345	.638	9	.986
1994—	Milwaukee (A.L.)	C	28	53	3	12	3	0	1	2	3	13	2	1	0-1	.226	.293	.340	.633	1	.989
—	New Orleans (A.A.)	C-1B-DH	57	177	20	39	10	1	4	21	16	39	4	5	1-1	.220	.284	.356	.655	5	.987
1995—	Milwaukee (A.L.)	C	80	166	13	41	9	1	0	21	12	28	2	3	2-1	.247	.306	.313	.619	4	.986
—	New Orleans (A.A.)	C	6	17	3	6	2	0	3	4	0	5	3	0	0-0	.353	.450	1.000	1.450	0	1.000
1996—	Milwaukee (A.L.)	C-DH	106	313	31	64	15	2	8	46	14	80	3	9	3-2	.204	.243	.342	.584	8	.985
—	New Orleans (A.A.)	C-DH	20	66	3	15	4	0	1	6	2	17	0	1	0-0	.227	.246	.333	.580	0	1.000
1997—	Milwaukee (A.L.)	C-1B	123	320	29	78	16	1	4	32	17	68	7	6	0-1	.244	.294	.338	.631	5	.993
1998—	Milwaukee (N.L.)	C	108	320	24	76	13	0	6	27	11	63	7	6	1-0	.238	.278	.334	.612	8	.987
—	Beloit (Midw.)	C-DH	2	8	1	2	1	0	0	0	1	3	0	0	0-0	.250	.333	.375	.708	0	1.000
1999—	Toronto (A.L.)	C	57	163	16	35	6	0	3	17	12	37	1	3	0-0	.215	.271	.307	.578	2	.995
2000—	St. Louis (N.L.)	C-1B	128	417	43	109	22	1	6	47	32	96	4	11	0-0	.261	.317	.362	.679	5	.994
2001—	St. Louis (N.L.)	C-1B	121	381	40	83	17	0	7	42	28	76	4	11	0-0	.218	.276	.304	.581	4	.995
2002—	St. Louis (N.L.)	C-1B	110	315	31	77	12	1	3	35	32	49	2	3	1-3	.244	.313	.317	.630	4	.994
2003—	St. Louis (N.L.)	C-1B	141	441	43	111	18	2	8	47	44	81	2	11	1-1	.252	.320	.356	.676	1	1.000
2004—	St. Louis (N.L.)	C-1B	122	385	28	95	22	1	5	50	23	83	3	12	0-2	.247	.292	.348	.640	1	.999
2005—	San Francisco (N.L.)	C	134	443	42	107	34	0	13	59	29	91	6	11	0-2	.242	.295	.406	.701	1	.999
2006—	San Francisco (N.L.)	C	47	160	10	37	8	0	3	18	9	30	2	7	0-0	.231	.278	.338	.613	1	.996
	American League totals (5 years)		394	1015	92	230	49	4	16	118	58	226	15	25	5-5	.227	.276	.330	.607	20	.990
	National League totals (8 years)		911	2862	261	695	141	6	51	325	208	569	30	72	3-9	.243	.298	.349	.648	24	.996
	Major League totals (13 years)		1305	3877	353	925	190	9	67	443	266	795	45	97	8-14	.239	.293	.344	.637	44	.994

DIVISION SERIES RECORD

Year	Team (League)	Pos.	G	AB	R	H	2B	3B	HR	RBI	BB	SO	HBP	GDP	SB-CS	Avg.	OBP	SLG	OPS	E	Avg.
2000—	St. Louis (N.L.)		Did not play.																		
2001—	St. Louis (N.L.)	C	4	5	0	1	0	0	0	0	0	3	0	0	0-0	.200	.200	.200	.400	0	1.000
2002—	St. Louis (N.L.)	C	3	9	3	4	1	0	0	2	2	1	0	0	0-0	.444	.545	.556	1.101	0	1.000
2004—	St. Louis (N.L.)	C	4	14	1	4	0	0	1	5	0	2	0	0	0-0	.286	.286	.500	.786	0	1.000
	Division series totals (3 years)		11	33	4	10	1	0	1	7	2	6	0	0	0-0	.303	.343	.424	.767	0	1.000

CHAMPIONSHIP SERIES RECORD

Year	Team (League)	Pos.	G	AB	R	H	2B	3B	HR	RBI	BB	SO	HBP	GDP	SB-CS	Avg.	OBP	SLG	OPS	E	Avg.
2000—	St. Louis (N.L.)		Did not play.																		

Year Team (League)	Pos.	G	AB	R	H	2B	3B	HR	RBI	BB	SO	HBP	GDP	SB-CS	Avg.	OBP	SLG	OPS	E	Avg.
2002— St. Louis (N.L.)	C	5	19	2	6	2	0	1	1	0	2	0	0	0-0	.316	.316	.579	.895	0	1.000
2004— St. Louis (N.L.)	C	7	19	0	2	0	0	0	0	1	8	0	0	0-0	.105	.150	.105	.255	0	1.000
Champ. series totals (2 years)		12	38	2	8	2	0	1	1	1	10	0	0	0-0	.211	.231	.342	.573	0	1.000

WORLD SERIES RECORD

Year Team (League)	Pos.	G	AB	R	H	2B	3B	HR	RBI	BB	SO	HBP	GDP	SB-CS	Avg.	OBP	SLG	OPS	E	Avg.
2004— St. Louis (N.L.)	C	4	8	0	2	0	0	0	2	0	3	0	0	0-0	.250	.200	.250	.450	0	1.000

2006 LEFTY-RIGHTY SPLITS

vs.	Avg.	AB	H	2B	3B	HR	RBI	BB	SO	OBP	Slg.	vs.	Avg.	AB	H	2B	3B	HR	RBI	BB	SO	OBP	Slg.
L	.364	44	16	3	0	1	8	3	3	.404	.500	R	.181	116	21	5	0	2	10	6	27	.228	.276

MATHIESON, SCOTT   P

PERSONAL: Born February 27, 1984, in Vancouver, British Columbia. ... 6-3/190. ... Throws right, bats right. ... Full name: Scott William Mathieson.
TRANSACTIONS/CAREER NOTES: Selected by Philadelphia Phillies organization in 17th round of 2002 free-agent draft. ... On disabled list (September 3, 2006-remainder of season).
CAREER HITTING: 1-for-7 (.143), 0 R, 0 2B, 0 3B, 0 HR, 0 RBI.

Year Team (League)	W	L	Pct.	ERA	WHIP	G	GS	CG	ShO	Hld.	Sv.-Opp.	IP	H	R	ER	HR	BB-IBB	SO	Avg.
2002— GC Phillies (GCL)	0	2	.000	5.40	1.80	7	2	0	0	...	0-...	16.2	24	11	10	0	6-0	14	.338
2003— GC Phillies (GCL)	2	7	.222	5.52	1.23	11	11	0	0	...	0-...	58.2	59	42	36	5	13-0	51	.247
— Batavia (NY-Penn)	0	0		0.00	0.00	2	0	0	0	...	1-...	6.0	0	0	0	0	0-0	7	.000
2004— Lakewood (S. Atl.)	8	9	.471	4.32	1.37	25	25	1	0	...	0-...	131.1	130	73	63	7	50-0	112	.260
2005— Clearwater (FSL)	3	8	.273	4.14	1.19	23	23	1	0	...	0-0	121.2	111	62	56	17	34-0	118	.241
2006— Reading (East.)	7	2	.778	3.21	1.10	14	14	0	0	0	0-0	92.2	73	35	33	8	29-1	99	.221
— Scran./W.B. (I.L.)	3	1	.750	3.93	1.05	5	5	0	0	0	0-0	34.1	26	16	15	2	10-0	36	.208
— Philadelphia (N.L.)	1	4	.200	7.47	1.71	9	8	0	0	0	0-0	37.1	48	36	31	8	16-1	28	.312
Major League totals (1 year)	1	4	.200	7.47	1.71	9	8	0	0	0	0-0	37.1	48	36	31	8	16-1	28	.312

2006 LEFTY-RIGHTY SPLITS

vs.	Avg.	AB	H	2B	3B	HR	RBI	BB	SO	OBP	Slg.	vs.	Avg.	AB	H	2B	3B	HR	RBI	BB	SO	OBP	Slg.
L	.279	68	19	4	1	4	16	7	17	.342	.544	R	.337	86	29	10	0	4	18	9	11	.406	.593

MATHIS, JEFF   C

PERSONAL: Born March 31, 1983, in Marianna, Fla. ... 6-0/180. ... Bats right, throws right. ... Full name: Jeffery Stephen Mathis. **TRANSACTIONS/CAREER NOTES:** Selected by Anaheim Angels organization in first round of 2001 free-agent draft. ... Angels franchise renamed Los Angeles Angels of Anaheim for 2005 season.
2006 GAMES PLAYED BY POSITION (MLB): C—20, DH—2.

Year Team (League)	Pos.	G	AB	R	H	2B	3B	HR	RBI	BB	SO	HBP	GDP	SB-CS	Avg.	OBP	SLG	OPS	E	Avg.
2001— Ariz. Angels (Ariz.)	C-OF	7	23	1	7	1	0	0	3	2	4	0	1	0-0	.304	.346	.348	.694	0	1.000
— Provo (Pion.)	C	22	77	14	23	6	3	0	18	11	13	2	1	1-0	.299	.387	.455	.842	2	.989
2002— Cedar Rap. (Midw.)	C	128	491	75	141	41	3	10	73	40	75	8	6	7-4	.287	.346	.444	.790	4	.994
2003— Rancho Cucamonga (Pion.)	C	97	378	73	122	28	3	11	54	35	74	5	4	5-3	.323	.384	.500	.884	...	...
— Arkansas (Texas)	C	24	95	19	27	11	0	2	14	12	16	1	2	1-2	.284	.364	.463	.827	1	.995
2004— Arkansas (Texas)	C	117	432	57	98	24	3	14	55	49	102	5	5	2-1	.227	.310	.394	.704	14	.979
2005— Salt Lake (PCL)	C-DH	112	427	78	118	26	3	21	73	42	85	1	7	4-3	.276	.340	.499	.838	9	.986
— Los Angeles (A.L.)	C-DH	5	3	1	1	0	0	0	0	0	1	0	0	0-0	.333	.333	.333	.667	0	1.000
2006— Salt Lake (PCL)	C	99	384	62	111	33	3	5	45	26	75	2	6	3-1	.289	.333	.430	.763	6	.990
— Los Angeles (A.L.)	C-DH	23	55	9	8	2	0	2	6	7	14	0	0	0-0	.145	.238	.291	.529	3	.970
Major League totals (2 years)		28	58	10	9	2	0	2	6	7	15	0	0	0-0	.155	.242	.293	.536	3	.971

2006 LEFTY-RIGHTY SPLITS

vs.	Avg.	AB	H	2B	3B	HR	RBI	BB	SO	OBP	Slg.	vs.	Avg.	AB	H	2B	3B	HR	RBI	BB	SO	OBP	Slg.
L	.133	15	2	0	0	0	0	2	3	.235	.133	R	.150	40	6	2	0	2	6	5	11	.239	.350

MATOS, LUIS   OF

PERSONAL: Born October 30, 1978, in Bayamon, Puerto Rico. ... 6-0/208. ... Bats right, throws right. ... Full name: Luis David Matos. ... Name pronounced: MAH-tose. ... High school: Disciple of Christ Academy (Bayamon, Puerto Rico). **TRANSACTIONS/CAREER NOTES:** Selected by Baltimore Orioles organization in 10th round of 1996 free-agent draft. ... On disabled list (March 30-August 24, 2001); included rehabilitation assignments to GCL Orioles, Frederick and Bowie. ... On disabled list (March 29-June 6, 2002); included rehabilitation assignment to Frederick. ... On disabled list (July 22, 2004-remainder of season). ... On disabled list (May 11-June 19, 2005); included rehabilitation assignment to Bowie. ... On disabled list (April 19-May 5, 2006); included rehabilitation assignment to Frederick. ... Released by Orioles (July 7, 2006). ... Signed by Washington Nationals (July 14, 2006). ... Released by Nationals (August 10, 2006).
2006 GAMES PLAYED BY POSITION (MLB): OF—51, DH—1.

Year Team (League)	Pos.	G	AB	R	H	2B	3B	HR	RBI	BB	SO	HBP	GDP	SB-CS	Avg.	OBP	SLG	OPS	E	Avg.
1996— GC Orioles (GCL)	OF	43	130	21	38	2	0	0	13	15	18	2	3	12-7	.292	.374	.308	.682	1	.983
1997— Delmarva (S. Atl.)	OF	36	119	10	25	1	2	0	13	9	21	2	2	8-5	.210	.275	.252	.527	2	.972
— Bluefield (Appal.)	OF	61	240	37	66	7	3	2	35	20	36	4	5	26-4	.275	.340	.354	.694	3	.977
1998— Delmarva (S. Atl.)	OF	133	503	73	137	26	6	7	32	38	90	7	5	42-14	.272	.328	.390	.718	10	.964
— Bowie (East.)	OF	5	19	2	5	0	0	1	3	1	1	0	0	1-1	.263	.300	.421	.721	1	.833
1999— Frederick (Carolina)	OF	68	273	40	81	15	1	7	41	20	35	2	6	27-6	.297	.343	.436	.779	2	.987
— Bowie (East.)	OF	66	283	41	67	11	5	9	36	15	39	1	4	14-4	.237	.272	.378	.650	3	.982
2000— Rochester (Int'l)		11	35	2	6	1	0	0	0	3	8	1	0	2-0	.171	.256	.200	.456	0	1.000
— Bowie (East.)	OF	50	181	26	49	7	5	2	33	17	23	5	3	8-8	.271	.345	.398	.742	2	.984
— Baltimore (A.L.)	OF-DH	72	182	21	41	6	3	1	17	12	30	3	7	13-4	.225	.281	.308	.589	2	.988
2001— GC Orioles (GCL)	DH	3	14	1	4	2	0	0	2	0	3	0	0	0-0	.286	.286	.429	.714	...	...
— Frederick (Carolina)	DH	2	7	3	3	0	0	1	2	1	3	0	0	0-0	.429	.500	.857	1.357	...	...
— Bowie (East.)	OF	13	46	6	14	5	0	1	8	5	7	1	0	0-1	.304	.385	.478	.863	1	.955
— Baltimore (A.L.)	OF	31	98	16	21	7	0	4	12	11	30	1	1	7-0	.214	.300	.408	.708	1	.985
2002— Frederick (Carolina)	OF	3	12	2	4	1	0	0	1	2	3	0	0	0-0	.333	.429	.417	.845	0	1.000
— Bowie (East.)	OF	62	218	34	60	14	2	9	30	32	45	2	6	14-4	.275	.370	.482	.852	1	.992
— Baltimore (A.L.)	OF-DH	17	31	0	4	1	0	0	1	1	6	0	1	0-0	.129	.156	.161	.318	0	1.000
2003— Ottawa (Int'l)	OF	45	175	28	53	16	4	1	25	13	34	1	6	6-1	.303	.347	.457	.804	1	.990
— Baltimore (A.L.)	OF-DH	109	439	70	133	23	3	13	45	28	90	7	9	15-7	.303	.353	.458	.811	4	.987
2004— Baltimore (A.L.)	OF	89	330	36	74	18	0	6	28	19	60	5	7	12-4	.224	.275	.333	.609	1	.992

Year Team (League)	Pos.	G	AB	R	H	2B	3B	HR	RBI	BB	SO	HBP	GDP	SB-CS	Avg.	OBP	SLG	OPS	E	Avg.
2005— Bowie (East.)	OF-DH	5	20	4	5	0	0	1	2	1	4	1	0	1-1	.250	.318	.400	.718	0	1.000
— Baltimore (A.L.)	OF	121	389	53	109	20	2	4	32	27	58	10	4	17-9	.280	.340	.373	.712	5	.984
2006— Frederick (Carolina)		2	9	1	3	0	0	1	2	0	1	0	0	1-0	.333	.333	.667	1.000	0	1.000
— Baltimore (A.L.)	OF-DH	55	121	14	25	7	1	2	5	10	21	2	3	7-0	.207	.278	.331	.609	0	1.000
— Wash. (N.L.)	OF	14	15	2	3	2	0	0	0	0	2	0	0	0-0	.200	.200	.333	.533	0	1.000
American League totals (7 years)		494	1590	210	407	82	9	30	140	108	295	28	32	72-24	.256	.313	.375	.688	13	.989
National League totals (1 year)		14	15	2	3	2	0	0	0	0	2	0	0	0-0	.200	.200	.333	.533	0	1.000
Major League totals (7 years)		508	1605	212	410	84	9	30	140	108	297	28	32	72-24	.255	.312	.375	.687	13	.989

2006 LEFTY-RIGHTY SPLITS

vs.	Avg.	AB	H	2B	3B	HR	RBI	BB	SO	OBP	Slg.	vs.	Avg.	AB	H	2B	3B	HR	RBI	BB	SO	OBP	Slg.
L	.219	64	14	3	1	1	2	3	13	.254	.344	R	.194	72	14	6	0	1	3	7	10	.284	.319

MATSUI, HIDEKI — OF

PERSONAL: Born June 12, 1974, in Kanazawa, Japan. ... 6-2/230. ... Bats left, throws right. ... Name pronounced: mat-SOO-ee. ... High school: Seiryo (Nagoya, Japan).
TRANSACTIONS/CAREER NOTES: Signed as a free agent by New York Yankees (December 19, 2002). ... On disabled list (May 12-September 12, 2006). **STATISTICAL NOTES:** Career major league grand slams: 4.
2006 GAMES PLAYED BY POSITION (MLB): OF—36, DH—13.

Year Team (League)	Pos.	G	AB	R	H	2B	3B	HR	RBI	BB	SO	HBP	GDP	SB-CS	Avg.	OBP	SLG	OPS	E	Avg.
1993— Yomiuri (Jp. Cen.)		57	184	27	41	9	0	11	27	...	...	...	...	1-0	.223	.296	.451	.747	1	...
1994— Yomiuri (Jp. Cen.)		130	503	70	148	23	4	20	66	57	101	4	...	6-3	.294	.368	.475	.843	5	...
1995— Yomiuri (Jp. Cen.)		131	501	76	142	31	1	22	80	62	93	4	...	9-7	.283	.363	.481	.844	3	...
1996— Yomiuri (Jp. Cen.)		130	487	97	153	34	1	38	99	71	98	4	...	7-2	.314	.401	.622	1.023	6	...
1997— Yomiuri (Jp. Cen.)		135	484	93	144	18	0	37	103	100	84	6	...	9-3	.298	.419	.564	.984	7	...
1998— Yomiuri (Jp. Cen.)		135	487	103	142	24	3	34	100	104	101	8	...	3-5	.292	.421	.563	.984	4	...
1999— Yomiuri (Jp. Cen.)		135	471	100	143	24	2	42	95	93	99	2	...	0-4	.304	.416	.631	1.047	1	...
2000— Yomiuri (Jp. Cen.)		135	474	116	150	32	1	42	108	106	108	2	...	5-2	.316	.438	.654	1.092	2	...
2001— Yomiuri (Jp. Cen.)		140	481	107	160	23	3	36	104	120	96	3	...	3-3	.333	.463	.617	1.081	6	...
2002— Yomiuri (Jp. Cen.)		140	500	112	167	27	1	50	107	114	104	6	...	3-4	.334	.461	.692	1.153	2	...
2003— New York (A.L.)	OF-DH	*163	623	82	179	42	1	16	106	63	86	3	25	2-2	.287	.353	.435	.788	8	.977
2004— New York (A.L.)	OF	•162	584	109	174	34	2	31	108	88	103	3	11	3-0	.298	.390	.522	.912	7	.978
2005— New York (A.L.)	OF-DH	•162	629	108	192	45	3	23	116	63	78	3	16	2-2	.305	.367	.496	.863	3	.990
2006— New York (A.L.)	OF-DH	51	172	32	52	9	0	8	29	27	23	0	6	1-0	.302	.393	.494	.887	1	.988
Major League totals (4 years)		538	2008	331	597	130	6	78	359	241	290	9	58	8-4	.297	.372	.485	.856	19	.982

DIVISION SERIES RECORD

Year Team (League)	Pos.	G	AB	R	H	2B	3B	HR	RBI	BB	SO	HBP	GDP	SB-CS	Avg.	OBP	SLG	OPS	E	Avg.
2003— New York (A.L.)	OF	4	15	2	4	1	0	1	3	2	3	0	1	0-0	.267	.353	.533	.886	0	1.000
2004— New York (A.L.)	OF	4	17	3	7	1	0	1	3	4	0	0	0	0-0	.412	.476	.647	1.123	0	1.000
2005— New York (A.L.)	OF	5	20	4	4	1	0	1	1	2	3	0	2	0-0	.200	.273	.400	.673	1	.909
2006— New York (A.L.)	OF-DH	4	16	1	4	1	0	0	1	0	2	0	0	0-0	.250	.250	.313	.563	0	1.000
Division series totals (4 years)		17	68	10	19	4	0	3	8	8	7	12	0	3	0-0	.279	.342	.471	.813	1	.970

CHAMPIONSHIP SERIES RECORD

Year Team (League)	Pos.	G	AB	R	H	2B	3B	HR	RBI	BB	SO	HBP	GDP	SB-CS	Avg.	OBP	SLG	OPS	E	Avg.
2003— New York (A.L.)	OF	7	26	3	8	3	0	0	4	1	3	0	1	0-0	.308	.321	.423	.745	1	.889
2004— New York (A.L.)	OF	7	34	9	14	6	1	2	10	2	4	0	0	0-0	.412	.444	.824	1.268	0	1.000
Champ. series totals (2 years)		14	60	12	22	9	1	2	14	3	7	0	1	0-0	.367	.391	.650	1.041	1	.960

WORLD SERIES RECORD

Year Team (League)	Pos.	G	AB	R	H	2B	3B	HR	RBI	BB	SO	HBP	GDP	SB-CS	Avg.	OBP	SLG	OPS	E	Avg.
2003— New York (A.L.)	OF	6	23	1	6	0	0	1	4	3	2	1	0	0-0	.261	.370	.391	.762	0	1.000

ALL-STAR GAME RECORD

		G	AB	R	H	2B	3B	HR	RBI	BB	SO	HBP	GDP	SB-CS	Avg.	OBP	SLG	OPS	E	Avg.
All-Star Game totals (2 years)		2	3	0	1	0	0	0	0	0	1	0	0	0-0	.333	.333	.333	.667	0	1.000

2006 LEFTY-RIGHTY SPLITS

vs.	Avg.	AB	H	2B	3B	HR	RBI	BB	SO	OBP	Slg.	vs.	Avg.	AB	H	2B	3B	HR	RBI	BB	SO	OBP	Slg.
L	.226	53	12	2	0	1	4	6	10	.305	.321	R	.336	119	40	7	0	7	25	21	13	.430	.571

MATSUI, KAZUO — 2B/SS

PERSONAL: Born October 23, 1975, in Osaka, Japan. ... 5-10/185. ... Bats both, throws right. ... Name pronounced: mat-SOO-ee. ... High school: PL Gakeun (Osaka, Japan).
TRANSACTIONS/CAREER NOTES: Signed as a free agent by New York Mets (December 10, 2003). ... On disabled list (August 9-September 24, 2004). ... On disabled list (June 21-August 9, 2005); included rehabilitation assignments to GCL Mets, Brooklyn and Binghamton. ... On disabled list (March 28-April 20, 2006); included rehabilitation assignments to St. Lucie and Norfolk. ... Traded by Mets to Colorado Rockies for OF Eli Marrero (June 9, 2006). **STATISTICAL NOTES:** Hit home run in first major league at-bat (April 6, 2004).
2006 GAMES PLAYED BY POSITION (MLB): 2B—52, SS—3.

Year Team (League)	Pos.	G	AB	R	H	2B	3B	HR	RBI	BB	SO	HBP	GDP	SB-CS	Avg.	OBP	SLG	OPS	E	Avg.
1995— Seibu (Jp. Pac.)		69	204	25	45	9	1	2	62	7	26	0	4	21-1	.221	.245	.304	.549	...	...
1996— Seibu (Jp. Pac.)		130	473	51	134	22	5	1	29	14	93	3	2	50-9	.283	.307	.357	.664	...	...
1997— Seibu (Jp. Pac.)		135	576	91	178	23	13	7	63	44	89	5	4	62-15	.309	.362	.431	.793	...	...
1998— Seibu (Jp. Pac.)		135	575	92	179	38	5	9	58	55	89	1	10	43-14	.311	.370	.442	.812	...	...
1999— Seibu (Jp. Pac.)		135	539	87	178	29	4	15	67	56	75	0	7	32-7	.330	.389	.482	.872	...	...
2000— Seibu (Jp. Pac.)		135	550	99	177	40	11	23	90	46	60	2	8	26-3	.322	.372	.560	.932	...	...
2001— Seibu (Jp. Pac.)		140	552	94	170	28	2	24	76	46	83	6	13	26-0	.308	.365	.496	.861	...	...
2002— Seibu (Jp. Pac.)		140	582	119	193	46	6	36	87	53	112	4	4	33-11	.332	.389	.617	1.006	...	...
2003— Seibu (Jp. Pac.)		140	587	104	179	36	4	33	84	55	124	4	4	13-0	.305	.365	.549	.914	...	...
2004— New York (N.L.)	SS-2B	114	460	65	125	32	4	7	44	40	97	2	3	14-3	.272	.331	.396	.727	24	.955
2005— GC Mets (GCL)	2B-DH	3	9	3	4	0	0	1	3	1	3	1	0	0-0	.444	.545	.778	1.323	0	1.000
— Brook. (N.Y.-Penn.)	2B	1	3	0	0	0	0	0	1	2	0	0	0	0-0	.000	.400	.000	.400	0	1.000
— Binghamton (East.)	2B	3	9	4	4	1	0	0	1	1	0	0	0	2-0	.444	.500	.556	1.056	0	1.000
— New York (N.L.)	2B	87	267	31	68	9	4	3	24	14	43	5	2	6-1	.255	.300	.352	.652	9	.970
2006— St. Lucie (Fla. St.)		2	7	1	2	0	0	0	0	0	0	0	0	0-0	.286	.375	.286	.661	0	.909

M

Year Team (League)	Pos.	G	AB	R	H	2B	3B	HR	RBI	BB	SO	HBP	GDP	SB-CS	Avg.	OBP	SLG	OPS	E	Avg.
— Norfolk (Int'l)		4	12	2	4	2	0	0	1	0	2	0	0	0-0	.333	.333	.500	.833	0	1.000
— New York (N.L.)	2B	38	130	10	26	6	0	1	7	6	19	0	1	2-0	.200	.235	.269	.505	1	.994
— Colo. Springs (PCL)		31	115	26	32	4	0	3	16	9	20	1	0	3-1	.278	.328	.391	.719	6	.961
— Colorado (N.L.)	2B-SS	32	113	22	39	6	3	2	19	10	27	0	0	8-1	.345	.392	.504	.896	2	.984
Major League totals (3 years)		271	970	128	258	53	9	13	94	70	186	7	6	30-5	.266	.318	.379	.697	36	.968

2006 LEFTY-RIGHTY SPLITS

vs.	Avg.	AB	H	2B	3B	HR	RBI	BB	SO	OBP	Slg.	vs.	Avg.	AB	H	2B	3B	HR	RBI	BB	SO	OBP	Slg.
L	.119	42	5	1	0	0	3	6	11	.229	.143	R	.299	201	60	11	3	3	23	10	35	.329	.428

MATTHEWS, GARY — OF

PERSONAL: Born August 25, 1974, in San Francisco. ... 6-3/225. ... Bats both, throws right. ... Full name: Gary Nathaniel Matthews Jr. ... High school: Granada Hills (Calif.). ... Junior college: Mission (Calif.) Community College. ... Son of Gary Matthews, outfielder with five major league teams (1972-87). **TRANSACTIONS/CAREER NOTES:** Selected by San Diego Padres organization in 13th round of 1993 free-agent draft. ... Traded by Padres to Chicago Cubs for P Rodney Myers (March 23, 2000). ... Claimed on waivers by Pittsburgh Pirates (August 10, 2001). ... Traded by Pirates to New York Mets for cash (December 28, 2001). ... Traded by Mets to Baltimore Orioles for P John Bale (April 3, 2002). ... On disabled list (August 25-September 11, 2002). ... Claimed on waivers by Padres (May 23, 2003). ... Claimed on waivers by Atlanta Braves (November 24, 2003). ... Released by Braves (March 31, 2004). ... Signed by Texas Rangers organization (April 7, 2004). ... On disabled list (May 15-June 8, 2005); included rehabilitation assignment to Frisco. ... On disabled list (March 24-April 12, 2006); included rehabilitation assignment to Oklahoma. **STATISTICAL NOTES:** Hit for the cycle (September 13, 2006). ... Career major league grand slams: 2.

2006 GAMES PLAYED BY POSITION (MLB): OF—145, DH—1.

Year Team (League)	Pos.	G	AB	R	H	2B	3B	HR	RBI	BB	SO	HBP	GDP	SB-CS	Avg.	OBP	SLG	OPS	E	Avg.
1994— Spokane (N'west)	2B-OF	52	191	23	40	6	1	0	18	19	58	2	4	3-5	.209	.286	.251	.538	4	.961
1995— Clinton (Midw.)	OF	128	421	57	100	18	4	2	40	68	109	6	8	28-8	.238	.349	.314	.663	9	.966
1996— Rancho Cuca. (Calif.)	OF	123	435	65	118	21	11	7	54	60	102	6	11	7-8	.271	.366	.418	.784	16	.934
1997— Rancho Cuca. (Calif.)	OF	69	268	66	81	15	4	8	40	49	57	3	4	10-4	.302	.416	.478	.893	5	.959
— Mobile (Sou.)	OF	28	90	14	22	4	1	2	12	15	29	1	1	3-1	.244	.352	.378	.730	2	.960
1998— Mobile (Sou.)	OF	72	254	62	78	15	4	7	51	55	50	1	6	11-1	.307	.428	.480	.908	1	.995
1999— Las Vegas (PCL)	OF	121	422	57	108	23	3	9	52	58	104	1	13	17-6	.256	.352	.386	.739	7	.976
— San Diego (N.L.)	OF	23	36	4	8	0	0	0	7	9	9	0	1	2-0	.222	.378	.222	.600	0	1.000
2000— Iowa (PCL)	OF	60	211	27	51	11	3	5	22	18	41	0	4	6-1	.242	.300	.393	.693	4	.970
— Chicago (N.L.)	OF	80	158	24	30	1	2	4	14	15	28	1	2	3-0	.190	.264	.297	.562	2	.978
2001— Chicago (N.L.)	OF	106	258	41	56	9	1	5	30	38	55	1	4	5-3	.217	.320	.364	.684	4	.970
— Pittsburgh (N.L.)	OF	46	147	22	36	6	1	5	14	22	45	0	4	3-2	.245	.341	.401	.743	3	.971
2002— New York (N.L.)		2	1	0	0	0	0	0	0	0	0	0	0	0-0	.000	.000	.000	.000	...	...
— Baltimore (A.L.)	OF-DH	109	344	54	95	25	3	7	38	43	69	1	4	15-5	.276	.355	.427	.782	6	.969
2003— Baltimore (A.L.)	OF-DH	41	162	21	33	12	1	2	20	9	29	1	4	0-3	.204	.250	.327	.577	0	1.000
— San Diego (N.L.)	OF	103	306	50	83	19	1	4	22	34	66	1	4	12-5	.271	.346	.379	.725	1	.993
2004— Oklahoma (PCL)	OF-DH	38	145	33	47	9	4	9	36	23	29	0	2	4-1	.324	.409	.628	1.037	2	.971
— Texas (A.L.)	OF-DH	87	280	37	77	17	1	11	36	33	64	1	1	5-1	.275	.350	.461	.811	2	.990
2005— Frisco (Texas)	OF	1	5	0	2	0	0	0	1	0	1	0	0	0-0	.400	.400	.800	.800	2	.500
— Texas (A.L.)	OF-DH	131	475	72	121	25	5	17	55	47	90	0	11	9-2	.255	.320	.436	.756	6	.982
2006— Oklahoma (PCL)		6	21	10	9	2	0	1	4	1	4	0	1	2-0	.429	.538	.524	1.062	2	.714
— Texas (A.L.)	OF-DH	147	620	102	194	44	6	19	79	58	99	4	8	10-7	.313	.371	.495	.866	7	.980
American League totals (5 years)		515	1881	286	520	123	16	56	228	190	351	7	28	39-18	.276	.342	.448	.790	21	.982
National League totals (5 years)		360	906	141	213	35	5	22	87	118	203	3	15	25-10	.235	.325	.358	.683	10	.981
Major League totals (8 years)		875	2787	427	733	158	21	78	315	308	554	10	43	64-28	.263	.336	.419	.755	31	.982

ALL-STAR GAME RECORD

	G	AB	R	H	2B	3B	HR	RBI	BB	SO	HBP	GDP	SB-CS	Avg.	OBP	SLG	OPS	E	Avg.
All-Star Game totals (1 year)	1	1	0	1	0	0	0	0	0	0	0	0	0-0	1.000	1.000	1.000	2.000	0	1.000

2006 LEFTY-RIGHTY SPLITS

vs.	Avg.	AB	H	2B	3B	HR	RBI	BB	SO	OBP	Slg.	vs.	Avg.	AB	H	2B	3B	HR	RBI	BB	SO	OBP	Slg.
L	.314	137	43	13	1	7	19	15	25	.374	.577	R	.313	483	151	31	5	12	60	43	74	.370	.472

MAUER, JOE — C

PERSONAL: Born April 19, 1983, in St. Paul, Minn. ... 6-4/220. ... Bats left, throws right. ... Full name: Joseph Patrick Mauer. ... High school: Cretin-Durham Hall (St. Paul). **TRANSACTIONS/CAREER NOTES:** Selected by Minnesota Twins organization in first round (first pick overall) of 2001 free-agent draft ... On disabled list (April 7-June 2 and July 16, 2004-remainder of season); included rehabilitation assignments to Fort Myers and Rochester. **HONORS:** Named catcher on SPORTING NEWS A.L. All-Star team (2006). ... Named catcher on A.L. Silver Slugger team (2006).

2006 GAMES PLAYED BY POSITION (MLB): C—120, DH—17.

Year Team (League)	Pos.	G	AB	R	H	2B	3B	HR	RBI	BB	SO	HBP	GDP	SB-CS	Avg.	OBP	SLG	OPS	E	Avg.
2001— Elizabethton (App.)	C	32	110	14	44	6	2	0	14	19	10	1	5	4-0	.400	.492	.491	.983	4	.980
2002— Quad City (Midw.)	C-1B	110	411	58	124	23	1	4	62	61	42	2	16	0-0	.302	.393	.392	.785	6	.993
2003— Fort Myers (FSL)	C-1B	62	233	25	78	13	1	1	44	24	24	1	11	3-0	.335	.395	.412	.807	0	1.000
— New Britain (East.)	C	73	276	48	94	17	1	4	41	25	25	5	10	0-0	.341	.400	.453	.853	3	.992
2004— Fort Myers (FSL)	C-DH	2	6	0	4	0	0	0	2	2	2	0	0	0-0	.667	.750	.667	1.417	0	1.000
— Rochester (Int'l)	DH-C	5	19	1	6	3	0	0	2	1	0	0	0	0-0	.316	.333	.474	.807	0	1.000
— Minnesota (A.L.)	C-DH	35	107	18	33	8	1	6	17	11	14	1	1	1-0	.308	.369	.570	.939	2	.991
2005— Minnesota (A.L.)	C-DH	131	489	61	144	26	3	9	55	61	64	1	9	13-1	.294	.372	.411	.783	5	.993
2006— Minnesota (A.L.)	C-DH	140	521	86	181	36	4	13	84	79	54	1	24	8-3	* .347	.429	.507	.936	4	.996
Major League totals (3 years)		306	1117	165	358	70	7	28	156	151	132	3	34	22-4	.321	.399	.471	.870	11	.994

DIVISION SERIES RECORD

Year Team (League)	Pos.	G	AB	R	H	2B	3B	HR	RBI	BB	SO	HBP	GDP	SB-CS	Avg.	OBP	SLG	OPS	E	Avg.
2006— Minnesota (A.L.)	C	3	11	0	2	0	0	0	0	0	1	0	0	0-0	.182	.250	.182	.432	0	1.000

ALL-STAR GAME RECORD

	G	AB	R	H	2B	3B	HR	RBI	BB	SO	HBP	GDP	SB-CS	Avg.	OBP	SLG	OPS	E	Avg.
All-Star Game totals (1 year)	1	2	0	0	0	0	0	0	0	1	0	0	0-0	.000	.000	.000	.000		

2006 LEFTY-RIGHTY SPLITS

vs.	Avg.	AB	H	2B	3B	HR	RBI	BB	SO	OBP	Slg.	vs.	Avg.	AB	H	2B	3B	HR	RBI	BB	SO	OBP	Slg.
L	.331	181	60	11	0	2	28	22	23	.401	.425	R	.356	340	121	25	4	11	56	57	31	.444	.550

MAYS, JOE — P

PERSONAL: Born December 10, 1975, in Flint, Mich. ... 6-1/192. ... Throws right, bats both. ... Full name: Joseph Emerson Mays. ... High school: Southeast (Bradenton, Fla.). ... Junior college: Manatee Community College (Bradenton, Fla.). **TRANSACTIONS/CAREER NOTES:** Selected by Seattle Mariners organization in sixth round of 1994 free-agent draft. ... Traded by Mariners to Minnesota Twins (October 8, 1997), completing deal in which Twins traded OF Roberto Kelly to Mariners for P Jeromy Palki and a player to be named (August 20, 1997). ... On disabled list (April 15-July 20, 2002); included rehabilitation assignments to Fort Myers and New Britain. ... On disabled list (March 23, 2004-entire season). ... Signed as a free agent by Kansas City Royals (January 3, 2006). ... Released by Royals (May 16, 2006).

CAREER HITTING: 6-for-24 (.250), 1 R, 2 2B, 0 3B, 0 HR, 3 RBI.

Year	Team (League)	W	L	Pct.	ERA	WHIP	G	GS	CG	ShO	Hld.	Sv.-Opp.	IP	H	R	ER	HR	BB-IBB	SO	Avg.
1995—	Ariz. Mariners (Ariz.)	2	3	.400	3.25	1.33	10	10	0	0	...	0-...	44.1	41	24	16	0	18-0	44	.247
1996—	Everett (N'west)	4	4	.500	3.08	1.20	13	10	0	0	...	0-...	64.1	55	33	22	3	22-0	56	.227
1997—	Wisconsin (Midw.)	9	3	.750	2.09	1.04	13	13	1	0	...	0-...	81.2	62	20	19	3	23-1	79	.214
—	Lancaster (Calif.)	7	4	.636	4.86	1.47	15	15	1	0	...	0-...	96.1	108	55	52	9	34-0	82	.290
1998—	Fort Myers (FSL)	7	2	.778	3.04	1.31	16	15	0	0	...	0-...	94.2	101	45	32	7	23-0	83	.276
—	New Britain (East.)	5	3	.625	4.99	1.46	11	10	0	0	...	0-...	57.2	63	40	32	4	21-0	45	.273
1999—	Minnesota (A.L.)	6	11	.353	4.37	1.44	49	20	2	1	2	0-0	171.0	179	92	83	24	67-2	115	.270
2000—	Minnesota (A.L.)	7	15	.318	5.56	1.62	31	28	2	1	0	0-0	160.1	193	105	99	20	67-1	102	.299
—	Salt Lake (PCL)	2	0	1.000	1.72	1.15	3	3	0	0	...	0-...	15.2	16	4	3	0	2-0	18	.267
2001—	Minnesota (A.L.)	17	13	.567	3.16	1.15	34	34	4	2	0	0-0	233.2	205	87	82	25	64-2	123	.235
2002—	Minnesota (A.L.)	4	8	.333	5.38	1.45	17	17	1	1	0	0-0	95.1	113	60	57	14	25-0	38	.292
—	Fort Myers (FSL)	0	1	.000	2.08	1.38	3	3	0	0	...	0-...	8.2	9	2	2	0	3-0	7	.273
—	New Britain (East.)	1	0	1.000	1.29	0.43	1	1	0	0	...	0-...	7.0	2	1	1	1	1-0	5	.087
2003—	Minnesota (A.L.)	8	8	.500	6.30	1.52	31	31	0	0	1	0-1	130.0	159	92	91	21	39-2	50	.302
2005—	Minnesota (A.L.)	6	10	.375	5.65	1.56	31	26	0	1	0	0-0	156.0	203	109	98	23	41-1	59	.318
2006—	Louisville (Int'l)	6	3	.667	3.07	1.20	10	10	1	0	0	0-0	67.1	68	27	23	4	13-0	40	.267
—	Kansas City (A.L.)	0	4	.000	10.27	2.20	6	6	0	0	0	0-0	23.2	38	33	27	7	14-0	9	.369
—	Cincinnati (N.L.)	0	1	.000	7.33	1.93	7	4	0	0	0	0-0	27.0	40	23	22	4	12-2	16	.342
American League totals (7 years)		48	69	.410	4.98	1.45	199	152	10	6	3	0-1	970.0	1090	578	537	134	317-8	496	.284
National League totals (1 year)		0	1	.000	7.33	1.93	7	4	0	0	0	0-0	27.0	40	23	22	4	12-2	16	.342
Major League totals (7 years)		48	70	.407	5.05	1.46	206	156	10	6	3	0-1	997.0	1130	601	559	138	329-10	512	.286

DIVISION SERIES RECORD

Year	Team (League)	W	L	Pct.	ERA	WHIP	G	GS	CG	ShO	Hld.	Sv.-Opp.	IP	H	R	ER	HR	BB-IBB	SO	Avg.
2002—	Minnesota (A.L.)	0	1	.000	14.73	3.00	1	1	0	0	...	0-0	3.2	9	6	6	1	2-1	1	.474

CHAMPIONSHIP SERIES RECORD

Year	Team (League)	W	L	Pct.	ERA	WHIP	G	GS	CG	ShO	Hld.	Sv.-Opp.	IP	H	R	ER	HR	BB-IBB	SO	Avg.
2002—	Minnesota (A.L.)	1	0	1.000	2.03	0.90	2	2	0	0	...	0-0	13.1	12	4	3	3	0-0	3	.235

ALL-STAR GAME RECORD

Year	Team (League)	W	L	Pct.	ERA	WHIP	G	GS	CG	ShO	Hld.	Sv.-Opp.	IP	H	R	ER	HR	BB-IBB	SO	Avg.
All-Star Game totals (1 year)		0	0	...	0.00	0.00	1	0	0	0	...	0-0	1.0	0	0	0	0	0-0	0	...

2006 LEFTY-RIGHTY SPLITS

vs.	Avg.	AB	H	2B	3B	HR	RBI	BB	SO	OBP	Slg.	vs.	Avg.	AB	H	2B	3B	HR	RBI	BB	SO	OBP	Slg.
L	.298	94	28	8	1	3	22	16	11	.400	.500	R	.397	126	50	13	0	8	31	10	14	.435	.690

MCANULTY, PAUL — OF

PERSONAL: Born February 24, 1981, in Oxnard, Calif. ... 5-10/220. ... Bats left, throws right. ... Full name: Paul Michael McAnulty. ... College: Long Beach State. **TRANSACTIONS/CAREER NOTES:** Selected by San Diego Padres organization in 12th round of 2002 free-agent draft.

2006 GAMES PLAYED BY POSITION (MLB): OF—1.

Year	Team (League)	Pos.	G	AB	R	H	2B	3B	HR	RBI	BB	SO	HBP	GDP	SB-CS	Avg.	OBP	SLG	OPS	E	Avg.
2002—	Idaho Falls (Pio.)	1B	67	235	56	89	29	0	8	51	49	43	4	5	7-2	.379	.488	.604	1.092	11	.979
2003—	Fort Wayne (Midw.)	1B-OF	133	455	48	124	27	0	7	73	67	82	9	7	5-3	.273	.370	.378	.748	16	.986
2004—	Lake Elsinore (Calif.)	OF-1B	133	495	98	147	36	3	23	87	88	106	4	5	3-1	.297	.404	.521	.925	8	.984
2005—	Mobile (Sou.)	OF-1B	79	298	39	84	17	2	10	42	34	66	6	3	5-2	.282	.364	.453	.817	10	.969
—	Portland (PCL)	1B-OF-DH	38	151	27	52	15	0	6	27	16	29	0	4	0-0	.344	.405	.563	.968	2	.992
—	San Diego (N.L.)	OF-1B	22	24	4	5	0	0	0	3	3	7	1	0	1-0	.208	.321	.208	.530	0	1.000
2006—	Portland (PCL)		125	478	76	148	34	5	19	79	62	79	4	14	1-2	.310	.388	.521	.909	21	.971
—	San Diego (N.L.)	OF	16	13	3	3	1	0	1	3	2	4	0	0	0-0	.231	.333	.538	.872	0	...
Major League totals (2 years)			38	37	7	8	1	0	1	3	5	11	1	0	1-0	.216	.326	.324	.650	0	1.000

2006 LEFTY-RIGHTY SPLITS

vs.	Avg.	AB	H	2B	3B	HR	RBI	BB	SO	OBP	Slg.	vs.	Avg.	AB	H	2B	3B	HR	RBI	BB	SO	OBP	Slg.
L	.000	1	0	0	0	0	0	0	0	.000	.000	R	.250	12	3	1	0	1	3	2	4	.357	.583

MCBRIDE, MACAY — P

PERSONAL: Born October 24, 1982, in Augusta, Ga. ... 5-11/210. ... Throws left, bats left. ... Full name: Joseph Macay McBride. **TRANSACTIONS/CAREER NOTES:** Selected by Atlanta Braves organization in first round (24th pick overall) of 2001 free-agent draft. ... On disabled list (April 1-30, 2006); included rehabilitation assignments to Mississippi and Richmond. **HONORS:** Named South Atlantic League Most Valuable Pitcher (2002).

CAREER HITTING: 0-for-0 (.000), 0 R, 0 2B, 0 3B, 0 HR, 0 RBI.

Year	Team (League)	W	L	Pct.	ERA	WHIP	G	GS	CG	ShO	Hld.	Sv.-Opp.	IP	H	R	ER	HR	BB-IBB	SO	Avg.
2001—	GC Braves (GCL)	4	4	.500	3.76	1.35	13	11	0	0	...	0-...	55.0	51	30	23	0	23-1	67	.248
2002—	Macon (S. Atl.)	12	8	.600	2.12	1.06	25	25	2	1	...	0-...	157.1	119	49	37	6	48-1	138	.209
2003—	Myrtle Beach (Carol.)	9	8	.529	2.95	1.29	27	27	1	0	...	0-...	164.2	164	63	54	5	49-0	139	.262
2004—	Greenville (Sou.)	1	7	.125	4.44	1.54	38	12	0	0	...	0-...	103.1	113	59	51	9	46-0	102	.277
2005—	Mississippi (Sou.)	3	1	.750	3.65	1.34	6	3	0	0	...	0-2	24.2	21	11	10	2	12-1	16	.233
—	Richmond (Int'l)	1	5	.167	4.33	1.63	25	1	0	0	4	2-3	43.2	49	27	21	5	22-2	47	.290
—	Atlanta (N.L.)	1	0	1.000	5.79	1.79	23	0	0	0	6	1-1	14.0	18	11	9	0	7-0	22	.305
2006—	Mississippi (Sou.)	0	0	...	9.64	1.93	4	2	0	0	...	0-0	4.2	8	5	5	1	1-0	6	.381
—	Richmond (Int'l)	0	0	...	0.00	0.67	3	0	0	0	1	0-0	3.0	1	0	0	0	1-0	3	.111
—	Atlanta (N.L.)	4	1	.800	3.65	1.40	71	0	0	0	10	1-2	56.2	53	28	23	2	32-4	46	.248
Major League totals (2 years)		5	1	.833	4.08	1.56	94	0	0	0	16	2-3	70.2	71	39	32	2	39-4	68	.260

DIVISION SERIES RECORD

Year	Team (League)	W	L	Pct.	ERA	WHIP	G	GS	CG	ShO	Hld.	Sv.-Opp.	IP	H	R	ER	HR	BB-IBB	SO	Avg.
2005—	Atlanta (N.L.)	0	0	...	0.00	0.00	1	0	0	0	0	0-0	1.0	0	0	0	0	0-0	1	.000

vs.	Avg.	AB	H	2B	3B	HR	RBI	BB	SO	OBP	Slg.	vs.	Avg.	AB	H	2B	3B	HR	RBI	BB	SO	OBP	Slg.
L	.181	105	19	4	1	2	10	9	30	.252	.295	R	.312	109	34	6	2	0	13	23	16	.432	.404

MCCANN, BRIAN — C

PERSONAL: Born February 20, 1984, in Athens, Ga. ... 6-3/210. ... Bats left, throws right. ... Full name: Brian Michael McCann. **TRANSACTIONS/CAREER NOTES:** Selected by Atlanta Braves organization in second round of 2002 free-agent draft. ... On disabled list (May 24-June 9, 2006); included rehabilitation assignment to Rome. **HONORS:** Named catcher on SPORTING NEWS N.L. All-Star team (2006). ... Named catcher on N.L. Silver Slugger team (2006). **STATISTICAL NOTES:** Career major league grand slams: 2.

2006 GAMES PLAYED BY POSITION (MLB): C—124.

Year Team (League)	Pos.	G	AB	R	H	2B	3B	HR	RBI	BB	SO	HBP	GDP	SB-CS	Avg.	OBP	SLG	OPS	E	Avg.
2002—GC Braves (GCL)	C	29	100	9	22	5	0	2	11	10	22	1	0	0-0	.220	.295	.330	.625	1	.993
2003—Rome (S. Atl.)	C	115	424	40	123	31	3	12	71	24	73	2	5	7-4	.290	.329	.462	.791	3	.995
2004—Myrtle Beach (Carol.)	C	111	385	45	107	35	0	16	66	31	54	4	6	2-2	.278	.337	.494	.831	7	.988
2005—Mississippi (Sou.)	C-DH	48	166	27	44	13	2	6	26	25	26	2	2	2-3	.265	.359	.476	.834	1	.997
—Atlanta (N.L.)	C	59	180	20	50	7	0	5	23	18	26	1	5	1-1	.278	.345	.400	.745	3	.991
2006—Rome (S. Atl.)		2	7	0	2	0	0	0	0	1	1	0	0	0-0	.286	.375	.286	.661	0	—
—Atlanta (N.L.)	C	130	442	61	147	34	0	24	93	41	54	3	12	2-0	.333	.388	.572	.961	9	.989
Major League totals (2 years)		189	622	81	197	41	0	29	116	59	80	4	17	3-1	.317	.376	.523	.898	12	.990

DIVISION SERIES RECORD

Year Team (League)	Pos.	G	AB	R	H	2B	3B	HR	RBI	BB	SO	HBP	GDP	SB-CS	Avg.	OBP	SLG	OPS	E	Avg.
2005—Atlanta (N.L.)	C	3	16	2	3	0	0	2	5	0	6	0	0	0-0	.188	.188	.563	.750	0	1.000

ALL-STAR GAME RECORD

		G	AB	R	H	2B	3B	HR	RBI	BB	SO	HBP	GDP	SB-CS	Avg.	OBP	SLG	OPS	E	Avg.
All-Star Game totals (1 year)		1	1	0	0	0	0	0	0	0	0	0	0	0-0	.000	.000	.000	.000	0	1.000

2006 LEFTY-RIGHTY SPLITS

vs.	Avg.	AB	H	2B	3B	HR	RBI	BB	SO	OBP	Slg.	vs.	Avg.	AB	H	2B	3B	HR	RBI	BB	SO	OBP	Slg.
L	.266	94	25	9	0	3	15	11	19	.352	.457	R	.351	348	122	25	0	21	78	30	35	.398	.603

MCCARTHY, BRANDON — P

PERSONAL: Born July 7, 1983, in Glendale, Calif. ... 6-7/190. ... Throws right, bats right. ... Full name: Brandon Patrick McCarthy. ... College: Lamar (CO) CC. **TRANSACTIONS/CAREER NOTES:** Selected by Chicago White Sox organization in 17th round of 2002 free-agent draft. **CAREER HITTING:** 0-for-3 (.000), 0 R, 0 2B, 0 3B, 0 HR, 0 RBI.

Year Team (League)	W	L	Pct.	ERA	WHIP	G	GS	CG	ShO	Hld.	Sv.-Opp.	IP	H	R	ER	HR	BB-IBB	SO	Avg.
2002—Ariz. White Sox (Ariz.)	4	4	.500	2.76	1.19	14	14	0	0	...	0-...	78.1	78	40	24	6	15-1	79	.255
2003—Great Falls (Pio.)	9	4	.692	3.65	1.19	16	15	1	0	...	0-...	101.0	105	49	41	7	15-0	125	.263
2004—Kannapolis (S. Atl.)	8	5	.615	3.64	1.07	15	15	3	1	...	0-...	94.0	80	41	38	10	21-0	113	.235
—Win.-Salem (Car.)	6	0	1.000	2.08	0.65	8	8	0	0	...	0-...	52.0	31	12	12	3	3-0	60	.171
—Birmingham (Sou.)	3	1	.750	3.46	1.12	4	4	0	0	...	0-...	26.0	23	10	10	2	6-1	29	.237
2005—Charlotte (Int'l)	7	7	.500	3.92	1.14	20	19	1	1	0	0-0	119.1	104	53	52	16	32-0	130	.233
—Chicago (A.L.)	3	2	.600	4.03	1.18	12	10	0	0	0	0-0	67.0	62	30	30	13	17-0	48	.242
2006—Chicago (A.L.)	4	7	.364	4.68	1.30	53	2	0	0	11	0-1	84.2	77	44	44	17	33-9	69	.243
Major League totals (2 years)	7	9	.438	4.39	1.25	65	12	0	0	11	0-1	151.2	139	74	74	30	50-9	117	.243

2006 LEFTY-RIGHTY SPLITS

vs.	Avg.	AB	H	2B	3B	HR	RBI	BB	SO	OBP	Slg.	vs.	Avg.	AB	H	2B	3B	HR	RBI	BB	SO	OBP	Slg.
L	.197	117	23	2	0	6	18	16	29	.291	.368	R	.270	200	54	5	3	11	31	17	40	.327	.490

MCCLUNG, SETH — P

PERSONAL: Born February 7, 1981, in Lewisburg, W.Va. ... 6-6/235. ... Throws right, bats left. ... Full name: Michael Seth McClung. ... High school: Greenbrier East (Lewisburg, W.Va.). **TRANSACTIONS/CAREER NOTES:** Selected by Tampa Bay Devil Rays organization in fifth round of free-agent draft (June 2, 1999). ... On disabled list (May 23, 2003-remainder of season; and February 23-August 3, 2004); included rehabilitation assignments to Charleston, S.C., and Montgomery. ... On bereavement list (August 31-September 3, 2005). **CAREER HITTING:** 0-for-1 (.000), 0 R, 0 2B, 0 3B, 0 HR, 0 RBI.

Year Team (League)	W	L	Pct.	ERA	WHIP	G	GS	CG	ShO	Hld.	Sv.-Opp.	IP	H	R	ER	HR	BB-IBB	SO	Avg.
1999—Princeton (Appal.)	2	4	.333	7.69	2.21	13	10	0	0	...	0-...	45.2	53	47	39	3	48-0	46	.285
2000—Char., S.C. (SAL)	2	1	.667	3.19	1.58	6	6	0	0	...	0-...	31.0	30	14	11	0	19-0	26	.246
—Hudson Valley (NYP)	2	2	.500	1.85	1.24	8	8	0	0	...	0-...	43.2	37	18	9	0	17-0	38	.227
2001—Char., S.C. (SAL)	10	11	.476	2.79	1.19	28	28	2	1	...	0-...	164.1	142	72	51	6	53-1	165	.231
2002—Bakersfield (Calif.)	3	2	.600	2.92	1.24	7	7	0	0	...	0-...	40.0	35	16	12	1	11-0	48	.243
—Orlando (South.)	5	7	.417	5.37	1.68	20	19	0	0	...	0-...	114.0	138	74	68	12	53-0	64	.299
2003—Tampa Bay (A.L.)	4	1	.800	5.35	1.50	12	5	0	0	1	0-0	38.2	33	23	23	6	25-1	25	.241
2004—Char., S.C. (SAL)	0	0	...	0.00	0.96	3	3	0	0	...	0-...	9.1	5	0	0	0	4-0	10	.152
—Montgom. (Sou.)	1	1	.500	4.73	1.05	3	3	0	0	...	0-...	13.1	10	7	7	3	4-0	8	.208
—Durham (Int'l)	2	1	.667	3.29	1.24	11	0	0	0	...	0-...	13.2	10	5	5	0	7-0	12	.196
2005—Durham (Int'l)	2	0	1.000	3.93	1.58	6	3	0	0	0	0-...	18.1	23	12	8	1	6-1	19	.303
—Tampa Bay (A.L.)	7	11	.389	6.59	1.54	34	17	0	0	0	0-1	109.1	106	85	80	20	62-1	92	.249
2006—Durham (Int'l)	1	0	1.000	2.20	1.10	14	0	0	0	0	5-5	16.1	16	5	4	1	2-0	26	.242
—Tampa Bay (A.L.)	6	12	.333	6.29	1.83	39	15	0	0	0	6-7	103.0	120	77	72	14	68-5	59	.294
Major League totals (3 years)	17	24	.415	6.27	1.65	85	37	0	0	3	6-8	251.0	259	185	175	40	155-7	176	.267

2006 LEFTY-RIGHTY SPLITS

vs.	Avg.	AB	H	2B	3B	HR	RBI	BB	SO	OBP	Slg.	vs.	Avg.	AB	H	2B	3B	HR	RBI	BB	SO	OBP	Slg.
L	.299	197	59	11	0	5	27	37	28	.406	.431	R	.289	211	61	10	0	9	41	31	31	.378	.464

MCCRACKEN, QUINTON — OF

PERSONAL: Born August 16, 1970, in Wilmington, N.C. ... 5-7/188. ... Bats both, throws right. ... Full name: Quinton Antoine McCracken. ... High school: South Brunswick (Southport, N.C.). ... College: Duke. **TRANSACTIONS/CAREER NOTES:** Selected by Colorado Rockies organization in 25th round of 1992 free-agent draft. ... Selected by Tampa Bay Devil Rays in first round (fourth pick overall) of expansion draft (November 18, 1997). ... On disabled list (May 25, 1999-remainder of season). ... Released by Devil Rays (November 27, 2000). ... Signed by St. Louis Cardinals (December 22, 2000). ... Released by Cardinals (March 28, 2001). ... Signed by Minnesota Twins organization (April 13, 2001). ... Signed as a free agent by Arizona Diamondbacks (January 9, 2002). ... Traded by Diamondbacks to Seattle Mariners for 1B Greg Colbrunn and cash

(December 15, 2003). ... Released by Mariners (June 7, 2004). ... Signed by Diamondbacks organization (June 11, 2004). ... Signed as free agent by Cincinnati Reds organization (February 14, 2006). ... Released by Reds (July 14, 2006). ... Signed by Minnesota Twins organization (July 22, 2006).

2006 GAMES PLAYED BY POSITION (MLB): OF—15.

Year Team (League)	Pos.	G	AB	R	H	2B	3B	HR	RBI	BB	SO	HBP	GDP	SB-CS	Avg.	OBP	SLG	OPS	E	Avg.
1992—Bend (N'west)	2B-OF	67	232	37	65	13	2	0	27	25	39	0	6	18-6	.280	.347	.353	.701	17	.930
1993—Central Valley (Cal.)	2B-OF	127	483	94	141	17	7	2	58	78	90	2	15	60-19	.292	.390	.369	.758	13	.946
1994—New Haven (East.)	OF	136	544	94	151	27	4	5	39	48	72	4	6	36-19	.278	.338	.369	.708	8	.972
1995—New Haven (East.)	OF-DH	55	221	33	79	11	4	1	26	21	32	3	2	26-8	.357	.419	.457	.876	3	.971
—Colo. Springs (PCL)	OF-DH	61	244	55	88	14	6	3	28	23	30	1	4	17-6	.361	.418	.504	.922	1	.991
—Colorado (N.L.)	OF	3	1	0	0	0	0	0	0	0	1	0	0	.000	.000	.000	.000	0	—
1996—Colorado (N.L.)	OF	124	283	50	82	13	6	3	40	32	62	1	5	17-6	.290	.363	.410	.773	6	.957
1997—Colorado (N.L.)	OF	147	325	69	95	11	1	3	36	42	62	1	6	28-11	.292	.374	.360	.734	4	.980
1998—Tampa Bay (A.L.)	OF	155	614	77	179	38	7	7	59	41	107	3	12	19-10	.292	.335	.410	.745	3	.992
1999—Tampa Bay (A.L.)	OF	40	148	20	37	6	1	1	18	14	23	1	7	6-5	.250	.317	.324	.641	1	.988
2000—Tampa Bay (A.L.)	OF	15	31	5	4	0	0	0	2	6	4	0	3	0-1	.129	.270	.129	.399	0	1.000
—Durham (Int'l)	OF	85	334	54	87	18	2	2	28	34	57	2	10	13-7	.260	.332	.344	.676	4	.977
2001—Edmonton (PCL)	OF	81	361	53	122	27	4	4	45	21	54	1	5	8-10	.338	.374	.468	.842	5	.971
—Minnesota (A.L.)	OF-DH	24	64	7	14	2	0	0	3	5	13	0	2	0-1	.219	.275	.313	.588	0	1.000
2002—Arizona (N.L.)	OF	123	349	60	108	27	8	3	40	32	68	2	3	5-4	.309	.367	.458	.825	1	.995
2003—Arizona (N.L.)	OF-DH	115	203	17	46	5	2	0	18	15	34	0	4	5-1	.227	.276	.271	.547	1	.983
2004—Seattle (A.L.)	OF-DH	19	20	6	3	0	0	0	0	2	4	0	1	1-1	.150	.227	.150	.377	0	1.000
—Tucson (PCL)	OF	15	58	7	19	5	1	1	8	3	5	0	1	2-2	.328	.361	.500	.861	0	1.000
—Arizona (N.L.)	OF	55	156	20	45	11	1	2	13	13	23	0	2	2-4	.288	.341	.410	.751	1	.979
2005—Arizona (N.L.)	OF	134	215	23	51	4	3	1	13	23	35	1	4	4-0	.237	.313	.298	.610	2	.975
2006—Rochester (Int'l)		31	109	10	31	4	0	1	11	9	17	0	4	2-1	.284	.339	.349	.688	0	1.000
—Sarasota (Fla. St.)		4	16	3	8	1	0	0	0	0	0	0	0	0-0	.500	.500	.625	1.125	0	1.000
—Cincinnati (N.L.)	OF	45	53	5	11	1	1	1	2	4	9	0	1	2-0	.208	.263	.321	.584	1	.955
American League totals (5 years)		253	877	115	237	46	10	8	82	68	151	4	25	26-18	.270	.323	.373	.695	4	.992
National League totals (8 years)		746	1585	244	438	72	22	13	162	161	294	5	25	63-26	.276	.343	.374	.717	16	.978
Major League totals (12 years)		999	2462	359	675	118	32	21	244	229	445	9	50	89-44	.274	.336	.374	.709	20	.984

DIVISION SERIES RECORD

Year Team (League)	Pos.	G	AB	R	H	2B	3B	HR	RBI	BB	SO	HBP	GDP	SB-CS	Avg.	OBP	SLG	OPS	E	Avg.
2002—Arizona (N.L.)	OF	3	11	1	4	1	0	0	2	1	2	0	0	0-0	.364	.417	.455	.871	0	1.000

2006 LEFTY-RIGHTY SPLITS

vs.	Avg.	AB	H	2B	3B	HR	RBI	BB	SO	OBP	Slg.	vs.	Avg.	AB	H	2B	3B	HR	RBI	BB	SO	OBP	Slg.
L	.143	7	1	0	0	0	0	0	3	.143	.143	R	.217	46	10	1	1	1	2	4	6	.280	.348

MCDONALD, JOHN   SS/2B

PERSONAL: Born September 24, 1974, in New London, Conn. ... 5-11/175. ... Bats right, throws right. ... Full name: John Joseph McDonald. ... High school: East Lyme (Conn.). ... College: Providence. **TRANSACTIONS/CAREER NOTES:** Selected by Cleveland Indians organization in 12th round of 1996 free-agent draft. ... On disabled list (June 30-July 17 and August 27, 2003-remainder of season); included rehabilitation assignments to Mahoning Valley and Lake County. ... Traded by Indians to Toronto Blue Jays for a player to be named (December 2, 2004); Indians acquired P Thomas Mastny to complete deal (December 14, 2004). ... Traded by Blue Jays to Detroit Tigers for player to be named (July 22, 2005); Blue Jays received cash to complete deal (November 3, 2005). ... Traded by Tigers to Blue Jays for cash (November 10, 2005). ... On disabled list (May 28-June 12, 2006). **STATISTICAL NOTES:** Career major league grand slams: 1.

2006 GAMES PLAYED BY POSITION (MLB): SS—90, 2B—10, 3B—2, DH—1.

Year Team (League)	Pos.	G	AB	R	H	2B	3B	HR	RBI	BB	SO	HBP	GDP	SB-CS	Avg.	OBP	SLG	OPS	E	Avg.
1996—Watertown (NYP)	SS	75	278	48	75	11	0	2	26	32	49	5	3	11-1	.270	.354	.331	.685	18	.946
1997—Kinston (Carol.)	SS	130	541	77	140	27	3	5	53	51	75	2	12	6-5	.259	.324	.348	.671	25	.961
1998—Akron (East.)	SS	132	514	68	118	18	2	2	43	43	61	6	7	17-6	.230	.293	.284	.578	23	.966
1999—Akron (East.)	SS-2B	55	226	31	67	12	0	1	26	19	26	2	5	7-3	.296	.351	.363	.713	8	.970
—Buffalo (Int'l)	SS-3B-2B	66	237	30	75	12	1	0	25	11	23	2	6	6-3	.316	.349	.376	.725	13	.956
—Cleveland (A.L.)	2B-SS	18	21	2	7	0	0	0	0	0	3	0	2	0-1	.333	.333	.333	.667	1	.967
2000—Buffalo (Int'l)	SS-2B	75	286	37	77	17	2	1	36	21	29	1	7	4-3	.269	.315	.353	.668	8	.975
—Mahoning Valley (N.Y.-Penn.)	SS	5	17	0	2	1	0	0	1	2	3	0	0	0-0	.118	.211	.176	.387	0	1.000
—Cleveland (A.L.)	SS	9	9	0	4	0	0	0	0	1	1	0	0	0-0	.444	.444	.444	.889	0	1.000
—Kinston (Carol.)	SS	1	3	0	1	0	0	0	0	0	0	0	0	0-0	.333	.333	.333	.667	0	1.000
2001—Cleveland (A.L.)	SS-2B-3B	17	22	1	2	1	0	0	0	1	7	1	0	0-0	.091	.167	.136	.303	1	.964
—Buffalo (Int'l)	SS-2B-3B	116	410	52	100	17	1	2	33	33	72	6	11	17-10	.244	.305	.305	.610	23	.957
2002—Cleveland (A.L.) 2B-SS-3B	DH	93	264	35	66	11	3	1	12	10	50	5	4	3-0	.250	.288	.326	.614	5	.979
2003—Mahoning Valley (N.Y.-Penn.)	SS	1	2	1	0	0	0	0	0	1	0	0	0	0-0	.000	.333	.000	.333	0	1.000
—Lake County (S.Atl.)	SS	1	3	0	0	0	0	0	0	0	0	0	0	0-0	.000	.000	.000	.000	0	1.000
—Cleveland (A.L.)	2B-SS-3B	82	214	21	46	9	1	1	14	11	31	2	4	3-3	.215	.258	.280	.538	10	.964
2004—Cleveland (A.L.) SS-2B-3B	DH	66	93	17	19	5	1	2	7	4	11	0	2	0-0	.204	.237	.344	.581	5	.965
2005—Toronto (A.L.)	SS-2B	37	93	8	27	3	0	0	12	6	12	2	3	5-0	.290	.340	.323	.662	3	.979
—Detroit (A.L.)	SS-2B-3B	31	73	10	19	3	1	0	4	5	12	0	1	1-1	.260	.308	.329	.636	5	.958
2006—Toronto (A.L.) SS-2B-3B	DH	104	260	35	58	7	3	0	23	16	41	2	8	7-2	.223	.271	.308	.579	14	.963
Major League totals (8 years)		457	1049	129	248	39	9	7	72	53	168	12	26	19-7	.236	.279	.311	.590	47	.969

2006 LEFTY-RIGHTY SPLITS

vs.	Avg.	AB	H	2B	3B	HR	RBI	BB	SO	OBP	Slg.	vs.	Avg.	AB	H	2B	3B	HR	RBI	BB	SO	OBP	Slg.
L	.230	87	20	4	0	1	12	9	11	.303	.310	R	.220	173	38	3	3	2	11	7	30	.254	.306

MCEWING, JOE   2B/SS

PERSONAL: Born October 19, 1972, in Bristol, Pa. ... 5-11/210. ... Bats right, throws right. ... Full name: Joseph Earl McEwing. ... High school: Bishop Egan (Fairless Hills, Pa.). ... Junior college: County College of Morris (Randolph, N.J.). **TRANSACTIONS/CAREER NOTES:** Selected by St. Louis Cardinals organization in 28th round of 1992 free-agent draft. ... Traded by Cardinals to New York Mets for P Jesse Orosco (March 18, 2000). ... On disabled list (July 14-31, 2002); included rehabilitation assignments to Brooklyn and Binghamton. ... On disabled list (August 20, 2004-remainder of season). ... Released by Mets (March 17, 2005). ... Signed by Kansas City Royals organization (March 22, 2005). ... Traded by Royals to Houston Astros for future considerations (March 30, 2006).

2006 GAMES PLAYED BY POSITION (MLB): 2B—2.

M

Year Team (League)	Pos.	G	AB	R	H	2B	3B	HR	RBI	BB	SO	HBP	GDP	SB-CS	Avg.	OBP	SLG	OPS	E	Avg.
1992—Ariz. Cardinals (Ariz.)	OF-SS	55	211	55	71	4	2	0	13	24	18	5	1	23-7	.336	.415	.374	.789	1	.991
1993—Savannah (S. Atl.)	OF	138	511	94	127	35	1	0	43	89	73	4	7	22-9	.249	.362	.321	.683	5	.982
1994—Madison (Midw.)	OF	90	346	58	112	24	2	4	47	32	53	1	5	18-15	.324	.380	.439	.819	5	.974
—St. Pete. (FSL)	2B-OF	50	197	22	49	7	0	1	20	19	32	1	4	8-4	.249	.314	.299	.613	2	.985
1995—St. Pete. (FSL)	2B-OF	75	281	33	64	13	0	1	23	25	49	1	5	2-3	.228	.289	.285	.574	15	.955
—Arkansas (Texas)	2B-OF	42	121	16	30	4	0	2	12	9	13	1	4	3-2	.248	.305	.331	.636	0	1.000
1996—Arkansas (Texas)	2B-OF	106	216	27	45	7	3	2	14	13	32	0	8	2-4	.208	.252	.296	.548	2	.987
1997—Arkansas (Texas)	P	103	263	33	68	6	3	4	35	19	39	1	6	2-4	.259	.309	.350	.659	2	.988
1998—Arkansas (Texas)	P	60	223	45	79	21	4	9	46	21	18	1	2	4-2	.354	.409	.605	1.014	1	.994
—Memphis (PCL)	2B-3B-OF																			
	SS	78	329	52	110	30	7	6	46	21	39	3	4	11-10	.334	.379	.523	.901	3	.982
—St. Louis (N.L.)	2B-OF	10	20	5	4	1	0	0	1	1	3	1	0	0-1	.200	.273	.250	.523	0	1.000
1999—St. Louis (N.L.)	2B-OF-3B																			
	1B-SS	152	513	65	141	28	4	9	44	41	87	6	3	7-4	.275	.333	.398	.730	11	.981
2000—Norfolk (Int'l)	OF-2B-3B																			
	SS	43	171	28	44	10	2	5	18	16	34	0	3	7-3	.257	.319	.427	.746	4	.973
—New York (N.L.)	OF-3B-2B																			
	SS	87	153	20	34	14	1	2	19	5	29	1	2	3-1	.222	.248	.366	.614	5	.957
2001—New York (N.L.)	OF-3B-SS																			
	2B-1B-DH	116	283	41	80	17	3	8	30	17	57	10	2	8-5	.283	.342	.449	.791	3	.981
2002—New York (N.L.)	OF-SS-1B																			
	2B-3B	105	196	22	39	8	1	3	26	9	50	3	0	4-4	.199	.242	.296	.538	7	.967
—Brook. N.Y.-Penn. (N.Y.-Penn.)	DH	1	4	0	1	0	0	0	1	0	0	0	0	0-0	.250	.250	.250	.500	...	...
—Binghamton (East.)	2B-3B	1	5	0	0	0	0	0	0	0	1	0	0	0-0	.000	.000	.000	.000	0	1.000
2003—Norfolk (Int'l)	OF-1B-2B																			
	3B	5	19	3	6	0	0	1	3	2	2	2	0	3-0	.316	.435	.474	.908	0	1.000
—New York (N.L.)	2B-SS-OF																			
	1B-3B	119	278	31	67	11	0	1	16	25	57	3	6	3-0	.241	.309	.291	.601	6	.984
2004—New York (N.L.)	2B-OF-SS																			
	1B-3B	75	138	17	35	3	1	1	16	9	32	0	1	4-1	.254	.297	.312	.609	3	.986
2005—Omaha (PCL)	3B-2B	5	18	4	3	1	0	0	1	4	2	0	1	0-0	.167	.318	.222	.540	1	.938
—Kansas City (A.L.)	3B-1B-2B																			
	SS-DH-OF	83	180	16	43	7	0	1	6	6	35	0	5	4-4	.239	.263	.294	.558	4	.984
2006—Round Rock (PCL)		112	422	64	133	21	1	10	46	23	65	3	5	16-7	.315	.351	.441	.792	13	.962
—Houston (N.L.)	2B	7	6	0	0	0	0	0	0	0	2	0	0	0-0	.000	.000	.000	.000	0	1.000
American League totals (1 year)		83	180	16	43	7	0	1	6	6	35	0	5	4-4	.239	.263	.294	.558	4	.984
National League totals (8 years)		671	1587	201	400	82	10	24	152	107	317	24	13	29-16	.252	.306	.362	.668	35	.979
Major League totals (9 years)		754	1767	217	443	89	10	25	158	113	352	24	18	33-20	.251	.302	.355	.657	39	.980

DIVISION SERIES RECORD

Year Team (League)	Pos.	G	AB	R	H	2B	3B	HR	RBI	BB	SO	HBP	GDP	SB-CS	Avg.	OBP	SLG	OPS	E	Avg.
2000—New York (N.L.)	3B-OF	4	1	0	1	0	0	0	0	0	0	0	0	0-0	1.000	1.000	1.000	2.000	0	...

CHAMPIONSHIP SERIES RECORD

Year Team (League)	Pos.	G	AB	R	H	2B	3B	HR	RBI	BB	SO	HBP	GDP	SB-CS	Avg.	OBP	SLG	OPS	E	Avg.
2000—New York (N.L.)	3B-OF	4	0	2	0	0	0	0	0	0	0	0	0	0-0	...	...	...	...	0	1.000

WORLD SERIES RECORD

Year Team (League)	Pos.	G	AB	R	H	2B	3B	HR	RBI	BB	SO	HBP	GDP	SB-CS	Avg.	OBP	SLG	OPS	E	Avg.
2000—New York (N.L.)	OF	3	1	1	0	0	0	0	0	0	0	0	0	0-0	.000	.000	.000	.000	0	1.000

2006 LEFTY-RIGHTY SPLITS

vs.	Avg.	AB	H	2B	3B	HR	RBI	BB	SO	OBP	Slg.	vs.	Avg.	AB	H	2B	3B	HR	RBI	BB	SO	OBP	Slg.
L	.000	1	0	0	0	0	0	0	0	.000	.000	R	.000	5	0	0	0	0	0	0	2	.000	.000

MCGOWAN, DUSTIN · P

PERSONAL: Born March 24, 1982, in Savannah, Ga. ... 6-3/220. ... Throws right, bats right. ... Full name: Dustin Michael McGowan. **TRANSACTIONS/CAREER NOTES:** Selected by Toronto Blue Jays organization in first round (33rd overall) of 2000 free-agent draft.
CAREER HITTING: 0-for-0 (.000), 0 R, 0 2B, 0 3B, 0 HR, 0 RBI.

Year Team (League)	W	L	Pct.	ERA	WHIP	G	GS	CG	ShO	Hld.	Sv.-Opp.	IP	H	R	ER	HR	BB-IBB	SO	Avg.
2000—Medicine Hat (Pio.)	0	3	.000	6.48	2.04	8	8	0	0	...	0-...	25.0	26	21	18	2	25-0	19	.274
2001—Auburn (NY-Penn)	3	6	.333	3.76	1.58	15	14	0	0	...	0-...	67.0	57	33	28	1	49-0	80	.234
2002—Char., W.Va. (SAL)	11	10	.524	4.19	1.36	28	28	1	0	...	0-...	148.1	143	77	69	10	59-0	163	.251
2003—Dunedin (Fla. St.)	5	6	.455	2.85	1.15	14	14	1	1	...	0-...	75.2	62	29	24	1	26-0	66	.223
—New Haven (East.)	7	0	1.000	3.17	1.27	14	14	1	0	...	0-...	76.2	78	28	27	1	19-0	72	.261
2004—New Hampshire (East.)	2	0	1.000	4.06	1.26	6	6	0	0	...	0-...	31.0	24	14	14	4	15-0	29	.209
2005—Dunedin (Fla. St.)	0	1	.000	4.29	1.24	5	5	0	0	0	0-0	21.0	21	12	10	2	5-0	20	.253
—New Hampshire (East.)	0	2	.000	3.34	1.29	6	6	0	0	0	0-0	35.0	35	16	13	6	15-0	33	.263
—Toronto (A.L.)	1	3	.250	6.35	1.46	13	7	0	0	1	0-0	45.1	49	34	32	7	17-0	34	.277
2006—Syracuse (Int'l)	4	5	.444	4.39	1.38	23	13	0	0	1	1-2	84.0	77	45	41	7	39-0	86	.238
—Toronto (A.L.)	1	2	.333	7.24	2.20	16	3	0	0	1	0-1	27.1	35	27	22	2	25-2	22	.304
Major League totals (2 years)	2	5	.286	6.69	1.73	29	10	0	0	2	0-1	72.2	84	61	54	9	42-2	56	.288

2006 LEFTY-RIGHTY SPLITS

vs.	Avg.	AB	H	2B	3B	HR	RBI	BB	SO	OBP	Slg.	vs.	Avg.	AB	H	2B	3B	HR	RBI	BB	SO	OBP	Slg.
L	.327	55	18	5	0	2	12	15	9	.472	.527	R	.283	60	17	3	0	0	12	10	13	.394	.333

MCLEARY, MARTY · P

PERSONAL: Born October 26, 1974, in Kettering, Ohio. ... 6-5/230. ... Throws right, bats right. ... Full name: Marty Lee McLeary. ... High school: Mansfield (Ohio) Christian. ... College: Mt. Vernon Nazarene (Ohio). **TRANSACTIONS/CAREER NOTES:** Selected by Boston Red Sox organization in 10th round of 1997 free-agent draft. ... Selected by Montreal Expos from Red Sox organization in Rule 5 major league draft (December 13, 1999). ... Returned to Red Sox organization (March 17, 2000). ... Released by Red Sox (April 15, 2003). ... Signed by Florida Marlins organization (April 29, 2003). ... Traded by Marlins to San Diego Padres for P Bryan Gaal (April 8, 2004). ... Signed as a free agent by Pittsburgh Pirates organization (November 27, 2005).
CAREER HITTING: 0-for-5 (.000), 0 R, 0 2B, 0 3B, 0 HR, 0 RBI.

Year Team (League)	W	L	Pct.	ERA	WHIP	G	GS	CG	ShO	Hld.	Sv.-Opp.	IP	H	R	ER	HR	BB-IBB	SO	Avg.
1997—Lowell (NY-Penn)	3	6	.333	3.75	1.43	13	13	0	0	...	0-...	62.1	53	38	26	2	36-1	43	.232

M

Year	Team (League)	W	L	Pct.	ERA	WHIP	G	GS	CG	ShO	Hld.	Sv.-Opp.	IP	H	R	ER	HR	BB-IBB	SO	Avg.
1998— Michigan (Midw.)		5	7	.417	4.16	1.51	37	7	0	0	...	0-...	88.2	99	58	41	4	35-2	54	.281
1999— Sarasota (Fla. St.)		1	0	1.000	12.08	2.84	8	0	0	0	...	0-...	12.2	29	20	17	1	7-0	11	.468
— Augusta (S. Atl.)		5	6	.455	3.12	1.21	35	9	0	0	...	3-...	80.2	73	34	28	8	25-1	90	.240
2000— Trenton (East.)		2	9	.182	4.56	1.73	43	8	0	0	...	5-...	96.2	114	66	49	5	53-3	53	.295
2001— Trenton (East.)		9	6	.600	3.46	1.61	35	0	0	0	...	2-...	54.2	58	30	21	2	30-5	42	.274
— Pawtucket (Int'l)		1	2	.333	3.00	1.43	18	0	0	0	...	0-...	30.0	28	13	10	4	15-1	20	.259
2002— Pawtucket (Int'l)		1	1	.500	7.32	1.88	18	1	0	0	...	0-...	35.2	44	30	29	6	23-0	19	.312
— Trenton (East.)		0	2	.000	4.86	1.68	11	0	0	0	...	0-...	16.2	20	12	9	0	8-2	10	.313
2003— Carolina (Southern)		1	1	.500	1.80	1.23	11	2	0	0	...	0-...	30.0	22	8	6	1	15-0	22	.208
— Albuquerque (PCL)		1	1	.500	4.32	1.74	20	1	0	0	...	0-...	33.1	40	22	16	3	18-1	17	.294
2004— Albuquerque (PCL)		0	1	.000	16.20	2.40	1	0	0	0	...	0-...	1.2	4	3	3	2	0-0	2	.500
— San Diego (N.L.)		0	0		14.73	2.45	3	0	0	0	0	0-0	3.2	7	6	6	2	2-0	4	.438
— Portland (PCL)		5	4	.556	2.99	1.27	44	7	0	0	...	13-...	84.1	65	30	28	4	42-1	81	.215
2005— Portland (Int'l)		5	8	.385	4.75	1.57	41	12	1	1	4	0-3	110.0	122	68	58	10	51-1	104	.280
2006— Indianapolis (Int'l)		3	4	.429	2.68	1.24	35	13	0	0	1	2-3	104.0	96	32	31	6	33-2	115	.242
— Pittsburgh (N.L.)		2	0	1.000	2.04	1.30	5	2	0	0	0	0-0	17.2	17	5	4	1	6-1	8	.258
Major League totals (2 years)		2	0	1.000	4.22	1.50	8	2	0	0	0	0-0	21.1	24	11	10	3	8-1	12	.293

2006 LEFTY-RIGHTY SPLITS

vs.	Avg.	AB	H	2B	3B	HR	RBI	BB	SO	OBP	Slg.	vs.	Avg.	AB	H	2B	3B	HR	RBI	BB	SO	OBP	Slg.
L	.167	30	5	0	0	1	1	3	2	.242	.267	R	.333	36	12	1	0	0	3	3	6	.375	.361

MCLOUTH, NATE — OF

PERSONAL: Born October 28, 1981, in Muskegon, Mich. ... 5-11/185. ... Bats left, throws right. ... Full name: Nathan Richard McLouth. **TRANSACTIONS/CAREER NOTES:** Selected by Pittsburgh Pirates organization in 25th round of 2000 free-agent draft. ... On disabled list (August 12, 2006-remainder of season).

2006 GAMES PLAYED BY POSITION (MLB): OF—75.

								BATTING										FIELDING	
Year	Team (League)	Pos.	G	AB	R	H	2B	3B	HR	RBI	BB	SO	HBP	GDP	SB-CS	Avg.	OBP	SLG	OPS	E	Avg.
2001— Hickory (S. Atl.)	OF-2B	96	351	59	100	17	5	12	54	43	54	7	5	21-5	.285	.371	.464	.835	5	.972
2002— Lynchburg (Caro.)	OF	114	393	58	96	23	4	9	46	41	48	8	12	20-7	.244	.324	.392	.716	5	.968
2003— Lynchburg (Caro.)	OF	117	440	85	132	27	2	6	33	55	68	7	4	40-4	.300	.386	.411	.797	5	.979
2004— Altoona (East.)	OF	133	515	93	166	40	4	8	73	48	62	8	8	31-7	.322	.384	.462	.846	7	.781
2005— Indianapolis (Int'l)	OF-DH	110	397	64	118	20	3	5	39	39	58	7	10	34-8	.297	.364	.401	.765	6	.986
— Pittsburgh (N.L.)	OF	41	109	20	28	6	0	5	12	3	20	5	3	2-0	.257	.305	.450	.755	2	.958
2006— Pittsburgh (N.L.)	OF	106	270	50	63	16	2	7	16	18	59	5	7	10-1	.233	.293	.385	.678	2	.982
Major League totals (2 years)		147	379	70	91	22	2	12	28	21	79	10	10	12-1	.240	.296	.404	.700	4	.975

2006 LEFTY-RIGHTY SPLITS

vs.	Avg.	AB	H	2B	3B	HR	RBI	BB	SO	OBP	Slg.	vs.	Avg.	AB	H	2B	3B	HR	RBI	BB	SO	OBP	Slg.
L	.260	50	13	2	1	3	6	1	8	.315	.520	R	.227	220	50	14	1	4	10	17	51	.288	.355

MCPHERSON, DALLAS — 3B

PERSONAL: Born July 23, 1980, in Greensboro, N.C. ... 6-4/230. ... Bats left, throws right. ... Full name: Dallas Lyle McPherson. ... High school: Randleman (N.C.). ... College: The Citadel. **TRANSACTIONS/CAREER NOTES:** Selected by Atlanta Braves organization in 44th round of 1998 free-agent draft; did not sign. ... Selected by Anaheim Angels organization in second round of 2001 free-agent draft. ... Angels franchise renamed Los Angeles Angels of Anaheim for 2005 season. ... On disabled list (July 9, 2005-remainder of season); included rehabilitation assignment to AZL Angels. ... On disabled list (June 24-September 1, 2006); included rehabilitation assignment to Salt Lake. **HONORS:** Named Minor League Player of the Year by THE SPORTING NEWS (2004).

2006 GAMES PLAYED BY POSITION (MLB): 3B—31, 1B—6, DH—2.

								BATTING										FIELDING	
Year	Team (League)	Pos.	G	AB	R	H	2B	3B	HR	RBI	BB	SO	HBP	GDP	SB-CS	Avg.	OBP	SLG	OPS	E	Avg.
2001— Provo (Pion.)	3B-1B	31	124	30	49	11	0	5	29	12	22	0	2	1-0	.395	.449	.605	1.053	11	.901
2002— Cedar Rap. (Midw.)	3B	132	499	71	138	24	3	15	88	78	128	7	9	30-6	.277	.381	.427	.807	31	.898
2003— Rancho Cuca. (Calif.)	3B	77	292	65	90	21	6	18	59	41	79	6	4	12-6	.308	.404	.606	1.010	14	.926
— Arkansas (Texas)	3B	28	102	22	32	9	1	5	27	19	25	1	4	4-0	.314	.426	.569	.995	2	.955
2004— Arkansas (Texas)	3B-DH	68	262	53	84	17	6	20	69	34	74	4	2	6-5	.321	.404	.660	1.056	12	.929
— Salt Lake (PCL) 3B-DH-OF	67	259	54	81	19	8	20	57	23	95	1	5	6-3	.313	.370	.680	1.047	17	.887
— Anaheim (A.L.)	3B	16	40	5	9	1	0	3	6	3	17	0	0	1-0	.225	.279	.475	.754	0	1.000
2005— Los Angeles (A.L.)	3B	61	205	29	50	14	2	8	26	14	64	1	5	3-3	.244	.295	.449	.744	7	.944
— Ariz. Angels (Ariz.)	3B	3	9	1	2	1	1	0	2	0	5	0	0	0-0	.222	.222	.556	.778	0	1.000
— Rancho Cuca. (Calif.)	3B-DH	5	16	3	7	2	0	2	5	3	4	1	0	1-1	.438	.550	.938	1.488	1	.857
— Salt Lake (PCL)	3B-DH	14	54	8	15	1	2	6	19	7	20	0	1	1-2	.278	.349	.704	1.053	2	.931
2006— Salt Lake (PCL)		56	208	35	52	11	5	17	45	15	88	4	0	3-1	.250	.307	.596	.904	7	.963
— Los Angeles (A.L.) 3B-1B-DH	40	115	16	30	4	0	7	13	6	40	0	3	1-0	.261	.298	.478	.776	3	.969
Major League totals (3 years)		117	360	50	89	19	2	18	45	23	121	1	8	5-3	.247	.294	.461	.755	10	.960

DIVISION SERIES RECORD

								BATTING										FIELDING	
Year	Team (League)	Pos.	G	AB	R	H	2B	3B	HR	RBI	BB	SO	HBP	GDP	SB-CS	Avg.	OBP	SLG	OPS	E	Avg.
2004— Anaheim (A.L.)	3B	3	9	0	1	0	0	0	0	0	4	0	0	0-0	.111	.111	.111	.222	0	1.000

2006 LEFTY-RIGHTY SPLITS

vs.	Avg.	AB	H	2B	3B	HR	RBI	BB	SO	OBP	Slg.	vs.	Avg.	AB	H	2B	3B	HR	RBI	BB	SO	OBP	Slg.
L	.231	13	3	0	0	2	2	1	6	.286	.692	R	.265	102	27	4	0	5	11	5	34	.299	.451

MEADOWS, BRIAN — P

PERSONAL: Born November 21, 1975, in Montgomery, Ala. ... 6-4/230. ... Throws right, bats right. ... Full name: Matthew Brian Meadows. ... High school: Charles Henderson (Troy, Ala.). **TRANSACTIONS/CAREER NOTES:** Selected by Florida Marlins organization in third round of 1994 free-agent draft; pick received as compensation for Colorado Rockies signing Type B free-agent SS Walt Weiss. ... On disabled list (July 28-August 13, 1998). ... Traded by Marlins to San Diego Padres for P Dan Miceli (November 15, 1999). ... Traded by Padres to Kansas City Royals for P Jay Witasick (July 31, 2000). ... Signed as a free agent by Minnesota Twins organization (January 15, 2002). ... Released by Twins (March 30, 2002). ... Signed by Pittsburgh Pirates organization (April 5, 2002). ... Signed as free agent by Tampa Bay Devil Rays (April 1, 2006). **CAREER HITTING:** 21-for-180 (.117), 12 R, 3 2B, 0 3B, 8 RBI.

Year	Team (League)	W	L	Pct.	ERA	WHIP	G	GS	CG	ShO	Hld.	Sv.-Opp.	IP	H	R	ER	HR	BB-IBB	SO	Avg.
1994— GC Marlins (GCL)		3	0	1.000	1.95	1.08	8	7	0	0	...	0-...	37.0	34	9	8	1	6-0	33	.236
1995— Kane Co. (Midw.)		9	9	.500	4.22	1.39	26	26	1	1	...	0-...	147.0	163	90	69	11	41-0	103	.281
1996— Brevard County (FSL)		8	7	.533	3.58	1.05	24	23	3	1	...	0-...	146.0	129	73	58	13	25-1	69	.231

- 317 -

Year	Team (League)	W	L	Pct.	ERA	WHIP	G	GS	CG	ShO	Hld.	Sv.-Opp.	IP	H	R	ER	HR	BB-IBB	SO	Avg.
—	Portland (East.)	0	1	.000	4.33	1.11	4	4	1	0	...	0-...	27.0	26	15	13	1	4-0	15	.263
1997—	Portland (East.)	9	7	.563	4.61	1.43	29	29	4	0	...	0-...	175.2	204	99	90	23	48-4	115	.292
1998—	Florida (N.L.)	11	13	.458	5.21	1.54	31	31	1	0	0	0-0	174.1	222	106	101	20	46-3	88	.315
1999—	Florida (N.L.)	11	15	.423	5.60	1.52	31	31	0	0	0	0-0	178.1	214	117	111	31	57-5	72	.302
2000—	San Diego (N.L.)	7	8	.467	5.34	1.60	22	22	0	0	0	0-0	124.2	150	80	74	24	50-6	53	.301
—	Kansas City (A.L.)	6	2	.750	4.77	1.37	11	10	2	0	0	0-0	71.2	84	39	38	8	14-0	26	.293
2001—	Kansas City (A.L.)	1	6	.143	6.97	1.69	10	10	0	0	0	0-0	50.1	73	41	39	12	12-2	21	.351
—	Omaha (PCL)	6	5	.545	6.17	1.55	18	18	0	0	0	0-...	105.0	143	73	72	21	20-1	74	.331
2002—	Nashville (PCL)	9	8	.529	4.27	1.25	23	22	1	1	...	0-...	126.1	132	69	60	15	26-1	98	.267
—	Pittsburgh (N.L.)	1	6	.143	3.88	1.21	11	11	0	0	0	0-0	62.2	62	29	27	7	14-8	31	.256
2003—	Nashville (PCL)	7	0	1.000	1.41	0.60	9	8	1	1	...	0-...	51.0	32	11	8	2	0-0	40	.178
—	Pittsburgh (N.L.)	2	1	.667	4.72	1.34	34	7	0	0	5	1-1	76.1	91	45	40	8	11-2	38	.290
2004—	Pittsburgh (N.L.)	2	4	.333	3.58	1.22	68	0	0	0	13	1-2	78.0	76	40	31	7	19-7	46	.259
2005—	Pittsburgh (N.L.)	3	1	.750	4.58	1.41	65	0	0	0	7	0-2	74.2	84	42	38	8	21-7	44	.287
2006—	Tampa Bay (A.L.)	3	6	.333	5.17	1.51	53	0	0	0	4	8-10	69.2	90	43	40	14	15-4	35	.313
American League totals (3 years)		10	14	.417	5.49	1.50	74	20	2	0	4	8-10	191.2	247	123	117	34	41-6	82	.315
National League totals (7 years)		37	48	.435	4.94	1.45	262	102	1	0	25	2-5	769.0	899	459	422	105	218-38	372	.294
Major League totals (9 years)		47	62	.431	5.05	1.46	336	122	3	0	29	10-15	960.2	1146	582	539	139	259-44	454	.299

2006 LEFTY-RIGHTY SPLITS

vs.	Avg.	AB	H	2B	3B	HR	RBI	BB	SO	OBP	Slg.	vs.	Avg.	AB	H	2B	3B	HR	RBI	BB	SO	OBP	Slg.
L	.254	130	33	7	2	6	22	10	22	.301	.477	R	.361	158	57	10	0	8	34	5	13	.373	.576

MECHE, GIL — P

PERSONAL: Born September 8, 1978, in Lafayette, La. ... 6-3/200. ... Throws right, bats right. ... Full name: Gilbert Allen Meche. ... Name pronounced: mesh. ... High school: Acadiana (Lafayette, La.). **TRANSACTIONS/CAREER NOTES:** Selected by Seattle Mariners organization in first round (22nd pick overall) of 1996 free-agent draft. ... On disabled list (May 29-June 13 and July 31, 2000-remainder of season); included rehabilitation assignments to Tacoma, Wisconsin and Everett. ... On disabled list (March 31, 2001-entire season; and August 20-September 16, 2005). **HONORS:** Named A.L. Comeback Player of the Year by THE SPORTING NEWS (2003).

CAREER HITTING: 2-for-13 (.154), 0 R, 0 2B, 0 3B, 0 HR, 1 RBI.

Year	Team (League)	W	L	Pct.	ERA	WHIP	G	GS	CG	ShO	Hld.	Sv.-Opp.	IP	H	R	ER	HR	BB-IBB	SO	Avg.
1996—	Ariz. Mariners (Ariz.)	0	1	.000	6.00	1.67	2	0	0	0	...	0-...	3.0	4	2	2	0	1-0	4	.333
1997—	Everett (N'west)	3	4	.429	3.98	1.33	12	12	1	0	...	0-...	74.2	75	40	33	7	24-0	62	.264
—	Wisconsin (Midw.)	0	2	.000	3.00	1.33	2	2	0	0	...	0-...	12.0	12	5	4	1	4-0	14	.261
1998—	Wisconsin (Midw.)	8	7	.533	3.44	1.34	26	0	0	0	...	0-...	149.0	136	77	57	9	63-0	168	.241
1999—	New Haven (East.)	3	4	.429	3.05	1.31	10	10	0	0	...	0-...	59.0	51	24	20	3	26-0	56	.231
—	Tacoma (PCL)	2	2	.500	3.19	1.42	6	6	0	0	...	0-...	31.0	31	12	11	3	13-0	24	.261
—	Seattle (A.L.)	8	4	.667	4.73	1.52	15	15	0	0	0	0-0	85.2	73	48	45	9	57-1	47	.240
2000—	Seattle (A.L.)	4	4	.500	3.78	1.34	15	15	1	1	0	0-0	85.2	75	37	36	7	40-0	60	.240
—	Tacoma (PCL)	1	1	.500	3.86	1.43	3	3	0	0	0	0-...	14.0	10	7	6	1	10-0	15	.200
—	Wisconsin (Midw.)	0	0	...	0.00	0.60	1	1	0	0	0	0-...	5.0	1	0	0	0	2-0	6	.067
—	Everett (N'west)	0	0	...	9.00	3.00	1	1	0	0	0	0-...	1.0	3	1	1	0	0-0	0	.600
2001—	Seattle (A.L.)			Did not play.																
2002—	San Antonio (Texas)	4	6	.400	6.51	1.54	25	13	0	0	...	0-...	65.0	68	49	47	8	32-0	56	.271
2003—	Seattle (A.L.)	15	13	.536	4.59	1.34	32	32	1	0	0	0-0	186.1	187	97	95	30	63-2	130	.263
2004—	Tacoma (PCL)	1	3	.250	5.05	1.44	10	10	0	0	0	0-...	57.0	55	37	32	8	27-1	45	.249
—	Seattle (A.L.)	7	7	.500	5.01	1.46	23	23	1	1	0	0-0	127.2	139	73	71	21	47-0	99	.273
2005—	Seattle (A.L.)	10	8	.556	5.09	1.57	29	26	0	0	0	0-0	143.1	153	92	81	18	72-1	83	.275
2006—	Seattle (A.L.)	11	8	.579	4.48	1.43	32	32	1	0	0	0-0	186.2	183	106	93	24	84-2	156	.256
Major League totals (6 years)		55	44	.556	4.65	1.44	147	143	4	2	0	0-0	815.1	810	453	421	109	363-6	575	.260

2006 LEFTY-RIGHTY SPLITS

vs.	Avg.	AB	H	2B	3B	HR	RBI	BB	SO	OBP	Slg.	vs.	Avg.	AB	H	2B	3B	HR	RBI	BB	SO	OBP	Slg.
L	.240	338	81	21	1	10	37	44	79	.334	.396	R	.271	376	102	21	3	14	49	40	77	.346	.455

MEDDERS, BRANDON — P

PERSONAL: Born January 26, 1980, in Tuscaloosa, Ala. ... 6-1/191. ... Throws right, bats right. ... Full name: Brandon Edward Medders. ... High school: Hillcrest (Ala.). ... College: Mississippi State. **TRANSACTIONS/CAREER NOTES:** Selected by Arizona Diamondbacks organization in eighth round of 2001 free-agent draft. ... On disabled list (April 1-19, 2006); included rehabilitation assignment to Tucson.

CAREER HITTING: 0-for-3 (.000), 0 R, 0 2B, 0 3B, 0 HR, 0 RBI.

Year	Team (League)	W	L	Pct.	ERA	WHIP	G	GS	CG	ShO	Hld.	Sv.-Opp.	IP	H	R	ER	HR	BB-IBB	SO	Avg.
2001—	Lancaster (Calif.)	1	2	.333	1.32	1.00	31	0	0	0	...	3-...	41.0	26	8	6	1	15-3	53	.182
2002—	Lancaster (Calif.)	4	8	.333	5.38	1.49	43	12	0	0	...	15-...	98.2	111	73	59	9	36-1	104	.282
2003—	El Paso (Texas)	5	3	.625	4.41	1.31	56	0	0	0	...	7-...	69.1	65	37	34	3	26-6	72	.244
2004—	Tucson (PCL)	0	0	...	4.26	1.50	11	0	0	0	...	0-...	12.2	15	7	6	3	4-1	17	.273
2005—	Tucson (PCL)	3	2	.600	2.48	1.35	36	0	0	0	1	8-10	36.1	31	11	10	3	18-3	44	.230
—	Arizona (N.L.)	4	1	.800	1.78	1.05	27	0	0	0	2	0-0	30.1	21	6	6	2	11-0	31	.194
2006—	Tucson (PCL)	0	1	.000	1.50	0.83	5	0	0	0	2	0-0	6.0	4	2	1	0	1-0	9	.200
—	Arizona (N.L.)	5	3	.625	3.64	1.45	60	0	0	0	10	0-1	71.2	76	37	29	5	28-3	47	.270
Major League totals (2 years)		9	4	.692	3.09	1.33	87	0	0	0	12	0-1	102.0	97	43	35	7	39-3	78	.249

2006 LEFTY-RIGHTY SPLITS

vs.	Avg.	AB	H	2B	3B	HR	RBI	BB	SO	OBP	Slg.	vs.	Avg.	AB	H	2B	3B	HR	RBI	BB	SO	OBP	Slg.
L	.348	138	48	12	1	2	23	14	10	.412	.493	R	.196	143	28	5	0	3	18	14	37	.269	.294

MELHUSE, ADAM — C

PERSONAL: Born March 27, 1972, in Santa Clara, Calif. ... 6-2/200. ... Bats both, throws right. ... Full name: Adam Michael Melhuse. ... High school: Lincoln (Stockton, Calif.). ... College: UCLA. **TRANSACTIONS/CAREER NOTES:** Selected by Toronto Blue Jays organization in 13th round of 1993 free-agent draft. ... Signed as a free agent by Los Angeles Dodgers organization (December 15, 1999). ... Traded by Dodgers to Colorado Rockies for cash (June 17, 2000). ... Signed as a free agent by Chicago Cubs organization (November 8, 2001). ... Released by Cubs (July 17, 2002). ... Signed by Rockies organization (July 18, 2002). ... Signed as a free agent by Oakland Athletics organization (November 6, 2002). **STATISTICAL NOTES:** Career major league grand slams: 2.

2006 GAMES PLAYED BY POSITION (MLB): C—24, DH—15, 3B—3, 1B—2.

Year	Team (League)	Pos.	G	AB	R	H	2B	3B	HR	RBI	BB	SO	HBP	GDP	SB-CS	Avg.	OBP	SLG	OPS	E	Avg.
						BATTING														FIELDING	
1993—	St. Catharines (NYP)	3B	73	266	40	68	14	2	5	32	45	61	0	4	4-0	.256	.360	.380	.740	14	.927

M

Year	Team (League)	Pos.	G	AB	R	H	2B	3B	HR	RBI	BB	SO	HBP	GDP	SB-CS	Avg.	OBP	SLG	OPS	E	Avg.
																BATTING				FIELDING	
1994— Hagerstown (SAL)		1B-C	118	422	61	109	16	3	11	58	53	77	1	13	6-8	.258	.338	.389	.727	13	.983
1995— Dunedin (Fla. St.)		1B-C-OF	123	428	43	92	20	0	4	41	61	87	1	7	6-1	.215	.312	.290	.601	13	.980
1996— Dunedin (Fla. St.)		1B-3B-C																			
		OF	97	315	50	78	23	2	13	51	69	68	3	5	3-1	.248	.384	.457	.841	15	.978
— Knoxville (Southern)		C	32	94	13	20	3	0	1	6	14	29	0	3	0-1	.213	.312	.277	.589	2	.989
1997— Knoxville (Southern)		1B-C-OF	31	87	14	20	3	0	3	10	19	19	0	1	0-0	.230	.364	.368	.732	2	.990
— Syracuse (Int'l)		2B-C-OF	118	118	7	28	5	1	2	9	12	18	1	2	1-1	.237	.311	.347	.658	2	.992
1998— Knoxville (Southern)		1B-C-OF	76	240	56	72	22	0	15	43	70	39	0	6	4-4	.300	.458	.579	1.037	11	.977
— Syracuse (Int'l)		3B-C	12	38	4	11	3	0	1	7	7	6	0	0	0-0	.289	.391	.447	.839	2	.965
1999— Knoxville (Southern)		1B-3B-C	107	374	79	110	25	0	19	69	108	76	4	10	5-6	.294	.454	.513	.967	4	.986
— Syracuse (Int'l)		C	21	71	15	20	5	0	2	16	10	20	0	1	1-1	.282	.370	.437	.807	0	1.000
2000— San Antonio (Texas)		C-OF-1B																			
		3B	16	58	17	23	7	0	2	9	11	9	2	2	3-0	.397	.500	.621	1.121	2	.973
— Albuquerque (PCL)		C-1B-3B																			
		OF	36	108	21	37	9	0	1	19	22	21	...	...	4-2	.343	...	.454	...	0	1.000
— Los Angeles (N.L.)			1	1	0	0	0	0	0	0	0	1	0	0	0-0	.000	.000	.000	.000	...	...
— Colorado (N.L.)		1B-C-OF	23	23	3	4	0	1	0	4	3	5	0	1	0-0	.174	.269	.261	.530	0	1.000
— Colo. Springs (PCL)		OF-C-1B	42	140	23	39	5	1	3	18	21	35	...	...	2-3	.279	...	.393	...	2	.987
2001— Colo. Springs (PCL)		C-1B-OF	54	184	26	49	10	1	7	32	31	42	2	8	0-1	.266	.378	.446	.824	5	.986
— Colorado (N.L.)		C-1B	40	71	5	13	2	0	1	8	6	18	0	3	1-0	.183	.241	.254	.494	1	.991
2002— Iowa (PCL)		C-3B-1B																			
		OF-SS	72	226	33	66	19	0	7	39	28	47	0	...	2-3	.292	.370	.469	.839	7	.983
— Colo. Springs (PCL)		C-1B	34	115	25	40	10	1	6	20	16	25	...	...	2-1	.348	.424	.609	1.033	4	.982
2003— Sacramento (PCL)		C-OF-3B																			
		DH	45	147	26	42	9	0	3	17	26	32	1	5	0-1	.286	.394	.408	.802	2	.992
— Oakland (A.L.)		C-3B-1B	40	77	13	23	7	0	5	14	9	19	0	2	0-1	.299	.372	.584	.957	2	.986
2004— Oakland (A.L.)		C-3B-1B	69	214	23	55	11	0	11	31	16	47	0	4	0-1	.257	.309	.463	.771	3	.992
2005— Oakland (A.L.)		C-DH	39	97	11	24	7	0	2	12	5	28	0	0	0-0	.247	.284	.381	.666	0	1.000
2006— Oakland (A.L.)		C-DH-3B																			
		1B	49	128	10	28	8	0	4	18	9	34	1	6	0-1	.219	.273	.375	.648	0	1.000
American League totals (4 years)			197	516	57	130	33	0	22	75	39	128	1	12	0-2	.252	.305	.444	.749	5	.994
National League totals (2 years)			64	95	8	17	2	1	1	12	9	24	0	4	1-0	.179	.245	.253	.498	1	.992
Major League totals (6 years)			261	611	65	147	35	1	23	87	48	152	1	16	1-2	.241	.296	.414	.710	6	.994

DIVISION SERIES RECORD

Year	Team (League)	Pos.	G	AB	R	H	2B	3B	HR	RBI	BB	SO	HBP	GDP	SB-CS	Avg.	OBP	SLG	OPS	E	Avg.
2003— Oakland (A.L.)		C	2	5	1	3	0	1	0	1	0	1	0	0	0-0	.600	.600	1.000	1.600	0	1.000

CHAMPIONSHIP SERIES RECORD

Year	Team (League)	Pos.	G	AB	R	H	2B	3B	HR	RBI	BB	SO	HBP	GDP	SB-CS	Avg.	OBP	SLG	OPS	E	Avg.
2006— Oakland (A.L.)			1	1	0	0	0	0	0	0	0	1	0	0	0-0	.000	.000	.000	.000	...	...

2006 LEFTY-RIGHTY SPLITS

vs.	Avg.	AB	H	2B	3B	HR	RBI	BB	SO	OBP	Slg.	vs.	Avg.	AB	H	2B	3B	HR	RBI	BB	SO	OBP	Slg.
L	.222	18	4	0	0	1	3	1	4	.250	.389	R	.218	110	24	8	0	3	15	8	30	.277	.373

MENCH, KEVIN — OF

PERSONAL: Born January 7, 1978, in Wilmington, Del. ... 6-0/225. ... Bats right, throws right. ... Full name: Kevin Ford Mench. ... High school: St. Mark's (Wilmington, Del.). ... College: Delaware. **TRANSACTIONS/CAREER NOTES:** Selected by Texas Rangers organization in fourth round of 1999 free-agent draft; pick received as part of compensation for Arizona Diamondbacks signing Type A free-agent P Todd Stottlemyre. ... On disabled list (March 21-April 17 and July 9, 2003-remainder of season); included rehabilitation assignment to Frisco. ... On disabled list (May 24-June 12, 2004); included rehabilitation assignment to Frisco. ... Traded by Rangers with OF Laynce Nix and Ps Francisco Cordero and Julian Cordero to Milwaukee Brewers for OFs Carlos Lee and Nelson Cruz (July 28, 2006). **STATISTICAL NOTES:** Hit three home runs in one game (June 30, 2005). ... Career major league grand slams: 3.

2006 GAMES PLAYED BY POSITION (MLB): OF—110, DH—15.

Year	Team (League)	Pos.	G	AB	R	H	2B	3B	HR	RBI	BB	SO	HBP	GDP	SB-CS	Avg.	OBP	SLG	OPS	E	Avg.
																BATTING				FIELDING	
1999— Pulaski (Appalachian)		OF	65	260	36	94	22	1	16	60	28	48	2	2	12-2	.362	.420	.638	1.059	1	.989
— Savannah (S. Atl.)		OF	6	23	4	7	1	1	2	8	2	4	0	1	0-0	.304	.360	.696	1.056	2	.900
2000— Charlotte (Fla. St.)		OF	132	491	118	164	39	9	27	121	78	72	7	9	19-7	.334	.427	.615	1.042	1	.996
2001— Tulsa (Texas)		OF	120	475	78	126	34	2	26	83	34	76	6	7	4-6	.265	.319	.509	.828	4	.983
2002— Oklahoma (PCL)		OF	26	98	17	21	8	0	6	15	17	33	2	7	0-0	.214	.342	.480	.821	2	.965
— Texas (A.L.)		OF-DH	110	366	52	95	20	2	15	60	31	83	8	4	1-1	.260	.327	.448	.775	2	.990
2003— Frisco (Texas)		OF	3	11	1	1	0	0	0	0	1	2	0	1	0-0	.091	.167	.091	.258	0	1.000
— Oklahoma (PCL)		OF	29	105	16	28	8	0	7	21	19	15	1	1	2-0	.267	.366	.457	.824	0	1.000
— Texas (A.L.)		OF	38	125	15	40	12	0	2	11	10	17	3	2	1-1	.320	.381	.464	.845	1	.984
2004— Frisco (Texas)		DH-OF	4	16	3	5	0	0	1	1	1	0	0	0	0-0	.313	.353	.500	.853	0	1.000
— Texas (A.L.)		OF-DH	125	438	69	122	30	3	26	71	33	63	6	6	0-0	.279	.335	.539	.874	1	.995
2005— Texas (A.L.)		OF-DH	150	557	71	147	33	3	25	73	50	68	5	6	4-3	.264	.328	.469	.797	4	.987
2006— Texas (A.L.)		OF-DH	87	320	36	91	18	1	12	50	23	42	4	4	1-0	.284	.338	.459	.797	1	.992
— Milwaukee (N.L.)		OF	40	126	9	29	6	1	1	18	4	17	0	4	0-0	.230	.248	.317	.566	1	.985
American League totals (5 years)			510	1806	243	495	113	9	80	265	147	273	26	22	7-5	.274	.335	.480	.815	9	.990
National League totals (1 year)			40	126	9	29	6	1	1	18	4	17	0	4	0-0	.230	.248	.317	.566	1	.985
Major League totals (5 years)			550	1932	252	524	119	10	81	283	151	290	26	26	7-5	.271	.330	.469	.799	10	.990

2006 LEFTY-RIGHTY SPLITS

vs.	Avg.	AB	H	2B	3B	HR	RBI	BB	SO	OBP	Slg.	vs.	Avg.	AB	H	2B	3B	HR	RBI	BB	SO	OBP	Slg.
L	.303	119	36	8	1	4		5	20	11	5	.364	.513	R	.257	327	84	16	1	8	48	16	54	.294	.385

MERCKER, KENT — P

PERSONAL: Born February 1, 1968, in Indianapolis. ... 6-2/205. ... Throws left, bats left. ... Full name: Kent Franklin Mercker. ... High school: Dublin (Ohio). **TRANSACTIONS/CAREER NOTES:** Selected by Atlanta Braves organization in first round (fifth pick overall) of June 1986 free-agent draft. ... On disabled list (August 9-24, 1991). ... Traded by Braves to Baltimore Orioles for Ps Joe Borowski and Rachaad Stewart (December 17, 1995). ... Traded by Orioles to Cleveland Indians for 1B Eddie Murray (July 21, 1996). ... Signed as a free agent by Cincinnati Reds (December 10, 1996). ... On disabled list (August 17-September 2, 1997). ... Signed as a free agent by St. Louis Cardinals (December 16, 1997). ... On disabled list (June 14-July 1, 1998). ... Traded by Cardinals to Boston Red Sox for P Mike Matthews and C David Benham (August 24,

1999). ... On disabled list (September 7-23, 1999). ... Signed as a free agent by Anaheim Angels organization (January 26, 2000). ... On disabled list (May 12-August 12, 2000); included rehabilitation assignment to Lake Elsinore. ... Signed as a free agent by Red Sox organization (January 5, 2001). ... Released by Red Sox (March 29, 2001). ... Signed by Colorado Rockies organization (January 31, 2002). ... On disabled list (June 6-July 30, 2002); included rehabilitation assignment to Colorado Springs. ... On suspended list (September 20-23, 2002). ... Signed as a free agent by Reds organization (January 7, 2003). ... On disabled list (June 25-July 10, 2003). ... Traded by Reds to Braves for a player to be named (August 12, 2003); Reds acquired P Matt Belisle to complete deal (August 14, 2003). ... Signed as a free agent by Chicago Cubs (December 19, 2003). ... On disabled list (May 16-June 4, 2004). ... On suspended list (September 13-15, 2004). ... Signed as a free agent by Reds (December 20, 2004). ... On disabled list (May 11-26; July 23-August 7, 2006 and August 12, 2006-remainder of season) **STATISTICAL NOTES:** Pitched six innings, combining with Mark Wohlers (two innings) and Alejandro Pena (one inning) in 1-0 no-hit victory against San Diego (September 11, 1991). ... Pitched 6-0 no-hit victory against Los Angeles (April 8, 1994). **MISCELLANEOUS NOTES:** Had a sacrifice hit and received a base on balls in two games as pinch hitter (1991). ... Appeared in one game as pinch hitter (1997). ... Appeared in one game as pinch runner (1998). ... Scored a run in only appearance as pinch runner with Cardinals (1999).

CAREER HITTING: 28-for-248 (.113), 12 R, 5 2B, 2 3B, 1 HR, 18 RBI.

Year — Team (League)	W	L	Pct.	ERA	WHIP	G	GS	CG	ShO	Hld.	Sv.-Opp.	IP	H	R	ER	HR	BB-IBB	SO	Avg.
1986—GC Braves (GCL)	4	3	.571	2.47	1.12	9	8	0	0	...	0-...	47.1	37	21	13	1	16-1	42	.200
1987—Durham (Carol.)	0	1	.000	5.40	1.46	3	3	0	0	...	0-...	11.2	11	8	7	1	6-0	14	.256
1988—Durham (Carol.)	11	4	.733	2.75	1.17	19	19	5	0	...	0-...	127.2	102	44	39	5	47-0	159	.214
—Greenville (Sou.)	3	1	.750	3.35	1.28	9	9	0	0	...	0-...	48.1	36	20	18	2	26-1	60	.201
1989—Richmond (Int'l)	9	12	.429	3.20	1.20	27	27	4	0	...	0-...	168.2	107	66	60	17	95-4	144	.183
—Atlanta (N.L.)	0	0	...	12.46	3.23	2	1	0	0	0	0-0	4.1	8	6	6	0	6-0	4	.400
1990—Richmond (Int'l)	5	4	.556	3.55	1.49	12	10	0	0	...	1-...	58.1	60	30	23	1	27-1	69	.260
—Atlanta (N.L.)	4	7	.364	3.17	1.39	36	0	0	0	...	7-10	48.1	43	22	17	6	24-3	39	.236
1991—Atlanta (N.L.)	5	3	.625	2.58	1.24	50	4	0	0	3	6-8	73.1	56	23	21	5	35-3	62	.211
1992—Atlanta (N.L.)	3	2	.600	3.42	1.26	53	0	0	0	6	6-9	68.1	51	27	26	4	35-1	49	.207
1993—Atlanta (N.L.)	3	1	.750	2.86	1.33	43	6	0	0	4	0-3	66.0	52	24	21	2	36-3	59	.214
1994—Atlanta (N.L.)	9	4	.692	3.45	1.20	20	17	2	1	0	0-0	112.1	90	46	43	16	45-3	111	.220
1995—Atlanta (N.L.)	7	8	.467	4.15	1.41	29	26	0	0	0	0-0	143.0	140	73	66	16	61-2	102	.258
1996—Baltimore (A.L.)	3	6	.333	7.76	1.86	14	12	0	0	0	0-0	58.0	73	56	50	12	35-1	22	.307
—Buffalo (A.A.)	0	2	.000	3.94	1.25	3	3	0	0	...	0-...	16.0	11	7	7	3	9-0	11	.193
—Cleveland (A.L.)	1	0	1.000	3.09	1.11	10	0	0	0	2	0-0	11.2	10	4	4	1	3-1	7	.244
1997—Cincinnati (N.L.)	8	11	.421	3.92	1.36	28	25	0	0	0	0-0	144.2	135	65	63	16	62-6	75	.250
1998—St. Louis (N.L.)	11	11	.500	5.07	1.56	30	29	0	0	0	0-0	161.2	199	99	91	11	53-4	72	.310
1999—St. Louis (N.L.)	6	5	.545	5.12	1.70	25	18	0	0	0	0-0	103.2	125	73	59	16	51-3	64	.303
—Boston (A.L.)	2	0	1.000	3.51	1.40	5	5	0	0	0	0-0	25.2	23	12	10	0	13-0	17	.235
2000—Anaheim (A.L.)	1	3	.250	6.52	1.78	21	7	0	0	1	0-0	48.1	57	35	35	12	29-3	30	.300
—Lake Elsinore (Calif.)	0	0	...	0.00	0.00	1	1	0	0	...	0-...	4.0	0	0	0	0	0-0	3	.000
2001—				Did not play.															
2002—Colorado (N.L.)	3	1	.750	6.14	1.75	58	0	0	0	9	0-3	44.0	55	33	30	12	22-2	37	.299
—Colo. Springs (PCL)	0	0	...	21.60	3.00	2	0	0	0	...	0-...	1.2	3	4	4	2	2-0	0	.429
2003—Cincinnati (N.L.)	0	2	.000	2.35	1.46	49	0	0	0	10	0-3	38.1	31	13	10	5	25-2	41	.225
—Atlanta (N.L.)	0	0	...	1.06	1.29	18	0	0	0	1	1-2	17.0	15	3	2	1	7-2	7	.231
2004—Chicago (N.L.)	3	1	.750	2.55	1.25	71	0	0	0	16	0-3	53.0	39	15	15	4	22-7	51	.205
2005—Cincinnati (N.L.)	3	1	.750	3.65	1.35	78	0	0	0	20	4-7	61.2	64	27	25	8	19-4	45	.270
2006—Cincinnati (N.L.)	1	1	.500	4.13	1.38	37	0	0	0	6	1-3	28.1	28	15	13	6	11-1	17	.259
American League totals (3 years)	7	9	.438	6.20	1.69	50	24	0	0	3	0-0	143.2	163	107	99	25	80-5	76	.287
National League totals (15 years)	66	58	.532	3.91	1.41	627	126	2	1	75	25-51	1168.0	1131	564	508	128	519-41	835	.256
Major League totals (17 years)	73	67	.521	4.16	1.44	677	150	2	1	78	25-51	1311.2	1294	671	607	153	599-46	911	.259

DIVISION SERIES RECORD

Year — Team (League)	W	L	Pct.	ERA	WHIP	G	GS	CG	ShO	Hld.	Sv.-Opp.	IP	H	R	ER	HR	BB-IBB	SO	Avg.
1995—Atlanta (N.L.)	0	0	...	0.00	0.00	1	0	0	0	0	0-0	0.1	0	0	0	0	0-0	0	.000
1999—Boston (A.L.)	0	0	...	10.80	3.60	1	1	0	0	0	0-0	1.2	3	2	2	0	3-0	1	.500
2003—Atlanta (N.L.)	0	0	...	0.00	1.00	1	0	0	0	0	0-0	1.0	0	0	0	0	1-0	1	.000
Division series totals (3 years)	0	0	...	6.00	2.33	3	1	0	0	0	0-0	3.0	3	2	2	0	4-0	2	.333

CHAMPIONSHIP SERIES RECORD

Year — Team (League)	W	L	Pct.	ERA	WHIP	G	GS	CG	ShO	Hld.	Sv.-Opp.	IP	H	R	ER	HR	BB-IBB	SO	Avg.
1991—Atlanta (N.L.)	0	1	.000	13.50	3.00	1	0	0	0	0	0-0	0.2	0	1	1	0	2-0	0	.000
1992—Atlanta (N.L.)	0	0	...	0.00	0.67	2	0	0	0	0	0-0	3.0	1	0	0	0	1-0	1	.100
1993—Atlanta (N.L.)	0	0	...	1.80	1.00	5	0	0	0	0	0-0	5.0	3	1	1	0	2-0	4	.176
1999—Boston (A.L.)	0	1	.000	4.70	2.09	2	2	0	0	0	0-0	7.2	12	4	4	2	4-0	5	.353
Champ. series totals (4 years)	0	2	.000	3.31	1.53	10	2	0	0	0	0-0	16.1	16	6	6	2	9-0	10	.254

WORLD SERIES RECORD

Year — Team (League)	W	L	Pct.	ERA	WHIP	G	GS	CG	ShO	Hld.	Sv.-Opp.	IP	H	R	ER	HR	BB-IBB	SO	Avg.
1991—Atlanta (N.L.)	0	0	...	0.00	0.00	2	0	0	0	1	0-0	1.0	0	0	0	0	0-0	1	.000
1995—Atlanta (N.L.)	0	0	...	4.50	1.50	1	0	0	0	0	0-0	2.0	1	1	1	0	2-0	2	.143
World series totals (2 years)	0	0	...	3.00	1.00	3	0	0	0	1	0-0	3.0	1	1	1	0	2-0	3	.100

2006 LEFTY-RIGHTY SPLITS

vs.	Avg.	AB	H	2B	3B	HR	RBI	BB	SO	OBP	Slg.	vs.	Avg.	AB	H	2B	3B	HR	RBI	BB	SO	OBP	Slg.
L	.260	50	13	4	0	5	9	5	9	.327	.640	R	.259	58	15	3	0	1	9	6	8	.323	.362

MEREDITH, CLA   P

PERSONAL: Born June 4, 1983, in Richmond, Va. ... 6-0/180. ... Throws right, bats right. ... Full name: Olise C. Meredith. ... College: Virginia Commonwealth. **TRANSACTIONS/CAREER NOTES:** Selected by Boston Red Sox organization in sixth round of 2004 free-agent draft. ... Traded by Red Sox with C Josh Bard and cash to San Diego Padres for C Doug Mirabelli (May 1, 2006).

CAREER HITTING: 0-for-0 (.000), 0 R, 0 2B, 0 3B, 0 HR, 0 RBI.

Year — Team (League)	W	L	Pct.	ERA	WHIP	G	GS	CG	ShO	Hld.	Sv.-Opp.	IP	H	R	ER	HR	BB-IBB	SO	Avg.
2004—Augusta (S. Atl.)	1	0	1.000	0.00	0.72	13	0	0	0	...	6-...	15.1	8	0	0	0	3-0	18	.148
—Sarasota (Fla. St.)	0	2	.000	2.20	1.10	16	0	0	0	...	12-...	16.1	15	4	4	0	3-0	16	.234
2005—Portland (East.)	1	0	1.000	0.00	0.53	12	0	0	0	...	9-9	15.0	5	0	0	0	3-1	12	.106
—Boston (A.L.)	0	0	...	27.00	4.29	3	0	0	0	0	0-0	2.1	6	7	7	1	4-0	0	.462
—Wilmington (Caro.)	0	0	...	0.00	1.00	1	0	0	0	0	0-0	1.0	1	0	0	0	0-0	2	.250
—Pawtucket (Int'l)	2	5	.286	5.59	1.55	40	0	0	0	2	10-20	48.1	63	30	30	6	12-2	42	.312
2006—Pawtucket (Int'l)	0	0	...	5.27	1.54	20	0	0	0	0	0-0	13.2	16	9	8	1	5-0	14	.302
—Portland (PCL)	3	0	1.000	1.39	0.93	24	0	0	0	3	2-5	32.1	26	5	5	2	4-1	25	.222
—San Diego (N.L.)	5	1	.833	1.07	0.71	45	0	0	0	16	0-2	50.2	30	6	6	3	6-3	37	.170
American League totals (1 year)	0	0	...	27.00	4.29	3	0	0	0	0	0-0	2.1	6	7	7	1	4-0	0	.462
National League totals (1 year)	5	1	.833	1.07	0.71	45	0	0	0	16	0-2	50.2	30	6	6	3	6-3	37	.170
Major League totals (2 years)	5	1	.833	2.21	0.87	48	0	0	0	16	0-2	53.0	36	13	13	4	10-3	37	.190

M

DIVISION SERIES RECORD

Year Team (League)	W	L	Pct.	ERA	WHIP	G	GS	CG	ShO	Hld.	Sv.-Opp.	IP	H	R	ER	HR	BB-IBB	SO	Avg.
2006— San Diego (N.L.)	0	0	...	0.00	0.82	2	0	0	0	0	0-0	3.2	3	2	0	0	0-0	3	.231

2006 LEFTY-RIGHTY SPLITS

vs.	Avg.	AB	H	2B	3B	HR	RBI	BB	SO	OBP	Slg.	vs.	Avg.	AB	H	2B	3B	HR	RBI	BB	SO	OBP	Slg.
L	.281	64	18	1	1	1	6	4	8	.333	.375	R	.107	112	12	1	0	2	9	2	29	.130	.170

MERLONI, LOU — IF

PERSONAL: Born April 6, 1971, in Framingham, Mass. ... 5-10/200. ... Bats right, throws right. ... Full name: Louis William Merloni. ... Name pronounced: mer-LONE-ee. ... High school: Framingham (Mass.) South. ... College: Providence. **TRANSACTIONS/CAREER NOTES:** Selected by Boston Red Sox organization in 10th round of 1993 free-agent draft. ... On disabled list (June 29-September 12, 1998); included rehabilitation assignment to GCL Red Sox. ... Contract sold by Red Sox to Yokohama of the Japan Central League (November 22, 1999). ... Signed as a free agent by Red Sox organization (July 28, 2000). ... On disabled list (June 6-21, 2001); included rehabilitation assignment to Pawtucket. ... Claimed on waivers by San Diego Padres (March 25, 2003). ... On disabled list (June 9-July 4, 2003); included rehabilitation assignment to Lake Elsinore. ... Traded by Padres to Red Sox for P Rene Miniel (August 28, 2003). ... Signed as a free agent by Cleveland Indians organization (January 12, 2004). ... On disabled list (August 9-September 1, 2004); included rehabilitation assignment to Mahoning Valley. ... Signed as a free agent by Los Angeles Angels of Anaheim organization (January 21, 2005). ... On disabled list (May 2, 2005-remainder of season); included rehabilitation assignments to Salt Lake and AZL Angels. ... Signed as a free agent by Indians organization (December 9, 2005).

2006 GAMES PLAYED BY POSITION (MLB): 2B—3, 3B—3, SS—3.

Year Team (League)	Pos.	G	AB	R	H	2B	3B	HR	RBI	BB	SO	HBP	GDP	SB-CS	Avg.	OBP	SLG	OPS	E	Avg.
1993— GC Red Sox (GCL)	SS	4	14	4	5	1	0	0	1	1	1	1	0	1-1	.357	.438	.429	.866	1	.952
— Fort Laud. (FSL)	3B-SS	44	156	14	38	1	1	2	21	13	26	1	6	1-1	.244	.299	.301	.600	8	.951
1994— Sarasota (Fla. St.)	2B-3B-SS	113	419	59	120	16	2	1	63	36	57	7	11	5-2	.286	.345	.341	.687	18	.965
1995— Trenton (East.)	2B-3B-SS	93	318	42	88	16	1	1	30	39	50	11	1	7-7	.277	.373	.343	.716	20	.951
1996— Trenton (East.)	1B-2B-3B-																			
	SS	28	95	11	22	6	1	3	16	9	18	5	2	0-2	.232	.330	.411	.741	8	.930
— GC Red Sox (GCL)	2B	1	4	1	1	0	0	0	1	0	0	0	0	0-0	.250	.250	.250	.450	0	1.000
— Pawtucket (Int'l)	2B-3B-SS	38	115	19	29	6	0	1	12	10	20	3	1	0-1	.252	.328	.330	.659	8	.945
1997— Trenton (East.)	2B-3B-SS	69	255	49	79	17	4	5	37	30	43	12	2	3-2	.310	.402	.467	.869	9	.957
— Pawtucket (Int'l)	2B-3B-SS	49	165	24	49	10	0	5	24	15	20	4	4	0-2	.297	.368	.448	.816	4	.979
1998— Pawtucket (Int'l)	2B-3B-SS	27	88	17	34	3	1	8	22	16	13	8	2	2-2	.386	.518	.716	1.234	2	.976
— Boston (A.L.)	2B-3B-SS	39	96	10	27	6	0	1	15	7	20	2	1	1-0	.281	.343	.375	.718	5	.962
— GC Red Sox (GCL)	2B	1	1	0	0	0	0	0	0	0	0	0	0	0-0	.000	.000	.000	.000	0	...
1999— Boston (A.L.)	DH-1B-OF	43	126	18	32	7	0	1	13	8	16	2	6	0-0	.254	.307	.333	.640	10	.940
— Pawtucket (Int'l)	SS-3B-DH																			
	1B-2B	66	229	45	64	14	1	7	36	30	38	9	4	1-1	.279	.383	.441	.824	12	.945
2000— Yo. Bay. (Jp. Cn.)	SS-1B-2B	42	94	10	20	4	0	1	3	7	15	...	•	0-...	.213	...	.287	...	...	...
— Pawtucket (Int'l)	3B	11	39	6	16	2	0	1	5	3	3	0	2	0-1	.410	.452	.538	.991	4	.897
— Boston (A.L.)	3B	40	128	10	41	11	2	0	18	4	12	1	8	1-0	.320	.341	.438	.778	7	.928
2001— Pawtucket (Int'l)	SS-2B-1B	52	195	30	51	12	0	4	20	15	37	5	6	2-0	.262	.330	.385	.715	10	.954
— Boston (A.L.)	1B	52	146	21	39	10	0	3	13	6	31	3	6	2-1	.267	.306	.397	.703	3	.983
2002— Boston (A.L.)	2B-3B-SS	84	194	28	48	12	2	4	18	20	35	5	4	1-2	.247	.332	.392	.724	5	.982
	1B-OF																			
— Pawtucket (Int'l)	3B-SS-OF	8	25	1	5	2	0	0	2	1	3	1	2	0-0	.200	.250	.280	.530	0	1.000
2003— Lake Elsinore (Calif.) ...	3B-SS-2B	5	19	3	9	3	0	1	7	1	0	0	0	0-0	.474	.476	.789	1.266	0	1.000
— San Diego (N.L.)	3B-SS																			
	1B-OF	65	151	20	41	7	2	1	17	22	33	1	3	2-3	.272	.362	.364	.726	6	.962
— Boston (A.L.)	2B-3B-OF	15	30	4	7	1	0	0	1	4	8	0	0	0-0	.233	.324	.267	.590	0	1.000
2004— Mahoning Valley (N.Y.-Penn.)	DH	2	8	1	2	1	0	0	1	4	0	3	0	0-0	.250	.250	.625	.875	0	...
— Cleveland (A.L.)	1B-3B-2B																			
	OF-DH	71	190	25	55	12	1	4	28	14	41	3	9	1-2	.289	.343	.426	.769	4	.989
2005— Los Angeles (A.L.)	3B-1B	5	5	1	0	0	0	0	1	1	2	0	0	0-0	.000	.143	.000	.143	0	1.000
— Ariz. Angels (Ariz.)	3B-DH	6	15	3	5	1	0	0	2	2	2	0	0	0-0	.333	.412	.400	.812	0	1.000
— Salt Lake (PCL)	3B-DH-2B	6	25	6	8	3	0	0	6	2	5	1	1	0-0	.320	.393	.440	.833	0	1.000
2006— Buffalo (Int'l)		91	330	33	94	22	0	7	38	29	49	11	9	0-2	.285	.361	.415	.776	9	.982
— Cleveland (A.L.)	2B-3B-SS	9	19	1	4	1	0	0	1	2	5	0	1	1-0	.211	.286	.263	.549	0	1.000
American League totals (9 years)		358	934	118	253	60	5	13	108	66	180	16	35	7-5	.271	.327	.388	.714	34	.973
National League totals (1 year)		65	151	20	41	7	2	1	17	22	33	1	3	2-3	.272	.362	.364	.726	6	.962
Major League totals (9 years)		423	1085	138	294	67	7	14	125	88	213	17	38	9-8	.271	.332	.384	.716	40	.972

DIVISION SERIES RECORD

Year Team (League)	Pos.	G	AB	R	H	2B	3B	HR	RBI	BB	SO	HBP	GDP	SB-CS	Avg.	OBP	SLG	OPS	E	Avg.
1999— Boston (A.L.)	SS	3	6	1	2	0	0	1	1	1	0	0	0	0-0	.333	.429	.333	.762	1	.833

CHAMPIONSHIP SERIES RECORD

Year Team (League)	Pos.	G	AB	R	H	2B	3B	HR	RBI	BB	SO	HBP	GDP	SB-CS	Avg.	OBP	SLG	OPS	E	Avg.
1999— Boston (A.L.)		1	0	0	0	0	0	0	0	0	1	0	0	0-0	1.000		1.000			

2006 LEFTY-RIGHTY SPLITS

vs.	Avg.	AB	H	2B	3B	HR	RBI	BB	SO	OBP	Slg.	vs.	Avg.	AB	H	2B	3B	HR	RBI	BB	SO	OBP	Slg.
L	.222	9	2	0	0	0	0	1	2	.300	.222	R	.200	10	2	1	0	0	1	1	3	.273	.300

MESA, JOSE — P

PERSONAL: Born May 22, 1966, in Azua, Dominican Republic. ... 6-3/232. ... Throws right, bats right. ... Full name: Jose Ramon Mesa. ... Name pronounced: MAY-sa. ... High school: Santa School (Azua, Dominican Republic). **TRANSACTIONS/CAREER NOTES:** Signed as a non-drafted free agent by Toronto Blue Jays organization (October 31, 1981). ... Traded by Blue Jays to Baltimore Orioles (September 4, 1987), completing deal in which Orioles traded P Mike Flanagan to Blue Jays for P Oswald Peraza and a player to be named (August 31, 1987). ... Traded by Orioles to Cleveland Indians for OF Kyle Washington (July 14, 1992). ... On suspended list (April 5-8, 1993). ... Traded by Indians with IF Shawon Dunston and P Alvin Morman to San Francisco Giants for P Steve Reed and OF Jacob Cruz (July 23, 1998). ... Signed as a free agent by Seattle Mariners (November 13, 1998). ... Signed as a free agent by Philadelphia Phillies (November 17, 2000). ... On suspended list (August 28-30, 2001). ... Signed as a free agent by Pittsburgh Pirates organization (January 29, 2004). ... Signed as a free agent by Colorado Rockies (December 8, 2005). ... On suspended list (June 14-17, 2006). **HONORS:** Named A.L. Fireman of the Year by THE SPORTING NEWS (1995). **MISCELLANEOUS NOTES:** Appeared in one game as pinch runner for Baltimore (1991). **CAREER HITTING:** 0-for-2 (.000), 1 R, 0 2B, 0 3B, 0 HR, 0 RBI.

M

Year	Team (League)	W	L	Pct.	ERA	WHIP	G	GS	CG	ShO	Hld.	Sv.-Opp.	IP	H	R	ER	HR	BB-IBB	SO	Avg.
1982	GC Jays (GCL)	6	4	.600	2.70	0.94	13	12	6	3	...	1-...	83.1	58	34	25	1	20-0	40	...
1983	Florence (S. Atl.)	6	12	.333	5.48	1.74	28	27	1	0	...	0-...	141.1	153	116	86	14	93-0	91	...
1984	Florence (S. Atl.)	4	3	.571	3.76	1.64	7	7	0	0	...	0-...	38.1	38	24	16	3	25-0	35	.255
—	Kinston (Carol.)	5	2	.714	3.91	1.56	10	9	0	0	...	0-...	50.2	51	23	22	2	28-0	24	.267
1985	Kinston (Carol.)	5	10	.333	6.16	1.77	30	20	0	0	...	1-...	106.2	110	89	73	11	79-2	71	.269
1986	Vent. Co. (Calif.)	10	6	.625	3.86	1.40	24	24	2	1	...	0-...	142.1	141	71	61	6	58-0	113	.256
—	Knoxville (Southern)	2	2	.500	4.35	1.52	9	8	2	1	...	0-...	41.1	40	32	20	6	23-0	30	.242
1987	Knoxville (Southern)	10	13	.435	5.21	1.60	35	35	4	2	...	0-...	193.1	206	131	112	19	104-0	115	.273
—	Baltimore (A.L.)	1	3	.250	6.03	1.69	6	5	0	0	1	0-0	31.1	38	23	21	7	15-0	17	.297
1988	Rochester (Int'l)	0	3	.000	8.62	2.23	11	2	0	0	...	0-...	15.2	.21	20	15	2	14-0	15	.328
1989	Rochester (Int'l)	0	2	.000	5.40	1.60	7	1	0	0	...	0-...	10.0	10	6	6	2	6-0	3	.263
—	Hagerstown (East.)	0	0	...	1.38	1.00	3	3	0	0	...	0-...	13.0	9	2	2	0	4-0	12	.191
1990	Hagerstown (East.)	5	5	.500	3.42	1.35	15	15	3	1	...	0-...	79.0	77	35	30	4	30-0	72	.258
—	Rochester (Int'l)	1	2	.333	2.42	1.27	4	4	0	0	...	0-...	26.0	21	11	7	2	12-0	23	.223
—	Baltimore (A.L.)	3	2	.600	3.86	1.37	7	7	0	0	...	0-0	46.2	37	20	20	2	27-2	24	.218
1991	Baltimore (A.L.)	6	11	.353	5.97	1.72	23	23	2	1	0	0-0	123.2	151	86	82	11	62-2	64	.307
—	Rochester (Int'l)	3	3	.500	3.86	1.31	8	8	1	1	...	0-...	51.1	37	25	22	4	30-0	48	.203
1992	Baltimore (A.L.)	3	8	.273	5.19	1.54	13	12	0	0	0	0-0	67.2	77	41	39	9	27-1	22	.287
—	Cleveland (A.L.)	4	4	.500	4.16	1.45	15	15	1	1	0	0-0	93.0	92	45	43	5	43-0	40	.262
1993	Cleveland (A.L.)	10	12	.455	4.92	1.41	34	33	3	0	0	0-0	208.2	232	122	114	21	62-2	118	.286
1994	Cleveland (A.L.)	7	5	.583	3.82	1.33	51	0	0	0	8	2-6	73.0	71	33	31	3	26-7	63	.254
1995	Cleveland (A.L.)	3	0	1.000	1.13	1.03	62	0	0	0	0	* 46-*48	64.0	49	9	8	3	17-2	58	.216
1996	Cleveland (A.L.)	2	7	.222	3.73	1.34	69	0	0	0	0	39-44	72.1	69	32	30	6	28-4	64	.257
1997	Cleveland (A.L.)	4	4	.500	2.40	1.35	66	0	0	0	9	16-21	82.1	83	28	22	7	28-3	69	.259
1998	Cleveland (A.L.)	3	4	.429	5.17	1.50	44	0	0	0	7	1-3	54.0	61	.36	31	7	20-3	35	.282
—	San Francisco (N.L.)	5	3	.625	3.52	1.57	32	0	0	0	6	0-1	30.2	30	14	12	1	18-2	28	.256
1999	Seattle (A.L.)	3	6	.333	4.98	1.81	68	0	0	0	1	33-38	68.2	84	42	38	11	40-4	42	.305
2000	Seattle (A.L.)	4	6	.400	5.36	1.61	66	0	0	0	11	1-3	80.2	89	48	48	11	41-0	84	.280
2001	Philadelphia (N.L.)	3	3	.500	2.34	1.23	71	0	0	0	1	42-46	69.1	65	26	18	4	20-2	59	.246
2002	Philadelphia (N.L.)	4	6	.400	2.97	1.37	74	0	0	0	0	45-54	75.2	65	26	25	5	39-7	64	.231
2003	Philadelphia (N.L.)	5	7	.417	6.52	1.76	61	0	0	0	2	24-28	58.0	71	44	42	7	31-2	45	.296
2004	Pittsburgh (N.L.)	5	2	.714	3.25	1.41	70	0	0	0	0	43-48	69.1	78	26	25	6	20-3	37	.291
2005	Pittsburgh (N.L.)	2	8	.200	4.76	1.54	55	0	0	0	1	27-34	56.2	61	30	30	7	26-3	37	.285
2006	Colorado (N.L.)	1	5	.167	3.86	1.51	79	0	0	0	19	1-8	72.1	73	32	31	9	36-6	39	.270
American League totals (12 years)		53	72	.424	4.45	1.47	524	95	6	2	37	138-163	1066.0	1133	565	527	103	436-30	700	.275
National League totals (7 years)		25	34	.424	3.81	1.47	442	0	0	0	29	182-219	432.0	443	198	183	39	190-25	309	.268
Major League totals (18 years)		78	106	.424	4.27	1.47	966	95	6	2	66	320-382	1498.0	1576	763	710	142	626-55	1009	.273

DIVISION SERIES RECORD

Year	Team (League)	W	L	Pct.	ERA	WHIP	G	GS	CG	ShO	Hld.	Sv.-Opp.	IP	H	R	ER	HR	BB-IBB	SO	Avg.
1995	Cleveland (A.L.)	0	0	...	0.00	1.00	2	0	0	0	0	...	2.0	0	0	0	0	2-0	0	.000
1996	Cleveland (A.L.)	0	1	.000	3.86	1.71	2	0	0	0	0	0-1	4.2	8	2	2	1	0-0	7	.381
1997	Cleveland (A.L.)	0	0	...	2.70	1.80	2	0	0	0	0	1-1	3.1	5	1	1	1	1-0	2	.333
2000	Seattle (A.L.)	1	0	1.000	0.00	0.50	2	0	0	0	1	0-0	2.0	0	0	0	0	1-1	2	.000
Division series totals (4 years)		1	1	.500	2.25	1.42	8	0	0	0	1	1-2	12.0	13	3	3	2	4-1	11	.277

CHAMPIONSHIP SERIES RECORD

Year	Team (League)	W	L	Pct.	ERA	WHIP	G	GS	CG	ShO	Hld.	Sv.-Opp.	IP	H	R	ER	HR	BB-IBB	SO	Avg.
1995	Cleveland (A.L.)	0	0	...	2.25	1.00	4	0	0	0	0	1-1	4.0	3	1	1	1	1-0	1	.214
1997	Cleveland (A.L.)	1	0	1.000	3.38	1.50	4	0	0	0	0	2-4	5.1	5	2	2	0	3-1	5	.238
2000	Seattle (A.L.)	0	0	...	12.46	1.85	3	0	0	0	0	0-0	4.1	5	6	6	2	3-0	3	.313
Champ. series totals (3 years)		1	0	1.000	5.93	1.46	11	0	0	0	0	3-5	13.2	13	9	9	3	7-1	9	.255

WORLD SERIES RECORD

Year	Team (League)	W	L	Pct.	ERA	WHIP	G	GS	CG	ShO	Hld.	Sv.-Opp.	IP	H	R	ER	HR	BB-IBB	SO	Avg.
1995	Cleveland (A.L.)	1	0	1.000	4.50	1.50	2	0	0	0	0	1-1	4.0	5	2	2	1	1-0	4	.333
1997	Cleveland (A.L.)	0	0	...	5.40	2.20	5	0	0	0	0	1-2	5.0	10	3	3	0	1-0	5	.417
World series totals (2 years)		1	0	1.000	5.00	1.89	7	0	0	0	0	2-3	9.0	15	5	5	1	2-0	9	.385

ALL-STAR GAME RECORD

		W	L	Pct.	ERA	WHIP	G	GS	CG	ShO	Hld.	Sv.-Opp.	IP	H	R	ER	HR	BB-IBB	SO	Avg.
All-Star Game totals (1 year)		0	0	...	0.00	0.00	1	0	0	0	0	0-0	1.0	0	0	0	0	0-0	1	.000

2006 LEFTY-RIGHTY SPLITS

vs.	Avg.	AB	H	2B	3B	HR	RBI	BB	SO	OBP	Slg.	vs.	Avg.	AB	H	2B	3B	HR	RBI	BB	SO	OBP	Slg.
L	.270	126	34	2	1	6	17	17	13	.378	.444	R	.271	144	39	10	0	3	24	19	26	.352	.403

MESSENGER, RANDY   P

PERSONAL: Born August 13, 1981, in Reno, Nev. ... 6-6/247. ... Throws right, bats right. ... Full name: Randall Jerome Messenger. **TRANSACTIONS/CAREER NOTES:** Selected by Florida Marlins organization in 11th round of 1999 free-agent draft.
CAREER HITTING: 1-for-5 (.200), 0 R, 0 2B, 0 3B, 0 HR, 0 RBI.

Year	Team (League)	W	L	Pct.	ERA	WHIP	G	GS	CG	ShO	Hld.	Sv.-Opp.	IP	H	R	ER	HR	BB-IBB	SO	Avg.
1999	GC Marlins (GCL)	0	3	.000	7.52	1.78	13	2	0	0	...	2-...	26.1	28	25	22	1	19-0	23	.283
2000	GC Marlins (GCL)	2	2	.500	4.83	1.47	12	12	0	0	...	0-...	59.2	66	37	32	6	22-0	29	.280
2001	Kane Co. (Midw.)	2	1	.667	3.93	1.47	14	0	0	0	...	0-...	18.1	22	13	8	0	5-0	14	.301
—	Brevard County (FSL)	7	4	.636	4.08	1.45	18	18	0	0	...	0-...	92.2	99	55	42	3	35-0	42	.277
2002	Jupiter (Fla. St.)	11	8	.579	4.37	1.51	28	27	1	0	...	0-...	156.2	178	94	.76	4	58-0	96	.284
2003	Carolina (Southern)	5	7	.417	5.46	1.65	29	23	0	0	...	0-...	113.2	137	83	69	7	51-1	78	.296
2004	Carolina (Southern)	6	3	.667	2.58	1.38	58	0	0	0	...	21-...	69.2	67	21	20	4	29-3	71	.245
2005	Albuquerque (PCL)	4	2	.667	3.88	1.29	39	0	0	0	9	7-11	48.2	46	25	21	5	17-1	35	.251
—	Florida (N.L.)	0	0	...	5.35	1.86	29	0	0	0	2	0-0	37.0	39	22	22	5	30-7	29	.273
2006	Jupiter (Fla. St.)	0	0	...	0.00	1.00	1	0	0	0	0	0-0	1.0	1	0	0	0	0-0	1	.250
—	Albuquerque (PCL)	0	0	...	9.00	1.33	4	0	0	0	0	0-0	3.0	1	3	3	0	3-0	1	.125
—	Florida (N.L.)	2	7	.222	5.67	1.59	59	0	0	0	9	0-1	60.1	72	42	38	8	24-2	45	.296
Major League totals (2 years)		2	7	.222	5.55	1.70	88	0	0	0	11	0-1	97.1	111	64	60	13	54-9	74	.288

2006 LEFTY-RIGHTY SPLITS

vs.	Avg.	AB	H	2B	3B	HR	RBI	BB	SO	OBP	Slg.	vs.	Avg.	AB	H	2B	3B	HR	RBI	BB	SO	OBP	Slg.
L	.333	108	36	11	0	7	30	8	22	.385	.630	R	.267	135	36	8	0	1	13	16	23	.340	.348

M

MEYER, DREW — 2B

PERSONAL: Born August 29, 1981, in Charleston, S.C. ... Bats left, throws right. ... Full name: Drew Edward Meyer. ... College: South Carolina. **TRANSACTIONS/CAREER NOTES:** Selected by Texas Rangers organization in first round (10th pick overall) of 2002 free-agent draft.

2006 GAMES PLAYED BY POSITION (MLB): 2B—3, SS—1, OF—1.

Year	Team (League)	Pos.	G	AB	R	H	2B	3B	HR	RBI	BB	SO	HBP	GDP	SB-CS	Avg.	OBP	SLG	OPS	E	Avg.
2002—	Savannah (S. Atl.)		54	214	15	52	5	4	1	24	10	53	0	2	7-6	.243	.274	.318	.592	...	...
—	Tulsa (Texas)		4	14	0	3	0	0	0	0	1	5	0	0	0-0	.214	.267	.214	.481	...	...
2003—	Stockton (Calif.)		94	398	59	112	16	9	5	53	32	92	0	6	24-10	.281	.330	.405	.735	...	...
—	Frisco (Texas)		26	98	14	31	1	1	0	6	11	23	0	1	9-1	.316	.385	.347	.732	...	...
2004—	Arizona Rangers (AZL)		15	62	15	24	2	0	0	5	3	8	0	2	4-1	.387	.415	.419	.834	...	...
—	Frisco (Texas)		59	232	35	56	6	2	2	13	22	43	1	2	4-2	.241	.309	.310	.619	...	...
2005—	Frisco (Texas)	2B-SS-3B																			
		OF	83	321	49	103	14	4	3	45	26	55	3	3	12-2	.321	.372	.417	.789	10	.975
—	Oklahoma (PCL)	SS-OF-2B																			
		3B	42	178	25	44	11	4	0	19	14	43	0	6	5-2	.247	.301	.354	.654	8	.958
2006—	Oklahoma (PCL)		95	364	37	83	14	4	2	28	27	91	0	10	9-11	.228	.278	.305	.583	10	.976
—	Texas (A.L.)	2B-SS-OF	5	14	1	3	0	0	0	0	0	8	0	0	0-0	.214	.214	.214	.429	1	.933
Major League totals (1 year)			5	14	1	3	0	0	0	0	0	8	0	0	0-0	.214	.214	.214	.429	1	.933

2006 LEFTY-RIGHTY SPLITS

vs.	Avg.	AB	H	2B	3B	HR	RBI	BB	SO	OBP	Slg.	vs.	Avg.	AB	H	2B	3B	HR	RBI	BB	SO	OBP	Slg.
L	.333	3	1	0	0	0	0	0	0	.333	.333	R	.182	11	2	0	0	0	0	0	8	.182	.182

MICELI, DAN — P

PERSONAL: Born September 9, 1970, in Newark, N.J. ... 6-0/215. ... Throws right, bats right. ... Full name: Daniel Miceli. ... Name pronounced: muh-SELL-ee. ... High school: Dr. Phillips (Orlando). **TRANSACTIONS/CAREER NOTES:** Signed as a non-drafted free agent by Kansas City Royals organization (March 7, 1990). ... Traded by Royals with P Jon Lieber to Pittsburgh Pirates for P Stan Belinda (July 31, 1993). ... Traded by Pirates to Detroit Tigers for P Clint Sodowsky (November 1, 1996). ... Traded by Tigers with P Donne Wall and 3B Ryan Balfe to San Diego Padres for P Tim Worrell and OF Trey Beamon (November 19, 1997). ... Traded by Padres to Florida Marlins for P Brian Meadows (November 15, 1999). ... On disabled list (May 30-July 19, 2000); included rehabilitation assignments to GCL Marlins and Brevard County. ... Released by Marlins (June 25, 2001). ... Signed by Colorado Rockies organization (July 2, 2001). ... Signed as a free agent by Texas Rangers organization (January 29, 2002). ... Released by Rangers (May 6, 2002). ... Signed by Rockies organization (December 19, 2002). ... Signed as a free agent by Cleveland Indians organization (May 15, 2003). ... Traded by Indians with OF Karim Garcia to New York Yankees for cash (June 25, 2003). ... Traded by Yankees to Houston Astros for cash (July 29, 2003). ... On disabled list (August 22-September 9, 2004). ... On disabled list (August 7, 2005-remainder of season). ... Signed as free agent by Tampa Bay Devil Rays (January 11, 2006). ... On disabled list (May 5-August 7, 2006); included rehabilitation assignment to Montgomery.

CAREER HITTING: 2-for-22 (.091), 0 R, 0 2B, 0 3B, 0 HR, 0 RBI.

Year	Team (League)	W	L	Pct.	ERA	WHIP	G	GS	CG	ShO	Hld.	Sv.-Opp.	IP	H	R	ER	HR	BB-IBB	SO	Avg.
1990—	GC Royals (GCL)	3	4	.429	3.91	1.40	27	0	0	0	...	4-...	53.0	45	27	23	0	29-5	48	.234
1991—	Eugene (Northwest)	0	1	.000	2.14	1.07	25	0	0	0	...	10-...	33.2	18	8	8	1	18-0	43	.158
1992—	Appleton (Midwest)	1	1	.500	1.93	0.69	23	0	0	0	...	9-...	23.1	12	6	5	0	4-1	44	.145
—	Memphis (Sou.)	3	0	1.000	1.91	0.88	32	0	0	0	...	4-...	37.2	20	10	8	5	13-0	46	.160
1993—	Memphis (Sou.)	6	4	.600	4.60	1.59	40	0	0	0	...	7-...	58.2	54	30	30	7	39-3	68	.242
—	Carolina (Southern)	0	2	.000	5.11	1.22	13	0	0	0	...	10-...	12.1	11	8	7	2	4-1	19	.234
—	Pittsburgh (N.L.)	0	0	...	5.06	1.69	9	0	0	0	...	0-0	5.1	6	3	3	0	3-0	4	.273
1994—	Buffalo (A.A.)	1	1	.500	1.88	0.88	19	0	0	0	...	2-...	24.0	15	5	5	2	6-0	31	.185
—	Pittsburgh (N.L.)	2	1	.667	5.93	1.43	28	0	0	0	4	2-3	27.1	28	19	18	5	11-2	27	.267
1995—	Pittsburgh (N.L.)	4	4	.500	4.66	1.53	58	0	0	0	2	21-27	58.0	61	30	30	7	28-5	56	.270
1996—	Pittsburgh (N.L.)	2	10	.167	5.78	1.68	44	9	0	0	4	1-1	85.2	99	65	55	15	45-5	66	.291
—	Carolina (Southern)	1	0	1.000	1.00	0.56	3	0	0	0	...	1-...	9.0	4	1	1	0	1-0	17	.125
1997—	Detroit (A.L.)	3	2	.600	5.01	1.39	71	0	0	0	11	3-8	82.2	77	49	46	13	38-4	79	.248
1998—	San Diego (N.L.)	10	5	.667	3.22	1.25	67	0	0	0	20	2-8	72.2	64	28	26	6	27-4	70	.238
1999—	San Diego (N.L.)	4	5	.444	4.46	1.50	66	0	0	0	9	2-4	68.2	67	39	34	7	36-5	59	.266
2000—	Florida (N.L.)	6	4	.600	4.25	1.29	45	0	0	0	11	0-3	48.2	45	23	23	4	18-2	40	.242
—	GC Marlins (GCL)	0	0	...	0.00	0.33	2	2	0	0	...	0-...	3.0	0	0	0	0	1-0	3	.000
—	Brevard County (FSL)	1	0	1.000	3.00	0.50	5	4	0	0	...	0-...	6.0	3	2	2	1	0-0	7	.143
2001—	Florida (N.L.)	0	5	.000	6.93	1.62	29	0	0	0	8	0-3	24.2	29	21	19	5	11-2	31	.287
—	Colo. Springs (PCL)	0	2	.000	6.00	1.00	4	0	0	0	...	0-...	3.0	2	2	2	0	1-1	4	.200
—	Colorado (N.L.)	2	0	1.000	2.21	1.13	22	0	0	0	0	1-1	20.1	18	8	5	2	5-0	17	.231
2002—	Texas (A.L.)	0	2	.000	8.64	1.92	9	0	0	0	1	0-1	8.1	13	8	8	1	3-0	5	.333
2003—	Colorado (N.L.)	0	2	.000	5.66	1.60	14	0	0	0	1	0-0	20.2	24	13	13	7	9-1	18	.286
—	Buffalo (Int'l)	0	1	.000	3.00	1.30	5	0	0	0	...	0-...	6.0	7	2	2	1	0-0	6	.280
—	Cleveland (A.L.)	1	1	.500	1.20	1.00	13	0	0	0	0	0-1	15.0	9	4	2	1	6-1	19	.164
—	New York (A.L.)	0	0	...	5.79	1.50	7	0	0	0	1	1-1	4.2	4	3	3	2	3-0	1	.211
—	Houston (N.L.)	1	1	.500	2.10	0.97	23	0	0	0	0	0-0	30.0	22	7	7	3	7-1	20	.208
2004—	Houston (N.L.)	6	6	.500	3.59	1.30	74	0	0	0	24	2-8	77.2	74	34	31	10	27-12	83	.247
2005—	Colo. Springs (PCL)	0	0	...	5.40	1.20	5	0	0	0	...	0-...	5.0	4	3	3	1	2-0	8	.200
—	Colorado (N.L.)	1	2	.333	5.89	1.75	19	0	0	0	5	0-2	18.1	19	12	12	1	13-0	19	.271
2006—	Montgom. (Sou.)	0	0	...	0.00	0.80	4	0	0	0	1	1-1	5.0	3	0	0	0	1-0	5	.176
—	Tampa Bay (A.L.)	1	2	.333	3.94	1.41	32	0	0	0	6	4-7	32.0	25	17	14	4	12-0	18	.217
American League totals (4 years)		5	7	.417	4.61	1.39	133	0	0	0	18	8-18	142.2	128	81	73	21	70-8	122	.238
National League totals (11 years)		38	45	.458	4.45	1.43	498	9	0	0	91	31-60	558.0	556	302	276	72	240-39	510	.260
Major League totals (14 years)		43	52	.453	4.48	1.42	631	9	0	0	109	39-78	700.2	684	383	349	93	310-47	632	.256

DIVISION SERIES RECORD

Year	Team (League)	W	L	Pct.	ERA	WHIP	G	GS	CG	ShO	Hld.	Sv.-Opp.	IP	H	R	ER	HR	BB-IBB	SO	Avg.
1998—	San Diego (N.L.)	1	1	.500	2.70	0.60	3	0	0	0	1	0-0	3.1	2	1	1	0	0-0	4	.200
2004—	Houston (N.L.)	0	1	.000	5.40	0.90	3	0	0	0	0	0-0	3.1	2	2	2	1	1-0	2	.167
Division series totals (2 years)		1	2	.333	4.05	0.75	6	0	0	0	1	0-0	6.2	4	3	3	1	1-0	6	.182

CHAMPIONSHIP SERIES RECORD

Year	Team (League)	W	L	Pct.	ERA	WHIP	G	GS	CG	ShO	Hld.	Sv.-Opp.	IP	H	R	ER	HR	BB-IBB	SO	Avg.
1998—	San Diego (N.L.)	0	0	...	13.50	6.00	3	0	0	0	0	0-0	0.2	4	1	1	0	0-0	1	.667
2004—	Houston (N.L.)	0	2	.000	27.00	3.00	2	0	0	0	1	0-0	1.1	3	4	4	3	1-0	0	.429
Champ. series totals (2 years)		0	2	.000	22.50	4.00	5	0	0	0	1	0-0	2.0	7	5	5	4	1-0	1	.538

M

WORLD SERIES RECORD

Year — Team (League)	W	L	Pct.	ERA	WHIP	G	GS	CG	ShO	Hld.	Sv.-Opp.	IP	H	R	ER	HR	BB-IBB	SO	Avg.
1998— San Diego (N.L.)	0	0	...	0.00	2.40	2	0	0	0	0	0-0	1.2	2	0	0	0	2-0	1	.286

2006 LEFTY-RIGHTY SPLITS

vs.	Avg.	AB	H	2B	3B	HR	RBI	BB	SO	OBP	Slg.	vs.	Avg.	AB	H	2B	3B	HR	RBI	BB	SO	OBP	Slg.
L	.130	54	7	2	0	2	9	13	12	.290	.278	R	.295	61	18	4	0	2	10	7	6	.371	.459

MICHAELS, JASON — OF

PERSONAL: Born May 4, 1976, in Tampa. ... 6-0/204. ... Bats right, throws right. ... Full name: Jason Drew Michaels. ... High school: Jesuit (Tampa). ... College: Miami. ... Grandson of John Michaels, pitcher with Boston Red Sox (1932). **TRANSACTIONS/CAREER NOTES:** Selected by San Diego Padres organization in 49th round of 1994 free-agent draft; did not sign. ... Selected by Tampa Bay Devil Rays organization in 44th round of 1996 free-agent draft; did not sign. ... Selected by St. Louis Cardinals organization in 15th round of 1997 free-agent draft; did not sign. ... Selected by Philadelphia Phillies organization in fourth round of 1998 free-agent draft. ... On disabled list (March 21-April 14, 2003); included rehabilitation assignment to Clearwater. ... Traded by Phillies to Cleveland Indians for P Arthur Rhodes (January 27, 2006). ... On disabled list (June 16-July 4, 2006); included rehabilitation assignment to Buffalo. **STATISTICAL NOTES:** Career major league grand slams: 2.

2006 GAMES PLAYED BY POSITION (MLB): OF—118, DH—2.

							BATTING												FIELDING	
Year — Team (League)	Pos.	G	AB	R	H	2B	3B	HR	RBI	BB	SO	HBP	GDP	SB-CS	Avg.	OBP	SLG	OPS	E	Avg.
1998— Batavia (NY-Penn)	OF	67	235	45	63	14	3	11	49	40	69	4	5	4-2	.268	.381	.494	.874	5	.949
1999— Clearwater (FSL)	OF	122	451	91	138	31	6	14	65	68	103	3	7	10-7	.306	.396	.494	.890	1	.996
2000— Reading (East.)	OF	113	437	71	129	30	4	10	74	28	87	3	9	7-4	.295	.337	.451	.788	6	.977
2001— Scran./W.B. (I.L.)	OF	109	418	58	109	19	3	17	69	37	126	8	7	11-3	.261	.332	.443	.774	0	1.000
— Philadelphia (N.L.)	OF	6	6	0	1	0	0	0	1	0	2	0	0	0-0	.167	.167	.167	.333	0	—
2002— Scran./W.B. (I.L.)	OF	9	32	3	9	2	0	0	7	5	5	0	0	1-3	.281	.359	.344	.703	0	1.000
— Philadelphia (N.L.)	OF-DH-3B	81	105	16	28	10	3	2	11	13	33	1	1	1-1	.267	.347	.476	.823	2	.923
2003— Clearwater (FSL)	OF	4	14	1	0	0	0	0	0	2	4	0	0	0-0	.000	.125	.000	.125	0	1.000
— Philadelphia (N.L.)	OF	76	109	20	36	11	0	5	17	15	22	1	3	0-0	.330	.416	.569	.985	1	.976
2004— Philadelphia (N.L.)	OF-DH	115	299	44	82	12	0	10	40	42	80	2	3	2-2	.274	.364	.415	.779	3	.983
2005— Philadelphia (N.L.)	OF	105	289	54	88	16	2	4	31	44	45	4	3	3-3	.304	.399	.415	.814	2	.990
2006— Buffalo (Int'l)		2	7	1	3	0	0	1	1	0	0	1	0	0-0	.429	.429	.857	1.286	0	1.000
— Cleveland (A.L.)	OF-DH	123	494	77	132	32	1	9	55	43	101	3	6	9-5	.267	.326	.391	.717	2	.991
American League totals (1 year)		123	494	77	132	32	1	9	55	43	101	3	6	9-5	.267	.326	.391	.717	2	.991
National League totals (5 years)		383	808	134	235	49	5	21	100	114	182	8	10	6-6	.291	.380	.442	.822	8	.982
Major league totals (6 years)		506	1302	211	367	81	6	30	155	157	283	11	16	15-11	.282	.360	.422	.783	10	.985

2006 LEFTY-RIGHTY SPLITS

vs.	Avg.	AB	H	2B	3B	HR	RBI	BB	SO	OBP	Slg.	vs.	Avg.	AB	H	2B	3B	HR	RBI	BB	SO	OBP	Slg.
L	.291	189	55	15	0	5	27	17	30	.349	.450	R	.252	305	77	17	1	4	28	26	71	.312	.354

MICHALAK, CHRIS — P

PERSONAL: Born January 4, 1971, in Joliet, Ill. ... 6-2/195. ... Throws left, bats left. ... Full name: Christian Matthew Michalak. ... High school: Joliet (Ill.) Catholic. ... College: Notre Dame. **TRANSACTIONS/CAREER NOTES:** Selected by Oakland Athletics organization in 12th round of 1993 free-agent draft. ... Released by A's (April 1, 1997). ... Signed by Arizona Diamondbacks organization (April 8, 1997). ... Loaned by Diamondbacks to Tulsa of the Texas Rangers organization (March 24-May 6, 1998). ... Signed as free agent by Anaheim Angels organization (January 25, 1999). ... Released by Angels (June 19, 1999). ... Signed by Diamondbacks organization (June 23, 1999). ... Signed as free agent by Tampa Bay Devil Rays organization (January 9, 2000). ... Released by Devil Rays (April 25, 2000). ... Signed by Los Angeles Dodgers organization (May 6, 2000). ... Signed as free agent by Toronto Blue Jays organization (December 13, 2000). ... Claimed on waivers by Rangers (August 22, 2001). ... Released by Rangers (May 31, 2002). ... Signed by Boston Red Sox organization (June 6, 2002). ... Signed as free agent by Colorado Rockies organization (November 24, 2002). ... Traded by Rockies to Cincinnati Reds for a player to be named (July 29, 2003). ... Signed as free agent by Milwaukee Brewers organization (February 20, 2004). ... Signed as free agent by Florida Marlins organization (July 16, 2004). ... Signed as free agent by Toronto Blue Jays organization (February 28, 2005). ... Released by Blue Jays (April 4, 2005). ... Signed by Diamondbacks organization (April 9, 2005). ... Signed as free agent by Reds organization (February 25, 2006). ... On bereavement list (August 20-23, 2006). ... Signed as free agent by Washington Nationals organization (November 6, 2006).

CAREER HITTING: 3-for-11 (.273), 0 R, 1 2B, 1 3B, 0 HR, 0 RBI.

Year — Team (League)	W	L	Pct.	ERA	WHIP	G	GS	CG	ShO	Hld.	Sv.-Opp.	IP	H	R	ER	HR	BB-IBB	SO	Avg.
1993— S. Oregon (N'west)	7	3	.700	2.85	1.43	16	15	0	0		0-...	79.0	77	41	25	2	36-0	57	.259
1994— W. Mich. (Mid.)	5	3	.625	3.90	1.40	15	10	0	0		0-...	67.0	66	32	29	3	28-0	38	.265
— Modesto (California)	5	3	.625	2.91	1.13	17	10	1	0		2-...	77.1	67	28	25	13	20-1	46	.238
1995— Huntsville (Sou.)	1	1	.500	11.12	2.65	7	0	0	0		1-...	5.2	10	7	7	1	5-0	4	.400
— Modesto (California)	3	2	.600	2.62	1.27	44	0	0	0		2-...	65.1	56	26	19	3	27-1	49	.246
1996— Modesto (California)	2	2	.500	3.03	1.40	21	0	0	0		4-...	38.2	37	21	13	4	17-0	39	.243
— Huntsville (Sou.)	4	0	1.000	7.71	2.49	21	0	0	0		0-...	23.1	32	29	20	2	26-4	15	.340
1997— High Desert (Calif.)	3	7	.300	2.65	1.26	49	0	0	0		4-...	85.0	76	36	25	4	31-1	74	.238
1998— Tulsa (Texas)	1	2	.333	1.84	0.61	10	0	0	0		0-...	19.2	10	4	4	2	2-0	15	.149
— Tucson (PCL)	3	8	.273	5.03	1.64	29	3	0	0		0-...	73.1	91	47	41	11	29-3	50	.318
— Arizona (N.L.)	0	0	...	11.81	2.44	5	0	0	0		0-0	5.1	9	7	7	1	4-0	5	.375
1999— Edmonton (PCL)	1	0	1.000	5.72	1.48	24	0	0	0		0-...	28.1	28	20	18	3	14-0	25	.259
— Tucson (PCL)	5	0	1.000	3.66	1.41	21	0	0	0		3-...	64.0	64	30	26	6	26-2	41	.268
2000— Durham (Int'l)	0	0	...	5.68	1.11	6	0	0	0		0-...	6.1	6	4	4	1	1-0	7	.240
— Albuquerque (PCL)	11	3	.786	4.26	1.66	23	21	0	0		0-...	133.0	166	72	63	18	55-0	83	.320
2001— Toronto (A.L.)	6	7	.462	4.62	1.58	24	18	0	0		0-0	115.0	133	66	59	14	49-5	57	.296
— Texas (A.L.)	2	2	.500	3.32	1.38	11	0	0	0		1-2	21.2	24	8	8	5	6-0	10	.279
2002— Oklahoma (PCL)	0	0	...	0.00		1	0	0	0		0-...	1.0	0	0	0	0	0-0	1	.000
— Texas (A.L.)	0	2	.000	4.40	2.09	13	0	0	0	2	0-0	14.1	20	7	7	1	10-2	5	.339
— Pawtucket (Int'l)	5	9	.357	5.77	1.67	17	16	0	0		0-...	93.2	125	68	60	15	31-0	52	.323
2003— Colo. Springs (PCL)	7	9	.438	4.41	1.51	24	18	0	0		1-...	120.1	138	76	59	22	44-3	72	.290
— Louisville (Int'l)	2	1	.667	5.13	1.52	9	3	0	0		0-...	26.1	35	15	15	3	5-0	15	.337
2004— Indianapolis (Int'l)	2	6	.250	5.18	1.71	37	0	0	0		1-...	48.2	65	37	28	3	18-2	29	.308
— Albuquerque (PCL)	1	1	.500	6.35	1.74	17	1	0	0		0-...	34.0	44	24	24	9	15-0	20	.317
2005— Tucson (PCL)	9	13	.409	4.47	1.31	26	25	3	0		0-0	165.0	174	88	82	27	42-0	74	.274
2006— Louisville (Int'l)	9	5	.643	2.99	1.28	23	22	0	0		0-...	132.1	142	56	44	17	28-0	61	.278
— Cincinnati (N.L.)	2	4	.333	4.89	1.66	8	6	0	0		0-0	35.0	42	21	19	6	16-2	10	.304
American League totals (2 years)	8	11	.421	4.41	1.60	48	18	0	0	2	1-2	151.0	177	81	74	20	65-7	72	.298
National League totals (2 years)	2	4	.333	5.80	1.76	13	6	0	0	0	0-0	40.1	51	28	26	7	20-2	15	.370
Major league totals (4 years)	10	15	.400	4.70	1.64	61	24	0	0	2	1-2	191.1	228	109	100	27	85-9	87	.311

2006 LEFTY-RIGHTY SPLITS

vs.	Avg.	AB	H	2B	3B	HR	RBI	BB	SO	OBP	Slg.	vs.	Avg.	AB	H	2B	3B	HR	RBI	BB	SO	OBP	Slg.
L	.276	29	8	0	0	1	2	2	3	.344	.379	R	.312	109	34	9	0	5	15	14	7	.400	.532

M

MIENTKIEWICZ, DOUG — 1B

PERSONAL: Born June 19, 1974, in Toledo, Ohio. ... 6-2/206. ... Bats left, throws right. ... Full name: Douglas Andrew Mientkiewicz. ... Name pronounced: mint-KAY-vich. ... High school: Westminster Christian (Miami). ... College: Florida State. **TRANSACTIONS/CAREER NOTES:** Selected by Minnesota Twins organization in fifth round of 1995 free-agent draft. ... On disabled list (July 7-23, 2004). ... Traded by Twins to Boston Red Sox as part of four-team deal in which Twins acquired P Justin Jones from Cubs, Red Sox acquired SS Orlando Cabrera from Expos, Expos acquired SS Alex S. Gonzalez, P Francis Beltran and IF Brendan Harris from Cubs, and Cubs acquired SS Nomar Garciaparra and Matt Murton from Red Sox (July 31, 2004). ... Traded by Red Sox to New York Mets for 1B Ian Bladergroen (January 26, 2005). ... On disabled list (June 26-July 16 and August 9-September 2, 2005); included rehabilitation assignments to GCL Mets and St. Lucie. ... Signed as a free agent by Kansas City Royals (December 16, 2005). ... On disabled list (July 26, 2006-remainder of season). **HONORS:** Won A.L. Gold Glove at first base (2001). **STATISTICAL NOTES:** Career major league grand slams: 1. **MISCELLANEOUS NOTES:** Member of 2000 U.S. Olympic baseball team.

2006 GAMES PLAYED BY POSITION (MLB): 1B—90.

Year Team (League)	Pos.	G	AB	R	H	2B	3B	HR	RBI	BB	SO	HBP	GDP	SB-CS	Avg.	OBP	SLG	OPS	E	Avg.
1995—Fort Myers (FSL)	1B	38	110	9	27	6	1	1	15	18	19	1	1	2-2	.245	.357	.345	.702	1	.994
1996—Fort Myers (FSL)	1B	133	492	69	143	36	4	5	79	66	47	3	10	12-2	.291	.374	.411	.784	3	.998
1997—New Britain (East.)	1B-OF	132	467	87	119	28	2	15	61	98	67	7	8	21-8	.255	.390	.420	.810	5	.995
1998—New Britain (East.)	1B-OF	139	502	96	162	45	0	16	88	96	58	6	6	11-4	.323	.432	.508	.940	12	.991
—Minnesota (A.L.)	1B	8	25	1	5	1	0	0	2	4	3	0	0	1-1	.200	.310	.240	.550	0	1.000
1999—Minnesota (A.L.)	1B	118	327	34	75	21	3	2	32	43	51	4	13	1-1	.229	.324	.330	.655	3	.997
2000—Salt Lake (PCL)	1B-3B-2B-OF	130	485	96	162	32	3	18	96	61	68	3	17	9-5	.334	.406	.524	.929	10	.989
—Minnesota (A.L.)	1B	3	14	0	6	0	0	0	4	0	0	0	1	0-0	.429	.400	.429	.829	0	1.000
2001—Minnesota (A.L.)	1B-DH	151	543	77	166	39	1	15	74	67	92	9	10	2-6	.306	.387	.464	.851	4	.997
2002—Minnesota (A.L.)	1B	143	467	60	122	29	1	10	64	74	69	6	7	1-2	.261	.365	.392	.756	5	.996
2003—Minnesota (A.L.)	1B-OF-2B-3B-DH	142	487	67	146	38	1	11	65	74	55	5	9	4-1	.300	.393	.450	.843	4	.997
2004—Minnesota (A.L.)	1B	78	284	34	70	18	0	5	25	38	38	3	9	2-2	.246	.340	.363	.703	4	.994
—Boston (A.L.)	1B-2B	49	107	13	23	6	1	1	10	10	18	1	4	0-0	.215	.286	.318	.603	1	.997
2005—GC Mets (GCL)	1B-DH	4	10	2	5	1	0	1	5	4	1	0	0	0-0	.500	.643	.900	1.543	0	1.000
—St. Lucie (Fla. St.)	1B-DH	8	27	3	7	4	0	0	2	7	7	0	0	0-0	.259	.412	.407	.819	1	.985
—New York (N.L.)	1B	87	275	36	66	13	0	11	29	32	39	2	11	0-1	.240	.322	.407	.729	4	.995
2006—Kansas City (A.L.)	1B	91	314	37	89	24	2	4	43	35	50	5	6	3-0	.283	.359	.411	.770	3	.996
American League totals (8 years)		783	2568	323	702	176	9	48	319	345	376	33	58	14-14	.273	.363	.405	.768	24	.996
National League totals (1 year)		87	275	36	66	13	0	11	29	32	39	2	11	0-1	.240	.322	.407	.729	4	.995
Major League totals (9 years)		870	2843	359	768	189	9	59	348	377	415	35	69	14-15	.270	.359	.405	.764	28	.996

DIVISION SERIES RECORD

Year Team (League)	Pos.	G	AB	R	H	2B	3B	HR	RBI	BB	SO	HBP	GDP	SB-CS	Avg.	OBP	SLG	OPS	E	Avg.
2002—Minnesota (A.L.)	1B	5	20	3	5	0	0	0	4	1	1	0	0	0-0	.250	.286	.550	.836	0	1.000
2003—Minnesota (A.L.)	1B	4	15	0	2	0	0	0	1	2	0	0	0	0-0	.133	.188	.133	.321	0	1.000
2004—Boston (A.L.)	1B	3	4	0	2	0	0	0	1	0	0	0	0	0-0	.500	.500	.500	1.000	0	1.000
Division series totals (3 years)		12	39	3	9	0	0	0	2	5	2	0	0	0-0	.231	.268	.385	.653	0	1.000

CHAMPIONSHIP SERIES RECORD

Year Team (League)	Pos.	G	AB	R	H	2B	3B	HR	RBI	BB	SO	HBP	GDP	SB-CS	Avg.	OBP	SLG	OPS	E	Avg.
2002—Minnesota (A.L.)	1B	5	18	1	5	1	0	0	2	1	2	0	0	0-0	.278	.316	.333	.649	0	1.000
2004—Boston (A.L.)	1B	4	4	0	2	1	0	0	0	0	1	0	0	0-0	.500	.500	.750	1.250	0	1.000
Champ. series totals (2 years)		9	22	1	7	2	0	0	2	1	3	0	0	0-0	.318	.348	.409	.757	0	1.000

WORLD SERIES RECORD

Year Team (League)	Pos.	G	AB	R	H	2B	3B	HR	RBI	BB	SO	HBP	GDP	SB-CS	Avg.	OBP	SLG	OPS	E	Avg.
2004—Boston (A.L.)	1B	4	1	0	0	0	0	0	0	0	0	0	0	0-0	.000	.000	.000	.000	0	1.000

2006 LEFTY-RIGHTY SPLITS

vs.	Avg.	AB	H	2B	3B	HR	RBI	BB	SO	OBP	Slg.	vs.	Avg.	AB	H	2B	3B	HR	RBI	BB	SO	OBP	Slg.
L	.274	62	17	6	0	1	10	7	12	.375	.419	R	.286	252	72	18	2	3	33	28	38	.355	.409

MILES, AARON — 2B

PERSONAL: Born December 15, 1976, in Pittsburg, Calif. ... 5-7/180. ... Bats both, throws right. ... Full name: Aaron Wade Miles. ... High school: Antioch (Calif.). **TRANSACTIONS/CAREER NOTES:** Selected by Houston Astros organization in 19th round of 1995 free-agent draft. ... Selected by Chicago White Sox organization from Astros organization in Rule 5 minor league draft (December 11, 2000). ... Traded by White Sox to Colorado Rockies for IF Juan Uribe (December 2, 2003). ... On disabled list (May 26-June 28, 2005); included rehabilitation assignment to Colorado Springs. ... Traded by Rockies with OF Larry Bigbie to St. Louis Cardinals for P Ray King (December 7, 2005). **STATISTICAL NOTES:** Career major league grand slams: 1.

2006 GAMES PLAYED BY POSITION (MLB): 2B—88, SS—39, 3B—1.

Year Team (League)	Pos.	G	AB	R	H	2B	3B	HR	RBI	BB	SO	HBP	GDP	SB-CS	Avg.	OBP	SLG	OPS	E	Avg.
1995—GC Astros (GCL)	SS-2B	47	171	32	44	9	3	0	18	14	14	0	3	9-6	.257	.312	.345	.657	14	.916
1996—GC Astros (GCL)	2B	55	214	48	63	3	2	0	15	20	18	1	3	14-7	.294	.357	.327	.685	10	.947
1997—Quad City (Midw.)	2B	97	370	55	97	13	2	1	35	30	45	2	8	18-11	.262	.318	.316	.634	14	.961
1998—Quad City (Midw.)	2B-3B-OF	108	369	42	90	22	6	2	37	25	52	1	7	28-13	.244	.293	.352	.645	28	.945
1999—Michigan (Midw.)	2B	112	470	72	149	28	8	10	71	28	33	2	8	17-12	.317	.353	.474	.828	11	.964
2000—Kissimmee (Fla. St.)	2B	75	295	40	86	20	1	2	36	28	29	0	7	11-6	.292	.352	.386	.738	17	.950
2001—Birmingham (Sou.)	3B-2B	84	343	53	89	16	3	8	42	26	35	2	10	3-5	.259	.313	.394	.706	6	.948
2002—Birmingham (Sou.)	2B-3B	138	531	67	171	39	1	9	68	40	45	2	4	25-16	.322	.369	.450	.819	26	.956
2003—Charlotte (Int'l)	2B-DH-3B	133	546	80	166	34	5	11	50	40	52	1	9	8-9	.304	.351	.445	.796	15	.973
—Chicago (A.L.)	2B-DH	8	12	3	4	3	0	0	2	0	0	0	0	0-0	.333	.333	.583	.917	0	1.000
2004—Colo. Springs (PCL)	2B	12	54	8	18	3	0	0	8	2	4	0	1	2-2	.333	.345	.389	.734	2	.968
—Colorado (N.L.)	2B	134	522	75	153	15	3	6	47	29	53	2	12	12-7	.293	.329	.368	.697	10	.984
2005—Colo. Springs (PCL)	2B	8	32	6	7	0	1	0	8	3	5	0	0	1-0	.219	.242	.281	.524	1	.978
—Colorado (N.L.)	2B-SS	99	324	37	91	12	3	2	28	8	38	4	6	4-2	.281	.306	.355	.661	7	.981
2006—St. Louis (N.L.)	2B-SS-3B	135	426	48	112	20	5	2	30	38	42	2	8	2-1	.263	.324	.347	.672	17	.970
American League totals (1 year)		8	12	3	4	3	0	0	2	0	0	0	0	0-0	.333	.333	.583	.917	0	1.000
National League totals (3 years)		368	1272	160	356	47	11	10	105	75	133	8	26	18-10	.280	.322	.358	.679	34	.978
Major League totals (4 years)		376	1284	163	360	50	11	10	107	75	133	8	26	18-10	.280	.322	.360	.682	34	.979

DIVISION SERIES RECORD

Year Team (League)	Pos.	G	AB	R	H	2B	3B	HR	RBI	BB	SO	HBP	GDP	SB-CS	Avg.	OBP	SLG	OPS	E	Avg.
2006—St. Louis (N.L.)	2B	2	2	0	1	0	0	0	0	0	0	0	0	0-0	.500	.500	.500	1.000	0	...

M

CHAMPIONSHIP SERIES RECORD

Year Team (League)	Pos.	G	AB	R	H	2B	3B	HR	RBI	BB	SO	HBP	GDP	SB-CS	Avg.	OBP	SLG	OPS	E	Avg.
2006— St. Louis (N.L.)	2B	3	3	0	2	0	1	0	0	0	0	0	0	0-0	.667	.667	1.333	2.000	0	—

WORLD SERIES RECORD

Year Team (League)	Pos.	G	AB	R	H	2B	3B	HR	RBI	BB	SO	HBP	GDP	SB-CS	Avg.	OBP	SLG	OPS	E	Avg.
2006— St. Louis (N.L.)	2B	2	6	2	1	0	0	0	0	1	2	0	0	1-0	.167	.286	.167	.452	0	1.000

2006 LEFTY-RIGHTY SPLITS

vs.	Avg.	AB	H	2B	3B	HR	RBI	BB	SO	OBP	Slg.	vs.	Avg.	AB	H	2B	3B	HR	RBI	BB	SO	OBP	Slg.
L	.291	86	25	6	0	0	7	12	17	.378	.360	R	.256	340	87	14	5	2	23	26	25	.310	.344

MILLAR, KEVIN — 1B

PERSONAL: Born September 24, 1971, in Los Angeles. ... 6-0/210. ... Bats right, throws right. ... Full name: Kevin Charles Millar. ... Name pronounced: mi-LAR. ... High school: University (Los Angeles). ... College: Lamar. ... Nephew of Wayne Nordhagen, outfielder with four major league teams (1976-83). **TRANSACTIONS/CAREER NOTES:** Contract purchased by Florida Marlins organization from Saint Paul of the independent Northern League (September 20, 1993). ... On disabled list (April 19, 1998-remainder of season); included rehabilitation assignment to Charlotte. ... On disabled list (May 4-28, 2002); included rehabilitation assignment to Portland. ... Claimed on waivers by Boston Red Sox (January 14, 2003); rejected claim. ... Traded by Marlins to Red Sox for cash considerations (February 15, 2003). ... Signed as a free agent by Baltimore Orioles (January 13, 2006). **STATISTICAL NOTES:** Hit three home runs in one game (July 23, 2004). ... Career major league grand slams: 3.

2006 GAMES PLAYED BY POSITION (MLB): 1B—98, DH—30.

										BATTING								FIELDING	
Year Team (League)	Pos.	G	AB	R	H	2B	3B	HR	RBI	BB	SO	HBP	GDP	SB-CS	Avg.	OBP	SLG	OPS	E	Avg.
1993— St. Paul (North.)	2B-3B	63	227	33	59	11	1	5	30	24	27	...	...	2-...	.260	...	.383	...	18	.911
1994— Kane Co. (Midw.)	1B	135	477	75	144	35	2	19	93	74	88	13	12	3-3	.302	.405	.503	.908	11	.990
1995— Brevard County (FSL)	1B	129	459	53	132	32	2	13	68	70	66	12	8	4-4	.288	.388	.451	.839	12	.991
1996— Portland (East.)	1B-3B	130	472	69	150	32	0	18	86	37	53	9	13	6-5	.318	.375	.500	.875	15	.987
1997— Portland (East.)	1B-3B	135	511	94	175	34	2	32	131	66	53	10	11	2-3	.342	.423	.605	1.027	17	.987
1998— Florida (N.L.)	3B	2	2	1	1	0	0	0	0	1	0	0	0	0-0	.500	.667	.500	1.167	1	.833
—Charlotte (Int'l)	1B-3B	14	46	14	15	3	0	4	15	9	7	2	3	1-0	.326	.448	.652	1.100	4	.930
1999— Calgary (PCL)	OF-3B-1B	36	143	24	43	11	1	7	26	11	19	0	5	2-0	.301	.348	.538	.887	2	.973
—Florida (N.L.)	1B-3B-OF	105	351	48	100	17	4	9	67	40	64	7	7	1-0	.285	.362	.433	.795	4	.995
2000— Florida (N.L.)	1B-OF-3B DH	123	259	36	67	14	3	14	42	36	47	8	5	0-0	.259	.364	.498	.862	5	.985
2001— Florida (N.L.)	OF-1B-3B	144	449	62	141	39	5	20	85	39	70	5	8	0-0	.314	.374	.557	.931	2	.981
2002— Portland (East.)	DH	3	12	1	1	0	0	1	3	0	5	0	0	0-0	.083	.077	.333	.410	0	1.000
—Florida (N.L.)	OF-DH-1B 3B	126	438	58	134	41	0	16	57	40	74	5	15	0-2	.306	.366	.509	.875	4	.981
2003— Boston (A.L.)	1B-OF-DH	148	544	83	150	30	1	25	96	60	108	5	14	3-2	.276	.348	.472	.820	5	.995
2004— Boston (A.L.)	OF-1B-DH	150	508	74	151	36	0	18	74	57	91	•17	16	1-1	.297	.383	.474	.857	9	.986
2005— Boston (A.L.)	1B-OF	134	449	57	122	28	1	9	50	54	74	8	12	0-1	.272	.355	.399	.753	7	.992
2006— Baltimore (A.L.)	1B-DH	132	430	64	117	20	0	15	64	59	74	12	14	1-1	.272	.374	.437	.811	4	.995
American League totals (4 years)		564	1931	278	540	120	2	67	284	230	347	42	56	5-5	.280	.364	.448	.812	25	.993
National League totals (5 years)		500	1499	205	443	111	12	59	251	156	255	25	35	1-2	.296	.367	.504	.871	16	.990
Major League totals (9 years)		1064	3430	483	983	231	14	126	535	386	602	67	91	6-7	.287	.366	.472	.838	41	.992

DIVISION SERIES RECORD

Year Team (League)	Pos.	G	AB	R	H	2B	3B	HR	RBI	BB	SO	HBP	GDP	SB-CS	Avg.	OBP	SLG	OPS	E	Avg.
2003— Boston (A.L.)	1B	5	21	0	5	0	0	0	2	4	0	0	0	0-0	.238	.304	.238	.542	0	1.000
2004— Boston (A.L.)	1B	3	10	2	3	0	0	1	4	1	1	0	0	0-0	.300	.364	.600	.964	0	1.000
2005— Boston (A.L.)	1B	2	3	0	1	1	0	0	1	1	0	0	0	0-0	.333	.333	.667	1.000	0	1.000
Division series totals (3 years)		10	34	2	9	1	0	1	5	3	6	0	0	0-0	.265	.324	.382	.707	0	1.000

CHAMPIONSHIP SERIES RECORD

Year Team (League)	Pos.	G	AB	R	H	2B	3B	HR	RBI	BB	SO	HBP	GDP	SB-CS	Avg.	OBP	SLG	OPS	E	Avg.
2003— Boston (A.L.)	1B	7	29	3	7	0	0	1	3	1	9	0	1	0-0	.241	.267	.345	.611	1	.986
2004— Boston (A.L.)	1B	7	24	4	6	3	0	0	2	5	4	0	1	0-0	.250	.379	.375	.754	0	1.000
Champ. series totals (2 years)		14	53	7	13	3	0	1	5	6	13	0	2	0-0	.245	.322	.358	.681	1	.992

WORLD SERIES RECORD

Year Team (League)	Pos.	G	AB	R	H	2B	3B	HR	RBI	BB	SO	HBP	GDP	SB-CS	Avg.	OBP	SLG	OPS	E	Avg.
2004— Boston (A.L.)	1B	4	8	2	1	1	0	0	0	2	2	1	0	0-0	.125	.364	.250	.614	1	.900

2006 LEFTY-RIGHTY SPLITS

vs.	Avg.	AB	H	2B	3B	HR	RBI	BB	SO	OBP	Slg.	vs.	Avg.	AB	H	2B	3B	HR	RBI	BB	SO	OBP	Slg.
L	.244	119	29	8	0	3	12	16	18	.336	.387	R	.283	311	88	18	0	12	52	43	56	.388	.457

MILLEDGE, LASTINGS — OF

PERSONAL: Born April 5, 1985, in Bradenton, Fla. ... Bats right, throws right. ... Full name: Lastings Darnell Milledge. **TRANSACTIONS/CAREER NOTES:** Selected by New York Mets organization in first round (12th pick overall) of 2003 free-agent draft.

2006 GAMES PLAYED BY POSITION (MLB): OF—50.

										BATTING								FIELDING	
Year Team (League)	Pos.	G	AB	R	H	2B	3B	HR	RBI	BB	SO	HBP	GDP	SB-CS	Avg.	OBP	SLG	OPS	E	Avg.
2003— Kingsport (Appalachian)		7	26	4	6	2	0	0	2	3	4	1	0	5-1	.231	.323	.308	.631	...	...
2004— St. Lucie (Fla. St.)		22	81	6	19	6	2	2	8	9	21	1	3	3-2	.235	.319	.432	.751	.:.	...
—Capital City (SAL)		65	261	66	88	22	1	13	58	17	53	12	3	23-6	.337	.399	.579	.978	...	...
2005— St. Lucie (Fla. St.)	OF	62	232	48	70	15	0	4	22	19	41	13	5	18-13	.302	.385	.418	.803	10	.968
—Binghamton (East.)	OF-DH	48	193	33	65	17	0	4	24	14	47	4	1	11-5	.337	.392	.487	.879	4	.979
2006— Norfolk (Int'l)		84	307	52	85	21	4	7	36	43	67	14	1	13-10	.277	.388	.440	.828	2	.990
—New York (N.L.)	OF	56	166	14	40	7	2	4	22	12	39	5	4	1-2	.241	.310	.380	.689	2	.977
Major League totals (1 year)		56	166	14	40	7	2	4	22	12	39	5	4	1-2	.241	.310	.380	.689	2	.977

2006 LEFTY-RIGHTY SPLITS

vs.	Avg.	AB	H	2B	3B	HR	RBI	BB	SO	OBP	Slg.	vs.	Avg.	AB	H	2B	3B	HR	RBI	BB	SO	OBP	Slg.
L	.241	54	13	2	1	0	3	6	11	.349	.315	R	.241	112	27	5	1	4	19	6	28	.289	.411

MILLER, ANDREW — P

PERSONAL: Born May 21, 1985, in Gainesville, Fla. ... 6-6/210. ... Throws left, bats right. ... Full name: Andrew Mark Miller. ... College: North Carolina. **TRANSACTIONS/CAREER NOTES:** Selected by Tampa Bay Devil Rays organization in third round of 2003 free-agent draft; did not sign. ... Selected by Detroit Tigers organization in first round (sixth pick overall) of 2006 free-agent draft.

CAREER HITTING: 0-for-0 (.000), 0 R, 0 2B, 0 3B, 0 HR, 0 RBI.

Year Team (League)	W	L	Pct.	ERA	WHIP	G	GS	CG	ShO	Hld.	Sv.-Opp.	IP	H	R	ER	HR	BB-IBB	SO	Avg.
2006— Lakeland (Fla. St.)	0	0	...	0.00	0.60	3	0	0	0	...	0-0	5.0	2	0	0	0	1-0	9	.118
— Detroit (A.L.)	0	1	.000	6.10	1.74	8	0	0	0	1	0-0	10.1	8	9	7	0	10-0	6	.205
Major League totals (1 year)	0	1	.000	6.10	1.74	8	0	0	0	1	0-0	10.1	8	9	7	0	10-0	6	.205

2006 LEFTY-RIGHTY SPLITS

vs.	Avg.	AB	H	2B	3B	HR	RBI	BB	SO	OBP	Slg.	vs.	Avg.	AB	H	2B	3B	HR	RBI	BB	SO	OBP	Slg.
L	.333	9	3	0	1	0	3	7	1	.625	.556	R	.167	30	5	2	0	0	1	3	5	.286	.233

MILLER, CORKY — C

PERSONAL: Born March 18, 1976, in Yucaipa, Calif. ... 6-1/225. ... Bats right, throws right. ... Full name: Corky Abraham Philip Miller. ... High school: Yucaipa (Calif.). ... College: Nevada-Reno. **TRANSACTIONS/CAREER NOTES:** Selected by California Angels organization in 23rd round of 1994 free-agent draft; did not sign. ... Signed as a non-drafted free agent by Cincinnati Reds organization (June 5, 1998). ... Claimed on waivers by Minnesota Twins (October 4, 2004). ... Signed as a free agent by Boston Red Sox organization (April 25, 2006).

2006 GAMES PLAYED BY POSITION (MLB): C—1.

									BATTING									FIELDING	
Year Team (League)	Pos.	G	AB	R	H	2B	3B	HR	RBI	BB	SO	HBP	GDP	SB-CS	Avg.	OBP	SLG	OPS	E	Avg.
1998— Billings (Pion.)	C	45	129	28	35	8	0	5	24	24	24	21	2	1-4	.271	.455	.450	.904	14	.963
1999— Rockford (Midwest)	C	66	195	43	56	10	1	10	40	33	42	20	5	3-6	.287	.438	.503	.940	14	.975
— Chattanooga (Sou.)	C	33	104	20	23	10	0	4	16	11	30	11	3	0-0	.221	.354	.433	.787	3	.989
2000— Chattanooga (Sou.)	C	103	317	40	74	18	0	9	44	41	51	30	12	5-8	.233	.373	.375	.748	16	.981
2001— Chattanooga (Sou.)	C	59	170	25	47	12	0	9	42	25	32	19	1	1-2	.276	.425	.506	.931	7	.985
— Louisville (Int'l)	C	44	144	30	50	11	0	7	28	10	19	12	2	2-0	.347	.431	.569	1.001	2	.994
— Cincinnati (N.L.)	C	17	49	5	9	2	0	3	7	4	16	2	1	1-0	.184	.263	.408	.671	1	.991
2002— Louisville (Int'l)	C	43	134	14	31	5	0	6	21	16	21	6	6	1-2	.231	.340	.403	.743	2	.993
— Cincinnati (N.L.)	C	39	114	9	29	10	0	3	15	9	20	4	7	0-0	.254	.328	.421	.749	2	.992
2003— Louisville (Int'l)	C-DH	103	354	49	88	28	0	11	43	35	58	7	12	0-0	.249	.326	.421	.747	7	.989
— Cincinnati (N.L.)	C	14	30	4	8	0	0	1	5	7	7	2	1	0-0	.267	.395	.267	.661	0	1.000
2004— Louisville (Int'l)	C-DH	74	227	31	50	14	0	6	37	25	44	9	4	0-0	.220	.316	.361	.677	4	.990
— Cincinnati (N.L.)	C	13	39	2	1	0	0	0	3	6	12	3	3	0-0	.026	.204	.026	.230	1	.989
2005— Minnesota (A.L.)	C-DH	5	12	0	0	0	0	0	0	0	2	0	0	0-0	.000	.000	.000	.000	1	1.000
— Rochester (Int'l)	C-DH-1B																			
	P	59	170	35	39	7	0	11	25	27	30	14	4	0-2	.229	.379	.465	.844	3	.994
2006— Pawtucket (Int'l)		63	198	29	51	11	0	13	36	22	43	6	6	0-0	.258	.343	.510	.854	6	.986
— Tacoma (PCL)		2	6	1	2	0	0	0	1	1	0	0	0	0-0	.333	.429	.333	.762	0	1.000
— Boston (A.L.)	C	1	4	0	0	0	0	0	0	0	1	0	0	0-0	.000	.000	.000	.000	0	1.000
American League totals (2 years)		6	16	0	0	0	0	0	0	0	3	0	0	0-0	.000	.000	.000	.000	1	1.000
National League totals (4 years)		83	232	20	47	12	0	6	26	24	55	11	12	1-0	.203	.301	.332	.633	4	.992
Major League totals (6 years)		89	248	20	47	12	0	6	26	24	58	11	12	1-0	.190	.285	.310	.595	4	.993

2006 LEFTY-RIGHTY SPLITS

vs.	Avg.	AB	H	2B	3B	HR	RBI	BB	SO	OBP	Slg.	vs.	Avg.	AB	H	2B	3B	HR	RBI	BB	SO	OBP	Slg.
L	.000	2	0	0	0	0	0	0	1	.000	.000	R	.000	2	0	0	0	0	0	0	0	.000	.000

MILLER, DAMIAN — C

PERSONAL: Born October 13, 1969, in La Crosse, Wis. ... 6-3/220. ... Bats right, throws right. ... Full name: Damian Donald Miller. ... High school: West Salem (Wis.). ... College: Viterbo (Wis.). **TRANSACTIONS/CAREER NOTES:** Selected by Minnesota Twins organization in 20th round of 1990 free-agent draft. ... Selected by Arizona Diamondbacks in second round (47th pick overall) of expansion draft (November 18, 1997). ... On disabled list (July 24-August 14, 2002); included rehabilitation assignment to Tucson. ... Traded by Diamondbacks to Chicago Cubs for P David Noyce and OF Gary Johnson (November 13, 2002). ... Traded by Cubs to Oakland Athletics for C Michael Barrett (December 21, 2003). ... Signed as a free agent by Milwaukee Brewers (November 24, 2004). **STATISTICAL NOTES:** Career major league grand slams: 5.

2006 GAMES PLAYED BY POSITION (MLB): C—98.

									BATTING									FIELDING	
Year Team (League)	Pos.	G	AB	R	H	2B	3B	HR	RBI	BB	SO	HBP	GDP	SB-CS	Avg.	OBP	SLG	OPS	E	Avg.
1990— Elizabethton (App.)	C	14	45	7	10	1	0	1	6	9	3	0	2	1-0	.222	.352	.311	.663	2	.982
1991— Kenosha (Midw.)	1B-C-OF	80	267	28	62	11	1	3	34	24	53	2	4	3-2	.232	.297	.315	.612	4	.990
1992— Kenosha (Midw.)	C	115	377	53	110	27	2	5	56	53	66	7	13	0-0	.292	.385	.414	.799	9	.989
1993— Fort Myers (FSL)	C	87	325	31	69	12	1	1	26	31	44	0	5	6-3	.212	.281	.265	.546	8	.985
— Nashville (Southern)	C	4	13	0	3	0	0	0	0	2	4	0	0	0-0	.231	.333	.231	.564	0	1.000
1994— Nashville (Southern)	C	103	328	36	88	10	0	8	35	35	51	1	11	4-6	.268	.336	.372	.708	8	.989
1995— Salt Lake (PCL)	C-OF	83	295	39	84	23	1	3	41	15	39	3	11	2-4	.285	.324	.400	.724	1	.998
1996— Salt Lake (PCL)	1B-C	104	385	54	110	27	1	7	55	25	58	6	13	1-4	.286	.336	.416	.751	6	.992
1997— Salt Lake (PCL)	C-DH	85	314	48	106	19	3	11	82	29	62	3	7	6-1	.338	.395	.522	.918	6	.988
— Minnesota (A.L.)	C-DH	25	66	5	18	1	0	2	13	2	12	0	2	0-0	.273	.282	.379	.660	0	1.000
1998— Tucson (PCL)	C	18	63	14	22	7	1	0	11	9	9	2	2	0-0	.349	.434	.492	.926	3	.973
— Arizona (N.L.)	C-DH-OF																			
	1B	57	168	17	48	14	2	3	14	11	43	2	0	1-0	.286	.337	.446	.783	4	.986
1999— Arizona (N.L.)	C	86	296	35	80	19	0	11	47	19	78	2	6	0-0	.270	.316	.446	.762	6	.991
2000— Arizona (N.L.)	C-1B	100	324	43	89	24	0	10	44	36	74	1	6	2-2	.275	.347	.441	.788	7	.991
2001— Arizona (N.L.)	C	123	380	45	103	19	0	13	47	35	80	4	9	0-1	.271	.337	.424	.761	7	.993
2002— Arizona (N.L.)	C	101	297	40	74	22	0	11	42	38	88	3	14	0-0	.249	.340	.434	.775	2	.997
— Tucson (PCL)	C	3	9	1	3	1	0	0	0	1	4	0	1	0-0	.333	.333	.444	.778	0	1.000
2003— Chicago (N.L.)	C	114	352	34	82	19	1	9	36	39	91	1	15	1-0	.233	.310	.369	.680	3	.997
2004— Oakland (A.L.)	C	110	397	39	108	25	0	9	58	39	87	2	19	0-1	.272	.339	.403	.742	1	.999
2005— Milwaukee (N.L.)	C	114	385	50	105	25	1	9	43	37	94	4	11	0-1	.273	.340	.413	.753	3	.996
2006— Milwaukee (N.L.)	C	101	331	34	83	28	0	6	38	33	86	4	11	0-0	.251	.322	.390	.711	2	.997
American League totals (2 years)		135	463	44	126	26	0	11	71	41	99	2	21	0-1	.272	.331	.400	.730	1	.999
National League totals (8 years)		796	2533	298	664	170	4	72	311	248	634	21	79	4-4	.262	.331	.418	.749	34	.994
Major League totals (10 years)		931	2996	342	790	196	4	83	382	289	733	23	100	4-5	.264	.331	.415	.746	35	.995

DIVISION SERIES RECORD

Year Team (League)	Pos.	G	AB	R	H	2B	3B	HR	RBI	BB	SO	HBP	GDP	SB-CS	Avg.	OBP	SLG	OPS	E	Avg.
2001— Arizona (N.L.)	C	5	15	1	4	0	0	0	0	1	3	1	0	0-0	.267	.353	.267	.620	0	1.000
2002— Arizona (N.L.)	C	1	2	0	1	1	0	0	1	0	0	0	0	0-0	.500	.750	1.000	1.750	0	1.000
2003— Chicago (N.L.)	C	4	11	0	1	1	0	0	0	4	5	0	0	0-0	.091	.231	.182	.413	0	1.000
Division series totals (3 years)		10	28	1	6	2	0	0	1	5	8	1	0	0-0	.214	.353	.286	.639	0	1.000

M

CHAMPIONSHIP SERIES RECORD

Year Team (League)	Pos.	G	AB	R	H	2B	3B	HR	RBI	BB	SO	HBP	GDP	SB-CS	Avg.	OBP	SLG	OPS	E	Avg.
2001— Arizona (N.L.)	C	5	17	0	3	0	0	0	0	2	5	0	2	0-0	.176	.263	.176	.440	0	1.000
2003— Chicago (N.L.)	C	4	10	0	2	1	0	0	1	2	2	0	0	0-0	.200	.333	.300	.633	0	1.000
Champ. series totals (2 years)		9	27	0	5	1	0	0	1	4	7	0	2	0-0	.185	.290	.222	.513	0	1.000

WORLD SERIES RECORD

Year Team (League)	Pos.	G	AB	R	H	2B	3B	HR	RBI	BB	SO	HBP	GDP	SB-CS	Avg.	OBP	SLG	OPS	E	Avg.
2001— Arizona (N.L.)	C	6	20	3	4	2	0	0	2	1	11	1	1	0-0	.200	.273	.300	.573	1	.982

ALL-STAR GAME RECORD

		G	AB	R	H	2B	3B	HR	RBI	BB	SO	HBP	GDP	SB-CS	Avg.	OBP	SLG	OPS	E	Avg.
All-Star Game totals (1 year)		1	3	1	2	1	0	0	1	0	0	0	0	0-0	.667	.667	1.333	2.000	0	1.000

2006 LEFTY-RIGHTY SPLITS

vs.	Avg.	AB	H	2B	3B	HR	RBI	BB	SO	OBP	Slg.	vs.	Avg.	AB	H	2B	3B	HR	RBI	BB	SO	OBP	Slg.
L	.280	82	23	15	0	1	10	12	22	.365	.500	R	.241	249	60	13	0	5	28	21	64	.307	.353

MILLER, MATT — P

PERSONAL: Born November 23, 1971, in Greenwood, Miss. ... 6-3/215. ... Throws right, bats right. ... Full name: Matt Jacob Miller. ... High school: Monterey (Lubbock, Texas). ... College: Delta State. **TRANSACTIONS/CAREER NOTES:** Signed as a free agent by Texas Rangers organization (December 1, 1997). ... Released by Rangers (March 29, 1998). ... Contract purchased by Rangers organization from Greenville of the independent Big South League (June 27, 1998). ... Signed as a free agent by San Diego Padres organization (November 5, 2000). ... Signed as a free agent by Oakland Athletics organization (November 19, 2001). ... Signed as a free agent by Colorado Rockies organization (November 20, 2002). ... Signed as a free agent by Cleveland Indians organization (January 5, 2004). ... On disabled list (July 16, 2005-remainder of season); included rehabilitation assignments to Mahoning Valley and Akron. ... On disabled list (April 20-September 5, 2006); included rehabilitation assignments to Buffalo and Akron.

CAREER HITTING: 0-for-0 (.000), 0 R, 0 2B, 0 3B, 0 HR, 0 RBI.

Year Team (League)	W	L	Pct.	ERA	WHIP	G	GS	CG	ShO	Hld.	Sv.-Opp.	IP	H	R	ER	HR	BB-IBB	SO	Avg.
1996— Greenville (BSL)	5	2	.714	6.07	1.82	19	6	0	0	...	1-...	69.2	77	51	47	2	50-0	54	.286
1997— Greenville (BSL)	12	3	.800	2.26	1.16	15	15	5	3	...	0-...	107.1	76	34	27	0	49-0	129	.203
1998— Greenville (BSL)	1	7	.125	2.85	1.21	8	8	4	0	...	0-...	53.2	46	26	17	1	19-1	49	.230
— Savannah (S. Atl.)	3	1	.750	2.29	0.99	17	0	0	0	...	3-...	35.1	25	9	9	0	10-0	46	.203
1999— Charlotte (Fla. St.)	1	2	.333	3.03	1.35	22	0	0	0	...	8-...	29.2	27	12	10	0	13-1	39	.231
— Tulsa (Texas)	6	4	.600	3.38	1.25	34	0	0	0	...	7-...	56.0	42	24	21	2	28-2	83	.213
2000— GC Rangers (GCL)	0	0	...	4.50	1.00	1	0	0	0	...	0-...	2.0	2	1	1	0	0-0	4	.250
— Tulsa (Texas)	0	0	...	14.73	3.00	3	0	0	0	...	0-...	3.2	7	7	6	0	4-0	4	.412
— Oklahoma (PCL)	3	3	.500	3.58	1.57	39	0	0	0	...	4-...	60.1	61	29	24	6	34-4	69	.264
2001— Portland (PCL)	1	7	.125	3.63	1.30	44	0	0	0	...	17-...	44.2	44	22	18	1	14-2	43	.254
2002— Sacramento (PCL)	3	7	.300	4.31	1.54	54	0	0	0	...	6-...	71.0	81	42	34	5	28-8	63	.286
2003— Colorado (N.L.)	0	0	...	2.08	1.62	4	0	0	0	...	0-...	4.1	5	1	1	0	2-0	5	.313
— Colo. Springs (PCL)	5	0	1.000	2.13	1.09	61	0	0	0	...	3-...	63.1	46	17	15	0	23-1	83	.204
2004— Buffalo (Int'l)	1	2	.333	1.93	1.14	13	0	0	0	...	2-...	14.0	10	4	3	0	6-1	17	.196
— Cleveland (A.L.)	4	1	.800	3.09	1.17	57	0	0	0	7	1-2	55.1	42	22	19	1	23-8	55	.216
2005— Buffalo (Int'l)	0	0	...	0.87	0.48	9	0	0	0	1	3-3	10.1	3	1	1	0	2-0	15	.088
— Cleveland (A.L.)	1	0	1.000	1.82	1.08	23	0	0	0	4	1-2	29.2	22	6	6	1	10-3	23	.212
— Mahoning Valley (N.Y.-Penn.)	0	0	...	54.00	7.50	1	1	0	0	...	0-0	0.2	5	4	4	0	1-0	0	.714
— Akron (East.)	0	0	...	0.00	0.00	1	0	0	0	...	0-0	1.0	0	0	0	0	0-0	0	.000
2006— Akron (East.)	0	0	...	0.00	1.50	2	0	0	0	...	0-0	2.0	2	0	0	0	1-0	0	.286
— Buffalo (Int'l)	0	0	...	0.00	0.00	1	1	0	0	...	0-0	1.0	0	0	0	0	0-0	2	...
— Cleveland (A.L.)	1	0	1.000	3.45	1.28	14	0	0	0	1	0-0	15.2	11	6	6	2	9-0	12	.212
American League totals (3 years)	6	1	.857	2.77	1.16	94	0	0	0	12	2-4	100.2	75	34	31	4	42-11	90	.214
National League totals (1 year)	0	0	...	2.08	1.62	4	0	0	0	0	0-0	4.1	5	1	1	0	2-0	5	.313
Major League totals (4 years)	6	1	.857	2.74	1.18	98	0	0	0	12	2-4	105.0	80	35	32	4	44-11	95	.219

2006 LEFTY-RIGHTY SPLITS

vs.	Avg.	AB	H	2B	3B	HR	RBI	BB	SO	OBP	Slg.	vs.	Avg.	AB	H	2B	3B	HR	RBI	BB	SO	OBP	Slg.
L	.250	20	5	0	0	2	4	4	2	.360	.550	R	.188	32	6	2	0	0	5	5	10	.325	.250

MILLER, TREVER — P

PERSONAL: Born May 29, 1973, in Louisville, Ky. ... 6-3/200. ... Throws left, bats right. ... Full name: Trever Douglas Miller. ... High school: Trinity (Louisville, Ky.). **TRANSACTIONS/CAREER NOTES:** Selected by Detroit Tigers organization in supplemental round ("sandwich pick" between first and second rounds, 41st pick overall) of 1991 free-agent draft; pick received as part of compensation for Atlanta Braves signing Type A free-agent C Mike Heath. ... Traded by Tigers with C Brad Ausmus, Ps Jose Lima and C.J. Nitkowski and 1B Daryle Ward to Houston Astros for OF Brian Hunter, IF Orlando Miller, Ps Doug Brocail and Todd Jones and cash (December 10, 1996). ... On disabled list (August 23-September 7, 1998). ... Traded by Astros to Philadelphia Phillies for P Yorkis Perez (March 29, 2000). ... Claimed on waivers by Los Angeles Dodgers (May 19, 2000). ... Signed as a free agent by Boston Red Sox organization (January 22, 2001). ... Signed as a free agent by Cincinnati Reds organization (December 21, 2001). ... Released by Reds (September 4, 2002). ... Signed by Toronto Blue Jays organization (October 30, 2002). ... Signed as a free agent by Tampa Bay Devil Rays (January 7, 2004). ... On disabled list (June 13-28, 2005). ... Signed as free agent by Houston Astros (January 10, 2006). ... On disabled list (April 19-May 12, 2006); included rehabilitation assignment to Round Rock.

CAREER HITTING: 1-for-6 (.167), 1 R, 1 2B, 0 3B, 0 HR, 0 RBI.

Year Team (League)	W	L	Pct.	ERA	WHIP	G	GS	CG	ShO	Hld.	Sv.-Opp.	IP	H	R	ER	HR	BB-IBB	SO	Avg.
1991— Bristol (Appal.)	2	7	.222	5.67	1.65	13	13	0	0	...	0-...	54.0	60	44	34	7	29-0	46	.278
1992— Bristol (Appal.)	3	8	.273	4.93	1.47	12	12	1	0	...	0-...	69.1	75	45	38	4	27-0	64	.271
1993— Fayetteville (SAL)	8	13	.381	4.19	1.35	28	28	2	0	...	0-...	161.0	151	99	75	7	67-0	116	.245
1994— Trenton (East.)	7	16	.304	4.39	1.43	26	26	6	0	...	0-...	174.1	198	95	85	9	51-0	73	.290
1995— Jacksonville (Sou.)	8	2	.800	2.72	1.28	31	16	3	2	...	0-...	122.1	122	46	37	5	34-0	77	.261
1996— Toledo (Int'l)	13	6	.684	4.90	1.40	27	27	0	0	...	0-...	165.1	167	98	90	19	65-1	115	.260
— Detroit (A.L.)	0	4	.000	9.18	2.22	5	4	0	0	0	0-0	16.2	28	17	17	3	9-0	8	.384
1997— New Orleans (A.A.)	6	7	.462	3.30	1.41	29	27	2	0	...	0-...	163.2	177	71	60	15	54-1	99	.283
1998— Houston (N.L.)	2	0	1.000	3.04	1.44	37	1	0	0	1	1-2	53.1	57	21	18	4	20-1	30	.266
1999— Houston (N.L.)	3	2	.600	5.07	1.75	47	0	0	0	4	1-1	49.2	58	29	28	6	29-1	37	.299
2000— Philadelphia (N.L.)	0	0	...	8.36	2.00	14	0	0	0	0	0-0	14.0	19	16	13	3	9-1	10	.317
— Los Angeles (N.L.)	0	0	...	23.14	4.71	2	0	0	0	0	0-0	2.1	8	6	6	0	3-0	1	.571
— Albuquerque (PCL)	4	2	.667	3.41	1.38	12	9	1	1	...	0-...	58.0	60	29	22	5	20-0	39	.268
2001— Sarasota (Fla. St.)	0	0	...	2.25	0.50	3	2	0	0	...	0-...	8.0	3	2	2	0	1-0	6	.115
— Pawtucket (Int'l)	3	11	.214	5.20	1.52	33	15	0	0	...	0-...	116.0	142	79	67	16	34-2	93	.307
2002— Louisville (Int'l)	9	5	.643	3.18	1.21	65	0	0	0	...	0-...	82.0	76	30	29	6	23-4	80	.242
2003— Toronto (A.L.)	2	2	.500	4.61	1.41	*79	0	0	0	16	3-4	52.2	46	30	27	7	28-3	44	.231

M

Year Team (League)	W	L	Pct.	ERA	WHIP	G	GS	CG	ShO	Hld.	Sv.-Opp.	IP	H	R	ER	HR	BB-IBB	SO	Avg.
2004— Tampa Bay (A.L.)	1	1	.500	3.12	1.29	60	0	0	0		9	1-3	49.0	48	21	17	3	15-4	43	.257
2005— Tampa Bay (A.L.)	2	2	.500	4.06	1.67	61	0	0	0		11	0-3	44.1	45	23	20	4	29-6	35	.278
2006— Round Rock (PCL)	0	0		0.00	0.00	2	2	0	0		0	0-0	2.0	0	0	0	0	0-0	3	
— Houston (N.L.)	2	3	.400	3.02	1.09	70	0	0	0		12	1-3	50.2	42	17	17	7	13-2	56	.225
American League totals (4 years)	5	9	.357	4.48	1.52	205	4	0	0		36	4-10	162.2	167	91	81	17	81-13	130	.269
National League totals (4 years)	7	5	.583	4.34	1.52	170	1	0	0		17	3-6	170.0	184	89	82	20	74-5	134	.275
Major League totals (8 years)	12	14	.462	4.41	1.52	375	5	0	0		53	7-16	332.2	351	180	163	37	155-18	264	.272

DIVISION SERIES RECORD

Year Team (League)	W	L	Pct.	ERA	WHIP	G	GS	CG	ShO	Hld.	Sv.-Opp.	IP	H	R	ER	HR	BB-IBB	SO	Avg.
1998— Houston (N.L.)	0	0	...			1	0	0	0		0	0-0	0.0	0	0	0	0	1-0	0	
1999— Houston (N.L.)	0	0	...	0.00	0.75	2	0	0	0		1	0-0	1.1	1	0	0	0	0-0	2	.200
Division series totals (2 years)	0	0	...	0.00	1.50	3	0	0	0		1	0-0	1.1	1	0	0	0	1-0	2	.200

2006 LEFTY-RIGHTY SPLITS

vs.	Avg.	AB	H	2B	3B	HR	RBI	BB	SO	OBP	Slg.	vs.	Avg.	AB	H	2B	3B	HR	RBI	BB	SO	OBP	Slg.
L	.224	85	19	2	0	4	9	7	31	.280	.388	R	.225	102	23	7	0	3	9	6	25	.292	.382

MILLER, WADE   P

PERSONAL: Born September 13, 1976, in Reading, Pa. ... 6-2/220. ... Throws right, bats right. ... Full name: Wade T. Miller. ... High school: Brandywine Heights (Pa.). ... College: Alvernia (Pa.). **TRANSACTIONS/CAREER NOTES:** Selected by Houston Astros organization in 20th round of 1996 free-agent draft. ... On disabled list (April 15-May 29, 2002); included rehabilitation assignment to New Orleans. ... On disabled list (June 26, 2004-remainder of season). ... Signed as a free agent by Boston Red Sox (December 22, 2004). ... On disabled list (April 1-May 8 and August 8, 2005-remainder of season); inlcuded rehabilitation assignment to Pawtucket. ... Signed as free agent by Chicago Cubs (January 23, 2006). ... On disabled list (April 1-September 1, 2006); included rehabilitation assignments to Peoria, West Tenn and Iowa. **MISCELLANEOUS NOTES:** Received a base on balls and struck out twice in three appearances as pinch hitter (2003). ... Struck out in only appearance as pinch hitter (2004). **CAREER HITTING:** 46-for-269 (.171), 20 R, 9 2B, 0 3B, 0 HR, 17 RBI.

Year Team (League)	W	L	Pct.	ERA	WHIP	G	GS	CG	ShO	Hld.	Sv.-Opp.	IP	H	R	ER	HR	BB-IBB	SO	Avg.
1996— GC Astros (GCL)	3	4	.429	3.79	1.07	11	10	0	0	...	0-...	57.0	49	26	24	1	12-0	53	.233
— Auburn (NY-Penn)	1	1	.500	5.00	1.33	2	2	0	0	...	0-...	9.0	8	9	5	0	4-0	11	.216
1997— Quad City (Midw.)	5	3	.625	3.36	0.93	10	8	2	0	...	0-...	59.0	45	27	22	7	10-0	50	.201
— Kissimmee (Fla. St.)	10	2	.833	1.80	0.93	14	14	4	1	...	0-...	100.0	79	28	20	3	14-1	76	.214
1998— Jackson (Texas)	5	0	1.000	2.32	1.23	10	10	0	0	...	0-...	62.0	49	23	16	7	27-2	48	.213
1999— New Orleans (PCL)	11	9	.550	4.38	1.36	26	26	0	0	...	0-...	162.1	156	85	79	16	64-0	135	.248
— Houston (N.L.)	0	1	.000	9.58	2.13	5	1	0	0	0	0-0	10.1	17	11	11	4	5-0	8	.362
2000— New Orleans (PCL)	4	5	.444	3.67	1.26	16	15	0	0	...	0-...	105.1	95	46	43	6	38-1	81	.245
— Houston (N.L.)	6	6	.500	5.14	1.39	16	16	2	0	0	0-0	105.0	104	66	60	14	42-1	89	.257
2001— Houston (N.L.)	16	8	.667	3.40	1.22	32	32	1	0	0	0-0	212.0	183	91	80	31	76-3	183	.234
2002— Houston (N.L.)	15	4	.789	3.28	1.29	26	26	1	1	0	0-0	164.2	151	63	60	14	62-9	144	.249
— New Orleans (PCL)	0	0		2.25	1.38	2	2	0	0	...	0-...	8.0	10	4	2	0	1-0	9	.323
2003— Houston (N.L.)	14	13	.519	4.13	1.31	33	33	1	0	0	0-0	187.1	168	96	86	17	77-1	161	.242
2004— Houston (N.L.)	7	7	.500	3.35	1.35	15	15	0	0	0	0-0	88.2	76	35	33	11	44-0	74	.228
2005— Greenville (SAL)	0	0		3.86	1.07	1	1	0	0	0	0-0	4.2	4	2	2	1	1-0	4	.222
— Wilmington (Caro.)	0	0		1.80	1.20	1	1	0	0	0	0-0	5.0	6	1	1	1	0-0	6	.316
— Pawtucket (Int'l)	0	0		2.53	1.50	2	2	0	0	0	0-0	10.2	10	4	3	1	6-0	10	.250
— Boston (A.L.)	4	4	.500	4.95	1.57	16	16	0	0	0	0-0	91.0	96	53	50	8	47-0	64	.267
2006— Peoria (Midw.)	0	0		2.50	1.22	5	5	0	0	0	0-0	18.0	17	5	5	0	5-0	15	.254
— West Tenn (Sou.)	1	0	1.000	1.50	0.67	1	1	0	0	0	0-0	6.0	3	1	1	0	1-0	4	.143
— Iowa (PCL)	1	0	1.000	6.55	1.91	2	2	0	0	0	0-0	11.0	18	8	8	2	3-0	9	.383
— Chicago (N.L.)	0	2	.000	4.57	1.71	5	5	0	0	0	0-0	21.2	19	12	11	4	18-1	20	.232
American League totals (1 year)	4	4	.500	4.95	1.57	16	16	0	0	0	0-0	91.0	96	53	50	8	47-0	64	.267
National League totals (7 years)	58	41	.586	3.89	1.32	132	128	5	1	0	0-0	789.2	718	374	341	95	324-15	679	.243
Major League totals (8 years)	62	45	.579	4.00	1.35	148	144	5	1	0	0-0	880.2	814	427	391	103	371-15	743	.246

DIVISION SERIES RECORD

Year Team (League)	W	L	Pct.	ERA	WHIP	G	GS	CG	ShO	Hld.	Sv.-Opp.	IP	H	R	ER	HR	BB-IBB	SO	Avg.
2001— Houston (N.L.)	0	0	...	2.57	1.00	1	1	0	0	0	0-0	7.0	7	2	2	1	0-0	6	.292

2006 LEFTY-RIGHTY SPLITS

vs.	Avg.	AB	H	2B	3B	HR	RBI	BB	SO	OBP	Slg.	vs.	Avg.	AB	H	2B	3B	HR	RBI	BB	SO	OBP	Slg.
L	.273	44	12	2	0	4	11	14	12	.458	.591	R	.184	38	7	0	0	0	0	4	8	.262	.184

MILLWOOD, KEVIN   P

PERSONAL: Born December 24, 1974, in Gastonia, N.C. ... 6-4/235. ... Throws right, bats right. ... Full name: Kevin Austin Millwood. ... High school: Bessemer City (N.C.). **TRANSACTIONS/CAREER NOTES:** Selected by Atlanta Braves organization in 11th round of 1993 free-agent draft. ... On disabled list (May 7-July 20, 2001); included rehabilitation assignments to Macon and Greenville. ... Traded by Braves to Philadelphia Phillies for C Johnny Estrada (December 20, 2002). ... On disabled list (August 6-September 12, 2004). ... Signed as a free agent by Cleveland Indians (January 6, 2005). ... On disabled list (May 26-June 16, 2005). ... On suspended list (August 5-11, 2005). ... Signed as a free agent by Texas Rangers (December 29, 2005). **STATISTICAL NOTES:** Pitched 1-0 no-hit victory against San Francisco (April 27, 2003). **CAREER HITTING:** 53-for-433 (.122), 18 R, 14 2B, 0 3B, 2 HR, 24 RBI.

Year Team (League)	W	L	Pct.	ERA	WHIP	G	GS	CG	ShO	Hld.	Sv.-Opp.	IP	H	R	ER	HR	BB-IBB	SO	Avg.
1993— GC Braves (GCL)	3	3	.500	3.06	1.28	12	9	0	0	...	0-...	50.0	36	27	17	3	28-0	49	.196
1994— Danville (Appal.)	3	3	.500	3.72	1.65	13	5	0	0	...	1-...	46.0	42	25	19	4	34-2	56	.247
— Macon (S. Atl.)	0	5	.000	5.79	1.93	12	4	0	0	...	1-...	32.2	31	31	21	4	32-1	24	.242
1995— Macon (S. Atl.)	5	6	.455	4.63	1.39	29	12	0	0	...	1-...	103.0	86	65	53	10	57-0	89	.219
1996— Durham (Carol.)	6	9	.400	4.28	1.31	33	20	1	0	...	1-...	149.1	138	77	71	17	58-0	139	.248
1997— Greenville (Sou.)	3	5	.375	4.11	1.35	11	11	0	0	...	0-...	61.1	59	37	28	8	24-0	61	.250
— Richmond (Int'l)	7	0	1.000	1.93	0.89	9	9	1	0	...	0-...	60.2	38	13	13	2	16-0	46	.178
— Atlanta (N.L.)	5	3	.625	4.03	1.48	12	8	0	0	0	0-0	51.1	55	26	23	1	21-1	42	.282
1998— Atlanta (N.L.)	17	8	.680	4.08	1.33	31	29	3	1	1	0-0	174.1	175	86	79	18	56-3	163	.258
1999— Atlanta (N.L.)	18	7	.720	2.68	1.00	33	33	0	0	0	0-0	228.0	168	80	68	24	59-2	205	* .202
2000— Atlanta (N.L.)	10	13	.435	4.66	1.29	36	• 35	0	0	0	0-0	212.2	213	115	110	26	62-2	168	.258
2001— Atlanta (N.L.)	7	7	.500	4.31	1.33	21	21	0	0	0	0-0	121.0	121	66	58	20	40-6	84	.260
— Macon (S. Atl.)	0	0		0.00	0.00	1	1	0	0	...	0-...	3.0	0	0	0	0	0-0	5	.000
— Greenville (Sou.)	0	1	.000	4.50	1.20	2	2	0	0	...	0-...	10.0	9	6	5	2	3-0	10	.243
2002— Atlanta (N.L.)	18	8	.692	3.24	1.16	35	34	1	1	0	0-0	217.0	186	83	78	16	65-7	178	.230
2003— Philadelphia (N.L.)	14	12	.538	4.01	1.25	35	35	5	• 3	0	0-0	222.0	210	103	99	19	68-6	169	.250
2004— Philadelphia (N.L.)	9	6	.600	4.85	1.46	25	25	0	0	0	0-0	141.0	155	81	76	14	51-5	125	.278

Year Team (League)	W	L	Pct.	ERA	WHIP	G	GS	CG	ShO	Hld.	Sv.-Opp.	IP	H	R	ER	HR	BB-IBB	SO	Avg.
2005— Cleveland (A.L.)	9	11	.450	*2.86	1.22	30	30	1	0	0	0-0	192.0	182	72	61	20	52-0	146	.248
2006— Texas (A.L.)	16	12	.571	4.52	1.31	34	•34	2	0	0	0-0	215.0	228	114	108	23	53-4	157	.272
American League totals (2 years)	25	23	.521	3.74	1.27	64	64	3	0	0	0-0	407.0	410	186	169	43	105-4	303	.261
National League totals (8 years)	98	64	.605	3.89	1.25	228	220	11	5	1	0-0	1367.1	1283	640	591	138	422-32	1134	.247
Major League totals (10 years)	123	87	.586	3.85	1.25	292	284	14	5	1	0-0	1774.1	1693	826	760	181	527-36	1437	.250

DIVISION SERIES RECORD

Year Team (League)	W	L	Pct.	ERA	WHIP	G	GS	CG	ShO	Hld.	Sv.-Opp.	IP	H	R	ER	HR	BB-IBB	SO	Avg.
1999— Atlanta (N.L.)	1	0	1.000	0.90	0.10	2	1	1	0	0	1-1	10.0	1	1	1	1	0-0	9	.031
2000— Atlanta (N.L.)	0	1	.000	7.71	1.50	1	1	0	0	0	0-0	4.2	4	4	4	2	3-0	3	.222
2001— Atlanta (N.L.)	Did not play.																		
2002— Atlanta (N.L.)	1	1	.500	3.27	0.64	2	2	0	0	0	0-0	11.0	7	4	4	3	0-0	14	.175
Division series totals (3 years)	2	2	.500	3.16	0.58	5	4	1	0	0	1-1	25.2	12	9	9	6	3-0	26	.133

CHAMPIONSHIP SERIES RECORD

Year Team (League)	W	L	Pct.	ERA	WHIP	G	GS	CG	ShO	Hld.	Sv.-Opp.	IP	H	R	ER	HR	BB-IBB	SO	Avg.
1999— Atlanta (N.L.)	1	0	1.000	3.55	1.11	2	2	0	0	0	0-0	12.2	13	6	5	1	1-0	9	.260
2001— Atlanta (N.L.)	0	0	...	0.00	0.00	1	0	0	0	0	0-0	1.0	0	0	0	0	0-0	1	.000
Champ. series totals (2 years)	1	0	1.000	3.29	1.02	3	2	0	0	0	0-0	13.2	13	6	5	1	1-0	10	.245

WORLD SERIES RECORD

Year Team (League)	W	L	Pct.	ERA	WHIP	G	GS	CG	ShO	Hld.	Sv.-Opp.	IP	H	R	ER	HR	BB-IBB	SO	Avg.
1999— Atlanta (N.L.)	0	1	.000	18.00	5.00	1	1	0	0	0	0-0	2.0	8	5	4	0	2-0	2	.615

ALL-STAR GAME RECORD

	W	L	Pct.	ERA	WHIP	G	GS	CG	ShO	Hld.	Sv.-Opp.	IP	H	R	ER	HR	BB-IBB	SO	Avg.
All-Star Game totals (1 year)	0	0	...	0.00	1.00	1	0	0	0	0	0-0	1.0	1	0	0	0	0-0	1	.250

2006 LEFTY-RIGHTY SPLITS

vs.	Avg.	AB	H	2B	3B	HR	RBI	BB	SO	OBP	Slg.	vs.	Avg.	AB	H	2B	3B	HR	RBI	BB	SO	OBP	Slg.
L	.285	417	119	20	1	13	52	38	89	.347	.432	R	.258	422	109	22	5	10	49	15	68	.286	.405

MILTON, ERIC — P

PERSONAL: Born August 4, 1975, in State College, Pa. ... 6-3/208. ... Throws left, bats left. ... Full name: Eric Robert Milton. ... High school: Bellefonte (Pa.). ... College: Maryland. **TRANSACTIONS/CAREER NOTES:** Selected by New York Yankees organization in first round (20th pick overall) of 1996 free-agent draft. ... Traded by Yankees with P Danny Mota, OF Brian Buchanan, SS Cristian Guzman and cash to Minnesota Twins for 2B Chuck Knoblauch (February 6, 1998). ... On disabled list (August 7-September 2, 2002). ... On disabled list (March 13-September 14, 2003); included rehabilitation assignments to Fort Myers and New Britain. ... Traded by Twins to Philadelphia Phillies for P Carlos Silva, IF Nick Punto and a player to be named (December 3, 2003); Twins acquired P Bobby Korecky to complete deal (December 16, 2003). ... Signed as a free agent by Cincinnati Reds (December 27, 2004). ... On disabled list (April 19-May 20, 2006). **STATISTICAL NOTES:** Pitched 7-0 no-hit victory against Anaheim (September 11, 1999). **MISCELLANEOUS NOTES:** Singled in only appearance as pinch hitter and scored a run in only appearance as pinch runner (2006).
CAREER HITTING: 35-for-190 (.184), 20 R, 5 2B, 1 3B, 2 HR, 14 RBI.

Year Team (League)	W	L	Pct.	ERA	WHIP	G	GS	CG	ShO	Hld.	Sv.-Opp.	IP	H	R	ER	HR	BB-IBB	SO	Avg.
1997— Tampa (Fla. St.)	8	3	.727	3.09	0.99	14	14	1	0	...	0-...	93.1	78	35	32	8	14-0	95	.223
— Norwich (East.)	6	3	.667	3.13	1.22	14	14	1	0	...	0-...	77.2	59	29	27	2	36-0	67	.210
1998— Minnesota (A.L.)	8	14	.364	5.64	1.54	32	32	1	0	0	0-0	172.1	195	113	108	25	70-0	107	.282
1999— Minnesota (A.L.)	7	11	.389	4.49	1.23	34	34	5	2	0	0-0	206.1	190	111	103	28	63-2	163	.243
2000— Minnesota (A.L.)	13	10	.565	4.86	1.25	33	33	0	0	0	0-0	200.0	205	123	108	35	44-0	160	.260
2001— Minnesota (A.L.)	15	7	.682	4.32	1.28	35	34	2	1	0	0-0	220.2	222	109	106	35	61-0	157	.257
2002— Minnesota (A.L.)	13	9	.591	4.84	1.19	29	29	2	1	0	0-0	171.0	173	96	92	24	30-0	121	.258
2003— Fort Myers (FSL)	0	0	...	0.00	1.50	1	1	0	0	...	0-...	2.0	1	0	0	0	2-0	2	.143
— Minnesota (A.L.)	1	0	1.000	2.65	0.94	3	3	0	0	0	0-0	17.0	15	5	5	2	1-0	7	.234
2004— Philadelphia (N.L.)	14	6	.700	4.75	1.35	34	34	0	0	0	0-0	201.0	196	110	106	*43	75-6	161	.255
2005— Cincinnati (N.L.)	8	15	.348	6.47	1.55	34	34	0	0	0	0-0	186.1	237	*141	134	*40	52-2	123	.302
2006— Cincinnati (N.L.)	8	8	.500	5.19	1.34	26	26	0	0	0	0-0	152.2	163	94	88	29	42-4	90	.269
American League totals (6 years)	57	51	.528	4.76	1.29	166	165	10	4	0	0-0	987.1	1000	557	522	149	269-2	715	.259
National League totals (3 years)	30	29	.508	5.47	1.42	94	94	0	0	0	0-0	540.0	596	345	328	112	169-12	374	.276
Major League totals (9 years)	87	80	.521	5.01	1.33	260	259	10	4	0	0-0	1527.1	1596	902	850	261	438-14	1089	.265

DIVISION SERIES RECORD

Year Team (League)	W	L	Pct.	ERA	WHIP	G	GS	CG	ShO	Hld.	Sv.-Opp.	IP	H	R	ER	HR	BB-IBB	SO	Avg.
2002— Minnesota (A.L.)	1	0	1.000	2.57	1.00	1	1	0	0	0	0-0	7.0	6	2	2	1	1-0	3	.222
2003— Minnesota (A.L.)	0	0	...	0.00	0.60	1	1	0	0	0	0-0	3.1	2	0	0	0	0-0	2	.167
Division series totals (2 years)	1	0	1.000	1.74	0.87	2	2	0	0	0	0-0	10.1	8	2	2	1	1-0	5	.205

CHAMPIONSHIP SERIES RECORD

Year Team (League)	W	L	Pct.	ERA	WHIP	G	GS	CG	ShO	Hld.	Sv.-Opp.	IP	H	R	ER	HR	BB-IBB	SO	Avg.
2002— Minnesota (A.L.)	0	0	...	1.50	1.17	1	1	0	0	0	0-0	6.0	5	1	1	0	2-0	4	.217

ALL-STAR GAME RECORD

	W	L	Pct.	ERA	WHIP	G	GS	CG	ShO	Hld.	Sv.-Opp.	IP	H	R	ER	HR	BB-IBB	SO	Avg.

2006 LEFTY-RIGHTY SPLITS

vs.	Avg.	AB	H	2B	3B	HR	RBI	BB	SO	OBP	Slg.	vs.	Avg.	AB	H	2B	3B	HR	RBI	BB	SO	OBP	Slg.
L	.216	148	32	2	1	6	18	5	32	.245	.365	R	.286	458	131	33	1	23	67	37	58	.343	.513

MINER, ZACH — P

PERSONAL: Born March 12, 1982, in St. Louis, Mo. ... Throws right, bats right. ... Full name: Zachary Charles Miner. **TRANSACTIONS/CAREER NOTES:** Selected by Atlanta Braves organization in fourth round of 2000 free-agent draft. ... Traded by Braves with P Roman Colon to Detroit Tigers for P Kyle Farnsworth (July 31, 2005).
CAREER HITTING: 1-for-6 (.167), 1 R, 1 2B, 0 3B, 0 HR, 0 RBI.

Year Team (League)	W	L	Pct.	ERA	WHIP	G	GS	CG	ShO	Hld.	Sv.-Opp.	IP	H	R	ER	HR	BB-IBB	SO	Avg.
2001— Jamestown (NYP)	3	4	.429	1.89	1.01	15	15	0	0	...	0-...	90.2	76	26	19	6	16-0	68	.226
2002— Macon (S. Atl.)	8	9	.471	3.28	1.22	29	28	1	1	...	0-...	159.0	143	73	58	10	51-1	131	.243
2003— Myrtle Beach (Carol.)	6	10	.375	3.69	1.37	27	27	2	0	...	0-...	153.2	150	74	63	10	61-1	88	.262
2004— Greenville (Sou.)	6	10	.375	5.22	1.45	27	22	1	0	...	0-...	129.1	132	87	75	14	55-0	111	.278
2005— Mississippi (Sou.)	0	1	.000	4.32	1.56	4	2	0	0	0	1-1	16.2	21	10	8	0	5-0	18	.313
— Richmond (Int'l)	2	7	.222	4.23	1.59	17	17	0	0	0	0-0	89.1	97	47	42	6	45-0	63	.275
— Toledo (Int'l)	3	1	.750	2.36	1.40	6	6	0	0	0	0-0	34.1	28	10	9	4	20-0	20	.230
2006— Toledo (Int'l)	6	0	1.000	2.82	1.25	9	9	1	0	0	0-0	51.0	43	18	16	2	21-0	40	.232
— Detroit (A.L.)	7	6	.538	4.84	1.42	27	16	1	0	1	0-0	93.0	100	53	50	11	32-1	59	.276
Major League totals (1 year)	7	6	.538	4.84	1.42	27	16	1	0	1	0-0	93.0	100	53	50	11	32-1	59	.276

Year Team (League)	W	L	Pct.	ERA	WHIP	G	GS	CG	ShO	Hld.	Sv.-Opp.	IP	H	R	ER	HR	BB-IBB	SO	Avg.
2006— Detroit (A.L.)	0	0	...	0.00	0.00	1	0	0	0	0	0-0	0.2	0	0	0	0	0-0	0	.000

2006 LEFTY-RIGHTY SPLITS

vs.	Avg.	AB	H	2B	3B	HR	RBI	BB	SO	OBP	Slg.	vs.	Avg.	AB	H	2B	3B	HR	RBI	BB	SO	OBP	Slg.
L	.320	150	48	10	2	5	23	19	23	.396	.513	R	.245	212	52	8	0	6	27	13	36	.286	.368

MIRABELLI, DOUG   C

PERSONAL: Born October 18, 1970, in Kingman, Ariz. ... 6-1/220. ... Bats right, throws right. ... Full name: Douglas Anthony Mirabelli. ... Name pronounced: mirr-uh-BEL-ee. ... High school: Valley (Las Vegas). ... College: Wichita State. **TRANSACTIONS/CAREER NOTES:** Selected by Detroit Tigers organization in sixth round of 1989 free-agent draft; did not sign. ... Selected by San Francisco Giants organization in fifth round of 1992 free-agent draft. ... Traded by Giants to Texas Rangers for cash (March 27, 2001). ... Traded by Rangers to Boston Red Sox for P Justin Duchscherer (June 12, 2001). ... On disabled list (May 20-June 12, 2005). ... Traded by Red Sox to San Diego Padres for 2B Mark Loretta (December 7, 2005). ... Traded by Padres to Red Sox for C Josh Bard, RHP Cla Meredith and a player to be named or cash (May 1, 2006). **STATISTICAL NOTES:** Career major league grand slams: 3.

2006 GAMES PLAYED BY POSITION (MLB): C—66, DH—2.

Year Team (League)	Pos.	G	AB	R	H	2B	3B	HR	RBI	BB	SO	HBP	GDP	SB-CS	Avg.	OBP	SLG	OPS	E	Avg.
1992— San Jose (Calif.)	C	53	177	30	41	11	1	0	21	24	18	4	7	1-3	.232	.333	.305	.638	10	.973
1993— San Jose (Calif.)	C	113	371	58	100	19	2	1	48	72	55	4	7	0-4	.270	.390	.340	.730	9	.989
1994— Shreveport (Texas)	1B-C	85	255	23	56	8	0	4	24	36	48	0	6	3-1	.220	.316	.298	.614	3	.993
1995— Phoenix (PCL)	C	23	66	3	11	0	1	0	7	12	10	1	5	1-0	.167	.296	.197	.493	2	.985
— Shreveport (Texas)	1B-C	40	126	14	38	13	0	0	16	20	14	0	3	1-0	.302	.397	.405	.802	3	.986
1996— Shreveport (Texas)	C-DH-1B	115	380	60	112	23	0	21	70	76	49	6	9	0-1	.295	.419	.521	.940	7	.989
— Phoenix (PCL)	C	14	47	10	14	7	0	0	7	4	7	1	1	0-0	.298	.365	.447	.812	2	.982
— San Francisco (N.L.)	C	9	18	2	4	1	0	0	1	3	4	0	0	0-0	.222	.333	.278	.611	0	1.000
1997— Phoenix (PCL)	C-DH	100	332	49	88	23	2	8	48	58	69	7	9	1-2	.265	.384	.419	.803	4	.994
— San Francisco (N.L.)	C	6	7	0	1	0	0	0	0	1	3	0	0	0-0	.143	.250	.143	.393	0	1.000
1998— Fresno (PCL)	C-DH	85	265	45	69	12	2	13	53	52	55	3	9	2-0	.260	.386	.468	.854	3	.995
— San Francisco (N.L.)	C	10	17	2	4	2	0	1	4	2	6	0	0	0-0	.235	.316	.529	.845	1	.974
1999— Fresno (PCL)	C-1B-DH	86	320	63	100	24	1	14	51	48	56	1	6	8-2	.313	.398	.525	.923	5	.993
— San Francisco (N.L.)	C	33	87	10	22	6	0	1	10	9	25	1	1	0-0	.253	.327	.356	.683	0	1.000
2000— San Francisco (N.L.)	C	82	230	23	53	10	2	6	28	36	57	2	6	1-0	.230	.337	.370	.707	7	.985
2001— Texas (A.L.)	C-DH	23	49	4	5	2	0	2	3	10	21	0	1	0-0	.102	.254	.265	.520	1	.990
— Boston (A.L.)	C-DH	54	141	16	38	8	0	9	26	17	36	4	2	0-0	.270	.360	.518	.877	2	.995
2002— Boston (A.L.)	C	57	151	17	34	7	0	7	25	17	33	3	6	0-0	.225	.312	.411	.723	0	1.000
2003— Boston (A.L.)	C-DH-1B	62	163	23	42	13	0	6	18	11	36	1	3	0-0	.258	.307	.448	.755	5	.986
2004— Boston (A.L.)	C-DH	59	160	27	45	12	0	9	32	19	46	3	5	0-0	.281	.368	.525	.893	2	.993
2005— Boston (A.L.)	C-DH	50	136	16	31	7	0	6	18	14	48	2	2	2-0	.228	.309	.412	.721	3	.988
2006— San Diego (N.L.)	C	14	22	1	4	1	0	0	4	4	14	0	0	0-0	.182	.308	.227	.535	1	1.000
— Boston (A.L.)	C-DH	59	161	12	31	6	0	6	25	11	54	4	2	0-0	.193	.261	.342	.603	2	.994
American League totals (6 years)		364	961	115	226	55	0	45	147	99	274	17	21	2-0	.235	.316	.433	.749	15	.992
National League totals (6 years)		154	381	38	88	20	2	8	43	55	100	3	7	1-0	.231	.330	.357	.687	8	.990
Major League totals (11 years)		518	1342	153	314	75	2	53	190	154	374	20	28	3-0	.234	.320	.411	.732	23	.992

DIVISION SERIES RECORD

Year Team (League)	Pos.	G	AB	R	H	2B	3B	HR	RBI	BB	SO	HBP	GDP	SB-CS	Avg.	OBP	SLG	OPS	E	Avg.
2000— San Francisco (N.L.)	C	2	2	0	0	0	0	0	0	1	1	0	0	0-0	.000	.333	.000	.333	0	1.000
2003— Boston (A.L.)	C	2	4	2	2	1	0	0	0	2	0	0	0	0-0	.500	.500	.750	1.250	0	1.000
2005— Boston (A.L.)	C	1	2	0	0	0	0	0	0	0	1	0	0	0-0	.000	.000	.000	.000	0	1.000
Division series totals (3 years)		5	8	2	2	1	0	0	0	3	2	0	0	0-0	.250	.333	.375	.708	0	1.000

CHAMPIONSHIP SERIES RECORD

Year Team (League)	Pos.	G	AB	R	H	2B	3B	HR	RBI	BB	SO	HBP	GDP	SB-CS	Avg.	OBP	SLG	OPS	E	Avg.
2003— Boston (A.L.)	C	3	7	2	2	0	0	0	0	0	0	0	0	0-0·	.286	.286	.286	.571	0	1.000
2004— Boston (A.L.)	C	1	1	0	0	0	0	0	0	0	0	0	0	0-0	.000	.000	.000	.000	0	1.000
Champ. series totals (2 years)		4	8	2	2	0	0	0	0	0	0	0	0	0-0	.250	.250	.250	.500	0	1.000

WORLD SERIES RECORD

Year Team (League)	Pos.	G	AB	R	H	2B	3B	HR	RBI	BB	SO	HBP	GDP	SB-CS	Avg.	OBP	SLG	OPS	E	Avg.
2004— Boston (A.L.)	C	1	3	1	1	0	0	0	0	1	0	0	0	0-0	.333	.333	.333	.667	0	1.000

2006 LEFTY-RIGHTY SPLITS

vs.	Avg.	AB	H	2B	3B	HR	RBI	BB	SO	OBP	Slg.	vs.	Avg.	AB	H	2B	3B	HR	RBI	BB	SO	OBP	Slg.
L	.200	55	11	4	0	1	2	7	19	.302	.327	R	.188	128	24	3	0	5	23	8	40	.252	.328

MISCH, PATRICK   P

PERSONAL: Born August 18, 1981, in Northbrook, Ill. ... Throws left, bats right. ... Full name: Patrick Theodore Joseph Misch. ... College: Western Michigan. **TRANSACTIONS/CAREER NOTES:** Selected by San Francisco Giants organization in seventh round of 2003 free-agent draft. ...
CAREER HITTING: 0-for-0 (.000), 0 R, 0 2B, 0 3B, 0 HR, 0 RBI.

Year Team (League)	W	L	Pct.	ERA	WHIP	G	GS	CG	ShO	Hld.	Sv.-Opp.	IP	H	R	ER	HR	BB-IBB	SO	Avg.
2003— Salem-Keizer (N'west)	7	5	.583	2.18	1.13	14	14	0	0	...	0-...	86.2	78	33	21	3	20-0	61	.247
2004— Norwich (East.)	7	6	.538	3.06	1.09	26	26	4	3	...	0-...	159.0	138	61	54	13	35-0	123	.243
2005— Fresno (PCL)	3	9	.250	6.35	1.72	19	19	1	0	0	0-0	102.0	135	80	72	18	40-0	69	.325
— Norwich (East.)	4	2	.667	3.52	1.14	9	9	1	0	0	0-0	61.1	63	25	24	7	7-0	43	.270
2006— Connecticut (East.)	5	4	.556	2.26	1.15	18	17	0	0	0	0-0	103.2	95	32	26	7	24-0	79	.247
— Fresno (PCL)	4	2	.667	4.02	1.31	10	10	1	0	0	0-0	65.0	74	32	29	7	11-0	57	.287
— San Francisco (N.L.)	0	0	...	0.00	2.00	1	0	0	0	0	0-0	1.0	2	0	0	0	0-0	1	.400
Major League totals (1 year)	0	0	...	0.00	2.00	1	0	0	0	0	0-0	1.0	2	0	0	0	0-0	1	.400

2006 LEFTY-RIGHTY SPLITS

vs.	Avg.	AB	H	2B	3B	HR	RBI	BB	SO	OBP	Slg.	vs.	Avg.	AB	H	2B	3B	HR	RBI	BB	SO	OBP	Slg.
L	.000	2	0	0	0	0	0	0	1	.000	.000	R	.667	3	2	0	0	0	0	0	0	.667	.667

MITRE, SERGIO   P

PERSONAL: Born February 16, 1981, in Los Angeles. ... 6-4/210. ... Throws right, bats right. ... Full name: Sergio Armando Mitre. ... High school: Montgomery (Chula Vista, Calif.). ... Junior college: San Diego City College. **TRANSACTIONS/CAREER NOTES:** Selected by Chicago Cubs organization in seventh round of 2001 free-agent draft. ...

M

Traded by Cubs with Ps Ricky Nolasco and Renyel Pinto to Florida Marlins for OF Juan Pierre (December 7, 2005). ... On disabled list (May 13-August 9, 2006); included rehabilitation assignment to GCL Marlins. **MISCELLANEOUS NOTES:** Appeared in one game as pinch runner (2004). ... Scored a run and had a sacrifice hit in only appearance as pinch hitter (2006).

CAREER HITTING: 8-for-40 (.200), 5 R, 3 2B, 0 3B, 0 HR, 2 RBI.

Year Team (League)	W	L	Pct.	ERA	WHIP	G	GS	CG	ShO	Hld.	Sv.-Opp.	IP	H	R	ER	HR	BB-IBB	SO	Avg.
2001— Boise (N'west)	8	4	.667	3.07	1.13	15	15	1	1	...	0-...	91.0	85	37	31	2	18-1	71	.243
2002— Lansing (Midw.)	8	10	.444	2.83	1.14	27	27	2	0	...	0-...	168.2	166	72	53	7	27-1	96	.261
2003— West Tenn (Sou.)	7	9	.438	3.34	1.39	25	24	0	0	...	0-...	145.2	162	75	54	6	41-0	128	.282
—Chicago (N.L.)	0	1	.000	8.31	2.19	3	2	0	0	0	0-0	8.2	15	8	8	1	4-1	3	.395
2004— Iowa (PCL)	6	4	.600	2.98	1.32	18	15	1	1	...	1-...	102.2	97	38	34	9	39-1	95	.255
—Chicago (N.L.)	2	4	.333	6.62	1.76	12	9	0	0	0	0-0	51.2	71	38	38	6	20-1	37	.327
2005— Iowa (PCL)	5	6	.455	4.33	1.33	13	13	1	0	...	0-0	70.2	-72	34	34	5	22-0	55	.263
—Chicago (N.L.)	2	5	.286	5.37	1.41	21	7	1	1	0	0-0	60.1	62	37	36	11	23-2	37	.261
2006— GC Marlins (GCL)	0	0	...	0.00	1.00	1	1	0	0	0	0-0	1.0	0	0	0	0	1-0	0	...
—Florida (N.L.)	1	5	.167	5.71	1.56	15	7	0	0	0	0-1	41.0	44	28	26	7	20-3	31	.275
Major League totals (4 years)	5	15	.250	6.01	1.60	51	25	1	1	2	0-1	161.2	192	111	108	25	67-7	108	.294

2006 LEFTY-RIGHTY SPLITS

vs.	Avg.	AB	H	2B	3B	HR	RBI	BB	SO	OBP	Slg.	vs.	Avg.	AB	H	2B	3B	HR	RBI	BB	SO	OBP	Slg.
L	.344	61	21	0	1	4	8	14	11	.474	.574	R	.232	99	23	2	0	3	14	6	20	.306	.343

MOEHLER, BRIAN — P

PERSONAL: Born December 31, 1971, in Rockingham, N.C. ... 6-3/235. ... Throws right, bats right. ... Full name: Brian Merritt Moehler. ... Name pronounced: MOLE-er. ... High school: Richmond (N.C.) South. ... College: North Carolina-Greensboro. **TRANSACTIONS/CAREER NOTES:** Selected by Detroit Tigers organization in sixth round of free-agent draft (June 3, 1993). ... On disabled list (August 7-22, 1997). ... On suspended list (May 3-13, 1999). ... On disabled list (April 17-May 19, 2000); included rehabilitation assignment to West Michigan. ... On disabled list (April 7, 2001-remainder of season); included rehabilitation assignment to Toledo. ... On disabled list (March 22-July 3, 2002); included rehabilitation assignment to Lakeland and Toledo. ... Traded by Tigers with IF Matt Boone to Cincinnati Reds for SS David Espinosa and two players to be named (July 23, 2002); Tigers acquired OF Gary Varner (August 30, 2002) and P Jorge Cordova (September 24, 2002) to complete deal. ... On disabled list (August 28-September 13, 2002). ... Signed as a free agent by Houston Astros (January 17, 2003). ... On disabled list (April 17, 2003-remainder of season); included rehabilitation assignment to New Orleans. ... Signed as a free agent by Atlanta Braves organization (February 17, 2004). ... Signed as a free agent by Florida Marlins organization (December 14, 2004). ... On disabled list (July 2-30, 2006); included rehabilitation assignment to GCL Marlins. **MISCELLANEOUS NOTES:** Was hit by a pitch and had a sacrifice hit in two appearances as pinch hitter (2006).

CAREER HITTING: 5-for-101 (.050), 3 R, 1 2B, 0 3B, 0 HR, 5 RBI.

Year Team (League)	W	L	Pct.	ERA	WHIP	G	GS	CG	ShO	Hld.	Sv.-Opp.	IP	H	R	ER	HR	BB-IBB	SO	Avg.
1993— Niagara Falls (NYP)	6	5	.545	3.22	1.33	12	11	0	0	...	0-...	58.2	51	33	21	3	27-0	38	.225
1994— Lakeland (Fla. St.)	12	12	.500	3.01	1.32	26	25	5	2	...	0-...	164.2	153	66	55	3	65-0	92	.254
1995— Jacksonville (Sou.)	8	10	.444	4.82	1.40	28	27	0	0	...	0-...	162.1	176	94	87	14	52-1	89	.279
1996— Jacksonville (Sou.)	15	6	.714	3.48	1.36	28	28	1	0	...	0-...	173.1	186	80	67	9	50-2	120	.272
—Detroit (A.L.)	0	1	.000	4.35	1.84	2	2	0	0	0	0-0	10.1	11	10	5	1	8-1	2	.262
1997— Detroit (A.L.)	11	12	.478	4.67	1.48	31	31	2	1	0	0-0	175.1	198	97	91	22	61-1	97	.285
1998— Detroit (A.L.)	14	13	.519	3.90	1.25	33	33	4	3	0	0-0	221.1	220	103	96	30	56-1	123	.259
1999— Detroit (A.L.)	10	*16	.385	5.04	1.47	32	32	2	2	0	0-0	196.1	229	116	110	22	59-5	106	.294
2000— Detroit (A.L.)	12	9	.571	4.50	1.47	29	29	2	0	0	0-0	178.0	222	99	89	20	40-0	103	.305
—W. Mich. (Mid.)	0	1	.000	4.26	0.95	1	1	0	0	0	0-0	6.1	5	3	3	0	1-0	4	.217
2001— Detroit (A.L.)	0	0	...	3.38	0.88	1	1	0	0	0	0-0	8.0	6	3	3	0	1-0	2	.207
—Toledo (Int'l)	0	2	.000	4.35	1.35	2	2	0	0	0	0-0	10.1	12	6	5	2	2-0	6	.279
2002— Lakeland (Fla. St.)	1	1	.500	2.92	0.89	2	2	0	0	0	0-0	12.1	10	4	4	2	1-0	7	.208
—Toledo (Int'l)	2	1	.667	4.88	1.29	4	4	0	0	0	0-0	24.0	28	15	13	3	3-0	7	.277
—Detroit (A.L.)	1	1	.500	2.29	0.97	3	3	0	0	0	0-0	19.2	17	5	5	3	2-0	13	.233
—Cincinnati (N.L.)	2	4	.333	6.02	1.66	10	9	0	0	0	0-0	43.1	61	34	29	8	11-0	18	.330
2003— Houston (N.L.)	0	0	...	7.90	2.05	3	3	0	0	0	0-0	13.2	22	12	12	4	6-0	5	.379
—New Orleans (PCL)	0	0	...	4.50	1.50	1	1	0	0	0	0-0	2.0	3	1	1	0	0-0	3	.375
2004— Greenville (Sou.)	3	9	.250	4.17	1.30	20	20	0	0	0	0-0	108.0	113	58	50	8	27-1	57	.276
2005— Florida (N.L.)	6	12	.333	4.55	1.52	37	25	0	0	1	0-0	158.1	198	82	80	16	42-9	95	.311
2006— GC Marlins (GCL)	0	1	.000	3.60	1.60	1	1	0	0	0	0-0	5.0	8	2	2	0	0-0	4	.348
—Florida (N.L.)	7	11	.389	6.57	1.66	29	21	0	0	0	0-1	122.0	164	95	89	19	38-3	58	.325
American League totals (7 years)	48	52	.480	4.44	1.40	131	131	10	6	0	0-0	809.0	903	433	399	98	227-8	446	.283
National League totals (4 years)	15	27	.357	5.60	1.61	79	58	0	0	1	0-1	337.1	445	223	210	47	97-12	176	.323
Major League totals (10 years)	63	79	.444	4.78	1.46	210	189	10	6	1	0-1	1146.1	1348	656	609	145	324-20	622	.295

2006 LEFTY-RIGHTY SPLITS

vs.	Avg.	AB	H	2B	3B	HR	RBI	BB	SO	OBP	Slg.	vs.	Avg.	AB	H	2B	3B	HR	RBI	BB	SO	OBP	Slg.
L	.351	268	94	17	4	9	47	21	23	.401	.545	R	.297	236	70	16	3	10	40	17	35	.350	.517

MOELLER, CHAD — C

PERSONAL: Born February 18, 1975, in Upland, Calif. ... 6-3/210. ... Bats right, throws right. ... Full name: Chad Edward Moeller. ... Name pronounced: MOE-ler. ... High school: Upland (Calif.). ... College: Southern California. **TRANSACTIONS/CAREER NOTES:** Selected by New York Yankees organization in 25th round of 1993 free-agent draft; did not sign. ... Selected by Minnesota Twins organization in seventh round of 1996 free-agent draft. ... On disabled list (August 12-30, 2000). ... Traded by Twins to Arizona Diamondbacks for SS Hanley Frias (March 28, 2001). ... Traded by Diamondbacks with SS Craig Counsell, 2B Junior Spivey, 1B Lyle Overbay and Ps Chris Capuano and Jorge de la Rosa to Milwaukee Brewers for 1B Richie Sexson, P Shane Nance and a player to be named (December 1, 2003); Diamondbacks acquired OF Noochie Varner to complete deal (December 15, 2003). **STATISTICAL NOTES:** Hit for the cycle (April 27, 2004). ... Career major league grand slams: 1.

2006 GAMES PLAYED BY POSITION (MLB): C—29.

										BATTING											FIELDING		
Year Team (League)	Pos.	G	AB	R	H	2B	3B	HR	RBI	BB	SO	HBP	GDP	SB-CS	Avg.	OBP	SLG	OPS			E	Avg.
1996— Elizabethton (App.)	C	17	59	17	21	4	0	4	13	18	9	2	3	1-2	.356	.519	.627	1.146			1	.991
1997— Fort Wayne (Midw.)	C	108	384	58	111	18	3	9	39	48	76	13	8	11-8	.289	.386	.422	.808			15	.984
1998— Fort Myers (FSL)	C	66	254	37	83	24	1	6	39	31	37	3	8	2-3	.327	.406	.500	.906			4	.980
—New Britain (East.)	C	58	187	21	44	10	0	6	23	24	41	3	4	2-1	.235	.332	.385	.717			6	.987
1999— New Britain (East.)	C	89	250	29	62	11	3	4	24	21	44	3	6	0-0	.248	.317	.364	.681			10	.994
2000— Salt Lake (PCL)	C	47	167	30	48	13	1	5	20	9	45	0	6	0-1	.287	.322	.467	.789			2	.993
—Minnesota (A.L.)	C	48	128	13	27	3	1	1	9	9	33	0	4	1-0	.211	.261	.273	.534			6	.979
2001— Tucson (PCL)	C	78	274	41	75	20	6	8	36	25	54	2	8	1-4	.274	.337	.434	.771			5	.989
—Arizona (N.L.)	C	25	56	8	13	0	1	1	6	6	14	0	0	0-0	.232	.306	.321	.628			0	1.000
2002— Tucson (PCL)	C	60	211	37	67	8	2	10	48	29	46	3	4	1-0	.318	.401	.517	.917			3	.994
—Arizona (N.L.)	C	37	105	10	30	11	1	2	16	17	23	0	6	0-1	.286	.385	.467	.852			1	.997

		BATTING																FIELDING	
Year Team (League)	Pos.	G	AB	R	H	2B	3B	HR	RBI	BB	SO	HBP	GDP	SB-CS	Avg.	OBP	SLG	OPS	E	Avg.
2003— Arizona (N.L.)	C	78	239	29	64	17	1	7	29	23	59	2	7	1-2	.268	.335	.435	.770	7	.987
2004— Milwaukee (N.L.)	C	101	317	25	66	13	1	5	27	21	74	4	12	0-1	.208	.265	.303	.568	1	.999
2005— Milwaukee (N.L.)	C	66	199	23	41	9	1	7	23	13	48	1	9	0-0	.206	.257	.367	.624	3	.994
2006— Nashville (PCL)		41	132	10	29	6	0	2	18	15	28	3	4	0-2	.220	.307	.311	.618	4	.986
— Milwaukee (N.L.)	C	29	98	9	18	3	0	2	5	4	26	2	3	0-0	.184	.231	.276	.506	1	.995
American League totals (1 year)		48	128	13	27	3	1	1	9	9	33	0	4	1-0	.211	.261	.273	.534	6	.979
National League totals (6 years)		336	1014	104	232	53	5	24	102	84	242	9	39	1-4	.229	.293	.362	.654	13	.995
Major League totals (7 years)		384	1142	117	259	56	6	25	111	93	275	9	43	2-4	.227	.289	.352	.641	19	.993

DIVISION SERIES RECORD

Year Team (League)	Pos.	G	AB	R	H	2B	3B	HR	RBI	BB	SO	HBP	GDP	SB-CS	Avg.	OBP	SLG	OPS	E	Avg.
2002— Arizona (N.L.)	C	3	5	0	2	0	0	0	0	0	1	0	0	0-0	.400	.400	.400	.800	0	1.000

2006 LEFTY-RIGHTY SPLITS

vs.	Avg.	AB	H	2B	3B	HR	RBI	BB	SO	OBP	Slg.	vs.	Avg.	AB	H	2B	3B	HR	RBI	BB	SO	OBP	Slg.
L	.211	19	4	0	0	1	2	2	4	.286	.368	R	.177	79	14	3	0	1	3	2	22	.217	.253

MOHR, DUSTAN — OF

PERSONAL: Born June 19, 1976, in Hattiesburg, Miss. ... 6-1/214. ... Bats right, throws right. ... Full name: Dustan Kyle Mohr. ... High school: Oak Grove (Miss.). ... College: Alabama. TRANSACTIONS/CAREER NOTES: Selected by California Angels organization in 20th round of 1994 free-agent draft; did not sign. ... Selected by Cleveland Indians organization in ninth round of 1997 free-agent draft. ... Released by Indians (March 31, 2000). ... Signed by Minnesota Twins organization (April 1, 2000). ... Traded by Twins to San Francisco Giants for P J.T. Thomas (December 15, 2003). ... Signed as free agent by Colorado Rockies (January 6, 2005). ... On disabled list (April 6-28, 2005); included rehabilitation assignment to Colorado Springs. ... Signed as a free agent by Boston Red Sox organization (January 27, 2006). ... Signed as a free agent by Detroit Tigers organization (June 28, 2006).

2006 GAMES PLAYED BY POSITION (MLB): OF—20.

		BATTING																FIELDING	
Year Team (League)	Pos.	G	AB	R	H	2B	3B	HR	RBI	BB	SO	HBP	GDP	SB-CS	Avg.	OBP	SLG	OPS	E	Avg.
1997— Watertown (NYP)	OF	74	275	52	80	20	2	7	53	31	76	4	1	3-6	.291	.366	.455	.821	1	.993
1998— Kinston (Carol.)	OF	134	491	60	119	23	9	19	65	39	146	9	7	8-4	.242	.309	.442	.751	7	.968
1999— Akron (East.)	OF	12	42	3	7	2	1	0	2	5	7	0	1	0-1	.167	.255	.262	.517	0	1.000
— Kinston (Carol.)	OF	112	429	46	120	29	3	8	60	26	104	1	13	6-6	.280	.322	.417	.739	6	.973
2000— Fort Myers (FSL)	OF	101	370	58	98	19	2	11	75	35	65	8	11	7-4	.265	.338	.416	.754	4	.978
2001— New Britain (East.)	OF	135	518	90	174	41	3	24	91	49	111	4	6	9-9	.336	.395	.566	.961	6	.978
— Minnesota (A.L.)	OF-DH	20	51	6	12	2	0	0	4	5	17	0	1	1-1	.235	.298	.275	.573	1	1.000
2002— Minnesota (A.L.)	OF-DH	120	383	55	103	23	2	12	45	31	86	1	5	6-3	.269	.325	.433	.759	2	.992
2003— Minnesota (A.L.)	OF-DH	121	348	50	87	22	0	10	36	33	106	1	10	5-2	.250	.314	.399	.714	6	.976
2004— San Francisco (N.L.)	OF-DH	117	263	52	72	20	1	7	28	46	64	8	5	0-3	.274	.394	.437	.831	3	.981
2005— Colo. Springs (PCL)	OF	3	12	2	3	2	0	1	4	0	4	0	1	0-0	.250	.250	.667	.917	0	1.000
— Colorado (N.L.)	OF	98	266	34	57	10	3	17	38	23	94	2	3	1-2	.214	.280	.466	.746	2	.987
2006— Toledo (Int'l)		54	187	21	49	11	4	6	25	22	70	0	2	1-4	.262	.338	.460	.798	0	1.000
— Boston (A.L.)	OF	21	40	5	7	1	0	2	3	3	20	0	0	0-0	.175	.233	.350	.583	0	1.000
— Pawtucket (Int'l)		22	65	10	11	2	0	1	6	21	23	0	0	0-0	.169	.368	.246	.614	0	1.000
American League totals (4 years)		282	822	116	209	48	2	24	88	72	229	2	15	12-6	.254	.314	.405	.720	8	.986
National League totals (2 years)		215	529	86	129	30	4	24	66	69	158	10	8	1-5	.244	.339	.452	.791	5	.984
Major League totals (6 years)		497	1351	202	338	78	6	48	154	141	387	12	23	13-11	.250	.325	.423	.748	13	.985

DIVISION SERIES RECORD

Year Team (League)	Pos.	G	AB	R	H	2B	3B	HR	RBI	BB	SO	HBP	GDP	SB-CS	Avg.	OBP	SLG	OPS	E	Avg.
2002— Minnesota (A.L.)	OF	4	2	1	2	1	0	0	0	1	0	0	0	0-0	1.000	1.000	1.500	2.500	0	1.000

CHAMPIONSHIP SERIES RECORD

Year Team (League)	Pos.	G	AB	R	H	2B	3B	HR	RBI	BB	SO	HBP	GDP	SB-CS	Avg.	OBP	SLG	OPS	E	Avg.
2002— Minnesota (A.L.)	OF	5	12	3	5	1	0	0	0	4	0	0	0	1-0	.417	.417	.500	.917	0	1.000

2006 LEFTY-RIGHTY SPLITS

vs.	Avg.	AB	H	2B	3B	HR	RBI	BB	SO	OBP	Slg.	vs.	Avg.	AB	H	2B	3B	HR	RBI	BB	SO	OBP	Slg.
L	.250	28	7	1	0	2	3	3	13	.323	.500	R	.000	12	0	0	0	0	0	0	7	.000	.000

MOLINA, BENGIE — C

PERSONAL: Born July 20, 1974, in Rio Piedras, Puerto Rico. ... 5-11/220. ... Bats right, throws right. ... Full name: Benjamin Jose Molina. ... Name pronounced: mo-LEE-nah. ... High school: Maestro Ladi (Vega Alta, Puerto Rico). ... Junior college: Arizona Western Community College. ... Brother of Jose Molina, catcher, Los Angeles Angels of Anaheim; and of Yadier Molina, catcher, St. Louis Cardinals. TRANSACTIONS/CAREER NOTES: Signed as a non-drafted free agent by California Angels organization (May 23, 1993). ... Angels franchise renamed Anaheim Angels for 1997 season. ... On disabled list (May 5-June 27, 2001); included rehabilitation assignments to Rancho Cucamonga and Salt Lake. ... On disabled list (July 17-August 1, 2002); included rehabilitation assignment to Rancho Cucamonga. ... On disabled list (September 5, 2003-remainder of season; and June 4-19 and August 1-17, 2004). ... Angels franchise renamed Los Angeles Angels of Anaheim for 2005 season. ... On disabled list (April 18-May 13, 2005). ... Signed as free agent by Toronto Blue Jays (February 6, 2006). HONORS: Won A.L. Gold Glove at catcher (2002 and 2003). STATISTICAL NOTES: Career major league grand slams: 3.

2006 GAMES PLAYED BY POSITION (MLB): C—99, DH—16.

		BATTING																FIELDING	
Year Team (League)	Pos.	G	AB	R	H	2B	3B	HR	RBI	BB	SO	HBP	GDP	SB-CS	Avg.	OBP	SLG	OPS	E	Avg.
1993— Ariz. Angels (Ariz.)	C	27	80	9	21	6	2	0	10	10	4	1	1	0-2	.263	.348	.388	.735	0	1.000
1994— Cedar Rap. (Midw.)	C	48	171	14	48	8	0	3	16	8	12	3	3	1-2	.281	.324	.380	.704	10	.975
1995— Vancouver (PCL)		2	2	0	0	0	0	0	0	0	1	0	0	0-0	.000	.000	.000	.000	0	1.000
— Cedar Rap. (Midw.)	C	39	133	15	39	9	0	4	17	15	11	1	4	1-1	.293	.367	.451	.818	7	.978
— Lake Elsinore (Calif.)	C	27	96	21	37	7	2	2	12	8	7	4	2	0-0	.385	.450	.563	1.012	1	.995
1996— Midland (Texas)	C	108	365	45	100	21	2	8	54	25	25	6	16	0-1	.274	.327	.408	.735	7	.990
1997— Lake Elsinore (Calif.)	C	36	149	18	42	10	2	4	33	7	9	0	5	0-1	.282	.308	.456	.765	1	.996
— Midland (Texas)	C	29	106	18	35	8	0	6	30	10	7	0	2	0-0	.330	.381	.575	.957	2	.978
1998— Vancouver (PCL)	C	49	184	13	54	9	1	1	22	5	14	0	6	1-1	.293	.311	.370	.680	5	.986
— Midland (Texas)	C	41	154	28	55	8	0	9	39	14	7	3	2	0-0	.357	.419	.584	1.003	3	.988
— Anaheim (A.L.)	C	2	1	0	0	0	0	0	0	0	0	0	0	0-0	.000	.000	.000	.000	0	1.000
1999— Edmonton (PCL)	C-DH	65	241	28	69	16	0	7	41	15	17	6	1	1-2	.286	.338	.440	.778	3	.993
— Anaheim (A.L.)	C	31	101	8	26	5	0	1	10	6	6	2	0	0-1	.257	.312	.337	.649	5	.991
2000— Anaheim (A.L.)	C-DH	130	473	59	133	20	2	14	71	23	33	6	17	1-0	.281	.318	.421	.739	7	.991
2001— Anaheim (A.L.)	C-DH	96	325	31	85	11	0	6	40	16	51	4	8	0-1	.262	.309	.351	.660	5	.991

M

Year	Team (League)	Pos.	G	AB	R	H	2B	3B	HR	RBI	BB	SO	HBP	GDP	SB-CS	Avg.	OBP	SLG	OPS	E	Avg.
																BATTING				**FIELDING**	
—Rancho Cuca. (Calif.)		C	3	11	1	6	1	0	0	2		0	1	0		0-0	.545	.545	.636	1.182	0	1.000
—Salt Lake (PCL)		C	5	18	2	5	1	0	0	3	2	3	0	2	0-0	.278	.350	.333	.683	0	1.000
2002—Anaheim (A.L.)		C	122	428	34	105	18	0	5	47	15	34	4	15	0-0	.245	.274	.322	.596	1	.999
—Rancho Cuca. (Calif.)		C	1	2	0	1	0	0	0	0	1	0	1	0	0-0	.500	.750	.500	1.250	0	1.000
2003—Anaheim (A.L.)		C	119	409	37	115	24	0	14	71	13	31	2	17	1-1	.281	.304	.443	.746	5	.993
2004—Anaheim (A.L.)		C-DH	97	337	36	93	13	0	10	54	18	35	2	18	0-1	.276	.313	.404	.717	3	.995
2005—Los Angeles (A.L.)		C-DH	119	410	45	121	17	0	15	69	27	41	1	14	0-2	.295	.336	.446	.782	3	.996
2006—Toronto (A.L.)		C-DH	117	433	44	123	20	1	19	57	19	47	4	15	1-1	.284	.319	.467	.785	2	.997
Major League totals (9 years)			833	2917	294	801	128	3	84	419	137	278	29	109	3-7	.275	.310	.407	.717	28	.994

DIVISION SERIES RECORD

Year	Team (League)	Pos.	G	AB	R	H	2B	3B	HR	RBI	BB	SO	HBP	GDP	SB-CS	Avg.	OBP	SLG	OPS	E	Avg.
2002—Anaheim (A.L.)		C	4	15	0	4	2	0	0	2	0	1	0	1	0-0	.267	.267	.400	.667	0	1.000
2004—Anaheim (A.L.)		C	3	6	0	1	0	0	0	0	0	2	0	0	0-0	.167	.167	.167	.333	1	1.000
2005—Los Angeles (A.L.)		C	5	18	5	8	0	0	3	5	0	0	1	0	0-0	.444	.474	.944	1.418	0	1.000
Division series totals (3 years)			12	39	5	13	2	0	3	7	0	3	1	1	0-0	.333	.350	.615	.965	1	1.000

CHAMPIONSHIP SERIES RECORD

Year	Team (League)	Pos.	G	AB	R	H	2B	3B	HR	RBI	BB	SO	HBP	GDP	SB-CS	Avg.	OBP	SLG	OPS	E	Avg.
2002—Anaheim (A.L.)		C	5	14	0	3	0	1	0	2	1	2	1	0	0-0	.214	.313	.357	.670	1	1.000
2005—Los Angeles (A.L.)		C-DH	5	17	0	2	0	0	0	1	0	2	1	0	0-0	.118	.167	.118	.284	1	1.000
Champ. series totals (2 years)			10	31	0	5	0	1	0	3	1	4	2	0	0-0	.161	.235	.226	.461	0	1.000

WORLD SERIES RECORD

Year	Team (League)	Pos.	G	AB	R	H	2B	3B	HR	RBI	BB	SO	HBP	GDP	SB-CS	Avg.	OBP	SLG	OPS	E	Avg.
2002—Anaheim (A.L.)		C	7	21	2	6	2	0	0	2	3	1	0	2	0-0	.286	.375	.381	.756	1	.979

2006 LEFTY-RIGHTY SPLITS

vs.	Avg.	AB	H	2B	3B	HR	RBI	BB	SO	OBP	Slg.	vs.	Avg.	AB	H	2B	3B	HR	RBI	BB	SO	OBP	Slg.
L	.358	148	53	6	1	10	28	5	12	.383	.615	R	.246	285	70	14	0	9	29	14	35	.286	.389

MOLINA, JOSE — C

PERSONAL: Born June 3, 1975, in Bayamon, Puerto Rico. ... 6-2/220. ... Bats right, throws right. ... Full name: Jose Benjamin Molina. ... Name pronounced: mo-LEE-nah. ... High school: Maestro Ladi (Vega Alta, Puerto Rico). ... Brother of Bengie Molina, catcher, Toronto Blue Jays; and of Yadier Molina, catcher, St. Louis Cardinals. **TRANSACTIONS/CAREER NOTES:** Selected by Chicago Cubs organization in 14th round of 1993 free-agent draft. ... Released by Cubs (November 27, 2000). ... Signed by Anaheim Angels organization (May 17, 2001). ... On disabled list (May 21-July 1, 2001); included rehabilitation assignment to Salt Lake. ... Angels franchise renamed Los Angeles Angels of Anaheim for 2005 season. **STATISTICAL NOTES:** Career major league grand slams: 1.

2006 GAMES PLAYED BY POSITION (MLB): C—76, 1B—3.

Year	Team (League)	Pos.	G	AB	R	H	2B	3B	HR	RBI	BB	SO	HBP	GDP	SB-CS	Avg.	OBP	SLG	OPS	E	Avg.
																BATTING				**FIELDING**	
1993—GC Cubs (GCL)		1B-C	33	78	5	17	2	0	0	4	12	12	0	2	3-2	.218	.322	.244	.566	7	.960
—Daytona (Fla. St.)		C	3	7	0	1	0	0	0	1	2	0	0	0	0-1	.143	.333	.143	.476	0	1.000
1994—Peoria (Midw.)		C	78	253	31	58	13	1	1	33	24	61	1	4	4-3	.229	.302	.300	.602	13	.980
1995—Daytona (Fla. St.)		C	82	233	27	55	9	1	1	19	29	53	7	7	1-0	.236	.336	.296	.632	8	.987
1996—Rockford (Midwest)		C	96	305	35	69	10	1	2	27	36	71	3	8	2-4	.226	.310	.285	.596	11	.985
1997—Daytona (Fla. St.)		C	55	179	17	45	9	1	0	23	14	25	1	5	4-0	.251	.306	.313	.619	8	.981
—Iowa (Am. Assoc.)		C	1	3	0	1	0	0	0	1	1	1	0	1	0-0	.333	.500	.333	.833	0	1.000
—Orlando (South.)		C	37	99	10	17	3	0	1	15	12	28	2	4	0-1	.172	.267	.232	.500	2	.993
1998—West Tenn (Sou.)		1B-C	109	320	33	71	10	1	2	28	32	74	3	10	1-5	.222	.296	.278	.574	8	.991
1999—West Tenn (Sou.)		C	14	35	2	6	3	0	0	5	2	14	0	1	0-0	.171	.211	.257	.468	2	.982
—Iowa (PCL)		C	74	240	24	63	11	1	4	26	20	54	4	3	0-1	.263	.327	.367	.694	7	.987
—Chicago (N.L.)		C	10	19	3	5	1	0	0	1	2	4	0	0	0-0	.263	.333	.316	.649	0	1.000
2000—Iowa (PCL)		C-1B	76	248	22	58	9	0	1	17	23	61	0	6	1-4	.234	.296	.282	.578	11	.981
2001—Salt Lake (PCL)		C	61	213	29	64	11	1	5	31	14	49	2	7	1-2	.300	.349	.432	.781	4	.992
—Anaheim (A.L.)		C	15	37	8	10	3	0	2	4	3	8	0	2	0-0	.270	.325	.514	.839	0	1.000
2002—Salt Lake (PCL)		C	79	290	30	89	14	2	4	43	12	60	4	4	0-3	.307	.341	.410	.751	4	.994
—Anaheim (A.L.)		C	29	70	5	19	3	0	1	6	5	15	0	2	0-2	.271	.312	.314	.626	3	.983
2003—Anaheim (A.L.)		C	53	114	12	21	4	0	0	6	1	26	3	1	0-0	.184	.210	.219	.429	1	.996
2004—Anaheim (A.L.)		C-1B-DH	73	203	26	53	14	0	3	25	10	52	0	6	4-1	.261	.296	.374	.670	3	.994
2005—Los Angeles (A.L.)		C-DH-1B	75	184	14	42	4	0	6	25	13	41	2	5	2-0	.228	.286	.348	.634	3	.994
2006—Los Angeles (A.L.)		C-1B	78	225	18	54	17	0	4	22	9	49	2	6	1-0	.240	.273	.369	.642	8	.986
American League totals (6 years)			323	833	83	199	41	2	15	87	41	191	7	22	7-3	.239	.279	.347	.626	18	.991
National League totals (1 year)			10	19	3	5	1	0	0	1	2	4	0	0	0-0	.263	.333	.316	.649	0	1.000
Major League totals (7 years)			333	852	86	204	42	2	15	88	43	195	7	22	7-3	.239	.280	.346	.626	18	.991

DIVISION SERIES RECORD

Year	Team (League)	Pos.	G	AB	R	H	2B	3B	HR	RBI	BB	SO	HBP	GDP	SB-CS	Avg.	OBP	SLG	OPS	E	Avg.
2004—Anaheim (A.L.)		C	2	3	2	1	0	0	0	0	2	0	0	0	0-0	.333	.600	.333	.933	0	1.000
2005—Los Angeles (A.L.)		C	1	1	1	1	0	0	0	1	0	0	0	0	0-0	1.000	1.000	1.000	2.000	0	1.000
Division series totals (2 years)			3	4	3	2	0	0	0	1	2	0	0	0	0-0	.500	.667	.500	1.167	0	1.000

CHAMPIONSHIP SERIES RECORD

Year	Team (League)	Pos.	G	AB	R	H	2B	3B	HR	RBI	BB	SO	HBP	GDP	SB-CS	Avg.	OBP	SLG	OPS	E	Avg.
2002—Anaheim (A.L.)		C	1	1	0	0	0	0	0	0	0	0	0	0	0-0	.000	.000	.000	.000	0	1.000
2005—Los Angeles (A.L.)		C	1	3	0	1	0	0	0	0	0	1	0	0	0-0	.333	.333	.333	.667	0	1.000
Champ. series totals (2 years)			4	4	0	1	0	0	0	0	0	1	0	0	0-0	.250	.250	.250	.500	0	1.000

WORLD SERIES RECORD

Year	Team (League)	Pos.	G	AB	R	H	2B	3B	HR	RBI	BB	SO	HBP	GDP	SB-CS	Avg.	OBP	SLG	OPS	E	Avg.
2002—Anaheim (A.L.)		C	3	0	0	0	0	0	0	0	0	0	0	0	0-0	...	...	...	...	0	1.000

2006 LEFTY-RIGHTY SPLITS

vs.	Avg.	AB	H	2B	3B	HR	RBI	BB	SO	OBP	Slg.	vs.	Avg.	AB	H	2B	3B	HR	RBI	BB	SO	OBP	Slg.
L	.218	87	19	6	0	2	7	5	15	.261	.356	R	.254	138	35	11	0	2	15	4	34	.281	.377

MOLINA, YADIER — C

PERSONAL: Born July 13, 1982, in Bayamon, Puerto Rico. ... 5-11/225. ... Bats right, throws right. ... Full name: Yadier B. Molina. ... Name pronounced: mo-LEE-nah. ... High school: Escuela Superior Maestro Ladi (Vega Alta, P.R.). ... Brother of Bengie Molina, catcher, Toronto Blue Jays, and Jose Molina, catcher, Los Angeles Angels of

Anaheim. **TRANSACTIONS/CAREER NOTES:** Selected by St. Louis Cardinals organization in fourth round of 2000 free-agent draft. ... On disabled list (July 17-August 18, 2005).

2006 GAMES PLAYED BY POSITION (MLB): C—127, 1B—4.

Year Team (League)	Pos.	G	AB	R	H	2B	3B	HR	RBI	BB	SO	HBP	GDP	SB-CS	Avg.	OBP	SLG	OPS	E	Avg.
2001—Johnson City (App.)	C	44	158	18	41	11	0	4	18	12	23	3	4	1-1	.259	.320	.405	.725	7	.986
2002—Peoria (Midw.)	C	112	393	39	110	20	0	7	50	21	36	10	14	2-7	.280	.331	.384	.715	14	.985
2003—Tennessee (Sou.)	C	104	364	32	100	13	1	2	51	25	45	5	11	0-1	.275	.327	.332	.660	8	.991
2004—Memphis (PCL)	C	37	129	19	39	6	0	1	14	17	14	2	2	0-0	.302	.387	.372	.750	0	1.000
—St. Louis (N.L.)	C	51	135	12	36	6	0	2	15	13	20	0	4	0-1	.267	.329	.356	.684	2	.993
2005—St. Louis (N.L.)	C-1B	114	385	36	97	15	1	8	49	23	30	2	10	2-3	.252	.295	.358	.654	7	.991
2006—St. Louis (N.L.)	C-1B	129	417	29	90	26	0	6	49	26	41	8	15	1-2	.216	.274	.321	.595	5	.994
Major League totals (3 years)		294	937	77	223	47	1	16	113	62	91	10	29	3-6	.238	.291	.342	.632	14	.992

DIVISION SERIES RECORD

Year Team (League)	Pos.	G	AB	R	H	2B	3B	HR	RBI	BB	SO	HBP	GDP	SB-CS	Avg.	OBP	SLG	OPS	E	Avg.
2005—St. Louis (N.L.)	C	3	13	1	3	0	0	0	3	0	1	0	0	0-0	.231	.231	.231	.462	0	1.000
2006—St. Louis (N.L.)	C	4	13	0	4	1	0	0	1	0	2	0	2	0-1	.308	.308	.385	.692	1	.974
Division series totals (2 years)		7	26	1	7	1	0	0	4	0	3	0	2	0-1	.269	.269	.308	.577	1	.982

CHAMPIONSHIP SERIES RECORD

Year Team (League)	Pos.	G	AB	R	H	2B	3B	HR	RBI	BB	SO	HBP	GDP	SB-CS	Avg.	OBP	SLG	OPS	E	Avg.
2004—St. Louis (N.L.)	C	1	4	0	1	0	0	0	0	0	0	0	0	0-0	.250	.250	.250	.500	0	1.000
2005—St. Louis (N.L.)	C	6	22	1	7	3	0	0	0	0	2	0	1	0-0	.318	.318	.455	.773	0	1.000
2006—St. Louis (N.L.)	C	7	23	2	8	1	0	2	6	3	2	0	0	0-0	.348	.423	.652	1.075	0	1.000
Champ. series totals (3 years)		14	49	3	16	4	0	2	6	3	4	0	1	0-0	.327	.365	.531	.896	0	1.000

WORLD SERIES RECORD

Year Team (League)	Pos.	G	AB	R	H	2B	3B	HR	RBI	BB	SO	HBP	GDP	SB-CS	Avg.	OBP	SLG	OPS	E	Avg.
2004—St. Louis (N.L.)	C	3	3	0	0	0	0	0	0	0	0	0	0	0-0	.000	.000	.000	.000	0	1.000
2006—St. Louis (N.L.)	C	5	17	3	7	2	0	0	3	1	0	0	0	0-0	.412	.500	.529	1.029	0	1.000
World series totals (2 years)		8	20	3	7	2	0	0	3	2	0	0	0	0-0	.350	.435	.450	.885	0	1.000

2006 LEFTY-RIGHTY SPLITS

vs.	Avg.	AB	H	2B	3B	HR	RBI	BB	SO	OBP	Slg.	vs.	Avg.	AB	H	2B	3B	HR	RBI	BB	SO	OBP	Slg.
L	.213	127	27	9	0	1	10	11	11	.296	.307	R	.217	290	63	17	0	5	39	15	30	.264	.328

MONROE, CRAIG — OF

PERSONAL: Born February 27, 1977, in Texarkana, Texas. ... 6-1/220. ... Bats right, throws right. ... Full name: Craig Keystone Monroe. ... High school: Texas (Texarkana, Texas). **TRANSACTIONS/CAREER NOTES:** Selected by Texas Rangers organization in eighth round of 1995 free-agent draft. ... Claimed on waivers by Detroit Tigers (February 1, 2002). ... On disabled list (July 21-August 7, 2004); included rehabilitation assignment to Toledo. **STATISTICAL NOTES:** Career major league grand slams: 2.

2006 GAMES PLAYED BY POSITION (MLB): OF—116, DH—30.

Year Team (League)	Pos.	G	AB	R	H	2B	3B	HR	RBI	BB	SO	HBP	GDP	SB-CS	Avg.	OBP	SLG	OPS	E	Avg.
1995—GC Rangers (GCL)	OF	54	193	22	48	6	2	0	33	18	25	2	1	13-2	.249	.316	.301	.617	4	.962
1996—Char., S.C. (SAL)	OF	49	153	11	23	11	1	0	9	18	48	3	3	2-2	.150	.253	.235	.488	4	.954
—Hudson Valley (NYP)	OF	67	268	53	74	16	6	5	29	23	63	2	4	21-7	.276	.336	.437	.772	6	.938
1997—Charlotte (Fla. St.)	OF	92	328	54	77	23	1	7	41	44	80	0	5	24-1	.235	.320	.375	.695	7	.959
1998—Charlotte (Fla. St.)	OF	132	472	73	114	26	7	17	76	66	102	3	15	50-13	.242	.334	.434	.768	11	.951
1999—Charlotte (Fla. St.)	OF	130	480	77	125	21	1	17	81	42	102	4	8	40-15	.260	.321	.415	.735	7	.980
—Oklahoma (PCL)	OF	6	16	2	4	1	0	0	1	1	4	4	0	0-0	.250	.429	.313	.741	0	1.000
2000—Tulsa (Texas)	OF	120	464	89	131	34	5	20	89	64	91	2	12	12-13	.282	.366	.506	.873	12	.948
2001—Oklahoma (PCL)	OF	114	410	60	115	25	5	20	75	46	85	5	11	10-8	.280	.358	.512	.870	5	.975
—Texas (A.L.)	OF-DH	27	52	8	11	1	0	2	5	6	18	0	1	0-1	.212	.293	.346	.639	0	1.000
2002—Toledo (Int'l)	OF	99	358	61	115	30	4	10	49	35	57	2	8	7-3	.321	.379	.511	.890	3	.983
—Detroit (A.L.)	OF	13	25	3	3	1	0	1	1	0	5	1	1	0-2	.120	.154	.280	.434	1	.950
2003—Toledo (Int'l)	OF-DH	14	47	14	19	4	1	2	6	4	10	0	0	1-0	.404	.451	.660	1.111	0	1.000
—Detroit (A.L.)	OF-DH	128	425	51	102	18	1	23	70	27	89	2	10	4-2	.240	.287	.449	.736	7	.970
2004—Toledo (Int'l)	OF-DH	6	25	4	8	4	0	2	6	0	6	0	0	0-0	.320	.320	.720	1.028	0	1.000
—Detroit (A.L.)	OF-DH	128	447	65	131	27	3	18	72	29	79	2	8	3-4	.293	.337	.488	.824	11	.960
2005—Detroit (A.L.)	OF-DH	157	567	69	157	30	3	20	89	40	95	3	16	8-3	.277	.322	.446	.768	6	.981
2006—Detroit (A.L.)	OF-DH	147	541	89	138	35	2	28	92	37	126	1	14	2-2	.255	.301	.482	.783	4	.980
Major League totals (6 years)		600	2057	285	542	112	9	92	329	139	412	9	50	19-13	.263	.310	.461	.770	29	.973

DIVISION SERIES RECORD

Year Team (League)	Pos.	G	AB	R	H	2B	3B	HR	RBI	BB	SO	HBP	GDP	SB-CS	Avg.	OBP	SLG	OPS	E	Avg.
2006—Detroit (A.L.)	OF	4	16	3	3	1	0	2	3	0	3	0	0	0-0	.188	.188	.625	.813	0	1.000

CHAMPIONSHIP SERIES RECORD

Year Team (League)	Pos.	G	AB	R	H	2B	3B	HR	RBI	BB	SO	HBP	GDP	SB-CS	Avg.	OBP	SLG	OPS	E	Avg.
2006—Detroit (A.L.)	OF	4	14	5	6	2	0	1	4	3	4	0	0	0-0	.429	.500	.786	1.286	0	1.000

WORLD SERIES RECORD

Year Team (League)	Pos.	G	AB	R	H	2B	3B	HR	RBI	BB	SO	HBP	GDP	SB-CS	Avg.	OBP	SLG	OPS	E	Avg.
2006—Detroit (A.L.)	OF	5	20	3	3	1	0	2	2	1	5	0	0	0-0	.150	.190	.500	.690	0	1.000

2006 LEFTY-RIGHTY SPLITS

vs.	Avg.	AB	H	2B	3B	HR	RBI	BB	SO	OBP	Slg.	vs.	Avg.	AB	H	2B	3B	HR	RBI	BB	SO	OBP	Slg.
L	.271	140	38	13	0	2	21	12	33	.327	.407	R	.249	401	100	22	2	26	71	25	93	.292	.509

MONTERO, AGUSTIN — P

PERSONAL: Born August 26, 1977, in San Pedro de Macoris, Dominican Republic. ... Throws right, bats right. ... Full name: Agustin Alcantara Montero. **TRANSACTIONS/CAREER NOTES:** Signed as a non-drafted free agent by Oakland Athletics organization (January 20, 1995). ... Released by Athletics (January 7, 1999). ... Signed by Los Angeles Dodgers organization (September 30, 1999). ... Signed as a free agent by Texas Rangers organization (October 28, 2004). ... On suspended list (April 20-30, 2005). ... Signed as a free agent by Chicago White Sox organization (January 19, 2006).

CAREER HITTING: 0-for-0 (.000), 0 R, 0 2B, 0 3B, 0 HR, 0 RBI.

Year Team (League)	W	L	Pct.	ERA	WHIP	G	GS	CG	ShO	Hld.	Sv.-Opp.	IP	H	R	ER	HR	BB-IBB	SO	Avg.
1995—Dom. Athletics (DSL)	0	1	.000	11.57	3.86	1				...	0-...	2.1	7	6	3	1	2-0	2	.500
1996—Dom. Athletics (DSL)	8	2	.800	2.21	1.42	17	12	2	0	...	1-...	85.2	64	29	21	1	58-0	71	.208

M

Year Team (League)	W	L	Pct.	ERA	WHIP	G	GS	CG	ShO	Hld.	Sv.-Opp.	IP	H	R	ER	HR	BB-IBB	SO	Avg.
1997—Ariz. A's (Ariz.)	3	2	.600	3.59	1.42	14	13	0	0	...	0-...	72.2	72	38	29	3	31-0	88	.251
—S. Oregon (N'west)	0	0	...	6.75	2.63	2	0	0	0	...	0-...	2.2	4	2	2	0	3-0	1	.400
1998—S. Oregon (N'west)	2	3	.400	8.68	1.96	14	3	0	0	...	0-...	37.1	47	42	36	5	26-0	28	.301
2000—Vero Beach (FSL)	0	0	...	6.00	2.67	3	0	0	0	...	0-...	3.0	2	2	2	0	6-0	4	.182
—San Bern. (Calif.)	0	2	.000	9.72	3.00	7	0	0	0	...	0-...	8.1	13	14	9	0	12-0	10	.351
—Great Falls (Pio.)	2	1	.667	3.93	1.53	11	0	0	0	...	0-...	18.1	16	10	8	1	12-0	21	.225
—Yakima (N'west)	1	0	1.000	6.08	1.43	7	0	0	0	...	0-...	13.1	12	9	9	0	7-1	21	.240
2001—Wilmington (S. Atl.)	2	1	.667	3.29	1.17	18	0	0	0	...	1-...	27.1	13	11	10	1	19-1	30	.148
—Vero Beach (FSL)	1	0	1.000	3.45	1.34	16	0	0	0	...	1-...	31.1	29	14	12	7	13-0	23	.250
2002—Vero Beach (FSL)	1	0	1.000	3.46	1.08	7	0	0	0	...	0-...	13.0	10	5	5	1	4-0	14	.217
—Jacksonville (Sou.)	1	3	.250	3.95	1.63	31	0	0	0	...	0-...	41.0	38	21	18	5	29-6	25	.260
2003—Jacksonville (Sou.)	2	1	.667	3.04	1.39	16	0	0	0	...	0-...	26.2	24	10	9	1	13-1	22	.244
—Las Vegas (PCL)	2	2	.500	4.97	1.74	35	0	0	0	...	1-...	50.2	57	32	28	4	31-3	30	.298
2004—Las Vegas (PCL)	1	4	.200	7.69	1.77	42	0	0	0	...	3-...	45.2	55	47	39	9	26-1	38	.285
—Jacksonville (Sou.)	2	0	1.000	2.40	1.20	21	0	0	0	...	4-...	30.0	20	10	8	1	16-0	36	.182
2005—Oklahoma (PCL)	0	0	...	5.40	1.80	4	0	0	0	...	0-0	5.0	6	3	3	0	3-0	4	.333
—Frisco (Texas)	2	4	.333	5.46	1.59	40	0	0	0	1	2-8	61.0	64	40	37	9	33-0	69	.263
2006—Charlotte (Int'l)	2	3	.400	4.85	1.25	39	0	0	0	9	1-3	59.1	54	33	32	8	20-4	55	.244
—Chicago (A.L.)	1	0	1.000	5.14	1.21	11	0	0	0	2	0-0	14.0	15	10	8	3	2-0	7	.278
Major League totals (1 year)	1	0	1.000	5.14	1.21	11	0	0	0	2	0-0	14.0	15	10	8	3	2-0	7	.278

2006 LEFTY-RIGHTY SPLITS

vs.	Avg.	AB	H	2B	3B	HR	RBI	BB	SO	OBP	Slg.	vs.	Avg.	AB	H	2B	3B	HR	RBI	BB	SO	OBP	Slg.
L	.368	19	7	0	0	2	9	1	3	.364	.684	R	.229	35	8	1	0	1	5	1	4	.243	.343

MONTERO, MIGUEL — C

PERSONAL: Born July 9, 1983, in Caracas, Venezuela. ... 5-11/195. ... Bats left, throws right. ... Full name: Miguel Angel Montero. **TRANSACTIONS/CAREER NOTES:** Signed as a non-drafted free agent by Arizona Diamondbacks organization (April 23, 2001).

2006 GAMES PLAYED BY POSITION (MLB): C—5.

Year Team (League)	Pos.	G	AB	R	H	2B	3B	HR	RBI	BB	SO	HBP	GDP	SB-CS	Avg.	OBP	SLG	OPS	E	Avg.
2001—Dominican Diamondbacks (DSL)		43	118	15	26	5	1	1	17	17	19	6	2	7-4	.220	.343	.305	.648	...	...
2002—Missoula (Pion.)		50	152	21	40	10	1	3	14	17	26	3	5	2-1	.263	.343	.401	.744	...	...
2003—Missoula (Pion.)		59	196	24	59	10	2	4	32	9	15	8	6	2-3	.301	.352	.434	.786	...	...
2004—South Bend (Mid.)		115	403	47	106	22	2	11	59	36	74	6	6	8-2	.263	.330	.409	.739	...	...
2005—Lancaster (Calif.)	C-DH-1B	85	355	73	124	24	1	24	82	26	52	10	5	1-2	.349	.403	.625	1.028	8	.983
—Tennessee (Sou.)	C-1B	30	108	13	27	1	2	2	13	7	26	3	2	1-0	.250	.311	.352	.663	4	.983
2006—Tennessee (Sou.)		81	289	24	78	18	0	10	46	39	44	5	3	0-3	.270	.362	.436	.798	2	.997
—Tucson (PCL)		36	134	21	43	5	0	7	29	14	21	4	4	1-1	.321	.396	.515	.911	5	.976
—Arizona (N.L.)	C	6	16	0	4	1	0	0	3	1	3	0	0	0-0	.250	.294	.313	.607	0	1.000
Major League totals (1 year)		6	16	0	4	1	0	0	3	1	3	0	0	0-0	.250	.294	.313	.607	0	1.000

2006 LEFTY-RIGHTY SPLITS

vs.	Avg.	AB	H	2B	3B	HR	RBI	BB	SO	OBP	Slg.	vs.	Avg.	AB	H	2B	3B	HR	RBI	BB	SO	OBP	Slg.
L	.333	3	1	0	0	0	2	0	0	.333	.333	R	.231	13	3	1	0	0	1	1	3	.286	.308

MOORE, SCOTT — IF

PERSONAL: Born November 17, 1983, in Long Beach, Calif. ... 6-4/210. ... Bats left, throws right. ... Full name: Scott Alan Moore. **TRANSACTIONS/CAREER NOTES:** Selected by Detroit Tigers organization in first round (eighth pick overall) of 2002 free-agent draft. ... Traded by Tigers with P Roberto Novoa and Bo Flowers to Chicago Cubs for P Kyle Farnsworth (February 9, 2005).

2006 GAMES PLAYED BY POSITION (MLB): 1B—6, 3B—5.

Year Team (League)	Pos.	G	AB	R	H	2B	3B	HR	RBI	BB	SO	HBP	GDP	SB-CS	Avg.	OBP	SLG	OPS	E	Avg.
2002—GC Tigers (GCL)		40	133	18	39	6	2	4	25	10	31	3	2	1-2	.293	.349	.459	.808	...	...
2003—W. Mich. (Mid.)		107	372	40	89	16	6	6	45	41	110	7	9	2-4	.239	.325	.363	.688	...	...
2004—Lakeland (Fla. St.)		118	391	52	87	13	4	14	56	49	125	10	10	2-4	.223	.322	.384	.706	...	...
2005—Daytona (Fla. St.)	3B-DH	128	466	77	131	31	2	20	82	55	134	6	7	22-7	.281	.358	.485	.843	30	.904
2006—West Tenn. (Sou.)		132	463	52	128	28	0	22	75	55	126	8	7	12-7	.276	.360	.479	.839	19	.943
—Iowa (PCL)		1	4	1	1	0	0	0	0	0	1	0	0	0-0	.250	.250	.500	.750	2	.714
—Chicago (N.L.)	1B-3B	16	38	6	10	2	0	2	5	2	10	1	1	0-0	.263	.317	.474	.791	1	.981
Major League totals (1 year)		16	38	6	10	2	0	2	5	2	10	1	1	0-0	.263	.317	.474	.791	1	.981

2006 LEFTY-RIGHTY SPLITS

vs.	Avg.	AB	H	2B	3B	HR	RBI	BB	SO	OBP	Slg.	vs.	Avg.	AB	H	2B	3B	HR	RBI	BB	SO	OBP	Slg.
L	.000	4	0	0	0	0	0		0	2	.200	.000	R	.294	34	10	2	0	2	5	2	8	.333	.529

MORA, MELVIN — 3B

PERSONAL: Born February 2, 1972, in Agua Negra, Venezuela. ... 5-11/200. ... Bats right, throws right. ... Name pronounced: MORE-a. ... High school: Libertador (Valencia, Venezuela). **TRANSACTIONS/CAREER NOTES:** Signed as a non-drafted free agent by Houston Astros organization (March 30, 1991). ... Signed as a free agent by New York Mets organization (July 24, 1998). ... On disabled list (May 13-30, 2000); included rehabilitation assignment to Norfolk. ... Traded by Mets with 3B Mike Kinkade and Ps Leslie Brea and Pat Gorman to Baltimore Orioles for SS Mike Bordick (July 28, 2000). ... On suspended list (September 13-16, 2002). ... On disabled list (August 1-September 2, 2003); included rehabilitation assignment to Bowie. ... On disabled list (July 3-18, 2004). **RECORDS:** Shares major league record for most times hit by pitch, game (3, July 18, 2002). **HONORS:** Named third baseman on THE SPORTING NEWS A.L. All-Star team (2004). ... Named third baseman on A.L. Silver Slugger team (2004). **STATISTICAL NOTES:** Career major league grand slams: 2.

2006 GAMES PLAYED BY POSITION (MLB): 3B—154, 2B—1, DH—1.

Year Team (League)	Pos.	G	AB	R	H	2B	3B	HR	RBI	BB	SO	HBP	GDP	SB-CS	Avg.	OBP	SLG	OPS	E	Avg.
1991—Dom. Astros (DSL)		58	211	38	63	18	1	0	20	19	22	...	...	21-...	.299		.393	...	...	...
1992—GC Astros (GCL)	2B-3B-OF	49	144	28	32	3	0	0	18	18	16	5	2	16-3	.222	.327	.243	.570	4	.961
1993—Asheville (S. Atl.)		108	365	66	104	22	2	2	31	36	46	9	7	20-13	.285	.356	.373	.729	17	.936
1994—Osceola (Fla. St.)	3B-OF	118	425	57	120	29	4	8	46	37	60	10	8	24-16	.282	.352	.426	.777	15	.947
1995—Jackson (Texas)	2B-3B-OF	123	467	63	139	32	4	5	45	32	57	9	11	22-11	.298	.350	.385	.735	6	.977
—Tucson (PCL)	OF	2	5	3	3	0	1	0	1	2	0	0	0	1-0	.600	.714	1.000	1.714	0	1.000

Year Team (League)	Pos.	G	AB	R	H	2B	3B	HR	RBI	BB	SO	HBP	GDP	SB-CS	Avg.	OBP	SLG	OPS	E	Avg.
1996— Jackson (Texas)	2B-3B-OF																			
	SS	70	255	36	73	6	1	5	23	14	23	6	4	4-7	.286	.336	.376	.712	7	.959
— Tucson (PCL)	2B-3B-OF	62	228	35	64	11	2	3	26	17	27	1	7	3-5	.281	.328	.386	.714	14	.912
1997— New Orleans (A.A.)		119	370	55	95	15	3	2	38	47	52	11	7	7-7	.257	.356	.330	.686	11	.956
1998— Mercury (Tai.)			164	34	54	11	2	3	11	...	...	...	...	...-...	.335		.482		...	
— St. Lucie (Fla. St.)	2B-OF-SS	17	55	5	15	0	0	0	8	5	9	0	0	1-1	.273	.328	.273	.601	1	.985
— Norfolk (Int'l)	2B-3B-OF	11	28	5	5	1	0	0	2	5	7	0	0	0-0	.179	.303	.214	.517	2	.875
1999— Norfolk (Int'l)	SS-OF-2B																			
	3B	82	304	55	92	17	2	8	36	41	54	7	8	18-8	.303	.393	.451	.844	16	.942
— New York (N.L.)	OF-2B-3B																			
	SS	66	31	6	5	0	0	0	1	4	7	1	0	2-1	.161	.278	.161	.439	0	1.000
2000— New York (N.L.)	SS-OF-2B	79	215	35	56	13	2	6	30	18	48	2	3	7-3	.260	.317	.423	.740	8	.962
— Norfolk (Int'l)	OF-2B-SS	8	27	7	9	2	0	0	7	7	3	0	0	2-0	.333	.471	.407	.878	1	1.000
— Baltimore (A.L.)	SS-2B	53	199	25	58	9	3	2	17	17	32	4	2	5-8	.291	.359	.397	.756	12	.953
2001— Baltimore (A.L.)	OF-SS-2B	128	436	49	109	28	0	7	48	41	91	14	6	11-4	.250	.329	.362	.692	11	.974
2002— Baltimore (A.L.)	OF-SS-2B																			
	DH	149	557	86	130	30	4	19	64	70	108	20	7	0-0	.233	.338	.404	.742	12	.976
2003— Bowie (East.)	OF	6	21	3	6	0	0	2	5	2	4	0	0	0-0	.286	.348	.571	.919	0	1.000
— Baltimore (A.L.)	OF-SS-2B																			
	1B	96	344	68	109	17	1	15	48	49	71	12	3	6-3	.317	.418	.503	.921	2	.992
2004— Baltimore (A.L.)	3B-DH-SS	140	550	111	187	41	0	27	104	66	95	11	10	11-6	.340 *	.419	.562	.981	21	.948
2005— Baltimore (A.L.)	3B-DH	149	593	86	168	30	1	27	88	50	112	10	9	7-4	.283	.348	.474	.821	18	.957
2006— Baltimore (A.L.)	3B-2B-DH	155	624	96	171	25	0	16	83	54	99	14	9	11-1	.274	.342	.391	.733	17	.959
American League totals (7 years)		870	3303	521	932	180	9	113	452	347	608	85	46	67-36	.282	.363	.445	.807	93	.965
National League totals (2 years)		145	246	41	61	13	2	6	31	22	55	3	3	9-4	.248	.312	.390	.702	8	.967
Major League totals (8 years)		1015	3549	562	993	193	11	119	483	369	663	88	49	76-40	.280	.359	.441	.800	101	.965

DIVISION SERIES RECORD

Year Team (League)	Pos.	G	AB	R	H	2B	3B	HR	RBI	BB	SO	HBP	GDP	SB-CS	Avg.	OBP	SLG	OPS	E	Avg.
1999— New York (N.L.)	OF	3	1	1	0	0	0	0	0	1	0	0	0	0-0	.000	.500	.000	.500	0	1.000

CHAMPIONSHIP SERIES RECORD

Year Team (League)	Pos.	G	AB	R	H	2B	3B	HR	RBI	BB	SO	HBP	GDP	SB-CS	Avg.	OBP	SLG	OPS	E	Avg.
1999— New York (N.L.)	OF	6	14	3	6	0	0	1	2	2	2	0	0	2-0	.429	.500	.643	1.143	0	1.000

ALL-STAR GAME RECORD

		G	AB	R	H	2B	3B	HR	RBI	BB	SO	HBP	GDP	SB-CS	Avg.	OBP	SLG	OPS	E	Avg.
All-Star Game totals (2 years)		2	1	1	0	0	0	0	0	0	0	0	0	0-0	.000	.000	.000	.000	1	1.000

2006 LEFTY-RIGHTY SPLITS

vs.	Avg.	AB	H	2B	3B	HR	RBI	BB	SO	OBP	Slg.	vs.	Avg.	AB	H	2B	3B	HR	RBI	BB	SO	OBP	Slg.
L	.253	166	42	6	0	7	23	19	26	.339	.416	R	.282	458	129	19	0	9	60	35	73	.343	.382

MORALES, KENDRY IF

PERSONAL: Born June 20, 1983, in Fomento, Cuba. ... 6-1/220. ... Bats both, throws right. ... Full name: Kendrys Morales. **TRANSACTIONS/CAREER NOTES:** Signed as a non-drafted free agent by Los Angeles Angels of Anaheim (December 16, 2004).
2006 GAMES PLAYED BY POSITION (MLB): 1B—56.

Year Team (League)	Pos.	G	AB	R	H	2B	3B	HR	RBI	BB	SO	HBP	GDP	SB-CS	Avg.	OBP	SLG	OPS	E	Avg.
2005— Rancho Cuca. (Calif.)	1B-3B-OF																			
	DH	22	90	18	31	3	0	5	17	6	11	3	3	0-0	.344	.400	.544	.944	5	.969
— Arkansas (Texas)	1B-DH-OF	74	281	47	86	12	0	17	54	17	43	2	7	2-0	.306	.349	.530	.879	7	.988
2006— Salt Lake (PCL)		66	256	41	82	13	1	12	52	14	40	2	6	0-3	.320	.359	.520	.879	1	.998
— Los Angeles (A.L.)	1B	57	197	21	46	10	1	5	22	17	28	0	11	1-1	.234	.293	.371	.664	5	.989
Major League totals (1 year)		57	197	21	46	10	1	5	22	17	28	0	11	1-1	.234	.293	.371	.664	5	.989

2006 LEFTY-RIGHTY SPLITS

vs.	Avg.	AB	H	2B	3B	HR	RBI	BB	SO	OBP	Slg.	vs.	Avg.	AB	H	2B	3B	HR	RBI	BB	SO	OBP	Slg.
L	.229	48	11	4	0	1	7	0	6	.229	.375	R	.235	149	35	6	1	4	15	17	22	.311	.369

MORILLO, JUAN P

PERSONAL: Born November 5, 1983, in San Pedro de Macoris, Dominican Republic. ... 6-3/190. ... Throws right, bats right. ... Full name: Juan Bautista Morillo. **TRANSACTIONS/CAREER NOTES:** Signed as a non-drafted free agent by Colorado Rockies organization (April 26, 2001).
CAREER HITTING: 0-for-1 (.000), 0 R, 0 2B, 0 3B, 0 RBI.

Year Team (League)	W	L	Pct.	ERA	WHIP	G	GS	CG	ShO	Hld.	Sv.-Opp.	IP	H	R	ER	HR	BB-IBB	SO	Avg.
2001— Dom. Rockies (DSL)	2	4	.333	6.81	2.05	14	7	0	0		0-...	35.2	35	31	27	1	38-0	20	.248
2002— Dom. Rockies (DSL)	1	5	.167	4.75	1.49	14	11	0	0		0-...	55.0	49	44	29	1	33-0	43	.230
2003— Casper (Pion.)	1	6	.143	5.91	1.95	15	15	0	0		0-...	64.0	85	73	42	6	40-0	44	.318
2004— Tri-City (N'west)	3	2	.600	2.98	1.46	14	14	0	0		0-...	66.1	56	34	22	0	41-0	73	.226
2005— Asheville (S. Atl.)	1	3	.250	4.54	1.57	7	7	0	0	0	0-0	33.2	40	24	17	2	13-0	43	.290
— Modesto (California)	6	5	.545	4.41	1.53	20	20	0	0	0	0-0	112.1	107	69	55	10	65-0	101	.258
2006— Tulsa (Texas)	12	8	.600	4.62	1.48	27	27	1	0	0	0-0	140.1	128	82	72	13	80-1	132	.248
— Colorado (N.L.)	0	0	...	15.75	2.75	1	1	0	0	0	0-0	4.0	8	7	7	3	3-0	4	.421
Major League totals (1 year)	0	0	...	15.75	2.75	1	1	0	0	0	0-0	4.0	8	7	7	3	3-0	4	.421

2006 LEFTY-RIGHTY SPLITS

vs.	Avg.	AB	H	2B	3B	HR	RBI	BB	SO	OBP	Slg.	vs.	Avg.	AB	H	2B	3B	HR	RBI	BB	SO	OBP	Slg.
L	.625	8	5	1	0	3	6	1	1	.667	1.875	R	.273	11	3	1	0	0	1	2	3	.429	.364

MORNEAU, JUSTIN 1B

PERSONAL: Born May 15, 1981, in New Westminster, British Columbia. ... 6-4/228. ... Bats left, throws right. ... Full name: Justin Ernest Morneau. ... Name pronounced: more-no. ... High school: New Westminster Academy (British Columbia). **TRANSACTIONS/CAREER NOTES:** Selected by Minnesota Twins organization in third round of 1999 free-agent draft. ... On disabled list (April 7-22, 2005). **HONORS:** Named first baseman on SPORTING NEWS A.L. All-Star team (2006). ... Named A.L. Most Valuable Player by Baseball Writers' Association of America (2006). ... Named first baseman on A.L. Silver Slugger team (2006). **STATISTICAL NOTES:** Career major league grand slams: 2.

2006 GAMES PLAYED BY POSITION (MLB): 1B—153, DH—4.

Year Team (League)	Pos.	G	AB	R	H	2B	3B	HR	RBI	BB	SO	HBP	GDP	SB-CS	Avg.	OBP	SLG	OPS	E	FIELDING Avg.
1999— GC Twins (GCL)	DH	17	53	3	16	4	0	0	10	10	15	1	...	1-1	.302	.333	.377	.710	0	...
2000— GC Twins (GCL)	1B-C-OF	52	194	47	48	21	0	10	58	30	18	0	...	3-1	.402	.478	.510	.988	3	.992
— Elizabethton (App.)	C	6	23	4	5	0	0	1	3	1	6	0	0	0-0	.217	.250	.348	.598	0	1.000
2001— Quad City (Midw.)	1B	64	236	50	84	17	2	12	53	26	38	3	4	0-0	.356	.420	.597	1.018	8	.985
— Fort Myers (FSL)	1B	53	197	25	58	10	3	4	40	24	41	8	1	0-0	.294	.385	.437	.821	3	.994
— New Britain (East.)	1B	10	38	3	6	1	0	0	4	3	8	0	1	0-0	.158	.214	.184	.399	0	1.000
2002— New Britain (East.)	1B	126	494	72	147	31	4	16	80	42	88	6	8	7-0	.298	.356	.474	.830	13	.989
2003— New Britain (East.)	1B	20	79	14	26	3	1	6	13	7	14	0	0	0-0	.329	.384	.620	1.004	0	1.000
— Rochester (Int'l)	1B-DH	71	265	39	71	11	1	16	42	28	56	4	2	0-2	.268	.344	.498	.843	4	.993
— Minnesota (A.L.)	DH-1B	40	106	14	24	4	0	4	16	9	30	0	4	0-0	.226	.287	.377	.664	1	.971
2004— Rochester (Int'l)	1B-DH	72	288	51	88	23	0	22	63	32	47	3	7	1-1	.306	.377	.615	.992	4	.993
— Minnesota (A.L.)	1B-DH	74	280	39	76	17	0	19	58	28	54	2	4	0-0	.271	.340	.536	.875	3	.995
2005— Minnesota (A.L.)	1B-DH	141	490	62	117	23	4	22	79	44	94	4	12	0-2	.239	.304	.437	.741	8	.994
2006— Minnesota (A.L.)	1B-DH	157	592	97	190	37	1	34	130	53	93	5	10	3-3	.321	.375	.559	.934	8	.994
Major League totals (4 years)		412	1468	212	407	81	5	79	283	134	271	11	30	3-5	.277	.338	.501	.839	20	.994

DIVISION SERIES RECORD

Year Team (League)	Pos.	G	AB	R	H	2B	3B	HR	RBI	BB	SO	HBP	GDP	SB-CS	Avg.	OBP	SLG	OPS	E	Avg.
2004— Minnesota (A.L.)	1B	4	17	1	4	2	0	0	2	0	3	0	0	0-0	.235	.235	.353	.588	0	1.000
2006— Minnesota (A.L.)	1B	3	12	3	5	1	0	2	2	0	0	0	0	0-0	.417	.417	1.000	1.417	1	.969
Division series totals (2 years)		7	29	4	9	3	0	2	4	0	3	0	0	0-0	.310	.310	.621	.931	1	.986

2006 LEFTY-RIGHTY SPLITS

vs.	Avg.	AB	H	2B	3B	HR	RBI	BB	SO	OBP	Slg.	vs.	Avg.	AB	H	2B	3B	HR	RBI	BB	SO	OBP	Slg.
L	.315	213	67	13	0	13	47	12	32	.345	.559	R	.325	379	123	24	1	21	83	41	61	.391	.559

MORRIS, MATT   P

PERSONAL: Born August 9, 1974, in Middletown, N.Y. ... 6-5/220. ... Throws right, bats right. ... Full name: Matthew Christian Morris. ... High school: Valley Central (Montgomery, N.Y.). ... College: Seton Hall. **TRANSACTIONS/CAREER NOTES:** Selected by Milwaukee Brewers organization in 25th round of 1992 free-agent draft; did not sign. ... Selected by St. Louis Cardinals organization in first round (12th pick overall) of 1995 free-agent draft. ... On disabled list (March 24-April 11 and April 12-July 10, 1998); included rehabilitation assignments to Arkansas and Memphis. ... On disabled list (March 26, 1999-entire season). ... On disabled list (April 2-May 28, 2000); included rehabilitation assignments to Arkansas and Memphis. ... On disabled list (August 24-September 10, 2002; and July 22-August 23, 2003). ... On disabled list (April 3-19, 2005); included rehabilitation assignment to Palm Beach. ... Signed as a free agent by San Francisco Giants (December 12, 2005). **HONORS:** Named N.L. Rookie Pitcher of the Year by THE SPORTING NEWS (1997). ... Named N.L. Comeback Player of the Year by THE SPORTING NEWS (2001). **MISCELLANEOUS NOTES:** Struck out in only appearance as pinch hitter (1997). ... Appeared in one game as pinch runner (2000).

CAREER HITTING: 77-for-479 (.161), 29 R, 15 2B, 0 3B, 1 HR, 34 RBI.

Year Team (League)	W	L	Pct.	ERA	WHIP	G	GS	CG	ShO	Hld.	Sv.-Opp.	IP	H	R	ER	HR	BB-IBB	SO	Avg.
1995— New Jersey (NYP)	2	0	1.000	1.64	1.36	2	2	0	0	...	0-...	11.0	12	3	2	1	3-0	13	.286
— St. Pete. (FSL)	3	2	.600	2.38	0.97	6	6	1	1	...	0-...	34.0	22	16	9	1	11-0	31	.182
1996— Arkansas (Texas)	12	12	.500	3.88	1.35	27	27	4	4	...	0-...	167.0	178	79	72	14	48-1	120	.274
— Louisville (A.A.)	0	1	.000	3.38	1.13	1	1	0	0	...	0-...	8.0	8	3	3	0	1-0	9	.258
1997— St. Louis (N.L.)	12	9	.571	3.19	1.28	33	33	3	0	0	0-0	217.0	208	88	77	12	69-2	149	.258
1998— Arkansas (Texas)	0	0	...	0.00	1.00	1	0	0	0	0	1-...	4.0	4	0	0	0	0-0	2	.235
— St. Louis (N.L.)	7	5	.583	2.53	1.26	17	17	2	1	0	0-0	113.2	101	37	32	8	42-6	79	.243
— Memphis (PCL)	1	0	1.000	4.50	1.43	4	4	0	0	...	0-0	14.0	16	8	7	1	4-0	21	.306
1999— Arkansas (Texas)			Did not play.																
2000— Arkansas (Texas)	0	0	...	6.43	1.71	2	2	0	0		0-...	7.0	8	5	5	0	4-0	7	.296
— Memphis (PCL)	1	2	.333	7.98	1.77	3	3	0	0	...	0-...	14.2	20	13	13	2	6-1	8	.351
— St. Louis (N.L.)	3	3	.500	3.57	1.32	31	0	0	0	7	4-7	53.0	53	22	21	3	17-1	34	.261
2001— St. Louis (N.L.)	•22	8	.733	3.16	1.26	34	34	2	1	0	0-0	216.1	218	86	76	13	54-3	185	.265
2002— St. Louis (N.L.)	17	9	.654	3.42	1.30	32	32	1	1	0	0-0	210.1	210	86	80	16	64-3	171	.261
2003— St. Louis (N.L.)	11	8	.579	3.76	1.18	27	27	5	•3	0	0-0	172.1	164	76	72	20	39-1	120	.252
2004— St. Louis (N.L.)	15	10	.600	4.72	1.29	32	32	3	2	0	0-0	202.0	205	116	106	35	56-3	131	.266
2005— Palm Beach (FSL)	0	1	.000	6.52	1.45	2	2	0	0	0	0-0	9.2	12	7	7	0	2-0	15	.300
— St. Louis (N.L.)	14	10	.583	4.11	1.28	31	31	2	0	0	0-0	192.2	209	101	88	22	37-3	117	.277
2006— San Francisco (N.L.)	10	15	.400	4.98	1.35	33	33	2	0	0	0-0	207.2	218	123	115	22	63-9	117	.268
Major League totals (9 years)	111	77	.590	3.79	1.28	270	239	20	8	7	4-7	1585.0	1586	735	667	151	441-31	1103	.262

DIVISION SERIES RECORD

Year Team (League)	W	L	Pct.	ERA	WHIP	G	GS	CG	ShO	Hld.	Sv.-Opp.	IP	H	R	ER	HR	BB-IBB	SO	Avg.
2000— St. Louis (N.L.)	0	0	...	0.00	0.50	2	0	0	0	0	0-0	2.0	0	0	0	0	1-0	0	.000
2001— St. Louis (N.L.)	0	1	.000	1.20	1.20	2	2	0	0	0	0-0	15.0	13	2	2	1	5-0	12	.236
2002— St. Louis (N.L.)	1	0	1.000	1.29	1.29	1	1	0	0	0	0-0	7.0	7	2	1	0	2-0	3	.259
2004— St. Louis (N.L.)	0	1	.000	5.14	1.14	1	1	0	0	0	0-0	7.0	6	4	4	2	2-1	5	.231
2005— St. Louis (N.L.)	1	0	1.000	3.00	1.33	1	1	0	0	0	0-0	6.0	5	2	2	0	3-0	4	.217
Division series totals (5 years)	2	2	.500	2.19	1.19	7	5	0	0	0	0-0	37.0	31	10	9	3	13-1	24	.226

CHAMPIONSHIP SERIES RECORD

Year Team (League)	W	L	Pct.	ERA	WHIP	G	GS	CG	ShO	Hld.	Sv.-Opp.	IP	H	R	ER	HR	BB-IBB	SO	Avg.
2000— St. Louis (N.L.)	0	0	...	4.91	1.36	2	2	0	0	0	0-0	3.2	3	2	2	0	2-1	2	.214
2002— St. Louis (N.L.)	0	2	.000	6.23	1.69	2	2	0	0	0	0-0	13.0	16	9	9	2	6-1	6	.320
2004— St. Louis (N.L.)	0	0	...	5.40	1.90	2	2	0	0	0	0-0	10.0	11	6	6	3	8-1	6	.297
2005— St. Louis (N.L.)	0	1	.000	5.06	1.69	1	1	0	0	0	0-0	5.1	8	4	3	1	1-0	3	.333
Champ. series totals (4 years)	0	3	.000	5.63	1.72	7	5	0	0	0	0-0	32.0	38	21	20	6	17-3	17	.304

WORLD SERIES RECORD

Year Team (League)	W	L	Pct.	ERA	WHIP	G	GS	CG	ShO	Hld.	Sv.-Opp.	IP	H	R	ER	HR	BB-IBB	SO	Avg.
2004— St. Louis (N.L.)	0	1	.000	8.31	1.85	1	1	0	0	0	0-0	4.1	4	4	4	0	4-0	5	.250

ALL-STAR GAME RECORD

	W	L	Pct.	ERA	WHIP	G	GS	CG	ShO	Hld.	Sv.-Opp.	IP	H	R	ER	HR	BB-IBB	SO	Avg.
All-Star Game totals (1 year)	0	0	...	0.00	1.00	1	0	0	0	0	0-0	1.0	1	0	0	0	0-0	1	

2006 LEFTY-RIGHTY SPLITS

vs.	Avg.	AB	H	2B	3B	HR	RBI	BB	SO	OBP	Slg.	vs.	Avg.	AB	H	2B	3B	HR	RBI	BB	SO	OBP	Slg.
L	.277	394	109	25	7	9	56	28	63	.332	.444	R	.261	418	109	29	2	13	56	35	54	.328	.433

MORSE, MIKE — SS/3B

PERSONAL: Born March 22, 1982, in Fort Lauderdale, Fla. ... 6-4/220. ... Bats right, throws right. ... Full name: Michael John Morse. **TRANSACTIONS/CAREER NOTES:** Selected by Chicago White Sox organization in third round of 2000 free-agent draft. ... Traded by White Sox with OF Jeremy Reed and C Miguel Olivo to Seattle Mariners for P Freddy Garcia, C Ben Davis and cash (June 27, 2004). ... On suspended list (September 7-17, 2005).

2006 GAMES PLAYED BY POSITION (MLB): OF—9, 3B—5, DH—4, 1B—2, SS—1.

									BATTING									FIELDING	
Year — Team (League)	Pos.	G	AB	R	H	2B	3B	HR	RBI	BB	SO	HBP	GDP	SB-CS	Avg.	OBP	SLG	OPS	E	Avg.
2000— Ariz. White Sox (Ariz.)	SS	45	180	32	46	6	1	2	24	15	29	1	6	5-2	.256	.308	.333	.641	18	.897
2001— Bristol (Appal.)	SS	57	181	23	41	7	3	4	27	17	57	9	4	6-2	.227	.324	.365	.689	14	.940
2002— Kannapolis (S. Atl.)	SS-3B	113	417	43	107	30	4	2	56	25	73	8	16	7-6	.257	.310	.362	.672	32	.934
2003— Win.-Salem (Car.)	SS	122	432	45	106	30	2	10	55	25	91	7	12	4-4	.245	.296	.394	.690	19	.959
2004— Birmingham (Sou.)	SS	54	209	30	60	9	5	11	38	15	46	1	4	0-3	.287	.336	.536	.872	11	.831
— San Antonio (Texas)	SS	41	157	18	43	10	1	6	33	9	27	4	8	0-2	.274	.326	.465	.791	9	.000
2005— Tacoma (PCL)	SS	49	182	20	46	12	2	4	23	16	36	2	6	1-0	.253	.317	.407	.723	4	.981
— Seattle (A.L.)	SS-DH-OF	72	230	41	64	10	1	3	23	18	50	8	9	3-1	.278	.349	.370	.718	12	.949
2006— Tacoma (PCL)	SS	57	206	23	51	15	1	5	34	14	46	3	7	0-1	.248	.300	.403	.702	3	.988
— Seattle (A.L.)	OF-3B-DH 1B-SS	21	43	5	16	5	0	0	11	3	7	0	2	1-0	.372	.396	.488	.884	0	1.000
Major League totals (2 years)		93	273	32	80	15	1	3	34	21	57	8	11	4-1	.293	.356	.388	.744	12	.953

2006 LEFTY-RIGHTY SPLITS

vs.	Avg.	AB	H	2B	3B	HR	RBI	BB	SO	OBP	Slg.	vs.	Avg.	AB	H	2B	3B	HR	RBI	BB	SO	OBP	Slg.
L	.438	32	14	4	0	0	9	2	4	.457	.563	R	.182	11	2	1	0	0	2	1	3	.231	.273

MOSELEY, DUSTIN — P

PERSONAL: Born December 26, 1981, in Texarkana, Ark. ... Throws right, bats right. ... Full name: Dustin Aaron Moseley. **TRANSACTIONS/CAREER NOTES:** Selected by Cincinnati Reds organization in supplemental round ("sandwich" pick between first and second rounds, 34th pick overall) of 2000 free-agent draft; pick received as compensation for Tampa Bay Devil Rays signing Type A free-agent P Juan Guzman. ... Traded by Reds to Anaheim Angels for P Ramon Ortiz (December 14, 2004). ... Angels franchise renamed Los Angeles Angels of Anaheim for 2005 season.

CAREER HITTING: 0-for-0 (.000), 0 R, 0 2B, 0 3B, 0 HR, 0 RBI.

Year — Team (League)	W	L	Pct.	ERA	WHIP	G	GS	CG	ShO	Hld.	Sv.-Opp.	IP	H	R	ER	HR	BB-IBB	SO	Avg.
2001— Dayton (Midw.)	10	8	.556	4.20	1.35	25	25	0	0	...	0-...	148.0	158	83	69	10	42-0	108	.271
2002— Stockton (Calif.)	6	3	.667	2.74	0.91	14	14	2	2	...	0-...	88.2	60	28	27	3	21-0	80	.188
— Chattanooga (Sou.)	5	6	.455	4.13	1.59	13	13	0	0	...	0-...	80.2	91	47	37	5	37-0	52	.293
2003— Chattanooga (Sou.)	5	6	.455	3.83	1.28	18	18	0	0	...	0-...	112.2	116	55	48	10	28-0	73	.264
— Louisville (Int'l)	2	3	.400	2.70	1.20	8	8	0	0	...	0-...	50.0	46	19	15	5	14-0	27	.245
2004— Chattanooga (Sou.)	3	2	.600	2.66	0.91	8	8	0	0	...	0-...	47.1	36	16	14	4	10-0	40	.198
— Louisville (Int'l)	2	4	.333	4.65	1.56	12	12	0	0	...	0-...	71.2	78	38	37	7	34-0	48	.294
2005— Salt Lake (PCL)	4	6	.400	5.03	1.60	17	17	0	0	0	0-0	82.1	102	51	46	11	30-0	38	.312
2006— Salt Lake (PCL)	13	8	.619	4.69	1.44	26	26	3	0	0	0-0	149.2	164	89	78	16	51-0	114	.283
— Los Angeles (A.L.)	1	0	1.000	9.00	2.18	3	2	0	0	0	0-0	11.0	22	11	11	3	2-0	3	.440
Major League totals (1 year)	1	0	1.000	9.00	2.18	3	2	0	0	0	0-0	11.0	22	11	11	3	2-0	3	.440

2006 LEFTY-RIGHTY SPLITS

vs.	Avg.	AB	H	2B	3B	HR	RBI	BB	SO	OBP	Slg.	vs.	Avg.	AB	H	2B	3B	HR	RBI	BB	SO	OBP	Slg.
L	.500	26	13	3	0	1	4	1	3	.519	.731	R	.375	24	9	0	0	2	7	1	0	.385	.625

MOTA, GUILLERMO — P

PERSONAL: Born July 25, 1973, in San Pedro de Macoris, Dominican Republic. ... 6-4/205. ... Throws right, bats right. ... Full name: Guillermo Reynoso Mota. ... Name pronounced: mo-TAH. ... High school: Jose Joaquin Perez (San Pedro de Macoris, Dominican Republic). **TRANSACTIONS/CAREER NOTES:** Signed as a non-drafted free agent by New York Mets organization (September 7, 1990). ... Played infield in Mets organization (1991-96). ... Selected by Montreal Expos organization from Mets organization in Rule 5 minor league draft (December 9, 1996). ... On disabled list (July 13-September 1, 2001); included rehabilitation assignment to Ottawa. ... Traded by Expos with OF Wilkin Ruan to Los Angeles Dodgers for P Matt Herges and IF Jorge Nunez (March 24, 2002). ... On suspended list (March 30-April 4, 2003). ... Traded by Dodgers with C Paul Lo Duca and OF Juan Encarnacion to Florida Marlins for Ps Brad Penny and Bill Murphy and 1B Hee Seop Choi (July 30, 2004). ... On disabled list (May 1-27, 2005); included rehabilitation assignment to Jupiter. ... Traded by Marlins with P Josh Beckett and 3B Mike Lowell to Boston Red Sox for SS Hanley Ramirez and Ps Anibal Sanchez, Harvey Garcia and Jesus Delgado (November 24, 2005). ... Traded by Red Sox with 3B Andy Marte and C Kelly Shoppach to Cleveland Indians for OF Coco Crisp, C Josh Bard and P David Riske (January 27, 2006). ... Traded by Indians to Mets for a player to be named or cash (August 20, 2006). **STATISTICAL NOTES:** Hit home run in first major league at-bat (June 9, 1999).

CAREER HITTING: 7-for-33 (.212), 4 R, 1 2B, 0 3B, 2 HR, 6 RBI.

Year — Team (League)	W	L	Pct.	ERA	WHIP	G	GS	CG	ShO	Hld.	Sv.-Opp.	IP	H	R	ER	HR	BB-IBB	SO	Avg.
1997— Cape Fear (S. Atl.)	5	10	.333	4.36	1.33	25	23	0	0	...	0-...	126.0	135	65	61	8	33-0	112	.278
1998— Jupiter (Fla. St.)	3	2	.600	0.66	0.59	20	0	0	0	...	2-...	41.0	18	6	3	0	6-0	27	.130
— Harrisburg (East.)	2	0	1.000	1.06	0.71	12	0	0	0	...	4-...	17.0	10	2	2	0	2-0	19	.172
1999— Ottawa (Int'l)	2	0	1.000	1.89	1.11	14	0	0	0	...	5-...	19.0	16	6	4	0	5-0	17	.235
— Montreal (N.L.)	2	4	.333	2.93	1.43	51	0	0	0	3	0-1	55.1	54	24	18	5	25-3	27	.257
2000— Ottawa (Int'l)	2	2	.444	2.29	1.27	35	0	0	0	...	7-...	63.0	49	16	16	4	31-3	35	.220
— Montreal (N.L.)	1	1	.500	6.00	1.30	29	0	0	0	5	0-0	30.0	27	21	20	3	12-0	24	.245
2001— Montreal (N.L.)	1	3	.250	5.26	1.39	53	0	0	0	12	0-3	49.2	51	30	29	9	18-1	31	.271
— Ottawa (Int'l)	0	0	...	2.25	0.25	4	0	0	0	...	0-...	4.0	1	1	1	0	1-0	4	.077
2002— Las Vegas (PCL)	1	3	.250	2.95	1.15	20	0	0	0	...	1-...	36.2	34	13	12	1	8-1	38	.260
— Los Angeles (N.L.)	1	3	.250	4.15	1.19	43	0	0	0	4	0-1	60.2	45	30	28	4	27-6	49	.202
2003— Los Angeles (N.L.)	6	3	.667	1.97	0.99	76	0	0	0	13	1-3	105.0	78	23	23	7	26-4	99	.206
2004— Los Angeles (N.L.)	8	4	.667	2.14	1.24	52	0	0	0	17	1-1	63.0	51	15	15	4	27-5	52	.228
— Florida (N.L.)	1	0	.200	4.81	1.01	26	0	0	0	13	3-7	33.2	24	18	18	4	10-1	31	.200
2005— Jupiter (Fla. St.)	0	0	...	0.00	1.13	2	0	0	0	...	0-0	2.2	3	1	0	0	0-0	4	.300
— Florida (N.L.)	2	2	.500	4.70	1.45	56	0	0	0	14	2-4	67.0	65	38	35	5	32-7	60	.254
2006— Cleveland (A.L.)	1	3	.250	6.21	1.70	34	0	0	0	5	0-0	37.2	45	27	26	9	19-3	27	.298
— New York (N.L.)	3	1	1.000	1.00	0.83	18	0	0	0	4	0-0	18.0	10	2	2	2	5-1	19	.159
American League totals (1 year)	1	3	.250	6.21	1.70	34	0	0	0	5	0-0	37.2	45	27	26	9	19-3	27	.298
National League totals (8 years)	25	24	.510	3.51	1.22	404	0	0	0	85	7-20	482.1	405	201	188	43	182-28	394	.228
Major League totals (8 years)	26	27	.491	3.70	1.25	438	0	0	0	90	7-20	520.0	450	228	214	52	201-31	421	.234

M

Year Team (League)	W	L	Pct.	ERA	WHIP	G	GS	CG	ShO	Hld.	Sv.-Opp.	IP	H	R	ER	HR	BB-IBB	SO	Avg.
DIVISION SERIES RECORD																			
2006—New York (N.L.)	1	0	1.000	6.75	1.50	2	0	0	0	1	0-1	4.0	6	3	3	0	0-0	5	.316
CHAMPIONSHIP SERIES RECORD																			
2006—New York (N.L.)	0	0	...	4.15	1.38	5	0	0	0	2	0-1	4.1	4	2	2	0	2-0	2	.267

2006 LEFTY-RIGHTY SPLITS

vs.	Avg.	AB	H	2B	3B	HR	RBI	BB	SO	OBP	Slg.	vs.	Avg.	AB	H	2B	3B	HR	RBI	BB	SO	OBP	Slg.
L	.252	103	26	5	2	6	22	14	21	.336	.515	R	.261	111	29	4	0	5	13	10	25	.320	.432

MOTTOLA, CHAD — OF

PERSONAL: Born October 15, 1971, in Augusta, Ga. ... 6-3/220. ... Bats right, throws right. ... Full name: Charles Edward Mottola. ... Name pronounced: muh-TOE-lah. ... High school: St. Thomas Aquinas (Fort Lauderdale, Fla.). ... College: Central Florida. **TRANSACTIONS/CAREER NOTES:** Selected by Baltimore Orioles organization in 10th round of 1989 free-agent draft; did not sign. ... Selected by Cincinnati Reds organization in first round (fifth pick overall) of 1992 free-agent draft. ... Traded by Reds to Texas Rangers for a player to be named (April 18, 1998); Reds acquired OF Andrew Vessel to complete deal (November 4, 1998). ... Traded by Blue Jays to Florida Marlins for cash (December 17, 1998). ... Signed as a free agent by Toronto Blue Jays organization (November 17, 1999). ... Traded by Blue Jays to Florida Marlins for cash (January 16, 2001). ... Signed as a free agent by Blue Jays organization (December 18, 2001). ... Signed as a free agent by Tampa Bay Devil Rays organization (November 1, 2002). ... Released by Devil Rays (June 8, 2003). ... Signed by Boston Red Sox organization (June 12, 2003). ... Signed as a free agent by Baltimore Orioles organization (December 29, 2003). ... Signed as a free agent by Blue Jays organization (January 8, 2005).

2006 GAMES PLAYED BY POSITION (MLB): OF—5, DH—2.

Year Team (League)	Pos.	G	AB	R	H	2B	3B	HR	RBI	BB	SO	HBP	GDP	SB-CS	Avg.	OBP	SLG	OPS	E	Avg.
1992—Billings (Pion.)	OF	57	213	53	61	8	3	12	37	25	43	0	4	12-3	.286	.361	.521	.882	3	.970
1993—Win.-Salem (Car.)	OF	137	493	76	138	25	3	21	91	62	109	2	9	13-7	.280	.361	.471	.831	15	.940
1994—Chattanooga (Sou.)	OF	118	402	44	97	19	1	7	41	30	68	1	12	9-12	.241	.294	.346	.640	1	.996
1995—Chattanooga (Sou.)	OF	51	181	32	53	13	1	10	39	13	32	1	2	1-2	.293	.342	.541	.883	3	.974
—Indianapolis (A.A.)	OF	69	239	40	62	11	1	8	37	20	50	0	6	8-1	.259	.315	.414	.730	4	.976
1996—Indianapolis (A.A.)	OF-DH	103	362	45	95	24	3	9	47	21	93	4	10	9-6	.262	.307	.420	.727	6	.968
—Cincinnati (N.L.)	OF	35	79	10	17	3	0	3	6	6	16	0	0	2-2	.215	.271	.367	.638	0	1.000
1997—Indianapolis (A.A.)	OF-DH	83	284	33	82	10	6	7	45	16	43	4	6	12-4	.289	.333	.440	.773	8	.947
—Chattanooga (Sou.)	OF-DH	46	174	35	63	9	3	5	32	16	23	1	3	7-1	.362	.408	.534	.943	3	.963
1998—Indianapolis (Int'l)	OF	5	12	2	5	0	0	1	2	4	0	0	0	0-2	.417	.563	.667	1.229	0	1.000
—Tulsa (Texas)	DH-OF	8	26	9	13	1	0	1	7	10	1	0	0	3-0	.500	.639	.654	1.293	0	1.000
—Oklahoma (PCL)	OF-DH	74	257	29	68	13	1	2	22	18	49	1	7	8-3	.265	.313	.346	.659	6	.981
1999—Charlotte (Int'l)	OF-DH	140	511	95	164	32	4	20	94	60	83	3	7	18-6	.321	.391	.517	.907	6	.981
2000—Syracuse (Int'l)	OF	134	505	85	156	25	3	33	102	37	99	5	11	30-15	.309	.359	.566	.925	10	.964
—Toronto (A.L.)	OF	3	9	1	2	0	0	0	2	0	4	0	0	0-0	.222	.300	.222	.522	0	1.000
2001—Calgary (PCL)	OF	119	457	66	135	23	2	15	66	30	85	4	5	11-5	.295	.343	.453	.796	8	.968
—Florida (N.L.)	OF	5	7	1	0	0	0	0	0	1	2	0	0	0-0	.000	.200	.000	.200	0	1.000
2002—Syracuse (Int'l)	OF	122	476	77	124	35	1	13	67	51	87	4	9	12-2	.261	.333	.420	.753	12	.946
2003—Durham (Int'l)	OF-DH	56	213	24	55	7	1	6	28	19	37	1	4	6-3	.258	.319	.385	.704	1	.988
—Pawtucket (Int'l)	OF-DH	21	72	11	23	3	2	3	18	6	10	1	1	0-1	.319	.380	.542	.922	1	.966
2004—Baltimore (A.L.)	OF	6	14	2	2	1	0	1	3	2	3	0	1	0-0	.143	.250	.429	.679	0	1.000
—Ottawa (Int'l)	OF-1B-DH	117	457	60	121	22	0	22	69	22	90	9	13	8-0	.265	.308	.457	.766	7	.979
2005—Syracuse (Int'l)	OF-DH-1B	125	478	67	122	27	3	21	69	35	100	4	2	2-5	.255	.310	.456	.766	8	.977
2006—Syracuse (Int'l)		110	431	48	114	27	2	16	65	30	103	6	9	8-0	.265	.315	.448	.762	4	.977
—Toronto (A.L.)	OF-DH	10	16	3	4	0	0	0	0	0	6	0	0	0-0	.250	.250	.375	.625	0	1.000
American League totals (3 years)		19	39	6	8	1	0	1	5	2	10	1	1	0-0	.205	.262	.359	.621	0	1.000
National League totals (2 years)		40	86	11	17	3	0	3	7	8	18	0	0	2-2	.198	.263	.337	.600	0	1.000
Major League totals (5 years)		59	125	17	25	4	0	4	12	10	28	1	1	2-2	.200	.263	.344	.607	0	1.000

2006 LEFTY-RIGHTY SPLITS

vs.	Avg.	AB	H	2B	3B	HR	RBI	BB	SO	OBP	Slg.	vs.	Avg.	AB	H	2B	3B	HR	RBI	BB	SO	OBP	Slg.
L	.182	11	2	1	0	0	0	0	1	.182	.273	R	.400	5	2	1	0	0	0	0	2	.400	.600

MOYER, JAMIE — P

PERSONAL: Born November 18, 1962, in Sellersville, Pa. ... 6-0/175. ... Throws left, bats left. ... High school: Souderton (Pa.) Area. ... College: St. Joseph's (Pa.). ... Son-in-law of Digger Phelps, ESPN college basketball analyst and Notre Dame basketball coach (1971-72 through 1990-91). **TRANSACTIONS/CAREER NOTES:** Selected by Chicago Cubs organization in sixth round of June 1984 free-agent draft. ... Traded by Cubs with OF Rafael Palmeiro and P Drew Hall to Texas Rangers for Ps Mitch Williams, Paul Kilgus and Steve Wilson, IFs Curtis Wilkerson and Luis Benitez and OF Pablo Delgado (December 5, 1988). ... On disabled list (May 31-September 1, 1989); included rehabilitation assignments to GCL Rangers and Tulsa. ... Released by Rangers (November 13, 1990). ... Signed by St. Louis Cardinals organization (January 9, 1991). ... Released by Cardinals (October 14, 1991). ... Signed by Cubs organization (January 8, 1992). ... Released by Cubs (March 30, 1992). ... Signed by Detroit Tigers organization (May 24, 1992). ... Signed as a free agent by Baltimore Orioles organization (December 14, 1992). ... Signed as a free agent by Boston Red Sox (January 2, 1996). ... Traded by Red Sox to Seattle Mariners for OF Darren Bragg (July 30, 1996). ... On disabled list (March 23-April 29, 1997); included rehabilitation assignment to Tacoma. ... On disabled list (April 15-June 2, 2000). ... Traded by Mariners to Philadelphia Phillies for Ps Andrew Baldwin and Andrew Barb (August 20, 2006). **STATISTICAL NOTES:** Led A.L. in winning percentage with .813 in 1996. **HONORS:** Named lefthanded pitcher on THE SPORTING NEWS A.L. All-Star team (1999).

CAREER HITTING: 29-for-195 (.149), 12 R, 2 2B, 0 3B, 0 HR, 7 RBI.

Year Team (League)	W	L	Pct.	ERA	WHIP	G	GS	CG	ShO	Hld.	Sv.-Opp.	IP	H	R	ER	HR	BB-IBB	SO	Avg.
1984—Geneva (NY-Penn)	9	3	.750	1.89	0.86	14	14	5	2	...	0-...	104.2	59	27	22	5	31-0	120	.160
1985—Win.-Salem (Car.)	8	2	.800	2.30	1.11	12	12	6	2	...	0-...	94.0	82	36	24	1	22-3	94	.232
—Pittsfield (East.)	7	6	.538	3.72	1.36	15	15	3	0	...	0-...	96.2	99	49	40	4	32-1	51	.265
1986—Pittsfield (East.)	3	1	.750	0.88	1.05	6	6	0	0	...	0-...	41.0	27	10	4	2	16-0	42	.184
—Iowa (Am. Assoc.)	3	2	.600	2.55	0.85	6	6	2	0	...	0-...	42.1	25	14	12	2	11-0	25	.162
—Chicago (N.L.)	7	4	.636	5.05	1.71	16	16	1	1	...	0-0	87.1	107	52	49	10	42-1	45	.311
1987—Chicago (N.L.)	12	15	.444	5.10	1.53	35	33	1	0	...	0-0	201.0	210	127	*114	28	97-9	147	.271
1988—Chicago (N.L.)	9	15	.375	3.48	1.32	34	30	3	1	...	0-2	202.0	212	84	78	20	55-7	121	.272
1989—Texas (A.L.)	4	9	.308	4.86	1.54	15	15	1	0	...	0-0	76.0	84	51	41	10	33-0	44	.283
—GC Rangers (GCL)	1	0	1.000	1.64	0.82	3	2	0	0	...	0-0	11.0	8	4	2	0	1-0	18	.195
—Tulsa (Texas)	1	1	.500	5.11	1.54	2	2	1	0	...	0-0	12.1	16	8	7	1	3-0	9	.320
1990—Texas (A.L.)	2	6	.250	4.66	1.50	33	10	1	0	...	0-0	102.1	115	59	53	6	39-4	58	.290
1991—St. Louis (N.L.)	0	5	.000	5.74	1.72	8	7	0	0	...	0-0	31.1	38	21	20	5	16-0	20	.319
—Louisville (A.A.)	5	10	.333	3.80	1.34	20	20	1	0	...	0-0	125.2	125	64	53	16	43-4	69	.260
1992—Toledo (Int'l)	10	8	.556	2.86	1.19	21	20	5	1	...	0-0	138.2	128	48	44	8	37-3	80	.246
1993—Rochester (Int'l)	6	0	1.000	1.67	1.02	8	8	1	1	...	0-0	54.0	42	13	10	2	13-0	41	.211

Year	Team (League)	W	L	Pct.	ERA	WHIP	G	GS	CG	ShO	Hld.	Sv.-Opp.	IP	H	R	ER	HR	BB-IBB	SO	Avg.
—	Baltimore (A.L.)	12	9	.571	3.43	1.26	25	25	3	1	0	0-0	152.0	154	63	58	11	38-2	90	.265
1994—	Baltimore (A.L.)	5	7	.417	4.77	1.32	23	23	0	0	0	0-0	149.0	158	81	79	23	38-3	87	.271
1995—	Baltimore (A.L.)	8	6	.571	5.21	1.27	27	18	0	0	0	0-0	115.2	117	70	67	18	30-0	65	.265
1996—	Boston (A.L.)	7	1	.875	4.50	1.53	23	10	0	0	1	0-0	90.0	111	50	45	14	27-2	50	.300
—	Seattle (A.L.)	6	2	.750	3.31	1.20	11	11	0	0	0	0-0	70.2	66	36	26	9	19-3	29	.243
1997—	Tacoma (PCL)	1	0	1.000	0.00	0.20	1	1	0	0	...	0-...	5.0	1	0	0	0	0-0	6	.063
—	Seattle (A.L.)	17	5	.773	3.86	1.22	30	30	2	0	0	0-0	188.2	187	82	81	21	43-2	113	.256
1998—	Seattle (A.L.)	15	9	.625	3.53	1.18	34	34	4	3	0	0-0	234.1	234	99	92	23	42-2	158	.256
1999—	Seattle (A.L.)	14	8	.636	3.87	1.24	32	32	4	0	0	0-0	228.0	235	108	98	23	48-1	137	.267
2000—	Seattle (A.L.)	13	10	.565	5.49	1.47	26	26	0	0	0	0-0	154.0	173	103	94	22	53-2	98	.281
2001—	Seattle (A.L.)	20	6	.769	3.43	1.10	33	33	1	0	0	0-0	209.2	187	84	80	24	44-4	119	.239
2002—	Seattle (A.L.)	13	8	.619	3.32	1.08	34	34	4	2	0	0-0	230.2	198	89	85	28	50-4	147	.230
2003—	Seattle (A.L.)	21	7	.750	3.27	1.23	33	33	1	0	0	0-0	215.0	199	83	78	19	66-3	129	.246
2004—	Seattle (A.L.)	7	13	.350	5.21	1.39	34	33	1	0	0	0-0	202.0	217	127	117	*44	63-3	125	.272
2005—	Seattle (A.L.)	13	7	.650	4.28	1.39	32	32	1	0	0	0-0	200.0	225	99	95	23	52-2	102	.283
2006—	Seattle (A.L.)	6	12	.333	4.39	1.39	25	25	2	1	0	0-0	160.0	179	85	78	25	44-3	82	.285
—	Philadelphia (N.L.)	5	2	.714	4.03	1.09	8	8	0	0	0	0-0	51.1	49	25	23	8	7-2	26	.251
American League totals (16 years)		183	125	.594	4.10	1.28	470	424	25	7	2	0-0	2778.0	2839	1369	1267	343	729-40	1633	.264
National League totals (5 years)		33	41	.446	4.46	1.45	101	94	5	2	0	0-2	573.0	616	309	284	71	217-19	359	.278
Major League totals (20 years)		216	166	.565	4.17	1.31	571	518	30	9	2	0-2	3351.0	3455	1678	1551	414	946-59	1992	.266

DIVISION SERIES RECORD

Year	Team (League)	W	L	Pct.	ERA	WHIP	G	GS	CG	ShO	Hld.	Sv.-Opp.	IP	H	R	ER	HR	BB-IBB	SO	Avg.
1997—	Seattle (A.L.)	0	1	.000	5.79	1.29	1	1	0	0	0	0-0	4.2	5	3	3	1	1-0	2	.278
2001—	Seattle (A.L.)	2	0	1.000	1.50	0.83	2	2	0	0	0	0-0	12.0	8	2	2	0	2-0	10	.186
Division series totals (2 years)		2	1	.667	2.70	0.96	3	3	0	0	0	0-0	16.2	13	5	5	1	3-0	12	.213

CHAMPIONSHIP SERIES RECORD

Year	Team (League)	W	L	Pct.	ERA	WHIP	G	GS	CG	ShO	Hld.	Sv.-Opp.	IP	H	R	ER	HR	BB-IBB	SO	Avg.
2001—	Seattle (A.L.)	1	0	1.000	2.57	0.71	1	1	0	0	0	0-0	7.0	4	2	2	1	1-0	5	.167

ALL-STAR GAME RECORD

	W	L	Pct.	ERA	WHIP	G	GS	CG	ShO	Hld.	Sv.-Opp.	IP	H	R	ER	HR	BB-IBB	SO	Avg.
All-Star Game totals (1 year)	0	0	...	0.00	0.00	1	0	0	0	0	0-0	1.0	0	0	0	0	0-0	1	.000

2006 LEFTY-RIGHTY SPLITS

vs.	Avg.	AB	H	2B	3B	HR	RBI	BB	SO	OBP	Slg.	vs.	Avg.	AB	H	2B	3B	HR	RBI	BB	SO	OBP	Slg.
L	.251	191	48	9	3	3	19	8	28	.289	.377	R	.285	632	180	43	4	30	81	43	80	.329	.508

MOYLAN, PETER — P

PERSONAL: Born December 2, 1978, in Attadale, Australia. ... 6-2/200. ... Throws right, bats right. ... Full name: Peter Michael Moylan. **TRANSACTIONS/CAREER NOTES:** Signed as a non-drafted free agent by Minnesota Twins organization (1996). ... Signed as a free agent by Atlanta Braves organization (March 17, 2006).
CAREER HITTING: 0-for-0 (.000), 0 R, 0 2B, 0 3B, 0 HR, 0 RBI.

Year	Team (League)	W	L	Pct.	ERA	WHIP	G	GS	CG	ShO	Hld.	Sv.-Opp.	IP	H	R	ER	HR	BB-IBB	SO	Avg.
1996—	GC Twins (GCL)	1	1	.500	4.08	1.50	13	0	0	0	...	1-...	28.2	34	16	13	3	9-0	16	.301
1997—	GC Twins (GCL)	4	2	.667	4.05	1.40	12	7	0	0	...	0-...	40.0	46	21	18	0	10-0	40	.282
2006—	Richmond (Int'l)	1	7	.125	6.35	1.75	35	0	0	0	...	1-7	56.2	61	43	40	4	38-6	54	.272
—	Atlanta (N.L.)	0	0	...	4.80	1.53	15	0	0	0	0	0-0	15.0	18	8	8	1	5-1	14	.290
Major League totals (1 year)		0	0	...	4.80	1.53	15	0	0	0	0	0-0	15.0	18	8	8	1	5-1	14	.290

2006 LEFTY-RIGHTY SPLITS

vs.	Avg.	AB	H	2B	3B	HR	RBI	BB	SO	OBP	Slg.	vs.	Avg.	AB	H	2B	3B	HR	RBI	BB	SO	OBP	Slg.
L	.192	26	5	0	0	1	5	3	3	.276	.308	R	.361	36	13	4	0	0	4	2	11	.395	.472

MUELLER, BILL — 3B

PERSONAL: Born March 17, 1971, in Maryland Heights, Mo. ... 5-10/180. ... Bats both, throws right. ... Full name: William Richard Mueller. ... Name pronounced: MILL-er. ... High school: DeSmet (Creve Coeur, Mo.). ... College: Southwest Missouri State. **TRANSACTIONS/CAREER NOTES:** Selected by San Francisco Giants organization in 15th round of 1993 free-agent draft. ... On disabled list (July 1-16, 1997). ... On disabled list (April 6-May 17, 1999); included rehabilitation assignment to Fresno. ... Traded by Giants to Chicago Cubs for P Tim Worrell (November 19, 2000). ... On disabled list (May 14-August 13, 2001); included rehabilitation assignment to Iowa. ... On disabled list (March 28-May 6, 2002); included rehabilitation assignment to Iowa. ... Traded by Cubs with cash to Giants for P Jeff Verplancke (September 3, 2002). ... Signed as a free agent by Boston Red Sox (January 14, 2003). ... Signed as a free agent by Los Angeles Dodgers (December 14, 2005). ... On disabled list (May 12, 2006-remainder of season). **HONORS:** Named third baseman on THE SPORTING NEWS A.L. All-Star team (2003). ... Named third baseman on A.L. Silver Slugger team (2003). **STATISTICAL NOTES:** Hit three home runs in one game (July 29, 2003). ... Career major league grand slams: 4.

2006 GAMES PLAYED BY POSITION (MLB): 3B—30.

Year	Team (League)	Pos.	G	AB	R	H	2B	3B	HR	RBI	BB	SO	HBP	GDP	SB-CS	Avg.	OBP	SLG	OPS	E	Avg.
1993—	Everett (N'west)	2B	58	200	31	60	8	2	1	24	42	17	3	3	13-6	.300	.425	.375	.800	8	.966
1994—	San Jose (Calif.)	2B-3B-SS	120	431	79	130	20	9	5	72	103	47	3	15	4-8	.302	.435	.425	.859	29	.925
1995—	Shreveport (Texas)	2B-3B	88	330	56	102	16	2	1	39	53	36	4	9	6-5	.309	.406	.379	.784	5	.978
—	Phoenix (PCL)	2B-3B	41	172	23	51	13	6	2	19	19	31	0	7	0-0	.297	.365	.477	.841	7	.941
1996—	Phoenix (PCL)	3B-SS-2B-DH	106	440	73	133	14	6	4	36	44	40	1	11	2-5	.302	.365	.389	.753	11	.969
—	San Francisco (N.L.)	3B-2B	55	200	31	66	15	1	0	19	24	26	1	1	0-0	.330	.401	.415	.816	6	.962
1997—	San Francisco (N.L.)	3B	128	390	51	114	26	3	7	44	48	71	3	10	4-3	.292	.369	.428	.797	14	.956
1998—	San Francisco (N.L.)	3B-2B	145	534	93	157	27	0	9	59	79	83	1	12	3-3	.294	.383	.395	.778	19	.953
1999—	San Francisco (N.L.)	3B-2B	116	414	61	120	24	0	2	36	65	52	0	11	4-2	.290	.388	.362	.751	12	.959
—	Fresno (PCL)	3B	3	12	3	5	0	1	0	6	3	5	0	0	0-0	.417	.385	.583	.968	3	.800
2000—	San Francisco (N.L.)	3B-2B	153	560	97	150	29	4	10	55	52	62	6	16	4-2	.268	.333	.388	.721	9	.975
2001—	Chicago (N.L.)	3B-2B	70	210	38	62	12	1	6	23	37	19	3	4	1-1	.295	.403	.448	.851	6	.942
—	Iowa (PCL)	3B	8	26	3	11	3	0	0	4	5	3	1	0	0-0	.423	.444	.538	.983	0	1.000
2002—	Iowa (PCL)	3B	6	16	2	6	1	0	1	5	3	1	0	0	0-1	.375	.474	.625	1.099	1	.909
—	Chicago (N.L.)	3B	103	353	51	94	19	4	7	37	55	41	0	6	0-0	.266	.355	.402	.757	6	.973
—	San Francisco (N.L.)	3B	8	13	0	2	0	0	0	1	1	1	0	1	0-0	.154	.214	.154	.368	0	1.000
2003—	Boston (A.L.)	3B-2B-DH-SS	146	524	85	171	45	5	19	85	59	77	7	11	1-4	*.326	.398	.540	.938	16	.956

M

Year	Team (League)	Pos.	G	AB	R	H	2B	3B	HR	RBI	BB	SO	HBP	GDP	SB-CS	Avg.	OBP	SLG	OPS	E	Avg.
									BATTING											FIELDING	
2004— Pawtucket (Int'l)		3B	4	13	1	4	2	0	0	2	2	0	0	0	0-0	.308	.400	.462	.862	1	.857
— Boston (A.L.)		3B-2B	110	399	75	113	27	1	12	57	51	56	4	8	2-2	.283	.365	.446	.811	17	.944
2005— Boston (A.L.)		3B-2B	150	519	69	153	34	3	10	62	59	74	6	22	0-0	.295	.369	.430	.799	11	.972
2006— Los Angeles (N.L.)		3B	32	107	12	27	7	0	3	15	17	9	1	1	1-1	.252	.357	.402	.759	8	.905
American League totals (3 years)			406	1442	229	437	106	9	41	204	169	207	17	41	3-6	.303	.378	.474	.853	44	.958
National League totals (8 years)			810	2781	434	792	159	13	44	289	374	364	18	64	17-12	.285	.370	.399	.768	82	.958
Major League totals (11 years)			1216	4223	663	1229	265	22	85	493	543	571	35	105	20-18	.291	.373	.425	.797	126	.958

DIVISION SERIES RECORD

Year	Team (League)	Pos.	G	AB	R	H	2B	3B	HR	RBI	BB	SO	HBP	GDP	SB-CS	Avg.	OBP	SLG	OPS	E	Avg.
1997— San Francisco (N.L.)		3B	3	12	1	3	0	0	1	1	0	0	0	1	0-1	.250	.250	.500	.750	0	1.000
2000— San Francisco (N.L.)		3B	4	20	2	5	2	0	0	0	0	4	0	1	0-0	.250	.250	.350	.600	0	1.000
2003— Boston (A.L.)		3B	5	19	0	2	1	0	0	0	3	4	0	1	0-0	.105	.227	.158	.385	0	1.000
2004— Boston (A.L.)		3B	3	12	3	4	0	0	0	0	1	1	0	0	0-0	.333	.385	.333	.718	0	1.000
2005— Boston (A.L.)		3B	3	11	0	0	0	0	0	0	1	2	0	0	0-0	.000	.083	.000	.083	0	1.000
Division series totals (5 years)			18	74	6	14	3	0	1	1	5	11	0	3	0-1	.189	.241	.270	.511	0	1.000

CHAMPIONSHIP SERIES RECORD

Year	Team (League)	Pos.	G	AB	R	H	2B	3B	HR	RBI	BB	SO	HBP	GDP	SB-CS	Avg.	OBP	SLG	OPS	E	Avg.
2003— Boston (A.L.)		3B	7	27	1	6	2	0	0	0	2	7	0	1	0-0	.222	.276	.296	.572	0	1.000
2004— Boston (A.L.)		3B	7	30	4	8	1	0	0	1	2	1	1	3	0-0	.267	.333	.300	.633	0	1.000
Champ. series totals (2 years)			14	57	5	14	3	0	1	1	4	8	1	4	0-0	.246	.306	.298	.605	0	1.000

WORLD SERIES RECORD

Year	Team (League)	Pos.	G	AB	R	H	2B	3B	HR	RBI	BB	SO	HBP	GDP	SB-CS	Avg.	OBP	SLG	OPS	E	Avg.
2004— Boston (A.L.)		3B	4	14	3	6	2	0	0	4	0	0	0	1	0-0	.429	.556	.571	1.127	3	.850

2006 LEFTY-RIGHTY SPLITS

vs.	Avg.	AB	H	2B	3B	HR	RBI	BB	SO	OBP	Slg.	vs.	Avg.	AB	H	2B	3B	HR	RBI	BB	SO	OBP	Slg.
L	.280	25	7	1	0	0	2	2	1	.333	.320	R	.244	82	20	6	0	3	13	15	8	.364	.427

MUJICA, EDWARD — P

PERSONAL: Born May 10, 1984, in Valencia, Venezuela. ... 6-2/220. ... Throws right, bats right. ... Full name: Edward Mujica. **TRANSACTIONS/CAREER NOTES:** Signed as a non-drafted free agent by Cleveland Indians organization (October 22, 2001).
CAREER HITTING: 0-for-0 (.000), 0 R, 0 2B, 0 3B, 0 HR, 0 RBI.

Year	Team (League)	W	L	Pct.	ERA	WHIP	G	GS	CG	ShO	Hld.	Sv.-Opp.	IP	H	R	ER	HR	BB-IBB	SO	Avg.
2002— San Felipe (VSL)		2	0	1.000	1.78	0.89	10	5	0	0		1-...	30.1	22	7	6	0	5-0	18	.202
2003— Burlington (Appal.)		2	6	.250	4.37	1.38	14	10	0	0		0-...	55.2	57	31	27	3	20-0	41	.275
2004— Lake County (S.Atl.)		7	7	.500	4.65	1.31	26	19	1	0		2-...	124.0	130	77	64	18	32-1	89	.278
2005— Kinston (Carol.)		1	0	1.000	2.08	0.73	25	0	0	0	0	14-14	26.0	17	6	6	3	2-0	32	.183
— Akron (East.)		2	1	.667	2.88	1.19	27	0	0	0	2	10-13	34.1	36	11	11	2	5-0	33	.273
2006— Akron (East.)		1	0	1.000	0.00	1.05	12	0	0	0	1	8-8	19.0	11	1	0	0	5-0	29	.169
— Buffalo (Int'l)		3	1	.750	2.48	1.10	22	0	0	0	0	5-7	32.2	31	10	9	1	5-0	29	.258
— Cleveland (A.L.)		0	1	.000	2.95	1.36	10	0	0	0	0	0-0	18.1	25	6	6	1	0-0	12	.333
Major League totals (1 year)		0	1	.000	2.95	1.36	10	0	0	0	0	0-0	18.1	25	6	6	1	0-0	12	.333

2006 LEFTY-RIGHTY SPLITS

vs.	Avg.	AB	H	2B	3B	HR	RBI	BB	SO	OBP	Slg.	vs.	Avg.	AB	H	2B	3B	HR	RBI	BB	SO	OBP	Slg.
L	.324	34	11	3	0	0	4	0	4	.324	.412	R	.341	41	14	2	0	1	9	0	8	.341	.463

MULDER, MARK — P

PERSONAL: Born August 5, 1977, in South Holland, Ill. ... 6-6/208. ... Throws left, bats left. ... Full name: Mark Alan Mulder. ... High school: Thornwood (South Holland, Ill.). ... College: Michigan State. **TRANSACTIONS/CAREER NOTES:** Selected by Detroit Tigers organization in 55th round of 1995 free-agent draft; did not sign. ... Selected by Oakland Athletics organization in first round (second pick overall) of 1998 free-agent draft. ... On disabled list (April 12-May 10, 2002; remainder of season). ... Traded by A's to St. Louis Cardinals for Ps Kiko Calero and Danny Haren and C Daric Barton (December 19, 2004). ... On disabled list (June 22-August 23, 2006); included rehabilitation assignments to Quad City and Memphis. ... On disabled list (August 30, 2006-remainder of season). **HONORS:** Named lefthanded pitcher on THE SPORTING NEWS A.L. All-Star team (2001).
CAREER HITTING: 17-for-109 (.156), 10 R, 2 2B, 0 3B, 1 HR, 9 RBI.

Year	Team (League)	W	L	Pct.	ERA	WHIP	G	GS	CG	ShO	Hld.	Sv.-Opp.	IP	H	R	ER	HR	BB-IBB	SO	Avg.
1999— Vancouver (PCL)		6	7	.462	4.06	1.42	22	22	1	0	...	0-...	128.2	152	69	58	13	31-0	81	.300
2000— Sacramento (PCL)		1	1	.500	5.40	2.28	2	2	0	0	...	0-...	8.1	15	11	5	1	4-0	6	.375
— Oakland (A.L.)		9	10	.474	5.44	1.69	27	27	0	0	0	0-0	154.0	191	106	93	22	69-3	88	.308
2001— Oakland (A.L.)		*21	8	.724	3.45	1.16	34	34	6	*4	0	0-0	229.1	214	92	88	16	51-4	153	.249
2002— Oakland (A.L.)		19	7	.731	3.47	1.14	30	30	2	1	0	0-0	207.1	182	88	80	21	55-3	159	.232
2003— Oakland (A.L.)		15	9	.625	3.13	1.18	26	26	•9	•2	0	0-0	186.2	180	66	65	15	40-2	128	.259
2004— Oakland (A.L.)		17	8	.680	4.43	1.36	33	33	•5	1	0	0-0	225.2	223	119	111	25	83-1	140	.264
2005— St. Louis (N.L.)		16	8	.667	3.64	1.38	32	32	3	2	0	0-0	205.0	212	90	83	19	70-1	111	.273
2006— Quad Cities (Mid.)		0	0	...	1.80	0.80	1	1	0	0	0	0-0	5.0	2	2	1	1	2-0	5	.125
— Memphis (PCL)		0	1	.000	9.00	2.50	2	2	0	0	0	0-0	8.0	11	9	8	2	9-0	5	.324
— St. Louis (N.L.)		6	7	.462	7.14	1.70	17	17	0	0	0	0-0	93.1	124	77	74	19	35-1	50	.327
American League totals (5 years)		81	42	.659	3.92	1.28	150	150	22	8	0	0-0	1003.0	990	471	437	99	298-13	668	.260
National League totals (2 years)		22	15	.595	4.74	1.48	49	49	3	2	0	0-0	298.1	336	167	157	38	105-2	161	.291
Major League totals (7 years)		103	57	.644	4.11	1.33	199	199	25	10	0	0-0	1301.1	1326	638	594	137	403-15	829	.267

DIVISION SERIES RECORD

Year	Team (League)	W	L	Pct.	ERA	WHIP	G	GS	CG	ShO	Hld.	Sv.-Opp.	IP	H	R	ER	HR	BB-IBB	SO	Avg.
2000— Oakland (A.L.)		Did not play.																		
2001— Oakland (A.L.)		1	1	.500	2.45	1.45	2	2	0	0	0	0-0	11.0	14	5	3	0	2-0	7	.318
2002— Oakland (A.L.)		1	1	.500	2.08	1.31	2	2	0	0	0	0-0	13.0	14	3	3	1	3-1	12	.280
2005— St. Louis (N.L.)		1	0	1.000	1.35	1.35	1	1	0	0	0	0-0	6.2	8	1	1	0	1-0	2	.333
Division series totals (3 years)		3	2	.600	2.05	1.37	5	5	0	0	0	0-0	30.2	36	9	7	1	6-1	21	.305

CHAMPIONSHIP SERIES RECORD

Year	Team (League)	W	L	Pct.	ERA	WHIP	G	GS	CG	ShO	Hld.	Sv.-Opp.	IP	H	R	ER	HR	BB-IBB	SO	Avg.
2005— St. Louis (N.L.)		0	2	.000	3.09	1.46	2	2	0	0	0	0-0	11.2	14	5	4	1	3-1	8	.311

M

	W	L	Pct.	ERA	WHIP	G	GS	CG	ShO	Hld.	Sv.-Opp.	IP	H	R	ER	HR	BB-IBB	SO	Avg.
ALL-STAR GAME RECORD																			
All-Star Game totals (2 years)	1	0	1.000	4.50	1.75	2	1	0	0	0	0-0	4.0	7	2	2	1	0-0	2	.412

2006 LEFTY-RIGHTY SPLITS

vs.	Avg.	AB	H	2B	3B	HR	RBI	BB	SO	OBP	Slg.	vs.	Avg.	AB	H	2B	3B	HR	RBI	BB	SO	OBP	Slg.
L	.241	83	20	4	0	2	8	5	19	.312	.361	R	.351	296	104	25	1	17	65	30	31	.413	.615

MULHOLLAND, TERRY — P

PERSONAL: Born March 9, 1963, in Uniontown, Pa. ... 6-3/220. ... Throws left, bats right. ... Full name: Terence John Mulholland. ... Name pronounced: mul-HOLLAND. ... High school: Laurel Highlands (Uniontown, Pa.). ... College: Marietta (Ohio). **TRANSACTIONS/CAREER NOTES:** Selected by San Francisco Giants organization in first round (24th pick overall) of June 1984 free-agent draft; pick received as compensation for Detroit Tigers signing free-agent IF Darrell Evans. ... On disabled list (August 1, 1988-remainder of season). ... Traded by Giants with P Dennis Cook and 3B Charlie Hayes to Philadelphia Phillies for P Steve Bedrosian and a player to be named (June 18, 1989); Giants acquired IF Rick Parker to complete deal (August 7, 1989). ... On disabled list (June 12-28, 1990); included rehabilitation assignment to Scranton/Wilkes-Barre. ... Traded by Phillies with a player to be named to New York Yankees for Ps Bobby Munoz and Ryan Karp and 2B Kevin Jordan (February 9, 1994); Yankees acquired P Jeff Patterson to complete deal (November 8, 1994). ... Signed as a free agent by Giants (April 8, 1995). ... On disabled list (June 6-July 4, 1995); included rehabilitation assignment to Phoenix. ... Signed as a free agent by Phillies organization (February 17, 1996). ... Traded by Phillies to Seattle Mariners for IF Desi Relaford (July 31, 1996). ... Signed as a free agent by Chicago Cubs (December 10, 1996). ... Claimed on waivers by Giants (August 8, 1997). ... Signed as a free agent by Cubs (February 2, 1998). ... Traded by Cubs with IF Jose Hernandez to Atlanta Braves for Ps Micah Bowie and Ruben Quevedo and a player to be named (July 31, 1999); Cubs acquired P Joey Nation to complete deal (August 24, 1999). ... Signed as a free agent by Pittsburgh Pirates (December 10, 2000). ... On disabled list (April 5-20 and June 12-August 1, 2001); included rehabilitation assignment to Altoona. ... Traded by Pirates to Los Angeles Dodgers for Ps Mike Fetters and Adrian Burnside (July 31, 2001). ... On disabled list (May 3-June 4, 2002). ... Traded by Dodgers with Ps Ricardo Rodriguez and Francisco Cruceta to Cleveland Indians for P Paul Shuey (July 28, 2002). ... Signed as a free agent by Mariners organization (February 10, 2004). ... Traded by Mariners to Minnesota Twins for cash (April 13, 2004). ... Signed as free agent by Arizona Diamondbacks organization (January 12, 2006). ... On disabled list (April 12-June 3, 2006); included rehabilitation assignment to Tucson. ... On disabled list (June 6-21, 2006). ... Released by Diamondbacks (June 21, 2006). **STATISTICAL NOTES:** Pitched 6-0 no-hit victory for Philadelphia against San Francisco (August 15, 1990). **MISCELLANEOUS NOTES:** Appeared in one game as pinch runner (1991). ... Appeared in one game as pinch runner with San Francisco (1995).

CAREER HITTING: 69-for-619 (.111), 26 R, 13 2B, 1 3B, 2 HR, 23 RBI.

Year	Team (League)	W	L	Pct.	ERA	WHIP	G	GS	CG	ShO	Hld.	Sv.-Opp.	IP	H	R	ER	HR	BB-IBB	SO	Avg.
1984—	Everett (N'west)	1	0	1.000	0.00	0.74	3	3	0	0	...	0-...	19.0	10	2	0	0	4-0	15	...
	Fresno (Calif.)	5	2	.714	2.95	1.59	9	9	0	0	...	0-...	42.2	32	17	14	1	36-0	39	...
1985—	Shreveport (Texas)	9	8	.529	2.90	1.43	26	26	8	3	...	0-...	176.2	166	79	57	9	87-2	122	.250
1986—	Phoenix (PCL)	8	5	.615	4.46	1.51	17	17	3	0	...	0-...	111.0	112	60	55	6	56-4	77	.269
	San Francisco (N.L.)	1	7	.125	4.94	1.57	15	10	0	0	0	0-0	54.2	51	33	30	3	35-2	27	.251
1987—	Phoenix (PCL)	7	12	.368	5.07	1.68	37	29	3	1	...	1-...	172.1	200	124	97	7	90-0	94	.289
1988—	Phoenix (PCL)	7	3	.700	3.58	1.59	19	14	3	2	...	0-...	100.2	116	45	40	2	44-0	57	.291
	San Francisco (N.L.)	2	1	.667	3.72	1.24	9	6	2	1	1	0-0	46.0	50	20	19	3	7-0	18	.281
1989—	Phoenix (PCL)	4	5	.444	2.99	1.19	13	10	3	0	...	0-...	78.1	67	30	26	3	26-2	61	.242
	San Francisco (N.L.)	0	0	...	4.09	1.73	5	1	0	0	1	0-0	11.0	15	5	5	0	4-0	6	.319
	Philadelphia (N.L.)	4	7	.364	5.00	1.48	20	17	2	1	0	0-0	104.1	122	61	58	8	32-3	60	.292
1990—	Philadelphia (N.L.)	9	10	.474	3.34	1.18	33	26	6	1	0	0-1	180.2	172	78	67	15	42-7	75	.252
	Scran./W.B. (I.L.)	0	1	.000	3.00	1.83	1	1	0	0	...	0-...	6.0	9	4	2	0	2-0	2	.360
1991—	Philadelphia (N.L.)	16	13	.552	3.61	1.21	34	34	8	3	0	0-0	232.0	231	100	93	15	49-2	142	.260
1992—	Philadelphia (N.L.)	13	11	.542	3.81	1.19	32	32	*12	0	0	0-0	229.0	227	101	97	14	46-3	125	.261
1993—	Philadelphia (N.L.)	12	9	.571	3.25	1.14	29	28	7	2	0	0-0	191.0	177	80	69	20	40-2	116	.241
1994—	New York (A.L.)	6	7	.462	6.49	1.55	24	19	2	0	0	0-0	120.2	150	94	87	24	37-1	72	.303
1995—	San Francisco (N.L.)	5	13	.278	5.80	1.53	29	24	2	0	0	0-0	149.0	190	112	96	25	38-1	65	.313
	Phoenix (PCL)	0	0	...	2.25	1.25	1	1	0	0	...	0-...	4.0	4	3	1	0	1-0	4	.235
1996—	Philadelphia (N.L.)	8	7	.533	4.66	1.34	21	21	0	0	0	0-0	133.1	157	74	69	17	21-1	52	.293
	Seattle (A.L.)	5	4	.556	4.67	1.49	12	12	0	0	0	0-0	69.1	75	38	36	5	28-3	34	.286
1997—	Chicago (N.L.)	6	12	.333	4.07	1.32	25	25	1	0	0	0-0	157.0	162	79	71	20	45-2	74	.271
	San Francisco (N.L.)	0	1	.000	5.16	1.15	15	2	0	0	1	0-0	29.2	28	21	17	4	6-1	25	.248
1998—	Chicago (N.L.)	6	5	.545	2.89	1.24	70	6	0	0	19	3-5	112.0	100	49	36	7	39-7	72	.235
1999—	Chicago (N.L.)	6	6	.500	5.15	1.54	26	16	0	0	1	0-0	110.0	137	71	63	16	32-4	44	.309
	Atlanta (N.L.)	4	2	.667	2.98	1.28	16	8	0	0	3	1-1	60.1	64	24	20	8	13-2	39	.274
2000—	Atlanta (N.L.)	9	9	.500	5.11	1.53	54	20	1	0	2	1-3	156.2	198	96	89	24	41-7	78	.308
2001—	Pittsburgh (N.L.)	0	0	...	3.72	1.32	22	1	0	0	3	0-0	36.1	38	15	15	5	10-1	17	.277
	Altoona (East.)	0	2	.000	3.86	2.57	2	2	0	0	...	0-...	2.1	5	3	1	0	1-0	3	.417
	Los Angeles (N.L.)	1	1	.500	5.83	1.60	19	3	0	0	4	0-0	29.1	40	20	19	7	7-0	25	.315
2002—	Los Angeles (N.L.)	0	0	...	7.31	1.63	21	0	0	0	1	0-0	32.0	45	29	26	10	7-0	17	.331
	Cleveland (A.L.)	3	2	.600	4.60	1.49	16	3	0	0	2	0-0	47.0	56	27	24	5	14-3	21	.301
2003—	Cleveland (A.L.)	3	4	.429	4.91	1.56	34	5	0	0	2	0-2	99.0	117	60	54	17	37-6	42	.295
2004—	Minnesota (A.L.)	5	9	.357	5.18	1.59	39	15	0	0	0	0-0	123.1	163	76	71	17	33-3	60	.327
2005—	Minnesota (A.L.)	0	2	.000	4.27	1.32	49	0	0	0	3	0-1	59.0	61	30	28	6	17-4	18	.276
2006—	Tucson (PCL)	1	1	.500	3.38	1.13	3	1	0	0	0	0-1	10.2	9	4	4	0	4-0	5	.257
	Arizona (N.L.)	0	0	...	9.00	2.67	5	0	0	0	1	0-1	3.0	7	3	3	1	1-0	1	.500
American League totals (6 years)		22	28	.440	5.21	1.52	185	52	2	0	9	0-3	518.1	622	325	300	74	166-20	247	.302
National League totals (16 years)		102	114	.472	4.21	1.33	500	280	44	10	36	5-11	2057.1	2211	1071	962	219	515-45	1078	.275
Major League totals (20 years)		124	142	.466	4.41	1.36	685	332	46	10	45	5-14	2575.2	2833	1396	1262	293	681-65	1325	.281

DIVISION SERIES RECORD

Year	Team (League)	W	L	Pct.	ERA	WHIP	G	GS	CG	ShO	Hld.	Sv.-Opp.	IP	H	R	ER	HR	BB-IBB	SO	Avg.
1998—	Chicago (N.L.)	0	1	.000	11.57	1.71	2	0	0	0	0	0-0	2.1	2	3	3	0	2-0	2	.222
1999—	Atlanta (N.L.)	0	0	...	27.00	4.50	2	0	0	0	0	0-0	0.2	3	2	2	0	0-0	0	.600
2000—	Atlanta (N.L.)	0	0	...	5.40	0.90	2	0	0	0	0	0-0	3.1	1	2	2	0	2-0	1	.100
2004—	Minnesota (A.L.)	0	0	...	3.00	1.00	1	0	0	0	0	0-0	3.0	3	1	1	1	0-0	0	.250
Division series totals (4 years)		0	1	.000	7.71	1.39	7	0	0	0	0	0-2	9.1	9	8	8	1	4-0	3	.250

CHAMPIONSHIP SERIES RECORD

Year	Team (League)	W	L	Pct.	ERA	WHIP	G	GS	CG	ShO	Hld.	Sv.-Opp.	IP	H	R	ER	HR	BB-IBB	SO	Avg.
1993—	Philadelphia (N.L.)	0	1	.000	7.20	2.00	1	1	0	0	0	0-0	5.0	9	5	4	0	1-0	2	.391
1999—	Atlanta (N.L.)	0	0	...	0.00	0.75	2	0	0	0	1	0-0	2.2	1	0	0	0	1-0	2	.143
Champ. series totals (2 years)		0	1	.000	4.70	1.57	3	1	0	0	1	0-0	7.2	10	5	4	0	2-0	4	.333

WORLD SERIES RECORD

Year	Team (League)	W	L	Pct.	ERA	WHIP	G	GS	CG	ShO	Hld.	Sv.-Opp.	IP	H	R	ER	HR	BB-IBB	SO	Avg.
1993—	Philadelphia (N.L.)	1	0	1.000	6.75	1.59	2	0	0	0	0	0-0	10.2	14	8	8	2	3-0	5	.326
1999—	Atlanta (N.L.)	0	0	...	7.36	1.64	2	0	0	0	0	0-0	3.2	5	3	3	1	1-1	3	.313
World series totals (2 years)		1	0	1.000	6.91	1.60	4	0	0	0	0	0-0	14.1	19	11	11	3	4-1	8	.322

M

	W	L	Pct.	ERA	WHIP	G	GS	CG	ShO	Hld.	Sv.-Opp.	IP	H	R	ER	HR	BB-IBB	SO	Avg.
All-Star Game totals (1 year)	0	0	...	4.50	1.50	1	1	0	0	0	0-0	2.0	1	1	1	1	2-0	0	.143

2006 LEFTY-RIGHTY SPLITS

vs.	Avg.	AB	H	2B	3B	HR	RBI	BB	SO	OBP	Slg.	vs.	Avg.	AB	H	2B	3B	HR	RBI	BB	SO	OBP	Slg.
L	.250	8	2	2	0	0	2	0	1	.250	.500	R	.833	6	5	1	0	1	2	1	0	.857	1.500

MUNSON, ERIC — 3B/1B

PERSONAL: Born October 3, 1977, in San Diego. ... 6-3/225. ... Bats left, throws right. ... Full name: Eric Walter Munson. ... High school: Mount Carmel (San Diego). ... College: Southern California. **TRANSACTIONS/CAREER NOTES:** Selected by Atlanta Braves organization in second round of 1996 free-agent draft; did not sign. ... Selected by Detroit Tigers organization in first round (third pick overall) of 1999 free-agent draft. ... On disabled list (August 12, 2003-remainder of season). ... Signed as a free agent by Minnesota Twins organization (January 17, 2005). ... Released by Twins (March 27, 2005). ... Signed by Tampa Bay Devil Rays organization (April 3, 2005). ... On disabled list (July 2-August 3, 2005); included rehabilitation assignment to Durham. ... Released by Devil Rays (October 7, 2005). ... Signed by Houston Astros organization (December 22, 2005).

2006 GAMES PLAYED BY POSITION (MLB): C—37, 1B—4, DH—1.

Year Team (League)	Pos.	G	AB	R	H	2B	3B	HR	RBI	BB	SO	HBP	GDP	SB-CS	Avg.	OBP	SLG	OPS	E	Avg.
1999—Lakeland (Fla. St.)	DH	2	6	0	2	0	0	0	1	1	1	0	0	0-0	.333	.429	.333	.762	...	...
—W. Mich. (Mid.)	1B-C	67	252	42	67	16	1	14	44	37	47	9	4	3-1	.266	.378	.504	.882	3	.991
2000—Jacksonville (Sou.)	1B	98	365	52	92	21	4	15	68	39	96	18	8	5-2	.252	.348	.455	.803	8	.989
—Detroit (A.L.)	1B	3	5	0	0	0	0	0	1	0	1	0	0	0-0	.000	.000	.000	.000	1	.941
2001—Erie (East.)	1B	142	519	88	135	35	1	26	102	84	141	11	6	0-3	.260	.371	.482	.853	17	.985
—Detroit (A.L.)	1B	17	66	4	10	3	1	1	6	3	21	0	2	0-1	.152	.188	.273	.461	1	.994
2002—Toledo (Int'l)	1B	136	477	77	125	30	4	24	84	77	114	7	9	1-3	.262	.367	.493	.860	12	.990
—Detroit (A.L.)	DH-1B	18	59	3	11	0	0	2	5	6	11	1	1	0-0	.186	.269	.288	.557	1	.970
2003—Detroit (A.L.)	3B-DH	99	313	28	75	9	0	18	50	35	61	1	4	3-0	.240	.312	.441	.753	19	.920
2004—Detroit (A.L.)	3B-DH-C	109	321	36	68	14	2	19	49	29	90	6	1	1-1	.212	.289	.445	.735	16	.934
2005—Durham (Int'l)	DH-3B-1B	100	382	67	109	22	0	25	71	38	81	2	11	1-1	.285	.351	.539	.891	16	.982
—Tampa Bay (A.L.)	OF	11	18	2	3	1	0	0	2	4	3	1	0	0-0	.167	.333	.222	.556	0	1.000
2006— Round Rock (PCL)		9	32	6	8	1	0	2	8	3	4	2	1	0-0	.250	.351	.820	.820	1	.980
—Houston (N.L.)	C-1B-DH	53	141	10	28	6	0	5	19	11	32	3	2	0-0	.199	.269	.348	.617	1	.996
American League totals (6 years)		257	782	73	167	27	3	40	113	77	187	9	10	4-2	.214	.288	.409	.698	38	.945
National League totals (1 year)		53	141	10	28	6	0	5	19	11	32	3	2	0-0	.199	.269	.348	.617	1	.996
Major League totals (7 years)		310	923	83	195	33	3	45	132	88	219	12	12	4-2	.211	.286	.400	.685	39	.958

2006 LEFTY-RIGHTY SPLITS

vs.	Avg.	AB	H	2B	3B	HR	RBI	BB	SO	OBP	Slg.	vs.	Avg.	AB	H	2B	3B	HR	RBI	BB	SO	OBP	Slg.
L	.318	22	7	3	0	1	7	1	5	.375	.591	R	.176	119	21	3	0	4	12	10	27	.250	.303

MUNTER, SCOTT — P

PERSONAL: Born March 7, 1980, in Norfolk, Neb. ... 6-6/240. ... Throws right, bats right. ... Full name: Scott Munter. ... Junior college: Butler County C.C. (Kan.). **TRANSACTIONS/CAREER NOTES:** Selected by San Francisco Giants organization in 47th round of 2001 free-agent draft. ... On disabled list (August 12-September 2, 2005).

CAREER HITTING: 1-for-1 (1.000), 1 R, 1 2B, 0 3B, 0 HR, 1 RBI.

Year Team (League)	W	L	Pct.	ERA	WHIP	G	GS	CG	ShO	Hld.	Sv.-Opp.	IP	H	R	ER	HR	BB-IBB	SO	Avg.
2001—Salem-Keizer (N'west)	1	2	.333	5.91	1.54	15	0	0	0	...	0-...	35.0	42	26	23	3	12-0	28	.296
—Hagerstown (SAL)	1	0	1.000	3.38	1.13	1	1	0	0	...	0-...	5.1	5	3	2	0	1-0	2	.278
2002—Salem-Keizer (N'west)	1	1	.500	6.98	1.79	10	4	0	0	...	0-...	29.2	33	24	23	0	20-0	20	.287
—San Jose (Calif.)	0	0	...	10.38	3.69	3	0	0	0	...	0-...	4.1	12	5	5	0	4-0	2	.571
2003—Hagerstown (SAL)	3	5	.375	2.36	1.30	40	0	0	0	...	5-...	68.2	61	28	18	3	28-0	47	.230
2004—Norwich (East.)	2	4	.333	2.35	1.31	42	0	0	0	...	3-...	65.0	63	19	17	4	22-5	30	.246
—Fresno (PCL)	1	1	.500	3.45	1.53	13	0	0	0	...	1-...	15.2	20	8	6	1	4-0	5	.299
2005—Fresno (PCL)	1	3	.250	5.11	1.70	12	0	0	0	1	0-1	12.1	17	8	7	0	4-0	5	.362
—San Francisco (N.L.)	2	0	1.000	2.56	1.34	45	0	0	0	12	0-3	38.2	40	15	11	1	12-1	11	.280
2006—Connecticut (East.)	1	4	.200	4.73	1.50	28	0	0	0	3	1-2	40.0	45	24	21	1	15-0	22	.292
—San Francisco (N.L.)	0	1	.000	8.74	2.12	27	0	0	0	5	0-0	22.2	30	22	22	1	18-2	7	.366
Major League totals (2 years)	2	1	.667	4.84	1.63	72	0	0	0	17	0-3	61.1	70	37	33	2	30-3	18	.311

2006 LEFTY-RIGHTY SPLITS

vs.	Avg.	AB	H	2B	3B	HR	RBI	BB	SO	OBP	Slg.	vs.	Avg.	AB	H	2B	3B	HR	RBI	BB	SO	OBP	Slg.
L	.405	37	15	4	0	1	13	9	5	.511	.595	R	.333	45	15	3	0	0	13	9	2	.464	.400

MURPHY, DAVID — OF

PERSONAL: Born October 18, 1981, in Houston, Texas. ... 6-4/190. ... Bats left, throws left. ... Full name: David Matthew Murphy. ... College: Baylor.
TRANSACTIONS/CAREER NOTES: Selected by Boston Red Sox organization in first round (17th pick overall) of 2003 free-agent draft.
2006 GAMES PLAYED BY POSITION (MLB): OF—16, DH—1.

Year Team (League)	Pos.	G	AB	R	H	2B	3B	HR	RBI	BB	SO	HBP	GDP	SB-CS	Avg.	OBP	SLG	OPS	E	Avg.
2003—Lowell (NY-Penn)		21	78	13	27	4	0	0	13	16	9	0	1	4-1	.346	.453	.397	.850	...	...
—Sarasota (Fla. St.)		45	153	18	37	5	1	1	18	20	33	0	3	6-2	.242	.329	.307	.636	...	...
2004—GC Red Sox (GCL)		5	18	3	5	1	0	0	1	1	2	0	1	1-0	.278	.316	.333	.649	...	...
—Sarasota (Fla. St.)		73	272	35	71	11	0	4	38	25	46	0	5	3-5	.261	.323	.346	.669	...	...
2005—Portland (East.)	OF-DH	135	484	71	133	25	4	14	75	46	83	1	11	13-6	.275	.337	.430	.767	8	.985
2006—Portland (East.)		42	172	22	47	17	1	3	25	11	29	0	3	4-2	.273	.315	.436	.751	3	.969
—Pawtucket (Int'l)		84	318	45	85	23	5	8	44	45	53	0	13	3-3	.267	.355	.447	.802	5	.972
—Boston (A.L.)	OF-DH	20	22	4	5	1	0	1	2	4	4	0	1	0-0	.227	.346	.409	.755	0	1.000
Major League totals (1 year)		20	22	4	5	1	0	1	2	4	4	0	1	0-0	.227	.346	.409	.755	0	1.000

2006 LEFTY-RIGHTY SPLITS

vs.	Avg.	AB	H	2B	3B	HR	RBI	BB	SO	OBP	Slg.	vs.	Avg.	AB	H	2B	3B	HR	RBI	BB	SO	OBP	Slg.
L	.000	1	0	0	0	0	0	0	0	.000	.000	R	.238	21	5	1	0	1	2	4	4	.360	.429

M

MURPHY, TOMMY — OF

PERSONAL: Born August 27, 1979, in Suffern, N.Y. ... 6-0/185. ... Bats both, throws right. ... Full name: Thomas Christian Murphy. ... College: Florida Atlantic. **TRANSACTIONS/CAREER NOTES:** Selected by Anaheim Angels organization in third round of 2000 free-agent draft. ... Angels franchise renamed Los Angeles Angels of Anaheim for 2005 season.

2006 GAMES PLAYED BY POSITION (MLB): OF—42, DH—2.

										BATTING										FIELDING	
Year	Team (League)	Pos.	G	AB	R	H	2B	3B	HR	RBI	BB	SO	HBP	GDP	SB-CS	Avg.	OBP	SLG	OPS	E	Avg.
2000— Boise (N'west)			55	213	38	48	18	1	2	25	15	52	5	1	14-7	.225	.291	.347	.638	...	...
2001— Cedar Rap. (Midw.)			74	280	32	57	15	3	4	31	16	94	6	5	7-10	.204	.259	.321	.580	...	...
— Rancho Cuca. (Calif.)			50	200	16	38	8	0	0	11	5	69	1	4	7-3	.190	.214	.230	.444	...	...
2002— Cedar Rap. (Midw.)			128	485	72	131	20	2	3	48	40	115	1	8	31-11	.270	.324	.338	.662	...	...
2003— Rancho Cuca. (Calif.)			132	565	74	151	25	6	11	43	31	138	8	7	24-12	.267	.313	.391	.704	...	...
2004— Arkansas (Texas)			129	477	77	124	24	6	7	45	36	113	1	9	27-5	.260	.310	.379	.689	...	...
2005— Arkansas (Texas)	OF-DH-1B		135	500	85	144	24	11	17	76	43	97	5	11	26-12	.288	.346	.482	.828	7	.989
2006— Salt Lake (PCL)			73	285	43	86	16	3	7	36	19	62	3	1	6-13	.302	.351	.453	.803	2	.986
— Los Angeles (A.L.)	OF-DH		48	70	12	16	4	1	1	6	5	21	0	0	4-1	.229	.276	.357	.633	0	1.000
Major League totals (1 year)			48	70	12	16	4	1	1	6	5	21	0	0	4-1	.229	.276	.357	.633	0	1.000

2006 LEFTY-RIGHTY SPLITS

vs.	Avg.	AB	H	2B	3B	HR	RBI	BB	SO	OBP	Slg.	vs.	Avg.	AB	H	2B	3B	HR	RBI	BB	SO	OBP	Slg.
L	.318	22	7	2	0	1	2	0	5	.318	.545	R	.188	48	9	2	1	0	4	5	16	.259	.271

MURTON, MATT — OF

PERSONAL: Born October 3, 1981, in Fort Lauderdale, Fla. ... 6-1/215. ... Bats right, throws right. ... Full name: Matthew Henry Murton. ... College: Georgia Tech. **TRANSACTIONS/CAREER NOTES:** Selected by Boston Red Sox organization in first round (32nd pick overall) of 2003 free-agent draft. ... Traded by Red Sox with SS Nomar Garciaparra to Chicago Cubs in four-team deal in which Cubs sent 3B Brendan Harris, RHP Francis Beltran and SS Alex Gonzalez to Montreal Expos, Expos sent SS Orlando Cabrera to Red Sox, Twins sent 1B Doug Mientkiewicz to Red Sox and Cubs sent LHP Justin Jones to Minnesota Twins (July 31, 2004). **RECORDS:** Shares major league record for most doubles, game (4, August 3, 2006).

2006 GAMES PLAYED BY POSITION (MLB): OF—133.

										BATTING										FIELDING	
Year	Team (League)	Pos.	G	AB	R	H	2B	3B	HR	RBI	BB	SO	HBP	GDP	SB-CS	Avg.	OBP	SLG	OPS	E	Avg.
2003— Lowell (NY-Penn)	OF		53	189	30	54	11	2	2	29	27	39	4	5	9-3	.286	.374	.397	.771	2	.976
2004— Sarasota (Fla. St.)	OF		102	376	60	113	16	4	11	55	42	61	3	7	5-4	.301	.372	.452	.824	2	.857
— Daytona (Fla. St.)	OF		24	79	13	20	1	1	2	8	8	10	1	3	2-0	.253	.326	.367	.693	0	...
2005— West Tenn (Sou.)	OF		78	313	46	107	17	4	8	46	29	42	4	11	18-5	.342	.403	.498	.902	8	.971
— Iowa (PCL)	OF		9	34	4	12	2	0	1	3	4	8	0	2	0-0	.353	.421	.500	.921	2	.923
— Chicago (N.L.)	OF		51	140	19	45	3	2	7	14	16	22	0	4	2-1	.321	.386	.521	.908	2	.969
2006— Chicago (N.L.)	OF		144	455	70	135	22	3	13	62	45	62	5	16	5-2	.297	.365	.444	.809	3	.988
Major League totals (2 years)			195	595	89	180	25	5	20	76	61	84	5	20	7-3	.303	.370	.462	.832	5	.984

2006 LEFTY-RIGHTY SPLITS

vs.	Avg.	AB	H	2B	3B	HR	RBI	BB	SO	OBP	Slg.	vs.	Avg.	AB	H	2B	3B	HR	RBI	BB	SO	OBP	Slg.
L	.301	136	41	7	0	6	19	18	11	.385	.485	R	.295	319	94	15	3	7	43	27	51	.356	.426

MUSSINA, MIKE — P

PERSONAL: Born December 8, 1968, in Williamsport, Pa. ... 6-2/185. ... Throws right, bats left. ... Full name: Michael Cole Mussina. ... Name pronounced: myoo-SEE-nuh. ... High school: Montoursville (Pa.). ... College: Stanford. **TRANSACTIONS/CAREER NOTES:** Selected by Baltimore Orioles organization in 11th round of 1987 free-agent draft; did not sign. ... Selected by Orioles organization in first round (20th pick overall) of 1990 free-agent draft. ... On disabled list (July 22-August 20, 1993); included rehabilitation assignment to Bowie. ... On disabled list (April 17-May 3 and May 15-June 6, 1998). ... Signed as a free agent by New York Yankees (November 30, 2000). ... On disabled list (July 7-August 18, 2004); included rehabilitation assignment to Columbus. ... On disabled list (August 21-September 5, 2006). **HONORS:** Named righthanded pitcher on THE SPORTING NEWS A.L. All-Star team (1995). ... Won A.L. Gold Glove at pitcher (1996-99, 2001 and 2003).

CAREER HITTING: 8-for-45 (.178), 3 R, 1 2B, 0 3B, 0 HR, 5 RBI.

Year	Team (League)	W	L	Pct.	ERA	WHIP	G	GS	CG	ShO	Hld.	Sv.-Opp.	IP	H	R	ER	HR	BB-IBB	SO	Avg.
1990— Hagerstown (East.)		3	0	1.000	1.49	0.97	7	7	2	1	...	0-...	42.1	34	10	7	1	7-0	40	.214
— Rochester (Int'l)		0	0	...	1.35	0.90	2	2	0	0	...	0-...	13.1	8	2	2	2	4-0	15	.174
1991— Rochester (Int'l)		10	4	.714	2.87	1.14	19	19	3	1	...	0-...	122.1	108	42	39	9	31-0	107	.235
— Baltimore (A.L.)		4	5	.444	2.87	1.12	12	12	2	0	0	0-0	87.2	77	31	28	7	21-0	52	.239
1992— Baltimore (A.L.)		18	5	*.783	2.54	1.08	32	32	8	4	0	0-0	241.0	212	70	68	16	48-2	130	.239
1993— Baltimore (A.L.)		14	6	.700	4.46	1.23	25	25	3	2	0	0-0	167.2	163	84	83	20	44-2	117	.256
— Bowie (East.)		1	0	1.000	2.25	0.75	2	2	0	0	...	0-...	8.0	5	2	2	0	1-0	10	.172
1994— Baltimore (A.L.)		16	5	.762	3.06	1.16	24	24	3	0	0	0-0	176.1	163	63	60	19	42-1	99	.248
1995— Baltimore (A.L.)		* 19	9	.679	3.29	1.07	32	32	7	* 4	0	0-0	221.2	187	86	81	24	50-4	158	.226
1996— Baltimore (A.L.)		19	11	.633	4.81	1.37	36	* 36	4	1	0	0-0	243.1	264	137	130	31	69-0	204	.275
1997— Baltimore (A.L.)		15	8	.652	3.20	1.12	33	33	4	1	0	0-0	224.2	197	87	80	27	54-3	218	.234
1998— Baltimore (A.L.)		13	10	.565	3.49	1.11	29	29	4	2	0	0-0	206.1	189	85	80	20	41-3	175	.242
1999— Baltimore (A.L.)		18	7	.720	3.50	1.27	31	31	4	0	0	0-0	203.1	207	88	79	16	52-0	172	.268
2000— Baltimore (A.L.)		11	15	.423	3.79	1.19	34	34	6	1	0	* 237.2	237.2	236	105	100	28	46-0	210	.255
2001— New York (A.L.)		17	11	.607	3.15	1.07	34	34	4	3	0	0-0	228.2	202	87	80	20	42-2	214	.237
2002— New York (A.L.)		18	10	.643	4.05	1.19	33	33	2	2	0	0-0	215.2	208	103	97	27	48-1	182	.253
2003— New York (A.L.)		17	8	.680	3.40	1.08	31	31	2	1	0	0-0	214.2	192	86	81	21	40-4	195	.238
2004— Columbus (Int'l)		0	0	...	0.00	0.67	1	1	0	0	...	0-...	3.0	2	0	0	0	0-0	5	.182
— New York (A.L.)		12	9	.571	4.59	1.32	27	27	1	0	0	0-0	164.2	178	91	84	22	40-1	132	.276
2005— New York (A.L.)		13	8	.619	4.41	1.37	30	30	2	0	0	0-0	179.2	199	93	88	23	47-0	142	.284
2006— New York (A.L.)		15	7	.682	3.51	1.11	32	32	1	0	0	0-0	197.1	184	88	77	22	35-1	172	.241
Major League totals (16 years)		239	134	.641	3.63	1.18	475	475	57	23	0	0-0	3210.1	3058	1384	1296	345	719-24	2572	.251

DIVISION SERIES RECORD

Year	Team (League)	W	L	Pct.	ERA	WHIP	G	GS	CG	ShO	Hld.	Sv.-Opp.	IP	H	R	ER	HR	BB-IBB	SO	Avg.
1996— Baltimore (A.L.)		0	0	...	4.50	1.50	1	1	0	0	0	0-0	6.0	7	4	3	1	2-0	6	.280
1997— Baltimore (A.L.)		2	0	1.000	1.93	0.71	2	2	0	0	0	0-0	14.0	7	3	3	3	3-0	16	.143
2001— New York (A.L.)		1	0	1.000	0.00	0.71	1	1	0	0	0	0-0	7.0	4	0	0	0	1-0	4	.167
2002— New York (A.L.)		0	0	...	9.00	1.50	1	1	0	0	0	0-0	4.0	6	4	4	1	0-0	2	.333
2003— New York (A.L.)		0	0	.000	3.86	1.43	1	1	0	0	0	0-0	7.0	7	3	3	0	3-1	6	.280
2004— New York (A.L.)		0	1	.000	2.57	1.14	1	1	0	0	0	0-0	7.0	7	2	2	1	1-0	7	.280

M

Year	Team (League)	W	L	Pct.	ERA	WHIP	G	GS	CG	ShO	Hld.	Sv.-Opp.	IP	H	R	ER	HR	BB-IBB	SO	Avg.
2005— New York (A.L.)		1	1	.500	5.40	1.44	2	2	0	0	0	0-0	8.1	11	5	5	1	1-0	7	.306
2006— New York (A.L.)		0	1	.000	5.14	1.14	1	1	0	0	0	0-0	7.0	8	4	4	1	0-0	5	.286
Division series totals (8 years)		4	4	.500	3.58	1.13	10	10	0	0	0	0-0	60.1	57	25	24	8	11-1	53	.248

CHAMPIONSHIP SERIES RECORD

Year	Team (League)	W	L	Pct.	ERA	WHIP	G	GS	CG	ShO	Hld.	Sv.-Opp.	IP	H	R	ER	HR	BB-IBB	SO	Avg.
1996— Baltimore (A.L.)		0	1	.000	5.87	1.30	1	1	0	0	0	0-0	7.2	8	5	5	1	2-0	6	.267
1997— Baltimore (A.L.)		0	0	...	0.60	0.53	2	2	0	0	0	0-0	15.0	4	1	1	0	4-0	25	.082
2001— New York (A.L.)		1	0	1.000	3.00	0.83	1	1	0	0	0	0-0	6.0	4	2	2	1	1-0	3	.182
2003— New York (A.L.)		0	2	.000	4.11	1.30	3	2	0	0	0	0-0	15.1	16	7	7	5	4-1	17	.267
2004— New York (A.L.)		1	0	1.000	4.26	0.95	2	2	0	0	0	0-0	12.2	10	6	6	0	2-0	15	.204
Champ. series totals (5 years)		2	3	.400	3.34	0.97	9	8	0	0	0	0-0	56.2	42	21	21	7	13-1	66	.200

WORLD SERIES RECORD

Year	Team (League)	W	L	Pct.	ERA	WHIP	G	GS	CG	ShO	Hld.	Sv.-Opp.	IP	H	R	ER	HR	BB-IBB	SO	Avg.
2001— New York (A.L.)		0	1	.000	4.09	1.36	2	2	0	0	0	0-0	11.0	11	7	5	4	4-3	14	.256
2003— New York (A.L.)		1	0	1.000	1.29	1.14	1	1	0	0	0	0-0	7.0	7	1	1	0	1-1	9	.259
World series totals (2 years)		1	1	.500	3.00	1.28	3	3	0	0	0	0-0	18.0	18	8	6	4	5-4	23	.257

ALL-STAR GAME RECORD

Year	Team (League)	W	L	Pct.	ERA	WHIP	G	GS	CG	ShO	Hld.	Sv.-Opp.	IP	H	R	ER	HR	BB-IBB	SO	Avg.
All-Star Game totals (3 years)		0	0	...	0.00	1.00	3	0	0	0	0	0-0	3.0	2	0	0	0	1-0	3	.182

2006 LEFTY-RIGHTY SPLITS

vs.	Avg.	AB	H	2B	3B	HR	RBI	BB	SO	OBP	Slg.	vs.	Avg.	AB	H	2B	3B	HR	RBI	BB	SO	OBP	Slg.
L	.223	359	80	11	1	13	47	19	90	.266	.368	R	.258	403	104	22	0	9	35	16	82	.291	.380

MYERS, BRETT   P

PERSONAL: Born August 17, 1980, in Jacksonville. ... 6-4/223. ... Throws right, bats right. ... Full name: Brett Allen Myers. ... High school: Englewood (Jacksonville).
TRANSACTIONS/CAREER NOTES: Selected by Philadelphia Phillies organization in first round (12th pick overall) of 1999 free-agent draft. **MISCELLANEOUS NOTES:** Had a sacrifice hit in only appearance as pinch hitter (2003).
CAREER HITTING: 34-for-264 (.129), 11 R, 7 2B, 0 HR, 9 RBI.

Year	Team (League)	W	L	Pct.	ERA	WHIP	G	GS	CG	ShO	Hld.	Sv.-Opp.	IP	H	R	ER	HR	BB-IBB	SO	Avg.
1999— GC Phillies (GCL)		2	1	.667	2.33	0.89	7	5	0	0	...	0-...	27.0	17	8	7	0	7-0	30	.177
2000— Piedmont (S. Atl.)		13	7	.650	3.18	1.33	27	27	1	1	...	0-...	175.1	165	78	62	7	69-0	140	.252
2001— Reading (East.)		13	4	.765	3.87	1.28	26	23	1	1	...	0-...	156.0	156	71	67	21	43-1	130	.258
2002— Scran./W.B. (I.L.)		9	6	.600	3.59	1.10	19	19	4	1	...	0-...	128.0	121	54	51	9	20-0	97	.252
— Philadelphia (N.L.)		4	5	.444	4.25	1.42	12	12	1	0	0	0-0	72.0	73	38	34	11	29-1	34	.277
2003— Philadelphia (N.L.)		14	9	.609	4.43	1.46	32	32	1	0	0	0-0	193.0	205	99	95	20	76-8	143	.272
2004— Philadelphia (N.L.)		11	11	.500	5.52	1.47	32	31	1	1	0	0-0	176.0	196	113	108	31	62-4	116	.281
2005— Philadelphia (N.L.)		13	8	.619	3.72	1.21	34	34	2	0	0	0-0	215.1	193	94	89	31	68-2	208	.237
2006— Philadelphia (N.L.)		12	7	.632	3.91	1.30	31	31	1	0	0	0-0	198.0	194	93	86	29	63-3	189	.257
Major League totals (5 years)		54	40	.574	4.34	1.36	141	140	6	2	0	0-0	854.1	861	437	412	122	298-18	690	.262

2006 LEFTY-RIGHTY SPLITS

vs.	Avg.	AB	H	2B	3B	HR	RBI	BB	SO	OBP	Slg.	vs.	Avg.	AB	H	2B	3B	HR	RBI	BB	SO	OBP	Slg.
L	.259	343	89	19	3	8	26	43	86	.342	.402	R	.254	413	105	16	2	21	59	20	103	.291	.455

MYERS, MIKE   P

PERSONAL: Born June 26, 1969, in Arlington Heights, Ill. ... 6-3/219. ... Throws left, bats left. ... Full name: Michael Stanley Myers. ... High school: Crystal Lake (Ill.) Central. ... College: Iowa State. **TRANSACTIONS/CAREER NOTES:** Selected by San Francisco Giants organization in fourth round of 1990 free-agent draft. ... Selected by Florida Marlins from Giants organization in Rule 5 major league draft (December 7, 1992). ... On disabled list (June 7-August 5, 1994); included rehabilitation assignment to Brevard County. ... Traded by Marlins to Detroit Tigers (August 9, 1995), completing deal in which Tigers traded P Buddy Groom to Marlins for a player to be named (August 7, 1995). ... Traded by Tigers with P Rick Greene and SS Santiago Perez to Milwaukee Brewers for P Bryce Florie and a player to be named (November 20, 1997). ... Traded by Brewers to Colorado Rockies for P Curtis Leskanic (November 17, 1999). ... Traded by Rockies to Arizona Diamondbacks for OF Jack Cust and C J.D. Closser (January 7, 2002). ... Signed as a free agent by Seattle Mariners organization (January 16, 2004). ... Traded by Mariners to Boston Red Sox for a player to be named or cash (August 6, 2004). ... Signed as a free agent by St. Louis Cardinals (December 22, 2004). ... Traded by Cardinals to Red Sox for P Kevin Ool and OF Carlos De La Cruz (March 29, 2005). ... Signed as a free agent by New York Yankees (December 15, 2005).
CAREER HITTING: 0-for-1 (.000), 0 R, 0 2B, 0 3B, 0 HR, 0 RBI.

Year	Team (League)	W	L	Pct.	ERA	WHIP	G	GS	CG	ShO	Hld.	Sv.-Opp.	IP	H	R	ER	HR	BB-IBB	SO	Avg.
1990— Everett (N'west)		4	5	.444	3.90	1.42	15	14	1	0	...	0-...	85.1	91	43	37	9	30-0	73	.269
1991— Clinton (Midw.)		5	3	.625	2.62	1.21	11	11	1	0	...	0-...	65.1	61	23	19	3	18-0	59	.253
— Ariz. Giants (Ariz.)		0	1	.000	12.00	2.33	1	0	0	0	...	0-...	3.0	5	5	4	0	2-0	2	.357
1992— San Jose (Calif.)		5	1	.833	2.30	1.10	8	8	0	0	...	0-...	54.2	43	20	14	1	17-0	40	.221
— Clinton (Midw.)		1	2	.333	1.19	0.96	7	7	0	0	...	0-...	37.2	28	11	5	0	8-0	32	.207
1993— Edmonton (PCL)		7	14	.333	5.18	1.53	27	27	3	0	...	0-...	161.2	195	109	93	20	52-1	112	.296
1994— Edmonton (PCL)		1	5	.167	5.55	1.65	12	11	0	0	...	0-...	60.0	78	42	37	9	21-0	55	.307
— Brevard County (FSL)		0	0	...	0.79	0.97	3	2	0	0	...	0-...	11.1	7	1	1	1	4-0	15	.184
1995— Florida (N.L.)		0	0	...	0.00	2.00	2	0	0	0	0	0-0	2.0	1	0	0	0	3-0	0	.167
— Charlotte (Int'l)		0	5	.000	5.65	1.53	37	0	0	0	...	0-...	36.2	41	25	23	6	15-1	24	.283
— Toledo (Int'l)		0	0	...	4.32	1.08	6	0	0	0	...	0-...	8.1	6	4	4	1	3-0	8	.194
— Detroit (A.L.)		1	0	1.000	9.95	2.21	11	0	0	0	1	0-1	6.1	10	7	7	1	4-0	4	.385
1996— Detroit (A.L.)		1	5	.167	5.01	1.61	83	0	0	0	17	6-8	64.2	70	41	36	6	34-8	69	.272
1997— Detroit (A.L.)		0	4	.000	5.70	1.55	88	0	0	0	18	2-5	53.2	58	36	34	12	25-2	50	.274
1998— Milwaukee (N.L.)		2	2	.500	2.70	1.32	70	0	0	0	* 23	1-3	50.0	44	19	15	5	22-1	40	.249
1999— Milwaukee (N.L.)		2	1	.667	5.23	1.43	71	0	0	0	14	0-3	41.1	46	24	24	7	13-1	35	.291
2000— Colorado (N.L.)		0	1	.000	1.99	1.06	78	0	0	0	15	1-2	45.1	24	10	10	2	24-3	41	.160
2001— Colorado (N.L.)		2	3	.400	3.60	1.40	73	0	0	0	10	0-2	40.0	32	17	16	2	24-7	35	.225
2002— Arizona (N.L.)		4	3	.571	4.38	1.51	69	0	0	0	17	4-9	37.0	39	18	18	7	17-0	31	.275
2003— Arizona (N.L.)		0	1	.000	5.70	1.62	64	0	0	0	6	0-3	36.1	38	23	23	4	21-1	21	.262
2004— Seattle (A.L.)		4	1	.800	4.88	1.66	50	0	0	0	8	0-0	27.2	29	15	15	4	17-4	23	.279
— Boston (A.L.)		1	0	1.000	4.20	1.47	25	0	0	0	4	0-0	15.0	16	7	7	0	6-1	9	.271
2005— Boston (A.L.)		3	1	.750	3.13	1.15	65	0	0	0	9	0-1	37.1	30	14	13	3	13-2	21	.224
2006— New York (A.L.)		1	2	.333	3.23	1.27	62	0	0	0	18	0-1	30.2	29	14	11	6	10-1	22	.244
American League totals (6 years)		11	13	.458	4.70	1.49	384	0	0	0	73	8-16	235.1	242	134	123	30	109-18	198	.265
National League totals (7 years)		10	11	.476	3.79	1.38	427	0	0	0	85	6-22	252.0	224	111	106	22	124-13	204	.243
Major League totals (12 years)		21	24	.467	4.23	1.43	811	0	0	0	158	14-38	487.1	466	245	229	52	233-31	402	.254

M

DIVISION SERIES RECORD

Year Team (League)	W	L	Pct.	ERA	WHIP	G	GS	CG	ShO	Hld.	Sv.-Opp.	IP	H	R	ER	HR	BB-IBB	SO	Avg.
2002— Arizona (N.L.)	0	0	...	0.00	1.20	1	0	0	0	0	0-0	1.2	2	0	0	0	0-0	1	.333
2004— Boston (A.L.)	0	0	...	27.00	3.00	2	0	0	0	1	0-0	0.1	0	1	1	0	1-0	1	.000
2005— Boston (A.L.)	0	0	...	...	...	1	0	0	0	0	0-0	0.0	0	0	0	0	1-0	0	...
2006— New York (A.L.)	0	0	...	...	...	1	0	0	0	0	0-0	0.0	1	1	1	1	0-0	0	1.000
Division series totals (4 years)	0	0	...	9.00	2.50	6	0	0	0	1	0-0	2.0	3	2	2	1	2-0	2	.375

CHAMPIONSHIP SERIES RECORD

Year Team (League)	W	L	Pct.	ERA	WHIP	G	GS	CG	ShO	Hld.	Sv.-Opp.	IP	H	R'	ER	HR	BB-IBB	SO	Avg.
2004— Boston (A.L.)	0	0	...	7.71	2.57	3	0	0	0	0	0-0	2.1	5	2	2	1	1-0	4	.455

2006 LEFTY-RIGHTY SPLITS

vs.	Avg.	AB	H	2B	3B	HR	RBI	BB	SO	OBP	Slg.	vs.	Avg.	AB	H	2B	3B	HR	RBI	BB	SO	OBP	Slg.
L	.257	70	18	3	2	2	14	4	17	.297	.443	R	.224	49	11	0	0	1	8	6	5	.345	.286

NADY, XAVIER — OF/1B

PERSONAL: Born November 14, 1978, in Carmel, Calif. ... 6-2/205. ... Bats right, throws right. ... Full name: Xavier Clifford Nady. ... Name pronounced: ZAV-yer NAY-dee. ... High school: Salinas (Calif.). ... College: California. **TRANSACTIONS/CAREER NOTES:** Selected by St. Louis Cardinals organization in fourth round of 1997 free-agent draft; did not sign. ... Selected by San Diego Padres organization in second round of 2000 free-agent draft. ... Traded by Padres to New York Mets for OF Mike Cameron (November 18, 2005). ... On disabled list (May 30-June 18, 2006); included rehabilitation assignment to Norfolk. ... Traded by Mets to Pittsburgh Pirates for Ps Roberto Hernandez and Oliver Perez (July 31, 2006). **STATISTICAL NOTES:** Career major league grand slams: 1.

2006 GAMES PLAYED BY POSITION (MLB): OF—99, 1B—35.

								BATTING										FIELDING	
Year Team (League)	Pos.	G	AB	R	H	2B	3B	HR	RBI	BB	SO	HBP	GDP	SB-CS	Avg.	OBP	SLG	OPS	E	Avg.
2000— San Diego (N.L.)		1	1	1	1	0	0	0	0	0	0	0	0	0-0	1.000	1.000	1.000	2.000	...	...
2001— Lake Elsinore (Calif.)	1B	137	524	96	158	38	1	26	100	62	109	10	14	6-0	.302	.381	.527	.908	10	.989
2002— Lake Elsinore (Calif.)	OF	45	169	41	47	6	3	13	37	28	40	1	2	2-0	.278	.382	.580	.962	0	1.000
— Portland (PCL)	OF	85	315	46	89	12	1	10	43	20	60	3	11	0-1	.283	.329	.422	.752	2	.981
2003— Portland (PCL)	OF-DH	37	136	19	36	7	0	7	23	12	28	2	2	0-0	.265	.329	.471	.800	3	.954
— San Diego (N.L.)	OF	110	371	50	99	17	1	9	39	24	74	6	14	6-2	.267	.321	.391	.712	6	.968
2004— Portland (PCL)	OF-1B-DH	74	291	52	97	19	1	22	70	22	42	7	7	3-0	.333	.394	.632	1.026	4	.981
— San Diego (N.L.)	OF-DH	34	77	7	19	4	0	3	9	5	13	1	4	0-0	.247	.301	.416	.717	2	.923
2005— San Diego (N.L.)	OF-1B-3B DH	124	326	40	85	15	2	13	43	22	67	7	6	2-1	.261	.321	.439	.760	6	.984
2006— Norfolk (Int'l)		3	11	2	4	1	0	0	3	1	3	0	0	0-0	.364	.417	.455	.871	0	1.000
— New York (N.L.)	OF-1B	75	265	37	70	15	1	14	40	19	51	6	7	2-1	.264	.326	.487	.813	4	.973
— Pittsburgh (N.L.)	1B-OF	55	203	20	61	13	0	3	23	11	34	5	5	1-2	.300	.352	.409	.760	2	.994
Major League totals (5 years)		399	1243	155	335	64	4	42	154	81	239	25	35	11-6	.270	.326	.429	.755	20	.981

DIVISION SERIES RECORD

								BATTING										FIELDING	
Year Team (League)	Pos.	G	AB	R	H	2B	3B	HR	RBI	BB	SO	HBP	GDP	SB-CS	Avg.	OBP	SLG	OPS	E	Avg.
2005— San Diego (N.L.)	1B	2	3	0	1	0	0	0	0	0	1	2	0	0-0	.333	.600	.333	.933	0	1.000

2006 LEFTY-RIGHTY SPLITS

vs.	Avg.	AB	H	2B	3B	HR	RBI	BB	SO	OBP	Slg.	vs.	Avg.	AB	H	2B	3B	HR	RBI	BB	SO	OBP	Slg.
L	.336	107	36	5	0	6	20	13	16	.418	.551	R	.263	361	95	23	1	11	43	17	69	.312	.424

NAGEOTTE, CLINT — P

PERSONAL: Born October 25, 1980, in Parma, Ohio. ... 6-3/200. ... Throws right, bats right. ... Full name: Clinton Scott Nageotte. ... High school: Brooklyn (Ohio). **TRANSACTIONS/CAREER NOTES:** Selected by Seattle Mariners organization in fifth round of 1999 free-agent draft. ... On disabled list (August 28, 2004-remainder of season). **CAREER HITTING:** 0-for-2 (.000), 0 R, 0 2B, 0 3B, 0 HR, 0 RBI.

Year Team (League)	W	L	Pct.	ERA	WHIP	G	GS	CG	ShO	Hld.	Sv.-Opp.	IP	H	R	ER	HR	BB-IBB	SO	Avg.
2000— Ariz. Mariners (Ariz.)	4	1	.800	2.16	1.14	12	7	0	0	...	1-...	50.0	29	15	12	0	28-0	59	.167
2001— Wisconsin (Midw.)	11	8	.579	3.13	1.25	28	26	0	0	...	0-...	152.1	141	65	53	10	50-1	187	.246
2002— San Bern. (Calif.)	9	6	.600	4.54	1.34	29	29	1	0	...	0-...	164.2	153	101	83	10	68-0	214	.241
2003— San Antonio (Texas)	11	7	.611	3.10	1.26	27	27	2	1	...	0-...	154.0	127	60	53	10	67-1	157	.224
2004— Tacoma (PCL)	6	6	.500	4.46	1.40	14	14	0	0	...	0-...	80.2	78	42	40	9	35-0	63	.256
— Seattle (A.L.)	1	6	.143	7.36	2.05	12	5	0	0	0	0-0	36.2	48	31	30	3	27-1	24	.324
2005— Ariz. Mariners (Ariz.)	0	0	...	0.00	0.00	1	1	0	0	0	0-0	3.0	0	0	0	0	0-0	6	.000
— Seattle (A.L.)	0	0	...	6.75	1.75	3	0	0	0	0	0-0	4.0	6	3	3	0	1-0	1	.353
— Tacoma (PCL)	2	1	.667	2.65	1.26	19	0	0	0	4	2-4	34.0	21	16	10	2	22-0	35	.176
2006— Seattle (A.L.)	0	0	...	27.00	4.00	1	0	0	0	0	0-0	1.0	2	3	3	1	2-1	1	.400
— Ariz. Mariners (Ariz.)	0	0	...	1.80	1.20	2	2	0	0	0	0-0	5.0	4	1	1	0	2-0	2	.222
— Tacoma (PCL)	7	7	.500	5.74	1.74	19	19	0	0	0	0-0	89.1	102	63	57	6	53-0	51	.295
Major league totals (3 years)	1	6	.143	7.78	2.06	16	5	0	0	0	0-0	41.2	56	37	36	4	30-2	26	.329

2006 LEFTY-RIGHTY SPLITS

vs.	Avg.	AB	H	2B	3B	HR	RBI	BB	SO	OBP	Slg.	vs.	Avg.	AB	H	2B	3B	HR	RBI	BB	SO	OBP	Slg.
L	.500	2	1	0	0	0	0	1	0	.667	.500	R	.333	3	1	0	0	1	3	1	1	.500	1.333

NAPOLI, MIKE — C

PERSONAL: Born October 31, 1981, in Hollywood, Fla. ... 6-0/205. ... Bats right, throws right. ... Full name: Michael Anthony Napoli. **TRANSACTIONS/CAREER NOTES:** Selected by Anaheim Angels organization in 17th round of 2000 free-agent draft. ... Angels franchise renamed Los Angeles Angels of Anaheim for 2005 season. **STATISTICAL NOTES:** Hit home run in first major league at-bat (May 4, 2006).

2006 GAMES PLAYED BY POSITION (MLB): C—94, DH—1.

								BATTING										FIELDING	
Year Team (League)	Pos.	G	AB	R	H	2B	3B	HR	RBI	BB	SO	HBP	GDP	SB-CS	Avg.	OBP	SLG	OPS	E	Avg.
2000— Butte (Pion.)		10	26	3	6	2	0	0	3	8	8	0	2	1-0	.231	.400	.308	.708	...	...
2001— Rancho Cuca. (Calif.)		7	20	3	4	0	0	1	4	8	11	0	0	0-0	.200	.429	.350	.779	...	...
— Cedar Rap. (Midw.)		43	155	23	36	10	1	5	18	24	54	2	1	3-2	.232	.341	.406	.747	...	...
2002— Cedar Rap. (Midw.)		106	362	57	91	19	1	10	50	62	104	4	9	6-5	.251	.362	.392	.754	...	...
2003— Rancho Cuca. (Calif.)		47	165	28	44	10	1	4	26	23	32	4	3	5-0	.267	.364	.412	.776	...	...
2004— Rancho Cuca. (Calif.)		132	482	94	136	29	4	29	118	88	166	5	4	9-5	.282	.393	.539	.932	...	...
2005— Arkansas (Texas)	C-DH-1B	131	439	96	104	22	2	31	99	88	140	9	8	12-4	.237	.372	.508	.880	14	.981
2006— Salt Lake (PCL)		21	78	12	19	6	0	3	10	8	29	4	1	1-1	.244	.344	.436	.780	1	.994

– 347 –

N

Year Team (League)	Pos.	G	AB	R	H	2B	3B	HR	RBI	BB	SO	HBP	GDP	SB-CS	Avg.	OBP	SLG	OPS	E	Avg.
— Los Angeles (A.L.)	C-DH	99	268	47	61	13	0	16	42	51	90	5	2	2-3	.228	.360	.455	.815	8	.987
Major League totals (1 year)		99	268	47	61	13	0	16	42	51	90	5	2	2-3	.228	.360	.455	.815	8	.987

2006 LEFTY-RIGHTY SPLITS

vs.	Avg.	AB	H	2B	3B	HR	RBI	BB	SO	OBP	Slg.	vs.	Avg.	AB	H	2B	3B	HR	RBI	BB	SO	OBP	Slg.
L	.185	65	12	0	0	5	9	15	24	.346	.415	R	.241	203	49	13	0	11	33	36	66	.365	.468

NARVESON, CHRIS — P

PERSONAL: Born December 20, 1981, in Englewood, Colo. ... 6-3/205. ... Throws left, bats left. ... Full name: Christopher Gregg Narveson. **TRANSACTIONS/CAREER NOTES:** Selected by St. Louis Cardinals organization in second round of 2000 free-agent draft. ... Traded by Cardinals with P Luis Martinez to Colorado Rockies (August 11, 2004), completing deal in which Rockies traded OF Larry Walker and cash to Cardinals for P Jason Burch and two players to be named (August 6, 2004). ... Traded by Rockies with C Charles Johnson to Boston Red Sox for P Byung-Hyun Kim (March 30, 2005). ... Claimed on waivers by Cardinals (August 8, 2005).

CAREER HITTING: 0-for-1 (.000), 0 R, 0 2B, 0 3B, 0 HR, 0 RBI.

Year Team (League)	W	L	Pct.	ERA	WHIP	G	GS	CG	ShO	Hld.	Sv.-Opp.	IP	H	R	ER	HR	BB-IBB	SO	Avg.
2000— Johnson City (App.)	2	4	.333	3.27	1.49	12	12	0	0	...	0-...	55.0	57	33	20	7	25-0	63	.263
2001— Peoria (Midw.)	3	3	.500	1.98	0.86	8	8	0	0	...	0-...	50.0	32	14	11	3	11-0	53	.185
— Potomac (Carol.)	4	3	.571	2.57	0.98	11	11	1	0	...	0-...	66.2	52	22	19	4	13-1	53	.212
2002— Johnson City (App.)	0	2	.000	4.91	1.58	6	6	0	0	...	0-...	18.1	23	12	10	2	6-0	16	.307
— Peoria (Midw.)	2	1	.667	4.46	1.35	9	9	0	0	...	0-...	42.1	49	24	21	5	8-0	36	.283
2003— Palm Beach (FSL)	7	7	.500	2.86	1.12	15	14	1	0	...	0-...	91.1	83	34	29	4	19-0	65	.242
— Tennessee (Sou.)	4	3	.571	3.00	1.44	10	10	0	0	...	0-...	57.0	56	21	19	6	26-2	34	.262
2004— Tennessee (Sou.)	5	10	.333	4.16	1.29	23	23	0	0	...	0-...	127.2	114	64	59	11	51-0	121	.244
— Tulsa (Texas)	0	3	.000	3.15	1.45	4	4	0	0	...	0-...	20.0	16	14	7	1	13-0	14	.235
2005— Pawtucket (Int'l)	4	5	.444	4.77	1.39	21	20	0	0	0	0-0	111.1	109	62	59	15	46-0	66	.253
— Memphis (PCL)	0	1	.000	12.15	2.70	2	2	0	0	0	0-0	6.2	11	9	9	2	7-0	8	.379
2006— Palm Beach (FSL)	0	0	...	2.12	0.59	3	3	0	0	0	0-0	17.0	9	4	4	2	1-0	13	.150
— Memphis (PCL)	8	5	.615	2.81	1.29	15	15	0	0	0	0-0	80.0	70	26	25	9	33-2	58	.238
— St. Louis (N.L.)	0	0	...	4.82	1.18	5	1	0	0	0	0-0	9.1	6	5	5	1	5-0	12	.176
Major League totals (1 year)	0	0	...	4.82	1.18	5	1	0	0	0	0-0	9.1	6	5	5	1	5-0	12	.176

2006 LEFTY-RIGHTY SPLITS

vs.	Avg.	AB	H	2B	3B	HR	RBI	BB	SO	OBP	Slg.	vs.	Avg.	AB	H	2B	3B	HR	RBI	BB	SO	OBP	Slg.
L	.000	6	0	0	0	0	0	2	3	.333	.000	R	.214	28	6	3	0	1	4	3	9	.290	.429

NATHAN, JOE — P

PERSONAL: Born November 22, 1974, in Houston. ... 6-4/205. ... Throws right, bats right. ... Full name: Joseph Michael Nathan. ... High school: Pine Bush (N.Y.). ... College: SUNY-Stony Brook. **TRANSACTIONS/CAREER NOTES:** Selected by San Francisco Giants organization in sixth round of 1995 free-agent draft. ... Played shortstop in Giants' organization (1995). ... On disabled list (May 13-June 6 and July 14-August 19, 2000); included rehabilitation assignments to San Jose, Bakersfield and Fresno. ... Traded by Giants with Ps Boof Bonser and Francisco Liriano to Minnesota Twins for C A.J. Pierzynski and cash (November 14, 2003). **HONORS:** Named co-A.L. Fireman of the Year by the SPORTING NEWS (2005).

CAREER HITTING: 10-for-63 (.159), 4 R, 3 2B, 0 3B, 2 HR, 4 RBI.

Year Team (League)	W	L	Pct.	ERA	WHIP	G	GS	CG	ShO	Hld.	Sv.-Opp.	IP	H	R	ER	HR	BB-IBB	SO	Avg.
1996—						Did not play.													
1997— Salem-Keizer (N'west)	2	1	.667	2.47	1.27	18	5	0	0	...	2-...	62.0	53	22	17	7	26-0	44	.243
1998— San Jose (Calif.)	8	6	.571	3.32	1.21	22	22	0	0	...	0-...	122.0	100	51	45	13	48-0	118	.224
— Shreveport (Texas)	1	3	.250	8.80	1.89	4	4	0·	0	...	0-...	15.1	20	15	15	4	9-0	10	.317
1999— Shreveport (Texas)	0	1	.000	3.12	1.38	2	2	0	0	...	0-...	8.2	5	4	3	0	7-0	7	.179
— San Francisco (N.L.)	7	4	.636	4.18	1.44	19	14	0	0	0	1-1	90.1	84	45	42	17	46-0	54	.243
— Fresno (PCL)	6	4	.600	4.46	1.39	13	13	1	0	...	0-...	74.2	68	44	37	11	36-0	82	.244
2000— San Francisco (N.L.)	5	2	.714	5.21	1.63	20	15	0	0	0	0-1	93.1	89	63	54	12	63-4	61	.255
— San Jose (Calif.)	0	1	.000	3.60	1.00	1	1	0	0	...	0-...	5.0	4	2	2	1	1-0	2	.235
— Bakersfield (Calif.)	1	0	1.000	5.06	1.69	1	1	0	0	...	0-...	5.1	2	3	3	0	7-0	6	.118
— Fresno (PCL)	0	2	.000	4.40	1.53	3	3	0	0	...	0-...	14.1	15	8	7	4	7-0	9	.268
2001— Fresno (PCL)	0	5	.000	7.77	2.07	10	10	0	0	...	0-...	46.1	63	47	40	13	33-0	21	.333
— Shreveport (Texas)	3	6	.333	6.93	1.76	21	7	0	0	...	0-...	62.1	73	49	48	11	37-5	33	.299
2002— Fresno (PCL)	6	12	.333	5.60	1.65	31	25	1	0	...	0-...	146.1	167	97	91	20	74-0	117	.283
— San Francisco (N.L.)	0	0	...	0.00	0.27	4	0	0	0	0	0-0	3.2	1	0	0	0	0-0	2	.083
2003— San Francisco (N.L.)	12	4	.750	2.96	1.06	78	0	0	0	20	0-3	79.0	51	26	26	7	33-3	83	.186
2004— Minnesota (A.L.)	1	2	.333	1.62	0.98	73	0	0	0	0	44-47	72.1	48	14	13	3	23-3	89	.187
2005— Minnesota (A.L.)	7	4	.636	2.70	0.97	69	0	0	0	0	43-48	70.0	48	22	21	5	22-1	94	.183
2006— Minnesota (A.L.)	7	0	1.000	1.58	0.79	64	0	0	0	0	36-38	68.1	38	12	12	3	16-4	95	.158
American League totals (3 years)	15	6	.714	1.97	0.92	206	0	0	0	0	123-133	210.2	132	48	46	11	61-8	278	.176
National League totals (4 years)	24	10	.706	4.12	1.38	121	29	0	0	20	1-5	266.1	225	134	122	36	142-7	200	.229
Major League totals (7 years)	39	16	.709	3.17	1.17	327	29	0	0	20	124-138	477.0	357	182	168	47	203-15	478	.206

DIVISION SERIES RECORD

Year Team (League)	W	L	Pct.	ERA	WHIP	G	GS	CG	ShO	Hld.	Sv.-Opp.	IP	H	R	ER	HR	BB-IBB	SO	Avg.
2003— San Francisco (N.L.)	0	1	.000	81.00	15.00	2	0	0	0	0	0-1	0.1	4	3	3	1	1-0	1	.800
2004— Minnesota (A.L.)	0	1	.000	3.60	1.40	3	0	0	0	0	1-1	5.0	2	2	2	0	5-2	6	.118
2006— Minnesota (A.L.)	0	0	...	0.00	1.50	1	0	0	0	0	0-0	0.2	1	0	0	0	0-0	1	.333
Division series totals (3 years)	0	2	.000	7.50	2.17	6	0	0	0	0	1-2	6.0	7	5	5	1	6-2	8	.280

ALL-STAR GAME RECORD

	W	L	Pct.	ERA	WHIP	G	GS	CG	ShO	Hld.	Sv.-Opp.	IP	H	R	ER	HR	BB-IBB	SO	Avg.
All-Star Game totals (2 years)	0	0	...	4.50	1.00	2	0	0	0	0	0-0	2.0	2	1	1	0	0-0	2	.250

2006 LEFTY-RIGHTY SPLITS

vs.	Avg.	AB	H	2B	3B	HR	RBI	BB	SO	OBP	Slg.	vs.	Avg.	AB	H	2B	3B	HR	RBI	BB	SO	OBP	Slg.
L	.193	109	21	5	0	3	6	8	41	.244	.239	R	.130	131	17	2	2	3	7	8	54	.186	.244

NAVARRO, DIONER — C

PERSONAL: Born February 9, 1984, in Caracas, Venezuela. ... 5-10/190. ... Bats both, throws right. ... Full name: Dioner Faviau Navarro. ... Name pronounced: dee-o-nair. **TRANSACTIONS/CAREER NOTES:** Signed as a non-drafted free agent by New York Yankees organization (August 21, 2000). ... Traded by Yankees with Ps Javier Vazquez and Brad Halsey and cash to Arizona Diamondbacks for P Randy Johnson (January 11, 2005). ... Traded by Diamondbacks with Ps William Juarez, Danny Muegge and

Beltran Perez to Los Angeles Dodgers for OF Shawn Green and cash (January 11, 2005). ... On disabled list (May 5-June 15, 2006); included rehabilitation assignment to Las Vegas. ... Traded by Dodgers with P Jae Seo and a player to be named to Tampa Bay Devil Rays for C Toby Hall, P Mark Hendrickson and cash (June 27, 2006).

2006 GAMES PLAYED BY POSITION (MLB): C—78.

Year Team (League)	Pos.	G	AB	R	H	2B	3B	HR	RBI	BB	SO	HBP	GDP	SB-CS	Avg.	OBP	SLG	OPS	E	Avg.
2001— GC Yankees (GCL)	C	43	143	27	40	10	1	2	22	17	23	0	4	6-0	.280	.345	.406	.751	3	.991
2002— Greensboro (S. Atl.)	C	92	328	41	78	12	2	8	36	39	61	5	9	1-2	.238	.326	.360	.686	8	.987
— Tampa (Fla. St.)	C	0	1	2	1	1	0	0	0	0	0	0	0	1.000	.500	2.000	3.000	0	1.000
2003— Tampa (Fla. St.)	C	52	197	28	59	16	4	3	28	17	27	4	4	1-0	.299	.364	.467	.831	3	.992
— Trenton (East.)	C	58	208	28	71	15	0	4	37	18	26	1	6	2-3	.341	.388	.471	.859	4	.986
2004— Trenton (East.)	C-DH	70	255	32	69	14	1	3	29	33	44	1	6	1-0	.271	.354	.369	.720	7	.984
— Columbus (Int'l)	C-DH	40	136	18	34	8	2	1	16	14	17	1	4	1-0	.250	.316	.360	.672	2	.994
— New York (A.L.)	C	5	7	2	3	0	0	0	1	0	0	0	1	0-0	.429	.429	.429	.857	0	1.000
2005— Las Vegas (PCL)	C-DH	75	241	31	64	12	0	6	29	38	24	2	9	2-2	.266	.366	.390	.756	1	.998
— Los Angeles (N.L.)	C	50	176	21	48	9	0	3	14	20	21	2	3	0-0	.273	.354	.375	.729	2	.995
2006— Los Angeles (N.L.)	C	25	75	5	21	2	0	2	8	11	18	0	1	1-0	.280	.372	.387	.759	1	.993
— Las Vegas (PCL)		11	40	3	7	2	0	0	2	3	7	0	1	1-0	.175	.233	.225	.458	0	1.000
— Tampa Bay (A.L.)	C	56	193	23	47	7	0	4	20	20	33	1	6	1-1	.244	.316	.342	.658	7	.981
American League totals (2 years)		61	200	25	50	7	0	4	21	20	33	1	7	1-1	.250	.320	.345	.665	7	.982
National League totals (2 years)		75	251	26	69	11	0	5	22	31	39	2	4	1-0	.275	.359	.378	.738	3	.994
Major League totals (3 years)		136	451	51	119	18	0	9	43	51	72	3	11	2-1	.264	.342	.364	.706	10	.989

2006 LEFTY-RIGHTY SPLITS

vs.	Avg.	AB	H	2B	3B	HR	RBI	BB	SO	OBP	Slg.	vs.	Avg.	AB	H	2B	3B	HR	RBI	BB	SO	OBP	Slg.
L	.286	56	16	2	0	1	7	11	10	.403	.375	R	.245	212	52	7	0	5	21	20	41	.312	.349

NAVARRO, OSWALDO — IF

PERSONAL: Born October 2, 1984, in Villa de Cura, Venezuela. ... 6-0/155. ... Bats both, throws right. ... Full name: Oswaldo Ramses Navarro. **TRANSACTIONS/CAREER NOTES:** Signed as a non-drafted free agent by Seattle Mariners organization (August 12, 2001).

2006 GAMES PLAYED BY POSITION (MLB): SS—2, DH—1.

Year Team (League)	Pos.	G	AB	R	H	2B	3B	HR	RBI	BB	SO	HBP	GDP	SB-CS	Avg.	OBP	SLG	OPS	E	Avg.
2002— Aguirre (VSL)		37	119	13	31	4	1	0	9	12	21	2	3	3-6	.261	.338	.311	.649	...	...
2003— Everett (N'west)		61	233	42	60	12	1	0	23	10	39	5	4	16-3	.258	.302	.318	.620	...	...
2004— Wisconsin (Midw.)		40	109	13	23	4	0	0	7	11	19	2	4	4-1	.211	.295	.248	.543	...	...
— Everett (N'west)		68	267	38	73	27	1	1	30	21	59	3	3	17-4	.273	.331	.393	.724	...	...
2005— Wisconsin (Midw.)	2B-SS-DH																			
	3B	120	450	57	121	29	0	9	69	39	60	6	9	11-7	.269	.329	.393	.722	27	.954
2006— Tacoma (PCL)		55	183	15	45	9	0	2	21	19	33	1	6	1-2	.246	.314	.328	.642	7	.971
— San Antonio (Texas)		79	266	27	71	13	1	1	24	39	57	5	5	7-6	.267	.371	.335	.706	13	.968
— Seattle (A.L.)	SS-DH	4	3	0	2	0	0	0	0	0	1	0	0	0-0	.667	.667	.667	1.333	1	.750
Major League totals (1 year)		4	3	0	2	0	0	0	0	0	1	0	0	0-0	.667	.667	.667	1.333	1	.750

2006 LEFTY-RIGHTY SPLITS

vs.	Avg.	AB	H	2B	3B	HR	RBI	BB	SO	OBP	Slg.	vs.	Avg.	AB	H	2B	3B	HR	RBI	BB	SO	OBP	Slg.
L	.000	0	0	0	0	0	0	0	0	.000	.000	R	.667	3	2	0	0	0	0	0	1	.667	.667

NELSON, JEFF — P

PERSONAL: Born November 17, 1966, in Baltimore. ... 6-8/225. ... Throws right, bats right. ... Full name: Jeffrey Allan Nelson. ... High school: Catonsville (Md.). ... Junior college: Catonsville (Md.) C.C. **TRANSACTIONS/CAREER NOTES:** Selected by Los Angeles Dodgers organization in 22nd round of June 1984 free-agent draft. ... Selected by Seattle Mariners organization from Dodgers organization in Rule 5 minor league draft (December 9, 1986). ... On disabled list (July 16, 1989-remainder of season). ... Traded by Mariners with 1B Tino Martinez and P Jim Mecir to New York Yankees for P Sterling Hitchcock and 3B Russ Davis (December 7, 1995). ... On suspended list (September 3-5, 1996; and May 28-29, 1998). ... On disabled list (June 26-September 4, 1998); included rehabilitation assignment to Tampa. ... On disabled list (May 3-20 and June 3-August 11, 1999); included rehabilitation assignments to GCL Yankees and Tampa. ... On disabled list (May 8-June 27, 2002); included rehabilitation assignment to Everett. ... Traded by Mariners to Yankees for P Armando Benitez (August 6, 2003). ... Signed as a free agent by Texas Rangers (January 14, 2004). ... On disabled list (May 13-July 26 and August 1-September 1, 2004); included rehabilitation assignments to Frisco and Oklahoma. ... Signed as a free agent by Mariners organization (January 31, 2005). ... On bereavement list (August 2-5). ... Signed as free agent by St. Louis Cardinals organization (January 16, 2006). ... Released by Cardinals (March 26, 2006). ... Signed by Chicago White Sox organization (May 2, 2006). ... On disabled list (June 4, 2006-remainder of season). **MISCELLANEOUS NOTES:** Appeared in one game as outfielder with no chances for Seattle (1993).
CAREER HITTING: 0-for-2 (.000), 0 R, 0 2B, 0 3B, 0 HR, 0 RBI.

Year Team (League)	W	L	Pct.	ERA	WHIP	G	GS	CG	ShO	Hld.	Sv.-Opp.	IP	H	R	ER	HR	BB-IBB	SO	Avg.
1984— Great Falls (Pio.)	0	0	...	54.00	9.00	1	0	0	0	...	0-...	0.2	3	4	4	1	3-0	1	...
— GC Dodgers (GCL)	0	0	...	1.35	0.90	9	0	0	0	...	0-...	13.1	6	3	2	0	6-0	7	.122
1985— GC Dodgers (GCL)	0	5	.000	5.51	2.20	14	7	0	0	...	0-...	47.1	72	50	29	1	32-0	31	.344
1986— Bakersfield (Calif.)	0	7	.000	6.69	2.29	24	11	0	0	...	0-...	71.1	79	83	53	9	84-1	37	.252
— Great Falls (Pio.)	0	0	...	13.50	4.00	3	0	0	0	...	0-...	2.0	5	3	3	0	3-2	1	...
1987— Salinas (Calif.)	3	7	.300	5.74	1.89	17	16	1	0	...	0-...	80.0	80	61	51	2	71-0	43	.261
1988— San Bern. (Calif.)	8	9	.471	5.54	1.70	27	27	1	1	...	0-...	149.1	163	115	92	9	91-2	94	.287
1989— Williamsport (East.)	7	5	.583	3.31	1.35	15	15	2	0	...	0-...	92.1	72	41	34	2	53-1	61	.217
1990— Williamsport (East.)	1	4	.200	6.44	1.92	10	10	0	0	...	0-...	43.1	65	35	31	2	18-1	14	.359
— Peninsula (Caro.)	2	2	.500	3.15	1.20	18	7	1	1	...	6-...	60.0	47	21	21	5	25-1	49	.214
1991— Jacksonville (Sou.)	4	0	1.000	1.27	1.13	21	0	0	0	...	12-...	28.1	23	5	4	0	9-0	34	.225
— Calgary (PCL)	3	4	.429	3.90	1.67	28	0	0	0	...	21-...	32.1	39	19	14	1	15-3	26	.310
1992— Calgary (PCL)	1	0	1.000	0.00	0.27	2	0	0	0	...	0-...	3.2	0	0	0	0	1-0	0	.000
— Seattle (A.L.)	1	7	.125	3.44	1.42	66	0	0	0	6	6-14	81.0	71	34	31	7	44-12	46	.245
1993— Calgary (PCL)	1	0	1.000	1.17	1.04	5	0	0	0	...	1-...	7.2	6	1	1	0	2-0	6	.222
— Seattle (A.L.)	5	3	.625	4.35	1.52	71	0	0	0	17	1-11	60.0	57	30	29	5	34-10	61	.258
1994— Seattle (A.L.)	0	0	...	2.76	1.30	28	0	0	0	2	0-0	42.1	35	18	13	3	20-4	44	.226
— Calgary (PCL)	1	4	.200	2.84	1.11	18	0	0	0	...	8-...	25.1	21	9	8	1	7-1	30	.236
1995— Seattle (A.L.)	7	3	.700	2.17	1.08	62	0	0	0	14	2-4	78.2	58	21	19	4	27-5	96	.209
1996— New York (A.L.)	4	4	.500	4.36	1.49	73	0	0	0	10	2-4	74.1	75	38	36	6	36-1	91	.262
1997— New York (A.L.)	3	7	.300	2.86	1.14	77	0	0	0	22	2-8	78.2	53	32	25	7	37-12	81	.191
1998— Seattle (A.L.)	5	3	.625	3.79	1.64	45	0	0	0	10	3-6	40.1	44	18	17	1	22-4	35	.278
— Tampa (Fla. St.)	0	0	...	0.00	1.00	2	1	0	0	...	0-...	2.0	1	0	0	0	1-0	4	.143

Year Team (League)	W	L	Pct.	ERA	WHIP	G	GS	CG	ShO	Hld.	Sv.-Opp.	IP	H	R	ER	HR	BB-IBB	SO	Avg.
1999— New York (A.L.)	2	1	.667	4.15	1.62	39	0	0	0	10	1-2	30.1	27	14	14	2	22-2	35	.245
— GC Yankees (GCL)	0	0	...	0.00	1.00	2	2	0	0	...	0-...	2.0	1	0	0	0	1-0	3	.143
— Tampa (Fla. St.)	0	0	...	0.00	1.00	3	3	0	0	...	0-...	3.0	1	0	0	0	2-0	5	.100
2000— New York (A.L.)	8	4	.667	2.45	1.28	73	0	0	0	15	0-4	69.2	44	24	19	2	45-1	71	.183
2001— Seattle (A.L.)	4	3	.571	2.76	1.13	69	0	0	0	26	4-5	65.1	30	21	20	3	44-1	88	.136
2002— Seattle (A.L.)	3	2	.600	3.94	1.38	41	0	0	0	12	2-4	45.2	36	20	20	4	27-3	55	.221
— Everett (N'west)	0	1	.000	0.00	0.75	1	1	0	0	...	0-...	1.1	1	1	0	0	0-0	4	.200
2003— Seattle (A.L.)	3	2	.600	3.35	1.27	46	0	0	0	6	7-11	37.2	34	16	14	3	14-1	47	.248
— New York (A.L.)	1	0	1.000	4.58	1.53	24	0	0	0	8	1-3	17.2	17	9	9	1	10-2	21	.246
2004— Oklahoma (PCL)	0	1	.000	16.20	1.80	2	2	0	0	...	0-...	1.2	3	3	3	0	0-0	3	.375
— Frisco (Texas)	0	0	...	2.46	0.82	3	3	0	0	...	0-...	3.2	2	1	1	0	1-0	3	.154
— Texas (A.L.)	1	2	.333	5.32	1.52	29	0	0	0	9	1-1	23.2	17	16	14	3	19-0	22	.207
2005— Seattle (A.L.)	1	3	.250	3.93	1.47	49	0	0	0	4	1-4	36.2	32	17	16	3	22-0	34	.237
2006— Charlotte (Int'l)	1	0	1.000	0.00	1.50	4	0	0	0	1	0-0	5.1	4	1	0	0	4-0	7	.222
— Chicago (A.L.)	0	1	.000	3.38	3.00	6	0	0	0	0	0-1	2.2	3	1	1	1	5-1	2	.300
Major League totals (15 years)	48	45	.516	3.41	1.35	798	0	0	0	176	33-82	784.2	633	329	297	55	428-59	829	.224

DIVISION SERIES RECORD

Year Team (League)	W	L	Pct.	ERA	WHIP	G	GS	CG	ShO	Hld.	Sv.-Opp.	IP	H	R	ER	HR	BB-IBB	SO	Avg.
1995— Seattle (A.L.)	0	1	.000	3.18	1.76	2	0	0	0	0	0-0	5.2	7	2	2	0	3-0	7	.304
1996— New York (A.L.)	1	0	1.000	0.00	1.09	2	0	0	0	0	0-0	3.2	2	0	0	0	2-1	5	.154
1997— New York (A.L.)	0	0	...	0.00	1.50	4	0	0	0	2	0-0	4.0	4	0	0	0	2-0	0	.267
1998— New York (A.L.)	0	0	...	0.00	1.13	2	0	0	0	1	0-0	2.2	2	0	0	0	1-0	2	.222
1999— New York (A.L.)	0	0	...	0.00	1.20	3	0	0	0	1	0-0	1.2	1	0	0	0	1-0	3	.167
2000— New York (A.L.)	0	0	...	0.00	0.00	2	0	0	0	1	0-0	2.0	0	0	0	0	0-0	2	.000
2001— Seattle (A.L.)	0	0	...	0.00	0.67	3	0	0	0	2	0-0	3.0	1	0	0	0	1-0	5	.100
2003— New York (A.L.)	0	0	...	...	...	1	0	0	0	0	0-0	0.0	0	0	0	0	1-0	0	...
Division series totals (8 years)	1	1	.500	0.79	1.24	20	0	0	0	7	0-0	22.2	17	2	2	0	11-1	24	.207

CHAMPIONSHIP SERIES RECORD

Year Team (League)	W	L	Pct.	ERA	WHIP	G	GS	CG	ShO	Hld.	Sv.-Opp.	IP	H	R	ER	HR	BB-IBB	SO	Avg.
1995— Seattle (A.L.)	0	0	...	0.00	2.67	3	0	0	0	1	0-0	3.0	3	0	0	0	5-1	3	.333
1996— New York (A.L.)	0	1	.000	11.57	2.14	2	0	0	0	0	0-0	2.1	5	3	3	0	0-0	3	.385
1998— New York (A.L.)	0	1	.000	20.25	3.00	3	0	0	0	0	0-0	1.1	3	3	3	0	1-0	3	.429
1999— New York (A.L.)	0	0	...	0.00	0.00	2	0	0	0	2	0-0	0.2	0	0	0	0	0-0	0	.000
2000— New York (A.L.)	0	0	...	9.00	1.67	3	0	0	0	1	0-0	3.0	5	3	3	2	0-0	6	.357
2001— Seattle (A.L.)	0	0	...	0.00	0.86	2	0	0	0	0	0-0	2.1	1	0	0	0	1-0	3	.143
2003— New York (A.L.)	0	0	...	6.00	1.33	4	0	0	0	0	0-0	3.0	4	2	2	0	0-0	3	.364
Champ. series totals (7 years)	0	2	.000	6.32	1.79	19	0	0	0	4	0-0	15.2	21	11	11	3	7-1	20	.339

WORLD SERIES RECORD

Year Team (League)	W	L	Pct.	ERA	WHIP	G	GS	CG	ShO	Hld.	Sv.-Opp.	IP	H	R	ER	HR	BB-IBB	SO	Avg.
1996— New York (A.L.)	0	0	...	0.00	0.46	3	0	0	0	0	0-0	4.1	1	0	0	0	1-0	5	.071
1998— New York (A.L.)	0	0	...	0.00	1.29	2	0	0	0	1	0-0	2.1	2	1	0	0	1-0	4	.222
1999— New York (A.L.)	0	0	...	0.00	1.13	4	0	0	0	1	0-0	2.2	2	0	0	0	1-0	3	.200
2000— New York (A.L.)	1	0	1.000	10.13	2.25	3	0	0	0	0	0-0	2.2	5	3	3	1	1-0	1	.417
2003— New York (A.L.)	0	0	...	0.00	1.50	3	0	0	0	1	0-0	4.0	4	0	0	0	2-0	5	.267
World series totals (5 years)	1	0	1.000	1.69	1.25	16	0	0	0	3	0-0	16.0	14	4	3	1	6-0	18	.233

ALL-STAR GAME RECORD

Year Team (League)	W	L	Pct.	ERA	WHIP	G	GS	CG	ShO	Hld.	Sv.-Opp.	IP	H	R	ER	HR	BB-IBB	SO	Avg.
All-Star Game totals (1 year)	0	0	...	0.00	1.00	1	0	0	0	1	0-0	1.0	0	0	0	0	1-0	1	.000

2006 LEFTY-RIGHTY SPLITS

vs.	Avg.	AB	H	2B	3B	HR	RBI	BB	SO	OBP	Slg.	vs.	Avg.	AB	H	2B	3B	HR	RBI	BB	SO	OBP	Slg.
L	.000	3	0	0	0	0	0	2	1	.400	.000	R	.429	7	3	1	0	1	2	3	1	.600	1.000

NELSON, JOE — P

PERSONAL: Born October 25, 1974, in Alameda, Calif. ... 6-2/185. ... Throws right, bats right. ... Full name: Joseph Georrge Nelson. ... College: San Francisco. **TRANSACTIONS/CAREER NOTES:** Selected by Atlanta Braves organization in fourth round of 1996 free-agent draft. ... On disabled list (June 20, 2001-remainder of season). ... Released by Braves (August 2, 2002). ... Signed by Boston Red Sox organization (August 10, 2002). ... Released by Red Sox (August 27, 2002). ... Signed as a free agent by New York Mets organization (December 28, 2004). ... Released by Mets (April 1, 2005). ... Signed by Tampa Bay Devil Rays organization (April 15, 2005). ... Released by Devil Rays (July 25, 2005). ... Signed by St. Louis Cardinals organization (July 31, 2005). ... Signed as a free agent by Kansas City Royals organization (November 15, 2005).
CAREER HITTING: 0-for-0 (.000), 0 R, 0 2B, 0 3B, 0 HR, 0 RBI.

Year Team (League)	W	L	Pct.	ERA	WHIP	G	GS	CG	ShO	Hld.	Sv.-Opp.	IP	H	R	ER	HR	BB-IBB	SO	Avg.
1996— Eugene (Northwest)	5	3	.625	4.37	1.40	14	13	0	0	...	0-...	70.0	69	43	34	5	29-1	67	.255
1997— Durham (Carol.)	10	6	.625	4.76	1.40	25	24	0	0	...	0-...	124.2	114	74	66	17	61-1	99	.247
1998— Greenville (Sou.)	6	9	.400	4.98	1.78	45	12	1	1	...	0-...	108.1	124	76	60	9	69-2	74	.295
1999— Greenville (Sou.)	1	1	.500	2.37	1.09	25	0	0	0	...	8-...	30.1	19	15	8	2	14-2	37	.173
— Richmond (Int'l)	2	3	.400	4.54	1.43	12	3	0	0	...	1-...	33.2	33	18	17	2	15-0	31	.254
2000— GC Braves (GCL)	1	0	1.000	2.25	1.50	4	0	0	0	...	1-...	4.0	3	1	1	0	3-0	7	.088
— Jamestown (NYP)	0	0	...	2.25	1.00	3	0	0	0	...	0-...	4.0	3	3	1	0	1-0	7	.200
2001— Richmond (Int'l)	1	2	.333	1.13	0.93	29	0	0	0	...	8-...	39.2	23	5	5	1	14-2	40	.172
— Atlanta (N.L.)	0	0	...	36.00	4.50	2	0	0	0	0	0-0	2.0	7	9	8	1	2-0	0	.583
2002— Trenton (East.)	0	0	...	14.54	2.54	4	0	0	0	...	0-...	4.1	9	8	7	1	2-0	3	.409
2003—			Did not play.																
2004— Portland (East.)	3	2	.600	1.78	1.02	25	0	0	0	...	13-...	30.1	16	8	6	1	15-0	49	.152
— Boston (A.L.)	0	0	...	16.88	2.63	3	0	0	0	0	0-0	2.2	4	5	5	0	3-0	5	.364
— Pawtucket (Int'l)	0	0	...	4.64	1.69	16	0	0	0	...	0-...	21.1	27	14	11	1	9-0	31	.307
2005— Durham (Int'l)	0	3	.000	4.11	1.35	35	0	0	0	2	6-9	46.0	41	25	21	9	21-1	62	.229
— Springfield (Texas)	0	0	...	2.03	0.83	9	0	0	0	1	1-1	13.1	4	3	3	1	7-0	22	.093
2006— Omaha (PCL)	2	2	.500	1.97	0.97	24	0	0	0	1	7-9	32.0	19	9	7	4	12-2	39	.181
— Kansas City (A.L.)	1	1	.500	4.43	1.37	43	0	0	0	5	9-10	44.2	37	22	22	5	24-4	44	.226
American League totals (2 years)	1	1	.500	5.13	1.44	46	0	0	0	5	9-10	47.1	41	27	27	5	27-4	49	.234
National League totals (1 year)	0	0	...	36.00	4.50	2	0	0	0	0	0-0	2.0	7	9	8	1	2-0	0	.583
Major League totals (3 years)	1	1	.500	6.39	1.56	48	0	0	0	5	9-10	49.1	48	36	35	6	29-4	49	.257

2006 LEFTY-RIGHTY SPLITS

vs.	Avg.	AB	H	2B	3B	HR	RBI	BB	SO	OBP	Slg.	vs.	Avg.	AB	H	2B	3B	HR	RBI	BB	SO	OBP	Slg.
L	.180	61	11	1	0	1	5	10	20	.296	.246	R	.252	103	26	13	1	4	16	14	24	.345	.515

NELSON, JOHN — SS

PERSONAL: Born March 3, 1979, in Denton, Texas. ... Bats right, throws right. ... Full name: John C. Nelson. ... College: Kansas. **TRANSACTIONS/CAREER NOTES:** Selected by St. Louis Cardinals organization in eighth round of 2001 free-agent draft.

2006 GAMES PLAYED BY POSITION (MLB): SS—1, 1B—1.

Year	Team (League)	Pos.	G	AB	R	H	2B	3B	HR	RBI	BB	SO	HBP	GDP	SB-CS	Avg.	OBP	SLG	OPS	E	Avg.
																		BATTING		FIELDING	
2001—	New Jersey (NYP)		66	252	43	60	16	3	8	26	35	76	3	3	14-3	.238	.332	.421	.753	...	...
2002—	Peoria (Midw.)		132	481	85	132	28	5	16	63	54	123	3	8	16-3	.274	.349	.453	.802	...	...
2003—	Tennessee (Sou.)		136	506	60	120	22	1	5	42	44	117	3	14	10-5	.237	.301	.314	.615	...	...
2004—	Tennessee (Sou.)		63	206	41	62	16	3	8	29	31	56	2	0	6-2	.301	.396	.524	.920	...	...
2005—	Memphis (PCL)	SS-OF	128	427	56	103	27	1	14	49	51	141	4	4	2-3	.241	.326	.407	.734	15	.971
2006—	Memphis (PCL)		125	423	55	91	16	2	21	48	42	153	5	4	12-2	.215	.291	.411	.702	21	.958
—	St. Louis (N.L.)	1B-SS	8	5	2	0	0	0	0	0	0	4	0	0	0-0	.000	.000	.000	.000	0	1.000
Major League totals (1 year)			8	5	2	0	0	0	0	0	0	4	0	0	0-0	.000	.000	.000	.000	0	1.000

2006 LEFTY-RIGHTY SPLITS

vs.	Avg.	AB	H	2B	3B	HR	RBI	BB	SO	OBP	Slg.	vs.	Avg.	AB	H	2B	3B	HR	RBI	BB	SO	OBP	Slg.
L	.000	0	0	0	0	0	0	0	0	.000	.000	R	.000	5	0	0	0	0	0	0	4	.000	.000

NESHEK, PAT — P

PERSONAL: Born September 4, 1980, in Madison, Wis. ... 6-2/200. ... Throws right, bats both. ... Full name: Patrick J. Neshek. ... College: Butler. **TRANSACTIONS/CAREER NOTES:** Selected by Minnesota Twins organization in sixth round of 2002 free-agent draft.

CAREER HITTING: 0-for-0 (.000), 0 R, 0 2B, 0 3B, 0 HR, 0 RBI.

Year	Team (League)	W	L	Pct.	ERA	WHIP	G	GS	CG	ShO	Hld.	Sv.-Opp.	IP	H	R	ER	HR	BB-IBB	SO	Avg.
2002—	Elizabethton (App.)	0	2	.000	0.99	0.70	23	0	0	...	...	15-...	27.1	13	6	3	0	6-0	41	.141
2003—	Quad City (Midw.)	3	2	.600	0.52	0.90	28	0	0	0	...	14-...	34.1	20	3	2	0	11-2	53	.165
—	Fort Myers (FSL)	4	1	.800	2.15	0.95	20	0	0	0	...	2-...	29.1	22	8	7	2	6-1	29	.202
—	New Britain (East.)	1	1	.500	5.87	1.30	5	1	0	0	...	0-...	7.2	7	5	5	2	3-0	5	.233
2004—	New Britain (East.)	2	1	.667	3.82	1.47	26	0	0	0	...	2-...	35.1	34	15	15	2	18-5	38	.246
—	Fort Myers (FSL)	0	1	.000	2.95	0.98	16	0	0	0	...	10-...	18.1	16	7	6	2	2-0	19	.225
2005—	New Britain (East.)	6	4	.600	2.19	1.09	55	0	0	0	0	24-29	82.1	69	25	20	9	21-0	95	.225
2006—	Rochester (Int'l)	6	2	.750	1.95	0.92	33	0	0	0	0	14-19	60.0	41	13	13	7	14-4	87	.189
—	Minnesota (A.L.)	4	2	.667	2.19	0.78	32	0	0	0	10	0-2	37.0	23	9	9	6	6-0	53	.176
Major League totals (1 year)		4	2	.667	2.19	0.78	32	0	0	0	10	0-2	37.0	23	9	9	6	6-0	53	.176

DIVISION SERIES RECORD

Year	Team (League)	W	L	Pct.	ERA	WHIP	G	GS	CG	ShO	Hld.	Sv.-Opp.	IP	H	R	ER	HR	BB-IBB	SO	Avg.
2006—	Minnesota (A.L.)	0	1	.000	9.00	1.00	2	0	0	0	0	0-0	1.0	1	1	1	0	0-0	1	.250

2006 LEFTY-RIGHTY SPLITS

vs.	Avg.	AB	H	2B	3B	HR	RBI	BB	SO	OBP	Slg.	vs.	Avg.	AB	H	2B	3B	HR	RBI	BB	SO	OBP	Slg.
L	.244	45	11	0	0	4	6	4	16	.300	.511	R	.140	86	12	1	0	2	5	2	37	.159	.221

NEVIN, PHIL — 1B

PERSONAL: Born January 19, 1971, in Fullerton, Calif. ... 6-2/231. ... Bats right, throws right. ... Full name: Phillip Joseph Nevin. ... High school: El Dorado (Placentia, Calif.). ... College: Cal State Fullerton. **TRANSACTIONS/CAREER NOTES:** Selected by Los Angeles Dodgers organization in third round of 1989 free-agent draft; did not sign. ... Selected by Houston Astros organization in first round (first pick overall) of 1992 free-agent draft. ... Traded by Astros to Detroit Tigers (August 15, 1995), completing deal in which Tigers traded P Mike Henneman to Astros for a player to be named (August 10, 1995). ... On disabled list (March 21-April 16, 1997); included rehabilitation assignment to Lakeland. ... Traded by Tigers with C Matt Walbeck to Anaheim Angels for P Nick Skuse (November 20, 1997). ... On suspended list (June 12-15, 1998). ... Traded by Angels with P Keith Volkman to San Diego Padres for IF Andy Sheets and OF Gus Kennedy (March 29, 1999). ... On disabled list (April 1-16, 1999); included rehabilitation assignment to Las Vegas. ... On disabled list (May 12-27 and May 30-July 12, 2002); included rehabilitation assignment to Lake Elsinore. ... On disabled list (March 25-July 23, 2003); included rehabilitation assignments to Lake Elsinore and Portland. ... On disabled list (July 5-21, 2004). ... On disabled list (June 26-July 18, 2005); included rehabilitation assignment to Portland. ... Traded by Padres to Texas Rangers for P Chan Ho Park (July 29, 2005). ... Traded by Rangers with cash to Chicago Cubs for IF Jerry Hairston (May 31, 2006). ... Traded by Cubs with cash to Minnesota Twins for a player to be named (August 31, 2006); Cubs acquired P Adam Harben to complete deal (September 5, 2006). **STATISTICAL NOTES:** Hit three home runs in one game (October 6, 2001). ... Career major league grand slams: 7. **MISCELLANEOUS NOTES:** Member of 1992 U.S. Olympic baseball team.

2006 GAMES PLAYED BY POSITION (MLB): DH—54, 1B—44, OF—10, C—1.

Year	Team (League)	Pos.	G	AB	R	H	2B	3B	HR	RBI	BB	SO	HBP	GDP	SB-CS	Avg.	OBP	SLG	OPS	E	Avg.
																	BATTING			FIELDING	
1993—	Tucson (PCL)	3B-OF	123	448	67	128	21	3	10	93	52	99	3	12	8-1	.286	.359	.413	.772	29	.898
1994—	Tucson (PCL)	3B-OF	118	445	67	117	20	1	12	79	55	101	1	21	3-2	.263	.343	.393	.736	32	.907
1995—	Tucson (PCL)	3B-DH	62	223	31	65	16	0	7	41	27	39	1	9	2-3	.291	.371	.457	.828	14	.923
—	Houston (N.L.)	3B	18	60	4	7	1	0	0	1	7	13	1	2	0-0	.117	.221	.133	.354	3	.933
—	Toledo (Int'l)	OF-DH	7	23	3	7	2	0	1	3	1	5	0	2	0-0	.304	.333	.522	.855	0	1.000
—	Detroit (A.L.)	OF-DH	29	96	9	21	3	1	2	12	11	27	3	3	0-0	.219	.318	.333	.652	2	.963
1996—	Jacksonville (Sou.)	C-DH-3B																			
		OF-1B	98	344	77	101	18	1	24	69	60	83	3	9	6-2	.294	.397	.561	.958	11	.977
—	Detroit (A.L.)	3B-OF-C																			
		DH	38	120	15	35	5	0	8	19	8	39	1	1	1-0	.292	.338	.533	.872	5	.951
1997—	Lakeland (Fla. St.)	1B-3B-DH	3	9	3	5	1	0	1	4	3	2	0	0	0-0	.556	.667	1.000	1.667	1	.929
—	Toledo (Int'l)	1B-3B-DH	5	19	1	3	0	0	1	3	2	9	0	1	0-0	.158	.238	.316	.554	0	1.000
—	Detroit (A.L.)	OF-DH-3B																			
		3B-C	93	251	32	59	16	1	9	35	25	68	1	5	0-1	.235	.306	.414	.720	2	.982
1998—	Anaheim (A.L.)	C-DH-1B	75	237	27	54	8	1	8	27	.17	67	5	6	0-0	.228	.291	.371	.663	5	.989
1999—	Las Vegas (PCL)	3B-C-OF	3	10	2	2	0	0	2	4	1	5	0	0	0-0	.200	.200	.800	1.000	0	1.000
—	San Diego (N.L.)	3B-C-OF																			
		1B	128	383	52	103	27	0	24	85	51	82	1	7	1-0	.269	.352	.527	.880	5	.989
2000—	San Diego (N.L.)	3B	143	538	87	163	34	1	31	107	59	121	4	17	2-0	.303	.374	.543	.916	*26	.929
2001—	San Diego (N.L.)	3B-DH	149	546	97	167	31	0	41	126	71	147	4	13	0-0	.306	.388	.588	.976	27	.930
2002—	San Diego (N.L.)	3B-1B	107	407	53	116	16	0	12	57	38	87	1	12	4-0	.285	.344	.413	.757	18	.963
—	Lake Elsinore (Calif.)	3B	2	3	1	1	0	0	0	6	1	2	0	0	0-0	.333	.375	1.000	1.375	2	.000
2003—	Lake Elsinore (Calif.)	DH	5	15	1	4	1	0	0	3	1	1	0	0	0-0	.267	.313	.333	.633	0	...
—	Portland (PCL)	1B-DH-OF	6	18	0	2	0	0	0	1	1	1	0	2	0-0	.111	.158	.111	.269	0	1.000
—	San Diego (N.L.)	1B-OF	59	226	30	63	13	0	13	46	21	44	0	9	2-0	.279	.339	.487	.825	2	.994

N

Year	Team (League)	Pos.	G	AB	R	H	2B	3B	HR	RBI	BB	SO	HBP	GDP	SB-CS	Avg.	OBP	SLG	OPS	E	Avg.
												BATTING								FIELDING	
2004—San Diego (N.L.)	1B-DH-C	147	547	78	158	31	1	26	105	66	121	5	16	0-0	.289	.368	.492	.859	13	.990
2005—Portland (PCL)	1B	2	7	0	1	0	0	0	1	0	2	0	1	0-0	.143	.143	.143	.286	0	1.000
—San Diego (N.L.)	1B-C	73	281	31	72	11	1	9	47	19	67	1	2	1-0	.256	.301	.399	.699	4	.994
—Texas (A.L.)	DH-1B-3B	29	99	15	18	5	0	3	8	8	30	1	6	2-0	.182	.250	.323	.573	0	1.000
2006—Texas (A.L.)	DH-1B	46	176	26	38	8	0	9	31	21	39	2	9	0-0	.216	.307	.415	.721	0	1.000
—Chicago (N.L.)	1B-OF-C	67	179	26	49	4	0	12	33	17	52	0	4	0-0	.274	.335	.497	.832	0	1.000
—Minnesota (A.L.)	DH-1B	16	42	2	8	1	0	1	4	10	15	0	0	0-0	.190	.340	.286	.625	0	1.000
American League totals (6 years)		326	1021	126	233	46	3	40	136	100	285	13	30	3-1	.228	.304	.397	.700	14	.982
National League totals (9 years)		891	3167	458	898	163	3	168	607	349	734	17	82	15-4	.284	.355	.496	.851	98	.977
Major League totals (12 years)		1217	4188	584	1131	209	6	208	743	449	1019	30	112	18-5	.270	.343	.472	.814	112	.977

DIVISION SERIES RECORD

Year	Team (League)	Pos.	G	AB	R	H	2B	3B	HR	RBI	BB	SO	HBP	GDP	SB-CS	Avg.	OBP	SLG	OPS	E	Avg.
2006—Minnesota (A.L.)	DH	1	3	0	0	0	0	0	0	0	0	0	0	0-0	.000	.000	.000	.000	0	...

ALL-STAR GAME RECORD

		G	AB	R	H	2B	3B	HR	RBI	BB	SO	HBP	GDP	SB-CS	Avg.	OBP	SLG	OPS	E	Avg.
All-Star Game totals (1 year)		1	1	0	0	0	0	0	0	0	0	0	0	0-0	.000	.000	.000	.000	0	...

2006 LEFTY-RIGHTY SPLITS

vs.	Avg.	AB	H	2B	3B	HR	RBI	BB	SO	OBP	Slg.	vs.	Avg.	AB	H	2B	3B	HR	RBI	BB	SO	OBP	Slg.
L	.226	133	30	4	0	7	17	19	28	.325	.414	R	.246	264	65	9	0	15	51	29	78	.322	.451

NEWHAN, DAVID — OF/3B

PERSONAL: Born September 7, 1973, in Fullerton, Calif. ... 5-10/180. ... Bats left, throws right. ... Full name: David Matthew Newhan. ... High school: Esperanza (Calif.). ... College: Pepperdine. **TRANSACTIONS/CAREER NOTES:** Selected by Oakland Athletics organization in 17th round of 1995 free-agent draft. ... Traded by A's with P Don Wengert to San Diego Padres for P Doug Bochtler and SS Jorge Velandia (December 15, 1997). ... Traded by Padres to Philadelphia Phillies (August 7, 2000), completing deal in which Phillies traded SS Desi Relaford to Padres for a player to be named (August 4, 2000). ... On disabled list (April 15, 2001-remainder of season); included rehabilitation assignments to Scranton/Wilkes-Barre. ... Signed as a free agent by Los Angeles Dodgers organization (February 5, 2002). ... Signed as a free agent by Colorado Rockies organization (May 8, 2003). ... Signed as a free agent by Texas Rangers organization (November 10, 2003). ... Released by Rangers (June 17, 2004) ... Signed by Baltimore Orioles (June 18, 2004). ... On disabled list (April 18-August 29, 2006); included rehabilitation assignment to Bowie. **STATISTICAL NOTES:** Career major league grand slams: 1.

2006 GAMES PLAYED BY POSITION (MLB): OF—37, DH—1, 1B—1.

Year	Team (League)	Pos.	G	AB	R	H	2B	3B	HR	RBI	BB	SO	HBP	GDP	SB-CS	Avg.	OBP	SLG	OPS	E	Avg.
1995—S. Oregon (N'west)	OF	42	145	25	39	8	1	6	21	29	30	1	2	10-5	.269	.388	.462	.850	9	.964
—W. Mich. (Mid.)	OF	25	96	9	21	5	0	3	8	13	26	1	2	3-2	.219	.315	.365	.680	1	.976
1996—Modesto (California)	OF	117	455	96	137	27	3	25	75	62	106	2	8	17-8	.301	.386	.538	.924	5	.964
1997—Visalia (Calif.)	2B	67	241	52	67	15	2	7	48	44	58	3	5	9-3	.278	.389	.444	.833	10	.966
—Huntsville (Sou.)	2B	57	212	40	67	13	2	5	35	28	59	2	4	5-5	.316	.398	.467	.865	16	.954
1998—Mobile (Sou.)	2B-3B-SS	121	491	89	128	26	3	12	45	68	110	2	8	27-8	.261	.352	.399	.751	14	.975
1999—Las Vegas (PCL)	2B-SS	98	374	49	107	25	1	14	49	30	84	2	8	22-4	.286	.342	.471	.812	20	.952
—San Diego (N.L.)	2B-1B-3B	32	43	7	6	1	0	2	6	1	11	0	0	2-1	.140	.159	.302	.461	2	.970
2000—San Diego (N.L.)	OF-2B-3B	14	20	5	3	1	0	1	2	6	7	0	0	0-0	.150	.346	.350	.696	0	1.000
—Las Vegas (PCL)	2B-OF	66	244	41	62	5	2	5	35	37	61	0	4	9-3	.254	.351	.352	.704	7	.975
—Scran./W.B. (I.L.)	2B	25	83	10	21	3	0	3	8	11	15	0	0	3-1	.253	.337	.398	.734	1	.991
—Philadelphia (N.L.)	2B	10	17	3	3	0	0	0	0	2	6	0	2	0-0	.176	.263	.176	.440	0	1.000
2001—Philadelphia (N.L.)	2B	7	6	2	2	1	0	0	1	1	0	0	0	0-0	.333	.375	.500	.875	0	1.000
—Scran./W.B. (I.L.)	2B	13	55	4	6	1	0	2	4	4	11	1	1	0-0	.109	.183	.127	.311	1	.969
2002—Los Angeles (N.L.)	Did not play.																			
2003—Colo. Springs (PCL)	2B-1B-OF-DH	72	244	43	85	17	2	3	28	16	36	2	6	6-4	.348	.392	.471	.863	14	.959
2004—Oklahoma (PCL)	2B-DH-3B-1B	61	262	57	86	21	6	3	38	26	55	1	3	10-0	.328	.387	.557	.944	10	.967
—Baltimore (A.L.)	OF-DH-1B	95	373	66	116	15	7	8	54	27	72	4	4	11-1	.311	.361	.453	.814	5	.960
2005—Ottawa (Int'l)	OF	11	41	11	15	4	0	1	8	2	6	1	0	2-0	.366	.400	.537	.937	0	1.000
—Baltimore (A.L.)	OF-3B-DH	96	218	31	44	9	0	5	21	22	45	2	2	9-2	.202	.279	.312	.591	1	.990
2006—Bowie (East.)		6	17	4	4	0	0	0	3	4	3	1	1	1-0	.235	.409	.353	.762	2	.800
—Baltimore (A.L.)	OF-1B-DH	39	131	14	33	4	0	4	18	7	22	2	4	4-2	.252	.294	.374	.668	2	.972
American League totals (3 years)		230	722	111	193	28	7	17	93	56	139	8	10	24-5	.267	.324	.396	.720	8	.974
National League totals (3 years)		63	86	17	14	3	0	3	9	10	24	0	2	2-1	.163	.247	.302	.550	2	.981
Major League totals (6 years)		293	808	128	207	31	7	20	102	66	163	8	12	26-6	.256	.315	.386	.702	10	.975

2006 LEFTY-RIGHTY SPLITS

vs.	Avg.	AB	H	2B	3B	HR	RBI	BB	SO	OBP	Slg.	vs.	Avg.	AB	H	2B	3B	HR	RBI	BB	SO	OBP	Slg.
L	.182	22	4	0	0	1	3	1	6	.250	.318	R	.266	109	29	4	0	3	15	6	16	.303	.385

NIEKRO, LANCE — 3B

PERSONAL: Born January 29, 1979, in Winter Haven, Fla. ... 6-3/210. ... Bats right, throws right. ... Full name: Lance Joseph Niekro. ... High school: George Jenkins (Lakeland, Florida). ... College: Florida Southern. ... Son of Joe Niekro, pitcher with seven major league teams (1967-88); nephew of Phil Niekro, pitcher with four major league teams (1964-87). **TRANSACTIONS/CAREER NOTES:** Selected by Philadelphia Phillies organization in 13th round of 1997 free-agent draft; did not sign. ... Selected by San Francisco Giants organization in second round of 2000 free-agent draft. ... On disabled list (March 26-April 10, 2004). ... On bereavement list (April 17-20, 2006). ... On disabled list (May 15-30, 2006). ... On disabled list (June 13-28, 2006); included rehabilitation assignment to Fresno.

2006 GAMES PLAYED BY POSITION (MLB): 1B—58.

Year	Team (League)	Pos.	G	AB	R	H	2B	3B	HR	RBI	BB	SO	HBP	GDP	SB-CS	Avg.	OBP	SLG	OPS	E	Avg.
2000—Salem-Keizer (N'west)	3B-3B	49	196	27	71	14	4	5	44	11	25	4	6	2-0	.362	.404	.551	.955	5	.939
2001—San Jose (Calif.)	3B-1B	42	163	18	47	11	0	3	34	4	14	0	2	4-2	.288	.298	.411	.709	8	.927
2002—Shreveport (Texas)	1B-1B-3B-3B	79	297	33	92	20	1	4	34	7	32	2	11	0-2	.310	.327	.424	.751	11	.979
2003—Fresno (PCL)	3B-1B-3B-1B-DH	98	381	43	115	15	2	4	41	19	39	1	12	3-3	.302	.334	.383	.717	15	.954
—San Francisco (N.L.)	1B	5	5	2	1	1	0	0	2	0	1	0	0	0-0	.200	.200	.400	.600	0	1.000

Year Team (League)	Pos.	G	AB	R	H	2B	3B	HR	RBI	BB	SO	HBP	GDP	SB-CS	Avg.	OBP	SLG	OPS	E	Avg.
2004—San Jose (Calif.)	1B	15	61	13	19	7	1	1	14	2	5	0	5	0-0	.311	.328	.508	.836	1	.997
—Fresno (PCL)	1B-3B	67	241	42	72	21	4	12	47	14	32	1	5	1-1	.299	.339	.568	.907	6	.992
2005—Fresno (PCL)	1B	1	4	0	1	0	0	0	0	0	1	0	0	0-0	.250	.250	.250	.500	0	1.000
—San Francisco (N.L.)	1B-DH	113	278	32	70	16	3	12	46	17	53	2	11	0-2	.252	.295	.460	.755	5	.991
2006—Fresno (PCL)		36	144	27	46	7	0	14	34	7	23	0	5	0-0	.319	.348	.660	1.008	6	.979
—San Francisco (N.L.)	1B	66	199	27	49	9	2	5	31	11	32	0	7	0-0	.246	.286	.387	.673	5	.989
Major League totals (3 years)		184	482	61	120	26	5	17	79	28	86	2	18	0-2	.249	.290	.429	.720	10	.990

2006 LEFTY-RIGHTY SPLITS

vs.	Avg.	AB	H	2B	3B	HR	RBI	BB	SO	OBP	Slg.	vs.	Avg.	AB	H	2B	3B	HR	RBI	BB	SO	OBP	Slg.
L	.246	61	15	6	1	1	8	2	11	.270	.426	R	.246	138	34	3	1	4	23	9	21	.293	.370

NIEVE, FERNANDO — P

PERSONAL: Born July 15, 1982, in Puerto Cabello, Venezuela. ... 6-0/195. ... Throws right, bats right. ... Full name: Fernando Alexis Nieve. **TRANSACTIONS/CAREER NOTES:** Signed as a non-drafted free agent by Houston Astros organization (May 11, 1999). ... On disabled list (August 20-September 6, 2006).
CAREER HITTING: 2-for-16 (.125), 0 R, 0 2B, 0 3B, 0 HR, 1 RBI.

Year Team (League)	W	L	Pct.	ERA	WHIP	G	GS	CG	ShO	Hld.	Sv.-Opp.	IP	H	R	ER	HR	BB-IBB	SO	Avg.
1999—La Pradera (VSL)	0	6	.000	4.55	1.47	11	7	0	0	...	0-...	32.0	31	22	16	0	16-0	41	...
2000—Venoco (VSL)	3	4	.429	2.71	1.05	14	13	0	0	...	0-...	79.2	56	29	24	5	28-0	64	.199
2001—Martinsville (App.)	4	2	.667	3.79	1.26	12	8	1	0	...	0-...	38.0	27	20	16	2	21-0	49	.197
2002—Martinsville (App.)	4	1	.800	2.39	1.08	13	13	0	0	...	0-...	67.2	46	23	18	5	27-0	60	.185
—Lexington (S. Atl.)	0	1	.000	6.00	2.00	1	1	0	0	...	0-...	3.0	6	5	2	0	0-0	2	.353
2003—Lexington (S. Atl.)	14	9	.609	3.65	1.32	28	28	1	0	...	0-...	150.1	133	69	61	10	65-0	144	.238
2004—Salem (Carol.)	10	6	.625	2.96	1.18	24	24	2	2	...	0-...	149.0	136	52	49	9	40-0	117	.251
—Round Rock (Texas)	2	0	1.000	1.56	1.15	3	3	0	0	...	0-...	17.1	12	4	3	0	8-0	17	.203
2005—Corpus Christi (Texas)	4	3	.571	2.65	1.07	14	14	0	0	0	0-0	85.0	62	27	25	7	29-0	96	.205
—Round Rock (PCL)	4	4	.500	4.83	1.52	13	13	2	2	0	0-0	82.0	92	45	44	10	33-0	75	.281
2006—Round Rock (PCL)	0	0	...	0.00	0.38	4	0	0	0	0	2-2	5.1	2	0	0	0	4-0	7	.105
—Houston (N.L.)	3	3	.500	4.20	1.33	40	11	0	0	0	0-0	96.1	87	46	45	18	41-5	70	.242
Major League totals (1 year)	3	3	.500	4.20	1.33	40	11	0	0	0	0-0	96.1	87	46	45	18	41-5	70	.242

2006 LEFTY-RIGHTY SPLITS

vs.	Avg.	AB	H	2B	3B	HR	RBI	BB	SO	OBP	Slg.	vs.	Avg.	AB	H	2B	3B	HR	RBI	BB	SO	OBP	Slg.
L	.262	164	43	7	0	8	19	29	27	.373	.451	R	.224	196	44	13	1	10	30	12	43	.272	.454

NIEVES, WIL — C

PERSONAL: Born September 25, 1977, in San Juan, Puerto Rico. ... 5-11/190. ... Bats right, throws right. ... Full name: Wilbert Nieves. ... Name pronounced: nee-AY-vas. ... Brother of Melvin Nieves, outfielder with four major league teams (1992-98). **TRANSACTIONS/CAREER NOTES:** Selected by San Diego Padres organization in 47th round of 1995 free-agent draft. ... Claimed on waivers by Anaheim Angels (December 18, 2002). ... Angels franchise renamed Los Angeles Angels of Anaheim for 2005 season. ... Traded by Angels to New York Yankees for P Bret Prinz (March 29, 2005).
2006 GAMES PLAYED BY POSITION (MLB): C—6.

Year Team (League)	Pos.	G	AB	R	H	2B	3B	HR	RBI	BB	SO	HBP	GDP	SB-CS	Avg.	OBP	SLG	OPS	E	Avg.
1996—Ariz. Padres (Ariz.)	C-3B-OF	43	113	23	39	5	0	2	22	13	19	0	1	3-4	.345	.413	.442	.855	10	.960
1997—Ariz. Padres (Ariz.)	C-OF-3B	8	27	2	8	2	0	0	2	5	5	0	0	2-1	.296	.406	.370	.776	0	1.000
—Clinton (Midw.)	C	18	55	6	12	1	1	1	7	6	10	0	0	2-1	.218	.290	.327	.617	7	.952
1998—Clinton (Midw.)	C	115	380	47	97	22	0	3	55	47	69	7	16	7-9	.255	.343	.337	.680	14	.982
1999—Rancho Cuca. (Calif.)	C	120	427	58	140	26	2	7	61	40	54	5	12	2-7	.328	.389	.447	.836	5	.995
2000—Las Vegas (PCL)	C	1	1	0	0	0	0	0	0	0	0	0	0	0-0	.000	.000	.000	.000	0	...
—Mobile (Sou.)	C-1B-2B	68	214	18	57	4	0	4	30	16	22	1	9	1-1	.266	.319	.341	.660	4	.991
—Rancho Cuca. (Calif.)	C-C	31	101	16	26	5	0	0	9	15	17	0	3	2-0	.257	.350	.307	.657	5	.984
2001—Mobile (Sou.)	C-1B-2B	95	330	28	99	24	0	3	41	18	40	2	8	1-0	.300	.336	.400	.736	3	.996
2002—Portland (PCL)	C-1B	70	237	24	73	20	2	7	29	5	40	0	7	0-0	.308	.321	.498	.819	3	.993
—San Diego (N.L.)	C	28	72	2	13	3	1	0	3	4	15	0		1-0	.181	.224	.250	.474	5	.971
2003—Salt Lake (PCL)	C-1B-3B	102	361	48	102	16	2	4	38	25	53	1	8	1-2	.283	.327	.371	.698	8	.988
2004—Salt Lake (PCL)	C-1B-3B	108	421	60	125	22	8	10	53	12	64	0	11	3-6	.297	.316	.458	.774	7	.993
2005—Columbus (Int'l)	C-DH	102	380	45	110	22	3	4	37	13	38	2	16	1-1	.289	.313	.395	.707	7	.991
—New York (A.L.)	C	3	4	0	0	0	0	0	0	0	1	0	0	0-0	.000	.000	.000	.000	0	1.000
2006—Columbus (Int'l)		88	321	29	83	13	0	5	34	18	29	1	13	2-1	.259	.298	.346	.644	13	.979
—New York (A.L.)	C	6	6	0	0	0	0	0	0	0	1	0	0	0-0	.000	.000	.000	.000	0	1.000
American League totals (2 years)		9	10	0	0	0	0	0	0	0	2	0	0	0-0	.000	.000	.000	.000	0	1.000
National League totals (1 year)		28	72	2	13	3	1	0	3	4	15	0		1-0	.181	.224	.250	.474	5	.971
Major League totals (3 years)		37	82	2	13	3	1	0	3	4	17	0		1-0	.159	.198	.220	.417	5	.975

2006 LEFTY-RIGHTY SPLITS

vs.	Avg.	AB	H	2B	3B	HR	RBI	BB	SO	OBP	Slg.	vs.	Avg.	AB	H	2B	3B	HR	RBI	BB	SO	OBP	Slg.
L	.000	2	0	0	0	0	0	0	1	.000	.000	R	.000	4	0	0	0	0	0	0	0	.000	.000

NIPPERT, DUSTIN — P

PERSONAL: Born May 6, 1981, in Wheeling, W.Va. ... 6-7/217. ... Throws right, bats right. ... Full name: Dustin David Nippert. ... High school: Beallsville (Ohio). ... College: Ohio Valley College (Vienna, W. Va.), then West Virginia. **TRANSACTIONS/CAREER NOTES:** Selected by Arizona Diamondbacks organization in 15th round of 2002 free-agent draft.
CAREER HITTING: 1-for-6 (.167), 0 R, 0 2B, 0 3B, 0 HR, 0 RBI.

Year Team (League)	W	L	Pct.	ERA	WHIP	G	GS	CG	ShO	Hld.	Sv.-Opp.	IP	H	R	ER	HR	BB-IBB	SO	Avg.
2002—Missoula (Pion.)	4	2	.667	1.65	0.93	17	11	0	0	...	0-...	54.2	42	12	10	2	9-0	77	.208
2003—South Bend (Mid.)	6	4	.600	2.82	1.02	17	17	0	0	...	0-...	95.2	66	32	30	4	32-3	96	.191
2004—El Paso (Texas)	2	5	.286	3.64	1.63	14	14	0	0	...	0-...	71.2	77	45	29	0	40-1	73	.273
2005—Tennessee (Sou.)	8	3	.727	2.38	1.17	18	18	3	2	...	0-0	117.1	95	33	31	4	42-1	97	.226
—Missoula (Pion.)	1	1	.500	6.56	1.57	15	3	0	0	3	0-0	35.2	44	27	26	4	12-0	35	.291
—Arizona (N.L.)	1	0	1.000	5.52	1.57	3	3	0	0	0	0-0	14.2	10	9	9	1	13-0	11	.185
2006—Arizona (N.L.)	0	2	.000	11.70	2.20	2	2	0	0	0	0-0	10.0	15	13	13	5	7-0	9	.349
Major League totals (2 years)	1	2	.333	8.03	1.82	5	5	0	0	0	0-0	24.2	25	22	22	6	20-0	20	.258

N

vs.	Avg.	AB	H	2B	3B	HR	RBI	BB	SO	OBP	Slg.	vs.	Avg.	AB	H	2B	3B	HR	RBI	BB	SO	OBP	Slg.
L	.333	27	9	1	0	4	9	4	7	.419	.815	R	.375	16	6	1	0	1	4	3	2	.474	.625

NIX, LAYNCE — OF

PERSONAL: Born October 30, 1980, in Houston. ... 6-0/200. ... Bats left, throws left. ... Full name: Laynce Michael Nix. ... Name pronounced: nicks. ... High school: Midland (Texas). **TRANSACTIONS/CAREER NOTES:** Selected by Texas Rangers organization in fourth round of 2000 free-agent draft. ... On disabled list (June 14-July 10, 2004); included rehabilitation assignment to Frisco. ... On disabled list (July 17, 2005-remainder of season). ... Traded by Rangers with OF Kevin Mench and Ps Francisco Cordero and Julian Cordero to Milwaukee Brewers for OFs Carlos Lee and Nelson Cruz (July 28, 2006). ... On disabled list (September 9, 2006-remainder of season).

2006 GAMES PLAYED BY POSITION (MLB): OF—18.

										BATTING								FIELDING	
Year	Team (League)	Pos.	G	AB	R	H	2B	3B	HR	RBI	BB	SO	HBP	GDP	SB-CS	Avg.	OBP	SLG	OPS	E	Avg.
2000—GC Rangers (GCL)	OF	51	199	34	45	7	1	2	25	23	37	2	3	4-2	.226	.307	.302	.609	1	.991
2001—Savannah (S. Atl.)	OF	104	407	50	113	26	8	8	59	37	94	2	1	9-6	.278	.337	.440	.777	4	.976
—Charlotte (Fla. St.)	OF	9	37	4	11	3	1	0	2	1	13	0	2	0-0	.297	.316	.432	.748	0	1.000
2002—Charlotte (Fla. St.)	OF	137	512	86	146	27	3	21	110	72	105	6	9	17-1	.285	.374	.473	.847	3	.988
2003—Frisco (Texas)	OF-DH	87	335	52	95	23	0	15	63	34	68	0	4	9-2	.284	.344	.487	.831	3	.984
—Texas (A.L.)	OF-DH	53	184	25	47	10	0	8	30	9	53	0	1	3-0	.255	.289	.440	.729	5	.963
2004—Frisco (Texas)	OF	7	26	2	7	1	0	0	2	1	10	0	1	0-1	.269	.296	.308	.604	0	1.000
—Texas (A.L.)	OF	115	371	58	92	20	4	14	46	23	113	2	6	1-1	.248	.293	.437	.730	1	.996
2005—Oklahoma (PCL)	OF	10	36	8	12	1	1	3	6	9	6	0	0	0-1	.333	.467	.667	1.133	0	1.000
—Texas (A.L.)	OF	63	229	28	55	12	3	6	32	9	45	0	3	2-0	.240	.267	.397	.664	2	.988
2006—Texas (A.L.)	OF	9	32	1	3	1	0	0	4	0	17	1	0	0-0	.094	.118	.125	.243	0	1.000
—Oklahoma (PCL)		77	286	39	77	14	1	10	55	18	77	6	2	4-1	.269	.323	.490	.753	2	.986
—Nashville (PCL)		18	68	16	28	5	1	7	13	4	18	1	0	0-0	.412	.452	.824	1.276	0	1.000
—Milwaukee (N.L.)	OF	10	35	2	8	1	0	1	6	0	11	1	1	0-0	.229	.250	.343	.593	0	1.000
American League totals (4 years)		240	816	112	197	43	7	28	112	41	228	3	10	6-1	.241	.278	.414	.692	8	.986
National League totals (1 year)		10	35	2	8	1	0	1	6	0	11	1	1	0-0	.229	.250	.343	.593	0	1.000
Major League totals (4 years)		250	851	114	205	44	7	29	118	41	239	4	11	6-1	.241	.277	.411	.688	8	.986

vs.	Avg.	AB	H	2B	3B	HR	RBI	BB	SO	OBP	Slg.	vs.	Avg.	AB	H	2B	3B	HR	RBI	BB	SO	OBP	Slg.
L	.125	8	1	0	0	0	3	0	5	.125	.125	R	.169	59	10	2	0	1	7	0	23	.194	.254

NIXON, TROT — OF

PERSONAL: Born April 11, 1974, in Durham, N.C. ... 6-2/211. ... Bats left, throws left. ... Full name: Christopher Trotman Nixon. ... High school: New Hanover (Wilmington, N.C.). **TRANSACTIONS/CAREER NOTES:** Selected by Boston Red Sox organization in first round (seventh pick overall) of 1993 free-agent draft. ... On disabled list (June 27-July 25, 2000); included rehabilitation assignment to GCL Red Sox. ... On disabled list (March 26-June 16 and July 25-September 7, 2004); included rehabilitation assignments to Pawtucket. ... On suspended list (May 3-5, 2005). ... On disabled list (July 27-August 23, 2005); included rehabilitation assignment to Pawtucket. ... On disabled list (July 31-September 3, 2006); included rehabilitation assignment to Pawtucket. **STATISTICAL NOTES:** Hit three home runs in one game (July 24, 1999). ... Career major league grand slams: 8.

2006 GAMES PLAYED BY POSITION (MLB): OF—110.

										BATTING								FIELDING	
Year	Team (League)	Pos.	G	AB	R	H	2B	3B	HR	RBI	BB	SO	HBP	GDP	SB-CS	Avg.	OBP	SLG	OPS	E	Avg.
1994—Lynchburg (Caro.)	OF	71	264	33	65	12	0	12	43	44	53	3	5	10-3	.246	.357	.428	.785	4	.974
1995—Sarasota (Fla. St.)	OF	73	264	43	80	11	4	5	39	45	46	1	5	7-5	.303	.404	.432	.836	2	.986
—Trenton (East.)	OF	25	94	9	15	3	1	2	8	7	20	0	0	2-1	.160	.214	.277	.490	0	1.000
1996—Trenton (East.)	OF-DH	123	438	55	110	11	4	11	63	50	65	3	6	7-9	.251	.329	.370	.698	5	.979
—Boston (A.L.)	OF	2	4	2	2	1	0	0	0	0	1	0	0	1-0	.500	.500	.750	1.250	0	1.000
1997—Pawtucket (Int'l)	OF	130	475	80	116	18	3	20	61	63	86	1	11	11-4	.244	.331	.421	.753	4	.986
1998—Pawtucket (Int'l)	OF-DH-1B	135	509	97	158	26	4	23	74	76	81	5	10	26-13	.310	.400	.513	.913	11	.957
—Boston (A.L.)	OF-DH	13	27	3	7	1	0	0	0	1	3	0	0	0-0	.259	.286	.296	.582	0	1.000
1999—Boston (A.L.)	OF	124	381	67	103	22	5	15	52	53	75	3	7	3-1	.270	.357	.472	.830	7	.968
2000—Boston (A.L.)	OF-DH	123	427	66	118	27	8	12	60	63	85	2	11	8-1	.276	.368	.461	.830	2	.991
—GC Red Sox (GCL)	OF	3	10	3	4	0	0	1	5	2	0	1	0	0-0	.400	.538	.700	1.238	0	1.000
2001—Boston (A.L.)	OF-DH	148	535	100	150	31	4	27	88	79	113	7	8	7-4	.280	.376	.505	.881	8	.973
2002—Boston (A.L.)	OF	152	532	81	136	36	3	24	94	65	109	5	7	4-2	.256	.338	.470	.808	5	.984
2003—Boston (A.L.)	OF	134	441	81	135	24	6	28	87	65	96	3	4	4-2	.306	.396	.578	.975	4	.983
2004—Sarasota (Fla. St.)	OF	1	3	1	2	1	0	0	1	0	0	0	0	0-0	.667	.667	1.000	1.667	0	...
—Pawtucket (Int'l)	OF	6	21	2	7	1	0	0	2	3	2	0	0	0-0	.333	.381	.381	.772	1	.750
—Boston (A.L.)	OF-DH	48	149	24	47	9	1	6	23	15	24	1	3	0-0	.315	.377	.510	.887	1	.985
2005—Pawtucket (Int'l)	OF-DH	2	6	3	3	0	0	1	2	2	2	0	0	0-0	.500	.556	1.000	1.556	0	1.000
—Boston (A.L.)	OF	124	408	64	112	29	1	13	67	53	59	3	7	2-1	.275	.357	.446	.804	1	.996
2006—Pawtucket (Int'l)		3	12	2	2	1	0	0	0	0	6	0	0	0-0	.167	.167	.250	.417	0	1.000
—Boston (A.L.)	OF	114	381	59	102	24	0	8	52	60	56	7	10	0-2	.268	.373	.394	.767	1	.995
Major League totals (10 years)		982	3285	547	912	204	28	133	523	454	621	31	56	29-13	.278	.366	.478	.845	29	.984

DIVISION SERIES RECORD

Year	Team (League)	Pos.	G	AB	R	H	2B	3B	HR	RBI	BB	SO	HBP	GDP	SB-CS	Avg.	OBP	SLG	OPS	E	Avg.
1998—Boston (A.L.)	OF	2	3	0	1	0	0	0	0	1	0	0	0	0-0	.333	.500	.333	.833	0	1.000
1999—Boston (A.L.)	OF	5	14	5	3	3	0	0	6	4	5	0	0	0-0	.214	.350	.429	.779	0	1.000
2003—Boston (A.L.)	OF	4	10	1	2	0	0	1	2	1	3	0	0	0-0	.200	.273	.500	.773	0	1.000
2004—Boston (A.L.)	OF	2	8	0	2	0	0	0	2	2	1	0	1	0-0	.250	.400	.250	.650	0	1.000
2005—Boston (A.L.)	OF	3	11	1	3	0	0	0	1	1	1	0	0	0-0	.273	.333	.273	.606	0	1.000
Division series totals (5 years)		16	46	7	11	3	0	1	11	9	10	0	1	0-0	.239	.351	.370	.720	0	1.000

CHAMPIONSHIP SERIES RECORD

Year	Team (League)	Pos.	G	AB	R	H	2B	3B	HR	RBI	BB	SO	HBP	GDP	SB-CS	Avg.	OBP	SLG	OPS	E	Avg.
1999—Boston (A.L.)	OF	4	14	2	4	0	0	0	0	1	5	0	0	0-0	.286	.333	.429	.762	0	1.000
2003—Boston (A.L.)	OF	7	24	3	8	1	0	3	5	3	7	1	1	1-2	.333	.429	.750	1.179	0	1.000
2004—Boston (A.L.)	OF	7	29	4	6	1	0	1	3	0	5	0	0	0-0	.207	.207	.345	.552	0	1.000
Champ. series totals (3 years)		18	67	9	18	4	0	4	8	4	17	1	1	1-2	.269	.319	.507	.827	0	1.000

WORLD SERIES RECORD

Year	Team (League)	Pos.	G	AB	R	H	2B	3B	HR	RBI	BB	SO	HBP	GDP	SB-CS	Avg.	OBP	SLG	OPS	E	Avg.
2004—Boston (A.L.)	OF	4	14	1	5	3	0	0	3	1	1	0	0	0-0	.357	.400	.571	.971	0	1.000

vs.	Avg.	AB	H	2B	3B	HR	RBI	BB	SO	OBP	Slg.	vs.	Avg.	AB	H	2B	3B	HR	RBI	BB	SO	OBP	Slg.
L	.204	93	19	4	0	2	10	16	20	.336	.312	R	.288	288	83	20	0	6	42	44	36	.385	.420

NOLASCO, RICKY — P

PERSONAL: Born December 13, 1982, in Corona, Calif. ... 6-2/220. ... Throws right, bats right. ... Full name: Carlos Enrique Nolasco. **TRANSACTIONS/CAREER NOTES:** Selected by Chicago Cubs organization in fourth round of 2001 free-agent draft. ... Traded by Cubs with Ps Sergio Mitre and Renyel Pinto to Florida Marlins for OF Juan Pierre (December 7, 2005).
CAREER HITTING: 7-for-41 (.171), 2 R, 0 2B, 0 3B, 1 HR, 5 RBI.

Year	Team (League)	W	L	Pct.	ERA	WHIP	G	GS	CG	ShO	Hld.	Sv.-Opp.	IP	H	R	ER	HR	BB-IBB	SO	Avg.
2001—Ariz. Cubs (Ariz.)		1	0	1.000	1.50	0.89	5	4	0	0	...	0-...	18.0	11	3	3	0	5-0	23	.175
2002—Boise (N'west)		7	2	.778	2.48	1.07	15	15	0	0	...	0-...	90.2	72	32	25	1	25-0	92	.214
2003—Daytona (Fla. St.)		11	5	.688	2.96	1.19	26	26	1	0	...	0-...	149.0	129	58	49	7	48-0	136	.232
2004—Iowa (PCL)		2	3	.400	9.30	2.07	9	9	0	0	...	0-...	40.2	68	42	42	7	16-1	28	.393
—West Tenn (Sou.)		6	4	.600	3.70	1.32	19	19	0	0	...	0-...	107.0	104	50	44	13	37-3	115	.260
2005—West Tenn (Sou.)		14	3	.824	2.89	1.22	27	27	1	0	0	0-0	161.2	151	57	52	13	46-0	173	.245
2006—Florida (N.L.)		11	11	.500	4.82	1.41	35	22	0	0	2	0-0	140.0	157	86	75	20	41-5	99	.286
Major League totals (1 year)		11	11	.500	4.82	1.41	35	22	0	0	2	0-0	140.0	157	86	75	20	41-5	99	.286

vs.	Avg.	AB	H	2B	3B	HR	RBI	BB	SO	OBP	Slg.	vs.	Avg.	AB	H	2B	3B	HR	RBI	BB	SO	OBP	Slg.
L	.338	260	88	12	3	12	49	24	35	.390	.546	R	.240	288	69	13	2	8	27	17	64	.302	.382

NORTON, GREG — 3B/1B

PERSONAL: Born July 6, 1972, in San Leandro, Calif. ... 6-1/200. ... Bats both, throws right. ... Full name: Gregory Blakemoor Norton. ... High school: Bishop O'Dowd (Oakland). ... College: Oklahoma. ... Son of Jerry Norton, outfielder with Pittsburgh Pirates organization. **TRANSACTIONS/CAREER NOTES:** Selected by San Francisco Giants organization in seventh round of 1990 free-agent draft; did not sign. ... Selected by Chicago White Sox organization in second round of 1993 free-agent draft. ... Signed as a free agent by Colorado Rockies (January 5, 2001). ... On disabled list (June 30-July 18, 2002); included rehabilitation assignment to Colorado Springs. ... Signed by Detroit Tigers organization (January 14, 2004). ... On disabled list (June 18-July 25, 2004); included rehabilitation assignment to Toledo. ... Signed as a free agent by Rockies (December 21, 2004). ... Signed as a free agent by White Sox organization (April 21, 2005). ... Signed as a free agent by Tampa Bay Devil Rays organization (January 11, 2006). **STATISTICAL NOTES:** Career major league grand slams: 2.
2006 GAMES PLAYED BY POSITION (MLB): DH—31, OF—31, 1B—25.

Year	Team (League)	Pos.	G	AB	R	H	2B	3B	HR	RBI	BB	SO	HBP	GDP	SB-CS	Avg.	OBP	SLG	OPS	E	Avg.
1993—GC Whi. Sox (GCL)	3B	3	9	1	2	0	0	0	2	1	1	0	0	0-0	.222	.300	.222	.522	0	1.000
—Hickory (S. Atl.)	3B-SS	71	254	36	62	12	2	4	36	41	44	1	6	0-2	.244	.347	.354	.701	17	.928
1994—South Bend (Mid.)	3B	127	477	73	137	22	2	6	64	62	71	2	7	5-3	.287	.369	.379	.749	30	.922
1995—Birmingham (Sou.)	3B	133	469	65	117	23	2	6	60	64	90	5	10	19-12	.249	.339	.345	.685	25	.938
1996—Birmingham (Sou.)	3B	76	287	40	81	14	3	8	44	33	55	1	5	5-5	.282	.357	.436	.793	17	.949
—Nashville (A.A.) SS-3B-DH		43	164	28	47	14	2	7	26	17	42	0	1	2-3	.287	.356	.524	.874	13	.914
—Chicago (A.L.) SS-3B-DH		11	23	4	5	0	0	1	3	4	6	0	0	0-1	.217	.333	.478	.812	2	.867
1997—Nashville (A.A.) 3B-SS-2B																				
	DH	114	414	82	114	27	1	26	76	57	101	4	9	3-5	.275	.366	.534	.900	38	.897
—Chicago (A.L.)	3B-DH	18	34	9	9	2	2	0	2	8	0	0	0	.265	.306	.441	.747	3	.864
1998—Chicago (A.L.) 1B-3B-DH																				
	2B	105	299	38	71	17	2	9	36	26	77	2	11	3-3	.237	.301	.398	.699	6	.991
1999—Chicago (A.L.) 3B-1B-DH		132	436	62	111	26	0	16	50	69	93	2	11	4-4	.255	.358	.424	.782	27	.931
2000—Chicago (A.L.) 3B-1B-DH		71	201	25	49	6	1	6	28	26	47	2	2	1-0	.244	.333	.373	.706	8	.960
—Charlotte (Int'l) 3B-1B-SS		29	97	18	28	4	0	5	17	24	23	2	0	1-0	.289	.435	.485	.920	1	.991
2001—Colorado (N.L.) OF-3B-1B																				
	DH	117	225	30	60	13	2	13	40	19	65	0	6	1-0	.267	.321	.516	.837	4	.968
2002—Colorado (N.L.) 3B-1B-OF		113	168	19	37	8	1	7	37	24	52	0	4	2-3	.220	.314	.405	.719	5	.955
—Colo. Springs (PCL) 1B-3B		3	12	2	1	0	0	0	0	3	5	0	0	0-0	.083	.267	.083	.350	1	1.000
2003—Colorado (N.L.) 3B-1B-OF		114	179	19	47	15	0	6	31	16	47	1	4	2-1	.263	.325	.447	.772	6	.941
2004—Detroit (A.L.) 3B-1B-DH																				
	OF	41	86	9	15	0	2	2	12	12	21	0	3	0-0	.174	.276	.256	.531	1	.985
—Toledo (Int'l)	3B-1B	53	184	26	38	6	1	4	16	24	48	0	4	1-1	.207	.297	.315	.612	4	.978
2005—Charlotte (Int'l) 3B-DH-1B		90	330	57	94	19	1	17	56	47	67	1	12	0-2	.285	.374	.503	.877	9	.955
2006—Durham (Int'l)		3	9	0	1	0	0	0	1	1	3	0	0	0-0	.111	.200	.111	.311	0	1.000
—Tampa Bay (A.L.) OF-DH-1B		98	294	47	87	15	0	17	45	35	69	3	2	1-5	.296	.374	.520	.895	3	.986
American League totals (7 years)		476	1373	190	347	67	5	52	165	174	321	9	29	9-13	.253	.339	.422	.761	50	.969
National League totals (3 years)		344	572	68	144	36	3	26	108	59	164	1	14	5-4	.252	.320	.462	.782	15	.955
Major League totals (10 years)		820	1945	258	491	103	8	78	273	233	485	10	43	14-17	.252	.333	.434	.767	65	.967

vs.	Avg.	AB	H	2B	3B	HR	RBI	BB	SO	OBP	Slg.	vs.	Avg.	AB	H	2B	3B	HR	RBI	BB	SO	OBP	Slg.
L	.283	60	17	1	0	3	10	12	16	.411	.450	R	.299	234	70	14	0	14	35	23	53	.364	.538

NOVOA, ROBERTO — P

PERSONAL: Born August 15, 1979, in Las Matas de Farfan, Dominican Republic. ... 6-5/200. ... Throws right, bats right. **TRANSACTIONS/CAREER NOTES:** Signed as a non-drafted free agent by Pittsburgh Pirates organization (July 3, 1999). ... Traded by Pirates to Detroit Tigers (December 17, 2002), as part of deal in which Pirates acquired 1B Randall Simon for P Adrian Burnside and two players to be named (November 25, 2002); Tigers acquired 3B Kody Kirkland to complete deal (May 24, 2003). ... Traded by Tigers with SS Scott Moore and OF Bo Flowers to Chicago Cubs for P Kyle Farnsworth (February 9, 2005).
CAREER HITTING: 1-for-6 (.167), 0 R, 1 2B, 0 3B, 0 HR, 1 RBI.

Year	Team (League)	W	L	Pct.	ERA	WHIP	G	GS	CG	ShO	Hld.	Sv.-Opp.	IP	H	R	ER	HR	BB-IBB	SO	Avg.
2000—Dom. Pirates (DSL)		4	6	.400	4.15	1.55	13	13	1	0	...	0-...	82.1	99	65	38	5	29-...	44	
2001—Will. (NYP)		5	5	.500	3.39	1.21	14	13	1	0	...	0-...	79.2	76	40	30	4	20-0	55	.255
2002—Hickory (S. Atl.)		1	5	.167	5.48	1.78	10	10	0	0	...	0-...	42.2	61	30	26	2	15-0	29	.335
—Will. (NYP)		8	3	.727	3.65	1.05	12	12	0	0	...	0-...	66.2	62	32	27	4	8-0	56	.240
2003—Lakeland (Fla. St.)		4	5	.444	3.73	1.19	19	15	2	0	...	0-...	99.0	93	45	41	8	25-0	71	.243
2004—Erie (East.)		7	0	1.000	2.96	1.03	41	0	0	0	...	4-...	79.0	63	32	26	4	18-1	59	.216
—Detroit (A.L.)		1	1	.500	5.57	1.48	16	0	0	0	3	0-1	21.0	25	15	13	4	6-0	15	.309

N

Year	Team (League)	W	L	Pct.	ERA	WHIP	G	GS	CG	ShO	Hld.	Sv.-Opp.	IP	H	R	ER	HR	BB-IBB	SO	Avg.
2005—Iowa (PCL)		2	2	.500	3.29	1.13	19	0	0	0		4-5	27.1	20	11	10	1	11-1	18	.217
—Chicago (N.L.)		4	5	.444	4.43	1.61	49	0	0	0	14	0-5	44.2	47	22	22	4	25-6	47	.264
2006—Iowa (PCL)		1	0	1.000	2.70	0.90	6	0	0	0	1	1-2	6.2	3	2	2	0	3-0	3	.136
—Chicago (N.L.)		2	1	.667	4.26	1.43	66	0	0	0	4	0-0	76.0	77	47	36	15	32-5	53	.262
American League totals (1 year)		1	1	.500	5.57	1.48	16	0	0	0	3	0-1	21.0	25	15	13	4	6-0	15	.309
National League totals (2 years)		6	6	.500	4.33	1.50	115	0	0	0	18	0-5	120.2	124	69	58	19	57-11	100	.263
Major League totals (3 years)		7	7	.500	4.51	1.50	131	0	0	0	21	0-6	141.2	149	84	71	23	63-11	115	.269

2006 LEFTY-RIGHTY SPLITS

vs.	Avg.	AB	H	2B	3B	HR	RBI	BB	SO	OBP	Slg.	vs.	Avg.	AB	H	2B	3B	HR	RBI	BB	SO	OBP	Slg.
L	.279	86	24	5	0	3	12	16	16	.404	.442	R	.255	208	53	10	1	12	36	16	37	.317	.486

NUNEZ, ABRAHAM O.　　IF

PERSONAL: Born March 16, 1976, in Santo Domingo, Dominican Republic. ... 5-11/190. ... Bats both, throws right. ... Full name: Abraham Orlando Nunez. ... Name pronounced: NOON-yez. ... High school: Emmanuel (Santo Domingo, Dominican Republic). **TRANSACTIONS/CAREER NOTES:** Signed as a non-drafted free agent by Toronto Blue Jays organization (May 5, 1994). ... Traded by Blue Jays with P Mike Halperin and C/OF Craig Wilson to Pittsburgh Pirates (December 11, 1996), completing deal in which Blue Jays traded Ps Jose Silva and Jose Pett, IF Brandon Cromer and three players to be named to Pirates for OF/1B Orlando Merced, IF Carlos Garcia and P Dan Plesac (November 14, 1996). ... Released by Pirates (November 29, 2004). ... Signed by St. Louis Cardinals organization (January 12, 2005). ... Signed as free agent by Philadelphia Phillies (November 29, 2005). **STATISTICAL NOTES:** Career major league pitching: 0-0, 0.00 ERA, 1 G, 0.1 IP, 0 H, 0 R, 0 ER, 0 BB, 0 SO.

2006 GAMES PLAYED BY POSITION (MLB): 3B—74, 2B—6, SS—3.

									BATTING											FIELDING	
Year	Team (League)	Pos.	G	AB	R	H	2B	3B	HR	RBI	BB	SO	HBP	GDP	SB-CS	Avg.	OBP	SLG	OPS	E	Avg.
1994—Dom. B. Jays (DSL)		2B	59	188	31	47	5	0	0	15	42	37	...	...	22-...	.250	...	.277	...	12	.938
1995—Dom. B. Jays (DSL)		2B	54	186	49	56	10	3	4	25	30	27	...	...	24-...	.301	...	.452	...	7	.962
1996—St. Catharines (NYP)		2B-SS	75	297	43	83	6	4	3	26	31	43	4	2	37-14	.279	.353	.357	.710	15	.962
1997—Lynchburg (Caro.)		SS	78	304	45	79	9	4	3	32	23	47	1	5	29-14	.260	.313	.345	.658	15	.955
—Carolina (Southern)		SS	47	198	31	65	6	1	1	14	20	28	0	2	10-5	.328	.385	.384	.768	11	.949
—Pittsburgh (N.L.)		SS-2B	19	40	3	9	2	2	0	6	3	10	1	1	1-0	.225	.289	.375	.664	0	1.000
1998—Nashville (PCL)		SS-2B	94	366	50	91	12	3	3	32	39	73	5	9	16-8	.249	.328	.322	.651	21	.953
—Lynchburg (Caro.)		SS-2B	5	18	2	4	1	0	0	2	3	1	0	2	1-0	.222	.333	.278	.611	1	.930
—Pittsburgh (N.L.)		SS	24	52	6	10	2	0	1	2	12	14	0	1	4-2	.192	.344	.288	.632	7	.930
1999—Pittsburgh (N.L.)		SS-2B	90	259	25	57	8	0	0	17	28	54	1	2	9-1	.220	.299	.251	.550	14	.959
—Nashville (PCL)		SS	15	58	12	18	0	0	0	3	5	8	0	2	1-0	.310	.365	.310	.675	2	.971
2000—Pittsburgh (N.L.)		SS-2B	40	91	10	20	1	0	1	8	8	14	0	3	0-0	.220	.283	.264	.547	2	.982
—Nashville (PCL)		SS-2B	90	351	49	97	11	3	3	29	36	46	1	7	20-6	.276	.344	.339	.683	13	.970
2001—Pittsburgh (N.L.)		2B-SS-3B-OF	115	301	30	79	11	4	1	21	28	53	1	0	8-2	.262	.326	.336	.662	4	.990
2002—Pittsburgh (N.L.)		2B-SS-DH	112	253	28	59	14	1	2	15	27	44	2	2	3-4	.233	.311	.320	.631	7	.977
—Nashville (PCL)		SS-2B-OF	5	18	3	4	0	0	0	2	7	0	0	1	4-1	.222	.300	.222	.522	0	1.000
2003—Pittsburgh (N.L.)		2B-SS-3B	118	311	37	77	8	7	4	35	26	53	3	8	9-3	.248	.310	.357	.667	8	.980
2004—Pittsburgh (N.L.)		2B-SS-3B-DH-P	112	182	17	43	9	0	2	13	10	36	0	1	1-3	.236	.275	.319	.593	3	.982
2005—St. Louis (N.L.)		3B-2B-SS	139	421	64	120	13	2	5	44	37	63	0	6	0-1	.285	.343	.361	.704	14	.963
2006—Philadelphia (N.L.)		3B-2B-SS	123	322	42	68	10	2	2	32	41	58	2	7	1-0	.211	.303	.273	.577	8	.963
Major League totals (10 years)			892	2232	262	542	78	18	18	193	220	399	10	38	36-16	.243	.313	.318	.631	67	.973

DIVISION SERIES RECORD

Year	Team (League)	Pos.	G	AB	R	H	2B	3B	HR	RBI	BB	SO	HBP	GDP	SB-CS	Avg.	OBP	SLG	OPS	E	Avg.
2005—St. Louis (N.L.)		3B	3	11	3	4	1	0	0	0	2	3	0	0	1-0	.364	.462	.455	.916	0	1.000

CHAMPIONSHIP SERIES RECORD

Year	Team (League)	Pos.	G	AB	R	H	2B	3B	HR	RBI	BB	SO	HBP	GDP	SB-CS	Avg.	OBP	SLG	OPS	E	Avg.
2005—St. Louis (N.L.)		3B	4	13	1	5	0	0	0	0	0	1	0	0	0-0	.385	.385	.385	.769	0	1.000

2006 LEFTY-RIGHTY SPLITS

vs.	Avg.	AB	H	2B	3B	HR	RBI	BB	SO	OBP	Slg.	vs.	Avg.	AB	H	2B	3B	HR	RBI	BB	SO	OBP	Slg.
L	.171	82	14	0	0	1	7	11	17	.274	.207	R	.225	240	54	10	2	1	25	30	41	.314	.296

NUNEZ, LEO　　P

PERSONAL: Born August 14, 1983, in Jamoa Norte, Dominican Republic. ... 6-1/160. ... Throws right, bats right. ... Full name: Leonel Nunez. **TRANSACTIONS/CAREER NOTES:** Signed as a non-drafted free agent by Pittsburgh Pirates organization (February 16, 2000). ... Traded by Pirates to Kansas City Royals for C Benito Santiago (December 16, 2004). **CAREER HITTING:** 0-for-0 (.000), 0 R, 0 2B, 0 3B, 0 HR, 0 RBI.

Year	Team (League)	W	L	Pct.	ERA	WHIP	G	GS	CG	ShO	Hld.	Sv.-Opp.	IP	H	R	ER	HR	BB-IBB	SO	Avg.
2000—Pittsburgh (DSL)		5	3	.625	2.19	1.12	14	14	1	0	...	0-...	86.0	69	26	21	0	27-0	82	...
2001—GC Pirates (GCL)		2	2	.500	4.39	1.33	10	7	1	1	...	0-...	53.1	62	28	26	4	9-0	34	.284
2002—GC Pirates (GCL)		4	2	.667	3.43	0.98	11	11	0	0	...	0-...	60.1	54	23	23	5	0-0	52	.238
—Hickory (S. Atl.)		0	0	...	0.00	2.00	1	1	0	0	...	0-...	4.0	5	0	0	0	3-0	1	.333
2003—Hickory (S. Atl.)		2	1	.667	5.59	1.51	13	7	0	0	...	0-...	48.1	59	34	30	6	14-0	37	.304
—Will. (NYP)		4	3	.571	3.05	1.12	8	8	0	0	...	0-...	38.1	31	14	13	0	12-0	41	.211
2004—Hickory (S. Atl.)		10	4	.714	3.06	1.16	27	20	3	0	...	1-...	144.0	121	53	49	16	46-0	140	.233
2005—High Desert (Calif.)		0	0	...	9.00	2.00	8	0	0	0	2	0-2	13.0	23	15	13	2	4-2	14	.377
—Wichita (Texas)		1	0	1.000	0.69	0.77	12	0	0	0	0	4-4	13.0	8	3	1	1	2-0	14	.170
—Kansas City (A.L.)		3	2	.600	7.55	1.70	41	0	0	0	0	0-1	53.2	73	45	45	9	18-2	32	.329
2006—Omaha (PCL)		2	2	.500	2.13	1.32	23	0	0	0	0	5-7	38.0	37	11	9	5	13-2	33	.255
—Wichita (Texas)		1	2	.333	4.29	1.43	15	0	0	0	0	3-6	21.0	18	10	10	3	12-1	22	.228
—Kansas City (A.L.)		0	0	...	4.73	1.50	7	0	0	0	0	0-0	13.1	15	7	7	2	5-0	7	.300
Major League totals (2 years)		3	2	.600	6.99	1.66	48	0	0	0	0	0-1	67.0	88	52	52	11	23-2	39	.324

2006 LEFTY-RIGHTY SPLITS

vs.	Avg.	AB	H	2B	3B	HR	RBI	BB	SO	OBP	Slg.	vs.	Avg.	AB	H	2B	3B	HR	RBI	BB	SO	OBP	Slg.
L	.211	19	4	0	0	0	2	4	1	.333	.211	R	.355	31	11	2	0	2	5	1	6	.412	.613

N

O'CONNOR, MIKE — P

PERSONAL: Born August 17, 1980, in Dallas, Texas. ... Throws left, bats left. ... Full name: Michael Patrick O'Connor. ... College: George Washington.
TRANSACTIONS/CAREER NOTES: Selected by Montreal Expos organization in seventh round of 2002 free-agent draft. ... Expos franchise relocated to Washington, D.C., and renamed Washington Nationals for 2005 season (December 3, 2004).
CAREER HITTING: 2-for-31 (.065), 2 R, 0 2B, 0 3B, 0 HR, 1 RBI.

Year — Team (League)	W	L	Pct.	ERA	WHIP	G	GS	CG	ShO	Hld.	Sv.-Opp.	IP	H	R	ER	HR	BB-IBB	SO	Avg.
2002— Vermont (NYP)	2	3	.400	3.14	1.21	21	0	0	0	...	4-...	43.0	25	17	15	2	27-2	66	.174
2003— Savannah (S. Atl.)	8	3	.727	3.86	1.30	42	0	0	0	...	1-...	70.0	56	36	30	6	35-1	83	.215
2004— Brevard County (FSL)	8	8	.500	4.11	1.36	26	14	0	0	...	0-...	103.0	98	51	47	5	42-0	104	.257
2005— Potomac (Carol.)	10	11	.476	3.54	1.15	26	26	2	1	0	0-0	167.2	144	73	66	14	48-0	158	.229
2006— New Orleans (PCL)	1	0	1.000	2.73	1.22	6	6	0	0	0	0-0	26.1	21	10	8	2	11-1	28	.221
— Wash. (N.L.)	3	8	.273	4.80	1.34	21	20	0	0	0	0-0	105.0	96	61	56	15	45-5	59	.244
Major League totals (1 year)	3	8	.273	4.80	1.34	21	20	0	0	0	0-0	105.0	96	61	56	15	45-5	59	.244

2006 LEFTY-RIGHTY SPLITS

vs.	Avg.	AB	H	2B	3B	HR	RBI	BB	SO	OBP	Slg.	vs.	Avg.	AB	H	2B	3B	HR	RBI	BB	SO	OBP	Slg.
L	.253	75	19	4	2	2	10	8	16	.352	.440	R	.242	318	77	13	3	13	39	37	43	.324	.425

O'FLAHERTY, ERIC — P

PERSONAL: Born February 5, 1985, in Walla Walla, Wash. ... Throws left, bats left. ... Full name: Eric G. O'Flaherty. **TRANSACTIONS/CAREER NOTES:** Selected by Seattle Mariners organization in sixth round of 2003 free-agent draft.
CAREER HITTING: 0-for-0 (.000), 0 R, 0 2B, 0 3B, 0 HR, 0 RBI.

Year — Team (League)	W	L	Pct.	ERA	WHIP	G	GS	CG	ShO	Hld.	Sv.-Opp.	IP	H	R	ER	HR	BB-IBB	SO	Avg.
2003— Ariz. Mariners (Ariz.)	3	0	1.000	1.95	0.87	13	1	0	0	...	0-...	27.2	17	10	6	1	7-1	20	.173
— Everett (N'west)	1	0	1.000	3.38	1.03	3	1	0	0	...	0-...	10.2	8	5	4	1	3-0	7	.235
2004— Wisconsin (Midw.)	3	3	.500	6.12	1.85	12	10	0	0	...	0-...	57.1	83	43	39	3	23-1	38	.344
2005— Wisconsin (Midw.)	4	4	.500	3.75	1.48	45	0	0	0	1	13-17	69.2	73	35	29	2	30-0	51	.268
2006— San Antonio (Texas)	2	2	.500	1.14	1.53	25	0	0	0	1	7-9	39.1	45	10	5	0	15-1	36	.300
— Inland Empire (Calif.)	0	1	.000	3.45	1.29	16	0	0	0	1	1-1	28.2	31	11	11	1	6-0	33	.292
— Tacoma (PCL)	1	0	1.000	0.00	1.09	2	0	0	0	0	0-0	3.2	3	0	0	0	1-0	4	.214
— Seattle (A.L.)	0	0	...	4.09	2.18	15	0	0	0	1	0-0	11.0	18	9	5	2	6-3	6	.360
Major League totals (1 year)	0	0	...	4.09	2.18	15	0	0	0	1	0-0	11.0	18	9	5	2	6-3	6	.360

2006 LEFTY-RIGHTY SPLITS

vs.	Avg.	AB	H	2B	3B	HR	RBI	BB	SO	OBP	Slg.	vs.	Avg.	AB	H	2B	3B	HR	RBI	BB	SO	OBP	Slg.
L	.238	21	5	2	0	0	1	0	3	.238	.333	R	.448	29	13	0	2	9	6	3	.543	.690

OHKA, TOMO — P

PERSONAL: Born March 18, 1976, in Kyoto, Japan. ... 6-1/200. ... Throws right, bats right. ... Full name: Tomokazu Ohka. ... Name pronounced: TOE-mo OH-kah. ... High school: Kyoto Siesio (Kyoto, Japan). **TRANSACTIONS/CAREER NOTES:** Contract purchased by Boston Red Sox from Yokohama of the Japan Central League (November 20, 1998). ... Traded by Red Sox with P Rich Rundles to Montreal Expos for P Ugueth Urbina (July 31, 2001). ... On suspended list (September 24-30, 2002). ... On disabled list (June 11-September 14, 2004). ... Expos franchise transferred to Washington, D.C., and renamed Washington Nationals for 2005 season (December 3, 2004). ... Traded by Nationals to Milwaukee Brewers for 2B Junior Spivey (June 10, 2005). ... On disabled list (May 4-July 18, 2006); included rehabilitation assignments to Brevard County and AZL Brewers. **MISCELLANEOUS NOTES:** Scored a run in only appearance as pinch runner (2003). ... Scored a run in only appearance as pinch runner (2005).
CAREER HITTING: 33-for-238 (.139), 8 R, 2 2B, 0 3B, 0 HR, 15 RBI.

Year — Team (League)	W	L	Pct.	ERA	WHIP	G	GS	CG	ShO	Hld.	Sv.-Opp.	IP	H	R	ER	HR	BB-IBB	SO	Avg.
1994— Yo. Bay. (Jp. Cn.)	1	1	.500	4.18	1.68	15	2	0	0	...	0-...	28.0	29	13	13	...	18-...	18	...
1995— Yo. Bay. (Jp. Cn.)	0	0	...	1.93	1.71	3	1	0	0	...	0-...	9.1	3	2	2	...	13-...	6	...
1996— Yo. Bay. (Jp. Cn.)	0	1	.000	9.50	2.28	14	1	0	0	...	0-...	18.0	27	19	19	...	14-...	11	...
1997—			Did not play.																
1998— Yo. Bay. (Jp. Cn.)	0	0	...	9.00	2.00	2	0	0	0	...	0-...	2.0	2	2	2	...	2-...	1	...
1999— Trenton (East.)	8	0	1.000	3.00	1.22	12	12	0	0	...	0-...	72.0	63	26	24	9	25-0	53	.233
— Pawtucket (Int'l)	7	0	1.000	1.58	1.04	12	12	1	1	...	0-...	68.1	60	17	12	5	11-0	63	.230
— Boston (A.L.)	1	2	.333	6.23	2.08	8	2	0	0	0	0-0	13.0	21	12	9	2	6-0	8	.362
2000— Pawtucket (Int'l)	9	6	.600	2.96	1.03	19	19	3	2	...	0-...	130.2	111	52	43	15	23-1	118	.232
— Boston (A.L.)	3	6	.333	3.12	1.38	13	12	0	0	0	0-0	69.1	70	25	24	7	26-0	40	.263
2001— Boston (A.L.)	2	5	.286	6.19	1.68	12	11	0	0	0	0-0	52.1	69	40	36	7	19-0	37	.317
— Pawtucket (Int'l)	2	5	.286	5.57	1.52	8	8	1	0	...	0-...	42.0	55	35	26	5	9-0	35	.322
— Montreal (N.L.)	1	4	.200	4.77	1.37	10	10	0	0	0	0-0	54.2	65	30	29	8	10-0	31	.302
2002— Montreal (N.L.)	13	8	.619	3.18	1.24	32	31	2	0	0	0-0	192.2	194	83	68	19	45-7	118	.264
2003— Montreal (N.L.)	10	12	.455	4.16	1.40	34	34	2	0	0	0-0	199.0	233	106	92	24	45-11	118	.292
2004— Montreal (N.L.)	3	7	.300	3.40	1.39	15	15	0	0	0	0-0	84.2	98	40	32	11	20-1	38	.288
2005— Wash. (N.L.)	4	3	.571	3.33	1.31	10	9	0	0	0	0-0	54.0	44	23	20	6	27-1	17	.224
— Milwaukee (N.L.)	7	6	.538	4.35	1.37	22	20	1	1	1	0-0	126.1	145	65	61	16	28-4	81	.285
2006— Brevard County (FSL)	1	0	1.000	0.00	1.22	2	2	0	0	0	0-0	10.2	12	2	0	0	1-0	10	.273
— Ariz. Brewers (Ariz.)	0	1	.000	6.00	2.33	1	1	0	0	0	0-0	3.0	7	4	2	0	0-0	0	.438
— Milwaukee (N.L.)	4	5	.444	4.82	1.37	18	18	0	0	0	0-0	97.0	98	58	52	12	35-1	50	.266
American League totals (3 years)	6	13	.316	4.61	1.57	33	25	0	0	0	0-0	134.2	160	77	69	16	51-0	85	.295
National League totals (6 years)	42	45	.483	3.94	1.34	141	137	5	1	1	0-0	808.1	877	405	354	96	210-25	453	.277
Major League totals (8 years)	48	58	.453	4.04	1.38	174	162	5	1	1	0-0	943.0	1037	482	423	112	261-25	538	.280

2006 LEFTY-RIGHTY SPLITS

vs.	Avg.	AB	H	2B	3B	HR	RBI	BB	SO	OBP	Slg.	vs.	Avg.	AB	H	2B	3B	HR	RBI	BB	SO	OBP	Slg.
L	.265	170	45	9	0	7	26	19	25	.337	.441	R	.266	199	53	12	0	5	22	16	25	.332	.402

OHMAN, WILL — P

PERSONAL: Born August 13, 1977, in Frankfurt, West Germany. ... 6-2/195. ... Throws left, bats left. ... Full name: William McDaniel Ohman. ... Name pronounced: OH-min. ... High school: Ponderos (Parker, Colo.). ... College: Pepperdine. **TRANSACTIONS/CAREER NOTES:** Selected by Chicago Cubs organization in eighth round of free-agent draft (June 2, 1998). ... On disabled list (March 15, 2002-entire season). ... On disabled list (March 28, 2003-entire season).
CAREER HITTING: 1-for-3 (.333), 0 R, 0 2B, 0 3B, 0 HR, 0 RBI.

Year — Team (League)	W	L	Pct.	ERA	WHIP	G	GS	CG	ShO	Hld.	Sv.-Opp.	IP	H	R	ER	HR	BB-IBB	SO	Avg.
1998— Will. (NYP)	4	4	.500	6.46	1.33	10	7	0	0	...	0-...	39.0	39	32	28	6	13-0	35	.260
— Rockford (Midwest)	1	1	.500	4.44	1.32	4	4	0	0	...	0-...	24.1	25	13	12	3	7-0	21	.269

O

Year	Team (League)	W	L	Pct.	ERA	WHIP	G	GS	CG	ShO	Hld.	Sv.-Opp.	IP	H	R	ER	HR	BB-IBB	SO	Avg.
1999—	Daytona (Fla. St.)	4	7	.364	3.46	1.34	31	15	2	2	...	5-...	106.2	102	59	41	11	41-1	97	.254
2000—	West Tenn. (Sou.)	6	4	.600	1.89	1.25	59	0	0	0	...	3-...	71.1	53	20	15	3	36-5	85	.200
	—Chicago (N.L.)	1	0	1.000	8.10	2.40	6	0	0	0	1	0-...	3.1	4	3	3	0	4-...	2	.308
2001—	Iowa (PCL)	5	2	.714	4.06	1.35	40	1	0	0	...	4-...	51.0	51	24	23	9	18-3	66	.259
	—Chicago (N.L.)	0	1	.000	7.71	1.71	11	0	0	0	1	0-...	11.2	14	10	10	2	6-...	12	.292
2002—	Chicago (N.L.)	Did not play.																		
2004—	Iowa (PCL)	3	3	.500	4.30	1.57	45	1	0	0	...	0-...	52.1	53	28	25	6	29-1	75	.249
2005—	Iowa (PCL)	1	0	1.000	4.15	0.69	8	0	0	0	0	1-1	8.2	4	4	4	2	2-0	12	.138
	—Chicago (N.L.)	2	2	.500	2.91	1.29	69	0	0	0	13	0-3	43.1	32	14	14	6	24-3	45	.201
2006—	Chicago (N.L.)	1	1	.500	4.13	1.30	78	0	0	0	9	0-0	65.1	51	30	30	6	34-2	74	.208
	Major League totals (4 years)	4	4	.500	4.15	1.37	164	0	0	0	24	0-3	123.2	101	57	57	14	68-5	133	.217

2006 LEFTY-RIGHTY SPLITS

vs.	Avg.	AB	H	2B	3B	HR	RBI	BB	SO	OBP	Slg.	vs.	Avg.	AB	H	2B	3B	HR	RBI	BB	SO	OBP	Slg.
L	.158	101	16	4	0	2	5	13	42	.277	.257	R	.243	144	35	7	1	4	28	21	32	.341	.389

OJEDA, MIGUEL — C

PERSONAL: Born January 29, 1975, in Sonora, Mexico. ... 6-2/190. ... Bats right, throws right. ... Full name: Miguel Arturo Ojeda. **TRANSACTIONS/CAREER NOTES:** Signed as a non-drafted free agent by Pittsburgh Pirates organization (May 28, 1993). ... Loaned by Pirates organization to Mexico City Reds of the Mexican League for the entire 1995, 1996 and 1997 seasons and part of the 1998 season. ... Traded by Pirates to Red Devils for future considerations (December 14, 1998). ... Signed as a free agent by San Diego Padres organization (January 12, 2003). ... Released by Padres (March 24, 2003). ... Contract purchased by Padres from Red Devils (May 17, 2003). ... On disabled list (August 16-September 1, 2004); included rehabilitation assignment to Portland. ... Traded by Padres with P Natanael Mateo to Seattle Mariners for C Miguel Olivo (July 30, 2005). ... Claimed on waivers by Colorado Rockies (October 11, 2005). ... Loaned by Rockies to Mexico City (June 27, 2006). ... Traded by Rockies to Texas Rangers for cash (July 30, 2006).

2006 GAMES PLAYED BY POSITION (MLB): C—29.

										BATTING										FIELDING	
Year	Team (League)	Pos.	G	AB	R	H	2B	3B	HR	RBI	BB	SO	HBP	GDP	SB-CS	Avg.	OBP	SLG	OPS	E	Avg.
1993—	GC Pirates (GCL)	C	27	97	9	27	3	1	3	11	10	18	0	1	2-0	.278	.339	.423	.762	3	.983
1994—	Welland (NYP)	C-1B-P	48	142	11	27	6	0	2	8	5	30	2	0	1-0	.190	.228	.275	.503	0	1.000
1995—	Mex. City (Mex.)		50	150	14	42	5	1	5	24	9	29	2	0	2-1	.280	.325	.427	.752	...	...
1996—	Mex. City (Mex.)		71	251	43	78	10	1	8	29	11	34	1	11	3-0	.311	.338	.454	.792	...	...
1997—	Mex. City (Mex.)		92	289	41	77	14	2	5	45	31	44	1	11	4-2	.266	.339	.381	.720	...	...
1998—	Carolina (Southern)	C	18	58	4	9	2	0	1	4	3	12	1	0	0-0	.155	.210	.241	.451	1	.991
	—Mex. City (Mex.)		68	236	39	68	11	3	5	34	21	34	3	6	3-3	.288	.352	.424	.776	...	...
1999—	Mex. City (Mex.)		89	316	60	87	17	2	10	45	51	35	2	6	5-2	.275	.375	.437	.812	...	...
2000—	Mex. City (Mex.)		92	330	59	105	25	4	25	73	43	47	1	14	1-1	.318	.396	.645	1.041	...	...
2001—	Mex. City (Mex.)		114	422	78	131	17	3	16	65	55	74	4	9	4-2	.310	.391	.479	.870	...	...
2002—	Mex. City (Mex.)		98	341	79	120	22	1	19	80	66	49	1	7	8-5	.352	.455	.589	1.044	...	...
2003—	Mex. City (Mex.)		43	159	30	52	14	2	10	41	24	23	2	7	4-1	.327	.417	.629	1.046	...	...
	—San Diego (N.L.)	C-1B	61	141	13	33	6	0	4	22	18	26	3	2	1-1	.234	.331	.362	.693	6	.982
2004—	Portland (PCL)	C	5	19	4	5	0	0	2	3	2	3	0	0	0-0	.263	.333	.579	.912	1	.974
	—San Diego (N.L.)	C	62	156	23	40	3	0	8	26	15	34	1	1	0-0	.256	.322	.429	.751	1	.996
2005—	San Diego (N.L.)	C-OF-DH	43	73	6	10	3	1	0	6	9	21	0	1	1-1	.137	.232	.205	.437	0	1.000
	—Portland (PCL)	C-OF-DH	17	57	8	11	1	0	3	5	7	16	1	0	0-0	.193	.292	.368	.661	1	.991
	—Tacoma (PCL)	C-DH-1B	9	33	7	11	1	0	3	11	1	5	1	0	0-0	.333	.371	.636	1.008	0	1.000
	—Seattle (A.L.)	C	16	29	2	5	0	0	1	3	6	3	0	0	0-1	.172	.314	.276	.590	1	.986
2006—	Oklahoma (PCL)	C	14	47	8	16	2	0	4	8	6	8	0	2	0-0	.340	.415	.383	.798	1	.991
	—Colorado (N.L.)	C	25	74	5	17	3	0	2	11	8	16	0	6	0-0	.230	.305	.351	.656	1	.993
	—Colo. Springs (PCL)		17	52	11	15	4	1	2	4	12	10	0	2	1-0	.288	.415	.519	.935	0	1.000
	—Mex. City (Mex.)		27	101	20	32	6	0	2	11	12	11	3	2	1-2	.317	.405	.436	.841	1	.994
	—Texas (A.L.)	C	5	13	0	4	2	0	0	4	0	3	0	0	0-0	.308	.308	.462	.769	0	1.000
	American League totals (2 years)		21	42	2	9	2	0	1	7	6	6	0	0	0-1	.214	.313	.333	.646	1	.990
	National League totals (4 years)		191	444	47	100	15	1	14	65	50	97	4	11	2-2	.225	.307	.358	.665	8	.990
	Major League totals (4 years)		212	486	49	109	17	1	15	72	56	103	4	11	2-3	.224	.308	.356	.664	9	.990

2006 LEFTY-RIGHTY SPLITS

vs.	Avg.	AB	H	2B	3B	HR	RBI	BB	SO	OBP	Slg.	vs.	Avg.	AB	H	2B	3B	HR	RBI	BB	SO	OBP	Slg.
L	.308	13	4	1	0	0	2	2	2	.400	.385	R	.230	74	17	4	0	2	13	6	17	.288	.365

OLIVER, DARREN — P

PERSONAL: Born October 6, 1970, in Kansas City, Mo. ... 6-2/220. ... Throws left, bats right. ... Full name: Darren Christopher Oliver. ... High school: Rio Linda (Calif.) Senior. ... Son of Bob Oliver, first baseman/outfielder with five major league teams (1965 and 1969-1975). **TRANSACTIONS/CAREER NOTES:** Selected by Texas Rangers organization in third round of 1988 free-agent draft. ... On disabled list (June 27, 1995-remainder of season). ... On disabled list (June 11-26, 1998); included rehabilitation assignment to Oklahoma City. ... Traded by Rangers with 3B Fernando Tatis and a player to be named to St. Louis Cardinals for P Todd Stottlemyre and SS Royce Clayton (July 31, 1998); Cardinals acquired OF Mark Little to complete deal (August 9, 1998). ... Signed as a free agent by Rangers (January 27, 2000). ... On disabled list (June 21-July 20 and August 1-September 1, 2000); included rehabilitation assignments to Oklahoma and Tulsa. ... On disabled list (May 8-June 6, 2001); included rehabilitation assignments to Oklahoma and Tulsa. ... Traded by Rangers to Boston Red Sox for OF Carl Everett (December 13, 2001). ... Released by Red Sox (July 2, 2002). ... Signed by Cardinals organization (July 19, 2002). ... Released by Cardinals (August 13, 2002). ... Signed by Colorado Rockies organization (January 29, 2003). ... Signed by Florida Marlins (February 6, 2004). ... Traded by Marlins to Houston Astros for future considerations (July 22, 2004). ... Signed as a free agent by Rockies organization (January 11, 2005). ... Released by Rockies (March 31, 2005). ... Signed by Arizona Diamondbacks organization (April 16, 2005). ... Released by Diamondbacks (May 3, 2005). ... Signed by Chicago Cubs organization (May 7, 2005). ... Announced retirement (May 21, 2005). ... Signed by New York Mets organization (December 19, 2005). **MISCELLANEOUS NOTES:** Made an out in only appearance as pinch hitter (1998). ... Had a sacrifice hit and struck out in five appearances as pinch hitter (1999). ... Made outs in both appearances as pinch hitter (2003). ... Made an out and struck out in two appearances as pinch hitter (2004). **CAREER HITTING:** 48-for-217 (.221), 17 R, 11 2B, 0 3B, 1 HR, 20 RBI.

Year	Team (League)	W	L	Pct.	ERA	WHIP	G	GS	CG	ShO	Hld.	Sv.-Opp.	IP	H	R	ER	HR	BB-IBB	SO	Avg.
1988—	GC Rangers (GCL)	5	1	.833	2.15	1.05	12	9	0	0	...	0-...	54.1	39	16	13	0	18-0	59	.203
1989—	Gastonia (S. Atl.)	8	7	.533	3.16	1.37	24	23	2	1	...	0-...	122.1	86	54	43	4	82-1	108	.199
1990—	GC Rangers (GCL)	0	0	...	0.00	0.33	3	3	0	0	...	0-...	6.0	1	1	0	0	1-0	7	.053
	—Gastonia (S. Atl.)	0	0	...	13.50	2.50	1	1	0	0	...	0-...	2.0	1	3	3	0	4-0	1	.143
1991—	Charlotte (Fla. St.)	0	1	.000	4.50	1.13	2	2	0	0	...	0-...	8.0	6	4	4	1	3-0	12	.200
1992—	Charlotte (Fla. St.)	1	0	1.000	0.72	0.84	3	3	0	0	...	0-...	25.0	11	2	2	0	10-2	33	.133
	—Tulsa (Texas)	0	1	.000	3.14	1.33	3	3	0	0	...	0-...	14.1	15	9	5	1	4-0	14	.246
1993—	Tulsa (Texas)	7	5	.583	1.96	1.25	46	0	0	0	...	6-...	73.1	51	18	16	1	41-5	77	.197
	—Texas (A.L.)	0	0	...	2.70	0.90	2	0	0	0	...	0-0	3.1	2	1	1	0	1-1	4	.154

— 358 —

Year Team (League)	W	L	Pct.	ERA	WHIP	G	GS	CG	ShO	Hld.	Sv.-Opp.	IP	H	R	ER	HR	BB-IBB	SO	Avg.
1994— Texas (A.L.)	4	0	1.000	3.42	1.50	43	0	0	0	9	2-3	50.0	40	24	19	4	35-4	50	.223
— Okla. City (A.A.)	0	0	...	0.00	0.55	6	0	0	0	...	1-...	7.1	1	0	0	0	3-2	6	.045
1995— Texas (A.L.)	4	2	.667	4.22	1.61	17	7	0	0	0	0-0	49.0	47	25	23	3	32-1	39	.257
1996— Charlotte (Fla. St.)	0	1	.000	3.00	0.92	2	1	0	0	...	0-...	12.0	8	4	4	1	3-0	9	.190
— Texas (A.L.)	14	6	.700	4.66	1.53	30	30	1	1	0	0-0	173.2	190	97	90	20	76-3	112	.279
1997— Texas (A.L.)	13	12	.520	4.20	1.47	32	32	3	1	0	0-0	201.1	213	111	94	29	82-3	104	.271
1998— Texas (A.L.)	6	7	.462	6.53	1.77	19	19	2	0	0	0-0	103.1	140	84	75	11	43-1	58	.325
— Oklahoma (PCL)	0	0	...	0.00	0.60	1	1	0	0	...	0-...	5.0	2	0	0	0	1-0	1	.118
— St. Louis (N.L.)	4	4	.500	4.26	1.53	10	10	0	0	0	0-0	57.0	64	31	27	7	23-1	29	.283
1999— St. Louis (N.L.)	9	9	.500	4.26	1.38	30	30	2	1	0	0-0	196.1	197	96	93	16	74-4	119	.266
2000— Texas (A.L.)	2	9	.182	7.42	1.79	21	21	0	0	0	0-0	108.0	151	95	89	16	42-3	49	.339
— Oklahoma (PCL)	2	1	.667	1.97	1.13	7	7	1	1	...	0-...	32.0	22	11	7	2	14-0	28	.196
— Tulsa (Texas)	0	1	.000	11.57	2.57	1	1	0	0	...	0-...	4.2	10	7	6	0	2-0	5	.417
2001— Texas (A.L.)	11	11	.500	6.02	1.65	28	28	1	0	0	0-0	154.0	189	109	103	23	65-0	104	.306
— Oklahoma (PCL)	0	0	...	0.00	1.00	1	1	0	0	...	0-...	3.0	3	0	0	0	0-0	3	.250
— Tulsa (Texas)	0	1	.000	5.40	1.20	1	1	0	0	...	0-...	5.0	4	3	3	1	1-0	5	.235
2002— Boston (A.L.)	4	5	.444	4.66	1.67	14	9	1	0	0	0-0	58.0	70	30	30	7	27-0	32	.317
— Memphis (PCL)	0	2	.000	7.88	2.13	5	5	0	0	...	0-...	16.0	17	16	14	1	17-0	9	.298
2003— Colorado (N.L.)	13	11	.542	5.04	1.45	33	32	1	0	0	0-0	180.1	201	108	101	21	61-3	88	.284
2004— Florida (N.L.)	2	3	.400	6.44	1.57	18	8	0	0	0	0-0	58.2	75	44	42	13	17-1	33	.319
— Houston (N.L.)	1	0	1.000	3.86	1.14	9	2	0	0	0	0-0	14.0	12	6	6	1	4-0	13	.240
2005— Tucson (PCL)	1	0	1.000	6.38	1.96	4	4	0	0	...	0-...	18.1	33	14	13	3	3-0	8	.393
— Iowa (PCL)	0	3	.000	13.50	2.48	3	3	0	0	...	0-...	13.1	28	20	20	3	5-0	10	.444
2006— New York (N.L.)	4	1	.800	3.44	1.12	45	0	0	0	13	0-0	81.0	70	33	31	13	21-2	60	.231
American League totals (9 years)	58	52	.527	5.24	1.60	206	146	8	3	9	2-3	900.2	1042	576	524	114	403-16	552	.293
National League totals (5 years)	33	28	.541	4.60	1.39	145	82	3	1	0	0-0	587.1	619	318	300	71	200-11	342	.273
Major League totals (13 years)	91	80	.532	4.98	1.52	351	228	11	4	12	2-3	1488.0	1661	894	824	185	603-27	894	.285

DIVISION SERIES RECORD

Year Team (League)	W	L	Pct.	ERA	WHIP	G	GS	CG	ShO	Hld.	Sv.-Opp.	IP	H	R	ER	HR	BB-IBB	SO	Avg.
1996— Texas (A.L.)	0	1	.000	3.38	1.00	1	1	0	0	0	0-0	8.0	6	3	3	1	2-0	3	.231
2006— New York (N.L.)	0	0	...	20.25	2.25	1	0	0	0	0	0-0	1.1	3	3	3	1	0-0	0	.500
Division series totals (2 years)	0	1	.000	5.79	1.18	2	1	0	0	0	0-0	9.1	9	6	6	2	2-0	3	.281

CHAMPIONSHIP SERIES RECORD

Year Team (League)	W	L	Pct.	ERA	WHIP	G	GS	CG	ShO	Hld.	Sv.-Opp.	IP	H	R	ER	HR	BB-IBB	SO	Avg.
2006— New York (N.L.)	0	0	...	0.00	0.67	1	0	0	0	0	0-0	6.0	3	0	0	0	1-0	3	.158

2006 LEFTY-RIGHTY SPLITS

vs.	Avg.	AB	H	2B	3B	HR	RBI	BB	SO	OBP	Slg.	vs.	Avg.	AB	H	2B	3B	HR	RBI	BB	SO	OBP	Slg.
L	.208	106	22	7	0	5	14	5	25	.252	.415	R	.244	197	48	8	1	8	26	16	35	.301	.416

OLIVO, MIGUEL — C

PERSONAL: Born July 15, 1978, in Villa Vasquez, Dominican Republic. ... 6-0/215. ... Bats right, throws right. ... Full name: Miguel Eduardo Olivo. **TRANSACTIONS/CAREER NOTES:** Signed as a non-drafted free agent by Oakland Athletics organization (September 30, 1996). ... Traded by A's to Chicago White Sox (December 12, 2000); completing deal in which White Sox traded P Chad Bradford to A's for player to be named (December 7, 2000). ... Traded by White Sox with OF Jeremy Reed and SS Michael Morse to Seattle Mariners for RHP Freddy Garcia and C Ben Davis (June 27, 2004). ... On disabled list (June 30-July 15, 2004); included rehabilitation assignment to Everett. ... On suspended list (October 2-3, 2004). ... Traded by Mariners to San Diego Padres for C Miguel Ojeda and P Natanael Mateo (July 30, 2005). ... Signed as a free agent by Florida Marlins (January 3, 2006). **STATISTICAL NOTES:** Hit home run in first major league at-bat (September 15, 2002). ... Career major league grand slams: 1.

2006 GAMES PLAYED BY POSITION (MLB): C—124, 1B—5.

							BATTING										FIELDING	
Year Team (League)	Pos.	G	AB	R	H	2B	3B	HR	RBI	BB	SO	HBP	GDP	SB-CS	Avg.	OBP	SLG	OPS	E	Avg.
1997— Dom. Athletics (DSL)		63	221	37	60	11	4	6	57	34	36	...	...	6-...	.271	.439	...		.977
1998— Ariz. A's (Ariz.)	C-OF	46	164	30	51	11	3	2	23	8	43	4	5	2-2	.311	.356	.451	.807	8	.974
1999— Modesto (California)	C	73	243	46	74	13	6	9	42	21	60	2	6	4-5	.305	.363	.519	.882	15	.959
2000— Modesto (California)	C	58	227	40	64	11	5	5	35	16	53	2	8	5-2	.282	.332	.441	.773	19	.980
— Midland (Texas)	C	19	59	8	14	2	0	1	9	5	15	0	3	0-0	.237	.297	.322	.619	2	.980
2001— Birmingham (Sou.)	C	93	316	45	82	23	1	14	55	37	62	7	4	6-3	.259	.347	.472	.819	9	.988
2002— Birmingham (Sou.)	C	106	359	51	110	24	10	6	49	40	66	5	11	29-13	.306	.381	.479	.860	13	.983
— Chicago (A.L.)	C	6	19	2	4	1	0	1	5	2	5	1	0	0-0	.211	.286	.421	.707	0	1.000
2003— Chicago (A.L.)	C	114	317	37	75	19	1	6	27	19	80	4	3	6-4	.237	.287	.360	.646	8	.988
2004— Chicago (A.L.)	C	46	141	21	38	7	2	7	26	10	29	0	2	5-4	.270	.316	.496	.812	4	.984
— Everett (N'west)	C	2	6	0	0	0	0	0	0	0	2	0	0	0-0	.000	.000	.000	.000	1	.909
— Seattle (A.L.)	C	50	160	25	32	8	2	6	14	10	55	3	2	2-2	.200	.260	.388	.648	1	.997
2005— Tacoma (PCL)	C-DH	24	90	13	21	4	1	3	21	7	19	1	1	8-1	.233	.293	.400	.693	0	1.000
— Seattle (A.L.)	C	54	152	14	23	4	0	5	18	4	49	0	3	1-1	.151	.172	.276	.448	4	.987
— San Diego (N.L.)	C	37	115	16	35	7	1	4	16	4	31	3	4	6-1	.304	.341	.487	.828	5	.979
2006— Florida (N.L.)	C-1B	127	430	52	113	22	3	16	58	9	103	7	9	2-3	.263	.287	.440	.727	7	.991
American League totals (4 years)		270	789	99	172	39	5	25	90	45	218	7	11	14-11	.218	.265	.375	.640	18	.989
National League totals (2 years)		164	545	68	148	29	4	20	74	13	134	10	13	8-4	.272	.299	.450	.748	12	.989
Major League totals (5 years)		434	1334	167	320	68	9	45	164	58	352	17	24	22-15	.240	.279	.406	.684	30	.989

DIVISION SERIES RECORD

Year Team (League)	Pos.	G	AB	R	H	2B	3B	HR	RBI	BB	SO	HBP	GDP	SB-CS	Avg.	OBP	SLG	OPS	E	Avg.
2005— San Diego (N.L.)		1	1	0	0	0	0	0	0	0	0	0	0	0-0	.000	.000	.000	.000	0	...

2006 LEFTY-RIGHTY SPLITS

vs.	Avg.	AB	H	2B	3B	HR	RBI	BB	SO	OBP	Slg.	vs.	Avg.	AB	H	2B	3B	HR	RBI	BB	SO	OBP	Slg.
L	.273	128	35	6	1	5	14	2	32	.285	.453	R	.258	302	78	16	2	11	44	7	71	.288	.434

OLMEDO, RANIER — SS

PERSONAL: Born May 31, 1981, in Maracay, Venezuela. ... 5-11/155. ... Bats right, throws right. ... Full name: Ranier G. Olmedo. **TRANSACTIONS/CAREER NOTES:** Signed as a non-drafted free agent by Cincinnati Reds organization (January 21, 1999). ... On disabled list (April 2-June 17, 2005); included rehabilitation assignment to Louisville.

2006 GAMES PLAYED BY POSITION (MLB): 2B—5, SS—4, 3B—3, OF—1.

							BATTING										FIELDING	
Year Team (League)	Pos.	G	AB	R	H	2B	3B	HR	RBI	BB	SO	HBP	GDP	SB-CS	Avg.	OBP	SLG	OPS	E	Avg.
1999— GC Reds (GCL)		54	195	30	46	12	1	1	19	12	28	1	1	13-7	.236	.281	.323	.604	...	...
2000— Dayton (Midw.)		111	369	50	94	19	1	4	41	30	70	1	11	17-11	.255	.309	.344	.653	...	...
2001— Mudville California (Calif.)		129	536	57	131	23	4	0	28	24	121	8	15	38-17	.244	.285	.302	.587	...	...
2002— Chattanooga (Sou.)	2B-SS	132	478	62	118	21	1	3	30	53	86	7	4	15-16	.247	.331	.314	.645	25	.961

Year	Team (League)	Pos.	G	AB	R	H	2B	3B	HR	RBI	BB	SO	HBP	GDP	SB-CS	Avg.	OBP	SLG	OPS	E	Avg.
2003—	Cincinnati (N.L.)	2B-SS	79	230	24	55	6	1	0	17	13	46	0	4	1-1	.239	.280	.274	.554	...	...
	—Chattanooga (Sou.)		49	160	23	47	11	0	2	15	14	29	0	3	3-3	.294	.349	.400	.749	...	...
	—Louisville (Int'l)		9	25	4	6	1	0	1	4	2	6	0	0	0-0	.240	.296	.400	.696	...	...
2004—	Cincinnati (N.L.)	SS	8	1	0	0	0	0	0	0	1	0	0	0	0-0	.000	.500	.000	.500	...	...
	—Louisville (Int'l)		82	294	33	84	13	7	2	26	23	40	2	8	2-3	.286	.342	.398	.740	...	...
2005—	Cincinnati (N.L.)	2B-SS	54	77	10	17	4	1	1	5	4	22	1	1	4-0	.221	.282	.338	.620	...	...
	—Louisville (Int'l)	2B-SS	14	58	8	16	3	0	1	5	1	11	1	0	2-2	.276	.300	.379	.679	0	1.000
2006—	Cincinnati (N.L.)	2B-SS-3B-OF	30	44	5	9	2	0	1	4	4	0	0	0	1-0	.205	.271	.318	.589	...	...
	—Louisville (Int'l)		100	383	47	108	20	3	3	29	34	71	3	11	17-6	.282	.344	.373	.717	20	.961
	Major League totals (4 years)		171	352	39	81	12	2	2	25	24	72	1	5	6-1	.230	.280	.293	.573	...	...

2006 LEFTY-RIGHTY SPLITS

vs.	Avg.	AB	H	2B	3B	HR	RBI	BB	SO	OBP	Slg.	vs.	Avg.	AB	H	2B	3B	HR	RBI	BB	SO	OBP	Slg.
L	.333	6	2	1	0	0	0	1	1	.429	.500	R	.184	38	7	1	0	1	4	3	3	.244	.289

OLSEN, SCOTT — P

PERSONAL: Born January 12, 1984, in Kalamazoo, Mich. ... 6-4/198. ... Throws left, bats left. ... Full name: Scott M. Olsen. **TRANSACTIONS/CAREER NOTES:** Selected by Florida Marlins organization in sixth round of 2002 free-agent draft. **MISCELLANEOUS NOTES:** Appeared in one game as pinch runner (2006).
CAREER HITTING: 11-for-61 (.180), 3 R, 2 2B, 0 3B, 0 HR, 8 RBI.

Year	Team (League)	W	L	Pct.	ERA	WHIP	G	GS	CG	ShO	Hld.	Sv.-Opp.	IP	H	R	ER	HR	BB-IBB	SO	Avg.
2002—	GC Marlins (GCL)	2	3	.400	2.96	1.08	13	11	0	0	...	0-...	51.2	39	18	17	0	17-0	50	.204
2003—	Greensboro (S. Atl.)	7	9	.438	2.81	1.25	25	24	0	0	...	0-...	128.1	101	51	40	4	59-0	129	.252
2004—	Jupiter (Fla. St.)	7	6	.538	2.97	1.32	25	25	1	1	...	0-...	136.1	127	57	45	8	53-0	158	.252
2005—	Carolina (Southern)	6	4	.600	3.92	1.27	14	14	1	1	0	0-0	80.1	75	38	35	7	27-0	94	.251
	—Florida (N.L.)	1	1	.500	3.98	1.52	5	4	0	0	0	0-0	20.1	21	13	9	5	10-0	21	.227
2006—	Albuquerque (PCL)	0	0	...	0.00	1.26	1	1	0	0	0	0-0	6.1	5	1	0	0	3-0	5	.227
	—Florida (N.L.)	12	10	.545	4.04	1.30	31	31	0	0	0	0-0	180.2	160	94	81	23	75-1	166	.239
	Major League totals (2 years)	13	11	.542	4.03	1.32	36	35	0	0	0	0-0	201.0	181	107	90	28	85-1	187	.241

2006 LEFTY-RIGHTY SPLITS

vs.	Avg.	AB	H	2B	3B	HR	RBI	BB	SO	OBP	Slg.	vs.	Avg.	AB	H	2B	3B	HR	RBI	BB	SO	OBP	Slg.
L	.182	148	27	6	1	4	12	11	46	.262	.318	R	.255	522	133	22	8	19	66	64	120	.337	.437

O'MALLEY, RYAN — P

PERSONAL: Born April 9, 1980, in Springfield, Ill. ... Throws left, bats right. ... Full name: Ryan Joseph O'Malley. ... College: Memphis. **TRANSACTIONS/CAREER NOTES:** Signed as a non-drafted free agent by Chicago Cubs organization (June 7, 2002). ... On disabled list (August 23-September 7, 2006).
CAREER HITTING: 0-for-4 (.000), 0 R, 0 2B, 0 3B, 0 HR, 0 RBI.

Year	Team (League)	W	L	Pct.	ERA	WHIP	G	GS	CG	ShO	Hld.	Sv.-Opp.	IP	H	R	ER	HR	BB-IBB	SO	Avg.
2002—	Boise (N'west)	3	1	.750	2.52	1.19	23	0	0	0	...	1-...	39.1	32	16	11	3	15-1	26	.227
2003—	Lansing (Midw.)	6	4	.600	2.88	1.25	40	3	0	0	...	0-...	81.1	85	34	26	3	17-1	55	.269
2004—	Daytona (Fla. St.)	4	1	.800	2.64	1.08	16	1	0	0	...	0-...	30.2	27	9	9	1	6-1	28	.233
	—Iowa (PCL)	0	2	.000	8.62	1.85	8	3	0	0	...	0-...	15.2	23	15	15	5	6-0	8	.383
	—West Tenn. (Sou.)	2	3	.400	3.72	1.24	16	7	0	0	...	0-...	55.2	49	25	23	6	20-1	37	.241
2005—	Iowa (PCL)	3	2	.600	6.33	1.89	7	4	0	0	0	0-0	27.0	40	19	19	6	11-0	26	.351
	—West Tenn. (Sou.)	3	3	.500	3.91	1.31	31	9	0	0	5	0-0	78.1	78	41	34	7	25-0	55	.257
2006—	Iowa (PCL)	7	7	.500	4.08	1.33	26	19	0	0	1	0-0	123.2	135	62	56	9	30-1	71	.284
	—Chicago (N.L.)	1	1	.500	2.13	1.34	2	2	0	0	0	0-0	12.2	10	3	3	0	7-0	4	.213
	Major League totals (1 year)	1	1	.500	2.13	1.34	2	2	0	0	0	0-0	12.2	10	3	3	0	7-0	4	.213

2006 LEFTY-RIGHTY SPLITS

vs.	Avg.	AB	H	2B	3B	HR	RBI	BB	SO	OBP	Slg.	vs.	Avg.	AB	H	2B	3B	HR	RBI	BB	SO	OBP	Slg.
L	.000	12	0	0	0	0	1	1	2	.143	.000	R	.286	35	10	0	1	0	2	6	2	.390	.343

ORDAZ, LUIS — SS

PERSONAL: Born August 12, 1975, in Maracaibo, Venezuela. ... 5-11/170. ... Bats right, throws right. ... Full name: Luis Javier Ordaz. ... Name pronounced: ORE-daz. ... High school: Santa Maria Gorette (Maracaibo, Venezuela). **TRANSACTIONS/CAREER NOTES:** Signed as non-drafted free agent by Cincinnati Reds organization (January 27, 1993). ... Traded by Reds to St. Louis Cardinals as part of three-team deal in which Reds sent P Mike Remlinger to Kansas City Royals, Cardinals sent OF Andre King to Reds and Royals sent OF Miguel Mejia to Cardinals (December 4, 1995). ... Traded by Cardinals to Arizona Diamondbacks for OF Dante Powell (December 15, 1999). ... Claimed on waivers by Kansas City Royals (April 5, 2000). ... On disabled list (May 18-July 1, 2001); included rehabilitation assignment to Omaha. ... Signed as a free agent by Chicago Cubs organization (December 7, 2001). ... Released by Cubs (July 1, 2002). ... Signed by Royals organization (July 1, 2002). ... Signed as a free agent by Tampa Bay Devil Rays organization (Feburary 9, 2004). ... On disabled list (April 5-August 22, 2006); included rehabilitation assignment to Durham.
2006 GAMES PLAYED BY POSITION (MLB): SS—1.

Year	Team (League)	Pos.	G	AB	R	H	2B	3B	HR	RBI	BB	SO	HBP	GDP	SB-CS	Avg.	OBP	SLG	OPS	E	Avg.
1993—	Princeton (Appal.)	2B-3B-SS	57	217	28	65	9	7	2	39	7	32	2	2	3-1	.300	.320	.433	.754	13	.931
1994—	Char., W.Va. (SAL)	SS	9	31	3	7	0	0	0	0	1	4	1	1	1-0	.226	.273	.226	.499	7	.829
	—Princeton (Appal.)	2B-SS	60	211	33	52	12	3	0	12	10	27	2	2	7-5	.246	.286	.332	.617	24	.914
1995—	Char., W.Va. (SAL)	SS	112	359	43	83	14	7	2	42	13	47	6	10	12-5	.231	.267	.326	.593	22	.954
1996—	St. Pete. (FSL)	SS	126	423	46	115	13	3	3	49	30	53	1	10	10-5	.272	.317	.338	.655	21	.963
1997—	Arkansas (Texas)	SS-DH	115	390	44	112	20	6	4	58	22	39	2	19	11-10	.287	.324	.400	.724	33	.935
	—St. Louis (N.L.)	SS	12	22	3	6	1	0	0	1	2	2	0	...	3-0	.273	.304	.318	.623	1	.963
1998—	Memphis (PCL)	SS-2B	59	214	29	62	9	2	6	35	16	20	1	6	3-3	.290	.341	.435	.775	14	.952
	—St. Louis (N.L.)	SS-3B-2B	57	153	9	31	5	0	0	8	12	18	0	...	2-0	.203	.261	.235	.496	13	.946
1999—	St. Louis (N.L.)	SS-2B-3B	10	9	1	1	0	0	0	2	1	2	0	...	1-0	.111	.200	.111	.311	3	.800
	—Memphis (PCL)	SS	107	362	31	103	25	4	1	45	24	40	4	3	3-4	.285	.328	.384	.712	23	.956
2000—	Kansas City (A.L.)	SS-2B	65	104	17	23	2	0	0	11	5	10	1	...	4-2	.221	.257	.240	.497	1	.992
2001—	Kansas City (A.L.)	2B-SS-3B-DH	28	56	8	14	0	0	0	4	8	1	1	...	0-0	.250	.295	.304	.599	3	.969
	—Omaha (PCL)	SS-2B-3B	14	52	5	16	1	0	1	4	2	10	3	2	3-0	.308	.368	.385	.753	2	.947
2002—	Iowa (PCL)	SS-2B	61	194	22	53	10	0	1	14	9	21	1	2	5-2	.273	.309	.340	.649	12	.948
	—Omaha (PCL)	SS	35	136	25	42	11	4	2	19	9	16	1	6	4-1	.309	.351	.493	.844	3	.983
	—Kansas City (A.L.)	2B-3B-SS	33	94	11	21	2	0	0	4	12	13	0	...	2-3	.223	.308	.245	.553	2	.984

Year Team (League)	Pos.	G	AB	R	H	2B	3B	HR	RBI	BB	SO	HBP	GDP	SB-CS	Avg.	OBP	SLG	OPS	E	Avg.
											BATTING								**FIELDING**	
2003— Omaha (PCL)		49	178	15	43	13	0	0	21	11	19	1	8	3-0	.242	.284	.315	.599	...	...
2004— Durham (Int'l)		103	361	39	92	27	6	3	34	11	51	2	11	1-4	.255	.278	.388	.666	...	...
2005— Durham (Int'l)	2B-3B-SS	39	125	17	36	8	0	1	19	6	13	0	4	0-0	.288	.313	.376	.689	8	.951
2006— Durham (Int'l)		17	59	5	20	4	1	1	6	1	3	0	3	1-0	.339	.344	.492	.836	0	1.000
— Tampa Bay (A.L.)	SS	1	2	0	0	0	0	0	0	0	0	0	0	0-0	.000	.000	.000	.000	0	1.000
American League totals (4 years)		127	256	36	58	7	0	0	19	20	31	2	0	6-5	.227	.283	.254	.537	6	.983
National League totals (3 years)		79	184	15	38	6	0	0	11	14	22	0	...	6-0	.207	.263	.239	.502	17	.940
Major League totals (7 years)		206	440	51	96	13	0	0	30	34	53	2	0	12-5	.218	.274	.248	.522	23	.964

2006 LEFTY-RIGHTY SPLITS

vs.	Avg.	AB	H	2B	3B	HR	RBI	BB	SO	OBP	Slg.	vs.	Avg.	AB	H	2B	3B	HR	RBI	BB	SO	OBP	Slg.
L	.000	0	0	0	0	0	0	0	0	.000	.000	R	.000	2	0	0	0	0	0	0	0	.000	.000

ORDONEZ, MAGGLIO — OF

PERSONAL: Born January 28, 1974, in Caracas, Venezuela. ... 6-0/215. ... Bats right, throws right. ... Full name: Magglio Jose Ordonez. ... Name pronounced: or-DOAN-yez. **TRANSACTIONS/CAREER NOTES:** Signed as a non-drafted free agent by Chicago White Sox organization (May 18, 1991). ... On suspended list (May 1-6, 2000). ... On disabled list (May 26-July 8 and July 22, 2004-remainder of season). ... Signed as a free agent by Detroit Tigers (February 7, 2005). ... On disabled list (April 15-July 1, 2005); included rehabilitation assignment to Toledo. **HONORS:** Named outfielder on THE SPORTING NEWS A.L. All-Star team (2000 and 2003). ... Named outfielder on A.L. Silver Slugger team (2000 and 2002). **STATISTICAL NOTES:** Career major league grand slams: 6.
2006 GAMES PLAYED BY POSITION (MLB): OF—148, DH—6.

Year Team (League)	Pos.	G	AB	R	H	2B	3B	HR	RBI	BB	SO	HBP	GDP	SB-CS	Avg.	OBP	SLG	OPS	E	Avg.
											BATTING								**FIELDING**	
1991— Dominican Orioles/W.S. (DSL)			25	94	17	28	3	1	0	8	6	12	...	4-...	.298		.351		...	...
1992— GC Whi. Sox (GCL)	OF	38	111	17	20	10	2	1	14	13	26	2	2	6-4	.180	.276	.333	.609	0	1.000
1993— Hickory (S. Atl.)	OF	84	273	32	59	14	4	3	20	26	66	0	6	5-5	.216	.284	.330	.614	6	.959
1994— Hickory (S. Atl.)	OF	132	490	86	144	24	5	11	69	45	57	1	11	16-7	.294	.353	.431	.783	6	.980
1995— Prince Will. (Car.)	OF	131	487	61	116	24	2	12	65	41	71	3	16	11-5	.238	.299	.370	.669	6	.978
1996— Birmingham (Sou.)	OF	130	479	66	126	41	0	18	67	39	74	9	16	9-10	.263	.330	.461	.792	6	.976
1997— Nashville (A.A.)	OF-DH	135	523	65	172	29	3	14	90	32	61	2	18	14-10	.329	.364	.476	.840	5	.983
— Chicago (A.L.)	OF	21	69	12	22	6	0	4	11	2	8	0	1	1-2	.319	.338	.580	.918	0	1.000
1998— Chicago (A.L.)	OF	145	535	70	151	25	2	14	65	28	53	9	19	9-7	.282	.326	.415	.741	5	.985
1999— Chicago (A.L.)	OF-DH	157	624	100	188	34	3	30	117	47	64	1	24	13-6	.301	.349	.510	.858	3	.991
2000— Chicago (A.L.)	OF	153	588	102	185	34	3	32	126	60	64	2	28	18-4	.315	.371	.546	.917	5	.983
2001— Chicago (A.L.)	OF-DH	160	593	97	181	40	1	31	113	70	70	5	14	25-7	.305	.382	.533	.914	5	.983
2002— Chicago (A.L.)	OF-DH	153	590	116	189	47	1	38	135	53	77	7	* 21	7-5	.320	.381	.597	.978	4	.986
2003— Chicago (A.L.)	OF-DH	160	606	95	192	46	3	29	99	57	73	7	20	9-5	.317	.380	.546	.926	2	.994
2004— Chicago (A.L.)	OF-DH	52	202	32	59	8	2	9	37	16	22	3	4	0-2	.292	.351	.485	.837	1	.990
2005— Toledo (Int'l)	OF-DH	4	14	3	3	1	0	1	2	3	0	0	0	0-0	.214	.313	.500	.813	0	1.000
— Detroit (A.L.)	OF-DH	82	305	38	92	17	0	8	46	30	35	1	8	0-0	.302	.359	.436	.795	1	.993
2006— Detroit (A.L.)	OF-DH	155	593	82	177	32	1	24	104	45	87	4	13	1-4	.298	.350	.477	.827	7	.974
Major League totals (10 years)		1238	4705	744	1436	289	16	219	853	408	553	39	152	83-42	.305	.362	.513	.875	33	.987

DIVISION SERIES RECORD

Year Team (League)	Pos.	G	AB	R	H	2B	3B	HR	RBI	BB	SO	HBP	GDP	SB-CS	Avg.	OBP	SLG	OPS	E	Avg.
2000— Chicago (A.L.)	OF	3	11	0	2	0	1	0	1	2	2	0	1	1-0	.182	.308	.364	.671	0	1.000
2006— Detroit (A.L.)	OF	4	15	3	4	1	0	1	2	1	2	0	1	0-1	.267	.313	.533	.846	0	1.000
Division series totals (2 years)		7	26	3	6	1	1	1	3	3	4	0	2	1-1	.231	.310	.462	.772	0	1.000

CHAMPIONSHIP SERIES RECORD

Year Team (League)	Pos.	G	AB	R	H	2B	3B	HR	RBI	BB	SO	HBP	GDP	SB-CS	Avg.	OBP	SLG	OPS	E	Avg.
2006— Detroit (A.L.)	OF	4	17	3	4	0	0	2	6	2	2	0	1	0-0	.235	.316	.588	.904	0	1.000

WORLD SERIES RECORD

Year Team (League)	Pos.	G	AB	R	H	2B	3B	HR	RBI	BB	SO	HBP	GDP	SB-CS	Avg.	OBP	SLG	OPS	E	Avg.
2006— Detroit (A.L.)	OF	5	19	2	2	0	0	0	0	1	4	0	0	0-0	.105	.150	.105	.255	0	1.000

ALL-STAR GAME RECORD

Year Team (League)	Pos.	G	AB	R	H	2B	3B	HR	RBI	BB	SO	HBP	GDP	SB-CS	Avg.	OBP	SLG	OPS	E	Avg.
All-Star Game totals (5 years)		5	7	1	3	1	0	1	2	1	0	0	0	0-0	.429	.375	1.000	1.375	0	1.000

2006 LEFTY-RIGHTY SPLITS

vs.	Avg.	AB	H	2B	3B	HR	RBI	BB	SO	OBP	Slg.	vs.	Avg.	AB	H	2B	3B	HR	RBI	BB	SO	OBP	Slg.
L	.294	163	48	10	1	9	32	9	20	.333	.534	R	.300	430	129	22	0	15	72	36	67	.356	.456

ORR, PETE — 2B/3B

PERSONAL: Born June 8, 1979, in Richmond Hill, Ontario. ... 6-1/185. ... Bats left, throws right. ... Full name: Peterson T. Orr. ... Junior college: Galveston (Texas) C.C. **TRANSACTIONS/CAREER NOTES:** Signed as a non-drafted free agent by Atlanta Braves (July 3, 1999).
2006 GAMES PLAYED BY POSITION (MLB): 2B—32, 3B—10.

Year Team (League)	Pos.	G	AB	R	H	2B	3B	HR	RBI	BB	SO	HBP	GDP	SB-CS	Avg.	OBP	SLG	OPS	E	Avg.
											BATTING								**FIELDING**	
2000— Jamestown (NYP)	2B-3B-SS	69	265	40	64	8	1	2	15	24	51	6	4	9-5	.242	.314	.302	.616	18	.934
2001— Myrtle Beach (Carol.)	SS-OF-2B 3B	92	317	38	74	10	1	4	23	19	70	11	3	17-6	.233	.299	.309	.608	11	.965
2002— Greenville (Sou.)	SS-2B-OF 3B	89	305	36	76	10	2	2	36	21	47	3	8	23-4	.249	.302	.315	.617	9	.976
— Myrtle Beach (Carol.)	SS-OF-2B 3B	17	51	8	20	0	2	0	8	3	6	1	0	3-0	.392	.436	.471	.907	2	.960
2003— Greenville (Sou.)	SS-2B-OF 3B	98	257	22	58	10	2	2	31	25	48	3	6	14-5	.226	.299	.304	.603	13	.956
2004— Richmond (Int'l)	2B-3B-OF SS	115	460	69	147	16	10	1	35	20	41	2	7	24-11	.320	.349	.404	.753	4	.940
2005— Atlanta (N.L.)	2B-3B-OF SS-DH	112	150	32	45	8	1	1	8	6	23	1	6	7-1	.300	.331	.387	.718	6	.950
2006— Atlanta (N.L.)	2B-3B	102	154	22	39	3	4	1	8	5	30	0	1	2-4	.253	.277	.344	.621	0	1.000
Major League totals (2 years)		214	304	54	84	11	5	2	16	11	53	1	9-5		.276	.304	.365	.669	6	.974

O

Year Team (League)	Pos.	G	AB	R	H	2B	3B	HR	RBI	BB	SO	HBP	GDP	SB-CS	Avg.	OBP	SLG	OPS	E	Avg.
2005—Atlanta (N.L.)		3	2	0	0	0	0	0	0	0	0	0	0	0-0	.000	.000	.000	.000	0	.000

2006 LEFTY-RIGHTY SPLITS

vs.	Avg.	AB	H	2B	3B	HR	RBI	BB	SO	OBP	Slg.	vs.	Avg.	AB	H	2B	3B	HR	RBI	BB	SO	OBP	Slg.
L	.182	22	4	0	0	0	0	2	6	.250	.182	R	.265	132	35	3	4	1	8	3	24	.281	.371

ORTIZ, DAVID — 1B/DH

PERSONAL: Born November 18, 1975, in Santo Domingo, Dominican Republic. ... 6-4/230. ... Bats left, throws left. ... Full name: David Americo Ortiz. ... Name pronounced: or-TEEZ. ... High school: Estudia Espallat (Dominican Republic). ... Formerly known as David Arias. **TRANSACTIONS/CAREER NOTES:** Signed as a non-drafted free agent by Seattle Mariners organization (November 28, 1992). ... Traded by Mariners to Minnesota Twins (September 13, 1996), completing deal in which Twins traded 3B Dave Hollins to Mariners for a player to be named (August 29, 1996). ... On disabled list (May 10-July 9, 1998); included rehabilitation assignment to Salt Lake. ... On disabled list (May 5-July 21, 2001); included rehabilitation assignments to GCL Twins, Fort Myers and New Britain. ... On disabled list (April 19-May 12, 2002). ... Released by Twins (December 16, 2002). ... Signed by Boston Red Sox (January 22, 2003). ... On suspended list (August 1-7, 2004). **HONORS:** Named designated hitter on THE SPORTING NEWS A.L. All-Star team (2004-06). ... Named designated hitter on A.L. Silver Slugger team (2004-06). **STATISTICAL NOTES:** Career major league grand slams: 6.

2006 GAMES PLAYED BY POSITION (MLB): DH—138, 1B—10.

								BATTING											FIELDING	
Year Team (League)	Pos.	G	AB	R	H	2B	3B	HR	RBI	BB	SO	HBP	GDP	SB-CS	Avg.	OBP	SLG	OPS	E	Avg.
1993— Dom. Mariners (DSL)		61	201	61	53	17	1	7	31	34	44			1-...	.264		.463			
1994— Ariz. Mariners (Ariz.)	1B	53	167	14	41	10	1	2	20	14	46	2	2	1-4	.246	.305	.353	.658	6	.985
1995— Ariz. Mariners (Ariz.)	1B	48	184	30	61	18	4	4	37	23	52	1	2	2-0	.332	.403	.538	.941	5	.989
1996— Wisconsin (Midw.)	1B-DH-3B	129	485	89	156	34	2	18	93	52	108	5	5	3-4	.322	.390	.511	.901	13	.989
1997— Fort Myers (FSL)	1B-DH	61	239	45	79	15	0	13	58	22	53	1	3	2-1	.331	.385	.556	.941	9	.984
— New Britain (East.)	DH-1B	69	258	40	83	22	2	14	56	21	78	4	6	2-6	.322	.379	.585	.964	3	.990
— Salt Lake (PCL)	1B-DH	10	42	5	9	1	0	4	10	2	11	0	4	0-1	.214	.250	.524	.774	0	1.000
— Minnesota (A.L.)	1B	15	49	10	16	3	0	1	6	2	19	0	1	0-0	.327	.353	.449	.802	1	.989
1998— Minnesota (A.L.)	1B-DH	86	278	47	77	20	0	9	46	39	72	5	8	1-0	.277	.371	.446	.817	6	.989
— Salt Lake (PCL)	1B-DH	11	37	5	9	3	0	2	6	3	9	0	0	0-0	.243	.300	.486	.786	3	.966
1999— Salt Lake (PCL)	1B-DH	130	476	85	150	35	3	30	110	79	105	3	8	2-2	.315	.412	.590	1.002	20	.980
— Minnesota (A.L.)	DH-1B-OF	10	20	1	0	0	0	0	0	5	12	0	2	0-0	.000	.200	.000	.200	0	1.000
2000— Minnesota (A.L.)	DH-1B	130	415	59	117	36	1	10	63	57	81	0	13	1-0	.282	.364	.446	.810	1	.996
2001— Minnesota (A.L.)	DH-1B	89	303	46	71	17	1	18	48	40	68	1	6	1-0	.234	.324	.475	.799	0	1.000
— GC Twins (GCL)	DH	4	10	3	4	0	0	0	1	3	1	0	0	1-0	.400	.538	.400	.938	...	...
— Fort Myers (FSL)	1B	1	3	0	0	0	0	0	0	1	0	0	0	0-0	.000	.250	.000	.250	0	1.000
— New Britain (East.)	1B	9	37	3	9	4	0	0	1	3	9	0	1	0-0	.243	.293	.351	.644	0	1.000
2002— Minnesota (A.L.)	DH-1B	125	412	52	112	32	1	20	75	43	87	3	5	1-2	.272	.339	.500	.839	1	.990
2003— Boston (A.L.)	DH-1B	128	448	79	129	39	2	31	101	58	83	1	9	0-0	.288	.369	.592	.961	3	.992
2004— Boston (A.L.)	DH-1B	150	582	94	175	47	3	41	139	75	133	4	12	0-0	.301	.380	.603	.983	4	.986
2005— Boston (A.L.)	DH-1B	159	601	119	180	40	1	* 47	* 148	102	124	1	13	1-0	.300	.397	.604	1.001	2	.976
2006— Boston (A.L.)	DH-1B	151	558	115	160	29	2	* 54	* 137	* 119	117	4	12	1-0	.287	.413	.636	1.049	2	.971
Major League totals (10 years)		1043	3666	622	1037	263	11	231	763	540	796	19	81	6-2	.283	.374	.550	.924	20	.989

DIVISION SERIES RECORD

Year Team (League)	Pos.	G	AB	R	H	2B	3B	HR	RBI	BB	SO	HBP	GDP	SB-CS	Avg.	OBP	SLG	OPS	E	Avg.
2002— Minnesota (A.L.)	DH	4	13	0	3	2	0	0	2	0	5	0	0	0-0	.231	.231	.385	.615	...	...
2003— Boston (A.L.)	DH	5	21	0	2	1	0	0	2	2	7	0	0	0-0	.095	.174	.143	.317	0	...
2004— Boston (A.L.)	DH	3	11	4	6	2	0	1	4	5	2	0	0	0-0	.545	.688	1.000	1.688	0	...
2005— Boston (A.L.)	DH	3	12	2	4	2	0	1	1	0	3	0	0	0-0	.333	.333	.750	1.083	0	...
Division series totals (4 years)		15	57	6	15	7	0	2	9	7	17	0	0	0-0	.263	.344	.491	.835	0	...

CHAMPIONSHIP SERIES RECORD

Year Team (League)	Pos.	G	AB	R	H	2B	3B	HR	RBI	BB	SO	HBP	GDP	SB-CS	Avg.	OBP	SLG	OPS	E	Avg.
2002— Minnesota (A.L.)	DH	5	16	0	5	1	0	0	2	0	5	0	0	0-0	.313	.313	.375	.688	...	...
2003— Boston (A.L.)	DH	7	26	4	7	1	0	2	6	3	8	1	1	0-0	.269	.367	.538	.905	0	...
2004— Boston (A.L.)	DH	7	31	6	12	0	1	3	11	4	7	0	0	0-1	.387	.457	.742	1.199	0	...
Champ. series totals (3 years)		19	73	10	24	2	1	5	19	7	20	1	1	0-1	.329	.395	.589	.984	0	...

WORLD SERIES RECORD

Year Team (League)	Pos.	G	AB	R	H	2B	3B	HR	RBI	BB	SO	HBP	GDP	SB-CS	Avg.	OBP	SLG	OPS	E	Avg.
2004— Boston (A.L.)	1B-DH	4	13	3	4	1	0	1	4	4	1	0	0	0-0	.308	.471	.615	1.086	0	1.000

ALL-STAR GAME RECORD

	G	AB	R	H	2B	3B	HR	RBI	BB	SO	HBP	GDP	SB-CS	Avg.	OBP	SLG	OPS	E	Avg.
All-Star Game totals (3 years)	3	6	2	3	0	0	1	3	2	1	0	0	0-0	.500	.625	1.000	1.625	0	1.000

2006 LEFTY-RIGHTY SPLITS

vs.	Avg.	AB	H	2B	3B	HR	RBI	BB	SO	OBP	Slg.	vs.	Avg.	AB	H	2B	3B	HR	RBI	BB	SO	OBP	Slg.
L	.278	205	57	13	1	18	44	30	48	.373	.615	R	.292	353	103	16	1	36	93	89	69	.434	.649

ORTIZ, RAMON — P

PERSONAL: Born May 23, 1973, in Cotui, Dominican Republic. ... 6-0/175. ... Throws right, bats right. ... Full name: Ramon Diogenes Ortiz. ... Name pronounced: or-TEEZ. ... High school: 8th Intermedian (Dominican Republic). ... Cousin of Pedro Liriano, pitcher with two major league teams (2004-05). **TRANSACTIONS/CAREER NOTES:** Signed as a non-drafted free agent by California Angels organization (June 20, 1995). ... Angels franchise renamed Anaheim Angels for 1997 season. ... On disabled list (March 20-April 11, 2000); included rehabilitation assignment to Lake Elsinore. ... Traded by Angels to Cincinnati Reds for P Dustin Moseley (December 14, 2004). ... On disabled list (April 9-May 1, 2005). ... Signed as a free agent by Washington Nationals (December 29, 2005). **MISCELLANEOUS NOTES:** Scored a run in five appearances as pinch runner (2006).

CAREER HITTING: 10-for-132 (.076), 7 R, 2 2B, 0 3B, 1 HR, 3 RBI.

Year Team (League)	W	L	Pct.	ERA	WHIP	G	GS	CG	ShO	Hld.	Sv.-Opp.	IP	H	R	ER	HR	BB-IBB	SO	Avg.
1995— Dom. Angels (DSL)	8	6	.571	2.23	1.37	16	16	7	0	...	0-...	97.0	79	44	24		54-...	100	...
1996— Ariz. Angels (Ariz.)	5	4	.556	2.12	1.21	16	8	2	2	...	1-...	68.0	55	28	16	5	27-0	78	.216
— Boise (N'west)	1	1	.500	3.66	1.37	3	3	0	0	...	0-...	19.2	21	10	8	3	6-0	18	.263
1997— Cedar Rap. (Midw.)	11	10	.524	3.58	1.15	27	27	8	4	...	0-...	181.0	156	78	72	22	53-0	225	.230
1998— Midland (Texas)	2	1	.667	5.55	1.40	7	7	0	0	...	0-...	47.0	50	31	29	10	16-0	53	.275
1999— Erie (East.)	9	4	.692	2.82	1.25	15	15	2	2	...	0-...	102.0	88	38	32	12	40-0	86	.237
— Edmonton (PCL)	5	3	.625	4.05	1.22	9	9	0	0	...	0-...	53.1	46	26	24	7	19-0	64	.227
— Anaheim (A.L.)	2	3	.400	6.52	1.55	9	9	0	0	...	0-0	48.1	50	35	35	7	25-0	44	.265
2000— Lake Elsinore (Calif.)	1	0	1.000	3.00	1.67	1	1	0	0	...	0-...	6.0	8	2	2	0	2-0	7	.333

0

Year · Team (League)	W	L	Pct.	ERA	WHIP	G	GS	CG	ShO	Hld.	Sv.-Opp.	IP	H	R	ER	HR	BB-IBB	SO	Avg.
—Anaheim (A.L.)	8	6	.571	5.09	1.36	18	18	2	0	...	0-0	111.1	96	69	63	18	55-0	73	.236
—Edmonton (PCL)	6	6	.500	4.55	1.25	15	15	1	0	...	0-	89.0	74	49	45	7	37-0	76	.223
2001—Anaheim (A.L.)	13	11	.542	4.36	1.43	32	32	2	0	0	0-0	208.2	223	114	101	25	76-6	135	.274
2002—Anaheim (A.L.)	15	9	.625	3.77	1.18	32	32	4	1	0	0-0	217.1	188	97	91	*40	68-0	162	.230
2003—Anaheim (A.L.)	16	13	.552	5.20	1.51	32	32	1	0	0	0-0	180.0	209	121	104	28	63-0	94	.287
2004—Anaheim (A.L.)	5	7	.417	4.43	1.38	34	14	0	0	0	0-0	128.0	139	64	63	18	38-4	82	.280
2005—Sarasota (Fla. St.)	0	1	.000	9.00	2.33	1	1	0	0	0	0-0	3.0	7	4	3	1	0-0	3	.412
—Cincinnati (N.L.)	9	11	.450	5.36	1.50	30	30	1	0	0	0-0	171.1	206	110	102	34	51-1	96	.302
2006—Wash. (N.L.)	11	•16	.407	5.57	1.54	33	33	0	0	0	0-0	190.2	230	127	118	31	64-14	104	.297
American League totals (6 years)	59	49	.546	4.60	1.38	157	137	9	1	0	0-0	893.2	905	500	457	136	325-10	590	.262
National League totals (2 years)	20	27	.426	5.47	1.52	63	63	1	0	0	0-0	362.0	436	237	220	65	115-15	200	.299
Major League totals (8 years)	79	76	.510	4.85	1.42	220	200	10	1	0	0-0	1255.2	1341	737	677	201	440-25	790	.273

DIVISION SERIES RECORD

Year · Team (League)	W	L	Pct.	ERA	WHIP	G	GS	CG	ShO	Hld.	Sv.-Opp.	IP	H	R	ER	HR	BB-IBB	SO	Avg.
2002—Anaheim (A.L.)	0	0	...	20.25	2.63	1	1	0	0	0	0-0	2.2	3	6	6	0	4-0	1	.333
2004—Anaheim (A.L.)	0	0	...	4.50	1.50	1	0	0	0	0	0-0	2.0	2	1	1	0	1-1	0	.250
Division series totals (2 years)	0	0	...	13.50	2.14	2	1	0	0	0	0-0	4.2	5	7	7	0	5-1	1	.294

CHAMPIONSHIP SERIES RECORD

Year · Team (League)	W	L	Pct.	ERA	WHIP	G	GS	CG	ShO	Hld.	Sv.-Opp.	IP	H	R	ER	HR	BB-IBB	SO	Avg.
2002—Anaheim (A.L.)	1	0	1.000	5.06	2.06	1	1	0	0	0	0-0	5.1	10	3	3	0	1-0	3	.435

WORLD SERIES RECORD

Year · Team (League)	W	L	Pct.	ERA	WHIP	G	GS	CG	ShO	Hld.	Sv.-Opp.	IP	H	R	ER	HR	BB-IBB	SO	Avg.
2002—Anaheim (A.L.)	1	0	1.000	7.20	1.80	1	1	0	0	0	0-0	5.0	5	4	4	2	4-1	3	.263

2006 LEFTY-RIGHTY SPLITS

vs.	Avg.	AB	H	2B	3B	HR	RBI	BB	SO	OBP	Slg.	vs.	Avg.	AB	H	2B	3B	HR	RBI	BB	SO	OBP	Slg.
L	.316	376	119	27	1	16	60	39	41	.389	.521	R	.278	399	111	19	3	15	55	25	63	.336	.454

ORTIZ, RUSS   P

PERSONAL: Born June 5, 1974, in Encino, Calif. ... 6-1/208. ... Throws right, bats right. ... Full name: Russell Reid Ortiz. ... Name pronounced: or-TEEZ. ... High school: Montclair Prep (Van Nuys, Calif.). ... College: Oklahoma. **TRANSACTIONS/CAREER NOTES:** Selected by San Francisco Giants organization in fourth round of 1995 free-agent draft. ... Traded by Giants to Atlanta Braves for Ps Damian Moss and Merkin Valdez (December 17, 2002). ... Signed as a free agent by Arizona Diamondbacks (December 10, 2004). ... On disabled list (June 18-August 13, 2005); included rehabilitation assignments to Lancaster and Tucson. ... On disabled list (May 2-June 6, 2006); included rehabilitation assignment to Tucson. ... Released by Diamondbacks (June 21, 2006). ... Signed by Baltimore Orioles (June 25, 2006). **MISCELLANEOUS NOTES:** Made an out in only appearance as pinch hitter (2003). ... Had a sacrifice hit and made an out in two appearances as pinch hitter (2005).
CAREER HITTING: 96-for-462 (.208), 43 R, 22 2B, 0 3B, 6 HR, 44 RBI.

Year · Team (League)	W	L	Pct.	ERA	WHIP	G	GS	CG	ShO	Hld.	Sv.-Opp.	IP	H	R	ER	HR	BB-IBB	SO	Avg.
1995—Bellingham (N'west)	2	0	1.000	0.52	0.93	25	0	0	0	...	11-...	34.1	19	4	2	1	13-0	55	.162
—San Jose (Calif.)	0	1	.000	1.50	1.00	5	0	0	0	...	0-...	6.0	4	1	1	0	2-0	7	.190
1996—San Jose (Calif.)	0	0	...	0.25	0.98	34	0	0	0	...	23-...	36.2	16	2	1	0	20-0	63	.131
—Shreveport (Texas)	1	2	.333	4.05	1.61	26	0	0	0	...	13-...	26.2	22	14	12	0	21-3	29	.220
1997—Shreveport (Texas)	2	3	.400	4.13	1.57	12	12	0	0	...	0-...	56.2	52	28	26	3	37-0	50	.252
—Phoenix (PCL)	4	3	.571	5.51	1.53	14	14	0	0	...	0-...	85.0	96	57	52	11	34-0	70	.287
1998—San Francisco (N.L.)	4	4	.500	4.99	1.54	22	13	0	1	0	0-...	88.1	90	51	49	11	46-1	75	.269
—Fresno (PCL)	3	1	.750	1.60	1.13	10	10	0	0	...	0-...	50.2	35	10	9	3	22-0	59	.198
1999—San Francisco (N.L.)	18	9	.667	3.81	1.51	33	33	3	0	0	0-0	207.2	189	109	88	24	*125-5	164	.244
2000—San Francisco (N.L.)	14	12	.538	5.01	1.55	33	32	0	0	0	0-0	195.2	192	117	109	28	112-1	167	.261
2001—San Francisco (N.L.)	17	9	.654	3.29	1.27	33	33	1	1	0	0-0	218.2	187	90	80	13	91-3	169	.232
2002—San Francisco (N.L.)	14	10	.583	3.61	1.33	33	33	2	0	0	0-0	214.1	191	89	86	15	94-5	137	.241
2003—Atlanta (N.L.)	*21	7	.750	3.81	1.31	34	34	1	1	0	0-0	212.1	177	101	90	17	*102-7	149	.223
2004—Atlanta (N.L.)	15	9	.625	4.13	1.51	34	34	2	1	0	0-0	204.2	197	98	94	23	112-7	143	.258
2005—Lancaster (Calif.)	0	1	.000	42.43	5.57	1	1	0	0	...	0-0	2.1	12	11	11	2	1-0	1	.706
—Tucson (PCL)	0	1	.000	13.00	2.11	2	2	0	0	...	0-0	9.0	14	14	13	4	5-0	5	.341
—Arizona (N.L.)	5	11	.313	6.89	1.84	22	22	0	0	0	0-0	115.0	147	92	88	18	65-3	46	.313
2006—Tucson (PCL)	1	0	1.000	2.61	1.31	4	4	0	0	...	0-0	20.2	22	7	6	1	5-0	10	.268
—Arizona (N.L.)	0	5	.000	7.54	2.16	6	6	0	0	0	0-0	22.2	27	21	19	3	22-1	21	.303
—Baltimore (A.L.)	0	3	.000	8.48	2.11	20	5	0	0	0	0-0	40.1	59	39	38	15	18-0	23	.349
American League totals (1 year)	0	3	.000	8.48	1.91	20	5	0	0	0	0-0	40.1	59	39	38	15	18-0	23	.349
National League totals (9 years)	108	76	.587	4.28	1.46	250	240	9	3	1	0-0	1479.1	1397	768	703	152	769-33	1071	.251
Major League totals (9 years)	108	79	.578	4.39	1.48	270	245	9	3	1	0-0	1519.2	1456	807	741	167	787-33	1094	.254

DIVISION SERIES RECORD

Year · Team (League)	W	L	Pct.	ERA	WHIP	G	GS	CG	ShO	Hld.	Sv.-Opp.	IP	H	R	ER	HR	BB-IBB	SO	Avg.
2000—San Francisco (N.L.)	0	0	...	1.69	1.13	1	1	0	0	0	0-0	5.1	2	1	1	0	4-1	4	.118
2002—San Francisco (N.L.)	2	0	1.000	2.19	1.38	2	2	0	0	0	0-0	12.1	9	3	3	0	8-1	8	.200
2003—Atlanta (N.L.)	1	1	.500	5.06	2.06	2	2	0	0	0	0-0	10.2	15	6	6	1	7-1	9	.333
2004—Atlanta (N.L.)	0	0	...	15.00	2.67	1	1	0	0	0	0-0	3.0	7	5	5	1	1-0	1	.467
Division series totals (4 years)	3	1	.750	4.31	1.69	6	6	0	0	0	0-0	31.1	33	15	15	2	20-3	22	.270

CHAMPIONSHIP SERIES RECORD

Year · Team (League)	W	L	Pct.	ERA	WHIP	G	GS	CG	ShO	Hld.	Sv.-Opp.	IP	H	R	ER	HR	BB-IBB	SO	Avg.
2002—San Francisco (N.L.)	0	0	...	7.71	1.71	1	1	0	0	0	0-0	4.2	5	4	4	2	3-0	3	.263

WORLD SERIES RECORD

Year · Team (League)	W	L	Pct.	ERA	WHIP	G	GS	CG	ShO	Hld.	Sv.-Opp.	IP	H	R	ER	HR	BB-IBB	SO	Avg.
2002—San Francisco (N.L.)	0	0	...	10.13	1.88	2	2	0	0	0	0-0	8.0	13	9	9	1	2-0	2	.361

ALL-STAR GAME RECORD

Year · Team (League)	W	L	Pct.	ERA	WHIP	G	GS	CG	ShO	Hld.	Sv.-Opp.	IP	H	R	ER	HR	BB-IBB	SO	Avg.
All-Star Game totals (1 year)	0	0	...	0.00	1.00	1						1.0	0	0	0	0	1-0	2	.000

2006 LEFTY-RIGHTY SPLITS

vs.	Avg.	AB	H	2B	3B	HR	RBI	BB	SO	OBP	Slg.	vs.	Avg.	AB	H	2B	3B	HR	RBI	BB	SO	OBP	Slg.
L	.378	111	42	11	0	8	30	23	17	.485	.694	R	.299	147	44	12	3	10	32	17	27	.380	.626

ORTMEIER, DAN   OF

PERSONAL: Born May 11, 1981, in Chattanooga, Tenn. ... 6-4/220. ... Bats both, throws left. ... Full name: Daniel D. Ortmeier. ... College: Texas-Arlington.
TRANSACTIONS/CAREER NOTES: Selected by San Francisco Giants organization in third round of 2002 free-agent draft.
2006 GAMES PLAYED BY POSITION (MLB): OF-3, DH-2.

Year Team (League)	Pos.	G	AB	R	H	2B	3B	HR	RBI	BB	SO	HBP	GDP	SB-CS	Avg.	OBP	SLG	OPS	FIELDING E	Avg.
2002—Salem-Keizer (N'west)	OF	49	195	32	57	9	1	5	31	18	37	1	5	3-0	.292	.352	.426	.778	1	.984
2003—San Jose (Calif.)	OF	115	408	62	124	32	6	8	56	39	89	11	13	13-6	.304	.378	.471	.849	3	.979
2004—Norwich (East.)	OF	106	377	55	95	23	6	10	48	47	110	12	5	18-2	.252	.352	.424	.776	2	.952
2005—Norwich (East.)	OF-DH	135	503	85	138	23	6	20	79	48	115	21	2	35-12	.274	.360	.463	.823	8	.983
—San Francisco (N.L.)	OF	15	22	1	3	0	0	0	1	3	5	1	2	1-0	.136	.269	.136	.406	0	1.000
2006—Fresno (PCL)		68	262	37	64	14	3	6	33	16	40	3	2	8-6	.244	.293	.389	.683	3	.977
—Connecticut (East.)		47	167	17	42	9	1	2	11	17	38	3	4	7-4	.251	.328	.353	.681	1	.990
—San Francisco (N.L.)	OF-DH	9	12	0	3	1	0	0	2	0	4	0	0	0-0	.250	.250	.333	.583	0	1.000
Major League totals (2 years)		24	34	1	6	1	0	0	3	3	9	1	2	1-0	.176	.263	.206	.469	0	1.000

2006 LEFTY-RIGHTY SPLITS

vs.	Avg.	AB	H	2B	3B	HR	RBI	BB	SO	OBP	Slg.	vs.	Avg.	AB	H	2B	3B	HR	RBI	BB	SO	OBP	Slg.
L	.000	2	0	0	0	0	0	0	1	.000	.000	R	.300	10	3	1	0	0	2	0	3	.300	.400

ORVELLA, CHAD — P

PERSONAL: Born October 1, 1980, in Renton, Wash. ... 5-11/190. ... Throws right, bats right. ... Full name: Chad Robert Orvella. ... College: North Carolina State. **TRANSACTIONS/CAREER NOTES:** Selected by Tampa Bay Devil Rays organization in 13th round of 2003 free-agent draft.
CAREER HITTING: 0-for-0 (.000), 0 R, 0 2B, 0 3B, 0 HR, 0 RBI.

Year Team (League)	W	L	Pct.	ERA	WHIP	G	GS	CG	ShO	Hld.	Sv.-Opp.	IP	H	R	ER	HR	BB-IBB	SO	Avg.
2003—Hudson Valley (NYP)	0	0		0.00	0.57	10	0	0	0	...	8-...	12.1	6	0	0	0	1-0	15	.140
2004—Char., S.C. (SAL)	1	0	1.000	1.33	0.70	22	0	0	0	...	4-...	47.1	28	9	7	4	5-0	76	.164
—Bakersfield (Calif.)	0	1	.000	3.06	0.96	15	0	0	0	...	4-...	17.2	13	7	6	2	4-1	24	.197
—Montgom. (Sou.)	0	0		0.00	0.00	6	0	0	0	...	4-...	7.0	0	0	0	0	0-0	14	.000
—Durham (Int'l)	0	0		5.40	1.20	2	0	0	0	...	0-...	1.2	1	1	1	1	1-0	2	.167
2005—Montgom. (Sou.)	0	0		0.36	0.84	16	0	0	0	0	9-10	25.0	15	1	1	0	6-0	29	.169
—Tampa Bay (A.L.)	3	3	.500	3.60	1.40	37	0	0	0	14	1-2	50.0	47	26	20	4	23-2	43	.244
2006—Durham (Int'l)	4	0	1.000	1.86	1.03	27	0	0	0	4	1-2	38.2	31	11	8	2	9-0	55	.217
—Tampa Bay (A.L.)	1	5	.167	7.40	2.30	22	0	0	0	1	0-3	24.1	36	23	20	6	20-0	17	.346
Major League totals (2 years)	4	8	.333	4.84	1.70	59	0	0	0	15	1-5	74.1	83	49	40	10	43-2	60	.281

2006 LEFTY-RIGHTY SPLITS

vs.	Avg.	AB	H	2B	3B	HR	RBI	BB	SO	OBP	Slg.	vs.	Avg.	AB	H	2B	3B	HR	RBI	BB	SO	OBP	Slg.
L	.275	40	11	2	0	2	9	12	8	.442	.475	R	.391	64	25	6	1	4	21	8	9	.474	.703

OSORIA, FRANQUELIS — P

PERSONAL: Born September 12, 1981, in Santiago, Dominican Republic. ... 6-0/165. ... Throws right, bats right. ... Full name: Franquelis Antonio Osoria.
TRANSACTIONS/CAREER NOTES: Signed as a non-drafted free agent by Los Angeles Dodgers organization (December 28, 1999).
CAREER HITTING: 0-for-5 (.000), 0 R, 0 2B, 0 3B, 0 HR, 0 RBI.

Year Team (League)	W	L	Pct.	ERA	WHIP	G	GS	CG	ShO	Hld.	Sv.-Opp.	IP	H	R	ER	HR	BB-IBB	SO	Avg.
2000—Los Angeles (DSL)	3	4	.429	2.52	1.26	13	12	0	0	...	0-...	64.1	58	33	18	1	23-1	46	.230
2001—Los Angeles (DSL)	4	4	.500	3.16	1.10	15	11	0	0	...	0-...	77.0	69	38	27	5	16-0	67	.237
2002—Vero Beach (FSL)	0	1	.000	2.45	0.82	3	0	0	0	...	0-...	7.1	4	2	2	0	2-0	10	.154
—South Georgia (S. Atl.)	2	2	.500	3.32	1.22	21	1	0	0	...	1-...	43.1	40	22	16	1	13-1	30	.244
2003—Vero Beach (FSL)	3	6	.333	3.00	1.17	33	3	0	0	...	0-...	75.0	69	34	25	4	19-5	53	.244
2004—Jacksonville (Sou.)	8	5	.615	3.67	1.10	51	0	0	0	...	5-...	81.0	71	36	33	2	18-4	73	.229
—Las Vegas (PCL)	0	0		6.48	1.68	4	0	0	0	...	0-...	8.1	13	6	6	0	1-0	3	.342
2005—Las Vegas (PCL)	6	4	.600	2.62	1.38	40	0	0	0	8	9-13	55.0	63	18	16	3	13-6	35	.299
—Los Angeles (N.L.)	0	2	.000	3.94	1.21	24	0	0	0	3	0-2	29.2	28	14	13	3	8-0	15	.259
2006—Las Vegas (PCL)	2	2	.500	4.35	1.97	44	0	0	0	5	2-8	51.2	81	31	25	2	21-3	28	.362
—Los Angeles (N.L.)	0	2	.000	7.13	2.04	12	0	0	0	0	0-0	17.2	27	14	14	4	9-1	13	.360
Major League totals (2 years)	0	4	.000	5.13	1.52	36	0	0	0	3	0-2	47.1	55	28	27	7	17-1	28	.301

2006 LEFTY-RIGHTY SPLITS

vs.	Avg.	AB	H	2B	3B	HR	RBI	BB	SO	OBP	Slg.	vs.	Avg.	AB	H	2B	3B	HR	RBI	BB	SO	OBP	Slg.
L	.500	26	13	2	0	3	7	2	3	.536	.923	R	.286	49	14	1	0	1	4	7	10	.386	.367

OSWALT, ROY — P

PERSONAL: Born August 29, 1977, in Weir, Miss. ... 6-0/185. ... Throws right, bats right. ... Full name: Roy Edward Oswalt. ... Name pronounced: OWES-walt. ... High school: Weir (Miss.). ... Junior college: Holmes (Miss.). **TRANSACTIONS/CAREER NOTES:** Selected by Houston Astros organization in 23rd round of 1996 free-agent draft. ... On suspended list (August 29-September 3, 2002). ... On disabled list (May 16-31, June 12-July 7 and July 30-September 8, 2003); included rehabilitation assignment to New Orleans. ... On disabled list (May 30-June 14, 2006). **HONORS:** Named N.L. Rookie Pitcher of the Year by THE SPORTING NEWS (2001). **STATISTICAL NOTES:** Pitched one inning, combining with Peter Munro (2 2/3 innings), Kirk Saarloos (1 1/3 innings), Brad Lidge (two innings), Octavio Dotel (one inning) and Billy Wagner (one inning) on 8-0 no-hitter against New York Yankees (June 11, 2003). **MISCELLANEOUS NOTES:** Member of 2000 U.S. Olympic baseball team. ... Made an out and struck out in two appearances as pinch hitter (2006).
CAREER HITTING: 59-for-373 (.158), 17 R, 6 2B, 0 3B, 1 HR, 23 RBI.

Year Team (League)	W	L	Pct.	ERA	WHIP	G	GS	CG	ShO	Hld.	Sv.-Opp.	IP	H	R	ER	HR	BB-IBB	SO	Avg.
1997—GC Astros (GCL)	1	1	.500	0.64	1.13	5	5	0	0	...	0-...	28.1	25	7	2	2	7-0	28	.227
—Auburn (NY-Penn)	2	4	.333	4.53	1.26	9	9	1	1	...	0-...	51.2	50	29	26	1	15-1	44	.253
1998—GC Astros (GCL)	1	1	.500	2.25	0.69	4	4	0	0	...	0-...	16.0	10	6	4	2	1-0	27	.182
—Auburn (NY-Penn)	4	5	.444	2.18	1.14	11	11	0	0	...	0-...	70.1	49	24	17	3	31-0	67	.194
1999—Michigan (Midw.)	13	4	.765	4.46	1.31	22	22	2	0	...	0-...	151.1	144	78	75	8	54-0	143	.250
2000—Kissimmee (Fla. St.)	4	3	.571	2.98	1.39	8	8	0	0	...	0-...	45.1	52	15	15	1	11-0	47	.294
—Round Rock (Texas)	11	4	.733	1.94	0.99	19	18	2	2	...	0-...	129.2	106	37	28	5	22-1	141	.223
2001—New Orleans (PCL)	2	3	.400	4.35	1.23	5	5	0	0	...	0-...	31.0	32	16	15	4	6-0	34	.267
—Houston (N.L.)	14	3	.824	2.73	1.06	28	20	3	1	0	0-0	141.2	126	48	43	13	24-2	144	.235
2002—Houston (N.L.)	19	9	.679	3.01	1.19	35	34	0	0	0	0-0	233.0	215	86	78	17	62-4	208	.247
2003—New Orleans (PCL)	0	0		3.00	1.00	1	1	0	0	...	0-...	3.0	3	1	1	0	0-0	2	.250
—Houston (N.L.)	10	5	.667	2.97	1.14	21	21	0	0	0	0-0	127.1	116	48	42	15	29-0	108	.246
2004—Houston (N.L.)	* 20	10	.667	3.49	1.24	36	• 35	2	0	0	0-0	237.0	233	100	92	17	62-5	206	.260
2005—Houston (N.L.)	20	12	.625	2.94	1.20	35	• 35	4	1	0	0-0	241.2	243	85	79	18	48-3	184	.262
2006—Houston (N.L.)	15	8	.652	* 2.98	1.17	33	32	0	0	0	0-0	220.2	220	76	73	18	38-4	166	.263
Major League totals (6 years)	98	47	.676	3.05	1.18	188	177	11	4	0	0-0	1201.1	1153	443	407	98	263-18	1016	.254

DIVISION SERIES RECORD

Year — Team (League)	W	L	Pct.	ERA	WHIP	G	GS	CG	ShO	Hld.	Sv.-Opp.	IP	H	R	ER	HR	BB-IBB	SO	Avg.
2004— Houston (N.L.)	1	0	1.000	2.38	1.68	2	2	0	0	0	0-0	11.1	15	3	3	2	4-0	8	.313
2005— Houston (N.L.)	1	0	1.000	3.68	1.09	1	1	0	0	0	0-0	7.1	6	3	3	0	2-0	7	.222
Division series totals (2 years)	2	0	1.000	2.89	1.45	3	3	0	0	0	0-0	18.2	21	6	6	2	6-0	15	.280

CHAMPIONSHIP SERIES RECORD

Year — Team (League)	W	L	Pct.	ERA	WHIP	G	GS	CG	ShO	Hld.	Sv.-Opp.	IP	H	R	ER	HR	BB-IBB	SO	Avg.
2004— Houston (N.L.)	0	0	...	6.75	1.88	2	1	0	0	0	0-0	8.0	11	6	6	1	4-0	2	.367
2005— Houston (N.L.)	2	0	1.000	1.29	0.86	2	2	0	0	0	0-0	14.0	8	2	2	1	4-0	12	.163
Champ. series totals (2 years)	2	0	1.000	3.27	1.23	4	3	0	0	0	0-0	22.0	19	8	8	2	8-0	14	.241

WORLD SERIES RECORD

Year — Team (League)	W	L	Pct.	ERA	WHIP	G	GS	CG	ShO	Hld.	Sv.-Opp.	IP	H	R	ER	HR	BB-IBB	SO	Avg.
2005— Houston (N.L.)	0	0	...	7.50	2.17	1	1	0	0	0	0-0	6.0	8	5	5	1	5-0	3	.320

ALL-STAR GAME RECORD

Year — Team (League)	W	L	Pct.	ERA	WHIP	G	GS	CG	ShO	Hld.	Sv.-Opp.	IP	H	R	ER	HR	BB-IBB	SO	Avg.
All-Star Game totals (2 years)	0	0	...	9.00	1.50	2	0	0	0	0	0-0	2.0	2	2	2	0	1-0	2	.250

2006 LEFTY-RIGHTY SPLITS

vs.	Avg.	AB	H	2B	3B	HR	RBI	BB	SO	OBP	Slg.	vs.	Avg.	AB	H	2B	3B	HR	RBI	BB	SO	OBP	Slg.
L	.264	367	97	23	2	6	32	19	75	.302	.387	R	.262	469	123	32	2	12	38	19	91	.296	.416

OTSUKA, AKINORI   P

PERSONAL: Born January 13, 1972, in Chiba, Japan. ... 6-0/200. ... Throws right, bats right. ... Name pronounced: oats-kah. ... High school: Yokoshiba (Japan). ... College: Tokai University. **TRANSACTIONS/CAREER NOTES:** Signed as a free agent by San Diego Padres (December 9, 2003). ... Traded by Padres with P Adam Eaton and C Billy Killian to Texas Rangers for 1B Adrian Gonzalez, OF Terrmel Sledge and P Chris Young (January 4, 2006).
CAREER HITTING: 0-for-2 (.000), 0 R, 0 2B, 0 3B, 0 HR, 0 RBI.

Year — Team (League)	W	L	Pct.	ERA	WHIP	G	GS	CG	ShO	Hld.	Sv.-Opp.	IP	H	R	ER	HR	BB-IBB	SO	Avg.
1997— Kintetsu (Jp. Pac.)	4	5	.444	2.07	1.09	52	0	0	0	...	7-...	82.2	44	22	19	2	46-0	127	...
1998— Kintetsu (Jp. Pac.)	3	2	.600	2.11	1.23	49	0	0	0	...	35-...	55.1	43	19	13	5	25-0	74	...
1999— Kintetsu (Jp. Pac.)	1	4	.200	2.73	1.15	25	0	0	0	...	6-...	29.2	24	12	9	1	10-0	32	...
2000— Kintetsu (Jp. Pac.)	1	3	.250	2.38	1.06	39	0	0	0	...	24-...	41.2	31	11	11	3	13-0	49	...
2001— Kintetsu (Jp. Pac.)	2	5	.286	4.02	1.02	48	0	0	0	...	26-...	56.0	42	25	25	7	15-0	82	...
2002— Kintetsu (Jp. Pac.)	2	1	.667	1.28	0.59	41	0	0	0	...	22-...	42.1	22	7	6	4	3-0	54	...
2003— Chunichi (Jp. Cn.)	1	3	.250	2.09	0.84	51	0	0	0	...	17-...	43.0	31	10	10	4	5-0	56	.199
2004— San Diego (N.L.)	7	2	.778	1.75	1.06	73	0	0	0	* 34	2-7	77.1	56	16	15	6	26-6	87	.199
2005— San Diego (N.L.)	2	8	.200	3.59	1.42	66	0	0	0	22	1-7	62.2	55	28	25	3	34-8	60	.234
2006— Texas (A.L.)	2	4	.333	2.11	1.07	63	0	0	0	7	32-36	59.2	53	17	14	3	11-0	47	.241
American League totals (1 year)	2	4	.333	2.11	1.07	63	0	0	0	7	32-36	59.2	53	17	14	3	11-0	47	.241
National League totals (2 years)	9	10	.474	2.57	1.22	139	0	0	0	56	3-14	140.0	111	44	40	9	60-14	147	.215
Major League totals (3 years)	11	14	.440	2.43	1.18	202	0	0	0	63	35-50	199.2	164	61	54	12	71-14	194	.223

DIVISION SERIES RECORD

Year — Team (League)	W	L	Pct.	ERA	WHIP	G	GS	CG	ShO	Hld.	Sv.-Opp.	IP	H	R	ER	HR	BB-IBB	SO	Avg.
2005— San Diego (N.L.)	0	0	...	0.00	0.67	3	0	0	0	0	0-0	3.0	1	0	0	0	1-1	0	.100

2006 LEFTY-RIGHTY SPLITS

vs.	Avg.	AB	H	2B	3B	HR	RBI	BB	SO	OBP	Slg.	vs.	Avg.	AB	H	2B	3B	HR	RBI	BB	SO	OBP	Slg.
L	.287	115	33	3	1	3	17	4	23	.308	.409	R	.190	105	20	1	1	0	7	24	.241	.219

OVERBAY, LYLE   1B

PERSONAL: Born January 28, 1977, in Centralia, Wash. ... 6-2/225. ... Bats left, throws left. ... Full name: Lyle Stefan Overbay. ... High school: Centralia (Wash.). ... College: Nevada. **TRANSACTIONS/CAREER NOTES:** Selected by Arizona Diamondbacks organization in 18th round of 1999 free-agent draft. ... Traded by Diamondbacks with SS Craig Counsell, 2B Junior Spivey, C Chad Moeller and Ps Chris Capuano and Jorge de la Rosa to Milwaukee Brewers for 1B Richie Sexson, P Shane Nance and a player to be named (December 1, 2003); Diamondbacks acquired OF Noochie Varner to complete deal (December 15, 2003). ... Traded by Brewers with a player to be named to Toronto Blue Jays for Ps Dave Bush, Zach Jackson and OF Gabe Gross (December 7, 2005); Blue Jays acquired P Ty Taubenheim to complete the deal (December 8, 2005). **STATISTICAL NOTES:** Career major league grand slams: 3.
2006 GAMES PLAYED BY POSITION (MLB): 1B—145, DH—11.

Year — Team (League)	Pos.	G	AB	R	H	2B	3B	HR	RBI	BB	SO	HBP	GDP	SB-CS	Avg.	OBP	SLG	OPS	E	Avg.
1999— Missoula (Pion.)	1B-OF	75	306	66	105	25	7	12	101	40	53	2	14	10-3	.343	.418	.588	1.006	10	.986
2000— South Bend (Mid.)	1B	71	259	47	86	19	3	6	47	27	36	2	2	9-2	.332	.397	.498	.895	11	.983
— El Paso (Texas)	1B	62	244	43	86	16	2	8	49	28	39	2	6	3-2	.352	.420	.533	.953	12	.979
2001— El Paso (Texas)	1B-OF	138	532	82	187	49	3	13	100	67	92	5	6	5-4	.352	.423	.528	.951	13	.987
— Arizona (N.L.)		2	2	0	1	0	0	0	0	0	1	0	0	0-0	.500	.500	.500	1.000	...	...
2002— Tucson (PCL)	1B	134	525	83	180	40	0	19	109	42	86	7	12	0-0	.343	.396	.528	.923	10	.991
— Arizona (N.L.)		10	10	0	1	0	0	0	1	0	5	0	0	0-0	.100	.100	.100	.200	0	...
2003— Tucson (PCL)	1B-DH	35	119	24	34	11	0	4	16	28	19	0	2	1-0	.286	.419	.479	.898	5	.985
— Arizona (N.L.)	1B	86	254	23	70	20	0	4	28	35	67	2	8	1-0	.276	.365	.402	.767	2	.997
2004— Milwaukee (N.L.)	1B	159	579	83	174	* 53	1	16	87	81	128	2	11	2-1	.301	.385	.478	.863	11	.992
2005— Milwaukee (N.L.)	1B	158	537	80	148	34	1	19	72	78	98	2	17	1-0	.276	.367	.449	.816	10	.992
2006— Toronto (A.L.)	1B-DH	157	581	82	181	46	1	22	92	55	96	2	19	5-3	.312	.372	.508	.880	9	.994
American League totals (1 year)		157	581	82	181	46	1	22	92	55	96	2	19	5-3	.312	.372	.508	.880	9	.994
National League totals (5 years)		415	1382	186	394	107	2	39	188	194	299	6	36	4-1	.285	.373	.450	.823	23	.993
Major League totals (6 years)		572	1963	268	575	153	3	61	280	249	395	8	55	9-4	.293	.372	.467	.840	32	.993

2006 LEFTY-RIGHTY SPLITS

vs.	Avg.	AB	H	2B	3B	HR	RBI	BB	SO	OBP	Slg.	vs.	Avg.	AB	H	2B	3B	HR	RBI	BB	SO	OBP	Slg.
L	.284	162	46	8	0	3	18	4	31	.305	.389	R	.322	419	135	38	1	19	74	51	65	.395	.554

OWENS, HENRY   P

PERSONAL: Born April 23, 1979, in Miami, Fla. ... 6-3/230. ... Throws right, bats right. ... Full name: Henry Jay Owens. ... College: Barry. **TRANSACTIONS/CAREER NOTES:** Signed as a non-drafted free agent by Pittsburgh Pirates organization (June 7, 2001). ... Selected by New York Mets organization from Pirates organization in Rule 5 minor league draft (December 13, 2004).
CAREER HITTING: 0-for-0 (.000), 0 R, 0 2B, 0 3B, 0 HR, 0 RBI.

O

Year Team (League)	W	L	Pct.	ERA	WHIP	G	GS	CG	ShO	Hld.	Sv.-Opp.	IP	H	R	ER	HR	BB-IBB	SO	Avg.
2001— GC Pirates (GCL)	1	0	1.000	1.29	1.00	6	0	0	0	...	1-...	7.0	5	1	1	0	2-0	8	.192
2002— Will. (NYP)	0	3	.000	2.62	0.94	23	0	0	0	...	7-...	44.2	26	18	13	4	16-0	63	.166
2003— Hickory (S. Atl.)	2	1	.667	2.91	1.12	22	0	0	0	...	9-...	34.0	21	14	11	0	17-0	52	.176
— Lynchburg (Caro.)	1	2	.333	2.45	1.36	13	0	0	0	...	5-...	14.2	9	6	4	0	11-0	21	.176
2004— Lynchburg (Caro.)	3	4	.429	4.28	1.32	39	0	0	0	...	4-...	54.2	46	26	26	4	26-1	49	.219
2005— St. Lucie (Fla. St.)	2	5	.286	3.15	1.34	38	1	0	0	1	4-6	54.1	49	29	19	2	24-0	74	.233
2006— New York (N.L.)	0	0	...	9.00	2.00	3	0	0	0	0	0-0	4.0	4	4	4	0	4-0	2	.286
— Binghamton (East.)	2	2	.500	1.58	0.73	37	0	0	0	0	20-22	40.0	19	9	7	1	10-1	74	.137
Major League totals (1 year)	0	0	...	9.00	2.00	3	0	0	0	0	0-0	4.0	4	4	4	0	4-0	2	.286

2006 LEFTY-RIGHTY SPLITS

vs.	Avg.	AB	H	2B	3B	HR	RBI	BB	SO	OBP	Slg.	vs.	Avg.	AB	H	2B	3B	HR	RBI	BB	SO	OBP	Slg.
L	.167	6	1	0	0	0	2	1	2	.250	.167	R	.375	8	3	0	0	0	2	3	0	.545	.375

OWENS, JERRY — OF

PERSONAL: Born February 16, 1981, in Hollywood, Calif. ... 6-3/195. ... Bats left, throws left. ... Full name: Jerry Lee Owens. ... College: Masters (Calif.) College. **TRANSACTIONS/CAREER NOTES:** Selected by Montreal Expos organization in second round of 2003 free-agent draft. ... Expos franchise transferred to Washington, D.C., and renamed Nationals for 2005 season (December 3, 2004). ... Traded by Nationals to Chicago White Sox for OF Alex Escobar (February 13, 2005). ... On disabled list (August 26-September 10, 2006); included rehabilitation assignment to Charlotte SC.

2006 GAMES PLAYED BY POSITION (MLB): DH—6, OF—5.

Year Team (League)	Pos.	G	AB	R	H	2B	3B	HR	RBI	BB	SO	HBP	GDP	SB-CS	Avg.	OBP	SLG	OPS	E	Avg.
2003— Vermont (NYP)		2	8	0	1	0	0	0	0	0	2	0	0	1-0	.125	.125	.125	.250	...	...
2004— Savannah (S. Atl.)		108	418	69	122	17	2	1	37	46	59	3	3	30-13	.292	.365	.349	.714	...	...
2005— Birmingham (Sou.)	OF-DH	130	522	99	173	21	6	2	52	52	72	5	5	38-20	.331	.393	.406	.799	6	.987
2006— Charlotte (Int'l)		112	439	75	115	15	5	4	48	45	61	1	5	40-12	.262	.330	.346	.676	4	.984
— Chicago (A.L.)	DH-OF	12	9	4	3	1	0	0	0	0	2	0	0	1-0	.333	.333	.444	.778	0	1.000
Major League totals (1 year)		12	9	4	3	1	0	0	0	0	2	0	0	1-0	.333	.333	.444	.778	0	1.000

2006 LEFTY-RIGHTY SPLITS

vs.	Avg.	AB	H	2B	3B	HR	RBI	BB	SO	OBP	Slg.	vs.	Avg.	AB	H	2B	3B	HR	RBI	BB	SO	OBP	Slg.
L	.000	1	0	0	0	0	0	0	1	.000	.000	R	.375	8	3	1	0	0	0	0	1	.375	.500

OZUNA, PABLO — OF/3B

PERSONAL: Born August 25, 1974, in Santo Domingo, Dominican Republic. ... 5-10/186. ... Bats right, throws right. ... Full name: Pablo Jose Ozuna. ... Name pronounced: oh-ZU-na. **TRANSACTIONS/CAREER NOTES:** Signed as non-drafted free agent by St. Louis Cardinals orgnaization (April 8, 1996). ... Traded by Cardinals with P Braden Looper and P Armando Almanza to Florida Marlins for SS Edgar Renteria (December 14, 1998). ... On disabled list (March 23, 2001-entire season). ... Traded by Marlins with C Charles Johnson, P Vic Darensbourg and OF Preston Wilson to Colorado Rockies for P Mike Hampton, OF Juan Pierre and cash (November 16, 2002). ... On disabled list (March 29-June 6, 2003); included rehabilitation assignment to Visalia. ... Released by Rockies (December 14, 2003). ... Signed by Detroit Tigers organization (January 14, 2004). ... Traded by Tigers to Philadelphia Phillies for cash (March 28, 2004). ... Signed as a free agent by Chicago White Sox organization (January 19, 2005).

2006 GAMES PLAYED BY POSITION (MLB): OF—39, 3B—17, DH—9, 2B—6.

Year Team (League)	Pos.	G	AB	R	H	2B	3B	HR	RBI	BB	SO	HBP	GDP	SB-CS	Avg.	OBP	SLG	OPS	E	Avg.
1996— Dom. Cardinals (DSL)	SS	74	295	57	107	12	4	6	60	23	19			19-...	.363	...	.492	...	32	.915
— St. Louis (DSL)		74	295	57	107	12	4	6	60	23	19	6	0	18-5	.363	.415	.492	.907	...	...
1997— Johnson City (App.)	SS	56	232	40	75	13	1	5	24	10	24	1	2	23-5	.323	.351	.453	.804	25	.898
1998— Peoria (Midw.)	SS	133	538	122	192	27	10	9	62	29	56	11	4	62-26	.357	.400	.494	.894	45	.929
1999— Portland (East.)	SS	117	502	62	141	25	7	7	46	13	50	13	8	31-16	.281	.315	.400	.715	28	.946
2000— Portland (East.)	SS-2B	118	464	74	143	25	6	7	59	40	55	7	9	35-24	.308	.368	.433	.801	25	.956
— Florida (N.L.)	2B	14	24	2	8	1	0	0	0	0	2	0	0	1-0	.333	.333	.375	.708	1	.967
2001— Florida (N.L.)		Did not play.																		
2002— Calgary (PCL)	2B-2B-OF	77	261	37	85	16	1	7	33	17	37	3	5	16-3	.326	.371	.475	.846	9	.961
— Florida (N.L.)	2B-OF	34	47	4	13	2	2	0	3	1	3	1	2	1-1	.277	.300	.404	.704	1	.967
2003— Visalia (Calif.)	2B-SS-2B	2	8	1	5	0	0	0	1	1	1	0	2	1-1	.625	.667	.625	1.292	0	1.000
— Tulsa (Texas)	2B-SS-3B	12	59	4	15	3	0	0	4	2	1	0	0	4-2	.254	.279	.305	.584	3	.943
— Colo. Springs (PCL)	2B-OF-SS 3B	56	219	30	59	13	7	1	17	9	23	1	4	12-6	.269	.300	.406	.706	6	.970
— Colorado (N.L.)	2B-SS-OF	17	40	5	8	1	0	0	2	2	4	1	1	3-0	.200	.273	.225	.498	2	.969
2004— Scran./W.B. (I.L.)	2B-SS-OF	126	472	77	145	27	3	6	76	22	43	7	11	31-12	.307	.344	.415	.759	15	.786
2005— Chicago (A.L.)	3B-SS-OF 2B-DH-1B	70	203	27	56	7	0	0	11	7	26	4	5	14-7	.276	.313	.330	.643	1	.951
2006— Chicago (A.L.)	OF-3B-DH 2B	79	189	25	62	12	2	0	7	7	16	4	3	6-6	.328	.365	.444	.809	1	.988
American League totals (2 years)		149	392	52	118	19	4	2	28	14	42	8	8	20-13	.301	.338	.385	.723	10	.962
National League totals (3 years)		65	111	11	29	4	2	0	5	3	11	3	3	5-1	.261	.297	.333	.630	4	.968
Major League totals (5 years)		214	503	63	147	23	6	2	33	17	53	11	11	25-14	.292	.329	.374	.703	14	.964

CHAMPIONSHIP SERIES RECORD

Year Team (League)	Pos.	G	AB	R	H	2B	3B	HR	RBI	BB	SO	HBP	GDP	SB-CS	Avg.	OBP	SLG	OPS	E	Avg.
2005— Chicago (A.L.)	DH	2	0	1	0	0	0	0	0	0	0	0	0	1-0	...	...	...	...	0	...

2006 LEFTY-RIGHTY SPLITS

vs.	Avg.	AB	H	2B	3B	HR	RBI	BB	SO	OBP	Slg.	vs.	Avg.	AB	H	2B	3B	HR	RBI	BB	SO	OBP	Slg.
L	.322	143	46	11	2		15	6	11	.358	.469		R	.348	46	16	1	0	0	2	1	5	.388	.370

PADILLA, JUAN — P

PERSONAL: Born February 17, 1977, in Rio Piedras, Puerto Rico. ... 6-0/200. ... Throws right, bats right. ... Full name: Juan Miguel Padilla. ... Name pronounced: pa-DEE-ya. ... High school: Visual Arts (Santurce, Puerto Rico). ... Junior college: Tallahassee (Fla.) Community College. ... College: Jacksonville. **TRANSACTIONS/CAREER NOTES:** Selected by Minnesota Twins in 24th round of 1998 free-agent draft. ... Traded by Twins to New York Yankees (September 2, 2003), completing deal in which Twins acquired P Jesse Orosco for a player to be named (August 31, 2003). ... Claimed on waivers by Cincinnati Reds (September 3, 2004). ... Signed as a free agent by New York Mets organization (December 2, 2004). ... On disabled list (March 22, 2006-entire season).

CAREER HITTING: 1-for-2 (.500), 0 R, 0 2B, 0 3B, 0 HR, 0 RBI.

Year Team (League)	W	L	Pct.	ERA	WHIP	G	GS	CG	ShO	Hld.	Sv.-Opp.	IP	H	R	ER	HR	BB-IBB	SO	Avg.
1998— GC Twins (GCL)	1	1	.500	1.40	0.78	17	0	0	0		10-...	25.2	19	4	4	1	1-0	27	.202
1999— Quad City (Midw.)	0	2	.000	2.40	1.60	12	0	0	0		0-...	15.0	18	8	4	0	6-2	16	.290
— New Britain (East.)	1	1	.500	6.63	2.00	11	0	0	0		2-...	19.0	31	15	14	3	7-0	12	.383
— Fort Myers (FSL)	2	2	.500	3.48	1.46	22	0	0	0		0-...	33.2	32	14	13	1	17-2	28	.260
2000— Quad City (Midw.)	2	2	.500	1.91	1.00	32	0	0	0		16-...	33.0	24	7	7	0	9-2	40	.200
— New Britain (East.)	0	1	.000	3.74	1.37	23	0	0	0		0-...	33.2	35	15	14	1	11-0	24	.269
2001— Fort Myers (FSL)	6	4	.600	2.99	1.40	56	0	0	0		23-...	69.1	72	35	23	2	25-6	77	.261
2002— New Britain (East.)	3	5	.375	3.31	1.33	54	0	0	0		29-...	65.1	69	30	24	2	18-6	52	.267
2003— Rochester (Int'l)	7	4	.636	3.36	1.22	57	0	0	0		6-...	91.0	94	40	34	7	17-3	68	.266
2004— Trenton (East.)	0	0		9.00	1.75	3	0	0	0		0-...	4.0	4	4	4	1	3-0	4	.267
— New York (A.L.)	0	0		3.97	1.76	6	0	0	0	0	0-0	11.1	16	5	5	1	4-0	5	.348
— Columbus (Int'l)	2	1	.667	2.03	0.95	44	0	0	0		0-...	57.2	49	20	13	1	6-2	52	.232
— Cincinnati (N.L.)	1	0	1.000	10.67	2.16	12	0	0	0	0	0-...	14.1	23	17	17	6	8-0	12	.359
2005— Norfolk (Int'l)	3	2	.600	1.42	0.85	37	0	0	0		11-14	63.1	45	13	10	4	9-0	59	.197
— New York (N.L.)	3	1	.750	1.49	1.02	24	0	0	0	6	1-2	36.1	24	7	6	0	13-2	17	.180
2006— New York (N.L.)				Did not play.															
American League totals (1 year)	0	0		3.97	1.76	6	0	0	0	0	0-0	11.1	16	5	5	1	4-0	5	.348
National League totals (2 years)	4	1	.800	4.09	1.34	36	0	0	0	6	1-2	50.2	47	24	23	6	21-2	29	.239
Major League totals (2 years)	4	1	.800	4.06	1.42	42	0	0	0	6	1-2	62.0	63	29	28	7	25-2	34	.259

PADILLA, VICENTE   P

PERSONAL: Born September 27, 1977, in Chinandega, Nicaragua. ... 6-2/219. ... Throws right, bats right. ... Full name: Vicente D. Padilla. ... Name pronounced: pa-DEE-ya. ... High school: Ruben Dario (Nicaragua). **TRANSACTIONS/CAREER NOTES:** Signed as a non-drafted free agent by Arizona Diamondbacks organization (August 31, 1998). ... Traded by Diamondbacks with 1B/OF Travis Lee and Ps Omar Daal and Nelson Figueroa to Philadelphia Phillies for P Curt Schilling (July 26, 2000). ... On disabled list (May 4-30, 2001); included rehabilitation assignment to Scranton/Wilkes-Barre. ... On disabled list (May 30-August 10, 2004); included rehabilitation assignments to Scranton/Wilkes-Barre and Clearwater. ... On disabled list (March 30-April 19, 2005). ... Traded by Phillies to Texas Rangers for a player to be named (December 12, 2005); Phillies acquired P Ricardo Rodriguez to complete deal (December 19, 2005). ... On suspended list (August 17-22, 2006).

CAREER HITTING: 19-for-206 (.092), 7 R, 3 2B, 1 3B, 0 HR, 13 RBI.

Year Team (League)	W	L	Pct.	ERA	WHIP	G	GS	CG	ShO	Hld.	Sv.-Opp.	IP	H	R	ER	HR	BB-IBB	SO	Avg.
1999— High Desert (Calif.)	4	1	.800	3.73	1.32	9	9	0	0		0-...	50.2	50	27	21	3	17-0	55	.253
— Tucson (PCL)	7	4	.636	3.75	1.40	18	14	0	0	...	0-...	93.2	107	47	39	6	24-7	58	.292
— Arizona (N.L.)	0	1	.000	16.88	3.75	5	0	0	0	1	0-1	2.2	7	5	5	1	4-0	2	.467
2000— Tucson (PCL)	0	1	.000	4.42	1.64	12	3	0	0	...	1-...	18.1	22	9	9	2	8-0	22	.306
— Arizona (N.L.)	2	1	.667	2.31	1.20	27	0	0	0	7	0-1	35.0	32	10	9	0	10-2	30	.242
— Philadelphia (N.L.)	2	6	.250	5.34	1.91	28	0	0	0	8	2-6	30.1	40	23	18	3	18-5	21	.328
2001— Philadelphia (N.L.)	3	1	.750	4.24	1.41	23	0	0	0	1	0-3	34.0	36	18	16	1	12-0	29	.273
— Scran./W.B. (I.L.)	7	0	1.000	2.42	0.92	16	16	0	0		0-...	81.2	64	24	22	8	11-0	75	.217
2002— Philadelphia (N.L.)	14	11	.560	3.28	1.22	32	32	1	1	0	0-0	206.0	198	83	75	16	53-5	128	.254
2003— Philadelphia (N.L.)	14	12	.538	3.62	1.24	32	32	1	1	0	0-0	208.2	196	94	84	22	62-4	133	.251
2004— Clearwater (FSL)	0	1	.000	9.00	2.00	1	1	0	0		0-...	2.0	3	2	2	0	1-0	1	.333
— Scran./W.B. (I.L.)	0	0		13.50	2.36	2	2	0	0		0-...	4.2	6	7	7	1	5-0	6	.286
— Philadelphia (N.L.)	7	7	.500	4.53	1.34	20	20	0	0	0	0-0	115.1	119	63	58	16	36-6	82	.267
2005— Clearwater (FSL)	0	1	.000	1.80	1.00	1	1	0	0		0-...	5.0	4	1	1	0	1-0	3	.200
— Scran./W.B. (I.L.)	1	0	1.000	3.60	1.60	1	1	0	0		0-...	5.0	6	2	2	0	2-0	4	.316
— Philadelphia (N.L.)	9	12	.429	4.71	1.50	27	27	0	0	0	0-0	147.0	146	79	77	22	74-9	103	.260
2006— Texas (A.L.)	15	10	.600	4.50	1.38	33	33	0	0	0	0-0	200.0	206	108	100	21	70-2	156	.266
American League totals (1 year)	15	10	.600	4.50	1.38	33	33	0	0	0	0-0	200.0	206	108	100	21	70-2	156	.266
National League totals (7 years)	51	51	.500	3.95	1.34	194	111	2	2	17	2-11	779.0	774	375	342	81	268-31	526	.261
Major League totals (8 years)	66	61	.520	4.06	1.35	227	144	2	2	17	2-11	979.0	980	483	442	102	338-33	682	.262

ALL-STAR GAME RECORD

	W	L	Pct.	ERA	WHIP	G	GS	CG	ShO	Hld.	Sv.-Opp.	IP	H	R	ER	HR	BB-IBB	SO	Avg.
All-Star Game totals (1 year)	0	0	...	0.00	0.50	1	0	0	0		0-0	2.0	1	0	0	0	1-0	0	.000

2006 LEFTY-RIGHTY SPLITS

vs.	Avg.	AB	H	2B	3B	HR	RBI	BB	SO	OBP	Slg.	vs.	Avg.	AB	H	2B	3B	HR	RBI	BB	SO	OBP	Slg.
L	.305	387	118	26	3	13	54	53	72	.401	.488	R	.228	386	88	21	1	8	41	17	84	.268	.350

PAGAN, ANGEL   OF

PERSONAL: Born July 2, 1981, in Rio Piedras, Puerto Rico. ... 6-1/180. ... Bats both, throws right. ... Full name: Angel Anthony Pagan. ... College: Indian River (FL) CC. **TRANSACTIONS/CAREER NOTES:** Selected by New York Mets organization in fourth round of 1999 free-agent draft. ... Traded by Mets to Chicago Cubs for cash (January 25, 2006). ... On disabled list (April 17-June 30, 2006); included rehabilitation assignments to Iowa and AZL Cubs.

2006 GAMES PLAYED BY POSITION (MLB): OF—58.

									BATTING									FIELDING	
Year Team (League)	Pos.	G	AB	R	H	2B	3B	HR	RBI	BB	SO	HBP	GDP	SB-CS	Avg.	OBP	SLG	OPS	E	Avg.
2000— Kingsport (Appalachian)		19	72	13	26	5	1	0	8	6	8	0	1	6-1	.361	.410	.458	.868	...	
2001— Columbia (S. Atl.)		15	57	4	17	1	1	0	5	6	5	0	1	3-2	.298	.365	.351	.716	...	
— Brook. N.Y.-Penn. (N.Y.-Penn.)		62	238	46	75	10	2	0	15	22	30	7	3	30-18	.315	.388	.374	.762	...	
2002— St. Lucie (Fla. St.)		16	67	12	23	2	1	1	7	7	9	0	5	10-2	.343	.405	.448	.853	...	
— Columbia (S. Atl.)		108	458	79	128	14	5	1	36	32	87	0	5	52-21	.279	.325	.338	.663	...	
2003— St. Lucie (Fla. St.)		113	441	64	110	15	5	1	33	35	80	2	5	35-15	.249	.307	.313	.620	...	
2004— Norfolk (Int'l)		12	45	13	13	3	3	0	1	4	8	0	0	4-1	.289	.347	.489	.836	...	
— Binghamton (East.)		112	449	71	129	25	8	4	63	42	96	1	6	29-5	.287	.346	.405	.751	...	
2005— Norfolk (Int'l)	OF-DH	129	516	69	140	20	6	8	44	49	111	1	7	27-15	.271	.333	.395	.729	18	.972
2006— Ariz. Cubs (Ariz.)		3	9	1	1	0	0	0	0	2	3	0	0	1-0	.111	.273	.111	.384	0	1.000
— Iowa (PCL)		4	15	2	4	0	0	0	1	1	4	0	0	1-0	.267	.313	.333	.646	1	.889
— Chicago (N.L.)	OF	77	170	28	42	6	2	5	18	15	28	0	4	4-2	.247	.306	.394	.701	1	.989
Major League totals (1 year)		77	170	28	42	6	2	5	18	15	28	0	4	4-2	.247	.306	.394	.701	1	.989

2006 LEFTY-RIGHTY SPLITS

vs.	Avg.	AB	H	2B	3B	HR	RBI	BB	SO	OBP	Slg.	vs.	Avg.	AB	H	2B	3B	HR	RBI	BB	SO	OBP	Slg.
L	.196	56	11	1	1	1	8	8	7	.292	.304	R	.272	114	31	5	1	4	10	7	21	.314	.439

P

PALMEIRO, ORLANDO   OF

PERSONAL: Born January 19, 1969, in Hoboken, N.J. ... 5-11/180. ... Bats left, throws left. ... Name pronounced: pahl-MARE-oh. ... High school: Southridge (Miami). ... College: Miami. ... Cousin of Rafael Palmeiro, first baseman with three teams (1986-2005). **TRANSACTIONS/CAREER NOTES:** Selected by California Angels organization in 33rd round of 1991 free-agent draft. ... On disabled list (September 1-26, 1994). ... Angels franchise renamed Anaheim Angels for 1997 season. ... On disabled list (August 23-September 7, 1997). ... Signed as a free agent by St. Louis Cardinals (February 2, 2003). ... Signed as a free agent by Houston Astros (January 19, 2004). ... On bereavement list (July 26-August 2, 2006).

2006 GAMES PLAYED BY POSITION (MLB): OF—23.

											BATTING									FIELDING	
Year	Team (League)	Pos.	G	AB	R	H	2B	3B	HR	RBI	BB	SO	HBP	GDP	SB-CS	Avg.	OBP	SLG	OPS	E	Avg.
1991— Boise (N'west)		OF	70	277	56	77	11	2	1	24	33	22	3	8	8-8	.278	.358	.343	.701	2	.986
1992— Quad City (Midw.)		OF	127	451	83	143	22	4	0	41	56	41	5	5	31-13	.317	.393	.384	.777	6	.973
1993— Midland (Texas)		OF	131	535	85	163	19	5	0	64	42	35	2	13	18-14	.305	.356	.359	.715	9	.973
1994— Vancouver (PCL)		OF	117	458	79	150	28	4	1	47	58	46	1	7	21-16	.328	.402	.413	.815	1	.996
1995— Vancouver (PCL)		OF-DH	107	398	66	122	21	4	0	47	41	34	3	11	16-7	.307	.371	.379	.751	1	.995
— California (A.L.)		OF-DH	15	20	3	7	0	0	0	1	1	1	0	0	0-0	.350	.381	.350	.731	0	1.000
1996— Vancouver (PCL)		OF	62	245	40	75	13	4	0	33	30	19	4	4	7-3	.306	.384	.392	.776	5	.959
— California (A.L.)		OF-DH	50	87	6	25	6	1	0	6	8	13	2	1	0-1	.287	.361	.379	.740	0	1.000
1997— Anaheim (A.L.)		OF-DH	74	134	19	29	2	2	0	8	17	11	1	4	2-2	.216	.307	.261	.568	2	.975
1998— Vancouver (PCL)		OF	43	140	21	42	13	3	1	29	16	10	0	2	3-1	.300	.363	.457	.820	0	1.000
— Anaheim (A.L.)		OF-DH	75	165	28	53	7	2	0	21	20	11	0	2	5-4	.321	.395	.388	.782	0	1.000
1999— Anaheim (A.L.)		OF-DH	109	317	46	88	12	1	1	23	39	30	6	4	5-5	.278	.364	.331	.696	1	.994
2000— Anaheim (A.L.)		OF-DH	108	243	38	73	20	2	0	25	38	20	2	4	4-1	.300	.395	.399	.794	2	.984
2001— Anaheim (A.L.)		OF-DH	104	230	29	56	10	1	2	23	25	24	3	3	6-6	.243	.319	.322	.641	1	.989
2002— Anaheim (A.L.)		OF-DH	110	263	35	79	12	1	0	31	30	22	0	7	7-2	.300	.368	.354	.722	1	.993
2003— St. Louis (N.L.)		OF	141	317	37	86	13	1	3	33	32	31	2	1	3-3	.271	.336	.347	.683	0	1.000
2004— Houston (N.L.)		OF	102	133	19	32	5	0	3	12	18	19	3	1	2-1	.241	.344	.346	.690	0	1.000
2005— Houston (N.L.)		OF	114	204	22	58	17	2	3	20	15	23	4	4	3-1	.284	.341	.431	.772	1	.986
2006— Houston (N.L.)		OF	103	119	12	30	6	1	0	17	6	17	1	2	0-1	.252	.294	.319	.613	0	1.000
American League totals (8 years)			645	1459	204	410	69	10	3	138	178	132	14	25	29-21	.281	.361	.348	.710	7	.991
National League totals (4 years)			460	773	90	206	41	4	9	82	71	90	10	8	8-6	.266	.333	.365	.697	1	.997
Major League totals (12 years)			1105	2232	294	616	110	14	12	220	249	222	24	33	37-27	.276	.352	.354	.705	8	.992

DIVISION SERIES RECORD

Year	Team (League)	Pos.	G	AB	R	H	2B	3B	HR	RBI	BB	SO	HBP	GDP	SB-CS	Avg.	OBP	SLG	OPS	E	Avg.
2004— Houston (N.L.)		OF	5	4	0	1	0	0	0	0	0	0	0	0	0-0	.250	.250	.250	.500	0	...
2005— Houston (N.L.)		OF	4	7	0	1	0	0	0	3	2	0	1	0	0-0	.143	.364	.143	.506	0	1.000
Division series totals (2 years)			9	11	0	2	0	0	0	3	2	0	1	0	0-0	.182	.333	.182	.515	0	...

CHAMPIONSHIP SERIES RECORD

Year	Team (League)	Pos.	G	AB	R	H	2B	3B	HR	RBI	BB	SO	HBP	GDP	SB-CS	Avg.	OBP	SLG	OPS	E	Avg.
2002— Anaheim (A.L.)		OF	2	2	0	0	0	0	0	0	0	1	0	0	0-0	.000	.000	.000	.000	0	...
2004— Houston (N.L.)		OF	7	6	0	2	1	0	0	0	0	0	1	0	0-0	.333	.429	.500	.929	0	...
2005— Houston (N.L.)			4	3	0	1	0	0	0	0	1	0	0	0	0-0	.333	.500	.333	.833	0	...
Champ. series totals (3 years)			13	11	0	3	1	0	0	0	1	1	1	0	0-0	.273	.385	.364	.748	0	...

WORLD SERIES RECORD

Year	Team (League)	Pos.	G	AB	R	H	2B	3B	HR	RBI	BB	SO	HBP	GDP	SB-CS	Avg.	OBP	SLG	OPS	E	Avg.
2002— Anaheim (A.L.)			4	4	1	1	1	0	0	0	2	0		0	0-0	.250	.250	.500	.750	0	...
2005— Houston (N.L.)		OF	2	2	0	0	0	0	0	0	2		0	0	0-0	.000	.500	.000	.500	0	...
World series totals (2 years)			6	6	1	1	1	0	0	0	2	2	0	0	0-0	.167	.375	.333	.708	0	...

2006 LEFTY-RIGHTY SPLITS

vs.	Avg.	AB	H	2B	3B	HR	RBI	BB	SO	OBP	Slg.	vs.	Avg.	AB	H	2B	3B	HR	RBI	BB	SO	OBP	Slg.
L	.000	3	0	0	0	0	0	0	1	.000	.000	R	.259	116	30	6	1	0	17	6	16	.301	.328

PAPELBON, JONATHAN   P

PERSONAL: Born November 23, 1980, in Baton Rouge, La. ... 6-4/230. ... Throws right, bats right. ... Full name: Jonathan Robert Papelbon. ... High school: Bishop Kenny (Jacksonville). ... College: Mississippi State. **TRANSACTIONS/CAREER NOTES:** Selected by Boston Red Sox organization in fourth round of 2003 free-agent draft.

CAREER HITTING: 0-for-0 (.000), 0 R, 0 2B, 0 3B, 0 HR, 0 RBI.

Year	Team (League)	W	L	Pct.	ERA	WHIP	G	GS	CG	ShO	Hld.	Sv.-Opp.	IP	H	R	ER	HR	BB-IBB	SO	Avg.
2003— Lowell (NY-Penn)		1	2	.333	6.34	1.59	13	6	0	0	...	0-...	32.2	43	23	23	2	9-0	36	.312
2004— Sarasota (Fla. St.)		12	7	.632	2.64	1.08	24	24	2	0	...	0-...	129.2	97	43	38	6	43-2	153	.210
2005— Portland (East.)		5	2	.714	2.48	0.94	14	14	0	0	0	0-0	87.0	59	28	24	9	23-3	83	.193
— Pawtucket (Int'l)		1	2	.333	2.93	0.87	7	4	0	0	0	1-1	27.2	21	9	9	2	3-0	27	.208
— Boston (A.L.)		3	1	.750	2.65	1.47	17	3	0	0	4	0-1	34.0	33	11	10	4	17-2	34	.260
2006— Boston (A.L.)		4	2	.667	0.92	0.78	59	0	0	0	1	35-41	68.1	40	8	7	3	13-2	75	.167
Major League totals (2 years)		7	3	.700	1.50	1.01	76	3	0	0	5	35-42	102.1	73	19	17	7	30-4	109	.199

DIVISION SERIES RECORD

Year	Team (League)	W	L	Pct.	ERA	WHIP	G	GS	CG	ShO	Hld.	Sv.-Opp.	IP	H	R	ER	HR	BB-IBB	SO	Avg.
2005— Boston (A.L.)		0	0	...	0.00	0.50	2	0	0	0	0	0-0	4.0	2	0	0	0	0-0	2	.143

2006 LEFTY-RIGHTY SPLITS

vs.	Avg.	AB	H	2B	3B	HR	RBI	BB	SO	OBP	Slg.	vs.	Avg.	AB	H	2B	3B	HR	RBI	BB	SO	OBP	Slg.
L	.203	123	25	7	0	2	7	8	37	.248	.309	R	.128	117	15	3	1	1	4	5	38	.171	.197

PARK, CHAN HO   P

PERSONAL: Born June 30, 1973, in Kong Ju City, South Korea. ... 6-2/210. ... Throws right, bats right. ... Full name: Chan Ho Park. ... High school: Kong Ju (Kong Ju City, South Korea). ... College: Hanyang University (South Korea). **TRANSACTIONS/CAREER NOTES:** Signed as a non-drafted free agent by Los Angeles Dodgers organization (January 14, 1994). ... On suspended list (June 8-17, 1999). ... Signed as a free agent by Texas Rangers (December 23, 2001). ... On disabled list (April 2-May 12 and August 7-23, 2002). ... On disabled list (April 28-June 7 and June 8, 2003-remainder of season); included rehabilitation assignments to Frisco and Oklahoma. ... On disabled list (May 20-August 26, 2004); included rehabilitation assignments to AZL Rangers, Frisco and Oklahoma. ... Traded by Rangers to San Diego Padres for IF Phil Nevin (July 29, 2005). ... On disabled list (July 26-August 11, 2006 and August 21-September 22, 2006). **MISCELLANEOUS NOTES:** Had a sacrifice hit and made an out in two appearances as pinch hitter (2006).

CAREER HITTING: 74-for-405 (.183), 26 R, 15 2B, 1 3B, 2 HR, 30 RBI.

Year Team (League)	W	L	Pct.	ERA	WHIP	G	GS	CG	ShO	Hld.	Sv.-Opp.	IP	H	R	ER	HR	BB-IBB	SO	Avg.
1994— Los Angeles (N.L.)	0	0	...	11.25	2.50	2	0	0	0	0	0-0	4.0	5	5	5	1	5-0	6	.294
— San Antonio (Texas)	5	7	.417	3.55	1.46	20	20	0	0	...	0-...	101.1	91	52	40	4	57-0	100	.241
1995— Albuquerque (PCL)	6	7	.462	4.91	1.54	23	22	0	0	...	0-...	110.0	93	64	60	10	76-2	101	.233
— Los Angeles (N.L.)	0	0	...	4.50	1.00	2	1	0	0	0	0-0	4.0	2	2	2	1	2-0	7	.143
1996— Los Angeles (N.L.)	5	5	.500	3.64	1.41	48	10	0	0	0	0-4	108.2	82	48	44	7	71-3	119	.209
1997— Los Angeles (N.L.)	14	8	.636	3.38	1.14	32	29	2	0	0	0-0	192.0	149	80	72	24	70-1	166	.213
1998— Los Angeles (N.L.)	15	9	.625	3.71	1.34	34	34	2	0	0	0-0	220.2	199	101	91	16	97-1	191	.244
1999— Los Angeles (N.L.)	13	11	.542	5.23	1.58	33	33	0	0	0	0-0	194.1	208	120	113	31	100-4	174	.276
2000— Los Angeles (N.L.)	18	10	.643	3.27	1.31	34	34	3	1	0	0-0	226.0	173	92	82	21	124-4	217	.214
2001— Los Angeles (N.L.)	15	11	.577	3.50	1.17	36	•35	2	1	0	0-0	234.0	183	98	91	23	91-1	218	.216
2002— Texas (A.L.)	9	8	.529	5.75	1.59	25	25	0	0	0	0-0	145.2	154	95	93	20	78-2	121	.273
— Oklahoma (PCL)	0	1	.000	27.00	4.00	1	1	0	0	...	0-...	3.0	9	9	9	0	3-0	3	.500
2003— Frisco (Texas)	1	0	1.000	2.45	1.30	2	2	0	0	...	0-...	11.0	10	5	3	0	4-0	6	.238
— Oklahoma (PCL)	1	0	1.000	5.89	1.90	3	3	0	0	...	0-...	18.1	27	12	12	4	8-0	15	.346
— Texas (A.L.)	1	3	.250	7.58	1.99	7	7	0	0	0	0-...	29.2	34	26	25	5	25-0	16	.306
2004— Rangers (Ariz.)	1	1	.500	1.71	1.00	4	4	0	0	...	0-...	21.0	15	6	4	0	6-0	20	.197
— Frisco (Texas)	0	2	.000	8.74	1.85	2	2	0	0	...	0-...	11.1	16	11	11	1	5-0	5	.356
— Oklahoma (PCL)	0	2	.000	3.72	1.24	4	4	0	0	...	0-...	19.1	21	8	8	4	3-0	19	.273
— Texas (A.L.)	4	7	.364	5.46	1.44	16	16	0	0	0	0-0	95.2	105	63	58	22	33-0	63	.281
2005— Texas (A.L.)	8	5	.615	5.66	1.68	20	20	0	0	0	0-0	109.2	130	70	69	8	54-1	80	.299
— San Diego (N.L.)	4	3	.571	5.91	1.66	10	9	0	0	0	0-0	45.2	50	33	30	3	26-0	33	.278
2006— San Diego (N.L.)	7	7	.500	4.81	1.39	24	21	1	1	0	0-0	136.2	146	81	73	20	44-7	96	.271
American League totals (4 years)	22	23	.489	5.79	1.61	68	68	0	0	0	0-0	380.2	423	254	245	55	190-3	280	.285
National League totals (10 years)	91	64	.587	3.97	1.34	255	206	10	3	4	0-0	1366.0	1197	660	603	147	630-21	1227	.236
Major League totals (13 years)	113	87	.565	4.37	1.40	323	274	10	3	4	0-0	1746.2	1620	914	848	202	820-24	1507	.247

DIVISION SERIES RECORD

Year Team (League)	W	L	Pct.	ERA	WHIP	G	GS	CG	ShO	Hld.	Sv.-Opp.	IP	H	R	ER	HR	BB-IBB	SO	Avg.
2006— San Diego (N.L.)	0	0	...	0.00	0.50	1	0	0	0	0	0-0	2.0	1	0	0	0	0-0	0	.200

ALL-STAR GAME RECORD

	W	L	Pct.	ERA	WHIP	G	GS	CG	ShO	Hld.	Sv.-Opp.	IP	H	R	ER	HR	BB-IBB	SO	Avg.
All-Star Game totals (1 year)	0	1	.000	9.00	1.00	1	0	0	0	0	0-0	1.0	1	1	1	1	0-0	1	.250

2006 LEFTY-RIGHTY SPLITS

vs.	Avg.	AB	H	2B	3B	HR	RBI	BB	SO	OBP	Slg.	vs.	Avg.	AB	H	2B	3B	HR	RBI	BB	SO	OBP	Slg.
L	.266	290	77	21	2	12	42	30	49	.341	.476	R	.278	248	69	10	2	8	30	14	47	.328	.431

PARONTO, CHAD — P

PERSONAL: Born July 28, 1975, in Woodsville, N.H. ... 6-5/250. ... Throws right, bats right. ... Full name: Chad Michael Paronto. ... Name pronounced: pah-RON-toe. ... High school: Woodsville (N.H.). ... College: Massachusetts. **TRANSACTIONS/CAREER NOTES:** Selected by Baltimore Orioles organization in eighth round of free-agent draft (June 4, 1996). ... Claimed on waivers by Cleveland Indians (November 19, 2001). ... On disabled list (July 29, 2002-remainder of season); included rehabilitation assignment to Akron. ... Signed as a free agent by St. Louis Cardinals organization (November 24, 2003). ... Signed as a free agent by Milwaukee Brewers organization (March 1, 2005). ... Released by Brewers (June 17, 2005). ... Signed by Atlanta Braves organization (June 21, 2005).

CAREER HITTING: 0-for-1 (.000), 0 R, 0 2B, 0 3B, 0 HR, 0 RBI.

Year Team (League)	W	L	Pct.	ERA	WHIP	G	GS	CG	ShO	Hld.	Sv.-Opp.	IP	H	R	ER	HR	BB-IBB	SO	Avg.
1996— Bluefield (Appal.)	1	1	.500	1.69	0.98	9	2	0	0	...	1-...	21.1	16	4	4	0	5-0	24	.208
— Frederick (Carolina)	0	1	.000	4.80	1.27	8	1	0	0	...	0-...	15.0	11	9	8	0	8-0	6	.208
1997— Delmarva (S. Atl.)	6	9	.400	4.74	1.48	28	23	0	0	...	0-...	127.1	133	95	67	9	56-1	93	.265
1998— Frederick (Carolina)	7	6	.538	3.13	1.50	18	18	0	0	...	0-...	103.2	116	44	36	4	39-0	87	.287
— Bowie (East.)	1	3	.250	5.80	1.71	8	7	0	0	...	1-...	35.2	38	30	23	1	23-0	28	.275
1999— Bowie (East.)	0	4	.000	8.12	2.22	15	9	0	0	...	0-...	41.0	59	39	37	3	32-1	27	.345
— Frederick (Carolina)	3	5	.375	4.73	1.48	13	13	1	0	...	0-...	72.1	81	46	38	7	26-1	55	.280
2000— Rochester (Int'l)	1	1	.500	5.75	1.53	12	6	0	0	...	0-...	36.0	40	26	23	5	15-0	18	.280
— Bowie (East.)	4	2	.667	2.87	0.96	8	8	1	0	...	0-...	47.0	29	19	15	2	16-0	31	.180
2001— Rochester (Int'l)	3	3	.500	4.57	1.57	33	0	0	0	...	0-...	43.1	44	28	22	5	24-4	39	.263
— Baltimore (A.L.)	1	3	.250	5.00	1.63	24	0	0	0	5	0-1	27.0	33	24	15	5	11-0	16	.289
2002— Buffalo (Int'l)	0	0	...	0.00	0.85	8	0	0	0	...	1-...	13.0	10	0	0	0	1-1	7	.213
— Cleveland (A.L.)	0	2	.000	4.04	1.26	29	0	0	0	0	0-0	35.2	34	19	16	3	11-1	23	.248
— Akron (East.)	0	0	...	27.00	6.00	1	1	0	0	...	0-...	0.1	1	1	1	0	1-0	0	.500
2003— Cleveland (A.L.)	0	2	.000	9.45	1.50	6	0	0	0	0	0-0	6.2	7	8	7	1	3-0	6	.292
— Buffalo (Int'l)	3	5	.375	4.34	1.50	49	0	0	0	...	18-...	56.0	64	36	27	2	22-7	48	.275
2004— Memphis (PCL)	5	3	.625	2.13	1.29	47	0	0	0	...	4-...	55.0	46	20	13	3	25-3	38	.218
2005— Nashville (PCL)	3	1	.750	2.75	1.50	27	0	0	0	...	4-5	39.1	40	17	12	1	19-0	38	.263
— Richmond (Int'l)	3	1	.750	3.95	1.46	26	0	0	0	5	0-3	41.0	43	18	18	4	17-0	28	.281
2006— Richmond (Int'l)	1	1	.500	1.02	1.13	12	0	0	0	...	4-5	17.2	17	3	2	1	3-0	15	.250
— Atlanta (N.L.)	2	3	.400	3.18	1.27	65	0	0	0	8	0-2	56.2	53	23	20	5	19-3	41	.252
American League totals (3 years)	1	7	.125	4.93	1.43	59	0	0	0	5	0-1	69.1	74	51	38	9	25-1	45	.269
National League totals (1 year)	2	3	.400	3.18	1.27	65	0	0	0	8	0-2	56.2	53	23	20	5	19-3	41	.252
Major League totals (4 years)	3	10	.231	4.14	1.36	124	0	0	0	13	0-3	126.0	127	74	58	14	44-4	86	.262

2006 LEFTY-RIGHTY SPLITS

vs.	Avg.	AB	H	2B	3B	HR	RBI	BB	SO	OBP	Slg.	vs.	Avg.	AB	H	2B	3B	HR	RBI	BB	SO	OBP	Slg.
L	.288	73	21	2	1	1	8	6	11	.342	.384	R	.234	137	32	6	0	4	21	13	30	.312	.365

PARRISH, JOHN — P

PERSONAL: Born November 26, 1977, in Lancaster, Pa. ... 5-11/192. ... Throws left, bats left. ... Full name: John Henry Parrish Jr. ... High school: J.P. McCaskey (Lancaster, Pa.). **TRANSACTIONS/CAREER NOTES:** Selected by Baltimore Orioles organization in 25th round of 1996 free-agent draft. ... On disabled list (March 30, 2002-entire season). ... On disabled list (September 6, 2005-remainder of season). ... On disabled list (April 1, 2006-entire season). **MISCELLANEOUS NOTES:** Appeared in one game as pinch runner (2005).

CAREER HITTING: 0-for-1 (.000), 0 R, 0 2B, 0 3B, 0 HR, 0 RBI.

Year Team (League)	W	L	Pct.	ERA	WHIP	G	GS	CG	ShO	Hld.	Sv.-Opp.	IP	H	R	ER	HR	BB-IBB	SO	Avg.
1996— GC Orioles (GCL)	2	0	1.000	1.86	1.24	19	0	0	0	...	2-...	19.1	13	5	4	0	11-0	33	.181
— Bluefield (Appal.)	2	1	.667	2.70	1.50	8	0	0	0	...	1-...	13.1	11	6	4	0	9-1	18	.229
1997— Delmarva (S. Atl.)	3	3	.500	3.84	1.39	23	10	0	0	...	1-...	72.2	69	39	31	7	32-3	76	.250
— Bowie (East.)	1	0	1.000	1.80	1.00	1	1	0	0	...	0-...	5.0	3	1	1	0	2-0	3	.167

Year	Team (League)	W	L	Pct.	ERA	WHIP	G	GS	CG	ShO	Hld.	Sv.-Opp.	IP	H	R	ER	HR	BB-IBB	SO	Avg.
—	Frederick (Carolina)	1	3	.250	6.04	1.75	5	5	0	0	...	0-...	22.1	23	18	15	3	16-0	17	.274
1998—	Frederick (Carolina)	4	4	.500	3.27	1.26	16	16	1	0	...	0-...	82.2	77	39	30	5	27-1	81	.246
1999—	Delmarva (S. Atl.)	0	1	.000	7.20	1.50	4	0	0	0	...	0-...	10.0	9	8	8	1	6-1	10	.225
—	Frederick (Carolina)	2	2	.500	4.17	1.25	6	6	0	0	...	0-...	36.2	34	17	17	4	12-0	44	.250
—	Bowie (East.)	0	2	.000	4.04	1.65	12	10	0	0	...	0-...	55.2	49	28	25	4	43-1	42	.258
2000—	Bowie (East.)	2	0	1.000	1.69	1.19	3	3	0	0	...	0-...	16.0	12	3	3	0	7-0	16	.214
—	Rochester (Int'l)	6	7	.462	4.24	1.36	18	18	0	0	...	0-...	104.0	85	54	49	10	56-1	87	.235
—	Baltimore (A.L.)	2	4	.333	7.18	2.06	8	8	0	0	0	0-0	36.1	40	32	29	6	35-0	28	.288
2001—	Rochester (Int'l)	7	7	.500	3.52	1.25	26	19	1	0	...	0-...	133.0	115	68	52	11	51-4	126	.231
—	Baltimore (A.L.)	1	2	.333	6.14	1.77	16	1	0	0	0	0-0	22.0	22	17	15	5	17-1	20	.256
2002—	Baltimore (A.L.)			Did not play.																
2003—	Bowie (East.)	3	3	.500	2.00	1.20	49	0	0	0	...	6-...	76.1	58	22	17	5	33-0	85	.214
—	Baltimore (A.L.)	0	1	.000	1.90	1.06	14	0	0	0	1	0-2	23.2	17	7	5	2	8-2	15	.205
2004—	Baltimore (A.L.)	6	3	.667	3.46	1.58	56	1	0	0	2	1-1	78.0	68	39	30	4	55-6	71	.238
2005—	Baltimore (A.L.)	1	0	1.000	3.12	2.08	14	0	0	0	1	0-0	17.1	19	6	6	1	17-1	25	.279
—	Bowie (East.)	0	0	...	2.89	1.39	6	0	0	0	...	0-0	9.1	7	3	3	0	6-0	13	.212
2006—	Baltimore (A.L.)			Did not play.																
Major League totals (5 years)		10	10	.500	4.31	1.68	108	10	0	0	6	1-3	177.1	166	101	85	18	132-10	159	.251

PATTERSON, COREY   OF

PERSONAL: Born August 13, 1979, in Atlanta. ... 5-9/180. ... Bats left, throws right. ... Full name: Donald Corey Patterson. ... High school: Harrison (Kennesaw, Ga.). ... Son of Don Patterson, defensive back with Detroit Lions (1979) and New York Giants (1980). **TRANSACTIONS/CAREER NOTES:** Selected by Chicago Cubs organization in first round (third pick overall) of 1998 free-agent draft. ... On disabled list (July 7, 2003-remainder of season). ... Traded by Cubs to Baltimore Orioles for P Carlos Perez and 2B Nate Spears (January 9, 2006).

2006 GAMES PLAYED BY POSITION (MLB): OF—134.

											BATTING							FIELDING	
Year	Team (League)	Pos.	G	AB	R	H	2B	3B	HR	RBI	BB	SO	HBP	GDP	SB-CS	Avg.	OBP	SLG	OPS	E	Avg.
1999—	Lansing (Midw.)	OF	112	475	94	152	35	17	20	79	25	85	5	5	33-9	.320	.358	.592	.949	9	.965
2000—	West Tenn. (Sou.)	OF	118	444	73	116	26	5	22	82	45	115	10	7	27-15	.261	.338	.491	.829	3	.990
—	Chicago (N.L.)	OF	11	42	9	7	1	0	2	2	3	14	1	0	1-1	.167	.239	.333	.572	1	.963
2001—	Iowa (PCL)	OF	89	367	63	93	22	3	7	32	29	65	1	2	19-8	.253	.308	.387	.694	6	.968
—	Chicago (N.L.)	OF	59	131	26	29	3	0	4	14	6	33	1	1	4-0	.221	.266	.336	.602	2	.976
2002—	Chicago (N.L.)	OF	153	592	71	150	30	5	14	54	19	142	8	8	18-3	.253	.284	.392	.676	3	.990
2003—	Chicago (N.L.)	OF	83	329	49	98	17	7	13	55	15	77	1	5	16-5	.298	.329	.511	.839	4	.975
2004—	Chicago (N.L.)	OF	157	631	91	168	33	6	24	72	45	168	5	7	32-9	.266	.320	.452	.771	1	.991
2005—	Iowa (PCL)	OF	24	91	16	27	4	0	5	12	8	19	0	0	6-1	.297	.366	.505	.872	0	1.000
—	Chicago (N.L.)	OF	126	451	47	97	15	3	13	34	23	118	1	5	15-5	.215	.254	.348	.602	5	.980
2006—	Baltimore (A.L.)	OF	135	463	75	128	19	5	16	53	21	94	5	0	45-9	.276	.314	.443	.757	4	.989
American League totals (1 year)			135	463	75	128	19	5	16	53	21	94	5	0	45-9	.276	.314	.443	.757	4	.989
National League totals (6 years)			589	2176	293	549	99	21	70	231	111	552	19	26	86-23	.252	.293	.414	.707	16	.987
Major League totals (7 years)			724	2639	368	677	118	26	86	284	132	646	24	26	131-32	.257	.297	.419	.715	20	.987

2006 LEFTY-RIGHTY SPLITS

vs.	Avg.	AB	H	2B	3B	HR	RBI	BB	SO	OBP	Slg.	vs.	Avg.	AB	H	2B	3B	HR	RBI	BB	SO	OBP	Slg.
L	.207	121	25	1	2	3	14	4	29	.238	.322	R	.301	342	103	18	3	13	39	17	65	.341	.485

PATTERSON, JOHN   P

PERSONAL: Born January 30, 1978, in Orange, Texas. ... 6-5/208. ... Throws right, bats right. ... Full name: John Hollis Patterson. ... High school: West Orange-Stark (Orange, Texas). **TRANSACTIONS/CAREER NOTES:** Signed as a non-drafted free agent by Arizona Diamondbacks organization (November 7, 1996). ... On disabled list (April 6-24 and May 6-September 8, 2000). ... Traded by Diamondbacks to Montreal Expos for P Randy Choate (March 27, 2004). ... On disabled list (April 28-July 15, 2004); included rehabilitation assignments to Brevard County and Harrisburg. ... Expos franchise transferred to Washington, D.C., and renamed Washington Nationals for 2005 season (December 3, 2004). ... On disabled list (May 16-31, 2005). ... On disabled list (April 28-June 23, 2006); included rehabilitation assignments to Potomac and New Orleans. ... On disabled list (July 15, 2006-remainder of season).

CAREER HITTING: 14-for-123 (.114), 4 R, 3 2B, 0 3B, 0 HR, 2 RBI.

Year	Team (League)	W	L	Pct.	ERA	WHIP	G	GS	CG	ShO	Hld.	Sv.-Opp.	IP	H	R	ER	HR	BB-IBB	SO	Avg.
1997—	South Bend (Mid.)	1	9	.100	3.23	1.24	18	18	0	0	...	0-...	78.0	63	32	28	3	34-0	95	.221
1998—	High Desert (Calif.)	8	7	.533	2.83	1.13	25	25	0	0	...	0-...	127.0	102	54	40	12	42-0	148	.217
1999—	El Paso (Texas)	8	6	.571	4.77	1.40	18	18	2	0	...	0-...	100.0	98	61	53	16	42-0	117	.256
—	Tucson (PCL)	1	5	.167	7.04	1.99	7	6	0	0	...	0-...	30.2	43	26	24	3	18-0	29	.331
2000—	Tucson (PCL)	0	2	.000	7.80	2.00	3	2	0	0	...	0-...	15.0	21	14	13	1	9-0	13	.323
2001—	Lancaster (Calif.)	0	0	...	5.79	1.29	2	2	0	0	...	0-...	9.1	9	6	6	3	3-0	9	.243
—	El Paso (Texas)	1	2	.333	4.26	1.54	5	5	0	0	...	0-...	25.1	30	15	12	2	9-0	19	.291
—	Tucson (PCL)	2	7	.222	5.85	1.67	13	12	0	0	...	0-...	67.2	82	50	44	9	31-3	40	.301
2002—	Tucson (PCL)	10	5	.667	4.23	1.44	19	18	0	0	...	0-...	112.2	117	59	53	14	45-1	104	.265
—	Arizona (N.L.)	2	0	1.000	3.23	1.11	19	0	0	0	0	0-0	30.2	27	11	11	7	7-0	31	.235
2003—	Tucson (PCL)	10	5	.667	2.63	1.30	18	18	2	2	...	0-...	109.1	100	48	32	6	43-0	74	.241
—	Arizona (N.L.)	1	4	.200	6.05	1.65	16	8	0	0	0	1-1	55.0	61	39	37	7	30-5	43	.281
2004—	Harrisburg (East.)	0	0	...	0.00	0.50	1	1	0	0	...	0-...	4.0	0	0	0	0	2-0	9	.000
—	Brevard County (FSL)	0	0	...	0.00	0.52	2	2	0	0	...	0-...	7.2	3	0	0	0	1-0	7	.111
—	Montreal (N.L.)	4	7	.364	5.03	1.48	19	19	0	0	...	0-0	98.1	100	58	55	18	46-4	99	.260
2005—	Wash. (N.L.)	9	7	.563	3.13	1.19	31	31	2	1	0	0-0	198.1	172	71	69	19	65-11	185	.233
2006—	New Orleans (PCL)	0	0	...	1.93	1.29	1	1	0	0	...	0-...	4.2	4	2	1	0	2-0	3	.222
—	Potomac (Carol.)	1	0	1.000	5.19	1.62	2	2	0	0	...	0-...	8.2	12	7	5	1	2-0	11	.324
—	Wash. (N.L.)	1	2	.333	4.43	1.11	8	8	0	0	...	0-0	40.2	36	21	20	4	9-1	42	.237
Major League totals (5 years)		17	20	.459	4.09	1.31	81	71	2	1	0	1-1	423.0	396	200	192	55	157-21	400	.246

2006 LEFTY-RIGHTY SPLITS

vs.	Avg.	AB	H	2B	3B	HR	RBI	BB	SO	OBP	Slg.	vs.	Avg.	AB	H	2B	3B	HR	RBI	BB	SO	OBP	Slg.
L	.299	67	20	5	2	2	11	5	22	.355	.522	R	.188	85	16	4	0	2	9	4	20	.228	.306

PAUL, JOSH   C

PERSONAL: Born May 19, 1975, in Evanston, Ill. ... 6-1/200. ... Bats right, throws right. ... Full name: Joshua William Paul. ... High school: Buffalo Grove (Ill.). ... College: Vanderbilt. **TRANSACTIONS/CAREER NOTES:** Selected by Chicago White Sox organization in second round of 1996 free-agent draft. ... Signed as a free agent by Chicago Cubs organization (July 4, 2003). ... Released by Cubs (October 31, 2003). ... Signed by Anaheim Angels organization (January 15, 2004). ... Angels franchise renamed Los Angeles Angels of Anaheim for 2005 season. ... On disabled list (August 12-September 1, 2005). ... Traded by Angels to Tampa Bay Devil Rays for 3B Travis Schlichting (December 19, 2005). **STATISTICAL NOTES:** Career major league grand slams: 1.

2006 GAMES PLAYED BY POSITION (MLB): C—52, DH—1, OF—1.

Year Team (League)	Pos.	G	AB	R	H	2B	3B	HR	RBI	BB	SO	HBP	GDP	SB-CS	Avg.	OBP	SLG	OPS	E	Avg.
1996—GC Whi. Sox (GCL)		1	0	0	0	0	0	0	0	1	0	0	0	0-0	...	1.000	...	1.000	...	...
—Hickory (S. Atl.)	C	59	226	41	74	16	0	8	37	21	53	1	2	13-4	.327	.386	.504	.890	2	.991
1997—Birmingham (Sou.)	C	34	115	18	34	5	0	1	16	12	25	1	4	6-2	.296	.367	.365	.732	3	.988
—GC Whi. Sox (GCL)	C	5	14	3	6	0	1	0	0	1	3	0	1	1-0	.429	.467	.571	1.038	3	.900
1998—Win.-Salem (Car.)	C	123	444	66	113	20	7	11	63	38	91	5	11	20-8	.255	.319	.405	.724	3	.997
1999—Birmingham (Sou.)	C-DH	93	319	47	89	19	3	4	42	29	68	5	6	6-6	.279	.345	.395	.740	5	.992
—Chicago (A.L.)	C	6	18	2	4	1	0	0	1	0	4	0	0	0-0	.222	.222	.278	.500	0	1.000
2000—Chicago (A.L.)	C-OF	36	71	15	20	3	2	1	8	5	17	1	3	1-0	.282	.338	.423	.760	4	.974
—Charlotte (Int'l)	C-OF	51	168	28	40	5	1	4	19	13	38	2	3	6-2	.238	.299	.351	.650	2	.994
2001—Chicago (A.L.)	C	57	139	20	37	11	0	3	18	13	25	0	3	6-2	.266	.327	.410	.737	6	.980
—Charlotte (Int'l)	C	22	75	11	21	4	0	0	7	7	18	0	0	0-0	.280	.337	.493	.831	0	1.000
2002—Charlotte (Int'l)	C-1B-OF	65	231	18	63	15	2	0	17	17	45	1	7	10-4	.273	.323	.355	.678	3	.993
—Chicago (A.L.)	C-OF	33	104	11	25	4	0	0	11	9	22	1	1	2-0	.240	.302	.279	.581	2	.991
2003—Charlotte (Int'l)	C-2B-DH	19	64	6	12	0	1	2	5	5	14	0	1	1-1	.188	.243	.313	.555	2	.982
—Chicago (A.L.)	C-DH	13	17	6	6	0	0	0	3	3	3	0	0	0-0	.353	.450	.353	.803	0	1.000
—Iowa (PCL)	C-OF-DH 1B	47	146	12	37	4	0	2	15	8	30	1	5	0-2	.253	.297	.322	.619	1	.995
—Chicago (N.L.)	C	3	6	0	0	0	0	0	0	0	3	0	0	0-0	.000	.000	.000	.000	1	1.000
2004—Anaheim (A.L.)	C-OF-DH	46	70	11	17	3	0	2	10	7	17	0	2	2-1	.243	.308	.371	.679	1	.993
2005—Salt Lake (PCL)	DH-C	9	33	6	9	4	0	0	6	6	7	0	0	1-0	.273	.385	.394	.779	0	1.000
—Los Angeles (A.L.)	C	34	37	4	7	1	0	2	4	2	9	0	1	0-0	.189	.231	.378	.609	1	.989
2006—Tampa Bay (A.L.)	C-OF-DH	58	146	15	38	9	0	1	8	14	39	1	2	1-2	.260	.327	.342	.670	0	1.000
American League totals (8 years)		283	602	84	154	32	2	9	64	53	136	3	12	12-5	.256	.317	.360	.677	14	.989
National League totals (1 year)		3	6	0	0	0	0	0	0	0	3	0	0	0-0	.000	.000	.000	.000	1	1.000
Major League totals (8 years)		286	608	84	154	32	2	9	64	53	139	3	12	12-5	.253	.314	.357	.671	14	.989

DIVISION SERIES RECORD

Year Team (League)	Pos.	G	AB	R	H	2B	3B	HR	RBI	BB	SO	HBP	GDP	SB-CS	Avg.	OBP	SLG	OPS	E	Avg.
2000—Chicago (A.L.)	C	1	0	0	0	0	0	0	0	0	0	0	0	0-0	...	...	...	...	0	1.000
2005—Los Angeles (A.L.)		1	0	0	0	0	0	0	0	0	0	0	0	0-0	...	...	...	...	0	...
Division series totals (2 years)		2	0	0	0	0	0	0	0	0	0	0	0	0-0	...	...	...	...	0	1.000

CHAMPIONSHIP SERIES RECORD

Year Team (League)	Pos.	G	AB	R	H	2B	3B	HR	RBI	BB	SO	HBP	GDP	SB-CS	Avg.	OBP	SLG	OPS	E	Avg.
2005—Los Angeles (A.L.)	C	1	0	0	0	0	0	0	0	0	0	0	0	0-0	...	...	...	...	1	.800

2006 LEFTY-RIGHTY SPLITS

vs.	Avg.	AB	H	2B	3B	HR	RBI	BB	SO	OBP	Slg.	vs.	Avg.	AB	H	2B	3B	HR	RBI	BB	SO	OBP	Slg.
L	.333	39	13	1	0	0	2	6	11	.426	.359	R	.234	107	25	8	0	1	6		28	.287	.336

PAULEY, DAVID — P

PERSONAL: Born June 17, 1983, in Longmont, Colo. ... 6-2/185. ... Throws right, bats right. ... Full name: David Wayne Pauley. **TRANSACTIONS/CAREER NOTES:** Selected by San Diego Padres organization in eighth round of 2001 free-agent draft. ... Traded by Padres with OF Jay Payton, IF Ramon Vazquez and cash to Boston Red Sox for OF Dave Roberts (December 20, 2004). ... On disabled list (August 29, 2006-remainder of season).

CAREER HITTING: 0-for-0 (.000), 0 R, 0 2B, 0 3B, 0 HR, 0 RBI.

Year Team (League)	W	L	Pct.	ERA	WHIP	G	GS	CG	ShO	Hld.	Sv.-Opp.	IP	H	R	ER	HR	BB-IBB	SO	Avg.
2001—Idaho Falls (Pio.)	4	9	.308	6.03	1.63	15	15	0	0	...	0-...	68.2	88	57	46	8	24-0	53	.308
2002—Eugene (Northwest)	6	1	.857	2.81	1.24	15	15	0	0	...	0-...	80.0	81	32	25	6	18-1	62	.266
2003—Fort Wayne (Midw.)	7	7	.500	3.29	1.25	22	21	0	0	...	1-...	117.2	109	51	43	9	38-0	117	.245
2004—Lake Elsinore (Calif.)	7	12	.368	4.17	1.40	27	26	0	0	...	0-...	153.1	155	89	71	8	60-0	128	.268
2005—Portland (East.)	9	7	.563	3.81	1.30	27	27	1	0	...	0-0	156.0	169	86	66	18	34-0	104	.274
2006—Portland (East.)	2	3	.400	2.39	1.18	10	10	0	0	...	0-0	60.1	54	20	16	6	17-1	47	.248
—Boston (A.L.)	0	2	.000	7.88	2.31	3	3	0	0	...	0-0	16.0	31	14	14	1	6-1	10	.419
—Pawtucket (Int'l)	1	3	.250	5.54	1.55	9	9	0	0	...	0-0	50.1	60	40	31	10	18-0	25	.303
Major League totals (1 year)	0	2	.000	7.88	2.31	3	3	0	0	...	0-0	16.0	31	14	14	1	6-1	10	.419

2006 LEFTY-RIGHTY SPLITS

vs.	Avg.	AB	H	2B	3B	HR	RBI	BB	SO	OBP	Slg.	vs.	Avg.	AB	H	2B	3B	HR	RBI	BB	SO	OBP	Slg.
L	.450	40	18	5	0	1	4	4	4	.500	.650	R	.382	34	13	1	0	1	7	2	6	.447	.471

PAULINO, RONNY — C

PERSONAL: Born April 21, 1981, in Santo Domingo, Dominican Republic. ... 6-3/235. ... Bats right, throws right. ... Full name: Ronny Leonel Paulino. ... High school: Escuela (Santo Domingo, Dominican Republic). **TRANSACTIONS/CAREER NOTES:** Signed as non-drafted free agent by Pittsburgh Pirates organization (December 29, 1997). ... Selected by Kansas City Royals from Pirates organization in Rule 5 major league draft (December 16, 2002). ... Returned to Pirates organization (March 13, 2003).

2006 GAMES PLAYED BY POSITION (MLB): C—124.

Year Team (League)	Pos.	G	AB	R	H	2B	3B	HR	RBI	BB	SO	HBP	GDP	SB-CS	Avg.	OBP	SLG	OPS	E	Avg.
1998—Pittsburgh (DSL)		53	170	18	40	5	0	4	26	17	27	4	2	6-4	.235	.318	.335	.653	...	...
1999—GC Pirates (GCL)	C	29	83	6	21	2	4	1	13	8	19	1	0	1-2	.253	.319	.410	.729	5	.974
2000—Hickory (S. Atl.)	C-1B-3B	88	301	38	87	16	2	6	39	27	71	4	9	3-2	.289	.354	.415	.769	9	.982
2001—Lynchburg (Caro.)	C	103	352	30	102	16	1	6	51	36	76	2	11	4-1	.290	.353	.392	.745	4	.994
2002—Lynchburg (Caro.)	1B-C-C	119	442	63	116	26	2	12	55	39	87	1	15	2-1	.262	.321	.412	.733	18	.982
2003—Altoona (East.)	C-1B	46	159	19	36	4	1	6	19	12	35	1	4	0-2	.226	.283	.390	.673	4	.988
—Lynchburg (Caro.)	C	23	81	8	19	3	0	1	12	8	8	1	6	1-0	.235	.308	.309	.617	2	.983
2004—Altoona (East.)	C-1B	99	369	54	105	23	2	15	60	32	62	3	7	3-2	.285	.344	.480	.824	10	.987
2005—Altoona (East.)	C-DH	43	168	24	49	6	0	6	20	15	30	0	3	3-0	.292	.350	.435	.784	3	.991
—Indianapolis (Int'l)	C-DH	77	273	49	86	18	2	13	42	26	48	0	11	3-0	.315	.372	.538	.911	5	.989
—Pittsburgh (N.L.)	C	2	4	1	2	0	0	0	0	1	0	0	0	0-0	.500	.600	.500	1.100	0	1.000
2006—Indianapolis (Int'l)		8	29	2	7	3	0	0	4	3	8	0	2	1-0	.241	.313	.345	.657	0	1.000
—Pittsburgh (N.L.)	C	129	442	37	137	19	0	6	55	34	79	2	17	0-0	.310	.360	.394	.754	11	.988
Major League totals (2 years)		131	446	38	139	19	0	6	55	35	79	2	17	0-0	.312	.363	.395	.758	11	.988

2006 LEFTY-RIGHTY SPLITS

vs.	Avg.	AB	H	2B	3B	HR	RBI	BB	SO	OBP	Slg.	vs.	Avg.	AB	H	2B	3B	HR	RBI	BB	SO	OBP	Slg.
L	.339	115	39	6	0	1	15	11	15	.402	.443	R	.300	327	98	13	0	4	40	23	64	.346	.376

P

PAVANO, CARL   P

PERSONAL: Born January 8, 1976, in New Britain, Conn. ... 6-5/241. ... Throws right, bats right. ... Full name: Carl Anthony Pavano. ... Name pronounced: pa-VAH-no. ... High school: Southington (Conn.). **TRANSACTIONS/CAREER NOTES:** Selected by Boston Red Sox organization in 13th round of 1994 free-agent draft. ... Traded by Red Sox with a player to be named to Montreal Expos for P Pedro Martinez (November 18, 1997); Expos acquired P Tony Armas to complete deal (December 18, 1997). ... On disabled list (July 12-September 11, 1999); included rehabilitation assignment to Ottawa. ... On disabled list (June 25, 2000-remainder of season). ... On disabled list (March 23-August 15, 2001); included rehabilitation assignments to Jupiter and Ottawa. ... Traded by Expos with Ps Graeme Lloyd and Justin Wayne and IF Mike Mordecai to Florida Marlins for OF Cliff Floyd, P Claudio Vargas, 2B/OF Wilton Guerrero, cash and a player to be named (July 11, 2002); Expos acquired P Don Levinski to complete deal (August 6, 2002). ... Signed as a free agent by New York Yankees (December 20, 2004). ... On disabled list (June 28, 2005-remainder of season); included rehabilitation assignment to GCL Yankees. ... On disabled list (April 1, 2006-entire season); included rehabilitation assignments to Tampa, Trenton and Columbus.

CAREER HITTING: 41-for-295 (.139), 14 R, 8 2B, 2 3B, 2 HR, 14 RBI.

Year	Team (League)	W	L	Pct.	ERA	WHIP	G	GS	CG	ShO	Hld.	Sv.-Opp.	IP	H	R	ER	HR	BB-IBB	SO	Avg.
1994—	GC Red Sox (GCL)	4	3	.571	1.84	0.86	9	7	0	0	...	0-...	44.0	31	14	9	1	7-0	47	.186
1995—	Michigan (Midw.)	6	6	.500	3.45	1.21	22	22	1	0	...	0-...	141.0	118	63	54	7	52-0	138	.227
1996—	Trenton (East.)	16	5	.762	2.63	1.09	27	26	6	2	...	0-...	185.0	154	66	54	16	47-2	146	.230
1997—	Pawtucket (Int'l)	11	6	.647	3.12	1.13	23	23	3	0	...	0-...	161.2	148	62	56	13	34-2	147	.248
1998—	Jupiter (Fla. St.)	0	0	...	6.60	1.53	4	4	0	0	...	0-...	15.0	20	11	11	1	3-0	14	.333
—	Ottawa (Int'l)	1	0	1.000	2.41	1.02	3	3	0	0	...	0-...	18.2	12	5	5	1	7-0	14	.190
—	Montreal (N.L.)	6	9	.400	4.21	1.28	24	23	0	0	...	0-0	134.2	130	70	63	18	43-1	83	.251
1999—	Montreal (N.L.)	6	8	.429	5.63	1.46	19	18	1	1	...	0-0	104.0	117	66	65	8	35-1	70	.285
—	Ottawa (Int'l)	0	1	.000	9.00	1.40	2	2	0	0	...	0-...	5.0	7	5	5	1	0-0	3	.318
2000—	Montreal (N.L.)	8	4	.667	3.06	1.27	15	15	0	0	...	0-0	97.0	89	40	33	8	34-1	64	.248
2001—	Jupiter (Fla. St.)	1	1	.500	2.19	0.97	3	3	0	0	...	0-...	12.1	10	7	3	1	2-0	11	.213
—	Ottawa (Int'l)	2	1	.667	3.58	1.16	4	4	0	0	...	0-...	27.2	27	13	11	4	5-0	19	.248
—	Montreal (N.L.)	1	6	.143	6.33	1.76	8	8	0	0	...	0-0	42.2	59	33	30	7	16-1	36	.331
2002—	Florida (N.L.)	3	8	.273	6.30	1.74	15	14	0	0	...	0-0	74.1	98	55	52	14	31-5	51	.318
—	Ottawa (Int'l)	3	0	1.000	3.10	1.23	3	3	0	0	...	0-...	20.1	23	8	7	2	2-0	9	.295
—	Florida (N.L.)	3	2	.600	3.79	1.46	22	8	0	0	3	0-0	61.2	76	33	26	5	14-3	41	.306
2003—	Florida (N.L.)	12	13	.480	4.30	1.26	33	32	2	0	0	0-0	201.0	204	99	96	19	49-10	133	.265
2004—	Florida (N.L.)	18	8	.692	3.00	1.17	31	31	2	2	0	0-0	222.1	212	80	74	16	49-13	139	.253
2005—	New York (A.L.)	4	6	.400	4.77	1.47	17	17	1	1	0	0-0	100.0	129	66	53	17	18-1	56	.315
—	GC Yankees (GCL)	0	0	...	1.80	0.40	1	1	0	0	0	0-0	5.0	2	2	1	1	0-0	5	.118
—	Tampa (Fla. St.)	0	1	.000	4.50	1.00	1	1	0	0	0	0-0	6.0	6	3	3	1	0-0	3	.250
2006—	Tampa (Fla. St.)	0	2	.000	2.31	1.11	3	3	0	0	0	0-0	11.2	10	6	3	2	3-1	10	.238
—	Trenton (East.)	1	0	1.000	1.64	0.55	3	3	0	0	0	0-0	11.0	6	2	2	0	0-0	12	.150
—	Columbus (Int'l)	1	0	1.000	3.00	1.50	1	1	0	0	0	0-0	6.0	8	2	2	0	1-0	5	.381
	American League totals (1 year)	4	6	.400	4.77	1.47	17	17	1	1	0	0-0	100.0	129	66	53	17	18-1	56	.315
	National League totals (7 years)	57	58	.496	4.21	1.34	167	149	5	3	3	0-0	937.2	985	476	439	95	271-35	617	.271
	Major League totals (8 years)	61	64	.488	4.27	1.35	184	166	6	4	3	0-0	1037.2	1114	542	492	112	289-36	673	.276

DIVISION SERIES RECORD

Year	Team (League)	W	L	Pct.	ERA	WHIP	G	GS	CG	ShO	Hld.	Sv.-Opp.	IP	H	R	ER	HR	BB-IBB	SO	Avg.
2003—	Florida (N.L.)	2	0	1.000	0.00	0.75	3	0	0	0	0	0-0	2.2	1	0	0	0	1-1	1	.111

CHAMPIONSHIP SERIES RECORD

Year	Team (League)	W	L	Pct.	ERA	WHIP	G	GS	CG	ShO	Hld.	Sv.-Opp.	IP	H	R	ER	HR	BB-IBB	SO	Avg.
2003—	Florida (N.L.)	0	0	...	2.35	1.17	3	1	0	0	0	0-0	7.2	8	2	2	0	1-0	8	.286

WORLD SERIES RECORD

Year	Team (League)	W	L	Pct.	ERA	WHIP	G	GS	CG	ShO	Hld.	Sv.-Opp.	IP	H	R	ER	HR	BB-IBB	SO	Avg.
2003—	Florida (N.L.)	0	0	...	1.00	1.00	2	1	0	0	0	0-0	9.0	8	1	1	0	1-0	6	.250

ALL-STAR GAME RECORD

	Year	W	L	Pct.	ERA	WHIP	G	GS	CG	ShO	Hld.	Sv.-Opp.	IP	H	R	ER	HR	BB-IBB	SO	Avg.
	All-Star Game totals (1 year)	0	0	...	9.00	1.50	1	0	0	0	0	0-0	2.0	3	2	2	1	0-0	1	.333

PAYTON, JAY   OF

PERSONAL: Born November 22, 1972, in Zanesville, Ohio. ... 5-10/185. ... Bats right, throws right. ... Full name: Jason Lee Payton. ... High school: Zanesville (Ohio). ... College: Georgia Tech. **TRANSACTIONS/CAREER NOTES:** Selected by New York Mets organization in supplemental round ("sandwich pick" between first and second rounds, 29th pick overall) of 1994 free-agent draft; pick received as part of compensation for Baltimore Orioles signing Type A free-agent P Sid Fernandez. ... On disabled list (April 3, 1997-entire season). ... On disabled list (March 21-June 8, 1999); included rehabilitation assignment to St. Lucie. ... On disabled list (May 8-June 26, 2001); included rehabilitation assignment to St. Lucie. ... Traded by Mets with P Mark Corey and OF Robert Stratton to Colorado Rockies for P John Thomson and OF Mark Little (July 31, 2002). ... Signed as a free agent by San Diego Padres (January 13, 2004). ... Traded by Padres with SS Ramon Vazquez, P David Pauley and cash to Boston Red Sox for OF Dave Roberts (December 20, 2004). ... Traded by Red Sox to Oakland Athletics for P Chad Bradford (July 13, 2005). **STATISTICAL NOTES:** Career major league grand slams: 3.

2006 GAMES PLAYED BY POSITION (MLB): OF—137, DH—4.

Year	Team (League)	Pos.	G	AB	R	H	2B	3B	HR	RBI	BB	SO	HBP	GDP	SB-CS	Avg.	OBP	SLG	OPS	E	Avg.
1994—	Pittsfield (NYP)	OF	58	219	47	80	16	2	3	37	23	18	9	1	10-2	.365	.439	.498	.937	5	.964
—	Binghamton (East.)	OF	8	25	3	7	1	0	0	1	2	3	1	1	1-1	.280	.357	.320	.677	1	.917
1995—	Binghamton (East.)	OF	85	357	59	123	20	3	14	54	29	32	2	11	16-7	.345	.395	.535	.930	3	.988
—	Norfolk (Int'l)	OF	50	196	33	47	11	4	4	30	11	22	2	5	11-3	.240	.284	.398	.682	2	.982
1996—	Norfolk (Int'l)	DH-OF	55	153	30	47	6	3	6	26	11	26	3	3	10-1	.307	.363	.503	.866	0	1.000
—	GC Mets (GCL)	DH	3	13	3	5	1	0	1	2	0	1	0	0	1-0	.385	.385	.692	1.077	...	...
—	St. Lucie (Fla. St.)	DH	9	26	4	8	2	0	0	1	4	5	0	1	2-1	.308	.400	.385	.785	...	...
—	Binghamton (East.)	DH	4	10	0	2	0	0	2	2	2	1	0	0	0-1	.200	.286	.200	.486	...	...
1997—							Did not play.														
1998—	Norfolk (Int'l)	OF-1B-DH	82	322	45	84	14	4	8	30	26	50	1	5	12-7	.261	.318	.404	.722	7	.980
—	St. Lucie (Fla. St.)	OF	3	7	0	1	0	0	0	0	3	1	0	0	0-0	.143	.400	.143	.543	0	1.000
—	New York (N.L.)	OF	15	22	2	7	1	0	0	1	1	4	0	0	0-0	.318	.348	.364	.711	0	1.000
1999—	St. Lucie (Fla. St.)	OF	7	26	3	9	1	1	0	4	1	4	0	0	0-1	.346	.433	.462	.895	1	.955
—	Norfolk (Int'l)	OF-DH	38	144	27	56	13	2	8	35	12	13	1	2	2-2	.389	.437	.674	1.110	1	.984
—	New York (N.L.)	OF	13	8	1	2	1	0	0	1	0	2	1	0	1-2	.250	.333	.375	.708	0	1.000
2000—	New York (N.L.)	OF	149	488	63	142	23	4	17	62	30	60	3	9	5-11	.291	.331	.447	.778	6	.981
2001—	New York (N.L.)	OF	104	361	44	92	16	1	8	34	18	52	5	11	4-3	.255	.298	.371	.669	4	.984
—	St. Lucie (Fla. St.)	OF	4	16	7	6	3	0	0	4	1	0	0	0	0-0	.375	.500	.563	1.063	0	1.000
2002—	New York (N.L.)	OF	87	275	33	78	6	3	8	31	21	34	1	9	4-1	.284	.336	.415	.750	1	.994
—	Colorado (N.L.)	OF	47	170	36	57	14	4	8	28	8	20	3	3	3-3	.335	.376	.606	.982	0	1.000

P

Year Team (League)	Pos.	G	AB	R	H	2B	3B	HR	RBI	BB	SO	HBP	GDP	SB-CS	Avg.	OBP	SLG	OPS	E	Avg.
2003—Colorado (N.L.)	OF	157	600	93	181	32	5	28	89	43	77	7	*27	6-4	.302	.354	.512	.865	4	.987
2004—San Diego (N.L.)	OF-DH	143	458	57	119	17	4	8	55	43	56	4	12	2-0	.260	.326	.367	.693	4	.989
2005—Boston (A.L.)	OF	55	133	24	35	7	0	5	21	10	14	0	4	0-0	.263	.313	.429	.741	0	1.000
—Oakland (A.L.)	OF	69	275	38	74	9	1	13	42	14	33	0	4	0-1	.269	.302	.451	.753	0	1.000
2006—Oakland (A.L.)	OF-DH	142	557	78	165	32	3	10	59	22	52	4	12	8-4	.296	.325	.418	.743	7	.978
American League totals (2 years)		266	965	140	274	48	4	28	122	46	99	4	20	8-5	.284	.317	.429	.746	7	.988
National League totals (7 years)		715	2382	329	678	110	18	77	300	164	305	24	70	25-24	.285	.335	.443	.778	19	.987
Major League totals (9 years)		981	3347	469	952	158	22	105	422	210	404	28	90	33-29	.284	.330	.439	.768	26	.987

DIVISION SERIES RECORD

Year Team (League)	Pos.	G	AB	R	H	2B	3B	HR	RBI	BB	SO	HBP	GDP	SB-CS	Avg.	OBP	SLG	OPS	E	Avg.
2000—New York (N.L.)	OF	4	17	1	3	0	0	0	2	0	4	0	1	1-1	.176	.167	.176	.343	0	1.000
2006—Oakland (A.L.)	OF	3	12	3	4	0	0	0	0	0	1	0	0	0-0	.333	.333	.333	.667	0	1.000
Division series totals (2 years)		7	29	4	7	0	0	0	2	0	5	0	1	1-1	.241	.233	.241	.475	0	1.000

CHAMPIONSHIP SERIES RECORD

Year Team (League)	Pos.	G	AB	R	H	2B	3B	HR	RBI	BB	SO	HBP	GDP	SB-CS	Avg.	OBP	SLG	OPS	E	Avg.
2000—New York (N.L.)	OF	5	19	1	3	0	0	1	3	2	5	1	1	0-0	.158	.273	.316	.589	0	1.000
2006—Oakland (A.L.)	OF	4	14	1	4	2	0	1	2	1	2	0	0	0-0	.286	.333	.643	.976	0	1.000
Champ. series totals (2 years)		9	33	2	7	2	0	2	5	3	7	1	1	0-0	.212	.297	.455	.752	0	1.000

WORLD SERIES RECORD

Year Team (League)	Pos.	G	AB	R	H	2B	3B	HR	RBI	BB	SO	HBP	GDP	SB-CS	Avg.	OBP	SLG	OPS	E	Avg.
2000—New York (N.L.)	OF	5	21	3	7	0	0	1	3	0	5	0	0	0-0	.333	.333	.476	.810	2	.895

2006 LEFTY-RIGHTY SPLITS

vs.	Avg.	AB	H	2B	3B	HR	RBI	BB	SO	OBP	Slg.	vs.	Avg.	AB	H	2B	3B	HR	RBI	BB	SO	OBP	Slg.
L	.296	142	42	6	1	6	22	9	11	.338	.479	R	.296	415	123	26	2	4	37	13	41	.320	.398

PEAVY, JAKE — P

PERSONAL: Born May 31, 1981, in Mobile, Ala. ... 6-1/180. ... Throws right, bats right. ... Full name: Jacob Edward Peavy. ... Name pronounced: PEE-vee. ... High school: St. Paul (Mobile, Ala.). **TRANSACTIONS/CAREER NOTES:** Selected by San Diego Padres organization in 15th round of 1999 free-agent draft. ... On disabled list (May 20-July 2, 2004); included rehabilitation assignment to Mobile.

CAREER HITTING: 41-for-260 (.158), 24 R, 8 2B, 0 3B, 2 HR, 17 RBI.

Year Team (League)	W	L	Pct.	ERA	WHIP	G	GS	CG	ShO	Hld.	Sv.-Opp.	IP	H	R	ER	HR	BB-IBB	SO	Avg.
1999—Ariz. Padres (Ariz.)	7	1	.875	1.34	1.02	13	11	1	0	...	0-...	73.2	52	16	11	4	23-0	90	.202
—Idaho Falls (Pio.)	2	0	1.000	0.00	0.55	2	2	0	0	...	0-...	11.0	5	0	0	0	1-0	13	.135
2000—Fort Wayne (Midw.)	13	8	.619	2.90	1.20	26	25	0	0	...	0-...	133.2	107	61	43	6	53-0	164	.216
2001—Lake Elsinore (Calif.)	7	5	.583	3.08	1.03	19	19	0	0	...	0-...	105.1	76	41	36	6	33-1	144	.200
—Mobile (Sou.)	2	1	.667	2.57	1.11	5	5	0	0	...	0-...	28.0	19	8	8	3	12-1	44	.192
2002—San Diego (N.L.)	4	5	.444	2.80	1.18	14	14	0	0	0	0-0	80.1	65	26	25	4	30-0	89	.220
—San Diego (N.L.)	6	7	.462	4.52	1.42	17	17	0	0	0	0-0	97.2	106	54	49	11	33-4	90	.274
2003—San Diego (N.L.)	12	11	.522	4.11	1.31	32	32	0	0	0	0-0	194.2	173	94	89	33	82-3	156	.238
2004—Mobile (Sou.)	0	1	.000	5.79	1.93	1	1	0	0	...	0-...	4.2	7	4	3	1	2-0	4	.318
—San Diego (N.L.)	15	6	.714	*2.27	1.20	27	27	0	0	0	0-0	166.1	146	49	42	13	53-4	173	.236
2005—San Diego (N.L.)	13	7	.650	2.88	1.04	30	30	3	3	0	0-0	203.0	162	70	65	18	50-3	*216	.217
2006—San Diego (N.L.)	11	14	.440	4.09	1.23	32	32	2	0	0	0-0	202.1	187	93	92	23	62-11	215	.242
Major League totals (5 years)	57	45	.559	3.51	1.22	138	138	5	3	0	0-0	864.0	774	360	337	98	280-25	850	.238

DIVISION SERIES RECORD

Year Team (League)	W	L	Pct.	ERA	WHIP	G	GS	CG	ShO	Hld.	Sv.-Opp.	IP	H	R	ER	HR	BB-IBB	SO	Avg.
2005—San Diego (N.L.)	0	1	.000	16.62	2.54	1	1	0	0	0	0-0	4.1	8	8	8	2	3-2	3	.400
2006—San Diego (N.L.)	0	1	.000	8.44	2.25	1	1	0	0	0	0-0	5.1	11	5	5	1	1-1	2	.478
Division series totals (2 years)	0	2	.000	12.10	2.38	2	2	0	0	0	0-0	9.2	19	13	13	3	4-3	5	.442

ALL-STAR GAME RECORD

	W	L	Pct.	ERA	WHIP	G	GS	CG	ShO	Hld.	Sv.-Opp.	IP	H	R	ER	HR	BB-IBB	SO	Avg.
All-Star Game totals (1 year)	0	0	...	0.00	1.50	1	0	0	0	0	0-0	0.2	1	0	0	0	0-0	1	.333

2006 LEFTY-RIGHTY SPLITS

vs.	Avg.	AB	H	2B	3B	HR	RBI	BB	SO	OBP	Slg.	vs.	Avg.	AB	H	2B	3B	HR	RBI	BB	SO	OBP	Slg.
L	.242	372	90	24	4	16	44	37	97	.317	.457	R	.243	400	97	24	3	7	43	25	118	.290	.370

PEDROIA, DUSTIN — 2B/SS

PERSONAL: Born August 17, 1983, in Woodland, Calif. ... Bats right, throws right. ... Full name: Dustin Luis Pedroia. ... College: Arizona State. **TRANSACTIONS/CAREER NOTES:** Selected by Boston Red Sox organization in second round of 2004 free-agent draft.

2006 GAMES PLAYED BY POSITION (MLB): 2B—27, SS—6.

Year Team (League)	Pos.	G	AB	R	H	2B	3B	HR	RBI	BB	SO	HBP	GDP	SB-CS	Avg.	OBP	SLG	OPS	E	Avg.
2004—Augusta (S. Atl.)		12	50	11	20	5	0	1	5	6	3	1	1	2-0	.400	.474	.560	1.034		...
—Sarasota (Fla. St.)		30	107	23	36	8	3	2	14	13	4	4	3	0-2	.336	.417	.523	.940		...
2005—Portland (East.)	2B-SS-DH	66	256	39	83	19	2	8	40	34	26	4	7	7-3	.324	.409	.508	.917	5	.982
—Pawtucket (Int'l)	2B-SS-DH	51	204	39	52	9	1	5	24	24	17	9	6	1-0	.255	.356	.382	.738	2	.991
2006—Pawtucket (Int'l)		111	423	55	129	30	3	5	50	48	27	9	9	1-4	.305	.384	.426	.810	7	.986
—Boston (A.L.)	2B-SS	31	89	5	17	4	0	2	7	7	7	1	1	0-1	.191	.258	.303	.561	4	.972
Major League totals (1 year)		31	89	5	17	4	0	2	7	7	7	1	1	0-1	.191	.258	.303	.561	4	.972

2006 LEFTY-RIGHTY SPLITS

vs.	Avg.	AB	H	2B	3B	HR	RBI	BB	SO	OBP	Slg.	vs.	Avg.	AB	H	2B	3B	HR	RBI	BB	SO	OBP	Slg.
L	.162	37	6	3	0	0	3	4	1	.262	.243	R	.212	52	11	1	0	2	4	3	6	.255	.346

PELFREY, MIKE — P

PERSONAL: Born January 14, 1984, in Wright Patterson AFB, Ohio. ... 6-7/190. ... Throws right, bats right. ... Full name: Michael Alan Pelfrey. ... College: Wichita State. **TRANSACTIONS/CAREER NOTES:** Selected by New York Mets organization in first round (ninth pick overall) of 2005 free-agent draft. **CAREER HITTING:** 0-for-9 (.000), 0 R, 0 2B, 0 3B, 0 HR, 0 RBI.

P

Year Team (League)	W	L	Pct.	ERA	WHIP	G	GS	CG	ShO	Hld.	Sv.-Opp.	IP	H	R	ER	HR	BB-IBB	SO	Avg.
2006—St. Lucie (Fla. St.)	2	1	.667	1.64	0.86	4	4	0	0	...	0-0	22.0	17	5	4	1	2-0	26	.224
—New York (N.L.)	2	1	.667	5.48	1.73	4	4	0	0	0	0-0	21.1	25	14	13	1	12-0	13	.305
—Norfolk (Int'l)	1	0	1.000	2.25	1.13	2	2	0	0	0	0-0	8.0	4	2	2	1	5-0	6	.148
—Binghamton (East.)	4	2	.667	2.71	1.30	12	12	0	0	...	0-0	66.1	60	23	20	2	26-1	77	.244
Major League totals (1 year)	2	1	.667	5.48	1.73	4	4	0	0	0	0-0	21.1	25	14	13	1	12-0	13	.305

2006 LEFTY-RIGHTY SPLITS

vs.	Avg.	AB	H	2B	3B	HR	RBI	BB	SO	OBP	Slg.	vs.	Avg.	AB	H	2B	3B	HR	RBI	BB	SO	OBP	Slg.
L	.278	36	10	2	0	0	5	7	6	.409	.333	R	.326	46	15	4	0	1	7	5	7	.407	.478

PENA, BRAYAN   C

PERSONAL: Born January 7, 1982, in Havana, Cuba. ... 5-11/220. ... Bats both, throws right. ... Full name: Brayan Eduardo Pena. ... Junior college: Espa Julio Trigo (Costa Rica). **TRANSACTIONS/CAREER NOTES:** Signed as a non-drafted free agent by Atlanta Braves (November 2, 2000).
2006 GAMES PLAYED BY POSITION (MLB): C—15, 3B—1.

Year Team (League)	Pos.	G	AB	R	H	2B	3B	HR	RBI	BB	SO	HBP	GDP	SB-CS	Avg.	OBP	SLG	OPS	E	Avg.
2001—Danville (Appal.)	C	64	235	39	87	16	2	1	33	31	30	0	5	3-1	.370	.440	.468	.908	5	.984
2002—Macon (S. Atl.)	C	81	271	26	62	10	0	3	25	22	37	2	5	0-3	.229	.290	.299	.589	5	.990
—Myrtle Beach (Carol.)	C	6	19	3	4	1	0	0	1	3	4	0	0	0-0	.211	.318	.263	.581	0	1.000
2003—Myrtle Beach (Carol.)	C	82	286	24	84	14	1	2	27	11	28	1	8	2-5	.294	.320	.371	.691	2	.996
2004—Greenville (Sou.)	C	77	277	30	87	10	4	2	30	15	29	1	6	3-4	.314	.349	.401	.750	8	.986
2005—Richmond (Int'l)	C-DH-1B	81	282	27	92	21	2	0	25	28	19	0	15	3-1	.326	.383	.415	.798	4	.991
—Atlanta (N.L.)	C	18	39	2	7	2	0	0	4	1	7	0	1	0-0	.179	.200	.231	.431	0	1.000
2006—Richmond (Int'l)	C	87	325	32	98	18	1	1	33	21	28	1	7	6-6	.302	.342	.372	.714	4	.993
—Atlanta (N.L.)	C-3B	23	41	9	11	2	0	1	5	2	5	0	2	0-0	.268	.302	.390	.693	0	1.000
Major League totals (2 years)		41	80	11	18	4	0	1	9	3	12	0	3	0-0	.225	.253	.313	.566	0	1.000

2006 LEFTY-RIGHTY SPLITS

vs.	Avg.	AB	H	2B	3B	HR	RBI	BB	SO	OBP	Slg.	vs.	Avg.	AB	H	2B	3B	HR	RBI	BB	SO	OBP	Slg.
L	.200	15	3	1	0	0	1	2	1	.294	.267	R	.308	26	8	1	0	1	4	0	4	.308	.462

PENA, CARLOS   1B

PERSONAL: Born May 17, 1978, in Santo Domingo, Dominican Republic. ... 6-2/215. ... Bats left, throws left. ... Full name: Carlos Felipe Pena. ... Name pronounced: PAIN-yuh. ... High school: Haverhill (Mass.). ... College: Northeastern. **TRANSACTIONS/CAREER NOTES:** Selected by Texas Rangers organization in first round (10th pick overall) of 1998 free-agent draft. ... Traded by Rangers with P Mike Venafro to Oakland Athletics for 1B Jason Hart, P Mario Ramos, C Gerald Laird and OF Ryan Ludwick (January 14, 2002). ... Traded by A's to Detroit Tigers with P Franklyn German and a player to be named as part of three-team deal in which New York Yankees acquired P Jeff Weaver from Tigers and A's acquired P Ted Lilly, OF John-Ford Griffin and P Jason Arnold from Yankees (July 5, 2002); Tigers acquired P Jeremy Bonderman to complete deal (August 22, 2002). ... On disabled list (June 2-27, 2003); included rehabilitation assignment to Toledo. ... Released by Tigers (March 26, 2006). ... Signed by Boston Red Sox organization (August 17, 2006). **STATISTICAL NOTES:** Hit three home runs in one game (May 19, 2003). ... Career major league grand slams: 3.
2006 GAMES PLAYED BY POSITION (MLB): 1B—17, OF—1.

Year Team (League)	Pos.	G	AB	R	H	2B	3B	HR	RBI	BB	SO	HBP	GDP	SB-CS	Avg.	OBP	SLG	OPS	E	Avg.
1998—GC Rangers (GCL)	1B	2	5	1	2	0	0	0	0	3	1	0	0	1-1	.400	.625	.400	1.025	0	1.000
—Savannah (S. Atl.)	1B-OF	30	117	22	38	14	0	6	20	8	26	4	0	3-2	.325	.385	.598	.983	3	.986
—Charlotte (Fla. St.)	1B	7	22	1	6	1	0	0	3	2	8	1	0	0-1	.273	.360	.318	.678	1	.977
1999—Charlotte (Fla. St.)	1B	136	501	85	128	31	8	18	103	74	135	16	7	2-5	.255	.365	.457	.822	16	.986
2000—Tulsa (Texas)	1B	138	529	117	158	36	2	28	105	101	108	9	7	12-0	.299	.414	.533	.947	22	.982
2001—Oklahoma (PCL)	1B	119	431	71	124	38	3	23	74	80	127	8	6	11-3	.288	.408	.550	.958	11	.989
—Texas (A.L.)	1B-DH	22	62	6	16	4	1	3	12	10	17	0	1	0-0	.258	.361	.500	.861	2	.987
2002—Oakland (A.L.)	1B	40	124	12	27	4	0	7	16	15	38	1	2	0-0	.218	.305	.419	.724	1	.997
—Sacramento (PCL)	1B	44	175	30	42	10	1	10	33	24	49	4	3	3-0	.240	.340	.480	.820	3	.992
—Detroit (A.L.)	1B-DH	75	273	31	69	13	4	12	36	26	73	2	5	2-2	.253	.321	.462	.783	3	.996
2003—Toledo (Int'l)	1B-DH	8	30	4	10	4	1	0	5	4	7	1	0	0-0	.333	.429	.533	.962	1	.986
—Detroit (A.L.)	1B-DH	131	452	51	112	21	6	18	50	53	123	6	6	4-5	.248	.332	.440	.772	13	.990
2004—Detroit (A.L.)	1B-DH	142	481	89	116	22	4	27	82	70	146	3	11	7-1	.241	.338	.472	.810	6	.995
2005—Toledo (Int'l)	1B-DH	71	257	43	80	17	1	12	45	45	65	6	4	3-4	.311	.414	.525	.949	8	.986
—Detroit (A.L.)	1B-DH	79	260	37	61	9	0	18	44	31	95	4	3	0-1	.235	.325	.477	.802	3	.993
2006—Columbus (Int'l)	1B	105	381	65	99	17	0	19	66	63	89	9	3	4-0	.260	.370	.454	.824	9	.984
—Pawtucket (Int'l)		11	37	7	17	3	0	4	8	5	5	1	0	0-0	.459	.523	.865	1.388	1	.986
—Boston (A.L.)	1B-OF	18	33	3	9	2	0	1	3	4	10	0	1	0-0	.273	.351	.424	.776	1	.989
Major League totals (6 years)		507	1685	229	410	75	15	86	243	209	502	16	29	13-9	.243	.331	.459	.789	29	.993

2006 LEFTY-RIGHTY SPLITS

vs.	Avg.	AB	H	2B	3B	HR	RBI	BB	SO	OBP	Slg.	vs.	Avg.	AB	H	2B	3B	HR	RBI	BB	SO	OBP	Slg.
L	.273	11	3	0	0	0	0	0	5	.273	.273	R	.273	22	6	2	0	1	3	4	5	.385	.500

PENA, TONY   P

PERSONAL: Born January 9, 1982, in Santo Domingo, Dominican Republic. ... 6-2/190. ... Throws right, bats right. ... Full name: Ramon Antonio Pena.
TRANSACTIONS/CAREER NOTES: Signed as a non-drafted free agent by Arizona Diamondbacks organization (June 13, 2002).
CAREER HITTING: 0-for-2 (.000), 0 R, 0 2B, 0 3B, 0 HR, 0 RBI.

Year Team (League)	W	L	Pct.	ERA	WHIP	G	GS	CG	ShO	Hld.	Sv.-Opp.	IP	H	R	ER	HR	BB-IBB	SO	Avg.
2004—Dom. D'backs (DSL)	1	0	1.000	0.64	0.79	3	1	0	0	...	2-...	14.0	11	2	1	0	0-0	17	.216
2005—Tennessee (Sou.)	7	13	.350	4.43	1.38	25	25	2	1	0	0-0	148.1	165	86	73	17	40-0	95	.283
2006—Tennessee (Sou.)	2	0	1.000	0.89	1.13	17	0	0	0	1	6-8	20.1	18	2	2	0	5-1	17	.231
—Tucson (PCL)	3	1	.750	1.71	0.72	24	0	0	0	0	7-9	26.1	17	6	5	1	2-0	21	.183
—Arizona (N.L.)	3	4	.429	5.58	1.43	25	0	0	0	2	1-1	30.2	36	21	19	6	8-0	21	.290
Major League totals (1 year)	3	4	.429	5.58	1.43	25	0	0	0	2	1-1	30.2	36	21	19	6	8-0	21	.290

2006 LEFTY-RIGHTY SPLITS

vs.	Avg.	AB	H	2B	3B	HR	RBI	BB	SO	OBP	Slg.	vs.	Avg.	AB	H	2B	3B	HR	RBI	BB	SO	OBP	Slg.
L	.382	68	26	7	1	4	14	5	12	.419	.691	R	.179	56	10	1	2	2	5	3	9	.220	.375

P

PENA, TONY F.   IF

PERSONAL: Born March 23, 1981, in Santiago, Dominican Republic. ... 6-1/180. ... Bats right, throws right. ... Full name: Tony Francisco Pena. ... Son of Tony Pena, catcher/first baseman with six teams (1980-97) and manager of Kansas City (2002-05); and nephew of Ramon Pena, pitcher with Detroit Tigers (1989). **TRANSACTIONS/CAREER NOTES:** Signed as a non-drafted free agent by Atlanta Braves organization (July 21, 1999).

2006 GAMES PLAYED BY POSITION (MLB): SS—22, 3B—1.

Year Team (League)	Pos.	G	AB	R	H	2B	3B	HR	RBI	BB	SO	HBP	GDP	SB-CS	Avg.	OBP	SLG	OPS	E	Avg.
2000—Danville (Appal.)		55	215	22	46	5	0	2	20	5	53	0	8	6-2	.214	.230	.265	.495	...	...
2001—Jamestown (NYP)		72	264	26	65	12	2	0	18	10	48	2	7	8-6	.246	.278	.307	.585	...	...
2002—Macon (S. Atl.)		118	405	42	101	9	5	2	36	14	68	5	6	11-15	.249	.282	.311	.593	...	...
2003—Myrtle Beach (Carol.)		120	405	43	105	14	1	4	30	24	82	2	9	17-12	.259	.304	.328	.632	...	...
2004—Greenville (Sou.)		130	495	65	126	22	0	11	34	16	108	4	6	25-13	.255	.282	.366	.648	...	...
2005—Richmond (Int'l)	SS	138	490	49	122	25	4	5	40	21	113	5	7	17-15	.249	.285	.347	.632	32	.953
2006—Richmond (Int'l)		81	298	38	84	12	4	1	23	12	56	2	6	12-3	.282	.312	.359	.671	13	.966
—Atlanta (N.L.)	SS-3B	40	44	12	10	2	0	1	3	2	10	0	1	0-0	.227	.261	.341	.602	1	.977
Major League totals (1 year)		40	44	12	10	2	0	1	3	2	10	0	1	0-0	.227	.261	.341	.602	1	.977

2006 LEFTY-RIGHTY SPLITS

vs.	Avg.	AB	H	2B	3B	HR	RBI	BB	SO	OBP	Slg.	vs.	Avg.	AB	H	2B	3B	HR	RBI	BB	SO	OBP	Slg.
L	.278	18	5	2	0	0	1	1	6	.316	.389	R	.192	26	5	0	0	1	2	1	4	.222	.308

PENA, WILY MO   OF

PERSONAL: Born January 23, 1982, in Laguna Salada, Dominican Republic. ... 6-3/215. ... Bats right, throws right. ... Full name: Wily Modesto Pena. ... Name pronounced: willie. **TRANSACTIONS/CAREER NOTES:** Signed as a non-drafted free agent by New York Mets organization (July 15, 1998); contract nullified by commissioner's office; was declared a free agent (February 26, 1999). ... Signed by New York Yankees organization (April 5, 1999). ... On disabled list (July 13, 2000-remainder of season). ... Traded by Yankees to Cincinnati Reds for 3B Drew Henson and OF Michael Coleman (March 21, 2001). ... On disabled list (July 5-30, 2003); included rehabilitation assignment to Louisville. ... On disabled list (May 9-June 7, 2005); included rehabilitation assignment to Louisville. ... Traded by Reds to Boston Red Sox for P Bronson Arroyo (March 20, 2006). ... On disabled list (May 28-July 18, 2006); included rehabilitation assignments to Lowell and Pawtucket. **STATISTICAL NOTES:** Career major league grand slams: 2.

2006 GAMES PLAYED BY POSITION (MLB): OF—76, DH—5.

Year Team (League)	Pos.	G	AB	R	H	2B	3B	HR	RBI	BB	SO	HBP	GDP	SB-CS	Avg.	OBP	SLG	OPS	E	Avg.
1999—GC Yankees (GCL)	OF	45	166	21	41	10	1	7	26	12	54	7	2	3-2	.247	.323	.446	.768	2	.947
2000—Greensboro (S. Atl.)	OF	67	249	41	51	7	1	10	28	18	91	5	9	6-5	.205	.268	.361	.630	4	.964
—Staten Is. (N.Y.-Penn)	OF	20	73	7	22	1	2	0	10	2	23	4	1	2-0	.301	.354	.370	.724	0	1.000
2001—Dayton (Midw.)	OF	135	511	87	135	25	5	26	113	33	177	17	6	26-10	.264	.327	.485	.813	9	.972
2002—Chattanooga (Sou.)	OF	105	388	47	99	23	1	11	47	36	126	9	9	8-0	.255	.330	.405	.735	4	.979
—Cincinnati (N.L.)	OF	13	18	1	4	0	0	1	1	0	11	0	0	0-0	.222	.222	.389	.611	0	1.000
2003—Louisville (Int'l)	OF	14	51	16	19	3	0	4	14	5	13	3	0	0-0	.373	.450	.667	1.117	2	.933
—Cincinnati (N.L.)	OF-3B	80	165	20	36	6	1	5	16	12	53	3	2	3-2	.218	.283	.358	.641	2	.978
2004—Cincinnati (N.L.)	OF	110	336	45	87	10	1	26	66	22	108	6	7	5-2	.259	.316	.527	.843	7	.969
2005—Louisville (Int'l)	OF-DH	7	24	1	7	1	0	1	4	1	10	0	0	0-0	.292	.320	.458	.778	2	.889
—Cincinnati (N.L.)	OF	99	311	46	79	17	0	19	51	20	116	3	7	2-1	.254	.304	.492	.796	4	.976
2006—Lowell (NY-Penn)		2	6	1	1	0	0	0	0	0	1	0	0	0-0	.167	.167	.167	.333	0	1.000
—Pawtucket (Int'l)		12	41	8	10	1	0	2	7	7	10	3	2	0-0	.244	.385	.415	.799	2	.950
—Boston (A.L.)	OF-DH	84	276	36	83	15	2	11	42	20	90	3	7	0-1	.301	.349	.489	.838	3	.981
American League totals (1 year)		84	276	36	83	15	2	11	42	20	90	3	7	0-1	.301	.349	.489	.838	3	.981
National League totals (4 years)		302	830	108	206	33	2	51	134	54	288	12	16	10-5	.248	.303	.477	.780	13	.973
Major League totals (5 years)		386	1106	144	289	48	4	62	176	74	378	15	23	10-6	.261	.315	.480	.795	16	.975

2006 LEFTY-RIGHTY SPLITS

vs.	Avg.	AB	H	2B	3B	HR	RBI	BB	SO	OBP	Slg.	vs.	Avg.	AB	H	2B	3B	HR	RBI	BB	SO	OBP	Slg.
L	.260	104	27	4	0	1	11	11	42	.333	.327	R	.326	172	56	11	2	10	31	9	48	.359	.587

PENN, HAYDEN   P

PERSONAL: Born October 13, 1984, in La Jolla, Calif. ... 6-3/185. ... Throws right, bats right. ... Full name: Hayden Andrew Penn. ... High school: Santana (Santee, Calif.). **TRANSACTIONS/CAREER NOTES:** Selected by Baltimore Orioles organization in fifth round of 2002 free-agent draft. ... On disabled list (May 23-July 20, 2006); included rehabilitation assignments to Bowie and Ottawa.

CAREER HITTING: 0-for-1 (.000), 0 R, 0 2B, 0 3B, 0 HR, 0 RBI.

Year Team (League)	W	L	Pct.	ERA	WHIP	G	GS	CG	ShO	Hld.	Sv.-Opp.	IP	H	R	ER	HR	BB-IBB	SO	Avg.
2003—GC Orioles (GCL)	0	0	...	2.70	1.20	1	1	0	0		0-...	3.1	3	1	1	0	1-0	4	.273
—Bluefield (Appal.)	1	4	.200	4.30	1.47	12	11	0	0		0-...	52.1	58	27	25	4	19-0	38	.283
2004—Delmarva (S. Atl.)	4	1	.800	3.32	1.13	13	6	0	0		1-...	43.1	30	18	16	4	19-1	41	.201
—Frederick (Carolina)	6	5	.545	3.80	1.08	13	13	0	0		0-...	73.1	59	33	31	7	20-0	61	.224
—Bowie (East.)	3	0	1.000	4.87	1.52	4	4	0	0		0-...	20.1	22	12	11	0	9-0	20	.278
2005—Bowie (East.)	7	6	.538	3.83	1.25	20	19	1	0		0-0	110.1	101	51	47	11	37-0	120	.248
—Baltimore (A.L.)	3	2	.600	6.34	1.75	8	8	0	0		0-0	38.1	46	30	27	6	21-3	18	.295
2006—Bowie (East.)	0	0	...	9.00	2.50	1	1	0	0		0-0	2.0	3	2	2	1	2-0	1	.375
—Ottawa (Int'l)	7	4	.636	2.26	1.12	14	14	2	1		0-0	87.2	71	25	22	5	27-1	85	.221
—Baltimore (A.L.)	0	4	.000	15.10	2.59	6	6	0	0		0-0	19.2	38	33	33	8	13-0	8	.392
Major League totals (2 years)	3	6	.333	9.31	2.03	14	14	0	0		0-0	58.0	84	63	60	14	34-3	26	.332

2006 LEFTY-RIGHTY SPLITS

vs.	Avg.	AB	H	2B	3B	HR	RBI	BB	SO	OBP	Slg.	vs.	Avg.	AB	H	2B	3B	HR	RBI	BB	SO	OBP	Slg.
L	.327	52	17	3	0	3	10	7	6	.407	.558	R	.467	45	21	4	1	5	19	6	2	.547	.933

PENNY, BRAD   P

PERSONAL: Born May 24, 1978, in Broken Arrow, Okla. ... 6-4/250. ... Throws right, bats right. ... Full name: Bradley Wayne Penny. ... High school: Broken Arrow (Okla.). **TRANSACTIONS/CAREER NOTES:** Selected by Arizona Diamondbacks organization in fifth round of 1996 free-agent draft. ... Traded by Diamondbacks with P Vladimir Nunez and a player to be named to Florida Marlins for P Matt Mantei (July 9, 1999). Marlins acquired OF Abraham Nunez to complete deal (December 13, 1999). ... On disabled list (July 20-September 2, 2000); included rehabilitation assignments to Brevard County and Calgary. ... On disabled list (May 19-July 2, 2002); included rehabilitation assignment to Jupiter. ... On suspended list (March 30-April 6, 2003). ... Traded with 1B Hee Seop Choi and P Bill Murphy to Los Angeles Dodgers for C Paul Lo Duca, P Guillermo Mota and OF Juan Encarnacion (July 30, 2004). ... On disabled list (August 9-September 22, 2004). ... On suspended list (August 31-September 6, 2005). **MISCELLANEOUS NOTES:** Made an out in only appearance as pinch hitter (2000). ... Struck out in only appearance as pinch hitter (2003).

P

CAREER HITTING: 55-for-389 (.141), 16 R, 10 2B, 2 3B, 2 HR, 21 RBI.

Year	Team (League)	W	L	Pct.	ERA	WHIP	G	GS	CG	ShO	Hld.	Sv.-Opp.	IP	H	R	ER	HR	BB-IBB	SO	Avg.
1996—	Ariz. D'backs (Ariz.)	2	2	.500	2.36	1.01	11	8	0	0	...	0-...	49.2	36	18	13	1	14-0	52	.197
1997—	South Bend (Mid.)	10	5	.667	2.73	1.13	25	25	0	0	...	0-...	118.2	91	44	36	4	43-2	116	.208
1998—	High Desert (Calif.)	14	5	.737	2.96	1.05	28	28	1	0	...	0-...	164.0	138	65	54	15	35-0	207	.225
1999—	El Paso (Texas)	2	7	.222	4.80	1.49	17	17	0	0	...	0-...	90.0	109	56	48	9	25-0	100	.303
	—Portland (East.)	1	0	1.000	3.90	1.30	6	6	0	0	...	0-...	32.1	28	15	14	3	14-0	35	.231
2000—	Florida (N.L.)	8	7	.533	4.81	1.50	23	22	0	0	0	0-0	119.2	120	70	64	13	60-4	80	.263
	—Brevard County (FSL)	0	1	.000	1.13	1.13	2	2	0	0	...	0-...	8.0	5	2	1	0	4-0	11	.172
	—Calgary (PCL)	2	0	1.000	1.80	1.20	3	3	0	0	...	0-...	15.0	8	8	3	1	10-0	16	.157
2001—	Florida (N.L.)	10	10	.500	3.69	1.16	31	31	1	1	0	0-0	205.0	183	92	84	15	54-3	154	.240
2002—	Florida (N.L.)	8	7	.533	4.66	1.53	24	24	1	1	0	0-0	129.1	148	76	67	18	50-7	93	.289
	—Jupiter (Fla. St.)	0	0	...	0.00	0.65	2	2	0	0	...	0-...	7.2	5	0	0	0	0-0	9	.179
2003—	Florida (N.L.)	14	10	.583	4.13	1.28	32	32	0	0	0	0-0	196.1	195	96	90	21	56-6	138	.264
2004—	Florida (N.L.)	8	8	.500	3.15	1.24	21	21	0	0	0	0-0	131.1	124	50	46	10	39-6	105	.250
	—Los Angeles (N.L.)	1	2	.333	3.09	1.03	3	3	0	0	0	0-0	11.2	6	5	4	2	6-0	6	.154
2005—	Vero Beach (FSL)	1	0	1.000	1.80	0.60	1	1	0	0	0	0-0	5.0	2	1	1	1	1-0	3	.125
	—Las Vegas (PCL)	1	0	1.000	3.00	1.17	1	1	0	0	0	0-0	6.0	5	2	2	1	2-0	9	.217
	—Los Angeles (N.L.)	7	9	.438	3.90	1.29	29	29	1	0	0	0-0	175.1	185	78	76	17	41-2	122	.270
2006—	Los Angeles (N.L.)	•16	9	.640	4.33	1.38	34	33	0	0	1	0-0	189.0	206	94	91	19	54-4	148	.279
Major League totals (7 years)		72	62	.537	4.06	1.32	197	195	3	2	1	0-0	1157.2	1167	561	522	115	360-32	846	.263

DIVISION SERIES RECORD

Year	Team (League)	W	L	Pct.	ERA	WHIP	G	GS	CG	ShO	Hld.	Sv.-Opp.	IP	H	R	ER	HR	BB-IBB	SO	Avg.
2003—	Florida (N.L.)	0	0	...	6.35	1.06	2	1	0	0	0	0-1	5.2	5	4	4	0	1-0	6	.250
2006—	Los Angeles (N.L.)	0	1	.000	18.00	4.00	1	0	0	0	0	0-0	1.0	2	2	2	0	2-0	1	.400
Division series totals (2 years)		0	1	.000	8.10	1.50	3	1	0	0	0	0-1	6.2	7	6	6	0	3-0	7	.280

CHAMPIONSHIP SERIES RECORD

Year	Team (League)	W	L	Pct.	ERA	WHIP	G	GS	CG	ShO	Hld.	Sv.-Opp.	IP	H	R	ER	HR	BB-IBB	SO	Avg.
2003—	Florida (N.L.)	1	1	.500	15.75	3.00	3	1	0	0	0	0-0	4.0	9	7	7	2	3-1	0	.450

WORLD SERIES RECORD

Year	Team (League)	W	L	Pct.	ERA	WHIP	G	GS	CG	ShO	Hld.	Sv.-Opp.	IP	H	R	ER	HR	BB-IBB	SO	Avg.
2003—	Florida (N.L.)	2	0	1.000	2.19	1.62	2	2	0	0	0	0-0	12.1	15	4	3	1	5-0	7	.319

ALL-STAR GAME RECORD

	W	L	Pct.	ERA	WHIP	G	GS	CG	ShO	Hld.	Sv.-Opp.	IP	H	R	ER	HR	BB-IBB	SO	Avg.
All-Star Game totals (1 year)	0	0	...	4.50	0.50	1	1	0	0	0	0-0	2.0	1	1	1	1	0-0	3	.143

2006 LEFTY-RIGHTY SPLITS

vs.	Avg.	AB	H	2B	3B	HR	RBI	BB	SO	OBP	Slg.	vs.	Avg.	AB	H	2B	3B	HR	RBI	BB	SO	OBP	Slg.
L	.275	378	104	23	0	11	45	30	70	.331	.423	R	.283	361	102	30	1	8	44	24	78	.338	.438

PERALTA, JHONNY — SS

PERSONAL: Born May 28, 1982, in Santiago, Dominican Republic. ... 6-1/185. ... Bats right, throws right. ... Full name: Jhonny Antonio Peralta. ... Name pronounced: johnny pah-RALL-tah. ... College: Collejo Pedagojico (Santiago, Dominican Republic). **TRANSACTIONS/CAREER NOTES:** Signed as a non-drafted free agent by Cleveland Indians organization (April 14, 1999). **STATISTICAL NOTES:** Career major league grand slams: 1.

2006 GAMES PLAYED BY POSITION (MLB): SS—147, DH—1.

			BATTING																	FIELDING	
Year	Team (League)	Pos.	G	AB	R	H	2B	3B	HR	RBI	BB	SO	HBP	GDP	SB-CS	Avg.	OBP	SLG	OPS	E	Avg.
1999—	Dom. Inds. (DSL)		62	208	48	63	14	6	6	43	33	49	2	...	14-3	.303	.397	.514	.911	...	...
2000—	Columbus (S. Atl.)	SS-3B	106	349	52	84	13	1	3	34	59	102	2	13	7-6	.241	.352	.309	.661	26	.948
2001—	Kinston (Carol.)	SS	125	441	57	106	24	2	7	47	58	148	1	9	4-8	.240	.328	.351	.680	27	.952
2002—	Akron (East.)	SS	130	470	62	132	28	5	15	62	45	97	5	6	4-2	.281	.343	.457	.800	21	.965
2003—	Buffalo (Int'l)	SS-3B	63	237	25	61	12	1	1	21	15	45	3	6	1-3	.257	.310	.329	.639	10	.969
	—Cleveland (A.L.)	SS-3B	77	242	24	55	10	1	4	21	20	65	4	5	1-3	.227	.295	.326	.621	8	.977
2004—	Buffalo (Int'l)	SS-3B-DH	138	556	109	181	44	2	15	86	54	126	4	16	8-4	.326	.384	.493	.876	27	.948
	—Cleveland (A.L.)	SS-3B	8	25	2	6	1	0	0	2	3	6	0	0	0-1	.240	.321	.280	.601	3	.900
2005—	Cleveland (A.L.)	SS	141	504	82	147	35	4	24	78	58	128	3	12	0-2	.292	.366	.520	.885	19	.970
2006—	Cleveland (A.L.)	SS-DH	149	569	84	146	28	3	13	68	56	152	1	19	0-1	.257	.323	.385	.708	16	.977
Major League totals (4 years)			375	1340	192	354	74	8	41	169	137	351	8	36	1-7	.264	.334	.423	.757	46	.973

2006 LEFTY-RIGHTY SPLITS

vs.	Avg.	AB	H	2B	3B	HR	RBI	BB	SO	OBP	Slg.	vs.	Avg.	AB	H	2B	3B	HR	RBI	BB	SO	OBP	Slg.
L	.267	176	47	9	0	5	17	13	57	.321	.403	R	.252	393	99	19	3	8	51	43	95	.323	.377

PERALTA, JOEL — P

PERSONAL: Born March 23, 1976, in Bonao, Dominican Republic. ... 5-11/170. ... Throws right, bats right. ... Full name: Joel Peralta. ... High school: 4th Bachillerato (Dominican Republic). ... Junior college: Ventura (Calif.) Community College. **TRANSACTIONS/CAREER NOTES:** Signed as a non-drafted free agent by Oakland Athletics organization (July 4, 1996). ... Released by A's (June 4, 1998). ... Signed by Anaheim Angels organization (February 25, 1999). ... Angels franchise renamed Los Angeles Angels of Anaheim for 2005 season. ... Claimed on waivers by Kansas City Royals (October 7, 2005).

CAREER HITTING: 0-for-0 (.000), 0 R, 0 2B, 0 3B, 0 HR, 0 RBI.

Year	Team (League)	W	L	Pct.	ERA	WHIP	G	GS	CG	ShO	Hld.	Sv.-Opp.	IP	H	R	ER	HR	BB-IBB	SO	Avg.
1999—	Anaheim SP (DSL)	2	3	.400	2.50	1.19	24	0	0	0	...	12-...	36.0	27	14	10	0	16-1	35	.201
2000—	Butte (Pion.)	2	1	.667	6.63	1.79	10	1	0	0	...	1-...	19.0	24	15	14	2	10-1	17	.333
	—Boise (N'west)	0	0	...	6.48	1.89	4	0	0	0	...	0-...	9.0	12	6	6	0	5-0	9	.353
2001—	Cedar Rap. (Midw.)	0	0	...	2.13	0.74	41	0	0	0	...	23-...	43.0	27	13	10	3	5-0	53	.175
	—Arkansas (Texas)	0	1	.000	6.30	2.00	9	0	0	0	...	2-...	10.0	15	10	7	2	5-0	14	.333
2002—	Arkansas (Texas)	0	0	...	6.62	1.98	12	0	0	0	...	0-...	17.2	25	15	13	5	10-0	11	.338
	—Cedar Rap. (Midw.)	5	0	1.000	0.95	0.81	41	0	0	0	...	21-...	48.0	28	7	5	2	11-3	53	.164
2003—	Arkansas (Texas)	5	4	.556	2.24	0.96	47	0	0	0	...	20-...	53.0	39	13	13	3	12-2	48	.205
	—Salt Lake (PCL)	0	0	...	...	...	1	0	0	0	...	0-...	0.0	0	0	0	0	1-0	0	...
2004—	Salt Lake (PCL)	4	2	.667	4.98	1.46	39	0	0	0	...	1-...	56.0	64	33	31	6	18-0	68	.276
	—Ariz. Angels (Ariz.)	0	0	...	2.08	0.20	2	0	0	0	...	0-...	5.0	1	1	1	0	0-0	9	.077
	—Rancho Cuca. (Calif.)	0	0	...	9.00	3.00	1	0	0	0	...	0-...	2.0	5	2	2	1	1-0	1	.455
2005—	Los Angeles (A.L.)	1	0	1.000	3.89	1.21	28	0	0	0	0	0-0	34.2	28	15	15	6	14-2	30	.219
	—Salt Lake (PCL)	4	1	.800	2.70	0.85	19	0	0	0	0	10-13	20.0	11	6	6	0	6-0	18	.159

P

Year	Team (League)	W	L	Pct.	ERA	WHIP	G	GS	CG	ShO	Hld.	Sv.-Opp.	IP	H	R	ER	HR	BB-IBB	SO	Avg.
2006— Omaha (PCL)		1	0	1.000	1.43	1.43	6	0	0	0	...	2-2	7.2	8	2	2	1	3-0	8	.296
— Kansas City (A.L.)		1	3	.250	4.40	1.24	64	0	0	0	17	1-3	73.2	74	37	36	10	17-2	57	.263
Major League totals (2 years)		2	3	.400	4.24	1.23	92	0	0	0	17	1-3	108.1	102	52	51	16	31-4	87	.249

2006 LEFTY-RIGHTY SPLITS

vs.	Avg.	AB	H	2B	3B	HR	RBI	BB	SO	OBP	Slg.	vs.	Avg.	AB	H	2B	3B	HR	RBI	BB	SO	OBP	Slg.
L	.338	80	27	6	2	4	23	9	13	.400	.613	R	.234	201	47	14	1	6	27	8	44	.268	.403

PERCIVAL, TROY — P

PERSONAL: Born August 9, 1969, in Fontana, Calif. ... 6-3/235. ... Throws right, bats right. ... Full name: Troy Eugene Percival. ... High school: Moreno Valley (Calif.). ... College: UC-Riverside. **TRANSACTIONS/CAREER NOTES:** Selected by California Angels organization in sixth round of 1990 free-agent draft. ... Played one season as a catcher in Angels organization (1990). ... Angels franchise renamed Anaheim Angels for 1997 season. ... On disabled list (April 7-May 16, 1997); included rehabilitation assignment to Lake Elsinore. ... On disabled list (August 5-26, 2000); included rehabilitation assignment to Lake Elsinore. ... On disabled list (April 3-18 and July 12-27, 2002; May 23-June 7, 2003; and June 2-27, 2004). ... Signed as a free agent by Detroit Tigers (November 17, 2004). ... On disabled list (May 9-June 5 and July 14, 2005-remainder of season). ... On disabled list (April 1, 2006-entire season). **MISCELLANEOUS NOTES:** Played catcher (1990). ... Struck out in only appearance as pinch hitter (1996).

CAREER HITTING: 0-for-1 (.000), 0 R, 0 2B, 0 3B, 0 HR, 0 RBI.

Year	Team (League)	W	L	Pct.	ERA	WHIP	G	GS	CG	ShO	Hld.	Sv.-Opp.	IP	H	R	ER	HR	BB-IBB	SO	Avg.
1991— Boise (N'west)	2	0	1.000	1.41	1.07	28	0	0	0	...	12-...	38.1	23	7	6	0	18-1	63	.172
1992— Palm Springs (Calif.)	1	1	.500	5.06	1.31	11	0	0	0	...	2-...	10.2	6	7	6	0	8-1	16	.188
— Midland (Texas)	3	0	1.000	2.37	1.53	20	0	0	0	...	5-...	19.0	18	5	5	1	11-1	21	.254
1993— Vancouver (PCL)	0	1	.000	6.27	1.98	18	0	0	0	...	4-...	18.2	24	14	13	0	13-1	19	.320
1994— Vancouver (PCL)	2	6	.250	4.13	1.51	49	0	0	0	...	15-...	61.0	63	31	28	4	29-5	73	.285
1995— California (A.L.)	3	2	.600	1.95	0.85	62	0	0	0	* 29	3-6	74.0	37	19	16	6	26-2	94	.147
1996— California (A.L.)	0	2	.000	2.31	0.93	62	0	0	0	2	36-39	74.0	38	20	19	8	31-4	100	.149
1997— Anaheim (A.L.)	5	5	.500	3.46	1.19	55	0	0	0	0	27-31	52.0	40	20	20	6	22-2	72	.205
— Lake Elsinore (Calif.)	0	0	...	0.00	0.50	2	1	0	0	...	0-...	2.0	1	0	0	0	0-3	3	.143
1998— Anaheim (A.L.)	2	7	.222	3.65	1.23	67	0	0	0	0	42-48	66.2	45	31	27	5	37-4	87	.186
1999— Anaheim (A.L.)	4	6	.400	3.79	1.05	60	0	0	0	0	31-39	57.0	38	24	24	9	22-0	58	.186
2000— Anaheim (A.L.)	5	5	.500	4.50	1.44	54	0	0	0	0	32-42	50.0	42	27	25	7	30-4	49	.228
— Lake Elsinore (Calif.)	0	0	...	4.50	1.00	2	0	0	0	0	0-...	2.0	1	1	1	0	1-0	1	.143
2001— Anaheim (A.L.)	4	2	.667	2.65	0.99	57	0	0	0	0	39-42	57.2	39	19	17	3	18-1	71	.187
2002— Anaheim (A.L.)	4	1	.800	1.92	1.12	58	0	0	0	0	40-44	56.1	38	12	12	5	25-1	68	.188
2003— Anaheim (A.L.)	0	5	.000	3.47	1.14	52	0	0	0	0	33-37	49.1	33	22	19	7	23-1	48	.184
2004— Anaheim (A.L.)	2	3	.400	2.90	1.25	52	0	0	0	0	33-38	49.2	43	19	16	7	19-3	33	.230
2005— Detroit (A.L.)	1	3	.250	5.76	1.20	26	0	0	0	0	8-11	25.0	19	16	16	7	11-3	20	.207
2006— Detroit (A.L.)			Did not play.																	
Major League totals (11 years)	30	41	.423	3.10	1.11	605	0	0	0	31	324-377	611.2	412	229	211	70	264-25	700	.187

DIVISION SERIES RECORD

Year	Team (League)	W	L	Pct.	ERA	WHIP	G	GS	CG	ShO	Hld.	Sv.-Opp.	IP	H	R	ER	HR	BB-IBB	SO	Avg.
2002— Anaheim (A.L.)	0	0	...	5.40	1.80	3	0	0	0	0	2-2	3.1	6	2	2	0	0-0	4	.375

CHAMPIONSHIP SERIES RECORD

Year	Team (League)	W	L	Pct.	ERA	WHIP	G	GS	CG	ShO	Hld.	Sv.-Opp.	IP	H	R	ER	HR	BB-IBB	SO	Avg.
2002— Anaheim (A.L.)	0	0	...	0.00	0.00	3	0	0	0	0	2-2	3.1	0	0	0	0	0-0	3	.000

WORLD SERIES RECORD

Year	Team (League)	W	L	Pct.	ERA	WHIP	G	GS	CG	ShO	Hld.	Sv.-Opp.	IP	H	R	ER	HR	BB-IBB	SO	Avg.
2002— Anaheim (A.L.)	0	0	...	3.00	1.00	3	0	0	0	0	3-3	3.0	2	1	1	1	1-0	3	.182

ALL-STAR GAME RECORD

Year	Team (League)	W	L	Pct.	ERA	WHIP	G	GS	CG	ShO	Hld.	Sv.-Opp.	IP	H	R	ER	HR	BB-IBB	SO	Avg.
All-Star Game totals (3 years)	0	0	...	0.00	1.00	3	0	0	0	0	0-0	3.0	2	0	0	0	1-0	4	.182

PEREZ, ANTONIO — 3B/SS

PERSONAL: Born January 26, 1980, in Bani, Dominican Republic. ... 5-11/170. ... Bats right, throws right. ... Full name: Antonio Miguel Perez. **TRANSACTIONS/CAREER NOTES:** Signed as a non-drafted free agent by Cincinnati Reds organization (March 21, 1998). ... Traded by Reds with OF Mike Cameron and Ps Brett Tomko and Jake Meyer to Seattle Mariners for OF Ken Griffey (February 10, 2000). ... Traded by Mariners to Tampa Bay Devil Rays for OF Randy Winn (October 28, 2002). ... Traded by Devil Rays to Los Angeles Dodgers for OF/IF Jason Romano (April 9-May 18, 2005); included rehabilitation assignment to Las Vegas. ... Traded by Dodgers with OF Milton Bradley to Oakland Athletics for OF Andre Ethier (December 13, 2005).

2006 GAMES PLAYED BY POSITION (MLB): 3B—27, DH—21, SS—4, 2B—2.

Year	Team (League)	Pos.	G	AB	R	H	2B	3B	HR	RBI	BB	SO	HBP	GDP	SB-CS	Avg.	OBP	SLG	OPS	E	Avg.
1998— Dom. Reds (DSL)		63	212	57	54	11	0	2	24	53	33	4	...	58-16	.255	.408	.335	.743	...	...
1999— Rockford (Midwest)	SS-2B	119	385	69	111	20	3	7	41	43	80	13	3	35-24	.288	.376	.410	.787	36	.929
2000— Lancaster (Calif.)	SS	98	395	90	109	36	6	17	63	58	99	8	3	28-16	.276	.376	.527	.903	27	.939
2001— San Antonio (Texas)	SS	5	21	3	3	0	0	0	0	0	7	0	0	0-0	.143	.143	.143	.286	6	.818
2002— Ariz. Mariners (Ariz.)	2B-SS	6	15	3	5	1	0	1	3	4	2	1	0	4-0	.333	.476	.600	1.076	0	1.000
— San Antonio (Texas)	2B-SS	72	240	30	62	8	2	2	24	11	64	10	3	15-9	.258	.312	.333	.645	13	.955
2003— Orlando (South.)	2B-DH	24	81	16	22	5	1	2	10	18	18	4	0	3-1	.272	.423	.432	.855	3	.967
— Durham (Int'l)	2B-DH	34	134	27	38	12	2	6	20	10	38	3	2	3-1	.284	.345	.537	.882	8	.958
— Tampa Bay (A.L.) 2B-3B-SS	DH	48	125	19	31	6	1	2	12	18	34	1	1	4-1	.248	.345	.360	.705	2	.985
2004— Las Vegas (PCL)	SS-2B-DH	125	476	92	141	24	6	22	88	61	87	7	1	23-12	.296	.379	.511	.890	20	.963
— Los Angeles (N.L.)	2B-SS	13	13	5	3	1	0	0	2	1	0	5	1	0	1-0	.231	.308	.308	.593	1	.857
2005— Las Vegas (PCL) 3B-2B-SS	3B-SS	16	56	8	13	3	0	2	6	3	20	1	1	2-1	.232	.279	.393	.672	2	.941
— Los Angeles (N.L.) 3B-2B-SS	OF-DH	98	259	28	77	13	2	3	23	21	61	5	4	11-4	.297	.360	.398	.758	9	.961
2006— Oakland (A.L.) 3B-DH-SS	2B	57	98	10	10	1	1	1	8	10	44	0	0	0-1	.102	.185	.204	.389	4	.954
American League totals (2 years)		105	223	29	41	11	2	3	20	28	78	1	1	4-2	.184	.277	.291	.568	6	.973
National League totals (2 years)		111	272	33	80	14	2	3	23	21	66	6	4	12-4	.294	.357	.393	.750	10	.958
Major League totals (4 years)		216	495	62	121	25	4	6	43	49	144	7	5	16-6	.244	.320	.347	.668	16	.965

2006 LEFTY-RIGHTY SPLITS

vs.	Avg.	AB	H	2B	3B	HR	RBI	BB	SO	OBP	Slg.	vs.	Avg.	AB	H	2B	3B	HR	RBI	BB	SO	OBP	Slg.
L	.129	31	4	2	0	1	4	5	14	.250	.290	R	.090	67	6	3	1	0	4	5	30	.153	.164

P

PEREZ, BELTRAN   P

PERSONAL: Born October 24, 1981, in San Francisco de Macoris, Dominican Republic. ... Throws right, bats right. ... Full name: Beltran Perez. **TRANSACTIONS/CAREER NOTES:** Signed as a non-drafted free agent by Arizona Diamondbacks organization (February 2, 1999). ... Traded by Diamondbacks with C Dioner Navarro and Ps William Juarez and Danny Muegge to Los Angeles Dodgers for OF Shawn Green and cash (January 11, 2005). ... Signed as a free agent by Washington Nationals organization (February 10, 2006). **MISCELLANEOUS NOTES:** Singled in only appearance as pinch hitter (2006). **CAREER HITTING:** 3-for-6 (.500), 0 R, 0 2B, 0 3B, 0 HR, 0 RBI.

Year Team (League)	W	L	Pct.	ERA	WHIP	G	GS	CG	ShO	Hld.	Sv.-Opp.	IP	H	R	ER	HR	BB-IBB	SO	Avg.
1999— Dominican Diamondbacks (DSL)	6	0	1.000	2.45	1.13	18	0	0	0	...	0-...	29.1	24	12	8	1	9-1	31	.216
2000— Ariz. D'backs (Ariz.)	5	1	.833	5.81	1.79	11	4	0	0	...	0-...	48.0	61	37	31	1	25-1	47	.321
— High Desert (Calif.)	0	1	.000	3.60	1.30	2	2	0	0	...	0-...	10.0	8	4	4	3	5-0	11	.211
2001— South Bend (Mid.)	12	4	.750	2.81	1.11	27	27	2	0	...	0-...	160.0	142	59	50	10	35-0	157	.236
2002— El Paso (Texas)	3	8	.273	5.47	1.52	20	19	1	0	...	0-...	97.0	114	70	59	10	33-2	77	.292
— Lancaster (Calif.)	3	2	.600	2.51	1.05	5	5	0	0	...	0-...	32.1	31	11	9	1	3-0	30	.263
2003— El Paso (Texas)	2	11	.154	5.30	1.58	29	20	0	0	...	0-...	147.2	180	94	87	13	54-1	88	.310
2004— El Paso (Texas)	2	6	.250	4.41	1.42	37	8	0	0	...	3-...	104.0	102	56	51	14	46-1	77	.256
2005— Vero Beach (FSL)	3	2	.600	3.78	1.38	19	0	0	0	0	0-2	33.1	31	15	14	3	15-0	33	.256
— Jacksonville (Sou.)	2	3	.400	2.90	1.23	17	1	0	0	0	3-4	31.0	22	11	10	1	16-0	32	.200
2006— Harrisburg (East.)	8	6	.571	3.11	1.37	31	16	1	0	1	1-3	121.2	127	53	42	8	40-5	107	.267
— Wash. (N.L.)	2	1	.667	3.86	1.38	8	3	0	0	0	0-0	21.0	16	9	9	3	13-2	9	.222
Major League totals (1 year)	2	1	.667	3.86	1.38	8	3	0	0	0	0-0	21.0	16	9	9	3	13-2	9	.222

2006 LEFTY-RIGHTY SPLITS

vs.	Avg.	AB	H	2B	3B	HR	RBI	BB	SO	OBP	Slg.	vs.	Avg.	AB	H	2B	3B	HR	RBI	BB	SO	OBP	Slg.
L	.270	37	10	1	0	2	5	9	4	.413	.459	R	.171	35	6	1	0	1	5	4	5	.256	.286

PEREZ, EDUARDO   1B/OF

PERSONAL: Born September 11, 1969, in Cincinnati. ... 6-4/240. ... Bats right, throws right. ... Full name: Eduardo Atanasio Perez. ... High school: Robinson (Santurce, Puerto Rico). ... College: Florida State. ... Son of Tony Perez, infielder with four major league teams (1964-86) and manager of Cincinnati Reds (1993). **TRANSACTIONS/CAREER NOTES:** Selected by California Angels organization in first round (17th pick overall) of 1991 free-agent draft. ... Traded by Angels to Cincinnati Reds for OF Will Pennyfeather (April 5, 1996). ... Released by Reds (December 14, 1998). ... Signed by St. Louis Cardinals organization (February 16, 1999). ... On disabled list (June 25-July 13 and August 13-September 1, 2000); included rehabilitation assignment to Memphis. ... Contract sold by Cardinals to Hanshin of the Japan Central League (December 20, 2000). ... Signed as a free agent by Cardinals organization (February 8, 2002). ... Signed as a free agent by Tampa Bay Devil Rays (December 11, 2003). ... On disabled list (May 10, 2004-remainder of season). ... Signed as free agent by Cleveland Indians (January 12, 2006). ... Traded by Indians to Seattle Mariners for SS Asdrubal Cabrera (June 30, 2006). **STATISTICAL NOTES:** Career major league grand slams: 2. **2006 GAMES PLAYED BY POSITION (MLB):** DH—36, 1B—34, OF—5.

Year Team (League)	Pos.	G	AB	R	H	2B	3B	HR	RBI	BB	SO	HBP	GDP	SB-CS	Avg.	OBP	SLG	OPS	E	Avg.
1991— Boise (N'west)	1B-OF	46	160	35	46	13	0	1	22	19	39	4	4	12-3	.288	.375	.388	.763	3	.969
1992— Palm Springs (Calif.)	3B-OF-SS	54	204	37	64	8	4	3	35	23	33	3	5	14-3	.314	.386	.436	.823	16	.882
— Midland (Texas)	1B-3B-OF	62	235	27	54	8	1	3	23	22	49	1	7	19-7	.230	.295	.311	.606	13	.920
1993— Vancouver (PCL)	3B-1B-OF	96	363	66	111	23	6	12	70	28	83	3	5	21-7	.306	.360	.501	.862	23	.922
— California (A.L.)	3B-DH	52	180	16	45	6	2	4	30	9	39	2	4	5-4	.250	.292	.372	.664	5	.962
1994— California (A.L.)	1B	38	129	10	27	7	0	5	16	12	29	0	5	3-0	.209	.275	.380	.654	1	.997
— Vancouver (PCL)	3B-DH	61	219	37	65	14	3	7	38	34	53	3	7	9-4	.297	.394	.484	.878	12	.926
— Ariz. Angels (Ariz.)	3B	1	3	0	0	0	0	0	0	1	1	0	0	0-0	.000	.250	.000	.250	1	1.000
1995— California (A.L.)	3B-DH	29	71	9	12	4	1	1	7	12	9	2	3	0-2	.169	.302	.296	.598	7	.883
— Vancouver (PCL)	3B-DH-1B	69	246	39	80	12	7	6	37	25	34	2	5	6-2	.325	.386	.504	.890	6	.968
1996— Indianapolis (A.A.)	3B-1B-OF	122	451	84	132	29	5	21	84	51	69	6	11	11-0	.293	.371	.519	.890	21	.939
— Cincinnati (N.L.)	1B-OF-3B	18	36	8	8	0	0	3	9	5	9	0	2	0-0	.222	.317	.472	.789	0	1.000
1997— Cincinnati (N.L.)	1B-OF-3B-DH	106	297	44	75	19	0	16	52	29	76	2	6	5-1	.253	.321	.475	.796	2	.996
1998— Cincinnati (N.L.)	1B-3B-OF	84	172	20	41	4	0	4	30	21	45	2	2	0-1	.238	.325	.331	.656	5	.985
1999— Memphis (PCL)	1B-3B-DH	119	416	67	133	31	0	18	82	45	92	6	11	7-8	.320	.393	.524	.917	9	.989
— St. Louis (N.L.)	OF-1B	21	32	6	11	2	0	1	9	7	6	0	0	0-0	.344	.462	.500	.962	1	.970
2000— St. Louis (N.L.)	1B-OF-3B	35	91	9	27	4	0	3	16	5	19	2	1	1-0	.297	.350	.440	.790	0	1.000
— Memphis (PCL)	1B-3B-OF	77	277	57	80	12	3	19	66	43	48	1	9	10-4	.289	.383	.560	.942	8	.980
2001— Hanshin (Jp. Cn.)		52	167	20	37	11	0	3	19	21	48	...	...	3-...	.222	.341	...	...	...	...
2002— St. Louis (N.L.)	OF-1B-3B-DH	96	154	22	31	9	0	10	26	17	36	3	7	0-0	.201	.290	.455	.744	2	.982
2003— St. Louis (N.L.)	OF-3B-1B-DH	105	253	47	72	16	0	11	41	29	53	4	7	5-2	.285	.365	.478	.843	7	.951
2004— Tampa Bay (A.L.)	1B-DH-OF-3B	13	38	2	8	2	0	1	7	4	9	0	1	0-0	.211	.286	.342	.628	0	1.000
2005— Tampa Bay (A.L.)	1B-DH-OF-3B	77	161	23	41	6	0	11	28	26	30	3	6	0-2	.255	.368	.497	.865	2	.993
2006— Cleveland (A.L.)	1B-OF	37	99	16	30	9	0	8	22	5	11	2	5	0-0	.303	.343	.636	.979	2	.991
— Seattle (A.L.)	DH-1B	43	87	6	17	1	0	1	11	13	22	1	3	0-0	.195	.304	.241	.545	0	1.000
American League totals (6 years)		289	765	82	180	35	3	31	121	81	149	10	27	8-9	.235	.314	.414	.725	17	.984
National League totals (7 years)		465	1035	156	265	53	0	48	173	113	244	14	26	11-4	.256	.335	.446	.781	17	.988
Major League totals (13 years)		754	1800	238	445	88	3	79	294	194	393	24	53	19-13	.247	.326	.431	.757	34	.987

DIVISION SERIES RECORD

Year Team (League)	Pos.	G	AB	R	H	2B	3B	HR	RBI	BB	SO	HBP	GDP	SB-CS	Avg.	OBP	SLG	OPS	E	Avg.
2002— St. Louis (N.L.)		1	1	0	0	0	0	0	0	0	0	0	0	0-0	.000	.000	.000	.000	0	...

CHAMPIONSHIP SERIES RECORD

Year Team (League)	Pos.	G	AB	R	H	2B	3B	HR	RBI	BB	SO	HBP	GDP	SB-CS	Avg.	OBP	SLG	OPS	E	Avg.
2002— St. Louis (N.L.)	OF	3	4	1	1	0	0	1	1	0	0	0	0	0-0	.250	.400	1.000	1.400	0	1.000

2006 LEFTY-RIGHTY SPLITS

vs.	Avg.	AB	H	2B	3B	HR	RBI	BB	SO	OBP	Slg.	vs.	Avg.	AB	H	2B	3B	HR	RBI	BB	SO	OBP	Slg.
L	.275	153	42	8	0	9	28	13	26	.331	.503	R	.152	33	5	2	0	0	5	5	7	.293	.212

PEREZ, JUAN   P

PERSONAL: Born September 3, 1978, in Villa Rivas, Dominican Republic. ... 6-1/170. ... Throws left, bats right. ... Full name: Juan P. Perez. **TRANSACTIONS/CAREER NOTES:** Signed as non-drafted free agent by Boston Red Sox organization (September 2, 1998). ... Signed as free agent by New York Mets organization (October 28, 2005). ... Claimed on waivers by Pittsburgh Pirates (August 23, 2006). **CAREER HITTING:** 0-for-0 (.000), 0 R, 0 2B, 0 3B, 0 HR, 0 RBI.

Year	Team (League)	W	L	Pct.	ERA	WHIP	G	GS	CG	ShO	Hld.	Sv.-Opp.	IP	H	R	ER	HR	BB-IBB	SO	Avg.
1999—	Dom. Red Sox (DSL)	6	6	.500	1.94	0.98	13	13	1	1	...	0-...	69.2	38	29	15	1	30-0	107	.159
2000—	GC Red Sox (GCL)	3	1	.750	2.36	1.08	9	5	0	0	...	1-...	34.1	24	12	9	2	13-0	43	.192
2001—	Augusta (S. Atl.)	8	8	.500	3.58	1.27	26	25	0	0	...	0-...	125.2	118	69	50	14	42-0	113	.251
2002—	Sarasota (Fla. St.)	0	6	.000	3.78	1.35	16	14	0	0	...	0-...	66.2	71	34	28	4	19-0	39	.274
2003—	Sarasota (Fla. St.)	3	4	.429	2.37	1.21	33	0	0	0	...	18-...	38.0	34	15	10	0	12-2	37	.230
—	Portland (East.)	3	3	.500	3.82	1.57	18	0	0	0	...	0-...	30.2	37	19	13	4	11-1	24	.306
2004—	Portland (East.)	5	1	.833	4.14	1.39	46	0	0	0	...	6-...	78.1	72	46	36	12	37-5	79	.237
2005—	Pawtucket (Int'l)	4	5	.444	4.50	1.45	40	1	0	0	7	1-4	62.0	61	31	31	7	29-0	74	.261
2006—	Indianapolis (Int'l)	0	0	...	0.00	0.86	4	0	0	0	2	0-0	7.0	3	0	0	0	3-0	6	.136
—	Norfolk (Int'l)	0	1	.000	2.86	1.57	43	0	0	0	9	0-1	63.0	65	24	20	4	34-0	55	.266
—	Pittsburgh (N.L.)	0	1	.000	8.10	1.80	7	0	0	0	0	0-0	3.1	5	3	3	1	1-0	3	.385
Major League totals (1 year)		0	1	.000	8.10	1.80	7	0	0	0	0	0-0	3.1	5	3	3	1	1-0	3	.385

2006 LEFTY-RIGHTY SPLITS

vs.	Avg.	AB	H	2B	3B	HR	RBI	BB	SO	OBP	Slg.	vs.	Avg.	AB	H	2B	3B	HR	RBI	BB	SO	OBP	Slg.
L	.286	7	2	0	0	0	3	0	2	.375	.286	R	.500	6	3	0	1	1	3	1	1	.556	1.333

PEREZ, NEIFI — SS/2B

PERSONAL: Born June 2, 1973, in Villa Mella, Dominican Republic. ... 6-0/197. ... Bats both, throws right. ... Full name: Neifi Neftali Perez. ... Name pronounced: NAY-fee PAIR-ez. **TRANSACTIONS/CAREER NOTES:** Signed as a non-drafted free agent by Colorado Rockies organization (November 9, 1992). ... On disabled list (April 8-23, 2001). ... Traded by Rockies to Kansas City Royals for OF Jermaine Dye (July 25, 2001). ... Claimed on waivers by San Francisco Giants (November 20, 2002). ... Released by Giants (August 13, 2004). ... Signed by Chicago Cubs organization (August 19, 2004). ... Traded by Cubs to Detroit Tigers for C Chris Robinson (August 20, 2006). **HONORS:** Won N.L. Gold Glove as shortstop (2000). **STATISTICAL NOTES:** Hit for the cycle (July 25, 1998). ... Career major league grand slams: 2.
2006 GAMES PLAYED BY POSITION (MLB): 2B—67, SS—28, 3B—11, DH—1.

Year	Team (League)	Pos.	G	AB	R	H	2B	3B	HR	RBI	BB	SO	HBP	GDP	SB-CS	Avg.	OBP	SLG	OPS	E	Avg.
1993—	Bend (N'west)	2B-SS	75	296	35	77	11	4	3	32	19	43	2	3	19-14	.260	.306	.355	.661	25	.937
1994—	Central Valley (Cal.)	SS	134	506	64	121	16	7	1	35	32	79	2	6	9-7	.239	.284	.304	.589	39	.940
1995—	Colo. Springs (PCL)	SS	11	36	4	10	4	0	0	2	0	5	0	0	1-1	.278	.278	.389	.667	3	.936
—	New Haven (East.)	SS	116	427	59	108	28	3	5	43	24	52	2	6	5-2	.253	.295	.368	.663	18	.967
1996—	Colo. Springs (PCL)	SS	133	570	77	180	28	12	7	72	21	48	2	13	16-13	.316	.337	.444	.781	25	.963
—	Colorado (N.L.)	SS-2B	17	45	4	7	0	0	0	3	0	8	0	2	2-2	.156	.156	.200	.356	2	.961
1997—	Colo. Springs (PCL)	SS	68	303	68	110	24	3	8	46	17	27	0	3	8-2	.363	.393	.541	.934	8	.975
—	Colorado (N.L.)	SS-2B-3B	83	313	46	91	13	10	5	31	21	43	1	3	4-3	.291	.333	.444	.777	9	.981
1998—	Colorado (N.L.)	SS-C	•162	647	80	177	25	9	9	59	38	70	1	8	5-6	.274	.313	.382	.695	20	.975
1999—	Colorado (N.L.)	SS	157	*690	108	193	27	•11	12	70	28	54	1	4	13-5	.280	.307	.403	.710	14	.981
2000—	Colorado (N.L.)	SS	•162	651	92	187	39	11	10	71	30	63	0	9	3-6	.287	.314	.427	.741	18	.978
2001—	Colorado (N.L.)	SS	87	382	65	114	19	8	7	47	16	49	0	8	6-2	.298	.326	.445	.771	10	.976
—	Kansas City (A.L.)	SS-2B	49	199	18	48	7	1	1	12	10	19	1	2	3-4	.241	.277	.302	.579	5	.980
2002—	Kansas City (A.L.)	SS-2B	145	554	65	131	20	4	3	37	20	53	0	11	8-9	.236	.260	.303	.564	20	.971
2003—	San Francisco (N.L.)	2B-SS-3B	120	328	27	84	19	4	1	31	14	23	0	9	3-2	.256	.285	.348	.632	5	.989
2004—	San Francisco (N.L.)	SS-2B-3B	103	319	28	74	12	1	2	33	21	35	0	7	0-1	.232	.276	.295	.571	6	.986
—	Iowa (PCL)	SS	10	34	1	7	1	0	0	3	0	5	0	0	0-0	.206	.206	.235	.441	0	1.000
—	Chicago (N.L.)	SS-2B	23	62	12	23	5	0	2	6	3	6	0	1	1-0	.371	.400	.548	.948	2	.972
2005—	Chicago (N.L.)	SS-2B-3B	154	572	59	157	33	1	9	54	18	47	3	22	8-4	.274	.298	.383	.681	12	.982
2006—	Chicago (N.L.)	SS-2B-3B	87	236	27	60	13	1	2	24	5	21	0	3	0-1	.254	.266	.343	.610	7	.973
—	Detroit (A.L.)	2B-SS-3B DH	21	65	4	13	1	0	0	5	3	4	0	2	1-0	.200	.235	.215	.451	1	.990
American League totals (3 years)			215	818	87	192	28	5	4	54	33	76	1	15	12-13	.235	.262	.296	.558	26	.975
National League totals (10 years)			1155	4245	548	1167	207	56	59	429	194	419	6	76	45-32	.275	.305	.392	.697	105	.980
Major League totals (11 years)			1370	5063	635	1359	235	61	63	483	227	495	7	91	57-45	.268	.298	.376	.674	131	.979

DIVISION SERIES RECORD

Year	Team (League)	Pos.	G	AB	R	H	2B	3B	HR	RBI	BB	SO	HBP	GDP	SB-CS	Avg.	OBP	SLG	OPS	E	Avg.
2003—	San Francisco (N.L.)	2B	3	3	1	1	1	0	0	0	0	0	0	0	0-0	.333	.500	.667	1.167	0	1.000

CHAMPIONSHIP SERIES RECORD

Year	Team (League)	Pos.	G	AB	R	H	2B	3B	HR	RBI	BB	SO	HBP	GDP	SB-CS	Avg.	OBP	SLG	OPS	E	Avg.
2006—	Detroit (A.L.)	SS	1	4	0	0	0	0	0	0	0	1	0	0	0-0	.000	.000	.000	.000	0	1.000

WORLD SERIES RECORD

Year	Team (League)	Pos.	G	AB	R	H	2B	3B	HR	RBI	BB	SO	HBP	GDP	SB-CS	Avg.	OBP	SLG	OPS	E	Avg.
2006—	Detroit (A.L.)	3B-SS	2	0	0	0	0	0	0	0	0	0	0	0	0-0	...	...	...	...	0	1.000

2006 LEFTY-RIGHTY SPLITS

vs.	Avg.	AB	H	2B	3B	HR	RBI	BB	SO	OBP	Slg.	vs.	Avg.	AB	H	2B	3B	HR	RBI	BB	SO	OBP	Slg.
L	.265	98	26	8	0	2	8	2	14	.275	.408	R	.232	203	47	6	1	0	21	6	11	.252	.271

PEREZ, ODALIS — P

PERSONAL: Born June 7, 1977, in Las Matas de Farfan, Dominican Republic. ... 6-0/150. ... Throws left, bats left. ... Full name: Odalis Amadol Perez. ... Name pronounced: oh-DALL-iss. ... High school: Damian Davis Ortiz (Las Matas de Farfan, Dominican Republic). **TRANSACTIONS/CAREER NOTES:** Signed as a non-drafted free agent by Atlanta Braves organization (July 2, 1994). ... On disabled list (July 23, 1999-remainder of season; and April 2, 2000-entire season). ... On disabled list (July 22-September 1, 2001); included rehabilitation assignment to Richmond. ... Traded by Braves with OF Brian Jordan and P Andrew Brown to Los Angeles Dodgers for OF Gary Sheffield (January 15, 2002). ... On disabled list (June 27-July 17, 2004). ... On disabled list (May 24-July 5 and August 22-September 24, 2005); included rehabilitation assignment to Las Vegas. ... On bereavement list (May 6-9, 2006). ... Traded by Dodgers with Ps Blake Johnson and Julio Pimentel to Kansas City Royals for P Elmer Dessens (July 25, 2006). **MISCELLANEOUS NOTES:** Made an out in only appearance as pinch hitter (2006).
CAREER HITTING: 36-for-282 (.128), 20 R, 8 2B, 0 3B, 1 HR, 10 RBI.

Year	Team (League)	W	L	Pct.	ERA	WHIP	G	GS	CG	ShO	Hld.	Sv.-Opp.	IP	H	R	ER	HR	BB-IBB	SO	Avg.
1995—	GC Braves (GCL)	3	5	.375	2.22	1.02	12	12	1	1	...	0-...	65.0	48	22	16	0	18-0	62	.200
1996—	Eugene (Northwest)	2	1	.667	3.80	1.56	10	6	0	0	...	0-...	23.2	26	16	10	2	11-0	38	.268
1997—	Macon (S. Atl.)	4	5	.444	1.65	1.08	36	0	0	0	...	5-...	87.1	67	31	16	4	27-1	100	.209
1998—	Greenville (Sou.)	6	5	.545	4.02	1.36	23	21	0	0	...	0-...	132.0	127	67	59	15	53-2	143	.256
—	Richmond (Int'l)	1	2	.333	2.96	1.36	13	0	0	0	...	3-...	24.1	26	10	8	4	7-1	22	• .283
—	Atlanta (N.L.)	1	0	.000	4.22	1.31	10	0	0	0	5	0-1	10.2	10	5	5	1	4-0	5	.244
1999—	Atlanta (N.L.)	4	6	.400	6.00	1.65	18	17	0	0	0	0-0	93.0	100	65	62	12	53-2	82	.275
2000—	Atlanta (N.L.)	Did not play.																		
2001—	Atlanta (N.L.)	7	8	.467	4.91	1.54	24	16	0	0	0	0-0	95.1	108	55	52	7	39-0	71	.290

P

Year	Team (League)	W	L	Pct.	ERA	WHIP	G	GS	CG	ShO	Hld.	Sv.-Opp.	IP	H	R	ER	HR	BB-IBB	SO	Avg.
	—Richmond (Int'l)	1	0	1.000	2.74	1.09	5	5	0	0	...	0-...	23.0	23	7	7	1	2-0	22	.256
2002—	Los Angeles (N.L.)	15	10	.600	3.00	0.99	32	32	4	2	0	0-0	222.1	182	76	74	21	38-5	155	.226
2003—	Los Angeles (N.L.)	12	12	.500	4.52	1.28	30	30	0	0	0	0-0	185.1	191	98	93	28	46-4	141	.267
2004—	Los Angeles (N.L.)	7	6	.538	3.25	1.14	31	31	0	0	0	0-0	196.1	180	76	71	26	44-4	128	.250
2005—	Las Vegas (PCL)	1	0	1.000	4.30	1.23	4	4	0	0	0	0-0	14.2	14	7	7	1	4-0	11	.255
	—Los Angeles (N.L.)	7	8	.467	4.56	1.26	19	19	0	0	0	0-0	108.2	109	59	55	13	28-2	74	.262
2006—	Los Angeles (N.L.)	4	4	.500	6.83	1.72	20	8	0	0	0	0-1	59.1	89	49	45	9	13-1	33	.346
	—Kansas City (A.L.)	2	4	.333	5.64	1.46	12	12	0	0	0	0-0	67.0	80	44	42	9	18-1	48	.295
American League totals (1 year)		2	4	.333	5.64	1.46	12	12	0	0	0	0-0	67.0	80	44	42	9	18-1	48	.295
National League totals (8 years)		56	55	.505	4.24	1.27	184	153	4	2	5	0-2	971.0	969	483	457	117	265-18	689	.262
Major League totals (8 years)		58	59	.496	4.33	1.28	196	165	4	2	5	0-2	1038.0	1049	527	499	126	283-19	737	.265

DIVISION SERIES RECORD

Year	Team (League)	W	L	Pct.	ERA	WHIP	G	GS	CG	ShO	Hld.	Sv.-Opp.	IP	H	R	ER	HR	BB-IBB	SO	Avg.
1998—	Atlanta (N.L.)	1	0	1.000	0.00	0.00	1	0	0	0	0	0-0	0.2	0	0	0	0	0-0	1	.000
2004—	Los Angeles (N.L.)	0	1	.000	14.40	3.00	2	2	0	0	0	0-0	5.0	8	8	8	4	7-0	3	.364
Division series totals (2 years)		1	1	.500	12.71	2.65	3	2	0	0	0	0-0	5.2	8	8	8	4	7-0	4	.348

CHAMPIONSHIP SERIES RECORD

Year	Team (League)	W	L	Pct.	ERA	WHIP	G	GS	CG	ShO	Hld.	Sv.-Opp.	IP	H	R	ER	HR	BB-IBB	SO	Avg.
1998—	Atlanta (N.L.)	0	0	...	54.00	21.00	2	0	0	0	0	0-0	0.1	5	2	2	0	2-1	0	1.000

ALL-STAR GAME RECORD

		W	L	Pct.	ERA	WHIP	G	GS	CG	ShO	Hld.	Sv.-Opp.	IP	H	R	ER	HR	BB-IBB	SO	Avg.
All-Star Game totals (1 year)		0	0	...	0.00	2.00	1	0	0	0	0	0-0	1.0	2	1	0	0	0-0	2	.400

2006 LEFTY-RIGHTY SPLITS

vs.	Avg.	AB	H	2B	3B	HR	RBI	BB	SO	OBP	Slg.	vs.	Avg.	AB	H	2B	3B	HR	RBI	BB	SO	OBP	Slg.
L	.336	113	38	8	3	4	18	8	21	.390	.566	R	.316	415	131	31	3	14	69	23	60	.348	.506

PEREZ, OLIVER   P

PERSONAL: Born August 15, 1981, in Culiacan, Mexico. ... 6-0/190. ... Throws left, bats left. ... High school: Cobales (Culiacan, Mexico). **TRANSACTIONS/CAREER NOTES:** Signed as a non-drafted free agent by San Diego Padres organization (March 4, 1999). ... Loaned by Padres organization to Yucatan of the Mexican League (June 2-22 and July 18, 2000-remainder of season). ... On disabled list (August 7-September 2, 2002). ... Traded by Padres with OF Jason Bay and a player to be named to Pittsburgh Pirates for OF Brian Giles (August 26, 2003); Pirates acquired P Cory Stewart to complete deal (October 2, 2003). ... On disabled list (June 28-September 3, 2005); included rehabilitation assignment to Indianapolis. ... Traded by Pirates with P Roberto Hernandez to New York Mets for OF Xavier Nady (July 31, 2006). **MISCELLANEOUS NOTES:** Appeared in one game as pinch runner (2004). ... Appeared in one game as pinch runner (2006).
CAREER HITTING: 32-for-198 (.162), 4 R, 0 2B, 0 3B, 0 HR, 10 RBI.

Year	Team (League)	W	L	Pct.	ERA	WHIP	G	GS	CG	ShO	Hld.	Sv.-Opp.	IP	H	R	ER	HR	BB-IBB	SO	Avg.
1999—	Ariz. Padres (Ariz.)	1	2	.333	5.08	1.55	15	2	0	0	...	3-...	28.1	28	20	16	1	16-0	37	.243
2000—	Yucatan (Mex.)	3	2	.600	4.40	1.30	11	6	0	0	...	1-...	43.0	39	24	21	...	17-...	37	...
	—Idaho Falls (Pio.)	3	1	.750	4.07	1.36	5	5	0	0	...	0-...	24.1	24	14	11	1	9-0	27	.270
2001—	Fort Wayne (Midw.)	8	5	.615	3.46	1.25	19	19	0	0	...	0-...	101.1	84	46	39	9	43-0	98	.230
	—Lake Elsinore (Calif.)	2	4	.333	2.72	1.32	9	9	0	0	...	0-...	53.0	45	22	16	4	25-0	62	.225
2002—	Lake Elsinore (Calif.)	3	3	.500	1.85	1.23	9	8	0	0	...	0-...	48.2	36	13	10	0	24-0	66	.209
	—Mobile (Sou.)	1	0	1.000	1.17	1.17	4	4	0	0	...	0-...	23.0	11	3	3	1	16-0	34	.147
	—San Diego (N.L.)	4	5	.444	3.50	1.32	16	15	0	0	0	0-0	90.0	71	37	35	13	48-1	94	.218
2003—	Portland (PCL)	3	3	.500	3.02	1.20	8	8	0	0	0	0-0	47.2	44	20	16	6	12-0	48	.246
	—San Diego (N.L.)	4	7	.364	5.38	1.62	19	19	0	0	0	0-0	103.2	103	65	62	20	65-2	117	.258
	—Pittsburgh (N.L.)	0	3	.000	5.87	1.65	5	5	0	0	0	0-0	23.0	26	15	15	2	12-1	24	.283
2004—	Pittsburgh (N.L.)	12	10	.545	2.98	1.15	30	30	2	1	0	0-0	196.0	145	71	65	22	81-2	239	.207
2005—	Indianapolis (Int'l)	0	1	.000	9.90	2.60	3	3	0	0	0	0-0	10.0	14	11	11	3	12-1	4	.326
	—Pittsburgh (N.L.)	7	5	.583	5.85	1.67	20	20	0	0	0	0-0	103.0	102	68	67	23	70-1	97	.264
2006—	Pittsburgh (N.L.)	2	10	.167	6.63	1.83	15	15	0	0	0	0-0	76.0	88	64	56	13	51-0	61	.296
	—Indianapolis (Int'l)	1	3	.250	5.63	1.22	6	6	0	0	0	0-0	32.0	28	21	20	6	11-0	34	.233
	—Norfolk (Int'l)	1	2	.333	6.05	1.55	4	4	0	0	0	0-0	19.1	18	13	13	4	12-0	26	.250
	—New York (N.L.)	1	3	.250	6.38	1.58	7	7	1	1	0	0-0	36.2	41	26	26	7	17-0	41	.287
Major League totals (5 years)		30	43	.411	4.67	1.46	112	111	3	2	0	0-0	628.1	576	346	326	100	344-7	673	.246

CHAMPIONSHIP SERIES RECORD

Year	Team (League)	W	L	Pct.	ERA	WHIP	G	GS	CG	ShO	Hld.	Sv.-Opp.	IP	H	R	ER	HR	BB-IBB	SO	Avg.
2006—	New York (N.L.)	1	0	1.000	4.63	1.37	2	2	0	0	0	0-0	11.2	13	6	6	3	3-1	7	.295

2006 LEFTY-RIGHTY SPLITS

vs.	Avg.	AB	H	2B	3B	HR	RBI	BB	SO	OBP	Slg.	vs.	Avg.	AB	H	2B	3B	HR	RBI	BB	SO	OBP	Slg.
L	.260	77	20	1	0	3	16	12	28	.355	.390	R	.300	363	109	18	1	17	66	56	74	.394	.496

PEREZ, RAFAEL   P

PERSONAL: Born May 15, 1982, in Santo Domingo, Dominican Republic. ... 6-3/184. ... Throws left, bats left. ... Full name: Rafael E. Perez. **TRANSACTIONS/CAREER NOTES:** Signed as a non-drafted free agent by Cleveland Indians organization (January 25, 2002).
CAREER HITTING: 0-for-0 (.000), 0 R, 0 2B, 0 3B, 0 HR, 0 RBI.

Year	Team (League)	W	L	Pct.	ERA	WHIP	G	GS	CG	ShO	Hld.	Sv.-Opp.	IP	H	R	ER	HR	BB-IBB	SO	Avg.
2002—	Dom. Indians (DSL)	7	1	.875	0.96	0.98	13	13	1	0	...	0-...	75.1	58	14	8	3	16-0	81	.208
2003—	Burlington (Appal.)	9	3	.750	1.70	1.04	13	12	0	0	...	0-...	69.0	56	23	13	1	16-0	63	.220
2004—	Lake County (S.Atl.)	7	6	.538	4.85	1.46	23	22	0	0	...	0-...	115.0	121	75	62	9	47-0	99	.277
	—Kinston (Carol.)	0	0	...	11.57	2.57	1	1	0	0	...	0-...	4.2	10	6	6	1	2-1	3	.435
2005—	Kinston (Carol.)	8	5	.615	3.36	1.11	14	14	0	0	0	0-0	77.2	54	33	29	6	32-0	48	.194
	—Akron (East.)	4	3	.571	1.76	0.98	15	8	0	0	0	1-1	66.2	53	22	13	5	12-0	46	.215
2006—	Akron (East.)	4	5	.444	2.81	1.11	12	12	1	1	0	0-0	67.1	53	25	21	3	22-1	53	.218
	—Buffalo (Int'l)	3	0	1.000	2.63	1.02	13	0	0	0	4	0-3	27.1	20	11	8	0	8-1	33	.202
	—Cleveland (A.L.)	0	0	...	4.38	1.30	18	0	0	0	1	0-1	12.1	10	6	6	2	6-1	15	.204
Major League totals (1 year)		0	0	...	4.38	1.30	18	0	0	0	1	0-1	12.1	10	6	6	2	6-1	15	.204

2006 LEFTY-RIGHTY SPLITS

vs.	Avg.	AB	H	2B	3B	HR	RBI	BB	SO	OBP	Slg.	vs.	Avg.	AB	H	2B	3B	HR	RBI	BB	SO	OBP	Slg.
L	.130	23	3	0	0	0	1	3	7	.231	.130	R	.269	26	7	0	0	2	5	3	8	.345	.500

P

PEREZ, TIMO — OF

PERSONAL: Born April 8, 1975, in Bani, Dominican Republic. ... 5-9/167. ... Bats left, throws left. ... Full name: Timoniel Perez. ... High school: Juan Baron Palanque (Bani, Dominican Republic). **TRANSACTIONS/CAREER NOTES:** Signed as a free agent by New York Mets organization (March 17, 2000). ... On disabled list (April 9-27, 2001); included rehabilitation assignment to Norfolk. ... On disabled list (May 26-June 10, 2003); included rehabilitation assignment to Norfolk. ... Traded by Mets to Chicago White Sox for P Matt Ginter (March 27, 2004). ... Signed as free agent by Cincinnati Reds organization (February 9, 2006). ... Traded by Reds to St. Louis Cardinals for cash (April 21, 2006). ... Released by Cardinals (August 28, 2006).

2006 GAMES PLAYED BY POSITION (MLB): OF—7, DH—1.

Year	Team (League)	Pos.	G	AB	R	H	2B	3B	HR	RBI	BB	SO	HBP	GDP	SB-CS	Avg.	OBP	SLG	OPS	E	Avg.
1994—Hiroshima (DSL)			51	206	40	70	9	8	0	21	31	7	...	...	8-...	.340	...	.461	...	...	...
1995—			Did not play.																		
1996—Hiroshima (Jp. Cn.)			31	54	8	15	1	0	1	7	2	7	...	...	3-...	.278	...	.352	...	...	...
1997—Hiroshima (Jap. West.)			19	69	9	21	3	1	2	12	10	3	...	...	9-...	.304	...	.464	...	...	...
—Hiroshima (Jp. Cn.)			86	139	17	34	4	2	3	15	10	16	...	...	4-...	.245	...	.367	...	...	...
1998—Hiroshima (Jap. West.)			2	7	0	2	0	0	0	0	0	0	...	...	0-...	.286	...	.286	...	...	...
—Hiroshima (Jp. Cn.)			98	230	22	68	8	1	5	35	20	21	...	...	2-...	.296	...	.404	...	...	...
1999—Hiroshima (Jap. West.)			60	160	19	58	13	4	1	24	34	13	...	...	6-...	.363	...	.513	...	...	...
—Hiroshima (Jp. Cn.)			12	23	2	4	0	0	0	2	3	3	...	...	0-...	.174	...	.174	...	...	...
2000—St. Lucie (Fla. St.)	OF		8	31	3	11	4	0	1	8	2	1	1	0	3-3	.355	.400	.581	.981	0	1.000
—Norfolk (Int'l)	OF		72	291	45	104	17	5	6	37	16	25	3	4	13-7	.357	.392	.512	.904	5	.976
—New York (N.L.)	OF		24	49	11	14	4	1	1	3	3	5	1	0	1-1	.286	.333	.469	*.803	1	.970
2001—New York (N.L.)	OF		85	239	26	59	9	1	5	22	12	25	2	1	1-6	.247	.287	.356	.643	0	1.000
—Norfolk (Int'l)	OF		48	192	37	69	10	2	6	19	12	18	2	1	15-2	.359	.399	.526	.925	5	.951
2002—Norfolk (Int'l)	OF		5	21	5	12	2	1	1	5	2	2	0	1	3-1	.571	.609	.905	1.513	0	1.000
—New York (N.L.)	OF		136	444	52	131	27	6	8	47	23	36	2	10	10-6	.295	.331	.437	.768	6	.979
2003—Norfolk (Int'l)	OF		3	9	2	2	0	0	1	1	1	0	0	0	0-0	.222	.300	.556	.856	0	1.000
—New York (N.L.)	OF		127	346	32	93	21	4	4	42	18	29	2	5	5-6	.269	.301	.364	.666	2	.989
2004—Chicago (A.L.)	OF-DH		103	293	38	72	12	0	5	40	15	29	2	9	3-1	.246	.285	.338	.623	2	.986
2005—Chicago (A.L.)	OF-DH-1B		76	179	13	39	8	0	2	15	12	25	0	3	2-2	.218	.266	.296	.562	4	.959
2006—Memphis (PCL)			75	268	42	79	16	2	13	41	21	27	2	3	4-2	.295	.349	.515	.864	3	.975
—St. Louis (N.L.)	OF-DH		23	31	3	6	1	0	1	3	4	1	0	0	0-0	.194	.286	.323	.608	0	1.000
American League totals (2 years)			179	472	51	111	20	0	7	55	27	54	2	12	5-3	.235	.278	.322	.600	6	.975
National League totals (5 years)			395	1109	124	303	62	8	19	117	59	99	8	16	17-19	.273	.311	.395	.706	9	.986
Major League totals (7 years)			574	1581	175	414	82	8	26	172	86	153	10	28	22-22	.262	.301	.373	.674	15	.983

DIVISION SERIES RECORD

Year	Team (League)	Pos.	G	AB	R	H	2B	3B	HR	RBI	BB	SO	HBP	GDP	SB-CS	Avg.	OBP	SLG	OPS	E	Avg.
2000—New York (N.L.)			4	17	2	5	1	0	0	3	0	2	0	0	1-0	.294	.294	.353	.647	0	1.000
2005—Chicago (A.L.)	OF		1	1	0	0	0	0	0	0	0	0	0	0	0-0	.000	.000	.000	.000	0	...
Division series totals (2 years)			5	18	2	5	1	0	0	3	0	2	0	0	1-0	.278	.278	.333	.611	0	1.000

CHAMPIONSHIP SERIES RECORD

Year	Team (League)	Pos.	G	AB	R	H	2B	3B	HR	RBI	BB	SO	HBP	GDP	SB-CS	Avg.	OBP	SLG	OPS	E	Avg.
2000—New York (N.L.)	OF		5	23	8	7	2	0	0	1	0	1	3	0	1	2-1	.304	.333	.391	.725	1	.947

WORLD SERIES RECORD

Year	Team (League)	Pos.	G	AB	R	H	2B	3B	HR	RBI	BB	SO	HBP	GDP	SB-CS	Avg.	OBP	SLG	OPS	E	Avg.
2000—New York (N.L.)	OF		5	16	1	2	0	0	0	1	4	0	0	0	0-0	.125	.176	.125	.301	1	.900
2005—Chicago (A.L.)			1	1	0	0	0	0	0	0	0	0	0	0	0-0	.000	.000	.000	.000	0	...
World series totals (2 years)			6	17	1	2	0	0	0	1	4	0	0	0	0-0	.118	.167	.118	.284	1	.900

2006 LEFTY-RIGHTY SPLITS

vs.	Avg.	AB	H	2B	3B	HR	RBI	BB	SO	OBP	Slg.	vs.	Avg.	AB	H	2B	3B	HR	RBI	BB	SO	OBP	Slg.
L	.400	5	2	0	0	1	1	0	2	.500	1.000	R	.154	26	4	1	0	0	2	3	2	.241	.192

PEREZ, TOMAS — 2B/3B

PERSONAL: Born December 29, 1973, in Barquisimeto, Venezuela. ... 5-11/192. ... Bats both, throws right. ... Full name: Tomas Orlando Perez. **TRANSACTIONS/CAREER NOTES:** Signed as a non-drafted free agent by Montreal Expos organization (July 11, 1991). ... Selected by California Angels from Expos organization in Rule 5 major league draft (December 5, 1994). ... Traded by Angels to Toronto Blue Jays for cash (December 5, 1994). ... On disabled list (June 25-July 25, 1997); included rehabilitation assignment to Syracuse. ... Traded by Blue Jays to Angels for IF Dave Hollins and cash (March 30, 1999). ... Signed as a free agent by Philadelphia Phillies organization (December 15, 1999). ... On disabled list (March 26-April 16, 2002); included rehabilitation assignment to Reading. ... Released by Phillies (April 1, 2006). ... Signed by Tampa Bay Devil Rays (April 6, 2006). **RECORDS:** Shares major league record for most doubles, game (4, July 29, 2006). ...Career major league pitching: 0-0, 0.00 ERA, 1 G, 0.1 IP, 0 H, 0 R, 0 ER, 0 BB, 0 SO. **STATISTICAL NOTES:** Career major league grand slams: 1.

2006 GAMES PLAYED BY POSITION (MLB): 3B—40, SS—36, 2B—22, OF—5, 1B—1.

Year	Team (League)	Pos.	G	AB	R	H	2B	3B	HR	RBI	BB	SO	HBP	GDP	SB-CS	Avg.	OBP	SLG	OPS	E	Avg.
1992—Dom. Expos (DSL)	IF		44	151	35	46	7	0	1	19	27	20	...	...	12-...	.305	...	.371	...	12	.954
1993—GC Expos (GCL)	SS		52	189	27	46	3	1	2	21	23	25	0	5	8-3	.243	.322	.302	.624	12	.965
1994—Burlington (Midw.)	2B-SS		119	465	76	122	22	1	8	47	48	78	1	2	8-10	.262	.329	.366	.695	34	.944
1995—Toronto (A.L.)	SS-2B-3B		41	98	12	24	3	1	1	8	7	18	0	6	0-1	.245	.292	.327	.619	5	.962
1996—Syracuse (Int'l)	SS-2B		40	123	15	34	10	1	1	13	7	19	0	2	8-1	.276	.313	.398	.711	7	.962
—Toronto (A.L.)	2B-3B-SS		91	295	24	74	13	4	1	19	25	29	1	10	1-2	.251	.311	.332	.643	15	.964
1997—Syracuse (Int'l)	SS-2B		89	303	32	68	13	1	0	20	37	67	0	9	3-4	.224	.308	.277	.585	12	.973
—Toronto (A.L.)	SS-2B		40	123	9	24	3	2	0	9	11	28	1	2	1-1	.195	.267	.252	.519	3	.984
1998—Syracuse (Int'l)	SS-2B		116	404	40	102	15	4	3	37	18	67	0	10	4-7	.252	.284	.332	.616	15	.977
—Toronto (A.L.)	SS-2B		6	9	1	1	0	0	0	0	1	3	0	1	0-0	.111	.200	.111	.311	0	1.000
1999—Edmonton (PCL)	SS-2B		83	296	31	77	17	1	4	19	43	52	1	5	2-2	.260	.306	.365	.671	11	.973
2000—Philadelphia (N.L.)	SS		45	140	17	31	7	1	0	13	11	30	0	3	1-1	.221	.278	.307	.585	4	.976
—Scran./W.B. (I.L.)	3B-SS-2B		77	279	44	82	16	2	10	56	16	48	2	5	4-1	.294	.334	.473	.808	9	.962
2001—Philadelphia (N.L.)	2B-3B-SS																				
	OF		62	135	11	41	7	1	3	19	7	22	0	2	0-1	.304	.347	.437	.784	1	.993
2002—Reading (East.)	2B-SS		2	9	2	4	0	0	1	0	1	0	0	0	0-0	.444	.444	.444	.889	0	1.000
—Philadelphia (N.L.)	SS-2B-SS																				
	1B-P		92	212	22	53	13	1	5	20	21	40	1	5	1-0	.250	.319	.392	.711	4	.985
2003—Philadelphia (N.L.)	3B-2B-1B																				
	SS		125	298	39	79	18	1	5	33	23	54	0	7	0-1	.265	.316	.383	.698	9	.969

P

Year Team (League)	Pos.	G	AB	R	H	2B	3B	HR	RBI	BB	SO	HBP	GDP	SB-CS	Avg.	OBP	SLG	OPS	E	Avg.
2004— Philadelphia (N.L.) ...3B-2B-1B																				
SS		86	176	22	38	13	2	6	21	9	44	1	2	0-0	.216	.257	.415	.671	6	.969
2005— Philadelphia (N.L.) ...1B-3B-SS		94	159	17	37	7	0	0	22	11	27	2	6	1-0	.233	.289	.277	.566	0	1.000
2006— Tampa Bay (A.L.) ...3B-SS-2B																				
OF-1B		99	241	31	51	12	0	2	16	5	44	0	3	1-0	.212	.224	.286	.510	8	.974
American League totals (5 years)		277	766	77	174	31	7	4	52	49	122	2	22	3-4	.227	.273	.302	.575	31	.970
National League totals (6 years)		504	1120	128	279	65	6	20	128	82	217	6	25	3-3	.249	.303	.371	.674	24	.981
Major League totals (11 years)		781	1886	205	453	96	13	24	180	131	339	8	47	6-7	.240	.291	.343	.634	55	.976

2006 LEFTY-RIGHTY SPLITS

vs.	Avg.	AB	H	2B	3B	HR	RBI	BB	SO	OBP	Slg.	vs.	Avg.	AB	H	2B	3B	HR	RBI	BB	SO	OBP	Slg.
L	.178	73	13	4	0	1	6	4	19	.218	.274	R	.226	168	38	8	0	1	10	1	25	.227	.292

PERKINS, GLEN   P

PERSONAL: Born March 2, 1983, in Saint Paul, Minn. ... Throws left, bats left. ... Full name: Glen Weston Perkins. ... College: Minnesota. **TRANSACTIONS/CAREER NOTES:** Selected by Minnesota Twins organization in first round (22nd pick overall) of the 2004 free-agent draft.
CAREER HITTING: 0-for-0 (.000), 0 R, 0 2B, 0 3B, 0 HR, 0 RBI.

Year Team (League)	W	L	Pct.	ERA	WHIP	G	GS	CG	ShO	Hld.	Sv.-Opp.	IP	H	R	ER	HR	BB-IBB	SO	Avg.
2004— Elizabethton (App.)	1	0	1.000	2.25	1.00	3	3	0	0	...	0-...	12.0	8	3	3	0	4-0	22	.186
— Quad City (Midw.)	2	1	.667	1.30	0.93	9	9	0	0	...	0-...	48.1	33	9	7	2	12-0	49	.205
2005— Fort Myers (FSL)	3	2	.600	2.13	0.98	10	9	2	1	0	0-0	55.0	41	14	13	2	13-0	66	.205
— New Britain (East.)	4	4	.500	4.90	1.46	14	14	0	0	0	0-0	79.0	80	45	43	4	35-0	67	.263
2006— Rochester (Int'l)	0	1	.000	2.08	2.54	1	1	0	0	0	0-0	4.1	6	1	1	0	5-0	3	.333
— New Britain (East.)	4	11	.267	3.91	1.31	23	23	2	1	0	0-0	117.1	109	60	51	11	45-0	131	.243
— Minnesota (A.L.)	0	0	...	1.59	0.53	4	0	0	0	1	0-0	5.2	3	1	1	0	0-0	6	.150
Major League totals (1 year)	0	0	...	1.59	0.53	4	0	0	0	1	0-0	5.2	3	1	1	0	0-0	6	.150

DIVISION SERIES RECORD

Year Team (League)	W	L	Pct.	ERA	WHIP	G	GS	CG	ShO	Hld.	Sv.-Opp.	IP	H	R	ER	HR	BB-IBB	SO	Avg.
2006— Minnesota (A.L.)	0	0	...	0.00	6.00	1	0	0	0	0	0-0	0.1	2	0	0	0	0-0	0	.667

2006 LEFTY-RIGHTY SPLITS

vs.	Avg.	AB	H	2B	3B	HR	RBI	BB	SO	OBP	Slg.	vs.	Avg.	AB	H	2B	3B	HR	RBI	BB	SO	OBP	Slg.
L	.250	8	2	0	0	0	0	0	5	.250	.250	R	.083	12	1	1	0	0	0	0	1	.083	.167

PETAGINE, ROBERTO   1B

PERSONAL: Born June 2, 1971, in New York. ... 6-1/215. ... Bats left, throws left. ... Full name: Roberto Antonio Petagine. ... Name pronounced: PET-uh-GHEEN. **TRANSACTIONS/CAREER NOTES:** Signed as non-drafted free agent by Houston Astros organization (February 13, 1990). ... Traded by Astros with 3B Ken Caminiti, OF Steve Finley, SS Andujar Cedeno, P Brian Williams and a player to be named to San Diego Padres for OFs Phil Plantier and Derek Bell, Ps Pedro A. Martinez and Doug Brocail, IF Craig Shipley and SS Ricky Gutierrez (December 28, 1994); Padres acquired P Sean Fesh to complete deal (May 1, 1995). ... Traded by Padres with P Scott Adair to New York Mets for Ps Luis Arroyo and Pete Walker (March 17, 1996). ... Traded by Mets to Cincinnati Reds for SS Yuri Sanchez (February 5, 1998). ... Contract sold by Reds to Yakult of Japan Central League (December 2, 1998). ... Signed as a free agent by Boston Red Sox organization (February 8, 2005). ... Released by Red Sox (February 14, 2006). ... Signed by Seattle Mariners organization (February 21, 2006).
2006 GAMES PLAYED BY POSITION (MLB): 1B—9.

Year Team (League)	Pos.	G	AB	R	H	2B	3B	HR	RBI	BB	SO	HBP	GDP	SB-CS	Avg.	OBP	SLG	OPS	E	Avg.
1990— GC Astros (GCL)	1B-OF	55	187	35	54	5	4	2	24	26	23	2	4	9-7	.289	.378	.390	.768	5	.990
1991— Burlington (Midw.)	1B	124	432	72	112	24	1	12	58	71	74	4	9	7-5	.259	.368	.403	.771	22	.978
1992— Osceola (Fla. St.)	1B	86	307	52	90	22	4	7	49	47	47	5	5	3-1	.293	.391	.459	.850	10	.987
— Jackson (Texas)	1B	21	70	8	21	4	0	4	12	6	15	2	4	1-0	.300	.363	.529	.892	0	1.000
1993— Jackson (Texas)	1B	128	437	73	146	36	2	15	90	84	89	4	4	6-5	.334	.442	.529	.971	14	.988
1994— Houston (N.L.)	1B	8	7	0	0	0	0	0	0	1	3	...	...	0-0	.000	.125	.000	.125	0	1.000
— Tucson (PCL)	1B	65	247	53	78	19	0	10	44	35	54	1	7	3-1	.316	.399	.514	.913	10	.984
1995— San Diego (N.L.)	1B-DH	89	124	15	29	8	0	3	17	26	41	...	...	0-0	.234	.367	.371	.738	1	.997
— Las Vegas (PCL)	1B-DH	19	56	8	12	2	1	1	5	13	17	0	0	1-0	.214	.362	.339	.701	3	.975
1996— Norfolk (Int'l)	1B-DH	95	314	49	100	24	3	12	65	51	75	7	3	4-1	.318	.421	.529	.950	15	.982
— New York (N.L.)	1B	50	99	10	23	3	0	4	17	9	27	...	...	0-2	.232	.296	.384	.680	1	.996
1997— Norfolk (Int'l)	1B-OF	129	441	90	140	32	1	31	100	85	92	8	6	0-1	.317	.430	.605	1.035	11	.990
— New York (N.L.)	1B-OF	12	15	2	1	0	0	0	2	3	6	...	...	0-0	.067	.222	.067	.289	0	1.000
1998— Indianapolis (Int'l)	1B-OF-DH	102	363	79	120	30	1	24	109	70	71	3	14	3-1	.331	.436	.617	1.053	6	.992
— Cincinnati (N.L.)	1B-OF	34	62	14	16	2	1	3	7	16	11	...	...	1-0	.258	.410	.468	.878	0	1.000
1999— Yakult (Jp. Cen.)	1B	134	452	97	147	23	2	44	112	116	91	7	...	10-1	.325	.469	.677	1.146	5	.996
2000— Yakult (Jp. Cen.)	1B	136	484	91	153	30	0	36	96	97	116	4	...	7-2	.316	.432	.601	1.033	5	.996
2001— Yakult (Jp. Cen.)	1B	138	463	93	149	27	0	39	127	120	89	...	...	4-1	.322	...	.633	...	6	.996
2002— Yakult (Jp. Cen.)	1B	131	453	90	146	23	1	41	94	85	106	11	...	0-1	.322	.438	.649	1.087	9	.992
2003— Yomiuri (Jp. Cen.)	OF-1B	100	331	70	107	17	0	34	81	77	72	5	...	1-0	.323	.457	.683	1.139	5	.982
2004— Yomiuri (Jp. Cen.)	1B	117	383	70	111	17	0	29	84	75	76	5	...	2-...	.290	...	.561	...	10	.989
2005— Pawtucket (Int'l)	1B-DH	74	266	54	87	18	2	20	69	63	46	2	9	0-3	.327	.452	.635	1.088	3	.994
— Boston (A.L.)	1B-DH-OF	18	32	4	9	2	0	1	9	4	5	0	3	0-0	.281	.361	.438	.799	1	.983
2006— Seattle (A.L.)	1B	31	27	3	5	2	0	1	2	4	10	1	0	0-0	.185	.313	.370	.683	0	1.000
— Tacoma (PCL)		4	6	1	1	0	0	0	0	4	1	0	0	0-0	.167	.500	.167	.667	0	1.000
American League totals (2 years)		49	59	7	14	4	0	2	11	8	15	1	3	0-0	.237	.338	.407	.745	1	.988
National League totals (5 years)		193	307	41	69	13	1	10	43	55	88	...	...	1-2	.225	...	.371	...	2	.997
Major League totals (7 years)		242	366	48	83	17	1	12	54	63	103	1	3	1-2	.227	.342	.377	.719	3	.996

2006 LEFTY-RIGHTY SPLITS

vs.	Avg.	AB	H	2B	3B	HR	RBI	BB	SO	OBP	Slg.	vs.	Avg.	AB	H	2B	3B	HR	RBI	BB	SO	OBP	Slg.
L	.000	2	0	0	0	0	0	0	2	.333	.000	R	.200	25	5	2	0	1	2	4	8	.310	.400

PETIT, YUSMEIRO   P

PERSONAL: Born November 22, 1984, in Maracaibo, Venezuela. ... 6-0/230. ... Throws right, bats right. ... Full name: Yusmeiro Alberto Petit. **TRANSACTIONS/CAREER NOTES:** Signed as a non-drafted free agent by New York Mets organization (November 15, 2001). ... Traded by Mets with 1B Mike Jacobs and IF Grant Psomas to Florida Marlins for 1B Carlos Delgado and cash (November 24, 2005).

CAREER HITTING: 1-for-5 (.200), 1 R, 0 2B, 0 3B, 0 HR, 1 RBI.

Year	Team (League)	W	L	Pct.	ERA	WHIP	G	GS	CG	ShO	Hld.	Sv.-Opp.	IP	H	R	ER	HR	BB-IBB	SO	Avg.
2002—	Universidad (VSL)	3	5	.375	2.43	1.24	12	11	0	0	...	0-...	55.2	53	25	15	1	16-0	62	.252
2003—	Kingsport (Appalachian)	3	3	.500	2.32	0.89	12	12	0	0	...	0-...	62.0	47	19	16	2	8-0	65	.219
—	Brook. N.Y.-Penn. (N.Y.-Penn.)	1	0	1.000	2.19	0.57	2	2	0	0	...	0-...	12.1	5	3	3	0	2-0	20	.119
2004—	Capital City (SAL)	9	2	.818	2.39	0.83	15	15	0	0	...	0-...	83.0	47	29	22	8	22-0	122	.162
—	St. Lucie (Fla. St.)	2	3	.400	1.22	0.92	9	9	1	1	...	0-...	44.1	27	9	6	0	14-1	62	.174
—	Binghamton (East.)	1	1	.500	4.50	1.25	2	2	0	0	...	0-...	12.0	10	6	6	0	5-0	16	.233
2005—	Binghamton (East.)	9	3	.750	2.91	0.92	21	21	2	0	0	0-0	117.2	90	41	38	15	18-0	130	.209
—	Norfolk (Int'l)	0	3	.000	9.20	2.05	3	3	0	0	0	0-0	14.2	24	16	15	5	6-0	14	.375
2006—	Albuquerque (PCL)	4	6	.400	4.28	1.25	17	17	0	0	0	0-0	96.2	101	53	46	14	20-1	68	.268
—	Florida (N.L.)	1	1	.500	9.57	2.09	15	1	0	0	0	0-0	26.1	46	28	28	7	9-1	20	.390
Major League totals (1 year)		1	1	.500	9.57	2.09	15	1	0	0	0	0-0	26.1	46	28	28	7	9-1	20	.390

2006 LEFTY-RIGHTY SPLITS

vs.	Avg.	AB	H	2B	3B	HR	RBI	BB	SO	OBP	Slg.	vs.	Avg.	AB	H	2B	3B	HR	RBI	BB	SO	OBP	Slg.
L	.381	63	24	2	4	2	13	7	10	.443	.635	R	.400	55	22	5	0	5	12	2	10	.414	.764

PETTITTE, ANDY — P

PERSONAL: Born June 15, 1972, in Baton Rouge, La. ... 6-5/225. ... Throws left, bats left. ... Full name: Andrew Eugene Pettitte. ... Name pronounced: pet-it. ... High school: Deer Park (Texas). ... Junior college: San Jacinto (Texas). **TRANSACTIONS/CAREER NOTES:** Selected by New York Yankees organization in 22nd round of 1990 free-agent draft; did not sign. ... Signed as a non-drafted free agent by Yankees organization (May 25, 1991). ... On disabled list (March 26-April 17, 1999); included rehabilitation assignment to Tampa. ... On disabled list (April 8-26, 2000; and June 15-July 1, 2001). ... On disabled list (April 16-June 14, 2002); included rehabilitation assignments to Tampa and Norwich. ... Signed as a free agent by Houston Astros (December 16, 2003). ... On disabled list (April 7-29, May 27-June 29 and August 18, 2004-remainder of season); included rehabilitation assignment to Round Rock. **HONORS:** Named lefthanded pitcher on THE SPORTING NEWS A.L. All-Star team (1996 and 2003). **MISCELLANEOUS NOTES:** Made an out and struck out in two appearances as pinch hitter (2006).

CAREER HITTING: 24-for-175 (.137), 5 R, 5 2B, 0 3B, 1 HR, 12 RBI.

Year	Team (League)	W	L	Pct.	ERA	WHIP	G	GS	CG	ShO	Hld.	Sv.-Opp.	IP	H	R	ER	HR	BB-IBB	SO	Avg.
1991—	GC Yankees (GCL)	4	1	.800	0.98	0.65	6	6	0	0	...	0-...	36.2	16	6	4	0	8-0	51	.127
—	Oneonta (NYP)	2	2	.500	2.18	1.48	6	6	1	0	...	0-...	33.0	33	18	8	1	16-0	32	.252
1992—	Greensboro (S. Atl.)	10	4	.714	2.20	1.17	27	27	2	1	...	0-...	168.0	141	53	41	4	55-0	130	.232
1993—	Prince Will. (Car.)	11	9	.550	3.04	1.21	26	26	2	1	...	0-...	159.2	146	68	54	7	47-0	129	.248
—	Albany (East.)	1	0	1.000	3.60	1.40	1	1	0	0	...	0-...	5.0	5	4	2	0	2-0	6	.250
1994—	Alb./Colon. (East.)	7	2	.778	2.71	1.07	11	11	0	0	...	0-...	73.0	60	32	22	5	18-1	50	.220
—	Columbus (Int'l)	7	2	.778	2.98	1.26	16	16	3	0	...	0-...	96.2	101	40	32	3	21-0	61	.272
1995—	New York (A.L.)	12	9	.571	4.17	1.41	31	26	3	0	0	0-0	175.0	183	86	81	15	63-3	114	.272
—	Columbus (Int'l)	0	0	...	0.00	0.60	2	2	0	0	...	0-...	11.2	7	0	0	0	0-0	8	.184
1996—	New York (A.L.)	*21	8	.724	3.87	1.36	35	34	2	0	0	0-0	221.0	229	105	95	23	72-2	162	.271
1997—	New York (A.L.)	18	7	.720	2.88	1.24	35	•35	4	1	0	0-0	240.1	233	86	77	7	65-0	166	.256
1998—	New York (A.L.)	16	11	.593	4.24	1.45	33	32	5	0	0	0-0	216.1	226	110	102	20	87-1	146	.274
1999—	Tampa (Fla. St.)	1	0	1.000	0.00	1.20	1	1	0	0	...	0-...	5.0	4	0	0	0	2-0	8	.222
—	New York (A.L.)	14	11	.560	4.70	1.59	31	31	0	0	0	0-0	191.2	216	105	100	20	89-3	121	.289
2000—	New York (A.L.)	19	9	.679	4.35	1.46	32	32	3	1	0	0-0	204.2	219	111	99	17	80-4	125	.271
2001—	New York (A.L.)	15	10	.600	3.99	1.32	31	31	2	0	0	0-0	200.2	224	103	89	14	41-3	•164	.281
2002—	New York (A.L.)	13	5	.722	3.27	1.31	22	22	3	1	0	0-0	134.2	144	58	49	6	32-2	97	.272
—	Tampa (Fla. St.)	0	0	...	0.00	0.60	2	2	0	0	...	0-...	5.0	3	0	0	0	0-0	4	.167
—	Norwich (East.)	0	0	...	1.42	0.32	1	1	0	0	...	0-...	6.1	2	1	1	0	0-0	5	.095
2003—	New York (A.L.)	21	8	.724	4.02	1.33	33	33	1	0	0	0-0	208.1	227	109	93	21	50-3	180	.272
2004—	Round Rock (Texas)	0	0	...	2.25	0.75	2	2	0	0	...	0-...	8.0	4	2	2	1	2-0	9	.143
—	Houston (N.L.)	6	4	.600	3.90	1.23	15	15	0	0	0	0-0	83.0	71	37	36	8	31-2	79	.226
2005—	Houston (N.L.)	17	9	.654	2.39	1.03	33	33	0	0	0	0-0	222.1	188	66	59	17	41-0	171	.230
2006—	Houston (N.L.)	14	13	.519	4.20	1.44	36	•35	2	1	0	0-0	214.1	238	114	100	27	70-9	178	.284
American League totals (9 years)		149	78	.656	3.94	1.38	283	276	23	3	0	0-0	1792.2	1901	873	785	143	579-21	1275	.273
National League totals (3 years)		37	26	.587	3.38	1.23	84	83	2	1	0	0-0	519.2	497	217	195	52	142-11	428	.252
Major League totals (12 years)		186	104	.641	3.81	1.35	367	359	25	4	0	0-0	2312.1	2398	1090	980	195	721-32	1703	.268

DIVISION SERIES RECORD

Year	Team (League)	W	L	Pct.	ERA	WHIP	G	GS	CG	ShO	Hld.	Sv.-Opp.	IP	H	R	ER	HR	BB-IBB	SO	Avg.
1995—	New York (A.L.)	0	0	...	5.14	1.71	1	1	0	0	0	0-0	7.0	9	4	4	1	3-0	0	.346
1996—	New York (A.L.)	0	0	...	5.68	1.58	1	1	0	0	0	0-0	6.1	4	4	4	2	6-0	3	.190
1997—	New York (A.L.)	0	2	.000	8.49	1.37	2	2	0	0	0	0-0	11.2	15	11	11	1	1-0	5	.333
1998—	New York (A.L.)	1	0	1.000	1.29	0.43	1	1	0	0	0	0-0	7.0	3	1	1	0	0-0	8	.125
1999—	New York (A.L.)	1	0	1.000	1.23	0.95	1	1	0	0	0	0-0	7.1	7	1	1	1	0-0	5	.241
2000—	New York (A.L.)	1	0	1.000	3.97	1.59	2	2	0	0	0	0-0	11.1	15	5	5	0	3-0	7	.326
2001—	New York (A.L.)	0	1	.000	1.42	1.42	1	1	0	0	0	0-0	6.1	7	1	1	1	2-0	4	.269
2002—	New York (A.L.)	0	0	...	12.00	2.67	1	1	0	0	0	0-0	3.0	8	4	4	2	0-0	1	.471
2003—	New York (A.L.)	1	0	1.000	1.29	1.00	1	1	0	0	0	0-0	7.0	4	1	1	1	3-0	10	.154
2005—	Houston (N.L.)	1	0	1.000	3.86	0.86	1	1	0	0	0	0-0	7.0	4	3	3	2	2-0	6	.167
Division series totals (10 years)		5	3	.625	4.26	1.30	12	12	0	0	0	0-0	74.0	76	35	35	11	20-0	49	.268

CHAMPIONSHIP SERIES RECORD

Year	Team (League)	W	L	Pct.	ERA	WHIP	G	GS	CG	ShO	Hld.	Sv.-Opp.	IP	H	R	ER	HR	BB-IBB	SO	Avg.
1996—	New York (A.L.)	1	0	1.000	3.60	1.00	2	2	0	0	0	0-0	15.0	10	6	6	4	5-0	7	.185
1998—	New York (A.L.)	0	1	.000	11.57	2.36	1	1	0	0	0	0-0	4.2	8	6	6	4	3-0	1	.364
1999—	New York (A.L.)	1	0	1.000	2.45	1.23	1	1	0	0	0	0-0	7.1	8	2	2	0	1-0	5	.296
2000—	New York (A.L.)	1	0	1.000	2.70	1.50	1	1	0	0	0	0-0	6.2	9	2	2	0	1-0	2	.346
2001—	New York (A.L.)	2	0	1.000	2.51	0.91	2	2	0	0	0	0-0	14.1	11	4	4	0	2-0	8	.216
2003—	New York (A.L.)	1	0	1.000	4.63	1.80	2	2	0	0	0	0-0	11.2	17	6	6	2	4-0	10	.340
2005—	Houston (N.L.)	0	1	.000	5.11	1.54	2	2	0	0	0	0-0	12.1	15	7	7	1	4-0	6	.313
Champ. series totals (7 years)		6	2	.750	4.13	1.36	11	11	0	0	0	0-0	72.0	78	33	33	11	20-0	39	.281

WORLD SERIES RECORD

Year	Team (League)	W	L	Pct.	ERA	WHIP	G	GS	CG	ShO	Hld.	Sv.-Opp.	IP	H	R	ER	HR	BB-IBB	SO	Avg.
1996—	New York (A.L.)	1	1	.500	5.91	1.41	2	2	0	0	0	0-0	10.2	11	7	7	1	4-0	5	.275
1998—	New York (A.L.)	1	0	1.000	0.00	1.09	1	1	0	0	0	0-0	7.1	5	0	0	0	3-0	4	.192
1999—	New York (A.L.)	0	0	...	12.27	3.00	1	1	0	0	0	0-0	3.2	10	5	5	0	1-0	1	.500
2000—	New York (A.L.)	0	0	...	1.98	1.46	2	2	0	0	0	0-0	13.2	16	5	3	0	4-1	9	.302
2001—	New York (A.L.)	0	2	.000	10.00	1.56	2	2	0	0	0	0-0	9.0	12	10	10	1	2-1	9	.324

Year Team (League)	W	L	Pct.	ERA	WHIP	G	GS	CG	ShO	Hld.	Sv.-Opp.	IP	H	R	ER	HR	BB-IBB	SO	Avg.
2003— New York (A.L.)	1	1	.500	0.57	1.02	2	2	0	0	0	0-0	15.2	12	3	1	0	4-1	14	.207
2005— Houston (N.L.)	0	0	...	3.00	1.33	1	1	0	0	0	0-0	6.0	8	2	2	0	0-0	4	.320
World series totals (7 years)	3	4	.429	3.82	1.39	11	11	0	0	0	0-0	66.0	74	32	28	2	18-3	46	.286

ALL-STAR GAME RECORD

	W	L	Pct.	ERA	WHIP	G	GS	CG	ShO	Hld.	Sv.-Opp.	IP	H	R	ER	HR	BB-IBB	SO	Avg.
All-Star Game totals (1 year)	0	0	...	0.00	1.00	1	0	0	0	0	0	1.0	1	0	0	0	0-0	1	.250

2006 LEFTY-RIGHTY SPLITS

vs.	Avg.	AB	H	2B	3B	HR	RBI	BB	SO	OBP	Slg.	vs.	Avg.	AB	H	2B	3B	HR	RBI	BB	SO	OBP	Slg.
L	.259	158	41	12	1	5	19	14	33	.318	.443	R	.290	680	197	41	3	22	83	56	145	.344	.456

PHILLIPS, ANDY — 2B

PERSONAL: Born April 6, 1977, in Tuscaloosa, Ala. ... 6-0/205. ... Bats right, throws right. ... Full name: George Andrew Phillips. ... High school: Demopolis Academy (Demopolis, Ala.). ... College: Alabama. **TRANSACTIONS/CAREER NOTES:** Selected by New York Yankees organization in seventh round of 1999 free-agent draft. ... On disabled list (August 18-September 2, 2006). **RECORDS:** Shares major league record for most strikeouts, game (5, May 2, 2005). **STATISTICAL NOTES:** Hit home run in first major league at-bat (September 26, 2004).

2006 GAMES PLAYED BY POSITION (MLB): 1B—94, 3B—10, DH—4, 2B—1.

										BATTING										FIELDING	
Year Team (League)	Pos.	G	AB	R	H	2B	3B	HR	RBI	BB	SO	HBP	GDP	SB-CS	Avg.	OBP	SLG	OPS	E	Avg.
1999— Staten Is. (N.Y.-Penn)	3B	64	233	35	75	11	7	7	48	37	40	3	4	3-3	.322	.417	.519	.936	16	.904
2000— Tampa (Fla. St.)	3B	127	478	66	137	33	2	13	58	46	98	2	9	2-0	.287	.346	.446	.792	30	.913
— Norwich (East.)	3B	7	28	5	7	2	1	0	3	3	11	0	1	1-0	.250	.323	.393	.715	2	.913
2001— Norwich (East.)	2B	51	183	23	49	9	2	6	25	21	54	0	6	1-0	.268	.340	.437	.777	17	.915
— Tampa (Fla. St.)	2B	75	288	43	87	17	4	11	50	25	55	3	6	3-3	.302	.353	.503	.856	10	.948
2002— Norwich (East.)	2B	73	272	58	83	24	2	19	51	33	56	3	6	4-3	.305	.381	.618	.999	7	.979
— Columbus (Int'l)	2B-1B	51	205	32	54	11	1	9	36	10	46	0	8	0-1	.263	.296	.459	.755	3	.985
2003— Columbus (Int'l)	2B	17	67	7	14	4	0	2	5	5	17	0	4	0-0	.209	.264	.358	.622	2	.955
2004— Trenton (East.)	3B-1B	10	42	8	15	2	1	4	16	3	1	0	0	3-0	.357	.383	.738	1.121	1	.982
— Columbus (Int'l)	1B-DH-3B																			
	3B	115	434	82	137	19	6	25	84	51	61	2	19	2-1	.316	.386	.560	.955	13	.984
— New York (A.L.)	3B-DH	5	8	1	2	0	0	1	2	0	1	0	1	0-0	.250	.250	.625	.875	0	1.000
2005— Columbus (Int'l)	3B-1B-DH																			
	2B	75	300	60	90	14	1	22	54	36	61	3	15	2-0	.300	.379	.573	.953	7	.979
— New York (A.L.)	1B-DH-3B																			
	OF	27	40	7	6	4	0	1	4	1	13	0	1	0-0	.150	.171	.325	.496	1	.987
2006— New York (A.L.)	1B-3B-DH																			
	2B	110	246	30	59	11	3	7	29	15	56	0	9	3-2	.240	.281	.394	.676	7	.988
Major League totals (3 years)		142	294	38	67	15	3	9	35	16	70	0	11	3-2	.228	.266	.391	.657	8	.988

DIVISION SERIES RECORD

Year Team (League)	Pos.	G	AB	R	H	2B	3B	HR	RBI	BB	SO	HBP	GDP	SB-CS	Avg.	OBP	SLG	OPS	E	Avg.
2006— New York (A.L.)	1B	1	1	0	0	0	0	0	0	0	0	0	0	0-0	.000	.000	.000	.000	0	1.000

2006 LEFTY-RIGHTY SPLITS

vs.	Avg.	AB	H	2B	3B	HR	RBI	BB	SO	OBP	Slg.	vs.	Avg.	AB	H	2B	3B	HR	RBI	BB	SO	OBP	Slg.
L	.195	82	16	1	0	1	4	4	18	.233	.244	R	.262	164	43	10	3	6	25	11	38	.305	.470

PHILLIPS, BRANDON — 2B

PERSONAL: Born June 28, 1981, in Raleigh, N.C. ... 5-11/185. ... Bats right, throws right. ... Full name: Brandon Emil Phillips. ... High school: Redan (Stone Mountain, Ga.). **TRANSACTIONS/CAREER NOTES:** Selected by Montreal Expos organization in second round of 1999 free-agent draft. ... Traded by Expos with 1B Lee Stevens, P Cliff Lee and OF Grady Sizemore to Cleveland Indians for P Bartolo Colon and future considerations (June 27, 2002); Expos acquired P Tim Drew to complete deal (June 28, 2002). ... Traded by Indians to Cincinnati Reds for cash or a player to be named (April 7, 2006); Indians acquired P Jeff Stevens to complete deal (June 13, 2006). **STATISTICAL NOTES:** Career major league grand slams: 1.

2006 GAMES PLAYED BY POSITION (MLB): 2B—142, SS—3.

										BATTING										FIELDING	
Year Team (League)	Pos.	G	AB	R	H	2B	3B	HR	RBI	BB	SO	HBP	GDP	SB-CS	Avg.	OBP	SLG	OPS	E	Avg.
1999— GC Expos (GCL)	SS	47	169	23	49	11	3	1	21	15	35	3	6	12-3	.290	.358	.408	.767	17	.915
2000— Cape Fear (S. Atl.)	SS-2B	126	484	74	117	17	8	11	72	38	97	9	11	23-8	.242	.306	.378	.684	36	.941
2001— Jupiter (Fla. St.)	SS	55	194	36	55	12	2	4	23	38	45	6	3	17-3	.284	.414	.428	.842	18	.930
— Harrisburg (East.)	SS-2B-3B	55	265	35	79	19	0	7	36	12	42	4	9	13-6	.298	.337	.449	.786	12	.958
2002— Harrisburg (East.)	SS	60	245	40	80	13	2	9	35	16	33	5	7	6-3	.327	.380	.506	.886	14	.936
— Ottawa (Int'l)	SS	10	35	1	9	4	0	1	5	2	6	0	...	0-0	.257	.297	.457	.754	0	1.000
— Buffalo (Int'l)	SS-2B	55	223	30	63	14	0	8	27	14	39	1		8-2	.283	.321	.453	.774	15	.957
— Cleveland (A.L.)	2B	11	31	5	8	3	1	0	4	3	6	1	0	0-0	.258	.343	.419	.762	2	.957
2003— Buffalo (Int'l)	2B	43	154	14	27	7	0	3	13	12	22	3	3	7-3	.175	.247	.279	.526	3	.958
— Cleveland (A.L.)	2B	112	370	36	77	18	1	6	33	14	77	3	12	4-5	.208	.242	.311	.553	11	.981
2004— Buffalo (Int'l)	2B-SS	135	521	83	158	34	4	8	50	44	56	8	12	14-11	.303	.363	.430	.793	28	.955
— Cleveland (A.L.)	2B	6	22	1	4	2	0	0	1	2	5	0	1	0-2	.182	.250	.273	.523	1	.957
2005— Cleveland (A.L.)	2B-SS-DH	6	9	1	0	0	0	0	0	0	4	0	0	0-0	.000	.000	.000	.000	1	.923
— Buffalo (Int'l)	SS-DH	112	465	79	119	24	1	15	46	39	90	10	11	7-5	.256	.326	.409	.734	21	.958
2006— Cincinnati (N.L.)	2B-SS	149	536	65	148	28	1	17	75	35	88	6	19	25-2	.276	.324	.427	.751	17	.975
American League totals (4 years)		135	432	43	89	23	2	6	38	19	92	4	13	4-7	.206	.246	.310	.556	15	.978
National League totals (1 year)		149	536	65	148	28	1	17	75	35	88	6	19	25-2	.276	.324	.427	.751	17	.975
Major League totals (5 years)		284	968	108	237	51	3	23	113	54	180	10	32	29-9	.245	.290	.375	.665	32	.976

2006 LEFTY-RIGHTY SPLITS

vs.	Avg.	AB	H	2B	3B	HR	RBI	BB	SO	OBP	Slg.	vs.	Avg.	AB	H	2B	3B	HR	RBI	BB	SO	OBP	Slg.
L	.299	137	41	5	0	4	16	12	21	.351	.423	R	.268	399	107	23	1	13	59	23	67	.315	.429

PHILLIPS, JASON — 1B/C

PERSONAL: Born September 27, 1976, in La Mesa, Calif. ... 6-1/177. ... Bats right, throws right. ... Full name: Jason Lloyd Phillips. ... High school: El Capitan (Lakeside, Calif.). ... College: San Diego State. **TRANSACTIONS/CAREER NOTES:** Selected by New York Mets organization in 24th round of 1997 free-agent draft. ... Traded by Mets to Los Angeles Dodgers for P Kazuhisa Ishii (March 20, 2005). ... Signed as a free agent by Toronto Blue Jays organization (January 3, 2006).

2006 GAMES PLAYED BY POSITION (MLB): DH—9, C—9, 1B—6.

								BATTING												FIELDING	
Year	Team (League)	Pos.	G	AB	R	H	2B	3B	HR	RBI	BB	SO	HBP	GDP	SB-CS	Avg.	OBP	SLG	OPS	E	Avg.
1997— Pittsfield (NYP)		C	48	155	15	32	9	0	2	17	13	24	4	2	4-0	.206	.282	.303	.585	4	.990
1998— Capital City (SAL)		C	69	251	36	68	15	1	5	37	23	35	5	3	5-2	.271	.343	.398	.741	4	.994
— St. Lucie (Fla. St.)		C	8	28	4	13	2	0	0	2	2	1	0	1	0-0	.464	.500	.536	1.036	0	1.000
1999— St. Lucie (Fla. St.)		C	81	283	36	73	12	1	9	48	43	28	8	10	0-1	.258	.367	.403	.770	4	.992
— Binghamton (East.)		C	39	141	13	32	5	0	7	23	13	20	3	4	0-0	.227	.304	.411	.715	5	.984
2000— St. Lucie (Fla. St.)		C	80	297	53	82	21	0	6	41	23	19	8	12	1-1	.276	.343	.407	.751	6	.989
— Binghamton (East.)		C	27	98	16	38	4	0	0	13	7	9	2	3	0-0	.388	.435	.429	.864	3	.983
2001— Binghamton (East.)		C	93	317	42	93	21	0	11	55	31	25	5	9	0-1	.293	.362	.464	.826	3	.995
— New York (N.L.)		C	6	7	2	1	1	0	0	0	0	1	0	0	0-0	.143	.143	.286	.429	1	1.000
— Norfolk (Int'l)		C	19	66	8	20	2	0	2	14	7	8	0	2	0-0	.303	.365	.424	.789	0	1.000
2002— Norfolk (Int'l)		C	88	323	35	91	22	1	13	65	24	29	2	10	1-0	.282	.327	.477	.804	4	.993
— New York (N.L.)		C	11	19	4	7	0	0	1	3	1	1	1	1	0-0	.368	.409	.526	.935	0	1.000
2003— Norfolk (Int'l)		C-1B-DH	22	78	13	27	5	0	4	20	11	9	2	4	0-0	.346	.435	.564	.999	0	1.000
— New York (N.L.)		1B-C	119	403	45	120	25	0	11	58	39	50	10	21	0-1	.298	.373	.442	.815	8	.991
2004— New York (N.L.)		C-1B	128	362	34	79	18	0	7	34	35	42	8	11	0-1	.218	.298	.326	.624	1	.999
2005— Los Angeles (N.L.)		C-1B	121	399	38	95	20	0	10	55	25	50	4	16	0-1	.238	.287	.363	.650	5	.993
2006— Syracuse (Int'l)			70	249	31	68	11	0	7	40	22	43	4	12	1-1	.273	.341	.402	.742	6	.990
— Toronto (A.L.)		C-DH-1B	25	48	4	12	6	0	0	6	1	5	1	2	0-1	.250	.275	.375	.650	1	.985
American League totals (1 year)			25	48	4	12	6	0	0	6	1	5	1	2	0-1	.250	.275	.375	.650	1	.985
National League totals (5 years)			385	1190	123	302	64	0	29	150	100	144	23	49	0-3	.254	.321	.381	.702	14	.994
Major League totals (6 years)			410	1238	127	314	70	0	29	156	101	149	24	51	0-4	.254	.319	.380	.700	15	.994

2006 LEFTY-RIGHTY SPLITS

vs.	Avg.	AB	H	2B	3B	HR	RBI	BB	SO	OBP	Slg.	vs.	Avg.	AB	H	2B	3B	HR	RBI	BB	SO	OBP	Slg.
L	.290	31	9	4	0	0	4	1	3	.303	.419	R	.176	17	3	2	0	0	2	0	2	.222	.294

PHILLIPS, PAUL   C

PERSONAL: Born April 15, 1977, in Demopolis, Ala. ... 5-11/185. ... Bats right, throws right. ... Full name: Paul Anthony Phillips. ... High school: West Lauderdale (Collinsville, Miss.). ... Junior college: Meridian. ... College: Alabama. **TRANSACTIONS/CAREER NOTES:** Selected by Kansas City Royals organization in 59th round of 1995 free-agent draft; did not sign. ... Selected by Houston Astros organization in 25th round of 1996 free-agent draft; did not sign. ... Selected by Royals organization in ninth round of 1998 free-agent draft. ... On disabled list (April 5, 2001-entire season).

2006 GAMES PLAYED BY POSITION (MLB): C—13, 1B—5, DH—2.

								BATTING												FIELDING	
Year	Team (League)	Pos.	G	AB	R	H	2B	3B	HR	RBI	BB	SO	HBP	GDP	SB-CS	Avg.	OBP	SLG	OPS	E	Avg.
1998— Spokane (N'west)		1B-C-OF	59	234	55	72	12	2	4	25	18	19	4	2	12-1	.308	.366	.427	.793	10	.978
— Wilmington (Caro.)		C	2	5	0	2	0	0	0	2	0	1	0	0	0-0	.400	.333	.400	.733	0	1.000
1999— Wichita (Texas)		C-OF-3B	108	393	58	105	20	2	3	56	26	38	2	8	8-9	.267	.314	.351	.665	10	.984
2000— Wichita (Texas)		C-OF	82	291	49	85	11	5	4	30	21	22	1	11	4-5	.292	.338	.405	.743	9	.983
2001— Kansas City (A.L.)				Did not play.																	
2002—				Did not play.																	
2003— Royals-1 (Ariz.)		C	4	13	3	6	2	0	1	2	1	0	0	0	0-0	.462	.500	.846	1.346	1	.967
— Wilmington (Caro.)		C	13	46	1	11	1	0	0	6	1	6	1	3	0-1	.239	.271	.261	.532	1	.988
2004— Omaha (PCL)		C-DH-OF	86	311	40	97	17	1	6	41	20	36	3	10	4-3	.312	.358	.431	.783	3	.995
— Kansas City (A.L.)		C	4	5	2	1	0	0	0	0	0	1	1	0	0-0	.200	.333	.200	.533	0	1.000
2005— Omaha (PCL)		C-DH	87	332	45	89	21	1	7	42	21	44	4	7	1-4	.268	.317	.401	.717	6	.990
— Kansas City (A.L.)		C-DH	23	67	6	18	4	1	1	9	0	5	0	4	0-0	.269	.269	.403	.672	1	.990
2006— Omaha (PCL)		C	91	345	43	84	11	1	9	39	22	37	1	15	0-0	.243	.286	.359	.646	10	.984
— Kansas City (A.L.)		C-1B-DH	23	65	8	18	3	0	1	5	1	8	0	0	0-0	.277	.284	.369	.653	1	.992
Major League totals (3 years)			50	137	16	37	7	1	2	14	1	14	1	4	0-0	.270	.279	.380	.658	2	.991

2006 LEFTY-RIGHTY SPLITS

vs.	Avg.	AB	H	2B	3B	HR	RBI	BB	SO	OBP	Slg.	vs.	Avg.	AB	H	2B	3B	HR	RBI	BB	SO	OBP	Slg.
L	.304	23	7	1	0	1	3	1	2	.333	.478	R	.262	42	11	2	0	0	2	0	6	.256	.310

PIAZZA, MIKE   C

PERSONAL: Born September 4, 1968, in Norristown, Pa. ... 6-3/215. ... Bats right, throws right. ... Full name: Michael Joseph Piazza. ... Name pronounced: pee-AH-zuh. ... High school: Phoenixville (Pa.) Area. ... Junior college: Miami-Dade Community College North. **TRANSACTIONS/CAREER NOTES:** Selected by Los Angeles Dodgers organization in 62nd round of 1988 free-agent draft. ... On disabled list (May 11-June 4, 1995). ... Traded by Dodgers with 3B Todd Zeile to Florida Marlins for OFs Gary Sheffield and Jim Eisenreich, 3B Bobby Bonilla, C Charles Johnson and P Manuel Barrios (May 15, 1998). ... Traded by Marlins to New York Mets for OF Preston Wilson and Ps Ed Yarnall and Geoff Goetz (May 22, 1998). ... On disabled list (April 10-25, 1999). ... On suspended list (April 2-6, 2003). ... On disabled list (May 17-August 13, 2003); included rehabilitation assignment to Norfolk. ... On disabled list (August 7-30, 2004); included rehabilitation assignment to St. Lucie. ... On disabled list (August 22-September 10, 2005). ... Signed as a free agent by San Diego Padres (February 9, 2006). **RECORDS:** Holds major league record for most home runs as a catcher, career (396). **HONORS:** Named N.L. Rookie Player of the Year by THE SPORTING NEWS (1993). ... Named catcher on THE SPORTING NEWS N.L. All-Star team (1993-2002). ... Named N.L. Rookie of the Year by Baseball Writers' Association of America (1993). ... Named catcher on N.L. Silver Slugger team (1993-2002). **STATISTICAL NOTES:** Hit three home runs in one game (June 29, 1996). ... Career major league grand slams: 14.

2006 GAMES PLAYED BY POSITION (MLB): C—99, DH—8.

								BATTING												FIELDING	
Year	Team (League)	Pos.	G	AB	R	H	2B	3B	HR	RBI	BB	SO	HBP	GDP	SB-CS	Avg.	OBP	SLG	OPS	E	Avg.
1989— Salem (N'west)		C	57	198	22	53	11	0	8	25	13	51	2	11	0-0	.268	.318	.444	.762	6	.977
1990— Vero Beach (FSL)		1B-C	88	272	27	68	20	0	6	45	11	68	1	6	0-1	.250	.281	.390	.670	16	.967
1991— Bakersfield (Calif.)		1B-C	117	448	71	124	27	2	29	80	47	83	3	19	0-3	.277	.344	.540	.884	15	.981
1992— San Antonio (Texas)		C	31	114	18	43	11	0	7	21	13	18	0	2	0-0	.377	.441	.658	1.099	4	.981
— Albuquerque (PCL)		C-1B	94	358	54	122	22	5	16	69	37	57	2	9	1-3	.341	.405	.564	.969	9	.985
— Los Angeles (N.L.)		C	21	69	5	16	3	0	1	7	4	12	1	1	0-0	.232	.284	.319	.603	1	.990
1993— Los Angeles (N.L.)		C-1B	149	547	81	174	24	2	35	112	46	86	3	10	3-4	.318	.370	.561	.932	11	.989
1994— Los Angeles (N.L.)		C	107	405	64	129	18	0	24	92	33	65	1	11	1-3	.319	.370	.541	.910	* 10	.985
1995— Los Angeles (N.L.)		C	112	434	82	150	17	0	32	93	39	80	1	10	1-0	.346	.400	1.006	1.006	9	.990
1996— Los Angeles (N.L.)		C	148	547	87	184	16	0	36	105	81	93	1	21	0-3	.336	.422	.563	.985	9	.992
1997— Los Angeles (N.L.)		C-DH	152	556	104	201	32	1	40	124	69	77	3	5	5-1	.362	.431	.638	1.070	* 16	.986
1998— Los Angeles (N.L.)		C	37	149	20	42	5	0	9	30	11	27	0	3	0-0	.282	.329	.497	.826	2	.993
— Florida (N.L.)		C	5	18	1	5	0	0	0	5	0	0	0	0	0-0	.278	.263	.278	.652	1	.968
— New York (N.L.)		C-DH	109	394	67	137	33	0	23	76	47	53	2	12	1-0	.348	.417	.607	1.024	8	.989

P

Year Team (League)	Pos.	G	AB	R	H	2B	3B	HR	RBI	BB	SO	HBP	GDP	SB-CS	Avg.	OBP	SLG	OPS	E	Avg.
1999— New York (N.L.)	C-DH	141	534	100	162	25	0	40	124	51	70	1	*27	2-2	.303	.361	.575	.936	11	.989
2000— New York (N.L.)	C-DH	136	482	90	156	26	0	38	113	58	69	3	15	4-2	.324	.398	.614	1.012	3	.997
2001— New York (N.L.)	C-DH	141	503	81	151	29	0	36	94	67	87	2	20	0-2	.300	.384	.573	.957	9	.991
2002— New York (N.L.)	C-DH	135	478	69	134	23	2	33	98	57	82	3	26	0-3	.280	.359	.544	.903	*12	.986
2003— Norfolk (Int'l)	C-1B-DH	5	17	2	3	0	0	1	2	1	3	0	0	0-0	.176	.222	.353	.575	0	1.000
— New York (N.L.)	C-1B	68	234	37	67	13	0	11	34	35	40	1	11	0-0	.286	.377	.483	.860	7	.982
2004— St. Lucie (Fla. St.)	1B-DH	2	6	0	3	1	0	0	2	1	0	0	0	0-0	.500	.500	.667	1.167	0	1.000
— New York (N.L.)	1B-C-DH	129	455	47	121	21	0	20	54	68	78	2	14	0-0	.266	.362	.444	.806	13	.984
2005— New York (N.L.)	C-DH	113	398	41	100	23	0	19	62	41	67	3	7	0-0	.251	.326	.452	.778	2	.997
2006— San Diego (N.L.)	C-DH	126	399	39	113	19	1	22	68	34	66	3	13	0-0	.283	.342	.501	.843	8	.987
Major League totals (15 years)		1829	6602	1015	2042	327	7	419	1291	741	1052	30	220	17-20	.309	.379	.551	.931	132	.989

DIVISION SERIES RECORD

Year Team (League)	Pos.	G	AB	R	H	2B	3B	HR	RBI	BB	SO	HBP	GDP	SB-CS	Avg.	OBP	SLG	OPS	E	Avg.
1995— Los Angeles (N.L.)	C	3	14	1	3	1	0	1	1	0	2	0	0	0-0	.214	.214	.500	.714	0	1.000
1996— Los Angeles (N.L.)	C	3	10	1	3	0	0	0	2	1	2	0	0	0-0	.300	.333	.300	.633	0	1.000
1999— New York (N.L.)	C	2	9	0	2	0	0	0	0	0	4	0	0	0-0	.222	.222	.222	.444	0	1.000
2000— New York (N.L.)	C	4	14	1	3	1	0	0	0	4	3	0	0	0-0	.214	.389	.286	.675	0	1.000
2006— San Diego (N.L.)	C	4	10	0	1	1	0	0	0	0	1	0	1	0-0	.100	.100	.200	.300	0	1.000
Division series totals (5 years)		16	57	3	12	3	0	1	3	5	12	0	1	0-0	.211	.270	.316	.586	0	1.000

CHAMPIONSHIP SERIES RECORD

Year Team (League)	Pos.	G	AB	R	H	2B	3B	HR	RBI	BB	SO	HBP	GDP	SB-CS	Avg.	OBP	SLG	OPS	E	Avg.
1999— New York (N.L.)	C	6	24	1	4	0	0	1	4	1	6	0	0	0-0	.167	.192	.292	.484	3	.940
2000— New York (N.L.)	C	5	17	7	7	3	0	2	4	5	0	0	1	0-0	.412	.545	.941	1.487	0	1.000
Champ. series totals (2 years)		11	41	8	11	3	0	3	8	6	6	0	1	0-0	.268	.354	.561	.915	3	.967

WORLD SERIES RECORD

Year Team (League)	Pos.	G	AB	R	H	2B	3B	HR	RBI	BB	SO	HBP	GDP	SB-CS	Avg.	OBP	SLG	OPS	E	Avg.
2000— New York (N.L.)	C-DH	5	22	3	6	2	0	2	4	0	4	0	0	0-1	.273	.273	.636	.909	0	1.000

ALL-STAR GAME RECORD

		G	AB	R	H	2B	3B	HR	RBI	BB	SO	HBP	GDP	SB-CS	Avg.	OBP	SLG	OPS	E	Avg.
All-Star Game totals (11 years)			11	25	2	6	1	0	2	5	1	5	0	0	0-0	.240	.269	.520	.789	0	1.000

2006 LEFTY-RIGHTY SPLITS

vs.	Avg.	AB	H	2B	3B	HR	RBI	BB	SO	OBP	Slg.	vs.	Avg.	AB	H	2B	3B	HR	RBI	BB	SO	OBP	Slg.
L	.359	103	37	6	0	8	20	11	12	.421	.650	R	.257	296	76	13	1	14	48	23	54	.314	.449

PIEDRA, JORGE — OF

PERSONAL: Born April 17, 1979, in Sun Valley, Calif. ... 6-0/190. ... Bats left, throws left. ... Full name: Jorge Moises Piedra. ... Name pronounced: pea-AY-dra. ... High school: Notre Dame (Van Nuys, Calif.). **TRANSACTIONS/CAREER NOTES:** Signed as a non-drafted free agent by Los Angeles Dodgers organization (August 14, 1997). ... Traded by Dodgers with P Jamie Arnold to Chicago Cubs for P Ismael Valdez (July 26, 2000). ... Traded by Cubs to Colorado Rockies for cash (May 3, 2002). ... On disabled list (March 28-May 2, 2006); included rehabilitation assignment to Colorado Springs.

2006 GAMES PLAYED BY POSITION (MLB): DH—5, OF—5.

Year Team (League)	Pos.	G	AB	R	H	2B	3B	HR	RBI	BB	SO	HBP	GDP	SB-CS	Avg.	OBP	SLG	OPS	E	Avg.
1998— Great Falls (Pio.)	OF	72	282	72	108	22	7	2	33	39	29	1	4	16-7	.383	.460	.532	.992	7	.949
1999— San Bern. (Calif.)	OF	8	30	6	9	2	0	0	3	3	3	0	0	1-0	.300	.343	.367	.710	0	1.000
— Vero Beach (FSL)	OF	15	59	13	17	3	1	1	6	7	9	0	0	2-2	.288	.358	.424	.782	2	.933
2000— Vero Beach (FSL)	OF	92	360	59	102	11	6	6	52	29	57	5	6	21-5	.283	.339	.397	.736	6	.974
— Daytona (Fla. St.)	OF	34	139	24	48	11	1	1	17	6	15	0	0	8-4	.345	.367	.460	.828	0	1.000
2001— West Tenn. (Sou.)	OF	124	441	55	108	26	6	8	54	37	80	8	8	12-5	.245	.310	.385	.696	5	.980
2002— West Tenn. (Sou.)	OF	23	60	5	10	3	1	0	4	3	11	1	1	2-0	.167	.219	.250	.469	1	.971
— Salem (Carol.)	OF	104	392	64	118	37	12	13	64	37	55	8	4	10-2	.301	.366	.556	.922	5	.975
2003— Tulsa (Texas)	OF	96	357	56	98	17	7	18	53	31	50	8	6	5-2	.275	.342	.513	.854	5	.973
2004— Colo. Springs (PCL)	OF-DH	99	377	71	126	29	5	15	55	23	56	3	7	4-3	.334	.372	.557	.924	4	.978
— Colorado (N.L.)	OF	38	91	15	27	8	0	3	10	5	19	1	1	0-1	.297	.340	.484	.824	0	1.000
2005— Colo. Springs (PCL)	OF	47	186	35	58	20	1	6	45	18	23	1	4	4-2	.312	.372	.527	.899	6	.960
— Colorado (N.L.)	OF-DH	61	112	19	35	8	1	6	16	10	15	1	2	2-1	.313	.371	.563	.933	0	1.000
2006— Colo. Springs (PCL)		41	138	15	33	8	0	6	18	15	31	1	2	0-2	.239	.314	.428	.742	3	.957
— Colorado (N.L.)	OF-DH	43	59	4	10	2	0	3	10	3	22	1	2	1-0	.169	.222	.356	.578	0	1.000
Major League totals (3 years)		142	262	38	72	18	1	12	36	18	56	3	5	3-2	.275	.327	.489	.816	0	1.000

2006 LEFTY-RIGHTY SPLITS

vs.	Avg.	AB	H	2B	3B	HR	RBI	BB	SO	OBP	Slg.	vs.	Avg.	AB	H	2B	3B	HR	RBI	BB	SO	OBP	Slg.
L	.000	6	0	0	0	0	0	0	3	.000	.000	R	.189	53	10	2	0	3	10	3	19	.246	.396

PIERRE, JUAN — OF

PERSONAL: Born August 14, 1977, in Mobile, Ala. ... 6-0/180. ... Bats left, throws left. ... Full name: Juan D'Vaughn Pierre. ... Name pronounced: pee-AIR. ... High school: Alexandria (La.). ... College: South Alabama. **TRANSACTIONS/CAREER NOTES:** Selected by Seattle Mariners organization in 30th round of 1995 free-agent draft; did not sign. ... Selected by Mariners organization in 48th round of 1996 free-agent draft; did not sign. ... Selected by Colorado Rockies organization in 13th round of 1998 free-agent draft. ... Traded by Rockies with P Mike Hampton and cash to Florida Marlins for C Charles Johnson, P Vic Darensbourg, OF Preston Wilson and 2B Pablo Ozuna (November 16, 2002). ... Traded by Marlins to Chicago Cubs for Ps Sergio Mitre, Ricky Nolasco and Renyel Pinto (December 7, 2005).

2006 GAMES PLAYED BY POSITION (MLB): OF—162.

Year Team (League)	Pos.	G	AB	R	H	2B	3B	HR	RBI	BB	SO	HBP	GDP	SB-CS	Avg.	OBP	SLG	OPS	E	Avg.
1998— Portland (N'west)	OF	64	264	55	93	9	2	0	30	19	11	2	3	38-9	.352	.399	.402	.800	5	.955
1999— Asheville (S. Atl.)	OF	140	585	93	187	28	5	1	55	38	37	8	12	66-19	.320	.366	.390	.756	4	.981
2000— Carolina (Southern)	OF	107	439	63	143	16	4	0	32	33	26	5	4	46-12	.326	.376	.380	.757	2	.992
— Colo. Springs (PCL)	OF	4	17	3	8	0	1	0	1	0	0	0	0	1-1	.471	.471	.588	1.059	0	1.000
— Colorado (N.L.)	OF	51	200	26	62	2	0	0	20	13	15	1	2	7-6	.310	.353	.320	.673	3	.975
2001— Colorado (N.L.)	OF	156	617	108	202	26	11	2	55	41	29	10	6	•46-*17	.327	.378	.415	.793	8	.991
2002— Colorado (N.L.)	OF	152	592	90	170	20	5	1	35	31	52	9	7	47-12	.287	.332	.343	.675	2	.995
2003— Florida (N.L.)	OF	162	*668	100	204	28	7	1	41	55	35	5	9	*65-* 20	.305	.361	.373	.734	3	.993
2004— Florida (N.L.)	OF	162	*678	100	*221	22	•12	3	49	45	35	6	9	45-24	.326	.374	.407	.781	2	.995

Year	Team (League)	Pos.	G	AB	R	H	2B	3B	HR	RBI	BB	SO	HBP	GDP	SB-CS	Avg.	OBP	SLG	OPS	E	Avg.
										BATTING										FIELDING	
2005— Florida (N.L.)		OF	•162	656	96	181	19	13	2	47	41	45	9	10	57-* 17	.276	.326	.354	.680	4	.988
2006— Chicago (N.L.)		OF	•162	* 699	87	* 204	32	13	3	40	32	38	8	6	58-* 20	.292	.330	.388	.717	0	1.000
Major League totals (7 years)			1007	4110	607	1244	149	61	12	287	258	249	50	49	325-116	.303	.350	.377	.728	22	.991

DIVISION SERIES RECORD

Year	Team (League)	Pos.	G	AB	R	H	2B	3B	HR	RBI	BB	SO	HBP	GDP	SB-CS	Avg.	OBP	SLG	OPS	E	Avg.
2003— Florida (N.L.)		OF	4	19	5	5	1	0	0	3	1	1	0	0	1-0	.263	.300	.316	.616	0	1.000

CHAMPIONSHIP SERIES RECORD

Year	Team (League)	Pos.	G	AB	R	H	2B	3B	HR	RBI	BB	SO	HBP	GDP	SB-CS	Avg.	OBP	SLG	OPS	E	Avg.
2003— Florida (N.L.)		OF	7	33	5	10	1	2	0	1	2	1	0	0	1-3	.303	.343	.455	.797	0	1.000

WORLD SERIES RECORD

Year	Team (League)	Pos.	G	AB	R	H	2B	3B	HR	RBI	BB	SO	HBP	GDP	SB-CS	Avg.	OBP	SLG	OPS	E	Avg.
2003— Florida (N.L.)		OF	6	21	2	7	2	0	0	3	5	2	0	0	1-1	.333	.481	.429	.910	0	1.000

2006 LEFTY-RIGHTY SPLITS

vs.	Avg.	AB	H	2B	3B	HR	RBI	BB	SO	OBP	Slg.	vs.	Avg.	AB	H	2B	3B	HR	RBI	BB	SO	OBP	Slg.
L	.293	246	72	12	2	0	17	11	15	.341	.358	R	.291	453	132	20	11	3	23	21	23	.324	.404

PIERZYNSKI, A.J.   C

PERSONAL: Born December 30, 1976, in Bridgehampton, N.Y. ... 6-3/245. ... Bats left, throws right. ... Full name: Anthony John Pierzynski. ... Name pronounced: PEER-zin-skee. ... High school: Dr. Phillips (Orlando). **TRANSACTIONS/CAREER NOTES:** Selected by Minnesota Twins organization in third round of 1994 free-agent draft. ... Traded by Twins with cash to San Francisco Giants for Ps Joe Nathan, Boof Bonser and Francisco Liriano (November 14, 2003). ... Released by Giants (December 16, 2004). ... Signed by Chicago White Sox (January 6, 2005). **STATISTICAL NOTES:** Career major league grand slams: 5.

2006 GAMES PLAYED BY POSITION (MLB): C—132.

Year	Team (League)	Pos.	G	AB	R	H	2B	3B	HR	RBI	BB	SO	HBP	GDP	SB-CS	Avg.	OBP	SLG	OPS	E	Avg.
										BATTING										FIELDING	
1994— GC Twins (GCL)		C-DH	43	152	21	44	8	1	1	19	12	19	0	3	0-2	.289	.337	.375	.712	8	.966
1995— Fort Wayne (Midw.)		C	22	84	10	26	5	1	2	14	2	10	0	1	0-0	.310	.322	.464	.786	10	.939
— Elizabethton (App.)		1B-C	56	205	29	68	13	1	7	45	14	23	0	6	0-2	.332	.373	.507	.880	12	.974
1996— Fort Wayne (Midw.)		C-DH-OF	114	431	48	118	30	3	7	70	22	53	2	10	0-4	.274	.308	.406	.714	21	.972
1997— Fort Myers (FSL)		C-DH-1B	118	412	49	115	23	1	9	64	16	59	6	9	2-1	.279	.313	.405	.718	10	.987
1998— New Britain (East.)		C-DH	59	212	30	63	11	0	3	17	10	25	2	4	0-2	.297	.333	.392	.725	2	.996
— Salt Lake (PCL)		C	59	208	29	53	7	2	7	30	9	24	0	4	3-1	.255	.284	.409	.693	7	.983
— Minnesota (A.L.)		C	7	10	1	3	0	0	0	1	1	2	1	0	0-0	.300	.385	.300	.685	0	1.000
1999— Salt Lake (PCL)		C	67	228	29	59	10	0	1	25	16	29	0	11	0-0	.259	.307	.316	.623	7	.984
— Minnesota (A.L.)		C	9	22	3	6	2	0	0	3	1	4	1	0	0-0	.273	.333	.364	.697	0	1.000
2000— New Britain (East.)		C	62	228	36	68	17	2	4	34	8	22	0	9	13-0	.298	.341	.443	.784	6	.982
— Salt Lake (PCL)		C	41	155	22	52	14	1	4	25	5	21	1	3	1-1	.335	.354	.516	.870	3	.990
— Minnesota (A.L.)		C	33	88	12	27	5	1	2	11	5	14	2	1	1-0	.307	.354	.455	.809	0	1.000
2001— Minnesota (A.L.)		C-DH	114	381	51	110	33	2	7	55	16	57	4	7	1-7	.289	.322	.441	.763	10	.985
2002— Minnesota (A.L.)		C	130	440	54	132	31	6	6	49	13	61	11	14	1-2	.300	.334	.439	.773	3	.996
2003— Minnesota (A.L.)		C	137	487	63	152	35	3	11	74	24	55	15	13	3-1	.312	.360	.464	.824	6	.993
2004— San Francisco (N.L.)		C	131	471	45	128	28	2	11	77	19	27	15	* 27	0-1	.272	.319	.410	.729	1	.999
2005— Chicago (A.L.)		C	128	460	61	118	21	0	18	56	23	68	12	13	0-2	.257	.308	.420	.728	1	.999
2006— Chicago (A.L.)		C	140	509	65	150	24	0	16	64	22	72	8	10	1-0	.295	.333	.436	.769	3	.997
American League totals (8 years)			698	2397	310	698	151	12	60	313	105	333	54	58	7-12	.291	.333	.439	.773	23	.995
National League totals (1 year)			131	471	45	128	28	2	11	77	19	27	15	27	0-1	.272	.319	.410	.729	1	.999
Major League totals (9 years)			829	2868	355	826	179	14	71	390	124	360	69	85	7-13	.288	.331	.434	.765	24	.995

DIVISION SERIES RECORD

Year	Team (League)	Pos.	G	AB	R	H	2B	3B	HR	RBI	BB	SO	HBP	GDP	SB-CS	Avg.	OBP	SLG	OPS	E	Avg.
2002— Minnesota (A.L.)		C	5	16	4	7	0	1	1	4	2	2	0	0	0-0	.438	.500	.750	1.250	1	.969
2003— Minnesota (A.L.)		C	4	13	1	3	0	0	1	1	2	0	0	1	0-0	.231	.333	.462	.795	0	1.000
2005— Chicago (A.L.)		C	3	9	5	4	2	0	2	4	1	0	0	1	1-0	.444	.545	1.333	1.879	0	1.000
Division series totals (3 years)			12	38	10	14	2	1	4	9	5	2	0	2	1-0	.368	.455	.789	1.244	1	.987

CHAMPIONSHIP SERIES RECORD

Year	Team (League)	Pos.	G	AB	R	H	2B	3B	HR	RBI	BB	SO	HBP	GDP	SB-CS	Avg.	OBP	SLG	OPS	E	Avg.
2002— Minnesota (A.L.)		C	5	16	1	4	0	0	0	2	0	2	0	0	0-1	.250	.250	.250	.500	2	.938
2005— Chicago (A.L.)		C	5	18	1	3	0	0	1	4	1	6	0	0	0-1	.167	.211	.333	.544	0	1.000
Champ. series totals (2 years)			10	34	2	7	0	0	1	4	1	8	0	0	0-2	*206	.222	.294	.516	2	.964

WORLD SERIES RECORD

Year	Team (League)	Pos.	G	AB	R	H	2B	3B	HR	RBI	BB	SO	HBP	GDP	SB-CS	Avg.	OBP	SLG	OPS	E	Avg.
2005— Chicago (A.L.)		C	4	15	3	4	0	0	0	3	2	2	0	1	1-0	.267	.353	.400	.753	0	1.000

ALL-STAR GAME RECORD

			G	AB	R	H	2B	3B	HR	RBI	BB	SO	HBP	GDP	SB-CS	Avg.	OBP	SLG	OPS	E	Avg.
All-Star Game totals (1 year)			1	3	0	0	0	0	0	0	0	0	0	0	0-0	.000	.000	.000	.000	0	1.000

2006 LEFTY-RIGHTY SPLITS

vs.	Avg.	AB	H	2B	3B	HR	RBI	BB	SO	OBP	Slg.	vs.	Avg.	AB	H	2B	3B	HR	RBI	BB	SO	OBP	Slg.
L	.270	141	38	4	0	1	14	4	22	.304	.319	R	.304	368	112	20	0	15	50	18	50	.344	.481

PINEIRO, JOEL   P

PERSONAL: Born September 25, 1978, in Rio Padres, Puerto Rico. ... 6-1/200. ... Throws right, bats right. ... Full name: Joel Alberto Pineiro. ... Name pronounced: pin-YER-oh. ... High school: Colonial (Orlando). ... Junior college: Edison (Fla.) C.C. **TRANSACTIONS/CAREER NOTES:** Selected by Seattle Mariners organization in 12th round of 1997 free-agent draft. ... On suspended list (October 3-6, 2001). ... On disabled list (July 26, 2004-remainder of season).

CAREER HITTING: 2-for-24 (.083), 1 R, 1 2B, 0 3B, 0 HR, 2 RBI.

Year	Team (League)	W	L	Pct.	ERA	WHIP	G	GS	CG	ShO	Hld.	Sv.-Opp.	IP	H	R	ER	HR	BB-IBB	SO	Avg.
1997— Ariz. Mariners (Ariz.)		1	0	1.000	0.00	0.33	1	0	0	0		0-...	3.0	1	0	0	0	0-0	4	.100
— Everett (N'west)		4	2	.667	5.33	1.47	18	6	0	0		2-...	49.0	54	33	29	2	18-1	59	.267
1998— Wisconsin (Midw.)		8	4	.667	3.19	1.25	16	16	1	0		0-...	96.0	92	40	34	8	28-1	84	.252
— Lancaster (Calif.)		2	0	1.000	7.80	1.78	9	9	1	1		0-...	45.0	58	40	39	6	22-0	48	.307
— Orlando (South.)		1	0	1.000	5.40	1.80	1	1	0	0		0-...	5.0	7	4	3	0	2-0	2	.368
1999— New Haven (East.)		10	15	.400	4.72	1.46	28	25	4	1		0-...	166.0	190	105	87	18	52-0	116	.290
2000— New Haven (East.)		2	1	.667	4.13	1.03	9	9	0	0		0-...	52.1	42	25	24	6	12-0	43	.218

P

Year	Team (League)	W	L	Pct.	ERA	WHIP	G	GS	CG	ShO	Hld.	Sv.-Opp.	IP	H	R	ER	HR	BB-IBB	SO	Avg.
—Tacoma (PCL)		7	1	.875	2.80	1.23	10	9	2	2	...	0-...	61.0	53	20	19	3	22-1	41	.232
—Seattle (A.L.)		1	0	1.000	5.59	1.97	8	1	0	0	0	0-0	19.1	25	13	12	3	13-0	21	.316
2001—Tacoma (PCL)		6	3	.667	3.62	1.31	18	10	0	0	...	0-...	77.0	68	31	31	8	33-0	64	.242
—Seattle (A.L.)		6	2	.750	2.03	0.94	17	11	0	0	2	0-0	75.1	50	24	17	2	21-0	56	.191
2002—Seattle (A.L.)		14	7	.667	3.24	1.25	37	28	2	1	3	0-0	194.1	189	75	70	24	54-1	136	.256
2003—Seattle (A.L.)		16	11	.593	3.78	1.27	32	32	3	•2	0	0-0	211.2	192	94	89	19	76-3	151	.241
2004—Seattle (A.L.)		6	11	.353	4.67	1.33	21	21	1	0	0	0-0	140.2	144	77	73	21	43-1	111	.265
2005—Tacoma (PCL)		0	0	...	1.29	0.71	1	1	0	0	0	0-0*	7.0	5	1	1	1	0-0	6	.192
—Seattle (A.L.)		7	11	.389	5.62	1.48	30	30	2	0	0	0-0	189.0	224	148	118	23	56-4	107	.300
2006—Seattle (A.L.)		8	13	.381	6.36	1.65	40	25	1	0	4	1-2	165.2	209	123	117	23	64-13	87	.311
Major League totals (7 years)		58	55	.513	4.48	1.37	185	148	9	3	9	1-2	996.0	1033	524	496	115	327-22	658	.269

DIVISION SERIES RECORD

Year	Team (League)	W	L	Pct.	ERA	WHIP	G	GS	CG	ShO	Hld.	Sv.-Opp.	IP	H	R	ER	HR	BB-IBB	SO	Avg.
2001—Seattle (A.L.)		Did not play.																		

CHAMPIONSHIP SERIES RECORD

Year	Team (League)	W	L	Pct.	ERA	WHIP	G	GS	CG	ShO	Hld.	Sv.-Opp.	IP	H	R	ER	HR	BB-IBB	SO	Avg.
2001—Seattle (A.L.)		0	0	...	4.50	3.00	1	0	0	0	0	0-0	2.0	4	1	1	0	2-0	5	.400

2006 LEFTY-RIGHTY SPLITS

vs.	Avg.	AB	H	2B	3B	HR	RBI	BB	SO	OBP	Slg.	vs.	Avg.	AB	H	2B	3B	HR	RBI	BB	SO	OBP	Slg.
L	.287	307	88	27	2	10	50	39	38	.364	.485	R	.332	365	121	22	1	13	60	25	49	.388	.504

PINTO, RENYEL — P

PERSONAL: Born July 8, 1982, in Miranda, Venezuela. ... 6-4/195. ... Throws left, bats left. ... Full name: Renyel Eligio Pinto. **TRANSACTIONS/CAREER NOTES:** Signed as a non-drafted free agent by Chicago Cubs organization (January 31, 1999). ... Traded by Cubs with Ps Sergio Mitre and Ricky Nolasco to Florida Marlins for OF Juan Pierre (December 7, 2005).
CAREER HITTING: 0-for-1 (.000), 0 R, 0 2B, 0 3B, 0 HR, 0 RBI.

Year	Team (League)	W	L	Pct.	ERA	WHIP	G	GS	CG	ShO	Hld.	Sv.-Opp.	IP	H	R	ER	HR	BB-IBB	SO	Avg.
1999—Dominican Cubs (DSL)		4	5	.444	4.38	1.45	13	13	1	0		0-...	63.2	70	35	31	5	22-0	62	.289
2000—Ariz. Cubs (Ariz.)		0	2	.000	6.30	1.93	9	4	0	0		0-...	30.0	42	29	21	3	16-0	23	.326
2001—Lansing (Midw.)		4	8	.333	5.22	1.57	20	20	1	0		0-...	88.0	94	64	51	9	44-1	69	.278
2002—Daytona (Fla. St.)		3	3	.500	5.51	1.71	7	7	0	0		0-...	32.2	45	23	20	5	11-0	24	.338
—Lansing (Midw.)		7	5	.583	3.31	1.09	17	16	0	0		0-...	98.0	79	39	36	9	28-0	92	.221
2003—Daytona (Fla. St.)		3	8	.273	3.22	1.19	20	19	0	0		0-...	114.2	91	47	41	4	45-1	104	.221
2004—West Tenn (Sou.)		11	8	.579	2.92	1.26	25	25	0	0		0-...	141.2	107	50	46	10	72-0	179	.216
—Iowa (PCL)		1	1	.500	7.71	1.82	2	2	0	0		0-...	9.1	9	9	8	2	8-0	9	.257
2005—Iowa (PCL)		1	2	.333	9.53	2.43	6	6	0	0		0-0	22.2	31	30	24	3	24-0	24	.348
—West Tenn (Sou.)		10	3	.769	2.71	1.23	22	21	1	0		0-0	129.2	101	43	39	8	58-0	123	.223
2006—Albuquerque (PCL)		8	2	.800	3.40	1.35	18	18	1	0	0	0-0	95.1	82	40	36	8	47-1	96	.232
—Florida (N.L.)		0	0	...	3.03	1.58	27	0	0	0	3	1-1	29.2	20	12	10	3	27-0	36	.190
Major League totals (1 year)		0	0	...	3.03	1.58	27	0	0	0	3	1-1	29.2	20	12	10	3	27-0	36	.190

2006 LEFTY-RIGHTY SPLITS

vs.	Avg.	AB	H	2B	3B	HR	RBI	BB	SO	OBP	Slg.	vs.	Avg.	AB	H	2B	3B	HR	RBI	BB	SO	OBP	Slg.
L	.171	35	6	1	0	1	4	11	15	.383	.286	R	.200	70	14	3	0	2	9	16	21	.345	.329

PODSEDNIK, SCOTT — OF

PERSONAL: Born March 18, 1976, in West, Texas. ... 6-0/188. ... Bats left, throws left. ... Full name: Scott Eric Podsednik. ... Name pronounced: pod-SED-nik. ... High school: West (Texas). **TRANSACTIONS/CAREER NOTES:** Selected by Texas Rangers organization in third round of 1994 free-agent draft. ... Traded by Rangers to Florida Marlins (October 8, 1995), completing deal in which Marlins traded P Bobby Witt to Texas Rangers for two players to be named (August 8, 1995); Marlins acquired P Wilson Heredia as part of deal (August 11, 1995). ... Selected by Rangers organization from Marlins organization in Rule 5 minor league draft (December 15, 1997). ... Signed as a free agent by Seattle Mariners organization (November 1, 2000). ... Claimed on waivers by Milwaukee Brewers (October 13, 2002). ... Traded by Brewers with P Luis Vizcaino and a player to be named to Chicago White Sox for OF Carlos Lee (December 13, 2004). White Sox acquired 1B Travis Hinton to complete deal (January 10, 2005). ... On disabled list (August 13-29, 2005); included rehabilitation assignment to Charlotte. **HONORS:** Named N.L. Rookie Player of the Year by THE SPORTING NEWS (2003). **STATISTICAL NOTES:** Career major league grand slams: 1.
2006 GAMES PLAYED BY POSITION (MLB): OF—135, DH—2.

Year	Team (League)	Pos.	G	AB	R	H	2B	3B	HR	RBI	BB	SO	HBP	GDP	SB-CS	Avg.	OBP	SLG	OPS	E	Avg.
1994—GC Rangers (GCL)		OF	60	211	34	48	7	1	1	17	41	34	3	1	18-5	.227	.357	.284	.641	0	1.000
1995—Hudson Valley (NYP)		OF	65	252	42	67	3	0	0	20	35	31	1	9	20-6	.266	.355	.278	.633	3	.978
1996—Brevard County (FSL)		OF	108	383	39	100	9	2	0	30	45	65	3	8	20-10	.261	.343	.295	.638	4	.984
1997—Kane Co. (Midw.)		OF	135	531	80	147	23	4	3	49	60	72	3	5	28-11	.277	.352	.352	.704	5	.977
1998—Charlotte (Fla. St.)		OF	81	302	55	86	12	4	4	39	44	32	0	2	26-8	.285	.369	.391	.760	2	.986
—Tulsa (Texas)		OF	17	75	9	18	4	1	0	4	6	11	0	3	5-2	.240	.296	.320	.616	0	1.000
1999—GC Rangers (GCL)		OF	5	17	6	7	0	2	0	5	2	3	0	1	1-0	.412	.474	.529	1.003	0	1.000
—Tulsa (Texas)		OF	37	116	10	18	4	0	0	1	·5	13	0	3	6-2	.155	.190	.190	.380	1	.987
2000—Tulsa (Texas)		OF	49	169	20	42	7	2	2	13	30	33	1	4	19-4	.249	.361	.349	.710	3	.968
2001—Tacoma (PCL)		OF	66	269	46	78	15	4	3	30	13	46	2	0	12-5	.290	.327	.409	.736	5	.967
—Seattle (A.L.)		OF	5	6	1	1	0	0	0	3	0	1	0	0	0-0	.167	.167	.500	.667	0	1.000
2002—Tacoma (PCL)		OF	125	438	63	122	25	6	9	61	43	70	9	18	35-13	.279	.347	.425	.772	5	.985
—Seattle (A.L.)		OF-DH	14	20	2	4	0	0	1	5	4	6	2	1	2-0	.200	.320	.350	.670	1	.938
2003—Milwaukee (N.L.)		OF	154	558	100	175	29	8	9	58	56	91	4	11	43-10	.314	.379	.443	.822	3	.992
2004—Milwaukee (N.L.)		OF	154	640	85	156	27	4	12	39	58	105	7	7	*70-13	.244	.313	.364	.677	4	.990
2005—Charlotte (Int'l)		OF	2	9	2	2	0	0	0	1	0	2	0	0	0-0	.222	.444	.667	1.000	0	1.000
—Chicago (A.L.)		OF	129	507	80	147	28	4	0	25	47	75	3	6	59-* 23	.290	.351	.349	.700	3	.989
2006—Chicago (A.L.)		OF-DH	139	524	86	137	27	6	3	45	54	96	2	7	40-* 19	.261	.330	.353	.684	8	.969
American League totals (4 years)			287	1057	169	289	55	8	4	78	105	178	5	16	99-42	.273	.339	.352	.691	12	.978
National League totals (2 years)			308	1198	185	331	56	15	21	97	114	196	11	18	113-23	.276	.344	.401	.745	7	.991
Major League totals (6 years)			595	2255	354	620	111	23	25	175	219	374	16	34	212-65	.275	.342	.378	.719	19	.985

DIVISION SERIES RECORD

Year	Team (League)	Pos.	G	AB	R	H	2B	3B	HR	RBI	BB	SO	HBP	GDP	SB-CS	Avg.	OBP	SLG	OPS	E	Avg.
2005—Chicago (A.L.)		OF	3	11	3	3	1	0	0	1	4	1	2	0	1-2	.273	.429	.636	1.065	0	1.000

P

Year	Team (League)	Pos.	G	AB	R	H	2B	3B	HR	RBI	BB	SO	HBP	GDP	SB-CS	Avg.	OBP	SLG	OPS	E	Avg.
	CHAMPIONSHIP SERIES RECORD																				
2005— Chicago (A.L.)		OF	5	17	4	5	0	1	0	0	6	5	0	0	3-1	.294	.478	.412	.890	0	1.000

Year	Team (League)	Pos.	G	AB	R	H	2B	3B	HR	RBI	BB	SO	HBP	GDP	SB-CS	Avg.	OBP	SLG	OPS	E	Avg.
	WORLD SERIES RECORD																				
2005— Chicago (A.L.)		OF	4	21	2	6	0	2	1	2	0	4	0	1	2-0	.286	.286	.619	.905	0	1.000

			G	AB	R	H	2B	3B	HR	RBI	BB	SO	HBP	GDP	SB-CS	Avg.	OBP	SLG	OPS	E	Avg.
	ALL-STAR GAME RECORD																				
All-Star Game totals (1 year)			1	0	0	0	0	0	0	0	0	0	0	0	0-0	...	...	...	...	0	...

2006 LEFTY-RIGHTY SPLITS

vs.	Avg.	AB	H	2B	3B	HR	RBI	BB	SO	OBP	Slg.	vs.	Avg.	AB	H	2B	3B	HR	RBI	BB	SO	OBP	Slg.
L	.216	139	30	4	1	1	8	12	30	.281	.281	R	.278	385	107	23	5	2	37	42	66	.348	.379

POLANCO, PLACIDO — 2B/3B

PERSONAL: Born October 10, 1975, in Santo Domingo, Dominican Republic. ... 5-10/190. ... Bats right, throws right. ... Full name: Placido Enrique Polanco. ... Name pronounced: PLAH-si-doh poh-LAHN-co. ... High school: Santo Clara (Santo Domingo, Dominican Republic). ... Junior college: Miami-Dade Community College Wolfson.
TRANSACTIONS/CAREER NOTES: Selected by St. Louis Cardinals in 19th round of 1994 free-agent draft. ... On disabled list (July 1-16, 2000). ... Traded by Cardinals with Ps Bud Smith and Mike Timlin to Philadelphia Phillies for 3B Scott Rolen and P Doug Nickle (July 29, 2002). ... On disabled list (April 16-May 1, 2003). ... On disabled list (May 8-June 7, 2004); included rehabilitation assignments to Reading and Scranton/Wilkes-Barre. ... Traded by Phillies to Detroit Tigers for 2B Ramon Martinez and P Ugueth Urbina (June 8, 2005). ... On disabled list (July 12-27, 2005 and August 16-September 22, 2006). **STATISTICAL NOTES:** Career major league grand slams: 1.
2006 GAMES PLAYED BY POSITION (MLB): 2B—108.

								BATTING												FIELDING	
Year	Team (League)	Pos.	G	AB	R	H	2B	3B	HR	RBI	BB	SO	HBP	GDP	SB-CS	Avg.	OBP	SLG	OPS	E	Avg.
1994— Ariz. Cardinals (Ariz.)		2B-SS	32	127	17	27	4	0	1	10	7	15	1	2	4-2	.213	.259	.268	.527	10	.932
1995— Peoria (Midw.)		2B-SS	103	361	43	96	7	4	2	41	18	30	2	8	7-6	.266	.303	.324	.627	21	.950
1996— St. Pete. (FSL)		2B	137	540	65	157	29	5	0	51	24	34	5	31	4-4	.291	.323	.363	.686	4	.993
1997— Arkansas (Texas)		2B	129	508	71	148	16	3	2	51	29	51	3	11	19-5	.291	.331	.346	.678	14	.979
1998— Memphis (PCL)		2B-SS	70	246	36	69	19	1	1	21	16	15	3	8	6-3	.280	.331	.378	.709	5	.984
— St. Louis (N.L.)		SS-2B	45	114	10	29	3	2	1	11	5	9	1	1	2-0	.254	.292	.342	.634	7	.961
1999— St. Louis (N.L.)		2B-3B-SS	88	220	24	61	9	3	1	19	15	24	0	7	1-3	.277	.321	.359	.680	8	.972
— Memphis (PCL)		2B-SS-3B	29	120	18	33	4	1	0	10	3	11	1	7	2-0	.275	.296	.325	.621	2	.985
2000— St. Louis (N.L.)		2B-3B-SS																			
		1B	118	323	50	102	12	3	5	39	16	26	1	8	4-4	.316	.347	.418	.765	3	.991
2001— St. Louis (N.L.)		3B-SS-2B																			
		DH	144	564	87	173	26	4	3	38	25	43	6	22	12-3	.307	.342	.383	.725	4	.992
2002— St. Louis (N.L.)		3B	53	206	28	61	13	1	4	22	14	14	4	3	2-2	.296	.353	.427	.780	3	.983
— Philadelphia (N.L.)		2B-3B	122	492	87	142	30	3	14	63	42	38	8	16	14-2	.289	.352	.447	.799	6	.989
2003— Philadelphia (N.L.)		2B-3B																			
2004— Reading (East.)		2B	1	3	0	2	0	0	0	0	0	0	0	0	0-0	.667	.667	.667	1.333	0	1.000
— Scran./W.B. (I.L.)		2B	1	3	1	0	0	0	0	0	0	1	0	0	0-0	.000	.250	.000	.250	0	1.000
— Philadelphia (N.L.)		2B-3B	126	503	74	150	21	0	17	55	27	39	12	13	7-4	.298	.345	.441	.786	3	.995
2005— Philadelphia (N.L.)		2B-3B-OF																			
		SS	43	158	26	50	7	0	3	20	12	9	3	3	0-0	.316	.376	.418	.793	1	1.000
— Detroit (A.L.)		2B-3B	86	343	58	116	20	2	6	36	21	16	8	9	4-3	.338	.386	.461	.846	3	.993
2006— Detroit (A.L.)		2B	110	461	58	136	18	1	4	52	17	27	7	18	1-2	.295	.329	.364	.693	6	.989
American League totals (2 years)			196	804	116	252	38	3	10	88	38	43	15	27	5-5	.313	.353	.405	.759	9	.991
National League totals (8 years)			833	2922	433	865	140	17	53	294	168	229	39	85	45-19	.296	.341	.410	.751	40	.987
Major League totals (9 years)			1029	3726	549	1117	178	20	63	382	206	272	54	112	50-24	.300	.344	.409	.753	49	.988

Year	Team (League)	Pos.	G	AB	R	H	2B	3B	HR	RBI	BB	SO	HBP	GDP	SB-CS	Avg.	OBP	SLG	OPS	E	Avg.
	DIVISION SERIES RECORD																				
2000— St. Louis (N.L.)		3B	3	10	1	3	0	0	0	3	1	0	0	0	1-0	.300	.364	.300	.664	0	1.000
2001— St. Louis (N.L.)		3B	5	15	1	4	0	0	0	1	1	1	0	1	1-0	.267	.294	.267	.561	1	.941
2006— Detroit (A.L.)		2B	4	17	3	7	1	0	0	2	1	2	0	2	0-1	.412	.444	.471	.915	0	1.000
Division series totals (3 years)			12	42	5	14	1	0	0	6	3	3	0	3	2-1	.333	.370	.357	.727	1	.977

Year	Team (League)	Pos.	G	AB	R	H	2B	3B	HR	RBI	BB	SO	HBP	GDP	SB-CS	Avg.	OBP	SLG	OPS	E	Avg.
	CHAMPIONSHIP SERIES RECORD																				
2000— St. Louis (N.L.)		3B	4	5	0	1	0	0	0	0	2	1	0	0	0-0	.200	.429	.200	.629	0	1.000
2006— Detroit (A.L.)		2B	4	17	2	9	1	0	2	2	2	1	0	0	0-0	.529	.579	.588	1.167	0	1.000
Champ. series totals (2 years)			8	22	2	10	1	0	2	2	4	2	0	0	0-0	.455	.538	.500	1.038	0	1.000

Year	Team (League)	Pos.	G	AB	R	H	2B	3B	HR	RBI	BB	SO	HBP	GDP	SB-CS	Avg.	OBP	SLG	OPS	E	Avg.
	WORLD SERIES RECORD																				
2006— Detroit (A.L.)		2B	5	17	0	0	0	0	0	0	1	1	1	0	0-0	.000	.105	.000	.105	0	1.000

2006 LEFTY-RIGHTY SPLITS

vs.	Avg.	AB	H	2B	3B	HR	RBI	BB	SO	OBP	Slg.	vs.	Avg.	AB	H	2B	3B	HR	RBI	BB	SO	OBP	Slg.
L	.272	136	37	8	1	2	20	8	12	.313	.390	R	.305	325	99	10	0	2	32	9	15	.335	.354

POLITTE, CLIFF — P

PERSONAL: Born February 27, 1974, in St. Louis. ... 5-11/200. ... Throws right, bats right. ... Full name: Cliff Anthony Politte. ... Name pronounced: po-LEET. ... High school: Vianney (Kirkwood, Mo.). ... Junior college: Jefferson (Hillsboro, Mo.). **TRANSACTIONS/CAREER NOTES:** Selected by St. Louis Cardinals organization in 54th round of 1995 free-agent draft. ... Traded by Cardinals with OF Ron Gant and P Jeff Brantley to Philadelphia Phillies for Ps Ricky Bottalico and Garrett Stephenson (November 19, 1998). ... On disabled list (March 31-July 6, 2001); included rehabilitation assignment to Clearwater. ... Traded by Phillies to Toronto Blue Jays for P Dan Plesac (May 26, 2002). ... On disabled list (June 29-July 25, 2003); included rehabilitation assignment to Syracuse. ... Signed as a free agent by Chicago White Sox (January 7, 2004). ... On disabled list (June 7-29, 2006); included rehabilitation assignment to Charlotte SC. ... Released by White Sox (July 20, 2006).
CAREER HITTING: 4-for-33 (.121), 3 R, 1 2B, 0 3B, 0 HR, 3 RBI.

Year	Team (League)	W	L	Pct.	ERA	WHIP	G	GS	CG	ShO	Hld.	Sv.-Opp.	IP	H	R	ER	HR	BB-IBB	SO	Avg.
1996— Peoria (Midw.)		14	6	.700	2.59	1.04	25	25	0	...	...	0-...	149.2	108	50	43	8	47-0	151	.199
1997— Prince Will. (Car.)		11	1	.917	2.24	1.00	19	19	0	0	...	0-...	120.1	89	37	30	11	31-0	118	.203
— Arkansas (Texas)		4	1	.800	2.15	1.17	6	6	0	0	...	0-...	37.2	35	15	9	3	9-1	26	.257
1998— St. Louis (N.L.)		2	3	.400	6.32	1.70	8	8	0	0	0	0-0	37.0	45	32	26	6	18-0	22	.304
— Memphis (PCL)		1	4	.200	7.64	1.88	10	10	0	0	...	0-...	50.2	71	46	43	10	24-0	42	.332
— Arkansas (Texas)		5	3	.625	2.96	1.07	10	10	1	1	...	0-...	67.0	56	25	22	6	16-0	61	.230
1999— Reading (East.)		9	8	.529	3.63	1.33	37	13	1	0	...	5-...	109.0	112	45	44	12	33-3	97	.270

P

Year Team (League)	W	L	Pct.	ERA	WHIP	G	GS	CG	ShO	Hld.	Sv.-Opp.	IP	H	R	ER	HR	BB-IBB	SO	Avg.
—Philadelphia (N.L.)	1	0	1.000	7.13	1.92	13	0	0	0	1	0-0	17.2	19	14	14	2	15-0	15	.275
2000—Scran./W.B. (I.L.)	8	4	.667	3.12	1.20	21	20	1	0		0-...	112.2	94	45	39	8	41-2	106	.224
—Philadelphia (N.L.)	4	3	.571	3.66	1.39	12	8	0	0	0	0-0	59.0	55	24	24	8	27-1	50	.248
2001—Clearwater (FSL)	0	1	.000	2.45	1.00	7	7	0	0		0-...	11.0	8	4	3	0	3-0	15	.200
—Philadelphia (N.L.)	2	3	.400	2.42	1.23	23	0	0	0	1	0-0	26.0	24	8	7	2	8-3	23	.250
2002—Philadelphia (N.L.)	2	0	1.000	3.86	1.71	13	0	0	0	0	0-1	16.1	19	10	7	0	9-1	15	.301
—Toronto (A.L.)	1	3	.250	3.61	0.99	55	0	0	0	25	1-3	57.1	38	23	23	5	19-1	57	.186
2003—Syracuse (Int'l)	0	0	...	0.00	0.00	1	0	0	0		0-...	1.0	0	0	0	0	0-0	1	.000
—Toronto (A.L.)	1	5	.167	5.66	1.40	54	0	0	0	8	12-18	49.1	52	32	31	11	17-4	40	.269
2004—Chicago (A.L.)	0	3	.000	4.38	1.44	54	0	0	0	19	1-1	51.1	52	26	25	6	22-5	48	.261
2005—Chicago (A.L.)	7	1	.875	2.00	0.94	68	0	0	0	23	1-2	67.1	42	15	15	7	21-4	57	.181
2006—Charlotte (Int'l)	0	0	...	1.93	1.29	3	2	0	0	0	0-0	4.2	5	1	1	0	1-0	5	.263
—Chicago (A.L.)	2	2	.500	8.70	2.07	30	0	0	0	4	0-2	30.0	47	30	29	9	15-7	15	.353
American League totals (5 years)	11	14	.440	4.34	1.27	261	0	0	0	79	15-26	255.1	231	126	123	38	94-21	217	.240
National League totals (5 years)	11	9	.550	4.50	1.53	69	16	0	0	2	0-1	156.0	162	88	78	18	77-5	125	.270
Major League totals (9 years)	22	23	.489	4.40	1.37	330	16	0	0	81	15-27	411.1	393	214	201	56	171-26	342	.252

DIVISION SERIES RECORD

Year Team (League)	W	L	Pct.	ERA	WHIP	G	GS	CG	ShO	Hld.	Sv.-Opp.	IP	H	R	ER	HR	BB-IBB	SO	Avg.
2005—Chicago (A.L.)	0	0	...	0.00	1.00	1	0	0	0		0-0	1.0	1	0	0	0	0-0	1	.250

WORLD SERIES RECORD

Year Team (League)	W	L	Pct.	ERA	WHIP	G	GS	CG	ShO	Hld.	Sv.-Opp.	IP	H	R	ER	HR	BB-IBB	SO	Avg.
2005—Chicago (A.L.)	0	0	...	3.86	0.86	3	0	0	0	3	0-0	2.1	1	1	1	0	2-1	2	.000

2006 LEFTY-RIGHTY SPLITS

vs.	Avg.	AB	H	2B	3B	HR	RBI	BB	SO	OBP	Slg.	vs.	Avg.	AB	H	2B	3B	HR	RBI	BB	SO	OBP	Slg.
L	.385	39	15	4	0	4	9	9	2	.500	.795	R	.340	94	32	9	0	5	20	6	13	.379	.596

PONSON, SIDNEY — P

PERSONAL: Born November 2, 1976, in Noord, Aruba. ... 6-1/255. ... Throws right, bats right. ... Full name: Sidney Alton Ponson. ... Name pronounced: pon-SONE. ... High school: Maria College (Aruba). ... College: Maria College (Aruba). **TRANSACTIONS/CAREER NOTES:** Signed as a non-drafted free agent by Baltimore Orioles organization (August 17, 1993). ... On disabled list (April 16-May 9, 2001); included rehabilitation assignment to Bowie. ... On disabled list (August 7-September 1, 2002). ... Traded by Orioles to San Francisco Giants for Ps Kurt Ainsworth, Damian Moss and Ryan Hannaman (July 31, 2003). ... Signed as a free agent by Orioles (January 26, 2004). ... On disabled list (August 9-September 1, 2005). ... Released by Orioles (September 1, 2005). ... Signed by St. Louis Cardinals (December 21, 2005). ... On disabled list (May 9-27, 2006). ... Released by Cardinals (July 11, 2006). ... Signed by New York Yankees (July 14, 2006). ... Released by Yankees (August 21, 2006).

CAREER HITTING: 9-for-63 (.143), 4 R, 3 2B, 0 3B, 0 HR, 1 RBI.

Year Team (League)	W	L	Pct.	ERA	WHIP	G	GS	CG	ShO	Hld.	Sv.-Opp.	IP	H	R	ER	HR	BB-IBB	SO	Avg.
1994—GC Orioles (GCL)	4	3	.571	2.96	1.16	12	10	1	0	...	0-...	73.0	68	30	24	5	17-0	53	.245
1995—Bluefield (Appal.)	6	3	.667	4.17	1.22	13	13	0	0	...	0-...	77.2	79	44	36	7	16-0	56	.262
1996—Frederick (Carolina)	7	6	.538	3.45	1.18	18	16	3	0	...	0-...	107.0	98	56	41	6	28-0	110	.244
1997—Bowie (East.)	2	7	.222	5.42	1.46	13	13	1	1	...	0-...	74.2	77	51	45	11	32-2	56	.269
—GC Orioles (GCL)	1	0	1.000	0.00	0.00	1	1	0	0	...	0-...	2.0	0	0	0	0	0-0	1	.000
1998—Rochester (Int'l)	1	0	1.000	0.00	1.00	1	1	0	0	...	0-...	5.0	4	0	0	0	3-0	3	.211
—Baltimore (A.L.)	8	9	.471	5.27	1.47	31	20	0	0	0	1-2	135.0	157	82	79	19	42-2	85	.293
1999—Baltimore (A.L.)	12	12	.500	4.71	1.46	32	32	6	0	0	0-0	210.0	227	118	110	35	80-2	112	.284
2000—Baltimore (A.L.)	9	13	.409	4.82	1.38	32	32	6	1	0	0-0	222.0	223	125	119	30	83-0	152	.258
2001—Baltimore (A.L.)	5	10	.333	4.94	1.43	23	23	3	1	0	0-0	138.1	161	83	76	21	37-0	84	.289
—Bowie (East.)	0	0	...	0.00	1.00	1	1	0	0	...	0-...	4.0	3	0	0	0	1-0	2	.231
2002—Baltimore (A.L.)	7	9	.438	4.09	1.34	28	28	3	0	0	0-0	176.0	172	84	80	26	63-1	120	.258
2003—Baltimore (A.L.)	14	6	.700	3.77	1.28	21	21	4	0	0	0-0	148.0	147	65	62	10	43-2	100	.258
—San Francisco (N.L.)	3	6	.333	3.71	1.21	10	10	0	0	0	0-0	68.0	64	29	28	6	18-3	34	.255
2004—Baltimore (A.L.)	11	15	.423	5.30	1.55	33	33	*5	*2	0	0-0	215.2	*265	136	*127	23	69-3	115	.305
2005—Baltimore (A.L.)	7	11	.389	6.21	1.73	23	23	1	0	0	0-0	130.1	177	97	90	16	48-1	68	.331
2006—St. Louis (N.L.)	4	4	.500	5.24	1.62	14	13	0	0	0	0-0	68.2	82	42	40	7	29-1	33	.308
—New York (A.L.)	0	1	.000	10.47	2.02	5	3	0	0	0	0-0	16.1	26	20	19	3	7-0	15	.351
American League totals (9 years)	73	86	.459	4.93	1.46	228	215	28	4	0	1-2	1391.2	1555	810	762	183	472-11	851	.284
National League totals (2 years)	7	10	.412	4.48	1.41	24	23	0	0	0	0-0	136.2	146	71	68	13	47-4	67	.282
Major League totals (9 years)	80	96	.455	4.89	1.45	252	238	28	4	0	1-2	1528.1	1701	881	830	196	519-15	918	.284

DIVISION SERIES RECORD

Year Team (League)	W	L	Pct.	ERA	WHIP	G	GS	CG	ShO	Hld.	Sv.-Opp.	IP	H	R	ER	HR	BB-IBB	SO	Avg.
2003—San Francisco (N.L.)	0	0	...	7.20	1.40	1	1	0	0	0	0-0	5.0	7	4	4	0	0-0	3	.318

2006 LEFTY-RIGHTY SPLITS

vs.	Avg.	AB	H	2B	3B	HR	RBI	BB	SO	OBP	Slg.	vs.	Avg.	AB	H	2B	3B	HR	RBI	BB	SO	OBP	Slg.
L	.304	148	45	9	0	6	23	22	20	.398	.486	R	.328	192	63	18	0	4	25	14	28	.383	.484

POSADA, JORGE — C

PERSONAL: Born August 17, 1971, in Santurce, Puerto Rico. ... 6-2/205. ... Bats both, throws right. ... Full name: Jorge Rafael Posada. ... Name pronounced: hor-hay po-sa-da. ... High school: Colegio Alejandrino (Puerto Rico). ... Junior college: Calhoun (Ala.) C.C. **TRANSACTIONS/CAREER NOTES:** Selected by New York Yankees organization in 24th round of 1990 free-agent draft. ... On suspended list (July 17-18, 2000; and September 26-October 2, 2001). **HONORS:** Named catcher on THE SPORTING NEWS A.L. All-Star team (2000-02). ... Named catcher on A.L. Silver Slugger team (2000-03). **STATISTICAL NOTES:** Career major league grand slams: 7.

2006 GAMES PLAYED BY POSITION (MLB): C—134, DH—2, 1B—1.

Year Team (League)	Pos.	G	AB	R	H	2B	3B	HR	RBI	BB	SO	HBP	GDP	SB-CS	Avg.	OBP	SLG	OPS	E	Avg.
1991—Oneonta (NYP)	2B-C	71	217	34	51	5	5	4	33	51	51	4	3	6-4	.235	.388	.359	.748	21	.947
1992—Greensboro (S. Atl.)	3B-C	101	339	60	94	22	4	12	58	58	87	6	8	11-6	.277	.389	.472	.861	11	.965
1993—Prince Will. (Car.)	3B-C	118	410	71	106	27	2	17	61	67	90	6	7	17-5	.259	.366	.459	.825	15	.981
—Albany (East.)	C	7	25	3	7	0	0	0	0	2	7	0	1	0-0	.280	.333	.280	.613	1	.958
1994—Columbus (Int'l)	C-OF	92	313	46	75	13	3	11	48	32	81	1	3	5-5	.240	.308	.406	.713	11	.977
1995—Columbus (Int'l)	C-DH	108	368	60	94	32	5	8	51	54	101	1	14	4-4	.255	.350	.435	.785	4	.993
—New York (A.L.)	C	1	0	0	0	0	0	0	0	0	0	0	0	0-0	...	...	...	...	0	1.000
1996—Columbus (Int'l)	C-DH-OF	106	354	76	96	22	6	11	62	79	86	3	13	3-3	.271	.405	.460	.866	10	.985
—New York (A.L.)	C-DH	8	14	1	1	0	0	0	0	1	6	0	1	0-0	.071	.133	.071	.205	0	1.000
1997—New York (A.L.)	C	60	188	29	47	12	0	6	25	30	33	2	4	1-2	.250	.359	.410	.768	3	.992
1998—New York (A.L.)	C-DH-1B	111	358	56	96	23	0	17	63	47	92	6	14	0-1	.268	.350	.475	.824	4	.994

Year	Team (League)	Pos.	G	AB	R	H	2B	3B	HR	RBI	BB	SO	HBP	GDP	SB-CS	Avg.	OBP	SLG	OPS	E	Avg.
										BATTING										FIELDING	
1999—New York (A.L.)	C-1B-DH	112	379	50	93	19	2	12	57	53	91	3	9	1-0	.245	.341	.401	.742	5	.993	
2000—New York (A.L.)	C-1B-DH	151	505	92	145	35	1	28	86	107	151	8	11	2-2	.287	.417	.527	.943	8	.992	
2001—New York (A.L.)	C-DH-1B	138	484	59	134	28	1	22	95	62	132	6	10	2-6	.277	.363	.475	.838	11	.990	
2002—New York (A.L.)	C-DH	143	511	79	137	40	1	20	99	81	143	3	*23	1-0	.268	.370	.468	.837	12	.988	
2003—New York (A.L.)	C-DH	142	481	83	135	24	0	30	101	93	110	10	13	2-4	.281	.405	.518	.922	6	.994	
2004—New York (A.L.)	C	137	449	72	122	31	0	21	81	88	92	9	•24	1-3	.272	.400	.481	.881	9	.990	
2005—New York (A.L.)	C-DH	142	474	67	124	23	0	19	71	66	94	2	8	1-0	.262	.352	.430	.782	3	.996	
2006—New York (A.L.)	C-DH-1B	143	465	65	129	27	2	23	93	64	97	11	10	3-0	.277	.374	.492	.867	9	.990	
Major League totals (12 years)		1288	4308	653	1163	262	7	198	771	692	1041	55	125	14-18	.270	.375	.472	.847	70	.992	

DIVISION SERIES RECORD

Year	Team (League)	Pos.	G	AB	R	H	2B	3B	HR	RBI	BB	SO	HBP	GDP	SB-CS	Avg.	OBP	SLG	OPS	E	Avg.
1995—New York (A.L.)		1	0	1	0	0	0	0	0	0	0	0	0	0-0	...	...	...	...	0	...
1997—New York (A.L.)	C	2	2	0	0	0	0	0	0	0	1	0	0	0-0	.000	.000	.000	.000	0	1.000
1998—New York (A.L.)	C	2	2	1	0	0	0	0	0	1	2	0	0	0-0	.000	.333	.000	.333	0	1.000
1999—New York (A.L.)	C	1	4	0	1	1	0	0	0	0	0	0	0	0-0	.250	.250	.500	.750	0	1.000
2000—New York (A.L.)	C	5	17	2	4	2	0	0	1	3	5	0	0	0-0	.235	.350	.353	.703	0	1.000
2001—New York (A.L.)	C	5	18	3	8	1	0	1	2	2	2	0	1	1-0	.444	.500	.667	1.167	0	1.000
2002—New York (A.L.)	C	4	17	2	4	0	0	1	3	0	3	0	1	0-0	.235	.222	.412	.634	1	.955
2003—New York (A.L.)	C	4	17	1	3	1	0	0	0	6	0	0	0	0-0	.176	.176	.235	.412	0	1.000
2004—New York (A.L.)	C	4	18	2	4	0	0	0	0	6	0	0	1	0-0	.222	.222	.222	.444	0	1.000
2005—New York (A.L.)	C	5	13	3	3	1	0	1	2	6	2	0	0	0-0	.231	.474	.538	1.012	0	1.000
2006—New York (A.L.)	C	4	14	2	7	1	0	1	2	2	2	0	0	0-0	.500	.563	.786	1.348	0	1.000
Division series totals (11 years)		36	122	17	34	7	0	4	10	14	29	0	3	1-0	.279	.350	.434	.785	1	.996

CHAMPIONSHIP SERIES RECORD

Year	Team (League)	Pos.	G	AB	R	H	2B	3B	HR	RBI	BB	SO	HBP	GDP	SB-CS	Avg.	OBP	SLG	OPS	E	Avg.
1998—New York (A.L.)	C	5	11	1	2	0	0	1	2	4	2	0	1	0-1	.182	.400	.455	.855	0	1.000
1999—New York (A.L.)	C	3	10	1	1	0	0	1	2	1	2	0	0	0-0	.100	.182	.400	.582	1	.955
2000—New York (A.L.)	C	6	19	2	3	1	0	0	3	5	5	1	0	0-1	.158	.360	.211	.571	0	1.000
2001—New York (A.L.)	C	5	14	4	3	1	0	0	0	6	7	0	0	0-0	.214	.450	.286	.736	0	1.000
2003—New York (A.L.)	C	7	27	5	8	4	0	1	6	3	4	0	1	0-0	.296	.367	.556	.922	0	1.000
2004—New York (A.L.)	C	7	27	4	7	1	0	0	2	7	1	1	1	0-0	.259	.417	.296	.713	0	1.000
Champ. series totals (6 years)		33	108	17	24	7	0	3	15	26	21	2	3	0-2	.222	.380	.370	.750	1	.996

WORLD SERIES RECORD

Year	Team (League)	Pos.	G	AB	R	H	2B	3B	HR	RBI	BB	SO	HBP	GDP	SB-CS	Avg.	OBP	SLG	OPS	E	Avg.
1998—New York (A.L.)	C	3	9	2	3	0	0	1	2	2	2	0	1	0-0	.333	.455	.667	1.121	0	1.000
1999—New York (A.L.)	C	2	8	0	2	1	0	0	1	0	3	0	1	0-0	.250	.250	.375	.625	0	1.000
2000—New York (A.L.)	C	5	18	2	4	0	0	1	1	5	4	0	1	0-0	.222	.391	.278	.669	1	.986
2001—New York (A.L.)	C	7	23	2	4	1	0	1	1	4	8	0	2	0-0	.174	.269	.348	.617	1	1.000
2003—New York (A.L.)	C	6	19	0	3	1	0	0	1	5	7	0	0	1-1	.158	.333	.211	.544	0	1.000
World series totals (5 years)		23	77	6	16	3	0	2	6	15	24	0	5	1-1	.208	.337	.338	.675	1	.995

ALL-STAR GAME RECORD

	G	AB	R	H	2B	3B	HR	RBI	BB	SO	HBP	GDP	SB-CS	Avg.	OBP	SLG	OPS	E	Avg.
All-Star Game totals (4 years)	4	8	0	1	1	0	0	0	0	5	0	0	0-0	.125	.125	.250	.375	0	1.000

2006 LEFTY-RIGHTY SPLITS

vs.	Avg.	AB	H	2B	3B	HR	RBI	BB	SO	OBP	Slg.	vs.	Avg.	AB	H	2B	3B	HR	RBI	BB	SO	OBP	Slg.
L	.263	137	36	5	1	3	15	15	32	.348	.380	R	.284	328	93	22	1	20	78	49	65	.385	.540

PRADO, MARTIN — IF

PERSONAL: Born October 27, 1983, in Maracay, Venezuela. ... 6-1/170. ... Bats right, throws right. ... Full name: Martin M. Prado. **TRANSACTIONS/CAREER NOTES:** Signed as a non-drafted free agent by Atlanta Braves organization (February 13, 2001).
2006 GAMES PLAYED BY POSITION (MLB): 2B—11, 3B—8.

Year	Team (League)	Pos.	G	AB	R	H	2B	3B	HR	RBI	BB	SO	HBP	GDP	SB-CS	Avg.	OBP	SLG	OPS	E	Avg.
										BATTING										FIELDING	
2001—Dominican Braves2 (DSL)		61	187	25	56	4	2	0	21	25	33	4	2	19-6	.299	.388	.342	.730	...	...	
2002—Dominican Braves2 (DSL)		59	222	35	71	18	3	1	26	17	16	3	7	13-5	.320	.373	.441	.814	...	...	
2003—GC Braves (GCL)		59	220	28	63	2	6	0	23	24	30	1	4	9-9	.286	.358	.350	.708	...	...	
2004—Rome (S. Atl.)		107	429	68	135	25	6	3	38	30	47	3	10	14-10	.315	.363	.422	.785	...	...	
2005—Myrtle Beach (Carol.)	2B-DH	75	297	44	91	13	3	4	34	24	48	0	7	9-6	.306	.353	.411	.764	9	.974	
—Mississippi (Sou.)	2B	39	143	17	40	7	1	1	11	17	17	0	5	3-3	.280	.354	.364	.718	2	.989	
2006—Mississippi (Sou.)		43	176	17	49	6	2	1	15	14	35	0	5	2-2	.278	.330	.352	.682	9	.947	
—Richmond (Int'l)		60	241	30	68	12	1	2	23	12	28	0	8	2-2	.282	.314	.365	.679	4	.985	
—Atlanta (N.L.)	2B-3B	24	42	3	11	1	1	1	9	5	7	0	2	0-0	.262	.340	.405	.745	2	.959	
Major League totals (1 year)		24	42	3	11	1	1	1	9	5	7	0	2	0-0	.262	.340	.405	.745	2	.959	

2006 LEFTY-RIGHTY SPLITS

vs.	Avg.	AB	H	2B	3B	HR	RBI	BB	SO	OBP	Slg.	vs.	Avg.	AB	H	2B	3B	HR	RBI	BB	SO	OBP	Slg.
L	.310	29	9	1	0	1	7	4	5	.394	.448	R	.154	13	2	0	1	0	2	1	2	.214	.308

PRATT, TODD — C

PERSONAL: Born February 9, 1967, in Bellevue, Neb. ... 6-3/236. ... Bats right, throws right. ... Full name: Todd Alan Pratt. ... High school: Hilltop (Chula Vista, Calif.). **TRANSACTIONS/CAREER NOTES:** Selected by Boston Red Sox organization in sixth round of June 1985 free-agent draft. ... Selected by Cleveland Indians organization from Red Sox organization in Rule 5 minor league draft (December 7, 1987). ... Returned to Red Sox organization (March 28, 1988). ... Signed as a free agent by Baltimore Orioles organization (November 13, 1991). ... Selected by Philadelphia Phillies from Orioles organization in Rule 5 major league draft (December 9, 1991). ... On disabled list (April 28-May 27, 1993); included rehabilitation assignment to Scranton/Wilkes-Barre. ... Signed as a free agent by Chicago Cubs organization (April 8, 1995). ... Signed as a free agent by Seattle Mariners organization (January 25, 1996). ... Released by Mariners (March 27, 1996). ... Signed by New York Mets organization (December 23, 1996). ... On disabled list (May 7-June 23, 1998); included rehabilitation assignments to St. Lucie, GCL Mets and Norfolk. ... Traded by Mets to Phillies for C Gary Bennett (July 23, 2001). ... On suspended list (May 17-20, 2004). ... Signed as a free agent by Atlanta Braves (December 9, 2005). **STATISTICAL NOTES:** Career major league grand slams: 1.
2006 GAMES PLAYED BY POSITION (MLB): C—54.

Year	Team (League)	Pos.	G	AB	R	H	2B	3B	HR	RBI	BB	SO	HBP	GDP	SB-CS	Avg.	OBP	SLG	OPS	E	Avg.
										BATTING										FIELDING	
1985—Elmira (N.Y.-Penn)	C	39	119	7	16	1	1	0	5	10	27	1	6	0-1	.134	.206	.160	.366	6	.979

P

Year Team (League)	Pos.	G	AB	R	H	2B	3B	HR	RBI	BB	SO	HBP	GDP	SB-CS	Avg.	OBP	SLG	OPS	E	Avg.
1986— Greensboro (S. Atl.)	1B-C	107	348	63	84	16	0	12	56	75	114	5	10	0-1	.241	.380	.391	.770	15	.983
1987— Winter Haven (FSL)	1B-C-OF	118	407	57	105	22	0	12	65	70	94	1	10	0-1	.258	.364	.400	.764	15	.980
1988— New Britain (East.)	1B-C	124	395	41	89	15	2	8	49	41	110	3	7	1-4	.225	.299	.334	.633	15	.975
1989— New Britain (East.)	1B-C	109	338	30	77	17	1	2	35	44	66	7	10	1-2	.228	.325	.302	.627	11	.977
1990— New Britain (East.)	1B-C	70	195	15	45	14	1	2	22	18	56	0	7	0-1	.231	.293	.344	.637	4	.978
1991— Pawtucket (Int'l)	1B-C	68	219	68	64	16	0	11	41	23	42	3	9	0-3	.292	.367	.516	.883	4	.985
1992— Reading (East.)	C	41	132	20	44	6	1	6	26	24	28	0	1	2-0	.333	.436	.530	.966	3	.977
— Scran./W.B. (I.L.)	C-1B	41	125	20	40	9	1	7	28	30	14	0	5	1-0	.320	.446	.576	1.022	4	.977
— Philadelphia (N.L.)	C	16	46	6	13	1	0	2	10	4	12	0	2	0-0	.283	.340	.435	.775	2	.972
1993— Philadelphia (N.L.)	C	33	87	8	25	6	0	5	13	5	19	1	2	0-0	.287	.330	.529	.859	2	.989
— Scran./W.B. (I.L.)	C	3	9	1	2	1	0	0	1	3	1	0	0	0-0	.222	.417	.333	.750	0	1.000
1994— Philadelphia (N.L.)	C	28	102	10	20	6	1	2	9	12	29	0	3	0-1	.196	.281	.333	.614	0	1.000
1995— Chicago (N.L.)	C	25	60	3	8	2	0	0	4	6	21	0	1	0-0	.133	.209	.167	.376	3	.981
— Iowa (Am. Assoc.)	C-1B-DH	23	58	3	19	1	0	0	5	4	17	0	0	0-0	.328	.371	.345	.716	2	.978
1996—	Did not play.																			
1997— Norfolk (Int'l)	C-DH	59	206	42	62	8	3	9	34	26	48	2	8	1-2	.301	.383	.500	.883	4	.988
— New York (N.L.)	C	39	106	12	30	6	0	2	19	13	32	1	0	0-1	.283	.372	.396	.768	2	.990
1998— Norfolk (Int'l)	DH-C-OF-1B	35	118	16	42	6	0	7	30	15	19	4	4	2-0	.356	.442	.585	1.027	2	.984
— New York (N.L.)	C-1B	41	69	9	19	9	1	2	18	2	20	0	0	0-0	.275	.296	.522	.818	2	.976
— St. Lucie (Fla. St.)	1B-C-OF	5	20	2	9	1	0	1	3	1	5	2	0	1-0	.450	.522	.650	1.172	0	1.000
— GC Mets (GCL)	C-OF	2	4	1	1	0	0	0	0	4	1	0	0	0-0	.250	.625	.250	.875	0	1.000
1999— New York (N.L.)	C-1B-OF	71	140	18	41	4	0	3	21	15	32	3	1	2-0	.293	.369	.386	.754	1	.996
2000— New York (N.L.)	C-DH	80	160	33	44	6	0	8	25	22	31	5	5	0-0	.275	.378	.463	.840	1	.997
2001— New York (N.L.)	C	45	80	6	13	5	0	2	4	15	36	2	4	1-0	.163	.306	.300	.606	1	.994
— Philadelphia (N.L.)	C-1B	35	93	12	19	3	0	2	7	19	25	1	2	0-0	.204	.345	.301	.646	3	.998
2002— Philadelphia (N.L.)	C-1B	39	106	14	33	11	0	3	16	24	28	4	3	2-0	.311	.449	.500	.949	0	1.000
2003— Philadelphia (N.L.)	C-1B	43	125	16	34	10	1	4	20	22	38	6	3	0-0	.272	.400	.464	.864	1	.997
2004— Philadelphia (N.L.)	C	45	128	16	33	5	0	3	16	18	38	1	5	0-0	.258	.351	.367	.719	0	1.000
2005— Philadelphia (N.L.)	C	60	175	17	44	7	0	7	23	19	50	2	3	0-0	.251	.332	.394	.726	1	.997
2006— Atlanta (N.L.)	C	62	135	14	28	6	0	4	19	12	43	1	4	1-0	.207	.272	.341	.612	4	.986
Major League totals (14 years)		662	1612	194	404	84	3	49	224	208	454	28	39	6-2	.251	.344	.398	.741	23	.993

DIVISION SERIES RECORD

Year Team (League)	Pos.	G	AB	R	H	2B	3B	HR	RBI	BB	SO	HBP	GDP	SB-CS	Avg.	OBP	SLG	OPS	E	Avg.
1999— New York (N.L.)	C	3	8	2	1	0	0	1	1	2	1	0	0	0-0	.125	.300	.500	.800	0	1.000
2000— New York (N.L.)	C	1	1	0	0	0	0	0	0	0	0	0	0	0-0	.000	.000	.000	.000	0	1.000
Division series totals (2 years)		4	9	2	1	0	0	1	1	2	1	0	0	0-0	.111	.273	.444	.717	0	1.000

CHAMPIONSHIP SERIES RECORD

Year Team (League)	Pos.	G	AB	R	H	2B	3B	HR	RBI	BB	SO	HBP	GDP	SB-CS	Avg.	OBP	SLG	OPS	E	Avg.
1993— Philadelphia (N.L.)	C	1	1	0	0	0	0	0	0	0	1	0	0	0-0	.000	.000	.000	.000	0	1.000
1999— New York (N.L.)	C	4	2	0	1	0	0	0	3	1	1	0	0	0-0	.500	.500	.500	1.000	0	1.000
Champ. series totals (2 years)		5	3	0	1	0	0	0	3	1	2	0	0	0-0	.333	.400	.333	.733	0	1.000

WORLD SERIES RECORD

Year Team (League)	Pos.	G	AB	R	H	2B	3B	HR	RBI	BB	SO	HBP	GDP	SB-CS	Avg.	OBP	SLG	OPS	E	Avg.
1993— Philadelphia (N.L.)		Did not play.																		
2000— New York (N.L.)	C	1	2	0	0	0	0	0	0	1	2	2	0	0-0	.000	.600	.000	.600	0	1.000

2006 LEFTY-RIGHTY SPLITS

vs.	Avg.	AB	H	2B	3B	HR	RBI	BB	SO	OBP	Slg.	vs.	Avg.	AB	H	2B	3B	HR	RBI	BB	SO	OBP	Slg.
L	.176	68	12	5	0	4	12	8	25	.260	.426	R	.239	67	16	1	0	0	7	4	18	.284	.254

PRIDE, CURTIS — OF

PERSONAL: Born December 17, 1968, in Washington, D.C. ... 6-0/210. ... Bats left, throws right. ... Full name: Curtis John Pride. ... High school: John F. Kennedy (Silver Spring, Md.). ... College: William & Mary (Va.). **TRANSACTIONS/CAREER NOTES:** Selected by New York Mets organization in 10th round of June 1986 free-agent draft. ... Signed as a free agent by Montreal Expos organization (December 8, 1992). ... Signed as a free agent by Detroit Tigers (March 31, 1996). ... On disabled list (April 13-May 10, 1996); included rehabilitation assignment to Toledo. ... Signed as a free agent by Boston Red Sox organization (August 30, 1997). ... Signed as a free agent by Atlanta Braves organization (February 6, 1998). ... On suspended list (May 27-28, 1998). ... On disabled list (June 28-July 14, 1998); included rehabilitation assignment to Richmond. ... Released by Braves (December 1, 1998). ... Signed by Kansas City Royals organization (February 24, 1999). ... Released by Royals (March 4, 1999). ... Signed by Mets organization (January 20, 2000). ... Traded by Mets to Red Sox for a player to be named (April 26, 2000); Mets acquired SS Gavin Jackson to complete deal (July 9, 2000). ... Released by Red Sox (July 8, 2000). ... Signed by Los Angeles Dodgers organization (July 18, 2000). ... Signed as a free agent by Expos organization (December 21, 2000). ... On disabled list (June 18-August 21, 2001); included rehabilitation assignments to Jupiter and Ottawa. ... Signed as a free agent by Pittsburgh Pirates organization (March 5, 2002). ... Contract purchased by New York Yankees organization from Nashua of the independent Atlantic League (May 23, 2003). ... Signed as a free agent by Anaheim Angels organization (May 31, 2004). ... Angels franchise renamed Los Angeles Angels of Anaheim prior to 2005 season. ... On disabled list (May 30-June 22, 2005); included rehabilitation assignment to Salt Lake. ... On disabled list (August 16-September 1, 2006); included rehabilitation assignment to Salt Lake. ... Waived by Angels (October 23, 2006).

2006 GAMES PLAYED BY POSITION (MLB): OF—11, DH—4.

Year Team (League)	Pos.	G	AB	R	H	2B	3B	HR	RBI	BB	SO	HBP	GDP	SB-CS	Avg.	OBP	SLG	OPS	E	Avg.
1986— Kingsport (Appalachian)	OF	27	46	5	5	0	0	1	4	6	24	1	0	5-0	.109	.226	.174	.400	0	1.000
1987— Kingsport (Appalachian)	OF	31	104	22	25	4	0	1	9	16	34	1	0	14-5	.240	.347	.308	.655	5	.894
1988— Kingsport (Appalachian)	OF	70	268	59	76	13	1	8	27	50	48	1	2	23-7	.284	.397	.429	.826	5	.961
1989— Pittsfield (NYP)	OF	55	212	35	55	7	3	6	23	25	47	2	1	9-2	.259	.342	.406	.747	4	.964
1990— Columbia (S. Atl.)	OF	53	191	38	51	4	4	6	25	21	45	0	3	11-8	.267	.338	.424	.762	11	.874
1991— St. Lucie (Fla. St.)	OF	116	392	57	102	21	7	9	37	43	94	2	8	24-5	.260	.336	.418	.755	4	.981
1992— Binghamton (East.)	OF	118	388	54	88	15	3	10	42	47	110	4	5	14-11	.227	.316	.358	.674	8	.964
1993— Harrisburg (East.)	OF	50	180	51	64	6	3	15	39	12	36	4	2	21-6	.356	.404	.672	1.076	2	.972
— Ottawa (Int'l)	OF	69	262	55	79	11	4	6	22	34	61	3	3	29-12	.302	.384	.443	.831	2	.986
— Montreal (N.L.)	OF	10	9	3	4	1	1	1	5	0	3	0	0	1-0	.444	.444	1.111	1.556	0	1.000
1994— W.P. Beach (FSL)	OF	3	8	5	6	1	0	1	3	4	2	0	0	2-2	.750	.833	1.250	2.083	0	1.000
— Ottawa (Int'l)	OF-DH	82	300	56	77	16	4	9	32	39	81	2	3	22-6	.257	.345	.427	.772	3	.982
1995— Ottawa (Int'l)	OF-DH	42	154	25	43	8	3	4	24	12	35	2	2	8-4	.279	.339	.448	.787	2	.974
— Montreal (N.L.)	OF	48	63	10	11	1	0	0	2	5	16	0	2	3-2	.175	.235	.190	.426	2	.920
1996— Detroit (A.L.)	OF-DH	95	267	52	80	17	5	10	31	31	63	0	1	11-6	.300	.372	.513	.886	3	.967

Year	Team (League)	Pos.	G	AB	R	H	2B	3B	HR	RBI	BB	SO	HBP	GDP	SB-CS	Avg.	OBP	SLG	OPS	E	Avg.
	—Toledo (Int'l)	DH-OF	9	26	4	6	1	0	1	2	1	...	0	1	4-1	.231	.444	.385	.829	0	1.000
1997	—Detroit (A.L.)	OF-DH	79	162	21	34	4	4	2	19	24	45	1	4	6-4	.210	.314	.321	.635	1	.980
	—Pawtucket (Int'l)	OF	1	3	0	0	0	0	0	0	0	2	0	0	0-0	.000	.000	.000	.000	0	1.000
	—Boston (A.L.)		2	2	1	1	0	0	1	1	0	1	0	0	0-0	.500	.500	2.000	2.500	...	...
1998	—Atlanta (N.L.)	OF-DH	70	107	19	27	6	1	3	9	9	29	3	2	4-0	.252	.325	.411	.736	0	1.000
	—Richmond (Int'l)	OF-DH	21	78	11	19	2	1	2	6	15	17	0	3	8-0	.244	.366	.372	.737	0	1.000
1999	—Nashua (Atl.)	DH	14	32	0	2	0	0	0	0	7	11	...	...	0-0	.063	...	.063	...	...	...
2000	—Norfolk (Atl.)	OF	15	31	9	9	2	2	1	4	11	7	2	2	3-2	.290	.500	.581	1.081	1	.929
	—Pawtucket (Int'l)	OF	48	154	44	47	10	2	9	31	38	31	0	3	12-1	.305	.443	.571	1.014	1	.990
	—Boston (A.L.)	OF-DH	9	20	4	5	1	0	0	0	1	7	0	0	0-0	.250	.286	.300	.586	0	1.000
	—Albuquerque (PCL)	OF	38	133	30	39	7	3	6	17	20	37	0	2	7-5	.293	.383	.526	.909	3	.959
2001	—Ottawa (Int'l)	OF	22	81	14	27	4	1	5	15	12	26	2	2	6-1	.333	.432	.593	1.024	1	.963
	—Montreal (N.L.)	OF-DH	36	76	8	19	3	1	1	9	9	22	2	4	3-2	.250	.345	.355	.700	0	1.000
	—Jupiter (Fla. St.)	OF	6	21	3	4	1	0	0	0	3	3	0	0	1-0	.190	.292	.238	.530	0	1.000
2002	—Nashville (PCL)	OF	110	385	71	114	22	1	10	46	33	75	7	7	22-8	.296	.362	.436	.798	6	.968
2003	—Nashua (Atl.)		16	61	10	21	5	1	5	25	4	12	2	1	5-1	.344	.391	.705	1.096	1	...
	—New York (A.L.)	OF	4	12	1	1	0	0	1	1	0	2	0	1	0-0	.083	.083	.333	.417	0	1.000
	—Columbus (Int'l)	OF-DH	55	225	44	65	11	4	7	34	20	48	4	7	7-7	.289	.357	.467	.824	1	.991
2004	—Nashua (Atl.)		17	65	12	29	9	0	1	12	10	5	0	1	4-0	.446	.513	.631	1.144	1	...
	—Ariz. Angels (Ariz.)	DH	4	14	1	3	1	0	0	3	1	6	0	0	1-0	.214	.250	.286	.536	0	1.000
	—Salt Lake (PCL)	OF-DH	19	65	13	28	8	1	2	10	4	12	1	0	2-0	.431	.465	.677	1.142	0	1.000
	—Anaheim (A.L.)	OF-DH	35	40	5	10	3	0	0	3	0	11	1	1	0-0	.250	.268	.325	.593	0	1.000
2005	—Salt Lake (PCL)	OF-DH	82	280	44	81	17	6	9	56	49	65	1	6	10-5	.289	.397	.489	.886	4	.978
	—Los Angeles (A.L.)	OF-DH	11	11	2	1	1	0	0	0	0	4	0	0	0-0	.091	.091	.182	.273	0	1.000
2006	—Salt Lake (PCL)	OF-DH	87	273	54	85	18	0	8	44	54	75	1	10	21-6	.311	.424	.465	.889	3	.975
	—Los Angeles (A.L.)	OF-DH	22	27	6	6	2	0	1	2	2	6	8	0	1-0	.222	.364	.407	.771	0	1.000
	American League totals (7 years)		257	541	92	138	28	9	15	57	62	141	2	9	18-10	.255	.333	.423	.757	4	.980
	National League totals (4 years)		164	255	40	61	11	3	5	25	23	70	5	8	11-4	.239	.313	.365	.678	2	.980
	Major League totals (11 years)		421	796	132	199	39	12	20	82	85	211	7	17	29-14	.250	.327	.405	.731	6	.980

DIVISION SERIES RECORD

Year	Team (League)	Pos.	G	AB	R	H	2B	3B	HR	RBI	BB	SO	HBP	GDP	SB-CS	Avg.	OBP	SLG	OPS	E	Avg.
2004	—Anaheim (A.L.)		2	2	0	0	0	0	0	0	0	1	0	0	0-0	.000	.000	.000	.000	0	...

2006 LEFTY-RIGHTY SPLITS

vs.	Avg.	AB	H	2B	3B	HR	RBI	BB	SO	OBP	Slg.	vs.	Avg.	AB	H	2B	3B	HR	RBI	BB	SO	OBP	Slg.
L	.000	2	0	0	0	0	0	0	1	.000	.000	R	.240	25	6	2	0	1	2	6	7	.387	.440

PRIOR, MARK — P

PERSONAL: Born September 7, 1980, in San Diego. ... 6-5/230. ... Throws right, bats right. ... Full name: Mark William Prior. ... High school: University of San Diego High (Calif.). ... College: Southern California. TRANSACTIONS/CAREER NOTES: Selected by New York Yankees organization in supplemental round ("sandwich" pick between first and second rounds, 43rd pick overall) of 1998 free-agent draft; did not sign; pick received as compensation for Yankees' failure to sign 1997 first-round pick of Tyrell Godwin. ... Selected by Chicago Cubs organization in first round (second pick overall) of 2001 free-agent draft. ... On disabled list (September 2-17, 2002; and July 12-August 4, 2003). ... On disabled list (March 26-June 4, 2004); included rehabilitation assignments to Lansing and Iowa. ... On disabled list (March 25-April 12 and May 28-June 26, 2005); included rehabilitation assignment to Iowa. ... On disabled list (March 27-June 18, 2006); included rehabilitation assignments to Peoria, West Tenn and Iowa. ... On disabled list (July 5-21, 2006). ... On disabled list (August 11-September 10, 2006). MISCELLANEOUS NOTES: Struck out in both appearances as pinch hitter (2003).

CAREER HITTING: 41-for-204 (.201), 19 R, 10 2B, 0 3B, 1 HR, 13 RBI.

Year	Team (League)	W	L	Pct.	ERA	WHIP	G	GS	CG	ShO	Hld.	Sv.-Opp.	IP	H	R	ER	HR	BB-IBB	SO	Avg.
2002	—West Tenn (Sou.)	4	1	.800	2.60	1.04	6	6	0	0	...	0-...	34.2	26	16	10	0	10-0	55	.198
	—Iowa (PCL)	1	1	.500	1.65	1.29	3	3	0	0	...	0-...	16.1	13	10	3	1	8-0	24	.203
	—Chicago (N.L.)	6	6	.500	3.32	1.17	19	19	1	0	...	0-0	116.2	98	45	43	14	38-0	147	.226
2003	—Chicago (N.L.)	18	6	.750	2.43	1.10	30	30	3	1	0	0-0	211.1	183	67	57	15	50-4	245	.231
2004	—Lansing (Midw.)	0	0	...	1.23	0.41	2	2	0	0	...	0-...	7.1	2	1	1	0	1-0	13	.087
	—Iowa (PCL)	1	0	1.000	3.38	0.75	1	1	0	0	...	0-...	5.1	3	2	2	2	1-0	11	.158
	—Chicago (N.L.)	6	4	.600	4.02	1.35	21	21	0	0	...	0-0	118.2	112	53	53	12	48-2	139	.251
2005	—Iowa (PCL)	0	1	.000	10.50	1.67	1	1	0	0	...	0-0	6.0	9	7	7	0	1-0	7	.360
	—Chicago (N.L.)	11	7	.611	3.67	1.21	27	27	1	0	...	0-0	166.2	143	73	68	25	59-2	188	.227
2006	—Peoria (Midw.)	0	2	.000	3.86	1.00	2	2	0	0	...	0-0	7.0	7	4	3	1	0-0	8	.241
	—West Tenn (Sou.)	1	0	1.000	5.40	1.20	1	1	0	0	...	0-0	5.0	4	3	3	1	2-0	4	.211
	—Iowa (PCL)	0	0	...	0.00	0.75	1	1	0	0	...	0-0	6.2	4	1	0	0	1-0	10	.174
	—Chicago (N.L.)	1	6	.143	7.21	1.69	9	9	0	0	0	0-0	43.2	46	39	35	9	28-2	38	.269
	Major League totals (5 years)	42	29	.592	3.51	1.23	106	106	5	1	0	0-0	657.0	582	277	256	77	223-10	757	.235

DIVISION SERIES RECORD

Year	Team (League)	W	L	Pct.	ERA	WHIP	G	GS	CG	ShO	Hld.	Sv.-Opp.	IP	H	R	ER	HR	BB-IBB	SO	Avg.
2003	—Chicago (N.L.)	1	0	1.000	1.00	0.67	1	1	0	0	...	0-0	9.0	7	1	1	0	4-0	7	.071

CHAMPIONSHIP SERIES RECORD

Year	Team (League)	W	L	Pct.	ERA	WHIP	G	GS	CG	ShO	Hld.	Sv.-Opp.	IP	H	R	ER	HR	BB-IBB	SO	Avg.
2003	—Chicago (N.L.)	1	1	.500	3.14	1.33	2	2	0	0	...	0-0	14.1	14	8	5	2	5-0	11	.241

2006 LEFTY-RIGHTY SPLITS

vs.	Avg.	AB	H	2B	3B	HR	RBI	BB	SO	OBP	Slg.	vs.	Avg.	AB	H	2B	3B	HR	RBI	BB	SO	OBP	Slg.
L	.321	78	25	4	0	6	21	12	16	.419	.603	R	.226	93	21	4	0	3	15	16	22	.371	.366

PROCTOR, SCOTT — P

PERSONAL: Born January 2, 1977, in Stuart, Fla. ... 6-1/198. ... Throws right, bats right. ... Full name: Scott Christopher Proctor. ... High school: Martin County (Stuart, Fla.). ... College: Florida State. TRANSACTIONS/CAREER NOTES: Selected by New York Mets organization in 17th round of 1995 free-agent draft; did not sign. ... Selected by Los Angeles Dodgers organization in fifth round of 1998 free-agent draft. ... Traded by Dodgers with OF Bubba Crosby to New York Yankees for IF Robin Ventura (July 31, 2003).

CAREER HITTING: 0-for-0 (.000), 0 R, 0 2B, 0 3B, 0 HR, 0 RBI.

Year	Team (League)	W	L	Pct.	ERA	WHIP	G	GS	CG	ShO	Hld.	Sv.-Opp.	IP	H	R	ER	HR	BB-IBB	SO	Avg.
1998	—Yakima (N'west)	0	1	.000	10.80	2.00	3	1	0	0	...	2-...	5.0	9	8	6	1	1-0	4	.391
1999	—Yakima (N'west)	4	2	.667	7.20	1.66	16	6	0	0	...	0-...	50.0	57	45	40	4	26-0	41	.286
2000	—Vero Beach (FSL)	3	7	.300	5.16	1.65	35	5	0	0	...	1-...	89.0	93	65	51	13	54-1	70	.268
2001	—Vero Beach (FSL)	6	4	.600	2.48	1.14	15	15	0	0	...	0-...	90.2	73	30	25	8	30-1	79	.226
	—Jacksonville (Sou.)	4	3	.571	4.17	1.41	10	9	0	0	...	0-...	49.2	39	26	23	6	31-1	48	.220

P

Year Team (League)	W	L	Pct.	ERA	WHIP	G	GS	CG	ShO	Hld.	Sv.-Opp.	IP	H	R	ER	HR	BB-IBB	SO	Avg.
2002—Jacksonville (Sou.)	7	9	.438	3.51	1.47	26	25	0	0	...	0-...	133.1	111	63	52	10	85-1	131	.227
2003—Jacksonville (Sou.)	1	2	.333	1.00	1.00	17	0	0	0	...	0-...	27.0	20	6	3	0	7-3	24	.208
—Las Vegas (PCL)	4	2	.667	3.66	1.22	24	0	0	0	...	1-...	39.1	35	17	16	2	13-13	35	.246
—Columbus (Int'l)	2	0	1.000	1.42	0.84	10	0	0	0	...	0-...	19.0	13	3	3	2	3-0	26	.197
2004—Columbus (Int'l)	2	3	.400	2.86	1.25	35	0	0	0	...	4-...	44.0	37	15	14	4	18-2	42	.233
—New York (A.L.)	2	1	.667	5.40	1.72	26	0	0	0	2	0-0	25.0	29	18	15	5	14-0	21	.284
2005—Columbus (Int'l)	6	1	.857	4.22	1.36	35	1	0	0		14-19	42.2	47	20	20	8	11-0	54	.280
—New York (A.L.)	1	0	1.000	6.04	1.41	29	0	0	0	0	0-0	44.2	46	32	30	10	17-4	36	.257
2006—New York (A.L.)	6	4	.600	3.52	1.19	*83	0	0	0	26	1-8	102.1	89	41	40	12	33-6	89	.232
Major League totals (3 years)	9	5	.643	4.45	1.33	138	1	0	0	28	1-8	172.0	164	91	85	27	64-10	146	.247

DIVISION SERIES RECORD

Year Team (League)	W	L	Pct.	ERA	WHIP	G	GS	CG	ShO	Hld.	Sv.-Opp.	IP	H	R	ER	HR	BB-IBB	SO	Avg.
2005—New York (A.L.)	0	0	...	0.00	1.50	2	0	0	0	...	0-0	2.0	3	0	0	0	0-0	1	.375
2006—New York (A.L.)	0	0	...	2.25	1.50	3	0	0	0	1	0-0	4.0	5	1	1	0	1-0	1	.294
Division series totals (2 years)	0	0	...	1.50	1.50	5	0	0	0	1	0-0	6.0	8	1	1	0	1-0	2	.320

2006 LEFTY-RIGHTY SPLITS

vs.	Avg.	AB	H	2B	3B	HR	RBI	BB	SO	OBP	Slg.	vs.	Avg.	AB	H	2B	3B	HR	RBI	BB	SO	OBP	Slg.
L	.204	147	30	5	1	5	18	13	37	.269	.354	R	.250	236	59	12	0	7	36	20	52	.307	.390

PUJOLS, ALBERT — 1B

PERSONAL: Born January 16, 1980, in Santo Domingo, Dominican Republic. ... 6-3/225. ... Bats right, throws right. ... Full name: Jose Albert Pujols. ... Name pronounced: POO-holes. ... High school: Fort Osage (Independence, Mo.). ... Junior college: Maple Woods (Mo.) C.C. **TRANSACTIONS/CAREER NOTES:** Selected by St. Louis Cardinals organization in 13th round of 1999 free-agent draft. ... On suspended list (August 19-21, 2003). ... On disabled list (June 4-22, 2006). **HONORS:** Named N.L. Rookie Player of the Year by THE SPORTING NEWS (2001). ... Named Major League Player of the Year by the SPORTING NEWS (2003). ... Named outfielder on THE SPORTING NEWS N.L. All-Star team (2003). ... Named first baseman on THE SPORTING NEWS N.L. All-Star team (2004 and 2005). ... Named N.L. Rookie of the Year by Baseball Writers' Association of America (2001). ... Named N.L. Most Valuable Player by Baseball Writers' Association of America (2005). ... Named third baseman on N.L. Silver Slugger team (2001). ... Named outfielder on N.L. Silver Slugger team (2003). ... Named first baseman on N.L. Silver Slugger team (2004 and 2005). ... Won N.L. Gold Glove at first base (2006). **STATISTICAL NOTES:** Hit three home runs in one game (July 20, 2004; and April 16 and September 3, 2006). ... Career major league grand slams: 5.

2006 GAMES PLAYED BY POSITION (MLB): 1B—143.

										BATTING									FIELDING	
Year Team (League)	Pos.	G	AB	R	H	2B	3B	HR	RBI	BB	SO	HBP	GDP	SB-CS	Avg.	OBP	SLG	OPS	E	Avg.
2000—Peoria (Midw.)	3B	109	395	62	128	32	6	17	84	38	37	5	10	2-4	.324	.389	.565	.953	19	.948
—Potomac (Carol.)	3B	21	81	11	23	8	1	2	10	7	8	0	3	1-1	.284	.341	.481	.822	3	.957
—Memphis (PCL)	3B-OF	3	14	1	3	1	0	0	2	1	2	0	0	1-0	.214	.267	.286	.552	0	1.000
2001—St. Louis (N.L.)	OF-3B-1B-DH	161	590	112	194	47	4	37	130	69	93	9	21	1-3	.329	.403	.610	1.013	20	.967
2002—St. Louis (N.L.)	OF-3B-1B-DH-SS	157	590	118	185	40	2	34	127	72	69	9	20	2-4	.314	.394	.561	.955	11	.975
2003—St. Louis (N.L.)	OF-1B-DH	157	591	*137	*212	*51	1	43	124	79	65	10	13	5-1	.359	.439	.667	1.106	4	.993
2004—St. Louis (N.L.)	1B-DH	154	592	*133	196	51	2	46	123	84	52	7	21	5-5	.331	.415	.657	1.072	10	.994
2005—St. Louis (N.L.)	1B	161	591	*129	195	38	2	41	117	97	65	9	14	16-2	.330	.430	.609	1.039	14	.992
2006—St. Louis (N.L.)	1B	143	535	119	177	33	1	49	137	92	50	4	20	7-2	.331	*.431	*.671*	1.102	6	.996
Major League totals (6 years)		933	3489	748	1159	260	12	250	758	493	394	48	114	36-17	.332	.419	.629	1.047	65	.990

DIVISION SERIES RECORD

Year Team (League)	Pos.	G	AB	R	H	2B	3B	HR	RBI	BB	SO	HBP	GDP	SB-CS	Avg.	OBP	SLG	OPS	E	Avg.
2001—St. Louis (N.L.)	1B-OF	5	18	1	2	0	0	1	2	2	2	0	1	0-0	.111	.200	.278	.478	1	.964
2002—St. Louis (N.L.)	OF-1B-3B	3	10	3	3	0	1	0	3	3	1	0	0	0-0	.300	.462	.500	.962	1	.833
2004—St. Louis (N.L.)	1B	4	15	4	5	0	0	2	5	3	0	0	1	0-0	.333	.444	.733	1.178	0	1.000
2005—St. Louis (N.L.)	1B	3	9	4	5	2	0	0	2	4	0	0	1	0-0	.556	.692	.778	1.470	0	1.000
2006—St. Louis (N.L.)	1B	4	15	3	5	1	0	1	3	1	4	0	2	0-0	.333	.375	.600	.975	0	1.000
Division series totals (5 years)		19	67	15	20	3	1	4	15	13	7	0	5	0-0	.299	.413	.552	.965	2	.986

CHAMPIONSHIP SERIES RECORD

Year Team (League)	Pos.	G	AB	R	H	2B	3B	HR	RBI	BB	SO	HBP	GDP	SB-CS	Avg.	OBP	SLG	OPS	E	Avg.
2002—St. Louis (N.L.)	OF	5	19	2	5	1	0	1	2	2	5	1	0	0-0	.263	.364	.474	.837	0	1.000
2004—St. Louis (N.L.)	1B	7	28	10	14	2	0	4	9	4	3	0	0	0-0	.500	.563	1.000	1.563	0	1.000
2005—St. Louis (N.L.)	1B	6	23	3	7	0	0	2	6	1	3	0	0	0-0	.304	.320	.565	.885	0	1.000
2006—St. Louis (N.L.)	1B	7	22	5	7	1	0	1	1	7	3	0	0	0-0	.318	.483	.500	.983	0	1.000
Champ. series totals (4 years)		25	92	20	33	4	0	8	18	14	14	1	0	0-0	.359	.444	.663	1.107	0	1.000

WORLD SERIES RECORD

Year Team (League)	Pos.	G	AB	R	H	2B	3B	HR	RBI	BB	SO	HBP	GDP	SB-CS	Avg.	OBP	SLG	OPS	E	Avg.
2004—St. Louis (N.L.)	1B	4	15	1	5	2	0	0	1	3	1	0	0	0-0	.333	.412	.467	.878	0	1.000
2006—St. Louis (N.L.)	1B	5	15	3	3	1	0	1	2	5	3	1	0	0-1	.200	.429	.467	.895	1	.980
World series totals (2 years)		9	30	4	8	3	0	1	2	6	6	2	0	0-1	.267	.421	.467	.888	1	.989

ALL-STAR GAME RECORD

	G	AB	R	H	2B	3B	HR	RBI	BB	SO	HBP	GDP	SB-CS	Avg.	OBP	SLG	OPS	E	Avg.
All-Star Game totals (5 years)	5	11	1	4	2	0	0	3	1	1	0	0	0-0	.364	.417	.545	.962	0	1.000

2006 LEFTY-RIGHTY SPLITS

vs.	Avg.	AB	H	2B	3B	HR	RBI	BB	SO	OBP	Slg.	vs.	Avg.	AB	H	2B	3B	HR	RBI	BB	SO	OBP	Slg.
L	.336	137	46	9	0	10	26	24	10	.435	.620	R	.329	398	131	24	1	39	111	68	40	.429	.688

PUNTO, NICK — IF

PERSONAL: Born November 8, 1977, in San Diego. ... 5-9/176. ... Bats both, throws right. ... Full name: Nicholas Paul Punto. ... Name pronounced: POON-toh. ... High school: Trabuco Hills (Mission Vieh Vijo, Calif.). ... Junior college: Saddleback (Calif.) Community College. **TRANSACTIONS/CAREER NOTES:** Selected by Minnesota Twins organization in 33rd round of 1997 free-agent draft. ... Selected by Philadelphia Phillies organization in 21st round of 1998 free-agent draft. ... Traded by Phillies with RHP Carlos Silva and a player to be named to Minnesota Twins for LHP Eric Milton (December 3, 2003); Twins acquired P Bobby Korecky to complete deal (December 16, 2003). ... On disabled list (May 9-June 30 and July 27, 2004-remainder of season); included rehabilitation assignment to Quad Cities. ... On disabled list (June 3-July 3, 2005); included rehabilitation assignment to Rochester. **STATISTICAL NOTES:** Career major league grand slams: 1.

2006 GAMES PLAYED BY POSITION (MLB): 3B—89, SS—26, 2B—17, OF—3, DH—2.

										BATTING									FIELDING	
Year Team (League)	Pos.	G	AB	R	H	2B	3B	HR	RBI	BB	SO	HBP	GDP	SB-CS	Avg.	OBP	SLG	OPS	E	Avg.
1998—Batavia (NY-Penn)	2B-SS	72	279	51	69	9	4	1	20	42	48	1	4	19-7	.247	.347	.319	.666	27	.924
1999—Clearwater (FSL)	SS	106	400	65	122	18	6	1	48	67	53	3	13	16-6	.305	.404	.388	.792	24	.958
2000—Reading (East.)	SS	121	456	77	116	15	4	5	47	69	71	2	5	33-10	.254	.351	.338	.689	20	.963
2001—Scran./W.B. (I.L.)	SS	123	463	57	106	19	5	1	39	68	114	0	15	33-9	.229	.327	.298	.625	21	.964

Year	Team (League)	Pos.	G	AB	R	H	2B	3B	HR	RBI	BB	SO	HBP	GDP	SB-CS	Avg.	OBP	SLG	OPS	E	Avg.
—Philadelphia (N.L.)	SS	4	5	0	2	0	0	0	0	0	0	0	0	0-0	.400	.400	.400	.800	0	1.000
002—Philadelphia (N.L.)	2B-SS	9	6	0	1	0	0	0	0	0	3	0	0	0-0	.167	.167	.167	.333	1	.750
—Scran./W.B. (I.L.)	SS	115	443	74	120	12	5	1	29	76	84	2	5	42-8	.271	.378	.327	.705	19	.967
003—Scran./W.B. (I.L.)	SS	25	111	19	35	7	1	0	9	7	13	0	0	7-1	.315	.353	.396	.749	4	.969
—Philadelphia (N.L.)	2B-3B-SS	64	92	14	20	2	0	1	4	7	22	0	0	2-1	.217	.273	.272	.544	2	.980
004—Quad Cities (Mid.)	SS-2B-3B	4	16	4	7	1	0	1	6	2	2	0	0	1-0	.438	.500	.688	1.188	0	1.000
—Minnesota (A.L.)	2B-SS-DH																			
	3B-OF	38	91	17	23	0	0	2	12	12	19	0	2	6-0	.253	.340	.319	.658	1	.991
005—Rochester (Int'l)	2B	4	15	2	3	1	0	0	1	2	2	0	0	0-0	.200	.294	.267	.561	2	.900
—Minnesota (A.L.)	2B-SS-3B																			
	DH-2B	112	394	45	94	18	4	4	26	36	86	0	9	13-8	.239	.301	.335	.636	9	.981
006—Minnesota (A.L.)	3B-SS-2B																			
	OF-DH	135	459	73	133	21	7	1	45	47	68	1	8	17-5	.290	.352	.373	.725	13	.966
American League totals (3 years)		285	944	135	250	39	11	7	83	95	173	1	19	36-13	.265	.330	.352	.682	23	.976
National League totals (3 years)		77	103	14	23	2	0	1	4	7	25	0	0	2-1	.223	.273	.272	.545	3	.972
Major League totals (6 years)		362	1047	149	273	41	11	8	87	102	198	1	19	38-14	.261	.324	.344	.668	26	.976

DIVISION SERIES RECORD

Year	Team (League)	Pos.	G	AB	R	H	2B	3B	HR	RBI	BB	SO	HBP	GDP	SB-CS	Avg.	OBP	SLG	OPS	E	Avg.
2006—Minnesota (A.L.)	3B	3	12	0	2	0	0	0	0	0	1	0	0	0-0	.167	.167	.167	.333	0	1.000

2006 LEFTY-RIGHTY SPLITS

vs.	Avg.	AB	H	2B	3B	HR	RBI	BB	SO	OBP	Slg.	vs.	Avg.	AB	H	2B	3B	HR	RBI	BB	SO	OBP	Slg.
L	.331	163	54	6	3	0	12	16	15	.392	.405	R	.267	296	79	15	4	1	33	31	53	.330	.355

PUTZ, J.J.   P

PERSONAL: Born February 22, 1977, in Trenton, Mich. ... 6-5/220. ... Throws right, bats right. ... Full name: Joseph Jason Putz. ... Name pronounced: pootz. ... High school: Trenton (Mich.). ... College: Michigan. **TRANSACTIONS/CAREER NOTES:** Selected by Chicago White Sox organization in third round of 1995 free-agent draft; did not sign. ... Selected by Minnesota Twins organization in 17th round of 1998 free-agent draft; did not sign. ... Selected by Seattle Mariners organization in sixth round of 1999 free-agent draft.

CAREER HITTING: 0-for-0 (.000), 0 R, 0 2B, 0 3B, 0 HR, 0 RBI.

Year	Team (League)	W	L	Pct.	ERA	WHIP	G	GS	CG	ShO	Hld.	Sv.-Opp.	IP	H	R	ER	HR	BB-IBB	SO	Avg.
1999—Everett (N'west)	0	0	...	4.84	1.52	10	0	0	0	...	2-...	22.1	23	13	12	2	11-1	17	.288
2000—Wisconsin (Midw.)	12	6	.667	3.15	1.35	26	25	3	2	...	0-...	142.2	130	71	50	4	63-2	105	.247
2001—San Antonio (Texas)	7	9	.438	3.83	1.38	27	26	0	0	...	0-...	148.0	145	80	63	11	59-2	135	.259
2002—San Antonio (Texas)	3	10	.231	3.64	1.33	15	15	1	1	...	0-...	84.0	84	41	34	7	28-0	60	.264
—Tacoma (PCL)	2	4	.333	3.83	1.33	9	9	0	0	...	0-...	54.0	51	23	23	4	21-0	39	.258
2003—Tacoma (PCL)	0	3	.000	2.51	1.20	41	0	0	0	...	11-...	86.0	69	30	24	4	34-0	60	.225
—Seattle (A.L.)	0	0	...	4.91	1.91	3	0	0	0	0	0-0	3.2	4	2	2	0	3-0	3	.267
2004—Tacoma (PCL)	0	0	...	4.32	1.56	7	0	0	0	...	3-...	8.1	10	5	4	2	3-0	13	.278
—Seattle (A.L.)	0	3	.000	4.71	1.43	54	0	0	0	3	9-13	63.0	66	35	33	10	24-4	47	.274
2005—Seattle (A.L.)	6	5	.545	3.60	1.35	64	0	0	0	21	1-4	60.0	58	27	24	8	23-2	45	.254
2006—Seattle (A.L.)	4	1	.800	2.30	0.92	72	0	0	0	5	36-43	78.1	59	20	20	4	13-1	104	.207
Major League totals (4 years)	10	9	.526	3.47	1.22	193	0	0	0	29	46-60	205.0	187	84	79	22	63-7	199	.243

2006 LEFTY-RIGHTY SPLITS

vs.	Avg.	AB	H	2B	3B	HR	RBI	BB	SO	OBP	Slg.	vs.	Avg.	AB	H	2B	3B	HR	RBI	BB	SO	OBP	Slg.
L	.211	133	28	6	1	3	13	7	45	.254	.338	R	.204	152	31	2	0	1	12	6	59	.238	.237

QUALLS, CHAD   P

PERSONAL: Born August 17, 1978, in Lomita, Calif. ... 6-5/220. ... Throws right, bats right. ... Full name: Chad Michael Qualls. ... High school: Narbonne (Harbor City, Calif.). ... Junior college: Los Angeles Harbor. ... College: Nevada. **TRANSACTIONS/CAREER NOTES:** Selected by Toronto Blue Jays organization in 52nd round of 1997 free-agent draft; did not sign. ... Selected by Houston Astros organization in second round of 2000 free-agent draft.

CAREER HITTING: 0-for-2 (.000), 0 R, 0 2B, 0 3B, 0 HR, 0 RBI.

Year	Team (League)	W	L	Pct.	ERA	WHIP	G	GS	CG	ShO	Hld.	Sv.-Opp.	IP	H	R	ER	HR	BB-IBB	SO	Avg.
2001—Michigan (Midw.)	15	6	.714	3.72	1.11	26	26	3	2	...	0-...	162.0	149	77	67	8	31-0	125	.239
2002—Round Rock (Texas)	6	13	.316	4.36	1.48	29	29	0	0	...	0-...	163.0	174	92	79	9	67-3	142	.273
2003—Round Rock (Texas)	8	11	.421	3.85	1.34	28	28	3	2	...	0-...	175.1	174	85	75	12	61-0	132	.264
2004—New Orleans (PCL)	3	6	.333	5.57	1.54	32	14	0	0	...	1-...	106.2	134	69	66	8	30-3	72	.312
—Houston (N.L.)	4	0	1.000	3.55	1.27	25	0	0	0	9	1-2	33.0	34	13	13	3	8-1	24	.266
2005—Houston (N.L.)	6	4	.600	3.28	1.21	77	0	0	0	22	0-0	79.2	73	33	29	7	23-2	60	.249
2006—Houston (N.L.)	7	3	.700	3.76	1.17	81	0	0	0	23	0-6	88.2	76	38	37	10	28-6	56	.242
Major League totals (3 years)	17	7	.708	3.53	1.20	183	0	0	0	54	1-8	201.1	183	84	79	20	59-9	140	.249

DIVISION SERIES RECORD

Year	Team (League)	W	L	Pct.	ERA	WHIP	G	GS	CG	ShO	Hld.	Sv.-Opp.	IP	H	R	ER	HR	BB-IBB	SO	Avg.
2004—Houston (N.L.)	0	0	...	6.75	1.25	4	0	0	0	1	0-1	4.0	4	3	3	1	1-0	3	.250
2005—Houston (N.L.)	0	0	...	6.00	2.33	2	0	0	0	0	0-0	3.0	5	2	2	0	2-1	1	.455
Division series totals (2 years)	0	0	...	6.43	1.71	6	0	0	0	1	0-1	7.0	9	5	5	1	3-1	4	.333

CHAMPIONSHIP SERIES RECORD

Year	Team (League)	W	L	Pct.	ERA	WHIP	G	GS	CG	ShO	Hld.	Sv.-Opp.	IP	H	R	ER	HR	BB-IBB	SO	Avg.
2004—Houston (N.L.)	0	1	.000	11.25	2.50	2	0	0	0	0	0-0	4.0	8	5	5	0	2-1	4	.444
2005—Houston (N.L.)	1	0	1.000	0.00	0.00	4	0	0	0	1	0-0	4.2	0	0	0	0	0-0	4	.000
Champ. series totals (2 years)	1	1	.500	5.19	1.15	6	0	0	0	1	0-0	8.2	8	5	5	0	2-1	8	.250

WORLD SERIES RECORD

Year	Team (League)	W	L	Pct.	ERA	WHIP	G	GS	CG	ShO	Hld.	Sv.-Opp.	IP	H	R	ER	HR	BB-IBB	SO	Avg.
2005—Houston (N.L.)	0	0	...	1.69	0.94	3	0	0	0	1	0-1	5.1	3	1	1	1	2-1	5	.167

2006 LEFTY-RIGHTY SPLITS

vs.	Avg.	AB	H	2B	3B	HR	RBI	BB	SO	OBP	Slg.	vs.	Avg.	AB	H	2B	3B	HR	RBI	BB	SO	OBP	Slg.
L	.229	131	30	6	0	4	16	10	25	.285	.366	R	.251	183	46	6	1	6	33	18	31	.332	.393

QUENTIN, CARLOS   OF

PERSONAL: Born August 28, 1982, in Bellflower, Calif. ... Bats right, throws right. ... Full name: Carlos J. Quentin. ... College: Stanford. **TRANSACTIONS/CAREER NOTES:** Selected by Arizona Diamondbacks organization in first round (29th pick overall) of 2003 free-agent draft.

2006 GAMES PLAYED BY POSITION (MLB): OF—46.

Year Team (League)	Pos.	G	AB	R	H	2B	3B	HR	RBI	BB	SO	HBP	GDP	SB-CS	Avg.	OBP	SLG	OPS	FIELDING E	Avg.
2004—Lancaster (Calif.)		65	242	64	75	14	1	15	51	25	33	27	10	5-1	.310	.428	.562	.990	...	...
—El Paso (Texas)		60	210	39	75	19	0	6	38	18	23	16	6	0-6	.357	.443	.533	.976	...	...
2005—Tucson (PCL)	OF-DH	136	452	98	136	28	4	21	89	72	71	29	14	9-1	.301	.422	.520	.942	2	.996
2006—Tucson (PCL)		85	318	66	92	30	3	9	52	45	46	31	13	5-0	.289	.424	.487	.912	3	.981
—Arizona (N.L.)	OF	57	166	23	42	13	3	9	32	15	34	8	6	1-0	.253	.342	.530	.872	2	.980
Major League totals (1 year)		57	166	23	42	13	3	9	32	15	34	8	6	1-0	.253	.342	.530	.872	2	.980

2006 LEFTY-RIGHTY SPLITS

vs.	Avg.	AB	H	2B	3B	HR	RBI	BB	SO	OBP	Slg.	vs.	Avg.	AB	H	2B	3B	HR	RBI	BB	SO	OBP	Slg.
L	.171	41	7	2	1	2	10	4	8	.277	.415	R	.280	125	35	11	2	7	22	11	26	.364	.568

QUINLAN, ROBB — 3B/1B

PERSONAL: Born March 17, 1977, in St. Paul, Minn. ... 6-1/200. ... Bats right, throws right. ... Full name: Robb William Quinlan. ... High school: Hill-Murray (Maplewood, Minn.). ... College: Minnesota. ... Brother of Tom Quinlan, infielder with three major league teams (1990, 1992, 1994 and 1996). **TRANSACTIONS/CAREER NOTES:** Selected by California Angels organization in 33rd round of 1995 free-agent draft; did not sign. ... Selected by Anaheim Angels organization in 10th round of 1999 free-agent draft. ... On disabled list (August 16, 2004-remainder of season). ... Angels franchise renamed Los Angeles Angels of Anaheim for 2005 season. ... On disabled list (July 1-August 23, 2005); included rehabilitation assignments to AZL Angels and Salt Lake.

2006 GAMES PLAYED BY POSITION (MLB): 1B—54, 3B—18, OF—16, DH—2.

Year Team (League)	Pos.	G	AB	R	H	2B	3B	HR	RBI	BB	SO	HBP	GDP	SB-CS	Avg.	OBP	SLG	OPS	FIELDING E	Avg.
1999—Boise (N'west)	3B-2B-1B	73	295	51	95	20	1	9	77	35	52	4	5	5-3	.322	.400	.488	.888	27	.892
2000—Lake Elsinore (Calif.)	1B-OF	127	482	79	153	35	5	5	85	67	82	2	7	6-4	.317	.396	.442	.838	16	.986
2001—Arkansas (Texas)	1B-OF	129	492	82	145	33	7	14	79	53	84	6	12	0-4	.295	.366	.476	.841	8	.993
2002—Salt Lake (PCL)	OF-1B	136	528	95	176	31	13	20	112	41	93	4	16	8-2	.333	.376	.555	.931	3	.988
2003—Salt Lake (PCL)	1B-OF-DH	95	393	55	122	18	4	9	68	25	59	1	9	10-3	.310	.352	.445	.797	1	1.000
—Anaheim (A.L.)	1B-DH-OF	38	94	13	27	4	2	0	4	6	16	0	3	1-2	.287	.330	.372	.702	2	.988
2004—Salt Lake (PCL)	1B-3B-OF	27	108	15	32	9	1	2	17	14	14	0	2	1-1	.296	.377	.454	.831	3	.987
—Anaheim (A.L.)	3B-1B-OF DH	56	160	23	55	14	0	5	23	14	26	2	1	3-1	.344	.401	.525	.926	1	.994
2005—Ariz. Angels (Ariz.)	DH-1B-3B	4	12	3	3	2	0	0	3	2	3	0	0	1-0	.250	.333	.417	.750	0	1.000
—Salt Lake (PCL)	1B-3B-DH	15	60	13	23	6	0	1	4	2	8	0	4	0-0	.383	.403	.533	.937	1	.986
—Los Angeles (A.L.)	3B-1B-OF	54	134	17	31	8	0	5	14	7	26	1	4	0-1	.231	.273	.403	.676	7	.943
2006—Los Angeles (A.L.)	1B-3B-OF DH	86	234	28	75	11	1	9	32	7	28	2	6	2-1	.321	.344	.491	.836	4	.991
Major League totals (4 years)		234	622	81	188	37	3	19	73	34	96	5	14	6-5	.302	.342	.463	.805	14	.984

DIVISION SERIES RECORD

Year Team (League)	Pos.	G	AB	R	H	2B	3B	HR	RBI	BB	SO	HBP	GDP	SB-CS	Avg.	OBP	SLG	OPS	E	Avg.
2005—Los Angeles (A.L.)	3B-DH	2	2	0	1	0	0	0	0	0	0	0	0	0-0	.500	.500	.500	1.000	0	1.000

CHAMPIONSHIP SERIES RECORD

Year Team (League)	Pos.	G	AB	R	H	2B	3B	HR	RBI	BB	SO	HBP	GDP	SB-CS	Avg.	OBP	SLG	OPS	E	Avg.
2005—Los Angeles (A.L.)	3B	1	3	1	1	0	0	1	1	0	2	0	0	0-0	.333	.333	1.333	1.667	0	1.000

2006 LEFTY-RIGHTY SPLITS

vs.	Avg.	AB	H	2B	3B	HR	RBI	BB	SO	OBP	Slg.	vs.	Avg.	AB	H	2B	3B	HR	RBI	BB	SO	OBP	Slg.
L	.326	138	45	8	0	7	19	6	17	.356	.536	R	.313	96	30	3	1	2	13	1	11	.327	.427

QUINTANILLA, OMAR — SS/2B

PERSONAL: Born October 24, 1981, in El Paso, Texas. ... 5-9/190. ... Bats left, throws right. ... Full name: Omar Quintanilla. ... High school: Socorro (El Paso, Texas). ... College: Texas. **TRANSACTIONS/CAREER NOTES:** Selected by Oakland Athletics organization in first round (33rd pick overall) of 2003 free-agent draft. ... Traded by Athletics with OF Eric Byrnes to Colorado Rockies for Ps Joe Kennedy and Jay Witasick (July 13, 2005). ... On disabled list (July 18-August 4, 2006); included rehabilitation assignment to Colorado Springs.

2006 GAMES PLAYED BY POSITION (MLB): SS—8, 2B—3.

Year Team (League)	Pos.	G	AB	R	H	2B	3B	HR	RBI	BB	SO	HBP	GDP	SB-CS	Avg.	OBP	SLG	OPS	FIELDING E	Avg.
2003—Vancouver (N'west)	SS	32	129	22	44	5	4	0	14	12	20	1	3	7-1	.341	.401	.442	.843	2	.983
—Modesto (Pion.)		8	36	9	15	3	0	2	6	3	6	0	1	0-0	.417	.462	.667	1.129	...	...
2004—Modesto (Pion.)		108	452	75	142	32	5	11	72	37	54	1	11	1-3	.314	.370	.480	.850	...	...
—Midland (Texas)		23	94	20	33	10	0	2	20	10	9	1	1	2-0	.351	.419	.521	.940	4	.000
2005—Midland (Texas)	SS	78	294	46	86	14	2	4	25	23	40	2	5	2-3	.293	.347	.395	.741	14	.960
—Colo. Springs (PCL)	SS	13	52	14	18	3	2	1	7	3	8	0	1	0-0	.346	.375	.538	.913	1	1.000
—Colorado (N.L.)	SS-2B	39	128	16	28	1	1	0	7	9	15	0	3	2-1	.219	.270	.242	.512	1	.993
2006—Colo. Springs (PCL)		82	308	48	85	23	2	4	29	28	55	4	6	4-1	.276	.342	.403	.745	1	.995
—Colorado (N.L.)	SS-2B	11	34	3	6	1	1	0	3	3	9	0	1	1-1	.176	.243	.265	.508	0	1.000
Major League totals (2 years)		50	162	19	34	2	2	0	10	12	24	0	4	3-2	.210	.264	.247	.511	1	.995

2006 LEFTY-RIGHTY SPLITS

vs.	Avg.	AB	H	2B	3B	HR	RBI	BB	SO	OBP	Slg.	vs.	Avg.	AB	H	2B	3B	HR	RBI	BB	SO	OBP	Slg.
L	.250	4	1	0	0	0	0		0	1	.250	.250	R	.167	30	5	1	1	0	3	3	8	.242	.267

QUINTERO, HUMBERTO — C

PERSONAL: Born August 8, 1979, in Maracaibo, Venezuela. ... 6-1/190. ... Bats right, throws right. ... High school: Andres Bello (Maracaibo, Venezuela). **TRANSACTIONS/CAREER NOTES:** Signed as a non-drafted free agent by Chicago White Sox organization (January 16, 1997). ... Traded by White Sox with OF Alex Fernandez to San Diego Padres for IF D'Angelo Jimenez (July 12, 2002). ... Traded by Padres to Houston Astros for P Tim Redding (March 28, 2005). ... On disabled list (June 19-July 16, 2005); included rehabilitation assignments to Round Rock and Corpus Christi.

2006 GAMES PLAYED BY POSITION (MLB): C—10.

Year Team (League)	Pos.	G	AB	R	H	2B	3B	HR	RBI	BB	SO	HBP	GDP	SB-CS	Avg.	OBP	SLG	OPS	FIELDING E	Avg.
1999—Bristol (Appal.)	C	48	155	30	43	5	2	0	15	9	19	6	8	11-1	.277	.341	.335	.677	6	.987
2000—Burlington (Midw.)	C	75	248	23	59	12	2	0	24	15	31	3	8	10-6	.238	.287	.302	.590	8	.986
—Ariz. White Sox (Ariz.)	C-OF	15	56	13	22	2	2	0	8	0	3	2	2	1-0	.393	.414	.500	.914	3	.976
2001—Kannapolis (S. Atl.)	C	60	197	32	53	7	1	1	20	8	20	7	5	7-3	.269	.321	.330	.651	7	.989
—Win.-Salem (Car.)	C	43	154	15	37	6	0	0	12	5	19	2	3	9-3	.240	.268	.279	.548	3	.992

Year — Team (League)	Pos.	G	AB	R	H	2B	3B	HR	RBI	BB	SO	HBP	GDP	SB-CS	Avg.	OBP	SLG	OPS	E	Avg.
— Birmingham (Sou.)	C	5	19	0	4	0	0	0	2	2	1	0	0	0-0	.211	.250	.211	.461	1	.971
2002— Birmingham (Sou.)	C	4	12	1	6	0	0	0	3	0	1	1	0	1-0	.500	.538	.500	1.038	0	1.000
— Charlotte (Int'l)	C	15	41	2	9	1	0	0	5	3	8	0	3	0-0	.220	.273	.244	.517	3	.964
— Win.-Salem (Car.)	C	52	160	15	31	1	1	0	12	8	23	4	4	2-3	.194	.247	.213	.460	4	.990
— Mobile (Sou.)	C	37	125	11	30	8	0	1	14	5	12	3	3	0-3	.240	.286	.328	.614	5	.983
2003— Mobile (Sou.)	C-DH	110	386	37	115	26	0	3	52	19	41	9	17	0-0	.298	.343	.389	.732	5	.995
— San Diego (N.L.)	C	12	23	1	5	0	0	0	2	1	6	0	0	0-0	.217	.250	.217	.467	1	.982
2004— Portland (PCL)	C-DH	68	259	36	82	25	0	5	30	8	18	5	7	0-0	.317	.348	.471	.819	6	.989
— San Diego (N.L.)	C	23	72	7	18	3	0	2	10	5	16	0	5	0-2	.250	.295	.375	.670	0	1.000
2005— Corpus Christi (Texas)	C	4	11	0	2	1	0	0	1	1	2	0	2	0-0	.182	.250	.273	.523	0	1.000
— Round Rock (PCL)	C-DH	52	191	23	55	13	0	8	31	10	30	2	3	2-1	.288	.327	.482	.809	2	.994
— Houston (N.L.)	C-1B	18	54	6	10	1	0	1	8	1	10	0	3	0-0	.185	.200	.259	.459	1	.989
2006— Round Rock (PCL)	C	82	292	39	87	21	2	4	37	19	48	0	16	4-0	.298	.352	.425	.777	4	.993
— Houston (N.L.)	C	11	21	2	7	2	0	0	2	1	3	0	0	0-0	.333	.364	.429	.792	0	1.000
Major League totals (4 years)		64	170	16	40	6	0	3	22	8	35	0	10	0-2	.235	.268	.324	.592	2	.994

2006 LEFTY-RIGHTY SPLITS

vs.	Avg.	AB	H	2B	3B	HR	RBI	BB	SO	OBP	Slg.	vs.	Avg.	AB	H	2B	3B	HR	RBI	BB	SO	OBP	Slg.
L	.571	7	4	1	0	0	2	1	0	.625	.714	R	.214	14	3	1	0	0	0	0	3	.214	.286

QUIROZ, GUILLERMO — C

PERSONAL: Born November 29, 1981, in Maracaibo, Venezuela. ... 6-1/202. ... Bats right, throws right. ... Full name: Guillermo Antonio Quiroz. **TRANSACTIONS/CAREER NOTES:** Signed as non-drafted free agent by Toronto Blue Jays organization (September 25, 1998). ... Claimed on waivers by Seattle Mariners (March 31, 2006).
2006 GAMES PLAYED BY POSITION (MLB): C—1.

Year — Team (League)	Pos.	G	AB	R	H	2B	3B	HR	RBI	BB	SO	HBP	GDP	SB-CS	Avg.	OBP	SLG	OPS	E	Avg.
1999— Medicine Hat (Pio.)	C	63	208	25	46	7	0	9	28	18	55	4	4	0-2	.221	.296	.385	.680	10	.981
2000— Hagerstown (SAL)	C	43	136	14	22	4	0	1	12	16	44	4	4	0-1	.162	.269	.213	.482	2	.994
— Queens (N.Y.-Penn.)	C	55	196	27	44	9	0	5	29	27	48	4	4	1-2	.224	.329	.347	.676	7	.987
2001— Char., W.Va. (SAL)	C	82	261	25	52	12	0	7	25	29	67	6	5	5-1	.199	.294	.326	.620	9	.986
2002— Dunedin (Fla. St.)	C	111	411	50	107	28	1	12	68	35	91	9	18	1-0	.260	.330	.421	.751	11	.984
— Syracuse (Int'l)	C	13	45	7	10	4	0	1	6	3	14	0	1	0-0	.222	.271	.378	.649	2	.956
2003— New Haven (East.)	C	108	369	63	104	27	0	20	79	44	83	12	13	0-0	.282	.372	.518	.889	4	.994
2004— Syracuse (Int'l)	C-DH	76	255	32	58	19	1	8	32	28	54	3	8	1-0	.227	.309	.404	.706	3	.994
— Toronto (A.L.)	C-DH	17	52	2	11	2	0	0	6	2	8	2	1	1-0	.212	.263	.250	.513	2	.976
2005— Dunedin (Fla. St.)	DH-C	11	38	4	9	1	0	2	8	2	8	3	1	0-0	.237	.326	.421	.747	0	1.000
— Syracuse (Int'l)	C-DH	25	83	11	19	3	0	6	18	9	19	1	5	0-0	.229	.309	.482	.790	1	.988
— Toronto (A.L.)	C-DH	12	36	3	7	2	0	0	4	2	13	1	0	0-0	.194	.256	.250	.506	0	1.000
2006— San Antonio (Texas)	C	16	64	5	12	3	0	3	9	3	15	1	2	0-0	.188	.235	.375	.610	4	.966
— Seattle (A.L.)	C	1	2	0	0	0	0	0	0	0	0	0	0	0-0	.000	.000	.000	.000	0	1.000
— Tacoma (PCL)		38	138	15	42	8	0	3	28	11	29	2	5	0-0	.304	.359	.428	.787	0	1.000
Major League totals (3 years)		30	90	5	18	4	0	0	10	4	23	3	1	1-0	.200	.255	.244	.500	2	.987

2006 LEFTY-RIGHTY SPLITS

vs.	Avg.	AB	H	2B	3B	HR	RBI	BB	SO	OBP	Slg.	vs.	Avg.	AB	H	2B	3B	HR	RBI	BB	SO	OBP	Slg.
L	.000	0	0	0	0	0	0	0	0	.000	.000	R	.000	2	0	0	0	0	0	0	2	.000	.000

RABE, JOSH — OF

PERSONAL: Born October 15, 1978, in Quincy, Ill. ... Bats right, throws right. ... Full name: Joshua Wayne Rabe. ... College: Quincy. **TRANSACTIONS/CAREER NOTES:** Selected by Minnesota Twins organization in 11th round of 2000 free-agent draft.
2006 GAMES PLAYED BY POSITION (MLB): DH—12, OF—11.

Year — Team (League)	Pos.	G	AB	R	H	2B	3B	HR	RBI	BB	SO	HBP	GDP	SB-CS	Avg.	OBP	SLG	OPS	E	Avg.
2000— Elizabethton (App.)		44	154	33	34	5	0	3	11	25	34	4	6	2-0	.221	.344	.312	.656	...	...
2001— Quad City (Midw.)		119	397	58	112	25	3	6	44	32	64	8	9	9-7	.282	.345	.406	.751	...	...
2002— Fort Myers (FSL)		85	297	60	101	23	2	5	40	44	36	3	10	16-4	.340	.427	.481	.908	...	...
— New Britain (East.)		46	183	21	43	10	0	1	18	10	30	2	5	4-1	.235	.282	.306	.588	...	...
2003— New Britain (East.)		94	366	63	111	15	2	11	72	30	63	6	10	19-3	.303	.361	.445	.806	...	...
— Rochester (Int'l)		38	131	15	31	6	0	5	11	11	22	1	7	2-1	.237	.301	.397	.698	...	...
2004— Rochester (Int'l)		122	429	54	113	27	0	4	45	40	76	6	9	26-5	.263	.333	.375	.708	...	...
2005— Rochester (Int'l)	OF-DH	90	285	50	68	17	0	11	49	29	57	.3	7	5-2	.239	.313	.414	.728	6	.972
2006— Rochester (Int'l)		93	355	51	106	20	1	6	47	35	37	3	5	7-4	.299	.362	.411	.773	3	.983
— Minnesota (A.L.)	DH-OF	24	49	8	14	1	0	3	7	2	11	0	3	0-1	.286	.314	.490	.804	2	.917
Major League totals (1 year)		24	49	8	14	1	0	3	7	2	11	0	3	0-1	.286	.314	.490	.804	2	.917

2006 LEFTY-RIGHTY SPLITS

vs.	Avg.	AB	H	2B	3B	HR	RBI	BB	SO	OBP	Slg.	vs.	Avg.	AB	H	2B	3B	HR	RBI	BB	SO	OBP	Slg.
L	.375	24	9	4	0	2	5	2	2	.423	.667	R	.200	25	5	0	0	1	2	0	9	.200	.320

RABELO, MIKE — C

PERSONAL: Born January 17, 1980, in New Port Richey, Fla. ... Bats both, throws right. ... Full name: Michael Gregory Rabelo. ... College: Tampa (Fla.).
TRANSACTIONS/CAREER NOTES: Selected by Boston Red Sox organization in 13th round of 1998 free-agent draft; did not sign. ... Selected by Detroit Tigers organization in fourth round of 2001 free-agent draft.
2006 GAMES PLAYED BY POSITION (MLB): DH—1.

Year — Team (League)	Pos.	G	AB	R	H	2B	3B	HR	RBI	BB	SO	HBP	GDP	SB-CS	Avg.	OBP	SLG	OPS	E	Avg.
2001— Oneonta (NYP)		53	194	27	63	4	2	0	32	23	45	4	4	1-2	.325	.405	.366	.771	...	...
2002— W. Mich. (Mid.)		123	410	42	80	13	1	2	41	42	91	8	21	3-1	.195	.281	.246	.527	...	...
2003— W. Mich. (Mid.)		123	394	41	108	16	0	5	40	31	62	3	13	9-4	.274	.328	.353	.681	...	...
2004— Erie (East.)		5	20	0	2	0	0	0	2	1	4	1	0	0-0	.100	.182	.100	.282	...	...
— Lakeland (Fla. St.)		92	327	36	94	20	2	0	38	25	56	7	9	3-2	.287	.349	.361	.710	...	...
2005— Erie (East.)	C-1B-DH / 3B	77	282	33	77	18	1	2	26	18	42	9	6	0-1	.273	.334	.365	.700	7	.987

Year Team (League)	Pos.	G	AB	R	H	2B	3B	HR	RBI	BB	SO	HBP	GDP	SB-CS	Avg.	OBP	SLG	OPS	E	Avg.
2006— Toledo (Int'l)		38	137	19	37	12	0	3	22	11	33	3	3	1-1	.270	.333	.423	.757	1	.996
— Erie (East.)		62	213	31	59	13	1	6	28	19	38	9	7	2-1	.277	.361	.432	.793	3	.992
— Detroit (A.L.)	DH	1	1	0	0	0	0	0	0	0	1	0	0	0-0	.000	.000	.000	.000	0	...
Major League totals (1 year)		1	1	0	0	0	0	0	0	0	1	0	0	0-0	.000	.000	.000	.000	0	...

2006 LEFTY-RIGHTY SPLITS

vs.	Avg.	AB	H	2B	3B	HR	RBI	BB	SO	OBP	Slg.	vs.	Avg.	AB	H	2B	3B	HR	RBI	BB	SO	OBP	Slg.
L	.000	1	0	0	0	0	0	0	1	.000	.000	R	.000	0	0	0	0	0	0	0	0	.000	.000

RADKE, BRAD P

PERSONAL: Born October 27, 1972, in Eau Claire, Wis. ... 6-2/184. ... Throws right, bats right. ... Full name: Brad William Radke. ... Name pronounced: RAD-key. ... High school: Jesuit (Tampa). **TRANSACTIONS/CAREER NOTES:** Selected by Minnesota Twins organization in eighth round of 1991 free-agent draft. ... On disabled list (August 4-21, 2001). ... On disabled list (May 14-30 and May 31-August 3, 2002); included rehabilitation assignments to GCL Twins and Fort Myers. ... On suspended list (May 17-23, 2003).
CAREER HITTING: 3-for-29 (.103), 0 R, 0 2B, 0 3B, 0 HR, 0 RBI.

Year Team (League)	W	L	Pct.	ERA	WHIP	G	GS	CG	ShO	Hld.	Sv.-Opp.	IP	H	R	ER	HR	BB-IBB	SO	Avg.
1991— GC Twins (GCL)	3	4	.429	3.08	1.11	10	9	1	0	...	1-...	49.2	41	21	17	0	14-0	46	.220
1992— Kenosha (Midw.)	10	10	.500	2.93	1.18	26	25	4	1	...	0-...	165.2	149	70	54	8	47-1	127	.243
1993— Fort Myers (FSL)	3	5	.375	3.82	1.15	14	14	0	0	...	0-...	92.0	85	42	39	3	21-1	69	.243
— Nashville (Southern)	2	6	.250	4.62	1.28	13	13	1	0	...	0-...	76.0	81	42	39	6	16-0	76	.267
1994— Nashville (Southern)	12	9	.571	2.66	1.08	29	28	5	1	...	0-...	186.1	167	66	55	9	34-0	123	.240
1995— Minnesota (A.L.)	11	14	.440	5.32	1.34	29	28	2	1	0	0-0	181.0	195	112	107	* 32	47-0	75	.275
1996— Minnesota (A.L.)	11	16	.407	4.46	1.24	35	35	3	0	0	0-0	232.0	231	125	115	* 40	57-2	148	.256
1997— Minnesota (A.L.)	20	10	.667	3.87	1.19	35	• 35	4	1	0	0-0	239.2	238	114	103	28	48-1	174	.257
1998— Minnesota (A.L.)	12	14	.462	4.30	1.32	32	32	5	1	0	0-0	213.2	238	109	102	23	43-1	146	.283
1999— Minnesota (A.L.)	12	14	.462	3.75	1.29	33	33	4	0	0	0-0	218.2	239	97	91	28	44-0	121	.280
2000— Minnesota (A.L.)	12	* 16	.429	4.45	1.38	34	34	4	1	0	0-0	226.2	261	119	112	27	51-1	141	.287
2001— Minnesota (A.L.)	15	11	.577	3.94	1.15	33	33	6	2	0	0-0	226.0	235	105	99	24	26-0	137	.271
2002— Minnesota (A.L.)	9	5	.643	4.72	1.22	21	21	2	1	0	0-0	118.1	124	64	62	12	20-0	62	.272
— GC Twins (GCL)	0	0	...	0.00	0.67	1	1	0	0	...	0-...	3.0	2	0	0	0	0-0	4	.182
— Fort Myers (FSL)	0	1	.000	3.12	1.27	2	2	0	0	...	0-...	8.2	11	6	3	1	0-0	6	.289
2003— Minnesota (A.L.)	14	10	.583	4.49	1.27	33	33	3	1	0	0-0	212.1	242	111	106	32	28-2	120	.288
2004— Minnesota (A.L.)	11	8	.579	3.48	1.16	34	34	1	1	0	0-0	219.2	229	92	85	23	26-1	143	.267
2005— Minnesota (A.L.)	9	12	.429	4.04	1.18	31	31	3	1	0	0-0	200.2	214	98	90	33	23-1	117	.272
2006— Minnesota (A.L.)	12	9	.571	4.32	1.41	28	28	0	0	0	0-0	162.1	197	87	78	24	32-3	83	.307
Major League totals (12 years)	148	139	.516	4.22	1.26	378	377	37	10	0	0-0	2451.0	2643	1233	1150	326	445-12	1467	.276

DIVISION SERIES RECORD

Year Team (League)	W	L	Pct.	ERA	WHIP	G	GS	CG	ShO	Hld.	Sv.-Opp.	IP	H	R	ER	HR	BB-IBB	SO	Avg.
2002— Minnesota (A.L.)	2	0	1.000	1.54	1.29	2	2	0	0	0	0-0	11.2	14	6	2	1	1-0	7	.280
2003— Minnesota (A.L.)	0	1	.000	2.84	1.11	1	1	0	0	0	0-0	6.1	5	2	2	0	2-0	4	.227
2004— Minnesota (A.L.)	0	0	...	7.11	1.74	1	1	0	0	0	0-0	6.1	8	5	5	3	3-0	3	.320
2006— Minnesota (A.L.)	0	1	.000	6.75	1.50	1	1	0	0	0	0-0	4.0	5	4	3	2	1-0	2	.263
Division series totals (4 years)	2	2	.500	3.81	1.38	5	5	0	0	0	0-0	28.1	32	17	12	6	7-0	13	.276

CHAMPIONSHIP SERIES RECORD

Year Team (League)	W	L	Pct.	ERA	WHIP	G	GS	CG	ShO	Hld.	Sv.-Opp.	IP	H	R	ER	HR	BB-IBB	SO	Avg.
2002— Minnesota (A.L.)	0	1	.000	2.70	0.90	1	1	0	0	0	0-0	6.2	5	2	2	0	1-0	4	.217

ALL-STAR GAME RECORD

	W	L	Pct.	ERA	WHIP	G	GS	CG	ShO	Hld.	Sv.-Opp.	IP	H	R	ER	HR	BB-IBB	SO	Avg.
All-Star Game totals (1 year)	0	0	...	9.00	3.00	1	0	0	0	0	0-0	1.0	2	1	1	0	1-0	1	.400

2006 LEFTY-RIGHTY SPLITS

vs.	Avg.	AB	H	2B	3B	HR	RBI	BB	SO	OBP	Slg.	vs.	Avg.	AB	H	2B	3B	HR	RBI	BB	SO	OBP	Slg.
L	.303	297	90	20	3	10	45	13	37	.325	.492	R	.311	344	107	16	0	14	37	19	46	.346	.480

RAKERS, AARON P

PERSONAL: Born January 22, 1977, in Highland, Ill. ... 6-3/205. ... Throws right, bats right. ... Full name: Aaron James Rakers. ... Name pronounced: Rockers. ... High school: Wesclin (Trenton, Ill.). ... College: Southern Illinois University-Edwardsville. **TRANSACTIONS/CAREER NOTES:** Selected by Baltimore Orioles organization in 23rd round of 1999 free-agent draft. ... On disabled list (March 28, 2006-entire season).
CAREER HITTING: 0-for-0 (.000), 0 R, 0 2B, 0 3B, 0 HR, 0 RBI.

Year Team (League)	W	L	Pct.	ERA	WHIP	G	GS	CG	ShO	Hld.	Sv.-Opp.	IP	H	R	ER	HR	BB-IBB	SO	Avg.
1999— Bluefield (Appal.)	0	0	...	2.57	1.14	3	0	0	0	...	0-...	7.0	5	2	2	1	3-0	12	.200
— Delmarva (S. Atl.)	4	1	.800	1.42	0.87	18	0	0	0	...	8-...	25.1	9	6	4	0	13-0	38	.108
2000— Frederick (Carolina)	1	1	.500	1.55	0.86	26	0	0	0	...	8-...	40.2	23	8	7	2	12-1	57	.163
— Bowie (East.)	3	2	.600	2.79	1.03	24	0	0	0	...	8-...	29.0	20	11	9	5	10-0	21	.194
2001— Bowie (East.)	4	4	.500	2.39	1.21	51	0	0	0	...	14-...	60.1	53	21	16	8	20-1	74	.227
2002— Bowie (East.)	5	1	.833	2.06	1.06	36	0	0	0	...	10-...	48.0	39	12	11	3	12-2	45	.232
2003— Bowie (East.)	5	0	1.000	2.75	1.17	31	0	0	0	...	10-...	39.1	27	12	12	7	19-1	42	.196
— Ottawa (Int'l)	2	4	.333	5.13	1.14	21	0	0	0	...	1-...	26.1	19	18	15	1	11-2	26	.202
2004— Ottawa (Int'l)	4	5	.444	2.75	1.14	54	1	0	0	...	1-...	78.2	65	27	24	8	25-4	80	.229
— Baltimore (A.L.)	0	0	...	4.15	1.38	3	0	0	0	...	0-...	4.1	5	2	2	0	1-0	3	.278
2005— Ottawa (Int'l)	6	5	.545	2.57	1.17	57	0	0	0	7	7-11	77.0	69	26	22	8	21-4	92	.235
— Baltimore (A.L.)	1	0	1.000	3.29	1.02	10	0	0		1	0-0	13.2	11	5	5	3	3-0	11	.220
2006— Baltimore (A.L.)	Did not play.																		
Major League totals (2 years)	1	0	1.000	3.50	1.11	13	0	0	0	1	0-0	18.0	16	7	7	3	4-0	14	.235

RAMIREZ, ARAMIS 3B

PERSONAL: Born June 25, 1978, in Santo Domingo, Dominican Republic. ... 6-1/215. ... Bats right, throws right. ... Full name: Aramis Nin Ramirez. ... Name pronounced: ah-RAH-mis. ... High school: Aida Cartagena Portalatin (Santo Domingo, Dominican Republic). **TRANSACTIONS/CAREER NOTES:** Signed as a non-drafted free agent by Pittsburgh Pirates organization (November 7, 1994). ... On suspended list (July 24-29, 1998). ... On disabled list (August 10-September 4, 1998); included rehabilitation assignment to Nashville. ... On disabled list (August 29, 2000-remainder of season). ... Traded by Pirates with OF Kenny Lofton to Chicago Cubs for IF Jose Hernandez, P Matt Bruback and a player to be named (July 23, 2003); Pirates acquired IF Bobby Hill to complete deal (August 15, 2003). ... On disabled list (August 26, 2005-remainder of season). **STATISTICAL NOTES:** Hit three home runs in one game (April 8, 2001; and July 30 and September 16, 2004). ... Career major league grand slams: 6.

2006 GAMES PLAYED BY POSITION (MLB): 3B—156.

Year	Team (League)	Pos.	G	AB	R	H	2B	3B	HR	RBI	BB	SO	HBP	GDP	SB-CS	Avg.	OBP	SLG	OPS	E	Avg.
											BATTING									**FIELDING**	
1995—	Dom. Pirates (DSL)	3B	64	214	41	63	13	0	11	54	42	26	...		2-...	.294		.509		19	.886
1996—	Erie (N.Y.-Penn)	3B	61	223	37	68	14	4	9	42	31	41	7	7	0-0	.305	.403	.525	.928	17	.896
—	Augusta (S. Atl.)	3B	6	20	3	4	1	0	1	2	1	7	2	0	0-2	.200	.304	.400	.704	2	.833
1997—	Lynchburg (Caro.)	3B-DH	137	482	85	134	24	2	29	114	80	103	12	12	5-3	.278	.390	.517	.907	39	.897
1998—	Nashville (PCL)	3B-DH-SS	47	168	19	46	10	0	5	18	24	28	4	3	0-2	.274	.374	.423	.796	8	.932
—	Pittsburgh (N.L.)	3B	72	251	23	59	9	1	6	24	18	72	4	3	0-1	.235	.296	.351	.646	9	.941
1999—	Nashville (PCL)	3B	131	460	92	151	35	1	21	74	73	56	9	11	5-3	.328	.425	.546	.971	42	.884
—	Pittsburgh (N.L.)	3B	18	56	2	10	2	1	0	7	6	9	0	0	0-0	.179	.254	.250	.504	3	.930
2000—	Pittsburgh (N.L.)	3B	73	254	19	65	15	2	6	35	10	36	5	9	0-0	.256	.293	.402	.695	14	.917
—	Nashville (PCL)	3B	44	167	28	59	12	2	4	26	11	26	4	5	2-1	.353	.407	.521	.928	9	.930
2001—	Pittsburgh (N.L.)	3B	158	603	83	181	40	0	34	112	40	100	8	9	5-4	.300	.350	.536	.885	25	.945
2002—	Pittsburgh (N.L.)	3B-DH	142	522	51	122	26	0	18	71	29	95	8	17	2-0	.234	.279	.387	.666	19	.946
2003—	Pittsburgh (N.L.)	3B	96	375	44	105	25	1	12	67	25	68	7	17	1-1	.280	.330	.448	.778	23	.924
—	Chicago (N.L.)	3B	63	232	30	60	7	1	15	39	17	31	3	4	1-1	.259	.314	.491	.805	10	.939
2004—	Chicago (N.L.)	3B	145	547	99	174	32	1	36	103	49	62	3	25	0-2	.318	.373	.578	.951	10	.969
2005—	Chicago (N.L.)	3B	123	463	72	140	30	0	31	92	35	60	6	15	0-1	.302	.358	.568	.926	16	.947
2006—	Chicago (N.L.)	3B	157	594	93	173	38	4	38	119	50	63	9	15	2-1	.291	.352	.561	.912	13	.965
Major League totals (9 years)			1047	3897	517	1089	224	11	196	669	279	596	53	114	11-11	.279	.332	.493	.826	142	.946

DIVISION SERIES RECORD

Year	Team (League)	Pos.	G	AB	R	H	2B	3B	HR	RBI	BB	SO	HBP	GDP	SB-CS	Avg.	OBP	SLG	OPS	E	Avg.
2003—	Chicago (N.L.)	3B	5	18	2	5	1	0	1	3	2	2	0	1	0-0	.278	.350	.500	.850	0	1.000

CHAMPIONSHIP SERIES RECORD

Year	Team (League)	Pos.	G	AB	R	H	2B	3B	HR	RBI	BB	SO	HBP	GDP	SB-CS	Avg.	OBP	SLG	OPS	E	Avg.
2003—	Chicago (N.L.)	3B	7	26	4	6	0	1	3	7	5	6	1	1	0-0	.231	.375	.654	1.029	0	1.000

ALL-STAR GAME RECORD

G	AB	R	H	2B	3B	HR	RBI	BB	SO	HBP	GDP	SB-CS	Avg.	OBP	SLG	OPS	E	Avg.
1	2	0	1	0	0	0	0	1	0			0-0	.500	.667	.500	1.167	0	1.000

All-Star Game totals (1 year)

2006 LEFTY-RIGHTY SPLITS

vs.	Avg.	AB	H	2B	3B	HR	RBI	BB	SO	OBP	Slg.	vs.	Avg.	AB	H	2B	3B	HR	RBI	BB	SO	OBP	Slg.
L	.261	142	37	8	1	9	32	17	21	.345	.521	R	.301	452	136	30	3	29	87	33	42	.354	.573

RAMIREZ, ELIZARDO — P

PERSONAL: Born January 28, 1983, in Villa Mella, Dominican Republic. ... 6-0/180. ... Throws right, bats both. ... High school: Liceo Pedregal (Dominican Republic).
TRANSACTIONS/CAREER NOTES: Signed as a non-drafted free agent by Philadelphia Phillies organization (July 2, 1999). ... Traded by Phillies to Cincinnati Reds (August 11, 2004) to complete deal in which Phillies acquired P Cory Lidle from Reds for OF Javon Moran, P Joe Wilson and a player to be named (August 9, 2004). ... On disabled list (September 4, 2006-remainder of season).
CAREER HITTING: 5-for-34 (.147), 2 R, 1 2B, 0 3B, 0 HR, 3 RBI.

Year	Team (League)	W	L	Pct.	ERA	WHIP	G	GS	CG	ShO	Hld.	Sv.-Opp.	IP	H	R	ER	HR	BB-IBB	SO	Avg.
2000—	Dom. Phillies (DSL)	5	2	.714	1.88	0.91	11	9	0	0	...	1-...	57.1	47	19	12	1	5-...	67	...
2001—	Dom. Phillies (DSL)	9	0	1.000	1.48	0.87	12	12	1	1	...	0-...	79.0	61	21	13	0	8-...	70	...
2002—	GC Phillies (GCL)	7	1	.875	1.10	0.63	11	11	2	1	...	0-...	73.1	44	18	9	3	2-0	73	.165
2003—	Clearwater (FSL)	13	9	.591	3.78	1.36	27	25	1	0	...	0-...	157.1	181	85	66	4	33-0	101	.290
2004—	Clearwater (FSL)	5	1	.833	2.44	1.07	9	9	1	0	...	0-...	59.0	55	17	16	3	8-0	33	.249
—	Philadelphia (N.L.)	0	0	...	4.80	1.47	7	0	0	0	0	0-0	15.0	17	8	8	3	5-1	9	.283
—	Reading (East.)	2	5	.286	6.68	1.93	8	8	1	0	...	0-...	33.2	51	34	25	4	14-1	20	.345
—	Chattanooga (Sou.)	1	0	1.000	3.19	1.26	5	5	1	1	...	0-...	31.0	35	11	11	6	4-1	23	.282
2005—	Cincinnati (N.L.)	0	3	.000	8.46	1.93	6	4	0	0	0	0-0	22.1	33	22	21	5	10-2	9	.344
—	Louisville (Int'l)	7	7	.500	3.77	1.28	21	21	0	0	...	0-...	131.1	150	63	55	14	18-1	82	.287
2006—	Dayton (Midw.)	0	0	...	4.50	1.00	1	1	0	0	...	0-...	6.0	6	3	3	1	0-0	3	.250
—	Cincinnati (N.L.)	4	9	.308	5.37	1.46	21	19	0	0	...	0-...	104.0	123	70	62	14	29-2	69	.293
—	Louisville (Int'l)	0	1	.000	4.05	1.20	4	4	0	0	.0	0-...	20.0	22	9	9	2	2-0	19	.272
Major League totals (3 years)		4	12	.250	5.79	1.54	34	23	0	0	0	0-0	141.1	173	100	91	22	44-5	87	.300

2006 LEFTY-RIGHTY SPLITS

vs.	Avg.	AB	H	2B	3B	HR	RBI	BB	SO	OBP	Slg.	vs.	Avg.	AB	H	2B	3B	HR	RBI	BB	SO	OBP	Slg.
L	.291	199	58	14	1	8	36	18	30	.355	.492	R	.294	221	65	18	2	6	28	11	39	.342	.475

RAMIREZ, HANLEY — SS

PERSONAL: Born December 23, 1983, in Samana, Dominican Republic. ... 6-3/195. ... Bats right, throws right. ... Full name: Hanley Ramirez. **TRANSACTIONS/CAREER NOTES:** Signed as a non-drafted free agent by Boston Red Sox organization (July 2, 2000). ... Traded by Red Sox with Ps Anibal Sanchez, Harvey Garcia and Jesus Delgado to the Florida Marlins for Ps Josh Beckett, Guillermo Mota and 3B Mike Lowell (November 24, 2005). **HONORS:** Named N.L. Rookie of the Year by the Baseball Writers' Association of America (2006).

2006 GAMES PLAYED BY POSITION (MLB): SS—154.

Year	Team (League)	Pos.	G	AB	R	H	2B	3B	HR	RBI	BB	SO	HBP	GDP	SB-CS	Avg.	OBP	SLG	OPS	E	Avg.
2001—	Boston (GCL)	SS	54	197	32	68	18	2	5	34	15	22	4	9	13-4	.345	.397	.533	.930	...	...
2002—	GC Red Sox (GCL)	SS-2B-3B	45	164	29	56	11	3	6	26	16	15	2	5	8-6	.341	.402	.555	.957	20	.915
—	Lowell (NY-Penn)	SS	22	97	17	36	9	2	1	19	4	14	2	2	4-3	.371	.400	.536	.936	7	.935
2003—	Sarasota (Fla. St.)	SS	111	422	69	116	24	3	8	50	32	73	2	12	36-13	.275	.327	.403	.730	36	.926
2004—	Sarasota (Fla. St.)	SS	62	239	33	74	8	4	1	24	17	39	4	2	12-7	.310	.364	.389	.753	17	.485
—	GC Red Sox (GCL)	SS-2B-3B	6	20	5	8	0	1	0	7	2	3	2	1	1-0	.400	.462	.500	.962	3	.885
—	Portland (East.)	SS-2B-3B	32	129	26	40	7	2	5	15	10	26	0	0	12-3	.310	.360	.512	.872	3	.000
2005—	Portland (East.)	SS-2B-3B-DH	122	465	66	126	21	7	6	52	39	62	7	12	26-13	.271	.335	.385	.720	22	.957
—	Boston (A.L.)	SS	2	2	0	0	0	0	0	0	0	0	0	0	0-0	.000	.000	.000	.000	1	1.000
2006—	Florida (N.L.)	SS	158	633	119	185	46	11	17	59	56	128	4	7	51-15	.292	.353	.480	.833	26	.963
American League totals (1 year)			2	2	0	0	0	0	0	0	0	0	0	0	0-0	.000	.000	.000	.000	1	1.000
National League totals (1 year)			158	633	119	185	46	11	17	59	56	128	4	7	51-15	.292	.353	.480	.833	26	.963
Major League totals (2 years)			160	635	119	185	46	11	17	59	56	130	4	7	51-15	.291	.352	.479	.830	26	.963

R

2006 LEFTY-RIGHTY SPLITS

vs.	Avg.	AB	H	2B	3B	HR	RBI	BB	SO	OBP	Slg.	vs.	Avg.	AB	H	2B	3B	HR	RBI	BB	SO	OBP	Slg.
L	.307	153	47	15	5	6	19	19	28	.385	.588	R	.288	480	138	31	6	11	40	37	100	.342	.446

RAMIREZ, HORACIO   P

PERSONAL: Born November 24, 1979, in Carson, Calif. ... 6-1/219. ... Throws left, bats left. ... High school: Inglewood (Calif.). **TRANSACTIONS/CAREER NOTES:** Selected by Atlanta Braves organization in fifth round of 1997 free-agent draft. ... On disabled list (March 22-June 18, 2002); included rehabilitation assignment to Macon and Greenville. ... On disabled list (May 26-September 25, 2004); included rehabilitation assignment to Greenville. ... On disabled list (April 6-May 6, 2006). ... On disabled list (May 7-21, 2006); included rehabilitation assignments to Richmond and Rome. ... On disabled list (August 8, 2006-remainder of season). **MISCELLANEOUS NOTES:** Appeared in one game as pinch runner (2004). ... Popped out in only appearance as pinch hitter (2005).

CAREER HITTING: 27-for-179 (.151), 9 R, 3 2B, 1 3B, 0 HR, 5 RBI.

Year	Team (League)	W	L	Pct.	ERA	WHIP	G	GS	CG	ShO	Hld.	Sv.-Opp.	IP	H	R	ER	HR	BB-IBB	SO	Avg.
1997— GC Braves (GCL)		3	3	.500	2.25	1.09	11	8	0	0	...	0-...	44.0	30	13	11	1	18-0	61	.192
1998— Macon (S. Atl.)		1	7	.125	5.86	1.55	12	12	0	0	...	0-...	55.1	70	50	36	8	16-0	38	.310
— Eugene (Northwest)		2	7	.222	6.31	1.81	16	8	0	0	...	0-...	55.2	84	51	39	4	17-0	39	.346
1999— Macon (S. Atl.)		6	3	.667	2.67	1.22	17	14	1	1	...	0-...	77.2	70	30	23	6	25-0	43	.248
2000— Myrtle Beach (Carol.)		15	8	.652	3.22	1.20	27	26	3	2	...	0-...	148.1	136	57	53	14	42-0	125	.242
2001— Greenville (Sou.)		1	1	.500	4.91	1.70	3	3	0	0	...	0-...	14.2	17	8	8	2	8-0	17	.309
2002— Macon (S. Atl.)		0	2	.000	6.00	2.17	2	1	0	0	...	0-...	6.0	11	10	4	0	2-0	5	.355
— Greenville (Sou.)		9	5	.643	3.03	1.27	16	16	0	0	...	0-...	92.0	85	41	31	5	32-0	64	.253
2003— Atlanta (N.L.)		12	4	.750	4.00	1.39	29	29	1	0	...	0-0	182.1	181	91	81	21	72-10	100	.263
2004— Greenville (Sou.)		2	0	1.000	3.09	1.54	3	2	0	0	...	0-...	11.2	15	4	4	0	3-0	2	.349
— Richmond (Int'l)		0	0	...	8.00	1.78	2	2	0	0	...	0-...	9.0	15	8	8	1	1-0	3	.385
— Atlanta (N.L.)		2	4	.333	2.39	1.34	10	9	1	0	0	0-0	60.1	51	24	16	7	30-5	31	.226
2005— Atlanta (N.L.)		11	9	.550	4.63	1.39	33	32	1	1	0	0-0	202.1	214	108	104	31	67-4	80	.282
2006— Rome (S. Atl.)		0	0	...	3.86	1.71	1	1	0	0	...	0-...	4.2	5	2	2	1	3-0	1	.294
— Richmond (Int'l)		1	1	.500	5.68	1.50	3	3	0	0	...	0-...	12.2	18	8	8	1	1-0	10	.327
— Atlanta (N.L.)		5	5	.500	4.48	1.52	14	14	0	0	...	0-0	76.1	85	42	38	6	31-2	37	.270
Major League totals (4 years)		30	22	.577	4.13	1.40	86	84	3	1	0	0-0	521.1	531	265	239	65	200-21	248	.270

2006 LEFTY-RIGHTY SPLITS

vs.	Avg.	AB	H	2B	3B	HR	RBI	BB	SO	OBP	Slg.	vs.	Avg.	AB	H	2B	3B	HR	RBI	BB	SO	OBP	Slg.
L	.286	70	20	2	0	2	9	2	13	.315	.400	R	.288	226	65	11	0	4	25	29	24	.372	.389

RAMIREZ, MANNY   OF

PERSONAL: Born May 30, 1972, in Santo Domingo, Dominican Republic. ... 6-0/213. ... Bats right, throws right. ... Full name: Manuel Aristides Ramirez. ... Name pronounced: ruh-MEER-ez. ... High school: George Washington (New York). **TRANSACTIONS/CAREER NOTES:** Selected by Cleveland Indians organization in first round (13th pick overall) of 1991 free-agent draft. ... On suspended list (June 8-11, 1999). ... On disabled list (May 30-July 13, 2000); included rehabilitation assignments to Akron and Buffalo. ... Signed as a free agent by Boston Red Sox (December 13, 2000). ... On disabled list (May 14-June 25, 2002); included rehabilitation assignment to Pawtucket. **HONORS:** Named outfielder on THE SPORTING NEWS A.L. All-Star team (1995, 2001, 2004-06). ... Named designated hitter on THE SPORTING NEWS A.L. All-Star team (2002). ... Named outfielder on A.L. Silver Slugger team (1995, 1999-2001, 2003-06). ... Named designated hitter on A.L. Silver Slugger team (2002). **STATISTICAL NOTES:** Hit three home runs in one game (September 15, 1998 and August 25, 1999). ... Career major league grand slams: 20.

2006 GAMES PLAYED BY POSITION (MLB): OF—123, DH—5.

Year	Team (League)	Pos.	G	AB	R	H	2B	3B	HR	RBI	BB	SO	HBP	GDP	SB-CS	Avg.	OBP	SLG	OPS	E	Avg.
1991— Burlington (Appal.)		OF	59	215	44	70	11	4	19	63	34	41	6	4	7-8	.326	.426	.679	1.105	3	.966
1992— Kinston (Carol.)		OF	81	291	52	81	18	4	13	63	45	74	4	9	1-3	.278	.379	.502	.881	5	.956
1993— Cant./Akr. (Eastern)		OF	89	344	67	117	32	0	17	79	45	68	2	11	2-2	.340	.414	.581	.996	6	.967
— Charlotte (Int'l)		OF	40	145	38	46	12	0	14	36	27	35	2	1	1-1	.317	.424	.600	1.113	3	.961
— Cleveland (A.L.)		DH-OF	22	53	5	9	1	0	2	5	2	8	0	3	0-0	.170	.200	.302	.502	0	1.000
1994— Cleveland (A.L.)		OF-DH	91	290	51	78	22	0	17	60	42	72	0	6	4-2	.269	.357	.521	.878	1	.994
1995— Cleveland (A.L.)		OF-DH	137	484	85	149	26	1	31	107	75	112	5	13	6-6	.308	.402	.558	.960	5	.978
1996— Cleveland (A.L.)		OF-DH	152	550	94	170	45	3	33	112	85	104	3	18	8-5	.309	.399	.582	.981	9	.970
1997— Cleveland (A.L.)		OF-DH	150	561	99	184	40	0	26	88	79	115	7	19	2-3	.328	.415	.538	.953	7	.975
1998— Cleveland (A.L.)		OF-DH	150	571	108	168	35	2	45	145	76	121	6	18	5-3	.294	.377	.599	.976	7	.977
1999— Cleveland (A.L.)		OF-DH	147	522	131	174	34	3	44	*165	96	131	13	12	2-4	.333	.442	*.663	1.105	7	.975
2000— Cleveland (A.L.)		OF-DH	118	439	92	154	34	2	38	122	86	117	3	9	1-1	.351	.457	*.697	1.154	2	.986
— Akron (East.)		DH	1	2	1	1	0	0	1	2	2	1	0	0	0-0	.500	.750	2.000	2.750	...	...
— Buffalo (Int'l)		DH	5	11	5	5	1	0	3	7	6	1	0	1	0-0	.455	.647	1.364	2.011	...	...
2001— Boston (A.L.)		DH-OF	142	529	93	162	33	2	41	125	81	147	8	9	0-1	.306	.405	.609	1.014	0	1.000
2002— Boston (A.L.)		OF-DH	120	436	84	152	31	0	33	107	73	85	8	13	0-0	*.349	*.450	.647	1.097	5	.959
— Pawtucket (Int'l)		OF	11	30	2	3	1	0	1	2	8	9	1	1	0-0	.100	.308	.233	.541	0	1.000
2003— Boston (A.L.)		OF-DH	154	569	117	185	36	1	37	104	97	94	8	22	3-1	.325	*.427	.587	1.014	4	.982
2004— Boston (A.L.)		OF-DH	152	568	108	175	44	0	*43	130	82	124	6	17	2-4	.308	.397	*.613	1.009	7	.967
2005— Boston (A.L.)		OF-DH	152	554	112	162	30	1	45	144	80	119	10	20	1-0	.292	.388	.594	.982	7	.974
2006— Boston (A.L.)		OF-DH	130	449	79	144	27	1	35	102	100	102	1	13	0-1	.321	*.439	.619	1.058	2	.989
Major League totals (14 years)			1817	6575	1258	2066	438	16	470	1516	1054	1451	78	192	34-31	.314	.411	.600	1.011	63	.978

DIVISION SERIES RECORD

Year	Team (League)	Pos.	G	AB	R	H	2B	3B	HR	RBI	BB	SO	HBP	GDP	SB-CS	Avg.	OBP	SLG	OPS	E	Avg.
1995— Cleveland (A.L.)		OF	3	12	1	0	0	0	0	0	1	2	1	0	0-0	.000	.143	.000	.143	0	1.000
1996— Cleveland (A.L.)		OF	4	16	4	6	2	0	2	2	1	4	0	1	0-0	.375	.412	.875	1.287	0	1.000
1997— Cleveland (A.L.)		OF	5	21	2	3	1	0	0	3	0	3	0	0	0-0	.143	.143	.190	.333	1	.750
1998— Cleveland (A.L.)		OF	4	14	2	5	0	0	2	3	1	4	2	0	0-0	.357	.471	.929	1.399	0	1.000
1999— Cleveland (A.L.)		OF	5	18	5	1	1	0	0	1	4	8	1	0	0-0	.056	.261	.111	.372	0	1.000
2003— Boston (A.L.)		OF	5	20	2	4	0	0	1	3	3	7	0	0	0-0	.200	.304	.350	.654	0	1.000
2004— Boston (A.L.)		OF	3	13	3	5	2	0	1	7	1	4	0	0	0-0	.385	.375	.769	1.144	0	1.000
2005— Boston (A.L.)		OF	3	10	2	3	2	0	2	4	2	0	0	0	0-0	.300	.417	.900	1.317	0	1.000
Division series totals (8 years)			32	124	21	27	8	0	8	23	13	32	4	1	0-0	.218	.308	.476	.783	1	.978

CHAMPIONSHIP SERIES RECORD

Year	Team (League)	Pos.	G	AB	R	H	2B	3B	HR	RBI	BB	SO	HBP	GDP	SB-CS	Avg.	OBP	SLG	OPS	E	Avg.
1995— Cleveland (A.L.)		OF	6	21	2	6	0	0	2	2	5	6	0	0	0-0	.286	.348	.571	.919	0	1.000
1997— Cleveland (A.L.)		OF	6	21	3	6	1	0	2	3	5	5	1	1	0-0	.286	.444	.619	1.063	1	.933
1998— Cleveland (A.L.)		OF	6	21	2	7	0	0	2	4	4	5	0	0	0-0	.333	.423	.667	1.090	0	1.000
2003— Boston (A.L.)		OF	7	29	3	9	1	0	2	4	4	4	0	1	0-1	.310	.333	.552	.885	0	1.000

Year Team (League)	Pos.	G	AB	R	H	2B	3B	HR	RBI	BB	SO	HBP	GDP	SB-CS	Avg.	OBP	SLG	OPS	E	Avg.
2004— Boston (A.L.)	OF	7	30	3	9	1	0	0	5	4	0	1		0-0	.300	.400	.333	.733	1	.947
Champ. series totals (5 years)		32	122	16	37	4	0	8	13	17	27	1	6	0-1	.303	.390	.533	.923	2	.971

WORLD SERIES RECORD

Year Team (League)	Pos.	G	AB	R	H	2B	3B	HR	RBI	BB	SO	HBP	GDP	SB-CS	Avg.	OBP	SLG	OPS	E	Avg.
1995— Cleveland (A.L.)	OF	6	18	2	4	0	0	1	2	4	5	0	1	1-0	.222	.364	.389	.753	0	1.000
1997— Cleveland (A.L.)	OF	7	26	3	4	0	0	2	6	6	5	0	2	0-0	.154	.294	.385	.679	1	.944
2004— Boston (A.L.)	OF	4	17	2	7	0	0	1	4	3	3	0	0	0-0	.412	.500	.588	1.088	2	.750
World series totals (3 years)		17	61	7	15	0	0	4	12	13	13	0	3	1-0	.246	.368	.443	.811	3	.912

ALL-STAR GAME RECORD

		G	AB	R	H	2B	3B	HR	RBI	BB	SO	HBP	GDP	SB-CS	Avg.	OBP	SLG	OPS	E	Avg.
All-Star Game totals (7 years)			7	9	2	3	0	0	1	4	3	3	0	1	0-0	.333	.462	.667	1.128	0	1.000

2006 LEFTY-RIGHTY SPLITS

vs.	Avg.	AB	H	2B	3B	HR	RBI	BB	SO	OBP	Slg.	vs.	Avg.	AB	H	2B	3B	HR	RBI	BB	SO	OBP	Slg.
L	.326	132	43	9	0	10	35	39	27	.477	.621	R	.319	317	101	18	1	25	67	61	75	.422	.618

RAMIREZ, RAMON — P

PERSONAL: Born August 31, 1981, in Puerto Plata, Dominican Republic. ... 5-11/190. ... Throws right, bats right. ... Full name: Ramon Ramirez. **TRANSACTIONS/CAREER NOTES:** Signed as a non-drafted free agent by Texas Rangers organization (December 27, 1996). ... Played one season as an outfielder in Rangers organization (1997). ... Released by Rangers (June 4, 1998). ... Acquired by New York Yankees organization from Hiroshima of the Japan Central League for cash (March 2003). ... Traded by Yankees with P Eduardo Sierra to Colorado Rockies for P Shawn Chacon (July 28, 2005).

CAREER HITTING: 2-for-4 (.500), 0 R, 0 2B, 0 3B, 0 HR, 0 RBI.

Year Team (League)	W	L	Pct.	ERA	WHIP	G	GS	CG	ShO	Hld.	Sv.-Opp.	IP	H	R	ER	HR	BB-IBB	SO	Avg.
1998—			Did not play.																
1999—			Did not play.																
2000—			Did not play.																
2001—			Did not play.																
2002—Hiroshima (Jp. Cn.)	0	0	...	3.00	1.67	2	0	0	0	...	0-0	3.0	3	1	1	0	2-0	3	...
2003— Tampa (Fla. St.)	2	8	.200	5.21	1.45	14	14	0	0	...	0-...	74.1	88	47	43	7	20-2	70	.291
—Trenton (East.)	1	1	.500	1.69	1.22	4	3	0	0	...	0-...	21.1	18	8	4	3	8-1	21	.231
—Columbus (Int'l)	0	1	.000	4.50	1.00	2	1	0	0	...	0-...	6.0	5	5	3	1	1-0	5	.208
2004—Columbus (Int'l)	0	3	.000	8.50	1.83	4	4	0	0	...	0-...	18.0	25	19	17	3	8-1	17	.329
—Trenton (East.)	4	6	.400	4.62	1.29	18	18	2	0	...	0-...	115.0	116	60	59	11	32-0	128	.264
2005—Columbus (Int'l)	1	3	.250	5.33	1.52	6	6	0	0	0	0-0	27.0	32	16	16	3	9-0	26	.305
—Trenton (East.)	6	5	.545	3.84	1.28	15	15	0	0	0	0-0	89.0	79	44	38	10	35-0	82	.236
—Tulsa (Texas)	2	1	.667	5.33	1.38	9	3	0	0	0	0-0	25.1	27	17	15	6	8-0	23	.273
2006— Colo. Springs (PCL)	0	0	0.00	0.00	0.00	1	0	0	0	0	0-0	1.0	0	0	0	0	0-0	1	.000
—Colorado (N.L.)	4	3	.571	3.46	1.26	61	0	0	0	10	0-2	67.2	58	28	26	5	27-3	61	.230
Major League totals (1 year)	4	3	.571	3.46	1.26	61	0	0	0	10	0-2	67.2	58	28	26	5	27-3	61	.230

2006 LEFTY-RIGHTY SPLITS

vs.	Avg.	AB	H	2B	3B	HR	RBI	BB	SO	OBP	Slg.	vs.	Avg.	AB	H	2B	3B	HR	RBI	BB	SO	OBP	Slg.
L	.274	113	31	8	2	3	12	12	18	.341	.460	R	.194	139	27	9	0	2	18	15	43	.274	.302

RAMIREZ, SANTIAGO — P

PERSONAL: Born August 15, 1978, in Bonao, Dominican Republic. ... 5-11/160. ... Throws right, bats right. ... Full name: Santiago Ramirez. **TRANSACTIONS/CAREER NOTES:** Signed as non-drafted free agent by Houston Astros organization (June 23, 1997). ... Signed as a non-drafted free agent by Houston Astros organization (June 16, 1997). ... Signed as free agent by Kansas City Royals organization (November 2, 2004). ... Signed as free agent by Washington Nationals organization (February 10, 2006). ... On disabled list (June 2-July 1, 2006). ... Released by Nationals (July 1, 2006).

CAREER HITTING: 0-for-0 (.000), 0 R, 0 2B, 0 3B, 0 HR, 0 RBI.

Year Team (League)	W	L	Pct.	ERA	WHIP	G	GS	CG	ShO	Hld.	Sv.-Opp.	IP	H	R	ER	HR	BB-IBB	SO	Avg.
1997—Dominican Astros (DSL) ...	4	1	.800	2.65	0.94	15	2	0	0	...	0-...	34.0	26	13	10	1	6-0	24	.217
1998—Dominican Astros (DSL) ...	6	5	.545	2.17	0.99	14	13	0	1	...	0-...	83.0	64	32	20	1	18-0	62	.203
1999—Martinsville (App.)	2	1	.667	1.45	1.29	25	0	0	0	...	17-...	31.0	26	9	5	1	14-1	35	.232
2000—Michigan (Midw.)	3	3	.500	6.07	1.99	23	0	0	0	...	5-...	29.2	27	28	20	6	32-1	22	.245
—Auburn (NY-Penn)	3	6	.333	4.25	1.42	20	0	0	0	...	2-...	53.0	36	34	25	3	39-1	57	.197
2001—Lexington (S. Atl.)	8	2	.800	3.63	1.22	45	0	0	0	...	4-...	79.1	69	35	32	2	28-1	85	.237
2002—Round Rock (Texas)	5	2	.714	2.56	1.12	33	0	0	0	...	4-...	63.1	45	19	18	3	26-3	73	.199
—New Orleans (PCL)	2	0	1.000	3.38	1.31	18	0	0	0	...	1-...	21.1	17	8	8	2	11-0	15	.221
2003—New Orleans (PCL)	4	0	1.000	4.26	1.26	10	0	0	0	...	0-...	12.2	7	7	6	1	9-0	9	.175
—Round Rock (Texas)	0	0	...	0.00	1.93	6	1	0	0	...	1-...	4.2	5	0	0	0	4-0	3	.278
2004—Round Rock (Texas)	6	4	.600	2.63	1.39	55	0	0	0	...	32-...	78.2	71	24	23	2	38-6	83	.233
2005—Omaha (PCL)	5	5	.500	5.21	1.51	50	1	0	0	1	17-21	67.1	81	43	39	11	21-0	53	.299
2006—New Orleans (PCL)	2	1	.667	0.99	0.73	19	0	0	0	2	7-7	27.1	16	3	3	1	4-1	28	.174
—Wash. (N.L.)	0	0	...	8.10	2.40	4	0	0	0	0	0-0	3.1	6	3	3	1	2-0	5	.375
Major League totals (1 year)	0	0	...	8.10	2.40	4	0	0	0	0	0-0	3.1	6	3	3	1	2-0	5	.375

2006 LEFTY-RIGHTY SPLITS

vs.	Avg.	AB	H	2B	3B	HR	RBI	BB	SO	OBP	Slg.	vs.	Avg.	AB	H	2B	3B	HR	RBI	BB	SO	OBP	Slg.
L	.500	6	3	0	0	1	1	0	0	.500	1.000	R	.300	10	3	1	0	0	5	2	1	.417	.400

RANDA, JOE — 3B

PERSONAL: Born December 18, 1969, in Milwaukee. ... 5-11/190. ... Bats right, throws right. ... Full name: Joseph Gregory Randa. ... High school: Kettle-Moraine (Wales, Wis.). ... College: Tennessee. **TRANSACTIONS/CAREER NOTES:** Selected by California Angels organization in 30th round of 1989 free-agent draft; did not sign. ... Selected by Kansas City Royals organization in 11th round of 1991 free-agent draft. ... On disabled list (May 5-27, 1996); included rehabilitation assignment to Omaha. ... Traded by Royals with Ps Jeff Granger, Jeff Martin and Jeff Wallace to Pittsburgh Pirates for SS Jay Bell and 1B Jeff King (December 13, 1996). ... On disabled list (June 28-July 27, 1997); included rehabilitation assignment to Calgary. ... Selected by Arizona Diamondbacks in third round (57th pick overall) of expansion draft (November 18, 1997). ... Traded by Diamondbacks with P Matt Drews and 3B Gabe Alvarez to Detroit Tigers for 3B Travis Fryman (November 18, 1997). ... Traded by Tigers to New York Mets for P Willie Blair (December 4, 1998). ... Traded by Mets to Royals for OF Juan LeBron (December 10, 1998). ... On disabled list (July 8-23, 2003; and June 28-July 24, 2004). ... Signed as a free agent by Cincinnati Reds (December 21, 2004). ... Traded by Reds to San Diego Padres for Ps Travis Chick and Justin Germano (July 23, 2005). ... Signed as a free agent by Pirates (January 3, 2006). ... On disabled list (May 7-June 13, 2006); included rehabilitation assignment to Indianapolis. ... On bereavement list (June 29-July 2, 2006). **STATISTICAL NOTES:** Career major league grand slams: 2.

2006 GAMES PLAYED BY POSITION (MLB): 3B—42, 1B—15, DH—3.

R

BATTING / FIELDING

Year	Team (League)	Pos.	G	AB	R	H	2B	3B	HR	RBI	BB	SO	HBP	GDP	SB-CS	Avg.	OBP	SLG	OPS	E	Avg.
1991—	Eugene (Northwest)	3B	72	275	53	93	20	2	11	59	46	29	6	8	6-1	.338	.438	.545	.984	14	.923
1992—	Appleton (Midwest)	3B	72	266	55	80	13	0	5	43	34	37	6	6	6-2	.301	.385	.406	.791	12	.941
	—Baseball City (FSL)	3B-SS	51	189	22	52	7	0	1	12	12	21	2	4	4-3	.275	.324	.328	.652	6	.961
1993—	Memphis (Sou.)	3B	131	505	74	149	31	5	11	72	39	64	3	10	8-7	.295	.343	.442	.784	25	.942
1994—	Omaha (A.A.)	3B	127	455	65	125	27	2	10	51	30	49	8	18	5-2	.275	.327	.409	.736	24	.945
1995—	Kansas City (A.L.)	3B-2B-DH	34	70	6	12	2	0	1	5	6	17	0	2	0-1	.171	.237	.243	.480	3	.952
	—Omaha (A.A.)	3B	64	233	33	64	10	2	8	33	22	33	2	9	2-2	.275	.341	.438	.779	6	.958
1996—	Kansas City (A.L.)	3B-2B-1B																			
		DH	110	337	36	102	24	1	6	47	26	47	1	10	13-4	.303	.351	.433	.784	10	.948
	—Omaha (A.A.)	3B	3	9	1	1	0	1	0	0	1	1	0	1	0-0	.111	.200	.333	.533	0	1.000
1997—	Pittsburgh (N.L.)	3B-2B	126	443	58	134	27	9	7	60	41	64	6	10	4-2	.302	.366	.451	.817	21	.948
	—Calgary (PCL)	3B	3	11	4	4	1	0	1	4	3	4	0	1	0-0	.364	.500	.727	1.227	1	.900
1998—	Detroit (A.L.)	3B-2B-1B																			
		DH	138	460	56	117	21	2	9	50	41	70	7	9	8-7	.254	.323	.367	.690	7	.981
1999—	Kansas City (A.L.)	3B	156	628	92	197	36	8	16	84	50	80	3	15	5-4	.314	.363	.473	.836	22	.952
2000—	Kansas City (A.L.)	3B-DH	158	612	88	186	29	4	15	106	36	66	6	19	6-3	.304	.343	.438	.781	19	.966
2001—	Kansas City (A.L.)	3B-DH-2B	151	581	59	147	34	2	13	83	42	80	6	15	3-2	.253	.307	.386	.693	13	.966
2002—	Kansas City (A.L.)	3B-DH	151	549	63	155	36	5	11	80	46	69	9	13	2-1	.282	.341	.426	.768	10	.972
2003—	Kansas City (A.L.)	3B-DH	131	502	80	146	31	1	16	72	41	61	7	12	1-0	.291	.348	.452	.800	7	.968
2004—	Kansas City (A.L.)	3B-DH-1B	128	485	65	139	31	2	8	56	40	77	6	11	0-1	.287	.343	.408	.751	11	.969
2005—	Cincinnati (N.L.)	3B-DH	92	332	44	96	26	1	13	48	33	52	2	6	0-0	.289	.356	.491	.847	6	.974
	—San Diego (N.L.)	3B	58	223	27	57	17	1	4	20	14	29	2	5	0-1	.256	.303	.395	.698	6	.974
2006—	Indianapolis (Int'l)		2	8	1	4	0	0	0	0	1	1	0	0	0-0	.500	.556	.500	1.056	1	.889
	—Pittsburgh (N.L.)	3B-1B-DH	89	206	23	55	13	0	4	28	16	26	0	12	0-0	.267	.316	.388	.704	5	.974
	American League totals (9 years)		1157	4224	545	1201	244	25	95	583	328	567	45	106	38-23	.284	.338	.421	.760	102	.966
	National League totals (3 years)		365	1204	152	342	83	11	28	156	104	171	10	33	4-3	.284	.343	.441	.784	38	.960
	Major League totals (12 years)		1522	5428	697	1543	327	36	123	739	432	738	55	139	42-26	.284	.339	.426	.765	140	.965

DIVISION SERIES RECORD

Year	Team (League)	Pos.	G	AB	R	H	2B	3B	HR	RBI	BB	SO	HBP	GDP	SB-CS	Avg.	OBP	SLG	OPS	E	Avg.
2005—	San Diego (N.L.)	3B	3	11	1	4	1	0	0	0	1	0	0	2	0-0	.364	.417	.455	.871	0	1.000

2006 LEFTY-RIGHTY SPLITS

vs.	Avg.	AB	H	2B	3B	HR	RBI	BB	SO	OBP	Slg.	vs.	Avg.	AB	H	2B	3B	HR	RBI	BB	SO	OBP	Slg.
L	.275	69	19	3	0	1	11	4	7	.307	.362	R	.263	137	36	10	0	3	17	12	19	.320	.401

RASNER, DARRELL — P

PERSONAL: Born January 13, 1981, in Carson City, Nev. ... 6-3/210. ... Throws right, bats right. ... Full name: Darrell Wayne Rasner. ... High school: Carson City (Nev.). ... College: Nevada. **TRANSACTIONS/CAREER NOTES:** Selected by Montreal Expos organization in second round of 2002 free-agent draft. ... Expos franchise transferred to Washington, D.C., and renamed Washington Nationals for 2005 season (December 3, 2004). ... Claimed on waivers by New York Yankees (February 10, 2006). ... On disabled list (June 3-August 24, 2006); included rehabilitation assignments to GCL Yankees and Tampa.

CAREER HITTING: 0-for-0 (.000), 0 R, 0 2B, 0 3B, 0 HR, 0 RBI.

Year	Team (League)	W	L	Pct.	ERA	WHIP	G	GS	CG	ShO	Hld.	Sv.-Opp.	IP	H	R	ER	HR	BB-IBB	SO	Avg.
2002—	Vermont (NYP)	2	5	.286	4.33	1.42	10	10	0	0	...	0-...	43.2	44	27	21	1	18-0	49	.262
2003—	Savannah (S. Atl.)	7	7	.500	4.19	1.35	22	22	2	0	...	0-...	105.1	106	53	49	8	36-0	90	.268
2004—	Brevard County (FSL)	6	5	.545	3.17	1.37	22	21	0	0	...	0-...	119.1	133	55	42	6	31-0	88	.295
	—Harrisburg (East.)	1	1	.500	1.21	1.01	5	5	0	0	...	0-...	29.2	21	4	4	1	9-1	15	.201
2005—	Harrisburg (East.)	6	7	.462	3.59	1.19	27	26	1	0	1	0-0	150.1	150	66	60	10	29-2	96	.260
	—Wash. (N.L.)	0	1	.000	3.68	0.95	5	1	0	0	0	0-0	7.1	5	3	3	0	2-1	4	.192
2006—	GC Yankees (GCL)	0	0		4.50	1.00	2	2	0	0	0	0-0	6.0	5	3	3	0	1-0	6	.217
	—Tampa (Fla. St.)	0	0		2.57	2.14	2*	2	0	0	0	0-0	7.0	12	3	2	0	3-0	6	.387
	—Columbus (Int'l)	4	0	1.000	2.76	1.21	10	10	0	0	0	0-0	58.2	60	22	18	4	11-0	47	.263
	—New York (A.L.)	3	1	.750	4.43	1.13	6	3	0	0	0	0-0	20.1	18	10	10	2	5-0	11	.237
	American League totals (1 year)	3	1	.750	4.43	1.13	6	3	0	0	0	0-0	20.1	18	10	10	2	5-0	11	.237
	National League totals (1 year)	0	1	.000	3.68	0.95	5	1	0	0	0	0-0	7.1	5	3	3	0	2-1	4	.192
	Major League totals (2 years)	3	2	.600	4.23	1.08	11	4	0	0	0	0-0	27.2	23	13	13	2	7-1	15	.225

2006 LEFTY-RIGHTY SPLITS

vs.	Avg.	AB	H	2B	3B	HR	RBI	BB	SO	OBP	Slg.	vs.	Avg.	AB	H	2B	3B	HR	RBI	BB	SO	OBP	Slg.
L	.189	37	7	2	1	0	0		5	.211	.297	R	.282	39	11	1	1	2	13	4	6	.364	.513

RAUCH, JON — P

PERSONAL: Born September 27, 1978, in Louisville, Ky. ... 6-11/260. ... Throws right, bats right. ... Full name: Jon Erich Rauch. ... Name pronounced: ROUSH. ... High school: Oldham County (Buckner, Ky.). ... College: Morehead State. **TRANSACTIONS/CAREER NOTES:** Selected by Chicago White Sox organization in third round of 1999 free-agent draft. ... Traded by White Sox with P Gary Majewski to Montreal Expos for OF Carl Everett (July 18, 2004). ... On disabled list (August 14-September 14, 2004). ... Franchise transferred to Washington, D.C., and renamed Washington Nationals for 2005 season (December 3, 2004). ... On disabled list (May 26-September 6, 2005); included rehabilitation assignment to New Orleans. **HONORS:** Named Minor League Player of the Year by THE SPORTING NEWS (2000). **MISCELLANEOUS NOTES:** Member of 2000 Olympic baseball team.

CAREER HITTING: 2-for-17 (.118), 2 R, 0 2B, 0 3B, 1 HR, 3 RBI.

Year	Team (League)	W	L	Pct.	ERA	WHIP	G	GS	CG	ShO	Hld.	Sv.-Opp.	IP	H	R	ER	HR	BB-IBB	SO	Avg.
1999—	Bristol (Appal.)	4	4	.500	4.45	1.43	14	9	0	0	...	2-...	56.2	65	44	28	4	16-1	66	.269
	—Win.-Salem (Car.)	0	0		3.00	1.17	1	1	0	0	...	0-...	6.0	4	3	2	1	3-0	7	.174
2000—	Win.-Salem (Car.)	11	3	.786	2.86	1.23	18	18	1	0	...	0-...	110.0	102	49	35	10	33-0	124	.249
	—Birmingham (Sou.)	5	1	.833	2.25	0.93	8	8	2	2	...	0-...	56.0	36	18	14	4	16-0	63	.179
2001—	Charlotte (Int'l)	1	3	.250	5.79	1.25	6	6	0	0	...	0-...	28.0	28	20	18	8	7-0	27	.248
2002—	Chicago (A.L.)	2	1	.667	6.59	1.47	8	6	0	0	0	0-0	28.2	28	26	21	7	14-2	19	.248
	—Charlotte (Int'l)	7	8	.467	4.28	1.22	19	19	1	0	...	0-...	109.1	91	60	52	14	42-2	97	.226
2003—	Charlotte (Int'l)	7	1	.875	4.11	1.30	24	23	1	0	...	0-...	124.2	121	60	57	16	35-1	94	.258
2004—	Chicago (A.L.)	1	1	.500	6.23	2.31	2	2	0	0	0	0-0	8.2	16	6	6	0	4-0	4	.432
	—Charlotte (Int'l)	6	3	.667	3.11	1.13	14	13	0	0	...	0-...	72.1	57	27	25	0	25-0	61	.218
	—Edmonton (PCL)	1	1	.500	4.50	1.06	3	3	0	0	...	0-...	18.0	17	9	9	3	2-0	13	.246
	—Montreal (N.L.)	3	0	1.000	1.54	0.90	3	2	0	0	0	0-0	23.1	14	4	4	1	7-2	18	.175
2005—	New Orleans (PCL)	1	1	.500	2.53	0.98	7	5	0	0	...	0-...	21.1	19	7	6	3	2-0	25	.232
	—Wash. (N.L.)	2	4	.333	3.60	1.17	15	1	0	0	0	0-0	30.0	24	12	12	3	11-2	23	.218

Year Team (League)	W	L	Pct.	ERA	WHIP	G	GS	CG	ShO	Hld.	Sv.-Opp.	IP	H	R	ER	HR	BB-IBB	SO	Avg.
2006— Wash. (N.L.)	4	5	.444	3.35	1.25	85	0	0	0	18	2-5	91.1	78	37	34	13	36-6	86	.231
American League totals (2 years)	3	2	.600	6.51	1.66	10	8	0	0	0	0-0	37.1	44	32	27	7	18-2	23	.293
National League totals (3 years)	9	9	.500	3.11	1.18	109	3	0	0	18	2-5	144.2	116	53	50	17	54-10	127	.220
Major League totals (4 years)	12	11	.522	3.81	1.27	119	11	0	0	18	2-5	182.0	160	85	77	24	72-12	150	.236

2006 LEFTY-RIGHTY SPLITS

vs.	Avg.	AB	H	2B	3B	HR	RBI	BB	SO	OBP	Slg.	vs.	Avg.	AB	H	2B	3B	HR	RBI	BB	SO	OBP	Slg.
L	.254	134	34	7	1	5	20	20	32	.344	.433	R	.216	204	44	6	0	8	19	16	54	.275	.363

RAY, CHRIS　　　　　　　P

PERSONAL: Born January 12, 1982, in Tampa. ... 6-3/200. ... Throws right, bats right. ... Full name: Christopher T. Ray. ... College: William & Mary. **TRANSACTIONS/CAREER NOTES:** Selected by Baltimore Orioles organization in third round of 2003 free-agent draft.
CAREER HITTING: 0-for-0 (.000), 0 R, 0 2B, 0 3B, 0 HR, 0 RBI.

Year Team (League)	W	L	Pct.	ERA	WHIP	G	GS	CG	ShO	Hld.	Sv.-Opp.	IP	H	R	ER	HR	BB-IBB	SO	Avg.
2003— Aberdeen (N.Y.-Penn.)	2	0	1.000	2.82	1.10	9	8	0	0	...	0-...	38.1	32	15	12	0	10-0	44	.225
2004— Delmarva (S. Atl.)	2	3	.400	3.42	1.20	10	9	0	0	...	0-...	50.0	43	21	19	3	17-0	46	.240
— Frederick (Carolina)	6	3	.667	3.80	1.39	14	14	1	1	...	0-...	73.1	82	31	31	6	20-0	74	.296
2005— Bowie (East.)	1	2	.333	0.96	0.64	31	0	0	0	0	18-18	37.1	17	5	4	3	7-0	40	.140
— Baltimore (A.L.)	1	3	.250	2.66	1.28	41	0	0	0	8	0-4	40.2	34	15	12	5	18-3	43	.222
2006— Baltimore (A.L.)	4	4	.500	2.73	1.09	61	0	0	0	0	33-38	66.0	45	22	20	10	27-2	51	.193
Major League totals (2 years)	5	7	.417	2.70	1.16	102	0	0	0	8	33-42	106.2	79	37	32	15	45-5	94	.205

2006 LEFTY-RIGHTY SPLITS

vs.	Avg.	AB	H	2B	3B	HR	RBI	BB	SO	OBP	Slg.	vs.	Avg.	AB	H	2B	3B	HR	RBI	BB	SO	OBP	Slg.
L	.184	114	21	2	1	8	20	18	27	.296	.430	R	.202	119	24	3	0	2	9	9	24	.254	.277

RAY, KEN　　　　　　　P

PERSONAL: Born November 27, 1974, in Atlanta. ... 6-2/200. ... Throws right, bats right. ... Full name: Kenneth Alan Ray. ... High school: Roswell (Ga.).
TRANSACTIONS/CAREER NOTES: Selected by Kansas City Royals organization in 18th round of 1993 free-agent draft. ... On disabled list (April 7-23, 1996). ... Traded by Royals to San Francisco Giants (January 7, 2000), completing deal in which Giants traded Jerry Spradlin to Royals for a player to be named (December 13, 1999). ... Signed by Yuba-Sutter of the independent Western League (2002). ... Signed by Long Island of the independent Atlantic League (2002). ... Signed as a free agent by Milwaukee Brewers organization (April 20, 2003). ... Signed as a free agent by Chicago White Sox organization (May 1, 2004). ... Released by White Sox (March 23, 2005). ... Signed by North Shore of the independent Can-Am League (2005). ... Contract purchased by Atlanta Braves organization from North Shore (June 13, 2005). ... Claimed on waivers by Kansas City Royals (October 12, 2006).
CAREER HITTING: 0-for-1 (.000), 0 R, 0 2B, 0 3B, 0 HR, 0 RBI.

Year Team (League)	W	L	Pct.	ERA	WHIP	G	GS	CG	ShO	Hld.	Sv.-Opp.	IP	H	R	ER	HR	BB-IBB	SO	Avg.
1993— GC Royals (GCL)	2	3	.400	2.28	1.29	13	7	0	0	...	0-...	47.1	44	21	12	1	17-0	45	.240
1994— Rockford (Midwest)	10	4	.714	1.82	1.17	27	18	0	0	...	3-...	128.2	94	34	26	5	56-2	128	.207
1995— Wichita (Texas)	4	5	.444	5.97	1.71	14	14	0	0	...	0-...	75.1	83	55	50	7	46-0	53	.282
— Wilmington (Caro.)	6	4	.600	2.69	1.25	13	13	1	0	...	0-...	77.0	74	32	23	3	22-2	63	.254
1996— Wichita (Texas)	4	12	.250	6.12	1.72	22	22	1	0	...	0-...	120.2	151	94	82	17	57-1	79	.312
1997— Omaha (A.A.)	5	12	.294	6.37	1.72	25	21	2	0	...	0-...	113.0	131	86	80	21	63-2	96	.296
1998— Wichita (Texas)	10	5	.667	5.20	1.67	24	21	0	0	...	0-...	117.2	149	79	68	7	47-2	71	.317
1999— Wichita (Texas)	0	0	...	5.06	1.54	14	0	0	0	...	0-...	21.1	23	12	12	2	10-0	18	.295
— Omaha (PCL)	1	0	1.000	5.19	1.22	27	0	0	0	...	8-...	43.1	41	27	25	9	12-1	36	.244
— Kansas City (A.L.)	1	0	1.000	8.74	2.56	13	0	0	0	1	0-...	11.1	23	12	11	2	6-...	0	.460
2000— Fresno (PCL)	0	0	...	7.45	2.17	7	0	0	0	...	0-...	9.2	13	10	8	4	8-0	8	.333
2001—			Did not play.																
2002— Yuba Sutter (West.)	2	0	1.000	2.38	1.15	12	0	0	0	...	3-...	11.1	10	3	3	...	3-...	11	...
— Long Island (Atl.)	0	0	...	11.12	1.76	4	0	0	0	...	0-...	5.2	10	7	7	...	0-...	6	...
2003— Huntsville (Sou.)	2	1	.667	2.93	1.47	31	0	0	0	...	4-...	61.1	65	25	20	6	25-0	49	.286
— High Desert (Calif.)	1	1	.500	7.71	2.00	7	0	0	0	...	0-...	14.0	22	13	12	4	6-0	18	.349
2004— Win.-Salem (Car.)	12	8	.600	4.08	1.35	29	18	0	0	...	1-...	123.2	124	63	56	12	43-2	99	.273
2005— North Shore (Can.-Am.)	2	0	1.000	2.75	1.02	3	3	0	0	...	0-...	19.2	10	6	6	4	10-...	22	...
— Richmond (Int'l)	2	4	.333	3.90	1.54	17	10	0	0	...	0-...	67.0	68	34	29	6	35-0	40	.274
2006— Atlanta (N.L.)	1	1	.500	4.52	1.54	69	0	0	0	7	5-8	67.2	66	36	34	9	38-4	50	.259
American League totals (1 year)	1	0	1.000	8.74	2.56	13	0	0	0	1	0-...	11.1	23	12	11	2	6-...	0	.460
National League totals (1 year)	1	1	.500	4.52	1.54	69	0	0	0	7	5-8	67.2	66	36	34	9	38-4	50	.259
Major League totals (2 years)	2	1	.667	5.13	1.68	82	0	0	0	8	5-8	79.0	89	48	45	11	44-4	50	.292

2006 LEFTY-RIGHTY SPLITS

vs.	Avg.	AB	H	2B	3B	HR	RBI	BB	SO	OBP	Slg.	vs.	Avg.	AB	H	2B	3B	HR	RBI	BB	SO	OBP	Slg.
L	.282	124	35	5	0	4	20	26	25	.404	.419	R	.237	131	31	7	0	5	21	12	25	.299	.405

REAMES, BRITT　　　　　　　P

PERSONAL: Born August 19, 1973, in Seneca, S.C. ... 5-10/180. ... Throws right, bats right. ... Full name: William Britt Reames. ... Name pronounced: REEMS. ... High school: Seneca (S.C.). ... College: The Citadel. **TRANSACTIONS/CAREER NOTES:** Selected by St. Louis Cardinals organization in 17th round of 1995 free-agent draft. ... On disabled list (April 4, 1997-entire season; and April 10, 1998-entire season). ... Traded by Cardinals with 3B Fernando Tatis to Montreal Expos for Ps Dustin Hermanson and Steve Kline (December 14, 2000). ... Signed as a free agent by Oakland Athletics organization (January 8, 2004). ... Signed as a free agent by Pittsburgh Pirates organization (November 29, 2005). **MISCELLANEOUS NOTES:** Appeared in two games as pinch runner (2000).
CAREER HITTING: 5-for-39 (.128), 3 R, 0 2B, 0 3B, 1 HR, 3 RBI.

Year Team (League)	W	L	Pct.	ERA	WHIP	G	GS	CG	ShO	Hld.	Sv.-Opp.	IP	H	R	ER	HR	BB-IBB	SO	Avg.
1995— New Jersey (NYP)	2	1	.667	1.52	1.04	5	5	0	0	...	0-...	29.2	19	7	5	1	12-0	42	.181
— Savannah (S. Atl.)	3	5	.375	3.46	1.02	10	10	1	0	...	0-...	54.2	41	23	21	7	15-0	63	.198
1996— Peoria (Midw.)	15	7	.682	1.90	0.86	25	25	2	1	...	0-...	161.0	97	43	34	5	41-0	167	.170
1997—			Did not play.																
1998—			Did not play.																
1999— Potomac (Carol.)	3	2	.600	3.19	1.50	10	8	0	0	...	0-...	36.2	34	21	13	2	21-0	22	.250
2000— Arkansas (Texas)	3	4	.400	6.13	1.61	8	8	0	0	...	0-...	39.2	46	28	27	4	18-0	39	.291
— Memphis (PCL)	6	2	.750	2.28	1.00	13	13	2	1	...	0-...	75.0	55	20	19	2	20-0	77	.212
— St. Louis (N.L.)	2	1	.667	2.88	1.30	8	7	0	0	...	0-0	40.2	30	17	13	4	23-1	31	.207
2001— Montreal (N.L.)	4	8	.333	5.59	1.57	41	13	0	0	...	0-1	95.0	101	68	59	16	48-3	86	.273
— Ottawa (Int'l)	4	3	.571	3.50	1.11	8	8	1	0	...	0-...	54.0	47	24	21	4	13-0	38	.242

Year Team (League)	W	L	Pct.	ERA	WHIP	G	GS	CG	ShO	Hld.	Sv.-Opp.	IP	H	R	ER	HR	BB-IBB	SO	Avg.
2002—Montreal (N.L.)	1	4	.200	5.03	1.59	42	6	0	0	6	0-1	68.0	70	42	38	8	38-6	76	.266
—Ottawa (Int'l)	3	2	.600	2.79	1.07	7	7	0	0	...	0-...	42.0	31	16	13	3	14-0	26	.207
2003—Montreal (N.L.)	0	0	...	27.00	4.50	2	0	0	0	...	0-0	1.1	4	4	4	0	2-0	1	.500
—Edmonton (PCL)	5	13	.278	5.42	1.63	25	20	0	0	...	0-...	118.0	146	80	71	8	46-1	86	.299
2004—Sacramento (PCL)	3	5	.375	4.67	1.60	34	3	0	0	...	8-...	52.0	55	27	27	5	28-5	57	.262
2005—Sacramento (PCL)	6	6	.500	3.31	1.36	42	7	0	0	4	8-12	92.1	91	46	34	3	35-3	85	.253
—Oakland (A.L.)	0	0	...	9.53	2.12	2	0	0	0	0	0-0	5.2	10	6	6	2	2-0	4	.400
2006—Indianapolis (Int'l)	4	2	.667	2.80	1.18	14	11	0	0	1	0-0	64.1	62	22	20	3	14-2	43	.261
—Pittsburgh (N.L.)	0	0	...	9.82	2.18	6	0	0	0	0	0-0	7.1	11	8	8	2	5-1	6	.355
American League totals (1 year)	0	0	...	9.53	2.12	2	0	0	0	0	0-0	5.2	10	6	6	2	2-0	4	.400
National League totals (5 years)	7	13	.350	5.17	1.56	99	26	0	0	12	0-2	212.1	216	139	122	30	116-11	200	.264
Major League totals (6 years)	7	13	.350	5.28	1.58	101	26	0	0	12	0-2	218.0	226	145	128	32	118-11	204	.268

DIVISION SERIES RECORD

Year Team (League)	W	L	Pct.	ERA	WHIP	G	GS	CG	ShO	Hld.	Sv.-Opp.	IP	H	R	ER	HR	BB-IBB	SO	Avg.
2000—St. Louis (N.L.)	1	0	1.000	0.00	0.90	2	0	0	0	...	0-0	3.1	0	0	0	0	3-0	2	...

CHAMPIONSHIP SERIES RECORD

Year Team (League)	W	L	Pct.	ERA	WHIP	G	GS	CG	ShO	Hld.	Sv.-Opp.	IP	H	R	ER	HR	BB-IBB	SO	Avg.
2000—St. Louis (N.L.)	0	0	...	1.42	1.42	2	0	0	0	...	0-0	6.1	5	1	1	1	4-1	6	...

2006 LEFTY-RIGHTY SPLITS

vs.	Avg.	AB	H	2B	3B	HR	RBI	BB	SO	OBP	Slg.	vs.	Avg.	AB	H	2B	3B	HR	RBI	BB	SO	OBP	Slg.
L	.444	9	4	0	0	1	3	3	1	.538	.778	R	.318	22	7	2	0	1	6	2	5	.375	.545

REDMAN, MARK P

PERSONAL: Born January 5, 1974, in San Diego. ... 6-5/245. ... Throws left, bats left. ... Full name: Mark Allen Redman. ... High school: Escondido (Calif.). ... College: Oklahoma. **TRANSACTIONS/CAREER NOTES:** Selected by Detroit Tigers organization in 41st round of 1992 free-agent draft; did not sign. ... Selected by Minnesota Twins organization in first round (13th pick overall) of 1995 free-agent draft. ... On disabled list (July 25-August 10, 1999). ... On disabled list (May 21-July 28, 2001); included rehabilitation assignment to Edmonton. ... Traded by Twins to Tigers for P Todd Jones (July 28, 2001). ... On disabled list (July 28-August 22, 2001); included rehabilitation assignment to Toledo. ... Traded by Tigers with P Jerrod Fuell to Florida Marlins for Ps Gary Knotts, Nate Robertson and Rob Henkel (January 11, 2003). ... On disabled list (April 30-May 30, 2003). ... Traded by Marlins to Oakland Athletics for Ps Mike Neu and Bill Murphy (December 16, 2003). ... Traded by A's with P Arthur Rhodes to Pittsburgh Pirates for C Jason Kendall and cash (November 29, 2004). ... Traded by Pirates to Kansas City Royals for P Jonah Bayliss and a player to be named (December 7, 2005); Pirates acquired P Chad Blackwell to complete deal (December 8, 2005). ... On disabled list (April 1-16, 2006); included rehabilitation assignment to Wichita. ... On bereavement list (May 24-31, 2006).

CAREER HITTING: 8-for-129 (.062), 2 R, 0 2B, 0 3B, 0 HR, 3 RBI.

Year Team (League)	W	L	Pct.	ERA	WHIP	G	GS	CG	ShO	Hld.	Sv.-Opp.	IP	H	R	ER	HR	BB-IBB	SO	Avg.
1995—Fort Myers (FSL)	2	1	.667	2.76	1.26	8	5	0	0	...	0-...	32.2	28	13	10	4	13-0	26	.239
1996—Fort Myers (FSL)	3	4	.429	1.85	1.17	13	13	0	0	...	0-...	82.2	63	24	17	1	34-0	75	.220
—New Britain (East.)	7	7	.500	3.81	1.42	16	16	3	0	...	0-...	106.1	101	51	45	5	50-1	96	.251
—Salt Lake (PCL)	0	0	...	9.00	2.25	1	1	0	0	...	0-...	4.0	7	4	4	1	2-0	4	.389
1997—Salt Lake (PCL)	8	15	.348	6.31	1.79	29	28	0	0	...	1-...	158.1	204	123	111	19	80-3	125	.316
1998—New Britain (East.)	4	2	.667	1.52	1.20	8	8	0	0	...	0-...	47.1	40	11	8	3	17-0	51	.237
—Salt Lake (PCL)	6	7	.462	5.53	1.53	19	18	0	0	...	0-...	99.1	111	75	61	13	41-1	88	.282
1999—Salt Lake (PCL)	9	9	.500	5.05	1.44	24	24	1	0	...	0-...	133.2	141	87	75	12	51-1	114	.272
—Minnesota (A.L.)	1	0	1.000	8.53	1.89	5	1	0	0	0	0-0	12.2	17	13	12	3	7-0	11	.298
2000—Minnesota (A.L.)	12	9	.571	4.76	1.41	32	24	0	0	0	0-0	151.1	168	81	80	22	45-0	117	.281
2001—Minnesota (A.L.)	2	4	.333	4.22	1.55	9	9	0	0	0	0-0	49.0	57	26	23	6	19-0	29	.286
—Edmonton (PCL)	0	0	...	13.50	3.00	1	1	0	0	...	0-...	1.1	3	2	2	0	1-0	0	.500
—Toledo (Int'l)	0	1	.000	5.27	1.10	3	3	0	0	...	0-...	13.2	14	10	8	3	1-0	12	.259
—Detroit (A.L.)	0	2	.000	6.00	1.67	2	2	0	0	0	0-0	9.0	11	6	6	1	4-0	4	.306
2002—Detroit (A.L.)	8	15	.348	4.21	1.29	30	30	3	0	0	0-0	203.0	211	107	95	15	51-2	109	.268
2003—Florida (N.L.)	14	9	.609	3.59	1.22	29	29	3	0	0	0-0	190.2	172	82	76	16	61-3	151	.239
2004—Oakland (A.L.)	11	12	.478	4.71	1.50	32	32	2	0	0	0-0	191.0	218	110	100	28	68-6	102	.292
2005—Pittsburgh (N.L.)	5	15	.250	4.90	1.37	30	30	2	1	0	0-0	178.1	188	100	97	18	56-3	101	.278
2006—Wichita (Texas)	0	0	...	0.90	0.70	2	2	0	0	0	0-0	10.0	6	2	1	0	1-0	9	.162
—Kansas City (A.L.)	11	10	.524	5.71	1.59	29	29	2	1	0	0-0	167.0	202	110	106	19	63-1	76	.307
American League totals (6 years)	45	52	.464	4.85	1.46	139	127	7	1	0	0-0	783.0	884	453	422	94	257-9	448	.287
National League totals (2 years)	19	24	.442	4.22	1.29	59	59	5	1	0	0-0	369.0	360	182	173	34	117-6	252	.258
Major League totals (8 years)	64	76	.457	4.65	1.40	198	186	12	2	0	0-0	1152.0	1244	635	595	128	374-15	700	.278

DIVISION SERIES RECORD

Year Team (League)	W	L	Pct.	ERA	WHIP	G	GS	CG	ShO	Hld.	Sv.-Opp.	IP	H	R	ER	HR	BB-IBB	SO	Avg.
2003—Florida (N.L.)	0	0	...	3.00	1.67	1	1	0	0	0	0-0	6.0	7	2	2	0	3-1	4	.280

CHAMPIONSHIP SERIES RECORD

Year Team (League)	W	L	Pct.	ERA	WHIP	G	GS	CG	ShO	Hld.	Sv.-Opp.	IP	H	R	ER	HR	BB-IBB	SO	Avg.
2003—Florida (N.L.)	0	0	...	6.52	1.76	2	2	0	0	0	0-0	9.2	13	7	7	2	4-0	4	.342

WORLD SERIES RECORD

Year Team (League)	W	L	Pct.	ERA	WHIP	G	GS	CG	ShO	Hld.	Sv.-Opp.	IP	H	R	ER	HR	BB-IBB	SO	Avg.
2003—Florida (N.L.)	0	1	.000	15.43	3.00	1	1	0	0	0	0-0	2.1	5	4	4	1	2-0	2	.500

2006 LEFTY-RIGHTY SPLITS

vs.	Avg.	AB	H	2B	3B	HR	RBI	BB	SO	OBP	Slg.	vs.	Avg.	AB	H	2B	3B	HR	RBI	BB	SO	OBP	Slg.
L	.229	131	30	6	1	2	14	6	18	.261	.336	R	.326	528	172	36	4	17	83	57	58	.398	.506

REDMOND, MIKE C

PERSONAL: Born May 5, 1971, in Seattle. ... 5-11/200. ... Bats right, throws right. ... Full name: Michael Patrick Redmond. ... High school: Gonzaga Prep (Spokane, Wash.). ... College: Gonzaga. **TRANSACTIONS/CAREER NOTES:** Signed as a non-drafted free agent by Florida Marlins organization (August 18, 1992). ... On disabled list (August 24-September 8, 1998). ... Signed as a free agent by Minnesota Twins (November 24, 2004).

2006 GAMES PLAYED BY POSITION (MLB): C—43, DH—2.

Year Team (League)	Pos.	G	AB	R	H	2B	3B	HR	RBI	BB	SO	HBP	GDP	SB-CS	Avg.	OBP	SLG	OPS	E	Avg.
							BATTING												FIELDING	
1993—Kane Co. (Midw.)	C	43	100	10	20	2	0	0	10	6	17	4	1	2-0	.200	.273	.220	.493	1	.996
1994—Kane Co. (Midw.)	C	92	306	39	83	10	0	1	24	26	31	9	10	3-4	.271	.344	.314	.658	6	.992
—Brevard County (FSL)	C	12	42	4	11	4	0	2	2	3	4	1		0-0	.262	.326	.357	.683	0	1.000
1995—Portland (East.)	3B-C	105	333	37	85	11	1	3	39	22	27	3	9	2-2	.255	.305	.321	.626	6	.992

Year	Team (League)	Pos.	G	AB	R	H	2B	3B	HR	RBI	BB	SO	HBP	GDP	SB-CS	Avg.	OBP	SLG	OPS	E	Avg.
1996—	Portland (East.)	C	120	394	43	113	22	0	4	44	26	45	5	12	3-4	.287	.335	.373	.708	4	.996
1997—	Charlotte (Int'l)	C	22	61	8	13	1	1	1	2	1	10	3	1	0-1	.213	.262	.377	.639	2	.985
	—GC Marlins (GCL)	DH	16	55	7	19	3	0	0	5	9	5	3	1	2-0	.345	.463	.400	.863	...	...
	—Brevard County (FSL)	1B	5	17	2	0	0	0	0	0	2	2	0	2	0-0	.000	.105	.000	.105	0	1.000
1998—	Portland (East.)	C	8	28	7	9	4	0	1	7	2	2	2	2	0-0	.321	.406	.571	.978	1	.983
	—Charlotte (Int'l)	C	18	58	4	14	2	0	2	7	0	3	1	3	0-0	.241	.246	.379	.625	0	1.000
	—Florida (N.L.)	C	37	118	10	39	9	0	2	12	5	16	2	6	0-0	.331	.368	.458	.826	2	.992
1999—	Florida (N.L.)	C	84	242	22	73	9	0	1	27	26	34	5	8	0-0	.302	.381	.351	.732	4	.992
2000—	Florida (N.L.)	C	87	210	17	53	8	1	0	15	13	19	8	5	0-0	.252	.315	.300	.616	2	.996
2001—	Florida (N.L.)	C	48	141	19	44	4	0	4	14	13	13	2	6	0-0	.312	.376	.426	.801	7	.994
2002—	Florida (N.L.)	C-1B	89	256	19	78	15	0	2	28	21	34	8	8	0-2	.305	.372	.387	.758	4	.993
2003—	Florida (N.L.)	C-1B-3B	59	125	12	30	7	1	0	11	7	16	5	2	0-0	.240	.302	.312	.614	1	.995
2004—	Florida (N.L.)	C	81	246	19	63	15	0	2	25	14	28	8	10	1-0	.256	.315	.341	.656	2	.996
2005—	Minnesota (A.L.)	C	45	148	17	46	9	0	1	26	6	14	3	9	0-0	.311	.350	.392	.742	0	1.000
2006—	Minnesota (A.L.)	C-DH	47	179	20	61	13	0	0	23	4	18	4	9	0-0	.341	.365	.413	.778	0	1.000
	American League totals (2 years)		92	327	37	107	22	0	1	49	10	32	7	18	0-0	.327	.358	.404	.762	0	1.000
	National League totals (7 years)		485	1338	118	380	67	2	11	132	99	160	38	41	1-2	.284	.348	.362	.710	17	.994
	Major League totals (9 years)		577	1665	155	487	89	2	12	181	109	192	45	59	1-2	.292	.350	.370	.720	17	.995

CHAMPIONSHIP SERIES RECORD

Year	Team (League)	Pos.	G	AB	R	H	2B	3B	HR	RBI	BB	SO	HBP	GDP	SB-CS	Avg.	OBP	SLG	OPS	E	Avg.
2003—	Florida (N.L.)	C	1	0	1	0	0	0	0	0	0	0	0	0	0-0	...	1.000	...	1.000	0	1.000

WORLD SERIES RECORD

Year	Team (League)	Pos.	G	AB	R	H	2B	3B	HR	RBI	BB	SO	HBP	GDP	SB-CS	Avg.	OBP	SLG	OPS	E	Avg.
2003—	Florida (N.L.)	C	1	1	0	0	0	0	0	0	0	0	0	0	0-0	.000	.000	.000	.000	0	1.000

2006 LEFTY-RIGHTY SPLITS

vs.	Avg.	AB	H	2B	3B	HR	RBI	BB	SO	OBP	Slg.
L	.443	70	31	7	0	0	9	3	1	.467	.543
R	.275	109	30	6	0	0	14	1	17	.298	.330

REED, ERIC — OF

PERSONAL: Born December 2, 1980, in Little Rock, Ark. ... 5-11/170. ... Bats left, throws left. ... Full name: Eric Shane Reed. ... College: Texas A&M.
TRANSACTIONS/CAREER NOTES: Selected by Florida Marlins organization in ninth round of 2002 free-agent draft.
2006 GAMES PLAYED BY POSITION (MLB): OF—32.

Year	Team (League)	Pos.	G	AB	R	H	2B	3B	HR	RBI	BB	SO	HBP	GDP	SB-CS	Avg.	OBP	SLG	OPS	E	Avg.
2002—	Jamestown (NYP)		60	250	35	77	5	1	0	17	17	30	0	3	19-10	.308	.348	.336	.684	...	...
	—Kane Co. (Midw.)		12	50	11	18	1	0	0	2	3	11	0	1	7-1	.360	.396	.380	.776	...	...
2003—	Jupiter (Fla. St.)		134	514	86	154	15	8	0	25	52	83	3	4	53-18	.300	.367	.360	.727	...	...
2004—	Carolina (Southern)		55	222	32	68	9	6	3	14	14	55	0	2	24-6	.306	.345	.441	.786	...	...
2005—	Carolina (Southern)	OF	71	271	35	69	9	0	1	15	17	62	4	2	23-8	.255	.305	.299	.604	2	.994
	—Albuquerque (PCL)	OF	39	171	19	53	5	4	1	20	3	31	4	1	17-7	.310	.335	.404	.739	2	.989
2006—	Albuquerque (PCL)		95	390	68	118	20	9	5	39	24	94	2	7	20-9	.303	.344	.438	.782	3	.987
	—Florida (N.L.)	OF	42	41	6	4	0	0	0	0	2	10	2	1	3-1	.098	.178	.098	.275	0	1.000
	Major League totals (1 year)		42	41	6	4	0	0	0	0	2	10	2	1	3-1	.098	.178	.098	.275	0	1.000

2006 LEFTY-RIGHTY SPLITS

vs.	Avg.	AB	H	2B	3B	HR	RBI	BB	SO	OBP	Slg.
L	.000	1	0	0	0	0	0	0	1	.500	.000
R	.100	40	4	0	0	0	0	2	9	.163	.100

REED, JEREMY — OF

PERSONAL: Born June 15, 1981, in San Dimas, Calif. ... 6-0/185. ... Bats left, throws left. ... Full name: Jeremy Thomas Reed. ... High school: Bonita (LaVerne, Calif.). ... College: Long Beach State. **TRANSACTIONS/CAREER NOTES:** Selected by Chicago White Sox organization in second round of 2002 free-agent draft. ... Traded by White Sox with C Miguel Olivo and SS Michael Morse to Seattle Mariners for P Freddy Garcia and C Ben Davis (June 27, 2004). ... On disabled list (July 3, 2006-remainder of season).
2006 GAMES PLAYED BY POSITION (MLB): OF—64.

Year	Team (League)	Pos.	G	AB	R	H	2B	3B	HR	RBI	BB	SO	HBP	GDP	SB-CS	Avg.	OBP	SLG	OPS	E	Avg.
2002—	Kannapolis (S. Atl.)	OF	57	210	37	67	15	0	4	32	11	24	11	7	17-5	.319	.377	.448	.825	0	1.000
2003—	Win.-Salem (Car.)	OF	65	222	37	74	18	1	4	52	41	17	1	5	27-6	.333	.431	.477	.909	3	.979
	—Birmingham (Sou.)	OF	66	242	51	99	17	3	7	43	29	19	2	7	18-13	.409	.454	.591	1.065	0	1.000
2004—	Charlotte (Int'l)	OF-DH	73	276	44	76	14	1	8	37	36	34	3	7	12-7	.275	.357	.420	.771	1	.995
	—Tacoma (PCL)	OF	61	233	40	71	10	5	5	36	23	22	0	6	14-2	.305	.366	.455	.821	3	.982
	—Seattle (A.L.)	OF	18	58	14	23	4	0	0	5	7	4	1	2	3-1	.397	.470	.466	.935	1	.981
2005—	Seattle (A.L.)	OF	141	488	61	124	33	3	3	45	48	74	2	10	12-11	.254	.322	.352	.675	3	.992
2006—	Seattle (A.L.)	OF	67	212	27	46	6	5	6	17	11	31	2	5	2-3	.217	.260	.377	.637	1	.992
	Major League totals (3 years)		226	758	99	193	43	8	9	67	66	109	5	17	17-15	.255	.317	.368	.685	5	.991

2006 LEFTY-RIGHTY SPLITS

vs.	Avg.	AB	H	2B	3B	HR	RBI	BB	SO	OBP	Slg.
L	.000	23	0	0	0	0	0	1	6	.042	.000
R	.243	189	46	6	5	6	17	10	25	.286	.423

REESE, KEVIN — OF

PERSONAL: Born March 11, 1978, in San Diego. ... 5-11/195. ... Bats left, throws left. ... Full name: Kevin Patrick Reese. ... College: San Diego. **TRANSACTIONS/CAREER NOTES:** Selected by San Diego Padres organization in 27th round of 2000 free-agent draft. ... Traded by Padres to New York Yankees for 2B Bernie Castro (December 18, 2001).
2006 GAMES PLAYED BY POSITION (MLB): OF—4, DH—2.

Year	Team (League)	Pos.	G	AB	R	H	2B	3B	HR	RBI	BB	SO	HBP	GDP	SB-CS	Avg.	OBP	SLG	OPS	E	Avg.
2000—	Idaho Falls (Pio.)	OF	53	201	51	72	14	4	2	36	43	30	3	5	12-3	.358	.474	.498	.972	5	.925
2001—	Fort Wayne (Midw.)	OF	125	459	84	151	30	6	13	73	54	62	5	5	30-10	.329	.402	.505	.907	4	.984
2002—	Norwich (East.)	OF	138	514	80	149	24	6	4	45	77	87	4	6	22-14	.290	.385	.383	.768	6	.980
2003—	Columbus (Int'l)	OF	15	55	11	12	1	0	1	3	6	8	0	0	1-0	.218	.295	.291	.586	1	.963

Year	Team (League)	Pos.	G	AB	R	H	2B	3B	HR	RBI	BB	SO	HBP	GDP	SB-CS	Avg.	OBP	SLG	OPS	E	Avg.
—Trenton (East.)	OF	86	309	42	84	13	2	4	21	25	58	2	4	27-5	.272	.328	.366	.694	4	.980
2004—Trenton (East.)	OF	78	329	57	98	37	4	6	40	23	48	3	5	13-5	.298	.348	.489	.837	2	.966
—Columbus (Int'l)	OF	53	217	41	70	13	3	8	28	12	34	5	5	4-4	.323	.370	.521	.891	2	.000
2005—New York (A.L.)	OF	2	1	0	0	0	0	0	0	1	1	0	0	0-0	.000	.500	.000	.500	1	1.000
—Columbus (Int'l)	OF-DH	133	540	92	149	38	7	14	69	63	86	10	10	16-5	.276	.359	.450	.809	8	.984
2006—New York (A.L.)	OF-DH	10	12	2	5	0	0	0	1	1	1	.1	0	1-0	.417	.500	.417	.917	1	.667
—Columbus (Int'l)		53	212	30	60	8	2	5	21	15	37	10	5	4-6	.283	.354	.410	.765	3	.972
Major League totals (2 years)		12	13	2	5	0	0	0	1	2	2	1	0	1-0	.385	.500	.385	.885	1	.800

2006 LEFTY-RIGHTY SPLITS

vs.	Avg.	AB	H	2B	3B	HR	RBI	BB	SO	OBP	Slg.	vs.	Avg.	AB	H	2B	3B	HR	RBI	BB	SO	OBP	Slg.
L	.000	0	0	0	0	0	0	0	0	1.000	.000	R	.417	12	5	0	0	0	1	1	1	.462	.417

R

REITSMA, CHRIS — P

PERSONAL: Born December 31, 1977, in Minneapolis. ... 6-5/235. ... Throws right, bats right. ... Full name: Christopher Michael Reitsma. ... Name pronounced: REETS-muh. ... High school: Calgary (Alberta) Christian. **TRANSACTIONS/CAREER NOTES:** Selected by Boston Red Sox organization in supplemental round ("sandwich pick" between first and second rounds, 34th pick overall) of 1996 free-agent draft; pick received as compensation for Toronto Blue Jays signing free-agent P Erik Hanson. ... Selected by Tampa Bay Devil Rays from Red Sox organization in Rule 5 major league draft (December 13, 1999). ... Returned to Red Sox (March 28, 2000). ... Traded by Red Sox with P John Curtice to Cincinnati Reds for OF Dante Bichette (August 31, 2000). ... Traded by Reds to Atlanta Braves for Ps Jung Bong and Bubba Nelson (March 26, 2004). ... On disabled list (June 14-30, 2006). ... On disabled list (July 2, 2006-remainder of season). **MISCELLANEOUS NOTES:** Appeared in two games as pinch runner (2001).

CAREER HITTING: 9-for-87 (.103), 3 R, 1 2B, 0 3B, 0 HR, 5 RBI.

Year	Team (League)	W	L	Pct.	ERA	WHIP	G	GS	CG	ShO	Hld.	Sv.-Opp.	IP	H	R	ER	HR	BB-IBB	SO	Avg.
1996—GC Red Sox (GCL)	3	1	.750	1.35	0.94	7	6	0	0	...	0-...	26.2	24	7	4	0	1-0	32	.229
1997—Michigan (Midw.)	4	1	.800	2.90	1.41	9	9	0	0	...	0-...	49.2	57	23	16	4	13-0	41	.285
1998—Sarasota (Fla. St.)	0	0	...	2.84	1.34	8	8	0	0	...	0-...	12.2	12	6	4	0	5-0	9	.245
1999—Sarasota (Fla. St.)	4	10	.286	5.61	1.53	19	19	0	0	...	0-...	96.1	116	71	60	11	31-1	79	.294
2000—Sarasota (Fla. St.)	3	4	.429	3.66	1.16	11	11	0	0	...	0-...	64.0	57	29	26	3	17-0	47	.238
—Trenton (East.)	7	2	.778	2.58	1.09	14	14	1	0	...	0-...	90.2	78	28	26	7	21-1	58	.232
2001—Cincinnati (N.L.)	7	15	.318	5.29	1.42	36	29	0	0	1	0-0	182.0	209	121	107	23	49-6	96	.288
2002—Cincinnati (N.L.)	6	12	.333	3.64	1.37	32	21	1	1	0	0-0	138.1	144	73	56	17	45-5	84	.267
—Louisville (Int'l)	2	0	1.000	3.86	1.19	3	3	1	0	...	0-...	21.0	17	10	9	2	8-1	13	.224
2003—Louisville (Int'l)	1	2	.333	4.00	1.50	4	4	0	0	...	0-...	18.0	22	10	8	1	5-0	11	.293
—Cincinnati (N.L.)	9	5	.643	4.29	1.32	57	3	0	0	3	12-18	84.0	92	41	40	14	19-6	53	.281
2004—Atlanta (N.L.)	6	4	.600	4.07	1.37	84	0	0	0	31	2-9	79.2	89	38	36	9	20-3	60	.284
2005—Atlanta (N.L.)	3	6	.333	3.93	1.27	76	0	0	0	13	15-24	73.1	79	32	32	8	14-3	42	.272
2006—Atlanta (N.L.)	1	2	.333	8.68	1.93	27	0	0	0	3	1-8	28.0	46	27	27	7	8-3	13	.362
Major League totals (6 years)	32	44	.421	4.58	1.39	312	53	1	1	51	37-63	585.1	659	332	298	73	155-26	348	.284

DIVISION SERIES RECORD

Year	Team (League)	W	L	Pct.	ERA	WHIP	G	GS	CG	ShO	Hld.	Sv.-Opp.	IP	H	R	ER	HR	BB-IBB	SO	Avg.
2004—Atlanta (N.L.)	0	0	...	18.00	2.00	3	0	0	0	0	0-0	3.0	5	6	6	2	1-0	2	.417
2005—Atlanta (N.L.)	0	0	...	16.20	2.70	4	0	0	0	0	0-0	3.1	7	6	6	0	2-2	0	.438
Division series totals (2 years)	0	0	...	17.05	2.37	7	0	0	0	0	0-0	6.1	12	12	12	2	3-2	2	.429

2006 LEFTY-RIGHTY SPLITS

vs.	Avg.	AB	H	2B	3B	HR	RBI	BB	SO	OBP	Slg.	vs.	Avg.	AB	H	2B	3B	HR	RBI	BB	SO	OBP	Slg.
L	.422	64	27	6	2	4	18	4	4	.457	.766	R	.302	63	19	4	0	3	11	4	9	.362	.508

REMLINGER, MIKE — P

PERSONAL: Born March 23, 1966, in Middletown, N.Y. ... 6-1/215. ... Throws left, bats left. ... Full name: Michael John Remlinger. ... Name pronounced: REM-lin-jurr. ... High school: Carver (Plymouth, Mass.). ... College: Dartmouth. **TRANSACTIONS/CAREER NOTES:** Selected by San Francisco Giants organization in first round (16th pick overall) of 1987 free-agent draft. ... Traded by Giants with OF Kevin Mitchell to Seattle Mariners for Ps Bill Swift, Mike Jackson and Dave Burba (December 11, 1991). ... Signed as a free agent by New York Mets organization (November 22, 1993). ... Traded by Mets to Cincinnati Reds for OF Cobi Cradle (May 11, 1995). ... Traded to Kansas City Royals as part of three-team deal in which Reds acquired OF Andre King from St. Louis Cardinals and Cardinals acquired SS Luis Ordaz from Reds and OF Miguel Mejia from Royals (December 4, 1995). ... Claimed on waivers by Reds (April 4, 1996). ... Traded by Reds with 2B Bret Boone to Atlanta Braves for Ps Denny Neagle and Rob Bell and OF Michael Tucker (November 10, 1998). ... On disabled list (April 3-18, 1999; June 23-July 13, 2000; and August 8-24, 2002). ... Signed as a free agent by Chicago Cubs (December 3, 2002). ... On disabled list (March 26-May 22 and June 24-July 11, 2004; included rehabilitation assignment to Iowa. ... On disabled list (May 25-June 5, 2005). ... Traded by Cubs to Boston Red Sox for P Olivo Astacio (August 9, 2005). ... Released by Red Sox (August 29, 2005). ... Signed by Atlanta Braves organization (January 23, 2006). ... Released by Braves (June 26, 2006). **MISCELLANEOUS NOTES:** Appeared in two games as pinch runner (1997).

CAREER HITTING: 8-for-110 (.073), 5 R, 3 2B, 0 3B, 0 HR, 8 RBI.

Year	Team (League)	W	L	Pct.	ERA	WHIP	G	GS	CG	ShO	Hld.	Sv.-Opp.	IP	H	R	ER	HR	BB-IBB	SO	Avg.
1987—Everett (N'west)	0	0	...	3.60	1.20	2	1	0	0	...	0-...	5.0	1	2	2	0	5-0	11	.071
—Clinton (Midw.)	2	1	.667	3.30	1.17	6	5	0	0	...	0-...	30.0	21	12	11	2	14-0	43	.196
—Shreveport (Texas)	4	2	.667	2.36	1.05	6	6	0	0	...	0-...	34.1	14	11	9	2	22-0	51	.120
1988—Shreveport (Texas)	1	0	1.000	0.69	0.85	3	3	0	0	...	0-...	13.0	7	4	1	0	4-0	18	.163
1989—Shreveport (Texas)	4	6	.400	2.98	1.56	16	16	0	0	...	0-...	90.2	68	43	30	2	73-0	92	.212
—Phoenix (PCL)	1	6	.143	9.21	2.40	11	10	0	0	...	0-...	43.0	51	47	44	8	52-0	28	.290
1990—Shreveport (Texas)	9	11	.450	3.90	1.50	25	25	2	1	...	0-...	147.2	149	82	64	9	72-1	75	.270
1991—Phoenix (PCL)	5	5	.500	6.38	1.78	19	19	1	1	...	0-...	108.2	134	86	77	15	59-0	68	.305
—San Francisco (N.L.)	2	1	.667	4.37	1.60	8	6	1	1	0	0-0	35.0	36	17	17	5	20-1	19	.271
1992—Calgary (PCL)	1	7	.125	6.65	2.06	21	11	0	0	...	0-...	70.1	97	65	52	7	48-1	24	.342
—Jacksonville (Sou.)	1	1	.500	3.46	1.38	5	5	0	0	...	0-...	26.0	25	15	10	1	11-0	21	.250
1993—Calgary (PCL)	4	3	.571	5.53	1.80	19	18	0	0	...	0-...	84.2	100	57	52	8	52-0	51	.300
—Jacksonville (Sou.)	1	3	.250	6.58	1.49	7	7	0	0	...	0-...	39.2	40	30	29	7	19-0	23	.261
1994—Norfolk (Int'l)	2	4	.333	3.14	1.30	12	9	0	0	...	0-...	63.0	57	29	22	5	25-0	45	.242
—New York (N.L.)	1	5	.167	4.61	1.65	10	9	0	0	1	0-0	54.2	55	30	28	9	35-4	33	.261
1995—New York (N.L.)	0	1	.000	6.35	1.59	5	0	0	0	1	0-1	5.2	7	5	4	1	2-0	6	.292
—Cincinnati (N.L.)	0	0	...	9.00	3.00	1	0	0	0	0	0-0	1.0	2	1	1	0	1-0	1	.500
—Indianapolis (A.A.)	5	3	.625	4.05	1.54	41	1	0	0	...	0-...	46.2	40	24	21	4	32-1	58	.231
1996—Indianapolis (A.A.)	4	3	.571	2.52	1.21	28	13	0	0	...	0-...	89.1	64	29	25	4	44-0	97	.203
—Cincinnati (N.L.)	0	1	.000	5.60	1.57	19	4	0	0	1	0-0	27.1	24	17	17	4	19-2	19	.245
1997—Cincinnati (N.L.)	8	8	.500	4.14	1.29	69	12	0	0	14	2-2	124.0	100	61	57	11	60-6	145	.223
1998—Cincinnati (N.L.)	8	15	.348	4.82	1.53	35	28	1	0	0	0-0	164.1	164	96	88	23	87-1	144	.266
1999—Atlanta (N.L.)	10	1	.909	2.37	1.21	73	0	0	0	21	1-3	83.2	66	24	22	9	35-5	81	.215

Year Team (League)	W	L	Pct.	ERA	WHIP	G	GS	CG	ShO	Hld.	Sv.-Opp.	IP	H	R	ER	HR	BB-IBB	SO	Avg.
2000—Atlanta (N.L.)	5	3	.625	3.47	1.27	71	0	0	0	23	12-16	72.2	55	29	28	6	37-1	72	.207
2001—Atlanta (N.L.)	3	3	.500	2.76	1.20	74	0	0	0	31	1-5	75.0	67	25	23	9	23-4	93	.234
2002—Atlanta (N.L.)	7	3	.700	1.99	1.12	73	0	0	0	30	0-5	68.0	48	17	15	3	28-3	69	.198
2003—Chicago (N.L.)	6	5	.545	3.65	1.35	73	0	0	0	17	0-1	69.0	54	30	28	11	39-4	83	.211
2004—Iowa (PCL)	0	0	...	16.20	1.80	2	0	0	0	...	0-...	1.2	3	3	3	1	0-0	1	.375
—Chicago (N.L.)	1	2	.333	3.44	1.34	48	0	0	0	13	2-6	36.2	33	16	14	3	16-3	35	.246
2005—Chicago (N.L.)	0	3	.000	4.91	1.30	35	0	0	0	5	0-1	33.0	31	19	18	5	12-2	30	.250
—Boston (A.L.)	0	0	...	14.85	3.00	8	0	0	0	0	0-0	6.2	15	14	11	2	5-0	5	.417
2006—Atlanta (N.L.)	2	4	.333	4.03	1.61	36	0	0	0	2	2-5	22.1	27	11	10	2	9-2	19	.293
American League totals (1 year)	0	0	...	14.85	3.00	8	0	0	0	0	0-0	6.2	15	14	11	2	5-0	5	.417
National League totals (14 years)	53	55	.491	3.82	1.37	631	59	4	2	158	20-45	872.1	769	398	370	101	425-38	849	.237
Major League totals (14 years)	53	55	.491	3.90	1.38	639	59	4	2	158	20-45	879.0	784	412	381	103	430-38	854	.239

DIVISION SERIES RECORD

Year Team (League)	W	L	Pct.	ERA	WHIP	G	GS	CG	ShO	Hld.	Sv.-Opp.	IP	H	R	ER	HR	BB-IBB	SO	Avg.
1999—Atlanta (N.L.)	0	0	...	9.82	1.91	4	0	0	0	0	0-1	3.2	4	4	4	1	3-2	4	.308
2000—Atlanta (N.L.)	0	0	...	2.70	1.80	3	0	0	0	0	0-0	3.1	6	1	1	1	0-0	3	.375
2001—Atlanta (N.L.)	0	0	...	0.00	0.00	1	0	0	0	1	0-0	0.1	0	0	0	0	0-0	0	.000
2002—Atlanta (N.L.)	0	0	...	4.50	2.50	3	0	0	0	0	0-0	2.0	3	1	1	0	2-0	3	.333
2003—Chicago (N.L.)	0	0	...	0.00	1.50	2	0	0	0	0	0-0	0.2	0	0	0	0	1-0	1	.000
Division series totals (5 years)	0	0	...	5.40	1.90	11	0	0	0	2	0-1	10.0	13	6	6	2	6-2	11	.317

CHAMPIONSHIP SERIES RECORD

Year Team (League)	W	L	Pct.	ERA	WHIP	G	GS	CG	ShO	Hld.	Sv.-Opp.	IP	H	R	ER	HR	BB-IBB	SO	Avg.
1999—Atlanta (N.L.)	0	1	.000	3.18	1.06	5	0	0	0	3	0-0	5.2	3	2	2	0	3-0	4	.158
2001—Atlanta (N.L.)	0	0	...	2.14	0	0	0	0	0	0-0	2.1	3	0	0	0	2-0	2	.333
2003—Chicago (N.L.)	0	0	...	2.70	1.20	5	0	0	0	0	1-1	3.1	3	1	1	1	1-0	2	.214
Champ. series totals (3 years)	0	1	.000	2.38	1.32	13	0	0	0	3	1-1	11.1	9	3	3	1	6-0	8	.214

WORLD SERIES RECORD

Year Team (League)	W	L	Pct.	ERA	WHIP	G	GS	CG	ShO	Hld.	Sv.-Opp.	IP	H	R	ER	HR	BB-IBB	SO	Avg.
1999—Atlanta (N.L.)	0	1	.000	9.00	2.00	2	0	0	0	0	0-0	1.0	1	1	1	1	1-0	0	.333

ALL-STAR GAME RECORD

	W	L	Pct.	ERA	WHIP	G	GS	CG	ShO	Hld.	Sv.-Opp.	IP	H	R	ER	HR	BB-IBB	SO	Avg.
All-Star Game totals (1 year)	0	0	...	27.00	3.00	1	0	0	0	1	0-0	0.2	1	2	2	0	1-0	0	.333

2006 LEFTY-RIGHTY SPLITS

vs.	Avg.	AB	H	2B	3B	HR	RBI	BB	SO	OBP	Slg.	vs.	Avg.	AB	H	2B	3B	HR	RBI	BB	SO	OBP	Slg.
L	.289	45	13	0	1	1	7	2	7	.347	.400	R	.298	47	14	3	0	1	6	7	12	.389	.426

RENTERIA, EDGAR — SS

PERSONAL: Born August 7, 1975, in Barranquilla, Colombia. ... 6-1/200. ... Bats right, throws right. ... Full name: Edgar Enrique Renteria. ... Name pronounced: ren-ter-REE-ah. ... High school: Instituto Los Alpes (Barranquilla, Colombia). **TRANSACTIONS/CAREER NOTES:** Signed as a non-drafted free agent by Florida Marlins organization (February 14, 1992). ... On disabled list (June 24-July 11, 1996); included rehabilitation assignment to Charlotte. ... On disabled list (August 25-September 9, 1998). ... Traded by Marlins to St. Louis Cardinals for Ps Braden Looper and Armando Almanza and SS Pablo Ozuna (December 14, 1998). ... Signed as a free agent by Boston Red Sox (December 17, 2004). ... Traded by Red Sox to Atlanta Braves for 3B Andy Marte (December 8, 2005). **HONORS:** Named shortstop on THE SPORTING NEWS N.L. All-Star team (2000, 2002-04). ... Won N.L. Gold Glove at shortstop (2002 and 2003). ... Named shortstop on N.L. Silver Slugger team (2000, 2002 and 2003). **STATISTICAL NOTES:** Career major league grand slams: 4.

2006 GAMES PLAYED BY POSITION (MLB): SS—146, DH—1.

Year Team (League)	Pos.	G	AB	R	H	2B	3B	HR	RBI	BB	SO	HBP	GDP	SB-CS	Avg.	OBP	SLG	OPS	E	Avg.
1992—GC Marlins (GCL)	SS	43	163	25	47	8	1	0	9	8	29	2	1	10-6	.288	.329	.350	.679	24	.897
1993—Kane Co. (Midw.)	SS	116	384	40	78	8	0	1	35	35	94	0	3	7-8	.203	.268	.232	.500	34	.934
1994—Brevard County (FSL)	SS	128	439	46	111	15	1	0	36	35	56	0	14	6-11	.253	.307	.292	.598	23	.959
1995—Portland (East.)	SS	135	508	70	147	15	7	7	68	32	85	2	10	30-11	.289	.329	.388	.717	33	.944
1996—Charlotte (Int'l)	SS	35	132	17	37	8	0	2	16	9	17	0	4	10-4	.280	.326	.386	.713	7	.959
—Florida (N.L.)	SS	106	431	68	133	18	3	5	31	33	68	2	12	16-2	.309	.358	.399	.757	11	.979
1997—Florida (N.L.)	SS	154	617	90	171	21	3	4	52	45	108	4	17	32-15	.277	.327	.340	.668	17	.975
1998—Florida (N.L.)	SS	133	517	79	146	18	2	3	31	48	78	4	13	41-22	.282	.347	.342	.689	20	.966
1999—St. Louis (N.L.)	SS	154	585	92	161	36	2	11	63	53	82	2	16	37-8	.275	.334	.400	.734	26	.959
2000—St. Louis (N.L.)	SS	150	562	94	156	32	1	16	76	63	77	1	19	21-13	.278	.346	.423	.770	27	.958
2001—St. Louis (N.L.) SS-1B-DH		141	493	54	128	19	3	10	57	39	73	3	15	17-4	.260	.314	.371	.685	24	.961
2002—St. Louis (N.L.)	SS	152	544	77	166	36	2	11	83	49	57	4	17	22-7	.305	.364	.439	.803	19	.970
2003—St. Louis (N.L.)	SS	157	587	96	194	47	1	13	100	65	54	1	21	34-7	.330	.394	.480	.874	16	.975
2004—St. Louis (N.L.)	SS	149	586	84	168	37	0	10	72	39	78	1	14	17-11	.287	.327	.401	.728	11	.983
2005—Boston (A.L.)	SS	153	623	100	172	36	4	8	70	55	100	3	15	9-4	.276	.335	.385	.721	30	.954
2006—Atlanta (N.L.)	SS-DH	149	598	100	175	40	2	14	70	62	89	3	17	17-6	.293	.361	.436	.797	13	.978
American League totals (1 year)		153	623	100	172	36	4	8	70	55	100	3	15	9-4	.276	.335	.385	.721	30	.954
National League totals (10 years)		1445	5520	834	1598	304	19	97	635	496	764	25	161	254-95	.289	.347	.404	.752	184	.970
Major League totals (11 years)		1598	6143	934	1770	340	23	105	705	551	864	28	176	263-99	.288	.346	.402	.749	214	.969

DIVISION SERIES RECORD

Year Team (League)	Pos.	G	AB	R	H	2B	3B	HR	RBI	BB	SO	HBP	GDP	SB-CS	Avg.	OBP	SLG	OPS	E	Avg.
1997—Florida (N.L.)	SS	3	13	1	2	0	0	0	1	2	4	0	1	0-0	.154	.267	.154	.421	2	.909
2000—St. Louis (N.L.)	SS	3	10	5	2	0	0	0	4	1	0	0	0	2-0	.200	.429	.200	.629	1	.909
2001—St. Louis (N.L.)	SS	5	17	2	4	1	0	1	1	2	4	0	1	0-0	.235	.316	.471	.786	1	.955
2002—St. Louis (N.L.)	SS	3	12	3	3	0	0	0	1	1	1	0	1	2-0	.250	.308	.250	.558	1	.909
2004—St. Louis (N.L.)	SS	4	11	4	5	2	0	0	6	1	2	1	0	1-1	.455	.500	.636	1.236	0	1.000
2005—Boston (A.L.)	SS	3	13	1	3	2	0	0	0	1	1	0	0	0-0	.231	.286	.385	.670	0	1.000
Division series totals (6 years)		21	76	16	19	5	0	1	6	13	12	1	3	5-1	.250	.367	.355	.722	5	.949

CHAMPIONSHIP SERIES RECORD

Year Team (League)	Pos.	G	AB	R	H	2B	3B	HR	RBI	BB	SO	HBP	GDP	SB-CS	Avg.	OBP	SLG	OPS	E	Avg.
1997—Florida (N.L.)	SS	6	22	4	5	1	0	0	3	6	1	1	1	1-0	.227	.346	.273	.619	0	1.000
2000—St. Louis (N.L.)	SS	5	20	4	6	1	0	0	4	0	2	0	0	3-0	.300	.286	.350	.636	0	1.000
2002—St. Louis (N.L.)	SS	5	19	0	3	0	0	0	0	1	1	0	0	0-0	.158	.190	.158	.348	1	.900
2004—St. Louis (N.L.)	SS	7	24	1	4	0	0	0	0	2	5	0	0	0-0	.167	.231	.167	.397	0	1.000
Champ. series totals (4 years)		23	85	9	18	2	0	0	7	5	15	2	2	4-0	.212	.266	.235	.501	1	.989

WORLD SERIES RECORD

Year Team (League)	Pos.	G	AB	R	H	2B	3B	HR	RBI	BB	SO	HBP	GDP	SB-CS	Avg.	OBP	SLG	OPS	E	Avg.
1997— Florida (N.L.)	SS	7	31	3	9	2	0	0	3	3	5	0	0	0-0	.290	.353	.355	.708	1	.974
2004— St. Louis (N.L.)	SS	4	15	2	5	3	0	0	1	2	2	0	1	0-0	.333	.412	.533	.945	1	.941
World series totals (2 years)		11	46	5	14	5	0	0	4	5	7	0	1	0-0	.304	.373	.413	.786	2	.964

ALL-STAR GAME RECORD

		G	AB	R	H	2B	3B	HR	RBI	BB	SO	HBP	GDP	SB-CS	Avg.	OBP	SLG	OPS	E	Avg.
All-Star Game totals (5 years)		5	10	2	1	1	0	1	1	0	1	0	2	0-0	.100	.100	.200	.300	0	1.000

2006 LEFTY-RIGHTY SPLITS

vs.	Avg.	AB	H	2B	3B	HR	RBI	BB	SO	OBP	Slg.	vs.	Avg.	AB	H	2B	3B	HR	RBI	BB	SO	OBP	Slg.
L	.333	132	44	14	0	4	15	20	20	.418	.530	R	.281	466	131	26	2	10	55	42	69	.344	.410

REPKO, JASON — OF

PERSONAL: Born December 27, 1980, in East Chicago, Ind. ... 5-11/175. ... Bats right, throws right. ... Full name: Jason Edward Repko. ... High school: Hanford (Wash.). **TRANSACTIONS/CAREER NOTES:** Selected by Los Angeles Dodgers organization in first round (37th pick overall) of 1999 free-agent draft. ... On disabled list (May 10-July 24, 2006); included rehabilitation assignment to Las Vegas.
2006 GAMES PLAYED BY POSITION (MLB): OF—62.

Year Team (League)	Pos.	G	AB	R	H	2B	3B	HR	RBI	BB	SO	HBP	GDP	SB-CS	Avg.	OBP	SLG	OPS	E	Avg.
1999— Great Falls (Pio.)	SS	49	207	51	63	9	9	8	32	21	43	3	1	12-5	.304	.375	.551	.926	38	.859
2000— Yakima (N'west)	SS	8	17	3	5	2	0	0	1	1	7	0	0	0-0	.294	.333	.412	.745	3	.813
2001— Wilmington (S. Atl.)	SS	88	337	36	74	17	4	4	32	15	68	3	2	17-8	.220	.257	.329	.586	26	.921
2002— Vero Beach (FSL)	OF	120	470	73	128	29	5	9	53	25	92	8	3	29-13	.272	.319	.413	.732	7	.973
2003— Jacksonville (Sou.)	OF	119	416	62	100	14	5	10	23	42	89	6	1	21-8	.240	.317	.370	.687	5	.980
2004— Jacksonville (Sou.)	OF	46	189	26	55	11	2	6	19	13	43	2	1	10-5	.291	.341	.466	.807	3	.936
—Las Vegas (PCL)	OF	75	302	55	94	26	4	7	41	18	57	3	4	13-5	.311	.355	.493	.848	2	1.000
2005— Las Vegas (PCL)	OF	8	31	6	12	0	0	3	6	0	4	0	0	1-0	.387	.387	.677	1.065	0	1.000
—Los Angeles (N.L.)	OF-DH	129	276	43	61	15	3	8	30	16	80	7	7	5-0	.221	.281	.384	.665	6	.968
2006— Las Vegas (PCL)		9	29	2	8	2	0	2	3	6	2	1	1	1-0	.276	.382	.345	.727	1	.944
—Los Angeles (N.L.)	OF	69	130	21	33	5	1	3	16	15	24	3	2	10-4	.254	.345	.377	.722	2	.977
Major League totals (2 years)		198	406	64	94	20	4	11	46	31	104	10	9	15-4	.232	.302	.382	.684	8	.971

DIVISION SERIES RECORD

Year Team (League)	Pos.	G	AB	R	H	2B	3B	HR	RBI	BB	SO	HBP	GDP	SB-CS	Avg.	OBP	SLG	OPS	E	Avg.
2006— Los Angeles (N.L.)		1	0	0	0	0	0	0	0	0	0	0	0	0-0	...	...	...	...	0	...

2006 LEFTY-RIGHTY SPLITS

vs.	Avg.	AB	H	2B	3B	HR	RBI	BB	SO	OBP	Slg.	vs.	Avg.	AB	H	2B	3B	HR	RBI	BB	SO	OBP	Slg.
L	.239	46	11	1	1	3	8	8	7	.375	.500	R	.262	84	22	4	0	0	8	7	17	.326	.310

RESOP, CHRIS — P

PERSONAL: Born November 4, 1982, in Naples, Fla. ... 6-3/222. ... Throws right, bats right. ... Full name: Christopher Paul Resop. ... High school: Barron Collier (Naples, Fla.). **TRANSACTIONS/CAREER NOTES:** Selected by Florida Marlins organization in fourth round of 2001 free-agent draft.
CAREER HITTING: 0-for-1 (.000), 0 R, 0 2B, 0 3B, 0 HR, 0 RBI.

Year Team (League)	W	L	Pct.	ERA	WHIP	G	GS	CG	ShO	Hld.	Sv.-Opp.	IP	H	R	ER	HR	BB-IBB	SO	Avg.
2003— Greensboro (S. Atl.)	0	1	.000	4.97	1.26	11	0	0	0	...	0-...	12.2	11	7	7	1	5-0	15	.224
2004— Greensboro (S. Atl.)	3	1	.750	1.94	0.79	41	0	0	0	...	13-...	41.2	26	11	9	1	7-0	68	.173
2005— Carolina (Southern)	3	2	.600	2.57	1.29	43	0	0	0	1	24-26	49.0	47	15	14	2	16-1	56	.242
—Florida (N.L.)	2	0	1.000	8.47	1.82	15	0	0	0	0	0-0	17.0	22	16	16	1	9-0	15	.324
2006— Albuquerque (PCL)	4	0	1.000	3.81	1.29	40	0	0	0	5	2-4	49.2	49	21	21	4	15-2	43	.258
—Florida (N.L.)	1	2	.333	3.38	1.97	22	0	0	0	2	0-1	21.1	26	9	8	1	16-5	10	.310
Major League totals (2 years)	3	2	.600	5.63	1.90	37	0	0	0	2	0-1	38.1	48	25	24	2	25-5	25	.316

2006 LEFTY-RIGHTY SPLITS

vs.	Avg.	AB	H	2B	3B	HR	RBI	BB	SO	OBP	Slg.	vs.	Avg.	AB	H	2B	3B	HR	RBI	BB	SO	OBP	Slg.
L	.279	43	12	3	1	1	3	10	7	.426	.465	R	.341	41	14	5	0	0	4	6	3	.426	.463

RESTOVICH, MICHAEL — OF

PERSONAL: Born January 3, 1979, in Rochester, Minn. ... 6-4/257. ... Bats right, throws right. ... Full name: Michael Jerome Restovich. ... Name pronounced: ress-TO-vich. ... High school: Mayo (Rochester, Minn.). **TRANSACTIONS/CAREER NOTES:** Selected by Minnesota Twins organization in second round of 1997 free-agent draft. ... Claimed on waivers by Tampa Bay Devil Rays (March 30, 2005). ... Claimed on waivers by Colorado Rockies (April 6, 2005). ... Traded by Rockies to Pittsburgh Pirates for a player to be named later or cash considerations (May 11, 2005). ... Released by Pirates (November 28, 2005). ... Signed by Chicago Cubs organization (January 3, 2006). ... Signed as free agent by Washington Nationals (November 6, 2006).
2006 GAMES PLAYED BY POSITION (MLB): OF—3.

Year Team (League)	Pos.	G	AB	R	H	2B	3B	HR	RBI	BB	SO	HBP	GDP	SB-CS	Avg.	OBP	SLG	OPS	E	Avg.
1998— Elizabethton (App.)	OF	65	242	68	86	20	1	13	64	54	58	9	10	5-2	.355	.489	.607	1.096	9	.912
—Fort Wayne (Midw.)	OF	11	45	9	20	5	2	0	6	4	12	0	1	0-0	.444	.490	.644	1.134	0	1.000
1999— Quad City (Midw.)	3B-OF	131	493	91	154	30	6	19	107	74	100	13	9	7-9	.312	.412	.513	.925	9	.958
2000— Fort Myers (FSL)	OF	135	475	73	125	27	9	8	64	61	100	4	11	19-7	.263	.350	.408	.758	6	.975
2001— New Britain (East.)	1B-OF	140	501	69	135	33	4	23	84	54	125	6	8	15-7	.269	.345	.489	.834	3	.989
2002— Edmonton (PCL)	OF-DH	138	518	95	148	32	7	29	98	53	151	4	11	11-7	.286	.353	.542	.896	6	.976
—Minnesota (A.L.)	OF-DH	8	13	3	4	0	0	1	1	1	4	0	2	1-0	.308	.357	.538	.896	0	1.000
2003— Rochester (Int'l)	OF-DH	119	454	75	125	34	2	16	72	47	117	4	10	10-3	.275	.346	.465	.811	3	.989
—Minnesota (A.L.)	OF-DH	24	53	10	15	3	2	0	4	10	12	1	3	0-0	.283	.406	.415	.821	0	1.000
2004— Rochester (Int'l)	OF-DH	106	425	65	105	20	3	20	63	25	104	2	13	4-3	.247	.291	.449	.740	5	.975
—Minnesota (A.L.)	OF-DH	29	47	9	12	3	0	1	4	4	10	0	0	0-0	.255	.314	.447	.761	0	1.000
2005— Colorado (N.L.)	OF	14	31	5	9	0	1	3	3	5	5	0	0	0-0	.290	.353	.452	.805	0	1.000
—Pittsburgh (N.L.)	OF	52	84	10	18	3	1	2	5	8	24	0	3	0-0	.214	.283	.345	.628	1	.976
2006— Iowa (PCL)		120	443	75	130	29	4	27	85	52	121	7	9	2-1	.293	.374	.560	.933	3	.986
—Chicago (N.L.)	OF	10	12	0	2	1	0	0	1	1	5	0	0	0-0	.167	.231	.250	.481	0	1.000
American League totals (3 years)		61	113	22	31	6	2	3	11	15	26	1	5	1-0	.274	.364	.442	.807	0	1.000
National League totals (2 years)		76	127	15	29	6	1	3	9	12	34	0	5	0-0	.228	.295	.362	.657	1	.983
Major League totals (5 years)		137	240	37	60	12	3	6	20	27	60	1	10	1-0	.250	.328	.400	.728	1	.991

2006 LEFTY-RIGHTY SPLITS

vs.	Avg.	AB	H	2B	3B	HR	RBI	BB	SO	OBP	Slg.	vs.	Avg.	AB	H	2B	3B	HR	RBI	BB	SO	OBP	Slg.
L	.222	9	2	1	0	0	1	0	3	.222	.333	R	.000	3	0	0	0	0	0	1	2	.250	.000

REYES, AL — P

PERSONAL: Born April 10, 1970, in San Cristobal, Dominican Republic. ... 6-1/212. ... Throws right, bats right. ... Full name: Rafael Alberto Reyes. ... Name pronounced: RAY-ess. ... High school: Francisco del Rosario Sanche (Santo Domingo, Dominican Republic). **TRANSACTIONS/CAREER NOTES:** Signed as a non-drafted free agent by Montreal Expos organization (February 17, 1988). ... Selected by Milwaukee Brewers from Expos organization in Rule 5 major league draft (December 5, 1994). ... On disabled list (July 19, 1995-remainder of season). ... On disabled list (July 25-September 8, 1998); included rehabilitation assignment to Louisville. ... Traded by Brewers to Baltimore Orioles (July 21, 1999), completing deal in which Orioles traded P Rocky Coppinger to Brewers for a player to be named (July 16, 1999). ... Traded by Orioles to Los Angeles Dodgers for P Alan Mills and cash (June 13, 2000). ... Signed as a free agent by Pittsburgh Pirates organization (January 25, 2002). ... Released by Pirates (March 10, 2003). ... Signed by New York Yankees organization (March 19, 2003). ... Released by Yankees (July 25, 2003). ... Signed by Tampa Bay Devil Rays organization (January 12, 2004). ... Released by Devil Rays (June 1, 2004). ... Signed by St. Louis Cardinals organization (June 3, 2004).
CAREER HITTING: 3-for-12 (.250), 2 R, 0 2B, 0 3B, 0 HR, 0 RBI.

Year	Team (League)	W	L	Pct.	ERA	WHIP	G	GS	CG	ShO	Hld.	Sv.-Opp.	IP	H	R	ER	HR	BB-IBB	SO	Avg.
1989— Dom. Expos (DSL)	3	4	.429	2.79	1.42	12	10	1	0	...	0-...	71.0	68	36	22	...	33-...	49	
1990— W.P. Beach (FSL)	5	4	.556	4.74	1.58	16	10	0	0	...	1-...	57.0	58	32	30	4	32-2	47	.272
1991— Rockford (Midwest)	0	1	.000	5.56	1.41	3	3	0	0	...	0-...	11.1	14	8	7	1	2-0	10	.304
1992— Albany (S. Atl.)	0	2	.000	3.95	1.35	27	0	0	0	...	4-...	27.1	24	14	12	0	13-0	29	.226
1993— Burlington (Midw.)	7	6	.538	2.68	1.05	53	0	0	0	...	11-...	74.0	52	33	22	7	26-3	80	.193
1994— Harrisburg (East.)	2	2	.500	3.25	1.17	60	0	0	0	...	35-...	69.1	68	26	25	4	13-0	60	.257
1995— Milwaukee (A.L.)	1	1	.500	2.43	1.11	27	0	0	0	4	1-1	33.1	19	9	9	3	18-2	29	.167
1996— Beloit (Midw.)	1	0	1.000	1.83	1.17	13	0	0	0	...	0-...	19.2	17	7	4	1	6-0	22	.227
— Milwaukee (A.L.)	1	0	1.000	7.94	1.76	5	0	0	0	0	0-0	5.2	8	5	5	1	2-0	2	.333
1997— Tucson (PCL)	2	4	.333	5.02	1.50	38	0	0	0	...	7-...	57.1	52	39	32	12	34-2	70	.243
— Milwaukee (A.L.)	1	2	.333	5.46	1.38	19	0	0	0	1	1-1	29.2	32	19	18	4	9-0	25	.274
1998— Milwaukee (A.L.)	5	1	.833	3.95	1.51	50	0	0	0	10	0-1	57.0	55	26	25	9	31-1	58	.255
— Louisville (Int'l)	0	1	.000	8.31	1.62	3	2	0	0	...	0-...	4.1	5	5	4	1	2-0	5	.294
1999— Louisville (Int'l)	0	2	.000	8.38	1.97	6	0	0	0	...	0-...	9.2	12	9	9	0	7-2	8	.343
— Milwaukee (A.L.)	2	0	1.000	4.25	1.44	26	0	0	0	2	0-1	36.0	27	17	17	5	25-1	39	.206
— Baltimore (A.L.)	2	3	.400	4.85	1.31	27	0	0	0	4	0-3	29.2	23	16	16	4	16-2	28	.225
2000— Rochester (Int'l)	0	1	.000	7.71	1.89	9	0	0	0	...	2-...	11.2	13	11	10	2	9-1	17	.271
— Baltimore (A.L.)	1	0	1.000	6.92	1.85	13	0	0	0	2	0-0	13.0	13	10	10	2	11-1	10	.271
— Albuquerque (PCL)	3	2	.600	3.72	1.40	30	0	0	0	...	8-...	38.2	33	20	16	5	21-0	39	.226
— Los Angeles (N.L.)	0	0	...	0.00	0.45	6	0	0	0	1	0-0	6.2	2	0	0	0	1-0	8	.087
2001— Las Vegas (PCL)	0	1	.000	3.38	1.16	19	0	0	0	...	0-...	29.1	24	11	11	3	10-1	37	.218
— Los Angeles (N.L.)	2	1	.667	3.86	1.60	19	0	0	0	0	1-2	25.2	28	13	11	3	13-1	23	.269
2002— Nashville (PCL)	7	3	.700	2.70	0.93	43	0	0	0	...	1-...	66.2	40	21	20	5	22-2	90	.167
— Pittsburgh (N.L.)	0	0	...	2.65	0.94	15	0	0	0	3	0-1	17.0	9	5	5	1	7-0	21	.161
2003— Columbus (Int'l)	1	1	.500	3.71	1.20	15	0	0	0	...	2-...	17.0	16	7	7	1	5-0	21	.239
— New York (A.L.)	0	0	...	3.18	1.29	13	0	0	0	0	0-1	17.0	13	7	6	1	9-1	9	.203
2004— Durham (Int'l)	2	1	.667	2.46	1.23	20	0	0	0	...	10-...	22.0	22	6	6	0	5-1	22	.265
— Memphis (PCL)	2	2	.500	2.95	1.16	37	0	0	0	...	23-...	39.2	32	13	13	7	14-3	47	.219
— St. Louis (N.L.)	0	0	...	0.75	0.42	12	0	0	0	0	0-0	12.0	3	1	1	0	2-0	11	.081
2005— St. Louis (N.L.)	4	2	.667	2.15	0.93	65	0	0	0	16	3-3	62.2	38	15	15	5	20-2	67	.177
2006— St. Louis (N.L.)									Did not play.										
American League totals (6 years)	6	6	.500	4.49	1.35	104	0	0	0	11	2-7	128.1	108	66	64	15	65-6	106	.230
National League totals (7 years)	13	4	.765	3.07	1.20	193	0	0	0	32	4-8	217.0	162	77	74	23	99-5	227	.207
Major League totals (11 years)	19	10	.655	3.60	1.26	297	2	0	0	43	6-15	345.1	270	143	138	38	164-11	333	.216

WORLD SERIES RECORD

Year	Team (League)	W	L	Pct.	ERA	WHIP	G	GS	CG	ShO	Hld.	Sv.-Opp.	IP	H	R	ER	HR	BB-IBB	SO	Avg.
2004— St. Louis (N.L.)	0	0	...	0.00	0.00	2	0	0	0	0	0-0	1.1	0	0	0	0	0-0	0	.000

2006 LEFTY-RIGHTY SPLITS

vs.	Avg.	AB	H	2B	3B	HR	RBI	BB	SO	OBP	Slg.	vs.	Avg.	AB	H	2B	3B	HR	RBI	BB	SO	OBP	Slg.
L												R											

REYES, ANTHONY — P

PERSONAL: Born October 16, 1981, in Downey, Calif. ... 6-2/215. ... Throws right, bats right. ... Full name: Anthony Loza Reyes. ... High school: California (Whittier, Calif.). ... College: Southern California. **TRANSACTIONS/CAREER NOTES:** Selected by St. Louis Cardinals organization in 15th round of 2003 free-agent draft. **MISCELLANEOUS NOTES:** Appeared in one game as pinch runner (2006).
CAREER HITTING: 3-for-29 (.103), 1 R, 0 2B, 0 3B, 0 HR, 0 RBI.

Year	Team (League)	W	L	Pct.	ERA	WHIP	G	GS	CG	ShO	Hld.	Sv.-Opp.	IP	H	R	ER	HR	BB-IBB	SO	Avg.
2004— Palm Beach (FSL)	3	0	1.000	4.66	1.31	7	7	0	0	...	0-...	36.2	41	21	19	5	7-0	38	.297
— Tennessee (Sou.)	6	2	.750	2.91	1.01	12	12	0	0	...	0-...	74.1	62	27	24	3	13-1	102	.230
2005— Memphis (PCL)	7	6	.538	3.64	1.08	23	23	2	1	...	0-0	128.2	105	55	52	13	34-1	136	.222
— St. Louis (N.L.)	1	1	.500	2.70	0.75	4	1	0	0	0	0-0	13.1	6	4	4	2	4-1	12	.133
2006— Memphis (PCL)	6	1	.857	2.57	0.96	13	13	0	0	0	0-0	84.0	70	27	24	9	11-0	82	.221
— St. Louis (N.L.)	5	8	.385	5.06	1.38	17	17	1	0	0	0-0	85.1	84	48	48	17	34-0	72	.262
Major League totals (2 years)	6	9	.400	4.74	1.30	21	18	1	0	0	0-0	98.2	90	52	52	19	38-1	84	.246

CHAMPIONSHIP SERIES RECORD

Year	Team (League)	W	L	Pct.	ERA	WHIP	G	GS	CG	ShO	Hld.	Sv.-Opp.	IP	H	R	ER	HR	BB-IBB	SO	Avg.
2006— St. Louis (N.L.)	0	0	...	4.50	1.75	1	1	0	0	0	0-0	4.0	3	2	2	2	4-0	4	.200

WORLD SERIES RECORD

Year	Team (League)	W	L	Pct.	ERA	WHIP	G	GS	CG	ShO	Hld.	Sv.-Opp.	IP	H	R	ER	HR	BB-IBB	SO	Avg.
2006— St. Louis (N.L.)	1	0	1.000	2.25	0.63	1	1	0	0	0	0-0	8.0	4	2	2	1	1-0	4	.143

2006 LEFTY-RIGHTY SPLITS

vs.	Avg.	AB	H	2B	3B	HR	RBI	BB	SO	OBP	Slg.	vs.	Avg.	AB	H	2B	3B	HR	RBI	BB	SO	OBP	Slg.
L	.278	144	40	6	2	7	16	14	25	.340	.493	R	.249	177	44	11	4	10	27	20	47	.345	.525

REYES, DENNYS — P

PERSONAL: Born April 19, 1977, in Higuera de Zaragoza, Mexico. ... 6-3/245. ... Throws left, bats right. ... Name pronounced: RAY-ess. ... High school: Ignacio Zaragoza (Higuera de Zaragoza, Mexico). **TRANSACTIONS/CAREER NOTES:** Signed as a non-drafted free agent by Los Angeles Dodgers organization (July 5, 1993). ... Loaned by

R

Dodgers organization to Mexico City Red Devils of the Mexican League (March 28-August 22, 1995). ... Traded by Dodgers with 1B/3B Paul Konerko to Cincinnati Reds for P Jeff Shaw (July 4, 1998). ... On disabled list (May 30-July 2, 2001). ... Traded by Reds with SS Pokey Reese to Colorado Rockies for Ps Gabe White and Luke Hudson (December 18, 2001). ... Traded by Rockies with OF Todd Hollandsworth to Texas Rangers for OF Gabe Kapler and 2B Jason Romano (July 31, 2002). ... Signed as a free agent by Pittsburgh Pirates organization (January 24, 2003). ... Signed as a free agent by Arizona Diamondbacks organization (June 11, 2003). ... Signed as a free agent by Kansas City Royals organization (October 30, 2003). ... Signed as a free agent by San Diego Padres (November 29, 2004). ... Released by Padres (July 17, 2005). ... Signed by New York Yankees organization (August 2, 2005). ... Signed as a free agent by Minnesota Twins organization (December 23, 2005).
CAREER HITTING: 4-for-54 (.074), 2 R, 1 2B, 0 3B, 0 HR, 0 RBI.

Year	Team (League)	W	L	Pct.	ERA	WHIP	G	GS	CG	ShO	Hld.	Sv.-Opp.	IP	H	R	ER	HR	BB-IBB	SO	Avg.
1993—	M.C. R. Dev. (Mex.)	0	1	.000	5.06	2.44	7	1	0	0		0-...	5.1	4	4	3	1	9-...	5	
1994—	Vero Beach (FSL)	2	4	.333	6.70	1.82	9	9	0	0		0-...	41.2	58	37	31	6	18-0	25	.324
—	Great Falls (Pio.)	7	1	.875	3.78	1.44	14	9	0	0		0-...	66.2	71	37	28	0	25-0	70	.267
1995—	M.C. R. Dev. (Mex.)	5	5	.500	6.60	1.99	17	15	1	0		0-...	58.2	76	49	43	4	41-...	44	
—	Vero Beach (FSL)	1	0	1.000	1.80	1.40	3	2	0	0		0-...	10.0	8	2	2	0	6-0	9	.222
1996—	San Bern. (Calif.)	11	12	.478	4.17	1.46	29	28	0	0		0-...	166.0	166	106	77	11	77-0	176	.259
1997—	San Antonio (Texas)	8	1	.889	3.02	1.33	12	12	1	0		0-...	80.1	79	33	27	6	28-1	66	.262
—	Albuquerque (PCL)	6	3	.667	5.65	1.80	10	10	1	0		0-...	57.1	70	40	36	4	33-0	45	.303
—	Los Angeles (N.L.)	1	4	.200	5.83	1.47	14	5	0	0		0-0	47.0	51	31	20	4	18-3	36	.280
1998—	Albuquerque (PCL)	1	4	.200	1.44	1.12	7	7	1	1		0-...	43.2	31	13	7	5	18-0	58	.197
—	Los Angeles (N.L.)	0	4	.000	4.71	1.64	11	3	0	0		0-0	28.2	27	17	15	1	20-4	33	.255
—	Indianapolis (Int'l)	2	0	1.000	3.00	1.42	4	4	0	0		0-...	24.0	20	10	8	1	14-0	27	.233
—	Cincinnati (N.L.)	3	1	.750	4.42	1.60	8	7	0	0	0	0-0	38.2	35	19	19	2	27-1	44	.255
1999—	Cincinnati (N.L.)	2	2	.500	3.79	1.49	65	1	0	0	14	2-3	61.2	53	30	26	5	39-1	72	.232
2000—	Cincinnati (N.L.)	2	1	.667	4.53	1.65	62	0	0	0	10	0-1	43.2	43	31	22	5	29-0	36	.262
2001—	Cincinnati (N.L.)	2	6	.250	4.92	1.62	35	6	0	0	6	0-0	53.0	51	35	29	5	35-1	52	.248
—	Louisville (Int'l)	4	2	.667	3.67	1.46	7	6	0	0		0-...	34.1	34	15	14	3	16-0	34	.260
2002—	Colorado (N.L.)	0	1	.000	4.24	1.66	43	0	0	0	4	0-0	40.1	43	19	19	1	24-3	30	.279
—	Texas (A.L.)	4	3	.571	6.38	1.80	15	5	0	0	0	0-0	42.1	55	33	30	9	21-1	29	.316
2003—	Pittsburgh (N.L.)	0	0	...	10.45	1.84	12	0	0	0	2	0-0	10.1	10	13	12	1	9-1	11	.263
—	Tucson (PCL)	2	1	.667	2.84	1.50	33	0	0	0		2-...	31.2	24	16	10	0	22-2	30	.207
—	Arizona (N.L.)	0	0	...	11.57	2.57	3	0	0	0	0	0-0	2.1	5	3	3	1	1-0	5	.417
2004—	Kansas City (A.L.)	4	8	.333	4.75	1.52	40	12	0	0	5	0-1	108.0	114	64	57	12	50-3	91	.273
2005—	San Diego (N.L.)	3	2	.600	5.15	2.04	36	1	0	0	6	0-1	43.2	57	30	25	3	32-2	35	.315
2006—	Rochester (Int'l)	1	0	1.000	0.50	0.78	4	3	0	0	1	0-0	18.0	11	1	1	0	3-0	13	.183
—	Minnesota (A.L.)	5	0	1.000	0.89	0.99	66	0	0	0	16	0-1	50.2	35	8	5	3	15-2	49	.197
American League totals (3 years)		13	11	.542	4.12	1.44	121	17	0	0	21	0-2	201.0	204	105	92	24	86-6	169	.265
National League totals (8 years)		14	20	.412	4.63	1.65	289	23	0	0	36	2-5	369.1	375	218	190	28	234-16	354	.266
Major League totals (10 years)		27	31	.466	4.45	1.58	410	40	0	0	57	2-7	570.1	579	323	282	52	320-22	523	.266

DIVISION SERIES RECORD

Year	Team (League)	W	L	Pct.	ERA	WHIP	G	GS	CG	ShO	Hld.	Sv.-Opp.	IP	H	R	ER	HR	BB-IBB	SO	Avg.
2006—	Minnesota (A.L.)	0	0	...	9.00	3.00	2	0	0	0	0	0-0	1.0	1	3	1	0	2-1	1	.250

2006 LEFTY-RIGHTY SPLITS

vs.	Avg.	AB	H	2B	3B	HR	RBI	BB	SO	OBP	Slg.		vs.	Avg.	AB	H	2B	3B	HR	RBI	BB	SO	OBP	Slg.
L	.148	88	13	2	0	1	4	8	28	.219	.205		R	.244	90	22	3	0	2	5	7	21	.299	.344

REYES, JOSE — SS

PERSONAL: Born June 11, 1983, in Villa Gonzalez, Dominican Republic. ... 6-0/160. ... Bats both, throws right. ... Full name: Jose Bernabe Reyes. ... Name pronounced: RAY-ess. ... High school: Attended Liceoi Delia Reyes, played for Felix de Leon (Dominican Republic). **TRANSACTIONS/CAREER NOTES:** Signed as a non-drafted free agent by New York Mets organization (August 16, 1999). ... On disabled list (September 1, 2003-remainder of season). ... On disabled list (March 26-June 19 and August 13-September 24, 2004); included rehabilitation assignments to St. Lucie and Binghamton. **HONORS:** Named shortstop on SPORTING NEWS N.L. All-Star team (2006). ... Named shortstop on N.L. Silver Slugger team (2006). **STATISTICAL NOTES:** Hit three home runs in one game (August 15, 2006). :.. Hit for the cycle (June 21, 2006). ... Career major league grand slams: 2.

2006 GAMES PLAYED BY POSITION (MLB): SS—149.

Year	Team (League)	Pos.	G	AB	R	H	2B	3B	HR	RBI	BB	SO	HBP	GDP	SB-CS	Avg.	OBP	SLG	OPS	E	Avg.
									BATTING											FIELDING	
2000—	Kingsport (Appalachian)	SS-3B-2B OF	49	132	22	33	3	3	0	8	20	37	3	1	10-4	.250	.359	.318	.677	11	.942
2001—	Capital City (SAL)	SS	108	407	71	125	22	15	5	48	18	71	2	4	30-10	.307	.337	.472	.809	18	.964
2002—	St. Lucie (Fla. St.)	SS	69	288	58	83	10	11	6	38	30	35	1	5	31-13	.288	.353	.462	.815	12	.967
—	Binghamton (East.)	SS	65	275	46	79	16	8	2	24	16	42	2	2	27-11	.287	.331	.425	.757	17	.940
2003—	Norfolk (Int'l)	SS-DH	42	160	28	43	6	4	0	13	15	25	1	2	26-5	.269	.333	.356	.690	5	.969
—	New York (N.L.)	SS	69	274	47	84	12	4	5	32	13	36	0	1	13-3	.307	.334	.434	.769	9	.973
2004—	St. Lucie (Fla. St.)	2B	6	23	3	6	2	0	0	1	0	3	0	1	2-0	.261	.261	.348	.609	2	.917
—	Binghamton (East.)	2B	4	18	2	2	0	0	0	3	2	4	0	0	3-1	.111	.190	.111	.302	0	1.000
—	New York (N.L.)	2B-SS	53	220	33	56	16	2	2	14	5	31	0	1	19-2	.255	.271	.373	.644	6	.975
2005—	New York (N.L.)	SS	161	*696	99	190	24	*17	7	58	27	78	2	7	*60-15	.273	.300	.386	.687	18	.974
2006—	New York (N.L.)	SS	153	647	122	194	*30	*17	19	81	53	81	1	6	*64-17	.300	.354	.487	.841	17	.971
Major League totals (4 years)			436	1837	301	524	82	40	33	185	98	226	3	15	156-37	.285	.321	.427	.749	50	.973

DIVISION SERIES RECORD

Year	Team (League)	Pos.	G	AB	R	H	2B	3B	HR	RBI	BB	SO	HBP	GDP	SB-CS	Avg.	OBP	SLG	OPS	E	Avg.
2006—	New York (N.L.)	SS	3	12	2	2	0	0	0	3	2	2	0	0	1-1	.167	.286	.167	.452	0	1.000

CHAMPIONSHIP SERIES RECORD

Year	Team (League)	Pos.	G	AB	R	H	2B	3B	HR	RBI	BB	SO	HBP	GDP	SB-CS	Avg.	OBP	SLG	OPS	E	Avg.
2006—	New York (N.L.)	SS	7	32	5	9	1	1	1	2	1	3	0	0	2-0	.281	.303	.469	.772	0	1.000

2006 LEFTY-RIGHTY SPLITS

vs.	Avg.	AB	H	2B	3B	HR	RBI	BB	SO	OBP	Slg.		vs.	Avg.	AB	H	2B	3B	HR	RBI	BB	SO	OBP	Slg.
L	.330	182	60	9	3	6	25	14	20	.378	.511		R	.288	465	134	21	14	13	56	39	61	.345	.477

REYES, JOSE A. — C

PERSONAL: Born February 26, 1984, in Barahona, Dominican Republic. ... 5-11/180. ... Bats both, throws right. ... Full name: Jose Ariel Reyes. **TRANSACTIONS/CAREER NOTES:** Signed as a non-drafted free agent by Chicago Cubs organization (May 29, 1999).
2006 GAMES PLAYED BY POSITION (MLB): C—2.

Year Team (League)	Pos.	G	AB	R	H	2B	3B	HR	RBI	BB	SO	HBP	GDP	SB-CS	Avg.	OBP	SLG	OPS	E	Avg.
2000— Dominican Cubs (DSL)		24	85	15	23	4	2	3	12	16	16	0	3	0-1	.271	.386	.471	.857	...	...
2001— Dominican Cubs (DSL)		67	250	38	72	12	4	4	36	34	26	4	6	12-3	.288	.379	.416	.795	...	...
2002— West Tenn (Sou.)		1	5	0	2	0	0	0	0	0	3	0	0	0-0	.400	.400	.400	.800	...	...
— Ariz. Cubs (Ariz.)		19	50	4	9	0	1	0	7	6	13	1	1	3-1	.180	.276	.220	.496	...	...
2003— Boise (N'west)		11	36	4	10	0	0	0	5	1	4	0	0	0-1	.278	.297	.278	.575	...	...
— Lansing (Midw.)		70	234	18	56	9	0	0	20	16	37	3	3	2-1	.239	.295	.278	.573	...	...
2004— Daytona (Fla. St.)		80	261	27	59	12	1	2	17	13	54	5	6	1-4	.226	.276	.303	.579	...	...
2005— West Tenn (Sou.)	C-1B	97	319	27	82	10	0	3	50	27	48	1	16	6-3	.257	.314	.317	.631	5	.994
2006— Iowa (PCL)		37	108	10	27	6	0	0	11	14	11	2	5	0-1	.250	.347	.306	.652	2	.992
— West Tenn (Sou.)		47	144	15	33	3	0	0	11	9	25	0	6	0-1	.229	.275	.250	.525	1	.997
— Chicago (N.L.)	C	4	5	0	1	0	0	0	2	0	3	0	0	0-0	.200	.200	.200	.400	0	1.000
Major League totals (1 year)		4	5	0	1	0	0	0	2	0	3	0	0	0-0	.200	.200	.200	.400	0	1.000

2006 LEFTY-RIGHTY SPLITS

vs.	Avg.	AB	H	2B	3B	HR	RBI	BB	SO	OBP	Slg.	vs.	Avg.	AB	H	2B	3B	HR	RBI	BB	SO	OBP	Slg.
L	.000	2	0	0	0	0	0	0	1	.000	.000	R	.333	3	1	0	0	0	2	0	2	.333	.333

RHEINECKER, JOHN   P

PERSONAL: Born May 29, 1979, in Belleville, Ill. ... 6-2/215. ... Throws left, bats left. ... Full name: John Philip Rheinecker. ... College: Southwest Missouri State. **TRANSACTIONS/CAREER NOTES:** Selected by Oakland Athletics organization in supplemental round ("sandwich pick" between first and second rounds, 37th pick overall) of 2001 free-agent draft; pick received as compensation for New York Mets signing Type A free-agent P Kevin Appier. ... Traded by Athletics with IF/OF Freddie Bynum to Texas Rangers for P Juan Dominguez as part of a three-team deal in which Rangers acquired P John Koronka from Chicago Cubs for Bynum (March 31, 2006).

CAREER HITTING: 0-for-0 (.000), 0 R, 0 2B, 0 3B, 0 HR, 0 RBI.

Year Team (League)	W	L	Pct.	ERA	WHIP	G	GS	CG	ShO	Hld.	Sv.-Opp.	IP	H	R	ER	HR	BB-IBB	SO	Avg.
2001— Vancouver (N'west)	0	1	.000	1.59	0.75	5	5	0	0	...	0-...	22.2	13	5	4	0	4-0	17	.160
— Modesto (California)	0	1	.000	6.30	1.50	2	2	0	0	...	0-...	10.0	10	7	7	1	5-1	5	.256
2002— Visalia (Calif.)	3	0	1.000	2.31	1.01	9	9	0	0	...	0-...	50.2	41	16	13	2	16-0	42	.216
— Midland (Texas)	7	7	.500	3.38	1.26	20	20	1	1	...	0-...	128.0	137	63	48	7	24-1	100	.274
2003— Midland (Texas)	9	6	.600	4.74	1.53	23	23	1	1	...	0-...	142.1	186	90	75	13	32-1	89	.313
— Sacramento (PCL)	2	0	1.000	3.79	1.55	6	6	0	0	...	0-...	38.0	47	19	16	1	12-1	26	.303
2004— Sacramento (PCL)	11	9	.550	4.44	1.41	28	27	0	0	...	0-...	172.1	192	102	85	22	51-3	129	.284
2005— Sacramento (PCL)	4	0	1.000	1.77	0.94	7	7	0	0	...	0-0	45.2	29	15	9	0	14-0	24	.181
2006— Oklahoma (PCL)	4	5	.444	2.52	1.26	15	15	2	2	0	0-0	93.0	93	33	26	5	24-0	68	.266
— Texas (A.L.)	4	6	.400	5.86	1.74	21	13	0	0	1	0-0	70.2	104	46	46	6	19-0	28	.349
Major League totals (1 year)	4	6	.400	5.86	1.74	21	13	0	0	1	0-0	70.2	104	46	46	6	19-0	28	.349

2006 LEFTY-RIGHTY SPLITS

vs.	Avg.	AB	H	2B	3B	HR	RBI	BB	SO	OBP	Slg.	vs.	Avg.	AB	H	2B	3B	HR	RBI	BB	SO	OBP	Slg.
L	.197	66	13	1	0	0	7	9	.284	.212		R	.392	232	91	19	0	6	38	12	19	.425	.552

RHODES, ARTHUR   P

PERSONAL: Born October 24, 1969, in Waco, Texas. ... 6-2/212. ... Throws left, bats left. ... Full name: Arthur Lee Rhodes. ... High school: LaVega (Waco, Texas). **TRANSACTIONS/CAREER NOTES:** Selected by Baltimore Orioles organization in second round of 1988 free-agent draft. ... On disabled list (May 16-August 2, 1993); included rehabilitation assignment to Rochester. ... On disabled list (May 2-20, 1994); included rehabilitation assignment to Frederick. ... On disabled list (August 25, 1995-remainder of season; and July 14-August 2 and August 6-September 27, 1996). ... On disabled list (July 5-August 17, 1998); included rehabilitation assignment to Rochester. ... Signed as a free agent by Seattle Mariners (December 21, 1999). ... Signed as a free agent by Oakland Athletics (December 23, 2003). ... On disabled list (June 28-August 18, 2004); included rehabilitation assignment to Sacramento. ... Traded by A's with P Mark Redman to Pittsburgh Pirates for C Jason Kendall and cash (November 29, 2004). ... Traded by Pirates with cash to Cleveland Indians for OF Matt Lawton and cash (December 11, 2004). ... On bereavement list (August 5-12, 2005). ... On disabled list (August 13-September 2, 2005); included rehabilitation assignment to Akron. ... Traded by Indians to Philadelphia Phillies for OF Jason Michaels (January 27, 2006). **MISCELLANEOUS NOTES:** Appeared in one game as pinch runner (1997).

CAREER HITTING: 1-for-4 (.250), 0 R, 0 2B, 0 3B, 0 HR, 0 RBI.

Year Team (League)	W	L	Pct.	ERA	WHIP	G	GS	CG	ShO	Hld.	Sv.-Opp.	IP	H	R	ER	HR	BB-IBB	SO	Avg.
1988— Bluefield (Appal.)	3	4	.429	3.31	1.25	11	7	0	0	...	0-...	35.1	29	17	13	1	15-0	44	.210
1989— Erie (N.Y.-Penn)	2	0	1.000	1.16	0.74	5	5	1	0	...	0-...	31.0	13	7	4	1	10-0	45	.124
— Frederick (Carolina)	2	2	.500	5.18	1.56	7	6	0	0	...	0-...	24.1	19	16	14	2	19-0	28	.213
1990— Frederick (Carolina)	4	6	.400	2.12	1.03	13	13	3	0	...	0-...	80.2	62	25	19	6	21-0	103	.207
— Hagerstown (East.)	3	4	.429	3.73	1.40	12	12	0	0	...	0-...	72.1	62	32	30	3	39-0	60	.238
1991— Hagerstown (East.)	7	4	.636	2.70	1.13	19	19	2	2	...	0-...	106.2	73	37	32	2	47-1	115	.194
— Baltimore (A.L.)	0	3	.000	8.00	1.94	8	8	0	0	0	0-0	36.0	47	35	32	4	23-0	23	.320
1992— Rochester (Int'l)	6	6	.500	3.72	1.28	17	17	1	0	...	0-...	101.2	84	48	42	7	46-0	115	.220
— Baltimore (A.L.)	7	5	.583	3.63	1.33	15	15	2	1	0	0-0	94.1	87	39	38	6	38-2	77	.250
1993— Baltimore (A.L.)	5	6	.455	6.51	1.63	17	17	0	0	0	0-0	85.2	91	62	62	16	49-1	49	.274
— Rochester (Int'l)	1	1	.500	4.05	1.54	6	6	0	0	...	0-...	26.2	26	12	12	5	15-0	33	.260
1994— Baltimore (A.L.)	3	5	.375	5.81	1.54	10	10	0	0	0	0-0	52.2	51	34	34	8	30-1	47	.254
— Frederick (Carolina)	0	0	...	0.00	0.60	1	1	0	0	...	0-...	5.0	3	0	0	0	1-0	7	.176
— Rochester (Int'l)	7	5	.583	2.79	1.15	15	15	3	0	...	0-...	90.1	70	41	28	7	34-1	86	.208
1995— Baltimore (A.L.)	2	5	.286	6.21	1.54	19	9	0	0	0	0-1	75.1	68	53	52	13	48-1	77	.239
— Rochester (Int'l)	2	1	.667	2.70	1.17	4	4	1	0	...	0-...	30.0	27	12	9	2	8-0	33	.239
1996— Baltimore (A.L.)	9	1	.900	4.08	1.34	28	9	0	0	2	1-1	53.0	48	28	24	6	23-3	62	.241
1997— Baltimore (A.L.)	10	3	.769	3.02	1.06	53	0	0	0	9	1-2	95.1	75	32	32	9	26-5	102	.218
1998— Baltimore (A.L.)	4	4	.500	3.51	1.29	45	0	0	0	4-8		77.0	65	30	30	8	34-2	83	.233
— Rochester (Int'l)	0	0	...	4.50	2.00	1	0	0	0	...	0-...	2.0	3	1	1	0	1-0	1	.333
1999— Baltimore (A.L.)	3	4	.429	5.43	1.66	43	0	0	0	5	3-5	59.0	53	43	37	9	45-6	59	.221
2000— Seattle (A.L.)	5	8	.385	4.28	1.15	72	0	0	0	24	0-7	69.1	51	34	33	6	29-3	77	.205
2001— Seattle (A.L.)	8	0	1.000	1.72	0.85	71	0	0	0	* 32	3-7	68.0	46	14	13	5	12-0	83	.189
2002— Seattle (A.L.)	10	4	.714	2.33	0.83	66	0	0	0	27	0-2	69.2	45	18	18	4	13-1	81	.181
2003— Seattle (A.L.)	3	3	.500	4.17	1.31	67	0	0	0	27	3-6	54.0	53	25	25	8	18-2	48	.256
2004— Sacramento (PCL)	0	0	...	0.00	0.50	2	2	0	0	...	0-...	2.0	0	0	0	0	0-0	3	.000
— Oakland (A.L.)	3	3	.500	5.12	1.73	37	0	0	0	3	9-14	38.2	46	23	22	9	21-4	34	.293
2005— Akron (East.)	0	0	...	0.00	0.00	1	0	0	0	0	0-0	1.0	0	0	0	0	0-0	0	.000
— Cleveland (A.L.)	3	1	.750	2.08	1.04	47	0	0	0	16	0-3	43.1	33	13	10	2	42-3	43	.206
2006— Philadelphia (N.L.)	0	5	.000	5.32	1.69	55	0	0	0	23	4-7	45.2	47	27	27	3	30-7	48	.261
American League totals (15 years)	75	55	.577	4.26	1.32	598	61	5	3	146	26-61	965.1	849	477	457	109	421-33	945	.237
National League totals (1 year)	0	5	.000	5.32	1.69	55	0	0	0	23	4-7	45.2	47	27	27	3	30-7	48	.261
Major League totals (16 years)	75	60	.556	4.31	1.33	653	61	5	3	169	30-68	1011.0	896	504	484	111	451-40	993	.238

DIVISION SERIES RECORD

Year Team (League)	W	L	Pct.	ERA	WHIP	G	GS	CG	ShO	Hld.	Sv.-Opp.	IP	H	R	ER	HR	BB-IBB	SO	Avg.
1996— Baltimore (A.L.)	0	0	...	9.00	2.00	2	0	0	0	0	0-0	1.0	1	1	1	0	1-0	1	.250
1997— Baltimore (A.L.)	0	0	...	0.00	0.00	1	0	0	0	0	0-0	2.1	0	0	0	0	0-0	4	.000
2000— Seattle (A.L.)	0	0	...	0.00	0.75	3	0	0	0	1	0-0	2.2	0	0	0	0	2-0	2	.000
2001— Seattle (A.L.)	0	0	...	0.00	0.38	3	0	0	0	2	0-0	2.2	1	0	0	0	0-0	1	.111
Division series totals (4 years)	0	0	...	1.04	0.58	9	0	0	0	3	0-0	8.2	2	1	1	0	3-0	8	.077

CHAMPIONSHIP SERIES RECORD

Year Team (League)	W	L	Pct.	ERA	WHIP	G	GS	CG	ShO	Hld.	Sv.-Opp.	IP	H	R	ER	HR	BB-IBB	SO	Avg.
1996— Baltimore (A.L.)	0	0	...	0.00	1.00	3	0	0	0	0	0-0	2.0	2	0	0	0	0-0	2	.286
1997— Baltimore (A.L.)	0	0	...	0.00	2.14	2	0	0	0	0	0-0	2.1	2	0	0	0	3-1	2	.250
2000— Seattle (A.L.)	0	1	.000	31.50	6.00	4	0	0	0	1	0-2	2.0	8	7	7	1	4-1	5	.615
2001— Seattle (A.L.)	0	0	...	4.50	1.00	2	0	0	0	1	0-1	2.0	2	1	1	1	0-0	2	.250
Champ. series totals (4 years)	0	1	.000	8.64	2.52	11	0	0	0	2	0-3	8.1	14	8	8	2	7-2	11	.389

2006 LEFTY-RIGHTY SPLITS

vs.	Avg.	AB	H	2B	3B	HR	RBI	BB	SO	OBP	Slg.		vs.	Avg.	AB	H	2B	3B	HR	RBI	BB	SO	OBP	Slg.
L	.290	62	18	5	1	2	13	5	17	.353	.500		R	.246	118	29	9	0	0	9	25	31	.382	.322

RIGGANS, SHAWN — C

PERSONAL: Born July 25, 1980, in Fort Lauderdale, Fla. ... 6-2/190. ... Bats right, throws right. ... Full name: Shawn Willis Riggans. ... Junior college: Indian River (Fla.) Community College. **TRANSACTIONS/CAREER NOTES:** Selected by Tampa Bay Devil Rays organization in 24th round of 2000 free-agent draft.

2006 GAMES PLAYED BY POSITION (MLB): C—8, DH—1.

									BATTING										FIELDING	
Year Team (League)	Pos.	G	AB	R	H	2B	3B	HR	RBI	BB	SO	HBP	GDP	SB-CS	Avg.	OBP	SLG	OPS	E	Avg.
2001— Princeton (Appal.)		15	58	15	20	4	0	8	17	9	18	0	0	1-0	.345	.433	.828	1.261	...	...
2002— Hudson Valley (NYP)		73	266	34	70	13	0	9	48	32	72	1	0	2-2	.263	.343	.414	.757	...	...
2003— Char., S.C. (SAL)		68	232	33	65	17	0	3	34	19	35	4	8	3-4	.280	.340	.392	.732	...	...
— Orlando (South.)		22	62	7	17	6	0	1	11	4	14	1	0	0-0	.274	.319	.419	.738	...	...
2004— Bakersfield (Calif.)		34	127	20	44	11	0	5	22	15	23	1	3	0-1	.346	.417	.551	.968	...	...
— Mohtgom. (Sou.)		10	36	3	8	1	0	2	7	2	14	1	2	0-0	.222	.282	.417	.699	...	...
2005— Montgom. (Sou'l)	C-DH	89	313	40	97	21	0	8	53	26	69	4	11	1-2	.310	.365	.454	.819	9	.983
2006— Durham (Int'l)		115	417	43	122	26	2	11	54	27	88	5	11	2-2	.293	.341	.444	.785	12	.984
— Tampa Bay (A.L.)	C-DH	10	29	3	5	1	0	0	1	4	7	0	1	0-0	.172	.273	.207	.480	0	1.000
Major League totals (1 year)		10	29	3	5	1	0	0	1	4	7	0	1	0-0	.172	.273	.207	.480	0	1.000

2006 LEFTY-RIGHTY SPLITS

vs.	Avg.	AB	H	2B	3B	HR	RBI	BB	SO	OBP	Slg.		vs.	Avg.	AB	H	2B	3B	HR	RBI	BB	SO	OBP	Slg.
L	.000	10	0	0	0	0	0	0	1	3	.091	.000		R	.263	19	5	1	0	0	1	3	4	.364	.316

RINCON, JUAN — P

PERSONAL: Born January 23, 1979, in Maracaibo, Venezuela. ... 5-11/201. ... Throws right, bats right. ... Full name: Juan Manuel Rincon. ... Name pronounced: rin-CONE. ... High school: Instituto Cervantes (Maracaibo, Venezuela). **TRANSACTIONS/CAREER NOTES:** Signed as a non-drafted free agent by Minnesota Twins organization (November 15, 1996). ... On restricted list (May 2-12, 2005).

CAREER HITTING: 1-for-2 (.500), 0 R, 0 2B, 0 3B, 0 HR, 0 RBI.

Year Team (League)	W	L	Pct.	ERA	WHIP	G	GS	CG	ShO	Hld.	Sv.-Opp.	IP	H	R	ER	HR	BB-IBB	SO	Avg.
1997— GC Twins (GCL)	3	3	.500	2.95	1.36	11	10	1	0	...	0-...	58.0	55	21	19	0	24-0	46	.259
— Elizabethton (App.)	0	1	.000	3.86	1.50	2	1	0	0	...	0-...	9.1	11	4	4	0	3-0	7	.289
1998— Fort Wayne (Midw.)	6	4	.600	3.83	1.43	37	13	0	0	...	6-...	96.1	84	51	41	6	54-1	74	.232
1999— Quad City (Midw.)	14	8	.636	2.92	1.30	28	28	0	0	...	0-...	163.1	146	67	53	8	66-3	153	.239
2000— Fort Myers (FSL)	5	3	.625	2.13	1.18	13	13	0	0	...	0-...	76.0	67	26	18	3	23-2	55	.238
— New Britain (East.)	3	9	.250	4.65	1.52	15	15	2	0	...	0-...	89.0	96	55	46	9	39-0	79	.267
2001— New Britain (East.)	14	6	.700	2.88	1.22	29	23	2	1	...	0-...	153.1	130	60	49	9	57-5	133	.226
— Minnesota (A.L.)	0	0	...	6.35	2.12	4	0	0	0	0	0-0	5.2	7	5	4	1	5-0	4	.318
2002— Edmonton (PCL)	7	4	.636	4.78	1.44	19	16	3	0	...	0-...	101.2	111	56	54	12	35-0	75	.278
— Minnesota (A.L.)	0	2	.000	6.28	1.85	10	3	0	0	0	0-...	28.2	44	23	20	5	9-0	21	.352
2003— Rochester (Int'l)	0	2	.000	7.56	2.00	2	2	0	0	...	0-...	8.1	12	7	7	0	5-0	8	.364
— Minnesota (A.L.)	5	6	.455	3.68	1.31	58	0	0	0	5	0-1	85.2	74	38	35	5	38-7	63	.231
2004— Minnesota (A.L.)	11	6	.647	2.63	1.02	77	0	0	0	16	2-6	82.0	52	27	24	5	32-1	106	.181
2005— Minnesota (A.L.)	6	6	.500	2.45	1.21	75	0	0	0	25	0-5	77.0	63	26	21	2	30-3	84	.224
2006— Minnesota (A.L.)	3	1	.750	2.91	1.35	75	0	0	0	26	1-3	74.1	76	30	24	2	24-3	65	.270
Major League totals (6 years)	25	21	.543	3.26	1.28	299	3	0	0	72	3-16	353.1	316	149	128	20	138-14	343	.240

DIVISION SERIES RECORD

Year Team (League)	W	L	Pct.	ERA	WHIP	G	GS	CG	ShO	Hld.	Sv.-Opp.	IP	H	R	ER	HR	BB-IBB	SO	Avg.
2003— Minnesota (A.L.)	0	0	...	0.00	2.14	3	0	0	0	0	0-0	2.1	1	0	0	0	4-0	1	.143
2004— Minnesota (A.L.)	0	0	...	10.80	1.80	3	0	0	0	1	0-0	3.1	4	4	4	1	2-0	5	.308
2006— Minnesota (A.L.)	0	0	...	3.00	0.33	2	0	0	0	0	0-0	3.0	1	1	1	0	0-0	3	.100
Division series totals (3 years)	0	0	...	5.19	1.38	8	0	0	0	1	0-0	8.2	6	5	5	1	6-0	9	.200

2006 LEFTY-RIGHTY SPLITS

vs.	Avg.	AB	H	2B	3B	HR	RBI	BB	SO	OBP	Slg.		vs.	Avg.	AB	H	2B	3B	HR	RBI	BB	SO	OBP	Slg.
L	.222	117	26	2	0	0	5	9	27	.283	.239		R	.303	165	50	11	0	2	23	15	38	.366	.406

RINCON, RICARDO — P

PERSONAL: Born April 13, 1970, in Veracruz, Mexico. ... 5-9/190. ... Throws left, bats left. ... Full name: Ricardo Rincon (Espinoza). ... Name pronounced: rin-CONE. **TRANSACTIONS/CAREER NOTES:** Contract purchased by Pittsburgh Pirates organization from Mexico City Red Devils of the Mexican League (March 30, 1997). ... On disabled list (March 22-April 14, 1998); included rehabilitation assignments to Carolina and Nashville. ... Traded by Pirates to Cleveland Indians for OF Brian Giles (November 18, 1998). ... On disabled list (April 12-May 14, 1999); included rehabilitation assignment to Akron. ... On disabled list (May 17-August 23, 2000); included rehabilitation assignment to Buffalo. ... Traded by Indians to Oakland Athletics for IF Marshall McDougall (July 30, 2002). ... Signed as a free agent by St. Louis Cardinals (December 13, 2005). ... On disabled list (April 28, 2006-remainder of season). **STATISTICAL NOTES:** Pitched one inning, combining with Francisco Cordova (eight innings) in 3-0 no-hit victory against Houston (July 12, 1997).

CAREER HITTING: 0-for-4 (.000), 0 R, 0 2B, 0 3B, 0 HR, 0 RBI.

Year Team (League)	W	L	Pct.	ERA	WHIP	G	GS	CG	ShO	Hld.	Sv.-Opp.	IP	H	R	ER	HR	BB-IBB	SO	Avg.
1990— Union Lag. (Mx.)	3	0	1.000	3.78	1.78	19	4	0	0	...	0-...	47.2	53	22	20	6	32-...	29	...

Year	Team (League)	W	L	Pct.	ERA	WHIP	G	GS	CG	ShO	Hld.	Sv.-Opp.	IP	H	R	ER	HR	BB-IBB	SO	Avg.
1991—	Union Lag. (Mx.)	2	8	.200	6.54	1.98	32	9	0	0	...	1-...	74.1	99	60	54	12	48-...	66	...
1992—	Union Lag. (Mx.)	6	5	.545	3.91	1.48	49	9	0	0	...	4-...	89.2	87	45	39	4	46-...	91	...
1993—	Torreon (Mex.)	7	3	.700	3.17	1.41	57	4	0	0	...	8-...	82.1	80	33	29	8	36-...	81	...
1994—	M.C. R. Dev. (Mex.)	2	4	.333	3.21	1.44	20	9	0	0	...	1-...	53.1	57	23	19	4	20-...	38	...
1995—	M.C. R. Dev. (Mex.)	6	6	.500	5.16	1.69	27	11	0	0	...	3-...	75.0	86	45	43	7	41-...	41	...
1996—	M.C. R. Dev. (Mex.)	5	3	.625	2.97	1.08	50	0	0	0	...	10-...	78.2	58	28	26	2	27-...	60	...
1997—	Pittsburgh (N.L.)	4	8	.333	3.45	1.25	62	0	0	0	18	4-6	60.0	51	26	23	5	24-6	71	.230
1998—	Carolina (Southern)	0	0	...	6.00	2.33	2	0	0	0	...	0-...	3.0	5	2	2	1	2-0	1	.385
—	Nashville (PCL)	0	0	...	0.00	0.00	1	0	0	0	...	0-...	1.0	0	0	0	0	0-0	1	.000
—	Pittsburgh (N.L.)	0	2	.000	2.91	1.22	60	0	0	0	11	14-17	65.0	50	31	21	6	29-2	64	.208
1999—	Cleveland (A.L.)	2	3	.400	4.43	1.46	59	0	0	0	11	0-2	44.2	41	22	22	6	24-5	30	.248
—	Akron (East.)	0	0	...	5.40	1.20	2	2	0	0	...	0-...	1.2	2	1	1	0	0-0	2	.250
2000—	Cleveland (A.L.)	2	0	1.000	2.70	1.50	35	0	0	0	10	0-0	20.0	17	7	6	1	13-1	20	.224
—	Buffalo (Int'l)	0	0	...	0.00	0.50	2	0	0	0	...	0-...	2.0	1	0	0	0	0-0	6	.111
2001—	Cleveland (A.L.)	2	1	.667	2.83	1.20	67	0	0	0	12	2-4	54.0	44	18	17	3	21-5	50	.223
2002—	Cleveland (A.L.)	1	4	.200	4.79	1.23	46	0	0	0	11	0-3	35.2	36	21	19	3	8-1	30	.263
—	Oakland (A.L.)	0	0	...	3.10	0.69	25	0	0	0	16	1-2	20.1	11	7	7	1	3-0	19	.164
2003—	Oakland (A.L.)	8	4	.667	3.25	1.39	64	0	0	0	13	0-3	55.1	45	21	20	4	32-4	40	.230
2004—	Oakland (A.L.)	1	1	.500	3.68	1.52	67	0	0	0	18	0-4	44.0	45	22	18	3	22-4	40	.256
2005—	Oakland (A.L.)	1	1	.500	4.34	1.45	67	0	0	0	16	0-2	37.1	34	19	18	7	20-4	27	.246
2006—	St. Louis (N.L.)	0	0	...	10.80	3.00	5	0	0	0	2	0-0	3.1	6	4	4	1	4-0	6	.375
	American League totals (7 years)	17	14	.548	3.67	1.34	430	0	0	0	107	3-20	311.1	273	137	127	28	143-24	256	.237
	National League totals (3 years)	4	10	.286	3.37	1.28	127	0	0	0	31	18-23	128.1	107	61	48	12	57-8	141	.224
	Major League totals (10 years)	21	24	.467	3.58	1.32	557	0	0	0	138	21-43	439.2	380	198	175	40	200-32	397	.233

DIVISION SERIES RECORD

Year	Team (League)	W	L	Pct.	ERA	WHIP	G	GS	CG	ShO	Hld.	Sv.-Opp.	IP	H	R	ER	HR	BB-IBB	SO	Avg.
1999—	Cleveland (A.L.)	0	0	...	40.50	4.50	1	0	0	0	0	0-0	0.2	2	3	3	1	1-0	1	.500
2001—	Cleveland (A.L.)	0	0	...	9.00	1.00	3	0	0	0	0	0-0	2.0	2	2	2	0	0-0	3	.286
2002—	Oakland (A.L.)	0	0	...	0.00	0.67	2	0	0	0	1	0-0	3.0	2	0	0	0	0-0	2	.182
2003—	Oakland (A.L.)	0	0	...	4.50	1.25	4	0	0	0	1	0-1	4.0	4	2	2	2	1-0	3	.267
	Division series totals (4 years)	0	0	...	6.52	1.24	10	0	0	0	2	0-1	9.2	10	7	7	3	2-0	9	.270

2006 LEFTY-RIGHTY SPLITS

vs.	Avg.	AB	H	2B	3B	HR	RBI	BB	SO	OBP	Slg.	vs.	Avg.	AB	H	2B	3B	HR	RBI	BB	SO	OBP	Slg.
L	.111	9	1	0	0	1	2	1	5	.200	.444	R	.714	7	5	2	0	0	2	3	1	.818	1.000

RING, ROYCE — P

PERSONAL: Born December 21, 1980, in La Mesa, Calif. ... 6-0/220. ... Throws left, bats left. ... Full name: Roger Royce Ring. ... High school: Monte Vista (Spring Valley, Calif.). ... College: San Diego State. **TRANSACTIONS/CAREER NOTES:** Selected by Chicago White Sox organization in first round (18th pick overall) of 2002 free-agent draft. ... Traded by White Sox with P Edwin Almonte and 2B Andrew Salvo to New York Mets for 2B Roberto Alomar (July 1, 2003).
CAREER HITTING: 0-for-0 (.000), 0 R, 0 2B, 0 3B, 0 HR, 0 RBI.

Year	Team (League)	W	L	Pct.	ERA	WHIP	G	GS	CG	ShO	Hld.	Sv.-Opp.	IP	H	R	ER	HR	BB-IBB	SO	Avg.
2002—	Ariz. White Sox (Ariz.)	0	0	...	0.00	0.40	3	0	0	0	...	0-...	5.0	2	0	0	0	0-0	9	.118
—	Win.-Salem (Car.)	2	0	1.000	3.91	1.35	21	0	0	0	...	5-...	23.0	20	11	10	2	11-2	22	.247
2003—	Birmingham (Sou.)	1	4	.200	2.52	1.32	36	0	0	0	...	19-...	35.2	33	11	10	1	14-1	44	.237
—	Binghamton (East.)	3	0	1.000	1.66	1.11	18	0	0	0	...	7-...	21.2	13	4	4	2	11-0	18	.176
2004—	Norfolk (Int'l)	3	1	.750	3.63	1.41	29	0	0	0	...	0-...	34.2	37	15	14	5	12-1	22	.266
—	Binghamton (East.)	2	2	.500	3.77	1.26	19	0	0	0	...	2-...	28.2	25	13	12	5	11-1	23	.225
2005—	New York (N.L.)	0	2	.000	5.06	1.88	15	0	0	0	3	0-0	10.2	10	6	6	0	10-1	8	.250
—	Norfolk (Int'l)	3	0	1.000	3.26	1.22	33	0	0	0	9	2-2	38.2	34	16	14	2	13-1	26	.239
2006—	Norfolk (Int'l)	2	2	.500	2.97	1.14	36	0	0	0	...	11-13	39.1	30	14	13	2	15-2	40	.210
—	New York (N.L.)	0	0	...	2.13	0.79	11	0	0	0	2	0-0	12.2	7	3	3	3	3-0	8	.156
	Major League totals (2 years)	0	2	.000	3.47	1.29	26	0	0	0	5	0-0	23.1	17	9	9	2	13-1	16	.200

2006 LEFTY-RIGHTY SPLITS

vs.	Avg.	AB	H	2B	3B	HR	RBI	BB	SO	OBP	Slg.	vs.	Avg.	AB	H	2B	3B	HR	RBI	BB	SO	OBP	Slg.
L	.150	20	3	1	0	0	2	2	7	.227	.200	R	.160	25	4	1	0	2	4	1	1	.192	.440

RIOS, ALEX — OF

PERSONAL: Born February 18, 1981, in Coffee, Ala. ... 6-5/195. ... Bats right, throws right. ... Full name: Alexis Israel Rios. ... High school: San Pedro Martin (Guaynabo, Puerto Rico). **TRANSACTIONS/CAREER NOTES:** Selected by Toronto Blue Jays organization in first round (19th pick overall) of 1999 free-agent draft. ... On disabled list (July 1-28, 2006); included rehabilitation assignment to Syracuse. **RECORDS:** Shares major league record for most strikeouts, 9-inning game (5, July 29, 2006).
2006 GAMES PLAYED BY POSITION (MLB): OF—125.

Year	Team (League)	Pos.	G	AB	R	H	2B	3B	HR	RBI	BB	SO	HBP	GDP	SB-CS	Avg.	OBP	SLG	OPS	E	Avg.
								BATTING												FIELDING	
1999—	Medicine Hat (Pio.)	OF	67	234	35	63	7	3	0	13	17	31	1	6	8-4	.269	.321	.325	.646	6	.955
2000—	Hagerstown (SAL)		22	74	5	17	3	1	0	5	2	14	1	0	2-3	.230	.256	.297	.554	...	...
—	Queens (N.Y.-Penn.)	OF	50	206	22	55	9	2	1	25	11	22	4	5	5-5	.267	.314	.345	.659	3	.957
2001—	Char., W.Va. (SAL)	OF	130	480	40	126	20	9	2	58	25	59	4	16	22-14	.263	.296	.354	.651	13	.944
2002—	Dunedin (Fla. St.)	OF	111	456	60	139	22	8	3	61	27	55	3	19	14-8	.305	.344	.408	.752	8	.967
2003—	New Haven (East.)	OF	127	514	86	181	32	11	11	82	39	85	6	22	11-3	.352	.402	.521	.924	3	.990
2004—	Syracuse (Int'l)	OF	46	185	14	48	10	1	3	23	9	30	0	10	2-1	.259	.292	.373	.665	4	.964
—	Toronto (A.L.)	OF	111	426	55	122	24	7	1	28	31	84	2	14	15-3	.286	.338	.383	.720	4	.991
2005—	Toronto (A.L.)	OF-DH	146	481	71	126	23	6	10	59	28	101	5	14	14-9	.262	.306	.397	.703	2	.992
2006—	Syracuse (Int'l)		3	10	0	3	1	0	0	1	1	3	0	0	0-0	.300	.364	.400	.764	0	1.000
—	Toronto (A.L.)	OF	128	450	68	136	33	6	17	82	35	89	3	10	15-6	.302	.349	.516	.865	1	.996
	Major League totals (3 years)		385	1357	194	384	80	19	28	169	94	274	10	38	44-18	.283	.331	.432	.762	5	.993

2006 LEFTY-RIGHTY SPLITS

vs.	Avg.	AB	H	2B	3B	HR	RBI	BB	SO	OBP	Slg.	vs.	Avg.	AB	H	2B	3B	HR	RBI	BB	SO	OBP	Slg.
L	.295	122	36	9	1	6	29	10	23	.341	.533	R	.305	328	100	24	5	11	53	25	66	.353	.509

RISKE, DAVID — P

PERSONAL: Born October 23, 1976, in Renton, Wash. ... 6-2/190. ... Throws right, bats right. ... Full name: David Richard Riske. ... Name pronounced: RISK-ee. ... High school: Lindbergh (Renton, Wash.). ... Junior college: Green River (Wash.) C.C. **TRANSACTIONS/CAREER NOTES:** Selected by Cleveland Indians organization in 56th round of 1996 free-agent draft. ... On disabled list (March 25-April 28, May 29-September 4 and September 14, 2000-remainder of season); included rehabilitation assignment to Akron. ... On disabled list (June 19-July 17, 2002); included rehabilitation assignment to Akron. ... On suspended list (September 2-5, 2005). ... Traded by Indians with OF

R

Coco Crisp and C Josh Bard to Boston Red Sox for 3B Andy Marte, P Guillermo Mota and C Kelly Shoppach (January 27, 2006). ... On disabled list (April 12-May 22, 2006); included rehabilitation assignment to Pawtucket. ... Traded by Red Sox to Chicago White Sox for P Javier Lopez (June 15, 2006). ... On suspended list (June 25-29).

CAREER HITTING: 0-for-0 (.000), 0 R, 0 2B, 0 3B, 0 HR, 0 RBI.

Year Team (League)	W	L	Pct.	ERA	WHIP	G	GS	CG	ShO	Hld.	Sv.-Opp.	IP	H	R	ER	HR	BB-IBB	SO	Avg.
1997— Kinston (Carol.)	4	4	.500	2.25	1.26	39	0	0	0	...	2-...	72.0	58	22	18	3	33-4	90	.227
1998— Kinston (Carol.)	1	1	.500	2.33	1.17	53	0	0	0	...	33-...	54.0	48	15	14	4	15-0	67	.241
— Akron (East.)	0	0		0.00	0.67	2	0	0	0	...	1-...	3.0	1	0	0	0	1-0	5	.100
1999— Akron (East.)	0	0		1.90	0.76	23	0	0	0	...	12-...	23.2	5	6	5	1	13-0	33	.067
— Buffalo (Int'l)	3	0	1.000	0.65	0.76	23	0	0	0	...	6-...	27.2	14	3	2	0	7-0	22	.151
— Cleveland (A.L.)	1	1	.500	8.36	1.86	12	0	0	0	0	0-1	14.0	20	15	13	2	6-0	16	.333
2000— Buffalo (Int'l)	0	0		0.00	0.50	3	1	0	0	...	1-...	4.0	2	0	0	0	0-0	4	.143
— Buffalo (Int'l)	0	0		3.00	1.33	2	0	0	0	...	0-...	3.0	2	1	1	0	2-0	2	.182
2001— Buffalo (Int'l)	1	2	.333	2.36	1.16	38	0	0	0	...	15-...	53.1	45	16	14	2	17-0	72	.232
— Cleveland (A.L.)	2	0	1.000	1.98	1.39	26	0	0	0	3	1-1	27.1	20	7	6	3	18-3	29	.206
2002— Cleveland (A.L.)	2	2	.500	5.26	1.64	51	0	0	0	0	1-1	51.1	49	32	30	8	35-4	65	.257
— Akron (East.)	0	0		3.00	1.00	4	2	0	0	...	0-...	6.0	5	2	2	1	1-0	10	.217
— Buffalo (Int'l)	0	1	.000	3.72	1.03	9	0	0	0	...	3-...	9.2	6	4	4	2	4-0	17	.182
2003— Cleveland (A.L.)	2	2	.500	2.29	0.96	68	0	0	0	17	8-13	74.2	52	21	19	9	20-3	82	.196
2004— Cleveland (A.L.)	7	3	.700	3.72	1.42	72	0	0	0	9	5-12	77.1	69	32	32	11	41-4	78	.240
2005— Cleveland (A.L.)	3	4	.429	3.10	0.96	58	0	0	0	0	1-1	72.2	55	28	25	11	15-0	48	.208
2006— Pawtucket (Int'l)	0	1	.000	5.40	2.00	5	2	0	0	...	0-0	5.0	5	3	3	0	5-0	8	.250
— Boston (A.L.)	0	1	.000	3.72	1.14	8	0	0	0	0	0-0	9.2	8	4	4	2	3-0	5	.222
— Chicago (A.L.)	1	0	1.000	5.00	3.93	1.34	33	0	0	0	2	0-1	34.1	32	16	15	4	14-1	23	.246
Major League totals (7 years)	18	14	.563	3.59	1.26	328	0	0	0	36	16-30	361.1	305	155	144	50	152-15	346	.229

DIVISION SERIES RECORD

Year Team (League)	W	L	Pct.	ERA	WHIP	G	GS	CG	ShO	Hld.	Sv.-Opp.	IP	H	R	ER	HR	BB-IBB	SO	Avg.
2001— Cleveland (A.L.)	0	0		0.00	0.82	3	0	0	0	0	0-...	3.2	2	0	0	0	1-0	5	.154

2006 LEFTY-RIGHTY SPLITS

vs.	Avg.	AB	H	2B	3B	HR	RBI	BB	SO	OBP	Slg.	vs.	Avg.	AB	H	2B	3B	HR	RBI	BB	SO	OBP	Slg.
L	.280	50	14	2	0	1	7	12	8	.438	.380	R	.224	116	26	8	0	5	21	5	20	.258	.422

RIVERA, JUAN — OF

PERSONAL: Born July 3, 1978, in Guarenas, Venezuela. ... 6-2/205. ... Bats right, throws right. ... Full name: Juan Luis Rivera. **TRANSACTIONS/CAREER NOTES:** Signed as a non-drafted free agent by New York Yankees organization (April 12, 1996). ... On disabled list (June 9-August 19, 2002); included rehabilitation assignments to GCL Yankees and Columbus. ... Traded by Yankees with 1B Nick Johnson and P Randy Choate to Montreal Expos for Javier Vazquez (December 16, 2003). ... Traded by Expos with SS Maicer Izturis to Anaheim Angels for OF Jose Guillen (November 23, 2004). ... Angels franchise renamed Los Angeles Angels of Anaheim for 2005 season. ... On disabled list (April 22-May 8, 2006); included rehabilitation assignment to Salt Lake. **STATISTICAL NOTES:** Career major league grand slams: 3.

2006 GAMES PLAYED BY POSITION (MLB): OF—103, DH—18.

Year Team (League)	Pos.	G	AB	R	H	2B	3B	HR	RBI	BB	SO	HBP	GDP	SB-CS	Avg.	OBP	SLG	OPS	E	Avg.
1996— Dom. Yankees (DSL)	OF	10	18	0	3	0	0	0	2	0	1			0-...	.167		.167		0	1.000
1997— Maracay 1 (VSL)		52	142	25	40	9	0	0	14	12	16			12-...	.282		.345		...	...
1998— GC Yankees (GCL)	OF	57	210	43	70	9	1	12	45	26	27	1	10	8-5	.333	.408	.557	.965	2	.979
— Oneonta (NYP)	OF	6	18	2	5	0	0	1	3	1	4	0	0	1-1	.278	.316	.444	.760	0	1.000
1999— Tampa (Fla. St.)	OF	109	426	50	112	20	2	14	77	26	67	5	13	5-3	.263	.308	.418	.725	4	.979
— GC Yankees (GCL)	OF	5	18	7	6	0	0	1	4	4	1	0	1	0-0	.333	.455	.500	.955	0	1.000
2000— Norwich (East.)	OF	17	62	9	14	5	0	2	12	6	15	0	2	0-0	.226	.294	.403	.697	1	.955
— Tampa (Fla. St.)	1B-OF	115	409	62	113	26	1	14	69	33	56	6	9	11-7	.276	.336	.447	.783	5	.978
2001— Norwich (East.)	OF	77	316	50	101	18	3	14	58	15	50	3	10	5-7	.320	.353	.528	.882	6	.963
— Columbus (Int'l)	OF	55	199	39	65	11	1	14	40	15	31	1	7	4-5	.327	.372	.603	.975	4	.970
— New York (A.L.)	OF	3	4	0	0	0	0	0	0	0	1	0	0	0-0	.000	.000	.000	.000	0	1.000
2002— Columbus (Int'l)	OF	65	265	40	86	21	1	8	47	13	39	1	4	5-1	.325	.355	.502	.856	6	.955
— New York (A.L.)	OF	28	83	9	22	5	0	1	6	1	14	1	1	1-1	.265	.311	.361	.673	2	.966
— GC Yankees (GCL)	OF	4	13	1	4	2	0	0	4	2	3	1	1	0-0	.308	.438	.462	.899	0	1.000
2003— Columbus (Int'l)	OF	79	308	47	100	21	0	7	37	26	37	0	8	1-3	.325	.374	.461	.835	3	.982
— New York (A.L.)	OF	57	173	22	46	14	0	7	26	10	27	0	8	0-0	.266	.304	.468	.773	2	.979
2004— Montreal (N.L.)	OF-DH	134	391	48	120	24	1	12	49	34	45	1	11	6-2	.307	.364	.465	.829	3	.986
2005— Los Angeles (A.L.)	OF-DH	106	350	46	95	17	1	15	59	23	44	0	15	1-9	.271	.316	.454	.770	1	.992
2006— Salt Lake (PCL)	OF	2	9	3	5	3	0	1	6	1	0	0	1	0-0	.556	.600	1.222	1.822	6	.600
— Los Angeles (A.L.)	OF-DH	124	448	65	139	27	0	23	85	33	59	7	14	0-4	.310	.362	.525	.887	6	.974
American League totals (5 years)		318	1058	142	302	63	1	46	176	72	140	7	41	2-14	.285	.332	.477	.810	11	.979
National League totals (1 year)		134	391	48	120	24	1	12	49	34	45	1	11	6-2	.307	.364	.465	.829	3	.986
Major League totals (6 years)		452	1449	190	422	87	2	58	225	106	185	8	52	8-16	.291	.341	.474	.815	14	.981

DIVISION SERIES RECORD

Year Team (League)	Pos.	G	AB	R	H	2B	3B	HR	RBI	BB	SO	HBP	GDP	SB-CS	Avg.	OBP	SLG	OPS	E	Avg.
2002— New York (A.L.)	OF	4	12	2	3	0	0	0	3	1	3	0	0	0-0	.250	.308	.250	.558	0	1.000
2003— New York (A.L.)	OF	4	12	2	4	0	0	0	0	0	1	0	0	0-0	.333	.385	.333	.718	0	1.000
2005— Los Angeles (A.L.)	DH	5	17	3	6	1	0	1	1	2	1	0	0	0-0	.353	.389	.588	.977	0	...
Division series totals (3 years)		13	41	7	13	1	0	1	4	3	5	0	1	0-0	.317	.364	.415	.778	0	1.000

CHAMPIONSHIP SERIES RECORD

Year Team (League)	Pos.	G	AB	R	H	2B	3B	HR	RBI	BB	SO	HBP	GDP	SB-CS	Avg.	OBP	SLG	OPS	E	Avg.
2003— New York (A.L.)	OF	2	2	0	0	0	0	0	0	0	1	0	0	0-0	.000	.000	.000	.000	0	1.000
2005— Los Angeles (A.L.)	OF-DH	3	9	1	1	1	0	0	0	0	1	0	0	0-0	.111	.111	.222	.333	0	1.000
Champ. series totals (2 years)		5	11	1	1	1	0	0	0	0	2	0	0	0-0	.091	.091	.182	.273	0	1.000

WORLD SERIES RECORD

Year Team (League)	Pos.	G	AB	R	H	2B	3B	HR	RBI	BB	SO	HBP	GDP	SB-CS	Avg.	OBP	SLG	OPS	E	Avg.
2003— New York (A.L.)	OF	4	6	0	1	1	0	0	1	1	0	0	0	0-0	.167	.286	.333	.619	0	1.000

2006 LEFTY-RIGHTY SPLITS

vs.	Avg.	AB	H	2B	3B	HR	RBI	BB	SO	OBP	Slg.	vs.	Avg.	AB	H	2B	3B	HR	RBI	BB	SO	OBP	Slg.
L	.351	134	47	11	0	7	27	7	14	.380	.590	R	.293	314	92	16	0	16	58	26	45	.355	.497

RIVERA, MARIANO — P

PERSONAL: Born November 29, 1969, in Panama City, Panama. ... 6-2/170. ... Throws right, bats right. ... Cousin of Ruben Rivera, outfielder with five major league teams (1995-2003). **TRANSACTIONS/CAREER NOTES:** Signed as a non-drafted free agent by New York Yankees organization (February 17, 1990). ... On disabled list (April 6-24, 1998). ... On disabled list (June 10-25, July 21-August 8 and August 18-September 21, 2002); included rehabilitation assignment to GCL Yankees. ... On disabled list (March

25-April 29, 2003). **HONORS:** Named A.L. Fireman of the Year by THE SPORTING NEWS (1997 and 1999). ... Named A.L. Reliever of the Year by THE SPORTING NEWS (2001 and 2004). ... Named co-A.L. Fireman of the Year by the SPORTING NEWS (2005).

CAREER HITTING: 0-for-1 (.000), 0 R, 0 2B, 0 3B, 0 HR, 0 RBI.

Year	Team (League)	W	L	Pct.	ERA	WHIP	G	GS	CG	ShO	Hld.	Sv.-Opp.	IP	H	R	ER	HR	BB-IBB	SO	Avg.
1990—	GC Yankees (GCL)	5	1	.833	0.17	0.46	22	1	1	1	...	1-...	52.0	17	3	1	0	7-0	58	.102
1991—	Greensboro (S. Atl.)	4	9	.308	2.75	1.21	29	15	1	0	...	0-...	114.2	103	48	35	2	36-0	123	.237
1992—	Fort Laud. (FSL)	5	3	.625	2.28	0.76	10	10	3	1	...	0-...	59.1	40	17	15	5	5-0	42	.191
1993—	Greensboro (S. Atl.)	1	0	1.000	2.06	1.17	10	10	0	0	...	0-...	39.1	31	12	9	0	15-0	32	.214
—	GC Yankees (GCL)	0	1	.000	2.25	0.75	2	2	0	0	...	0-...	4.0	2	1	1	0	1-0	6	.143
1994—	Tampa (Fla. St.)	3	0	1.000	2.21	1.25	7	7	0	0	...	0-...	36.2	34	12	9	2	12-0	27	.258
—	Alb./Colon. (East.)	3	0	1.000	2.27	1.04	9	9	0	0	...	0-...	63.1	58	20	16	5	8-0	39	.242
—	Columbus (Int'l)	4	2	.667	5.81	1.42	6	6	1	0	...	0-...	31.0	34	22	20	5	10-0	23	.268
1995—	Columbus (Int'l)	2	2	.500	2.10	0.93	7	7	1	1	...	0-...	30.0	25	10	7	2	3-0	30	.227
—	New York (A.L.)	5	3	.625	5.51	1.51	19	10	0	0	...	0-1	67.0	71	43	41	11	30-0	51	.266
1996—	New York (A.L.)	8	3	.727	2.09	0.99.	61	0	0	0	* 27	5-8	107.2	73	25	25	1	34-3	130	.189
1997—	New York (A.L.)	6	4	.600	1.88	1.19	66	0	0	0		43-52	·71.2	65	17	15	5	20-6	68	.237
1998—	New York (A.L.)	3	0	1.000	1.91	1.06	54	0	0	0		36-41	61.1	48	13	13	3	17-1	36	.215
1999—	New York (A.L.)	4	3	.571	1.83	0.88	66	0	0	0	*	45-49	69.0	43	15	14	2	18-3	52	.176
2000—	New York (A.L.)	7	4	.636	2.85	1.10	66	0	0	0		36-41	75.2	58	26	24	4	25-3	58	.208
2001—	New York (A.L.)	4	6	.400	2.34	0.90	71	0	0	0	*	50-57	80.2	61	24	21	5	12-2	83	.209
2002—	New York (A.L.)	1	4	.200	2.74	1.00	45	0	0	0	2	28-32	46.0	35	16	14	3	11-2	41	.203
—	GC Yankees (GCL)	0	0	...	0.00	1.50	1	1	0	0		0-...	2.0	2	0	0	0	1-0	2	.286
2003—	New York (A.L.)	5	2	.714	1.66	1.00	64	0	0	0		40-46	70.2	61	15	13	3	10-1	63	.235
2004—	New York (A.L.)	4	2	.667	1.94	1.08	74	0	0	0	*	53-57	78.2	65	17	17	3	20-3	66	.225
2005—	New York (A.L.)	7	4	.636	1.38	0.87	71	0	0	0		43-47	78.1	50	18	12	2	18-0	80	.177
2006—	New York (A.L.)	5	5	.500	1.80	0.96	63	0	0	0		34-37	75.0	61	16	15	3	11-4	55	.223
Major League totals (12 years)		59	40	.596	2.29	1.04	720	10	0	0	29	413-468	881.2	691	245	224	45	226-28	783	.213

DIVISION SERIES RECORD

Year	Team (League)	W	L	Pct.	ERA	WHIP	G	GS	CG	ShO	Hld.	Sv.-Opp.	IP	H	R	ER	HR	BB-IBB	SO	Avg.
1995—	New York (A.L.)	1	0	1.000	0.00	0.75	3	0	0	0	0	0-0	5.1	3	0	0	0	1-1	8	.167
1996—	New York (A.L.)	0	0	...	0.00	0.21	2	0	0	0	1	0-0	·4.2	1	0	0	0	1-0	1	.000
1997—	New York (A.L.)	0	0	...	4.50	1.00	2	0	0	0	0	1-2	2.0	2	1	1	1	0-0	1	.250
1998—	New York (A.L.)	0	0	...	0.00	0.60	3	0	0	0	0	2-2	3.1	1	0	0	0	1-0	2	.091
1999—	New York (A.L.)	0	0	...	0.00	0.33	2	0	0	0	0	2-2	3.0	1	0	0	0	0-0	3	.111
2000—	New York (A.L.)	0	0	...	0.00	0.40	3	0	0	0	0	3-3	5.0	2	0	0	0	0-0	3	.111
2001—	New York (A.L.)	0	0	...	0.00	0.80	3	0	0	0	0	2-2	5.0	4	1	0	0	0-0	4	.211
2002—	New York (A.L.)	0	0	...	0.00	1.00	1	0	0	0	0	1-1	1.0	1	0	0	0	0-0	1	.250
2003—	New York (A.L.)	0	0	...	0.00	0.00	2	0	0	0	0	2-2	4.0	0	0	0	0	0-0	4	.000
2004—	New York (A.L.)	1	0	1.000	0.00	0.35	4	0	0	0	0	0-1	5.2	2	0	0	0	0-0	2	.111
2005—	New York (A.L.)	0	0	...	3.00	0.67	2	0	0	0	0	2-2	3.0	1	1	1	0	1-0	2	.100
2006—	New York (A.L.)	0	0	...	0.00	1.00	1	0	0	0	0	1-1	1.0	·1	0	0	0	0-0	1	.333
Division series totals (12 years)		2	0	1.000	0.42	0.51	28	0	0	0	1	15-17	43.0	18	3	2	1	4-1	29	.125

CHAMPIONSHIP SERIES RECORD

Year	Team (League)	W	L	Pct.	ERA	WHIP	G	GS	CG	ShO	Hld.	Sv.-Opp.	IP	H	R	ER	HR	BB-IBB	SO	Avg.
1996—	New York (A.L.)	1	0	1.000	0.00	1.75	2	0	0	0	1	0-0	4.0	6	0	0	0	1-0	5	.333
1998—	New York (A.L.)	0	0	...	0.00	0.18	4	0	0	0	0	1-1	5.2	0	0	0	0	1-0	5	.000
1999—	New York (A.L.)	1	0	1.000	0.00	1.07	3	0	0	0	0	2-2	4.2	5	0	0	0	0-0	3	.294
2000—	New York (A.L.)	0	0	...	1.93	0.86	4	0	0	0	0	1-1	4.2	4	1	1	0	0-0	1	.222
2001—	New York (A.L.)	1	0	1.000	1.93	0.64	4	0	0	0	0	2-2	4.2	2	1	1	0	1-0	3	.125
2003—	New York (A.L.)	1	0	1.000	1.13	0.63	4	0	0	0	0	2-2	8.0	5	1	1	0	1-0	6	.172
2004—	New York (A.L.)	0	1	...	1.29	1.14	5	0	0	0	0	2-4	7.0	6	1	1	0	2-0	6	.250
Champ. series totals (7 years)		4	1	1.000	0.93	0.85	25	0	0	0	1	10-12	38.2	28	4	4	0	5-0	29	.203

WORLD SERIES RECORD

Year	Team (League)	W	L	Pct.	ERA	WHIP	G	GS	CG	ShO	Hld.	Sv.-Opp.	IP	H	R	ER	HR	BB-IBB	SO	Avg.
1996—	New York (A.L.)	0	0	...	1.59	1.24	4	0	0	0	2	0-0	5.2	4	1	1	0	3-0	4	.211
1998—	New York (A.L.)	0	0	...	0.00	1.15	3	0	0	0	0	3-3	4.1	5	0	0	0	0-0	4	.294
1999—	New York (A.L.)	1	0	1.000	0.00	0.86	3	0	0	0	0	2-2	4.2	3	0	0	0	1-0	3	.188
2000—	New York (A.L.)	0	0	...	3.00	0.83	4	0	0	0	0	2-2	6.0	4	2	2	1	1-0	7	.182
2001—	New York (A.L.)	1	1	.500	1.42	1.11	4	0	0	0	0	1-2	6.1	6	2	1	0	1-1	7	.250
2003—	New York (A.L.)	0	0	...	0.00	0.50	2	0	0	0	0	1-1	4.0	2	0	0	0	0-0	4	.143
World series totals (6 years)		2	1	.667	1.16	0.97	20	0	0	0	2	9-10	31.0	24	5	4	1	6-1	29	.214

ALL-STAR GAME RECORD

	W	L	Pct.	ERA	WHIP	G	GS	CG	ShO	Hld.	Sv.-Opp.	IP	H	R	ER	HR	BB-IBB	SO	Avg.
All-Star Game totals (6 years)	0	0	...	0.00	0.56	6	0	0	0	0	3-3	5.1	3	1	0	0	0-0	2	.158

2006 LEFTY-RIGHTY SPLITS

vs.	Avg.	AB	H	2B	3B	HR	RBI	BB	SO	OBP	Slg.	vs.	Avg.	AB	H	2B	3B	HR	RBI	BB	SO	OBP	Slg.
L	.194	129	25	2		1	9	4	22	.224	.233	R	.248	145	36	5	1	2	12	7	33	.297	.338

RIVERA, MICHAEL — C

PERSONAL: Born September 8, 1976, in Rio Piedras, Puerto Rico. ... 6-0/210. ... Bats right, throws right. ... Full name: Michael R. Rivera. ... High school: Dr. Augustin Stahl (Bayamon, Puerto Rico). ... College: Troy State. **TRANSACTIONS/CAREER NOTES:** Signed as a non-drafted free agent by Detroit Tigers organization (January 20, 1997). ... Traded by Tigers to San Diego Padres for OF Gene Kingsale (November 15, 2002). ... Claimed on waivers by Chicago White Sox (June 9, 2003). ... Claimed on waivers by Oakland Athletics (April 22, 2004). ... Signed as a free agent by Tigers organization (January 6, 2005). ... Released by Tigers (April 1, 2005). ... Signed by Milwaukee Brewers organization (May 17, 2005).

2006 GAMES PLAYED BY POSITION (MLB): C—44.

Year	Team (League)	Pos.	G	AB	R	H	2B	3B	HR	RBI	BB	SO	HBP	GDP	SB-CS	Avg.	OBP	SLG	OPS	E	Avg.
1997—	GC Tigers (GCL)	1B-C	47	154	34	44	9	2	10	36	18	25	3	2	0-0	.286	.367	.565	.932	1	.996
1998—	W. Mich. (Mid.)	C	108	403	40	111	34	3	9	67	15	68	2	8	0-2	.275	.301	.442	.743	10	.990
1999—	Lakeland (Fla. St.)	C	104	370	44	103	20	2	14	72	20	59	3	10	1-1	.278	.314	.457	.771	8	.989
—	Jacksonville (Sou.)	C	7	23	3	4	1	0	2	6	2	5	0	0	0-0	.174	.240	.478	.718	0	1.000
2000—	Lakeland (Fla. St.)	C	64	243	30	71	19	4	11	53	16	45	0	8	2-0	.292	.336	.539	.875	5	.988
—	Toledo (Int'l)	C	4	13	0	3	3	0	0	1	0	2	0	0	0-0	.231	.231	.462	.692	1	.968
—	Jacksonville (Sou.)	C	39	150	10	29	8	1	2	9	7	30	0	4	0-0	.193	.228	.300	.528	4	.969

R

Year Team (League)	Pos.	G	AB	R	H	2B	3B	HR	RBI	BB	SO	HBP	GDP	SB-CS	Avg.	OBP	SLG	OPS	E	Avg.
2001— Erie (East.)	C	112	415	76	120	19	1	33	101	44	96	10	9	2-2	.289	.368	.578	.946	10	.989
— Detroit (A.L.)	C	4	12	2	4	2	0	0	1	0	2	0	0	0-0	.333	.333	.500	.833	2	.929
2002— Detroit (A.L.)	C-DH	39	132	11	30	8	1	1	11	4	35	1	5	0-0	.227	.254	.326	.579	2	.990
— Toledo (Int'l)	C	74	265	43	66	11	1	20	53	35	64	3	6	0-1	.249	.341	.525	.866	3	.993
2003— San Diego (N.L.)	C-1B	19	53	2	9	1	0	1	2	5	11	0	4	0-0	.170	.241	.245	.487	2	.986
— Portland (PCL)	C	13	50	0	8	1	0	0	2	1	21	0	1	0-1	.160	.176	.180	.356	1	.990
— Charlotte (Int'l)	C-DH-1B	68	245	38	76	11	0	12	52	16	50	9	4	0-1	.310	.373	.502	.875	2	.992
2004— Charlotte (Int'l)		11	40	3	4	0	1	0	2	3	12	1	0	0-0	.100	.178	.150	.328	...	...
— Sacramento (PCL)		49	170	12	38	7	2	5	20	10	34	0	2	1-1	.224	.262	.376	.638	...	...
2005— Nashville (PCL)	C-1B	60	214	34	61	12	1	16	43	9	37	3	9	3-1	.285	.320	.575	.895	6	.988
2006— Nashville (PCL)		60	213	30	63	11	0	10	46	13	40	4	5	3-3	.296	.339	.488	.827	6	.986
— Milwaukee (N.L.)	C	46	142	16	38	9	0	6	24	10	21	3	3	0-0	.268	.325	.458	.783	3	.991
American League totals (2 years)		43	144	13	34	10	1	1	12	4	37	1	5	0-0	.236	.260	.340	.600	4	.983
National League totals (2 years)		65	195	18	47	10	0	7	26	15	32	3	7	0-0	.241	.302	.400	.702	5	.990
Major League totals (4 years)		108	339	31	81	20	1	8	38	19	69	4	12	0-0	.239	.285	.375	.660	9	.987

2006 LEFTY-RIGHTY SPLITS

vs.	Avg.	AB	H	2B	3B	HR	RBI	BB	SO	OBP	Slg.	vs.	Avg.	AB	H	2B	3B	HR	RBI	BB	SO	OBP	Slg.
L	.226	31	7	1	0	0	5	2	4	.273	.258	R	.279	111	31	8	0	6	19	8	17	.339	.514

RIVERA, RENE — C

PERSONAL: Born July 31, 1983, in Bayamon, Puerto Rico. ... 5-10/190. ... Bats right, throws right. ... High school: Papa Juan XXIII (Bayamon, Puerto Rico.). **TRANSACTIONS/CAREER NOTES:** Selected by Seattle Mariners organization in second round of 2001 free-agent draft.
2006 GAMES PLAYED BY POSITION (MLB): C—35.

Year Team (League)	Pos.	G	AB	R	H	2B	3B	HR	RBI	BB	SO	HBP	GDP	SB-CS	Avg.	OBP	SLG	OPS	E	Avg.
2001— Everett (N'west)	C	15	45	3	4	1	0	2	3	1	19	0	1	0-0	.089	.106	.244	.351	1	.992
— Ariz. Mariners (Ariz.)	C	21	71	13	24	4	0	2	12	2	11	1	0	0-0	.338	.360	.479	.839	4	.977
2002— Everett (N'west)	C	62	227	29	55	18	1	1	26	16	38	9	3	5-2	.242	.314	.344	.657	7	.987
2003— Wisconsin (Midw.)	C	116	407	39	112	19	0	9	54	38	81	7	6	2-2	.275	.344	.388	.732	11	.987
2004— Tacoma (PCL)	C	4	15	3	6	1	0	1	1	0	3	0	0	0-0	.400	.400	.667	1.067	0	1.000
— Inland Empire (Calif.)	C-DH	107	379	41	89	22	1	6	53	28	70	9	17	0-1	.235	.300	.346	.646	7	.993
— Seattle (A.L.)	C	2	3	0	0	0	0	0	0	0	1	0	0	0-0	.000	.000	.000	.000	1	1.000
2005— San Antonio (Texas)	C	57	212	20	59	14	1	2	21	7	35	1	6	1-0	.278	.305	.382	.687	4	.990
— Tacoma (PCL)	C-DH	14	49	3	10	3	0	1	6	2	12	0	2	0-1	.204	.235	.327	.562	0	1.000
— Seattle (A.L.)	C	16	48	3	19	3	0	1	6	1	11	0	0	0-0	.396	.408	.521	.929	3	.961
2006— Tacoma (PCL)		1	3	1	2	1	0	0	0	0	1	0	0	0-0	.667	.667	1.000	1.667	0	1.000
— Seattle (A.L.)	C	35	99	8	15	4	0	2	4	3	29	1	2	1-0	.152	.184	.253	.437	3	.987
Major League totals (3 years)		53	150	11	34	7	0	3	10	4	41	1	2	1-0	.227	.252	.333	.585	6	.981

2006 LEFTY-RIGHTY SPLITS

vs.	Avg.	AB	H	2B	3B	HR	RBI	BB	SO	OBP	Slg.	vs.	Avg.	AB	H	2B	3B	HR	RBI	BB	SO	OBP	Slg.
L	.087	23	2	0	0	1	2	1	9	.125	.217	R	.171	76	13	4	0	1	2	2	20	.203	.263

RIVERA, SAUL — P

PERSONAL: Born December 7, 1977, in San Juan, Puerto Rico. ... 5-11/155. ... Throws right, bats right. ... Full name: Rabell Saul Rivera. ... High school: Escuela Superial Rafael Cordero (San Juan, Puerto . ... College: Mobile. **TRANSACTIONS/CAREER NOTES:** Selected by Minnesota Twins organization in ninth round of free-agent draft (June 2, 1998). ... Claimed on waivers by New York Mets (November 20, 2001). ... Traded by Mets to Montreal Expos (July 14, 2002), completing deal in which Expos traded Ps Scott Strickland and Phil Seibel and OF Matt Watson to Mets for P Bruce Chen, IF Luis Figueroa and a player to be named (April 5, 2002). ... Traded by Expos to Milwaukee Brewers (June 18, 2004), completing deal in which Brewers traded P Jason Childers and OF Jason Belcher to Expos for OF Peter Bergeron and a player to be named (June 6, 2004). ... Signed as a free agent by Expos organization (November 16, 2004). ... Franchise transferred to Washington, D.C., and renamed Washington Nationals for 2005 season (December 3, 2004).
CAREER HITTING: 0-for-4 (.000), 0 R, 0 2B, 0 3B, 0 HR, 0 RBI.

Year Team (League)	W	L	Pct.	ERA	WHIP	G	GS	CG	ShO	Hld.	Sv.-Opp.	IP	H	R	ER	HR	BB-IBB	SO	Avg.
1998— Elizabethton (App.)	3	3	.500	2.25	1.06	23	0	0	0	...	7-...	36.0	19	10	9	4	19-2	65	.151
1999— Quad City (Midw.)	4	1	.800	1.42	1.12	60	0	0	0	...	23-...	69.2	42	12	11	0	36-5	102	.171
2000— Fort Myers (FSL)	8	1	.889	3.58	1.41	29	0	0	0	...	5-...	37.2	34	15	15	0	19-3	45	.234
— New Britain (East.)	1	0	1.000	3.89	1.35	22	0	0	0	...	0-...	37.0	28	16	16	0	22-0	47	.206
2001— New Britain (East.)	5	2	.714	3.16	1.24	33	0	0	0	...	13-...	42.2	35	16	15	3	18-1	55	.220
— GC Twins (GCL)	0	0	...	0.00	1.00	3	0	0	0	...	0-...	3.0	2	0	0	0	1-0	4	.167
2002— Binghamton (East.)	2	3	.400	3.03	1.24	30	0	0	0	...	13-...	38.2	25	18	13	2	23-2	32	.182
— Harrisburg (East.)	0	2	.000	3.32	1.58	15	0	0	0	...	3-...	19.0	21	8	7	0	9-1	15	.288
2003—	Did not play.																		
2004— Harrisburg (East.)	0	2	.000	7.71	1.86	18	0	0	0	...	3-...	21.0	27	22	18	3	12-2	15	.307
— Huntsville (Sou.)	2	1	.667	1.62	1.38	26	0	0	0	...	1-...	33.1	30	11	6	1	16-1	25	.231
2005— Harrisburg (East.)	3	3	.500	2.47	1.20	40	0	0	0	2	9-11	76.2	72	30	21	3	20-0	70	.236
2006— New Orleans (PCL)	1	1	.500	1.59	1.31	12	2	0	0	0	1-1	28.1	25	7	5	1	12-1	25	.236
— Wash. (N.L.)	3	0	1.000	3.43	1.51	54	0	0	0	9	1-3	60.1	59	28	23	4	32-6	41	.250
Major League totals (1 year)	3	0	1.000	3.43	1.51	54	0	0	0	9	1-3	60.1	59	28	23	4	32-6	41	.250

2006 LEFTY-RIGHTY SPLITS

vs.	Avg.	AB	H	2B	3B	HR	RBI	BB	SO	OBP	Slg.	vs.	Avg.	AB	H	2B	3B	HR	RBI	BB	SO	OBP	Slg.
L	.194	98	19	4	0	2	11	20	26	.333	.296	R	.290	138	40	4	0	2	21	12	15	.359	.377

RLEAL, SENDY — P

PERSONAL: Born June 21, 1980, in San Pedro de Macoris, Dominican Republic. ... 6-1/165. ... Throws right, bats right. ... Full name: Sendy Rleal. **TRANSACTIONS/CAREER NOTES:** Signed as a non-drafted free agent by Baltimore Orioles organization (June 30, 1999).
CAREER HITTING: 0-for-0 (.000), 0 R, 0 2B, 0 3B, 0 HR, 0 RBI.

Year Team (League)	W	L	Pct.	ERA	WHIP	G	GS	CG	ShO	Hld.	Sv.-Opp.	IP	H	R	ER	HR	BB-IBB	SO	Avg.
1999— Dom. Orioles (DSL)	4	3	.571	3.47	1.35	9	9	0	0	...	0-...	46.2	43	24	18	3	20-0	43	.243
2000— Bluefield (Appal.)	6	2	.750	3.39	1.41	13	12	0	0	...	0-...	61.0	61	26	23	5	25-0	55	.268
— Delmarva (S. Atl.)	0	1	.000	10.80	1.80	1	1	0	0	...	0-...	3.1	3	5	4	0	3-0	4	.214

Year Team (League)	W	L	Pct.	ERA	WHIP	G	GS	CG	ShO	Hld.	Sv.-Opp.	IP	H	R	ER	HR	BB-IBB	SO	Avg.
2001— Delmarva (S. Atl.)	3	6	.333	3.57	1.03	20	20	1	0	...	0-...	103.1	79	50	41	9	27-0	83	.207
2002— Delmarva (S. Atl.)	1	0	1.000	6.10	1.65	28	1	0	0	...	1-...	41.1	53	28	28	4	15-0	34	.317
2003— Frederick (Carolina)	3	5	.375	3.16	1.02	44	0	0	0	· 0	11-...	57.0	35	20	20	8	23-7	59	.177
2004— Bowie (East.)	4	0	1.000	2.66	1.12	39	0	0	0	...	3-...	47.1	41	16	14	7	12-0	60	.227
2005— Bowie (East.)	4	4	.500	2.04	0.91	56	0	0	0	7	16-19	70.2	46	19	16	4	18-0	75	.187
2006— Ottawa (Int'l)	2	2	.500	6.65	1.48	19	0	0	0	5	0-2	23.0	29	18	17	4	5-0	14	.315
— Baltimore (A.L.)	1	1	.500	4.44	1.52	42	0	0	0	3	0-1	46.2	48	25	23	10	23-1	19	.274
Major League totals (1 year)	1	1	.500	4.44	1.52	42	0	0	0	3	0-1	46.2	48	25	23	10	23-1	19	.274

2006 LEFTY-RIGHTY SPLITS

vs.	Avg.	AB	H	2B	3B	HR	RBI	BB	SO	OBP	Slg.	vs.	Avg.	AB	H	2B	3B	HR	RBI	BB	SO	OBP	Slg.
L	.242	91	22	3	1	3	13	11	6	.317	.396	R	.310	84	26	5	0	7	21	12	13	.392	.619

ROBERSON, CHRIS — OF

PERSONAL: Born August 23, 1979, in Oakland, Calif. ... Bats right, throws right. ... Full name: Christopher William Roberson. ... College: Feather River (Calif.). **TRANSACTIONS/CAREER NOTES:** Selected by Philadelphia Phillies organization in ninth round of 2001 free-agent draft.
2006 GAMES PLAYED BY POSITION (MLB): OF—45.

Year Team (League)	Pos.	G	AB	R	H	2B	3B	HR	RBI	BB	SO	HBP	GDP	SB-CS	Avg.	OBP	SLG	OPS	E	Avg.
2001— GC Phillies (GCL)		38	133	17	33	8	1	0	13	16	30	2	3	6-2	.248	.336	.323	.659	...	...
2002— Batavia (NY-Penn)		62	214	29	59	8	3	2	24	26	51	10	2	17-8	.276	.377	.369	.746	...	...
2003— Lakewood (S. Atl.)		132	470	64	110	19	5	2	32	57	108	12	9	59-16	.234	.331	.309	.640	...	...
2004— Clearwater (FSL)		83	313	52	96	13	6	9	38	27	71	5	5	16-12	.307	.371	.473	.844	...	...
2005— Reading (East.)	OF-DH	139	553	90	172	24	8	15	70	40	112	9	6	34-14	.311	.365	.465	.829	12	.982
2006— Scran./W.B. (I.L.)		74	284	44	83	14	2	1	17	23	57	3	7	25-9	.292	.349	.366	.716	8	.957
— Philadelphia (N.L.)	OF	57	41	9	8	0	1	0	1	0	9	1	0	3-0	.195	.214	.244	.458	0	1.000
Major League totals (1 year)		57	41	9	8	0	1	0	1	0	9	1	0	3-0	.195	.214	.244	.458	0	1.000

2006 LEFTY-RIGHTY SPLITS

vs.	Avg.	AB	H	2B	3B	HR	RBI	BB	SO	OBP	Slg.	vs.	Avg.	AB	H	2B	3B	HR	RBI	BB	SO	OBP	Slg.
L	.111	18	2	0	0	0	1	0	6	.158	.111	R	.261	23	6	0	1	0	0	0	3	.261	.348

ROBERTS, BRIAN — 2B

PERSONAL: Born October 9, 1977, in Durham, N.C. ... 5-9/176. ... Bats both, throws right. ... Full name: Brian Michael Roberts. ... High school: Chapel Hill (N.C.). ... College: North Carolina, then South Carolina. **TRANSACTIONS/CAREER NOTES:** Selected by Baltimore Orioles organization in supplemental round ("sandwich pick" between first and second rounds, 50th pick overall) of 1999 free-agent draft; pick received as part of compensation for Texas Rangers signing Type A free-agent 1B Rafael Palmeiro. ... On disabled list (April 30-May 24, 2006); included rehabilitation assignment to Bowie. **HONORS:** Named second baseman on the SPORTING NEWS A.L. All-Star team (2005). **STATISTICAL NOTES:** Career major league grand slams: 3.
2006 GAMES PLAYED BY POSITION (MLB): 2B—137, DH—1.

Year Team (League)	Pos.	G	AB	R	H	2B	3B	HR	RBI	BB	SO	HBP	GDP	SB-CS	Avg.	OBP	SLG	OPS	E	Avg.
1999— Delmarva (S. Atl.)	SS	47	167	22	40	12	1	0	21	27	42	1	0	17-5	.240	.347	.323	.670	8	.964
2000— Frederick (Carolina)	SS	48	163	27	49	6	3	0	16	27	24	1	4	13-10	.301	.403	.374	.777	8	.952
— GC Orioles (GCL)	SS	9	29	8	9	1	2	1	3	7	4	0	0	7-1	.310	.432	.586	1.019	2	.905
2001— Bowie (East.)	2B-SS	22	81	12	24	7	0	1	7	9	12	1	2	10-0	.296	.366	.420	.785	3	.968
— Rochester (Int'l)	SS	44	161	16	43	4	1	1	12	28	22	0	0	23-3	.267	.376	.323	.699	13	.927
— Baltimore (A.L.)	SS-2B-DH	75	273	42	69	12	3	2	17	13	36	0	3	12-3	.253	.284	.341	.624	16	.941
2002— Rochester (Int'l)	2B	78	313	49	86	9	7	3	30	40	46	3	3	22-4	.275	.361	.377	.738	7	.978
— Baltimore (A.L.)	2B-DH	38	128	19	29	6	0	1	11	15	21	1	3	9-2	.227	.308	.297	.605	3	.977
2003— Ottawa (Int'l)	2B-SS	44	178	36	56	13	1	0	15	27	12	0	1	19-6	.315	.401	.399	.800	4	.979
— Baltimore (A.L.) 2B-DH-SS		112	460	65	124	22	4	5	41	46	58	1	9	23-6	.270	.337	.367	.704	9	.983
2004— Baltimore (A.L.)	2B-DH	159	641	107	175	*50	2	4	53	71	95	1	9	29-12	.273	.344	.376	.720	8	.988
2005— Baltimore (A.L.)	2B	143	561	92	176	45	7	18	73	67	83	3	6	27-10	.314	.387	.515	.903	8	.988
2006— Bowie (East.)		2	5	0	1	0	0	0	0	2	0	0	0	0-0	.200	.429	.200	.629	0	1.000
— Baltimore (A.L.)	2B-DH	138	563	85	161	34	3	10	55	55	66	0	16	36-7	.286	.347	.410	.757	9	.985
Major League totals (6 years)		665	2626	409	734	169	19	40	250	267	359	6	40	136-40	.280	.345	.404	.749	53	.981

ALL-STAR GAME RECORD

	G	AB	R	H	2B	3B	HR	RBI	BB	SO	HBP	GDP	SB-CS	Avg.	OBP	SLG	OPS	E	Avg.
All-Star Game totals (1 year)	1	2	1	1	0	0	0	0	0	0	0	0	0-0	.500	.500	1.000	1.500	0	1.000

2006 LEFTY-RIGHTY SPLITS

vs.	Avg.	AB	H	2B	3B	HR	RBI	BB	SO	OBP	Slg.	vs.	Avg.	AB	H	2B	3B	HR	RBI	BB	SO	OBP	Slg.
L	.235	170	40	10	1	1	11	25	32	.332	.324	R	.308	393	121	24	2	9	44	30	34	.354	.448

ROBERTS, DAVE — OF

PERSONAL: Born May 31, 1972, in Okinawa, Japan. ... 5-10/180. ... Bats left, throws left. ... Full name: David Ray Roberts. ... High school: Rancho Buena Vista (Oceanside, Calif.). ... College: UCLA. **TRANSACTIONS/CAREER NOTES:** Selected by Cleveland Indians organization in 47th round of 1993 free-agent draft; did not sign. ... Selected by Detroit Tigers organization in 28th round of 1994 free-agent draft. ... Loaned by Tigers organization to Oakland Athletics organization (March 30-August 30, 1996). ... Traded by Tigers with P Tim Worrell to Cleveland Indians for OF Geronimo Berroa (June 24, 1998). ... On disabled list (March 31-June 24, 2001); included rehabilitation assignment to Akron. ... Traded by Indians to Los Angeles Dodgers for Ps Christian Bridenbaugh and Nial Hughes (December 21, 2001). ... On disabled list (May 17-June 1 and July 2-26, 2003); included rehabilitation assignments to Las Vegas and Ogden. ... On disabled list (May 5-28, 2004); included rehabilitation assignment to Vero Beach. ... Traded by Dodgers to Boston Red Sox for OF Henri Stanley (July 31, 2004). ... Traded by Red Sox to San Diego Padres for OF Jay Payton, SS Ramon Vazquez, P David Pauley and cash (December 20, 2004). ... On disabled list (March 30-April 18, 2005); included rehabilitation assignment to Lake Elsinore. ... On disabled list (June 20-July 5, 2006); included rehabilitation assignment to Lake Elsinore. **STATISTICAL NOTES:** Career major league grand slams: 2.
2006 GAMES PLAYED BY POSITION (MLB): OF—127.

Year Team (League)	Pos.	G	AB	R	H	2B	3B	HR	RBI	BB	SO	HBP	GDP	SB-CS	Avg.	OBP	SLG	OPS	E	Avg.
1994— Jamestown (NYP)	OF	54	178	33	52	7	2	0	12	29	27	1	0	12-8	.292	.392	.354	.746	0	1.000
1995— Lakeland (Fla. St.)	OF	92	357	67	108	10	5	3	30	39	43	1	7	30-8	.303	.371	.384	.755	1	.985
1996— Visalia (Calif.)	OF	126	482	112	131	24	7	5	37	98	105	1	6	65-21	.272	.391	.382	.773	5	.977
— Jacksonville (Sou.)	OF	3	9	0	2	0	0	0	1	0	0	0	0	0-1	.222	.300	.222	.522	0	1.000
1997— Jacksonville (Sou.)	OF	105	415	76	123	24	2	4	41	45	62	2	5	23-5	.296	.366	.393	.759	4	.954

R

Year	Team (League)	Pos.	G	AB	R	H	2B	3B	HR	RBI	BB	SO	HBP	GDP	SB-CS	Avg.	OBP	SLG	OPS	E	Avg.
1998—	Jacksonville (Sou.)	OF	69	279	71	91	14	5	5	42	53	59	3	4	21-9	.326	.434	.466	.900	0	1.000
—	Akron (East.)	OF	56	227	49	82	10	5	7	33	35	30	1	3	28-6	.361	.447	.542	.989	1	.992
—	Buffalo (Int'l)	OF	5	15	2	2	0	0	0	2	0	3	0	0	2-0	.133	.125	.133	.258	0	1.000
1999—	Buffalo (Int'l)	OF-DH	89	350	65	95	17	10	0	38	43	52	2	1	39-3	.271	.351	.377	.728	1	.996
—	Cleveland (A.L.)	OF	41	143	26	34	4	0	2	12	9	16	0	0	11-3	.238	.281	.308	.589	0	1.000
2000—	Buffalo (Int'l)	OF	120	462	93	135	16	3	13	55	59	68	2	3	39-11	.292	.373	.424	.798	1	.997
—	Cleveland (A.L.)	OF	19	10	1	2	0	0	0	0	2	2	0	0	1-1	.200	.333	.200	.533	0	1.000
2001—	Akron (East.)	OF	17	64	9	13	5	0	0	2	9	8	1	1	4-0	.203	.307	.281	.588	1	.969
—	Buffalo (Int'l)	OF	62	241	34	73	12	4	0	22	18	44	2	2	17-6	.303	.352	.386	.738	3	.978
—	Cleveland (A.L.)	OF-DH	15	12	3	4	1	0	0	2	1	2	0	0	0-1	.333	.385	.417	.801	0	1.000
2002—	Los Angeles (N.L.)	OF	127	422	63	117	14	7	3	34	48	51	2	1	45-10	.277	.353	.354	.718	0	1.000
2003—	Las Vegas (PCL)	OF	2	5	2	0	0	0	0	0	1	0	0	0	1-0	.000	.167	.000	.167	0	...
—	Ogden (Pion.)	OF	3	10	4	4	0	0	0	1	0	0	0	0	1-0	.400	.455	.400	.855	0	1.000
—	Los Angeles (N.L.)	OF	107	388	56	97	6	5	2	16	43	39	4	0	40-14	.250	.331	.307	.638	5	.976
2004—	Vero Beach (FSL)	OF	2	8	0	0	0	0	0	0	0	0	0	0	0-0	.000	.000	.000	.000	0	1.000
—	Los Angeles (N.L.)	OF	68	233	45	59	4	7	2	21	28	31	4	2	33-1	.253	.340	.356	.696	3	.976
—	Boston (A.L.)	OF-DH	45	86	19	22	10	0	2	14	10	17	1	2	5-2	.256	.330	.442	.772	1	.982
2005—	Lake Elsinore (Calif.)	OF	3	10	2	2	1	0	0	0	3	1	0	0	0-1	.200	.385	.300	.685	0	1.000
—	San Diego (N.L.)	OF	115	411	65	113	19	10	8	38	53	59	1	9	23-12	.275	.356	.428	.784	2	.992
2006—	Lake Elsinore (Calif.)		1	3	0	1	0	0	0	0	0	2	0	0	0-0	.333	.333	.333	.667	0	...
—	San Diego (N.L.)	OF	129	499	80	146	18	13	2	44	51	61	4	5	49-6	.293	.360	.393	.752	0	1.000
	American League totals (4 years)		120	251	49	62	15	0	4	28	22	37	1	2	17-7	.247	.306	.355	.660	1	.994
	National League totals (5 years)		546	1953	309	532	61	42	17	153	223	241	15	17	190-43	.272	.349	.373	.722	10	.991
	Major League totals (8 years)		666	2204	358	594	76	42	21	181	245	278	16	19	207-50	.270	.344	.371	.715	11	.991

DIVISION SERIES RECORD

Year	Team (League)	Pos.	G	AB	R	H	2B	3B	HR	RBI	BB	SO	HBP	GDP	SB-CS	Avg.	OBP	SLG	OPS	E	Avg.
1999—	Cleveland (A.L.)	OF	2	3	0	0	0	0	0	0	0	2	0	0	0-0	.000	.000	.000	.000	0	1.000
2004—	Boston (A.L.)		1	0	0	0	0	0	0	0	0	0	0	0	0-0	...	...	...	...	0	...
2005—	San Diego (N.L.)	OF	3	9	1	2	0	0	1	1	0	1	0	0	0-0	.222	.222	.556	.778	0	1.000
2006—	San Diego (N.L.)	OF	4	16	1	7	0	1	0	0	1	4	0	0	1-1	.438	.471	.563	1.033	0	1.000
	Division series totals (4 years)		10	28	2	9	0	1	1	1	1	7	0	0	1-1	.321	.345	.500	.845	0	1.000

CHAMPIONSHIP SERIES RECORD

Year	Team (League)	Pos.	G	AB	R	H	2B	3B	HR	RBI	BB	SO	HBP	GDP	SB-CS	Avg.	OBP	SLG	OPS	E	Avg.
2004—	Boston (A.L.)		2	0	2	0	0	0	0	0	0	0	0	0	1-0	...	...	...	...	0	...

WORLD SERIES RECORD

Year	Team (League)	Pos.	G	AB	R	H	2B	3B	HR	RBI	BB	SO	HBP	GDP	SB-CS	Avg.	OBP	SLG	OPS	E	Avg.
2004—	Boston (A.L.)		Did not play.																			

2006 LEFTY-RIGHTY SPLITS

vs.	Avg.	AB	H	2B	3B	HR	RBI	BB	SO	OBP	Slg.	vs.	Avg.	AB	H	2B	3B	HR	RBI	BB	SO	OBP	Slg.
L	.292	65	19	2	3	0	11	2	10	.310	.415	R	.293	434	127	16	10	2	33	49	51	.367	.389

ROBERTS, RYAN — IF

PERSONAL: Born September 19, 1980, in Fort Worth, Texas. ... 5-11/190. ... Bats right, throws right. ... Full name: Ryan Alan Roberts. ... College: Texas.
TRANSACTIONS/CAREER NOTES: Selected by Toronto Blue Jays organization in 18th round of 2003 free-agent draft.
2006 GAMES PLAYED BY POSITION (MLB): 2B—8, DH—1.

Year	Team (League)	Pos.	G	AB	R	H	2B	3B	HR	RBI	BB	SO	HBP	GDP	SB-CS	Avg.	OBP	SLG	OPS	E	Avg.
2003—	Auburn (NY-Penn)		66	248	52	69	10	3	8	36	35	63	4	10	7-3	.278	.374	.440	.814	...	...
2004—	Char., W.Va. (SAL)		64	226	38	64	9	0	13	39	55	50	9	6	0-0	.283	.440	.496	.936	...	...
—	Dunedin (Fla. St.)		59	205	29	49	1	1	7	25	36	51	1	8	0-3	.239	.350	.356	.706	...	...
2005—	Dunedin (Fla. St.)	2B-DH	42	164	33	47	9	0	9	35	24	27	2	5	6-1	.287	.380	.506	.886	11	.949
—	New Hampshire (East.)	2B-DH	92	338	54	92	19	3	15	44	55	94	4	6	5-1	.272	.379	.479	.859	5	.988
2006—	Syracuse (Int'l)	2B-DH	98	362	44	99	28	1	10	49	30	86	2	5	5-3	.273	.330	.439	.769	11	.972
—	Toronto (A.L.)	2B-DH	9	13	1	1	0	0	1	1	1	4	0	1	0-0	.077	.143	.308	.451	0	1.000
	Major League totals (1 year)		9	13	1	1	0	0	1	1	1	4	0	1	0-0	.077	.143	.308	.451	0	1.000

2006 LEFTY-RIGHTY SPLITS

vs.	Avg.	AB	H	2B	3B	HR	RBI	BB	SO	OBP	Slg.	vs.	Avg.	AB	H	2B	3B	HR	RBI	BB	SO	OBP	Slg.
L	.000	0	0	0	0	0	0	0	0	.000	.000	R	.077	13	1	0	0	1	1	1	4	.143	.308

ROBERTSON, NATE — P

PERSONAL: Born September 3, 1977, in Wichita, Kan. ... 6-2/215. ... Throws left, bats right. ... Full name: Nathan Daniel Robertson. ... High school: Maize (Kan.). ... College: Wichita State. **TRANSACTIONS/CAREER NOTES:** Selected by Chicago White Sox organization in 35th round of 1995 free-agent draft; did not sign. ... Selected by White Sox organization in 15th round of 1998 free-agent draft; did not sign. ... Selected by Florida Marlins organization in fifth round of 1999 free-agent draft. ... Traded by Marlins with Ps Gary Knotts and Rob Henkel to Detroit Tigers for Ps Mark Redman and Jerrod Fuell (January 11, 2003).
CAREER HITTING: 1-for-14 (.071), 0 R, 0 2B, 0 3B, 0 HR, 1 RBI.

Year	Team (League)	W	L	Pct.	ERA	WHIP	G	GS	CG	ShO	Hld.	Sv.-Opp.	IP	H	R	ER	HR	BB-IBB	SO	Avg.
1999—	Kane Co. (Midw.)	6	1	.857	2.29	1.06	8	8	1	1	...	0-...	51.0	42	14	13	1	12-0	33	.230
—	Utica (N.Y.-Penn)	2	0	1.000	2.77	1.15	5	5	0	0	...	0-...	26.0	22	9	8	0	8-0	26	.244
2000—	Kane Co. (Midw.)	0	2	.000	5.09	1.70	6	6	0	0	...	0-...	17.2	24	13	10	0	6-0	15	.324
2001—	Brevard County (FSL)	11	4	.733	2.88	1.30	19	19	2	0	...	0-...	106.1	95	44	34	3	43-1	67	.244
2002—	Portland (East.)	10	9	.526	3.42	1.26	27	27	3	0	...	0-...	163.0	156	77	62	12	50-2	109	.260
—	Florida (N.L.)	0	1	.000	11.88	2.28	6	1	0	0	0	0-0	8.1	15	11	11	3	4-1	3	.375
2003—	Toledo (Int'l)	9	7	.563	3.14	1.20	24	23	3	1	...	0-...	155.0	145	62	54	14	47-2	102	.250
—	Detroit (A.L.)	1	2	.333	5.44	1.75	8	8	0	0	0	0-0	44.2	55	27	27	6	23-2	33	.306
2004—	Detroit (A.L.)	12	10	.545	4.90	1.40	34	32	1	0	0	1-1	196.2	210	116	107	30	66-1	155	.274
2005—	Detroit (A.L.)	7	16	.304	4.48	·1.36	32	32	2	0	0	0-0	196.2	202	113	98	28	65-2	122	.266
2006—	Detroit (A.L.)	13	13	.500	3.84	1.31	32	32	1	0	0	0-0	208.2	206	98	89	29	67-2	137	.259
	American League totals (4 years)	33	41	.446	4.47	1.38	106	104	4	0	0	1-1	646.2	673	354	321	93	221-7	447	.269
	National League totals (1 year)	0	1	.000	11.88	2.28	6	1	0	0	0	0-0	8.1	15	11	11	3	4-1	3	.375
	Major League totals (5 years)	33	42	.440	4.56	1.39	112	105	4	0	0	1-1	655.0	688	365	332	96	225-8	450	.271

DIVISION SERIES RECORD

Year	Team (League)	W	L	Pct.	ERA	WHIP	G	GS	CG	ShO	Hld.	Sv.-Opp.	IP	H	R	ER	HR	BB-IBB	SO	Avg.
2006— Detroit (A.L.)		0	1	.000	11.12	2.12	1	1	0	0	0	0-0	5.2	12	7	7	1	0-0	1	.429

CHAMPIONSHIP SERIES RECORD

Year	Team (League)	W	L	Pct.	ERA	WHIP	G	GS	CG	ShO	Hld.	Sv.-Opp.	IP	H	R	ER	HR	BB-IBB	SO	Avg.
2006— Detroit (A.L.)		1	0	1.000	0.00	1.80	1	1	0	0	0	0-0	5.0	6	0	0	0	3-0	4	.333

WORLD SERIES RECORD

Year	Team (League)	W	L	Pct.	ERA	WHIP	G	GS	CG	ShO	Hld.	Sv.-Opp.	IP	H	R	ER	HR	BB-IBB	SO	Avg.
2006— Detroit (A.L.)		0	1	.000	3.60	1.60	1	1	0	0	0	0-0	5.0	5	2	2	0	3-1	3	.250

2006 LEFTY-RIGHTY SPLITS

vs.	Avg.	AB	H	2B	3B	HR	RBI	BB	SO	OBP	Slg.	vs.	Avg.	AB	H	2B	3B	HR	RBI	BB	SO	OBP	Slg.
L	.181	193	35	9	1	2	9	5	44	.221	.269	R	.284	602	171	29	2	27	76	62	93	.351	.473

ROBINSON, KERRY — OF

PERSONAL: Born October 3, 1973, in St. Louis, Mo. ... 6-0/175. ... Bats left, throws left. ... Full name: Kerry Keith Robinson. ... High school: Hazelwood East (St. Louis). ... College: Southeast Missouri State. **TRANSACTIONS/CAREER NOTES:** Selected by St. Louis Cardinals organization in 34th round of 1995 free-agent draft. ... Selected by Tampa Bay Devil Rays in second round (44th pick overall) of expansion draft (November 18, 1997). ... Claimed on waivers by Seattle Mariners (November 19, 1998). ... Traded by Mariners to Cincinnati Reds for P Todd Williams (July 22, 1999). ... Released by Reds (March 30, 2000). ... Signed by New York Yankees organization (April 9, 2000). ... Signed as a free agent by Cardinals organization (December 7, 2000). ... Traded by Cardinals to San Diego Padres for OF Brian L. Hunter (March 29, 2004). ... Signed as a free agent by New York Mets organization (December 23, 2004). ... Released by Mets (March 31, 2005). ... Signed by Padres organization (April 7, 2005). ... Released by Padres (June 15, 2005). ... Signed by Atlanta Braves organization (June 22, 2005). ... Released by Braves (September 1, 2005). ... Signed by Kansas City Royals organization (November 18, 2005).

2006 GAMES PLAYED BY POSITION (MLB): OF—16.

Year	Team (League)	Pos.	G	AB	R	H	2B	3B	HR	RBI	BB	SO	HBP	GDP	SB-CS	Avg.	OBP	SLG	OPS	FIELDING E	Avg.
1995— Johnson City (App.)	OF	60	250	44	74	12	8	1	26	16	30	0	3	14-10	.296	.336	.420	.756	6	.938
1996— Peoria (Midw.)	OF	123	440	98	158	17	4	2	47	51	51	3	2	50-26	.359	.422	.430	.852	7	.962
1997— Arkansas (Texas)	OF	135	523	80	168	16	3	2	62	54	64	2	7	40-23	.321	.386	.375	.760	7	.966
— Louisville (A.A.)	OF	2	9	0	1	0	0	0	0	0	1	0	0	0-0	.111	.111	.111	.222	0	1.000
1998— Orlando (South.)	OF	72	309	45	83	7	5	2	26	27	28	0	6	28-9	.269	.325	.343	.668	0	1.000
— Durham (Int'l)	OF	58	242	28	73	7	4	1	28	23	30	0	1	18-11	.302	.361	.376	.737	2	.987
— Tampa Bay (A.L.)	OF	2	3	0	0	0	0	0	0	0	1	0	0	0-0	.000	.000	.000	.000	0	1.000
1999— Tacoma (PCL)	OF-DH	79	335	53	108	16	9	0	34	14	44	0	4	30-7	.322	.348	.424	.771	4	.974
— Indianapolis (Int'l)	OF	34	129	24	34	3	2	1	14	4	12	1	2	14-4	.264	.285	.341	.626	2	.977
— Cincinnati (N.L.)	OF	9	1	4	0	0	0	0	0	0	1	0	0	0-0	.000	.000	.000	.000	0	—
2000— Columbus (Int'l)	OF	119	437	71	139	17	9	0	32	41	40	2	5	37-18	.318	.378	.398	.777	3	.988
2001— Memphis (PCL)	OF	10	40	4	13	1	0	0	3	4	10	0	1	4-1	.325	.386	.350	.736	0	1.000
— St. Louis (N.L.)	OF	114	186	34	53	6	1	1	15	12	20	2	1	11-2	.285	.330	.344	.674	2	.981
2002— Memphis (PCL)	OF-DH	16	61	14	21	2	1	0	3	1	7	0	0	5-0	.344	.355	.410	.765	1	.979
— St. Louis (N.L.)	OF	124	181	27	47	7	4	1	15	11	29	0	1	7-4	.260	.301	.359	.660	2	.977
2003— Memphis (PCL)	OF	116	208	19	52	6	3	1	16	8	27	1	3	6-1	.250	.281	.322	.603	0	1.000
— St. Louis (N.L.)	OF-DH	42	170	31	52	6	3	2	20	19	15	3	4	25-1	.306	.383	.412	.795	1	.986
2004— Portland (PCL)	OF-DH	80	92	20	27	4	0	0	5	5	8	1	0	11-4	.293	.330	.337	.667	0	1.000
— San Diego (N.L.)	OF	61	253	40	73	5	2	2	17	10	26	1	4	26-7	.289	.316	.348	.664	2	.992
2005— Portland (PCL)	OF	58	204	29	67	9	1	1	12	13	23	1	2	13-6	.328	.370	.397	.767	2	.990
— Richmond (Int'l)	OF	100	396	68	123	24	3	2	40	33	36	4	10	17-14	.311	.370	.402	.771	2	.992
2006— Omaha (PCL)	OF	18	64	8	17	2	1	0	5	1	7	0	1	1-1	.266	.277	.328	.605	0	1.000
— Kansas City (A.L.)																					
American League totals (2 years)		20	67	8	17	2	1	0	5	1	8	0	1	1-1	.254	.265	.313	.578	0	1.000
National League totals (5 years)		443	668	104	179	23	8	3	51	36	85	4	5	35-12	.268	.307	.340	.647	4	.988
Major League totals (7 years)		463	735	112	196	25	9	3	56	37	93	4	6	36-13	.267	.303	.337	.640	4	.989

DIVISION SERIES RECORD

Year	Team (League)	Pos.	G	AB	R	H	2B	3B	HR	RBI	BB	SO	HBP	GDP	SB-CS	Avg.	OBP	SLG	OPS	E	Avg.
2001— St. Louis (N.L.)	OF	4	2	0	1	0	0	0	1	0	0	0	0	0-0	.500	.500	.500	1.000	0	...
2002— St. Louis (N.L.)		2	2	0	1	0	0	0	2	0	0	0	0	0-0	.500	.500	.500	1.000	0	...
Division series totals (2 years)		6	4	0	2	0	0	0	3	0	0	0	0	0-0	.500	.500	.500	1.000	0	

CHAMPIONSHIP SERIES RECORD

Year	Team (League)	Pos.	G	AB	R	H	2B	3B	HR	RBI	BB	SO	HBP	GDP	SB-CS	Avg.	OBP	SLG	OPS	E	Avg.
2002— St. Louis (N.L.)	OF	3	2	1	0	0	0	0	0	1	0	0	0	0-1	.000	.333	.000	.333	0	...

2006 LEFTY-RIGHTY SPLITS

vs.	Avg.	AB	H	2B	3B	HR	RBI	BB	SO	OBP	Slg.	vs.	Avg.	AB	H	2B	3B	HR	RBI	BB	SO	OBP	Slg.
L	.182	11	2	0	0	0	0	0	1	.182	.182	R	.283	53	15	2	1	0	5	1	6	.296	.358

ROBLES, OSCAR — 2B/3B

PERSONAL: Born April 9, 1976, in Tijuana, Mexico. ... 5-11/155. ... Bats left, throws right. ... Full name: Oscar M. Robles. ... High school: Montgomery (San Diego). **TRANSACTIONS/CAREER NOTES:** Selected by Houston Astros organization in third round of 1994 free-agent draft. ... Signed by Mexico City of Mexican League (April 2000). ... Contract purchased by Los Angeles Dodgers from Mexico City Red Devils (May 9, 2005).

2006 GAMES PLAYED BY POSITION (MLB): 2B—13, 3B—6.

Year	Team (League)	Pos.	G	AB	R	H	2B	3B	HR	RBI	BB	SO	HBP	GDP	SB-CS	Avg.	OBP	SLG	OPS	FIELDING E	Avg.
1994— GC Astros (GCL)	SS-3B-2B	55	165	40	54	5	1	0	19	32	17	2	5	14-10	.327	.442	.370	.812	14	.930
1995— Auburn (NY-Penn)	SS	58	216	49	62	9	1	0	19	39	15	0	5	8-2	.287	.395	.338	.733	16	.949
1996— Kissimmee (Fla. St.)	2B	125	427	57	115	13	2	0	29	74	37	6	13	10-8	.269	.383	.309	.692	26	.957
1997— Kissimmee (Fla. St.)	2B	66	236	39	53	4	0	0	21	43	28	1	4	0-1	.225	.344	.242	.586	8	.973
— New Orleans (A.A.)	2B	2	3	0	1	0	0	0	0	1	1	0	0	0-0	.333	.500	.333	.833	0	1.000
1998— Kissimmee (Fla. St.)	2B	66	207	31	56	7	1	0	24	38	14	3	1	6-2	.271	.390	.314	.704	13	.954
— Jackson (Texas)	2B	4	5	0	1	0	0	0	1	1	0	0	0	0-0	.200	.333	.200	.533	0	1.000
2000— Mexico (Mex.)	2B-3B	1	0	1	0	0	0	0	0	0	0	0	0	0-0	...	1.000	...	1.000	0	1.000
— Oaxaca (Mex.)	3B-SS-2B																			
		OF	84	310	62	108	14	1	4	45	68	35	0	10	3-3	.348	.461	.439	.900	10	.970
2001— Oaxaca (Mex.)	3B-SS-2B																			
		OF	118	466	71	138	26	2	5	51	59	50	1	16	4-5	.296	.373	.393	.766	14	.971
2002— Oaxaca (Mex.)	3B-SS-2B																			
		OF	105	368	67	128	25	0	9	76	74	35	5	7	4-3	.348	.452	.489	.941	18	.960

R

Year Team (League)	Pos.	G	AB	R	H	2B	3B	HR	RBI	BB	SO	HBP	GDP	SB-CS	Avg.	OBP	SLG	OPS	E	Avg.
2003—Mexico (Mex.)	2B-3B	99	398	81	123	13	9	8	53	69	29	0	10	6-3	.309	.404	.447	.851	10	.982
2004—Mexico (Mex.)	2B-3B	97	335	72	128	23	5	8	64	62	11	0	8	8-6	.382	.473	.552	1.025	11	.933
2005—Mexico (Mex.)	2B-OF	30	118	27	46	7	0	4	21	19	8	1	6	1-1	.390	.475	.551	1.026	2	.989
—Los Angeles (N.L.)	SS-3B-2B-DH	110	364	44	99	18	1	5	34	31	33	2	8	0-8	.272	.332	.368	.700	7	.977
2006—Las Vegas (PCL)		86	275	29	79	10	0	0	28	36	20	0	6	0-1	.287	.366	.324	.690	2	.994
—Los Angeles (N.L.)	2B-3B	29	33	6	5	0	1	0	0	5	5	0	0	0-0	.152	.263	.212	.475	1	.962
Major League totals (2 years)		139	397	50	104	18	2	5	34	36	38	2	8	0-8	.262	.326	.355	.681	8	.976

2006 LEFTY-RIGHTY SPLITS

vs.	Avg.	AB	H	2B	3B	HR	RBI	BB	SO	OBP	Slg.	vs.	Avg.	AB	H	2B	3B	HR	RBI	BB	SO	OBP	Slg.
L	.000	4	0	0	0	0	0	1	2	.200	.000	R	.172	29	5	0	1	0	0	4	3	.273	.241

RODNEY, FERNANDO — P

PERSONAL: Born March 18, 1977, in Samana, Dominican Republic. ... 5-11/208. ... Throws right, bats right. **TRANSACTIONS/CAREER NOTES:** Signed as a non-drafted free agent by Detroit Tigers organization (November 1, 1997). ... On disabled list (March 26, 2004-entire season). ... On disabled list (March 29-June 9, 2005); included rehabilitation assignment to Toledo.

CAREER HITTING: 0-for-1 (.000), 0 R, 0 2B, 0 3B, 0 HR, 0 RBI.

Year Team (League)	W	L	Pct.	ERA	WHIP	G	GS	CG	ShO	Hld.	Sv.-Opp.	IP	H	R	ER	HR	BB-IBB	SO	Avg.
1998—Dom. Tigers (DSL)	1	3	.250	3.38	1.38	11	5	0	0	...	1-...	32.0	25	16	12	...	19-...	37	...
—Detroit (DSL)	1	3	.250	3.38	1.38	11	5	0	0	...	1-...	32.0	25	16	12	4	19-2	37	.214
1999—GC Tigers (GCL)	3	3	.500	2.40	1.37	22	0	0	0	...	9-...	30.0	20	8	8	1	21-0	39	.200
—Lakeland (Fla. St.)	1	0	1.000	1.42	1.26	4	0	0	0	...	2-...	6.1	7	1	1	0	1-0	5	.304
2000—W. Mich. (Mid.)	6	4	.600	2.94	1.32	22	10	0	0	...	0-...	82.2	74	34	27	2	35-0	56	.238
2001—Lakeland (Fla. St.)	4	2	.667	3.42	1.30	16	9	0	0	...	0-...	55.1	53	26	21	2	19-1	44	.249
—GC Tigers (GCL)	0	0	...	0.00	1.00	1	1	0	0	...	0-...	1.0	0	0	0	0	1-0	1	.000
—Erie (East.)	0	0	...	4.26	1.58	4	0	0	0	...	1-...	6.1	7	3	3	1	3-0	8	.292
2002—Erie (East.)	1	0	1.000	1.33	0.93	21	0	0	0	...	11-...	20.1	14	4	3	0	5-0	18	.194
—Detroit (A.L.)	1	3	.250	6.00	1.94	20	0	0	0	0	0-4	18.0	25	15	12	2	10-2	10	.329
—Toledo (Int'l)	1	1	.500	0.81	0.99	20	0	0	0	...	4-...	22.1	13	4	2	1	9-0	25	.171
2003—Toledo (Int'l)	1	1	.500	1.33	0.86	38	0	0	0	...	23-...	40.2	22	6	6	0	13-0	58	.163
—Detroit (A.L.)	1	3	.250	6.07	1.75	27	0	0	0	3	3-6	29.2	35	20	20	2	17-1	33	.294
2003—Detroit (A.L.)	Did not play																		
2005—Toledo (Int'l)	0	0	...	3.00	1.00	3	0	0	0	1	0-1	3.0	2	1	1	0	1-0	4	.182
—Detroit (A.L.)	2	3	.400	2.86	1.27	39	0	0	0	3	9-15	44.0	39	14	14	5	17-3	42	.238
2006—Detroit (A.L.)	7	4	.636	3.52	1.19	63	0	0	0	18	7-11	71.2	51	36	28	6	34-4	65	.196
Major League totals (4 years)	11	13	.458	4.08	1.40	149	0	0	0	24	19-36	163.1	150	85	74	15	78-10	150	.242

CHAMPIONSHIP SERIES RECORD

Year Team (League)	W	L	Pct.	ERA	WHIP	G	GS	CG	ShO	Hld.	Sv.-Opp.	IP	H	R	ER	HR	BB-IBB	SO	Avg.
2006—Detroit (A.L.)	0	0	...	0.00	0.55	3	0	0	0	2	0-0	3.2	1	0	0	0	1-0	4	.091

WORLD SERIES RECORD

Year Team (League)	W	L	Pct.	ERA	WHIP	G	GS	CG	ShO	Hld.	Sv.-Opp.	IP	H	R	ER	HR	BB-IBB	SO	Avg.
2006—Detroit (A.L.)	0	0	...	4.50	2.25	4	0	0	0	0	0-1	4.0	5	4	2	0	4-1	5	.333

2006 LEFTY-RIGHTY SPLITS

vs.	Avg.	AB	H	2B	3B	HR	RBI	BB	SO	OBP	Slg.	vs.	Avg.	AB	H	2B	3B	HR	RBI	BB	SO	OBP	Slg.
L	.202	109	22	2	0	4	11	16	25	.320	.330	R	.192	151	29	7	0	2	22	18	40	.299	.278

RODRIGUEZ, ALEX — 3B

PERSONAL: Born July 27, 1975, in New York. ... 6-3/210. ... Bats right, throws right. ... Full name: Alexander Emmanuel Rodriguez. ... Name pronounced: rod-RI-guez. ... High school: Westminster Christian (Miami). **TRANSACTIONS/CAREER NOTES:** Selected by Seattle Mariners organization in first round (first pick overall) of 1993 free-agent draft. ... On disabled list (April 22-May 7, 1996); included rehabilitation assignment to Tacoma. ... On disabled list (June 12-27, 1997; April 7-May 14, 1999; and July 8-24, 2000). ... Signed as a free agent by Texas Rangers (December 11, 2000). ... Traded by Rangers to New York Yankees for 2B Alfonso Soriano and a player to be named (Feburary 16, 2004); Rangers acquired SS Joaquin Arias to complete deal (March 23, 2005). ... On suspended list (August 14-19, 2004). **HONORS:** Named Major League Player of the Year by THE SPORTING NEWS (1996 and 2002). ... Named shortstop on THE SPORTING NEWS A.L. All-Star team (1996, 1998 and 2000-03). ... Named third baseman on the SPORTING NEWS A.L. All-Star team (2005). ... Named A.L. Most Valuable Player by Baseball Writers' Association of America (2003 and 2005). ... Won A.L. Gold Glove at shortstop (2002 and 2003). ... Named shortstop on A.L. Silver Slugger team (1996, 1998-2003). ... Named third baseman on A.L. Silver Slugger team (2005). **STATISTICAL NOTES:** Hit for the cycle (June 5, 1997). ... Hit three home runs in one game (April 16, 2000; August 17, 2002; and April 26, 2005). ... Career major league grand slams: 13.

2006 GAMES PLAYED BY POSITION (MLB): 3B—151, DH—3.

Year Team (League)	Pos.	G	AB	R	H	2B	3B	HR	RBI	BB	SO	HBP	GDP	SB-CS	Avg.	OBP	SLG	OPS	E	Avg.
1994—Appleton (Midwest)	SS-DH	65	248	49	79	17	6	14	55	24	44	2	7	16-5	.319	.379	.605	.984	19	.934
—Jacksonville (Sou.)	SS	17	59	7	17	4	1	1	8	10	13	0	1	2-1	.288	.391	.441	.832	3	.964
—Seattle (A.L.)	SS	17	54	4	11	0	0	0	2	3	20	0	0	3-0	.204	.241	.204	.445	6	.915
—Calgary (PCL)	SS	32	119	22	37	7	4	6	21	8	25	1	0	2-4	.311	.359	.588	.948	3	.980
1995—Tacoma (PCL)	SS-DH	54	214	37	77	12	3	15	45	18	44	2	2	2-4	.360	.411	.654	1.065	10	.961
—Seattle (A.L.)	SS-DH	48	142	15	33	6	2	5	19	6	42	0	0	4-2	.232	.264	.408	.672	8	.953
1996—Seattle (A.L.)	SS	146	601	*141	215	*54	1	36	123	59	104	4	15	15-4	*.358	.414	.631	1.045	15	.977
—Tacoma (PCL)	SS	2	5	*0	1	0	0	0	0	2	1	0	0	0-0	.200	.429	.200	.629	1	.833
1997—Seattle (A.L.)	SS-DH	141	587	100	176	40	3	23	84	41	99	5	14	29-6	.300	.350	.496	.846	*24	.962
1998—Seattle (A.L.)	SS-DH	161	*686	123	*213	35	5	42	124	45	121	10	12	46-13	.310	.360	.560	.920	18	.975
1999—Seattle (A.L.)	SS	129	502	110	143	25	0	42	111	56	109	5	12	21-7	.285	.357	.586	.943	14	.977
2000—Seattle (A.L.)	SS	148	554	134	175	34	2	41	132	100	121	7	10	15-4	.316	.420	.607	1.026	10	.986
2001—Texas (A.L.)	SS-DH	•162	632	*133	201	34	1	*52	135	75	131	16	17	18-3	.318	.399	.622	1.021	18	.976
2002—Texas (A.L.)	SS	•162	624	125	187	27	2	*57	*142	87	122	10	14	9-4	.300	.392	.623	1.015	10	.987
2003—Texas (A.L.)	SS-DH	161	607	*124	181	30	6	*47	118	87	126	15	14	17-3	.298	.396	.600	.995	8	.989
2004—New York (A.L.)	3B-SS	155	601	112	172	24	2	36	106	80	131	10	18	28-4	.286	.375	.512	.888	13	.966
2005—New York (A.L.)	3B-SS	•162	605	*124	194	29	1	*48	130	91	139	16	8	21-6	.321	.421	*.610	1.031	12	.971
2006—New York (A.L.)	3B-DH	154	572	113	166	26	1	35	121	90	139	8	22	15-4	.290	.392	.523	.914	24	.937
Major League totals (13 years)		1746	6767	1358	2067	364	26	464	1347	820	1404	106	158	241-60	.305	.386	.573	.958	180	.974

DIVISION SERIES RECORD

Year — Team (League)	Pos.	G	AB	R	H	2B	3B	HR	RBI	BB	SO	HBP	GDP	SB-CS	Avg.	OBP	SLG	OPS	E	Avg.
1995— Seattle (A.L.)	SS	1	1	1	0	0	0	0	0	0	0	0	0	0-0	.000	.000	.000	.000	0	...
1997— Seattle (A.L.)	SS	4	16	1	5	1	0	1	1	0	5	0	0	0-0	.313	.313	.563	.875	0	1.000
2000— Seattle (A.L.)	SS	3	13	0	4	0	0	0	2	0	2	0	1	0-1	.308	.308	.308	.615	0	1.000
2004— New York (A.L.)	3B	4	19	3	8	3	0	1	3	2	1	0	0	2-1	.421	.476	.737	1.213	0	1.000
2005— New York (A.L.)	3B	5	15	2	2	1	0	0	0	6	5	2	2	1-1	.133	.435	.200	.635	1	.933
2006— New York (A.L.)	3B	4	14	0	1	0	0	0	0	0	4	1	0	0-0	.071	.133	.071	.205	1	.917
Division series totals (6 years)		21	78	7	20	5	0	2	6	8	17	3	3	3-3	.256	.348	.397	.746	2	.973

CHAMPIONSHIP SERIES RECORD

Year — Team (League)	Pos.	G	AB	R	H	2B	3B	HR	RBI	BB	SO	HBP	GDP	SB-CS	Avg.	OBP	SLG	OPS	E	Avg.
1995— Seattle (A.L.)		1	1	0	0	0	0	0	0	0	1	0	0	0-0	.000	.000	.000	.000	...	...
2000— Seattle (A.L.)	SS	6	22	4	9	2	0	2	5	3	8	0	0	1-0	.409	.480	.773	1.253	0	1.000
2004— New York (A.L.)	3B	7	31	8	8	2	0	2	5	4	6	2	1	0-0	.258	.378	.516	.895	0	1.000
Champ. series totals (3 years)		14	54	12	17	4	0	4	10	7	15	2	1	1-0	.315	.413	.611	1.024	0	1.000

ALL-STAR GAME RECORD

	G	AB	R	H	2B	3B	HR	RBI	BB	SO	HBP	GDP	SB-CS	Avg.	OBP	SLG	OPS	E	Avg.
All-Star Game totals (9 years)	9	21	4	6	0	1	1	2	1	9	0	0	0-0	.286	.318	.524	.842	0	1.000

2006 LEFTY-RIGHTY SPLITS

vs.	Avg.	AB	H	2B	3B	HR	RBI	BB	SO	OBP	Slg.	vs.	Avg.	AB	H	2B	3B	HR	RBI	BB	SO	OBP	Slg.
L	.294	136	40	6	1	10	30	33	29	.434	.574	R	.289	436	126	20	0	25	91	57	110	.377	.507

RODRIGUEZ, EDDY — P

PERSONAL: Born August 8, 1981, in San Pedro de Macoris, Dominican Republic. ... 6-1/194. ... Throws right, bats right. **TRANSACTIONS/CAREER NOTES:** Signed as a non-drafted free agent by Baltimore Orioles organization (March 15, 1999).

CAREER HITTING: 0-for-1 (.000), 0 R, 0 2B, 0 3B, 0 HR, 0 RBI.

Year — Team (League)	W	L	Pct.	ERA	WHIP	G	GS	CG	ShO	Hld.	Sv.-Opp.	IP	H	R	ER	HR	BB-IBB	SO	Avg.
1999— Dom. Orioles (DSL)	4	1	.800	3.02	0.77	17	...	...	...	...	5-...	20.2	16	...	7	...	...-...	...	.170
2000— GC Orioles (GCL)	2	1	.667	2.00	1.33	18	0	0	0	...	6-...	27.0	17	8	6	0	19-1	31	.185
— Delmarva (S. Atl.)	0	0	...	1.80	1.40	4	0	0	0	...	...	5.0	5	1	1	1	2-0	3	.263
2001— Delmarva (S. Atl.)	5	3	.625	3.39	1.33	41	0	0	0	...	1-...	61.0	58	27	23	4	23-0	64	.247
— Bowie (East.)	1	1	.500	2.08	1.50	5	0	0	0	...	2-...	8.2	7	2	2	0	6-1	10	.241
2002— Frederick (Carolina)	0	3	.000	2.23	0.99	38	0	0	0	...	11-...	48.1	28	14	12	3	20-3	58	.169
— Bowie (East.)	0	0	...	5.63	1.63	6	0	0	0	...	1-...	8.0	6	6	5	1	7-0	7	.200
2003— Bowie (East.)	3	4	.429	2.34	1.15	56	0	0	0	...	13-...	73.0	49	26	19	3	35-2	66	.188
2004— Ottawa (Int'l)	1	0	1.000	5.12	1.64	28	0	0	0	...	3-...	31.2	34	19	18	4	18-0	31	.266
— Baltimore (A.L.)	1	0	1.000	4.78	1.52	29	0	0	0	0	0-0	43.1	36	23	23	5	30-5	37	.231
2005— Ottawa (Int'l)	2	3	.400	3.77	1.50	50	0	0	0	6	3-5	62.0	57	30	26	2	36-4	51	.248
2006— Baltimore (A.L.)	1	1	.500	7.20	1.80	9	0	0	0	0	0-0	15.0	17	14	12	5	10-0	11	.283
— Ottawa (Int'l)	3	1	.750	1.71	1.08	42	0	0	0	7	12-13	47.1	33	13	9	0	18-0	55	.191
Major League totals (2 years)	2	1	.667	5.40	1.59	38	0	0	0	0	0-0	58.1	53	37	35	10	40-5	48	.245

2006 LEFTY-RIGHTY SPLITS

vs.	Avg.	AB	H	2B	3B	HR	RBI	BB	SO	OBP	Slg.	vs.	Avg.	AB	H	2B	3B	HR	RBI	BB	SO	OBP	Slg.
L	.318	22	7	2	0	1	4	3	2	.385	.545	R	.263	38	10	1	0	4	12	7	9	.370	.605

RODRIGUEZ, FELIX — P

PERSONAL: Born September 9, 1972, in Monte Cristi, Dominican Republic. ... 6-1/210. ... Throws right, bats right. ... Full name: Felix Antonio Rodriguez. ... High school: Liceo Bijiador (Monte Cristi, Dominican Republic). **TRANSACTIONS/CAREER NOTES:** Signed as a non-drafted free agent by Los Angeles Dodgers organization (October 17, 1989). ... Played catcher in Dodgers organization (1990-92). ... Claimed on waivers by Cincinnati Reds (December 18, 1996). ... Traded by Reds to Arizona Diamondbacks for a player to be named (November 11, 1997); Reds acquired P Scott Winchester to complete deal (November 18, 1997). ... On disabled list (June 21-July 30, 1998); included rehabilitation assignments to AZL Diamondbacks and Tucson. ... Traded by Diamondbacks to San Francisco Giants for future considerations (December 8, 1998); Diamondbacks acquired P Troy Brohawn and OF Chris Van Rossum to complete deal (December 21, 1998). ... On disabled list (August 3-18, 2003). ... Traded by Giants to Philadelphia Phillies for OF Ricky Ledee and P Alfredo Simon (July 30, 2004). ... Traded by Phillies to New York Yankees for OF Kenny Lofton and cash (December 3, 2004). ... On disabled list (May 11-July 19, 2005); included rehabilitation assignments to Staten Island and Trenton. ... Signed as free agent by Washington Nationals (January 31, 2006). ... On suspended list (May 1-4, 2006). ... On disabled list (May 26-September 5, 2006); included rehabilitation assignments to Potomac and New Orleans. ... Released by Nationals (October 3, 2006).

CAREER HITTING: 4-for-17 (.235), 4 R, 1 2B, 0 3B, 1 HR, 3 RBI.

Year — Team (League)	W	L	Pct.	ERA	WHIP	G	GS	CG	ShO	Hld.	Sv.-Opp.	IP	H	R	ER	HR	BB-IBB	SO	Avg.
1993— Vero Beach (FSL)	8	8	.500	3.75	1.36	32	20	2	1	...	0-...	132.0	109	71	55	15	71-1	80	.225
1994— San Antonio (Texas)	6	8	.429	4.03	1.42	26	26	0	0	...	0-...	136.1	106	70	61	8	88-3	126	.219
1995— Albuquerque (PCL)	3	2	.600	4.24	1.53	14	11	0	0	...	0-...	51.0	52	29	24	5	26-0	46	.269
— Los Angeles (N.L.)	1	1	.500	2.53	1.50	11	0	0	0	...	0-1	10.2	11	3	3	2	5-0	5	.275
1996— Albuquerque (PCL)	3	9	.250	5.53	1.59	27	19	0	0	...	0-...	107.1	111	70	66	17	60-1	65	.280
1997— Indianapolis (A.A.)	3	3	.500	1.01	1.43	23	0	0	0	...	1-...	26.2	22	10	3	0	16-1	26	.212
— Cincinnati (N.L.)	0	0	...	4.30	1.65	26	1	0	0	...	0-0	46.0	48	23	22	2	28-2	34	.271
1998— Arizona (N.L.)	0	2	.000	6.14	1.66	43	0	0	0	...	5-8	44.0	44	31	30	5	29-1	36	.259
— Ariz. D'backs (Ariz.)	0	0	...	4.15	1.15	3	2	0	0	...	0-...	4.1	3	4	2	0	2-0	5	.200
— Tucson (PCL)	0	0	...	9.00	3.00	1	0	0	0	...	0-...	1.0	1	1	1	0	2-0	0	.250
1999— San Francisco (N.L.)	2	3	.400	3.80	1.45	47	0	0	0	3	0-1	66.1	67	32	28	6	29-2	55	.262
2000— San Francisco (N.L.)	4	2	.667	2.64	1.31	76	0	0	0	* 30	3-8	81.2	65	29	24	5	42-2	95	.220
2001— San Francisco (N.L.)	9	1	.900	1.68	1.00	80	0	0	0	* 32	0-3	80.1	53	16	15	5	27-2	91	.188
2002— San Francisco (N.L.)	8	6	.571	4.17	1.19	71	0	0	0	24	0-6	69.0	53	33	32	2	29-1	58	.212
2003— San Francisco (N.L.)	8	2	.800	3.10	1.44	68	0	0	0	19	2-3	61.0	59	21	21	5	29-2	64	.259
2004— San Francisco (N.L.)	3	5	.375	3.43	1.39	53	0	0	0	13	0-3	44.2	43	18	17	7	19-2	31	.250
— Philadelphia (N.L.)	2	3	.400	3.00	1.33	23	0	0	0	7	1-1	21.0	18	7	7	1	10-2	28	.231
2005— Staten Is. (N.Y.-Penn)	0	0	...	3.00	1.33	2	0	0	0	...	0-0	3.0	1	1	1	1	0-0	5	.308
— Trenton (East.)	0	0	...	0.00	1.33	2	0	0	0	...	0-0	3.0	4	0	0	0	3-0	3	.125
— New York (A.L.)	0	0	...	5.01	1.64	34	0	0	0	3	0-0	32.1	33	18	18	2	20-0	18	.264
2006— New Orleans (PCL)	0	0	...	7.84	2.32	8	0	0	0	2	0-0	10.1	14	10	9	1	10-1	7	.326
— Potomac (Carol.)	0	0	...	9.00	2.00	1	0	0	0	...	0-0	1.0	2	2	1	1	0-0	0	.400
— Wash. (N.L.)	1	1	.500	7.67	1.64	29	0	0	0	3	0-0	29.1	32	25	25	5	16-3	15	.281
American League totals (1 year)	0	0	...	5.01	1.64	34	0	0	0	3	0-0	32.1	33	18	18	2	20-0	18	.264
National League totals (10 years)	38	26	.594	3.64	1.36	529	1	0	0	131	11-34	554.0	493	238	224	48	263-19	494	.239
Major League totals (11 years)	38	26	.594	3.71	1.38	563	1	0	0	134	11-34	586.1	526	256	242	50	283-19	512	.240

R

DIVISION SERIES RECORD

Year Team (League)	W	L	Pct.	ERA	WHIP	G	GS	CG	ShO	Hld.	Sv.-Opp.	IP	H	R	ER	HR	BB-IBB	SO	Avg.
2000— San Francisco (N.L.)	0	1	.000	6.23	1.62	3	0	0	0	1	0-0	4.1	6	3	3	1	1-0	6	.316
2002— San Francisco (N.L.)	0	0	...	0.00	1.00	3	0	0	0	1	0-0	3.0	1	0	0	0	2-0	2	.111
2003— San Francisco (N.L.)	0	1	.000	2.25	1.25	3	0	0	0	0	0-0	4.0	4	3	1	0	1-1	5	.235
Division series totals (3 years)	0	2	.000	3.18	1.32	9	0	0	0	2	0-0	11.1	11	6	4	1	4-1	13	.244

CHAMPIONSHIP SERIES RECORD

Year Team (League)	W	L	Pct.	ERA	WHIP	G	GS	CG	ShO	Hld.	Sv.-Opp.	IP	H	R	ER	HR	BB-IBB	SO	Avg.
2002— San Francisco (N.L.)	0	0		1.93	1.07	4	0	0	0	1	0-0	4.2	3	1	1	0	2-0	2	.200

WORLD SERIES RECORD

Year Team (League)	W	L	Pct.	ERA	WHIP	G	GS	CG	ShO	Hld.	Sv.-Opp.	IP	H	R	ER	HR	BB-IBB	SO	Avg.
2002— San Francisco (N.L.)	0	1	.000	4.76	0.88	6	0	0	0	2	0-0	5.2	4	3	3	2	1-0	3	.190

2006 LEFTY-RIGHTY SPLITS

vs.	Avg.	AB	H	2B	3B	HR	RBI	BB	SO	OBP	Slg.	vs.	Avg.	AB	H	2B	3B	HR	RBI	BB	SO	OBP	Slg.
L	.314	51	16	4	2	2	11	11	6	.422	.588	R	.254	63	16	4	0	3	12	5	9	.342	.460

R

RODRIGUEZ, FRANCISCO   P

PERSONAL: Born January 7, 1982, in Caracas, Venezuela. ... 6-0/185. ... Throws right, bats right. ... Full name: Francisco Jose Rodriguez. ... High school: Juan Lovera (Venezuela). **TRANSACTIONS/CAREER NOTES:** Signed as a non-drafted free agent by Anaheim Angels organization (September 24, 1998). ... Angels franchise renamed Los Angeles Angels of Anaheim for 2005 season. ... On disabled list (May 15-June 1, 2005). **HONORS:** Named A.L. Fireman of the Year by the SPORTING NEWS (2006).
CAREER HITTING: 0-for-0 (.000), 0 R, 0 2B, 0 3B, 0 HR, 0 RBI.

Year Team (League)	W	L	Pct.	ERA	WHIP	G	GS	CG	ShO	Hld.	Sv.-Opp.	IP	H	R	ER	HR	BB-IBB	SO	Avg.
1999— Butte (Pion.)	1	1	.500	3.31	1.05	12	9	1	0	...	0-	51.2	33	21	19	1	21-1	69	.179
— Boise (N'west)	1	0	1.000	5.40	0.80	1	1	0	0	...	0-	5.0	3	4	3	0	1-0	6	.150
2000— Lake Elsinore (Calif.)	4	4	.500	2.81	1.17	13	12	0	0	...	0-	64.0	43	29	20	2	32-0	79	.189
2001— Rancho Cuca. (Calif.)	5	7	.417	5.38	1.60	20	20	1	1	...	0-	113.2	127	72	68	13	55-1	147	.277
2002— Arkansas (Texas)	3	3	.500	1.96	1.14	23	0	0	0	...	2-6	41.1	32	13	9	2	15-0	61	.206
— Salt Lake (PCL)	2	3	.400	2.57	1.02	27	0	0	0	...	6-	42.0	30	13	12	1	13-0	59	.204
— Anaheim (A.L.)	0	0	...	0.00	0.88	5	0	0	0	0	0-0	5.2	3	0	0	0	2-1	13	.167
2003— Anaheim (A.L.)	8	3	.727	3.03	0.99	59	0	0	0	7	2-6	86.0	50	30	29	12	35-5	95	.172
2004— Anaheim (A.L.)	4	1	.800	1.82	1.00	69	0	0	0	27	12-19	84.0	51	21	17	2	33-1	123	.172
2005— Los Angeles (A.L.)	2	5	.286	2.67	1.14	66	0	0	0	0	• 45-50	67.1	45	20	20	7	32-3	91	.184
2006— Los Angeles (A.L.)	2	3	.400	1.73	1.10	69	0	0	0	0	* 47-* 51	73.0	52	16	14	6	28-5	98	.197
Major League totals (5 years)	16	12	.571	2.28	1.05	268	0	0	0	34	106-126	316.0	201	87	80	27	130-15	420	.180

DIVISION SERIES RECORD

Year Team (League)	W	L	Pct.	ERA	WHIP	G	GS	CG	ShO	Hld.	Sv.-Opp.	IP	H	R	ER	HR	BB-IBB	SO	Avg.
2002— Anaheim (A.L.)	2	0	1.000	3.18	0.71	3	0	0	0	0	0-1	5.2	2	2	2	1	2-0	8	.105
2004— Anaheim (A.L.)	0	2	.000	3.86	1.50	2	0	0	0	0	0-0	4.2	4	2	2	0	3-1	5	.235
2005— Los Angeles (A.L.)	0	0	...	2.70	1.50	3	0	0	0	0	2-2	3.1	5	1	1	1	0-0	2	.357
Division series totals (3 years)	2	2	.500	3.29	1.17	8	0	0	0	0	2-3	13.2	11	5	5	2	5-1	15	.220

CHAMPIONSHIP SERIES RECORD

Year Team (League)	W	L	Pct.	ERA	WHIP	G	GS	CG	ShO	Hld.	Sv.-Opp.	IP	H	R	ER	HR	BB-IBB	SO	Avg.
2002— Anaheim (A.L.)	2	0	1.000	0.00	0.92	4	0	0	0	2	0-1	4.1	2	0	0	0	2-0	7	.143
2005— Los Angeles (A.L.)	0	0	...	0.00	2.14	2	0	0	0	0	1-1	2.1	2	2	0	0	3-0	3	.250
Champ. series totals (2 years)	2	0	1.000	0.00	1.35	6	0	0	0	2	1-2	6.2	4	2	0	0	5-0	10	.182

WORLD SERIES RECORD

Year Team (League)	W	L	Pct.	ERA	WHIP	G	GS	CG	ShO	Hld.	Sv.-Opp.	IP	H	R	ER	HR	BB-IBB	SO	Avg.
2002— Anaheim (A.L.)	1	1	.500	2.08	0.81	4	0	0	0	1	0-0	8.2	6	3	2	1	1-0	13	.194

ALL-STAR GAME RECORD

Year Team (League)	W	L	Pct.	ERA	WHIP	G	GS	CG	ShO	Hld.	Sv.-Opp.	IP	H	R	ER	HR	BB-IBB	SO	Avg.
All-Star Game totals (1 year)	0	0	...	0.00	0.00	1	0	0	0	0	0-0	0.2	0	0	0	0	0-0	0	.000

2006 LEFTY-RIGHTY SPLITS

vs.	Avg.	AB	H	2B	3B	HR	RBI	BB	SO	OBP	Slg.	vs.	Avg.	AB	H	2B	3B	HR	RBI	BB	SO	OBP	Slg.
L	.215	130	28	9	0	5	11	13	42	.287	.400	R	.179	134	24	9	0	1	10	15	56	.267	.269

RODRIGUEZ, IVAN   C

PERSONAL: Born November 30, 1971, in Vega Baja, Puerto Rico. ... 5-9/218. ... Bats right, throws right. ... Name pronounced: rod-RI-gez. ... High school: Lina Padron Rivera (Vega Baja, Puerto Rico). **TRANSACTIONS/CAREER NOTES:** Signed as a non-drafted free agent by Texas Rangers organization (July 27, 1988). ... On disabled list (June 6-27, 1992; July 25, 2000-remainder of season; May 2-17 and August 31, 2001-remainder of season). ... On disabled list (April 15-June 7, 2002); included rehabilitation assignment to Charlotte. ... On suspended list (September 28-29, 2002). ... Signed as a free agent by Florida Marlins (January 22, 2003). ... Signed as a free agent by Detroit Tigers (February 6, 2004). ... On suspended list (August 8-12, 2005). **HONORS:** Named catcher on THE SPORTING NEWS A.L. All-Star team (1994-99 and 2004). ... Named A.L. Most Valuable Player by Baseball Writers' Association of America (1999). ... Won A.L. Gold Glove at catcher (1992-2001, 2004 and 2006). ... Named catcher on A.L. Silver Slugger team (1994-99 and 2004). **STATISTICAL NOTES:** Hit three home runs in one game (September 11, 1997). ... Career major league grand slams: 5.
2006 GAMES PLAYED BY POSITION (MLB): C—123, 1B—7, DH—5, 2B—1.

Year Team (League)	Pos.	G	AB	R	H	2B	3B	HR	RBI	BB	SO	HBP	GDP	SB-CS	Avg.	OBP	SLG	OPS	E	Avg.
1989— Gastonia (S. Atl.)	C	112	386	38	92	22	1	7	42	21	58	2	6	2-5	.238	.278	.355	.633	11	.986
1990— Charlotte (Fla. St.)	C	109	408	48	117	17	7	2	55	12	50	7	6	1-0	.287	.316	.377	.693	14	.983
1991— Tulsa (Texas)	C	50	175	16	48	7	2	3	28	6	27	1	5	1-2	.274	.294	.389	.683	3	.988
— Texas (A.L.)	C	88	280	24	74	16	0	3	27	5	42	0	10	0-1	.264	.276	.354	.630	10	.983
1992— Texas (A.L.)	C-DH	123	420	39	109	16	1	8	37	24	73	1	15	0-0	.260	.300	.360	.659	* 15	.983
1993— Texas (A.L.)	C-DH	137	473	56	129	28	4	10	66	29	70	4	16	8-7	.273	.315	.412	.727	8	.991
1994— Texas (A.L.)	C	99	363	56	108	19	1	16	57	31	42	7	10	6-3	.298	.360	.488	.848	5	.992
1995— Texas (A.L.)	C-DH	130	492	56	149	32	2	12	67	16	48	4	11	0-2	.303	.327	.449	.776	8	.990
1996— Texas (A.L.)	C-DH	153	639	116	192	47	3	19	86	38	55	4	5-0	.300	.342	.473	.814	• 10	.989
1997— Texas (A.L.)	C-DH	150	597	98	187	34	4	20	77	38	89	8	10	7-3	.313	.360	.484	.844	7	.992
1998— Texas (A.L.)	C-DH	145	579	88	186	40	4	21	91	32	88	13	9	10-3	.321	.358	.513	.871	6	.994
1999— Texas (A.L.)	C-DH	144	600	116	199	29	1	35	113	24	64	1	* 31	25-12	.332	.356	.558	.914	7	.993
2000— Texas (A.L.)	C-DH	91	363	66	126	27	4	27	83	19	48	1	17	5-5	.347	.375	.667	1.042	2	.996
2001— Texas (A.L.)	C-DH	111	442	70	136	24	2	25	65	23	73	4	13	10-3	.308	.347	.541	.888	7	.990
2002— Texas (A.L.)	C-DH	108	408	67	128	32	2	19	60	25	71	2	14	5-4	.314	.353	.542	.895	7	.990
— Charlotte (Fla. St.)	C	3	9	1	3	0	0	0	0	0	0	0	0-0	.333	.333	.333	.667	0	1.000

Year Team (League)	Pos.	G	AB	R	H	2B	3B	HR	RBI	BB	SO	HBP	GDP	SB-CS	Avg.	OBP	SLG	OPS	E	Avg.
						BATTING													**FIELDING**	
2003— Florida (N.L.)	C-DH	144	511	90	152	36	3	16	85	55	92	6	18	10-6	.297	.369	.474	.843	8	.992
2004— Detroit (A.L.)	C-DH	135	527	72	176	32	2	19	86	41	91	3	15	7-4	.334	.383	.510	.893	11	.987
2005— Detroit (A.L.)	C-DH	129	504	71	139	33	5	14	50	11	93	2	19	7-3	.276	.290	.444	.735	4	.995
2006— Detroit (A.L.)	C-1B-DH 2B	136	547	74	164	28	4	13	69	26	86	1	16	8-3	.300	.332	.437	.769	3	.997
American League totals (15 years)		1879	7234	1069	2202	437	39	261	1034	382	1033	45	237	102-50	.304	.340	.484	.824	110	.991
National League totals (1 year)		144	511	90	152	36	3	16	85	55	92	6	18	10-6	.297	.369	.474	.843	8	.992
Major League totals (16 years)		2023	7745	1159	2354	473	42	277	1119	437	1125	51	255	112-56	.304	.342	.483	.826	118	.991

DIVISION SERIES RECORD

Year Team (League)	Pos.	G	AB	R	H	2B	3B	HR	RBI	BB	SO	HBP	GDP	SB-CS	Avg.	OBP	SLG	OPS	E	Avg.
1996— Texas (A.L.)	C	4	16	1	6	1	0	0	2	2	3	0	0	0-0	.375	.444	.438	.882	0	1.000
1998— Texas (A.L.)	C	3	10	1	1	0	0	0	1	0	5	0	0	0-0	.100	.100	.100	.200	0	1.000
1999— Texas (A.L.)	C	3	12	0	3	1	0	0	0	0	2	0	1	1-0	.250	.250	.333	.583	0	1.000
2003— Florida (N.L.)	C	4	17	3	6	1	0	1	3	3	0	0	0	0-0	.353	.450	.588	1.038	0	1.000
2006— Detroit (A.L.)	C	4	13	3	3	1	0	0	3	2	3	0	0	1-0	.231	.313	.308	.620	0	1.000
Division series totals (5 years)		18	68	7	19	4	0	1	12	7	14	0	1	1-0	.279	.342	.382	.724	0	1.000

CHAMPIONSHIP SERIES RECORD

Year Team (League)	Pos.	G	AB	R	H	2B	3B	HR	RBI	BB	SO	HBP	GDP	SB-CS	Avg.	OBP	SLG	OPS	E	Avg.
2003— Florida (N.L.)	C	7	28	5	9	2	0	2	10	5	7	0	0	0-0	.321	.424	.607	1.031	1	.983
2006— Detroit (A.L.)	C	4	16	2	2	0	0	1	1	1	4	0	0	0-0	.125	.176	.313	.489	0	1.000
Champ. series totals (2 years)		11	44	7	11	2	0	3	11	6	11	0	0	0-0	.250	.340	.500	.840	1	.989

WORLD SERIES RECORD

Year Team (League)	Pos.	G	AB	R	H	2B	3B	HR	RBI	BB	SO	HBP	GDP	SB-CS	Avg.	OBP	SLG	OPS	E	Avg.
2003— Florida (N.L.)	C	6	22	2	6	2	0	0	1	1	4	0	1	0-0	.273	.292	.364	.655	0	1.000
2006— Detroit (A.L.)	C	5	19	1	3	1	0	0	1	0	3	0	1	0-0	.158	.158	.211	.368	0	1.000
World series totals (2 years)		11	41	3	9	3	0	0	2	1	7	0	2	0-0	.220	.233	.293	.525	0	1.000

ALL-STAR GAME RECORD

	Pos.	G	AB	R	H	2B	3B	HR	RBI	BB	SO	HBP	GDP	SB-CS	Avg.	OBP	SLG	OPS	E	Avg.
All-Star Game totals (13 years)		13	34	4	10	1	1	0	3	1	6	0	0	1-0	.294	.314	.382	.697	0	1.000

2006 LEFTY-RIGHTY SPLITS

vs.	Avg.	AB	H	2B	3B	HR	RBI*	BB	SO	OBP	Slg.	vs.	Avg.	AB	H	2B	3B	HR	RBI	BB	SO	OBP	Slg.
L	.340	156	53	11	0	5	22	12	28	.385	.506	R	.284	391	111	17	4	8	47	14	58	.310	.409

RODRIGUEZ, JOHN — OF

PERSONAL: Born January 20, 1978, in New York. ... 6-0/205. ... Bats left, throws left. ... Full name: John Joseph Rodriguez. ... High school: Brandeis (New York). **TRANS-ACTIONS/CAREER NOTES:** Signed as a non-drafted free agent by New York Yankees organization (November 17, 1996). ... Signed as a free agent by Cleveland Indians (November 16, 2004). ... Traded by Indians to St. Louis Cardinals for C Javier Cardona (June 11, 2005).
2006 GAMES PLAYED BY POSITION (MLB): OF—51, DH—1.

Year Team (League)	Pos.	G	AB	R	H	2B	3B	HR	RBI	BB	SO	HBP	GDP	SB-CS	Avg.	OBP	SLG	OPS	E	Avg.
						BATTING													**FIELDING**	
1997— GC Yankees (GCL)	OF	46	157	31	47	10	2	3	23	30	32	0	3	7-0	.299	.405	.446	.851	1	.985
1998— Greensboro (S. Atl.)	OF	119	408	64	103	18	4	10	49	64	93	4	7	14-3	.252	.357	.390	.747	6	.958
1999— Tampa (Fla. St.)	OF	71	269	37	82	14	3	8	43	41	52	3	5	2-5	.305	.394	.468	.867	4	.966
— GC Yankees (GCL)	OF	3	7	1	2	0	1	0	1	3	0	0	0	0-0	.286	.500	.571	1.071	0	1.000
2000— Norwich (East.)	1B	17	56	4	11	4	0	1	10	8	22	1	1	0-0	.196	.308	.321	.629	2	.969
— Tampa (Fla. St.)	OF	105	362	59	97	14	2	16	44	40	81	8	6	3-2	.268	.354	.450	.804	2	.986
2001— Norwich (East.)	1B	103	393	64	112	31	1	22	66	26	117	11	7	2-3	.285	.345	.537	.882	4	.976
— GC Yankees (GCL)	OF	2	6	2	5	0	0	0	2	0	0	0	0	0-0	.833	.833	.833	1.666	0	—
2002— Norwich (East.)	1B	103	354	51	76	18	3	15	63	35	94	11	4	13-3	.215	.302	.410	.712	3	.985
2003— Columbus (Int'l)	OF	79	232	35	61	9	2	10	33	24	50	1	2	6-0	.263	.333	.448	.781	3	.981
2004— Columbus (Int'l)	OF	112	378	78	111	26	10	16	68	48	84	8	7	10-3	.294	.382	.542	.924	7	.865
2005— Buffalo (Int'l)	OF-DH	46	170	25	42	13	3	5	23	15	40	6	1	5-0	.247	.323	.447	.770	2	.989
— Memphis (PCL)	OF	34	120	24	41	5	0	17	47	13	28	3	2	1-1	.342	.419	.808	1.227	2	.983
— St. Louis (N.L.)	OF	56	149	15	44	6	0	5	24	19	45	3	0	2-0	.295	.382	.436	.818	2	.973
2006— Memphis (PCL)	OF	20	64	10	17	4	1	3	7	11	18	0	1	0-0	.266	.373	.500	.873	0	1.000
— St. Louis (N.L.)	OF-DH	102	183	31	55	12	3	2	19	21	45	3	9	0-0	.301	.374	.432	.806	1	.986
Major League totals (2 years)		158	332	46	99	18	3	7	43	40	90	6	9	2-0	.298	.378	.434	.811	3	.979

DIVISION SERIES RECORD

Year Team (League)	Pos.	G	AB	R	H	2B	3B	HR	RBI	BB	SO	HBP	GDP	SB-CS	Avg.	OBP	SLG	OPS	E	Avg.
2005— St. Louis (N.L.)		1	1	0	0	0	0	0	0	0	0	0	0	0-0	.000	.000	.000	.000	0	—
2006— St. Louis (N.L.)		1	1	0	0	0	0	0	0	0	0	0	0	0-0	.000	.000	.000	.000	0	—
Division series totals (2 years)		2	2	0	0	0	0	0	0	0	0	0	0	0-0	.000	.000	.000	.000	0	—

CHAMPIONSHIP SERIES RECORD

Year Team (League)	Pos.	G	AB	R	H	2B	3B	HR	RBI	BB	SO	HBP	GDP	SB-CS	Avg.	OBP	SLG	OPS	E	Avg.
2005— St. Louis (N.L.)		5	2	1	0	0	0	0	1	2	1	0	0	0-0	.000	.400	.000	.400	0	—
2006— St. Louis (N.L.)		4	4	0	0	0	0	0	1	0	1	0	1	0-0	.000	.000	.000	.000	0	—
Champ. series totals (2 years)		9	6	1	0	0	0	0	2	2	2	0	1	0-0	.000	.222	.000	.222	0	—

WORLD SERIES RECORD

Year Team (League)	Pos.	G	AB	R	H	2B	3B	HR	RBI	BB	SO	HBP	GDP	SB-CS	Avg.	OBP	SLG	OPS	E	Avg.
2006— St. Louis (N.L.)		1	1	0	0	0	0	0	0	0	1	0	0	0-0	.000	.000	.000	.000	0	—

2006 LEFTY-RIGHTY SPLITS

vs.	Avg.	AB	H	2B	3B	HR	RBI	BB	SO	OBP	Slg.	vs.	Avg.	AB	H	2B	3B	HR	RBI	BB	SO	OBP	Slg.
L	.308	13	4	1	1	0	2	3	6	.471	.769	R	.300	170	51	11	2	2	17	18	39	.366	.406

RODRIGUEZ, LUIS — 3B/2B

PERSONAL: Born June 27, 1980, in San Carlos, Venezuela. ... 5-9/180. ... Bats both, throws right. ... Full name: Luis Orlando Rodriguez. ... High school: Sixto Sosa (Cojedos, Venezuela). **TRANSACTIONS/CAREER NOTES:** Signed as a non-drafted free agent by Minnesota Twins organization (June 1, 1997).
2006 GAMES PLAYED BY POSITION (MLB): 3B—29, 2B—14, DH—3, SS—2, 1B—1.

Year	Team (League)	Pos.	G	AB	R	H	2B	3B	HR	RBI	BB	SO	HBP	GDP	SB-CS	Avg.	OBP	SLG	OPS	E	Avg.
1997—Maracay-1 (Pion.)			51	107	21	33	6	1	0	12	12	6	0	2	5-0	.308	.357	.383	.740	...	...
1998—GC Twins (GCL)	2B-SS-3B		52	180	33	50	11	1	1	15	22	17	0	4	14-3	.278	.353	.367	.720	12	.949
1999—Quad City (Midw.)	2B-3B		119	434	63	117	20	4	3	50	53	49	4	10	8-4	.270	.348	.336	.684	11	.978
2000—Quad City (Midw.)	2B-3B		106	342	35	77	11	2	0	28	40	29	5	10	4-5	.225	.314	.269	.583	14	.971
2001—Fort Myers (FSL)	SS-2B-3B		125	463	71	127	21	3	4	64	82	42	6	14	11-8	.274	.387	.359	.746	21	.968
2002—New Britain (East.)	SS-2B		129	455	60	117	18	2	8	40	61	44	5	8	3-2	.257	.349	.358	.707	19	.970
2003—Rochester (Int'l)	2B-SS		131	518	65	153	35	2	1	44	46	46	3	15	6-8	.295	.354	.376	.730	13	.978
2004—Rochester (Int'l)	2B-SS		127	486	73	139	33	1	5	52	53	49	1	17	3-3	.286	.353	.389	.742	10	.878
2005—Rochester (Int'l)	2B-SS-3B		40	138	19	42	10	0	1	17	16	14	1	3	0-1	.304	.381	.399	.779	1	.994
—Minnesota (A.L.)	2B-3B-SS																				
	DH		79	175	21	47	10	2	2	20	18	23	1	4	2-2	.269	.335	.383	.718	3	.986
2006—Minnesota (A.L.)	3B-2B-DH																				
	SS-1B		59	115	11	27	4	0	2	6	14	16	0	3	0-0	.235	.315	.322	.637	2	.980
Major League totals (2 years)			138	290	32	74	14	2	4	26	32	39	1	7	2-2	.255	.327	.359	.686	5	.984

2006 LEFTY-RIGHTY SPLITS

vs.	Avg.	AB	H	2B	3B	HR	RBI	BB	SO	OBP	Slg.	vs.	Avg.	AB	H	2B	3B	HR	RBI	BB	SO	OBP	Slg.
L	.250	24	6	0	0	0	1	3	3	.333	.250	R	.231	91	21	4	0	2	5	11	13	.311	.341

RODRIGUEZ, WANDY — P

PERSONAL: Born January 18, 1979, in Santiago, Dominican Republic. ... 5-11/160. ... Throws left, bats both. ... Full name: Wandy E. Rodriguez. **TRANSACTIONS/CAREER NOTES:** Signed as a non-drafted free agent by Houston Astros organization (January 12, 1999).
CAREER HITTING: 9-for-77 (.117), 7 R, 0 2B, 0 3B, 0 HR, 2 RBI.

Year	Team (League)	W	L	Pct.	ERA	WHIP	G	GS	CG	ShO	Hld.	Sv.-Opp.	IP	H	R	ER	HR	BB-IBB	SO	Avg.
1999—Houston SP (DSL)	3	1	.750	3.61	1.59	19	7	0	0	...	2-...	52.1	61	27	21	1	22-0	51	.302
2000—Houston (DSL)	3	3	.500	2.19	1.21	14	14	0	0	...	0-...	78.0	65	31	19	2	29-0	86	.226
2001—Martinsville (App.)	4	3	.571	1.58	1.00	12	12	1	0	...	0-...	74.0	54	19	13	6	20-0	67	.208
2002—Lexington (S. Atl.)	11	4	.733	3.78	1.32	28	28	0	0	...	0-...	159.1	167	74	67	12	44-0	137	.275
2003—Salem (Carol.)	8	7	.533	3.49	1.29	20	20	1	1	...	0-...	111.0	102	51	43	9	41-1	72	.239
2004—Round Rock (Texas)	11	6	.647	4.48	1.51	26	25	1	0	...	0-...	142.1	159	77	71	15	57-1	115	.286
2005—Round Rock (PCL)	4	2	.667	3.69	1.27	8	8	0	0	0	0-0	46.1	43	20	19	7	16-0	48	.246
—Corpus Christi (Texas)	0	0	...	2.70	1.50	1	1	0	0	0	0-0	3.1	3	1	1	0	2-1	3	.273
—Houston (N.L.)	10	10	.500	5.53	1.46	25	22	0	0	0	0-0	128.2	135	82	79	19	53-2	80	.274
2006—Round Rock (PCL)	2	2	.500	6.92	1.73	5	5	0	0	0	0-0	26.0	32	21	20	2	13-1	13	.305
—Houston (N.L.)	9	10	.474	5.64	1.60	30	24	0	0	0	0-0	135.2	154	96	85	17	63-7	98	.290
Major League totals (2 years)	19	20	.487	5.58	1.53	55	46	0	0	0	0-0	264.1	289	178	164	36	116-9	178	.282

DIVISION SERIES RECORD

Year	Team (League)	W	L	Pct.	ERA	WHIP	G	GS	CG	ShO	Hld.	Sv.-Opp.	IP	H	R	ER	HR	BB-IBB	SO	Avg.
2005—Houston (N.L.)	0	0	...	9.00	1.00	1	0	0	0	0	0-0	1.0	1	1	1	1	0-0	2	.250

WORLD SERIES RECORD

Year	Team (League)	W	L	Pct.	ERA	WHIP	G	GS	CG	ShO	Hld.	Sv.-Opp.	IP	H	R	ER	HR	BB-IBB	SO	Avg.
2005—Houston (N.L.)	0	1	.000	2.45	2.45	2	0	0	0	0	0-0	3.2	4	1	1	1	5-1	2	.333

2006 LEFTY-RIGHTY SPLITS

vs.	Avg.	AB	H	2B	3B	HR	RBI	BB	SO	OBP	Slg.	vs.	Avg.	AB	H	2B	3B	HR	RBI	BB	SO	OBP	Slg.
L	.262	122	32	2	1	2	12	19	21	.366	.344	R	.298	409	122	35	4	15	70	44	77	.370	.513

ROGERS, BRIAN — P

PERSONAL: Born July 17, 1982, in Dallas. ... 6-4/190. ... Throws right, bats right. ... Full name: Brian A. Rogers. ... College: Georgia Southern. **TRANSACTIONS/CAREER NOTES:** Selected by Detroit Tigers organization in 11th round of 2003 free-agent draft. ... Traded by Tigers to Pittsburgh Pirates for 1B Sean Casey (July 31, 2006).
CAREER HITTING: 0-for-0 (.000), 0 R, 0 2B, 0 3B, 0 HR, 0 RBI.

Year	Team (League)	W	L	Pct.	ERA	WHIP	G	GS	CG	ShO	Hld.	Sv.-Opp.	IP	H	R	ER	HR	BB-IBB	SO	Avg.
2003—Oneonta (NYP)	3	2	.600	3.34	1.18	12	12	0	0	...	0-...	56.2	49	23	21	2	18-0	66	.232
2004—W. Mich. (Mid.)	6	8	.429	4.55	1.45	25	25	0	0	...	0-...	142.1	163	76	72	9	44-1	120	.293
2005—Lakeland (Fla. St.)	4	1	.800	2.06	1.08	52	1	0	0	12	2-6	65.2	50	16	15	2	21-0	65	.212
2006—Altoona (East.)	0	0	...	0.00	1.00	2	0	0	0	0	1-1	4.0	2	0	0	0	2-1	5	.167
—Erie (East.)	3	2	.600	2.39	0.98	37	0	0	0	7	1-4	64.0	49	19	17	7	14-1	69	.210
—Indianapolis (Int'l)	1	1	.500	1.08	0.36	7	0	0	0	1	1-1	8.1	2	1	1	1	1-0	8	.077
—Pittsburgh (N.L.)	0	0	...	8.31	1.50	10	0	0	0	0	0-0	8.2	11	8	8	2	2-0	7	.324
Major League totals (1 year)	0	0	...	8.31	1.50	10	0	0	0	0	0-0	8.2	11	8	8	2	2-0	7	.324

2006 LEFTY-RIGHTY SPLITS

vs.	Avg.	AB	H	2B	3B	HR	RBI	BB	SO	OBP	Slg.	vs.	Avg.	AB	H	2B	3B	HR	RBI	BB	SO	OBP	Slg.
L	.444	9	4	0	0	0	2	4	0	.444	1.111	R	.280	25	7	0	0	0	2	0	7	.357	.440

ROGERS, EDDIE — IF

PERSONAL: Born August 29, 1978, in San Pedro de Macoris, Dominican Republic. ... 6-1/172. ... Bats right, throws right. ... Full name: Edward Antonio Rogers. **TRANSACTIONS/CAREER NOTES:** Signed as non-drafted free agent by Baltimore Orioles organization (November 1, 1997).
2006 GAMES PLAYED BY POSITION (MLB): 2B—4, 3B—4, OF—4, SS—1, DH—1.

Year	Team (League)	Pos.	G	AB	R	H	2B	3B	HR	RBI	BB	SO	HBP	GDP	SB-CS	Avg.	OBP	SLG	OPS	E	Avg.
1998—Dom. Orioles/W.S. (DSL) ..			58	194	33	56	9	2	2	27	26	29			8-...	.289		.387		...	...
—Baltimore SP (DSL)			58	194	33	56	9	2	2	27	26	29	2	5	8-5	.289	.373	.387	.760	...	...
1999—GC Orioles (GCL)	2B-3B-SS		53	177	34	51	5	1	1	19	23	22	4	2	20-3	.288	.379	.345	.724	10	.947
2000—Delmarva (S. Atl.)	2B-SS-SS		80	332	46	91	14	5	5	42	22	63	0	3	27-6	.274	.317	.392	.709	19	.947
—Bowie (East.)	SS		13	49	4	14	3	0	1	8	3	15	0	0	1-1	.286	.321	.408	.729	0	1.000
2001—Bowie (East.)	SS		53	191	11	38	10	1	0	13	6	40	2	4	10-2	.199	.231	.262	.493	10	.960
—Frederick (Carolina)	SS		73	292	39	76	20	3	8	41	14	47	8	8	18-6	.260	.310	.432	.742	14	.958
2002—Bowie (East.)	SS		112	422	59	110	26	2	11	57	16	70	10	9	14-4	.261	.300	.410	.710	20	.958
—Baltimore (A.L.)	SS		5	5	0	0	0	0	0	0	0	3	0	0	0-0	.000	.000	.000	.000	0	1.000
2003—Bowie (East.)	SS		97	340	48	72	13	1	6	35	12	64	6	7	27-8	.212	.249	.309	.558	17	.957
—Aberdeen (N.Y.-Penn.)	SS		3	14	2	5	2	0	1	6	2	1	0	0	0-0	.357	.333	.714	1.047	1	.929

			BATTING																	FIELDING	
Year Team (League)	Pos.	G	AB	R	H	2B	3B	HR	RBI	BB	SO	HBP	GDP	SB-CS	Avg.	OBP	SLG	OPS		E	Avg.
2004—Bowie (East.) 3B-2B-SS																					
	OF	124	482	71	137	32	1	4	37	37	78	4	4	20-7	.284	.340	.380	.720		14	.860
2005—Ottawa (Int'l) SS-3B-2B																					
	OF	125	431	52	113	21	3	7	48	17	66	1	9	14-6	.262	.291	.374	.665		17	.967
—Baltimore (A.L.)	DH-SS	8	1	4	1	0	0	1	2	0	0	0	0	0-2	1.000	1.000	4.000	5.000		0	...
2006—Ottawa (Int'l) 2B-3B-OF		86	339	40	101	18	1	5	30	13	52	1	6	12-7	.298	.324	.401	.725		10	.970
—Baltimore (A.L.)	SS-DH	17	25	1	5	0	0	0	2	0	3	0	0	0-0	.200	.192	.200	.392		2	.867
Major League totals (3 years)		30	29	5	6	0	0	1	4	0	3	0	0	0-2	.207	.200	.310	.510		2	.909

2006 LEFTY-RIGHTY SPLITS

vs.	Avg.	AB	H	2B	3B	HR	RBI	BB	SO	OBP	Slg.	vs.	Avg.	AB	H	2B	3B	HR	RBI	BB	SO	OBP	Slg.
L	.154	13	2	0	0	0	0	1	0	1	.143	.154	R	.250	12	3	0	0	0	1	0	2	.250	.250

ROGERS, KENNY — P — R

PERSONAL: Born November 10, 1964, in Savannah, Ga. ... 6-1/211. ... Throws left, bats left. ... Full name: Kenneth Scott Rogers. ... High school: Plant City (Fla.). **TRANSACTIONS/CAREER NOTES:** Selected by Texas Rangers organization in 39th round of June 1982 free-agent draft. ... Signed as a free agent by New York Yankees (December 30, 1995). ... Traded by Yankees with IF Mariano Duncan and P Kevin Henthorne to San Diego Padres for OF Greg Vaughn and Ps Kerry Taylor and Chris Clark (July 4, 1997); trade voided because Vaughn failed physical (July 6, 1997). ... Traded by Yankees with cash to Oakland Athletics for a player to be named (November 7, 1997); Yankees acquired 3B Scott Brosius to complete deal (November 18, 1997). ... Traded by A's to New York Mets for OF Terrence Long and P Leo Vasquez (July 23, 1999). ... Signed as a free agent by Rangers (December 29, 1999). ... On disabled list (July 24, 2001-remainder of season). ... Signed as a free agent by Minnesota Twins (March 17, 2003). ... On suspended list (July 11-19, 2003). ... Signed as a free agent by Rangers (January 14, 2004). ... On suspended list (July 27-August 10, 2005). ... Signed as a free agent by Detroit Tigers (December 12, 2005). **HONORS:** Won A.L. Gold Glove as pitcher (2000, 2002 and 2004-06). **STATISTICAL NOTES:** Pitched 4-0 perfect game against California (July 28, 1994). **MISCELLANEOUS NOTES:** Appeared in one game as pinch runner (2002).

CAREER HITTING: 9-for-63 (.143), 5 R, 1 2B, 1 3B, 0 HR, 4 RBI.

Year Team (League)	W	L	Pct.	ERA	WHIP	G	GS	CG	ShO	Hld.	Sv.-Opp.	IP	H	R	ER	HR	BB-IBB	SO	Avg.
1982—GC Rangers (GCL)	0	0	...	0.00	0.00	2	0	0	0	...	0-...	3.0	0	0	0	0	0-0	4	...
1983—GC Rangers (GCL)	4	1	.800	2.36	1.13	15	6	0	0	...	1-...	53.1	40	21	14	0	20-0	36	...
1984—Burlington (Midw.)	4	7	.364	3.98	1.29	39	4	1	0	...	3-...	92.2	87	52	41	0	33-3	93	.246
1985—Daytona Beach (FSL)	0	1	.000	7.20	2.30	6	0	0	0	...	0-...	10.0	12	9	8	0	11-1	9	.300
—Burlington (Midw.)	2	5	.286	2.84	1.36	33	4	2	1	...	4-...	95.0	67	34	30	3	62-9	96	.202
1986—Tulsa (Texas)	0	3	.000	9.91	2.16	10	4	0	0	...	0-...	26.1	39	30	29	4	18-1	23	.333
—Salem (Carol.)	2	7	.222	6.27	1.53	12	12	0	0	...	0-...	66.0	75	54	46	9	26-0	46	.282
1987—Charlotte (Fla. St.)	0	3	.000	4.76	1.47	5	3	0	0	...	0-...	17.0	17	13	9	1	8-0	14	.258
—Tulsa (Texas)	1	5	.167	5.35	1.67	28	6	0	0	...	2-...	69.0	80	51	41	5	35-3	59	.291
1988—Charlotte (Fla. St.)	2	0	1.000	1.27	0.93	8	6	0	0	...	1-...	35.1	22	8	5	1	11-0	26	.179
—Tulsa (Texas)	4	6	.400	4.00	1.28	13	13	2	0	...	0-...	83.1	73	43	37	6	34-0	76	.233
1989—Texas (A.L.)	3	4	.429	2.93	1.38	73	0	0	0	15	2-5	73.2	60	28	24	2	42-9	63	.232
1990—Texas (A.L.)	10	6	.625	3.13	1.38	69	3	0	0	6	15-23	97.2	93	40	34	6	42-5	74	.249
1991—Texas (A.L.)	10	10	.500	5.42	1.66	63	9	0	0	11	5-6	109.2	121	80	66	14	61-7	73	.281
1992—Texas (A.L.)	3	6	.333	3.09	1.35	81	0	0	0	16	6-10	78.2	80	32	27	7	26-8	70	.261
1993—Texas (A.L.)	16	10	.615	4.10	1.35	35	33	5	0	1	0-0	208.1	210	108	95	18	71-2	140	.263
1994—Texas (A.L.)	11	8	.579	4.46	1.32	24	24	6	2	0	0-0	167.1	169	93	83	24	52-1	120	.260
1995—Texas (A.L.)	17	7	.708	3.38	1.29	31	31	3	1	0	0-0	208.0	192	87	78	26	76-1	140	.243
1996—New York (A.L.)	12	8	.600	4.68	1.46	30	30	2	1	0	0-0	179.0	179	97	93	16	83-2	92	.261
1997—New York (A.L.)	6	7	.462	5.65	1.54	31	24	1	0	1	0-0	145.0	161	100	91	18	62-1	78	.280
1998—Oakland (A.L.)	16	8	.667	3.17	1.18	34	34	7	1	0	0-0	238.2	215	96	84	19	67-0	138	.242
1999—Oakland (A.L.)	5	3	.625	4.30	1.47	19	19	3	0	0	0-0	119.1	135	66	57	8	41-0	68	.288
—New York (N.L.)	5	1	.833	4.03	1.30	12	12	2	1	0	0-0	76.0	71	35	34	8	28-1	58	.253
2000—Texas (A.L.)	13	13	.500	4.55	1.47	34	34	2	0	0	0-0	227.1	257	126	115	20	78-2	127	.285
2001—Texas (A.L.)	5	7	.417	6.19	1.65	20	20	0	0	0	0-0	120.2	150	88	83	18	49-2	74	.307
2002—Texas (A.L.)	13	8	.619	3.84	1.34	33	33	2	1	0	0-0	210.2	212	101	90	21	70-1	107	.261
2003—Minnesota (A.L.)	13	8	.619	4.57	1.42	33	31	0	0	0	0-0	195.0	227	108	99	22	50-5	116	.292
2004—Texas (A.L.)	18	9	.667	4.76	1.48	35	35	2	1	0	0-0	211.2	248	117	112	24	66-0	126	.292
2005—Texas (A.L.)	14	8	.636	3.46	1.32	30	30	1	1	0	0-0	195.1	205	86	75	15	53-1	87	.271
2006—Detroit (A.L.)	17	8	.680	3.84	1.26	34	33	0	0	0	0-0	204.0	195	97	87	23	62-2	99	.253
American League totals (18 years)	202	138	.594	4.19	1.39	709	421	34	8	50	28-44	2990.0	3109	1550	1393	301	1051-49	1792	.269
National League totals (1 year)	5	1	.833	4.03	1.30	12	12	2	1	0	0-0	76.0	71	35	34	8	28-1	58	.253
Major League totals (18 years)	207	139	.598	4.19	1.39	721	433	36	9	50	28-44	3066.0	3180	1585	1427	309	1079-50	1850	.268

DIVISION SERIES RECORD

Year Team (League)	W	L	Pct.	ERA	WHIP	G	GS	CG	ShO	Hld.	Sv.-Opp.	IP	H	R	ER	HR	BB-IBB	SO	Avg.
1996—New York (A.L.)	0	0	...	9.00	3.50	2	1	0	0	0	0-0	2.0	5	2	2	0	2-0	1	.455
1999—New York (N.L.)	0	1	.000	8.31	1.62	1	1	0	0	0	0-0	4.1	5	4	4	0	2-0	6	.278
2003—Minnesota (A.L.)	0	0	...	0.00	1.50	1	0	0	0	0	0-0	1.1	1	0	0	0	1-1	3	.200
2006—Detroit (A.L.)	1	0	1.000	0.00	0.91	1	1	0	0	0	0-0	7.2	5	0	0	0	2-0	8	.185
Division series totals (4 years)	1	1	.500	3.52	1.50	5	3	0	0	0	0-0	15.1	16	6	6	0	7-1	18	.262

CHAMPIONSHIP SERIES RECORD

Year Team (League)	W	L	Pct.	ERA	WHIP	G	GS	CG	ShO	Hld.	Sv.-Opp.	IP	H	R	ER	HR	BB-IBB	SO	Avg.
1996—New York (A.L.)	0	0	...	12.00	2.33	1	1	0	0	0	0-0	3.0	5	4	4	1	2-0	3	.385
1999—New York (N.L.)	0	2	.000	5.87	2.35	3	1	0	0	0	0-0	7.2	11	5	5	2	7-2	2	.393
2006—Detroit (A.L.)	1	0	1.000	0.00	0.55	1	1	0	0	0	0-0	7.1	2	0	0	0	2-0	6	.087
Champ. series totals (3 years)	1	2	.333	4.50	1.61	5	3	0	0	0	0-0	18.0	18	9	9	3	11-2	11	.281

WORLD SERIES RECORD

Year Team (League)	W	L	Pct.	ERA	WHIP	G	GS	CG	ShO	Hld.	Sv.-Opp.	IP	H	R	ER	HR	BB-IBB	SO	Avg.
1996—New York (A.L.)	0	0	...	22.50	3.50	1	1	0	0	0	0-0	2.0	5	5	5	1	2-0	5	.500
2006—Detroit (A.L.)	1	0	1.000	0.00	0.63	1	1	0	0	0	0-0	8.0	2	0	0	0	3-0	5	.080
World series totals (2 years)	1	0	1.000	4.50	1.20	2	2	0	0	0	0-0	10.0	7	5	5	1	5-0	5	.200

ALL-STAR GAME RECORD

	W	L	Pct.	ERA	WHIP	G	GS	CG	ShO	Hld.	Sv.-Opp.	IP	H	R	ER	HR	BB-IBB	SO	Avg.
All-Star Game totals (3 years)	0	0	...	9.00	1.75	3	1	0	0	0	0-1	4.0	7	4	4	3	0-0	4	.412

2006 LEFTY-RIGHTY SPLITS

vs.	Avg.	AB	H	2B	3B	HR	RBI	BB	SO	OBP	Slg.	vs.	Avg.	AB	H	2B	3B	HR	RBI	BB	SO	OBP	Slg.
L	.200	165	33	13	0	4	20	20	43	.296	.352	R	.268	605	162	28	2	19	66	42	56	.319	.415

ROLEN, SCOTT — 3B

PERSONAL: Born April 4, 1975, in Jasper, Ind. ... 6-4/240. ... Bats right, throws right. ... Full name: Scott Bruce Rolen. ... Name pronounced: ROH-len. ... High school: Jasper (Ind.). **TRANSACTIONS/CAREER NOTES:** Selected by Philadelphia Phillies organization in second round of 1993 free-agent draft. ... On disabled list (May 24-June 8, 2000). ... Traded by Phillies with P Doug Nickle to St. Louis Cardinals for IF/OF Placido Polanco and Ps Bud Smith and Mike Timlin (July 29, 2002). ... On disabled list (May 12-June 18 and July 22-remainder of season, 2005). **RECORDS:** Shares major league record for most strikeouts, 9-inning game (5, August 23, 1999). **HONORS:** Named N.L. Rookie Player of the Year by THE SPORTING NEWS (1997). ... Named third baseman on THE SPORTING NEWS N.L. All-Star team (2002-04). ... Named N.L. Rookie of the Year by Baseball Writers' Association of America (1997). ... Won N.L. Gold Glove at third base (1998, 2000-04 and 2006). ... Named third baseman on N.L. Silver Slugger team (2003). **STATISTICAL NOTES:** Career major league grand slams: 4.

2006 GAMES PLAYED BY POSITION (MLB): 3B—142.

Year — Team (League)	Pos.	G	AB	R	H	2B	3B	HR	RBI	BB	SO	HBP	GDP	SB-CS	Avg.	OBP	SLG	OPS	E	Avg.
1993— Martinsville (App.)	3B	25	80	8	25	5	0	0	12	10	15	7	3	3-4	.313	.429	.375	.804	10	.889
1994— Spartanburg (SAL)	3B	138	513	83	151	34	5	14	72	55	90	4	8	6-8	.294	.363	.462	.825	38	.917
1995— Clearwater (FSL)	3B	66	238	45	69	13	2	10	39	37	46	5	4	4-0	.290	.392	.487	.880	20	.899
— Reading (East.)	3B	20	76	16	22	3	0	3	15	7	14	1	2	1-0	.289	.353	.447	.800	4	.934
1996— Reading (East.)	3B	61	230	44	83	22	2	9	42	34	32	5	5	8-3	.361	.445	.591	1.037	9	.949
— Scran./W.B. (I.L.)	3B	45	168	23	46	17	0	2	19	28	28	0	9	4-5	.274	.376	.411	.786	6	.952
— Philadelphia (N.L.)	3B	37	130	10	33	7	0	4	18	13	27	1	4	0-2	.254	.322	.400	.722	4	.954
1997— Philadelphia (N.L.)	3B	156	561	93	159	35	3	21	92	76	138	13	6	16-6	.283	.377	.469	.846	24	.948
1998— Philadelphia (N.L.)	3B	160	601	120	174	45	4	31	110	93	141	11	10	14-7	.290	.391	.532	.923	14	.970
1999— Philadelphia (N.L.)	3B	112	421	74	113	28	1	26	77	67	114	3	8	12-2	.268	.368	.525	.893	14	.960
2000— Philadelphia (N.L.)	3B	128	483	88	144	32	6	26	89	51	99	5	4	8-1	.298	.370	.551	.920	10	.971
2001— Philadelphia (N.L.)	3B	151	554	96	160	39	1	25	107	74	127	13	6	16-5	.289	.378	.498	.876	12	.973
2002— Philadelphia (N.L.)	3B	100	375	52	97	21	4	17	66	52	68	8	12	5-2	.259	.358	.472	.830	8	.973
— St. Louis (N.L.)	3B	55	205	37	57	8	4	14	44	20	34	4	10	3-2	.278	.354	.561	.915	8	.958
2003— St. Louis (N.L.)	3B	154	559	98	160	49	1	28	104	82	104	9	19	13-3	.286	.382	.528	.910	13	.969
2004— St. Louis (N.L.)	3B	142	500	109	157	32	4	34	124	72	92	13	8	4-3	.314	.409	.598	1.007	10	.977
2005— St. Louis (N.L.)	3B	56	196	28	46	12	1	5	28	25	28	1	3	1-2	.235	.323	.383	.706	6	.966
2006— St. Louis (N.L.)	3B	142	521	94	154	48	1	22	95	56	69	9	10	7-4	.296	.369	.518	.887	15	.965
Major League totals (11 years)		1393	5106	899	1454	356	30	253	954	681	1041	90	100	99-39	.285	.375	.515	.890	138	.966

DIVISION SERIES RECORD

Year — Team (League)	Pos.	G	AB	R	H	2B	3B	HR	RBI	BB	SO	HBP	GDP	SB-CS	Avg.	OBP	SLG	OPS	E	Avg.
2002— St. Louis (N.L.)	3B	2	7	1	3	0	0	1	2	0	2	1	0	0-0	.429	.500	.857	1.357	0	1.000
2004— St. Louis (N.L.)	3B	4	12	1	0	0	0	0	0	6	3	0	0	0-0	.000	.333	.000	.333	0	1.000
2006— St. Louis (N.L.)	3B	3	11	0	1	1	0	0	0	0	2	1	1	0-0	.091	.167	.182	.348	0	1.000
Division series totals (3 years)		9	30	2	4	1	0	1	2	6	7	2	1	0-0	.133	.316	.267	.582	0	1.000

CHAMPIONSHIP SERIES RECORD

Year — Team (League)	Pos.	G	AB	R	H	2B	3B	HR	RBI	BB	SO	HBP	GDP	SB-CS	Avg.	OBP	SLG	OPS	E	Avg.
2004— St. Louis (N.L.)	3B	7	29	6	9	3	0	3	6	2	9	0	1	0-0	.310	.355	.690	1.044	0	1.000
2006— St. Louis (N.L.)	3B	7	21	4	5	0	0	0	0	3	1	0	1	0-1	.238	.333	.286	.619	2	.882
Champ. series totals (2 years)		14	50	10	14	3	0	3	6	5	10	0	2	0-1	.280	.345	.520	.865	2	.950

WORLD SERIES RECORD

Year — Team (League)	Pos.	G	AB	R	H	2B	3B	HR	RBI	BB	SO	HBP	GDP	SB-CS	Avg.	OBP	SLG	OPS	E	Avg.
2004— St. Louis (N.L.)	3B	4	15	0	0	0	0	0	1	1	1	0	1	0-0	.000	.059	.000	.059	0	1.000
2006— St. Louis (N.L.)	3B	5	19	5	8	3	0	1	2	2	4	0	1	0-0	.421	.476	.737	1.213	1	.923
World series totals (2 years)		9	34	5	8	3	0	1	3	3	5	0	2	0-0	.235	.289	.412	.701	1	.962

ALL-STAR GAME RECORD

		G	AB	R	H	2B	3B	HR	RBI	BB	SO	HBP	GDP	SB-CS	Avg.	OBP	SLG	OPS	E	Avg.
All-Star Game totals (3 years)		3	6	1	2	0	0	0	0	0	1	0	0	0-0	.333	.429	.333	.762	0	1.000

2006 LEFTY-RIGHTY SPLITS

vs.	Avg.	AB	H	2B	3B	HR	RBI	BB	SO	OBP	Slg.	vs.	Avg.	AB	H	2B	3B	HR	RBI	BB	SO	OBP	Slg.
L	.259	143	37	12	1	5	17	18	18	.335	.462	R	.310	378	117	36	0	17	78	38	51	.381	.540

ROLLINS, JIMMY — SS

PERSONAL: Born November 27, 1978, in Oakland. ... 5-8/167. ... Bats both, throws right. ... Full name: James Calvin Rollins. ... High school: Encinal (Alameda, Calif.). ... Cousin of Tony Tarasco, outfielder with six major league teams (1988-99). **TRANSACTIONS/CAREER NOTES:** Selected by Philadelphia Phillies organization in second round of 1996 free-agent draft. **STATISTICAL NOTES:** Career major league grand slams: 1.

2006 GAMES PLAYED BY POSITION (MLB): SS—157.

Year — Team (League)	Pos.	G	AB	R	H	2B	3B	HR	RBI	BB	SO	HBP	GDP	SB-CS	Avg.	OBP	SLG	OPS	E	Avg.
1996— Martinsville (App.)	SS	49	172	22	41	3	1	1	16	28	20	2	2	11-5	.238	.351	.285	.636	20	.906
1997— Piedmont (S. Atl.)	SS	139	560	94	151	22	8	6	59	52	80	0	4	46-6	.270	.330	.370	.700	26	.960
1998— Clearwater (FSL)	SS	119	495	72	121	18	9	6	35	41	62	4	9	23-9	.244	.306	.354	.659	29	.952
1999— Reading (East.)	SS	133	532	81	145	21	8	11	56	51	47	1	8	24-12	.273	.336	.404	.740	22	.965
— Scran./W.B. (I.L.)	SS	4	13	0	1	1	0	0	1	1	1	0	0	1-0	.077	.143	.154	.297	1	.960
2000— Scran./W.B. (I.L.)	SS	133	470	67	129	28	11	12	69	49	55	2	4	24-7	.274	.341	.457	.798	26	.958
— Philadelphia (N.L.)	SS	14	53	5	17	1	1	0	8	2	7	0	0	3-0	.321	.345	.377	.723	1	.978
2001— Philadelphia (N.L.)	SS	158	656	97	180	29	* 12	14	54	48	108	2	5	• 46-8	.274	.323	.419	.743	14	.979
2002— Philadelphia (N.L.)	SS-2B	154	* 637	82	156	33	* 10	11	60	54	103	4	14	31-13	.245	.306	.380	.686	14	.980
2003— Philadelphia (N.L.)	SS	156	628	85	165	42	6	8	62	54	113	0	9	20-12	.263	.320	.387	.707	14	.979
2004— Philadelphia (N.L.)	SS	154	657	119	190	43	• 12	14	73	57	73	3	4	30-9	.289	.348	.455	.803	9	.986
2005— Philadelphia (N.L.)	SS	158	677	115	196	38	11	12	54	47	71	4	9	41-6	.290	.338	.431	.770	12	.981
2006— Philadelphia (N.L.)	SS	158	689	127	191	45	9	25	83	57	80	5	12	36-4	.277	.334	.478	.811	11	.984
Major League totals (7 years)		952	3997	630	1095	231	61	84	391	319	555	18	53	207-52	.274	.329	.425	.754	75	.981

ALL-STAR GAME RECORD

		G	AB	R	H	2B	3B	HR	RBI	BB	SO	HBP	GDP	SB-CS	Avg.	OBP	SLG	OPS	E	Avg.
All-Star Game totals (3 years)		3	3	2	3	0	0	0	0	1	0	0	0	1-0	1.000	1.000	1.000	2.000	0	1.000

2006 LEFTY-RIGHTY SPLITS

vs.	Avg.	AB	H	2B	3B	HR	RBI	BB	SO	OBP	Slg.	vs.	Avg.	AB	H	2B	3B	HR	RBI	BB	SO	OBP	Slg.
L	.277	177	49	2	9	17	15	18	.335	.503		R	.277	512	142	36	7	16	66	42	62	.333	.469

ROMERO, DAVIS P

PERSONAL: Born March 30, 1983, in Aguadulce, Panama. ... Throws left, bats left. ... Full name: Davis Javier Rodriguez Romero. **TRANSACTIONS/CAREER NOTES:** Signed as non-drafted free agent by Toronto Blue Jays organization (July 3, 1999).
CAREER HITTING: 0-for-0 (.000), 0 R, 0 2B, 0 3B, 0 HR, 0 RBI.

Year	Team (League)	W	L	Pct.	ERA	WHIP	G	GS	CG	ShO	Hld.	Sv.-Opp.	IP	H	R	ER	HR	BB-IBB	SO	Avg.
2000—	Dom. B. Jays (DSL)	1	0	1.000	2.65	0.74	13	2	0	0	...	4-...	34.0	15	10	10	1	10-0	45	.129
2001—	Dom. B. Jays (DSL)	4	3	.571	2.47	0.92	10	9	0	0	...	0-...	51.0	35	19	14	1	12-0	85	.187
2002—	Medicine Hat (Pio.)	3	2	.600	5.19	1.33	27	4	0	0	...	2-...	50.1	49	38	29	7	18-0	76	.249
2003—	Auburn (NY-Penn)	4	1	.800	2.38	0.94	30	0	0	0	...	2-...	41.2	31	13	11	1	8-1	53	.199
2004—	Char., W.Va. (SAL)	5	4	.556	2.53	1.04	32	14	0	0	...	1-...	103.1	77	36	29	6	30-0	108	.209
2005—	Dunedin (Fla. St.)	9	6	.600	3.47	1.34	34	18	0	0	1	1-1	124.2	133	60	48	10	34-0	136	.273
2006—	New Hampshire (East.)	6	5	.545	2.93	1.03	12	12	1	1	0	0-0	73.2	57	27	24	3	19-1	70	.213
—	Syracuse (Int'l)	4	4	.500	3.83	1.19	18	3	0	0	...	1-3	44.2	46	25	19	3	7-0	36	.264
—	Toronto (A.L.)	1	0	1.000	3.86	1.53	7	0	0	0	...	0-0	16.1	19	7	7	1	6-1	10	.297
	Major League totals (1 year)	1	0	1.000	3.86	1.53	7	0	0	0	...	0-0	16.1	19	7	7	1	6-1	10	.297

2006 LEFTY-RIGHTY SPLITS

vs.	Avg.	AB	H	2B	3B	HR	RBI	BB	SO	OBP	Slg.	vs.	Avg.	AB	H	2B	3B	HR	RBI	BB	SO	OBP	Slg.
L	.318	22	7	1	0	0	0	1	4	.348	.364	R	.286	42	12	4	0	1	5	5	6	.375	.452

ROMERO, J.C. P

PERSONAL: Born June 4, 1976, in Rio Piedras, Puerto Rico. ... 5-11/198. ... Throws left, bats both. ... Full name: Juan Carlos Romero. ... High school: Berwing (San Juan, Puerto Rico). ... College: Mobile (Ala.). **TRANSACTIONS/CAREER NOTES:** Selected by Minnesota Twins organization in 21st round of 1997 free-agent draft. ... On disabled list (March 25-May 10, 2000); included rehabilitation assignment to Fort Myers. ... Traded by Twins to Los Angeles Angels of Anaheim for IF Alexi Casilla (December 9, 2005).
CAREER HITTING: 1-for-3 (.333), 1 R, 1 2B, 0 3B, 0 HR, 0 RBI.

Year	Team (League)	W	L	Pct.	ERA	WHIP	G	GS	CG	ShO	Hld.	Sv.-Opp.	IP	H	R	ER	HR	BB-IBB	SO	Avg.
1997—	Elizabethton (App.)	3	2	.600	4.88	1.42	18	0	0	0	...	3-...	24.0	27	16	13	4	7-0	29	.276
—	Fort Myers (FSL)	1	1	.500	4.38	1.22	7	1	0	0	...	0-...	12.1	11	6	6	1	4-0	9	.244
1998—	New Britain (East.)	6	3	.667	2.19	1.17	51	1	0	0	...	2-...	78.0	48	28	19	3	43-3	79	.178
1999—	New Britain (East.)	4	4	.500	3.40	1.60	36	1	0	0	...	7-...	53.0	51	25	20	6	34-0	53	.254
—	Salt Lake (PCL)	4	1	.800	3.20	1.63	15	0	0	0	...	1-...	19.2	18	11	7	1	14-0	20	.250
—	Minnesota (A.L.)	0	0	...	3.72	1.34	5	0	0	0	0	0-0	9.2	13	4	4	0	0-0	4	.333
2000—	Fort Myers (FSL)	0	0	...	1.93	1.07	2	0	0	0	...	0-...	4.2	4	1	1	0	1-0	3	.222
—	Salt Lake (PCL)	4	2	.667	3.44	1.30	17	11	1	0	...	4-...	65.1	60	40	25	6	25-0	38	.244
—	Minnesota (A.L.)	2	7	.222	7.02	1.77	12	11	0	0	...	0-...	57.2	72	51	45	8	30-0	50	.312
2001—	Minnesota (A.L.)	1	4	.200	6.23	1.46	14	11	0	0	...	0-...	65.0	71	48	45	10	24-1	39	.277
—	Edmonton (PCL)	3	3	.500	3.68	1.43	12	10	0	0	...	0-...	63.2	67	33	26	4	24-0	55	.276
2002—	Minnesota (A.L.)	9	2	.818	1.89	1.21	81	0	0	0	* 33	1-5	81.0	62	17	17	3	36-4	76	.213
2003—	Minnesota (A.L.)	2	0	1.000	5.00	1.71	73	0	0	0	22	0-4	63.0	66	37	35	7	42-7	50	.272
2004—	Rochester (Int'l)	0	0	...	2.25	1.13	3	3	0	0	...	0-...	8.0	4	2	2	1	5-0	11	.143
—	Minnesota (A.L.)	7	4	.636	3.51	1.33	74	0	0	0	16	1-8	74.1	61	32	29	4	38-6	69	.224
2005—	Minnesota (A.L.)	4	3	.571	3.47	1.56	68	0	0	0	11	0-1	57.0	50	26	22	6	39-8	48	.235
2006—	Los Angeles (A.L.)	1	2	.333	6.70	1.76	65	0	0	0	7	0-1	48.1	57	40	36	3	28-2	31	.298
	Major League totals (8 years)	26	22	.542	4.60	1.51	392	22	0	0	89	2-19	456.0	452	255	233	41	237-28	367	.260

DIVISION SERIES RECORD

Year	Team (League)	W	L	Pct.	ERA	WHIP	G	GS	CG	ShO	Hld.	Sv.-Opp.	IP	H	R	ER	HR	BB-IBB	SO	Avg.
2002—	Minnesota (A.L.)	0	0	...	0.00	1.20	3	0	0	0	2	0-0	3.1	3	0	0	0	1-0	2	.231
2003—	Minnesota (A.L.)	0	0	...	0.00	1.50	3	0	0	0	0	0-0	3.1	3	0	0	0	2-1	1	.250
2004—	Minnesota (A.L.)	0	0	...	9.00	1.00	2	0	0	0	0	0-0	1.0	0	1	1	0	1-0	1	.000
	Division series totals (3 years)	0	0	...	1.17	1.30	8	0	0	0	2	0-0	7.2	6	1	1	0	4-1	4	.231

CHAMPIONSHIP SERIES RECORD

Year	Team (League)	W	L	Pct.	ERA	WHIP	G	GS	CG	ShO	Hld.	Sv.-Opp.	IP	H	R	ER	HR	BB-IBB	SO	Avg.
2002—	Minnesota (A.L.)	0	1	.000	22.50	3.00	4	0	0	0	0	0-0	2.0	4	5	5	1	2-0	3	.400

2006 LEFTY-RIGHTY SPLITS

vs.	Avg.	AB	H	2B	3B	HR	RBI	BB	SO	OBP	Slg.	vs.	Avg.	AB	H	2B	3B	HR	RBI	BB	SO	OBP	Slg.
L	.202	89	18	6	0	1	15	13	13	.298	.303	R	.382	102	39	12	1	2	21	15	18	.455	.578

RONEY, MATT P

PERSONAL: Born January 10, 1980, in Tulsa, Okla. ... 6-3/230. ... Throws right, bats right. ... Full name: Matthew S. Roney. ... High school: Edmond North (Edmond, Okla.). **TRANSACTIONS/CAREER NOTES:** Selected by Colorado Rockies organization in first round (28th pick overall) of 1998 free-agent draft. ... Selected by Pittsburgh Pirates from Rockies organization in Rule 5 major league draft (December 16, 2002). ... Traded by Pirates to Detroit Tigers for cash (December 16, 2002). ... Released by Tigers (July 3, 2005). ... Signed by Texas Rangers organization (July 7, 2005). ... Signed as free agent by Oakland Athletics (November 15, 2005).
CAREER HITTING: 1-for-2 (.500), 0 R, 0 2B, 0 3B, 0 HR, 0 RBI.

Year	Team (League)	W	L	Pct.	ERA	WHIP	G	GS	CG	ShO	Hld.	Sv.-Opp.	IP	H	R	ER	HR	BB-IBB	SO	Avg.
1998—	Ariz. Rockies (Ariz.)	1	1	.500	5.80	1.51	9	9	1	1	...	0-...	40.1	50	31	26	1	11-0	49	.291
1999—				Did not play.																
2000—	Portland (N'west)	7	5	.583	3.14	1.48	15	15	0	0	...	0-...	80.1	75	35	28	6	44-0	85	.244
2001—	Asheville (S. Atl.)	8	10	.444	4.98	1.44	23	23	1	0	...	0-...	121.0	131	74	67	16	43-0	115	.275
2002—	Asheville (S. Atl.)	4	6	.400	3.48	1.29	14	14	1	1	...	0-...	82.2	82	39	32	7	25-1	88	.261
—	Carolina (Southern)	3	6	.333	6.11	1.50	13	13	0	0	...	0-...	70.2	73	52	48	6	33-1	65	.265
2003—	Detroit (A.L.)	1	9	.100	5.45	1.49	45	11	0	0	6	0-2	100.2	102	67	61	17	48-4	47	.262
2004—	Erie (East.)	9	9	.500	4.93	1.47	22	22	3	1	...	0-...	133.1	163	79	73	20	33-0	89	.304
—	Toledo (Int'l)	2	1	.667	3.86	1.32	5	5	0	0	...	0-...	30.1	30	13	13	3	10-0	18	.280
2005—	Erie (East.)	0	1	.000	1.25	0.88	11	0	0	0	3	1-2	21.2	13	3	3	1	6-0	23	.173
—	Toledo (Int'l)	1	1	.500	0.95	1.20	14	0	0	0	3	3-4	28.1	23	3	3	0	11-0	27	.225
2006—	Oakland (A.L.)	4	1	.800	3.03	1.29	24	0	0	0	4	1-2	32.2	34	11	11	3	8-0	32	.272
—	Sacramento (PCL)	0	1	.000	4.50	1.50	3	0	0	0	0	0-0	4.0	5	2	2	0	1-1	0	.333
2006—	Sacramento (PCL)	4	3	.571	2.95	1.33	47	0	0	0	9	6-9	58.0	58	26	19	4	19-1	65	.260
	Major League totals (2 years)	1	10	.091	5.42	1.49	48	11	0	0	6	0-2	104.2	107	69	63	17	49-5	47	.265

2006 LEFTY-RIGHTY SPLITS

vs.	Avg.	AB	H	2B	3B	HR	RBI	BB	SO	OBP	Slg.	vs.	Avg.	AB	H	2B	3B	HR	RBI	BB	SO	OBP	Slg.
L	.250	4	1	0	0	0	1	0	.400	.250		R	.364	11	4	2	0	0	2	0	0	.333	.545

R

ROSARIO, FRANCISCO — P

PERSONAL: Born September 28, 1980, in San Rafael, Dominican Republic. ... 6-0/195. ... Throws right, bats right. ... Full name: Francisco A. Rosario.
TRANSACTIONS/CAREER NOTES: Signed as non-drafted free agent by Toronto Blue Jays organization (January 11, 1999).
CAREER HITTING: 0-for-1 (.000), 0 R, 0 2B, 0 3B, 0 HR, 0 RBI.

Year Team (League)	W	L	Pct.	ERA	WHIP	G	GS	CG	ShO	Hld.	Sv.-Opp.	IP	H	R	ER	HR	BB-IBB	SO	Avg.
1999— Dom. B. Jays (DSL)	1	0	1.000	3.06	1.14	18	0	0	0	...	3-...	32.1	26	16	11	0	11-2	38	.208
2000— Dom. B. Jays (DSL)	2	0	1.000	1.21	0.75	26	0	0	0	...	16-...	37.1	21	5	5	0	7-0	51	.160
2001— Medicine Hat (Pio.)	3	7	.300	5.59	1.55	16	15	0	0	...	0-...	75.2	79	61	47	8	38-0	55	.271
2002— Char., W.Va. (SAL)	6	1	.857	2.57	0.96	13	13	1	0	...	0-...	66.2	50	22	19	5	14-0	78	.206
— Dunedin (Fla. St.)	3	3	.500	1.29	0.92	13	12	0	0	...	0-...	63.0	33	10	9	3	25-0	65	.151
2004— Dunedin (Fla. St.)	1	1	.500	4.67	1.56	6	6	0	0	...	0-...	17.1	16	12	9	2	11-0	16	.239
— New Hampshire (East.) ...	2	4	.333	4.31	1.33	12	12	0	0	...	0-...	48.0	48	25	23	6	16-0	45	.271
2005— Syracuse (Int'l)	2	7	.222	3.95	1.32	30	18	0	0	4	2-2	116.1	111	59	51	16	42-0	80	.258
2006— Syracuse (Int'l)	0	3	.000	2.79	1.00	14	8	0	0	1	1-1	42.0	29	14	13	2	13-0	50	.196
— Toronto (A.L.)	1	2	.333	6.65	1.74	17	1	0	0	1	0-0	23.0	24	17	17	4	16-2	21	.264
Major League totals (1 year)	1	2	.333	6.65	1.74	17	1	0	0	1	0-0	23.0	24	17	17	4	16-2	21	.264

2006 LEFTY-RIGHTY SPLITS

vs.	Avg.	AB	H	2B	3B	HR	RBI	BB	SO	OBP	Slg.	vs.	Avg.	AB	H	2B	3B	HR	RBI	BB	SO	OBP	Slg.
L	.310	29	9	0	0	2	5	8	8	.459	.517	R	.242	62	15	2	1	2	9	8	13	.338	.403

ROSE, MIKE — C

PERSONAL: Born August 25, 1976, in Sacramento. ... 6-1/185. ... Bats both, throws right. ... Full name: Michael John-Ferrero Rose. ... High school: Jesuit (Sacramento).
TRANSACTIONS/CAREER NOTES: Selected by Houston Astros organization in fifth round of 1995 free-agent draft. ... Released by Astros (March 16, 2000). ... Signed by Arizona Diamondbacks organization (March 21, 2000). ... Traded by Diamondbacks to Boston Red Sox for cash (August 18, 2001). ... Released by Red Sox (April 26, 2002). ... Signed by Kansas City Royals organization (May 1, 2002). ... Signed as a free agent by Oakland Athletics organization (November 6, 2002). ... Signed as a free agent by Los Angeles Dodgers organization (November 16, 2004). ... Claimed on waivers by Tampa Bay Devil Rays (October 14, 2005). ... Signed as free agent by St. Louis Cardinals organization (May 3, 2006). ... Signed as free agent by Cleveland Indians organization (November 9, 2006).
2006 GAMES PLAYED BY POSITION (MLB): C—4.

Year Team (League)	Pos.	G	AB	R	H	2B	3B	HR	RBI	BB	SO	HBP	GDP	SB-CS	Avg.	OBP	SLG	OPS	E	Avg.
1995— GC Astros (GCL)	C-1B	35	89	13	23	2	1	1	9	11	18	3	1	2-1	.258	.359	.337	.696	1	.996
1996— Kissimmee (Fla. St.)	C	2	1	0	0	0	0	0	0	0	1	0	0	0-0	.000	.000	.000	.000	0	1.000
— Auburn (NY-Penn)	C	61	180	20	45	5	1	2	11	30	41	1	5	9-3	.250	.360	.322	.682	7	.984
1997— Quad City (Midw.)	C	79	234	22	60	6	1	3	27	28	62	4	1	3-1	.256	.342	.329	.671	10	.983
1998— Kissimmee (Fla. St.)	C	18	62	9	14	4	0	3	9	8	14	0	2	1-0	.226	.314	.435	.750	3	.973
— Quad City (Midw.)	C-OF	88	267	48	81	13	2	7	40	52	56	1	5	10-8	.303	.417	.446	.863	8	.988
1999— Kissimmee (Fla. St.)	C	95	303	61	84	16	2	11	32	59	64	3	7	12-6	.277	.398	.452	.850	13	.981
— Jackson (Texas)	C	15	45	8	11	0	0	3	8	13	10	0	1	0-2	.244	.414	.444	.858	2	.983
2000— El Paso (Texas)	C-OF	117	352	58	100	22	1	10	62	68	70	1	16	8-11	.284	.398	.438	.835	16	.980
2001— Tucson (PCL)	C	20	55	9	10	0	0	0	8	12	16	0	3	0-0	.182	.324	.273	.596	0	1.000
— El Paso (Texas)	C-OF-3B	62	205	28	53	13	1	3	23	37	40	0	8	4-4	.259	.370	.376	.746	4	.984
— Trenton (East.)	C	9	24	3	4	0	0	1	2	6	10	0	0	0-1	.167	.333	.292	.625	0	1.000
2002— Trenton (East.)	C	10	29	1	3	1	1	0	5	7	0	0	2	0-0	.103	.235	.207	.442	0	1.000
— Omaha (PCL)	C	52	177	22	46	12	2	3	17	28	40	1	7	2-3	.260	.364	.401	.765	6	.981
— Wichita (Texas)	C-OF	14	59	13	18	5	0	2	14	7	11	0	3	0-1	.305	.379	.492	.870	1	.977
2003— Sacramento (PCL)	C-OF	70	221	44	58	10	1	8	30	44	50	4	6	2-1	.262	.390	.425	.815	8	.982
2004— Sacramento (PCL)	C-DH	107	349	56	98	20	2	6	49	76	80	3	14	0-0	.281	.407	.401	.808	8	.988
— Oakland (A.L.)	C	2	2	1	0	0	0	0	0	0	2	0	0	0-0	.000	.000	.000	.000	1	1.000
2005— Las Vegas (PCL)	C-OF-DH	69	205	31	53	20	1	5	36	25	51	3	3	2-0	.259	.343	.439	.782	2	.995
— Los Angeles (N.L.)	C	15	43	2	9	2	0	1	1	3	6	0	3	0-0	.209	.261	.326	.586	2	.978
2006— Durham (Int'l)		20	67	4	7	1	0	2	5	5	21	0	0	0-0	.104	.164	.209	.373	2	.969
— Memphis (PCL)		82	271	38	71	19	0	15	36	40	83	2	7	2-1	.262	.361	.498	.859	5	.985
— St. Louis (N.L.)	C	10	9	0	2	0	0	0	1	0	4	0	0	0-0	.222	.222	.222	.444	0	1.000
American League totals (1 year)		2	2	1	0	0	0	0	0	0	2	0	0	0-0	.000	.000	.000	.000	1	1.000
National League totals (2 years)		25	52	2	11	2	0	1	2	3	10	0	3	0-0	.212	.255	.308	.562	2	.980
Major League totals (3 years)		27	54	3	11	2	0	1	2	3	12	0	3	0-0	.204	.246	.296	.542	2	.980

2006 LEFTY-RIGHTY SPLITS

vs.	Avg.	AB	H	2B	3B	HR	RBI	BB	SO	OBP	Slg.	vs.	Avg.	AB	H	2B	3B	HR	RBI	BB	SO	OBP	Slg.
L	.000	2	0	0	0	0	0	0	0	.000	.000	R	.286	7	2	0	0	0	1	0	4	.286	.286

ROSS, CODY — OF

PERSONAL: Born December 23, 1980, in Portales, N.M. ... 5-11/180. ... Bats right, throws left. ... Full name: Cody Joseph Ross. ... High school: Carlsbad (N.M.). **TRANSACTIONS/CAREER NOTES:** Selected by Detroit Tigers organization in fourth round of 1999 free-agent draft. ... Traded by Tigers to Los Angeles Dodgers for P Steve Colyer and cash (April 1, 2004). ... Traded by Dodgers to Cincinnati Reds for a player to be named (April 24, 2006); Dodgers acquired P Ben Kozlowski to complete the deal (June 1, 2006). ... Traded by Reds to Florida Marlins for cash (May 26, 2006). **STATISTICAL NOTES:** Hit three home runs in one game (September 11, 2006). ... Career major league grand slams: 2.
2006 GAMES PLAYED BY POSITION (MLB): OF—83.

Year Team (League)	Pos.	G	AB	R	H	2B	3B	HR	RBI	BB	SO	HBP	GDP	SB-CS	Avg.	OBP	SLG	OPS	E	Avg.
1999— GC Tigers (GCL)	OF	42	142	19	31	8	3	4	18	16	28	2	3	3-1	.218	.304	.401	.705	4	.980
2000— W. Mich. (Mid.)	OF-OF	122	434	71	116	17	9	7	68	55	83	9	14	11-3	.267	.356	.396	.752	6	.978
2001— Lakeland (Fla. St.)	OF-OF	127	482	84	133	34	5	15	80	44	96	5	9	28-5	.276	.337	.461	.798	4	.984
2002— Erie (East.)	OF-OF	105	400	73	112	28	3	19	72	44	86	3	11	16-2	.280	.352	.508	.860	6	.975
2003— Toledo (Int'l)	OF-OF-DH	124	470	74	135	35	6	20	61	32	90	5	12	15-6	.287	.333	.515	.848	6	.977
— Detroit (A.L.)	OF	6	19	1	4	1	0	1	5	1	3	1	0	0-0	.211	.286	.421	.707	2	.882
2004— Las Vegas (PCL)	OF	60	238	44	65	17	2	14	49	18	43	2	11	0-0	.273	.328	.538	.866	3	.500
2005— Los Angeles (N.L.)	OF	14	25	1	4	1	0	1	1	1	10	0	1	0-0	.160	.192	.200	.392	1	.933
— Las Vegas (PCL)	OF	115	393	79	105	21	4	22	63	49	103	0	8	4-2	.267	.348	.509	.857	2	.995
2006— Los Angeles (N.L.)	OF	8	14	4	7	1	0	2	9	0	2	0	0	1-0	.500	.500	1.143	1.643	0	1.000
— Louisville (Int'l)		15	50	11	17	0	0	3	16	13	12	1	4	0-2	.340	.484	.540	1.024	1	.968

Year	Team (League)	Pos.	G	AB	R	H	2B	3B	HR	RBI	BB	SO	HBP	GDP	SB-CS	Avg.	OBP	SLG	OPS	E	Avg.
	—Cincinnati (N.L.)	OF	2	5	0	1	0	0	0	0	2	0	0		0-0	.200	.200	.200	.400	0	1.000
	—Florida (N.L.)	OF	91	250	30	53	11	1	11	37	22	61	4	8	0-1	.212	.284	.396	.680	2	.985
American League totals (1 year)			6	19	1	4	1	0	1	5	1	3	1	0	0-0	.211	.286	.421	.707	2	.882
National League totals (2 years)			115	294	35	65	13	2	13	47	23	75	4	9	1-1	.221	.285	.412	.696	3	.980
Major League totals (3 years)			121	313	36	69	14	2	14	52	24	78	5	9	1-1	.220	.285	.412	.697	5	.970

2006 LEFTY-RIGHTY SPLITS

vs.	Avg.	AB	H	2B	3B	HR	RBI	BB	SO	OBP	Slg.	vs.	Avg.	AB	H	2B	3B	HR	RBI	BB	SO	OBP	Slg.
L	.245	102	25	6	1	9	28	8	25	.300	.588	R	.216	167	36	6	1	4	18	14	40	.289	.335

ROSS, DAVID — C

PERSONAL: Born March 19, 1977, in Bainbridge, Ga. ... 6-2/205. ... Bats right, throws right. ... Full name: David Wade Ross. ... High school: Florida (Tallahassee, Fla.). ... College: Florida. **TRANSACTIONS/CAREER NOTES:** Selected by Los Angeles Dodgers organization in 19th round of 1995 free-agent draft; did not sign. ... Selected by Dodgers organization in seventh round of 1998 free-agent draft. ... Traded by Dodgers to Pittsburgh Pirates for cash (March 30, 2005). ... Traded by Pirates to San Diego Padres for IF J.J. Furmaniak (July 28, 2005). ... Traded by Padres to Cincinnati Reds for P Robert Basham (March 21, 2006). ... On disabled list (July 8-26, 2006); included rehabilitation assignment to Chattanooga.

2006 GAMES PLAYED BY POSITION (MLB): C—75.

Year	Team (League)	Pos.	G	AB	R	H	2B	3B	HR	RBI	BB	SO	HBP	GDP	SB-CS	Avg.	OBP	SLG	OPS	E	Avg.
1998—Yakima (N'west)		C	59	191	31	59	14	1	6	25	34	49	1	5	2-2	.309	.412	.487	.899	10	.979
1999—Vero Beach (FSL)		C-1B-OF	114	375	47	85	19	1	7	39	46	111	7	10	5-9	.227	.318	.339	.657	16	.979
2000—San Bern. (Calif.)		C	51	191	27	49	11	1	7	21	17	43	1	3	3-2	.257	.319	.435	.754	3	.992
—San Antonio (Texas)		C	24	67	11	14	2	1	3	12	9	17	1	0	1-0	.209	.308	.403	.711	1	.994
2001—Jacksonville (Sou.)		C	74	246	35	65	13	1	11	45	34	72	10	5	1-1	.264	.372	.459	.831	9	.985
2002—Las Vegas (PCL)		C	92	293	48	87	16	2	15	68	35	86	9	4	1-1	.297	.384	.519	.903	7	.989
—Los Angeles (N.L.)		C	8	10	2	2	1	0	1	2	2	4	1	0	0-0	.200	.385	.600	.985	1	1.000
2003—Las Vegas (PCL)		C	24	86	12	19	4	0	5	16	11	27	1	0	0-2	.221	.313	.442	.755	2	.989
—Los Angeles (N.L.)		C	40	124	19	32	7	0	10	18	13	42	2	4	0-0	.258	.336	.556	.892	4	.986
2004—Los Angeles (N.L.)		C	70	165	13	28	3	1	5	15	15	62	5	3	0-0	.170	.253	.291	.544	3	.992
2005—Pittsburgh (N.L.)		C	40	108	9	24	8	0	3	15	6	24	1	3	0-0	.222	.263	.380	.642	3	.986
—Indianapolis (Int'l)		C	6	19	1	4	1	0	0	1	3	7	0	0	0-0	.211	.304	.263	.568	1	.971
—Portland (PCL)		C	6	21	3	6	1	0	0	1	2	4	1	0	0-0	.353	.389	.471	.859	0	1.000
—San Diego (N.L.)		C	11	17	2	6	0	1	0	2	2	4	0	0	0-0	.353	.500	.333	.833	0	1.000
2006—Chattanooga (Sou.)		C	2	6	0	2	0	0	0	2	2	2	0	0	0-0	.333	.500	.333	.833	0	1.000
—Cincinnati (N.L.)		C	90	247	37	63	15	1	21	52	37	75	3	4	0-0	.255	.353	.579	.932	8	.985
Major League totals (5 years)			259	671	82	155	34	3	40	102	73	211	13	14	0-0	.231	.313	.469	.782	18	.988

DIVISION SERIES RECORD

Year	Team (League)	Pos.	G	AB	R	H	2B	3B	HR	RBI	BB	SO	HBP	GDP	SB-CS	Avg.	OBP	SLG	OPS	E	Avg.
2004—Los Angeles (N.L.)		C	3	3	0	0	0	0	0	0	1	0	0	0	0-0	.000	.250	.000	.250	1	.923

2006 LEFTY-RIGHTY SPLITS

vs.	Avg.	AB	H	2B	3B	HR	RBI	BB	SO	OBP	Slg.	vs.	Avg.	AB	H	2B	3B	HR	RBI	BB	SO	OBP	Slg.
L	.316	76	24	4	1	11	19	12	22	.404	.829	R	.228	171	39	11	0	10	33	25	53	.330	.468

ROTTINO, VINNY — 3B

PERSONAL: Born April 7, 1980, in Racine, Wis. ... Bats right, throws right. ... Full name: Vincent Antonio Rottino. ... College: Wisconsin-La Crosse. **TRANSACTIONS/CAREER NOTES:** Signed as a non-drafted free agent by Milwaukee Brewers organization (February 3, 2003).

2006 GAMES PLAYED BY POSITION (MLB): 3B—3, OF—2, C—1.

Year	Team (League)	Pos.	G	AB	R	H	2B	3B	HR	RBI	BB	SO	HBP	GDP	SB-CS	Avg.	OBP	SLG	OPS	E	Avg.
2003—Helena (Pion.)			64	222	42	69	10	0	1	20	28	25	8	4	5-2	.311	.404	.369	.773	...	...
2004—Beloit (Midw.)			140	529	78	161	25	9	17	124	40	71	4	12	5-1	.304	.352	.482	.834	...	...
2005—Huntsville (Sou.)	3B-C-1B OF-DH		120	469	63	139	20	6	6	52	40	68	2	14	2-1	.296	.351	.403	.754	15	.974
—Nashville (PCL)	3B-C-1B OF		9	29	4	10	1	0	1	2	3	6	0	1	0-1	.345	.406	.483	.889	0	1.000
2006—Nashville (PCL)			117	398	55	125	25	2	7	42	40	74	5	9	12-7	.314	.379	.440	.819	17	.959
—Milwaukee (N.L.)	3B-OF-C		9	14	1	3	1	0	0	1	1	2	0	0	1-0	.214	.267	.286	.552	0	1.000
Major League totals (1 year)			9	14	1	3	1	0	0	1	1	2	0	0	1-0	.214	.267	.286	.552	0	1.000

2006 LEFTY-RIGHTY SPLITS

vs.	Avg.	AB	H	2B	3B	HR	RBI	BB	SO	OBP	Slg.	vs.	Avg.	AB	H	2B	3B	HR	RBI	BB	SO	OBP	Slg.
L	.143	7	1	1	0	0	0	1	0	.250	.286	R	.286	7	2	0	0	0	0	0	2	.286	.286

ROUSE, MIKE — IF

PERSONAL: Born April 25, 1980, in San Jose, Calif. ... 5-11/185. ... Bats left, throws right. ... Full name: Michael Gregory Rouse. ... College: Cal State Fullerton. **TRANSACTIONS/CAREER NOTES:** Selected by Toronto Blue Jays organization in fifth round of 2001 free-agent draft. ... Traded by Blue Jays to Oakland Athletics for Ps Cory Lidle and Chris Mowday (November 16, 2002). ... Claimed on waivers by Cleveland Indians (September 13, 2006).

2006 GAMES PLAYED BY POSITION (MLB): 2B—7.

Year	Team (League)	Pos.	G	AB	R	H	2B	3B	HR	RBI	BB	SO	HBP	GDP	SB-CS	Avg.	OBP	SLG	OPS	E	Avg.
2001—Dunedin (Fla. St.)			48	180	27	49	17	2	5	24	13	45	2	2	3-1	.272	.327	.472	.799	...	...
2002—Tennessee (Sou.)			71	231	35	60	11	0	9	43	29	47	2	3	7-6	.260	.342	.424	.766	...	...
2003—Midland (Texas)			129	457	75	137	33	3	3	53	63	83	9	16	7-2	.300	.392	.405	.797	...	...
—Sacramento (PCL)			2	7	2	3	0	0	0	1	0	0	0	0	0-0	.429	.429	.429	.858	...	...
2004—Sacramento (PCL)			99	323	63	89	11	2	10	40	50	68	5	5	0-4	.276	.379	.415	.794	...	...
2005—Sacramento (PCL)	SS-2B-DH		130	469	69	126	30	3	7	72	59	115	7	6	2-4	.269	.358	.390	.748	19	.964
2006—Sacramento (PCL)			99	345	59	89	21	1	6	47	42	67	6	8	4-1	.258	.347	.391	.724	8	.980
—Oakland (A.L.)	2B		8	24	2	7	3	0	0	2	1	4	1	1	1-0	.292	.346	.417	.763	0	1.000
Major League totals (1 year)			8	24	2	7	3	0	0	2	1	4	1	1	1-0	.292	.346	.417	.763	0	1.000

2006 LEFTY-RIGHTY SPLITS

vs.	Avg.	AB	H	2B	3B	HR	RBI	BB	SO	OBP	Slg.	vs.	Avg.	AB	H	2B	3B	HR	RBI	BB	SO	OBP	Slg.
L	.200	5	1	0	0	0	0	0	1	.333	.200	R	.316	19	6	3	0	0	2	0	3	.350	.474

R

ROWAND, AARON — OF

PERSONAL: Born August 29, 1977, in Portland, Ore. ... 6-0/205. ... Bats right, throws right. ... Full name: Aaron Ryan Rowand. ... Name pronounced: ROE-und. ... High school: Glendora (Calif.). ... College: Cal State Fullerton. ... Cousin of James Shields, pitcher, Tampa Bay Devil Rays. **TRANSACTIONS/CAREER NOTES:** Selected by New York Mets organization in 40th round of 1995 free-agent draft; did not sign. ... Selected by Chicago White Sox organization in supplemental round ("sandwich pick" between first and second rounds, 35th pick overall) of 1998 free-agent draft; pick received as part of compensation for Tampa Bay Devil Rays signing Type A free-agent OF Dave Martinez. ... Traded by White Sox with P Daniel Haigwood and a player to be named to Philadelphia Phillies for 1B Jim Thome and cash (November 25, 2005); Phillies acquired P Gio Gonzalez to complete deal (December 8, 2005). ... On disabled list (May 12-27, 2006). ... On disabled list (August 22, 2006-remainder of season). **STATISTICAL NOTES:** Career major league grand slams: 1.

2006 GAMES PLAYED BY POSITION (MLB): OF—107.

Year	Team (League)	Pos.	G	AB	R	H	2B	3B	HR	RBI	BB	SO	HBP	GDP	SB-CS	Avg.	OBP	SLG	OPS	E	Avg.
1998—	Hickory (S. Atl.)	OF	61	222	42	76	13	3	5	32	21	36	6	5	7-3	.342	.410	.496	.906	3	.966
1999—	Win.-Salem (Car.)	OF	133	512	96	143	37	3	24	88	33	94	13	13	15-9	.279	.336	.504	.840	5	.973
2000—	Birmingham (Sou.)	OF	139	532	80	137	26	5	20	98	38	117	14	12	22-7	.258	.321	.438	.759	8	.975
2001—	Charlotte (Int'l)	OF	82	329	54	97	28	0	16	48	21	47	9	9	8-2	.295	.353	.526	.879	6	.966
—	Chicago (A.L.)	OF	63	123	21	36	5	0	4	20	15	24	2	5	5-1	.293	.385	.431	.816	1	.991
2002—	Chicago (A.L.)	OF	126	302	41	78	16	2	7	29	12	54	6	8	0-1	.258	.298	.394	.692	4	.983
2003—	Charlotte (Int'l)	OF	32	120	15	29	9	0	3	13	11	12	2	3	0-0	.242	.316	.392	.707	5	.950
—	Chicago (A.L.)	OF-DH	93	157	22	45	8	0	6	24	7	21	3	1	0-0	.287	.327	.452	.780	5	1.000
2004—	Chicago (A.L.)	OF	140	487	94	151	38	2	24	69	30	91	10	5	17-5	.310	.361	.544	.905	8	.975
2005—	Chicago (A.L.)	OF	157	578	77	156	30	5	13	69	32	116	21	17	16-5	.270	.329	.407	.736	3	.992
2006—	Philadelphia (N.L.)	OF	109	405	59	106	24	3	12	47	18	76	18	13	10-4	.262	.321	.425	.745	5	.981
	American League totals (5 years)		579	1647	255	466	97	9	54	211	96	310	44	33	38-12	.283	.337	.451	.788	16	.986
	National League totals (1 year)		109	405	59	106	24	3	12	47	18	76	18	13	10-4	.262	.321	.425	.745	5	.981
	Major League totals (6 years)		688	2052	314	572	121	12	66	258	114	386	62	46	48-16	.279	.334	.446	.780	21	.985

DIVISION SERIES RECORD

Year	Team (League)	Pos.	G	AB	R	H	2B	3B	HR	RBI	BB	SO	HBP	GDP	SB-CS	Avg.	OBP	SLG	OPS	E	Avg.
2005—	Chicago (A.L.)	OF	3	10	3	4	2	0	0	2	1	1	0	2	1-0	.400	.455	.600	1.055	0	1.000

CHAMPIONSHIP SERIES RECORD

Year	Team (League)	Pos.	G	AB	R	H	2B	3B	HR	RBI	BB	SO	HBP	GDP	SB-CS	Avg.	OBP	SLG	OPS	E	Avg.
2005—	Chicago (A.L.)	OF	5	18	3	3	3	0	0	1	1	2	1	1	0-0	.167	.238	.333	.571	0	1.000

WORLD SERIES RECORD

Year	Team (League)	Pos.	G	AB	R	H	2B	3B	HR	RBI	BB	SO	HBP	GDP	SB-CS	Avg.	OBP	SLG	OPS	E	Avg.
2005—	Chicago (A.L.)	OF	4	17	2	5	1	0	0	0	2	6	0	0	0-0	.294	.368	.353	.721	0	1.000

2006 LEFTY-RIGHTY SPLITS

vs.	Avg.	AB	H	2B	3B	HR	RBI	BB	SO	OBP	Slg.	vs.	Avg.	AB	H	2B	3B	HR	RBI	BB	SO	OBP	Slg.
L	.222	99	22	7	0	5	16	9	18	.304	.444	R	.275	306	84	17	3	7	31	9	58	.326	.418

RUIZ, CARLOS — C

PERSONAL: Born January 22, 1979, in David, Panama. ... 5-10/180. ... Bats right, throws right. ... Full name: Carlos Joaquin Ruiz. **TRANSACTIONS/CAREER NOTES:** Signed as a non-drafted free agent by Philadelphia Phillies organization (December 4, 1998).

2006 GAMES PLAYED BY POSITION (MLB): C—24.

Year	Team (League)	Pos.	G	AB	R	H	2B	3B	HR	RBI	BB	SO	HBP	GDP	SB-CS	Avg.	OBP	SLG	OPS	E	Avg.
1999—	Dom. Phillies (DSL)		60	226	39	69	15	5	4	35	9	11	8	9	3-7	.305	.351	.469	.820	...	...
2000—	GC Phillies (GCL)		38	130	11	36	7	1	1	22	9	9	2	5	3-0	.277	.329	.369	.698	...	...
2001—	Lakewood (S. Atl.)		73	249	21	65	14	3	4	32	10	27	1	5	5-4	.261	.290	.390	.680	...	...
2002—	Clearwater (FSL)		92	342	35	73	18	3	5	32	18	30	6	16	3-1	.213	.264	.327	.591	...	...
2003—	Clearwater (FSL)		15	54	5	17	0	0	2	9	2	5	0	5	2-2	.315	.339	.426	.765	...	...
—	Reading (East.)		52	169	22	45	6	0	2	16	12	15	3	10	1-1	.266	.321	.337	.658	...	...
2004—	Reading (East.)		101	349	45	99	15	2	17	50	22	37	8	15	8-4	.284	.338	.484	.822	...	...
2005—	Scran./W.B. (I.L.)	C-DH-1B	100	347	50	104	25	9	4	40	30	48	3	14	4-5	.300	.354	.458	.812	4	.991
2006—	Scran./W.B. (I.L.)		100	368	56	113	25	0	16	69	42	56	9	13	4-3	.307	.389	.505	.894	3	.995
—	Philadelphia (N.L.)	C	27	69	5	18	1	1	1	10	5	8	1	3	0-0	.261	.316	.435	.751	3	.981
	Major League totals (1 year)		27	69	5	18	1	1	1	10	5	8	1	3	0-0	.261	.316	.435	.751	3	.981

2006 LEFTY-RIGHTY SPLITS

vs.	Avg.	AB	H	2B	3B	HR	RBI	BB	SO	OBP	Slg.	vs.	Avg.	AB	H	2B	3B	HR	RBI	BB	SO	OBP	Slg.
L	.263	19	5	1	1	1	3	2	.364	.526		R	.260	50	13	1	0	2	9	2	6	.296	.400

RUPE, JOSH — P

PERSONAL: Born August 18, 1982, in Portsmouth, Va. ... 6-2/200. ... Throws right, bats right. ... Full name: Joshua Matthew Rupe. ... Junior college: Louisburg (NC). **TRANSACTIONS/CAREER NOTES:** Selected by Chicago White Sox organization in third round of 2002 free-agent draft. ... Traded by White Sox with OF Anthony Webster and P Frank Francisco to Texas Rangers (July 24, 2003); completed deal in which Rangers sent OF Carl Everett and cash to White Sox for three players to be named (July 1, 2003). ... On disabled list (March 31-June 29, 2006); included rehabilitation assignment to Frisco. **CAREER HITTING:** 0-for-0 (.000), 0 R, 0 2B, 0 3B, 0 HR, 0 RBI.

Year	Team (League)	W	L	Pct.	ERA	WHIP	G	GS	CG	ShO	Hld.	Sv.-Opp.	IP	H	R	ER	HR	BB-IBB	SO	Avg.
2002—	Bristol (Appal.)	3	3	.500	5.26	1.59	17	2	0	0	...	0-	37.2	38	23	22	4	22-1	40	.260
2003—	Kannapolis (S. Atl.)	5	5	.500	3.02	1.31	26	7	2	0	...	6-	65.2	50	27	22	0	36-2	69	.212
—	Clinton (Midw.)	4	1	.800	3.90	1.30	6	5	0	0	...	0-	27.2	29	14	12	1	7-0	23	.266
2004—	Stockton (Calif.)	2	0	1.000	0.98	0.87	4	3	0	0	...	0-	18.1	12	4	2	0	4-0	14	.182
—	Spokane (N'west)	2	0	1.000	1.50	0.94	4	3	0	0	...	0-	18.0	14	3	3	1	3-0	19	.209
—	Frisco (Texas)	2	2	.500	4.38	1.54	7	6	0	0	...	0-	37.0	41	23	18	5	16-1	16	.281
2005—	Frisco (Texas)	4	3	.571	3.74	1.38	11	10	0	0	...	0-0	65.0	64	29	27	7	26-0	55	.261
—	Oklahoma (PCL)	6	7	.462	6.25	1.64	17	17	0	0	...	0-0	93.2	116	75	65	12	38-1	62	.306
—	Texas (A.L.)	1	0	1.000	1.96	1.14	4	1	0	0	...	0-0	9.2	7	4	3	0	4-0	6	.219
2006—	Frisco (Texas)	0	0	...	10.50	1.83	6	0	0	0	1	0-0	6.0	7	7	7	2	4-0	4	.280
—	Oklahoma (PCL)	1	1	.500	3.38	1.43	12	0	0	0	1	2-2	13.1	13	6	5	0	6-0	4	.271
—	Texas (A.L.)	0	1	.000	3.41	1.45	16	0	0	0	1	0-1	29.0	33	11	11	2	9-0	14	.287
	Major League totals (2 years)	1	1	.500	3.26	1.37	20	1	0	0	1	0-1	38.2	40	15	14	2	13-0	20	.272

2006 LEFTY-RIGHTY SPLITS

vs.	Avg.	AB	H	2B	3B	HR	RBI	BB	SO	OBP	Slg.	vs.	Avg.	AB	H	2B	3B	HR	RBI	BB	SO	OBP	Slg.
L	.225	40	9	1	0	1	7	4	6	.311	.325	R	.320	75	24	3	0	1	8	5	8	.363	.400

RUSCH, GLENDON   P

PERSONAL: Born November 7, 1974, in Seattle. ... 6-1/220. ... Throws left, bats left. ... Full name: Glendon James Rusch. ... Name pronounced: RUSH. ... High school: Shorecrest (Seattle). **TRANSACTIONS/CAREER NOTES:** Selected by Kansas City Royals organization in 17th round of 1993 free-agent draft. ... On disabled list (June 16-July 1, 1997); included rehabilitation assignment to Omaha. ... On disabled list (August 9-September 4, 1998); included rehabilitation assignment to Omaha. ... Traded by Royals to New York Mets for P Dan Murray (September 14, 1999). ... Traded by Mets with IF Lenny Harris to Milwaukee Brewers as part of three-team deal in which Brewers acquired OF Alex Ochoa from Colorado Rockies, Mets acquired P Jeff D'Amico, OF Jeromy Burnitz, IF Lou Collier, OF/1B Mark Sweeney from Brewers and 1B/OF Ross Gload and P Craig House from Rockies and Rockies acquired 1B/3B Todd Zeile, OF Benny Agbayani and cash from Mets (January 21, 2002). ... Signed as a free agent by Texas Rangers organization (January 21, 2004). ... Signed as a free agent by Chicago Cubs organization (April 1, 2004). ... On disabled list (June 18-July 3, 2006); included rehabilitation assignment to Iowa. ... On disabled list (August 1-21, 2006). **MISCELLANEOUS NOTES:** Had two sacrifice hits and struck out in three appearances as pinch hitter (2002). ... Singled and drove in a run in only appearance as pinch hitter (2003). ... Made an out in only appearance as pinch hitter (2004).

CAREER HITTING: 47-for-305 (.154), 16 R, 4 2B, 0 3B, 3 HR, 19 RBI.

Year Team (League)	W	L	Pct.	ERA	WHIP	G	GS	CG	ShO	Hld.	Sv.-Opp.	IP	H	R	ER	HR	BB-IBB	SO	Avg.
1993— GC Royals (GCL)	4	2	.667	1.60	0.87	11	10	0	0	...	0-...	62.0	43	14	11	0	11-0	48	.197
— Rockford (Midwest)	0	1	.000	3.38	2.13	2	2	0	0	...	0-...	8.0	10	6	3	0	7-0	8	.313
1994— Rockford (Midwest)	8	5	.615	4.66	1.27	28	17	1	1	...	1-...	114.0	111	61	59	5	34-2	122	.256
1995— Wilmington (Caro.)	14	6	.700	1.74	0.87	26	26	1	1	...	0-...	165.2	110	41	32	5	34-3	147	.188
1996— Omaha (A.A.)	11	9	.550	3.98	1.28	28	28	1	0	...	0-...	169.2	177	88	75	15	40-3	117	.267
1997— Kansas City (A.L.)	6	9	.400	5.50	1.51	30	27	1	0	0	0-0	170.1	206	111	104	28	52-0	116	.301
— Omaha (A.A.)	0	1	.000	4.50	1.33	1	1	0	0	...	0-...	6.0	7	3	3	3	1-0	2	.292
1998— Kansas City (A.L.)	6	15	.286	5.88	1.56	29	24	1	1	0	1-1	154.2	191	104	101	22	50-0	94	.304
— Omaha (PCL)	1	1	.500	7.98	1.77	3	3	0	0	...	0-...	14.2	20	18	13	4	6-0	14	.317
1999— Omaha (PCL)	4	7	.364	4.42	1.54	20	20	1	0	...	0-...	114.0	143	68	56	10	33-0	102	.307
— GC Royals (GCL)	0	0	...	1.50	1.00	2	2	0	0	...	0-...	6.0	3	1	1	0	3-0	9	.136
— Kansas City (A.L.)	0	1	.000	15.75	2.50	3	0	0	0	0	0-0	4.0	7	7	7	1	3-0	4	.368
— New York (N.L.)	1	0	.000	0.00	1.00	1	0	0	0	0	0-0	1.0	1	0	0	0	0-0	0	.333
2000— New York (N.L.)	11	11	.500	4.01	1.26	31	30	2	0	0	0-0	190.2	196	91	85	18	44-2	157	.267
2001— New York (N.L.)	8	12	.400	4.63	1.45	33	33	1	0	0	0-0	179.0	216	101	92	23	43-2	156	.301
2002— Milwaukee (N.L.)	10	•16	.385	4.70	1.44	34	34	4	1	0	0-0	210.2	227	118	110	30	76-1	140	.279
2003— Indianapolis (Int'l)	1	1	.500	3.86	1.00	4	3	1	0	...	0-...	21.0	17	9	9	4	4-0	20	.218
— Milwaukee (N.L.)	1	12	.077	6.42	1.75	32	19	1	0	7	1-1	123.1	171	93	88	11	45-3	93	.331
2004— Iowa (PCL)	2	0	1.000	1.90	1.00	4	4	0	0	...	0-...	19.0	18	6	4	0	1-0	16	.257
— Chicago (N.L.)	6	2	.750	3.47	1.23	32	16	0	0	4	2-2	129.2	127	54	50	10	33-1	90	.256
2005— Chicago (N.L.)	9	8	.529	4.52	1.57	46	16	1	1	3	0-1	145.1	175	79	73	14	53-8	111	.302
2006— Iowa (PCL)	0	0	...	2.25	0.50	1	1	0	0	...	0-...	4.0	2	1	1	0	0-0	2	.154
— Chicago (N.L.)	3	8	.273	7.46	1.79	25	9	0	0	0	0-0	66.1	86	57	55	21	33-2	59	.320
American League totals (3 years)	12	25	.324	5.80	1.55	62	51	2	1	0	1-1	329.0	404	222	212	51	105-0	214	.303
National League totals (8 years)	48	69	.410	4.76	1.46	234	160	9	2	13	3-4	1046.0	1199	593	553	127	327-19	806	.290
Major League totals (10 years)	60	94	.390	5.01	1.48	296	211	11	3	13	4-5	1375.0	1603	815	765	178	432-19	1020	.293

DIVISION SERIES RECORD

Year Team (League)	W	L	Pct.	ERA	WHIP	G	GS	CG	ShO	Hld.	Sv.-Opp.	IP	H	R	ER	HR	BB-IBB	SO	Avg.
2000— New York (N.L.)	0	0	...	0.00	0.00	1	0	0	0	0	0-0	0.2	0	0	0	0	0-0	2	.000

CHAMPIONSHIP SERIES RECORD

Year Team (League)	W	L	Pct.	ERA	WHIP	G	GS	CG	ShO	Hld.	Sv.-Opp.	IP	H	R	ER	HR	BB-IBB	SO	Avg.
2000— New York (N.L.)	1	0	1.000	0.00	0.82	2	0	0	0	0	0-0	3.2	3	0	0	0	0-0	3	.250

WORLD SERIES RECORD

Year Team (League)	W	L	Pct.	ERA	WHIP	G	GS	CG	ShO	Hld.	Sv.-Opp.	IP	H	R	ER	HR	BB-IBB	SO	Avg.
2000— New York (N.L.)	0	0	...	2.25	2.00	3	0	0	0	0	0-0	4.0	6	1	1	0	2-1	2	.353

2006 LEFTY-RIGHTY SPLITS

vs.	Avg.	AB	H	2B	3B	HR	RBI	BB	SO	OBP	Slg.	vs.	Avg.	AB	H	2B	3B	HR	RBI	BB	SO	OBP	Slg.
L	.348	69	24	6	1	6	16	5	14	.392	.725	R	.310	200	62	11	0	15	36	28	45	.396	.590

RYAN, B.J.   P

PERSONAL: Born December 28, 1975, in Bossier City, La. ... 6-6/249. ... Throws left, bats left. ... Full name: Robert Victor Ryan. ... High school: Airline (Bossier City, La.). ... College: Southwestern Louisiana. **TRANSACTIONS/CAREER NOTES:** Selected by Cincinnati Reds organization in 17th round of 1998 free-agent draft. ... Traded by Reds with P Jacobo Sequea to Baltimore Orioles for P Juan Guzman (July 31, 1999). ... Signed as a free agent by Toronto Blue Jays (November 28, 2005).

CAREER HITTING: 0-for-2 (.000), 0 R, 0 2B, 0 3B, 0 HR, 0 RBI.

Year Team (League)	W	L	Pct.	ERA	WHIP	G	GS	CG	ShO	Hld.	Sv.-Opp.	IP	H	R	ER	HR	BB-IBB	SO	Avg.
1998— Billings (Pion.)	2	1	.667	1.93	1.07	14	0	0	0	...	4-...	18.2	15	4	4	0	5-0	25	.211
— Char., W.Va. (SAL)	0	0	...	2.08	0.46	3	0	0	0	...	2-...	4.1	1	1	1	0	1-0	5	.077
— Chattanooga (Sou.)	1	0	1.000	2.20	1.16	16	0	0	0	...	4-...	16.1	13	4	4	0	6-0	21	.220
1999— Chattanooga (Sou.)	2	1	.667	2.59	1.20	35	0	0	0	...	6-...	41.2	33	13	12	1	17-0	46	.217
— Indianapolis (Int'l)	1	0	1.000	4.00	1.33	11	0	0	0	...	0-...	9.0	9	4	4	0	3-1	12	.265
— Cincinnati (N.L.)	0	0	...	4.50	2.50	1	0	0	0	...	1-...	2.0	4	1	1	0	1-0	1	.500
— Rochester (Int'l)	0	0	...	2.51	0.84	11	0	0	0	...	1-...	14.1	8	4	4	2	4-1	20	.160
— Baltimore (A.L.)	1	0	1.000	2.95	1.15	13	0	0	0	...	0-0	18.1	9	6	6	0	12-1	28	.150
2000— Baltimore (A.L.)	2	3	.400	5.91	1.57	42	0	0	0	7	0-3	42.2	36	29	28	7	31-1	41	.225
— Rochester (Int'l)	0	1	.000	4.74	1.30	14	4	0	0	...	0-...	24.2	23	13	13	4	9-0	28	.247
2001— Baltimore (A.L.)	2	4	.333	4.25	1.45	61	0	0	0	14	2-4	53.0	47	31	25	6	30-4	54	.233
2002— Baltimore (A.L.)	2	1	.667	4.68	1.46	67	0	0	0	12	1-2	57.2	51	31	30	7	33-4	56	.241
2003— Baltimore (A.L.)	4	1	.800	3.40	1.37	76	0	0	0	19	0-2	50.1	42	19	19	1	27-0	63	.227
2004— Baltimore (A.L.)	4	6	.400	2.28	1.14	76	0	0	0	21	3-7	87.0	64	24	22	4	35-9	122	.200
2005— Baltimore (A.L.)	1	4	.200	2.43	1.14	69	0	0	0	0	36-41	70.1	54	20	19	4	26-2	100	.208
2006— Toronto (A.L.)	2	2	.500	1.37	0.86	65	0	0	0	0	38-42	72.1	42	12	11	3	20-1	86	.169
American League totals (8 years)	18	21	.462	3.19	1.24	469	0	0	0	74	80-101	451.2	345	172	160	32	214-22	550	.209
National League totals (1 year)	0	0	...	4.50	2.50	1	0	0	0	0	0-0	2.0	4	1	1	0	1-0	1	.500
Major League totals (8 years)	18	21	.462	3.19	1.24	470	0	0	0	74	80-101	453.2	349	173	161	32	215-22	551	.211

ALL-STAR GAME RECORD

	W	L	Pct.	ERA	WHIP	G	GS	CG	ShO	Hld.	Sv.-Opp.	IP	H	R	ER	HR	BB-IBB	SO	Avg.
All-Star Game totals (2 years)	1	0	1.000	5.40	0.60	2	0	0	0	0	0-0	1.2	1	1	1	0	0-0	1	.167

2006 LEFTY-RIGHTY SPLITS

vs.	Avg.	AB	H	2B	3B	HR	RBI	BB	SO	OBP	Slg.	vs.	Avg.	AB	H	2B	3B	HR	RBI	BB	SO	OBP	Slg.
L	.120	50	6	0	0	0	2	3	19	.167	.120	R	.182	198	36	2	0	3	9	17	67	.247	.237

RYU, JAE KUK   P

PERSONAL: Born May 30, 1983, in Choon Chung Do, South Korea. ... 6-3/220. ... Throws right, bats right. ... Full name: Jae Kuk Ryu. **TRANSACTIONS/CAREER NOTES:** Signed as a non-drafted free agent by Chicago Cubs organization (June 1, 2001).
CAREER HITTING: 0-for-1 (.000), 0 R, 0 2B, 0 3B, 0 HR, 0 RBI.

Year Team (League)	W	L	Pct.	ERA	WHIP	G	GS	CG	ShO	Hld.	Sv.-Opp.	IP	H	R	ER	HR	BB-IBB	SO	Avg.
2001— Ariz. Cubs (Ariz.)	1	0	1.000	0.61	1.09	4	3	0	0	...	0-...	14.2	11	2	1	0	5-0	20	.196
2002— Boise (N'west)	6	1	.857	3.57	1.32	10	10	0	0	...	0-...	53.0	45	28	21	1	25-0	56	.223
— Lansing (Midw.)	1	2	.333	7.11	1.79	5	4	0	0	...	0-...	19.0	26	16	15	1	8-0	21	.333
2003— Daytona (Fla. St.)	0	1	.000	3.05	1.21	4	4	0	0	...	0-...	20.2	14	14	7	1	11-0	22	.187
— Lansing (Midw.)	6	1	.857	1.75	1.08	11	11	0	0	...	0-...	72.0	59	19	14	2	19-0	57	.227
— West Tenn (Sou.)	2	5	.286	5.43	1.52	11	11	1	0	...	0-...	58.0	63	37	35	3	25-0	45	.280
2004— Ariz. Cubs (Ariz.)	0	0	...	4.50	1.00	2	2	0	0	...	0-...	4.0	4	2	2	1	0-0	5	.250
— Boise (N'west)	0	2	.000	2.57	1.71	5	0	0	0	...	0-...	7.0	7	3	2	1	5-0	7	.250
— West Tenn (Sou.)	1	0	1.000	2.95	1.75	14	0	0	0	...	0-...	18.1	22	8	6	0	10-3	19	.286
— Iowa (PCL)	0	0	...	40.50	4.50	1	0	0	0	...	0-...	0.2	2	4	3	1	1-0	1	.500
2005— West Tenn (Sou.)	11	8	.579	3.34	1.20	27	27	0	0	1	0-0	169.2	154	67	63	12	49-0	133	.246
2006— Iowa (PCL)	8	8	.500	3.23	1.25	24	23	1	0	1	0-0	139.1	123	54	50	12	51-1	114	.237
— Chicago (N.L.)	0	1	.000	8.40	1.93	10	1	0	0	0	0-0	15.0	23	14	14	7	6-1	17	.348
Major League totals (1 year)	**0**	**1**	**.000**	**8.40**	**1.93**	**10**	**1**	**0**	**0**	**0**	**0-0**	**15.0**	**23**	**14**	**14**	**7**	**6-1**	**17**	**.348**

2006 LEFTY-RIGHTY SPLITS

vs.	Avg.	AB	H	2B	3B	HR	RBI	BB	SO	OBP	Slg.		vs.	Avg.	AB	H	2B	3B	HR	RBI	BB	SO	OBP	Slg.
L	.360	25	9	2	1	3	5	5	6	.484	.880		R	.341	41	14	2	0	4	10	1	11	.372	.683

S

SAARLOOS, KIRK   P

PERSONAL: Born May 23, 1979, in Long Beach, Calif. ... 6-0/180. ... Throws right, bats right. ... Full name: Kirk Craig Saarloos. ... Name pronounced: SAR-lohs. ... High school: Valley Christian (Cerritos, Calif.). ... College: Cal State Fullerton. **TRANSACTIONS/CAREER NOTES:** Selected by Houston Astros organization in third round of 2001 free-agent draft. ... Traded by Astros to Oakland Athletics for P Chad Harville (April 17, 2004). ... On disabled list (July 30, 2004-remainder of season). **STATISTICAL NOTES:** Pitched 1 1/3 innings, combining with Roy Oswalt (one inning), Peter Munro (2 2/3 innings), Brad Lidge (two innings), Octavio Dotel (one inning) and Billy Wagner (one inning) on 8-0 no-hitter against New York Yankees (June 11, 2003).
CAREER HITTING: 2-for-36 (.056), 0 R, 1 2B, 0 3B, 0 HR, 3 RBI.

Year Team (League)	W	L	Pct.	ERA	WHIP	G	GS	CG	ShO	Hld.	Sv.-Opp.	IP	H	R	ER	HR	BB-IBB	SO	Avg.
2001— Lexington (S. Atl.)	1	1	.500	1.17	0.82	22	0	0	0	...	11-...	30.2	18	5	4	1	7-0	40	.165
2002— Round Rock (Texas)	10	1	.909	1.40	0.83	13	13	1	1	...	0-...	83.1	48	17	13	1	21-0	82	.165
— New Orleans (PCL)	2	0	1.000	2.25	0.88	4	2	0	0	...	0-...	16.0	12	4	4	1	2-0	19	.211
— Houston (N.L.)	6	7	.462	6.01	1.49	17	17	1	1	0	0-0	85.1	100	59	57	12	27-5	54	.301
2003— New Orleans (PCL)	5	0	1.000	3.08	1.10	13	7	2	1	...	0-...	61.1	54	22	21	4	11-1	34	.242
— Houston (N.L.)	2	1	.667	4.93	1.46	36	4	0	0	4	0-0	49.1	55	31	27	4	17-3	43	.281
2004— New Orleans (PCL)	0	2	.000	15.43	2.57	2	2	0	0	...	0-...	7.0	17	15	12	4	1-0	6	.459
— Oakland (A.L.)	2	1	.667	4.44	1.60	6	5	0	0	...	0-...	24.1	27	13	12	4	12-0	10	.284
— Sacramento (PCL)	2	0	1.000	3.54	1.38	5	5	0	0	...	0-...	20.1	19	8	8	1	9-0	17	.250
2005— Oakland (A.L.)	10	9	.526	4.17	1.40	29	27	2	1	0	0-0	159.2	170	75	74	11	54-8	53	.278
2006— Oakland (A.L.)	7	7	.500	4.75	1.66	35	16	0	0	0	2-3	121.1	149	70	64	19	53-3	52	.308
American League totals (3 years)	**19**	**17**	**.528**	**4.42**	**1.52**	**70**	**48**	**2**	**1**	**0**	**2-3**	**305.1**	**346**	**158**	**150**	**34**	**119-11**	**115**	**.291**
National League totals (2 years)	**8**	**8**	**.500**	**5.61**	**1.48**	**53**	**21**	**1**	**1**	**4**	**0-0**	**134.2**	**155**	**90**	**84**	**16**	**44-8**	**97**	**.292**
Major League totals (5 years)	**27**	**25**	**.519**	**4.79**	**1.51**	**123**	**69**	**3**	**2**	**4**	**2-3**	**440.0**	**501**	**248**	**234**	**50**	**163-19**	**212**	**.292**

2006 LEFTY-RIGHTY SPLITS

vs.	Avg.	AB	H	2B	3B	HR	RBI	BB	SO	OBP	Slg.		vs.	Avg.	AB	H	2B	3B	HR	RBI	BB	SO	OBP	Slg.
L	.319	232	74	11	0	7	32	28	28	.396	.457		R	.298	252	75	17	3	12	40	25	24	.356	.532

SABATHIA, C.C.   P

PERSONAL: Born July 21, 1980, in Vallejo, Calif. ... 6-7/290. ... Throws left, bats left. ... Full name: Carsten Charles Sabathia. ... Name pronounced: sa-BATH-ee-a. ... High school: Vallejo (Calif.). **TRANSACTIONS/CAREER NOTES:** Selected by Cleveland Indians organization in first round (20th pick overall) of 1998 free-agent draft. ... On disabled list (March 25-April 16, 2005). ... On disabled list (April 4-May 2, 2006); included rehabilitation assignment to Buffalo. **HONORS:** Named A.L. Rookie Pitcher of the Year by THE SPORTING NEWS (2001). **MISCELLANEOUS NOTES:** Singled in only appearance as pinch hitter (2003).
CAREER HITTING: 9-for-34 (.265), 2 R, 1 2B, 0 3B, 1 HR, 6 RBI.

Year Team (League)	W	L	Pct.	ERA	WHIP	G	GS	CG	ShO	Hld.	Sv.-Opp.	IP	H	R	ER	HR	BB-IBB	SO	Avg.
1998— Burlington (Appal.)	1	0	1.000	4.50	1.56	5	5	0	0	...	0-...	18.0	20	14	9	1	8-0	35	.274
1999— Mahoning Valley (N.Y.-Penn.)	0	0	...	1.83	1.07	6	6	0	0	...	0-...	19.2	9	5	4	0	12-0	27	.143
— Columbus (S. Atl.)	2	0	1.000	1.08	0.78	3	3	0	0	...	0-...	16.2	8	2	2	1	5-0	20	.140
— Kinston (Carol.)	3	3	.500	5.34	1.53	7	7	0	0	...	0-...	32.0	30	22	19	3	19-0	29	.256
2000— Kinston (Carol.)	3	2	.600	3.54	1.29	10	10	2	2	...	0-...	56.0	48	23	22	4	24-0	69	.234
— Akron (East.)	3	7	.300	3.59	1.36	17	17	0	0	...	0-...	90.1	75	41	36	6	48-0	90	.223
2001— Cleveland (A.L.)	17	5	.773	4.39	1.35	33	33	0	0	...	0-0	180.1	149	93	88	19	95-1	171	.228
2002— Cleveland (A.L.)	13	11	.542	4.37	1.36	33	33	2	0	...	0-0	210.0	198	109	102	17	88-2	149	.252
2003— Cleveland (A.L.)	13	9	.591	3.60	1.30	30	30	2	1	0	0-0	197.2	190	85	79	19	66-3	141	.255
2004— Cleveland (A.L.)	11	10	.524	4.12	1.32	30	30	1	1	0	0-0	188.0	176	90	86	20	72-3	139	.252
2005— Akron (East.)	0	1	.000	1.00	0.67	2	2	0	0	0	0-0	9.0	4	3	1	0	2-0	9	.121
— Cleveland (A.L.)	15	10	.600	4.03	1.26	31	31	1	0	0	0-0	196.2	185	92	88	19	62-1	161	.248
2006— Buffalo (Int'l)	1	0	1.000	1.80	1.40	1	1	0	0	0	0-0	5.0	6	2	1	0	1-0	5	.300
— Cleveland (A.L.)	12	11	.522	3.22	1.17	28	28	*6	•2	0	0-0	192.2	182	83	69	17	44-3	172	.247
Major League totals (6 years)	**81**	**56**	**.591**	**3.95**	**1.29**	**185**	**185**	**12**	**4**	**0**	**0-0**	**1165.1**	**1080**	**552**	**512**	**111**	**427-13**	**933**	**.247**

DIVISION SERIES RECORD

Year Team (League)	W	L	Pct.	ERA	WHIP	G	GS	CG	ShO	Hld.	Sv.-Opp.	IP	H	R	ER	HR	BB-IBB	SO	Avg.
2001— Cleveland (A.L.)	1	0	1.000	3.00	1.83	1	1	0	0	...	0-0	6.0	6	2	2	0	5-1	5	.261

ALL-STAR GAME RECORD

	W	L	Pct.	ERA	WHIP	G	GS	CG	ShO	Hld.	Sv.-Opp.	IP	H	R	ER	HR	BB-IBB	SO	Avg.
All-Star Game totals (1 year)	0	0	...	27.00	4.00	1	0	0	0	...	0-0	1.0	4	3	3	0	0-0	0	.571

2006 LEFTY-RIGHTY SPLITS

vs.	Avg.	AB	H	2B	3B	HR	RBI	BB	SO	OBP	Slg.		vs.	Avg.	AB	H	2B	3B	HR	RBI	BB	SO	OBP	Slg.
L	.271	107	29	4	1	3	13	8	35	.328	.411		R	.242	631	153	27	4	14	62	36	137	.288	.355

SADLER, BILLY   P

PERSONAL: Born September 21, 1981, in Pensacola, Fla. ... Throws right, bats right. ... Full name: William H. Sadler. ... College: LSU. **TRANSACTIONS/CAREER NOTES:** Selected by San Francisco Giants organization in sixth round of 2003 free-agent draft.

CAREER HITTING: 0-for-0 (.000), 0 R, 0 2B, 0 3B, 0 HR, 0 RBI.

Year Team (League)	W	L	Pct.	ERA	WHIP	G	GS	CG	ShO	Hld.	Sv.-Opp.	IP	H	R	ER	HR	BB-IBB	SO	Avg.
2003— Hagerstown (SAL)	0	0	...	4.80	1.87	12	0	0	0	...	1-...	15.0	15	8	8	4	13-0	10	.263
2004— San Jose (Calif.)	2	2	.500	2.38	1.22	30	3	0	0	...	0-...	56.2	29	17	15	1	40-0	66	.149
— Norwich (East.)	0	3	.000	3.86	1.32	17	0	0	0	...	0-...	30.1	22	16	13	3	18-0	24	.195
2005— Norwich (East.)	6	5	.545	3.31	1.15	47	0	0	0	7	5-10	84.1	64	34	31	4	33-0	81	.208
2006— Fresno (PCL)	2	0	1.000	1.80	0.70	7	0	0	0	1	1-1	10.0	5	2	2	1	2-0	12	.156
— Connecticut (East.)	4	3	.571	2.56	1.14	44	0	0	0	1	20-23	45.2	23	14	13	1	29-2	67	.146
— San Francisco (N.L.)	0	0	...	6.75	1.75	5	0	0	0	0	0-0	4.0	5	3	3	2	2-0	6	.294
Major League totals (1 year)	0	0	...	6.75	1.75	5	0	0	0	0	0-0	4.0	5	3	3	2	2-0	6	.294

2006 LEFTY-RIGHTY SPLITS

vs.	Avg.	AB	H	2B	3B	HR	RBI	BB	SO	OBP	Slg.	vs.	Avg.	AB	H	2B	3B	HR	RBI	BB	SO	OBP	Slg.
L	.250	8	2	0	0	1	1	1	3	.333	.625	R	.333	9	3	2	0	1	4	1	3	.455	.889

SAENZ, OLMEDO   1B/3B

PERSONAL: Born October 8, 1970, in Chitre Herrera, Panama. ... 5-11/221. ... Bats right, throws right. ... Full name: Olmedo Sanchez Saenz. ... Name pronounced: SIGNS. **TRANSACTIONS/CAREER NOTES:** Signed as a non-drafted free agent by Chicago White Sox organization (May 11, 1990). ... Signed as a free agent by Oakland Athletics (November 13, 1998). ... On disabled list (July 26-August 16, 1999); included rehabilitation assignment to Vancouver. ... On disabled list (August 1-September 19, 2000); included rehabilitation assignment to Sacramento. ... Signed as a free agent by Los Angeles Dodgers organization (December 19, 2003). **STATISTICAL NOTES:** Career major league grand slams: 1.

2006 GAMES PLAYED BY POSITION (MLB): 1B—30, 3B—16, DH—3.

Year Team (League)	Pos.	G	AB	R	H	2B	3B	HR	RBI	BB	SO	HBP	GDP	SB-CS	Avg.	OBP	SLG	OPS	E	Avg.
1991— South Bend (Mid.)	3B	56	192	23	47	10	1	2	22	21	48	5	3	5-3	.245	.332	.339	.670	12	.890
— Sarasota (Fla. St.)	3B	5	19	1	2	0	1	0	2	2	0	0	1	0-1	.105	.190	.211	.401	3	.842
1992— South Bend (Mid.)	1B-3B	132	493	66	121	26	4	7	59	36	52	11	16	16-13	.245	.309	.357	.666	48	.895
1993— Sarasota (Fla. St.)	3B	33	121	13	31	9	4	0	27	9	18	2	1	3-1	.256	.316	.397	.712	5	.933
— South Bend (Mid.)	3B	13	50	3	18	4	1	0	7	7	7	0	1	1-1	.360	.439	.480	.919	4	.913
— Birmingham (Sou.)	3B	49	173	30	60	17	2	6	29	20	21	5	7	2-1	.347	.427	.572	.999	14	.899
1994— Nashville (A.A.)	3B-DH	107	383	48	100	27	2	12	59	30	57	9	5	3-2	.261	.326	.436	.762	22	.917
— Chicago (A.L.)	3B	5	14	2	2	0	0	0	0	0	5	0	0	0-0	.143	.143	.286	.429	0	1.000
1995— Nashville (A.A.)	3B	111	415	60	126	26	1	13	74	45	60	12	11	0-2	.304	.385	.465	.850	24	.939
1996— Nashville (A.A.)	3B-DH	134	476	86	124	29	1	18	63	53	80	13	5	4-2	.261	.350	.439	.789	22	.939
1997— GC Whi. Sox (GCL)	DH	2	1	0	1	0	0	0	0	0	1	0	0	0-0	1.000	1.000	2.000	3.000	...	...
1998— Calgary (PCL)	3B	124	466	89	146	29	0	29	102	45	49	22	16	3-3	.313	.394	.562	.957	21	.937
1999— Oakland (A.L.)	3B-1B-DH	97	255	41	70	18	0	11	41	22	47	15	6	1-1	.275	.363	.475	.837	8	.971
— Vancouver (PCL)	3B	2	5	1	3	1	0	0	2	0	0	0	0	0-0	.600	.571	.800	1.371	0	1.000
2000— Oakland (A.L.)	DH-3B-1B	76	214	40	67	12	2	9	33	25	40	7	6	1-1	.313	.401	.514	.915	4	.977
— Sacramento (PCL)	DH	1	4	1	2	0	0	0	1	0	0	0	0	0-0	.500	.500	.500	1.000	...	...
2001— Oakland (A.L.)	DH-1B-3B	106	305	33	67	21	1	9	32	19	64	13	9	0-1	.220	.291	.384	.675	5	.979
2002— Oakland (A.L.)	1B-3B-DH	68	156	15	43	10	1	6	18	13	31	7	2	1-1	.276	.354	.468	.822	5	.980
2003— Ariz. A's (Ariz.)	1B-3B-DH	13	45	13	15	2	0	2	8	8	6	2	1	1-0	.333	.455	.511	.966	1	.974
— Modesto (California)	DH	1	4	0	0	0	0	0	1	0	1	0	0	0-0	.000	.000	.000	.000	...	...
2004— Los Angeles (N.L.)	1B-DH-3B	77	111	17	31	1	0	8	22	12	33	2	4	0-0	.279	.352	.505	.856	2	.986
2005— Los Angeles (N.L.)	1B-3B-DH	109	319	30	84	24	0	15	63	27	63	3	12	0-1	.263	.325	.480	.804	3	.994
2006— Los Angeles (N.L.)	1B-3B-DH	103	179	30	53	15	0	11	48	14	47	7	4	0-0	.296	.363	.564	.927	4	.981
American League totals (5 years)		352	944	131	249	61	5	35	124	79	187	42	24	3-3	.264	.345	.450	.795	22	.977
National League totals (3 years)		289	609	86	168	40	0	34	133	53	143	12	20	0-1	.276	.341	.509	.850	9	.990
Major League totals (8 years)		641	1553	217	417	101	5	69	257	132	330	54	44	3-4	.269	.343	.473	.816	31	.983

DIVISION SERIES RECORD

Year Team (League)	Pos.	G	AB	R	H	2B	3B	HR	RBI	BB	SO	HBP	GDP	SB-CS	Avg.	OBP	SLG	OPS	E	Avg.
2000— Oakland (A.L.)	DH	4	13	1	3	0	1	0	4	0	2	1	1	0-0	.231	.267	.462	.728	...	...
2001— Oakland (A.L.)	DH	3	4	0	0	0	0	0	0	1	0	0	0	0-0	.000	.000	.000	.000	...	...
2002— Oakland (A.L.)	1B	1	0	0	0	0	0	0	0	1	0	0	0	0-0	...	1.000	...	1.000	0	1.000
2006— Los Angeles (N.L.)		2	2	0	0	0	0	0	0	1	2	0	0	0-0	.000	.000	.000	.000	0	...
Division series totals (4 years)		10	19	1	3	0	1	0	4	1	4	1	1	0-0	.158	.227	.316	.543	0	1.000

2006 LEFTY-RIGHTY SPLITS

vs.	Avg.	AB	H	2B	3B	HR	RBI	BB	SO	OBP	Slg.	vs.	Avg.	AB	H	2B	3B	HR	RBI	BB	SO	OBP	Slg.
L	.397	58	23	5	0	5	22	8	16	.457	.741	R	.248	121	30	10	0	6	26	6	31	.313	.479

SAITO, TAKASHI   P

PERSONAL: Born February 14, 1970, in Miyagi, Japan. ... 6-1/202. ... Throws right, bats left. ... Full name: Takashi Saito. ... College: Tohoku Fukushi Univ. (Japan). **TRANSACTIONS/CAREER NOTES:** Signed as non-drafted free agent by Los Angeles Dodgers (February 7, 2006).

CAREER HITTING: 0-for-0 (.000), 0 R, 0 2B, 0 3B, 0 HR, 0 RBI.

Year Team (League)	W	L	Pct.	ERA	WHIP	G	GS	CG	ShO	Hld.	Sv.-Opp.	IP	H	R	ER	HR	BB-IBB	SO	Avg.
2006— Los Angeles (N.L.)	6	2	.750	2.07	0.91	72	0	0	0	7	24-26	78.1	48	19	18	3	23-3	107	.177
Major League totals (1 year)	6	2	.750	2.07	0.91	72	0	0	0	7	24-26	78.1	48	19	18	3	23-3	107	.177

DIVISION SERIES RECORD

Year Team (League)	W	L	Pct.	ERA	WHIP	G	GS	CG	ShO	Hld.	Sv.-Opp.	IP	H	R	ER	HR	BB-IBB	SO	Avg.
2006— Los Angeles (N.L.)	0	0	...	0.00	0.00	2	0	0	0	0	0-0	2.2	0	0	0	0	0-0	4	.000

2006 LEFTY-RIGHTY SPLITS

vs.	Avg.	AB	H	2B	3B	HR	RBI	BB	SO	OBP	Slg.	vs.	Avg.	AB	H	2B	3B	HR	RBI	BB	SO	OBP	Slg.
L	.229	131	30	9	1	2	13	10	42	.285	.336	R	.129	140	18	3	0	2	12	13	65	.205	.193

SALAS, JUAN   P

PERSONAL: Born November 7, 1978, in Santo Domingo, Dominican Republic. ... Throws right, bats right. ... Full name: Juan Salas. **TRANSACTIONS/CAREER NOTES:** Signed as a non-drafted free agent by Tampa Bay Devil Rays organization (July 8, 1998). ... Played six seasons as a third baseman/outfielder in Devil Rays system (1999-2004).

CAREER HITTING: 0-for-0 (.000), 0 R, 0 2B, 0 3B, 0 HR, 0 RBI.

Year	Team (League)	W	L	Pct.	ERA	WHIP	G	GS	CG	ShO	Hld.	Sv-Opp.	IP	H	R	ER	HR	BB-IBB	SO	Avg.
2004— Princeton (Appal.)		1	0	1.000	4.82	1.71	8	0	0	0	...	0-...	9.1	10	7	5	2	6-1	6	.263
2005— Visalia (Calif.)		2	1	.667	3.52	1.25	25	0	0	0	3	1-3	38.1	30	19	15	6	18-0	47	.216
— Montgom. (Sou.)		1	0	1.000	3.68	1.68	15	0	0	0	2	0-0	22.0	25	12	9	2	12-0	18	.281
2006— Montgom. (Sou.)		3	0	1.000	0.00	0.78	23	0	0	0	14-17		34.2	13	4	0	0	14-0	52	.110
— Durham (Int'l)		1	1	.500	1.57	0.91	27	0	0	0	2	3-3	28.2	15	5	5	3	11-0	33	.149
— Tampa Bay (A.L.)		0	0	...	5.40	1.60	8	0	0	0	1	0-1	10.0	13	7	6	1	3-0	8	.295
Major League totals (1 year)		0	0	...	5.40	1.60	8	0	0	0	1	0-1	10.0	13	7	6	1	3-0	8	.295

2006 LEFTY-RIGHTY SPLITS

vs.	Avg.	AB	H	2B	3B	HR	RBI	BB	SO	OBP	Slg.	vs.	Avg.	AB	H	2B	3B	HR	RBI	BB	SO	OBP	Slg.
L	.200	25	5	1	1	0	2	2	6	.259	.320	R	.421	19	8	4	0	1	5	1	2	.429	.789

SALAZAR, JEFF — OF

PERSONAL: Born November 24, 1980, in Oklahoma City, Okla. .., 6-0/190. ... Bats left, throws left. ... Full name: Jeffrey Dewan Salazar. ... College: Oklahoma State. **TRANS-ACTIONS/CAREER NOTES:** Selected by Colorado Rockies organization in eighth round of 2002 free-agent draft.

2006 GAMES PLAYED BY POSITION (MLB): OF—14.

Year	Team (League)	Pos.	G	AB	R	H	2B	3B	HR	RBI	BB	SO	HBP	GDP	SB-CS	Avg.	OBP	SLG	OPS	E	Avg.
2002— Tri-City (N'west)			72	268	38	63	5	4	4	21	47	43	2	2	10-6	.235	.351	.328	.679	...	...
2003— Asheville (S. Atl.)			129	486	109	138	23	4	29	98	77	74	7	5	28-14	.284	.387	.523	.914	...	...
— Visalia (Calif.)			1	5	1	0	0	0	0	0	0	0	0	0	0-0	.000	.000	.000	.000	...	...
2004— Visalia (Calif.)			75	314	79	109	18	9	13	44	38	33	2	4	17-2	.347	.419	.586	1.005	...	...
— Tulsa (Texas)			58	224	39	50	13	2	1	17	35	31	2	1	10-3	.223	.331	.313	.644	...	...
2005— Tulsa (Texas)	OF-DH		69	266	47	74	13	2	6	35	44	49	2	1	12-8	.278	.381	.410	.791	2	.994
— Colo. Springs (PCL)	OF-DH		59	236	42	62	17	3	6	26	32	58	0	1	5-2	.263	.349	.436	.786	0	1.000
2006— Colo. Springs (PCL)			85	328	62	87	14	7	9	39	46	64	2	0	12-5	.265	.357	.433	.790	5	.973
— Colorado (N.L.)	OF		19	53	13	15	4	0	1	8	11	16	1	0	2-0	.283	.409	.415	.824	0	1.000
Major League totals (1 year)			19	53	13	15	4	0	1	8	11	16	1	0	2-0	.283	.409	.415	.824	0	1.000

2006 LEFTY-RIGHTY SPLITS

vs.	Avg.	AB	H	2B	3B	HR	RBI	BB	SO	OBP	Slg.	vs.	Avg.	AB	H	2B	3B	HR	RBI	BB	SO	OBP	Slg.
L	.000	2	0	0	0	0	0	0	1	.000	.000	R	.294	51	15	4	0	1	8	11	15	.422	.431

SALMON, TIM — DH/OF

PERSONAL: Born August 24, 1968, in Long Beach, Calif. ... 6-3/235. ... Bats right, throws right. ... Full name: Timothy James Salmon. ... Name pronounced: SAM-en. ... High school: Greenway (Phoenix). ... College: Grand Canyon (Ariz.). ... Brother of Mike Salmon, safety with San Francisco 49ers (1997). **TRANSACTIONS/CAREER NOTES:** Selected by Atlanta Braves organization in 18th round of June 1986 free-agent draft; did not sign. ... Selected by California Angels organization in third round of 1989 free-agent draft. ... On disabled list (July 18-August 3, 1994). ... Angels franchise renamed Anaheim Angels for 1997 season. ... On disabled list (April 23-May 9, 1998). ... On disabled list (May 4-July 17, 1999); included rehabilitation assignment to Lake Elsinore. ... On disabled list (July 1-19, 2001); included rehabilitation assignment to Rancho Cucamonga. ... On disabled list (August 14-September 1, 2002). ... On disabled list (April 30-June 9 and August 24, 2004-remainder of season); included rehabilitation assignments to Rancho Cucamonga. ... Angels franchise renamed Los Angeles Angels of Anaheim for 2005 season. ... On disabled list (March 28, 2005-entire season). **HONORS:** Named Minor League Player of the Year by THE SPORTING NEWS (1992). ... Named A.L. Rookie Player of the Year by THE SPORTING NEWS (1993). ... Named outfielder on THE SPORTING NEWS A.L. All-Star team (1995 and 1997). ... Named A.L. Rookie of the Year by Baseball Writers' Association of America (1993). ... Named outfielder on A.L. Silver Slugger team (1995). **STATISTICAL NOTES:** Career major league grand slams: 6.

2006 GAMES PLAYED BY POSITION (MLB): DH—54, OF—4.

Year	Team (League)	Pos.	G	AB	R	H	2B	3B	HR	RBI	BB	SO	HBP	GDP	SB-CS	Avg.	OBP	SLG	OPS	E	Avg.
1989— Bend (N'west)	OF	55	196	37	48	6	5	6	31	33	60	6	2	2-4	.245	.367	.418	.785	*4	.958
1990— Palm Springs (Calif.)	OF	36	118	19	34	6	0	2	21	21	44	4	1	11-1	.288	.413	.390	.802	1	.985
— Midland (Texas)	OF	27	97	17	26	3	1	3	16	18	38	1	1	1-0	.268	.385	.412	.797	3	.950
1991— Midland (Texas)	OF	131	465	100	114	26	4	23	94	89	166	6	6	12-6	.245	.372	.467	.839	10	.966
1992— Edmonton (PCL)	OF	118	409	101	142	38	4	29	105	91	103	6	9	9-7	.347	.469	.672	1.141	3	.988
— California (A.L.)	OF	23	79	8	14	1	0	2	6	11	23	1	1	1-1	.177	.283	.266	.548	2	.953
1993— California (A.L.)	OF-DH	142	515	93	146	35	1	31	95	82	135	5	6	5-6	.284	.382	.536	.918	7	.980
1994— California (A.L.)	OF	100	373	67	107	18	2	23	70	54	102	5	3	1-3	.287	.382	.531	.912	8	.966
1995— California (A.L.)	OF-DH	143	537	111	177	34	3	34	105	91	111	6	9	5-5	.330	.429	.594	1.024	4	.988
1996— California (A.L.)	OF-DH	156	581	90	166	27	4	30	98	93	125	4	8	4-2	.286	.386	.501	.887	8	.975
1997— Anaheim (A.L.)	OF-DH	157	582	95	172	28	1	33	129	95	142	7	7	9-12	.296	.394	.517	.911	11	.971
1998— Anaheim (A.L.)	DH-OF	136	463	84	139	28	1	26	88	90	100	3	4	0-1	.300	.410	.533	.943	2	.959
1999— Anaheim (A.L.)	OF-DH	98	353	60	94	24	2	17	69	63	82	0	1	4-1	.266	.372	.490	.862	4	.981
— Lake Elsinore (Calif.)	DH	1	5	0	3	2	0	0	2	0	1	0	0	0-0	.600	.600	1.000	1.600	...	...
2000— Anaheim (A.L.)	OF-DH	158	568	108	165	36	2	34	97	104	139	6	14	0-2	.290	.404	.540	.945	6	.979
2001— Anaheim (A.L.)	OF-DH	137	475	63	108	21	1	17	49	96	121	8	11	9-3	.227	.365	.383	.748	3	.989
— Rancho Cuca. (Calif.)	OF	2	7	1	1	1	0	0	0	1	4	0	0	0-0	.143	.250	.286	.536	1	.667
2002— Anaheim (A.L.)	OF-DH	138	483	84	138	37	1	22	88	71	102	7	6	6-3	.286	.380	.503	.883	3	.986
2003— Anaheim (A.L.)	OF-DH	148	528	78	145	35	4	19	72	77	93	10	12	3-1	.275	.374	.464	.838	6	.958
2004— Rancho Cuca. (Calif.)	DH	7	23	5	8	1	1	2	6	4	6	0	0	0-0	.348	.444	.739	1.184	0	...
— Anaheim (A.L.)	DH-OF	60	186	15	47	7	0	2	23	14	41	2	1	1-0	.253	.306	.323	.628	0	1.000
2005—							Did not play.														
2006— Los Angeles (A.L.)	DH-OF	76	211	30	56	8	2	9	27	29	44	3	6	0-2	.265	.361	.450	.811	0	1.000
Major League totals (14 years)		1672	5934	986	1674	339	24	299	1016	970	1360	67	98	48-42	.282	.385	.498	.884	64	.978

DIVISION SERIES RECORD

Year	Team (League)	Pos.	G	AB	R	H	2B	3B	HR	RBI	BB	SO	HBP	GDP	SB-CS	Avg.	OBP	SLG	OPS	E	Avg.
2002— Anaheim (A.L.)	OF	4	19	3	5	1	0	2	7	1	5	0	0	0-0	.263	.300	.632	.932	0	1.000

CHAMPIONSHIP SERIES RECORD

Year	Team (League)	Pos.	G	AB	R	H	2B	3B	HR	RBI	BB	SO	HBP	GDP	SB-CS	Avg.	OBP	SLG	OPS	E	Avg.
2002— Anaheim (A.L.)	OF	5	14	0	3	0	0	0	0	3	1	0	1	0-0	.214	.353	.214	.567	0	1.000

WORLD SERIES RECORD

Year	Team (League)	Pos.	G	AB	R	H	2B	3B	HR	RBI	BB	SO	HBP	GDP	SB-CS	Avg.	OBP	SLG	OPS	E	Avg.
2002— Anaheim (A.L.)	OF	7	26	7	9	1	0	2	5	4	7	1	0	1-0	.346	.452	.615	1.067	1	.917

2006 LEFTY-RIGHTY SPLITS

vs.	Avg.	AB	H	2B	3B	HR	RBI	BB	SO	OBP	Slg.	vs.	Avg.	AB	H	2B	3B	HR	RBI	BB	SO	OBP	Slg.
L	.298	104	31	5	1	7	15	15	19	.392	.567	R	.234	107	25	3	1	2	12	14	25	.331	.336

SAMPSON, CHRIS   P

PERSONAL: Born May 23, 1978, in Pasadena, Texas. ... Throws right, bats right. ... Full name: Christopher K. Sampson. ... College: Texas Tech. **TRANSACTIONS/CAREER NOTES:** Selected by Houston Astros organization in eighth round of 1999 free-agent draft. ... Played one season as a shortstop in Astros organization (1999).
CAREER HITTING: 0-for-5 (.000), 0 R, 0 2B, 0 3B, 0 HR, 0 RBI.

Year	Team (League)	W	L	Pct.	ERA	WHIP	G	GS	CG	ShO	Hld.	Sv.-Opp.	IP	H	R	ER	HR	BB-IBB	SO	Avg.
2003—	Salem (Carol.)	1	1	.500	5.91	1.78	9	0	0	0	...	1-...	10.2	14	8	7	0	5-2	6	.326
—Lexington (S. Atl.)		4	3	.571	1.39	0.95	22	14	0	0	...	1-...	84.0	66	17	13	2	26-0	66	.212
2004—	Salem (Carol.)	7	11	.389	3.80	1.29	27	27	2	2	...	0-...	151.2	170	72	64	8	26-0	101	.295
—Round Rock (Texas)		0	0	...	0.00	1.50	1	0	0	0	...	0-...	2.0	3	0	0	0	0-0	1	.333
2005—	Corpus Christi (Texas)	4	12	.250	3.12	1.11	32	19	2	1	0	4-4	150.0	147	67	52	11	19-0	92	.256
2006—	Round Rock (PCL)	12	3	.800	2.51	0.99	27	18	2	0	0	4-4	125.2	110	48	35	12	14-0	68	.234
—Houston (N.L.)		2	1	.667	2.12	0.88	12	3	0	0	0	0-0	34.0	25	10	8	3	5-1	15	.205
Major League totals (1 year)		2	1	.667	2.12	0.88	12	3	0	0	0	0-0	34.0	25	10	8	3	5-1	15	.205

2006 LEFTY-RIGHTY SPLITS

vs.	Avg.	AB	H	2B	3B	HR	RBI	BB	SO	OBP	Slg.	vs.	Avg.	AB	H	2B	3B	HR	RBI	BB	SO	OBP	Slg.
L	.154	52	8	0	0	0	1	2	5	.200	.154	R	.243	70	17	2	0	3	8	3	10	.270	.400

SANCHES, BRIAN   P

PERSONAL: Born August 8, 1978, in Beaumont, Texas. ... Throws right, bats right. ... Full name: Brian Lee Sanches. ... College: Lamar. **TRANSACTIONS/CAREER NOTES:** Selected by Kansas City Royals organization in second round of 1999 free-agent draft. ... Traded by Royals with P Chris Tierney to San Diego Padres for OF Rondell White (August 26, 2003). ... Traded by Padres to Philadelphia Phillies for a player to be named (April 1, 2004); Padres acquired C Mauber Lopez to complete deal (August 2, 2004).
CAREER HITTING: 0-for-0 (.000), 0 R, 0 2B, 0 3B, 0 HR, 0 RBI.

Year	Team (League)	W	L	Pct.	ERA	WHIP	G	GS	CG	ShO	Hld.	Sv.-Opp.	IP	H	R	ER	HR	BB-IBB	SO	Avg.
1999—	Spokane (N'west)	1	1	.500	4.76	1.29	9	9	0	0	...	0-...	34.0	32	19	18	2	12-0	51	.241
2000—	Wilmington (Caro.)	6	12	.333	3.53	1.27	28	27	2	1	...	0-...	158.0	132	77	62	9	69-0	122	.233
2001—	Wichita (Texas)	7	9	.438	5.98	1.59	29	21	0	0	...	0-...	134.0	152	96	89	12	61-4	95	.289
2002—	Wichita (Texas)	10	6	.625	4.40	1.32	33	15	0	0	...	0-...	116.2	111	60	57	8	43-5	101	.252
2003—	Wichita (Texas)	1	5	.167	3.16	1.18	38	6	0	0	...	0-...	85.1	84	38	30	8	17-2	73	.260
2004—	Reading (East.)	4	2	.667	2.71	1.15	41	0	0	0	...	3-...	69.2	55	22	21	10	25-1	60	.211
—Scran./W.B. (I.L.)		0	0	...	7.50	2.00	4	0	0	0	...	0-...	6.0	9	5	5	1	3-0	4	.333
2005—	Scran./W.B. (I.L.)	5	3	.625	3.69	1.30	51	2	0	0	6	1-3	83.0	81	36	34	9	27-0	75	.260
2006—	Scran./W.B. (I.L.)	3	2	.600	1.85	0.85	36	0	0	0	4	19-20	43.2	24	9	9	2	13-1	52	.164
—Philadelphia (N.L.)		0	0	...	5.91	1.69	18	0	0	0	0	0-0	21.1	23	14	14	5	13-3	22	.271
Major League totals (1 year)		0	0	...	5.91	1.69	18	0	0	0	0	0-0	21.1	23	14	14	5	13-3	22	.271

2006 LEFTY-RIGHTY SPLITS

vs.	Avg.	AB	H	2B	3B	HR	RBI	BB	SO	OBP	Slg.	vs.	Avg.	AB	H	2B	3B	HR	RBI	BB	SO	OBP	Slg.
L	.282	39	11	4	0	3	4	6	11	.378	.615	R	.261	46	12	3	1	2	10	7	11	.358	.500

SANCHEZ, ANGEL   IF

PERSONAL: Born September 20, 1983, in Humacao, Puerto Rico. ... 6-2/180. ... Bats right, throws right. ... Full name: Angel Luis Sanchez.
2006 GAMES PLAYED BY POSITION (MLB): 2B—4, SS—4.

Year	Team (League)	Pos.	G	AB	R	H	2B	3B	HR	RBI	BB	SO	HBP	GDP	SB-CS	Avg.	OBP	SLG	OPS	E	Avg.
2001—	GC Royals (GCL)		30	95	10	23	4	0	0	6	6	28	0	2	3-1	.242	.287	.284	.571	...	...
2002—	GC Royals (GCL)		49	175	21	44	4	0	0	12	10	24	4	1	9-2	.251	.302	.274	.576	...	...
2003—	Burlington (Midw.)		106	408	54	110	8	1	2	35	28	52	4	10	14-5	.270	.321	.309	.630	...	...
2004—	Burlington (Midw.)		90	337	34	85	12	1	2	24	15	47	9	5	16-7	.252	.300	.312	.612	...	...
2005—	High Desert (Calif.)	SS	133	585	102	183	33	4	5	70	39	54	3	11	10-5	.313	.356	.409	.765	26	.964
2006—	Wichita (Texas)		133	542	105	153	24	1	4	57	44	63	7	12	8-9	.282	.339	.352	.692	26	.960
—Kansas City (A.L.)		2B-SS	8	27	2	6	0	0	0	1	0	4	0	0	0-0	.222	.214	.222	.437	0	1.000
Major League totals (1 year)			8	27	2	6	0	0	0	1	0	4	0	0	0-0	.222	.214	.222	.437	0	1.000

2006 LEFTY-RIGHTY SPLITS

vs.	Avg.	AB	H	2B	3B	HR	RBI	BB	SO	OBP	Slg.	vs.	Avg.	AB	H	2B	3B	HR	RBI	BB	SO	OBP	Slg.
L	.250	12	3	0	0	0	0	0	3	.250	.250	R	.200	15	3	0	0	0	1	0	1	.188	.200

SANCHEZ, ANIBAL   P

PERSONAL: Born February 27, 1984, in Maracay, Venezuela. ... 6-0/180. ... Throws right, bats right. ... Full name: Anibal Alejandro Sanchez. **TRANSACTIONS/CAREER NOTES:** Signed as a non-drafted free agent by Boston Red Sox organization (January 3, 2001). ... Traded by Red Sox with SS Hanley Ramirez and Ps Harvey Garcia and Jesus Delgado to the Florida Marlins for Ps Josh Beckett and Guillermo Mota and 3B Mike Lowell (November 24, 2005). **STATISTICAL NOTES:** Pitched 2-0 no-hit victory against Arizona (September 6, 2006).
CAREER HITTING: 4-for-35 (.114), 1 R, 0 2B, 0 3B, 0 HR, 2 RBI.

Year	Team (League)	W	L	Pct.	ERA	WHIP	G	GS	CG	ShO	Hld.	Sv.-Opp.	IP	H	R	ER	HR	BB-IBB	SO	Avg.
2001—	San Joaquin (VSL)	4	3	.571	3.19	1.17	24	1	0	0	...	3-...	53.2	40	23	19	0	23-0	64	...
2002—	Ciudad Alianza (VSL)	5	3	.625	3.50	0.99	11	11	1	0	...	0-...	61.2	50	31	24	3	11-0	73	.222
2004—	Lowell (NY-Penn)	3	4	.429	1.77	0.94	15	15	0	0	...	0-...	76.1	43	24	15	3	29-0	101	.160
2005—	Wilmington (Caro.)	6	1	.857	2.40	0.98	14	14	0	0	0	0-0	78.2	53	25	21	7	24-0	95	.187
—Portland (East.)		3	5	.375	3.45	1.20	11	11	0	0	0	0-0	57.1	53	28	22	5	16-0	63	.244
2006—	Carolina (Southern)	3	6	.333	3.15	1.27	15	15	2	1	0	0-0	85.2	82	41	30	7	27-1	92	.246
—Florida (N.L.)		10	3	.769	2.83	1.19	18	17	2	1	0	0-0	114.1	90	39	36	9	46-1	72	.217
Major League totals (1 year)		10	3	.769	2.83	1.19	18	17	2	1	0	0-0	114.1	90	39	36	9	46-1	72	.217

2006 LEFTY-RIGHTY SPLITS

vs.	Avg.	AB	H	2B	3B	HR	RBI	BB	SO	OBP	Slg.	vs.	Avg.	AB	H	2B	3B	HR	RBI	BB	SO	OBP	Slg.
L	.229	227	52	9	2	5	14	26	36	.310	.352	R	.202	188	38	7	1	4	20	20	36	.289	.314

SANCHEZ, DUANER   P

PERSONAL: Born October 14, 1979, in Cotui, Dominican Republic. ... 6-0/190. ... Throws right, bats right. ... High school: Francisco H. Carvajal (Cotui, Dominican Repblic). **TRANSACTIONS/CAREER NOTES:** Signed as a non-drafted free agent by Arizona Diamondbacks organization (October 16, 1996). ... Traded by Diamondbacks to Pittsbugh Pirates for P Mike Fetters (July 6, 2002). ... Claimed on waivers by Los Angeles Dodgers (November 20, 2003). ... Traded by Dodgers with P Steve Schmoll to New York Mets for Ps Jae Seo and Tim Hamulack (January 4, 2006). ... On disabled list (July 30, 2006-remainder of season).

CAREER HITTING: 1-for-9 (.111), 2 R, 1 2B, 0 3B, 0 HR, 2 RBI.

Year	Team (League)	W	L	Pct.	ERA	WHIP	G	GS	CG	ShO	Hld.	Sv.-Opp.	IP	H	R	ER	HR	BB-IBB	SO	Avg.
1997—	Dominican Diamondbacks (DSL)	4	4	.500	5.13	1.76	21	6	0	0	...	1-...	59.2	57	50	34	...	48-...	44	
1998—	Dominican Diamondbacks (DSL)	2	3	.400	1.79	1.19	14	8	1	0	...	1-...	50.1	36	19	10	...	24-...	44	
1999—	High Desert (Calif.)	0	0		7.53	1.67	3	3	0	0	...	0-...	14.1	15	13	12	2	9-0	9	.288
	Missoula (Pion.)	5	3	.625	3.13	1.22	13	11	0	0	...	0-...	63.1	54	34	22	3	23-0	51	.224
2000—	South Bend (Mid.)	8	9	.471	3.65	1.25	28	28	0	0	...	0-...	165.1	152	80	67	6	54-1	121	.243
2001—	El Paso (Texas)	3	7	.300	6.78	1.66	13	13	0	0	...	0-...	70.1	92	56	53	5	25-1	41	.324
	Lancaster (Calif.)	2	4	.333	4.58	1.41	10	10	1	0	...	0-...	59.0	65	44	30	7	18-0	49	.274
2002—	El Paso (Texas)	4	3	.571	3.03	1.23	31	0	0	0	...	13-...	35.2	31	16	12	1	13-1	37	.223
	Arizona (N.L.)	0	0		4.91	2.18	6	0	0	0	1	0-1	3.2	3	2	2	1	5-0	4	.214
	Tucson (PCL)	1	1	.500	6.75	1.31	4	0	0	0	...	1-...	5.1	6	4	4	1	1-0	9	.261
	Nashville (PCL)	0	3	.000	4.76	1.50	20	0	0	0	...	6-...	22.2	23	12	12	2	11-2	20	.274
	Pittsburgh (N.L.)	0	0		15.43	2.14	3	0	0	0	0	0-0	2.1	3	4	4	1	2-0	2	.300
2003—	Nashville (PCL)	4	4	.500	3.69	1.50	41	1	0	0	...	1-...	61.0	63	28	25	3	27-5	34	.266
	Pittsburgh (N.L.)	1	0	1.000	16.50	2.67	6	0	0	0	0	0-0	6.0	15	11	11	2	1-0	3	.500
2004—	Los Angeles (N.L.)	3	1	.750	3.38	1.35	67	0	0	0	4	0-1	80.0	81	34	30	9	27-2	44	.266
2005—	Los Angeles (N.L.)	4	7	.364	3.73	1.35	79	0	0	0	13	8-12	82.0	75	36	34	8	36-6	71	.243
2006—	New York (N.L.)	5	1	.833	2.60	1.21	49	0	0	0	14	0-1	55.1	43	19	16	3	24-6	44	.223
Major League totals (5 years)		13	9	.591	3.81	1.37	210	0	0	0	32	8-15	229.1	220	106	97	24	95-14	168	.258

DIVISION SERIES RECORD

Year	Team (League)	W	L	Pct.	ERA	WHIP	G	GS	CG	ShO	Hld.	Sv.-Opp.	IP	H	R	ER	HR	BB-IBB	SO	Avg.
2004—	Los Angeles (N.L.)	0	0		0.00	1.00	2	0	0	0	0	0-0	2.0	1	0	0	0	1-0	3	.143

2006 LEFTY-RIGHTY SPLITS

vs.	Avg.	AB	H	2B	3B	HR	RBI	BB	SO	OBP	Slg.		vs.	Avg.	AB	H	2B	3B	HR	RBI	BB	SO	OBP	Slg.
L	.276	87	24	7	0	2	16	13	18	.362	.425		R	.179	106	19	2	0	1	5	11	26	.275	.226

S

SANCHEZ, FREDDY   2B/3B

PERSONAL: Born December 21, 1977, in Hollywood, Calif. ... 5-10/192. ... Bats right, throws right. ... Full name: Frederick Philip Sanchez. ... High school: Burbank (Calif.). ... Junior college: Oklahoma City C.C. ... College: Oklahoma City. **TRANSACTIONS/CAREER NOTES:** Selected by Boston Red Sox organization in 11th round of 2000 free-agent draft. ... Traded by Red Sox with P Mike Gonzalez and cash to Pittsburgh Pirates for Ps Jeff Suppan, Brandon Lyon and Anastacio Martinez (July 31, 2003). ... On disabled list (March 26-July 9, 2004); included rehabilitation assignment to Nashville.

2006 GAMES PLAYED BY POSITION (MLB): 3B—99, SS—28, 2B—23.

Year	Team (League)	Pos.	G	AB	R	H	2B	3B	HR	RBI	BB	SO	HBP	GDP	SB-CS	Avg.	OBP	SLG	OPS	E	Avg.
2000—	Lowell (NY-Penn)	SS	34	132	24	38	13	2	1	14	9	16	3	1	2-4	.288	.347	.439	.787	4	.974
	Augusta (S. Atl.)	SS	30	109	17	33	7	0	0	15	11	19	1	1	4-0	.303	.372	.367	.739	3	.976
2001—	Sarasota (Fla. St.)	SS	69	280	40	95	19	4	1	24	22	30	2	3	5-3	.339	.388	.464	.834	17	.944
	Trenton (East.)	SS	44	178	25	58	20	0	2	19	9	21	2	6	3-1	.326	.363	.472	.835	9	.948
2002—	Trenton (East.)	SS-2B	80	311	60	102	23	1	3	38	37	45	5	9	19-3	.328	.403	.437	.841	16	.955
	Pawtucket (Int'l)	SS-2B	45	183	25	55	10	1	4	28	12	21	3	3	5-3	.301	.350	.432	.782	13	.942
	Boston (A.L.)	2B-SS-DH	12	16	3	3	0	0	0	2	2	3	0	0	0-0	.188	.278	.188	.465	0	1.000
2003—	Boston (A.L.)	3B-SS-2B	20	34	6	8	2	0	0	2	0	8	0	0	0-0	.235	.235	.294	.529	0	1.000
		DH	58	211	46	72	17	0	5	25	31	36	2	7	8-0	.341	.430	.493	.923	4	.983
	Nashville (PCL)	P	1	5	1	2	1	0	0	0	0	1	0	0	0-0	.400	.400	.600	1.000	0	1.000
2004—	Nashville (PCL)	2B-SS-3B	44	125	10	33	7	1	1	11	11	17	1	3	4-1	.264	.326	.360	.686	2	.983
	Pittsburgh (N.L.)	SS-2B-3B	9	19	2	3	0	0	0	2	0	4	0	0	0-0	.158	.158	.158	.316	1	.917
2005—	Pittsburgh (N.L.)	3B-2B-SS	132	453	54	132	26	4	5	35	27	36	5	6	2-2	.291	.336	.400	.736	6	.986
2006—	Pittsburgh (N.L.)	3B-SS-2B	157	582	85	200	* 53	2	6	85	31	52	7	12	3-2	* .344	.378	.473	.851	10	.981
American League totals (2 years)			32	50	9	11	2	0	0	4	2	11	0	0	0-0	.220	.250	.260	.510	0	1.000
National League totals (3 years)			298	1054	141	335	79	6	11	122	58	91	12	18	5-4	.318	.357	.435	.792	17	.983
Major League totals (5 years)			330	1104	150	346	81	6	11	126	60	102	12	18	5-4	.313	.352	.428	.779	17	.984

ALL-STAR GAME RECORD

		G	AB	R	H	2B	3B	HR	RBI	BB	SO	HBP	GDP	SB-CS	Avg.	OBP	SLG	OPS	E	Avg.
All-Star Game totals (1 year)		1	2	0	0	0	0	0	0	0	0	0	0	0-0	.000	.000	.000	.000	0	1.000

2006 LEFTY-RIGHTY SPLITS

vs.	Avg.	AB	H	2B	3B	HR	RBI	BB	SO	OBP	Slg.		vs.	Avg.	AB	H	2B	3B	HR	RBI	BB	SO	OBP	Slg.
L	.442	129	57	10	1	2	20	7	14	.460	.581		R	.316	453	143	43	1	4	65	24	38	.355	.442

SANCHEZ, JONATHAN   P

PERSONAL: Born November 19, 1982, in Mayaguez, Puerto Rico. ... Throws left, bats left. ... Full name: Jonathan O. Sanchez. ... College: Ohio Dominican. **TRANSACTIONS/CAREER NOTES:** Selected by San Francisco Giants organization in 27th round of 2004 free-agent draft.

CAREER HITTING: 0-for-7 (.000), 1 R, 0 2B, 0 3B, 0 HR, 0 RBI.

Year	Team (League)	W	L	Pct.	ERA	WHIP	G	GS	CG	ShO	Hld.	Sv.-Opp.	IP	H	R	ER	HR	BB-IBB	SO	Avg.
2004—	Ariz. Giants (Ariz.)	5	0	1.000	2.77	1.19	9	3	0	0	...	1-...	26.0	22	9	8	0	9-1	27	.229
	Salem-Keizer (N'west)	2	1	.667	4.84	1.57	6	6	0	0	...	0-...	22.1	16	13	12	3	19-0	34	.203
2005—	Augusta (S. Atl.)	5	7	.417	4.08	1.28	25	25	0	0	0	0-0	125.2	122	59	57	8	39-0	166	.254
2006—	Connecticut (East.)	2	1	.667	1.15	0.73	13	3	0	0	1	2-2	31.1	14	7	4	0	9-0	46	.137
	Fresno (PCL)	2	2	.500	3.80	1.10	6	6	0	0	0	0-0	23.2	13	10	10	1	13-0	28	.163
	San Francisco (N.L.)	3	1	.750	4.95	1.55	27	4	0	0	5	0-0	40.0	39	26	22	2	23-0	33	.250
Major League totals (1 year)		3	1	.750	4.95	1.55	27	4	0	0	5	0-0	40.0	39	26	22	2	23-0	33	.250

2006 LEFTY-RIGHTY SPLITS

vs.	Avg.	AB	H	2B	3B	HR	RBI	BB	SO	OBP	Slg.		vs.	Avg.	AB	H	2B	3B	HR	RBI	BB	SO	OBP	Slg.
L	.256	39	10	3	0	0	6	3	6	.333	.333		R	.248	117	29	7	1	2	23	20	27	.364	.376

SANDERS, REGGIE   OF

PERSONAL: Born December 1, 1967, in Florence, S.C. ... 6-1/205. ... Bats right, throws right. ... Full name: Reginald Laverne Sanders. ... High school: Wilson (Florence, S.C.). ... Junior college: Spartanburg Methodist (S.C.). ... College: Spartanburg Methodist (S.C.). **TRANSACTIONS/CAREER NOTES:** Selected by Cincinnati Reds organization in seventh round of 1987 free-agent draft. ... On disabled list (August 24-September 20, 1991; and May 13-29 and July 17-August 2, 1992). ... On suspended list (June 3-9, 1994). ... On disabled list (April 20-May 22, May 31-June 15 and September 17, 1996-remainder of season); included rehabilitation assignment to Indianapolis. ... On disabled list (April 19-May 6 and May 24-July 23, 1997); included rehabilitation assignments to Chattanooga and Indianapolis. ... Traded by Reds with SS Damian Jackson and P Josh Harris to San Diego Padres for OF Greg Vaughn and OF/1B Mark Sweeney (February 2, 1999). ... On disabled list (June 3-18, 1999). ... Traded by Padres with 2B Quilvio Veras and 1B Wally Joyner to Atlanta Braves for OF/1B Ryan Klesko, 2B Bret Boone and P Jason Shiell (December 22, 1999). ... On disabled list (April 30-May 23 and July 28-August 15, 2000). ... Signed as a free agent by Arizona Diamondbacks (January 5, 2001). ... On disabled list (March 23-April 8, 2001); included rehabilitation assignment to Tucson. ... Signed as a free agent by San Francisco Giants (January 8, 2002). ... Signed as a free agent by Pittsburgh Pirates (February 25, 2003). ... Signed as a free agent by St. Louis Cardinals (December 19, 2003). ... On disabled list (July 18-September 12, 2005). ... Signed as a free agent by Kansas City Royals (January 6, 2006). ... On disabled list (July 16-31 and August 25, 2006-remainder of season). **HONORS:** Named outfielder on THE SPORTING NEWS N.L. All-Star team (1995). **STATISTICAL NOTES:** Hit three home runs in one game (August 15, 1995). ... Career major league grand slams: 5.

2006 GAMES PLAYED BY POSITION (MLB): OF—73, DH—13.

Year Team (League)	Pos.	G	AB	R	H	2B	3B	HR	RBI	BB	SO	HBP	GDP	SB-CS	Avg.	OBP	SLG	OPS	E	Avg.
1988—Billings (Pion.)	SS	17	64	11	15	1	1	0	3	6	4	0	1	10-2	.234	.296	.281	.577	3	.944
1989—Greensboro (S. Atl.)	SS	81	315	53	91	18	5	9	53	29	63	3	3	21-7	.289	.353	.463	.817	42	.875
1990—Cedar Rap. (Midw.)	OF	127	466	89	133	21	4	17	63	59	97	4	8	40-15	.285	.370	.457	.827	10	.962
1991—Chattanooga (Sou.)	OF	86	302	50	95	15	8	8	49	41	67	1	5	15-2	.315	.394	.497	.890	3	.982
—Cincinnati (N.L.)	OF	9	40	6	8	0	0	1	3	0	9	0	1	1-1	.200	.200	.275	.475	0	1.000
1992—Cincinnati (N.L.)	OF	116	385	62	104	26	6	12	36	48	98	4	6	16-7	.270	.356	.462	.819	6	.978
1993—Cincinnati (N.L.)	OF	138	496	90	136	16	4	20	83	51	118	5	10	27-10	.274	.343	.444	.786	8	.975
1994—Cincinnati (N.L.)	OF	107	400	66	105	20	8	17	62	41 *	114	2	2	21-9	.263	.332	.480	.812	6	.975
1995—Cincinnati (N.L.)	OF	133	484	91	148	36	4	28	99	69	122	8	9	36-12	.306	.397	.579	.975	5	.982
1996—Cincinnati (N.L.)	OF	81	287	49	72	17	1	14	33	44	86	2	8	24-8	.251	.353	.463	.817	2	.988
—Indianapolis (A.A.)	OF-DH	4	12	3	5	2	0	0	1	1	4	1	0	0-1	.417	.500	.583	1.083	1	1.000
1997—Cincinnati (N.L.)	OF	86	312	52	79	19	2	19	56	42	93	3	9	13-7	.253	.347	.510	.857	5	.974
—Chattanooga (Sou.)	OF	3	11	3	6	1	1	1	3	1	2	1	0	0-0	.545	.615	1.091	1.706	0	1.000
—Indianapolis (A.A.)	OF	5	19	1	4	0	0	0	1	1	6	0	0	0-0	.211	.250	.211	.461	2	.750
1998—Cincinnati (N.L.)	OF	135	481	83	129	18	6	14	59	51	137	7	10	20-9	.268	.346	.418	.764	6	.978
1999—San Diego (N.L.)	OF-DH	133	478	92	136	24	7	26	72	65	108	6	10	36-13	.285	.376	.527	.904	6	.975
2000—Atlanta (N.L.)	OF	103	340	43	79	23	1	11	37	32	78	2	9	21-4	.232	.302	.403	.705	6	.964
2001—Tucson (PCL)	OF	2	6	0	2	1	0	0	1	2	0	0	2	1-0	.333	.500	.500	1.000	0	1.000
—Arizona (N.L.)	OF	126	441	84	116	21	3	33	90	46	126	5	2	14-10	.263	.337	.549	.886	1	.996
2002—San Francisco (N.L.)	OF	140	505	75	126	23	6	23	85	47	121	12	10	18-6	.250	.324	.455	.779	5	.984
2003—Pittsburgh (N.L.)	OF-DH	130	453	74	129	27	4	31	87	38	110	5	10	15-5	.285	.345	.567	.913	4	.983
2004—St. Louis (N.L.)	OF-DH	135	446	64	116	27	3	22	67	33	118	4	5	21-5	.260	.315	.482	.797	4	.981
2005—St. Louis (N.L.)	OF-DH	93	295	49	80	14	2	21	54	28	75	4	8	14-1	.271	.340	.546	.886	2	.983
2006—Kansas City (A.L.)	OF-DH	88	325	45	80	23	1	11	49	28	86	1	10	7-7	.246	.304	.425	.729	2	.989
American League totals (1 year)		88	325	45	80	23	1	11	49	28	86	1	10	7-7	.246	.304	.425	.729	2	.989
National League totals (15 years)		1665	5843	980	1563	311	59	292	923	635	1513	69	109	297-107	.267	.344	.491	.835	66	.980
Major League totals (16 years)		1753	6168	1025	1643	334	60	303	972	663	1599	70	119	304-114	.266	.342	.487	.830	68	.980

DIVISION SERIES RECORD

Year Team (League)	Pos.	G	AB	R	H	2B	3B	HR	RBI	BB	SO	HBP	GDP	SB-CS	Avg.	OBP	SLG	OPS	E	Avg.
1995—Cincinnati (N.L.)	OF	3	13	3	2	1	0	1	2	1	9	0	0	2-0	.154	.214	.462	.676	1	.875
2000—Atlanta (N.L.)	OF	3	9*	0	0	0	0	0	0	2	5	0	0	0-0	.000	.182	.000	.182	0	1.000
2001—Arizona (N.L.)	OF	5	14	2	5	1	0	1	3	3	3	0	0	1-0	.357	.471	.643	1.113	0	1.000
2002—San Francisco (N.L.)	OF	5	18	1	4	1	0	0	1	3	5	0	1	0-0	.222	.333	.278	.611	0	1.000
2004—St. Louis (N.L.)	OF	4	14	3	4	0	0	1	1	0	2	1	2	1-0	.286	.333	.500	.833	0	1.000
2005—St. Louis (N.L.)	OF	3	12	1	4	2	0	1	10	1	2	1	0	0-0	.333	.385	.750	1.135	0	1.000
Division series totals (6 years)		23	80	10	19	5	0	4	15	10	26	1	3	4-0	.238	.330	.450	.780	1	.981

CHAMPIONSHIP SERIES RECORD

Year Team (League)	Pos.	G	AB	R	H	2B	3B	HR	RBI	BB	SO	HBP	GDP	SB-CS	Avg.	OBP	SLG	OPS	E	Avg.
1995—Cincinnati (N.L.)	OF	4	16	0	2	0	0	0	0	2	10	0	2	0-1	.125	.222	.125	.347	1	.875
2001—Arizona (N.L.)	OF	5	17	2	2	0	0	0	1	5	5	0	0	1-0	.118	.318	.118	.436	0	1.000
2002—San Francisco (N.L.)	OF	4	16	0	1	0	0	0	0	0	4	0	0	0-0	.063	.063	.063	.125	0	1.000
2004—St. Louis (N.L.)	OF	6	21	1	4	2	0	0	0	1	5	0	1	0-0	.190	.227	.286	.513	0	1.000
2005—St. Louis (N.L.)	OF	5	18	1	3	0	0	1	2	1	8	0	1	1-0	.167	.211	.333	.544	0	1.000
Champ. series totals (5 years)		24	88	4	12	2	0	1	3	9	32	0	4	2-1	.136	.216	.193	.410	1	.983

WORLD SERIES RECORD

Year Team (League)	Pos.	G	AB	R	H	2B	3B	HR	RBI	BB	SO	HBP	GDP	SB-CS	Avg.	OBP	SLG	OPS	E	Avg.
2001—Arizona (N.L.)	OF	6	23	6	7	1	0	0	1	1	7	1	1	1-0	.304	.360	.348	.708	0	1.000
2002—San Francisco (N.L.)	OF	7	21	3	.5	0	0	2	6	2	9	0	0	1-0	.238	.280	.524	.804	0	1.000
2004—St. Louis (N.L.)	OF-DH	4	9	1	0	0	0	0	0	4	5	0	0	1-0	.000	.308	.000	.308	0	1.000
World series totals (3 years)		17	53	10	12	1	0	2	7	7	21	1	1	3-0	.226	.317	.358	.676	0	1.000

ALL-STAR GAME RECORD

	G	AB	R	H	2B	3B	HR	RBI	BB	SO	HBP	GDP	SB-CS	Avg.	OBP	SLG	OPS	E	Avg.
All-Star Game totals (1 year)	1	1	0	0	0	0	0	0	0	1	0	0	0-0	.000	.000	.000	.000	0	...

2006 LEFTY-RIGHTY SPLITS

vs.	Avg.	AB	2B	3B	HR	RBI	BB	SO	OBP	Slg.	vs.	Avg.	AB	H	2B	3B	HR	RBI	BB	SO	OBP	Slg.
L	.268	97	26	8	0	3	16	19	23	.385	.443	R	.237	228	54	15	1	8	33	9	63	.266	.417

SANDOVAL, DANNY — 2B

PERSONAL: Born April 7, 1979, in Lara, Venezuela. ... 5-11/192. ... Bats both, throws right. ... Full name: Danny E. Sandoval. **TRANSACTIONS/CAREER NOTES:** Signed as a non-drafted free agent by Chicago White Sox organization (December 8, 1996). ... Signed as a free agent by Philadelphia Phillies organization (November 14, 2003). ... Selected by Colorado Rockies from Phillies organization in Rule 5 minor league draft (December 15, 2003). ... Signed as a free agent by Phillies (October 29, 2004).

2006 GAMES PLAYED BY POSITION (MLB): 2B—8, SS—6.

Year Team (League)	Pos.	G	AB	R	H	2B	3B	HR	RBI	BB	SO	HBP	GDP	SB-CS	Avg.	OBP	SLG	OPS	E	Avg.
1997—Guacara-1 (Pion.)		31	82	16	28	0	1	0	9	11	7	0	2	8-0	.341	.398	.366	.764		...
1998—Hickory (S. Atl.)	SS	126	430	43	99	12	2	0	30	29	88	5	10	13-15	.230	.285	.267	.552	57	.912
1999—Burlington (Midw.)	SS	76	255	34	58	5	1	3	37	17	39	0	7	8-5	.227	.274	.290	.564	26	.929
2000—Burlington (Midw.)	SS	75	269	34	87	9	3	0	34	18	22	2	6	37-18	.323	.369	.379	.748	24	.927
—Win.-Salem (Car.)	2B-3B-SS	52	199	29	53	11	2	2	17	18	21	1	7	11-7	.266	.330	.372	.702	9	.956
—Charlotte (Int'l)	SS	2	8	0	1	0	0	0	1	1	1	0	0	0-0	.125	.222	.125	.347	1	.800
2001—Win.-Salem (Car.)	2B-3B-SS	48	176	25	48	11	0	3	14	11	31	3	3	11-2	.273	.323	.386	.709	16	.929
—Birmingham (Sou.)	SS-OF-3B	58	203	24	57	7	1	0	29	17	26	1	5	17-4	.281	.335	.325	.660	9	.948

Year Team (League)	Pos.	G	AB	R	H	2B	3B	HR	RBI	BB	SO	HBP	GDP	SB-CS	Avg.	OBP	SLG	OPS	E	Avg.
																		BATTING		FIELDING
2002— Birmingham (Sou.)	SS-OF-3B	135	504	86	133	30	2	5	45	45	56	5	12	39-24	.264	.329	.361	.690	23	.958
2003— Birmingham (Sou.)	SS-OF-3B	130	478	62	137	30	2	3	49	43	67	3	10	21-11	.287	.343	.377	.720	15	.972
2004— Tulsa (Texas)	SS	133	530	73	169	37	4	8	66	37	64	2	12	22-10	.319	.365	.449	.814	29	.726
2005— Philadelphia (N.L.)	SS	3	2	1	0	0	0	0	0	0	1	0	0	0-0	.000	.000	.000	.000	0	1.000
— Scran./W.B. (I.L.)	SS-2B	104	390	53	129	20	0	7	48	31	49	2	16	11-11	.331	.379	.436	.815	12	.976
2006— Reading (East.)		8	31	1	9	1	0	0	2	1	4	0	0	2-0	.290	.313	.323	.635	1	.969
— Scran./W.B. (I.L.)		91	345	31	88	17	1	2	39	14	50	3	8	1-1	.255	.288	.328	.616	14	.959
— Philadelphia (N.L.)	2B-SS	28	38	1	8	1	0	0	4	4	3	0	2	0-0	.211	.279	.237	.516	1	.966
Major League totals (2 years)		31	40	2	8	1	0	0	4	4	4	0	2	0-0	.200	.267	.225	.492	1	.967

2006 LEFTY-RIGHTY SPLITS

vs.	Avg.	AB	H	2B	3B	HR	RBI	BB	SO	OBP	Slg.	vs.	Avg.	AB	H	2B	3B	HR	RBI	BB	SO	OBP	Slg.
L	.286	14	4	0	0	0	0	2	1	.375	.286	R	.167	24	4	1	0	0	4	2	2	.222	.208

SANTANA, ERVIN — P

PERSONAL: Born January 10, 1983, in La Romana, Dominican Republic. ... 6-2/160. ... Throws right, bats right. ... Full name: Ervin Ramon Santana.
TRANSACTIONS/CAREER NOTES: Signed as a non-drafted free agent by Anaheim Angels organization (September 2, 2000). ... Angels franchise renamed Los Angeles Angels of Anaheim for 2005 season.
CAREER HITTING: 1-for-4 (.250), 0 R, 0 2B, 0 3B, 0 HR, 0 RBI.

Year Team (League)	W	L	Pct.	ERA	WHIP	G	GS	CG	ShO	Hld.	Sv.-Opp.	IP	H	R	ER	HR	BB-IBB	SO	Avg.
2001— Ariz. Angels (Ariz.)	3	2	.600	3.22	1.28	10	9	1	1	...	0-...	58.2	40	27	21	0	35-0	69	.184
— Provo (Pion.)	2	1	.667	7.71	1.66	4	4	0	0	...	0-...	18.2	19	17	16	1	12-1	22	.247
2002— Cedar Rap. (Midw.)	14	8	.636	4.16	1.23	27	27	0	0	...	0-...	147.0	133	75	68	10	48-3	146	.240
2003— Rancho Cuca. (Calif.)	10	2	.833	2.53	1.07	20	20	1	0	...	0-...	124.2	98	44	35	9	36-0	130	.212
— Arkansas (Texas)	1	1	.500	3.94	1.18	6	6	0	0	...	0-...	29.2	23	15	13	4	12-0	23	.211
2004— Arkansas (Texas)	2	1	.667	3.30	1.35	8	8	0	0	...	0-...	43.2	41	19	16	3	18-0	48	.247
2005— Arkansas (Texas)	5	1	.833	2.31	1.26	7	7	0	0	...	0-...	39.0	34	12	10	2	15-0	32	.234
— Salt Lake (PCL)	1	0	1.000	4.19	1.09	3	3	0	0	...	0-0	19.1	19	11	9	2	2-0	17	.260
— Los Angeles (A.L.)	12	8	.600	4.65	1.39	23	23	1	1	0	0-0	133.2	139	73	69	17	47-2	99	.266
2006— Los Angeles (A.L.)	16	8	.667	4.28	1.23	33	33	0	0	0	0-0	204.0	181	106	97	21	70-2	141	.241
Major League totals (2 years)	28	16	.636	4.42	1.29	56	56	1	1	0	0-0	337.2	320	179	166	38	117-4	240	.251

DIVISION SERIES RECORD

Year Team (League)	W	L	Pct.	ERA	WHIP	G	GS	CG	ShO	Hld.	Sv.-Opp.	IP	H	R	ER	HR	BB-IBB	SO	Avg.
2005— Los Angeles (A.L.)	1	0	1.000	5.06	1.31	1	0	0	0	0	0-0	5.1	5	3	3	1	2-0	2	.263

CHAMPIONSHIP SERIES RECORD

Year Team (League)	W	L	Pct.	ERA	WHIP	G	GS	CG	ShO	Hld.	Sv.-Opp.	IP	H	R	ER	HR	BB-IBB	SO	Avg.
2005— Los Angeles (A.L.)	0	1	.000	10.38	1.38	1	1	0	0	0	0-0	4.1	3	6	5	2	3-0	2	.188

2006 LEFTY-RIGHTY SPLITS

vs.	Avg.	AB	H	2B	3B	HR	RBI	BB	SO	OBP	Slg.	vs.	Avg.	AB	H	2B	3B	HR	RBI	BB	SO	OBP	Slg.
L	.254	350	89	17	3	12	46	46	54	.339	.423	R	.229	401	92	24	3	9	49	24	87	.286	.372

SANTANA, JOHAN — P

PERSONAL: Born March 13, 1979, in Tovar Merida, Venezuela. ... 6-0/206. ... Throws left, bats left. ... Full name: Johan Alexander Santana. ... Name pronounced: YO-hahn. ... High school: Liceo Nucete Sardi (Venezuela). **TRANSACTIONS/CAREER NOTES:** Signed as a non-drafted free agent by Houston Astros organization (July 2, 1995). ... Selected by Florida Marlins from Astros organization in Rule 5 major league draft (December 13, 1999). ... Traded by Marlins with cash to Minnesota Twins for P Jared Camp (December 13, 1999). ... On disabled list (July 7-September 21, 2001). **HONORS:** Named A.L. Pitcher of the Year by the SPORTING NEWS (2004 and 2006). ... Named pitcher on THE SPORTING NEWS A.L. All-Star team (2004). ... Named A.L. Cy Young Award winner by Baseball Writers' Association of America (2004 and 2006).
CAREER HITTING: 6-for-24 (.250), 1 R, 0 2B, 0 3B, 0 HR, 2 RBI.

Year Team (League)	W	L	Pct.	ERA	WHIP	G	GS	CG	ShO	Hld.	Sv.-Opp.	IP	H	R	ER	HR	BB-IBB	SO	Avg.
1996— Dom. Astros (DSL)	4	3	.571	2.70	1.20	23	1	0	0	...	3-...	40.0	26	16	12	...	22-...	51	...
1997— GC Astros (GCL)	0	4	.000	7.93	1.84	9	5	1	0	...	0-...	36.1	49	36	32	2	18-0	25	.322
— Auburn (NY-Penn)	0	0	...	2.25	1.75	1	1	0	0	...	0-...	4.0	1	1	1	0	6-0	5	.083
1998— Quad City (Midw.)	0	1	.000	9.45	2.55	2	1	0	0	...	0-...	6.2	14	7	7	1	3-0	6	.452
— Auburn (NY-Penn)	7	5	.583	4.36	1.18	15	15	1	1	...	0-...	86.2	81	52	42	9	21-0	88	.243
1999— Michigan (Midw.)	8	8	.500	4.66	1.35	27	26	1	0	...	0-...	160.1	162	94	83	14	55-0	150	.263
2000— Minnesota (A.L.)	2	3	.400	6.49	1.81	30	5	0	0	...	0-0	86.0	102	64	62	11	54-0	64	.302
2001— Minnesota (A.L.)	1	0	1.000	4.74	1.51	15	4	0	0	0	0-0	43.2	50	25	23	6	16-0	28	.292
2002— Edmonton (PCL)	5	2	.714	3.14	1.32	11	9	0	0	...	0-...	48.2	37	24	17	7	27-0	75	.202
— Minnesota (A.L.)	8	6	.571	2.99	1.23	27	14	0	0	3	1-1	108.1	84	41	36	7	49-0	137	.212
2003— Minnesota (A.L.)	12	3	.800	3.07	1.10	45	18	0	0	5	0-0	158.1	127	56	54	17	47-1	169	.216
2004— Minnesota (A.L.)	20	6	.769	* 2.61	0.92	34	34	1	1	0	0-0	228.0	156	70	66	24	54-0	* 265	* .192
2005— Minnesota (A.L.)	16	7	.696	2.87	0.97	33	33	3	2	0	0-0	231.2	180	77	74	22	45-1	* 238	* .210
2006— Minnesota (A.L.)	19	6	.760	* 2.77	1.00	34	* 34	0	0	0	* 233.2	186	79	72	24	47-0	* 245	* .216
Major League totals (7 years)	78	31	.716	3.20	1.10	218	142	5	3	8	1-1	1089.2	885	412	387	111	312-2	1146	.220

DIVISION SERIES RECORD

Year Team (League)	W	L	Pct.	ERA	WHIP	G	GS	CG	ShO	Hld.	Sv.-Opp.	IP	H	R	ER	HR	BB-IBB	SO	Avg.
2002— Minnesota (A.L.)	0	0	...	6.00	1.67	2	0	0	0	1	0-0	3.0	3	2	2	0	2-0	2	.250
2003— Minnesota (A.L.)	0	1	.000	7.04	1.57	2	2	0	0	0	0-0	7.2	9	6	6	0	3-1	6	.290
2004— Minnesota (A.L.)	1	0	1.000	0.75	1.50	2	2	0	0	0	0-0	12.0	14	1	1	0	4-0	12	.304
2006— Minnesota (A.L.)	0	1	.000	2.25	0.75	1	1	0	0	0	0-0	8.0	5	2	2	1	1-0	8	.172
Division series totals (4 years)	1	2	.333	3.23	1.34	7	5	0	0	1	0-0	30.2	31	11	11	1	10-1	28	.263

CHAMPIONSHIP SERIES RECORD

Year Team (League)	W	L	Pct.	ERA	WHIP	G	GS	CG	ShO	Hld.	Sv.-Opp.	IP	H	R	ER	HR	BB-IBB	SO	Avg.
2002— Minnesota (A.L.)	0	1	.000	10.80	1.20	4	0	0	0	0	0-0	3.1	4	4	4	1	0-0	4	.286

ALL-STAR GAME RECORD

	W	L	Pct.	ERA	WHIP	G	GS	CG	ShO	Hld.	Sv.-Opp.	IP	H	R	ER	HR	BB-IBB	SO	Avg.
All-Star Game totals (2 years)	0	0	...	0.00	1.50	2	0	0	0	0	0-0	2.0	1	0	0	0	2-0	1	.200

2006 LEFTY-RIGHTY SPLITS

vs.	Avg.	AB	H	2B	3B	HR	RBI	BB	SO	OBP	Slg.	vs.	Avg.	AB	H	2B	3B	HR	RBI	BB	SO	OBP	Slg.
L	.254	169	43	8	2	6	18	12	37	.306	.432	R	.206	693	143	34	3	18	54	35	208	.247	.342

S

SANTANA, JULIO   P

PERSONAL: Born January 20, 1974, in San Pedro de Macoris, Dominican Republic. ... 6-0/225. ... Throws right, bats right. ... Full name: Julio Franklin Santana. ... High school: Divina Providence (Dominican Republic). ... Nephew of Rico Carty, outfielder with seven major league teams (1963-79). **TRANSACTIONS/CAREER NOTES:** Signed as a non-drafted free agent by Texas Rangers organization (February 18, 1990). ... On disabled list (July 15-August 10, 1997). ... Claimed on waivers by Tampa Bay Devil Rays (April 27, 1998). ... On disabled list (May 3-24, 1999). ... Traded by Devil Rays to Boston Red Sox for a player to be named and cash (July 21, 1999); Devil Rays acquired P Will Silverthorn to complete deal (July 30, 1999). ... On disabled list (July 22, 1999-remainder of season). ... Released by Red Sox (June 15, 2000). ... Signed by Montreal Expos (June 18, 2000). ... Signed as a free agent by San Francisco Giants organization (November 11, 2000). ... Selected by New York Mets from Giants organization in Rule 5 major league draft (December 11, 2000). ... Returned to Giants organization (March 30, 2001). ... Signed as a free agent by Detroit Tigers organization (November 16, 2001). ... On disabled list (August 11, 2002-remainder of season). ... Released by Tigers (March 23, 2003). ... Signed by Philadelphia Phillies organization (March 30, 2003). ... Contract sold to Yomiuri of the Japan Central League by Phillies (June 9, 2003). ... Signed as free agent by Milwaukee Brewers organization (December 22, 2005). ... On disabled list (August 14-September 22, 2005). ... Signed as a free agent by Philadelphia Phillies (November 29, 2005). ... On disabled list (April 21-May 6, 2006); included rehabilitation assignment to Reading. ... On disabled list (May 13, 2006-remainder of season). ... Released by Phillies (October 11, 2006).

CAREER HITTING: 2-for-16 (.125), 0 R, 0 2B, 0 3B, 0 HR, 1 RBI.

Year Team (League)	W	L	Pct.	ERA	WHIP	G	GS	CG	ShO	Hld.	Sv.-Opp.	IP	H	R	ER	HR	BB-IBB	SO	Avg.
1992— San Pedro (DSL)	0	1	.000	3.24	1.80	17	1	0	0	...	0-...	8.1	8	5	3	...	7-...	5	
— Texas (DSL)	0	1	.000	3.24	1.67	4	4	0	0	...	0-...	9.0	8	5	3	0	7-0	5	.222
1993— GC Rangers (GCL)	4	1	.800	1.38	0.97	26	0	0	0	...	7-...	39.0	31	9	6	0	7-0	50	.214
1994— Char., W.Va. (SAL)	6	7	.462	2.46	1.19	16	16	0	0	...	0-...	91.1	65	38	25	3	44-...	103	
— Tulsa (Texas)	7	2	.778	2.90	1.26	11	11	2	0	...	0-...	72.0	50	26	23	1	41-0	45	.205
— Char., S.C. (SAL)	6	7	.462	2.46	1.18	16	16	0	0	...	0-...	92.0	65	38	25	3	44-0	103	.198
1995— Okla. City (A.A.)	0	2	.000	39.00	5.33	2	2	0	0	...	0-...	3.0	9	14	13	3	7-0	6	.500
— Charlotte (Fla. St.)	0	3	.000	3.73	1.50	5	5	1	0	...	0-...	32.0	32	16	13	1	16-0	27	.271
— Tulsa (Texas)	6	4	.600	3.15	1.39	15	15	3	0	...	0-...	103.0	91	40	36	8	52-2	71	.239
1996— Okla. City (A.A.)	11	12	.478	4.02	1.28	29	29	4	1	...	0-...	185.2	171	102	83	12	66-1	113	.244
1997— Texas (A.L.)	4	6	.400	6.75	1.83	30	14	0	0	...	0-1	104.0	141	86	78	16	49-2	64	.323
— Okla. City (A.A.)	0	0	...	15.00	3.67	1	1	0	0	...	0-...	3.0	9	6	5	0	1-0	5	.500
1998— Texas (A.L.)	0	0	...	8.44	2.06	3	0	0	0	...	0-0	5.1	7	5	5	0	4-1	1	.304
— Tampa Bay (A.L.)	5	6	.455	4.23	1.44	32	19	1	0	...	0-0	140.1	144	72	66	18	58-2	60	.270
1999— Tampa Bay (A.L.)	1	4	.200	7.32	1.77	22	5	0	0	0	0-0	55.1	66	49	45	10	32-0	34	.300
2000— Pawtucket (Int'l)	5	3	.625	4.71	1.29	12	12	0	0	...	0-...	65.0	61	34	34	7	23-0	55	.249
— Montreal (N.L.)	1	5	.167	5.67	1.53	36	4	0	0	1	0-2	66.2	69	45	42	11	33-2	58	.271
2001— Fresno (PCL)	8	8	.500	5.83	1.58	25	25	0	0	...	0-...	132.2	160	94	86	28	50-0	125	.299
2002— Toledo (Int'l)	0	1	.000	2.13	1.18	7	0	0	0	...	1-...	12.2	12	5	3	1	3-0	12	.250
— Detroit (A.L.)	3	5	.375	2.84	1.35	38	0	0	0	7	0-1	57.0	49	19	18	8	28-2	38	.238
2003— Scran./W.B. (I.L.)	1	1	.500	3.64	1.38	19	0	0	0	...	3-...	29.2	29	12	12	0	12-0	26	.261
— Yomiuri (Jp. Cen.)	2	1	.667	4.94	1.46	25	0	0	0	...	5-...	28.0	35	15	15	3	6-0	21	
2005— Nashville (PCL)	2	0	1.000	1.50	1.00	8	0	0	0	...	1-1	12.0	8	2	2	0	4-0	15	.190
— Milwaukee (N.L.)	3	5	.375	4.50	1.26	41	0	0	0	11	1-4	42.0	34	21	21	6	19-4	49	.221
2006— Reading (East.)	0	0	...	0.00	0.50	2	0	0	0	1	0-0	2.0	1	1	0	0	0-0	3	.111
— Philadelphia (N.L.)	0	0	...	7.56	2.04	7	0	0	0	0	0-0	8.1	8	9	7	1	9-1	4	.258
American League totals (4 years)	**13**	**21**	**.382**	**5.27**	**1.60**	**125**	**38**	**1**	**0**	**7**	**0-2**	**362.0**	**407**	**231**	**212**	**52**	**171-7**	**197**	**.955**
National League totals (3 years)	**4**	**10**	**.286**	**5.38**	**1.47**	**84**	**4**	**0**	**0**	**12**	**1-6**	**117.0**	**111**	**75**	**70**	**18**	**61-7**	**111**	**.252**
Major League totals (7 years)	**17**	**31**	**.354**	**5.30**	**1.57**	**209**	**42**	**1**	**0**	**19**	**1-8**	**479.0**	**518**	**306**	**282**	**70**	**232-14**	**308**	**.598**

2006 LEFTY-RIGHTY SPLITS

vs.	Avg.	AB	H	2B	3B	HR	RBI	BB	SO	OBP	Slg.	vs.	Avg.	AB	H	2B	3B	HR	RBI	BB	SO	OBP	Slg.
L	.143	14	2	0	0	0	1	7	1	.429	.143	R	.353	17	6	3	0	1	9	2	3	.409	.706

SANTIAGO, RAMON   SS/2B

PERSONAL: Born August 31, 1979, in Las Matas de Farfan, Dominican Republic. ... 5-11/167. ... Bats both, throws right. ... Full name: Ramon D. Santiago. **TRANSACTIONS/CAREER NOTES:** Signed as a non-drafted free agent by Detroit Tigers organization (July 29, 1998). ... On disabled list (July 24-September 1, 2002). ... Traded by Tigers with SS Juan Gonzalez to Seattle Mariners for SS Carlos Guillen (January 8, 2004). ... Released by Mariners (November 18, 2005). ... Signed as a free agent by Tigers organization (January 4, 2006).

2006 GAMES PLAYED BY POSITION (MLB): SS—27, 2B—12, 3B—1, DH—1.

Year Team (League)	Pos.	G	AB	R	H	2B	3B	HR	RBI	BB	SO	HBP	GDP	SB-CS	Avg.	OBP	SLG	OPS	E	Avg.
1999— GC Tigers (GCL)	SS	35	134	25	43	9	2	0	11	9	17	1	3	20-7	.321	.361	.418	.778	4	.974
— Oneonta (NYP)	SS	12	50	9	17	1	2	1	8	2	12	1	0	5-0	.340	.377	.500	.877	1	.979
2000— W. Mich. (Mid.)	SS	98	379	69	103	15	1	1	42	34	60	12	10	39-12	.272	.346	.325	.670	8	.976
2001— Lakeland (Fla. St.)	DH	120	429	64	115	15	3	2	46	54	60	11	7	34-8	.268	.361	.331	.692	...	...
2002— Erie (East.)	SS	22	75	9	21	0	2	1	7	3	12	3	2	6-0	.280	.329	.373	.703	3	.966
— Toledo (Int'l)	SS	9	28	8	12	1	0	2	6	3	4	2	0	0-2	.429	.515	.679	1.194	2	.956
— Detroit (A.L.)	SS-DH	65	222	33	54	5	5	4	20	13	48	8	2	8-5	.243	.306	.365	.671	7	.977
2003— Detroit (A.L.)	SS-2B	141	444	41	100	18	1	2	29	33	66	10	10	10-4	.225	.292	.284	.576	20	.970
2004— Tacoma (PCL)	SS-2B	71	243	35	47	7	2	1	24	24	31	10	3	9-6	.193	.288	.251	.539	6	.981
— Seattle (A.L.)	SS-DH	19	39	8	7	1	0	0	2	3	3	1	1	0-0	.179	.256	.205	.461	3	.946
2005— Tacoma (PCL)	2B-SS-3B	129	441	68	111	22	3	10	50	38	62	15	11	18-7	.252	.328	.383	.711	6	.990
— Seattle (A.L.)	2B-SS	8	8	2	1	0	0	0	0	1	2	3	0	0-0	.125	.417	.125	.542	1	.833
2006— Toledo (Int'l)	SS-2B-3B	25	83	13	21	6	0	2	12	9	18	1	0	2-1	.253	.333	.398	.731	3	.976
— Detroit (A.L.)	DH	43	80	9	18	1	1	0	3	1	14	1	1	2-0	.225	.244	.263	.506	0	1.000
Major League totals (5 years)		**276**	**793**	**93**	**180**	**25**	**7**	**6**	**54**	**51**	**133**	**23**	**13**	**20-9**	**.227**	**.292**	**.299**	**.590**	**31**	**.973**

CHAMPIONSHIP SERIES RECORD

Year Team (League)	Pos.	G	AB	R	H	2B	3B	HR	RBI	BB	SO	HBP	GDP	SB-CS	Avg.	OBP	SLG	OPS	E	Avg.
2006— Detroit (A.L.)	SS	3	7	0	0	0	0	0	0	1	0	0	0	0-0	.000	.125	.000	.125	0	1.000

WORLD SERIES RECORD

Year Team (League)	Pos.	G	AB	R	H	2B	3B	HR	RBI	BB	SO	HBP	GDP	SB-CS	Avg.	OBP	SLG	OPS	E	Avg.
2006— Detroit (A.L.)	SS	3	5	0	1	0	0	0	0	0	2	0	0	0-0	.200	.200	.200	.400	0	1.000

2006 LEFTY-RIGHTY SPLITS

vs.	Avg.	AB	H	2B	3B	HR	RBI	BB	SO	OBP	Slg.	vs.	Avg.	AB	H	2B	3B	HR	RBI	BB	SO	OBP	Slg.
L	.208	24	5	1	0	0	0	5	.208	.250		R	.232	56	13	0	1	0	2	1	9	.259	.268

SANTOS, CHAD — 1B

PERSONAL: Born April 28, 1981, in Honolulu, Hawaii. ... Bats left, throws left. ... Full name: Chad Roque Santos. **TRANSACTIONS/CAREER NOTES:** Selected by Kansas City Royals organization in 22nd round of 1999 free-agent draft. ... Signed as a free agent by San Francisco Giants organization (December 15, 2005).

2006 GAMES PLAYED BY POSITION (MLB): 1B—3.

Year	Team (League)	Pos.	G	AB	R	H	2B	3B	HR	RBI	BB	SO	HBP	GDP	SB-CS	Avg.	OBP	SLG	OPS	E	Avg.
1999—GC Royals (GCL)			48	177	20	48	9	0	4	35	12	54	1	...	1-0	.271	.319	.390	.709	8	...
2000—Charleston (SAL)			59	187	16	39	9	2	4	18	27	62	0	...	0-1	.209	.307	.342	.649	7	...
—Spokane (N'west)			73	267	40	67	18	0	14	47	36	103	2	...	1-0	.251	.344	.476	.820	13	...
2001—Burlington (Mid.)			121	444	58	112	32	0	16	83	52	101	6	...	0-1	.252	.337	.432	.769	14	...
2002—Wilmington (Car.)			110	379	46	91	21	0	9	54	46	122	6	...	0-0	.240	.330	.367	.697	11	...
2003—Wichita (Texas)			111	396	48	107	21	3	11	49	35	116	3	...	3-0	.270	.332	.422	.754	13	...
2004—Wichita (Texas)			130	471	59	123	27	3	21	68	46	119	4	...	3-1	.261	.330	.465	.795	16	...
2005—Omaha (PCL)			120	433	50	112	26	0	16	64	38	133	5	17	2-1	.259	.325	.430	.755	11	.987
2006—San Jose (Calif.)			14	55	5	13	3	1	2	11	2	18	1	1	0-0	.236	.271	.436	.708	2	.984
—Fresno (PCL)			91	353	40	92	18	1	14	70	24	86	1	13	0-0	.261	.307	.436	.743	12	.985
—San Francisco (N.L.)	1B		3	7	2	3	0	0	1	2	1	2	0	0	0-0	.429	.500	.857	1.357	1	.947
Major League totals (1 year)			3	7	2	3	0	0	1	2	1	2	0	0	0-0	.429	.500	.857	1.357	1	.947

2006 LEFTY-RIGHTY SPLITS

vs.	Avg.	AB	H	2B	3B	HR	RBI	BB	SO	OBP	Slg.	vs.	Avg.	AB	H	2B	3B	HR	RBI	BB	SO	OBP	Slg.
L	.667	3	2	0	0	0	0	0	0	.667	.667	R	.250	4	1	0	0	1	2	1	2	.400	1.000

SANTOS, VICTOR — P

PERSONAL: Born October 2, 1976, in San Pedro de Macoris, Dominican Republic. ... 6-3/190. ... Throws right, bats right. ... Full name: Victor Irving Santos. ... High school: Passaic (N.J.). ... College: St. Peter's. **TRANSACTIONS/CAREER NOTES:** Signed as a non-drafted free agent by Detroit Tigers organization (June 11, 1995). ... Traded by Tigers with IF Ronnie Merrill to Colorado Rockies for P Jose Paniagua (March 25, 2002). ... Released by Rockies (October 9, 2002). ... Signed by Texas Rangers organization (November 13, 2002). ... Signed as a free agent by Milwaukee Brewers organization (December 3, 2003). ... Signed as a free agent by Kansas City Royals organization (November 18, 2005). ... Selected by Pittsburgh Pirates from Royals organization in Rule 5 major league draft (December 8, 2005). ... On disabled list (June 18-July 13, 2006); included rehabilitation assignment to Indianapolis.

CAREER HITTING: 12-for-121 (.099), 5 R, 2 2B, 0 3B, 0 HR, 2 RBI.

Year	Team (League)	W	L	Pct.	ERA	WHIP	G	GS	CG	ShO	Hld.	Sv.-Opp.	IP	H	R	ER	HR	BB-IBB	SO	Avg.
1995— Dom. Tigers (DSL)		7	5	.583	3.72	1.37	15	12	3	2	...	0-...	77.1	88	46	32		18-...	75	...
1996— Lakeland (Fla. St.)		2	2	.500	2.22	0.99	5	4	0	0	...	0-...	28.1	19	11	7	2	9-0	25	.194
— GC Tigers (GCL)		3	2	.600	1.98	1.14	9	9	0	0	...	0-...	50.0	44	12	11	1	13-0	39	.251
1997— Lakeland (Fla. St.)		10	5	.667	3.23	1.34	26	26	4	2	...	0-...	145.0	136	74	52	10	59-1	108	.248
1998— Lakeland (Fla. St.)		5	2	.714	2.51	1.12	16	15	0	0	...	1-...	100.1	88	38	28	9	24-1	74	.235
— Toledo (Int'l)		1	2	.333	11.05	2.32	5	3	0	0	...	0-...	14.2	24	22	18	5	10-0	12	.353
— Jacksonville (Sou.)		4	2	.667	4.17	1.50	6	6	0	0	...	0-...	36.2	40	20	17	2	15-1	37	.284
1999— Jacksonville (Sou.)		12	6	.667	3.49	1.20	28	28	2	1	...	0-...	173.0	150	86	67	16	58-2	146	.230
2000— GC Tigers (GCL)		0	0	...	0.00	1.33	1	1	0	0	...	0-...	3.0	2	1	0	0	2-0	5	.182
— Lakeland (Fla. St.)		1	0	1.000	0.00	1.20	1	1	0	0	...	0-...	5.0	5	0	0	0	1-0	4	.263
— Toledo (Int'l)		0	1	.000	11.37	2.05	2	2	0	0	...	0-...	6.1	7	8	8	4	6-0	2	.280
2001— Detroit (A.L.)		2	2	.500	3.30	1.45	33	7	0	0	2	0-0	76.1	62	33	28	9	49-4	52	.222
— Toledo (Int'l)		2	1	.667	6.37	1.75	6	6	0	0	...	0-0	35.1	50	27	25	6	12-0	22	.340
2002— Colo. Springs (PCL)		4	9	.308	5.72	1.61	21	21	1	1	...	0-0	118.0	147	81	75	17	43-0	134	.311
— Colorado (N.L.)		0	4	.000	10.38	2.42	24	2	0	0	1	0-0	26.0	41	30	30	3	22-3	25	.360
2003— Texas (A.L.)		0	2	.000	7.01	1.75	14	3	0	0	...	0-0	25.2	29	21	20	5	16-1	15	.299
— Oklahoma (PCL)		5	4	.556	3.41	1.40	20	16	1	1	...	1-...	108.1	112	54	41	6	35-0	65	.264
2004— Indianapolis (Int'l)		0	0	...	3.48	1.55	3	3	0	0	...	0-...	10.1	12	4	4	1	4-0	11	.308
— Milwaukee (N.L.)		11	12	.478	4.97	1.47	31	28	0	0	...	0-0	154.0	169	95	85	18	57-5	115	.278
2005— Milwaukee (N.L.)		4	13	.235	4.57	1.50	29	24	1	1	0	0-0	141.2	153	87	72	20	60-8	89	.269
2006— Indianapolis (Int'l)		1	0	1.000	0.00	0.20	1	1	0	0	...	0-0	5.0	1	0	0	0	0-0	0	.067
— Pittsburgh (N.L.)		5	9	.357	5.70	1.66	25	19	0	0	0	0-0	115.1	150	80	73	16	42-3	81	.321
American League totals (2 years)		2	4	.333	4.24	1.53	41	11	0	0	2	0-0	102.0	91	54	48	14	65-5	67	.242
National League totals (4 years)		20	38	.345	5.35	1.59	109	73	1	1	1	0-0	437.0	513	292	260	57	181-19	310	.292
Major League totals (6 years)		22	42	.344	5.14	1.58	150	84	1	1	3	0-0	539.0	604	346	308	71	246-24	377	.283

2006 LEFTY-RIGHTY SPLITS

vs.	Avg.	AB	H	2B	3B	HR	RBI	BB	SO	OBP	Slg.	vs.	Avg.	AB	H	2B	3B	HR	RBI	BB	SO	OBP	Slg.
L	.264	193	51	9	2	7	26	19	41	.327	.440	R	.361	274	99	17	5	9	50	23	40	.416	.558

SARFATE, DENNIS — P

PERSONAL: Born April 9, 1981, in Queens, N.Y. ... 6-4/210. ... Throws right, bats right. ... Full name: Dennis Scott Sarfate. ... College: Chandler-Gilbert C.C. **TRANSACTIONS/CAREER NOTES:** Selected by Milwaukee Brewers organization in ninth round of 2001 free-agent draft.

CAREER HITTING: 0-for-0 (.000), 0 R, 0 2B, 0 3B, 0 HR, 0 RBI.

Year	Team (League)	W	L	Pct.	ERA	WHIP	G	GS	CG	ShO	Hld.	Sv.-Opp.	IP	H	R	ER	HR	BB-IBB	SO	Avg.
2001— Ogden (Pion.)		1	2	.333	4.63	1.29	9	4	0	0	...	1-...	23.1	20	13	12	4	10-0	32	.230
2002— Ariz. Brewers (Ariz.)		0	0	...	2.57	0.93	5	5	0	0	...	0-...	14.0	6	4	4	0	7-0	22	.125
— Ogden (Pion.)		0	0	...	9.00	3.00	1	0	0	0	...	0-...	1.0	2	1	1	0	1-0	2	.400
2003— Beloit (Midw.)		12	2	.857	2.84	1.29	26	26	0	0	...	0-...	139.2	114	50	44	11	66-0	140	.227
2004— Huntsville (Sou.)		7	12	.368	4.05	1.60	28	25	0	0	...	0-...	129.0	128	71	58	12	78-0	113	.278
2005— Huntsville (Sou.)		9	9	.500	3.88	1.38	24	24	1	0	0	0-0	130.0	120	65	56	13	59-0	110	.245
— Nashville (PCL)		0	1	.000	2.25	0.83	2	1	0	0	0	0-0	12.0	6	3	3	1	4-0	10	.150
2006— Nashville (PCL)		10	7	.588	3.67	1.62	34	21	0	0	0	0-2	125.0	125	63	51	7	78-0	117	.265
— Milwaukee (N.L.)		0	0	...	4.32	1.56	8	0	0	0	0	0-0	8.1	9	4	4	0	4-1	11	.265
Major League totals (1 year)		0	0	...	4.32	1.56	8	0	0	0	0	0-0	8.1	9	4	4	0	4-1	11	.265

2006 LEFTY-RIGHTY SPLITS

vs.	Avg.	AB	H	2B	3B	HR	RBI	BB	SO	OBP	Slg.	vs.	Avg.	AB	H	2B	3B	HR	RBI	BB	SO	OBP	Slg.
L	.267	15	4	2	0	0	2	1	4	.313	.400	R	.263	19	5	2	0	0	2	3	7	.364	.368

SAUERBECK, SCOTT — P

PERSONAL: Born November 9, 1971, in Cincinnati. ... 6-3/200. ... Throws left, bats right. ... Full name: Scott William Sauerbeck. ... Name pronounced: SOW-er-beck. ... High school: Northwest (Cincinnati). ... College: Miami (Ohio). **TRANSACTIONS/CAREER NOTES:** Selected by New York Mets organization in 23rd round of 1994 free-agent draft. ... Selected by Pittsburgh Pirates from Mets organization in Rule 5 major league draft (December 14, 1998). ... On disabled list (June 14-July 3, 2000); included rehabilitation

S

assignment to Nashville. ... Traded by Pirates with P Jeff Suppan to Boston Red Sox for 2B Freddy Sanchez (July 31, 2003). ... Signed as a free agent by Cleveland Indians organization (March 20, 2004). ... Released by Indians (June 14, 2006). ... Signed by Oakland Athletics (June 19, 2006). ... On disabled list (July 26-August 10, 2006); included rehabilitation assignments to Sacramento and Stockton. ... Released by Athletics (October 10, 2006).

CAREER HITTING: 0-for-7 (.000), 0 R, 0 2B, 0 3B, 0 HR, 0 RBI.

Year Team (League)	W	L	Pct.	ERA	WHIP	G	GS	CG	ShO	Hld.	Sv.-Opp.	IP	H	R	ER	HR	BB-IBB	SO	Avg.
1994— Pittsfield (NYP)	3	1	.750	2.05	1.20	21	0	0	0	...	1-...	48.1	39	16	11	0	19-2	39	.222
1995— St. Lucie (Fla. St.)	0	1	.000	2.03	1.50	20	1	0	0	...	0-...	26.2	26	10	6	0	14-1	25	.260
— Capital City (SAL)	5	4	.556	3.27	1.27	19	0	0	0	...	2-...	33.0	28	14	12	2	14-1	33	.230
1996— St. Lucie (Fla. St.)	6	6	.500	2.27	1.29	17	16	2	2	...	0-...	99.1	101	37	25	1	27-0	62	.269
— Binghamton (East.)	3	3	.500	3.47	1.29	8	8	2	0	...	0-...	46.2	48	24	18	4	12-0	30	.274
1997— Binghamton (East.)	8	9	.471	4.93	1.48	27	20	2	0	...	0-...	131.1	144	89	72	15	50-0	88	.280
— Norfolk (Int'l)	1	0	1.000	3.60	1.40	1	1	0	0	...	0-...	5.0	3	2	2	0	4-0	4	.200
1998— Norfolk (Int'l)	7	13	.350	3.93	1.54	27	27	2	0	...	0-...	160.1	178	82	70	8	69-1	119	.287
1999— Pittsburgh (N.L.)	4	1	.800	2.00	1.34	65	0	0	0	10	2-5	67.2	53	19	15	6	38-5	55	.220
2000— Pittsburgh (N.L.)	5	4	.556	4.04	1.81	75	0	0	0	13	1-4	75.2	76	36	34	4	61-8	83	.270
— Nashville (PCL)	0	0	...	0.00	0.50	2	0	0	0	...	0-...	2.0	1	0	0	0	0-0	1	.167
2001— Pittsburgh (N.L.)	2	2	.500	5.60	1.61	70	0	0	0	19	2-4	62.2	61	41	39	4	40-6	79	.257
2002— Pittsburgh (N.L.)	5	4	.556	2.30	1.23	78	0	0	0	28	0-0	62.2	50	18	16	4	27-4	70	.220
2003— Pittsburgh (N.L.)	3	4	.429	4.05	1.38	53	0	0	0	16	0-0	40.0	30	20	18	5	25-2	32	.207
— Boston (A.L.)	0	1	.000	6.48	2.10	26	0	0	0	2	0-1	16.2	17	14	12	1	18-3	18	.266
2004— Cleveland (A.L.)							Did not play.												
2005— Cleveland (A.L.)	1	0	1.000	4.04	1.43	58	0	0	0	14	0-2	35.2	35	18	16	4	16-2	35	.259
2006— Sacramento (PCL)	0	0	...	0.00	1.50	1	0	0	0	0	0-0	2.0	2	0	0	0	1-0	2	.286
— Stockton (Calif.)	0	0	...	0.00	2.00	1	0	0	0	0	0-0	1.0	2	0	0	0	0-0	0	.667
— Cleveland (A.L.)	0	1	.000	6.23	1.38	24	0	0	0	2	0-2	13.0	9	9	9	2	9-1	11	.196
— Oakland (A.L.)	0	0	...	3.65	1.78	22	0	0	0	3	0-0	12.1	13	8	5	1	9-0	6	.271
American League totals (3 years)	1	2	.333	4.87	1.62	130	0	0	0	21	0-5	77.2	74	49	42	8	52-6	70	.253
National League totals (5 years)	19	15	.559	3.56	1.49	341	0	0	0	86	5-17	308.2	270	134	122	23	191-25	319	.239
Major League totals (7 years)	20	17	.541	3.82	1.52	471	0	0	0	107	5-22	386.1	344	183	164	31	243-31	389	.242

CHAMPIONSHIP SERIES RECORD

Year Team (League)	W	L	Pct.	ERA	WHIP	G	GS	CG	ShO	Hld.	Sv.-Opp.	IP	H	R	ER	HR	BB-IBB	SO	Avg.
2003— Boston (A.L.)	0	0	...	0.00	6.00	1	0	0	0	...	0-0	0.1	1	0	0	0	1-0	0	.500

2006 LEFTY-RIGHTY SPLITS

vs.	Avg.	AB	H	2B	3B	HR	RBI	BB	SO	OBP	Slg.	vs.	Avg.	AB	H	2B	3B	HR	RBI	BB	SO	OBP	Slg.
L	.234	47	11	3	0	3	10	11	12	.419	.489	R	.234	47	11	2	1	0	5	7	5	.368	.319

SAUNDERS, JOE — P

PERSONAL: Born June 16, 1981, in Falls Church, Va. ... 6-3/210. ... Throws left, bats left. ... Full name: Joseph Francis Saunders. ... High school: West Springfield (Va.). ... College: Virginia Tech. **TRANSACTIONS/CAREER NOTES:** Selected by Anaheim Angels organization in first round (12th pick overall) of 2002 free-agent draft. ... Angels franchise renamed Los Angeles Angels of Anaheim for 2005 season.

CAREER HITTING: 0-for-0 (.000), 0 R, 0 2B, 0 3B, 0 HR, 0 RBI.

Year Team (League)	W	L	Pct.	ERA	WHIP	G	GS	CG	ShO	Hld.	Sv.-Opp.	IP	H	R	ER	HR	BB-IBB	SO	Avg.
2002— Provo (Pion.)	2	1	.667	3.62	1.58	8	8	0	0	...	0-...	32.1	40	19	13	1	11-0	21	.305
— Cedar Rap. (Midw.)	3	1	.750	1.88	0.87	5	5	0	0	...	0-...	28.2	16	7	6	2	9-0	27	.168
2004— Rancho Cuca. (Calif.)	9	7	.563	3.41	1.22	19	19	0	0	...	0-...	105.2	106	49	40	13	23-0	76	.265
— Arkansas (Texas)	4	3	.571	5.77	1.67	8	8	0	0	...	0-...	39.0	51	26	25	5	14-0	25	.327
2005— Arkansas (Texas)	7	4	.636	3.49	1.32	18	18	2	1	0	0-0	105.2	107	52	41	9	32-0	80	.263
— Salt Lake (PCL)	3	3	.500	4.58	1.56	9	9	1	1	0	0-0	55.0	65	38	28	3	21-0	29	.304
— Los Angeles (A.L.)	0	0	...	7.71	1.50	2	2	0	0	0	0-0	9.1	10	8	8	3	4-0	4	.270
2006— Salt Lake (PCL)	10	4	.714	2.67	1.15	21	20	1	1	0	0-0	135.0	117	44	40	12	38-0	97	.234
— Los Angeles (A.L.)	7	3	.700	4.71	1.42	13	13	0	0	0	0-0	70.2	71	42	37	6	29-1	51	.264
Major League totals (2 years)	7	3	.700	5.06	1.43	15	15	0	0	0	0-0	80.0	81	50	45	9	33-1	55	.265

2006 LEFTY-RIGHTY SPLITS

vs.	Avg.	AB	H	2B	3B	HR	RBI	BB	SO	OBP	Slg.	vs.	Avg.	AB	H	2B	3B	HR	RBI	BB	SO	OBP	Slg.
L	.220	50	11	2	0	0	4	3	11	.278	.260	R	.274	219	60	11	0	6	28	26	40	.348	.406

SCHILLING, CURT — P

PERSONAL: Born November 14, 1966, in Anchorage, Alaska. ... 6-5/235. ... Throws right, bats right. ... Full name: Curtis Montague Schilling. ... Name pronounced: SHILL-ing. ... High school: Shadow Mountain (Phoenix). ... Junior college: Yavapai (Ariz.). **TRANSACTIONS/CAREER NOTES:** Selected by Boston Red Sox organization in second round of January 1986 free-agent draft. ... Traded by Red Sox with OF Brady Anderson to Baltimore Orioles for P Mike Boddicker (July 29, 1988). ... Traded by Orioles with P Pete Harnisch and OF Steve Finley to Houston Astros for 1B Glenn Davis (January 10, 1991). ... Traded by Astros to Philadelphia Phillies for P Jason Grimsley (April 2, 1992). ... On disabled list (May 17-July 25, 1994); included rehabilitation assignments to Scranton/Wilkes-Barre and Reading. ... On disabled list (July 19, 1995-remainder of season). ... On disabled list (March 23-May 14, 1996); included rehabilitation assignments to Clearwater and Scranton/Wilkes-Barre. ... On disabled list (August 8-September 3, 1999). ... On disabled list (March 25-April 30, 2000); included rehabilitation assignments to Clearwater and Scranton/Wilkes-Barre. ... Traded by Phillies to Arizona Diamondbacks for 1B/OF Travis Lee and Ps Omar Daal, Vicente Padilla and Nelson Figueroa (July 26, 2000). ... On disabled list (April 18-May 3 and May 31-July 12, 2003); included rehabilitation assignment to Tucson. ... Traded by Diamondbacks to Boston Red Sox for Ps Casey Fossum, Brandon Lyon and Jorge de la Rosa and a player to be named (November 28, 2003); Diamondbacks acquired OF Michael Goss to complete deal (December 15, 2003). ... On disabled list (March 30-April 13 and April 24-July 13, 2005); included rehabilitation assignment to Pawtucket. **HONORS:** Named N.L. Pitcher of the Year by THE SPORTING NEWS (2001 and 2002). ... Named righthanded pitcher on THE SPORTING NEWS N.L. All-Star team (2001 and 2002). **MISCELLANEOUS NOTES:** Struck out once in two appearances as pinch hitter with Philadelphia (1996).

CAREER HITTING: 116-for-771 (.150), 39 R, 13 2B, 1 3B, 0 HR, 29 RBI.

Year Team (League)	W	L	Pct.	ERA	WHIP	G	GS	CG	ShO	Hld.	Sv.-Opp.	IP	H	R	ER	HR	BB-IBB	SO	Avg.
1986— Elmira (N.Y.-Penn)	7	3	.700	2.59	1.30	16	15	2	1	...	0-...	93.2	92	34	27	3	30-1	75	.254
1987— Greensboro (S. Atl.)	8	15	.348	3.82	1.33	29	28	7	3	...	0-...	184.0	179	96	78	10	65-8	189	.255
1988— New Britain (East.)	8	5	.615	2.97	1.24	21	17	4	1	...	0-...	106.0	91	44	35	3	40-0	62	.232
— Charlotte (Sou.)	5	2	.714	3.18	1.30	7	7	2	1	...	0-...	45.1	36	19	16	3	23-0	32	.217
— Baltimore (A.L.)	0	3	.000	9.82	2.18	4	4	0	0	...	0-0	14.2	22	19	16	3	10-1	4	.355
1989— Rochester (Int'l)	13	11	.542	3.21	1.27	27	27	9	3	...	0-...	185.1	176	76	66	11	59-0	109	.254
— Baltimore (A.L.)	0	1	.000	6.23	1.50	5	1	0	0	...	0-...	8.2	10	6	6	2	3-0	6	.286
1990— Rochester (Int'l)	4	4	.500	3.92	1.37	15	14	1	0	...	0-...	87.1	95	46	38	10	25-1	83	.277
— Baltimore (A.L.)	1	2	.333	2.54	1.24	35	0	0	0	...	3-9	46.0	38	13	13	1	19-0	32	.229
1991— Houston (N.L.)	3	5	.375	3.81	1.56	56	0	0	0	...	8-11	75.2	79	35	32	2	39-7	71	.271
— Tucson (PCL)	0	1	.000	3.42	1.18	13	0	0	0	...	3-...	23.2	16	9	9	0	12-1	21	.186
1992— Philadelphia (N.L.)	14	11	.560	2.35	0.99	42	26	10	4	0	2-3	226.1	165	67	59	11	59-4	147	* .201

Year Team (League)	W	L	Pct.	ERA	WHIP	G	GS	CG	ShO	Hld.	Sv.-Opp.	IP	H	R	ER	HR	BB-IBB	SO	Avg.
1993—Philadelphia (N.L.)	16	7	.696	4.02	1.24	34	34	7	2	0	0-0	235.1	234	114	105	23	57-6	186	.259
1994—Philadelphia (N.L.)	2	8	.200	4.48	1.40	13	13	1	0	0	0-0	82.1	87	42	41	10	28-3	58	.270
—Scran./W.B. (I.L.)	0	*0	...	1.80	1.10	2	2	0	0	...	0-...	10.0	6	2	2	0	5-0	6	.171
—Reading (East.)	0	0	...	0.00	1.75	1	1	0	0	...	0-...	4.0	6	0	0	0	1-0	4	.375
1995—Philadelphia (N.L.)	7	5	.583	3.57	1.05	17	17	1	0	0	0-0	116.0	96	52	46	12	26-2	114	.220
1996—Clearwater (FSL)	2	0	1.000	1.29	0.71	2	2	0	0	0	0-0	14.0	9	2	2	0	1-0	17	.173
—Scran./W.B. (I.L.)	1	0	1.000	1.38	1.08	2	2	0	0	0	0-0	13.0	9	2	2	0	5-0	10	.200
—Philadelphia (N.L.)	9	10	.474	3.19	1.09	26	26	*8	2	0	0-0	183.1	149	69	65	16	50-5	182	.223
1997—Philadelphia (N.L.)	17	11	.607	2.97	1.05	35	•35	7	2	0	0-0	254.1	208	96	84	25	58-3	*319	.236
1998—Philadelphia (N.L.)	15	14	.517	3.25	1.11	35	•35	*15	2	0		*268.2	236	101	97	23	61-3	*300	.236
1999—Philadelphia (N.L.)	15	6	.714	3.54	1.13	24	24	8	1	0	0-0	180.1	159	74	71	25	44-0	152	.223
2000—Clearwater (FSL)	1	0	1.000	1.31	0.58	4	4	0	0	0	0-...	20.2	10	3	3	0	2-0	23	.137
—Scran./W.B. (I.L.)	0	0	...	3.60	2.00	1	1	0	0	...	0-...	5.0	9	2	2	0	1-0	7	.375
—Philadelphia (N.L.)	6	6	.500	3.91	1.26	16	16	0	0	0	0-...	112.2	110	49	49	17	32-4	96	.253
—Arizona (N.L.)	5	6	.455	3.69	1.10	13	13	§4	1	0	0-...	97.2	94	41	40	10	13-0	72	.257
2001—Arizona (N.L.)	•22	6	.786	2.98	1.08	35	•35	*6	1	0		*256.2	237	86	85	• 37	39-0	293	.245
2002—Arizona (N.L.)	23	7	.767	3.23	0.97	36	35	0	0	0	0-0	259.1	218	95	93	•29	33-1	316	.228
2003—Tucson (PCL)	1	0	1.000	4.50	1.30	2	2	0	0	0	0-...	10.0	10	5	5	3	3-0	15	.256
—Arizona (N.L.)	8	9	.471	2.95	1.05	24	24	·3	2	0	0-...	168.0	144	58	55	17	32-2	194	.239
2004—Boston (A.L.)	*21	6	.778	3.26	1.06	32	32	3	0	0	0-0	226.2	206	84	82	23	35-0	203	.239
2005—Pawtucket (Int'l)	0	2	.000	6.63	1.58	6	3	0	0	0	0-0	19.0	27	15	14	3	3-0	21	.321
—Boston (A.L.)	8	8	.500	5.69	1.53	32	11	0	0	0	9-11	93.1	121	59	59	12	22-0	87	.314
2006—Boston (A.L.)	15	7	.682	3.97	1.22	31	31	0	0	0	0-0	204.0	220	90	90	28	28-1	183	.276
American League totals (6 years)	45	27	.625	4.03	1.24	139	79	3	0	5	12-20	593.1	617	271	266	69	117-2	515	.268
National League totals (13 years)	162	111	.593	3.30	1.11	406	333	79	19	5	10-14	2516.2	2216	979	922	257	571-40	2500	.242
Major League totals (19 years)	207	138	.600	3.44	1.13	545	412	82	19	10	22-34	3110.0	2833	1250	1188	326	688-42	3015	.242

DIVISION SERIES RECORD

Year Team (League)	W	L	Pct.	ERA	WHIP	G	GS	CG	ShO	Hld.	Sv.-Opp.	IP	H	R	ER	HR	BB-IBB	SO	Avg.
2001—Arizona (N.L.)	2	0	1.000	0.50	0.61	2	2	2	1	0	0-0	18.0	9	1	1	1	2-0	18	.143
2002—Arizona (N.L.)	0	0	...	1.29	1.14	1	1	0	0	0	0-0	7.0	7	1	1	1	1-0	7	.250
2004—Boston (A.L.)	1	0	1.000	2.70	1.65	1	1	0	0	0	0-0	6.2	9	3	2	2	2-0	4	.300
Division series totals (3 years)	3	0	1.000	1.14	0.95	4	4	2	1	0	0-0	31.2	25	5	4	4	5-0	29	.207

CHAMPIONSHIP SERIES RECORD

Year Team (League)	W	L	Pct.	ERA	WHIP	G	GS	CG	ShO	Hld.	Sv.-Opp.	IP	H	R	ER	HR	BB-IBB	SO	Avg.
1993—Philadelphia (N.L.)	0	0	...	1.69	1.00	2	2	0	0	0	0-0	16.0	11	4	3	0	5-0	19	.193
2001—Arizona (N.L.)	1	0	1.000	1.00	0.67	1	1	1	0	0	0-0	9.0	4	1	1	0	2-0	12	.133
2004—Boston (A.L.)	1	1	.500	6.30	1.20	2	2	0	0	0	0-0	10.0	10	7	7	1	2-0	5	.256
Champ. series totals (3 years)	2	1	.667	2.83	0.97	5	5	1	0	0	0-0	35.0	25	12	11	1	9-0	36	.198

WORLD SERIES RECORD

Year Team (League)	W	L	Pct.	ERA	WHIP	G	GS	CG	ShO	Hld.	Sv.-Opp.	IP	H	R	ER	HR	BB-IBB	SO	Avg.
1993—Philadelphia (N.L.)	1	1	.500	3.52	1.17	2	2	1	1	0	0-0	15.1	13	7	6	2	5-0	19	.236
2001—Arizona (N.L.)	1	0	1.000	1.69	0.66	3	3	0	0	0	0-0	21.1	12	4	4	2	2-0	26	.162
2004—Boston (A.L.)	1	0	1.000	0.00	0.83	1	1	•0	0	0	0-0	6.0	4	1	0	0	1-0	4	.174
World series totals (3 years)	3	1	.750	2.11	0.87	6	6	1	1	0	0-0	42.2	29	12	10	4	8-0	39	.191

ALL-STAR GAME RECORD

	W	L	Pct.	ERA	WHIP	G	GS	CG	ShO	Hld.	Sv.-Opp.	IP	H	R	ER	HR	BB-IBB	SO	Avg.
All-Star Game totals (3 years)	0	1	.000	3.00	1.17	3	2	0	0	0	0-0	6.0	6	2	2	0	1-0	9	.261

2006 LEFTY-RIGHTY SPLITS

vs.	Avg.	AB	H	2B	3B	HR	RBI	BB	SO	OBP	Slg.	vs.	Avg.	AB	H	2B	3B	HR	RBI	BB	SO	OBP	Slg.
L	.277	382	106	28	3	13	49	14	87	.304	.469	R	.275	414	114	23	2	15	38	14	96	.302	.449

SCHMIDT, JASON   P

PERSONAL: Born January 29, 1973, in Lewiston, Idaho. ... 6-5/205. ... Throws right, bats right. ... Full name: Jason David Schmidt. ... High school: Kelso (Wash.). **TRANSACTIONS/CAREER NOTES:** Selected by Atlanta Braves organization in eighth round of 1991 free-agent draft. ... On disabled list (July 15-August 30, 1996); included rehabilitation assignment to Greenville. ... Traded by Braves to Pittsburgh Pirates (August 30, 1996), completing deal in which Pirates traded P Denny Neagle to Braves for a player to be named (August 28, 1996). ... On disabled list (April 15-May 1 and June 10, 2000-remainder of season); included rehabilitation assignment to GCL Pirates. ... On disabled list (March 31-May 10, 2001); included rehabilitation assignments to Altoona and Nashville. ... Traded by Pirates with OF John Vander Wal to San Francisco Giants for OF Armando Rios and P Ryan Vogelsong (July 30, 2001). ... On disabled list (March 21-April 24, 2002); included rehabilitation assignment to Fresno. ... On disabled list (March 26-April 16, 2004); included rehabilitation assignment to San Jose. ... On disabled list (May 10-28, 2005). **HONORS:** Named N.L. Pitcher of the Year by THE SPORTING NEWS (2004). ... Named pitcher on THE SPORTING NEWS N.L. All-Star team (2004). **MISCELLANEOUS NOTES:** Received base on balls in only appearance as pinch hitter with Atlanta (1995).

CAREER HITTING: 61-for-584 (.104), 27 R, 9 2B, 0 3B, 6 HR, 20 RBI.

Year Team (League)	W	L	Pct.	ERA	WHIP	G	GS	CG	ShO	Hld.	Sv.-Opp.	IP	H	R	ER	HR	BB-IBB	SO	Avg.
1991—GC Braves (GCL)	3	4	.429	2.38	1.21	11	11	0	0	...	0-...	45.1	32	21	12	0	23-0	44	.189
1992—Pulaski (Appalachian)	3	4	.429	4.01	1.18	11	11	0	0	...	0-...	58.1	38	36	26	4	31-0	56	.170
—Macon (S. Atl.)	0	3	.000	4.01	2.03	7	7	0	0	...	0-...	24.2	31	18	11	2	19-0	33	.316
1993—Durham (Carol.)	7	11	.389	4.94	1.50	22	22	0	0	...	0-...	116.2	128	69	64	12	47-3	110	.286
1994—Greenville (Sou.)	8	7	.533	3.65	1.34	24	24	1	0	...	0-...	140.2	135	64	57	9	54-1	131	.255
1995—Atlanta (N.L.)	2	2	.500	5.76	1.80	9	2	0	0	0	0-1	25.0	27	17	16	2	18-3	19	.287
—Richmond (Int'l)	8	6	.571	2.25	1.25	19	19	0	0	0	0-0	116.0	97	40	29	2	48-3	95	.233
1996—Atlanta (N.L.)	3	4	.429	6.75	1.72	13	11	0	0	0	0-0	58.2	69	48	44	8	32-0	48	.296
—Richmond (Int'l)	3	0	1.000	2.56	1.20	7	7	0	0	0	0-0	45.2	36	17	13	2	19-1	41	.220
—Greenville (Sou.)	0	0	...	9.00	2.00	1	1	0	0	0	0-0	2.0	4	2	2	0	0-0	2	.444
—Pittsburgh (N.L.)	2	2	.500	4.06	1.59	6	6	1	0	0	0-0	37.2	39	19	17	2	21-0	26	.271
1997—Pittsburgh (N.L.)	10	9	.526	4.60	1.43	32	32	2	0	0	0-0	187.2	193	106	96	16	76-2	136	.265
1998—Pittsburgh (N.L.)	11	14	.440	4.07	1.40	33	33	0	0	0	0-0	214.1	228	106	97	24	71-3	158	.275
1999—Pittsburgh (N.L.)	13	11	.542	4.19	1.43	33	33	2	0	0	0-0	212.2	219	110	99	24	85-4	148	.262
2000—Pittsburgh (N.L.)	2	5	.286	5.40	1.77	11	11	0	0	0	0-0	63.1	71	43	38	6	41-2	51	.287
—GC Pirates (GCL)	0	0	...	2.25	1.25	1	1	0	0	0	0-...	4.0	4	2	1	0	1-0	5	.267
2001—Altoona (East.)	0	1	.000	0.96	0.86	3	3	0	0	0	0-...	9.1	7	1	1	0	1-0	17	.200
—Nashville (PCL)	1	0	1.000	0.00	0.57	1	1	0	0	0	0-...	7.0	4	0	0	0	0-0	6	.160
—Pittsburgh (N.L.)	6	6	.500	4.61	1.30	14	14	1	0	0	0-0	84.0	81	46	43	11	28-2	77	.256
—San Francisco (N.L.)	7	1	.875	3.39	1.36	11	11	0	0	0	0-0	66.1	57	29	25	2	33-1	65	.243

Year— Team (League)	W	L	Pct.	ERA	WHIP	G	GS	CG	ShO	Hld.	Sv.-Opp.	IP	H	R	ER	HR	BB-IBB	SO	Avg.
2002— Fresno (PCL)	2	0	1.000	3.00	1.08	2	2	0	0	...	0-...	12.0	11	4	4	0	2-0	12	.262
— San-Francisco (N.L.)	13	8	.619	3.45	1.19	29	29	2	2	0	0-0	185.1	148	78	71	15	73-1	196	.218
2003— San Francisco (N.L.)	17	5	.773	* 2.34	0.95	29	29	5	•3	0	0-0	207.2	152	56	54	14	46-1	208	* .200
2004— San Jose (Calif.)	1	0	1.000	0.00	0.60	1	1	0	0	...	0-...	5.0	2	0	0	0	1-0	7	.118
— San Francisco (N.L.)	18	7	.720	3.20	1.08	32	32	4	•3	0	0-0	225.0	165	84	80	18	77-3	251	.202
2005— San Francisco (N.L.)	12	7	.632	4.40	1.42	29	29	0	0	0	0-0	172.0	160	90	84	16	85-4	165	.246
2006— San Francisco (N.L.)	11	9	.550	3.59	1.26	32	32	3	1	0	0-0	213.1	189	94	85	21	80-6	180	.238
Major League totals (12 years)	127	90	.585	3.91	1.31	313	304	20	9	0	0-1	1953.0	1798	926	849	179	766-32	1728	.244

DIVISION SERIES RECORD

Year— Team (League)	W	L	Pct.	ERA	WHIP	G	GS	CG	ShO	Hld.	Sv.-Opp.	IP	H	R	ER	HR	BB-IBB	SO	Avg.
2002— San Francisco (N.L.)	0	1	.000	6.75	1.31	1	1	0	0	0	0-0	5.1	3	4	4	0	4-1	5	.158
2003— San Francisco (N.L.)	1	0	1.000	0.00	0.33	1	1	1	1	0	0-0	9.0	3	0	0	0	0-0	5	.100
Division series totals (2 years)	1	1	.500	2.51	0.70	2	2	1	1	0	0-0	14.1	6	4	4	0	4-1	10	.122

CHAMPIONSHIP SERIES RECORD

Year— Team (League)	W	L	Pct.	ERA	WHIP	G	GS	CG	ShO	Hld.	Sv.-Opp.	IP	H	R	ER	HR	BB-IBB	SO	Avg.
2002— San Francisco (N.L.)	1	0	1.000	1.17	0.65	1	1	0	0	0	0-0	7.2	4	1	1	1	1-0	8	.160

WORLD SERIES RECORD

Year— Team (League)	W	L	Pct.	ERA	WHIP	G	GS	CG	ShO	Hld.	Sv.-Opp.	IP	H	R	ER	HR	BB-IBB	SO	Avg.
2002— San Francisco (N.L.)	1	0	1.000	5.23	1.94	2	2	0	0	0	0-0	10.1	16	6	6	2	4-0	14	.348

ALL-STAR GAME RECORD

Year— Team (League)	W	L	Pct.	ERA	WHIP	G	GS	CG	ShO	Hld.	Sv.-Opp.	IP	H	R	ER	HR	BB-IBB	SO	Avg.
All-Star Game totals (1 year)	0	0	...	0.00	0.50	1	1	0	0	0	0-0	2.0	1	0	0	0	0-0	3	.143

2006 LEFTY-RIGHTY SPLITS

vs.	Avg.	AB	H	2B	3B	HR	RBI	BB	SO	OBP	Slg.	vs.	Avg.	AB	H	2B	3B	HR	RBI	BB	SO	OBP	Slg.
L	.262	390	102	16	3	6	37	50	95	.345	.364	R	.215	404	87	19	4	15	48	30	85	.275	.394

SCHNEIDER, BRIAN — C

PERSONAL: Born November 26, 1976, in Jacksonville. ... 6-1/196. ... Bats left, throws right. ... Full name: Brian Duncan Schneider. ... High school: Northampton (Pa.).
TRANSACTIONS/CAREER NOTES: Selected by Montreal Expos organization in fifth round of 1995 free-agent draft. ... Expos franchise transferred to Washington, D.C., and renamed Washington Nationals for 2005 season (December 3, 2004). ... On disabled list (May 13-26, 2006); included rehabilitation assignment to Potomac. **STATISTICAL NOTES:** Career major league grand slams: 2.
2006 GAMES PLAYED BY POSITION (MLB): C—123, 1B—1.

Year— Team (League)	Pos.	G	AB	R	H	2B	3B	HR	RBI	BB	SO	HBP	GDP	SB-CS	Avg.	OBP	SLG	OPS	E	Avg.
1995— GC Expos (GCL)	C	30	97	7	22	3	0	0	4	14	23	1	1	2-4	.227	.330	.258	.588	3	.982
1996— GC Expos (GCL)	C	52	144	26	44	5	2	0	23	24	15	3	3	2-3	.306	.415	.368	.783	3	.988
— Delmarva (S. Atl.)	C	5	9	0	3	0	0	1	1	1	1	1	0-0	.333	.455	.333	.788	0	1.000
1997— Cape Fear (S. Atl.)	C	113	381	46	96	20	1	4	49	53	45	4	9	3-6	.252	.345	.341	.687	10	.988
1998— Cape Fear (S. Atl.)	C	38	134	33	40	7	2	7	30	16	9	3	4	6-3	.299	.381	.537	.918	6	.980
— Jupiter (Fla. St.)	C	82	302	32	82	12	1	3	30	22	38	1	9	4-4	.272	.321	.348	.669	11	.981
1999— Harrisburg (East.)	C-1B	121	421	48	111	19	1	17	66	32	56	2	6	2-2	.264	.318	.435	.753	6	.992
2000— Ottawa (Int'l)	C-1B	67	238	22	59	22	3	4	31	16	42	0	5	1-0	.248	.285	.416	.701	8	.982
— Montreal (N.L.)	C	45	115	6	27	6	0	0	11	7	24	0	1	0-1	.235	.276	.287	.563	6	.974
2001— Ottawa (Int'l)	C	97	338	33	93	27	1	6	43	27	55	0	5	2-0	.275	.336	.414	.750	4	.994
— Montreal (N.L.)	C	27	41	4	13	3	0	1	6	3	0	0	0	0-0	.317	.396	.463	.859	0	1.000
2002— Montreal (N.L.)	C-OF	73	207	21	57	19	2	5	29	21	41	0	7	1-2	.275	.339	.459	.798	3	.993
2003— Montreal (N.L.)	C-DH	108	335	34	77	26	1	9	46	37	75	2	12	0-2	.230	.309	.394	.703	3	.996
2004— Montreal (N.L.)	C	135	436	40	112	20	3	12	49	42	63	3	8	0-0	.257	.325	.399	.724	2	.998
2005— Wash. (N.L.)	C	116	369	38	99	20	1	10	44	29	48	6	10	1-0	.268	.330	.409	.739	5	.993
2006— Potomac (Carol.)		2	9	1	2	1	0	0	1	0	2	0	0	0-0	.222	.222	.333	.556	0	...
— Wash. (N.L.)	C-1B	124	410	30	105	18	0	4	55	38	67	2	14	2-2	.256	.320	.329	.649	5	.993
Major League totals (7 years)		628	1913	173	490	112	7	41	240	180	321	13	52	4-8	.256	.322	.386	.709	24	.994

2006 LEFTY-RIGHTY SPLITS

vs.	Avg.	AB	H	2B	3B	HR	RBI	BB	SO	OBP	Slg.	vs.	Avg.	AB	H	2B	3B	HR	RBI	BB	SO	OBP	Slg.
L	.271	107	29	5	0	0	16	5	22	.304	.318	R	.251	303	76	13	0	4	39	33	45	.325	.333

SCHOENEWEIS, SCOTT — P

PERSONAL: Born October 2, 1973, in Long Branch, N.J. ... 6-0/195. ... Throws left, bats left. ... Full name: Scott David Schoeneweis. ... Name pronounced: show-en-weiss. ... High school: Lenape (Medford, N.J.). ... College: Duke. **TRANSACTIONS/CAREER NOTES:** Selected by California Angels organization in third round of 1996 free-agent draft. ... Angels franchise renamed Anaheim Angels for 1997 season. ... On disabled list (June 17-July 26, 2000); included rehabilitation assignments to Lake Elsinore and Edmonton. ... Traded by Anaheim Angels with P Doug Nickle to Chicago White Sox for Ps Gary Glover, Scott Dunn, and Tim Bittner (July 29, 2003). ... On disabled list (June 22-July 7 and August 5-September 30, 2004). ... Signed as a free agent by Toronto Blue Jays (January 10, 2005). ... Traded by Blue Jays to Cincinnati Reds for a player to be named (August 16, 2006); Blue Jays acquired 2B Trevor Lawhorn to complete deal (October 13, 2006).
CAREER HITTING: 2-for-7 (.286), 0 R, 1 2B, 0 3B, 0 HR, 1 RBI.

Year— Team (League)	W	L	Pct.	ERA	WHIP	G	GS	CG	ShO	Hld.	Sv.-Opp.	IP	H	R	ER	HR	BB-IBB	SO	Avg.
1996— Lake Elsinore (Calif.)	8	3	.727	3.94	1.21	14	12	0	0	...	0-...	93.2	86	47	41	6	27-0	83	.244
1997— Midland (Texas)	7	5	.583	5.96	1.62	20	20	3	0	...	0-...	113.1	145	84	75	7	39-0	84	.313
1998— Vancouver (PCL)	11	8	.579	4.50	1.37	27	27	2	0	.	0-...	180.0	188	102	90	18	59-0	133	.266
1999— Anaheim (A.L.)	1	1	.500	5.49	1.55	31	0	0	0	3	0-0	39.1	47	27	24	4	14-1	22	.294
— Edmonton (PCL)	2	4	.333	7.64	1.98	9	7	0	0	...	0-...	35.1	58	35	30	6	12-0	29	.360
2000— Anaheim (A.L.)	7	10	.412	5.45	1.47	27	27	1	0	0	0-0	170.0	183	112	103	21	67-2	78	.276
— Lake Elsinore (Calif.)	0	0	...	1.93	1.29	1	1	0	0	...	0-0	4.2	3	1	1	0	3-0	3	.200
— Edmonton (PCL)	0	0	...	0.00	0.43	1	1	0	0	...	0-...	7.0	2	0	0	0	1-0	6	.083
2001— Anaheim (A.L.)	10	11	.476	5.08	1.48	32	32	1	0	0	0-0	205.1	227	122	116	21	77-2	104	.281
2002— Anaheim (A.L.)	9	8	.529	4.88	1.42	54	15	0	0	11	1-4	118.0	119	68	64	17	49-4	65	.264
2003— Anaheim (A.L.)	1	1	.500	3.96	1.22	39	0	0	0	4	0-1	38.2	37	19	17	2	10-3	29	.250
— Chicago (A.L.)	2	1	.667	4.50	1.35	20	0	0	0	1	0-0	26.0	26	16	13	1	9-2	27	.255
2004— Chicago (A.L.)	6	9	.400	5.59	1.58	20	19	0	0	0	0-0	112.2	129	74	70	17	49-0	69	.291
2005— Toronto (A.L.)	3	4	.429	3.32	1.39	80	0	0	0	21	1-4	57.0	54	23	21	2	25-5	43	.245
2006— Toronto (A.L.)	2	2	.500	6.51	1.47	55	0	0	0	18	1-3	37.1	39	27	27	3	16-5	18	.273
— Cincinnati (N.L.)	2	0	1.000	0.63	1.19	16	0	0	0	1	3-3	14.1	9	1	1	1	8-1	11	.176
American League totals (8 years)	41	47	.466	5.09	1.46	358	93	2	1	57	3-13	804.1	861	488	455	88	316-24	455	.275
National League totals (1 year)	2	0	1.000	0.63	1.19	16	0	0	0	1	3-3	14.1	9	1	1	1	8-1	11	.176
Major League totals (8 years)	43	47	.478	5.01	1.46	374	93	2	1	58	6-16	818.2	870	489	456	89	324-25	466	.273

S

DIVISION SERIES RECORD

Year Team (League)	W	L	Pct.	ERA	WHIP	G	GS	CG	ShO	Hld.	Sv.-Opp.	IP	H	R	ER	HR	BB-IBB	SO	Avg.
2002— Anaheim (A.L.)	0	0	...	27.00	6.00	3	0	0	0	...	0-1	0.1	2	1	1	0	0-0	0	.667

CHAMPIONSHIP SERIES RECORD

Year Team (League)	W	L	Pct.	ERA	WHIP	G	GS	CG	ShO	Hld.	Sv.-Opp.	IP	H	R	ER	HR	BB-IBB	SO	Avg.
2002— Anaheim (A.L.)	0	0	...	0.00	0.00	1	0	0	0	...	0-0	0.2	0	0	0	0	0-0	0	.000

WORLD SERIES RECORD

Year Team (League)	W	L	Pct.	ERA	WHIP	G	GS	CG	ShO	Hld.	Sv.-Opp.	IP	H	R	ER	HR	BB-IBB	SO	Avg.
2002— Anaheim (A.L.)	0	0	...	0.00	1.00	2	0	0	0	...	0-0	2.0	1	0	0	0	1-0	2	.167

2006 LEFTY-RIGHTY SPLITS

vs.	Avg.	AB	H	2B	3B	HR	RBI	BB	SO	OBP	Slg.	vs.	Avg.	AB	H	2B	3B	HR	RBI	BB	SO	OBP	Slg.
L	.236	89	21	5	0	0	13	11	15	.333	.292	R	.257	105	27	4	1	4	13	13	14	.339	.429

SCHRODER, CHRIS — P

PERSONAL: Born August 20, 1978, in Okarche, Okla. ... Throws right, bats right. ... Full name: Christopher K. Schroder. ... College: Oklahoma City University. **TRANSAC-TIONS/CAREER NOTES:** Selected by Montreal Expos organization in 19th round of 2001 free-agent draft.
CAREER HITTING: 0-for-2 (.000), 0 R, 0 2B, 0 3B, 0 HR, 0 RBI.

Year Team (League)	W	L	Pct.	ERA	WHIP	G	GS	CG	ShO	Hld.	Sv.-Opp.	IP	H	R	ER	HR	BB-IBB	SO	Avg.
2001— Vermont (NYP)	0	0	...	1.50	1.08	11	0	0	0	...	2-...	12.0	8	2	2	1	5-0	18	.186
— Jupiter (Fla. St.)	1	0	1.000	2.30	1.02	10	0	0	0	...	0-...	15.2	12	5	4	1	4-0	20	.200
2002— Clinton (Midw.)	1	3	.250	1.65	1.06	22	0	0	0	...	10-...	27.1	15	7	5	1	14-1	42	.156
— Brevard County (FSL)	2	2	.500	1.52	1.08	23	0	0	0	...	6-...	29.2	13	6	5	2	19-1	36	.133
2003— Harrisburg (East.)	9	2	.818	2.84	1.40	49	0	0	0	...	4-...	82.1	68	29	26	5	47-1	81	.231
2004— Harrisburg (East.)	2	2	.500	2.42	1.16	32	0	0	0	...	11-...	48.1	39	13	13	3	17-2	51	.213
— Edmonton (PCL)	2	1	.667	4.39	1.46	17	1	0	0	...	0-...	26.2	24	13	13	3	15-0	32	.231
2005— t (GCL)	0	0	...	9.00	2.00	1	0	0	0	0	0-0	1.0	2	1	1	0	0-0	3	.400
— Potomac (Carol.)	0	0	...	0.00	1.29	5	0	0	0	1	1-2	7.0	7	3	0	0	2-0	10	.250
— Harrisburg (East.)	2	3	.400	4.70	1.35	16	0	0	0	0	0-2	23.0	20	13	12	4	11-0	28	.238
— New Orleans (PCL)	2	0	1.000	7.83	1.57	19	0	0	0	2	4-5	23.0	21	21	20	6	15-0	29	.239
2006— New Orleans (PCL)	2	1	.667	1.52	0.87	28	0	0	0	1	1-1	47.1	25	9	8	2	16-1	60	.152
— Harrisburg (East.)	2	0	1.000	5.02	1.67	9	0	0	0	1	1-2	14.1	18	9	-8	2	6-2	13	.300
— Wash. (N.L.)	0	2	.000	6.35	1.34	21	0	0	0	1	0-1	28.1	23	21	20	7	15-3	39	.223
Major League totals (1 year)	0	2	.000	6.35	1.34	21	0	0	0	1	0-1	28.1	23	21	20	7	15-3	39	.223

2006 LEFTY-RIGHTY SPLITS

vs.	Avg.	AB	H	2B	3B	HR	RBI	BB	SO	OBP	Slg.	vs.	Avg.	AB	H	2B	3B	HR	RBI	BB	SO	OBP	Slg.
L	.261	46	12	3	0	4	16	12	15	.400	.587	R	.193	57	11	2	0	3	8	3	24	.288	.386

SCHUMAKER, SKIP — OF

PERSONAL: Born February 3, 1980, in Torrance, Calif. ... 5-10/175. ... Bats left, throws right. ... Full name: Jared Michael Schumaker. ... High school: Aliso Niguel (Aliso Viejo, Calif.). ... College: California-Santa Barbara. **TRANSACTIONS/CAREER NOTES:** Selected by St. Louis Cardinals organization in fifth round of 2001 free-agent draft.
2006 GAMES PLAYED BY POSITION (MLB): OF—25.

Year Team (League)	Pos.	G	AB	R	H	2B	3B	HR	RBI	BB	SO	HBP	GDP	SB-CS	Avg.	OBP	SLG	OPS	E	Avg.
2001— New Jersey (NYP)	OF	49	162	22	41	10	1	0	14	29	33	1	4	11-2	.253	.368	.327	.695	2	.971
2002— Potomac (Carol.)	OF	136	551	71	158	22	4	2	44	45	84	2	10	26-16	.287	.342	.352	.694	3	.988
2003— Tennessee (Sou.)	OF-3B	91	342	43	86	20	3	2	22	37	54	4	6	6-6	.251	.330	.345	.675	1	.994
2004— Tennessee (Sou.)	OF-3B	138	516	78	163	29	6	4	43	60	61	2	7	19-14	.316	.389	.419	.808	7	.821
2005— Memphis (PCL)	OF	115	443	66	127	24	3	7	34	29	54	2	14	14-3	.287	.330	.402	.732	2	.996
— St. Louis (N.L.)	OF	27	24	9	6	1	0	0	1	2	2	0	0	1-0	.250	.308	.292	.599	0	1.000
2006— Memphis (PCL)		95	369	47	113	13	3	3	27	23	48	3	12	11-4	.306	.348	.382	.730	2	.991
— St. Louis (N.L.)	OF	28	54	3	10	1	0	1	2	5	6	0	1	2-1	.185	.254	.259	.513	0	1.000
Major League totals (2 years)		55	78	12	16	2	0	1	3	7	8	0	1	3-1	.205	.271	.269	.540	0	1.000

2006 LEFTY-RIGHTY SPLITS

vs.	Avg.	AB	H	2B	3B	HR	RBI	BB	SO	OBP	Slg.	vs.	Avg.	AB	H	2B	3B	HR	RBI	BB	SO	OBP	Slg.
L	.000	9	0	0	0	0	0	0	2	.000	.000	R	.222	45	10	1	0	1	2	5	4	.300	.311

SCOTT, LUKE — OF

PERSONAL: Born June 25, 1978, in Deleon Springs, Fla. ... 6-0/210. ... Bats left, throws right. ... Full name: Luke Brandon Scott. ... High school: DeLand (Fla.). ... Junior college: Indian River (Fla.). ... College: Oklahoma State. **TRANSACTIONS/CAREER NOTES:** Selected by Cleveland Indians organization in ninth round of 2001 free-agent draft. Traded by Indians with OF Willy Taveras to Houston Astros for P Jeriome Robertson (March 31, 2004). **STATISTICAL NOTES:** Hit for the cycle (July 28, 2006).
2006 GAMES PLAYED BY POSITION (MLB): OF—60.

Year Team (League)	Pos.	G	AB	R	H	2B	3B	HR	RBI	BB	SO	HBP	GDP	SB-CS	Avg.	OBP	SLG	OPS	E	Avg.
2002— Columbus (S. Atl.)	OF	49	171	28	44	15	4	7	32	21	58	3	3	9-1	.257	.345	.515	.860	1	.971
— Kinston (Carol.)	OF-1B	48	163	22	39	7	1	8	30	16	47	5	2	2-1	.239	.326	.442	.768	2	.973
2003— Kinston (Carol.)	OF-1B	67	241	37	67	12	1	13	44	27	62	4	0	6-3	.278	.360	.498	.858	1	.989
— Akron (East.)	OF	50	183	21	50	13	1	7	37	11	37	2	2	0-1	.273	.317	.470	.787	2	.947
2004— Salem (Carol.)	OF	66	241	45	67	20	1	8	35	41	58	0	5	6-1	.278	.376	.469	.845	1	.500
— Round Rock (Texas)	OF	63	208	45	62	17	0	19	62	33	43	6	4	0-2	.298	.401	.654	1.055	1	.000
2005— Round Rock (PCL)	OF-DH	103	398	69	114	25	4	31	87	43	96	6	4	2-2	.286	.363	.603	.966	2	.996
— Houston (N.L.)	OF	34	80	6	15	4	2	0	4	9	23	0	1	1-1	.188	.270	.288	.557	1	.963
2006— Round Rock (PCL)		87	318	63	95	15	1	20	63	52	66	5	3	6-1	.299	.400	.541	.941	1	.994
— Houston (N.L.)	OF	65	214	31	72	19	6	10	37	30	43	4	2	2-1	.336	.426	.621	1.047	0	1.000
Major League totals (2 years)		99	294	37	87	23	8	10	41	39	66	4	3	3-2	.296	.385	.531	.915	1	.992

DIVISION SERIES RECORD

Year Team (League)	Pos.	G	AB	R	H	2B	3B	HR	RBI	BB	SO	HBP	GDP	SB-CS	Avg.	OBP	SLG	OPS	E	Avg.
2005— Houston (N.L.)	OF	2	2	1	0	0	0	0	0	1	1	0	0	0-0	.000	.333	.000	.333	0	...

2006 LEFTY-RIGHTY SPLITS

vs.	Avg.	AB	H	2B	3B	HR	RBI	BB	SO	OBP	Slg.	vs.	Avg.	AB	H	2B	3B	HR	RBI	BB	SO	OBP	Slg.
L	.240	50	12	2	1	1	6	11	17	.397	.380	R	.366	164	60	17	5	9	31	19	26	.435	.695

S

SCUTARO, MARCO 2B/SS

PERSONAL: Born October 30, 1975, in San Felipe, Venezuela. ... 5-10/170. ... Bats right, throws right. ... Full name: Marcos Scutaro. ... Name pronounced: scoot-AH-roh. ... High school: Frederico Quiroz (Venezuela). **TRANSACTIONS/CAREER NOTES:** Signed as a non-drafted free agent by Cleveland Indians organization (July 26, 1994). ... Traded by Indians to Milwaukee Brewers (August 30, 2000); completing deal in which Indians traded 1B Richie Sexson, Ps Paul Rigdon and Kane Davis and a player to be named to Brewers for Ps Bob Wickman, Jason Bere and Steve Woodard (July 28, 2000). ... Claimed on waivers by New York Mets (April 5, 2002). ... Claimed on waivers by Oakland Athletics (October 9, 2003).

2006 GAMES PLAYED BY POSITION (MLB): SS—69, 2B—37, 3B—12, OF—2.

Year	Team (League)	Pos.	G	AB	R	H	2B	3B	HR	RBI	BB	SO	HBP	GDP	SB-CS	Avg.	OBP	SLG	OPS	E	Avg.
1995—	Dom. Inds. (DSL)	3B	66	262	71	103	18	6	0	38	20	11			32-...	.393		.508		17	.931
1996—	Columbus (S. Atl.)	2B-3B-SS	85	315	66	79	12	3	10	45	38	86	4	6	6-3	.251	.334	.403	.737	17	.959
1997—	Kinston (Carol.)	2B-3B-SS	97	378	58	103	17	6	10	59	35	72	9	3	23-7	.272	.346	.429	.774	11	.972
	— Buffalo (A.A.)	2B-3B-SS	21	57	8	15	3	0	1	6	6	8	0	4	0-1	.263	.328	.368	.697	3	.959
1998—	Akron (East.)	2B-SS	124	462	68	146	27	6	11	62	47	71	10	8	33-16	.316	.387	.472	.859	15	.976
	— Buffalo (Int'l)	2B-SS	8	26	3	6	3	0	0	4	0	2	0	0	0-0	.231	.231	.346	.577	2	.939
1999—	Buffalo (Int'l)	2B-SS	129	462	76	126	24	2	8	51	61	69	6	5	21-6	.273	.362	.385	.747	16	.974
2000—	Buffalo (Int'l)	2B-SS	124	425	67	117	20	5	5	54	61	53	9		9-6	.275	.373	.381	.754	15	.976
	— Indianapolis (Int'l)	2B-SS	4	13	5	7	1	1	1	3	1	2	0		1-0	.538	.571	1.000	1.571	0	1.000
2001—	Indianapolis (Int'l)	2B-3B-SS	132	495	87	146	29	3	11	50	62	83	10	9	11-11	.295	.382	.432	.815	19	.968
2002—	Norfolk (Int'l)	2B-SS-OF 3B	97	354	48	113	22	6	7	28	30	61	2	7	7-8	.319	.375	.475	.849	10	.974
	— New York (N.L.)	OF	27	36	2	8	0	1	1	6	0	11	0	1	0-1	.222	.216	.361	.577	1	.968
2003—	Norfolk (Int'l)	3B-2B-SS OF-DH	70	244	42	76	18	3	9	32	33	34	6	6	11-6	.311	.401	.520	.921	7	.970
	— New York (N.L.)	2B-SS	48	75	10	16	4	0	2	6	13	14	1	1	2-0	.213	.333	.347	.680	2	.981
2004—	Oakland (A.L.)	2B-SS-3B	137	455	50	124	32	1	7	43	16	58	0	9	0-0	.273	.297	.393	.690	5	.992
2005—	Oakland (A.L.)	SS-2B OF	118	381	48	94	22	3	9	37	36	48	0	6	5-2	.247	.310	.391	.701	9	.982
2006—	Oakland (A.L.)	SS-2B-3B OF	117	365	52	97	21	6	5	41	50	66	0	16	5-1	.266	.350	.397	.747	13	.972
	American League totals (3 years)		372	1201	150	315	75	10	21	121	102	172	0	31	10-3	.262	.318	.394	.712	27	.983
	National League totals (2 years)		75	111	12	24	4	1	3	12	13	25	1	2	2-1	.216	.299	.351	.651	3	.978
	Major League totals (5 years)		447	1312	162	339	79	11	24	133	115	197	1	33	12-4	.258	.316	.390	.707	30	.982

DIVISION SERIES RECORD

Year	Team (League)	Pos.	G	AB	R	H	2B	3B	HR	RBI	BB	SO	HBP	GDP	SB-CS	Avg.	OBP	SLG	OPS	E	Avg.
2006—	Oakland (A.L.)	SS	3	12	1	4	0	0	0	0	0	0			0-0	.333	.333	.667	1.000	0	1.000

CHAMPIONSHIP SERIES RECORD

Year	Team (League)	Pos.	G	AB	R	H	2B	3B	HR	RBI	BB	SO	HBP	GDP	SB-CS	Avg.	OBP	SLG	OPS	E	Avg.
2006—	Oakland (A.L.)	SS	4	15	1	1	0	0	0	0	0	3	0	1	0-0	.067	.067	.067	.133	0	1.000

2006 LEFTY-RIGHTY SPLITS

vs.	Avg.	AB	H	2B	3B	HR	RBI	BB	SO	OBP	Slg.	vs.	Avg.	AB	H	2B	3B	HR	RBI	BB	SO	OBP	Slg.
L	.218	78	17	4	0	2	10	15	19	.340	.346	R	.279	287	80	17	6	3	31	35	47	.353	.411

SEANEZ, RUDY P

PERSONAL: Born October 20, 1968, in Brawley, Calif. ... 5-11/200. ... Throws right, bats right. ... Full name: Rudy Caballero Seanez. ... Name pronounced: SEE-ahn-ez. ... High school: Brawley (Calif.) Union. **TRANSACTIONS/CAREER NOTES:** Selected by Cleveland Indians organization in fourth round of June 1986 free-agent draft. ... On disabled list (April 1-16 and July 30-September 2, 1991); included rehabilitation assignment to Colorado Springs. ... Traded by Indians to Los Angeles Dodgers for Ps Dennis Cook and Mike Christopher (December 10, 1991). ... On disabled list (March 29, 1992-entire season). ... Traded by Dodgers to Colorado Rockies for 2B Jody Reed (November 17, 1992). ... On disabled list (April 4-July 16, 1993); included rehabilitation assignments to Central Valley and Colorado Springs. ... Signed as a free agent by San Diego Padres organization (July 22, 1993). ... Released by Padres (November 18, 1993). ... Signed by Dodgers organization (January 12, 1994). ... On disabled list (May 28-June 16, 1995); included rehabilitation assignment to San Bernardino. ... Signed as a free agent by New York Mets organization (January 15, 1997). ... Traded by Mets to Kansas City Royals for future considerations (May 30, 1997). ... Signed as a free agent by Atlanta Braves organization (December 9, 1997). ... On disabled list (August 21, 1999-remainder of season). ... On disabled list (March 23-April 27, 2000 and June 14-remainder of season); included rehabilitation assignment to Greenville. ... Signed as a free agent by Padres organization (February 14, 2001). ... On disabled list (June 6-21, 2001). ... Traded by Padres to Braves for a player to be named (August 31, 2001); Padres acquired P Winston Abreu to complete deal (September 6, 2001). ... Signed as a free agent by Texas Rangers (January 28, 2002). ... On disabled list (May 30-September 2, 2002); included rehabilitation assignment to Oklahoma. ... Released by Rangers (May 3, 2003). ... Signed by Boston Red Sox organization (May 6, 2003). ... Released by Red Sox (July 30, 2003). ... Signed by Chicago Cubs organization (August 1, 2003). ... Signed by Kansas City Royals organization (February 12, 2004). ... Traded by Royals to Florida Marlins for OF Abraham Nunez (July 31, 2004). ... Signed as a free agent by Padres (November 24, 2004). ... On disabled list (July 18-August 12, 2005); included rehabilitation assignment to Lake Elsinore. ... Signed as a free agent by Red Sox (December 20, 2005). ... Released by Red Sox (August 28, 2006). ... Signed by Padres (August 31, 2006).

CAREER HITTING: 0-for-4 (.000), 1 R, 0 2B, 0 3B, 0 HR, 0 RBI.

Year	Team (League)	W	L	Pct.	ERA	WHIP	G	GS	CG	ShO	Hld.	Sv.-Opp.	IP	H	R	ER	HR	BB-IBB	SO	Avg.
1986—	Burlington (Appal.)	5	2	.714	3.20	1.20	13	12	1	1	...	0-...	76.0	59	37	27	5	32-0	56	.212
1987—	Waterloo (Midw.)	0	4	.000	6.75	1.67	10	10	0	0	...	0-...	34.2	35	29	26	6	23-0	23	.263
1988—	Waterloo (Midw.)	6	6	.500	4.69	1.46	22	22	1	1	...	0-...	113.1	98	69	59	10	68-0	93	.230
1989—	Kinston (Carol.)	8	10	.444	4.14	1.81	25	25	1	0	...	0-...	113.0	94	66	52	0	111-1	149	.223
	— Colo. Springs (PCL)	0	0		0.00	1.00	1	0	0	0	0	0-...	1.0	1	0	0	0	0-0	0	.250
	— Cleveland (A.L.)	0	0		3.60	1.00	5	0	0	0	0	0-...	5.0	1	2	2	0	4-1	7	.071
1990—	Cant./Akr. (Eastern)	1	0	1.000	2.16	1.26	15	0	0	0		5-...	16.2	9	4	4	0	12-0	27	.170
	— Cleveland (A.L.)	2	1	.667	5.60	1.72	24	0	0	0	3	0-0	27.1	22	17	17	2	25-1	24	.220
	— Colo. Springs (PCL)	1	4	.200	6.75	2.08	12	0	0	0		1-...	12.0	15	10	9	2	10-0	7	.313
1991—	Colo. Springs (PCL)	0	0		7.27	2.25	16	0	0	0		0-...	17.1	17	14	14	2	22-0	19	.274
	— Cant./Akr. (Eastern)	4	2	.667	2.58	1.23	25	0	0	0		7-...	38.1	17	12	11	2	30-1	73	.132
	— Cleveland (A.L.)	0	1	.000	16.20	3.40	5	0	0	0	0	0-1	5.0	10	12	9	2	7-0	7	.385
1992—	Los Angeles (N.L.)			Did not play.																
1993—	Central Valley (Cal.)	0	0	.000	9.72	2.40	5	1	0	0		0-...	8.1	9	9	9	0	11-0	7	.265
	— Colo. Springs (PCL)	0	0		9.00	1.33	3	0	0	0		0-...	3.0	3	3	3	1	1-0	5	.250
	— Las Vegas (PCL)	0	1	.000	6.41	1.78	14	0	0	0		0-...	19.2	24	15	14	2	11-0	14	.308
	— San Diego (N.L.)	0	0		13.50	3.00	3	0	0	0	0	0-...	3.1	8	6	5	1	2-0	1	.471
1994—	Albuquerque (PCL)	2	1	.667	5.32	1.86	20	0	0	0		9-...	22.0	22	14	13	3	13-1	26	.308
	— Los Angeles (N.L.)	1	1	.500	2.66	1.39	17	0	0	0	1	0-1	23.2	24	7	7	2	9-1	18	.273

Year	Team (League)	W	L	Pct.	ERA	WHIP	G	GS	CG	ShO	Hld.	Sv.-Opp.	IP	H	R	ER	HR	BB-IBB	SO	Avg.
1995—	Los Angeles (N.L.)	1	3	.250	6.75	1.64	37	0	0	0	6	3-4	34.2	39	27	26	5	18-3	29	.285
	—San Bern. (Calif.)	2	0	1.000	0.00	0.83	4	0	0	0	...	1-...	6.0	2	0	0	0	3-0	5	.100
1996—	Albuquerque (PCL)	0	2	.000	6.52	1.97	21	0	0	0	...	6-...	19.1	27	18	14	0	11-1	20	.325
1997—	Norfolk (Int'l)	1	0	1.000	4.05	1.73	9	0	0	0	...	0-...	13.1	12	8	6	1	11-0	17	.231
	—Omaha (A.A.)	2	5	.286	6.51	1.66	28	3	0	0	...	0-...	47.0	53	42	34	13	25-0	46	.270
1998—	Richmond (Int'l)	2	0	1.000	1.29	0.95	16	0	0	0	...	7-...	21.0	13	9	3	1	7-1	33	.169
	—Atlanta (N.L.)	4	1	.800	2.75	1.14	34	0	0	0	8	2-4	36.0	25	13	11	2	16-0	50	.195
1999—	Atlanta (N.L.)	6	1	.857	3.35	1.27	56	0	0	0	18	3-8	53.2	47	21	20	3	21-1	41	.234
2000—	Greenville (Sou.)	0	0	...	0.00	1.00	2	1	0	0	...	0-...	2.0	2	0	0	0	0-0	3	.250
	—Atlanta (N.L.)	2	4	.333	4.29	1.14	23	0	0	0	6	2-3	21.0	15	11	10	3	9-1	20	.192
2001—	Lake Elsinore (Calif.)	0	1	.000	2.08	1.04	7	0	0	0	...	0-...	8.2	7	3	2	1	2-0	8	.219
	—San Diego (N.L.)	0	0	.000	2.63	1.25	26	0	0	0	5	1-3	24.0	15	8	7	3	15-0	24	.176
	—Atlanta (N.L.)	0	0	...	3.00	1.00	12	0	0	0	4	0-0	12.0	8	4	4	1	4-0	17	.182
2002—	Texas (A.L.)	1	3	.250	5.73	1.58	33	0	0	0	10	0-...	33.0	28	25	21	5	24-1	40	.230
	—Oklahoma (PCL)	0	0	...	4.50	1.00	4	0	0	0	...	0-...	4.0	4	2	2	0	0-0	3	.267
2003—	Oklahoma (PCL)	0	1	.000	2.08	1.80	5	0	0	0	...	0-...	4.1	3	4	1	0	5-0	7	.176
	—Boston (A.L.)	0	1	.000	6.23	1.96	9	0	0	0	0	0-1	8.2	11	7	6	2	6-1	9	.297
	—Pawtucket (Int'l)	2	2	.500	6.10	1.50	17	0	0	0	...	3-...	20.2	20	14	14	5	10-1	24	.253
	—Iowa (PCL)	1	2	.333	3.46	1.60	13	0	0	0	...	2-...	13.0	12	10	5	1	9-2	13	.235
2004—	Omaha (PCL)	1	2	.667	1.57	0.90	24	0	0	0	...	3-...	34.1	19	8	6	3	12-0	41	.152
	—Kansas City (A.L.)	0	1	.000	3.91	1.39	16	0	0	0	1	0-1	23.0	21	10	10	0	11-2	21	.244
	—Florida (N.L.)	3	1	.750	2.74	1.13	23	0	0	0	3	0-1	23.0	18	7	7	3	8-1	25	.212
2005—	Lake Elsinore (Calif.)	0	1	.000	36.00	4.00	1	0	0	0	...	0-0	1.0	3	4	4	2	1-0	0	.500
	—San Diego (N.L.)	7	1	.875	2.69	1.18	57	0	0	0	11	0-2	60.1	49	19	18	4	22-4	84	.222
2006—	Boston (A.L.)	2	1	.667	4.82	1.65	41	0	0	0	3	0-1	46.2	51	28	25	6	26-1	48	.271
	—San Diego (N.L.)	1	2	.333	5.68	2.05	8	0	0	0	0	0-1	6.1	7	4	4	2	6-3	6	.259
	American League totals (7 years)	5	7	.417	5.45	1.66	133	0	0	0	17	0-8	148.2	144	101	90	17	103-7	156	.251
	National League totals (10 years)	25	16	.610	3.59	1.29	296	0	0	0	62	11-27	298.0	255	127	119	29	130-14	315	.230
	Major League totals (15 years)	30	23	.566	4.21	1.41	429	0	0	0	79	11-35	446.2	399	228	209	46	233-21	471	.237

DIVISION SERIES RECORD

Year	Team (League)	W	L	Pct.	ERA	WHIP	G	GS	CG	ShO	Hld.	Sv.-Opp.	IP	H	R	ER	HR	BB-IBB	SO	Avg.
1998—	Atlanta (N.L.)	0	0	...	0.00	1.00	1	0	0	0	...	0-0	1.0	0	0	0	0	1-0	0	.000
2001—	Atlanta (N.L.)	1	0	1.000	0.00	1.00	1	0	0	0	...	0-0	1.0	0	0	0	0	1-0	0	.000
2005—	San Diego (N.L.)	0	0	...	6.00	1.33	2	0	0	0	...	0-0	3.0	3	2	2	0	1-0	4	.250
2006—	San Diego (N.L.)	0	0	...	0.00	0.00	1	0	0	0	...	0-0	1.2	0	0	0	0	0-0	2	.000
	Division series totals (4 years)	1	0	1.000	2.70	0.75	5	0	0	0	...	0-0	6.2	3	2	2	0	2-0	6	.130

CHAMPIONSHIP SERIES RECORD

Year	Team (League)	W	L	Pct.	ERA	WHIP	G	GS	CG	ShO	Hld.	Sv.-Opp.	IP	H	R	ER	HR	BB-IBB	SO	Avg.
1998—	Atlanta (N.L.)	0	0	...	6.00	1.00	4	0	0	0	1	0-0	3.0	2	2	2	0	1-0	4	.200
2001—	Atlanta (N.L.)	0	0	...	0.00	2.00	2	0	0	0	0	0-0	2.0	1	0	0	0	3-2	3	.143
	Champ. series totals (2 years)	0	0	...	3.60	1.40	6	0	0	0	1	0-0	5.0	3	2	2	0	4-2	7	.176

2006 LEFTY-RIGHTY SPLITS

vs.	Avg.	AB	H	2B	3B	HR	RBI	BB	SO	OBP	Slg.	vs.	Avg.	AB	H	2B	3B	HR	RBI	BB	SO	OBP	Slg.
L	.266	94	25	3	2	3	18	17	23	.378	.436	R	.273	121	33	5	0	5	20	15	31	.355	.438

SEAY, BOBBY   P

PERSONAL: Born June 20, 1978, in Sarasota, Fla. ... 6-2/235. ... Throws left, bats left. ... Full name: Robert Michael Seay. ... Name pronounced: see. ... High school: Sarasota (Fla.). **TRANSACTIONS/CAREER NOTES:** Selected by Chicago White Sox organization in first round (12th pick overall) of 1996 free-agent draft. ... Rights relinquished by White Sox (August 15, 1996). ... Signed by Tampa Bay Devil Rays organization (November 8, 1996). ... On disabled list (March 22-June 3, 2002); included rehabilitation assignment to Orlando. ... On disabled list (April 24-June 3, 2003). ... Traded by Devil Rays to Colorado Rockies for OF Reggie Taylor (April 8, 2005). ... On disabled list (April 18-June 5, 2005); inlcuded rehabilitation assignments to Tulsa and Colorado Springs. ... Signed as a free agent by Detroit Tigers organization (November 29, 2005). **MISCELLANEOUS NOTES:** Member of 2000 U.S. Olympic baseball team.
CAREER HITTING: 0-for-0 (.000), 0 R, 0 2B, 0 3B, 0 HR, 0 RBI.

Year	Team (League)	W	L	Pct.	ERA	WHIP	G	GS	CG	ShO	Hld.	Sv.-Opp.	IP	H	R	ER	HR	BB-IBB	SO	Avg.
1997—	Char., S.C. (SAL)	3	4	.429	4.55	1.52	13	13	0	0	...	0-...	61.1	56	35	31	2	37-0	64	.249
1998—	Char., S.C. (SAL)	1	7	.125	4.30	1.28	15	15	0	0	...	0-...	69.0	59	40	33	10	29-0	74	.236
1999—	St. Pete. (FSL)	2	6	.250	3.00	1.39	12	11	0	0	...	0-...	57.0	56	25	19	0	23-0	45	.271
	—Orlando (South.)	1	2	.333	7.94	2.18	6	6	0	0	...	0-...	17.0	22	15	15	2	15-0	16	.319
2000—	Orlando (South.)	8	7	.533	3.88	1.40	24	24	0	0	...	0-...	132.1	132	64	57	13	53-1	106	.265
2001—	Orlando (South.)	2	5	.286	5.98	1.65	15	13	0	0	...	0-...	64.2	81	48	43	9	26-0	49	.310
	—Tampa Bay (A.L.)	1	1	.500	6.23	1.38	12	0	0	0	...	0-...	13.0	13	11	9	2	5-1	12	.260
2002—	Orlando (South.)	2	0	1.000	3.28	1.29	15	3	0	0	...	0-...	35.2	31	16	13	2	15-0	24	.237
	—Durham (Int'l)	0	0	...	6.00	1.13	10	0	0	0	...	0-...	15.0	15	10	10	1	2-0	14	.254
2003—	Tampa Bay (A.L.)	0	0	...	3.00	1.44	12	0	0	0	...	0-1	9.0	7	3	3	0	6-0	5	.226
	—Durham (Int'l)	3	0	1.000	2.10	1.30	25	0	0	0	...	0-...	30.0	23	10	7	1	15-0	29	.195
2004—	Durham (Int'l)	1	2	.667	1.72	0.95	29	0	0	0	...	1-...	36.2	26	9	7	3	9-0	35	.195
	—Tampa Bay (A.L.)	0	0	...	2.38	1.15	21	0	0	0	...	0-...	22.2	21	6	6	2	5-1	17	.239
2005—	Tulsa (Texas)	1	0	1.000	1.80	0.60	4	0	0	0	...	1-1	5.0	3	1	1	0	0-0	3	.188
	—Colorado (N.L.)	0	0	...	8.49	2.23	17	0	0	0	...	0-1	11.2	18	11	11	3	8-1	11	.367
	—Colo. Springs (PCL)	1	0	1.000	2.38	1.46	17	0	0	0	...	3-3	22.2	23	8	6	2	10-0	24	.271
2006—	Toledo (Int'l)	1	2	.333	4.74	1.26	24	1	0	0	...	0-0	24.2	25	15	13	3	6-2	14	.278
	—Detroit (A.L.)	0	0	...	6.46	1.50	14	0	0	0	...	0-...	15.1	14	11	11	1	9-1	12	.246
	American League totals (4 years)	1	1	.500	4.35	1.33	59	0	0	0	...	0-1	60.0	55	31	29	6	25-3	46	.243
	National League totals (1 year)	0	0	...	8.49	2.23	17	0	0	0	...	0-1	11.2	18	11	11	3	8-1	11	.367
	Major League totals (5 years)	1	1	.500	5.02	1.48	76	0	0	0	...	0-2	71.2	73	42	40	9	33-4	57	.265

2006 LEFTY-RIGHTY SPLITS

vs.	Avg.	AB	H	2B	3B	HR	RBI	BB	SO	OBP	Slg.	vs.	Avg.	AB	H	2B	3B	HR	RBI	BB	SO	OBP	Slg.
L	.227	22	5	3	0	0	1	4	5	.414	.364	R	.257	35	9	0	0	1	6	5	7	.341	.343

SELE, AARON   P

PERSONAL: Born June 25, 1970, in Golden Valley, Minn. ... 6-5/230. ... Throws right, bats right. ... Full name: Aaron Helmer Sele. ... Name pronounced: SEE-lee. ... High school: North Kitsap (Poulsbo, Wash.). ... College: Washington State. **TRANSACTIONS/CAREER NOTES:** Selected by Minnesota Twins organization in 37th round of 1988 free-agent draft; did not sign. ... Selected by Boston Red Sox organization in first round (23rd pick overall) of 1991 free-agent draft. ... On disabled list (May 24, 1995-remainder of season); included rehabilitation assignments to Trenton, Sarasota and Pawtucket. ... On disabled list (August 14-September 1, 1996); included rehabilitation assignment to Pawtucket. ... Traded by Red Sox with P Mark Brandenburg and C Bill Haselman to Texas Rangers for C Jim Leyritz and OF Damon Buford (November 6, 1997). ... Signed as a free agent by Seattle Mariners (January 10, 2000). ... Signed as a free agent by Anaheim Angels (January 4, 2002). ... On disabled list (August 21-September 29, 2002). ... On disabled list (March 21-May 9, 2003); included rehabilitation assignments to Rancho Cucamonga and Salt Lake. ... On disabled list (June 11-26, 2004). ... Signed as a free agent by Seattle Mariners organization (January 19, 2005). ... Released by Mariners (July 31, 2005). ... Signed by Texas Rangers organization (August 6, 2005). ... Released by Rangers (August 16, 2005). ... Signed by Los Angeles Dodgers organization (January 14, 2006). **HONORS:** Named A.L. Rookie Pitcher of the Year by THE SPORTING NEWS (1993).

CAREER HITTING: 9-for-54 (.167), 5 R, 2 2B, 0 3B, 0 HR, 1 RBI.

Year	Team (League)	W	L	Pct.	ERA	WHIP	G	GS	CG	ShO	Hld.	Sv.-Opp.	IP	H	R	ER	HR	BB-IBB	SO	Avg.
1991—	Winter Haven (FSL)	3	6	.333	4.96	1.41	13	11	4	0	...	1-...	69.0	65	42	38	2	32-2	51	.247
1992—	Lynchburg (Caro.)	13	5	.722	2.91	1.18	20	19	2	1	...	0-...	127.0	104	51	41	5	46-0	112	.222
—	New Britain (East.)	2	1	.667	6.27	1.76	7	6	1	0	...	0-...	33.0	43	29	23	2	15-0	29	.305
1993—	Pawtucket (Int'l)	8	2	.800	2.19	1.03	14	14	2	1	...	0-...	94.1	74	30	23	8	23-0	87	.216
—	Boston (A.L.)	7	2	.778	2.74	1.33	18	18	0	0	...	0-0	111.2	100	42	34	5	48-2	93	.237
1994—	Boston (A.L.)	8	7	.533	3.83	1.40	22	22	0	0	...	0-0	143.1	140	68	61	13	60-2	105	.261
1995—	Boston (A.L.)	3	1	.750	3.06	1.42	6	6	0	0	...	0-0	32.1	32	14	11	3	14-0	21	.252
—	Trenton (East.)	0	1	.000	3.38	1.25	2	2	0	0	...	0-0	8.0	8	3	3	0	2-0	9	.286
—	Sarasota (Fla. St.)	0	0	...	0.00	1.00	2	2	0	0	...	0-0	7.0	6	0	0	0	1-0	8	.231
—	Pawtucket (Int'l)	0	0	...	9.00	2.20	2	2	0	0	...	0-0	5.0	9	5	5	3	2-0	1	.409
1996—	Boston (A.L.)	7	11	.389	5.32	1.65	29	29	1	0	0	0-0	157.1	192	110	93	14	67-2	137	.303
—	Pawtucket (Int'l)	0	0	...	6.00	1.33	1	1	0	0	...	0-0	3.0	3	2	2	0	1-0	4	.250
1997—	Boston (A.L.)	13	12	.520	5.38	1.56	33	33	1	0	0	0-0	177.1	196	115	106	25	80-4	122	.279
1998—	Texas (A.L.)	19	11	.633	4.23	1.52	33	33	3	2	0	0-0	212.2	239	116	100	14	84-6	167	.283
1999—	Texas (A.L.)	18	9	.667	4.79	1.53	33	33	2	2	0	0-0	205.0	244	115	109	21	70-3	186	.293
2000—	Seattle (A.L.)	17	10	.630	4.51	1.39	34	34	2	0	0	0-0	211.2	221	110	106	27	74-7	137	.271
2001—	Seattle (A.L.)	15	5	.750	3.60	1.24	34	33	2	1	0	0-0	215.0	216	93	86	25	51-2	114	.261
2002—	Anaheim (A.L.)	8	9	.471	4.89	1.49	26	26	1	1	0	0-0	160.0	190	92	87	21	49-2	82	.299
2003—	Rancho Cuca. (Calif.)	0	0	...	4.50	1.90	3	2	0	0	...	0-...	8.0	12	4	4	0	3-0	7	.375
—	Salt Lake (PCL)	1	2	.333	6.43	1.80	3	3	0	0	...	0-...	14.0	16	10	10	2	4-0	8	.296
—	Anaheim (A.L.)	7	11	.389	5.77	1.59	25	25	0	0	0	0-0	121.2	135	82	78	17	58-1	53	.284
2004—	Anaheim (A.L.)	9	4	.692	5.05	1.62	28	24	0	0	0	0-0	132.0	163	84	74	16	51-2	51	.310
2005—	Seattle (A.L.)	6	12	.333	5.66	1.62	21	21	1	1	0	0-0	116.0	147	76	73	18	41-2	53	.315
—	Oklahoma (PCL)	1	1	.500	8.03	1.95	2	2	0	0	...	0-...	12.1	22	12	11	2	2-0	6	.400
2006—	Las Vegas (PCL)	3	0	1.000	2.43	1.01	5	5	0	0	...	0-...	29.2	25	8	8	1	5-0	28	.227
—	Los Angeles (N.L.)	8	6	.571	4.53	1.45	28	15	0	0	0	0-1	103.1	120	57	52	11	30-2	57	.290
	American League totals (13 years)	137	104	.568	4.59	1.48	342	337	15	9	0	0-0	1996.0	2215	1117	1018	209	747-35	1321	.282
	National League totals (1 year)	8	6	.571	4.53	1.45	28	15	0	0	0	0-1	103.1	120	57	52	11	30-2	57	.290
	Major League totals (14 years)	145	110	.569	4.59	1.48	370	352	15	9	0	0-1	2099.1	2335	1174	1070	220	777-37	1378	.283

DIVISION SERIES RECORD

Year	Team (League)	W	L	Pct.	ERA	WHIP	G	GS	CG	ShO	Hld.	Sv.-Opp.	IP	H	R	ER	HR	BB-IBB	SO	Avg.
1998—	Texas (A.L.)	0	1	.000	6.00	1.50	1	1	0	0	0	0-0	6.0	8	4	4	2	1-0	4	.320
1999—	Texas (A.L.)	0	1	.000	5.40	2.20	1	1	0	0	0	0-0	5.0	6	4	3	0	5-2	3	.286
2000—	Seattle (A.L.)	0	0	...	1.23	0.82	1	1	0	0	0	0-0	7.1	3	1	1	0	3-0	1	.143
2001—	Seattle (A.L.)	0	1	.000	9.00	2.50	1	1	0	0	0	0-0	2.0	5	4	2	0	0-0	0	.417
	Division series totals (4 years)	0	3	.000	4.43	1.52	4	4	0	0	0	0-0	20.1	22	13	10	2	9-2	8	.278

CHAMPIONSHIP SERIES RECORD

Year	Team (League)	W	L	Pct.	ERA	WHIP	G	GS	CG	ShO	Hld.	Sv.-Opp.	IP	H	R	ER	HR	BB-IBB	SO	Avg.
2000—	Seattle (A.L.)	0	1	.000	6.00	1.50	1	1	0	0	0	0-0	6.0	9	4	4	2	0-0	4	.333
2001—	Seattle (A.L.)	0	2	.000	3.60	1.50	2	2	0	0	0	0-0	10.0	11	8	4	3	4-0	5	.282
	Champ. series totals (2 years)	0	3	.000	4.50	1.50	3	3	0	0	0	0-0	16.0	20	12	8	5	4-0	9	.303

ALL-STAR GAME RECORD

Year	Team (League)	W	L	Pct.	ERA	WHIP	G	GS	CG	ShO	Hld.	Sv.-Opp.	IP	H	R	ER	HR	BB-IBB	SO	Avg.
	All-Star Game totals (1 year)	0	0	...	0.00	1.00	1	0	0	0	0	0-0	1.0	0	0	0	0	0-0	0	.250

2006 LEFTY-RIGHTY SPLITS

vs.	Avg.	AB	H	2B	3B	HR	RBI	BB	SO	OBP	Slg.	vs.	Avg.	AB	H	2B	3B	HR	RBI	BB	SO	OBP	Slg.
L	.280	186	52	11	4	7	25	18	28	.346	.495	R	.298	228	68	17	1	4	27	12	29	.335	.434

SEO, JAE — P

PERSONAL: Born May 24, 1977, in Kwanju, South Korea. ... 6-1/215. ... Throws right, bats right. ... Full name: Jae Weong Seo. ... Name pronounced: jay wong sew. ... High school: First (Kwanju, South Korea). ... College: Inha (South Korea). **TRANSACTIONS/CAREER NOTES:** Signed as a non-drafted free agent by New York Mets organization (December 17, 1997). ... On disabled list (April 6, 2000-entire season). ... Traded by Mets with P Tim Hamulack to Los Angeles Dodgers for Ps Duaner Sanchez and Steve Schmoll (January 4, 2006). ... Traded by Dodgers with C Dioner Navarro and a player to be named to Tampa Bay Devil Rays for C Toby Hall, P Mark Hendrickson and cash (June 27, 2006). ... On disabled list (August 21-September 5, 2006). **MISCELLANEOUS NOTES:** Scored a run in three appearances as pinch runner (2003). ... Scored a run in two appearances as pinch runner (2004).

CAREER HITTING: 15-for-131 (.115), 7 R, 3 2B, 0 3B, 0 HR, 5 RBI.

Year	Team (League)	W	L	Pct.	ERA	WHIP	G	GS	CG	ShO	Hld.	Sv.-Opp.	IP	H	R	ER	HR	BB-IBB	SO	Avg.
1998—	St. Lucie (Fla. St.)	3	1	.750	2.27	1.01	8	7	0	0	...	0-...	35.2	26	13	9	2	10-0	37	.206
—	GC Mets (GCL)	0	0	...	0.00	0.80	2	0	0	0	...	0-...	5.0	4	0	0	0	0-0	0	.235
1999—	St. Lucie (Fla. St.)	2	0	1.000	1.84	0.68	3	3	0	0	...	0-...	14.2	8	3	3	0	2-0	14	.154
2000—	St. Lucie (Fla. St.)			Did not play.																
2001—	St. Lucie (Fla. St.)	2	3	.400	3.55	1.07	6	5	0	0	...	0-...	25.1	21	11	10	2	6-0	19	.221
—	Binghamton (East.)	5	1	.833	1.94	0.91	12	10	0	0	...	0-...	60.1	44	14	13	3	11-1	47	.206
—	Norfolk (Int'l)	2	2	.500	3.42	1.25	9	9	0	0	...	0-...	47.1	53	18	18	4	6-1	25	.296
2002—	Binghamton (East.)	0	0	...	5.40	1.20	1	0	0	0	...	0-...	5.0	5	3	3	1	1-0	6	.250
—	Norfolk (Int'l)	6	9	.400	3.99	1.30	26	24	1	0	...	0-...	128.2	145	66	57	14	22-1	87	.284
—	New York (N.L.)	0	0	...	0.00	0.00	1	0	0	0	0	0-0	1.0	0	0	0	0	0-0	1	.000
2003—	New York (N.L.)	9	12	.429	3.82	1.27	32	31	0	0	0	0-0	188.1	193	94	80	18	46-11	110	.260
2004—	Norfolk (Int'l)	0	2	.000	2.82	1.34	4	4	0	0	...	0-...	22.1	22	7	7	1	8-0	20	.272
—	New York (N.L.)	5	10	.333	4.90	1.56	24	21	0	0	0	0-0	117.2	133	67	64	17	50-7	54	.299
2005—	Norfolk (Int'l)	7	4	.636	4.29	1.28	19	19	0	0	...	0-...	121.2	126	64	58	13	30-0	111	.268
—	New York (N.L.)	8	2	.800	2.59	1.11	14	14	1	0	0	0-0	90.1	84	26	26	9	16-0	59	.251
2006—	Los Angeles (N.L.)	2	4	.333	5.78	1.49	19	10	0	0	0	0-0	67.0	75	45	43	14	25-1	49	.284
—	Tampa Bay (A.L.)	1	8	.111	5.00	1.70	17	16	0	0	1	0-0	90.0	122	56	50	17	31-3	39	.331
	American League totals (1 year)	1	8	.111	5.00	1.70	17	16	0	0	1	0-0	90.0	122	56	50	17	31-3	39	.331
	National League totals (5 years)	24	28	.462	4.13	1.34	90	76	1	0	0	0-0	464.1	485	232	213	58	137-19	273	.271
	Major League totals (5 years)	25	36	.410	4.27	1.40	107	92	1	0	1	0-0	554.1	607	288	263	75	168-22	312	.281

S

vs.	Avg.	AB	H	2B	3B	HR	RBI	BB	SO	OBP	Slg.	vs.	Avg.	AB	H	2B	3B	HR	RBI	BB	SO	OBP	Slg.
L	.310	297	92	24	3	13	44	28	37	.367	.542	R	.313	336	105	20	1	18	50	28	51	.367	.539

SEXSON, RICHIE — 1B

PERSONAL: Born December 29, 1974, in Portland. ... 6-8/235. ... Bats right, throws right. ... Full name: Richmond Lockwood Sexson. ... Name pronounced: SECKS-un. ... High school: Prairie (Brush Prairie, Wash.). **TRANSACTIONS/CAREER NOTES:** Selected by Cleveland Indians organization in 24th round of 1993 free-agent draft. ... Traded by Indians with Ps Paul Rigdon and Kane Davis and a player to be named to Milwaukee Brewers for Ps Bob Wickman, Steve Woodard and Jason Bere (July 28, 2000); Brewers acquired P Marco Scutaro to complete deal (August 30, 2000). ... Traded by Brewers with P Shane Nance and a player to be named to Arizona Diamondbacks for SS Craig Counsell, 2B Junior Spivey, 1B Lyle Overbay, C Chad Moeller and Ps Chris Capuano and Jorge de la Rosa (December 1, 2003); Diamondbacks acquired OF Noochie Varner to complete deal (December 15, 2003). ... On disabled list (April 29-May 21 and May 23, 2004-remainder of season). ... On suspended list (September 23-24, 2005). ... Signed as a free agent by Seattle Mariners (December 15, 2004). ... On bereavement list (August 14-17, 2006). **RECORDS:** Shares major league record for most strikeouts, 9-inning game (5, May 29, 2001). **STATISTICAL NOTES:** Hit three home runs in one game (September 25, 2001; and April 25, 2003). ... Career major league grand slams: 14.
2006 GAMES PLAYED BY POSITION (MLB): 1B—150, DH—8.

									BATTING							FIELDING	
Year	Team (League)	Pos.	G	AB	R	H	2B	3B	HR	RBI	BB	SO	HBP	GDP	SB-CS	Avg.	OBP	SLG	OPS	E	Avg.
1993— Burlington (Appal.)	1B	40	97	11	18	3	0	1	5	18	21	1	1	1-1	.186	.316	.247	.564	4	.988
1994— Columbus (S. Atl.)	1B	130	488	88	133	25	2	14	77	37	87	14	5	7-3	.273	.338	.418	.756	10	.990
1995— Kinston (Carol.)	1B	131	494	80	151	34	0	22	85	43	115	10	8	4-6	.306	.368	.508	.876	12	.990
1996— Cant./Akr. (Eastern)	1B	133	518	85	143	33	3	16	76	39	118	6	13	2-1	.276	.331	.444	.775	11	.989
1997— Buffalo (A.A.)	1B-DH	115	434	57	113	20	2	31	88	27	87	4	11	5-1	.260	.307	.530	.837	4	.996
— Cleveland (A.L.)	1B-DH	5	11	1	3	0	0	0	0	0	2	0	2	0-0	.273	.273	.273	.545	0	1.000
1998— Buffalo (Int'l)	OF-1B-DH	89	344	58	102	20	1	21	74	50	68	3	11	1-2	.297	.386	.544	.929	3	.990
— Cleveland (A.L.)	1B-DH	49	174	28	54	14	1	11	35	6	42	3	3	1-1	.310	.344	.592	.936	6	.984
1999— Cleveland (A.L.)	1B-OF-DH	134	479	72	122	17	7	31	116	34	117	4	19	3-3	.255	.305	.514	.818	7	.989
2000— Cleveland (A.L.)	OF-1B-DH	91	324	45	83	16	1	16	44	25	96	4	8	1-0	.256	.315	.460	.774	1	.997
— Milwaukee (N.L.)	1B	57	213	44	63	14	0	14	47	34	63	3	3	1-0	.296	.398	.559	.957	5	.991
2001— Milwaukee (N.L.)	1B	158	598	94	162	24	3	45	125	60	178	6	20	2-4	.271	.342	.547	.889	8	.995
2002— Milwaukee (N.L.)	1B-DH	157	570	86	159	37	2	29	102	70	136	8	17	0-0	.279	.364	.504	.867	7	.995
2003— Milwaukee (N.L.)	1B	162	606	97	165	28	2	45	124	98	151	9	18	2-3	.272	.379	.548	.927	11	.993
2004— Arizona (N.L.)	1B	23	90	20	21	4	0	9	23	14	21	0	2	0-0	.233	.337	.578	.914	1	.996
2005— Seattle (A.L.)	1B-DH	156	558	99	147	36	1	39	121	89 *	167	6	14	1-1	.263	.369	.541	.910	7	.995
2006— Seattle (A.L.)	1B-DH	158	591	75	156	40	0	34	107	64	154	4	17	1-1	.264	.338	.504	.842	4	.997
American League totals (6 years)		593	2137	320	565	123	10	131	423	218	578	21	63	7-6	.264	.336	.515	.851	25	.994
National League totals (5 years)		557	2077	341	570	107	7	142	421	276	549	26	60	5-7	.274	.365	.538	.902	32	.994
Major League totals (10 years)		1150	4214	661	1135	230	17	273	844	494	1127	47	123	12-13	.269	.350	.526	.877	57	.994

DIVISION SERIES RECORD

Year	Team (League)	Pos.	G	AB	R	H	2B	3B	HR	RBI	BB	SO	HBP	GDP	SB-CS	Avg.	OBP	SLG	OPS	E	Avg.
1998— Cleveland (A.L.)	1B	3	2	0	0	0	0	0	0	2	1	0	0	0-0	.000	.500	.000	.500	0	1.000
1999— Cleveland (A.L.)	1B-OF	3	6	1	1	0	0	0	1	1	3	0	0	0-0	.167	.286	.167	.452	0	1.000
Division series totals (2 years)		6	8	1	1	0	0	0	1	3	4	0	0	0-0	.125	.364	.125	.489	0	1.000

CHAMPIONSHIP SERIES RECORD

Year	Team (League)	Pos.	G	AB	R	H	2B	3B	HR	RBI	BB	SO	HBP	GDP	SB-CS	Avg.	OBP	SLG	OPS	E	Avg.
1998— Cleveland (A.L.)	1B	3	6	0	0	0	0	0	0	0	3	0	1	0-0	.000	.000	.000	.000	0	1.000

ALL-STAR GAME RECORD

		G	AB	R	H	2B	3B	HR	RBI	BB	SO	HBP	GDP	SB-CS	Avg.	OBP	SLG	OPS	E	Avg.
All-Star Game totals (2 years)		2	3	0	0	0	0	0	0	0	0	0	0	0-0	.000	.000	.000	.000	0	1.000

2006 LEFTY-RIGHTY SPLITS

vs.	Avg.	AB	H	2B	3B	HR	RBI	BB	SO	OBP	Slg.	vs.	Avg.	AB	H	2B	3B	HR	RBI	BB	SO	OBP	Slg.
L	.204	137	28	11	0	7	20	25	40	.325	.438	R	.282	454	128	29	0	27	87	39	114	.342	.524

SHACKELFORD, BRIAN — P

PERSONAL: Born August 30, 1976, in McAlester, Okla. ... 6-1/195. ... Throws left, bats left. ... Full name: Brian Wesley Shackelford. ... High school: McAlester (Okla.). ... College: Oklahoma. **TRANSACTIONS/CAREER NOTES:** Selected by Kansas City Royals organization in 13th round of 1998 free-agent draft. ... Played five seasons as a first baseman/outfielder in Royals organization (1998-2002). ... Traded by Royals with P Jeff Austin to Cincinnati Reds for 3B Damaso Espino and OF Alan Moye (March 6, 2003).
CAREER HITTING: 0-for-1 (.000), 0 R, 0 2B, 0 3B, 0 HR, 0 RBI.

Year	Team (League)	W	L	Pct.	ERA	WHIP	G	GS	CG	ShO	Hld.	Sv.-Opp.	IP	H	R	ER	HR	BB-IBB	SO	Avg.
2001— Wichita (Texas)	0	0	...	18.00	4.00	1	0	0	0	...	0-...	1.0	3	2	2	0	1-0	0	.500
2002— Wichita (Texas)	3	1	.750	3.51	1.91	22	0	0	0	...	0-...	25.2	23	12	10	1	26-2	15	.258
2003— Chattanooga (Sou.)	3	2	.600	6.30	2.00	13	1	0	0	...	1-...	20.0	26	18	14	3	14-2	19	.313
— Potomac (Carol.)	0	1	.000	1.98	0.91	18	0	0	0	...	1-...	27.1	17	6	6	1	8-0	20	.181
— Louisville (Int'l)	1	0	1.000	2.30	1.40	12	0	0	0	...	0-...	15.2	15	4	4	0	7-0	11	.259
2004— Louisville (Int'l)	8	1	.889	3.58	1.37	59	0	0	0	...	0-...	73.0	58	31	29	6	42-1	63	.213
2005— Louisville (Int'l)	1	6	.143	5.23	1.38	31	0	0	0	9	1-2	32.2	35	19	19	1	10-0	21	.282
— Cincinnati (N.L.)	1	0	1.000	2.43	1.01	37	0	0	0	3	0-0	29.2	21	9	8	2	9-1	17	.204
2006— Louisville (Int'l)	1	0	1.000	1.82	1.45	34	0	0	0	1-4	29.2	29	6	6	0	14-0	23	.259
— Cincinnati (N.L.)	1	0	1.000	7.16	1.71	26	0	0	0	2	0-0	16.1	18	13	13	4	10-0	15	.269
Major League totals (2 years)	2	0	1.000	4.11	1.26	63	0	0	0	5	0-0	46.0	39	22	21	6	19-1	32	.229

2006 LEFTY-RIGHTY SPLITS

vs.	Avg.	AB	H	2B	3B	HR	RBI	BB	SO	OBP	Slg.	vs.	Avg.	AB	H	2B	3B	HR	RBI	BB	SO	OBP	Slg.
L	.175	40	7	1	1	0	4	3	10	.267	.250	R	.407	27	11	1	0	4	11	7	5	.529	.889

SHARPLESS, JOSH — P

PERSONAL: Born January 26, 1981, in Beaver, Pa. ... 6-5/235. ... Throws right, bats right. ... Full name: Joshua David Sharpless. ... College: Allegheny. **TRANSACTIONS/CAREER NOTES:** Selected by Pittsburgh Pirates organization in 24th round of 2003 free-agent draft. ... On disabled list (August 10-September 1, 2006).
CAREER HITTING: 0-for-0 (.000), 0 R, 0 2B, 0 3B, 0 HR, 0 RBI.

Year	Team (League)	W	L	Pct.	ERA	WHIP	G	GS	CG	ShO	Hld.	Sv.-Opp.	IP	H	R	ER	HR	BB-IBB	SO	Avg.
2003— Will. (NYP)	1	1	.500	2.59	1.15	22	0	0	0	...	5-...	31.1	19	9	9	2	17-0	45	.173
2004— Hickory (S. Atl.)	6	2	.750	3.03	1.30	44	0	0	0	...	4-...	74.1	42	28	25	4	55-2	109	.158
2005— Lynchburg (Caro.)	3	0	1.000	0.67	1.13	17	0	0	0	5-5	27.0	7	1	0	0	11-0	46	.081

Year Team (League)	W	L	Pct.	ERA	WHIP	G	GS	CG	ShO	Hld.	Sv.-Opp.	IP	H	R	ER	HR	BB-IBB	SO	Avg.
— Altoona (East.)	1	0	1.000	2.89	0.96	7	0	0	0	4	0-1	9.1	6	3	3	0	3-0	13	.171
2006—Altoona (East.)	2	0	1.000	0.86	0.81	14	0	0	0	8	8-8	21.0	8	2	2	0	9-0	30	.114
— Indianapolis (Int'l)	1	1	.500	2.45	1.42	23	0	0	0	4	1-1	33.0	32	11	9	1	15-2	30	.250
— Pittsburgh (N.L.)	0	0	...	1.50	1.50	14	0	0	0	2	0-0	12.0	7	2	2	0	11-1	7	.175
Major League totals (1 year)	0	0	...	1.50	1.50	14	0	0	0	2	0-0	12.0	7	2	2	0	11-1	7	.175

2006 LEFTY-RIGHTY SPLITS

vs.	Avg.	AB	H	2B	3B	HR	RBI	BB	SO	OBP	Slg.	vs.	Avg.	AB	H	2B	3B	HR	RBI	BB	SO	OBP	Slg.
L	.000	8	0	0	0	0	1	5	1	.385	.000	R	.219	32	7	1	0	0	3	6	6	.333	.250

SHEALY, RYAN — 1B

PERSONAL: Born August 29, 1979, in Fort Lauderdale, Fla. ... 6-5/240. ... Bats right, throws right. ... Full name: Ryan Nelson Shealy. ... High school: Cardinal Gibbons (Fort Lauderdale, Fla.). ... College: Florida. **TRANSACTIONS/CAREER NOTES:** Selected by Colorado Rockies organization in 11th round of 2002 free-agent draft. ... On disabled list (March 28-May 12, 2006); included rehabilitation assignment to Colorado Springs. ... Traded by Rockies with P Scott Dohmann to Kansas City Royals for Ps Denny Bautista and Jeremy Affeldt (July 31, 2006). **STATISTICAL NOTES:** Career major league grand slams: 1.

2006 GAMES PLAYED BY POSITION (MLB): 1B—53.

Year Team (League)	Pos.	G	AB	R	H	2B	3B	HR	RBI	BB	SO	HBP	GDP	SB-CS	Avg.	OBP	SLG	OPS	E	Avg.
2002—Casper (Pion.)	1B	69	231	55	85	21	1	19	70	50	52	18	7	0-0	.368	.497	.714	1.211	6	.991
2003—Visalia (Calif.)		93	341	70	102	31	1	14	73	42	72	14	5	0-0	.299	.391	.519	.910	...	...
2004—Tulsa (Texas)	1B	132	469	88	149	32	3	29	99	61	123	16	10	1-1	.318	.411	.584	.995	4	.998
2005—Colo. Springs (PCL)	1B-DH-OF	108	411	85	135	30	2	26	88	41	81	7	13	4-0	.328	.393	.601	.994	13	.987
— Colorado (N.L.)	1B-DH	36	91	14	30	7	0	2	16	13	22	0	6	1-0	.330	.413	.473	.886	0	1.000
2006—Colo. Springs (PCL)		58	222	37	63	16	1	15	55	20	34	4	9	0-0	.284	.351	.568	.918	2	.996
— Colorado (N.L.)	1B	5	9	2	2	0	0	0	1	0	4	0	0	0-0	.222	.222	.444	.667	0	1.000
— Kansas City (A.L.)	1B	51	193	29	54	10	1	7	36	15	50	2	5	1-1	.280	.338	.451	.789	3	.993
American League totals (1 year)		51	193	29	54	10	1	7	36	15	50	2	5	1-1	.280	.338	.451	.789	3	.993
National League totals (2 years)		41	100	16	32	9	0	2	17	13	26	0	6	1-0	.320	.398	.470	.868	0	1.000
Major League totals (2 years)		92	293	45	86	19	1	9	53	28	76	2	11	2-1	.294	.359	.457	.816	3	.995

2006 LEFTY-RIGHTY SPLITS

vs.	Avg.	AB	H	2B	3B	HR	RBI	BB	SO	OBP	Slg.	vs.	Avg.	AB	H	2B	3B	HR	RBI	BB	SO	OBP	Slg.
L	.185	54	10	5	0	1	6	7	17	.279	.333	R	.311	148	46	7	1	6	31	8	37	.354	.493

SHEETS, BEN — P

PERSONAL: Born July 18, 1978, in Baton Rouge, La. ... 6-1/220. ... Throws right, bats right. ... Full name: Ben M. Sheets. ... High school: St. Amant (La.). ... College: Northeast Louisiana. **TRANSACTIONS/CAREER NOTES:** Selected by Milwaukee Brewers organization in first round (10th pick overall) of 1999 free-agent draft. ... On disabled list (August 6-September 21, 2001; April 21-May 28 and August 27, 2005-remainder of season). ... On disabled list (March 30-April 16, 2006); included rehabilitation assignments to Huntsville and Nashville. ... On disabled list (May 10-July 25, 2006); included rehabilitation assignments to Nashville, Huntsville and AZL Brewers. **MISCELLANEOUS NOTES:** Member of 2000 U.S. Olympic baseball team.

CAREER HITTING: 25-for-321 (.078), 9 R, 1 2B, 0 3B, 0 HR, 7 RBI.

Year Team (League)	W	L	Pct.	ERA	WHIP	G	GS	CG	ShO	Hld.	Sv.-Opp.	IP	H	R	ER	HR	BB-IBB	SO	Avg.
1999—Ogden (Pion.)	0	1	.000	5.63	1.25	2	2	0	0	...	0-...	8.0	8	5	5	2	2-0	12	.267
— Stockton (Calif.)	1	0	1.000	3.58	1.34	5	5	0	0	...	0-...	27.2	23	11	11	1	14-0	28	.232
2000—Huntsville (Sou.)	5	3	.625	1.88	1.11	13	13	0	0	...	0-...	72.0	55	17	15	4	25-0	60	.215
— Indianapolis (Int'l)	3	5	.375	2.87	1.32	14	13	1	0	...	0-...	81.2	77	31	26	4	31-0	59	.251
2001—Milwaukee (N.L.)	11	10	.524	4.76	1.41	25	25	1	1	0	0-0	151.1	166	89	80	23	48-6	94	.283
— Indianapolis (Int'l)	1	1	.500	3.38	1.59	2	2	0	0	...	0-...	10.2	14	5	4	0	3-0	6	.318
2002—Milwaukee (N.L.)	11	•16	.407	4.15	1.42	34	34	1	0	0	0-0	216.2	237	105	100	21	70-10	170	.281
2003—Milwaukee (N.L.)	11	13	.458	4.45	1.25	34	34	1	0	0	0-0	220.2	232	122	109	29	43-2	157	.268
2004—Milwaukee (N.L.)	12	14	.462	2.70	0.98	34	34	5	0	0	0-0	237.0	201	85	71	25	32-1	264	.226
2005—Milwaukee (N.L.)	10	9	.526	3.33	1.07	22	22	3	0	0	0-0	156.2	142	66	58	19	25-1	141	.237
2006—Huntsville (Sou.)	0	0	...	3.38	1.50	1	1	0	0	...	0-...	2.2	4	1	1	0	0-0	5	.308
— Ariz. Brewers (Ariz.)	0	0	...	10.38	1.62	1	1	0	0	...	0-...	4.1	5	5	5	0	2-0	8	.294
— Nashville (PCL)	2	1	.667	2.40	0.93	3	3	0	0	...	0-0	15.0	9	4	4	1	5-0	15	.173
— Milwaukee (N.L.)	6	7	.462	3.82	1.09	17	17	0	0	0	0-0	106.0	105	47	45	9	11-1	116	.259
Major League totals (6 years)	61	69	.469	3.83	1.21	166	166	11	1	0	0-0	1088.1	1083	514	463	126	229-21	942	.258

ALL-STAR GAME RECORD

	W	L	Pct.	ERA	WHIP	G	GS	CG	ShO	Hld.	Sv.-Opp.	IP	H	R	ER	HR	BB-IBB	SO	Avg.
All-Star Game totals (2 years)	0	0	...	0.00	0.00	2	0	0	0	...	0-0	1.1	0	0	0	0	0-0	1	.000

2006 LEFTY-RIGHTY SPLITS

vs.	Avg.	AB	H	2B	3B	HR	RBI	BB	SO	OBP	Slg.	vs.	Avg.	AB	H	2B	3B	HR	RBI	BB	SO	OBP	Slg.
L	.248	165	41	11	3	6	17	5	58	.270	.461	R	.266	241	64	22	0	3	25	6	58	.284	.394

SHEFFIELD, GARY — OF/1B

PERSONAL: Born November 18, 1968, in Tampa. ... 6-0/205. ... Bats right, throws right. ... Full name: Gary Antonian Sheffield. ... High school: Hillsborough (Tampa). ... Nephew of Dwight Gooden, pitcher with five major league teams (1984-2000). **TRANSACTIONS/CAREER NOTES:** Selected by Milwaukee Brewers organization in first round (sixth pick overall) of June 1986 free-agent draft. ... On disabled list (July 14-September 9, 1989). ... On suspended list (August 31-September 3, 1990). ... On disabled list (June 15-July 3 and July 25, 1991-remainder of season). ... Traded by Brewers with P Geoff Kellogg to San Diego Padres for P Ricky Bones, SS Jose Valentin and OF Matt Mieske (March 27, 1992). ... Traded by Padres with P Rich Rodriguez to Florida Marlins for Ps Trevor Hoffman, Jose Martinez and Andres Berumen (June 24, 1993). ... On suspended list (July 9-12, 1993). ... On disabled list (May 10-25 and May 28-June 12, 1994); included rehabilitation assignment to Portland. ... On disabled list (June 11-September 1, 1995; and May 14-29, 1997). ... Traded by Marlins with 3B Bobby Bonilla, C Charles Johnson, OF Jim Eisenreich and P Manuel Barrios to Los Angeles Dodgers for C Mike Piazza and 3B Todd Zeile (May 15, 1998). ... On suspended list (August 4-6, 1998; and August 23-27, 2000). ... On disabled list (May 24-June 8, 2001). ... Traded by Dodgers to Atlanta Braves for OF Brian Jordan and Ps Odalis Perez and Andrew Brown (January 15, 2002). ... Signed as a free agent by New York Yankees (December 19, 2003). ... On suspended list (August 30-31, 2005). ... On disabled list (May 6-23 and May 30-September 19, 2006); included rehabilitation assignment to Trenton. ... Traded by Yankees to Detroit Tigers for Ps Humberto Sanchez, Kevin Whelan and Anthony Claggett (November 10, 2006). **HONORS:** Named Minor League co-Player of the Year by THE SPORTING NEWS (1988). ... Named Major League Player of the Year by THE SPORTING NEWS (1992). ... Named N.L. Comeback Player of the Year by THE SPORTING NEWS (1992). ... Named third baseman on THE SPORTING NEWS N.L. All-Star team (1992). ... Named outfielder on THE SPORTING NEWS N.L. All-Star team (1996 and 2003). ... Named third baseman on N.L. Silver Slugger team (1992). ... Named outfielder on N.L. Silver Slugger team (1996 and 2003). ... Named outfielder on A.L. Silver Slugger team (2004 and 2005). **STATISTICAL NOTES:** Career major league grand slams: 11.

2006 GAMES PLAYED BY POSITION (MLB): OF—21, DH—9, 1B—9.

Year	Team (League)	Pos.	G	AB	R	H	2B	3B	HR	RBI	BB	SO	HBP	GDP	SB-CS	Avg.	OBP	SLG	OPS	E	Avg.
								BATTING												FIELDING	
1986—Helena (Pion.)		SS	57	222	53	81	12	2	15	71	20	14	3	3	14-4	.365	.413	.640	1.052	24	.911
1987—Stockton (Calif.)		SS	129	469	84	130	23	3	17	103	81	49	8	7	25-15	.277	.388	.448	.836	39	.937
1988—El Paso (Texas)		3B-OF-SS	77	296	70	93	19	3	19	65	35	41	3	9	5-4	.314	.386	.591	.978	23	.936
—Denver (A.A.)		3B-SS	57	212	42	73	9	5	9	54	21	22	5	3	8-4	.344	.407	.561	.969	8	.950
—Milwaukee (A.L.)		SS	24	80	12	19	1	0	4	12	7	7	0	5	3-1	.238	.295	.400	.695	3	.967
1989—Milwaukee (A.L.)		3B-DH-SS	95	368	34	91	18	0	5	32	27	33	4	4	10-6	.247	.303	.337	.640	16	.955
—Denver (A.A.)		SS	7	29	3	4	1	1	0	0	2	0	0	1	0-0	.138	.194	.241	.435	0	1.000
1990—Milwaukee (A.L.)		3B	125	487	67	143	30	1	10	67	44	41	3	11	25-10	.294	.350	.421	.771	25	.934
1991—Milwaukee (A.L.)		3B-DH	50	175	25	34	12	2	2	22	19	15	3	3	5-5	.194	.277	.320	.597	8	.922
1992—San Diego (N.L.)		3B	146	557	87	184	34	3	33	100	48	40	6	19	5-6	.330	.385	.580	.965	16	.961
1993—San Diego (N.L.)		3B	68	258	34	76	12	2	10	36	18	30	3	9	5-1	.295	.344	.473	.817	15	.905
—Florida (N.L.)		3B	72	236	33	69	8	3	10	37	29	34	6	2	12-4	.292	.378	.479	.857	19	.894
1994—Florida (N.L.)		OF	87	322	61	89	16	1	27	78	51	50	6	10	12-6	.276	.380	.584	.964	5	.970
—Portland (East.)		OF	2	7	1	2	1	0	0	0	1	3	0	0	0-0	.286	.375	.429	.804	0	1.000
1995—Florida (N.L.)		OF	63	213	46	69	8	0	16	46	55	45	4	3	19-4	.324	.467	.587	1.054	7	.942
1996—Florida (N.L.)		OF	161	519	118	163	33	1	42	120	142	66	10	16	16-9	.314*	.465	.624	1.090	6	.976
1997—Florida (N.L.)		OF-DH	135	444	86	111	22	1	21	71	121	79	15	7	11-7	.250	.424	.446	.870	5	.980
1998—Florida (N.L.)		OF	40	136	21	37	11	1	6	28	26	16	2	3	4-2	.272	.392	.500	.892	1	.986
—Los Angeles (N.L.)		OF	90	301	52	95	16	1	16	57	69	30	6	4	18-5	.316	.444	.535	.979	1	.994
1999—Los Angeles (N.L.)		OF-DH	152	549	103	165	20	0	34	101	101	64	4	10	11-5	.301	.407	.523	.930	7	.972
2000—Los Angeles (N.L.)		OF-DH	141	501	105	163	24	3	43	109	101	71	4	13	4-6	.325	.438	.643	1.081	•10	.954
2001—Los Angeles (N.L.)		OF-DH	143	515	98	160	28	2	36	100	94	67	4	12	10-4	.311	.417	.583	1.000	6	.972
2002—Atlanta (N.L.)		OF-DH	135	492	82	151	26	0	25	84	72	53	11	16	18-2	.307	.404	.512	.916	4	.984
2003—Atlanta (N.L.)		OF	155	576	126	190	37	2	39	132	86	55	8	16	18-4	.330	.419	.604	1.023	4	.986
2004—New York (A.L.)		OF-DH-3B	154	537	117	166	30	1	36	121	92	83	11	16	5-6	.290	.393	.534	.927	6	.979
2005—New York (A.L.)		OF-DH	154	584	104	170	27	0	34	123	78	76	8	11	10-2	.291	.379	.512	.891	3	.988
2006—Trenton (East.)			1	3	0	1	0	0	0	1	0	1	0	0	0-0	.333	.250	.333	.583	0	...
—New York (A.L.)		OF-1B-DH	39	151	22	45	5	0	6	25	13	16	1	6	5-1	.298	.355	.450	.806	2	.980
American League totals (7 years)			641	2418	381	668	123	4	97	402	280	271	30	56	63-31	.276	.354	.451	.805	63	.960
National League totals (12 years)			1588	5619	1052	1722	295	20	358	1099	1013	700	89	140	157-65	.306	.416	.557	.973	106	.965
Major League totals (19 years)			2229	8037	1433	2390	418	24	455	1501	1293	971	119	196	220-96	.297	.398	.525	.923	169	.963

DIVISION SERIES RECORD

Year	Team (League)	Pos.	G	AB	R	H	2B	3B	HR	RBI	BB	SO	HBP	GDP	SB-CS	Avg.	OBP	SLG	OPS	E	Avg.
1997—Florida (N.L.)		OF	3	9	3	5	1	0	1	1	5	0	0	0	1-0	.556	.714	1.000	1.714	0	1.000
2002—Atlanta (N.L.)		OF	5	16	3	1	0	0	1	1	7	3	0	1	0-0	.063	.348	.250	.598	0	1.000
2003—Atlanta (N.L.)		OF	4	14	0	2	0	0	0	1	2	0	0	1	0-0	.143	.294	.143	.437	0	1.000
2004—New York (A.L.)		OF	4	18	2	4	1	0	1	2	3	1	0	1	0-1	.222	.333	.444	.778	0	1.000
2005—New York (A.L.)		OF	5	21	1	6	0	0	0	2	1	2	0	0	0-0	.286	.318	.286	.604	1	.900
2006—New York (A.L.)		1B	3	12	1	1	0	0	0	1	0	4	1	0	0-0	.083	.083	.083	.167	1	.962
Division series totals (6 years)			24	90	10	19	2	0	3	8	18	10	1	3	1-1	.211	.349	.333	.682	2	.967

CHAMPIONSHIP SERIES RECORD

Year	Team (League)	Pos.	G	AB	R	H	2B	3B	HR	RBI	BB	SO	HBP	GDP	SB-CS	Avg.	OBP	SLG	OPS	E	Avg.
1997—Florida (N.L.)		OF	6	17	6	4	0	0	1	1	7	1	0	1	0-0	.235	.458	.412	.870	0	1.000
2004—New York (A.L.)		OF	7	30	7	10	3	0	1	5	6	8	0	1	0-0	.333	.444	.533	.978	0	1.000
Champ. series totals (2 years)			13	47	13	14	3	0	2	6	13	11	0	1	0-0	.298	.450	.489	.939	0	1.000

WORLD SERIES RECORD

Year	Team (League)	Pos.	G	AB	R	H	2B	3B	HR	RBI	BB	SO	HBP	GDP	SB-CS	Avg.	OBP	SLG	OPS	E	Avg.
1997—Florida (N.L.)		OF	7	24	4	7	1	0	1	5	5	1	2	0	0-0	.292	.485	.458	.943	1	.941

ALL-STAR GAME RECORD

	G	AB	R	H	2B	3B	HR	RBI	BB	SO	HBP	GDP	SB-CS	Avg.	OBP	SLG	OPS	E	Avg.
All-Star Game totals (9 years)	9	12	3	1	0	0	1	2	2	0	0	0	0-0	.167	.286	.417	.702	0	1.000

2006 LEFTY-RIGHTY SPLITS

vs.	Avg.	AB	H	2B	3B	HR	RBI	BB	SO	OBP	Slg.	vs.	Avg.	AB	H	2B	3B	HR	RBI	BB	SO	OBP	Slg.
L	.344	32	11	0	0	2	8	4	1	.417	.531	R	.286	119	34	5	0	4	17	9	15	.338	.429

SHELTON, CHRIS — 1B

PERSONAL: Born June 26, 1980, in Salt Lake City. ... 6-0/220. ... Bats right, throws right. ... Full name: Christopher Bob Shelton. ... High school: Cottonwood (Salt Lake City). ... Junior college: Salt Lake C.C. (Salt Lake City). ... College: Utah. **TRANSACTIONS/CAREER NOTES:** Selected by Pittsburgh Pirates organization in 33rd round of 2001 free-agent draft. ... Selected by Detroit Tigers from Pirates organization in Rule 5 major league draft (December 15, 2003). ... On disabled list (May 31-July 10, 2004); included rehabilitation assignment to Toledo.

2006 GAMES PLAYED BY POSITION (MLB): 1B—115.

Year	Team (League)	Pos.	G	AB	R	H	2B	3B	HR	RBI	BB	SO	HBP	GDP	SB-CS	Avg.	OBP	SLG	OPS	E	Avg.
								BATTING												FIELDING	
2001—Will. (NYP)		C-1B	50	174	22	53	11	0	2	33	33	31	2	1	4-1	.305	.415	.402	.817	7	.985
2002—Hickory (S. Atl.)		1B-C-OF	93	332	72	113	27	2	17	65	47	74	5	1	0-0	.340	.425	.587	1.013	1	.998
2003—Lynchburg (Caro.)		1B-C	95	315	71	113	24	1	21	69	68	67	5	6	1-4	.359	.478	.641	1.119	4	.993
—Altoona (East.)		1B-C	35	122	17	34	10	1	0	14	8	23	2	1	0-1	.279	.331	.377	.708	2	.993
2004—Toledo (Int'l)		1B-DH	18	62	5	21	2	0	0	7	10	13	0	0	0-0	.339	.425	.371	.796	2	.973
—Detroit (A.L.)		DH-1B-C-OF	27	46	6	9	1	0	1	3	9	14	2	8	0-0	.196	.321	.283	.604	0	1.000
2005—Toledo (Int'l)		1B-DH-C	48	181	34	60	19	0	8	39	25	33	3	3	0-2	.331	.417	.569	.986	4	.987
—Detroit (A.L.)		1B-DH-OF	107	388	61	116	22	3	18	59	34	87	5	11	0-0	.299	.360	.510	.870	6	.993
2006—Toledo (Int'l)			28	109	20	29	6	2	3	14	18	37	1	2	1-0	.266	.372	.440	.812	6	.976
—Detroit (A.L.)		1B	115	373	50	102	16	4	16	47	34	107	2	4	1-2	.273	.340	.466	.806	6	.994
Major League totals (3 years)			249	807	117	227	39	7	35	109	77	208	9	23	1-2	.281	.348	.477	.825	12	.994

2006 LEFTY-RIGHTY SPLITS

vs.	Avg.	AB	H	2B	3B	HR	RBI	BB	SO	OBP	Slg.	vs.	Avg.	AB	H	2B	3B	HR	RBI	BB	SO	OBP	Slg.
L	.276	98	27	4	1	3	10	14	25	.377	.429	R	.273	275	75	12	3	13	37	20	82	.326	.480

SHERRILL, GEORGE — P

PERSONAL: Born April 19, 1977, in Memphis. ... 6-0/210. ... Throws left, bats left. ... Full name: George Friederich Sherrill. ... High school: Evangelical Christian (Memphis). ... Junior college: Jackson State C.C. ... College: Austin Peay. **TRANSACTIONS/CAREER NOTES:** Signed by Evansville of the independent Frontier League (1999). ... Signed by Sioux City of the independent Norther League (2001). ... Signed by Winnipeg of the independent Northern League. ... Signed as a free agent by Seattle Mariners organization (July 2, 2003). ... On disabled list (September 17, 2004-remainder of season).

CAREER HITTING: 0-for-0 (.000), 0 R, 0 2B, 0 3B, 0 HR, 0 RBI.

Year	Team (League)	W	L	Pct.	ERA	WHIP	G	GS	CG	ShO	Hld.	Sv.-Opp.	IP	H	R	ER	HR	BB-IBB	SO	Avg.
1999— Evansville (Fron.)		2	4	.333	3.15	1.45	22	4	1	1	...	2-...	40.0	40	20	14	3	18-...	33	...
2000— Evansville (Fron.)		3	5	.375	4.66	1.41	13	13	1	0	...	0-...	75.1	71	45	39	5	35-...	61	...
2001— Sioux Falls (Nor.)		4	4	.500	2.45	1.14	48	2	0	0	...	0-...	58.2	53	20	16	3	14-...	45	...
2002— Winnipeg (North.)		3	5	.375	3.07	1.17	38	0	0	0	...	2-...	41.0	35	16	14	6	13-...	61	...
2003— Winnipeg (North.)		1	0	1.000	1.13	0.75	16	0	0	0	...	1-...	16.0	8	2	2	0	4-...	30	...
— San Antonio (Texas)		3	0	1.000	0.33	1.13	16	0	0	0	...	0-...	27.1	19	2	1	1	12-1	31	.198
2004— Tacoma (PCL)		4	2	.667	2.33	1.01	36	0	0	0	...	13-...	50.1	42	13	13	4	9-1	62	.223
— Seattle (A.L.)		2	1	.667	3.80	1.39	21	0	0	0	3	0-0	23.2	24	12	10	3	9-1	16	.258
2005— Ariz. Mariners (Ariz.)		0	0	...	0.00	0.00	3	2	0	0	0	0-0	4.0	0	0	0	0	0-0	5	.000
— Tacoma (PCL)		1	3	.250	2.28	1.06	22	0	0	0	1	7-9	23.2	19	7	6	0	6-0	38	.209
— Seattle (A.L.)		4	3	.571	5.21	1.05	29	0	0	0	9	0-0	19.0	13	12	11	3	7-2	24	.194
2006— Seattle (A.L.)		2	4	.333	4.28	1.43	72	0	0	0	17	1-1	40.0	30	19	19	0	27-4	42	.213
Major League totals (3 years)		8	8	.500	4.35	1.33	122	0	0	0	29	1-1	82.2	67	43	40	6	43-7	82	.223

2006 LEFTY-RIGHTY SPLITS

vs.	Avg.	AB	H	2B	3B	HR	RBI	BB	SO	OBP	Slg.	vs.	Avg.	AB	H	2B	3B	HR	RBI	BB	SO	OBP	Slg.
L	.143	77	11	3	0	0	6	9	29	.230	.182	R	.297	64	19	4	0	0	9	18	13	.446	.359

SHIELDS, JAMES — P

PERSONAL: Born December 20, 1981, in Newhall, Calif. ... 6-3/215. ... Throws right, bats right. ... Full name: James Anthony Shields. ... Cousin of Aaron Rowand, outfielder, Philadelphia Phillies. **TRANSACTIONS/CAREER NOTES:** Selected by Tampa Bay Devil Rays organization in 16th round of 2000 free-agent draft.
CAREER HITTING: 3-for-8 (.375), 2 R, 0 2B, 0 3B, 0 HR, 0 RBI.

Year	Team (League)	W	L	Pct.	ERA	WHIP	G	GS	CG	ShO	Hld.	Sv.-Opp.	IP	H	R	ER	HR	BB-IBB	SO	Avg.
2001— Hudson Valley (NYP)		2	1	.667	2.30	1.17	5	5	0	0	...	0-...	27.1	27	8	7	1	5-0	25	.255
— Char., S.C. (SAL)		4	5	.444	2.65	1.02	10	10	2	1	...	0-...	71.1	63	24	21	7	10-0	60	.236
2003— Bakersfield (Calif.)		10	10	.500	4.45	1.39	26	24	0	0	...	1-...	143.2	161	85	71	19	38-0	119	.279
2004— Montgom. (Sou.)		0	3	.000	7.85	1.75	4	4	0	0	...	0-...	18.1	24	16	16	4	8-0	14	.329
— Bakersfield (Calif.)		8	5	.615	4.23	1.30	20	20	1	1	...	0-...	117.0	119	61	55	13	33-0	92	.273
2005— Montgom. (Sou.)		7	5	.583	2.80	1.15	17	16	0	0	0	0-0	109.1	95	36	34	6	31-0	104	.244
— Durham (Int'l)		1	0	1.000	6.00	2.00	1	1	0	0	0	0-0	6.0	9	4	4	0	3-0	6	.346
2006— Durham (Int'l)		3	2	.600	2.64	1.08	10	10	0	0	0	0-0	61.1	60	24	18	3	6-0	64	.262
— Tampa Bay (A.L.)		6	8	.429	4.84	1.44	21	21	1	0	0	0-0	124.2	141	69	67	18	38-5	104	.288
Major League totals (1 year)		6	8	.429	4.84	1.44	21	21	1	0	0	0-0	124.2	141	69	67	18	38-5	104	.288

2006 LEFTY-RIGHTY SPLITS

vs.	Avg.	AB	H	2B	3B	HR	RBI	BB	SO	OBP	Slg.	vs.	Avg.	AB	H	2B	3B	HR	RBI	BB	SO	OBP	Slg.
L	.266	241	64	13	0	10	34	19	43	.323	.444	R	.309	249	77	20	0	8	31	19	61	.363	.486

SHIELDS, SCOT — P

PERSONAL: Born July 22, 1975, in Fort Lauderdale, Fla. ... 6-1/170. ... Throws right, bats right. ... Full name: Robert Scot Shields. ... High school: Fort Lauderdale (Fla.). ... College: Lincoln Memorial (Tenn.). **TRANSACTIONS/CAREER NOTES:** Selected by Anaheim Angels organization in 38th round of 1997 free-agent draft. ... Angels franchise renamed Los Angeles Angels of Anaheim for 2005 season.
CAREER HITTING: 0-for-3 (.000), 0 R, 0 2B, 0 3B, 0 HR, 0 RBI.

Year	Team (League)	W	L	Pct.	ERA	WHIP	G	GS	CG	ShO	Hld.	Sv.-Opp.	IP	H	R	ER	HR	BB-IBB	SO	Avg.
1997— Boise (N'west)		7	2	.778	2.94	1.33	30	0	0	0	...	2-...	52.0	45	20	17	1	24-4	61	.233
1998— Cedar Rap. (Midw.)		6	5	.545	3.65	1.23	58	0	0	0	...	7-...	74.0	62	33	30	5	29-0	81	.232
1999— Lake Elsinore (Calif.)		10	3	.769	2.52	1.21	24	9	2	1	...	1-...	107.1	91	37	30	1	39-4	113	.233
— Erie (East.)		4	4	.500	2.89	1.41	10	10	1	1	...	0-...	74.2	57	26	24	10	26-0	81	.216
2000— Edmonton (PCL)		7	13	.350	5.41	1.47	27	27	4	1	...	0-...	163.0	158	114	98	16	82-0	156	.250
2001— Salt Lake (PCL)		6	11	.353	4.97	1.25	21	21	4	0	...	0-...	137.2	141	84	76	24	31-0	104	.267
— Anaheim (A.L.)		0	0	...	0.00	1.36	8	0	0	0	0	0-0	11.0	8	1	0	0	7-0	7	.200
2002— Salt Lake (PCL)		2	2	.500	3.06	0.96	28	1	0	0	...	1-...	47.0	39	18	16	5	6-0	50	.223
— Anaheim (A.L.)		5	3	.625	2.20	1.06	29	1	0	0	3	0-0	49.0	31	13	12	4	21-1	30	.188
2003— Anaheim (A.L.)		5	6	.455	2.85	1.19	44	13	0	0	3	1-1	148.1	138	56	47	12	38-6	111	.247
2004— Anaheim (A.L.)		8	2	.800	3.33	1.30	60	0	0	0	17	4-7	105.1	97	42	39	6	40-5	109	.238
2005— Los Angeles (A.L.)		10	11	.476	2.75	1.12	78	0	0	0	• 33	7-13	91.2	66	33	28	5	37-2	98	.201
2006— Los Angeles (A.L.)		7	7	.500	2.87	1.07	74	0	0	0	31	2-8	87.2	70	30	28	8	24-4	84	.217
Major League totals (6 years)		35	29	.547	2.81	1.17	293	14	0	0	87	14-29	493.0	410	175	154	35	167-18	439	.225

DIVISION SERIES RECORD

Year	Team (League)	W	L	Pct.	ERA	WHIP	G	GS	CG	ShO	Hld.	Sv.-Opp.	IP	H	R	ER	HR	BB-IBB	SO	Avg.
2004— Anaheim (A.L.)		0	0	...	6.00	2.33	2	0	0	0	0	0-0	3.0	5	2	2	1	2-1	3	.357
2005— Los Angeles (A.L.)		1	1	.500	3.60	1.40	4	0	0	0	0	0-1	5.0	4	2	2	0	3-0	5	.211
Division series totals (2 years)		1	1	.500	4.50	1.75	6	0	0	0	0	0-1	8.0	9	4	4	1	5-1	8	.273

CHAMPIONSHIP SERIES RECORD

Year	Team (League)	W	L	Pct.	ERA	WHIP	G	GS	CG	ShO	Hld.	Sv.-Opp.	IP	H	R	ER	HR	BB-IBB	SO	Avg.
2005— Los Angeles (A.L.)		0	0	...	0.00	0.83	4	0	0	0	1	0-0	6.0	4	0	0	0	1-1	5	.200

WORLD SERIES RECORD

Year	Team (League)	W	L	Pct.	ERA	WHIP	G	GS	CG	ShO	Hld.	Sv.-Opp.	IP	H	R	ER	HR	BB-IBB	SO	Avg.
2002— Anaheim (A.L.)		0	0	...	5.40	3.00	1	0	0	0	0	0-0	1.2	5	5	1	2	0-0	1	.455

2006 LEFTY-RIGHTY SPLITS

vs.	Avg.	AB	H	2B	3B	HR	RBI	BB	SO	OBP	Slg.	vs.	Avg.	AB	H	2B	3B	HR	RBI	BB	SO	OBP	Slg.
L	.207	150	31	6	0	4	12	14	45	.274	.327	R	.227	172	39	9	0	4	21	10	39	.272	.349

SHIELL, JASON — P

PERSONAL: Born October 19, 1976, in Savannah, Ga. ... 6-0/180. ... Throws right, bats right. ... Full name: Jason Alexander Shiell. ... High school: Windsor-Forest (Savannah, Ga.). **TRANSACTIONS/CAREER NOTES:** Selected by Atlanta Braves organization in 48th round of 1995 free-agent draft. ... Traded by Braves with OF/1B Ryan Klesko and 2B Bret Boone to San Diego Padres for 2B Quilvio Veras, 1B Wally Joyner and OF Reggie Sanders (December 22, 1999). ... Claimed on waivers by Boston Red Sox (October 2, 2002). ... On disabled list (March 26, 2004-entire season). ... Signed by Somerset of the independent Atlantic League (2006). ... Signed as a free agent by Atlanta Braves organization (June 25, 2006).
CAREER HITTING: 0-for-4 (.000), 0 R, 0 2B, 0 3B, 0 HR, 0 RBI.

Year Team (League)	W	L	Pct.	ERA	WHIP	G	GS	CG	ShO	Hld.	Sv.-Opp.	IP	H	R	ER	HR	BB-IBB	SO	Avg.
1995—GC Braves (GCL)	1	3	.250	4.43	1.48	12	0	0	0	...	2-...	22.1	23	16	11	0	10-1	13	.258
1996—Danville (Appal.)	3	1	.750	1.97	1.06	12	12	0	0	...	0-...	59.1	44	14	13	1	19-0	57	.210
1997—Macon (S. Atl.)	10	5	.667	2.86	1.12	27	24	0	0	...	0-...	129.0	113	53	41	12	32-0	101	.238
1998—Macon (S. Atl.)	0	1	.000	4.50	1.00	4	3	0	0	...	0-...	8.0	7	4	4	2	1-0	8	.226
1999—Myrtle Beach (Carol.)	6	7	.462	3.77	1.34	26	17	0	0	...	0-...	114.2	118	51	48	5	36-0	90	.268
2000—Rancho Cuca. (Calif.)	7	5	.583	5.33	1.41	16	14	0	0	...	0-...	81.0	73	54	48	9	41-0	80	.239
2001—Mobile (Sou.)	2	3	.400	4.44	1.52	45	2	0	0	...	0-...	81.0	91	46	40	5	32-2	60	.295
2002—Portland (PCL)	4	3	.571	2.78	1.22	56	0	0	0	...	6-...	74.1	62	26	23	4	29-0	74	.219
—San Diego (N.L.)	0	0	...	27.00	7.50	3	0	0	0	0	0-...	1.1	7	4	4	0	3-0	1	.700
2003—Boston (A.L.)	2	0	1.000	4.63	1.71	17	0	0	0	0	1-2	23.1	23	13	12	4	17-2	23	.253
—Pawtucket (Int'l)	3	2	.600	2.42	1.20	20	0	0	0	...	2-...	26.0	26	11	7	0	6-0	22	.263
2004—	Did not play.									*									
2005—	Did not play.																		
2006—Somerset (Atl.)	3	2	.600	2.92	1.38	9	9	0	0	...	0-0	52.1	54	18	17	4	18-...	32	
—Richmond (Int'l)	2	4	.333	4.50	1.29	9	9	0	0	...	0-0	52.0	51	26	26	3	16-0	34	.263
—Atlanta (N.L.)	0	2	.000	8.62	2.04	4	3	0	0	...	0-0	15.2	23	15	15	5	9-1	14	.343
American League totals (1 year)	2	0	1.000	4.63	1.71	17	0	0	0	0	1-2	23.1	23	13	12	4	17-2	23	.253
National League totals (2 years)	0	2	.000	10.06	2.47	7	3	0	0	0	0-...	17.0	30	19	19	5	12-1	15	.390
Major League totals (3 years)	2	2	.500	6.92	2.03	24	3	0	0	0	1-2	40.1	53	32	31	9	29-3	38	.315

2006 LEFTY-RIGHTY SPLITS

vs.	Avg.	AB	H	2B	3B	HR	RBI	BB	SO	OBP	Slg.	vs.	Avg.	AB	H	2B	3B	HR	RBI	BB	SO	OBP	Slg.
L	.423	26	11	4	0	3	8	2	4	.464	.923	R	.293	41	12	3	0	1	7	7	10	.400	.512

SHOPPACH, KELLY — C

PERSONAL: Born April 29, 1980, in Fort Worth, Texas. ... 6-1/210. ... Bats right, throws right. ... Full name: Kelly Brian Shoppach. ... High school: Brewer (Fort Worth, Texas). ... College: Baylor. **TRANSACTIONS/CAREER NOTES:** Selected by Boston Red Sox organization in second round of 2001 free-agent draft. ... Traded by Red Sox with P Guillermo Mota and 3B Andy Marte to Cleveland Indians for OF Coco Crisp, C Josh Bard and P David Riske (January 27, 2006).

2006 GAMES PLAYED BY POSITION (MLB): C—40.

Year Team (League)	Pos.	G	AB	R	H	2B	3B	HR	RBI	BB	SO	HBP	GDP	SB-CS	Avg.	OBP	SLG	OPS	E	Avg.
2002—Sarasota (Fla. St.)	C	116	414	54	112	35	1	10	66	59	112	6	11	2-1	.271	.369	.432	.801	9	.986
2003—Portland (East.)	C	92	340	45	96	30	2	12	60	35	83	5	10	0-0	.282	.353	.488	.841	11	.982
2004—Pawtucket (Int'l)	C	113	399	62	93	25	0	22	64	46	138	6	7	0-0	.233	.320	.461	.781	8	.988
2005—Pawtucket (Int'l)	C-DH	102	371	60	94	16	0	26	75	46	116	12	9	0-0	.253	.352	.507	.859	5	.993
—Boston (A.L.)	C-DH	9	15	1	0	0	0	0	0	0	7	1	0	0-0	.000	.063	.000	.063	0	1.000
2006—Buffalo (Int'l)		21	78	11	22	8	0	4	9	6	25	3	1	0-1	.282	.336	.538	.895	4	.975
—Cleveland (A.L.)	C	41	110	7	27	6	0	3	16	8	45	0	2	0-0	.245	.297	.382	.678	2	.991
Major League totals (2 years)		50	125	8	27	6	0	3	16	8	52	1	2	0-0	.216	.269	.336	.605	2	.992

2006 LEFTY-RIGHTY SPLITS

vs.	Avg.	AB	H	2B	3B	HR	RBI	BB	SO	OBP	Slg.	vs.	Avg.	AB	H	2B	3B	HR	RBI	BB	SO	OBP	Slg.
L	.314	35	11	5	0	2	7	3	10	.368	.629	R	.213	75	16	1	0	1	9	5	35	.263	.267

SHOUSE, BRIAN — P

PERSONAL: Born September 26, 1968, in Effingham, Ill. ... 5-11/190. ... Throws left, bats left. ... Full name: Brian Douglas Shouse. ... High school: Effingham (Ill.). ... College: Bradley. **TRANSACTIONS/CAREER NOTES:** Selected by Pittsburgh Pirates organization in 13th round of 1990 free-agent draft. ... Released by Pirates (May 16, 1996). ... Signed by Baltimore Orioles organization (May 22, 1996). ... Signed as a free agent by Boston Red Sox organization (October 28, 1997). ... Contract sold by Red Sox to Kintetsu Buffaloes of the Japan Pacific League (June 25, 1998). ... Signed as a free agent by Arizona Diamondbacks organization (November 19, 1998). ... On disabled list (September 18, 1999-remainder of season). ... Signed as a free agent by New York Mets organization (December 2, 1999). ... Released by Mets (April 14, 2000). ... Signed by Orioles organization (May 13, 2000). ... Signed as a free agent by Houston Astros organization (December 22, 2000). ... Signed as a free agent by Kansas City Royals organization (December 7, 2001). ... On disabled list (April 28-May 13, 2002). ... Released by Royals (June 27, 2002). ... Signed by Astros organization (July 22, 2002). ... Signed as a free agent by Texas Rangers organization (November 13, 2002). ... On disabled list (March 27-May 13, 2004; included rehabilitation assignment to Oklahoma. ... On disabled list (April 22-May 8, 2006; included rehabilitation assignments to Oklahoma and Frisco. ... Traded by Rangers to Milwaukee Brewers for SS Enrique Cruz and cash (May 13, 2006).

CAREER HITTING: 0-for-0 (.000), 0 R, 0 2B, 0 3B, 0 HR, 0 RBI.

Year Team (League)	W	L	Pct.	ERA	WHIP	G	GS	CG	ShO	Hld.	Sv.-Opp.	IP	H	R	ER	HR	BB-IBB	SO	Avg.
1990—Welland (NYP)	4	3	.571	5.22	1.44	17	1	0	0	...	2-...	39.2	50	27	23	2	7-0	39	.309
1991—Augusta (S. Atl.)	2	3	.400	3.19	1.00	26	0	0	0	...	8-...	31.0	22	13	11	1	9-1	32	.200
—Salem (Carol.)	2	1	.667	2.94	1.49	17	0	0	0	...	2-...	33.2	35	12	11	2	15-2	25	.269
1992—Carolina (Southern)	5	6	.455	2.44	1.28	59	0	0	0	...	4-...	77.1	71	31	21	3	28-4	79	.252
1993—Buffalo (A.A.)	1	0	1.000	3.83	1.37	48	0	0	0	...	2-...	51.2	54	24	22	7	17-2	25	.276
—Pittsburgh (N.L.)	0	0	...	9.00	2.25	6	0	0	0	0	0-0	4.0	7	4	4	1	2-0	3	.368
1994—Buffalo (A.A.)	3	4	.429	3.63	1.13	43	0	0	0	...	3-...	52.0	44	22	21	6	15-4	31	.232
1995—Carolina (Southern)	7	6	.538	4.47	1.26	21	20	0	0	...	0-...	114.2	126	64	57	14	19-2	76	.281
—Calgary (PCL)	4	4	.500	6.18	1.75	8	8	1	0	...	0-...	39.1	62	35	27	2	7-0	17	.354
1996—Calgary (PCL)	1	0	1.000	10.66	2.05	12	1	0	0	...	0-...	12.2	22	15	15	4	4-1	12	.367
—Rochester (Int'l)	1	2	.333	4.50	1.38	32	0	0	0	...	0-...	50.0	53	27	25	6	16-1	45	.270
1997—Rochester (Int'l)	6	2	.750	2.27	0.97	54	0	0	0	...	9-...	71.1	48	21	18	6	21-4	81	.191
1998—Pawtucket (Int'l)	2	0	1.000	2.90	0.90	22	1	0	0	...	6-...	31.0	21	11	10	7	7-0	25	.188
—Boston (A.L.)	0	1	.000	5.63	1.63	7	0	0	0	1	0-0	8.0	9	5	5	2	4-0	5	.281
—Kintetsu (Jp. Pac.)	0	2	.000	6.58	2.04	18	3	0	0	...	0-...	26.0	40	20	19	...	13-...	20	...
—Kintetsu (Jp. West.)	1	0	1.000	1.38	1.23	5	2	0	0	...	0-...	13.0	9	2	2	...	7-...	9	...
1999—Tucson (PCL)	3	4	.429	6.25	1.81	30	0	0	0	...	0-...	44.2	63	35	31	4	18-3	32	.339
2000—Norfolk (Int'l)	0	1	.000	15.00	2.67	4	0	0	0	...	0-...	3.0	6	5	5	2	2-0	1	.429
—Rochester (Int'l)	4	4	.500	2.79	1.33	43	0	0	0	...	2-...	58.0	63	20	18	4	14-1	52	.279
2001—New Orleans (PCL)	2	2	.500	2.89	1.25	56	1	0	0	...	1-...	53.0	51	21	17	4	15-0	56	.249
2002—Kansas City (A.L.)	0	0	...	6.14	1.64	23	0	0	0	2	0-...	14.2	15	10	10	3	9-1	11	.259
—Omaha (PCL)	0	0	...	11.57	3.43	5	0	0	0	...	0-...	2.1	7	3	3	0	1-0	3	.538
—New Orleans (PCL)	1	0	1.000	3.43	0.95	19	0	0	0	...	0-...	21.0	17	10	8	2	3-0	20	.215
2003—Oklahoma (PCL)	0	1	.000	3.68	1.50	6	0	0	0	...	1-...	7.1	8	3	3	0	3-0	2	.286
—Texas (A.L.)	0	0	...	3.10	1.25	62	0	0	0	10	1-1	61.0	62	24	21	1	14-6	40	.267
2004—Oklahoma (PCL)	0	0	...	6.14	2.18	9	0	0	0	...	0-...	7.1	12	5	5	1	4-1	3	.375
—Texas (A.L.)	2	0	1.000	2.23	1.22	53	0	0	0	12	0-...	44.1	36	12	11	3	18-3	34	.224

Year Team (League)	W	L	Pct.	ERA	WHIP	G	GS	CG	ShO	Hld.	Sv.-Opp.	IP	H	R	ER	HR	BB-IBB	SO	Avg.
2005— Texas (A.L.)	3	2	.600	5.23	1.37	64	0	0	0	11	0-2	53.1	55	37	31	7	18-4	35	.266
2006— Oklahoma (PCL)	0	1	.000	5.40	2.20	5	0	0	0	0	0-0	5.0	7	5	3	1	4-0	3	.318
— Frisco (Texas)	0	0	...	0.00	1.50	2	0	0	0	1	0-0	2.0	2	0	0	0	1-1	1	.286
— Texas (A.L.)	0	0	...	4.15	1.62	6	0	0	0	1	0-1	4.1	6	2	2	1	1-1	3	.316
— Milwaukee (N.L.)	1	3	.250	3.97	1.50	59	0	0	0	14	2-4	34.0	34	16	15	3	17-4	20	.264
American League totals (6 years)	5	4	.556	3.88	1.33	215	0	0	0	37	1-4	185.2	183	90	80	17	64-15	128	.258
National League totals (2 years)	1	3	.250	4.50	1.58	65	0	0	0	14	2-4	38.0	41	20	19	4	19-4	23	.277
Major League totals (7 years)	6	7	.462	3.98	1.37	280	0	0	0	51	3-8	223.2	224	110	99	21	83-19	151	.261

2006 LEFTY-RIGHTY SPLITS

vs.	Avg.	AB	H	2B	3B	HR	RBI	BB	SO	OBP	Slg.	vs.	Avg.	AB	H	2B	3B	HR	RBI	BB	SO	OBP	Slg.
L	.238	80	19	6	0	1	13	6	19	.319	.350	R	.309	68	21	3	1	3	14	12	4	.427	.515

SIERRA, RUBEN — DH/OF

PERSONAL: Born October 6, 1965, in Rio Piedras, Puerto Rico. ... 6-1/215. ... Bats both, throws right. ... Full name: Ruben Angel Sierra. ... High school: Dr. Secario Rosario (Rio Piedras, Puerto Rico). **TRANSACTIONS/CAREER NOTES:** Signed as a non-drafted free agent by Texas Rangers organization (November 21, 1982). ... Traded by Rangers with Ps Jeff Russell and Bobby Witt and cash to Oakland Athletics for OF Jose Canseco (August 31, 1992). ... On disabled list (July 7-22, 1995). ... Traded by A's with P Jason Beverlin to New York Yankees for OF/DH Danny Tartabull (July 28, 1995). ... Signed by Campeche of the Mexican League. ... Traded by Yankees with P Matt Drews to Detroit Tigers for 1B/DH Cecil Fielder (July 31, 1996). ... Traded by Tigers to Cincinnati Reds for OF Decomba Conner and P Ben Bailey (October 28, 1996). ... Released by Reds (May 9, 1997). ... Signed by Toronto Blue Jays organization (May 11, 1997). ... Released by Blue Jays (June 16, 1997). ... Signed by Chicago White Sox organization (January 9, 1998). ... Released by White Sox (May 29, 1998). ... Signed by New York Mets organization (June 20, 1998). ... Signed by Atlantic City of the independent Atlantic League (May 6, 1999). ... Signed as a free agent by Cleveland Indians organization (December 23, 1999). ... Released by Indians (March 20, 2000). ... Signed by Cancun of the Mexican Leagu (April 3, 2000). ... Signed as a free agent by Rangers organization (May 1, 2000). ... On disabled list (July 27-August 11, 2001). ... Signed as a free agent by Seattle Mariners (January 3, 2002). ... Signed as a free agent by Rangers organization (January 27, 2003). ... Traded by Rangers to Yankees for OF Marcus Thames (June 6, 2003). ... On disabled list (April 21-May 20 and July 19-September 1, 2005). ... Signed as free agent by Minnesota Twins (January 31, 2006). ... On disabled list (April 30-June 16, 2006; included rehabilitation assignment to Rochester. ... Released by Twins (July 10, 2006). **HONORS:** Named A.L. Player of the Year by THE SPORTING NEWS (1989). ... Named A.L. Comeback Player of the Year by THE SPORTING NEWS (2001). **STATISTICAL NOTES:** Career major league grand slams: 9. **MISCELLANEOUS NOTES:** Batted righthanded only (1983).

2006 GAMES PLAYED BY POSITION (MLB): DH—7.

Year Team (League)	Pos.	G	AB	R	H	2B	3B	HR	RBI	BB	SO	HBP	GDP	SB-CS	Avg.	OBP	SLG	OPS	E	Avg.
1983— GC Rangers (GCL)	OF	48	182	26	44	7	3	1	26	16	38	1	...	3-4	.242	.300	.330	.630	4	.948
1984— Burlington (Midw.)	OF	138	482	55	127	33	5	6	75	49	97	1	9	13-9	.263	.331	.390	.721	20	.928
1985— Tulsa (Texas)	OF	137	545	63	138	34	8	13	74	35	111	1	8	22-7	.253	.297	.417	.713	15	.943
1986— Okla. City (A.A.)	OF	46	189	31	56	11	2	9	41	15	27	0	5	8-2	.296	.341	.519	.860	2	.983
— Texas (A.L.)	DH-OF	113	382	50	101	13	10	16	55	22	65	1	8	7-8	.264	.302	.476	.779	6	.972
1987— Texas (A.L.)	OF	158	*643	97	169	35	4	30	109	39	114	2	18	16-11	.263	.302	.470	.771	11	.963
1988— Texas (A.L.)	DH-OF	156	615	77	156	32	2	23	91	44	91	1	15	18-4	.254	.301	.424	.725	7	.979
1989— Texas (A.L.)		• 162	634	101	194	35	*14	29	*119	43	82	2	7	8-2	.306	.347	*.543	.889	9	.973
1990— Texas (A.L.)	DH-OF	159	608	70	170	37	2	16	96	49	86	1	15	9-0	.280	.330	.426	.756	10	.967
1991— Texas (A.L.)	OF	161	661	110	203	44	5	25	116	56	91	0	17	16-4	.307	.357	.502	.859	7	.979
1992— Texas (A.L.)	OF-DH	124	500	66	139	30	6	14	70	31	59	0	9	12-4	.278	.315	.446	.761	7	.970
— Oakland (A.L.)	OF-DH	27	101	17	28	4	1	3	17	14	9	0	2	2-0	.277	.359	.426	.785	0	1.000
1993— Oakland (A.L.)	OF-DH	158	630	77	147	23	5	22	101	52	97	1	17	25-5	.233	.288	.390	.678	7	.977
1994— Oakland (A.L.)	OF-DH	110	426	71	114	21	1	23	92	23	64	0	15	8-5	.268	.298	.484	.781	*9	.948
1995— Oakland (A.L.)	OF-DH	70	264	40	70	17	0	12	42	24	54	0	2	4-4	.265	.323	.466	.789	4	.957
— New York (A.L.)	DH-OF	56	215	33	56	15	0	7	44	22	34	0	6	1-0	.260	.322	.428	.750	1	.950
1996— Campeche (Mex.)	DH	1	0	1	0	0	0	0	0	0	0	0	...	0-0	.000	...	.000	...	...	...
— New York (A.L.)	DH-OF	96	360	39	93	17	1	11	52	40	58	0	10	1-3	.258	.327	.403	.730	1	.984
— Detroit (A.L.)	OF-DH	46	158	22	35	9	1	1	20	20	25	0	2	3-1	.222	.306	.310	.616	5	.914
1997— Cincinnati (N.L.)	OF	25	90	6	22	5	1	2	7	6	21	0	1	0-0	.244	.292	.389	.681	0	1.000
— Syracuse (Int'l)	OF	8	32	5	7	2	0	1	5	2	6	0	0	0-0	.219	.265	.375	.640	1	.923
— Toronto (Int'l)	OF-DH	14	48	4	10	0	2	1	5	3	13	0	0	0-0	.208	.250	.354	.604	1	.929
1998— Chicago (A.L.)	OF-DH	27	74	7	16	4	1	4	11	3	11	0	2	2-0	.216	.247	.459	.706	0	1.000
— Norfolk (Int'l)	OF-DH	28	108	16	28	5	0	3	19	13	18	0	4	3-0	.259	.331	.389	.720	0	1.000
1999— Atlantic City (Atl.)	DH-OF	112	422	76	124	22	2	28	82	59	63	...	...	3-2	.294	...	.555	...	3	.960
2000— Cancun (Mex.)	OF	16	62	8	22	2	1	3	12	10	10	...	...	0-1	.355	...	.565	...	0	1.000
— Oklahoma (PCL)	OF	112	439	70	143	26	3	18	82	55	63	0	24	5-2	.326	.398	.522	.919	6	.962
— Texas (A.L.)	DH	20	60	5	14	0	0	1	7	4	9	0	1	1-0	.233	.281	.283	.565	...	...
2001— Oklahoma (PCL)	OF	24	94	14	25	7	1	3	12	10	14	0	5	2-0	.266	.337	.404	.741	0	1.000
— Texas (A.L.)	DH-OF	94	344	55	100	21	1	23	67	19	52	0	13	2-0	.291	.322	.561	.884	4	.937
2002— Seattle (A.L.)	OF-DH	122	419	47	113	23	0	13	60	31	66	0	17	4-0	.270	.319	.418	.736	2	.979
2003— Seattle (A.L.)	OF-DH	43	133	14	35	9	1	3	16	14	27	0	2	1-1	.263	.333	.399	.732	1	.962
— New York (A.L.)	DH-OF	63	174	19	48	8	1	6	31	13	20	0	7	1-0	.276	.323	.437	.760	1	1.000
2004— New York (A.L.)	DH-OF	107	307	40	75	12	1	17	65	25	55	0	5	1-0	.244	.296	.456	.752	1	.977
2005— Columbus (Int'l)		3	11	2	2	0	0	1	1	2	3	0	0	0-0	.182	.308	.455	.762	0	...
— New York (A.L.)	DH-OF	61	170	14	39	12	4	4	29	9	41	0	2	0-0	.229	.265	.371	.636	1	.958
2006— Fort Myers (FSL)		3	12	2	3	1	0	1	3	1	3	0	0	0-0	.250	.308	.333	.641	0	1.000
— Rochester (Int'l)		2	6	1	2	0	0	0	2	2	1	0	0	0-0	.333	.500	.333	.833	0	...
— Minnesota (A.L.)	DH	14	28	3	5	1	0	0	4	4	7	0	0	0-0	.179	.273	.214	.487	0	...
American League totals (20 years)		2161	7954	1078	2130	423	58	304	1315	604	1218	7	192	142-52	.268	.316	.450	.766	94	.970
National League totals (1 year)		25	90	6	22	5	1	2	7	6	21	0	1	0-0	.244	.292	.389	.681	0	1.000
Major League totals (20 years)		2186	8044	1084	2152	428	59	306	1322	610	1239	7	193	142-52	.268	.315	.450	.765	94	.970

DIVISION SERIES RECORD

Year Team (League)	Pos.	G	AB	R	H	2B	3B	HR	RBI	BB	SO	HBP	GDP	SB-CS	Avg.	OBP	SLG	OPS	E	Avg.
1995— New York (A.L.)	DH	5	23	2	4	2	0	2	5	2	7	0	0	0-0	.174	.231	.522	.753	...	...
2003— New York (A.L.)	OF	1	2	0	0	0	0	0	0	0	0	0	0	0-0	.000	.000	.000	.000	...	...
2004— New York (A.L.)	DH	3	12	1	2	0	0	1	3	2	3	0	0	1-0	.167	.286	.417	.702	0	...
2005— New York (A.L.)	OF	3	3	0	1	0	0	0	1	0	1	0	0	0-0	.333	.333	.333	.667	0	...
Division series totals (4 years)		12	40	3	7	2	0	3	9	4	11	0	0	1-0	.175	.244	.450	.694	0	...

CHAMPIONSHIP SERIES RECORD

Year Team (League)	Pos.	G	AB	R	H	2B	3B	HR	RBI	BB	SO	HBP	GDP	SB-CS	Avg.	OBP	SLG	OPS	E	Avg.
1992— Oakland (A.L.)	OF	6	24	4	8	3	1	0	7	3	4	0	1	1-2	.333	.357	.625	.982	0	1.000
2003— New York (A.L.)	OF	3	2	1	1	0	0	1	1	0	0	0	0	0-0	.500	.667	2.000	2.667	0	...
2004— New York (A.L.)	DH	5	21	1	7	1	1	1	2	3	3	0	0	0-0	.333	.417	.476	.893	0	...
Champ. series totals (3 years)		14	47	6	16	3	2	2	10	6	9	0	1	1-2	.340	.400	.617	1.017	0	1.000

S

WORLD SERIES RECORD

Year	Team (League)	Pos.	G	AB	R	H	2B	3B	HR	RBI	BB	SO	HBP	GDP	SB-CS	Avg.	OBP	SLG	OPS	E	Avg.
2003— New York (A.L.)		OF	5	4	0	1	0	1	0	2	1	3	0	0	0-0	.250	.400	.750	1.150	0	...

ALL-STAR GAME RECORD

			G	AB	R	H	2B	3B	HR	RBI	BB	SO	HBP	GDP	SB-CS	Avg.	OBP	SLG	OPS	E	Avg.
All-Star Game totals (4 years)			4	9	3	4	0	0	1	3	0	2	0	0	0-0	.444	.444	.778	1.222	0	1.000

2006 LEFTY-RIGHTY SPLITS

vs.	Avg.	AB	H	2B	3B	HR	RBI	BB	SO	OBP	Slg.	vs.	Avg.	AB	H	2B	3B	HR	RBI	BB	SO	OBP	Slg.
L	.250	8	2	0	0	0	2	0	1	.250	.250	R	.150	20	3	1	0	0	2	4	6	.280	.200

SIKORSKI, BRIAN — P

PERSONAL: Born July 27, 1974, in Detroit. ... 6-1/190. ... Throws right, bats right. ... Full name: Brian Patrick Sikorski. ... Name pronounced: si-CORE-ski. ... High school: Roseville (Mich.). ... College: Western Michigan. **TRANSACTIONS/CAREER NOTES:** Selected by Houston Astros organization in fourth round of 1995 free-agent draft. ... Claimed on waivers by Texas Rangers (November 9, 1999). ... Contract sold by Rangers to Chiba Lotte Marines of the Japan Pacific League (June 26, 2001). ... Signed by Yomiuri Giants of the Japan Pacific League (2004). ...Signed as a free agent by San Diego Padres (December 22, 2005). ... Released by Padres (March 27, 2006). ... Re-signed by Padres organization (March 30, 2006). ... Traded by Padres to Cleveland Indians for P Mike Adams (July 18, 2006).

CAREER HITTING: 0-for-0 (.000), 0 R, 0 2B, 0 3B, 0 HR, 0 RBI.

Year	Team (League)	W	L	Pct.	ERA	WHIP	G	GS	CG	ShO	Hld.	Sv.-Opp.	IP	H	R	ER	HR	BB-IBB	SO	Avg.
1995— Auburn (NY-Penn)		1	2	.333	2.10	1.05	23	0	0	0	...	12-...	34.1	22	8	8	...	14-...	35	...
— Quad City (Midw.)		1	0	1.000	0.00	0.33	2	0	0	0	...	0-...	3.0	1	1	0	...	0-...	4	...
1996— Quad City (Midw.)		11	8	.579	3.13	1.26	26	25	1	0	...	0-...	166.2	140	79	58	...	70-...	150	...
1997— Kissimmee (Fla. St.)		8	2	.800	3.06	1.18	11	11	0	0	...	0-...	67.2	64	29	23	...	16-...	46	...
— Jackson (Texas)		5	5	.500	4.63	1.31	17	17	0	0	...	0-...	93.1	.91	55	48	...	31-...	74	...
1998— Jackson (Texas)		6	4	.600	4.07	1.30	15	15	0	0	...	0-...	97.1	83	50	44	...	44-...	80	...
— New Orleans (PCL)		5	8	.385	5.79	1.40	15	14	1	0	...	0-...	84.0	86	57	54	...	32-...	64	...
1999— New Orleans (PCL)		7	10	.412	4.95	1.43	28	27	2	1	...	0-...	158.1	169	92	87	25	58-...	122	...
2000— Oklahoma (PCL)		10	9	.526	4.04	1.36	24	23	5	2	...	0-...	140.1	131	73	63	9	60-...	99	...
— Texas (A.L.)		1	3	.250	5.73	1.88	10	5	0	0	0	0-...	37.2	46	31	24	9	25-...	32	.288
2001— Oklahoma (PCL)		6	4	.600	3.61	1.28	14	14	1	0	...	0-...	87.1	89	37	35	8	23-...	73	...
— Chiba Lotte (Jap. Pac.)		1	4	.200	6.43	1.56	12	6	1	0	...	0-...	42.1	48	36	30	9	18-...	31	...
2002— Chiba Lotte (Jap. Pac.)		4	6	.400	3.44	0.99	47	7	0	0	...	2-...	96.2	76	38	37	14	20-...	102	...
2003— Chiba Lotte (Jap. Pac.)		4	6	.400	3.16	1.25	47	5	0	0	...	1-...	82.2	80	35	29	4	23-...	71	...
2004— Yomiuri (Jp. Cen.)		5	3	.625	2.67	1.26	62	0	0	0	...	5-...	77.2	76	25	23	9	22-...	83	...
2005— Yomiuri (Jp. Cen.)		7	1	.875	3.29	1.23	70	0	0	0	...	0-...	87.2	75	33	32	4	33-...	100	...
2006— Portland (PCL)		2	3	.400	3.14	1.12	22	0	0	0	7-9		28.2	25	12	10	3	7-1	44	.225
— San Diego (N.L.)		1	1	.500	5.65	1.33	13	0	0	0	0	0-0	14.1	16	9	9	4	3-1	14	.281
— Cleveland (A.L.)		2	1	.667	4.58	1.22	17	0	0	0	2	0-1	19.2	20	10	10	4	4-0	24	.267
American League totals (2 years)		3	4	.429	5.34	1.66	27	5	0	0	2	0-1	57.1	66	41	34	13	29-0	56	.281
National League totals (1 year)		1	1	.500	5.65	1.33	13	0	0	0	0	0-0	14.1	16	9	9	4	3-1	14	.281
Major League totals (2 years)		4	5	.444	5.40	1.59	40	5	0	0	2	0-1	71.2	82	50	43	17	32-1	70	.281

2006 LEFTY-RIGHTY SPLITS

vs.	Avg.	AB	H	2B	3B	HR	RBI	BB	SO	OBP	Slg.	vs.	Avg.	AB	H	2B	3B	HR	RBI	BB	SO	OBP	Slg.
L	.346	52	18	3	0	5	13	4	15	.404	.692	R	.225	80	18	5	0	3	7	3	23	.250	.400

SILVA, CARLOS — P

PERSONAL: Born April 23, 1979, in Bolivar, Venezuela. ... 6-4/240. ... Throws right, bats right. ... High school: U.E. General Ezequiel Zamora Bolivar (Venezuela). **TRANSACTIONS/CAREER NOTES:** Signed as a non-drafted free agent by Philadelphia Phillies organization (March 22, 1996). ... On disabled list (May 27-June 14, 2002); included rehabilitation assignment to Reading. ... On suspended list (July 17-22, 2003). ... Traded by Phillies with IF Nick Punto and a player to be named to Minnesota Twins for P Eric Milton (December 3, 2003); Twins acquired P Bobby Korecky to complete deal (December 16, 2003). ... On disabled list (April 7-22, 2005); included rehabilitation assignment to Beloit.

CAREER HITTING: 3-for-19 (.158), 0 R, 1 2B, 0 3B, 0 HR, 1 RBI.

Year	Team (League)	W	L	Pct.	ERA	WHIP	G	GS	CG	ShO	Hld.	Sv.-Opp.	IP	H	R	ER	HR	BB-IBB	SO	Avg.
1996— Martinsville (App.)		0	0	...	4.00	1.39	7	1	0	0	...	0-...	18.0	20	11	8	1	5-0	16	.299
1997— Martinsville (App.)		2	2	.500	5.15	1.39	11	11	0	0	...	0-...	57.2	66	46	33	9	14-0	31	.284
1998— Martinsville (App.)		1	4	.200	5.05	1.27	7	7	1	0	...	0-...	41.0	48	24	23	2	4-0	21	.284
— Batavia (NY-Penn)		2	3	.400	6.35	1.54	9	7	0	0	...	0-...	45.1	61	37	32	4	9-0	27	.314
1999— Piedmont (S. Atl.)		11	8	.579	3.12	1.32	26	26	3	1	...	0-...	164.1	176	79	57	6	41-2	99	.273
2000— Clearwater (FSL)		8	13	.381	3.57	1.45	26	24	4	0	...	0-...	176.1	229	99	70	7	26-1	82	.314
2001— Reading (East.)		15	8	.652	3.90	1.24	28	28	4	1	...	0-...	180.0	197	85	78	20	27-0	100	.284
2002— Philadelphia (N.L.)		5	0	1.000	3.21	1.31	68	0	0	0	8	1-5	84.0	88	34	30	4	22-6	41	.282
— Reading (East.)		0	0	...	0.00	0.00	2	0	0	0	...	1-...	3.0	0	0	0	0	0-0	1	.000
2003— Philadelphia (N.L.)		3	1	.750	4.43	1.48	62	1	0	0	4	1-3	87.1	92	43	43	· 7	37-5	48	.280
2004— Minnesota (A.L.)		14	8	.636	4.21	1.43	33	33	1	1	0	0-0	203.0	255	100	95	23	35-2	76	.310
2005— Beloit (Midw.)		0	0	...	1.80	1.00	1	1	0	0	...	0-0	5.0	5	1	1	1	0-0	3	.263
— Minnesota (A.L.)		9	8	.529	3.44	1.17	27	27	2	0	0	0-0	188.1	212	83	72	25	9-2	71	.290
2006— Minnesota (A.L.)		11	15	.423	5.94	1.54	36	31	0	0	2	0-0	180.1	246	* 130	119	* 38	32-4	70	.324
American League totals (3 years)		34	31	.523	4.50	1.38	96	91	3	1	2	0-0	571.2	713	313	286	86	76-8	217	.308
National League totals (2 years)		8	1	.889	3.83	1.39	130	1	0	0	12	2-8	171.1	180	77	73	11	59-11	89	.281
Major League totals (5 years)		42	32	.568	4.35	1.38	226	92	3	1	14	2-8	743.0	893	390	359	97	135-19	306	.302

DIVISION SERIES RECORD

Year	Team (League)	W	L	Pct.	ERA	WHIP	G	GS	CG	ShO	Hld.	Sv.-Opp.	IP	H	R	ER	HR	BB-IBB	SO	Avg.
2004— Minnesota (A.L.)		0	1	.000	10.80	2.00	1	1	0	0	...	0-0	5.0	10	6	6	1	0-0	1	.417

2006 LEFTY-RIGHTY SPLITS

vs.	Avg.	AB	H	2B	3B	HR	RBI	BB	SO	OBP	Slg.	vs.	Avg.	AB	H	2B	3B	HR	RBI	BB	SO	OBP	Slg.
L	.329	362	119	23	2	22	60	19	39	.363	.586	R	.320	397	127	21	0	16	54	13	31	.345	.494

SIMON, RANDALL — 1B

PERSONAL: Born May 25, 1975, in Willemstad, Curacao. ... 6-0/240. ... Bats left, throws left. ... Full name: Randall Carlito Simon. ... High school: Juan Pablo Duarte Tech (Willemstad, Curacao). **TRANSACTIONS/CAREER NOTES:** Signed as a non-drafted free agent by Atlanta Braves organization (July 17, 1992). ... Released by Braves (March 31, 2000). ... Signed by Florida Marlins organization (April 5, 2000). ... Released by Marlins (May 8, 2000). ... Signed by New York Yankees organization (May 14, 2000). ... Signed as a free agent by Detroit Tigers organization (January 18, 2001). ... Traded by Tigers to Pittsburgh Pirates for P Adrian Burnside and two players to be named

(November 25, 2002); Tigers acquired P Roberto Novoa (December 16, 2002) and IF Kody Kirkland (May 24, 2003) to complete deal. ... On disabled list (June 21-July 7, 2003); included rehabilitation assignment to Nashville. ... On suspended list (July 10-13, 2003). ... Traded by Pirates to Chicago Cubs for OF Ray Sadler (August 17, 2003). ... Signed as a free agent by Pirates (February 19, 2004). ... On disabled list (April 25-May 28, 2004); included rehabilitation assignment to Nashville. ... Released by Pirates (August 14, 2004). ... Signed by Tampa Bay Devil Rays (August 19, 2004). ... Released by Devil Rays (September 8, 2004). ... Signed by Tijuana of the Mexican League (2005). ... Contract purchased by Texas Rangers organization from Tijuana (August 2006). ... Traded by Rangers to Philadelphia Phillies for cash (September 1, 2006). **STA-TISTICAL NOTES:** Career major league grand slams: 2.

| | | | | | | | | | | BATTING | | | | | | | | | | FIELDING | |
Year Team (League)	Pos.	G	AB	R	H	2B	3B	HR	RBI	BB	SO	HBP	GDP	SB-CS	Avg.	OBP	SLG	OPS	E	Avg.
1992— Dominican Braves (DSL) ...	C	11	43	7	12	4	2	0	7	5	6			1-...	.279		.465		4	.979
1993— Danville (Appal.)	1B	61	232	28	59	17	1	3	31	10	34	2	4	1-1	.254	.289	.375	.664	10	.980
1994— Macon (S. Atl.)	1B	106	358	48	105	23	1	10	54	6	56	1	7	7-6	.293	.305	.447	.752	9	.986
1995— Durham (Carol.)	1B	122	420	56	111	18	1	18	79	36	63	5	15	6-5	.264	.326	.440	.767	10	.989
1996— Greenville (Sou.)	1B-OF	134	498	74	139	26	2	18	77	37	61	4	13	4-9	.279	.331	.448	.779	16	.980
1997— Richmond (Int'l)	1B-DH	133	519	62	160	45	1	14	102	17	76	4	18	1-6	.308	.335	.480	.814	14	.988
— Atlanta (N.L.)	1B	13	14	2	6	1	0	0	1	1	2	0	1	0-0	.429	.467	.500	.967	0	1.000
1998— Richmond (Int'l)	1B-DH	126	484	52	124	20	1	13	70	24	62	2	22	4-4	.256	.292	.382	.674	11	.989
— Atlanta (N.L.)	1B	7	16	2	3	0	0	0	0	0	1	0	0	0-0	.188	.176	.188	.364	0	1.000
1999— Atlanta (N.L.)	1B	90	218	26	69	16	0	5	25	17	25	1	10	2-2	.317	.367	.459	.826	3	.994
— Richmond (Int'l)	1B-DH	15	59	7	16	4	0	1	8	3	10	0	0	0-1	.271	.302	.390	.691	0	1.000
2000— Calgary (PCL)	1B	22	68	5	20	3	0	1	11	0	3	0	1	0-0	.294	.290	.382	.672	4	.966
— Columbus (Int'l)	1B-OF	94	364	52	97	20	4	17	74	35	42	0	17	6-5	.266	.325	.484	.809	9	.987
2001— Toledo (Int'l)	1B	59	222	27	75	13	0	10	31	21	21	2	8	0-3	.338	.400	.532	.932	7	.986
— Detroit (A.L.)	1B-DH	81	256	28	78	14	2	6	37	15	28	0	9	0-1	.305	.341	.445	.786	3	.992
2002— Detroit (A.L.)	DH-1B	130	482	51	145	17	1	19	82	13	30	4	13	0-1	.301	.320	.459	.779	7	.988
2003— Nashville (PCL)	1B	2	8	3	3	1	0	1	2	0	0	0	1	0-0	.375	.375	.875	1.250	0	1.000
— Pittsburgh (N.L.)	1B	91	307	34	84	14	0	10	51	12	30	2	6	0-0	.274	.305	.417	.722	4	.994
— Chicago (N.L.)	1B	33	103	13	29	3	0	6	21	4	7	2	1	0-0	.282	.318	.485	.804	2	.991
2004— Nashville (PCL)	1B-DH	17	64	5	17	4	0	1	6	2	8	1	4	1-0	.266	.294	.375	.669	1	1.000
— Pittsburgh (N.L.)	1B-DH	61	175	14	34	6	0	3	14	15	17	2	8	0-0	.194	.264	.280	.544	3	.992
— Tampa Bay (A.L.)	DH-1B	8	17	2	2	0	0	0	0	3	2	1	0	0-0	.118	.286	.118	.403	0	...
2005— Tijuana (Mex.)	1B-DH	64	273	52	99	17	0	19	71	13	32	3	7	2-0	.363	.394	.634	1.028	6	.988
2006— Tijuana (Mex.)		63	233	46	81	13	0	18	69	29	18	4	10	1-0	.348	.422	.635	1.057	7	.989
— Arizona Rangers (AZL)		5	18	2	5	1	0	0	3	1	0	0	1	0-0	.278	.316	.333	.649	0	1.000
— Oklahoma (PCL)		19	63	3	20	5	0	1	7	7	1	0	3	0-0	.317	.389	.444	.833	1	.977
— Philadelphia (N.L.)		23	21	0	5	0	0	0	2	2	6	0	0	0-0	.238	.304	.238	.542	0	...
American League totals (3 years)		219	755	81	225	31	3	25	119	31	60	5	22	0-2	.298	.326	.446	.773	10	.990
National League totals (6 years)		318	854	91	230	40	0	24	118	51	88	7	26	2-2	.269	.314	.400	.715	12	.994
Major League totals (8 years)		537	1609	172	455	71	3	49	237	82	148	12	48	2-4	.283	.320	.422	.742	22	.992

DIVISION SERIES RECORD

Year Team (League)	Pos.	G	AB	R	H	2B	3B	HR	RBI	BB	SO	HBP	GDP	SB-CS	Avg.	OBP	SLG	OPS	E	Avg.
1999— Atlanta (N.L.)		Did not play.																		
2003— Chicago (N.L.)	1B	4	7	1	3	1	0	0	2	0	2	0	0	0-0	.429	.429	.571	1.000	0	1.000

CHAMPIONSHIP SERIES RECORD

Year Team (League)	Pos.	G	AB	R	H	2B	3B	HR	RBI	BB	SO	HBP	GDP	SB-CS	Avg.	OBP	SLG	OPS	E	Avg.
1999— Atlanta (N.L.)		Did not play.																		
2003— Chicago (N.L.)	1B	6	17	3	5	2	0	1	4	0	1	0	1	0-0	.294	.294	.588	.882	1	.970

WORLD SERIES RECORD

Year Team (League)	Pos.	G	AB	R	H	2B	3B	HR	RBI	BB	SO	HBP	GDP	SB-CS	Avg.	OBP	SLG	OPS	E	Avg.
1999— Atlanta (N.L.)		Did not play.																		

2006 LEFTY-RIGHTY SPLITS

vs.	Avg.	AB	H	2B	3B	HR	RBI	BB	SO	OBP	Slg.	vs.	Avg.	AB	H	2B	3B	HR	RBI	BB	SO	OBP	Slg.
L	.000	0	0	0	0	0	0	0	0	.000	.000	R	.238	21	5	0	0	0	2	2	6	.304	.238

SIMPSON, ALLAN — P

PERSONAL: Born August 26, 1977, in Springfield, Ill. ... 6-4/185. ... Throws right, bats right. ... Full name: Larry Allan Simpson. ... High school: Cheyenne (North Las Vegas, Nev.). ... Junior college: Taft (Calif.). ... College: Long Beach State. **TRANSACTIONS/CAREER NOTES:** Selected by Seattle Mariners organization in eighth round of 1997 free-agent draft. ... Traded by Mariners to Colorado Rockies for P Chris Buglovsky (December 15, 2003). ... Traded by Rockies to Cincinnati Reds for P Jose Acevedo (April 9, 2005). ... Released by Reds (March 15, 2006). ... Signed by Milwaukee Brewers organization (March 19, 2006).

CAREER HITTING: 0-for-1 (.000), 0 R, 0 2B, 0 3B, 0 HR, 0 RBI.

Year Team (League)	W	L	Pct.	ERA	WHIP	G	GS	CG	ShO	Hld.	Sv.-Opp.	IP	H	R	ER	HR	BB-IBB	SO	Avg.
1997— Everett (N'west)	0	3	.000	6.84	1.90	16	0	0	0	...	0-...	26.1	26	23	20	1	24-1	26	.263
1998— Wisconsin (Midw.)	3	5	.375	4.44	1.61	19	19	0	0	...	0-...	93.1	89	52	46	5	61-0	86	.257
— Ariz. Mariners (Ariz.)	1	0	1.000	0.96	1.18	3	0	0	0	...	1-...	9.1	8	2	1	1	3-0	12	.235
1999— Wisconsin (Midw.)	2	9	.182	4.38	1.45	24	13	1	0	...	0-...	90.1	83	56	44	4	48-0	88	.245
— Lancaster (Calif.)	0	0	...	6.33	1.45	9	0	0	0	...	0-...	21.1	17	16	15	4	14-0	25	.218
2000— Lancaster (Calif.)	3	2	.600	2.08	1.17	46	0	0	0	...	6-...	52.0	34	17	12	1	27-1	67	.184
2001— San Bern. (Calif.)	1	0	1.000	1.80	1.03	16	0	0	0	...	1-...	30.0	19	7	6	1	12-0	40	.178
— San Antonio (Texas)	2	1	.667	1.86	1.03	22	0	0	0	...	9-...	38.2	25	8	8	1	15-1	37	.184
2002— San Antonio (Texas)	10	5	.667	3.06	1.25	56	0	0	0	...	7-...	82.1	53	33	28	4	50-5	99	.189
2003— Tacoma (PCL)	2	5	.286	4.16	1.63	43	0	0	0	...	0-...	62.2	60	30	29	7	42-1	69	.251
2004— Colo. Springs (PCL)	2	1	.667	2.80	1.13	27	0	0	0	...	4-...	35.1	30	14	11	1	10-0	43	.236
— Colorado (N.L.)	2	1	.667	5.08	1.64	32	0	0	0	1	0-1	39.0	44	26	22	4	20-0	46	.289
2005— Colorado (N.L.)	0	0	...	67.50	9.00	2	0	0	0	...	0-0	0.2	3	5	5	0	3-0	0	.750
— Louisville (Int'l)	4	4	.500	4.06	1.38	50	0	0	0	9	1-5	64.1	51	30	29	5	38-1	89	.213
— Cincinnati (N.L.)	0	1	.000	6.75	1.20	9	0	0	0	...	0-1	6.2	3	5	5	1	5-0	6	.136
2006— Nashville (PCL)	2	4	.333	3.34	1.27	42	0	0	0		10-14	56.2	45	26	21	7	27-1	53	.223
— Milwaukee (N.L.)	0	0	...	3.38	1.88	2	0	0	0	...	0-0	2.2	1	2	1	0	4-0	5	.111
Major League totals (3 years)	2	2	.500	6.06	1.69	45	0	0	0	1	0-2	49.0	51	38	33	5	32-0	57	.273

2006 LEFTY-RIGHTY SPLITS

vs.	Avg.	AB	H	2B	3B	HR	RBI	BB	SO	OBP	Slg.	vs.	Avg.	AB	H	2B	3B	HR	RBI	BB	SO	OBP	Slg.
L	.167	6	1	0	0	0	0	1	3	.286	.167	R	.000	3	0	0	0	0	1	3	2	.429	.000

SISCO, ANDREW — P

PERSONAL: Born January 13, 1983, in Steamboat Springs, Colo. ... 6-10/270. ... Throws left, bats left. ... Full name: Andrew Frank Sisco. **TRANSACTIONS/CAREER NOTES:** Selected by Chicago Cubs organization in second round of 2001 free-agent draft. ... Selected by Kansas City Royals from Cubs organization in Rule 5 major league draft (December 13, 2004).

CAREER HITTING: 0-for-1 (.000), 0 R, 0 2B, 0 3B, 0 HR, 0 RBI.

Year	Team (League)	W	L	Pct.	ERA	WHIP	G	GS	CG	ShO	Hld.	Sv.-Opp.	IP	H	R	ER	HR	BB-IBB	SO	Avg.
2001—	Ariz. Cubs (Ariz.)	1	0	1.000	5.24	1.34	10	7	0	0	...	0-...	34.1	36	28	20	1	10-0	31	.267
2002—	Boise (N'west)	7	2	.778	2.43	1.16	14	14	0	0	...	0-...	77.2	51	23	21	3	39-0	101	.188
2003—	Lansing (Midw.)	6	8	.429	3.54	1.14	19	19	3	0	...	0-...	94.0	76	44	37	3	31-0	99	.220
2004—	Daytona (Fla. St.)	4	10	.286	4.21	1.45	26	25	0	0	...	0-...	126.0	118	64	59	11	65-1	134	.262
2005—	Kansas City (A.L.)	2	5	.286	3.11	1.46	67	0	0	0	14	0-5	75.1	68	27	26	6	42-4	76	.243
2006—	Omaha (PCL)	0	0	...	1.93	0.86	3	0	0	0	0	1-1	4.2	3	1	1	1	1-0	6	.176
	—Kansas City (A.L.)	1	3	.250	7.10	1.82	65	0	0	0	5	1-5	58.1	66	47	46	8	40-6	52	.289
Major League totals (2 years)		3	8	.273	4.85	1.62	132	0	0	0	19	1-10	133.2	134	74	72	14	82-10	128	.264

2006 LEFTY-RIGHTY SPLITS

vs.	Avg.	AB	H	2B	3B	HR	RBI	BB	SO	OBP	Slg.	vs.	Avg.	AB	H	2B	3B	HR	RBI	BB	SO	OBP	Slg.
L	.318	88	28	6	0	3	24	17	20	.430	.489	R	.271	140	38	4	0	5	32	23	32	.365	.407

SIZEMORE, GRADY — OF

PERSONAL: Born August 2, 1982, in Seattle, Wash. ... 6-2/200. ... Bats left, throws left. ... Full name: Grady Sizemore III. ... High school: Cascade (Everett, Wash.). **TRANSACTIONS/CAREER NOTES:** Selected by Montreal Expos organization in third round of 2000 free-agent draft. ... Traded by Expos with 1B Lee Stevens, IF Brandon Phillips and P Cliff Lee to Cleveland Indians for P Bartolo Colon and future considerations (June 27, 2002); Expos acquired P Tim Drew to complete deal (June 28, 2002). **STATISTICAL NOTES:** Career major league grand slams: 1.

2006 GAMES PLAYED BY POSITION (MLB): OF—160, DH—1.

					BATTING																FIELDING	
Year	Team (League)	Pos.	G	AB	R	H	2B	3B	HR	RBI	BB	SO	HBP	GDP	SB-CS	Avg.	OBP	SLG	OPS	E	Avg.
2000—	GC Expos (GCL)	OF-1B	55	205	31	60	8	3	1	14	23	24	6	1	16-2	.293	.380	.376	.756	3	.975
2001—	Clinton (Midw.)	OF	123	451	64	121	16	4	2	61	81	92	4	7	32-11	.268	.381	.335	.716	7	.972
2002—	Brevard County (FSL)	OF	75	256	37	66	15	4	0	26	36	41	2	6	9-9	.258	.351	.348	.699	3	.977
	—Kinston (Carol.)	OF	47	172	31	59	9	3	3	20	33	30	1	1	14-7	.343	.451	.483	.934	4	.949
2003—	Akron (East.)	OF	128	496	96	151	26	11	13	78	46	73	11	5	10-9	.304	.373	.480	.853	4	.986
2004—	Buffalo (Int'l)	OF-DH	101	418	73	120	23	8	8	51	42	72	8	6	15-10	.287	.360	.438	.787	1	.996
	—Cleveland (A.L.)	OF	43	138	15	34	6	2	4	24	14	34	5	0	2-0	.246	.333	.406	.739	1	.991
2005—	Cleveland (A.L.)	OF	158	640	111	185	37	11	22	81	52	132	7	17	22-10	.289	.348	.484	.832	3	.992
2006—	Cleveland (A.L.)	OF-DH	• 162	655	* 134	190	* 53	11	28	76	78	153	13	2	22-6	.290	.375	.533	.907	3	.993
Major League totals (3 years)			363	1433	260	409	96	24	54	181	144	319	25	19	46-16	.285	.359	.499	.858	7	.992

ALL-STAR GAME RECORD

	G	AB	R	H	2B	3B	HR	RBI	BB	SO	HBP	GDP	SB-CS	Avg.	OBP	SLG	OPS	E	Avg.
All-Star Game totals (1 year)	1	2	0	0	0	0	0	0	0	1	0	0	0-0	.000	.000	.000	.000	0	1.000

2006 LEFTY-RIGHTY SPLITS

vs.	Avg.	AB	H	2B	3B	HR	RBI	BB	SO	OBP	Slg.	vs.	Avg.	AB	H	2B	3B	HR	RBI	BB	SO	OBP	Slg.
L	.214	220	47	13	2	10	25	19	54	.290	.427	R	.329	435	143	40	9	18	51	59	99	.416	.586

SLATEN, DOUG — P

PERSONAL: Born February 4, 1980, in Venice, Calif. ... 6-5/200. ... Throws left, bats left. ... Full name: Douglas Slaten. ... Junior college: Los Angeles Pierce. **TRANSACTIONS/CAREER NOTES:** Selected by Arizona Diamondbacks organization in 17th round of 2000 free-agent draft.

CAREER HITTING: 0-for-0 (.000), 0 R, 0 2B, 0 3B, 0 HR, 0 RBI.

Year	Team (League)	W	L	Pct.	ERA	WHIP	G	GS	CG	ShO	Hld.	Sv.-Opp.	IP	H	R	ER	HR	BB-IBB	SO	Avg.
2000—	Ariz. D'backs (Ariz.)	0	0	...	0.96	1.07	9	4	0	0	...	0-...	9.1	7	1	1	0	3-0	7	.200
2001—	Lancaster (Calif.)	9	8	.529	4.79	1.60	28	27	1	0	...	0-...	157.2	207	105	84	16	45-3	110	.312
2002—	Lancaster (Calif.)	1	6	.143	9.00	2.03	8	8	0	0	...	0-...	35.0	59	43	35	4	12-0	23	.360
	—South Bend (Mid.)	0	0	...	4.40	1.53	7	0	0	0	...	0-...	14.1	18	8	7	0	4-0	5	.310
2003—	Lancaster (Calif.)	6	7	.462	6.03	1.70	32	19	0	0	...	0-...	119.1	156	94	80	13	47-0	78	.316
2004—	El Paso (Texas)	0	1	.000	10.00	2.89	11	0	0	0	...	0-...	9.0	16	13	10	1	10-0	6	.390
	—South Bend (Mid.)	5	2	.714	2.25	1.30	36	0	0	0	...	5-...	44.0	44	13	11	2	13-1	40	.250
2005—	Tennessee (Sou.)	2	2	.500	4.26	1.42	58	0	0	0	6	1-3	61.1	61	45	29	2	26-0	72	.262
2006—	Tennessee (Sou.)	2	3	.400	1.88	1.07	40	0	0	0	6	8-10	43.0	31	12	9	1	15-0	59	.209
	—Tucson (PCL)	2	1	.667	0.45	0.85	18	0	0	0	4	2-2	20.0	10	2	1	0	7-0	21	.152
	—Arizona (N.L.)	0	0	...	0.00	0.88	9	0	0	0	2	0-0	5.2	3	0	0	0	2-1	3	.167
Major League totals (1 year)		0	0	...	0.00	0.88	9	0	0	0	2	0-0	5.2	3	0	0	0	2-1	3	.167

2006 LEFTY-RIGHTY SPLITS

vs.	Avg.	AB	H	2B	3B	HR	RBI	BB	SO	OBP	Slg.	vs.	Avg.	AB	H	2B	3B	HR	RBI	BB	SO	OBP	Slg.
L	.111	9	1	0	0	0	0	0	3	.111	.111	R	.222	9	2	0	0	0	0	2	0	.364	.222

SLEDGE, TERRMEL — OF

PERSONAL: Born March 18, 1977, in Fayetteville, N.C. ... 6-0/185. ... Bats left, throws left. ... Full name: Terrmel Sledge. ... Name pronounced: tur-MEL. ... High school: John F. Kennedy (Granada Hills, Calif.). ... College: Long Beach State. **TRANSACTIONS/CAREER NOTES:** Selected by Cincinnati Reds organization in 45th round of 1998 free-agent draft; did not sign. ... Selected by Seattle Mariners organization in eighth round of 1999 free-agent draft. ... Traded by Mariners to Montreal Expos (September 27, 2000), completing deal in which Expos traded C Chris Widger to Mariners for two players to be named (August 8, 2000); Expos acquired P Sean Spencer as part of deal (August 10, 2000). ... Expos franchise transferred to Washington, D.C., and renamed Washington Nationals for 2005 season (December 3, 2004). ... On disabled list (May 3, 2005-remainder of season). ... Traded by Nationals with OF Brad Wilkerson and P Armando Galarraga to Texas Rangers for 2B Alfonso Soriano (December 13, 2005). ... Traded by Rangers with 1B Adrian Gonzalez and P Chris Young to San Diego Padres for Ps Adam Eaton and Akinori Otsuka and C Billy Killian (January 4, 2006). **STATISTICAL NOTES:** Career major league grand slams: 1.

2006 GAMES PLAYED BY POSITION (MLB): OF—22.

					BATTING																FIELDING	
Year	Team (League)	Pos.	G	AB	R	H	2B	3B	HR	RBI	BB	SO	HBP	GDP	SB-CS	Avg.	OBP	SLG	OPS	E	Avg.
1999—	Everett (N'west)	OF	62	233	43	74	8	3	5	32	27	35	9	2	9-8	.318	.406	.442	.848	4	.958
2000—	Wisconsin (Midw.)	OF	7	23	5	5	2	2	0	3	3	3	1	1	1-0	.217	.333	.478	.812	0	1.000
	—Lancaster (Calif.)	OF	103	384	90	130	22	7	11	75	72	49	17	4	35-11	.339	.458	.518	.976	3	.981
2001—	Harrisburg (East.)	1B-OF	129	448	66	124	22	6	9	48	51	72	9	5	30-8	.277	.359	.413	.772	15	.985
2002—	Harrisburg (East.)	OF-1B	102	396	74	119	18	6	8	43	55	70	12	4	11-8	.301	.401	.437	.838	1	.996
	—Ottawa (Int'l)	OF-1B	24	80	12	21	5	2	1	11	11	15	1	2	1-1	.263	.359	.413	.771	2	.972
2003—	Edmonton (PCL)	OF-1B	131	497	95	161	26	9	22	92	61	93	5	10	13-5	.324	.397	.545	.942	8	.972
2004—	Montreal (N.L.)	OF-1B	133	398	45	107	20	6	15	62	40	66	1	2	3-3	.269	.336	.462	.799	3	.990
2005—	Wash. (N.L.)	OF	20	37	7	9	0	1	1	8	7	8	0	3	2-1	.243	.348	.378	.726	0	1.000

Year Team (League)	Pos.	G	AB	R	H	2B	3B	HR	RBI	BB	SO	HBP	GDP	SB-CS	Avg.	OBP	SLG	OPS	E	FIELDING Avg.
2006— Portland (PCL)		101	367	69	114	18	5	24	73	59	75	1	9	5-3	.311	.402	.583	.985	4	.975
— San Diego (N.L.)	OF	38	70	7	16	3	0	2	7	8	17	0	1	0-0	.229	.308	.357	.665	1	.971
Major League totals (3 years)		191	505	59	132	23	7	18	77	55	91	1	6	5-4	.261	.333	.442	.775	4	.989

2006 LEFTY-RIGHTY SPLITS

vs.	Avg.	AB	H	2B	3B	HR	RBI	BB	SO	OBP	Slg.	vs.	Avg.	AB	H	2B	3B	HR	RBI	BB	SO	OBP	Slg.
L	.400	5	2	0	0	0	1	0	1	.400	.400	R	.215	65	14	3	0	2	6	8	16	.301	.354

SLOCUM, BRIAN — P

PERSONAL: Born March 27, 1981, in New Rochelle, N.Y. ... 6-4/200. ... Throws right, bats right. ... Full name: Brian John Slocum. ... College: Villanova.
TRANSACTIONS/CAREER NOTES: Selected by Minnesota Twins organization in 14th round of 1999 free-agent draft; did not sign. ... Selected by Cleveland Indians organization in second round of 2002 free-agent draft.
CAREER HITTING: 0-for-0 (.000), 0 R, 0 2B, 0 3B, 0 HR, 0 RBI.

Year Team (League)	W	L	Pct.	ERA	WHIP	G	GS	CG	ShO	Hld.	Sv.-Opp.	IP	H	R	ER	HR	BB-IBB	SO	Avg.
2002— Mahoning Valley (N.Y.-Penn.)	5	2	.714	2.60	1.10	11	11	0	0	...	0-...	55.1	47	19	16	1	14-0	48	.230
2003— Kinston (Carol.)	6	7	.462	4.46	1.43	22	21	0	0	...	1-...	107.0	112	61	53	7	41-0	66	.266
2004— Kinston (Carol.)	15	6	.714	4.33	1.31	25	25	2	2	...	0-...	135.0	136	66	65	13	41-0	102	.267
2005— Akron (East.)	7	5	.583	4.40	1.31	21	18	1	0	0	0-1	102.1	98	52	50	9	36-0	95	.255
2006— Buffalo (Int'l)	6	3	.667	3.35	1.22	27	15	0	0	1	1-2	94.0	78	42	35	5	37-2	91	.227
— Cleveland (A.L.)	0	0	...	5.60	2.04	8	2	0	0	0	0-0	17.2	27	11	11	3	9-0	11	.360
Major League totals (1 year)	0	0	...	5.60	2.04	8	2	0	0	0	0-0	17.2	27	11	11	3	9-0	11	.360

2006 LEFTY-RIGHTY SPLITS

vs.	Avg.	AB	H	2B	3B	HR	RBI	BB	SO	OBP	Slg.	vs.	Avg.	AB	H	2B	3B	HR	RBI	BB	SO	OBP	Slg.
L	.367	30	11	2	0	0	2	4	4	.457	.433	R	.356	45	16	3	1	3	8	5	7	.420	.667

SMALL, AARON — P

PERSONAL: Born November 23, 1971, in Oxnard, Calif. ... 6-5/225. ... Throws right, bats right. ... Full name: Aaron James Small. ... High school: South Hills (Covina, Calif.).
TRANSACTIONS/CAREER NOTES: Selected by Toronto Blue Jays organization in 22nd round of 1989 free-agent draft. ... Traded by Blue Jays to Florida Marlins for a player to be named (April 26, 1995); Blue Jays acquired P Ernie Delgado to complete deal (September 19, 1995). ... Claimed on waivers by Seattle Mariners (January 23, 1996). ... Claimed on waivers by Oakland Athletics (January 29, 1996). ... Claimed on waivers by Arizona Diamondbacks (June 26, 1998). ... Released by Diamondbacks (March 30, 1999). ... Signed by Milwaukee Brewers organization (April 12, 1999). ... Released by Brewers (May 23, 1999). ... Signed by Tampa Bay Devil Rays organization (May 27, 1999). ... Signed as a free agent by Colorado Rockies organization (January 5, 2000). ... Signed as a free agent by Anaheim Angels organization (December 21, 2000). ... Released by Angels (May 4, 2001). ... Signed by Atlanta Braves organization (May 10, 2001). ... Released by Braves (September 30, 2002). ... Signed by Chicago Cubs organization (January 13, 2003). ... Released by Cubs (March 29, 2003). ... Signed by Marlins organization (April 30, 2003). ... Signed as a free agent by New York Yankees organization (January 28, 2005). ... On disabled list (April 1-May 1, 2006); included rehabilitation assignment to Columbus.
CAREER HITTING: 0-for-4 (.000), 0 R, 0 2B, 0 3B, 0 HR, 0 RBI.

Year Team (League)	W	L	Pct.	ERA	WHIP	G	GS	CG	ShO	Hld.	Sv.-Opp.	IP	H	R	ER	HR	BB-IBB	SO	Avg.
1989— Medicine Hat (Pio.)	1	7	.125	5.86	1.57	15	14	0	0	...	0-...	70.2	80	55	46	2	31-1	40	.279
1990— Myrtle Beach (SAL)	9	9	.500	2.80	1.40	27	27	1	0	...	0-...	147.2	150	72	46	6	56-2	96	.262
1991— Dunedin (Fla. St.)	8	7	.533	2.73	1.15	24	23	1	0	...	0-...	148.1	129	51	45	5	42-1	92	.240
1992— Knoxville (Southern) ..	5	12	.294	5.27	1.58	27	24	2	1	...	0-...	135.0	152	94	79	13	61-0	79	.283
1993— Knoxville (Southern) ..	4	4	.500	3.39	1.49	48	9	0	0	...	16-...	93.0	99	44	35	5	40-4	44	.273
1994— Knoxville (Southern) ..	5	5	.500	2.99	1.35	29	11	1	1	...	5-...	96.1	92	37	32	4	38-0	75	.258
— Syracuse (Int'l)	3	2	.600	2.22	1.15	13	0	0	0	...	0-...	24.1	19	8	6	2	9-2	15	.218
— Toronto (A.L.)	0	0	...	9.00	3.50	1	0	0	0	0	0-0	2.0	5	2	2	1	2-0	0	.500
1995— Syracuse (Int'l)	0	0	...	5.40	2.40	1	0	0	0	0	0-0	1.2	3	1	1	1	1-0	2	.375
— Charlotte (Int'l)	2	1	.667	2.88	1.13	33	0	0	0	...	10-...	40.2	36	15	13	2	10-1	31	.229
— Florida (N.L.)	1	0	1.000	1.42	2.05	7	0	0	0	0	0-0	6.1	7	2	1	1	6-0	5	.269
1996— Oakland (A.L.)	1	3	.250	8.16	2.06	12	3	0	0	0	0-0	28.2	37	28	26	3	22-1	17	.308
— Edmonton (PCL)	8	6	.571	4.29	1.16	25	19	1	1	...	1-...	119.2	111	65	57	9	28-0	83	.244
1997— Edmonton (PCL)	1	0	1.000	0.00	0.20	1	1	0	0	...	0-...	5.0	1	0	0	0	0-0	4	.063
— Oakland (A.L.)	9	5	.643	4.28	1.54	71	0	0	0	8	4-6	96.2	109	50	46	6	40-6	57	.294
1998— Oakland (A.L.)	1	1	.500	7.25	1.81	24	0	0	0	3	0-0	36.0	51	34	29	3	14-3	19	.333
— Arizona (N.L.)	3	1	.750	3.69	1.26	23	0	0	0	1	0-2	31.2	32	14	13	5	8-1	14	.269
1999— Louisville (Int'l)	1	1	.500	9.43	2.52	11	0	0	0	...	0-...	21.0	38	23	22	3	15-1	11	.400
— Durham (Int'l)	4	6	.400	6.34	1.51	21	18	0	0	...	0-...	99.1	118	81	70	16	32-2	52	.295
2000— Colo. Springs (PCL) ...	11	6	.647	5.61	1.48	36	18	0	0	...	0-...	131.2	152	87	82	14	43-0	85	.285
2001— Salt Lake (PCL)	0	1	.000	1.69	1.69	3	0	0	0	...	0-...	5.1	8	1	1	1	1-0	5	.364
— Richmond (Int'l)	10	7	.588	3.83	1.33	41	11	0	0	...	0-...	96.1	97	50	41	14	31-5	61	.257
2002— Richmond (Int'l)	0	3	.000	6.39	2.00	14	4	0	0	...	0-...	31.0	48	27	22	2	14-1	19	.364
— Atlanta (N.L.)	0	0	...	27.00	12.00	1	0	0	0	0	0-0	0.1	2	1	1	0	2-0	1	.667
— GC Braves (GCL)	0	0	...	6.00	1.50	5	5	0	0	...	0-...	6.0	9	4	4	0	0-0	3	.360
2003— Carolina (Southern)	3	4	.429	4.83	1.50	8	7	0	0	...	0-...	41.0	47	23	22	5	14-0	24	.290
— Albuquerque (PCL)	6	4	.600	4.63	1.30	14	14	0	0	...	0-...	89.1	95	50	46	12	18-0	56	.270
2004— Albuquerque (PCL)	9	9	.500	5.06	1.47	27	24	2	0	...	0-...	154.2	199	95	87	18	29-2	109	.315
— Florida (N.L.)	0	0	...	8.27	1.90	7	0	0	0	1	0-0	16.1	24	15	15	5	7-0	8	.343
2005— Trenton (East.)	1	0	1.000	3.60	1.60	1	1	0	0	...	0-0	5.0	7	3	2	1	1-0	3	.333
— Columbus (Int'l)	1	4	.200	4.96	1.43	11	10	0	0	...	0-...	49.0	62	30	27	5	8-0	21	.310
— New York (A.L.)	10	0	1.000	3.20	1.25	15	9	1	1	0	0-0	76.0	71	27	27	8	24-0	37	.250
2006— Columbus (Int'l)	2	4	.333	5.62	1.82	11	8	0	0	...	0-...	41.2	64	29	26	4	12-0	17	.350
— New York (A.L.)	0	3	.000	8.46	1.95	11	3	0	0	0	0-0	27.2	42	29	26	7	12-1	12	.341
American League totals (6 years)	21	12	.636	5.26	1.61	134	15	1	1	11	4-7	267.0	315	170	156	26	114-11	142	.297
National League totals (4 years)	4	1	.800	4.94	1.61	38	0	0	0	2	0-2	54.2	65	32	30	11	23-1	28	.298
Major League totals (9 years)	25	13	.658	5.20	1.61	172	15	1	1	13	4-9	321.2	380	202	186	37	137-12	170	.297

DIVISION SERIES RECORD

Year Team (League)	W	L	Pct.	ERA	WHIP	G	GS	CG	ShO	Hld.	Sv.-Opp.	IP	H	R	ER	HR	BB-IBB	SO	Avg.
2005→New York (A.L.)	0	1	.000	6.75	1.50	1	0	0	0	0	0-0	2.2	4	2	2	0	0-0	2	.364

2006 LEFTY-RIGHTY SPLITS

vs.	Avg.	AB	H	2B	3B	HR	RBI	BB	SO	OBP	Slg.	vs.	Avg.	AB	H	2B	3B	HR	RBI	BB	SO	OBP	Slg.
L	.358	53	19	4	1	3	9	7	6	.433	.642	R	.329	70	23	3	1	6	17	5	6	.377	.657

SMITH, JASON — 2B/SS

PERSONAL: Born July 24, 1977, in Meridian, Miss. ... 6-3/199. ... Bats left, throws right. ... Full name: Jason William Smith. ... High school: Demopolis (Ala.). ... Junior college: Meridian (Miss.) C.C. **TRANSACTIONS/CAREER NOTES:** Selected by Los Angeles Dodgers organization in 42nd round of 1995 free-agent draft; did not sign. ... Selected by Chicago Cubs organization in 23rd round of 1996 free-agent draft. ... Traded by Cubs to Tampa Bay Devil Rays (August 5, 2001), completing deal in which Devil Rays traded 1B Fred McGriff to Cubs for P Manny Aybar and a player to be named (July 27, 2001). ... Signed as a free agent by Detroit Tigers organization (December 8, 2003). ... Signed as a free agent by Colorado Rockies organization (November 8, 2005).

2006 GAMES PLAYED BY POSITION (MLB): 2B—18, 1B—6, 3B—3, SS—1.

Year Team (League)	Pos.	G	AB	R	H	2B	3B	HR	RBI	BB	SO	HBP	GDP	SB-CS	Avg.	OBP	SLG	OPS	E	Fielding Avg.
1997—Will. (NYP)	SS	51	205	25	59	5	2	0	11	10	44	0	0	9-2	.288	.321	.332	.653	19	.930
—Rockford (Midwest)	SS	9	33	4	6	0	1	0	3	2	11	0	1	1-0	.182	.229	.242	.471	5	.884
1998—Rockford (Midwest)	SS	126	464	67	111	15	9	7	60	31	122	1	2	23-6	.239	.286	.356	.642	38	.939
1999—Daytona (Fla. St.)	SS	39	142	22	37	5	2	5	26	12	29	3	2	9-3	.261	.329	.430	.759	7	.953
2000—West Tenn (Sou.)	SS	119	481	55	114	22	7	12	61	22	130	2	7	16-10	.237	.273	.387	.659	37	.927
2001—Iowa (PCL)	SS	70	240	31	56	8	6	4	15	12	71	1	4	6-3	.233	.271	.367	.637	19	.942
—Chicago (N.L.)	SS	2	1	0	0	0	0	0	0	0	1	0	0	0-0	.000	.000	.000	.000	0	1.000
—Durham (Int'l)	SS	8	31	2	6	1	0	0	3	0	11	0	0	0-0	.194	.194	.226	.419	3	.917
2002—Tampa Bay (A.L.) 3B-SS-2B	DH	26	65	9	13	1	2	1	6	2	24	0	0	3-0	.200	.224	.323	.547	6	.905
—Durham (Int'l)	SS-3B	54	206	29	57	11	2	4	28	10	44	1	2	5-1	.277	.312	.408	.720	16	.936
2003—Tampa Bay (A.L.)	3B	1	4	0	1	0	0	0	0	0	0	0	0	0-0	.250	.250	.250	.500	2	.500
—Durham (Int'l) SS-2B-3B	DH	130	515	76	147	20	14	15	71	11	128	5	1	14-9	.285	.304	.466	.770	23	.959
2004—Toledo (Int'l)	3B	33	122	18	33	8	2	3	13	6	26	0	1	5-1	.270	.300	.443	.743	6	.938
—Detroit (A.L.) 2B-SS-3B	DH	61	155	20	37	7	4	5	19	8	37	1	0	1-2	.239	.280	.432	.713	5	.977
2005—Detroit (A.L.) SS-2B-3B	1B-DH	27	58	4	11	1	2	0	2	0	16	1	0	2-1	.190	.203	.276	.479	1	.989
—Toledo (Int'l) 1B-2B-3B	SS-OF-DH	55	187	24	43	11	2	6	25	11	53	0	1	8-4	.230	.269	.406	.675	5	.977
2006—Colo. Springs (PCL)		41	141	26	41	9	5	4	23	15	41	0	3	3-1	.291	.354	.511	.865	5	.968
—Colorado (N.L.) 2B-1B-3B	SS	49	99	9	26	1	0	5	13	7	29	2	1	3-0	.263	.324	.424	.748	2	.984
American League totals (4 years)		115	282	33	62	9	8	6	27	10	77	2	0	6-3	.220	.252	.372	.624	14	.963
National League totals (2 years)		51	100	9	26	1	0	5	13	7	30	2	1	3-0	.260	.321	.420	.741	2	.984
Major League totals (6 years)		166	382	42	88	10	8	11	40	17	107	4	1	9-3	.230	.270	.385	.655	16	.968

2006 LEFTY-RIGHTY SPLITS

vs.	Avg.	AB	H	2B	3B	HR	RBI	BB	SO	OBP	Slg.	vs.	Avg.	AB	H	2B	3B	HR	RBI	BB	SO	OBP	Slg.
L	.400	5	2	0	0	2	3	2	0	.571	1.600	R	.255	94	24	1	0	3	10	5	29	.307	.362

SMITH, MATT — P

PERSONAL: Born June 15, 1979, in Las Vegas, Nev. ... 6-5/225. ... Throws left, bats left. ... Full name: Matthew J. Smith. ... College: Oklahoma State. **TRANSACTIONS/CAREER NOTES:** Selected by New York Yankees organization in fourth round of 2000 free-agent draft. ... Traded by Yankees with SS C.J. Henry, C Jesus Sanchez and P Carlos Monastrios to Philadelphia Phillies for OF Bobby Abreu and P Cory Lidle (July 30, 2006).

CAREER HITTING: 0-for-0 (.000), 0 R, 0 2B, 0 3B, 0 HR, 0 RBI.

Year Team (League)	W	L	Pct.	ERA	WHIP	G	GS	CG	ShO	Hld.	Sv.-Opp.	IP	H	R	ER	HR	BB-IBB	SO	Avg.
2000—Staten Is. (N.Y.-Penn)	5	4	.556	2.38	1.24	14	14	0	0	...	0-...	75.2	74	32	20	1	20-0	59	.261
2001—Greensboro (S. Atl.)	5	3	.625	2.59	1.04	16	16	1	1	...	0-...	97.1	69	37	28	1	32-0	116	.197
—Tampa (Fla. St.)	6	2	.750	2.24	1.11	11	11	0	0	...	0-...	68.1	54	21	17	2	22-0	71	.215
2002—Norwich (East.)	3	8	.273	5.44	1.67	17	17	0	0	...	0-...	89.1	112	63	54	8	37-0	70	.305
—Tampa (Fla. St.)	0	4	.000	6.59	1.98	8	6	0	0	...	0-...	27.1	37	23	20	1	17-0	20	.330
2003—Tampa (Fla. St.)	2	3	.400	2.23	0.99	6	6	0	0	...	0-...	32.1	20	11	8	0	12-0	25	.175
—Trenton (East.)	2	3	.400	4.26	1.60	9	9	0	0	...	0-...	50.2	57	29	24	6	24-0	36	.291
2004—Trenton (East.)	4	4	.500	4.96	1.59	14	11	0	0	...	0-...	61.2	67	34	34	5	31-1	56	.285
2005—Trenton (East.)	3	4	.429	2.80	1.26	22	4	0	0	3	2-2	54.2	46	24	17	2	23-0	59	.230
—Columbus (Int'l)	2	0	1.000	2.60	1.34	25	0	0	0	5	1-1	27.2	24	9	8	3	13-0	33	.226
2006—New York (A.L.)	0	0	...	0.00	1.00	12	0	0	0	4	0-0	12.0	4	0	0	0	8-1	9	.105
—Columbus (Int'l)	0	1	.000	2.08	1.35	24	0	0	0		0-3	26.0	27	9	6	3	8-1	22	.267
—Clearwater (FSL)	0	0	...	0.00	0.00	2	0	0	0		0-0	2.0	0	0	0	0	0-0	6	.000
—Scran./W.B. (I.L.)	0	0	...	2.00	1.22	9	0	0	0		4-4	9.0	5	2	2	1	6-0	6	.161
—Philadelphia (N.L.)	0	1	.000	2.08	0.81	14	0	0	0	6	0-0	8.2	3	2	2	0	4-0	12	.111
American League totals (1 year)	0	0	...	0.00	1.00	12	0	0	0		0-0	12.0	4	0	0	0	8-1	9	.105
National League totals (1 year)	0	1	.000	2.08	0.81	14	0	0	0		0-0	8.2	3	2	2	0	4-0	12	.111
Major League totals (1 year)	0	1	.000	0.87	0.92	26	0	0	0	6	0-0	20.2	7	2	2	0	12-1	21	.108

2006 LEFTY-RIGHTY SPLITS

vs.	Avg.	AB	H	2B	3B	HR	RBI	BB	SO	OBP	Slg.	vs.	Avg.	AB	H	2B	3B	HR	RBI	BB	SO	OBP	Slg.
L	.167	18	3	0	0	0	2	8	6	.423	.167	R	.085	47	4	0	0	0	0	4	15	.157	.085

SMITH, MIKE — P

PERSONAL: Born September 19, 1977, in Norwood, Mass. ... 5-11/195. ... Throws right, bats right. ... Full name: Michael Anthony Smith. ... College: Richmond. **TRANSACTIONS/CAREER NOTES:** Selected by Toronto Blue Jays organization in fifth round of 2000 free-agent draft. ... Signed as a free agent by Philadelphia Phillies organization (April 5, 2005). ... Signed as a free agent by Minnesota Twins organization (December 23, 2005).

CAREER HITTING: 0-for-0 (.000), 0 R, 0 2B, 0 3B, 0 HR, 0 RBI.

Year Team (League)	W	L	Pct.	ERA	WHIP	G	GS	CG	ShO	Hld.	Sv.-Opp.	IP	H	R	ER	HR	BB-IBB	SO	Avg.
2000—Queens (N.Y.-Penn.)	2	2	.500	2.29	1.14	14	12	0	0	...	0-...	51.0	41	18	13	1	17-0	55	...
2001—Char., W.Va. (SAL)	5	5	.500	2.10	1.05	14	14	2	1	...	0-...	94.1	78	32	22	2	21-0	85	...
—Tennessee (Sou.)	6	2	.750	2.42	1.14	14	14	1	0	...	0-...	93.0	80	32	25	7	26-2	77	...
2002—Syracuse (Int'l)	8	4	.667	3.48	1.22	20	20	1	1	...	0-...	121.2	106	51	47	10	43-0	76	...
—Toronto (A.L.)	0	3	.000	6.62	1.78	14	6	0	0	...	0-...	35.1	43	28	26	3	20-0	16	.301
2005—Reading (East.)	5	14	.263	4.48	1.43	28	28	1	0	0	0-0	170.2	162	97	85	18	82-0	113	.254
—Scran./W.B. (I.L.)	0	0	...	9.82	2.18	1	1	0	0	0	0-0	3.2	6	4	4	1	3-0	2	.313

Year Team (League)	W	L	Pct.	ERA	WHIP	G	GS	CG	ShO	Hld.	Sv.-Opp.	IP	H	R	ER	HR	BB-IBB	SO	Avg.
2006—Rochester (Int'l)	11	5	.688	3.88	1.39	28	24	2	1	0	0-1	150.2	152	76	65	12	57-1	110	.261
—Minnesota (A.L.)	0	0	...	12.00	2.67	1	1	0	0	0	0-0	3.0	5	4	4	1	3-0	1	.357
Major League totals (2 years)	0	3	.000	7.04	1.85	15	7	0	0	0	0-0	38.1	48	32	30	4	23-0	17	.306

2006 LEFTY-RIGHTY SPLITS

vs.	Avg.	AB	H	2B	3B	HR	RBI	BB	SO	OBP	Slg.	vs.	Avg.	AB	H	2B	3B	HR	RBI	BB	SO	OBP	Slg.
L	.375	8	3	1	0	0	1	1	1	.500	.500	R	.333	6	2	0	1	1	3	2	0	.500	1.167

SMITH, TRAVIS — P

PERSONAL: Born November 7, 1972, in Springfield, Ore. ... 5-10/165. ... Throws right, bats right. ... Full name: Travis William Smith. ... High school: Bend (Ore.). ... College: Texas Tech. **TRANSACTIONS/CAREER NOTES:** Selected by Milwaukee Brewers organization in 19th round of 1995 free-agent draft. ... On disabled list (June 23, 1998-remainder of season). ... Signed as a free agent by Houston Astros organization (November 1, 2000). ... Signed as a free agent by St. Louis Cardinals organization (November 21, 2001). ... Signed as a free agent by Atlanta Braves organization (November 10, 2003). ... Signed as a free agent by Florida Marlins organization (November 11, 2004). ... Signed as a free agent by Braves organization (November 1, 2005). ... Signed as a free agent by Cardinals organization (May 30, 2006).

CAREER HITTING: 4-for-28 (.143), 0 R, 0 2B, 0 3B, 0 HR, 2 RBI.

Year Team (League)	W	L	Pct.	ERA	WHIP	G	GS	CG	ShO	Hld.	Sv.-Opp.	IP	H	R	ER	HR	BB-IBB	SO	Avg.
1995—Helena (Pion.)	4	2	.667	2.41	1.07	20	7	0	0	...	5-...	56.0	41	16	15	4	19-0	63	.207
1996—Stockton (Calif.)	6	1	.857	1.84	1.31	14	6	0	0	...	1-...	58.2	56	17	12	4	21-0	48	.260
—El Paso (Texas)	7	4	.636	4.18	1.47	17	17	3	1	...	0-...	107.2	119	56	50	6	39-0	68	.281
1997—El Paso (Texas)	16	3	.842	4.15	1.45	28	28	5	1	...	0-...	184.1	210	106	85	12	58-2	107	.288
1998—Louisville (Int'l)	4	6	.400	5.32	1.51	12	11	0	0	...	0-...	67.2	77	44	40	9	25-1	36	.294
—Milwaukee (N.L.)	0	0	...	0.00	0.50	1	0	0	0	0	0-0	2.0	1	0	0	0	0-0	1	.143
1999—Ogden (Pion.)	0	0	...	0.00	0.00	1	1	0	0	0	0-0	1.0	0	1	0	0	0-0	3	.000
—Stockton (Calif.)	0	2	.000	6.14	1.64	3	3	0	0	0	0-0	7.1	9	6	5	1	3-0	8	.300
—Huntsville (Sou.)	3	2	.600	5.87	1.51	7	7	0	0	0	0-0	38.1	40	27	25	3	18-0	23	.268
2000—Huntsville (Sou.)	12	7	.632	3.73	1.15	27	24	1	1	...	0-...	154.1	141	77	64	13	37-0	113	.242
—Indianapolis (Int'l)	1	1	.500	12.66	2.63	3	3	0	0	0	0-0	10.2	19	18	15	6	9-1	5	.413
2001—Round Rock (Texas)	15	8	.652	3.09	1.12	29	22	1	1	...	1-...	160.1	154	66	55	7	26-0	85	.251
—New Orleans (PCL)	0	0	...	0.00	2.00	1	0	0	0	0	0-0	2.0	3	0	0	0	1-0	0	.333
2002—Memphis (PCL)	4	7	.364	2.31	1.05	16	13	1	0	0	0-0	85.2	76	24	22	7	14-1	62	.238
—St. Louis (N.L.)	4	2	.667	7.17	1.65	12	10	0	0	0	0-0	54.0	69	44	43	10	20-0	32	.322
2004—Richmond (Int'l)	10	2	.833	2.59	1.15	20	19	1	0	0	0-0	107.2	98	31	31	6	26-0	93	.246
—Atlanta (N.L.)	2	3	.400	6.20	1.48	16	4	0	0	1	0-0	40.2	48	28	28	12	12-2	26	.293
2005—Florida (N.L.)	0	0	...	6.75	2.06	12	0	0	0	0	0-0	10.2	17	8	8	1	5-1	9	.370
—Albuquerque (PCL)	7	8	.467	4.08	1.33	18	17	0	0	0	0-0	103.2	107	54	47	12	31-1	73	.268
2006—Richmond (Int'l)	3	1	.750	2.91	1.23	8	8	0	0	0	0-0	46.1	41	15	15	2	16-1	44	.234
—Atlanta (N.L.)	0	1	.000	4.15	1.38	1	1	0	0	0	0-0	4.1	5	4	2	0	1-0	1	.313
—Memphis (PCL)	5	6	.455	5.66	1.52	15	15	1	0	0	0-0	89.0	109	60	56	9	26-3	49	.306
Major League totals (5 years)	6	6	.500	6.53	1.59	42	15	0	0	0	0-0	111.2	140	84	81	23	38-3	69	.313

2006 LEFTY-RIGHTY SPLITS

vs.	Avg.	AB	H	2B	3B	HR	RBI	BB	SO	OBP	Slg.	vs.	Avg.	AB	H	2B	3B	HR	RBI	BB	SO	OBP	Slg.
L	.364	11	4	1	0	0	3	1	1	.385	.455	R	.200	5	1	1	0	0	0	0	0	.200	.400

SMOLTZ, JOHN — P

PERSONAL: Born May 15, 1967, in Warren, Mich. ... 6-3/220. ... Throws right, bats right. ... Full name: John Andrew Smoltz. ... High school: Waverly (Lansing, Mich.). **TRANSACTIONS/CAREER NOTES:** Selected by Detroit Tigers organization in 22nd round of June 1985 free-agent draft. ... Traded by Tigers to Atlanta Braves for P Doyle Alexander (August 12, 1987). ... On disabled list (March 29-April 15 and May 24-June 20, 1998); included rehabilitation assignments to Greenville and Macon. ... On disabled list (May 17-June 1 and July 5-24, 1999); included rehabilitation assignment to Greenville. ... On disabled list (April 2, 2000-entire season). ... On disabled list (March 23-May 17 and June 10-July 22, 2001); included rehabilitation assignments to Macon and Greenville. ... On disabled list (August 27-September 20, 2003). **HONORS:** Named N.L. Pitcher of the Year by THE SPORTING NEWS (1996). ... Named righthanded pitcher on THE SPORTING NEWS N.L. All-Star team (1996). ... Named N.L. Reliever of the Year by THE SPORTING NEWS (2002). ... Named N.L. Cy Young Award winner by Baseball Writers' Association of America (1996). ... Named pitcher on N.L. Silver Slugger team (1997). **STATISTICAL NOTES:** Tied for Florida State League lead with six balks in 1986. ... Led N.L. with 14 wild pitches in 1990, 20 in 1991 and 17 in 1992. ... Struck out 15 batters in one game (May 24, 1992). ... Pitched 3-0 one-hit, complete-game victory against Cincinnati (May 28, 1997). ... Led N.L. with 59 save opportunities in 2002. **MISCELLANEOUS NOTES:** Appeared in three games as pinch runner and struck out in only appearance in pinch hitter (1989). ... Appeared in four games as pinch runner (1990). ... Appeared in two games as pinch runner (1991). ... Struck out in only appearance as pinch hitter (1992). ... Appeared in one game as pinch runner (1997).

CAREER HITTING: 145-for-871 (.166), 75 R, 25 2B, 2 3B, 5 HR, 58 RBI.

Year Team (League)	W	L	Pct.	ERA	WHIP	G	GS	CG	ShO	Hld.	Sv.-Opp.	IP	H	R	ER	HR	BB-IBB	SO	Avg.
1986—Lakeland (Fla. St.)	7	8	.467	3.56	1.22	17	14	2	1	...	0-...	96.0	86	44	38	7	31-0	47	.242
1987—Glens Falls (East.)	4	10	.286	5.68	1.63	21	21	0	0	...	0-...	130.0	131	89	82	17	81-2	86	.268
—Richmond (Int'l)	0	1	.000	6.19	1.75	3	3	0	0	...	0-...	16.0	17	11	11	2	11-0	5	.266
1988—Richmond (Int'l)	10	5	.667	2.79	1.15	20	20	3	0	...	0-...	135.1	118	49	42	5	37-1	115	.233
—Atlanta (N.L.)	2	7	.222	5.48	1.67	12	12	0	0	0	0-0	64.0	74	40	39	10	33-4	37	.285
1989—Atlanta (N.L.)	12	11	.522	2.94	1.12	29	29	5	0	0	0-0	208.0	160	79	68	15	72-2	168	.212
1990—Atlanta (N.L.)	14	11	.560	3.85	1.28	34	34	6	2	0	0-0	231.1	206	109	99	20	• 90-3	170	.240
1991—Atlanta (N.L.)	14	13	.519	3.80	1.23	36	36	5	0	0	0-0	229.2	206	101	97	16	77-1	148	.243
1992—Atlanta (N.L.)	15	12	.556	2.85	1.16	35	•35	9	3	0	0-0	246.2	206	90	78	17	80-5 •	215	.224
1993—Atlanta (N.L.)	15	11	.577	3.62	1.26	35	35	3	1	0	0-0	243.2	208	104	98	23	100-12	208	.230
1994—Atlanta (N.L.)	6	10	.375	4.14	1.25	21	21	0	0	0	0-0	134.2	120	69	62	15	48-4	113	.239
1995—Atlanta (N.L.)	12	7	.632	3.18	1.24	29	29	2	1	0	0-0	192.2	166	76	68	15	72-8	193	.232
1996—Atlanta (N.L.)	• 24	8	.750	2.94	1.00	35	35	6	2	0	0-0	• 253.2	199	93	83	19	55-3 •	• 276	.216
1997—Atlanta (N.L.)	15	12	.556	3.02	1.16	35	•35	7	2	0	0-0	• 256.0	• 234	97	86	21	63-9	241	.242
1998—Greenville (Sou.)	0	1	.000	2.57	1.00	3	3	0	0	0	0-...	14.0	11	4	4	1	3-0	16	.216
—Macon (S. Atl.)	0	0	...	3.60	0.80	2	2	0	0	0	0-...	10.0	7	4	4	1	1-0	14	.179
—Atlanta (N.L.)	17	3	.850	2.90	1.13	26	26	2	2	0	0-0	167.2	145	58	54	10	44-2	173	.231
1999—Atlanta (N.L.)	11	8	.579	3.19	1.12	29	29	1	1	0	0-0	186.1	168	70	66	14	40-2	156	.245
—Greenville (Sou.)	0	0	...	4.50	1.50	2	1	0	0	0	0-...	4.0	5	2	2	0	1-0	7	.294
2000—Atlanta (N.L.)	Did not play.																		
2001—Greenville (Sou.)	0	0	...	0.00	0.50	3	1	0	0	0	0-...	6.0	3	0	0	0	0-0	6	.150
—Macon (S. Atl.)	0	0	...	1.80	0.80	1	0	0	0	0	0-...	5.0	4	1	1	0	0-0	5	.235
—Atlanta (N.L.)	3	3	.500	3.36	1.07	36	5	0	0	5	10-11	59.0	53	24	22	7	10-2	57	.238
2002—Atlanta (N.L.)	3	2	.600	3.25	1.03	75	0	0	0	0	• 55-•59	80.1	59	30	29	4	24-1	85	.206
2003—Atlanta (N.L.)	0	2	.000	1.12	0.87	62	0	0	0	0	45-49	64.1	48	9	8	2	8-1	73	.204
2004—Atlanta (N.L.)	0	1	.000	2.76	1.08	73	0	0	0	0	44-49	81.2	75	25	25	8	13-2	85	.245

S

Year Team (League)	W	L	Pct.	ERA	WHIP	G	GS	CG	ShO	Hld.	Sv.-Opp.	IP	H	R	ER	HR	BB-IBB	SO	Avg.
2005— Atlanta (N.L.)	14	7	.667	3.06	1.15	33	33	3	1	0	0-0	229.2	210	83	78	18	53-7	169	.243
2006— Atlanta (N.L.)	•16	9	.640	3.49	1.19	35	•35	3	1	0	0-0	232.0	221	93	90	23	55-4	211	.251
Major League totals (18 years)	193	137	.585	3.27	1.17	670	429	53	16	5	154-168	3161.1	2758	1250	1150	257	937-72	2778	.234

DIVISION SERIES RECORD

Year Team (League)	W	L	Pct.	ERA	WHIP	G	GS	CG	ShO	Hld.	Sv.-Opp.	IP	H	R	ER	HR	BB-IBB	SO	Avg.
1995— Atlanta (N.L.)	0	0	...	7.94	1.06	1	1	0	0	0	0-0	5.2	5	5	5	2	1-0	6	.238
1996— Atlanta (N.L.)	1	0	1.000	1.00	0.67	1	1	0	0	0	0-0	9.0	4	1	1	0	2-0	7	.129
1997— Atlanta (N.L.)	1	0	1.000	1.00	0.44	1	1	0	0	0	0-0	9.0	3	1	1	0	1-0	11	.097
1998— Atlanta (N.L.)	1	0	1.000	1.17	0.65	1	1	0	0	0	0-0	7.2	5	1	1	1	0-0	6	.185
1999— Atlanta (N.L.)	1	0	1.000	5.14	1.29	1	1	0	0	0	0-0	7.0	6	4	4	2	3-0	3	.222
2001— Atlanta (N.L.)	0	0	...	2.25	0.75	3	0	0	0	0	2-2	4.0	3	1	1	0	0-0	3	.214
2002— Atlanta (N.L.)	0	0	...	2.70	1.20	2	0	0	0	0	0-0	3.1	2	1	1	1	2-0	7	.182
2003— Atlanta (N.L.)	1	0	1.000	6.00	1.33	2	0	0	0	0	1-2	3.0	4	2	2	0	0-0	1	.364
2004— Atlanta (N.L.)	1	0	1.000	0.00	1.20	2	0	0	0	0	0-0	5.0	4	0	0	0	2-0	5	.235
2005— Atlanta (N.L.)	1	0	1.000	1.29	1.14	1	1	0	0	0	0-0	7.0	7	1	1	0	1-1	5	.259
Division series totals (10 years)	7	0	1.000	2.52	0.91	15	6	0	0	0	3-4	60.2	43	17	17	8	12-1	53	.198

CHAMPIONSHIP SERIES RECORD

Year Team (League)	W	L	Pct.	ERA	WHIP	G	GS	CG	ShO	Hld.	Sv.-Opp.	IP	H	R	ER	HR	BB-IBB	SO	Avg.
1991— Atlanta (N.L.)	2	0	1.000	1.76	1.11	2	2	1	1	0	0-0	15.1	14	3	3	2	3-0	15	.230
1992— Atlanta (N.L.)	2	0	1.000	2.66	1.18	3	3	0	0	0	0-0	20.1	14	7	6	1	10-2	19	.194
1993— Atlanta (N.L.)	0	1	.000	0.00	2.05	1	1	0	0	0	0-0	6.1	8	2	0	0	5-0	10	.296
1995— Atlanta (N.L.)	0	0	...	2.57	1.29	1	1	0	0	0	0-0	7.0	7	2	2	0	2-0	2	.269
1996— Atlanta (N.L.)	2	0	1.000	1.20	1.00	2	2	0	0	0	0-0	15.0	12	2	2	0	3-0	12	.214
1997— Atlanta (N.L.)	0	1	.000	7.50	1.67	1	1	0	0	0	0-0	6.0	5	5	5	1	5-2	9	.227
1998— Atlanta (N.L.)	0	0	...	3.95	1.39	2	2	0	0	0	0-0	13.2	13	6	6	0	6-0	13	.250
1999— Atlanta (N.L.)	0	0	...	6.23	0.92	3	1	0	0	0	1-1	8.2	8	6	6	2	0-0	8	.257
2001— Atlanta (N.L.)	0	0	...	0.00	0.00	2	0	0	0	0	0-0	3.0	0	0	0	0	0-0	1	.000
Champ. series totals (9 years)	6	2	.750	2.83	1.21	17	13	1	1	0	1-1	95.1	81	33	30	8	34-4	89	.226

WORLD SERIES RECORD

Year Team (League)	W	L	Pct.	ERA	WHIP	G	GS	CG	ShO	Hld.	Sv.-Opp.	IP	H	R	ER	HR	BB-IBB	SO	Avg.
1991— Atlanta (N.L.)	0	0	...	1.26	0.98	2	2	0	0	0	0-0	14.1	13	2	2	1	1-0	11	.241
1992— Atlanta (N.L.)	1	0	1.000	2.70	1.50	2	2	0	0	0	0-0	13.1	13	5	4	0	7-0	12	.255
1995— Atlanta (N.L.)	0	0	...	15.43	3.43	1	1	0	0	0	0-0	2.1	6	4	4	0	2-0	4	.462
1996— Atlanta (N.L.)	1	1	.500	0.64	1.00	2	2	0	0	0	0-0	14.0	6	2	1	0	8-0	14	.125
1999— Atlanta (N.L.)	0	1	.000	3.86	1.29	1	1	0	0	0	0-0	7.0	6	3	3	0	3-1	11	.228
World series totals (5 years)	2	2	.500	2.47	1.27	8	8	0	0	0	0-0	51.0	44	16	14	1	21-1	52	.228

ALL-STAR GAME RECORD

	W	L	Pct.	ERA	WHIP	G	GS	CG	ShO	Hld.	Sv.-Opp.	IP	H	R	ER	HR	BB-IBB	SO	Avg.
All-Star Game totals (6 years)	1	2	.333	3.18	1.41	6	1	0	0	0	0-0	5.2	7	2	2	1	1-0	2	.304

2006 LEFTY-RIGHTY SPLITS

vs.	Avg.	AB	H	2B	3B	HR	RBI	BB	SO	OBP	Slg.	vs.	Avg.	AB	H	2B	3B	HR	RBI	BB	SO	OBP	Slg.
L	.278	414	115	27	1	12	49	41	83	.348	.435	R	.226	468	106	22	3	11	37	14	128	.251	.357

SNELL, IAN — P

PERSONAL: Born October 30, 1981, in Dover, Del. ... 5-11/170. ... Throws right, bats right. ... Full name: Ian Dante Snell, formerly Ian Oquendo. ... High school: Caesar Rodney (Camden, Del.). **TRANSACTIONS/CAREER NOTES:** Selected by Pittsburgh Pirates organization in 26th round of 2000 free-agent draft. **MISCELLANEOUS NOTES:** Scored a run in five appearances as pinch runner (2006).

CAREER HITTING: 3-for-64 (.047), 2 R, 1 2B, 0 3B, 0 HR, 2 RBI.

Year Team (League)	W	L	Pct.	ERA	WHIP	G	GS	CG	ShO	Hld.	Sv.-Opp.	IP	H	R	ER	HR	BB-IBB	SO	Avg.
2000— GC Pirates (GCL)	1	0	1.000	2.35	0.78	4	0	0	0	...	0-...	7.2	5	2	2	1	1-0	8	.200
2001— GC Pirates (GCL)	3	0	1.000	0.47	0.89	3	3	0	0	...	0-...	19.0	12	2	1	0	5-0	13	.185
— Will. (NYP)	7	1	1.000	1.39	1.01	10	9	1	0	...	0-...	64.2	55	16	10	2	10-0	56	.230
2002— Hickory (S. Atl.)	11	6	.647	2.71	1.23	24	22	0	0	...	0-...	139.2	127	49	42	8	45-0	149	.243
2003— Lynchburg (Caro.)	10	3	.769	3.33	1.19	20	20	1	1	...	0-...	116.1	105	46	43	3	33-1	122	.244
— Altoona (East.)	4	0	1.000	1.96	1.25	6	6	0	0	...	0-...	36.2	36	13	8	2	10-0	23	.252
2004— Altoona (East.)	11	7	.611	3.16	1.24	26	26	3	2	...	0-...	151.0	147	54	53	16	40-2	142	.259
— Pittsburgh (N.L.)	0	1	.000	7.50	1.92	3	1	0	0	0	0-0	12.0	14	10	10	2	9-0	8	.298
2005— Indianapolis (Int'l)	11	3	.786	3.70	1.01	18	18	2	1	0	0-0	112.0	90	49	46	14	23-0	104	.216
— Pittsburgh (N.L.)	1	2	.333	5.14	1.60	15	5	0	0	1	0-0	42.0	43	25	24	5	24-3	34	.267
2006— Pittsburgh (N.L.)	14	11	.560	4.74	1.46	32	32	0	0	0	0-0	186.0	198	104	98	29	74-4	169	.277
Major League totals (3 years)	15	14	.517	4.95	1.51	50	38	0	0	1	0-0	240.0	255	139	132	36	107-7	212	.276

2006 LEFTY-RIGHTY SPLITS

vs.	Avg.	AB	H	2B	3B	HR	RBI	BB	SO	OBP	Slg.	vs.	Avg.	AB	H	2B	3B	HR	RBI	BB	SO	OBP	Slg.
L	.305	344	105	18	2	18	49	47	76	.386	.526	R	.251	371	93	25	1	11	49	27	93	.303	.412

SNELLING, CHRIS — OF

PERSONAL: Born December 3, 1981, in North Miami, Fla. ... 5-10/165. ... Bats left, throws left. ... Full name: Christopher Doyle Snelling. ... High school: Corpus Christi College Tuggerah (Australia). **TRANSACTIONS/CAREER NOTES:** Signed as a non-drafted free agent by Seattle Mariners organization (March 2, 1999). ... On disabled list (June 5, 2002-remainder of season; and March 21-April 29, 2003). ... On disabled list (March 26, 2004-entire season; included rehabilitation assignment to AZL Mariners. ... On disabled list (March 25-April 14 and August 12, 2005-remainder of season); included rehabilitation assignment to Tacoma. ... On disabled list (April 1-May 20 and July 26-August 17, 2006); included rehabilitation assignment to Tacoma.

2006 GAMES PLAYED BY POSITION (MLB): OF—34.

									BATTING									FIELDING	
Year Team (League)	Pos.	G	AB	R	H	2B	3B	HR	RBI	BB	SO	HBP	GDP	SB-CS	Avg.	OBP	SLG	OPS	E	Avg.
1999— Everett (N'west)	OF-OF	69	265	46	81	15	3	10	50	33	24	6	4	8-9	.306	.388	.498	.886	1	.993
2000— Wisconsin (Midw.)	OF-OF	72	259	44	79	9	5	9	56	34	34	6	2	7-4	.305	.386	.483	.869	2	.983
2001— San Bern. (Calif.)	OF-OF	114	450	90	151	29	10	7	73	45	63	21	4	12-5	.336	.418	.491	.909	4	.978
2002— San Antonio (Texas)	OF-OF	23	89	10	29	9	2	1	12	12	11	4	1	5-1	.326	.429	.506	.935	0	1.000
— Seattle (A.L.)	OF	8	27	2	4	0	0	1	3	2	4	0	2	0-0	.148	.207	.259	.466	0	1.000
2003— San Antonio (Texas)	OF	47	186	24	62	12	3	3	25	8	30	5	0	1-7	.333	.371	.468	.839	0	1.000
— Tacoma (PCL)	OF	18	67	11	18	2	0	3	10	5	12	2	0	1-0	.269	.333	.433	.766	0	1.000

Year Team (League)	Pos.	G	AB	R	H	2B	3B	HR	RBI	BB	SO	HBP	GDP	SB-CS	Avg.	OBP	SLG	OPS	E	Avg.
2004— Ariz. Mariners (Ariz.)	OF	10	32	8	10	4	1	0	9	7	3	3	2	1-0	.313	.476	.500	.976	2	.846
2005— Tacoma (PCL)	OF-DH	65	246	50	91	17	2	8	46	36	43	4	1	2-3	.370	.452	.553	1.005	4	.976
— Seattle (A.L.)	OF	15	29	4	8	2	0	1	1	5	2	0	0	0-2	.276	.382	.448	.831	0	1.000
2006— Tacoma (PCL)		69	241	36	52	13	1	5	39	31	60	11	4	4-2	.216	.326	.340	.667	2	.977
— Seattle (A.L.)	OF	36	96	14	24	6	1	3	8	13	38	4	0	2-1	.250	.360	.427	.787	1	.979
Major League totals (3 years)		59	152	20	36	8	1	5	12	20	44	4	2	2-3	.237	.339	.401	.740	1	.988

2006 LEFTY-RIGHTY SPLITS

vs.	Avg.	AB	H	2B	3B	HR	RBI	BB	SO	OBP	Slg.	vs.	Avg.	AB	H	2B	3B	HR	RBI	BB	SO	OBP	Slg.
L	.091	11	1	1	0	0	0	1	2	.231	.182	R	.271	85	23	5	1	3	8	12	36	.376	.459

SNOW, J.T.   1B

PERSONAL: Born February 26, 1968, in Long Beach, Calif. ... 6-2/209. ... Bats left, throws left. ... Full name: Jack Thomas Snow. ... High school: Los Alamitos (Calif.). ... College: Arizona. ... Son of Jack Snow, wide receiver with Los Angeles Rams (1965-75). **TRANSACTIONS/CAREER NOTES:** Selected by New York Yankees organization in fifth round of 1989 free-agent draft. ... Traded by Yankees with Ps Jerry Nielsen and Russ Springer to California Angels for P Jim Abbott (December 6, 1992). ... Traded to Angels by Yankees with Ps Allen Watson and Fausto Macey (November 27, 1996). ... On disabled list (May 27-June 14, June 24-July 15 and July 27-August 7, 2001); included rehabilitation assignments to Fresno. ... On disabled list (June 18-July 3 and August 17-September 1, 2003). ... On disabled list (May 22-June 25, 2004); included rehabilitation assignment to Fresno. ... Signed as a free agent by Boston Red Sox (January 9, 2006). ... Released by Red Sox (June 27, 2006). **HONORS:** Won A.L. Gold Glove at first base (1995-96). ... Won N.L. Gold Glove at first base (1997-2000). **STATISTICAL NOTES:** Hit three home runs in one game (August 13, 2004). ... Career major league grand slams: 7. **MISCELLANEOUS NOTES:** Batted as switch-hitter (1989-98).

2006 GAMES PLAYED BY POSITION (MLB): 1B—26, DH—1.

Year Team (League)	Pos.	G	AB	R	H	2B	3B	HR	RBI	BB	SO	HBP	GDP	SB-CS	Avg.	OBP	SLG	OPS	E	Avg.
1989— Oneonta (NYP)	1B	73	274	41	80	18	2	8	51	29	35	2	9	4-1	.292	.359	.460	.819	6	.991
1990— Prince Will. (Car.)	1B	138	520	57	133	25	1	8	72	46	65	5	20	2-0	.256	.318	.354	.672	12	.991
1991— Alb./Colon. (East.)	1B	132	477	78	133	33	3	13	76	67	78	3	10	5-1	.279	.364	.442	.807	8	.993
1992— Columbus (Int'l)	1B-OF	135	492	81	154	26	4	15	78	70	65	1	9	3-3	.313	.395	.474	.869	8	.993
— New York (A.L.)	1B-DH	7	14	1	2	1	0	0	2	5	5	0	0	0-0	.143	.368	.214	.583	0	1.000
1993— California (A.L.)	1B	129	419	60	101	18	2	16	57	55	88	2	10	3-0	.241	.328	.408	.736	6	.995
— Vancouver (PCL)	1B	23	94	19	32	9	1	5	24	10	13	1	2	0-0	.340	.410	.617	1.027	2	.991
1994— Vancouver (PCL)	1B-DH	53	189	35	56	13	2	8	43	22	32	0	5	1-2	.296	.364	.513	.878	1	.998
— California (A.L.)	1B	61	223	22	49	4	0	8	30	19	48	3	2	0-1	.220	.289	.345	.634	2	.996
1995— California (A.L.)	1B	143	544	80	157	22	1	24	102	52	91	3	16	2-1	.289	.353	.465	.818	4	.997
1996— California (A.L.)	1B	155	575	69	148	20	1	17	67	56	96	5	19	1-6	.257	.327	.384	.711	10	.993
1997— San Francisco (N.L.)	1B	157	531	81	149	36	1	28	104	96	124	1	8	6-4	.281	.387	.510	.898	7	.995
1998— San Francisco (N.L.)	1B	138	435	65	108	29	1	15	79	58	84	0	12	1-2	.248	.332	.423	.755	1	.999
1999— San Francisco (N.L.)	1B	161	570	93	156	25	2	24	98	86	121	5	16	0-4	.274	.370	.451	.821	6	.996
2000— San Francisco (N.L.)	1B	155	536	82	152	33	2	19	96	66	129	11	20	1-3	.284	.365	.459	.824	6	.995
2001— San Francisco (N.L.)	1B	101	285	43	70	12	1	8	34	55	81	4	2	0-0	.246	.371	.379	.750	7	.993
— Fresno (PCL)	1B	4	12	1	0	0	0	0	0	2	7	0	0	0-0	.000	.143	.000	.143	0	1.000
2002— San Francisco (N.L.)	1B	143	422	47	104	26	2	6	53	59	90	7	11	0-0	.246	.344	.360	.704	5	.994
2003— San Francisco (N.L.)	1B	103	330	48	90	18	3	8	51	55	55	8	7	1-2	.273	.387	.418	.806	3	.994
2004— Fresno (PCL)	1B	2	7	1	2	0	0	1	2	0	1	0	0	0-0	.286	.286	.714	1.000	0	1.000
— San Francisco (N.L.)	1B	107	346	62	113	32	1	12	60	58	61	7	5	0-0	.327	.429	.529	.958	4	.995
2005— San Francisco (N.L.)	1B	117	367	40	101	17	2	4	40	32	61	7	6	1-0	.275	.343	.365	.708	3	.997
2006— Boston (A.L.)	1B-DH	38	44	5	9	0	0	0	4	8	11	1	1	0-0	.205	.340	.205	.544	1	.990
American League totals (6 years)		533	1819	237	466	65	4	65	262	195	336	14	48	6-14	.256	.331	.404	.734	23	.995
National League totals (9 years)		1182	3822	561	1043	228	15	124	615	565	806	50	87	14-9	.273	.369	.438	.807	40	.996
Major League totals (15 years)		1715	5641	798	1509	293	19	189	877	760	1142	64	135	20-23	.268	.357	.427	.784	63	.995

DIVISION SERIES RECORD

Year Team (League)	Pos.	G	AB	R	H	2B	3B	HR	RBI	BB	SO	HBP	GDP	SB-CS	Avg.	OBP	SLG	OPS	E	Avg.
1997— San Francisco (N.L.)	1B	3	6	0	1	0	0	0	0	1	1	0	0	0-0	.167	.286	.167	.452	0	1.000
2000— San Francisco (N.L.)	1B	4	10	1	4	0	0	1	3	0	1	0	0	0-0	.400	.400	.700	1.271	0	1.000
2002— San Francisco (N.L.)	1B	5	19	3	6	2	0	1	3	1	5	0	0	0-0	.316	.350	.579	.929	0	1.000
2003— San Francisco (N.L.)	1B	4	16	0	5	0	0	0	3	0	3	0	0	0-0	.313	.313	.313	.625	2	.929
Division series totals (4 years)		16	51	4	16	2	0	2	9	6	10	0	0	0-0	.314	.386	.471	.857	2	.982

CHAMPIONSHIP SERIES RECORD

Year Team (League)	Pos.	G	AB	R	H	2B	3B	HR	RBI	BB	SO	HBP	GDP	SB-CS	Avg.	OBP	SLG	OPS	E	Avg.
2002— San Francisco (N.L.)	1B	5	20	1	5	1	1	0	2	1	4	0	0	0-0	.250	.286	.400	.686	0	1.000

WORLD SERIES RECORD

Year Team (League)	Pos.	G	AB	R	H	2B	3B	HR	RBI	BB	SO	HBP	GDP	SB-CS	Avg.	OBP	SLG	OPS	E	Avg.
2002— San Francisco (N.L.)	1B	7	27	6	11	1	0	1	4	2	1	0	0	0-0	.407	.448	.556	1.004	0	1.000

2006 LEFTY-RIGHTY SPLITS

vs.	Avg.	AB	H	2B	3B	HR	RBI	BB	SO	OBP	Slg.	vs.	Avg.	AB	H	2B	3B	HR	RBI	BB	SO	OBP	Slg.
L	.333	6	2	0	0	0	0	2	2	.500	.333	R	.184	38	7	0	0	0	3	6	6	.311	.184

SNYDER, CHRIS   C

PERSONAL: Born February 12, 1981, in Houston. ... 6-3/220. ... Bats right, throws right. ... Full name: Christopher Ryan Snyder. ... High school: Spring Woods (Houston). ... College: Houston. **TRANSACTIONS/CAREER NOTES:** Selected by Arizona Diamondbacks organization in second round of 2002 free-agent draft. **STATISTICAL NOTES:** Career major league grand slams: 1.

2006 GAMES PLAYED BY POSITION (MLB): C—60.

Year Team (League)	Pos.	G	AB	R	H	2B	3B	HR	RBI	BB	SO	HBP	GDP	SB-CS	Avg.	OBP	SLG	OPS	E	Avg.
2002— Lancaster (Calif.)	C-DH	60	217	31	56	16	0	9	44	25	54	3	7	0-0	.258	.337	.456	.794	3	.992
2003— Lancaster (Calif.)	C-DH	69	245	53	77	16	2	10	53	35	43	8	4	0-1	.314	.414	.518	.932	5	.984
— El Paso (Texas)	C-DH	53	188	21	38	14	0	4	26	19	29	4	9	0-0	.202	.286	.340	.627	3	.991
2004— El Paso (Texas)	C-DH-1B	99	346	66	104	31	0	15	57	46	57	6	7	3-1	.301	.389	.520	.909	9	.987
— Arizona (N.L.)	C	29	96	10	23	6	0	5	15	13	25	0	0	0-0	.240	.327	.458	.786	1	1.000
2005— Arizona (N.L.)	C	115	326	24	66	14	0	6	28	40	87	4	6	0-1	.202	.297	.301	.598	2	.997
2006— Arizona (N.L.)	C	61	184	19	51	9	0	6	32	22	39	1	6	0-0	.277	.349	.424	.773	2	.995
Major League totals (3 years)		205	606	53	140	29	0	17	75	75	151	5	11	0-1	.231	.318	.363	.681	4	.997

S

2006 LEFTY-RIGHTY SPLITS

vs.	Avg.	AB	H	2B	3B	HR	RBI	BB	SO	OBP	Slg.
L	.246	65	16	3	0	2	15	10	11	.333	.385
R	.294	119	35	6	0	4	17	12	28	.358	.445

SNYDER, KYLE   P

PERSONAL: Born September 9, 1977, in Houston. ... 6-8/220. ... Throws right, bats both. ... Full name: Kyle Ehren Snyder. ... High school: Riverview (Sarasota, Fla.). ... College: North Carolina. **TRANSACTIONS/CAREER NOTES:** Selected by Tampa Bay Devil Rays organization in 27th round of 1996 free-agent draft; did not sign. ... Selected by Kansas City Royals organization in first round (seventh pick overall) of 1999 free-agent draft. ... On disabled list (July 1-21 and August 6, 2003-remainder of season); included rehabilitation assignments to AZL Royals and Wichita. ... On disabled list (March 26, 2004-entire season). ... On disabled list (May 12-July 13, 2005); included rehabilitation assignments to Omaha and Wichita. ... Claimed on waivers by Boston Red Sox (June 16, 2006).

CAREER HITTING: 0-for-2 (.000), 0 R, 0 2B, 0 3B, 0 HR, 0 RBI.

Year Team (League)	W	L	Pct.	ERA	WHIP	G	GS	CG	ShO	Hld.	Sv.-Opp.	IP	H	R	ER	HR	BB-IBB	SO	Avg.
1999—Spokane (N'west)	0	1	1.000	4.13	1.13	7	7	0	0	...	0-...	24.0	20	13	11	1	7-0	25	.220
2000—GC Royals (GCL)	0	0	...	0.00	0.50	1	1	0	0	...	0-...	2.0	1	0	0	0	0-0	4	.143
—Wilmington (Caro.)	0	0	...	...	...	1	1	0	0	...	0-...	0.0	0	0	1	0	1-0	1	0
2001—											Did not play.								
2002—Wilmington (Caro.)	0	2	.000	2.98	1.24	15	15	0	0	...	0-...	48.1	49	19	16	1	11-0	48	.261
—Wichita (Texas)	2	2	.500	4.21	1.09	6	6	0	0	...	0-...	25.2	21	12	12	4	7-1	18	.226
2003—Omaha (PCL)	3	0	1.000	2.79	1.17	5	5	0	0	...	0-...	29.0	28	9	9	3	6-0	15	.259
—Arizona Royals 1 (AZL)	0	0	...	4.50	1.50	1	1	0	0	...	0-...	2.0	3	1	1	0	0-0	1	.375
—Wichita (Texas)	0	0	...	0.00	0.40	1	1	0	0	...	0-...	5.0	2	0	0	0	0-0	2	.125
—Kansas City (A.L.)	1	6	.143	5.17	1.35	15	15	0	0	0	0-0	85.1	94	52	49	11	21-3	39	.283
2004—											Did not play								
2005—Wichita (Texas)	1	0	1.000	5.40	1.20	1	1	0	0	0	0-0	5.0	5	3	3	1	1-0	1	.263
—Omaha (PCL)	2	3	.400	3.55	1.26	15	12	0	0	1	0-0	66.0	61	32	26	3	22-0	48	.263
—Kansas City (A.L.)	1	3	.250	6.75	1.81	13	13	0	0	0	0-0	36.0	55	29	27	3	10-1	19	.353
2006—Omaha (PCL)	0	4	...	3.88	1.19	10	9	0	0	1	1-1	60.1	63	36	26	4	9-0	43	.264
—Kansas City (A.L.)	0	0	...	22.50	5.50	1	1	0	0	0	0-0	2.0	10	5	5	1	1-0	2	.556
—Boston (A.L.)	4	5	.444	6.02	1.65	16	10	0	0	1	0-0	58.1	77	42	39	11	19-3	55	.314
—Pawtucket (Int'l)	1	1	.500	3.54	1.28	3	3	0	0	0	0-0	20.1	24	8	8	1	2-0	7	.314
Major League totals (3 years)	6	14	.300	5.94	1.58	45	29	0	0	0	0-0	181.2	236	132	120	26	51-7	115	.314

2006 LEFTY-RIGHTY SPLITS

vs.	Avg.	AB	H	2B	3B	HR	RBI	BB	SO	OBP	Slg.
L	.349	126	44	10	0	6	27	9	22	.399	.571
R	.314	137	43	10	0	6	18	11	35	.362	.518

SOLER, ALAY   P

PERSONAL: Born October 9, 1979, in Pinar del Rio, Cuba. ... 6-1/240. ... Throws right, bats right. ... Full name: Alain Soler. **TRANSACTIONS/CAREER NOTES:** Signed as a free agent by New York Mets (August 27, 2004). ... On restricted list (April 1, 2005-March 8, 2006).

CAREER HITTING: 1-for-11 (.091), 0 R, 0 2B, 0 3B, 0 HR, 0 RBI.

Year Team (League)	W	L	Pct.	ERA	WHIP	G	GS	CG	ShO	Hld.	Sv.-Opp.	IP	H	R	ER	HR	BB-IBB	SO	Avg.
2005—Dominican Mets (DSL)	0	1	.000	1.69	0.94	2	1	0	0	...	0-0	5.1	3	3	1	0	2-0	12	.143
2006—St. Lucie (Fla. St.)	2	0	1.000	0.60	0.73	6	6	0	0	...	0-0	30.0	13	2	2	0	9-0	33	.129
—Binghamton (East.)	1	0	1.000	2.75	0.97	3	3	0	0	...	0-0	19.2	16	6	6	0	3-0	22	.222
—New York (N.L.)	2	3	.400	6.00	1.58	9	8	1	1	0	0-0	45.0	50	33	30	7	21-1	23	.275
—Norfolk (Int'l)	1	1	.500	6.30	1.70	2	2	0	0	0	0-0	10.0	13	7	7	0	4-0	12	.317
—Brook.. (N.Y.-Penn.)	0	1	.000	6.23	0.92	1	1	0	0	0	0-0	4.1	3	3	3	1	2-0	9	.125
Major League totals (1 year)	2	3	.400	6.00	1.58	8	8	1	1	0	0-0	45.0	50	33	30	7	21-1	23	.275

2006 LEFTY-RIGHTY SPLITS

vs.	Avg.	AB	H	2B	3B	HR	RBI	BB	SO	OBP	Slg.
L	.252	107	27	7	2	2	13	13	12	.333	.411
R	.307	75	23	5	0	5	17	8	11	.373	.573

SORIANO, ALFONSO   OF/2B

PERSONAL: Born January 7, 1976, in San Pedro de Macoris, Dominican Republic. ... 6-1/180. ... Bats right, throws right. ... Full name: Alfonso Guilleard Soriano. ... Name pronounced: soar-ee-AH-no. ... High school: Eugenio Maria de Osto (Dominican Republic). **TRANSACTIONS/CAREER NOTES:** Signed by Hiroshima Carp of the Japan Central League (November 1994). ... Retired from Japan Central League and declared a free agent by Major League Baseball (1998). ... Signed by New York Yankees (September 29, 1998). ... Traded by Yankees with a player to be named to Texas Rangers for SS Alex Rodriguez (February 16, 2004); Rangers acquired SS Joaquin Arias to complete deal (March 13, 2005). ... Traded by Rangers to Washington Nationals for OFs Brad Wilkerson and Terrmel Sledge and P Armando Galarraga (December 13, 2005). **HONORS:** Named second baseman on THE SPORTING NEWS A.L. All-Star team (2002 and 2004). ... Named second baseman on A.L. Silver Slugger team (2002, 2004 and 2005). ... Named outfielder on SPORTING NEWS N.L. All-Star team (2006). ... Named outfielder on SPORTING NEWS N.L. Silver Slugger team (2006). **STATISTICAL NOTES:** Hit three home runs in one game (April 21, 2006). ... Career major league grand slams: 3.

2006 GAMES PLAYED BY POSITION (MLB): OF—158.

Year Team (League)	Pos.	G	AB	R	H	2B	3B	HR	RBI	BB	SO	HBP	GDP	SB-CS	Avg.	OBP	SLG	OPS	FIELDING E	Avg.
1995—Hiroshima (DSL)		63	227	52	83	12	3	4	55	30	19	...	...	8-...	.366	...	.498	...	...	...
1996—Hiroshima (Jap. West.)		57	131	11	28	...	...	0	13	...	...	...	...	-"-...	.214	...	.214	...	...	...
1997—Hiroshima (Jap. West.)		68	242	28	61	13	2	8	34	13	35	...	...	14-...	.252	...	.421	...	...	...
—Hiroshima (Jp. Cn.)	OF	9	17	2	2	0	0	0	0	2	4	...	...	0-...	.118	...	.118	...	...	...
1998—										Did not play.										
1999—Norwich (East.)	SS-DH	89	361	57	110	20	3	15	68	32	67	4	9	24-16	.305	.363	.501	.865	27	.937
—GC Yankees (GCL)	SS-DH	5	19	7	5	2	0	1	5	1	3	1	0	0-0	.263	.318	.526	.844	1	.929
—Columbus (Int'l)	SS-3B-2B	20	82	8	15	5	1	2	11	5	18	0	1	1-1	.183	.225	.341	.566	3	.955
—New York (A.L.)	DH-SS	9	8	2	1	0	0	1	1	0	3	0	0	0-1	.125	.125	.500	.625	1	.500
2000—Columbus (Int'l)	SS-2B	111	459	90	133	32	6	12	66	25	85	3	8	14-7	.290	.327	.464	.791	21	.952
—New York (A.L.)	3B-SS-2B DH	22	50	5	9	3	0	2	3	1	15	0	0	2-0	.180	.196	.360	.556	7	.837
2001—New York (A.L.)	2B-DH	158	574	77	154	34	3	18	73	29	125	14	7	43-14	.268	.304	.432	.736	19	.973
2002—New York (A.L.)	2B-DH	156	*696	*128	*209	51	2	39	102	23	157	14	8	*41-13	.300	.332	.547	.880	*23	.968
2003—New York (A.L.)	2B	156	*682	114	198	36	5	38	91	38	130	12	8	35-8	.290	.338	.525	.863	19	.975
2004—Texas (A.L.)	2B-DH	145	608	77	170	32	4	28	91	33	121	10	7	18-5	.280	.324	.484	.807	23	.969
2005—Texas (A.L.)	2B-DH	156	637	102	171	43	2	36	104	33	125	7	6	30-2	.268	.309	.512	.821	21	.972
2006—Wash. (N.L.)	OF	159	647	119	179	41	2	46	95	67	160	9	3	41-17	.277	.351	.560	.911	11	.969
American League totals (7 years)		802	3255	505	912	199	16	162	465	157	676	46	36	169-43	.280	.320	.500	.820	113	.970
National League totals (1 year)		159	647	119	179	41	2	46	95	67	160	9	3	41-17	.277	.351	.560	.911	11	.969
Major League totals (8 years)		961	3902	624	1091	240	18	208	560	224	836	55	39	210-60	.280	.325	.510	.836	124	.970

DIVISION SERIES RECORD

Year · Team (League)	Pos.	G	AB	R	H	2B	3B	HR	RBI	BB	SO	HBP	GDP	SB-CS	Avg.	OBP	SLG	OPS	E	Avg.
2001—New York (A.L.)	2B	5	18	2	4	0	0	0	3	1	5	0	0	2-1	.222	.263	.222	.485	0	1.000
2002—New York (A.L.)	2B	4	17	2	2	1	0	1	2	1	4	1	1	1-0	.118	.211	.353	.563	1	.958
2003—New York (A.L.)	2B	4	19	2	7	1	0	0	4	0	6	0	0	2-0	.368	.368	.421	.789	1	.938
Division series totals (3 years)		13	54	6	13	2	0	1	9	2	15	1	1	5-1	.241	.281	.333	.614	2	.964

CHAMPIONSHIP SERIES RECORD

Year Team (League)	Pos.	G	AB	R	H	2B	3B	HR	RBI	BB	SO	HBP	GDP	SB-CS	Avg.	OBP	SLG	OPS	E	Avg.
2001—New York (A.L.)	2B	5	15	5	6	0	0	1	2	3	3	1	0	2-0	.400	.526	.600	1.126	1	.955
2003—New York (A.L.)	2B	7	30	0	4	1	0	0	3	1	11	1	1	2-0	.133	.188	.167	.354	1	.973
Champ. series totals (2 years)		12	45	5	10	1	0	1	5	4	14	2	1	4-0	.222	.314	.311	.625	2	.966

WORLD SERIES RECORD

Year Team (League)	Pos.	G	AB	R	H	2B	3B	HR	RBI	BB	SO	HBP	GDP	SB-CS	Avg.	OBP	SLG	OPS	E	Avg.
2001—New York (A.L.)	2B	7	25	1	6	0	0	1	2	0	7	0	0	0-1	.240	.240	.360	.600	3	.927
2003—New York (A.L.)	2B-OF	6	22	2	5	0	0	1	2	2	9	0	1	1-1	.227	.292	.364	.655	0	1.000
World series totals (2 years)		13	47	3	11	0	0	2	4	2	16	0	1	1-2	.234	.265	.362	.627	3	.955

ALL-STAR GAME RECORD

		G	AB	R	H	2B	3B	HR	RBI	BB	SO	HBP	GDP	SB-CS	Avg.	OBP	SLG	OPS	E	Avg.
All-Star Game totals (5 years)		5	11	3	4	0	0	2	4	0	3	0	0	1-0	.364	.364	.909	1.273	0	1.000

2006 LEFTY-RIGHTY SPLITS

vs.	Avg.	AB	H	2B	3B	HR	RBI	BB	SO	OBP	Slg.	vs.	Avg.	AB	H	2B	3B	HR	RBI	BB	SO	OBP	Slg.
L	.293	167	49	10	1	12	23	29	43	.401	.581	R	.271	480	130	31	1	34	72	38	117	.333	.552

SORIANO, RAFAEL — P

PERSONAL: Born December 19, 1979, in San Jose, Dominican Republic. ... 6-1/175. ... Throws right, bats right. ... Full name: Rafael Soriano. ... Name pronounced: soar-ee-AH-no. **TRANSACTIONS/CAREER NOTES:** Signed as a non-drafted free agent by Seattle Mariners organization (August 30, 1996). ... Played first base and outfield for two seasons in Mariners organization (1997-98). ... On disabled list (July 3-August 2, 2002). ... On disabled list (May 10, 2004-remainder of season); included rehabilitation assignment to Tacoma. ... On disabled list (April 1-September 5, 2005); included rehabilitation assignments to Everett, Inland Empire, San Antonio and Tacoma. ... On disabled list (July 20-August 4, 2006). **HONORS:** Named A.L. Rookie Pitcher of the Year by THE SPORTING NEWS (2003). **MISCELLANEOUS NOTES:** Appeared in one game as pinch runner (2002).

CAREER HITTING: 0-for-4 (.000), 0 R, 0 2B, 0 3B, 0 HR, 0 RBI.

Year Team (League)	W	L	Pct.	ERA	WHIP	G	GS	CG	ShO	Hld.	Sv.-Opp.	IP	H	R	ER	HR	BB-IBB	SO	Avg.
1999—Everett (N'west)	5	4	.556	3.11	1.39	14	14	0	0	...	0-...	75.1	56	34	26	8	49-0	83	.208
2000—Wisconsin (Midw.)	8	4	.667	2.87	1.20	21	21	1	0	...	0-...	122.1	97	41	39	3	50-0	90	.225
2001—San Bern. (Calif.)	6	3	.667	2.53	0.99	15	15	2	1	...	0-...	89.0	49	28	25	4	39-0	98	.164
—San Antonio (Texas)	2	2	.500	3.35	0.99	8	8	0	0	...	0-...	48.1	34	18	18	5	14-0	53	.192
2002—San Antonio (Texas)	2	3	.400	2.31	1.01	10	8	0	0	...	0-...	46.2	32	13	12	6	15-0	52	.190
—Seattle (A.L.)	0	3	.000	4.56	1.29	10	8	0	0	0	1-1	47.1	45	25	24	8	16-1	32	.243
2003—Tacoma (PCL)	4	3	.571	3.19	0.90	11	10	0	0	...	0-...	62.0	43	24	22	2	12-0	63	.192
—Seattle (A.L.)	3	0	1.000	1.53	0.79	40	0	0	0	5	1-2	53.0	30	9	9	2	12-1	68	.162
2004—Inland Empire (Calif.)	0	0	...	2.25	1.00	2	1	0	0	...	0-...	8.0	7	3	2	1	1-0	9	.241
—San Antonio (Texas)	1	0	1.000	1.13	0.50	2	1	0	0	...	0-...	8.0	4	1	1	1	0-0	10	.154
—Seattle (A.L.)	0	3	.000	13.50	3.60	6	0	0	0	0	0-1	3.1	9	6	5	1	3-0	3	.450
—Tacoma (PCL)	0	0	...	2.46	1.09	3	0	0	0	...	0-...	3.2	2	1	1	1	2-0	5	.154
2005—Inland Empire (Calif.)	0	0	...	0.00	0.50	3	0	0	0	...	0-...	4.0	2	0	0	0	0-0	5	.154
—San Antonio (Texas)	0	0	...	0.00	1.00	1	0	0	0	...	0-...	1.0	0	0	0	0	0-0	0	.000
—Everett (N'west)	0	0	...	3.00	1.33	4	4	0	0	...	0-...	6.0	6	3	2	0	2-0	8	.250
—Tacoma (PCL)	1	0	1.000	0.00	0.75	5	0	0	0	1	0-0	5.1	3	0	0	0	1-0	9	.158
—Seattle (A.L.)	0	0	...	2.45	0.95	7	0	0	0	0	0-0	7.1	6	2	2	0	1-0	9	.222
2006—Seattle (A.L.)	1	2	.333	2.25	1.08	53	0	0	0	18	2-6	60.0	44	15	15	6	21-0	65	.204
Major League totals (5 years)	4	8	.333	2.89	1.09	116	8	0	0	24	4-10	171.0	134	57	55	16	53-2	177	.212

2006 LEFTY-RIGHTY SPLITS

vs.	Avg.	AB	H	2B	3B	HR	RBI	BB	SO	OBP	Slg.	vs.	Avg.	AB	H	2B	3B	HR	RBI	BB	SO	OBP	Slg.
L	.244	82	20	2	1	3	7	9	21	.315	.390	R	.179	134	24	5	1	3	16	12	44	.257	.299

SOSA, JORGE — P

PERSONAL: Born April 28, 1977, in Santo Domingo, Dominican Republic. ... 6-2/170. ... Throws right, bats both. ... Full name: Jorge Bolivar Sosa. ... Name pronounced: hor-hey. **TRANSACTIONS/CAREER NOTES:** Signed as a non-drafted free agent by Colorado Rockies organization (June 23, 1995). ... Played outfield for six seasons in Rockies organization (1995-2000). ... Selected by Seattle Mariners organization from Rockies organization in Rule 5 minor league draft (December 11, 2000). ... Selected by Milwaukee Brewers from Mariners organization in Rule 5 major league draft (December 13, 2001). ... Claimed on waivers by Tampa Bay Devil Rays (March 18, 2002). ... On disabled list (May 26-June 25, 2002); included rehabilitation assignment to Orlando. ... Traded by Devil Rays to Atlanta Braves for 2B Nick Green (March 31, 2005). ... Traded by Braves to St. Louis Cardinals for P Rich Scalamandre (July 31, 2006). **MISCELLANEOUS NOTES:** Appeared in one game as pinch runner (2005). ... Scored a run in only appearance as pinch runner (2006).

CAREER HITTING: 6-for-55 (.109), 5 R, 0 2B, 0 3B, 3 HR, 3 RBI.

Year Team (League)	W	L	Pct.	ERA	WHIP	G	GS	CG	ShO	Hld.	Sv.-Opp.	IP	H	R	ER	HR	BB-IBB	SO	Avg.
2001—Everett (N'west)	3	1	.750	1.69	1.09	21	7	0	0	...	7-...	58.2	45	22	11	2	19-0	57	.204
—Wisconsin (Midw.)	0	0	...	9.00	1.50	2	0	0	0	...	0-...	2.0	3	2	2	1	0-0	4	.333
2002—Tampa Bay (A.L.)	2	7	.222	5.53	1.43	31	14	0	1	...	0-0	99.1	88	63	61	16	54-0	48	.236
—Orlando (South.)	0	0	...	0.00	0.71	2	2	0	0	...	0-...	7.0	4	2	0	1	1-0	3	.167
2003—Durham (Int'l)	1	1	.500	5.47	1.70	4	4	0	0	...	0-...	24.2	32	15	15	2	9-0	17	.314
—Tampa Bay (A.L.)	5	12	.294	4.62	1.53	29	19	1	1	0	0-0	128.2	137	71	66	14	60-4	72	.278
2004—Durham (Int'l)	1	2	.333	2.77	0.85	3	3	0	0	...	0-...	13.0	11	5	4	0	0-0	23	.224
—Tampa Bay (A.L.)	4	7	.364	5.53	1.55	43	8	0	0	6	1-1	99.1	100	67	61	17	54-3	94	.259
2005—Atlanta (N.L.)	13	3	* .813	2.55	1.39	44	20	0	0	4	0-0	134.0	122	42	38	12	64-8	85	.241
2006—Atlanta (N.L.)	3	10	.231	5.46	1.57	26	13	0	0	0	3-6	87.1	105	61	53	20	32-5	58	.298
—St. Louis (N.L.)	0	1	.000	5.28	1.34	19	0	0	0	0	1-1	30.2	33	18	18	10	8-1	17	.275
American League totals (3 years)	11	26	.297	5.17	1.51	103	41	1	1	7	1-1	327.1	325	201	188	47	168-7	214	.260
National League totals (2 years)	16	14	.533	3.89	1.44	89	33	0	0	4	4-7	252.0	260	121	109	42	104-14	160	.266
Major League totals (5 years)	27	40	.403	4.61	1.48	192	74	1	1	11	5-8	579.1	585	322	297	89	272-21	374	.262

DIVISION SERIES RECORD

Year Team (League)	W	L	Pct.	ERA	WHIP	G	GS	CG	ShO	Hld.	Sv.-Opp.	IP	H	R	ER	HR	BB-IBB	SO	Avg.
2005—Atlanta (N.L.)	0	1	.000	4.50	1.50	1	1	0	0	...	0-...	6.0	7	3	3	1	2-2	3	.304

S

2006 LEFTY-RIGHTY SPLITS

vs.	Avg.	AB	H	2B	3B	HR	RBI	BB	SO	OBP	Slg.	vs.	Avg.	AB	H	2B	3B	HR	RBI	BB	SO	OBP	Slg.
L	.326	190	62	9	1	13	27	23	28	.399	.589	R	.270	282	76	18	0	17	48	17	47	.309	.514

SOTO, GEOVANY — C

PERSONAL: Born January 20, 1983, in San Juan, Puerto Rico. ... 6-1/195. ... Bats right, throws right. ... Full name: Geovany Soto. **TRANSACTIONS/CAREER NOTES:** Selected by Chicago Cubs organization in 11th round of 2001 free-agent draft.

2006 GAMES PLAYED BY POSITION (MLB): C—7.

Year Team (League)	Pos.	G	AB	R	H	2B	3B	HR	RBI	BB	SO	HBP	GDP	SB-CS	Avg.	OBP	SLG	OPS	FIELDING E	Avg.
2001— Ariz. Cubs (Ariz.)	C-1B-3B OF	41	150	18	39	16	0	1	20	15	33	3	3	1-0	.260	.339	.387	.726	7	.975
2002— Ariz. Cubs (Ariz.)	C-1B-3B OF	44	156	24	42	10	2	3	24	13	35	3	2	0-2	.269	.333	.417	.750	1	.992
— Boise (N'west)	C	1	5	1	2	0	0	0	0	0	1	0	0	0-0	.400	.400	.400	.800	0	1.000
2003— Daytona (Fla. St.)	C-3B	89	297	26	72	12	2	2	38	31	58	2	10	0-0	.242	.313	.316	.629	9	.987
2004— West Tenn (Sou.)	C-1B	104	332	47	90	16	0	9	48	40	71	5	10	1-2	.271	.355	.417	.756	6	.993
2005— Iowa (PCL)	C-DH	91	292	30	74	14	0	4	39	48	77	0	15	0-1	.253	.357	.342	.699	4	.995
— Chicago (N.L.)		1	0	1	0	0	0	0	0	0	0	0	0	0-0	.000	.000	.000	.000	0	...
2006— Iowa (PCL)		108	342	34	93	21	0	6	38	41	74	3	10	0-1	.272	.353	.386	.739	8	.990
— Chicago (N.L.)	C	11	25	1	5	1	0	0	2	0	5	1	0	0-0	.200	.231	.240	.471	1	.986
Major League totals (2 years)		12	26	1	5	1	0	0	2	0	5	1	0	0-0	.192	.222	.231	.453	1	.986

2006 LEFTY-RIGHTY SPLITS

vs.	Avg.	AB	H	2B	3B	HR	RBI	BB	SO	OBP	Slg.	vs.	Avg.	AB	H	2B	3B	HR	RBI	BB	SO	OBP	Slg.
L	.133	15	2	0	0	0	1	0	2	.133	.133	R	.300	10	3	1	0	0	1	0	3	.364	.400

SOWERS, JEREMY — P

PERSONAL: Born May 17, 1983, in St. Clairsville, Ohio. ... Throws right, bats right. ... Full name: Jeremy Bryan Sowers. ... College: Vanderbilt. **TRANSACTIONS/CAREER NOTES:** Selected by Cleveland Indians organization in first round (sixth overall pick) of 2000 free-agent draft.

CAREER HITTING: 0-for-0 (.000), 0 R, 2B, 0 3B, 0 HR, 0 RBI.

Year Team (League)	W	L	Pct.	ERA	WHIP	G	GS	CG	ShO	Hld.	Sv.-Opp.	IP	H	R	ER	HR	BB-IBB	SO	Avg.
2005— Kinston (Carol.)	8	3	.727	2.78	1.11	13	13	0	0	0	0-0	71.1	60	25	22	5	19-0	75	.223
— Akron (East.)	5	1	.833	2.08	1.01	13	13	0	0	0	0-0	82.1	74	25	19	8	9-1	70	.241
— Buffalo (Int'l)	1	0	1.000	1.59	1.41	1	1	0	0	0	0-0	5.2	7	1	1	0	1-0	4	.292
— Auburn (NY-Penn)	4	0	1.000	4.86	1.57	19	2	0	0	0	0-1	37.0	42	23	20	1	16-0	27	.284
2006— Lansing (Midw.)	0	2	.000	5.56	1.59	18	0	0	0	0	0-2	34.0	44	23	21	0	10-1	21	.317
— Dunedin (Fla. St.)	0	0		0.00	2.00	1	0	0	0	0	0-0	3.0	5	2	0	0	1-0	1	.455
— Auburn (NY-Penn)	1	0	1.000	0.00	0.86	1	0	0	0	0	0-0	2.1	1	0	0	0	1-0	1	.143
— Cleveland (A.L.)	7	4	.636	3.57	1.19	14	14	2	•2	0	0-0	88.1	85	36	35	10	20-1	35	.252
Major League totals (1 year)	7	4	.636	3.57	1.19	14	14	2	2	0	0-0	88.1	85	36	35	10	20-1	35	.252

2006 LEFTY-RIGHTY SPLITS

vs.	Avg.	AB	H	2B	3B	HR	RBI	BB	SO	OBP	Slg.	vs.	Avg.	AB	H	2B	3B	HR	RBI	BB	SO	OBP	Slg.
L	.225	71	16	1	0	4	9	3	12	.257	.408	R	.259	266	69	12	2	6	25	17	23	.309	.387

SPEIER, JUSTIN — P

PERSONAL: Born November 6, 1973, in Walnut Creek, Calif. ... 6-4/205. ... Throws right, bats right. ... Full name: Justin James Speier. ... Name pronounced: SPY-er. ... High school: Brophy College Prep (Phoenix). ... College: Nicholls State. ... Son of Chris Speier, infielder with five major league teams (1971-89). **TRANSACTIONS/CAREER NOTES:** Selected by Chicago Cubs organization in 55th round of 1995 free-agent draft. ... Traded by Cubs with 3B Kevin Orie and P Todd Noel to Florida Marlins for Ps Felix Heredia and Steve Hoff (July 31, 1998). ... Traded by Marlins to Atlanta Braves for a player to be named (April 1, 1999); Marlins acquired P Matthew Targac to complete deal (June 11, 1999). ... Claimed on waivers by Cleveland Indians (November 23, 1999). ... Traded by Indians to New York Mets for OF Brian Jenkins (May 19, 2001). ... Claimed on waivers by Colorado Rockies (May 29, 2002). ... On disabled list (March 31-May 6, 2002); included rehabilitation assignment to Colorado Springs. ... Traded by Rockies to Toronto Blue Jays as part of three-team deal in which Rockies acquired P Joe Kennedy from Devil Rays and a player to be named from Blue Jays, and Devil Rays acquired P Mark Hendrickson from Blue Jays (December 14, 2003); Rockies acquired P Sandy Nin to complete deal (December 15, 2003). ... On disabled list (May 11-June 8, 2004); included rehabilitation assignment to Dunedin. ... On disabled list (August 9-September 10, 2006).

CAREER HITTING: 3-for-17 (.176), 0 R, 2B, 0 3B, 0 HR, 0 RBI.

Year Team (League)	W	L	Pct.	ERA	WHIP	G	GS	CG	ShO	Hld.	Sv.-Opp.	IP	H	R	ER	HR	BB-IBB	SO	Avg.
1995— Will. (NYP)	2	1	.667	1.49	0.85	30	0	0	0	...	12-...	36.1	27	6	6	1	4-0	39	.203
1996— Daytona (Fla. St.)	2	4	.333	3.76	1.33	33	0	0	0	...	13-...	38.1	32	19	16	3	19-3	34	.225
— Orlando (South.)	4	1	.800	2.05	1.06	24	0	0	0	...	6-...	26.1	23	7	6	2	5-1	14	.228
1997— Orlando (South.)	6	5	.545	4.48	1.28	50	0	0	0	...	6-...	78.1	77	46	39	8	23-0	63	.260
— Iowa (Am. Assoc.)	2	0	1.000	0.00	0.49	9	0	0	0	...	1-...	12.1	5	0	0	0	1-0	9	.128
1998— Iowa (PCL)	3	3	.500	5.05	1.37	45	0	0	0	...	12-...	51.2	52	31	29	10	19-1	49	.261
— Chicago (N.L.)	0	0	...	13.50	2.25	1	0	0	0	0	0-0	1.1	2	2	2	0	1-0	2	.333
— Florida (N.L.)	0	3	.000	8.38	1.91	18	0	0	0	1	0-1	19.1	25	18	18	7	12-1	15	.325
1999— Richmond (Int'l)	2	4	.333	5.62	1.75	27	0	0	0	...	3-...	41.2	51	28	26	4	22-4	39	.293
— Atlanta (N.L.)	0	0	...	5.65	1.43	19	0	0	0	0	0-0	28.2	28	18	18	8	13-1	22	.248
2000— Buffalo (Int'l)	0	0	...	4.15	1.23	13	0	0	0	...	9-...	13.0	13	6	6	0	3-0	12	.255
— Cleveland (A.L.)	5	2	.714	3.29	1.24	47	0	0	0	6	0-1	68.1	57	27	25	9	28-3	69	.226
2001— Cleveland (A.L.)	2	0	1.000	6.97	1.55	12	0	0	0	0	0-0	20.2	24	16	16	5	8-0	15	.293
— Colorado (N.L.)	4	3	.571	3.70	1.05	42	0	0	0	4	0-1	56.0	47	24	23	8	12-3	47	.229
— Colo. Springs (PCL)	1	0	1.000	1.46	1.38	11	0	0	0	...	2-...	12.1	10	2	2	0	7-0	16	.227
2002— Colo. Springs (PCL)	2	0	1.000	3.86	1.64	12	0	0	0	...	2-...	14.0	20	7	6	2	3-1	14	.333
— Colorado (N.L.)	5	1	.833	4.33	1.12	63	0	0	0	18	1-4	62.1	51	31	30	9	19-4	47	.216
2003— Colorado (N.L.)	3	1	.750	4.05	1.31	72	0	0	0	12	9-12	73.1	73	37	33	11	23-6	66	.257
2004— Dunedin (Fla. St.)	0	0	...	4.50	1.50	2	0	0	0	...	0-...	2.0	3	1	1	1	0-0	2	.333
— Toronto (A.L.)	3	8	.273	3.91	1.25	62	0	0	0	7	7-11	69.0	61	32	30	8	25-6	52	.239
2005— Toronto (A.L.)	3	2	.600	2.57	0.95	65	0	0	0	11	0-4	66.2	48	20	19	10	15-2	56	.198
2006— Toronto (A.L.)	2	0	1.000	2.98	1.32	58	0	0	0	25	0-3	51.1	47	18	17	5	21-3	55	.235
American League totals (5 years)	15	12	.556	3.49	1.21	244	0	0	0	49	7-19	276.0	237	113	107	37	97-14	247	.230
National League totals (5 years)	12	8	.600	4.63	1.27	215	0	0	0	35	10-18	241.0	226	130	124	43	80-15	199	.245
Major League totals (9 years)	27	20	.574	4.02	1.24	459	0	0	0	84	17-37	517.0	463	243	231	80	177-29	446	.237

vs.	Avg.	AB	H	2B	3B	HR	RBI	BB	SO	OBP	Slg.	vs.	Avg.	AB	H	2B	3B	HR	RBI	BB	SO	OBP	Slg.
L	.183	71	13	1	1	3	12	6	23	.256	.352	R	.264	129	34	11	1	2	18	15	32	.340	.411

SPIEZIO, SCOTT — 3B/OF

PERSONAL: Born September 21, 1972, in Joliet, Ill. ... 6-2/220. ... Bats both, throws right. ... Full name: Scott Edward Spiezio. ... Name pronounced: SPEE-zee-oh. ... High school: Morris (Ill.). ... College: Illinois. ... Son of Ed Spiezio, third baseman with three major league teams (1964-72). **TRANSACTIONS/CAREER NOTES:** Selected by Oakland Athletics organization in sixth round of 1993 free-agent draft. ... On disabled list (June 8-25, 1997); included rehabilitation assignment to Southern Oregon. ... On disabled list (June 15-July 31, 1998); included rehabilitation assignment to Edmonton. ... Signed as a free agent by Anaheim Angels (January 11, 2000). ... Signed as a free agent by Seattle Mariners (December 19, 2003). ... On disabled list (March 28-April 17, 2004); included rehabilitation assignment to Inland Empire. ... On disabled list (April 19-July 1, 2005); included rehabilitation assignment to Tacoma. ... Released by Mariners (August 19, 2005). ... Signed by St. Louis Cardinals organization (February 17, 2006). **STATISTICAL NOTES:** Career major league grand slams: 5.

2006 GAMES PLAYED BY POSITION (MLB): 3B—38, OF—35, 1B—13, 2B—8, DH—5.

										BATTING								FIELDING	
Year	Team (League)	Pos.	G	AB	R	H	2B	3B	HR	RBI	BB	SO	HBP	GDP	SB-CS	Avg.	OBP	SLG	OPS	E	Avg.
1993—	S. Oregon (N'west)	1B-3B	31	125	32	41	10	2	3	19	16	18	0	1	0-1	.328	.404	.512	.916	9	.928
—	Modesto (California)	1B-3B	32	110	12	28	9	1	1	13	23	19	1	4	1-5	.255	.388	.382	.770	5	.949
1994—	Modesto (California)	1B-3B-SS	127	453	84	127	32	5	14	68	88	72	7	15	5-0	.280	.399	.466	.864	18	.951
1995—	Huntsville (Sou.)	1B-2B-3B	141	528	78	149	33	8	13	86	67	78	4	10	10-3	.282	.359	.449	.808	29	.935
1996—	Edmonton (PCL)	3B-1B-DH	140	523	87	137	30	4	20	91	56	66	4	5	6-5	.262	.335	.449	.784	15	.970
—	Oakland (A.L.)	3B-DH	9	29	6	9	2	0	2	8	4	4	0	0	0-1	.310	.394	.586	.980	2	.846
1997—	Oakland (A.L.)	2B-3B	147	538	58	131	28	4	14	65	44	75	1	13	9-3	.243	.300	.388	.688	7	.990
—	S. Oregon (N'west)	2B-DH	2	9	1	5	0	0	0	2	2	1	0	0	0-0	.556	.583	.556	1.139	1	.875
1998—	Oakland (A.L.)	2B-DH	114	406	54	105	19	1	9	50	44	56	2	10	1-3	.259	.333	.377	.710	13	.975
—	Edmonton (PCL)	2B-DH	5	13	3	3	1	0	1	4	3	2	0	0	0-0	.231	.375	.538	.913	1	.889
1999—	Oakland (A.L.)	2B-3B-1B DH	89	247	31	60	24	0	8	33	29	36	2	5	0-0	.243	.324	.437	.761	7	.976
—	Vancouver (PCL)	2B-3B-DH	28	105	27	41	7	1	6	27	15	16	2	3	0-0	.390	.475	.648	1.123	4	.969
2000—	Anaheim (A.L.)	DH-1B-3B OF-2B	123	297	47	72	11	2	17	49	40	56	3	5	1-2	.242	.334	.465	.799	3	.984
2001—	Anaheim (A.L.)	1B-DH-OF 3B	139	457	57	124	29	4	13	54	34	65	5	6	5-2	.271	.326	.438	.764	2	.998
2002—	Anaheim (A.L.)	2B	153	491	80	140	34	2	12	82	67	52	4	12	6-7	.285	.371	.436	.807	5	.996
2003—	Anaheim (A.L.)	1B-3B-OF	158	521	69	138	36	7	16	83	46	66	5	12	6-3	.265	.326	.453	.779	11	.988
2004—	Inland Empire (Calif.)	3B-DH	2	5	0	0	0	0	0	1	0	1	0	0	0-0	.000	.000	.000	.000	0	1.000
—	Seattle (A.L.)	3B-1B-DH	112	367	38	79	12	3	10	41	36	60	4	7	4-1	.215	.288	.346	.634	11	.977
2005—	Tacoma (PCL)	1B-DH-3B OF	14	58	11	19	3	1	2	9	1	9	1	2	0-0	.328	.333	.517	.851	0	1.000
—	Seattle (A.L.)	3B-DH-1B 2B	29	47	2	3	1	0	1	1	4	18	0	1	0-0	.064	.137	.149	.286	0	1.000
2006—	St. Louis (N.L.)	3B-OF-1B 2B-DH	119	276	44	75	15	4	13	52	37	66	5	1	1-0	.272	.366	.496	.862	5	.971
	American League totals (10 years)		1073	3400	442	861	196	23	102	466	348	488	26	71	32-22	.253	.324	.414	.739	61	.988
	National League totals (1 year)		119	276	44	75	15	4	13	52	37	66	5	1	1-0	.272	.366	.496	.862	5	.971
	Major League totals (11 years)		1192	3676	486	936	211	27	115	518	385	554	31	72	33-22	.255	.327	.421	.748	66	.988

DIVISION SERIES RECORD

Year	Team (League)	Pos.	G	AB	R	H	2B	3B	HR	RBI	BB	SO	HBP	GDP	SB-CS	Avg.	OBP	SLG	OPS	E	Avg.
2002—	Anaheim (A.L.)	1B	4	15	2	6	1	0	1	6	2	1	0	0	0-0	.400	.471	.667	1.137	0	1.000
2006—	St. Louis (N.L.)	3B	2	5	1	1	0	0	0	1	0	1	0	0	0-0	.200	.200	.200	.400	0	1.000
	Division series totals (2 years)		6	20	3	7	1	0	1	7	2	2	0	0	0-0	.350	.409	.550	.959	0	1.000

CHAMPIONSHIP SERIES RECORD

Year	Team (League)	Pos.	G	AB	R	H	2B	3B	HR	RBI	BB	SO	HBP	GDP	SB-CS	Avg.	OBP	SLG	OPS	E	Avg.
2002—	Anaheim (A.L.)	1B	5	17	5	6	2	0	1	5	2	5	0	1	1-0	.353	.421	.647	1.068	0	1.000
2006—	St. Louis (N.L.)	OF-3B	6	17	3	4	1	2	0	5	2	5	0	0	1-0	.235	.316	.529	.845	0	1.000
	Champ. series totals (2 years)		11	34	8	10	3	2	1	10	4	6	0	1	1-0	.294	.368	.588	.957	0	1.000

WORLD SERIES RECORD

Year	Team (League)	Pos.	G	AB	R	H	2B	3B	HR	RBI	BB	SO	HBP	GDP	SB-CS	Avg.	OBP	SLG	OPS	E	Avg.
2002—	Anaheim (A.L.)	1B	7	23	3	6	1	1	1	8	1	6	1	0	1-0	.261	.400	.522	.922	0	1.000
2006—	St. Louis (N.L.)	DH	2	4	0	0	0	0	0	0	1	1	0	0	0-0	.000	.200	.000	.200	0	...
	World series totals (2 years)		9	27	3	6	1	1	1	8	2	7	1	0	1-0	.222	.371	.444	.816	0	1.000

2006 LEFTY-RIGHTY SPLITS

vs.	Avg.	AB	H	2B	3B	HR	RBI	BB	SO	OBP	Slg.	vs.	Avg.	AB	H	2B	3B	HR	RBI	BB	SO	OBP	Slg.
L	.318	85	27	2	1	0	10	8	14	.372	.365	R	.251	191	48	13	3	13	42	29	52	.363	.555

SPILBORGHS, RYAN — OF

PERSONAL: Born September 5, 1979, in Santa Barbara, Calif. ... 6-1/190. ... Bats right, throws right. ... Full name: Ryan A. Spilborghs. ... College: Cal-Santa Barbara. **TRANSACTIONS/CAREER NOTES:** Selected by Colorado Rockies organization in seventh round of 2002 free-agent draft.

2006 GAMES PLAYED BY POSITION (MLB): OF—46, DH—1.

										BATTING								FIELDING	
Year	Team (League)	Pos.	G	AB	R	H	2B	3B	HR	RBI	BB	SO	HBP	GDP	SB-CS	Avg.	OBP	SLG	OPS	E	Avg.
2002—	Tri-Cities (NWL)		71	261	34	60	11	1	4	34	29	61	3	5	11-7	.230	.313	.326	.639	3	.977
2003—	Asheville (S. Atl.)	OF	119	434	78	122	22	2	15	61	63	96	8	4	10-11	.281	.379	.445	.824	4	.982
2004—	Visalia (Pion.)		125	444	59	115	26	3	8	57	64	98	6	13	8-6	.259	.357	.385	.742	...	...
2005—	Tulsa (Texas)	OF-DH	71	255	52	87	23	3	6	54	42	49	2	8	10-3	.341	.435	.525	.961	2	.991
—	Colorado (N.L.)	OF	1	4	0	2	0	0	0	1	0	1	0	0	0-0	.500	.500	.500	1.000	0	1.000
—	Colo. Springs (PCL)	OF	60	227	49	77	23	5	5	30	22	53	3	5	7-3	.339	.405	.551	.955	4	.979
2006—	Colo. Springs (PCL)		68	269	50	91	20	1	5	34	30	49	1	10	8-2	.338	.400	.476	.876	3	.979
—	Colorado (N.L.)	OF-DH	67	167	26	48	6	3	4	21	14	30	0	7	5-2	.287	.337	.431	.768	1	.988
	Major League totals (2 years)		68	171	26	50	6	3	4	22	14	31	0	7	5-2	.292	.340	.433	.773	1	.989

2006 LEFTY-RIGHTY SPLITS

vs.	Avg.	AB	H	2B	3B	HR	RBI	BB	SO	OBP	Slg.	vs.	Avg.	AB	H	2B	3B	HR	RBI	BB	SO	OBP	Slg.
L	.323	62	20	3	0	1	6	5	9	.362	.419	R	.267	105	28	3	3	3	15	9	21	.322	.438

S

SPRINGER, RUSS — P

PERSONAL: Born November 7, 1968, in Alexandria, La. ... 6-4/211. ... Throws right, bats right. ... Full name: Russell Paul Springer. ... High school: Grant (Dry Prong, La.). ... College: Louisiana State. **TRANSACTIONS/CAREER NOTES:** Selected by New York Yankees organization in seventh round of 1989 free-agent draft. ... Traded by Yankees with 1B J.T. Snow and P Jerry Nielsen to California Angels for P Jim Abbott (December 6, 1992). ... On disabled list (August 2, 1993-remainder of season). ... Traded by Angels to Philadelphia Phillies (August 15, 1995), completing deal in which Phillies traded OF Dave Gallagher to Angels for 2B Kevin Flora and a player to be named (August 9, 1995). ... Released by Phillies (December 20, 1996). ... Signed by Houston Astros organization (December 30, 1996). ... On disabled list (June 17-July 10, 1997); included rehabilitation assignment to Jackson. ... Selected by Arizona Diamondbacks in third round (61st pick overall) of expansion draft (November 18, 1997). ... Traded by Diamondbacks to Atlanta Braves for P Alan Embree (June 23, 1998). ... On disabled list (April 3-May 17, 1999); included rehabilitation assignment to Richmond. ... Signed as a free agent by Diamondbacks (December 3, 1999). ... On disabled list (May 23, 2001-remainder of season); included rehabilitation assignment to Tucson. ... Signed as a free agent by St. Louis Cardinals organization (December 19, 2002). ... On disabled list (May 1-August 30, 2003); included rehabilitation assignment to Memphis. ... Signed as a free agent by Astros organization (June 19, 2004). ... On suspended list (May 19-23, 2006).

CAREER HITTING: 2-for-26 (.077), 1 R, 0 2B, 0 3B, 0 HR, 0 RBI.

Year Team (League)	W	L	Pct.	ERA	WHIP	G	GS	CG	ShO	Hld.	Sv.-Opp.	IP	H	R	ER	HR	BB-IBB	SO	Avg.
1989— GC Yankees (GCL)	3	0	1.000	1.50	1.00	6	6	0	0	...	0-...	24.0	14	8	4	0	10-0	34	.167
1990— GC Yankees (GCL)	0	2	.000	1.20	0.93	4	4	0	0	...	0-...	15.0	10	6	2	0	4-0	17	.172
— Greensboro (S. Atl.)	2	3	.400	3.67	1.46	10	10	0	0	...	0-...	56.1	51	33	23	3	31-0	51	.236
1991— Fort Laud. (FSL)	5	9	.357	3.49	1.18	25	25	2	0	...	0-...	152.1	118	68	59	9	62-1	139	.213
— Alb./Colon. (East.)	1	0	1.000	1.80	1.00	2	2	0	0	...	0-...	15.0	9	4	3	0	6-1	16	.167
1992— Columbus (Int'l)	8	5	.615	2.69	1.16	20	20	1	0	...	0-...	123.2	89	46	37	11	54-0	95	.204
— New York (A.L.)	0	0	...	6.19	1.75	14	0	0	0	...	2	0-0	16.0	18	11	11	0	10-0	12	.281
1993— Vancouver (PCL)	5	4	.556	4.27	1.54	11	9	1	0	...	0-...	59.0	58	37	28	5	33-1	40	.250
— California (A.L.)	1	6	.143	7.20	1.75	14	9	1	0	0	0-0	60.0	73	48	48	11	32-1	31	.303
1994— Vancouver (PCL)	7	4	.636	3.04	1.16	12	12	4	0	...	0-...	83.0	77	35	28	7	19-0	58	.242
— California (A.L.)	2	2	.500	5.52	1.47	18	5	0	0	1	2-3	45.2	53	28	28	9	14-0	28	.290
1995— California (A.L.)	1	2	.333	6.10	1.65	19	6	0	0	0	1-2	51.2	60	37	35	11	25-1	38	.290
— Vancouver (PCL)	2	0	1.000	3.44	1.38	6	6	0	0	...	0-...	34.0	24	16	13	3	23-0	23	.227
— Philadelphia (N.L.)	0	0	...	3.71	1.20	14	0	0	0	0	0-0	26.2	22	11	11	5	10-3	32	.227
1996— Philadelphia (N.L.)	3	10	.231	4.66	1.49	51	7	0	0	6	0-3	96.2	106	60	50	12	38-6	94	.272
1997— Houston (N.L.)	3	3	.500	4.23	1.36	54	0	0	0	9	3-7	55.1	48	28	26	4	27-2	74	.232
— Jackson (Texas)	0	0	...	9.00	2.00	1	0	0	0	...	0-...	1.0	2	1	1	0	0-0	2	.400
1998— Arizona (N.L.)	4	3	.571	4.13	1.32	26	0	0	0	1	0-3	32.2	29	16	15	4	14-1	37	.232
— Atlanta (N.L.)	1	1	.500	4.05	1.90	22	0	0	0	6	0-1	20.0	22	10	9	0	16-3	19	.301
1999— Richmond (Int'l)	1	0	1.000	1.17	0.65	11	0	0	0	...	2-...	15.1	9	2	2	0	1-0	13	.170
— Atlanta (N.L.)	2	1	.667	3.42	1.12	49	0	0	0	8	1-1	47.1	31	20	18	5	22-2	49	.185
2000— Arizona (N.L.)	2	4	.333	5.08	1.56	52	0	0	0	3	0-2	62.0	63	36	35	11	34-6	59	.261
2001— Arizona (N.L.)	0	0	...	7.13	1.36	18	0	0	0	2	1-1	17.2	20	16	14	5	4-0	12	.274
— Tucson (PCL)	0	0	...	4.91	1.36	7	3	0	0	...	0-...	7.1	7	4	4	1	3-0	6	.241
2002—			Did not play.																
2003— Memphis (PCL)	0	0	...	1.42	0.90	7	0	0	0	...	0-...	6.1	2	1	1	1	4-0	5	.105
— St. Louis (N.L.)	1	1	.500	8.31	1.44	17	0	0	0	5	0-1	17.1	19	16	16	8	6-0	11	.271
2004— New Orleans (PCL)	1	2	.333	3.48	1.45	26	0	0	0	...	6-...	31.0	31	13	12	3	14-3	33	.263
— Houston (N.L.)	0	1	.000	2.63	1.54	16	0	0	0	5	0-0	13.2	15	4	4	1	6-0	9	.278
2005— Houston (N.L.)	4	4	.500	4.73	1.19	62	0	0	0	10	0-3	59.0	49	34	31	4	21-3	54	.222
2006— Houston (N.L.)	1	1	.500	3.47	1.04	72	0	0	0	9	0-0	59.2	46	23	23	10	16-1	46	.211
American League totals (4 years)	4	10	.286	6.33	1.64	65	20	1	0	3	3-5	173.1	204	124	122	31	81-2	109	.294
National League totals (11 years)	21	29	.420	4.46	1.35	453	7	0	0	64	5-22	508.0	470	274	252	74	214-27	496	.243
Major League totals (14 years)	25	39	.391	4.94	1.42	518	27	1	0	67	8-27	681.1	674	398	374	105	295-29	605	.256

DIVISION SERIES RECORD

Year Team (League)	W	L	Pct.	ERA	WHIP	G	GS	CG	ShO	Hld.	Sv.-Opp.	IP	H	R	ER	HR	BB-IBB	SO	Avg.
1997— Houston (N.L.)	0	0	...	5.40	1.80	2	0	0	0	0	0-0	1.2	2	1	1	0	1-0	3	.286
1998— Atlanta (N.L.)			Did not play.																
1999— Atlanta (N.L.)	0	0	...	0.00	3.00	1	0	0	0	0	0-0	1.0	2	0	0	0	1-0	1	.400
2004— Houston (N.L.)	0	1	.000	18.00	2.00	2	0	0	0	0	0-0	2.0	3	4	4	1	1-0	5	.333
2005— Houston (N.L.)	0	0	...	3.86	2.57	2	0	0	0	0	0-0	2.1	5	1	1	0	1-0	1	.556
Division series totals (4 years)	0	1	.000	7.71	2.29	7	0	0	0	0	0-0	7.0	12	6	6	1	4-0	10	.400

CHAMPIONSHIP SERIES RECORD

Year Team (League)	W	L	Pct.	ERA	WHIP	G	GS	CG	ShO	Hld.	Sv.-Opp.	IP	H	R	ER	HR	BB-IBB	SO	Avg.
1998— Atlanta (N.L.)			Did not play.																
1999— Atlanta (N.L.)	1	0	1.000	0.00	0.50	2	0	0	0	0	0-0	2.0	0	0	0	0	1-0	1	.000
2005— Houston (N.L.)	0	0	...	0.00	1.00	1	0	0	0	0	0-0	1.0	0	0	0	0	1-0	1	.000
Champ. series totals (2 years)	1	0	1.000	0.00	0.67	3	0	0	0	0	0-0	3.0	0	0	0	0	2-0	2	.000

WORLD SERIES RECORD

Year Team (League)	W	L	Pct.	ERA	WHIP	G	GS	CG	ShO	Hld.	Sv.-Opp.	IP	H	R	ER	HR	BB-IBB	SO	Avg.
1999— Atlanta (N.L.)	0	0	...	0.00	0.43	2	0	0	0	0	0-0	2.1	1	0	0	0	0-0	1	.125
2005— Houston (N.L.)	0	0	...	4.50	1.00	2	0	0	0	0	0-0	2.0	2	1	1	0	0-0	1	.250
World series totals (2 years)	0	0	...	2.08	0.69	4	0	0	0	0	0-0	4.1	3	1	1	0	0-0	2	.188

2006 LEFTY-RIGHTY SPLITS

vs.	Avg.	AB	H	2B	3B	HR	RBI	BB	SO	OBP	Slg.	vs.	Avg.	AB	H	2B	3B	HR	RBI	BB	SO	OBP	Slg.
L	.253	79	20	3	2	5	16	6	13	.314	.532	R	.187	139	26	3	0	5	15	10	33	.257	.317

SPURLING, CHRIS — P

PERSONAL: Born June 28, 1977, in Dayton, Ohio. ... 6-5/230. ... Throws right, bats right. ... Full name: Christopher Michael Spurling. ... High school: Northridge (Johnstown, Ohio). ... Junior college: Sinclair (Ohio) C.C. **TRANSACTIONS/CAREER NOTES:** Selected by New York Yankees organization in 41st round of 1997 free-agent draft. ... Traded by Yankees to Pittsburgh Pirates for IF Luis Sojo (August 7, 2000). ... Selected by Atlanta Braves from Pirates organization in Rule 5 major league draft (December 16, 2002). ... Traded by Braves to Detroit Tigers for P Matt Coenen (March 25, 2003). ... On disabled list (April 2, 2004-entire season). ... Claimed on waivers by Milwaukee Brewers (September 8, 2006).

CAREER HITTING: 0-for-0 (.000), 0 R, 0 2B, 0 3B, 0 HR, 0 RBI.

Year Team (League)	W	L	Pct.	ERA	WHIP	G	GS	CG	ShO	Hld.	Sv.-Opp.	IP	H	R	ER	HR	BB-IBB	SO	Avg.
1998— GC Yankees (GCL)	2	1	.667	2.28	1.32	13	6	0	0	...	1-...	51.1	57	21	13	3	11-0	44	.279
— Greensboro (S. Atl.)	1	0	1.000	3.00	1.33	1	1	0	0	...	0-...	6.0	7	2	2	1	1-0	5	.292
1999— Greensboro (S. Atl.)	4	6	.400	3.66	1.32	49	0	0	0	...	4-...	76.1	78	34	31	8	23-3	68	.265
2000— Lynchburg (Caro.)	1	0	1.000	0.98	0.60	9	0	0	0	...	5-...	18.1	8	2	2	1	3-0	17	.129
— Tampa (Fla. St.)	4	6	.400	3.79	1.26	34	0	0	0	...	1-...	57.0	50	27	24	1	22-5	55	.237

Year Team (League)	W	L	Pct.	ERA	WHIP	G	GS	CG	ShO	Hld.	Sv.-Opp.	IP	H	R	ER	HR	BB-IBB	SO	Avg.
2001—Altoona (East.)	5	7	.417	3.11	1.32	34	15	0	0	...	1-...	121.2	133	48	42	9	28-1	63	.279
2002—Altoona (East.)	4	3	.571	2.19	0.94	51	0	0	0	...	20-...	70.0	54	18	17	8	12-1	60	.210
2003—Detroit (A.L.)	1	3	.250	4.68	1.30	66	0	0	0	5	3-6	77.0	78	42	40	9	22-1	38	.266
2004—								Did not play											
2005—Toledo (Int'l)	2	1	.667	4.12	1.07	12	0	0	0	2	1-2	19.2	18	10	9	2	3-0	15	.243
—Detroit (A.L.)	3	4	.429	3.44	1.13	56	0	0	0	11	0-1	70.2	58	30	27	8	22-6	26	.230
2006—Toledo (Int'l)	1	4	.200	2.05	1.08	49	0	0	0	16	5-9	66.0	61	20	15	4	10-4	34	.254
—Detroit (A.L.)	0	0	...	3.18	1.50	9	0	0	0	0	0-0	11.1	13	4	4	2	4-2	4	.289
—Milwaukee (N.L.)	0	0	...	7.20	1.60	7	0	0	0	0	0-1	10.0	12	8	8	3	4-1	3	.286
American League totals (3 years)	4	7	.364	4.02	1.24	131	0	0	0	16	3-7	159.0	149	76	71	19	48-9	68	.253
National League totals (1 year)	0	0	...	7.20	1.60	7	0	0	0	0	0-1	10.0	12	8	8	3	4-1	3	.286
Major League totals (3 years)	4	7	.364	4.21	1.26	138	0	0	0	16	3-8	169.0	161	84	79	22	52-10	71	.255

2006 LEFTY-RIGHTY SPLITS

vs.	Avg.	AB	H	2B	3B	HR	RBI	BB	SO	OBP	Slg.	vs.	Avg.	AB	H	2B	3B	HR	RBI	BB	SO	OBP	Slg.
L	.263	38	10	2	0	2	6	6	2	.364	.474	R	.306	49	15	3	0	3	11	2	5	.333	.551

STAIRS, MATT — OF/DH

PERSONAL: Born February 27, 1968, in Saint John, New Brunswick. ... 5-9/210. ... Bats left, throws right. ... Full name: Matthew Wade Stairs. ... High school: Fredericton (New Brunswick). **TRANSACTIONS/CAREER NOTES:** Signed as a non-drafted free agent by Montreal Expos organization (January 17, 1989). ... Contract sold by Expos to Chunichi Dragons of the Japan Central League (June 8, 1993). ... Signed as a free agent by Expos organization (December 15, 1993). ... Traded by Expos with P Pete Young to Boston Red Sox for cash (February 18, 1994). ... Signed as a free agent by Oakland Athletics organization (December 1, 1995). ... Traded by A's to Chicago Cubs for P Eric Ireland (November 20, 2000). ... Signed as a free agent by Milwaukee Brewers (January 25, 2002). ... On disabled list (May 16-June 3, 2002). ... Signed as a free agent by Pittsburgh Pirates organization (December 18, 2002). ... On disabled list (May 19-June 10, 2003); included rehabilitation assignment to Nashville. ... Signed as a free agent by Kansas City Royals (December 9, 2003). ... On disabled list (August 7-22, 2004). ... Traded by Royals to Texas Rangers for P Jose Diaz (July 31, 2006). ... Claimed on waivers by Detroit Tigers (September 15, 2006). **STATISTICAL NOTES:** Career major league grand slams: 9. **MISCELLANEOUS NOTES:** Member of 1988 Canadian Olympic baseball team.

2006 GAMES PLAYED BY POSITION (MLB): DH—87, 1B—12, OF—3.

Year Team (League)	Pos.	G	AB	R	H	2B	3B	HR	RBI	BB	SO	HBP	GDP	SB-CS	Avg.	OBP	SLG	OPS	E	Avg.
1989—W.P. Beach (FSL)	2B-3B-SS	36	111	12	21	3	1	1	9	9	18	0	3	0-0	.189	.248	.261	.509	4	.956
—Jamestown (NYP)	2B-3B	14	43	8	11	1	0	1	5	3	5	0	0	1-2	.256	.304	.349	.653	6	.893
—Rockford (Midwest)	3B	44	141	20	40	9	2	2	14	15	29	2	4	5-4	.284	.358	.418	.777	7	.929
1990—W.P. Beach (FSL)	2B-3B	55	183	30	62	9	3	3	30	41	19	5	5	15-2	.339	.468	.470	.937	17	.899
—Jacksonville (Sou.)	2B-3B-OF-SS	79	280	26	71	17	0	3	34	22	43	3	6	5-3	.254	.310	.346	.656	22	.893
1991—Harrisburg (East.)	2B-3B-OF	129	505	87	168	30	10	13	78	66	47	3	14	23-11	.333	.411	.509	.920	22	.958
1992—Indianapolis (A.A.)	OF	110	401	57	107	23	4	11	56	49	61	4	10	11-11	.267	.351	.426	.777	3	.985
—Montreal (N.L.)	OF	13	30	2	5	0	0	0	7	7	7	0	0	0-0	.167	.316	.233	.549	1	.933
1993—Ottawa (Int'l)	OF	34	125	16	35	4	2	3	20	11	15	2	4	4-1	.280	.348	.416	.764	0	1.000
—Montreal (N.L.)	OF	6	8	1	3	1	0	0	1	1	0	0	0	0-0	.375	.375	.500	.875	0	1.000
—Chunichi (Jp. Cn.)		60	132	10	33	6	0	6	23	7	34	...	...	1-...	.250		.432			
1994—New Britain (East.)	OF-DH-1B	93	317	64	98	25	2	9	61	53	38	3	10	10-7	.309	.407	.486	.893	3	.975
1995—Pawtucket (Int'l)	OF-DH	75	271	40	77	17	0	13	56	29	41	1	3	3-3	.284	.352	.491	.843	0	1.000
—Boston (A.L.)	OF-DH	39	88	8	23	7	1	1	17	4	14	1	4	0-1	.261	.298	.398	.696	2	.913
1996—Oakland (A.L.)	OF-DH-1B	61	137	21	38	5	1	10	23	19	23	1	2	1-1	.277	.367	.547	.915	1	.987
—Edmonton (PCL)	DH-OF-1B	51	180	35	62	16	1	8	41	21	34	0	4	0-0	.344	.401	.578	.979	3	.944
1997—Oakland (A.L.)	OF-DH-1B	133	352	62	105	19	0	27	73	50	60	3	2	3-2	.298	.386	.582	.969	4	.974
1998—Oakland (A.L.)	DH-OF-1B	149	523	88	154	33	1	26	106	59	93	6	13	8-3	.294	.370	.511	.880	1	1.000
1999—Oakland (A.L.)	OF-DH-1B	146	531	94	137	26	3	38	102	89	124	4	8	2-7	.258	.366	.533	.899	4	.981
2000—Oakland (A.L.)	OF-DH-1B	143	476	74	108	26	0	21	81	78	122	1	5	2-5	.227	.333	.414	.747	4	.980
2001—Chicago (N.L.)	1B-OF-DH-2B	128	340	48	85	21	0	17	61	52	76	7	4	2-3	.250	.358	.462	.820	4	.993
2002—Milwaukee (N.L.)	OF	107	270	41	66	15	0	16	41	36	50	8	7	2-0	.244	.349	.478	.827	1	.993
2003—Nashville (PCL)	OF-1B-DH	7	18	3	3	0	0	2	3	7	2	2	1	0-0	.167	.444	.500	.944	0	1.000
—Pittsburgh (N.L.)	OF-1B-DH	121	305	49	89	20	1	20	57	45	64	5	7	0-1	.292	.389	.561	.950	3	.990
2004—Kansas City (A.L.)	OF-1B-DH	126	439	48	117	21	3	18	66	49	92	5	15	1-0	.267	.345	.451	.796	5	.986
2005—Kansas City (A.L.)	1B-DH-OF	127	396	55	109	26	1	13	66	60	69	5	9	1-2	.275	.373	.444	.818	4	.993
2006—Kansas City (A.L.)	DH-1B-OF	77	226	31	59	11	0	8	32	31	52	1	0	0-0	.261	.352	.429	.782	0	1.000
—Texas (A.L.)	DH-1B-OF	26	81	16	17	4	0	3	11	6	22	1	1	0-0	.210	.273	.370	.643	0	1.000
—Detroit (A.L.)	DH	14	41	5	10	3	0	2	8	3	12	0	1	0-0	.244	.295	.463	.759	0	...
American League totals (9 years)		1041	3290	492	877	184	10	167	585	448	683	27	71	21-18	.267	.357	.481	.837	25	.986
National League totals (5 years)		375	953	141	248	59	1	53	166	140	198	20	19	4-4	.260	.364	.491	.855	9	.991
Major League totals (14 years)		1416	4243	633	1125	243	11	220	751	588	881	47	90	25-22	.265	.358	.483	.841	34	.988

DIVISION SERIES RECORD

Year Team (League)	Pos.	G	AB	R	H	2B	3B	HR	RBI	BB	SO	HBP	GDP	SB-CS	Avg.	OBP	SLG	OPS	E	Avg.
1995—Boston (A.L.)		1	1	0	0	0	0	0	0	0	1	0	0	0-0	.000	.000	.000	.000		...
2000—Oakland (A.L.)	OF	3	9	0	1	1	0	0	0	0	1	0	0	0-0	.111	.111	.222	.333	0	1.000
Division series totals (2 years)		4	10	0	1	1	0	0	0	0	2	0	0	0-0	.100	.100	.200	.300	0	1.000

2006 LEFTY-RIGHTY SPLITS

vs.	Avg.	AB	H	2B	3B	HR	RBI	BB	SO	OBP	Slg.	vs.	Avg.	AB	H	2B	3B	HR	RBI	BB	SO	OBP	Slg.
L	.217	46	10	2	0	1	6	2	13	.265	.326	R	.252	302	76	19	0	12	45	38	73	.337	.434

STANDRIDGE, JASON — P

PERSONAL: Born November 9, 1978, in Birmingham, Ala. ... 6-4/230. ... Throws right, bats right. ... Full name: Jason Wayne Standridge. ... High school: Hewitt-Trussville (Ala.). **TRANSACTIONS/CAREER NOTES:** Selected by Tampa Bay Devil Rays organization in first round (31st pick overall) of 1997 free-agent draft. ... On disabled list (March 24-May 19, 2004); included rehabilitation assignments to Montgomery and Durham. ... Signed as a free agent by Texas Rangers organization (November 19, 2004). ... Signed as a free agent by Cincinnati Reds organization (July 1, 2005). ... On disabled list (August 7-September 1, 2006); included rehabilitation assignment to Louisville. ... Released by Reds (November 10, 2006).

CAREER HITTING: 0-for-0 (.000), 0 R, 0 2B, 0 3B, 0 HR, 0 RBI.

Year Team (League)	W	L	Pct.	ERA	WHIP	G	GS	CG	ShO	Hld.	Sv.-Opp.	IP	H	R	ER	HR	BB-IBB	SO	Avg.
1997—GC Devil Rays (GCL)	0	6	.000	3.59	1.20	13	13	0	.0	0	0-...	57.2	56	30	23	3	13-1	55	.250

Year Team (League)	W	L	Pct.	ERA	WHIP	G	GS	CG	ShO	Hld.	Sv.-Opp.	IP	H	R	ER	HR	BB-IBB	SO	Avg.
1998—Princeton (Appal.)	4	4	.500	7.00	1.75	12	12	0	0	...	0-...	63.0	82	61	49	4	28-0	47	.314
1999—Char., S.C. (SAL)	9	1	.900	2.02	0.96	18	18	3	3	...	0-...	116.0	80	35	26	5	31-1	84	.197
—St. Pete. (FSL)	4	4	.500	3.91	1.43	8	8	0	0	...	0-...	48.1	49	21	21	0	20-0	26	.268
2000—St. Pete. (FSL)	2	4	.333	3.38	1.36	10	10	1	0	...	0-...	56.0	45	28	21	4	31-0	41	.214
—Orlando (South.)	6	8	.429	3.62	1.32	17	17	2	0	...	0-...	97.0	85	46	39	4	43-0	55	.237
2001—Durham (Int'l)	5	10	.333	5.28	1.76	20	20	0	0	...	0-...	102.1	130	73	60	13	50-0	48	.315
—Tampa Bay (A.L.)	0	0	...	4.66	1.71	9	1	0	0	0	0-0	19.1	19	10	10	5	14-1	9	.260
—Orlando (South.)	0	2	.000	5.59	1.66	2	2	0	0	0	0-0	9.2	12	6	6	0	4-0	7	.300
2002—Durham (Int'l)	10	9	.526	3.12	1.34	29	29	0	0	...	0-...	173.0	168	71	60	12	64-1	111	.259
—Tampa Bay (A.L.)	0	0	...	9.00	3.67	1	0	0	0	0	0-0	3.0	7	3	3	1	4-0	1	.500
2003—Tampa Bay (A.L.)	0	5	.000	6.37	1.53	8	7	1	0	0	0-0	35.1	38	25	25	7	16-0	20	.275
—Durham (Int'l)	2	4	.333	4.50	1.50	12	10	0	0	0	1-...	60.0	62	32	30	5	28-0	37	.270
2004—Montgom. (Sou.)	1	0	1.000	3.60	1.70	2	2	0	0	0	0-...	10.0	13	4	4	1	4-0	8	.361
—Tampa Bay (A.L.)	0	0	...	9.00	1.80	3	1	0	0	0	0-0	10.0	14	10	10	5	4-0	7	.326
—Durham (Int'l)	8	4	.667	3.85	1.37	20	20	2	0	...	0-...	119.1	120	56	51	7	44-0	76	.265
2005—Oklahoma (PCL)	5	3	.625	4.50	1.57	15	10	0	0	...	0-...	76.0	83	41	38	3	36-0	47	.288
—Texas (A.L.)	0	0	...	11.57	3.43	2	0	0	0	0	0-0	2.1	7	3	3	0	1-1	2	.467
—Louisville (Int'l)	0	0	...	16.20	2.40	2	0	0	0	0	0-0	1.2	3	3	3	0	1-0	4	.375
—Cincinnati (N.L.)	2	2	.500	4.06	1.74	32	0	0	0	5	0-0	31.0	38	14	14	3	16-7	17	.314
2006—Louisville (Int'l)	2	2	.500	2.93	1.20	37	0	0	0	7	0-2	46.0	40	16	15	2	15-1	43	.233
—Cincinnati (N.L.)	1	1	.500	4.82	1.66	21	0	0	0	1	0-0	18.2	17	14	10	2	14-0	18	.243
American League totals (5 years)	0	5	.000	6.56	1.77	23	9	1	0	0	0-0	70.0	85	51	51	18	39-2	39	.300
National League totals (2 years)	3	3	.500	4.35	1.71	53	0	0	0	6	0-0	49.2	55	28	24	5	30-7	35	.288
Major League totals (6 years)	3	8	.273	5.64	1.75	76	9	1	0	6	0-0	119.2	140	79	75	23	69-9	74	.295

2006 LEFTY-RIGHTY SPLITS

vs.	Avg.	AB	H	2B	3B	HR	RBI	BB	SO	OBP	Slg.	vs.	Avg.	AB	H	2B	3B	HR	RBI	BB	SO	OBP	Slg.
L	.200	25	5	0	0	1	3	5	8	.355	.320	R	.267	45	12	2	0	1	4	9	10	.389	.378

S STANTON, MIKE — P

PERSONAL: Born June 2, 1967, in Houston. ... 6-1/215. ... Throws left, bats left. ... Full name: William Michael Stanton. ... High school: Midland (Texas). ... Junior college: Alvin (Texas) C.C. **TRANSACTIONS/CAREER NOTES:** Selected by Atlanta Braves organization in 13th round of 1987 free-agent draft. ... On disabled list (April 27, 1990-remainder of season); included rehabilitation assignments to Greenville. ... Traded by Braves with a player to be named to Boston Red Sox for two players to be named (July 31, 1995); Red Sox acquired P Matt Murray and Braves acquired OF Marc Lewis and P Mike Jacobs to complete deal (August 31, 1995). ... Traded by Red Sox to Texas Rangers for Ps Mark Brandenburg and Kerry Lacy (July 31, 1996). ... Signed as a free agent by New York Yankees (December 11, 1996). ... On suspended list (July 3-10, 1998). ... Signed as a free agent by New York Mets (December 16, 2002). ... On disabled list (May 22-June 6 and June 11-July 13, 2003); included rehabilitation assignments to Binghamton and Brooklyn. ... Traded by Mets with cash to Yankees for P Felix Heredia (December 3, 2004). ... Released by Yankees (July 11, 2005). ... Signed by Washington Nationals (July 13, 2005). ... Traded by Nationals to Boston Red Sox for Ps Rhys Taylor and Yader Peralta (September 29, 2005). ... Signed as a free agent by Nationals (December 24, 2005). ... Traded by Nationals to San Francisco Giants for P Shairon Martis (July 28, 2006).
CAREER HITTING: 8-for-22 (.364), 3 R, 1 2B, 0 3B, 0 HR, 3 RBI.

Year Team (League)	W	L	Pct.	ERA	WHIP	G	GS	CG	ShO	Hld.	Sv.-Opp.	IP	H	R	ER	HR	BB-IBB	SO	Avg.
1987—Pulaski (Appalachian)	4	8	.333	3.24	1.27	15	13	3	2	...	0-...	83.1	64	37	30	7	42-0	82	.212
1988—Burlington (Midw.)	11	5	.688	3.62	1.45	30	23	1	1	...	0-...	154.0	154	86	62	7	69-2	160	.258
—Durham (Carol.)	1	0	1.000	1.46	1.54	2	2	1	1	...	0-...	12.1	14	3	2	0	5-0	14	.280
1989—Greenville (Sou.)	4	1	.800	1.58	1.23	47	0	0	0	...	19-...	51.1	32	10	9	1	31-3	58	.189
—Richmond (Int'l)	2	0	1.000	0.00	0.95	13	0	0	0	...	8-...	20.0	6	0	0	0	13-2	20	.097
—Atlanta (N.L.)	0	1	.000	1.50	1.04	20	0	0	0	2	7-8	24.0	17	4	4	0	8-1	27	.207
1990—Atlanta (N.L.)	0	3	.000	18.00	2.86	7	0	0	0	0	2-3	7.0	16	16	14	1	4-2	7	.444
—Greenville (Sou.)	0	1	.000	1.59	1.76	4	4	0	0	0	0-...	5.2	7	1	1	0	3-0	4	.292
1991—Atlanta (N.L.)	5	5	.500	2.88	1.06	74	0	0	0	15	7-10	78.0	62	27	25	6	21-6	54	.217
1992—Atlanta (N.L.)	5	4	.556	4.10	1.24	65	0	0	0	15	8-11	63.2	59	32	29	6	20-2	44	.247
1993—Atlanta (N.L.)	4	6	.400	4.67	1.54	63	0	0	0	5	27-33	52.0	51	35	27	4	29-7	43	.255
1994—Atlanta (N.L.)	3	1	.750	3.55	1.47	49	0	0	0	10	3-4	45.2	41	18	18	2	26-3	35	.248
1995—Atlanta (N.L.)	1	1	.500	5.59	1.91	26	0	0	0	4	1-2	19.1	31	14	12	3	6-2	13	.369
—Boston (A.L.)	1	0	1.000	3.00	1.19	22	0	0	0	0	0-1	21.0	17	9	7	3	8-0	10	.224
1996—Boston (A.L.)	4	3	.571	3.83	1.44	59	0	0	0	15	1-5	56.1	58	24	24	9	23-4	46	.275
—Texas (A.L.)	0	1	.000	3.22	1.07	22	0	0	0	7	0-1	22.1	20	8	8	2	4-1	14	.241
1997—New York (A.L.)	6	1	.857	2.57	1.26	64	0	0	0	26	3-5	66.2	50	19	19	3	34-2	70	.205
1998—New York (A.L.)	4	1	.800	5.47	1.23	67	0	0	0	18	6-10	79.0	71	51	48	13	26-1	69	.239
1999—New York (A.L.)	2	2	.500	4.33	1.43	73	1	0	0	21	0-5	62.1	71	30	30	5	18-4	59	.289
2000—New York (A.L.)	2	3	.400	4.10	1.35	69	0	0	0	15	0-4	68.0	68	32	31	5	24-2	75	.263
2001—New York (A.L.)	9	4	.692	2.58	1.36	76	0	0	0	23	0-1	80.1	80	25	23	4	29-9	78	.263
2002—New York (A.L.)	7	1	.875	3.00	1.29	79	0	0	0	17	6-9	78.0	73	29	26	4	28-3	44	.256
2003—Binghamton (East.)	0	1	.000	9.00	6.00	1	1	0	0	...	0-...	1.0	6	3	1	0	0-0	1	.750
—Brook.. (N.Y.-Penn.)	0	0	...	0.00	0.50	1	1	0	0	0	0-...	1.0	2	1	0	0	0-0	1	.167
—New York (N.L.)	2	7	.222	4.57	1.24	50	0	0	0	10	5-7	45.1	37	25	23	6	19-4	34	.219
2004—New York (N.L.)	2	6	.250	3.16	1.34	83	0	0	0	25	0-6	77.0	70	32	27	6	33-6	58	.237
2005—New York (N.L.)	1	2	.333	7.07	1.64	28	0	0	0	4	0-0	14.0	17	11	11	1	6-0	12	.298
—Wash. (N.L.)	2	1	.667	3.58	1.45	30	0	0	0	5	0-1	27.2	31	13	11	2	9-4	14	.292
—Boston (A.L.)	0	0	...	0.00	1.00	1	0	0	0	0	0-0	1.0	1	0	0	0	1-0	0	.333
2006—Wash. (N.L.)	3	5	.375	4.47	1.53	56	0	0	0	10	0-3	44.1	47	22	22	1	21-11	30	.278
—San Francisco (N.L.)	4	2	.667	3.09	1.24	26	0	0	0	5	8-11	23.1	23	8	8	1	6-0	18	.267
American League totals (9 years)	36	18	.667	3.72	1.32	560	1	0	0	150	16-41	549.0	526	230	227	49	200-26	478	.255
National League totals (11 years)	31	42	.425	3.90	1.35	549	0	0	0	106	68-99	507.1	485	246	220	38	202-48	377	.253
Major League totals (18 years)	67	60	.528	3.81	1.34	1109	1	0	0	256	84-140	1056.1	1011	484	447	87	402-74	855	.254

DIVISION SERIES RECORD

Year Team (League)	W	L	Pct.	ERA	WHIP	G	GS	CG	ShO	Hld.	Sv.-Opp.	IP	H	R	ER	HR	BB-IBB	SO	Avg.
1995—Boston (A.L.)	0	0	...	0.00	0.43	1	0	0	0	0	0-0	2.1	1	0	0	0	0-0	4	.125
1996—Texas (A.L.)	0	1	.000	2.70	1.50	3	0	0	0	0	0-0	3.1	2	2	1	1	3-0	3	.200
1997—New York (A.L.)	0	0	...	0.00	2.00	3	0	0	0	1	0-0	1.0	1	0	0	0	1-0	3	.250
1998—New York (A.L.)	Did not play.																		
1999—New York (A.L.)	Did not play.																		
2000—New York (A.L.)	1	0	1.000	2.08	1.38	4	0	0	0	0	0-0	4.1	5	1	1	0	1-0	3	.294
2001—New York (A.L.)	1	0	1.000	0.00	0.64	3	0	0	0	0	0-0	4.2	3	0	0	0	0-0	1	.176
2002—New York (A.L.)	0	1	.000	10.13	2.63	2	0	0	0	0	0-1	2.2	6	3	3	0	1-1	1	.500
Division series totals (6 years)	2	2	.500	2.45	1.31	16	0	0	0	1	0-1	18.1	18	6	5	1	6-1	15	.265

CHAMPIONSHIP SERIES RECORD

Year Team (League)	W	L	Pct.	ERA	WHIP	G	GS	CG	ShO	Hld.	Sv.-Opp.	IP	H	R	ER	HR	BB-IBB	SO	Avg.
1991—Atlanta (N.L.)	0	0	...	2.45	1.91	3	0	0	0	1	0-0	3.2	4	1	1	0	3-1	3	.333
1992—Atlanta (N.L.)	0	0	...	0.00	0.92	5	0	0	0	2	0-0	4.1	2	1	0	0	2-1	5	.154
1993—Atlanta (N.L.)	0	0	...	0.00	2.00	1	0	0	0	0	0-0	1.0	1	0	0	0	1-0	0	.250
1998—New York (A.L.)	0	0	...	0.00	0.82	3	0	0	0	1	0-0	3.2	1	0	0	0	1-1	4	.167
1999—New York (A.L.)	0	0	...	0.00	6.00	3	0	0	0	0	0-0	0.1	1	0	0	0	1-0	0	.500
2000—New York (A.L.)	Did not play.																		
2001—New York (A.L.)	0	0	...	27.00	3.00	2	0	0	0	0	0-0	1.0	1	3	3	0	2-1	0	.200
Champ. series totals (6 years)	0	0	...	2.57	1.50	17	0	0	0	4	0-0	14.0	11	5	4	0	10-4	12	.229

WORLD SERIES RECORD

Year Team (League)	W	L	Pct.	ERA	WHIP	G	GS	CG	ShO	Hld.	Sv.-Opp.	IP	H	R	ER	HR	BB-IBB	SO	Avg.
1991—Atlanta (N.L.)	1	0	1.000	0.00	0.95	5	0	0	0	0	0-0	7.1	5	0	0	0	2-2	7	.200
1992—Atlanta (N.L.)	0	0	...	0.00	1.00	4	0	0	0	1	1-1	5.0	3	0	0	0	2-2	1	.188
1998—New York (A.L.)	0	0	...	27.00	4.50	1	0	0	0	0	0-0	0.2	3	2	2	0	0-0	1	.600
1999—New York (A.L.)	0	0	...	0.00	0.00	1	0	0	0	0	0-0	0.1	0	0	0	0	0-0	1	.000
2000—New York (A.L.)	2	0	1.000	0.00	0.00	4	0	0	0	0	0-0	4.1	0	0	0	0	0-0	7	.000
2001—New York (A.L.)	0	0	...	3.18	0.71	5	0	0	0	1	0-0	5.2	3	2	2	0	1-0	3	.167
World series totals (6 years)	3	0	1.000	1.54	0.81	20	0	0	0	3	1-1	23.1	14	4	4	0	5-4	20	.182

ALL-STAR GAME RECORD

	W	L	Pct.	ERA	WHIP	G	GS	CG	ShO	Hld.	Sv.-Opp.	IP	H	R	ER	HR	BB-IBB	SO	Avg.
All-Star Game totals (1 year)	0	0	...	0.00	0.00	1	0	0	0	1	0-0	0.2	0	0	0	0	0-0	0	.000

2006 LEFTY-RIGHTY SPLITS

vs.	Avg.	AB	H	2B	3B	HR	RBI	BB	SO	OBP	Slg.	vs.	Avg.	AB	H	2B	3B	HR	RBI	BB	SO	OBP	Slg.
L	.271	85	23	5	0	1	16	7	21	.330	.365	R	.276	170	47	13	0	1	20	20	27	.351	.371

STAUFFER, TIM   P

PERSONAL: Born June 2, 1982, in Portland, Maine. ... 6-1/214. ... Throws right, bats right. ... Full name: Timothy James Stauffer. ... College: Richmond.
TRANSACTIONS/CAREER NOTES: Selected by San Diego Padres organization in first round (fourth pick overall) of 2003 free-agent draft.
CAREER HITTING: 4-for-26 (.154), 1 R, 1 2B, 0 3B, 0 HR, 1 RBI.

Year Team (League)	W	L	Pct.	ERA	WHIP	G	GS	CG	ShO	Hld.	Sv.-Opp.	IP	H	R	ER	HR	BB-IBB	SO	Avg.
2004—Lake Elsinore (Calif.)	2	0	1.000	1.78	1.05	6	6	0	0	—	0-...	35.1	28	10	7	0	9-0	30	.222
—Mobile (Sou.)	3	2	.600	2.63	1.34	8	8	1	0	—	0-...	51.1	56	17	15	3	13-1	33	.290
—Portland (PCL)	6	3	.667	3.54	1.34	14	14	0	0	—	0-...	81.1	83	46	32	15	26-1	50	.269
2005—San Diego (N.L.)	3	6	.333	5.33	1.49	15	14	0	0	0	0-0	81.0	92	50	48	10	29-0	49	.286
—Portland (PCL)	3	5	.375	5.14	1.42	13	13	1	1	0	0-0	75.1	90	48	43	5	17-0	64	.296
2006—Portland (PCL)	7	12	.368	5.53	1.64	28	26	0	0	0	0-0	153.0	199	108	94	20	52-1	89	.320
—San Diego (N.L.)	1	0	1.000	1.50	0.67	1	1	0	0	0	0-0	6.0	3	2	1	0	1-0	2	.150
Major League totals (2 years)	4	6	.400	5.07	1.44	16	15	0	0	0	0-0	87.0	95	52	49	10	30-0	51	.278

2006 LEFTY-RIGHTY SPLITS

vs.	Avg.	AB	H	2B	3B	HR	RBI	BB	SO	OBP	Slg.	vs.	Avg.	AB	H	2B	3B	HR	RBI	BB	SO	OBP	Slg.
L	.091	11	1	0	0	0	1	0	1	.167	.091	R	.222	9	2	0	0	0	2	0	2	.222	.222

STEMLE, STEVE   P

PERSONAL: Born May 20, 1977, in Louisville, Ky. ... 6-4/200. ... Throws right, bats right. ... Full name: Stephen J. Stemle. ... College: Western Kentucky.
TRANSACTIONS/CAREER NOTES: Selected by St. Louis Cardinals organization in fifth round of 1998 free-agent draft. ... Signed as a free agent by Kansas City Royals organization (November 15, 2004). ... On disabled list (June 11, 2005-remainder of season). ... On disabled list (April 17, 2006-remainder of season). ... Released by Royals (October 9, 2006).
CAREER HITTING: 0-for-0 (.000), 0 R, 0 2B, 0 3B, 0 HR, 0 RBI.

Year Team (League)	W	L	Pct.	ERA	WHIP	G	GS	CG	ShO	Hld.	Sv.-Opp.	IP	H	R	ER	HR	BB-IBB	SO	Avg.
1998—New Jersey (NYP)	3	3	.500	1.83	1.15	9	9	0	0	...	0-...	44.1	37	17	9	1	14-0	47	.219
1999—Peoria (Midw.)	7	10	.412	5.47	1.65	28	28	0	0	...	0-...	148.0	177	104	90	11	67-0	113	.292
2000—Potomac (Carol.)	9	10	.474	4.80	1.52	26	26	1	0	...	0-...	150.0	169	89	80	15	59-1	84	.286
2001—New Haven (East.)	7	10	.412	4.77	1.51	26	25	0	0	...	0-...	134.0	159	76	71	12	43-2	75	.293
2002—New Haven (East.)	5	2	.714	4.36	1.38	8	7	0	0	...	0-...	43.1	45	24	21	3	15-1	26	.280
—Memphis (PCL)	7	4	.636	3.65	1.28	20	11	0	0	...	0-...	93.2	97	41	38	8	23-1	55	.266
2003—Memphis (PCL)	6	11	.353	3.46	1.22	26	26	1	0	...	0-...	156.0	155	71	60	12	36-4	89	.260
2004—Palm Beach (FSL)	2	0	1.000	1.50	0.83	3	1	0	0	...	0-...	6.0	5	1	1	0	0-0	2	.217
—Memphis (PCL)	6	3	.667	3.30	1.27	54	0	0	0	...	3-...	76.1	85	28	28	7	12-2	42	.269
2005—Omaha (PCL)	1	1	.500	0.45	0.80	14	0	0	0	3	3-3	20.0	13	3	1	0	3-0	12	.191
—Kansas City (A.L.)	0	0	...	5.06	1.31	6	0	0	0	1	0-0	10.2	10	6	6	0	4-0	9	.256
2006—Kansas City (A.L.)	0	1	.000	15.00	3.00	5	0	0	0	0	0-1	6.0	15	10	10	1	3-0	0	.455
Major League totals (2 years)	0	1	.000	8.64	1.92	11	0	0	0	1	0-1	16.2	25	16	16	1	7-0	9	.347

2006 LEFTY-RIGHTY SPLITS

vs.	Avg.	AB	H	2B	3B	HR	RBI	BB	SO	OBP	Slg.	vs.	Avg.	AB	H	2B	3B	HR	RBI	BB	SO	OBP	Slg.
L	.429	14	6	1	1	0	5	2	0	.500	.643	R	.474	19	9	4	0	1	6	1	0	.500	.842

STERN, ADAM   OF

PERSONAL: Born February 12, 1980, in London, Ontario. ... 5-11/180. ... Bats left, throws right. ... Full name: Adam James Stern. ... College: Nebraska.
TRANSACTIONS/CAREER NOTES: Selected by Atlanta Braves organization in third round of 2001 free-agent draft. ... Selected by Boston Red Sox organization from Braves organization in Rule 5 major league draft (December 13, 2004). ... On disabled list (April 1-July 7 and August 20-September 4, 2005); included rehabilitation assignment to Pawtucket. ... On disabled list (August 28, 2006-remainder of season). ... Traded by Red Sox to Baltimore Orioles (October 3, 2006); completing deal in which Orioles traded C Javy Lopez to Red Sox for a player to be named (August 4, 2006).
2006 GAMES PLAYED BY POSITION (MLB): OF—10.

									BATTING									FIELDING	
Year Team (League)	Pos.	G	AB	R	H	2B	3B	HR	RBI	BB	SO	HBP	GDP	SB-CS	Avg.	OBP	SLG	OPS	E	Avg.
2001—Jamestown (NYP)	OF	21	75	20	23	4	2	0	11	15	11	0	0	9-4	.307	.413	.413	.826	0	1.000
2002—Myrtle Beach (Carol.)	OF	119	462	65	117	22	10	3	47	27	89	3	3	40-8	.253	.298	.364	.662	3	.990
2003—GC Braves (GCL)	OF	7	29	6	10	1	0	1	6	6	3	0	1	2-2	.345	.457	.483	.940	0	1.000
—Myrtle Beach (Carol.)	OF	28	103	11	20	2	0	0	6	13	21	0	1	7-3	.194	.282	.214	.496	0	1.000
2004—Greenville (Sou.)		102	394	64	127	26	6	8	47	35	58	2	2	27-10	.322	.378	.480	.858	...	...

S

Year	Team (League)	Pos.	G	AB	R	H	2B	3B	HR	RBI	BB	SO	HBP	GDP	SB-CS	Avg.	OBP	SLG	OPS	E	Avg.
2005	— Pawtucket (Int'l)	OF	20	81	16	26	8	0	2	14	8	10	1	2	3-1	.321	.385	.494	.878	2	.980
	— Boston (A.L.)	OF	36	15	4	2	0	0	1	2	0	4	1	0	1-1	.133	.188	.333	.521	0	1.000
2006	— Boston (A.L.)	OF	10	20	3	3	1	0	0	4	0	4	1	0	1-0	.150	.190	.200	.390	0	1.000
	— Pawtucket (Int'l)		93	392	59	101	21	3	8	34	23	78	1	5	23-7	.258	.300	.388	.688	2	.991
Major League totals (2 years)			46	35	7	5	1	0	1	6	0	8	2	0	2-1	.143	.189	.257	.446	0	1.000

2006 LEFTY-RIGHTY SPLITS

vs.	Avg.	AB	H	2B	3B	HR	RBI	BB	SO	OBP	Slg.	vs.	Avg.	AB	H	2B	3B	HR	RBI	BB	SO	OBP	Slg.
L	.000	1	0	0	0	0	0	0	0	.000	.000	R	.158	19	3	1	0	0	4	0	4	.200	.211

STEWART, CHRIS — C

PERSONAL: Born February 19, 1982, in Fontana, Calif. ... 6-4/205. ... Bats right, throws right. ... Full name: Christopher David Stewart. ... Junior college: Riverside (Calif.) C.C. **TRANSACTIONS/CAREER NOTES:** Selected by Chicago White Sox organization in 12th round of 2001 free-agent draft.

2006 GAMES PLAYED BY POSITION (MLB): C—5, DH—1.

Year	Team (League)	Pos.	G	AB	R	H	2B	3B	HR	RBI	BB	SO	HBP	GDP	SB-CS	Avg.	OBP	SLG	OPS	E	Avg.
2002	— Bristol (Appal.)		42	158	25	44	9	0	1	12	14	23	4	2	0-0	.278	.350	.354	.704	...	...
2003	— Win.-Salem (Car.)		76	217	18	45	8	2	2	27	27	29	0	6	1-0	.207	.294	.290	.584	...	...
2004	— Charlotte (Int'l)		5	14	1	1	1	0	0	1	1	3	1	0	0-0	.071	.188	.143	.331	...	...
	— Birmingham (Sou.)		83	260	26	60	11	2	1	17	22	59	4	3	2-4	.231	.299	.300	.599	...	...
2005	— Birmingham (Sou.)	C-DH	95	311	39	89	21	0	11	51	24	37	3	7	3-3	.286	.341	.460	.801	8	.988
2006	— Charlotte (Int'l)		89	272	40	72	17	3	4	28	15	35	5	7	3-0	.265	.314	.393	.707	4	.994
	— Chicago (A.L.)	C-DH	6	8	0	0	0	0	0	0	0	2	0	0	0-0	.000	.000	.000	.000	0	1.000
Major League totals (1 year)			6	8	0	0	0	0	0	0	0	2	0	0	0-0	.000	.000	.000	.000	0	1.000

2006 LEFTY-RIGHTY SPLITS

vs.	Avg.	AB	H	2B	3B	HR	RBI	BB	SO	OBP	Slg.	vs.	Avg.	AB	H	2B	3B	HR	RBI	BB	SO	OBP	Slg.
L	.000	2	0	0	0	0	1	0	0	.000	.000	R	.000	6	0	0	0	0	0	0	1	.000	.000

STEWART, SHANNON — OF

PERSONAL: Born February 25, 1974, in Cincinnati. ... 5-11/200. ... Bats right, throws right. ... Full name: Shannon Harold Stewart. ... High school: Southridge Senior (Miami). **TRANSACTIONS/CAREER NOTES:** Selected by Toronto Blue Jays organization in first round (19th pick overall) of 1992 free-agent draft; pick received as part of compensation for Los Angeles Dodgers signing Type A free-agent P Tom Candiotti. ... On disabled list (April 29-May 14, 2000); included rehabilitation assignment to Dunedin. ... On disabled list (May 1-16, 2002). ... On disabled list (May 29-June 23, 2003); included rehabilitation assignment to Syracuse. ... Traded by Blue Jays to Minnesota Twins for OF Bobby Kielty (July 16, 2003). ... On disabled list (May 18-July 15, 2004); included rehabilitation assignment to Rochester. ... On disabled list (May 23-June 30, 2006); included rehabilitation assignment to Rochester. ... On disabled list (July 16, 2006-remainder of season). **RECORDS:** Shares major league record for most doubles, game (4, July 18, 2000).

2006 GAMES PLAYED BY POSITION (MLB): OF—34, DH—10.

Year	Team (League)	Pos.	G	AB	R	H	2B	3B	HR	RBI	BB	SO	HBP	GDP	SB-CS	Avg.	OBP	SLG	OPS	E	Avg.
1992	— GC Jays (GCL)	OF	50	172	44	40	1	0	1	11	24	27	3	3	32-5	.233	.333	.256	.589	1	.988
1993	— St. Catharines (NYP)	OF	75	301	53	84	15	2	3	29	33	43	2	7	25-10	.279	.351	.372	.723	1	1.000
1994	— Hagerstown (SAL)	OF	56	225	39	73	10	5	4	25	23	39	1	3	15-11	.324	.386	.467	.853	1	.990
1995	— Knoxville (Southern)	OF-DH	138	498	89	143	24	6	5	55	89	61	6	13	42-16	.287	.390	.398	.788	6	.980
	— Toronto (A.L.)	OF	12	38	2	8	0	0	0	1	5	5	1	0	2-0	.211	.318	.211	.529	1	.955
1996	— Syracuse (Int'l)	OF	112	420	77	125	26	8	6	42	54	61	2	6	35-8	.298	.377	.440	.818	5	.983
	— Toronto (A.L.)	OF	7	17	2	3	1	0	0	2	1	4	0	1	1-0	.176	.222	.235	.458	1	.800
1997	— Toronto (A.L.)	OF-DH	44	168	25	48	13	7	0	22	19	24	4	3	10-3	.286	.368	.446	.814	2	.980
	— Syracuse (Int'l)	OF	58	208	41	72	13	1	5	24	36	26	4	1	9-6	.346	.452	.490	.942	2	.983
1998	— Toronto (A.L.)	OF	144	516	90	144	29	3	12	55	67	77	15	5	51-18	.279	.377	.417	.794	6	.980
1999	— Toronto (A.L.)	OF-DH	145	608	102	185	28	2	11	67	59	83	8	12	37-•14	.304	.371	.411	.782	5	.981
2000	— Toronto (A.L.)	OF	136	583	107	186	43	5	21	69	37	79	6	12	20-5	.319	.363	.518	.882	2	.993
	— Dunedin (Fla. St.)	OF	1	3	2	3	1	0	0	1	2	0	0	0	0-1	1.000	1.000	1.333	2.333	0	—
2001	— Toronto (A.L.)	OF-DH	155	640	103	202	44	7	12	60	46	72	11	9	27-10	.316	.371	.463	.834	5	.981
2002	— Toronto (A.L.)	OF-DH	141	577	103	175	38	6	10	45	54	60	9	17	14-2	.303	.371	.442	.813	2	.990
2003	— Syracuse (Int'l)	OF	1	3	0	0	0	0	0	0	1	0	0	0	0-0	.000	.250	.000	.250	0	1.000
	— Toronto (A.L.)	OF-DH	71	303	47	89	22	2	7	35	27	30	2	6	1-2	.294	.347	.449	.796	4	.974
	— Minnesota (A.L.)	OF-DH	65	270	43	87	22	0	6	38	25	36	4	4	3-4	.322	.384	.470	.854	1	.993
2004	— Rochester (Int'l)	DH-OF	3	9	3	3	1	0	0	0	1	2	0	0	0-0	.333	.400	.444	.844	0	—
	— Minnesota (A.L.)	OF-DH	92	378	46	115	17	2	11	47	47	44	1	5	6-3	.304	.380	.447	.827	3	.972
2005	— Minnesota (A.L.)	OF-DH	132	551	69	151	27	3	10	56	34	73	8	11	7-5	.274	.323	.388	.711	4	.985
2006	— Rochester (Int'l)		5	18	2	5	1	0	0	1	0	1	0	0	1-0	.278	.333	.333	.667	0	1.000
	— Minnesota (A.L.)	OF-DH	44	174	21	51	5	1	2	21	14	19	1	7	3-1	.293	.347	.368	.715	1	.984
Major League totals (12 years)			1188	4823	760	1444	289	38	102	518	435	606	70	92	182-67	.299	.364	.439	.802	37	.983

DIVISION SERIES RECORD

Year	Team (League)	Pos.	G	AB	R	H	2B	3B	HR	RBI	BB	SO	HBP	GDP	SB-CS	Avg.	OBP	SLG	OPS	E	Avg.
2003	— Minnesota (A.L.)	OF	4	15	0	6	2	0	0	0	2	4	0	0	1-0	.400	.471	.533	1.004	0	1.000
2004	— Minnesota (A.L.)	OF-DH	4	20	1	4	0	0	0	2	0	2	0	0	0-0	.200	.190	.200	.390	0	1.000
Division series totals (2 years)			8	35	1	10	2	0	0	2	2	6	0	0	1-0	.286	.316	.343	.659	0	1.000

2006 LEFTY-RIGHTY SPLITS

vs.	Avg.	AB	H	2B	3B	HR	RBI	BB	SO	OBP	Slg.	vs.	Avg.	AB	H	2B	3B	HR	RBI	BB	SO	OBP	Slg.
L	.288	52	15	2	0	0	4	7	7	.373	.327	R	.295	122	36	3	1	2	17	7	12	.336	.385

STINNETT, KELLY — C

PERSONAL: Born February 4, 1970, in Lawton, Okla. ... 5-11/225. ... Bats right, throws right. ... Full name: Kelly Lee Stinnett. ... Name pronounced: sti-NETT. ... High school: Lawton (Okla.). ... Junior college: Seminole (Okla.). **TRANSACTIONS/CAREER NOTES:** Selected by Cleveland Indians organization in 11th round of 1989 free-agent draft. ... Selected by New York Mets from Indians organization in Rule 5 major league draft (December 13, 1993). ... Traded by Mets to Milwaukee Brewers for P Cory Lidle (January 17, 1996). ... On disabled list (July 27-September 2, 1997). ... Selected by Arizona Diamondbacks in third round (65th pick overall) of expansion draft (November 18, 1997). ... Signed as a free agent by Cincinnati Reds (January 9, 2001). ... On disabled list (September 4, 2001-remainder of season). ... On disabled list (April 6-July 15, 2002); included rehabilitation assignments to Louisville. ... Traded by Reds to Philadelphia Phillies for OF Eric Valent (August 31, 2003). ... Signed as a free agent by Kansas City Royals (December 19, 2003). ... On disabled list (June 20, 2004-remainder of season). ... Signed as a free agent by Diamondbacks organization (December 13, 2004). ...

Signed as a free agent by Mets organization (March 29, 2005). ... Released by Mets (April 1, 2005). ... Signed by Diamondbacks organization (May 10, 2005). ... On disabled list (July 19-August 9, 2005); included rehabilitation assignment to Lancaster. ... Signed as a free agent by New York Yankees (November 29, 2005). ... Released by Yankees (August 3, 2006). ... Signed by Mets organization (August 24, 2006). **STATISTICAL NOTES:** Career major league grand slams: 2.

2006 GAMES PLAYED BY POSITION (MLB): C—41.

Year	Team (League)	Pos.	G	AB	R	H	2B	3B	HR	RBI	BB	SO	HBP	GDP	SB-CS	Avg.	OBP	SLG	OPS	E	Avg.
1990—	Watertown (NYP)	1B-C	60	192	29	46	10	2	2	21	40	43	4	8	3-7	.240	.378	.344	.722	18	.957
1991—	Columbus (S. Atl.)	1B-C	102	384	49	101	15	1	14	74	26	70	9	17	4-1	.263	.321	.417	.737	28	.966
1992—	Cant./Akr. (Eastern)	C	91	296	37	84	10	0	6	32	16	43	4	8	7-6	.284	.326	.378	.704	13	.979
1993—	Charlotte (Int'l)	C	98	288	42	79	10	3	6	33	17	52	2	4	0-0	.274	.318	.392	.711	8	.985
1994—	New York (N.L.)	C	47	150	20	38	6	2	2	14	11	28	5	3	0-0	.253	.323	.360	.683	5	.979
1995—	New York (N.L.)	C	77	196	23	43	8	1	4	18	29	65	6	3	2-0	.219	.338	.332	.669	7	.983
1996—	Milwaukee (A.L.)	C-DH	14	26	1	2	0	0	0	0	2	11	1	0	0-0	.077	.172	.077	.249	2	.960
—	New Orleans (A.A.)	C-DH-3B	95	334	63	96	21	1	27	70	31	83	13	6	3-3	.287	.366	.599	.965	11	.980
1997—	Tucson (PCL)	C-DH-1B	64	209	50	67	15	3	10	43	42	46	6	2	1-1	.321	.444	.565	1.009	2	.993
—	Milwaukee (A.L.)	C-DH	30	36	2	9	4	0	0	3	3	9	0	0	0-0	.250	.308	.361	.669	1	.989
1998—	Arizona (N.L.)	C-DH	92	274	35	71	14	1	11	34	35	74	6	9	0-1	.259	.353	.438	.791	8	.984
1999—	Arizona (N.L.)	C	88	284	36	66	13	0	14	38	24	83	5	4	2-1	.232	.302	.426	.728	6	.990
2000—	Arizona (N.L.)	C	76	240	22	52	7	0	8	33	19	56	6	5	0-1	.217	.291	.346	.636	6	.990
2001—	Cincinnati (N.L.)	C-DH	63	187	27	48	11	0	9	25	17	61	5	5	2-2	.257	.333	.460	.793	12	.966
2002—	Cincinnati (N.L.)	C	34	93	10	21	5	0	3	13	15	25	0	1	2-0	.226	.333	.376	.710	2	.990
—	Louisville (Int'l)	C	30	86	6	17	6	0	0	5	3	24	0	1	0-0	.198	.225	.267	.492	2	.988
2003—	Cincinnati (N.L.)	C	60	179	14	41	13	0	3	19	13	51	4	3	0-0	.229	.294	.352	.646	2	.993
—	Philadelphia (N.L.)	C	7	7	0	3	0	0	0	0	1	1	0	0	0-0	.429	.500	.429	.929	0	1.000
2004—	Kansas City (A.L.)	C	20	59	10	18	0	0	3	7	5	16	2	0	0-0	.305	.379	.458	.836	3	.971
2005—	Tucson (PCL)	C	11	35	4	8	2	0	1	2	3	12	2	0	0-0	.229	.325	.371	.696	2	.973
—	Lancaster (Calif.)	C-DH	3	11	4	3	1	0	1	5	2	1	0	0	0-0	.273	.385	.636	1.021	0	1.000
—	Arizona (N.L.)	C	59	129	15	32	4	0	6	12	12	32	1	4	0-0	.248	.317	.419	.736	6	.977
2006—	Norfolk (Int'l)		5	16	2	6	1	0	1	1	2	2	0	0	0-0	.375	.444	.625	1.069	0	1.000
—	New York (A.L.)	C	34	79	6	18	3	0	1	9	5	29	1	0	0-0	.228	.282	.304	.586	2	.989
—	New York (N.L.)	C	7	12	0	1	0	0	0	0	0	5	0	0	0-0	.083	.083	.083	.167	1	.976
	American League totals (4 years)		98	200	19	47	7	0	4	19	15	65	4	0	0-0	.235	.301	.330	.631	8	.981
	National League totals (10 years)		610	1751	202	416	81	4	60	206	176	480	38	37	10-5	.238	.319	.391	.711	55	.984
	Major League totals (13 years)		708	1951	221	463	88	4	64	225	191	545	42	37	10-5	.237	.318	.385	.703	63	.984

DIVISION SERIES RECORD

Year	Team (League)	Pos.	G	AB	R	H	2B	3B	HR	RBI	BB	SO	HBP	GDP	SB-CS	Avg.	OBP	SLG	OPS	E	Avg.
1999—	Arizona (N.L.)	C	4	14	1	2	1	0	0	0	1	4	0	0	0-0	.143	.200	.214	.414	0	1.000

2006 LEFTY-RIGHTY SPLITS

vs.	Avg.	AB	H	2B	3B	HR	RBI	BB	SO	OBP	Slg.	vs.	Avg.	AB	H	2B	3B	HR	RBI	BB	SO	OBP	Slg.
L	.200	30	6	3	0	1	6	4	12	.294	.400	R	.213	61	13	0	0	1	3	1	21	.238	.213

STOCKMAN, PHIL   P

PERSONAL: Born January 25, 1980, in Oldham, England. ... Throws right, bats right. ... Full name: Phillip Matthew Stockman. **TRANSACTIONS/CAREER NOTES:** Signed as a non-drafted free agent by Arizona Diamondbacks organization (September 7, 1997). ... Signed as a free agent by Atlanta Braves organization (February 1, 2005). ... On disabled list (June 24, 2006-remainder of season); included rehabilitation assignments to Rome and Richmond.

CAREER HITTING: 0-for-0 (.000), 0 R, 0 2B, 0 3B, 0 HR, 0 RBI.

Year	Team (League)	W	L	Pct.	ERA	WHIP	G	GS	CG	ShO	Hld.	Sv.-Opp.	IP	H	R	ER	HR	BB-IBB	SO	Avg.
1998—	Ariz. D'backs (Ariz.)	0	0	...	0.00	6.00	1	0	0	0	...	0-...	0.1	0	0	0	0	2-0	1	.000
1999—		Did not play																		
2000—	Ariz. D'backs (Ariz.)	3	2	.600	2.59	1.51	14	2	0	0	...	1-...	41.2	40	22	12	2	23-0	40	.237
—	Missoula (Pion.)	2	0	1.000	2.45	1.18	2	2	0	0	...	0-...	11.0	10	3	3	0	3-0	4	.233
2001—	Lancaster (Calif.)	0	0	...	5.09	1.13	8	0	0	0	...	0-...	17.2	11	11	10	2	9-0	18	.200
—	Yakima (N'west)	3	4	.429	4.26	1.36	15	14	0	0	...	0-...	76.0	81	39	36	5	22-0	48	.272
2002—	Lancaster (Calif.)	7	5	.583	4.40	1.38	20	20	0	0	...	0-...	108.1	91	58	53	10	58-0	108	.232
2003—	Tucson (PCL)	1	1	.500	1.00	1.33	2	1	0	0	...	0-...	9.0	8	1	1	0	4-0	5	.258
—	El Paso (Texas)	11	7	.611	3.96	1.36	26	26	0	0	...	0-...	147.2	137	75	65	8	64-0	146	.244
2004—	Tucson (PCL)	3	2	.600	5.75	1.70	12	12	0	0	...	0-...	56.1	60	39	36	6	36-0	35	.288
—	El Paso (Texas)	1	3	.250	2.67	1.37	6	6	1	0	...	0-...	27.0	17	13	8	1	20-0	21	.185
2005—	Tucson (PCL)	1	1	.500	6.25	1.96	17	4	0	0	2	0-0	31.2	35	29	22	4	27-0	16	.285
—	Tennessee (Sou.)	1	3	.250	3.34	1.53	47	1	0	0	3	1-2	35.0	31	16	13	2	24-0	30	.237
2006—	Mississippi (Sou.)	0	0	...	0.00	0.41	3	0	0	0	1	0-0	7.1	1	0	0	0	2-0	12	.043
—	Atlanta (Int'l)	0	0	...	2.25	1.75	4	0	0	0	0	0-0	4.0	3	1	1	0	4-2	4	.231
—	Rome (S. Atl.)	0	1	.000	0.00	2.67	3	0	0	0	0	0-0	3.0	5	3	0	0	3-0	6	.417
—	Richmond (Int'l)	0	0	...	0.81	0.69	18	0	0	0	0	2-2	33.1	13	3	3	0	10-1	41	.123
	Major League totals (1 year)	0	0	...	2.25	1.75	4	0	0	0	0	0-0	4.0	3	1	1	0	4-2	4	.231

2006 LEFTY-RIGHTY SPLITS

vs.	Avg.	AB	H	2B	3B	HR	RBI	BB	SO	OBP	Slg.	vs.	Avg.	AB	H	2B	3B	HR	RBI	BB	SO	OBP	Slg.
L	.500	2	1	1	0	0	0	2	0	.750	1.000	R	.182	11	2	1	0	0	1	2	4	.308	.273

STOKES, BRIAN   P

PERSONAL: Born September 7, 1979, in Pomona, Calif. ... 6-1/203. ... Throws right, bats right. ... Full name: Brian Alexander Stokes. ... Junior college: Riverside (Calif.) C.C. **TRANSACTIONS/CAREER NOTES:** Signed as a non-drafted free agent by Tampa Bay Devil Rays organization (October 2, 1998).

CAREER HITTING: 0-for-0 (.000), 0 R, 0 2B, 0 3B, 0 HR, 0 RBI.

Year	Team (League)	W	L	Pct.	ERA	WHIP	G	GS	CG	ShO	Hld.	Sv.-Opp.	IP	H	R	ER	HR	BB-IBB	SO	Avg.
1999—	Princeton (Appal.)	2	3	.400	3.89	1.46	33	0	0	0	...	9-...	37.0	33	20	16	2	21-0	39	.239
2000—	Char., S.C. (SAL)	5	6	.455	2.56	1.12	46	0	0	0	...	5-...	70.1	45	24	20	1	34-2	66	.179
2001—	Bakersfield (Calif.)	8	6	.571	3.92	1.41	32	20	1	0	...	1-...	128.2	118	65	56	11	64-0	92	.244
2002—	Bakersfield (Calif.)	10	7	.588	3.26	1.29	28	28	1	1	...	0-...	165.2	156	79	60	13	57-1	152	.248
2003—	Orlando (South.)	2	5	.286	3.20	1.34	10	10	0	0	...	0-...	50.2	55	26	18	2	13-0	33	.274
2005—	Visalia (Calif.)	1	2	.333	4.24	1.18	4	4	0	0	...	0-...	17.0	15	8	8	3	5-0	21	.231
—	Montgom. (Sou.)	4	6	.400	3.47	1.18	16	16	1	0	...	0-...	93.1	82	36	36	8	28-0	70	.238
2006—	Durham (Int'l)	7	7	.500	4.11	1.37	29	23	0	0	...	0-...	133.2	134	75	61	8	49-0	103	.260
—	Tampa Bay (A.L.)	1	0	1.000	4.88	1.67	5	4	0	0	...	0-...	24.0	31	13	13	2	9-0	15	.320
	Major League totals (1 year)	1	0	1.000	4.88	1.67	5	4	0	0	...	0-...	24.0	31	13	13	2	9-0	15	.320

S

2006 LEFTY-RIGHTY SPLITS

vs.	Avg.	AB	H	2B	3B	HR	RBI	BB	SO	OBP	Slg.	vs.	Avg.	AB	H	2B	3B	HR	RBI	BB	SO	OBP	Slg.
L	.302	53	16	6	0	1	8	5	9	.350	.472	R	.341	44	15	2	0	1	7	4	6	.400	.455

STREET, HUSTON   P

PERSONAL: Born August 2, 1983, in Austin, Texas. ... 6-0/185. ... Throws right, bats right. ... Full name: Huston Lowell Street. ... High school: Westlake, (Austin, Texas). ... College: Texas. **TRANSACTIONS/CAREER NOTES:** Selected by Oakland Athletics organization in first round (40th pick overall) of 2004 free-agent draft. ... On disabled list (August 19-September 8, 2006). **HONORS:** Named A.L. Rookie of the Year by THE SPORTING NEWS (2005). ... Named A.L. Rookie of the Year by Baseball Writers' Association of America (2005).

CAREER HITTING: 0-for-0 (.000), 0 R, 0 2B, 0 3B, 0 HR, 0 RBI.

Year	Team (League)	W	L	Pct.	ERA	WHIP	G	GS	CG	ShO	Hld.	Sv.-Opp.	IP	H	R	ER	HR	BB-IBB	SO	Avg.
2004—	Kane Co. (Midw.)	0	1	.000	1.69	1.31	9	0	0	0	...	4-...	10.2	9	2	2	0	5-1	14	.220
—	Midland (Texas)	1	0	1.000	1.35	0.98	10	0	0	0	...	3-...	13.1	10	2	2	0	3-0	14	.200
—	Sacramento (PCL)	0	0	...	0.00	1.00	2	0	0	0	...	1-...	2.0	2	0	0	0	0-0	2	.250
2005—	Oakland (A.L.)	5	1	.833	1.72	1.01	67	0	0	0	0	23-27	78.1	53	17	15	3	26-4	72	.194
2006—	Oakland (A.L.)	4	4	.500	3.31	1.09	69	0	0	0	1	37-48	70.2	64	28	26	4	13-3	67	.238
	Major League totals (2 years)	9	5	.643	2.48	1.05	136	0	0	0	1	60-75	149.0	117	45	41	7	39-7	139	.216

DIVISION SERIES RECORD

Year	Team (League)	W	L	Pct.	ERA	WHIP	G	GS	CG	ShO	Hld.	Sv.-Opp.	IP	H	R	ER	HR	BB-IBB	SO	Avg.
2006—	Oakland (A.L.)	0	0	...	3.00	1.67	3	0	0	0	...	2-2	3.0	4	1	1	0	1-0	1	.333

CHAMPIONSHIP SERIES RECORD

Year	Team (League)	W	L	Pct.	ERA	WHIP	G	GS	CG	ShO	Hld.	Sv.-Opp.	IP	H	R	ER	HR	BB-IBB	SO	Avg.
2006—	Oakland (A.L.)	0	1	.000	10.80	1.20	2	0	0	0	...	0-0	3.1	4	4	4	2	0-0	3	.308

2006 LEFTY-RIGHTY SPLITS

vs.	Avg.	AB	H	2B	3B	HR	RBI	BB	SO	OBP	Slg.	vs.	Avg.	AB	H	2B	3B	HR	RBI	BB	SO	OBP	Slg.
L	.274	117	32	8	1	3	22	8	31	.325	.436	R	.211	152	32	7	0	1	12	5	36	.236	.276

STULTS, ERIC   P

PERSONAL: Born December 9, 1979, in Plymouth, Ind. ... 6-0/215. ... Throws left, bats left. ... Full name: Eric William Stults. ... High school: Argos (Ind.). ... College: Bethel (Ind.). **TRANSACTIONS/CAREER NOTES:** Selected by Los Angeles Dodgers organization in 15th round of 2002 free-agent draft.

CAREER HITTING: 3-for-5 (.600), 1 R, 0 2B, 0 3B, 0 HR, 0 RBI.

Year	Team (League)	W	L	Pct.	ERA	WHIP	G	GS	CG	ShO	Hld.	Sv.-Opp.	IP	H	R	ER	HR	BB-IBB	SO	Avg.
2002—	Great Falls (Pio.)	1	0	1.000	2.25	1.13	5	0	0	0	...	1-...	8.0	6	4	2	0	3-0	9	.200
—	Vero Beach (FSL)	3	1	.750	3.00	1.40	13	6	0	0	...	0-...	42.0	39	19	14	3	20-0	40	.244
—	Jacksonville (Sou.)	0	0	...	0.00	0.00	1	0	0	0	...	0-...	1.0	0	0	0	0	0-0	0	.000
2003—	Jacksonville (Sou.)	3	4	.429	4.97	1.55	9	7	0	0	...	1-...	38.0	46	23	21	5	13-0	14	.305
—	Vero Beach (FSL)	0	1	.000	6.00	2.33	1	1	0	0	...	0-...	3.0	6	2	2	0	1-0	1	.500
2004—	Columbus (S. Atl.)	1	2	.333	2.49	1.11	12	0	0	0	...	3-...	21.2	18	8	6	0	6-0	16	.217
—	Vero Beach (FSL)	2	1	.667	2.70	1.50	7	0	0	0	...	1-...	10.0	11	4	3	0	4-0	6	.268
2005—	Jacksonville (Sou.)	4	3	.571	3.31	1.28	12	12	0	0	0	0-0	68.0	73	33	25	6	14-0	58	.266
—	Las Vegas (PCL)	3	7	.300	6.58	1.68	15	14	0	0	0	0-0	78.0	107	60	57	15	24-0	60	.322
2006—	Las Vegas (PCL)	10	11	.476	4.23	1.44	26	26	1	0	0	0-0	153.1	153	85	72	10	68-5	128	.268
—	Los Angeles (N.L.)	1	0	1.000	5.60	1.36	6	2	0	0	0	0-0	17.2	17	12	11	4	7-0	5	.266
	Major League totals (1 year)	1	0	1.000	5.60	1.36	6	2	0	0	0	0-0	17.2	17	12	11	4	7-0	5	.266

2006 LEFTY-RIGHTY SPLITS

vs.	Avg.	AB	H	2B	3B	HR	RBI	BB	SO	OBP	Slg.	vs.	Avg.	AB	H	2B	3B	HR	RBI	BB	SO	OBP	Slg.
L	.467	15	7	3	0	1	2	4	0	.579	.867	R	.204	49	10	2	1	3	9	3	5	.250	.469

STURTZE, TANYON   P

PERSONAL: Born October 12, 1970, in Worcester, Mass. ... 6-5/200. ... Throws right, bats right. ... Full name: Tanyon James Sturtze. ... Name pronounced: sturts. ... High school: St. Peter-Marian (Worcester, Mass.). ... Junior college: Quinsigamond (Mass.) Community College. **TRANSACTIONS/CAREER NOTES:** Selected by Oakland Athletics organization in 23rd round of 1990 free-agent draft. ... Selected by Chicago Cubs from A's organization in Rule 5 major league draft (December 5, 1994). ... Signed as a free agent by Texas Rangers (November 20, 1996). ... Signed as a free agent by Chicago White Sox organization (November 23, 1998). ... On suspended list (May 1-3, 2000). ... Traded by White Sox to Tampa Bay Devil Rays for IF Tony Graffanino (May 31, 2000). ... On disabled list (August 27, 2000-remainder of season). ... Signed as a free agent by Toronto Blue Jays (December 22, 2002). ... On suspended list (September 26-28, 2003). ... Signed as a free agent by Los Angeles Dodgers organization (December 19, 2003). ... Released by Dodgers (March 29, 2004). ... Signed by Florida Marlins organization (March 30, 2004). ... Released by Marlins (April 2, 2004). ... Signed by Dodgers organization (April 14, 2004). ... Traded by Dodgers to New York Yankees for 1B Bryan Myrow (May 15, 2004). ... On suspended list (August 12-15, 2004). ... On disabled list (April 18-May 5, 2005); included rehabilitation assignment to Tampa. ... On disabled list (May 14, 2006-remainder of season).

CAREER HITTING: 1-for-16 (.063), 0 R, 0 2B, 0 3B, 0 HR, 0 RBI.

Year	Team (League)	W	L	Pct.	ERA	WHIP	G	GS	CG	ShO	Hld.	Sv.-Opp.	IP	H	R	ER	HR	BB-IBB	SO	Avg.
1990—	Ariz. A's (Ariz.)	2	5	.286	5.44	1.71	12	10	0	0	...	0-...	48.0	55	41	29	3	27-0	30	.276
1991—	Madison (Midw.)	10	5	.667	3.09	1.19	27	27	0	0	...	0-...	163.0	136	77	56	5	58-5	88	.223
1992—	Modesto (California)	7	11	.389	3.75	1.46	25	25	1	0	...	0-...	151.0	143	72	63	6	78-1	126	.254
1993—	Huntsville (Sou.)	5	12	.294	4.78	1.53	28	28	1	1	...	0-...	165.2	169	102	88	16	85-2	112	.269
1994—	Huntsville (Sou.)	6	3	.667	3.22	1.35	17	17	1	0	...	0-...	103.1	100	40	37	5	39-1	63	.259
—	Tacoma (PCL)	4	5	.444	4.04	1.65	11	9	0	0	...	0-...	64.2	73	36	29	5	34-2	28	.284
1995—	Chicago (N.L.)	0	0	...	9.00	1.50	2	0	0	0	0	0-0	2.0	2	2	2	1	1-0	0	.250
—	Iowa (Am. Assoc.)	4	7	.364	6.80	1.74	23	17	1	1	...	0-...	86.0	108	66	65	18	42-1	48	.314
1996—	Iowa (Am. Assoc.)	6	4	.600	4.85	1.56	51	1	0	0	...	4-...	72.1	80	42	39	7	33-2	51	.290
—	Chicago (N.L.)	1	0	1.000	9.00	1.91	6	0	0	0	0	0-0	11.0	16	11	11	3	5-0	7	.348
1997—	Okla. City (A.A.)	8	6	.571	5.10	1.57	25	19	1	0	...	0-...	114.2	133	76	65	10	47-1	79	.295
—	Texas (A.L.)	1	1	.500	8.27	1.93	9	5	0	0	0	0-0	32.2	45	30	30	6	18-0	18	.338
1998—	GC Rangers (GCL)	0	1	.000	7.71	2.29	3	3	0	0	...	0-...	7.0	12	7	6	1	4-0	10	.364
—	Charlotte (Fla. St.)	0	1	.000	6.00	1.00	1	1	0	0	...	0-...	3.0	2	3	2	0	1-0	3	.200
—	Tulsa (Texas)	1	0	1.000	5.40	2.40	1	0	0	0	...	0-...	1.2	2	1	1	1	2-0	3	.400
—	Oklahoma (PCL)	3	1	.750	3.34	1.46	13	3	0	0	...	0-...	35.0	33	13	13	3	18-0	31	.252
1999—	Charlotte (Int'l)	9	4	.692	4.05	1.19	33	14	2	1	...	3-...	104.1	83	53	47	7	41-1	107	.214
—	Chicago (A.L.)	0	0	...	0.00	1.00	1	1	0	0	0	0-0	6.0	4	0	0	0	2-0	2	.200
2000—	Chicago (A.L.)	1	2	.333	12.06	2.55	10	1	0	0	0	0-0	15.2	25	23	21	4	15-0	6	.379
—	Tampa Bay (A.L.)	4	0	1.000	2.56	1.16	19	5	0	0	0	0-0	52.2	47	16	15	4	14-1	38	.236
2001—	Tampa Bay (A.L.)	11	12	.478	4.42	1.43	39	27	3	3	0	1-3	195.1	200	98	96	23	79-0	110	.271
2002—	Tampa Bay (A.L.)	4	* 18	.182	5.18	1.61	33	33	4	0	0	0-0	224.0	* 271	* 141	* 129	33	* 89-2	137	.302

Year Team (League)	W	L	Pct.	ERA	WHIP	G	GS	CG	ShO	Hld.	Sv.-Opp.	IP	H	R	ER	HR	BB-IBB	SO	Avg.
2003— Toronto (A.L.)	7	6	.538	5.94	1.68	40	8	0	0	1	0-0	89.1	107	67	59	14	43-3	54	.296
2004— Las Vegas (PCL)	3	0	1.000	2.50	1.06	6	6	0	0	...	0-...	36.0	26	11	10	2	12-0	32	.203
— New York (A.L.)	6	2	.750	5.47	1.40	28	3	0	0	1	1-1	77.1	75	49	47	9	33-2	56	.254
2005— Tampa (Fla. St.)	0	1	.000	6.00	1.33	2	2	0	0	0	0-0	3.0	4	2	2	0	0-0	4	.286
— New York (A.L.)	5	3	.625	4.73	1.32	64	1	0	0	16	1-6	78.0	76	43	41	10	27-1	45	.257
2006— New York (A.L.)	0	0	...	7.59	2.16	18	0	0	0	3	0-0	10.2	17	10	9	3	6-0	6	.354
American League totals (9 years)	39	44	.470	5.15	1.53	261	84	4	0	24	3-10	781.2	867	477	447	106	326-9	472	.284
National League totals (2 years)	1	0	1.000	9.00	1.85	8	0	0	0	0	0-0	13.0	18	13	13	4	6-0	7	.333
Major League totals (11 years)	40	44	.476	5.21	1.53	269	84	4	0	24	3-10	794.2	885	490	460	110	332-9	479	.285

DIVISION SERIES RECORD

Year Team (League)	W	L	Pct.	ERA	WHIP	G	GS	CG	ShO	Hld.	Sv.-Opp.	IP	H	R	ER	HR	BB-IBB	SO	Avg.
2004— New York (A.L.)	0	0	...	6.75	2.63	2	0	0	0	0	0-0	2.2	4	2	2	1	3-0	4	.333
2005— New York (A.L.)	0	0	...	13.50	1.50	2	0	0	0	0	0-0	0.2	1	1	1	1	0-0	0	.333
Division series totals (2 years)	0	0	...	8.10	2.40	4	0	0	0	0	0-0	3.1	5	3	3	2	3-0	4	.333

CHAMPIONSHIP SERIES RECORD

Year Team (League)	W	L	Pct.	ERA	WHIP	G	GS	CG	ShO	Hld.	Sv.-Opp.	IP	H	R	ER	HR	BB-IBB	SO	Avg.
2004— New York (A.L.)	0	0	...	2.70	1.20	4	0	0	0	2	0-0	3.1	2	1	1	1	2-0	2	.182

2006 LEFTY-RIGHTY SPLITS

vs.	Avg.	AB	H	2B	3B	HR	RBI	BB	SO	OBP	Slg.	vs.	Avg.	AB	H	2B	3B	HR	RBI	BB	SO	OBP	Slg.
L	.333	12	4	0	0	1	3	3	0	.467	.583	R	.361	36	13	4	0	2	8	3	6	.415	.639

SULLIVAN, CORY — OF

PERSONAL: Born August 20, 1979, in Tulsa, Okla. ... 6-0/180. ... Bats left, throws left. ... Full name: Cory Sullivan. ... High school: North Allegheny (Pa.). ... Junior college: Cypress (Calif.). ... College: Wake Forest. **TRANSACTIONS/CAREER NOTES:** Selected by Colorado Rockies organization in seventh round of 2001 free-agent draft.

2006 GAMES PLAYED BY POSITION (MLB): OF—114.

									BATTING									FIELDING	
Year Team (League)	Pos.	G	AB	R	H	2B	3B	HR	RBI	BB	SO	HBP	GDP	SB-CS	Avg.	OBP	SLG	OPS	E	Avg.
2001— Asheville (S. Atl.)	OF	67	258	36	71	12	1	5	22	25	56	2	2	13-9	.275	.344	.388	.732	2	.985
2002— Salem (Carol.)	OF	138	560	90	161	42	6	12	67	36	70	12	8	26-5	.288	.340	.448	.788	4	.987
2003— Tulsa (Texas)	OF	135	557	81	167	34	8	5	61	39	83	4	4	17-13	.300	.347	.417	.764	2	.994
2004—	Did not play																			
2005— Colorado (N.L.)	OF	139	378	64	111	15	4	4	30	28	83	3	6	12-3	.294	.343	.386	.729	3	.986
2006— Colorado (N.L.)	OF	126	386	47	103	26	10	2	30	32	100	1	5	10-6	.267	.321	.402	.722	1	.996
Major League totals (2 years)		265	764	111	214	41	14	6	60	60	183	4	11	22-9	.280	.332	.394	.726	4	.991

2006 LEFTY-RIGHTY SPLITS

vs.	Avg.	AB	H	2B	3B	HR	RBI	BB	SO	OBP	Slg.	vs.	Avg.	AB	H	2B	3B	HR	RBI	BB	SO	OBP	Slg.
L	.280	25	7	1	1	1	4	2	9	.310	.520	R	.266	361	96	25	9	1	26	30	91	.322	.393

SUPPAN, JEFF — P

PERSONAL: Born January 2, 1975, in Oklahoma City. ... 6-2/220. ... Throws right, bats right. ... Full name: Jeffrey Scot Suppan. ... Name pronounced: SOO-pahn. ... High school: Crespi (Encino, Calif.). **TRANSACTIONS/CAREER NOTES:** Selected by Boston Red Sox organization in second round of 1993 free-agent draft. ... On disabled list (August 25, 1996-remainder of season). ... Selected by Arizona Diamondbacks in first round (third pick overall) of expansion draft (November 18, 1997). ... Traded by Diamondbacks to Kansas City Royals for cash (September 3, 1998). ... Signed as a free agent by Pittsburgh Pirates (January 31, 2003). ... Traded by Pirates with Ps Brandon Lyon and Anastacio Martinez to Boston Red Sox for 2B Freddy Sanchez, P Mike Gonzalez and cash (July 31, 2003). ... Signed as a free agent by St. Louis Cardinals (December 18, 2003).

CAREER HITTING: 49-for-251 (.195), 16 R, 4 2B, 0 3B, 1 HR, 15 RBI.

Year Team (League)	W	L	Pct.	ERA	WHIP	G	GS	CG	ShO	Hld.	Sv.-Opp.	IP	H	R	ER	HR	BB-IBB	SO	Avg.
1993— GC Red Sox (GCL)	4	3	.571	2.18	1.18	10	9	2	1	...	0-...	57.2	52	20	14	0	16-0	64	.237
1994— Sarasota (Fla. St.)	13	7	.650	3.26	1.17	27	27	4	2	...	0-...	174.0	153	74	63	10	50-0	173	.236
1995— Trenton (East.)	6	2	.750	2.36	1.13	15	15	1	1	...	0-...	99.0	86	35	26	8	26-1	88	.232
— Boston (A.L.)	1	2	.333	5.96	1.50	8	3	0	0	1	0-0	22.2	29	15	15	4	5-1	19	.312
— Pawtucket (Int'l)	2	3	.400	5.32	1.29	7	7	0	0	0	0-0	45.2	50	29	27	9	9-0	32	.278
1996— Boston (A.L.)	1	1	.500	7.54	1.85	8	4	0	0	0	0-0	22.2	29	19	19	3	13-0	13	.330
— Pawtucket (Int'l)	10	6	.625	3.22	1.07	22	22	7	1	0	0-...	145.1	130	66	52	16	25-1	142	.233
1997— Pawtucket (Int'l)	5	1	.833	3.71	1.09	9	9	2	1	...	0-...	60.2	51	26	25	7	15-0	40	.233
— Boston (A.L.)	7	3	.700	5.69	1.57	23	23	0	0	0	0-0	112.1	140	75	71	12	36-1	67	.305
1998— Arizona (N.L.)	1	7	.125	6.68	1.56	13	13	1	0	0	0-0	66.0	82	55	49	12	21-1	39	.301
— Tucson (PCL)	4	3	.571	3.63	1.37	13	12	0	0	0	0-...	67.0	75	29	27	4	17-1	62	.277
— Kansas City (A.L.)	0	0	...	0.71	0.79	4	1	0	0	0	0-0	12.2	9	1	1	1	1-0	12	.200
1999— Kansas City (A.L.)	10	12	.455	4.53	1.36	32	32	4	1	0	0-0	208.2	222	113	105	28	62-4	103	.274
2000— Kansas City (A.L.)	10	9	.526	4.94	1.49	35	33	3	1	0	0-0	217.0	240	121	119	* 36	84-3	128	.284
2001— Kansas City (A.L.)	10	14	.417	4.37	1.38	34	34	1	0	0	0-0	218.1	227	120	106	26	74-3	120	.267
2002— Kansas City (A.L.)	9	16	.360	5.32	1.43	33	33	3	1	0	0-0	208.0	229	134	123	32	68-3	109	.279
2003— Pittsburgh (N.L.)	10	7	.588	3.57	1.26	21	21	3	2	0	0-0	141.0	147	57	56	11	31-5	78	.268
— Boston (A.L.)	3	4	.429	5.57	1.43	11	10	0	0	0	0-0	63.0	70	41	39	12	20-0	32	.281
2004— St. Louis (N.L.)	16	9	.640	4.16	1.37	31	31	0	0	0	0-0	188.0	192	98	87	25	65-1	110	.265
2005— St. Louis (N.L.)	16	10	.615	3.57	1.38	32	32	0	0	0	0-0	194.1	206	93	77	24	63-11	114	.275
2006— St. Louis (N.L.)	12	7	.632	4.12	1.45	32	32	0	0	0	0-0	190.0	207	100	87	21	69-6	104	.277
American League totals (8 years)	51	61	.455	4.96	1.44	188	172	11	3	1	0-0	1085.1	1195	639	598	154	363-15	603	.280
National League totals (5 years)	55	40	.579	4.11	1.39	129	129	4	2	0	0-0	779.1	834	403	356	93	249-14	445	.274
Major League totals (12 years)	106	101	.512	4.60	1.42	317	301	15	5	1	0-0	1864.2	2029	1042	954	247	612-29	1048	.278

DIVISION SERIES RECORD

Year Team (League)	W	L	Pct.	ERA	WHIP	G	GS	CG	ShO	Hld.	Sv.-Opp.	IP	H	R	ER	HR	BB-IBB	SO	Avg.
2004— St. Louis (N.L.)	1	0	1.000	2.57	0.71	1	1	0	0	0	0-0	7.0	2	2	2	1	3-0	2	.091
2006— St. Louis (N.L.)	0	1	.000	6.23	2.08	1	1	0	0	0	0-0	4.1	6	3	3	0	3-1	3	.353
Division series totals (2 years)	1	1	.500	3.97	1.24	2	2	0	0	0	0-0	11.1	8	5	5	1	6-1	5	.205

CHAMPIONSHIP SERIES RECORD

Year Team (League)	W	L	Pct.	ERA	WHIP	G	GS	CG	ShO	Hld.	Sv.-Opp.	IP	H	R	ER	HR	BB-IBB	SO	Avg.
2004— St. Louis (N.L.)	1	1	.500	3.00	1.00	2	2	0	0	0	0-0	12.0	8	5	4	2	4-0	9	.186
2005— St. Louis (N.L.)	0	0	...	1.80	1.20	1	1	0	0	0	0-0	5.0	3	1	1	0	3-0	5	.167
2006— St. Louis (N.L.)	1	0	1.000	0.60	0.73	2	2	0	0	0	0-0	15.0	5	1	1	0	6-1	6	.100
Champ. series totals (3 years)	2	1	.667	1.69	0.91	5	5	0	0	0	0-0	32.0	16	7	6	3	13-1	20	.144

S

Year	Team (League)	W	L	Pct.	ERA	WHIP	G	GS	CG	ShO	Hld.	Sv.-Opp.	IP	H	R	ER	HR	BB-IBB	SO	Avg.
2004—	St. Louis (N.L.)	0	1	.000	7.71	1.93	1	1	0	0	0	0-0	4.2	8	4	4	1	1-0	4	.364
2006—	St. Louis (N.L.)	0	0		4.50	1.67	1	1	0	0	0	0-0	6.0	8	3	3	1	2-1	4	.320
	World series totals (2 years)	0	1	.000	5.91	1.78	2	2	0	0	0	0-0	10.2	16	7	7	2	3-1	8	.340

2006 LEFTY-RIGHTY SPLITS

vs.	Avg.	AB	H	2B	3B	HR	RBI	BB	SO	OBP	Slg.	vs.	Avg.	AB	H	2B	3B	HR	RBI	BB	SO	OBP	Slg.
L	.302	338	102	23	1	10	39	33	54	.370	.464	R	.257	409	105	26	4	11	49	36	50	.321	.421

SUZUKI, ICHIRO — OF

PERSONAL: Born October 22, 1973, in Kasugai, Japan. ... 5-9/172. ... Bats left, throws right. ... Name pronounced: ee-chee-row. ... High school: Aikoudai Meiden (Kasugai, Japan). **TRANSACTIONS/CAREER NOTES:** Signed as a free agent by Seattle Mariners (November 18, 2000). **RECORDS:** Holds major league record for most hits, season (262, 2004). **HONORS:** Named A.L. Rookie Player of the Year by THE SPORTING NEWS (2001). ... Named outfielder on THE SPORTING NEWS A.L. All-Star team (2001 and 2004). ... Named A.L. Rookie of the Year by Baseball Writers' Association of America (2001). ... Named A.L. Most Valuable Player by Baseball Writers' Association of America (2001). ... Won A.L. Gold Glove as outfielder (2001-06). ... Named outfielder on A.L. Silver Slugger team (2001). **STATISTICAL NOTES:** Career major league grand slams: 3.
2006 GAMES PLAYED BY POSITION (MLB): OF—159, DH—2.

											BATTING								FIELDING	
Year	Team (League)	Pos.	G	AB	R	H	2B	3B	HR	RBI	BB	SO	HBP	GDP	SB-CS	Avg.	OBP	SLG	OPS	E	Avg.
1992—	Orix (Jap. Pacific)		40	95	9	24	5	0	0	5	3	11	...	...	3-2	.253	...	.305	...	...	...
1993—	Orix (Jap. Pacific)		43	64	4	12	2	0	1	3	2	7	...	...	0-2	.188	...	.266	...	...	...
1994—	Orix (Jap. Pacific)		130	546	111	210	41	5	13	54	51	53	...	...	29-7	.385	...	.549	...	...	...
1995—	Orix (Jap. Pacific)		130	524	104	179	23	4	25	80	68	52	...	...	49-9	.342	...	.544	...	...	...
1996—	Orix (Jap. Pacific)		130	542	104	193	24	4	16	84	56	52	...	...	35-3	.356	...	.504	...	...	...
1997—	Orix (Jap. Pacific)		135	536	94	185	31	4	17	91	62	36	...	...	39-4	.345	...	.513	...	...	...
1998—	Orix (Jap. Pacific)		135	506	79	181	36	3	13	71	43	35	...	...	11-4	.358	...	.518	...	...	...
1999—	Orix (Jap. Pacific)		103	411	80	141	27	2	21	68	45	46	...	...	12-1	.343	...	.572	...	...	...
2000—	Orix (Jap. Pacific)		105	395	73	153	22	1	12	74	54	36	...	...	21-...	.387	...	.539	...	...	...
2001—	Seattle (A.L.)	OF-DH	157	* 692	127	* 242	34	8	8	69	30	53	8	3*	* 56-14	* .350	.381	.457	.838	1	.997
2002—	Seattle (A.L.)	OF-DH	157	647	111	208	27	8	8	51	68	62	5	8	31-15	.321	.388	.425	.813	3	.991
2003—	Seattle (A.L.)	OF	159	679	111	212	29	8	13	62	36	69	6	3	34-8	.312	.352	.436	.788	2	.994
2004—	Seattle (A.L.)	OF-DH	161	* 704	101	* 262	24	5	8	60	49	63	4	6	36-11	* .372	.414	.455	.869	3	.992
2005—	Seattle (A.L.)	OF-DH	* 162	679	111	206	21	12	15	68	48	66	4	5	33-8	.303	.350	.436	.786	2	.995
2006—	Seattle (A.L.)	OF-DH	161	695	110	* 224	20	9	9	49	49	71	5	2	45-2	.322	.370	.416	.786	3	.992
	Major League totals (6 years)		957	4096	671	1354	155	50	61	359	280	384	32	27	235-58	.331	.376	.438	.814	14	.994

DIVISION SERIES RECORD

Year	Team (League)	Pos.	G	AB	R	H	2B	3B	HR	RBI	BB	SO	HBP	GDP	SB-CS	Avg.	OBP	SLG	OPS	E	Avg.
2001—	Seattle (A.L.)	OF	5	20	4	12	1	0	0	2	1	0	0	0	1-2	.600	.619	.650	1.269	1	.900

CHAMPIONSHIP SERIES RECORD

Year	Team (League)	Pos.	G	AB	R	H	2B	3B	HR	RBI	BB	SO	HBP	GDP	SB-CS	Avg.	OBP	SLG	OPS	E	Avg.
2001—	Seattle (A.L.)	OF	5	18	3	4	1	0	0	1	4	4	0	0	2-0	.222	.364	.278	.641	0	1.000

ALL-STAR GAME RECORD

		G	AB	R	H	2B	3B	HR	RBI	BB	SO	HBP	GDP	SB-CS	Avg.	OBP	SLG	OPS	E	Avg.
	All-Star Game totals (6 years)	6	15	2	3	1	0	0	2	2	1	0	0	1-0	.200	.294	.267	.561	0	1.000

2006 LEFTY-RIGHTY SPLITS

vs.	Avg.	AB	H	2B	3B	HR	RBI	BB	SO	OBP	Slg.	vs.	Avg.	AB	H	2B	3B	HR	RBI	BB	SO	OBP	Slg.
L	.352	176	62	5	3	2	8	11	15	.397	.449	R	.312	519	162	15	6	7	41	38	56	.361	.405

SWEENEY, BRIAN — P

PERSONAL: Born June 13, 1974, in Yonkers, N.Y. ... 6-2/202. ... Throws right, bats right. ... Full name: Brian Edward Sweeney. ... High school: Yonkers (N.Y.). ... College: Mercy (N.Y.). **TRANSACTIONS/CAREER NOTES:** Signed as a non-drafted free agent by Seattle Mariners organization (September 17, 1996). ... Traded by Mariners with IF Jeff Cirillo and cash to San Diego Padres for P Kevin Jarvis, IF Dave Hansen, C Wiki Gonzalez and OF Vince Faison (January 6, 2004). ... Signed as a free agent by Tampa Bay Devil Rays organization (January 19, 2005). ... Released by Devil Rays (May 25, 2005). ... Signed by Padres organization (May 29, 2005).
CAREER HITTING: 0-for-5 (.000), 0 R, 0 2B, 0 3B, 0 HR, 0 RBI.

Year	Team (League)	W	L	Pct.	ERA	WHIP	G	GS	CG	ShO	Hld.	Sv.-Opp.	IP	H	R	ER	HR	BB-IBB	SO	Avg.
1997—	Lancaster (Calif.)	6	3	.667	3.80	1.22	40	0	0	0	...	1-...	85.1	83	39	36	11	21-1	73	.252
1998—	Lancaster (Calif.)	6	0	1.000	3.63	1.19	17	4	0	0	...	0-...	52.0	41	26	21	6	21-1	48	.218
1999—	Lancaster (Calif.)	0	0		6.75	1.82	5	0	0	0	...	0-...	9.1	14	7	7	4	3-0	14	.341
—	Tacoma (PCL)	0	2	.000	6.75	1.75	5	1	0	0	...	0-...	16.0	26	17	12	5	2-0	10	.366
—	New Haven (East.)	4	6	.400	4.69	1.40	23	18	0	0	...	1-...	111.1	125	65	58	18	31-1	83	.285
2000—	Tacoma (PCL)	0	1	.000	6.00	1.67	2	1	0	0	...	0-...	6.0	9	4	4	2	1-0	1	.360
—	New Haven (East.)	4	3	.571	3.40	1.43	19	7	0	0	...	1-...	47.2	49	20	18	3	19-0	27	.268
2001—	San Antonio (Texas)	7	4	.636	3.80	1.34	37	9	0	0	...	0-...	104.1	117	47	44	8	23-1	96	.283
2002—	Tacoma (PCL)	9	5	.643	3.80	1.30	30	23	0	1	...	2-...	142.0	157	67	60	16	28-0	113	.275
2003—	Tacoma (PCL)	11	10	.524	4.28	1.40	29	21	0	0	...	0-...	141.0	165	80	67	17	32-0	115	.288
—	Seattle (A.L.)	0	0		1.93	0.86	5	0	0	0	...	0-...	9.1	7	2	2	0	1-0	7	.212
2004—	Portland (PCL)	11	4	.733	3.83	1.24	24	23	0	0	...	0-...	138.2	130	65	59	16	42-1	110	.242
—	San Diego (N.L.)	1	0	1.000	5.65	1.53	7	2	0	0	0	0-0	14.1	20	9	9	1	2-0	10	.328
2005—	Durham (Int'l)	3	4	.429	4.06	1.76	10	10	0	0	...	0-...	51.0	70	30	23	6	20-1	39	.333
—	Portland (PCL)	4	5	.444	3.98	1.24	20	16	0	0	...	0-...	110.2	121	51	49	15	16-0	72	.281
2006—	Portland (PCL)	2	1	.667	4.70	1.30	7	5	0	0	...	0-1	30.2	33	17	16	3	7-0	22	.280
—	San Diego (N.L.)	2	0	1.000	3.20	1.22	37	0	0	0	...	2-3	56.1	53	22	20	6	16-5	23	.249
	American League totals (1 year)	0	0		1.93	0.86	5	0	0	0	...	0-0	9.1	7	2	2	0	1-0	7	.212
	National League totals (2 years)	3	0	1.000	3.69	1.29	44	2	0	0	...	2-3	70.2	73	31	29	7	18-5	33	.266
	Major League totals (3 years)	3	0	1.000	3.49	1.24	49	2	0	0	...	2-3	80.0	80	33	31	7	19-5	40	.261

2006 LEFTY-RIGHTY SPLITS

vs.	Avg.	AB	H	2B	3B	HR	RBI	BB	SO	OBP	Slg.	vs.	Avg.	AB	H	2B	3B	HR	RBI	BB	SO	OBP	Slg.
L	.263	99	26	1		3	11	7	8	.315	.384	R	.237	114	27	5	0	3	16	9	15	.290	.360

SWEENEY, MARK — 1B/OF

PERSONAL: Born October 26, 1969, in Framingham, Mass. ... 6-1/215. ... Bats left, throws left. ... Full name: Mark Patrick Sweeney. ... High school: Holliston (Mass.). ... College: Maine. **TRANSACTIONS/CAREER NOTES:** Selected by Los Angeles Dodgers organization in 39th round of 1990 free-agent draft; did not sign. ... Selected by

California Angels organization in ninth round of 1991 free-agent draft. ... Traded by Angels with a player to be named to St. Louis Cardinals for P John Habyan (July 8, 1995); Cardinals acquired IF Rod Correia to complete deal (January 31, 1996). ... Traded by Cardinals with Ps Danny Jackson and Rich Batchelor to San Diego Padres for P Fernando Valenzuela, 3B Scott Livingstone and OF Phil Plantier (June 13, 1997). ... Traded by Padres with OF Greg Vaughn to Cincinnati Reds for OF Reggie Sanders, SS Damian Jackson and P Josh Harris (February 2, 1999). ... Traded by Reds with a player to be named to Milwaukee Brewers for OF Alex Ochoa (January 14, 2000); Brewers acquired P Gene Altman to complete deal (May 15, 2000). ... On disabled list (March 31-May 7 and July 18-August 14, 2000); included rehabilitation assignments to Indianapolis. ... Traded by Brewers with P Jeff D'Amico, OF Jeromy Burnitz, IF Lou Collier and cash to New York Mets as part of three-team deal in which Mets also acquired 1B/OF Ross Gload and P Craig House from Colorado Rockies, Rockies acquired IF Todd Zeile, OF Benny Agbayani and cash from Mets and Brewers acquired P Glendon Rusch and IF/OF Lenny Harris from Mets and OF Alex Ochoa from Rockies (January 21, 2002). ... Released by Mets (March 13, 2002). ... Signed by Padres organization (March 16, 2002). ... On disabled list (June 6-26, 2002). ... Released by Padres (July 15, 2002). ... Signed as a free agent by Rockies organization (January 21, 2003). ... Signed as a free agent by Padres (December 22, 2004). ... Signed as a free agent by San Francisco Giants (December 8, 2005). **STATISTICAL NOTES:** Career major league grand slams: 1.

2006 GAMES PLAYED BY POSITION (MLB): 1B—53, OF—21.

									BATTING									FIELDING	
Year	Team (League)	Pos.	G	AB	R	H	2B	3B	HR	RBI	BB	SO	HBP	GDP	SB-CS	Avg.	OBP	SLG	OPS	E	Avg.
1991—Boise (N'west)		OF	70	234	45	66	10	3	4	34	51	42	5	7	9-5	.282	.416	.402	.818	4	.954
1992—Quad City (Midw.)		OF	120	424	65	115	20	5	14	76	47	85	4	6	15-11	.271	.346	.441	.787	4	.981
1993—Palm Springs (Calif.)		OF-1B	66	245	41	87	18	3	3	47	42	29	2	4	9-6	.355	.449	.490	.938	7	.955
—Midland (Texas)		OF	51	188	41	67	13	2	9	32	27	22	6	5	1-1	.356	.444	.590	1.035	1	.989
1994—Vancouver (PCL)		DH-1B-OF	103	344	59	98	12	3	8	49	59	50	5	3	3-3	.285	.394	.407	.801	2	.994
—Midland (Texas)		OF-1B-DH	14	50	13	15	3	0	3	18	10	10	0	3	1-1	.300	.403	.540	.943	2	.973
1995—Vancouver (PCL)		OF-DH-1B	69	226	48	78	14	2	7	59	43	33	2	6	3-1	.345	.452	.518	.970	2	.981
—Louisville (A.A.)		1B	22	76	15	28	8	0	2	22	14	8	2	0	2-0	.368	.468	.553	1.021	2	.990
—St. Louis (N.L.)		1B-OF	37	77	5	21	2	0	2	13	10	15	0	3	1-1	.273	.348	.377	.725	2	.988
1996—St. Louis (N.L.)		OF-1B	98	170	32	45	9	0	3	22	33	29	1	4	3-0	.265	.387	.371	.758	3	.977
1997—St. Louis (N.L.)		OF-1B	44	61	5	13	3	0	0	4	9	14	1	2	0-1	.213	.319	.262	.582	0	1.000
—San Diego (N.L.)		OF-1B	71	103	11	33	4	0	2	19	11	18	0	1	2-2	.320	.383	.417	.800	2	.957
1998—San Diego (N.L.)		OF-1B-DH	122	192	17	45	8	3	2	15	26	37	1	5	1-2	.234	.324	.339	.663	1	.994
1999—Cincinnati (N.L.)		1B-OF	37	31	6	11	3	0	2	7	4	9	0	2	0-0	.355	.429	.645	1.074	0	1.000
—Indianapolis (Int'l)		OF-DH-1B	86	311	66	100	17	1	12	51	59	40	4	7	3-2	.322	.432	.498	.931	5	.982
2000—Milwaukee (N.L.)		DH-OF-1B	71	73	9	16	6	0	1	6	12	18	1	1	0-0	.219	.337	.342	.680	0	1.000
—Indianapolis (Int'l)		1B-OF	18	55	13	28	8	0	2	14	10	8	0	3	0-0	.509	.585	.764	1.348	0	1.000
2001—Indianapolis (Int'l)		OF-1B	109	404	65	116	34	1	6	69	56	71	2	6	3-1	.287	.373	.421	.793	1	.994
—Milwaukee (N.L.)		OF-1B	48	89	9	23	3	1	3	11	12	23	0	0	2-1	.258	.347	.416	.762	1	.971
2002—San Diego (N.L.)		1B-OF-DH	48	65	3	11	3	0	1	4	4	19	0	1	0-0	.169	.217	.262	.479	2	.956
—Portland (PCL)		1B	1	1	0	1	0	0	0	0	0	0	0	0	0-0	1.000	1.000	1.000	2.000	0	...
2003—Colo. Springs (PCL)		OF-1B-DH	51	165	24	49	10	1	5	35	34	32	0	5	1-4	.297	.407	.461	.867	2	.985
—Colorado (N.L.)		OF-1B-DH	67	97	13	25	9	0	2	14	9	27	0	2	0-1	.258	.321	.412	.733	0	1.000
2004—Colorado (N.L.)		1B-OF-DH	122	177	25	47	12	2	9	40	32	51	2	2	1-0	.266	.377	.508	.885	0	1.000
2005—San Diego (N.L.)		1B-OF-DH	135	221	31	65	12	1	8	40	40	58	0	6	4-0	.294	.395	.466	.861	5	.986
2006—San Francisco		1B-OF	114	259	32	65	15	2	5	37	28	50	5	0	1-0	.251	.330	.382	.712	3	.993
Major League totals (12 years)			1014	1615	198	420	89	9	40	232	230	368	9	35	14-9	.260	.352	.401	.753	19	.988

	DIVISION SERIES RECORD																				
Year	Team (League)	Pos.	G	AB	R	H	2B	3B	HR	RBI	BB	SO	HBP	GDP	SB-CS	Avg.	OBP	SLG	OPS	E	Avg.
1996—St. Louis (N.L.)			1	1	0	1	0	0	0	0	0	0	0	0	0-0	1.000	1.000	1.000	2.000	...	...
1998—San Diego (N.L.)			2	1	0	0	0	0	0	0	1	0	0	0	0-1	.000	.500	.000	.500	...	...
2005—San Diego (N.L.)		1B	3	3	1	2	1	0	0	0	2	0	0	0	0-0	.667	.800	1.000	1.800	0	1.000
Division series totals (3 years)			6	5	1	3	1	0	0	0	3	0	0	0	0-1	.600	.750	.800	1.550	0	1.000

	CHAMPIONSHIP SERIES RECORD																				
Year	Team (League)	Pos.	G	AB	R	H	2B	3B	HR	RBI	BB	SO	HBP	GDP	SB-CS	Avg.	OBP	SLG	OPS	E	Avg.
1996—St. Louis (N.L.)		OF	5	4	1	0	0	0	0	0	0	0	0	0	0-0	.000	.000	.000	.000	0	1.000
1998—San Diego (N.L.)			3	2	1	0	0	0	0	0	1	0	0	0	0-0	.000	.333	.000	.333	...	...
Champ. series totals (2 years)			8	6	2	0	0	0	0	0	1	3	0	0	0-0	.000	.143	.000	.143	0	1.000

	WORLD SERIES RECORD																				
Year	Team (League)	Pos.	G	AB	R	H	2B	3B	HR	RBI	BB	SO	HBP	GDP	SB-CS	Avg.	OBP	SLG	OPS	E	Avg.
1998—San Diego (N.L.)			3	3	0	2	0	0	0	1	0	0	0	0	0-0	.667	.667	.667	1.333	...	...

2006 LEFTY-RIGHTY SPLITS

vs.	Avg.	AB	H	2B	3B	HR	RBI	BB	SO	OBP	Slg.	vs.	Avg.	AB	H	2B	3B	HR	RBI	BB	SO	OBP	Slg.
L	.135	37	5	0	0	0	2	4	12	.238	.135	R	.270	222	60	15	2	5	35	24	38	.345	.423

SWEENEY, MIKE   DH/1B

PERSONAL: Born July 22, 1973, in Orange, Calif. ... 6-3/225. ... Bats right, throws right. ... Full name: Michael John Sweeney. ... High school: Ontario (Calif.). **TRANSACTIONS/CAREER NOTES:** Selected by Kansas City Royals organization in 10th round of 1991 free-agent draft. ... On suspended list (August 17-27, 2001). ... On disabled list (July 14-August 13, 2002); included rehabilitation assignment to Omaha. ... On disabled list (June 21-August 8, 2003); included rehabilitation assignment to Omaha. ... On disabled list (August 22, 2004-remainder of season). ... On disabled list (June 20-July 1, 2005). ... On disabled list (May 3-August 8, 2006); included rehabilitation assignments to Burlington, Wichita and Omaha. **STATISTICAL NOTES:** Career major league grand slams: 3. **MISCELLANEOUS NOTES:** Holds Kansas City Royals all-time record for highest career batting average (.309).

2006 GAMES PLAYED BY POSITION (MLB): DH—59.

									BATTING									FIELDING	
Year	Team (League)	Pos.	G	AB	R	H	2B	3B	HR	RBI	BB	SO	HBP	GDP	SB-CS	Avg.	OBP	SLG	OPS	E	Avg.
1991—GC Royals (GCL)		1B-C	38	102	8	22	3	0	1	11	11	9	0	2	1-0	.216	.287	.275	.561	4	.972
1992—Eugene (Northwest)		C	59	199	17	44	12	1	4	28	13	54	4	0	3-3	.221	.280	.352	.632	14	.967
1993—Eugene (Northwest)		C	53	175	32	42	10	2	6	29	30	41	3	2	1-0	.240	.359	.423	.782	7	.983
1994—Rockford (Midwest)		C	86	276	47	83	20	3	10	52	55	44	9	8	0-1	.301	.427	.504	.931	6	.988
1995—Wilmington (Caro.)		C-DH-3B	99	332	61	103	23	1	18	53	60	39	9	4	6-1	.310	.424	.548	.972	7	.989
—Kansas City (A.L.)		C	4	4	1	1	0	0	0	0	0	0	0	0	0-0	.250	.250	.250	.500	1	.875
1996—Wichita (Texas)		DH-C	66	235	45	75	18	1	14	51	32	29	2	5	3-2	.319	.399	.583	.982	1	.995
—Omaha (A.A.)		C-DH	25	101	14	26	9	0	3	16	6	13	3	0	0-0	.257	.318	.436	.754	0	1.000
—Kansas City (A.L.)		C-DH	50	165	23	46	10	0	4	24	18	21	4	7	1-2	.279	.358	.412	.770	1	.994
1997—Kansas City (A.L.)		C-DH	84	240	30	58	8	0	7	31	17	33	6	8	3-2	.242	.306	.363	.668	3	.993
—Omaha (A.A.)		C-DH	40	144	22	34	8	1	10	29	18	20	2	2	0-2	.236	.323	.514	.837	1	.996
1998—Kansas City (A.L.)		C	92	282	32	73	18	0	8	35	24	38	2	7	2-3	.259	.320	.408	.728	•9	.984
1999—Kansas City (A.L.)		1B-DH-C	150	575	101	185	44	2	22	102	54	48	10	21	6-1	.322	.387	.520	.907	12	.981
2000—Kansas City (A.L.)		1B-DH	159	618	105	206	30	0	29	144	71	67	•15	15	8-3	.333	.407	.523	.930	9	.991

S

Year Team (League)	Pos.	G	AB	R	H	2B	3B	HR	RBI	BB	SO	HBP	GDP	SB-CS	Avg.	OBP	SLG	OPS		E	Avg.
																		BATTING		FIELDING	
2001— Kansas City (A.L.)	1B-DH	147	559	97	170	46	0	29	99	64	64	2	13	10-3	.304	.374	.542	.916		12	.989
2002— Kansas City (A.L.)	1B-DH	126	471	81	160	31	1	24	86	61	46	6	9	9-7	.340	.417	.563	.979		9	.991
— Omaha (PCL)	1B	3	12	2	3	1	0	1	4	1	2	0	1	0-0	.250	.286	.583	.869		0	1.000
2003— Omaha (PCL)	DH	2	8	3	2	1	0	1	1	1	1	0	0	0-0	.250	.333	.750	1.083		0	...
— Kansas City (A.L.)	DH-1B	108	392	62	115	18	1	16	83	64	56	2	13	3-2	.293	.391	.467	.858		4	.990
2004— Kansas City (A.L.)	1B-DH	106	411	56	118	23	0	22	79	33	44	6	7	3-2	.287	.347	.504	.851		4	.992
2005— Kansas City (A.L.)	DH-1B	122	470	63	141	39	0	21	83	33	61	4	16	3-0	.300	.347	.517	.864		1	.998
2006— Wichita (Texas)		4	13	3	5	1	0	2	5	2	2	0		0-0	.385	.467	.923	1.390		0	...
— Omaha (PCL)		5	15	3	5	2	0	1	4	5	1	0	2	0-0	.333	.476	.667	1.143		0	...
— Burlington (Midw.)		2	7	2	1	0	0	1	1	1	2	0		0-0	.143	.250	.571	.821		0	...
— Kansas City (A.L.)	DH	60	217	23	56	15	0	8	33	28	48	4	5	2-0	.258	.349	.438	.787		0	...
Major League totals (12 years)		1208	4404	674	1329	282	4	190	799	467	526	61	121	50-25	.302	.373	.497	.870		65	.990

ALL-STAR GAME RECORD

	G	AB	R	H	2B	3B	HR	RBI	BB	SO	HBP	GDP	SB-CS	Avg.	OBP	SLG	OPS	E	Avg.
All-Star Game totals (4 years)	4	4	0	0	0	0	0	0	0	1	0		0-0	.000	.000	.000	.000	0	1.000

2006 LEFTY-RIGHTY SPLITS

vs.	Avg.	AB	H	2B	3B	HR	RBI	BB	SO	OBP	Slg.	vs.	Avg.	AB	H	2B	3B	HR	RBI	BB	SO	OBP	Slg.
L	.266	64	17	3	0	2	7	10	12	.365	.406	R	.255	153	39	12	0	6	26	18	36	.343	.451

SWEENEY, RYAN — OF

PERSONAL: Born February 20, 1985, in Cedar Rapids, Iowa. ... Bats left, throws left. ... Full name: Ryan Joseph Sweeney. **TRANSACTIONS/CAREER NOTES:** Selected by Chicago White Sox organization in second round of 2003 free-agent draft.
2006 GAMES PLAYED BY POSITION (MLB): OF—15, DH—1.

Year Team (League)	Pos.	G	AB	R	H	2B	3B	HR	RBI	BB	SO	HBP	GDP	SB-CS	Avg.	OBP	SLG	OPS		E	Avg.
																		BATTING		FIELDING	
2003— Bristol (Appal.)		19	67	11	21	3	0	2	5	7	10	1	1	3-0	.313	.387	.448	.835		...	...
— Great Falls (Pio.)		10	34	0	12	2	0	0	4	2	3	0	1	0-2	.353	.389	.412	.801		...	...
2004— Win.-Salem (Car.)		134	515	71	146	22	3	7	66	40	65	7	3	8-6	.283	.342	.379	.721		...	...
2005— Birmingham (Sou.)	OF-DH	113	429	64	128	22	3	1	47	35	53	7	5	6-6	.298	.357	.371	.728		6	.987
2006— Charlotte (Int'l)		118	449	64	133	25	3	13	70	35	73	3	9	7-7	.296	.350	.452	.802		3	.988
— Chicago (A.L.)	OF-DH	18	35	1	8	0	0	0	5	0	7	0	1	0-0	.229	.229	.229	.457		0	1.000
Major League totals (1 year)		18	35	1	8	0	0	0	5	0	7	0	1	0-0	.229	.229	.229	.457		0	1.000

2006 LEFTY-RIGHTY SPLITS

vs.	Avg.	AB	H	2B	3B	HR	RBI	BB	SO	OBP	Slg.	vs.	Avg.	AB	H	2B	3B	HR	RBI	BB	SO	OBP	Slg.
L	.286	7	2	0	0	0	0	0	3	.286	.286	R	.214	28	6	0	0	0	5	0	4	.214	.214

SWISHER, NICK — OF/1B

PERSONAL: Born November 25, 1980, in Parkersburg, W.Va. ... 6-0/195. ... Bats both, throws left. ... Full name: Nicolas Thompson Swisher. ... High school: Parkersburg (W. Va.). ... College: Ohio State. ... Son of Steve Swisher, catcher with three major league teams (1974-82). **TRANSACTIONS/CAREER NOTES:** Selected by Oakland Athletics organization in first round (16th pick overall) of 2002 free-agent draft. ... On disabled list (May 2-25, 2005); included rehabilitation assignment to Sacramento. ... On bereavement list (August 14-19, 2005). **STATISTICAL NOTES:** Career major league grand slams: 2.
2006 GAMES PLAYED BY POSITION (MLB): 1B—90, OF—80, DH—2.

Year Team (League)	Pos.	G	AB	R	H	2B	3B	HR	RBI	BB	SO	HBP	GDP	SB-CS	Avg.	OBP	SLG	OPS		E	Avg.
																		BATTING		FIELDING	
2002— Vancouver (N'west)	OF	13	44	10	11	3	0	2	12	13	11	2	0	3-0	.250	.433	.455	.888		0	1.000
— Visalia (Calif.)	OF	49	183	22	44	13	2	4	23	26	48	2	6	3-1	.240	.340	.399	.739		4	.953
2003— Modesto (California)	OF-1B	51	189	38	56	14	2	10	43	41	49	2	4	0-2	.296	.418	.550	.968		4	.969
— Midland (Texas)	OF-1B	76	287	36	66	24	2	5	43	37	76	6	8	0-1	.230	.324	.380	.704		5	.971
2004— Sacramento (PCL)	OF-DH-1B	125	443	109	119	28	2	29	92	103	109	3	16	3-3	.269	.406	.537	.940		7	.977
— Oakland (A.L.)	OF-1B-DH	20	60	11	15	4	0	2	8	8	11	2	2	0-0	.250	.352	.417	.769		3	.935
2005— Oakland (A.L.)	OF-1B	131	462	66	109	32	1	21	74	55	110	4	9	0-1	.236	.322	.446	.768		2	.994
2006— Oakland (A.L.)	1B-OF-DH	157	556	106	141	24	2	35	95	97	152	11	13	1-2	.254	.372	.493	.864		8	.991
Major League totals (3 years)		308	1078	183	265	60	3	58	177	160	273	17	24	1-3	.246	.350	.468	.818		13	.990

DIVISION SERIES RECORD

Year Team (League)	Pos.	G	AB	R	H	2B	3B	HR	RBI	BB	SO	HBP	GDP	SB-CS	Avg.	OBP	SLG	OPS	E	Avg.
2006— Oakland (A.L.)	1B	3	10	3	3	2	0	0	2	2	2	0	0	0-0	.300	.417	.500	.917	0	1.000

CHAMPIONSHIP SERIES RECORD

Year Team (League)	Pos.	G	AB	R	H	2B	3B	HR	RBI	BB	SO	HBP	GDP	SB-CS	Avg.	OBP	SLG	OPS	E	Avg.
2006— Oakland (A.L.)	1B	4	10	0	1	0	0	0	0	5	5	0	0	0-0	.100	.400	.100	.500	0	1.000

2006 LEFTY-RIGHTY SPLITS

vs.	Avg.	AB	H	2B	3B	HR	RBI	BB	SO	OBP	Slg.	vs.	Avg.	AB	H	2B	3B	HR	RBI	BB	SO	OBP	Slg.
L	.291	141	41	6	0	8	26	25	29	.406	.504	R	.241	415	100	18	2	27	69	72	123	.360	.489

SWITZER, JON — P

PERSONAL: Born August 13, 1979, in Houston. ... 6-3/191. ... Throws left, bats left. ... Full name: Jon Michael Switzer. ... High school: Clear Lake (Texas). ... College: Arizona State. **TRANSACTIONS/CAREER NOTES:** Selected by Pittsburgh Pirates organization in 26th round of 1998 free-agent draft; did not sign. ... Selected by Tampa Bay Devil Rays organization in second round of 2001 free-agent draft. ... On disabled list (April 8, 2004-entire season).
CAREER HITTING: 0-for-0 (.000), 0 R, 0 2B, 0 3B, 0 HR, 0 RBI.

Year Team (League)	W	L	Pct.	ERA	WHIP	G	GS	CG	ShO	Hld.	Sv.-Opp.	IP	H	R	ER	HR	BB-IBB	SO	Avg.
2001— Hudson Valley (NYP)	2	0	1.000	0.63	0.77	5	0	0	0	...	0-...	14.1	9	3	1	0	2-0	20	.173
2002— Bakersfield (Calif.)	7	5	.583	4.27	1.30	20	20	0	0	...	0-...	103.1	108	55	49	8	26-0	129	.269
2003— Orlando (South.)	8	8	.500	3.43	1.18	22	22	0	0	...	0-...	126.0	117	63	48	10	32-1	100	.246
— Durham (Int'l)	1	0	1.000	1.80	1.20	1	1	0	0	...	0-...	5.0	6	1	1	1	0-0	3	.316
— Tampa Bay (A.L.)	0	0	...	7.45	1.66	5	0	0	0	0	0-0	9.2	13	8	8	2	3-0	7	.342
2004— Tampa Bay (A.L.)			Did not play																
2005— Montgom. (Sou.)	3	1	.750	3.45	1.21	6	6	0	0	0	0-0	31.1	33	14	12	2	5-0	20	.268
— Tampa Bay (A.L.)	0	0	...	6.75	3.00	2	0	0	0	0	0-0	4.0	5	4	3	0	7-0	5	.278
— Durham (Int'l)	0	5	.000	7.11	1.94	17	8	0	0	2	0-0	44.1	64	38	35	6	22-1	28	.342
2006— Durham (Int'l)	3	0	1.000	0.87	1.13	26	0	0	0	4	3-3	31.0	22	4	3	1	13-0	29	.191
— Tampa Bay (A.L.)	2	2	.500	4.54	1.69	40	0	0	0	5	0-3	33.2	38	19	17	5	19-3	18	.284
Major League totals (3 years)	2	2	.500	5.32	1.80	47	0	0	0	5	0-3	47.1	56	31	28	7	29-3	30	.295

vs.	Avg.	AB	H	2B	3B	HR	RBI	BB	SO	OBP	Slg.	vs.	Avg.	AB	H	2B	3B	HR	RBI	BB	SO	OBP	Slg.
L	.220	50	11	0	0	2	6	7	11	.310	.340	R	.321	84	27	6	0	3	10	12	7	.412	.500

TAGUCHI, SO — OF

PERSONAL: Born July 2, 1969, in Hyogo Prefecture, Japan. ... 5-10/163. ... Bats right, throws right. ... Name pronounced: tah-gu-chee. ... High school: Nishinomyia Kita (Osaka, Japan). ... College: Kansai Gakuin (Japan). **TRANSACTIONS/CAREER NOTES:** Signed as a free agent by St. Louis Cardinals (January 9, 2002).

2006 GAMES PLAYED BY POSITION (MLB): OF—123, 2B—1, DH—1.

Year Team (League)	Pos.	G	AB	R	H	2B	3B	HR	RBI	BB	SO	HBP	GDP	SB-CS	Avg.	OBP	SLG	OPS	E	Avg.
1992— Orix (Jap. Pacific)	OF	47	123	...	33	...	...	1	7	...	...	...	...	5-...	.268	...	.293	...	...	...
1993— Orix (Jap. Pacific)	OF	31	83	...	23	...	...	0	5	...	...	...	...	3-...	.277	...	.277	...	...	...
1994— Orix (Jap. Pacific)	OF	108	329	...	101	...	...	6	43	...	...	...	...	10-...	.307	...	.362	...	...	...
1995— Orix (Jap. Pacific)	OF	130	495	...	122	...	...	9	61	...	...	...	...	14-...	.246	...	.301	...	...	...
1996— Orix (Jap. Pacific)	OF	128	509	...	142	...	...	7	44	...	...	...	...	10-...	.279	...	.320	...	...	...
1997— Orix (Jap. Pacific)	OF	135	572	...	168	...	...	10	56	...	...	...	...	7-...	.294	...	.346	...	...	...
1998— Orix (Jap. Pacific)	OF	132	497	...	135	...	...	9	41	...	...	...	...	8-...	.272	...	.326	...	...	...
1999— Orix (Jap. Pacific)	OF	133	524	...	141	...	...	9	56	...	...	...	...	11-...	.269	...	.321	...	...	...
2000— Orix (Jap. Pacific)	OF	129	509	...	142	...	...	8	49	...	...	...	...	9-...	.279	...	.326	...	...	...
2001— Orix (Jap. Pacific)	OF	134	453	70	127	21	6	8	42	43	88	...	...	6-...	.280	...	.406	...	2	...
2002— Memphis (PCL)	OF	91	304	37	75	17	0	5	36	13	44	5	5	6-3	.247	.286	.352	.638	2	.990
— St. Louis (N.L.)	OF	19	15	4	6	0	0	0	2	2	1	0	0	1-0	.400	.471	.400	.871	1	.929
— New Haven (East.)	OF	26	107	21	33	10	0	1	15	9	15	3	1	3-1	.308	.375	.430	.805	2	.970
2003— Memphis (PCL)	OF-DH	90	258	31	66	8	2	2	24	22	36	2	5	14-5	.256	.318	.326	.644	1	.994
— St. Louis (N.L.)	OF-2B	43	54	9	14	3	1	3	13	4	11	0	2	1-0	.259	.310	.519	.829	1	1.000
2004— Memphis (PCL)	OF-DH	17	55	5	18	4	0	1	7	1	10	2	2	6-0	.327	.362	.455	.817	0	1.000
— St. Louis (N.L.)	OF	109	179	26	52	10	2	3	25	12	23	2	6	6-3	.291	.337	.419	.756	2	.980
2005— St. Louis (N.L.)	OF	143	396	45	114	21	2	8	53	20	62	2	11	11-2	.288	.322	.412	.734	2	.989
2006— St. Louis (N.L.)	OF-2B-DH	134	316	46	84	19	1	2	31	32	48	2	9	11-3	.266	.335	.351	.686	6	.969
Major League totals (5 years)		448	960	130	270	53	6	16	124	70	145	6	28	29-8	.281	.331	.399	.730	11	.979

DIVISION SERIES RECORD

Year Team (League)	Pos.	G	AB	R	H	2B	3B	HR	RBI	BB	SO	HBP	GDP	SB-CS	Avg.	OBP	SLG	OPS	E	Avg.
2004— St. Louis (N.L.)	OF	1	0	0	0	0	0	0	0	0	0	0	0	0-0	...	...	...	...	0	...
2005— St. Louis (N.L.)	OF	3	1	0	0	0	0	0	0	0	0	0	0	0-0	.000	.000	.000	.000	0	...
2006— St. Louis (N.L.)	OF	2	1	1	1	0	0	1	1	0	0	0	0	0-0	1.000	1.000	4.000	5.000	0	1.000
Division series totals (3 years)		6	2	1	1	0	0	1	1	0	0	0	0	0-0	.500	.500	2.000	2.500	0	1.000

CHAMPIONSHIP SERIES RECORD

Year Team (League)	Pos.	G	AB	R	H	2B	3B	HR	RBI	BB	SO	HBP	GDP	SB-CS	Avg.	OBP	SLG	OPS	E	Avg.
2004— St. Louis (N.L.)	OF	3	2	0	0	0	0	0	0	0	0	0	0	0-0	.000	.000	.000	.000	0	1.000
2005— St. Louis (N.L.)	OF	6	6	0	0	0	0	0	0	0	3	0	0	0-0	.000	.000	.000	.000	0	1.000
2006— St. Louis (N.L.)	OF	5	3	1	3	1	0	1	3	0	1	0	0	0-0	1.000	1.000	2.333	3.333	0	1.000
Champ. series totals (3 years)		14	11	1	3	1	0	1	3	0	4	0	0	0-0	.273	.273	.636	.909	0	1.000

WORLD SERIES RECORD

Year Team (League)	Pos.	G	AB	R	H	2B	3B	HR	RBI	BB	SO	HBP	GDP	SB-CS	Avg.	OBP	SLG	OPS	E	Avg.
2004— St. Louis (N.L.)	DH-OF	2	4	1	1	0	0	0	1	0	2	0	0	0-0	.250	.250	.250	.500	0	1.000
2006— St. Louis (N.L.)	OF	4	11	3	2	0	0	0	0	1	2	0	0	0-0	.182	.250	.182	.432	0	1.000
World series totals (2 years)		6	15	4	3	0	0	0	1	1	4	0	0	0-0	.200	.250	.200	.450	0	1.000

vs.	Avg.	AB	H	2B	3B	HR	RBI	BB	SO	OBP	Slg.	vs.	Avg.	AB	H	2B	3B	HR	RBI	BB	SO	OBP	Slg.
L	.280	157	44	12	1	1	21	14	20	.337	.389	R	.252	159	40	7	0	1	10	18	28	.333	.314

TALLET, BRIAN — P

PERSONAL: Born September 21, 1977, in Midwest City, Okla. ... 6-7/208. ... Throws left, bats left. ... Full name: Brian Curtis Tallet. ... Name pronounced: tal-ETT. ... High school: Putnam City West (Bethany, Okla.). ... College: Louisiana State. **TRANSACTIONS/CAREER NOTES:** Selected by Florida Marlins organization in 14th round of 1996 free-agent draft; did not sign. ... Selected by New York Yankees organization in 13th round of 1997 free-agent draft; did not sign. ... Selected by Pittsburgh Pirates organization in 19th round of 1999 free-agent draft; did not sign. ... Selected by Cleveland Indians organization in second round of 2000 free-agent draft. ... On disabled list (April 1-July 26, 2004); included rehabilitation assignments to Mahoning Valley, Lake County and Akron. ... Traded by Indians to Toronto Blue Jays for P Bubbie Buzachero (January 17, 2006).

CAREER HITTING: 0-for-2 (.000), 0 R, 0 2B, 0 3B, 0 HR, 0 RBI.

Year Team (League)	W	L	Pct.	ERA	WHIP	G	GS	CG	ShO	Hld.	Sv.-Opp.	IP	H	R	ER	HR	BB-IBB	SO	Avg.
2000— Mahoning Valley (N.Y.-Penn.)	0	0	...	1.15	0.83	6	6	0	0	...	0-...	15.2	10	2	2	0	3-0	20	.172
2001— Kinston (Carol.)	9	7	.563	3.04	1.08	27	27	2	0	...	0-...	160.0	134	62	54	12	38-0	164	.224
2002— Akron (East.)	10	1	.909	3.08	1.22	18	16	1	0	...	0-...	102.1	93	41	35	9	32-0	73	.243
— Buffalo (Int'l)	2	3	.400	3.07	1.43	8	7	0	0	...	0-...	44.0	47	17	15	1	16-0	25	.281
— Cleveland (A.L.)	1	0	1.000	1.50	1.08	2	1	0	0	0	0-0	12.0	9	3	2	0	4-0	5	.214
2003— Cleveland (A.L.)	0	2	.000	4.74	1.63	5	3	0	0	0	0-0	19.0	23	14	10	2	8-0	9	.303
— Buffalo (Int'l)	4	4	.500	5.14	1.46	15	15	0	0	...	0-...	84.0	89	50	48	10	34-1	67	.270
2004— Mahoning Valley (N.Y.-Penn.)	0	0	...	0.00	1.13	2	1	0	0	...	0-...	2.2	3	0	0	0	0-0	2	.273
— Lake County (S.Atl.)	0	0	...	0.00	0.50	2	1	0	0	...	0-...	2.0	1	0	0	0	0-0	1	.143
— Akron (East.)	1	1	.500	5.32	1.65	14	0	0	0	...	1-...	23.2	26	15	14	0	13-1	24	.268
— Buffalo (Int'l)	0	0	...	4.15	1.15	5	0	0	0	...	0-...	8.2	7	4	4	0	3-1	7	.212
2005— Cleveland (A.L.)	0	0	...	7.71	1.93	2	0	0	0	0	0-0	4.2	6	4	4	2	2-0	4	.300
— Buffalo (Int'l)	6	5	.545	4.05	1.26	22	17	0	0	...	0-0	97.2	98	51	44	17	25-0	61	.260
2006— Syracuse (Int'l)	1	2	.333	5.68	1.66	20	0	0	0	3	3-4	25.1	32	17	16	4	10-1	21	.317
— Toronto (A.L.)	3	0	1.000	3.81	1.40	44	1	0	0	5	0-0	54.1	45	24	23	5	31-4	37	.238
Major League totals (4 years)	4	2	.667	3.90	1.43	53	6	0	0	5	0-0	90.0	83	45	39	9	46-4	53	.254

vs.	Avg.	AB	H	2B	3B	HR	RBI	BB	SO	OBP	Slg.	vs.	Avg.	AB	H	2B	3B	HR	RBI	BB	SO	OBP	Slg.
L	.280	59	13	0	2	5	8	11	.319	.373		R	.246	130	32	9	0	3	20	23	26	.358	.385

TANKERSLEY, TAYLOR — P

PERSONAL: Born March 7, 1983, in Missoula, Mont. ... Throws left, bats left. ... Full name: Taylor M. Tankersley. ... College: Alabama. **TRANSACTIONS/CAREER NOTES:** Selected by Florida Marlins organization in first round (27th pick overall) of 2004 free-agent draft.

CAREER HITTING: 0-for-2 (.000), 0 R, 0 2B, 0 3B, 0 HR, 0 RBI.

Year Team (League)	W	L	Pct.	ERA	WHIP	G	GS	CG	ShO	Hld.	Sv.-Opp.	IP	H	R	ER	HR	BB-IBB	SO	Avg.
2004— Jamestown (NYP)	1	1	.500	3.38	1.09	6	6	0	0	...	0-...	26.2	21	14	10	2	8-0	32	.210
2005— Greensboro (S. Atl.)	2	7	.222	5.18	1.50	12	12	0	0	0	0-0	66.0	74	45	38	12	25-0	63	.279
— Jupiter (Fla. St.)	1	0	1.000	3.38	1.25	4	4	1	0	0	0-0	24.0	21	10	9	1	9-0	19	.247
2006— Carolina (Southern)	4	1	.800	0.95	0.88	22	0	0	0	3	6-7	28.1	11	4	3	0	14-1	40	.115
— Florida (N.L.)	2	1	.667	2.85	1.44	49	0	0	0	22	3-7	41.0	33	14	13	4	26-5	46	.228
Major League totals (1 year)	2	1	.667	2.85	1.44	49	0	0	0	22	3-7	41.0	33	14	13	4	26-5	46	.228

2006 LEFTY-RIGHTY SPLITS

vs.	Avg.	AB	H	2B	3B	HR	RBI	BB	SO	OBP	Slg.	vs.	Avg.	AB	H	2B	3B	HR	RBI	BB	SO	OBP	Slg.
L	.236	55	13	0	0	3	9	5	15	.295	.400	R	.222	90	20	2	1	1	16	21	31	.368	.300

TASCHNER, JACK   P

PERSONAL: Born April 21, 1978, in Milwaukee. ... 6-3/190. ... Throws left, bats left. ... Full name: Jack Gerard Taschner. ... High school: Racine (Wisc.). ... College: Wisconsin-Oshkosh. **TRANSACTIONS/CAREER NOTES:** Selected by San Francisco Giants organization in second round of 1999 free-agent draft.
CAREER HITTING: 0-for-0 (.000), 0 R, 0 2B, 0 3B, 0 HR, 0 RBI.

Year Team (League)	W	L	Pct.	ERA	WHIP	G	GS	CG	ShO	Hld.	Sv.-Opp.	IP	H	R	ER	HR	BB-IBB	SO	Avg.
1999— Salem-Keizer (N'west)	3	2	.600	2.51	1.26	7	6	0	0	...	0-...	28.2	26	12	8	1	10-0	36	.241
2000— San Jose (Calif.)	2	2	.500	4.10	1.52	10	2	0	0	...	1-...	26.1	23	17	12	0	17-0	22	.237
2001— San Jose (Calif.)	4	4	.500	4.11	1.39	14	14	0	0	...	0-...	65.2	62	33	30	7	29-0	72	.244
2003— Norwich (East.)	0	6	.000	5.71	1.63	34	12	0	0	...	0-...	75.2	78	53	48	7	45-0	46	.269
2004— Norwich (East.)	3	1	.750	2.48	1.09	14	10	0	0	...	0-...	58.0	47	17	16	5	16-0	55	.233
— Fresno (PCL)	4	7	.364	9.28	1.93	18	9	0	0	...	0-...	53.1	71	59	55	14	32-1	44	.323
2005— Fresno (PCL)	3	0	1.000	1.64	1.09	44	0	0	0	1	10-13	49.1	30	9	9	3	24-0	62	.173
— San Francisco (N.L.)	2	0	1.000	1.59	1.24	24	0	0	0	3	0-1	22.2	15	5	4	0	13-0	19	.185
2006— Fresno (PCL)	6	7	.462	3.65	1.34	45	0	0	0	1	14-19	49.1	49	21	20	5	17-0	68	.263
— San Francisco (N.L.)	0	1	.000	8.38	1.97	24	0	0	0	3	0-1	19.1	31	23	18	4	7-0	15	.344
Major League totals (2 years)	2	1	.667	4.71	1.57	48	0	0	0	6	0-2	42.0	46	28	22	4	20-0	34	.250

2006 LEFTY-RIGHTY SPLITS

vs.	Avg.	AB	H	2B	3B	HR	RBI	BB	SO	OBP	Slg.	vs.	Avg.	AB	H	2B	3B	HR	RBI	BB	SO	OBP	Slg.
L	.275	40	11	0	0	0	6	3	8	.318	.275	R	.400	50	20	6	0	4	17	4	7	.456	.760

TATA, JORDAN   P

PERSONAL: Born September 20, 1981, in Plano, Texas. ... Throws right, bats right. ... Full name: Jordan A. Tata. ... Name pronounced: TAY-ta ... College: Sam Houston State. **TRANSACTIONS/CAREER NOTES:** Selected by Detroit Tigers organization in 16th round of 2003 free-agent draft.
CAREER HITTING: 0-for-0 (.000), 0 R, 0 2B, 0 3B, 0 HR, 0 RBI.

Year Team (League)	W	L	Pct.	ERA	WHIP	G	GS	CG	ShO	Hld.	Sv.-Opp.	IP	H	R	ER	HR	BB-IBB	SO	Avg.
2003— Oneonta (NYP)	4	3	.571	2.58	1.15	16	12	0	0	...	1-...	73.1	64	32	21	1	20-0	60	.236
2004— W. Mich. (Mid.)	8	11	.421	3.35	1.41	28	28	1	0	...	0-...	166.1	167	77	62	7	68-2	116	.272
2005— Lakeland (Fla. St.)	13	2	.867	2.79	1.15	25	25	2	2	0	0-0	155.0	138	55	48	12	41-0	134	.239
2006— Toledo (Int'l)	10	6	.625	3.84	1.36	21	21	1	1	0	0-0	122.0	117	58	52	11	49-2	86	.252
— Detroit (A.L.)	0	0	...	6.14	1.43	8	0	0	0	0	0-0	14.2	14	11	10	1	7-1	6	.250
Major League totals (1 year)	0	0	...	6.14	1.43	8	0	0	0	0	0-0	14.2	14	11	10	1	7-1	6	.250

2006 LEFTY-RIGHTY SPLITS

vs.	Avg.	AB	H	2B	3B	HR	RBI	BB	SO	OBP	Slg.	vs.	Avg.	AB	H	2B	3B	HR	RBI	BB	SO	OBP	Slg.
L	.259	27	7	1	0	0	3	3	3	.323	.296	R	.241	29	7	0	0	1	5	4	3	.324	.345

TATIS, FERNANDO   3B

PERSONAL: Born January 1, 1975, in San Pedro de Macoris, Dominican Republic. ... 5-10/180. ... Bats right, throws right. ... Full name: Fernando Tatis Jr. ... Name pronounced: TAH-tece. **TRANSACTIONS/CAREER NOTES:** Signed as a non-drafted free agent by Texas Rangers organization (August 25, 1992). ... Traded by Rangers with P Darren Oliver and a player to be named to St. Louis Cardinals for P Todd Stottlemyre and SS Royce Clayton (July 31, 1998); Cardinals acquired OF Mark Little to complete deal (August 9, 1998). ... On disabled list (April 30-June 30, 2000); included rehabilitation assignment to Memphis. ... Traded by Cardinals with P Britt Reames to Montreal Expos for P Dustin Hermanson and P Steve Kline (December 14, 2000). ... On disabled list (May 11-26 and June 3, 2001-remainder of season). ... On suspended list (July 8-9, 2001). ... On disabled list (March 22-April 28, 2002); included rehabilitation assignment to Brevard County. ... On suspended list (August 31-September 3, 2002). ... On disabled list (June 16, 2003-remainder of season). ... Signed as a free agent by Tampa Bay Devil Rays organization (January 12, 2004). ... Released by Devil Rays (March 24, 2004). ... Signed by Baltimore Orioles organization (November 9, 2005). **RECORDS:** Holds major league single-inning records for most grand slams—2; and most runs batted in—8 (April 23, 1999, third inning). ... Shares major league single-game record for most grand slams—2 (April 23, 1999). ... Shares major league single-inning record for most home runs—2 (April 23, 1999, third inning). **STATISTICAL NOTES:** Career major league grand slams: 6.
2006 GAMES PLAYED BY POSITION (MLB): DH—9, 3B—5, 1B—4, OF—4, 2B—1.

Year Team (League)	Pos.	G	AB	R	H	2B	3B	HR	RBI	BB	SO	HBP	GDP	SB-CS	Avg.	OBP	SLG	OPS	E	Avg.
1993— Dom. Rangers (DSL)	IF	59	198	22	54	5	1	4	34	27	12			7-...	.273		.369		11	.940
1994— GC Rangers (GCL)	2B-3B	60	212	34	70	10	2	6	32	25	33	3	4	21-4	.330	.405	.481	.886	17	.927
1995— Char., S.C. (SAL)	3B	131	499	74	151	43	4	15	84	45	95	7	5	22-19	.303	.366	.495	.861	37	.900
1996— Charlotte (Fla. St.)	3B	85	325	46	93	25	0	12	53	30	48	6	9	9-3	.286	.353	.474	.827	24	.893
— Okla. City (A.A.)	3B	2	4	0	2	1	0	0	0	0	0	1	0	0-0	.500	.500	.750	1.250		1.000
1997— Tulsa (Texas)	3B-DH	102	382	73	120	26	1	24	61	46	72	3	15	17-8	.314	.390	.576	.966	21	.921
— Texas (A.L.)	3B	60	223	29	57	9	0	8	29	14	42	0	6	3-0	.256	.297	.404	.701	7	.951
1998— Texas (A.L.)	3B	95	330	41	89	17	2	3	32	12	66	4	10	6-2	.270	.303	.361	.664	15	.945
— St. Louis (N.L.)	3B-SS	55	202	28	58	16	2	8	26	24	57	2	6	7-3	.287	.367	.505	.872	12	.930
1999— St. Louis (N.L.)	3B	149	537	104	160	31	2	34	107	82	128	16	11	21-9	.298	.404	.553	.957	16	.958
2000— St. Louis (N.L.)	3B-DH-1B	96	324	59	82	21	1	18	64	57	94	10	13	2-3	.253	.379	.491	.870	9	.955
— Memphis (PCL)	3B	3	9	0	0	0	0	0	0	1	3	0	0	0-0	.000	.100	.000	.100	0	1.000
2001— Montreal (N.L.)	3B	41	145	20	37	9	0	2	11	16	43	4	5	0-0	.255	.339	.359	.698	9	.889
2002— Brevard County (FSL)	3B	6	17	2	4	1	0	2	4	2	9	2	1	0-0	.235	.391	.294	.685	1	.929
— Montreal (N.L.)	3B-DH	114	381	41	87	18	1	15	55	35	90	3	8	2-2	.228	.303	.399	.702	13	.948
2003— Montreal (N.L.)	3B	53	175	15	34	6	0	2	15	18	40	3	7	2-1	.194	.281	.263	.543	4	.968
2004—	Did not play.																			
2005—	Did not play.																			
2006— Ottawa (Int'l)		90	326	44	97	15	2	7	37	36	56	3		8-2	.298	.372	.420	.793	8	.968
— Baltimore (A.L.)	DH-3B-1B OF-2B	28	56	7	14	6	1	2	8	6	17	0	2	0-0	.250	.313	.500	.813	0	1.000
American League totals (3 years)		183	609	77	160	32	3	13	69	32	125	4	18	9-2	.263	.302	.389	.691	22	.954
National League totals (6 years)		508	1764	269	458	101	6	79	278	232	452	43	57	34-18	.260	.357	.458	.815	62	.948
Major League totals (8 years)		691	2373	346	618	133	9	92	347	264	577	47	75	43-20	.260	.344	.440	.784	84	.950

DIVISION SERIES RECORD

Year	Team (League)	Pos.	G	AB	R	H	2B	3B	HR	RBI	BB	SO	HBP	GDP	SB-CS	Avg.	OBP	SLG	OPS	E	Avg.
2000—	St. Louis (N.L.)		Did not play.																		

CHAMPIONSHIP SERIES RECORD

Year	Team (League)	Pos.	G	AB	R	H	2B	3B	HR	RBI	BB	SO	HBP	GDP	SB-CS	Avg.	OBP	SLG	OPS	E	Avg.
2000—	St. Louis (N.L.)	3B	5	13	1	3	2	0	0	2	1	5	0	...	0-0	.231	.267	.385	.651	2	.800

2006 LEFTY-RIGHTY SPLITS

vs.	Avg.	AB	H	2B	3B	HR	RBI	BB	SO	OBP	Slg.	vs.	Avg.	AB	H	2B	3B	HR	RBI	BB	SO	OBP	Slg.
L	.286	28	8	2	1	2	7	3	4	.333	.643	R	.214	28	6	4	0	0	1	3	13	.290	.357

TAUBENHEIM, TY — P

PERSONAL: Born November 17, 1982, in Bellingham, Wash. ... Throws right, bats right. ... Full name: Ty Andrew Taubenheim. ... College: Edmonds (Wash.) C.C. **TRANSACTIONS/CAREER NOTES:** Selected by Milwaukee Brewers organization in 19th round of 2003 free-agent draft. ... Traded by Brewers to Toronto Blue Jays for P Zach Jackson (December 8, 2005), completing deal in which Blue Jays traded P David Bush, OF Gabe Gross and a player to be named to Brewers for 1B Lyle Overbay and a player to be named (December 7, 2005). ... On disabled list (July 10-29, 2006); included rehabilitation assignment to Syracuse.

CAREER HITTING: 1-for-3 (.333), 0 R, 0 2B, 0 3B, 0 HR, 0 RBI.

Year	Team (League)	W	L	Pct.	ERA	WHIP	G	GS	CG	ShO	Hld.	Sv.-Opp.	IP	H	R	ER	HR	BB-IBB	SO	Avg.
2003—	Helena (Pion.)	6	1	.857	2.15	0.99	14	0	0	0	...	1-...	50.1	47	13	12	3	3-0	44	.251
2004—	Beloit (Midw.)	5	3	.625	3.61	1.06	47	0	0	0	...	12-...	92.1	81	41	37	10	17-0	106	.227
2005—	Brevard County (FSL)	10	2	.833	2.63	1.06	16	16	2	1	0	0-0	106.0	86	34	31	7	26-0	75	.224
—	Huntsville (Sou.)	2	6	.250	4.36	1.38	11	11	0	0	0	0-0	64.0	64	36	31	7	24-0	44	.269
2006—	Syracuse (Int'l)	2	4	.333	2.85	1.23	18	14	0	0	1	0-0	75.2	75	25	24	9	18-0	48	.261
—	Toronto (A.L.)	1	5	.167	4.89	1.66	12	7	0	0	0	0-0	35.0	40	22	19	5	18-0	26	.282
Major League totals (1 year)		1	5	.167	4.89	1.66	12	7	0	0	0	0-0	35.0	40	22	19	5	18-0	26	.282

2006 LEFTY-RIGHTY SPLITS

vs.	Avg.	AB	H	2B	3B	HR	RBI	BB	SO	OBP	Slg.	vs.	Avg.	AB	H	2B	3B	HR	RBI	BB	SO	OBP	Slg.
L	.262	61	16	3	2	2	12	13	11	.382	.475	R	.296	81	24	6	0	3	9	5	15	.367	.481

TAVAREZ, JULIAN — P

PERSONAL: Born May 22, 1973, in Santiago, Dominican Republic. ... 6-2/195. ... Throws right, bats left. ... Name pronounced: JOOL-ee-en tah-VAR-rez. ... High school: Santiago (Dominican Republic). **TRANSACTIONS/CAREER NOTES:** Signed as a non-drafted free agent by Cleveland Indians organization (March 16, 1990). ... On suspended list (June 18-21, 1996). ... Traded by Indians with 2B Jeff Kent, IF Jose Vizcaino and a player to be named to San Francisco Giants for 3B Matt Williams and a player to be named (November 13, 1996); Indians traded P Joe Roa to Giants for OF Trenidad Hubbard to complete deal (December 16, 1996). ... On disabled list (July 13-August 7, 1998); included rehabilitation assignment to Fresno. ... On suspended list (September 14-16, 1998). ... On disabled list (May 1-June 1, 1999); included rehabilitation assignment to Fresno. ... Claimed on waivers by Colorado Rockies (November 21, 1999). ... Signed as a free agent by Chicago Cubs (November 16, 2000). ... On suspended list (April 29-May 5, 2001). ... Traded by Cubs with Ps Jose Cueto and Dontrelle Willis and C Ryan Jorgensen to Florida Marlins for Ps Antonio Alfonseca and Matt Clement (March 27, 2002). ... On disabled list (April 17-May 12, 2002). ... Signed as a free agent by Pittsburgh Pirates organization (January 28, 2003). ... On suspended list (June 22-25, 2003). ... Signed as a free agent by St. Louis Cardinals (January 9, 2004). ... On suspended list (September 24-October 2, 2004). ... Signed as free agent by Boston Red Sox (January 18, 2006). ... On suspended list (April 3-13, 2006). **HONORS:** Named A.L. Rookie Pitcher of the Year by THE SPORTING NEWS (1995).

CAREER HITTING: 15-for-135 (.111), 8 R, 0 2B, 0 3B, 0 HR, 9 RBI.

Year	Team (League)	W	L	Pct.	ERA	WHIP	G	GS	CG	ShO	Hld.	Sv.-Opp.	IP	H	R	ER	HR	BB-IBB	SO	Avg.
1990—	Dom. Indians. (DSL)	5	5	.500	3.29	1.62	14	12	3	0	...	0-...	82.0	85	53	30	...	48-...	33	...
1991—	Dom. Indians. (DSL)	8	2	.800	2.67	1.01	19	18	1	0	...	0-...	121.1	95	41	36	...	28-...	75	...
1992—	Burlington (Appal.)	6	3	.667	2.68	1.12	14	14	2	2	...	0-...	87.1	86	41	26	3	12-0	69	.250
1993—	Kinston (Carol.)	11	5	.688	2.42	1.09	18	18	2	0	...	0-...	119.0	102	48	32	6	28-0	107	.228
—	Cant./Akr. (Eastern)	2	1	.667	0.95	0.79	3	2	1	1	...	0-...	19.0	14	2	2	0	1-0	11	.212
—	Cleveland (A.L.)	2	2	.500	6.57	1.78	8	7	0	0	0	0-0	37.0	53	29	27	7	13-2	19	.340
1994—	Charlotte (Int'l)	15	6	.714	3.48	1.19	26	26	2	2	...	0-...	176.0	167	79	68	15	43-0	102	.247
—	Cleveland (A.L.)	0	1	.000	21.60	4.20	1	1	0	0	0	0-0	1.2	6	8	4	1	1-1	0	.500
1995—	Cleveland (A.L.)	10	2	.833	2.44	1.14	57	0	0	0	19	0-4	85.0	76	36	23	7	21-0	68	.235
1996—	Cleveland (A.L.)	4	7	.364	5.36	1.52	51	4	0	0	13	0-0	80.2	101	49	48	9	22-5	46	.315
—	Buffalo (A.A.)	1	0	1.000	1.29	0.93	2	2	0	0	...	0-...	14.0	10	2	2	0	3-0	10	.200
1997—	San Francisco (N.L.)	6	4	.600	3.87	1.42	*89	0	0	0	26	0-3	88.1	91	43	38	6	34-5	38	.277
1998—	San Francisco (N.L.)	5	3	.625	3.80	1.55	60	0	0	0	10	1-6	85.1	96	41	36	5	36-11	52	.298
—	Fresno (PCL)	0	0	...	19.29	2.57	1	0	0	0	...	0-...	2.1	6	5	5	0	0-0	1	.500
1999—	San Francisco (N.L.)	2	0	1.000	5.93	1.65	47	0	0	0	5	0-2	54.2	65	38	36	7	25-3	33	.295
—	Fresno (PCL)	0	0	...	2.25	0.75	4	1	0	0	...	0-...	8.0	3	2	2	1	3-0	9	.115
—	San Jose (Calif.)	0	0	...	0.00	0.50	1	1	0	0	...	0-...	4.0	1	0	0	0	1-0	3	.091
2000—	Colorado (N.L.)	11	5	.688	4.43	1.48	51	12	1	0	6	1-1	120.0	124	68	59	11	53-9	62	.268
2001—	Chicago (N.L.)	10	9	.526	4.52	1.49	34	28	0	0	2	0-0	161.1	172	98	81	13	69-4	107	.277
2002—	Florida (N.L.)	10	12	.455	5.39	1.70	29	27	0	0	0	0-1	153.2	188	100	92	9	74-7	67	.308
2003—	Pittsburgh (N.L.)	3	3	.500	3.66	1.22	64	0	0	0	9	11-14	83.2	75	37	34	1	27-8	39	.244
2004—	St. Louis (N.L.)	7	4	.636	2.38	1.18	77	0	0	0	19	4-6	64.1	57	21	17	1	19-0	48	.238
2005—	St. Louis (N.L.)	2	3	.400	3.43	1.32	74	0	0	0	•32	4-6	65.2	68	28	25	6	19-4	47	.278
2006—	Boston (A.L.)	5	4	.556	4.47	1.56	58	6	1	0	2	1-3	98.2	110	54	49	10	44-3	56	.293
American League totals (5 years)		21	16	.568	4.49	1.48	175	18	1	0	34	1-7	303.0	346	176	151	34	101-11	189	.291
National League totals (9 years)		56	43	.566	4.29	1.47	525	67	1	0	109	21-39	877.0	936	474	418	59	356-51	493	.279
Major League totals (14 years)		77	59	.566	4.34	1.47	700	85	2	0	143	22-46	1180.0	1282	650	569	93	457-62	682	.282

DIVISION SERIES RECORD

Year	Team (League)	W	L	Pct.	ERA	WHIP	G	GS	CG	ShO	Hld.	Sv.-Opp.	IP	H	R	ER	HR	BB-IBB	SO	Avg.
1995—	Cleveland (A.L.)	0	0	...	6.75	1.88	3	0	0	0	1	0-1	2.2	5	2	2	1	0-0	3	.385
1996—	Cleveland (A.L.)	0	0	...	0.00	2.25	2	0	0	0	0	0-0	1.1	1	0	0	0	2-0	1	.250
1997—	San Francisco (N.L.)	0	1	.000	4.50	1.50	3	0	0	0	0	0-0	4.0	4	2	2	1	2-1	0	.267
2004—	St. Louis (N.L.)	0	0	...	0.00	0.86	2	0	0	0	0	0-0	2.1	2	0	0	0	0-0	3	.222
2005—	St. Louis (N.L.)	0	0	...	13.50	3.75	2	0	0	0	1	0-0	1.1	4	2	2	1	1-0	0	.500
Division series totals (5 years)		0	1	.000	4.63	1.80	12	0	0	0	2	0-1	11.2	16	6	6	3	5-1	7	.327

CHAMPIONSHIP SERIES RECORD

Year	Team (League)	W	L	Pct.	ERA	WHIP	G	GS	CG	ShO	Hld.	Sv.-Opp.	IP	H	R	ER	HR	BB-IBB	SO	Avg.
1995—	Cleveland (A.L.)	0	1	.000	2.70	1.20	4	0	0	0	1	0-0	3.1	3	1	1	0	1-1	2	.200
2004—	St. Louis (N.L.)	2	1	.667	3.00	0.83	5	0	0	0	1	0-0	6.0	3	2	2	2	2-1	3	.150
2005—	St. Louis (N.L.)	0	0	...	5.40	1.50	3	0	0	0	0	0-0	3.1	5	2	2	0	0-0	2	.333
Champ. series totals (3 years)		2	2	.500	3.55	1.11	12	0	0	0	2	0-0	12.2	11	5	5	2	3-2	7	.220

Year Team (League)	W	L	Pct.	ERA	WHIP	G	GS	CG	ShO	Hld.	Sv.-Opp.	IP	H	R	ER	HR	BB-IBB	SO	Avg.

WORLD SERIES RECORD

Year Team (League)	W	L	Pct.	ERA	WHIP	G	GS	CG	ShO	Hld.	Sv.-Opp.	IP	H	R	ER	HR	BB-IBB	SO	Avg.
1995— Cleveland (A.L.)	0	0	...	0.00	1.15	5	0	0	0	0	0-0	4.1	3	0	0	0	2-0	1	.250
2004— St. Louis (N.L.)	0	1	.000	4.50	0.50	2	0	0	0	0	0-0	2.0	1	2	1	1	0-0	1	.125
World series totals (2 years)	0	1	.000	1.42	0.95	7	0	0	0	0	0-0	6.1	4	2	1	1	2-0	2	.200

2006 LEFTY-RIGHTY SPLITS

vs.	Avg.	AB	H	2B	3B	HR	RBI	BB	SO	OBP	Slg.	vs.	Avg.	AB	H	2B	3B	HR	RBI	BB	SO	OBP	Slg.
L	.248	161	40	14	1	5	33	24	28	.344	.441	R	.327	214	70	11	1	5	26	20	28	.397	.458

TAVERAS, WILLY — OF

PERSONAL: Born December 25, 1981, in Tenares, Dominican Republic. ... 6-0/160. ... Bats right, throws right. **TRANSACTIONS/CAREER NOTES:** Signed as a non-drafted free agent by Cleveland Indians organization (May 27, 1999). ... Selected by Houston Astros from Indians organization in Rule 5 major league draft (December 15, 2003). ... Rights acquired by Astros as part of deal in which Astros traded P Jeriome Robertson to Indians for OF Luke Scott (March 31, 2005). **HONORS:** Named N.L. Rookie of the Year by the SPORTING NEWS (2005).

2006 GAMES PLAYED BY POSITION (MLB): OF—138.

									BATTING									FIELDING	
Year Team (League)	Pos.	G	AB	R	H	2B	3B	HR	RBI	BB	SO	HBP	GDP	SB-CS	Avg.	OBP	SLG	OPS	E	Avg.
1999— Dom. Indians. (DSL)	OF	68	277	57	98	19	6	3	44	32	32	10	...	26-10	.354	.435	.498	.933	0	...
2000— Burlington (Appal.)	OF	50	190	46	50	4	3	1	16	23	44	6	6	36-9	.263	.356	.332	.687	5	.961
2001— Columbus (S. Atl.)	OF	97	395	55	107	15	7	3	32	22	73	6	7	29-9	.271	.317	.367	.684	11	.952
2002— Columbus (S. Atl.)	OF	85	313	68	83	14	1	4	27	45	68	18	3	54-12	.265	.385	.355	.740	10	.944
2003— Kinston (Carol.)	OF	113	397	64	112	9	6	2	35	52	68	12	4	57-12	.282	.381	.350	.731	6	.978
2004— Round Rock (Texas)	OF-DH	103	409	76	137	13	1	2	27	38	76	9	2	55-11	.335	.402	.386	.776	6	.974
— Houston (N.L.)	OF	10	1	2	0	0	0	0	0	0	1	0	0	1-0	.000	.000	.000	.000	0	1.000
2005— Houston (N.L.)	OF	152	592	82	172	13	4	3	29	25	103	7	4	34-11	.291	.325	.341	.666	3	.991
2006— Houston (N.L.)	OF	149	529	83	147	19	5	1	30	34	88	11	6	33-9	.278	.333	.338	.672	5	.986
Major League totals (3 years)		311	1122	167	319	32	9	4	59	59	192	18	10	68-20	.284	.329	.340	.668	8	.988

DIVISION SERIES RECORD

									BATTING										
Year Team (League)	Pos.	G	AB	R	H	2B	3B	HR	RBI	BB	SO	HBP	GDP	SB-CS	Avg.	OBP	SLG	OPS	E	Avg.
2005— Houston (N.L.)	OF	4	14	2	5	1	0	0	1	1	0	0	0	0-0	.357	.400	.429	.829	0	1.000

CHAMPIONSHIP SERIES RECORD

Year Team (League)	Pos.	G	AB	R	H	2B	3B	HR	RBI	BB	SO	HBP	GDP	SB-CS	Avg.	OBP	SLG	OPS	E	Avg.
2005— Houston (N.L.)	OF	6	14	1	5	0	0	0	0	1	0	0	0	0-1	.357	.400	.357	.757	0	1.000

WORLD SERIES RECORD

Year Team (League)	Pos.	G	AB	R	H	2B	3B	HR	RBI	BB	SO	HBP	GDP	SB-CS	Avg.	OBP	SLG	OPS	E	Avg.
2005— Houston (N.L.)	OF	4	15	2	5	2	1	0	0	0	3	2	0	1-0	.333	.412	.600	1.012	0	1.000

2006 LEFTY-RIGHTY SPLITS

vs.	Avg.	AB	H	2B	3B	HR	RBI	BB	SO	OBP	Slg.	vs.	Avg.	AB	H	2B	3B	HR	RBI	BB	SO	OBP	Slg.
L	.254	118	30	5	1	0	6	9	18	.318	.314	R	.285	411	117	14	4	1	24	25	70	.338	.345

TEAHEN, MARK — 3B

PERSONAL: Born September 6, 1981, in Redlands, Calif. ... 6-3/210. ... Bats left, throws right. ... Full name: Mark Thomas Teahen. ... High school: Yucaipa (Calif.). ... College: St. Mary's (Calif.). **TRANSACTIONS/CAREER NOTES:** Selected by Oakland Athletics organization in first round (39th pick overall) of 2002 free-agent draft. ... Traded by Athletics with P Mike Wood to Kansas City Royals in three-team deal in which Royals traded OF Carlos Beltran to Houston Astros and Astros traded C John Buck to Royals and P Octavio Dotel to Athletics (June 24, 2004). ... On disabled list (April 13-May 3, 2005); included rehabilitation assignment to Omaha. **STATISTICAL NOTES:** Career major league grand slams: 1.

2006 GAMES PLAYED BY POSITION (MLB): 3B—109.

									BATTING									FIELDING	
Year Team (League)	Pos.	G	AB	R	H	2B	3B	HR	RBI	BB	SO	HBP	GDP	SB-CS	Avg.	OBP	SLG	OPS	E	Avg.
2002— Vancouver (N'west)	3B	13	57	10	23	5	1	0	6	5	9	0	0	4-1	.404	.444	.526	.970	4	.882
— Modesto (California)	3B	59	234	25	56	9	1	1	26	21	53	2	4	1-2	.239	.307	.299	.606	4	.971
2003— Modesto (California)	3B	121	453	68	128	27	4	3	71	66	113	6	19	4-0	.283	.377	.380	.757	22	.931
2004— Midland (Texas)	3B	53	197	31	66	15	4	6	36	29	44	1	12	0-0	.335	.419	.543	.962	5	.918
— Sacramento (PCL)	3B	20	69	9	19	8	0	0	10	11	22	1	1	0-1	.275	.383	.391	.774	1	.000
— Omaha (PCL)	3B	66	246	33	69	15	1	8	31	21	69	4	4	0-0	.280	.344	.447	.791	14	.000
2005— Omaha (PCL)	3B-DH	8	27	4	7	2	0	0	4	7	9	0	1	0-0	.259	.412	.333	.745	1	.923
— Kansas City (A.L.)	3B	130	447	60	110	29	4	7	55	40	107	1	13	7-2	.246	.309	.376	.685	20	.947
2006— Omaha (PCL)		24	79	14	30	8	4	2	14	19	12	0	2	0-0	.380	.500	.658	1.158	1	.981
— Kansas City (A.L.)	3B	109	393	70	114	21	7	18	69	40	85	2	5	10-0	.290	.357	.517	.874	14	.958
Major League totals (2 years)		239	840	130	224	50	11	25	124	80	192	3	18	17-2	.267	.332	.442	.773	34	.952

2006 LEFTY-RIGHTY SPLITS

vs.	Avg.	AB	H	2B	3B	HR	RBI	BB	SO	OBP	Slg.	vs.	Avg.	AB	H	2B	3B	HR	RBI	BB	SO	OBP	Slg.
L	.274	106	29	10	3	2	15	8	26	.333	.481	R	.296	287	85	11	4	16	54	32	59	.366	.530

TEIXEIRA, MARK — 1B

PERSONAL: Born April 11, 1980, in Annapolis, Md. ... 6-3/220. ... Bats both, throws right. ... Full name: Mark Charles Teixeira. ... Name pronounced: tuh-SHARE-uh. ... High school: Mount St. Joseph (Baltimore). ... College: Georgia Tech. **TRANSACTIONS/CAREER NOTES:** Selected by Boston Red Sox organization in ninth round of 1998 free-agent draft; did not sign. ... Selected by Texas Rangers organization in first round (fifth pick overall) of 2001 free-agent draft. ... On disabled list (April 13-29, 2004); included rehabilitation assignment to Frisco. **HONORS:** Named first baseman on the SPORTING NEWS A.L. All-Star team (2005). ... Won A.L. Gold Glove as first baseman (2005-06). ... Named first baseman on A.L. Silver Slugger team (2004 and 2005). **STATISTICAL NOTES:** Hit for the cycle (August 17, 2004). ... Hit three home runs in one game (July 13, 2006). ... Career major league grand slams: 3.

2006 GAMES PLAYED BY POSITION (MLB): 1B—159, DH—3.

									BATTING									FIELDING	
Year Team (League)	Pos.	G	AB	R	H	2B	3B	HR	RBI	BB	SO	HBP	GDP	SB-CS	Avg.	OBP	SLG	OPS	E	Avg.
2002— Charlotte (Fla. St.)	3B	38	150	32	48	10	2	9	41	21	24	3	4	2-0	.320	.411	.593	1.005	9	.902
— Tulsa (Texas)	3B	48	171	31	54	11	3	10	28	25	36	4	2	3-2	.316	.415	.591	1.006	12	.925
2003— Texas (A.L.)	1B-OF-3B																			
	DH	146	529	66	137	29	5	26	84	44	120	14	14	1-2	.259	.331	.480	.811	12	.989
2004— Frisco (Texas)	1B	3	10	0	0	0	0	0	0	1	1	0	0	0-0	.000	.250	.000	.250	0	1.000
— Texas (A.L.)	1B-OF-DH	145	545	101	153	34	2	38	112	68	117	10	6	4-1	.281	.370	.560	.929	10	.992

Year	Team (League)	Pos.	G	AB	R	H	2B	3B	HR	RBI	BB	SO	HBP	GDP	SB-CS	Avg.	OBP	SLG	OPS	E	Avg.
															BATTING					FIELDING	
2005—Texas (A.L.)		1B-DH	•162	644	112	194	41	3	43	144	72	124	11	18	4-0	.301	.379	.575	.954	3	.998
2006—Texas (A.L.)		1B-DH	•162	628	99	177	45	1	33	110	89	128	4	17	2-0	.282	.371	.514	.886	4	.997
Major League totals (4 years)			615	2346	378	661	149	11	140	450	273	489	39	55	11-3	.282	.364	.534	.898	29	.995

ALL-STAR GAME RECORD

			G	AB	R	H	2B	3B	HR	RBI	BB	SO	HBP	GDP	SB-CS	Avg.	OBP	SLG	OPS	E	Avg.
All-Star Game totals (1 year)			1	3	1	1	0	0	1	2	0	0	0	0	0-0	.333	.333	1.333	1.667	0	1.000

2006 LEFTY-RIGHTY SPLITS

vs.	Avg.	AB	H	2B	3B	HR	RBI	BB	SO	OBP	Slg.	vs.	Avg.	AB	H	2B	3B	HR	RBI	BB	SO	OBP	Slg.
L	.302	169	51	14	0	12	32	20	42	.379	.598	R	.275	459	126	31	1	21	78	69	86	.369	.484

TEJADA, MIGUEL — SS

PERSONAL: Born May 25, 1976, in Bani, Dominican Republic. ... 5-9/209. ... Bats right, throws right. ... Full name: Miguel Odalis Tejada. ... Name pronounced: tay-HA-duh.
TRANSACTIONS/CAREER NOTES: Signed as a non-drafted free agent by Oakland Athletics organization (July 17, 1993). ... On disabled list (March 22-May 20, 1998); included rehabilitation assignments to Edmonton and Huntsville. ... Signed as a free agent by Baltimore Orioles (December 18, 2003). **HONORS:** Named shortstop on THE SPORTING NEWS A.L. All-Star team (2004). ... Named A.L. Most Valuable Player by Baseball Writers' Association of America (2002). ... Named shortstop on A.L. Silver Slugger team (2004 and 2005). **STATISTICAL NOTES:** Hit three home runs in one game (June 11, 1999 and June 30, 2001). ... Hit for the cycle (September 29, 2001). ... Career major league grand slams: 9.
2006 GAMES PLAYED BY POSITION (MLB): SS—150, DH—12.

Year	Team (League)	Pos.	G	AB	R	H	2B	3B	HR	RBI	BB	SO	HBP	GDP	SB-CS	Avg.	OBP	SLG	OPS	E	Avg.
															BATTING					FIELDING	
1994—Dom. Athletics (DSL)		2B	74	218	51	64	9	1	18	62	37	36	...	...	13-...	.294	...	.592	...	16	.927
1995—S. Oregon (N'west)		SS	74	269	45	66	15	5	8	44	41	54	2	3	19-2	.245	.346	.428	.774	26	.930
1996—Modesto (California)		SS-DH-3B	114	458	97	128	12	5	20	72	51	93	4	9	27-16	.279	.352	.459	.810	45	.925
1997—Huntsville (Sou.)		SS	128	502	85	138	20	3	22	97	50	99	7	9	15-11	.275	.344	.458	.802	36	.948
—Oakland (A.L.)		SS	26	99	10	20	3	2	2	10	2	22	3	3	2-0	.202	.240	.333	.574	4	.969
1998—Edmonton (PCL)		SS	1	3	0	0	0	0	0	0	1	1	0	1	0-0	.000	.250	.000	.250	0	1.000
—Huntsville (Sou.)		SS-DH	15	52	9	17	6	0	2	7	4	8	0	2	1-0	.327	.362	.558	.920	5	.922
—Oakland (A.L.)		SS	105	365	53	85	20	1	11	45	28	86	7	8	5-6	.233	.298	.384	.681	26	.951
1999—Oakland (A.L.)		SS	159	593	93	149	33	4	21	84	57	94	10	11	8-7	.251	.325	.427	.751	21	.973
2000—Oakland (A.L.)		SS	160	607	105	167	32	1	30	115	66	102	4	15	6-0	.275	.349	.479	.828	21	.972
2001—Oakland (A.L.)		SS	•162	622	107	166	31	3	31	113	43	89	13	14	11-5	.267	.326	.476	.801	20	.973
2002—Oakland (A.L.)		SS	•162	662	108	204	30	0	34	131	38	84	11	*21	7-2	.308	.354	.508	.861	19	.975
2003—Oakland (A.L.)		SS	162	636	98	177	42	0	27	106	53	65	6	12	10-0	.278	.336	.472	.807	21	.972
2004—Baltimore (A.L.)		SS	162	653	107	203	40	2	34	*150	48	73	10	•24	4-1	.311	.360	.534	.894	24	.970
2005—Baltimore (A.L.)		SS-DH	•162	654	89	199	*50	5	26	98	40	83	7	•26	5-1	.304	.349	.515	.865	22	.971
2006—Baltimore (A.L.)		SS-DH	162	648	99	214	37	0	24	100	46	79	9	*28	6-2	.330	.379	.498	.878	19	.972
Major League totals (10 years)			1422	5539	869	1584	318	18	240	952	421	777	80	162	64-24	.286	.342	.480	.822	197	.971

DIVISION SERIES RECORD

Year	Team (League)	Pos.	G	AB	R	H	2B	3B	HR	RBI	BB	SO	HBP	GDP	SB-CS	Avg.	OBP	SLG	OPS	E	Avg.
2000—Oakland (A.L.)		SS	5	20	5	7	2	0	1	2	2	2	0	0	1-0	.350	.409	.450	.859	0	1.000
2001—Oakland (A.L.)		SS	5	21	1	6	3	0	1	0	3	3	1	0	0-0	.286	.304	.429	.733	1	.958
2002—Oakland (A.L.)		SS	5	21	3	3	1	0	1	4	1	7	0	0	0-0	.143	.174	.333	.507	1	.947
2003—Oakland (A.L.)		SS	5	23	0	2	1	0	0	2	0	4	0	0	0-0	.087	.087	.130	.217	1	.957
Division series totals (4 years)			20	85	9	18	7	0	3	8	3	16	1	0	1-0	.212	.242	.329	.571	3	.966

ALL-STAR GAME RECORD

			G	AB	R	H	2B	3B	HR	RBI	BB	SO	HBP	GDP	SB-CS	Avg.	OBP	SLG	OPS	E	Avg.
All-Star Game totals (4 years)			4	7	2	2	0	0	1	2	0	0	0	0	0-0	.286	.286	.714	1.000	0	1.000

2006 LEFTY-RIGHTY SPLITS

vs.	Avg.	AB	H	2B	3B	HR	RBI	BB	SO	OBP	Slg.	vs.	Avg.	AB	H	2B	3B	HR	RBI	BB	SO	OBP	Slg.
L	.335	161	54	9	0	6	23	12	19	.375	.503	R	.329	487	160	28	0	18	77	34	60	.381	.497

TEJEDA, ROBINSON — P

PERSONAL: Born March 24, 1982, in Bani, Dominican Republic. ... 6-3/188. ... Throws right, bats right. ... Full name: Robinson Garcia Tejeda. ... Name pronounced: tey-HEY-dah. ... High school: Liceo Club de Leones (Dominican Republic). **TRANSACTIONS/CAREER NOTES:** Signed as a non-drafted free agent by Philadelphia Phillies organization (November 24, 1998). ... Traded by Phillies with 3B Jake Blalock to Texas Rangers for OF David Dellucci (April 1, 2006).
CAREER HITTING: 2-for-22 (.091), 1 R, 0 2B, 1 3B, 0 HR, 0 RBI.

Year	Team (League)	W	L	Pct.	ERA	WHIP	G	GS	CG	ShO	Hld.	Sv.-Opp.	IP	H	R	ER	HR	BB-IBB	SO	Avg.
1999—GC Phillies (GCL)		1	3	.250	4.27	1.60	12	9	0	0	...	0-...	46.1	47	27	22	5	27-0	39	.273
2000—GC Phillies (GCL)		2	5	.286	5.54	1.44	10	6	1	1	...	0-...	39.0	44	30	24	3	12-0	22	.273
2001—Lakewood (S. Atl.)		8	9	.471	3.40	1.23	26	24	1	1	...	0-...	150.2	128	74	57	10	58-1	152	.228
2002—Clearwater (FSL)		4	8	.333	3.97	1.21	17	17	1	0	...	0-...	99.2	73	48	44	14	48-0	87	.204
2003—Lakewood (S. Atl.)		0	3	.000	5.30	1.77	5	4	0	0	...	0-...	18.2	17	11	11	4	16-0	20	.246
—Clearwater (FSL)		2	4	.333	3.20	1.18	11	11	0	0	...	0-...	64.2	53	25	23	4	23-0	42	.221
2004—Reading (East.)		8	14	.364	5.15	1.38	27	26	0	0	...	0-...	150.1	148	93	86	29	59-4	133	.256
2005—Scran./W.B. (I.L.)		2	0	1.000	2.22	1.20	5	5	0	0	...	0-0	28.1	21	8	7	0	13-0	28	.214
—Philadelphia (N.L.)		4	3	.571	3.57	1.38	26	13	0	0	1	0-0	85.2	67	36	34	5	51-4	72	.218
2006—Arizona Rangers (AZL)		0	0	...	6.75	1.00	2	2	0	0	0	0-0	4.0	4	3	3	0	0-0	6	.250
—Oklahoma (PCL)		6	2	.750	3.15	1.29	15	15	0	0	0	0-0	80.0	61	30	28	7	42-0	79	.210
—Texas (A.L.)		5	5	.500	4.28	1.56	14	14	0	0	0	0-0	73.2	83	40	35	10	32-1	40	.288
American League totals (1 year)		5	5	.500	4.28	1.56	14	14	0	0	0	0-0	73.2	83	40	35	10	32-1	40	.288
National League totals (1 year)		4	3	.571	3.57	1.38	26	13	0	0	1	0-0	85.2	67	36	34	5	51-4	72	.218
Major League totals (2 years)		9	8	.529	3.90	1.46	40	27	0	0	1	0-0	159.1	150	76	69	15	83-5	112	.252

2006 LEFTY-RIGHTY SPLITS

vs.	Avg.	AB	H	2B	3B	HR	RBI	BB	SO	OBP	Slg.	vs.	Avg.	AB	H	2B	3B	HR	RBI	BB	SO	OBP	Slg.
L	.331	136	45	8	0	6	17	15	17	.401	.522	R	.250	152	38	5	0	4	16	17	23	.324	.362

TERRERO, LUIS — OF

PERSONAL: Born May 18, 1980, in Barahona, Dominican Republic. ... 6-2/206. ... Bats right, throws right. ... Full name: Luis Enrique Terrero Gomez. ... Name pronounced: tuh-RARE-oh. ... High school: Barney Morgan (Barahona, Dominican Republic). **TRANSACTIONS/CAREER NOTES:** Signed as a non-drafted free agent by Arizona

T

Diamondbacks organization (October 15, 1997). ... On disabled list (June 8-28, 2005); included rehabilitation assignment to Tucson. ... Released by Diamondbacks (March 29, 2006). ... Signed by Baltimore Orioles organization (April 13, 2006). ... Signed by Chicago White Sox (November 3, 2006).

2006 GAMES PLAYED BY POSITION (MLB): OF—23, DH—1.

Year	Team (League)	Pos.	G	AB	R	H	2B	3B	HR	RBI	BB	SO	HBP	GDP	SB-CS	Avg.	OBP	SLG	OPS	E	Avg.
1998—	Dom. D'backs (DSL)	OF	56	169	19	39	7	1	2	15	13	44	4	...	9-6	.231	.301	.320	.621	4	...
1999—	Missoula (Pion.)	OF	71	272	74	78	13	7	8	40	32	91	5	2	27-10	.287	.365	.474	.839	11	.928
2000—	High Desert (Calif.)	OF	19	79	10	15	3	1	0	1	3	16	1	0	5-5	.190	.229	.253	.482	3	.941
—	Missoula (Pion.)	OF	68	276	48	72	10	0	8	44	10	75	8	5	23-11	.261	.305	.384	.689	5	.949
2001—	South Bend (Mid.)	OF	24	89	4	14	2	0	1	8	0	29	2	2	3-0	.157	.176	.213	.389	0	1.000
—	Yakima (N'west)	OF	11	41	7	13	2	1	0	0	2	8	0	0	0-3	.317	.349	.415	.763	0	1.000
—	Lancaster (Calif.)	OF	19	71	16	32	9	1	4	11	1	14	1	3	5-0	.451	.466	.775	1.240	1	.971
—	El Paso (Texas)	OF	34	147	29	44	13	3	3	8	4	45	3	2	9-2	.299	.331	.490	.821	5	.943
2002—	El Paso (Texas)	OF	104	360	49	103	20	6	8	54	23	89	3	9	18-22	.286	.342	.442	.784	7	.973
2003—	Arizona (N.L.)	OF	5	4	0	1	0	0	0	0	1	0	1	0	0-0	.250	.400	.250	.650	0	1.000
—	Tucson (PCL)	OF-DH	118	467	83	134	20	15	3	46	31	103	11	6	23-19	.287	.345	.413	.758	10	.968
2004—	Tucson (PCL)	OF-DH	58	217	36	68	9	6	9	35	17	48	4	7	15-3	.313	.374	.535	.909	3	.978
—	Arizona (N.L.)	OF	62	229	21	56	14	0	4	14	20	78	5	5	10-2	.245	.319	.358	.677	8	.938
2005—	Tucson (PCL)	OF	7	30	4	8	1	0	0	1	1	9	1	2	1-0	.267	.313	.300	.613	0	1.000
—	Arizona (N.L.)	OF	88	161	23	37	6	1	4	20	14	40	6	5	3-2	.230	.313	.354	.667	2	.984
2006—	Ottawa (Int'l)		84	302	52	96	21	2	16	44	16	61	8	4	18-9	.318	.367	.560	.927	4	.981
—	Baltimore (A.L.)	OF-DH	27	40	4	8	1	0	1	6	1	7	1	0	0-3	.200	.238	.300	.538	1	.973
American League totals (1 year)			27	40	4	8	1	0	1	6	1	7	1	0	0-3	.200	.238	.300	.538	1	.973
National League totals (3 years)			155	394	44	94	20	1	8	34	34	119	12	10	13-4	.239	.317	.355	.673	10	.961
Major League totals (4 years)			182	434	48	102	21	1	9	40	35	126	13	10	13-7	.235	.311	.350	.661	11	.963

2006 LEFTY-RIGHTY SPLITS

vs.	Avg.	AB	H	2B	3B	HR	RBI	BB	SO	OBP	Slg.	vs.	Avg.	AB	H	2B	3B	HR	RBI	BB	SO	OBP	Slg.
L	.182	33	6	1	0	1	2	0	6	.206	.303	R	.286	7	2	0	0	0	4	1	1	.375	.286

THAMES, MARCUS — OF

PERSONAL: Born March 6, 1977, in Louisville, Miss. ... 6-2/205. ... Bats right, throws right. ... Full name: Marcus Markey Thames. ... Name pronounced: timms. ... Junior college: East Central (Miss.). **TRANSACTIONS/CAREER NOTES:** Selected by New York Yankees organization in 30th round of 1996 free-agent draft. ... Traded by Yankees to Texas Rangers for OF Ruben Sierra (June 6, 2003). ... Signed as a free agent by Detroit Tigers organization (December 8, 2003) **STATISTICAL NOTES:** Hit home run in first major league at-bat (June 10, 2002). ... Career major league grand slams: 2.

2006 GAMES PLAYED BY POSITION (MLB): OF—59, DH—46.

Year	Team (League)	Pos.	G	AB	R	H	2B	3B	HR	RBI	BB	SO	HBP	GDP	SB-CS	Avg.	OBP	SLG	OPS	E	Avg.
1997—	GC Yankees (GCL)	OF	57	195	51	67	17	4	7	36	16	26	3	3	6-4	.344	.394	.579	.974	2	.978
—	Greensboro (S. Atl.)	OF	4	16	2	5	1	0	0	2	0	3	0	0	1-0	.313	.313	.375	.688	0	1.000
1998—	Tampa (Fla. St.)	OF	122	457	62	130	18	3	11	59	24	78	8	5	13-6	.284	.328	.409	.737	9	.970
1999—	Norwich (East.)	OF	51	182	25	41	6	2	4	26	22	40	3	2	0-1	.225	.316	.346	.662	7	.929
—	Tampa (Fla. St.)	OF	69	266	47	65	12	4	11	38	33	48	3	1	3-0	.244	.332	.444	.776	3	.974
2000—	Norwich (East.)	OF	131	474	72	114	30	2	15	79	50	89	4	13	1-5	.241	.313	.407	.721	9	.959
2001—	Norwich (East.)	OF	139	520	114	167	43	4	31	97	73	101	7	6	10-4	.321	.410	.598	1.008	8	.973
2002—	Columbus (Int'l)	OF	107	386	51	80	21	3	13	45	43	71	7	8	5-4	.207	.297	.378	.675	5	.983
—	New York (A.L.)	OF	7	13	2	3	1	0	1	2	0	4	0	0	0-0	.231	.231	.538	.769	0	1.000
2003—	Columbus (Int'l)	OF	52	194	26	54	15	2	2	28	17	48	1	4	3-4	.278	.332	.407	.739	3	.977
—	Oklahoma (PCL)	OF-DH	18	66	9	17	4	0	2	7	8	12	0	2	1-0	.258	.338	.409	.747	1	.968
—	Texas (A.L.)	OF-DH	30	73	12	15	2	0	1	4	8	18	2	2	0-1	.205	.298	.274	.572	0	1.000
2004—	Toledo (Int'l)	OF-DH	64	234	57	77	21	1	24	59	33	40	2	5	4-1	.329	.410	.735	1.145	2	.979
—	Detroit (A.L.)	OF-DH	61	165	24	42	12	0	10	33	16	42	2	3	0-1	.255	.326	.509	.835	0	1.000
2005—	Toledo (Int'l)	OF-DH	73	265	53	90	18	3	22	56	41	59	3	5	4-1	.340	.427	.679	1.106	4	.975
—	Detroit (A.L.)	OF-DH	38	107	11	21	2	0	7	16	9	38	1	1	0-0	.196	.263	.411	.674	1	.978
2006—	Detroit (A.L.)	OF-DH	110	348	61	89	20	2	26	60	37	92	4	0	1-1	.256	.333	.549	.882	2	.977
Major League totals (5 years)			246	706	110	170	37	2	45	115	70	194	9	6	1-3	.241	.316	.490	.806	3	.989

DIVISION SERIES RECORD

Year	Team (League)	Pos.	G	AB	R	H	2B	3B	HR	RBI	BB	SO	HBP	GDP	SB-CS	Avg.	OBP	SLG	OPS	E	Avg.
2006—	Detroit (A.L.)	DH	4	15	2	5	2	0	1	5	1	5	0	0	0-0	.333	.375	.467	.842	0	...

CHAMPIONSHIP SERIES RECORD

Year	Team (League)	Pos.	G	AB	R	H	2B	3B	HR	RBI	BB	SO	HBP	GDP	SB-CS	Avg.	OBP	SLG	OPS	E	Avg.
2006—	Detroit (A.L.)	DH	2	5	1	0	0	0	0	0	0	1	0	0	0-0	.000	.000	.000	.000	0	...

WORLD SERIES RECORD

Year	Team (League)	Pos.	G	AB	R	H	2B	3B	HR	RBI	BB	SO	HBP	GDP	SB-CS	Avg.	OBP	SLG	OPS	E	Avg.
2006—	Detroit (A.L.)	OF	2	1	0	0	0	0	0	0	0	0	0	0	0-0	.000	.000	.000	.000	0	...

2006 LEFTY-RIGHTY SPLITS

vs.	Avg.	AB	H	2B	3B	HR	RBI	BB	SO	OBP	Slg.	vs.	Avg.	AB	H	2B	3B	HR	RBI	BB	SO	OBP	Slg.
L	.238	130	31	8	2	8	19	17	31	.331	.515	R	.266	218	58	12	0	18	41	20	61	.335	.569

THERIOT, RYAN — SS/2B

PERSONAL: Born December 7, 1979, in Baton Rouge, La. ... 5-11/175. ... Bats right, throws right. ... Full name: Ryan Stewart Theriot. ... High school: Broadmoor (Baton Rouge, La.). ... College: Louisiana State. **TRANSACTIONS/CAREER NOTES:** Selected by Chicago Cubs organization in third round of 2001 free-agent draft.

2006 GAMES PLAYED BY POSITION (MLB): 2B—39, SS—2, 3B—1.

Year	Team (League)	Pos.	G	AB	R	H	2B	3B	HR	RBI	BB	SO	HBP	GDP	SB-CS	Avg.	OBP	SLG	OPS	E	Avg.
2001—	Daytona (Fla. St.)	SS	30	103	20	21	5	0	0	9	21	17	1	2	2-4	.204	.341	.252	.593	7	.944
2002—	Lansing (Midw.)	2B-SS	130	489	75	123	19	4	1	37	59	77	4	3	32-8	.252	.335	.313	.648	29	.957
2003—	Lansing (Midw.)	2B-SS	58	220	29	57	8	1	1	17	31	34	1	4	21-5	.259	.353	.318	.671	12	.961
—	West Tenn (Sou.)	SS	78	178	20	42	3	0	1	9	29	21	3	6	9-8	.236	.351	.270	.621	10	.953
2004—	Daytona (Fla. St.)	SS	103	330	47	90	14	3	1	34	48	43	3	4	13-11	.273	.367	.342	.709	18	.526
2005—	West Tenn (Sou.)	2B-SS-3B	120	448	52	136	28	4	1	53	45	38	1	9	24-10	.304	.365	.391	.755	13	.975
—	Chicago (N.L.)	2B	9	13	3	2	1	0	0	0	1	2	0	0	0-0	.154	.214	.231	.445	0	1.000
2006—	Iowa (PCL)		73	280	41	85	11	5	0	22	27	34	2	5	14-3	.304	.367	.379	.745	10	.966
—	Chicago (N.L.)	2B-SS-3B	53	134	34	44	11	3	3	16	17	18	2	5	13-2	.328	.412	.522	.934	3	.977
Major League totals (2 years)			62	147	37	46	12	3	3	16	18	20	2	5	13-2	.313	.395	.497	.892	3	.979

vs.	Avg.	AB	H	2B	3B	HR	RBI	BB	SO	OBP	Slg.	vs.	Avg.	AB	H	2B	3B	HR	RBI	BB	SO	OBP	Slg.
L	.346	52	18	4	1	1	6	11	3	.460	.519	R	.317	82	26	7	2	2	10	6	15	.378	.524

THOMAS, FRANK — DH/1B

PERSONAL: Born May 27, 1968, in Columbus, Ga. ... 6-5/275. ... Bats right, throws right. ... Full name: Frank Edward Thomas. ... High school: Columbus (Ga.). ... College: Auburn. **TRANSACTIONS/CAREER NOTES:** Selected by Chicago White Sox organization in first round (seventh pick overall) of 1989 free-agent draft. ... On disabled list (July 11-30, 1996; June 7-22, 1997; May 10, 2001-remainder of season; and July 7, 2004-remainder of season). ... On disabled list (April 2-May 30 and July 22, 2005-remainder of season); included rehabilitation assignment to Charlotte. ... Signed as free agent by Oakland Athletics (January 31, 2006). ... On disabled list (June 15-30, 2006). **HONORS:** Named first baseman on THE SPORTING NEWS college All-America team (1989). ... Named Major League Player of the Year by THE SPORTING NEWS (1993). ... Named A.L. Comeback Player of the Year by THE SPORTING NEWS (2000). ... Named first baseman on THE SPORTING NEWS A.L. All-Star team (1993-94). ... Named designated hitter on THE SPORTING NEWS A.L. All-Star team (2003). ... Named A.L. Most Valuable Player by Baseball Writers' Association of America (1993-94). ... Named designated hitter on A.L. Silver Slugger team (1991 and 2000). ... Named first baseman on A.L. Silver Slugger team (1993 and 1994). **STATISTICAL NOTES:** Hit three home runs in one game (September 15, 1996) ... Career major league grand slams: 8.
2006 GAMES PLAYED BY POSITION (MLB): DH—135.

									BATTING									FIELDING		
Year Team (League)	Pos.	G	AB	R	H	2B	3B	HR	RBI	BB	SO	HBP	GDP	SB-CS	Avg.	OBP	SLG	OPS	E	Avg.
1989— GC Whi. Sox (GCL)	1B	17	52	8	19	5	0	1	11	11	3	1	0	4-0	.365	.470	.519	.989	2	.986
—Sarasota (Fla. St.)	1B	55	188	27	52	9	1	4	30	31	33	3	6	0-1	.277	.386	.399	.785	7	.985
1990— Birmingham (Sou.)	1B	109	353	85	114	27	5	18	71	112	74	5	13	7-5	.323	.487	.581	1.068	14	.987
—Chicago (A.L.)	1B-DH	60	191	39	63	11	3	7	31	44	54	2	5	0-1	.330	.454	.529	.983	5	.989
1991— Chicago (A.L.)	1B-DH	158	559	104	178	31	2	32	109	*138	112	1	20	1-2	.318 *	.453	.553	1.006	2	.996
1992— Chicago (A.L.)	1B-DH	160	573	108	185	•46	2	24	115	•122	88	5	19	6-3	.323 *	.439	.536	.975	13	.992
1993— Chicago (A.L.)	1B-DH	153	549	106	174	36	0	41	128	112	54	2	10	4-2	.317	.426	.607	1.033	15	.989
1994— Chicago (A.L.)	1B-DH	113	399	*106	141	34	1	38	101	*109	61	2	15	2-3	.353 *	.487 *	.729	1.217	7	.991
1995— Chicago (A.L.)	1B-DH	•145	493	102	152	27	0	40	111	*136	74	6	14	3-2	.308	.454	.606	1.061	7	.991
1996— Chicago (A.L.)	1B	141	527	110	184	26	0	40	134	109	70	5	25	1-1	.349	.459	.626	1.085	9	.992
1997— Chicago (A.L.)	1B-DH	146	530	110	184	35	0	35	125	109	69	3	15	1-1	*.347 *	.456	.611	1.067	11	.986
1998— Chicago (A.L.)	DH-1B	160	585	109	155	35	2	29	109	110	93	6	14	7-0	.265	.381	.480	.861	2	.984
1999— Chicago (A.L.)	DH-1B	135	486	74	148	36	0	15	77	87	66	9	15	3-3	.305	.414	.471	.885	4	.996
2000— Chicago (A.L.)	DH-1B	159	582	115	191	44	0	43	143	112	94	5	13	1-3	.328	.436	.625	1.061	1	.996
2001— Chicago (A.L.)	DH-1B	20	68	8	15	3	0	4	10	10	12	0	0	0-0	.221	.316	.441	.758	1	.955
2002— Chicago (A.L.)	DH-1B	148	523	77	132	29	1	28	92	88	115	7	10	3-0	.252	.361	.472	.834	2	.955
2003— Chicago (A.L.)	DH-1B	153	546	87	146	35	0	42	105	100	115	12	11	0-0	.267	.390	.562	.952	1	.995
2004— Chicago (A.L.)	DH-1B	74	240	53	65	16	0	18	49	64	57	6	2	0-2	.271	.434	.563	.997	0	1.000
2005— Charlotte (Int'l)		11	42	3	8	1	0	1	4	4	9	0	2	0-0	.190	.261	.286	.547	0	...
—Chicago (A.L.)	DH	34	105	19	23	3	0	12	26	16	31	0	2	0-0	.219	.315	.590	.905	0	...
2006— Oakland (A.L.)	DH	137	466	77	126	11	0	39	114	81	81	6	13	0-0	.270	.381	.545	.926	0	...
Major League totals (17 years)		2096	7422	1404	2262	458	11	487	1579	1547	1246	77	203	32-23	.305	.424	.566	.990	80	.991

DIVISION SERIES RECORD

Year Team (League)	Pos.	G	AB	R	H	2B	3B	HR	RBI	BB	SO	HBP	GDP	SB-CS	Avg.	OBP	SLG	OPS	E	Avg.
2000— Chicago (A.L.)	1B-DH	3	9	0	0	0	0	0	0	4	0	0	0	0-0	.000	.308	.000	.308	0	1.000
2006— Oakland (A.L.)	DH	3	10	3	5	1	0	2	2	2	1	0	0	0-0	.500	.583	1.200	1.783	0	...
Division series totals (2 years)		6	19	3	5	1	0	2	2	6	1	0	0	0-0	.263	.440	.632	1.072	0	1.000

CHAMPIONSHIP SERIES RECORD

Year Team (League)	Pos.	G	AB	R	H	2B	3B	HR	RBI	BB	SO	HBP	GDP	SB-CS	Avg.	OBP	SLG	OPS	E	Avg.
1993— Chicago (A.L.)	1B-DH	.6	17	2	6	0	0	1	3	10	5	0	0	0-0	.353	.593	.529	1.122	0	1.000
2006— Oakland (A.L.)	DH	4	13	0	0	0	0	0	0	2	4	1	1	0-0	.000	.188	.000	.188	0	...
Champ. series totals (2 years)		10	30	2	6	0	0	1	3	12	9	1	1	0-0	.200	.442	.300	.742	0	1.000

ALL-STAR GAME RECORD

		G	AB	R	H	2B	3B	HR	RBI	BB	SO	HBP	GDP	SB-CS	Avg.	OBP	SLG	OPS	E	Avg.
All-Star Game totals (3 years)		3	5	2	4	0	1	1	3	1	0	0	0	0-0	.800	.833	1.400	2.233	0	1.000

2006 LEFTY-RIGHTY SPLITS

vs.	Avg.	AB	H	2B	3B	HR	RBI	BB	SO	OBP	Slg.	vs.	Avg.	AB	H	2B	3B	HR	RBI	BB	SO	OBP	Slg.
L	.245	106	26	4	0	9	18	31	23	.429	.538	R	.278	360	100	7	0	30	96	50	58	.365	.547

THOME, JIM — DH/1B

PERSONAL: Born August 27, 1970, in Peoria, Ill. ... 6-4/244. ... Bats left, throws right. ... Full name: James Howard Thome. ... Name pronounced: TOE-mee. ... High school: Limestone (Bartonville, Ill.). ... Junior college: Illinois Central. **TRANSACTIONS/CAREER NOTES:** Selected by Cleveland Indians organization in 13th round of 1989 free-agent draft. ... On disabled list (March 28-May 18, 1992); included rehabilitation assignment to Canton/Akron. ... On disabled list (May 20-June 15, 1992); included rehabilitation assignment to Canton/Akron. ... On disabled list (August 8-September 16, 1998). ... Signed as a free agent by Philadelphia Phillies (December 3, 2002). ... On disabled list (May 3-21 and July 1, 2005-remainder of season); included rehabilitation assignment to Clearwater. ... Traded by Phillies with cash to Chicago White Sox for OF Aaron Rowand, P Daniel Haigwood and a player to be named (November 25, 2005); Phillies acquired P Gio Gonzalez to complete deal (December 8, 2005). **RECORDS:** Shares major league record for most strikeouts, 9-inning game (5, April 9, 2000). **HONORS:** Named A.L. Comeback Player of the Year by the SPORTING NEWS (2006). ... Named third baseman on THE SPORTING NEWS A.L. All-Star team (1995-96). ... Named first baseman on THE SPORTING NEWS A.L. All-Star team (2001). ... Named third baseman on A.L. Silver Slugger team (1996). **STATISTICAL NOTES:** Hit three home runs in one game (July 22, 1994 and July 6, 2001). ... Career major league grand slams: 8.
2006 GAMES PLAYED BY POSITION (MLB): DH—136, 1B—3.

									BATTING									FIELDING		
Year Team (League)	Pos.	G	AB	R	H	2B	3B	HR	RBI	BB	SO	HBP	GDP	SB-CS	Avg.	OBP	SLG	OPS	E	Avg.
1989— GC Indians (GCL)	3B-SS	55	186	22	44	5	3	0	22	21	33	1	5	6-4	.237	.314	.296	.610	21	.909
1990— Burlington (Appal.)	3B	34	118	31	44	7	1	12	34	27	18	4	2	6-3	.373	.503	.754	1.258	11	.907
—Kinston (Carol.)	3B	33	117	19	36	4	1	4	16	24	26	1	4	4-1	.308	.427	.462	.888	8	.905
1991— Cant./Akr. (Eastern)	3B	84	294	47	99	20	2	5	45	44	58	4	7	8-2	.337	.426	.469	.895	17	.924
—Colo. Springs (PCL)	3B	41	151	20	43	7	3	2	28	12	29	0	4	0-0	.285	.331	.411	.742	6	.949
—Cleveland (A.L.)	3B	27	98	7	25	4	2	1	9	5	16	1	1	1-1	.255	.298	.367	.665	8	.900
1992— Colo. Springs (PCL)	3B	12	48	11	15	4	1	2	14	6	16	1	0	0-0	.313	.400	.563	.963	8	.784
—Cleveland (A.L.)	3B	40	117	8	24	3	1	2	12	10	34	2	3	2-0	.205	.275	.299	.574	11	.882
—Cant./Akr. (Eastern)	3B	30	107	16	36	9	2	1	14	24	30	1	0	0-2	.336	.462	.486	.948	4	.920
1993— Charlotte (Int'l)	3B	115	410	85	136	21	4	25	102	76	94	7	3	1-3	.332	.441	.585	1.026	15	.951
—Cleveland (A.L.)	3B	47	154	28	41	11	0	7	22	29	36	1	3	2-1	.266	.385	.474	.859	6	.950
1994— Cleveland (A.L.)	3B	98	321	58	86	20	1	20	52	46	84	0	8	3-3	.268	.359	.523	.882	15	.940
1995— Cleveland (A.L.)	3B-DH	137	452	92	142	29	3	25	73	97	113	6	4	4-3	.314	.438	.558	.996	16	.948

Year Team (League)	Pos.	G	AB	R	H	2B	3B	HR	RBI	BB	SO	HBP	GDP	SB-CS	Avg.	OBP	SLG	OPS	E	Avg.
1996— Cleveland (A.L.)	3B-DH	151	505	122	157	28	5	38	116	123	141	6	13	2-2	.311	.450	.612	1.062	17	.953
1997— Cleveland (A.L.)	1B	147	496	104	142	25	0	40	102	* 120	146	3	9	1-1	.286	.423	.579	1.001	10	.993
1998— Cleveland (A.L.)	1B-DH	123	440	89	129	34	2	30	85	89	141	4	7	1-0	.293	.413	.584	.998	10	.991
1999— Cleveland (A.L.)	1B-DH	146	494	101	137	27	2	33	108	* 127	* 171	4	6	0-0	.277	.426	.540	.967	6	.994
2000— Cleveland (A.L.)	1B-DH	158	557	106	150	33	1	37	106	118	171	4	8	1-0	.269	.398	.531	.929	5	.995
2001— Cleveland (A.L.)	1B-DH	156	526	101	153	26	1	49	124	111 *	185	4	9	0-1	.291	.416	.624	1.040	10	.992
2002— Cleveland (A.L.)	1B-DH	147	480	101	146	19	2	52	118	* 122	139	5	5	1-2	.304	.445	* .677	1.122	10	.991
2003— Philadelphia (N.L.)	1B-DH	159	578	111	154	30	3	* 47	131	111 *	182	4	5	0-3	.266	.385	.573	.958	5	.997
2004— Philadelphia (N.L.)	1B-DH	143	508	97	139	28	1	42	105	104	144	2	10	0-2	.274	.396	.581	.977	7	.994
2005— Philadelphia (N.L.)	1B-DH	59	193	26	40	7	0	7	30	45	59	2	5	0-0	.207	.360	.352	.712	0	1.000
— Clearwater (FSL)		5	12	2	4	0	0	1	3	6	1	0	0	0-0	.333	.556	.583	1.139	0	...
2006— Chicago (A.L.)	DH-1B	143	490	108	141	26	0	42	109	107	147	6	4	0-0	.288	.416	.598	1.014	0	1.000
American League totals (13 years)		1520	5130	1025	1473	285	20	376	1036	1104	1524	48	90	18-14	.287	.415	.570	.985	124	.985
National League totals (3 years)		361	1279	234	333	65	4	96	266	260	385	8	20	0-5	.260	.386	.543	.928	12	.996
Major League totals (16 years)		1881	6409	1259	1806	350	24	472	1302	1364	1909	56	110	18-19	.282	.409	.565	.974	136	.988

DIVISION SERIES RECORD

Year Team (League)	Pos.	G	AB	R	H	2B	3B	HR	RBI	BB	SO	HBP	GDP	SB-CS	Avg.	OBP	SLG	OPS	E	Avg.
1995— Cleveland (A.L.)	3B	3	13	1	2	0	0	1	3	1	6	0	0	0-0	.154	.214	.385	.599	0	1.000
1996— Cleveland (A.L.)	3B	4	10	1	3	0	0	0	0	1	5	1	0	0-0	.300	.417	.300	.717	0	1.000
1997— Cleveland (A.L.)	1B	4	15	1	3	0	0	0	1	0	5	0	0	0-0	.200	.200	.200	.400	0	1.000
1998— Cleveland (A.L.)	1B-DH	4	15	2	2	0	0	2	2	2	5	0	0	0-0	.133	.235	.533	.769	0	1.000
1999— Cleveland (A.L.)	1B	5	17	7	6	0	0	4	10	4	5	0	0	0-0	.353	.476	1.059	1.535	0	1.000
2001— Cleveland (A.L.)	1B	5	19	2	3	0	0	1	2	2	8	0	0	0-0	.158	.238	.316	.554	0	1.000
Division series totals (6 years)		25	89	14	19	0	0	8	17	10	34	1	0	0-0	.213	.300	.483	.783	0	1.000

CHAMPIONSHIP SERIES RECORD

Year Team (League)	Pos.	G	AB	R	H	2B	3B	HR	RBI	BB	SO	HBP	GDP	SB-CS	Avg.	OBP	SLG	OPS	E	Avg.
1995— Cleveland (A.L.)	3B	5	15	2	4	0	0	2	5	2	3	0	1	0-0	.267	.353	.667	1.020	1	.857
1997— Cleveland (A.L.)	1B	6	14	3	1	0	0	0	0	5	4	0	0	0-0	.071	.316	.071	.387	0	1.000
1998— Cleveland (A.L.)	1B-DH	6	23	4	7	0	0	4	8	1	8	1	0	0-0	.304	.360	.826	1.186	0	1.000
Champ. series totals (3 years)		17	52	9	12	0	0	6	13	8	15	1	1	0-0	.231	.344	.577	.921	1	.989

WORLD SERIES RECORD

Year Team (League)	Pos.	G	AB	R	H	2B	3B	HR	RBI	BB	SO	HBP	GDP	SB-CS	Avg.	OBP	SLG	OPS	E	Avg.
1995— Cleveland (A.L.)	3B	6	19	1	4	1	0	1	2	2	5	0	0	0-0	.211	.286	.421	.707	1	.889
1997— Cleveland (A.L.)	1B	7	28	8	8	0	1	2	4	5	7	0	2	0-0	.286	.394	.571	.965	1	.984
World series totals (2 years)		13	47	9	12	1	1	3	6	7	12	0	2	0-0	.255	.352	.511	.862	2	.972

ALL-STAR GAME RECORD

		G	AB	R	H	2B	3B	HR	RBI	BB	SO	HBP	GDP	SB-CS	Avg.	OBP	SLG	OPS	E	Avg.
All-Star Game totals (5 years)		5	8	2	1	0	0	0	1	3	2	0	0		.125	.364	.125	.489	0	1.000

2006 LEFTY-RIGHTY SPLITS

vs.	Avg.	AB	H	2B	3B	HR	RBI	BB	SO	OBP	Slg.	vs.	Avg.	AB	H	2B	3B	HR	RBI	BB	SO	OBP	Slg.
L	.236	191	45	6	0	6	24	31	66	.354	.361	R	.321	299	96	20	0	36	85	76	81	.454	.749

THOMPSON, BRAD — P

PERSONAL: Born January 31, 1982, in Las Vegas. ... 6-1/190. ... Throws right, bats right. ... Full name: Bradley Joseph Thompson. ... High school: Cimarron-Memorial (Las Vegas). ... Junior college: Dixie State (Utah). **TRANSACTIONS/CAREER NOTES:** Selected by St. Louis Cardinals organization in 16th round of 2002 free-agent draft. **MISCEL- LANEOUS NOTES:** Appeared in one game as pinch runner (2005).

CAREER HITTING: 2-for-8 (.250), 0 R, 0 2B, 0 3B, 0 HR, 0 RBI.

Year Team (League)	W	L	Pct.	ERA	WHIP	G	GS	CG	ShO	Hld.	Sv.-Opp.	IP	H	R	ER	HR	BB-IBB	SO	Avg.
2003— Peoria (Midw.)	5	3	.625	2.91	1.23	30	4	0	0	...	0-...	65.0	70	23	21	2	10-2	43	.273
— Palm Beach (FSL)	1	0	1.000	0.00	0.50	2	1	0	0	...	0-...	6.0	3	0	0	0	0-0	4	.158
2004— Tennessee (Sou.)	8	2	.800	2.36	1.20	13	12	2	2	...	0-...	72.1	56	19	19	6	11-0	57	.218
— Memphis (PCL)	1	0	1.000	5.52	1.57	3	3	0	0	...	0-...	14.2	20	10	9	3	3-0	10	.333
2005— Memphis (PCL)	2	1	.667	3.29	1.39	9	0	0	0	1	0-1	13.2	12	5	5	1	7-5	11	.240
— St. Louis (N.L.)	.4	0	1.000	2.95	1.11	40	0	0	0	7	1-1	55.0	46	22	18	5	15-2	29	.227
2006— Memphis (PCL)	2	0	1.000	2.11	0.98	14	5	0	0	2	0-0	42.2	36	12	10	3	6-1	33	.235
— St. Louis (N.L.)	1	2	.333	3.34	1.38	43	1	0	0	3	0-0	56.2	58	23	21	4	20-3	32	.267
Major League totals (2 years)	5	2	.714	3.14	1.24	83	1	0	0	10	1-1	111.2	104	45	39	9	35-5	61	.248

DIVISION SERIES RECORD

Year Team (League)	W	L	Pct.	ERA	WHIP	G	GS	CG	ShO	Hld.	Sv.-Opp.	IP	H	R	ER	HR	BB-IBB	SO	Avg.
2005— St. Louis (N.L.)	0	0	...	13.50	2.25	2	0	0	0	0	0-0	1.1	3	2	2	1	0-0	1	.500
2006— St. Louis (N.L.)	0	0	...	0.00	1.50	1	0	0	0	0	0-0	0.2	0	0	0	0	1-0	1	.000
Division series totals (2 years)	0	0	...	9.00	2.00	3	0	0	0	0	0-0	2.0	3	2	2	1	1-0	2	.375

CHAMPIONSHIP SERIES RECORD

Year Team (League)	W	L	Pct.	ERA	WHIP	G	GS	CG	ShO	Hld.	Sv.-Opp.	IP	H	R	ER	HR	BB-IBB	SO	Avg.
2005— St. Louis (N.L.)	0	0	...	0.00	2.00	2	0	0	0	0	0-0	1.0	2	0	0	0	0-0	0	.400
2006— St. Louis (N.L.)	0	1	.000	27.00	4.50	2	0	0	0	0	0-0	0.2	3	3	2	1	0-0	1	.500
Champ. series totals (2 years)	0	1	.000	10.80	3.00	4	0	0	0	0	0-0	1.2	5	3	2	1	0-0	1	.455

WORLD SERIES RECORD

Year Team (League)	W	L	Pct.	ERA	WHIP	G	GS	CG	ShO	Hld.	Sv.-Opp.	IP	H	R	ER	HR	BB-IBB	SO	Avg.
2006— St. Louis (N.L.)	0	0	...	0.00	0.00	1	0	0	0	0	0-0	0.2	0	0	0	0	0-0	1	.000

2006 LEFTY-RIGHTY SPLITS

vs.	Avg.	AB	H	2B	3B	HR	RBI	BB	SO	OBP	Slg.	vs.	Avg.	AB	H	2B	3B	HR	RBI	BB	SO	OBP	Slg.
L	.284	88	25	7	1	1	11	6	11	.337	.420	R	.256	129	33	6	0	3	16	14	21	.347	.372

THOMPSON, KEVIN — OF

PERSONAL: Born September 18, 1979, in Fort Worth, Texas. ... 5-10/185. ... Bats right, throws right. ... Full name: Kevin Deshawn Thompson. ... College: Grayson County (Texas) C.C. **TRANSACTIONS/CAREER NOTES:** Selected by New York Yankees organization in 31st round of 1999 free-agent draft.
2006 GAMES PLAYED BY POSITION (MLB): OF—15, DH—2.

Year Team (League)	Pos.	G	AB	R	H	2B	3B	HR	RBI	BB	SO	HBP	GDP	SB-CS	Avg.	OBP	SLG	OPS	FIELDING E	Avg.
2000— GC Yankees (GCL)		20	75	13	20	7	1	2	9	10	14	1	1	2-3	.267	.356	.467	.823	...	...
2001— Staten Is. (N.Y.-Penn)		68	260	46	68	11	4	6	33	36	48	5	5	11-5	.262	.360	.404	.764	...	...
2002— Greensboro (S. Atl.)		62	226	44	64	24	3	3	31	37	42	6	4	14-3	.283	.396	.456	.852	...	...
— Tampa (Fla. St.)		25	87	10	16	5	0	0	7	13	15	2	3	11-1	.184	.298	.241	.539	...	...
— Staten Is. (N.Y.-Penn) ...		36	139	25	42	5	2	4	14	17	24	0	1	6-3	.302	.376	.453	.829	...	...
2003— Tampa (Fla. St.)		44	163	42	54	13	4	5	25	32	27	2	3	16-5	.331	.433	.552	.985	...	...
— Trenton (East.)		86	328	48	74	16	2	5	20	37	57	4	5	47-8	.226	.310	.332	.642	...	...
2004— Tampa (Fla. St.)		11	45	12	16	4	0	2	6	4	7	1	0	9-2	.356	.420	.578	.998	...	...
— Trenton (East.)		69	270	43	76	17	0	9	17	30	40	4	8	29-10	.281	.362	.444	.806	...	...
2005— Trenton (East.)	OF-DH	81	313	59	103	28	5	12	43	53	68	6	5	25-6	.329	.432	.565	.997	6	.977
— Columbus (Int'l)	OF-DH	58	209	28	52	17	0	2	28	23	45	6	4	18-5	.249	.335	.359	.694	8	.967
2006— Columbus (Int'l)	OF-DH	91	362	69	96	22	5	9	44	44	63	2	3	17-7	.265	.345	.428	.773	6	.971
— New York (A.L.)	OF-DH	19	30	5	9	3	0	1	6	6	9	0	0	2-0	.300	.417	.500	.917	0	1.000
Major League totals (1 year)		19	30	5	9	3	0	1	6	6	9	0	0	2-0	.300	.417	.500	.917	0	1.000

2006 LEFTY-RIGHTY SPLITS

vs.	Avg.	AB	H	2B	3B	HR	RBI	BB	SO	OBP	Slg.	vs.	Avg.	AB	H	2B	3B	HR	RBI	BB	SO	OBP	Slg.
L	.182	11	2	0	0	0	0	4	6	.400	.182	R	.368	19	7	3	0	1	6	2	3	.429	.684

THOMPSON, MIKE P

PERSONAL: Born November 6, 1980, in Walsh, Colo. ... Throws right, bats right. ... Full name: Michael Paul Thompson. **TRANSACTIONS/CAREER NOTES:** Selected by San Diego Padres organization in fifth round of 1999 free-agent draft.

CAREER HITTING: 4-for-25 (.160), 2 R, 0 2B, 0 3B, 0 HR, 0 RBI.

Year Team (League)	W	L	Pct.	ERA	WHIP	G	GS	CG	ShO	Hld.	Sv.-Opp.	IP	H	R	ER	HR	BB-IBB	SO	Avg.
1999— Ariz. Padres (Ariz.)	1	7	.125	6.09	1.62	13	13	0	0	...	0-...	65.0	78	52	44	8	27-0	62	.295
2000— Fort Wayne (Midw.)	1	3	.250	5.13	1.63	6	6	0	0	...	0-...	26.1	28	19	15	1	15-0	17	.289
— Idaho Falls (Pio.)	6	4	.600	5.94	1.78	14	14	0	0	...	0-...	72.2	99	56	48	8	30-0	52	.331
2001— Fort Wayne (Midw.)	0	1	.000	6.00	1.67	1	1	0	0	...	0-...	6.0	8	4	4	0	2-0	1	.308
— Lake Elsinore (Calif.)	5	4	.556	5.35	1.45	19	12	0	0	...	0-...	74.0	82	46	44	7	25-0	39	.290
2002— Lake Elsinore (Calif.)	5	7	.417	5.56	1.60	25	22	0	0	...	0-...	123.0	144	93	76	14	53-0	79	.286
— Mobile (Sou.)	1	0	1.000	3.60	1.00	1	1	0	0	...	0-...	5.0	5	2	2	1	0-0	0	.263
2003— Lake Elsinore (Calif.)	10	11	.476	4.42	1.42	28	22	0	0	...	0-...	136.1	163	78	67	8	31-0	75	.298
2004— Mobile (Sou.)	10	2	.833	3.41	1.31	35	18	0	0	...	0-...	121.1	128	50	46	13	31-2	69	.290
2005— Mobile (Sou.)	6	6	.500	3.22	1.25	18	18	2	1	0	0-0	114.2	116	50	41	6	27-0	68	.269
— Portland (PCL)	4	2	.667	3.15	1.18	9	9	0	0	0	0-0	60.0	58	22	21	6	13-0	25	.258
2006— Portland (PCL)	6	1	.857	3.76	1.28	13	13	0	0	0	0-0	69.1	69	30	29	4	20-1	41	.263
— San Diego (N.L.)	4	5	.444	4.99	1.45	19	16	0	0	0	0-0	92.0	103	56	51	13	30-4	35	.285
Major League totals (1 year)	4	5	.444	4.99	1.45	19	16	0	0	0	0-0	92.0	103	56	51	13	30-4	35	.285

2006 LEFTY-RIGHTY SPLITS

vs.	Avg.	AB	H	2B	3B	HR	RBI	BB	SO	OBP	Slg.	vs.	Avg.	AB	H	2B	3B	HR	RBI	BB	SO	OBP	Slg.
L	.283	184	52	6	0	6	24	14	16	.340	.413	R	.288	177	51	13	0	7	26	16	19	.360	.480

THOMSON, JOHN P

PERSONAL: Born October 1, 1973, in Vicksburg, Miss. ... 6-3/220. ... Throws right, bats right. ... Full name: John Carl Thomson. ... Name pronounced: TOM-son. ... High school: Sulphur (La.). ... Junior college: Blinn (Texas). ... College: Blinn (TX) JC. **TRANSACTIONS/CAREER NOTES:** Selected by Colorado Rockies organization in seventh round of 1993 free-agent draft. ... On disabled list (June 16-July 26, 1998); included rehabilitation assignment to Asheville. ... On disabled list (May 19-July 19, 1999); included rehabilitation assignment to Salem. ... On disabled list (March 23, 2000-remainder of season); included rehabilitation assignment to Colorado Springs. ... On disabled list (March 23-May 12 and May 26-August 2, 2001); included rehabilitation assignments to Colorado Springs. ... Traded by Rockies with OF Mark Little to New York Mets for OFs Jay Payton and Robert Stratton and P Mark Corey (July 31, 2002). ... Signed as a free agent by Texas Rangers (January 3, 2002). ... Signed as a free agent by Atlanta Braves (December 10, 2003). ... On disabled list (May 17-August 13, 2005); included rehabilitation assignments to GCL Braves, Richmond, Mississippi and Rome. ... On disabled list (June 16-July 4 and July 15-September 26, 2006); included rehabilitation assignments to Rome and Mississippi.

CAREER HITTING: 63-for-318 (.198), 20 R, 6 2B, 1 3B, 0 HR, 22 RBI.

Year Team (League)	W	L	Pct.	ERA	WHIP	G	GS	CG	ShO	Hld.	Sv.-Opp.	IP	H	R	ER	HR	BB-IBB	SO	Avg.
1993— Ariz. Rockies (Ariz.)	3	5	.375	4.62	1.46	11	11	0	0	...	0-...	50.2	43	40	26	0	31-0	36	.225
1994— Asheville (S. Atl.)	6	6	.500	2.85	1.17	19	15	1	1	...	0-...	88.1	70	34	28	3	33-1	79	.219
— Central Valley (Cal.)	3	1	.750	3.28	1.24	9	8	0	0	...	0-...	49.1	43	20	18	0	18-1	41	.239
1995— New Haven (East.)	7	8	.467	4.18	1.43	26	24	0	0	...	0-...	131.1	132	69	61	8	56-0	82	.261
1996— New Haven (East.)	9	4	.692	2.86	1.12	16	16	1	0	...	0-...	97.2	82	35	31	8	27-1	86	.230
— Colo. Springs (PCL)	4	7	.364	5.04	1.46	11	11	0	0	...	0-...	69.2	76	45	39	6	26-2	62	.280
1997— Colo. Springs (PCL)	4	2	.667	3.43	1.19	7	7	0	0	...	0-...	42.0	36	18	16	4	14-1	49	.235
— Colorado (N.L.)	7	9	.438	4.71	1.47	27	27	2	1	0	0-0	166.1	193	94	87	15	51-0	106	.296
1998— Colorado (N.L.)	8	11	.421	4.81	1.39	26	26	0	0	0	0-0	161.0	174	86	86	21	49-0	106	.282
— Asheville (S. Atl.)	1	0	1.000	0.00	0.67	2	2	0	0	...	0-...	9.0	5	1	0	0	1-0	12	.161
1999— Colorado (N.L.)	1	10	.091	8.04	1.93	14	13	1	0	0	0-0	62.2	85	62	56	11	36-1	34	.324
— Colo. Springs (PCL)	0	2	.000	9.45	2.20	5	5	1	0	...	0-...	20.0	36	25	21	3	8-0	19	.414
— Salem (Carol.)	0	1	.000	9.00	2.00	1	1	0	0	...	0-...	2.0	4	2	2	0	0-0	2	.400
2000— Ariz. Rockies (Ariz.)	0	1	.000	13.50	2.25	3	3	0	0	...	0-...	5.1	8	8	8	0	4-0	7	.333
— Portland (N'west)	0	0	...	2.25	1.25	1	1	0	0	...	0-...	4.0	4	1	1	0	1-0	3	.250
2001— Colo. Springs (PCL)	5	3	.625	3.31	1.28	12	12	0	0	...	0-...	68.0	74	29	25	6	13-0	52	.274
— Colorado (N.L.)	4	5	.444	4.04	1.16	14	14	1	1	0	0-0	93.2	84	46	42	15	25-3	68	.239
2002— Colorado (N.L.)	7	8	.467	4.88	1.28	21	21	0	0	0	0-0	127.1	136	77	69	21	27-6	76	.268
— New York (N.L.)	2	6	.250	4.31	1.51	9	9	0	0	0	0-0	54.1	65	39	26	7	17-3	31	.290
2003— Texas (A.L.)	13	14	.481	4.85	1.30	35	35	3	1	0	0-0	217.0	234	125	117	27	49-2	136	.276
2004— Atlanta (N.L.)	14	8	.636	3.72	1.32	33	33	0	0	0	0-0	198.1	210	93	82	20	52-5	133	.276
2005— Rome (S. Atl.)	0	0	...	0.00	0.75	1	1	0	0	0	0-0	4.0	2	0	0	0	1-0	1	.143
— Richmond (Int'l)	0	0	...	4.91	1.64	1	1	0	0	0	0-0	3.2	5	2	2	0	1-0	2	.357
— Mississippi (Sou.)	1	0	1.000	1.50	0.67	1	1	0	0	0	0-0	6.0	4	1	1	0	0-0	4	.190
— Atlanta (N.L.)	4	6	.400	4.47	1.41	17	17	1	0	0	0-0	98.2	111	52	49	6	28-2	61	.284
2006— Rome (S. Atl.)	0	1	.000	10.80	1.80	1	1	0	0	0	0-0	1.2	3	2	2	0	0-0	0	.375
— Mississippi (Sou.)	0	0	...	9.00	3.00	1	1	0	0	0	0-0	1.0	2	1	1	0	1-0	1	.400
— Atlanta (N.L.)	2	7	.222	4.82	1.56	18	15	0	0	0	0-0	80.1	93	55	43	11	32-4	46	.295
American League totals (1 year)	13	14	.481	4.85	1.30	35	35	3	1	0	0-0	217.0	234	125	117	27	49-2	136	.276
National League totals (8 years)	49	70	.412	4.66	1.41	179	175	7	2	1	0-0	1042.2	1151	604	540	127	317-24	661	.282
Major League totals (9 years)	62	84	.425	4.69	1.39	214	210	10	3	1	0-0	1259.2	1385	729	657	154	366-26	797	.281

T

DIVISION SERIES RECORD

Year Team (League)	W	L	Pct.	ERA	WHIP	G	GS	CG	ShO	Hld.	Sv.-Opp.	IP	H	R	ER	HR	BB-IBB	SO	Avg.
2004—Atlanta (N.L.)	0	0	...	0.00	6.00	1	1	0	0	0	0-0	0.1	1	0	0	0	1-0	0	.500
2005—Atlanta (N.L.)	0	0	...	0.00	0.50	1	0	0	0	0	0-0	2.0	0	0	0	0	1-0	3	.000
Division series totals (2 years)	0	0	...	0.00	1.29	2	1	0	0	0	0-0	2.1	1	0	0	0	2-0	3	.125

2006 LEFTY-RIGHTY SPLITS

vs.	Avg.	AB	H	2B	3B	HR	RBI	BB	SO	OBP	Slg.	vs.	Avg.	AB	H	2B	3B	HR	RBI	BB	SO	OBP	Slg.
L	.276	152	42	8	1	5	23	19	22	.354	.441	R	.313	163	51	7	0	6	27	13	24	.359	.466

THORMAN, SCOTT — 1B/OF

PERSONAL: Born January 6, 1982, in Cambridge, Ontario. ... 6-3/225. ... Bats left, throws right. ... Full name: Scott Robert Thorman. **TRANSACTIONS/CAREER NOTES:** Selected by Atlanta Braves organization in first round (30th overall pick) of 2000 free-agent draft.

2006 GAMES PLAYED BY POSITION (MLB): OF—21, 1B—18.

Year Team (League)	Pos.	G	AB	R	H	2B	3B	HR	RBI	BB	SO	HBP	GDP	SB-CS	Avg.	OBP	SLG	OPS	E	Avg.
2000—GC Braves (GCL)		29	97	15	22	7	1	1	19	12	23	4	1	0-1	.227	.330	.351	.681	...	...
2001—									Did not play											
2002—Macon (S. Atl.)		127	470	57	138	38	3	16	82	51	83	7	16	2-2	.294	.367	.489	.856	...	...
2003—Myrtle Beach (Carol.)		124	445	44	108	26	2	12	56	42	79	4	13	0-0	.243	.311	.391	.702	...	...
2004—Myrtle Beach (Carol.)		43	154	20	46	11	1	4	29	12	19	5	1	1-0	.299	.358	.481	.819	...	...
—Greenville (Sou.)		94	345	31	87	14	3	11	51	39	73	0	3	5-3	.252	.326	.406	.732	...	...
2005—Mississippi (Sou.)	1B	90	348	49	106	21	2	15	65	28	76	4	3	2-2	.305	.360	.506	.866	9	.990
—Richmond (Int'l)	1B	52	210	23	58	10	3	6	27	9	42	3	3	0-0	.276	.313	.438	.751	4	.991
2006—Richmond (Int'l)		81	309	38	92	16	2	15	48	31	48	1	6	4-2	.298	.360	.508	.869	8	.984
—Atlanta (N.L.)	OF-1B	55	128	13	30	11	0	5	14	5	21	0	0	1-0	.234	.263	.438	.701	1	.993
Major League totals (1 year)		55	128	13	30	11	0	5	14	5	21	0	0	1-0	.234	.263	.438	.701	1	.993

2006 LEFTY-RIGHTY SPLITS

vs.	Avg.	AB	H	2B	3B	HR	RBI	BB	SO	OBP	Slg.	vs.	Avg.	AB	H	2B	3B	HR	RBI	BB	SO	OBP	Slg.
L	.189	37	7	4	0	1	3	2	11	.231	.378	R	.253	91	23	7	0	4	11	3	10	.277	.462

THORNTON, MATT — P

PERSONAL: Born September 15, 1976, in Three Rivers, Mich. ... 6-6/220. ... Throws left, bats left. ... Full name: Matthew J. Thornton. ... High school: Centreville High (Allendale,Mich.). ... College: Grand Valley State. **TRANSACTIONS/CAREER NOTES:** Selected by Detroit Tigers organization in 27th round of 1995 free-agent draft; did not sign. ... Selected by Seattle Mariners organization in first round (22nd pick overall) of 1998 free-agent draft. ... On disabled list (August 15, 2003-remainder of season). ... Traded by Mariners to Chicago White Sox for OF Joe Borchard (March 20, 2006).

CAREER HITTING: 0-for-0 (.000), 0 R, 0 2B, 0 3B, 0 HR, 0 RBI.

Year Team (League)	W	L	Pct.	ERA	WHIP	G	GS	CG	ShO	Hld.	Sv.-Opp.	IP	H	R	ER	HR	BB-IBB	SO	Avg.
1998—Everett (N'west)	0	0	...	27.00	3.00	2	0	0	0	...	0-...	1.1	1	4	4	0	3-0	0	.250
1999—Wisconsin (Midw.)	0	0	...	4.91	2.18	25	1	0	0	...	1-...	29.1	39	19	16	1	25-0	34	.320
2000—Wisconsin (Midw.)	6	9	.400	4.01	1.61	26	17	0	0	...	0-...	103.1	94	59	46	2	72-1	88	.245
2001—San Bern. (Calif.)	14	7	.667	2.52	1.18	27	27	0	0	...	0-...	157.0	126	56	44	9	60-0	192	.220
2002—San Antonio (Texas)	1	5	.167	3.63	1.31	12	12	0	0	...	0-...	62.0	52	31	25	3	29-0	44	.237
2003—Inland Empire (Calif.)	0	0	...	4.00	1.44	2	2	0	0	...	0-...	9.0	9	4	4	2	4-0	14	.265
—San Antonio (Texas)	3	0	1.000	0.36	0.67	4	4	0	0	...	0-...	25.1	8	3	1	0	9-0	18	.104
—Tacoma (PCL)	0	2	.000	8.00	1.89	2	2	0	0	...	0-...	9.0	14	11	8	2	3-0	5	.359
2004—Tacoma (PCL)	7	5	.583	5.42	1.80	16	15	1	0	...	0-...	83.0	86	58	50	4	63-1	74	.273
—Seattle (A.L.)	1	2	.333	4.13	1.68	19	1	0	0	...	0-0	32.2	30	15	15	2	25-1	30	.250
2005—Seattle (A.L.)	0	4	.000	5.21	1.68	55	0	0	0	5	0-1	57.0	54	33	33	13	42-2	57	.248
2006—Chicago (A.L.)	5	3	.625	3.33	1.24	63	0	0	0	18	2-5	54.0	46	20	20	5	21-4	49	.229
Major League totals (3 years)	6	9	.400	4.26	1.52	137	1	0	0	23	2-6	143.2	130	68	68	20	88-7	136	.241

2006 LEFTY-RIGHTY SPLITS

vs.	Avg.	AB	H	2B	3B	HR	RBI	BB	SO	OBP	Slg.	vs.	Avg.	AB	H	2B	3B	HR	RBI	BB	SO	OBP	Slg.
L	.211	76	16	5	0	1	13	5	23	.253	.316	R	.240	125	30	2	1	4	11	16	26	.329	.368

THURSTON, JOE — 2B/OF

PERSONAL: Born September 29, 1979, in Fairfield, Calif. ... 5-11/175. ... Bats left, throws right. ... Full name: Joseph William Thurston. ... High school: Vallejo (Calif.). ... Junior college: Sacramento (Calif.) City College. ... College: Sacramento (CA) CC. **TRANSACTIONS/CAREER NOTES:** Selected by Boston Red Sox organization in 45th round of 1997 free-agent draft; did not sign. ... Selected by Los Angeles Dodgers organization in fourth round of 1999 free-agent draft. ... Traded by Dodgers to New York Yankees for cash (July 29, 2005). ... Signed as a free agent by Philadelphia Phillies organization (December 20, 2005). ... Signed as a free agent by Washington Nationals organization (November 6, 2006).

2006 GAMES PLAYED BY POSITION (MLB): 2B—4, OF—3.

Year Team (League)	Pos.	G	AB	R	H	2B	3B	HR	RBI	BB	SO	HBP	GDP	SB-CS	Avg.	OBP	SLG	OPS	E	Avg.
1999—Yakima (N'west)	1B-SS	71	277	48	79	10	3	0	32	29	34	21	3	27-17	.285	.387	.343	.730	29	.899
—San Bern. (Calif.)	SS	2	3	0	0	0	0	0	0	0	1	1	0	0-0	.000	.250	.000	.250	0	1.000
2000—San Bern. (Calif.)	2B-SS	138	551	97	167	31	8	4	70	56	61	17	8	43-25	.303	.380	.410	.790	34	.953
2001—Jacksonville (Sou.)	2B-SS	134	544	80	145	25	7	7	46	48	65	12	5	20-18	.267	.338	.377	.715	17	.973
2002—Las Vegas (PCL)	2B-SS	136	587	106	196	39	13	12	55	25	60	12	10	22-9	.334	.372	.506	.878	21	.973
—Los Angeles (N.L.)	2B	8	13	1	6	1	0	0	1	0	1	0	0	0-0	.462	.429	.538	.967	0	1.000
2003—Las Vegas (PCL)	2B-SS	132	538	77	156	27	6	7	68	31	48	18	10	1-12	.290	.345	.401	.746	15	.978
—Los Angeles (N.L.)	2B	12	10	2	2	0	0	0	0	1	1	0	0	0-0	.200	.273	.200	.473	1	.857
2004—Las Vegas (PCL)	2B-DH	101	317	38	90	17	3	4	23	20	46	17	6	7-2	.284	.356	.394	.750	10	.977
—Los Angeles (N.L.)	2B	17	17	1	3	1	1	0	1	1	6	0	0	0-0	.176	.167	.353	.520	1	1.000
2005—Las Vegas (PCL)	2B	84	257	32	74	10	2	6	35	13	36	3	3	4-5	.288	.326	.412	.739	7	.981
—Columbus (Int'l)	2B	29	107	13	25	3	3	2	7	7	19	1	1	2-2	.234	.287	.374	.661	4	.969
2006—Scran./W.B. (Int'l)	2B	127	479	74	135	29	9	9	55	43	65	7	3	20-10	.282	.349	.436	.785	14	.979
—Philadelphia (N.L.)	2B-OF	18	18	3	4	1	0	0	0	1	2	1	0	0-0	.222	.300	.278	.578	0	1.000
Major League totals (4 years)		55	58	7	15	3	1	0	2	2	9	1	0	0-0	.259	.286	.345	.631	1	.972

2006 LEFTY-RIGHTY SPLITS

vs.	Avg.	AB	H	2B	3B	HR	RBI	BB	SO	OBP	Slg.	vs.	Avg.	AB	H	2B	3B	HR	RBI	BB	SO	OBP	Slg.
L	.000	0	0	0	0	0	0	0	0	.000	.000	R	.222	18	4	1	0	0	0	1	2	.300	.278

TIFFEE, TERRY — 3B

PERSONAL: Born April 21, 1979, in North Little Rock, Ark. ... 6-3/210. ... Bats both, throws right. ... Full name: Terry R. Tiffee. ... High school: Sylvan Hills (Sherwood, Ark.). ... Junior college: Pratt (Kan.) Community College. **TRANSACTIONS/CAREER NOTES:** Selected by Minnesota Twins organization in 26th round of 1999 free-agent draft.

2006 GAMES PLAYED BY POSITION (MLB): 3B—6, DH—5, 1B—3.

Year Team (League)	Pos.	G	AB	R	H	2B	3B	HR	RBI	BB	SO	HBP	GDP	SB-CS	Avg.	OBP	SLG	OPS	E	Avg.
2000— Quad City (Midw.)	3B-1B	129	493	59	125	25	0	7	60	29	73	0	14	2-0	.254	.292	.347	.639	31	.872
2001— Quad City (Midw.)	3B-1B	128	495	65	153	32	1	11	86	32	48	1	13	3-1	.309	.347	.444	.791	30	.942
2002— Fort Myers (FSL)	1B-3B	126	473	47	133	31	0	8	64	25	49	2	12	0-3	.281	.316	.397	.714	14	.982
2003— New Britain (East.)	3B-1B	139	530	77	167	31	3	14	93	31	49	2	13	4-1	.315	.351	.464	.815	21	.951
2004— Rochester (Int'l)	3B-1B-DH	82	316	42	97	26	3	12	68	21	26	4	9	0-0	.307	.357	.522	.871	14	.942
— Minnesota (A.L.)	3B-1B-DH	17	44	7	12	4	0	2	8	3	3	1	2	0-0	.273	.333	.500	.833	1	.968
2005— Rochester (Int'l)	3B-1B-DH	58	229	33	61	11	1	10	39	15	24	3	9	0-1	.266	.313	.454	.768	7	.965
— Minnesota (A.L.)	3B-1B-DH	54	150	9	31	8	1	1	15	8	15	0	10	1-0	.207	.245	.293	.539	6	.962
2006— Rochester (Int'l)		79	308	37	84	20	0	4	38	20	50	0	7	1-0	.273	.314	.377	.691	13	.936
— Minnesota (A.L.)	3B-DH-1B	20	45	4	11	1	0	2	6	4	8	0	2	0-1	.244	.306	.400	.706	2	.923
Major League totals (3 years)		91	239	20	54	13	1	5	29	15	26	1	14	1-1	.226	.273	.351	.625	9	.958

2006 LEFTY-RIGHTY SPLITS

vs.	Avg.	AB	H	2B	3B	HR	RBI	BB	SO	OBP	Slg.	vs.	Avg.	AB	H	2B	3B	HR	RBI	BB	SO	OBP	Slg.
L	.200	15	3	0	0	1	1	1	2	.250	.400	R	.267	30	8	1	0	1	5	3	6	.333	.400

TIMLIN, MIKE — P

PERSONAL: Born March 10, 1966, in Midland, Texas. ... 6-4/210. ... Throws right, bats right. ... Full name: Michael August Timlin. ... Name pronounced: TIM-lin. ... High school: Midland (Texas). ... College: Southwestern (Georgetown, Texas). **TRANSACTIONS/CAREER NOTES:** Selected by Toronto Blue Jays organization in fifth round of 1987 free-agent draft. ... On disabled list (August 2-17, 1991). ... On disabled list (March 27-June 12, 1992); included rehabilitation assignments to Dunedin and Syracuse. ... On disabled list (May 25-June 9, 1994). ... On disabled list (June 22-August 18, 1995); included rehabilitation assignment to Syracuse. ... Traded by Blue Jays with P Paul Spoljaric to Seattle Mariners for OF Jose Cruz (July 31, 1997). ... Signed as a free agent by Baltimore Orioles (November 16, 1998). ... On disabled list (April 2-17, 2000). ... Traded by Orioles with cash to St. Louis Cardinals for 1B Chris Richard and P Mark Nussbeck (July 29, 2000). ... On disabled list (July 26-August 17, 2001). ... Traded by Cardinals with IF/OF Placido Polanco and P Bud Smith to Philadelphia Phillies for 3B Scott Rolen and P Doug Nickle (July 29, 2002). ... Signed as a free agent by Boston Red Sox (December 18, 2002). ... On disabled list (May 28-June 13, 2006).

CAREER HITTING: 0-for-7 (.000), 0 R, 0 2B, 0 3B, 0 HR, 0 RBI.

Year Team (League)	W	L	Pct.	ERA	WHIP	G	GS	CG	ShO	Hld.	Sv.-Opp.	IP	H	R	ER	HR	BB-IBB	SO	Avg.
1987— Medicine Hat (Pio.)	4	8	.333	5.14	1.39	13	12	2	0	...	0-...	75.1	79	50	43	4	26-0	66	.271
1988— Myrtle Beach (SAL)	10	6	.625	2.86	1.30	35	22	0	0	...	0-...	151.0	119	68	48	4	77-2	106	.215
1989— Dunedin (Fla. St.)	5	8	.385	3.25	1.42	33	7	1	0	...	7-...	88.2	90	44	32	2	36-2	64	.262
1990— Dunedin (Fla. St.)	7	3	.778	1.43	1.03	42	0	0	0	...	22-...	50.1	36	11	8	0	16-2	46	.197
— Knoxville (Southern)	1	2	.333	1.73	1.04	17	0	0	0	...	8-...	26.0	20	6	5	0	7-1	21	.206
1991— Toronto (A.L.)	11	6	.647	3.16	1.33	63	3	0	0	9	3-8	108.1	94	43	38	6	50-11	85	.233
1992— Dunedin (Fla. St.)	0	0	...	0.90	1.10	6	1	0	0	...	0-...	10.0	9	2	1	0	2-0	7	.243
— Syracuse (Int'l)	0	1	.000	8.74	1.76	7	1	0	0	...	3-...	11.1	15	11	11	3	5-1	7	.333
— Toronto (A.L.)	0	2	.000	4.12	1.48	26	0	0	0	1	1-1	43.2	45	23	20	0	20-5	35	.271
1993— Toronto (A.L.)	4	2	.667	4.69	1.62	54	0	0	0	1	1-4	55.2	63	32	29	7	27-3	49	.284
— Dunedin (Fla. St.)	0	0	...	1.00	0.44	4	0	0	0	...	1-...	9.0	4	1	1	0	0-0	8	.133
1994— Toronto (A.L.)	0	1	.000	5.18	1.53	34	0	0	0	5	2-4	40.0	41	25	23	5	20-0	38	.261
1995— Toronto (A.L.)	4	3	.571	2.14	1.31	31	0	0	0	4	5-9	42.0	38	13	10	1	17-5	36	.242
— Syracuse (Int'l)	1	1	.500	1.04	0.98	8	1	0	0	...	4-...	17.1	13	6	2	2	4-0	13	.197
1996— Toronto (A.L.)	1	6	.143	3.65	1.15	59	0	0	0	2	31-38	56.2	47	25	23	4	18-4	52	.229
1997— Toronto (A.L.)	3	2	.600	2.87	1.19	38	0	0	0	2	9-13	47.0	41	17	15	6	15-4	36	.243
— Seattle (A.L.)	3	2	.600	3.86	1.29	26	0	0	0	7	1-5	25.2	28	13	11	2	5-1	9	.280
1998— Seattle (A.L.)	3	3	.500	2.95	1.18	70	0	0	0	6	19-24	79.1	78	26	26	5	16-2	60	.264
1999— Baltimore (A.L.)	3	9	.250	3.57	1.17	62	0	0	0	9	27-36	63.0	51	30	25	9	23-3	50	.221
2000— Baltimore (A.L.)	2	3	.400	4.89	1.49	37	0	0	0	1	11-15	35.0	37	22	19	6	15-3	26	.276
— St. Louis (N.L.)	3	1	.750	3.34	1.69	25	0	0	0	5	1-3	29.2	30	11	11	2	20-3	26	.265
2001— St. Louis (N.L.)	4	5	.444	4.09	1.33	67	0	0	0	12	3-7	72.2	78	35	33	6	19-4	47	.277
2002— St. Louis (N.L.)	1	3	.250	2.51	0.90	42	1	0	0	12	0-2	61.0	48	19	17	9	7-2	35	.215
— Philadelphia (N.L.)	3	3	.500	3.79	0.95	30	0	0	0	8	0-2	35.2	27	16	15	6	7-0	15	.206
2003— Boston (A.L.)	6	4	.600	3.55	1.03	72	0	0	0	17	2-6	83.2	77	37	33	11	9-3	65	.239
2004— Boston (A.L.)	5	4	.556	4.13	1.23	76	0	0	0	20	1-4	76.1	75	35	35	8	19-3	56	.257
2005— Boston (A.L.)	7	3	.700	2.24	1.32	* 81	0	0	0	24	13-20	80.1	86	23	20	2	20-5	59	.277
2006— Boston (A.L.)	6	6	.500	4.36	1.47	68	0	0	0	21	9-17	64.0	78	33	31	7	16-4	30	.305
American League totals (14 years)	58	56	.509	3.58	1.30	797	3	0	0	128	135-204	900.2	879	397	358	79	290-56	686	.255
National League totals (3 years)	11	12	.478	3.44	1.19	164	1	0	0	37	4-14	199.0	183	81	76	23	53-9	123	.244
Major League totals (16 years)	69	68	.504	3.55	1.28	961	4	0	0	165	139-218	1099.2	1062	478	434	102	343-65	809	.255

DIVISION SERIES RECORD

Year Team (League)	W	L	Pct.	ERA	WHIP	G	GS	CG	ShO	Hld.	Sv.-Opp.	IP	H	R	ER	HR	BB-IBB	SO	Avg.
1997— Seattle (A.L.)	0	0	...	54.00	6.00	1	0	0	0	0	0-0	0.2	3	4	4	1	1-1	1	.600
2000— St. Louis (N.L.)	0	0	...	10.80	3.60	2	0	0	0	0	0-0	1.2	5	2	2	1	1-0	2	.500
2001— St. Louis (N.L.)	0	0	...	0.00	0.75	1	0	0	0	0	0-0	1.1	1	0	0	0	0-0	1	.200
2003— Boston (A.L.)	0	0	...	0.00	0.00	2	0	0	0	2	0-0	4.1	0	0	0	0	0-0	5	.000
2004— Boston (A.L.)	0	0	...	9.00	1.33	3	0	0	0	0	0-0	3.0	3	3	3	1	1-0	5	.250
2005— Boston (A.L.)	0	0	...	9.00	1.00	2	0	0	0	0	0-0	1.0	1	1	1	0	0-0	1	.333
Division series totals (6 years)	0	0	...	7.50	1.33	11	0	0	0	4	0-0	12.0	13	10	10	3	3-1	14	.271

CHAMPIONSHIP SERIES RECORD

Year Team (League)	W	L	Pct.	ERA	WHIP	G	GS	CG	ShO	Hld.	Sv.-Opp.	IP	H	R	ER	HR	BB-IBB	SO	Avg.
1991— Toronto (A.L.)	0	1	.000	3.18	1.24	4	0	0	0	0	0-1	5.2	5	4	2	1	2-1	5	.208
1992— Toronto (A.L.)	0	0	...	6.75	3.00	2	0	0	0	1	0-0	1.1	4	1	1	0	0-0	1	.500
1993— Toronto (A.L.)	0	0	...	3.86	1.29	2	0	0	0	0	0-0	2.1	3	1	1	0	2-0	3	.300
2000— St. Louis (N.L.)	0	1	.000	0.00	0.90	3	0	0	0	0	0-0	3.1	1	3	0	0	2-0	4	.091
2003— Boston (A.L.)	0	0	...	0.00	0.56	5	0	0	0	0	0-0	5.1	1	0	0	0	2-1	1	.059
2004— Boston (A.L.)	0	0	...	4.76	2.65	4	0	0	0	0	0-1	5.2	10	3	3	0	5-0	2	.400
Champ. series totals (6 years)	0	2	.000	2.66	1.48	20	0	0	0	1	0-2	23.2	24	12	7	1	11-2	16	.253

WORLD SERIES RECORD

Year Team (League)	W	L	Pct.	ERA	WHIP	G	GS	CG	ShO	Hld.	Sv.-Opp.	IP	H	R	ER	HR	BB-IBB	SO	Avg.
1992— Toronto (A.L.)	0	0	...	0.00	0.00	2	0	0	0	0	1-1	1.1	0	0	0	0	0-0	0	.000
1993— Toronto (A.L.)	0	0	...	0.00	0.86	2	0	0	0	1	0-0	2.1	2	0	0	0	0-0	4	.250
2004— Boston (A.L.)	0	0	...	6.00	1.00	3	0	0	0	0	0-0	3.0	2	2	2	0	1-0	0	.200
World series totals (3 years)	0	0	...	2.70	0.75	7	0	0	0	1	1-1	6.2	4	2	2	0	1-0	4	.182

2006 LEFTY-RIGHTY SPLITS

vs.	Avg.	AB	H	2B	3B	HR	RBI	BB	SO	OBP	Slg.	vs.	Avg.	AB	H	2B	3B	HR	RBI	BB	SO	OBP	Slg.
L	.306	124	38	5	0	2	17	7	15	.341	.395	R	.303	132	40	11	0	5	23	9	15	.357	.500

TOMKO, BRETT   P

PERSONAL: Born April 7, 1973, in Euclid, Ohio. ... 6-4/215. ... Throws right, bats right. ... Full name: Brett Daniel Tomko. ... Name pronounced: TOM-koh. ... High school: El Dorado (Placentia, Calif.). ... College: Florida Southern. **TRANSACTIONS/CAREER NOTES:** Selected by Los Angeles Dodgers organization in 20th round of 1994 free-agent draft; did not sign. ... Selected by Cincinnati Reds organization in second round of 1995 free-agent draft. ... Traded by Reds with OF Mike Cameron, IF Antonio Perez and P Jake Meyer to Seattle Mariners for OF Ken Griffey (February 10, 2000). ... On disabled list (June 7-24, 2000). ... Traded by Mariners with C Tom Lampkin and SS Ramon Vazquez to San Diego Padres for C Ben Davis, P Wascar Serrano and SS Alex Arias (December 11, 2001). ... Traded by Padres to St. Louis Cardinals for P Luther Hackman and a player to be named (December 15, 2002); Padres acquired P Mike Wodnicki to complete deal (December 16, 2002). ... Signed as a free agent by San Francisco Giants (January 12, 2004). ... On disabled list (June 8-24, 2004); included rehabilitation assignment to Fresno. ... Signed as a free agent by Dodgers (January 3, 2006). ... On disabled list (June 27-July 28, 2006). **MISCELLANEOUS NOTES:** Appeared in two games as pinch runner (1997). ... Appeared in one game as pinch runner and struck out in only appearance as pinch hitter (1998). ... Singled and scored a run in two appearances as pinch hitter (2003). ... Struck out in only appearance as pinch hitter (2004). ... Struck out in only appearance as pinch hitter (2006).

CAREER HITTING: 71-for-419 (.169), 23 R, 9 2B, 0 3B, 0 HR, 28 RBI.

Year Team (League)	W	L	Pct.	ERA	WHIP	G	GS	CG	ShO	Hld.	Sv.-Opp.	IP	H	R	ER	HR	BB-IBB	SO	Avg.
1995— Char., W.Va. (SAL)	4	2	.667	1.84	1.02	9	7	0	0	...	0-...	49.0	41	12	10	1	9-1	46	.228
1996— Chattanooga (Sou.)	11	7	.611	3.88	1.17	27	27	0	0	...	0-...	157.2	131	73	68	20	54-4	164	.226
1997— Indianapolis (A.A.)	6	3	.667	2.95	1.02	10	10	0	0	...	0-...	61.0	53	21	20	7	9-0	60	.232
— Cincinnati (N.L.)	11	7	.611	3.43	1.21	22	19	0	0	0	0-...	126.0	106	50	48	14	47-4	95	.234
1998— Cincinnati (N.L.)	13	12	.520	4.44	1.24	34	34	1	0	0	0-...	210.2	198	111	104	22	64-3	162	.247
1999— Cincinnati (N.L.)	5	7	.417	4.92	1.37	33	26	1	0	1	0-0	172.0	175	103	94	31	60-10	132	.263
— Indianapolis (Int'l)	2	0	1.000	4.97	1.26	2	2	0	0	...	0-...	12.2	15	7	7	1	1-0	9	.288
2000— Tacoma (PCL)	1	0	1.000	2.84	1.42	2	2	0	0	...	0-...	12.2	13	4	4	1	5-1	8	.271
— Seattle (A.L.)	7	5	.583	4.68	1.43	32	8	0	0	3	1-2	92.1	92	53	48	12	40-4	59	.264
2001— Seattle (A.L.)	3	1	.750	5.19	1.64	11	4	0	0	0	0-1	34.2	42	24	20	9	15-2	22	.288
— Tacoma (PCL)	10	6	.625	4.04	1.17	19	18	3	2	...	0-...	127.0	124	64	57	12	25-1	117	.254
2002— San Diego (N.L.)	10	10	.500	4.49	1.33	32	32	3	0	0	0-...	204.1	212	107	102	31	60-9	126	.267
2003— St. Louis (N.L.)	13	9	.591	5.28	1.52	33	32	0	0	0	0-...	202.2	*252	126	•119	35	57-2	114	.305
2004— Fresno (PCL)	0	0	...	5.40	1.20	1	1	0	0	...	0-...	5.0	4	3	3	1	2-0	4	.211
— San Francisco (N.L.)	11	7	.611	4.04	1.34	32	31	-2	1	0	0-...	194.0	196	98	87	19	64-3	108	.260
2005— San Francisco (N.L.)	8	15	.348	4.48	1.37	33	30	3	0	1	1-1	190.2	205	99	95	20	57-11	114	.274
2006— Las Vegas (PCL)	0	0	...	0.00	2.00	2	0	0	0	0	0-...	2.0	3	0	0	0	4-0	3	.375
— Los Angeles (N.L.)	8	7	.533	4.73	1.35	44	15	0	0	5	0-3	112.1	123	67	59	17	29-0	76	.276
American League totals (2 years)	10	6	.625	4.82	1.49	43	12	0	0	3	1-3	127.0	134	77	68	21	55-6	81	.271
National League totals (8 years)	79	74	.516	4.51	1.35	263	219	12	1	7	1-4	1412.2	1467	761	708	189	438-42	927	.267
Major League totals (10 years)	89	80	.527	4.54	1.36	306	231	12	1	10	2-7	1539.2	1601	838	776	210	493-48	1008	.268

DIVISION SERIES RECORD

Year Team (League)	W	L	Pct.	ERA	WHIP	G	GS	CG	ShO	Hld.	Sv.-Opp.	IP	H	R	ER	HR	BB-IBB	SO	Avg.
2000— Seattle (A.L.)	0	0	...	0.00	0.75	1	0	0	0	0	0-0	2.2	1	0	0	0	1-0	0	.125
2006— Los Angeles (N.L.)	0	0	...	9.00	6.00	1	0	0	0	0	0-0	1.0	4	4	1	0	2-0	0	.667
Division series totals (2 years)	0	0	...	2.45	2.18	2	0	0	0	0	0-0	3.2	5	4	1	0	3-0	0	.357

CHAMPIONSHIP SERIES RECORD

Year Team (League)	W	L	Pct.	ERA	WHIP	G	GS	CG	ShO	Hld.	Sv.-Opp.	IP	H	R	ER	HR	BB-IBB	SO	Avg.
2000— Seattle (A.L.)	0	1	.000	7.20	1.40	2	0	0	0	0	0-0	5.0	3	4	4	0	4-1	4	.176

2006 LEFTY-RIGHTY SPLITS

vs.	Avg.	AB	H	2B	3B	HR	RBI	BB	SO	OBP	Slg.	vs.	Avg.	AB	H	2B	3B	HR	RBI	BB	SO	OBP	Slg.
L	.300	190	57	12	4	7	23	18	32	.362	.516	R	.258	256	66	12	2	10	40	11	44	.284	.438

TORREALBA, YORVIT   C

PERSONAL: Born July 19, 1978, in Caracas, Venezuela. ... 5-11/190. ... Bats right, throws right. ... Full name: Yorvit Adolfo Torrealba. ... Name pronounced: yor-VEET tor-ee-ALL-buh. ... High school: Vincente Emilio Sojo (Venezuela). **TRANSACTIONS/CAREER NOTES:** Signed as a non-drafted free agent by San Francisco Giants organization (September 14, 1994). ... Traded by Giants with P Jesse Foppert to Seattle Mariners for OF Randy Winn (July 30, 2005). ... Traded by Mariners to Colorado Rockies for a player to be named (December 7, 2005); Mariners acquired P Marcos Carvajal to Mariners to complete deal (December 8, 2005). ... On disabled list (April 2-June 2, 2006); included rehabilitation assignment to Colorado Springs. ... On disabled list (September 10, 2006-remainder of season). **STATISTICAL NOTES:** Career major league grand slams: 2.

2006 GAMES PLAYED BY POSITION (MLB): C—63.

Year Team (League)	Pos.	G	AB	R	H	2B	3B	HR	RBI	BB	SO	HBP	GDP	SB-CS	Avg.	OBP	SLG	OPS	E	Avg. (Fielding)
1995— Bellingham (N'west)	C	26	71	2	11	3	0	0	8	2	14	1	1	0-1	.155	.187	.197	.384	5	.973
1996— San Jose (Calif.)	C	2	5	0	0	0	0	0	0	1	1	0	0	0-0	.000	.167	.000	.167	0	1.000
— Burlington (Midw.)	C	1	4	0	0	0	0	0	0	0	1	0	1	0-0	.000	.000	.000	.000	0	1.000
— Bellingham (N'west)	C	48	150	23	40	4	0	1	10	9	27	0	7	4-1	.267	.304	.313	.618	2	.994
1997— Bakersfield (Calif.)	C	119	446	52	122	15	3	4	40	31	58	5	8	4-2	.274	.326	.348	.673	6	.993
1998— Shreveport (Texas)	C	59	196	18	46	7	0	4	13	18	30	4	3	0-5	.235	.311	.270	.581	2	.996
— San Jose (Calif.)	C	21	70	10	20	2	0	0	11	1	6	0	4	2-2	.286	.292	.314	.606	2	.989
— Fresno (PCL)	C	4	11	1	2	1	0	0	1	4	0	0	0	0-0	.182	.250	.273	.523	0	1.000
1999— Shreveport (Texas)	C	65	217	25	53	10	1	4	26	9	34	2	6	0-2	.244	.278	.355	.633	2	.994
— Fresno (PCL)	C	17	63	9	16	2	0	2	10	4	11	2	2	0-1	.254	.319	.381	.700	2	.988
— San Jose (Calif.)	C	19	73	10	23	3	2	4	14	6	15	1	2	2-0	.315	.370	.438	.809	5	.975
2000— Shreveport (Texas)	C	108	398	50	114	21	4	4	32	34	55	6	17	2-3	.286	.350	.374	.724	8	.990
2001— Fresno (PCL)	C	115	394	56	108	23	3	8	36	19	65	4	11	2-3	.274	.313	.409	.721	4	.989
— San Francisco (N.L.)	C	3	4	0	2	1	0	0	1	0	1	0	0	0-0	.500	.500	1.000	1.500	0	1.000
2002— San Francisco (N.L.)	C	53	136	17	38	10	2	2	14	14	20	2	11	0-0	.279	.355	.397	.752	3	.993
2003— San Francisco (N.L.)	C-OF	66	200	22	52	10	2	4	29	14	39	2	3	1-0	.260	.312	.390	.702	5	.997
2004— San Francisco (N.L.)	C	64	172	19	39	7	1	6	23	17	31	2	7	2-0	.227	.302	.407	.709	2	.995

Year	Team (League)	Pos.	G	AB	R	H	2B	3B	HR	RBI	BB	SO	HBP	GDP	SB-CS	Avg.	OBP	SLG	OPS	E	Avg.
																			BATTING		FIELDING
2005— San Francisco (N.L.)		C-DH	34	93	18	21	8	0	1	7	9	25	1	3	1-0	.226	.301	.344	.645	0	1.000
— Seattle (A.L.)		C	42	108	14	26	4	0	2	8	7	25	1	5	0-0	.241	.293	.333	.626	0	1.000
2006— Colo. Springs (PCL)			10	36	0	6	2	0	0	2	4	9	0	3	0-0	.167	.250	.222	.472	0	1.000
— Colorado (N.L.)		C	65	223	23	55	16	3	7	43	11	49	4	7	4-3	.247	.293	.439	.732	5	.987
American League totals (1 year)			42	108	14	26	4	0	2	8	7	25	1	5	0-0	.241	.293	.333	.626	0	1.000
National League totals (6 years)			285	828	99	207	51	9	20	118	65	164	11	31	8-3	.250	.310	.406	.717	10	.994
Major League totals (6 years)			327	936	113	233	55	9	22	126	72	189	12	36	8-3	.249	.310	.397	.707	10	.995

DIVISION SERIES RECORD

Year	Team (League)	Pos.	G	AB	R	H	2B	3B	HR	RBI	BB	SO	HBP	GDP	SB-CS	Avg.	OBP	SLG	OPS	E	Avg.
2003— San Francisco (N.L.)		C	2	3	0	0	0	0	0	1	0	0	0	0	0-0	.000	.000	.000	.000	1	.909

2006 LEFTY-RIGHTY SPLITS

vs.	Avg.	AB	H	2B	3B	HR	RBI	BB	SO	OBP	Slg.	vs.	Avg.	AB	H	2B	3B	HR	RBI	BB	SO	OBP	Slg.
L	.246	57	14	5	1	2	15	2	8	.283	.474	R	.247	166	41	11	2	5	28	9	41	.296	.428

TORRES, SALOMON — P

PERSONAL: Born March 11, 1972, in San Pedro de Macoris, Dominican Republic. ... 5-11/210. ... Throws right, bats right. ... Full name: Salomon Ramirez Torres. ... High school: Centro Academico Rogus (San Pedro de Macoris, Domi. **TRANSACTIONS/CAREER NOTES:** Signed as a non-drafted free agent by San Francisco Giants organization (September 15, 1989). ... Traded by Giants to Seattle Mariners for P Shawn Estes and IF Wilson Delgado (May 21, 1995). ... Claimed on waivers by Montreal Expos (April 18, 1997). ... On voluntarily retired list (August 1, 1997-January 29, 2001). ... Released by Expos (January 29, 2001). ... Signed by Samsung Lions of the Korean League. ... Signed as a free agent by Pittsburgh Pirates organization (January 8, 2002). ... On disabled list (August 6-29, 2003); included rehabilitation assignment to Nashville. ... On suspended list (July 19-22, 2004). **MISCELLANEOUS NOTES:** Struck out in only appearance as pinch hitter and appeared in one game as pinch runner (2003).

CAREER HITTING: 15-for-102 (.147), 5 R, 1 2B, 1 3B, 0 HR, 1 RBI.

Year	Team (League)	W	L	Pct.	ERA	WHIP	G	GS	CG	ShO	Hld.	Sv.-Opp.	IP	H	R	ER	HR	BB-IBB	SO	Avg.
1990— San Pedro (DSL)		11	1	.917	0.50	0.82	13	13	6	0	...	0-...	90.0	44	15	5		30-...	101	...
1991— Clinton (Midw.)		16	5	.762	1.41	0.93	28	28	8	3	...	0-...	210.1	148	48	33	4	47-2	214	.195
1992— Shreveport (Texas)		6	10	.375	4.21	1.24	25	25	4	2	...	0-...	162.1	167	93	76	10	34-2	151	.263
1993— Shreveport (Texas)		7	4	.636	2.70	0.95	12	12	2	1	...	0-...	83.1	67	27	25	6	12-0	67	.218
— Phoenix (PCL)		7	4	.636	3.50	1.25	14	14	4	1	...	0-...	105.1	105	43	41	5	27-0	99	.261
— San Francisco (N.L.)		3	5	.375	4.03	1.43	8	8	0	0	...	0-0	44.2	37	21	20	5	27-3	23	.231
1994— San Francisco (N.L.)		2	8	.200	5.44	1.53	16	14	1	0	...	0-0	84.1	95	55	51	10	34-2	42	.292
— Phoenix (PCL)		5	6	.455	4.22	1.47	13	13	0	0	...	0-0	79.0	85	49	37	7	31-0	64	.278
1995— San Francisco (N.L.)		0	1	.000	9.00	2.50	4	1	0	0	...	0-0	8.0	13	8	8	4	7-0	2	.394
— Phoenix (PCL)		0	0	...	0.00	1.00	1	0	0	0	...	0-...	2.0	2	0	0	0	0-0	5	.286
— Tacoma (PCL)		1	1	.500	3.21	1.18	5	4	0	0	...	0-...	28.0	20	10	10	2	13-1	19	.206
— Seattle (A.L.)		3	8	.273	6.00	1.79	16	13	1	0	0	0-0	72.0	87	53	48	12	42-3	45	.291
1996— Tacoma (PCL)		7	10	.412	5.29	1.50	22	21	3	1	...	0-...	134.1	150	87	79	16	52-1	121	.279
— Seattle (A.L.)		3	3	.500	4.59	1.37	10	7	1	1	0	0-0	49.0	44	27	25	5	23-2	36	.242
1997— Seattle (A.L.)		0	0	...	27.00	3.00	2	0	0	0	0	0-0	3.1	7	10	10	0	3-0	1	.412
— Montreal (N.L.)		0	0	...	7.25	1.66	12	0	0	0	0	0-0	22.1	25	19	18	2	12-0	11	.284
— Ottawa (Int'l)		0	0	...	5.40	1.80	2	1	0	0	...	0-...	5.0	7	5	3	0	2-0	2	.318
1998—				Did not play.																
1999—				Did not play.																
2000—				Did not play.																
2001— Samsung (Kor.)		0	2	.000		2.00	2					0-...	5.0					10-...	5	
2002— Nashville (PCL)		8	5	.615	3.83	1.28	26	24	2	1	...	0-...	162.1	169	78	69	12	39-2	136	.270
— Pittsburgh (N.L.)		2	1	.667	2.70	1.37	5	5	0	0	0	0-0	30.0	28	10	9	2	13-1	12	.257
2003— Nashville (PCL)		1	0	1.000	1.80	0.60	1	1	0	0	...	0-...	5.0	2	1	1	0	1-0	4	.118
— Pittsburgh (N.L.)		7	5	.583	4.76	1.40	41	16	0	0	6	2-3	121.0	128	65	64	19	42-5	84	.276
2004— Pittsburgh (N.L.)		7	7	.500	2.64	1.18	84	0	0	0	30	0-4	92.0	87	33	27	6	22-6	56	.256
2005— Pittsburgh (N.L.)		5	5	.500	2.76	1.18	78	0	0	0	8	3-3	94.2	76	34	29	7	36-7	55	.222
2006— Pittsburgh (N.L.)		3	6	.333	3.28	1.46	94	0	0	0	20	12-15	93.1	98	42	34	6	38-9	72	.274
American League totals (3 years)		6	11	.353	6.01	1.66	28	20	2	1	0	0-0	124.1	138	90	83	17	68-5	81	.277
National League totals (9 years)		29	38	.433	3.96	1.39	342	44	1	0	64	17-25	590.1	587	287	260	61	231-33	363	.265
Major League totals (10 years)		35	49	.417	4.32	1.43	370	64	3	1	64	17-25	714.2	725	377	343	78	299-38	444	.267

2006 LEFTY-RIGHTY SPLITS

vs.	Avg.	AB	H	2B	3B	HR	RBI	BB	SO	OBP	Slg.	vs.	Avg.	AB	H	2B	3B	HR	RBI	BB	SO	OBP	Slg.
L	.281	139	39	6	0	2	14	15	26	.363	.367	R	.269	219	59	10	0	4	25	23	46	.344	.370

TOWERS, JOSH — P

PERSONAL: Born February 26, 1977, in Port Hueneme, Calif. ... 6-1/188. ... Throws right, bats right. ... Full name: Joshua Eric Towers. ... High school: Hueneme (Oxnard, Calif.) ... Junior college: Oxnard (Calif.). **TRANSACTIONS/CAREER NOTES:** Selected by Baltimore Orioles organization in 15th round of 1996 free-agent draft. ... On disabled list (October 1, 2001-remainder of season). ... Signed as a free agent by Toronto Blue Jays organization (November 8, 2002).

CAREER HITTING: 1-for-15 (.067), 1 R, 0 2B, 0 3B, 0 HR, 0 RBI.

Year	Team (League)	W	L	Pct.	ERA	WHIP	G	GS	CG	ShO	Hld.	Sv.-Opp.	IP	H	R	ER	HR	BB-IBB	SO	Avg.
1996— Bluefield (Appal.)		4	1	.800	5.24	1.24	14	9	0	0	...	0-...	55.0	63	35	32	9	5-0	61	.278
1997— Delmarva (S. Atl.)		0	0	...	3.44	1.09	9	1	0	0	...	1-...	18.1	18	8	7	1	2-0	16	.261
— Frederick (Carolina)		6	2	.750	4.86	1.71	25	3	0	0	...	1-...	53.2	74	36	29	4	18-0	64	.323
1998— Frederick (Carolina)		8	7	.533	3.34	1.00	25	20	3	0	...	1-...	145.1	137	58	54	11	9-0	122	.247
— Bowie (East.)		2	1	.667	3.50	1.33	5	2	0	0	...	0-...	18.0	20	9	7	1	4-0	7	.270
1999— Bowie (East.)		12	7	.632	3.76	1.22	29	29	5	2	...	0-...	189.0	204	86	79	26	26-1	106	.276
2000— Rochester (Int'l)		8	6	.571	3.47	1.20	24	24	5	1	...	0-...	148.0	157	63	57	17	21-0	102	.269
2001— Rochester (Int'l)		3	1	.750	3.51	1.17	6	6	1	1	...	0-...	41.0	40	16	16	2	8-2	27	.255
— Baltimore (A.L.)		8	10	.444	4.49	1.29	24	24	1	1	0	0-0	140.1	165	74	70	21	16-0	58	.297
2002— Baltimore (A.L.)		0	3	.000	7.90	1.72	5	3	0	0	0	0-0	27.1	42	24	24	11	6-0	13	.362
— Rochester (Int'l)		0	9	.000	7.57	1.78	15	13	1	0	...	0-...	69.0	109	65	58	16	14-0	43	.353
2003— Syracuse (Int'l)		5	7	.417	3.32	1.20	21	20	1	1	...	0-...	64.1	67	34	32	15	7-1	42	.266
— Toronto (A.L.)		3	1	.889	4.48	1.15	14	8	1	0	0	1-1	36.0	33	11	10	7	5-0	25	.246
2004— Syracuse (Int'l)		3	1	.750	2.50	1.11	6	5	0	0	...	0-...	36.0	33	11	10	1	5-0	24	.246
— Toronto (A.L.)		9	9	.500	5.11	1.50	21	21	0	0	0	0-0	116.1	148	70	66	16	26-2	51	.310
2005— Toronto (A.L.)		13	12	.520	3.71	1.27	33	33	2	1	0	0-0	208.2	237	101	86	24	29-2	112	.285
2006— Syracuse (Int'l)		5	5	.500	4.00	1.30	15	15	0	0	...	0-...	101.0	121	53	45	12	11-...	76	.300
— Toronto (A.L.)		2	10	.167	8.42	1.77	15	12	0	0	0	0-0	62.0	93	62	58	17	17-3	35	.343
Major League totals (6 years)		40	45	.471	4.89	1.38	112	97	4	2	0	1-1	619.0	752	365	336	104	100-10	311	.300

T

2006 LEFTY-RIGHTY SPLITS

vs.	Avg.	AB	H	2B	3B	HR	RBI	BB	SO	OBP	Slg.	vs.	Avg.	AB	H	2B	3B	HR	RBI	BB	SO	OBP	Slg.
L	.325	114	37	5	1	9	27	7	16	.366	.623	R	.357	157	56	9	0	8	28	10	19	.398	.567

TRABER, BILLY — P

PERSONAL: Born September 18, 1979, in Torrance, Calif. ... 6-5/205. ... Throws left, bats left. ... Full name: William Henry Traber Jr.. ... High school: El Segundo (Calif.). ... College: Loyola Marymount. **TRANSACTIONS/CAREER NOTES:** Selected by Toronto Blue Jays organization in 58th round of 1997 free-agent draft; did not sign. ... Selected by New York Mets organization in first round (16th pick overall) of 2000 free-agent draft; pick received as part of compensation for Seattle Mariners signing Type A free-agent 1B John Olerud. ... Traded by Mets with OFs Matt Lawton and Alex Escobar, P Jerrod Riggan and 1B Earl Snyder to Cleveland Indians for 2B Roberto Alomar, P Mike Bascik and OF Danny Peoples (December 11, 2001). ... On disabled list (March 17, 2004-entire season). ... Claimed on waivers by Boston Red Sox (November 10, 2004). ... Signed as a free agent by Indians organization (January 14, 2005). ... Signed as free agent by Washington Nationals (November 15, 2005).
CAREER HITTING: 1-for-17 (.059), 1 R, 0 2B, 0 3B, 0 HR, 1 RBI.

Year	Team (League)	W	L	Pct.	ERA	WHIP	G	GS	CG	ShO	Hld.	Sv.-Opp.	IP	H	R	ER	HR	BB-IBB	SO	Avg.
2001—	St. Lucie (Fla. St.)	6	5	.545	2.66	1.06 *	18	18	0	0	...	0-...	101.2	85	36	30	2	23-0	79	.223
	—Binghamton (East.)	4	3	.571	4.43	1.48	8	8	0	0	...	0-...	42.2	50	25	21	4	13-1	45	.296
	—Norfolk (Int'l)	0	1	.000	1.29	0.71	1	1	0	0	...	0-...	7.0	5	3	1	0	0-0	0	.192
2002—	Akron (East.)	13	2	.867	2.76	1.11	18	17	2	2	...	0-...	107.2	99	38	33	8	20-0	82	.243
	—Buffalo (Int'l)	4	3	.571	3.29	1.28	9	9	0	0	...	0-...	54.2	58	22	20	3	12-0	33	.276
2003—	Cleveland (A.L.)	6	9	.400	5.24	1.54	33	18	1	1	1	0-0	111.2	132	67	65	15	40-4	88	.293
2004—					Did not play.															
2005—	Kinston (Carol.)	2	2	.500	4.98	1.15	4	4	0	0	0	0-0	21.2	19	12	12	2	6-0	13	.241
	—Akron (East.)	3	2	.600	2.65	0.88	5	5	0	0	0	0-0	34.0	25	11	10	2	5-0	27	.197
	—Buffalo (Int'l)	3	7	.300	5.75	1.64	19	12	0	0	2	0-0	76.2	96	59	49	7	30-1	55	.301
2006—	New Orleans (PCL)	7	7	.500	4.05	1.36	21	21	1	0	0	0-0	124.1	143	62	56	8	26-2	102	.289
	—Wash. (N.L.)	4	3	.571	6.44	1.55	15	8	0	0	2	0-0	43.1	53	33	31	5	14-2	25	.301
	American League totals (1 year)	6	9	.400	5.24	1.54	33	18	1	1	1	0-0	111.2	132	67	65	15	40-4	88	.293
	National League totals (1 year)	4	3	.571	6.44	1.55	15	8	0	0	2	0-0	43.1	53	33	31	5	14-2	25	.301
	Major League totals (2 years)	10	12	.455	5.57	1.54	48	26	1	1	3	0-0	155.0	185	100	96	20	54-6	113	.295

2006 LEFTY-RIGHTY SPLITS

vs.	Avg.	AB	H	2B	3B	HR	RBI	BB	SO	OBP	Slg.	vs.	Avg.	AB	H	2B	3B	HR	RBI	BB	SO	OBP	Slg.
L	.263	38	10	3	0	0	8	5	9	.391	.342	R	.312	138	43	11	1	5	23	9	16	.373	.514

TRACEY, SEAN — P

PERSONAL: Born November 14, 1980, in Upland, Calif. ... 6-3/210. ... Throws right, bats left. ... Full name: Sean Patrick Tracey. ... College: Cal-Irvine.
TRANSACTIONS/CAREER NOTES: Selected by Chicago White Sox organization in eighth round of 2002 free-agent draft.
CAREER HITTING: 0-for-0 (.000), 0 R, 0 2B, 0 3B, 0 HR, 0 RBI.

Year	Team (League)	W	L	Pct.	ERA	WHIP	G	GS	CG	ShO	Hld.	Sv.-Opp.	IP	H	R	ER	HR	BB-IBB	SO	Avg.
2002—	Bristol (Appal.)	5	2	.714	3.02	1.16	13	12	0	0	...	0-...	65.2	57	27	22	4	19-0	50	.241
2003—	Kannapolis (S. Atl.)	2	7	.222	9.50	2.33	14	9	0	0	...	0-...	41.2	51	54	44	4	46-0	28	.305
	—Great Falls (Pio.)	8	5	.615	3.69	1.21	16	12	1	0	...	0-...	92.2	90	45	38	5	22-0	74	.259
2004—	Win.-Salem (Car.)	9	8	.529	2.73	1.19	27	27	0	0	...	0-...	148.1	108	60	45	5	69-0	130	.213
2005—	Birmingham (Sou.)	14	6	.700	4.07	1.41	28	28	2	0	0	0-0	163.2	154	80	74	13	76-0	106	.257
2006—	Charlotte (Int'l)	8	9	.471	4.30	1.44	29	20	1	1	0	0-0	129.2	111	67	62	17	76-1	102	.238
	—Chicago (A.L.)	0	0	...	3.38	1.13	7	0	0	0	0	0-0	8.0	4	3	3	2	5-0	3	.143
	Major League totals (1 year)	0	0	...	3.38	1.13	7	0	0	0	0	0-0	8.0	4	3	3	2	5-0	3	.143

2006 LEFTY-RIGHTY SPLITS

vs.	Avg.	AB	H	2B	3B	HR	RBI	BB	SO	OBP	Slg.	vs.	Avg.	AB	H	2B	3B	HR	RBI	BB	SO	OBP	Slg.
L	.091	11	1	0	0	1	2	2	1	.286	.364	R	.176	17	3	0	0	1	3	3	2	.300	.353

TRACHSEL, STEVE — P

PERSONAL: Born October 31, 1970, in Oxnard, Calif. ... 6-4/205. ... Throws right, bats right. ... Full name: Stephen Christopher Trachsel. ... Name pronounced: TRACKS-ul. ... High school: Troy (Fullerton, Calif.). ... College: Long Beach State. **TRANSACTIONS/CAREER NOTES:** Selected by Chicago Cubs organization in eighth round of 1991 free-agent draft. ... On disabled list (July 20-August 4, 1994). ... Signed as a free agent by Tampa Bay Devil Rays (January 28, 2000). ... Traded by Devil Rays with P Mark Guthrie to Toronto Blue Jays for 2B Brent Abernathy and cash (July 31, 2000). ... Signed as a free agent by New York Mets (December 11, 2000). ... On disabled list (July 1-22, 2002); included rehabilitation assignment to Binghamton. ... On disabled list (March 30-August 23, 2005); included rehabilitation assignments to St. Lucie, Binghamton and Norfolk. **HONORS:** Named N.L. Rookie Pitcher of the Year by THE SPORTING NEWS (1994). **MISCELLANEOUS NOTES:** Grounded out in only appearance as pinch hitter (2002). ... Appeared in three games as pinch runner (2003). ... Grounded out in only appearance as pinch hitter and scored a run in only appearance as pinch runner (2004).
CAREER HITTING: 105-for-639 (.164), 49 R, 17 2B, 1 3B, 3 HR, 40 RBI.

Year	Team (League)	W	L	Pct.	ERA	WHIP	G	GS	CG	ShO	Hld.	Sv.-Opp.	IP	H	R	ER	HR	BB-IBB	SO	Avg.
1991—	Geneva (NY-Penn)	1	0	1.000	1.26	1.12	2	2	0	0	...	0-...	14.1 *	10	2	2	0	6-0	7	.217
	—Win.-Salem (Car.)	4	4	.500	3.67	1.21	12	12	1	0	...	0-...	73.2	70	38	30	3	19-0	69	.245
1992—	Charlotte (Sou.)	13	8	.619	3.06	1.13	29	29	5	2	...	0-...	191.0	180	76	65	19	35-3	135	.250
1993—	Iowa (Am. Assoc.)	13	6	.684	3.96	1.26	27	26	1	1	...	0-...	170.2	170	78	75	20	45-0	135	.264
	—Chicago (N.L.)	0	2	.000	4.58	0.97	3	3	0	0	0	0-0	19.2	16	10	10	4	3-0	14	.219
1994—	Chicago (N.L.)	9	7	.563	3.21	1.28	22	22	1	0	0	0-0	146.0	133	57	52	19	54-4	108	.242
	—Iowa (Am. Assoc.)	0	2	.000	10.00	2.00	2	2	0	0	...	0-...	9.0	11	10	10	1	7-0	8	.289
1995—	Chicago (N.L.)	7	13	.350	5.15	1.56	30	29	2	0	0	0-0	160.2	174	104	92	25	76-8	117	.277
1996—	Orlando (South.)	0	1	.000	2.77	0.85	2	2	0	0	...	0-...	13.0	11	6	4	0	0-0	12	.220
	—Chicago (N.L.)	13	9	.591	3.03	1.19	31	31	3	2	0	0-...	205.0	181	82	69	30	62-3	132	.235
1997—	Chicago (N.L.)	8	12	.400	4.51	1.46	34	34	0	0	0	0-...	201.1	225	110	101	* 32	69-6	160	.287
1998—	Chicago (N.L.)	15	8	.652	4.46	1.38	33	33	1	0	0	0-0	208.0	204	107	103	27	84-5	149	.260
1999—	Chicago (N.L.)	8	* 18	.308	5.56	1.41	34	34	4	0	0	0-0	205.2	226	133	127	32	64-4	149	.280
2000—	Tampa Bay (A.L.)	6	10	.375	4.58	1.52	23	23	3	1	0	0-0	137.2	160	76	70	16	49-1	78	.294
	—Toronto (A.L.)	2	5	.286	5.29	1.54	11	11	0	0	0	0-0	63.0	72	40	37	10	25-1	32	.293
2001—	New York (N.L.)	11	13	.458	4.46	1.24	28	28	1	1	0	0-0	173.2	168	90	86	28	47-7	144	.254
	—Norfolk (Int'l)	2	0	1.000	2.79	0.98	3	3	1	1	...	0-...	19.1	13	6	6	0	6-0	12	.188
2002—	New York (N.L.)	11	11	.500	3.37	1.38	30	30	1	1	0	0-0	173.2	170	80	65	16	69-4	105	.258
	—Binghamton (East.)	0	1	.000	0.00	1.24	1	1	0	0	...	0-...	5.2	3	1	0	0	4-0	5	.150
2003—	New York (N.L.)	16	10	.615	3.78	1.31	33	33	2	1	0	0-0	204.2	204	90	86	26	65-9	111	.264
2004—	New York (N.L.)	12	13	.480	4.00	1.41	33	33	0	0	0	0-0	202.2	203	104	90	25	83-9	117	.262
2005—	St. Lucie (Fla. St.)	0	1	.000	1.35	0.90	2	2	0	0	0	0-0	6.2	5	2	1	0	1-0	5	.208
	—Binghamton (East.)	1	0	1.000	3.00	1.00	2	2	1	0	0	0-0	12.0	8	4	4	2	4-0	7	.190

Year Team (League)	W	L	Pct.	ERA	WHIP	G	GS	CG	ShO	Hld.	Sv.-Opp.	IP	H	R	ER	HR	BB-IBB	SO	Avg.
— Norfolk (Int'l)	0	1	.000	2.57	0.86	2	2	0	0	0	0-0	14.0	10	4	4	2	2-0	12	.192
— New York (N.L.)	1	4	.200	4.14	1.32	6	6	0	0	0	0-0	37.0	37	20	17	6	12-0	24	.264
2006— New York (N.L.)	15	8	.652	4.97	1.60	30	30	1	0	0	0-0	164.2	185	94	91	23	78-1	79	.288
American League totals (1 year)	8	15	.348	4.80	1.52	34	34	3	1	0	0-0	200.2	232	116	107	26	74-2	110	.294
National League totals (13 years)	126	128	.496	4.23	1.38	347	346	16	6	0	0-0	2102.2	2126	1081	989	293	766-60	1409	.264
Major League totals (14 years)	134	143	.484	4.28	1.39	381	380	19	7	0	0-0	2303.1	2358	1197	1096	319	840-62	1519	.267

DIVISION SERIES RECORD

Year Team (League)	W	L	Pct.	ERA	WHIP	G	GS	CG	ShO	Hld.	Sv.-Opp.	IP	H	R	ER	HR	BB-IBB	SO	Avg.
2006— New York (N.L.)	0	0	...	5.40	2.10	1	1	0	0	0	0-0	3.1	6	2	2	0	1-0	2	.375

CHAMPIONSHIP SERIES RECORD

Year Team (League)	W	L	Pct.	ERA	WHIP	G	GS	CG	ShO	Hld.	Sv.-Opp.	IP	H	R	ER	HR	BB-IBB	SO	Avg.
2006— New York (N.L.)	0	1	.000	45.00	10.00	1	1	0	0	0	0-0	1.0	5	5	5	1	5-0	1	.714

ALL-STAR GAME RECORD

Year Team (League)	W	L	Pct.	ERA	WHIP	G	GS	CG	ShO	Hld.	Sv.-Opp.	IP	H	R	ER	HR	BB-IBB	SO	Avg.
All-Star Game totals (1 year)	0	0	...	0.00	0.00	1	0	0	0	0	0-0	1.0	0	0	0	0	0-0	3	.000

2006 LEFTY-RIGHTY SPLITS

vs.	Avg.	AB	H	2B	3B	HR	RBI	BB	SO	OBP	Slg.	vs.	Avg.	AB	H	2B	3B	HR	RBI	BB	SO	OBP	Slg.
L	.267	300	80	9	3	8	33	35	31	.340	.397	R	.306	343	105	30		15	51	43	48	.386	.525

TRACY, CHAD — 3B

PERSONAL: Born May 22, 1980, in Charlotte, N.C. ... 6-2/200. ... Bats left, throws right. ... Full name: Chad Austin Tracy. ... High school: West Mecklenburg (Charlotte). ... College: East Carolina. **TRANSACTIONS/CAREER NOTES:** Selected by Arizona Diamondbacks organization in seventh round of 2001 free-agent draft. **STATISTICAL NOTES:** Career major league grand slams: 2.

2006 GAMES PLAYED BY POSITION (MLB): 3B—147, 1B—6, DH—2.

Year Team (League)	Pos.	G	AB	R	H	2B	3B	HR	RBI	BB	SO	HBP	GDP	SB-CS	Avg.	OBP	SLG	OPS	E	Avg.
2001— Yakima (N'west)	3B	10	36	2	10	1	0	0	5	3	5	1	1	1-0	.278	.350	.306	.656	0	1.000
— South Bend (Mid.)	3B-1B	54	215	43	73	11	0	4	36	19	19	2	4	3-0	.340	.393	.447	.840	17	.896
2002— El Paso (Texas)	3B-1B	129	514	80	177	39	5	8	74	38	51	4	10	2-3	.344	.389	.486	.875	26	.931
2003— Tucson (PCL)	3B	133	522	91	169	31	4	10	80	41	52	4	7	0-2	.324	.372	.456	.827	20	.951
2004— Tucson (PCL)	3B-OF	11	40	7	16	4	0	2	11	8	5	0	0	2-0	.400	.490	.650	1.140	3	.921
— Arizona (N.L.)	3B-1B-OF	143	481	45	137	29	3	8	53	45	60	0	11	2-3	.285	.343	.407	.750	26	.938
2005— Arizona (N.L.)	1B-OF-DH	145	503	73	155	34	4	27	72	35	78	8	10	3-1	.308	.359	.553	.911	5	.994
2006— Spokane (N'west)		66	252	41	66	14	1	11	35	23	46	7	8	4-1	.262	.330	.456	.796	4	.986
— Arizona (N.L.)	3B-1B-DH	154	597	91	168	41	0	20	80	54	129	5	11	5-1	.281	.343	.451	.794	26	.937
Major League totals (3 years)		442	1581	209	460	104	7	55	205	134	267	13	32	10-5	.291	.348	.470	.818	57	.966

2006 LEFTY-RIGHTY SPLITS

vs.	Avg.	AB	H	2B	3B	HR	RBI	BB	SO	OBP	Slg.	vs.	Avg.	AB	H	2B	3B	HR	RBI	BB	SO	OBP	Slg.
L	.231	182	42	9	0	4	23	13	48	.281	.346	R	.304	415	126	32	0	16	57	41	81	.370	.496

TREANOR, MATT — C

PERSONAL: Born March 3, 1976, in Garden Grove, Calif. ... 6-2/220. ... Bats right, throws right. ... Full name: Matthew Aaron Treanor. ... Name pronounced: TRAY-ner. ... High school: Mater Dei (Calif.). **TRANSACTIONS/CAREER NOTES:** Selected by Kansas City Royals organization in fourth round of 1994 free-agent draft. ... Traded by Royals to Florida Marlins for P Matt Whisenant (July 29, 1997). ... On disabled list (August 1-16, 2006).

2006 GAMES PLAYED BY POSITION (MLB): C—61.

Year Team (League)	Pos.	G	AB	R	H	2B	3B	HR	RBI	BB	SO	HBP	GDP	SB-CS	Avg.	OBP	SLG	OPS	E	Avg.
1994— GC Royals (GCL)	C-2B-OF	46	99	17	18	5	0	1	12	14	23	3	2	1-1	.182	.299	.263	.562	6	.968
1995— Springfield (Midw.)	C	75	211	17	39	6	2	3	19	21	59	4	1	1-1	.185	.269	.275	.544	11	.976
1996— Lansing (Midw.)	C-OF	119	384	56	100	18	2	6	33	35	63	13	9	5-3	.260	.342	.365	.706	16	.978
1997— Wilmington (Caro.)	C	80	257	22	51	6	1	5	25	25	59	2	4	1-6	.198	.275	.288	.563	12	.978
— Brevard County (FSL)	C	23	70	11	15	4	1	0	3	12	14	2	1	0-0	.214	.345	.300	.645	0	1.000
1998— Brevard County (FSL)	C-1B-3B	80	243	24	57	8	0	3	28	38	45	5	4	3-2	.235	.346	.305	.651	4	.989
1999— Kane Co. (Midw.)	C	86	308	56	88	21	1	10	53	36	65	15	6	4-1	.286	.385	.458	.843	8	.988
2000— Brevard County (FSL)	C-1B	109	350	51	86	17	0	3	37	48	65	14	6	3-3	.246	.357	.320	.677	12	.986
2001— GC Marlins (GCL)	C	11	34	10	14	4	0	1	4	7	7	0	1	0-0	.412	.512	.618	1.130	1	.968
— Kane Co. (Midw.)	C	1	1	2	1	0	0	0	0	3	0	0	0	0-0	1.000	1.000	1.000	2.000	0	1.000
— Portland (East.)	C-1B	35	89	7	14	2	0	2	8	13	18	9	2	1-1	.157	.347	.247	.572	1	.996
2002— Portland (East.)	C	50	156	24	39	5	1	9	28	28	33	7	5	3-0	.250	.387	.468	.855	9	.977
— Calgary (PCL)	C-1B	36	95	10	27	8	1	1	18	12	13	5	4	1-1	.284	.393	.400	.793	3	.984
2003— Albuquerque (PCL)	C	98	315	46	86	18	1	11	40	39	44	17	8	9-4	.273	.380	.441	.821	11	.984
2004— Albuquerque (PCL)	C	62	198	32	51	8	0	8	38	33	44	10	2	2-0	.258	.385	.419	.781	4	.991
— Florida (N.L.)	C	29	55	7	13	2	0	0	4	4	13	2	3	0-0	.236	.311	.273	.584	3	.976
2005— Florida (N.L.)	C	58	134	10	27	8	0	0	13	16	28	3	5	0-0	.201	.301	.261	.562	5	.985
2006— Florida (N.L.)	C	67	157	12	36	6	1	2	14	19	34	5	4	0-1	.229	.328	.318	.646	3	.993
Major League totals (3 years)		154	346	29	76	16	1	2	28	39	75	10	12	0-1	.220	.315	.289	.604	11	.987

2006 LEFTY-RIGHTY SPLITS

vs.	Avg.	AB	H	2B	3B	HR	RBI	BB	SO	OBP	Slg.	vs.	Avg.	AB	H	2B	3B	HR	RBI	BB	SO	OBP	Slg.
L	.268	41	11	2	1	0	3	4	8	.348	.366	R	.216	116	25	4	0	2	11	15	26	.321	.302

TSAO, CHIN-HUI — P

PERSONAL: Born June 2, 1981, in Hua-Lien, Taiwan. ... 6-2/177. ... Throws right, bats right. ... Full name: Chin-Hui Tsao. ... Name pronounced: chin-wee sow. **TRANSACTIONS/CAREER NOTES:** Signed as a non-drafted free agent by Colorado Rockies organization (October 7, 1999). ... On disabled list (August 27-September 16, 2003). ... On disabled list (March 25-April 12, 2005); included rehabilitation assignment to Colorado Springs and Modesto. ... On disabled list (May 12, 2005-remainder of season and March 1, 2006-entire season).

CAREER HITTING: 2-for-13 (.154), 2-R, 1 2B, 0 3B, 0 HR, 0 RBI.

Year Team (League)	W	L	Pct.	ERA	WHIP	G	GS	CG	ShO	Hld.	Sv.-Opp.	IP	H	R	ER	HR	BB-IBB	SO	Avg.
2000— Asheville (S. Atl.)	11	8	.579	2.73	1.10	24	24	0	0		0-...	145.0	119	54	44	8	40-0	187	.220
2001— Salem (Carol.)	0	4	.000	4.67	1.62	4	4	0	0		0-...	17.1	23	11	9	1	5-0	18	.333

Year Team (League)	W	L	Pct.	ERA	WHIP	G	GS	CG	ShO	Hld.	Sv.-Opp.	IP	H	R	ER	HR	BB-IBB	SO	Avg.
2002—Tri-Cities (NWL)	0	0	...	0.00	0.73	3	3	0	0	...	0-...	11.0	6	2	0	0	2-0	16	.150
—Salem (Carol.)	4	2	.667	2.09	0.97	9	9	0	0	...	0-...	47.1	34	13	11	3	12-0	45	.204
2003—Tulsa (Texas)	11	4	.733	2.46	1.01	18	18	0	0	...	0-...	113.1	88	34	31	7	26-0	125	.214
—Colorado (N.L.)	3	3	.500	6.02	1.57	9	8	0	0	0	0-0	43.1	48	30	29	11	20-1	29	.284
2004—Asheville (S. Atl.)	1	0	1.000	1.80	0.90	2	2	0	0	...	0-0	10.0	8	2	2	1	1-0	14	.211
—Tulsa (Texas)	1	1	.500	2.77	1.08	2	2	0	0	...	0-0	13.0	12	4	4	1	2-0	10	.261
—Colo. Springs (PCL)	1	1	.500	8.53	2.13	4	4	0	0	...	0-0	12.2	22	12	12	5	5-0	14	.379
—Colorado (N.L.)	0	0	...	3.86	0.86	10	0	0	0	1	1-2	9.1	7	4	4	2	1-0	11	.200
2005—Colo. Springs (PCL)	0	0	...	0.00	1.00	1	1	0	0	0	0-0	1.0	1	0	0	0	0-0	1	.250
—Modesto (California)	0	0	...	0.00	0.00	1	0	0	0	0	0-0	1.0	0	0	0	0	0-0	1	.000
—Colorado (N.L.)	1	0	1.000	6.55	1.91	10	0	0	0	0	3-4	11.0	16	8	8	3	5-1	4	.333
2006—Colorado (N.L.)	Did not play.																		
Major League totals (3 years)	4	3	.571	5.80	1.52	29	8	0	0	1	4-6	63.2	71	42	41	16	26-2	44	.282

TUCKER, MICHAEL — OF

PERSONAL: Born June 25, 1971, in South Boston, Va. ... 6-2/195. ... Bats left, throws right. ... Full name: Michael Anthony Tucker. ... High school: Bluestone (Skipwith, Va.). ... College: Longwood (Va.). **TRANSACTIONS/CAREER NOTES:** Selected by Kansas City Royals organization in first round (10th pick overall) of 1992 free-agent draft. ... On disabled list (June 4-21 and August 28, 1996-remainder of season); included rehabilitation assignment to Wichita. ... Traded by Royals with IF Keith Lockhart to Atlanta Braves for OF Jermaine Dye and P Jamie Walker (March 27, 1997). ... Traded by Braves with Ps Denny Neagle and Rob Bell to Cincinnati Reds for 2B Bret Boone and P Mike Remlinger (November 10, 1998). ... Traded by Reds to Chicago Cubs for Ps Chris Booker and Ben Shaffar (July 20, 2001). ... Traded by Cubs to Royals for a player to be named (December 19, 2001); Cubs acquired P Shawn Sonnier to complete deal (March 15, 2002). ... On disabled list (August 5-September 24, 2003). ... Signed as a free agent by San Francisco Giants (December 7, 2003). ... Traded by Giants to Philadelphia Phillies for P Kelvin Pichardo (August 27, 2005). ... Signed as free agent by Washington Nationals (January 11, 2006). ... Released by Nationals (March 30, 2006). ... Signed by New York Mets organization (April 26, 2006). **STATISTICAL NOTES:** Career major league grand slams: 2.

2006 GAMES PLAYED BY POSITION (MLB): OF—18, 1B—1.

Year Team (League)	Pos.	G	AB	R	H	2B	3B	HR	RBI	BB	SO	HBP	GDP	SB-CS	Avg.	OBP	SLG	OPS	E	Avg.
1993—Wilmington (Caro.)	2B	61	239	42	73	14	2	6	44	34	49	2	0	12-2	.305	.391	.456	.847	10	.965
—Memphis (Sou.)	2B	72	244	38	68	7	4	9	35	42	51	6	1	12-5	.279	.392	.451	.843	13	.962
1994—Omaha (A.A.)	OF	132	485	75	134	16	7	21	77	69	111	3	6	11-3	.276	.366	.468	.834	7	.967
1995—Kansas City (A.L.)	OF-DH	62	177	23	46	10	0	4	17	18	51	1	3	2-3	.260	.332	.384	.716	1	.986
—Omaha (A.A.)	OF	71	275	37	84	18	4	4	28	24	39	4	3	11-4	.305	.367	.444	.811	2	.986
1996—Kansas City (A.L.)	OF-1B-DH	108	339	55	88	18	4	12	53	40	69	7	7	10-4	.260	.346	.442	.789	2	.992
—Wichita (Texas)	OF-1B	6	20	4	9	1	3	0	7	5	4	0	0	0-2	.450	.538	.800	1.338	0	1.000
1997—Atlanta (N.L.)	OF	138	499	80	141	25	7	14	56	44	116	6	7	12-7	.283	.347	.445	.792	5	.980
1998—Atlanta (N.L.)	OF	130	414	54	101	27	3	13	46	49	112	4	4	8-3	.244	.327	.418	.745	1	.980
1999—Cincinnati (N.L.)	OF	133	296	55	75	8	5	11	44	37	81	3	5	11-4	.253	.338	.426	.764	2	.990
2000—Cincinnati (N.L.)	OF-2B	148	270	55	72	13	4	15	36	44	64	7	6	13-6	.267	.381	.511	.892	5	.969
2001—Cincinnati (N.L.)	OF	86	231	31	56	10	1	7	30	23	55	1	4	12-5	.242	.308	.385	.693	3	.978
—Chicago (N.L.)	OF-1B	63	205	31	54	9	7	5	31	23	47	1	4	4-3	.263	.339	.449	.788	3	.978
2002—Kansas City (A.L.)	OF-DH-1B-2B	144	475	65	118	27	6	12	56	56	105	3	5	23-9	.248	.330	.406	.737	4	.985
2003—Kansas City (A.L.)	OF-DH	104	389	61	102	20	5	13	55	39	88	2	8	8-10	.262	.331	.440	.771	2	.989
2004—San Francisco (N.L.)	OF	140	464	77	119	21	6	13	62	70	106	2	5	5-2	.256	.353	.412	.765	6	.978
2005—San Francisco (N.L.)	OF-DH	104	250	32	60	16	1	5	33	28	48	2	6	4-0	.240	.317	.372	.689	1	.983
—Philadelphia (N.L.)	OF	22	18	3	4	0	0	0	3	3	4	0	1	0-0	.222	.333	.222	.556	0	...
2006—Norfolk (Int'l)		83	275	44	73	18	2	6	33	49	45	5	5	10-3	.265	.381	.411	.792	2	.985
—New York (N.L.)	OF-1B	35	56	3	11	4	0	1	6	16	14	1	2	2-0	.196	.378	.321	.700	0	1.000
American League totals (4 years)		418	1380	204	354	75	15	41	181	153	313	13	23	43-26	.257	.335	.422	.756	9	.985
National League totals (8 years)		999	2703	421	693	133	34	84	347	337	647	26	44	71-30	.256	.342	.424	.766	27	.982
Major League totals (12 years)		1417	4083	625	1047	208	49	125	528	490	960	39	67	114-56	.256	.339	.423	.763	36	.984

DIVISION SERIES RECORD

Year Team (League)	Pos.	G	AB	R	H	2B	3B	HR	RBI	BB	SO	HBP	GDP	SB-CS	Avg.	OBP	SLG	OPS	E	Avg.
1997—Atlanta (N.L.)	OF	2	6	0	1	0	0	0	1	0	1	0	0	0-0	.167	.167	.167	.333	0	1.000
1998—Atlanta (N.L.)	OF	3	8	1	2	0	0	1	2	2	0	0	0	1-0	.250	.400	.625	1.025	0	1.000
2006—New York (N.L.)		2	1	1	0	0	0	0	0	1	0	1	0	0-0	.000	.500	.000	.500	0	...
Division series totals (3 years)		7	15	2	3	0	0	1	3	3	1	1	0	1-0	.200	.333	.400	.733	0	1.000

CHAMPIONSHIP SERIES RECORD

Year Team (League)	Pos.	G	AB	R	H	2B	3B	HR	RBI	BB	SO	HBP	GDP	SB-CS	Avg.	OBP	SLG	OPS	E	Avg.
1997—Atlanta (N.L.)	OF	5	10	1	1	0	0	0	1	3	4	0	0	0-0	.100	.308	.400	.708	0	1.000
1998—Atlanta (N.L.)	OF	6	13	1	5	1	0	1	5	2	5	0	0	0-0	.385	.467	.692	1.159	0	1.000
2006—New York (N.L.)		6	5	1	2	0	0	0	0	0	1	1	0	1-0	.400	.500	.400	.900	0	...
Champ. series totals (3 years)		17	28	3	8	1	0	2	6	5	10	1	0	1-0	.286	.412	.536	.947	0	1.000

2006 LEFTY-RIGHTY SPLITS

vs.	Avg.	AB	H	2B	3B	HR	RBI	BB	SO	OBP	Slg.	vs.	Avg.	AB	H	2B	3B	HR	RBI	BB	SO	OBP	Slg.
L	.294	17	5	2	0	0	0	3	3	.429	.412	R	.154	39	6	2	0	1	4	13	11	.358	.282

TULOWITZKI, TROY — SS

PERSONAL: Born October 10, 1984, in Santa Clara, Calif. ... Bats right, throws right. ... Full name: Troy T. Tulowitzki. ... College: Long Beach State. **TRANSACTIONS/CAREER NOTES:** Selected by Colorado Rockies organization in first round (seventh pick overall) of 2005 free-agent draft.

2006 GAMES PLAYED BY POSITION (MLB): SS—25.

Year Team (League)	Pos.	G	AB	R	H	2B	3B	HR	RBI	BB	SO	HBP	GDP	SB-CS	Avg.	OBP	SLG	OPS	E	Avg.
2005—Modesto (California)	SS-DH	22	94	17	25	6	0	4	14	9	18	2	2	1-0	.266	.343	.457	.800	5	.948
2006—Tulsa (Texas)		104	423	75	123	34	2	13	61	46	71	10	8	6-5	.291	.370	.473	.843	25	.948
—Colorado (N.L.)	SS	25	96	15	23	2	0	1	6	10	25	1	1	3-0	.240	.318	.292	.609	2	.983
Major League totals (1 year)		25	96	15	23	2	0	1	6	10	25	1	1	3-0	.240	.318	.292	.609	2	.983

2006 LEFTY-RIGHTY SPLITS

vs.	Avg.	AB	H	2B	3B	HR	RBI	BB	SO	OBP	Slg.	vs.	Avg.	AB	H	2B	3B	HR	RBI	BB	SO	OBP	Slg.
L	.150	20	3	1	0	0	0	2	5	.227	.200	R	.263	76	20	1	0	1	6	8	20	.341	.316

TURNBOW, DERRICK — P

PERSONAL: Born January 25, 1978, in Union City, Tenn. ... 6-3/210. ... Throws right, bats right. ... Full name: Thomas Derrick Turnbow. ... High school: Franklin (Tenn.).
TRANSACTIONS/CAREER NOTES: Selected by Philadelphia Phillies organization in fifth round of 1997 free-agent draft. ... Selected by Anaheim Angels from Phillies organization in Rule 5 major league draft (December 13, 1999). ... On disabled list (April 20, 2001-remainder of season). ... Claimed on waivers by Milwaukee Brewers (October 14, 2004).
CAREER HITTING: 0-for-2 (.000), 0 R, 0 2B, 0 3B, 0 HR, 0 RBI.

Year Team (League)	W	L	Pct.	ERA	WHIP	G	GS	CG	ShO	Hld.	Sv.-Opp.	IP	H	R	ER	HR	BB-IBB	SO	Avg.
1997—Martinsville (App.)	1	3	.250	7.40	2.05	7	7	0	0	...	0-...	24.1	34	29	20	5	16-1	7	.354
1998—Martinsville (App.)	2	6	.250	5.01	1.31	13	13	1	0	...	0-...	70.0	66	44	39	7	26-1	45	.249
1999—Piedmont (S. Atl.)	12	8	.600	3.35	1.14	26	26	4	1	...	0-...	161.0	130	67	60	10	53-0	149	.221
2000—Anaheim (A.L.)	0	0		4.74	1.89	24	1	0	0	...	0-...	38.0	36	21	20	7	36-...	25	.254
2001—Arkansas (Texas)	0	0		2.57	1.21	3	3	0	0	...	0-...	14.0	12	4	4	0	5-0	11	.240
2002—Ariz. Angels (Ariz.)	0	1	.000	4.50	1.00	3	3	0	0	...	0-..:	8.0	5	5	4	0	3-0	12	.161
—Rancho Cuca. (Calif.)	0	0		5.25	2.08	13	0	0	0	...	0-...	12.0	16	11	7	1	9-0	14	.320
2003—Arkansas (Texas)	1	0	1.000	0.00	0.60	7	0	0	0	...	3-...	14.0	4	0	0	0	5-0	19	.087
—Salt Lake (PCL)	1	2	.333	5.73	1.70	35	0	0	0	...	2-...	55.0	68	36	35	5	24-0	63	.300
—Anaheim (A.L.)	2	0	1.000	0.59	0.65	11	0	0	0	0	0-0	15.1	7	1	1	0	3-0	15	.140
2004—Anaheim (A.L.)	0	0		0.00	1.42	4	0	0	0	0	0-0	6.1	2	0	0	0	7-0	3	.105
—Salt Lake (PCL)	2	6	.250	5.06	1.57	46	3	0	0	...	6-...	74.2	75	46	42	8	42-0	56	.275
2005—Milwaukee (N.L.)	7	1	.875	1.74	1.08	69	0	0	0	2	39-43	67.1	49	15	13	5	24-2	64	.199
2006—Milwaukee (N.L.)	4	9	.308	6.87	1.69	64	0	0	0	4	24-32	56.1	56	51	43	8	39-2	69	.255
American League totals (3 years)	2	0	1.000	3.17	1.53	39	1	0	0	1	0-0	59.2	45	22	21	7	46-0	43	.213
National League totals (2 years)	11	10	.524	4.08	1.36	133	0	0	0	6	63-75	123.2	105	66	56	13	63-4	133	.225
Major League totals (5 years)	13	10	.565	3.78	1.41	172	1	0	0	7	63-75	183.1	150	88	77	20	109-4	176	.222

ALL-STAR GAME RECORD

	W	L	Pct.	ERA	WHIP	G	GS	CG	ShO	Hld.	Sv.-Opp.	IP	H	R	ER	HR	BB-IBB	SO	Avg.
All-Star Game totals (1 year)	0	0	...	0.00	1.00	1	0	0	0	1	0-0	1.0	1	0	0	0	0-0	0	.333

2006 LEFTY-RIGHTY SPLITS

vs.	Avg.	AB	H	2B	3B	HR	RBI	BB	SO	OBP	Slg.	vs.	Avg.	AB	H	2B	3B	HR	RBI	BB	SO	OBP	Slg.
L	.245	106	26	6	1	3	18	16	32	.341	.406	R	.263	114	30	6	2	5	18	23	37	.404	.482

TYNER, JASON — OF

PERSONAL: Born April 23, 1977, in Beaumont, Texas. ... 6-1/168. ... Bats left, throws left. ... Full name: Jason Renyt Tyner. ... Name pronounced: tie-ner. ... High school: Westbrook (Beaumont, Texas). ... College: Texas A&M. **TRANSACTIONS/CAREER NOTES:** Selected by New York Mets organization in first round (21st pick overall) of 1998 free-agent draft. ... Traded by Mets with P Paul Wilson to Tampa Bay Devil Rays for P Rick White and OF Bubba Trammell (July 28, 2000). ... Signed by Atlanta Braves organization (April 27, 2004). ... Released by Braves (July 25, 2004). ... Signed by Cleveland Indians organization (July 28, 2004). ... Signed as a free agent by Minnesota Twins organization (November 10, 2004).
2006 GAMES PLAYED BY POSITION (MLB): OF—50, DH—12.

Year Team (League)	Pos.	G	AB	R	H	2B	3B	HR	RBI	BB	SO	HBP	GDP	SB-CS	Avg.	OBP	SLG	OPS	E	Avg.
1998—St. Lucie (Fla. St.)	OF-OF	50	201	30	61	2	3	0	16	17	20	1	3	15-11	.303	.361	.343	.704	2	.976
1999—Binghamton (East.)	OF-OF	129	518	91	162	19	5	0	33	62	46	1	8	49-16	.313	.387	.369	.756	2	.993
—Norfolk (Int'l)	OF-OF	3	8	0	0	0	0	0	0	0	5	0	0	0-0	.000	.000	.000	.000	0	1.000
2000—Norfolk (Int'l)	OF-OF	84	327	54	105	5	2	0	28	30	32	1	8	33-14	.321	.380	.349	.729	1	.995
—New York (N.L.)	OF	13	41	3	8	2	0	0	5	1	4	1	4	1-1	.195	.222	.244	.466	2	.920
—Tampa Bay (A.L.)	OF-DH	37	83	6	20	2	0	0	8	4	12	1	1	6-1	.241	.281	.265	.546	0	1.000
2001—Durham (Int'l)	OF-OF	39	157	25	49	4	5	0	12	15	10	2	1	11-5	.312	.371	.338	.709	5	.978
—Tampa Bay (A.L.)	OF	105	396	51	111	8	5	0	31	15	42	3	6	31-6	.280	.311	.326	.637	5	.978
2002—Tampa Bay (A.L.)	OF-DH	44	168	17	36	2	1	0	9	7	19	1	1	7-1	.214	.249	.238	.487	1	.990
—Durham (Int'l)	OF-OF	88	351	59	102	12	4	0	27	34	27	6	3	20-7	.291	.362	.348	.710	1	.994
2003—Tampa Bay (A.L.)	OF-DH	46	90	12	25	1	0	0	6	10	12	0	1	2-1	.278	.350	.356	.706	2	.962
—Durham (Int'l)	OF-OF-OF	65	275	34	89	11	5	0	24	22	25	1	5	10-7	.324	.372	.400	.772	1	.993
2004—Richmond (Int'l)	OF	64	243	40	70	12	1	1	16	15	22	7	4	18-6	.288	.346	.358	.704	0	...
—Buffalo (Int'l)	OF	38	139	26	48	4	1	0	16	18	15	2	0	5-0	.345	.417	.388	.805	0	...
2005—Rochester (Int'l)	OF-DH	133	524	81	150	18	2	1	36	48	57	5	9	18-6	.286	.351	.334	.685	2	.996
—Minnesota (A.L.)	OF-DH	18	56	8	18	1	1	0	4	4	4	0	2	2-0	.321	.367	.375	.742	0	1.000
2006—Rochester (Int'l)	OF-DH	80	316	52	104	14	5	0	22	25	39	3	2	8-2	.329	.379	.405	.784	2	.989
—Minnesota (A.L.)	OF-DH	62	218	29	68	5	2	0	18	11	18	1	5	4-2	.312	.345	.353	.698	1	.993
American League totals (6 years)		312	1011	123	278	25	9	0	67	51	107	6	16	52-11	.275	.312	.318	.630	9	.985
National League totals (1 year)		13	41	3	8	2	0	0	5	1	4	1	1	1-1	.195	.222	.244	.466	2	.920
Major League totals (6 years)		325	1052	126	286	27	9	0	72	52	111	7	17	53-12	.272	.309	.315	.623	11	.983

DIVISION SERIES RECORD

Year Team (League)	Pos.	G	AB	R	H	2B	3B	HR	RBI	BB	SO	HBP	GDP	SB-CS	Avg.	OBP	SLG	OPS	E	Avg.
2006—Minnesota (A.L.)	DH	2	6	0	0	0	0	0	0	2	2	0	1	1-0	.000	.250	.000	.250	0	...

2006 LEFTY-RIGHTY SPLITS

vs.	Avg.	AB	H	2B	3B	HR	RBI	BB	SO	OBP	Slg.	vs.	Avg.	AB	H	2B	3B	HR	RBI	BB	SO	OBP	Slg.
L	.269	52	14	0	0	0	5	1	9	.283	.269	R	.325	166	54	5	2	0	13	10	9	.363	.380

UGGLA, DAN — IF

PERSONAL: Born March 11, 1980, in Louisville, Ky. ... 5-10/200. ... Bats right, throws right. ... Full name: Daniel Cooley Uggla. ... College: Memphis.
TRANSACTIONS/CAREER NOTES: Selected by Arizona Diamondbacks organization in 11th round of 2001 free-agent draft ... Selected by Florida Marlins from Diamondbacks organization in Rule 5 major league draft (December 8, 2005). **HONORS:** Named N.L. Rookie of the Year by the SPORTING NEWS (2006).
2006 GAMES PLAYED BY POSITION (MLB): 2B—151, DH—1.

Year Team (League)	Pos.	G	AB	R	H	2B	3B	HR	RBI	BB	SO	HBP	GDP	SB-CS	Avg.	OBP	SLG	OPS	E	Avg.
2001—Yakima (N'west)		72	278	39	77	21	0	5	40	20	52	9	9	8-4	.277	.341	.406	.747	...	...
2002—Lancaster (Calif.)		54	184	21	42	7	2	3	16	21	51	2	3	3-2	.228	.311	.413	.648	...	...
—South Bend (Mid.)		53	171	16	34	5	1	2	10	23	34	0	2	0-2	.199	.291	.275	.566	...	...
2003—Lancaster (Calif.)		134	534	104	155	31	7	23	90	46	105	11	7	24-9	.290	.355	.504	.859	...	...
2004—El Paso (Texas)		83	294	29	76	12	2	4	30	15	55	4	6	10-7	.259	.302	.354	.656	...	...
—Lancaster (Calif.)		37	140	29	47	13	3	6	38	17	21	4	0	2-4	.336	.422	.600	1.022	...	...

U

Year Team (League)	Pos.	G	AB	R	H	2B	3B	HR	RBI	BB	SO	HBP	GDP	SB-CS	Avg.	OBP	SLG	OPS	E	Avg.
2005—Tennessee (Sou.) 2B-3B-1B																				
SS-DH		135	498	88	148	33	3	21	87	52	103	14	10	15-8	.297	.378	.502	.880	25	.959
2006—Florida (N.L.)	2B-DH	154	611	105	172	26	7	27	90	48	123	9	5	6-6	.282	.339	.480	.818	15	.980
Major League totals (1 year)		154	611	105	172	26	7	27	90	48	123	9	5	6-6	.282	.339	.480	.818	15	.980

2006 LEFTY-RIGHTY SPLITS

vs.	Avg.	AB	H	2B	3B	HR	RBI	BB	SO	OBP	Slg.	vs.	Avg.	AB	H	2B	3B	HR	RBI	BB	SO	OBP	Slg.
L	.307	153	47	11	0	4	13	12	25	.363	.458	R	.273	458	125	15	7	23	77	36	98	.331	.487

UPTON, B.J.   3B

PERSONAL: Born August 21, 1984, in Norfolk, Va. ... 6-3/180. ... Bats right, throws right. ... Full name: Melvin Emanuel Upton. ... High school: Greenbrier Christian Academy (Chesapeake, Va.). **TRANSACTIONS/CAREER NOTES:** Selected by Tampa Bay Devil Rays organization in first round (second pick overall) of 2002 free-agent draft.
2006 GAMES PLAYED BY POSITION (MLB): 3B—50.

Year Team (League)	Pos.	G	AB	R	H	2B	3B	HR	RBI	BB	SO	HBP	GDP	SB-CS	Avg.	OBP	SLG	OPS	E	Avg.
2003—Char., S.C. (SAL)	SS	101	384	70	116	22	6	7	46	57	80	5	8	38-17	.302	.394	.445	.839	42	.907
—Orlando (South.)	SS	29	105	14	29	8	0	1	16	16	25	2	1	2-4	.276	.376	.381	.757	14	.879
2004—Montgom. (Sou.)	SS-DH	29	104	21	34	7	1	2	15	14	28	0	0	3-0	.327	.407	.471	.878	10	.900
—Durham (Int'l)	SS-DH	69	264	65	82	17	1	12	36	42	72	3	9	17-5	.311	.411	.519	.924	25	.916
—Tampa Bay (A.L.) SS-DH-3B																				
OF		45	159	19	41	8	2	4	12	15	46	1	1	4-1	.258	.324	.409	.733	9	.905
2005—Durham (Int'l)	SS-DH	139	545	98	165	36	6	18	74	78	124	4	15	44-13	.303	.392	.490	.882	53	.921
2006—Durham (Int'l)		106	398	72	107	18	4	8	41	65	89	4	6	46-17	.269	.374	.394	.769	33	.926
—Tampa Bay (A.L.)	3B	50	175	20	43	5	0	1	10	13	40	1	1	11-3	.246	.302	.291	.593	13	.906
Major League totals (2 years)		95	334	39	84	13	2	5	22	28	86	2	2	15-4	.251	.312	.347	.660	22	.906

2006 LEFTY-RIGHTY SPLITS

vs.	Avg.	AB	H	2B	3B	HR	RBI	BB	SO	OBP	Slg.	vs.	Avg.	AB	H	2B	3B	HR	RBI	BB	SO	OBP	Slg.
L	.298	47	14	1	0	1	5	2	10	.327	.383	R	.227	128	29	4	0	0	5	11	30	.293	.258

URIBE, JUAN   SS

PERSONAL: Born July 22, 1979, in Bani, Dominican Republic. ... 5-11/175. ... Bats right, throws right. ... Full name: Juan C. Tena Uribe. ... Name pronounced: ohh-ree-bay. ... High school: Abel Uribe (Dominican Republic). **TRANSACTIONS/CAREER NOTES:** Signed as a non-drafted free agent by Colorado Rockies organization (January 15, 1997). ... On disabled list (March 18-June 3, 2003); included rehabilitation assignments to Visalia and Tulsa. ... Traded by Rockies to Chicago White Sox for 2B Aaron Miles (December 2, 2003). **STATISTICAL NOTES:** Career major league grand slams: 2.
2006 GAMES PLAYED BY POSITION (MLB): SS—132.

Year Team (League)	Pos.	G	AB	R	H	2B	3B	HR	RBI	BB	SO	HBP	GDP	SB-CS	Avg.	OBP	SLG	OPS	E	Avg.
1997—DSL Rockies (DSL)		65	234	32	63	12	0	0	29	31	22	...	...	7-...	.269	...	.321	...	...	...
1998—Ariz. Rockies (Ariz.)	SS	40	148	25	41	5	3	0	17	12	25	3	1	8-1	.277	.339	.351	.691	14	.927
1999—Asheville (S. Atl.)	SS	125	430	57	115	28	3	9	46	20	79	6	12	11-7	.267	.307	.409	.716	38	.938
2000—Salem (Carol.)	SS	134	485	64	124	22	7	13	65	38	100	4	11	22-5	.256	.314	.410	.724	26	.961
2001—Carolina (Southern)	SS	3	13	1	3	1	0	0	1	0	4	0	1	1-0	.231	.231	.308	.538	2	.833
—Colorado (N.L.)	SS	72	273	32	82	15	11	8	53	8	55	2	6	33-0	.300	.325	.524	.849	5	.983
—Colo. Springs (PCL)	SS	74	281	40	87	27	7	7	48	12	43	2	8	11-8	.310	.340	.530	.870	16	.960
2002—Colorado (N.L.)	SS	155	566	69	136	25	7	6	49	34	120	5	17	9-2	.240	.286	.341	.627	27	.966
2003—Visalia (Calif.)	2B-SS	2	9	4	5	1	0	0	1	1	0	0	1	0-0	.556	.600	.667	1.267	0	1.000
—Tulsa (Texas) 2B-3B-OF																				
SS		5	20	3	5	2	0	1	4	0	2	0	0	0-0	.250	.238	.500	.738	0	1.000
—Colorado (N.L.) SS-2B-OF		87	316	45	80	19	3	10	33	17	60	3	3	7-2	.253	.297	.427	.724	12	.974
2004—Chicago (A.L.) 2B-SS-3B																				
DH		134	502	82	142	31	6	23	74	32	96	3	10	9-11	.283	.327	.506	.833	11	.982
2005—Chicago (A.L.)	SS	146	481	58	121	23	3	16	71	34	77	4	7	4-6	.252	.301	.412	.712	16	.977
2006—Chicago (A.L.)	SS	132	463	53	109	28	2	21	71	13	82	3	10	1-1	.235	.257	.441	.698	14	.977
American League totals (3 years)		412	1446	193	372	82	11	60	216	79	255	10	27	14-18	.257	.296	.454	.750	41	.978
National League totals (3 years)		314	1155	146	298	59	21	24	135	59	235	10	26	19-4	.258	.297	.408	.706	44	.972
Major League totals (6 years)		726	2601	339	670	141	32	84	351	138	490	20	53	33-22	.258	.297	.433	.730	85	.975

DIVISION SERIES RECORD

Year Team (League)	Pos.	G	AB	R	H	2B	3B	HR	RBI	BB	SO	HBP	GDP	SB-CS	Avg.	OBP	SLG	OPS	E	Avg.
2005—Chicago (A.L.)	SS	3	10	4	4	1	0	1	4	0	2	0	0	0-0	.400	.400	.800	1.200	0	1.000

CHAMPIONSHIP SERIES RECORD

Year Team (League)	Pos.	G	AB	R	H	2B	3B	HR	RBI	BB	SO	HBP	GDP	SB-CS	Avg.	OBP	SLG	OPS	E	Avg.
2005—Chicago (A.L.)	SS	5	16	1	4	1	0	0	2	3	0	1		0-0	.250	.333	.313	.646	1	.971

WORLD SERIES RECORD

Year Team (League)	Pos.	G	AB	R	H	2B	3B	HR	RBI	BB	SO	HBP	GDP	SB-CS	Avg.	OBP	SLG	OPS	E	Avg.
2005—Chicago (A.L.)	SS	4	16	2	4	3	0	0	2	3	3	0	0	1-0	.250	.368	.438	.806	2	.923

2006 LEFTY-RIGHTY SPLITS

vs.	Avg.	AB	H	2B	3B	HR	RBI	BB	SO	OBP	Slg.	vs.	Avg.	AB	H	2B	3B	HR	RBI	BB	SO	OBP	Slg.
L	.224	192	43	12	1	4	27	5	41	.241	.359	R	.244	271	66	16	1	17	44	8	41	.268	.498

UTLEY, CHASE   2B

PERSONAL: Born December 17, 1978, in Pasadena, Calif. ... 6-1/183. ... Bats left, throws right. ... Full name: Chase Cameron Utley. ... High school: Long Beach Poly (California). ... College: UCLA. **TRANSACTIONS/CAREER NOTES:** Selected by Los Angeles Dodgers organization in second round of 1997 free-agent draft; did not sign. ... Selected by Philadelphia Phillies organization in first round (15th pick overall) of 2000 free-agent draft. **HONORS:** Named second baseman on SPORTING NEWS N.L. All-Star team (2006). ... Named second baseman on N.L. Silver Slugger team (2006). **STATISTICAL NOTES:** Career major league grand slams: 3.
2006 GAMES PLAYED BY POSITION (MLB): 2B—156, 1B—2, DH—1.

Year Team (League)	Pos.	G	AB	R	H	2B	3B	HR	RBI	BB	SO	HBP	GDP	SB-CS	Avg.	OBP	SLG	OPS	E	Avg.
2000—Batavia (NY-Penn)	2B	40	153	21	47	13	1	2	22	18	23	2	3	5-3	.307	.383	.444	.827	3	.983
2001—Clearwater (FSL)	2B	122	467	65	120	25	2	16	59	37	88	12	6	19-8	.257	.324	.422	.746	17	.970

Year Team (League)	Pos.	G	AB	R	H	2B	3B	HR	RBI	BB	SO	HBP	GDP	SB-CS	Avg.	OBP	SLG	OPS	E	Avg.
2002—Scran./W.B. (I.L.)	3B	125	464	73	122	39	1	17	70	46	89	20	5	8-3	.263	.352	.461	.813	28	.918
2003—Scran./W.B. (I.L.)	2B	113	431	80	139	26	2	18	77	41	75	11	3	10-4	.323	.390	.517	.907	13	.978
—Philadelphia (N.L.)	2B	43	134	13	32	10	1	2	21	11	22	6	3	2-0	.239	.322	.373	.696	3	.983
2004—Scran./W.B. (I.L.)	2B	33	123	23	35	8	1	6	25	18	29	0	2	4-2	.285	.368	.512	.880	5	.970
—Philadelphia (N.L.)	2B-1B	94	267	36	71	11	2	13	57	15	40	2	6	4-1	.266	.308	.468	.776	4	.988
2005—Philadelphia (N.L.)	2B-1B	147	543	93	158	39	6	28	105	69	109	9	10	16-3	.291	.376	.540	.915	16	.978
2006—Philadelphia (N.L.)	2B-1B-DH	160	658	*131	203	40	4	32	102	63	132	14	9	15-4	.309	.379	.527	.906	18	.978
Major League totals (4 years)		444	1602	273	464	100	13	75	285	158	303	31	28	37-8	.290	.362	.509	.871	41	.980

ALL-STAR GAME RECORD

	G	AB	R	H	2B	3B	HR	RBI	BB	SO	HBP	GDP	SB-CS	Avg.	OBP	SLG	OPS	E	Avg.
All-Star Game totals (1 year)	1	2	0	1	0	0	0	0	0	0	0	0	0-0	.500	.500	.500	1.000	0	1.000

2006 LEFTY-RIGHTY SPLITS

vs.	Avg.	AB	H	2B	3B	HR	RBI	BB	SO	OBP	Slg.	vs.	Avg.	AB	H	2B	3B	HR	RBI	BB	SO	OBP	Slg.
L	.301	216	65	14	3	5	24	25	63	.394	.463	R	.312	442	138	26	1	27	78	38	69	.371	.559

VALENTIN, JAVIER — C

PERSONAL: Born September 19, 1975, in Manati, Puerto Rico. ... 5-10/192. ... Bats both, throws right. ... Full name: Jose Javier Valentin. ... Name pronounced: val-en-TEEN. ... High school: Fernando Callejo (Manati, Puerto Rico). ... Brother of Jose Valentin, infielder, New York Mets. **TRANSACTIONS/CAREER NOTES:** Selected by Minnesota Twins organization in third round of 1993 free-agent draft. ... Traded by Twins with P Matt Kinney to Milwaukee Brewers for Ps Matt Yeatman and Gerard Oakes (November 15, 2002). ... Traded by Brewers to Tampa Bay Devil Rays for OF Jason Conti (March 24, 2003). ... Signed as a free agent by Cincinnati Reds organization (January 9, 2004). **STATISTICAL NOTES:** Career major league grand slams: 1.
2006 GAMES PLAYED BY POSITION (MLB): C—46, 1B—2, DH—1.

Year Team (League)	Pos.	G	AB	R	H	2B	3B	HR	RBI	BB	SO	HBP	GDP	SB-CS	Avg.	OBP	SLG	OPS	E	Avg.
1993—GC Twins (GCL)	3B-C-DH	32	103	18	27	6	1	1	19	14	19	1	1	0-2	.262	.344	.369	.713	5	.966
—Elizabethton (App.)	C	9	24	3	5	1	0	0	3	4	2	1	0	0-0	.208	.345	.250	.595	2	.977
1994—Elizabethton (App.)	3B-C	54	210	23	44	5	0	9	27	15	44	2	9	0-1	.210	.263	.362	.625	12	.966
1995—Fort Wayne (Midw.)	3B-C	112	383	59	124	26	5	19	65	47	75	2	7	0-5	.324	.400	.567	.967	23	.974
1996—Fort Myers (FSL)	C-DH-3B	87	338	34	89	26	1	7	54	32	65	4	5	1-0	.263	.330	.408	.738	4	.991
—New Britain (East.)	C-3B-DH	48	165	22	39	8	0	3	14	16	35	1	2	0-3	.236	.308	.339	.647	5	.978
1997—New Britain (East.)	C-DH-3B	102	370	41	90	17	0	8	50	30	61	1	5	2-3	.243	.297	.354	.651	6	.990
—Minnesota (A.L.)	C	4	7	1	2	0	0	0	0	0	3	0	0	0-0	.286	.286	.286	.571	0	1.000
1998—Minnesota (A.L.)	C-DH	55	162	11	32	7	1	3	18	11	30	0	7	0-0	.198	.247	.309	.556	5	.984
1999—Minnesota (A.L.)	C	78	218	22	54	12	1	5	28	22	39	1	2	0-0	.248	.313	.381	.694	1	.998
2000—Salt Lake (PCL)	C	39	140	25	50	16	2	7	35	9	27	1	1	1-0	.357	.397	.650	1.047	1	.994
2001—Edmonton (PCL)	C-3B-1B	121	431	53	121	29	2	17	71	47	108	4	14	0-1	.281	.352	.476	.827	14	.977
2002—Edmonton (PCL)	C-3B-1B	127	455	69	130	33	1	21	80	41	96	5	15	0-1	.286	.346	.501	.847	9	.984
—Minnesota (A.L.)	C	4	4	0	2	0	0	0	0	0	0	0	0	0-0	.500	.500	.500	1.000	0	1.000
2003—Tampa Bay (A.L.)	C-DH	49	135	13	30	7	1	3	15	5	31	1	7	0-0	.222	.254	.356	.609	0	1.000
2004—Cincinnati (N.L.)	C-1B	82	202	18	47	10	1	6	20	17	36	1	4	0-0	.233	.293	.381	.674	4	.989
2005—Cincinnati (N.L.)	C-1B	76	221	36	62	11	0	14	50	30	37	0	5	0-0	.281	.362	.520	.883	3	.992
2006—Cincinnati (N.L.)	C-1B-DH	92	186	24	50	6	1	8	27	13	29	0	5	0-0	.269	.313	.441	.754	7	.974
American League totals (5 years)		190	526	47	120	26	3	11	61	38	103	2	16	0-0	.228	.279	.352	.631	6	.994
National League totals (3 years)		250	609	78	159	27	2	28	97	60	102	1	14	0-0	.261	.325	.450	.775	14	.987
Major League totals (8 years)		440	1135	125	279	53	5	39	158	98	205	3	30	0-0	.246	.304	.404	.708	20	.990

2006 LEFTY-RIGHTY SPLITS

vs.	Avg.	AB	H	2B	3B	HR	RBI	BB	SO	OBP	Slg.	vs.	Avg.	AB	H	2B	3B	HR	RBI	BB	SO	OBP	Slg.
L	.111	18	2	0	0	0	0	2	4	6	.273	.111	R	.286	168	48	6	1	8	25	9	23	.318	.476

VALENTIN, JOSE — IF/OF

PERSONAL: Born October 12, 1969, in Manati, Puerto Rico. ... 5-10/195. ... Bats left, throws right. ... Full name: Jose Antonio Valentin. ... Name pronounced: val-en-TEEN. ... High school: Fernando Callejo (Manati, Puerto Rico). ... Brother of Javier Valentin, catcher, Cincinnati Reds. **TRANSACTIONS/CAREER NOTES:** Signed as a non-drafted free agent by San Diego Padres organization (October 12, 1986). ... Traded by Padres with P Ricky Bones and OF Matt Mieske to Milwaukee Brewers for 3B Gary Sheffield and P Geoff Kellogg (March 27, 1992). ... On disabled list (April 14-May 5, 1997); included rehabilitation assignment to Beloit. ... On disabled list (April 13-June 16, 1999). ... Traded by Brewers with P Cal Eldred to Chicago White Sox for Ps Jaime Navarro and John Snyder (January 12, 2000). ... On disabled list (June 8-24, 2001). ... On disabled list (April 19-May 7, 2004); included rehabilitation assignment to Charlotte. ... Signed as a free agent by Los Angeles Dodgers (December 21, 2004). ... On disabled list (May 4-July 31, 2005); included rehabilitation assignment to Las Vegas. ... Signed as a free agent by New York Mets organization (December 8, 2005). **STATISTICAL NOTES:** Hit three home runs in one game (April 3, 1998; and July 30, 2003). ... Hit for the cycle (April 27, 2000). ... Career major league grand slams: 9.
2006 GAMES PLAYED BY POSITION (MLB): 2B—94, OF—7, 3B—1, 1B—1.

Year Team (League)	Pos.	G	AB	R	H	2B	3B	HR	RBI	BB	SO	HBP	GDP	SB-CS	Avg.	OBP	SLG	OPS	E	Avg.
1987—Spokane (N'west)	SS	70	244	52	61	8	2	2	24	35	38	1	4	8-5	.250	.346	.324	.670	26	.914
1988—Char., S.C. (SAL)	SS	133	444	56	103	20	1	6	44	45	83	3	10	11-4	.232	.304	.322	.627	60	.911
1989—Riverside (Calif.)	SS	114	381	40	74	10	5	10	41	37	93	5	4	8-7	.194	.273	.325	.598	46	.924
—Wichita (Texas)	3B-SS	18	49	8	12	1	0	2	5	5	12	0	1	1-0	.245	.315	.388	.703	8	.899
1990—Wichita (Texas)	SS	11	36	4	10	2	0	0	2	5	7	0	1	2-1	.278	.366	.333	.699	2	.959
1991—Wichita (Texas)	SS	129	447	73	112	22	5	17	68	55	115	4	5	8-6	.251	.335	.436	.771	40	.939
1992—Denver (A.A.)	SS	139	492	78	118	19	11	3	45	53	99	5	8	9-4	.240	.317	.341	.658	38	.941
—Milwaukee (A.L.)	2B-SS	4	3	1	0	0	0	0	1	0	0	0	0	0-0	.000	.000	.000	.000	1	.667
1993—New Orleans (A.A.)	SS-1B	122	389	56	96	22	5	9	53	47	87	8	3	9-10	.247	.337	.396	.736	29	.951
—Milwaukee (A.L.)	SS	19	53	10	13	1	2	1	7	7	16	1	1	1-0	.245	.344	.396	.740	6	.922
1994—Milwaukee (A.L.)	SS-2B-3B-DH	97	285	47	68	19	0	11	46	38	75	2	1	12-3	.239	.330	.421	.751	20	.961
1995—Milwaukee (A.L.)	SS-DH-3B	112	338	62	74	23	3	11	49	37	83	0	0	16-8	.219	.293	.402	.695	15	.971
1996—Milwaukee (A.L.)	SS	154	552	90	143	33	7	24	95	66	145	1	1	17-4	.259	.336	.475	.811	*37	.950
1997—Milwaukee (A.L.)	SS-DH	136	494	58	125	23	1	17	58	39	109	4	5	19-8	.253	.310	.447	.757	20	.967
—Beloit (Midw.)	SS	2	6	3	3	1	0	0	1	2	1	0	0	0-0	.500	.625	.667	1.292	0	1.000
1998—Milwaukee (N.L.)	SS-DH	151	428	65	96	24	0	16	49	63	105	1	2	10-7	.224	.323	.393	.716	21	.963
1999—Milwaukee (N.L.)	SS	89	256	45	58	9	5	10	38	48	52	2	3	3-2	.227	.347	.418	.765	22	.937
—Louisville (Int'l)	SS	6	20	6	5	3	0	3	3	4	3	0	0	0-1	.250	.375	.700	1.075	0	1.000

V

Year Team (League)	Pos.	G	AB	R	H	2B	3B	HR	RBI	BB	SO	HBP	GDP	SB-CS	Avg.	OBP	SLG	OPS	E	Avg.
										BATTING									**FIELDING**	
2000—Chicago (A.L.)	SS-OF	144	568	107	155	37	6	25	92	59	106	4	11	19-2	.273	.343	.491	.835	36	.950
2001—Chicago (A.L.)	3B-SS-OF	124	438	74	113	22	2	28	68	50	114	3	7	9-6	.258	.336	.509	.845	22	.947
2002—Chicago (A.L.)	3B-SS-DH	135	474	70	118	26	4	25	75	43	99	2	9	3-3	.249	.311	.479	.790	19	.957
2003—Chicago (A.L.)	SS	144	503	79	119	26	2	28	74	54	114	3	6	8-3	.237	.313	.463	.776	20	.969
2004—Charlotte (Int'l)	DH-SS	8	31	1	2	0	0	0	2	2	15	0	0	0-0	.065	.121	.065	.186	2	.895
—Chicago (A.L.)	SS-OF-SS	125	450	73	97	20	3	30	70	43	139	3	5	8-6	.216	.287	.473	.760	20	.965
2005—Las Vegas (PCL)	3B-OF-DH																			
	2B	12	35	8	14	3	0	2	5	7	6	1	0	1-0	.400	.512	.657	1.169	0	1.000
—Los Angeles (N.L.)	3B-OF-SS	56	147	17	25	4	2	2	14	31	38	4	2	3-1	.170	.326	.265	.591	8	.932
2006—New York (N.L.)	2B-OF-1B																			
	3B	137	384	56	104	24	3	18	62	37	71	0	5	6-2	.271	.330	.490	.820	6	.988
American League totals (11 years)		1194	4158	671	1025	230	30	200	635	436	1000	22	49	112-43	.247	.319	.461	.780	216	.950
National League totals (4 years)		433	1215	183	283	61	10	46	163	179	266	7	12	22-12	.233	.331	.413	.744	57	.963
Major League totals (15 years)		1627	5373	854	1308	291	40	246	798	615	1266	29	61	134-55	.243	.322	.450	.772	273	.960

DIVISION SERIES RECORD

Year Team (League)	Pos.	G	AB	R	H	2B	3B	HR	RBI	BB	SO	HBP	GDP	SB-CS	Avg.	OBP	SLG	OPS	E	Avg.
2000—Chicago (A.L.)	SS	3	10	2	3	2	0	0	1	2	2	0	0	3-0	.300	.417	.500	.917	1	.964
2006—New York (N.L.)	2B	3	9	2	0	0	0	0	0	2	4	1	0	0-0	.000	.250	.000	.250	1	.900
Division series totals (2 years)		6	19	4	3	2	0	0	1	4	6	1	0	3-0	.158	.333	.263	.596	2	.947

CHAMPIONSHIP SERIES RECORD

Year Team (League)	Pos.	G	AB	R	H	2B	3B	HR	RBI	BB	SO	HBP	GDP	SB-CS	Avg.	OBP	SLG	OPS	E	Avg.
2006—New York (N.L.)	2B	7	24	0	6	2	0	0	5	2	5	1	2	0-0	.250	.333	.333	.667	0	1.000

2006 LEFTY-RIGHTY SPLITS

vs.	Avg.	AB	H	2B	3B	HR	RBI	BB	SO	OBP	Slg.		vs.	Avg.	AB	H	2B	3B	HR	RBI	BB	SO	OBP	Slg.
L	.219	96	21	6	0	2	11	12	18	.300	.344		R	.288	288	83	18	3	16	51	25	53	.341	.538

VALVERDE, JOSE — P

PERSONAL: Born July 24, 1979, in San Pedro de Macoris, Dominican Republic. ... 6-4/254. ... Throws right, bats right. ... Full name: Jose Rafael Valverde. ... Name pronounced: val-VARE-day. ... High school: Wscuela San Lorenzo (El Seybo, Dominican Republic). **TRANSACTIONS/CAREER NOTES:** Signed as a non-drafted free agent by Arizona Diamondbacks organization (February 6, 1997). ... On disabled list (June 14, 2004-remainder of season); included rehabilitation assignment to Tucson. ... On disabled list (March 25-May 2, 2005); included rehabilitation assignment to Tucson.
CAREER HITTING: 1-for-1 (1.000), 1 R, 1 2B, 0 3B, 0 HR, 0 RBI.

Year Team (League)	W	L	Pct.	ERA	WHIP	G	GS	CG	ShO	Hld.	Sv.-Opp.	IP	H	R	ER	HR	BB-IBB	SO	Avg.
1997—Dom. Diamondbacks (DSL)	0	0	...	5.30	1.77	14	0	0	0	...	0-...	18.2	20	12	11	1	13-...	19	...
1998—Dom. Diamondbacks (DSL)	1	3	.250	1.75	1.03	23	4	0	0	...	7-...	51.1	31	14	10	2	22-...	56	...
1999—Ariz. D'backs (Ariz.)	1	2	.333	4.08	1.53	20	0	0	0	...	8-...	28.2	34	21	13	1	10-0	47	.274
—South Bend (Mid.)	0	0	...	0.00	1.50	2	0	0	0	...	0-...	2.2	2	0	0	0	2-0	3	.250
2000—South Bend (Mid.)	0	5	.000	5.40	1.77	31	0	0	0	...	14-...	31.2	31	20	19	1	25-0	39	.254
—Missoula (Pion.)	1	0	1.000	0.00	0.60	12	0	0	0	...	4-...	11.2	3	0	0	0	4-0	24	.075
2001—El Paso (Texas)	2	2	.500	3.92	1.52	39	0	0	0	...	13-...	41.1	36	19	18	1	27-0	72	.225
2002—Tucson (PCL)	2	4	.333	5.85	1.43	49	0	0	0	...	5-...	47.2	45	33	31	8	23-1	65	.250
2003—Tucson (PCL)	1	1	.500	3.10	1.38	22	0	0	0	...	5-...	29.0	26	11	10	1	14-1	26	.236
—Arizona (N.L.)	2	1	.667	2.15	0.99	54	0	0	0	8	10-11	50.1	24	16	12	4	26-2	71	.137
2004—Arizona (N.L.)	1	2	.333	4.25	1.35	29	0	0	0	5	8-10	29.2	23	17	14	7	17-4	38	.213
—Tucson (PCL)	1	1	.500	4.22	1.31	10	1	0	0	...	3-...	10.2	9	5	5	0	5-0	5	.225
2005—Tucson (PCL)	0	0	...	0.00	1.00	2	0	0	0	...	0-0	2.0	1	0	0	0	1-0	3	.143
—Arizona (N.L.)	3	4	.429	2.44	1.07	61	0	0	0	7	15-17	66.1	51	19	18	5	20-1	75	.211
2006—Tucson (PCL)	1	0	1.000	3.06	1.30	15	0	0	0	2	3-3	17.2	13	9	6	1	10-0	18	.200
—Arizona (N.L.)	2	3	.400	5.84	1.46	44	0	0	0	1	18-22	49.1	50	32	32	6	22-3	69	.256
Major League totals (4 years)	8	10	.444	3.50	1.19	188	0	0	0	21	51-60	195.2	148	84	76	22	85-10	253	.206

2006 LEFTY-RIGHTY SPLITS

vs.	Avg.	AB	H	2B	3B	HR	RBI	BB	SO	OBP	Slg.		vs.	Avg.	AB	H	2B	3B	HR	RBI	BB	SO	OBP	Slg.
L	.323	96	31	6	0	5	19	15	25	.407	.542		R	.192	99	19	3	1	1	13	7	44	.257	.273

VAN BENSCHOTEN, JOHN — P

PERSONAL: Born April 14, 1980, in San Diego, Calif. ... 6-4/217. ... Throws right, bats right. ... Full name: John Wesley Van Benschoten. ... High school: Milford (Ohio). ... College: Kent State. **TRANSACTIONS/CAREER NOTES:** Selected by Pittsburgh Pirates organization in first round (eighth overall pick) of 2001 free-agent draft. ... On disabled list (April 1, 2005-entire season). ... On disabled list (March 24-August 16, 2006); included rehabilitation assignments to GCL Pirates and Altoona.
CAREER HITTING: 1-for-8 (.125), 2 R, 0 2B, 0 3B, 1 HR, 2 RBI.

Year Team (League)	W	L	Pct.	ERA	WHIP	G	GS	CG	ShO	Hld.	Sv.-Opp.	IP	H	R	ER	HR	BB-IBB	SO	Avg.
2001—Will. (NYP)	0	2	.000	3.51	1.29	9	9	0	0	...	0-...	25.2	23	11	10	0	10-0	19	.247
2002—Hickory (S. Atl.)	11	4	.733	2.80	1.22	27	27	0	0	...	0-...	148.0	119	57	46	6	62-1	145	.219
2003—Lynchburg (Caro.)	6	0	1.000	2.22	1.05	9	9	0	0	...	0-...	48.2	33	14	12	1	18-0	49	.192
—Altoona (East.)	7	6	.538	3.69	1.43	17	17	1	0	...	0-...	90.1	95	46	37	5	34-1	78	.268
2004—Nashville (PCL)	4	11	.267	4.72	1.40	23	23	0	0	...	0-...	131.2	135	75	69	16	49-1	101	.261
—Pittsburgh (N.L.)	1	3	.250	6.91	1.81	6	5	0	0	0	0-0	28.2	33	27	22	3	19-0	18	.300
2005—Pittsburgh (N.L.)					Did not play.														
2006—GC Pirates (GCL)	0	1	.000	4.50	0.50	1	1	0	0	...	0-0	6.0	1	3	3	1	2-0	4	.053
—Indianapolis (Int'l)	1	1	.500	5.40	1.46	3	3	0	0	...	0-0	11.2	10	7	7	2	7-0	13	.233
—Altoona (East.)	1	0	1.000	3.60	1.20	1	1	0	0	...	0-0	5.0	3	2	2	0	3-0	3	.176
Major League totals (1 year)	1	3	.250	6.91	1.81	6	5	0	0	0	0-0	28.2	33	27	22	3	19-0	18	.300

VAN BUREN, JERMAINE — P

PERSONAL: Born July 2, 1980, in Laurel, Miss. ... 6-1/220. ... Throws right, bats right. ... Full name: Jermaine Russell Van Buren. ... High school: Hattiesburg (Ms.). ... **TRANSACTIONS/CAREER NOTES:** Selected by Colorado Rockies organization in second round of 1998 free-agent draft. ... Released by Rockies (March 23, 2003). ... Signed by independent Fort Worth of Central league (May 2003). ... Signed as a free agent by Chicago Cubs (January 24, 2004). ... Traded by Cubs to Boston Red Sox for cash (December 1, 2005). ... Signed as free agent by Washington Nationals organization (November 6, 2006).
CAREER HITTING: 0-for-0 (.000), 0 R, 0 2B, 0 3B, 0 HR, 0 RBI.

V

Year Team (League)	W	L	Pct.	ERA	WHIP	G	GS	CG	ShO	Hld.	Sv.-Opp.	IP	H	R	ER	HR	BB-IBB	SO	Avg.
1998— Ariz. Rockies (Ariz.)	7	2	.778	2.22	0.98	12	11	1	1	...	0-...	65.0	42	20	16	2	22-0	92	.182
— Portland (N'west)	0	0	...	3.60	1.40	2	2	0	0	...	0-...	10.0	7	4	4	0	7-0	9	.212
1999— Asheville (S. Atl.)	7	10	.412	4.91	1.49	28	28	0	0	...	0-...	143.0	143	87	78	16	70-0	133	.266
2000— Portland (N'west)	4	5	.444	2.61	1.22	13	13	0	0	...	0-...	69.0	54	27	20	1	30-0	41	.214
2001— Casper (Pion.)	3	0	1.000	5.32	1.48	6	3	1	0	...	0-...	23.2	25	15	14	2	10-0	25	.275
— Tri-Cities (NWL)	1	0	1.000	7.20	2.00	1	1	0	0	...	0-...	5.0	7	4	4	0	3-0	2	.304
2002— Asheville (S. Atl.)	6	9	.400	4.96	1.49	30	17	0	0	...	0-...	107.0	115	71	59	13	44-1	88	.276
2003— Fort Worth (Central)	9	4	.692	3.07	1.29	18	18	1	0	...	0-...	111.1	107	45	38	4	37-0	113	.255
2004— Lansing (Midw.)	0	1	.000	1.80	2.20	3	0	0	0	...	0-...	5.0	6	1	1	0	5-0	7	.300
— West Tenn (Sou.)	3	2	.600	1.87	0.89	51	0	0	0	...	21-...	53.0	23	11	11	2	24-0	64	.128
— Iowa (PCL)	0	0	...	2.08	0.69	3	0	0	0	...	1-...	4.1	3	1	1	1	0-0	5	.188
2005— Iowa (PCL)	2	3	.400	1.98	1.01	52	0	0	0	...	25-28	54.2	33	13	12	5	22-2	65	.181
— Chicago (N.L.)	0	0	...	3.00	1.83	6	0	0	0	0	0-0	6.0	2	2	2	0	9-2	3	.118
2006— Pawtucket (Int'l)	4	0	1.000	2.98	1.21	33	0	0	0	1	16-20	45.1	37	16	15	2	18-0	46	.233
— Boston (A.L.)	1	0	1.000	11.77	2.23	10	0	0	0	2	0-0	13.0	14	17	17	1	15-1	8	.292
American League totals (1 year)	1	0	1.000	11.77	2.23	10	0	0	0	2	0-0	13.0	14	17	17	1	15-1	8	.292
National League totals (1 year)	0	0	.000	3.00	1.83	6	0	0	0	0	0-0	6.0	2	2	2	0	9-2	3	.118
Major League totals (2 years)	1	2	.333	9.00	2.11	16	0	0	0	2	0-0	19.0	16	19	19	1	24-3	11	.246

2006 LEFTY-RIGHTY SPLITS

vs.	Avg.	AB	H	2B	3B	HR	RBI	BB	SO	OBP	Slg.	vs.	Avg.	AB	H	2B	3B	HR	RBI	BB	SO	OBP	Slg.
L	.350	20	7	3	0	1	6	9	3	.552	.650	R	.250	28	7	0	1	0	4	6	5	.371	.321

VARGAS, CLAUDIO — P

PERSONAL: Born June 19, 1978, in Valverde Mao, Dominican Republic. ... 6-3/228. ... Throws right, bats right. ... Full name: Claudio Almonte Vargas.
TRANSACTIONS/CAREER NOTES: Signed as a non-drafted free agent by Florida Marlins organization (August 25, 1995). ... Traded by Marlins with OF Cliff Floyd, OF/2B Wilton Guerrero and cash to Montreal Expos for Ps Carl Pavano, Graeme Lloyd and Justin Wayne, IF Mike Mordecai and a player to be named (July 11, 2002); Marlins acquired P Don Levinski to complete deal (August 6, 2002). ... On disabled list (August 6-September 15, 2003). ... Expos franchise transferred to Washington, D.C., and renamed Washington Nationals for 2005 season (December 3, 2004). ... On disabled list (March 16-May 11, 2005); included rehabilitation assignment to New Orleans. ... Claimed on waivers by Arizona Diamondbacks (June 3, 2005). **MISCELLANEOUS NOTES:** Appeared in one game as pinch runner (2004).
CAREER HITTING: 10-for-139 (.072), 3 R, 3 2B, 0 3B, 0 HR, 7 RBI.

Year Team (League)	W	L	Pct.	ERA	WHIP	G	GS	CG	ShO	Hld.	Sv.-Opp.	IP	H	R	ER	HR	BB-IBB	SO	Avg.
1996— Dom. Marlins (DSL)	2	3	.400	3.09	1.44	15	4	0	0	...	0-...	46.2	41	25	16	1	26-...	37	...
1997— Dom. Marlins (DSL)	6	0	1.000	2.50	1.29	13	10	3	1	...	0-...	72.0	62	32	20	3	31-...	81	...
1998— Brevard County (FSL)	0	1	.000	4.66	1.97	2	2	0	0	...	0-...	9.2	15	5	5	1	4-0	9	.366
— GC Marlins (GCL)	0	4	.000	4.08	1.08	5	4	0	0	...	0-...	28.2	24	15	13	1	7-0	27	.226
1999— Kane Co. (Midw.)	5	5	.500	3.88	1.38	19	19	1	0	...	0-...	99.2	97	47	43	8	41-0	88	.255
2000— Brevard County (FSL)	10	5	.667	3.28	1.17	24	23	0	0	...	0-...	145.1	126	64	53	10	44-3	143	.234
— Portland (East.)	1	1	.500	3.60	1.47	3	2	0	0	...	0-...	15.0	16	9	6	1	6-0	13	.276
2001— Portland (East.)	8	9	.471	4.19	1.19	27	27	0	0	...	0-...	159.0	122	77	74	25	67-1	151	.211
2002— Calgary (PCL)	4	11	.267	6.72	1.61	17	16	1	0	...	0-...	76.1	88	63	57	18	35-0	34	.286
— Harrisburg (East.)	2	2	.500	4.64	1.42	8	8	0	0	...	0-...	33.0	38	17	17	2	9-0	34	.189
2003— Edmonton (PCL)	0	0	...	2.79	1.24	2	2	0	0	...	0-...	9.2	7	3	3	1	5-2	12	.189
— Harrisburg (East.)	1	0	1.000	0.75	0.83	2	2	0	0	...	0-...	12.0	7	1	1	0	3-0	13	.171
— Montreal (N.L.)	6	8	.429	4.34	1.33	23	20	0	0	...	0-0	114.0	111	59	55	16	41-5	62	.255
2004— Montreal (N.L.)	5	5	.500	5.25	1.55	45	14	0	0	...	0-0	118.1	120	75	69	26	64-7	89	.266
2005— New Orleans (PCL)	2	2	.500	4.18	1.29	5	5	0	0	...	0-0	28.0	24	13	13	4	12-0	35	.231
— Wash. (N.L.)	0	3	.000	9.24	2.29	4	4	0	0	...	0-0	12.2	22	15	13	4	7-2	15	.373
— Arizona (N.L.)	9	6	.600	4.81	1.37	21	19	0	0	...	0-0	119.2	124	66	64	21	40-3	90	.266
2006— Arizona (N.L.)	12	10	.545	4.83	1.41	31	30	0	0	...	0-0	167.2	185	101	90	27	52-2	123	.274
Major League totals (4 years)	32	32	.500	4.92	1.44	124	87	0	0	...	0-0	532.1	562	316	291	94	204-19	369	.269

2006 LEFTY-RIGHTY SPLITS

vs.	Avg.	AB	H	2B	3B	HR	RBI	BB	SO	OBP	Slg.	vs.	Avg.	AB	H	2B	3B	HR	RBI	BB	SO	OBP	Slg.
L	.275	327	90	19	4	14	46	25	46	.328	.486	R	.272	349	95	23	1	13	44	27	77	.335	.461

VARGAS, JASON — P

PERSONAL: Born February 2, 1983, in Seattle. ... 6-0/215. ... Throws left, bats left. ... Full name: Jason M. Vargas. ... High school: Apple Valley (Calif.). ... College: Long Beach State. **TRANSACTIONS/CAREER NOTES:** Selected by Florida Marlins organization in second round of 2004 free-agent draft. **MISCELLANEOUS NOTES:** Scored a run in only appearance as pinch runner (2005).
CAREER HITTING: 13-for-42 (.310), 4 R, 3 2B, 0 3B, 0 HR, 3 RBI.

Year Team (League)	W	L	Pct.	ERA	WHIP	G	GS	CG	ShO	Hld.	Sv.-Opp.	IP	H	R	ER	HR	BB-IBB	SO	Avg.
2004— Jamestown (NYP)	3	1	.750	1.96	1.16	8	8	0	0	...	0-...	41.1	35	17	9	2	13-0	41	.235
— Greensboro (S. Atl.)	2	1	.667	2.37	0.58	3	3	0	0	...	0-...	19.0	9	5	5	1	2-0	17	.143
2005— Greensboro (S. Atl.)	4	1	.800	0.80	0.77	5	5	0	0	...	0-...	33.2	16	4	3	1	10-0	33	.140
— Jupiter (Fla. St.)	2	3	.400	3.42	1.10	9	9	0	0	...	0-...	55.1	47	24	21	6	14-0	60	.225
— Carolina (Southern)	1	0	1.000	2.84	1.05	3	3	0	0	...	0-...	19.0	13	6	6	3	7-0	25	.194
— Florida (N.L.)	5	5	.500	4.03	1.38	17	13	1	0	...	0-0	73.2	71	34	33	4	31-4	59	.249
2006— Albuquerque (PCL)	3	6	.333	7.43	1.83	13	13	0	0	...	0-...	69.0	98	60	57	11	28-3	51	.348
— Florida (N.L.)	1	2	.333	7.33	1.86	12	5	0	0	...	0-0	43.0	50	39	35	8	30-3	25	.292
Major League totals (2 years)	6	7	.462	5.25	1.56	29	18	1	0	...	0-0	116.2	121	73	68	13	61-7	84	.265

2006 LEFTY-RIGHTY SPLITS

vs.	Avg.	AB	H	2B	3B	HR	RBI	BB	SO	OBP	Slg.	vs.	Avg.	AB	H	2B	3B	HR	RBI	BB	SO	OBP	Slg.
L	.262	42	11	3	0	2	7	4	6	.360	.476	R	.302	129	39	10	2	7	31	26	19	.415	.574

V

VARITEK, JASON — C

PERSONAL: Born April 11, 1972, in Rochester, Mich. ... 6-2/230. ... Bats both, throws right. ... Full name: Jason Andrew Varitek. ... Name pronounced: VAIR-eh-teck. ... High school: Lake Brantley (Longwood, Fla.). ... College: Georgia Tech. **TRANSACTIONS/CAREER NOTES:** Selected by Minnesota Twins organization in first round (21st pick overall) of 1993 free-agent draft; did not sign. ... Selected by Seattle Mariners organization in first round (14th pick overall) of 1994 free-agent draft. ... Traded by Mariners with P Derek Lowe to Boston Red Sox for P Heathcliff Slocumb (July 31, 1997). ... On disabled list (June 8, 2001-remainder of season). ... On suspended list (September 16-20, 2002). ... On disabled list (August 1-September 3, 2006); included rehabilitation assignment to Pawtucket. **HONORS:** Named catcher on the SPORTING NEWS A.L. All-Star team (2005). ... Won A.L. Gold Glove as catcher (2005). ... Named catcher on A.L. Silver Slugger team (2005). **STATISTICAL NOTES:** Hit three home runs in one game (May 20, 2001). ... Career major league grand slams: 2.

Year Team (League)	Pos.	G	AB	R	H	2B	3B	HR	RBI	BB	SO	HBP	GDP	SB-CS	Avg.	OBP	SLG	OPS	E	Avg.
															BATTING				FIELDING	
1995— Port City (Sou.)	C	104	352	42	79	14	3	10	44	61	126	2	8	0-1	.224	.340	.366	.706	8	.988
1996— Port City (Sou.)	C-DH-3B																			
	OF	134	503	63	132	34	1	12	67	66	93	4	14	7-6	.262	.350	.406	.756	5	.993
1997— Tacoma (PCL)	C-DH	87	307	54	78	13	0	15	48	34	71	2	13	0-1	.254	.329	.443	.772	3	.995
— Pawtucket (Int'l)	C	20	66	6	13	5	0	1	5	8	12	0	4	0-0	.197	.284	.318	.602	1	.993
— Boston (A.L.)	C	1	1	0	1	0	0	0	0	0	0	0	0	0-0	1.000	1.000	1.000	2.000	0	1.000
1998— Boston (A.L.)	C-DH	86	221	31	56	13	0	7	33	17	45	2	8	2-2	.253	.309	.407	.716	5	.988
1999— Boston (A.L.)	C-DH	144	483	70	130	39	2	20	76	46	85	2	13	1-2	.269	.330	.482	.813	* 11	.987
2000— Boston (A.L.)	C-DH	139	448	55	111	31	1	10	65	60	84	6	16	1-1	.248	.342	.388	.730	7	.992
2001— Boston (A.L.)	C-DH	51	174	19	51	11	1	7	25	21	35	1	6	0-0	.293	.371	.489	.859	2	.996
2002— Boston (A.L.)	C-DH	132	467	58	124	27	1	10	61	41	95	7	13	4-3	.266	.332	.392	.724	4	.996
2003— Boston (A.L.)	C-DH	142	451	63	123	31	1	25	85	51	106	7	10	3-2	.273	.351	.512	.863	9	.990
2004— Boston (A.L.)	C-DH	137	463	67	137	30	1	18	73	62	126	10	11	10-3	.296	.390	.482	.872	2	.998
2005— Boston (A.L.)	C	133	470	70	132	30	1	22	70	62	117	3	10	2-0	.281	.366	.489	.866	8	.990
2006— Pawtucket (Int'l)		2	7	2	3	0	0	1	1	0	3	0	0	0-0	.429	.429	.857	1.286	0	1.000
— Boston (A.L.)	C	103	365	46	87	19	2	⁻12	55	46	87	2	10	1-2	.238	.325	.400	.725	4	.994
Major League totals (10 years)		1068	3543	479	952	231	10	131	543	406	780	40	97	24-15	.269	.348	.450	.798	52	.993

DIVISION SERIES RECORD

Year Team (League)	Pos.	G	AB	R	H	2B	3B	HR	RBI	BB	SO	HBP	GDP	SB-CS	Avg.	OBP	SLG	OPS	E	Avg.
1998— Boston (A.L.)	C	1	4	0	1	0	0	0	1	0	1	0	0	0-0	.250	.250	.250	.500	0	1.000
1999— Boston (A.L.)	C	5	21	7	5	3	0	1	3	0	4	1	0	0-0	.238	.273	.524	.797	0	1.000
2003— Boston (A.L.)	C	5	14	4	4	0	0	2	2	2	2	0	0	0-0	.286	.375	.714	1.089	0	1.000
2004— Boston (A.L.)	C	3	12	3	2	0	0	1	2	2	5	1	1	0-0	.167	.333	.417	.750	0	1.000
2005— Boston (A.L.)	C	3	10	1	3	0	0	0	1	0	2	0	0	0-0	.300	.300	.300	.600	0	1.000
Division series totals (5 years)		17	61	15	15	3	0	4	9	4	14	2	1	0-0	.246	.313	.492	.805	0	1.000

CHAMPIONSHIP SERIES RECORD

Year Team (League)	Pos.	G	AB	R	H	2B	3B	HR	RBI	BB	SO	HBP	GDP	SB-CS	Avg.	OBP	SLG	OPS	E	Avg.
1999— Boston (A.L.)	C	5	20	1	4	1	1	.1	1	1	4	0	1	0-0	.200	.238	.500	.738	1	.978
2003— Boston (A.L.)	C	6	20	4	6	2	0	2	3	1	5	0	0	0-0	.300	.333	.700	1.033	0	1.000
2004— Boston (A.L.)	C	7	28	5	9	1	0	2	7	2	6	0	0	0-0	.321	.355	.571	.926	0	1.000
Champ. series totals (3 years)		18	68	10	19	4	1	5	11	4	15	0	1	0-0	.279	.315	.588	.903	1	.993

WORLD SERIES RECORD

Year Team (League)	Pos.	G	AB	R	H	2B	3B	HR	RBI	BB	SO	HBP	GDP	SB-CS	Avg.	OBP	SLG	OPS	E	Avg.
2004— Boston (A.L.)	C	4	13	2	2	0	0	1	1	4	1	0	0	0-0	.154	.267	.308	.574	0	1.000

ALL-STAR GAME RECORD

		G	AB	R	H	2B	3B	HR	RBI	BB	SO	HBP	GDP	SB-CS	Avg.	OBP	SLG	OPS	E	Avg.
All-Star Game totals (1 year)		1	1	1	1	0	0	0	0	0	0	0	0	0-0	1.000	1.000	1.000	2.000	0	1.000

2006 LEFTY-RIGHTY SPLITS

vs.	Avg.	AB	H	2B	3B	HR	RBI	BB	SO	OBP	Slg.	vs.	Avg.	AB	H	2B	3B	HR	RBI	BB	SO	OBP	Slg.
L	.229	131	30	7	1	4	15	13	35	.299	.389	R	.244	234	57	12	1	8	40	33	52	.339	.406

VAZQUEZ, JAVIER — P

PERSONAL: Born July 25, 1976, in Ponce, Puerto Rico. ... 6-2/205. ... Throws right, bats right. ... Full name: Javier Carlos Vazquez. ... Name pronounced: VAS-kez. ... High school: Colegio de Ponce (Ponce, Puerto Rico). **TRANSACTIONS/CAREER NOTES:** Selected by Montreal Expos organization in fifth round of 1994 free-agent draft. ... On suspended list (July 23-27, 1998). ... Traded by Expos to New York Yankees for 1B Nick Johnson, OF Juan Rivera and P Randy Choate (December 16, 2003). ... Traded by Yankees with P Brad Halsey, C Dioner Navarro and cash to Arizona Diamondbacks for P Randy Johnson (January 11, 2005). ... Traded by Diamondbacks with cash to Chicago White Sox for Ps Orlando Hernandez, Luis Vizcaino and OF Chris Young (December 20, 2005).

CAREER HITTING: 92-for-427 (.215), 32 R, 10 2B, 2 3B, 1 HR, 24 RBI.

Year Team (League)	W	L	Pct.	ERA	WHIP	G	GS	CG	ShO	Hld.	Sv.-Opp.	IP	H	R	ER	HR	BB-IBB	SO	Avg.
1994— GC Expos (GCL)	5	2	.714	2.53	0.77	15	11	1	1	...	0-...	67.2	37	25	19	0	15-0	56	.155
1995— Albany (S. Atl.)	6	6	.500	5.08	1.52	21	21	1	0	...	0-...	102.2	109	67	58	8	47-0	87	.273
1996— Delmarva (S. Atl.)	14	3	.824	2.68	1.19	27	27	1	0	...	0-...	164.1	138	64	49	12	57-0	173	.229
1997— W.P. Beach (FSL)	6	3	.667	2.16	1.12	19	19	1	0	...	0-...	112.2	98	40	27	8	28-0	100	.231
— Harrisburg (East.)	4	0	1.000	1.07	0.64	6	6	1	0	...	0-...	42.0	15	5	5	2	12-0	47	.107
1998— Montreal (N.L.)	5	15	.250	6.06	1.53	33	32	0	0	0	0-0	172.1	196	121	116	31	68-2	139	.292
1999— Montreal (N.L.)	9	8	.529	5.00	1.33	26	26	3	1	0	0-0	154.2	154	98	86	20	52-4	113	.255
— Ottawa (Int'l)	4	2	.667	4.85	1.43	7	7	0	0	...	0-...	42.2	45	24	23	7	16-0	46	.280
2000— Montreal (N.L.)	11	9	.550	4.05	1.42	33	33	2	1	0	0-0	217.2	247	104	98	24	61-10	196	.286
2001— Montreal (N.L.)	16	11	.593	3.42	1.08	32	32	5	• 3	0	0-0	223.2	197	92	85	24	44-4	208	.235
2002— Montreal (N.L.)	10	13	.435	3.91	1.27	34	34	2	0	0	0-0	230.1	* 243	111	100	28	49-6	179	.271
2003— Montreal (N.L.)	13	12	.520	3.24	1.11	34	34	4	1	0	0-0	230.2	198	93	83	28	57-5	241	.229
2004— New York (A.L.)	14	10	.583	4.91	1.29	32	32	0	0	0	0-0	198.0	195	114	108	33	60-3	150	.255
2005— Arizona (N.L.)	11	15	.423	4.42	1.25	33	33	3	1	0	0-0	215.2	223	112	106	35	46-4	192	.266
2006— Chicago (A.L.)	11	12	.478	4.84	1.29	33	32	1	0	0	0-0	202.2	206	116	109	23	56-2	184	.259
American League totals (2 years)	25	22	.532	4.87	1.29	65	64	1	0	0	0-0	400.2	401	230	217	56	116-5	334	.257
National League totals (7 years)	75	83	.475	4.20	1.27	225	224	19	7	0	0-0	1445.0	1458	731	674	190	377-35	1268	.261
Major League totals (9 years)	100	105	.488	4.34	1.27	290	288	20	7	0	0-0	1845.2	1859	961	891	246	493-40	1602	.261

DIVISION SERIES RECORD

Year Team (League)	W	L	Pct.	ERA	WHIP	G	GS	CG	ShO	Hld.	Sv.-Opp.	IP	H	R	ER	HR	BB-IBB	SO	Avg.
2004— New York (A.L.)	0	0	...	9.00	1.80	1	1	0	0	0	0-0	5.0	7	5	5	1	2-0	6	.368

CHAMPIONSHIP SERIES RECORD

Year Team (League)	W	L	Pct.	ERA	WHIP	G	GS	CG	ShO	Hld.	Sv.-Opp.	IP	H	R	ER	HR	BB-IBB	SO	Avg.
2004— New York (A.L.)	1	0	1.000	9.95	2.53	2	0	0	0	0	0-0	6.1	9	7	7	3	7-0	6	.360

ALL-STAR GAME RECORD

	W	L	Pct.	ERA	WHIP	G	GS	CG	ShO	Hld.	Sv.-Opp.	IP	H	R	ER	HR	BB-IBB	SO	Avg.
All-Star Game totals (1 year)	0	0	...	0.00	0.00	1	0	0	0	0	0-0	1.0	0	0	0	0	0-0	2	.000

2006 LEFTY-RIGHTY SPLITS

vs.	Avg.	AB	H	2B	3B	HR	RBI	BB	SO	OBP	Slg.	vs.	Avg.	AB	H	2B	3B	HR	RBI	BB	SO	OBP	Slg.
L	.256	359	92	20	2	13	42	31	76	.321	.432	R	.261	436	114	22	2	10	56	25	108	.316	.390

V

VAZQUEZ, RAMON — IF

PERSONAL: Born August 21, 1976, in Aibonito, Puerto Rico. ... 5-11/170. ... Bats left, throws right. ... Full name: Ramon Luis Vazquez. ... Name pronounced: VAS-kez. ... Junior college: Indian Hills (Iowa) Community College. **TRANSACTIONS/CAREER NOTES:** Selected by Seattle Mariners organization in 27th round of 1995 free-agent draft. ... Traded by Mariners with P Brett Tomko and C Tom Lampkin to San Diego Padres for C Ben Davis, P Wascar Serrano and SS Alex Arias (December 11, 2001). ... On disabled list (June 1-July 7, 2003); included rehabilitation assignment to Lake Elsinore. ... On disabled list (May 20-June 20, 2004); included rehabilitation assignment to Portland. ... Traded by Padres with OF Jay Payton, P David Pauley and cash to Boston Red Sox for OF Dave Roberts (December 20, 2004). ... Traded by Red Sox to Cleveland Indians for SS Alex Cora (July 7, 2005). **STATISTICAL NOTES:** Career major league grand slams: 1.

2006 GAMES PLAYED BY POSITION (MLB): 3B—14, 2B—7, SS—7.

Year	Team (League)	Pos.	G	AB	R	H	2B	3B	HR	RBI	BB	SO	HBP	GDP	SB-CS	Avg.	OBP	SLG	OPS	E	Avg.
1995—	Ariz. Mariners (Ariz.)	2B-3B-SS	39	141	20	29	3	1	0	11	19	27	2	2	4-3	.206	.309	.241	.550	11	.941
1996—	Everett (N'west)	SS	33	126	25	35	5	2	1	18	26	26	1	3	7-2	.278	.392	.373	.765	20	.873
—	Tacoma (PCL)	2B-SS	18	49	7	11	2	1	0	4	4	12	1	2	0-0	.224	.296	.306	.602	1	.985
—	Wisconsin (Midw.)	3B	3	10	1	3	1	0	0	1	2	2	0	1	0-0	.300	.417	.400	.817	2	.818
1997—	Wisconsin (Midw.)	SS	131	479	79	129	25	5	8	49	78	93	3	8	16-10	.269	.373	.392	.765	35	.935
1998—	Lancaster (Calif.)	SS	121	468	77	129	26	4	2	72	81	66	2	6	15-11	.276	.384	.361	.745	31	.944
1999—	New Haven (East.)	2B-3B-SS	127	438	58	113	27	3	5	45	62	77	5	11	8-1	.258	.354	.368	.722	31	.942
2000—	New Haven (East.)	SS	124	405	58	116	25	4	8	59	52	76	2	6	1-6	.286	.367	.427	.794	22	.961
2001—	Tacoma (PCL)	SS	127	466	85	140	28	1	10	79	76	84	1	13	9-7	.300	.397	.429	.827	12	.979
—	Seattle (A.L.)																				
		DH	17	35	5	8	0	0	0	4	0	3	0	0	0-0	.229	.222	.229	.451	1	.969
2002—	San Diego (N.L.)	2B-SS-3B	128	423	50	116	21	5	2	32	45	79	1	6	7-2	.274	.344	.362	.706	7	.986
2003—	Lake Elsinore (Calif.)	SS	5	16	3	3	0	0	1	4	3	3	1	1	0-1	.188	.350	.375	.725	1	.950
—	San Diego (N.L.)	SS-3B-2B	116	422	56	110	17	4	3	30	52	88	2	4	10-3	.261	.342	.341	.684	14	.968
2004—	Portland (PCL)	2B-3B-SS	53	184	36	55	21	1	8	34	33	28	0	2	2-0	.299	.402	.554	.956	2	.991
—	San Diego (N.L.)	SS-2B-3B																			
		1B	52	115	12	27	3	2	1	13	11	24	0	2	1-1	.235	.297	.322	.619	1	.991
2005—	Boston (A.L.)	SS-3B-2B																			
		DH	27	61	6	12	2	0	0	4	3	14	0	0	0-0	.197	.234	.230	.464	3	.950
—	Buffalo (Int'l)	SS-2B-3B	21	84	13	18	3	1	0	4	7	16	0	2	1-1	.214	.275	.274	.549	4	.959
—	Cleveland (A.L.)	2B-SS	12	24	1	6	3	0	0	1	2	3	0	0	0-0	.250	.308	.375	.683	0	1.000
2006—	Cleveland (A.L.)	3B-2B-SS	34	67	11	14	2	0	1	8	6	18	0	3	0-0	.209	.267	.284	.550	4	.949
—	Buffalo (Int'l)		28	99	19	24	2	1	2	11	22	27	0		2-1	.242	.377	.343	.720	3	.977
American League totals (3 years)			**90**	**187**	**23**	**40**	**7**	**0**	**1**	**17**	**11**	**38**	**0**	**3**	**0-0**	**.214**	**.254**	**.267**	**.521**	**8**	**.961**
National League totals (3 years)			**296**	**960**	**118**	**253**	**41**	**11**	**6**	**75**	**108**	**191**	**3**	**12**	**18-6**	**.264**	**.338**	**.348**	**.686**	**22**	**.979**
Major League totals (6 years)			**386**	**1147**	**141**	**293**	**48**	**11**	**7**	**92**	**119**	**229**	**3**	**15**	**18-6**	**.255**	**.324**	**.335**	**.659**	**30**	**.976**

DIVISION SERIES RECORD

Year	Team (League)	Pos.	G	AB	R	H	2B	3B	HR	RBI	BB	SO	HBP	GDP	SB-CS	Avg.	OBP	SLG	OPS	E	Avg.
2001—	Seattle (A.L.)		Did not play.																		

CHAMPIONSHIP SERIES RECORD

Year	Team (League)	Pos.	G	AB	R	H	2B	3B	HR	RBI	BB	SO	HBP	GDP	SB-CS	Avg.	OBP	SLG	OPS	E	Avg.
2001—	Seattle (A.L.)		Did not play.																		

2006 LEFTY-RIGHTY SPLITS

vs.	Avg.	AB	H	2B	3B	HR	RBI	BB	SO	OBP	Slg.	vs.	Avg.	AB	H	2B	3B	HR	RBI	BB	SO	OBP	Slg.
L	.286	7	2	1	0	0	0	0	3	.286	.429	R	.200	60	12	1	0	1	8	6	15	.265	.267

VENAFRO, MIKE — P

PERSONAL: Born August 2, 1973, in Takoma Park, Md. ... 5-10/180. ... Throws left, bats left. ... Full name: Michael Robert Venafro. ... Name pronounced: VEN-a-fro. ... High school: Paul VI (Fairfax, Va.). ... College: James Madison (Va.). **TRANSACTIONS/CAREER NOTES:** Selected by Texas Rangers organization in 29th round of 1995 free-agent draft. ... Traded by Rangers with 1B Carlos Pena to Oakland Athletics for 1B Jason Hart, P Mario Ramos, C Gerald Laird and OF Ryan Ludwick (January 14, 2002). ... Signed as a free agent by Atlanta Braves (January 13, 2003). ... Released by Braves (March 26, 2003). ... Signed by Tampa Bay Devil Rays (March 28, 2003). ... Released by Devil Rays (June 30, 2003). ... Signed by Houston Astros organization (July 10, 2003). ... Released by Astros (August 29, 2003). ... Signed by Kansas City Royals organization (November 21, 2003). ... Traded by Royals to Los Angeles Dodgers for P Elvin Nina (August 10, 2004). ... Signed as a free agent by Cincinnati Reds organization (April 14, 2006). ... Released by Reds (July 17, 2006). ... Signed by Colorado Rockies organization (July 21, 2006).

CAREER HITTING: 0-for-0 (.000), 0 R, 0 2B, 0 3B, 0 HR, 0 RBI.

Year	Team (League)	W	L	Pct.	ERA	WHIP	G	GS	CG	ShO	Hld.	Sv.-Opp.	IP	H	R	ER	HR	BB-IBB	SO	Avg.
1995—	Hudson Valley (NYP)	9	1	.900	2.13	1.14	32	0	0	0	...	2-...	50.2	37	13	12	0	21-2	32	.216
1996—	Char., S.C. (SAL)	1	3	.250	3.51	1.32	50	0	0	0	...	19-...	59.0	57	27	23	0	21-3	62	.250
1997—	Charlotte (Fla. St.)	4	2	.667	3.43	1.61	35	0	0	0	...	10-...	44.2	51	17	17	2	21-1	35	.305
—	Tulsa (Texas)	0	1	.000	3.45	1.60	11	0	0	0	...	1-...	15.2	13	12	6	1	12-0	13	.220
1998—	Tulsa (Texas)	3	4	.429	3.10	1.30	46	0	0	0	...	14-...	52.1	42	21	18	5	26-0	45	.219
—	Okla. City (PCL)	0	0	...	6.35	1.71	13	0	0	0	...	1-...	17.0	19	12	12	3	10-0	15	.271
1999—	Oklahoma (PCL)	0	0	...	5.40	1.37	6	0	0	0	...	1-...	11.2	16	7	7	2	0-0	7	.348
—	Texas (A.L.)	3	2	.600	3.29	1.24	65	0	0	0	19	0-1	68.1	63	29	25	4	22-0	37	.251
2000—	Texas (A.L.)	3	1	.750	3.83	1.51	77	0	0	0	17	1-2	56.1	64	27	24	2	21-4	32	.295
2001—	Texas (A.L.)	5	5	.500	4.80	1.37	70	0	0	0	21	4-8	60.0	54	35	32	2	28-4	29	.240
2002—	Oakland (A.L.)	2	2	.500	4.62	1.59	47	0	0	0	15	0-0	37.0	45	22	19	5	14-2	16	.308
—	Sacramento (PCL)	0	1	.000	6.97	1.26	8	0	0	0	...	0-...	10.1	12	8	8	2	1-0	14	.293
2003—	Tampa Bay (A.L.)	1	0	1.000	4.74	1.42	24	0	0	0	4	0-0	19.0	24	10	10	1	3-0	9	.308
—	New Orleans (PCL)	2	1	.667	3.54	1.40	23	0	0	0	...	0-...	20.0	35	11	11	0	5-1	11	.310
2004—	Omaha (PCL)	2	4	.333	4.37	1.54	35	0	0	0	...	2-...	57.2	70	30	28	8	19-2	41	.308
—	Las Vegas (PCL)	0	1	.000	7.11	1.58	6	0	0	0	...	1-...	6.1	8	5	5	0	2-0	4	.320
—	Los Angeles (N.L.)	0	0	...	4.00	1.56	17	0	0	0	2	0-0	9.0	11	5	4	1	3-1	6	.306
2005—	Las Vegas (PCL)	0	1	.000	6.85	2.13	53	0	0	0	11	1-3	44.2	60	38	34	0	35-5	24	.335
—	Louisville (Int'l)	0	0	...	2.45	1.23	36	0	0	0	9	2-3	22.0	19	6	6	0	8-3	18	.232
2006—	Colo. Springs (PCL)	3	1	.750	2.20	0.92	20	0	0	0	8	0-2	16.1	10	4	4	1	5-0	10	.175
—	Colorado (N.L.)	1	0	1.000	2.45	1.64	7	0	0	0	0	0-0	3.2	3	1	1	0	3-2	2	.250
American League totals (5 years)		**14**	**10**	**.583**	**4.11**	**1.40**	**283**	**0**	**0**	**0**	**76**	**5-11**	**240.2**	**250**	**123**	**110**	**14**	**88-10**	**123**	**.273**
National League totals (2 years)		**1**	**0**	**1.000**	**3.55**	**1.58**	**24**	**0**	**0**	**0**	**2**	**0-0**	**12.2**	**14**	**6**	**5**	**1**	**6-1**	**8**	**.292**
Major League totals (7 years)		**15**	**10**	**.600**	**4.09**	**1.41**	**307**	**0**	**0**	**0**	**78**	**5-11**	**253.1**	**264**	**129**	**115**	**15**	**94-11**	**131**	**.274**

DIVISION SERIES RECORD

Year	Team (League)	W	L	Pct.	ERA	WHIP	G	GS	CG	ShO	Hld.	Sv.-Opp.	IP	H	R	ER	HR	BB-IBB	SO	Avg.
1999—	Texas (A.L.)	0	0	...	0.00	3.00	2	0	0	0	0	0-0	1.0	2	2	0	0	1-0	1	.333
2004—	Los Angeles (N.L.)	0	0	...	0.00	0.00	2	0	0	0	0	0-0	0.2	0	0	0	0	0-0	1	.000
Division series totals (2 years)		**0**	**0**	**...**	**0.00**	**1.80**	**4**	**0**	**0**	**0**	**0**	**0-0**	**1.2**	**2**	**2**	**0**	**0**	**1-0**	**2**	**.250**

V

vs.	Avg.	AB	H	2B	3B	HR	RBI	BB	SO	OBP	Slg.	vs.	Avg.	AB	H	2B	3B	HR	RBI	BB	SO	OBP	Slg.
L	.200	5	1	0	0	0	1	2	2	.429	.200	R	.286	7	2	1	0	0	2	1	0	.375	.429

VENTO, MIKE — OF

PERSONAL: Born May 25, 1978, in Albuquerque, N.M. ... 6-0/195. ... Bats right, throws right. ... Full name: Michael Vento. ... High school: Cibola (N.M.). ... Junior college: New Mexico, then Santa Ana (Calif.) J.C. **TRANSACTIONS/CAREER NOTES:** Selected by New York Yankees organization in 40th round of 1997 free-agent draft. ... Signed as a free agent by Washington Nationals organization (December 1, 2005).

2006 GAMES PLAYED BY POSITION (MLB): OF—8.

Year	Team (League)	Pos.	G	AB	R	H	2B	3B	HR	RBI	BB	SO	HBP	GDP	SB-CS	Avg.	OBP	SLG	OPS	E	Avg.
1998— Oneonta (NYP)		OF	43	148	25	45	9	3	1	23	14	28	5	1	8-3	.304	.379	.426	.805	0	1.000
1999— Tampa (Fla. St.)		OF-1B	70	255	37	66	10	1	7	28	17	69	3	1	2-3	.259	.310	.388	.698	1	.990
— Greensboro (S. Atl.)		OF	40	148	20	37	11	1	3	16	14	46	2	1	3-1	.250	.321	.399	.720	2	.938
2000— Tampa (Fla. St.)		OF	10	30	1	5	0	0	1	4	4	12	1	0	1-0	.167	.278	.267	.545	0	1.000
— Greensboro (S. Atl.)		OF	84	318	49	83	15	2	6	52	47	66	11	11	13-8	.261	.372	.377	.749	5	.956
2001— Tampa (Fla. St.)		OF-OF	130	457	71	137	20	10	20	87	45	88	9	9	13-10	.300	.372	.519	.891	12	.945
2002— Norwich (East.)		OF-OF	64	227	29	54	16	2	4	26	25	49	1	6	3-3	.238	.314	.379	.693	3	.977
2003— Trenton (East.)		OF	81	314	46	95	19	3	9	56	22	52	5	6	4-4	.303	.354	.468	.822	5	.966
— Columbus (Int'l)		OF	51	184	28	56	14	1	5	31	14	36	3	6	1-2	.304	.363	.473	.836	1	.992
2004— Columbus (Int'l)		OF	122	451	64	124	28	1	15	72	34	77	9	8	2-3	.275	.333	.441	.774	4	.982
2005— Columbus (Int'l)		OF-DH	130	501	62	146	37	2	12	84	49	96	13	13	1-4	.291	.365	.445	.810	8	.982
— New York (A.L.)		OF	2	2	0	0	0	0	0	0	0	1	0	0	0-0	.000	.000	.000	.000	0	1.000
2006— New Orleans (PCL)			62	217	34	74	14	0	7	33	20	35	1	5	3-4	.341	.396	.502	.898	2	.986
— Wash. (N.L.)		OF	9	18	3	5	1	0	1	4	4	5	0	0	0-0	.278	.409	.333	.742	0	1.000
— GC Nationals (GCL)			6	20	3	5	0	0	1	4	4	1	0	0	0-0	.250	.375	.400	.775	0	1.000
American League totals (1 year)			2	2	0	0	0	0	0	0	0	1	0	0	0-0	.000	.000	.000	.000	0	1.000
National League totals (1 year)			9	18	3	5	1	0	1	4	4	5	0	0	0-0	.278	.409	.333	.742	0	1.000
Major League totals (2 years)			11	20	3	5	1	0	1	4	4	6	0	0	0-0	.250	.375	.300	.675	0	1.000

2006 LEFTY-RIGHTY SPLITS

vs.	Avg.	AB	H	2B	3B	HR	RBI	BB	SO	OBP	Slg.	vs.	Avg.	AB	H	2B	3B	HR	RBI	BB	SO	OBP	Slg.
L	.250	8	2	1	0	0	0	2	1	.400	.375	R	.300	10	3	0	0	0	1	2	4	.417	.300

VERAS, JOSE — P

PERSONAL: Born October 20, 1980, in Santo Domingo, Dominican Republic. ... 6-5/230. ... Throws right, bats right. ... Full name: Jose Enger Veras. **TRANSACTIONS/CAREER NOTES:** Signed as a non-drafted free agent by Tampa Bay Devil Rays organization (January 19, 1998). ... Signed as a free agent by Texas Rangers organization (November 15, 2004). ... Signed as a free agent by New York Yankees organization (January 6, 2006).

CAREER HITTING: 0-for-0 (.000), 0 R, 0 2B, 0 3B, 0 HR, 0 RBI.

Year	Team (League)	W	L	Pct.	ERA	WHIP	G	GS	CG	ShO	Hld.	Sv.-Opp.	IP	H	R	ER	HR	BB-IBB	SO	Avg.
1998— GC Devil Rays (GCL)		1	1	.500	6.75	1.94	5	4	0	0	...	0-...	16.0	19	14	12	1	12-0	19	.288
1999— Princeton (Appal.)		3	5	.375	7.12	2.04	14	14	0	0	...	0-...	60.2	74	57	48	5	50-1	48	.312
2000— Char., S.C. (SAL)		8	8	.500	4.81	1.56	20	20	1	0	...	0-...	106.2	125	74	57	7	41-0	102	.285
2001— Bakersfield (Calif.)		9	8	.529	4.53	1.42	27	27	0	0	...	0-...	153.0	163	104	77	13	55-0	138	.272
2002— Hudson Valley (NYP)		0	0	...	0.00	1.00	2	2	0	0	...	0-...	7.0	2	0	0	0	5-0	7	.087
— Bakersfield (Calif.)		3	4	.429	5.34	1.81	11	11	0	0	...	0-...	59.0	77	44	35	10	30-0	57	.316
2003— Orlando (South.)		6	9	.400	3.45	1.24	27	22	1	1	...	0-...	130.1	108	59	50	11	53-0	118	.222
— Durham (Int'l)		0	0	...	8.44	1.88	3	0	0	0	...	0-...	5.1	9	5	5	2	1-0	3	.360
2004— Montgom. (Sou.)		1	0	1.000	6.30	1.70	3	3	0	0	...	0-...	10.0	10	7	7	2	7-0	6	.286
— Durham (Int'l)		6	5	.545	5.23	1.59	30	10	0	0	...	0-...	84.1	101	55	49	9	33-3	63	.294
2005— Oklahoma (PCL)		3	5	.375	3.79	1.56	57	0	0	0	2	24-29	61.2	63	27	26	4	33-0	72	.266
2006— Columbus (Int'l)		5	3	.625	2.41	1.14	50	0	0	0	4	21-24	59.2	49	17	16	3	19-2	68	.224
— New York (A.L.)		0	0	...	4.09	1.18	12	0	0	0	1	1-1	11.0	8	5	5	2	5-0	6	.211
Major League totals (1 year)		0	0	...	4.09	1.18	12	0	0	0	1	1-1	11.0	8	5	5	2	5-0	6	.211

2006 LEFTY-RIGHTY SPLITS

vs.	Avg.	AB	H	2B	3B	HR	RBI	BB	SO	OBP	Slg.	vs.	Avg.	AB	H	2B	3B	HR	RBI	BB	SO	OBP	Slg.
L	.188	16	3	0	0	1	4	2	4	.278	.375	R	.227	22	5	1	0	1	3	3	2	.320	.409

VERLANDER, JUSTIN — P

PERSONAL: Born February 20, 1983, in Manakin-Sabot, Va. ... 6-5/200. ... Throws right, bats right. ... Full name: Justin Brooks Verlander. ... High school: Goochland (Va.). ... College: Old Dominion. **TRANSACTIONS/CAREER NOTES:** Selected by Detroit Tigers organization in first round (second pick overall) of 2004 free-agent draft. **HONORS:** Named A.L. Rookie of the Year by the SPORTING NEWS (2006). ... Named A.L. Rookie of the Year by the Baseball Writers' Association of America (2006).

CAREER HITTING: 0-for-1 (.000), 0 R, 0 2B, 0 3B, 0 HR, 0 RBI.

Year	Team (League)	W	L	Pct.	ERA	WHIP	G	GS	CG	ShO	Hld.	Sv.-Opp.	IP	H	R	ER	HR	BB-IBB	SO	Avg.
2005— Lakeland (Fla. St.)		9	2	.818	1.67	1.03	13	13	2	0	0	0-0	86.0	70	19	16	3	19-0	104	.230
— Detroit (A.L.)		0	2	.000	7.15	1.76	2	2	0	0	0	0-0	11.1	15	9	9	1	5-0	7	.313
— Erie (East.)		2	0	1.000	0.28	0.55	7	7	0	0	0	0-0	32.2	11	1	1	1	7-0	32	.103
2006— Detroit (A.L.)		17	9	.654	3.63	1.33	30	30	1	1	0	0-0	186.0	187	78	75	21	60-1	124	.266
Major League totals (2 years)		17	11	.607	3.83	1.35	32	32	1	1	0	0-0	197.1	202	87	84	22	65-1	131	.269

DIVISION SERIES RECORD

Year	Team (League)	W	L	Pct.	ERA	WHIP	G	GS	CG	ShO	Hld.	Sv.-Opp.	IP	H	R	ER	HR	BB-IBB	SO	Avg.
2006— Detroit (A.L.)		0	0	...	5.06	2.06	1	1	0	0	0	0-0	5.1	7	3	3	1	4-0	5	.318

CHAMPIONSHIP SERIES RECORD

Year	Team (League)	W	L	Pct.	ERA	WHIP	G	GS	CG	ShO	Hld.	Sv.-Opp.	IP	H	R	ER	HR	BB-IBB	SO	Avg.
2006— Detroit (A.L.)		1	0	1.000	6.75	1.50	1	1	0	0	0	0-0	5.1	7	4	4	2	1-0	6	.304

WORLD SERIES RECORD

Year	Team (League)	W	L	Pct.	ERA	WHIP	G	GS	CG	ShO	Hld.	Sv.-Opp.	IP	H	R	ER	HR	BB-IBB	SO	Avg.
2006— Detroit (A.L.)		0	2	.000	5.73	1.55	2	2	0	0	0	0-0	11.0	12	10	7	2	5-0	12	.273

2006 LEFTY-RIGHTY SPLITS

vs.	Avg.	AB	H	2B	3B	HR	RBI	BB	SO	OBP	Slg.	vs.	Avg.	AB	H	2B	3B	HR	RBI	BB	SO	OBP	Slg.
L	.279	340	95	15	4	13	41	33	58	.343	.462	R	.253	363	92	18	0	8	30	27	66	.313	.369

V

VICTORINO, SHANE — OF

PERSONAL: Born November 30, 1980, in Wailuku, Hawaii. ... 5-9/160. ... Bats both, throws right. ... Full name: Shane Patrick Victorino. ... High school: St. Anthony (Wailuku, Hawaii). **TRANSACTIONS/CAREER NOTES:** Selected by Los Angeles Dodgers organization in sixth round of 1999 free-agent draft. ... Selected by San Diego Padres from Dodgers organization in Rule 5 major league draft (December 16, 2002). ... Claimed on waivers by Dodgers (May 28, 2003). ... Selected by Philadelphia Phillies from Dodgers organization in Rule 5 major league draft (December 13, 2004).

2006 GAMES PLAYED BY POSITION (MLB): OF—122.

Year	Team (League)	Pos.	G	AB	R	H	2B	3B	HR	RBI	BB	SO	HBP	GDP	SB-CS	Avg.	OBP	SLG	OPS	E	Avg.
1999— Great Falls (Pio.)		OF	55	225	53	63	7	6	2	25	20	31	0	3	20-5	.280	.335	.391	.726	2	.986
2000— Yakima (N'west)		2B-2B-SS																			
		SS	61	236	32	58	7	2	2	20	20	44	3	3	21-9	.246	.310	.318	.628	11	.964
2001— Wilmington (S. Atl.)		OF	112	435	71	123	21	9	4	32	36	61	5	3	47-13	.283	.344	.400	.744	6	.976
— Vero Beach (FSL)		OF-OF	2	6	2	1	0	0	0	0	3	1	0	0	0-0	.167	.444	.167	.611	0	1.000
2002— Jacksonville (Sou.)		OF-OF	122	481	61	124	15	1	4	34	47	49	4	6	45-16	.258	.328	.318	.646	4	.986
2003— San Diego (N.L.)		OF	36	73	8	11	2	0	0	4	7	17	1	5	7-2	.151	.232	.178	.410	0	1.000
— Jacksonville (Sou.)		OF-OF	66	266	37	75	9	4	2	15	21	41	3	3	16-7	.282	.340	.368	.708	4	.978
— Las Vegas (PCL)		OF-OF-2B	11	41	6	16	1	2	1	9	1	5	0	1	0-1	.390	.395	.585	.980	1	.966
2004— Las Vegas (PCL)		OF-2B	55	200	28	47	9	1	3	20	11	37	1	3	7-2	.235	.278	.335	.613	2	.959
— Jacksonville (Sou.)		OF	75	293	70	96	13	7	16	43	20	64	5	0	9-7	.328	.375	.584	.959	2	.000
2005— Scran./W.B. (I.L.)		OF	126	494	93	153	25	16	18	70	51	74	5	4	17-9	.310	.377	.534	.912	6	.991
— Philadelphia (N.L.)		OF	21	17	5	5	0	0	2	8	0	3	0	0	0-0	.294	.263	.647	.910	0	
2006— Philadelphia (N.L.)		OF	153	415	70	119	19	8	6	46	24	54	14	5	4-3	.287	.346	.414	.760	1	1.000
Major League totals (3 years)			210	505	83	135	21	8	8	58	31	74	15	10	11-5	.267	.326	.388	.714	0	1.000

2006 LEFTY-RIGHTY SPLITS

vs.	Avg.	AB	H	2B	3B	HR	RBI	BB	SO	OBP	Slg.	vs.	Avg.	AB	H	2B	3B	HR	RBI	BB	SO	OBP	Slg.
L	.273	132	36	9	1	3	16	5	16	.340	.424	R	.293	283	83	10	7	3	30	19	38	.349	.410

VIDRO, JOSE — 2B

PERSONAL: Born August 27, 1974, in Mayaguez, Puerto Rico. ... 5-11/193. ... Bats both, throws right. ... Full name: Jose Angel Vidro. ... Name pronounced: VEE-dro. ... High school: Blanco Morales (Sabana Grande, Puerto Rico). **TRANSACTIONS/CAREER NOTES:** Selected by Montreal Expos organization in sixth round of 1992 free-agent draft. ... On disabled list (May 20-June 12, 2001; and August 26, 2004-remainder of season). ... Expos franchise transferred to Washington, D.C., and renamed Washington Nationals for 2005 season (December 3, 2004). ... On disabled list (May 5-July 5, 2005); included rehabilitation assignment to Potomac. ... On disabled list (July 25-August 18, 2006); included rehabilitation assignments to Potomac and Harrisburg. **HONORS:** Named second baseman on N.L. Silver Slugger team (2003). **STATISTICAL NOTES:** Career major league grand slams: 3.

2006 GAMES PLAYED BY POSITION (MLB): 2B—107, 1B—8, DH—2.

Year	Team (League)	Pos.	G	AB	R	H	2B	3B	HR	RBI	BB	SO	HBP	GDP	SB-CS	Avg.	OBP	SLG	OPS	E	Avg.
1992— GC Expos (GCL)		2B	54	200	29	66	6	2	4	31	16	31	0	5	10-1	.330	.376	.440	.816	4	.982
1993— Burlington (Midw.)		2B	76	287	39	69	19	0	2	34	28	54	1	7	3-2	.240	.317	.328	.644	7	.974
1994— W.P. Beach (FSL)		2B	125	465	57	124	30	2	4	49	51	56	5	5	8-2	.267	.344	.366	.709	20	.964
1995— W.P. Beach (FSL)		IF	44	163	20	53	15	2	3	24	8	21	2	5	0-1	.325	.360	.497	.857	4	.981
— Harrisburg (East.)		IF	64	246	33	64	16	2	4	38	20	37	1	5	7-7	.260	.315	.390	.705	9	.966
1996— Harrisburg (East.)		IF	126	452	57	117	25	3	18	82	29	71	2	6	3-1	.259	.300	.447	.747	15	.964
1997— Ottawa (Int'l)		3B-2B-DH	73	279	40	90	17	0	13	47	22	40	1	6	2-0	.323	.370	.523	.894	8	.967
— Montreal (N.L.)		3B-2B-DH	67	169	19	42	12	1	2	17	11	20	2	1	1-0	.249	.297	.367	.664	4	.955
1998— Montreal (N.L.)		2B-3B	83	205	24	45	12	0	0	18	27	33	4	5	2-2	.220	.318	.278	.596	6	.972
— Ottawa (Int'l)		2B-3B-DH	63	235	35	68	14	2	2	32	24	25	4	4	5-2	.289	.361	.391	.752	6	.973
1999— Montreal (N.L.)		2B-1B-OF																			
		3B	140	494	67	150	45	2	12	59	29	51	4	12	0-4	.304	.346	.476	.822	11	.981
2000— Montreal (N.L.)		2B	153	606	101	200	51	2	24	97	49	69	2	17	5-4	.330	.379	.540	.918	10	.986
2001— Montreal (N.L.)		2B-DH	124	486	82	155	34	1	15	59	60	70	3	12	4-1	.319	.371	.486	.856	9	.983
2002— Montreal (N.L.)		2B	152	604	103	190	43	3	19	96	60	70	3	12	2-1	.315	.378	.490	.868	11	.983
2003— Montreal (N.L.)		2B	144	509	77	158	36	0	15	65	69	50	7	16	3-2	.310	.397	.470	.866	10	.983
2004— Montreal (N.L.)		2B	110	412	51	121	24	0	14	60	49	43	0	14	3-1	.294	.367	.454	.821	6	.987
2005— Potomac (Carol.)		DH-2B	5	13	3	2	1	0	0	3	4	2	0	0	0-0	.154	.353	.231	.584	0	1.000
— Wash. (N.L.)		2B	87	309	38	85	21	2	7	32	31	30	1	8	0-0	.275	.339	.424	.763	5	.985
2006— Potomac (Carol.)			1	3	0	1	0	0	0	0	0	0	0	0	0-0	.333	.333	.333	1.000	0	
— Harrisburg (East.)			3	8	0	2	0	0	0	1	2	0	1	0	0-0	.250	.400	.250	.650	0	1.000
— Wash. (N.L.)		2B-1B-DH	126	463	52	134	26	1	7	47	41	48	3	16	1-0	.289	.348	.395	.744	5	.991
Major League totals (10 years)			1186	4257	614	1280	304	12	115	550	397	463	36	119	21-15	.301	.363	.459	.821	77	.984

ALL-STAR GAME RECORD

			G	AB	R	H	2B	3B	HR	RBI	BB	SO	HBP	GDP	SB-CS	Avg.	OBP	SLG	OPS	E	Avg.
All-Star Game totals (3 years)			3	5	0	0	0	0	0	0	0	2	0	0	0-0	.000	.000	.000	.000	1	.750

2006 LEFTY-RIGHTY SPLITS

vs.	Avg.	AB	H	2B	3B	HR	RBI	BB	SO	OBP	Slg.	vs.	Avg.	AB	H	2B	3B	HR	RBI	BB	SO	OBP	Slg.
L	.323	133	43	13	0	3	13	10	15	.372	.444	R	.276	330	91	19	1	4	34	31	33	.339	.376

VILLANUEVA, CARLOS — P

PERSONAL: Born November 28, 1983, in Santiago, Dominican Republic. ... 6-2/190. ... Throws right, bats both. ... Full name: Carlos Manuel Villanueva. **TRANSACTIONS/CAREER NOTES:** Signed as a non-drafted free agent by San Francisco Giants organization (March 4, 2002). ... Traded by Giants with P Glenn Woolard to Milwaukee Brewers for Ps Wayne Franklin and Leo Estrella (March 30, 2004).

CAREER HITTING: 1-for-15 (.067), 0 R, 0 2B, 0 3B, 0 HR, 1 RBI.

Year	Team (League)	W	L	Pct.	ERA	WHIP	G	GS	CG	ShO	Hld.	Sv.-Opp.	IP	H	R	ER	HR	BB-IBB	SO	Avg.
2002— Ariz. Giants (Ariz.)		4	0	1.000	0.59	0.89	19	0	0	0	...	3-...	30.1	24	3	2	1	3-0	23	.220
2003— Ariz. Giants (Ariz.)		3	6	.333	3.97	1.31	12	10	0	0	...	0-...	59.0	64	31	26	1	13-0	67	.277
2004— Beloit (Midw.)		8	8	.500	3.77	1.15	25	21	1	1	...	1-...	114.2	102	67	48	20	30-1	113	.236
2005— Brevard County (FSL)		8	1	.889	2.32	0.98	21	21	0	0	0	0-0	112.1	78	31	29	11	32-0	124	.195
— Huntsville (Sou.)		1	3	.250	7.40	1.45	4	4	0	0	0	0-0	20.2	21	18	17	3	9-0	14	.256
2006— Huntsville (Sou.)		4	5	.444	3.75	1.19	11	10	1	1	0	0-0	62.1	60	31	26	6	14-0	59	.247
— Nashville (PCL)		7	1	.875	2.71	1.03	11	9	1	0	0	0-0	66.1	42	20	20	6	26-0	61	.182
— Milwaukee (N.L.)		2	2	.500	3.69	1.01	10	6	0	0	0	0-0	53.2	43	22	22	8	11-1	39	.216
Major League totals (1 year)		2	2	.500	3.69	1.01	10	6	0	0	0	0-0	53.2	43	22	22	8	11-1	39	.216

vs.	Avg.	AB	H	2B	3B	HR	RBI	BB	SO	OBP	Slg.	vs.	Avg.	AB	H	2B	3B	HR	RBI	BB	SO	OBP	Slg.
L	.226	106	24	6	2	4	9	6	24	.268	.434	R	.204	93	19	5	1	4	13	5	15	.275	.409

VILLARREAL, OSCAR P

PERSONAL: Born November 22, 1981, in Nuevo Leon, Mexico. ... 6-0/205. ... Throws right, bats left. ... Full name: Oscar Eduardo Villarreal. ... Name pronounced: VEE-yuh-ray-al. ... High school: Prepa High School No. 16 (Nuevo Leon, Mexico). **TRANSACTIONS/CAREER NOTES:** Signed as a non-drafted free agent by Arizona Diamondbacks organization (November 6, 1998). ... On disabled list (May 10, 2004-remainder of season); included rehabilitation assignment to Tucson. ... On disabled list (April 11-September 2, 2005); included rehabilitation assignment to Tucson. ... Traded by Diamondbacks with Lance Cormier to Atlanta Braves for C Johnny Estrada (December 7, 2005).

CAREER HITTING: 0-for-10 (.000), 0 R, 0 2B, 0 3B, 0 HR, 0 RBI.

Year	Team (League)	W	L	Pct.	ERA	WHIP	G	GS	CG	ShO	Hld.	Sv.-Opp.	IP	H	R	ER	HR	BB-IBB	SO	Avg.
1999—	Ariz. D'backs (Ariz.)	1	5	.167	3.78	1.38	14	11	0	0	...	0-...	64.1	64	39	27	1	25-0	51	.260
2000—	Ariz. D'backs (Ariz.)	1	0	1.000	2.08	1.85	2	0	0	0	...	0-...	4.1	6	1	1	0	2-0	4	.353
—	South Bend (Mid.)	1	3	.250	4.41	1.65	13	5	0	0	...	0-...	32.2	37	19	16	0	17-3	30	.274
—	Ariz. D'backs (Ariz.)	0	0	...	9.00	2.00	1	0	0	0	...	0-...	1.0	2	1	1	0	0-0	1	.400
—	High Desert (Calif.)	0	2	.000	3.65	1.54	9	4	0	0	...	0-...	24.2	24	20	10	4	14-0	18	.253
2001—	El Paso (Texas)	6	9	.400	4.41	1.54	27	27	0	0	...	0-...	140.2	154	96	69	10	63-1	108	.274
2002—	El Paso (Texas)	6	3	.667	3.74	1.17	14	12	1	0	...	0-...	84.1	73	36	35	2	26-0	85	.233
—	Tucson (PCL)	3	3	.500	4.36	1.41	10	10	0	0	...	0-...	64.0	68	33	31	8	22-0	40	.278
2003—	Arizona (N.L.)	10	7	.588	2.57	1.29	86	1	0	0	10	0-4	98.0	80	40	28	8	46-10	80	.222
2004—	Arizona (N.L.)	0	2	.000	7.00	1.78	17	0	0	0	2	0-0	18.0	25	14	14	3	7-1	17	.342
—	Tucson (PCL)	0	2	.000	14.34	2.25	6	5	0	0	...	0-...	10.2	20	17	17	3	4-0	12	.385
2005—	Tucson (PCL)	0	3	.000	5.19	1.33	12	8	0	0	0	0-0	17.1	19	12	10	1	4-0	8	.292
—	Arizona (N.L.)	2	0	1.000	5.27	1.24	11	0	0	0	0	0-2	13.2	11	8	8	2	6-2	5	.234
2006—	Atlanta (N.L.)	9	1	.900	3.61	1.30	58	4	0	0	2	0-4	92.1	93	41	37	13	27-3	55	.261
	Major League totals (4 years)	21	10	.677	3.53	1.33	172	5	0	0	16	0-10	222.0	209	103	87	24	86-16	157	.250

vs.	Avg.	AB	H	2B	3B	HR	RBI	BB	SO	OBP	Slg.	vs.	Avg.	AB	H	2B	3B	HR	RBI	BB	SO	OBP	Slg.
L	.264	163	43	8	2	8	21	16	25	.328	.485	R	.259	193	50	10	0	5	26	11	30	.311	.389

VILLONE, RON P

PERSONAL: Born January 16, 1970, in Englewood, N.J. ... 6-3/230. ... Throws left, bats left. ... Full name: Ronald Thomas Villone. ... Name pronounced: vill-OWN. ... High school: Bergenfield (N.J.). ... College: Massachusetts. **TRANSACTIONS/CAREER NOTES:** Selected by Seattle Mariners in first round (14th pick overall) of 1992 free-agent draft. ... Traded by Mariners with OF Marc Newfield to San Diego Padres for P Andy Benes and a player to be named (July 31, 1995); Mariners acquired P Greg Keagle to complete deal (September 16, 1995). ... Traded by Padres with P Bryce Florie and OF Marc Newfield to Milwaukee Brewers for OF Greg Vaughn and a player to be named (July 31, 1996); Padres acquired OF Gerald Parent to complete deal (September 16, 1996). ... Traded by Brewers with Ps Ben McDonald and Mike Fetters to Cleveland Indians for OF Marquis Grissom and P Jeff Juden (December 8, 1997). ... On disabled list (August 15-September 1, 1998); included rehabilitation assignment to Buffalo. ... Released by Indians (April 2, 1999). ... Signed by Cincinnati Reds organization (April 5, 1999). ... Traded by Reds to Colorado Rockies for two players to be named (November 8, 2000); Reds acquired Ps Jeff Taglienti and Justin Carter to complete deal (December 20, 2000). ... Traded by Rockies to Houston Astros for P Jay Powell (June 27, 2001). ... Signed as a free agent by Pittsburgh Pirates organization (February 12, 2002). ... On disabled list (August 15-September 1, 2002). ... Signed as a free agent by Arizona Diamondbacks organization (January 29, 2003). ... Released by Diamondbacks (May 15, 2003). ... Signed by Astros organization (May 19, 2003). ... Signed as a free agent by Mariners (February 10, 2004). ... Traded by Mariners to Florida Marlins for Ps Yorman Bazardo and Michael Flannery (July 31, 2005). ... Traded by Marlins to New York Yankees for P Ben Julianel (December 16, 2005). **MISCELLANEOUS NOTES:** Member of 1992 U.S. Olympic baseball team.

CAREER HITTING: 22-for-169 (.130), 7 R, 3 2B, 1 3B, 1 HR, 7 RBI.

Year	Team (League)	W	L	Pct.	ERA	WHIP	G	GS	CG	ShO	Hld.	Sv.-Opp.	IP	H	R	ER	HR	BB-IBB	SO	Avg.
1993—	Riverside (Calif.)	7	4	.636	4.21	1.63	16	16	0	0	...	0-...	83.1	74	47	39	5	62-0	82	.241
—	Jacksonville (Sou.)	3	4	.429	4.38	1.41	11	11	0	0	...	0-...	63.2	49	34	31	6	41-3	66	.219
1994—	Jacksonville (Sou.)	6	7	.462	3.86	1.56	41	5	0	0	...	8-...	79.1	56	37	34	7	68-3	94	.199
1995—	Seattle (A.L.)	0	2	.000	7.91	2.22	19	0	0	0	3	0-3	19.1	20	19	17	6	23-0	26	.270
—	Tacoma (PCL)	1	0	1.000	0.61	0.94	22	0	0	0	...	13-...	29.2	9	6	2	1	19-0	43	.095
—	San Diego (N.L.)	2	1	.667	4.21	1.36	19	0	0	0	3	1-2	25.2	24	12	12	5	11-0	37	.242
1996—	Las Vegas (PCL)	2	1	.667	1.64	1.00	23	0	0	0	...	3-...	22.0	13	5	4	0	9-0	29	.169
—	San Diego (N.L.)	1	1	.500	2.95	1.31	21	0	0	0	4	0-1	18.1	17	6	6	2	7-0	19	.243
—	Milwaukee (A.L.)	0	0	...	3.28	1.30	23	0	0	0	5	2-2	24.2	14	9	9	4	18-0	19	.175
1997—	Milwaukee (A.L.)	1	0	1.000	3.42	1.71	50	0	0	0	8	0-2	52.2	54	23	20	4	36-2	40	.271
1998—	Buffalo (Int'l)	0	0	...	2.01	1.39	23	0	0	0	...	7-...	22.1	20	11	5	2	11-1	28	.235
—	Cleveland (A.L.)	0	0	...	6.00	1.93	25	0	0	0	1	0-0	27.0	30	18	18	3	22-0	15	.297
1999—	Indianapolis (Int'l)	2	0	1.000	1.42	1.16	18	0	0	0	...	1-...	19.0	9	3	3	1	13-1	23	.155
—	Cincinnati (N.L.)	9	7	.563	4.23	1.31	29	22	0	0	0	0-0	142.2	114	70	67	8	73-2	97	.219
2000—	Cincinnati (N.L.)	10	10	.500	5.43	1.65	35	23	2	0	0	0-0	141.0	154	95	85	22	78-3	77	.286
2001—	Colorado (N.L.)	1	3	.250	6.36	1.82	22	6	0	0	2	0-0	46.2	56	35	33	6	29-4	48	.295
—	Houston (N.L.)	5	7	.417	5.56	1.49	31	6	0	0	4	0-0	68.0	77	46	42	12	24-1	65	.282
2002—	Pittsburgh (N.L.)	4	6	.400	5.81	1.39	45	7	0	0	6	0-1	93.0	95	63	60	8	34-3	55	.270
2003—	Tucson (PCL)	1	1	.500	3.55	1.30	15	0	0	0	...	1-...	25.1	20	14	10	2	12-1	22	.233
—	New Orleans (PCL)	3	1	.750	1.23	1.20	5	5	0	0	...	0-...	29.1	24	5	4	0	10-0	18	.233
—	Houston (N.L.)	6	6	.500	4.13	1.30	19	19	0	0	0	0-0	106.2	91	51	49	16	48-1	91	.233
2004—	Seattle (A.L.)	8	6	.571	4.08	1.42	56	10	0	0	7	0-1	117.0	102	64	53	12	64-3	86	.232
2005—	Seattle (A.L.)	2	3	.400	2.45	1.39	52	0	0	0	17	1-6	40.1	33	14	11	2	23-1	41	.226
—	Florida (N.L.)	3	2	.600	6.85	1.52	27	0	0	0	4	0-3	23.2	24	20	18	2	12-1	29	.264
2006—	New York (A.L.)	3	3	.500	5.04	1.57	70	0	0	0	6	0-1	80.1	75	48	45	9	51-9	72	.250
	American League totals (7 years)	14	14	.500	4.31	1.56	295	10	0	0	47	3-15	361.1	328	195	173	40	237-15	299	.245
	National League totals (8 years)	41	43	.488	5.03	1.45	248	83	2	0	18	3-9	665.2	652	398	372	81	316-15	518	.258
	Major League totals (12 years)	55	57	.491	4.78	1.49	543	93	2	0	65	6-24	1027.0	980	593	545	121	553-30	817	.254

DIVISION SERIES RECORD

Year	Team (League)	W	L	Pct.	ERA	WHIP	G	GS	CG	ShO	Hld.	Sv.-Opp.	IP	H	R	ER	HR	BB-IBB	SO	Avg.
2001—	Houston (N.L.)	0	0	...	0.00	0.00	1	0	0	0	0	0-0	0.2	0	0	0	0	0-0	0	.000
2006—	New York (A.L.)	0	0	...	0.00	2.00	1	0	0	0	0	0-0	1.0	1	0	0	0	1-0	1	.250
	Division series totals (2 years)	0	0	...	0.00	1.20	2	0	0	0	0	0-0	1.2	1	0	0	0	1-0	1	.167

vs.	Avg.	AB	H	2B	3B	HR	RBI	BB	SO	OBP	Slg.	vs.	Avg.	AB	H	2B	3B	HR	RBI	BB	SO	OBP	Slg.
L	.179	106	19	4	0	4	15	12	37	.281	.330	R	.289	194	56	14	0	5	27	39	35	.403	.438

V

VIZCAINO, JOSE — IF

PERSONAL: Born March 26, 1968, in San Cristobal, Dominican Republic. ... 6-1/190. ... Bats both, throws right. ... Full name: Jose Luis Vizcaino. ... Name pronounced: vis-ky-ee-no. ... High school: Americo Tolentino (Palenque de San Cristobal, Dominican Republic). **TRANSACTIONS/CAREER NOTES:** Signed as a non-drafted free agent by Los Angeles Dodgers organization (February 18, 1986). ... Traded by Dodgers to Chicago Cubs for IF Greg Smith (December 14, 1990). ... On disabled list (April 20-May 6 and August 26-September 16, 1992). ... Traded by Cubs to New York Mets for Ps Anthony Young and Ottis Smith (March 30, 1994). ... Traded by Mets with 2B Jeff Kent to Cleveland Indians for 2B Carlos Baerga and IF Alvaro Espinoza (July 29, 1996). ... Traded by Indians with 2B Jeff Kent, P Julian Tavarez and a player to be named to San Francisco Giants for 3B Matt Williams and a player to be named (November 13, 1996); Indians traded P Joe Roa to Giants for OF Trenidad Hubbard to complete deal (December 16, 1996). ... Signed as a free agent by Dodgers (December 8, 1997). ... On disabled list (June 22-September 9, 1998; and May 19-June 4, 1999). ... Traded by Dodgers to New York Yankees for IF/DH Jim Leyritz (June 20, 2000). ... Signed as a free agent by Houston Astros (November 20, 2000). ... On disabled list (June 25-August 21, 2003); included rehabilitation assignment to New Orleans. ... Signed as a free agent by San Francisco Giants (January 3, 2006). ... Released by Giants (August 17, 2006). ... Signed by St. Louis Cardinals (August 23, 2006).

2006 GAMES PLAYED BY POSITION (MLB): SS—26, 2B—18, 1B—11, 3B—2.

Year—Team (League)	Pos.	G	AB	R	H	2B	3B	HR	RBI	BB	SO	HBP	GDP	SB-CS	Avg.	OBP	SLG	OPS	E	Avg.
1987— GC Dodgers (GCL)	1B-SS	49	150	26	38	5	1	0	12	22	24	0	1	8-5	.253	.347	.300	.647	13	.933
1988— Bakersfield (Calif.)	SS	122	433	77	126	11	4	0	38	50	54	7	6	13-14	.291	.372	.335	.707	30	.946
1989— Albuquerque (PCL)	SS	129	434	60	123	10	4	1	44	33	41	1	10	16-14	.283	.333	.332	.665	30	.951
— Los Angeles (N.L.)	SS	7	10	2	2	0	0	0	0	0	1	0	0	0-0	.200	.200	.200	.400	2	.882
1990— Albuquerque (PCL)	2B-SS	81	276	46	77	10	2	2	38	30	33	0	6	13-6	.279	.346	.351	.698	14	.964
— Los Angeles (N.L.)	2B-SS	37	51	3	14	1	1	0	2	4	8	0	1	1-1	.275	.327	.333	.661	2	.962
1991— Chicago (N.L.)	2B-3B-SS	93	145	7	38	5	0	0	10	5	18	0	1	2-1	.262	.283	.297	.579	7	.960
1992— Chicago (N.L.)	SS-3B-2B	86	285	25	64	10	4	1	17	14	35	0	4	3-0	.225	.260	.298	.558	9	.970
1993— Chicago (N.L.)	SS-3B-2B	151	551	74	158	19	4	4	54	46	71	3	9	12-9	.287	.340	.358	.697	17	.974
1994— New York (N.L.)	SS	103	410	47	105	13	3	3	33	33	62	2	5	1-11	.256	.310	.324	.635	13	.970
1995— New York (N.L.)	SS-2B	135	509	66	146	21	5	3	56	35	76	1	14	8-3	.287	.332	.365	.698	10	.984
1996— New York (N.L.)	SS-2B	96	363	47	110	12	6	1	32	28	58	3	6	9-5	.303	.356	.377	.733	6	.986
— Cleveland (A.L.)	2B-SS-DH	48	179	23	51	5	2	0	13	7	24	0	2	6-2	.285	.310	.335	.645	4	.982
1997— San Francisco (N.L.)	SS-2B	151	568	77	151	19	7	5	50	48	87	0	13	8-8	.266	.323	.350	.673	16	.976
1998— Los Angeles (N.L.)	SS-2B	67	237	30	62	9	0	3	29	17	35	1	4	7-3	.262	.311	.338	.649	4	.985
1999— Los Angeles (N.L.)	SS-2B-3B																			
	OF	94	266	27	67	9	0	1	29	20	23	1	9	2-1	.252	.305	.297	.601	7	.976
2000— Los Angeles (N.L.)	SS-3B-2B																			
	1B-DH	40	93	9	19	2	1	0	4	10	15	1	3	1-0	.204	.288	.247	.536	2	.978
— New York (A.L.)	2B-3B-DH																			
	SS	73	174	23	48	8	1	0	10	12	28	0	3	5-7	.276	.319	.333	.652	2	.991
2001— Houston (N.L.)	SS-2B-3B	107	256	38	71	8	3	1	14	15	33	2	6	3-2	.277	.322	.344	.666	14	.939
2002— Houston (N.L.)	SS-3B-2B																			
	1B	125	406	53	123	19	2	5	37	24	40	1	5	3-5	.303	.342	.397	.738	4	.989
2003— New Orleans (PCL)	2B-SS	2	8	1	2	0	0	1	1	1	0	0	0	0-0	.250	.333	.625	.958	1	.889
— Houston (N.L.)	SS-3B-2B																			
	1B	91	189	14	47	7	3	3	26	8	22	1	5	0-1	.249	.281	.365	.646	5	.970
2004— Houston (N.L.)	SS-3B-2B																			
	1B	138	358	34	98	21	3	3	20	23	39	0	4	1-1	.274	.311	.374	.685	11	.972
2005— Houston (N.L.)	2B-SS-1B																			
	3B	98	187	15	46	10	2	1	23	15	40	0	2	2-0	.246	.299	.337	.636	5	.974
2006— San Francisco (N.L.)	SS-2B-1B																			
	3B	64	119	16	25	3	0	1	5	16	10	0	3	0-2	.210	.304	.261	.564	4	.980
— St. Louis (N.L.)	SS-2B-1B	16	23	3	8	3	0	1	3	1	4	0	2	0-0	.348	.375	.609	.984	2	.913
American League totals (2 years)		121	353	46	99	13	3	0	23	19	52	0	5	11-9	.280	.315	.334	.649	6	.986
National League totals (18 years)		1699	5026	587	1354	191	44	36	457	359	677	16	100	63-53	.269	.318	.346	.664	140	.975
Major League totals (18 years)		1820	5379	633	1453	204	47	36	480	378	729	16	105	74-62	.270	.318	.346	.663	146	.976

DIVISION SERIES RECORD

Year—Team (League)	Pos.	G	AB	R	H	2B	3B	HR	RBI	BB	SO	HBP	GDP	SB-CS	Avg.	OBP	SLG	OPS	E	Avg.
1996— Cleveland (A.L.)	2B	3	12	1	4	2	0	0	1	1	1	0	0	0-0	.333	.385	.500	.885	1	.875
1997— San Francisco (N.L.)	SS	3	11	1	2	1	0	0	0	0	5	0	0	0-0	.182	.182	.273	.455	0	1.000
2000— New York (A.L.)	2B	1	0	1	0	0	0	0	0	0	0	0	0	0-0	...	...	...	...	0	1.000
2001— Houston (N.L.)	SS	3	6	0	1	0	0	0	0	0	1	0	0	0-0	.167	.167	.167	.333	0	1.000
2004— Houston (N.L.)	2B	5	19	2	2	0	0	0	1	1	2	0	1	0-0	.105	.143	.105	.248	0	1.000
2005— Houston (N.L.)	1B-2B-SS	2	5	0	0	0	0	0	0	0	1	0	0	0-0	.000	.000	.000	.000	1	.857
Division series totals (6 years)		17	53	5	9	3	0	0	2	2	10	0	1	0-0	.170	.196	.226	.423	2	.962

CHAMPIONSHIP SERIES RECORD

Year—Team (League)	Pos.	G	AB	R	H	2B	3B	HR	RBI	BB	SO	HBP	GDP	SB-CS	Avg.	OBP	SLG	OPS	E	Avg.
2000— New York (A.L.)	2B	4	2	3	2	1	0	0	2	0	0	0	0	2-0	1.000	.667	1.500	2.167	0	1.000
2004— Houston (N.L.)	SS-2B	7	28	1	7	1	0	0	0	0	7	0	0	0-1	.250	.250	.286	.536	1	.963
2005— Houston (N.L.)		2	2	0	0	0	0	0	0	0	0	0	0	0-0	.000	.000	.000	.000	0	...
Champ. series totals (3 years)		13	32	4	9	2	0	0	2	0	7	0	0	2-1	.281	.273	.344	.616	1	.966

WORLD SERIES RECORD

Year—Team (League)	Pos.	G	AB	R	H	2B	3B	HR	RBI	BB	SO	HBP	GDP	SB-CS	Avg.	OBP	SLG	OPS	E	Avg.
2000— New York (A.L.)	2B	4	17	0	4	0	0	0	1	0	5	0	0	0-1	.235	.235	.235	.471	0	1.000
2005— Houston (N.L.)	1B-2B-SS	3	2	0	1	0	0	0	2	1	0	0	0	0-0	.500	.667	.500	1.167	0	1.000
World series totals (2 years)		7	19	0	5	0	0	0	3	1	5	0	0	0-1	.263	.300	.263	.563	0	1.000

2006 LEFTY-RIGHTY SPLITS

vs.	Avg.	AB	H	2B	3B	HR	RBI	BB	SO	OBP	Slg.	vs.	Avg.	AB	H	2B	3B	HR	RBI	BB	SO	OBP	Slg.
L	.214	42	9	1	0	1	3	8	6	.340	.310	R	.240	100	24	5	0	1	5	9	8	.303	.320

VIZCAINO, LUIS — P

PERSONAL: Born August 6, 1974, in Bani, Dominican Republic. ... 5-11/185. ... Throws right, bats right. ... Full name: Luis Arias Vizcaino. ... Name pronounced: vis-ky-ee-no. **TRANSACTIONS/CAREER NOTES:** Signed as a non-drafted free agent by Oakland Athletics organization (December 9, 1994). ... Traded by A's to Texas Rangers for P Justin Duchscherer (March 18, 2002). ... Traded by Rangers to Milwaukee Brewers for P Jesus Pena (March 24, 2002). ... Traded by Brewers with OF Scott Podsednik and a player to be named to Chicago White Sox for OF Carlos Lee (December 13, 2004); White Sox acquired P Travis Hinton to complete the deal (January 10, 2005). ... Traded by White Sox with P Orlando Hernandez and OF Chris Young to Arizona Diamondbacks for P Javier Vazquez and cash (December 20, 2005).

CAREER HITTING: 0-for-2 (.000), 0 R, 0 2B, 0 3B, 0 HR, 0 RBI.

Year Team (League)	W	L	Pct.	ERA	WHIP	G	GS	CG	ShO	Hld.	Sv.-Opp.	IP	H	R	ER	HR	BB-IBB	SO	Avg.
1995— Dom. Athletics (DSL)	10	2	.833	2.27	1.06	16	15	5	1	...	0-...	115.0	93	41	29	...	29-...	89	...
1996— Ariz. A's (Ariz.)	6	3	.667	4.07	1.37	15	10	0	0	...	1-...	59.2	58	36	27	1	24-1	52	.247
1997— Modesto (California)	0	3	.000	13.19	2.58	7	0	0	0	...	0-...	14.1	24	24	21	4	13-4	15	.387
— S. Oregon (N'west)	1	6	.143	7.93	1.87	22	5	0	0	...	0-...	47.2	62	51	42	5	27-0	42	.308
1998— Modesto (California)	6	3	.667	2.74	1.13	23	16	0	0	...	0-...	102.0	72	39	31	5	43-1	108	.196
— Huntsville (Sou.)	3	2	.600	4.66	1.68	7	7	0	0	...	0-...	38.2	43	27	20	8	22-0	26	.279
1999— Midland (Texas)	8	7	.533	5.85	1.61	25	19	0	0	...	0-...	104.2	120	74	68	18	48-2	88	.287
— Oakland (A.L.)	0	0	...	5.40	1.80	1	0	0	0	0	0-0	3.1	3	2	2	1	.3-0	2	.231
— Vancouver (PCL)	0	1	.000	1.38	1.46	7	0	0	0	0	0-0	13.0	13	4	2	0	6-0	7	.260
2000— Oakland (A.L.)	0	1	.000	7.45	1.86	12	0	0	0	0	0-0	19.1	25	17	16	2	11-0	18	.305
— Sacramento (PCL)	6	2	.750	5.03	1.43	33	2	0	0	...	5-...	48.1	48	27	27	4	21-0	41	.255
2001— Sacramento (PCL)	2	2	.500	2.14	1.07	27	0	0	0	...	7-...	42.0	35	10	10	5	10-4	56	.220
— Oakland (A.L.)	2	1	.667	4.66	1.36	36	0	0	0	3	1-1	36.2	38	19	19	8	12-1	31	.266
2002— Milwaukee (N.L.)	5	3	.625	2.99	1.05	76	0	0	0	19	5-6	81.1	55	27	27	6	30-4	79	.194
2003— Milwaukee (N.L.)	4	3	.571	6.39	1.44	75	0	0	0	9	0-6	62.0	64	45	44	16	25-3	61	.263
2004— Milwaukee (N.L.)	4	4	.500	3.75	1.18	73	0	0	0	21	1-5	72.0	61	35	30	12	24-3	63	.228
2005— Chicago (A.L.)	6	5	.545	3.73	1.47	65	0	0	0	9	0-3	70.0	74	30	29	8	29-6	43	.275
2006— Arizona (N.L.)	4	6	.400	3.58	1.22	70	0	0	0	25	0-2	65.1	51	26	26	8	29-6	72	.215
American League totals (4 years)	8	7	.533	4.59	1.51	114	0	0	0	12	1-4	129.1	140	68	66	19	55-7	94	.276
National League totals (4 years)	17	16	.515	4.07	1.21	294	0	0	0	74	6-19	280.2	231	133	127	42	108-16	275	.223
Major League totals (8 years)	25	23	.521	4.24	1.30	408	0	0	0	86	7-23	410.0	371	201	193	61	163-23	369	.241

WORLD SERIES RECORD

Year Team (League)	W	L	Pct.	ERA	WHIP	G	GS	CG	ShO	Hld.	Sv.-Opp.	IP	H	R	ER	HR	BB-IBB	SO	Avg.
2005— Chicago (A.L.)	0	0	...	0.00	1.00	1	0	0	0	0	0-0	1.0	0	0	0	0	1-0	0	.000

2006 LEFTY-RIGHTY SPLITS

vs.	Avg.	AB	H	2B	3B	HR	RBI	BB	SO	OBP	Slg.	vs.	Avg.	AB	H	2B	3B	HR	RBI	BB	SO	OBP	Slg.
L	.163	104	17	3	2	2	10	15	29	.281	.288	R	.256	133	34	8	2	6	17	14	43	.336	.481

VIZQUEL, OMAR   SS

PERSONAL: Born April 24, 1967, in Caracas, Venezuela. ... 5-9/175. ... Bats both, throws right. ... Full name: Omar Enrique Vizquel. ... Name pronounced: viz-KELL. ... High school: Francisco Espejo (Caracas, Venezuela). **TRANSACTIONS/CAREER NOTES:** Signed as a non-drafted free agent by Seattle Mariners organization (April 1, 1984). ... On disabled list (April 7-May 13, 1990); included rehabilitation assignments to Calgary and San Bernardino. ... On disabled list (April 13-May 11, 1992); included rehabilitation assignment to Calgary. ... Traded by Mariners to Cleveland Indians for SS Felix Fermin, 1B Reggie Jefferson and cash (December 20, 1993). ... On disabled list (April 23-June 13, 1994); included rehabilitation assignment to Charlotte. ... On suspended list (September 17-18, 1998). ... On disabled list (June 12-August 26 and September 6, 2003-remainder of season); included rehabilitation assignment to Lake County. ... Signed as a free agent by San Francisco Giants (November 16, 2004). **HONORS:** Won A.L. Gold Glove at shortstop (1993-2001). ... Won N.L. Gold Glove at shortstop (2005-06). **STATISTICAL NOTES:** Career major league grand slams: 4. **MISCELLANEOUS NOTES:** Batted righthanded only (1984-88).

2006 GAMES PLAYED BY POSITION (MLB): SS—152.

Year Team (League)	Pos.	G	AB	R	H	2B	3B	HR	RBI	BB	SO	HBP	GDP	SB-CS	Avg.	OBP	SLG	OPS	E	Avg.
1984— Butte (Pion.)	2B-SS	15	45	7	14	2	0	0	4	3	8	0	0	2-0	.311	.347	.356	.702	5	.894
1985— Bellingham (N'west)	2B-SS	50	187	24	42	9	0	5	17	12	27	0	0	4-3	.225	.270	.353	.623	19	.932
1986— Wausau (Midw.)	2B-SS	105	352	60	75	13	2	4	28	64	56	2	6	19-6	.213	.333	.295	.629	16	.968
1987— Salinas (Calif.)	2B-SS	114	407	61	107	12	8	0	38	57	55	0	5	25-19	.263	.350	.332	.682	25	.938
1988— Vermont (East.)	SS	103	374	54	95	18	2	2	35	42	44	3	6	30-11	.254	.328	.329	.657	19	.959
— Calgary (PCL)	SS	33	107	10	24	2	3	1	12	5	14	0	1	2-4	.224	.259	.327	.586	6	.957
1989— Seattle (A.L.)	SS	143	387	45	85	7	3	1	20	28	40	1	6	1-4	.220	.273	.261	.534	18	.971
— Calgary (PCL)	SS	7	28	3	6	2	0	0	3	3	4	1	1	0-2	.214	.313	.286	.598	0	1.000
1990— Seattle (A.L.)	SS	48	150	19	35	6	2	0	8	13	10	2	3	4-3	.233	.299	.300	.599	6	.972
— San Bern. (Calif.)	SS	6	28	5	7	0	0	0	3	3	1	0	0	1-2	.250	.323	.250	.573	3	.914
— Seattle (A.L.)	SS	81	255	19	63	3	2	1	18	18	22	0	7	4-1	.247	.295	.298	.593	7	.980
1991— Seattle (A.L.)	2B-SS	142	426	42	98	16	4	1	41	45	37	0	8	7-2	.230	.302	.293	.595	13	.980
1992— Seattle (A.L.)	SS	136	483	49	142	20	4	0	21	32	38	2	14	15-13	.294	.340	.352	.692	7	.989
— Calgary (PCL)	SS	6	22	0	6	1	0	0	2	1	3	1	3	0-1	.273	.333	.318	.652	1	.972
1993— Seattle (A.L.)	SS-DH	158	560	68	143	14	2	2	31	50	71	4	7	12-14	.255	.319	.298	.618	15	.980
— Charlotte (Int'l)	SS	7	26	3	7	1	0	0	1	2	1	0	0	1-0	.269	.321	.308	.629	1	.967
1994— Cleveland (A.L.)	SS	69	286	39	78	10	1	1	33	23	23	0	4	13-4	.273	.325	.325	.650	6	.981
1995— Cleveland (A.L.)	SS	136	542	87	144	28	0	6	56	59	59	1	4	29-11	.266	.333	.351	.684	9	.986
1996— Cleveland (A.L.)	SS	151	542	98	161	36	1	9	64	56	42	4	10	35-9	.297	.362	.417	.779	20	.971
1997— Cleveland (A.L.)	SS	153	565	89	158	23	6	5	49	57	58	2	16	43-12	.280	.347	.368	.715	10	.985
1998— Cleveland (A.L.)	SS	151	576	86	166	30	6	2	50	62	64	4	10	37-12	.288	.358	.372	.730	5	.993
1999— Cleveland (A.L.)	SS-OF	144	574	112	191	36	4	5	66	65	50	1	8	42-9	.333	.397	.436	.833	15	.976
2000— Cleveland (A.L.)	SS	156	613	101	176	27	3	7	66	87	72	5	13	22-10	.287	.377	.375	.753	3	.995
2001— Cleveland (A.L.)	SS	155	611	84	156	26	8	2	50	61	72	2	14	13-9	.255	.323	.334	.657	7	.989
2002— Cleveland (A.L.)	SS	151	582	85	160	31	5	14	72	56	64	4	7	18-10	.275	.341	.418	.759	7	.990
2003— Lake County (S.Atl.)	SS	4	14	1	1	0	0	0	2	1	2	0	0	1-0	.071	.133	.071	.205	0	1.000
— Cleveland (A.L.)	SS	64	250	43	61	13	2	2	19	29	20	0	11	8-3	.244	.321	.336	.657	7	.978
2004— Cleveland (A.L.)	SS	148	567	82	165	24	3	7	59	57	62	1	12	19-6	.291	.353	.388	.741	11	.982
2005— San Francisco (N.L.)	SS	152	568	66	154	28	4	3	45	56	58	5	10	24-10	.271	.341	.350	.691	8	.988
2006— San Francisco (N.L.)	SS	153	579	88	171	22	10	4	58	56	51	6	13	24-7	.295	.361	.389	.749	4	.993
American League totals (16 years)		2138	7819	1129	2147	348	54	66	715	785	794	35	151	318-129	.275	.341	.358	.699	160	.983
National League totals (2 years)		305	1147	154	325	50	14	7	103	112	109	11	23	48-17	.283	.351	.370	.720	12	.991
Major League totals (18 years)		2443	8966	1283	2472	398	68	73	818	897	903	46	174	366-146	.276	.342	.360	.702	172	.984

DIVISION SERIES RECORD

Year Team (League)	Pos.	G	AB	R	H	2B	3B	HR	RBI	BB	SO	HBP	GDP	SB-CS	Avg.	OBP	SLG	OPS	E	Avg.
1995— Cleveland (A.L.)	SS	3	12	2	2	1	0	0	4	2	2	0	0	1-0	.167	.286	.250	.536	0	1.000
1996— Cleveland (A.L.)	SS	4	14	4	6	1	0	0	2	3	4	0	0	4-2	.429	.500	.500	1.000	0	1.000
1997— Cleveland (A.L.)	SS	5	18	3	9	0	0	0	2	1	1	0	0	4-0	.500	.550	.500	1.050	0	1.000
1998— Cleveland (A.L.)	SS	4	15	1	1	0	0	0	1	0	0	0	0	0-0	.067	.125	.067	.192	0	1.000
1999— Cleveland (A.L.)	SS	5	21	3	5	1	1	0	3	2	3	0	0	0-0	.238	.304	.381	.685	0	1.000
2001— Cleveland (A.L.)	SS	5	22	2	9	1	1	0	4	3	1	0	0	1-0	.409	.435	.545	.980	1	.964
Division series totals (6 years)		26	102	15	32	4	2	0	16	11	11	0	0	10-2	.314	.377	.392	.769	1	.992

CHAMPIONSHIP SERIES RECORD

Year	Team (League)	Pos.	G	AB	R	H	2B	3B	HR	RBI	BB	SO	HBP	GDP	SB-CS	Avg.	OBP	SLG	OPS	E	Avg.
1995—	Cleveland (A.L.)	SS	6	23	2	2	1	0	0	2	5	2	0	0	3-0	.087	.241	.130	.372	0	1.000
1997—	Cleveland (A.L.)	SS	6	25	1	1	0	0	0	0	2	10	1	0	0-0	.040	.143	.040	.183	0	1.000
1998—	Cleveland (A.L.)	SS	6	25	2	11	0	1	0	0	1	3	1	0	4-1	.440	.481	.520	1.001	1	.974
	Champ. series totals (3 years)		18	73	5	14	1	1	0	2	8	15	2	0	7-1	.192	.286	.233	.519	1	.990

WORLD SERIES RECORD

Year	Team (League)	Pos.	G	AB	R	H	2B	3B	HR	RBI	BB	SO	HBP	GDP	SB-CS	Avg.	OBP	SLG	OPS	E	Avg.
1995—	Cleveland (A.L.)	SS	6	23	3	4	0	1	0	1	3	5	0	0	1-0	.174	.269	.261	.530	0	1.000
1997—	Cleveland (A.L.)	SS	7	30	5	7	2	0	0	1	3	5	0	0	5-0	.233	.303	.300	.603	0	1.000
	World series totals (2 years)		13	53	8	11	2	1	0	2	6	10	0	0	6-0	.208	.288	.283	.571	0	1.000

ALL-STAR GAME RECORD

		G	AB	R	H	2B	3B	HR	RBI	BB	SO	HBP	GDP	SB-CS	Avg.	OBP	SLG	OPS	E	Avg.
	All-Star Game totals (3 years)	3	5	0	2	0	1	0	1	1	0	0	0	0-0	.400	.500	.800	1.300	0	1.000

2006 LEFTY-RIGHTY SPLITS

vs.	Avg.	AB	H	2B	3B	HR	RBI	BB	SO	OBP	Slg.	vs.	Avg.	AB	H	2B	3B	HR	RBI	BB	SO	OBP	Slg.
L	.340	141	48	-7	0	0	7	19	10	.423	.390	R	.281	438	123	15	10	4	51	37	41	.340	.388

VOGELSONG, RYAN — P

PERSONAL: Born July 22, 1977, in Charlotte. ... 6-3/213. ... Throws right, bats right. ... Full name: Ryan Andrew Vogelsong. ... High school: Octorara Area (Atglen, Pa.). ... College: Kutztown (Pa.). **TRANSACTIONS/CAREER NOTES:** Selected by San Francisco Giants organization in fifth round of 1998 free-agent draft. ... Traded by Giants with OF Armando Rios to Pittsburgh Pirates for P Jason Schmidt (July 30, 2001). ... On disabled list (March 30-August 1, 2002); included rehabilitation assignments to Lynchburg and Altoona. **MISCELLANEOUS NOTES:** Had a sacrifice hit and struck out in two appearances as pinch hitter (2004).

CAREER HITTING: 11-for-59 (.186), 3 R, 4 2B, 0 3B, 0 HR, 3 RBI.

Year	Team (League)	W	L	Pct.	ERA	WHIP	G	GS	CG	ShO	Hld.	Sv.-Opp.	IP	H	R	ER	HR	BB-IBB	SO	Avg.
1998—	Salem-Keizer (N'west)	6	1	.857	1.77	0.95	10	10	0	0	...	0-...	56.0	37	15	11	5	16-0	66	.186
	San Jose (Calif.)	0	0	...	7.58	1.42	4	4	0	0	...	0-...	19.0	23	16	16	3	4-0	26	.307
1999—	San Jose (Calif.)	4	4	.500	2.45	0.92	13	13	0	0	...	0-...	69.2	37	26	19	3	27-0	86	.154
	Shreveport (Texas)	0	2	.000	7.31	1.94	6	6	0	0	...	0-...	28.1	40	25	23	7	15-0	23	.336
2000—	Shreveport (Texas)	6	10	.375	4.23	1.43	27	27	1	0	...	0-...	155.1	•153	82	73	15	69-2	147	.260
	San Francisco (N.L.)	0	0	...	0.00	1.00	4	0	0	0	0	0-0	6.0	4	0	0	0	2-0	6	.182
2001—	Fresno (PCL)	3	3	.500	2.79	0.91	10	10	0	0	...	0-...	58.0	35	18	18	6	18-0	53	.170
	San Francisco (N.L.)	0	3	.000	5.65	1.50	13	0	0	0	1	0-0	28.2	29	21	18	5	14-0	17	.257
	Nashville (PCL)	2	3	.400	3.98	1.29	6	6	0	0	...	0-...	31.2	26	15	14	2	15-0	33	.230
	Pittsburgh (N.L.)	0	2	.000	12.00	2.67	2	2	0	0	0	0-0	6.0	10	10	8	1	6-1	7	.357
2002—	Lynchburg (Caro.)	1	1	.500	8.04	1.66	4	4	0	0	...	0-...	15.2	19	14	14	0	7-0	20	.297
	Altoona (East.)	1	5	.167	5.56	1.31	8	8	0	0	...	0-...	43.2	47	27	27	5	10-0	35	.278
2003—	Nashville (PCL)	12	8	.600	4.29	1.30	26	26	1	1	...	0-...	149.0	142	75	71	12	54-5	146	.250
	Pittsburgh (N.L.)	2	2	.500	6.55	1.77	6	5	0	0	0	0-0	22.0	30	19	16	1	9-3	15	.323
2004—	Pittsburgh (N.L.)	6	13	.316	6.50	1.62	31	26	0	0	0	0-0	133.0	148	97	96	22	67-7	92	.285
2005—	Pittsburgh (N.L.)	2	2	.500	4.43	1.50	44	0	0	0	1	0-1	81.1	82	43	40	5	40-1	52	.259
2006—	Indianapolis (Int'l)	4	5	.444	2.66	0.98	11	10	1	0	0	0-0	67.2	54	23	20	5	12-3	43	.217
	Pittsburgh (N.L.)	0	0	...	6.39	1.58	20	0	0	0	0	0-0	38.0	44	27	27	2	16-2	27	.301
	Major League totals (6 years)	10	22	.313	5.86	1.59	120	33	0	0	2	0-1	315.0	347	217	205	36	154-14	216	.281

2006 LEFTY-RIGHTY SPLITS

vs.	Avg.	AB	H	2B	3B	HR	RBI	BB	SO	OBP	Slg.	vs.	Avg.	AB	H	2B	3B	HR	RBI	BB	SO	OBP	Slg.
L	.239	46	11	2	0	2	10	3	10	.379	.413	R	.330	100	33	5	1	0	16	9	17	.391	.400

VOLQUEZ, EDISON — P

PERSONAL: Born July 3, 1983, in La Segunda, Dominican Republic. ... 6-1/190. ... Throws right, bats right. ... Full name: Edison Volquez. **TRANSACTIONS/CAREER NOTES:** Signed as a non-drafted free agent by Texas Rangers organization (October 29, 2001).

CAREER HITTING: 0-for-0 (.000), 0 R, 0 2B, 0 3B, 0 HR, 0 RBI.

Year	Team (League)	W	L	Pct.	ERA	WHIP	G	GS	CG	ShO	Hld.	Sv.-Opp.	IP	H	R	ER	HR	BB-IBB	SO	Avg.
2002—	Texas (DSL)	1	2	.333	2.68	1.26	14	8	0	0	...	0-...	47.0	45	19	14	1	14-1	58	.254
2003—	Arizona Rangers (AZL)	2	1	.667	4.00	1.30	10	4	0	0	...	1-...	27.0	24	14	12	1	11-0	28	.245
2004—	Clinton (Midw.)	4	4	.500	4.21	1.24	21	15	0	0	...	3-...	87.2	82	49	41	8	27-1	74	.246
	Stockton (Calif.)	4	1	.800	2.95	1.13	8	8	0	0	...	0-...	39.2	31	16	13	6	14-0	34	.221
2005—	Bakersfield (Calif.)	5	4	.556	4.14	1.14	11	11	1	0	0	0-0	66.2	64	34	31	9	12-0	77	.252
	Arizona Rangers (AZL)	0	0	...	0.00	1.00	1	1	0	0	0	0-0	2.0	2	0	0	0	0-0	2	.222
	Frisco (Texas)	1	5	.167	4.14	1.28	10	10	1	1	0	0-0	58.2	58	29	27	6	17-0	49	.258
	Texas (A.L.)	0	4	.000	14.21	2.76	6	3	0	0	0	0-0	12.2	25	22	20	•3	10-0	11	.403
2006—	Oklahoma (PCL)	6	6	.500	3.21	1.31	21	21	0	0	0	0-0	120.2	86	51	43	9	72-0	130	.203
	Texas (A.L.)	1	6	.143	7.29	2.07	8	8	0	0	0	0-0	33.1	52	28	27	7	17-0	15	.359
	Major League totals (2 years)	1	10	.091	9.20	2.26	14	11	0	0	0	0-0	46.0	77	50	47	10	27-0	26	.372

2006 LEFTY-RIGHTY SPLITS

vs.	Avg.	AB	H	2B	3B	HR	RBI	BB	SO	OBP	Slg.	vs.	Avg.	AB	H	2B	3B	HR	RBI	BB	SO	OBP	Slg.
L	.361	61	22	1	0	2	10	4	7	.394	.475	R	.357	84	30	4	0	5	16	13	8	.449	.583

WAECHTER, DOUG — P

PERSONAL: Born January 28, 1981, in St. Petersburg, Fla. ... 6-4/210. ... Throws right, bats right. ... Full name: Douglas Michael Waechter. ... Name pronounced: WACK-ter. ... High school: Northeast Senior (St. Petersburg, Fla.). **TRANSACTIONS/CAREER NOTES:** Selected by Tampa Bay Devil Rays organization in third round of 1999 free-agent draft. ... On disabled list (June 9-September 6, 2004); included rehabilitation assignment to Durham. ... On disabled list (July 3-25, 2005); included rehabilitation assignment to Durham.

CAREER HITTING: 0-for-2 (.000), 1 R, 0 2B, 0 3B, 0 HR, 0 RBI.

Year	Team (League)	W	L	Pct.	ERA	WHIP	G	GS	CG	ShO	Hld.	Sv.-Opp.	IP	H	R	ER	HR	BB-IBB	SO	Avg.
1999—	Princeton (Appal.)	0	5	.000	9.77	2.31	11	7	0	0	...	0-...	35.0	46	45	38	2	35-0	38	.317
2000—	Hudson Valley (NYP)	4	4	.500	2.35	1.24	14	14	2	2	...	0-...	72.2	53	23	19	2	37-0	58	.205
2001—	Char., S.C. (SAL)	8	11	.421	4.34	1.42	26	26	1	0	...	0-...	153.1	179	97	74	14	38-1	107	.285
2002—	Char., S.C. (SAL)	3	3	.500	3.47	1.51	7	7	0	0	...	0-...	36.1	39	20	14	2	16-3	36	.277
	Bakersfield (Calif.)	6	3	.667	2.66	1.32	17	17	0	0	...	0-...	108.1	114	43	32	9	29-0	101	.267
	Orlando (South.)	1	3	.250	9.00	2.22	4	4	1	0	...	0-...	18.0	27	20	18	4	13-0	18	.338

W

Year Team (League)	W	L	Pct.	ERA	WHIP	G	GS	CG	ShO	Hld.	Sv.-Opp.	IP	H	R	ER	HR	BB-IBB	SO	Avg.
2003— Orlando (South.)	5	3	.625	4.13	1.22	13	12	0	0	...	0-...	76.1	74	39	35	6	19-0	45	.257
— Durham (Int'l)	3	3	.500	3.33	1.23	10	10	0	0	...	0-...	51.1	51	25	19	9	12-0	35	.262
— Tampa Bay (A.L.)	3	2	.600	3.31	1.25	6	5	1	1	0	0-0	35.1	29	13	13	4	15-0	29	.225
2004— Durham (Int'l)	0	2	.000	6.75	1.70	8	8	0	0	...	0-...	29.1	33	22	22	11	17-0	22	.277
— Tampa Bay (A.L.)	5	7	.417	6.01	1.44	14	14	0	0	0	0-0	70.1	68	54	47	20	33-1	36	.252
2005— Durham (Int'l)	0	2	.000	9.22	1.61	3	3	0	0	...	0-0	13.2	17	14	14	3	5-0	16	.304
— Tampa Bay (A.L.)	5	12	.294	5.62	1.46	29	25	0	0	0	0-0	157.0	191	109	98	29	38-5	87	.298
2006— Durham (Int'l)	1	12	.077	8.32	1.94	17	15	1	0	0	0-0	79.0	129	82	73	7	24-1	45	.366
— Tampa Bay (A.L.)	1	4	.200	6.62	1.62	11	10	0	0	0	0-0	53.0	67	40	39	6	19-1	25	.310
Major League totals (4 years)	14	25	.359	5.62	1.46	60	54	1	1	0	0-0	315.2	355	216	197	59	105-7	177	.282

2006 LEFTY-RIGHTY SPLITS

vs.	Avg.	AB	H	2B	3B	HR	RBI	BB	SO	OBP	Slg.	vs.	Avg.	AB	H	2B	3B	HR	RBI	BB	SO	OBP	Slg.
L	.284	95	27	5	0	3	15	5	9	.327	.432	R	.331	121	40	9	1	3	18	14	16	.401	.496

WAGNER, BILLY — P

PERSONAL: Born July 25, 1971, in Tannersville, Va. ... 5-11/195. ... Throws left, bats left. ... Full name: William Edward Wagner. ... High school: Tazewell (Va.). ... Junior college: Ferrum (Va.). **TRANSACTIONS/CAREER NOTES:** Selected by Houston Astros organization in first round (12th pick overall) of 1993 free-agent draft. ... On disabled list (August 23-September 7, 1996). ... On disabled list (July 16-August 7, 1998); included rehabilitation assignment to Jackson. ... On disabled list (June 21, 2000-remainder of season). ... On disabled list (June 4-June 19, 2001); included rehabilitation assignment to Round Rock. ... Traded by Astros to Philadelphia Phillies for Ps Brandon Duckworth, Taylor Buchholz and Ezequiel Astascio (November 3, 2003). ... On disabled list (May 8-June 8 and July 22-September 4, 2004); included rehabilitation assignment to Reading. ... On suspended list (September 17-19, 2004). ... Signed as a free agent by New York Mets (November 29, 2005). **STATISTICAL NOTES:** Pitched one inning, combining with Roy Oswalt (one inning), Peter Munro (2 2/3 innings), Kirk Saarloos (1 1/3 innings), Brad Lidge (two innings) and Octavio Dotel (one inning) on 8-0 no-hitter against New York Yankees (June 11, 2003).

CAREER HITTING: 2-for-20 (.100), 1 R, 0 2B, 0 3B, 0 HR, 1 RBI.

Year Team (League)	W	L	Pct.	ERA	WHIP	G	GS	CG	ShO	Hld.	Sv.-Opp.	IP	H	R	ER	HR	BB-IBB	SO	Avg.
1993— Auburn (NY-Penn)	1	3	.250	4.08	1.74	7	7	0	0	...	0-...	28.2	25	19	13	2	25-0	31	.231
1994— Quad City (Midw.)	8	9	.471	3.29	1.24	26	26	2	0	...	0-...	153.0	99	71	56	9	91-0	204	.188
1995— Jackson (Texas)	2	2	.500	2.57	1.21	12	12	0	0	...	0-...	70.0	49	25	20	7	36-1	77	.199
— Tucson (PCL)	5	3	.625	3.18	1.34	13	13	0	0	...	0-0	76.1	70	28	27	3	32-0	80	.245
— Houston (N.L.)	0	0	...	0.00	0.00	1	0	0	0	...	0-0	0.1	0	0	0	0	0-0	0	.000
1996— Tucson (PCL)	6	2	.750	3.28	1.28	12	12	1	1	...	0-...	74.0	62	32	27	2	33-0	86	.225
— Houston (N.L.)	2	2	.500	2.44	1.12	37	0	0	0	3	9-13	51.2	28	16	14	6	30-2	67	.165
1997— Houston (N.L.)	7	8	.467	2.85	1.19	62	0	0	0	1	23-29	66.1	49	23	21	5	30-1	106	.204
1998— Houston (N.L.)	4	3	.571	2.70	1.18	58	0	0	0	1	30-35	60.0	46	19	18	6	25-1	97	.211
— Jackson (Texas)	0	0	...	0.00	0.33	3	1	0	0	...	0-0	3.0	1	0	0	0	0-0	7	.100
1999— Houston (N.L.)	4	1	.800	1.57	0.78	66	0	0	0	1	39-42	74.2	35	14	13	5	23-1	124	.135
2000— Houston (N.L.)	2	4	.333	6.18	1.66	28	0	0	0	...	6-15	27.2	28	19	19	6	18-0	28	.255
2001— Houston (N.L.)	2	5	.286	2.73	1.02	64	0	0	0	1	39-41	62.2	44	19	19	5	20-0	79	.198
— Round Rock (Texas)	0	0	...	0.00	0.00	1	0	0	0	...	0-0	1.0	0	0	0	0	0-0	2	.000
2002— Houston (N.L.)	4	2	.667	2.52	0.97	70	0	0	0	1	35-41	75.0	51	21	21	7	22-5	88	.196
2003— Houston (N.L.)	1	4	.200	1.78	0.87	78	0	0	0	1	44-47	86.0	52	18	17	8	23-5	105	.169
2004— Reading (East.)	0	0	...	0.00	1.00	1	1	0	0	...	0-0	1.0	1	0	0	0	0-0	2	.250
— Philadelphia (N.L.)	4	0	1.000	2.42	0.77	45	0	0	0	1	21-25	48.1	31	16	13	6	6-1	59	.181
2005— Philadelphia (N.L.)	4	3	.571	1.51	0.84	75	0	0	0	1	38-41	77.2	45	17	13	6	20-2	87	.165
2006— New York (N.L.)	3	2	.600	2.24	1.11	70	0	0	0	1	40-45	72.1	59	22	18	7	21-1	94	.219
Major League totals (12 years)	37	34	.521	2.38	1.00	654	0	0	0	7	324-374	702.2	468	204	186	66	238-19	934	.187

DIVISION SERIES RECORD

Year Team (League)	W	L	Pct.	ERA	WHIP	G	GS	CG	ShO	Hld.	Sv.-Opp.	IP	H	R	ER	HR	BB-IBB	SO	Avg.
1997— Houston (N.L.)	0	0	...	18.00	3.00	1	0	0	0	0	0-0	1.0	3	2	2	0	0-0	2	.500
1998— Houston (N.L.)	1	0	1.000	18.00	4.00	1	0	0	0	0	0-1	1.0	4	2	2	1	0-0	1	.571
1999— Houston (N.L.)	0	0	...	0.00	0.00	1	0	0	0	0	0-0	1.0	0	0	0	0	0-0	1	.000
2001— Houston (N.L.)	0	0	...	5.40	0.60	2	0	0	0	0	0-0	1.2	1	1	1	0	0-0	3	.167
2006— New York (N.L.)	0	0	...	3.00	1.00	3	0	0	0	0	2-2	3.0	3	1	1	0	0-0	4	.250
Division series totals (5 years)	1	0	1.000	7.04	1.43	8	0	0	0	0	2-3	7.2	11	6	6	2	0-0	11	.324

CHAMPIONSHIP SERIES RECORD

Year Team (League)	W	L	Pct.	ERA	WHIP	G	GS	CG	ShO	Hld.	Sv.-Opp.	IP	H	R	ER	HR	BB-IBB	SO	Avg.
2006— New York (N.L.)	0	1	.000	16.88	3.00	3	0	0	0	0	1-1	2.2	7	5	5	1	1-0	0	.467

ALL-STAR GAME RECORD

	W	L	Pct.	ERA	WHIP	G	GS	CG	ShO	Hld.	Sv.-Opp.	IP	H	R	ER	HR	BB-IBB	SO	Avg.
All-Star Game totals (3 years)	0	0	...	4.50	0.50	3	0	0	0	0	0-0	2.0	1	1	1	0	1-0	2	.143

2006 LEFTY-RIGHTY SPLITS

vs.	Avg.	AB	H	2B	3B	HR	RBI	BB	SO	OBP	Slg.	vs.	Avg.	AB	H	2B	3B	HR	RBI	BB	SO	OBP	Slg.
L	.161	56	9	0	0	1	4	2	19	.190	.214	R	.234	214	50	5	0	6	17	19	75	.308	.341

WAGNER, RYAN — P

PERSONAL: Born July 15, 1982, in Yoakum, Texas. ... 6-4/210. ... Throws right, bats right. ... Full name: Ryan Scott Wagner. ... High school: Yoakum (Texas). ... College: Houston. **TRANSACTIONS/CAREER NOTES:** Selected by Cincinnati Reds organization in first round (14th pick overall) of 2003 free-agent draft. ... On bereavement list (Sept. 20-24, 2004). ... On disabled list (July 15, 2005-remainder of season). ... Traded by Reds with SS Felipe Lopez and OF Austin Kearns to Washington Nationals for Ps Gary Majewski, Bill Bray and Daryl Thompson, SS Royce Clayton and IF Brendan Harris (July 13, 2006).

CAREER HITTING: 1-for-4 (.250), 1 R, 0 2B, 0 3B, 0 HR, 0 RBI.

Year Team (League)	W	L	Pct.	ERA	WHIP	G	GS	CG	ShO	Hld.	Sv.-Opp.	IP	H	R	ER	HR	BB-IBB	SO	Avg.
2003— Chattanooga (Sou.)	1	0	1.000	0.00	0.80	5	0	0	0	...	0-...	5.0	2	1	0	0	2-0	6	.125
— Louisville (Int'l)	0	1	.000	4.50	1.25	4	0	0	0	...	0-0	4.0	5	2	2	0	0-0	4	.313
— Cincinnati (N.L.)	2	0	1.000	1.66	1.15	17	0	0	0	6	0-1	21.2	13	4	4	2	12-1	25	.173
2004— Louisville (Int'l)	1	0	1.000	2.70	1.32	15	0	0	0	...	1-...	16.2	13	5	5	0	9-0	19	.210
— Cincinnati (N.L.)	3	2	.600	4.70	1.66	49	0	0	0	8	0-3	51.2	59	31	27	7	27-2	37	.284
2005— Cincinnati (N.L.)	3	2	.600	6.11	1.60	42	0	0	0	12	0-1	45.2	56	33	31	4	17-1	39	.303
2006— Louisville (Int'l)	1	3	.250	6.34	1.80	35	0	0	0	6	1-4	38.1	55	29	27	3	14-1	28	.344
— New Orleans (PCL)	0	0	...	4.00	1.11	6	0	0	0	1	0-0	9.0	8	4	4	0	2-0	5	.250
— Wash. (N.L.)	3	3	.500	4.70	1.66	26	0	0	0	3	0-2	30.2	36	21	16	3	15-3	20	.293
Major League totals (4 years)	11	7	.611	4.69	1.57	134	0	0	0	29	0-7	149.2	164	89	78	16	71-7	121	.277

W

2006 LEFTY-RIGHTY SPLITS

vs.	Avg.	AB	H	2B	3B	HR	RBI	BB	SO	OBP	Slg.	vs.	Avg.	AB	H	2B	3B	HR	RBI	BB	SO	OBP	Slg.
L	.197	61	12	2	0	1	10	9	7	.300	.279	R	.387	62	24	3	0	2	9	6	13	.457	.532

WAINWRIGHT, ADAM　　　　　　　　　P

PERSONAL: Born August 30, 1981, in Brunswick, Ga. ... 6-7/205. ... Throws right, bats right. ... Full name: Adam Parrish Wainwright. ... High school: Glynn Academy (Brunswick, Ga.). **TRANSACTIONS/CAREER NOTES:** Selected by Atlanta Braves organization in first round (29th pick overall) of 2000 free-agent draft. ... Traded by Braves with Ps Ray King and Jason Marquis to St. Louis Cardinals for OFs J.D. Drew and Eli Marrero (December 14, 2003). **STATISTICAL NOTES:** Hit a home run in first major league at-bat (May 24, 2006). **MISCELLANEOUS NOTES:** Appeared in one game as pinch runner (2005).
CAREER HITTING: 3-for-6 (.500), 2 R, 1 2B, 0 3B, 1 HR, 1 RBI.

Year , Team (League)	W	L	Pct.	ERA	WHIP	G	GS	CG	ShO	Hld.	Sv.-Opp.	IP	H	R	ER	HR	BB-IBB	SO	Avg.
2000— GC Braves (GCL)	4	0	1.000	1.13	0.78	7	5	0	0	...	0-...	32.0	15	5	4	1	10-0	42	.136
— Danville (Appal.)	2	2	.500	3.68	1.02	6	6	0	0	...	0-...	29.1	28	13	12	3	2-0	39	.252
2001— Macon (S. Atl.)	10	10	.500	3.77	1.17	28	28	1	0	...	0-...	164.2	144	89	69	9	48-1	184	.230
2002— Myrtle Beach (Carol.)	9	6	.600	3.31	1.32	28	28	1	0	...	0-...	163.1	149	67	60	7	66-0	167	.240
2003— Greenville (Sou.)	10	8	.556	3.37	1.14	27	27	1	0	...	0-...	149.2	133	59	56	9	37-0	128	.242
2004— Memphis (PCL)	4	4	.500	5.37	1.51	12	12	0	0	...	0-...	63.2	68	47	38	12	28-0	64	.280
2005— Memphis (PCL)	10	10	.500	4.40	1.40	29	29	0	0	...	0-0	182.0	204	98	89	18	51-6	147	.282
— St. Louis (N.L.)	0	0	...	13.50	1.50	2	0	0	0	0	0-...	2.0	2	3	3	1	1-0	0	.250
2006— St. Louis (N.L.)	2	1	.667	3.12	1.15	61	0	0	0	17	3-5	75.0	64	26	26	6	22-2	72	.230
Major League totals (2 years)	2	1	.667	3.39	1.16	63	0	0	0	17	3-5	77.0	66	29	29	7	23-2	72	.231

DIVISION SERIES RECORD

Year Team (League)	W	L	Pct.	ERA	WHIP	G	GS	CG	ShO	Hld.	Sv.-Opp.	IP	H	R	ER	HR	BB-IBB	SO	Avg.
2006— St. Louis (N.L.)	0	0	...	0.00	0.82	3	0	0	0	...	1-1	3.2	3	0	0	0	0-0	6	.214

CHAMPIONSHIP SERIES RECORD

Year Team (League)	W	L	Pct.	ERA	WHIP	G	GS	CG	ShO	Hld.	Sv.-Opp.	IP	H	R	ER	HR	BB-IBB	SO	Avg.
2006— St. Louis (N.L.)	0	0	...	0.00	1.00	3	0	0	0	...	2-2	3.0	2	0	0	0	1-0	4	.182

WORLD SERIES RECORD

Year Team (League)	W	L	Pct.	ERA	WHIP	G	GS	CG	ShO	Hld.	Sv.-Opp.	IP	H	R	ER	HR	BB-IBB	SO	Avg.
2006— St. Louis (N.L.)	1	0	1.000	0.00	1.00	3	0	0	0	...	1-2	3.0	2	0	0	0	1-0	5	.182

2006 LEFTY-RIGHTY SPLITS

vs.	Avg.	AB	H	2B	3B	HR	RBI	BB	SO	OBP	Slg.	vs.	Avg.	AB	H	2B	3B	HR	RBI	BB	SO	OBP	Slg.
L	.301	113	34	6	0	5	16	14	38	.380	.487	R	.182	165	30	9	0	1	9	8	34	.233	.255

WAKEFIELD, TIM　　　　　　　　　P

PERSONAL: Born August 2, 1966, in Melbourne, Fla. ... 6-2/210. ... Throws right, bats right. ... Full name: Timothy Stephen Wakefield. ... High school: Eau Gallie (Melbourne, Fla.). ... College: Florida Tech. **TRANSACTIONS/CAREER NOTES:** Selected by Pittsburgh Pirates organization in eighth round of 1988 free-agent draft. ... Played infield in Pirates organization (1988-89). ... Released by Pirates (April 20, 1995). ... Signed by Boston Red Sox organization (April 26, 1995). ... On disabled list (April 15-May 6, 1997 and July 22-September 13, 2006). **HONORS:** Named N.L. Rookie Pitcher of the Year by THE SPORTING NEWS (1992). ... Named A.L. Comeback Player of the Year by THE SPORTING NEWS (1995). **MISCELLANEOUS NOTES:** Appeared in one game as pinch runner with Pittsburgh (1992). ... Had a sacrifice hit in only appearance as pinch hitter (1998). ... Had a sacrifice hit in only appearance as pinch hitter (2000).
CAREER HITTING: 12-for-96 (.125), 4 R, 2 2B, 0 3B, 1 HR, 4 RBI.

Year Team (League)	W	L	Pct.	ERA	WHIP	G	GS	CG	ShO	Hld.	Sv.-Opp.	IP	H	R	ER	HR	BB-IBB	SO	Avg.
1989— Welland (NYP)	1	1	.500	3.40	1.29	36	1	0	0	...	2-...	39.2	30	17	15	1	21-0	42	.211
1990— Salem (Carol.)	10	14	.417	4.73	1.43	28	28	2	0	...	0-...	190.1	187	109	100	24	85-2	127	.261
1991— Carolina (Southern)	15	8	.652	2.90	1.13	26	25	8	1	...	0-...	183.0	155	68	59	13	51-6	120	.231
— Buffalo (A.A.)	0	1	.000	11.57	1.93	1	1	0	0	...	0-...	4.2	8	6	6	3	1-0	4	.364
1992— Buffalo (A.A.)	10	3	.769	3.06	1.28	20	20	6	1	...	0-...	135.1	122	52	46	10	51-1	71	.246
— Pittsburgh (N.L.)	8	1	.889	2.15	1.21	13	13	4	1	0	0-0	92.0	76	26	22	3	35-1	51	.232
1993— Pittsburgh (N.L.)	6	11	.353	5.61	1.71	24	20	3	2	0	0-0	128.1	145	83	80	14	75-2	59	.291
— Carolina (Southern)	3	5	.375	6.99	1.59	9	9	1	0	...	0-...	56.2	68	48	44	5	22-0	36	.293
1994— Buffalo (A.A.)	5	15	.250	5.84	1.68	30	29	4	1	...	0-...	175.2	197	127	114	27	98-0	83	.290
1995— Pawtucket (Int'l)	2	1	.667	2.52	1.28	4	4	0	0	...	0-...	25.0	23	10	7	1	9-0	14	.253
— Boston (A.L.)	16	8	.667	2.95	1.18	27	27	6	1	0	0-...	195.1	163	76	64	22	68-0	119	.227
1996— Boston (A.L.)	14	13	.519	5.14	1.55	32	32	6	0	0	0-0	211.2	238 *	151	121	38	90-0	140	.280
1997— Boston (A.L.)	12	• 15	.444	4.25	1.39	35	29	4	2	1	0-0	201.1	193	109	95	24	87-5	151	.256
1998— Boston (A.L.)	17	8	.680	4.58	1.34	36	33	2	0	0	0-0	216.0	211	123	110	30	79-1	146	.252
1999— Boston (A.L.)	6	11	.353	5.08	1.56	49	17	0	0	...	15-18	140.0	146	93	79	19	72-2	104	.266
2000— Boston (A.L.)	6	10	.375	5.48	1.47	51	17	0	0	3	0-1	159.1	170	107	97	31	65-3	102	.272
2001— Boston (A.L.)	9	12	.429	3.90	1.36	45	17	0	0	3	3-5	168.2	156	84	73	13	73-5	148	.248
2002— Boston (A.L.)	11	5	.688	2.81	1.05	45	15	0	0	5	3-5	163.1	121	57	51	15	51-2	134	.204
2003— Boston (A.L.)	11	7	.611	4.09	1.30	35	33	0	0	1	1-1	202.1	193	106	92	23	71-0	169	.246
2004— Boston (A.L.)	12	10	.545	4.87	1.38	32	30	0	0	0	0-0	188.1	197	121	102	29	63-3	116	.264
2005— Boston (A.L.)	16	12	.571	4.15	1.23	33	33	3	0	0	0-0	225.1	210	113	104	* 35	68-4	151	.246
2006— Boston (A.L.)	7	11	.389	4.63	1.33	23	23	1	0	0	0-0	140.0	135	80	72	19	51-0	90	.248
American League totals (12 years)	137	122	.529	4.31	1.34	443	306	22	3	13	22-30	2211.2	2133	1220	1060	298	838-25	1570	.251
National League totals (2 years)	14	12	.538	4.17	1.50	37	33	7	3	0	0-0	220.1	221	109	102	17	110-3	110	.268
Major League totals (14 years)	151	134	.530	4.30	1.36	480	339	29	6	13	22-30	2432.0	2354	1329	1162	315	948-28	1680	.253

DIVISION SERIES RECORD

Year Team (League)	W	L	Pct.	ERA	WHIP	G	GS	CG	ShO	Hld.	Sv.-Opp.	IP	H	R	ER	HR	BB-IBB	SO	Avg.
1995— Boston (A.L.)	0	1	.000	11.81	1.88	1	1	0	0	0	0-0	5.1	5	7	7	1	5-0	4	.238
1998— Boston (A.L.)	0	1	.000	33.75	3.75	1	1	0	0	0	0-0	1.1	3	5	5	0	2-0	1	.500
1999— Boston (A.L.)	0	0	...	13.50	3.50	2	0	0	0	0	0-0	2.0	3	3	3	0	4-0	4	.300
2003— Boston (A.L.)	0	1	.000	3.52	1.17	2	1	0	0	0	0-0	7.2	6	5	3	0	3-0	7	.207
2005— Boston (A.L.)	0	1	.000	6.75	1.31	1	1	0	0	0	0-0	5.1	6	4	4	1	1-0	4	.300
Division series totals (5 years)	0	4	.000	9.14	1.75	7	4	0	0	0	0-0	21.2	23	24	22	2	15-0	20	.267

CHAMPIONSHIP SERIES RECORD

Year Team (League)	W	L	Pct.	ERA	WHIP	G	GS	CG	ShO	Hld.	Sv.-Opp.	IP	H	R	ER	HR	BB-IBB	SO	Avg.
1992— Pittsburgh (N.L.)	2	0	1.000	3.00	1.06	2	2	2	0	0	0-0	18.0	14	6	6	4	5-0	7	.206
1999— Boston (A.L.)			Did not play.																
2003— Boston (A.L.)	2	1	.667	2.57	1.00	3	2	0	0	0	0-0	14.0	8	4	4	1	6-0	10	.163
2004— Boston (A.L.)	1	0	1.000	8.59	1.64	3	0	0	0	0	0-0	7.1	9	7	7	1	3-2	6	.281
Champ. series totals (3 years)	5	1	.833	3.89	1.14	8	4	2	0	0	0-0	39.1	31	17	17	6	14-2	23	.208

W

Year Team (League)	W	L	Pct.	ERA	WHIP	G	GS	CG	ShO	Hld.	Sv.-Opp.	IP	H	R	ER	HR	BB-IBB	SO	Avg.

WORLD SERIES RECORD

Year Team (League)	W	L	Pct.	ERA	WHIP	G	GS	CG	ShO	Hld.	Sv.-Opp.	IP	H	R	ER	HR	BB-IBB	SO	Avg.
2004— Boston (A.L.)	0	0		12.27	2.18	1	1	0	0	0	0-0	3.2	3	5	5	1	5-0	2	.300

2006 LEFTY-RIGHTY SPLITS

vs.	Avg.	AB	H	2B	3B	HR	RBI	BB	SO	OBP	Slg.	vs.	Avg.	AB	H	2B	3B	HR	RBI	BB	SO	OBP	Slg.
L	.221	217	48	11	1	4	17	20	35	.286	.336	R	.265	328	87	20	0	15	52	31	55	.345	.463

WALKER, JAMIE — P

PERSONAL: Born July 1, 1971, in McMinnville, Tenn. ... 6-2/195. ... Throws left, bats left. ... Full name: Jamie Ross Walker. ... High school: Warren County (McMinnville, Tenn.). ... College: Austin Peay. **TRANSACTIONS/CAREER NOTES:** Selected by Houston Astros organization in 10th round of 1992 free-agent draft. ... Selected by Atlanta Braves from Astros organization in Rule 5 major league draft (December 9, 1996). ... Traded by Braves with OF Jermaine Dye to Kansas City Royals for OF Michael Tucker and IF Keith Lockhart (March 27, 1997). ... On disabled list (June 5-24, 1997; included rehabilitation assignment to Wichita. ... On disabled list (June 1, 1998-remainder of season). ... Released by Royals (July 27, 2000). ... Signed by Cleveland Indians organization (February 9, 2001). ... Signed as a free agent by Detroit Tigers organization (December 19, 2001).

CAREER HITTING: 0-for-0 (.000), 0 R, 0 2B, 0 3B, 0 HR, 0 RBI.

Year Team (League)	W	L	Pct.	ERA	WHIP	G	GS	CG	ShO	Hld.	Sv.-Opp.	IP	H	R	ER	HR	BB-IBB	SO	Avg.
1992— Auburn (NY-Penn)	4	6	.400	3.13	1.15	15	14	0	0	...	0-...	83.1	75	35	29	4	21-0	67	.243
1993— Quad City (Midw.)	3	11	.214	5.13	1.43	25	24	1	1	...	0-...	131.2	140	92	75	12	48-1	121	.271
1994— Quad City (Midw.)	8	10	.444	4.18	1.40	32	18	0	0	...	1-...	125.0	133	80	58	10	42-2	104	.269
1995— Jackson (Texas)	4	2	.667	4.50	1.43	50	0	0	0	...	2-...	58.0	59	29	29	6	24-5	38	.269
1996— Jackson (Texas)	5	1	.833	2.50	1.28	45	7	0	0	...	2-...	101.0	94	34	28	7	35-2	79	.249
1997— Kansas City (A.L.)	3	3	.500	5.44	1.53	50	0	0	0	3	0-1	43.0	46	28	26	6	20-3	24	.271
— Wichita (Texas)	0	1	.000	9.45	1.65	5	0	0	0	...	0-...	6.2	6	8	7	1	5-0	6	.261
1998— Omaha (PCL)	5	1	.833	2.70	1.46	7	7	0	0	...	0-...	46.2	57	15	14	3	11-1	21	.313
— Kansas City (A.L.)	0	1	.000	9.87	1.90	6	2	0	0	1	0-0	17.1	30	20	19	5	3-0	15	.380
1999— Omaha (PCL)	0	1	.000	4.67	1.50	4	4	0	0	...	0-...	17.1	22	12	9	1	4-0	11	.314
— GC Royals (GCL)	1	0	1.000	3.38	1.25	2	2	0	0	...	0-...	8.0	10	3	3	1	0-0	9	.286
2000— Omaha (PCL)	3	10	.231	5.22	1.60	24	15	0	0	...	0-...	101.2	138	65	59	25	25-1	52	.336
2001— Buffalo (Int'l)	7	2	.778	3.87	1.41	38	8	0	0	...	2-...	93.0	104	44	40	12	27-1	51	.282
2002— Toledo (Int'l)	0	1	.000	1.98	0.73	10	0	0	0	...	1-...	13.2	7	3	3	2	3-0	9	.156
— Detroit (A.L.)	1	1	.500	3.71	0.94	57	0	0	0	5	1-4	43.2	32	19	18	9	9-1	40	.199
2003— Detroit (A.L.)	4	3	.571	3.32	1.20	78	0	0	0	12	3-7	65.0	61	30	24	6	17-1	45	.247
2004— Detroit (A.L.)	3	4	.429	3.20	1.25	70	0	0	0	18	1-7	64.2	69	28	23	8	12-3	53	.263
2005— Detroit (A.L.)	4	3	.571	3.70	1.27	66	0	0	0	14	0-2	48.2	49	22	20	5	13-3	30	.257
2006— Detroit (A.L.)	0	1	.000	2.81	1.15	56	0	0	0	11	0-0	48.0	47	15	15	8	8-3	37	.251
Major League totals (7 years)	**15**	**16**	**.484**	**3.95**	**1.26**	**383**	**2**	**0**	**0**	**64**	**5-21**	**330.1**	**334**	**162**	**145**	**50**	**82-14**	**244**	**.258**

DIVISION SERIES RECORD

Year Team (League)	W	L	Pct.	ERA	WHIP	G	GS	CG	ShO	Hld.	Sv.-Opp.	IP	H	R	ER	HR	BB-IBB	SO	Avg.
2006— Detroit (A.L.)	1	0	1.000	4.91	1.09	3	0	0	0	0	0-0	3.2	3	2	2	2	1-0	1	.231

CHAMPIONSHIP SERIES RECORD

Year Team (League)	W	L	Pct.	ERA	WHIP	G	GS	CG	ShO	Hld.	Sv.-Opp.	IP	H	R	ER	HR	BB-IBB	SO	Avg.
2006— Detroit (A.L.)	0	0	...	0.00	0.00	1	0	0	0	0	0-0	0.1	0	0	0	0	0-0	1	.000

WORLD SERIES RECORD

Year Team (League)	W	L	Pct.	ERA	WHIP	G	GS	CG	ShO	Hld.	Sv.-Opp.	IP	H	R	ER	HR	BB-IBB	SO	Avg.
2006— Detroit (A.L.)	0	0	...	0.00	0.00	1	0	0	0	0	0-0	0.1	0	0	0	0	0-0	1	.000

2006 LEFTY-RIGHTY SPLITS

vs.	Avg.	AB	H	2B	3B	HR	RBI	BB	SO	OBP	Slg.	vs.	Avg.	AB	H	2B	3B	HR	RBI	BB	SO	OBP	Slg.
L	.235	81	19	9	0	3	8	3	24	.262	.457	R	.264	106	28	2	1	5	13	5	13	.297	.443

WALKER, PETE — P

PERSONAL: Born April 8, 1969, in Beverly, Mass. ... 6-2/195. ... Throws right, bats right. ... Full name: Peter Brian Walker. ... High school: East Lyme (Conn.). ... College: Connecticut. **TRANSACTIONS/CAREER NOTES:** Selected by New York Mets organization in seventh round of free-agent draft (June 4, 1990). ... Traded by Mets with P Luis Arroyo to San Diego Padres for 1B Roberto Petagine and P Scott Adair (March 17, 1996). ... Signed as a free agent by Boston Red Sox organization (June 30, 1997). ... Signed as a free agent by Colorado Rockies organization (February 8, 1999). ... Released by Rockies (November 13, 2000). ... Signed by Mets organization (December 26, 2000). ... Claimed on waivers by Toronto Blue Jays (May 3, 2002). ... On disabled list (June 10-27, 2006). ... On disabled list (July 8, 2006-remainder of season).

CAREER HITTING: 0-for-1 (.000), 0 R, 0 2B, 0 3B, 0 HR, 0 RBI.

Year Team (League)	W	L	Pct.	ERA	WHIP	G	GS	CG	ShO	Hld.	Sv.-Opp.	IP	H	R	ER	HR	BB-IBB	SO	Avg.
1990— Pittsfield (NYP)	5	7	.417	4.16	1.50	16	13	1	0	...	0-...	80.0	74	43	37	1	46-0	73	.253
1991— St. Lucie (Fla. St.)	10	12	.455	3.21	1.30	26	25	1	0	...	0-...	152.0	145	77	54	9	52-2	95	.254
1992— Binghamton (East.)	7	12	.368	4.12	1.47	24	23	4	0	...	0-...	139.2	159	77	64	9	46-0	72	.289
1993— Binghamton (East.)	4	9	.308	3.44	1.35	45	10	0	0	...	19-...	100.0	89	45	38	6	46-1	89	.244
1994— St. Lucie (Fla. St.)	0	0	...	2.25	1.00	3	0	0	0	...	0-...	4.0	3	2	1	1	1-0	5	.200
— Norfolk (Int'l)	2	4	.333	3.97	1.51	37	0	0	0	...	0-...	47.2	48	22	21	3	24-2	42	.270
1995— Norfolk (Int'l)	5	2	.714	3.91	1.37	34	1	0	0	...	8-...	49.0	51	24	21	4	16-1	39	.274
— New York (N.L.)	1	0	1.000	4.58	1.64	13	0	0	0	1	0-0	17.2	24	9	9	3	5-0	5	.329
1996— Las Vegas (PCL)	5	1	.833	6.83	1.84	26	0	0	0	...	0-...	27.2	37	22	21	7	14-2	23	.336
— Ariz. Padres (Ariz.)	0	1	.000	2.25	1.00	2	2	0	0	...	0-...	4.0	4	1	1	0	0-0	5	.250
— San Diego (N.L.)	0	0	...	0.00	4.50	1	0	0	0	...	0-0	2.0	0	0	0	0	3-0	1	.000
1997— GC Red Sox (GCL)	0	0	...	0.96	0.60	4	3	0	0	...	0-...	10.0	5	1	1	0	1-0	14	.147
— Trenton (East.)	0	0	...	4.05	1.50	8	0	0	0	...	3-...	14.0	14	6	6	1	7-0	13	.275
— Pawtucket (Int'l)	0	0	...	5.40	1.80	7	0	0	0	...	0-...	11.2	14	8	7	2	7-0	8	.280
1998— Pawtucket (Int'l)	1	4	.200	5.94	1.50	22	0	0	0	...	0-...	34.0	34	26	22	8	17-1	19	.272
1999— Colo. Springs (PCL)	8	4	.667	4.48	1.46	48	0	0	0	...	5-...	63.0	64	37	31	9	28-3	57	.268
2000— Colo. Springs (PCL)	7	3	.700	3.07	1.27	58	0	0	0	...	5-...	74.0	64	29	25	3	30-1	61	.231
— Colorado (N.L.)	0	0	...	17.36	3.00	3	0	0	0	...	0-...	4.2	10	9	9	1	4-0	2	.435
2001— Norfolk (Int'l)	13	4	.765	2.99	1.13	26	26	0	0	...	0-...	169.0	145	64	56	12	46-5	106	.234
— New York (N.L.)	0	0	...	2.70	0.90	2	0	0	0	...	0-0	6.2	6	2	2	0	0-0	4	.240
2002— Norfolk (Int'l)	0	0	...	3.00	1.11	2	2	0	0	...	0-...	9.0	9	3	3	1	1-0	5	.243
— New York (N.L.)	0	0	...	9.00	2.00	1	0	0	0	...	0-0	1.0	2	1	1	0	0-0	0	.400
— Toronto (A.L.)	10	5	.667	4.33	1.39	37	20	0	0	3	1-1	139.1	143	72	67	18	51-5	80	.270
2003— New Haven (East.)	0	1	.000	9.00	1.50	2	0	0	0	...	0-...	2.0	3	2	2	0	0-0	4	.375
— Syracuse (Int'l)	0	1	.000	6.75	1.29	5	5	0	0	...	0-...	14.0	15	10	10	2	3-0	8	.278
— Toronto (A.L.)	2	2	.500	4.88	1.50	23	7	0	0	2	0-0	55.1	59	31	30	11	24-2	29	.277

Year Team (League)	W	L	Pct.	ERA	WHIP	G	GS	CG	ShO	Hld.	Sv.-Opp.	IP	H	R	ER	HR	BB-IBB	SO	Avg.
2005— Toronto (A.L.)	6	6	.500	3.54	1.36	41	4	0	0	4	2-5	84.0	81	33	33	10	33-0	43	.254
2006— Toronto (A.L.)	1	1	.500	5.40	1.67	23	0	0	0	3	1-1	30.0	37	24	18	5	13-2	27	.296
American League totals (4 years)	19	14	.576	4.32	1.43	124	31	0	0	12	4-7	308.2	320	160	148	44	121-9	179	.270
National League totals (5 years)	1	0	1.000	6.16	1.76	20	0	0	0	1	0-0	30.2	42	21	21	4	12-0	12	.328
Major League totals (8 years)	20	14	.588	4.48	1.46	144	31	0	0	13	4-7	339.1	362	181	169	48	133-9	191	.275

2006 LEFTY-RIGHTY SPLITS

vs.	Avg.	AB	H	2B	3B	HR	RBI	BB	SO	OBP	Slg.	vs.	Avg.	AB	H	2B	3B	HR	RBI	BB	SO	OBP	Slg.
L	.318	44	14	2	1	3	9	8	12	.423	.614	R	.284	81	23	4	0	2	12	5	15	.326	.407

WALKER, TODD — IF

PERSONAL: Born May 25, 1973, in Bakersfield, Calif. ... 6-0/185. ... Bats left, throws right. ... Full name: Todd Arthur Walker. ... High school: Airline (Bossier City, La.). ... College: Louisiana State. **TRANSACTIONS/CAREER NOTES:** Selected by Texas Rangers organization in 51st round of 1991 free-agent draft; did not sign. ... Selected by Minnesota Twins organization in first round (eighth pick overall) of 1994 free-agent draft. ... Traded by Twins with OF/1B Butch Huskey to Colorado Rockies for 2B Todd Sears and cash (July 16, 2000). ... Traded by Rockies with OF Robin Jennings to Cincinnati Reds for OF Alex Ochoa (July 19, 2001). ... Traded by Reds to Boston Red Sox for two players to be named (December 12, 2002); Reds acquired P Josh Thigpen and 3B Tony Blanco to complete deal (December 16, 2002). ... Signed as a free agent by Chicago Cubs (January 6, 2004). ... On disabled list (April 11-May 25, 2005); included rehabilitation assignment to Iowa. ... Traded by Cubs to San Diego Padres for P Jose Ceda (July 31, 2006). **STATISTICAL NOTES:** Career major league grand slams: 2.

2006 GAMES PLAYED BY POSITION (MLB): 2B—60, 1B—40, 3B—23, DH—5.

Year Team (League)	Pos.	G	AB	R	H	2B	3B	HR	RBI	BB	SO	HBP	GDP	SB-CS	Avg.	OBP	SLG	OPS	E	Avg.
1994— Fort Myers (FSL)	2B	46	171	29	52	5	2	10	34	32	15	0	4	6-3	.304	.406	.532	.938	9	.959
1995— New Britain (East.)	2B-3B	137	513	83	149	27	3	21	85	63	101	2	13	23-9	.290	.365	.478	.843	27	.955
1996— Salt Lake (PCL) 3B-2B-DH		135	551	94	187	41	9	28	111	57	91	5	17	13-8	.339	.400	.599	.999	19	.955
— Minnesota (A.L.) 3B-2B-DH		25	82	8	21	6	0	0	6	4	13	0	4	2-0	.256	.281	.329	.610	2	.965
1997— Minnesota (A.L.) 3B-2B-DH		52	156	15	37	7	1	3	16	11	30	1	5	7-0	.237	.288	.353	.641	4	.968
— Salt Lake (PCL)	3B-DH	83	322	69	111	20	1	11	53	46	49	1	10	5-5	.345	.420	.516	.936	24	.901
1998— Minnesota (A.L.)	2B-DH	143	528	85	167	41	3	12	62	47	65	2	13	19-7	.316	.372	.473	.845	13	.978
1999— Minnesota (A.L.)	2B-DH	143	531	62	148	37	4	6	46	52	83	1	15	18-10	.279	.343	.397	.740	7	.984
2000— Minnesota (A.L.)	2B-DH	23	77	14	18	1	0	2	8	7	10	0	3	3-0	.234	.287	.325	.612	4	.946
— Salt Lake (PCL)	2B	63	249	51	81	14	1	2	37	32	32	0	6	8-3	.325	.398	.414	.812	11	.964
— Colorado (N.L.)	2B	57	171	28	54	10	4	7	36	20	19	1	2	4-1	.316	.385	.544	.928	5	.975
2001— Colorado (N.L.)	2B	85	290	52	86	18	2	12	43	25	40	0	8	1-3	.297	.349	.497	.846	7	.981
— Cincinnati (N.L.)	2B-SS	66	261	41	77	17	0	5	32	26	42	1	6	0-5	.295	.361	.418	.779	4	.987
2002— Cincinnati (N.L.)	2B	155	612	79	183	42	3	11	64	50	81	3	9	8-5	.299	.353	.431	.785	8	.989
2003— Boston (A.L.)	2B	144	587	92	166	38	4	13	85	48	54	1	17	1-1	.283	.333	.428	.760	16	.975
2004— Chicago (N.L.) 2B-1B-OF		129	372	60	102	19	4	15	50	43	52	4	2	0-3	.274	.352	.468	.820	7	.982
2005— Iowa (PCL)	2B-DH	9	37	3	8	3	0	0	3	1	4	0	4	0-0	.216	.237	.297	.534	0	1.000
— Chicago (N.L.) 2B-1B-DH		110	397	50	121	25	3	12	40	31	40	1	8	1-1	.305	.355	.474	.829	6	.986
2006— Chicago (N.L.) 2B-1B-DH		94	318	38	88	16	1	6	40	38	27	1	7	0-1	.277	.352	.390	.742	7	.985
— San Diego (N.L.) 3B-2B-1B		44	124	18	35	6	1	3	13	17	11	0	1	2-0	.282	.366	.419	.786	6	.953
American League totals (6 years)		530	1961	276	557	130	12	36	223	169	255	5	57	50-18	.284	.339	.418	.756	46	.976
National League totals (6 years)		740	2545	366	746	153	18	71	318	250	312	11	43	16-19	.293	.356	.451	.807	50	.984
Major League totals (11 years)		1270	4506	642	1303	283	30	107	541	419	567	16	100	66-37	.289	.349	.437	.785	96	.981

DIVISION SERIES RECORD

Year Team (League)	Pos.	G	AB	R	H	2B	3B	HR	RBI	BB	SO	HBP	GDP	SB-CS	Avg.	OBP	SLG	OPS	E	Avg.
2003— Boston (A.L.)	2B	5	16	4	5	0	0	3	4	0	1	1	0	0-0	.313	.353	.875	1.228	2	.857
2006— San Diego (N.L.)	2B	3	9	0	0	0	0	0	0	0	0	0	1	0-0	.000	.000	.000	.000	0	1.000
Division series totals (2 years)		8	25	4	5	0	0	3	4	0	1	1	1	0-0	.200	.231	.560	.791	2	.929

CHAMPIONSHIP SERIES RECORD

Year Team (League)	Pos.	G	AB	R	H	2B	3B	HR	RBI	BB	SO	HBP	GDP	SB-CS	Avg.	OBP	SLG	OPS	E	Avg.
2003— Boston (A.L.)	2B	7	27	5	10	1	1	2	2	1	2	1	0	0-0	.370	.414	.704	1.118	0	1.000

2006 LEFTY-RIGHTY SPLITS

vs.	Avg.	AB	H	2B	3B	HR	RBI	BB	SO	OBP	Slg.	vs.	Avg.	AB	H	2B	3B	HR	RBI	BB	SO	OBP	Slg.
L	.204	108	22	3	0	1	8	16	19	10	.320	.315	R	.302	334	101	19	2	6	37	36	28	.368	.425

WALKER, TYLER — P

PERSONAL: Born May 15, 1976, in San Francisco. ... 6-3/255. ... Throws right, bats right. ... Full name: Tyler Lanier Walker. ... High school: University (San Francisco). ... College: California. **TRANSACTIONS/CAREER NOTES:** Selected by New York Mets organization in second round of 1997 free-agent draft. ... Claimed on waivers by Detroit Tigers (April 3, 2003). ... Signed as a free agent by San Francisco Giants organization (December 6, 2003). ... On disabled list (August 21-September 7, 2005). ... Traded by Giants to Tampa Bay Devil Rays for RHP Carlos Hines (April 28, 2006). ... On disabled list (June 14, 2006-reamainder of season). ... Released by Devil Rays (November 10, 2006). **CAREER HITTING:** 0-for-10 (.000), 0 R, 0 2B, 0 3B, 0 HR, 0 RBI.

Year Team (League)	W	L	Pct.	ERA	WHIP	G	GS	CG	ShO	Hld.	Sv.-Opp.	IP	H	R	ER	HR	BB-IBB	SO	Avg.
1997— GC Mets (GCL)	0	0	...	1.00	1.11	5	0	0	0	...	3-...	9.0	8	1	1	0	2-1	9	.235
— Pittsfield (NYP)	0	0	...	13.50	4.50	1	0	0	0	...	0-...	0.2	2	1	1	0	1-0	1	.400
1998— Capital City (SAL)	5	5	.500	4.12	1.38	34	13	0	0	...	1-...	115.2	122	63	53	9	38-0	110	.268
1999— St. Lucie (Fla. St.)	6	5	.545	2.94	1.17	13	13	2	0	...	0-...	79.2	64	31	26	6	29-2	64	.219
— Binghamton (East.)	6	4	.600	6.22	1.62	13	13	0	0	...	0-...	68.0	78	49	47	11	32-0	59	.292
2000— Binghamton (East.)	7	6	.538	2.75	1.13	22	22	0	0	...	0-...	121.0	82	43	37	3	55-1	111	.191
— Norfolk (Int'l)	1	3	.250	2.39	1.44	5	5	0	0	...	0-...	26.1	9	7	7	1	9-0	17	.290
2001— St. Lucie (Fla. St.)	0	2	.000	8.04	1.40	4	4	0	0	...	0-...	15.2	19	14	14	0	3-0	11	.288
— Binghamton (East.)	1	0	1.000	0.40	0.99	4	3	0	0	...	0-...	22.1	9	2	1	1	13-1	13	.127
— Norfolk (Int'l)	3	2	.600	4.02	1.04	8	8	0	0	...	0-...	40.1	34	19	18	7	8-0	35	.230
2002— Norfolk (Int'l)	10	5	.667	3.99	1.34	28	25	0	1	...	1-...	142.0	152	65	63	13	38-3	109	.275
— New York (N.L.)	1	0	1.000	5.91	1.50	5	1	0	0	...	0-...	10.2	11	7	7	3	5-1	7	.250
2003— Toledo (Int'l)	2	9	.182	4.45	1.40	26	22	0	0	...	0-...	131.1	139	73	65	13	47-5	117	.270
2004— Fresno (PCL)	1	1	.500	1.72	1.15	9	1	0	0	...	0-...	15.2	16	5	3	1	2-0	15	.250
— San Francisco (N.L.)	5	1	.833	4.24	1.46	52	0	0	0	...	1-1	63.2	69	31	30	8	24-1	48	.288
2005— San Francisco (N.L.)	6	4	.600	4.23	1.54	67	0	0	0	2	23-28	61.2	68	31	29	9	27-6	54	.281
2006— San Francisco (N.L.)	0	0	.000	15.19	2.63	6	0	0	0	1	0-2	5.1	9	9	9	1	5-0	3	.391
— Tampa Bay (A.L.)	1	3	.250	4.95	1.25	20	0	0	0	0	10-12	20.0	18	11	11	0	7-0	16	.240
American League totals (1 year)	1	3	.250	4.95	1.25	20	0	0	0	0	10-12	20.0	18	11	11	0	7-0	16	.240
National League totals (4 years)	12	6	.667	4.78	1.54	130	1	0	0	8	24-31	141.1	157	78	75	21	61-8	112	.286
Major League totals (4 years)	13	9	.591	4.80	1.51	150	1	0	0	8	34-43	161.1	175	89	86	21	68-8	128	.280

W

vs.	Avg.	AB	H	2B	3B	HR	RBI	BB	SO	OBP	Slg.	vs.	Avg.	AB	H	2B	3B	HR	RBI	BB	SO	OBP	Slg.
L	.333	45	15	3	0	1	8	6	8	.412	.467	R	.226	53	12	2	0	0	6	6	11	.305	.264

WALROND, LES — P

PERSONAL: Born November 7, 1976, in Muskogee, Okla. ... 6-0/210. ... Throws left, bats left. ... Full name: Leslie Dale Walrond. ... Name pronounced: WALL-run. ... High school: Union (Tulsa, Okla.). ... College: Kansas. **TRANSACTIONS/CAREER NOTES:** Selected by St. Louis Cardinals organization in 13th round of 1998 free-agent draft. ... On disabled list (May 12-July 20, 2001). ... Claimed on waivers by Kansas City Royals (May 29, 2003). ... Signed as a free agent by Florida Marlins organization (December 24, 2004). ... Released by Marlins (June 24, 2005). ... Signed by Chicago Cubs organization (January 11, 2006).

CAREER HITTING: 0-for-2 (.000), 0 R, 0 2B, 0 3B, 0 HR, 0 RBI.

Year — Team (League)	W	L	Pct.	ERA	WHIP	G	GS	CG	ShO	Hld.	Sv.-Opp.	IP	H	R	ER	HR	BB-IBB	SO	Avg.
1998— New Jersey (NYP)	2	4	.333	4.01	1.47	13	10	0	0	...	0-...	51.2	52	31	23	1	24-0	52	.259
1999— Peoria (Midw.)	7	10	.412	5.70	1.60	21	20	0	0	...	0-...	109.0	115	77	69	12	59-0	78	.274
2000— Potomac (Carol.)	10	5	.667	3.34	1.25	27	27	0	0	...	0-...	151.0	134	66	56	9	54-0	153	.236
2001— New Haven (East.)	2	8	.200	3.87	1.40	16	16	1	0	...	0-...	81.1	68	41	35	5	46-0	67	.227
2002— New Haven (East.)	2	1	.667	2.42	1.30	4	4	0	0	...	0-...	22.1	19	8	6	2	10-0	31	.221
— Memphis (PCL)	8	7	.533	4.98	1.54	28	18	0	0	...	0-...	123.0	127	75	68	20	63-2	111	.270
2003— Memphis (PCL)	0	0	...	1.04	1.10	10	1	0	0	...	0-...	17.1	12	2	2	0	7-1	14	.194
— Tennessee (Sou.)	0	0	...	2.70	1.20	4	0	0	0	...	0-...	6.2	4	2	2	1	4-0	7	.167
— Kansas City (A.L.)	0	2	.000	10.13	2.25	7	0	0	0	...	1	0-0	8.0	11	9	9	2	7-1	6	.324
— Omaha (PCL)	3	1	.750	2.45	1.10	18	0	0	0	...	2-...	25.2	19	9	7	1	9-0	20	.196
— Wichita (Texas)	2	0	1.000	3.27	0.80	2	2	0	0	...	0-...	11.0	7	4	4	2	2-0	9	.171
2004— Wichita (Texas)	3	3	.500	4.38	1.21	8	6	0	0	...	0-...	39.0	30	19	19	2	17-0	34	.213
— Omaha (PCL)	11	5	.688	3.06	1.25	19	19	1	1	...	0-...	123.2	114	46	42	12	41-0	107	.247
2005— Albuquerque (PCL)	4	5	.444	4.57	1.55	15	15	2	2	0	0-0	86.2	97	50	44	13	37-0	61	.291
2006— Iowa (PCL)	10	5	.667	3.98	1.45	31	20	0	0	2	0-1	133.1	134	72	59	11	59-6	104	.265
— Chicago (N.L.)	0	1	.000	6.23	1.79	10	2	0	0	0	0-0	17.1	19	13	12	2	12-1	21	.271
American League totals (1 year)	0	2	.000	10.13	2.25	7	0	0	0	1	0-0	8.0	11	9	9	2	7-1	6	.324
National League totals (1 year)	0	1	.000	6.23	1.79	10	2	0	0	0	0-0	17.1	19	13	12	2	12-1	21	.271
Major League totals (2 years)	0	3	.000	7.46	1.93	17	2	0	0	1	0-0	25.1	30	22	21	4	19-2	27	.288

vs.	Avg.	AB	H	2B	3B	HR	RBI	BB	SO	OBP	Slg.	vs.	Avg.	AB	H	2B	3B	HR	RBI	BB	SO	OBP	Slg.
L	.136	22	3	0	0	2	3	2	10	.200	.409	R	.333	48	16	4	0	0	8	10	11	.448	.417

WANG, CHIEN-MING — P

PERSONAL: Born March 31, 1980, in Tainan, Taiwan. ... 6-3/200. ... Throws right, bats right. ... Full name: Chien-Ming Wang. ... College: Taipei College of Physical Education. **TRANSACTIONS/CAREER NOTES:** Signed as a non-drafted free agent by New York Yankees organization (May 5, 2000). ... On disabled list (July 14-September 6, 2005).

CAREER HITTING: 0-for-5 (.000), 0 R, 0 2B, 0 3B, 0 HR, 0 RBI.

Year — Team (League)	W	L	Pct.	ERA	WHIP	G	GS	CG	ShO	Hld.	Sv.-Opp.	IP	H	R	ER	HR	BB-IBB	SO	Avg.
2000— Staten Is. (N.Y.-Penn)	4	4	.500	2.48	1.13	14	14	2	1	...	0-...	87.0	77	34	24	2	21-1	75	.233
2002— Staten Is. (N.Y.-Penn)	6	1	.857	1.72	0.98	13	13	0	0	...	0-...	78.1	63	23	15	2	14-0	64	.219
2003— Trenton (East.)	7	6	.538	4.65	1.43	21	21	2	1	...	0-...	122.0	143	71	63	7	32-2	84	.294
— GC Yankees (GCL)	0	0	...	0.00	0.67	1	1	0	0	...	0-...	3.0	2	0	0	0	0-0	2	.182
2004— Trenton (East.)	6	5	.545	4.05	1.27	18	18	0	0	...	0-...	109.0	112	53	49	6	26-0	90	.274
— Columbus (Int'l)	5	1	.833	2.01	0.97	6	5	2	1	...	0-...	40.1	31	9	9	3	8-0	35	.215
2005— Columbus (Int'l)	2	1	.667	4.24	1.35	6	6	0	0	0	0-0	34.0	40	16	16	4	6-0	21	.301
— New York (A.L.)	8	5	.615	4.02	1.25	18	17	0	0	0	0-0	116.1	113	58	52	9	32-3	47	.256
2006— New York (A.L.)	19	6	.760	3.63	1.31	34	33	2	1	0	1-1	218.0	233	92	88	12	52-4	76	.277
Major League totals (2 years)	27	11	.711	3.77	1.29	52	50	2	1	0	1-1	334.1	346	150	140	21	84-7	123	.270

DIVISION SERIES RECORD

Year — Team (League)	W	L	Pct.	ERA	WHIP	G	GS	CG	ShO	Hld.	Sv.-Opp.	IP	H	R	ER	HR	BB-IBB	SO	Avg.
2005— New York (A.L.)	0	1	.000	1.35	0.90	1	1	0	0	0	0-0	6.2	6	4	1	1	0-0	1	.231
2006— New York (A.L.)	1	0	1.000	4.05	1.35	1	1	0	0	0	0-0	6.2	8	3	3	1	1-0	4	.308
Division series totals (2 years)	1	1	.500	2.70	1.13	2	2	0	0	0	0-0	13.1	14	7	4	2	1-0	5	.269

vs.	Avg.	AB	H	2B	3B	HR	RBI	BB	SO	OBP	Slg.	vs.	Avg.	AB	H	2B	3B	HR	RBI	BB	SO	OBP	Slg.
L	.275	375	103	24	1	5	35	25	27	.321	.384	R	.279	466	130	20	0	7	48	27	49	.319	.367

WARD, DARYLE — 1B/OF

PERSONAL: Born June 27, 1975, in Lynwood, Calif. ... 6-2/230. ... Bats left, throws left. ... Full name: Daryle Lamar Ward. ... High school: Brethren Christian (Riverside, Calif.). ... Junior college: Rancho Santiago (Calif.). ... College: Santa Ana (CA) JC. ... Son of Gary Ward, outfielder with four major league teams (1979-90) and coach, Chicago White Sox (2001-03). **TRANSACTIONS/CAREER NOTES:** Selected by Detroit Tigers organization in 15th round of 1994 free-agent draft. ... Traded by Tigers with C Brad Ausmus and Ps Jose Lima, C.J. Nitkowski and Trever Miller to Houston Astros for OF Brian Hunter, IF Orlando Miller, Ps Doug Brocail and Todd Jones and cash (December 10, 1996). ... Traded by Astros to Los Angeles Dodgers for P Ruddy Lugo (January 25, 2003). ... Signed as a free agent by Pittsburgh Pirates organization (December 8, 2003). ... On disabled list (June 26-August 15, 2004); included rehabilitation assignment to Nashville. ... Signed as free agent by Washington Nationals organization (January 27, 2006).... Traded by Nationals to Atlanta Braves for P Luis Atilano (August 31, 2006). **STATISTICAL NOTES:** Hit for the cycle (May 26, 2004). ... Career major league grand slams: 2.

2006 GAMES PLAYED BY POSITION (MLB): OF—14, 1B—10, DH—4.

Year — Team (League)	Pos.	G	AB	R	H	2B	3B	HR	RBI	BB	SO	HBP	GDP	SB-CS	Avg.	OBP	SLG	OPS	E	Avg.
1994— Bristol (Appal.)	1B	48	161	17	43	6	0	5	30	19	33	0	3	5-1	.267	.343	.398	.740	11	.968
1995— Fayetteville (SAL)	1B	137	524	75	149	32	0	14	106	46	111	5	13	1-2	.284	.344	.426	.769	14	.987
1996— Lakeland (Fla. St.)	1B-DH	128	464	65	135	29	4	10	68	57	77	6	9	1-1	.291	.373	.435	.808	8	.993
— Toledo (Int'l)	1B	6	23	1	4	0	0	1	3	0	3	0	2	0-0	.174	.174	.174	.348	1	.979
1997— Jackson (Texas)	1B-DH	114	422	72	139	25	0	19	90	46	68	3	11	4-2	.329	.398	.524	.922	12	.988
— New Orleans (A.A.)	1B	14	48	4	18	1	0	2	8	7	7	0	0	0-0	.375	.455	.521	.975	2	.976
1998— New Orleans (PCL)	OF-1B-DH	116	463	78	141	31	1	23	96	41	78	2	17	2-0	.305	.361	.525	.886	5	.976
— Houston (N.L.)		4	3	1	1	0	0	0	0	1	2	0	0	0-0	.333	.500	.333	.833	...	...
1999— New Orleans (PCL)	1B-OF	61	241	56	85	15	1	28	65	23	43	3	3	1-1	.353	.416	.772	1.188	5	.991
— Houston (N.L.)	OF-1B-DH	64	150	11	41	6	0	8	30	9	31	0	3	0-0	.273	.311	.473	.784	2	.973
2000— Houston (N.L.)	OF-1B-DH	119	264	36	68	10	2	20	47	15	61	0	6	0-0	.258	.295	.538	.833	1	.992
2001— Houston (N.L.)	OF-1B-DH	95	213	21	56	15	0	9	39	19	48	1	4	0-0	.263	.323	.460	.784	1	.988

W

Year	Team (League)	Pos.	G	AB	R	H	2B	3B	HR	RBI	BB	SO	HBP	GDP	SB-CS	Avg.	OBP	SLG	OPS	E	Avg.
																			BATTING		**FIELDING**
2002— Houston (N.L.)		OF-DH	136	453	41	125	31	0	12	72	33	82	1	9	1-3	.276	.324	.424	.748	3	.981
2003— Jacksonville (Squ.)		1B-OF	4	16	0	2	0	0	0	1	0	3	0	0	0-0	.125	.125	.125	.250	0	.950
— Los Angeles (N.L.)		1B-OF	52	109	6	20	1	0	0	9	3	19	1	4	0-0	.183	.211	.193	.403	1	.992
— Las Vegas (PCL)		1B-DH	34	128	16	38	9	0	4	24	10	22	0	1	0-0	.297	.343	.461	.804	2	.992
2004— Nashville (PCL) 1B-DH-OF			28	96	14	27	7	0	7	17	5	16	0	1	0-0	.281	.317	.573	.890	0	1.000
— Pittsburgh (N.L.)		1B-OF	79	293	39	73	17	2	15	57	22	45	3	8	0-0	.249	.305	.474	.780	5	.992
2005— Pittsburgh (N.L.)		1B	133	407	46	106	21	1	12	63	37	60	1	18	0-2	.260	.318	.405	.723	6	.994
2006— Wash. (N.L.) OF-1B-DH			78	104	15	32	9	0	6	19	14	21	2	5	0-1	.308	.390	.567	.958	1	.980
— Atlanta (N.L.)		1B-OF	20	26	2	8	1	0	1	7	1	6	0	0	0-0	.308	.333	.462	.795	0	1.000
Major League totals (9 years)			780	2022	218	530	111	5	83	343	154	375	9	56	1-6	.262	.314	.445	.759	20	.991

DIVISION SERIES RECORD

Year	Team (League)	Pos.	G	AB	R	H	2B	3B	HR	RBI	BB	SO	HBP	GDP	SB-CS	Avg.	OBP	SLG	OPS	E	Avg.
1999— Houston (N.L.)		OF	3	7	1	1	0	0	1	1	0	2	0	0	0-0	.143	.143	.571	.714	1	.750
2001— Houston (N.L.)			2	2	1	1	0	0	1	2	0	0	0	0	0-0	.500	.500	2.000	2.500	...	...
Division series totals (2 years)			5	9	2	2	0	0	2	3	0	2	0	0	0-0	.222	.222	.889	1.111	1	.750

2006 LEFTY-RIGHTY SPLITS

vs.	Avg.	AB	H	2B	3B	HR	RBI	BB	SO	OBP	Slg.	vs.	Avg.	AB	H	2B	3B	HR	RBI	BB	SO	OBP	Slg.
L	.059	17	1	0	0	0	0	2	10	.158	.059	R	.345	113	39	10	0	7	26	13	17	.412	.619

WASDIN, JOHN   P

PERSONAL: Born August 5, 1972, in Fort Belvoir, Va. ... 6-2/190. ... Throws right, bats right. ... Full name: John Truman Wasdin. ... Name pronounced: WAAZ-din. ... High school: Amos P. Godby (Tallahassee, Fla.). ... College: Florida State. **TRANSACTIONS/CAREER NOTES:** Selected by New York Yankees organization in 41st round of 1990 free-agent draft; did not sign. ... Selected by Oakland Athletics organization in first round (25th pick overall) of 1993 free-agent draft. ... Traded by A's with cash to Boston Red Sox for OF Jose Canseco (January 27, 1997). ... On disabled list (July 18-August 5, 1999); included rehabilitation assignment to GCL Red Sox. ... Traded by Red Sox with Ps Brian Rose and Jeff Taglienti and 2B Jeff Frye to Colorado Rockies for Ps Rolando Arrojo and Rick Croushore, 2B Mike Lansing and cash (July 27, 2000). ... On suspended list (September 8-10, 2000). ... Released by Rockies (June 7, 2001). ... Signed by Baltimore Orioles organization (July 18, 2001). ... Traded by Orioles to Philadelphia Phillies for P Chris Brock (December 13, 2001). ... Signed as a free agent by Yomiuri of the Japan Central League (January 9, 2002). ... Signed as a free agent by Pittsburgh Pirates organization (December 1, 2002). ... Traded by Pirates to Toronto Blue Jays for OF Rich Thompson (July 8, 2003). ... Signed as a free agent by Texas Rangers organization (October 21, 2003). ... Released by Rangers (March 29, 2006). ... Re-signed by Rangers organization (April 1, 2006). ... On disabled list (June 16-July 1, 2006); included rehabilitation assignment to Oklahoma. ... Released by Rangers (August 3, 2006).

CAREER HITTING: 3-for-15 (.200), 2 R, 1 2B, 0 3B, 0 HR, 1 RBI.

Year	Team (League)	W	L	Pct.	ERA	WHIP	G	GS	CG	ShO	Hld.	Sv.-Opp.	IP	H	R	ER	HR	BB-IBB	SO	Avg.
1993— Ariz. A's (Ariz.)		0	0	...	3.00	1.00	1	1	0	0	...	0-...	3.0	3	1	1	0	0-0	1	.250
— Madison (Midw.)		2	3	.400	1.86	0.85	9	9	0	0	...	0-...	48.1	32	11	10	1	9-1	40	.186
— Modesto (California)		0	3	.000	3.86	1.29	3	3	0	0	...	0-...	16.1	17	9	7	0	4-0	11	.266
1994— Modesto (California)		3	1	.750	1.69	0.83	6	4	0	0	...	0-...	26.2	17	6	5	2	5-0	30	.179
— Huntsville (Sou.)		12	3	.800	3.43	1.09	21	21	0	0	...	0-...	141.2	126	61	54	13	29-2	108	.236
1995— Edmonton (PCL)		12	8	.600	5.52	1.33	29	28	2	1	...	0-...	174.1	193	117	107	26	38-3	111	.281
— Oakland (A.L.)		1	1	.500	4.67	0.98	5	2	0	0	0	0-0	17.1	14	9	9	4	3-0	6	.215
1996— Edmonton (PCL)		2	1	.667	4.14	1.38	9	9	0	0	...	0-...	50.0	52	23	23	6	17-2	30	.267
— Oakland (A.L.)		8	7	.533	5.96	1.48	25	21	1	0	0	0-1	131.1	145	96	87	24	50-5	75	.283
1997— Boston (A.L.)		4	6	.400	4.40	1.28	53	7	0	0	11	0-2	124.2	121	68	61	18	38-4	84	.251
1998— Boston (A.L.)		6	4	.600	5.25	1.44	47	8	0	0	4	0-1	96.0	111	57	56	14	27-8	59	.288
— Pawtucket (Int'l)		1	0	1.000	3.00	1.33	4	2	0	0	...	0-...	12.0	11	6	4	0	5-0	10	.239
1999— Pawtucket (Int'l)		1	1	.500	2.12	0.88	5	5	0	0	...	0-...	29.2	19	9	7	1	7-0	28	.184
— Boston (A.L.)		8	3	.727	4.12	1.33	45	0	0	0	2	2-5	74.1	66	38	34	14	18-0	57	.236
— GC Red Sox (GCL)		0	0	...	0.00	0.50	1	1	0	0	...	0-...	2.0	1	0	0	0	0-0	4	.143
2000— Boston (A.L.)		1	3	.250	5.04	1.41	25	1	0	0	0	1-2	44.2	48	25	25	8	15-1	36	.273
— Pawtucket (Int'l)		1	0	1.000	2.25	0.56	5	3	0	0	...	0-...	16.0	7	4	4	0	2-0	11	.130
— Colorado (N.L.)		0	3	.000	5.80	1.43	14	3	0	0	0	0-0	35.2	42	23	23	6	9-2	35	.302
2001— Colorado (N.L.)		2	1	.667	7.03	1.64	18	0	0	0	0	0-3	24.1	32	19	19	7	8-2	17	.320
— Rochester (Int'l)		2	1	.667	3.98	1.57	5	3	0	0	...	0-...	20.1	27	9	9	3	5-0	20	.321
— Baltimore (A.L.)		1	1	.500	4.17	1.41	26	0	0	0	4	0-2	49.2	54	25	23	4	16-4	47	.277
2003— Nashville (PCL)		8	4	.667	3.04	1.10	18	18	3	1	...	0-...	112.1	101	46	38	4	24-4	116	.238
— Toronto (A.L.)		0	1	.000	23.40	4.00	3	2	0	0	0	0-0	5.0	16	13	13	2	4-0	5	.533
— Syracuse (Int'l)		2	1	.667	5.23	1.40	10	1	0	0	...	0-...	20.2	28	13	12	1	1-0	21	.318
2004— Oklahoma (PCL)		7	1	.875	3.46	1.10	19	18	14	2	1	0-...	104.0	94	43	40	10	19-0	81	.242
— Texas (A.L.)		2	4	.333	6.78	1.63	15	10	0	0	0	0-0	65.0	83	52	49	18	23-2	36	.305
2005— Oklahoma (PCL)		9	2	.818	4.93	1.48	13	11	0	0	0	0-1	73.0	84	43	40	11	24-1	57	.286
— Texas (A.L.)		3	2	.600	4.28	1.28	31	6	0	0	4	4-6	75.2	77	37	36	9	20-2	44	.261
2006— Oklahoma (PCL)		3	3	.500	2.00	1.10	13	9	1	1	2	0-1	63.0	52	23	14	2	17-1	62	.225
— Texas (A.L.)		2	2	.500	5.10	1.53	9	5	0	0	0	0-0	30.0	33	19	17	6	13-0	16	.266
American League totals (11 years)		36	34	.514	5.17	1.39	284	62	1	0	25	7-19	713.2	768	439	410	121	227-26	465	.273
National League totals (2 years)		2	4	.333	6.30	1.52	32	3	0	0	0	0-3	60.0	74	42	42	13	17-4	52	.310
Major League totals (11 years)		38	38	.500	5.26	1.40	316	65	1	0	25	7-22	773.2	842	481	452	134	244-30	517	.276

DIVISION SERIES RECORD

Year	Team (League)	W	L	Pct.	ERA	WHIP	G	GS	CG	ShO	Hld.	Sv.-Opp.	IP	H	R	ER	HR	BB-IBB	SO	Avg.
1998— Boston (A.L.)		0	0	...	10.80	1.80	1	0	0	0	0	0-0	1.2	2	2	2	1	1-0	2	.286
1999— Boston (A.L.)		0	0	...	27.00	3.60	2	0	0	0	0	0-0	1.2	2	5	5	1	4-0	1	.400
Division series totals (2 years)		0	0	...	18.90	2.70	3	0	0	0	0	0-0	3.1	4	7	7	2	5-0	3	.333

CHAMPIONSHIP SERIES RECORD

Year	Team (League)	W	L	Pct.	ERA	WHIP	G	GS	CG	ShO	Hld.	Sv.-Opp.	IP	H	R	ER	HR	BB-IBB	SO	Avg.
1999— Boston (A.L.)				Did not play.																

2006 LEFTY-RIGHTY SPLITS

vs.	Avg.	AB	H	2B	3B	HR	RBI	BB	SO	OBP	Slg.	vs.	Avg.	AB	H	2B	3B	HR	RBI	BB	SO	OBP	Slg.
L	.328	58	19	4	0	5	9	8	7	.435	.655	R	.212	66	14	3	0	1	8	5	9	.278	.303

WASHBURN, JARROD   P

PERSONAL: Born August 13, 1974, in La Crosse, Wis. ... 6-1/195. ... Full name: Jarrod Michael Washburn. ... High school: Webster (Wis.). ... College: Wisconsin-Oshkosh. **TRANSACTIONS/CAREER NOTES:** Selected by California Angels organizaiton in second round of 1995 free-agent draft. ... Angels franchise renamed Anaheim Angels for 1997 season. ... On disabled list (March 25-April 9, July 22-August 7 and August 8, 2000-remainder of season); included rehabilitation assign-

W

ment to Lake Elsinore. ... On disabled list (March 23-April 16, 2001); included rehabilitation assignment to Salt Lake. ... On disabled list (July 21-September 2, 2004); included rehabilitation assignment to Rancho Cucamonga. ... Angels franchise renamed Los Angeles Angels of Anaheim for 2005 season. ... On disabled list (July 25-August 12, 2005). ... Signed as a free agent by Seattle Mariners (December 20, 2005).
CAREER HITTING: 8-for-30 (.267), 2 R, 0 2B, 0 3B, 0 HR, 3 RBI.

Year — Team (League)	W	L	Pct.	ERA	WHIP	G	GS	CG	ShO	Hld.	Sv.-Opp.	IP	H	R	ER	HR	BB-IBB	SO	Avg.
1995— Boise (N'west)	3	2	.600	3.33	1.07	8	8	0	0	...	0-...	46.0	35	17	17	1	14-0	54	.208
— Cedar Rap. (Midw.)	0	1	.000	3.44	1.31	3	3	0	0	...	0-...	18.1	17	7	7	1	7-0	20	.258
1996— Lake Elsinore (Calif.)	6	3	.667	3.30	1.21	14	14	3	0	...	0-...	92.2	79	38	34	5	33-0	93	.229
— Midland (Texas)	5	6	.455	4.40	1.16	13	13	1	0	...	0-...	88.0	77	44	43	11	25-0	58	.235
— Vancouver (PCL)	0	2	.000	10.80	2.88	2	2	0	0	...	0-...	8.1	12	16	10	1	12-0	5	.333
1997— Midland (Texas)	15	12	.556	4.80	1.46	29	29	5	1	...	0-...	189.1	211	115	101	23	65-0	146	.288
— Vancouver (PCL)	0	0	...	3.60	1.20	1	1	0	0	...	0-...	5.0	4	2	2	0	2-0	6	.211
1998— Vancouver (PCL)	4	5	.444	4.32	1.46	14	14	2	0	...	0-...	91.2	91	44	44	7	43-0	66	.261
— Anaheim (A.L.)	6	3	.667	4.62	1.31	15	11	0	0	1	0-0	74.0	70	40	38	11	27-1	48	.248
— Midland (Texas)	0	1	.000	6.23	1.73	1	1	0	0	...	0-0	8.2	13	8	6	2	2-0	8	.351
1999— Edmonton (PCL)	1	5	.167	4.73	1.14	11	11	1	0	...	0-0	59.0	50	31	31	6	17-0	55	.226
— Anaheim (A.L.)	4	5	.444	5.25	1.41	16	10	0	0	1	0-0	61.2	61	36	36	6	26-0	39	.261
2000— Lake Elsinore (Calif.)	0	0	...	6.00	1.67	1	1	0	0	...	0-0	3.0	3	2	2	0	2-0	7	.250
— Edmonton (PCL)	3	0	1.000	3.52	1.57	5	5	0	0	...	0-0	30.2	35	13	12	2	13-0	23	.299
— Anaheim (A.L.)	7	2	.778	3.74	1.20	14	14	0	0	0	0-0	84.1	64	38	35	16	37-0	49	.215
2001— Salt Lake (PCL)	0	1	.000	5.87	1.30	1	1	0	0	...	0-0	7.2	9	5	5	1	1-0	5	.300
— Anaheim (A.L.)	11	10	.524	3.77	1.29	30	30	1	0	0	0-0	193.1	196	89	81	25	54-4	126	.263
2002— Anaheim (A.L.)	18	6	.750	3.15	1.17	32	32	1	0	0	0-0	206.0	183	75	72	19	59-1	139	.235
2003— Anaheim (A.L.)	10	15	.400	4.43	1.25	32	32	2	0	0	0-0	207.1	205	106	102	•34	54-4	118	.256
2004— Rancho Cuca. (Calif.)	0	0	...	2.25	1.75	1	1	0	0	...	0-0	4.0	4	1	1	0	3-0	5	.250
— Anaheim (A.L.)	11	8	.579	4.64	1.33	25	25	1	1	0	0-0	149.1	159	81	77	20	40-1	86	.269
2005— Los Angeles (A.L.)	8	8	.500	3.20	1.33	29	29	1	1	0	0-0	177.1	184	66	63	19	51-0	94	.274
2006— Seattle (A.L.)	8	14	.364	4.67	1.35	31	31	0	0	0	0-0	187.0	198	103	97	25	55-2	103	.268
Major League totals (9 years)	**83**	**71**	**.539**	**4.04**	**1.29**	**224**	**214**	**6**	**2**	**2**	**0-0**	**1340.1**	**1320**	**634**	**601**	**175**	**403-13**	**802**	**.257**

DIVISION SERIES RECORD

Year — Team (League)	W	L	Pct.	ERA	WHIP	G	GS	CG	ShO	Hld.	Sv.-Opp.	IP	H	R	ER	HR	BB-IBB	SO	Avg.
2002— Anaheim (A.L.)	1	0	1.000	3.75	1.25	2	2	0	0	0	0-0	12.0	12	6	5	3	3-0	4	.286
2004— Anaheim (A.L.)	0	1	.000	10.80	2.70	2	1	0	0	0	0-0	3.1	6	8	4	2	3-0	3	.353
Division series totals (2 years)	**1**	**1**	**.500**	**5.28**	**1.57**	**4**	**3**	**0**	**0**	**0**	**0-0**	**15.1**	**18**	**14**	**9**	**5**	**6-0**	**7**	**.305**

CHAMPIONSHIP SERIES RECORD

Year — Team (League)	W	L	Pct.	ERA	WHIP	G	GS	CG	ShO	Hld.	Sv.-Opp.	IP	H	R	ER	HR	BB-IBB	SO	Avg.
2002— Anaheim (A.L.)	0	0	...	1.29	0.86	1	1	0	0	0	0-0	7.0	6	1	1	0	0-0	7	.207
2005— Los Angeles (A.L.)	0	0	...	0.00	1.07	1	1	0	0	0	0-0	4.2	4	1	0	0	1-0	1	.235
Champ. series totals (2 years)	**0**	**0**	**...**	**0.77**	**0.94**	**2**	**2**	**0**	**0**	**0**	**0-0**	**11.2**	**10**	**2**	**1**	**0**	**1-0**	**8**	**.217**

WORLD SERIES RECORD

Year — Team (League)	W	L	Pct.	ERA	WHIP	G	GS	CG	ShO	Hld.	Sv.-Opp.	IP	H	R	ER	HR	BB-IBB	SO	Avg.
2002— Anaheim (A.L.)	0	2	.000	9.31	1.97	2	2	0	0	0	0-0	9.2	12	10	10	3	7-2	6	.324

2006 LEFTY-RIGHTY SPLITS

vs.	Avg.	AB	H	2B	3B	HR	RBI	BB	SO	OBP	Slg.	vs.	Avg.	AB	H	2B	3B	HR	RBI	BB	SO	OBP	Slg.
L	.317	139	44	9	0	6	18	11	25	.364	.511	R	.257	599	154	41	2	19	75	44	78	.313	.427

WATSON, BRANDON — OF

PERSONAL: Born September 30, 1981, in Los Angeles. ... 6-1/170. ... Bats left, throws right. ... Full name: Brandon Eric Watson. ... High school: Westchester (Los Angeles).
TRANSACTIONS/CAREER NOTES: Selected by Montreal Expos organization in ninth round of 1999 free-agent draft. ... Expos franchise relocated to Washington, D.C., and renamed Washington Nationals for 2005 season (December 3, 2004). ... Claimed on waivers by Cincinnati Reds (July 14, 2006).
2006 GAMES PLAYED BY POSITION (MLB): OF—8.

Year — Team (League)	Pos.	G	AB	R	H	2B	3B	HR	RBI	BB	SO	HBP	GDP	SB-CS	Avg.	OBP	SLG	OPS	E	Avg.
1999— GC Expos (GCL)	OF	33	119	15	36	2	0	0	12	11	11	1	0	4-2	.303	.361	.319	.680	1	.986
2000— Vermont (NYP)	OF	69	278	53	81	9	1	0	30	25	38	3	4	26-9	.291	.354	.331	.685	7	.948
2001— Clinton (Midw.)	OF	117	489	74	160	16	9	2	38	29	65	1	6	33-20	.327	.364	.409	.773	4	.980
2002— Brevard County (FSL)	OF	111	424	57	113	16	2	0	24	27	53	3	5	22-13	.267	.314	.314	.628	5	.983
— Harrisburg (East.)	OF	2	6	2	2	0	0	0	0	1	0	0	0	0-0	.333	.429	.333	.762	0	1.000
2003— Harrisburg (East.)	OF	139	565	86	180	17	6	1	39	38	60	3	7	18-17	.319	.362	.375	.737	7	.983
2004— Edmonton (PCL)	OF	139	526	74	154	17	3	2	41	31	68	1	3	22-10	.293	.332	.348	.680	6	.870
2005— Harrisburg (East.)	OF	34	146	13	36	1	0	0	6	7	21	2	2	7-5	.247	.290	.253	.544	4	.973
— New Orleans (PCL)	OF-DH	88	372	69	132	15	3	1	25	28	33	1	5	31-13	.355	.400	.419	.819	6	.986
— Wash. (N.L.)	OF	25	40	8	7	1	1	1	5	4	8	0	0	0-2	.175	.250	.325	.575	1	.933
2006— Louisville (Int'l)		42	137	16	37	3	0	0	8	11	12	0	1	6-2	.270	.324	.292	.616	2	.975
— Wash. (N.L.)	OF	9	28	0	5	0	0	0	0	1	3	0	0	0-2	.179	.207	.179	.385	0	1.000
— New Orleans (PCL)		21	82	11	25	3	1	0	13	3	10	0	2	2-1	.305	.326	.366	.691	0	1.000
— GC Nationals (GCL)		2	6	1	2	0	0	0	0	1	1	0	0	0-0	.333	.429	.333	.762	0	1.000
— Cincinnati (N.L.)		1	0	0	0	0	0	0	0	0	0	0	0	1-0	...	...	...	...	0	...
Major League totals (2 years)		**35**	**68**	**8**	**12**	**1**	**1**	**1**	**5**	**5**	**11**	**0**	**0**	**1-4**	**.176**	**.233**	**.265**	**.498**	**1**	**.969**

2006 LEFTY-RIGHTY SPLITS

vs.	Avg.	AB	H	2B	3B	HR	RBI	BB	SO	OBP	Slg.	vs.	Avg.	AB	H	2B	3B	HR	RBI	BB	SO	OBP	Slg.
L	.000	4	0	0	0	0	0	0	1	.000	.000	R	.208	24	5	0	0	0	0	1	2	.240	.208

WEATHERS, DAVID — P

PERSONAL: Born September 25, 1969, in Lawrenceburg, Tenn. ... 6-3/230. ... Throws right, bats right. ... Full name: John David Weathers. ... High school: Loretto (Tenn.). ... Junior college: Motlow State (Tenn.) Community College. **TRANSACTIONS/CAREER NOTES:** Selected by Toronto Blue Jays organization in third round of 1988 free-agent draft. ... Selected by Florida Marlins in second round (29th pick overall) of expansion draft (November 17, 1992). ... On disabled list (June 26-July 13, 1995); included rehabilitation assignments to Brevard County and Charlotte. ... Traded by Marlins to New York Yankees for P Mark Hutton (July 31, 1996). ... Traded by Yankees to Cleveland Indians for OF Chad Curtis (June 9, 1997). ... Claimed on waivers by Cincinnati Reds (December 20, 1997). ... Claimed on waivers by Milwaukee Brewers (June 24, 1998). ... On disabled list (August 2-22, 2000). ... Traded by Brewers with P Roberto Miniel to Chicago Cubs for P Ruben Quevedo and OF Pete Zoccolillo (July 30, 2001). ... Signed as a free agent by New York Mets (December 13, 2001). ... On suspended list (September 20-22, 2002). ... Traded by Mets with P Jeremy Griffiths to Houston Astros for OF Richard Hidalgo (June 17, 2004). ... Released by Astros (September 3, 2004). ... Signed by Marlins (September 8, 2004). ... Signed as a free agent by Reds (December 15,

W

2004). **MISCELLANEOUS NOTES:** Appeared in two games as pinch runner (1994). ... Appeared in one game as pinch runner with Florida (1996). ... Struck out in only appearance as pinch hitter (1999).

CAREER HITTING: 14-for-139 (.101), 7 R, 0 2B, 0 3B, 2 HR, 4 RBI.

Year Team (League)	W	L	Pct.	ERA	WHIP	G	GS	CG	ShO	Hld.	Sv.-Opp.	IP	H	R	ER	HR	BB-IBB	SO	Avg.
1988—St. Catharines (NYP)	4	4	.500	3.02	1.34	15	12	0	0	...	0-...	62.2	58	30	21	3	26-0	36	.245
1989—Myrtle Beach (SAL)	11	13	.458	3.86	1.44	31	31	2	0	...	0-...	172.2	163	99	74	3	86-2	111	.247
1990—Dunedin (Fla. St.)	10	7	.588	3.70	1.37	27	27	2	0	...	0-...	158.0	158	82	65	2	59-0	96	.266
1991—Knoxville (Southern)	10	7	.588	2.45	1.22	24	22	5	2	...	0-...	139.1	121	51	38	3	49-1	114	.236
—Toronto (A.L.)	1	0	1.000	4.91	2.18	15	0	0	0	1	0-0	14.2	15	9	8	1	17-3	13	.263
1992—Syracuse (Int'l)	1	4	.200	4.66	1.43	12	10	0	0	...	0-0	48.1	48	29	25	3	21-2	30	.254
—Toronto (A.L.)	0	0	...	8.10	2.10	2	0	0	0	0	0-0	3.1	5	3	3	1	2-0	3	.385
1993—Edmonton (PCL)	11	4	.733	3.83	1.40	22	22	3	1	...	0-...	141.0	150	77	60	12	47-2	117	.271
—Florida (N.L.)	2	3	.400	5.12	1.53	14	6	0	0	...	0-...	45.2	57	26	26	3	13-1	34	.306
1994—Florida (N.L.)	8	12	.400	5.27	1.67	24	24	0	0	...	0-...	135.0	166	87	79	13	59-9	72	.306
1995—Florida (N.L.)	4	5	.444	5.98	1.73	28	15	0	0	1	0-...	90.1	104	68	60	8	52-3	60	.295
—Brevard County (FSL)	0	0	...	0.00	1.25	1	1	0	0	...	0-...	4.0	4	0	0	0	1-0	3	.286
—Charlotte (Int'l)	0	1	.000	9.00	3.00	1	1	0	0	...	0-...	5.0	10	5	5	0	5-0	4	.455
1996—Florida (N.L.)	2	2	.500	4.54	1.58	31	8	0	0	3	0-0	71.1	85	41	36	7	28-4	40	.302
—Charlotte (Int'l)	0	0	...	7.71	3.43	1	1	0	0	...	0-...	2.1	5	2	2	0	3-0	0	.500
—New York (A.L.)	0	2	.000	9.35	2.13	11	4	0	0	...	0-...	17.1	23	19	18	1	14-1	13	.315
—Columbus (Int'l)	0	2	.000	5.40	1.50	3	3	0	0	...	0-...	16.2	20	13	10	1	5-0	7	.299
1997—New York (A.L.)	0	1	.000	10.00	2.44	10	0	0	0	...	0-1	9.0	15	10	10	1	7-0	4	.375
—Columbus (Int'l)	2	2	.500	3.19	1.15	5	5	1	0	...	0-0	36.2	35	18	13	3	7-0	35	.250
—Buffalo (A.A.)	4	3	.571	3.15	1.28	11	11	2	1	...	0-...	68.2	71	37	24	7	17-0	51	.266
—Cleveland (A.L.)	1	2	.333	7.56	1.86	9	1	0	0	...	0-0	16.2	23	14	14	2	8-0	14	.343
1998—Cincinnati (N.L.)	2	4	.333	6.21	1.81	16	9	0	0	...	0-...	62.1	86	47	43	3	27-2	51	.330
—Milwaukee (N.L.)	4	1	.800	3.21	1.22	28	0	0	0	...	0-1	47.2	44	22	17	3	14-1	43	.264
1999—Milwaukee (N.L.)	7	4	.636	4.65	1.51	63	0	0	0	9	2-6	93.0	102	49	48	14	38-3	74	.279
2000—Milwaukee (N.L.)	3	5	.375	3.07	1.38	69	0	0	0	14	1-7	76.1	73	29	26	7	32-8	50	.260
2001—Milwaukee (N.L.)	3	4	.429	2.03	1.08	52	0	0	0	10	4-7	57.2	37	14	13	3	25-7	46	.188
—Chicago (N.L.)	1	1	.500	3.18	1.31	28	0	0	0	6	0-3	28.1	28	10	10	3	9-1	20	.269
2002—New York (N.L.)	6	3	.667	2.91	1.36	71	0	0	0	18	0-5	77.1	69	30	25	0	36-7	61	.245
2003—New York (N.L.)	1	6	.143	3.08	1.45	77	0	0	0	26	7-9	87.2	87	33	30	6	40-6	75	.264
2004—New York (N.L.)	5	3	.625	4.28	1.66	32	0	0	0	6	0-1	33.2	41	19	16	5	23-0	25	.304
—Houston (N.L.)	1	4	.200	4.78	1.38	26	0	0	0	5	0-3	32.0	31	20	17	5	13-1	26	.261
—Florida (N.L.)	1	0	1.000	2.70	1.20	8	2	0	0	1	0-0	16.2	13	5	5	2	7-1	10	.232
2005—Cincinnati (N.L.)	7	4	.636	3.94	1.29	73	0	0	0	8	15-19	77.2	71	36	34	7	29-2	61	.241
2006—Cincinnati (N.L.)	4	4	.500	3.54	1.29	67	0	0	0	9	12-19	73.2	61	31	29	12	34-4	50	.226
American League totals (4 years)	2	5	.286	7.82	2.11	47	5	0	0	1		61.0	81	55	53	6	48-4	47	.324
National League totals (13 years)	61	65	.484	4.18	1.47	707	64	0	0	119	41-80	1106.1	1155	567	514	107	471-60	798	.273
Major League totals (16 years)	63	70	.474	4.37	1.50	754	69	0	0	120	41-81	1167.1	1236	622	567	113	519-64	845	.276

DIVISION SERIES RECORD

Year Team (League)	W	L	Pct.	ERA	WHIP	G	GS	CG	ShO	Hld.	Sv.-Opp.	IP	H	R	ER	HR	BB-IBB	SO	Avg.
1996—New York (A.L.)	1	0	1.000	0.00	0.20	2	0	0	0	...	0-0	5.0	1	0	0	0	0-0	5	.071

CHAMPIONSHIP SERIES RECORD

Year Team (League)	W	L	Pct.	ERA	WHIP	G	GS	CG	ShO	Hld.	Sv.-Opp.	IP	H	R	ER	HR	BB-IBB	SO	Avg.
1996—New York (A.L.)	1	0	1.000	0.00	1.00	2	0	0	0	...	0-0	3.0	3	0	0	0	0-0	0	.250

WORLD SERIES RECORD

Year Team (League)	W	L	Pct.	ERA	WHIP	G	GS	CG	ShO	Hld.	Sv.-Opp.	IP	H	R	ER	HR	BB-IBB	SO	Avg.
1996—New York (A.L.)	0	0	...	3.00	1.67	3	0	0	0	...	1 0-0	3.0	2	1	1	0	3-1	3	.200

2006 LEFTY-RIGHTY SPLITS

vs.	Avg.	AB	H	2B	3B	HR	RBI	BB	SO	OBP	Slg.	vs.	Avg.	AB	H	2B	3B	HR	RBI	BB	SO	OBP	Slg.
L	.219	105	23	2	0	4	9	21	16	.352	.352	R	.230	165	38	10	0	8	24	13	34	.287	.436

WEAVER, JEFF — P

PERSONAL: Born August 22, 1976, in Northridge, Calif. ... 6-5/200. ... Throws right, bats right. ... Full name: Jeffrey Charles Weaver. ... High school: Simi Valley (Calif.). ... College: Fresno State. ... Brother of Jered Weaver, pitcher, Los Angeles Angels of Anaheim. **TRANSACTIONS/CAREER NOTES:** Selected by Chicago White Sox organziation in second-round of 1997 free-agent draft; did not sign; pick received as part of compensation for Chicago Cubs signing Type A free-agent P Kevin Tapani. ... Selected by Detroit Tigers organization in first round (14th pick overall) of 1998 free-agent draft. ... Traded by Tigers to New York Yankees as part of three-team deal in which Oakland Athletics acquired Ps Ted Lilly and Jason Arnold and OF John-Ford Griffin from Yankees and Tigers acquired 1B Carlos Pena, P Franklyn German and a player to be named from A's (July 5, 2002); Tigers acquired P Jeremy Bonderman to complete deal (August 22, 2002). ... Traded by Yankees with Ps Yhency Brazoban and Brandon Wheedon and cash to Los Angeles Dodgers for P Kevin Brown (December 13, 2003). ... Traded by Angels with cash considerations to St. Louis Cardinals for OF Terry Evans (July 5, 2006).
MISCELLANEOUS NOTES: Member of 1996 U.S. Olympic baseball team. ... Appeared in one game as pinch runner (1999). ... Appeared in one game as pinch runner (2004). ... Struck out in only appearance as pinch hitter and scored a run in four appearances as pinch runner (2005). ... Struck out in only appearance as pinch hitter and made one appearance as pinch runner (2006).
CAREER HITTING: 39-for-189 (.206), 12 R, 6 2B, 1 3B, 0 HR, 13 RBI.

Year Team (League)	W	L	Pct.	ERA	WHIP	G	GS	CG	ShO	Hld.	Sv.-Opp.	IP	H	R	ER	HR	BB-IBB	SO	Avg.
1998—Jamestown (NYP)	1	0	1.000	1.50	0.58	3	3	0	0	...	0-...	12.0	6	4	2	0	1-0	12	.143
—W. Mich. (Mid.)	1	0	1.000	1.38	0.62	2	2	0	0	...	0-...	13.0	8	3	2	1	0-0	21	.182
1999—Jacksonville (Sou.)	0	0	...	3.00	0.83	1	1	0	0	...	0-...	6.0	5	2	2	0	0-0	6	.227
—Detroit (A.L.)	9	12	.429	5.55	1.42	30	29	0	0	0	0-0	163.2	176	104	101	27	56-2	114	.278
2000—Toledo (Int'l)	0	1	.000	3.38	1.13	1	1	0	0	...	0-0	5.1	5	2	2	1	1-0	10	.250
—Detroit (A.L.)	11	15	.423	4.32	1.29	31	30	2	0	0	0-0	200.0	205	102	96	26	52-2	136	.267
2001—Detroit (A.L.)	13	16	.448	4.08	1.32	33	33	5	0	0	0-0	229.1	235	116	104	19	68-4	152	.266
2002—Detroit (A.L.)	6	8	.429	3.18	1.19	17	17	§3	0	0	0-0	121.2	112	50	43	4	33-1	75	.243
—New York (A.L.)	5	3	.625	4.04	1.23	15	8	0	0	0	2-2	78.0	81	38	35	12	15-3	57	.260
2003—New York (A.L.)	7	9	.438	5.99	1.62	32	24	0	0	1	0-0	159.1	211	113	106	16	47-2	93	.330
2004—Los Angeles (N.L.)	13	13	.500	4.01	1.30	34	34	0	0	0	0-0	220.0	219	103	98	21	67-9	153	.260
2005—Los Angeles (N.L.)	14	11	.560	4.22	1.17	34	34	3	2	0	0-0	224.0	220	111	105	35	43-1	157	.256
2006—Los Angeles (N.L.)	3	10	.231	6.29	1.52	16	16	0	0	0	0-0	88.2	114	68	62	18	21-0	62	.309
—St. Louis (N.L.)	5	4	.556	5.18	1.50	15	15	0	0	0	0-0	83.1	99	49	48	16	26-1	45	.297
American League totals (6 years)	54	73	.425	4.73	1.37	174	157	10	3	1	2-2	1040.2	1134	591	547	122	292-14	689	.275
National League totals (3 years)	32	28	.533	4.28	1.28	83	83	3	2	0	0-0	527.1	538	263	251	70	136-11	355	.265
Major League totals (8 years)	86	101	.460	4.58	1.34	257	240	13	5	1	2-2	1568.0	1672	854	798	192	428-25	1044	.273

W

DIVISION SERIES RECORD

Year Team (League)	W	L	Pct.	ERA	WHIP	G	GS	CG	ShO	Hld.	Sv.-Opp.	IP	H	R	ER	HR	BB-IBB	SO	Avg.
2002— New York (A.L.)	0	0	...	6.75	2.63	2	0	0	0	0	0-0	2.2	4	2	2	0	3-1	1	.444
2004— Los Angeles (N.L.)	0	1	.000	11.57	2.14	1	1	0	0	0	0-0	4.2	8	6	6	0	2-0	4	.381
2006— St. Louis (N.L.)	1	0	1.000	0.00	1.00	1	1	0	0	0	0-0	5.0	2	0	0	0	3-0	3	.125
Division series totals (3 years)	1	1	.500	5.84	1.78	4	2	0	0	0	0-0	12.1	14	8	8	0	8-1	8	.304

CHAMPIONSHIP SERIES RECORD

Year Team (League)	W	L	Pct.	ERA	WHIP	G	GS	CG	ShO	Hld.	Sv.-Opp.	IP	H	R	ER	HR	BB-IBB	SO	Avg.
2006— St. Louis (N.L.)	1	1	.500	3.09	1.20	2	2	0	0	0	0-0	11.2	10	4	4	1	4-1	2	.222

WORLD SERIES RECORD

Year Team (League)	W	L	Pct.	ERA	WHIP	G	GS	CG	ShO	Hld.	Sv.-Opp.	IP	H	R	ER	HR	BB-IBB	SO	Avg.
2003— New York (A.L.)	0	1	.000	9.00	1.00	1	0	0	0	0	0-0	1.0	1	1	1	1	0-0	0	.250
2006— St. Louis (N.L.)	1	1	.500	2.77	1.15	2	2	0	0	0	0-0	13.0	13	5	4	2	2-0	14	.250
World series totals (2 years)	1	2	.333	3.21	1.14	3	2	0	0	0	0-0	14.0	14	6	5	3	2-0	14	.250

2006 LEFTY-RIGHTY SPLITS

vs.	Avg.	AB	H	2B	3B	HR	RBI	BB	SO	OBP	Slg.	vs.	Avg.	AB	H	2B	3B	HR	RBI	BB	SO	OBP	Slg.
L	.340	350	119	24	2	22	58	29	47	.396	.609	R	.267	352	94	18	3	12	48	18	60	.310	.438

WEAVER, JERED — P

PERSONAL: Born October 4, 1982, in Northridge, Calif. ... Throws right, bats right. ... Full name: Jered David Weaver. ... College: Long Beach State. ... Brother of Jeff Weaver, pitcher with Los Angeles Angels of Anaheim and St. Louis Cardinals in 2006. **TRANSACTIONS/CAREER NOTES:** Selected by Anaheim Angels organization in first round (12th pick overall) of 2004 draft. ... Angels franchise renamed Los Angeles Angels of Anaheim for 2005 season.
CAREER HITTING: 0-for-0 (.000), 0 R, 0 2B, 0 3B, 0 HR, 0 RBI.

Year Team (League)	W	L	Pct.	ERA	WHIP	G	GS	CG	ShO	Hld.	Sv.-Opp.	IP	H	R	ER	HR	BB-IBB	SO	Avg.
2005— Rancho Cuca. (Calif.)	4	1	.800	3.82	0.97	7	7	0	0	0	0-0	33.0	25	18	14	3	7-0	49	.205
— Arkansas (Texas)	3	3	.500	3.98	1.44	8	8	0	0	0	0-0	43.0	43	22	19	5	19-0	46	.250
2006— Salt Lake (PCL)	6	1	.857	2.10	0.95	12	11	2	2	0	0-0	77.0	63	19	18	7	10-0	93	.223
— Los Angeles (A.L.)	11	2	.846	2.56	1.03	19	19	0	0	0	0-0	123.0	94	36	35	15	33-1	105	.209
Major League totals (1 year)	11	2	.846	2.56	1.03	19	19	0	0	0	0-0	123.0	94	36	35	15	33-1	105	.209

2006 LEFTY-RIGHTY SPLITS

vs.	Avg.	AB	H	2B	3B	HR	RBI	BB	SO	OBP	Slg.	vs.	Avg.	AB	H	2B	3B	HR	RBI	BB	SO	OBP	Slg.
L	.250	208	52	10	1	13	26	15	49	.299	.495	R	.174	242	42	9	1	2	8	18	56	.239	.244

WEBB, BRANDON — P

PERSONAL: Born May 9, 1979, in Ashland, Ky. ... 6-2/228. ... Throws right, bats right. ... Full name: Brandon Tyler Webb. ... High school: Ashland (Ky.). ... College: Kentucky. **TRANSACTIONS/CAREER NOTES:** Selected by Arizona Diamondbacks organization in eighth round of 2000 free-agent draft. **HONORS:** Named N.L. Cy Young Award winner by the Baseball Writers' Association of America (2006).
CAREER HITTING: 28-for-249 (.112), 9 R, 3 2B, 0 3B, 0 HR, 15 RBI.

Year Team (League)	W	L	Pct.	ERA	WHIP	G	GS	CG	ShO	Hld.	Sv.-Opp.	IP	H	R	ER	HR	BB-IBB	SO	Avg.
2000— Ariz. D'backs (Ariz.)	0	0	...	9.00	2.00	1	1	0	0	...	0-...	1.0	2	1	1	0	0-0	3	.400
— South Bend (Mid.)	0	0	...	3.24	1.14	12	0	0	0	...	2-...	16.2	10	7	6	0	9-1	18	.172
2001— Lancaster (Calif.)	6	10	.375	3.99	1.34	29	28	0	0	...	0-...	162.1	174	90	72	9	44-0	158	.276
2002— Tucson (PCL)	0	1	.000	3.86	1.29	1	1	0	0	...	0-...	7.0	5	3	3	0	4-0	5	.200
— El Paso (Texas)	10	6	.625	3.14	1.32	26	25	1	1	...	0-...	152.0	141	66	53	4	59-1	122	.247
2003— Tucson (PCL)	1	1	.500	6.00	1.50	3	3	0	0	...	0-...	18.0	18	17	12	0	9-0	17	.257
— Arizona (N.L.)	10	9	.526	2.84	1.15	29	28	1	1	0	0-0	180.2	140	65	57	12	68-4	172	.212
2004— Arizona (N.L.)	7	*16	.304	3.59	1.50	35	*35	1	0	0	0-0	208.0	194	111	83	17	*119-11	164	.248
2005— Arizona (N.L.)	14	12	.538	3.54	1.26	33	33	1	0	0	0-0	229.0	229	98	90	21	59-4	172	.265
2006— Arizona (N.L.)	• 16	8	.667	3.10	1.13	33	33	5	*3	0	0-0	235.0	216	91	81	15	50-4	178	.246
Major League totals (4 years)	47	45	.511	3.28	1.26	130	129	8	4	0	0-0	852.2	779	365	311	65	296-23	686	.245

ALL-STAR GAME RECORD

	W	L	Pct.	ERA	WHIP	G	GS	CG	ShO	Hld.	Sv.-Opp.	IP	H	R	ER	HR	BB-IBB	SO	Avg.
All-Star Game totals (1 year)	0	0	...	0.00	0.00	1	0	0	0	0	0-0	1.0	0	0	0	0	0-0	1	.000

2006 LEFTY-RIGHTY SPLITS

vs.	Avg.	AB	H	2B	3B	HR	RBI	BB	SO	OBP	Slg.	vs.	Avg.	AB	H	2B	3B	HR	RBI	BB	SO	OBP	Slg.
L	.261	440	115	20	4	9	44	39	74	.321	.386	R	.231	438	101	24	2	6	35	11	104	.256	.336

WEEKS, RICKIE — 2B

PERSONAL: Born September 13, 1982, in Daytona Beach, Fla. ... 6-0/195. ... Bats right, throws right. ... Full name: Rickie Darnell Weeks. ... High school: Lake Brantley (Altamonte Springs, Fla.). ... College: Southern University. **TRANSACTIONS/CAREER NOTES:** Selected by Milwaukee Brewers organization in first round (second pick overall) of 2003 free-agent draft. ... On disabled list (July 25, 2006-remainder of season).
2006 GAMES PLAYED BY POSITION (MLB): 2B—92, DH—1.

Year Team (League)	Pos.	G	AB	R	H	2B	3B	HR	RBI	BB	SO	HBP	GDP	SB-CS	Avg.	OBP	SLG	OPS	E	Avg.
								BATTING										FIELDING		
2003— Ariz. Brewers (Ariz.)	DH	4	4	0	2	0	0	0	4	0	2	1	0	1-0	.500	.600	.500	1.100	0	...
— Beloit (Midw.) 2B-2B-DH		20	63	13	22	8	1	1	16	15	9	6	1	2-0	.349	.494	.556	1.050	7	.923
— Milwaukee (N.L.)	2B	7	12	1	2	1	0	0	1	1	6	1	0	0-0	.167	.286	.250	.536	1	.667
2004— Huntsville (Sou.)	2B	133	479	67	124	35	6	8	42	55	107	28	5	11-12	.259	.366	.407	.773	17	.795
2005— Nashville (PCL)	2B	55	203	43	65	14	9	12	48	28	51	14	3	10-1	.320	.435	.655	1.090	10	.961
— Milwaukee (N.L.)	2B	96	360	56	86	13	2	13	42	40	96	11	11	15-2	.239	.333	.394	.727	21	.951
2006— Milwaukee (N.L.)	2B-DH	95	359	73	100	15	3	8	34	30	92	*19	6	19-5	.279	.363	.404	.766	22	.952
Major League totals (3 years)		198	731	130	188	29	5	21	76	71	194	31	17	34-7	.257	.346	.397	.743	44	.951

2006 LEFTY-RIGHTY SPLITS

vs.	Avg.	AB	H	2B	3B	HR	RBI	BB	SO	OBP	Slg.	vs.	Avg.	AB	H	2B	3B	HR	RBI	BB	SO	OBP	Slg.
L	.271	70	19	5	0	3	9	9	21	.369	.471	R	.280	289	81	10	3	5	25	21	71	.361	.388

WELLEMEYER, TODD — P

PERSONAL: Born August 30, 1978, in Louisville, Ky. ... 6-3/205. ... Throws right, bats right. ... Full name: Todd Allen Wellemeyer. ... Name pronounced: WELL-my-er. ... High school: Eastern (Louisville, Ky.). ... College: Bellarmine (Ky.). **TRANSACTIONS/CAREER NOTES:** Selected by Chicago Cubs organization in fourth round of 2000 free-agent draft. ... On disabled list (May 22-July 16, 2004); included rehabilitation assignment to Iowa. ... Traded by Cubs to Florida Marlins for Ps Lincoln Holdzkom and Zach McCormack (March 28, 2006). ... Claimed on waivers by Kansas City Royals (June 9, 2006).

CAREER HITTING: 1-for-7 (.143), 1 R, 0 2B, 0 3B, 0 HR, 0 RBI.

Year Team (League)	W	L	Pct.	ERA	WHIP	G	GS	CG	ShO	Hld.	Sv.-Opp.	IP	H	R	ER	HR	BB-IBB	SO	Avg.
2000— Eugene (Northwest)	4	4	.500	3.67	1.25	15	15	0	0	...	0-...	76.0	62	35	31	3	33-2	85	.225
2001— Lansing (Midw.)	13	9	.591	4.16	1.63	27	27	1	0	...	0-...	147.0	165	85	68	14	74-0	167	.288
2002— Daytona (Fla. St.)	2	4	.333	3.79	1.11	14	14	0	0	...	0-...	73.2	63	33	31	7	19-1	87	.230
— West Tenn (Sou.)	3	3	.500	4.70	1.11	8	8	1	1	...	0-...	46.0	33	25	24	2	18-0	37	.204
2003— West Tenn (Sou.)	1	1	.500	5.48	1.36	4	4	0	0	...	0-...	21.1	19	13	13	1	10-0	34	.238
— Iowa (PCL)	5	5	.500	5.18	1.53	13	12	0	0	...	0-...	66.0	68	39	38	7	33-4	56	.272
— Chicago (N.L.)	1	1	.500	6.51	1.59	15	0	0	0	1	1-1	27.2	25	22	20	5	19-1	30	.245
2004— Iowa (PCL)	1	1	.500	3.91	1.57	14	4	0	0	0	0-0	23.0	24	11	10	2	12-0	23	.273
— Chicago (N.L.)	2	1	.667	5.92	1.93	20	0	0	0	0	0-0	24.1	27	16	16	1	20-2	30	.287
2005— Iowa (PCL)	3	2	.600	3.02	1.34	12	12	0	0	0	0-0	53.2	47	21	18	8	25-0	48	.235
— Chicago (N.L.)	2	1	.667	6.12	1.67	22	0	0	0	3	1-1	32.1	32	23	22	7	22-1	32	.264
2006— Florida (N.L.)	0	2	.000	5.48	1.55	18	0	0	0	0	0-0	21.1	20	13	13	1	13-1	17	.256
— Kansas City (A.L.)	1	2	.333	3.63	1.49	28	0	0	0	3	1-1	57.0	48	25	23	5	37-2	37	.235
American League totals (1 year)	1	2	.333	3.63	1.49	28	0	0	0	3	1-1	57.0	48	25	23	5	37-2	37	.235
National League totals (4 years)	5	5	.500	6.05	1.68	75	0	0	0	4	2-2	105.2	104	74	71	14	74-5	109	.263
Major League totals (4 years)	6	7	.462	5.20	1.62	103	0	0	0	7	3-3	162.2	152	99	94	19	111-7	146	.254

2006 LEFTY-RIGHTY SPLITS

vs.	Avg.	AB	H	2B	3B	HR	RBI	BB	SO	OBP	Slg.	vs.	Avg.	AB	H	2B	3B	HR	RBI	BB	SO	OBP	Slg.
L	.208	120	25	6	1	3	13	18	22	.312	.350	R	.265	162	43	11	1	3	24	32	32	.387	.401

WELLS, DAVID   P

PERSONAL: Born May 20, 1963, in Torrance, Calif. ... 6-4/248. ... Throws left, bats left. ... Full name: David Lee Wells. ... High school: Point Loma (San Diego). **TRANSACTIONS/CAREER NOTES:** Selected by Toronto Blue Jays organization in second round of June 1982 free-agent draft. ... Released by Blue Jays (March 30, 1993). ... Signed by Detroit Tigers (April 3, 1993). ... On disabled list (August 1-20, 1993). ... On disabled list (April 19-June 6, 1994); included rehabilitation assignment to Lakeland. ... Traded by Tigers to Cincinnati Reds for Ps C.J. Nitkowski and David Tuttle and a player to be named (July 31, 1995); Tigers acquired IF Mark Lewis to complete deal (November 16, 1995). ... Traded by Reds to Baltimore Orioles for OFs Curtis Goodwin and Trovin Valdez (December 26, 1995). ... Signed as a free agent by New York Yankees (December 24, 1996). ... Traded by Yankees with P Graeme Lloyd and 2B Homer Bush to Blue Jays for P Roger Clemens (February 18, 1999). ... Traded by Blue Jays with P Matt DeWitt to Chicago White Sox for Ps Mike Sirotka, Kevin Beirne and Mike Williams and OF Brian Simmons (January 14, 2001). ... On disabled list (July 2, 2001-remainder of season). ... Signed as a free agent by Yankees (January 17, 2002). ... Signed as a free agent by San Diego Padres (January 6, 2004). ... On disabled list (May 17-June 7, 2004). ... Signed as a free agent by Boston Red Sox (December 17, 2004). ... On disabled list (April 26-May 18, 2005). ... On suspended list (August 29-September 4, 2005). ... On disabled list (March 28-April 12, 2006); included rehabilitation assignment to Pawtucket. ... On disabled list (April 13-May 26, 2006); included rehabilitation assignment to Pawtucket. ... On disabled list (May 31-July 31, 2006). ... Traded by Red Sox to San Diego Padres for a player to be named or cash (August 31, 2006). **HONORS:** Named lefthanded pitcher on THE SPORTING NEWS A.L. All-Star team (1998 and 2000). **STATISTICAL NOTES:** Pitched 4-0 perfect game against Minnesota (May 17, 1998).

CAREER HITTING: 15-for-125 (.120), 5 R, 1 2B, 0 3B, 0 HR, 4 RBI.

Year Team (League)	W	L	Pct.	ERA	WHIP	G	GS	CG	ShO	Hld.	Sv.-Opp.	IP	H	R	ER	HR	BB-IBB	SO	Avg.
1982— Medicine Hat (Pio.)	4	3	.571	5.18	1.60	12	12	1	0	...	0-...	64.1	71	42	37	5	32-1	53	...
1983— Kinston (Carol.)	6	5	.545	3.73	1.35	25	25	5	0	...	0-...	157.0	141	81	65	13	71-2	115	.238
1984— Kinston (Carol.)	1	6	.143	4.71	1.67	7	7	0	0	...	0-...	42.0	51	29	22	1	19-1	44	.302
— Knoxville (Southern)	3	2	.600	2.59	1.27	8	8	3	1	...	0-...	59.0	58	22	17	3	17-0	34	.262
1985— Syracuse (Int'l)			Did not play.																
1986— Florence (S. Atl.)	0	0	...	3.55	1.26	4	1	0	0	...	0-...	12.2	7	6	5	0	9-0	14	.159
— Ventura (Calif.)	2	1	.667	1.89	0.89	5	2	0	0	...	0-...	19.0	13	5	4	0	4-0	26	.200
— Knoxville (Southern)	1	3	.250	4.05	1.50	10	7	1	0	...	0-...	40.0	42	24	18	1	18-0	32	.280
— Syracuse (Int'l)	0	1	.000	9.82	1.91	3	0	0	0	...	0-...	3.2	6	4	4	0	1-0	2	.400
1987— Syracuse (Int'l)	4	6	.400	3.87	1.23	43	12	0	0	...	6-...	109.1	102	49	47	9	32-0	106	.248
— Toronto (A.L.)	4	3	.571	3.99	1.67	18	2	0	0	...	1-2	29.1	37	14	13	0	12-0	32	.311
1988— Toronto (A.L.)	3	5	.375	4.62	1.49	41	0	0	0	...	4-6	64.1	65	36	33	12	31-9	56	.269
— Syracuse (Int'l)	0	0	...	0.00	1.59	6	0	0	0	...	3-...	5.2	7	1	0	0	2-1	8	.269
1989— Toronto (A.L.)	7	4	.636	2.40	1.09	54	0	0	0	...	2-9	86.1	66	25	23	5	28-7	78	.207
1990— Toronto (A.L.)	11	6	.647	3.14	1.11	43	25	0	0	3	3-3	189.0	165	72	66	14	45-3	115	.239
1991— Toronto (A.L.)	15	10	.600	3.72	1.19	40	28	2	0	3	1-2	198.1	188	88	82	24	49-1	106	.252
1992— Toronto (A.L.)	7	9	.438	5.40	1.45	41	14	0	0	3	2-4	120.0	138	84	72	16	36-6	62	.289
1993— Detroit (A.L.)	11	9	.550	4.19	1.20	32	30	0	0	1	0-0	187.0	183	93	87	26	42-6	71	.260
1994— Detroit (A.L.)	5	7	.417	3.96	1.23	16	16	5	1	0	0-0	111.1	113	54	49	13	24-6	71	.260
— Lakeland (Fla. St.)	0	0	...	0.00	0.83	2	2	0	0	...	0-...	6.0	5	1	0	0	0-0	3	.217
1995— Detroit (A.L.)	10	3	.769	3.04	1.20	18	18	3	0	0	0-0	130.1	120	54	44	17	37-5	83	.242
— Cincinnati (N.L.)	6	5	.545	3.59	1.24	11	11	3	0	0	0-0	72.2	74	34	29	6	16-4	50	.265
1996— Baltimore (A.L.)	11	14	.440	5.14	1.33	34	34	3	0	0	0-0	224.1	247	132	128	32	51-7	130	.285
1997— New York (A.L.)	16	10	.615	4.21	1.30	32	32	5	2	0	0-0	218.0	239	109	102	24	45-0	156	.278
1998— New York (A.L.)	18	4	.818	3.49	1.05	30	30	8	*5	0	0-0	214.1	195	86	83	29	29-0	163	.239
1999— Toronto (A.L.)	17	10	.630	4.82	1.33	34	34	*7	1	0	0-0	*231.2	*246	132	124	32	62-2	169	.271
2000— Toronto (A.L.)	•20	8	.714	4.11	1.29	35	•35	*9	1	0	0-0	229.2	*266	115	105	23	31-0	166	.289
2001— Chicago (A.L.)	5	7	.417	4.47	1.40	16	16	1	0	0	0-0	100.2	120	55	50	12	21-1	59	.297
2002— New York (A.L.)	19	7	.731	3.75	1.24	31	31	2	1	0	0-0	206.1	210	100	86	21	45-2	137	.259
2003— New York (A.L.)	15	7	.682	4.14	1.23	31	30	4	1	0	0-0	213.0	242	101	98	24	20-0	101	.286
2004— San Diego (N.L.)	12	8	.600	3.73	1.14	31	31	0	0	0	0-0	195.2	203	85	81	23	20-1	101	.266
2005— Boston (A.L.)	15	7	.682	4.45	1.31	30	30	2	0	0	0-0	184.0	220	95	91	21	21-0	107	.296
2006— Pawtucket (Int'l)	1	1	.500	8.10	1.40	2	2	0	0	0	0-0	10.0	10	9	9	2	4-0	4	.263
— Boston (A.L.)	2	3	.400	4.98	1.53	8	8	0	0	0	0-0	47.0	64	30	26	10	8-0	24	.327
— San Diego (N.L.)	1	2	.333	3.49	1.31	5	5	0	0	0	0-0	28.1	33	11	11	4	4-0	14	.292
American League totals (19 years)	211	133	.613	4.11	1.26	584	413	51	12	28	13-26	2985.0	3124	1475	1362	355	637-55	1954	.268
National League totals (3 years)	19	15	.559	3.67	1.18	47	47	3	0	0	0-0	296.2	310	130	121	30	40-5	165	.268
Major League totals (20 years)	230	148	.608	4.07	1.25	631	460	54	12	28	13-26	3281.2	3434	1605	1483	385	677-60	2119	.269

DIVISION SERIES RECORD

Year Team (League)	W	L	Pct.	ERA	WHIP	G	GS	CG	ShO	Hld.	Sv.-Opp.	IP	H	R	ER	HR	BB-IBB	SO	Avg.
1995— Cincinnati (N.L.)	1	0	1.000	0.00	1.11	1	1	0	0	0	0-0	6.1	6	1	0	0	1-0	8	.231
1996— Baltimore (A.L.)	1	0	1.000	4.61	1.39	2	2	0	0	0	0-0	13.2	15	7	7	1	4-1	6	.288
1997— New York (A.L.)	1	0	1.000	1.00	0.56	1	1	1	0	0	0-0	9.0	5	1	1	0	0-0	6	.152
1998— New York (A.L.)	1	0	1.000	0.00	0.75	1	1	0	0	0	0-0	8.0	5	0	0	0	1-0	9	.172
2002— New York (A.L.)	0	1	.000	15.43	2.14	1	1	0	0	0	0-0	4.2	10	8	8	1	0-0	4	.435
2003— New York (A.L.)	1	0	1.000	1.17	1.04	1	1	0	0	0	0-0	7.2	5	1	1	0	3-0	5	.258

Year Team (League)	W	L	Pct.	ERA	WHIP	G	GS	CG	ShO	Hld.	Sv.-Opp.	IP	H	R	ER	HR	BB-IBB	SO	Avg.
2005— Boston (A.L.)	0	1	.000	2.70	1.05	1	1	0	0	0	0-0	6.2	7	5	2	1	0-0	2	.269
2006— San Diego (N.L.)	0	1	.000	3.60	1.40	1	1	0	0	0	0-0	5.0	7	2	2	0	0-0	2	.389
Division series totals (8 years)	5	3	.625	3.10	1.13	9	9	1	0	0	0-0	61.0	63	25	21	3	6-1	33	.265

CHAMPIONSHIP SERIES RECORD

Year Team (League)	W	L	Pct.	ERA	WHIP	G	GS	CG	ShO	Hld.	Sv.-Opp.	IP	H	R	ER	HR	BB-IBB	SO	Avg.
1989— Toronto (A.L.)	0	0	...	0.00	2.00	1	0	0	0	0	0-0	1.0	0	1	0	0	2-0	1	.000
1991— Toronto (A.L.)	0	0	...	2.35	1.04	4	0	0	0	0	0-0	7.2	6	2	2	0	2-1	9	.207
1992— Toronto (A.L.)		Did not play.																	
1995— Cincinnati (N.L.)	0	1	.000	4.50	1.67	1	1	0	0	0	0-0	6.0	8	3	3	1	2-0	3	.320
1996— Baltimore (A.L.)	1	0	1.000	4.05	1.65	1	1	0	0	0	0-0	6.2	8	3	3	0	3-0	6	.308
1998— New York (A.L.)	2	0	1.000	2.87	0.89	2	2	0	0	0	0-0	15.2	12	5	5	3	2-0	18	.218
2003— New York (A.L.)	1	0	1.000	2.35	0.91	2	1	0	0	0	0-0	7.2	5	2	2	2	2-0	5	.179
Champ. series totals (6 years)	4	1	.800	3.02	1.16	11	5	0	0	0	0-0	44.2	39	16	15	6	13-1	42	.235

WORLD SERIES RECORD

Year Team (League)	W	L	Pct.	ERA	WHIP	G	GS	CG	ShO	Hld.	Sv.-Opp.	IP	H	R	ER	HR	BB-IBB	SO	Avg.
1992— Toronto (A.L.)	0	0	...	0.00	0.69	4	0	0	0	0	0-1	4.1	1	0	0	0	2-0	3	.083
1998— New York (A.L.)	1	0	1.000	6.43	1.29	1	1	0	0	0	0-0	7.0	7	5	5	3	2-0	4	.269
2003— New York (A.L.)	0	1	.000	3.38	1.00	2	2	0	0	0	0-0	8.0	6	3	3	0	2-0	1	.222
World series totals (3 years)	1	1	.500	3.72	1.03	7	3	0	0	0	0-1	19.1	14	8	8	3	6-0	8	.215

ALL-STAR GAME RECORD

	W	L	Pct.	ERA	WHIP	G	GS	CG	ShO	Hld.	Sv.-Opp.	IP	H	R	ER	HR	BB-IBB	SO	Avg.
All-Star Game totals (3 years)	0	0	...	0.00	0.69	3	2	0	0	0	0-0	4.1	2	0	0	0	1-0	4	.143

2006 LEFTY-RIGHTY SPLITS

vs.	Avg.	AB	H	2B	3B	HR	RBI	BB	SO	OBP	Slg.	vs.	Avg.	AB	H	2B	3B	HR	RBI	BB	SO	OBP	Slg.
L	.303	66	20	6	0	2	7	3	8	.333	.485	R	.317	243	77	10	1	9	31	9	30	.340	.477

WELLS, KIP   P

PERSONAL: Born April 21, 1977, in Houston, Texas. ... 6-3/200. ... Throws right, bats right. ... Full name: Robert Kip Wells. ... High school: Elkins (Fort Bend, Texas). ... College: Baylor. **TRANSACTIONS/CAREER NOTES:** Selected by Milwaukee Brewers organization in 58th round of 1995 free-agent draft; did not sign. ... Selected by Chicago White Sox organization in first round (16th pick overall) of 1998 free-agent draft. ... Traded by White Sox with Ps Sean Lowe and Josh Fogg to Pittsburgh Pirates for P Todd Ritchie and C Lee Evans (December 13, 2001). ... On disabled list (August 14-September 5, 2004). ... On disabled list (April 1-June 18, 2006); included rehabilitation assignments to Lynchburg and Altoona. ... Traded by Pirates to Texas Rangers for P Jesse Chavez (July 31, 2006). ... On disabled list (August 12, 2006-remainder of season). **MISCELLANEOUS NOTES:** Struck out in only appearance as pinch hitter (2002). ... Singled, doubled and scored a run in two appearances as pinch hitter (2003). ... Had a sacrifice hit in only appearance as pinch hitter (2004). ... Grounded out in only appearance as pinch hitter (2005).
CAREER HITTING: 44-for-250 (.176), 21 R, 9 2B, 1 3B, 3 HR, 12 RBI.

Year Team (League)	W	L	Pct.	ERA	WHIP	G	GS	CG	ShO	Hld.	Sv.-Opp.	IP	H	R	ER	HR	BB-IBB	SO	Avg.
1999— Win.-Salem (Car.)	5	6	.455	3.57	1.31	14	14	0	0	...	0-...	85.2	78	39	34	4	34-1	95	.252
— Birmingham (Sou.)	8	2	.800	2.94	1.14	11	11	0	0	...	0-...	70.1	49	24	23	5	31-0	44	.198
— Chicago (A.L.)	4	1	.800	4.04	1.35	7	7	0	0	0	0-0	35.2	33	17	16	2	15-0	29	.248
2000— Chicago (A.L.)	6	9	.400	6.02	1.86	20	20	0	0	0	0-0	98.2	126	76	66	15	58-4	71	.312
— Charlotte (Int'l)	5	3	.625	5.37	1.52	12	12	2	1	0	0-...	62.0	67	38	37	10	27-1	38	.272
2001— Charlotte (Int'l)	2	1	.667	3.55	1.34	4	4	0	0	0	0-...	25.1	26	11	10	2	8-0	24	.260
— Chicago (A.L.)	10	11	.476	4.79	1.55	40	20	0	0	6	0-2	133.1	145	80	71	14	61-5	99	.281
2002— Pittsburgh (N.L.)	12	14	.462	3.58	1.35	33	33	1	1	0	0-0	198.1	197	92	79	21	71-11	134	.261
2003— Pittsburgh (N.L.)	10	9	.526	3.28	1.31	31	31	1	0	0	0-0	197.1	171	77	72	24	76-7	147	.233
2004— Pittsburgh (N.L.)	5	7	.417	4.55	1.53	24	24	0	0	0	0-0	138.1	145	71	70	14	66-4	116	.270
2005— Pittsburgh (N.L.)	8	* 18	.308	5.09	1.57	33	33	1	1	0	0-0	182.0	186	116	103	23	* 99-8	132	.266
2006— Lynchburg (Caro.)	1	0	1.000	0.00	0.83	1	1	0	0	0	0-0	6.0	3	0	0	0	2-0	5	.158
— Altoona (East.)	1	0	1.000	3.68	0.95	1	1	0	0	0	0-0	7.1	6	3	3	1	1-0	4	.231
— Pittsburgh (N.L.)	1	5	.167	6.69	1.88	7	7	0	0	0	0-0	36.1	46	27	27	3	18-1	16	.319
— Texas (A.L.)	1	0	1.000	5.63	2.25	2	2	0	0	0	0-0	8.0	15	6	5	0	3-0	4	.405
American League totals (4 years)	21	21	.500	5.16	1.65	69	49	0	0	6	0-2	275.2	319	179	158	31	137-9	203	.293
National League totals (5 years)	36	53	.404	4.20	1.43	128	128	3	2	0	0-0	752.1	745	383	351	85	330-31	545	.260
Major League totals (8 years)	57	74	.435	4.46	1.49	197	177	3	2	6	0-2	1028.0	1064	562	509	116	467-40	748	.269

2006 LEFTY-RIGHTY SPLITS

vs.	Avg.	AB	H	2B	3B	HR	RBI	BB	SO	OBP	Slg.	vs.	Avg.	AB	H	2B	3B	HR	RBI	BB	SO	OBP	Slg.
L	.353	85	30	3	3	0	11	15	8	.455	.459	R	.323	96	31	9	0	3	15	6	12	.377	.510

WELLS, VERNON   OF

PERSONAL: Born December 8, 1978, in Shreveport, La. ... 6-1/225. ... Bats right, throws right. ... Full name: Vernon Wells III. ... High school: Bowie (Arlington, Texas). **TRANSACTIONS/CAREER NOTES:** Selected by Toronto Blue Jays organization in first round (fifth pick overall) of 1997 free-agent draft. ... On disabled list (June 16-July 16, 2004). **HONORS:** Named outfielder on THE SPORTING NEWS A.L. All-Star team (2003 and 2006). ... Won A.L. Gold Glove as outfielder (2004-06). ... Named outfielder on A.L. Silver Slugger team (2003). **STATISTICAL NOTES:** Career major league grand slams: 4. ... Hit three home runs in one game (May 30, 2006).
2006 GAMES PLAYED BY POSITION (MLB): OF—150, DH—4.

									BATTING										FIELDING	
Year Team (League)	Pos.	G	AB	R	H	2B	3B	HR	RBI	BB	SO	HBP	GDP	SB-CS	Avg.	OBP	SLG	OPS	E	Avg.
1997— St. Catharines (NYP)	OF	66	264	52	81	20	1	10	31	30	44	1	2	8-6	.307	.377	.504	.881	7	.953
1998— Hagerstown (SAL)	OF	134	509	86	145	35	2	11	65	49	84	1	8	13-8	.285	.348	.426	.774	5	.980
1999— Dunedin (Fla. St.)	OF-DH	70	265	43	91	16	2	11	43	26	34	1	6	13-2	.343	.403	.543	.946	1	.993
— Knoxville (Southern)	OF	26	106	18	36	6	2	3	17	12	15	0	6	6-2	.340	.400	.519	.919	0	1.000
— Syracuse (Int'l)	OF	33	129	20	40	8	1	4	21	10	22	1	3	5-1	.310	.357	.481	.837	2	.976
— Toronto (A.L.)	OF	24	88	8	23	5	0	1	8	4	18	0	1	1-1	.261	.293	.352	.646	0	1.000
2000— Syracuse (Int'l)	OF	127	493	76	120	31	2	16	66	48	88	4	8	23-4	.243	.313	.432	.745	3	.990
— Toronto (A.L.)	OF	3	2	0	0	0	0	0	0	0	0	0	0	0-0	.000	.000	.000	.000	0	1.000
2001— Syracuse (Int'l)	OF	107	413	57	116	27	4	12	52	29	68	4	9	15-11	.281	.333	.453	.785	5	.978
— Toronto (A.L.)	OF	30	96	14	30	8	0	1	6	5	15	1	0	0-3	.313	.350	.427	.777	2	.969
2002— Toronto (A.L.)	OF	159	608	87	167	34	4	23	100	27	85	2	15	9-4	.275	.305	.457	.762	3	.990
2003— Toronto (A.L.)	OF	161	678	118	• 215	• 49	5	33	117	42	80	7	21	4-1	.317	.359	.550	.909	4	.990
2004— Toronto (A.L.)	OF-DH	134	536	82	146	34	2	23	67	51	83	2	17	9-2	.272	.337	.472	.809	1	.995
2005— Toronto (A.L.)	OF-DH	156	620	78	167	30	4	28	97	47	86	6	13	8-3	.269	.320	.463	.783	1	1.000
2006— Toronto (A.L.)	OF-DH	154	611	91	185	40	5	32	106	54	90	8	13	17-4	.303	.357	.542	.899	4	.988
Major League totals (8 years)		821	3239	478	933	200	19	141	501	230	457	26	85	53-15	.288	.336	.492	.828	14	.993

W

	G	AB	R	H	2B	3B	HR	RBI	BB	SO	HBP	GDP	SB-CS	Avg.	OBP	SLG	OPS	E	Avg.
All-Star Game totals (2 years)	2	4	1	2	1	0	0	1	0	0	0	0	0-0	.500	.500	.750	1.250	0	1.000

2006 LEFTY-RIGHTY SPLITS

vs.	Avg.	AB	H	2B	3B	HR	RBI	BB	SO	OBP	Slg.	vs.	Avg.	AB	H	2B	3B	HR	RBI	BB	SO	OBP	Slg.
L	.333	156	52	9	0	6	24	15	22	.392	.506	R	.292	455	133	31	5	26	82	39	68	.346	.554

WERTH, JAYSON — OF

PERSONAL: Born May 20, 1979, in Springfield, Ill. ... 6-5/215. ... Bats right, throws right. ... Full name: Jayson Richard Werth. ... High school: Chatham Glenwood (Chatham, Ill.). ... Stepson of Dennis Werth, outfielder/first baseman with two major league teams (1979-82); nephew of Dick Schofield, infielder with four major league teams (1983-96); grandson of Dick Schofield, infielder/outfielder with six major league teams (1953-71). **TRANSACTIONS/CAREER NOTES:** Selected by Baltimore Orioles organization in first round (22nd pick overall) of 1997 free-agent draft. ... Traded by Orioles to Toronto Blue Jays for P John Bale (December 11, 2000). ... On disabled list (March 21-April 13, 2003); included rehabilitation assignment Dunedin. ... Traded by Blue Jays to Los Angeles Dodgers for P Jason Frasor (March 29, 2004). ... On disabled list (April 6-June 4, 2004); included rehabilitation assignment to Las Vegas. ... On disabled list (April 2-May 25 and July 28-August 11, 2005); included rehabilitation assignments to Las Vegas. ... On disabled list (April 1, 2006-entire season).

									BATTING										FIELDING	
Year Team (League)	Pos.	G	AB	R	H	2B	3B	HR	RBI	BB	SO	HBP	GDP	SB-CS	Avg.	OBP	SLG	OPS	E	Avg.
1997— GC Orioles (GCL)	1B-C	32	88	16	26	6	0	1	8	22	22	0	0	7-1	.295	.432	.398	.830	9	.958
1998—Delmarva (S. Atl.)	C	120	408	71	108	20	3	8	53	50	92	15	14	21-6	.265	.364	.387	.751	9	.991
—Bowie (East.)	C	5	19	2	3	2	0	0	1	2	6	0	0	1-0	.158	.238	.263	.501	0	1.000
1999—Frederick (Carolina)	C	66	236	41	72	10	1	3	30	37	37	3	4	16-3	.305	.403	.394	.797	10	.981
—Bowie (East.)	C-OF	35	121	18	33	5	1	1	11	17	26	2	1	7-1	.273	.364	.355	.719	1	.996
2000—Bowie (East.)	C-OF	85	276	47	63	16	2	5	26	54	50	4	10	9-3	.228	.361	.355	.716	7	.988
—Frederick (Carolina)	C	24	83	16	23	3	0	2	18	10	15	0	3	5-1	.277	.347	.386	.733	2	.985
2001—Dunedin (Fla. St.)	C	21	70	9	14	3	0	2	14	17	19	0	2	1-1	.200	.356	.329	.685	0	1.000
—Tennessee (Sou.)	C-1B	104	369	51	105	23	1	18	69	63	93	3	5	12-3	.285	.387	.499	.886	7	.988
2002—Syracuse (Int'l)	OF-C	127	443	65	114	25	2	18	82	67	125	4	7	24-7	.257	.354	.445	.798	5	.985
—Toronto (A.L.)	OF	15	46	4	12	2	1	0	6	6	11	0	4	1-0	.261	.340	.348	.687	0	1.000
2003—Dunedin (Fla. St.)	OF-DH	18	62	10	23	5	0	4	18	3	14	0	2	1-0	.371	.388	.645	1.033	0	1.000
—Toronto (A.L.)	OF-DH	26	48	7	10	4	0	2	10	3	22	0	0	1-0	.208	.255	.417	.672	0	1.000
—Syracuse (Int'l)	OF-DH	64	236	37	56	19	1	5	34	15	68	2	7	11-1	.237	.285	.441	.726	7	.954
2004—Las Vegas (PCL)	OF-DH	14	51	13	21	2	1	5	20	8	10	1	2	2-0	.412	.500	.784	1.284	0	1.000
—Los Angeles (N.L.)	OF-DH	89	290	56	76	11	3	16	47	30	85	4	1	4-1	.262	.338	.486	.825	4	.974
2005—Las Vegas (PCL)	OF	15	49	9	18	0	0	3	10	13	17	2	0	6-1	.367	.516	.551	1.067	2	.957
—Los Angeles (N.L.)	OF-DH	102	337	46	79	22	2	7	43	48	114	6	10	11-2	.234	.338	.374	.711	3	.987
2006—Los Angeles (N.L.)		Did not play.																		
American League totals (2 years)		41	94	11	22	6	1	2	16	9	33	0	4	2-0	.234	.298	.383	.681	0	1.000
National League totals (2 years)		191	627	102	155	33	5	23	90	78	199	10	11	15-3	.247	.338	.426	.764	7	.982
Major League totals (4 years)		232	721	113	177	39	6	25	106	87	232	10	15	17-3	.245	.333	.420	.753	7	.984

DIVISION SERIES RECORD

Year Team (League)	Pos.	G	AB	R	H	2B	3B	HR	RBI	BB	SO	HBP	GDP	SB-CS	Avg.	OBP	SLG	OPS	E	Avg.
2004—Los Angeles (N.L.)	OF	4	14	3	4	1	0	2	3	3	4	0	0	0-0	.286	.412	.786	1.197	0	1.000

WESTBROOK, JAKE — P

PERSONAL: Born September 29, 1977, in Athens, Ga. ... 6-3/185. ... Throws right, bats right. ... Full name: Jacob Cauthen Westbrook. ... High school: Madison County (Danielsville, Ga.). **TRANSACTIONS/CAREER NOTES:** Selected by Colorado Rockies organization in first round (21st pick overall) of 1996 free-agent draft. ... Traded by Rockies with P John Nicholson and OF Mark Hamlin to Montreal Expos for 2B Mike Lansing (December 16, 1997). ... Traded by Expos with two players to be named to New York Yankees for P Hideki Irabu (December 22, 1999); Yankees acquired Ps Ted Lilly (March 17, 2000) and Christian Parker (March 22, 2000) to complete deal. ... Traded by Yankees with P Zach Day to Cleveland Indians (July 25, 2000), completing deal in which Indians traded OF Dave Justice to Yankees for OF Ricky Ledee and two players to be named (June 29, 2000). ... On disabled list (September 1, 2000-remainder of season). ... On disabled list (March 30-July 11 and August 26, 2002-remainder of season); included rehabilitation assignments to Akron and Buffalo.

CAREER HITTING: 2-for-10 (.200), 0 R, 1 2B, 0 3B, 0 HR, 1 RBI.

Year Team (League)	W	L	Pct.	ERA	WHIP	G	GS	CG	ShO	Hld.	Sv.-Opp.	IP	H	R	ER	HR	BB-IBB	SO	Avg.
1996— Ariz. Rockies (Ariz.)	4	2	.667	2.87	1.28	11	11	0	0	...	0-...	62.2	66	33	20	0	14-0	57	.269
—Portland (N'west)	1	1	.500	2.55	1.09	4	4	0	0	...	0-...	24.2	22	8	7	1	5-0	19	.237
1997— Asheville (S. Atl.)	14	11	.560	4.82	1.36	28	27	3	2	...	0-...	170.0	176	93	91	16	55-0	92	.269
1998— Jupiter (Fla. St.)	11	6	.647	3.26	1.34	27	27	2	0	...	0-...	171.0	169	70	62	11	60-0	79	.264
1999— Harrisburg (East.)	11	5	.688	3.92	1.39	27	27	2	0	...	0-...	174.2	180	88	76	14	63-1	90	.274
2000— Columbus (Int'l)	5	7	.417	4.65	1.48	16	15	2	0	...	0-...	89.0	94	53	46	3	38-0	61	.272
—New York (A.L.)	0	2	.000	13.50	2.85	3	2	0	0	0	0-0	6.2	15	10	10	1	4-1	1	.469
2001— Buffalo (Int'l)	8	1	.889	3.20	1.28	12	12	0	0	...	0-...	64.2	60	27	23	2	23-0	45	.249
—Cleveland (A.L.)	4	4	.500	5.85	1.56	23	6	0	0	5	0-0	64.2	79	43	42	6	22-4	48	.306
2002— Akron (East.)	0	0	.000	4.80	0.93	3	3	0	0	...	0-...	15.0	13	8	8	0	1-0	8	.228
—Buffalo (Int'l)	1	0	1.000	6.00	1.33	1	1	0	0	...	0-...	6.0	8	4	4	1	0-0	2	.333
—Cleveland (A.L.)	1	3	.250	5.83	1.49	11	4	0	0	1	0-2	41.2	50	30	27	6	12-1	20	.296
2003— Buffalo (Int'l)	1	0	1.000	0.00	0.40	2	2	0	0	...	0-...	10.0	0	0	0	0	4-0	7	.000
—Cleveland (A.L.)	7	10	.412	4.33	1.49	34	22	1	0	...	0-0	133.0	142	70	64	9	56-1	58	.281
2004— Cleveland (A.L.)	14	9	.609	3.38	1.25	33	30	•5	1	0	0-0	215.2	208	95	81	19	61-3	116	.255
2005— Cleveland (A.L.)	15	15	.500	4.49	1.30	34	34	2	0	0	0-0	210.2	218	121	105	19	56-3	119	.265
2006— Cleveland (A.L.)	15	10	.600	4.17	1.43	32	32	3	•2	0	0-0	211.1	•247	106	98	15	55-4	109	.296
Major League totals (7 years)	56	53	.514	4.35	1.39	170	130	11	3	7	0-2	883.2	959	475	427	75	266-17	471	.279

2006 LEFTY-RIGHTY SPLITS

vs.	Avg.	AB	H	2B	3B	HR	RBI	BB	SO	OBP	Slg.	vs.	Avg.	AB	H	2B	3B	HR	RBI	BB	SO	OBP	Slg.
L	.290	369	107	13	1	7	32	35	40	.355	.388	R	.300	466	140	27	1	8	58	20	69	.329	.414

WHEELER, DAN — P

PERSONAL: Born December 10, 1977, in Providence, R.I. ... 6-3/222. ... Throws right, bats right. ... Full name: Daniel Michael Wheeler. ... High school: Pilgrim (Warwick, R.I.). ... Junior college: Central Arizona. **TRANSACTIONS/CAREER NOTES:** Selected by Tampa Bay Devil Rays organization in 34th round of 1996 free-agent draft. ... Released by Devil Rays (December 13, 2001). ... Signed by Atlanta Braves organization (January 10, 2002). ... Signed as a free agent by New York Mets organization (January 27, 2003). ... Traded by Mets to Houston Astros for P Adam Seuss (August 27, 2004). ... On suspended list (September 24-27, 2004).

CAREER HITTING: 1-for-7 (.143), 1 R, 0 2B, 0 3B, 0 HR, 0 RBI.

W

Year Team (League)	W	L	Pct.	ERA	WHIP	G	GS	CG	ShO	Hld.	Sv.-Opp.	IP	H	R	ER	HR	BB-IBB	SO	Avg.
1997—Hudson Valley (NYP)	6	7	.462	3.00	1.10	15	15	0	0	...	0-...	84.0	75	38	28	2	17-0	81	.228
1998—Char., S.C. (SAL)	12	14	.462	4.43	1.30	29	29	3	1	...	0-...	181.0	206	96	89	16	29-0	136	.290
1999—Orlando (South.)	3	0	1.000	3.26	1.10	9	9	0	0	...	0-...	58.0	56	27	21	7	8-0	53	.252
—Durham (Int'l)	7	5	.583	4.92	1.55	14	14	2	1	...	0-...	82.1	103	59	45	16	25-0	58	.307
—Tampa Bay (A.L.)	0	4	.000	5.87	1.57	6	6	0	0	0	0-0	30.2	35	20	20	7	13-1	32	.287
2000—Tampa Bay (A.L.)	1	1	.500	5.48	1.74	11	2	0	0	1	0-1	23.0	29	14	14	2	11-2	17	.302
—Durham (Int'l)	5	11	.313	5.63	1.50	26	26	0	0	...	0-...	150.1	183	109	94	35	42-1	91	.300
2001—Durham (Int'l)	3	5	.375	5.23	1.27	18	10	0	0	...	0-...	65.1	72	51	38	11	11-0	39	.271
—Tampa Bay (A.L.)	1	0	1.000	8.66	1.98	13	0	0	0	0	0-0	17.2	30	17	17	3	5-0	12	.375
—Orlando (South.)	0	2	.000	2.81	1.31	3	3	0	0	...	0-...	16.0	15	5	5	2	6-1	12	.242
2002—Richmond (Int'l)	9	6	.600	4.65	1.32	27	25	0	0	...	0-...	155.0	163	87	80	23	42-0	110	.265
2003—Norfolk (Int'l)	4	2	.667	3.94	1.40	22	5	0	0	...	4-...	45.2	48	20	20	4	16-3	44	.265
—New York (N.L.)	1	3	.250	3.71	1.29	35	0	0	0	0	2-3	51.0	49	23	21	6	17-4	35	.253
2004—Norfolk (Int'l)	1	0	1.000	2.46	1.36	5	0	0	0	...	0-...	7.1	8	2	2	0	2-0	10	.271
—New York (N.L.)	3	1	.750	4.80	1.62	32	1	0	0	3	0-0	50.2	65	29	27	9	17-2	46	.307
—Houston (N.L.)	0	0	...	2.51	0.98	14	0	0	0	2	0-0	14.1	11	4	4	1	3-0	9	.215
2005—Houston (N.L.)	2	3	.400	2.21	0.98	71	0	0	0	17	3-5	73.1	53	18	18	7	19-3	69	.204
2006—Houston (N.L.)	3	5	.375	2.52	1.15	75	0	0	0	24	9-12	71.1	58	22	20	5	24-8	68	.221
American League totals (3 years)	2	5	.286	6.43	1.72	30	8	0	0	1	0-1	71.1	94	51	51	12	29-3	61	.315
National League totals (4 years)	9	12	.429	3.11	1.21	227	1	0	0	46	14-20	260.2	236	96	90	28	80-17	227	.241
Major League totals (7 years)	11	17	.393	3.82	1.32	257	9	0	0	47	14-21	332.0	330	147	141	40	109-20	288	.258

DIVISION SERIES RECORD

Year Team (League)	W	L	Pct.	ERA	WHIP	G	GS	CG	ShO	Hld.	Sv.-Opp.	IP	H	R	ER	HR	BB-IBB	SO	Avg.
2004—Houston (N.L.)	0	0	...	0.00	0.00	1	0	0	0	0	0-0	1.0	0	0	0	0	0-0	0	.000
2005—Houston (N.L.)	0	0	...	2.08	1.62	3	0	0	0	0	0-0	4.1	4	1	1	0	3-1	5	.235
Division series totals (2 years)	0	0	...	1.69	1.31	4	0	0	0	0	0-0	5.1	4	1	1	0	3-1	5	.190

CHAMPIONSHIP SERIES RECORD

Year Team (League)	W	L	Pct.	ERA	WHIP	G	GS	CG	ShO	Hld.	Sv.-Opp.	IP	H	R	ER	HR	BB-IBB	SO	Avg.
2004—Houston (N.L.)	1	0	1.000	0.00	0.57	4	0	0	0	0	0-0	7.0	4	0	0	0	0-0	9	.160
2005—Houston (N.L.)	0	0	...	0.00	0.75	3	0	0	0	2	0-0	2.2	2	0	0	0	0-0	2	.200
Champ. series totals (2 years)	1	0	1.000	0.00	0.62	7	0	0	0	2	0-0	9.2	6	0	0	0	0-0	11	.171

WORLD SERIES RECORD

Year Team (League)	W	L	Pct.	ERA	WHIP	G	GS	CG	ShO	Hld.	Sv.-Opp.	IP	H	R	ER	HR	BB-IBB	SO	Avg.
2005—Houston (N.L.)	0	0	...	13.50	1.50	2	0	0	0	0	0-0	2.0	2	3	3	0	1-0	1	.250

2006 LEFTY-RIGHTY SPLITS

vs.	Avg.	AB	H	2B	3B	HR	RBI	BB	SO	OBP	Slg.	vs.	Avg.	AB	H	2B	3B	HR	RBI	BB	SO	OBP	Slg.
L	.273	110	30	11	0	3	18	14	20	.357	.455	R	.183	153	28	9	1	2	11	10	48	.235	.294

WHITE, RICK   P

PERSONAL: Born December 23, 1968, in Springfield, Ohio. ... 6-4/230. ... Throws right, bats right. ... Full name: Richard Allen White. ... High school: Kenton Ridge (Springfield, Ohio). ... Junior college: Paducah (Ky.) Community College. **TRANSACTIONS/CAREER NOTES:** Selected by Pittsburgh Pirates organization in 15th round of 1990 free-agent draft. ... On disabled list (April 14-May 17, 1995); included rehabilitation assignment to GCL Pirates. ... Signed as a free agent by Tampa Bay Devil Rays organization (February 4, 1997). ... Loaned by Devil Rays organization to Chicago Cubs organization (April 3-September 11, 1997). ... Traded by Devil Rays with OF Bubba Trammell to New York Mets for OF Jason Tyner and P Paul Wilson (July 28, 2000). ... On disabled list (March 31-April 21 and May 1-17, 2001). ... Signed as a free agent by Colorado Rockies (January 10, 2002). ... On disabled list (May 27-June 18, 2002); included rehabilitation assignment to Colorado Springs. ... Released by Rockies (August 12, 2002). ... Signed by St. Louis Cardinals organization (August 17, 2002). ... Signed as a free agent by Chicago White Sox (January 22, 2003). ... Released by White Sox (August 11, 2003). ... Signed by Houston Astros (August 14, 2003). ... Signed as a free agent by Los Angeles Dodgers organization (January 16, 2004). ... Traded by Dodgers to Cleveland Indians for OF Trey Dyson (April 25, 2004). ... Signed as a free agent by Pirates organization (January 27, 2005). ... Signed as a free agent by Cincinnati Reds (February 1, 2006). ... Claimed on waivers by Philadelphia Phillies (June 23, 2006). **MISCELLANEOUS NOTES:** Struck out and grounded out in two appearances as pinch hitter with New York (2000).

CAREER HITTING: 4-for-42 (.095), 1 R, 1 2B, 0 3B, 0 HR, 1 RBI.

Year Team (League)	W	L	Pct.	ERA	WHIP	G	GS	CG	ShO	Hld.	Sv.-Opp.	IP	H	R	ER	HR	BB-IBB	SO	Avg.
1990—GC Pirates (GCL)	3	1	.750	0.76	0.84	7	6	0	0	...	0-...	35.2	26	11	3	0	4-0	27	.194
—Welland (NYP)	1	4	.200	3.26	1.37	9	5	1	0	...	0-...	38.2	39	19	14	2	14-2	43	.265
1991—Augusta (S. Atl.)	4	4	.500	3.00	1.37	34	0	0	0	...	6-...	63.0	68	26	21	2	18-2	52	.264
—Salem (Carol.)	2	3	.400	4.66	1.08	13	5	1	0	...	1-...	46.1	41	27	24	2	9-3	36	.233
1992—Salem (Carol.)	7	9	.438	3.80	1.16	18	18	5	0	...	0-...	120.2	116	58	51	15	24-1	70	.255
—Carolina (Southern)	1	7	.125	4.21	1.34	10	10	1	0	...	0-...	57.2	59	32	27	8	18-1	45	.265
1993—Carolina (Southern)	4	3	.571	3.50	1.02	12	12	1	0	...	0-...	69.1	59	29	27	5	12-0	52	.231
—Buffalo (A.A.)	0	3	.000	3.54	1.18	7	3	0	0	...	0-...	28.0	25	13	11	1	8-0	16	.238
1994—Pittsburgh (N.L.)	4	5	.444	3.82	1.27	43	5	0	0	3	6-9	75.1	79	35	32	9	17-3	38	.280
1995—Pittsburgh (N.L.)	2	3	.400	4.75	1.53	15	0	0	0	...	0-...	55.0	66	33	29	3	18-0	29	.299
—Calgary (PCL)	6	4	.600	4.20	1.35	14	11	1	0	...	0-...	79.1	97	40	37	13	10-0	56	.302
1996—GC Pirates (GCL)	0	0	...	2.25	0.92	3	3	0	0	...	0-...	12.0	8	4	3	0	3-0	8	.205
—Carolina (Southern)	0	1	.000	11.37	1.58	2	1	0	0	...	0-...	6.1	9	8	8	2	1-0	7	.321
1997—Orlando (South.)	5	7	.417	4.71	1.34	39	8	0	0	...	12-...	86.0	93	55	45	7	22-2	65	.275
1998—Durham (Int'l)	4	2	.667	4.22	1.39	9	9	1	0	...	0-...	53.1	63	29	25	3	11-0	31	.294
—Tampa Bay (A.L.)	2	6	.250	3.80	1.30	38	3	0	0	...	0-0	68.2	66	32	29	8	23-2	39	.253
1999—Tampa Bay (A.L.)	5	3	.625	4.08	1.57	63	1	0	0	4	0-2	108.0	132	56	49	8	38-5	81	.304
2000—Tampa Bay (A.L.)	3	6	.333	3.41	1.16	44	0	0	0	2	2-5	71.1	57	30	27	4	26-3	47	.220
—New York (N.L.)	2	3	.400	3.81	1.34	22	0	0	0	2	1-2	28.1	26	14	12	2	12-2	20	.232
2001—New York (N.L.)	4	5	.444	3.88	1.26	55	0	0	0	10	2-4	69.2	71	38	30	7	17-4	51	.257
2002—Memphis (PCL)	0	0	...	2.45	1.91	3	0	0	0	...	0-...	3.2	4	1	1	0	3-0	4	.286
—Colorado (N.L.)	2	6	.250	6.20	1.65	41	0	0	0	9	0-1	40.2	49	30	28	4	18-4	27	.310
—St. Louis (N.L.)	3	1	.750	0.82	0.73	20	0	0	0	0	0-0	22.0	13	3	2	0	3-1	14	.169
2003—Chicago (A.L.)	1	2	.333	6.61	1.45	34	0	0	0	3	1-1	56.0	56	39	35	11	13-2	37	.255
—Houston (N.L.)	0	0	...	3.72	1.34	15	0	0	0	1	0-0	19.1	18	9	8	2	8-0	17	.243
2004—Las Vegas (PCL)	0	0	...	0.00	0.43	6	0	0	0	...	2-...	11.2	4	0	0	0	1-0	14	.105
—Cleveland (A.L.)	5	5	.500	5.29	1.49	59	0	0	0	2	1-3	78.1	88	52	46	15	24-4	47	.293
2005—Pittsburgh (N.L.)	4	7	.364	3.72	1.59	71	0	0	0	2	2-3	75.0	90	39	31	3	29-10	40	.308
2006—Cincinnati (N.L.)	1	0	1.000	6.26	1.43	26	0	0	0	1	1-2	27.1	34	23	19	5	5-1	17	.318
—Philadelphia (N.L.)	3	1	.750	4.34	1.42	38	0	0	0	5	0-0	37.1	38	21	18	3	15-0	23	.273
American League totals (5 years)	16	22	.421	4.48	1.41	238	4	0	0	13	4-11	374.0	399	209	186	49	129-19	248	.276
National League totals (8 years)	25	31	.446	4.18	1.39	346	14	0	0	51	12-21	450.0	484	245	209	38	142-25	276	.278
Major League totals (11 years)	41	53	.436	4.31	1.40	584	18	0	0	64	16-32	824.0	883	454	395	87	271-44	524	.277

W

DIVISION SERIES RECORD

Year Team (League)	W	L	Pct.	ERA	WHIP	G	GS	CG	ShO	Hld.	Sv.-Opp.	IP	H	R	ER	HR	BB-IBB	SO	Avg.
2000— New York (N.L.)	1	0	1.000	0.00	3.00	2	0	0	0	0	0-0	2.2	6	0	0	0	2-0	4	.429
2002— St. Louis (N.L.)	0	0	...	0.00	1.00	2	0	0	0	1	0-1	2.0	1	0	0	0	1-0	1	.125
Division series totals (2 years)	1	0	1.000	0.00	2.14	4	0	0	0	1	0-1	4.2	7	1	0	0	3-0	5	.318

CHAMPIONSHIP SERIES RECORD

Year Team (League)	W	L	Pct.	ERA	WHIP	G	GS	CG	ShO	Hld.	Sv.-Opp.	IP	H	R	ER	HR	BB-IBB	SO	Avg.
2000— New York (N.L.)	0	0	...	9.00	2.00	1	0	0	0	0	0-0	3.0	5	3	3	0	1-0	1	.385
2002— St. Louis (N.L.)	0	1	.000	4.50	1.00	3	0	0	0	1	0-1	4.0	2	2	2	1	2-1	5	.143
Champ. series totals (2 years)	0	1	.000	6.43	1.43	4	0	0	0	1	0-1	7.0	7	5	5	1	3-1	6	.259

WORLD SERIES RECORD

Year Team (League)	W	L	Pct.	ERA	WHIP	G	GS	CG	ShO	Hld.	Sv.-Opp.	IP	H	R	ER	HR	BB-IBB	SO	Avg.
2000— New York (N.L.)	0	0	...	6.75	1.50	1	0	0	0	0	0-0	1.1	1	1	1	0	1-1	1	.250

2006 LEFTY-RIGHTY SPLITS

vs.	Avg.	AB	H	2B	3B	HR	RBI	BB	SO	OBP	Slg.	vs.	Avg.	AB	H	2B	3B	HR	RBI	BB	SO	OBP	Slg.
L	.295	78	23	5	1	4	17	10	14	.389	.538	R	.292	168	49	6	0	4	22	10	26	.331	.399

WHITE, RONDELL — OF/DH

PERSONAL: Born February 23, 1972, in Milledgeville, Ga. ... 6-1/225. ... Bats right, throws right. ... Full name: Rondell Bernard White. ... High school: Jones County (Gray, Ga.). **TRANSACTIONS/CAREER NOTES:** Selected by Montreal Expos organization in first round (24th pick overall) of 1990 free-agent draft; pick received as part of compensation for California Angels signing Type A free-agent P Mark Langston. ... On disabled list (April 28-July 16, 1996); included rehabilitation assignments to West Palm Beach, GCL Expos and Harrisburg. ... On disabled list (July 21, 1998-remainder of season; June 14-29 and July 2-17, 1999). ... On disabled list (July 8-August 6 and August 27, 2000-remainder of season). ... Traded by Expos to Chicago Cubs for P Scott Downs (July 31, 2000). ... On disabled list (June 26-July 12 and July 14-September 1, 2001); included rehabilitation assignment to West Tenn. ... Signed as a free agent by New York Yankees (December 21, 2001). ... Traded by Yankees to San Diego Padres for OF Bubba Trammell, P Mark Phillips and cash (March 19, 2003). ... Traded by Padres to Kansas City Royals for Ps Chris Tierney and Brian Sanches (August 26, 2003). ... Signed as a free agent by Detroit Tigers (December 19, 2003). ... On disabled list (August 15, 2005-remainder of season). ... Signed as a free agent by Minnesota Twins (December 22, 2005). ... On disabled list (June 30-July 16 and August 9-24, 2006); included rehabilitation assignment to Rochester. **STATISTICAL NOTES:** Hit for the cycle (June 11, 1995, 13 innings). ... Career major league grand slams: 4.

2006 GAMES PLAYED BY POSITION (MLB): DH—54, OF—38.

Year Team (League)	Pos.	G	AB	R	H	2B	3B	HR	RBI	BB	SO	HBP	GDP	SB-CS	Avg.	OBP	SLG	OPS	E	Avg.
1990— GC Expos (GCL)	OF	57	221	33	66	7	4	5	34	17	33	5	4	10-7	.299	.362	.434	.797	2	.973
1991— Sumter (S. Atl.)	OF	123	465	80	147	23	6	13	68	57	109	8	7	50-17	.316	.351	.422	.772	3	.987
1992— W.P. Beach (FSL)	OF	111	450	80	142	10	12	4	41	46	78	5	7	42-16	.316	.384	.418	.802	3	.984
— Harrisburg (East.)	OF	21	89	22	27	7	1	2	7	6	14	4	3	6-1	.303	.374	.472	.846	2	.938
1993— Harrisburg (East.)	OF	90	372	72	122	16	10	12	52	22	72	5	3	21-6	.328	.371	.522	.892	1	.995
— Ottawa (Int'l)	OF	37	150	28	57	8	2	7	32	12	20	3	4	10-1	.380	.436	.600	1.036	1	.988
— Montreal (N.L.)	OF	23	73	9	19	3	1	2	15	7	16	0	2	1-2	.260	.321	.411	.732	0	1.000
1994— Montreal (N.L.)	OF	40	97	16	27	10	1	2	13	9	18	3	1	1-1	.278	.358	.464	.822	2	.946
— Ottawa (Int'l)	OF	42	169	23	46	7	3	5	18	15	17	4	5	9-2	.272	.344	.438	.782	4	.979
1995— Montreal (N.L.)	OF	130	474	87	140	33	4	13	57	41	87	6	11	25-5	.295	.356	.464	.820	4	.986
1996— Montreal (N.L.)	OF	88	334	35	98	19	4	6	41	22	53	2	11	14-6	.293	.340	.428	.768	2	.990
— W.P. Beach (FSL)	DH-OF	3	10	0	2	1	0	0	2	0	4	0	0	0-1	.200	.200	.300	.500	1	1.000
— GC Expos (GCL)	OF	3	12	3	3	0	0	2	4	1	1	0	0	1-0	.250	.250	.750	1.000	1	1.000
— Harrisburg (East.)	OF	5	20	5	7	1	0	3	6	1	1	0	1	1-1	.350	.381	.850	1.231	0	1.000
1997— Montreal (N.L.)	OF	151	592	84	160	29	5	28	82	31	111	10	18	16-8	.270	.316	.478	.794	3	.992
1998— Montreal (N.L.)	OF-DH	97	357	54	107	21	2	17	58	30	57	7	7	16-7	.300	.363	.513	.875	4	.996
1999— Montreal (N.L.)	OF	138	539	83	168	26	6	22	64	32	85	11	17	10-6	.312	.359	.505	.863	11	.964
2000— Montreal (N.L.)	OF	75	290	52	89	24	0	11	54	28	67	2	4	5-1	.307	.370	.503	.873	1	.994
— Chicago (N.L.)	OF	19	67	7	22	2	0	2	7	5	12	2	0	0-2	.328	.392	.448	.840	0	1.000
2001— Chicago (N.L.)	OF	95	323	43	99	19	1	17	50	26	56	7	14	1-0	.307	.371	.529	.900	3	.979
— West Tenn (Sou.)	OF	9	28	2	4	1	0	2	4	1	7	2	1	0-0	.143	.226	.393	.619	0	1.000
2002— New York (A.L.)	OF-DH	126	455	59	109	21	0	14	62	25	86	8	11	1-2	.240	.288	.378	.666	0	1.000
2003— San Diego (N.L.)	OF-DH	115	413	49	115	17	3	18	66	25	71	8	11	1-1	.278	.330	.465	.795	4	.978
— Kansas City (A.L.)	OF-DH	22	75	13	26	6	1	4	21	6	8	2	2	0-0	.347	.400	.613	1.013	1	.978
2004— Detroit (A.L.)	OF-DH	121	448	76	121	21	2	19	67	39	77	4	8	1-2	.270	.337	.453	.790	3	.977
2005— Detroit (A.L.)	OF-DH	97	374	49	117	24	3	12	53	17	48	5	8	1-0	.313	.348	.489	.837	0	1.000
2006— Rochester (Int'l)		13	51	8	12	0	0	1	5	1	6	0	0	0-0	.235	.245	.294	.539	1	1.000
— Minnesota (N.L.)	DH-OF	99	337	32	83	17	1	7	38	11	54	4	11	1-1	.246	.276	.365	.641	0	1.000
American League totals (5 years)		465	1689	229	456	89	7	56	241	98	273	27	45	4-5	.270	.317	.430	.748	4	.993
National League totals (10 years)		971	3559	519	1044	203	27	138	507	256	633	58	96	90-42	.293	.348	.482	.830	31	.985
Major League totals (14 years)		1436	5248	748	1500	292	34	194	748	354	906	85	141	94-47	.286	.339	.465	.804	35	.987

DIVISION SERIES RECORD

Year Team (League)	Pos.	G	AB	R	H	2B	3B	HR	RBI	BB	SO	HBP	GDP	SB-CS	Avg.	OBP	SLG	OPS	E	Avg.
2002— New York (A.L.)	DH	1	3	1	1	0	0	1	1	0	0	0	0	0-0	.333	.333	1.333	1.667	0	...
2006— Minnesota (A.L.)	OF	3	12	1	5	1	0	1	2	0	0	0	0	0-0	.417	.417	.750	1.167	0	1.000
Division series totals (2 years)		4	15	2	6	1	0	2	3	0	0	0	0	0-0	.400	.400	.867	1.267	0	1.000

ALL-STAR GAME RECORD

	G	AB	R	H	2B	3B	HR	RBI	BB	SO	HBP	GDP	SB-CS	Avg.	OBP	SLG	OPS	E	Avg.
All-Star Game totals (1 year)	1	1	0	0	0	0	0	0	0	0	0	0	0-0	.000	.000	.000	.000	0	...

2006 LEFTY-RIGHTY SPLITS

vs.	Avg.	AB	H	2B	3B	HR	RBI	BB	SO	OBP	Slg.	vs.	Avg.	AB	H	2B	3B	HR	RBI	BB	SO	OBP	Slg.
L	.271	107	29	6	0	2	12	4	12	.301	.383	R	.235	230	54	11	1	5	26	7	42	.264	.357

WICKMAN, BOB — P

PERSONAL: Born February 6, 1969, in Green Bay. ... 6-1/240. ... Throws right, bats right. ... Full name: Robert Joe Wickman. ... High school: Oconto Falls (Wis.). ... College: Wisconsin-Whitewater. **TRANSACTIONS/CAREER NOTES:** Selected by Chicago White Sox organization in second round of 1990 free-agent draft. ... Traded by White Sox with Ps Melido Perez and Domingo Jean to New York Yankees for 2B Steve Sax and cash (January 10, 1992). ... Traded by Yankees with OF Gerald Williams to Milwaukee Brewers for P Graeme Lloyd and OF Pat Listach (August 23, 1996). ... Traded by Brewers with Ps Steve Woodard and Jason Bere to Cleveland Indians for 1B/OF Richie Sexson, Ps Paul Rigdon and Kane Davis and a player to be named (July 28, 2000); Brewers acquired 2B Marco Scutaro to complete deal (August 30, 2000). ... On disabled list (July 22-August 10 and August 11, 2002-remainder of season). ... On disabled list (March 29, 2003-entire season); included rehabilitation assignments to Akron and Lake County. ... On disabled list (April 2-July 6, 2004); included rehabilitation assignments to Akron and Buffalo. ... Traded by Indians to Atlanta Braves for C Max Ramirez (July 20, 2006).

CAREER HITTING: 0-for-2 (.000), 0 R, 0 2B, 0 3B, 0 HR, 0 RBI.

Year	Team (League)	W	L	Pct.	ERA	WHIP	G	GS	CG	ShO	Hld.	Sv.-Opp.	IP	H	R	ER	HR	BB-IBB	SO	Avg.
1990—	GC Whi. Sox (GCL)	2	0	1.000	2.45	0.73	2	2	0	0	...	0-...	11.0	7	4	3	0	1-0	15	.175
	— Sarasota (Fla. St.)	0	1	.000	1.98	1.54	2	2	0	0	...	0-...	13.2	17	7	3	0	4-0	8	.304
	— South Bend (Mid.)	7	2	.778	1.38	1.01	9	9	3	0	...	0-...	65.1	50	16	10	1	16-0	50	.212
1991—	Sarasota (Fla. St.)	5	1	.833	2.05	1.23	7	7	1	1	...	0-...	44.0	43	16	10	2	11-0	32	.247
	— Birmingham (Sou.)	6	10	.375	3.56	1.35	20	20	4	1	...	0-...	131.1	127	68	52	5	50-0	81	.250
1992—	Columbus (Int'l)	12	5	.706	2.92	1.18	23	23	2	1	...	0-...	157.0	131	61	51	12	55-0	108	.225
	— New York (A.L.)	6	1	.857	4.11	1.41	8	8	0	0	0	0-0	50.1	51	25	23	2	20-0	21	.273
1993—	New York (A.L.)	14	4	.778	4.63	1.61	41	19	1	1	2	4-8	140.0	156	82	72	13	69-7	70	.283
1994—	New York (A.L.)	5	4	.556	3.09	1.16	53	0	0	0	11	6-10	70.0	54	26	24	3	27-3	56	.213
1995—	New York (A.L.)	2	4	.333	4.05	1.38	63	1	0	0	21	1-10	80.0	77	38	36	6	33-3	51	.253
1996—	New York (A.L.)	4	1	.800	4.67	1.62	58	0	0	0	6	0-3	79.0	94	41	41	7	34-1	61	.299
	— Milwaukee (A.L.)	3	0	1.000	3.24	1.32	12	0	0	0	4	0-1	16.2	12	9	6	3	10-2	14	.200
1997—	Milwaukee (A.L.)	7	6	.538	2.73	1.36	74	0	0	0	* 28	1-5	95.2	89	32	29	8	41-7	78	.251
1998—	Milwaukee (N.L.)	6	9	.400	3.72	1.43	72	0	0	0	9	25-32	82.1	79	38	34	4	39-2	71	.262
1999—	Milwaukee (N.L.)	3	8	.273	3.39	1.52	71	0	0	0	4	37-45	74.1	75	31	28	6	38-6	60	.262
2000—	Milwaukee (N.L.)	2	2	.500	2.93	1.24	43	0	0	0	9	16-20	46.0	37	18	15	1	20-2	44	.215
	— Cleveland (A.L.)	1	3	.250	3.38	1.46	26	0	0	0	4	14-17	26.2	27	12	10	0	12-3	11	.270
2001—	Cleveland (A.L.)	5	0	1.000	2.39	1.11	70	0	0	0	4	32-35	67.2	61	18	18	4	14-2	66	.240
2002—	Cleveland (A.L.)	1	3	.250	4.46	1.51	36	0	0	0	0	20-22	34.1	42	22	17	3	10-0	36	.284
2003—	Lake County (S.Atl.)	0	0	...	0.00	0.50	2	2	0	0	...	0-...	2.0	1	0	0	0	0-0	4	.143
	— Akron (East.)	0	0	...	16.20	2.40	2	2	0	0	...	0-...	1.2	3	3	3	0	1-0	2	.429
2004—	Akron (East.)	0	0	...	0.00	2.00	1	0	0	0	...	0-...	1.0	1	0	0	0	2-0	1	.000
	— Buffalo (Int'l)	1	0	1.000	10.13	1.50	6	1	0	0	...	0-...	5.1	4	6	6	0	4-0	4	.211
	— Cleveland (A.L.)	0	2	.000	4.25	1.45	30	0	0	0	4	13-14	29.2	33	14	14	4	10-0	26	.282
2005—	Cleveland (A.L.)	0	4	.000	2.47	1.26	64	0	0	0	0	• 45-50	62.0	57	17	17	9	21-3	41	.247
2006—	Cleveland (A.L.)	1	4	.200	4.18	1.43	29	0	0	0	0	15-18	28.0	29	15	13	1	11-0	17	.271
	— Atlanta (N.L.)	0	2	.000	1.04	1.00	28	0	0	0	0	18-19	26.0	24	7	3	1	2-0	25	.231
	American League totals (12 years)	49	36	.576	3.69	1.40	564	28	1	1	80	151-193	780.0	782	351	320	63	312-31	548	.263
	National League totals (4 years)	11	21	.344	3.15	1.37	214	0	0	0	9	96-116	228.2	215	94	80	13	99-10	200	.249
	Major League totals (14 years)	60	57	.513	3.57	1.40	778	28	1	1	89	247-309	1008.2	997	445	400	76	411-41	748	.260

Year	Team (League)	W	L	Pct.	ERA	WHIP	G	GS	CG	ShO	Hld.	Sv.-Opp.	IP	H	R	ER	HR	BB-IBB	SO	Avg.
	DIVISION SERIES RECORD																			
1995—	New York (A.L.)	0	0	...	0.00	1.67	3	0	0	0	0	0-0	3.0	5	0	0	0	0-0	3	.417
2001—	Cleveland (A.L.)	0	0	...	0.00	0.00	1	0	0	0	0	0-0	1.0	0	0	0	0	0-0	2	.000
	Division series totals (2 years)	0	0	...	0.00	1.25	4	0	0	0	0	0-0	4.0	5	0	0	0	0-0	5	.333

Year	Team (League)	W	L	Pct.	ERA	WHIP	G	GS	CG	ShO	Hld.	Sv.-Opp.	IP	H	R	ER	HR	BB-IBB	SO	Avg.
	ALL-STAR GAME RECORD																			
	All-Star Game totals (2 years)	0	0	...	9.00	1.00	2	0	0	0	0	0-0	1.0	0	1	1	0	1-0	1	.000

2006 LEFTY-RIGHTY SPLITS

vs.	Avg.	AB	H	2B	3B	HR	RBI	BB	SO	OBP	Slg.	vs.	Avg.	AB	H	2B	3B	HR	RBI	BB	SO	OBP	Slg.
L	.267	101	27	6	0	1	17	9	23	.324	.356	R	.236	110	26	5	0	1	5	4	19	.265	.309

WIDGER, CHRIS — C

PERSONAL: Born May 21, 1971, in Wilmington, Del. ... 6-2/210. ... Bats right, throws right. ... Full name: Christopher Jon Widger. ... High school: Pennsville (N.J.). ... College: George Mason. **TRANSACTIONS/CAREER NOTES:** Selected by Seattle Mariners organization in third round of 1992 free-agent draft. ... Traded by Mariners with Ps Trey Moore and Matt Wagner to Montreal Expos for Ps Jeff Fassero and Alex Pacheco (October 29, 1996). ... On disabled list (May 25-June 9, 2000). ... Traded by Expos to Mariners for two players to be named (August 8, 2000); Expos acquired OF Terrmel Sledge (September 28) and Sean Spencer (August 10) to complete deal. ... On disabled list (March 31, 2001-entire season); included rehabilitation assignment to Everett. ... Signed as a free agent by New York Yankees organization (February 1, 2002). ... Released by Yankees (April 7, 2003). ... Signed by St. Louis Cardinals organization (April 12, 2003). ... On disabled list (June 10-30, 2003); included rehabilitation assignment to Memphis. ... Traded by Cardinals with IF Wilson Delgado to New York Mets for OF Roger Cedeno (April 3, 2004). ... Released by Mets (April 5, 2004). ... Signed by Chicago White Sox organization (January 19, 2005). ... Released by White Sox (August 1, 2006). ... Signed by Baltimore Orioles (August 4, 2006). ... On disabled list (September 8, 2006-remainder of season). **STATISTICAL NOTES:** Career major league grand slams: 1.

2006 GAMES PLAYED BY POSITION (MLB): C—28, DH—5.

Year	Team (League)	Pos.	G	AB	R	H	2B	3B	HR	RBI	BB	SO	HBP	GDP	SB-CS	Avg.	OBP	SLG	OPS	E	Avg.
1992—	Bellingham (N'west)	C-C	51	166	28	43	7	2	5	30	22	36	1	4	8-1	.259	.340	.416	.756	4	.987
1993—	Riverside (Calif.)	C-OF-C																			
		OF	97	360	44	95	28	2	9	58	19	64	3	8	5-4	.264	.303	.428	.731	14	.974
1994—	Jacksonville (Sou.)	1B-C-OF	116	388	58	101	15	3	16	59	39	69	5	7	8-7	.260	.334	.438	.772	12	.979
1995—	Tacoma (PCL)	C-C-DH																			
		OF-OF	50	174	29	48	11	1	9	21	9	29	0	4	0-0	.276	.311	.506	.817	4	.980
	— Seattle (A.L.)	C-OF-OF	23	45	2	9	0	0	1	2	3	11	0	0	0-0	.200	.245	.267	.512	0	1.000
1996—	Tacoma (PCL)	C-C-DH	97	352	42	107	20	2	13	48	27	62	2	13	7-1	.304	.355	.483	.838	8	.988
	— Seattle (A.L.)	C	8	11	1	2	0	0	0	0	0	5	1	0	0-0	.182	.250	.182	.432	2	.905
1997—	Montreal (N.L.)	C	91	278	30	65	20	3	7	37	22	59	1	7	2-0	.234	.290	.403	.693	11	.981
1998—	Montreal (N.L.)	C	125	417	36	97	18	1	15	53	29	85	0	5	6-1	.233	.281	.388	.670	* 14	.983
1999—	Montreal (N.L.)	C	124	383	42	101	24	1	14	56	28	86	7	5	1-4	.264	.325	.441	.766	4	.992
2000—	Montreal (N.L.)	C	86	281	31	67	17	2	12	34	29	61	1	5	1-2	.238	.311	.441	.752	8	.985
	— Seattle (A.L.)	C-1B-DH																			
		OF	10	11	1	1	0	0	1	1	1	2	0	0	0-0	.091	.167	.364	.530	0	1.000
2001—	Everett (N'west)	1B-1B	5	13	2	1	0	0	0	0	1	6	0	0	0-0	.077	.368	.077	.445	0	1.000
2002—	Columbus (Int'l)	C-C-OF																			
		OF	61	217	26	53	14	1	10	39	17	31	1	3	0-3	.244	.300	.456	.756	4	.990
	— New York (A.L.)	C	21	64	4	19	5	0	0	5	2	9	2	0	0-0	.297	.338	.375	.713	2	.983
2003—	Memphis (PCL)	C-C-OF																			
		OF-1B-1B	23	71	8	17	7	0	2	10	7	12	0	0	1-0	.239	.304	.423	.727	4	.968
	— St. Louis (N.L.)	C-1B-OF	44	102	9	24	9	0	0	14	6	20	1	5	0-0	.235	.279	.324	.603	1	.995
2004—	Camden (Atl.)	C	55	202	37	54	12	1	16	43	20	27	2	10	5-0	.267	.336	.574	.910	3	.988
2005—	Chicago (A.L.)	C-1B-3B																			
		DH	45	141	18	34	8	0	4	11	10	22	1	5	0-2	.241	.296	.383	.679	5	.982

Year Team (League)	Pos.	G	AB	R	H	2B	3B	HR	RBI	BB	SO	HBP	GDP	SB-CS	Avg.	OBP	SLG	OPS	E	Avg.
2006—Chicago (A.L.)	C-DH	27	76	6	14	3	0	1	7	9	20	0	1	0-0	.184	.264	.263	.528	3	.973
—Baltimore (A.L.)	C-DH	9	17	0	2	0	0	0	2	2	4	0	1	0-0	.118	.211	.118	.328	1	1.000
American League totals (6 years)		143	365	32	81	16	0	7	28	27	73	4	7	0-2	.222	.281	.323	.604	12	.981
National League totals (5 years)		470	1461	148	354	88	7	48	194	114	311	10	27	10-7	.242	.300	.411	.711	40	.986
Major League totals (10 years)		613	1826	180	435	104	7	55	222	141	384	14	34	10-9	.238	.296	.393	.689	52	.985

DIVISION SERIES RECORD

Year Team (League)	Pos.	G	AB	R	H	2B	3B	HR	RBI	BB	SO	HBP	GDP	SB-CS	Avg.	OBP	SLG	OPS	E	Avg.
1995—Seattle (A.L.)	C	2	3	0	0	0	0	0	0	0	3	0	0	0-0	.000	.000	.000	.000	0	1.000
2000—Seattle (A.L.)		Did not play.																		

CHAMPIONSHIP SERIES RECORD

Year Team (League)	Pos.	G	AB	R	H	2B	3B	HR	RBI	BB	SO	HBP	GDP	SB-CS	Avg.	OBP	SLG	OPS	E	Avg.
1995—Seattle (A.L.)	C	3	1	0	0	0	0	0	0	0	1	0	...	0-0	.000	.000	.000	.000	0	1.000
2000—Seattle (A.L.)		Did not play.																		

WORLD SERIES RECORD

Year Team (League)	Pos.	G	AB	R	H	2B	3B	HR	RBI	BB	SO	HBP	GDP	SB-CS	Avg.	OBP	SLG	OPS	E	Avg.
2005—Chicago (A.L.)	C	1	1	0	0	0	0	0	0	0	1	0	0	0-0	.000	.667	.000	.667	0	1.000

2006 LEFTY-RIGHTY SPLITS

vs.	Avg.	AB	H	2B	3B	HR	RBI	BB	SO	OBP	Slg.	vs.	Avg.	AB	H	2B	3B	HR	RBI	BB	SO	OBP	Slg.
L	.154	52	8	2	0	0	1	6	13	.237	.192	R	.195	41	8	1	0	1	8	5	11	.277	.293

WIGGINTON, TY   IF/OF

PERSONAL: Born October 11, 1977, in San Diego. ... 6-0/200. ... Bats right, throws right. ... Full name: Ty Allen Wigginton. ... High school: Chula Vista (Calif.). ... College: North Carolina-Asheville. **TRANSACTIONS/CAREER NOTES:** Selected by New York Mets organization in 17th round of 1998 free-agent draft. ... On disabled list (April 21-May 7, 2004); included rehabilitation assignment to St. Lucie. ... Traded by Mets with IF Jose Bautista and P Matt Peterson to Pittsburgh Pirates for P Kris Benson and IF Jeff Keppinger (July 30, 2004). ... Released by Pirates (December 8, 2005). ... Signed by Tampa Bay Devil Rays (January 10, 2006). ... On disabled list (July 30-September 1, 2006); included rehabilitation assignment to Durham.

2006 GAMES PLAYED BY POSITION (MLB): 1B—45, 2B—43, 3B—34, OF—12, DH—1.

Year Team (League)	Pos.	G	AB	R	H	2B	3B	HR	RBI	BB	SO	HBP	GDP	SB-CS	Avg.	OBP	SLG	OPS	E	Avg.
1998—Pittsfield (NYP)	2B-3B	70	272	39	65	14	4	8	29	16	72	1	4	11-2	.239	.284	.408	.692	14	.949
1999—St. Lucie (Fla. St.)	2B	123	456	69	133	23	5	21	73	56	82	4	5	9-12	.292	.373	.502	.875	16	.974
2000—Binghamton (East.)	2B-3B	122	453	64	129	27	3	20	77	24	107	2	4	5-5	.285	.319	.490	.809	23	.943
2001—St. Lucie (Fla. St.)	2B	3	9	1	3	1	0	0	1	4	2	1	0	0-0	.333	.571	.444	1.016	0	1.000
—Binghamton (East.)	2B-3B	8	28	5	8	3	0	0	5	5	5	0	0	1-0	.286	.394	.393	.787	3	.870
—Norfolk (Int'l)	3B-2B-1B-C-OF	78	260	29	65	12	0	7	24	27	66	2	4	3-3	.250	.323	.377	.700	17	.924
2002—Norfolk (Int'l)	3B-2B-OF-1B	104	383	49	115	26	3	6	48	43	50	1	7	5-3	.300	.366	.431	.796	11	.967
—New York (N.L.)	OF	46	116	18	35	8	0	6	18	8	19	2	4	2-1	.302	.354	.526	.880	5	.966
2003—New York (N.L.)	3B	156	573	73	146	36	6	11	71	46	124	9	15	12-2	.255	.318	.396	.714	16	.962
2004—St. Lucie (Fla. St.)	3B	2	8	1	3	0	0	0	0	0	1	0	0	0-0	.375	.375	.375	.750	0	1.000
—New York (N.L.)	3B-2B-1B	86	312	46	89	23	2	12	42	23	48	1	11	6-1	.285	.334	.487	.822	16	.949
—Pittsburgh (N.L.)	3B	58	182	17	40	7	0	5	24	22	34	1	4	1-0	.220	.306	.341	.646	6	.955
2005—Indianapolis (Int'l)	3B-1B-DH-2B	72	280	53	82	18	0	14	52	45	56	1	4	8-5	.293	.390	.507	.897	7	.975
—Pittsburgh (N.L.)	3B-1B-2B	57	155	20	40	9	1	7	25	14	30	1	3	0-1	.258	.324	.465	.788	9	.921
2006—Durham (Int'l)		2	8	2	3	2	0	1	0	2	0	0	0	0-0	.375	.375	1.000	1.375	0	1.000
—Tampa Bay (A.L.)	1B-2B-3B-OF-DH	122	444	55	122	25	1	24	79	32	97	6	11	4-3	.275	.330	.498	.828	8	.987
American League totals (1 year)		122	444	55	122	25	1	24	79	32	97	6	11	4-3	.275	.330	.498	.828	8	.987
National League totals (4 years)		403	1338	174	350	83	9	41	180	113	255	14	37	21-5	.262	.324	.429	.753	52	.954
Major League totals (5 years)		525	1782	229	472	108	10	65	259	145	352	20	48	25-8	.265	.325	.446	.771	60	.966

2006 LEFTY-RIGHTY SPLITS

vs.	Avg.	AB	H	2B	3B	HR	RBI	BB	SO	OBP	Slg.	vs.	Avg.	AB	H	2B	3B	HR	RBI	BB	SO	OBP	Slg.
L	.316	117	37	8	0	5	21	13	29	.385	.513	R	.260	327	85	17	1	19	58	19	68	.310	.492

WILKERSON, BRAD   OF

PERSONAL: Born June 1, 1977, in Daviess, Ky. ... 6-0/206. ... Bats left, throws left. ... Full name: Stephen Bradley Wilkerson. ... High school: Apollo (Owensboro, Ky.). ... College: Florida. **TRANSACTIONS/CAREER NOTES:** Selected by Los Angeles Dodgers organization in 13th round of 1995 free-agent draft; did not sign. ... Selected by Montreal Expos organization in supplemental round ("sandwich pick" between first and second rounds, 33rd pick overall) of 1998 free-agent draft; pick received as part of compensation for Toronto Blue Jays signing Type A free-agent C Darrin Fletcher. ... Expos franchise transferred to Washington, D.C., and renamed Washington Nationals for 2005 season (December 3, 2004). ... Traded by Nationals with OF Terrmel Sledge and P Armando Galarraga to Texas Rangers for 2B Alfonso Soriano (December 13, 2005). ... On disabled list (August 10, 2006-remainder of season). **HONORS:** Named N.L. Rookie Player of the Year by THE SPORTING NEWS (2002). **STATISTICAL NOTES:** Hit for the cycle (June 24, 2003; and April 6, 2005). ... Career major league grand slams: 4.

2006 GAMES PLAYED BY POSITION (MLB): OF—82, DH—12.

Year Team (League)	Pos.	G	AB	R	H	2B	3B	HR	RBI	BB	SO	HBP	GDP	SB-CS	Avg.	OBP	SLG	OPS	E	Avg.
1999—Harrisburg (East.)	1B-OF	138	422	66	99	21	3	8	49	88	100	7	3	3-5	.235	.372	.355	.727	7	.972
2000—Harrisburg (East.)	1B-OF	66	229	53	77	36	2	6	44	42	38	4	4	8-4	.336	.442	.590	1.032	3	.983
—Ottawa (Int'l)	OF	63	212	40	53	11	1	12	35	45	60	3	0	5-4	.250	.387	.481	.868	6	.956
2001—Jupiter (Fla. St.)	DH	6	26	3	6	3	0	0	1	3	10	0	0	0-0	.231	.310	.346	.656	...	...
—Ottawa (Int'l)	OF	69	233	43	63	10	0	12	48	60	68	3	2	12-5	.270	.423	.468	.891	3	.973
—Montreal (N.L.)	OF	47	117	11	24	7	2	1	5	17	41	0	2	2-1	.205	.304	.325	.628	2	.970
2002—Montreal (N.L.)	OF-1B	153	507	92	135	27	8	20	59	81	161	5	5	13-10	.266	.370	.469	.840	7	.984
2003—Montreal (N.L.)	OF-1B	146	504	78	135	34	4	19	77	89	155	4	4	13-10	.268	.380	.464	.844	5	.988
2004—Montreal (N.L.)	1B-OF	160	572	112	146	39	2	32	67	106	152	4	4	13-6	.255	.374	.498	.872	7	.993
2005—Wash. (N.L.)	OF-1B	148	565	76	140	42	7	11	57	84	147	7	6	8-10	.248	.351	.405	.756	6	.988
2006—Texas (A.L.)	OF-DH	95	320	56	71	15	2	15	44	37	116	3	0	3-2	.222	.306	.422	.728	1	.993
American League totals (1 year)		95	320	56	71	15	2	15	44	37	116	3	0	3-2	.222	.306	.422	.728	1	.993
National League totals (5 years)		654	2265	369	580	149	23	83	265	377	656	20	30	43-35	.256	.365	.452	.817	27	.989
Major League totals (6 years)		749	2585	425	651	164	25	98	309	414	772	23	30	46-37	.252	.358	.448	.806	28	.989

W

vs.	Avg.	AB	H	2B	3B	HR	RBI	BB	SO	OBP	Slg.	vs.	Avg.	AB	H	2B	3B	HR	RBI	BB	SO	OBP	Slg.
L	.190	63	12	2	0	2	8	7	25	.278	.317	R	.230	257	59	13	2	13	36	30	91	.313	.447

WILLIAMS, BERNIE — OF

PERSONAL: Born September 13, 1968, in San Juan, Puerto Rico. ... 6-2/205. ... Bats both, throws right. ... Full name: Bernabe Figueroa Williams. ... High school: Escuela Libre de Musica (San Juan, Puerto Rico). ... College: University of Puerto Rico. **TRANSACTIONS/CAREER NOTES:** Signed as a non-drafted free agent by New York Yankees organization (September 13, 1985). ... On disabled list (May 13-June 7, 1993; May 11-May 26, 1996; June 16-July 2 and July 15-August 1, 1997). ... On disabled list (June 11-July 18, 1998); included rehabilitation assignments to Tampa and Norwich. ... On disabled list (May 23-July 9, 2003); included rehabilitation assignment to Trenton. **RECORDS:** Shares major league record for most strikeouts, 9-inning game (5, August 21, 1991). **HONORS:** Named outfielder on THE SPORTING NEWS A.L. All-Star team (2000 and 2002). ... Won A.L. Gold Glove as outfielder (1997-2000). **STATISTICAL NOTES:** Career major league grand slams: 11. **MISCELLANEOUS NOTES:** Batted righthanded only (1986-88).

2006 GAMES PLAYED BY POSITION (MLB): OF—89, DH—31.

Year Team (League)	Pos.	G	AB	R	H	2B	3B	HR	RBI	BB	SO	HBP	GDP	SB-CS	Avg.	OBP	SLG	OPS	E	Avg.
1986— GC Yankees (GCL)	OF	61	230	45	62	5	3	2	25	39	40	1	3	33-12	.270	.374	.343	.717	3	.976
1987— Fort Laud. (FSL)	OF	25	71	11	11	3	0	0	4	18	22	3	1	9-1	.155	.348	.197	.545	0	1.000
— Oneonta (NYP)	OF	25	93	13	32	4	0	0	15	10	14	1	0	9-3	.344	.410	.387	.797	2	.952
1988— Prince Will. (Car.)	OF	92	337	72	113	16	7	7	45	65	65	4	5	29-11	.335	.447	.487	.934	5	.975
1989— Columbus (Int'l)	OF	50	162	21	35	8	1	2	16	25	38	2	3	11-5	.216	.325	.315	.639	1	.991
— Alb./Colon. (East.)	OF	91	314	63	79	11	8	11	42	60	72	6	9	26-13	.252	.381	.443	.823	5	.987
1990— Alb./Colon. (East.)	OF	134	466	91	131	28	5	8	54	98	97	4	12	39-18	.281	.409	.414	.823	4	.987
1991— Columbus (Int'l)	OF	78	306	52	90	14	6	8	37	38	43	2	5	9-8	.294	.372	.458	.830	1	.994
— New York (A.L.)	OF	85	320	43	76	19	4	3	34	48	57	1	4	10-5	.238	.336	.350	.686	5	.979
1992— New York (A.L.)	OF	62	261	39	73	14	2	5	26	29	36	1	5	7-6	.280	.354	.406	.760	1	.995
— Columbus (Int'l)	OF	95	363	68	111	23	9	8	50	52	61	1	8	20-8	.306	.389	.485	.873	2	.990
1993— New York (A.L.)	OF	139	567	67	152	31	4	12	68	53	106	4	17	9-9	.268	.333	.400	.734	4	.989
1994— New York (A.L.)	OF	108	408	80	118	29	1	12	57	61	54	3	11	16-9	.289	.384	.453	.837	3	.990
1995— New York (A.L.)	OF	144	563	93	173	29	9	18	82	75	98	5	12	8-6	.307	.392	.487	.878	•8	.982
1996— New York (A.L.)	OF-DH	143	551	108	168	26	7	29	102	82	72	0	15	17-4	.305	.391	.535	.926	5	.986
1997— New York (A.L.)	OF	129	509	107	167	35	6	21	100	73	80	1	10	15-8	.328	.408	.544	.952	2	.993
1998— New York (A.L.)	OF-DH	128	499	101	169	30	5	26	97	74	81	1	19	15-9	.339	.422	.575	.997	3	.990
— Tampa (Fla. St.)	OF	1	2	0	1	0	0	0	0	1	0	0	0	0-0	.500	.667	1.000	1.667	0	1.000
— Norwich (East.)	OF	3	11	6	6	2	0	2	5	2	1	0	1	0-0	.545	.571	1.273	1.844	0	1.000
1999— New York (A.L.)	OF-DH	158	591	116	202	28	6	25	115	100	95	1	11	9-10	.342	.435	.536	.971	5	.987
2000— New York (A.L.)	OF-DH	141	537	108	165	37	6	30	121	71	84	5	15	13-5	.307	.391	.566	.957	0	1.000
2001— New York (A.L.)	OF-DH	146	540	102	166	38	0	26	94	78	67	6	15	11-5	.307	.395	.522	.917	2	.994
2002— New York (A.L.)	OF-DH	154	612	102	204	37	2	19	102	83	97	3	19	8-4	.333	.415	.493	.908	5	.986
2003— Trenton (East.)	OF-DH	5	15	4	5	2	0	0	4	4	1	1	1	0-1	.333	.476	.467	.943	0	1.000
— New York (A.L.)	OF-DH	119	445	77	117	19	1	15	64	71	61	3	21	5-0	.263	.367	.411	.778	1	.997
2004— New York (A.L.)	OF-DH	148	561	105	147	29	1	22	70	85	96	2	11	1-5	.262	.360	.435	.795	1	.995
2005— New York (A.L.)	OF-DH	141	485	53	121	19	1	12	64	53	75	1	16	1-2	.249	.321	.367	.688	2	.991
2006— New York (A.L.)	OF-DH	131	420	65	118	29	0	12	61	33	53	2	14	2-0	.281	.332	.436	.768	1	.994
Major League totals (16 years)		2076	7869	1366	2336	449	55	287	1257	1069	1212	39	223	147-87	.297	.381	.477	.858	48	.990

DIVISION SERIES RECORD

Year Team (League)	Pos.	G	AB	R	H	2B	3B	HR	RBI	BB	SO	HBP	GDP	SB-CS	Avg.	OBP	SLG	OPS	E	Avg.
1995— New York (A.L.)	OF	5	21	8	9	2	0	2	5	7	3	0	0	1-0	.429	.571	.810	1.381	0	1.000
1996— New York (A.L.)	OF	4	15	5	7	0	0	3	5	2	1	0	0	1-1	.467	.500	1.067	1.567	0	1.000
1997— New York (A.L.)	OF	5	17	3	2	1	0	0	1	4	3	1	1	0-0	.118	.318	.176	.495	0	1.000
1998— New York (A.L.)	OF	3	11	0	0	0	0	0	0	1	4	0	2	0-0	.000	.083	.000	.083	0	1.000
1999— New York (A.L.)	OF	3	11	2	4	1	0	1	6	1	2	1	0	0-0	.364	.462	.727	1.189	0	1.000
2000— New York (A.L.)	OF	5	20	3	5	0	0	1	1	1	4	0	0	0-1	.250	.273	.400	.673	0	1.000
2001— New York (A.L.)	OF	5	18	4	4	3	0	0	5	3	3	0	0	0-1	.222	.333	.389	.722	0	1.000
2002— New York (A.L.)	OF	4	15	4	5	1	0	1	3	3	2	0	2	0-0	.333	.444	.600	1.044	1	.900
2003— New York (A.L.)	OF	4	15	3	6	2	0	2	2	2	0	0	0	0-0	.400	.444	.533	.978	1	.900
2004— New York (A.L.)	OF	4	18	2	5	1	0	1	3	1	2	0	0	0-0	.278	.316	.500	.816	0	1.000
2005— New York (A.L.)	OF-DH	5	19	2	4	2	0	0	1	1	3	0	0	0-0	.211	.238	.316	.554	0	1.000
2006— New York (A.L.)	DH	1	3	0	0	0	0	0	0	0	2	0	0	0-0	.000	.000	.000	.000	0	...
Division series totals (12 years)		48	183	36	51	16	0	8	33	26	31	2	11	2-3	.279	.367	.497	.865	1	.991

CHAMPIONSHIP SERIES RECORD

Year Team (League)	Pos.	G	AB	R	H	2B	3B	HR	RBI	BB	SO	HBP	GDP	SB-CS	Avg.	OBP	SLG	OPS	E	Avg.
1996— New York (A.L.)	OF	5	19	6	9	3	0	2	6	5	4	0	0	1-0	.474	.583	.947	1.531	0	1.000
1998— New York (A.L.)	OF	6	21	4	8	1	0	0	5	7	4	0	1	1-1	.381	.536	.429	.964	0	1.000
1999— New York (A.L.)	OF	5	20	3	5	1	0	1	2	5	5	0	0	1-0	.250	.318	.450	.768	0	1.000
2000— New York (A.L.)		6	23	5	10	1	0	1	3	2	3	1	1	1-0	.435	.481	.609	1.090	0	1.000
2001— New York (A.L.)	OF	5	17	4	4	0	0	3	5	4	4	0	0	0-1	.235	.409	.765	1.174	1	.900
2003— New York (A.L.)	OF	7	26	5	5	1	0	0	2	4	3	0	0	0-0	.192	.300	.231	.531	0	1.000
2004— New York (A.L.)	OF	7	36	4	11	3	0	2	10	0	5	0	1	0-0	.306	.306	.556	.861	0	1.000
Champ. series totals (7 years)		41	162	31	52	10	0	9	33	25	28	1	3	4-2	.321	.413	.549	.962	1	.991

WORLD SERIES RECORD

Year Team (League)	Pos.	G	AB	R	H	2B	3B	HR	RBI	BB	SO	HBP	GDP	SB-CS	Avg.	OBP	SLG	OPS	E	Avg.
1996— New York (A.L.)	OF	6	24	3	4	0	0	1	4	3	6	0	1	1-0	.167	.259	.292	.551	0	1.000
1998— New York (A.L.)	OF	4	16	2	1	0	0	1	3	2	5	0	0	0-0	.063	.167	.250	.417	0	1.000
1999— New York (A.L.)	OF	4	13	2	3	0	0	0	0	5	2	0	0	0-0	.231	.412	.231	.643	0	1.000
2000— New York (A.L.)	OF	5	18	2	2	0	0	0	1	5	5	0	0	0-0	.111	.304	.278	.582	0	1.000
2001— New York (A.L.)	OF	7	24	2	5	1	0	0	1	4	6	0	0	0-0	.208	.321	.250	.571	0	1.000
2003— New York (A.L.)	OF	6	25	5	10	2	0	2	5	2	2	0	1	1-0	.400	.429	.720	1.149	0	1.000
World series totals (6 years)		32	120	16	25	3	0	5	14	20	26	0	2	2-0	.208	.319	.358	.677	0	1.000

ALL-STAR GAME RECORD

		G	AB	R	H	2B	3B	HR	RBI	BB	SO	HBP	GDP	SB-CS	Avg.	OBP	SLG	OPS	E	Avg.
All-Star Game totals (4 years)		4	5	1	0	0	0	0	0	1	1	0	0	.1-0	.000	.167	.000	.167	0	1.000

vs.	Avg.	AB	H	2B	3B	HR	RBI	BB	SO	OBP	Slg.	vs.	Avg.	AB	H	2B	3B	HR	RBI	BB	SO	OBP	Slg.
L	.323	133	43	9	0	7	26	14	11	.387	.549	R	.261	287	75	20	0	5	35	19	42	.305	.383

W

WILLIAMS, DAVE — P

PERSONAL: Born March 12, 1979, in Anchorage, Alaska. ... 6-2/219. ... Throws left, bats left. ... Full name: David Aaron Williams. ... High school: Caesar Rodney (Camden, Del.). ... Junior college: Delaware Tech & Community College. **TRANSACTIONS/CAREER NOTES:** Selected by Pittsburgh Pirates organization in 17th round of 1998 free-agent draft. ... On disabled list (May 28, 2002-remainder of season; March 24-June 3, 2003; and August 13-31, 2004). ... Traded by Pirates to Cincinnati Reds for 1B Sean Casey and cash (December 8, 2005). ... Traded by Reds with cash to New York Mets for P Robert Manuel (May 25, 2006). **MISCELLANEOUS NOTES:** Struck out in only appearance as pinch hitter (2002).

CAREER HITTING: 15-for-122 (.123), 5 R, 3 2B, 0 3B, 1 HR, 9 RBI.

Year—Team (League)	W	L	Pct.	ERA	WHIP	G	GS	CG	ShO	Hld.	Sv.-Opp.	IP	H	R	ER	HR	BB-IBB	SO	Avg.
1998—Erie (N.Y.-Penn)	2	2	.500	3.23	1.25	22	2	0	0	...	0-...	47.1	45	21	17	6	14-0	38	.245
1999—Will.'(NYP)	4	2	.667	2.56	0.96	7	7	1	1	...	0-...	45.2	33	17	13	2	11-0	47	.198
—Hickory (S. Atl.)	3	1	.750	3.20	0.90	9	9	1	1	...	0-...	59.0	42	22	21	5	11-0	46	.201
2000—Hickory (S. Atl.)	11	9	.550	2.96	1.08	24	24	1	1	...	0-...	170.0	145	66	56	14	39-2	193	.232
—Lynchburg (Caro.)	1	0	1.000	6.55	1.91	2	2	0	0	...	0-...	11.0	18	8	8	2	3-0	8	.383
2001—Altoona (East.)	5	2	.714	2.61	0.97	9	8	1	0	...	0-...	58.2	45	17	17	8	12-0	39	.211
—Nashville (PCL)	1	1	.500	3.38	1.31	2	2	0	0	...	0-...	10.2	9	5	4	3	5-0	6	.231
—Pittsburgh (N.L.)	3	7	.300	3.71	1.27	22	18	0	0	1	0-0	114.0	100	53	47	15	45-4	57	.244
2002—Pittsburgh (N.L.)	2	5	.286	4.98	1.43	9	9	0	0	0	0-0	43.1	38	26	24	9	24-2	33	.232
2003—Nashville (PCL)	7	4	.636	4.19	1.40	16	16	0	0	0	0-0	77.1	78	44	36	7	30-2	56	.260
—Pittsburgh (N.L.)	5	5	.500	4.42	1.14	10	6	0	0	0	0-0	38.2	31	21	19	4	13-2	33	.217
2004—Nashville (PCL)	6	2	.750	3.47	1.25	21	21	0	0	0	0-0	116.2	113	52	45	10	33-2	103	.252
—Pittsburgh (N.L.)	2	3	.400	7.20	1.75	8	8	0	0	0	0-0	40.0	54	34	32	9	16-0	16	.321
2005—Pittsburgh (N.L.)	10	11	.476	4.41	1.41	25	25	1	1	0	0-0	138.2	137	74	68	20	58-5	88	.261
2006—Cincinnati (N.L.)	2	3	.400	7.20	1.75	8	8	0	0	0	0-0	8.0	8	7	6	0	0-0	10	.080
—GC Mets (GCL)	1	0	1.000	0.00	0.25	2	2	0	0	0	0-0	8.0	5	0	0	0	0-0	10	.080
—Norfolk (Int'l)	2	2	.500	3.68	1.17	7	6	0	0	0	0-0	36.2	33	20	15	3	10-0	17	.236
—New York (N.L.)	3	1	.750	5.59	1.48	6	5	0	0	0	0-0	29.0	39	18	18	5	4-1	16	.333
Major League totals (5 years)	**22**	**30**	**.423**	**4.64**	**1.38**	**80**	**71**	**1**	**1**	**1**	**0-0**	**403.2**	**399**	**226**	**208**	**62**	**160-14**	**243**	**.261**

2006 LEFTY-RIGHTY SPLITS

vs.	Avg.	AB	H	2B	3B	HR	RBI	BB	SO	OBP	Slg.	vs.	Avg.	AB	H	2B	3B	HR	RBI	BB	SO	OBP	Slg.
L	.283	46	13	2	0	2	5	4	11	.353	.457	R	.335	239	80	14	1	12	41	16	21	.384	.552

WILLIAMS, JEROME — P

PERSONAL: Born December 4, 1981, in Honolulu. ... 6-3/246. ... Throws right, bats right. ... Full name: Jerome Lee Williams. ... High school: Waipahu (Hawaii). **TRANSACTIONS/CAREER NOTES:** Selected by San Francisco Giants organization in supplemental round ("sandwich") pick between first and second rounds, 39th pick overall) of 1999 free-agent draft; pick received as compensation for Seattle Mariners signing Type-A free-agent P Jose Mesa. ... On disabled list (July 31-September 16, 2004). ... Traded by Giants with P David Aardsma to Chicago Cubs for P LaTroy Hawkins (May 28, 2005). ... Claimed on waivers by Oakland Athletics (September 5, 2006).

CAREER HITTING: 12-for-109 (.110), 3 R, 2 2B, 0 3B, 0 HR, 1 RBI.

Year—Team (League)	W	L	Pct.	ERA	WHIP	G	GS	CG	ShO	Hld.	Sv.-Opp.	IP	H	R	ER	HR	BB-IBB	SO	Avg.
1999—Salem-Keizer (N'west)	1	1	.500	2.19	1.08	7	7	1	1	...	0-...	37.0	29	13	9	1	11-0	34	.213
2000—San Jose (Calif.)	7	6	.538	2.94	1.09	23	19	0	0	...	0-...	125.2	89	53	41	6	48-3	115	.201
2001—Shreveport (Texas)	9	7	.563	3.95	1.15	23	23	2	1	...	0-...	130.0	116	69	57	14	34-0	84	.235
2002—Fresno (PCL)	6	11	.353	3.59	1.18	28	28	0	0	...	0-...	160.2	140	76	64	16	50-1	130	.234
2003—Fresno (PCL)	4	2	.667	2.68	1.19	10	10	1	0	...	0-...	57.0	52	19	17	3	16-0	40	.237
—San Francisco (N.L.)	7	5	.583	3.30	1.26	21	21	2	1	0	0-0	131.0	116	54	48	10	49-3	88	.242
2004—San Francisco (N.L.)	10	7	.588	4.24	1.29	22	22	0	0	0	0-0	129.1	123	69	61	14	44-1	80	.254
2005—San Francisco (N.L.)	0	2	.000	6.48	1.50	4	3	0	0	0	0-0	16.2	21	12	12	2	4-1	11	.313
—Fresno (PCL)	1	4	.200	9.39	2.09	6	6	0	0	0	0-0	30.2	47	34	32	3	17-0	15	.364
—Iowa (PCL)	1	1	.500	2.22	1.36	4	4	0	0	0	0-0	24.1	27	10	6	1	7-0	21	.265
—Chicago (N.L.)	6	8	.429	3.91	1.35	18	17	0	0	0	0-0	106.0	98	50	46	12	45-0	59	.253
2006—Chicago (N.L.)	0	2	.000	7.30	2.11	6	6	0	0	0	0-0	12.1	15	12	10	2	11-1	5	.326
—Iowa (PCL)	5	7	.417	4.76	1.61	29	16	1	1	2	0-0	111.2	145	66	59	17	35-1	52	.324
Major League totals (4 years)	**23**	**24**	**.489**	**4.03**	**1.33**	**70**	**65**	**2**	**1**	**1**	**0-0**	**395.1**	**373**	**197**	**177**	**40**	**153-6**	**243**	**.255**

DIVISION SERIES RECORD

Year—Team (League)	W	L	Pct.	ERA	WHIP	G	GS	CG	ShO	Hld.	Sv.-Opp.	IP	H	R	ER	HR	BB-IBB	SO	Avg.
2003—San Francisco (N.L.)	0	0	...	13.50	3.00	1	1	0	0	0	0-0	2.0	5	3	3	0	1-0	1	.455

2006 LEFTY-RIGHTY SPLITS

vs.	Avg.	AB	H	2B	3B	HR	RBI	BB	SO	OBP	Slg.	vs.	Avg.	AB	H	2B	3B	HR	RBI	BB	SO	OBP	Slg.
L	.214	14	3	0	0	1	3	4	2	.368	.429	R	.375	32	12	3	1	1	7	7	3	.476	.625

WILLIAMS, TODD — P

PERSONAL: Born February 13, 1971, in Syracuse, N.Y. ... 6-3/210. ... Throws right, bats right. ... Full name: Todd Michael Williams. ... High school: Minoa (East Syracuse, N.Y.). ... Junior college: Onondaga (N.Y.) Community College. **TRANSACTIONS/CAREER NOTES:** Selected by Los Angeles Dodgers organization in 54th round of 1990 free-agent draft. ... Traded by Dodgers to Oakland Athletics for P Matt McDonald (September 8, 1995). ... Released by A's (January 16, 1997). ... Signed by Cincinnati Reds organization (February 3, 1997). ... Traded by Reds to Seattle Mariners for OF Kerry Robinson (July 22, 1999). ... Released by Mariners (November 16, 2000). ... Signed by New York Yankees organization (January 3, 2001). ... On disabled list (May 27-July 18, 2001); included rehabilitation assignment to GCL Yankees. ... Signed as a free agent by Dodgers organization (December 27, 2001). ... Released by Dodgers (March 26, 2002). ... Signed by Montreal Expos organization (May 3, 2002). ... Signed as a free agent by Tampa Bay Devil Rays (December 23, 2002). ... Signed as a free agent by Texas Rangers organization (December 4, 2003). ... Released by Rangers (June 14, 2004). ... Signed by Baltimore Orioles organization (June 15, 2004). ... On disabled list (April 1-29, 2006); included rehabilitation assignment to Bowie. **MISCELLANEOUS NOTES:** Member of 2000 U.S. Olympic baseball team.

CAREER HITTING: 1-for-4 (.250), 0 R, 0 2B, 0 3B, 0 HR, 0 RBI.

Year—Team (League)	W	L	Pct.	ERA	WHIP	G	GS	CG	ShO	Hld.	Sv.-Opp.	IP	H	R	ER	HR	BB-IBB	SO	Avg.
1991—Great Falls (Pio.)	5	2	.714	2.72	1.40	28	0	0	0	...	8-...	53.0	50	26	16	1	24-1	51	.242
1992—Bakersfield (Calif.)	0	0	...	2.30	1.15	13	0	0	0	...	9-...	15.2	11	4	4	1	7-1	11	.196
—San Antonio (Texas)	7	4	.636	3.27	1.59	39	0	0	0	...	13-...	44.0	47	17	16	0	23-6	35	.281
1993—Albuquerque (PCL)	5	5	.500	4.99	1.68	65	0	0	0	...	21-...	70.1	87	44	39	3	17-3	30	.302
1994—Albuquerque (PCL)	4	2	.667	3.11	1.31	59	0	0	0	...	13-...	72.1	78	29	25	0	17-3	30	.287
1995—Los Angeles (N.L.)	3	3	.500	5.12	1.34	16	0	0	0	0	0-1	19.1	19	11	11	3	7-2	8	.264
—Albuquerque (PCL)	4	1	.800	3.38	1.63	25	0	0	0	...	5-...	91.2	125	71	56	4	37-3	33	.329
1996—Edmonton (PCL)	5	3	.625	5.50	1.77	35	10	0	0	...	1-...	55.2	38	16	13	1	25-2	45	.186
1997—Chattanooga (Sou.)	3	3	.500	2.10	1.13	48	0	0	0	...	31-...	55.2	38	16	13	1	25-2	45	.186
—Indianapolis (A.A.)	1	0	1.000	2.13	1.34	12	0	0	0	...	2-...	12.2	11	4	3	0	6-1	11	.239
1998—Indianapolis (Int'l)	0	3	.000	2.31	1.34	53	0	0	0	...	26-...	58.1	54	19	15	0	24-2	35	.255
—Cincinnati (N.L.)	0	1	.000	7.71	2.25	6	0	0	0	0	0-0	9.1	15	8	8	1	6-0	4	.341

W

Year	Team (League)	W	L	Pct.	ERA	WHIP	G	GS	CG	ShO	Hld.	Sv.-Opp.	IP	H	R	ER	HR	BB-IBB	SO	Avg.
1999—	Indianapolis (Int'l)	1	3	.250	5.10	1.20	38	0	0	0	...	24-...	42.1	38	24	24	3	13-0	35	.250
	— Tacoma (PCL)	0	0	...	0.00	0.60	1	0	0	0	...	1-...	1.2	1	0	0	0	0-0	0	.200
	— Seattle (A.L.)	0	0	...	4.66	1.86	13	0	0	0	0	0-0	9.2	11	5	5	1	7-0	7	.289
2000—	Tacoma (PCL)	2	3	.400	2.98	1.34	50	0	0	0	...	32-...	51.1	51	20	17	2	18-1	26	.268
2001—	New York (A.L.)	1	0	1.000	4.70	2.02	15	0	0	0	1	0-0	15.1	22	9	8	1	9-2	13	.324
	— GC Yankees (GCL)	0	0	...	0.00	0.50	1	1	0	0	...	0-...	2.0	1	0	0	0	0-0	5	.143
	— Columbus (Int'l)	0	1	.000	7.11	2.11	17	0	0	0	...	2-...	19.0	31	19	15	5	9-3	14	.352
	— Norwich (East.)	1	0	1.000	0.00	0.50	6	0	0	0	...	1-...	8.0	4	0	0	0	0-0	5	.148
2002—	Ottawa (Int'l)	3	5	.375	3.75	1.42	46	0	0	0	...	24-...	48.0	56	26	20	4	12-3	21	.298
2003—	Durham (Int'l)	3	2	.600	1.55	1.00	56	0	0	0	...	4-...	69.2	55	12	12	2	14-2	36	.215
2004—	Oklahoma (PCL)	2	2	.500	3.03	1.48	27	0	0	0	...	9-...	29.2	37	15	10	2	7-2	11	.308
	— Ottawa (Int'l)	1	1	.500	3.05	1.06	14	0	0	0	...	2-...	20.2	19	7	7	0	3-1	11	.250
	— Baltimore (A.L.)	2	0	1.000	2.87	1.12	29	0	0	0	3	0-0	31.1	26	10	10	2	9-0	13	.232
2005—	Baltimore (A.L.)	5	5	.500	3.30	1.28	72	0	0	0	18	1-3	76.1	72	34	28	5	26-4	38	.252
2006—	Bowie (East.)	0	0	...	4.50	1.25	4	1	0	0	1	0-1	4.0	4	2	2	0	1-0	5	.252
	— Baltimore (A.L.)	2	4	.333	4.74	1.67	62	0	0	0	13	1-5	57.0	76	36	30	8	19-3	24	.323
American League totals (5 years)		10	9	.526	3.84	1.46	191	0	0	0	35	2-8	189.2	207	94	81	17	70-9	95	.280
National League totals (2 years)		2	3	.400	5.97	1.64	22	0	0	0	0	0-1	28.2	34	19	19	4	13-2	12	.293
Major League totals (7 years)		12	12	.500	4.12	1.48	213	0	0	0	35	2-9	218.1	241	113	100	21	83-11	107	.282

2006 LEFTY-RIGHTY SPLITS

vs.	Avg.	AB	H	2B	3B	HR	RBI	BB	SO	OBP	Slg.	vs.	Avg.	AB	H	2B	3B	HR	RBI	BB	SO	OBP	Slg.
L	.342	79	27	4	1	2	16	8	6	.402	.494	R	.314	156	49	6	1	6	30	11	18	.365	

WILLIAMS, WOODY   P

PERSONAL: Born August 19, 1966, in Houston. ... 6-0/200. ... Throws right, bats right. ... Full name: Gregory Scott Williams. ... High school: Cypress-Fairbanks (Houston). ... College: Houston. **TRANSACTIONS/CAREER NOTES:** Selected by Toronto Blue Jays organization in 28th round of 1988 free-agent draft. ... On disabled list (July 17, 1995-remainder of season); included rehabilitation assignment to Syracuse. ... On disabled list (March 22-May 31 and June 11-July 26, 1996); included rehabilitation assignments to Dunedin, Syracuse and St. Catharines. ... Traded by Blue Jays with P Carlos Almanzar and OF Peter Tucci to San Diego Padres for P Joey Hamilton (December 13, 1998). ... On disabled list (May 2-July 2, 2000); included rehabilitation assignments to Rancho Cucamonga and Las Vegas. ... Traded by Padres to St. Louis Cardinals for OF Ray Lankford and cash (August 2, 2001). ... On disabled list (April 6-May 15 and July 7-August 29, 2002); included rehabilitation assignment to,Memphis. ... Signed as a free agent by Padres (December 8, 2004). ... On disabled list (May 4-June 5, 2005). ... On disabled list (May 13-July 1, 2006); included rehabilitation assignments to Lake Elsinore and Portland. **MISCELLANEOUS NOTES:** Appeared in one game as pinch runner (1999). ... Scored three runs in four appearances as pinch runner (2000). ... Struck out twice in two appearances as pinch hitter (2000). ... Appeared in two games as pinch runner (2001). ... Struck out in only appearance as pinch hitter (2001). ... Struck out in only appearance as pinch hitter (2002). ... Made an out and struck out twice in three appearances as pinch hitter (2004). ... Had a sacrifice hit and struck out in two appearances as pinch hitter (2005). ... Made an out in only appearance as pinch hitter (2006).

CAREER HITTING: 99-for-481 (.206), 49 R, 25 2B, 1 3B, 3 HR, 41 RBI.

Year	Team (League)	W	L	Pct.	ERA	WHIP	G	GS	CG	ShO	Hld.	Sv.-Opp.	IP	H	R	ER	HR	BB-IBB	SO	Avg.
1988—	St. Catharines (NYP)	8	2	.800	1.54	0.91	12	12	2	0	...	0-...	76.0	48	22	13	1	21-0	58	.178
	— Knoxville (Southern)	2	2	.500	3.81	1.38	6	4	0	0	...	0-...	28.1	27	13	12	1	12-0	25	.250
1989—	Dunedin (Fla. St.)	3	5	.375	2.32	1.11	20	9	0	0	...	0-...	81.1	63	26	21	3	27-1	60	.217
	— Knoxville (Southern)	3	5	.375	3.55	1.32	14	12	2	2	...	1-...	71.0	61	32	28	6	33-2	51	.235
1990—	Knoxville (Southern)	7	9	.438	3.14	1.19	42	12	0	0	...	5-...	126.0	111	55	44	7	39-3	74	.236
	— Syracuse (Int'l)	0	1	.000	10.00	2.11	3	0	0	0	...	0-...	9.0	15	10	10	1	4-0	8	.375
1991—	Knoxville (Southern)	3	2	.600	3.59	1.31	18	1	0	0	...	3-...	42.2	42	18	17	1	14-0	37	.250
	— Syracuse (Int'l)	3	4	.429	4.12	1.45	31	0	0	0	...	6-...	54.2	52	27	25	2	27-3	37	.250
1992—	Syracuse (Int'l)	6	8	.429	3.13	1.29	25	16	1	0	...	1-...	120.2	115	46	42	4	41-0	81	.253
1993—	Syracuse (Int'l)	1	1	.500	2.20	1.22	12	0	0	0	...	3-...	16.1	15	5	4	2	5-3	16	.246
	— Toronto (A.L.)	3	1	.750	4.38	1.68	30	0	0	0	4	0-2	37.0	40	18	18	2	22-3	24	.274
	— Dunedin (Fla. St.)	0	0	...	0.00	0.50	2	0	0	0	...	0-...	4.0	0	0	0	0	2-0	2	.000
1994—	Toronto (A.L.)	1	3	.250	3.64	1.30	38	0	0	0	0	0-0	59.1	44	24	24	5	33-1	56	.205
	— Syracuse (Int'l)	0	0	...	0.00	0.00	1	0	0	0	...	1-...	2.0	0	0	0	0	0-0	1	.000
1995—	Toronto (A.L.)	1	2	.333	3.69	1.34	23	1	0	0	1	0-1	53.2	44	23	22	6	28-1	41	.220
	— Syracuse (Int'l)	0	0	...	3.52	1.30	5	1	0	0	...	1-...	7.2	5	3	3	0	5-0	13	.172
1996—	Dunedin (Fla. St.)	0	2	.000	8.22	1.43	2	2	0	0	...	0-...	7.2	9	7	7	1	2-0	11	.281
	— Toronto (A.L.)	4	5	.444	4.73	1.44	12	10	1	0	0	0-0	59.0	64	33	31	8	21-1	43	.278
	— St. Catharines (NYP)	0	0	...	3.68	1.50	2	2	0	0	...	0-...	7.1	7	3	3	0	2-0	7	.233
1997—	Toronto (A.L.)	9	14	.391	4.35	1.37	31	31	0	0	...	0-0	194.2	201	98	94	31	66-3	124	.269
1998—	Toronto (A.L.)	10	9	.526	4.46	1.32	32	32	1	1	...	0-0	209.2	196	112	104	36	81-3	151	.245
1999—	San Diego (N.L.)	12	12	.500	4.41	1.37	33	33	0	0	...	0-0	208.1	213	106	102	33	73-5	137	.268
2000—	San Diego (N.L.)	10	8	.556	3.75	1.23	23	23	4	0	...	0-0	168.0	152	74	70	23	54-2	111	.239
	— Rancho Cuca. (Calif.)	0	0	...	0.00	0.60	1	1	0	0	...	0-...	5.0	3	0	0	0	0-0	10	.167
	— Las Vegas (PCL)	0	0	...	1.50	1.17	1	1	0	0	...	0-...	6.0	7	2	1	1	0-0	5	.292
2001—	San Diego (N.L.)	8	8	.500	4.97	1.43	23	23	0	0	...	0-...	145.0	170	88	80	28	37-4	102	.296
	— St. Louis (N.L.)	7	1	.875	2.28	0.97	11	11	3	1	...	0-0	75.0	54	22	19	7	19-1	52	.205
2002—	St. Louis (N.L.)	9	4	.692	2.53	1.05	17	17	1	0	...	0-0	103.1	84	30	29	10	25-2	76	.222
	— Memphis (PCL)	1	0	1.000	1.80	0.40	1	1	0	0	...	0-...	5.0	1	1	1	0	1-0	7	.067
2003—	St. Louis (N.L.)	18	9	.667	3.87	1.25	34	33	0	0	...	0-1	220.2	220	101	95	20	55-2	153	.259
2004—	St. Louis (N.L.)	11	8	.579	4.18	1.32	31	31	0	0	...	0-0	189.2	193	93	88	20	58-3	131	.262
2005—	San Diego (N.L.)	9	12	.429	4.85	1.41	28	28	0	0	...	0-0	159.2	174	92	86	24	51-1	106	.275
2006—	Lake Elsinore (Calif.)	0	0	...	0.00	0.33	1	1	0	0	...	0-...	3.0	1	0	0	0	1-0	5	.091
	— Portland (PCL)	0	1	.000	20.25	3.75	1	1	0	0	...	0-0	2.2	8	6	6	1	2-0	2	.500
	— San Diego (N.L.)	12	5	.706	3.65	1.29	25	24	0	0	...	0-0	145.1	152	68	59	21	35-3	72	.267
American League totals (6 years)		28	34	.452	4.30	1.37	166	76	2	1	10	0-3	613.1	589	308	293	88	251-12	439	.252
National League totals (8 years)		96	67	.589	3.99	1.29	225	223	8	1	0	0-1	1415.0	1412	674	628	186	407-23	940	.259
Major League totals (14 years)		124	101	.551	4.09	1.31	391	299	10	2	10	0-4	2028.1	2001	982	921	274	658-35	1379	.257

DIVISION SERIES RECORD

Year	Team (League)	W	L	Pct.	ERA	WHIP	G	GS	CG	ShO	Hld.	Sv.-Opp.	IP	H	R	ER	HR	BB-IBB	SO	Avg.
2001—	St. Louis (N.L.)	1	0	1.000	1.29	0.71	1	1	0	0	...	0-0	7.0	4	1	1	0	1-0	9	.160
2004—	St. Louis (N.L.)	1	0	1.000	3.00	1.50	1	1	0	0	...	0-0	6.0	8	2	2	0	1-0	2	.320
2005—	San Diego (N.L.)	0	1	.000	27.00	4.80	1	1	0	0	...	0-0	1.2	6	5	5	0	2-1	2	.545
2006—	San Diego (N.L.)	0	1	.000	6.75	1.31	1	1	0	0	...	0-0	5.1	5	4	4	0	2-0	1	.250
Division series totals (4 years)		2	2	.500	5.40	1.45	4	4	0	0	...	0-0	20.0	23	12	12	0	6-1	14	.284

W

CHAMPIONSHIP SERIES RECORD

Year Team (League)	W	L	Pct.	ERA	WHIP	G	GS	CG	ShO	Hld.	Sv.-Opp.	IP	H	R	ER	HR	BB-IBB	SO	Avg.
2002— St. Louis (N.L.)	0	1	.000	4.50	1.17	1	1	0	0	0	0-0	6.0	6	3	3	2	1-0	7	.261
2004— St. Louis (N.L.)	1	0	1.000	2.77	0.62	2	2	0	0	0	0-0	13.0	5	4	4	2	3-0	9	.114
Champ. series totals (2 years)	1	1	.500	3.32	0.79	3	3	0	0	0	0-0	19.0	11	7	7	4	4-0	16	.164

WORLD SERIES RECORD

Year Team (League)	W	L	Pct.	ERA	WHIP	G	GS	CG	ShO	Hld.	Sv.-Opp.	IP	H	R	ER	HR	BB-IBB	SO	Avg.
2004— St. Louis (N.L.)	0	0	...	27.00	4.71	1	1	0	0	0	0-0	2.1	8	7	7	1	3-0	1	.533

ALL-STAR GAME RECORD

	W	L	Pct.	ERA	WHIP	G	GS	CG	ShO	Hld.	Sv.-Opp.	IP	H	R	ER	HR	BB-IBB	SO	Avg.
All-Star Game totals (1 year)	0	0	...	18.00	2.00	1	0	0	0	0	0-0	1.0	2	2	2	1	0-0	1	.400

2006 LEFTY-RIGHTY SPLITS

vs.	Avg.	AB	H	2B	3B	HR	RBI	BB	SO	OBP	Slg.	vs.	Avg.	AB	H	2B	3B	HR	RBI	BB	SO	OBP	Slg.
L	.245	274	67	12	2	10	23	21	38	.295	.412	R	.287	296	85	14	2	11	36	14	34	.332	.459

WILLIAMSON, SCOTT   P

PERSONAL: Born February 17, 1976, in Fort Polk, La. ... 6-0/180. ... Throws right, bats right. ... Full name: Scott Ryan Williamson. ... High school: Friendswood (Texas). ... College: Oklahoma State. **TRANSACTIONS/CAREER NOTES:** Selected by Cincinnati Reds organization in ninth round of 1997 free-agent draft. ... On disabled list (August 24-September 8, 2000; and April 4, 2001-remainder of season). ... Traded by Reds to Boston Red Sox for P Phil Dumatrait, a player to be named and cash (July 30, 2003); Reds acquired P Tyler Pelland to complete deal (August 18, 2003). ... On disabled list (May 19-June 11 and July 1-September 9, 2004); included rehabilitation assignment to Pawtucket. ... Signed as free agent by Chicago Cubs (January 18, 2005). ... On disabled list (March 30-August 5, 2005); included rehabilitation assignment to Iowa. ... On disabled list (June 4-27, 2006); included rehabilitation assignments to Peoria and Iowa. ... Traded by Cubs to San Diego Padres for Ps Fabian Jimenez and Joel Santo (July 22, 2006). ... On disabled list (August 26-September 22, 2006). ... Released by Padres (October 11, 2006). **HONORS:** Named N.L. Rookie Pitcher of the Year by THE SPORTING NEWS (1999). ... Named N.L. Rookie of the Year by Baseball Writers' Association of America (1999).

CAREER HITTING: 1-for-23 (.043), 1 R, 0 2B, 0 3B, 0 HR, 0 RBI.

Year Team (League)	W	L	Pct.	ERA	WHIP	G	GS	CG	ShO	Hld.	Sv.-Opp.	IP	H	R	ER	HR	BB-IBB	SO	Avg.
1997— Billings (Pion.)	8	2	.800	1.78	1.03	13	13	2	1		0-...	86.0	66	25	17	5	.23-0	101	.209
1998— Chattanooga (Sou.)	4	5	.444	3.78	1.31	18	18	0	0		0-...	100.0	85	49	42	4	46-4	105	.234
— Indianapolis (Int'l)	0	0	...	3.48	1.40	5	5	0	0		0-...	20.2	20	9	8	2	9-0	17	.260
1999— Cincinnati (N.L.)	12	7	.632	2.41	1.04	62	0	0	0	5	19-26	93.1	54	29	25	8	43-6	107	.171
2000— Cincinnati (N.L.)	5	8	.385	3.29	1.49	48	10	0	0	6	6-8	112.0	92	45	41	7	75-7	136	.224
2001— Cincinnati (N.L.)	0	0	...	0.00	4.50	2	0	0	0	1	0-0	0.2	1	0	0	0	2-0	0	.333
2002— Cincinnati (N.L.)	3	4	.429	2.92	1.11	63	0	0	0	8	8-12	74.0	46	27	24	5	36-5	84	.181
2003— Cincinnati (N.L.)	5	3	.625	3.19	1.39	42	0	0	0	5	21-26	42.1	34	15	15	6	25-4	53	.214
— Boston (A.L.)	0	1	.000	6.20	1.43	24	0	0	0	5	0-2	20.1	20	15	14	1	9-2	21	.253
2004— Pawtucket (Int'l)	1	0	1.000	12.27	2.45	4	1	0	0		0-...	3.2	5	5	5	0	6-0	6	.231
— Boston (A.L.)	1	1	.000	1.26	1.01	28	0	0	0	3	1-2	28.2	11	6	4	0	18-1	28	.115
2005— Ariz. Cubs (Ariz.)	0	2	.000	2.45	1.23	4	1	0	0		0-0	7.1	7	8	2	0	2-0	9	.226
— Iowa (PCL)	1	0	1.000	3.86	1.00	6	0	0	0	1	0-0	7.0	4	3	3	1	3-0	10	.154
— Chicago (N.L.)	0	0	...	5.65	1.47	17	0	0	0	1	0-0	14.1	15	9	9	3	6-0	23	.273
2006— Peoria (Midw.)	0	0	...	9.00	1.00	1	0	0	0		0-0	1.0	1	1	1	0	0-0	1	.222
— Iowa (PCL)	0	0	...	1.80	1.20	4	0	0	0	1	1-1	5.0	4	1	1	0	2-0	5	.248
— Chicago (N.L.)	2	3	.400	5.08	1.52	31	0	0	0	6	0-0	28.1	27	17	16	2	16-1	32	.333
— San Diego (N.L.)	0	1	.000	7.36	1.82	11	0	0	0	1	0-0	11.0	14	9	9	2	6-0	10	.333
American League totals (2 years)	0	2	.000	3.31	1.18	52	0	0	0	8	1-4	49.0	31	21	18	1	27-3	49	.177
National League totals (7 years)	27	26	.509	3.33	1.31	276	10	0	0	26	54-72	376.0	283	151	139	33	209-23	445	.210
Major League totals (8 years)	27	28	.491	3.32	1.29	328	10	0	0	34	55-76	425.0	314	172	157	34	236-26	494	.206

DIVISION SERIES RECORD

Year Team (League)	W	L	Pct.	ERA	WHIP	G	GS	CG	ShO	Hld.	Sv.-Opp.	IP	H	R	ER	HR	BB-IBB	SO	Avg.
2003— Boston (A.L.)	2	0	1.000	0.00	1.00	5	0	0	0		0-0	5.0	2	0	0	0	3-0	8	.125

CHAMPIONSHIP SERIES RECORD

Year Team (League)	W	L	Pct.	ERA	WHIP	G	GS	CG	ShO	Hld.	Sv.-Opp.	IP	H	R	ER	HR	BB-IBB	SO	Avg.
2003— Boston (A.L.)	0	0	...	3.00	0.33	3	0	0	0	3-3		3.0	1	1	1	0	0-0	6	.100

ALL-STAR GAME RECORD

Year Team (League)	W	L	Pct.	ERA	WHIP	G	GS	CG	ShO	Hld.	Sv.-Opp.	IP	H	R	ER	HR	BB-IBB	SO	Avg.

2006 LEFTY-RIGHTY SPLITS

vs.	Avg.	AB	H	2B	3B	HR	RBI	BB	SO	OBP	Slg.	vs.	Avg.	AB	H	2B	3B	HR	RBI	BB	SO	OBP	Slg.
L	.200	50	10	4	1	0	2	11	16	.339	.320	R	.307	101	31	6	0	4	18	11	26	.377	.485

WILLINGHAM, JOSH   OF

PERSONAL: Born February 17, 1979, in Florence, Ala. ... 6-1/200. ... Bats right, throws right. ... Full name: Joshua David Willingham. ... High school: Mars Hill Bible (Florence, Ala.). ... College: Northern Alabama. **TRANSACTIONS/CAREER NOTES:** Selected by Florida Marlins organization in third round of 2000 free-agent draft. ... On disabled list (July 6-September 2, 2005); included rehabilitation assignment to Albuquerque. ... On disabled list (June 7-22, 2006); included rehabilitation assignment to Carolina.

2006 GAMES PLAYED BY POSITION (MLB): OF—132, DH—3, 1B—2, C—2.

Year Team (League)	Pos.	G	AB	R	H	2B	3B	HR	RBI	BB	SO	HBP	GDP	SB-CS	Avg.	OBP	SLG	OPS	E	Avg.
2000— Utica (N.Y.-Penn)	OF-2B-3B																			
	SS-1B	65	205	37	54	16	0	6	29	39	55	9	2	9-5	.263	.400	.429	.829	2	.982
2001— Kane Co. (Midw.)	3B-OF-2B	97	320	57	83	20	2	7	36	53	85	13	7	24-2	.259	.382	.400	.782	15	.945
2002— Jupiter (Fla. St.)	1B-3B-OF	107	376	72	103	21	4	17	69	63	88	13	7	18-5	.274	.394	.487	.881	9	.975
2003— Jupiter (Fla. St.)	C-1B-OF																			
	3B	59	193	46	51	17	1	12	34	46	42	9	3	9-2	.264	.422	.549	.972	2	.994
— GC Marlins (GCL)		2	7	3	3	1	0	1	3	1	2	0	0	0-0	.429	.500	1.000	1.500	...	...
— Carolina (Southern)	1B-C-3B																			
	OF	22	67	15	20	2	1	5	14	13	20	3	0	0-0	.299	.434	.582	1.016	0	1.000
2004— Florida (N.L.)	C-OF	12	25	2	5	0	0	1	1	4	8	0	1	0-0	.200	.310	.320	.630	1	.955
— Carolina (Southern)	C-1B-OF																			
	DH-3B	112	338	81	95	24	0	24	76	91	87	18	5	6-3	.281	.449	.565	.992	5	.994
2005— Jupiter (Fla. St.)	C	2	9	1	2	1	0	0	1	0	2	1	0	0-0	.222	.300	.333	.633	0	1.000
— Albuquerque (PCL)	C-3B-DH	66	219	56	71	14	3	19	54	47	54	9	5	5-1	.324	.455	.676	1.131	5	.988
— Florida (N.L.)	C-OF-DH	16	23	3	7	1	0	0	4	2	5	1	0	0-0	.304	.407	.348	.755	0	1.000

W

Year Team (League)	Pos.	G	AB	R	H	2B	3B	HR	RBI	BB	SO	HBP	GDP	SB-CS	Avg.	OBP	SLG	OPS	E	Avg.
2006—Carolina (Southern)	2	8	0	2	0	0	0	0	0	3	0	0	0-0	.250	.250	.250	.500	0	1.000
— Florida (N.L.)	OF-DH-C 1B	142	502	62	139	28	2	26	74	54	109	11	13	2-0	.277	.356	.496	.852	7	.970
Major League totals (3 years)		170	550	67	151	29	2	27	79	60	122	13	15	2-0	.275	.356	.482	.838	8	.971

2006 LEFTY-RIGHTY SPLITS

vs.	Avg.	AB	H	2B	3B	HR	RBI	BB	SO	OBP	Slg.	vs.	Avg.	AB	H	2B	3B	HR	RBI	BB	SO	OBP	Slg.
L	.299	134	40	8	1	11	26	23	25	.411	.619	R	.269	368	99	20	1	15	48	31	84	.334	.451

WILLIS, DONTRELLE — P

PERSONAL: Born January 12, 1982, in Oakland. ... 6-4/239. ... Throws left, bats left. ... Full name: Dontrelle Wayne Willis. ... High school: Encinal (Alameda, Calif.). **TRANSACTIONS/CAREER NOTES:** Selected by Chicago Cubs organization in eighth round of 2000 free-agent draft. ... Traded by Cubs with Ps Julian Tavarez and Jose Cueto and C Ryan Jorgensen to Florida Marlins for Ps Antonio Alfonseca and Matt Clement (March 27, 2002). **HONORS:** Named N.L. Rookie Pitcher of the Year by THE SPORTING NEWS (2003). ... Named N.L. Rookie of the Year by Baseball Writers' Association of America (2003). **STATISTICAL NOTES:** Career major league grand slams: 1. **MISCELLANEOUS NOTES:** Was 3-for-8 with a triple, a base on balls, a sacrifice hit and three strikeouts in 10 appearances as pinch hitter (2004). ... Singled in only appearance as pinch hitter (2005). ... Singled, scored a run and struck out in six appearances as pinch hitter (2006).

CAREER HITTING: 64-for-288 (.222), 29 R, 8 2B, 2 3B, 6 HR, 28 RBI.

Year Team (League)	W	L	Pct.	ERA	WHIP	G	GS	CG	ShO	Hld.	Sv.-Opp.	IP	H	R	ER	HR	BB-IBB	SO	Avg.
2000—Ariz. Cubs (Ariz.)	3	1	.750	3.86	1.21	9	1	0	0	...	0-...	28.0	26	15	12	0	8-1	22	.245
2001—Boise (N'west)	8	2	.800	2.98	1.01	15	15	0	0	...	0-...	93.2	76	36	31	1	19-0	77	.217
2002—Kane Co. (Midw.)	10	2	.833	1.83	0.88	19	19	3	2	...	0-...	127.2	91	29	26	3	21-0	101	.200
— Jupiter (Fla. St.)	2	0	1.000	1.80	0.90	5	5	0	0	...	0-...	30.0	24	7	6	2	3-0	27	.216
2003—Carolina (Southern)	4	0	1.000	1.49	0.91	6	6	0	0	...	0-...	36.1	24	6	6	2	9-0	32	.194
— Florida (N.L.)	14	6	.700	3.30	1.28	27	27	2	2	0	0-0	160.2	148	61	59	13	58-0	142	.245
2004—Florida (N.L.)	10	11	.476	4.02	1.38	32	32	2	0	0	0-0	197.0	210	99	88	20	61-8	139	.273
2005—Florida (N.L.)	* 22	10	.688	2.63	1.13	34	34	•7	* 5	0	0-0	236.1	213	79	69	11	55-3	170	.243
2006—Florida (N.L.)	12	12	.500	3.87	1.42	34	34	4	1	0	0-0	223.1	234	106	96	21	83-6	160	.274
Major League totals (4 years)	58	39	.598	3.44	1.30	127	127	15	8	0	0-0	817.1	805	345	312	65	257-17	611	.259

DIVISION SERIES RECORD

Year Team (League)	W	L	Pct.	ERA	WHIP	G	GS	CG	ShO	Hld.	Sv.-Opp.	IP	H	R	ER	HR	BB-IBB	SO	Avg.
2003—Florida (N.L.)	0	0	...	7.94	1.59	2	1	0	0	0	0-0	5.2	7	5	5	0	2-0	3	.318

CHAMPIONSHIP SERIES RECORD

Year Team (League)	W	L	Pct.	ERA	WHIP	G	GS	CG	ShO	Hld.	Sv.-Opp.	IP	H	R	ER	HR	BB-IBB	SO	Avg.
2003—Florida (N.L.)	0	1	.000	18.90	3.00	2	1	0	0	0	0-0	3.1	4	7	7	1	6-0	4	.308

WORLD SERIES RECORD

Year Team (League)	W	L	Pct.	ERA	WHIP	G	GS	CG	ShO	Hld.	Sv.-Opp.	IP	H	R	ER	HR	BB-IBB	SO	Avg.
2003—Florida (N.L.)	0	0	...	0.00	1.64	3	0	0	0	1	0-0	3.2	4	0	0	0	2-0	3	.267

ALL-STAR GAME RECORD

Year Team (League)	W	L	Pct.	ERA	WHIP	G	GS	CG	ShO	Hld.	Sv.-Opp.	IP	H	R	ER	HR	BB-IBB	SO	Avg.
All-Star Game totals (1 year)	0	0	...	18.00	3.00	1	0	0	0	0	0-0	1.0	2	2	2	1	1-0	0	.500

2006 LEFTY-RIGHTY SPLITS

vs.	Avg.	AB	H	2B	3B	HR	RBI	BB	SO	OBP	Slg.	vs.	Avg.	AB	H	2B	3B	HR	RBI	BB	SO	OBP	Slg.
L	.231	121	28	3	0	3	17	12	41	.307	.331	R	.281	734	206	31	4	18	75	71	119	.356	.407

WILLITS, REGGIE — OF

PERSONAL: Born May 30, 1981, in Chickasha, Okla. ... 5-11/185. ... Bats both, throws right. ... Full name: Reggie Willits. ... College: Oklahoma. **TRANSACTIONS/CAREER NOTES:** Selected by Anaheim Angels organization in seventh round of 2003 free-agent draft. ... Angels franchise renamed Los Angeles Angels of Anaheim for 2005 season.

2006 GAMES PLAYED BY POSITION (MLB): OF—20, DH—2.

Year Team (League)	Pos.	G	AB	R	H	2B	3B	HR	RBI	BB	SO	HBP	GDP	SB-CS	Avg.	OBP	SLG	OPS	E	Avg.
2003—Provo (Pion.)		59	230	53	69	14	4	4	27	37	52	6	2	14-4	.300	.410	.448	.858	...	...
2004—Rancho Cuca. (Calif.)		135	526	99	150	17	5	5	52	73	112	8	9	44-15	.285	.374	.365	.739	...	...
2005—Arkansas (Texas)	OF-DH	123	487	75	148	23	6	2	46	54	78	8	5	40-14	.304	.377	.388	.765	8	.986
2006—Salt Lake (PCL)		97	352	85	115	18	4	3	39	77	50	2	5	31-15	.327	.448	.426	.874	4	.983
— Los Angeles (A.L.)	OF-DH	28	45	12	12	1	0	0	2	11	10	0	0	4-3	.267	.411	.289	.700	1	.974
Major League totals (1 year)		28	45	12	12	1	0	0	2	11	10	0	0	4-3	.267	.411	.289	.700	1	.974

2006 LEFTY-RIGHTY SPLITS

vs.	Avg.	AB	H	2B	3B	HR	RBI	BB	SO	OBP	Slg.	vs.	Avg.	AB	H	2B	3B	HR	RBI	BB	SO	OBP	Slg.
L	.083	12	1	0	0	0	0	4	1	.313	.083	R	.333	33	11	1	0	0	2	7	9	.450	.364

WILSON, BRIAN — P

PERSONAL: Born March 16, 1982, in Londonderry, N.H. ... Throws right, bats right. ... Full name: Brian P. Wilson. ... College: LSU. **TRANSACTIONS/CAREER NOTES:** Selected by San Francisco Giants organization in 24th round of 2003 free-agent draft. ... On disabled list (April 25-May 20, 2006); included rehabilitation assignments to San Jose and Fresno.

CAREER HITTING: 0-for-2 (.000), 0 R, 0 2B, 0 3B, 0 HR, 0 RBI.

Year Team (League)	W	L	Pct.	ERA	WHIP	G	GS	CG	ShO	Hld.	Sv.-Opp.	IP	H	R	ER	HR	BB-IBB	SO	Avg.
2004—Hagerstown (SAL)	2	5	.286	5.34	1.48	23	3	0	0	...	3-...	57.1	63	37	34	7	22-1	41	.269
2005—Augusta (S. Atl.)	5	1	.833	0.82	0.91	26	0	0	0	0	13-19	33.0	23	7	3	0	7-0	30	.190
— Norwich (East.)	0	0	...	0.57	0.70	15	0	0	0	0	8-8	15.2	6	1	1	0	5-0	22	.115
— Fresno (PCL)	1	1	.500	3.97	1.41	9	0	0	0	1	0-1	11.1	8	7	5	0	8-0	13	.190
2006—San Jose (Calif.)	0	0	...	9.00	2.00	1	0	0	0	0	0-0	1.0	1	1	1	0	1-0	1	.200
— Fresno (PCL)	1	3	.250	2.89	1.21	24	0	0	0	1	7-9	28.0	20	9	9	2	14-0	30	.202
— San Francisco (N.L.)	2	3	.400	5.40	1.77	31	0	0	0	4	1-2	30.0	32	19	18	1	21-2	23	.281
Major League totals (1 year)	2	3	.400	5.40	1.77	31	0	0	0	4	1-2	30.0	32	19	18	1	21-2	23	.281

2006 LEFTY-RIGHTY SPLITS

vs.	Avg.	AB	H	2B	3B	HR	RBI	BB	SO	OBP	Slg.	vs.	Avg.	AB	H	2B	3B	HR	RBI	BB	SO	OBP	Slg.
L	.348	46	16	4	1	0	4	13	9	.475	.478	R	.235	68	16	0	1	1	8	8	14	.316	.309

W

WILSON, C.J. — P

PERSONAL: Born November 18, 1980, in Newport Beach, Calif. ... 6-2/200. ... Throws left, bats left. ... Full name: Christopher John Wilson. ... High school: Fountain Valley (Calif.). ... Junior college: Santa Ana (Calif.). ... College: Loyola Marymount. **TRANSACTIONS/CAREER NOTES:** Selected by Texas Rangers organization in fifth round of 2001 free-agent draft. ... On disabled list (March 31-April 14, 2006); included rehabilitation assignment to Frisco.
CAREER HITTING: 0-for-0 (.000), 0 R, 0 2B, 0 3B, 0 HR, 0 RBI.

Year Team (League)	W	L	Pct.	ERA	WHIP	G	GS	CG	ShO	Hld.	Sv.-Opp.	IP	H	R	ER	HR	BB-IBB	SO	Avg.
2001—Puluski (Appalachian)	1	0	1.000	0.96	0.88	8	8	0	0	...	0-...	37.2	24	6	4	2	9-0	49	.178
—Savannah (S. Atl.)	1	2	.333	3.18	1.15	5	5	0	0	...	1-...	34.0	30	13	12	2	9-0	26	.252
2002—Charlotte (Fla. St.)	10	2	.833	3.06	1.20	26	15	0	0	...	1-...	106.0	86	48	36	4	41-1	76	.215
—Tulsa (Texas)	1	0	1.000	1.80	1.17	5	5	0	0	...	0-...	30.0	23	6	6	0	12-0	17	.211
2003—Frisco (Texas)	6	9	.400	5.05	1.41	22	21	0	0	...	0-...	123.0	135	79	69	11	38-3	89	.276
2005—Bakersfield (Calif.)	0	1	.000	3.29	1.02	4	4	0	0	...	0-0	13.2	10	5	5	2	4-0	14	.189
—Frisco (Texas)	0	4	.000	4.43	1.46	12	12	0	0	...	0-0	44.2	51	32	22	7	14-0	43	.290
—Texas (A.L.)	1	7	.125	6.94	1.69	24	6	0	0	4	1-1	48.0	63	39	37	5	18-1	30	.321
2006—Frisco (Texas)	0	0	...	2.70	1.50	4	0	0	0	...	0-0	3.1	3	1	1	0	2-0	6	.231
—Oklahoma (PCL)	1	0	1.000	2.45	1.36	9	0	0	0	7	2-2	11.0	10	3	3	0	5-0	17	.233
—Texas (A.L.)	2	4	.333	4.06	1.29	44	0	0	0	7	1-2	44.1	39	23	20	7	18-1	43	.234
Major League totals (2 years)	3	11	.214	5.56	1.49	68	6	0	0	11	2-3	92.1	102	62	57	12	36-2	73	.281

2006 LEFTY-RIGHTY SPLITS

vs.	Avg.	AB	H	2B	3B	HR	RBI	BB	SO	OBP	Slg.	vs.	Avg.	AB	H	2B	3B	HR	RBI	BB	SO	OBP	Slg.
L	.155	71	11	0	0	4	10	4	19	.241	.324	R	.292	96	28	6	0	3	19	14	24	.387	.448

WILSON, CRAIG — OF/1B

PERSONAL: Born November 30, 1976, in Fountain Valley, Calif. ... 6-2/220. ... Bats right, throws right. ... Full name: Craig Alan Wilson. ... High school: Marina (Huntington Beach, Calif.). **TRANSACTIONS/CAREER NOTES:** Selected by Toronto Blue Jays organization in second round of 1995 free-agent draft. ... Traded by Blue Jays with SS Abraham Nunez and P Mike Halperin to Pittsburgh Pirates (December 11, 1996), completing deal in which Pirates traded 2B Carlos Garcia, 1B Orlando Merced and P Dan Plesac to Blue Jays for Ps Jose Pett and Jose Silva, SS Brandon Cromer and three players to be named (November 14, 1996). ... On disabled list (May 8-July 9 and July 17-August 28, 2005); included rehabilitation assignment to Indianapolis. ... Traded by Pirates to New York Yankees for P Shawn Chacon (July 31, 2006). **STATISTICAL NOTES:** Career major league grand slams: 1.
2006 GAMES PLAYED BY POSITION (MLB): 1B—78, OF—32, DH—1.

									BATTING										FIELDING	
Year Team (League)	Pos.	G	AB	R	H	2B	3B	HR	RBI	BB	SO	HBP	GDP	SB-CS	Avg.	OBP	SLG	OPS	E	Avg.
1995—Medicine Hat (Pio.)	C	49	184	33	52	14	1	7	35	24	44	3	1	8-2	.283	.367	.484	.851	5	.982
1996—Hagerstown (SAL)	C-OF	131	495	66	129	27	5	11	70	32	120	10	12	17-11	.261	.316	.402	.718	9	.986
1997—Lynchburg (Caro.)	C	117	401	54	106	26	1	9	69	39	98	15	3	6-5	.264	.350	.476	.826	12	.985
1998—Lynchburg (Caro.)	1B-C	61	219	26	59	12	2	12	45	22	53	5	3	2-1	.269	.348	.507	.855	6	.986
—Carolina (Southern)	C	45	148	20	49	11	0	5	21	14	32	4	2	4-1	.331	.399	.507	.906	1	.995
1999—Altoona (East.)	1B-C-OF	111	362	57	97	21	3	20	69	40	104	19	8	1-3	.268	.367	.508	.875	9	.978
2000—Nashville (PCL)	1B-C	124	396	83	112	24	1	33	86	44	121	25	7	1-2	.283	.383	.598	.982	13	.982
2001—Nashville (PCL)	1B-C	11	45	4	13	2	1	1	3	2	14	1	1	0-0	.289	.333	.444	.778	2	.976
—Pittsburgh (N.L.)	1B-OF-C DH	88	158	27	49	3	1	13	32	15	53	7	4	3-1	.310	.390	.589	.979	3	.987
2002—Pittsburgh (N.L.)	OF-1B-C DH	131	368	48	97	16	1	16	57	32	116	* 21	10	2-3	.264	.355	.443	.798	5	.988
2003—Pittsburgh (N.L.)	OF-1B-C DH	116	309	49	81	15	4	18	48	35	89	13	6	3-1	.262	.360	.511	.872	6	.986
2004—Pittsburgh (N.L.)	OF-1B-DH	155	561	97	148	35	5	29	82	50	169	* 30	11	2-2	.264	.354	.499	.853	7	.990
2005—Indianapolis (Int'l)	OF-1B-DH	7	21	4	8	1	0	3	11	3	6	1	1	1-0	.381	.480	.857	1.337	2	.920
—Pittsburgh (N.L.)	OF-1B	59	197	23	52	14	1	5	22	30	69	10	6	3-0	.264	.387	.421	.808	2	.989
2006—Pittsburgh (N.L.)	1B-OF-DH	85	255	38	68	11	2	13	41	24	88	5	6	1-0	.267	.339	.478	.818	1	.998
—New York (A.L.)	1B-OF-DH	40	104	15	22	4	0	4	8	4	34	1	4	0-0	.212	.248	.365	.613	2	.992
American League totals (1 year)		40	104	15	22	4	0	4	8	4	34	1	4	0-0	.212	.248	.365	.613	2	.992
National League totals (6 years)		634	1848	282	495	94	14	94	282	186	584	86	43	14-7	.268	.360	.486	.846	24	.990
Major League totals (6 years)		674	1952	297	517	98	14	98	290	190	618	87	47	14-7	.265	.354	.480	.834	26	.990

2006 LEFTY-RIGHTY SPLITS

vs.	Avg.	AB	H	2B	3B	HR	RBI	BB	SO	OBP	Slg.	vs.	Avg.	AB	H	2B	3B	HR	RBI	BB	SO	OBP	Slg.
L	.278	133	37	6	1	7	24	12	38	.347	.496	R	.235	226	53	9	1	10	25	16	84	.294	.416

WILSON, JACK — SS

PERSONAL: Born December 29, 1977, in Westlake Village, Calif. ... 6-0/192. ... Bats right, throws right. ... Full name: Jack Eugene Wilson. ... High school: Thousand Oaks (Calif.). ... Junior college: Oxnard (Calif.). **TRANSACTIONS/CAREER NOTES:** Selected by St. Louis Cardinals organization in ninth round of 1998 free-agent draft. ... Traded by Cardinals to Pittsburgh Pirates for P Jason Christiansen (July 30, 2000). **HONORS:** Named shortstop on N.L. Silver Slugger team (2004). **STATISTICAL NOTES:** Career major league grand slams: 2.
2006 GAMES PLAYED BY POSITION (MLB): SS—131.

									BATTING										FIELDING	
Year Team (League)	Pos.	G	AB	R	H	2B	3B	HR	RBI	BB	SO	HBP	GDP	SB-CS	Avg.	OBP	SLG	OPS	E	Avg.
1998—Johnson City (App.)	SS	61	241	50	90	18	4	4	29	18	30	3	4	22-6	.373	.424	.531	.955	16	.940
1999—Peoria (Midw.)	SS	64	251	47	86	22	4	3	28	15	23	2	2	11-5	.343	.384	.498	.882	16	.943
—Potomac (Carol.)	SS	64	257	44	76	10	1	2	18	19	31	1	2	7-4	.296	.345	.366	.711	18	.941
2000—Potomac (Carol.)	SS	13	47	7	13	0	1	2	7	5	10	0	1	2-3	.277	.340	.447	.786	2	.967
—Arkansas (Texas)	SS	88	343	65	101	20	8	6	34	36	59	5	5	2-3	.294	.368	.452	.820	12	.971
—Altoona (East.)	SS	33	139	17	35	7	2	1	16	14	17	2	3	1-3	.252	.325	.353	.677	5	.966
2001—Pittsburgh (N.L.)	SS	108	390	44	87	17	3	3	25	16	70	1	4	2-2	.223	.255	.295	.550	16	.968
—Nashville (PCL)	SS	27	103	20	39	6	1	1	9	9	13	2	1	5-2	.252	.306	.332	.638	15	.977
2002—Pittsburgh (N.L.)	SS	147	527	77	133	22	4	6	47	37	74	4	7	5-2	.252	.306	.353	.656	17	.977
2003—Pittsburgh (N.L.)	SS	150	558	58	143	23	3	9	62	36	74	4	6	5-5	.256	.303	.413	.716	17	.977
2004—Pittsburgh (N.L.)	SS	157	652	82	201	41	• 12	11	59	26	71	3	15	8-4	.308	.335	.459	.794	14	.982
2005—Pittsburgh (N.L.)	SS	158	587	60	151	24	7	8	52	31	58	6	11	7-3	.273	.316	.370	.686	18	.972
2006—Pittsburgh (N.L.)	SS	142	543	70	148	27	1	8	35	33	65	2	13	3-5	.265	.306	.368	.674	19	.976
Major League totals (6 years)		862	3257	391	863	152	26	43	280	179	412	22	63	30-20	.265	.306	.368	.674	97	.976

W

All-Star Game totals (1 year)	G	AB	R	H	2B	3B	HR	RBI	BB	SO	HBP	GDP	SB-CS	Avg.	OBP	SLG	OPS	E	Avg.
	1	2	0	0	0	0	0	0	0	0	0	0	0-0	.000	.000	.000	.000	0	1.000

2006 LEFTY-RIGHTY SPLITS

vs.	Avg.	AB	H	2B	3B	HR	RBI	BB	SO	OBP	Slg.	vs.	Avg.	AB	H	2B	3B	HR	RBI	BB	SO	OBP	Slg.
L	.301	153	46	4	0	3	8	11	13	.348	.386	R	.262	390	102	23	1	5	27	22	52	.304	.364

WILSON, KRIS — P

PERSONAL: Born August 6, 1976, in Washington, D.C. ... 6-4/225. ... Throws right, bats right. ... Full name: Kristopher Kyle Wilson. ... High school: Tarpon Springs (Fla.). ... College: Georgia Tech. **TRANSACTIONS/CAREER NOTES:** Selected by New York Mets organization in 65th round of 1994 free-agent draft; did not sign. ... Selected by Kansas City Royals organization in ninth round of 1997 free-agent draft. ... On disabled list (March 22-May 26, 2002); included rehabilitation assignment to Omaha. ... Signed as a free agent by Boston Red Sox organization (December 9, 2004). ... Released by Red Sox (March 31, 2005). ... Signed by New York Yankees organization (May 9, 2005). **CAREER HITTING:** 1-for-3 (.333), 1 R, 0 2B, 0 3B, 0 HR, 0 RBI.

Year Team (League)	W	L	Pct.	ERA	WHIP	G	GS	CG	ShO	Hld.	Sv.-Opp.	IP	H	R	ER	HR	BB-IBB	SO	Avg.
1997— Spokane (N'west)	5	3	.625	4.52	1.66	15	15	0	0	...	0-...	73.2	101	50	37	6	21-1	72	.303
1998— Wilmington (Caro.)	0	3	.000	3.75	1.04	10	2	0	0	...	1-...	24.0	19	10	10	0	6-1	20	.229
— Lansing (Midw.)	10	5	.667	3.53	1.14	18	18	1	0	...	0-...	117.1	119	50	46	7	15-0	74	.267
1999— Wilmington (Caro.)	8	1	.889	1.13	0.75	14	4	0	0	...	0-...	48.0	25	7	6	0	11-0	45	.158
— Omaha (PCL)	0	1	.000	8.44	1.50	1	1	0	0	...	0-...	5.1	5	5	5	3	0-0	3	.348
— Wichita (Texas)	5	7	.417	5.45	1.41	23	10	0	0	...	0-...	74.1	91	51	45	11	14-0	45	.301
2000— Wichita (Texas)	7	3	.700	3.51	1.17	21	15	1	0	...	0-...	102.2	99	52	40	12	21-0	69	.252
— Kansas City (A.L.)	0	1	.000	4.19	1.43	20	0	0	0	...	0-1	34.1	38	16	16	3	11-3	17	.288
2001— Kansas City (A.L.)	6	5	.545	5.19	1.50	29	15	0	0	...	1-1	109.1	132	78	63	26	32-0	67	.297
— Omaha (PCL)	2	2	.500	2.79	1.28	6	5	0	0	...	0-...	29.0	31	9	9	2	6-0	18	.279
2002— Omaha (PCL)	2	0	1.000	3.08	1.48	8	3	0	0	...	1-...	26.1	38	9	9	4	1-0	17	.342
— Wichita (Texas)	3	3	.500	1.88	1.06	13	7	1	0	...	0-...	48.0	47	17	10	4	4-1	33	.260
— Kansas City (A.L.)	2	0	1.000	8.20	1.82	12	0	0	0	...	0-...	18.2	29	18	17	7	5-0	10	.354
2003— Omaha (PCL)	0	2	.000	8.03	1.90	5	0	0	0	...	0-...	12.1	21	12	11	2	3-0	9	.382
— Kansas City (A.L.)	6	3	.667	5.33	1.49	29	0	0	0	...	0-1	72.2	92	49	43	13	16-3	42	.305
2005— Columbus (Int'l)	4	1	.800	4.28	1.41	29	7	0	0	4	0-1	67.1	78	39	32	8	17-1	52	.288
2006— Columbus (Int'l)	9	6	.600	3.40	1.09	21	21	2	1	0	0-0	132.1	120	54	50	7	24-1	103	.240
— Trenton (East.)	0	2	.000	9.35	1.73	2	2	0	0	0	0-0	8.2	13	10	9	4	2-1	2	.342
— New York (A.L.)	0	0		8.64	2.16	5	1	0	0	0	0-0	8.1	14	8	8	4	4-0	6	.368
Major League totals (5 years)	14	9	.609	5.44	1.53	95	20	0	0	1	1-5	243.1	305	169	147	53	68-6	142	.306

2006 LEFTY-RIGHTY SPLITS

vs.	Avg.	AB	H	2B	3B	HR	RBI	BB	SO	OBP	Slg.	vs.	Avg.	AB	H	2B	3B	HR	RBI	BB	SO	OBP	Slg.
L	.200	15	3	0		2	6	1	5	.250	.600	R	.478	23	11	2	0	2	4	3	1	.538	.826

WILSON, PAUL — P

PERSONAL: Born March 28, 1973, in Orlando. ... 6-5/215. ... Throws right, bats right. ... Full name: Paul Anthony Wilson. ... High school: William R. Boone (Orlando). ... College: Florida State. **TRANSACTIONS/CAREER NOTES:** Selected by New York Mets organization in first round (first pick overall) of 1994 free-agent draft. ... On disabled list (June 5-July 15, 1996); included rehabilitation assignments to St. Lucie and Binghamton. ... On disabled list (March 27, 1997-entire season); included rehabilitation assignments to GCL Mets and St. Lucie. ... On disabled list (March 13-August 4, 1998); included rehabilitation assignment to St. Lucie. ... On disabled list (April 8, 1999-entire season). ... Traded by Mets with OF Jason Tyner to Tampa Bay Devil Rays for OF Bubba Trammell and P Rick White (July 28, 2000). ... Signed as a free agent by Cincinnati Reds (January 11, 2003). ... On disabled list (August 14-September 1, 2004). ... On disabled list (May 25, 2005-remainder of season). ... On disabled list (April 1, 2006-entire season); included rehabilitation assignments to Dayton, Louisville and Sarasota. **MISCELLANEOUS NOTES:** Made an out in only appearance as pinch hitter (2003). **CAREER HITTING:** 19-for-184 (.103), 7 R, 3 2B, 0 3B, 1 HR, 8 RBI.

Year Team (League)	W	L	Pct.	ERA	WHIP	G	GS	CG	ShO	Hld.	Sv.-Opp.	IP	H	R	ER	HR	BB-IBB	SO	Avg.
1994— GC Mets (GCL)	0	2	.000	3.00	1.00	3	3	0	0	...	0-...	12.0	8	4	4	0	4-0	13	.190
— St. Lucie (Fla. St.)	0	5	.000	5.06	1.31	8	8	0	0	...	0-...	37.1	32	23	21	3	17-1	37	.230
1995— Binghamton (East.)	6	3	.667	2.17	0.94	16	16	4	1	...	0-...	120.1	89	34	29	5	24-2	127	.208
— Norfolk (Int'l)	5	3	.625	2.85	1.19	10	10	4	2	...	0-...	66.1	59	25	21	3	20-0	67	.242
1996— New York (N.L.)	5	12	.294	5.38	1.53	26	26	1	0	0	0-0	149.0	157	102	89	15	71-11	109	.268
— St. Lucie (Fla. St.)	0	1	.000	3.38	1.25	2	2	0	0	...	0-0	8.0	6	5	3	0	4-3	5	.194
— Binghamton (East.)	0	1	.000	7.20	2.20	1	1	0	0	...	0-...	5.0	6	4	4	0	5-0	5	.316
1997— GC Mets (GCL)	1	0	1.000	1.45	0.96	4	3	0	0	...	1-...	18.2	14	7	3	0	4-0	18	.203
— St. Lucie (Fla. St.)	0	0		2.57	0.86	1	1	0	0	...	0-...	7.0	6	2	2	1	0-0	6	.231
1998— Norfolk (Int'l)	0	1	.000	6.38	1.47	5	5	0	0	...	0-...	18.1	23	13	13	2	4-0	16	.315
— Norfolk (Int'l)	4	1	.800	4.42	1.32	7	7	0	0	...	0-...	38.2	42	19	19	2	9-0	30	.273
1999— Did not play.																			
2000— St. Lucie (Fla. St.)	2	0	1.000	1.40	1.01	5	5	0	0	...	0-...	25.2	22	9	4	0	4-0	19	.234
— Norfolk (Int'l)	5	5	.500	4.23	1.33	15	13	0	0	...	0-...	83.0	85	40	39	7	25-1	56	.266
— Tampa Bay (A.L.)	1	4	.200	3.35	1.06	11	7	0	0	1	0-0	51.0	38	20	19	1	16-2	40	.209
2001— Tampa Bay (A.L.)	8	9	.471	4.88	1.43	37	24	0	0	0	0-1	151.1	165	94	82	21	52-2	119	.278
2002— Tampa Bay (A.L.)	6	12	.333	4.83	1.48	30	30	1	0	0	0-0	193.2	219	113	104	29	67-2	111	.287
2003— Cincinnati (N.L.)	8	10	.444	4.64	1.44	28	28	0	0	0	0-0	166.2	190	97	86	24	50-5	93	.285
2004— Cincinnati (N.L.)	11	6	.647	4.36	1.39	29	29	1	0	0	0-0	183.2	192	93	89	26	63-5	117	.271
2005— Cincinnati (N.L.)	1	5	.167	7.77	1.83	9	9	0	0	0	0-0	46.1	68	41	40	10	17-1	30	.343
2006— Dayton (Midw.)	0	1	.000	5.14	1.43	1	1	0	0	0	0-0	7.0	10	6	4	1	0-0	4	.313
— Sarasota (Fla. St.)	1	0	1.000	3.00	1.67	1	1	0	0	0	0-0	6.0	9	2	2	0	1-0	1	.360
— Louisville (Int'l)	0	2	.000	4.91	1.45	2	2	0	0	0	0-0	11.0	15	11	6	4	1-0	3	.300
American League totals (3 years)	15	25	.375	4.66	1.41	78	61	1	0	1	0-1	396.0	422	227	205	51	135-6	270	.274
National League totals (4 years)	25	33	.431	5.01	1.48	92	92	2	0	0	0-0	545.2	607	333	304	75	201-22	349	.281
Major League totals (7 years)	40	58	.408	4.86	1.45	170	153	3	0	1	0-1	941.2	1029	560	509	126	336-28	619	.278

WILSON, PRESTON — OF

PERSONAL: Born July 19, 1974, in Bamberg, S.C. ... 6-2/215. ... Bats right, throws right. ... Full name: Preston James Richard Wilson. ... High school: Bamberg Erhardt (Bamberg, S.C.). ... Stepson of Mookie Wilson, outfielder who played with two major league teams (1980-91) and coach with New York Mets (1996-2002). **TRANSACTIONS/CAREER NOTES:** Selected by Mets organization in first round (ninth pick overall) of 1992 free-agent draft. ... Traded by Mets with Ps Ed Yarnall and Geoff Goetz to Florida Marlins for C Mike Piazza (May 22, 1998). ... On disabled list (July 2-August 10, 2001); included rehabilitation assignment to Calgary. ... Traded by Marlins with C Charles Johnson, P Vic Darensbourg and 2B Pablo Ozuna to Colorado Rockies for P Mike Hampton, OF Juan Pierre and cash (November 16, 2002). ... On disabled list (April 13-June 18 and August 21, 2004-remainder of season); included rehabilitation assignment to Tulsa. ... Traded by Rockies to Washington Nationals for P Zach Day, OF J.J. Davis and a player

W

to be named (July 13, 2005); Rockies acquired OF Cedrick Brooks to complete deal (December 16, 2005). ... Signed as a free agent by Houston Astros (January 6, 2006). ... Released by Astros (August 15, 2006). ... Signed by St. Louis Cardinals (August 18, 2006). **RECORDS:** Shares major league record for most strikeouts, 9-inning game (5, April 17, 2006). **HONORS:** Named N.L. Rookie Player of the Year by THE SPORTING NEWS (1999). **STATISTICAL NOTES:** Career major league grand slams: 4.

2006 GAMES PLAYED BY POSITION (MLB): OF—128.

Year Team (League)	Pos.	G	AB	R	H	2B	3B	HR	RBI	BB	SO	HBP	GDP	SB-CS	Avg.	OBP	SLG	OPS	E	Avg.
1993— Kingsport (Appalachian)	3B	66	259	44	60	10	0	16	48	24	75	3	6	6-2	.232	.303	.456	.759	25	.873
— Pittsfield (NYP)	3B	8	29	6	16	5	1	1	12	2	7	1	0	1-0	.552	.576	.897	1.472	6	.700
1994— Capital City (SAL)	3B	131	474	55	108	17	4	14	58	20	135	3	4	10-10	.228	.262	.369	.631	47	.884
1995— Capital City (SAL)	OF	111	442	70	119	26	5	20	61	19	114	9	4	20-6	.269	.311	.486	.797	8	.961
1996— St. Lucie (Fla. St.)	OF	23	85	6	15	3	0	1	7	8	21	2	3	1-1	.176	.263	.247	.510	2	.956
1997— St. Lucie (Fla. St.)	OF-DH	63	245	32	60	12	1	11	48	8	66	1	4	3-4	.245	.267	.437	.704	3	.973
— Binghamton (East.) OF-DH-3B		70	259	37	74	12	1	19	47	21	71	2	5	7-1	.286	.340	.560	.900	6	.952
1998— Norfolk (Int'l)	OF	18	73	9	18	5	1	1	9	2	22	1	...	1-1	.247	.273	.384	.656	2	.958
— New York (N.L.)	OF	8	20	3	6	2	0	0	2	2	8	0	0	1-1	.300	.364	.400	.764	1	.909
— Charlotte (Int'l)	OF-DH	94	356	71	99	25	3	25	77	34	121	2	...	14-6	.278	.341	.576	.917	4	.979
— Florida (N.L.)	OF	14	31	4	2	0	0	1	1	4	13	1	0	0-0	.065	.194	.161	.356	0	1.000
1999— Florida (N.L.)	OF	149	482	67	135	21	4	26	71	46	156	9	15	11-4	.280	.350	.502	.852	9	.973
2000— Florida (N.L.)	OF	161	605	94	160	35	3	31	121	55 *	187	8	11	36-14	.264	.331	.486	.817	5	.988
2001— Florida (N.L.)	OF	123	468	70	128	30	2	23	71	36	107	6	14	20-8	.274	.331	.494	.825	2	.993
— Calgary (PCL)	OF	4	10	3	5	2	0	1	5	1	0	0	0	2-0	.500	.667	.700	1.367	0	1.000
2002— Florida (N.L.)	OF	141	510	80	124	22	2	23	65	58	140	9	17	20-11	.243	.329	.429	.759	6	.981
2003— Colorado (N.L.)	OF	155	600	94	169	43	1	36 *	141	54	139	4	23	14-7	.282	.343	.537	.880	7	.980
2004— Tulsa (Texas)	OF-DH	6	17	4	7	1	0	1	2	4	1	1	1	1-1	.412	.524	.647	1.171	0	1.000
— Colorado (N.L.)	OF	58	202	24	50	11	0	6	29	17	49	3	9	2-1	.248	.315	.391	.706	6	.953
2005— Colorado (N.L.)	OF	71	267	39	69	15	1	15	47	25	77	1	8	3-2	.258	.322	.491	.813	3	.979
— Wash. (N.L.)	OF	68	253	34	66	14	1	10	43	20	71	6	10	3-4	.261	.329	.443	.771	0	1.000
2006— Houston (N.L.)	OF	102	390	40	105	22	2	9	55	22	94	2	18	6-2	.269	.309	.405	.714	4	.960
— St. Louis (N.L.)	OF	33	111	18	27	3	0	8	17	7	27	2	2	6-0	.243	.300	.486	.786	2	.960
Major League totals (9 years)		1083	3939	567	1041	218	16	188	663	346	1068	51	127	122-54	.264	.330	.471	.801	41	.983

DIVISION SERIES RECORD

Year Team (League)	Pos.	G	AB	R	H	2B	3B	HR	RBI	BB	SO	HBP	GDP	SB-CS	Avg.	OBP	SLG	OPS	E	Avg.
2006— St. Louis (N.L.)	OF	2	8	2	2	1	0	0	0	0	1	0	0	0-0	.250	.250	.375	.625	0	1.000

CHAMPIONSHIP SERIES RECORD

Year Team (League)	Pos.	G	AB	R	H	2B	3B	HR	RBI	BB	SO	HBP	GDP	SB-CS	Avg.	OBP	SLG	OPS	E	Avg.
2006— St. Louis (N.L.)	OF	6	17	2	3	1	0	0	1	1	4	0	0	0-0	.176	.222	.235	.458	0	1.000

WORLD SERIES RECORD

Year Team (League)	Pos.	G	AB	R	H	2B	3B	HR	RBI	BB	SO	HBP	GDP	SB-CS	Avg.	OBP	SLG	OPS	E	Avg.
2006— St. Louis (N.L.)	OF-DH	5	10	1	2	0	0	0	1	3	2	1	0	0-0	.200	.429	.200	.629	0	1.000

ALL-STAR GAME RECORD

		G	AB	R	H	2B	3B	HR	RBI	BB	SO	HBP	GDP	SB-CS	Avg.	OBP	SLG	OPS	E	Avg.
All-Star Game totals (1 year)		1	2	0	1	0	0	0	0	0	1	0	0	0-0	.500	.500	.500	1.000	0	1.000

2006 LEFTY-RIGHTY SPLITS

vs.	Avg.	AB	H	2B	3B	HR	RBI	BB	SO	OBP	Slg.	vs.	Avg.	AB	H	2B	3B	HR	RBI	BB	SO	OBP	Slg.
L	.292	113	33	3	1	6	22	12	27	.362	.496	R	.255	388	99	22	1	11	50	17	94	.290	.402

WILSON, VANCE — C

PERSONAL: Born March 17, 1973, in Mesa, Ariz. ... 5-11/190. ... Bats right, throws right. ... Full name: Vance Allen Wilson. ... High school: Red Mountain (Mesa, Ariz.). ... Junior college: Mesa (Ariz.) Community College. **TRANSACTIONS/CAREER NOTES:** Selected by New York Mets organization in 44th round of 1993 free-agent draft. ... On disabled list (September 8, 1998-remainder of season; and August 28, 1999-remainder of season). ... On disabled list (June 16-July 7 and September 14, 2004-remainder of season); included rehabilitation assignments to Binghamton and Norfolk. ... Traded by Mets to Detroit Tigers for SS Anderson Hernandez (January 6, 2005).

2006 GAMES PLAYED BY POSITION (MLB): C—55.

Year Team (League)	Pos.	G	AB	R	H	2B	3B	HR	RBI	BB	SO	HBP	GDP	SB-CS	Avg.	OBP	SLG	OPS	E	Avg.
1994— Pittsfield (NYP)	C	44	166	22	51	12	0	2	20	5	27	5	1	4-1	.307	.343	.416	.758	5	.977
1995— Capital City (SAL)	C	91	324	34	81	11	0	6	32	19	45	8	6	4-3	.250	.306	.340	.645	14	.981
1996— St. Lucie (Fla. St.)	C	93	311	29	76	14	2	6	44	31	41	6	7	2-4	.244	.321	.360	.681	8	.987
1997— Binghamton (East.)	C	92	322	46	89	17	0	15	40	20	46	5	6	2-5	.276	.328	.469	.797	11	.984
1998— Norfolk (Int'l)	C	46	154	18	40	3	0	4	16	9	29	1	5	0-3	.260	.305	.357	.662	4	.990
— GC Mets (GCL)	C	10	28	5	10	5	0	2	9	0	1	2	0	0-1	.357	.367	.750	1.117	2	.957
— St. Lucie (Fla. St.)	C	4	16	0	1	0	0	0	0	0	5	0	0	0-0	.063	.063	.063	.125	0	1.000
1999— Norfolk (Int'l)	C	15	53	10	14	3	0	3	5	4	8	1	4	1-0	.264	.328	.491	.818	1	.991
— New York (N.L.)	C	1	0	0	0	0	0	0	0	0	0	0	0	...	...	...	...	...	0	...
2000— Norfolk (Int'l)	C	111	400	47	104	23	1	16	62	24	65	12	12	11-6	.260	.319	.443	.761	3	.996
— New York (N.L.)	C	4	4	0	0	0	0	0	0	0	2	0	0	0-0	.000	.000	.000	.000	1	1.000
2001— New York (N.L.)	C	65	228	24	56	14	0	6	31	12	34	9	7	0-1	.246	.306	.386	.692	8	.984
— New York (N.L.)	C	32	57	3	17	3	0	0	6	2	16	2	1	0-1	.298	.339	.351	.690	1	.993
2002— New York (N.L.)	C	74	163	19	40	7	0	5	26	5	32	8	4	0-1	.245	.301	.380	.682	6	.983
2003— New York (N.L.)	C-1B	96	268	28	65	9	1	8	39	15	56	5	6	1-2	.243	.293	.373	.666	5	.990
2004— Binghamton (East.)	C	1	3	2	1	0	0	1	1	0	0	1	0	0-0	.333	.500	1.333	1.833	0	1.000
— Norfolk (Int'l)	C	1	4	1	2	1	0	1	1	0	0	0	0	0-0	.500	.500	1.250	1.750	0	1.000
— New York (N.L.)	C	79	157	18	43	10	1	4	21	11	24	5	5	1-0	.274	.335	.427	.762	2	.993
2005— Detroit (A.L.)	C	61	152	18	30	4	0	3	19	11	26	6	6	0-0	.197	.275	.283	.558	3	.989
2006— Detroit (A.L.)	C	56	152	18	43	9	0	5	18	2	33	3	1	0-4	.283	.304	.441	.745	1	.997
American League totals (2 years)		117	304	36	73	13	0	8	37	13	59	9	7	0-4	.240	.289	.362	.651	4	.993
National League totals (6 years)		286	649	68	165	29	2	17	92	33	130	20	16	2-4	.254	.308	.384	.692	14	.989
Major League totals (8 years)		403	953	104	238	42	2	25	129	46	189	29	23	2-8	.250	.302	.377	.679	18	.990

2006 LEFTY-RIGHTY SPLITS

vs.	Avg.	AB	H	2B	3B	HR	RBI	BB	SO	OBP	Slg.	vs.	Avg.	AB	H	2B	3B	HR	RBI	BB	SO	OBP	Slg.
L	.326	43	14	4	0	1	6	2	13	.356	.488	R	.266	109	29	5	0	4	12	0	20	.283	.422

W

WINDSOR, JASON — P

PERSONAL: Born July 16, 1982, in San Bernardino, Calif. ... Throws right, bats right. ... Full name: Jason David Windsor. ... College: Cal State Fullerton.
TRANSACTIONS/CAREER NOTES: Selected by Oakland Athletics organization in third round of 2004 free-agent draft.
CAREER HITTING: 0-for-0 (.000), 0 R, 0 2B, 0 3B, 0 HR, 0 RBI.

Year — Team (League)	W	L	Pct.	ERA	WHIP	G	GS	CG	ShO	Hld.	Sv.-Opp.	IP	H	R	ER	HR	BB-IBB	SO	Avg.
2004— Vancouver (N'west)	0	0	...	0.00	0.80	4	0	0	0	...	1-...	5.0	4	0	0	0	0-0	5	.211
—Kane Co. (Midw.)	1	0	1.000	2.77	1.23	9	0	0	0	...	3-...	13.0	11	4	4	0	5-1	13	.220
2005— Stockton (Calif.)	2	2	.500	3.58	1.08	10	10	0	0	0	0-0	55.1	52	28	22	5	8-0	64	.244
— Midland (Texas)	3	6	.333	5.72	1.62	11	11	0	0	0	0-0	56.2	69	40	36	5	23-0	39	.303
2006— Midland (Texas)	4	1	.800	2.97	1.11	6	6	0	0	0	0-0	33.1	27	12	11	2	10-0	35	.227
— Sacramento (PCL)	13	1	.929	3.81	1.36	20	20	1	0	0	0-0	118.0	128	53	50	7	32-0	123	.272
— Oakland (A.L.)	0	1	.000	6.59	1.90	4	3	0	0	0	0-0	13.2	21	12	10	2	5-0	6	.375
Major League totals (1 year)	0	1	.000	6.59	1.90	4	3	0	0	0	0-0	13.2	21	12	10	2	5-0	6	.375

2006 LEFTY-RIGHTY SPLITS

vs.	Avg.	AB	H	2B	3B	HR	RBI	BB	SO	OBP	Slg.	vs.	Avg.	AB	H	2B	3B	HR	RBI	BB	SO	OBP	Slg.
L	.381	21	8	0	1	1	3	4	3	.462	.619	R	.371	35	13	2	0	1	8	1	3	.378	.514

WINKELSAS, JOE — P

PERSONAL: Born September 14, 1973, in Buffalo. ... 6-3/188. ... Throws right, bats right. ... Full name: Joseph Winkelsas. ... High school: Bishop Timon (Buffalo). ... Junior college: South Carolina-Salkehatchie. ... College: Elon College (N.C.). **TRANSACTIONS/CAREER NOTES:** Signed as a non-drafted free agent by Atlanta Braves organization (June 7, 1996). ... Released by Braves (July 9, 2003). ... Signed by Somerset of the independent Atlantic League (2004). ... Signed by Elmira of the independent Northeast League (2004). ... Contract purchased by Chicago White Sox organization from Elmira (June 21, 2004). ... Released by White Sox (April 20, 2005). ... Signed by Grays of the independent Can-Am League (August 9, 2005). ... Released by Grays (August 15, 2005). ... Signed by Milwaukee Brewers organization (January 2006). ... Announced retirement (July 2006).
CAREER HITTING: 0-for-0 (.000), 0 R, 0 2B, 0 3B, 0 HR, 0 RBI.

Year — Team (League)	W	L	Pct.	ERA	WHIP	G	GS	CG	ShO	Hld.	Sv.-Opp.	IP	H	R	ER	HR	BB-IBB	SO	Avg.
1996— Danville (Appal.)	1	1	.500	7.15	1.32	8	0	0	0	...	2-...	11.1	11	10	9	0	4-0	9	.239
1997— Macon (S. Atl.)	3	2	.600	2.01	0.91	38	0	0	0	...	5-...	62.2	44	17	14	1	13-0	45	.198
— Durham (Carol.)	1	4	.200	7.11	1.84	13	0	0	0	...	1-...	19.0	24	18	15	0	11-1	17	.338
1998— Danville (Carol.)	6	9	.400	2.22	1.30	50	0	0	0	...	22-...	69.0	66	26	17	3	24-8	53	.250
— Greenville (Sou.)	0	0	...	4.15	1.62	4	0	0	0	...	0-...	4.1	3	2	2	0	4-0	3	.188
1999— Greenville (Sou.)	4	4	.500	3.75	1.62	55	0	0	0	...	12-...	62.1	71	32	26	5	30-6	38	.290
— Atlanta (N.L.)	0	0	...	54.00	15.00	1	0	0	0	0	0-...	0.1	4	2	2	0	1-...	0	.500
2000— Richmond (Int'l)	0	1	.000	14.40	3.40	4	0	0	0	...	0-...	5.0	9	8	8	1	5-2	1	.480
2001— Greenville (Sou.)	4	2	.667	3.27	1.15	20	0	0	0	...	3-...	33.0	24	12	12	0	14-2	14	.205
— Myrtle Beach (Carol.)	1	0	1.000	0.00	0.53	4	0	0	0	...	3-...	5.2	2	0	0	0	1-0	5	.105
2002— Greenville (Sou.)	0	0	...	0.00	1.00	2	0	0	0	...	0-...	2.0	1	0	0	0	1-0	5	.143
— Richmond (Int'l)	1	2	.333	2.10	1.32	16	0	0	0	...	2-...	25.2	25	6	6	0	9-3	13	.258
2003— Greenville (Sou.)	1	1	.500	2.93	1.23	23	0	0	0	...	2-...	27.2	26	11	9	2	8-0	14	.257
2004— Somerset (Atl.)	0	0	...	7.36	2.00	7	0	0	0	...	1-...	11.0	18	9	9	0	4-0	4	...
— Win.-Salem (Car.)	0	0	...	6.75	3.00	1	0	0	0	...	0-...	1.1	4	1	1	0	0-0	1	.500
— Elmira (Northeast)	0	1	.000	14.73	2.45	3	0	0	0	...	1-...	3.2	8	6	6	0	0-0	4	.471
— Charlotte (Int'l)	0	0	...	6.30	1.80	5	0	0	0	...	0-...	10.0	15	7	7	1	3-0	5	.333
2005— Charlotte (Int'l)	0	0	...	6.48	1.80	4	0	0	0	...	0-...	8.1	11	6	6	2	4-0	3	.333
2006— Grays (Can-Am.)	0	0	...	10.80	3.00	1	0	0	0	0	0-0	1.0	3	3	2	0	0-0	2	...
— Nashville (PCL)	1	3	.250	5.06	1.22	8	0	0	0	0	1-2	10.2	11	6	6	0	2-0	7	.268
— Huntsville (Sou.)	1	1	.500	1.72	1.09	13	0	0	0	0	4-4	15.2	15	3	3	1	2-0	15	.242
— Milwaukee (N.L.)	0	1	.000	7.71	2.14	7	0	0	0	0	0-0	7.0	9	7	6	1	6-0	4	.310
Major League totals (2 years)	0	1	.000	9.82	2.73	8	0	0	0	0	0-0	7.1	13	9	8	1	7-0	4	.394

2006 LEFTY-RIGHTY SPLITS

vs.	Avg.	AB	H	2B	3B	HR	RBI	BB	SO	OBP	Slg.	vs.	Avg.	AB	H	2B	3B	HR	RBI	BB	SO	OBP	Slg.
L	.300	10	3	1	0	0	5	1	2	.364	.400	R	.316	19	6	0	0	1	9	5	2	.458	.474

WINN, RANDY — OF

PERSONAL: Born June 9, 1974, in Los Angeles. ... 6-2/197. ... Bats both, throws right. ... Full name: Dwight Randolph Winn. ... High school: San Ramon Valley (Danville, Calif.). ... College: Santa Clara. **TRANSACTIONS/CAREER NOTES:** Selected by Florida Marlins organization in third round of 1995 free-agent draft. ... Selected by Tampa Bay Devil Rays in third round (58th pick overall) of expansion draft (November 18, 1997). ... Traded by Devil Rays to Seattle Mariners for SS Antonio Perez (October 28, 2002). ... Traded by Mariners to San Francisco Giants for C Yorvit Torrealba and P Jesse Foppert (July 30, 2005). **STATISTICAL NOTES:** Hit for the cycle (August 15, 2005). ... Career major league grand slams: 5.
2006 GAMES PLAYED BY POSITION (MLB): OF—141.

Year — Team (League)	Pos.	G	AB	R	H	2B	3B	HR	RBI	BB	SO	HBP	GDP	SB-CS	Avg.	OBP	SLG	OPS	E	Avg.
1995— Elmira (N.Y.-Penn)	OF	51	213	38	67	7	4	0	22	15	31	3	1	19-7	.315	.365	.385	.750	4	.954
1996— Kane Co. (Midw.)	OF	130	514	90	139	16	3	0	35	47	115	8	3	30-18	.270	.340	.313	.654	8	.970
1997— Brevard County (FSL)	OF	36	143	26	45	8	2	0	15	16	28	5	3	16-8	.315	.400	.399	.799	0	1.000
— Portland (East.)	OF	96	384	66	112	15	6	4	36	42	92	7	4	35-20	.292	.371	.424	.795	4	.979
1998— Durham (Int'l)	OF	29	123	25	35	5	2	1	16	15	24	0	1	10-4	.285	.362	.382	.744	2	.966
— Tampa Bay (A.L.)	OF-DH	109	338	51	94	9	9	1	17	29	69	1	2	26-12	.278	.337	.367	.704	4	.980
1999— Tampa Bay (A.L.)	OF	79	303	44	81	16	4	2	24	17	63	1	3	9-9	.267	.307	.366	.673	1	.995
— Durham (Int'l)	OF	46	207	38	73	20	3	3	30	16	27	1	2	9-6	.353	.402	.522	.924	4	.960
2000— Durham (Int'l)	OF	79	303	67	100	24	5	7	40	48	53	3	5	18-5	.330	.425	.512	.937	5	.960
— Tampa Bay (A.L.)	OF-DH	51	159	28	40	5	0	1	16	26	25	2	2	6-7	.252	.362	.302	.664	1	.990
2001— Tampa Bay (A.L.)	OF-DH	128	429	54	117	25	6	6	50	38	81	6	10	12-10	.273	.339	.401	.740	5	.981
2002— Tampa Bay (A.L.)	OF-DH	152	607	87	181	39	14	14	75	55	109	4	9	27-8	.298	.360	.461	.821	3	.993
2003— Seattle (A.L.)	OF	157	600	103	177	37	4	11	75	41	108	6	9	23-5	.295	.346	.425	.771	3	.992
2004— Seattle (A.L.)	OF-DH	157	626	84	179	34	6	14	81	53	98	8	16	21-7	.286	.346	.427	.772	4	.991
2005— Seattle (A.L.)	OF-DH	102	386	46	106	25	1	6	37	37	53	4	7	12-6	.275	.342	.391	.733	0	1.000
— San Francisco (N.L.)	OF	58	231	39	83	22	5	14	26	11	48	3	0	7-5	.359	.391	.680	1.071	4	.994
2006— San Francisco (N.L.)	OF	149	573	82	150	34	5	11	56	48	63	7	7	10-8	.262	.324	.396	.721	3	.992
American League totals (8 years)		935	3448	497	975	190	39	55	375	296	606	36	58	136-64	.283	.343	.408	.752	21	.990
National League totals (2 years)		207	804	121	233	56	10	25	82	59	101	8	11	17-13	.290	.343	.478	.820	4	.992
Major League totals (9 years)		1142	4252	618	1208	246	49	80	457	355	707	44	69	153-77	.284	.343	.421	.765	25	.991

W

		G	AB	R	H	2B	3B	HR	RBI	BB	SO	HBP	GDP	SB-CS	Avg.	OBP	SLG	OPS	E	Avg.
ALL-STAR GAME RECORD																				
All-Star Game totals (1 year)		1	2	1	1	0	0	0	0	1	0	0		1-0	.500	.667	1.000	1.667	0	1.000

2006 LEFTY-RIGHTY SPLITS

vs.	Avg.	AB	H	2B	3B	HR	RBI	BB	SO	OBP	Slg.		vs.	Avg.	AB	H	2B	3B	HR	RBI	BB	SO	OBP	Slg.
L	.219	155	34	12	0	4	16	10	14	.280	.374		R	.278	418	116	22	5	7	40	38	49	.341	.404

WISE, DEWAYNE — OF

PERSONAL: Born February 24, 1978, in Columbia, S.C. ... 6-1/180. ... Bats left, throws left. ... Full name: Larry Dewayne Wise. ... High school: Chapin (S.C.). **TRANSACTIONS/CAREER NOTES:** Selected by Cincinnati Reds organization in fifth round of 1997 free-agent draft. ... Selected by Toronto Blue Jays from Reds organization in Rule 5 major league draft (December 13, 1999). ... On disabled list (June 6-September 1, 2000); included rehabilitation assignment to Tennessee. ... Refused minor league assignment and became a free agent (September 30, 2003). ... Signed by Atlanta Braves organization (November 18, 2003). ... On disabled list (June 23-July 15, 2004); included rehabilitation assignments to Rome and Myrtle Beach. ... Claimed on waivers by Detroit Tigers (October 15, 2004). ... Signed as a free agent by Cincinnati Reds organization (October 28, 2005).

2006 GAMES PLAYED BY POSITION (MLB): OF—18.

										BATTING										FIELDING	
Year	Team (League)	Pos.	G	AB	R	H	2B	3B	HR	RBI	BB	SO	HBP	GDP	SB-CS	Avg.	OBP	SLG	OPS	E	Avg.
1997— Billings (Pion.)		OF	62	268	53	84	13	9	7	41	9	47	2	2	18-8	.313	.337	.507	.844	13	.907
1998— Burlington (Midw.)		OF	127	496	61	111	15	9	2	44	41	111	1	4	27-17	.224	.280	.302	.582	7	.972
1999— Rockford (Midwest)		OF	131	502	70	127	20	13	11	81	42	81	7	6	35-13	.253	.312	.410	.722	8	.975
2000— Toronto (A.L.)		OF-DH	28	22	3	3	0	0	0	0	1	5	1	0	1-0	.136	.208	.136	.345	0	1.000
— Tennessee (Sou.)		OF	15	56	10	14	5	2	2	8	7	13	0	2	3-2	.250	.333	.518	.851	4	.882
2001— Tennessee (Sou.)		OF	87	351	44	84	13	6	8	44	21	58	1	6	13-5	.239	.283	.379	.662	5	.976
— Syracuse (Int'l)		OF	3	13	1	3	0	0	0	0	0	8	0	0	0-1	.231	.231	.231	.462	0	1.000
— Dunedin (Fla. St.)		OF	25	103	9	23	3	1	2	16	5	13	0	1	5-0	.223	.252	.330	.582	0	1.000
2002— Tennessee (Sou.)		OF	86	340	59	101	21	4	10	49	29	49	1	4	15-8	.297	.350	.471	.821	4	.981
— Toronto (A.L.)		OF-DH	42	112	14	20	4	1	3	13	4	15	0	0	5-0	.179	.207	.313	.519	0	1.000
2003— Syracuse (Int'l)		OF-DH	80	285	37	62	11	4	10	37	17	72	1	10	11-3	.218	.262	.389	.651	5	.974
2004— Myrtle Beach (Carol.)		OF-DH	4	16	1	4	0	1	0	0	0	5	0	0	1-0	.250	.250	.375	.625	0	1.000
— Rome (S. Atl.)		DH-OF	5	15	4	5	0	0	2	4	1	5	1	0	1-0	.333	.412	.733	1.145	0	1.000
— Richmond (Int'l)		OF	34	118	18	37	4	6	5	16	5	19	0	1	6-1	.228	.272	.444	.716	0	1.000
— Atlanta (N.L.)		OF	77	162	24	37	9	4	6	17	9	28	1	1	6-1	.228	.285	.354	.639	1	.980
2005— Toledo (Int'l)		OF-DH	108	384	42	90	12	5	8	45	23	76	5	8	22-7	.234	.285	.354	.639	2	.982
2006— Louisville (Int'l)			44	154	27	41	10	4	4	21	13	29	4	1	6-2	.266	.335	.461	.796	2	.982
— Chattanooga (Sou.)			13	50	11	21	7	0	3	7	3	9	1	0	1-0	.420	.455	.740	1.195	1	.967
— Cincinnati (N.L.)		OF	31	38	3	7	2	0	0	1	0	6	0	2	0-0	.184	.184	.237	.421	1	.950
American League totals (2 years)			70	134	17	23	4	1	3	13	5	20	1	0	6-0	.172	.207	.284	.491	0	1.000
National League totals (2 years)			108	200	27	44	11	4	6	18	9	34	1	3	6-1	.220	.256	.405	.661	1	.988
Major League totals (4 years)			178	334	44	67	15	5	9	31	14	54	2	3	12-1	.201	.236	.356	.593	1	.995

							DIVISION SERIES RECORD												
Year	Team (League)	Pos.	G	AB	R	H	2B	3B	HR	RBI	BB	SO	HBP	GDP	SB-CS	Avg.	OBP	SLG	OPS	E	Avg.
2004— Atlanta (N.L.)		OF	5	5	1	1	1	0	0	0	0	2	0	0	0-0	.200	.200	.400	.600	0	...

2006 LEFTY-RIGHTY SPLITS

vs.	Avg.	AB	H	2B	3B	HR	RBI	BB	SO	OBP	Slg.		vs.	Avg.	AB	H	2B	3B	HR	RBI	BB	SO	OBP	Slg.
L	.000	4	0	0	0	0	0	0	1	.000	.000		R	.206	34	7	2	0	0	1	0	5	.206	.265

WISE, MATT — P

PERSONAL: Born November 18, 1975, in Montclair, Calif. ... 6-4/200. ... Throws right, bats right. ... Full name: Matthew John Wise. ... Name pronounced: WIZE. ... High school: Bonita (Calif.). ... College: Cal State Fullerton. **TRANSACTIONS/CAREER NOTES:** Selected by Seattle Mariners organization in 54th round of 1993 free-agent draft; did not sign. ... Selected by Anaheim Angels organization in sixth round of 1997 free-agent draft. ... On disabled list (March 18, 2003-entire season). ... Released by Angels (October 6, 2003). ... Signed by Milwaukee Brewers organization (January 20, 2004). ... On disabled list (August 14-September 1, 2005 and August 14, 2006-remainder of season).

CAREER HITTING: 1-for-6 (.167), 0 R, 0 2B, 0 3B, 0 HR, 1 RBI.

Year	Team (League)	W	L	Pct.	ERA	WHIP	G	GS	CG	ShO	Hld.	Sv.-Opp.	IP	H	R	ER	HR	BB-IBB	SO	Avg.
1997— Boise (N'west)		9	1	.900	3.25	1.40	15	15	0	0	...	0-...	83.0	82	37	30	5	34-0	86	.269
1998— Midland (Texas)		9	10	.474	5.42	1.45	27	27	3	1	...	0-...	167.2	195	111	101	23	48-0	131	.289
1999— Erie (East.)		8	5	.615	3.77	1.29	16	16	3	0	...	0-...	98.0	102	48	41	10	24-0	72	.268
2000— Edmonton (PCL)		9	6	.600	3.69	1.19	19	19	2	1	...	0-...	124.1	122	54	51	10	26-0	82	.258
— Anaheim (A.L.)		3	3	.500	5.54	1.42	8	6	0	0	0	0-0	37.1	40	23	23	11	18-1	50	.250
2001— Anaheim (A.L.)		1	4	.200	4.38	1.32	11	9	0	0	0	0-0	49.1	47	27	24	11	18-1	25	.250
— Salt Lake (PCL)		9	9	.500	5.04	1.22	21	21	0	0	0	0-0	123.1	134	79	69	19	17-0	111	.271
2002— Anaheim (A.L.)		0	0	...	3.24	0.96	7	0	0	0	0	0-0	8.1	7	3	3	0	1-0	6	.233
— Salt Lake (PCL)		3	4	.429	5.42	1.50	16	16	0	0	0	0-0	78.0	102	51	47	12	15-0	76	.324
2003— Anaheim (A.L.)		Did not play.																		
2004— Indianapolis (Int'l)		1	0	1.000	1.80	0.80	7	1	0	0	0	0-...	20.0	12	4	4	3	4-0	25	.176
— Milwaukee (N.L.)		1	2	.333	4.44	1.25	30	3	0	0	3	0-0	52.2	51	27	26	3	15-1	30	.252
2005— Milwaukee (N.L.)		4	4	.500	3.36	0.96	49	0	0	0	10	1-3	64.1	37	25	24	6	25-5	62	.160
2006— Milwaukee (N.L.)		5	6	.455	3.86	1.33	40	0	0	0	14	0-4	44.1	45	24	19	6	14-2	27	.268
American League totals (3 years)		4	7	.364	4.74	1.33	26	15	0	0	0	0-0	95.0	94	53	50	18	32-2	76	.258
National League totals (3 years)		10	12	.455	3.85	1.16	119	3	0	0	27	1-7	161.1	133	76	69	15	54-8	119	.221
Major League totals (6 years)		14	19	.424	4.18	1.22	145	18	0	0	27	1-7	256.1	227	129	119	33	86-10	195	.235

2006 LEFTY-RIGHTY SPLITS

vs.	Avg.	AB	H	2B	3B	HR	RBI	BB	SO	OBP	Slg.		vs.	Avg.	AB	H	2B	3B	HR	RBI	BB	SO	OBP	Slg.
L	.206	68	14	6	0	3	10	4	11	.247	.353		R	.310	100	31	8	0	3	10	10	16	.384	.480

WITASICK, JAY — P

PERSONAL: Born August 28, 1972, in Baltimore. ... 6-4/235. ... Throws right, bats right. ... Full name: Gerald Alphonse Witasick. ... Name pronounced: wi-TASS-ik. ... High school: C. Milton Wright (Bel Air, Md.). ... College: Maryland-Baltimore County. **TRANSACTIONS/CAREER NOTES:** Selected by St. Louis Cardinals organization in second round of 1993 free-agent draft. ... Traded by Cardinals with OF Allen Battle and Ps Bret Wagner and Carl Dale to Oakland Athletics for P Todd Stottlemyre (January 9, 1996). ... On disabled list (March 31-June 14, 1997); included rehabilitation assignment to Modesto. ... Traded by A's to Kansas City Royals for a player to be named and cash (March 30, 1999); A's acquired P Scott Chiasson to complete deal (June 10, 1999). ... Traded by Royals to San Diego Padres for P Brian Meadows (July 31, 2000). ... Traded by Padres to New York Yankees for IF D'Angelo Jimenez (June 23, 2001). ... Traded by Yankees to San Francisco Giants for OF John Vander Wal (December 13, 2001). ... On disabled list (July 27-August 15, 2002); included rehabilitation assignment to Fresno. ... Signed as a free agent by Padres (December 24, 2002). ... On disabled list (March 21-June 9, 2003); included rehabilitation assignments to Lake Elsinore and Portland. ... On disabled list (August 16-September 18, 2004); included rehabilitation assignment to Portland. ... Released by Padres (October 7, 2004). ... Signed as a free agent by Baltimore Orioles (January 18, 2005). ... Released by Orioles (April 7, 2005). ... Signed by Colorado Rockies organization (April 8, 2005). ... Traded by Rockies with P Joe Kennedy to Oakland Athletics for OF Eric Byrnes and SS Omar Quintanilla (July 13, 2005). ... Signed as a free agent by Athletics (November 9, 2005). ... On disabled list (April 14-June 5, 2006); included rehabilitation assignments to Stockton and Sacramento. ... On disabled list (June 23-August 9, 2006); included rehabilitation assignments to Stockton and Sacramento.

CAREER HITTING: 3-for-42 (.071), 0 R, 0 2B, 0 3B, 0 HR, 3 RBI.

Year	Team (League)	W	L	Pct.	ERA	WHIP	G	GS	CG	ShO	Hld.	Sv.-Opp.	IP	H	R	ER	HR	BB-IBB	SO	Avg.
1993—	Johnson City (App.)	4	3	.571	4.12	1.24	12	12	0	0	...	0-...	67.2	65	42	31	8	19-0	74	.246
—	Savannah (S. Atl.)	1	0	1.000	4.50	1.50	1	1	0	0	...	0-...	6.0	7	3	3	0	2-0	8	.280
1994—	Madison (Midw.)	10	4	.714	2.32	1.03	18	18	2	0	...	0-...	112.1	74	36	29	5	42-0	141	.189
1995—	St. Pete. (FSL)	7	7	.500	2.74	1.10	18	18	1	1	...	0-...	105.0	80	39	32	4	36-1	109	.208
—	Arkansas (Texas)	2	4	.333	6.88	1.82	7	7	0	0	...	0-...	34.0	46	29	26	4	16-1	26	.317
1996—	Huntsville (Sou.)	0	3	.000	2.30	1.10	25	6	0	0	...	4-...	66.2	47	21	17	3	26-2	63	.195
—	Oakland (A.L.)	1	1	.500	6.23	1.31	12	0	0	0	0	0-1	13.0	12	9	9	5	5-0	12	.245
1997—	Modesto (California)	0	1	.000	4.15	1.21	9	2	0	0	...	1-...	17.1	19	9	8	1	5-0	29	.232
—	Edmonton (PCL)	3	2	.600	4.28	1.46	13	1	0	0	...	0-...	27.1	25	13	13	3	15-3	17	.243
—	Oakland (A.L.)	0	0	...	5.73	1.82	8	0	0	0	1	0-0	11.0	14	7	7	2	6-0	8	.304
1998—	Edmonton (PCL)	11	7	.611	3.87	1.17	27	26	2	1	...	0-...	149.0	126	74	64	19	49-0	155	.226
—	Oakland (A.L.)	1	3	.250	6.33	1.89	7	3	0	0	0	0-0	27.0	36	24	19	9	15-1	29	.317
1999—	Kansas City (A.L.)	9	12	.429	5.57	1.73	32	28	1	1	0	0-0	158.1	191	108	98	23	83-1	102	.304
2000—	Kansas City (A.L.)	3	8	.273	5.94	1.65	22	14	2	0	0	0-0	89.1	109	65	59	15	38-0	67	.301
—	San Diego (N.L.)	3	2	.600	5.64	1.71	11	11	0	0	0	0-0	60.2	69	42	38	9	35-5	54	.291
2001—	San Diego (N.L.)	5	2	.714	1.86	1.19	31	0	0	0	5	1-3	38.2	31	14	8	3	15-3	53	.218
—	New York (A.L.)	3	0	1.000	4.69	1.61	32	0	0	0	5	0-1	40.1	47	27	21	5	18-1	53	.283
2002—	San Francisco (N.L.)	1	0	1.000	2.37	1.16	44	0	0	0	4	0-0	68.1	58	19	18	3	21-3	54	.234
—	Fresno (PCL)	0	0	...	4.50	1.00	2	2	0	0	...	0-...	2.0	1	1	1	0	1-0	2	.143
2003—	Lake Elsinore (Calif.)	0	0	...	5.79	1.30	4	0	0	0	...	0-...	4.2	6	4	3	0	0-0	7	.300
—	Portland (PCL)	0	0	...	3.00	0.80	5	0	0	0	...	1-...	6.0	4	2	2	0	1-0	8	.182
—	San Diego (N.L.)	3	7	.300	4.53	1.47	46	0	0	0	12	2-7	45.2	42	24	23	6	25-4	42	.244
2004—	San Diego (N.L.)	0	1	.000	3.21	1.35	44	0	0	0	2	1-3	61.2	57	28	22	8	26-2	57	.244
2005—	Colo. Springs (PCL)	0	0	...	3.60	1.50	8	0	0	0	2	0-1	10.0	10	5	4	0	5-0	14	.270
—	Colorado (N.L.)	0	4	.000	2.52	1.09	32	0	0	0	11	0-1	35.2	27	11	10	2	12-3	40	.209
—	Oakland (A.L.)	1	1	.500	3.25	1.55	28	0	0	0	6	1-3	27.2	26	15	10	2	17-2	33	.253
2006—	Sacramento (PCL)	1	0	1.000	3.86	1.00	12	0	0	0	3	0-1	14.0	10	7	6	2	4-0	6	.196
—	Stockton (Calif.)	0	0	...	3.60	1.00	3	3	0	0	0	0-0	5.0	4	2	2	0	1-0	6	.222
—	Oakland (A.L.)	0	0	...	6.75	2.03	20	0	0	0	2	0-0	22.2	25	17	17	3	21-2	23	.281
American League totals (8 years)		19	25	.432	5.55	1.70	161	45	3	1	14	1-5	389.1	460	272	240	64	203-7	327	.294
National League totals (6 years)		12	16	.429	3.45	1.35	208	11	0	0	34	4-14	310.2	284	138	119	31	134-20	300	.243
Major League totals (11 years)		31	41	.431	4.62	1.54	369	56	3	1	48	5-19	700.0	744	410	359	95	337-27	627	.272

DIVISION SERIES RECORD

Year	Team (League)	W	L	Pct.	ERA	WHIP	G	GS	CG	ShO	Hld.	Sv.-Opp.	IP	H	R	ER	HR	BB-IBB	SO	Avg.
2001—	New York (A.L.)	0	0	...	13.50	3.00	1	0	0	0	0	0-0	0.2	1	1	1	0	1-0	0	.500
2002—	San Francisco (N.L.)	0	0	...	0.00	0.00	2	0	0	0	0	0-0	2.1	0	0	0	0	0-0	1	.000
Division series totals (2 years)		0	0	...	3.00	0.67	3	0	0	0	0	0-0	3.0	1	1	1	0	1-0	1	.111

CHAMPIONSHIP SERIES RECORD

Year	Team (League)	W	L	Pct.	ERA	WHIP	G	GS	CG	ShO	Hld.	Sv.-Opp.	IP	H	R	ER	HR	BB-IBB	SO	Avg.
2001—	New York (A.L.)	0	0	...	9.00	2.00	1	0	0	0	0	0-0	3.0	6	3	3	1	0-0	2	.375
2002—	San Francisco (N.L.)	0	1	.000	9.00	1.00	1	0	0	0	0	0-0	1.0	1	1	1	1	0-0	0	.250
Champ. series totals (2 years)		0	1	.000	9.00	1.75	2	0	0	0	0	0-0	4.0	7	4	4	2	0-0	2	.350

WORLD SERIES RECORD

Year	Team (League)	W	L	Pct.	ERA	WHIP	G	GS	CG	ShO	Hld.	Sv.-Opp.	IP	H	R	ER	HR	BB-IBB	SO	Avg.
2001—	New York (A.L.)	0	0	...	54.00	7.50	1	0	0	0	0	0-0	1.1	10	9	8	0	0-0	4	.714
2002—	San Francisco (N.L.)	0	0	...	54.00	15.00	2	0	0	0	0	0-0	0.1	3	2	2	0	2-0	1	.750
World series totals (2 years)		0	0	...	54.00	9.00	3	0	0	0	0	0-0	1.2	13	11	10	0	2-0	5	.722

2006 LEFTY-RIGHTY SPLITS

vs.	Avg.	AB	H	2B	3B	HR	RBI	BB	SO	OBP	Slg.	vs.	Avg.	AB	H	2B	3B	HR	RBI	BB	SO	OBP	Slg.
L	.138	29	4	2	0	0	1	12	7	.405	.207	R	.350	60	21	3	0	0	13	9	16	.435	.550

WITT, KEVIN — 1B

PERSONAL: Born January 5, 1976, in High Point, N.C. ... 6-4/220. ... Bats left, throws right. ... Full name: Kevin Joseph Witt. ... High school: Bishop Kenny (Jacksonville, Fla.). **TRANSACTIONS/CAREER NOTES:** Selected by Toronto Blue Jays organization in first round (28th pick overall) of 1994 free-agent draft. ... Signed as a free agent by San Diego Padres organization (December 15, 2000). ... Signed as a free agent by Cincinnati Reds organization (December 21, 2001). ... Signed as a free agent by Detroit Tigers organization (January 29, 2003). ... Signed as a free agent by St. Louis Cardinals organization (November 19, 2003). ... Signed by Yokohama Bay Stars of the Japan Central League (2005). ... Signed as a free agent by Tampa Bay Devil Rays organization (January 11, 2006). ... Released by Devil Rays (October 16, 2006).

2006 GAMES PLAYED BY POSITION (MLB): DH—10, 1B—5.

Year	Team (League)	Pos.	G	AB	R	H	2B	3B	HR	RBI	BB	SO	HBP	GDP	SB-CS	Avg.	OBP	SLG	OPS	E	Avg.
1994—	Medicine Hat (Pio.)	SS	60	243	37	62	10	4	7	36	15	52	1	3	4-1	.255	.300	.416	.716	25	.914
1995—	Hagerstown (SAL)	SS	119	479	58	111	35	1	14	50	28	148	4	5	1-5	.232	.280	.397	.677	48	.919
1996—	Dunedin (Fla. St.)	SS	124	446	63	121	18	6	13	70	39	96	6	9	9-4	.271	.335	.426	.761	48	.917
1997—	Knoxville (Southern)	1B-3B-DH OF-SS	127	501	76	145	27	4	30	91	44	109	3	13	1-0	.289	.349	.539	.888	15	.978
1998—	Syracuse (Int'l)	1B-OF-DH	126	455	71	124	20	3	23	67	53	124	7	5	3-3	.273	.354	.481	.835	4	.996
—	Toronto (A.L.)	1B	5	7	0	1	0	0	0	0	0	3	0	0	0-0	.143	.143	.143	.286	0	1.000
1999—	Syracuse (Int'l)	1B-OF	114	421	72	117	24	3	24	71	64	109	3	11	0-0	.278	.376	.520	.896	9	.994
—	Toronto (A.L.)	DH	15	34	3	7	1	0	1	5	2	9	0	0	0-0	.206	.250	.324	.574	0	...
2000—	Syracuse (Int'l)	1B-OF	135	489	58	121	24	5	26	72	45	132	4	9	1-1	.247	.316	.476	.792	14	.986
2001—	Portland (PCL)	1B-OF-3B	129	456	66	132	28	5	27	87	22	127	3	13	1-1	.289	.322	.550	.873	12	.984
—	San Diego (N.L.)	1B	14	27	5	5	0	0	1	5	2	7	0	0	0-0	.185	.233	.407	.641	0	1.000
2002—	Louisville (Int'l)	1B-OF-3B	131	509	77	134	32	1	24	107	34	140	6	18	0-1	.263	.314	.472	.786	9	.987
2003—	Toledo (Int'l)	1B-3B-DH	39	133	22	42	10	1	8	36	16	36	1	2	0-0	.316	.391	.594	.985	8	.967

Year	Team (League)	Pos.	G	AB	R	H	2B	3B	HR	RBI	BB	SO	HBP	GDP	SB-CS	Avg.	OBP	SLG	OPS	E	Avg.
— Detroit (A.L.)	DH-1B-OF																				
		3B	93	270	25	71	9	0	10	26	15	68	1	5	1-1	.263	.301	.407	.708	0	1.000
2004— Memphis (PCL)			131	477	81	146	30	1	36	107	28	112	8	12	2-0	.306	.353	.600	.953	...	...
2005— Yo. Bay. (Jp. Cn.)	1B-DH		25	64	4	11	1	1	4	7	3	28	0	2	0-...	.172	.206	.406	.612	0	...
2006— Durham (Int'l)			128	485	82	141	29	1	36	99	50	132	4	14	0-0	.291	.360	.577	.937	9	.988
— Tampa Bay (A.L.)	DH-1B		19	61	5	9	2	0	2	5	0	21	0	1	0-0	.148	.148	.279	.426	2	.935
American League totals (4 years)			132	372	33	88	12	0	13	36	17	101	1	6	1-1	.237	.270	.374	.643	2	.993
National League totals (1 year)			14	27	5	5	0	0	2	5	2	7	0	0	0-0	.185	.233	.407	.641	0	1.000
Major League totals (5 years)			146	399	38	93	12	0	15	41	19	108	1	6	1-1	.233	.267	.376	.643	2	.995

2006 LEFTY-RIGHTY SPLITS

vs.	Avg.	AB	H	2B	3B	HR	RBI	BB	SO	OBP	Slg.	vs.	Avg.	AB	H	2B	3B	HR	RBI	BB	SO	OBP	Slg.
L	.167	6	1	0	0	0	0	0	1	.167	.167	R	.145	55	8	2	0	2	5	0	20	.145	.291

WOLF, RANDY   P

PERSONAL: Born August 22, 1976, in Canoga Park, Calif. ... 6-0/200. ... Throws left, bats left. ... Full name: Randall Christopher Wolf. ... High school: El Camino Real (Woodland Hills, Calif.). ... College: Pepperdine. **TRANSACTIONS/CAREER NOTES:** Selected by Los Angeles Dodgers organization in 25th round of 1994 free-agent draft; did not sign. ... Selected by Philadelphia Phillies organization in second round of 1997 free-agent draft. ... On disabled list (August 2-September 1, 2001); included rehabilitation assignments to Scranton/Wilkes-Barre and Reading. ... On disabled list (March 25-April 12, 2002); included rehabilitation assignment to Clearwater. ... On disabled list (June 3-26 and August 29, 2004-remainder of season); included rehabilitation assignment to Reading. ... On disabled list (June 12, 2005-remainder of season). ... On disabled list (March 30-July 30, 2006); included rehabilitation assignments to Clearwater, Reading and Lakewater. **HONORS:** Named lefthanded pitcher on THE SPORTING NEWS N.L. All-Star team (2003). **MISCELLANEOUS NOTES:** Struck out in only appearance as pinch hitter (2002). ... Grounded out in only appearance as pinch hitter and scored a run in only appearance as pinch runner (2004). ... Flied out in only appearance as pinch hitter and appeared in one game as pinch runner (2005). ... Struck out in only appearance as pinch hitter (2006).

CAREER HITTING: 68-for-353 (.193), 34 R, 19 2B, 0 3B, 4 HR, 34 RBI.

Year	Team (League)	W	L	Pct.	ERA	WHIP	G	GS	CG	ShO	Hld.	Sv.-Opp.	IP	H	R	ER	HR	BB-IBB	SO	Avg.
1997— Batavia (NY-Penn)	4	0	1.000	1.58	0.93	7	7	0	0	...	0-...	40.0	29	8	7	1	8-0	53	.204
1998— Reading (East.)	2	0	1.000	1.44	0.76	4	4	0	0	...	0-...	25.0	15	4	4	0	4-0	33	.172
— Scran./W.B. (I.L.)	9	7	.563	4.62	1.45	24	23	1	0	...	0-...	148.0	167	88	76	16	48-4	118	.285
1999— Scran./W.B. (I.L.)	4	5	.444	3.61	1.32	12	12	0	0	...	0-...	77.1	73	36	31	8	29-1	72	.247
— Philadelphia (N.L.)	6	9	.400	5.55	1.59	22	21	0	0	0	0-0	121.2	126	78	75	20	67-0	116	.266
2000— Philadelphia (N.L.)	11	9	.550	4.36	1.42	32	32	1	0	0	0-0	206.1	210	107	100	25	83-2	160	.269
2001— Philadelphia (N.L.)	10	11	.476	3.70	1.23	28	25	4	2	0	0-0	163.0	150	74	67	15	51-4	152	.248
— Scran./W.B. (I.L.)	0	0	1.000	5.00	1.67	2	2	0	0	...	0-...	9.0	10	6	5	2	5-0	7	.286
— Reading (East.)	0	0	...	4.50	1.17	1	1	0	0	...	0-...	6.0	5	3	3	0	2-0	7	.208
2002— Clearwater (FSL)	0	0	...	0.00	0.40	1	1	0	0	...	0-...	5.0	1	0	0	0	1-0	8	.071
— Philadelphia (N.L.)	11	9	.550	3.20	1.12	31	31	3	2	0	0-0	210.2	172	77	75	23	63-5	172	.223
2003— Philadelphia (N.L.)	16	10	.615	4.23	1.27	33	33	2	2	0	0-0	200.0	176	101	94	27	78-4	177	.233
2004— Reading (East.)	0	0	...	2.25	1.25	1	1	0	0	...	0-...	4.0	5	1	1	0	0-0	4	.271
— Philadelphia (N.L.)	5	8	.385	4.28	1.32	23	23	1	1	0	0-0	136.2	145	73	65	20	36-4	89	.277
2005— Philadelphia (N.L.)	6	4	.600	4.39	1.41	13	13	0	0	0	0-0	80.0	87	40	39	14	26-2	61	.282
2006— Clearwater (FSL)	0	0	...	0.00	1.76	2	2	0	0	0	0-0	5.2	6	1	0	0	4-0	4	.300
— Reading (East.)	1	1	.500	6.75	1.83	3	3	0	0	0	0-0	12.0	15	10	9	0	7-0	11	.306
— Lakewood (S. Atl.)	0	0	...	1.13	0.63	2	2	0	0	0	0-0	8.0	2	1	1	0	3-0	7	.087
— Philadelphia (N.L.)	4	0	1.000	5.56	1.69	12	12	0	0	0	0-0	56.2	63	37	35	13	33-2	44	.285
Major League totals (8 years)	69	60	.535	4.21	1.33	194	190	11	7	0	0-0	1175.0	1129	587	550	157	437-23	971	.254

ALL-STAR GAME RECORD

	W	L	Pct.	ERA	WHIP	G	GS	CG	ShO	Hld.	Sv.-Opp.	IP	H	R	ER	HR	BB-IBB	SO	Avg.
All-Star Game totals (1 year)	0	0	...	9.00	2.00	1	0	0	0	0	0-0	1.0	1	1	1	0	1-0	2	.250

2006 LEFTY-RIGHTY SPLITS

vs.	Avg.	AB	H	2B	3B	HR	RBI	BB	SO	OBP	Slg.	vs.	Avg.	AB	H	2B	3B	HR	RBI	BB	SO	OBP	Slg.
L	.086	35	3	0	0	1	5	4	12	.175	.171	R	.323	186	60	12	2	12	27	29	32	.416	.602

WOMACK, TONY   2B

PERSONAL: Born September 25, 1969, in Danville, Va. ... 5-9/170. ... Bats left, throws right. ... Full name: Anthony Darrell Womack. ... Name pronounced: WO-mack. ... High school: Gretna (Va.). ... College: Guilford (N.C.). **TRANSACTIONS/CAREER NOTES:** Selected by Pittsburgh Pirates organization in seventh round of 1991 free-agent draft. ... Traded by Pirates to Arizona Diamondbacks for OF Paul Weichard and a player to be named (February 26, 1999); Pirates acquired P Jason Boyd to complete deal (August 25, 1999). ... On disabled list (March 26-April 12, 1999); included rehabilitation assignment to Tucson. ... On disabled list (July 22-August 6, 2001); included rehabilitation assignment to Tucson. ... On disabled list (June 29-July 18, 2003); included rehabilitation assignment to El Paso. ... Traded by Diamondbacks to Colorado Rockies for P Mike Watson (July 18, 2003). ... Traded by Rockies to Chicago Cubs for P Enmanuel Ramires (August 19, 2003). ... Signed by Boston Red Sox organization (January 24, 2004). ... Traded by Red Sox to St. Louis Cardinals for P Matt Duff (March 21, 2004). ... Signed as a free agent by New York Yankees (December 20, 2004). ... Traded by Yankees to Cincinnati Reds for IF Kevin Howard and OF Benjamin Himes (December 8, 2005). ... Released by Reds (May 2, 2006). ... Signed by Chicago Cubs organization (May 18, 2006). ... Released by Cubs (July 6, 2006). **STATISTICAL NOTES:** Career major league grand slams: 2.

2006 GAMES PLAYED BY POSITION (MLB): 2B—21.

Year	Team (League)	Pos.	G	AB	R	H	2B	3B	HR	RBI	BB	SO	HBP	GDP	SB-CS	Avg.	OBP	SLG	OPS	E	Avg.
1991— Welland (NYP)	2B-SS	45	166	30	46	3	1	0	8	17	39	0	1	26-5	.277	.344	.313	.658	16	.921
1992— Augusta (S. Atl.)	2B-SS	102	380	62	93	8	3	0	18	41	59	5	2	50-25	.245	.325	.282	.606	40	.923
1993— Salem (Carol.)	SS	72	304	41	91	11	3	2	18	13	34	2	2	28-14	.299	.331	.375	.706	28	.927
— Carolina (Southern)	SS	60	247	41	75	7	2	0	23	17	34	1	3	21-6	.304	.346	.348	.694	11	.961
— Pittsburgh (N.L.)	SS	15	24	5	2	0	0	0	0	3	3	0	0	2-0	.083	.185	.083	.269	1	.971
1994— Buffalo (A.A.)	SS-2B	106	421	40	93	9	2	0	18	19	76	0	2	41-10	.221	.253	.252	.505	22	.957
— Pittsburgh (N.L.)	2B-SS	5	12	4	4	0	0	0	1	1	4	0	0	0-0	.333	.429	.333	.762	2	.818
1995— Calgary (PCL)	2B-SS	30	107	12	30	3	2	0	6	12	11	0	1	7-5	.280	.353	.327	.680	5	.963
— Carolina (Southern)	SS-2B	82	332	52	85	9	4	1	19	19	36	2	1	27-10	.256	.300	.316	.617	18	.953
1996— Calgary (PCL)	SS-2B-OF																			
		DH	131	506	75	151	19	11	3	47	31	79	3	3	37-12	.298	.339	.385	.725	24	.961
— Pittsburgh (N.L.)	OF-2B	17	30	11	10	3	1	0	7	6	1	1	0	2-0	.333	.459	.500	.959	2	.905
1997— Pittsburgh (N.L.)	2B-SS	155	641	85	178	26	9	6	50	43	109	3	6	* 60-7	.278	.326	.374	.700	20	.975
1998— Pittsburgh (N.L.)	2B-OF-SS	159	655	85	185	26	7	3	45	38	94	0	4	* 58-6	.282	.319	.357	.677	17	.978
1999— Tucson (PCL)	OF	4	16	1	4	1	0	1	2	3	0	0	1	0-1	.250	.333	.500	.833	0	1.000
— Arizona (N.L.)	OF-2B-SS	144	614	111	170	25	10	4	41	52	68	2	4	* 72-13	.277	.332	.370	.702	6	.987

Year Team (League)	Pos.	G	AB	R	H	2B	3B	HR	RBI	BB	SO	HBP	GDP	SB-CS	Avg.	OBP	SLG	OPS	E	Avg.
							BATTING												FIELDING	
2000—Arizona (N.L.)	SS-OF	146	617	95	167	21	*14	7	57	30	74	5	6	45-11	.271	.307	.384	.692	18	.970
2001—Arizona (N.L.)	SS-OF	125	481	66	128	19	5	3	30	23	54	6	4	28-7	.266	.307	.345	.652	22	.955
—Tucson (PCL)	SS	4	13	1	5	0	1	0	2	0	1	0	0	0-1	.385	.385	.538	.923	2	.846
2002—Arizona (N.L.)	SS-OF	153	590	90	160	23	5	5	57	46	80	4	9	29-12	.271	.325	.353	.678	20	.964
2003—Arizona (N.L.)	SS	61	219	30	52	10	3	2	15	8	27	2	6	8-3	.237	.270	.338	.607	7	.966
—El Paso (Texas)	SS	4	17	3	5	0	0	0	2	2	2	0	0	3-0	.294	.368	.294	.663	1	.923
—Colorado (N.L.)	SS-2B-OF	21	79	9	15	2	0	0	5	0	9	1	1	3-1	.190	.200	.215	.415	2	.974
—Chicago (N.L.)	2B-SS	21	51	4	12	2	1	0	2	1	11	0	0	2-1	.235	.250	.314	.564	0	1.000
2004—St. Louis (N.L.)	SS	145	553	91	170	22	3	5	38	36	60	3	6	26-5	.307	.350	.385	.735	15	.976
2005—New York (A.L.)	OF-2B-DH	108	329	46	82	8	1	0	15	12	49	1	7	27-5	.249	.276	.280	.556	3	.988
2006—Cincinnati (N.L.)	2B	9	18	1	4	2	0	0	3	4	3	0	0	0-0	.222	.364	.333	.697	1	1.000
—Iowa (PCL)		5	15	2	7	1	0	0	1	3	3	0	0	3-1	.467	.556	.533	1.089	1	.955
—Chicago (N.L.)	2B	19	50	6	14	1	0	1	2	4	4	0	0	1-1	.280	.333	.360	.693	0	1.000
American League totals (1 year)		108	329	46	82	8	1	0	15	12	49	1	7	27-5	.249	.276	.280	.556	3	.988
National League totals (12 years)		1195	4634	693	1271	182	58	36	353	296	600	27	46	336-69	.274	.320	.362	.681	131	.972
Major League totals (13 years)		1303	4963	739	1353	190	59	36	368	308	649	28	53	363-74	.273	.317	.356	.673	134	.973

DIVISION SERIES RECORD

Year Team (League)	Pos.	G	AB	R	H	2B	3B	HR	RBI	BB	SO	HBP	GDP	SB-CS	Avg.	OBP	SLG	OPS	E	Avg.
1999—Arizona (N.L.)	OF-SS	4	18	2	2	0	1	0	0	0	6	0	0	0-0	.111	.111	.222	.333	2	.833
2001—Arizona (N.L.)	SS	5	17	1	5	1	0	0	1	3	2	0	0	0-1	.294	.400	.353	.753	2	.905
2002—Arizona (N.L.)	SS	3	13	1	2	0	0	0	0	1	1	0	0	0-0	.154	.214	.154	.368	1	.941
2004—St. Louis (N.L.)	2B	4	19	2	3	0	1	0	1	0	2	0	0	1-0	.158	.158	.263	.421	0	1.000
2005—New York (A.L.)		2	0	0	0	0	0	0	0	0	0	0	0	0-0	...	...	...	...	0	...
Division series totals (5 years)		18	67	6	12	1	2	0	2	4	11	0	0	1-1	.179	.225	.254	.479	5	.919

CHAMPIONSHIP SERIES RECORD

Year Team (League)	Pos.	G	AB	R	H	2B	3B	HR	RBI	BB	SO	HBP	GDP	SB-CS	Avg.	OBP	SLG	OPS	E	Avg.
2001—Arizona (N.L.)	SS	4	20	4	4	1	0	0	0	0	2	0	0	0-1	.200	.200	.250	.450	0	1.000
2004—St. Louis (N.L.)	2B	7	26	5	7	1	0	0	1	1	3	0	0	2-0	.269	.296	.308	.604	0	1.000
Champ. series totals (2 years)		11	46	9	11	2	0	0	1	1	5	0	0	2-1	.239	.255	.283	.538	0	1.000

WORLD SERIES RECORD

Year Team (League)	Pos.	G	AB	R	H	2B	3B	HR	RBI	BB	SO	HBP	GDP	SB-CS	Avg.	OBP	SLG	OPS	E	Avg.
2001—Arizona (N.L.)	SS	7	32	3	8	3	0	0	3	1	7	1	1	1-1	.250	.294	.344	.638	1	.968
2004—St. Louis (N.L.)	2B	4	11	1	2	0	0	0	0	1	2	0	0	0-0	.182	.250	.182	.432	0	1.000
World series totals (2 years)		11	43	4	10	3	0	0	3	2	9	1	1	1-1	.233	.283	.302	.585	1	.978

ALL-STAR GAME RECORD

Year Team (League)	Pos.	G	AB	R	H	2B	3B	HR	RBI	BB	SO	HBP	GDP	SB-CS	Avg.	OBP	SLG	OPS	E	Avg.
All-Star Game totals (1 year)		1	1	0	0	0	0	0	0	0	0	0	0	0-0	.000	.000	.000	.000	0	1.000

2006 LEFTY-RIGHTY SPLITS

vs.	Avg.	AB	H	2B	3B	HR	RBI	BB	SO	OBP	Slg.
L	.250	16	4	0	0	0	0	1	4	.294	.250
R	.269	52	14	3	0	1	5	7	3	.356	.385

WOOD, JASON — IF

PERSONAL: Born December 16, 1969, in San Bernadino, Calif. ... 6-1/200. ... Bats right, throws right. ... Full name: Jason William Wood. ... High school: McLane (Fresno, Calif.). ... Junior college: Fresno City College. ... College: Fresno State. **TRANSACTIONS/CAREER NOTES:** Selected by Oakland Athletics organzation in 11th round of 1991 free-agent draft. ... Traded by A's to Detroit Tigers (July 18, 1998), completing deal in which Tigers traded IF Bip Roberts to A's for a player to be named (June 23, 1998). ... On disabled list (March 29-May 11, 1999); included rehabilitation assignment to Lakeland. ... Signed as a free agent by Pittsburgh Pirates organization (December 7, 1999). ... Signed as a free agent by Florida Marlins organization (March 8, 2002).

2006 GAMES PLAYED BY POSITION (MLB): 1B—5, 2B—1.

Year Team (League)	Pos.	G	AB	R	H	2B	3B	HR	RBI	BB	SO	HBP	GDP	SB-CS	Avg.	OBP	SLG	OPS	E	Avg.
1991—S. Oregon (N'west)	2B-SS	44	142	30	44	3	4	3	23	28	30	...	...	5-...	.310		.451		14	.928
1992—Modesto (California)	SS	128	454	66	105	28	3	6	49	40	106	...	...	5-...	.231		.346		37	.938
1993—Huntsville (Sou.)	SS	103	370	44	85	21	2	3	36	33	97	...	...	2-...	.230		.322		32	.924
1994—Huntsville (Sou.)	SS	134	468	54	128	29	2	6	84	46	83	...	...	3-...	.274		.382		25	.957
1995—Edmonton (PCL)	2B-3B-SS	127	421	49	99	20	5	2	50	29	72	...	...	1-...	.235		.321		26	.951
1996—Huntsville (Sou.)	1B-3B-SS	133	491	77	128	21	1	20	84	72	87	...	...	2-...	.261		.430		20	.969
—Edmonton (PCL)	1B	3	12	0	0	0	0	0	0	5	6	...	...	0-...	.000		.000		1	.976
1997—Edmonton (PCL)	3B-SS	130	505	83	162	35	7	19	87	45	74	...	...	2-...	.321		.531		17	.956
1998—Oakland (A.L.)	SS-3B	3	1	1	0	0	0	0	0	0	1	...	...	0-0	.000		.000		0	1.000
—Edmonton (PCL)	2B-3B-SS / SS	80	307	52	86	20	0	18	73	37	71	...	...	1-1	.280		.521		10	.964
—Detroit (A.L.)	1B-DH-SS	10	23	5	8	2	0	1	1	3	4	...	...	0-1	.348	.423	.565	.988	0	1.000
—Toledo (Int'l)	1B-3B-SS	46	169	24	47	9	0	7	29	16	30	...	...	0-0	.278		.456		5	.971
1999—Lakeland (Fla. St.)	SS-1B-2B / 3B	5	17	0	4	0	0	0	1	4	2	...	...	0-1	.235		.235		2	.917
—Detroit (A.L.)	3B-SS-1B / 2B-DH	27	44	5	7	1	0	1	8	2	13	0	...	0-0	.159	.196	.250	.446	4	.932
—Toledo (Int'l)	2B-1B-SS / 2B-C-OF-DH	48	185	34	53	11	0	6	24	22	43	...	...	0-2	.286		.443		4	.979
2000—Nashville (PCL)	3B-SS-2B / 1B	88	316	40	75	18	0	7	45	28	84	...	...	2-2	.237		.361		4	.978
2001—Nashville (PCL)	3B-SS-2B / 1B	113	379	46	92	19	1	8	38	27	73	...	...	0-0	.243		.361		23	.940
2005—Albuquerque (PCL)	3B-1B-2B / DH-SS	129	452	75	136	18	3	21	77	48	81	8	24	5-3	.301	.374	.493	.867	9	.984
2006—Albuquerque (PCL)		123	441	64	127	23	3	11	77	42	92	2	22	1-1	.288	.347	.429	.775	13	.975
—Florida (N.L.)	1B-2B	12	13	3	6	2	0	0	1	1	2	0	0	1-0	.462	.500	.615	1.115	0	1.000
American League totals (2 years)		40	68	11	15	3	0	2	9	5	18	0	...	0-1	.221	.274	.353	.627	4	.961
National League totals (1 year)		12	13	3	6	2	0	0	1	1	2	0	0	1-0	.462	.500	.615	1.115	0	1.000
Major League totals (3 years)		52	81	14	21	5	0	2	10	6	20	0	0	1-1	.259	.310	.395	.705	4	.967

2006 LEFTY-RIGHTY SPLITS

vs.	Avg.	AB	H	2B	3B	HR	RBI	BB	SO	OBP	Slg.
L	.500	4	2	0	0	0	0	1	2	.500	.500
R	.444	9	4	2	0	0	0	1	0	.500	.667

W

WOOD, KERRY   P

PERSONAL: Born June 16, 1977, in Irving, Texas. ... 6-5/225. ... Throws right, bats right. ... Full name: Kerry Lee Wood. ... High school: Grand Prairie (Texas). **TRANSACTIONS/CAREER NOTES:** Selected by Chicago Cubs organization in first round (fourth pick overall) of 1995 free-agent draft. ... On disabled list (March 31, 1999-entire season). ... On disabled list (March 25-May 2 and July 30-August 22, 2000); included rehabilitation assignments to Daytona and Iowa. ... On suspended list (September 8-11, 2000). ... On disabled list (August 4-September 7, 2001). ... On suspended list (May 14-20, 2004). ... On disabled list (May 20-July 11, 2004); included rehabilitation assignment to Iowa. ... On suspended list (August 16-22, 2004). ... On disabled list (May 3-June 29, July 21-August 5 and August 30, 2005-remainder of season); included rehabilitation assignments to Iowa and Peoria. ... On disabled list (March 27-May 18, 2006); included rehabilitation assignments to Peoria and Iowa. ... On disabled list (June 9, 2006-remainder of season). **RECORDS:** Shares major league record for most strikeouts, 9-inning game (20, May 6, 1998). **HONORS:** Named N.L. Rookie Pitcher of the Year by THE SPORTING NEWS (1998). ... Named N.L. Rookie of the Year by Baseball Writers' Association of America (1998). **MISCELLANEOUS NOTES:** Struck out and had sacrifice hit in two appearances as pinch hitter (2000). ... Appeared in one game as pinch runner (2001).

CAREER HITTING: 59-for-344 (.172), 23 R, 6 2B, 0 3B, 7 HR, 32 RBI.

Year Team (League)	W	L	Pct.	ERA	WHIP	G	GS	CG	ShO	Hld.	Sv.-Opp.	IP	H	R	ER	HR	BB-IBB	SO	Avg.
1995—GC Cubs (GCL)	0	0	...	0.00	0.33	1	1	0	0	...	0-...	3.0	0	0	0	0	1-0	2	.000
—Will. (NYP)	0	0	...	10.38	2.31	2	2	0	0	...	0-...	4.1	5	8	5	0	5-0	5	.278
1996—Daytona (Fla. St.)	10	2	.833	2.91	1.24	22	22	0	0	...	0-...	114.1	72	51	37	6	70-0	136	.179
1997—Orlando (South.)	6	7	.462	4.50	1.46	19	19	0	0	...	0-...	94.0	58	49	47	2	79-2	106	.181
—Iowa (Am. Assoc.)	4	2	.667	4.68	1.51	10	10	0	0	...	0-...	57.2	35	35	30	2	52-0	80	.181
1998—Iowa (PCL)	1	0	1.000	0.00	0.60	1	1	0	0	...	0-...	5.0	1	0	0	0	0-0	6	.067
—Chicago (N.L.)	13	6	.684	3.40	1.21	26	26	1	1	0	0-0	166.2	117	69	63	14	85-1	233	* .196
1999—Chicago (N.L.)			Did not play.																
2000—Daytona (Fla. St.)	2	0	1.000	1.50	0.67	2	2	0	0	...	0-...	12.0	3	2	2	0	5-0	17	.081
—Iowa (PCL)	0	0	...	2.57	1.14	1	1	0	0	...	0-...	7.0	4	2	2	1	4-0	7	.174
—Chicago (N.L.)	8	7	.533	4.80	1.45	23	23	1	0	0	0-0	137.0	112	77	73	17	87-0	132	.226
2001—Chicago (N.L.)	12	6	.667	3.36	1.26	28	28	1	1	0	0-0	174.1	127	70	65	16	92-3	217	* .202
2002—Chicago (N.L.)	12	11	.522	3.66	1.24	33	33	4	1	0	0-0	213.2	169	92	87	22	97-5	217	.221
2003—Chicago (N.L.)	14	11	.560	3.20	1.19	32	32	4	2	0	0-0	211.0	152	97	75	24	100-2	* 266	.203
2004—Iowa (PCL)	1	0	1.000	0.00	0.60	1	1	0	0	...	0-...	5.0	2	0	0	0	1-0	4	.111
—Chicago (N.L.)	8	9	.471	3.72	1.27	22	22	0	0	0	0-0	140.1	127	62	58	16	51-0	144	.244
2005—Iowa (PCL)	0	0	...	2.84	1.34	3	3	0	0	0	0-...	12.2	11	4	4	1	6-0	18	.239
—Peoria (Midw.)	0	0	...	0.00	0.43	2	0	0	0	0	0-...	2.1	1	0	0	0	0-0	5	.125
—Chicago (N.L.)	3	4	.429	4.23	1.18	21	10	0	0	4	0-0	66.0	52	32	31	14	26-0	77	.215
2006—Peoria (Midw.)	0	0	...	0.00	0.40	1	1	0	0	0	0-...	5.0	1	0	0	0	1-0	12	.063
—Iowa (PCL)	0	1	.000	1.80	1.40	1	1	0	0	0	0-...	5.0	5	1	1	0	2-0	3	.250
—Chicago (N.L.)	1	2	.333	4.12	1.37	4	4	0	0	0	0-0	19.2	19	13	9	5	8-0	13	.253
Major League totals (8 years)	**71**	**56**	**.559**	**3.68**	**1.26**	**189**	**178**	**11**	**5**	**4**	**0-0**	**1128.2**	**875**	**492**	**461**	**128**	**546-11**	**1299**	**.215**

DIVISION SERIES RECORD

Year Team (League)	W	L	Pct.	ERA	WHIP	G	GS	CG	ShO	Hld.	Sv.-Opp.	IP	H	R	ER	HR	BB-IBB	SO	Avg.
1998—Chicago (N.L.)	0	1	.000	1.80	1.40	1	1	0	0	0	0-0	5.0	3	1	1	0	4-1	5	.167
2003—Chicago (N.L.)	2	0	1.000	1.76	0.91	2	2	0	0	0	0-0	15.1	7	3	3	1	7-0	18	.132
Division series totals (2 years)	**2**	**1**	**.667**	**1.77**	**1.03**	**3**	**3**	**0**	**0**	**0**	**0-0**	**20.1**	**10**	**4**	**4**	**1**	**11-1**	**23**	**.141**

CHAMPIONSHIP SERIES RECORD

Year Team (League)	W	L	Pct.	ERA	WHIP	G	GS	CG	ShO	Hld.	Sv.-Opp.	IP	H	R	ER	HR	BB-IBB	SO	Avg.
2003—Chicago (N.L.)	0	1	.000	7.30	1.70	2	2	0	0	0	0-0	12.1	14	10	10	1	7-0	13	.280

ALL-STAR GAME RECORD

Year Team (League)	W	L	Pct.	ERA	WHIP	G	GS	CG	ShO	Hld.	Sv.-Opp.	IP	H	R	ER	HR	BB-IBB	SO	Avg.
All-Star Game totals (1 year)	**0**	**0**	**...**	**0.00**	**1.00**	**1**	**0**	**0**	**0**	**0**	**0-0**	**1.0**	**1**	**0**	**0**	**0**	**0-0**	**2**	**.250**

2006 LEFTY-RIGHTY SPLITS

vs.	Avg.	AB	H	2B	3B	HR	RBI	BB	SO	OBP	Slg.	vs.	Avg.	AB	H	2B	3B	HR	RBI	BB	SO	OBP	Slg.
L	.206	34	7	0	0	1	2	1	7	.229	.294	R	.293	41	12	3	1	4	10	7	6	.392	.707

WOOD, MIKE   P

PERSONAL: Born April 26, 1980, in West Palm Beach, Fla. ... 6-3/210. ... Throws right, bats right. ... Full name: Michael Burton Wood. ... High school: Forest Hill Community (West Palm Beach, Fla.). ... College: North Florida. **TRANSACTIONS/CAREER NOTES:** Selected by Oakland Athletics organization in 10th round of 2001 free-agent draft. ... Traded by Oakland Athletics with 3B Mark Teahen to Kansas City Royals as part of three-team deal in which Royals acquired C John Buck and cash from Houston Astros, Athletics acquired P Octavio Dotel and cash from Astros and Astros acquired OF Carlos Beltran from Royals (June 24, 2004). ... On disabled list (July 3-September 5, 2006); included rehabilitation assignments to Wichita and Omaha. ... Claimed on waivers by Texas Rangers (October 11, 2006).

CAREER HITTING: 0-for-5 (.000), 0 R, 0 2B, 0 3B, 0 HR, 0 RBI.

Year Team (League)	W	L	Pct.	ERA	WHIP	G	GS	CG	ShO	Hld.	Sv.-Opp.	IP	H	R	ER	HR	BB-IBB	SO	Avg.
2001—Vancouver (N'west)	2	0	1.000	1.25	0.97	5	2	0	0	...	0-...	21.2	17	4	3	0	4-0	24	.210
—Modesto (California)	4	3	.571	3.09	0.96	10	9	0	0	...	0-...	58.1	46	22	20	6	10-3	52	.211
2002—Modesto (California)	3	3	.500	3.48	1.14	7	7	0	0	...	0-...	41.1	41	17	16	4	6-0	50	.265
—Midland (Texas)	11	3	.786	3.15	1.25	17	17	0	0	...	0-...	105.2	103	41	37	8	29-0	63	.259
2003—Sacramento (PCL)	9	3	.750	3.05	1.20	16	16	0	0	...	0-...	91.1	87	34	31	5	23-1	59	.257
—Oakland (A.L.)	2	1	.667	10.54	2.27	7	1	0	0	0	0-0	13.2	24	16	16	1	7-2	15	.387
2004—Sacramento (PCL)	11	3	.786	2.80	1.19	15	15	1	0	...	0-...	90.0	83	42	28	8	24-1	66	.241
—Kansas City (A.L.)	3	8	.273	5.94	1.40	17	17	0	0	0	0-0	100.0	112	67	66	16	28-3	54	.286
2005—Omaha (PCL)	0	0	...	2.00	1.33	2	2	0	0	0	0-...	9.0	10	2	2	0	2-0	8	.286
—Kansas City (A.L.)	5	8	.385	4.46	1.57	47	10	0	0	7	2-2	115.0	129	66	57	18	52-5	60	.287
2006—Omaha (PCL)	2	0	.000	6.32	1.60	4	4	0	0	0	0-...	15.2	22	12	11	3	3-0	5	.349
—Wichita (Texas)	0	0	...	6.75	1.25	2	2	0	0	0	0-...	4.0	5	4	3	0	0-0	3	.294
—Kansas City (A.L.)	3	3	.500	5.71	1.69	23	7	0	0	1	0-0	64.2	86	51	41	10	23-3	29	.314
Major League totals (4 years)	**13**	**20**	**.394**	**5.52**	**1.57**	**94**	**35**	**0**	**0**	**8**	**2-2**	**293.1**	**351**	**201**	**180**	**45**	**110-13**	**158**	**.298**

2006 LEFTY-RIGHTY SPLITS

vs.	Avg.	AB	H	2B	3B	HR	RBI	BB	SO	OBP	Slg.	vs.	Avg.	AB	H	2B	3B	HR	RBI	BB	SO	OBP	Slg.
L	.320	122	39	7	0	3	21	11	13	.382	.451	R	.309	152	47	9	1	7	27	12	16	.376	.520

WOODS, JAKE   P

PERSONAL: Born September 3, 1981, in Fresno, Calif. ... 6-1/190. ... Throws left, bats left. ... Full name: Jacob Thomas Woods. ... College: Bakersfield (CA). **TRANSACTIONS/CAREER NOTES:** Selected by Anaheim Angels organization in third round of 2001 free-agent draft. ... Angels franchise renamed Los Angeles Angels of Anaheim for 2005 season. ... Claimed on waivers by Mariners (December 20, 2005).

CAREER HITTING: 0-for-0 (.000), 0 R, 0 2B, 0 3B, 0 HR, 0 RBI.

W

Year Team (League)	W	L	Pct.	ERA	WHIP	G	GS	CG	ShO	Hld.	Sv.-Opp.	IP	H	R	ER	HR	BB-IBB	SO	Avg.
2001— Provo (Pion.)	4	3	.571	5.29	1.53	15	14	1	1	...	0-...	64.2	70	41	38	6	29-0	84	.275
2002— Cedar Rap. (Midw.)	10	5	.667	3.05	1.19	27	27	1	0	...	0-...	153.1	128	66	52	12	54-0	121	.228
2003— Rancho Cuca. (Calif.)	12	7	.632	3.99	1.35	28	28	2	1	...	0-...	171.1	178	90	76	9	54-0	109	.259
2004— Arkansas (Texas)	9	2	.818	2.70	1.17	14	14	1	0	...	0-...	90.0	86	29	27	5	19-0	60	.259
—Salt Lake (PCL)	6	4	.600	6.07	1.80	15	14	1	0	...	0-...	83.0	107	67	56	13	42-0	60	.317
2005— Los Angeles (A.L.)	1	1	.500	4.55	1.37	28	0	0	0	2	0-0	27.2	30	18	14	7	8-0	20	.278
—Salt Lake (PCL)	3	1	.750	5.89	1.83	15	5	0	0	1	0-2	36.2	50	27	24	7	17-2	36	.314
2006— Seattle (A.L.)	7	4	.636	4.20	1.60	37	8	0	0	2	1-1	105.0	115	51	49	12	53-5	66	.278
Major League totals (2 years)	8	5	.615	4.27	1.55	65	8	0	0	4	1-1	132.2	145	69	63	19	61-5	86	.276

2006 LEFTY-RIGHTY SPLITS

vs.	Avg.	AB	H	2B	3B	HR	RBI	BB	SO	OBP	Slg.	vs.	Avg.	AB	H	2B	3B	HR	RBI	BB	SO	OBP	Slg.
L	.291	117	34	5	2	3	12	9	19	.339	.444	R	.273	297	81	23	1	9	48	44	47	.369	.448

WOODWARD, CHRIS — IF/OF

PERSONAL: Born June 27, 1976, in Covina, Calif. ... 6-0/185. ... Bats right, throws right. ... Full name: Christopher Michael Woodward. ... High school: Northview (Covina, Calif.). ... Junior college: Mt. San Antonio (Calif.). ... College: Mt. San Antonio (CA). **TRANSACTIONS/CAREER NOTES:** Selected by Toronto Blue Jays organization in 54th round of 1994 free-agent draft. ... On disabled list (July 1-26, 2001); included rehabilitation assignment to Syracuse. ... On disabled list (June 21-July 11, 2002); included rehabilitation assignment to Dunedin. ... On disabled list (May 12-June 8, 2004); included rehabilitation assignment to Dunedin. ... Signed as a free agent by New York Mets organization (December 28, 2005). **STATISTICAL NOTES:** Hit three home runs in one game (August 7, 2002). ... Career major league grand slams: 1.

2006 GAMES PLAYED BY POSITION (MLB): 2B—39, SS—13, 3B—11, OF—9, 1B—1.

Year Team (League)	Pos.	G	AB	R	H	2B	3B	HR	RBI	BB	SO	HBP	GDP	SB-CS	Avg.	OBP	SLG	OPS	E	Avg.
1995— Medicine Hat (Pio.)	SS	72	241	44	56	8	0	3	21	33	41	6	1	9-4	.232	.336	.303	.639	30	.911
1996— Hagerstown (SAL)	SS	123	424	41	95	24	2	1	48	43	70	5	3	11-3	.224	.300	.297	.597	30	.951
1997— Dunedin (Fla. St.)	SS	91	314	38	92	13	4	1	38	52	52	5	3	4-8	.293	.397	.369	.767	12	.972
1998— Knoxville (Southern)	SS	73	253	36	62	12	0	3	27	26	47	3	4	3-5	.245	.319	.328	.647	11	.971
—Syracuse (Int'l)	SS	25	85	9	17	6	0	2	6	7	20	0	4	1-1	.200	.261	.341	.602	4	.961
1999— Syracuse (Int'l)	SS-2B	75	281	46	82	20	3	1	20	38	49	1	5	4-1	.292	.378	.395	.773	11	.966
—Toronto (A.L.)	SS-3B	14	26	1	6	1	0	0	2	2	6	0	1	0-0	.231	.276	.269	.545	2	.944
2000— Toronto (A.L.)	SS-3B-1B-2B	37	104	16	19	7	0	3	14	10	28	0	1	1-0	.183	.254	.337	.591	5	.963
—Syracuse (Int'l)	2B-3B-SS	37	143	23	46	13	2	5	25	11	30	0	2	2-0	.322	.370	.545	.916	2	.988
2001— Toronto (A.L.)	2B-3B-SS-1B-DH	37	63	9	12	3	2	2	5	1	14	0	1	0-1	.190	.203	.397	.600	8	.933
—Syracuse (Int'l)	3B-SS-1B-2B	51	193	29	59	14	3	11	31	26	16	1	4	3-0	.306	.360	.580	.941	9	.950
2002— Toronto (A.L.)	3B-DH-SS	90	312	48	86	13	4	13	45	26	72	3	8	3-0	.276	.330	.468	.797	15	.964
—Dunedin (Fla. St.)	SS	2	6	1	2	0	0	0	0	0	1	0	0	0-0	.333	.429	.333	.762	0	1.000
2003— Toronto (A.L.)	SS	104	349	49	91	22	2	7	45	28	72	3	6	1-2	.261	.316	.395	.711	17	.964
2004— Dunedin (Fla. St.)	SS	6	16	2	5	2	0	1	3	1	2	0	0	0-0	.313	.333	.625	.958	0	1.000
—Toronto (A.L.)	SS-DH	69	213	21	50	13	4	1	24	14	46	1	3	1-2	.235	.283	.347	.630	5	.981
2005— New York (N.L.)	1B-OF-SS-3B-2B-DH	81	173	16	49	10	0	3	18	13	46	2	2	0-0	.283	.337	.393	.730	6	.979
2006— New York (N.L.)	2B-SS-3B-OF-1B	83	222	25	48	10	1	3	25	23	55	1	2	1-1	.216	.289	.311	.600	5	.980
American League totals (6 years)		351	1067	144	264	59	12	26	135	81	238	7	20	6-5	.247	.300	.398	.699	52	.964
National League totals (2 years)		164	395	41	97	20	1	6	43	36	101	3	4	1-1	.246	.310	.347	.657	11	.980
Major League totals (8 years)		515	1462	185	361	79	13	32	178	117	339	10	24	7-6	.247	.300	.384	.687	63	.968

DIVISION SERIES RECORD

Year Team (League)	Pos.	G	AB	R	H	2B	3B	HR	RBI	BB	SO	HBP	GDP	SB-CS	Avg.	OBP	SLG	OPS	E	Avg.
2006— New York (N.L.)		1	1	1	1	1	0	0	0	0	0	0	0	0-0	1.000	1.000	2.000	3.000		...

2006 LEFTY-RIGHTY SPLITS

vs.	Avg.	AB	H	2B	3B	HR	RBI	BB	SO	OBP	Slg.	vs.	Avg.	AB	H	2B	3B	HR	RBI	BB	SO	OBP	Slg.
L	.226	93	21	4	0	2	12	11	23	.302	.333	R	.209	129	27	6	1	9	13	12	32	.280	.295

WORRELL, TIM — P

PERSONAL: Born July 5, 1967, in Pasadena, Calif. ... 6-4/230. ... Throws right, bats right. ... Full name: Timothy Howard Worrell. ... Name pronounced: wor-RELL. ... High school: Maranatha (Sierra Madre, Calif.). ... College: Biola (Calif.). ... Brother of Todd Worrell, pitcher with two major league teams (1985-97). **TRANSACTIONS/CAREER NOTES:** Selected by San Diego Padres organization in 20th round of 1989 free-agent draft. ... On disabled list (April 19, 1994-remainder of season). ... On disabled list (April 24-September 1, 1995); included rehabilitation assignments to Rancho Cucamonga and Las Vegas. ... Traded by Padres with OF Trey Beamon to Detroit Tigers for Ps Dan Miceli and Donne Wall and 3B Ryan Balfe (November 19, 1997). ... Traded by Tigers with OF Dave Roberts to Cleveland Indians for OF Geronimo Berroa (June 24, 1998). ... Traded by Indians to Oakland Athletics for a player to be named (July 12, 1998); Indians acquired SS Adam Robinson to complete deal (July 27, 1998). ... On disabled list (July 20-August 8, 1999); included rehabilitation assignment to Modesto. ... Signed as a free agent by Baltimore Orioles organization (February 4, 2000). ... Released by Orioles (May 1, 2000). ... Signed by Chicago Cubs organization (May 8, 2000). ... Traded by Cubs to San Francisco Giants for 3B Bill Mueller (November 19, 2000). ... On disabled list (July 9-26, 2001); included rehabilitation assignment to AZL Giants. ... Signed as a free agent by Philadelphia Phillies (December 10, 2003). ... On disabled list (May 6-July 4, 2005); included rehabilitation assignments to Lakewood and Reading. ... Traded by Phillies to Arizona Diamondbacks for IF Matt Kata (July 21, 2005). ... Signed as a free agent by San Francisco Giants (December 1, 2005). ... On disabled list (May 23-June 7, 2006 and July 1, 2006-remainder of season).
CAREER HITTING: 8-for-81 (.099), 6 R, 1 2B, 0 3B, 0 HR, 4 RBI.

Year Team (League)	W	L	Pct.	ERA	WHIP	G	GS	CG	ShO	Hld.	Sv.-Opp.	IP	H	R	ER	HR	BB-IBB	SO	Avg.
1990— Char., S.C. (SAL)	5	8	.385	4.64	1.34	20	19	3	0	...	0-...	110.2	120	65	57	6	28-2	68	.272
1991— Waterloo (Midw.)	8	4	.667	3.34	1.19	14	14	3	2	...	0-...	86.1	70	36	32	5	33-0	83	.217
—High Desert (Calif.)	5	2	.714	4.24	1.54	11	11	2	0	...	0-...	63.2	65	32	30	2	33-0	70	.267
1992— Wichita (Texas)	8	6	.571	2.86	1.17	19	19	1	1	...	0-...	125.2	115	46	40	8	32-0	109	.245
—Las Vegas (PCL)	4	2	.667	4.26	1.26	10	10	1	1	...	0-...	63.1	61	32	30	4	19-0	32	.253
1993— Las Vegas (PCL)	5	6	.455	5.48	1.47	15	14	2	0	...	0-...	87.0	102	61	53	13	26-1	89	.294
—San Diego (N.L.)	2	7	.222	4.92	1.46	21	16	0	0		0-0	100.2	104	63	55	11	43-5	52	.269
1994— San Diego (N.L.)	0	1	.000	3.68	0.95	3	0	0	0		0-0	14.2	9	7	6	1	5-0	14	.170
1995— Rancho Cuca. (Calif.)	0	2	.000	5.16	1.37	9	3	0	0		1-...	22.2	25	17	13	2	6-1	17	.266
—Las Vegas (PCL)	0	2	.000	6.00	1.83	10	3	0	0		0-...	24.0	27	21	16	1	17-0	18	.273
—San Diego (N.L.)	1	0	1.000	4.73	1.65	9	1	0	0		0-0	13.1	16	7	7	1	6-0	13	.291
1996— San Diego (N.L.)	9	7	.563	3.05	1.22	50	11	0	0	10	1-2	121.0	109	45	41	9	39-1	99	.236

Year Team (League)	W	L	Pct.	ERA	WHIP	G	GS	CG	ShO	Hld.	Sv.-Opp.	IP	H	R	ER	HR	BB-IBB	SO	Avg.
1997—San Diego (N.L.)	4	8	.333	5.16	1.56	60	10	0	0	16	3-7	106.1	116	67	61	14	50-2	81	.280
1998—Detroit (A.L.)	2	6	.250	5.98	1.38	15	9	0	0	0	0-1	61.2	66	42	41	11	19-2	47	.270
—Cleveland (A.L.)	0	0	...	5.06	1.50	3	0	0	0	0	0-0	5.1	6	3	3	0	2-0	2	.300
—Oakland (A.L.)	0	1	.000	4.00	1.17	25	0	0	0	6	0-2	36.0	34	17	16	5	8-1	33	.241
1999—Oakland (A.L.)	2	2	.500	4.15	1.49	53	0	0	0	5	0-5	69.1	69	38	32	6	34-1	62	.256
—Modesto (California)	0	0	...	0.00	0.00	1	1	0	0	0	0-...	2.0	0	0	0	0	0-0	5	.000
2000—Baltimore (A.L.)	2	2	.500	7.36	2.32	5	0	0	0	0	0-0	7.1	12	6	6	3	5-3	5	.353
—Iowa (PCL)	2	0	1.000	5.06	1.31	6	0	0	0	0	0-0	10.2	9	6	6	3	5-1	7	.237
—Chicago (N.L.)	3	4	.429	2.47	1.35	54	0	0	0	12	3-6	62.0	60	20	17	7	24-8	52	.252
2001—San Francisco (N.L.)	2	5	.286	3.45	1.33	73	0	0	0	13	0-3	78.1	71	33	30	4	33-4	63	.240
—Ariz. Giants (Ariz.)	0	0	...	0.00	0.67	1	1	0	0	0	0-...	3.0	1	0	0	0	1-0	2	.125
2002—San Francisco (N.L.)	8	2	.800	2.25	1.18	80	0	0	0	23	0-1	72.0	55	21	18	3	30-2	55	.212
2003—San Francisco (N.L.)	4	4	.500	2.87	1.30	76	0	0	0	1	38-45	78.1	74	35	25	5	28-6	65	.246
2004—Philadelphia (N.L.)	5	6	.455	3.68	1.23	77	0	0	0	20	19-27	78.1	75	36	32	10	21-4	64	.254
2005—Lakewood (S. Atl.)	0	0	...	2.08	1.62	3	3	0	0	0	0-0	4.1	7	3	1	0	0-0	6	.350
—Reading (East.)	0	0	...	0.00	0.00	2	1	0	0	0	0-0	3.0	0	0	0	0	0-0	3	.000
—Philadelphia (N.L.)	0	1	.000	7.41	1.88	19	0	0	0	3	1-3	17.0	29	17	14	4	3-0	17	.377
—Arizona (N.L.)	1	1	.500	2.27	1.23	32	0	0	0	9	0-1	31.2	30	13	8	4	9-2	22	.250
2006—San Francisco (N.L.)	3	2	.600	7.52	1.72	23	0	0	0	1	6-8	20.1	28	18	17	9	7-0	12	.308
American League totals (3 years)	6	11	.353	4.91	1.42	101	9	0	0	11	0-8	179.2	187	106	98	25	68-7	149	.264
National League totals (12 years)	42	48	.467	3.75	1.35	577	40	0	0	109	71-103	794.0	776	382	331	82	298-34	609	.255
Major League totals (14 years)	48	59	.449	3.97	1.36	678	49	0	0	120	71-111	973.2	963	488	429	107	366-41	758	.256

DIVISION SERIES RECORD

Year Team (League)	W	L	Pct.	ERA	WHIP	G	GS	CG	ShO	Hld.	Sv.-Opp.	IP	H	R	ER	HR	BB-IBB	SO	Avg.
1996—San Diego (N.L.)	0	0	...	2.45	1.36	2	0	0	0	0	0-1	3.2	4	1	1	0	1-0	2	.286
2002—San Francisco (N.L.)	0	0	...	12.00	3.00	3	0	0	0	1	0-0	3.0	7	6	4	2	2-0	3	.438
2003—San Francisco (N.L.)	0	1	.000	0.00	2.25	2	0	0	0	0	0-1	2.2	3	2	0	0	3-1	0	.273
Division series totals (3 years)	0	1	.000	4.82	2.14	7	0	0	0	1	0-1	9.1	14	9	5	2	6-1	5	.341

CHAMPIONSHIP SERIES RECORD

Year Team (League)	W	L	Pct.	ERA	WHIP	G	GS	CG	ShO	Hld.	Sv.-Opp.	IP	H	R	ER	HR	BB-IBB	SO	Avg.
2002—San Francisco (N.L.)	2	0	1.000	2.08	0.46	4	0	0	0	0	0-0	4.1	2	1	1	1	0-0	3	.133

WORLD SERIES RECORD

Year Team (League)	W	L	Pct.	ERA	WHIP	G	GS	CG	ShO	Hld.	Sv.-Opp.	IP	H	R	ER	HR	BB-IBB	SO	Avg.
2002—San Francisco (N.L.)	1	1	.500	3.18	0.88	6	0	0	0	2	0-0	5.2	4	3	2	1	1-0	4	.190

2006 LEFTY-RIGHTY SPLITS

vs.	Avg.	AB	H	2B	3B	HR	RBI	BB	SO	OBP	Slg.	vs.	Avg.	AB	H	2B	3B	HR	RBI	BB	SO	OBP	Slg.
L	.256	43	11	3	0	3	8	4	8	.333	.535	R	.354	48	17	1	0	6	14	3	4	.392	.750

WRIGHT, DAVID — 3B

PERSONAL: Born December 20, 1982, in Norfolk, Va. ... 6-0/200. ... Bats right, throws right. ... Full name: David Allen Wright. ... High school: Hickory (Chesapeake, Va.).
TRANSACTIONS/CAREER NOTES: Selected by New York Mets organization in supplemental round ("sandwich pick" between first and second rounds, 38th pick overall) of 2001 free-agent draft; pick acquired as compensation for Colorado Rockies signing Type A free-agent P Mike Hampton. **HONORS:** Named third baseman on SPORTING NEWS N.L. All-Star team (2006). **STATISTICAL NOTES:** Career major league grand slams: 4.
2006 GAMES PLAYED BY POSITION (MLB): 3B—153, DH—1.

									BATTING										FIELDING	
Year Team (League)	Pos.	G	AB	R	H	2B	3B	HR	RBI	BB	SO	HBP	GDP	SB-CS	Avg.	OBP	SLG	OPS	E	Avg.
2001—Kingsport (Appalachian)	3B	36	120	27	36	7	0	4	17	16	30	2	3	9-1	.300	.391	.458	.850	5	.939
2002—Capital City (SAL)		135	496	85	132	30	2	11	93	76	114	5	4	21-5	.266	.367	.401	.768	19	.942
2003—St. Lucie (Fla. St.)	3B	133	466	69	126	39	2	15	75	72	98	4	8	19-5	.270	.369	.459	.828	16	.951
2004—Binghamton (East.)	3B-DH	60	223	44	81	27	0	10	40	39	41	7	5	20-6	.363	.467	.619	1.072	8	.943
—Norfolk (Int'l)	3B	31	114	18	34	8	0	8	17	16	19	2	3	2-4	.298	.388	.579	.958	11	.933
—New York (N.L.)	3B	69	263	41	77	17	1	14	40	14	40	3	7	6-0	.293	.332	.525	.857	11	.942
2005—New York (N.L.)	3B	160	575	99	176	42	1	27	102	72	113	7	16	17-7	.306	.388	.523	.912	24	.948
2006—New York (N.L.)	3B-DH	154	582	96	181	40	5	26	116	66	113	5	15	20-5	.311	.381	.531	.912	19	.954
Major League totals (3 years)		383	1420	236	434	99	7	67	258	152	266	15	38	43-12	.306	.375	.527	.902	54	.949

DIVISION SERIES RECORD

Year Team (League)	Pos.	G	AB	R	H	2B	3B	HR	RBI	BB	SO	HBP	GDP	SB-CS	Avg.	OBP	SLG	OPS	E	Avg.
2006—New York (N.L.)	3B	3	12	1	4	2	0	0	4	1	4	0	0	0-0	.333	.385	.500	.885	1	.875

CHAMPIONSHIP SERIES RECORD

Year Team (League)	Pos.	G	AB	R	H	2B	3B	HR	RBI	BB	SO	HBP	GDP	SB-CS	Avg.	OBP	SLG	OPS	E	Avg.
2006—New York (N.L.)	3B	7	25	2	4	1	0	1	2	4	4	0	0	0-0	.160	.276	.320	.596	0	1.000

ALL-STAR GAME RECORD

	G	AB	R	H	2B	3B	HR	RBI	BB	SO	HBP	GDP	SB-CS	Avg.	OBP	SLG	OPS	E	Avg.
	1	3	1	1	0	1	0	1	0	0	0	0	0-0	.333	.333	1.333	1.667	0	1.000
All-Star Game totals (1 year)	1	3	1	1	0	1	0	1	0	0	0	0	0-0	.333	.333	1.333	1.667	0	1.000

2006 LEFTY-RIGHTY SPLITS

vs.	Avg.	AB	H	2B	3B	HR	RBI	BB	SO	OBP	Slg.	vs.	Avg.	AB	H	2B	3B	HR	RBI	BB	SO	OBP	Slg.
L	.285	165	47	13	1	6	28	27	29	.385	.485	R	.321	417	134	27	4	20	88	39	84	.380	.549

WRIGHT, JAMEY — P

PERSONAL: Born December 24, 1974, in Oklahoma City. ... 6-6/235. ... Throws right, bats right. ... Full name: Jamey Alan Wright. ... High school: Westmoore (Moore, Okla.).
TRANSACTIONS/CAREER NOTES: Selected by Colorado Rockies organization in first round (28th pick overall) of 1993 free-agent draft. ... On disabled list (May 15-June 8, 1997); included rehabilitation assignment to Salem. ... Traded by Rockies with C Henry Blanco to Milwaukee Brewers as part of three-team deal in which Rockies acquired 3B Jeff Cirillo, P Scott Karl and cash from Brewers, Oakland Athletics acquired P Justin Miller and cash from Rockies and Brewers acquired P Jimmy Haynes from A's (December 13, 1999). ... On disabled list (March 28-May 23, 2000); included rehabilitation assignments to Huntsville and Indianapolis. ... On disabled list (May 25-June 10, 2001). ... On disabled list (April 11-May 24, 2002); included rehabilitation assignment to Indianapolis. ... Traded by Brewers with cash to St. Louis Cardinals for P Chris Morris and a player to be named (August 29, 2002); Brewers acquired P Mike Matthews to complete deal (September 11, 2002). ... Signed as a free agent by Seattle Mariners organization (January 24, 2003). ... Released by Mariners (March 18, 2003). ... Signed by Brewers organization (March 26, 2003). ... Released by Brewers (April 28, 2003). ... Signed by Texas Rangers organization (May 7, 2003). ... Released by Rangers (June 15, 2003). ... Signed by Kansas City Royals organization (June 20, 2003). ... Signed as a free agent by Chicago Cubs organization (December 29, 2003). ... Signed as a free agent by Royals organization (March 27, 2004). ... Released by Royals (July 21, 2004). ... Signed by Rockies (July 22, 2004). ... Signed as free agent by San Francisco Giants organization (January 17, 2006). ... On suspended list (September 22-25, 2006).
MISCELLANEOUS NOTES: Struck out in only appearance as pinch hitter (2001). ... Appeared in one game as pinch runner (2005). ... Struck out in only appearance as pinch hitter (2006).

CAREER HITTING: 64-for-435 (.147), 26 R, 15 2B, 1 3B, 1 HR, 17 RBI.

Year	Team (League)	W	L	Pct.	ERA	WHIP	G	GS	CG	ShO	Hld.	Sv.-Opp.	IP	H	R	ER	HR	BB-IBB	SO	Avg.
1993—	Ariz. Rockies (Ariz.)	1	3	.250	4.00	1.22	8	8	0	0	...	0-...	36.0	35	19	16	1	9-0	26	.243
1994—	Asheville (S. Atl.)	7	14	.333	5.97	1.72	28	27	2	0	...	0-...	143.1	188	107	95	6	59-1	103	.329
1995—	Salem (Carol.)	10	8	.556	2.47	1.36	26	26	2	1	...	0-...	171.0	160	74	47	7	72-3	95	.251
	— New Haven (East.)	0	1	.000	9.00	3.00	1	1	0	0	...	0-...	3.0	6	6	3	0	3-0	0	.375
1996—	New Haven (East.)	5	1	.833	0.81	0.87	7	7	1	1	...	0-...	44.2	27	7	4	0	12-0	54	.180
	— Colo. Springs (PCL)	4	2	.667	2.72	1.26	9	9	0	0	...	0-...	59.2	53	20	18	3	22-0	40	.240
	— Colorado (N.L.)	4	4	.500	4.93	1.60	16	15	0	0	1	0-0	91.1	105	50	50	8	41-1	45	.298
1997—	Colorado (N.L.)	8	12	.400	6.25	1.80	26	26	1	0	0	0-0	149.2	198	113	104	19	71-3	59	.327
	— Salem (Carol.)	0	1	.000	9.00	2.00	1	1	0	0	...	0-...	1.0	1	1	1	0	1-0	1	.250
	— Colo. Springs (PCL)	1	0	1.000	1.64	1.27	2	2	0	0	...	0-...	11.0	9	3	2	1	5-0	11	.231
1998—	Colorado (N.L.)	9	14	.391	5.67	1.60	34	34	1	0	0	0-0	206.1	235	143	130	24	95-3	86	.294
1999—	Colorado (N.L.)	4	3	.571	4.87	1.74	16	16	0	0	0	0-0	94.1	110	52	51	10	54-3	49	.308
	— Colo. Springs (PCL)	5	7	.417	6.46	1.70	17	16	2	0	...	0-...	100.1	133	87	72	13	38-2	75	.324
2000—	Huntsville (Sou.)	2	0	1.000	0.00	0.97	2	2	0	0	...	0-...	12.1	7	0	0	0	5-0	10	.175
	— Indianapolis (Int'l)	0	0	...	1.80	2.20	1	1	0	0	...	0-...	5.0	8	5	1	0	3-0	7	.364
	— Milwaukee (N.L.)	7	9	.438	4.10	1.49	26	25	0	0	0	0-0	164.2	157	81	75	12	88-5	96	.261
2001—	Milwaukee (N.L.)	11	12	.478	4.90	1.54	33	33	1	1	0	0-0	194.2	201	115	106	26	98-10	129	.272
2002—	Milwaukee (N.L.)	5	13	.278	5.35	1.56	19	19	1	1	0	0-0	114.1	115	72	68	15	63-8	69	.270
	— Indianapolis (Int'l)	1	1	.500	4.11	1.37	3	3	0	0	...	0-...	15.1	16	7	7	3	5-0	13	.271
	— St. Louis (N.L.)	2	0	1.000	4.80	1.80	4	3	0	0	0	0-0	15.0	15	8	8	2	12-1	8	.259
2003—	Indianapolis (Int'l)	1	3	.250	7.36	1.90	7	4	0	0	...	0-...	22.0	32	21	18	5	10-0	17	.344
	— Oklahoma (PCL)	2	1	.667	4.12	1.50	7	7	0	0	...	0-...	39.1	38	18	18	1	21-0	40	.260
	— Omaha (PCL)	3	5	.375	3.64	1.40	13	12	1	0	...	0-...	76.2	70	35	31	10	38-0	65	.246
	— Kansas City (A.L.)	1	2	.333	4.26	1.34	4	4	2	1	0	0-...	25.1	23	14	12	1	11-0	19	.245
2004—	Omaha (PCL)	8	6	.571	4.21	1.39	18	18	1	1	...	0-...	104.2	111	58	49	13	35-0	70	.273
	— Colorado (N.L.)	2	3	.400	4.12	1.61	14	14	0	0	0	0-0	78.2	82	39	36	8	45-3	41	.266
2005—	Colorado (N.L.)	8	16	.333	5.46	1.65	34	27	0	0	1	0-0	171.1	201	119	104	22	81-4	101	.296
2006—	San Francisco (N.L.)	6	10	.375	5.19	1.48	34	21	0	0	0	0-0	156.0	167	95	90	16	64-4	79	.282
	American League totals (1 year)	1	2	.333	4.26	1.34	4	4	2	1	0	0-0	25.1	23	14	12	1	11-0	19	.245
	National League totals (10 years)	66	96	.407	5.15	1.60	256	233	4	2	2	0-0	1436.1	1586	897	822	162	712-45	762	.287
	Major League totals (11 years)	67	98	.406	5.14	1.60	260	237	6	3	2	0-0	1461.2	1609	911	834	163	723-45	781	.287

2006 LEFTY-RIGHTY SPLITS

vs.	Avg.	AB	H	2B	3B	HR	RBI	BB	SO	OBP	Slg.	vs.	Avg.	AB	H	2B	3B	HR	RBI	BB	SO	OBP	Slg.
L	.261	276	72	11	3	7	37	29	48	.335	.399	R	.300	317	95	12	4	9	49	35	31	.380	.448

WRIGHT, JARET   P

PERSONAL: Born December 29, 1975, in Anaheim. ... 6-2/230. ... Throws right, bats right. ... Full name: Jaret Samuel Wright. ... High school: Katella (Anaheim). ... Son of Clyde Wright, pitcher with three major league teams (1966-75). **TRANSACTIONS/CAREER NOTES:** Selected by Cleveland Indians organization in first round (10th pick overall) of 1994 free-agent draft. ... On suspended list (May 10-16, 1999). ... On disabled list (July 19-August 3 and August 9-September 10, 1999); included rehabilitation assignments to Buffalo and Akron. ... On disabled list (May 12-27 and June 3, 2000-remainder of season); included rehabilitation assignments to Buffalo and Akron. ... On disabled list (March 31-May 19 and September 1, 2001-remainder of season); included rehabilitation assignments to Buffalo and Akron. ... On disabled list (March 30-July 20, 2002); included rehabilitation assignment to Buffalo. ... Signed as a free agent by San Diego Padres (December 10, 2002). ... Claimed on waivers by Atlanta Braves (August 29, 2003). ... Signed as a free agent by New York Yankees (January 12, 2005). ... On disabled list (April 24-August 15, 2005); included rehabilitation assignments to GCL Yankees and Tampa. ... Traded by Yankees with cash to Baltimore Orioles for P Chris Britton (November 12, 2006). **MISCELLANEOUS NOTES:** Appeared in one game as pinch runner (2006).

CAREER HITTING: 11-for-78 (.141), 6 R, 2 2B, 0 3B, 1 HR, 6 RBI.

Year	Team (League)	W	L	Pct.	ERA	WHIP	G	GS	CG	ShO	Hld.	Sv.-Opp.	IP	H	R	ER	HR	BB-IBB	SO	Avg.
1994—	Burlington (Appal.)	0	1	.000	5.40	1.65	4	4	0	0	...	0-...	13.1	13	10	8	1	9-0	16	.260
1995—	Columbus (S. Atl.)	5	6	.455	3.00	1.33	24	24	0	0	...	0-...	129.0	93	55	43	9	79-0	113	.205
1996—	Kinston (Carol.)	7	4	.636	2.50	1.19	19	19	0	0	...	0-...	101.0	65	32	28	1	55-0	109	.190
1997—	Akron (East.)	3	3	.500	3.67	1.22	8	8	1	0	...	0-...	54.0	43	26	22	4	23-2	59	.223
	— Buffalo (A.A.)	4	1	.800	1.80	1.09	7	7	1	1	...	0-...	45.0	30	16	9	4	19-0	47	.185
	— Cleveland (A.L.)	8	3	.727	4.38	1.28	16	16	0	0	0	0-0	90.1	81	45	44	9	35-0	63	.238
1998—	Cleveland (A.L.)	12	10	.545	4.72	1.53	32	32	1	1	0	0-0	192.2	207	109	101	22	87-4	140	.277
1999—	Cleveland (A.L.)	8	10	.444	6.06	1.65	26	26	0	0	0	0-0	133.2	144	99	90	18	77-1	91	.277
	— Buffalo (Int'l)	0	0	...	0.00	0.00	1	1	0	0	...	0-...	3.0	0	0	0	0	0-0	4	.000
	— Akron (East.)	1	0	1.000	0.00	0.80	1	1	0	0	...	0-...	5.0	3	0	0	0	1-0	6	.167
2000—	Cleveland (A.L.)	3	4	.429	4.70	1.39	9	9	1	1	0	0-0	51.2	44	27	27	6	28-0	36	.235
	— Buffalo (Int'l)	0	0	...	0.00	0.50	1	1	0	0	...	0-...	2.0	0	0	0	0	1-0	1	.000
	— Akron (East.)	0	0	...	3.38	0.88	2	2	0	0	...	0-...	8.0	4	3	3	0	3-0	5	.133
2001—	Buffalo (Int'l)	3	1	.750	4.71	1.33	7	7	0	0	...	0-...	28.2	25	18	15	3	13-0	28	.234
	— Akron (East.)	0	0	...	1.29	0.29	1	1	0	0	...	0-...	7.0	2	1	1	1	0-0	4	.087
	— Cleveland (A.L.)	2	2	.500	6.52	2.00	7	7	0	0	0	0-0	29.0	36	22	21	2	22-0	18	.313
2002—	Buffalo (Int'l)	5	3	.625	3.88	1.46	10	10	1	0	...	0-...	55.2	57	27	24	5	24-0	43	.268
	— Cleveland (A.L.)	2	3	.400	15.71	3.22	8	6	0	0	0	0-0	18.1	40	34	32	3	19-0	12	.435
2003—	Portland (PCL)	2	1	.667	1.42	1.20	12	1	0	0	...	0-...	19.0	16	7	3	0	7-0	21	.222
	— San Diego (N.L.)	1	5	.167	8.37	2.05	39	0	0	0	1	2-4	47.1	69	44	44	9	28-2	41	.348
	— Atlanta (N.L.)	1	0	1.000	2.00	1.11	11	0	0	0	3	0-1	9.0	7	2	2	0	3-0	9	.226
2004—	Atlanta (N.L.)	15	8	.652	3.28	1.28	32	32	0	0	0	0-0	186.1	168	79	68	11	70-5	159	.242
2005—	GC Yankees (GCL)	0	1	.000	7.71	2.57	1	1	0	0	...	0-...	2.1	4	2	2	0	2-0	3	.364
	— Tampa (Fla. St.)	1	0	1.000	1.50	1.00	2	2	0	0	...	0-...	12.0	9	2	2	0	3-0	12	.220
	— New York (A.L.)	5	5	.500	6.08	1.77	13	13	0	0	0	0-0	63.2	81	51	43	8	32-1	34	.313
2006—	New York (A.L.)	11	7	.611	4.49	1.52	30	27	0	0	0	0-0	140.1	157	76	70	16	57-0	84	.283
	American League totals (8 years)	51	44	.537	5.35	1.59	141	136	2	2	1	0-0	719.2	790	463	428	78	357-6	478	.281
	National League totals (2 years)	17	13	.567	4.23	1.42	82	32	0	0	4	2-5	242.2	244	125	114	20	101-7	209	.264
	Major League totals (10 years)	68	57	.544	5.07	1.55	223	168	2	2	5	2-5	962.1	1034	588	542	98	458-13	687	.277

DIVISION SERIES RECORD

Year	Team (League)	W	L	Pct.	ERA	WHIP	G	GS	CG	ShO	Hld.	Sv.-Opp.	IP	H	R	ER	HR	BB-IBB	SO	Avg.
1997—	Cleveland (A.L.)	2	0	1.000	3.97	1.59	2	2	0	0	0	0-0	11.1	11	6	5	0	7-1	10	.256
1998—	Cleveland (A.L.)	0	1	.000	12.46	2.08	1	1	0	0	0	0-0	4.1	7	6	6	2	2-0	6	.350
1999—	Cleveland (A.L.)	0	1	.000	22.50	2.50	1	0	0	0	0	0-0	2.0	4	5	5	1	1-0	1	.444
2003—	Atlanta (N.L.)	0	0	...	0.00	0.50	4	0	0	0	0	0-0	4.0	0	0	0	0	2-0	4	.000
2004—	Atlanta (N.L.)	0	2	.000	9.31	1.55	2	2	0	0	0	0-0	9.2	14	10	10	5	1-0	7	.350

W

Year Team (League)	W	L	Pct.	ERA	WHIP	G	GS	CG	ShO	Hld.	Sv.-Opp.	IP	H	R	ER	HR	BB-IBB	SO	Avg.
2006— New York (A.L.)	0	1	.000	10.13	2.25	1	1	0	0	...	0-0	2.2	5	4	3	2	1-0	1	.357
Division series totals (6 years)	2	5	.286	7.68	1.62	11	6	0	0	1	0-0	34.0	41	31	29	10	14-1	29	.297

CHAMPIONSHIP SERIES RECORD

Year Team (League)	W	L	Pct.	ERA	WHIP	G	GS	CG	ShO	Hld.	Sv.-Opp.	IP	H	R	ER	HR	BB-IBB	SO	Avg.
1997— Cleveland (A.L.)	0	0	...	15.00	2.67	1	1	0	0	0	0-0	3.0	6	5	5	3	2-0	3	.400
1998— Cleveland (A.L.)	0	1	.000	8.10	2.25	2	1	0	0	0	0-0	6.2	7	6	6	1	8-0	4	.304
Champ. series totals (2 years)	0	1	.000	10.24	2.38	3	2	0	0	0	0-0	9.2	13	11	11	4	10-0	7	.342

WORLD SERIES RECORD

Year Team (League)	W	L	Pct.	ERA	WHIP	G	GS	CG	ShO	Hld.	Sv.-Opp.	IP	H	R	ER	HR	BB-IBB	SO	Avg.
1997— Cleveland (A.L.)	1	0	1.000	2.92	1.38	2	2	0	0	0	0-0	12.1	7	4	4	2	10-0	12	.167

2006 LEFTY-RIGHTY SPLITS

vs.	Avg.	AB	H	2B	3B	HR	RBI	BB	SO	OBP	Slg.	vs.	Avg.	AB	H	2B	3B	HR	RBI	BB	SO	OBP	Slg.
L	.314	261	82	18	3	7	29	33	41	.390	.487	R	.255	294	75	19	0	3	28	24	43	.324	.350

WUERTZ, MICHAEL   P

PERSONAL: Born December 15, 1978, in Austin, Minn. ... 6-3/205. ... Throws right, bats right. ... Full name: Michael James Wuertz. ... Name pronounced: werts. ... High school: Austin (Minn.). **TRANSACTIONS/CAREER NOTES:** Selected by Chicago Cubs organization in 11th round of 1997 free-agent draft.

CAREER HITTING: 0-for-3 (.000), 0 R, 0 2B, 0 3B, 0 HR, 0 RBI.

Year Team (League)	W	L	Pct.	ERA	WHIP	G	GS	CG	ShO	Hld.	Sv.-Opp.	IP	H	R	ER	HR	BB-IBB	SO	Avg.
1998— Will. (NYP)	7	5	.583	3.44	1.14	14	14	1	0	...	0-...	86.1	79	36	33	4	19-0	59	.236
1999— Lansing (Midw.)	11	12	.478	4.80	1.46	28	28	1	0	...	0-...	161.1	191	104	86	11	44-0	127	.290
2000— Daytona (Fla. St.)	12	7	.632	3.78	1.34	28	28	3	2	...	0-...	171.1	166	79	72	15	64-1	142	.253
2001— West Tenn (Sou.)	4	9	.308	3.99	1.36	27	27	1	1	...	0-...	160.0	160	80	71	20	58-2	135	.260
2002— Iowa (PCL)	9	5	.643	5.55	1.65	28	27	0	0	...	0-...	154.0	185	109	95	24	69-3	131	.295
2003— Iowa (PCL)	3	9	.250	4.57	1.41	43	16	0	0	...	1-...	124.0	140	70	63	16	35-8	92	.288
2004— Iowa (PCL)	1	1	.500	2.42	1.01	37	0	0	0	...	19-...	44.2	30	13	12	4	15-2	59	.186
— Chicago (N.L.)	1	0	1.000	4.34	1.34	31	0	0	0	1	1-1	29.0	22	14	14	4	17-1	30	.218
2005— Chicago (N.L.)	6	2	.750	3.81	1.32	75	0	0	0	18	0-3	75.2	60	36	32	6	40-7	89	.219
2006— Iowa (PCL)	6	0	1.000	1.73	0.94	30	0	0	0	1	10-13	41.2	30	10	8	2	9-1	67	.191
— Chicago (N.L.)	3	1	.750	2.66	1.25	41	0	0	0	6	0-1	40.2	35	14	12	5	16-2	42	.226
Major League totals (3 years)	10	3	.769	3.59	1.31	147	0	0	0	25	1-5	145.1	117	64	58	13	73-10	161	.221

2006 LEFTY-RIGHTY SPLITS

vs.	Avg.	AB	H	2B	3B	HR	RBI	BB	SO	OBP	Slg.	vs.	Avg.	AB	H	2B	3B	HR	RBI	BB	SO	OBP	Slg.
L	.184	49	9	2	1	1	5	4	14	.259	.327	R	.245	106	26	2	1	4	22	12	28	.322	.396

YAN, ESTEBAN   P

PERSONAL: Born June 22, 1975, in Campina del Seibo, Dominican Republic. ... 6-4/255. ... Throws right, bats right. ... Full name: Esteban Luis Yan. ... Name pronounced: YAHN. ... High school: Escuela Hicayagua (Dominican Republic). **TRANSACTIONS/CAREER NOTES:** Signed as a non-drafted free agent by Atlanta Braves organization (November 21, 1990). ... Traded by Braves with OFs Roberto Kelly and Tony Tarasco to Montreal Expos for OF Marquis Grissom (April 6, 1995). ... Traded by Expos to Baltimore Orioles for cash (April 6, 1996). ... Selected by Tampa Bay Devil Rays in first round (18th pick overall) of expansion draft (November 18, 1997). ... On disabled list (June 17-July 15, 1999); included rehabilitation assignment to St. Petersburg. ... On disabled list (June 22-July 12, 2001); included rehabilitation assignment to Orlando. ... Signed as a free agent by Texas Rangers (December 26, 2002). ... Traded by Rangers to St. Louis Cardinals for OF Rick Asadoorian (May 27, 2003). ... Released by Cardinals (August 23, 2003). ... Signed by Detroit Tigers organization (January 20, 2004). ... Signed as a free agent by Anaheim Angels (December 13, 2004). ... Angels franchise renamed Los Angeles Angels of Anaheim for 2005 season. ... Traded by Angels with cash to Cincinnati Reds for P Kyle Edens (May 30, 2006). ... Released by Reds (July 24, 2006). **STATISTICAL NOTES:** Hit home run in first major league at-bat (June 4, 2000).

CAREER HITTING: 2-for-2 (1.000), 1 R, 0 2B, 0 3B, 1 HR, 1 RBI.

Year Team (League)	W	L	Pct.	ERA	WHIP	G	GS	CG	ShO	Hld.	Sv.-Opp.	IP	H	R	ER	HR	BB-IBB	SO	Avg.
1991— San Pedro (DSL)	4	1	.800	3.63	1.21	18	11	0	0	...	0-...	72.0	61	36	29	...	26-...	34	...
1992— San Pedro (DSL)	12	3	.800	1.32	0.93	16	16	7	4	...	0-...	115.2	85	37	17	1	23-...	86	...
1993— Danville (Appal.)	4	7	.364	3.03	1.36	14	14	0	0	...	0-...	71.1	73	46	24	4	24-1	50	.253
1994— Macon (S. Atl.)	11	12	.478	3.27	1.11	28	28	4	3	...	0-...	170.2	155	85	62	15	34-1	121	.242
1995— W.P. Beach (FSL)	6	8	.429	3.07	1.25	24	21	1	0	...	1-...	137.2	139	63	47	3	33-0	89	.265
1996— Bowie (East.)	0	2	.000	5.63	1.63	9	1	0	0	...	0-...	16.0	18	12	10	2	8-0	15	.277
— Baltimore (A.L.)	0	0	...	5.79	1.71	4	0	0	0	0	0-0	9.1	13	7	6	3	3-1	7	.333
— Rochester (Int'l)	5	4	.556	4.27	1.30	22	10	0	0	...	1-...	71.2	75	37	34	6	18-0	61	.269
1997— Rochester (Int'l)	11	5	.688	3.10	1.21	34	12	0	0	...	2-...	119.0	107	54	41	13	37-0	131	.243
— Baltimore (A.L.)	0	1	.000	15.83	2.79	3	2	0	0	0	0-0	9.2	20	18	17	3	7-0	4	.417
1998— Tampa Bay (A.L.)	5	4	.556	3.86	1.34	64	0	0	0	8	1-5	88.2	78	41	38	11	41-2	77	.236
1999— Tampa Bay (A.L.)	3	4	.429	5.90	1.79	50	1	0	0	7	0-3	61.0	77	41	40	8	32-4	46	.326
— St. Pete. (FSL)	0	0	...	0.00	1.00	2	2	0	0	...	0-...	4.0	3	1	0	0	1-0	5	.214
2000— Tampa Bay (A.L.)	7	8	.467	6.21	1.45	43	20	0	0	3	0-2	137.2	158	98	95	26	42-0	111	.285
2001— Tampa Bay (A.L.)	4	6	.400	3.90	1.20	54	0	0	0	0	22-31	62.1	64	34	27	7	11-1	64	.267
— Orlando (South.)	0	0	...	3.00	1.00	3	0	0	0	...	0-...	3.0	3	1	1	0	0-0	4	.250
2002— Tampa Bay (A.L.)	7	8	.467	4.30	1.43	55	0	0	0	0	19-27	69.0	70	35	33	10	29-1	53	.259
2003— Texas (A.L.)	0	1	.000	6.94	1.63	15	0	0	0	1	0-0	23.1	31	19	18	5	7-1	25	.307
— St. Louis (N.L.)	2	0	1.000	6.02	1.59	39	0	0	0	3	1-1	43.1	53	29	29	8	16-4	28	.308
2004— Detroit (A.L.)	3	6	.333	3.83	1.43	69	0	0	0	11	7-17	87.0	92	43	37	8	32-5	69	.274
2005— Los Angeles (A.L.)	1	1	.500	4.59	1.44	49	0	0	0	1	0-0	66.2	66	36	34	8	30-4	45	.258
2006— Omaha (PCL)	0	1	.000	7.32	1.68	11	0	0	0	...	0-1	19.2	24	16	16	3	9-1	16	.292
— Los Angeles (A.L.)	0	0	...	6.85	1.43	14	0	0	0	0	0-0	22.1	19	18	17	4	13-2	16	.232
— Cincinnati (N.L.)	1	0	1.000	3.60	1.33	14	0	0	0	0	1-1	15.0	13	7	6	4	7-2	8	.245
American League totals (11 years)	30	39	.435	5.11	1.47	419	23	0	0	31	49-85	637.0	688	390	362	93	247-21	517	.275
National League totals (2 years)	3	0	1.000	5.40	1.53	53	0	0	0	3	2-2	58.1	66	36	35	12	23-6	36	.293
Major League totals (11 years)	33	39	.458	5.14	1.47	472	23	0	0	34	51-87	695.1	754	426	397	105	270-27	553	.277

CHAMPIONSHIP SERIES RECORD

Year Team (League)	W	L	Pct.	ERA	WHIP	G	GS	CG	ShO	Hld.	Sv.-Opp.	IP	H	R	ER	HR	BB-IBB	SO	Avg.
2005— Los Angeles (A.L.)	0	0	...	9.00	2.00	1	0	0	0	0	0-0	2.0	3	2	2	0	1-0	2	.375

2006 LEFTY-RIGHTY SPLITS

vs.	Avg.	AB	H	2B	3B	HR	RBI	BB	SO	OBP	Slg.	vs.	Avg.	AB	H	2B	3B	HR	RBI	BB	SO	OBP	Slg.
L	.294	51	15	2	0	4	16	10	10	.403	.569	R	.202	84	17	5	0	4	15	10	14	.289	.405

Y

YATES, TYLER   P

PERSONAL: Born August 7, 1977, in Lihue, Hawaii. ... 6-4/220. ... Throws right, bats right. ... Full name: Tyler Kali Yates. ... High school: Kauai High (Lihue Kauai, Hawaii). ... College: Hawaii-Hilo. **TRANSACTIONS/CAREER NOTES:** Selected by Oakland Athletics organization in 23rd round of 1998 free-agent draft. ... Traded by Athletics with P Mark Guthrie to New York Mets for OF David Justice (December 14, 2001). ... On disabled list (March 21-April 6, 2003); included rehabilitation assignment to St. Lucie. ... On disabled list (March 15, 2005-entire season). ... Signed as a free agent by Baltimore Orioles organization (February 15, 2006). ... Released by Orioles (April 28, 2006). ... Signed by Atlanta Braves organization (May 3, 2006).

CAREER HITTING: 1-for-11 (.091), 0 R, 0 2B, 0 3B, 0 HR, 0 RBI.

Year	Team (League)	W	L	Pct.	ERA	WHIP	G	GS	CG	ShO	Hld.	Sv.-Opp.	IP	H	R	ER	HR	BB-IBB	SO	Avg.
1998—	Ariz. A's (Ariz.)	0	0		3.91	1.83	15	0	0	0	...	2-...	23.0	28	12	10	0	14-0	20	.304
—	S. Oregon (N'west)	0	0		0.00	0.86	2	0	0	0	...	1-...	2.1	2	0	0	0	0-0	1	.222
1999—	Visalia (Calif.)	2	5	.286	5.47	1.62	47	1	0	0	...	4-...	82.1	98	64	50	12	35-3	74	.290
2000—	Modesto (California)	4	2	.667	2.86	1.29	30	0	0	0	...	1-...	56.2	50	23	18	2	23-4	61	.237
—	Midland (Texas)	1	1	.500	6.15	1.63	22	0	0	0	...	0-...	26.1	28	20	18	2	15-3	24	.275
2001—	Midland (Texas)	4	6	.400	4.31	1.48	56	0	0	0	...	17-...	62.2	66	39	30	4	27-8	61	.261
—	Sacramento (PCL)	1	0	1.000	0.00	0.75	4	0	0	0	...	1-...	5.1	3	0	0	0	1-0	3	.167
2002—	Norfolk (Int'l)	2	2	.500	1.32	1.24	24	0	0	0	...	6-...	34.0	29	10	5	1	13-1	34	.227
2003—	St. Lucie (Fla. St.)	1	2	.333	4.31	1.35	14	11	0	0	...	0-...	48.0	41	28	23	5	24-0	49	.232
—	Binghamton (East.)	1	2	.333	4.35	1.27	8	8	0	0	...	0-...	39.1	33	21	19	4	17-0	36	.223
—	Norfolk (Int'l)	1	2	.333	4.05	1.55	4	4	0	0	...	0-...	20.0	22	9	9	1	9-0	15	.289
2004—	Norfolk (Int'l)	6	2	.750	3.18	1.26	30	1	0	0	...	4-...	39.2	28	18	14	2	22-0	43	.194
—	New York (N.L.)	2	4	.333	6.36	1.84	21	7	0	0	0	0-0	46.2	61	36	33	6	25-3	35	.311
2005—	New York(N.L.)				Did not play															
2006—	Richmond (Int'l)	0	0		2.16	1.08	7	0	0	0	4	0-0	8.1	6	2	2	0	3-0	10	.214
—	Atlanta (N.L.)	2	5	.286	3.96	1.46	56	0	0	0	12	1-6	50.0	42	23	22	6	31-8	46	.228
Major League totals (2 years)		4	9	.308	5.12	1.64	77	7	0	0	14	1-6	96.2	103	59	55	12	56-11	81	.271

2006 LEFTY-RIGHTY SPLITS

vs.	Avg.	AB	H	2B	3B	HR	RBI	BB	SO	OBP	Slg.	vs.	Avg.	AB	H	2B	3B	HR	RBI	BB	SO	OBP	Slg.
L	.217	69	15	4	1	2	11	17	23	.372	.391	R	.235	115	27	5	2	4	14	14	23	.318	.417

YOUKILIS, KEVIN   1B/3B

PERSONAL: Born March 15, 1979, in Cincinnati. ... 6-1/220. ... Bats right, throws right. ... Full name: Kevin Edmund Youkilis. ... Name pronounced: YOU-ka-lis. ... High school: Sycamore (Cincinnati). ... College: Cincinnati. **TRANSACTIONS/CAREER NOTES:** Selected by Boston Red Sox organization in eighth round of 2001 free-agent draft. ... On disabled list (August 16-September 1, 2004); included rehabilitation assignment to Lowell.

2006 GAMES PLAYED BY POSITION (MLB): 1B—127, OF—18, 3B—16.

								BATTING													FIELDING	
Year	Team (League)	Pos.	G	AB	R	H	2B	3B	HR	RBI	BB	SO	HBP	GDP	SB-CS	Avg.	OBP	SLG	OPS	E	Avg.
2001—	Lowell (NY-Penn)	3B	59	183	52	58	14	2	3	28	70	28	5	0	4-3	.317	.512	.464	.976	12	.936
—	Augusta (S. Atl.)	3B	5	12	0	2	0	0	0	0	3	3	1	0	0-0	.167	.375	.167	.542	0	1.000
2002—	Augusta (S. Atl.)	3B	15	53	5	15	5	0	0	6	13	8	1	0	0-0	.283	.433	.377	.810	4	.913
—	Sarasota (Fla. St.)	1B-3B	76	268	45	79	16	0	3	48	49	37	15	5	0-2	.295	.422	.388	.810	12	.974
—	Trenton (East.)	3B	44	160	34	55	10	0	5	26	31	18	5	1	5-4	.344	.462	.500	.962	11	.916
2003—	Portland (East.)	3B	94	312	74	102	23	1	6	37	86	40	15	7	7-0	.327	.487	.465	.952	20	.925
—	Pawtucket (Int'l)	3B	32	109	9	18	3	0	2	15	18	21	3	2	0-1	.165	.295	.248	.543	4	.952
2004—	Pawtucket (Int'l)	3B-1B-DH	38	154	25	41	12	0	3	18	19	28	2	1	2-0	.266	.350	.403	.745	5	.955
—	Lowell (NY-Penn)	3B	2	4	1	3	1	1	0	2	2	0	1	0	0-0	.750	.857	1.500	2.333	0	1.000
—	Boston (A.L.)	3B-DH	72	208	38	54	11	0	7	35	33	45	4	1	0-1	.260	.367	.413	.780	5	.968
2005—	Pawtucket (Int'l)	3B-1B-2B DH	43	152	30	49	15	1	8	27	35	29	5	0	1-2	.322	.459	.592	1.051	5	.975
—	Boston (A.L.)	3B-1B-2B	44	79	11	22	7	0	1	9	14	19	2	0	0-1	.278	.400	.405	.805	0	1.000
2006—	Boston (A.L.)	1B-OF-3B	147	569	100	159	42	2	13	72	91	120	9	12	5-2	.279	.381	.429	.810	8	.993
Major League totals (3 years)			263	856	149	235	60	2	21	116	138	184	15	13	5-4	.275	.379	.423	.802	13	.991

DIVISION SERIES RECORD

Year	Team (League)	Pos.	G	AB	R	H	2B	3B	HR	RBI	BB	SO	HBP	GDP	SB-CS	Avg.	OBP	SLG	OPS	E	Avg.
2004—	Boston (A.L.)	3B	1	2	0	0	0	0	0	0	0	1	0	0	0-0	.000	.000	.000	.000	0	...

2006 LEFTY-RIGHTY SPLITS

vs.	Avg.	AB	H	2B	3B	HR	RBI	BB	SO	OBP	Slg.	vs.	Avg.	AB	H	2B	3B	HR	RBI	BB	SO	OBP	Slg.
L	.270	163	44	10	1	3	19	33	32	.392	.399	R	.283	406	115	32	1	10	53	58	88	.376	.441

YOUMAN, SHANE   P

PERSONAL: Born October 11, 1979, in New Iberia, La. ... Throws left, bats left. ... Full name: Shane Demond Youman. ... College: LSU. **TRANSACTIONS/CAREER NOTES:** Selected by Pittsburgh Pirates organization in 43rd round of 2001 free-agent draft.

CAREER HITTING: 3-for-7 (.429), 0 R, 0 2B, 0 3B, 0 HR, 1 RBI.

Year	Team (League)	W	L	Pct.	ERA	WHIP	G	GS	CG	ShO	Hld.	Sv.-Opp.	IP	H	R	ER	HR	BB-IBB	SO	Avg.
2002—	Will. (NYP)	4	0	1.000	1.45	0.88	20	0	0	0	...	5-...	37.1	25	7	6	1	8-0	48	.189
2003—	Hickory (S. Atl.)	6	3	.667	4.65	1.71	40	1	0	0	...	12-...	50.1	51	31	26	2	35-2	58	.263
2004—	Lynchburg (Caro.)	4	2	.667	3.16	1.38	47	0	0	0	...	2-...	74.0	67	28	26	5	35-5	62	.233
2005—	Altoona (East.)	8	6	.571	3.92	1.49	44	5	0	0	3	2-4	101.0	102	54	44	10	48-0	77	.258
2006—	Indianapolis (Int'l)	4	0	1.000	4.04	1.23	8	7	0	0	0	0-0	42.1	42	20	19	2	10-0	19	.259
—	Altoona (East.)	7	2	.778	1.51	0.94	23	11	0	0	2	1-1	95.1	70	27	16	4	20-1	64	.201
—	Pittsburgh (N.L.)	0	2	.000	2.91	1.15	5	3	0	0	0	0-0	21.2	15	7	7	1	10-0	5	.200
Major League totals (1 year)		0	2	.000	2.91	1.15	5	3	0	0	0	0-0	21.2	15	7	7	1	10-0	5	.200

2006 LEFTY-RIGHTY SPLITS

vs.	Avg.	AB	H	2B	3B	HR	RBI	BB	SO	OBP	Slg.	vs.	Avg.	AB	H	2B	3B	HR	RBI	BB	SO	OBP	Slg.
L	.250	16	4	0	0	0	2	3	0	.368	.250	R	.186	59	11	3	0	1	3	7	5	.269	.288

YOUNG, CHRIS   P

PERSONAL: Born May 25, 1979, in Dallas. ... 6-10/250. ... Throws right, bats right. ... Full name: Christopher Ryan Young. ... High school: Highland Park (Dallas). ... College: Princeton. **TRANSACTIONS/CAREER NOTES:** Selected by Pittsburgh Pirates organization in third round of 2000 free-agent draft. ... Traded by Pirates with P Jon Searles to Montreal Expos for P Matt Herges (December 20, 2002). ... Traded by Expos with OF Josh McKinley to Texas Rangers for C Einar Diaz and P Justin Echols (April 3, 2004). ... Traded by Rangers with 1B Adrian Gonzalez and OF Terrmel Sledge to San Diego Padres for Ps Adam Eaton and Akinori Otsuka and C Billy Killian (January 4, 2006).

Y

CAREER HITTING: 7-for-59 (.119), 2 R, 2 2B, 1 3B, 0 HR, 4 RBI.

Year Team (League)	W	L	Pct.	ERA	WHIP	G	GS	CG	ShO	Hld.	Sv.-Opp.	IP	H	R	ER	HR	BB-IBB	SO	Avg.
2001—Hickory (S. Atl.)	5	3	.625	4.12	1.33	12	12	2	0	...	0-...	74.1	79	39	34	6	20-0	72	.269
2002—Hickory (S. Atl.)	11	9	.550	3.11	1.11	26	26	1	0	...	0-...	144.2	127	57	50	11	34-1	136	.234
2003—Brevard County (FSL)	5	2	.714	1.62	0.62	8	8	0	0	...	0-...	50.0	26	9	9	3	5-0	39	.150
—Harrisburg (East.)	4	4	.500	4.01	1.27	15	15	0	0	...	0-...	83.0	83	39	37	9	22-0	64	.259
2004—Frisco (Texas)	6	5	.545	4.48	1.42	18	18	0	0	...	0-...	88.1	94	48	44	9	31-1	75	.269
—Oklahoma (PCL)	3	0	1.000	1.48	0.96	5	5	1	0	...	0-...	30.1	20	7	5	2	9-0	34	.189
—Texas (A.L.)	3	2	.600	4.71	1.27	7	7	0	0	0	0-0	36.1	36	21	19	7	10-0	27	.250
2005—Texas (A.L.)	12	7	.632	4.26	1.26	31	31	0	0	0	0-0	164.2	162	84	78	19	45-2	137	.252
2006—San Diego (N.L.)	11	5	.688	3.46	1.13	31	31	0	0	0	0-0	179.1	134	72	69	28	69-4	164	* .206
American League totals (2 years)	15	9	.625	4.34	1.26	38	38	0	0	0	0-0	201.0	198	105	97	26	55-2	164	.252
National League totals (1 year)	11	5	.688	3.46	1.13	31	31	0	0	0	0-0	179.1	134	72	69	28	69-4	164	.206
Major League totals (3 years)	26	14	.650	3.93	1.20	69	69	0	0	0	0-0	380.1	332	177	166	54	124-6	328	.231

DIVISION SERIES RECORD

Year Team (League)	W	L	Pct.	ERA	WHIP	G	GS	CG	ShO	Hld.	Sv.-Opp.	IP	H	R	ER	HR	BB-IBB	SO	Avg.
2006—San Diego (N.L.)	1	0	1.000	0.00	0.90	1	1	0	0	0	0-0	6.2	4	0	0	0	2-1	9	.174

2006 LEFTY-RIGHTY SPLITS

vs.	Avg.	AB	H	2B	3B	HR	RBI	BB	SO	OBP	Slg.	vs.	Avg.	AB	H	2B	3B	HR	RBI	BB	SO	OBP	Slg.
L	.175	303	53	8	2	11	24	34	81	.265	.323	R	.234	346	81	12	3	17	38	35	83	.307	.434

YOUNG, CHRIS — OF

PERSONAL: Born September 5, 1983, in Houston, Texas. ... 6-2/180. ... Bats right, throws right. ... Full name: Christopher Brandon Young. **TRANSACTIONS/CAREER NOTES:** Selected by Chicago White Sox organization in 16th round of 2001 free-agent draft. ... Traded by White Sox with Ps Orlando Hernandez and Luis Vizcaino to Arizona Diamondbacks for P Javier Vazquez and cash (December 20, 2005).

2006 GAMES PLAYED BY POSITION (MLB): OF—24.

							BATTING												FIELDING	
Year Team (League)	Pos.	G	AB	R	H	2B	3B	HR	RBI	BB	SO	HBP	GDP	SB-CS	Avg.	OBP	SLG	OPS	E	Avg.
2002—Ariz. White Sox (Ariz.)		55	184	26	40	13	1	5	17	19	54	5	1	7-8	.217	.308	.380	.688	...	...
2003—Bristol (Appal.)		64	238	47	69	18	3	7	28	23	40	4	0	21-7	.290	.357	.479	.836	...	...
—Great Falls (Pio.)		10	34	5	6	3	0	0	1	1	10	0	0	0-0	.176	.200	.265	.465	...	...
2004—Kannapolis (S. Atl.)		135	465	83	122	31	5	24	56	66	145	11	2	31-9	.262	.365	.505	.870	...	...
2005—Birmingham (Sou.)	OF-DH	126	466	100	129	41	3	26	77	70	129	7	4	32-6	.277	.377	.545	.922	6	.990
2006—Tucson (PCL)		100	402	78	111	32	4	21	77	52	71	6	6	17-5	.276	.363	.532	.896	5	.982
—Arizona (N.L.)	OF	30	70	10	17	4	0	2	10	6	12	1	0	2-1	.243	.308	.386	.693	0	1.000
Major League totals (1 year)		30	70	10	17	4	0	2	10	6	12	1	0	2-1	.243	.308	.386	.693	0	1.000

2006 LEFTY-RIGHTY SPLITS

vs.	Avg.	AB	H	2B	3B	HR	RBI	BB	SO	OBP	Slg.	vs.	Avg.	AB	H	2B	3B	HR	RBI	BB	SO	OBP	Slg.
L	.360	25	9	3	0	1	6	1	2	.385	.600	R	.178	45	8	1	0	1	4	5	10	.269	.267

YOUNG, DELMON — OF

PERSONAL: Born September 14, 1985, in Montgomery, Ala. ... 6-3/205. ... Bats right, throws right. ... Full name: Delmon Damarcus Young. ... Brother of Dmitri Young, outfielder/DH with Detroit Tigers in 2006. **TRANSACTIONS/CAREER NOTES:** Selected by Tampa Bay Devil Rays organization in first round (first pick overall) of 2003 free-agent draft.

2006 GAMES PLAYED BY POSITION (MLB): OF—30.

							BATTING												FIELDING	
Year Team (League)	Pos.	G	AB	R	H	2B	3B	HR	RBI	BB	SO	HBP	GDP	SB-CS	Avg.	OBP	SLG	OPS	E	Avg.
2004—Char., S.C. (SAL)		131	513	95	164	26	5	25	115	53	120	6	11	21-6	.320	.386	.536	.922	...	...
2005—Montgm. (Sou.)	OF-DH	84	330	59	111	13	4	20	71	25	66	7	10	25-8	.336	.386	.582	.968	14	.952
—Durham (Int'l)	OF-DH	52	228	33	65	13	3	6	28	4	33	2	6	7-4	.285	.303	.447	.751	12	.943
2006—Durham (Int'l)		86	342	50	108	22	4	8	59	15	65	3	12	22-4	.316	.341	.474	.814	2	.988
—Tampa Bay (A.L.)	OF	30	126	16	40	9	1	3	10	1	24	3	0	2-2	.317	.336	.476	.812	1	.983
Major League totals (1 year)		30	126	16	40	9	1	3	10	1	24	3	0	2-2	.317	.336	.476	.812	1	.983

2006 LEFTY-RIGHTY SPLITS

vs.	Avg.	AB	H	2B	3B	HR	RBI	BB	SO	OBP	Slg.	vs.	Avg.	AB	H	2B	3B	HR	RBI	BB	SO	OBP	Slg.
L	.379	29	11	4	0	1	2	0	4	.379	.621	R	.299	97	29	5	1	2	8	1	20	.324	.433

YOUNG, DELWYN — OF

PERSONAL: Born June 30, 1982, in Los Angeles. ... 5-8/210. ... Bats both, throws right. ... Full name: Delwyn Rudy Young. ... High school: Littlerock (Calif.). ... Junior college: Santa Barbara C.C. **TRANSACTIONS/CAREER NOTES:** Selected by Atlanta Braves organization in 31st round of 2000 free-agent draft; did not sign. ... Selected by Braves organization in 29th round of 2001 free-agent draft; did not sign. ... Selected by Los Angeles Dodgers organization in fourth round of 2002 free-agent draft.

2006 GAMES PLAYED BY POSITION (MLB): OF—2.

							BATTING												FIELDING	
Year Team (League)	Pos.	G	AB	R	H	2B	3B	HR	RBI	BB	SO	HBP	GDP	SB-CS	Avg.	OBP	SLG	OPS	E	Avg.
2002—Great Falls (Pio.)		59	240	42	72	18	1	10	41	27	60	4	2	4-2	.300	.380	.508	.888	...	...
2003—South Georgia (S. Atl.)		119	443	67	143	38	7	15	73	36	87	8	2	5-2	.323	.381	.542	.923	...	...
2004—Vero Beach (FSL)		129	470	76	132	36	3	22	85	57	134	7	13	11-4	.281	.364	.511	.875	...	...
2005—Jacksonville (Sou.)	2B-DH-3B-OF	95	371	52	110	25	1	16	62	27	86	3	9	1-3	.296	.346	.499	.844	12	.965
—Las Vegas (PCL)	2B	36	160	23	52	12	0	4	14	8	35	1	3	0-0	.325	.361	.475	.836	4	.980
2006—Las Vegas (PCL)		140	532	76	145	42	1	18	98	42	104	3	11	3-4	.273	.326	.457	.783	9	.958
—Los Angeles (N.L.)	OF	8	5	0	0	0	0	0	0	0	1	0	0	0-0	.000	.000	.000	.000	0	...
Major League totals (1 year)		8	5	0	0	0	0	0	0	0	1	0	0	0-0	.000	.000	.000	.000	0	...

2006 LEFTY-RIGHTY SPLITS

vs.	Avg.	AB	H	2B	3B	HR	RBI	BB	SO	OBP	Slg.	vs.	Avg.	AB	H	2B	3B	HR	RBI	BB	SO	OBP	Slg.
L	.000	0	0	0	0	0	0	0	0	.000	.000	R	.000	5	0	0	0	0	0	0	1	.000	.000

Y

YOUNG, DMITRI   1B/OF

PERSONAL: Born October 11, 1973, in Vicksburg, Miss. ... 6-2/245. ... Bats both, throws right. ... Full name: Dmitri Dell Young. ... High school: Rio Mesa (Oxnard, Calif.). ... Brother of Delmon Young, outfielder, Tampa Bay Devil Rays. **TRANSACTIONS/CAREER NOTES:** Selected by St. Louis Cardinals organization in first round (fourth pick overall) of 1991 free-agent draft. ... On disabled list (May 11-29, 1997); included rehabilitation assignment to Louisville. ... Traded by Cardinals to Cincinnati Reds for P Jeff Brantley (November 10, 1997). ... Selected by Tampa Bay Devil Rays in first round (16th pick overall) of expansion draft (November 18, 1997). ... Traded by Devil Rays to Reds (November 18, 1997), completing deal in which Reds traded OF Mike Kelly to Devil Rays for a player to be named (November 11, 1997). ... Traded by Reds to Detroit Tigers for OF Juan Encarnacion and P Luis Pineda (December 11, 2001). ... On disabled list (April 23-May 14 and July 6, 2002-remainder of season). ... On disabled list (April 7-May 31, 2004); included rehabilitation assignment to Toledo. ... On disabled list (April 15-May 5 and May 23-July 21, 2006); included rehabilitation assignments to Erie, Lakeland and Toledo. ... Released by Tigers (September 6, 2006). **STATISTICAL NOTES:** Hit three home runs in one game (April 4, 2005). ... Career major league grand slams: 5.

2006 GAMES PLAYED BY POSITION (MLB): DH—44, 1B—3.

Year	Team (League)	Pos.	G	AB	R	H	2B	3B	HR	RBI	BB	SO	HBP	GDP	SB-CS	Avg.	OBP	SLG	OPS	E	Avg.
1991— Johnson City (App.)		3B	37	129	22	33	10	0	2	22	21	28	2	1	2-1	.256	.364	.380	.743	5	.932
1992— Springfield (Midw.)		3B	135	493	74	153	36	6	14	72	51	94	5	9	14-13	.310	.378	.493	.871	42	.879
1993— St. Pete. (FSL)		1B-3B	69	270	31	85	13	3	5	43	24	28	2	7	3-4	.315	.369	.441	.810	10	.981
— Arkansas (Texas)		1B-3B	45	166	13	41	11	2	3	21	9	29	2	5	4-4	.247	.294	.392	.685	7	.982
1994— Arkansas (Texas)		1B-OF	125	453	53	123	33	2	8	54	36	60	5	6	0-3	.272	.330	.406	.736	16	.971
1995— Arkansas (Texas)		OF-DH	97	367	54	107	18	6	10	62	30	46	3	11	2-4	.292	.347	.455	.802	9	.931
— Louisville (A.A.)		OF	2	7	3	2	0	0	0	0	1	1	0	0	0-0	.286	.375	.286	.661	1	.750
1996— Louisville (A.A.)		1B	122	459	90	153	31	8	15	64	34	67	1	5	16-5	.333	.378	.534	.912	8	.993
— St. Louis (N.L.)		1B	16	29	3	7	0	0	0	2	4	5	1	0	0-1	.241	.353	.241	.594	1	.977
1997— St. Louis (N.L.)	1B-OF-DH		110	333	38	86	14	3	5	34	38	63	2	8	6-5	.258	.335	.363	.698	13	.981
— Louisville (A.A.)		OF-1B	24	84	10	23	7	0	4	14	13	15	0	1	1-1	.274	.371	.500	.871	1	.985
1998— Cincinnati (N.L.)		OF-1B	144	536	81	166	48	1	14	83	47	94	2	16	2-4	.310	.364	.481	.846	12	.981
1999— Cincinnati (N.L.)	OF-1B-DH		127	373	63	112	30	2	14	56	30	71	2	11	1-3	.300	.352	.504	.856	4	.982
2000— Cincinnati (N.L.)	OF-1B-DH		152	548	68	166	37	6	18	88	36	80	3	16	0-3	.303	.346	.491	.837	8	.981
2001— Cincinnati (N.L.)		OF-1B-3B	142	540	68	163	28	3	21	69	37	77	5	22	8-5	.302	.350	.481	.832	16	.967
2002— Detroit (A.L.)	DH-1B-3B																				
	OF		54	201	25	57	14	0	7	27	12	39	2	12	2-0	.284	.329	.458	.786	4	.972
2003— Detroit (A.L.)	DH-OF-3B																				
	1B		155	562	78	167	34	7	29	85	58	130	11	16	2-1	.297	.372	.537	.909	10	.947
2004— Toledo (Int'l)		DH	2	10	1	5	1	1	1	5	1	0	0	0	0-0	.500	.545	1.100	1.645	0	...
— Detroit (A.L.)	DH-1B-OF																				
	3B		104	389	72	106	23	2	18	60	33	71	6	8	0-1	.272	.336	.481	.816	0	1.000
2005— Detroit (A.L.)		DH-1B-OF	126	469	61	127	25	3	21	72	29	100	9	16	1-0	.271	.325	.471	.796	3	.991
2006— Lakeland (Fla. St.)			2	5	1	2	1	0	0	1	1	1	0	0	0-0	.400	.500	.600	1.100	0	...
— Erie (East.)			6	20	2	3	1	0	0	1	1	4	0	0	0-0	.150	.292	.200	.492	2	.935
— Toledo (Int'l)			8	31	4	14	3	0	1	6	4	4	0	0	0-0	.452	.514	.645	1.159	2	...
— Detroit (A.L.)		DH-1B	48	172	19	43	4	1	7	23	11	39	0	5	1-1	.250	.293	.407	.700	3	.889
American League totals (5 years)			487	1793	255	500	100	13	82	267	143	379	28	55	6-3	.279	.340	.486	.826	20	.978
National League totals (6 years)			691	2359	321	700	157	15	72	332	192	390	15	74	19-19	.297	.351	.468	.818	54	.977
Major League totals (11 years)			1178	4152	576	1200	257	28	154	599	335	769	43	129	25-22	.289	.346	.476	.822	74	.977

DIVISION SERIES RECORD

Year	Team (League)	Pos.	G	AB	R	H	2B	3B	HR	RBI	BB	SO	HBP	GDP	SB-CS	Avg.	OBP	SLG	OPS	E	Avg.
1996— St. Louis (N.L.)			Did not play.																		

CHAMPIONSHIP SERIES RECORD

Year	Team (League)	Pos.	G	AB	R	H	2B	3B	HR	RBI	BB	SO	HBP	GDP	SB-CS	Avg.	OBP	SLG	OPS	E	Avg.
1996— St. Louis (N.L.)		1B	4	7	1	2	0	1	0	2	0	2	0	0	0-0	.286	.286	.571	.857	0	1.000

2006 LEFTY-RIGHTY SPLITS

vs.	Avg.	AB	H	2B	3B	HR	RBI	BB	SO	OBP	Slg.	vs.	Avg.	AB	H	2B	3B	HR	RBI	BB	SO	OBP	Slg.
L	.136	22	3	1	0	0	1	2	7	.208	.182	R	.267	150	40	3	1	7	22	9	32	.306	.440

YOUNG, ERIC   OF/2B

PERSONAL: Born May 11, 1967, in New Brunswick, N.J. ... 5-8/186. ... Bats right, throws right. ... Full name: Eric Orlando Young. ... High school: New Brunswick (N.J.). ... College: Rutgers. **TRANSACTIONS/CAREER NOTES:** Selected by Los Angeles Dodgers organization in 43rd round of 1989 free-agent draft. ... Selected by Colorado Rockies organization in first round (11th pick overall) of expansion draft (November 17, 1992). ... On disabled list (March 22-April 22, 1996); included rehabilitation assignments to New Haven, Salem and Colorado Springs. ... Traded by Rockies to Dodgers for P Pedro Astacio (August 19, 1997). ... On disabled list (July 24-August 13, 1999); included rehabilitation assignment to San Bernardino. ... Traded by Dodgers with P Ismael Valdes to Chicago Cubs for Ps Terry Adams and Chad Ricketts and a player to be named (December 12, 1999); Dodgers acquired P Brian Stephenson to complete deal (December 16, 1999). ... Signed as a free agent by Milwaukee Brewers (January 17, 2002). ... Traded by Brewers to San Francisco Giants for P Greg Bruso (August 19, 2003). ... Signed as a free agent by Texas Rangers (January 6, 2004). ... Signed as a free agent by San Diego Padres (December 9, 2004). ... On disabled list (April 8-July 2, 2005); included rehabilitation assignment to Portland. ... Released by Padres (August 1, 2006). ... Signed by Texas Rangers organization (August 11, 2006). **HONORS:** Named second baseman on THE SPORTING NEWS N.L. All-Star team (1996). ... Named second baseman on N.L. Silver Slugger team (1996).

2006 GAMES PLAYED BY POSITION (MLB): OF—40, 2B—2, DH—1.

Year	Team (League)	Pos.	G	AB	R	H	2B	3B	HR	RBI	BB	SO	HBP	GDP	SB-CS	Avg.	OBP	SLG	OPS	E	Avg.
1989— GC Dodgers (GCL)		2B	56	197	56	65	11	5	2	22	33	16	3	1	41-10	.330	.432	.467	.899	15	.939
1990— Vero Beach (FSL)		2B-OF	127	460	101	132	23	7	2	50	69	35	6	4	76-16	.287	.384	.380	.764	25	.974
1991— San Antonio (Texas)		2B-OF	127	461	82	129	17	4	3	35	67	36	2	13	70-26	.280	.373	.354	.726	13	.974
— Albuquerque (PCL)		2B	1	5	0	2	0	0	0	0	0	0	0	0	0-0	.400	.400	.400	.800	0	1.000
1992— Albuquerque (PCL)		2B	94	350	61	118	16	5	3	49	33	18	4	10	28-11	.337	.393	.437	.831	20	.961
— Los Angeles (N.L.)		2B	49	132	9	34	1	0	1	11	8	14	0	3	6-1	.258	.300	.288	.588	3	.957
1993— Colorado (N.L.)		2B-OF	144	490	82	132	16	8	3	42	63	41	4	9	42-19	.269	.355	.353	.708	18	.964
1994— Colorado (N.L.)		OF-2B	90	228	37	62	13	1	7	30	38	17	2	3	18-7	.272	.378	.430	.808	2	.981
1995— Colorado (N.L.)		2B-OF	120	366	68	116	21	•9	6	36	49	29	5	4	35-12	.317	.404	.473	.876	11	.974
1996— New Haven (East.)		2B	3	15	0	1	0	0	0	0	0	3	0	0	0-0	.067	.067	.067	.133	0	1.000
— Salem (Carol.)		2B	3	10	2	3	3	0	0	0	3	1	0	0	2-0	.300	.462	.600	1.062	2	.875
— Colo. Springs (PCL)		2B	7	23	4	6	1	1	0	3	6	2	0	1	6-1	.261	.393	.391	.784	3	.917
— Colorado (N.L.)		2B	141	568	113	184	23	4	8	74	47	31	21	9	* 53-*19	.324	.393	.421	.814	12	.978
1997— Colorado (N.L.)		2B	118	468	78	132	29	6	6	45	57	37	5	16	32-12	.282	.363	.408	.771	15	.978
— Los Angeles (N.L.)		2B	37	154	28	42	4	2	1	16	14	17	4	2	13-2	.273	.347	.364	.710	3	.978

— 542 —

Year Team (League)	Pos.	G	AB	R	H	2B	3B	HR	RBI	BB	SO	HBP	GDP	SB-CS	Avg.	OBP	SLG	OPS	E	Avg.
1998— Los Angeles (N.L.)	2B-DH	117	452	78	129	24	1	8	43	45	32	5	4	42-13	.285	.355	.396	.751	13	.976
1999— Los Angeles (N.L.)	2B	119	456	73	128	24	2	2	41	63	26	5	12	51-*22	.281	.371	.355	.726	9	.984
—San Bern. (Calif.)	2B	3	12	0	3	0	0	0	0	0	2	0	0	0-0	.250	.250	.250	.500	2	.833
2000— Chicago (N.L.)	2B	153	607	98	180	40	2	6	47	63	39	8	12	54-7	.297	.368	.399	.766	15	.979
2001— Chicago (N.L.)	2B	149	603	98	168	43	4	6	42	42	45	9	15	31-14	.279	.333	.393	.726	12	.981
2002— Milwaukee (N.L.)	2B-DH-OF	138	496	57	139	29	3	3	28	39	38	6	14	31-11	.280	.338	.369	.707	12	.979
2003— Milwaukee (N.L.)	2B-DH	109	404	71	105	18	1	15	31	48	34	4	9	25-7	.260	.344	.421	.764	15	.967
—San Francisco (N.L.)	2B-OF	26	71	9	14	2	0	0	3	9	10	1	3	3-5	.197	.293	.225	.518	1	.989
2004— Texas (A.L.) OF-DH-2B-SS-3B		104	344	55	99	25	2	1	27	43	28	8	9	14-9	.288	.377	.381	.758	9	.952
2005— Portland (PCL)	DH-2B	5	16	3	0	0	0	0	0	6	2	0	0	0-0	.000	.273	.000	.273	0	1.000
—San Diego (N.L.)	OF-2B	56	142	22	39	9	0	2	12	19	12	0	6	7-6	.275	.356	.380	.737	3	.972
2006— San Diego (N.L.)	OF-2B	56	128	19	26	5	0	3	13	13	16	2	6	8-2	.203	.281	.313	.593	1	.980
—Oklahoma (PCL)		9	27	3	6	2	3	0	1	4	4	0	2	0-2	.222	.364	.519	.882	0	1.000
—Texas (A.L.)	2B-OF-DH	4	10	1	2	1	1	0	2	1	1	0	1	0-0	.200	.273	.500	.773	0	1.000
American League totals (2 years)		108	354	56	101	26	3	1	29	44	29	8	10	14-9	.285	.374	.384	.758	9	.955
National League totals (14 years)		1622	5765	940	1630	301	43	78	514	616	433	81	125	451-159	.283	.358	.390	.748	151	.977
Major League totals (15 years)		1730	6119	996	1731	327	46	79	543	660	462	89	135	465-168	.283	.359	.390	.749	160	.976

DIVISION SERIES RECORD

Year Team (League)	Pos.	G	AB	R	H	2B	3B	HR	RBI	BB	SO	HBP	GDP	SB-CS	Avg.	OBP	SLG	OPS	E	Avg.
1995— Colorado (N.L.)	2B	4	16	3	7	1	0	1	2	2	2	0	0	1-0	.438	.500	.688	1.188	3	.875
2005— San Diego (N.L.)	OF	3	6	2	2	0	0	1	3	0	0	0	1	0-0	.333	.333	.833	1.167	0	...
Division series totals (2 years)		7	22	5	9	1	0	2	5	2	2	0	1	1-0	.409	.458	.727	1.186	3	.875

ALL-STAR GAME RECORD

		G	AB	R	H	2B	3B	HR	RBI	BB	SO	HBP	GDP	SB-CS	Avg.	OBP	SLG	OPS	E	Avg.
All-Star Game totals (1 year)		1	1	0	0	0	0	0	0	0	0	0	0	0-0	.000	.000	.000	.000	0	1.000

2006 LEFTY-RIGHTY SPLITS

vs.	Avg.	AB	H	2B	3B	HR	RBI	BB	SO	OBP	Slg.	vs.	Avg.	AB	H	2B	3B	HR	RBI	BB	SO	OBP	Slg.
L	.268	71	19	4	1	3	12	5	8	.329	.479	R	.134	67	9	2	0	0	3	9	9	.231	.164

YOUNG, MICHAEL — SS

PERSONAL: Born October 19, 1976, in Covina, Calif. ... 6-1/190. ... Bats right, throws right. ... Full name: Michael Brian Young. ... High school: Bishop Amat (La Puente, Calif.). ... College: UC-Santa Barbara. **TRANSACTIONS/CAREER NOTES:** Selected by Baltimore Orioles organization in 25th round of 1994 free-agent draft; did not sign. ... Selected by Toronto Blue Jays organization in fifth round of 1997 free-agent draft. ... Traded by Blue Jays with P Darwin Cubillan to Texas Rangers for P Esteban Loaiza (July 19, 2000). **HONORS:** Named shortstop on the SPORTING NEWS A.L. All-Star team (2005). **STATISTICAL NOTES:** Career major league grand slams: 2.
2006 GAMES PLAYED BY POSITION (MLB): SS—155, DH—7.

Year Team (League)	Pos.	G	AB	R	H	2B	3B	HR	RBI	BB	SO	HBP	GDP	SB-CS	Avg.	OBP	SLG	OPS	E	Avg.
1997— St. Catharines (NYP)	2B-SS	74	276	49	85	18	3	9	48	33	59	7	6	9-5	.308	.392	.493	.886	18	.946
1998— Hagerstown (SAL)	2B-OF-SS	140	522	86	147	33	5	16	87	55	96	7	12	16-8	.282	.354	.456	.810	13	.977
1999— Dunedin (Fla. St.)	2B-SS	129	495	86	155	36	3	5	83	61	78	4	10	30-6	.313	.389	.428	.818	22	.961
2000— Tennessee (Sou.)	2B-SS	91	345	51	95	24	5	6	47	36	72	1	5	16-5	.275	.340	.426	.766	16	.965
—Tulsa (Texas)	SS	43	188	30	60	13	5	1	32	17	28	0	4	9-3	.319	.368	.457	.826	7	.965
—Texas (A.L.)	2B	2	2	0	0	0	0	0	0	0	0	0	0	0-0	.000	.000	.000	.000	0	...
2001— Oklahoma (PCL)	2B-SS	47	189	28	55	8	0	8	28	20	34	1	6	3-3	.291	.358	.460	.819	6	.968
—Texas (A.L.)	2B	106	386	57	96	18	4	11	49	26	91	3	9	3-1	.249	.298	.402	.699	8	.984
2002— Texas (A.L.) 2B-SS-3B-DH		156	573	77	150	26	8	9	62	41	112	0	14	6-7	.262	.308	.382	.690	9	.988
2003— Texas (A.L.)	2B-SS	160	666	106	204	33	9	14	72	36	103	1	14	13-2	.306	.339	.446	.785	10	.987
2004— Texas (A.L.)	SS-DH	160	690	114	216	33	9	22	99	44	89	1	11	12-3	.313	.353	.483	.836	19	.972
2005— Texas (A.L.)	SS-DH	159	668	114	*221	40	5	24	91	58	91	3	20	5-2	*.331	.385	.513	.899	18	.974
2006— Texas (A.L.)	SS-DH	•162	691	93	217	52	3	14	103	48	96	1	27	7-3	.314	.356	.459	.814	14	.981
Major League totals (7 years)		905	3676	561	1104	202	38	94	476	253	583	9	95	46-18	.300	.344	.453	.797	78	.981

ALL-STAR GAME RECORD

		G	AB	R	H	2B	3B	HR	RBI	BB	SO	HBP	GDP	SB-CS	Avg.	OBP	SLG	OPS	E	Avg.
All-Star Game totals (3 years)		3	5	0	2	1	1	0	2	0	0	0	0	0-0	.400	.400	1.000	1.400	0	1.000

2006 LEFTY-RIGHTY SPLITS

vs.	Avg.	AB	H	2B	3B	HR	RBI	BB	SO	OBP	Slg.	vs.	Avg.	AB	H	2B	3B	HR	RBI	BB	SO	OBP	Slg.
L	.295	166	49	16	0	4	17	15	24	.352	.464	R	.320	525	168	36	3	10	86	33	72	.357	.457

ZAMBRANO, CARLOS — P

PERSONAL: Born June 1, 1981, in Puerto Cabello, Venezuela. ... 6-5/255. ... Throws right, bats both. ... Full name: Carlos Alberto Zambrano. ... Name pronounced: zam-BRAH-no. ... High school: Unidad Educativa Creacion (Puerto Cabello, Venezuela). **TRANSACTIONS/CAREER NOTES:** Signed as a non-drafted free agent by Chicago Cubs organization (July 12, 1997). ... On disabled list (May 10-June 7, 2002); included rehabilitation assignment to Iowa. ... On suspended list (August 3-9, 2002; and August 5-11, 2004). **HONORS:** Named pitcher on N.L. Silver Slugger team (2006). **MISCELLANEOUS NOTES:** Scored a run in two appearances as pinch runner (2005). ... Struck out twice, grounded into double play and flied out in four appearances as pinch hitter (2006).
CAREER HITTING: 70-for-330 (.212), 34 R, 13 2B, 2 3B, 10 HR, 28 RBI.

Year Team (League)	W	L	Pct.	ERA	WHIP	G	GS	CG	ShO	Hld.	Sv.-Opp.	IP	H	R	ER	HR	BB-IBB	SO	Avg.
1998— Ariz. Cubs (Ariz.)	0	1	.000	3.15	1.60	14	2	0	0	...	1-...	40.0	39	17	14	0	25-3	36	.257
1999— Lansing (Midw.)	13	7	.650	4.17	1.38	27	24	2	1	...	0-...	153.1	150	87	71	9	62-1	98	.258
2000— West Tenn (Sou.)	3	1	.750	1.34	0.99	9	9	0	0	...	0-...	60.1	39	14	9	2	21-0	43	.181
—Iowa (PCL)	2	5	.286	3.97	1.66	34	0	0	0	...	6-...	56.2	54	30	25	3	40-2	46	.260
2001— Iowa (PCL)	10	5	.667	3.88	1.27	26	25	1	0	...	0-...	150.2	124	73	65	9	68-1	155	.226
—Chicago (N.L.)	1	2	.333	15.26	2.48	6	1	0	0	0	0-1	7.2	11	13	13	2	8-0	4	.355
2002— Iowa (PCL)	0	0	...	0.00	0.89	3	3	0	0	0	0-0	9.0	2	0	0	0	6-0	11	.069
—Chicago (N.L.)	4	8	.333	3.66	1.45	32	16	0	0	0	0-0	108.1	94	53	44	9	63-2	93	.235
2003— Chicago (N.L.)	13	11	.542	3.11	1.32	32	32	3	1	0	0-0	214.0	188	88	74	9	94-12	168	.239
2004— Chicago (N.L.)	16	8	.667	2.75	1.22	31	31	1	1	0	0-0	209.2	174	75	64	14	81-4	188	.225
2005— Chicago (N.L.)	14	6	.700	3.26	1.15	33	33	2	0	0	0-0	223.1	170	88	81	21	86-3	202	.212
2006— Chicago (N.L.)	•16	7	.696	3.41	1.29	33	33	0	0	0	0-0	214.0	162	91	81	20	*115-4	210	.208
Major League totals (6 years)	64	42	.604	3.29	1.28	167	146	6	2	0	0-1	977.0	799	406	357	75	447-25	865	.224

DIVISION SERIES RECORD

Year Team (League)	W	L	Pct.	ERA	WHIP	G	GS	CG	ShO	Hld.	Sv.-Opp.	IP	H	R	ER	HR	BB-IBB	SO	Avg.
2003— Chicago (N.L.)	0	0	...	4.76	1.94	1	1	0	0	0	0-0	5.2	11	3	3	0	0-0	4	.407

CHAMPIONSHIP SERIES RECORD

Year Team (League)	W	L	Pct.	ERA	WHIP	G	GS	CG	ShO	Hld.	Sv.-Opp.	IP	H	R	ER	HR	BB-IBB	SO	Avg.
2003— Chicago (N.L.)	0	1	.000	5.73	1.73	2	2	0	0	0	0-0	11.0	14	8	7	4	5-0	8	.311

ALL-STAR GAME RECORD

	W	L	Pct.	ERA	WHIP	G	GS	CG	ShO	Hld.	Sv.-Opp.	IP	H	R	ER	HR	BB-IBB	SO	Avg.
All-Star Game totals (1 year)	0	0	...	9.00	2.00	1	0	0	0	0	0-0	1.0	1	1	1	0	1-0	1	.250

2006 LEFTY-RIGHTY SPLITS

vs.	Avg.	AB	H	2B	3B	HR	RBI	BB	SO	OBP	Slg.	vs.	Avg.	AB	H	2B	3B	HR	RBI	BB	SO	OBP	Slg.
L	.247	369	91	22	4	10	36	75	79	.377	.409	R	.174	409	71	19	1	10	48	40	131	.255	.298

ZAMBRANO, VICTOR — P

PERSONAL: Born August 6, 1975, in Los Teques, Venezuela. ... 6-0/203. ... Throws right, bats both. ... Full name: Victor Manuel Zambrano. ... Name pronounced: zam-BRAH-no. ... High school: Manve Maria Billolobo (Los Teques, Venezuela). **TRANSACTIONS/CAREER NOTES:** Signed as a non-drafted free agent by New York Yankees organization (August 19, 1993). ... Played infield for two seasons in Yankees organization (1994-95). ... Released by Yankees (February 7, 1996). ... Signed by Tampa Bay Devil Rays organization (March 14, 1996). ... Traded by Devil Rays with P Bartolome Fortunato to New York Mets for Ps Scott Kazmir and Jose Diaz (July 30, 2004). ... On disabled list (August 18, 2004-remainder of season). ... On disabled list (May 7, 2006-remainder of season).

CAREER HITTING: 9-for-73 (.123), 3 R, 1 2B, 1 3B, 0 HR, 3 RBI.

Year Team (League)	W	L	Pct.	ERA	WHIP	G	GS	CG	ShO	Hld.	Sv.-Opp.	IP	H	R	ER	HR	BB-IBB	SO	Avg.
1996— GC Devil Rays (GCL)	0	0	...	8.10	1.20	1	0	0	0	...	0-...	3.1	4	4	3	0	0-0	6	.250
1997— GC Devil Rays (GCL)	0	0	...	0.00	0.33	2	0	0	0	...	0-...	3.0	1	0	0	0	0-0	2	.100
— Princeton (Appal.)	0	2	.000	1.82	0.91	20	0	0	0	...	0-...	29.2	18	13	6	1	9-1	36	.159
1998— Char., S.C. (SAL)	6	4	.600	3.38	1.19	48	2	0	0	...	0-...	77.1	72	32	29	5	20-1	89	.244
1999— St. Pete. (FSL)	0	2	.000	4.00	1.67	7	0	0	0	...	0-...	9.0	10	6	4	1	5-0	15	.278
— Orlando (South.)	7	2	.778	4.59	1.58	40	4	0	0	...	1-...	82.1	92	55	42	5	38-2	81	.280
2000— Durham (Int'l)	0	6	.000	5.03	1.61	53	0	0	0	...	8-...	62.2	72	38	35	9	29-2	55	.289
2001— Durham (Int'l)	1	2	.333	2.08	1.25	29	0	0	0	...	12-...	30.1	26	10	7	2	12-1	29	.232
— Tampa Bay (A.L.)	6	2	.750	3.16	1.09	36	0	0	0	5	2-6	51.1	38	21	18	6	18-0	58	.201
2002— Tampa Bay (A.L.)	8	8	.500	5.53	1.65	42	11	0	0	6	1-3	114.0	120	77	70	15	68-5	73	.278
— Durham (Int'l)	0	1	.000	1.93	0.93	10	0	0	0	...	0-...	14.0	9	4	3	2	4-0	15	.180
2003— Durham (Int'l)	0	1	.000	4.50	1.50	1	1	0	0	...	0-...	4.0	4	6	2	0	2-0	6	.222
— Tampa Bay (A.L.)	12	10	.545	4.21	1.44	34	28	1	0	2	0-0	188.1	165	97	88	21	* 106-2	132	.237
2004— Tampa Bay (A.L.)	9	7	.563	4.43	1.59	23	22	0	0	1	0-0	128.0	107	68	63	13	• 96-2	109	.230
— New York (N.L.)	2	0	1.000	3.86	1.29	3	3	0	0	0	0-0	14.0	12	9	6	0	6-0	14	.222
2005— New York (N.L.)	7	12	.368	4.17	1.48	31	27	0	0	0	0-0	166.1	170	85	77	12	77-2	112	.264
2006— New York (N.L.)	1	2	.333	6.75	1.69	5	5	0	0	0	0-0	21.1	25	16	16	5	11-0	15	.291
American League totals (4 years)	35	27	.565	4.47	1.49	135	61	1	0	14	3-9	481.2	430	263	239	55	288-9	372	.241
National League totals (3 years)	10	14	.417	4.42	1.49	39	35	0	0	0	0-0	201.2	207	110	99	17	94-2	141	.264
Major League totals (6 years)	45	41	.523	4.45	1.49	174	96	1	0	14	3-9	683.1	637	373	338	72	382-11	513	.248

2006 LEFTY-RIGHTY SPLITS

vs.	Avg.	AB	H	2B	3B	HR	RBI	BB	SO	OBP	Slg.	vs.	Avg.	AB	H	2B	3B	HR	RBI	BB	SO	OBP	Slg.
L	.344	32	11	3	0	2	8	7	3	.462	.625	R	.259	54	14	0	0	3	8	4	12	.310	.426

ZAUN, GREGG — C

PERSONAL: Born April 14, 1971, in Glendale, Calif. ... 5-10/190. ... Bats both, throws right. ... Full name: Gregory Owen Zaun. ... Name pronounced: ZAHN. ... High school: St. Francis (La Canada, Calif.). ... Nephew of Rick Dempsey, catcher with six major league teams (1969-92). **TRANSACTIONS/CAREER NOTES:** Selected by Baltimore Orioles organization in 17th round of 1989 free-agent draft. ... Traded by Orioles to Florida Marlins (August 23, 1996), completing deal in which Marlins traded P Terry Mathews to Orioles for a player to be named (August 21, 1996). ... Traded by Marlins to Texas Rangers for cash (November 23, 1998). ... Traded by Rangers with OF Juan Gonzalez and P Danny Patterson to Detroit Tigers for Ps Justin Thompson, Francisco Cordero and Alan Webb, OF Gabe Kapler, C Bill Haselman and 2B Frank Catalanotto (November 2, 1999). ... Traded by Tigers to Kansas City Royals for cash (March 7, 2000). ... On disabled list (April 15-May 29, 2000); included rehabilitation assignment to Omaha. ... On disabled list (March 31-July 23, 2001); included rehabilitation assignments to GCL Royals and Omaha. ... Signed as a free agent by Houston Astros (December 11, 2001). ... Released by Astros (August 21, 2003). ... Signed by Colorado Rockies (August 26, 2003). ... Signed as a free agent by Montreal Expos organization (January 13, 2004). ... Signed as a free agent by Toronto Blue Jays organization (April 10, 2004). ... On disabled list (May 9-24, 2005); included rehabilitation assignment to New Hampshire. ... On disabled list (March 24-April 8, 2006); included rehabilitation assignment to Dunedin. **STATISTICAL NOTES:** Career major league grand slams: 3.

2006 GAMES PLAYED BY POSITION (MLB): C—72, DH—19.

									BATTING									FIELDING		
Year Team (League)	Pos.	G	AB	R	H	2B	3B	HR	RBI	BB	SO	HBP	GDP	SB-CS	Avg.	OBP	SLG	OPS	E	Avg.
1990— Wausau (Midw.)	C	37	100	3	13	0	1	1	7	7	17	1	2	0-0	.130	.194	.180	.374	3	.990
— Bluefield (Appal.)	P	61	184	29	55	5	2	2	21	23	15	1	2	5-5	.299	.378	.380	.758	10	.980
1991— Kane Co. (Midw.)	C	113	409	67	112	17	5	4	51	50	41	2	10	4-4	.274	.353	.369	.722	12	.980
1992— Frederick (Carolina)	2B-C	108	383	54	96	18	6	6	52	42	45	3	10	3-5	.251	.324	.376	.700	18	.980
1993— Bowie (East.)	C-P	79	258	25	79	10	0	3	38	27	26	1	7	4-7	.306	.373	.380	.753	10	.979
— Rochester (Int'l)	C	21	78	10	20	4	2	1	11	6	11	0	1	0-0	.256	.302	.397	.700	4	.975
1994— Rochester (Int'l)	C	123	388	61	92	16	4	7	43	56	72	4	5	4-2	.237	.337	.353	.690	9	.989
1995— Rochester (Int'l)	C-DH	42	140	26	41	13	1	6	18	14	21	3	0	0-3	.293	.367	.529	.896	3	.989
— Baltimore (A.L.)	C	40	104	18	27	5	0	3	14	16	14	0	2	1-1	.260	.358	.394	.753	2	.987
1996— Baltimore (A.L.)	C	50	108	16	25	8	1	1	13	11	15	2	3	0-0	.231	.309	.352	.661	2	.987
— Rochester (Int'l)	C-DH	14	47	11	15	2	0	0	4	11	6	0	0	0-2	.319	.441	.362	.802	0	.975
— Florida (N.L.)	C	10	31	4	9	1	0	1	2	3	5	0	2	1-0	.290	.353	.419	.772	0	1.000
1997— Florida (N.L.)	C-1B	58	143	21	43	10	2	2	20	26	18	2	3	1-0	.301	.415	.441	.856	8	.978
1998— Florida (N.L.)	C-2B	106	298	19	56	12	2	5	29	35	52	1	7	5-2	.188	.274	.292	.566	8	.984
1999— Texas (A.L.)	C-DH	43	93	12	23	2	1	1	12	10	7	0	2	1-0	.247	.314	.323	.637	1	.984
2000— Kansas City (A.L.)	C-1B-2B	83	234	36	64	11	0	7	33	43	34	3	4	7-3	.274	.390	.410	.800	5	.994
— Omaha (PCL)	C	9	25	7	7	3	0	0	3	4	3	0	1	1-1	.280	.379	.400	.779	0	1.000
2001— GC Royals (GCL)	C	6	18	3	1	0	0	0	1	7	5	0	1	0-0	.056	.320	.056	.376	0	1.000
— Omaha (PCL)	C	11	43	5	12	2	0	2	7	4	5	0	2	0-0	.279	.333	.442	.775	1	.985
— Kansas City (A.L.)	C-DH	39	125	15	40	9	0	6	18	12	16	0	2	1-2	.320	.377	.536	.913	5	.987
2002— Houston (N.L.)	C	76	185	18	41	7	1	3	24	12	36	2	4	1-0	.222	.275	.319	.594	5	.985
2003— Houston (N.L.)	C	59	120	9	26	6	1	0	13	14	14	1	5	1-0	.217	.299	.300	.599	4	.973
— Colorado (N.L.)	C	15	46	6	12	1	0	3	8	5	7	0	0	0-1	.261	.333	.478	.812	2	.973
2004— Syracuse (Int'l)	C-DH	7	23	4	7	1	0	2	2	5	0	1	0	1-0	.304	.346	.348	.694	0	1.000

Year Team (League)	Pos.	G	AB	R	H	2B	3B	HR	RBI	BB	SO	HBP	GDP	SB-CS	Avg.	OBP	SLG	OPS	E	Avg.
—Toronto (A.L.)	C-DH	107	338	46	91	24	0	6	36	47	61	6	7	0-2	.269	.367	.393	.761	8	.987
2005—New Hampshire (East.)	C-DH	2	6	1	2	1	0	0	0	2	2	0	0	0-0	.333	.500	.500	1.000	0	1.000
—Toronto (A.L.)	C	133	434	61	109	18	1	11	61	73	70	0	11	2-3	.251	.355	.373	.729	8	.990
2006—Dunedin (Fla. St.)		1	4	0	0	0	0	0	0	0	1	0	0	0-0	.000	.000	.000	.000	0	1.000
—Toronto (A.L.)	C-DH	99	290	39	79	19	0	12	40	41	42	3	10	0-2	.272	.363	.462	.825	3	.994
American League totals (8 years)		594	1726	243	458	96	3	47	227	253	259	14	41	12-13	.265	.361	.406	.767	38	.988
National League totals (5 years)		324	823	77	187	38	5	15	96	95	132	6	21	9-3	.227	.310	.340	.650	27	.983
Major League totals (12 years)		918	2549	320	645	134	8	62	323	348	391	20	62	21-16	.253	.345	.385	.729	65	.986

DIVISION SERIES RECORD

Year Team (League)	Pos.	G	AB	R	H	2B	3B	HR	RBI	BB	SO	HBP	GDP	SB-CS	Avg.	OBP	SLG	OPS	E	Avg.
1997—Florida (N.L.)		Did not play.																		

CHAMPIONSHIP SERIES RECORD

Year Team (League)	Pos.	G	AB	R	H	2B	3B	HR	RBI	BB	SO	HBP	GDP	SB-CS	Avg.	OBP	SLG	OPS	E	Avg.
1997—Florida (N.L.)	C	1	0	0	0	0	0	0	0	0	0	0	0	0-0	...	...	...	...	0	1.000

WORLD SERIES RECORD

Year Team (League)	Pos.	G	AB	R	H	2B	3B	HR	RBI	BB	SO	HBP	GDP	SB-CS	Avg.	OBP	SLG	OPS	E	Avg.
1997—Florida (N.L.)	C	2	2	0	0	0	0	0	0	0	0	0	0	0-0	.000	.000	.000	.000	0	1.000

2006 LEFTY-RIGHTY SPLITS

vs.	Avg.	AB	H	2B	3B	HR	RBI	BB	SO	OBP	Slg.	vs.	Avg.	AB	H	2B	3B	HR	RBI	BB	SO	OBP	Slg.
L	.373	51	19	7	0	2	6	10	2	.492	.627	R	.251	239	60	12	0	10	34	31	40	.333	.427

ZIMMERMAN, RYAN — 3B

PERSONAL: Born September 28, 1984, in Washington, N.C. ... 6-3/210. ... Bats right, throws right. ... Full name: Ryan Wallace Zimmerman. ... High school: Kellam (Virginia Beach, Va.). ... College: Virginia. **TRANSACTIONS/CAREER NOTES:** Selected by Washington Nationals organization in first round (fourth pick overall) of 2005 free-agent draft.
2006 GAMES PLAYED BY POSITION (MLB): 3B—157.

Year Team (League)	Pos.	G	AB	R	H	2B	3B	HR	RBI	BB	SO	HBP	GDP	SB-CS	Avg.	OBP	SLG	OPS	E	Avg.
2005—Savannah (S. Atl.)	3B	4	17	5	8	2	1	2	6	0	3	0	0	0-1	.471	.471	1.059	1.529	0	1.000
—Harrisburg (East.)	3B-SS	63	233	40	76	20	0	9	32	15	34	2	3	1-5	.326	.371	.528	.898	10	.946
—Wash. (N.L.)	3B-SS	20	58	6	23	10	0	6	3	12	0	1	0-0	.397	.419	.569	.988	2	.951
2006—Wash. (N.L.)	3B	157	614	84	176	47	3	20	110	61	120	2	15	11-8	.287	.351	.471	.822	15	.965
Major League totals (2 years)		177	672	90	199	57	3	20	116	64	132	2	16	11-8	.296	.357	.479	.836	17	.964

2006 LEFTY-RIGHTY SPLITS

vs.	Avg.	AB	H	2B	3B	HR	RBI	BB	SO	OBP	Slg.	vs.	Avg.	AB	H	2B	3B	HR	RBI	BB	SO	OBP	Slg.
L	.280	150	42	13	0	4	25	21	25	.364	.447	R	.289	464	134	34	3	16	85	40	95	.346	.478

ZITO, BARRY — P

PERSONAL: Born May 13, 1978, in Las Vegas. ... 6-4/215. ... Throws left, bats left. ... Full name: Barry William Zito. ... Name pronounced: ZEE-toe. ... High school: University (San Diego). ... College: Southern California. **TRANSACTIONS/CAREER NOTES:** Selected by Seattle Mariners organization in 59th round of 1996 free-agent draft; did not sign. ... Selected by Texas Rangers organization in third round of 1998 free-agent draft; did not sign. ... Selected by Oakland Athletics organization in first round (ninth pick overall) of 1999 free-agent draft. **HONORS:** Named A.L. Pitcher of the Year by THE SPORTING NEWS (2002). ... Named lefthanded pitcher on THE SPORTING NEWS A.L. All-Star team (2002). ... Named A.L. Cy Young Award winner by Baseball Writers' Association of America (2002).
CAREER HITTING: 1-for-29 (.034), 0 R, 0 2B, 0 3B, 0 HR, 0 RBI.

Year Team (League)	W	L	Pct.	ERA	WHIP	G	GS	CG	ShO	Hld.	Sv.-Opp.	IP	H	R	ER	HR	BB-IBB	SO	Avg.
1999—Visalia (Calif.)	3	0	1.000	2.45	1.07	8	8	0	0	...	0-...	40.1	21	13	11	3	22-0	62	.157
—Midland (Texas)	2	1	.667	4.91	1.50	4	4	0	0	...	0-...	22.0	22	15	12	1	11-0	29	.253
—Vancouver (PCL)	1	0	1.000	1.50	1.17	1	1	0	0	...	0-...	6.0	5	1	1	0	2-0	6	.227
2000—Sacramento (PCL)	8	5	.615	3.19	1.31	18	18	0	0	...	0-...	101.2	88	44	36	4	45-0	91	.230
—Oakland (A.L.)	7	4	.636	2.72	1.18	14	14	1	1	0	0-0	92.2	64	30	28	6	45-2	78	.195
2001—Oakland (A.L.)	17	8	.680	3.49	1.23	35	35	3	2	0	0-0	214.1	184	92	83	18	80-0	205	.230
2002—Oakland (A.L.)	*23	5	.821	2.75	1.13	35	*35	1	0	0	0-0	229.1	182	79	70	24	78-2	182	.218
2003—Oakland (A.L.)	14	12	.538	3.30	1.18	35	35	4	1	0	0-0	231.2	186	98	85	19	88-3	146	.219
2004—Oakland (A.L.)	11	11	.500	4.48	1.39	34	34	0	0	0	0-0	213.0	216	116	106	28	81-2	163	.263
2005—Oakland (A.L.)	14	13	.519	3.86	1.20	35	•35	0	0	0	0-0	228.1	185	106	98	26	89-0	171	.221
2006—Oakland (A.L.)	16	10	.615	3.83	1.40	34	•34	0	0	0	0-0	221.0	211	99	94	27	99-5	151	.257
Major League totals (7 years)	102	63	.618	3.55	1.25	222	222	9	4	0	0-0	1430.1	1228	620	564	148	560-14	1096	.232

DIVISION SERIES RECORD

Year Team (League)	W	L	Pct.	ERA	WHIP	G	GS	CG	ShO	Hld.	Sv.-Opp.	IP	H	R	ER	HR	BB-IBB	SO	Avg.
2000—Oakland (A.L.)	1	0	1.000	1.59	1.59	1	1	0	0	0	0-0	5.2	7	1	1	0	2-0	5	.304
2001—Oakland (A.L.)	0	1	.000	1.13	0.38	1	1	0	0	0	0-0	8.0	2	1	1	0	1-0	6	.077
2002—Oakland (A.L.)	1	0	1.000	4.50	1.50	1	1	0	0	0	0-0	6.0	5	3	3	0	4-0	8	.217
2003—Oakland (A.L.)	1	1	.500	3.46	1.00	2	2	0	0	0	0-0	13.0	9	5	5	2	4-0	13	.191
2006—Oakland (A.L.)	1	0	1.000	1.13	0.88	1	1	0	0	0	0-0	8.0	4	1	1	0	3-0	1	.154
Division series totals (5 years)	4	2	.667	2.43	1.01	6	6	0	0	0	0-0	40.2	27	11	11	4	14-0	33	.186

CHAMPIONSHIP SERIES RECORD

Year Team (League)	W	L	Pct.	ERA	WHIP	G	GS	CG	ShO	Hld.	Sv.-Opp.	IP	H	R	ER	HR	BB-IBB	SO	Avg.
2006—Oakland (A.L.)	0	1	.000	12.27	2.73	1	1	0	0	0	0-0	3.2	7	5	5	2	3-0	0	.389

ALL-STAR GAME RECORD

	W	L	Pct.	ERA	WHIP	G	GS	CG	ShO	Hld.	Sv.-Opp.	IP	H	R	ER	HR	BB-IBB	SO	Avg.
All-Star Game totals (2 years)	0	0	...	0.00	0.00	2	0	0	0	0	0-0	1.1	0	0	0	0	0-0	0	.000

2006 LEFTY-RIGHTY SPLITS

vs.	Avg.	AB	H	2B	3B	HR	RBI	BB	SO	OBP	Slg.	vs.	Avg.	AB	H	2B	3B	HR	RBI	BB	SO	OBP	Slg.
L	.260	150	39	3	0	6	19	24	33	.369	.400	R	.257	670	172	39	3	21	74	75	118	.339	.418

ZOBRIST, BEN — SS

PERSONAL: Born May 26, 1981, in Eureka, Ill. ... Bats both, throws right. ... Full name: Benjamin T. Zobrist. ... College: Dallas Baptist. **TRANSACTIONS/CAREER NOTES:** Selected by Houston Astros organization in sixth round of 2004 free-agent draft. ... Traded by Astros with P Mitch Talbot to Tampa Bay Devil Rays for OF Aubrey Huff and cash (July 12, 2006).
2006 GAMES PLAYED BY POSITION (MLB): SS—52.

Year	Team (League)	Pos.	G	AB	R	H	2B	3B	HR	RBI	BB	SO	HBP	GDP	SB-CS	Avg.	OBP	SLG	OPS	E	Avg.
																				FIELDING	
2004—	Tri-City (N.Y.-Penn.)		68	257	50	87	14	3	4	45	43	31	4	5	15-4	.339	.438	.463	.901	...	...
2005—	Lexington (S. Atl.)	SS-DH	68	247	45	75	17	2	2	32	47	35	5	2	16-5	.304	.415	.413	.828	12	.962
—	Salem (Carol.)	SS-DH	42	141	25	47	12	1	3	13	37	17	1	3	2-1	.333	.475	.496	.971	3	.983
2006—	Corpus Christi (Texas)		83	315	57	103	25	6	3	30	55	46	5	7	9-5	.327	.434	.473	.907	16	.956
—	Durham (Int'l)		18	69	12	21	3	1	0	6	10	9	1	0	4-1	.304	.400	.377	.777	2	.968
—	Tampa Bay (A.L.)	SS	52	183	10	41	6	2	2	18	10	26	0	2	2-3	.224	.260	.311	.572	9	.963
	Major League totals (1 year)		52	183	10	41	6	2	2	18	10	26	0	2	2-3	.224	.260	.311	.572	9	.963

2006 LEFTY-RIGHTY SPLITS

vs.	Avg.	AB	H	2B	3B	HR	RBI	BB	SO	OBP	Slg.	vs.	Avg.	AB	H	2B	3B	HR	RBI	BB	SO	OBP	Slg.
L	.212	52	11	3	1	0	4	1	5	.226	.308	R	.229	131	30	3	1	2	14	9	21	.273	.313

ZUMAYA, JOEL   P

PERSONAL: Born November 9, 1984, in Chula Vista, Calif. ... 6-3/210. ... Throws right, bats right. ... Full name: Joel Martin Zumaya. **TRANSACTIONS/CAREER NOTES:** Selected by Detroit Tigers organization in 11th round of 2002 free-agent draft.
CAREER HITTING: 0-for-0 (.000), 0 R, 0 2B, 0 3B, 0 HR, 0 RBI.

Year	Team (League)	W	L	Pct.	ERA	WHIP	G	GS	CG	ShO	Hld.	Sv.-Opp.	IP	H	R	ER	HR	BB-IBB	SO	Avg.
2002—	GC Tigers (GCL)	2	1	.667	1.93	0.86	9	8	0	0	...	0-...	37.1	21	9	8	2	11-0	46	.163
2003—	W. Mich. (Mid.)	7	5	.583	2.79	1.18	19	19	0	0	...	0-...	90.1	69	35	28	3	38-0	126	.209
2004—	Lakeland (Fla. St.)	7	6	.538	4.15	1.23	19	19	1	1	...	0-...	110.2	81	55	51	7	55-0	104	.214
—	Erie (East.)	2	2	.500	6.30	1.45	4	4	0	0	...	0-...	20.0	19	20	14	6	10-0	29	.250
2005—	Erie (East.)	8	3	.727	2.77	1.15	18	18	0	0	0	0-0	107.1	71	40	33	7	52-0	143	.187
—	Toledo (Int'l)	1	2	.333	2.66	1.23	8	8	1	0	0	0-0	44.0	30	13	13	2	24-0	56	.194
2006—	Detroit (A.L.)	6	3	.667	1.94	1.18	62	0	0	0	30	1-6	83.1	56	20	18	6	42-2	97	.187
	Major League totals (1 year)	6	3	.667	1.94	1.18	62	0	0	0	30	1-6	83.1	56	20	18	6	42-2	97	.187

DIVISION SERIES RECORD

Year	Team (League)	W	L	Pct.	ERA	WHIP	G	GS	CG	ShO	Hld.	Sv.-Opp.	IP	H	R	ER	HR	BB-IBB	SO	Avg.
2006—	Detroit (A.L.)	0	0	...	0.00	0.00	2	0	0	0	1	0-0	2.0	0	0	0	0	0-0	3	.000

CHAMPIONSHIP SERIES RECORD

Year	Team (League)	W	L	Pct.	ERA	WHIP	G	GS	CG	ShO	Hld.	Sv.-Opp.	IP	H	R	ER	HR	BB-IBB	SO	Avg.
2006—	Detroit (A.L.)	0	0	...	9.00	1.00	1	0	0	0	0	0-0	1.0	1	1	1	0	0-0	0	.250

WORLD SERIES RECORD

Year	Team (League)	W	L	Pct.	ERA	WHIP	G	GS	CG	ShO	Hld.	Sv.-Opp.	IP	H	R	ER	HR	BB-IBB	SO	Avg.
2006—	Detroit (A.L.)	0	1	.000	3.00	1.33	3	0	0	0	0	0-0	3.0	1	3	1	0	3-0	3	.091

2006 LEFTY-RIGHTY SPLITS

vs.	Avg.	AB	H	2B	3B	HR	RBI	BB	SO	OBP	Slg.	vs.	Avg.	AB	H	2B	3B	HR	RBI	BB	SO	OBP	Slg.
L	.183	109	20	1	1	2	15	21	38	.311	.266	R	.188	191	36	2	1	4	17	21	59	.273	.272

2007 MANAGERS LIST

▶ Year-by-year major and minor league managing statistics

▶ Career major league playing totals

▶ Biographical information for all active major league managers

▶ Managerial tendencies from the 2006 season

ACTA, MANNY — NATIONALS

PERSONAL: Born January 11, 1969, in San Pedro de Macoris, Dominican Republic. ... 6-2/205. ... Full name: Manuel Elias Acta.

RECORD AS MANAGER

BACKGROUND: Coach, Asheville of South Atlantic League, Houston Astros organization (1992). ... Coach, New Orleans of PCL, Astros organization (2001). ... Coach, Montreal Expos (2002-04). ... Coach, New York Mets (2005-06).

Year Team (League)	W	L	Pct.	Pos	Year Team (League)	W	L	Pct.	Pos
1993—Auburn (NY-Penn.)	30	46	.395	4P	1998—Kissimmee (Fla. St.)	30	40	.429	4E
1994—Auburn (NY-Penn.)	45	31	.592	2P	—Second half	34	35	.493	3E
1995—Auburn (NY-Penn.)	40	34	.541	2P	1999—Kissimmee (Fla. St.)	30	37	.448	3E
1996—Auburn (NY-Penn.)	37	39	.487	3P	—Second half	41	29	.586	1E
1997—Quad City (Mid.)	26	38	.406	3W	2000—Kissimmee (Fla. St.)	38	32	.543	3E
—Second half	33	37	.471	T-2W	—Second half	35	34	.507	2E

NOTES:
1994—Defeated Watertown, 2-0, in semifinals; lost to New Jersey, 2-0, in league championship. ... **1999**—Defeated Jupiter, 2-1, in semifinals; defeated Dunedin, 3-1, in league championship.

BELL, BUDDY — ROYALS

PERSONAL: Born August 27, 1951, in Pittsburgh. ... 6-3/200. ... Full name: David Gus Bell. ... High school: Moeller (Cincinnati). ... College: Xavier, then Miami (Ohio). ... Father of David Bell, third baseman, Milwaukee Brewers; and Mike Bell, third baseman with Cincinnati Reds (2000); son of Gus Bell, outfielder with four major league teams (1950-64).

RECORD AS PLAYER

				— BATTING —								— FIELDING—			
	G	AB	R	H	2B	3B	HR	RBI	Avg.	BB	SO	SB	PO	A	E	Avg.
Major League totals (18 years)	2405	8995	1151	2514	425	56	201	1106	.279	836	776	55	2198	5009	262	.965

RECORD AS MANAGER

BACKGROUND: Minor league hitting instructor, Cleveland Indians (1990). ... Director of minor league instruction, Chicago White Sox (1991-93). ... Coach, Cleveland Indians (1994-95, 2002-05). ... Minor league field coordinator, Cincinnati Reds (1998-99). ... Director of player development, Reds (1999).

Year Team (League)	W	L	Pct.	Pos	Year Team (League)	W	L	Pct.	Pos
1996—Detroit (A.L.)	53	109	.327	5E	2005—Kansas City (A.L.)	43	69	.384	5C
1997—Detroit (A.L.)	79	83	.488	3E	2006—Kansas City (A.L.)	62	100	.383	5C
1998—Detroit (A.L.)	52	85	.380	...	American League totals (5 years)	289	446	.393	
2000—Colorado (N.L.)	82	80	.506	4W	National League totals (3 years)	161	185	.465	
2001—Colorado (N.L.)	73	89	.451	5W	Major League totals (8 years)	450	631	.416	
2002—Colorado (N.L.)	6	16	.273	...					

NOTES:
1998—Replaced as Detroit manager on interim basis by Larry Parrish with club in fifth place (September 1). ... **2002**—Replaced as Colorado manager by Clint Hurdle (April 26). ... **2005**—Replaced Kansas City manager Tony Pena (record of 8-25) and interim manager Bob Schaefer (5-12) with club in fifth place and a record of 13-37. On suspended list (July 22-23).

BLACK, BUD — PADRES

PERSONAL: Born June 30, 1957, in San Mateo, Calif. ... 6-2/188. ... Full name: Harry Ralston Black. ... High school: Mark Morris (Longview, Wash.). ... Junior college: Lower Columbia College (Wash.). ... College: San Diego State.

RECORD AS PLAYER

	W	L	ERA	G	GS	CG	ShO	Sv.-Opp.	IP	H	R	ER	HR	BB	SO	Avg.
Major League totals (15 years)	121	116	3.84	398	296	32	12	11-16	2053.1	1978	982	876	217	623	1039	.253

RECORD AS MANAGER

BACKGROUND: Coach, Buffalo of International League (1998). ... Special assistant to G.M., Cleveland Indians (1996-97 and 1999). ... Coach, Los Angeles Angels of Anaheim (2000-06).

BOCHY, BRUCE — GIANTS

PERSONAL: Born April 16, 1955, in Landes de Boussac, France. ... Full name: Bruce Douglas Bochy. ... Name pronounced: BO-chee. ... High school: Melbourne (Fla.). ... Junior college: Brevard Community College (Fla.). ... College: Florida State.

RECORD AS PLAYER

				— BATTING —								— FIELDING —			
	G	AB	R	H	2B	3B	HR	RBI	Avg.	BB	SO	SB	PO	A	E	Avg.
Major League totals (9 years)	358	802	75	192	37	2	26	93	.239	66	170	1	1220	130	29	.979

RECORD AS MANAGER

BACKGROUND: Player/coach, Las Vegas, San Diego Padres organization (1988). ... Coach, Padres (1993-94).
HONORS: Named N.L. Manager of the Year by Baseball Writers' Association of America (1996). ... Named N.L. Manager of the Year by THE SPORTING NEWS (1996 and 1998).

Year Team (League)	W	L	Pct.	Pos	Year Team (League)	W	L	Pct.	Pos
1989—Spokane (N'west)	41	34	.547	1N	1992—Wichita (Texas)	39	29	.574	1W
1990—Riverside (Calif.)	35	36	.493	4S	—Second half	31	37	.456	4W
—Second half	29	42	.408	5S	1995—San Diego (N.L.)	70	74	.486	3W
1991—High Desert (Calif.)	31	37	.456	3S	1996—San Diego (N.L.)	91	71	.562	1W
—Second half	42	26	.618	1S	1997—San Diego (N.L.)	76	86	.469	4W

Year Team (League)	W	L	Pct.	Pos	Year Team (League)	W	L	Pct.	Pos
1998—San Diego (N.L.)	98	64	.605	1W	2003—San Diego (N.L.)	64	98	.395	5W
1999—San Diego (N.L.)	74	88	.457	4W	2004—San Diego (N.L.)	87	75	.537	3W
2000—San Diego (N.L.)	76	86	.469	5W	2005—San Diego (N.L.)	82	80	.506	1W
2001—San Diego (N.L.)	79	83	.488	4W	2006—San Diego (N.L.)	88	74	.543	1W
2002—San Diego (N.L.)	66	96	.407	5W	Major League totals (12 years)	951	975	.494	

NOTES:
1989—Defeated Southern Oregon, 2-1, in league championship. ... 1991—Defeated Bakersfield, 3-0, in semifinals; defeated Stockton, 3-2, in league championship. ... 1992—Defeated El Paso, 2-1, in semifinals; defeated Shreveport, 4-0, in league championship. ... 1996—Lost to St. Louis, 3-0, in N.L. Division Series. ... 1998—Defeated Houston, 3-1, in N.L. Division Series; defeated Atlanta, 4-2, in N.L. Championship Series; lost to New York Yankees, 4-0, in World Series. ... 2005—Lost to St. Louis, 3-0, in N.L. Division Series. ... 2006—Lost to St. Louis, 3-1, in N.L. Division Series. ... Career major league postseason record: 8-16.

COX, BOBBY — BRAVES

PERSONAL: Born May 21, 1941, in Tulsa, Okla. ... Full name: Robert Joseph Cox. ... High school: Selma (Calif.). ... Junior college: Reedley Junior College (Calif.).

RECORD AS PLAYER

				BATTING									FIELDING		
	G	AB	R	H	2B	3B	HR	RBI	Avg.	BB	SO	SB	PO	A	E	Avg.
Major League totals (2 years)	220	628	50	141	22	2	9	58	.225	75	126	3	148	426	28	.953

RECORD AS MANAGER

BACKGROUND: Minor league instructor, New York Yankees (1970-71). ... Player/manager, Fort Lauderdale, Yankees organization (1971). ... Coach, Yankees (1977). ... General manager, Braves (1985-90).

HONORS: Named Major League Manager of the Year by THE SPORTING NEWS (1985). ... Named N.L. Manager of the Year by THE SPORTING NEWS (1991, 1993, 1999, 2002, 2003, 2004 and 2005). ... Named A.L. Manager of the Year by Baseball Writers' Association of America (1985). ... Named N.L. Manager of the Year by Baseball Writers' Association of America (1991, 2004 and 2005).

Year Team (League)	W	L	Pct.	Pos	Year Team (League)	W	L	Pct.	Pos
1971—Fort Laud. (FSL)	71	70	.504	4E	1993—Atlanta (N.L.)	104	58	.642	1W
1972—West Haven (East.)	84	56	.600	1A	1994—Atlanta (N.L.)	68	46	.596	...
1973—Syracuse (Int'l)	76	70	.521	3A	1995—Atlanta (N.L.)	90	54	.625	1E
1974—Syracuse (Int'l)	74	70	.514	2N	1996—Atlanta (N.L.)	96	66	.593	1E
1975—Syracuse (Int'l)	72	64	.529	3N	1997—Atlanta (N.L.)	101	61	.623	1E
1976—Syracuse (Int'l)	82	57	.590	2N	1998—Atlanta (N.L.)	106	56	.654	1E
1978—Atlanta (N.L.)	69	93	.426	6W	1999—Atlanta (N.L.)	103	59	.636	1E
1979—Atlanta (N.L.)	66	94	.413	6W	2000—Atlanta (N.L.)	95	67	.586	1E
1980—Atlanta (N.L.)	81	80	.503	4W	2001—Atlanta (N.L.)	88	74	.543	1E
1981—Atlanta (N.L.)	25	29	.463	4W	2002—Atlanta (N.L.)	101	59	.631	1E
—Second half	25	27	.481	5W	2003—Atlanta (N.L.)	101	61	.623	1E
1982—Toronto (A.L.)	78	84	.481	6E	2004—Atlanta (N.L.)	96	66	.593	1E
1983—Toronto (A.L.)	89	73	.549	4E	2005—Atlanta (N.L.)	90	72	.556	1E
1984—Toronto (A.L.)	89	73	.549	2E	2006—Atlanta (N.L.)	79	83	.488	3E
1985—Toronto (A.L.)	99	62	.615	1E	American League totals (4 years)	355	292	.549	
1990—Atlanta (N.L.)	40	57	.412	6W	National League totals (21 years)	1816	1394	.566	
1991—Atlanta (N.L.)	94	68	.580	1W	Major League totals (25 years)	2171	1686	.563	
1992—Atlanta (N.L.)	98	64	.605	1W					

NOTES:
1972—Defeated Three Rivers, 3-0, in league championship. ... 1976—Defeated Memphis, 3-0, in semifinals; defeated Richmond, 3-1, in league championship. ... 1985—Lost to Kansas City, 4-3, in A.L. Championship Series. ... 1990—Replaced Russ Nixon as Atlanta manager with club in sixth place and record of 25-40 (June 22). ... 1991—Defeated Pittsburgh, 4-3, in N.L. Championship Series; lost to Minnesota, 4-3, in World Series. ... 1992—Defeated Pittsburgh, 4-3, in N.L. Championship Series; lost to Toronto, 4-2, in World Series. ... 1993—Lost to Philadelphia, 4-2, in N.L. Championship Series. ... 1994—Atlanta was in second place in N.L. East at time of season-ending strike (August 12). ... 1995—Defeated Colorado, 3-1, in N.L. Division Series; defeated Cincinnati, 4-0, in N.L. Championship Series; defeated Cleveland, 4-2, in World Series. ... 1996—Defeated Los Angeles, 3-0, in N.L. Division Series; defeated St. Louis, 4-3, in N.L. Championship Series; lost to New York Yankees, 4-2, in World Series. ... 1997—Defeated Houston, 3-0, in N.L. Division Series; lost to Florida, 4-2, in N.L. Championship Series. ... 1998—Defeated Chicago Cubs, 3-0, in N.L. Division Series; lost to San Diego, 4-2, in N.L. Championship Series. ... 1999—Defeated Houston, 3-1, in N.L. Division Series; defeated New York Mets, 4-2, in N.L. Championship Series; lost to New York Yankees, 4-0, in World Series. ... 2000—Lost to St. Louis, 3-0, in N.L. Division Series. ... 2001—Defeated Houston, 3-0, in N.L. Division Series; lost to Arizona, 4-1, in N.L. Championship Series. ... 2002—Lost to San Francisco, 3-2, in N.L. Division Series. ... 2003—Lost to Chicago Cubs, 3-2, in N.L. Division Series. ... 2004—Lost to Houston, 3-2, in N.L. Division Series. ... 2005—Lost to Houston Astros, 3-1, in N.L. Division Series. ... Career major league postseason record: 66-66.

FRANCONA, TERRY — RED SOX

PERSONAL: Born April 22, 1959, in Aberdeen, S.D. ... 6-1/175. ... Full name: Terry Jon Francona. ... High school: New Brighton (Pa.). ... College: Arizona. ... Son of Tito Francona, outfielder and first baseman with nine major league teams (1956-70).

RECORD AS PLAYER

				BATTING									FIELDING		
	G	AB	R	H	2B	3B	HR	RBI	Avg.	BB	SO	SB	PO	A	E	Avg.
Major League totals (10 years)	708	1731	163	474	74	6	16	143	.274	65	119	12	2032	188	22	.990

RECORD AS MANAGER

BACKGROUND: Manager, Scottsdale Scorpions, Arizona Fall League (1994). ... Coach, Detroit Tigers (1996). ... Coach, Texas Rangers (2002). ... Coach, Oakland Athletics (2003).

Year Team (League)	W	L	Pct.	Pos	Year Team (League)	W	L	Pct.	Pos
1992—South Bend (Mid.)	35	33	.515	3N	1998—Philadelphia (N.L.)	75	87	.463	3E
—Second half	38	31	.556	2N	1999—Philadelphia (N.L.)	77	85	.475	3E
1993—Birmingham (Sou.)	35	36	.493	2W	2000—Philadelphia (N.L.)	65	97	.401	5E
—Second half	43	28	.606	1W	2004—Boston (A.L.)	98	64	.605	2E
1994—Birmingham (Sou.)	31	38	.449	4W	2005—Boston (A.L.)	95	67	.586	2E
—Second half	34	36	.486	5W	2006—Boston (A.L.)	86	76	.531	3E
1995—Birmingham (Sou.)	33	39	.458	4W	American League totals (3 years)	279	207	.574	
—Second half	47	25	.653	2W	National League totals (4 years)	285	363	.440	
1997—Philadelphia (N.L.)	68	94	.420	5E	Major League totals (7 years)	564	570	.497	

NOTES:
1993—Defeated Nashville, 3-0, in semifinals; defeated Knoxville, 3-1, in league championship. ... **2004**—Defeated Anaheim, 3-0, in A.L. Division Series; defeated New York Yankees, 4-3, in A.L. Championship Series; defeated St. Louis, 4-0, in World Series. ... **2005**—On suspended list (April 29-May 2). Lost to Chicago White Sox, 3-0, in A.L. Division Series. ... Career major league postseason record: 11-6.

GARDENHIRE, RON | TWINS

PERSONAL: Born October 24, 1957, in Butzbach, West Germany. ... Full name: Ronald Clyde Gardenhire. ... High school: Okmulgee (Okla.) ... Junior college: Paris (Texas). ... College: Texas.

RECORD AS PLAYER

	G	AB	R	H	2B	3B	HR	RBI	Avg.	BB	SO	SB	PO	A	E	Avg.
						BATTING								FIELDING		
Major League totals (5 years)	285	710	57	165	27	3	4	49	.232	46	122	13	395	665	47	.958

RECORD AS MANAGER

BACKGROUND: Coach, Minnesota Twins (1991-2001).
HONORS: Named co-A.L. Manager of the Year by THE SPORTING NEWS (2004).

Year Team (League)	W	L	Pct.	Pos	Year Team (League)	W	L	Pct.	Pos
1988—Kenosha (Midw.)	41	27	.603	1N	2002—Minnesota (A.L.)	94	67	.584	1C
—Second half	40	32	.556	2N	2003—Minnesota (A.L.)	90	72	.556	1C
1989—Orlando (South.)	40	31	.563	1E	2004—Minnesota (A.L.)	92	70	.568	1C
—Second half	39	34	.534	4E	2005—Minnesota (A.L.)	83	79	.512	3C
1990—Orlando (South.)	42	30	.583	1E	2006—Minnesota (A.L.)	96	66	.593	1C
—Second half	43	29	.597	2E	Major League totals (5 years)	455	354	.562	

NOTES:
1988—Defeated Rockford, 2-0, in semifinals; lost to Cedar Rapids, 3-1, in league championship. ... **1989**—Lost to Greenville, 3-1, in semifinals. ... **1990**—Defeated Jacksonville, 3-1, in semifinals; lost to Memphis, 3-2, in league championship. ... **2002**—Defeated Oakland, 3-2, in A.L. Division Series; lost to Anaheim, 4-1, in A.L. Championship Series. ... **2003**—Lost to New York Yankees, 3-1, in A.L. Division Series. ... **2004**—Lost to New York Yankees, 3-1, in A.L. Division Series. ... **2006**—Lost to Oakland, 3-0, in A.L. Division Series. ... Career major league postseason record: 6-15.

GARNER, PHIL | ASTROS

PERSONAL: Born April 30, 1949, in Jefferson City, Tenn. ... Full name: Philip Mason Garner. ... High school: Beardon (Knoxville, Tenn.). ... College: Tennessee

RECORD AS PLAYER

	G	AB	R	H	2B	3B	HR	RBI	Avg.	BB	SO	SB	PO	A	E	Avg.
						BATTING								FIELDING		
Major League totals (16 years)	1860	6136	780	1594	299	82	109	738	.260	564	842	225	2746	4356	259	.965

RECORD AS MANAGER

BACKGROUND: Coach, Houston Astros (1989-91).

Year Team (League)	W	L	Pct.	Pos	Year Team (League)	W	L	Pct.	Pos
1992—Milwaukee (A.L.)	92	70	.568	2E	2001—Detroit (A.L.)	66	96	.407	4C
1993—Milwaukee (A.L.)	69	93	.426	7E	2002—Detroit (A.L.)	0	6	.000	...
1994—Milwaukee (A.L.)	53	62	.461	...	2004—Houston (N.L.)	48	26	.649	2C
1995—Milwaukee (A.L.)	65	79	.451	4C	2005—Houston (N.L.)	89	73	.549	2C
1996—Milwaukee (A.L.)	80	82	.494	3C	2006—Houston (N.L.)	82	80	.506	2C
1997—Milwaukee (A.L.)	78	83	.484	3C	American League totals (9 years)	582	654	.471	
1998—Milwaukee (N.L.)	74	88	.457	5C	National League totals (5 years)	345	327	.513	
1999—Milwaukee (N.L.)	52	60	.464	...	Major League totals (14 years)	927	981	.486	
2000—Detroit (A.L.)	79	83	.488	3C					

NOTES:
1993—On suspended list (September 24-27). ... **1994**—Milwaukee was in fifth place in A.L. Central at time of season-ending strike (August 12). ... **1995**—On suspended list (July 27-31). ... **1999**—Replaced as Milwaukee manager on an interim basis by Joe Lefebvre (August 11). ... **2002**—Replaced as Detroit manager by interim manager Luis Pujols with club in fifth place (April 8). ... **2004**—Replaced Houston manager Jimy Williams on an interim basis with club in fifth place and record of 44-44 (July 14); on suspended list (August 13); defeated Atlanta, 3-2, in N.L. Division Series; lost to St. Louis, 4-3, in N.L. Championship Series. ... **2005**—Defeated Atlanta, 3-1, in N.L. Division Series; Defeated St. Louis, 4-2, in N.L. Championship Series; Lost to Chicago White Sox, 4-0, in World Series. ... Career major league postseason record: 13-13.

GEREN, BOB | ATHLETICS

PERSONAL: Born September 22, 1961 in San Diego. ... Full name: Robert Peter Geren. ... High school: Clairemont (San Diego).

RECORD AS PLAYER

	G	AB	R	H	2B	3B	HR	RBI	Avg.	BB	SO	SB	PO	A	E	Avg.
						BATTING								FIELDING		
Major League totals (5 years)	307	765	62	178	21	1	22	76	.233	49	179	0	1320	129	12	.992

RECORD AS MANAGER

BACKGROUND: Minor league roving catching instructor, Boston Red Sox organization (1994 and 1997). ... Coach, Oakland Athletics (2003-06).

Year Team (League)	W	L	Pct.	Pos	Year Team (League)	W	L	Pct.	Pos
1995—Utica (NY-Penn)	33	40	.452	5S					
1996—GC Red Sox (GCL)	24	36	.400	4SW	—Second half	44	26	.629	1N
1998—Sarasota (Fla. St.)	38	31	.551	4W	2000—Sacramento (PCL)	90	54	.625	1S
—Second half	38	30	.559	3W	2001—Sacramento (PCL)	75	69	.521	1S
1999—Modesto (Calif.)	44	26	.629	1N	2002—Sacramento (PCL)	66	78	.458	3S

NOTES:
1999—Lost to San Jose, 3-2, in semifinals. ... **2000**—Lost to Salt Lake, 3-2, in semifinals. ... **2001**—Lost to Tacoma, 3-2, in semifinals.

GIBBONS, JOHN — BLUE JAYS

PERSONAL: Born June 8, 1962, in Great Falls, Mont. ... Full name: John Michael Gibbons. ... High school: MacArthur (San Antonio).

RECORD AS MANAGER

BACKGROUND: Minor league instructor, New York Mets organization (1991-93). ... Minor league coach, Mets organization (1994). ... Coach, Toronto Blue Jays (2002-August 8, 2004).

Year Team (League)	W	L	Pct.	Pos	Year Team (League)	W	L	Pct.	Pos
1995—Kingsport (Appalachian)	48	18	.727	1S	2000—Norfolk (Int'l)	65	79	.451	3S
1996—St. Lucie (Fla. St.)	32	34	.485	3E	2001—Norfolk (Int'l)	85	57	.599	1S
—Second half	39	28	.582	1E	2003—Toronto (A.L.)	3	0	1.000	...
1997—St. Lucie (Fla. St.)	28	39	.418	4E	2004—Toronto (A.L.)	20	30	.400	5E
—Second half	26	42	.382	6E	2005—Toronto (A.L.)	80	82	.494	3E
1998—Binghamton (East.)	82	60	.577	2N	2006—Toronto (A.L.)	87	75	.537	2E
1999—Norfolk (Int'l)	77	63	.550	3S	Major League totals (4 years)	190	187	.504	

NOTES:
1995—Defeated Bluefield, 2-1, in league championship. ... **1996**—Defeated Vero Beach, 2-0, in semifinals; defeated Clearwater, 3-1, in league championship. ... **1998**—Lost to New Britain, 3-1, in semifinals. ... **2001**—Lost to Louisville, 3-2, in semifinals. ... **2003**—Managed Toronto on an interim basis for three games (May 2-3 and September 5). ... **2004**—Replaced Toronto manager Carlos Tosca on an interim basis with club in fifth place and record of 47-64 (August 9).

GONZALEZ, FREDI — MARLINS

PERSONAL: Born January 28, 1964, in Havana, Cuba.

RECORD AS MANAGER

BACKGROUND: Coach, Florida Marlins (1999-2001). ... Coach, Atlanta Braves (2003-06).

Year Team (League)	W	L	Pct.	Pos	Year Team (League)	W	L	Pct.	Pos
1990—Miami (Fla. St.)	10	10	.500	4E	1995—Brevard County (Fla. St.)	30	38	.441	4E
1991—Miami (Fla. St.)	35	29	.547	2E	—Second half	31	36	.463	3E
—Second half	28	38	.424	4E	1996—Brevard County (Fla. St.)	25	45	.357	6E
1992—Erie (N.Y.-Penn)	40	37	.519	2S	—Second half	22	47	.319	6E
1993—High Desert (Calif.)	44	24	.647	1S	1997—Portland (East.)	79	63	.556	1N
—Second half	41	28	.594	1S	1998—Charlotte (Int'l)	70	73	.490	3S
1994—Brevard County (Fla. St.)	44	26	.629	1E	2002—Richmond (Int'l)	75	67	.528	2S
—Second half	34	35	.493	2E					

NOTES:
1990—Replaced Mike Easler as Miami coach with record of 19-29 (August 14). ... **1994**—Defeated Riverside, 3-1, in semifinals; defeated Modesto, 3-2, in league championship. ... **1995**—Defeated West Palm Beach, 2-0; lost to Tampa, 3-1, in league championship.

GUILLEN, OZZIE — WHITE SOX

PERSONAL: Born January 20, 1964, in Ocumare del Tuy, Miranda, Venezuela. ... 5-11/165. ... Full name: Oswaldo Jose Barrios Guillen. ... Name pronounced: GHEE-un.

RECORD AS PLAYER

	G	AB	R	H	2B	3B	HR	RBI	Avg.	BB	SO	SB	PO	A	E	Avg.
						BATTING								**FIELDING**		
Major League totals (16 years)	1993	6686	773	1764	275	69	28	619	.264	239	511	169	2935	5376	222	.974

RECORD AS MANAGER

BACKGROUND: Coach, Montreal Expos (2001). ... Coach, Florida Marlins (2002-03).
HONORS: Named A.L. Manager of the Year by the SPORTING NEWS (2005). ... Named A.L. Manager of the year by Baseball Writers' Association of America (2005).

Year Team (League)	W	L	Pct.	Pos	Year Team (League)	W	L	Pct.	Pos
2004—Chicago (A.L.)	83	79	.512	2C	2006—Chicago (A.L.)	90	72	.556	3C
2005—Chicago (A.L.)	99	63	.611	1C	Major League totals (3 years)	272	214	.560	

NOTES:
2005—Defeated Boston, 3-0, in A.L. Division Series; Defeated Los Angeles Angels of Anaheim, 4-1, in A.L. Championship Series; Defeated Houston, 4-0, in World Series. ... Career major league postseason record: 11-1.

HARGROVE, MIKE — MARINERS

PERSONAL: Born October 26, 1949, in Perryton, Texas. ... Full name: Dudley Michael Hargrove. ... High school: Perryton (Texas). ... College: Northwestern State (Okla.).

RECORD AS PLAYER

	G	AB	R	H	2B	3B	HR	RBI	Avg.	BB	SO	SB	PO	A	E	Avg.
						BATTING								**FIELDING**		
Major League totals (12 years)	1666	5564	783	1614	266	28	80	686	.290	965	550	24	11603	1027	123	.990

RECORD AS MANAGER

BACKGROUND: Minor league coach, Cleveland Indians organization (1986). ... Coach, Indians (1990-91). ... Assistant to the general manager, Indians (2004).
HONORS: Named A.L. Manager of the Year by THE SPORTING NEWS (1995).

Year Team (League)	W	L	Pct.	Pos	Year Team (League)	W	L	Pct.	Pos
1987—Kinston (Carol.)	33	37	.471	T3S	1997—Cleveland (A.L.)	86	75	.534	1C
—Kinston (Carol.)	42	28	.600	1S	1998—Cleveland (A.L.)	89	73	.549	1C
1988—Williamsport (East.)	66	73	.475	3rd	1999—Cleveland (A.L.)	97	65	.599	1C
1989—Colo. Springs (PCL)	44	26	.629	1S	2000—Baltimore (A.L.)	74	88	.457	4E
—Colo. Springs (PCL)	34	38	.472	3S	2001—Baltimore (A.L.)	63	98	.391	4E
1991—Cleveland (A.L.)	32	53	.376	7E	2002—Baltimore (A.L.)	67	95	.414	4E
1992—Cleveland (A.L.)	76	86	.469	4E	2003—Baltimore (A.L.)	71	91	.438	4E
1993—Cleveland (A.L.)	76	86	.469	6E	2005—Seattle (A.L.)	69	93	.426	4W
1994—Cleveland (A.L.)	66	47	.584	...	2006—Seattle (A.L.)	78	84	.481	4W
1995—Cleveland (A.L.)	100	44	.694	1C	Major League totals (15 years)	1143	1140	.501	
1996—Cleveland (A.L.)	99	62	.615	1C					

NOTES:
1987—Defeated Winston-Salem, 2-0, in playoffs; lost to Salem, 3-1, in league championship. ... **1989**—Lost to Albuquerque, 3-2, in semifinals. ... **1991**—Replaced Cleveland manager John McNamara with club in seventh place and record of 25-52 (July 6). ... **1994**—Cleveland was in second place in A.L. Central at time of season-ending strike (August 12). ... **1995**—Defeated Boston, 3-0, in A.L. Division Series; defeated Seattle, 4-2, in A.L. Championship Series; lost to Atlanta, 4-2, in World Series. ... **1996**—Lost to Baltimore, 3-1, in A.L. Division Series. ... **1997**—Defeated New York Yankees, 3-2, in A.L. Division Series; defeated Baltimore, 4-2, in A.L. Championship Series; lost to Florida, 4-3, in World Series. ... **1998**—Defeated Boston, 3-1, in A.L. Division Series; lost to New York Yankees, 4-2, in A.L. Championship Series. ... **1999**—Lost to Boston, 3-2, in A.L. Division Series. ... Career major league postseason record: 27-25.

HURDLE, CLINT — ROCKIES

PERSONAL: Born July 30, 1957, in Big Rapids, Mich. ... Full name: Clinton Merrick Hurdle. ... High school: Merritt Island (Fla.).

RECORD AS PLAYER

	G	AB	R	H	2B	3B	HR	RBI	Avg.	BB	SO	SB	PO	A	E	Avg.
						BATTING								FIELDING		
Major League totals (10 years)	515	1391	162	360	81	12	32	193	.259	176	261	1	1384	96	34	.978

BACKGROUND: Roving hitting instructor, Colorado Rockies organization (1994-96). ... Coach, Rockies (1997-April 26, 2002).

RECORD AS MANAGER

Year Team (League)	W	L	Pct.	Pos	Year Team (League)	W	L	Pct.	Pos
1988—St. Lucie (Fla. St.)	36	34	.514	4E	1993—Norfolk (Int'l)	70	71	.496	4W
—Second half	38	31	.551	1E	2002—Colorado (N.L.)	67	73	.479	4W
1989—St. Lucie (Fla. St.)	42	28	.600	1E	2003—Colorado (N.L.)	74	88	.457	4W
—Second half	37	27	.578	1E	2004—Colorado (N.L.)	68	94	.420	4W
1990—Jackson (Texas)	35	32	.522	2E	2005—Colorado (N.L.)	67	95	.414	5W
—Second half	38	30	.559	1E	2006—Colorado (N.L.)	76	86	.469	5W
1991—Williamsport (East.)	60	79	.432	7th	**Major League totals (5 years)**	352	436	.447	
1992—Tidewater (Int'l)	56	86	.394	4W					

NOTES:
1988—Defeated Lakeland, 2-1, in first round; defeated Tampa, 2-0, in semifinals; defeated Osceola, 2-0, in league championship. ... **1989**—Lost to Port Charlotte, 2-1, in first round. ... **1990**—Lost to Shreveport, 2-0, in semifinals. ... **2002**—Replaced Buddy Bell as Colorado manager with club in fifth place and a record of 6-16 (April 26).

LA RUSSA, TONY — CARDINALS

PERSONAL: Born October 4, 1944, in Tampa. ... Full name: Anthony La Russa Jr.. ... High school: Jefferson (Tampa). ... College: University of Tampa, then South Florida.

RECORD AS PLAYER

	G	AB	R	H	2B	3B	HR	RBI	Avg.	BB	SO	SB	PO	A	E	Avg.
						BATTING								FIELDING		
Major League totals (6 years)	132	176	15	35	5	2	0	7	.199	23	37	0	112	127	10	.960

BACKGROUND: Coach, St. Louis Cardinals organization (1977). ... Coach, Chicago White Sox (July 3, 1978-remainder of season).
HONORS: Named Major League Manager of the Year by THE SPORTING NEWS (1983). ... Named A.L. Manager of the Year by THE SPORTING NEWS (1988 and 1992). ...Named A.L. Manager of the Year by Baseball Writers' Association of America (1983, 1988 and 1992). ... Named N.L. Manager of the Year by Baseball Writers' Association of America (2002).

RECORD AS MANAGER

Year Team (League)	W	L	Pct.	Pos	Year Team (League)	W	L	Pct.	Pos
1978—Knoxville (Southern)	49	21	.700	1st	1992—Oakland (A.L.)	96	66	.593	1W
—Second half	4	4	.500	...	1993—Oakland (A.L.)	68	94	.420	7W
1979—Chicago (A.L.)	27	27	.500	5th	1994—Oakland (A.L.)	51	63	.447	...
—Iowa (Am. Assoc.)	54	52	.509	...	1995—Oakland (A.L.)	67	77	.465	4W
—Second half	4	4	.500	...	1996—St. Louis (N.L.)	88	74	.543	1C
1980—Chicago (A.L.)	70	90	.438	5W	1997—St. Louis (N.L.)	73	89	.451	4C
1981—Chicago (A.L.)	31	22	.585	3W	1998—St. Louis (N.L.)	83	79	.512	3C
—Second half	23	30	.434	6W	1999—St. Louis (N.L.)	75	86	.466	4C
1982—Chicago (A.L.)	87	75	.537	3W	2000—St. Louis (N.L.)	95	67	.586	1C
1983—Chicago (A.L.)	99	63	.611	1W	2001—St. Louis (N.L.)	93	69	.574	2C
1984—Chicago (A.L.)	74	88	.457	5W	2002—St. Louis (N.L.)	97	65	.599	1C
1985—Chicago (A.L.)	85	77	.525	3W	2003—St. Louis (N.L.)	85	77	.525	3C
1986—Chicago (A.L.)	26	38	.406	...	2004—St. Louis (N.L.)	105	57	.648	1C
—Oakland (A.L.)	45	34	.570	3W	2005—St. Louis (N.L.)	100	62	.617	1C
1987—Oakland (A.L.)	81	81	.500	3W	2006—St. Louis (N.L.)	83	78	.516	1C
1988—Oakland (A.L.)	104	58	.642	1W	**American League totals (17 years)**	1320	1183	.527	
1989—Oakland (A.L.)	99	63	.611	1W	**National League totals (11 years)**	977	803	.549	
1990—Oakland (A.L.)	103	59	.636	1W	**Major League totals (28 years)**	2297	1986	.536	
1991—Oakland (A.L.)	84	78	.519	4W					

NOTES:
1978—Became Chicago White Sox coach and replaced as Knoxville manager by Joe Jones, with club in third place (July 3). ... **1979**—Replaced as Iowa manager by Joe Sparks with club in second place (August 3); replaced Chicago manager Don Kessinger with club in fifth place and record of 46-60 (August 3). ... **1983**—Lost to Baltimore, 3-1, in A.L. Championship Series. ... **1985**—On suspended list (August 10-11). ... **1986**—Replaced as Chicago manager by interim manager Doug Rader, with club in sixth place (June 20); replaced Oakland manager Jackie Moore (record of 29-44) and interim manager Jeff Newman (record of 2-8) with club in seventh place and record of 31-52 (July 7). ... **1988**—Defeated Boston, 4-0, in A.L. Championship Series; lost to Los Angeles, 4-1, in World Series. ... **1989**—Defeated Toronto, 4-1, in A.L. Championship Series; defeated San Francisco, 4-0, in World Series. ... **1990**—Defeated Boston, 4-0, in A.L. Championship Series; lost to Cincinnati, 4-0, in World Series. ... **1992**—Lost to Toronto, 4-2, in A.L. Championship Series. ... **1993**—On suspended list (October 1-remainder of season). ... **1994**—Oakland was in second place in A.L. West at time of season-ending strike (August 12). ... **1996**—Defeated San Diego, 3-0, in N.L. Division Series; lost to Atlanta, 4-3, in N.L. Championship Series. ... **2000**—Defeated Atlanta, 3-0, in N.L. Division Series; lost to New York Mets, 4-1, in N.L. Championship Series. ... **2001**—Lost to Arizona, 3-2, in N.L. Division Series. ... **2002**—Defeated Arizona, 3-0, in N.L. Division Series; lost to San Francisco, 4-1, in N.L. Championship Series. ... **2003**—On suspended list (September 26-27). ... **2004**—Defeated Los Angeles, 3-1, in N.L. Division Series; defeated Houston, 4-3, in N.L. Championship Series; lost to Boston, 4-0, in World Series. ... **2005**—Defeated San Diego, 3-0, in N.L Division Series; lost to Houston, 4-2, in N.L. Championship Series. ... **2006**—Defeated San Diego, 3-1, in N.L. Division Series; defeated New York Mets, 4-3, in N.L. Championship Series; defeated Detroit, 4-1, in World Series. ... Career major league postseason record: 59-48.

LEYLAND, JIM — TIGERS

PERSONAL: Born December 15, 1944, in Toledo, Ohio. ... Full name: James Richard Leyland. ... Name pronounced: LEE-lund. ... High school: Perrysburg (Ohio).

RECORD AS MANAGER

BACKGROUND: Coach, Detroit Tigers organization (1970-June 5, 1971); served as player/coach (1970). ... Coach, Chicago White Sox (1982-85). ... Special assignment scout, St. Louis Cardinals (2000-2005).

HONORS: Named N.L. co-Manager of the Year by THE SPORTING NEWS (1988). ... Named N.L. Manager of the Year by THE SPORTING NEWS (1990 and 1992). ... Named A.L. Manager of the Year by SPORTING NEWS (2006). ... Named N.L. Manager of the Year by the Baseball Writers' Association of America (1990 and 1992). ... Named A.L. Manager of the Year by the Baseball Writers' Association of America (2006).

Year	Team (League)	W	L	Pct.	Pos	Year	Team (League)	W	L	Pct.	Pos
1971—	Bristol (Appal.)	31	35	.470	3S	1988—	Pittsburgh (N.L.)	85	75	.531	2E
1972—	Clinton (Midw.)	22	41	.349	5N	1989—	Pittsburgh (N.L.)	74	88	.457	5E
	— Second half	27	36	.429	4N	1990—	Pittsburgh (N.L.)	95	67	.586	1E
1973—	Clinton (Midw.)	36	26	.581	2N	1991—	Pittsburgh (N.L.)	98	64	.605	1E
	— Clinton (Midw.)	37	25	.597	1N	1992—	Pittsburgh (N.L.)	96	66	.593	1E
1974—	Montgom. (Sou.)	61	76	.445	3W	1993—	Pittsburgh (N.L.)	73	84	.465	5E
1975—	Clinton (Midw.)	29	31	.483	4S	1994—	Pittsburgh (N.L.)	53	61	.465	
	— Clinton (Midw.)	38	30	.559	2S	1995—	Pittsburgh (N.L.)	58	86	.403	5C
1976—	Lakeland (Fla. St.)	74	64	.536	2N	1996—	Pittsburgh (N.L.)	73	89	.451	5C
1977—	Lakeland (Fla. St.)	85	53	.616	1N	1997—	Florida (N.L.)	92	70	.568	2E
1978—	Lakeland (Fla. St.)	31	38	.449	4N	1998—	Florida (N.L.)	54	108	.333	5E
	— Lakeland (Fla. St.)	47	22	.681	1N	1999—	Colorado (N.L.)	72	90	.444	5W
1979—	Evansville (A.A.)	78	58	.574	1E	2006—	Detroit (A.L.)	95	67	.586	2C
1980—	Evansville (A.A.)	61	74	.452	2E						
1981—	Evansville (A.A.)	73	63	.537	1E	**American League totals (1 year)**		95	67	.586	
1986—	Pittsburgh (N.L.)	64	98	.395	6E	**National League totals (14 years)**		1067	1128	.486	
1987—	Pittsburgh (N.L.)	80	82	.494	4E	**Major League totals (15 years)**		1162	1195	.493	

NOTES:
1973—Lost to Wisconsin Rapids, 2-0, in playoff. ... **1976**—Defeated Miami, 2-0, in semifinals; defeated Tampa, 2-0, in league championship. ... **1977**—Defeated Miami, 2-0, in semifinals; defeated St. Petersburg, 3-1, in league championship. ... **1978**—Defeated St. Petersburg, 1-0, in North Division playoff; lost to Miami, 2-0, in league championship. ... **1979**—Defeated Oklahoma City, 4-2, in league championship. ... **1981**—Lost to Denver, 3-1, in semifinals. ... **1985**—Served as acting manager of Chicago White Sox (record of 1-1), with club in fourth place, while manager Tony La Russa served a suspension (August 10-11). ... **1990**—Lost to Cincinnati, 4-2, in N.L. Championship Series. ... **1991**—Lost to Atlanta, 4-3, in N.L. Championship Series. ... **1992**—Lost to Atlanta, 4-3, in N.L. Championship Series. ... **1993**—On suspended list (August 27-September 1). ... **1994**—Pittsburgh was tied for fourth place in N.L. Central at time of season-ending baseball strike (August 12). ... **1997**—Defeated San Francisco, 3-0, in N.L. divisional playoff, defeated Atlanta, 4-2, in N.L. Championship Series; defeated Cleveland, 4-3, in World Series. ... **2006**—Defeated New York Yankees, 3-1, in A.L. Division Series; defeated Oakland, 4-0, in A.L. Championship Series; lost to St. Louis, 4-1, in World Series. ... Career major league postseason record: 27-22.

LITTLE, GRADY　　　　　　　　　　　　　　　　　　　　　　　　DODGERS

PERSONAL: Born March 3, 1950, in Abilene, Texas. ... Full name: William Grady Little. ... High school: Garinger (Charlotte, N.C.). ... Brother of Bryan Little, infielder with three major league teams (1982-86)

RECORD AS MANAGER

BACKGROUND: Coach, West Haven of Eastern League, New York Yankees organization (1974). ... Bullpen coach, San Diego Padres (1996). ... Coach, Boston Red Sox (1997-99). ... Coach, Cleveland Indians (2000-01). ... Special assistant to G.M. and roving catching instructor, Chicago Cubs (2004-05).

HONORS: Named Minor League Manager of the Year by THE SPORTING NEWS (1992).

Year	Team (League)	W	L	Pct.	Pos	Year	Team (League)	W	L	Pct.	Pos
1980—	Bluefield (Appal.)	29	39	.426	5th		— Second half	37	31	.544	1S
1981—	Hagerstown (Car.)	37	31	.544	1N	1990—	Durham (Carol.)	37	33	.529	3S
	— Second half	33	37	.471	3N		— Second half	34	35	.493	4S
1982—	Hagerstown (Car.)	38	29	.567	2N	1991—	Durham (Carol.)	38	29	.567	3S
	— Second half	33	36	.478	3N		— Second half	41	29	.586	2S
1983—	Charlotte (Fla. St.)	33	39	.458	4E	1992—	Greenville (Sou.)	49	23	.681	1E
	— Second half	36	38	.486	3E		— Second half	51	20	.718	1E
1984—	Charlotte (Sou.)	29	43	.403	5E	1993—	Richmond (Int'l)	80	62	.563	2W
	— Hagerstown (Car.)	1	3	.250	...	1994—	Richmond (Int'l)	80	61	.567	1W
1985—	Kinston (Carol.)	23	47	.329	4S	1995—	Richmond (Int'l)	75	66	.532	2W
	— Second half	41	26	.612	1S	2002—	Boston (A.L.)	93	69	.574	2E
1986—	Pulaski (Appalachian)	41	25	.621	1N	2003—	Boston (A.L.)	95	67	.586	2E
1987—	Pulaski (Appalachian)	39	31	.557	2N	2006—	Los Angeles (N.L.)	88	74	.543	2W
1988—	Burlington (Midw.)	20	22	.476	...						
	— Durham (Carol.)	14	14	.500	2S	**American League totals (2 years)**		188	136	.580	
	— Second half	38	32	.543	2S	**National League totals (1 year)**		88	74	.543	
1989—	Durham (Carol.)	47	23	.671	1S	**Major League totals (3 years)**		276	210	.568	

NOTES:
1981—Defeated Salem, 1-0, in playoffs; defeated Peninsula, 3-0, for league championship. ... **1985**—Lost to Winston Salem in playoffs. ... **1986**—Defeated Johnson City for league championship. ... **1989**—Lost to Durham in league championship. ... **1992**—Defeated Charlotte, 3-1, in playoffs; defeated Chattanooga, 3-2, for league championship. ... **1993**—Lost to Charlotte in playoffs. ... **1994**—Defeated Charlotte, 3-1, in playoffs; defeated Syracuse, 3-0, for league championship. ... **1995**—Lost to Norfolk in playoffs. ... **2003**—Defeated Oakland Athletics, 3-2, in A.L. Division Series; lost to New York Yankees, 4-3, in A.L. Championship Series. ... **2006**—Lost to New York Mets, 3-0, in N.L. Division Series. ... Career major league postseason record: 6-9.

MADDON, JOE　　　　　　　　　　　　　　　　　　　　　　　　DEVIL RAYS

PERSONAL: Born February 4, 1954, in Hazelton, Pa. ... Full name: Joseph John Maddon. ... Name pronounced: Madden. ... High school: Hazelton (Pa.). ... College: Lafayette.

RECORD AS MANAGER

BACKGROUND: Coordinator, Arizona Instructional League, California Angels organization (1984-93). ... Roving hitting instructor, Angels organization (1987-93). ... Minor league field coordinator, Angels (1992-94). ... Director of player development, Angels (1994). ... Coach, Angels (1994-2005).

Year	Team (League)	W	L	Pct.	Pos	Year	Team (League)	W	L	Pct.	Pos
1981—	Idaho Falls (Pio.)	27	43	.386	3S	1986—	Midland (Texas)	35	30	.538	2W
1982—	Salem (N'west)	34	36	.486	1N		— Second half	27	41	.397	4W
1983—	Salem (N'west)	31	39	.443	4N	1996—	California (A.L.)	8	14	.364	...
1984—	Peoria (Midw.)	66	73	.475	2S	1999—	Anaheim (A.L.)	19	10	.655	4W
1985—	Midland (Texas)	29	37	.439	4W	2006—	Tampa Bay (A.L.)	61	101	.377	5E
	— Second half	30	40	.429	3W	**Major League totals (3 years)**		88	125	.413	

NOTES:
1982—Defeated Medford, 2-0, in league championship. ... **1996**—Replaced California manager Marcel Lachemann (52-59) and interim manager John McNamara (5-9) on an interim basis with club in fourth place and a record of 57-68 (August 21). ... **1999**—Replaced Anaheim manager Terry Collins on an interim basis with club in fourth place and a record of 52-81 (September 3).

MANUEL, CHARLIE — PHILLIES

PERSONAL: Born January 4, 1944, in North Fork, W.Va. ... Full name: Charles Fuqua Manuel. ... Name pronounced: manual. ... High school: Parry McCluer (Buena Vista, W.Va.).

RECORD AS PLAYER

	G	AB	R	H	2B	3B	HR	RBI	Avg.	BB	SO	SB	PO	A	E	Avg.
													FIELDING			
Major League totals (6 years)	239	384	25	76	12	0	4	43	.198	40	77	1	103	6	3	.973

BACKGROUND: Scout, Minnesota Twins (1982). ... Coach, Cleveland Indians (1988-89 and 1994-99).

RECORD AS MANAGER

Year Team (League)	W	L	Pct.	Pos	Year Team (League)	W	L	Pct.	Pos
1983—Wisconsin (Midw.)	71	67	.514	2N	1992—Colo. Springs (PCL)	36	33	.522	2S
1984—Orlando (South.)	34	35	.493	3E	—Second half	48	24	.667	1S
—Second half	45	30	.600	2E	1993—Charlotte (Int'l)	86	55	.610	1W
1985—Orlando (South.)	29	35	.453	5E	2000—Cleveland (A.L.)	90	72	.556	2C
—Second half	43	36	.544	2E	2001—Cleveland (A.L.)	91	71	.562	1C
1986—Toledo (Int'l)	62	77	.446	6th	2002—Cleveland (A.L.)	39	47	.453	—
1987—Portland (PCL)	20	49	.290	5N	2005—Philadelphia (N.L.)	88	74	.543	2E
—Second half	25	47	.347	5N	2006—Philadelphia (N.L.)	85	77	.525	2E
1990—Colo. Springs (PCL)	39	33	.542	3S	American League totals (3 years)	220	190	.537	
1991—Colo. Springs (PCL)	30	41	.423	5S	National League totals (2 years)	173	151	.534	
—Second half	42	26	.618	1S	Major League totals (5 years)	393	341	.535	

NOTES:
1984—Lost to Charlotte in one-game playoff. ... **1990**—Replaced Colorado Springs manager Bobby Molinaro with club in second place and record of 37-34 (June 22). ... **1991**—Lost to Tucson, 3-1, in semifinals. ... **1992**—Defeated Las Vegas, 3-2, in semifinals; lost to Vancouver, 3-0, in league championship. ... **1993**—Defeated Richmond, 3-1, in semifinals; defeated Rochester, 3-2, in league championship. ... **2001**—Lost to Seattle, 3-2, in A.L. Division Series. ... **2002**—Replaced as Cleveland manager on an interim basis by Joel Skinner with club in third place (July 11). ... Career major league postseason record: 2-3.

MELVIN, BOB — DIAMONDBACKS

PERSONAL: Born October 28, 1961, in Palo Alto, Calif. ... Full name: Robert Paul Melvin. ... High school: Menlo-Atherton (Menlo Park, Calif.). ... Junior college: Canada College (Calif.). ... College: California-Berkeley.

RECORD AS PLAYER

	G	AB	R	H	2B	3B	HR	RBI	Avg.	BB	SO	SB	PO	A	E	Avg.
													FIELDING			
Major League totals (10 years)	692	1955	174	456	85	6	35	212	.233	98	396	4	2961	253	24	.993

BACKGROUND: Scout, Milwaukee Brewers (1996). ... Roving fielding instructor, Brewers organization (1997). ... Assistant to general manager, Brewers (1998). ... Coach, Brewers (1999). ... Coach, Detroit Tigers (2000). ... Coach, Arizona Diamondbacks (2001-02).

RECORD AS MANAGER

Year Team (League)	W	L	Pct.	Pos	Year Team (League)	W	L	Pct.	Pos
2003—Seattle (A.L.)	93	69	.574	2W	2006—Arizona (N.L.)	76	86	.469	4W
2004—Seattle (A.L.)	63	99	.389	4W	American League totals (2 years)	156	168	.481	
2005—Arizona (N.L.)	77	85	.475	2W	National League totals (2 years)	153	171	.472	
					Major League totals (4 years)	309	339	.477	

NARRON, JERRY — REDS

PERSONAL: Born January 15, 1956, in Goldsboro, N.C. ... 6-3/205. ... Full name: Jerry Austin Narron. ... High school: Goldsboro (N.C.). ... College: East Carolina. ... Cousin of Sam Narron, pitcher with Texas Rangers (2004); nephew of Sam Narron, catcher with St. Louis Cardinals (1935, 1942-43).

RECORD AS PLAYER

	G	AB	R	H	2B	3B	HR	RBI	Avg.	BB	SO	SB	PO	A	E	Avg.
													FIELDING			
Major League totals (8 years)	392	840	64	177	23	2	21	96	.211	67	127	0	1038	80	12	.989

BACKGROUND: Third base coach, Texas Rangers (1993-May 4, 2001). ... Coach, Red Sox (2003). ... Coach, Reds (December 23, 2003-June 21, 2005).

RECORD AS MANAGER

Year Team (League)	W	L	Pct.	Pos	Year Team (League)	W	L	Pct.	Pos
1989—Frederick (Carolina)	34	36	.486	2N	2002—Texas (A.L.)	72	90	.444	4W
—Second half	39	29	.574	2N	2005—Cincinnati (N.L.)	46	46	.500	5C
1990—Hagerstown (East.)	67	71	.486	6th	2006—Cincinnati (N.L.)	80	82	.494	3C
1991—Hagerstown (East.)	81	59	.579	2nd	American League totals (2 years)	134	162	.453	
1992—Rochester (Int'l)	70	74	.486	3E	National League totals (2 years)	126	128	.496	
2001—Texas (A.L.)	62	72	.463	4W	Major League totals (4 years)	260	290	.473	

NOTES:
1991—Lost to Albany, 3-0, in semifinals. ... **2001**—Replaced Texas manager Johnny Oates with club in third place and record of 11-17 (May 4). ... **2005**—Replaced Cincinnati manager Dave Miley with team in sixth place and record of 27-43 (June 21).

PERLOZZO, SAM — ORIOLES

PERSONAL: Born March 4, 1951, in Cumberland, Md. ...Full name: Samuel Benedict Perlozzo. ...High school: Bishop Walsh (Cumberland, Md.). ...College: George Washington.

RECORD AS PLAYER

	G	AB	R	H	2B	3B	HR	RBI	Avg.	BB	SO	SB	PO	A	E	Avg.
													FIELDING			
Major League totals (2 years)	12	26	6	7	0	2	0	0	.268	3	3	0	13	17	1	.968

RECORD AS MANAGER

BACKGROUND: Coach, New York Mets (1987-89). ... Coach, Cincinnati Reds (1990-92). ... Coach, Seattle Mariners (1993-95). ... Coach, Baltimore Orioles (1996-August 4, 2005).

Year Team (League)	W	L	Pct.	Pos	Year Team (League)	W	L	Pct.	Pos
1982—Little Falls (NYP)	38	38	.500	3E	—Second half	42	28	.600	1E
1983—Lynchburg (Caro.)	49	20	.710	1N	1986—Tidewater (Int'l)	74	66	.529	4th
—Second half	47	23	.671	1N	2005—Baltimore (A.L.)	23	32	.418	4E
1984—Jackson (Texas)	43	24	.642	1E	2006—Baltimore (A.L.)	70	92	.432	4E
—Second half	40	29	.580	1E	Major League totals (2 years)	93	124	.429	
1985—Jackson (Texas)	31	35	.470	3E					

NOTES:
1983—Defeated Winston-Salem, 3-0, in league championship. ... **1984**—Defeated Beaumont, 4-2, in league championship. ... **1985**—Jackson tied two games; defeated Arkansas, 2-0, in semifinals; defeated El Paso, 4-0, in league championship. ... **1986**—Lost to Richmond, 3-0, in semifinals. ... **2005**—Replaced Baltimore manager Lee Mazzilli on an interim basis with club in fourth place and record of 51-56 (August 4).

PINIELLA, LOU   CUBS

PERSONAL: Born August 28, 1943, in Tampa. ... Full name: Louis Victor Piniella. ... Name pronounced: pin-ELL-uh. ... High school: Jesuit (Tampa). ... College: Tampa.

RECORD AS PLAYER

	G	AB	R	H	2B	3B	HR	RBI	Avg.	BB	SO	SB	PO	A	E	Avg.
									BATTING					FIELDING		
Major League totals (18 years)	1747	5867	651	1705	305	41	102	766	.291	368	541	33	2639	112	54	.981

RECORD AS MANAGER

BACKGROUND: Coach, New York Yankees (June 25, 1984-85). ... Vice-president/general manager, Yankees (March 1988 season-June 22, 1988). ... Special adviser, Yankees (1989). ... Broadcaster, FOX (2006).
HONORS: Named A.L. Manager of the Year by THE SPORTING NEWS (2001). ...Named A.L. Manager of the Year by Baseball Writers' Association of America (1995 and 2001).

Year Team (League)	W	L	Pct.	Pos	Year Team (League)	W	L	Pct.	Pos
1986—New York (A.L.)	90	72	.556	2E	1998—Seattle (A.L.)	76	85	.472	3W
1987—New York (A.L.)	89	73	.549	4E	1999—Seattle (A.L.)	79	83	.488	3W
1988—New York (A.L.)	45	48	.484	5E	2000—Seattle (A.L.)	91	71	.562	2W
1990—Cincinnati (N.L.)	91	71	.562	1W	2001—Seattle (A.L.)	116	46	.716	1W
1991—Cincinnati (N.L.)	74	88	.457	5W	2002—Seattle (A.L.)	93	69	.574	3W
1992—Cincinnati (N.L.)	90	72	.556	2W	2003—Tampa Bay (A.L.)	63	99	.389	5E
1993—Seattle (A.L.)	82	80	.506	4W	2004—Tampa Bay (A.L.)	70	91	.435	4E
1994—Seattle (A.L.)	49	63	.438	...	2005—Tampa Bay (A.L.)	67	95	.414	5E
1995—Seattle (A.L.)	79	66	.545	1W	American League totals (16 years)	1264	1189	.515	
1996—Seattle (A.L.)	85	76	.528	2W	National League totals (3 years)	255	231	.525	
1997—Seattle (A.L.)	90	72	.556	1W	Major League totals (19 years)	1519	1420	.517	

NOTES:
1988—Replaced New York manager Billy Martin with club in second place and record of 40-28 (June 23). ... **1990**—Defeated Pittsburgh, 4-2, in N.L. Championship Series; defeated Oakland, 4-0, in World Series. ... **1994**—Seattle was in third place in A.L. West at time of season-ending strike (August 12). ... **1995**—Defeated New York Yankees, 3-2, in A.L. Division Series; lost to Cleveland, 4-2, in A.L. Championship Series. ... **1997**—Lost to Baltimore, 3-1, in A.L. Division Series. ... **2000**—Defeated Chicago White Sox, 3-0, in A.L. Division Series; lost to New York Yankees, 4-2, in A.L. Championship Series. ... **2001**—Defeated Cleveland, 3-1, in A.L. Division Series; lost to New York Yankees, 4-1, in A.L. Championship Series. ... Career major league postseason record: 23-21.

RANDOLPH, WILLIE   METS

PERSONAL: Born July 6, 1954, in Holly Hill, S.C. ... 5-11/171. ... Full name: William Larry Randolph Jr.. ... High school: Tilden (Brooklyn, N.Y.).

RECORD AS PLAYER

	G	AB	R	H	2B	3B	HR	RBI	Avg.	BB	SO	SB	PO	A	E	Avg.
									BATTING					FIELDING		
Major League totals (18 years)	2202	8018	1239	2210	316	65	54	687	.276	1243	675	271	4859	6339	237	.979

RECORD AS MANAGER

BACKGROUND: Assistant general manager, New York Yankees (1993). ... Coach, Yankees (1994-2004).

Year Team (League)	W	L	Pct.	Pos	Year Team (League)	W	L	Pct.	Pos
2005—New York (N.L.)	83	79	.512	4E	2006—New York (N.L.)	97	65	.599	1E
					Major League totals (2 years)	180	144	.556	

NOTES:
2006—Defeated Los Angeles Dodgers, 3-0, in N.L. Division Series; lost to St. Louis, 4-3, in N.L. Championship Series. ... Career major league postseason record: 6-4.

SCIOSCIA, MIKE   ANGELS

PERSONAL: Born November 27, 1958, in Upper Darby, Pa. ... Full name: Michael Lorri Scioscia. ... Name pronounced: SO-sha. ... High school: Springfield (Pa.). ... College: Penn State.

RECORD AS PLAYER

	G	AB	R	H	2B	3B	HR	RBI	Avg.	BB	SO	SB	PO	A	E	Avg.
									BATTING					FIELDING		
Major League totals (13 years)	1441	4373	398	1131	198	12	68	446	.259	567	307	29	8335	737	114	.988

RECORD AS MANAGER

BACKGROUND: Minor league catching coordinator, Dodgers organization (1995-96). ... Coach, Dodgers (1997-98). ... Manager, Peoria Javelinas, Arizona Fall League (1997).
HONORS: Named A.L. Manager of the Year by THE SPORTING NEWS (2002). ... Named A.L. Manager of the Year by Baseball Writers' Association of America (2002).

Year Team (League)	W	L	Pct.	Pos	Year Team (League)	W	L	Pct.	Pos
1999—Albuquerque (PCL)	65	74	.468	3C	2004—Anaheim (A.L.)	92	70	.568	1W
2000—Anaheim (A.L.)	82	80	.506	3W	2005—Los Angeles (A.L.)	95	67	.586	1W
2001—Anaheim (A.L.)	75	87	.463	3W	2006—Los Angeles (A.L.)	89	73	.549	2W
2002—Anaheim (A.L.)	99	63	.611	2W	Major League totals (7 years)	609	525	.537	
2003—Anaheim (A.L.)	77	85	.475	3W					

NOTES:
2002—Defeated New York Yankees, 3-1, in A.L. Division Series; defeated Minnesota, 4-1, in A.L. Championship Series; defeated San Francisco, 4-3, in World Series. ... **2004**—Lost to Boston, 3-0, in A.L. Division Series. ... **2005**—Defeated New York Yankees, 3-2, in A.L. Division Series; Lost to Chicago White Sox, 4-1, in A.L. Championship Series. ... Career major league postseason record: 15-14.

TORRE, JOE   YANKEES

PERSONAL: Born July 18, 1940, in Brooklyn, N.Y. ... Full name: Joseph Paul Torre. ... Name pronounced: TORE-ee. ... High school: St. Francis Prep (Brooklyn, N.Y.). ... Brother of Frank Torre, first baseman with two major league teams (1956-60, 1962-63).

RECORD AS PLAYER

	G	AB	R	H	2B	3B	HR	RBI	Avg.	BB	SO	SB	PO	A	E	Avg.
						BATTING								FIELDING		
Major League totals (18 years).........	2209	7874	996	2342	344	59	252	1185	.297	805	1058	25	11618	1731	163	.988

RECORD AS MANAGER

HONORS: Named Sportsman of the Year by THE SPORTING NEWS (1996). ... Named A.L. Manager of the Year by THE SPORTING NEWS (1998). ... Named co-A.L. Manager of the Year by Baseball Writers' Association of America (1996). ... Named A.L. Manager of the Year by Baseball Writers' Association of America (1998).

Year Team (League)	W	L	Pct.	Pos	Year Team (League)	W	L	Pct.	Pos
1977—New York (N.L.)	49	68	.419	6E	1996—New York (A.L.)	92	70	.568	1E
1978—New York (N.L.)	66	96	.407	6E	1997—New York (A.L.)	96	66	.593	2E
1979—New York (N.L.)	63	99	.389	6E	1998—New York (A.L.)	114	48	.704	1E
1980—New York (N.L.)	67	95	.414	5E	1999—New York (A.L.)	98	64	.605	1E
1981—New York (N.L.)	17	34	.333	5E	2000—New York (A.L.)	87	74	.540	1E
—Second half	24	28	.462	4E	2001—New York (A.L.)	95	65	.594	1E
1982—Atlanta (N.L.)	89	73	.549	1W	2002—New York (A.L.)	103	58	.640	1E
1983—Atlanta (N.L.)	88	74	.543	2W	2003—New York (A.L.)	101	61	.623	1E
1984—Atlanta (N.L.)	80	82	.494	2W	2004—New York (A.L.)	101	61	.623	1E
1990—St. Louis (N.L.)	24	34	.414	6E	2005—New York (A.L.)	95	67	.586	1E
1991—St. Louis (N.L.)	84	78	.519	2E	2006—New York (A.L.)	97	65	.599	1E
1992—St. Louis (N.L.)	83	79	.512	3E	American League totals (11 years)	1079	699	.607	
1993—St. Louis (N.L.)	87	75	.537	3E	National League totals (14 years)	894	1003	.471	
1994—St. Louis (N.L.)	53	61	.465	...	Major League totals (25 years)	1973	1702	.537	
1995—St. Louis (N.L.)	20	27	.426	4E					

NOTES:
1977—Replaced New York manager Joe Frazier with club in sixth place and record of 15-30 (May 31); served as player/manager (May 31-June 18, when released as player). ... **1982**—Lost to St. Louis, 3-0, in N.L. Championship Series. ... **1990**—Replaced St. Louis manager Whitey Herzog (33-47) and interim manager Red Schoendienst (13-11) with club in sixth place and record of 46-58 (August 1). ... **1994**—St. Louis was tied for third place in N.L. Central at time of season-ending strike (August 12). ... **1995**—Replaced as St. Louis manager by interim manager Mike Jorgensen, with club in fourth place (June 16). ... **1996**—Defeated Texas, 3-1, in A.L. Division Series; defeated Baltimore, 4-1, in A.L. Championship Series; defeated Atlanta, 4-2, in World Series. ... **1997**—Lost to Cleveland, 3-2, in A.L. Division Series. ... **1998**—Defeated Texas, 3-0, in A.L. Division Series; defeated Cleveland, 4-2, in A.L. Championship Series; defeated San Diego, 4-0, in World Series. ... **1999**—Defeated Texas, 3-0, in A.L. Division Series; defeated Boston, 4-1, in A.L. Championship Series; defeated Atlanta, 4-0, in World Series. ... **2000**—Defeated Oakland, 3-2, in A.L. Division Series; defeated Seattle, 4-2, in A.L. Championship Series; defeated New York Mets, 4-1, in World Series. ... **2001**—Defeated Oakland, 3-2, in A.L. Division Series; defeated Seattle, 4-1, in A.L. Championship Series; lost to Arizona, 4-3, in World Series. ... **2002**—Lost to Anaheim, 3-1, in A.L. Division Series. ... **2003**—Defeated Minnesota, 3-1, in A.L. Division Series; defeated Boston, 4-3, in A.L. Championship Series; lost to Florida, 4-2, in World Series. ... **2004**—Defeated Minnesota, 3-1, in A.L. Division Series; lost to Boston, 4-3, in A.L. Championship Series ... **2005**— Lost to Los Angeles Angels of Anaheim, 3-2, in A.L. Division Series. ... **2006**—Lost to Detroit, 3-1, in A.L. Division Series. ... Career major league postseason record: 75-47.

TRACY, JIM   PIRATES

PERSONAL: Born December 31, 1955, in Hamilton, Ohio. ... Full name: James Edwin Tracy. ... High school: Badin (Hamilton, Ohio). ... College: Marietta College (Ohio).

RECORD AS PLAYER

	G	AB	R	H	2B	3B	HR	RBI	Avg.	BB	SO	SB	PO	A	E	Avg.
						BATTING								FIELDING		
Major League totals (2 years).............	87	185	18	46	5	4	3	14	.249	25	51	3	60	0	2	.968

RECORD AS MANAGER

BACKGROUND: Minor league field coordinator, Cincinnati Reds (1992). ... Coach, Montreal Expos (1995-98). ... Coach, Los Angeles Dodgers (1999-2000).
HONORS: Named Minor League Manager of the Year by THE SPORTING NEWS (1993).

Year Team (League)	W	L	Pct.	Pos	Year Team (League)	W	L	Pct.	Pos
1987— Peoria (Midw.)	71	69	.507	2S	1993— Harrisburg (East.)	94	44	.681	1st
1988— Peoria (Midw.)	29	40	.420	6S	1994— Ottawa (Int'l)	70	72	.493	3W
—Second half	41	30	.577	3S	2001— Los Angeles (N.L.)	86	76	.531	3W
1989— Chattanooga (Sou.)	33	38	.465	4S	2002— Los Angeles (N.L.)	92	70	.568	3W
—Second half	25	43	.368	5S	2003— Los Angeles (N.L.)	85	77	.525	2W
1990— Chattanooga (Sou.)	35	36	.493	4W	2004— Los Angeles (N.L.)	93	69	.574	1W
—Second half	31	42	.425	4W	2005— Los Angeles (N.L.)	71	91	.438	4W
1991— Chattanooga (Sou.)	35	32	.522	2W	2006— Pittsburgh (N.L.)	67	95	.414	5C
—Second half	38	39	.494	3W	Major League totals (6 years)	494	478	.508	

NOTES:
1993—Defeated Albany, 3-1, in semifinals; defeated Canton-Akron, 3-2, in league championship. ... **2004**—Lost to St. Louis, 3-1, in N.L. Division Series. ... Career major league postseason record: 1-3.

WASHINGTON, RON   RANGERS

PERSONAL: Born April 29, 1952, in New Orleans. ... 5-11/170. ... Full name: Ronald Washington. ... High school: John McDonogh (New Orleans). ... Junior college: Manatee (Fla.) Community College.

RECORD AS PLAYER

	G	AB	R	H	2B	3B	HR	RBI	Avg.	BB	SO	SB	PO	A	E	Avg.
						BATTING								FIELDING		
Major League totals (10 years).........	564	1586	190	414	65	22	20	146	.261	65	266	28	673	1069	71	.961

RECORD AS MANAGER

BACKGROUND: Coach, Tidewater of Int'l League, New York Mets organization (1991-92) ... Coach, Norfolk of Int'l League, Mets organization (1995)....Coach, Oakland Athletics (1996-2006).

Year Team (League)	W	L	Pct.	Pos	Year Team (League)	W	L.	Pct.	Pos
1993—Capital City (S.Atl.)	28	41	.406	7S	1994—Columbia (S. Atl.)	31	37	.456	5S
— Second half	36	36	.500	3S	— Second half	28	39	.418	4S

WEDGE, ERIC   INDIANS

PERSONAL: Born January 27, 1968, in Fort Wayne, Ind. ... Full name: Eric Michael Wedge. ... High school: Northrop (Fort Wayne, Ind.). ... College: Wichita State.

RECORD AS PLAYER

				BATTING									FIELDING			
	G	AB	R	H	2B	3B	HR	RBI	Avg.	BB	SO	SB	PO	A	E	Avg.
Major League totals (4 years)	39	86	13	20	2	0	5	12	.233	14	25	0	25	3	0	1.000

RECORD AS MANAGER

Year Team (League)	W	L	Pct.	Pos	Year Team (League)	W	L	Pct.	Pos
1998— Columbus (S. Atl.)	28	42	.400	4S	2002—Buffalo (Int'l)	87	57	.604	2N
— Second half	31	39	.443	3S	2003—Cleveland (A.L.)	68	94	.420	4C
1999—Kinston (Carol.)	37	32	.536	1S	2004—Cleveland (A.L.)	80	82	.494	3C
— Second half	42	26	.618	2S	2005—Cleveland (A.L.)	93	69	.574	2C
2000—Akron (East.)	75	68	.524	3S	2006—Cleveland (A.L.)	78	84	.481	4C
2001—Buffalo (Int'l)	91	51	.641	1N	Major League totals (4 years)	319	329	.492	

NOTES:
1999—Lost to Myrtle Beach, 2-1, in semifinals. ... **2001**—Lost to Scranton/Wilkes-Barre, 3-2, in semifinals. ... **2002**—Defeated Scranton/Wilkes-Barre, 3-0, in semifinals; lost to Durham, 3-0, in league championship. ... **2005**—On suspended list (August 5-6).

YOST, NED   BREWERS

PERSONAL: Born August 19, 1954, in Eureka, Calif. ... Full name: Edgar Frederick Yost. ... Junior college: Chabot Junior College.

RECORD AS PLAYER

				BATTING									FIELDING			
	G	AB	R	H	2B	3B	HR	RBI	Avg.	BB	SO	SB	PO	A	E	Avg.
Major League totals (6 years)	219	605	54	128	15	4	16	64	.212	21	117	5	843	54	16	.982

BACKGROUND: Coach, Atlanta Braves (1991-02).

RECORD AS MANAGER

Year Team (League)	W	L	Pct.	Pos	Year Team (League)	W	L	Pct.	Pos
1988—Sumter (S. Atl.)	29	40	.420	6S	2003—Milwaukee (N.L.)	68	94	.420	5C
— Second half	35	33	.515	4S	2004—Milwaukee (N.L.)	67	94	.416	6C
1989—Sumter (S. Atl.)	30	40	.429	5S	2005—Milwaukee (N.L.)	81	81	.500	3C
— Second half	30	41	.423	6S	2006—Milwaukee (N.L.)	75	87	.463	4C
1990—Sumter (S. Atl.)	38	34	.528	4S	Major League totals (4 years)	291	356	.450	
— Second half	35	35	.500	4S					

2006 MANAGERIAL TENDENCIES

One of the things about baseball which appeals to many of us is the game's endless opportunity for analysis. . . and few things are analyzed more than managerial decisions. Major league skippers may not have batting averages and slugging percentages to point to at the end of the season, but when it comes time to judge their performance and production, there's no reason we can't take a look at their statistics.

Which manager posted the best stolen-base success rate?

Which skippers were constantly tinkering with their lineups?

Which managers wore out a path to the pitching mound?

It's questions like these that get our second-guessing juices going, and it's questions like these that inspired this look at managerial tendencies in a number of situations. Once again, the skippers are compared based on offense, defense, lineups and pitching use. We don't rank the managers; there is plenty of room for argument on whether certain moves are good or bad. We are simply providing fodder for the discussion.

Offensively, managers have control over bunting, stealing and the timing of hit-and-runs. This section looks at the quantity, timing and success of these moves.

Defensively, this section looks at the success of pitchouts, the frequency of intentional walks, and the pattern of defensive substitutions.

Most managers spend large amounts of their time devising lineups. Here you'll find the number of lineups used, as well as the platoon percentage. The use of pinch-hitters and pinch-runners also is explored.

Finally, how does the manager use pitchers? For starters, this section shows slow and quick hooks, along with the number of times a starter was allowed to throw more than 120 pitches or 140 pitches. For relievers, we look at the number of relief appearances, mid-inning changes and how often a pitcher gets a save going more than one inning (a rare occurrence these days).

For the purposes of this section, it is assumed that a coach filling in for his manager will make his decisions based on what the manager would do in a given situation.

The categories include:

Stolen Base Success Percentage: Stolen bases divided by attempts.

Pitchout Runners Moving: The number of times the opposition is running when a manager calls a pitchout.

Double Steals: The number of double steals attempted in 2006.

Out Percentage: The proportion of stolen bases with that number of outs.

Sacrifice Bunt Attempts: A bunt is considered a sac attempt if no runner is on third, there are no outs, or the pitcher attempts a bunt.

Sacrifice Bunt Success %: A bunt that results in a sacrifice or a hit, divided by the number of attempts.

Favorite Inning: The most common inning in which an event occurred.

Hit-and-Run Success: The hit-and-run results in baserunner advancement with no double play.

Intentional Walk Situation: Runners on base, first base open, and anyone but the pitcher up. The teams must be within two runs of each other, or the tying run must be on base, at bat or on deck.

Defensive Substitutions: Straight defensive substitutions, with the team leading by four runs or less.

Number of Lineups: Based on batting order, 1-8 for National Leaguers, 1-9 for American Leaguers.

Percent LHB vs. RHSP and RHB vs. LHSP: A measure of platooning. A batter is considered to always have the platoon advantage if he is a switch-hitter.

Percent PH platoon: Frequency the manager gets his pinch-hitter the platoon advantage. Switch-hitters always have the advantage.

Score Diff: The most common score differential on which an intentional walk is called for.

Slow and Quick Hooks: A quick hook is the removal of a pitcher who has pitched fewer than six innings and given up three runs or less. A slow hook occurs when a pitcher pitches more than nine innings, or allows seven or more runs, or whose combined innings pitched and runs allowed totals 13 or more.

Mid-Inning Change: The number of times a manager changed pitchers in the middle of an inning.

1-Batter Appearances: The number of times a pitcher was brought in to face only one batter. Called the "Tony La Russa special" because of his penchant for trying to orchestrate specific matchups for specific situations.

3 Pitchers (2 runs or less): The club gives up two runs or less in a game but uses at least three pitchers.

OFFENSE

	G	Att.	SB%	Pitchout Rn Mv	2nd SB-CS	3rd SB-CS	Home SB-CS	Dbl Stls	Out Percentage 0	1	2	SACRIFICE BUNTS Att.	Suc. %	Fav. Inn.	Sqz.	HIT & RUN Att.	Suc. %
AL MANAGERS																	
Bell, Buddy, KC	162	99	65.7	2	55-30	10-4	0-0	4	10.1	41.4	48.5	74	74.3	7	2	72	33.3
Francona, Terry, Bos	162	74	68.9	0	46-22	5-1	0-0	0	16.2	33.8	50.0	34	70.6	5	1	61	37.7
Gardenhire, Ron, Min	162	143	70.6	5	88-36	13-6	0-0	3	23.8	39.9	36.4	48	77.1	3	1	116	46.6
Gibbons, John, Tor	162	98	66.3	0	53-26	12-7	0-0	2	22.4	31.6	45.9	22	68.2	8	4	93	34.4
Guillen, Ozzie, CWS	162	141	66.0	5	83-43	10-4	0-1	2	22.7	29.8	47.5	63	74.6	3	5	76	35.5
Hargrove, Mike, Sea	162	143	74.1	2	90-34	16-3	0-0	3	18.2	33.6	48.3	43	86.0	7	3	94	34.0
Leyland, Jim, Det	162	100	60.0	3	49-32	11-6	0-2	4	15.0	45.0	40.0	59	83.1	7	2	93	39.8
Macha, Ken, Oak	162	81	75.3	1	56-19	4-1	1-0	1	9.9	37.0	53.1	29	53.7	7	0	42	33.3
Maddon, Joe, TB	162	186	72.0	7	109-45	24-7	1-0	2	20.4	37.4	41.9	58	77.6	5	7	105	33.3
Perlozzo, Sam, Bal	162	153	79.1	9	100-27	21-4	0-1	5	24.8	34.6	40.5	60	76.7	8	0	60	41.7
Scioscia, Mike, LAA	162	205	72.2	12	123-45	23-6	2-6	13	20.0	30.7	49.3	39	92.3	5	5	157	41.4
Showalter, Buck, Tex	162	77	68.8	1	47-23	6-1	0-0	2	22.1	33.8	44.2	30	83.3	7	1	41	29.3
Torre, Joe, NYY	162	174	79.9	5	121-30	18-4	0-1	8	16.7	30.5	52.9	50	82.0	7	0	71	33.8
Wedge, Eric, Cle	162	78	70.5	2	50-19	5-4	0-0	0	19.2	44.9	35.9	41	87.8	8	0	58	41.4
NL MANAGERS																	
Alou, Felipe, SF	161	83	69.9	1	47-22	10-3	1-0	3	22.9	43.4	33.7	98	83.7	3	9	63	42.9
Baker, Dusty, ChC	162	170	71.2	4	107-41	13-5	1-3	5	27.1	42.4	30.6	114	86.0	3	12	84	41.7
Bochy, Bruce, SD	162	154	79.9	3	111-26	12-4	0-1	0	18.8	41.6	39.6	77	81.8	3	2	71	31.0
Cox, Bobby, Atl	162	87	59.8	0	48-34	4-1	0-0	2	12.6	39.1	48.3	104	81.7	3	9	33	36.4
Garner, Phil, Hou	162	115	68.7	7	74-30	5-3	0-3	0	28.7	37.4	33.9	130	82.3	7	8	88	37.5
Girardi, Joe, Fla	162	168	65.5	6	95-50	13-6	2-2	5	21.4	32.7	45.8	99	80.8	3	10	82	36.6
Hurdle, Clint, Col	162	135	63.0	11	80-44	4-3	1-3	3	17.8	27.4	54.8	157	80.3	5	1	68	36.8
La Russa, Tony, StL	161	91	64.8	2	53-27	6-4	0-1	4	24.2	36.3	39.6	90	83.3	5	11	104	32.7
Little, Grady, LAD	162	177	72.3	5	116-42	12-5	0-2	3	24.3	33.3	42.4	83	84.3	2	6	105	32.4
Manuel, Charlie, Phi	162	117	78.6	3	87-25	5-0	0-0	1	22.2	23.1	54.7	80	73.8	8	3	38	42.1
Melvin, Bob, Ari	162	106	71.7	4	64-26	11-4	1-0	4	21.7	42.5	35.8	82	78.0	3	6	42	38.1
Narron, Jerry, Cin	162	157	79.0	5	98-24	26-5	0-4	10	15.3	43.3	41.4	85	80.0	4	7	55	16.4
Randolph, Willie, NYM	162	181	80.7	9	119-33	27-2	0-0	7	17.7	24.9	57.5	103	83.5	2	5	67	26.9
Robinson, Frank, Was	162	185	66.5	7	104-43	19-19	0-0	4	27.0	39.5	33.5	97	86.6	7	6	100	41.0
Tracy, Jim, Pit	162	91	74.7	5	63-18	5-3	0-2	1	28.6	37.4	34.1	81	82.7	3	5	60	31.7
Yost, Ned, Mil	162	108	65.7	3	60-33	10-4	1-0	5	17.6	34.3	48.1	80	73.8	5	5	62	40.3

DEFENSE

	G	PITCHOUT Total	Runners Moving	CS%	Non-PO CS%	INTENTIONAL BB IBB	Pct. of Situations	Fav. Score Diff.	DEFENSIVE SUBS Total	Favorite Inning	Pos. 1	Pos. 2	Pos. 3
AL MANAGERS													
Bell, Buddy, KC	162	14	2	50.0	33.7	31	4.5	0	16	8	cf-9	1b-4	c-1
Francona, Terry, Bos	162	16	2	100.0	16.3	19	2.9	4	36	9	1b-11	rf-8	cf-6
Gardenhire, Ron, Min	162	11	1	100.0	35.7	16	2.8	0	21	8	lf-15	3b-3	1b-1
Gibbons, John, Tor	162	40	6	50.0	18.6	43	6.9	-2	30	7	lf-12	1b-5	ss-5
Guillen, Ozzie, CWS	162	27	4	75.0	21.2	34	5.2	0	33	9	cf-16	lf-10	3b-2
Hargrove, Mike, Sea	162	17	3	66.7	33.6	31	4.8	-2	14	8	rf-8	cf-4	1b-1
Leyland, Jim, Det	162	9	3	66.7	40.7	25	4.5	-2	34	8	lf-14	cf-6	1b-5
Macha, Ken, Oak	162	24	2	50.0	31.5	31	5.2	0	18	8	1b-4	3b-3	ss-3
Maddon, Joe, TB	162	51	11	54.5	28.0	32	4.4	-2	47	9	rf-14	1b-11	3b-11
Perlozzo, Sam, Bal	162	30	4	50.0	38.1	18	3.0	-2	43	9	lf-14	1b-12	c-6
Scioscia, Mike, LAA	162	23	4	100.0	31.9	21	3.2	-1	27	8	1b-14	cf-7	3b-4
Showalter, Buck, Tex	162	8	3	33.3	37.5	11	1.9	-2	19	9	lf-10	rf-7	2b-1
Torre, Joe, NYY	162	52	7	42.9	33.3	30	5.1	-2	49	8	1b-17	rf-16	lf-5
Wedge, Eric, Cle	162	16	1	100.0	20.5	30	4.7	-1	11	8	1b-7	c-1	3b-1
NL MANAGERS													
Alou, Felipe, SF	161	15	7	57.1	27.5	27	4.3	-1	29	9	lf-12	cf-7	1b-3
Baker, Dusty, ChC	162	47	7	57.1	23.3	26	4.4	-2	6	8	2b-2	1b-1	3b-1
Bochy, Bruce, SD	162	21	2	50.0	14.4	48	7.6	-1	27	7	3b-12	c-11	1b-2
Cox, Bobby, Atl	162	26	8	75.0	19.5	50	8.1	-2	20	7	lf-13	1b-2	3b-2

	G	Total	Runners Moving	CS%	Non-PO CS%	IBB	Pct. of Situations	Fav. Score Diff.	Total	Favorite Inning	Pos. 1	Pos. 2	Pos. 3
		PITCHOUT					**INTENTIONAL BB**			**DEFENSIVE SUBS**			
Garner, Phil, Hou	162	24	3	33.3	26.2	43	6.9	4	30	9	2b-12	rf-6	c-5
Girardi, Joe, Fla	162	43	4	50.0	39.6	41	6.6	1	37	8	1b-15	cf-9	ss-4
Hurdle, Clint, Col	162	30	4	75.0	28.5	67	10.5	0	9	8	cf-4	rf-2	c-1
La Russa, Tony, StL	161	13	3	100.0	31.5	27	4.4	-1	24	7	lf-12	cf-5	rf-3
Little, Grady, LAD	162	65	12	50.0	23.5	32	4.9	0	8	7	1b-3	3b-2	cf-2
Manuel, Charlie, Phi	162	16	4	50.0	26.4	46	6.7	-2	25	9	lf-12	rf-7	c-3
Melvin, Bob, Ari	162	30	5	60.0	32.3	27	4.1	1	20	9	1b-11	cf-4	c-1
Narron, Jerry, Cin	162	13	4	100.0	38.3	32	5.4	-1	22	8	3b-7	lf-7	ss-4
Randolph, Willie, NYM	162	18	7	42.9	25.7	29	4.8	-1	11	8	lf-6	rf-3	2b-1
Robinson, Frank, Was	162	13	0	-	21.4	51	7.6	-1	13	7	cf-4	ss-3	rf-3
Tracy, Jim, Pit	162	11	3	0.0	34.4	50	7.2	-2	11	8	1b-7	3b-2	ss-1
Yost, Ned, Mil	162	17	3	33.3	24.0	24	3.4	-2	5	7	2b-1	3b-1	lf-1

LINEUPS

	G	Lineups Used	%LHB vs. RHSP	%RHB vs. LHSP	#PH	Percent PH Platoon	PH BA	PH HR	#PR	PR SB-CS
		STARTING LINEUP				**SUBSTITUTIONS**				
AL MANAGERS										
Bell, Buddy, KC	162	142	47.1	77.3	92	70.7	.250	1	29	1-1
Francona, Terry, Bos	162	116	44.9	84.1	93	77.4	.224	0	54	5-3
Gardenhire, Ron, Min	162	97	52.1	78.3	93	84.9	.145	2	36	1-1
Gibbons, John, Tor	162	117	40.1	85.8	112	80.4	.240	2	32	1-0
Guillen, Ozzie, CWS	162	86	47.5	77.9	135	90.4	.225	6	42	6-1
Hargrove, Mike, Sea	162	84	41.5	77.5	121	82.6	.206	2	21	1-0
Leyland, Jim, Det	162	120	35.4	90.6	81	67.9	.222	2	34	2-0
Macha, Ken, Oak	162	121	48.9	85.4	62	77.4	.154	1	33	0-1
Maddon, Joe, TB	162	145	49.0	75.4	81	75.3	.225	1	26	0-2
Perlozzo, Sam, Bal	162	123	45.7	79.4	72	58.3	.092	0	46	3-1
Scioscia, Mike, LAA	162	114	51.7	86.3	103	75.7	.171	4	45	2-1
Showalter, Buck, Tex	162	95	45.5	87.9	39	74.4	.171	0	34	1-0
Torre, Joe, NYY	162	120	64.4	68.8	108	78.7	.233	0	50	2-2
Wedge, Eric, Cle	162	110	49.3	75.8	98	81.6	.232	2	13	0-0
NL MANAGERS										
Alou, Felipe, SF	161	123	52.6	84.7	215	71.6	.225	3	57	3-0
Baker, Dusty, ChC	162	132	48.1	73.3	271	69.0	.216	5	9	0-0
Bochy, Bruce, SD	162	110	50.9	77.1	264	87.9	.260	8	63	0-1
Cox, Bobby, Atl	162	85	46.3	84.0	299	82.3	.277	8	24	1-0
Garner, Phil, Hou	162	110	33.2	91.5	287	67.2	.240	7	17	2-0
Girardi, Joe, Fla	162	117	34.6	86.8	250	62.8	.242	4	44	6-0
Hurdle, Clint, Col	162	111	40.3	82.0	259	56.0	.214	6	17	0-1
La Russa, Tony, StL	161	131	36.0	89.7	272	78.7	.235	7	11	0-0
Little, Grady, LAD	162	118	57.4	80.0	291	61.9	.195	7	34	6-4
Manuel, Charlie, Phi	162	81	61.4	67.7	301	83.7	.209	3	42	1-2
Melvin, Bob, Ari	162	114	65.4	71.1	278	65.5	.193	7	11	1-0
Narron, Jerry, Cin	162	140	45.6	77.3	273	74.0	.270	13	23	3-0
Randolph, Willie, NYM	162	101	59.9	77.5	246	67.9	.187	3	9	1-0
Robinson, Frank, Was	162	110	48.4	78.5	314	80.9	.263	8	37	3-1
Tracy, Jim, Pit	162	121	29.2	79.8	264	48.9	.226	5	22	0-2
Yost, Ned, Mil	162	105	37.3	82.3	238	54.2	.267	4	12	1-0

DEFENSE

	G	Slow Hooks	Quick Hooks	> 120 Pitches	> 140 Pitches	3 Days Rest	Relief App	Mid-Inning Change	Save > 1 IP	1st Batter Platoon Pct	1-Batter App	3 Pit. (<=2run)
		STARTERS					**RELIEVERS**					
AL MANAGERS												
Bell, Buddy, KC	162	12	30	5	0	1	473	226	6	63.8	37	13
Francona, Terry, Bos	162	16	27	2	0	1	454	164	9	57.7	19	19
Gardenhire, Ron, Min	162	11	26	0	0	2	421	152	5	62.9	36	41
Gibbons, John, Tor	162	9	38	2	0	0	482	216	16	60.7	36	23
Guillen, Ozzie, CWS	162	22	8	4	0	0	398	213	7	70.9	43	19

– 560 –

		STARTERS					RELIEVERS					
	G	Slow Hooks	Quick Hooks	> 120 Pitches	> 140 Pitches	3 Days Rest	Relief App	Mid-Inning Change	Save > 1 IP	1st Batter Platoon Pct	1-Batter App	3 Pit. (<=2run)
Hargrove, Mike, Sea	162	18	19	3	0	0	429	205	14	72.0	49	32
Leyland, Jim, Det	162	11	19	2	0	1	390	157	3	67.2	32	39
Macha, Ken, Oak	162	17	20	6	0	1	444	177	8	63.5	42	27
Maddon, Joe, TB	162	14	31	1	0	0	444	184	10	57.9	16	25
Perlozzo, Sam, Bal	162	23	27	2	0	3	472	171	10	63.6	42	22
Scioscia, Mike, LAA	162	17	9	2	0	0	380	133	9	61.8	17	39
Showalter, Buck, Tex	162	14	26	0	0	1	489	186	4	64.0	37	30
Torre, Joe, NYY	162	9	21	1	0	0	489	215	7	64.7	51	35
Wedge, Eric, Cle	162	21	15	2	0	0	377	125	1	61.7	28	24
NL MANAGERS												
Alou, Felipe, SF	161	15	16	9	0	2	438	177	5	61.9	55	23
Baker, Dusty, ChC	162	18	29	7	0	0	542	191	2	66.4	51	27
Bochy, Bruce, SD	162	11	22	5	0	0	475	125	2	58.1	33	42
Cox, Bobby, Atl	162	15	18	8	0	5	522	163	3	61.5	45	24
Garner, Phil, Hou	162	14	21	5	0	4	497	160	2	62.8	51	35
Girardi, Joe, Fla	162	17	22	3	0	0	438	129	3	57.1	34	35
Hurdle, Clint, Col	162	14	11	2	0	0	499	192	2	60.8	55	27
La Russa, Tony, StL	161	20	24	3	0	2	469	194	6	66.7	45	32
Little, Grady, LAD	162	10	24	2	0	2	454	114	9	55.5	10	38
Manuel, Charlie, Phi	162	15	26	2	0	2	500	154	2	57.4	37	22
Melvin, Bob, Ari	162	16	18	3	0	2	461	97	0	55.5	26	28
Narron, Jerry, Cin	162	12	12	4	0	3	476	147	2	66.7	36	22
Randolph, Willie, NYM	162	14	23	1	0	1	474	119	4	53.5	23	36
Robinson, Frank, Was	162	14	21	3	0	0	517	161	3	59.4	41	26
Tracy, Jim, Pit	162	15	20	2	0	0	505	170	3	63.3	51	32
Yost, Ned, Mil	162	16	18	3	0	1	427	140	4	63.5	39	21

AMERICAN LEAGUE BATTING LEADERS

BATTING AVERAGE
minimum 502 PA

Player, Team	AB	H	AVG
J Mauer, Min	521	181	.347
D Jeter, NYY	623	214	.343
R Cano, NYY	482	165	.342
M Tejada, Bal	648	214	.330
V Guerrero, LAA	607	200	.329
I Suzuki, Sea	695	224	.322
J Morneau, Min	592	190	.321
M Ramirez, Bos	449	144	.321
C Guillen, Det	543	174	.320
R Johnson, Tor	461	147	.319

ON-BASE PERCENTAGE
minimum 502 PA; * AB + BB + HBP + SF

Player, Team	*PA	OB	OBP
M Ramirez, Bos	558	245	.439
T Hafner, Cle	563	247	.439
J Mauer, Min	608	261	.429
D Jeter, NYY	708	295	.417
J Thome, CWS	610	254	.416
J Giambi, NYY	579	239	.413
D Ortiz, Bos	686	283	.413
C Guillen, Det	622	249	.400
A Rodriguez, NYY	674	264	.392
V Martinez, Cle	652	255	.391

SLUGGING PERCENTAGE
minimum 502 PA

Player, Team	AB	TB	SLG
T Hafner, Cle	454	299	.659
D Ortiz, Bos	558	355	.636
J Dye, CWS	539	335	.622
M Ramirez, Bos	449	278	.619
J Thome, CWS	490	293	.598
J Morneau, Min	592	331	.559
J Giambi, NYY	446	249	.558
V Guerrero, LAA	607	335	.552
P Konerko, CWS	566	312	.551
F Thomas, Oak	466	254	.545

GAMES
G Sizemore, Cle	162
M Teixeira, Tex	162
M Tejada, Bal	162
M Young, Tex	162
I Suzuki, Sea	161

PLATE APPEARANCES
I Suzuki, Sea	752
G Sizemore, Cle	751
M Young, Tex	748
M Teixeira, Tex	727
D Jeter, NYY	715

AT-BATS
I Suzuki, Sea	695
M Young, Tex	691
G Sizemore, Cle	655
M Tejada, Bal	648
M Loretta, Bos	635

HITS
I Suzuki, Sea	224
M Young, Tex	217
D Jeter, NYY	214
M Tejada, Bal	214
V Guerrero, LAA	200

SINGLES
I Suzuki, Sea	186
D Jeter, NYY	158
M Tejada, Bal	153
M Young, Tex	148
M Loretta, Bos	143

DOUBLES
G Sizemore, Cle	53
M Young, Tex	52
M Lowell, Bos	47
L Overbay, Tor	46
2 tied with	45

TRIPLES
C Crawford, TB	16
G Sizemore, Cle	11
C Granderson, Det	9
I Suzuki, Sea	9
2 tied with	8

HOME RUNS
D Ortiz, Bos	54
J Dye, CWS	44
T Hafner, Cle	42
J Thome, CWS	42
F Thomas, Oak	39

TOTAL BASES
D Ortiz, Bos	355
G Sizemore, Cle	349
J Dye, CWS	335
V Guerrero, LAA	335
2 tied with	331

RUNS SCORED
G Sizemore, Cle	134
D Jeter, NYY	118
J Damon, NYY	115
D Ortiz, Bos	115
A Rodriguez, NYY	113

RUNS BATTED IN
D Ortiz, Bos	137
J Morneau, Min	130
R Ibanez, Sea	123
A Rodriguez, NYY	121
J Dye, CWS	120

GDP
M Tejada, Bal	28
V Martinez, Cle	27
M Young, Tex	27
T Glaus, Tor	25
P Konerko, CWS	25

SACRIFICE HITS
J Lopez, Sea	12
N Punto, Min	10
V Wilson, Det	10
6 tied with	9

SACRIFICE FLIES
O Cabrera, LAA	11
J Morneau, Min	11
K Youkilis, Bos	11
E Brown, KC	10
A Rios, Tor	10

STOLEN BASES
C Crawford, TB	58
C Figgins, LAA	52
C Patterson, Bal	45
I Suzuki, Sea	45
S Podsednik, CWS	40

CAUGHT STEALING
S Podsednik, CWS	19
C Figgins, LAA	16
L Castillo, Min	11
J Damon, NYY	10
A Kennedy, LAA	10

WALKS
D Ortiz, Bos	119
J Giambi, NYY	110
J Thome, CWS	107
T Hafner, Cle	100
M Ramirez, Bos	100

INTENTIONAL WALKS
V Guerrero, LAA	25
D Ortiz, Bos	23
J Mauer, Min	21
3 tied with	16

HIT BY PITCH
R Johnson, Tor	21
J Giambi, NYY	16
M Mora, Bal	14
K Johjima, Sea	13
G Sizemore, Cle	13

STRIKEOUTS
C Granderson, Det	174
R Sexson, Sea	154
G Sizemore, Cle	153
J Peralta, Cle	152
N Swisher, Oak	152

SCORING POSITION AVG
minimum 100 PA

Player, Team	AB	H	AVG.
M Young, Tex	148	61	.412
P Polanco, Det	96	38	.396
D Jeter, NYY	155	59	.381
P Konerko, CWS	142	52	.366
A Rios, Tor	112	41	.366
J Mauer, Min	125	45	.360
J Dye, CWS	148	52	.351
M Teahen, KC	103	36	.350
J Rivera, LAA	109	38	.349
C Crawford, TB	138	48	.348

LEADOFF OBP
minimum 150 PA; * AB + BB + HBP + SF

Player, Team	PA*	OB	OBP
R Johnson, Tor	486	190	.391
K Youkilis, Bos	467	180	.385
G Sizemore, Cle	748	280	.374
J Kendall, Oak	426	159	.373
J Lugo, TB	319	119	.373
G Matthews Jr., Tex	689	256	.372
I Suzuki, Sea	751	278	.370
P Ozuna, CWS	154	57	.370
R Baldelli, TB	193	71	.368
D DeJesus, KC	513	188	.366

CLEANUP SLG
minimum 150 PA

Player, Team	AB	TB	SLG
T Hafner, Cle	263	174	.662
M Ramirez, Bos	448	278	.621
V Guerrero, LAA	297	184	.620
M Teixeira, Tex	214	122	.570
R Ibanez, Sea	399	221	.554
P Konerko, CWS	439	240	.547
F Thomas, Oak	361	197	.546
T Wigginton, TB	144	78	.542
T Glaus, Tor	491	256	.521
M Tejada, Bal	378	190	.503

AVG VS. LHP
minimum 125 PA

V Guerrero, LAA	401
D Jeter, NYY	390
B Molina, Tor	358
I Suzuki, Sea	352
J Rivera, LAA	351

AVG VS. RHP
minimum 377 PA

J Mauer, Min	356
V Martinez, Cle	332
C Guillen, Det	332
G Sizemore, Cle	329
M Tejada, Bal	329

AVG AT HOME
minimum 251 PA

M Tejada, Bal	357
M Ramirez, Bos	355
D Jeter, NYY	354
C Guillen, Det	344
R Johnson, Tor	342

AVG ON THE ROAD
minimum 251 PA

R Cano, NYY	364
J Mauer, Min	359
D Jeter, NYY	334
J Kendall, Oak	330
J Dye, CWS	324

OBP VS. LHP
minimum 125 PA

V Guerrero, LAA	483
M Ramirez, Bos	477
D Jeter, NYY	458
T Hafner, Cle	442
J Gomes, TB	438

OBP VS. RHP
minimum 377 PA

J Thome, CWS	454
J Mauer, Min	444
J Giambi, NYY	434
D Ortiz, Bos	434
M Ramirez, Bos	422

LATE & CLOSE
minimum 50 PA

W Bloomquist, Sea	431
T Hafner, Cle	411
G Matthews Jr., Tex	398
F Catalanotto, Tor	394
J Damon, NYY	361

BASES LOADED
minimum 10 PA

J Rivera, LAA	667
M Young, Tex	615
C Crawford, TB	600
T Hafner, Cle	571
A Pierzynski, CWS	571

SLG VS. LHP
minimum 125 PA

V Guerrero, LAA	687
T Hafner, Cle	658
J Dye, CWS	645
T Glaus, Tor	635
M Ramirez, Bos	621

SLG VS. RHP
minimum 377 PA

J Thome, CWS	749
D Ortiz, Bos	649
M Ramirez, Bos	618
J Dye, CWS	610
J Giambi, NYY	592

AB PER HR
minimum 502 PA

D Ortiz, Bos	10.3
T Hafner, Cle	10.8
J Thome, CWS	11.7
F Thomas, Oak	11.9
J Giambi, NYY	12.1

TIMES ON BASE

D Jeter, NYY	295
D Ortiz, Bos	283
G Sizemore, Cle	281
I Suzuki, Sea	278
M Teixeira, Tex	270

PITCHES SEEN

G Sizemore, Cle	3013
K Youkilis, Bos	3004
M Teixeira, Tex	2884
I Suzuki, Sea	2806
M Young, Tex	2802

PITCHES PER PA
minimum 502 PA

K Youkilis, Bos	4.42
J Giambi, NYY	4.37
F Thomas, Oak	4.36
J Thome, CWS	4.31
T Glaus, Tor	4.20

% PITCHES TAKEN
minimum 1500 pitches

K Youkilis, Bos	64.0
J Giambi, NYY	64.0
J Mauer, Min	63.4
L Castillo, Min	63.4
M Izturis, LAA	62.5

GROUND/FLY RATIO
minimum 502 PA

D Jeter, NYY	3.23
L Castillo, Min	3.01
M Grudzielanek, KC	2.34
J Kendall, Oak	2.00
M Tejada, Bal	1.97

GDP/GDP OPP
minimum 50 PA

C Patterson, Bal	0.00
M Thames, Det	0.00
I Suzuki, Sea	0.02
G Sizemore, Cle	0.02
J Thome, CWS	0.03

SB SUCCESS %
minimum 20 SB attempts

I Suzuki, Sea	95.7
O Cabrera, LAA	90.0
D Jeter, NYY	87.2
C Crawford, TB	86.6
C Crisp, Bos	84.6

STEALS OF THIRD

D Jeter, NYY	12
B Roberts, Bal	12
C Figgins, LAA	11
O Cabrera, LAA	9
S Podsednik, CWS	9

% CS BY CATCHERS
minimum 70 SB attempts

R Hernandez, Bal	38.9
J Posada, NYY	34.7
K Johjima, Sea	27.8
J Kendall, Oak	24.5
A Pierzynski, CWS	18.9

†**Scoring-Position Average** denotes batting average when a runner is at second and/or third base. **Leadoff OBP** denotes OBP for a player batting in the first position of the batting order. **Cleanup Slugging** denotes slugging percentage for a player batting in the fourth position of the batting order. **Late & Close Avg.** refers to batting average when the game is in the seventh inning or later and the batting team is either leading by one run, tied, or has the potential tying run on base, at bat or on deck (a batting situation coming close to a pitcher's save situation). **Ground/Fly Ratio** denotes ground balls hit divided by fly balls hit. All batted balls except line drives and bunts are included. **GDP/GDP Opp.** denotes the ratio of times grounding into double plays per opportunities to do so (any situation with a runner on first and less than two out).

EARNED RUN AVERAGE
minimum 162 IP

Player, Team	IP	ER	ERA
J Santana, Min	233.2	72	2.77
R Halladay, Tor	220.0	78	3.19
C Sabathia, Cle	192.2	69	3.22
M Mussina, NYY	197.1	77	3.51
J Lackey, LAA	217.2	86	3.56
K Escobar, LAA	189.1	76	3.61
J Verlander, Det	186.0	75	3.63
C Wang, NYY	218.0	88	3.63
E Bedard, Bal	196.1	82	3.76
B Zito, Oak	221.0	94	3.83

WON-LOST PERCENTAGE
minimum 15 decisions

Pitcher, Team	W	L	Pct
F Liriano, Min	12	3	.800
R Halladay, Tor	16	5	.762
J Santana, Min	19	6	.760
C Wang, NYY	19	6	.760
J Garland, CWS	18	7	.720
M Mussina, NYY	15	7	.682
C Schilling, Bos	15	7	.682
K Rogers, Det	17	8	.680
E Santana, LAA	16	8	.667
2 tied with			.654

OPPOSITION AVG
minimum 162 IP

Pitcher, Team	AB	H	AVG
J Santana, Min	862	186	.216
E Santana, LAA	751	181	.241
M Mussina, NYY	762	184	.241
J Beckett, Bos	780	191	.245
J Lackey, LAA	825	203	.246
C Sabathia, Cle	738	182	.247
R Johnson, NYY	777	194	.250
R Halladay, Tor	829	208	.251
K Rogers, Det	770	195	.253
T Lilly, Tor	706	179	.254

GAMES

S Proctor, NYY	83
S Camp, TB	75
J Rincon, Min	75
S Shields, LAA	74
3 tied with	72

GAMES STARTED

J Bonderman, Det	34
D Haren, Oak	34
K Millwood, Tex	34
J Santana, Min	34
B Zito, Oak	34

COMPLETE GAMES

C Sabathia, Cle	6
R Halladay, Tor	4
K Benson, Bal	3
J Lackey, LAA	3
J Westbrook, Cle	3

GAMES FINISHED

J Nathan, Min	61
M Rivera, NYY	59
B Jenks, CWS	58
F Rodriguez, LAA	58
2 tied with	57

WINS

J Santana, Min	19
C Wang, NYY	19
J Garland, CWS	18
4 tied with	17

LOSSES

R Lopez, Bal	18
C Silva, Min	15
K Escobar, LAA	14
F Hernandez, Sea	14
J Washburn, Sea	14

SAVES

F Rodriguez, LAA	47
B Jenks, CWS	41
B Ryan, Tor	38
T Jones, Det	37
H Street, Oak	37

SHUTOUTS

J Lackey, LAA	2
C Sabathia, Cle	2
J Sowers, Cle	2
J Westbrook, Cle	2
17 tied with	1

HITS ALLOWED

M Buehrle, CWS	247
J Garland, CWS	247
J Westbrook, Cle	247
C Silva, Min	246
J Blanton, Oak	241

DOUBLES ALLOWED

J Garland, CWS	51
C Schilling, Bos	51
J Blanton, Oak	50
J Washburn, Sea	50
2 tied with	49

TRIPLES ALLOWED

J Bonderman, Det	10
P Byrd, Cle	7
J Contreras, CWS	7
3 tied with	6

HOME RUNS ALLOWED

C Silva, Min	38
J Beckett, Bos	36
M Buehrle, CWS	36
K Benson, Bal	33
2 tied with	32

BATTERS FACED

B Zito, Oak	945
D Haren, Oak	930
J Santana, Min	923
J Lackey, LAA	922
F Garcia, CWS	917

INNINGS PITCHED

J Santana, Min	233.2
D Haren, Oak	223.0
B Zito, Oak	221.0
R Halladay, Tor	220.0
C Wang, NYY	218.0

RUNS ALLOWED

C Silva, Min	130
R Lopez, Bal	129
R Johnson, NYY	125
M Buehrle, CWS	124
J Pineiro, Sea	123

STRIKEOUTS

J Santana, Min	245
J Bonderman, Det	202
J Lackey, LAA	190
J Vazquez, CWS	184
C Schilling, Bos	183

WALKS ALLOWED

D Cabrera, Bal	104
B Zito, Oak	99
G Meche, Sea	84
T Lilly, Tor	81
J Beckett, Bos	74

HIT BATSMEN

V Padilla, Tex	17
J Vazquez, CWS	15
B Zito, Oak	13
C Fossum, TB	12
E Santana, LAA	11

WILD PITCHES

D Cabrera, Bal	17
J Contreras, CWS	16
J Lackey, LAA	16
M Redman, KC	12
3 tied with	11

BALKS

T Lilly, Tor	4
A Burgos, KC	3
12 tied with	2

AMERICAN LEAGUE RELIEF PITCHING LEADERS

SAVES

Player,Team	Saves
F Rodriguez, LAA	47
B Jenks, CWS	41
B Ryan, Tor	38
T Jones, Det	37
H Street, Oak	37
J Nathan, Min	36
J Putz, Sea	36
J Papelbon, Bos	35
M Rivera, NYY	34
C Ray, Bal	33

SAVE PERCENTAGE
minimum 20 SvOp

Player,Team	OPP.	SV.	PCT.
J Nathan, Min	38	36	94.7
F Rodriguez, LAA	51	47	92.2
M Rivera, NYY	37	34	91.9
B Jenks, CWS	45	41	91.1
B Ryan, Tor	42	38	90.5
A Otsuka, Tex	36	32	88.9
C Ray, Bal	38	33	86.8
T Jones, Det	43	37	86.0
J Papelbon, Bos	41	35	85.4
J Putz, Sea	43	36	83.7

RELIEF ERA
minimum 50 relief IP

Player,Team	IP	ER	ERA
D Reyes, Min	50.2	5	0.89
J Papelbon, Bos	68.1	7	0.92
B Ryan, Tor	72.1	11	1.37
J Nathan, Min	68.1	12	1.58
F Rodriguez, LAA	73.0	14	1.73
M Rivera, NYY	75.0	15	1.80
J Zumaya, Det	83.1	18	1.94
A Otsuka, Tex	59.2	14	2.11
R Soriano, Sea	60.0	15	2.25
J Putz, Sea	78.1	20	2.30

RELIEF WINS

J Mateo, Sea	9
6 tied with	7

RELIEF GAMES

S Proctor, NYY	83
S Camp, TB	75
J Rincon, Min	75
S Shields, LAA	74
3 tied with	72

OPPOSITION AVG
minimum 50 relief IP

J Nathan, Min	158
J Papelbon, Bos	167
B Ryan, Tor	169
J Zumaya, Det	187
C Ray, Bal	193

AVG VS. LHB
minimum 50 relief IP

B Ryan, Tor	120
D Reyes, Min	148
S Downs, Tor	177
R Villone, NYY	179
J Speier, Tor	183

EASY SAVES

T Jones, Det	26
B Jenks, CWS	25
F Rodriguez, LAA	25
J Nathan, Min	22
A Otsuka, Tex	22

RELIEF LOSSES

E Dessens, KC	7
S Shields, LAA	7
6 tied with	6

GAMES FINISHED

J Nathan, Min	61
M Rivera, NYY	59
B Jenks, CWS	58
F Rodriguez, LAA	58
2 tied with	57

OPPOSITION OBP
minimum 50 relief IP

J Papelbon, Bos	211
J Nathan, Min	212
B Ryan, Tor	230
J Putz, Sea	245
D Reyes, Min	259

AVG VS. RHB
minimum 50 relief IP

J Papelbon, Bos	128
J Nathan, Min	130
F Rodriguez, LAA	179
R Soriano, Sea	179
B Ryan, Tor	182

REGULAR SAVES

F Rodriguez, LAA	19
M Rivera, NYY	16
B Ryan, Tor	16
J Nathan, Min	13
B Jenks, CWS	12

HOLDS

S Shields, LAA	31
J Zumaya, Det	30
S Proctor, NYY	26
J Rincon, Min	26
J Speier, Tor	25

RELIEF INNINGS

S Proctor, NYY	102.1
S Shields, LAA	87.2
H Carrasco, LAA	86.1
R Lugo, TB	85.0
J Zumaya, Det	83.1

OPPOSITION SLG
minimum 50 relief IP

B Ryan, Tor	214
J Nathan, Min	242
J Papelbon, Bos	254
J Zumaya, Det	270
D Reyes, Min	275

AVG RUNNERS ON
minimum 50 relief IP

J Papelbon, Bos	112
S Downs, Tor	134
J Nathan, Min	141
B Ryan, Tor	142
D Reyes, Min	151

BLOWN SAVES

A Burgos, KC	12
H Street, Oak	11
F Cordero, Tex	9
M Timlin, Bos	8
2 tied with	7

% INH RUNNERS SCORED
minimum 30 inherited runners

D Reyes, Min	13.3
B Jenks, CWS	16.7
J Putz, Sea	17.5
C Gaudin, Oak	20.0
M Myers, NYY	22.4

1ST BATTER AVG
minimum 40 first BFP

J Duchscherer, Oak	115
C Britton, Bal	125
B Ryan, Tor	125
J Putz, Sea	143
S Downs, Tor	146

AVG ALLOWED SCPOS
minimum 50 relief IP

J Papelbon, Bos	082
S Downs, Tor	111
B Ryan, Tor	121
D Reyes, Min	135
J Nathan, Min	145

PITCHES PER BATTER
minimum 50 relief IP

S Camp, TB	3.38
J Davis, Cle	3.41
T Jones, Det	3.42
J Mateo, Sea	3.49
J Crain, Min	3.53

†**Holds** denote the number of times a relief pitcher enters the game in a save situation, records at least one out and leaves the game never having relinquished the lead. A pitcher cannot finish the game and receive credit for a hold, nor can he earn a hold and a save in the same game. **Blown Saves** denote the number of times a relief pitcher enters a game in a save situation and allows the tying or go-ahead run to score. **Pct. Inherited Scored** denotes the percent of inherited runners (those on base when a reliever enters the game) that score. **Avg., Runners On** denotes batting average allowed when runners are on base. **Avg., Scoring Pos.** denotes batting average allowed when a runner is at second and/or third base. **Easy Saves** denote saves in which the first batter faced doesn't represent the tying run and the reliever pitches one inning or less. **Regular Saves** denote those saves that are not Easy Saves or Tough Saves. **Tough Saves** denote saves which occur after the reliever enters with the tying run anywhere on base.

BASERUNNERS PER 9 IP
minimum 162 IP

Player,Team	IP	BR	BR/9
J Santana, Min	233.2	237	9.13
R Halladay, Tor	220.0	247	10.10
M Mussina, NYY	197.1	224	10.22
C Sabathia, Cle	192.2	233	10.88
C Schilling, Bos	204.0	251	11.07
D Haren, Oak	223.0	279	11.26
E Santana, LAA	204.0	262	11.56
R Johnson, NYY	205.0	264	11.59
K Escobar, LAA	189.1	246	11.69
K Rogers, Det	204.0	266	11.74

STRIKEOUTS PER 9 IP
minimum 162 IP

Player,Team	IP	SO	SO/9
J Santana, Min	233.2	245	9.44
J Bonderman, Det	214.0	202	8.50
F Hernandez, Sea	191.0	176	8.29
J Vazquez, CWS	202.2	184	8.17
C Schilling, Bos	204.0	183	8.07
C Sabathia, Cle	192.2	172	8.03
T Lilly, Tor	181.2	160	7.93
J Lackey, LAA	217.2	190	7.86
M Mussina, NYY	197.1	172	7.84
E Bedard, Bal	196.1	171	7.84

RUN SUPPORT PER 9 IP
minimum 162 IP

Player,Team	IP	R	R/9
R Johnson, NYY	205.0	171	7.51
J Verlander, Det	186.0	140	6.77
J Westbrook, Cle	211.1	158	6.73
P Byrd, Cle	179.0	131	6.59
M Mussina, NYY	197.1	143	6.52
C Lee, Cle	200.2	145	6.50
J Vazquez, CWS	202.2	146	6.48
K Rogers, Det	204.0	145	6.40
J Garland, CWS	211.1	150	6.39
V Padilla, Tex	200.0	141	6.34

OPPOSITION OBP
minimum 162 IP

J Santana, Min	258
M Mussina, NYY	279
R Halladay, Tor	283
C Sabathia, Cle	293
D Haren, Oak	301

OPPOSITION SLG
minimum 162 IP

J Santana, Min	360
J Lackey, LAA	360
C Sabathia, Cle	363
E Bedard, Bal	370
R Halladay, Tor	374

HITS PER 9 IP
minimum 162 IP

J Santana, Min	7.16
E Santana, LAA	7.99
M Mussina, NYY	8.39
J Lackey, LAA	8.39
J Beckett, Bos	8.40

HOME RUNS PER 9 IP
minimum 162 IP

C Wang, NYY	0.50
J Lackey, LAA	0.58
J Westbrook, Cle	0.64
E Bedard, Bal	0.73
J Bonderman, Det	0.76

AVG VS. LHB
minimum 125 BFP

N Robertson, Det	181
J Zumaya, Det	183
C Ray, Bal	184
J Benoit, Tex	191
M Rivera, NYY	194

AVG VS. RHB
minimum 225 BFP

J Weaver, LAA	174
F Liriano, Min	206
J Santana, Min	206
M Hendrickson, TB	223
V Padilla, Tex	228

AVG ALLOWED SCPOS
minimum 125 BFP

J Santana, Min	174
S Kazmir, TB	188
T Wakefield, Bos	193
N Robertson, Det	199
B Halsey, Oak	204

OBP LEAD OFF INNING
minimum 150 BFP

J Beckett, Bos	231
M Mussina, NYY	235
D Haren, Oak	241
J Contreras, CWS	255
J Lackey, LAA	271

K/BB RATIO
minimum 162 IP

C Schilling, Bos	6.54
J Santana, Min	5.21
M Mussina, NYY	4.91
D Haren, Oak	3.91
C Sabathia, Cle	3.91

GRD/FLY RATIO OFF
minimum 162 IP

C Wang, NYY	3.06
J Westbrook, Cle	3.01
F Hernandez, Sea	2.39
R Halladay, Tor	2.39
E Bedard, Bal	1.70

PITCHES PER START
minimum 30 games started

B Zito, Oak	107.8
J Lackey, LAA	106.7
C Schilling, Bos	104.8
J Garland, CWS	104.1
G Meche, Sea	103.1

PITCHES PER BATTER
minimum 162 IP

C Silva, Min	3.32
C Wang, NYY	3.40
R Halladay, Tor	3.48
N Robertson, Det	3.53
M Buehrle, CWS	3.54

STEALS ALLOWED

F Garcia, CWS	40
T Wakefield, Bos	24
J Contreras, CWS	21
R Johnson, NYY	21
R Halladay, Tor	20

CAUGHT STEALING OFF

B Zito, Oak	12
C Wang, NYY	11
K Escobar, LAA	10
R Johnson, NYY	10
R Lopez, Bal	10

SB% ALLOWED
minimum 162 IP

K Rogers, Det	14.3
J Verlander, Det	16.7
E Santana, LAA	35.7
M Buehrle, CWS	36.4
B Zito, Oak	40.0

PICKOFFS

M Buehrle, CWS	10
J Verlander, Det	8
J Lester, Bos	6
S Kazmir, TB	5
3 tied with	4

PKOF THROW/RUNNER
minimum 162 IP

D Haren, Oak	0.56
C Wang, NYY	0.53
K Rogers, Det	0.53
K Escobar, LAA	0.51
R Johnson, NYY	0.49

GDP INDUCED

J Westbrook, Cle	36
C Wang, NYY	33
B Zito, Oak	31
N Robertson, Det	30
K Rogers, Det	25

GDP PER 9 IP
minimum 162 IP

J Westbrook, Cle	1.5
C Wang, NYY	1.4
N Robertson, Det	1.3
B Zito, Oak	1.3
M Redman, KC	1.2

QUALITY STARTS

J Santana, Min	24
J Lackey, LAA	23
M Mussina, NYY	23
K Millwood, Tex	22
5 tied with	20

†**Run Support per 9 IP** denotes the number of runs scored by a pitcher's team while he was still in the game times nine divided by his innings pitched. **Avg. Allowed Sc. Pos.** denotes batting average allowed when a runner is at second and/or third base. **Grd/Fly Ratio Off** denotes ground balls allowed divided by fly balls allowed. All batted balls except line drives and bunts are included. **PkOf Throw/Runner** denotes the number of pickoff throws made by a pitcher divided by the number of runners on first base. **Quality Starts** denote the number of outings in which a starting pitcher works at least six innings and allows three or fewer earned runs.

2006 NATIONAL LEAGUE LEADERS

NATIONAL LEAGUE BATTING LEADERS

BATTING AVERAGE
minimum 502 PA

Player,Team	AB	H	AVG
F Sanchez, Pit	582	200	.344
M Cabrera, Fla	576	195	.339
A Pujols, StL	535	177	.331
G Atkins, Col	602	198	.329
M Holliday, Col	602	196	.326
P Lo Duca, NYM	512	163	.318
L Berkman, Hou	536	169	.315
R Howard, Phi	581	182	.313
D Wright, NYM	582	181	.311
C Utley, Phi	658	203	.309

ON-BASE PERCENTAGE
minimum 502 PA; * AB + BB + HBP + SF

Player,Team	PA*	OB	OBP
A Pujols, StL	634	273	.431
M Cabrera, Fla	676	291	.430
N Johnson, Was	626	268	.428
R Howard, Phi	704	299	.425
L Berkman, Hou	646	271	.420
G Atkins, Col	695	284	.409
T Helton, Col	649	262	.404
J Bay, Pit	689	273	.396
J Drew, LAD	593	233	.393
S Hatteberg, Cin	537	209	.389

SLUGGING PERCENTAGE
minimum 502 PA

Player,Team	AB	TB	SLG
A Pujols, StL	535	359	.671
R Howard, Phi	581	383	.659
L Berkman, Hou	536	333	.621
C Beltran, NYM	510	303	.594
M Holliday, Col	602	353	.586
M Cabrera, Fla	576	327	.568
A LaRoche, Atl	492	276	.561
A Ramirez, ChC	594	333	.561
A Soriano, Was	647	362	.560
G Atkins, Col	602	335	.556

GAMES

J Francoeur, Atl	162
J Pierre, ChC	162
A Dunn, Cin	160
P Feliz, SF	160
C Utley, Phi	160

PLATE APPEARANCES

J Rollins, Phi	758
J Pierre, ChC	750
C Utley, Phi	739
R Furcal, LAD	736
A Soriano, Was	728

AT-BATS

J Pierre, ChC	699
J Rollins, Phi	689
C Utley, Phi	658
R Furcal, LAD	654
J Francoeur, Atl	651

HITS

J Pierre, ChC	204
C Utley, Phi	203
F Sanchez, Pit	200
G Atkins, Col	198
2 tied with	196

SINGLES

J Pierre, ChC	156
R Furcal, LAD	140
F Sanchez, Pit	139
O Vizquel, SF	135
2 tied with	128

DOUBLES

F Sanchez, Pit	53
L Gonzalez, Ari	52
M Cabrera, Fla	50
G Atkins, Col	48
S Rolen, StL	48

TRIPLES

J Reyes, NYM	17
J Pierre, ChC	13
D Roberts, SD	13
S Finley, SF	12
K Lofton, LAD	12

HOME RUNS

R Howard, Phi	58
A Pujols, StL	49
A Soriano, Was	46
L Berkman, Hou	45
2 tied with	41

TOTAL BASES

R Howard, Phi	383
A Soriano, Was	362
A Pujols, StL	359
M Holliday, Col	353
C Utley, Phi	347

RUNS SCORED

C Utley, Phi	131
C Beltran, NYM	127
J Rollins, Phi	127
J Reyes, NYM	122
4 tied with	119

RUNS BATTED IN

R Howard, Phi	149
A Pujols, StL	137
L Berkman, Hou	136
A Jones, Atl	129
G Atkins, Col	120

GDP

G Atkins, Col	24
A Gonzalez, SD	24
J Castillo, Pit	22
M Holliday, Col	22
B Ausmus, Hou	21

SACRIFICE HITS

R Oswalt, Hou	20
C Barmes, Col	19
C Sullivan, Col	19
J Smoltz, Atl	18
2 tied with	15

SACRIFICE FLIES

C Delgado, NYM	10
J Bay, Pit	9
A Jones, Atl	9
F Sanchez, Pit	9
6 tied with	8

STOLEN BASES

J Reyes, NYM	64
J Pierre, ChC	58
H Ramirez, Fla	51
D Roberts, SD	49
F Lopez, Cin-Was	44

CAUGHT STEALING

J Pierre, ChC	20
J Reyes, NYM	17
A Soriano, Was	17
H Ramirez, Fla	15
R Furcal, LAD	13

WALKS

B Bonds, SF	115
A Dunn, Cin	112
N Johnson, Was	110
R Howard, Phi	108
B Giles, SD	104

INTENTIONAL WALKS

B Bonds, SF	38
R Howard, Phi	37
A Pujols, StL	28
M Cabrera, Fla	27
L Berkman, Hou	22

HIT BY PITCH

R Weeks, Mil	19
A Rowand, Phi	18
J Bautista, Pit	16
D Eckstein, StL	15
M Holliday, Col	15

STRIKEOUTS

A Dunn, Cin	194
R Howard, Phi	181
B Hall, Mil	162
A Soriano, Was	160
J Bay, Pit	156

SCORING POSITION AVG
minimum 100 PA

Player,Team	AB	H	AVG.
B Bonds, SF	78	33	.423
A Pujols, StL	126	50	.397
F Sanchez, Pit	153	59	.386
L Berkman, Hou	131	50	.382
M Cabrera, Fla	148	56	.378
N Garciaparra, LAD	125	46	.368
D Wright, NYM	167	61	.365
T Helton, Col	121	42	.347
C Lee, Mil	101	35	.347
2 tied with			.346

LEADOFF OBP
minimum 150 PA; * AB + BB + HBP + SF

Player,Team	PA*	OB	OBP
J Carroll, Col	419	156	.372
R Furcal, LAD	710	264	.372
A Soriano, Was	608	224	.368
R Weeks, Mil	339	122	.360
J Bautista, Pit	214	77	.360
R Freel, Cin	490	176	.359
D Roberts, SD	552	198	.359
H Ramirez, Fla	587	210	.358
J Reyes, NYM	697	247	.354
D Eckstein, StL	544	191	.351

CLEANUP SLG
minimum 150 PA

Player,Team	AB	TB	SLG
D Wright, NYM	138	95	.688
R Howard, Phi	273	184	.674
M Holliday, Col	464	268	.578
L Berkman, Hou	157	90	.573
C Lee, Mil	356	204	.573
E Encarnacion, Cin	144	82	.569
C Delgado, NYM	455	253	.556
J Bay, Pit	497	273	.549
B Bonds, SF	354	194	.548
J Edmonds, StL	127	69	.543

AVG VS. LHP
minimum 125 PA

F Sanchez, Pit	.442
R Aurilia, Cin	.347
R Durham, SF	.341
O Vizquel, SF	.340
R Paulino, Pit	.339

AVG VS. RHP
minimum 377 PA

B McCann, Atl	.351
M Cabrera, Fla	.344
L Berkman, Hou	.335
C Jones, Atl	.332
R Howard, Phi	.331

AVG AT HOME
minimum 251 PA

F Sanchez, Pit	.388
J Carroll, Col	.375
M Holliday, Col	.373
M Cabrera, Fla	.355
G Atkins, Col	.346

AVG ON THE ROAD
minimum 251 PA

C Jones, Atl	.355
M Cabrera, Fla	.323
K Lofton, LAD	.322
J Barfield, SD	.319
P Lo Duca, NYM	.318

OBP VS. LHP
minimum 125 PA

M Ensberg, Hou	.463
F Sanchez, Pit	.460
B Bonds, SF	.451
P Burrell, Phi	.440
N Johnson, Was	.438

OBP VS. RHP
minimum 377 PA

R Howard, Phi	.453
L Berkman, Hou	.438
C Jones, Atl	.434
A Pujols, StL	.429
M Cabrera, Fla	.429

LATE & CLOSE
minimum 50 PA

M Anderson, Was-LAD	.400
W Helms, Fla	.400
G Jenkins, Mil	.397
C Lee, Mil	.373
R Durham, SF	.364

BASES LOADED
minimum 10 PA

E Renteria, Atl	.818
J Pierre, ChC	.643
E Chavez, NYM	.625
G Atkins, Col	.571
T Helton, Col	.571

SLG VS. LHP
minimum 125 PA

R Aurilia, Cin	.680
R Durham, SF	.650
B Hall, Mil	.650
A Pujols, StL	.620
J Willingham, Fla	.619

SLG VS. RHP
minimum 377 PA

R Howard, Phi	.711
L Berkman, Hou	.704
A Pujols, StL	.688
C Beltran, NYM	.648
B McCann, Atl	.603

AB PER HR
minimum 502 PA

R Howard, Phi	10.0
A Pujols, StL	10.9
L Berkman, Hou	11.9
C Beltran, NYM	12.4
A Jones, Atl	13.8

TIMES ON BASE

R Howard, Phi	299
M Cabrera, Fla	291
G Atkins, Col	284
C Utley, Phi	280
2 tied with	273

PITCHES SEEN

F Lopez, Cin-Was	2938
C Utley, Phi	2926
R Howard, Phi	2859
A Dunn, Cin	2858
A Soriano, Was	2839

PITCHES PER PA
minimum 502 PA

P Burrell, Phi	4.32
N Johnson, Was	4.28
C Beltran, NYM	4.20
A Dunn, Cin	4.18
J Carroll, Col	4.15

% PITCHES TAKEN
minimum 1500 pitches

S Hatteberg, Cin	65.9
B Abreu, Phi	65.9
B Bonds, SF	65.5
N Johnson, Was	65.0
P Burrell, Phi	64.4

GROUND/FLY RATIO
minimum 502 PA

M Murton, ChC	2.40
J Jones, ChC	2.27
J Pierre, ChC	2.26
D Roberts, SD	2.24
P Wilson, Hou-StL	2.04

GDP/GDP OPP
minimum 50 PA

D Dellucci, Phi	0.02
S Spiezio, StL	0.02
S Drew, Ari	0.02
C Barmes, Col	0.02
A Soriano, Was	0.03

SB SUCCESS %
minimum 20 SB attempts

C Duffy, Pit	96.3
B Phillips, Cin	92.6
J Rollins, Phi	90.0
E Byrnes, Ari	89.3
D Roberts, SD	89.1

STEALS OF THIRD

A Soriano, Was	14
J Pierre, ChC	12
R Freel, Cin	10
B Phillips, Cin	8
J Reyes, NYM	8

% CS BY CATCHERS
minimum 70 SB attempts

M Olivo, Fla	34.2
B Schneider, Was	26.6
R Paulino, Pit	26.4
R Martin, LAD	26.0
J Estrada, Ari	24.1

†**Scoring-Position Average** denotes batting average when a runner is at second and/or third base. **Leadoff OBP** denotes OBP for a player batting in the first position of the batting order. **Cleanup Slugging** denotes slugging percentage for a player batting in the fourth position of the batting order. **Late & Close Avg.** refers to batting average when the game is in the seventh inning or later and the batting team is either leading by one run, tied, or has the potential tying run on base, at bat or on deck (a batting situation coming close to a pitcher's save situation). **Ground/Fly Ratio** denotes ground balls hit divided by fly balls hit. All batted balls except line drives and bunts are included. **GDP/GDP Opp.** denotes the ratio of times grounding into double plays per opportunities to do so (any situation with a runner on first and less than two out).

EARNED RUN AVERAGE
minimum 162 IP

Player,Team	IP	ER	ERA
R Oswalt, Hou	220.2	73	2.98
C Carpenter, StL	221.2	76	3.09
B Webb, Ari	235.0	81	3.10
B Arroyo, Cin	240.2	88	3.29
C Zambrano, ChC	214.0	81	3.41
C Young, SD	179.1	69	3.46
J Smoltz, Atl	232.0	90	3.49
J Schmidt, SF	213.1	85	3.59
D Lowe, LAD	218.0	88	3.63
C Hensley, SD	187.0	77	3.71

WON-LOST PERCENTAGE
minimum 15 decisions

Pitcher,Team	W	L	Pct
C James, Atl	11	4	.733
W Williams, SD	12	5	.706
C Zambrano, ChC	16	7	.696
C Young, SD	11	5	.688
T Glavine, NYM	15	7	.682
D Lowe, LAD	16	8	.667
B Webb, Ari	16	8	.667
C Carpenter, StL	15	8	.652
R Oswalt, Hou	15	8	.652
S Trachsel, NYM	15	8	.652

OPPOSITION AVG
minimum 162 IP

Pitcher,Team	AB	H	AVG
C Young, SD	649	134	.206
C Zambrano, ChC	778	162	.208
M Cain, SF	708	157	.222
C Carpenter, StL	827	194	.235
J Schmidt, SF	794	189	.238
S Olsen, Fla	670	160	.239
J Peavy, SD	772	187	.242
B Arroyo, Cin	912	222	.243
B Webb, Ari	878	216	.246
J Francis, Col	747	187	.250

GAMES

S Torres, Pit	94
M Capps, Pit	85
J Rauch, Was	85
B Howry, ChC	84
M Stanton, Was-SF	82

GAMES STARTED

B Arroyo, Cin	35
A Harang, Cin	35
T Hudson, Atl	35
A Pettitte, Hou	35
J Smoltz, Atl	35

COMPLETE GAMES

A Harang, Cin	6
C Carpenter, StL	5
B Webb, Ari	5
D Willis, Fla	4
7 tied with	3

GAMES FINISHED

R Dempster, ChC	64
J Borowski, Fla	60
C Cordero, Was	59
B Wagner, NYM	59
B Fuentes, Col	58

WINS

A Harang, Cin	16
D Lowe, LAD	16
B Penny, LAD	16
J Smoltz, Atl	16
B Webb, Ari	16
C Zambrano, ChC	16

LOSSES

J Marquis, StL	16
R Ortiz, Was	16
A Cook, Col	15
Z Duke, Pit	15
M Morris, SF	15

SAVES

T Hoffman, SD	46
B Wagner, NYM	40
J Borowski, Fla	36
T Gordon, Phi	34
J Isringhausen, StL	33

SHUTOUTS

C Carpenter, StL	3
B Webb, Ari	3
4 tied with	2

HITS ALLOWED

Z Duke, Pit	255
L Hernandez, Was-Ari	246
A Cook, Col	242
A Harang, Cin	242
A Pettitte, Hou	238

DOUBLES ALLOWED

C Capuano, Mil	66
Z Duke, Pit	60
R Oswalt, Hou	55
A Harang, Cin	54
M Morris, SF	54

TRIPLES ALLOWED

J Fogg, Col	10
J Marquis, StL	10
4 tied with	9

HOME RUNS ALLOWED

J Marquis, StL	35
B Arroyo, Cin	31
R Ortiz, Was	31
J Sosa, Atl-StL	30
5 tied with	29

BATTERS FACED

A Harang, Cin	993
B Arroyo, Cin	992
D Willis, Fla	975
J Smoltz, Atl	960
2 tied with	959

INNINGS PITCHED

B Arroyo, Cin	240.2
B Webb, Ari	235.0
A Harang, Cin	234.1
J Smoltz, Atl	232.0
D Willis, Fla	223.1

RUNS ALLOWED

J Marquis, StL	136
T Hudson, Atl	129
R Ortiz, Was	127
L Hernandez, Was-Ari	125
M Morris, SF	123

STRIKEOUTS

A Harang, Cin	216
J Peavy, SD	215
J Smoltz, Atl	211
C Zambrano, ChC	210
B Myers, Phi	189

WALKS ALLOWED

C Zambrano, ChC	115
D Davis, Mil	102
M Cain, SF	87
J Jennings, Col	85
M Batista, Ari	84

HIT BATSMEN

D Willis, Fla	19
D Bush, Mil	18
R Ortiz, Was	18
J Marquis, StL	16
M Morris, SF	14

WILD PITCHES

M Batista, Ari	14
R Madson, Phi	12
B Lidge, Hou	11
J Schmidt, SF	11
J Jennings, Col	10

BALKS

O Hernandez, Ari-NYM	3
M Morris, SF	3
R Ortiz, Was	3
E Ramirez, Cin	3
6 tied with	2

NATIONAL LEAGUE RELIEF PITCHING LEADERS

SAVES

Player,Team	Saves
T Hoffman, SD	46
B Wagner, NYM	40
J Borowski, Fla	36
T Gordon, Phi	34
J Isringhausen, StL	33
B Lidge, Hou	32
B Fuentes, Col	30
C Cordero, Was	29
4 tied with	24

SAVE PERCENTAGE
minimum 20 SvOp

Player,Team	OPP.	SV.	PCT.
M Gonzalez, Pit	24	24	100.0
T Saito, LAD	26	24	92.3
T Hoffman, SD	51	46	90.2
B Wagner, NYM	45	40	88.9
C Cordero, Was	33	29	87.9
T Gordon, Phi	39	34	87.2
B Lidge, Hou	38	32	84.2
J Borowski, Fla	43	36	83.7
B Fuentes, Col	36	30	83.3
J Valverde, Ari	22	18	81.8

RELIEF ERA
minimum 50 relief IP

Player,Team	IP	ER	ERA
C Meredith, SD	50.2	6	1.07
T Saito, LAD	78.1	18	2.07
P Feliciano, NYM	60.1	14	2.09
T Hoffman, SD	63.0	15	2.14
M Gonzalez, Pit	54.0	13	2.17
B Wagner, NYM	72.1	18	2.24
D Wheeler, Hou	71.1	20	2.52
J Broxton, LAD	76.1	22	2.59
D Sanchez, NYM	55.1	16	2.60
C Bradford, NYM	62.0	20	2.90

RELIEF WINS

M Capps, Pit	9
B Looper, StL	9
O Villarreal, Atl	8
6 tied with	7

RELIEF GAMES

S Torres, Pit	94
M Capps, Pit	85
J Rauch, Was	85
B Howry, ChC	84
M Stanton, Was-SF	82

OPPOSITION AVG
minimum 50 relief IP

C Meredith, SD	170
T Saito, LAD	177
T Hoffman, SD	205
W Ohman, ChC	208
B Fuentes, Col	209

AVG VS. LHB
minimum 50 relief IP

W Ohman, ChC	158
B Wagner, NYM	161
M Gonzalez, Pit	163
L Vizcaino, Ari	163
J Borowski, Fla	167

EASY SAVES

T Hoffman, SD	28
J Borowski, Fla	25
B Fuentes, Col	24
B Wagner, NYM	22
2 tied with	21

RELIEF LOSSES

R Dempster, ChC	9
D Turnbow, Mil	9
J Isringhausen, StL	8
5 tied with	7

GAMES FINISHED

R Dempster, ChC	64
J Borowski, Fla	60
C Cordero, Was	59
B Wagner, NYM	59
B Fuentes, Col	58

OPPOSITION OBP
minimum 50 relief IP

C Meredith, SD	207
T Saito, LAD	243
T Hoffman, SD	250
R Springer, Hou	277
C Cordero, Was	279

AVG VS. RHB
minimum 50 relief IP

C Meredith, SD	107
T Saito, LAD	129
D Sanchez, NYM	179
A Wainwright, StL	182
D Wheeler, Hou	183

REGULAR SAVES

T Hoffman, SD	18
B Wagner, NYM	18
T Gordon, Phi	13
B Lidge, Hou	12
3 tied with	11

HOLDS

S Linebrink, SD	36
A Heilman, NYM	27
L Vizcaino, Ari	25
D Wheeler, Hou	24
3 tied with	23

RELIEF INNINGS

S Torres, Pit	93.1
G Geary, Phi	91.1
J Rauch, Was	91.1
C Qualls, Hou	88.2
A Heilman, NYM	87.0

OPPOSITION SLG
minimum 50 relief IP

C Meredith, SD	244
M Gonzalez, Pit	259
T Saito, LAD	262
B Wagner, NYM	315
D Sanchez, NYM	316

AVG RUNNERS ON
minimum 50 relief IP

C Meredith, SD	114
T Hoffman, SD	122
B Wagner, NYM	171
J Broxton, LAD	172
B Fuentes, Col	173

TOUGH SAVES

C Cordero, Was	2
F Cordero, Mil	2
B Lidge, Hou	2
C Reitsma, Atl	2
M Remlinger, Atl	2
M Stanton, Was-SF	2
D Wheeler, Hou	2

BLOWN SAVES

J Isringhausen, StL	10
M Capps, Pit	9
R Dempster, ChC	9
S Linebrink, SD	9
3 tied with	8

% INH RUNNERS SCORED
minimum 30 inherited runners

J Grabow, Pit	17.5
T Miller, Hou	17.5
C Bradford, NYM	18.9
W Ohman, ChC	19.5
M Stanton, Was-SF	20.3

1ST BATTER AVG
minimum 40 first BFP

C Meredith, SD	140
D Aardsma, ChC	175
B Fuentes, Col	180
R Franklin, Phi-Cin	194
2 tied with	194

AVG ALLOWED SCPOS
minimum 50 relief IP

T Miller, Hou	063
J Broxton, LAD	159
C Meredith, SD	159
J Capellan, Mil	171
T Hoffman, SD	182

PITCHES PER BATTER
minimum 50 relief IP

C Qualls, Hou	3.33
O Villarreal, Atl	3.40
M Capps, Pit	3.48
B Thompson, StL	3.48
M Herges, Fla	3.53

†**Holds** denote the number of times a relief pitcher enters the game in a save situation, records at least one out and leaves the game never having relinquished the lead. A pitcher cannot finish the game and receive credit for a hold, nor can he earn a hold and a save in the same game. **Blown Saves** denote the number of times a relief pitcher enters a game in a save situation and allows the tying or go-ahead run to score. **Pct. Inherited Scored** denotes the percent of inherited runners (those on base when a reliever enters the game) that score. **Avg., Runners On** denotes batting average allowed when runners are on base. **Avg., Scoring Pos.** denotes batting average allowed when a runner is at second and/or third base. **Easy Saves** denote saves in which the first batter faced doesn't represent the tying run and the reliever pitches one inning or less. **Regular Saves** denote those saves that are not Easy Saves or Tough Saves. **Tough Saves** denote saves which occur after the reliever enters with the tying run anywhere on base.

BASERUNNERS PER 9 IP
minimum 162 IP

Player,Team	IP	BR	BR/9
C Carpenter, StL	221.2	247	10.03
B Webb, Ari	235.0	272	10.42
C Young, SD	179.1	209	10.49
R Oswalt, Hou	220.2	264	10.77
B Arroyo, Cin	240.2	291	10.88
G Maddux, ChC-LAD	210.0	256	10.97
D Bush, Mil	210.0	257	11.01
J Smoltz, Atl	232.0	285	11.06
J Peavy, SD	202.1	255	11.34
C Capuano, Mil	221.1	285	11.59

STRIKEOUTS PER 9 IP
minimum 162 IP

Player,Team	IP	SO	SO/9
J Peavy, SD	202.1	215	9.56
O Hernandez, Ari-NYM	162.1	164	9.09
C Zambrano, ChC	214.0	210	8.83
B Myers, Phi	198.0	189	8.59
M Cain, SF	190.2	179	8.45
A Harang, Cin	234.1	216	8.30
S Olsen, Fla	180.2	166	8.27
C Young, SD	179.1	164	8.23
J Smoltz, Atl	232.0	211	8.19
I Snell, Pit	186.0	169	8.18

RUN SUPPORT PER 9 IP
minimum 162 IP

Player,Team	IP	R	R/9
S Trachsel, NYM	164.2	121	6.61
J Fogg, Col	172.0	123	6.44
D Davis, Mil	203.1	140	6.20
T Hudson, Atl	218.1	148	6.10
C Zambrano, ChC	214.0	142	5.97
B Penny, LAD	189.0	125	5.95
T Glavine, NYM	198.0	130	5.91
J Francis, Col	199.0	129	5.83
M Batista, Ari	206.1	132	5.76
J Suppan, StL	190.0	121	5.73

OPPOSITION OBP
minimum 162 IP

C Carpenter, StL	279
C Young, SD	287
B Webb, Ari	289
B Arroyo, Cin	296
J Smoltz, Atl	298

OPPOSITION SLG
minimum 162 IP

C Zambrano, ChC	351
D Lowe, LAD	360
B Webb, Ari	361
C Carpenter, StL	364
M Cain, SF	371

HITS PER 9 IP
minimum 162 IP

C Young, SD	6.72
C Zambrano, ChC	6.81
M Cain, SF	7.41
C Carpenter, StL	7.88
S Olsen, Fla	7.97

HOME RUNS PER 9 IP
minimum 162 IP

B Webb, Ari	0.57
D Lowe, LAD	0.58
Z Duke, Pit	0.71
A Cook, Col	0.72
J Jennings, Col	0.72

AVG VS. LHB
minimum 125 BFP

J Borowski, Fla	167
C Young, SD	175
S Olsen, Fla	182
J Julio, NYM-Ari	185
T Glavine, NYM	200

AVG VS. RHB
minimum 225 BFP

C Zambrano, ChC	174
R Clemens, Hou	185
O Hernandez, Ari-NYM	199
B Arroyo, Cin	206
C Carpenter, StL	210

AVG ALLOWED SCPOS
minimum 125 BFP

C Young, SD	176
C Billingsley, LAD	191
J Schmidt, SF	197
J Cruz, Ari	216
J Smoltz, Atl	223

OBP LEAD OFF INNING
minimum 150 BFP

J Lieber, Phi	246
C Capuano, Mil	252
C Carpenter, StL	261
B Arroyo, Cin	262
M Cain, SF	264

K/BB RATIO
minimum 162 IP

D Bush, Mil	4.37
R Oswalt, Hou	4.37
C Carpenter, StL	4.28
J Lieber, Phi	4.17
A Harang, Cin	3.86

GRD/FLY RATIO OFF
minimum 162 IP

B Webb, Ari	4.06
D Lowe, LAD	3.99
A Cook, Col	2.77
T Hudson, Atl	2.22
C Hensley, SD	2.10

PITCHES PER START
minimum 30 games started

B Arroyo, Cin	110.1
C Zambrano, ChC	110.0
J Schmidt, SF	108.4
A Harang, Cin	106.6
D Willis, Fla	106.3

PITCHES PER BATTER
minimum 162 IP

G Maddux, ChC-LAD	3.26
A Cook, Col	3.41
D Bush, Mil	3.49
J Lieber, Phi	3.49
Z Duke, Pit	3.51

STEALS ALLOWED

C Young, SD	41
D Lowe, LAD	26
G Maddux, ChC-LAD	25
J Peavy, SD	25
2 tied with	24

CAUGHT STEALING OFF

Z Duke, Pit	12
P Maholm, Pit	11
T Glavine, NYM	9
B Webb, Ari	9
7 tied with	8

SB% ALLOWED
minimum 162 IP

C Capuano, Mil	25.0
C Carpenter, StL	30.0
T Glavine, NYM	40.0
C Zambrano, ChC	40.0
R Oswalt, Hou	45.5

PICKOFFS

P Maholm, Pit	9
Z Duke, Pit	7
J Wright, SF	7
J Beimel, LAD	6
C Capuano, Mil	6

PKOF THROW/RUNNER
minimum 162 IP

C Capuano, Mil	0.99
C Young, SD	0.75
C Vargas, Ari	0.69
S Trachsel, NYM	0.68
O Hernandez, Ari-NYM	0.64

GDP INDUCED

M Batista, Ari	32
D Willis, Fla	32
D Lowe, LAD	29
B Webb, Ari	29
A Cook, Col	28

GDP PER 9 IP
minimum 162 IP

M Batista, Ari	1.4
C Hensley, SD	1.3
D Willis, Fla	1.3
D Lowe, LAD	1.2
A Cook, Col	1.2

QUALITY STARTS

C Capuano, Mil	25
R Oswalt, Hou	25
J Smoltz, Atl	24
B Arroyo, Cin	23
B Webb, Ari	23

†**Run Support per 9 IP** denotes the number of runs scored by a pitcher's team while he was still in the game times nine divided by his innings pitched. **Avg. Allowed Sc. Pos.** denotes batting average allowed when a runner is at second and/or third base. **Grd/Fly Ratio Off** denotes ground balls allowed divided by fly balls allowed. All batted balls except line drives and bunts are included. **PkOf Throw/Runner** denotes the number of pickoff throws made by a pitcher divided by the number of runners on first base. **Quality Starts** denote the number of outings in which a starting pitcher works at least six innings and allows three or fewer earned runs.

2006 ACTIVE CAREER LEADERS

BATTING

BATTING AVERAGE
minimum 1000 PA

Rk.	Player	AB	H	AVG
1	Todd Helton	5106	1700	.333
2	Albert Pujols	3489	1159	.332
3	Ichiro Suzuki	4096	1354	.331
4	Vladimir Guerrero	5502	1786	.325
5	Joe Mauer	1117	358	.321
6	Robinson Cano	1004	320	.319
7	Nomar Garciaparra	4832	1537	.318
8	Derek Jeter	6790	2150	.317
9	Manny Ramirez	6575	2066	.314
10	Freddy Sanchez	1104	346	.313
11	Miguel Cabrera	2106	654	.311
12	Matt Holliday	1481	459	.310
13	Mike Piazza	6602	2042	.309
14	David Wright	1420	434	.306
15	Alex Rodriguez	6767	2067	.305
16	Magglio Ordonez	4705	1436	.305
17	Frank Thomas	7422	2262	.305
18	Chipper Jones	6385	1944	.304
19	Ivan Rodriguez	7745	2354	.304
20	Lance Berkman	3687	1120	.304
21	Ryan Howard	932	283	.304
22	Juan Pierre	4110	1244	.303
23	Bobby Abreu	5276	1595	.302
24	Garrett Atkins	1218	368	.302
25	Sean Casey	4414	1333	.302

ON-BASE PERCENTAGE
minimum 1000 PA; * AB + BB + HBP + SF

Rk.	Player	*PA	OB	OBP
1	Barry Bonds	12125	5370	.443
2	Todd Helton	6070	2610	.430
3	Frank Thomas	9161	3886	.424
4	Albert Pujols	4061	1700	.419
5	Lance Berkman	4458	1855	.416
6	Jason Giambi	6906	2855	.413
7	Bobby Abreu	6361	2623	.412
8	Manny Ramirez	7781	3198	.411
9	Jim Thome	7890	3226	.409
10	Brian Giles	6373	2602	.408
11	Travis Hafner	2108	847	.402
12	Chipper Jones	7540	3029	.402
13	Ryan Howard	1094	437	.399
14	Joe Mauer	1284	512	.399
15	Gary Sheffield	9551	3802	.398
16	Nick Johnson	2387	943	.395
17	J.D. Drew	3756	1475	.393
18	Carlos Delgado	7252	2831	.390
19	Jason Bay	1970	769	.390
20	Vladimir Guerrero	6159	2400	.390
21	Derek Jeter	7647	2970	.388
22	Alex Rodriguez	7758	2993	.386
23	Tim Salmon	7039	2711	.385
24	Miguel Cabrera	2388	917	.384
25	Jim Edmonds	6889	2633	.382

SLUGGING PERCENTAGE
minimum 1000 PA

Rk.	Player	AB	TB	SLG
1	Albert Pujols	3489	2193	.629
2	Ryan Howard	932	582	.624
3	Barry Bonds	9507	5784	.608
4	Manny Ramirez	6575	3946	.600
5	Todd Helton	5106	3029	.593
6	Vladimir Guerrero	5502	3206	.583
7	Travis Hafner	1775	1034	.583
8	Alex Rodriguez	6767	3875	.573
9	Lance Berkman	3687	2089	.567
10	Frank Thomas	7422	4203	.566
11	Jim Thome	6409	3620	.565
12	Carlos Delgado	6053	3376	.558
13	Ken Griffey Jr.	8298	4622	.557
14	Mike Piazza	6602	3640	.551
15	David Ortiz	3666	2015	.550
16	Jason Bay	1667	910	.546
17	Chipper Jones	6385	3458	.542
18	Jason Giambi	5620	3040	.541
19	Nomar Garciaparra	4832	2610	.540
20	Jim Edmonds	5907	3181	.539
21	Miguel Cabrera	2106	1127	.535
22	Mark Teixeira	2346	1252	.534
23	Matt Holliday	1481	790	.533
24	David Wright	1420	748	.527
25	Richie Sexson	4214	2218	.526

HITS

Craig Biggio	2930
Barry Bonds	2841
Julio Franco	2566
Steve Finley	2531
Omar Vizquel	2472
Ken Griffey Jr.	2412
Gary Sheffield	2390
Luis Gonzalez	2373
Ivan Rodriguez	2354
Bernie Williams	2336
Kenny Lofton	2283
Frank Thomas	2262
Jeff Kent	2189
Ruben Sierra	2152
Derek Jeter	2150
Garret Anderson	2081
Alex Rodriguez	2067
Manny Ramirez	2066
Mike Piazza	2042
Moises Alou	2005

HOME RUNS

Barry Bonds	734
Ken Griffey Jr.	563
Frank Thomas	487
Jim Thome	472
Manny Ramirez	470
Alex Rodriguez	464
Gary Sheffield	455
Mike Piazza	419
Carlos Delgado	407
Chipper Jones	357
Jim Edmonds	350
Jason Giambi	350
Jeff Kent	345
Andruw Jones	342
Vladimir Guerrero	338
Luis Gonzalez	331
Vinny Castilla	320
Moises Alou	319
Shawn Green	318
Jeromy Burnitz	315

RUNS BATTED IN

Barry Bonds	1930
Ken Griffey Jr.	1608
Frank Thomas	1579
Manny Ramirez	1516
Gary Sheffield	1501
Jeff Kent	1380
Alex Rodriguez	1347
Luis Gonzalez	1324
Ruben Sierra	1322
Jim Thome	1302
Mike Piazza	1291
Carlos Delgado	1287
Bernie Williams	1257
Moises Alou	1229
Chipper Jones	1197
Julio Franco	1178
Steve Finley	1165
Jason Giambi	1144
Garret Anderson	1128
Craig Biggio	1125

STOLEN BASES

Kenny Lofton	599
Barry Bonds	509
Eric Young	465
Craig Biggio	410
Omar Vizquel	366
Tony Womack	363
Juan Pierre	325
Steve Finley	320
Luis Castillo	306
Johnåny Damåon	306
Reggie Sanders	304
Julio Franco	279
Bobby Abreu	271
Edgar Renteria	263
Ray Durham	255
Mike Cameron	254
Derek Jeter	249
Alex Rodriguez	241
Ichiro Suzuki	235
Royce Clayton	229å

SEASONS PLAYED

Roger Clemens	23
Julio Franco	22
Barry Bonds	21
Greg Maddux	21
Ruben Sierra	20
Jamie Moyer	20
Terry Mulholland	20
David Wells	20
Tom Glavine	20
Craig Biggio	19
Sandy Alomar Jr	19
Randy Johnson	19
Curt Schilling	19
Gary Sheffield	19

DOUBLES

Craig Biggio	637
Barry Bonds	587
Luis Gonzalez	547
Jeff Kent	501
Ivan Rodriguez	473
Frank Thomas	458
Ken Griffey Jr.	449
Bernie Williams	449
Steve Finley	446
Manny Ramirez	438

TOTAL BASES

Craig Biggio	637
Barry Bonds	587
Luis Gonzalez	547
Jeff Kent	501
Ivan Rodriguez	473
Frank Thomas	458
Ken Griffey Jr.	449
Bernie Williams	449
Steve Finley	446
Manny Ramirez	438

STRIKEOUTS

Jim Thome	1909
Craig Biggio	1641
Reggie Sanders	1599
Jim Edmonds	1512
Ken Griffey Jr.	1494
Barry Bonds	1485
Carlos Delgado	1483
Manny Ramirez	1451
Jeff Kent	1409
Alex Rodriguez	1404

SB SUCCESS %
minimum 100 SB attempts

Carlos Beltran	87.6
Tony Womack	83.1
Carl Crawford	82.8
Jose Reyes	80.8
Orlando Cabrera	80.6
Dave Roberts	80.5
Corey Patterson	80.4
Ichiro Suzuki	80.2
Alex Rodriguez	80.1
Derek Jeter	80.1

GAMES

Barry Bonds	2860
Craig Biggio	2709
Steve Finley	2540
Julio Franco	2472
Omar Vizquel	2443
Luis Gonzalez	2316
Ken Griffey Jr.	2234
Gary Sheffield	2229
Ruben Sierra	2186
Frank Thomas	2096

TRIPLES

Steve Finley	124
Kenny Lofton	110
Johnny Damon	85
Barry Bonds	77
Ray Durham	77
Omar Vizquel	68
Carl Crawford	65
Luis Gonzalez	65
3 tied with	61

WALKS

Barry Bonds	2426
Frank Thomas	1547
Jim Thome	1364
Gary Sheffield	1293
Craig Biggio	1137
Jason Giambi	1089
Ken Griffey Jr.	1077
Chipper Jones	1070
Bernie Williams	1069
Luis Gonzalez	1058

K/BB RATIO
minimum 1000 AB

Barry Bonds	612
Brian Giles	687
Eric Young	700
Gary Sheffield	751
Todd Helton	794
Albert Pujols	799
Frank Thomas	805
Joe Mauer	874
Jason Kendall	890
Orlando Palmeiro	892

CAUGHT STEALING

Eric Young	168
Kenny Lofton	153
Omar Vizquel	146
Barry Bonds	141
Luis Castillo	125
Craig Biggio	121
Steve Finley	118
Juan Pierre	116
Reggie Sanders	114
Julio Franco	106

AT-BATS

Craig Biggio	10359
Barry Bonds	9507
Steve Finley	9303
Omar Vizquel	8966
Julio Franco	8587
Luis Gonzalez	8352
Ken Griffey Jr.	8298
Ruben Sierra	8044
Gary Sheffield	8037
Bernie Williams	7869

AB PER HR
minimum 1000 AB

Barry Bonds	13.0
Jim Thome	13.6
Albert Pujols	14.0
Manny Ramirez	14.0
Adam Dunn	14.3
Alex Rodriguez	14.6
Ken Griffey Jr.	14.7
Carlos Delgado	14.9
Travis Hafner	15.0
Frank Thomas	15.2

INTENTIONAL WALKS

Barry Bonds	645
Ken Griffey Jr.	216
Vladimir Guerrero	195
Frank Thomas	165
Carlos Delgado	159
Manny Ramirez	154
Todd Helton	146
Mike Piazza	146
Luis Gonzalez	145
Jim Thome	139

SACRIFICE HITS

Omar Vizquel	218
Tom Glavine	201
Greg Maddux	165
John Smoltz	122
Royce Clayton	110
Jose Vizcaino	107
Curt Schilling	102
Neifi Perez	96
Craig Biggio	94
Steve Finley	91

GDP

Julio Franco	310
Ivan Rodriguez	255
Vinny Castilla	224
Bernie Williams	223
Mike Piazza	220
Royce Clayton	208
Frank Thomas	203
Gary Sheffield	196
Jeff Kent	194
Ruben Sierra	193

RUNS SCORED

Barry Bonds	2152
Craig Biggio	1776
Ken Griffey Jr.	1467
Kenny Lofton	1442
Steve Finley	1434
Gary Sheffield	1433
Frank Thomas	1404
Bernie Williams	1366
Alex Rodriguez	1358
Luis Gonzalez	1312

AB PER RBI
minimum 1000 AB

Manny Ramirez	4.3
Albert Pujols	4.6
Travis Hafner	4.7
Frank Thomas	4.7
Carlos Delgado	4.7
David Ortiz	4.8
Lance Berkman	4.9
Jason Giambi	4.9
Jim Thome	4.9
Barry Bonds	4.9

HIT BY PITCH

Craig Biggio	282
Jason Kendall	209
Carlos Delgado	149
Jason Giambi	127
Damion Easley	120
Gary Sheffield	119
Derek Jeter	115
Jeff Kent	113
Luis Gonzalez	107
Alex Rodriguez	106

SACRIFICE FLIES

Ruben Sierra	120
Frank Thomas	115
Gary Sheffield	102
Jeff Conine	96
Jeff Kent	95
Luis Gonzalez	91
Barry Bonds	89
Ken Griffey Jr.	85
Omar Vizquel	80
2 tied with	78

AB PER GDP
minimum 1000 AB

Ichiro Suzuki	151.7
Rob Mackowiak	132.1
Greg Maddux	122.8
Jose Reyes	122.5
Dave Roberts	116.0
Russell Branyan	113.7
Willy Taveras	112.2
Carl Crawford	106.1
Johnny Damon	102.6
Corey Patterson	101.5

WINS

Roger Clemens	348
Greg Maddux	333
Tom Glavine	290
Randy Johnson	280
Mike Mussina	239
David Wells	230
Jamie Moyer	216
Kenny Rogers	207
Curt Schilling	207
Pedro Martinez	206

GAMES

Mike Stanton	1109
Jose Mesa	966
Mike Timlin	961
Roberto Hernandez	960
Todd Jones	874
Trevor Hoffman	821
Mike Myers	811
Tom Gordon	809
Jeff Nelson	798
Eddie Guardado	781

COMPLETE GAMES

Roger Clemens	118
Greg Maddux	108
Randy Johnson	98
Curt Schilling	82
Mike Mussina	57
Tom Glavine	55
David Wells	54
John Smoltz	53
Scott Erickson	51
2 tied with	46

STRIKEOUTS

Roger Clemens	4604
Randy Johnson	4544
Greg Maddux	3169
Curt Schilling	3015
Pedro Martinez	2998
John Smoltz	2778
Mike Mussina	2572
Tom Glavine	2481
David Wells	2119
Jamie Moyer	1992

LOSSES

Greg Maddux	203
Tom Glavine	191
Roger Clemens	178
Jamie Moyer	166
David Wells	148
Randy Johnson	147
Steve Trachsel	143
Terry Mulholland	142
Brad Radke	139
Kenny Rogers	139

GAMES STARTED

Roger Clemens	690
Greg Maddux	673
Tom Glavine	635
Randy Johnson	546
Jamie Moyer	518
Mike Mussina	475
David Wells	460
Kenny Rogers	433
John Smoltz	429
Curt Schilling	412

COMPLETE GAME %
minimum 100 GS

Curt Schilling	0.20
Randy Johnson	0.18
Roger Clemens	0.17
Greg Maddux	0.16
Scott Erickson	0.14
Terry Mulholland	0.14
Livan Hernandez	0.13
Roy Halladay	0.13
Mark Mulder	0.13
John Smoltz	0.12

WALKS ALLOWED

Roger Clemens	1549
Randy Johnson	1409
Tom Glavine	1399
Kenny Rogers	1079
Tim Wakefield	948
Jamie Moyer	946
Tom Gordon	944
Greg Maddux	944
John Smoltz	937
Scott Erickson	865

WINNING PERCENTAGE
minimum 100 decisions

Johan Santana	716
Pedro Martinez	691
Roy Oswalt	676
Tim Hudson	665
Roy Halladay	664
Roger Clemens	662
Randy Johnson	656
Mark Mulder	644
Andy Pettitte	641
Mike Mussina	641

INNINGS PITCHED

Roger Clemens	4817.2
Greg Maddux	4616.1
Tom Glavine	4149.2
Randy Johnson	3798.2
Jamie Moyer	3351.0
David Wells	3281.2
Mike Mussina	3210.1
John Smoltz	3161.1
Curt Schilling	3110.0
Kenny Rogers	3066.0

SHUTOUTS

Roger Clemens	46
Randy Johnson	37
Greg Maddux	35
Tom Glavine	24
Mike Mussina	23
Curt Schilling	19
Scott Erickson	17
Pedro Martinez	17
John Smoltz	16
3 tied with	12

STRIKEOUTS/9 IP
minimum 750 IP

Randy Johnson	10.77
Kerry Wood	10.36
Pedro Martinez	10.20
Trevor Hoffman	9.81
Jeff Nelson	9.51
Johan Santana	9.47
Jake Peavy	8.85
Arthur Rhodes	8.84
Mike Remlinger	8.74
Curt Schilling	8.73

ERA
minimum 750 IP

Mariano Rivera	2.29
Trevor Hoffman	2.71
Pedro Martinez	2.81
Roy Oswalt	3.05
Greg Maddux	3.07
Roger Clemens	3.10
Johan Santana	3.20
Randy Johnson	3.22
John Smoltz	3.27
Brandon Webb	3.28

BATTERS FACED

Roger Clemens	19820
Greg Maddux	18787
Tom Glavine	17468
Randy Johnson	15644
Jamie Moyer	14235
David Wells	13719
Kenny Rogers	13223
Mike Mussina	13118
John Smoltz	12957
Curt Schilling	12651

QUALITY START %
minimum 100 GS

Roy Oswalt	70.6
Pedro Martinez	69.9
Randy Johnson	68.3
Brandon Webb	66.7
Curt Schilling	66.5
Carlos Zambrano	66.4
Greg Maddux	66.1
Roger Clemens	65.9
Tom Glavine	64.3
Mark Prior	64.2

WALKS PER 9 INNINGS
minimum 750 IP

Brad Radke	1.63
Jon Lieber	1.71
Greg Maddux	1.84
David Wells	1.86
Ben Sheets	1.89
Roy Oswalt	1.97
Curt Schilling	1.99
Mike Mussina	2.02
Mark Buehrle	2.07
Keith Foulke	2.16

K/BB RATIO
minimum 750 IP

Curt Schilling	4.38
Pedro Martinez	4.28
Ben Sheets	4.11
Roy Oswalt	3.86
Trevor Hoffman	3.86
Keith Foulke	3.84
Jon Lieber	3.74
Johan Santana	3.67
Mike Mussina	3.58
Mariano Rivera	3.46

OPPOSITION AVG
minimum 750 IP

Trevor Hoffman	208
Pedro Martinez	209
Mariano Rivera	213
Kerry Wood	215
Randy Johnson	217
Johan Santana	220
Keith Foulke	223
Jeff Nelson	224
Carlos Zambrano	224
Roger Clemens	228

HIT BATSMEN

Randy Johnson	178
Roger Clemens	154
Tim Wakefield	146
Pedro Martinez	129
Chan Ho Park	126
Greg Maddux	125
Kenny Rogers	117
Jamey Wright	114
Jamie Moyer	112
Pedro Astacio	111

SAVES

Trevor Hoffman	482
Mariano Rivera	413
Roberto Hernandez	326
Billy Wagner	324
Jose Mesa	320
Armando Benitez	280
Todd Jones	263
Jason Isringhausen	249
Bob Wickman	247
Keith Foulke	190

†**Quality Starts** denote the number of outings in which a starting pitcher works at least six innings and allows three or fewer earned runs.

HITS PER 9 INNINGS
minimum 750 IP

Pedro Martinez	6.85
Trevor Hoffman	6.86
Kerry Wood	6.98
Mariano Rivera	7.05
Randy Johnson	7.14
Jeff Nelson	7.26
Johan Santana	7.31
Carlos Zambrano	7.36
Keith Foulke	7.43
Roger Clemens	7.63

OPPOSITION OBP
minimum 750 IP

Trevor Hoffman	264
Mariano Rivera	269
Pedro Martinez	270
Johan Santana	279
Keith Foulke	279
Curt Schilling	285
Greg Maddux	290
John Smoltz	292
Mike Mussina	293
Roger Clemens	294

WILD PITCHES

Roger Clemens	136
John Smoltz	135
Tom Gordon	105
Matt Clement	101
Randy Johnson	101
David Wells	100
Jason Grimsley	96
Jason Schmidt	91
Jeff Fassero	86
2 tied with	82

SAVE %
minimum 50 SvOp

Eric Gagne	96.4
John Smoltz	91.7
Joe Nathan	89.9
Trevor Hoffman	89.6
Bobby Jenks	88.7
Mariano Rivera	88.2
Billy Wagner	86.6
Chad Cordero	85.8
Jose Valverde	85.0
Jason Isringhausen	84.7

BASERUNNERS PER 9 INNINGS
minimum 750 IP

Trevor Hoffman	9.48
Mariano Rivera	9.66
Pedro Martinez	9.67
Johan Santana	10.08
Keith Foulke	10.10
Curt Schilling	10.33
Greg Maddux	10.47
John Smoltz	10.66
Mike Mussina	10.72
Roger Clemens	10.81

OPPOSITION SLG
minimum 750 IP

Mariano Rivera	290
Pedro Martinez	327
Jeff Nelson	331
Trevor Hoffman	336
Roger Clemens	340
Carlos Zambrano	344
Randy Johnson	346
Jason Isringhausen	351
Greg Maddux	353
John Smoltz	356

GDP INDUCED

Greg Maddux	392
Tom Glavine	392
Roger Clemens	321
Kenny Rogers	317
Scott Erickson	310
Jamie Moyer	273
Terry Mulholland	266
Andy Pettitte	262
David Wells	254
Mike Mussina	251

GAMES FINISHED

Trevor Hoffman	682
Roberto Hernandez	647
Jose Mesa	612
Mariano Rivera	600
Billy Wagner	546
Todd Jones	528
Armando Benitez	501
Bob Wickman	471
Mike Timlin	422
Keith Foulke	397

HOME RUNS/9 IP
minimum 750 IP

Mariano Rivera	0.46
Greg Maddux	0.62
Jeff Nelson	0.63
Roger Clemens	0.66
Bob Wickman	0.68
Brandon Webb	0.69
Carlos Zambrano	0.69
Hector Carrasco	0.69
Tom Glavine	0.70
Julian Tavarez	0.71

HOME RUNS ALLOWED

Jamie Moyer	414
David Wells	385
Randy Johnson	361
Roger Clemens	354
Mike Mussina	345
Brad Radke	326
Curt Schilling	326
Tom Glavine	322
Steve Trachsel	319
Greg Maddux	318

GDP/9 IP
minimum 750 IP

Julian Tavarez	1.30
Shawn Estes	1.29
Jake Westbrook	1.29
Jamey Wright	1.19
Scott Erickson	1.18
Bob Wickman	1.15
Scott Schoeneweis	1.13
Mark Mulder	1.12
Danny Graves	1.09
Jon Garland	1.07

SB % ALLOWED
minimum 750 IP

Chris Carpenter	38.3
Mike Maroth	40.0
Terry Mulholland	41.2
Mark Buehrle	41.4
Kenny Rogers	41.7
Carlos Zambrano	44.7
Gil Meche	45.5
Johan Santana	47.8
Roy Oswalt	49.1
Mark Redman	50.0